Routledge
Encyclopedia of
PHILOSOPHY

General Editor
EDWARD CRAIG

London and New York

First published 1998
by Routledge
ew Fetter Lane, London EC4P 4EE
Simultaneously published in the USA and Canada
by Routledge
29 West 35th Street, New York, NY 10001

Typeset in Monotype Times New Roman by
Routledge

Printed in England by
T J International Ltd, Padstow, Cornwall, England

Printed on acid-free paper which conforms to ANS1.Z39, 48-1992 and ISO 9706 standards

British Library Cataloguing-in-Publication Data
A catalogue record for this book is available from the British Library

The Library of Congress Cataloguing-in-Publication data is given in volume 10.

ISBN: 0415-07310-3 (10-volume set)
ISBN: 0415-18706-0 (volume 1)
ISBN: 0415-18707-9 (volume 2)
ISBN: 0415-18708-7 (volume 3)
ISBN: 0415-18709-5 (volume 4)
ISBN: 0415-18710-9 (volume 5)
ISBN: 0415-18711-7 (volume 6)
ISBN: 0415-18712-5 (volume 7)
ISBN: 0415-18713-3 (volume 8)
ISBN: 0415-18714-1 (volume 9)
ISBN: 0415-18715-X (volume 10)

ISBN: 0415-16916-X (CD-ROM)
ISBN: 0415-16917-8 (10-volume set and CD-ROM)

Contents

Using the *Encyclopedia*

List of entries

Using the *Encyclopedia*

The *Routledge Encyclopedia of Philosophy* is designed for ease of use. The following notes outline its organization and editorial approach and explain the ways of locating material. This will help readers make the most of the *Encyclopedia*.

SEQUENCE OF ENTRIES

The *Encyclopedia* contains 2,054 entries (from 500 to 19,000 words in length) arranged in nine volumes with a tenth volume for the index. Volumes 1–9 are arranged in a single alphabetical sequence, as follows:

Volume 1: A posteriori *to* Bradwardine, Thomas

Volume 2: Brahman *to* Derrida, Jacques

Volume 3: Descartes, René *to* Gender and science

Volume 4: Genealogy *to* Iqbal, Muhammad

Volume 5: Irigaray, Luce *to* Lushi chunqiu

Volume 6: Luther, Martin *to* Nifo, Agostino

Volume 7: Nihilism *to* Quantum mechanics, interpretation of

Volume 8: Questions *to* Sociobiology

Volume 9: Sociology of knowledge *to* Zoroastrianism

Alphabetical order

Entries are listed in alphabetical order by word rather than by letter with all words including *and*, *in*, *of* and *the* being given equal status. The exceptions to this rule are as follows:

- biographies: where the forenames and surname of a philosopher are inverted, the entry takes priority in the sequence, for example:

Alexander, Samuel (1859–1938)
Alexander of Aphrodisias (*c.* AD 200)
Alexander of Hales (*c.* 1185–1245)

- names with prefixes, which follow conventional alphabetical placing (see Transliteration and naming conventions below).

A complete alphabetical list of entries is given in each of the Volumes 1 to 9.

Inverted titles

Titles of entries consisting of more than one word are often inverted so that the key term (in a thematic or signpost entry) or the surname (in a biographical entry) determines the place of the entry in the alphabetical sequence, for example:

Law, philosophy of *or*
Market, ethics of the *or*
Hart, Herbert Lionel Adolphus (1907–93)

Conceptual organization

Several concerns have had a bearing on the sequence of entries where there is more than one key term.

In deciding on the sequence of entries we have tried, wherever possible, to integrate philosophy as it is known and studied in the USA and Europe with philosophy from around the world. This means that the reader will frequently find entries from different philosophical traditions or approaches to the same topic close to each other, for example, in the sequence:

Political philosophy [signpost entry]
Political philosophy, history of
Political philosophy in classical Islam
Political philosophy, Indian

Similarly, in entries where a philosophical tradition or approach is surveyed we have tried, whenever appropriate, to keep philosophical traditions from different countries together. An example is the sequence:

Confucian philosophy, Chinese
Confucian philosophy, Japanese
Confucian philosophy, Korean
Confucius (551–479 BC)

Finally, historical entries are usually placed with contemporary entries under the topic rather than the historical period. For example, in the sequence:

Language, ancient philosophy of
Language and gender
Language, conventionality of
Language, early modern philosophy of
Language, Indian theories of
Language, innateness of

DUMMY TITLES

The *Encyclopedia* has been extensively cross-referenced in order to help the reader locate their topic of interest. Dummy titles are placed throughout the alphabetical sequence of entries to direct the reader to the actual title of the entry where a topic is discussed. This may be under a different entry title, a synonym or as part of a larger entry. Wherever useful we have included the numbers of the sections (§§) in which a particular topic or subject is discussed. Examples of this type of cross-reference are:

AFRICAN AESTHETICS *see*
AESTHETICS, AFRICAN

CANGUILHEM, GEORGES *see*
FRENCH PHILOSOPHY OF SCIENCE §§3–4

TAO *see* DAO

GLOSSARY OF LOGICAL AND MATHEMATICAL TERMS

A glossary of logical and mathematical terms is provided to help users with terms from formal logic and mathematics. 'See also' cross-references to the glossary are provided at the end of entries where the user might benefit from help with unfamiliar terms. The glossary can be found in Volume 5 under L (LOGICAL AND MATHEMATICAL TERMS, GLOSSARY OF).

THE INDEX VOLUME

Volume 10 is devoted to a comprehensive index of key terms, concepts and names covered in Volumes 1–9, allowing readers to reap maximum benefit from the *Encyclopedia*. A guide to the index can be found at the beginning of the index. The index volume includes a full listing of contributors, their affiliations and the entries they have written. It also includes permission acknowledgements, listed in publisher order.

STRUCTURE OF ENTRIES

The *Routledge Encyclopedia of Philosophy* contains three types of entry:

- 'signpost' entries, for example, METAPHYSICS; SCIENCE, PHILOSOPHY OF; EAST ASIAN PHILOSOPHY. These entries provide an accessible overview of the sub-disciplines or regional coverage within the *Encyclopedia*; they provide a 'map' which directs the reader towards and around the many

entries relating to each topic;
- thematic entries, ranging from general entries such as KNOWLEDGE, CONCEPT OF, to specialized topics such as VIRTUE EPISTEMOLOGY;
- biographical entries, devoted to individual philosophers, emphasizing the work rather than the life of the subject and with a list of the subject's major works.

Overview

All thematic and biographical entries begin with an overview which provides a concise and accessible summary of the topic or subject. This can be referred to on its own if the reader does not require the depth and detail of the main part of the entry.

Table of contents

All thematic and biographical entries over 1000 words in length are divided into sections and have a numbered table of contents following the overview. This gives the headings of each of the sections of the entry, enabling the reader to see the scope and structure of the entry at a glance. For example, the table of contents in the entry on HERACLITUS:

1 Life and work
2 Methodology
3 Unity of opposites and perspectivism
4 Cosmology
5 Psychology, ethics and religion
6 Influence

Cross-references within an entry

Entries in the *Encyclopedia* have been extensively cross-referenced in order to indicate other entries that may be of interest to the reader. There are two types of cross-reference in the *Encyclopedia*:

1. 'See' cross-references

Cross-references within the text of an entry direct the reader to other entries on or closely related to the topic under discussion. For example, a reader may be directed from a conceptual entry to a biography of the philosopher whose work is under discussion or vice versa. These internal cross-references appear in small capital letters, either in parentheses, for example:

Opponents of naturalism before and since Wittgenstein have been animated by the notion that the aims of social science are not causal explanation and improving prediction, but uncovering rules that make social life intelligible to its participants (see EXPLANATION IN HISTORY AND SOCIAL SCIENCE).

or sometimes, when the reference is to a person who

has a biographical entry, as small capitals in the text itself, for example:

Thomas NAGEL emphasizes the discrepancy between the objective insignificance of our lives and projects and the seriousness and energy we devote to them.

For entries over 1,000 words in length we have included the numbers of the sections (§) in which a topic is discussed, wherever useful, for example:

In *Nicomachean Ethics*, Aristotle criticizes Plato's account for not telling us anything about particular kinds of goodness (see ARISTOTLE §§ 21–6).

2. 'See also' cross-references

At the end of the text of each entry, 'See also' cross-references guide the reader to other entries of related interest, such as more specialized entries, biographical entries, historical entries, geographical entries and so on. These cross-references appear in small capitals in alphabetical order.

References

References in the text are given in the Harvard style, for example, Kant (1788), Rawls (1971). Exceptions to this rule are made when presenting works with established conventions, for example, with some major works in ancient philosophy. Full bibliographical details are given in the 'List of works' and 'References and further reading'.

Bibliography

List of works

Biographical entries are followed by a list of works which gives full bibliographical details of the major works of the philosopher. This is in chronological order and includes items cited in the text, significant editions, dates of composition for pre-modern works (where known), preferred English-language translations and English translations for the titles of untranslated foreign-language works.

References and further reading

Both biographical and thematic entries have a list of references and further reading. Items are listed alphabetically by author's name. (Publications with joint authors are listed under the name of the first author and after any individual publications by that author). References cited in the text are preceded by an asterisk (*). Further reading which the reader may find particularly useful is also included.

The authors and editors have attempted to provide the fullest possible bibliographical information for every item.

Annotations

Publications in the 'List of works' and the 'References and further reading' have been annotated with a brief description of the content so that their relevance to readers' interests can be quickly assessed.

EDITORIAL STYLE

Spelling and punctuation in the *Encyclopedia* have been standardized to follow British English usage.

Transliteration and naming conventions

All names and terms from non-roman alphabets have been romanized in the *Encyclopedia*. Foreign names have been given according to the conventions within the particular language.

Arabic

Arabic has been transliterated in a simplified form, that is, without macrons or subscripts. Names of philosophers are given in their Arabic form rather than their Latinate form, for example, IBN RUSHD rather than AVERROES. Arabic names beginning with the prefix 'al-' are alphabetized under the substantive part of the name and not the prefix, for example:

KILWARDBY, ROBERT (d. 1279)
AL-KINDI, ABU YUSUF YAQUB IBN ISHAQ (d. *c*.866–73)
KNOWLEDGE AND JUSTIFICATION, COHERENCE THEORY OF

Arabic names beginning with the prefix 'Ibn' are alphabetized under 'I'.

Chinese, Korean and Japanese

Chinese has been transliterated using the Pinyin system. Dummy titles in the older Wade–Giles system are given for names and key terms; these direct the reader to the Pinyin titles.

Japanese has been transliterated using a modified version of the Hepburn system.

Chinese, Japanese and Korean names are given in Asian form, that is, surname preceding forenames, for example:

WANG FUZHI
NISHITANI KEIJI

The exception is where an author has chosen to present their own name in conventional Western form.

Hebrew

Hebrew has been transliterated in a simplified form, that is, without macrons or subscripts.

Russian

Cyrillic characters have been transliterated using the Library of Congress system. Russian names are usually given with their patronymic, for example, BAKUNIN, MIKHAIL ALEKSANDROVICH.

Sanskrit

A guide to the pronunciation of Sanskrit can be found in the INDIAN AND TIBETAN PHILOSOPHY signpost entry.

Tibetan

Tibetan has been transliterated using the Wylie system. Dummy titles in the Virginia system are given for names and key terms. A guide to Tibetan pronunciation can be found in the INDIAN AND TIBETAN PHILOSOPHY signpost entry.

European names

Names beginning with the prefixes 'de', 'von' or 'van' are usually alphabetized under the substantive part of the name. For example:

BEAUVOIR, SIMONE DE
HUMBOLDT, WILHELM VON

The exception to this rule is when the person is either a national of or has spent some time living or working in an English-speaking country. For example:

DE MORGAN, AUGUSTUS
VON WRIGHT, GEORG HENRIK

Names beginning with the prefix 'de la' or 'le' are alphabetized under the prefix 'la' or 'le'. For example:

LA FORGE, LOUIS DE
LE DOEUFF, MICHÈLE

Names beginning with 'Mc' or 'Mac' are treated as 'Mac' and appear before Ma.

Historical names

Medieval and Renaissance names where a person is not usually known by a surname are alphabetized under the forename, for example:

GILES OF ROME
JOHN OF SALISBURY

List of entries

Below is a complete list of entries in the order in which they appear in the *Routledge Encyclopedia of Philosophy*.

A posteriori
A priori
'Abduh, Muhammad
Abelard, Peter
Aberdeen Philosophical Society
Abhinavagupta
Abravanel, Isaac
Abravanel, Judah ben Isaac
Absolute, the
Absolutism
Abstract objects
Academy
Action
Adorno, Theodor Wiesengrund
Adverbs
Aenesidemus
Aesthetic attitude
Aesthetic concepts
Aesthetics
Aesthetics, African
Aesthetics and ethics
Aesthetics, Chinese
Aesthetics in Islamic philosophy
Aesthetics, Japanese
Affirmative action
al-Afghani, Jamal al-Din
African philosophy
African philosophy, anglophone
African philosophy, francophone
African traditional religions
Agnosticism
Agricola, Rudolph
Agricultural ethics
Agrippa
Agrippa von Nettesheim, Henricus
   Cornelius
Ailly, Pierre d'
Ajdukiewicz, Kazimierz
Akan philosophical psychology
Akrasia
Albert of Saxony
Albert the Great
Albo, Joseph
Alchemy

Alcinous
Alcmaeon
Alemanno, Yohanan ben Isaac
D'Alembert, Jean Le Rond
Alexander, Samuel
Alexander of Aphrodisias
Alexander of Hales
Alienation
Alighieri, Dante
Alison, Archibald
Alterity and identity, postmodern
   theories of
Althusser, Louis Pierre
Ambedkar, Bimrao Ramji
Ambiguity
American philosophy in the 18th and
   19th centuries
al-'Amiri, Abu'l Hasan Muhammad
   ibn Yusuf
Ammonius, son of Hermeas
Amo, Anton Wilhelm
Analysis, nonstandard
Analysis, philosophical issues in
Analytic ethics
Analytical philosophy
Analytical philosophy in Latin
   America
Analyticity
Anaphora
Anarchism
Anaxagoras
Anaxarchus
Anaximander
Anaximenes
Ancient philosophy
Anderson, John
Animal language and thought
Animals and ethics
Anomalous monism
Anscombe, Gertrude Elizabeth
   Margaret
Anselm of Canterbury
Anthropology, philosophy of
Antiochus

Antiphon
Anti-positivist thought in Latin
   America
Antirealism in the philosophy of
   mathematics
Anti-Semitism
Antisthenes
Applied ethics
Apuleius
Aquinas, Thomas
Arama, Isaac ben Moses
Arcesilaus
Archaeology, philosophy of
Archē
Architecture, aesthetics of
Archytas
Arendt, Hannah
Aretē
Argentina, philosophy in
Aristippus the Elder
Ariston of Chios
Aristotelianism in Islamic
   philosophy
Aristotelianism in the 17th century
Aristotelianism, medieval
Aristotelianism, Renaissance
Aristotle
Aristotle commentators
Arithmetic, philosophical issues in
Armstrong, David Malet
Arnauld, Antoine
Art, abstract
Art and morality
Art and truth
Art criticism
Art, definition of
Art, performing
Art, understanding of
Art, value of
Art works, ontology of
Artificial intelligence
Artistic expression
Artistic forgery
Artistic interpretation

An alphabetical list of contributors, their affiliations and the entries they have written can be found in the index volume (Volume 10).

NIHILISM

As its name implies (from Latin nihil, *'nothing'), philosophical nihilism is a philosophy of negation, rejection, or denial of some or all aspects of thought or life. Moral nihilism, for example, rejects any possibility of justifying or criticizing moral judgments, on grounds such as that morality is a cloak for egoistic self-seeking, and therefore a sham; that only descriptive claims can be rationally adjudicated and that moral (prescriptive) claims cannot be logically derived from descriptive ones; or that moral principles are nothing more than expressions of subjective choices, preferences or feelings of people who endorse them.*

Similarly, epistemological nihilism denies the possibility of justifying or criticizing claims to knowledge, because it assumes that a foundation of infallible, universal truths would be required for such assessments, and no such thing is available; because it views all claims to knowledge as entirely relative to historical epochs, cultural contexts or the vagaries of individual thought and experience, and therefore as ultimately arbitrary and incommensurable; because it sees all attempts at justification or criticism as useless, given centuries of unresolved disagreement about disputed basic beliefs even among the most intelligent thinkers; or because it notes that numerous widely accepted, unquestioned beliefs of the past are dismissed out of hand today and expects a similar fate in the future for many, if not all, of the most confident present beliefs.

Political nihilism calls for the complete destruction of existing political institutions, along with their supporting outlooks and social structures, but has no positive message of what should be put in their place. Cosmic nihilism regards nature as either wholly unintelligible and starkly indifferent to basic human concerns, or as knowable only in the sense of being amenable to scientific description and explanation. In either case, the cosmos is seen as giving no support to distinctively human aims or values, and it may even be regarded as actively hostile to human beings. Existential nihilism negates the meaning of human life, judging it to be irremediably pointless, futile and absurd. Cosmic and existential nihilism are the focus of this entry.

1   **Historical background**
2   **Cosmic nihilism**
3   **Existential nihilism**
4   **Critical comment**

1   Historical background

Scattered uses of the term 'nihilism' can be found in philosophical, theological, political and literary writings of the late eighteenth and early nineteenth centuries in Europe. In that period, the term was sometimes used to refer to atheism and its alleged inability to provide support for knowledge and morality, or to impart purpose to human life; sometimes to any sort of uncommitted, sceptical or despairing outlook on existence; sometimes to philosophical idealists (especially proponents of the 'critical' philosophy of Immanuel KANT), on the basis that they negate any possibility of knowing or relating to objective, in-itself facts of the world by insisting that all experienced objects are constructions of the mind; and sometimes to socialists or anarchists, because their revolutionary philosophies were judged to be destructive of all political and social order. But the term first came into wide use in the period extending from the 1870s into the early years of the twentieth century, due largely to the influence of three writers: the Russian novelists Ivan Turgenev and Fëdor DOSTOEVSKII, and the German philosopher Friedrich NIETZSCHE.

A character named Bazarov, in Turgenev's novel *Fathers and Sons* (1862), proclaims himself a nihilist and explains that nihilists 'act by virtue of what we recognize as beneficial'. What is most beneficial for the present, he continues, is 'negation, and we deny....everything'. Bazarov's nihilism quickly became famous in Russia and was warmly endorsed by certain revolutionary groups there in the 1860s, as well as being denounced by defenders of traditional beliefs and existing religious and political institutions. Dostoevskii was one such adamant defender, and his novel *The Possessed* (1871–2) gives a lurid portrayal of the lives of three members of a nihilist society, two of whom die by their own hand, the third at the hands of his comrades. Their existence is wretched and empty, the author implies, because they have lost faith in God and think that they must now arrogate to themselves God's absolute freedom. But theirs is an absurd freedom, without guidance or norms. It ravages their lives and brings them to pointless deaths. Dostoevskii propounded the theme of ruinous nihilism following inevitably from atheism through much of his literary career.

In notebooks composed between 1883 and 1888, parts of which were later published under the title *The Will to Power* (1901), Nietzsche announced 'the advent of nihilism' in European culture and ruminated at length on its character and causes (see NIETZSCHE, F.). There was one sense, he thought, in which nihilism could be attributed to the declining influence of Christianity and loss of faith in God, for without God human life seemed deprived of purpose and value. But in another sense, Western civilization was now coming to realize that Christianity had stripped the world of immanent meaning – thus containing in itself the seeds of the most thorough-going nihilism – by insisting on the necessity for a transcendent ground of truths and values, and focusing most of its attention on attainment of a paradise beyond the grave where the trials and sorrows of earthly existence would be redeemed.

The task to which Nietzsche devoted much of his writing, therefore, was twofold. The first part was to do relentless battle with Christianity and lay bare what he regarded as its implicit nihilism, thus freeing European culture from its spell. The second was to find some way to move beyond the nihilistic desolation that Nietzsche's character Zarathustra foresees in *Thus Spoke Zarathustra* (1883–85), following hard on the heels of his startling discovery of 'the death of God'. Nietzsche condemned as 'passive nihilism' the despairing resignation with which Arthur SCHOPEN-HAUER and other radical pessimists responded to the looming crisis of the West. He sought to develop a vision of an 'active nihilism' that would fully acknowledge important findings of epistemological, moral and cosmic nihilism, but convert them into stepping stones to a new affirmation of life.

2 Cosmic nihilism

The absolute form of cosmic nihilism denies to the universe any sort of intelligibility or meaning. It is blank and featureless, giving no response to the age-old human search for understanding and no support to distinctively human aims, aspirations or purposes. All attempts to comprehend the world, including those of the various natural sciences, are doomed to failure. Whatever meanings or values we may think we have found in it stem from unconscious projections of our own suppositions and wishes, because it contains no knowable traits, principles or patterns that would enable it to be understood, and it is utterly lacking in discernible value. This total alienation of human understanding and need from the surrounding universe is asserted by the German thinker Max STIRNER, when he states that the world 'cannot be regarded as a comprehensive structure of objective meanings' but must rather be seen 'as a metaphysical chaos'. This conclusion follows from Stirner's radical nominalism, which views the world as a loose aggregation of unique, self-contained particulars which exhibit no intelligible relations to one another. As for values, Stirner's nominalism led him to the view that we must fend for ourselves; individuals are left isolated in a chaotic world to find as much private enjoyment and achieve as much power over others as they can.

A similar bleak view of the cosmos is taken by Antoine Roquentin, a character in Jean-Paul Sartre's novel *Nausea* (1938). The fundamental discovery he makes is that 'the world of explanations and reasons is not the world of existence'. An uncrossable chasm yawns between the concepts, descriptions, explanations and valuations of human beings on the one hand, and the world on the other. From the perspective of his recurring experiences of 'nausea,' Roquentin perceives the world to be like a thick paste or oozing slime, without character or distinction, and impenetrable to the mind (see SARTRE, J.-P. §4). In much the same fashion, Albert CAMUS speaks in *The Myth of Sisyphus* (1942) of the world as 'dense' and 'strange', a 'vast irrational' wholly unresponsive to human attempts to find a home within it or to comprehend its meaning. Schopenhauer, in the early nineteenth century, went even further than these thinkers in denuding the world of value. He argues in *The World as Will and Idea* (1818) that the cosmos is steered by a blind impulse or energy that is not merely oblivious to matters of good and evil but actively hostile to human beings, generating a horrible preponderance of sufferings over pleasures and disappointments over satisfactions.

The relative form of cosmic nihilism sees the world as fully open to scientific understanding but denies to it any normative significance. The real universe, in this outlook, is the purely descriptive one being brought steadily into view by the natural sciences, a universe of factual principles and laws that gives no place or support to the moral, aesthetic and religious concerns that preoccupy human life. The French biochemist Jacques Monod develops this idea in *Chance and Necessity* (1970), where he identifies 'the essential message of science' as an objective portrayal of the cosmos that 'outrages values' by making them 'seem to melt into the world's uncaring emptiness'. Humans must somehow reconcile themselves to living 'on the boundary of an alien world' just as indifferent to their hopes as it is to their sufferings or crimes.

3 Existential nihilism

Existential nihilists contend that human existence has no purpose, value, or justification. There is no reason to live, and yet we persist in living. The human situation is therefore absurd. The philosophical position of existential nihilism is not just that this or that person may fail to find meaning in life; it is rather that a genuinely meaningful life is impossible. In the face of this conclusion, Schopenhauer counsels us to quench the flame of affirmation and desire, to resign ourselves to the span of our days without hope of respite and calmly await an annihilating death, the last sure sign of the utter futility of our existence.

Sartre too hammers at the absurdity of existence but counsels us in *Being and Nothingness* (1943) to invent meanings for our lives through sheer acts of freedom, creating those meanings – in the manner of the God of traditional religion – out of nothing. Camus, in *The Myth of Sisyphus*, finds the absurdity of the human situation to lie in our restless, futile search for comprehensive meaning in a universe that has no discoverable significance or value. He advises us not to commit suicide when we realize that our lives have no point – that would be the coward's way out. Instead, we should heroically rebel against the abyss of meaninglessness and in that very act of defiance find some semblance of a reason for being (see EXISTENTIALISM).

A relentless, uncompromising exponent of existential nihilism is the Romanian philosopher E.M. Cioran. In *A Short History of Decay* (1949), he notes that most of us strive throughout our lives to 'keep deep down inside a certitude superior to all the others: life has no meaning, it *cannot* have any such thing'. Civilizations, philosophies, religions – all are ways of masking this inescapable truth, of seeking to divert our attention from its shattering impact. How, then, can we cope with it? As against Schopenhauer, Cioran insists that we cannot escape torturing ourselves with awareness of the 'disease', 'shame' and 'curse' of our existence. Our probing, questioning minds give us no peace; only those living in shallowness and illusion can avoid their constant torture. As against Camus, Cioran argues that we all *should* commit suicide: this is the only consistent way of dealing with the absurdity of our lives. But we foolishly compound the absurdity by refusing, in our cowardice, to do away with ourselves. As against Sartre, Cioran contends that 'the intoxication of freedom is only a shudder within a fatality, the form of [our]... fate being no less regulated than that of a sonnet or a star'. For beings born only to experience the crushing inevitabilities of disappointment, suffering and death, a freedom thrown defiantly against the void can give no respite. From 'spermatozoon to sepulchre' we are pawns of a taunting fate that arbitrarily selects some for good fortune and others for bad. Each life is a useless 'hyphen' between birth and death. Human history, as evolutionary biology and scientific cosmology show, is that of one more organic species doomed, like all the rest, to extinction, and of a mere fleeting breath in the universe's onrush to entropic death. Analogous to Sartre's descriptions of 'nausea' is Cioran's acknowledgement of a sickening 'disgust' welling up from such recognitions: 'that *negative* superfluity which spares nothing... [and] shows us the inanity of life'.

4 Critical comment

That the threat of nihilism is still very much with us is indicated by Loyal Rue's book, *By the Grace of Guile: The Role of Deception in Natural History and Human Affairs* (1994). Rue states that he is convinced of two things: that nihilism is true and that human beings cannot live with its truth. Rue does not so much systematically argue for nihilism as confess himself to be firmly in its grasp. The solution he proposes is that of a 'Noble Lie', that is, a programme of mythical re-enchantment of the universe which will deceive people into believing that it and they both have significance, even though neither has. This desperate and implausible strategy shows the continuing power of nihilism, here regarded as a kind of foregone conclusion.

Martin Heidegger, a prominent critic of nihilism in its various forms, attributes what he regards as the nihilistic malaise of the West – astutely predicted by Nietzsche – to an inherited tangle of epistemological and metaphysical misconceptions that have led to a disastrous 'forgetfulness of being'. Only if we go back to the philosophical roots of the Western world, in the profound reflections of the Presocratic philosophers that Heidegger considers to have been distorted by Plato and Aristotle (these distortions having plagued us ever since), can we come to understand how the objectifying, separating, controlling and ego-centred modes of present thought and experience have led us to nihilism. Heidegger's solution lies in our learning radically to 're-vision' reality, to become receptive to the healing presence of being that shines through all beings and binds us to one another and to the world (Heidegger 1953). A powerful explication and defence of Heidegger's general approach to nihilism is contained in Levin (1988).

Arguments for cosmic and existential nihilism, like those for the other forms of nihilism, are complex and varied. Detailed analysis and criticism of some of them can be found in Crosby (1988), which probes beneath the arguments themselves to the crucial assumptions that underlie them, many of which stem from the legacy of seventeenth- and eighteenth-century Western thought (some examples of these assumptions are given below). The book concludes that, while philosophical nihilism has important lessons to teach us, it is ultimately a distorted and one-sided view of ourselves and the experienced world, one that turns on highly questionable assumptions.

Many such assumptions lie behind some of the arguments put forward in support of cosmic nihilism. Proponents believe that if claims about the universe cannot be convincingly shown to correspond to what it is in and of itself, apart from human experience and conceptualization, then we cannot be said to have any significant understanding of the universe. Additionally, they sometimes think that the presence of purposive activity in the universe (for example, in human beings and other animals on earth) is not enough to give it meaning – for this there must be a discernible purpose of the universe *as a whole*. Such thinkers often demand that the universe must have a 'human face', have its ground in a personal divine Being and be centred on humans and their distinctive concerns. Others rely on natural science as the final arbiter of the nature of nature and assume that, since science discovers no values in nature but only descriptive facts and relations, nature is devoid of value. Some suppose that if, as natural science claims, the universe had an accidental beginning (the Big Bang) and will eventually come to an absolute end (its inevitable entropic death, assuming that the universe is a closed system) then it follows that the universe can have no meaning.

Similarly, proponents of existential nihilism use arguments which are informed by a number of disputable assumptions. They may believe that a life which ends in annihilating death cannot be said to have meaning, or that there is too much suffering, or constant threat of suffering, in human life for it to be meaningful. They sometimes conceive of time as a series of disconnected moments, and hence believe that our lives in time can have no cumulative pattern or significance. Often they assume that meaningful values, including the existential ones that relate to the course and direction of our lives, must be conferred on us from on high and thus have a transcendent source and sanction. Others believe that values, including existential ones, can have no significance or weight unless they are absolute, unconditioned, timeless and universal, or that our lives are meaningless if they are the outcome of a process of biological evolution, guided by the principle of natural selection that is non-purposive and non-designed. That human beings are locked in their individual subjectivities and doomed to invent arbitrary meanings for themselves, with no objective rules or standards, is yet another assumption that often underlies the existential nihilist's argument.

All these suppositions are open to serious criticism. When they are brought under careful scrutiny, arguments that depend on them lose much of their force. Still, there is considerable truth about the world and the human condition that nihilistic arguments in general can bring home to us. Reflection on such arguments can sharpen our philosophical vision in fundamental and positive ways.

See also: ANARCHISM; LIFE, MEANING OF; MORAL SCEPTICISM; NISHITANI KEIJI; SCEPTICISM

References and further reading

* Camus, A. (1942) *The Myth of Sisyphus and Other Essays*, trans. J. O'Brien, New York: Alfred A. Knopf, 1955. (Sisyphus is a symbol of human beings learning to live defiantly despite their inability to find meaning in the universe; see §2 above; relatively easy.)

Carr, K. (1992) *The Banalization of Nihilism: Twentieth-Century Responses to Meaninglessness*, Albany, NY: State University of New York Press. (Examines Nietzsche's diagnosis of nihilism as an impending crisis of the West and compares responses to it given by Karl Barth and Richard Rorty; warns that nihilism has become so 'banal' in its postmodern form as to sanction a dangerous complacency about existing structures of thought, practice and value; moderately difficult.)

* Cioran, E.M. (1949) *A Short History of Decay*, trans. R. Howard, Oxford: Blackwell, 1975. (Plumbs the depths of the mood and outlook of existential nihilism; mentioned in §3 above; relatively easy.)

* Crosby, D.A. (1988) *The Specter of the Absurd: Sources and Criticisms of Modern Nihilism*, Albany, NY: State University of New York Press. (Explicates and critically examines arguments for moral, epistemological, cosmic and existential nihilism, with an emphasis on existential nihilism and ways the other types relate to it; see §4 above; moderately difficult.)

* Dostoevskii, F. (1871–2) *The Possessed*, trans. C. Garnett, New York: Heritage Press, 1959. (A novel about the destructive lives of members of a revolutionary nihilist society in nineteenth century Russia; see §1 above; relatively easy.)

Evans, F.J. (1993) *Psychology and Nihilism: A Genealogical Critique of the Computational Model of Mind*, Albany, NY: State University of New York Press. (Argues that cognitive psychology not only reflects the currents of nihilism rampant in our time, but also reinforces them with truncated, technocratic, inadequate conceptions of human mind, human language, human creativity and human beings themselves; moderately difficult.)

* Heidegger, M. (1953) *An Introduction to Metaphysics*, trans. R. Manheim, Garden City, NY: Doubleday & Company, Anchor Books, 1959. (Traces the rise of nihilism in the West to epistemological and metaphysical ideas going back to the Hellenic Age in Greece; see §4 above; difficult.)

* Levin, D.M. (1988) *The Opening of Vision: Nihilism and the Postmodern Situation*, New York and

London: Routledge. (Argues that the advent of nihilism is both cause and consequence of a corrupted egocentric and patriarchical vision; pleads for a new metaphysical and social vision that draws on the thought of Heidegger, Merleau-Ponty, Foucault and others; see §4 above; difficult.)

* Monod, J. (1970) *Chance and Necessity*, trans. A. Wainhouse, New York: Vintage Books, 1972. (Natural science's 'postulate of objectivity' shows the world and human life to be devoid of value, so values must be arbitrarily created; see §2 above; moderately difficult.)

* Nietzsche, F. (1883–5) *Thus Spoke Zarathustra*, trans. W. Kaufmann, New York: Viking, 1966. (Nietzsche's prophet Zarathustra proclaims the death of God and its consequences; see §1 above; moderately difficult.)

* —— (1901) *The Will to Power*, trans. W. Kaufmann and R.J. Hollingdale, ed. W. Kaufmann, New York: Vintage Books, 1968. (Excerpts from Nietzsche's notebooks in the 1880s that announce the advent of nihilism in the West and defend 'active' nihilism against 'passive' nihilism; see above §1; moderately difficult.)

Ritter, J. and Gründer, K. (eds) (1971–) 'Nihilismus', *Historisches Wörterbuch der Philosophie* (Historical dictionary of philosophy), Basel/Stuttgart: Schwabe & Company, vol. 6, 846–54. (Extensive survey of uses of the term 'nihilism' in literature, philosophy, theology and politics, going back to the twelfth century.)

Rosen, S. (1969) *Nihilism: A Philosophical Essay*, New Haven, CT: Yale University Press. (Attributes the presence of nihilism in today's world to a series of past philosophical decisions; especially attacks the modern detachment of 'reason' from its traditional close association with 'good'; moderately difficult.)

* Rue, L.D. (1994) *By the Grace of Guile: The Role of Deception in Natural History and Human Affairs*, New York: Oxford University Press. (Accepts the truth of what he regards as epistemological, moral and cosmic nihilism, and argues that only deception or illusion can enable human beings to live in the face of this truth; discussed in §4 above; moderately difficult.)

* Sartre, J.-P. (1938) *Nausea*, trans. L. Alexander, New York: New Directions, 1964. (A novel about a character who lives nihilism through in its various forms and experiences a sickening loathing for himself, other humans, and the world; see §2 above; relatively easy.)

* —— (1943) *Being and Nothingness*, trans. H. Barnes, New York: Washington Square Press, 1966. (An approach to existential meaning, epistemic truth and moral values that turns on a radical doctrine of human freedom; see §3 above; difficult.)

* Schopenhauer, A. (1818) *The World as Will and Idea*, trans. R.B. Haldane and J. Kemp, 2nd edn, London: Routledge & Kegan Paul, 3 vols, 1957. (Portrays the world and humans as expressions of the inexorable workings of a cosmic will that is without purpose or meaning and causes an overbalance of suffering in all forms of sentient life, including our own; see §2 above; difficult.)

* Stirner, M. (1845) *The Ego and His Own*, trans. J. Carroll, New York: Harper & Row, 1971. (Presents an ego-centred nominalism implying moral, epistemological and cosmic nihilism; see §2 above; relatively easy.)

Tillich, P. (1953) *The Courage to Be*, New Haven, CT: Yale University Press. (Draws on the ideas of Heidegger, among others, to discover resources for coping with the threats of 'non-being' in the forms of fate and death, guilt and moral self-condemnation, emptiness and meaninglessness. Finds 'the courage to be' in the 'God above God,' that is, the power of 'being-itself'; moderately difficult.)

* Turgenev, I. (1862) *Fathers and Sons*, trans. M.R. Katz, New York: W.W. Norton, 1994. (A novel about the seductions of nihilism for youths in nineteenth-century Russia; see §1 above; relatively easy.)

DONALD A. CROSBY

NIHILISM, RUSSIAN

The term 'Nihilist', although it was first used in Russian as early as 1829, only acquired its present significance in Turgenev's novel Ottsy i deti *(Fathers and Sons) (1862), where it is applied to the central character, Bazarov. Thereafter Nihilism quickly became the subject of polemical debate in the journal press and in works of literature. The Nihilists were the generation of young, radical, non-gentry intellectuals who espoused a thoroughgoing materialism, positivism and scientism. The major theorists of Russian Nihilism were Nikolai Chernyshevskii and Dmitrii Pisarev, although their authority and influence extended well beyond the realm of theory. Nihilism was a broad social and cultural movement as well as a doctrine.*

Russian Nihilism negated not the normative significance of the world or the general meaning of human existence, but rather a particular social, political and aesthetic order. Despite their name, the Russian Nihilists did hold beliefs – most notably in themselves and in the power of their doctrine to effect social change. It is, however, the vagueness of their positive programmes that distinguishes the Nihilists from the revolutionary socialists who followed them. Russian Nihilism is perhaps best regarded as the intellectual pool of the period 1855–66 out of which later radical movements emerged; it held the potential for both Jacobinism and anarchism.

1 The Nihilist movement: materialism as way of life
2 Nihilist doctrine

1 The Nihilist movement: materialism as way of life

Russian Nihilism is a phenomenon of cultural history just as much as a current in Russian thought. Educated Russians in the nineteenth century had a marked propensity not only to reflect on but also to live by ideas, and nowhere is this more evident than in the radical movement of the 1860s. In the decade following the death of Tsar Nicholas I the new class of educated commoners (the *raznochintsy*) felt the delayed intellectual impact of materialism, which they converted into an all-consuming worldview. Characteristic of the Nihilists was a rejection of all authorities other than materialism itself. In *Fathers and Sons* (1862) a Nihilist is defined as someone who 'does not bow down before any authorities, who does not take a single principle on faith'. Turgenev's Bazarov trusts only the exercise of his own rational faculties in the spirit of scientific inquiry.

The leading lights of Russian Nihilism were Nikolai CHERNYSHEVSKII and Dmitrii Pisarev, whose articles appeared in *Sovremennik* (The Contemporary) and *Russkoe slovo* (The Russian Word) (both of these radical journals were closed for good after the attempted assassination of the Tsar in 1866). Chernyshevskii wrote prolifically, but by far his most influential work was *Chto delat'* (What Is To Be Done?) (1863), which became the catechism of the Nihilist 'new men'.

This novel offered them less a utopian vision than a practical programme of social action and a code of moral conduct. The main characters embodied the Nihilist ideals of equality, personal liberation and 'rational egoism'. The novel's artlessness, moreover, provided an excellent illustration of the new 'realist' aesthetics propounded by the Nihilists. Among Pisarev's most famous essays is 'Bazarov' (1862), a review of *Fathers and Sons* where he accepted Turgenev's depiction of the younger generation and thereby sparked an acrimonious debate within the Nihilist camp. Pisarev argued that Bazarov had enormous significance as a representative of the new worldview, and drew particular attention to his rejection of abstraction and his commitment to immediate and concrete action. Bazarov, unlike the earlier socially alienated 'superfluous men' of Russian literature, had both the will to act and the knowledge to act effectively. The Nihilist movement belonged to the young. It contained an element of protest not only against the existing order but also against the older generation, the intellectual 'fathers' who had been brought up on German Idealism rather than Feuerbach. The Nihilists gave short shrift to anything that smacked of sentimentality or romanticism. Rather like protesting youth in the twentieth century, the Nihilists cultivated their own style of dress and behaviour, which is particularly evident in contemporary descriptions of women radicals (*nigilistki*). One conservative newspaper noted that they were:

> usually very plain, exceedingly ungracious, so that they have no need to cultivate curt, awkward manners; they dress with no taste and in impossibly filthy fashion, rarely wash their hands, never clean their nails, often wear glasses, always cut their hair, and sometimes even shave it off.
>
> (Moser 1964: 44)

The 'woman question' did in fact occupy a prominent place in Nihilist social thought. In *What Is To Be Done?* Chernyshevskii affirmed the importance of women's personal liberation and sexual freedom. The Nihilist striving for women's emancipation was reflected in the phenomenon of fictitious marriages: in the 1860s a young woman wanting to gain independence from her family might search out a young man willing to go through the nuptial rites with her, and would then be free to join a sewing cooperative or disappear abroad to study.

For the young Nihilists materialism was less a philosophical doctrine than an article of faith and a guide to action: it carried with it a new ethic of scientific inquiry, personal liberation and social activism. The Nihilists were convinced that the methods of the natural sciences would bring benefits if applied to the study of man, art and society. They asserted the prime social value of work and advocated the introduction of rational forms of social cooperation, most notably in the communal movement. But perhaps most importantly of all, they were blessed with boundless faith in themselves and their ideas. As Pisarev wrote in his essay 'Mysliashchii proletariat' ('The Thinking Proletariat') (1865), the new man 'believes in his reason and in his reason alone'. For the Nihilist the intellectual emancipation of the individual came before social emancipation. Enlightenment was to be spread throughout society by the actions of an elite group of 'new men'.

The contemporary observer Nikolai Strakhov suggested that 'Nihilism itself hardly exists, although there is no denying the fact that Nihilists do'. The Nihilists undoubtedly did form a significant social movement, but their activities were underpinned by a materialist doctrine. The philosophical content of Nihilism will be examined in greater detail in the next section.

2 Nihilist doctrine

The 1860s were once described by Trotsky as 'a brief eighteenth century' in Russian thought. The Nihilist thinkers sought to assimilate and resynthesize the main trends in Western materialism and positivism. As usual in Russia, imported ideas were treated selectively and deployed in quite distinctive intellectual formations.

The best-known and most scandalous statements of the Nihilist position came in the field of aesthetics. In Russia from the 1840s onwards literature could be both the instrument and the subject of social, philosophical and political debate: for the Nihilists too it was both a target and a weapon. Chernyshevskii's master's thesis, 'Esteticheskie otnosheniia iskusstva k deistvitel'nosti' ('The Aesthetic Relations of Art to Reality') (1855), identifies the main criteria of artistic value in the new 'realist' aesthetic. Chernyshevskii counters idealism in aesthetics, and argues that art is always aesthetically inferior to reality. Art's worth is thus defined by its faithfulness to reality. The artist, however, does more than provide naturalistic snapshots of life: the work of art contains not only accurate depiction, but also explanation and assessment of reality. Chernyshevskii's views helped to spawn a new school of civic-minded criticism which assessed works of literature for the faithfulness and 'typicality' of their depiction of contemporary Russian society. The most brilliant representative of this school was Chernyshevskii's friend and disciple Nikolai Dobroliubov, whose essays included an impassioned sociological reading of Goncharov's *Oblomov* (this novel contained perhaps the most celebrated Russian depiction of social superfluousness). Pisarev summed up well the demands the Nihilists made of the artist: 'The true, "useful" poet must know and understand everything that at a given moment interests the best, the most intelligent, and the most enlightened representatives of his age and nation'. Realist aesthetics, in its concept of the 'typical', did not in fact manage to part entirely with the Hegelian notion of the ideal: art was expected not simply to depict reality, but to single out the 'most real' part of reality.

For the Russian Nihilists, reality was the world of nineteenth-century science. Taking its lead from the contemporary German materialists BÜCHNER, Vogt

and Moleschott, their worldview left no room for anything other than force and matter. In his essay, 'Antropologicheskii printsip v filosofii' ('The Anthropological Principle in Philosophy') (1860), Chernyshevskii mounts an assault on philosophical dualism and abstraction, arguing that materialism proves the 'unity of the human organism'. He concedes the distinction between 'moral' and 'material' phenomena, but maintains that it is one of degree rather than of kind. Chernyshevskii's 'anthropological principle' was intended to prove that the methods of the natural sciences were applicable to the study of man. As these methods became more sophisticated, the moral sciences would inevitably attain complete understanding of the causes of human behaviour.

To his scientism and determinism Chernyshevskii added an ethics based on 'rational egoism'. 'Good' and 'bad', he argues, are not inherent in human nature. Man always acts in his own interests and does what is 'useful' for him. Good is thus defined as 'the superlative of utility'. Chernyshevskii's theory of rational self-interest is underpinned by the optimistic assumption that the interests of society and those of the individual naturally coincide. If individuals, acting as always in their own interests, commit 'bad' deeds, then it is the social order that must be at fault. Chernyshevskii's determinism was thus profoundly polemical. In his essay 'The Thinking Proletariat' (1865) Pisarev makes the similar argument that selfishness is useful if it is allowed to find a productive outlet, and that work is the best way of harmonizing the interests of all members of a society. Idleness and exploitation, on the other hand, lead man's natural selfishness to take destructive forms. In the Nihilist 'new men' individual qualities and the general interest are inseparable: 'goodness and truth, honesty and knowledge, character and reason are identical'.

Largely because of this faith in the natural state of harmony between the individual and society, the Nihilists tended to leave their social programmes vague. They were certainly committed to a form of secular socialist society with guaranteed rights for the individual, but their main contribution to social debate was their rejection of existing authority. The Nihilists were, however, unswerving in their commitment to social change through the spread of enlightenment and in particular the natural sciences. They believed that if true 'understanding' was brought to people through the dissemination of knowledge, social progress would inevitably follow. Pisarev laid particular emphasis on the role of education in social change. In his essay 'The Realists' (1864) he argues that science must find its way into the everyday life of the common people if they are to break out of the vicious circle of poverty and ignorance. With a characteristically Russian faith in the power of ideas, he asserts that the wise investment of 'intellectual capital' can 'diminish the quantity of human pains'.

See also: NIHILISM; POSITIVISM, RUSSIAN; RUSSIAN MATERIALISM: 'THE 1860S'

List of works

Chernyshevskii, N.G. (1939–53) *Polnoe sobranie sochinenii* (Collected Works), Moscow: Khudozhestvennaia literatura, 16 vols. (The standard Soviet edition of Chernyshevskii's works.)

—— (1863) *Chto delat'*, St Petersburg; trans. B.R. Tucker, *What Is To Be Done?*, New York: Vintage Books, 1961. (An English translation of Chernyshevskii's famous and highly influential novel.)

—— (1953) *Selected Philosophical Essays*, Moscow: Foreign Language Publishing House. (A useful selection of Chernyshevskii's main writings translated into English.)

Dobroliubov, N.A. (1956) *Selected Philosophical Essays*, Moscow: Foreign Language Publishing House. (A selection of essays by Chernyshevskii's friend and disciple.)

Pisarev, D.I. (1958) *Selected Philosophical, Social and Political Essays*, Moscow: Foreign Language Publishing House. (A useful selection of Pisarev's writings which includes all the essays mentioned in this entry.)

—— (1955) *Sochineniia v chetyrëkh tomakh* (Works in Four Volumes), Moscow: Khudozhestvennaia literatura. (The standard Soviet edition of Pisarev's works.)

References and further reading

Coquart, A. (1946) *Dmitri Pisarev (1840–68) et l'idéologie du nihilisme russe* (Dmitri Pisarev (1840–68) and the Ideology of Russian Nihilism), Paris. (A good, detailed account of Pisarev's thought and its place in the social and philosophical debate of the 1860s; has a useful bibliography.)

Edie, J.M. *et al.* (eds) (1965) *Russian Philosophy*, Chicago, IL: Quadrangle Books, 3 vols. (A very useful edited selection of Russian philosophy; vol. 2 contains extracts from important works by Chernyshevskii and Pisarev, along with short introductions.)

Masaryk, T.G. (1919) *The Spirit of Russia*, London: Allen & Unwin, 2 vols. (An old but excellent account of Russian philosophy, with a substantial chapter on Nihilism in vol. 2.)

Moser, C. (1964) *Antinihilism in the Russian Novel of the 1860's*, The Hague: Mouton. (Although the main focus of this book is anti-Nihilism, it has two excellent introductory chapters on the history and background of Nihilism itself.)

Paperno, I. (1988) *Chernyshevsky and the Age of Realism: A Study in the Semiotics of Behavior*, Stanford, CA: Stanford University Press. (An important study of the cultural significance of Chernyshevskii's *What Is To Be Done?*)

Stites, R. (1991) *The Women's Liberation Movement in Russia: Feminism, Nihilism, and Bolshevism 1860–1930*, Princeton, NJ: Princeton University Press, 2nd edn. (This fine social and intellectual history of the women's movement has an interesting chapter on the Nihilist contribution to the cause.)

* Turgenev, I. (1862) *Ottsy i deti*; trans. M.R. Katz, *Fathers and Sons*, New York: W.W. Norton, 1994. (Referred to in §1.)

STEPHEN LOVELL

NIPHUS, AUGUSTINUS *see* NIFO, AGOSTINO

NIRVĀṆA

The aim of the spiritual life was already described as nirvāṇa before the rise of Buddhism around the fifth century BC, but it is in the Buddhist context that it is most well known. In earlier Buddhist works and in popular usage to the present day it refers to the goal of Buddhist discipline, reached by systematic training in morality, meditation and intellect. That goal consists of the final removal of the disturbing mental elements which obstruct a peaceful and clear state of mind, together with a state of awakening from the mental sleep which they induce. Such an awakening (often referred to in English as 'enlightenment') enables a clear perception of fundamental truths, the understanding of which is essential to mental freedom. Later, the term was often applied more narrowly to a specific aspect of the awakened condition – that aspect of this experience which was considered to be unchanging, that is, an element which is not the product of either mental construction in particular, or of causes and conditions in general.

1   **Origins and etymology of the word *nirvāṇa***
2   **Earlier accounts**
3   **European understanding of the term**
4   **Schools of mainstream Buddhism**
5   **In the Mahāyāna systems**
6   **Synonyms for *nirvāṇa***

1 Origins and etymology of the word nirvāṇa

Nirvāṇa (or nibbāna in the Pāli language) means literally 'blowing out' or 'quenching'. However, since the term is probably pre-Buddhist, its etymology is not necessarily conclusive for determining its exact meaning as the highest goal of early Buddhism. In fact, many Buddhists have traditionally preferred to explain it as absence of the weaving (vāna) activity. Here weaving is a metaphorical description of the mind's manner of operation when distorted by ignorance of the true nature of things and by craving for possessions and states of being. It is probably not accidental that such a definition does not tell us what exactly nirvāṇa is. Buddhists have generally avoided any verbal description of their goal and have tended to doubt whether it is possible to describe it.

The earliest Buddhist texts seem to use the word nirvāṇa to designate the final end (accantaniṭṭhā) of the path taught by the Buddha. As such it is by definition supreme happiness and ultimate peace. Probably they shared this with other religious-philosophical schools of the period. The same texts generally go to great lengths to avoid discussing what happens to the attainer of this goal after death. The Buddha is presented as 'not having declared' that such a one exists after death or does not exist then. Nor did he declare that both of these were the case. Even a denial of both possibilities was ruled out as an option. Indeed, concern with the nature of that goal of happiness and ultimate peace is presented as unhelpful to the task of achieving it. The simile of the man injured by a poisoned arrow is commonly cited in this context: in the immediate situation he should focus upon obtaining medical treatment rather than be concerned with specific details of the arrow, poison or archer. Similarly the urgency of attaining nirvāṇa is such that it is better not to be overconcerned with details of its nature and consequences.

From the origins of the word itself it is possible to assess the earlier position which is being reacted to here. Nirvāṇa derives from the root 'to blow' and means the blowing out or quenching of a lamp flame or a fire. In one use it is the fires of passions, such as greed and hate, which are put out by the enlightened sage. In another usage, applicable to the time of death, the flame of the lamp covers all types of ordinary human activity. These cease at the death of the enlightened saint, like the flame of a lamp. In pre-Buddhist usage this would probably have been understood as meaning that the fire had returned to the latent or potential state from which it arose in the first place. Contrary to its modern ascription, the metaphor would not have had connotations of annihilation. The Buddha himself seems to have resisted this kind of understanding, perhaps because it was too closely associated with the pantheistic self of the Upaniṣads, or the life-monad of the Jains and others (see JAINA PHILOSOPHY). Rather, the Buddhist texts tend to suggest that language is inapplicable to the case since words are in the last analysis derived from sensory experience, which is taken to include memory and imagination.

2 Earlier accounts

Most mentions of nirvāṇa refer to it as the goal, or as supreme happiness with many synonyms which make clear that it is conceived as the ultimate security, purity and peace. A few of the early texts, mostly preserved in Pāli or Chinese translations, provide a little more information. Someone who experiences nirvāṇa is explicitly declared to be conscious, but not conscious of 'anything which the mind has seen, heard, sensed, felt, obtained, sought or explored' (Anguttara Nikāya (The Book of Gradual Sayings) IV 320; 353–8). This experience is differentiated from various kinds of meditative attainment.

Later a clear distinction between nirvāṇa attained in life and nirvāṇa entered into at the point of death begins to develop. The term parinirvāṇa is often used for the latter although it does not acquire this meaning until a later date – in the earliest sources it is simply an alternative to nirvāṇa. (Strictly, nirvāṇa is the state of release; parinirvāṇa is the act of attaining release.) However, relatively early sources (although not the very oldest) do contain the important simile of the ocean which shows no sign of filling or diminishing no matter how much water is poured into it by streams or rainfall. Similarly, even if many enter parinirvāṇa by means of the element of nirvāṇa without any remaining 'clinging', the element of nirvāṇa shows no sign of filling or diminishing. Here 'clinging' is a technical term referring to the appropriation or identification which occurs as a result of desire. Since ordinary human existence and mental process are understood as the result of such appropriation, there can be no continuation in the familiar conditions of existence once it has ceased. The point of the simile is no doubt to emphasize that nirvāṇa transcends normal rules.

3 European understanding of the term

The Oxford English Dictionary (first edition) defines nirvāṇa thus: 'In Buddhist theology, the extinction of individual existence and absorption into the supreme spirit, or the extinction of all desires and passions and attainment of perfect beatitude'. Although versions of this definition have been widely used, it confuses the

Buddhist with Jain and Hindu understandings of the term (see KARMA AND REBIRTH, INDIAN CONCEPTIONS OF). Such descriptions of *nirvāṇa* are rather old in European thought. By the seventeenth century the French ambassador to the Siamese court, Simon de La Loubère referred to Portuguese authors as having translated a closely related Siamese term as 'it is annihilated' and 'it has become a God'. He rightly indicated that in the opinion of the Siamese: 'this is not a real Annihilation, nor an Acquisition of any divine Nature'. In fact, La Loubère translated *nirvāṇa* as 'disappearance', meaning disappearance from the world of birth and death. This is a very accurate understanding of the term and cannot be bettered today.

However, little attention was paid to La Loubère's more reliable account of the term, and the views he corrected remained current. Part of the reason for this was the tendency, especially in the seventeenth and eighteenth centuries, but still current in some circles, to understand Buddhism as a form of paganism and then to apply to it the critique which the Church Fathers directed against pagan philosophy. While there are some similarities between the two areas, such as the belief in reincarnation characteristic of some forms of classical philosophy, overall this is inappropriate.

4 Schools of mainstream Buddhism

By the time of the development of the first forms of organized Buddhist exegesis in the third or fourth centuries BC slightly more systematic ideas were found (see BUDDHIST PHILOSOPHY, INDIAN). *Nirvāṇa* as the element 'without any remaining clinging' was contrasted with the element 'with remaining clinging' (*saupādisesa*). This latter perception of *nirvāṇa* connoted the stages of partial enlightenment known as 'entering the stream'. As earlier texts most often referred to *nirvāṇa* 'without any remaining clinging' in the context of the Buddha's death, it began to be assumed that if what was attained at the death of the saint was the element of *nirvāṇa* 'without any remaining clinging', then there must be a corresponding element which was achieved at enlightenment. Henceforth, the element of *nirvāṇa* 'with remaining clinging' regularly referred to the achievement of enlightenment, normally envisaged as followed by a life of compassionate teaching activity. As a result of a later mistranslation or misunderstanding, the word translated as 'clinging' is often replaced by a word which may refer to 'possessions' (*saupadhiśeṣa*) and taken as referring to the mind and body as possessions appropriated during the process of rebirth. Alternatively, both *saupādisesa* and *saupadhiśeṣa*

could derive from *upādhisesa and *upātisesa respectively, meaning 'small remainder'. Thus, originally the meaning of the terms connoting 'clinging' could have been a reference to the small number of defilements remaining after 'entering the stream'.

Older sources are reticent on the subject of *nirvāṇa*. However, the same is not quite true of the canonical *abhidhamma* literature which took form between the second and fourth centuries BC. A characteristic feature of this literature is the analysis of mind and body in terms of a changing process of interacting and multiple events. These were referred to as *dhammas*, that is, particular truths as opposed to truth in general. (Earlier the word was used for all objects of mental awareness other than sense objects themselves.) The *abhidhamma* texts compiled openended lists of these events and tried to analyse which events occurred in which mental states. In this analysis they included *nirvāṇa* which they explained as differing from all other events in that it was not categorizable in spatial or temporal terms. At this stage there does not seem to have been any controversy as to its fundamental nature, nor was it conceived as mere absence: '*Nibbāna* exists; it does not change its nature. *Nibbāna* is permanent, constant, eternal, not subject to change' (*Kathāvatthu* (Points of Controversy) 122).

It is probable that the main concern of the *abhidhamma* texts was with the experience of *nirvāṇa* in life in terms of awakening or enlightenment. In that context *nirvāṇa* would be understood as the object or support for the enlightened mind, itself a composite characterized by the repeated presence of such events as faith and wisdom. Like the texts which preceded them, the works of this period did not attempt to comment upon the fate of the enlightened saint after death. No doubt the tradition of the undeclared questions was still too firmly established to allow this.

5 In the Mahāyāna systems

New tendencies in Indian religion, developing over some time, led to the formation of a new kind of Buddhism in the period AD 100–300: the Mahāyāna or 'great vehicle'. Attracting only minor interest in the beginning, the new movement gradually became increasingly influential. Devotional elements were strong in this school which arose essentially from an elaboration of the idealized biography of the BUDDHA and an extension of that into an ideal for all. An important feature was the prolongation of the path to enlightenment in order to enable the development of the superior qualities seen as necessary to achieve Buddhahood and work more effectively for the benefit of others. A side effect of this shift in focus was that *nirvāṇa* receded somewhat into the background, although in some subsequent schools of Mahāyāna Buddhism, such as Chan/Zen or Tantra, it was ultimately to return to the foreground as something attainable in this life.

New schools of thought developed within the overall Mahāyāna with particular perspectives. Probably the oldest of these was the Madhyamaka (see BUDDHISM, MĀDHYAMIKA: INDIA AND TIBET). This laid stress on the idea that there was no difference between *nirvāṇa* and existence in the round of rebirths (*saṃsāra*). They seem to have meant by this that *nirvāṇa* is simply a name for ordinary existence with ignorance removed. In other words it is not to be viewed as an entity existing somewhere else. It is rather a transformation of normal experience.

Some later Mahāyāna writings placed an emphasis on '*nirvāṇa* without foundation' as part of the path to the highest goal. This means that true enlightenment involves neither acceptance nor rejection of birth and death. More remarkably, it implies neither accepting nor rejecting *nirvāṇa* itself, but instead encouraging minds to be free of dependency upon or need for any objects at all, whether those objects are internal or external.

6 Synonyms for *nirvāṇa*

A common error in examining a concept such as *nirvāṇa* is to focus too much on the exact denotation of the term at the expense of its wider associations and context, not taking into account the number of synonyms frequently used to describe it. In a practical, experiential context it is referred to as 'freedom' or 'awakening'; 'peace' or 'bliss'. In each case the implication is that it is this in the ultimate possible degree. Words which imply safety or complete protection are commonly used in relation to it, as are words which imply permanence, unchangingness or unendingness. These latter denotations are close to the general terms used in Indian religions to describe the highest goal of the spiritual life. Many such words are regularly used to describe *nirvāṇa*. So it is liberation (*mokkha/mokṣa*), wholeness (*kevala/kaivalya*), truth and the like; it is the deathless and the imperishable. Many of these terms are given a specific Buddhist sense, but their general connotation in the world at large should not be neglected. A specific example might be that *nirvāṇa* is the *amṛta*, or the deathless, but it is important that this refers to the nectar which confers immortality upon the gods. In the Buddhist context it refers to a condition in which there is no death, although it is clearly intended to have the positive associations of Indian myth.

See also: BUDDHISM, ĀBHIDHARMIKA SCHOOLS OF; BUDDHIST CONCEPT OF EMPTINESS; COSMOLOGY AND COSMOGONY, INDIAN THEORIES OF; GOD, INDIAN CONCEPTIONS OF; HEAVEN, INDIAN CONCEPTIONS OF; MOMENTARINESS, BUDDHIST DOCTRINE OF; TIBETAN PHILOSOPHY

References and further reading

Hare, E.M. (trans.) (1955) *Anguttara Nikāya, or More Numbered Suttas* (The Book of Gradual Sayings), vol. 4, *The Books of the Sevens, Eights and Nines*, London: Pāli Text Society, 1955. (One of the major Pāli canonical works.)

Harvey, P. (1995) *The Selfless Mind: Personality, Consciousness and Nirvāna in Early Buddhism*, Richmond: Curzon Press. (Analyses most of the early sources.)

Norman, K.R. (1991) 'Death and the Tathāgata', *Studies in Buddhism and Culture* (in honour of Professor Egaku Mayeda), Tokyo: 1–11. (An essay that appears in a volume in honour of Mayeda.)

—— (1994) 'Mistaken Ideas about *Nibbāna*', in T. Skorupski and U. Pagel (eds) *The Buddhist Forum*, London: School of Oriental and African Studies, vol. 3: 211–25. (Two technical discussions by a leading specialist.)

Rahula, W. (1967) *What the Buddha Taught*, Bedford: Gordon Fraser, 2nd edn, 1959. (An influential account of the basic issues by a Sinhalese Buddhist monk.)

Saddhātissa, H. (1970/1) *Buddhist Ethics*, London, New York: Allen & Unwin/Braziller. (A Sinhalese Buddhist monk taking a slightly more traditionalist approach. Chapter 8 is especially interesting.)

Slater, R.H.L. (1951) *Paradox and Nirvāna*, Chicago, IL: University of Chicago Press. (An older work which deserves to be better known.)

* Tissa Moggalīputta (*c.*246 BC) *Kathāvatthu* (Points of Controversy), trans. Shwe Zan Aung and C.A.F. Rhys Davids, London: The Pāli Text Society, 1979. (The standard English translation of the earliest collection of points disputed by Buddhists during the first two centuries after the Buddha's career, part of the *abhidhamma* section of the Pāli canon.)

Vajirañāna, P.M. (1962) *Buddhist Meditation in Theory and Practice: A General Exposition According to the Pāli Canon of the Theravāda School*, Colombo: M.D. Gunasena & Co. (Includes a convenient list of synonyms, some of which are discussed in §6. Pages 469–80 are especially interesting.)

Welbon, G.R. (1968) *The Buddhist Nirvāna and Its Western Interpreters*, Chicago, IL: University of Chicago Press. (Expansion of the material in §3.)

Williams, P. (1989) *Mahāyāna Buddhism: The Doctrinal Foundations*, London, New York: Routledge, esp. 52–4; 67–9; 181–4. (Presents the fundamental ideas of the Mahāyāna, as discussed in §4.)

L.S. COUSINS

NISHI AMANE (1829–97)

Among the campaigners for Japanese enlightenment in the early Meiji era, Nishi Amane was prominent for his philosophical achievements. He introduced European philosophy into Japan, especially the positivism of Auguste Comte and the utilitarianism of John Stuart Mill. The academic philosophy of modern Japan owes its origins to him.

The son of a court physician of the Tsuwano fief, Nishi was ordered by his lord to learn neo-Confucianism. Quite unsatisfied by this old-fashioned doctrine, he became aware of the necessity for studying Western science and fled the fief. In 1857 he was employed at the Foreign Books Research Institute by the Tokugawa government, and in 1862 he was sent by the government to Leiden in Holland on a mission to study the European social sciences. He studied law, statistics and economics formally under S. Vissering, but he also attended lectures by C.W. Opzoomer, then the leading historian of philosophy in Holland. Opzoomer introduced him to the works of Auguste COMTE and J.S. MILL.

Having returned home in 1865, Nishi continued to work for the Tokugawa government and, after the Restoration, was appointed to the Military Department of the Meiji government in 1870. He contributed much to the establishment of the modern Japanese military during his bureaucratic career, while as a private individual he introduced European philosophy and social sciences through his writing and teaching. From 1870 onwards he ran a private school called the Ikueisha. In 1873 he took part in the inauguration of the Meirokusha (the Meiji Six Society), an active scholarly society, and promoted the campaign for the enlightenment of the Japanese people.

Nishi's philosophical writings were motivated by criticism of Confucianism and praise for Western scientific thinking. In *Hyakuichi-shinron* (New Theory of the Hundred and One), published in 1874, he stressed the distinctions between morality and law and between human and natural principles. Embracing a dualistic attitude, he declared himself against the monism of the Confucians, especially the neo-Confucian world view. In *Jinsei-sanposetsu* (Theory of the Three Human Treasures), he enumerated health, knowledge and wealth as the *sine qua non* for happiness. He opposed these to the feudalistic values of docility, naivety, humility, deference, unselfishness and freedom from avarice. Thus he replaced the group-oriented morality with a utilitarian– individualistic one. In *Hyakugaku-renkan* (Links of All Sciences), which consists of drafts of his lectures at Ikueisha, he showed the classification and harmony of all disciplines, assigning the pivotal position to philosophy. He also explained Comte's theory of three stages and Mill's method of induction. Moreover, he published the first Japanese textbook on formal logic, *Chichi-keimo* (Logic and Enlightenment) in 1874, and a translation of Mill's *Utilitarianism* in 1877. As Thomas R.H. Havens states:

> Because Nishi's contributions... were the transmission of European ideologies and the invention of new academic terminology, rather than original thought systems of his own, Nishi did not found any new school of Japanese philosophy. However, his influence is to be found in the works of...various important philosophers in Meiji era.
>
> (Havens 1970: 218–9)

See also: JAPANESE PHILOSOPHY; LOGIC IN JAPAN

List of works

Nishi Amane (c.1866–89) *Nishi Amane zenshū* (The Complete Works of Nishi Amane), ed. T. Okubo, Tokyo: Munetaka Shobo, 1960–6, 3 vols. (Standard edition of Nishi's collected works.)

—— (1874) *Hyakuichi-shinron* (New Theory of the Hundred and One), in *Nishi Amane zenshū*, ed. T. Okubo, Tokyo: Munetaka Shobo, 1960–6. (Stresses the distinctions between morality and law and between human and natural principles.)

—— (1876) *Jinsei-sanposetsu* (Theory of the Three Human Treasures), in *Nishi Amane zenshū*, ed. T. Okubo, Tokyo: Munetaka Shobo, 1960–6. (Discusses the prerequisites for human happiness.)

—— (1877) *Hyakugaku-renkan* (Links of All Sciences), in *Nishi Amane zenshū*, ed. T. Okubo, Tokyo: Munetaka Shobo, 1960–6. (Drafts of lectures in which Nishi assigns positions to all the disciplines.)

—— (1874) *Chichi-keimo* (Logic and Enlightenment), in *Nishi Amane zenshū*, ed. T. Okubo, Tokyo: Munetaka Shobo, 1960–6. (The first Japanese textbook on formal logic.)

References and further reading

* Havens, T.R.H. (1970) *Nishi Amane and Modern Japanese Thought*, Princeton, NJ: Princeton University Press. (A detailed argument about Nishi's contribution to the Japanese revolution of ideas in the latter half of the nineteenth century.)

Miyagawa, T. (1962) *Kindai Nihon no Tetsugaku* (Japanese Modern Philosophy), Tokyo: Keisoshobo. (An explanation of the role played by Nishi at the beginning of modern Japanese philosophy; see especially pages 17–47.)

HIMI KIYOSHI

NISHIDA KITARŌ (1870–1945)

Considered Japan's first original modern philosopher, Nishida not only transmitted Western philosophical problems to his contemporaries but also used Buddhist philosophy and his own methods to subvert the basis of traditional dichotomies and propose novel integrations. His developmental philosophy began with the notion of unitary or pure experience before the split between subject and object. It developed to challenge other traditional opposites such as intuition and reflection, fact and value, art and morality, individual and universal, and relative and absolute. In its organic development, Nishida's philosophy reacted to critiques that it neglected the social dimension with political essays that sometimes aligned it with Japanese imperialism. It culminated in the 'logic of place', a form of thinking that would do justice to the contradictory world of human actions.

While a teacher in his twenties and thirties, Nishida fervently practiced Zen Buddhism under masters of the Rinzai lineage. After the publication in 1911 of his groundbreaking work *Zen no kenkyū* (An Inquiry Into the Good), he held professorships at Kyoto Imperial University until his retirement in 1929. Nishida produced numerous essays, developing a logic of consciousness and, from the 1930s, a philosophy of history and culture. In the 1940s, government leaders called upon the prestigious philosopher to write political tracts in support of Japanese expansionism. These writings were too abstract for politicians and military leaders, but were attacked as pro-Western by right-wing philosophers of the day, and later as imperialist by leftist critics. Because of his interest in Zen, his adaptation of Mahāyāna Buddhist logic and his influence on younger Kyoto colleagues such as TANABE HAJIME and students such as NISHITANI KEIJI, Nishida became known as the father of the 'Kyoto School' that dominated Japanese philosophy of religion up to the 1990s and informed much Buddhist–Christian dialogue (see KYOTO SCHOOL). It is possible, however, to understand 'Nishida philosophy' in a different light, as a systematic deconstruction of logical relations.

Four methods are evident in the development of Nishida's philosophy and help to clarify it. First is his way of laying a foundation; then, undermining or undergirding that foundation with something more basic, and ultimately, undermining any positive determination of a foundation. This method has similarities with that of NĀGĀRJUNA, except that Nishida works on broad foundations in several major treatises instead of particular propositions in a single analysis. Second, there is his way of subverting anthropocentric assumptions about the nature of knowledge and reality. Third, there is his method of exhibiting the self-reflective or self-mirroring structure of many logical and metaphysical categories. Fourth, there is his reversal of the order of things in many traditional hierarchies or explanatory schemes.

The preface to *Zen no kenkyū* expresses Nishida's initial project to explain everything on the basis of pure experience as the single reality. Pure or immediate experience is the moment or act of experiencing before there is an awareness of any difference between an object that is experienced and a subject who does the experiencing, before there is any thought, reflection or meaning. This singular and unitary foundation develops to include derivative and differentiated moments such as thought and reflection that seek a higher unity in reality. Reality objectified and unified as a whole is what is meant by nature, but as the activity of unifying it is spirit. Nishida undermines subjectivist views of experience by claiming that it precedes and founds the individual human subject; he subverts appeals to an ultimate difference between reality and consciousness, and he distances himself from anthropocentric views of consciousness by using the word 'God' for the infinite activity of unification. Unlike many commentators who see the notion of pure experience as the basis of all of Nishida's philosophy, however, he himself soon abandoned this notion, perhaps because of its psychological connotations, or perhaps because of its inherent logical difficulty in accounting for a meaningful world that arises from a meaning-less foundation.

Jikaku ni okeru chokkan to hansei (Intuition and Reflection in Self-Consciousness), written serially from 1913 to 1917, at first continues the project to explain immediate experience as a dynamic system that develops into reflective thought and judgment. Nishida follows neo-Kantians in undercutting the

13

traditional fact–value distinction; factual judgments intend truth that serves as a value or norm (see NEO-KANTIANISM). He appeals to the notion of intellectual intuition as a way to reconcile immediate experience with reflection, which coincide in the case of intuited self-awareness. By the end of this work he has shifted the foundation to what he considers the primary instance of self-awareness, namely absolute free will, because its activities of creating and valuing are more basic than intellectual knowing (see FREE WILL). In *Ishiki no mondai* (Problems of Consciousness), Nishida reverses the usual primacy not only of knowing over valuing, but also of feeling over willing and sensing over feeling, by proposing that the latter term of each pair is the more concrete reality. *Geijutsu to dōtoku* (Art and Morality) names the absolute will as the source of moral decision making and creative artistic activity. In later works, however, Nishida eventually abandons the notion of absolute will as a basis, because the activity of the will eludes reflection and thus would be an unknowable foundation.

Essays in *Hataraku mono kara miru mono e* (From That Which Acts to That Which Sees) and *Ippansha no jikakuteki taikei* (The Self-Conscious System of Universals) begin to develop Nishida's 'logic of place' (*basho*). His notion of a universal (see UNIVERSALS) as a place may be interpreted as a founding level of discourse that resolves contradictions on less comprehensive levels. Ultimately, the place that holds differences or contradictions together is absolute nothingness, the place beyond discursive determination. This notion undermines previous attempts to locate a foundation with a positive description such as pure experience, self-awareness, or absolute will. Yet the self-reflective structure of self-awareness, in which a whole is mirrored or reflected in a part of itself, is still evident in universals of all levels, including the ultimate nothingness. We may read 'self-reflective' for the term 'self-conscious' (*jikakuteki*) in the above works, or in *Mu no jikakuteki gentei* (The Self-Conscious Determination of Nothingness), published in 1932.

In *Tetsugaku no kompon mondai* (The Fundamental Problems of Philosophy) and seven volumes of *Tetsugaku ronbunshū* (Philosophical Essays), Nishida shifts from the scheme of place within place (in other words, less and more inclusive contexts) to the notions of 'absolutely contradictory self-identity' and 'the world as a dialectical universal'. The former notion lets opposites form unities through continual self-negation, for example, that of the world or the self, each a contradictory unity of many and one, and a 'continuity of absolute discontinuities'. The notion of the dialectical universal implies that the world is not another entity but rather a place of mediation

between individuals that co-arises and is codetermined with them. The exemplary case of individuality is not a material (and abstract) object like an atom, but rather the concrete human self, the focal point where the world reflects itself in itself. The self is not a subject that can be defined by adding specific differences to a genus (see ARISTOTLE §§7–8), but rather something that forms itself through continual self-negation of its previous identities, in other words, through 'acting intuition', acting arising from direct seeing. Self and world both find their immediate 'ground' in absolute nothingness, for nothing outside them can serve as their basis and yet they do not serve as a foundation for themselves.

Partially in tension with this individualism is the theme that the world in its most concrete manifestation is a historical world determined by the interaction of different selves. Nishida's turn towards a philosophy of history from 1931 onwards culminated in a political and cultural philosophy, pronounced in the early 1940s, that envisaged a new, truly global world of nation-states (see NATION AND NATIONALISM). Each has its own principle that forms it in difference from and in interaction with all others. The state is the source of moral values. Nishida's own warning that Japan should not become imperialist is belied in his view that Japan is the nation-state that can awaken other nations, particularly Asian ones, to their truly global identities. The historical position of the Emperor is the empty centre of the body of the nation (*kokutai*) and the place from which emerge the creative possibilities of Japan as a nation and of being Japanese. In contrast to a view of history that sees present circumstances determined by past events and decisions oriented toward the future, Nishida sees history forming out of the 'absolute present' in which past and future are simultaneously co-present, each negating the other to allow infinite possibilities.

Nishida's last writings continue this nationalism but also make more explicit the religious themes latent throughout. In particular, *Bashoteki ronri to shūkyōteki sekaikan* (The Logic of Place and the Religious Worldview), published in 1945, addresses personal concerns of religious awareness and the death of the individual self. There the basic Other to oneself is not another self, nor the world as dialectical universal, nor even absolute nothingness, but rather the absolute or God (see ABSOLUTE, THE; GOD, CONCEPTS OF). The relation between the individual self and God is a kind of contradictory self-identity, more properly called an 'inverse correspondence' (*gyakutaiō*). The self properly relates to God only by dying to itself, to ego (a death that is not the same thing as the nihilation of the person), and so becomes its true self. For its part, the absolute arises through its self-negation in the relative self; it does not exclude the relative, nor even evil. Although God 'is absolute being only because he is absolute nothingness', this essay's implicit accommodations to Christian theism and Pure Land Buddhist faith seem at odds with Nishida's earlier anti-foundation of absolute nothingness.

See also: JAPANESE PHILOSOPHY; LOGIC IN JAPAN; PERCEPTION, EPISTEMIC ISSUES IN; POLITICAL PHILOSOPHY, HISTORY OF

List of works

Nishida Kitarō (1911–45) *Nishida Kitarō zenshū* (Complete Works of Nishida Kitarō), Tokyo: Iwanami Shoten, 1987–89, 3rd edn. (Complete works of Nishida Kitarō in nineteen volumes.)

—— (1911) *Zen no kenkyū* (An Inquiry into the Good), in *Nishida Kitarō zenshū*, Tokyo: Iwanami Shoten, 1987–89, 3rd edn, vol. 1; trans. Masao Abe and C. Ives, *An Inquiry Into the Good*, New Haven, CN: Yale University Press, 1990. (Nishida's first major work on consciousness.)

—— (1915) *Shisaku to taiken* (Contemplation and Experience), in *Nishida Kitarō zenshū*, Tokyo: Iwanami Shoten, 1987–89, 3rd edn, vol. 1. (On consciousness and perception.)

—— (1917) *Jikaku ni okeru chokkan to hansei* (Intuition and Reflection in Self-Consciousness), in *Nishida Kitarō zenshū*, Tokyo: Iwanami Shoten, 1987–89, 3rd edn, vol. 2; trans. V. Viglielmo with Y. Takeuchi and J. O'Leary, Albany, NY: State University of New York Press, 1987. (Appeals to the notion of intellectual intuition in a further attempt to explain the relations of thought and experience.)

—— (1920) *Ishiki no mondai* (The Problem of Consciousness), in *Nishida Kitarō zenshū*, Tokyo: Iwanami Shoten, 1987–89, 3rd edn, vol. 3. (Proposes that valuing, willing and feeling are more concrete than knowing and sensing.)

—— (1923) *Geijutsu to dōtoku* (Art and Morality), in *Nishida Kitarō zenshū*, Tokyo: Iwanami Shoten, 1987–89, 3rd edn, vol. 3; trans. D. Dilworth and V. Viglielmo, Honolulu, HI: University Press of Hawaii, 1973. (Names the absolute will as the source of moral decision making and creative activity.)

—— (1927) *Hataraku mono kara miru mono e* (From That Which Acts to That Which Sees), in *Nishida Kitarō zenshū*, Tokyo: Iwanami Shoten, 1987–89, 3rd edn, vol. 4. (Early development of Nishida's logic of place.)

—— (1930) *Ippansha no jikakuteki taikei* (The Self-Conscious System of Universals), in *Nishida Kitarō zenshū*, Tokyo: Iwanami Shoten, 1987–89, 3rd edn, vol. 5; 'Sōsetsu' (General Summary) trans. in R. Wargo, 'The Logic of Basho and the Concept of Nothingness in the Philosophy of Nishida Kitarō', Ann Arbor, MI: University Microfilms, 1972; 'Eichiteki sekai' (The Intelligible World) trans. in R. Schinzinger, *Intelligibility and the Philosophy of Nothingness*, Westport, CN: Greenwood Press, 1973. (The translations are of two central essays of the volume.)

—— (1932) *Mu no jikakuteki gentei* (The Self-Conscious Determination of Nothingness), in *Nishida Kitarō zenshū*, Tokyo: Iwanami Shoten, 1987–89, 3rd edn, vol. 6. (On self-reflection and self-awareness.)

—— (1933–4) *Tetsugaku no kompon mondai* (Fundamental Problems of Philosophy), in *Nishida Kitarō zenshū*, Tokyo: Iwanami Shoten, 1987–89, 3rd edn, vol. 7; trans. D. Dilworth, *Fundamental Problems of Philosophy*, Tokyo: Sophia University, 1970. (Later work on universals and self-identity.)

—— (1935–46) *Tetsugaku ronbunshū I –VII* (Philosophical Essays I–VII), in *Nishida Kitarō zenshū*, Tokyo: Iwanami Shoten, 1987–89, 3rd edn, vols 8–11; 'Sekai no jikodōitsu to renzoku' and 'Rekishiteki keiseisayō toshite no geijutsuteki sōsaku', trans. E. Weinmayr as 'Selbstidentität und Kontinuität der Welt' and 'Das künstlerische Schaffen als Gestaltungsakt der Geschichte', in *Die Philosophie der Kyōto-Schule*, ed. R. Ohashi, Munich: Karl Alber, 1990; 'Kokka riyū no mondai', trans. A. Jacinto Zavala as 'El problema de la razón de estado', in Nishida Kitarō, *Estado y Filosophía*, Zamora: El Colegio de Michoacan, 1985; 'Basho-teki ronri to shūkyōteki sekaikan', trans. Michiko Yusa as 'The Logic of *Topos* and the Religious Worldview', *The Eastern Buddhist* 19 (2):1–29 and 20 (1): 81–119, 1986–7. (Further work on universals and the self.)

—— (1937) *Zoku shisaku to taiken* (Contemplation and Experience, Continued), in *Nishida Kitarō zenshū*, Tokyo: Iwanami Shoten, 1987–89, 3rd edn, vol. 12. (Revisiting earlier work on perception.)

—— (1938) *Zoku shisaku to taiken igo* (Sequel to Contemplation and Experience, Continued), in *Nishida Kitarō zenshū*, Tokyo: Iwanami Shoten, 1987–89, 3rd edn, vol. 12. (Follows on from *Zoku shisaku to taiken*.)

—— (1938) 'Nihon bunka no mondai' (The Problem of Japanese Culture) in *Nishida Kitarō zenshū*, Tokyo: Iwanami Shoten, 1987–89, 3rd edn, vol. 12; trans. A. Jacinto Zavala, 'La crisis de la cultura Japonesa', in Nishida Kitarō, *Estado y Filosophía*, Zamora: El Colegio de Michoacan, 1985; trans. P.

Lavelle, *La Culture Japonaise en Question*, Paris: Publications Orientalistes de France, 1991. (Essay on culture.)

References and further reading

Abe Masao (1988) 'Nishida's Philosophy of Place', *International Philosophical Quarterly* 28 (4): 355–71. (A clear exposition from a Zen philosopher's point of view. Includes a comprehensive bibliography of translations and works on Nishida.)

Arisaka, Y. (1996) 'The Nishida Enigma: "The Principle of the New World Order"', *Monumenta Nipponica* 51 (1): 81–105. (A clarification of the background of Nishida's political views and translation of his 1943 essay on the new world order.)

Dilworth, D. (1973) 'Nishida Kitarō: Nothingness as the Negative Space of Experiential Immediacy', *International Philosophical Quarterly* 13 (4): 463–84. (An advanced exposition of Nishida's philosophy of nothingness.)

—— (ed.) (1987) *Last Writings: Nothingness and the Religious Worldview*, Honolulu, HI: University of Hawaii Press. (Comparative essays on Nishida and a free translation of 'Bashoteki ronri to shūkyōteki sekaikan' and a fragment, 'Concerning My Logic'.)

Feenberg, A. and Arisaka, Y. (1990) 'Experiential Ontology: The Origins of the Nishida Philosophy in the Doctrine of Pure Experience', *International Philosophical Quarterly* 30 (2): 173–205. (A clear account of the main ideas of Nishida's philosophy in light of his first work.)

Heisig, J. and Maraldo, J. (ed.) (1994) *Rude Awakenings: Zen, the Kyoto School and the Question of Nationalism*, Honolulu, HI: University of Hawaii Press. (The articles by Ueda, Yusa, Jacinto Zavala and Feenberg in particular examine the role of politics in Nishida's philosophy.)

Mafli, P. (1996) *Nishida Kitarō's Denkweg* (Nishida Kitarō's Way of Thought), Munich: Icidium. (A systematic survey in German of Nishida's entire 'way of thought'.)

Maraldo, J. (1989) 'Translating Nishida', *Philosophy East and West* 39 (4): 465–96. (Summaries of some of Nishida's major works and terms, as well as a review of English translations.)

Nishitani Keiji (1991) *Nishida Kitarō*, trans. Yamamoto Seisaku and J. Heisig, Berkeley, CA: University of California Press. (Clearly translated essays on Nishida's person and thought, by a renowned student and successor.)

JOHN C. MARALDO

NISHITANI KEIJI (1900–90)

Nishitani Keiji is generally regarded as the leading light of the 'second generation' Kyoto School of modern Japanese philosophy. Influenced by Zen thinkers from Chinese and Japanese Buddhism as well as by figures from the Western mystical and existential traditions, he is a pre-eminent voice in East–West comparative philosophy and late twentieth-century Buddhist–Christian dialogue. Primarily a philosopher of religion, Nishitani strove throughout his career to formulate existential responses to the problem of nihilism.

A student of the foremost figure in modern Japanese philosophy, NISHIDA KITARŌ, Nishitani Keiji spent most of his life writing and teaching in Kyoto and became one of the most prominent members of the Kyoto School of philosophy (see KYOTO SCHOOL). His earliest thinking developed under two different sets of influences. A classical education acquainted him with the Chinese Confucian and Buddhist traditions as well as with the philosophies of the Japanese schools of Zen Buddhism (see BUDDHIST PHILOSOPHY, JAPANESE), where he found the thinking of Dōgen, Hakuin and Takuan most congenial. At the same time he read widely among Western authors (he mentions in particular NIETZSCHE and DOSTOEVSKII, EMERSON and CARLYLE, as well as the Bible and St. Francis), and soon began to tackle such thinkers as PLOTINUS, MEISTER ECKHART, SCHELLING and HEIDEGGER. By his own account, his engagement with philosophy was not the result of an intellectual decision but was precipitated by a severe existential crisis in his youth.

In 1936, Nishitani went to study philosophy in Germany and ended up in Freiburg, where he worked closely with Heidegger, returning to Japan on the eve of the Second World War. The next several years saw the publication of a number of texts on political themes (some of which were clearly written under external pressure). Although some internationalist elements in these writings provoked the ire of the right wing at the time, Nishitani was subsequently relieved of his teaching duties at Kyoto University for several years on the grounds of the inflammatory 'nationalist' tone of his wartime writings. While he has been reviled by Marxists in Japan and the USA for his 'rightwing' politics, Nishitani's published works of the period are mild compared to those of some other members of the Kyoto School; and among the critics, political innuendo has generally substituted for contextualized readings of the relevant texts.

Nishitani's long-standing engagement with the problem of nihilism was furthered in a series of talks subsequently published in 1949, the Japanese title of which was simply *Nihirizumu* (Nihilism). In the framework of a synoptic account of nihilism as a historical phenomenon arising in nineteenth-century Europe, the author goes on to take it as an immediately existential problem. With the main focus on Nietzsche and a secondary concern with such thinkers as Max STIRNER and Heidegger, he shows their common concern with the issue of what he calls 'the fundamental integration of creative nihilism and finitude'. By this is meant that when the self is plumbed to sufficient depth, and if one can endure the experience of the *nihilum*, or void, at its base, that 'nihility' may eventually be realized as a creative nothingness. Turning at the end of the book to nihilism in modern Japan, Nishitani argues that the Nietzschean project of 'the self-overcoming of nihilism' has close parallels to 'the standpoint of Buddhism, and in particular to the standpoint of emptiness in the Mahāyāna tradition' (see BUDDHIST CONCEPT OF EMPTINESS; BUDDHIST PHILOSOPHY, JAPANESE). On this view, the nothingness of the abyss in Nietzsche would be similar to the nothingness (*mu*) or fertile emptiness (*kū*) that is central to Japanese Buddhist thinking.

The text that is widely regarded as Nishitani's most important work, *Shūkyō to wa nani ka?* (What Is Religion?), came out of a series of essays written in the late 1950s and was first published in book form in 1961. The emphasis is now very much on the Zen Buddhist tradition, with a secondary focus on Christianity and certain figures in Western philosophy (Meister Eckhart, Nietzsche, Heidegger). Like his teacher Nishida and several other senior members of the Kyoto School, Nishitani sees the Zen notion of 'absolute nothingness' as central to both philosophy and religion. True to the Mahāyāna Buddhist tradition, he stresses that absolute nothingness cannot be properly grasped by intellect alone but must rather be thought and experienced as the field or place from which all our thoughts and actions can flow. He thereby elaborates a radically non-anthropocentric worldview that allows us to realize ourselves as fully human beings-in-the-world, and from which the nothingness discussed by Nietzsche and Heidegger can be seen to 'fall short' of the Mahāyāna notion. However, to avoid entering a debate in competitive (rather than comparative) philosophy, let it simply be said in conclusion that the 'double genealogy' of Nishitani's thinking – incorporating strains of Confucian, Daoist and Buddhist thinking on the one hand, and Neoplatonic, Christian mystical, and German idealist and existential philosophy on the other – gives rise to a uniquely formidable philosophy.

See also: BUDDHIST PHILOSOPHY, JAPANESE; DŌGEN; JAPANESE PHILOSOPHY; KYOTO SCHOOL; NIHILISM

List of works

Nishitani Keiji (1949) *Nihirizumu* (Nihilism), trans. G. Parkes and Setsuko Aihara, *The Self-Overcoming of Nihilism*, Albany, NY: State University of New York Press, 1990. (The main focus is Nietzsche, with chapters on Stirner, Heidegger and Russian authors.)

—— (1961) *Shūkyō to wa nani ka?* (What is Religion?), trans. J. Van Bragt, *Religion and Nothingness*, Berkeley, CA: University of California Press, 1985. (The excellent translator's introduction includes a brief biographical account.)

—— (1985) *Nishida Kitarō*, trans. Yamamoto Seisaku and J.W. Heisig, Berkeley, CA: University of California Press, 1991. (A collection of essays from several decades, beginning in the mid-1930s.)

References and further reading

In Memoriam Nishitani Keiji (1992), special edition of *The Eastern Buddhist* 25 (1). (A collection of essays and personal reminiscences conveying a lively sense of Nishitani's personality.)

Unno Taitetsu (ed.) (1989) *The Religious Philosophy of Nishitani Keiji: Encounter with Emptiness*, Berkeley, CA: Asian Humanities Press. (A collection of conference papers; of broad range but uneven quality.)

Waldenfels, H. (1980) *Absolute Nothingness: Foundations for a Buddhist–Christian Dialogue*, trans. J.W. Heisig, New York: Paulist Press. (A pioneering work, now out of print but still a good introduction.)

GRAHAM PARKES

NOMINALISM

'Nominalism' refers to a reductionist approach to problems about the existence and nature of abstract entities; it thus stands opposed to Platonism and realism. Whereas the Platonist defends an ontological framework in which things like properties, kinds, relations, propositions, sets and states of affairs are taken to be primitive and irreducible, the nominalist denies the existence of abstract entities and typically seeks to show that discourse about abstract entities is analysable in terms of discourse about familiar concrete particulars.

In different periods, different issues have provided the focus for the debate between nominalists and Platonists. In the Middle Ages, the problem of universals was pivotal. Nominalists like Abelard and Ockham insisted that everything that exists is a particular. They argued that talk of universals is talk about certain linguistic expressions – those with generality of application – and they attempted to provide an account of the semantics of general terms rich enough to accommodate the view that universals are to be identified with them.

The classical empiricists followed medieval nominalists in being particularists, and they sought to identify the kinds of mental representations associated with general terms. Locke argued that these representations have a special content. He called them abstract ideas and claimed that they are formed by removing from ideas of particulars those features peculiar to the particulars in question. Berkeley and Hume, however, attacked Locke's doctrine of abstraction and insisted that the ideas corresponding to general terms are ideas whose content is fully determinate and particular, but which the mind uses as proxies for other particular ideas of the same sort.

A wider range of issues has dominated recent ontological discussion, and concern over the existence and status of things like sets, propositions, events and states of affairs has come to be every bit as significant as concern over universals. Furthermore, the nature of the debate has changed. While there are philosophers who endorse a nominalist approach to all abstract entities, a more typical brand of nominalism is that which recognizes the existence of sets and attempts to reduce talk about other kinds of abstract entities to talk about set-theoretical structures whose ultimate constituents are concrete particulars.

1   Introduction

In one use, 'nominalism' refers to a cluster of loosely-related philosophical and theological themes articulated by certain late fourteenth-century thinkers who were influenced by WILLIAM OF OCKHAM. These thinkers expressed doubts about the Aristotelian metaphysics, in particular its use in proving God's existence. They gave priority to faith over reason and emphasized the omnipotence of God in ways that often led to a Divine Command theory in ethics and a general scepticism about our knowledge of both causal relations and the substance–accident distinction.

Used this way, the term has its roots in the more common use which refers to a general theoretical orientation to questions about the existence and nature of abstract entities, an orientation exemplified in the work of Ockham himself. Those who are nominalists in this sense reject a Platonistic or realistic interpretation of discourse about things as diverse as properties, kinds, relations, propositions, sets, states of affairs and modality. Sometimes the nominalist is said to endorse the view that discourse of the sort in question is metalinguistic and that talk about the so-called abstract entities is really just talk about *nomina* or linguistic expressions. Characterized in this way, nominalism is sometimes said to stand opposed to conceptualism, another reductionist approach to ontological questions about abstract entities. The claim is that while the conceptualist insists that it is necessary to make reference to the activity of conceptual representation to accommodate the recalcitrant discourse, the nominalist denies this. But, first, not all of those who are called nominalists endorse a metalinguistic interpretation of the disputed discourse; and, second, since few philosophers have thought it possible to characterize language without referring to conceptual activity, to take nominalism as a view opposed to conceptualism yields the result that few of those thinkers normally taken to be nominalists turn out to deserve that label. Accordingly, it has become customary to construe as nominalistic any reductive approach to ontological questions about abstract entities that stands opposed to the Platonistic view.

2   The medieval period

The orientation we call nominalism is typically traced back to medieval debates over universals. A major source of these debates was Boethius' commentary on Porphyry's *Isagoge*, where we find a detailed discussion of the ontological status of universals (see BOETHIUS, A.M.S.; PORPHYRY §1). Boethius' commentary became a pivotal text for medieval philosophers, and by the twelfth century the debate over universals had become a dominant topic of philosophical concern. Two opposing views emerged. One, championed by WILLIAM OF CHAMPEAUX, was an extreme form of realism. On this view, a genus or a species is literally the same in all its members; the individuals falling under the kind are rendered distinct by the addition of forms to the common essence, and those forms are predicates of the essence. The opposing view, defended by ROSCELIN OF COMPIÈGNE, represented an extreme version of nominalism. Insisting that all entities are particulars, Roscelin argued that talk of universals is merely talk about linguistic expressions that can be applied to a number of different particulars, and he held to an austere interpretation of linguistic expressions where universals are mere *flatus vocis* or vocalizations.

Abelard attacked both views (see ABELARD, P. §5). He argued that since the forms which allegedly diversify any common essence are contraries, William's realism commits us to the view that a single entity can simultaneously exhibit incompatible properties; and he appealed to Aristotle's definition of the universal as that which can be predicated of many to call into question the claim that nonlinguistic entities can be universals. That definition, he contended, applies exclusively to things that can function as predicates in subject-predicate sentences, to what we nowadays call general terms. But while agreeing with Roscelin that we can 'ascribe universality to words alone' Abelard rejected Rocelin's claim that universals are mere *flatus vocis*, insisting that they are expressions that are significative or meaningful; and he argued that any adequate account of universals must show how, in the absence of a common essence, general terms can be meaningful. In doing so, it must answer two questions: (1) what is the cause of the imposition of a common name; and (2) what is it that we grasp when we grasp the signification of a common name?

Abelard's answer to the first question is disarming. The things to which the term 'man' applies, for example, all agree in being men. Their being men is the ground of the imposition of the common name 'man'. Abelard denies, however, that this agreement involves any common entity. He takes it to be an irreducibly primitive fact that all the things called men agree in that they are all men. In response to the second question, Abelard argues that what we grasp when we understand the common name 'man' is not any of the particular men named by that term; nor is it the collection consisting of all those particulars. To explain the kind of cognition associated with general terms, Abelard appeals to the distinction between perception and intellection. In perception, we grasp the particular named by a proper name; the cognition associated with general terms is, however, intellective. Here, the mind is directed toward an object of its own making, a *res ficta*. The *res ficta* is a kind of image, one that is *communis et confusa* (common and indifferent). It is common to all the items named by the associated general term and proper to none. Accordingly, it represents them all indifferently. Since it is something distinct from any of the particulars that fall under the Aristotelian categories, it is neither a substance nor an accident. It is the product of the intellect's activity of abstraction, and it is what is signified by the associated general term – it is what we grasp when we understand such a term.

The century after Abelard brought a number of different developments. The appearance of the complete Aristotelian corpus gave a clearer picture of Aristotle's views on universals, and the rich framework of semantical concepts associated with the developing terminist logic made possible the articulation of a more powerful form of nominalism than those defended by Roscelin and Abelard. That articulation came from William of Ockham (see WILLIAM OF OCKHAM §6). Following terminist logicians, Ockham distinguished between categorematic and syncategorematic terms. Categorematic terms are expressions whose significance derives from their having a 'definite and determinate signification'. Syncategorematic terms, by contrast, do not serve as signs of objects; their significance derives from the roles they play when used in conjunction with categorematic terms. Categorematic terms are further divided into discrete and common terms, where this is the contrast between expressions that signify just one object and expressions that signify many and so are predicable of many.

Like Abelard, Ockham identifies universals with common terms. Insisting that every existing thing is a particular, he construes the distinction between universals and particulars as a distinction between categorematic terms that signify just one thing and those that signify many. But where Abelard takes conceptual representations to be nonlinguistic items that function as the significata of the various common terms, Ockham wants to claim that a common term like 'man' signifies the various particulars of which it is truly predicable, and that the conceptual representation corresponding to the term 'man' is itself a linguistic entity. His idea is that thinking is inner dialogue, best understood by way of the familiar concepts appropriate to spoken and written language. Thus, concepts are mental terms, judgments are mental propositions, and inferences are mental syllogisms. Conceptual linguistic items differ, however, from spoken or written words in that while the latter are only conventionally significant, the former are natural signs. The phoneme 'man' has the meaning it does only by virtue of a complicated system of conventions, but the concept *man* is something whose intrinsic nature it is to play the linguistic role it does; and although we describe conceptual representations by the use of concepts derived from our characterization of spoken and written language, mental language is prior to both. Just as written language is an outgrowth of spoken language, spoken language is an extension of mental language, a sort of 'thinking out loud'.

The distinction between discrete and common terms, therefore, applies to conceptual representations, so that there are conceptual universals – conceptual representations that are predicable of many – and these are the genuine universals. Since they are naturally significant, the common terms of mental language are in their intrinsic nature items predicated of many; and their universality is the root of the merely conventional universality of the common terms of spoken and written language. Corresponding to the spoken/written term 'universal' there is a mental common term *universal*. To bring out the contrast between his own form of nominalism and its realist alternatives, Ockham tells us that this mental term is a term of second rather than first intention; it is a term that signifies not extramental entities but, rather, intentions of the soul, those that are in their intrinsic nature signs of many.

In characterizing the conceptual items that are in their intrinsic nature universals, Ockham mentions three possible views. One harkens back to Abelard and construes the mental term as a *res ficta* not found in any Aristotelian category; a second construes mental terms as qualities of the soul that serve as objects of its acts of understanding; the third identifies the mental term with the act of understanding itself. Over the course of his career, Ockham wavers between these views, but he ultimately comes to endorse the third view on grounds of theoretical simplicity.

Ockham's nominalism extends beyond a concern with universals and the distinction between common and discrete terms. He is also interested in the distinction between concrete and abstract terms, between terms like 'man' and 'humanity', 'courageous' and 'courage', and he is concerned to undermine what initially appears to be a plausible account of this distinction. A natural response to the distinction is to say that whereas concrete terms signify familiar concrete particulars (the particulars which are men and courageous), their abstract counterparts signify the abstract entities (humanity and courage) those particulars exhibit. Since the distinction between concrete and abstract terms is found in all ten Aristotelian categories, the view unfolds into the claim that for each category there is a categorically different kind of abstract entity such that, in virtue of exhibiting an entity of that kind, a particular comes to be characterized by the appropriate concrete term.

In combating this view, Ockham argues that the categories do not represent a classification of nonlinguistic objects; they are, rather, a classification of linguistic expressions according to their mode of signification. As he sees it, there are nonlinguistic objects corresponding only to the categories of substance and quality, and the entities in question are all particulars. So there are particular substances (like this man) and particular qualities (like the whiteness of this piece of paper). Abstract terms from the category of substance do not signify anything distinct from the particular substances signified by their concrete counterparts. Abstract terms from the category of quality do tend to signify entities distinct from the familiar substances that we say are white and courageous; but a term like 'courage' does not signify some one quality that all courageous individuals share. 'Courage' is better construed as a general term signifying individual qualities, the various courages in virtue of which individual human beings are called courageous. In none of the other Aristotelian categories do abstract terms signify any entities distinct from those signified by their concrete counterparts. Indeed, Ockham wanted to claim that abstract terms from categories other than that of quality are eliminable from discourse, that sentences incorporating terms like 'paternity' and 'burglary' can be replaced, without loss of content, by sentences in which those terms do not appear, but their concrete counterparts ('father' and 'burglar') do; and a significant portion of his ontological/logical works is dedicated to showing how these translations are to go (see ARISTOTELIANISM, MEDIEVAL §6).

3 Classical British empiricism

The classical empiricists followed Abelard and Ockham in denying that general terms signify universals. Thus, Hobbes sounds a familiar theme when he tells us that the only things that exist are particulars and that the terms 'general' and 'universal' are just 'names of names'. Like their medieval forbears, the empiricists recognized that the plausibility of this view hinges on our ability to provide a satisfactory account of the relation between general terms and the inner representations or ideas corresponding to them. Locke, who agrees that extramental entities are one and all particulars, argues that words signify ideas and that the ideas corresponding to general terms are abstract ideas – ideas formed from our ideas of particulars by separating out the features peculiar to this or that particular, retaining 'only what is common' to all the things to which a given general term applies. Berkeley goes further in his nominalism, denying that we have abstract ideas of the sort Locke describes. On Locke's view, the process of forming an abstract idea of a triangle, for example, consists in separating out all those features with respect to which triangles differ; and the result of this process is an idea of a triangle that is 'neither oblique nor rectangle, neither equilateral nor equicrural nor scalenon, but all and none of these at once'. Berkeley challenges us to identify an idea that corresponds to this characterization. As he sees it, our ideas are determinate in all their features and, accordingly, particular in their content (see HOBBES, T. §3; LOCKE, J. §6; BERKELEY, G. §2).

While Berkeley attacks the view that ideas are general in virtue of being abstract, he concedes that there are general ideas; but he insists that the generality of an idea is a function of its role in thinking rather than any special kind of content. Ideas are general not because they result from abstraction in Locke's sense, but because the idea is made 'to represent or stand for all other particular ideas of the same sort'. So the mind takes an idea that is fully determinate and particular in its content and makes it stand for other ideas of the same kind. Hume wholeheartedly endorses Berkeley's attack on abstraction and his account of generality, telling us that general ideas are 'in themselves individual, however they may become general in their representation. The image in the mind is only that of a particular object, though the application of it in our reasoning be the same as if it were universal' (Hume [1740] 1978: 20).

4 The twentieth century

Like ontological debates in earlier periods, ontological discussions in early analytic philosophy typically focused on the problem of universals. Thus, Frege, Moore and Russell were all anxious to undermine nominalistic theories that seek to analyse subject-predicate discourse without reference to nonlinguistic universals; and when the later Wittgenstein attacks the view that the use of a general term like 'game' is grounded in the antecedent recognition of a property or set of properties common to all the items to which the term applies, he is, among other things, challenging their Platonistic accounts of subject–predicate discourse (see WITTGENSTEIN, L. §9). Although concern with universals has continued throughout the twentieth century, the investigations of recent nominalists bear on a wider range of issues than those of their medieval and classical modern forbears. In addition to concern with universals, contemporary nominalists attempt to provide reductive accounts of things as diverse as the mathematician's sets, propositions, states of affairs, events and possible worlds, and philosophers of a nominalistic spirit take different attitudes towards different items on this list. Some, for example, are nominalists with regard to the traditional universals while insisting on a Platonistic account of sets; others insist on the irreducibility of events while providing reductive accounts of discourse apparently about propositions, states of affairs and

universals. Indeed, few philosophers have been willing to defend a nominalistic approach to all of the so-called abstract entities. One exception is Wilfred Sellars (see SELLARS, W. §2).

The account given by Sellars is an elaboration of Ockham's suggestion that talk about abstract entities is metalinguistic discourse. This suggestion had previously been elaborated in a proposal by Rudolf Carnap *The Logical Syntax of Language* that we construe talk about abstract entities as pseudo-material mode discourse, discourse apparently, but not really about nonlinguistic objects (see CARNAP, R. §3). Carnap's concern is with sentences of the following sort:

(1) Courage is a property.
(2) Mankind is a kind.
(3) Paternity is a relation.
(4) That two plus two equals four is a proposition

His proposal is that we treat these sentences as disguised ways of making claims about the syntax of certain linguistic expressions. Thus, (1)–(4) become:

(1') 'Courage' is an adjective.
(2') 'Man' is a common noun.
(3') 'Father of' is a many-place predicate.
(4') 'Two plus two equals four' is a declarative sentence

The difficulty with this proposal is that (1)–(4) turn out to be claims about *English* expressions. The proposal forces us to take the Spanish counterparts of (1)–(4), for example, to be claims about *Spanish* words, so that (1)–(4) and what are supposed to be their Spanish translations do not even agree in reference. Sellars responds to this problem by introducing a kind of quotation that cuts across languages, called dot quotation. Whereas standard quotation of the sort we meet in (1')–(4') creates metalinguistic expressions that apply exclusively to words in the quoting language, the application of Sellars' dot quotation to an expression creates a metalinguistic common noun that is true of all those expressions, regardless of language, which play the same linguistic role that the quoted expression plays in the base language. Thus, '·man·' is a common noun true of 'hombre', 'homme', and 'Mensch'. In their respective languages, these terms play the same role that 'man' plays in English; they are all '·man·'s. Now, Sellars wants to claim that using the machinery of dot quotation, we can provide a satisfactory reconstruction of (1)–(4) as:

(1'') ·Red·s are adjectives.
(2'') ·Man·s are common nouns.
(3'') ·Father of·s are many-place predicates.

(4″) ·Two plus two equals four·s are declarative sentences.

As Sellars understands them, (1″)–(4″) represent claims about linguistic expressions construed as tokens rather than types; and talk of linguistic tokens can be recast as talk about speakers and inscribers. Even the apparent Platonism involved in talk about linguistic roles is illusory since talk about linguistic roles can be eliminated by reference to talk about the linguistic rules that govern the use of terms. Accordingly, talk apparently about abstract entities is consistent with the most austere nominalism; it is merely metalinguistic discourse that cuts across languages.

Sellars believes that the sort of account he proposes for (1)–(4) can be extended to handle all discourse involving the so-called abstract entities. A slightly less radical form of nominalism is found in the writings of W.V. Quine (see QUINE, W.V. §6). Early in his career, Quine espoused a nominalism as austere as that developed by Sellars, but by the time he wrote *Word & Object* (1960), he had concluded that there is one kind of abstract entity whose existence we have to acknowledge, the mathematician's set or class. Quine remains unwilling to recognize things like properties, relations, kinds, and propositions, however. Unlike sets, these alleged entities lack clear-cut identity conditions and should play no role in our ontology.

Most contemporary philosophers agree with Quine that we must endorse an ontology of sets. This view provides the backdrop for the reductive approach to universals defended by G.F. Stout and D.C. Williams. They hold that there are particular as opposed to general qualities or properties, things like the whiteness of this piece of paper. So there are abstract entities besides sets; but they are one and all particulars. Williams calls these abstract particulars *tropes* and he tells us that they constitute 'the alphabet of being'. Tropes are ontologically primitive, and items from other categories are constructions out of them. Thus, the universal of the Platonist is a set of resembling tropes; and familiar concrete objects are bundles of tropes that contingently enter into a relation of 'collocation'.

Although Williams' trope-theoretic nominalism continues to enjoy some popularity, the most prominent form of nominalism in the contemporary arena is that influenced by developments in the semantics of modal logic, where we meet the idea that the actual world is just one of infinitely many possible worlds and that the totality of possible worlds constitutes the subject matter for talk about necessity and possibility (see POSSIBLE WORLDS). Contemporary nominalists claim that the framework of possible worlds provides the resources for a genuinely reductive account of things like properties and propositions. These philosophers propose that we take possible worlds as primitive. Each such world, they claim, can be characterized in nominalist terms as a totality of concrete particulars, and they argue that we can provide a nominalist treatment of things like properties and propositions by identifying them with set-theoretical entities of a transworld sort. We can identify properties with functions from worlds to sets of objects, relations with functions from worlds to sets of ordered n-tuples and propositions with sets of worlds or functions from worlds to the truth values. The most prominent proponent of this sort of view is David Lewis (see LEWIS, D. §3). He has invoked the framework of possible worlds not simply to provide an account of properties and propositions, but to clarify the concept of meaning, to state truth conditions for counterfactuals, and to provide an analysis of causation (1986).

See also: ABSTRACT OBJECTS; INTENSIONAL ENTITIES; NOMINALISM, BUDDHIST DOCTRINE OF; UNIVERSALS

References and further reading

Abelard, P. (before 1120) 'Logica "Ingredientibus"', in R. McKeon (ed.) *Selections from Medieval Philosophers*, New York: Scribners, 1959, 202–58. (Provides a survey of Abelard's approach as outlined in §2 above.)

Armstrong, D. (1978) *Universals and Scientific Realism*, Cambridge: Cambridge University Press, 2 vols. (Contains useful discussions of nominalism.)

Berkeley, G. (1710) *A Treatise Concerning the Principles of Human Knowledge* in C. Turbayne (ed.) *Principles, Dialogues, and Correspondence*, New York: Bobbs-Merrill, 1965. (The introduction to this work is especially relevant.)

* Carnap, R. (1934) *Logische Syntax der Sprache* (The Logical Syntax of Language), trans. A. Smeaton, Patterson, NJ: Littlefield & Adams, 1959. (Carnap's attempt to clarify the structure of language.)

Goodman, N. (1956) *The Problem of Universals*, Notre Dame, IN: University of Notre Dame Press. (The chapter entitled 'A World of Universals' is especially relevant.)

* Hobbes, T. (1651) *Leviathan*, ed. M. Oakeshott and R. Peters, New York: Collier, 1962. (Part 1, chapter 4 contains Hobbes' exposition of the topic.)

* Hume, D. (1740) *A Treatise of Human Nature*, ed. L.A. Selby-Bigge, 2nd edn (with revisions by P.H. Nidditch), Oxford: Clarendon, 1978. (Book I, part

1, section 7 contains Hume's response to Berkeley on abstract ideas.)

* Lewis, D. (1986) *On the Plurality of Worlds*, Oxford: Blackwell. (Uses possible worlds as the framework for a new perspective, as outlined at the end of §4 above.)

Locke, J. (1689) *An Essay Concerning Human Understanding*, collated and annotated by A.C. Fraser, Oxford: Oxford University Press, 1894. (See Book II, chapter 9, sects 9–10 and Book III, chapters 3 and 4.)

Loux, M.J. (1978) *Substance and Attribute*, Dordrecht: Reidel. (Contains discussions of a variety of different forms of nominalism.)

Ockham, William of (*c.*1329) 'Summa Logicae', part I, in M.J. Loux, *Ockham's Theory of Terms*, Notre Dame, IN: Notre Dame University Press, 1974. (A translation of the clearest formulation of Ockham's approach to ontology.)

Quine, W.V. (1953) *From a Logical Point of View*, Cambridge, MA: Harvard University Press. (The essays in this volume express the earliest and most austere form of Quine's nominalism.)

* —— (1960) *Word and Object*, Cambridge, MA: MIT Press. (Gives the 'sets only' doctrine.)

Sellars, W. (1967) 'Abstract Entities', in *Philosophical Perspectives*, Springfield, IL: Charles C. Thomas. (Exposition of the line of thought outlined in §4 above.)

Stout, G.F. (1921) *The Nature of Universals and Propositions*, London Oxford University Press. (British Academy Lecture which discusses 'Trope Theory', outlined in §4 above.)

Williams, D.C. (1953) 'Elements of Being', parts I and II, *Review of Metaphysics*, 6: 3–18, 171–93. ('Trope theory' outlined in §4 above.)

Wittgenstein, L. (1953) *Philosophical Investigations*, trans. G.E.M. Anscombe, London: Macmillan. (The famous passage on 'family resemblances' begins at §65.)

MICHAEL J. LOUX

NOMINALISM, BUDDHIST DOCTRINE OF

Buddhist nominalism refers to the nominalist ontology and semantics developed especially by the Indian Buddhist philosophers Dignāga and Dharmakīrti. Elaborating on the arguments of their Buddhist predecessor Vasubandhu, they critically examine the notions of spatial and temporal extension. For Dignāga and Dharmakīrti, spatially and temporally composite entities are constructed through concepts and language and as such those entities exist only nominally or conventionally. Their semantics rejects the realist position that expressions refer to real, extra-mental universals that are instantiated in each particular of the class formed by the respective universal. Instead, these philosophers developed the unique theory of 'exclusion' whereby expressions convey meaning by the exclusion of some particulars from those which do not have the expected causal capacities. Dharmakīrti's nominalism is credited with a greater impact on Indian philosophy than Dignāga's.

1 Ontology
2 Critique of universals
3 Theory of meaning

1 Ontology

One can reduce the concerns of Buddhist philosophers to a central preoccupation: the cessation of suffering. According to Buddhist philosophers, the elimination of suffering (*duḥkha*) requires the elimination of its cause, which is thought to be the belief in entities that in fact do not exist (see SUFFERING, BUDDHIST VIEWS OF ORIGINATION OF). Of particular concern is the belief in an eternal, unchanging self or soul (*ātman*), for this belief motivates the behaviour that produces suffering. Buddhists before DHARMAKĪRTI often employed part or whole arguments to refute the notion of self and eventually to reject all composite entities. These arguments, which inform much of Dharmakīrti's nominalism, can be summarized by briefly examining a composite entity, such as a table.

Although a table is apparently a single entity composed of various parts, Buddhists question whether any such entity actually exists. They ask whether the whole that is the table is the same as or different from its parts. If the whole differs from its parts, what evidence do we have for its existence? Immediate sensory perception yields information only about the parts. If the whole is the same as its parts, then it must be either fully or partially instantiated in each part. If it is fully instantiated in each part, then any single part is an entire table. If the table is only partially instantiated in its parts, then we should speak of many partial tables rather than one single table. If we were to claim that all the parts together are the table, then a heap of table-parts should be a table. Finally if the parts in a particular configuration are the table, one could again ask whether that configuration is the same as or different from the configured parts: an infinite regress ensues.

Expanding on this critique of spatial extension,

Dharmakīrti also attacks temporal extension. In doing so, he affirms the doctrine of momentariness, whereby an ultimately real entity can only exist for an infinitesimal period of time (see MOMENTARINESS, BUDDHIST DOCTRINE OF). This doctrine is supported in part by the argument that an entity which does not change over time cannot produce any effects, for a cause must change from a pre-production state to a post-production state; otherwise, it would either produce its effects at all times eternally, or it would never produce any effect. Furthermore, Dharmakīrti maintained a causal model of sense perception whereby a sensed entity causes the content of one's sensory cognition. Since a nonmomentary entity could never act as a cause, it could never be perceived. As a result, one could never indubitably establish its existence, for in Dharmakīrti's words, 'to exist is to be perceived' (*sattvam upalabdhir eva*) (*Pramāṇavārttikasvopajñavṛtti on Pramāṇavārttika* I.3ab).

In short, Dharmakīrti denies that any composite entity can be real in the strictest sense. However, following his predecessors, he admits that composite entities can be said to exist from the perspective of conceptual and linguistic conventions. These modes of existence yield two important categories: things that exist in the strictest sense are 'ultimately' real (*paramārthasat*), while those contingent upon linguistic and conceptual conventions are only 'nominally' (*prajñaptisat*) or 'conventionally' real (*saṃvṛtisat*).

2 Critique of universals

Dharmakīrti's most thorough analysis of semantic issues appears in the *Svopajñavṛtti* (Interpretative Commentary), his lengthy remarks on the first chapter of his *Pramāṇavārttika* (Comments on Instrumental Knowledge). Much of his work concerns the problem of repeatability or universality (*anvaya*). In other words, when I use the expression 'cow', for example, what is it about all cows that allows me to apply this one word to all of them? On the pre-reflective intuitions suggested by language, it seems that there is something the same about all cows. Elaborating on this intuition, most Indian philosophers maintained that there is in fact some real entity – in this case, 'cowness' – that is instantiated in each cow. Entities such as 'cowness' are called 'universals' (*sāmānya, jāti*) and they are instantiated in 'particulars' (*vyakti, svalakṣaṇa*), the things that impinge on our senses and which we seem to identify as 'cows'. Here, the technical term 'referent' might be used in a way that differs from some of its more common uses in Western philosophy. That is, to describe the view of Indian realism, the actual referent of the expression

'cow' might best be considered the universal 'cowness' itself (see UNIVERSALS, INDIAN THEORIES OF).

When Dharmakīrti attacks this view, he maintains that an expression is successful in its semantic function only when it has induced an action (*pravṛtti*) towards the intended particular in the person who has apprehended that expression. Such action might be some physical manipulation of the particular or a mere cognitive act such as recognition. That being the case, ultimately real universals make meaning impossible because expressions which refer to ultimately real universals would be incapable of inducing action towards particulars.

To demonstrate this conclusion, Dharmakīrti raises the problem of identity and difference as a species of the part or whole analyses previously mentioned. He asks whether the universal is the same as or different from the particulars in which it is instantiated. If the universal is different, then the expression 'cow' would not induce acts towards any particular because it refers only to the universal 'cowness', which is entirely distinct from any particular. One might still insist that the expression can induce action towards the intended particular, but then one must admit that an expression can induce action towards any entity, whether it be the same as or different from its referent.

On the other hand, if the universal is identical with the particulars, then the universal would lose its universality or repeatability. In other words, a cow-particular must be distinct from all other cow-particulars, otherwise, one would be unable to distinguish one cow from any other. Hence, a cow-particular is not repeatable – one cow-particular does not occur in or as any other cow-particular. But if the universal 'cowness' is identical with any cow-particular, then it would also be unrepeatable. One would need a new universal for every instance and the expression 'cow' could only be applied to that one particular, which is identical to the universal 'cowness'.

In response, some Indian realists admit that the particular and universal must be distinct, but they claim that an expression which refers to a universal can induce action towards a particular by virtue of the particular's relation to the universal. Among the more compelling criticisms of this position is Dharmakīrti's contention that any form of relation necessarily leads to either a contradiction or an infinite regress. That is, a relation's relata must be either the same or different. If they are the same, then there is no relation, for relations presuppose difference. If, on the other hand, the relata are different, then they cannot be in relation, for if entirely distinct entities can stand in relation, then one can haphazardly relate any entity to any other entity. The notion of relation would thus be meaningless. Only a contradiction remains: the relata are both the same and different. If in response one posits a subsistent relation that 'ties' the relata together, one must then explain how the relata are related to the relation. If one then speaks of some second-order relation that connects the relata to the relation, one falls into an infinite regress.

3 Theory of meaning

Dharmakīrti's ontology can be reduced to the claim that the ultimately real is necessarily unique and unrepeatable. Hence, he rejects realist semantics because a universal must be in some sense repeatable in each of its instances. Yet without real universals, how do we explain our ability to use language? The Buddhist answer is that expressions convey meaning by the exclusion of some particulars from those which do not have the expected causal capacities. In this respect, meaning has three components: the cognitive image (*pratibhāsa, ākāra*), the particular and the exclusion (*vyāṛtti*).

For Dharmakīrti, language operates in the same fashion as conceptual thought. We can most easily examine the role of cognitive images by turning to the cognition called 'recognition' (*pratyabhijñāna*) – the conceptual act whereby a sensed object is identified or labelled. For recognition to occur, one must have learned the conventions that govern the appropriate expression or concept. If, for example, one knows the conventions that govern 'cow', one can have the recognition, 'that is a cow'. For Indian philosophers the important question is, what is it that we label with concepts or expressions such as 'cow'?

In discussing recognition, Dharmakīrti assumes a causal model of sense perception: when some particular impinges upon the senses, that particular creates an image in the mind. This image or sensum is what one knows in sense perception. This means that what we recognize as a 'cow' is not some particular that impinged upon the senses; rather, it is the image produced in our minds by that particular. Hence, if expressions and concepts give us any knowledge of particulars, they do so only by the mediation of the cognitive images caused by those particulars.

Objectors to this position point out that if concepts and language yield knowledge just of cognitive images, then actions based on such knowledge would be focused upon images and not upon particulars. Dharmakīrti responds that ordinary persons have a deeply inculcated cognitive habit of mistaking the images that arise from particulars for those particulars themselves. This claim leads to his assertion that all linguistic and conceptual knowledge is flawed in that it rests upon the conflation of the image with the particular that caused it. Dharmakīrti remarks that this psychological apparatus explains how images can induce action towards particulars. He further notes that an image nevertheless can yield useful information because it directs one only towards the particular which acted as its cause.

In appealing to the causal link between images and particulars, Dharmakīrti makes a crucial statement about images. That is, Dharmakīrti argues that any entity which acts as a cause or effect is a particular and since images are effects, they must be mental particulars. As particulars, images are never repeatable, so images cannot be the same in all cases when we use a given concept or expression. Instead, Dharmakīrti maintains that what is actually the same in all cases are 'exclusions'.

His theory begins with the claim in the *Pramāṇavārttikasvopajñavṛtti on Pramāṇavārttika* (I, V 107–9; 119–43) that all images of tables, for example, produce an effect that no non-table produces: a second-order cognition called the 'determination of sameness' (*ekapratyavamarśajñāna*) in which any table-image is determined to be the same as every other table-image in that they are all imagined to be tables. Hence, all table-images are the same in that they all produce a cognition of their sameness. Since those images were produced by certain particulars, we can likewise say that those particulars are the same because they all produce images that all produce a second-order cognition of their sameness.

Some Indian realists maintain that this claim leads to an infinite regress. That is, in this respect all images of tables are the same because they produce the same effect, namely, second-order cognitions of their sameness. But since those second-order cognitions are all effects, they must be unique mental particulars. Thus, we must also prove that those second-order cognitions are the same. To do so, we must show that they all produce the same third-order cognition and an infinite regress ensues. In response, Dharmakīrti admits that the sameness of a certain set of images is constituted by their production of the same second-order cognitions. Nevertheless, the sameness of the second-order cognitions is not constituted by the sameness of their effects. Rather, they are all said to be the same in that they determine the first-order cognitions to be the same. This is an appeal to experience: the fact that the second-order cognitions include this determination of sameness is established by the apperceptive aspect of those second-order cognitions themselves.

It might appear that Dharmakīrti has opted for a realist theory of resemblance: certain particulars are the same in that they have the same causal capacity to produce images that in turn produce a determination of their sameness. But he rejects the notion of some shared causal capacity precisely for the reasons mentioned above: such an entity would have to be either the same as or different from the particulars in which it is instantiated and neither possibility makes sense.

Given that there can be no single entity that is the same in all cases, how then can we use this information that all tables, for example, produce the same effect? If we cannot even conclude that there is some repeatable causal capacity, then what will provide the commonality in all table-particulars such that we can use the expression 'table' for each one of them? Dharmakīrti answers that we need not find any repeatable entity at all. Instead, we need only admit that if all tables produce the same effect, this necessarily distinguishes them from all other particulars. In short, what is the same about all tables is that they are excluded from non-tables.

This move seems tantamount to calling a table a non-non-table and one might wonder why we should resort to this double negative: why not simply say that a table is a table? Although modern interpreters have taken this objection seriously, Dharmakīrti noted that this qualm is misplaced for it fails to see how anti-realist ontological claims inform his semantics. Dharmakīrti's theory rests on the argument that repeatable entities are impossible. Since we undeniably experience particulars in such a way that we are able to classify them, our cognitions must group particulars into classes without having to pinpoint any repeatable entity. But since it is impossible to group particulars positively, we must do so negatively. The point here is that while we cannot posit any single, repeated entity that accounts for the fact that the particulars of a given class produce cognitive images that in turn produce the determination of their sameness, we are still able to distinguish between particulars that lead to that determination and particulars that do not.

The Mīmāṃsaka philosopher Kumārila (*fl. c.*625) responds that the reasoning employed is circular. That is, if Buddhists define 'tree' as the negation of 'non-tree', then one must be able to specify non-trees. Either this requires that one has already specified what trees are, or that one is somehow able to specify directly what non-trees are. In the former case, the theory of exclusion is superfluous since one can specify trees before excluding them from non-trees. In the latter case, one has specified what are non-trees without the negation of their complement. If this is possible in the case of non-trees, why should it not also be possible in the case of trees? The answer is the one stated above: we know that images are different by the apperceptive second-order cognitions that they

induce. Nevertheless, we cannot specify any repeatable entity possessed by a certain set of images and not possessed by the set of all other images. We can only appeal to the difference and we use that difference to define both sets. Dharmakīrti suggests that if this theory is circular, then no theory of semantics will be able to avoid circularity.

Clearly, the theory of exclusion assumes some cognitive means of comparing images. Dharmakīrti notes that this process involves imprints (*vāsanā*) placed in the mind by previous experiences and that in the act of comparison those imprints become active. Another crucial factor enters into comparison: the intentions and expectations present in one's mind when one uses concepts and expressions. That is, since any cognitive image is necessarily unique it can be excluded from an infinite range of other images. For example, any table-image is unique and one can focus on its uniqueness by excluding it from all other images, even other table-images. If we wish to say that the particular which produced that image is a 'table', we ignore that image's difference from other table-images. Also, if we wish to speak of it as 'furniture' we widen our scope by ignoring its difference from chairs and such while maintaining its difference from all non-furniture, such as ping-pong balls. This process is a function of the goals, expectations and other disposition that we bring to any use of language and concepts. While accounting for the importance of dispositions in the determination of meaning, the theory of exclusion also allows Dharmakīrti to account for repeatability and reference without making any ontological commitments to universals. As far as the Indian realist account is concerned, it would seem that exclusions are universals instantiated in images. Hence, Dharmakīrti would face the same identity/difference objection that he levelled against the realists. To avoid this problem, Dharmakīrti resorts to the aforementioned distinction between ultimate and conventional reality. As a species of negation, exclusions cannot exist ultimately. Hence, no expression has any real referent. Nevertheless, in conventional terms exclusions can be said to qualify cognitive images and since any image is the unique effect of some particular, that causal link enables Dharmakīrti to claim that the particulars which cause images are the indirect referents of expressions. His semantic theory enables him to avoid the realist doctrine of universals when he claims that the information derived from language can lead to successful activity in the world.

See also: BUDDHIST PHILOSOPHY, INDIAN; DIGNĀGA; MEANING, INDIAN THEORIES OF; NOMINALISM; VASUBANDHU

References and further reading

* Dharmakīrti (*c*.625) *Pramāṇavārttikasvopajñavṛtti on Pramāṇavārttika (Svopajñavṛtti)* (Pramāṇavārttikam: The First Chapter with Autocommentary), Serie Orientale Roma 23, ed. R. Gnoli, Rome: Istituto Italiano per il Medio ed Estremo Oriente, 1960. (Sanskrit edition of the most important source for views discussed in §2 and §3. Relevant portions translated in Dunne (1997).)

—— (*c*.625) *Pramāṇavārttika of Ācārya Dharmakīrti with Manorathanandin's Commentary*, ed. S. Dvārikādāsa Śāstrī, Bauddha Bharata Series 3, Varanasi: Bauddha Bharati, 2nd edn, 1984. (Sanskrit edition; portions of the chapter on direct awareness (*pratyakṣa*) are particularly relevant to §1.)

Dreyfus, G. (1997) *Recognizing Reality: Dharmakīrti's Philosophy and its Tibetan Interpretations*, Albany, NY: State University of New York Press. (An important work that offers some competing interpretations on these issues.)

Dunne, J.D. (1997) 'Rending the Web of Concepts: Dharmakīrti's Nonessentialist Approach to Language and Concepts', unpublished Ph.D. dissertation, Harvard University, MA. (Expands on the presented here; includes a translation of Dharmakīrti's *Pramāṇavārttikasvopajñavṛtti* up to verse 231.)

Hayes, R.P. (1988) *Dignāga on the Interpretation of Signs*, Dordrecht: Kluwer. (An excellent study of Dharmakīrti's predecessor. Chapters 2, 3 and 5 are particularly relevant.)

Kumārila Bhaṭṭa (7th century) *Ślokavārttika: Translated from the Original Sanskrit with Extracts from the Commentaries 'Kāśikā' of Sucarita Miśra and 'Nyāyaratnākara' of Pārthasārathi Miśra*, trans. G. Jha, New Delhi: Sri Satguru Publications, 1983. (Reprint of 1908 edition; although at points problematic, this translation provides access to the views of an influential opponent of Buddhist nominalism.)

Shah, N.J. (1967) *Akalaṅka's Criticism of Dharmakīrti's Philosophy: A Study*, Lalbhai Dalpatbhai Series 11, D. Malvania and A.P. Shah (eds), Ahmedabad: L.D. Institute of Indology. (Includes a useful summary of Dharmakīrti's views relevant to §§2–3.)

Siderits, M. (1991) *Indian Philosophy of Language: Studies in Selected Issues*, Studies in Linguistics and Philosophy 46, Dordrecht: Kluwer. (Discusses the issues raised in §3, while presenting a different approach to the apparent problem of double negation).

Steinkellner, E. (1971) 'Wirklichkeit und Begriff bei Dharmakīrti' (Reality and Concept in Dharmakīrti), *Wiener Zeitschrift für die Kunde Südasiens und Archiv für Indische Philosophie* 15: 179–211. (This seminal article, although technical at points, expands on §1 and §3.)

JOHN D. DUNNE

NOMOS *see* PHYSIS AND NOMOS

NON-CONCEPTUAL CONTENT *see* CONTENT, NON-CONCEPTUAL

NON-CONSTRUCTIVE RULES OF INFERENCE

For some theoretical purposes, generalized deductive systems (or, 'semi-formal' systems) are considered, having rules with an infinite number of premises. The best-known of these rules is the 'ω-rule', or rule of infinite induction. This rule allows the inference of $\forall n \Phi(n)$ from the infinitely many premises $\Phi(0)$, $\Phi(1), \ldots$ that result from replacing the numerical variable n in $\Phi(n)$ with the numeral for each natural number. About 1930, in part as a response to Gödel's demonstration that no formal deductive system had as theorems all and only the true formulas of arithmetic, several writers (most notably, Carnap) suggested considering the semi-formal systems obtained, from some formulation of arithmetic, by adding this rule. Since no finite notation can provide terms for all sets of natural numbers, no comparable rule can be formulated for higher-order arithmetic. In effect, the ω-rule is valid just in case the relevant quantifier can be interpreted substitutionally; looked at from the other side, the validity of some analogue of the ω-rule is the essential mathematical characteristic of substitutional quantification.

1 The ω-rule
2 Related rules

1 The ω-rule

In a standard formalized deductive system, the axioms form a decidable set of formulas (or, under Gödel-numbering, a recursive set of numbers), and each rule is a decidable relation between (conclusion) formulas and finite sets of (premise) formulas. (A set, or relation, is 'decidable' if there is an algorithm for determining whether a given item belongs to it, or given items stand in it.) A proof in the system can therefore be thought of as a tree of formulas, with the theorem to be proved at the root, axioms at the leaves, and at each node a formula which follows by a rule from its predecessors.

For some theoretical purposes, however, 'semiformal' systems (generalized deductive systems) are considered, having rules with an infinite number of premises. The best-known of these rules is that called the rule of infinite induction, or the 'ω-rule'. This rule allows the inference of $\forall n \Phi(n)$ from the infinitely many premises $\Phi(0), \Phi(1), \ldots$ that result from replacing the numerical variable n in $\Phi(n)$ with the numeral for each natural number. About 1930, in part as a response to Gödel's demonstration that no formal deductive system had as theorems all and only the true formulas of arithmetic, several writers (most notably, Carnap) suggested considering the semiformal systems obtained, from some formulation of arithmetic, by adding this rule.

An axiomatic system enriched with the ω-rule can, obviously, prove all the truths of first-order arithmetic: without loss of generality we may think of the atomic sentences of arithmetic as equations between terms made up out of numerals and the signs for addition and multiplication, so propositional logic and elementary algorithms (which can be simulated in standard axiomatic systems) suffice to prove all quantifier-free sentences of arithmetic, after which any true existential quantification can be inferred by the standard rule of existential quantifier introduction from one of its true instances, and any true universal quantification by the ω-rule from the set of all its true instances. (Proofs of true 'prenex' sentences (that is, those made up of a string of quantifiers followed by an atomic sentence) have this form exactly; other truths can be deduced from their prenex equivalents by standard means.)

If the language of the system goes beyond firstorder arithmetic the situation is more complicated. Within a few years of its proposal, Rosser (1937) showed that the addition of the ω-rule to a standard system of higher-order arithmetic did not suffice to render the system complete. There are, however, some partial completeness results. Schütte (1960) showed that standard axioms and rules enriched with the ω-rule remain complete when the language of first-order arithmetic is supplemented with free variables for sets of numbers. Earlier, Orey (1956) had shown that any set of sentences of second-order arithmetic consistent with the ω-rule has an 'ω-model', that is, a model in

which the second-order quantification (quantification over sets of numbers) can have a nonstandard interpretation in the manner of Henkin (1950), but in which the first-order quantifiers range over the genuine natural numbers. (Note that Schütte's result is that every sentence true in the standard model is a theorem of a certain theory, whereas Orey's is more analogous to completeness theorems for logics in specifying only a kind of model.)

The finite trees of formulas counting as proofs in a given formal system themselves form a decidable set of arrays, and can be Gödel-numbered; the set of (Gödel-numbers of) theorems of the system is thus defined by a Σ_1^0 formula, that is, a formula obtained from one expressing a recursive relation by existentially quantifying over numbers (see RECURSIONTHEORETIC HIERARCHIES). This is the general form of a definition of a recursively enumerable set, and, as shown most elegantly by Smullyan (1961), any recursively enumerable set can be represented by the set of theorems of a formal system. A proof in a semiformal system can be represented by a set of numbers, so it is tempting to define the set of (Gödel numbers of) theorems of a semi-formal system by a formula starting with an existential quantifier over sets, by analogy with the definition of a recursively enumerable set by existential quantification over numbers.

But an ω-proof is a *well-founded* tree of formulas: it may have infinitely many branches, though each branch is only finitely long. So specifying just which sets of numbers correspond to infinite proofs would require a second quantifier over sets, and this would yield a Σ_2^1 formula as definiens. It is better to define the set of theorems directly, without reference to the infinite proofs, as the set of formulas belonging to every set which contains the axioms, is closed under the ordinary rules of inference, and contains a universal (numerical) quantification if it contains all its instances. This yields a Π_1^1 formula (a formula obtained by prefixing existential quantifiers over sets to a formula containing at most first-order quantifiers) as a definiens. Since Frege (1879) it has been standard to use a formula of this form in giving an explicit definition of an inductively defined notion, and sets definable by Π_1^1 formulas are sometimes called 'inductive' sets (see Aczel (1977) or Moschovakis (1974) for details). Any Π_1^1 set can be represented by the set of theorems of a semi-formal system.

Formal systems of arithmetic can be given an elegant formulation analogous to natural deduction or sequent-calculus formulations of pure logic, with the principle of mathematical induction taking the form of a rule of inference similar to the rules for the quantifiers. When this is done, it turns out that Gentzen's cut-elimination theorem for pure logic

(1935) does not extend in its general form to arithmetic, but his later proof of the consistency of arithmetic can be seen as proceeding via a special case of cut-elimination that does hold. Kurt Schütte noted that it was possible to modify Gentzen's methods to prove a general cut-elimination theorem for various systems of arithmetic, provided that the cut-free proofs are allowed to employ the ω-rule. He and his colleagues have developed this into a useful tool for analysing formal systems of arithmetic: the complexity of the cut-free ω-proofs corresponding to proofs in a particular formal system turns out to be a measure of the strength of that system, correlating in particular with the class of number-theoretic functions whose totality can be proved in the system.

2 Related rules

Stronger infinitary rules, producing semi-formal systems of second-order arithmetic which are still incomplete but are stronger than those formed by adding the ω-rule to standard formal systems, have been studied by Mostowski (1961) and Enderton (1967). No satisfactory analogue of the ω-rule for introducing the universal quantifications over sets in classical higher-order arithmetic or set theory is possible because a formal language cannot contain terms for all the uncountably many sets in the standard model, but higher-order analogues of the ω-rule have been studied in the context of non-classical set theories. Schütte (1960) describes a type-free theory inspired by Ackermann; and Fitch, in publications starting in the late 1940s, obtained results closely related to those of later workers on the inductive semantics of type-free theories by studying semi-formal systems with rules similar to the ω-rule.

In the other direction, various weaker forms of the ω-rule have been studied. It is sometimes possible to prove in a finitary metatheory (or in a theory like Peano arithmetic used as its own syntactic metatheory) that all the instances of a certain quantification are provable in a formal system. A rule allowing the inference of a universal (numerical) quantification from the statement that all its instances are provable is sometimes called the 'formalized' ω-rule. Such a rule, unlike those discussed above, is of finitary character; added to a formalized system of arithmetic it amounts to a kind of reflection principle. Feferman (1962) showed that every true sentence of first-order arithmetic is provable in some formal system in a transfinite hierarchy of systems obtained from a standard axiomatic system by iterated addition of reflection principles. (Much earlier, Hilbert (1931) had proposed a restricted version of the formalized ω-rule

in what seems to have been an attempt to get around Gödel's incompleteness theorems.)

A somewhat related idea is the 'constructive' ω-rule: take $\forall n\Phi(n)$ to be a theorem if there is a recursive function assigning to each natural number (the Gödel number of) a formal proof of the corresponding instance of $\Phi(n)$. Despite the name, this is a non-constructive rule, since it is not in general a decidable matter whether or not there is a recursive function of the sort required: Shoenfield (1959) shows that all truths of first-order arithmetic are provable with it.

References and further reading

* Aczel, P. (1977) 'An Introduction to Inductive Definitions', in J. Barwise (ed.) *Handbook of Mathematical Logic*, Amsterdam: North Holland, 739–82. (A survey of results on inductive definability; shorter than Moschovakis (1974).)

Carnap, R. (1935) 'Ein Gültigskeitskriterium für die Sätze der klassischen Mathematik', *Monatshefte für Mathematik und Physik* 42: 163–90; incorporated in *The Logical Syntax of Language*, trans. A. Smeaton, London: Kegan Paul, 1937. (Uses the ω-rule to give a definition of mathematical 'validity'.)

Dunn, J.M. and Belnap, N.D. (1968) 'The Substitution Interpretation of the Quantifiers', *Noûs* 2: 177–85. (An influential study of the notion of substitutional quantification, pointing out that analogues of the ω-rule are valid for it.)

* Enderton, H. (1967) 'An Infinitistic Rule of Proof', *Journal of Symbolic Logic*, 32: 447–51. (Treats a non-constructive rule more nearly analogous to the ω-rule than, but weaker than, that studied in Mostowski (1961).)

* Feferman, S. (1962) 'Transfinite Recursive Progressions of Axiomatic Theories', *Journal of Symbolic Logic* 27: 259–316. (Study of iterated addition of reflection principles.)

—— (1984) 'Toward Useful Type-Free Systems I', *Journal of Symbolic Logic* 49: 75–111. (Includes a historical survey describing the Ackermann–Schütte and Fitch type-free systems.)

* Frege, G. (1879) *Begriffsschrift, eine der arithmetischen nachgebildete Formelsprache des reinen Denkens*, Halle: Nebert; trans. '*Begriffsschrift*, a Formula Language, Modelled Upon That of Arithmetic, for Pure Thought', in J. van Heijenoort (ed.) *From Frege to Gödel: A Source Book in Mathematical Logic, 1879–1931*, Cambridge, MA: Harvard University Press, 1967, 1–82. (First formalization of second-order logic; replacement of recursive definitions with explicit definitions quantifying over sets.)

* Gentzen, G. (1935) 'Untersuchungen über das

logische Schließen', *Mathematische Zeitschrift* 39: 176– 210, 405–565; repr. Darmstadt: Wissenschaftliche Buchgesellschaft, 1969; trans. 'Investigations into Logical Deduction', *American Philosophical Quarterly* 1: 288–306, 2: 204–18, 1964; repr. in *The Collected Papers of Gerhard Gentzen*, ed. M.E. Szabo, Amsterdam and London: North Holland, 1969, 68–131. (Cut elimination.)

—— (1936) 'Die Widerspruchsfreiheit der reinen Zahlentheorie', *Mathematische Annalen* 112: 493– 565; trans. 'The Consistency of Elementary Number Theory', in *The Collected Papers of Gerhard Gentzen*, ed. M.E. Szabo, Amsterdam and London: North Holland, 1969, 132–213. (Proof of consistency of arithmetic.)

* Henkin, L. (1950) 'Completeness in the Theory of Types', *Journal of Symbolic Logic* 15: 81–91. (Introduces nonstandard models for higher-order logic and arithmetic.)

* Hilbert, D. (1931) 'Die Grundlegung der elementaren Zahlenlehre', *Mathematische Annalen* 104: 485–94. (An early proposal of a restricted version of the formalized ω-rule.)

* Moschovakis, Y.N. (1974) *Elementary Induction on Abstract Structures*, Amsterdam: North Holland. (Inductive definition.)

* Mostowski, A. (1961) 'Formal Systems of Analysis Based on an Infinitistic Rule of Proof', in *Infinitistic Methods: Proceedings of Symposium on Foundations of Mathematics*, Warsaw: PWN, and New York, Oxford, London, Paris: Pergamon Press, 141–66; repr. in *Foundational Studies* vol. 1, Amsterdam: North Holland, 1979. (Investigates systems of second-order arithmetic validated by a certain subclass of ω-models.)

* Orey, S. (1956) 'On ω-Consistency and Related Properties', *Journal of Symbolic Logic* 21: 246–56. (Completeness theorem.)

Pohlers, W. (1987) 'Contributions of the Schütte School', appendix in G. Takeuti, *Proof Theory*, Amsterdam: North Holland, 2nd edn. (Survey of work by Schütte and colleagues.)

—— (1989) *Proof Theory: An Introduction*, Berlin: Springer. (Introductory textbook on the work of the Schütte school.)

* Rosser, J. (1937) 'Gödel Theorems for Non-Constructive Logics', *Journal of Symbolic Logic* 2: 129– 37. (Incompleteness theorem.)

Schmerl, U. (1982) 'Iterated Reflection Principles and the ω-Rule', *Journal of Symbolic Logic* 47: 721–33. (Relates ideas of Feferman (1962) to more explicitly stated rules.)

* Schütte, K. (1960) *Beweistheorie*, Berlin: Springer; trans. J.N. Crossley, *Proof Theory*, Berlin and New York: Springer, 1997; also trans. with modifica-

tions, S. Toledo, *Tableau Systems for First Order Number Theory and Certain Higher Order Theories*, Berlin: Springer, 1975 (Treatise on proof theory. Toledo's book is a 'pseudo-translation' of the first edition, helpfully substituting Beth–Smullyan tableaux for Schütte's idiosyncratic formulation of basic logic.)

* Shoenfield, J. (1959) 'On a Restricted ω-Rule', *Bulletin de l'Académie Polonaise des Sciences* 7: 405– 7. (Result on effective ω-rule.)

* Smullyan, R. (1961) *Theory of Formal Systems*, Princeton, NJ: Princeton University Press. (Elegant presentation of basic recursion theory in terms of simple formal systems.)

Tarski, A. (1933) 'Einige Betrachtungen über die Begriffe ω-Widerspruchsfreiheit und der ω-Vollständigkeit', *Monatshefte für Mathematik und Physik* 40: 97–112; trans. 'Some Observations on the Concepts of ω-Consistency and ω-Completeness', in *Logic, Semantics, Metamathematics: Papers from 1923 to 1938*, ed. J.H. Woodger, Oxford: Oxford University Press, 1956. (Introduces the ω-rule.)

A.P. HAZEN

NON-MONOTONIC LOGIC

A relation of inference is 'monotonic' if the addition of premises does not undermine previously reached conclusions; otherwise the relation is non-monotonic. Deductive inference, at least according to the canons of classical logic, is monotonic: if a conclusion is reached on the basis of a certain set of premises, then that conclusion still holds if more premises are added.

By contrast, everyday reasoning is mostly non-monotonic because it involves risk: we jump to conclusions from deductively insufficient premises. We know when it is worthwhile or even necessary (for example, in medical diagnosis) to take the risk. Yet we are also aware that such inference is 'defeasible' – that new information may undermine old conclusions. Various kinds of defeasible but remarkably successful inference have traditionally captured the attention of philosophers (theories of induction, Peirce's theory of abduction, inference to the best explanation, and so on). More recently logicians have begun to approach the phenomenon from a formal point of view. The result is a large body of theories at the interface of philosophy, logic and artificial intelligence.

1   **Sources of non-monotonicity**
2   **Patterns and models of non-monotonic inference**
3   **Related work**

1 Sources of non-monotonicity

A relation of inference is 'monotonic' if the addition of premises does not undermine previously reached conclusions; otherwise the relation is non-monotonic. Theories of non-monotonic inference locate the source of non-monotonicity in various forms of calculated risk-taking in the course of seeking information. Many kinds of reasoning involving 'degrees of belief' provide familiar examples. Suppose that a set A of assumptions raises the credibility of an event described by a sentence b above a certain threshold. (Lower case letters will stand for sentences in a given language, upper case letters denote sets of sentences.) Then it is quite possible that the credibility of b falls below that threshold if further assumptions are added to A. Thus, while one may be prepared to accept b on the assumptions A, one may prefer to remain agnostic about b given additional information. Credibility here may be measured by ordinary probability or by more general measures, such as Shackle's (1979) non-additive degrees of belief (where the credence of mutually exclusive and jointly exhaustive alternatives need not add up to unity). Indeed, most advocates of non-monotonic formalisms insist that they model a wider class of phenomena than can be captured by ordinary probability functions.

A particularly simple source of non-monotonicity is the 'closed world assumption' (CWA). With respect to a given collection of data about some subject matter it states that the collection is complete; that no relevant information is left out. Hence, if a is not part of the collection, it is safe to assume $\neg a$. Since a may be derivable from a larger set of data, derivability under the CWA is non-monotonic. The CWA is behind the treatment of 'negation as failure' in Prolog ('Programming in logic', a programming language): Prolog derives $\neg a$ from a set of data D just in case a query for a given D fails. (Caution: a must be of a suitably simple syntactic kind. For complex sentences, negation as failure is a delicate and potentially hazardous matter.)

Another source of non-monotonicity is the licence to draw from a pool of presumptions ('defaults') as long as these are 'safe' to use (that is, consistent). For example, if one is told that tea is served, one will naturally act on the presumption that it is served plain or with milk and/or sugar. That presumption may become unsafe as additional information is supplied (such as that tea is served with brake fluid or salt).

Default logic (Reiter 1980) is one of the first and most influential theories responding to this source of non-monotonicity. It serves well as a principal example of a non-monotonic logic because it exhibits very clearly three characteristic features of almost all theories of non-monotonic reasoning: first, closure under rules with premises that require tests for non-derivability ('non-Horn' rules); second, a non-unique process of extending premises using defaults; and third, some method for reducing the multitude of extensions and for specifying a univocal set of conclusions.

A 'default theory' (D, A) (giving rise to a default logic) consists of a set A of premises (or 'facts') and a set D of default rules ('defaults' for short), each of the form

(1) $(B : C) \Rightarrow a.$

These rules are to be read as follows: infer a from B unless C is inconsistent with what can be known by default on the basis of A.

A similar and, under certain conditions, equivalent way of expressing defaults is by modal formulas such as

(1′) $\Box b \wedge \neg \Box \neg c \rightarrow a,$

as in Moore's (1985) auto-epistemic logic, where $\Box a$ may be read 'a is known'.

The rule (1) is non-Horn, since the 'unless' clause must be verified by showing that no contradiction can be derived from C together with the closure of A under the default rules.

Closing the premises A under the default rules in D issues in an extension of the default theory (D, A). More precisely, let $\Sigma = (S_0, S_1, \ldots)$ be a sequence of sets of formulas with $S_0 = A$, let S be the union of all its members, and let each S_i in Σ be such that

$$S_{i+1} = \{a: \text{there is a default } (B : C) \Rightarrow a \text{ in } D,$$
$$B \subseteq Cn(S_i) \text{ and}$$
$$C \text{ is consistent with } S\}$$

(where Cn denotes the operation of generating the deductive consequence of a given set). For each such sequence Σ, $Cn(S)$ is called an 'extension' of the default theory (D, A).

To see how a single default theory (D, A) gives rise to a multitude of extensions, let $A = \{a\}$ and consider a set D of two defaults,

(2) $(a : \neg b) \Rightarrow c$
(3) $(a : \neg c) \Rightarrow b$

If we first close A under (2), we obtain a set A_1 containing c, so b cannot be inferred using (3). If we first close A under (3) we obtain a set A_2 containing b, so c cannot be inferred using (2). Thus, the result of extending a set of premises ('facts') by using default rules depends on the order in which the rules are applied. In general there are many extensions of a set of facts under default rules; sometimes there are none (Poole 1994: §7).

The multiplicity can be resolved by intersecting a set of selected extensions. There are three basic options for selecting: according to the 'sceptical' (full meet) solution, all extensions should be selected; the 'brave' (maxi-choice) approach recommends selecting a single extension; and the 'cautious' (partial meet) approach is less committal in requiring only that some extensions be selected. In each case a set of premises A is said to entail a conclusion b by default D just in case b follows deductively from the intersection of all selected extensions of A under D. How should one select among possible extensions? Some approaches recommend that the basis should be syntactic information about the applied defaults: for example, that extensions generated by more specific defaults should take precedence over those generated by more high-handed ones. Others assume that defaults are to be ordered, either by a qualitative preference ranking or by a numerical assignment of degrees of belief.

2 Patterns and models of non-monotonic inference

Inference is 'defeasible' if new information may undermine old conclusions. Formal theories of non-monotonic reasoning differ greatly both as to the kind of defeasibility they focus on and as to their chosen level of generality. They also differ, at first sight, from what are typically referred to as 'logics'. Still, the term logic is appropriate because all these theories can be used to specify a relation in some formal language which exhibits many of the patterns usually associated with relations of inference.

It is not enough to characterize defeasible inference negatively by the possible failure of monotonicity. We also need to ask: which conditions are compatible with defeasibility and which conditions should be satisfied by any relation of inference? These questions point towards continuing the abstract study of consequence relations (or operations) initiated by Tarski (1930). By abstracting from the particular ways in which inference relations are generated we turn to properties they may share.

Let $Cn(A)$ stand for the set of classical and $C(A)$ for the set of defeasible consequences of some set A. Among the more stable properties for C that have emerged are the following:

$A \subseteq C(A)$	(inclusion)
$C(A) = C(C(A))$	(idempotence)
If $A \subseteq B \subseteq C(A)$ then $C(A) = C(B)$	(cumulativity)
$Cn(A) \subseteq C(A)$	(supraclassicality)

$$C(A) \cap C(B) \subseteq C(Cn(A) \cap Cn(B)) \qquad \text{(distribution)}$$

In the presence of the other conditions, cumulativity is equivalent to the slightly more perspicuous: from $A \subseteq C(B)$ infer $C(A \cup B) = C(A)$. The properties of C may be recast in terms of a relation $A \hspace{-0.3em}\mid\hspace{-0.6em}\sim b$, defined to mean $b \in C(A)$. For example, cumulativity combines the classical principles of cut,

$$\text{If } (\forall b \in B)A \hspace{-0.3em}\mid\hspace{-0.6em}\sim b \text{ and } A \cup B \hspace{-0.3em}\mid\hspace{-0.6em}\sim c, \text{ then } A \hspace{-0.3em}\mid\hspace{-0.6em}\sim c \qquad \text{(cut)}$$

with a cautious form of monotonicity,

$$\text{If } (\forall b \in B)A \hspace{-0.3em}\mid\hspace{-0.6em}\sim b \text{ and } A \hspace{-0.3em}\mid\hspace{-0.6em}\sim c, \text{ then } A \cup B \hspace{-0.3em}\mid\hspace{-0.6em}\sim c.$$

$$\text{(cautious monotonicity)}$$

Inference operations (and their associated relations) satisfying the first three conditions are called 'cumulative'; if they also satisfy the last two conditions, they are called 'classically cumulative'. Note that although the above list describes the common core of various theories of non-monotonic inference, theories based on high probability rules for acceptance are not among them. If $A \hspace{-0.3em}\mid\hspace{-0.6em}\sim b$ is defined to hold just in case the probability of b given all members of A reaches a certain threshold, then $\hspace{-0.3em}\mid\hspace{-0.6em}\sim$ satisfies neither cut nor cautious monotonicity, nor can $\hspace{-0.3em}\mid\hspace{-0.6em}\sim$ be both idempotent and supraclassical; for that would entail the objectionable left absorption principle $C = CnC$. (Objectionable because of 'lottery paradoxes' where both a and b are accepted, while their logical consequence $a \wedge b$ is not (see Kyburg 1961).) Still, high probability accounts of $\hspace{-0.3em}\mid\hspace{-0.6em}\sim$ can be made to score better on the above properties, if the probability required for acceptance is pushed high enough, that is, infinitely close to unity. Such accounts have been developed by Adams (1975) and Pearl (1988).

Cumulative inference can be characterized in terms of *preferential models* (see Shoham 1987; Kraus, Lehmann and Magidor 1990; Makinson 1994). These consist of a set of 'states' ordered by some relation $<$ and a mapping $| \ |$ assigning to each sentence a set of states. Intuitively, the mapping takes a sentence to a state just in case the sentence truly describes the state, and the relation $<$ orders states with respect to their 'extravagance' (conversely, 'naturalness'). For example, a state in which tea is served with a dash of brake fluid is less natural (more extravagant) than a state in which tea is served with salt, which in turn is still less natural than serving tea with sugar or with milk or with both. The most natural states are the states we can expect to obtain unless there is evidence to the contrary.

If $|a|$ is the set of all states at which a holds, then the minimal elements of $|a|$ under $<$ represent the most natural ('preferred') ways for a to be true. The condition of 'stopperedness' (sometimes called 'smoothness'; see also the 'limit' assumption in Lewis 1973) requires that there always are minimal elements.

For each set A of sentences, let $|A|_<$ denote the set of minimal states at which all sentences in A hold. Then A *preferentially* entails b just in case $|A|_< \subseteq |b|$. In contrast to ordinary entailment, preferential entailment restricts the domain of quantification: not all possible but only the most natural ways in which all elements of A can be true are considered. Since a most natural way for A to be true may not be a most natural way for $A \cup B$ to be true, preferential entailment is not monotonic. To illustrate: we may find that all most natural ways of making the sentence 'tea is served' true will please someone in the room. But that finding may well be undermined, if we move to considering all 'natural' ways of serving tea with brake fluid.

It can be shown that (stoppered) preferential entailment is a cumulative inference relation and that every cumulative inference relation can be presented as a relation of preferential entailment. (For the representation results mentioned here see Makinson 1994: §3.4.) The condition of stopperedness guarantees that preferential entailment will be cautiously monotonic. (To see how cautious monotonicity may fail in non-stoppered models let the states be indexed by the natural numbers and let s_m be more natural than s_n just in case m is greater than n. Consider three sentences a, b, c such that a holds everywhere, c fails everywhere and b holds at the first state only. Then $|a|_< = \emptyset$ because there is no most natural state for a. So, on the one hand we have both $|a|_< \subseteq |b|$ and $|a|_< \subseteq |c|$ vacuously. On the other hand, there is exactly one state – namely the first – that satisfies both a and b. Hence, $|\{a, b\}|_<$ – having the first state as its (only) member – cannot be contained in $|c|$ since the latter was assumed to be empty.)

If the mapping $|\ |$ is classically well-behaved (that is, satisfies the equations $|a \wedge b| = |a| \cap |b|$ and $|\neg a| = \overline{|a|}$), then each state will be closed under classical consequence whence preferential entailment will be supraclassical. Moreover, it will also be distributive and thus satisfy the conditions for being classically cumulative. Conversely, each classically cumulative inference can be represented as preferential entailment in preferential models that respect the truth-functional connectives.

Supraclassicality is a rather common property of non-monotonic reasoning. It gives formal expression to the idea that such reasoning goes beyond what can be inferred 'safely' (deductively) from a given body of knowledge. However, some theories of non-monotonic inference (like those based on defeasible

inheritance nets or on reason maintenance systems) fail to fully extend classical logic because they operate in impoverished fragments of classical languages. Such restrictions are usually introduced for computational reasons; they are not based on principled objections to supraclassicality.

Note also that in so far as non-monotonic logics are supraclassical, they are not rivals but extensions of classical logic. This sets them apart from certain other logics which fail to be monotonic, such as relevance, linear and many paraconsistent logics. These logics are *sub*classical and their source of non-monotonicity is different, having nothing to do with 'risk-taking'.

3 Related work

A sentence b may be (defeasibly) inferred from a set A in the light of background assumptions B just in case b follows logically from A together with as much of B as is compatible with A. The right-hand side of this equivalence can be seen as involving a step of belief change: from the background beliefs B to a *revision* of B so as to accommodate A (with a minimal amount of change). Belief revision and defeasible inference thus appear to be two sides of the same coin.

The correspondence between belief revision and non-monotonic reasoning has been investigated in depth by Gärdenfors and Makinson (1994). In contrast, Levi (1995) argues that the correspondence can only be partial because the sole purpose of belief revision is to accommodate belief-contravening evidence. Such accommodation obeys a maxim of minimal change. But in so far as non-monotonic reasoning also covers ampliative inference, it must go beyond the maxim of minimal change governing belief revision. Hence, according to Levi, properties of non-monotonic inference as generated by belief revision on the one hand and as generated by ampliative inference on the other hand cannot be expected to coincide.

There is a close relation between counterfactual conditionals and belief revision via the 'Ramsey test': accept a conditional 'If a were the case, then b would be the case' in a state of belief A just in case you would accept b if A had to be revised so as to contain a. Given the correspondence, noted in the last paragraph, between belief revision and non-monotonic reasoning, one expects – and will not be disappointed – to find similarities between counterfactuals and non-monotonic reasoning.

A more direct route to such similarities is opened by comparing preferential models with the Stalnaker–Lewis semantics for counterfactuals (see COUNTERFACTUAL CONDITIONALS §§3–4). In this semantics a counterfactual is pronounced true in a 'world' w just in case the consequent is true in all the closest possible worlds (that is, those worlds which depart as little as possible from w) that make the antecedent true. There is an obvious similarity between the condition for evaluating preferential entailments and that for evaluating counterfactuals: not all antecedent-worlds are examined but only those that are minimal under a certain relation. But there are also differences. Because each model for counterfactuals is equipped with as many relations of closeness as there are worlds to be close to, counterfactuals can be evaluated (differently) at single worlds. By contrast, preferential models have only one relation; accordingly, preferential entailments are assessed not with respect to single worlds but only in a model as a whole. It is a controversial matter how to interpret such subtle differences (see Makinson 1993): whether preferential entailments are essentially valid counterfactuals frozen at the first degree (that is, with the conditional connective joining truth-functional formulas only) or whether the differences are more substantial.

See also: LOGICAL AND MATHEMATICAL TERMS, GLOSSARY OF

References and further reading

* Adams, E. (1975) *The Logic of Conditionals*, Dordrecht: Reidel. (Derives a relation of defeasible inference (p-entailment) from limiting probability valuations.)

Brewka, G. (1991) *Non-Monotonic Reasoning: Logical Foundations of Commonsense*, Cambridge: Cambridge University Press. (A concise introduction to the topic.)

Gabbay, D.M., Hogger, C.J. and Robinson, J.A. (eds) (1994) *Handbook of Logic in Artificial Intelligence and Logic Programming*, vol. 3, *Non-Monotonic Reasoning*, Oxford: Oxford University Press. (A collection of authoritative surveys.)

* Gärdenfors, P. and Makinson, D. (1994) 'Non-Monotonic Inference Based on Expectations', *Artificial Intelligence* 65: 197–245. (Investigates correspondences between belief change and non-monotonic reasoning.)

* Kraus, S., Lehmann, D. and Magidor, M. (1990) 'Non-Monotonic Reasoning, Preferential Models and Cumulative Logics', *Artificial Intelligence* 44: 167–207. (A study of models for non-monotonic inference relations extending the approach of Shoham (1987).)

* Kyburg, H. (1961) *Probability and the Logic of Rational Belief*, Middleton, CT: Wesleyan University Press. (An early treatise of defeasible inference

as in high probability accounts of acceptance. See also Kyburg's contribution to Gabbay *et al.* (1994).)

* Levi, I. (1995) *For the Sake of the Argument: Ramsey Test Conditionals, Inductive Inference and Non-monotonic Reasoning*, Cambridge: Cambridge University Press. (Critically examines non-monotonic logic in the light of philosophical studies of inductive inference and rational belief change.)

* Lewis, D.K. (1973) *Counterfactuals*, Oxford: Blackwell. (Seminal study of models for counterfactual conditionals.)

* Makinson, D. (1993) 'Five Faces of Minimality', *Studia Logica* 52: 339–79. (Compares various ways of using the notion of 'minimality' in semantics for non-monotonic logic, semantics for conditionals and for conditional obligation, belief change and updating.)

* —— (1994) 'General Patterns in Non-Monotonic Reasoning', in D.M. Gabbay, C.J. Hogger and J.A. Robinson (eds) *Handbook of Logic in Artificial Intelligence and Logic Programming*, vol. 3, *Non-Monotonic Reasoning*, Oxford: Oxford University Press. (Focuses on the material of §2.)

* Moore, R.C. (1985) 'Semantical Considerations on Non-Monotonic Logic', *Artificial Intelligence* 25: 75–94. (Develops the modal version of default logic.)

* Pearl, J. (1988) *Probabilistic Reasoning in Intelligent Systems*, San Mateo, CA: Morgan Kaufmann. (Derives non-monotonic inference from limiting probability valuations. Rediscovers and further develops Adams' (1975) theory of p-entailment (under the name of ε-entailment).)

* Poole, D. (1994) 'Default Logic', in D.M. Gabbay, C.J. Hogger and J.A. Robinson (eds) *Handbook of Logic in Artificial Intelligence and Logic Programming*, vol. 3, *Non-Monotonic Reasoning*, Oxford: Oxford University Press. (A survey of default logics.)

* Reiter, R. (1980) 'A Logic for Default Reasoning', *Artificial Intelligence* 13: 81–132. (Classic presentation of default logic.)

* Shackle, G.L.S. (1979) *Imagination and the Nature of Choice*, Edinburgh: Edinburgh University Press. (Shackle's writings have informally anticipated many of the models of non-monotonic reasoning.)

* Shoham, Y. (1987) 'A Semantical Approach to Non-Monotonic Logics', in *Readings on Non-Monotonic Reasoning*, ed. M. Ginsberg, Los Altos, CA: Morgan Kaufmann. (First presentation of preferential models.)

* Tarski, A. (1930) 'Fundamentale Begriffe der Methodologie der deduktiven Wissenschaften I', *Monatshefte für Mathematik und Physik* 37: 361–404; trans. J.H. Woodger (1956), 'Fundamental Con-

cepts of the Methodology of Deductive Sciences', in *Logic, Semantics, Metamathematics: Papers from 1923 to 1938*, ed. J. Corcoran, Indianapolis, IN: Hackett Publishing Company, 2nd edn, 1983, 60–109. (Classic study of abstract consequence operations.)

Ullman-Margalit, E. (1973) 'On Presumptions', *Journal of Philosophy* 80: 143–63. (Develops informally many of the ideas underlying formal theories of non-probabilistic non-monotonic reasoning.)

ANDRÉ FUHRMANN

NONSTANDARD MODELS

see LÖWENHEIM–SKOLEM THEOREMS AND NONSTANDARD MODELS

NORMATIVE EPISTEMOLOGY

There are three kinds of normative work in epistemology. The first is the provision of epistemic advice, which offers guidance towards improving the cognitive condition of an individual or community. This advice often concerns science. Philosophers in the tradition of Francis Bacon have sought to identify and advocate proper forms of scientific research and explanation. More generally, according to some philosophers, a principal epistemological task is that of finding and recommending ways to improve the whole range of our individual and collective cognitive activities.

A second kind of epistemology is classified as normative because evaluative concepts figure in explanations. For example, A.J. Ayer explains knowledge partly in terms of having a right to be sure. Other evaluative notions enter into work in this category, such as intellectual duties, responsibilities and virtues. Some of these are specifically ethical notions; some are non-ethical evaluative notions such as proper cognitive functioning and intellectual excellence.

Epistemic concepts such as justification and rationality appear to be normative, or at least evaluative, in a way that contrasts with purely descriptive concepts. One tendency in naturalistic epistemology is to seek either to explain away this appearance or to reconcile it with a scientific worldview. Non-naturalistic efforts in epistemology commonly find no reason to undertake this project, and are consequently often counted as normative. Most historical epistemology is normative by this standard.

1 **Advisory epistemology**
2 **Evaluative epistemology**
3 **Non-naturalistic epistemology**

1 Advisory epistemology

Francis Bacon and René Descartes are among the prominent historical philosophers who advocated methods of cognitive improvement. Bacon (1620) defended methodological departures from the scholastic intellectual traditions that prevailed in Europe in his time. The investigative practices that Bacon recommended constituted early modern scientific methodology (see BACON, F. §§4–8).

Descartes (1701) elaborated a system of rules to guide inquiry. His most characteristic enterprise was a search for certainty in his beliefs. He advocated a method of doubt for achieving certainty. In Descartes' view, beliefs that withstand the strongest reasons for doubt are certain. Such beliefs are distinguished by being clearly and distinctly perceived. His rules are designed to facilitate achieving this (see DESCARTES, R. §4).

In the twentieth century, Alvin Goldman among others has supported advisory projects for epistemologists. Goldman (1986) has championed 'epistemics': an alliance between epistemology and cognitive psychology. Epistemologists contribute to the joint effort by identifying epistemically desirable magnitudes that apply to belief formation process types, such as the truth-to-falsehood ratio of the doxastic output of a process type. Psychologists determine the degree to which actual psychological processes exemplify these magnitudes. They also contribute to epistemics by studying how, and to what extent, our cognitive capacities allow the magnitudes to be exemplified to other degrees. In light of such psychological findings epistemologists engaged in epistemics propose strategies for effecting cognitive improvements.

Advisory epistemology has problematic characteristics. For one thing, philosophical thought does not seem to constitute a suitable preparation for recommending successful ways to conduct empirical science. Effective ways to learn the contingent facts that are the subject matter of science seem themselves to be matters of contingent empirical fact. Bacon and other philosophers of science may well have happened to acquire the empirical information useful in making helpful recommendations in this area. But the actual efficacy of any given empirical research strategy seems to be an empirical question rather than a philosophical one.

More fundamental difficulties affect epistemological advice on all topics. These problems concern whether there is some distinctive epistemic standard, and whether there is any general justification for recommending cognitive conditions or processes that have some positive epistemic status. Epistemic advice seems to include identifying and asserting effective techniques for gaining various epistemically favourable outcomes, such as reasonable beliefs, justified beliefs, true beliefs, and knowledge. This multiplicity of positive potential outcomes does not always coincide, and that leads to the first problem. Note that it might be feasible to get someone to believe some difficult truth for a bad reason and feasible to give them good reason to believe the negation of that truth, but not feasible to get them to believe the truth for a good reason. When there is some such competition between apparently valuable epistemic states, what is 'epistemically advisable'? A single overriding ranking of epistemic outcomes would answer this sort of question. But does such a ranking exist, and if so, why does it override?

The other fundamental problem concerns justification for issuing any epistemic advice. Is some such advice somehow justified even when the advised outcome is not sought and is not an effective means for attaining anything that is sought? For instance, suppose that a friend is interested in forming a belief about what fraction of the inhabitants of Tibet are Buddhists. It might seem to be sensible epistemic advice to recommend forming this belief on the basis of a large and randomly selected sample. Believing on this sort of basis may well give such beliefs a relatively high truth-to-falsehood ratio. Does this make that basis 'epistemically advisable'? Suppose that a friend wants to form a fanciful belief on the topic, with no concern for its truth. If so, what justification would there be for offering the hypothesized advice? Or suppose that the friend seeks certainty and nothing less. The advised procedure will not yield that. Would the same recommendation be apposite, and if so, why?

Recommendations can be justified in various ways. Advice can be justified for the sake of meeting several sorts of standards, such as moral ones, legal ones and goal-oriented ones. So various beliefs and inferences might be morally, legally or instrumentally advisable. But there seems not to be any unified notion of 'cognitive betterment' that could provide some distinctively epistemic standard justifying the issuing of doxastic advice (see SCIENTIFIC METHOD).

2 Evaluative epistemology

In a tradition which is traceable to John Locke, some philosophers have theorized about epistemic notions in plainly evaluative terms. One line of thinking, directly initiated by Locke and recently represented by Roderick Chisholm, appeals to intellectual duty. Another approach, stemming from Cartesian and Lockean origins and present in recent work by Laurence BonJour (1985) and Hilary Kornblith (1980), explains a kind of epistemic justification for belief in terms of responsible doxastic conduct.

Criticism has been offered of requiring any such duty fulfilment or responsible conduct in order for believing to have some positive epistemic status. Some objections are based on the assumption that epistemic duties or responsibilities are limited by our ability to comply with them. A common sort of objection adds the premise that we seldom if ever have control over what we believe. These assumptions together imply that we seldom if ever have such duties or responsibilities to believe otherwise than we actually do. Yet believing otherwise frequently does have some positive epistemic status. Thus dutiful or responsible doxastic conduct is not required for having this status.

There is a reasonable reply to this criticism. It is doubtful that all duties are limited by the ability to comply with them. Duties from various sources seem to exceed this limit. Political entities appear to impose legal duties beyond the abilities of their citizens always to comply. The duties taken on by agreeing to perform a job with certain assigned responsibilities may turn out not to be feasible to accomplish. So the general principle that duties can always be met seems unacceptable. Even within the sphere of purely ethical duties, it has been credibly argued that obligations can exceed abilities. Consequently, the principle that epistemic duties in particular are limited by ability stands in need of some special defence.

Alvin Plantinga (1993) has offered a different criticism of a reliance on intellectual duties in a theory of knowledge. Plantinga's topic is a theory of warrant. 'Warrant' is his term for a magnitude the bearing of enough of which by a true belief constitutes a case of knowledge. Plantinga objects to the thought, derived from work by Chisholm, that believing a proposition as a result of trying one's best to fulfil one's epistemic duties is sufficient for being warranted in the belief to some significant extent. Plantinga describes the following case. Paul is given by a malicious demon a nearly overwhelming tendency to believe that whenever it sounds to him as though a church bell is ringing what he is hearing is orange in colour. All who are around Paul have been given this same tendency. Plantinga contends that, by acceding to this strong inclination when hearing a church bell sound and believing that what he hears is orange, Paul would fulfil his epistemic duties. Yet this belief would have little or no warrant for Paul. Plantinga concludes that complying with intellectual duty is not sufficient for being significantly warranted in the resulting belief.

There is a promising reply to this objection. It can be maintained that having even a nearly overwhelming tendency to believe something does not generate an intellectual duty to believe it. What intellectual duties require is conformity to epistemic reason. A sound and a colour are conspicuously diverse. In Plantinga's example Paul is ascribed no *reason* for thinking that the two go together. So, intellectual duty calls for Paul to refrain from forming the colour belief. He would thereby respond rationally to the manifest lack of any evidential connection with the sound. He has no epistemic ground, and hence no duty, to give in here to a powerful but unreasonable impulse. Thus, this sort of case does not seem to pose an insuperable problem for the claim in question that complying with intellectual duty is sufficient for having significant warrant.

3 Non-naturalistic epistemology

Naturalism in epistemology has no widely accepted definition. Naturalistic epistemologists variously ally themselves with science in ontology or method. They tend to seek explanations of epistemic facts that employ properties with actually or prospectively good scientific credentials, such as causal relations and statistical probabilities, and they tend to classify the epistemological claims that they make as empirical rather than a priori (see NATURALIZED EPISTEMOLOGY). Sometimes it is counted as adequately naturalistic to postulate entities that have some suitable sort of ontological dependence on physical reality, whether or not the postulated entities themselves play a role in physical science (see SUPERVENIENCE).

It is notoriously difficult to see how ethical features such as intrinsic goodness and moral obligation can be part of the sort of reality that science describes. Like such ethical evaluations, some epistemological categories seem to resist assimilation to a scientific worldview. Several of the main epistemological characterizations, such as 'justified', 'rational' and 'reasonable', seem to make comparably evaluative appraisals of the mental states or processes to which they are applied. It is comparably unclear how such epistemic attributes of belief and reasoning fit into the world of natural science. Naturalistic epistemologists characteristically attempt to clarify this fit or eliminate the recalcitrant epistemic features.

Other epistemologists do not make this attempt. At one non-naturalistic extreme there is work like that of Alvin Plantinga, who argues that God plays a role in the nature of warrant. Plantinga conceives of warrant in terms of properly functioning cognitive mechan-isms. He argues that only the intentional design of these mechanisms by God is adequate to explain their proper function. This sort of view relies on a defiantly non-naturalistic ontology.

Many non-naturalist epistemologists simply theorize in terms of whatever concepts they find adequate to their theoretical tasks, without paying heed to naturalistic constraints. For instance, a coherence relation among propositions figures in some theories of epistemic justification, and often no effort is made to square the existence of this coherence relation with a scientific ontology (see KNOWLEDGE AND JUSTIFICATION, COHERENCE THEORY OF).

Non-naturalistic methodology is common in epistemology. Explicit appeals are made to a priori considerations in defence of epistemological theses, typically by claiming support by appeal to intuitive judgments about hypothetical cases. This methodological departure from natural science marks the work as non-naturalistic.

Some epistemologists thus do not abide by the ontological and methodological constraints that are characteristic of naturalism. This is unproblematic to the extent that these constraints are inadequately defended. Notably, they seem to have no credible defence when applied to the analogous field of pure mathematics. To ban from mathematical research a priori considerations or ontological commitments beyond the foreseeable domain of natural science would abolish the discipline. This would be unwise. Unconstrained mathematics efforts yield some of our clearest and most secure knowledge.

It seems similarly unwise to burden epistemological inquiry with naturalistic constraints. Much non-naturalistic epistemological work is relevantly similar in method and subject matter to mathematical work that yields knowledge. Although established results are rare in epistemology, the example of mathematics shows that we have good reason not to blame the paucity of such success on a violation of naturalistic constraints.

See also: EPISTEMOLOGY AND ETHICS

References and further reading

Alston, W. (1985) 'Concepts of Epistemic Justification', *The Monist* 68 (1): 57–89. (Argues against theories of justification that appeal to intellectual duty.)

Ayer, A.J. (1956) *The Problem of Knowledge*, London: Macmillan. (Employs the evaluative primitive of having a right to be sure in an analysis of knowledge. See especially chapter 1.)

* Bacon, F. (1620) *Novum Organum*, trans. J. Spedding,

R.L. Ellis and D.D. Heath as *The New Organon*, ed. Fulton Anderson, Indianapolis, IN: Bobbs-Merrill, 1960. (Advocates an early form of modern scientific methodology.)

* BonJour, L. (1985) *The Structure of Empirical Knowledge*, Cambridge, MA: Harvard University Press. (Widely discussed presentation of a coherentist theory of justification, where justification is said to be ultimately determined by a sort of intellectual responsibility.)

Chisholm, R. (1966) *Theory of Knowledge*, New York: Prentice Hall, 2nd edn, 1977. (Classic effort in analytical epistemology, one that makes irreducible use of a notion of intellectual duty.)

* Descartes, R. (1701) *Rules for the Direction of the Mind*, trans. and ed. E.S. Haldane and G.R.T. Ross, London: Cambridge University Press, 1967. (Recommends rules for discovering the truth with clarity and distinctness.)

* Goldman, A. (1986) *Epistemology and Cognition*, Cambridge, MA: Harvard University Press. (Contains an extended exposition and defence of the partially advisory discipline of epistemics.)

* Kornblith, H. (1983) 'Justified Belief and Epistemically Responsible Action', *The Philosophical Review* 92: 33–48. (Explains epistemic justification for belief in terms of responsible conduct.)

Locke, J. (1689) *Essay Concerning Human Understanding*, ed. A.C. Fraser, New York: Dover, 1959. (Contains a classic statement of empiricist evaluative epistemology.)

* Plantinga, A. (1993) *Warrant: The Current Debate*, New York: Oxford University Press. (Contains a useful survey and critique of literature on epistemic justification, and includes a brief sketch of Plantinga's proper functionalist theory of warrant.)

Stich, S. (1990) *The Fragmentation of Reason*, Cambridge, MA: MIT Press. (Attacks analytic epistemology and advocates a pragmatic sort of advisory epistemology.)

EARL CONEE

NORMS, LEGAL

A legal norm sets a standard of behaviour. As a norm, it thus can remain in existence even though it is broken. Norms can be distinguished from causal laws which need to be reinterpreted if an exception is found. Linguistic signals help us determine what the norm is. Thus 'ought', 'must', 'shall', 'have to', 'right', 'wrong', 'good', 'bad', and so on, characteristically belong to the statement of norms, whereas words like 'is', 'are', 'were', 'will be' 'possible', 'impossible' tend to show descriptive rules. These linguistic signals reflect a difference, they do not constitute it. There are many counterexamples: thus 'swimming is forbidden' and 'we ought to be at the col now' express normativity and description respectively.

Whatever is for someone a standard for their conduct is normative for them. One might say that the idea stems from the notion of measurement. That we 'run the rule' over someone or 'get the measure of them' stems from the idea of measuring, of imposing a standard on them or on oneself.

Where does the legal norm stem from? There are two main views: the practice theory holds that norms are expressions or articulations of people's behaviour; the interpretive theory holds that norms are not connected to behaviour in the way the practice theory holds but are the means whereby we make sense of such behaviour. But the connection between the two groups is much closer than appears at first sight.

1   **Normativity and description**
2   **The practice theory**
3   **The norm as interpretation**

1   Normativity and description

The law prohibiting murder seems both different from, and more mysterious than, the law of gravity. Why? One can break the former and it will still be valid and in existence but we still have to follow it. There is still something that constrains us, that binds us. The fact that the murder rate has gone up will not be taken as evidence that it does not exist. However, if objects started to float away into space then the law of gravity would have to be revised, an exception to the scientific law must modify it. The law cannot be broken.

We can explain this by looking at the difference between 'doing something as a rule' and 'having a rule about something', as Hart posed it (1961). Take the behaviour of a group of cars at a traffic intersection. We could say that they stop at the red traffic lights 'as a rule'. This would imply that there is a certain regularity of behaviour but that if there is a departure from it this will be merely something unusual, a departure from the average. Scientific laws stem from this sort of observation. They generalize into a rule what normally happens, what people do 'as a rule'. This will take the form of some causal explanation about the nature of the world. But we can give another explanation. We may say that the cars' behaviour is governed by the Road Traffic Act. There is a difference between that law and the causal one we observed earlier. The former is provisional. If we find that cars do not stop at red lights any more that means that our causal law is invalid and we have to amend it. Whereas the fact that cars do not stop at red traffic lights does not make the Road Traffic Act invalid. We ought to obey even if we do not. We are not looking at the generalization of 'as a rule' behaviour. Rather we are looking at a standard of behaviour, departure from which would not just be seen as unusual but as a reason for criticism. Here there is a prescription as to what behaviour is required. In the first case there was not. The former is a normative law while the causal law is descriptive.

We now turn to asking what the legal norm is and how we can recognize it. This is closely tied up with where normativity itself comes from. The question as to whether something is a religious norm, a moral norm or a legal norm is mainly a formal question. Thus, as we will see below, the basic question when looking at the legal norm is to understand its normativity.

2   The practice theory

We may first of all think of the norm as stemming from simple iteration; that is, what is done once will be done again, and will through repetition induce expectation, in this way producing normativity. Thus, *per* Hayek (1969), normativity comes from custom which is generalized into abstract and general rules. This is the best way because it reflects that what people should have as standards of behaviour is what over a long period of time they have done. What is important here is the iteration. Something happening over and over again is what imparts normativity. The legal norm is the abstraction of that.

Hayek's theory is a modern version of older theories that stressed custom as the source of law. John AUSTIN thought that custom missed out the element of the will: the legal norm was a species of command. The norm is the imposition of the will of one person, who sets the standard of behaviour, on another. Thus Austin (1971) gives a definition of law (the legal norm) as the command of a sovereign backed by a sanction. Laws are thus a species of commands, directed by sovereigns to their subjects. They are an exercise of political will or power and necessarily involve the imposition of sanctions in the case of disobedience. But, behind obedience to this will, there re-enter descriptive regularities of custom and usage in the shape of what Austin calls habit.

Austin defines the sovereign as the 'political superior' towards whom the population exhibits a 'habit of obedience'. As a political superior the sovereign's power and authority is based in social practices and in the social fact of habitual obedience –

the social source of law. The normativity of law, one might say, comes ultimately from the barrel of the gun which people habitually obey (see SOVEREIGNTY §2).

H.L.A. HART is more complicated. He wants to reject the command theory but still claim that normativity comes from social practice. For him norms are not merely commands but can be seen as rules. The key is in his famous distinction between being obliged and having an obligation. Austin's version of the legal norm misses the idea of obligation. It can be best likened to the gunman who demands money from you. You are obliged to give it to him, but only as long as he is pointing the gun at you. The legal norm lasts after the gunman has gone. It is something more than merely a habit of obedience to some commander. Habits refer only to the external regularities of behaviour. By contrast there is an internal aspect in the case of rules of conduct shared by members of a social group. This depends upon the attitude (a critical reflective attitude) of insiders of the group. For them a certain regular pattern of behaviour is not merely observable regularity. It is a standard for the criticism of conduct which contravenes the pattern in question. This is expressed in the idea of obligation. This comes both from people's behaviour and from their attitude. To say that someone has an obligation implies two statements, a cognitive statement that there are observed regularities and a volitional one that people have the critically reflective attitude to that regularity.

The above are examples of a general way of seeing the legal norm that can be called the practice theory; the norm must be inextricably connected to real action in the world. Normativity then stems from people's practices. But this idea has also been criticized. One can always intelligibly ask of a practice whether one ought to follow it and therefore the norm cannot be constituted by the practice. For Hart this does not make sense. If there is a critically reflective practice it would be unintelligible for someone within that to ask whether they ought to follow it. It would be like asking if the standard metre bar in Paris (by which the metre used to be defined) is really a metre. However, for Kelsen (1960) it would make sense because, in following this practice, we assume that is how a metre ought to be defined. And this explains why for Kelsen the *Grundnorm* (the norm from which all other norms in the system get validity) has to be presupposed to be valid while the equivalent for Hart (the ultimate rule of recognition) just is.

3   The norm as interpretation

For KELSEN, then, the legal norm is the meaning of an act of will. It is not the police waving the car down but the meaning of the police's act as saying that 'you ought, by the authority vested in me by the Road Traffic Act, to stop' that is the legal norm. The content of the norm must not be confused with its physical expression. But behaviour still has some importance in the sense that one can only derive a legal norm in the context of efficacious behaviour. It only makes sense to understand the physical activities that constitute the parliamentary process as law-making behaviour when people by and large do treat them as such and obey them.

In separating the norm more and more from behaviour in the physical world, we can see the legal norm as a standard of judgment. Thus Dworkin (1986) attacks the rule-based theory of law and sees principles and latterly rights as being the key to the legal norm (see DWORKIN, R.). But where do they come from? In his interpretivist turn we see the return of practice. For the rights are our interpretation of the community's practice. We can thus say that they are the meaning of the community's practice. Now this sounds remarkably like Kelsen's version of the legal norm. For it is the meaning of the practices that is important and that is what gives us the rights. If however we think of the practices as constituting the rights then we see something more like Hart, even though Dworkin, ironically, started his professional life by attacking Hart. The meaning of the practices is locked into the practices that we do and we cannot go beyond them; the legal norm (in the form of rights) comes from our interpretation of them. For him too it makes no sense for someone inside the practice to question its validity.

This shows the difficulties of making a rigid separation between the normative and the descriptive, at least in the way that the normative is generated. Because, even for Kelsen, it makes no sense to generate a meaning except in the context of by-and-large efficacy. We have a sort of spectrum then. The norm is custom or habit and is thus fully expressed in the practice or, more complicatedly, in a critically reflective practice. Kelsen separates the critically reflective from the practice in order to separate the meaning of the norm from the act of will that generates it. But that separation does not work totally because we can, as Dworkin does, construct the hermeneutic circle and see the meaning as constituting the practice (see COMMON LAW).

That one cannot get totally away from practice can also be seen in another critic of the practice theory, Joseph Raz (1979). For him the legal norm is a species of reason for action, specifically an exclusionary or content-independent reason for action. We can explain it in this way. Someone is telephoned late at night by a friend and offered the chance of a

speculative but potentially highly lucrative investment. The only drawback is that they have to make up their mind immediately. Knowing he is a bit drunk and tired, and thus not trusting his judgement, what should he do? He could make the decisions on the balance of all the reasons *pro* and all the reasons *contra* including the reason that he is tired and a little drunk. He could, on the other hand, say that he makes it a rule not to take investment decisions late at night. The former way of doing it would be to make the judgment on the balance of reasons. The latter would use the rule 'do not take investment decisions late at night' as a reason for excluding consideration of the investment decision on the balance of reasons, even though that decision might be to make the investment. His decision would operate at a second-order level in respect to the reasons of substance as to whether to take the investment decision or not. It would thus be an exclusionary reason or a content-independent reason. We would have a reason for not thinking about the substance of the case because of this second-order reason.

But where does that reason come from? From where is, in Raz's terms, the 'legal point of view' generated? In the end we can find the generation of these only in the institutions of law as they are. We thus see that the standard criticism of natural law theories that they conflate the descriptive with the normative is, in some sense, replicated among other, more positivistically inclined, legal theorists. They both face similar problems – where is normativity generated from?

John Finnis (1980) in his natural law theory sees the legal norm, on Razian lines, as an exclusionary reason. But it is a reason for action because it instantiates the objective values of the universe, more specifically the values of practical reason and human sociability, and it is these that generate legal norms. But how do we know these values? It is not our drives which are the goods. The good of life is not to be reduced to our sexual drive. We are not animals. Rather it is the way in which the drives are transformed through our intelligent understanding that makes them basic values. For example, our drive to survive is not what the good of life is. Survival is not a basic good. Rather it is our understanding of this which enables us to see that we should not survive at all costs and that is not what the good of life means. The problems here are the same as they are in positivist theories.

For Finnis legal norms instantiate moral norms and are *determinationes* of ultimately self-evident values. We can then say that most theories of the legal norm see it as in some way connected to the things that people do. The 'ought' comes in some way from causal regularities in the world, as bearer, constituter or condition of the norm. So we can see that the norm comes in the end from people's behaviour or their understanding of it. We ought to do X because in some way we *do* do it. And this appears true even in apparently metaphysical accounts such as those of the natural law. Normativity then is something connected to what people do and not something mysterious at all (see NATURAL LAW §3).

But for some there was still a mystery to be explained. The template or measure way of looking at the norm was not the best. More important were metaphors of chain and yoke. What made us do things? What yoked us to rules and legal norms? In Judaism we speak of the 'yoke' of the law. This seems a metaphysical question that for the Scandinavian legal realists remained unanswered (see LEGAL REALISM §1). Hence they answered it in a naturalistic way: by reducing the norm to our psychological feelings of constraint and being bound, which stemmed from an earlier, more magical age. Thus the magic was reduced to psychological states; the Freudian theory of normativity, as it were.

See also: LAW, PHILOSOPHY OF; LEGAL POSITIVISM

References and further reading

* Austin, J.L. (1971) *The Province of Jurisprudence Determined*, London: Weidenfeld and Nicolson. (A statement of the law as command theory.)
* Dworkin, R. (1986) *Law's Empire*, London: Fontana. (An interpretivist view of law.)
* Finnis, J. (1980) *Natural Law and Natural Rights*, Oxford: Clarendon Press. (A natural law theory.)
  Hägerström, A. (1953) *An Enquiry into the Nature of Law and Morals*, Stockholm: Almquist and Wiksell. (A psychologistic account from a strong Scandinavian realist perspective.)
* Hart, H.L.A. (1961) *The Concept of Law*, 2nd edn, with postscript, P. Bullock and J. Raz (eds), Oxford: Clarendon Press, 1994. (The *locus classicus* in English of the practice theory.)
* Hayek, F. (1969) *Law, Legislation and Liberty*, London: Routledge & Kegan Paul. (A customary theory of law.)
* Kelsen, H. (1960) *Reine Rechtslehre*, 2nd edn, Vienna: Deuticke; trans. M. Knight, *Pure Theory of Law*, Berkeley, CA: University of California Press, 1967. (The main continental theory of the norm as a scheme of interpretation.)
* Raz, J. (1979) *The Authority of Law*, Oxford: Clarendon Press. (A statement of the theory of exclusionary reasons.)
  Ross, A. (1968) *Directives and Norms*, London: Routledge & Kegan Paul. (An acute positivist account, from a mild Scandinavian realist perspective.)
  Schauer, F. (1991) *Playing by the Rules*, Oxford: Clarendon Press. (An acute positivist account, from a mild Scandinavian realist perspective.)
  Shiner, R. (1992) *Norm and Nature*, Oxford: Clarendon Press. (A general account with anti-positivist leanings.)

ZENON BAŃKOWSKI

NORRIS, JOHN (1657–1711)

John Norris was a philosopher in the Platonic tradition of the seventeenth century. His philosophy combines elements from both the French and English aspects of that tradition: he was an admirer of Henry More and was the leading English disciple of Malebranche, whose philosophy he did much to popularize in England. A churchman by profession, much of his writing is concerned with the practical application of divinity. Central to Norris' thought is his theory that the proper and immediate object of both human knowledge and human love is God, who is identified with truth. Thus necessary truths are known directly in God and, conversely, to know eternal and necessary truth is to know God.

John Norris was born at Collingbourne Kingston in Wiltshire, England. He was educated at Winchester College and Exeter College, Oxford, becoming fellow of All Souls College in 1680. In 1689, he was appointed rector of Newton St Loe. In 1692, through the good offices of Lady MASHAM and John LOCKE, he was appointed vicar of Bemerton near Salisbury, where he remained for the rest of his life. Norris' high regard for the Cambridge Platonists is evident from his brief correspondence with Henry MORE, published as *Letters Philosophical and Moral* and appended to his 1688 *The Theory and Regulation of Love* (see CAMBRIDGE PLATONISM). It is likely that Norris' early Platonist leanings combined with Augustinian strands in his theology to predispose him towards the philosophy of MALEBRANCHE. Norris himself denied that his discovery of Malebranche changed his philosophical standpoint (Acworth 1979: 64). None the less the impact of Malebranche is both clearly evident and duly acknowledged in his mature writings. But there were important aspects of Malebranche's philosophy which Norris did not accept, notably Malebranche's account of the distribution of Grace. Nor did he change his view that God acts out of pure benevolence in dealing with created things. It is perhaps truer to say, therefore, that Norris' reading of Malebranche enabled him to articulate his own analogous views more fully and more precisely.

His early writings (later published in *Miscellanies* in 1687) anticipate some of the main themes of his later, Malebranchian phase. For example, his essay 'Of the Advantages of Thinking' argues that ideas and necessary and eternal truths are in God, and are immediately present to the human mind as the proper object of human knowledge. Norris' concern in this essay is with proving the existence of God rather than with epistemology. The arguments are more fully stated in *Reason and Religion* (1689), which propounds Malebranche's theory of the 'vision in God', and are most fully developed in *An Essay towards the Theory of the Ideal or Intelligible World* (1701–4), which he had originally conceived while at Oxford as a *Metaphysica Platonica*. In this, his most substantial book, Norris argues for the existence of an ideal world of intelligible and unchanging entities which serve as the archetypes of the natural world. This ideal world exists in God as the 'omniform Essence' of God. Only the ideal world can be truly known. Since the mind cannot know matter directly, we have no certain knowledge of the physical world. Our knowledge of physical nature derives not from perception of physical bodies, but from our seeing the essences of things in God. It is this Malebranchean idealism which underlies Norris' critique of Locke in his *Cursory Reflections upon a Book Called an Essay Concerning Human Understanding* (1690), where he criticizes Locke for deriving the idea of God from sense knowledge.

Just as God is the proper object of human knowledge, according to Norris, so also, is God the proper object of human love. In *The Theory and Regulation of Love* (1688) Norris distinguishes two kinds of love: love of God and love of things. The former he calls love of concupiscence or desire, that is 'a motion of the Soul towards good' (10). The latter he calls love of benevolence, or disinterested love. The former is irresistible, uniting the soul with the good, which it lacks, that is, with God. Love of benevolence includes self-love and charity, and is the love most perfectly exemplified by God. Later, in his *Discourse concerning the Measure of Divine Love* (1693) he introduced an important modification to his account of human love of God, invoking Malebranche's occasionalist account of sensation. The proper object of desire is that which causes us pleasure, including pleasurable sensations. Since sensations are sense impressions planted in the mind by God on the occasion of the presence of corporeal objects, God is the cause of our pleasure. Therefore, as the true cause of our pleasure, God is the proper object of the love of concupiscence.

Norris' importance as a philosopher derives from his continuing the Platonic tradition of seventeenth-century English philosophy into the eighteenth century, and his popularizing the philosophy of Malebranche in England. He also played a role as a mediator of philosophy to a growing lay readership through his books and his association with the journal *The Athenian Mercury*. By writing accessibly on philosophical themes, Norris was probably more influential than can be specifically documented, though particular mention might be made of John Wesley and Arthur COLLIER. He is also notable for the encouragement he gave to women interested in philosophy, among them Mary Chudleigh, Catharine COCKBURN and Mary ASTELL.

List of works

Norris, J. (1687) *A Collection of Miscellanies*, London. (Early essays, including 'Of the Advantages of Thinking. A Metaphysical Essay towards a Demonstration of a God from the Steady and Immutable Nature of Truth'.)

—— (1688) *The Theory and Regulation of Love, a Moral Essay*, Oxford. (His brief correspondence with Henry More was appended to this work, published as *Letters Philosophical and Moral*.)

—— (1689) *Reason and Religion*, London. (A Malebranchian discussion of divine and human nature.)

—— (1690) *Cursory Reflections upon a Book called, An Essay Concerning Human Understanding, in Christian Blessedness*, London. (A critique of Locke's *Essay*.)

—— (1690) *Reflections on the Conduct of Human Life*, London. (Dedicated to Lady Masham: emphasizes the pious goal of philosophy.)

—— (1693) *Discourse concerning the Measure of Divine Love*, in *Practical Discourses upon Several Divine Subjects*, London, 4 vols, 1691–8.

—— (1697) *An Account of Reason and Faith*, London. (Reply to Toland's, *Christianity not mysterious* (1696).)

—— (1701–4) *An Essay towards the Theory of the Ideal or Intelligible World*, 2 parts, London; repr. Hildesheim: Olms, 1974; repr. New York: Garland, 1978. (Metaphysics strongly influenced by Malebranche.)

—— (1708) *A Philosophical Discourse concerning the Natural Immortality of the Soul*, London. (On the immortality of the soul.)

Norris, J. and Astell M. (1695) *Letters Concerning the*

Love of God, London. (Correspondence with Mary Astell.)

References and further reading

Acworth, R. (1977) 'Malebranche and his Heirs', *Journal of the History of Ideas* 38: 673–6. (On Norris and his influence.)

* —— (1979) *The Philosophy of John Norris of Bemerton (1657–1712)*, Hildesheim: Olms. (A comprehensive study of Norris' life, theology and philosophy.)

MacKinnon, F.I. (1910) *The Philosophy of John Norris of Bemerton*, Baltimore, MD: Psychological Monographs of the Philosophical Review. (On Norris' philosophy.)

McCracken, C.J. (1983) *Malebranche and British Philosophy*, Oxford: Clarendon Press. (Norris as the principal conduit for Malebranchism in Britain.)

SARAH HUTTON

NORWAY, PHILOSOPHY OF

see SCANDINAVIA, PHILOSOPHY IN

NOUS

Commonly translated as 'mind' or 'intellect', the Greek word nous *is a key term in the philosophies of Plato, Aristotle and Plotinus. What gives* nous *its special significance there is not primarily its dictionary meaning – other nouns in Greek can also signify the mind – but the value attributed to its activity and to the metaphysical status of things that are 'noetic' (intelligible and incorporeal) as distinct from being perceptible and corporeal. In Plato's later dialogues, and more systematically in Aristotle and Plotinus,* nous *is not only the highest activity of the human soul but also the divine and transcendent principle of cosmic order.*

In its pre-philosophical usage *nous* is only one among a number of terms for mind. It is chiefly distinguished from these other words by its tendency to signify 'intelligent' activity – realizing, understanding, planning, visualizing – rather than mental processes more generally, including the emotions.

The earliest Greek philosophers traded on this usage of the term. HERACLITUS complained that 'much learning does not teach *nous*'. In PARMENIDES, the cognate verb *noein* and other related words

(*noēma*, 'thought' and *noētos*, 'thinkable') are crucial to his argument. Drawing an absolute distinction between 'opinion' (*doxa*) based upon sense perception and 'truth' (*alētheia*), Parmenides argues that 'noetic' activity, properly speaking, is indissolubly linked to true discourse, valid reasoning and the cognition of reality. What is not true cannot be spoken or 'thought', a rule that applies not only to 'nothing' but also to the illusory data of sense perception. The reality that Parmenides' *nous* deduces and apprehends is unqualified 'being', homogeneous and invariant in time and place.

ANAXAGORAS (§4), with a cosmology strongly influenced by Parmenides, adopted *nous* as the controlling principle of the universe. Making *nous* quite separate from everything else, he characterized it as 'the finest and purest of all things, which has all knowledge about everything and the greatest power'. *Nous* causes the primordial mixture of other things to rotate and separate into distinct beings.

In the dialogues of PLATO the treatment of *nous* was powerfully influenced by these antecedent conceptions. In his *Phaedo*, Socrates favours the idea that *nous* has organized the universe in the best possible way (an idea, he suggests, that Anaxagoras failed to carry through). This conception of *nous* was fully developed in other Platonic dialogues including the *Timaeus*, where it is figuratively expressed in the teleological thinking of the world's divine manufacturer (demiurge). In the *Republic*, the three great images of sun, divided line and cave are ways of distinguishing levels of reality and modes of cognition. Common to all three images is a distinction between the visible world of 'unknowable' phenomena and the 'noetic' world of stable and intelligible Forms. *Noēsis* – the highest activity of the soul's rational component – has cognition of the Forms as its objective, which it pursues by seeking understanding that is unhypothetical and absolutely secure. In ethical and psychological contexts Plato also uses *nous* as a term for the soul's 'rational component', with meanings that may be as broad as 'mind' in everyday English.

Although Plato's special uses of *nous* left their mark on Aristotle, the latter arrived at systematic ideas concerning *nous* as the distinctive faculty of the human soul (see ARISTOTLE §19). In Aristotle's general model of the soul, psychic functions are realizations of bodily potentialities. *Nous*, by contrast, 'has no actual existence before it thinks', and it has no corresponding organ as 'perception' has in being the function of eye, ear, and so on. Like Plato, Aristotle links *nous* to the thinking of incorporeal 'forms' – the definable essences of things; but in contrast to Plato's independently existing 'Forms', those of Aristotle only become actual 'thought objects' in being thought since *nous* is identical in its actuality to what it thinks. For Aristotle, in contrast again with Plato, *nous* can only perform its activity with the help of data provided by 'imagination' (*phantasia*), which is the soul's capacity to represent sensory information, and it functions as the agent not only of theoretical activity but also of purposive action in everyday life.

In a notoriously obscure chapter (III 5) of his work *On the Soul*, Aristotle distinguishes *nous* as 'a capacity to become everything' from *nous* as 'a capacity to make everything', in the way that light makes potential colours actual. This 'active' *nous*, called 'immortal', has often been identified with the Aristotelian Unmoved Mover, whose life is 'a thinking of thinking' (see ARISTOTLE §16). But Aristotle probably regarded human thought as being godlike rather than as being a product of the Unmoved Mover, who exists as an eternally transcendent thinker.

For PLOTINUS (§4), *nous* comprises 'primary reality', the domain of intelligence and intelligible beings. He construes this domain as an 'emanation' from the ineffable One, the ultimate principle of everything. Taken universally, *nous* corresponds more or less to a syncretism of Plato's Forms with Aristotle's Unmoved Mover. Everlastingly contemplating the One, *nous* is construed as an equivalence between thought thinking itself and intelligible beings as the only true thinkables. The activity of *nous* 'overflows' into 'soul', the principle of embodied life. As a lower level of reality, soul can only think things by treating them successively and separately. Human beings live primarily at the level of 'soul', but they also, by virtue of their immortal and 'undescended' self, have access to identification with *nous* and thereby to a mode of being in which thinker and thought are completely unified. In this transcendent condition, the mind is reality itself.

Stoics and Epicureans tend to use other words for the mind, probably because as rigorous physicalists they found *nous* too strongly tinged by Platonic metaphysics.

See also: ALEXANDER OF APHRODISIAS §2; MARCUS AURELIUS §2; NEOPLATONISM §3; NUMENIUS §2; PLATONISM, EARLY AND MIDDLE §5; PROCLUS §5; PSYCHĒ; PTOLEMY; THEOPHRASTUS §3

References and further reading

* Aristotle (*c.* mid fourth century BC) *On the Soul*, trans. H. Lawson-Tancred, Harmondsworth: Penguin, 1986. (The main treatment of *nous* is found in book III.)
Everson, S. (ed.) (1991) *Companions to Ancient Thought 2: Psychology*, Cambridge: Cambridge University Press. (Includes chapters on Plato, Aristotle and Plotinus.)
Kirk, G.S., Raven, J.E. and Schofield, M. (1983) *The Presocratic Philosophers*, Cambridge: Cambridge University Press, 2nd edn. (Greek text, with translation and commentary, of Heraclitus, Parmenides and Anaxagoras.)
* Plato (*c.*380s BC) *Phaedo*, trans. D. Gallop, Oxford: Clarendon Press, 1975. (Includes notes; see *Phaedo* 97–9 for the cosmic role of *nous*.)
* —— (*c.*370s BC) *Republic*, trans. R. Waterfield, Oxford: Oxford University Press, 1993. (Plato's main discussion of *nous* is found in books VI–VII.)
* —— (*c.*360s BC) *Timaeus*, trans. H.D.P. Lee, Harmondsworth: Penguin, 1963. (Plato's seminal account of the interplay of *nous* and necessity in the formation of the world.)
* Plotinus (*c.* AD 250–66) *Enneads*, V 1–9 trans. A.H. Armstrong, *Plotinus*, vol. 5, Loeb Classical Library, Cambridge, MA: Harvard University Press and London: Heinemann, 1984. (Greek text with facing translation.)

A.A. LONG

NOVUM ORGANUM
see ARISTOTLE

NOZICK, ROBERT (1938–)

Although Robert Nozick has published on an enormous range of topics, he is best known as a political philosopher, and especially for his powerful and entertaining statement of libertarianism. In Anarchy, State, and Utopia *(1974), Nozick presents an image of a fully voluntary society, in which people cooperate only on terms which violate no one's rights.*

Nozick's other major contributions to philosophy include an analysis of knowledge, and an accompanying response to scepticism, an account of personal identity and contributions to decision theory and the theory of rationality.

1 Introduction
2 *Anarchy, State, and Utopia*
3 *Philosophical Explanations*
4 *The Examined Life* and *The Nature of Rationality*

1 Introduction

Robert Nozick was born in Brooklyn and studied at Columbia and Princeton Universities. He has taught at Harvard since 1969, and was appointed Arthur Kingsley Porter Professor of Philosophy in 1985.

Although he first came to prominence with two papers published in 1969, 'Newcomb's Problem and Two Principles of Choice' and 'Coercion', Nozick's first book (his defence of libertarianism), *Anarchy, State, and Utopia* (1974), is considered his most important work to date. This was followed by *Philosophical Explanations* (1981), *The Examined Life* (1989) (in which he remarks that he no longer considers himself to be a libertarian) and *The Nature of Rationality* (1993).

Nozick's eclecticism is accompanied by a particularly engaging writing style. He regrets the increasingly technical turn taken by recent intellectual work and has done much to make his own research accessible to a general readership without compromising its philosophical content. His openness appears in another way also: Nozick is often the first to point out the difficulties with his own position, believing that 'there is room for words on subjects other than last words' (1974: xii). Yet, in his search to break new ground he has rarely returned to a subject to answer critics or to fill in the gaps he admits are exposed.

2 *Anarchy, State, and Utopia*

Anarchy, State, and Utopia begins with the words: 'Individuals have rights, and there are things no person or group may do to them (without violating their rights)' (1974: ix). His conclusions fall into three parts: a defence of the minimal state; a theory of economic justice; and a utopian vision of society.

Nozick claims – in opposition to the anarchist – that the existence of a minimal state (the 'nightwatchman' state of classical liberalism) is consistent with individual (negative) natural rights to life, liberty and property. To defend this claim he uses an 'invisible hand' argument to show how the state could emerge.

In Locke's state of nature (see LOCKE, J. §10), individuals have a natural right of self-defence and a right to punish those who violate their rights. Nozick argues that such people would rationally band together in groups to enforce their claims of justice. Commercial protection agencies would follow and, Nozick argues, such agencies would merge or join federations until a single 'dominant protection agency' exists. This yields what Nozick terms an ultra-minimal state, for not all individuals need join.

However, Nozick believes that the dominant protection agency has the right to prohibit individuals from exercising their natural right to punish, provided it compensates them for this by offering protection services. Thus, ultimately the protection agency would satisfy two conditions Nozick believes sufficient to constitute a state: it (virtually) monopolizes legitimate coercion within its territory, and it offers protection to almost all. By showing that a minimal state could come into existence without violating rights, Nozick believes he has demonstrated that *at least* a minimal state is justified.

The centrepiece of Nozick's libertarianism, however, is his theory of distributive justice. Nozick argues that the more-than-minimal state – a welfare state, for example – would violate people's rights. Nozick's own theory of justice – the entitlement theory – falls into three parts: principles of justice in the initial acquisition of property; in transfer; and in rectification, which simply concerns how to rectify violations of the first two principles (see JUSTICE §5; PROPERTY §3). The principle of justice in acquisition is not fully stated, although Nozick remarks that it must include one element taken from Locke: an individual's appropriation must not worsen any third party's condition. Nozick instead gives most attention to the principle of justice in transfer, which essentially states that a transfer is just if, and only if, it is voluntary. His contention is that only his theory properly respects liberty. All others, he claims, are defeated by his notorious 'Wilt Chamberlain' example.

In this example, Nozick claims that any 'pattern' of holdings – each according to their needs, for example – will inevitably be destroyed by the free and voluntary trading and gift-giving behaviour of individuals. The only way of enforcing a pattern involves 'constantly interfering' in individuals' lives: either by prohibiting certain transfers or by intrusively redistributing property. Even a system of taxation and welfare payments is rejected by Nozick on the grounds that it forces some people to labour for the benefit of others, without choice or reward. Accordingly, taxation is 'on a par with forced labour'. Hence, any state more extensive than the minimal state will violate individual rights to liberty: 'The socialist society would have to forbid capitalist acts between consenting adults' (1974: 163).

The third part of Nozick's project is to show that the minimal state is 'inspiring as well as right'. Here he makes it clear that libertarianism is intended to provide a set of background rights and duties for society, but people may enter into whatever voluntary arrangements they wish. Thus Nozick argues that a group may set up any type of community they wish, provided they have the resources and do not coerce

45

others to join them. Thus libertarianism is viewed as a 'framework for utopia' in which individuals can act out their own model of utopia, in company with like-minded others (see LIBERTARIANISM §§1, 3).

Nozick's views have generated an enormous critical literature. Critics claim that the entire weight of his position stands on the justification of the initial acquisition of individual property rights. And on this point Nozick is particularly weak, doing so little to state and defend his principle of justice in acquisition. Critics have also doubted that Nozick can justify even the minimal state, given the very strong assumptions of individual freedom with which he starts. Nozick has not published a response to these criticisms.

3 Philosophical Explanations

Nozick's second book, *Philosophical Explanations*, ranges unconfined over topics in metaphysics, epistemology and the philosophy of value. While here he makes important contributions to the issues of personal identity and the foundations of ethics, his treatments of knowledge and scepticism have attracted the greatest attention.

What is it to know something, as distinct, for example, from guessing correctly? The traditional analysis of knowledge asserts that knowledge is justified true belief. Yet this seems to have been refuted by 'Gettier examples': once we appreciate that some beliefs, while justified, are nevertheless false, it is a short step to realize that a justified belief might be true by accident or fluke (see GETTIER PROBLEMS).

To avoid such problems Nozick presents the 'truth-tracking' theory. This is an externalist theory, and Nozick's own approach is a variety of reliabilism (see RELIABILISM), in which, broadly, one has knowledge if one's true beliefs are generated by a reliable mechanism. Nozick claims that, if '*S* knows that *p*', then four conditions are individually necessary and jointly sufficient:

(1) *p* is true.
(2) *S* believes that *p*.
(3) If *p* were not true then *S* would not believe it.
(4) If *p* were true then *S* would believe it.

Conditional statements (3) and (4) replace the appeal to justification in the traditional account. These are to be interpreted as subjunctive or counterfactual conditionals rather than as material implications. Using possible worlds semantics for counterfactual conditionals (see COUNTERFACTUAL CONDITIONALS §3), the third condition can be read as: 'In close possible worlds where *p* is not true, *S* does not believe *p*'. If your belief is true by accident, there will be a

close possible world in which you still have that belief, even though it is false. The belief fails therefore to meet the third condition, and so does not count as knowledge.

We can now see why Nozick calls his theory the 'truth-tracking' theory: knowledge requires not just that you believe the truth, but that your belief 'tracks' the truth among close possible worlds. Together the third and fourth conditions require that, not only do you believe the truth, but in reasonably similar situations where it is false you would not believe it, and where it is true you would.

Nozick's analysis gives him a reply to the sceptic about knowledge. If we grant that you cannot know that you are not now a brain in a vat on Alpha Centauri, then it seems to follow that you cannot know anything else: for example, that you are now on Earth, reading. Nozick's reply is to point out that the sceptic's argument presupposes that 'knowledge is closed under known logical implication', and that his own analysis of knowledge shows that this assumption is false.

The closure principle is a relatively simple idea. If you know that *p*, and that *p* logically entails *q*, then according to the closure principle it follows that you know that *q*. The sceptic uses this principle (in reverse) to argue that we have no knowledge. If I am reading on Earth, then it logically follows (and I know that it follows) that I am not a brain in a vat on Alpha Centauri. Hence, according to the closure principle, if I know that I am reading on Earth, then I know that I am not a brain in a vat. But, the sceptic claims, as I do not know that, I do not know that I am reading on Earth. Indeed, I cannot know anything known to be inconsistent with my being a brain in a vat on Alpha Centauri.

The closure principle is central to the sceptic's case. But on Nozick's analysis the principle is false. Nozick points out that whether or not an individual knows a proposition depends on how their beliefs vary over a set of close possible worlds. But the possible worlds to take into account differ according to the proposition under consideration. Hence, I can know that *p*, and know that *p* entails *q* without knowing that *q*, and the sceptic's argument falls.

While an ingenious response, critics argue that Nozick's analysis of knowledge should be rejected. For it has the peculiar consequence that I can know a conjunction '*p* and *q*' without knowing one of the conjuncts *q* for the set of possible worlds in which '*p* and *q*' is true is not identical to the set of possible worlds in which '*q*' is true. Although this is a consequence Nozick points out himself, for many it is a *reductio ad absurdum* of his approach.

4 *The Examined Life* and *The Nature of Rationality*

The Examined Life, Nozick's third book – a book about 'living and what is important in life' (1989: 11) – has not made much impact on the philosophical world. However, his fourth, *The Nature of Rationality* (1993), marks a return to issues of decision theory and rationality, and so contributes to ongoing debates within the analytic tradition.

Nozick was the first to present Newcomb's problem to the philosophical world, and his discussion has remained a classic work in decision theory, emphasizing the distinction between evidential and causal decision theory. In *The Nature of Rationality* he introduces a new idea: symbolic utility. An action or decision may be symbolic – expressive of an emotion or attitude, for example – and so may have value not so much in its effects, but by its standing as a symbol. To illustrate, Nozick points out that for some people minimum wage legislation may have value as a way of symbolizing the idea of helping the poor, even if it turns out to be ineffective as a policy. Acting rationally, on Nozick's view, is a matter of 'maximizing decision-value', which is a weighted sum of causal, evidential and symbolic utility (see DECISION AND GAME THEORY).

See also: KNOWLEDGE, CONCEPT OF; PERSONAL IDENTITY; RATIONAL CHOICE THEORY; SCEPTICISM

List of works

Nozick, R. (1969a) 'Newcomb's Problem and Two Principles of Choice', in N. Rescher (ed.) *Essays in Honour of Carl G. Hempel*, Reidel: Dordrecht. (First philosophical discussion of Newcomb's problem.)
—— (1969b) 'Coercion', in S. Morgenbesser, P. Suppes and M. White *Philosophy, Science and Method*, New York: St Martin's Press. (Influential analysis of the concept of coercion.)
—— (1974) *Anarchy, State, and Utopia*, Oxford: Blackwell. (Powerful statement of libertarianism.)
—— (1981) *Philosophical Explanations*, Oxford: Oxford University Press. (Wide-ranging discussion of topics in metaphysics, epistemology and ethics.)
—— (1989) *The Examined Life*, New York: Simon & Schuster. (A book about 'living and what is important in life'.)
—— (1993) *The Nature of Rationality*, Princeton, NJ: Princeton University Press. (Presents a theory of rational action.)

References and further reading

Luper-Foy, S. (ed.) (1987) *The Possibility of Knowledge*, Totowa, NJ: Rowman & Littlefield. (Contains critical discussions of Nozick's views on knowledge and scepticism.)
Paul, J. (ed.) (1982) *Reading Nozick*, Oxford: Blackwell. (Collection of essays discussing *Anarchy, State, and Utopia*.)
Wolff, J. (1991) *Robert Nozick*, Cambridge: Polity Press. (Critical analysis of Nozick's libertarianism.)

JONATHAN WOLFF

NUMBERS

Numbers are, in general, mathematical entities whose function is to express the size, order or magnitude of something or other. Historically, starting from the most basic kind of number, the positive integers (1, 2, 3, . . .), which appear in the earliest written records, the notion of number has been generalized and extended in several different directions – often in the face of considerable opposition.

Other than the positive integers, the most venerable are the rational numbers (fractions), which were known to the Egyptians and Mesopotamians. The discovery, by Pythagorean mathematicians, that there are lengths that cannot be expressed as fractions occasioned the introduction of irrational numbers, such as the square root of 2, though the Greeks managed only a geometric understanding of these. The number zero was recognized, first in Indian mathematics, by the seventh century; the use of negative numbers evolved after this time; and complex numbers, such as the square root of −1, appeared first at the end of the Middle Ages. Infinitesimal numbers were developed by the founders of the calculus, Newton and Leibniz, in the seventeenth century (and were later to disappear from mathematics – for a time); and infinite numbers (ordinals and cardinals) were introduced by the founder of modern set theory, Cantor, in the nineteenth century.

The introductions of three of these kinds of number, in particular, occasioned crises in the foundations of mathematics. The first (concerning irrational numbers) was finally resolved in the nineteenth century by the work of Cauchy and Weierstrass. The second (concerning infinitesimals) was also resolved then, by the work of Weierstrass and Dedekind. The third (concerning infinite numbers), which involves paradoxes such as Russell's, still awaits a convincing solution.

It is seemingly impossible to give a rigorous definition of what it is to be a number. The closest

one can get is a family-resemblance notion, with very ill-defined boundaries.

1   Natural numbers

All human societies would appear to have some form of counting, however limited, both for size – cardinality (one, two, three,...) – and for order – ordinality (first, second, third,...). The recognition that an infinitude of positive integers could be used for these purposes was already in place in the earliest civilization from which we have written records, that of Egypt *circa* the fourth millennium BC. The investigation of basic arithmetic operations (addition, multiplication and so on) was also well under way then. This was continued in the next great Middle Eastern civilization, that of Mesopotamia (Babylon), *circa* the second millennium BC. The investigations were greatly facilitated by the Mesopotamian invention of place-notation, that is, the idea that a single numeral can represent different quantities depending on where it occurs in a string of numerals. Thus, for example, in decimal notation, the first '2' of '2,121' represents two thousands and the second represents two tens. (The Mesopotamians actually preferred a sexagesimal to a decimal base.)

The *natural* numbers comprise the positive integers together with zero. The idea of zero as a number was not to be found in either of these civilizations, although the Mesopotamians did sometimes leave a gap where we would now write a zero. (Thus '2 2' might represent 202 or 2,020, and so on.) Though the origin of the idea is uncertain, zero was certainly being used by the seventh century AD by Indian mathematicians, who had also developed place-notation and used a decimal base. They therefore possessed, in effect, our modern number system (though the symbols they used were different). This system was taken up in the Arabian civilization around the eighth century, and thence passed into Europe around the twelfth.

2   Rational and irrational numbers

Positive integers quantify wholes. Once one starts to measure, it becomes clear that a way is required to quantify parts. *Rational* numbers, as ratios of natural numbers (with non-zero denominator), clearly serve this function. These were known to the Egyptians, at least in the form of unit fractions (of the form $1/n$) and, in a more sophisticated and general form, to the Mesopotamians. Decimal fractions (of the form 0.23) appear to have been developed by Arabic mathematicians, and by the time we reach Stevin in late sixteenth-century Europe, the modern computational system for rational numbers is essentially in place.

The creation of modern mathematics is usually reckoned to have occurred in Ancient Greece in the second half of the first millennium BC. What was distinctive about the Greek approach was that mathematics was freed from its practical roots and took on a purely theoretical form. In particular, the central concern of Greek mathematics was proof, especially proofs in geometry. As far as arithmetic goes, the first part of this epoch was dominated by Pythagoreanism, according to which everything can be explained in terms of the positive integers. (It follows that rational numbers are of little theoretical importance: given two lengths to compare, if one chooses one's unit of measurement small enough, the lengths will be integral.)

The discovery that the Pythagorean assumption was wrong came as a distinct shock. Most simply, the diagonal of a unit square (whose length is the square root of two) is not commensurable with its sides. The proof of this (one of the first *reductio* arguments in the history of mathematics) is now celebrated. It is not known who discovered it, though it was probably one of the later Pythagoreans, *c.*400 BC. At any rate, it inaugurated the first of three crises in the foundations of mathematics that have been associated with the introduction of a new kind of number.

The new numbers in this case are *irrational* numbers (that is, numbers which cannot be written as a ratio of integers – written as decimals they are infinite and non-repeating), such as the square root of two (and pi (π), although the irrationality of this was not proved until the eighteenth century by Lambert). They are required, together with rational numbers, for general quantification of length: in fact, the only conception of such magnitudes available to the Greeks was as geometric lengths. Given this representation, some geometric account of arithmetic operations had to be given. The hardest of these is division, which was solved by Eudoxus (*c.*360 BC) in his theory of proportions, given in book 5 of Euclid's *Elements*. But even for Eudoxus, ratios were not entities in their own right. Operations which treat irrational numbers in the form of surds (expressed in ways such as $\sqrt{2}$, $\sqrt[3]{71}$), as bona fide entities, can be found in Indian mathematics and, in particular, in the seventh-century mathematician Brahmagupta. Some use of surds was made by Arabic mathematicians, but their use did not become common until the sixteenth century (for example, in the work of Stevin and Cardan). A clear statement to the effect that irrational numbers are first-class numerical citizens can be found in Newton, in the seventeenth century; however, an adequate understanding of what this citizenship amounted to had to wait until the nineteenth century.

3 Negative and complex numbers

Subtraction had been familiar to mathematicians since the earliest times. The idea that a sensible quantity might itself be negative, however – and what the sense of it might be – took a long time to catch on. *Negative* numbers, the rules for operating with them, and their use as roots of equations appear in Brahmagupta, and were consequently known to Arabic mathematicians – though they did not use them as roots of equations. The first time they appear in this way in European mathematics is in the work of fifteenth-century mathematician Nicholas of Chuquet (who, however, did not allow zero to be a root!). Even Cardan, a century later, who employed negative roots extensively, called them 'fictional'. The idea that negative numbers might correspond to direction reversal is to be found in the early seventeenth-century mathematician, Girard; but, even after the invention of analytic geometry by Descartes a little later, many mathematicians simply ignored the negative parts of the plane. And even as late as the middle of the eighteenth century some textbook writers were still disputing the claim that the product of a pair of negative numbers is positive.

Once the use of negative numbers became common mathematical practice, the thought that there might be a new kind of number to provide for their square roots was not far behind. If we call all of the numbers mentioned so far *real* numbers, and write the square root of -1 as i (following Euler), the product of i with any real number is called an *imaginary* number. More generally, the sum of a real number and an imaginary number $(a + ib)$ is called a *complex* number. One of the earliest occurrences of complex numbers in mathematics is in the work of Cardan, who observed, as we would now put it, that a cubic equation with a real root may also have complex roots, though Cardan himself regarded this observation as useless. A few years later, Bombelli articulated the use of complex numbers (in the same context) much further. Opposition to them did not then cease, however; for example, their use was frowned upon by Newton. But

by the time of, and especially in the work of, Euler, in the eighteenth century, complex numbers had been shown to have numerous uses, both as the solutions of equations and elsewhere – for example, in important relationships between trigonometric functions. And by the time that Gauss, in the early nineteenth century, showed that every polynomial equation with complex coefficients has complex roots, complex numbers were well entrenched. With the development of electromagnetic theory later in the century, complex numbers were shown to be capable of representing even physical quantities (for example, impedance).

The problem of what sense to make of complex numbers was also solved by Gauss and later contemporaries, such as Argand. The complex number $x + iy$ could be thought of as the point (x, y) in two-dimensional Euclidean space (now usually called the Argand plane), with the arithmetic operations on complex numbers defined in a suitable way. This prompted the idea that points in a higher-dimensional space could also be thought of as numbers of a certain kind. Defining a suitable notion of multiplication for points in a three-dimensional space turned out to be impossible, but the problem was solved for four dimensions by the Irish mathematician William Hamilton later in the nineteenth century. Hamilton defined a class of numbers known as 'quaternions', of the form $x + iy + jz + kw$, where $ijk = i^2 = j^2 = k^2 = -1$. The properties of quaternions were investigated for some years, but no real use was found for them, so the investigations lapsed. By this time, the observation that a somewhat different set of operations on points in Euclidean space might be fruitful had been made, and vector algebra was born. (If one thinks of complex numbers as two-dimensional vectors, then complex addition and vector addition are the same thing, but complex multiplication and the various vector multiplications are distinct.)

4 Infinitesimal numbers

The numbers discussed so far have all been finite. But numbers of some kinds are infinite – or their intuitive inverse; infinitesimal. It is sometimes (dubiously) claimed that infinitesimals can be found in Greek mathematics. What certainly can be found, from about the third century BC on, is a method called 'the method of exhaustion', (probably) invented by Eudoxus and developed by Archimedes. The main purpose of this method is the computation of areas and volumes of non-rectilinear geometric figures, and requires their approximation by rectilinear figures. For example, a circle is approximated by a regular polygon inscribed within it. As the length of the sides of the polygon decreases (and the number of sides increases) the approximation gets closer. By the late sixteenth century we find mathematicians such as Stevin and Wallis suggesting, in effect, that if we make the sides of the polygon infinitesimally small, the approximation will be exact – or, at least, will differ only infinitesimally from the true value. Hence, a new kind of number, *infinitesimals*, had to be recognized, to quantify infinitesimal lengths.

The use of infinitesimals in essentially this way was developed by Newton and Leibniz in the next century as the foundation of modern calculus (see ANALYSIS, PHILOSOPHICAL ISSUES IN §1). Though their inventions were independent, and used quite different notations, the essential ideas were the same. For example, to determine the gradient of the curve $y = x^2$ at the point $x = a$, we consider a point on the curve an infinitesimal distance d away along the x-axis. The slope of the line joining these two points is

$$\frac{(a+d)^2 - a^2}{d} = \frac{2ad + d^2}{d}$$
$$= 2a + d$$

but since d is infinitesimally small, we can disregard it. Hence the gradient is $2a$.

The power of infinitesimal methods was so great, in both pure and applied mathematics, that they soon became entrenched. However, many people – most notably Berkeley – were severely critical. In particular, infinitesimals had at the same time to be both non-zero (since one divided by them) and zero (since one ignored them). This dilemma inaugurated the second foundational crisis in mathematics associated with the introduction of a new kind of number. But this one would have to wait only 200 years for a solution.

5 Transfinite numbers

It is clear that there are infinite quantities in mathematics, and hence that there must be a size that these quantities can be, namely, infinite. But for most of the history of mathematics, infinitude was thought of as mathematically indeterminate, and hence there was little to be said about the quantity 'infinity'. (One does, however, sometimes find mathematicians – even of the stature of Euler – taking it as a definite quantity, in particular, as the reciprocal of zero.) Even in the heyday of the infinitesimal calculus, infinite numbers played little part (though Leibniz certainly held that the reciprocals of distinct infinitesimals were distinct infinite numbers). The recognition of different orders of infinity, and consequently of the sense of

infinite numbers, therefore came as another highly contentious idea.

This recognition is almost entirely due to Georg Cantor in the late nineteenth century. He realized that, given some iterable operation (for example, forming the set of topological limit points of some set of points), it made sense to consider the result of having applied the operation an infinite number of times, and then to apply the operation again, and again ... indefinitely (see CANTOR, G. §1). To quantify this ordering, Cantor introduced a new class of infinite numbers, *transfinite ordinals*, the least of which he denoted by a lower-case omega, ω (see SET THEORY §2). He also defined arithmetic operations on these numbers which generalize the operations on finite numbers, but which have rather unusual properties. For example, addition is not commutative: $\omega + 1 \neq 1 + \omega$.

Having generalized the notion of order into the infinite, Cantor next generalized the notion of size. To do this he needed a criterion of size that would work (even) in infinite domains. He adopted the criterion (also suggested by FREGE (§8)) that two collections have the same size just if their members can be put into one-to-one correspondence (that is, each member of either collection corresponds to exactly one member of the other). He observed that adding members to an infinite set may not increase its size. (This fact had been noted by some previous mathematicians – for example, Galileo – who thought it so absurd that they rejected infinity as a quantity.) In another of the most famous *reductio* arguments in the history of mathematics, Cantor also established that for any infinite collection, there is one of greater size. This is now called 'Cantor's theorem' (see CANTOR'S THEOREM). To quantify the different sizes Cantor introduced a new kind of infinite number, *transfinite cardinals* (see SET THEORY §3), denoted by the Hebrew letter aleph ($\aleph$) with a subscript ($\aleph_0$ being the smallest, the size of the natural numbers); and defined arithmetic operations on these which, again, generalize the finite case. These operations also have striking properties: for example, double any aleph and you get what you started with.

It should be noted that natural numbers can be thought of indifferently as ordinals or cardinals. This is because, canonically, we count the size of a finite collection by ordering, and its cardinality is n just if the last object in the ordering is the nth. However, transfinite ordinals and cardinals are quite distinct since, as just observed, if one adds further objects to an ordered set, the size may remain the same. Transfinite ordinal and cardinal arithmetics are also quite distinct. Cardinal addition, for example, is commutative, where ordinal addition is not. It is worth noting that there are very simple questions concerning basic transfinite arithmetic operations that are still unanswered (see CONTINUUM HYPOTHESIS).

Cantor's introduction of transfinite numbers into mathematics did not entail the use of infinitesimals. This is because the unusual properties of (cardinal and ordinal) multiplication allow no obvious sense to be given to the notion of division, and so not to reciprocation. However, the use of infinite numbers brought its own problems. In particular, the totality of all ordinal numbers is an ordered collection and hence must have an ordinal, which must be greater than, and so distinct from, all ordinals. Similarly, the totality of all objects must have the largest possible cardinal, but, by Cantor's theorem, there is a larger. These paradoxes are now called the Burali-Forti paradox and Cantor's paradox, respectively; Russell's paradox, concerning the set of all sets that are not members of themselves, is a stripped-down version of Cantor's (see PARADOXES OF SET AND PROPERTY §4). They heralded the third crisis in the foundations of mathematics associated with the introduction of a new kind of number; a crisis which, unlike the first two, is as yet not satisfactorily resolved. These paradoxes fuelled the rejection of Cantor's ideas by some, including Kroneker; but despite this, they were absorbed into orthodox mathematics within about fifty years.

6   Weierstrass and Dedekind

The final resolution of the first two crises we met (concerning irrationals and infinitesimals) took place in the nineteenth century, a period when mathematicians became particularly concerned with the rigorous foundations of their subject. In this context, the work of Weierstrass and DEDEKIND is particularly significant.

Early in the nineteenth century, the notion of a 'limit' appeared in Cauchy's formulation of the calculus. His method differed from that set out in §4 above as follows: instead of taking d to be some infinitesimal quantity, we let it be a finite quantity, and then consider the limit of what happens when d approaches zero (the limit being a quantity that may be approached as close as we please, though never, perhaps, attained). Despite the fact that Cauchy possessed the notion of a limit, he mixed both infinitesimal and limit terminology, and it was left to Weierstrass, later in the century, to replace all appeals to infinitesimals by appeals to limits. At this point infinitesimal numbers disappeared from mathematics (though they would return, as we shall see).

Weierstrass also gave the first modern account of negative numbers, defining them as signed reals, that is, pairs whose first members are reals and whose second members are 'sign bits' ('+' or '−'), subject to suitable operations.

A contemporary of Weierstrass, Tannery, gave the first modern account of rational numbers. An 'equivalence relation' is a relation R that is reflexive (xRx), symmetric (if xRy then yRx) and transitive (if xRy and yRz then xRz). Given an equivalence relation on a domain of objects, an 'equivalence class' is the set of all those things in the domain related to some fixed object. Tannery defined the rationals as equivalence classes of pairs of natural numbers (the second of which is non-zero), under the equivalence relation '∼' (tilde), defined as follows.

$$\langle m,n \rangle \sim \langle r,s \rangle \text{ iff } m.s = r.n$$

The problem of irrational numbers was finally solved independently by Weierstrass, Cantor and Dedekind, who gave different but equivalent constructions of real numbers. Weierstrass' is in terms of infinite decimal expansions; Cantor's is in terms of convergent infinite sequences of rationals. Dedekind's construction is the simplest: consider any splitting of the rational numbers (which can be taken to include the integers, since the integer n may be identified with the rational number $n/1$) into two non-empty disjoint collections L ('left') and R ('right'), such that anything less than a member of L is in L, and anything greater than a member of R is in R. This pair is now called a 'Dedekind cut' (or 'section'). Real numbers (including irrational numbers) can be thought of as such sections (or just one of their parts).

Dedekind also gave the first axiom system for the natural numbers, in terms of an initial number and the successor operation (+1). In modern form, the axioms are as follows:

(1)   0 is a number.

(2)   The successor of any number is a number.

(3)   0 is the successor of no number.

(4)   Any two numbers with the same successor are the same.

(5)   If 0 has some property, and the successor of any number with that property also has it, then all numbers have it.

These axioms, together with the recursive definitions for addition and multiplication (also given by Dedekind), are now usually named after Peano, who gave a formalized version a few years later.

7   Set-theoretic reduction

The drive for rigour in the foundations of number theory reached its height in the reduction of all numbers to sets, due to the logicists Frege, Russell and Whitehead at the turn of the twentieth century (see LOGICISM). The key to this was a set-theoretic definition of cardinal and ordinal numbers. The cardinal numbers were defined as equivalence classes of sets under the equivalence relation 'can be put into one-to-one correspondence with'. (For Russell and Whitehead, this was restricted to sets of fixed type, in an attempt to avoid the paradoxes of infinite number – see THEORY OF TYPES.) A 'well-ordering' on a set is an ordering such that every non-empty subset has a least member in the ordering (see SET THEORY §2). Two well-ordered sets are 'order-isomorphic' if they can be put into a one-to-one correspondence that preserves the ordering. The ordinal numbers were defined as the equivalence classes of well-ordered sets (of a given type) under the equivalence relation of order-isomorphism. Cardinal and ordinal arithmetic operations were defined in an appropriate fashion.

Given the ordinals, other numbers could then be defined in a relatively straightforward way. Natural numbers are the finite ordinals (which can be shown to satisfy the Peano axioms – see §6 above); rational numbers can be defined by the Tannery construction; real numbers as Dedekind sections; negative numbers as Weierstrassian pairs; complex numbers can be defined as pairs of signed reals, thought of as points on the Argand plane. In each case, arithmetic operations can be defined in natural ways.

Since the Frege/Russell reduction, several other non-equivalent, but equally good, definitions of the cardinal and ordinal numbers have been discovered (and in virtue of this, the claim that these numbers just *are* certain sets is difficult to maintain). The most elegant of these is due to von Neumann. According to this, each ordinal is simply the collection of all smaller ordinals. (Thus, zero is simply the empty set, the least infinite ordinal is the set of natural numbers, and so on.) Cardinal numbers are identified with 'initial' ordinals, that is, least ordinals of each size.

8 Developments from logic

Work in mathematical logic in the twentieth century has provided several notable developments bearing on numbers. Three are particularly important. The first was the proof by Gödel in 1931 that the Peano axioms, and all other consistent axiom systems for arithmetic, are incomplete, in the sense that there are truths of arithmetic that cannot be proved from the axioms – at least if the underlying logic is first-order (see GÖDEL'S THEOREMS). The axioms are complete if the underlying logic is second-order and the induction principle (5) is formulated as a second-order axiom and not just a first-order schema; but second-order

logic is not itself axiomatizable (see SECOND- AND HIGHER-ORDER LOGICS §1). This raises profound questions about the nature of both numbers and our knowledge thereof, that fall outside the bounds of this entry.

The second development concerns the paradoxes surrounding transfinite numbers. The orthodox view that has emerged this century is that embedded in Zermelo–Fraenkel set theory (ZF). According to this, there just is no totality of all ordinals, all sets or other 'large' collections, and so the question of their size does not arise. Although this account provides enough set theory for most mathematics (though not all: category theory appears to require large sets of just this kind), it can hardly be said to be conceptually adequate. For example, standard logic defines the sense of a quantifier in terms of the domain (totality) over which it ranges. It is therefore unclear what the sense of the quantifiers of ZF is, if, as it claims, there is no such totality. (See Priest 1987.)

The third development is due to Robinson and is called 'nonstandard analysis' (see ANALYSIS, NON-STANDARD). As was proved originally by Löwenheim and Skolem, (first-order) theories of number have nonstandard models (see LÖWENHEIM–SKOLEM THE-OREMS AND NONSTANDARD MODELS). In particular, any theory of the reals will have such models. Robinson showed that in all of these models, there are non-zero numbers that are smaller than any real number: infinitesimals. Using these, he demonstrated that the reasoning of the infinitesimal calculus (which is much more intuitive than limit reasoning) can be interpreted in a perfectly consistent manner. Hence, infinitesimals have been rehabilitated as perfectly good numbers.

9 Number in general

The preceding review of the development of the notion of number naturally prompts the question of what a number is. One might interpret this as the question of whether numbers are Platonic objects, mental constructions, or nothing more than mystified numerals. This is a central issue in the philosophy of mathematics.

Alternatively, in virtue of the plethora of kinds of numbers we have seen, one might interpret the question as asking what makes entities of certain kinds, but not others, numbers. Beyond the rather vague characterization with which this article began, it seems difficult to give a general characterization of number. The most fundamental numbers (both historically and conceptually), the natural numbers, measured size (or order), were subject to distinctive operations (such as addition) and could be the roots of equations. Each of these central features has played a role in generating new kinds of numbers (different concerns being dominant on different occasions). The result is a collection of entities which are related by family resemblance (as observed by Wittgenstein in §67 of *Philosophical Investigations*), though the boundaries of the family seem somewhat arbitrary. It is difficult to see why, for example, complex numbers (or quaternions) should be called numbers, but not vectors or numerical matrices; both of these share the central features of natural numbers.

This conclusion is reinforced by recent work by Conway (1976). He gives a (transfinite) recursive construction that generalizes both the Dedekind construction of the reals and the von Neumann construction of ordinals. Essentially, a number is any pair, $\langle L, R \rangle$, such that all the members of L and R are numbers, and every member of R is greater than or equal to ($\geqslant$) every member of L (see ANALYSIS, PHILOSOPHICAL ISSUES IN §2). '$\geqslant$' and the arithmetic operations are also defined in a natural recursive manner. The construction generates virtually all the numbers we have met in this article, including infinitesimals, but excluding, notably, the complex numbers (and if cardinals are to be identified with initial ordinals, a non-uniform definition of arithmetic operations is necessary). Moreover, the construction generates many novel numbers, for example, notably, numbers obtained by applying the full range of real-number operations to infinite numbers, for example, $\omega - 1$, $\sqrt{\omega}$, which make no sense on the usual understanding. Moreover, a simple generalization of the construction (dropping the ordering condition on L and R), produces even more number-like objects (which Conway calls 'games', because, in a certain sense, they code the strategic possibilities in a two-person game).

Just conceivably, a unifying account of number might eventually be found, but in the meantime the emergence of new kinds of numbers seems likely. For example, there are nonstandard inconsistent models of arithmetic which contain inconsistent numbers (natural numbers with inconsistent properties). These have some notable applications. For example, some of them can be shown to provide solutions for arbitrary sets of simultaneous linear equations. (See Mortensen 1995.) And just as the existence of nonstandard models of analysis made infinitesimals legitimate, so might these legitimize the notion of an inconsistent number.

See also: ANALYSIS, PHILOSOPHICAL ISSUES IN; ANTIREALISM IN THE PHILOSOPHY OF MATHEMATICS; ARITHMETIC, PHILOSOPHICAL ISSUES IN; LOGICAL AND MATHEMATICAL TERMS, GLOSSARY OF; REALISM IN THE PHILOSOPHY OF MATHEMATICS; SET THEORY, DIFFERENT SYSTEMS OF

References and further reading

Bell, J.L. and Machover, M. (1977) *A Course in Mathematical Logic*, Amsterdam: North Holland. (Chapter 10 gives a clear account of the modern set-theoretic reduction of cardinal and ordinal numbers.)

Benacerraf, P. (1965) 'What Numbers Could Not Be', *Philosophical Review* 74: 47–73; repr. in P. Benacerraf and H. Putnam (eds) *Philosophy of Mathematics: Selected Readings*, Cambridge: Cambridge University Press, 2nd edn, 1983. (A standard critique of set-theoretic reductionism.)

Boyer, C.B. and Merzbach, U.C. (1968) *A History of Mathematics*, New York and London: Wiley & Sons; 2nd edn, 1989, repr. 1991. (An excellent reference on the history of mathematics, recently updated.)

Cajori, F. (1919) *A History of Mathematics*, London: Macmillan; 5th edn, New York: Chelsea, 1991. (A classic on the history of mathematics. Now a bit dated, but still good value.)

* Conway, J.H. (1976) *On Numbers and Games*, London: Academic Press. (Provides a unified construction of many different kinds of number. Cited in §9.)

Crossley, J.N. (1980) *The Emergence of Number*, Singapore: World Scientific. (A very readable history of number.)

Dedekind, R. (1963) *Essays on the Theory of Numbers*, New York: Dover. (Includes English translations of two of the most important essays on numbers ever written.)

Lakatos, I. (1978) 'Cauchy and the Continuum', in *Collected Papers*, vol. 2, *Mathematics, Science and Epistemology*, Cambridge: Cambridge University Press, ch. 3. (A perceptive analysis of the infinitesimal calculus, its downfall and its relationship to nonstandard analysis.)

* Mortensen, C. (1995) *Inconsistent Mathematics*, Dordrecht: Kluwer. (Chapters 2 and 8 include discussions of inconsistent numbers and their use in solving inconsistent sets of linear equations. Cited in §9.)

Nechaev, I.V. (1987) 'Number', in M. Hazewinkel (ed.) *Encyclopaedia of Mathematics: An Updated and Annotated Translation of the Soviet Mathematical Encyclopaedia*, Dordrecht: Kluwer. (A clear but more technical account of number.)

* Priest, G. (1987) *In Contradiction*, The Hague: Martinus Nijhoff. (Chapter 2 includes a discussion of problems of ZF. Cited in §8.)

* Wittgenstein, L.J.J. (1953) *Philosophical Investigations*, ed. G.E.M. Anscombe and R. Rhees, trans. G.E.M. Anscombe, Oxford: Blackwell. (Numbers illustrate Wittgenstein's notion of family resemblance. Cited in §9.)

GRAHAM PRIEST

NUMENIUS (*fl. c.* mid 2nd century AD)

Numenius was a Platonist philosopher. He came from Apamea (Syria) and wrote in Greek. His work – now lost – is usually considered Neo-Pythagorean in tendency, and exercised a major influence on the emergence of Neoplatonism in the third century. A radical dualist, he postulated the twin principles of god – a transcendent and changeless intellect, equated with the Good of Plato's Republic *– and matter, identified as the Pythagorean Indefinite Dyad: god is good, matter evil. In addition to this supreme god, he added at a secondary level a creator-god, one of whose aspects is the world-soul, itself further distinguished into a good and an evil world-soul. He had a strong interest in Oriental wisdom, especially Judaic, and famously called Plato 'Moses speaking Attic'.*

1 Life, work and influence
2 Metaphysics

1 Life, work and influence

Nothing is known of Numenius' life, but he can be dated with reasonable accuracy by the fact that he is attested as the teacher of one Harpocration, who was also influenced by the Athenian Platonist Atticus, who in turn flourished in the AD 170s. He is often mentioned in conjunction with a 'companion', Cronius, who was presumably associated with his school, and who may possibly be the addressee of Lucian's treatise on Peregrinus.

Of his works none has survived, but some extracts of his dialogue *On the Good* are preserved by Eusebius in his *Preparation for the Gospel*, as also are some considerable passages from a lively polemical work, *On the Apostasy ['Diastasis'] of the Academics from Plato*, which helps to clarify Numenius' own position, while providing some useful data on the New Academy. Alongside this, we know of the works *On the Indestructibility of the Soul* and *On the Secret Doctrines of Plato*, treatises *On Numbers* and *On Place*, and a work called *Epops*, or 'The Hoopoe', which probably embodies a pun on *epopteia* (mystical vision). We also have an extended account of his doctrine on matter preserved by the late Roman commentator on Plato's *Timaeus*, CALCIDIUS, who may well be more extensively indebted to him than he acknowledges.

His philosophical importance is considerable. He was a major influence, through the mediation of Ammonius Saccas (not to be confused with Ammonius, son of Hermias), on the father of Neoplatonism Plotinus and his followers Amelius and Porphyry, as well as the Christian theologian Origen (see NEOPLATONISM §1; PORPHYRY §4; ORIGEN). His Pythagoreanism consists of presenting Plato as a disciple of Pythagoras (see, for example, fragments 7, 24.57), although without derogating from Plato's greatness (as was done by more extreme Pythagoreans, such as Moderatus of Gades).

Numenius was much interested in the wisdom of the East and in comparative religion. He attracted the interest of Church Fathers by his references to Jahveh, Moses and even Jesus (fr. 1). Indeed, he described Plato as 'Moses speaking Attic' (fr. 8), which seems to imply an acceptance of something like Philo's wholesale allegorization of the Pentateuch (see PHILO OF ALEXANDRIA §1). There has been speculation that he was himself of Jewish stock – his hospitality to the Jewish tradition is certainly notable – but this is not a necessary inference. Numenius may simply be reflecting the syncretistic religious and philosophical milieu in which he lived.

2 Metaphysics

Numenius' views on ethics and logic are not known (although his ethical stance may be assumed to be austere), so we may confine ourselves to his metaphysics and psychology. He is at odds with previous Pythagoreans in maintaining a radical dualism between the first principles of god (the Monad, the Good) and matter (the Dyad), instead of subordinating the material Dyad to the all-generating Monad, as is done by his Pythagoreanizing predecessors from Eudorus through Moderatus to Nicomachus of Gerasa. Numenius' dualism allies him rather with Plutarch and Atticus, and leads him, like them, to postulate an evil world-soul, derived from a reading of Plato (*Laws* X) to balance the beneficent world-soul (see PLUTARCH OF CHAERONEA §§3–4).

Numenius proffered a system of three levels of spiritual reality: a primal god (the Good, or the Father), who is almost supra-intellectual; a secondary, creator-god (the demiurge of Plato's *Timaeus*); and a world-soul. In this he anticipates to some extent Plotinus, although he was more strongly dualist than Plotinus in his attitude to the physical world and matter, and does not take the radical step of declaring his first principle to be above intellect – although his intellect is an intellect *at rest*, as opposed to the secondary intellect, which is *in motion* (fr. 15). Numenius does seem to have felt the awkwardness of attributing both intellectual and creative activity to a first principle which is utterly transcendent and completely unitary (in fragment 12, he is insistent that the first god is 'inactive in respect of all activity'), but he was no more willing than his predecessors to declare it to be 'beyond being *and* intellection'. Indeed, mindful of Plato (*Sophist* 248e) he is even unwilling to deny it a form of motion, speaking of the 'rest' (*stasis*) of the first god as 'an innate motion' – ancestor of the 'spiritual motion' of intellect in later Neoplatonism.

The distinction between his second and third gods is rather subtle, and has led to confusion. In fragment 11 he declares that the second and third gods are 'one', but a division results from the demiurgic activity of the second god with regard to matter. This difference splits the god into two aspects, similar to the 'transcendent' and 'immanent' aspects of the *logos* of god in the philosophies of Philo of Alexandria and Plutarch (at least in the latter's treatise *On Isis and Osiris*). The 'lower' aspect of the demiurgic intellect may be viewed as a 'third god', and constitutes a rational world-soul, which bestows form on the chaos of matter to create the physical world at the price of suffering multiplicity itself.

Numenius is, like any later Platonist, concerned with basing his doctrine on suitable Platonic proof-texts. His doctrine of three gods he derives primarily from the Platonic *Second Letter*, which he would have naturally taken as genuine, but he derives confirmation also from a well-known passage of the *Timaeus*, where he takes 'the essential living being' (*auto ho esti zōon*) as the primal god (equated in turn with the 'Good' of the *Republic*). This essential living being the demiurgic intellect contemplates, thus bringing into being the world of Forms, while also 'discursively intelligizing' (*dienoēthē*) the physical world, thus constituting itself, or a lower projection of itself, as the world-soul (fr. 22). The fact that the *Timaeus* myth presents the demiurge as creating the world-soul may have led Numenius to describe his third god as a 'creation' (*poiēma*), as Proclus alleges (fr. 21) it is certainly an active principle.

Adumbrated in this fragment is his doctrine of *proschrēsis* ('calling in the help of . . .') which, although obscure, may anticipate Neoplatonic doctrines of the interaction between *hypostases* (see PLOTINUS §3). Each level of being (the primal god, the demiurge) performs its proper role only by *proschrēsis* of the level of being below it. This serves

to link up the entire spiritual world into a dynamic whole. It may be behind the rather bombastic imagery of 'grandfather, son, and grandson', which Proclus criticizes (fr. 21), and which Numenius seems to have used to characterize the relations between the three principles.

It is in his doctrine of matter (Calcidius, fr. 52) that Numenius' dualism emerges most strongly. Matter, as the Pythagorean Indefinite Dyad, is coeval with the primal god, and is a positively evil force. Numenius is scornful of his predecessors' attempts to derive the Dyad from the Monad by one formula or another (fr. 52.15–). He discerns the postulation of a maleficent, 'material' soul in Plato *Laws* (X 896e), which, like Plutarch before him, he sees as represented also by the 'disorderly cause' of the *Timaeus* (see PLUTARCH §§3–4). This can be brought to order by the demiurgic intellect, but never completely neutralized.

This 'evil' soul is represented in each individual also (frs 43–4), although how exactly its functions are distinguished from those of the rational soul is less than clear. It is not a simple distinction between rational and irrational soul, since Numenius also envisages the rational soul as picking up a series of 'garments' as it descends through the heavenly spheres to incarnation, some of which are irrational. But later evidence from Porphyry and Iamblichus indicates that Numenius' psychology was regarded as distinctive and strongly dualist. Finally, Numenius, like Middle Platonists in general, had no objection to postulating transmigration into animals if a soul became excessively corrupt.

See also: NEO-PYTHAGOREANISM ; PLATONISM, EARLY AND MIDDLE §§1, 4

References and further reading

Beutler, R. (1940) 'Noumenios', *Realencyclopädie der klassischen Altertumswissenschaft*, suppl. 7: 664–78 (A useful general account, now superseded in large part by Frede (1987).)

Dillon, J.M. (1977) *The Middle Platonists*, London: Duckworth. (Pages 361–79 offer an introductory account of Numenius.)

Dodds, E.R. (1960) 'Numenius and Ammonius', *Entretiens Fondation Hardt* 5: 3–32. (Good discussion of the problem of Numenius' influence on Ammonius Saccas.)

Frede, M. (1987) 'Numenius', in W. Haase (ed.) *Aufstieg und Niedergang der römischen Welt*, Berlin and New York: de Gruyter, II 36 (2) 1,034–75. (An excellent discussion of problematic aspects of Numenius' thought.)

* Numenius (*fl. c.* mid 2nd century AD) Fragments, in

E. des Places (ed.) *Numénius*, Paris: Les Belles Lettres, 1973. (The standard edition with French translation.)

JOHN DILLON

NURSING ETHICS

Nursing ethics may be defined simply in relation to what nurses do that doctors and others do not characteristically do; or in relation to the nursing perspective on any issues in health care and medicine. More radically, it claims to employ a distinctive conceptual framework, regarding care, rather than cure, as fundamental. Nursing ethics concerns itself with the relationship between 'carer' and 'cared for' and the meanings embedded in that relationship. It is the moral exploration of an illness or disability as a personal life crisis rather than an instance of a biomedical generalization.

The divergence of medical and nursing ethics took its cue from a distinction between curing and caring. Curing, involving diagnosis, treatment and prognosis, was taken to be characteristic of medicine (with surgery as the paradigm), while caring, involving preparation for treatment, maintenance, and recuperation, was characteristic of nursing (with, perhaps, palliative or domiciliary care as paradigmatic). These were soon taken to be more than just two aspects of physical management of patients but conceptually distinct kinds of activity, one directed to a 'distanced' biology-based approach to dysfunctional specimens, or even parts of specimens, of *Homo sapiens*, and the other a humanities-based intimate approach to individual persons with unique life crises. Whereas this distinction is not sustainable as an absolute it does provide enlightening analytic comparisons of emphasis or tendency.

The distinction has continued to develop as a philosophical one and has merged with gender debates. Nursing ethics has taken up the notion of 'care' formulated by Carol Gilligan (1982) and Nel Noddings (1984) (see FEMINIST ETHICS §1). The debate is largely an engagement with the 'principalism' founded by Beauchamp and Childress (1979) (see MEDICAL ETHICS §6). Some nursing ethicists have developed the idea that the 'ethics of care', rooted in a feminine response to life, is a superior alternative to a masculine 'ethics of justice'. Certainly the overwhelming majority of nurses are female, but while some take this as evidence of an advantageous feminine moral attitude others have thought it reflects only political contingencies.

Some insist that rationalistic, abstract and liberal 'impartiality' and 'distance' lead to indifference and unresponsiveness in modern medicine, and expound a contrasting 'partialist' nursing ethics of context, personal engagement and unique human relationships (see IMPARTIALITY). Nursing theorists influenced by Gilligan, such as Fry and Watson, take up her suggestion that whereas a principles approach seeks agreement, the caring approach seeks mutual understanding through an exploration of the meaning of a personal crisis (illness, disability, infirmity). Gadow (1980) has a distinctively nursing notion of care in her concept of 'existential advocacy': a true nursing relationship involves helping patients make sense of their life experiences so as to regain some control, clarifying the patients' values so as authentically to exercise their freedom of self-determination. The emphasis on the 'carer/cared for' relationship has led one stream of nursing ethics, influenced by Benner, into phenomenological methods.

Other writers have attempted to integrate principles-based approaches with 'caring relationship' approaches. Beauchamp and Childress, admitting that principles may be insufficient for health care ethics, have responded with a clarification of 'mutual interdependence' and 'emotional response' in the 'ethics of care' and still regard the notion of caring as too undeveloped to be integrated coherently. One empirical study finds no significant difference in the distribution of 'impartialist' and 'partialist' modes of thinking among doctors and nurses and suggests the modes really operate together but at different levels.

The question of a difference between medical and nursing ethics, whether a sharp one or merely one of emphasis and tendency, is carried into questions about which health care issues nurses identify as ethically problematic and how they approach them. Nurse ethicists often do, and *qua* nurses arguably should, select issues which concern nursing activity (the assessment, planning, implementation and evaluation of care) as opposed to medical activity (diagnosis, treatment, prognosis). Such issues would be found in, for example, health promotion and preventative nursing, continuing care of the elderly, and residential and hospice care. Given the intimate and ongoing nature of the nursing process (as opposed to the transitory medical intervention) ethical issues are identified in everyday and routine issues, such as incontinence and toileting, falls among the elderly, and choice of clothing and sleep periods.

Ethically aware nurses may more readily see the human, personal, cultural and social aspects of any issue, whether medical or nursing, such as patient self-esteem and privacy, pain alleviation and comfort, empowering and encouraging self-care, security and general wellbeing. Ethical issues in nursing research may relate in content to clinical nursing (such as wound or bed sore management) or may, in form, approach issues through meanings and relationships employing the methods of ethnography or 'action theory'.

The considerations above also apply to ethical issues in the organization and professional development of nursing. The themes of 'nurse autonomy' and 'advocacy' are particularly strong. The first concerns the degree to which nurses can exercise moral choice as employees and as the subordinates of doctors. Thus, professional and contractual obligations may come into conflict, for example, over informing the patient in their interest about a matter the employer may regard as commercially confidential (see PROFESSIONAL ETHICS); and medical judgment and nursing judgment may conflict, for example, over when to discharge a patient. In these contexts the rights and wrongs of 'blowing the whistle' may arise. This may even be entailed by the demand that the nurse act as 'advocate' of the patient. The interpretation of this notion is controversial. While it requires that the nurse plead the cause of the patient, it is not always clear whether this is to be given the 'banal' interpretation that the patient by definition is someone who needs another to do what they would do if able, or the 'radical' interpretation that the nurse must challenge and speak up to defend the patient against any obstacle whatsoever to their autonomy (see AUTONOMY, ETHICAL).

'Nursing ethics' may be taken as a generic term to cover the concerns of all the professions allied to medicine. In midwifery ethical issues emerge from maternal choice, the professional autonomy of the midwife vis-à-vis obstetrics, and 'natural childbirth'. In physiotherapy there are questions around delimiting potentially coercive or unavoidably uncomfortable or even futile procedures, such as chest physiotherapy on terminally ill patients.

See also: APPLIED ETHICS; BIOETHICS; HELP AND BENEFICENCE

References and further reading

* Beauchamp, T.L. and Childress, J.F. (1979) *Principles of Biomedical Ethics*, Oxford: Oxford University Press; 4th edn, 1994. (Definitive work of 'principalism', criticized by many nursing ethicists.)
Benner, P. (ed.) (1994) *Interpretive Phenomenology: Embodiment, Caring and Ethics in Health and Illness*, London: Sage. (A phenomenological approach to nursing ethics. Not easy reading.)
Fry, F.T. (1989) 'Toward a Theory of Nursing Ethics', *Advances in Nursing Science* 11 (4): 9–22. (Argues for a moral-point-of-view theory with caring as a fundamental value.)
* Gadow, S. (1980) 'Existential Advocacy: Philosophical Foundations of Nursing', in S.F. Spiker and S. Gadow (eds) *Nursing Images and Ideals: Opening Dialogue with the Humanities*, New York: Springer. (Draws on existentialist assumptions.)
* Gilligan, C. (1982) *In a Different Voice: Psychological Theory and Women's Development*, Cambridge, MA: Harvard University Press. (Very strong influence on nursing ethics.)
Hunt, G. (1994) *Ethical Issues in Nursing*, London: Routledge. (Attempts to identify obstacles to good practice rather than formulate a theory of good practice as such.)
* Noddings, N. (1984) *Caring: A Feminine Approach to Ethics and Moral Education*, Berkeley, CA: University of California Press. (Strong influence on nursing ethics.)
Rickard, M., Kuhse, H. and Singer, P. (1996) 'Caring and Justice: A Study of Two Approaches to Health Care Ethics', *Nursing Ethics* 3 (3): 212–23. (An empirical study of approaches to ethical decision-making in nurses and doctors.)
Watson, J. (1988) *Nursing: Human Science and Human Care: A Theory of Nursing*, New York: National League for Nursing. (An exploration of the meanings embedded in caring.)
Nursing Ethics: An International Journal for Healthcare Professionals. (Six issues a year, covering all aspects of nursing ethics and philosophy, with some law).

GEOFFREY HUNT

NYĀYA *see* NYĀYA-VAIŚEṢIKA

NYĀYA-VAIŚEṢIKA

The Nyāya school of philosophy developed out of the ancient Indian tradition of debate; its name, often translated as 'logic', relates to its original and primary concern with the method (nyāya) of proof. The fully fledged classical school presents its interests in a list of sixteen categories of debate, of which the first two are central: the means of valid cognition (perception, inference, analogy and verbal testimony) and the soteriologically relevant objects of valid cognition (self, body, senses, sense objects, cognition, and so on). The latter reflect an early philosophy of nature added to an original eristic-dialectic tradition. On the whole, classical Nyāya adopts, affirms and further develops, next to its epistemology and logic, the ontology of Vaiśeṣika. The soteriological relevance of the school is grounded in the claim that adequate knowledge of the sixteen categories, aided by contemplation, yogic exercises and philosophical debate, leads to release from rebirth. Vaiśeṣika, on the other hand, is a philosophy of nature most concerned with the comprehensive enumeration and identification of all distinct and irreducible world constituents, aiming to provide a real basis for all cognitive and linguistic acts. This endeavour for distinction (viśeṣa) may well account for the school's name. Into the atomistic and mechanistic worldview of Vaiśeṣika a soteriology and orthodox ethics are fitted, but not without tensions; still later the notion of a supreme god, whose function is at first mainly regulative but later expanded to the creation of the world, is introduced. In the classical period the Vaiśeṣika philosophy of nature, including the highly developed doctrine of causality, is cast into a rigorous system of six, later seven, categories (substance, quality, motion, universal, particularity, inherence, nonexistence). Nyāya epistemology increasingly influences that of Vaiśeṣika.

The interaction and mutual influences between Nyāya and Vaiśeṣika finally led to the formation of what may be styled a syncretistic school, called Nyāya-Vaiśeṣika in modern scholarly publications. This step, facilitated by the common religious affiliation to Śaivism, occurs with Udayana (eleventh century), who commented on texts of both schools. Subsequently, numerous syncretistic manuals attained high popularity. Udayana also inaugurated the period of Navya-Nyāya, 'New Logic', which developed and refined sophisticated methods of philosophical analysis.

1 **Sources**
2 **Origin and orientation of Vaiśeṣika**
3 **Origin and formation of Nyāya**
4 **Ontology: the three older categories**
5 **Ontology: the younger categories**
6 **Epistemology, logic and dialectics**
7 **Soteriology and ethics**

1 Sources

The basic Vaiśeṣika text is the *Vaiśeṣikasūtra*, ascribed to the legendary founder of the school, Kaṇāda ('grain-eater'; also Kaṇabhuj, and Kāśyapa by clan name). This compilation of some 400 concise and often enigmatic mnemonic sentences contains materials from several developmental stages of the system; substantial parts of it may have been in existence already during the first two centuries AD. Old commentaries are referred to in later works, but have for the most part been lost. Mainstream classical Vaiśeṣika largely goes back to the *Padārthadharmasaṅgraha* (Compendium of Properties of the Categories) – also called *Praśastapādabhāṣya* (Praśastapāda's Commentary) – of Praśastapāda (early sixth century), the great systematizer and scholiast of the school. Another compendium from approximately the same period, the innovative *Treatise on the Ten Categories* by Candramati (surviving in Chinese translation), had no lasting impact. The major works of the classical period are commentaries on the *Padārthadharmasaṅgraha*: the *Vyomavatī* (The Spacious [Commentary]) by Vyomaśiva (ninth century), the *Nyāyakandalī* (The White-Flowered Tree of Nyāya) by Śrīdhara (late tenth century) and the *Kiraṇāvalī* (A Sequence of Rays) by Udayana (early eleventh century). A commentary on the *Vaiśeṣikasūtra* by Candrānanda (probably ninth or tenth century) was published only in 1961; although strongly influenced by the *Padārthadharmasaṅgraha*, it preserves a more genuine version of the text than the until then standard commentary by Śaṅkara Miśra, the *Vaiśeṣikasūtra-Upaskāra* (The Ornament of the *Vaiśeṣikasūtra*; fifteenth century).

At the basis of Nyāya is the *Nyāyasūtra*, ascribed to Akṣapāda. Its earliest preserved commentary, Pakṣilasvāmin Vātsyāyana's *Nyāyabhāṣya* (A Commentary on Nyāya), dates from the second half of the fifth century. Its subcommentary, the *Nyāyavārttika* (A Supplementary Commentary on Nyāya) by Uddyotakara Bhāradvāja (sixth century), represents a defence and renewal of Nyāya in response to Buddhist logic. Of many commentaries on these two texts, only Vācaspati Miśra I's voluminous *Nyāyavārttikatātparyaṭīkā* (A Commentary on the True Intention of the *Nyāyavārttika*; tenth century) has survived. It is commented upon by Udayana in his *Nyāyavārttikatātparyapariśuddhi* (The Clarification of the True Intention of the *Nyāyavārttika*). Important independently composed treatises of the classical period are Jayanta Bhaṭṭa's *Nyāyamañjarī* (A Cluster of Blossoms of Nyāya; late ninth century) and Bhāsarvajña's *Nyāyasāra* (The Essence of Nyāya), with the author's own extensive commentary, *Nyāyabhūṣaṇa* (The Ornament of Nyāya; tenth century). Udayana's *Ātmatattvaviveka* (The Discernment of the True Nature/Reality of the Self) mainly defends the notion of a permanent self against Buddhist criticism, whereas his *Nyāyakusumāñjali* (A Handful of Flowers of Nyāya) establishes the existence of a supreme god. Of Navya-Nyāya works, Gaṅgeśa's monumental *Tattvacintāmaṇi* (The Jewel of Reflection on the True Nature [of Things]/Reality; fourteenth century) deserves special mention (see

GAUTAMA, AKṢAPĀDA; VĀTSYĀYANA; UDDYOTAKARA; UDAYANA; GAṄGEŚA).

2 Origin and orientation of Vaiśeṣika

The beginnings and development of Vaiśeṣika prior to its classical form are still largely obscure. The most valuable and knowledgeable attempt so far at a comprehensive 'archaeology' of Vaiśeṣika is the brilliant, though necessarily speculative and sometimes intuitive reconstruction of the school's formation by Erich Frauwallner. About thirty years after the publication of his *Geschichte der indischen Philosophie* (History of Indian Philosophy), volume II (1956), Vaiśeṣika studies experienced a renaissance, and scholars turned again to his stimulating reconstruction. Some developments traced by him have been reconsidered; his evaluation of the original orientation of the school has also become the subject of debate. According to Frauwallner, early Vaiśeṣika is an outstanding example of a philosophy of nature that strives systematically to understand and explain the world out of a pure philosophical urge for knowledge, without mythological, theological or soteriological interests. Within the broader tradition of philosophy of nature in which Vaiśeṣika arose, Frauwallner also locates the materialist schools (see MATERIALISM, INDIAN SCHOOL OF). Other philosophical schools belonging to that tradition, however, notably Jainism, Nyāya and Mīmāṃsā, combined philosophy of nature with soteriological and ethical teachings. Frauwallner assumes that Vaiśeṣika too, during its development, was influenced by the religious and moralistic tendencies of contemporary philosophies and eventually added a soteriology, still later a theology, to its teachings. These developments he perceives in stark contrast to the school's original spirit and considers them to have had negative consequences for it. Some modern Indian interpreters, notably Anantalal Thakur (1969), also stress the purely scientific attitude of the *Vaiśeṣikasūtra*.

The other extreme lies in ascribing an original and primary soteriological concern to early Vaiśeṣika (for example, Madeleine Biardeau) or a general religious orientation by claiming its main purpose to be the defence of the Vedas and of orthodox ritualism and ethics against heterodox challenges (Jan Houben 1994). Because sources for the school's early history are lacking, it is safer to assume a middle stand, leaning towards Frauwallner's side. The basic orientation of early and even classical Vaiśeṣika is certainly towards cosmology, the systematic and comprehensive explanation of the world, its origin and the processes, natural, psychological, and so forth, occurring through the interaction of its constituents.

Some rudimentary soteriology, however, may have been attached already to the early teachings, even if it was an extraneous element of minor importance. The very acceptance of the notion of an individual soul would necessitate in its historical context some ideas about the soul's involvement in rebirth and its possible release from it.

A similar situation can be assumed for those teachings in the epic *Mahābhārata* that have a pronounced character of philosophies of nature. Their predominant topics are the origin and constitution of the world, centring around the concept of the five 'great elements', earth, water, fire/light, wind/air and space/'ether'. The elements are respectively characterized by firmness, moistness, and so on, and, among other qualities, by the 'special qualities' that are the five sense objects, namely, smell, flavour, form, touch and sound, which are sometimes conceived as the emanations of the elements. Various qualities to be subsumed under these five 'special qualities' are enumerated in long and heterogenous lists. All things of this world, including the body and the five senses, are made up of the five elements. The generally strong interest in the empirical human being is manifest in theories about the formation of the body, its constitution by the elements and its internal processes, such as digestion. Attention is also paid to the explanation of cognitive processes. The five senses are recognized as different from their seats, that is, the sense organs; according to the principle 'like grasps like', they grasp the five 'special' elementary qualities and consist of the element which possesses the respective quality. An internal organ or sense (*manas*) functions in non-sensory cognitive processes and rules over the activities of the external senses. Further entities in the world are the individual souls, the sentient and active subjects within the bodies. They are responsible for life, and due to involvement with the sense objects and nescience they become the subjects of transmigration. Time and the cardinal directions appear also as important factors in the world.

It is within the milieu of these teachings that one can situate the beginning of Vaiśeṣika. During its formation they were further developed and refined; in particular, the entities perceived as primary constituents of the world were systematized, some of them subsumed elsewhere, some accorded independent status, and some eliminated, towards an ordered and complete enumeration of irreducible world constituents.

3 Origin and formation of Nyāya

The roots of the Nyāya school are in the ancient

Indian tradition of debate (*vāda*). In the Vedic period, priests already held verbal contests as part of ritual, to discover and appropriately formulate the enigmatic true nature of the world and of the rituals themselves. Subsequently, the Upaniṣads refer to religious-philosophical debates at the assemblies of local rulers. The winners were rewarded not only with recognition and fame, but also with material goods and royal patronage. Thus rules of debate had to be fixed, and guidelines were compiled to assure an orderly and fair procedure. They also provided criteria to determine sound and unsound arguments and thus winners and losers. These early guidelines developed into manuals which covered heterogenous points, such as the characteristics of the opponent and composition of the audience with respect to psychological tactics, types of debate, manner of speech, the parts of an argument and their order, means of valid cognition employed in an argument, types of faulty reasons, unfair criticism, and various points of defeat. The central position, however, was occupied increasingly by consideration of the method (*nyāya*) of proof. Epic references to numerous 'models of method' (*nyāya-tantra*) pronounced by debaters may point to this tradition.

The tradition of debate was closely related to the branch of knowledge or 'science' concerned with principled and reasoned reflection (*ānvīkṣikī vidyā*), or even led to its development. Further designations related to this 'science' of argumentative corroboration or disproof also refer to its special concern and general method, which, like the term 'nyāya', is often rendered as 'logic': 'the science of turning around (in examination)' (*tarkavidyā, tarkaśāstra*), 'the science of (formal and logical) coherence' (*yuktiśāstra*) and 'the science of reasons' (*hetuvidyā, hetuśāstra*).

At first the manuals of debate and reasoned examination may have been formulated without presupposing specific metaphysics, and therefore could be used by different religious and nascent philosophical traditions. However, the central concern with the method of proof led to increasing reflection on the means of valid cognition and logical issues, and eventually certain traditions of debate became associated with certain philosophical outlooks. Further, in the case of Nyāya, the reflection on the *objects* of valid cognition, one of the categories of debate, initiated the inclusion of an early philosophy of nature, similar to the one from which Vaiśeṣika developed, into an originally eristic-dialectic tradition. With the addition of a plain soteriology, the process of the formation of a separate philosophical school was concluded.

4 Ontology: the three older categories

The *Vaiśeṣikasūtra* presents a developed philosophy of nature clad in a rigorous doctrine of categories (*padārtha*, literally 'meaning of a word'). The six categories fall into two triads, of which the first may historically precede the second: (I) substance, (II) quality and (III) motion; (IV) universal, (V) particularity and (VI) inherence. Further categories, namely potentiality and nonpotentiality, existence (the highest universal) and nonexistence, were introduced by Candramati, but not generally accepted. Nonexistence (*abhāva*), though, increasingly attracted philosophical interest and was finally adopted as a seventh category in the eleventh century (see NEGATIVE FACTS IN CLASSICAL INDIAN PHILOSOPHY §5). As elaborated by Wilhelm Halbfass (1992), common to everything comprised by the six classical or seven postclassical categories are the three abstract attributes of 'is-ness' (*astitva*), that is, objectivity or factual identifiability, knowability and nameability. This points to the basic endeavour of Vaiśeṣika, the enumeration and identification of what there is in order to provide a real basis for all cognitive and linguistic acts. However, only substances, qualities and motions exist in the fullest sense, that is, as concrete 'objects' or 'things' (*artha*), because the highest universal, existence (*sattā*, literally 'being-ness', 'real-ness'; or *bhāva*, literally 'becoming', but used synonymously), inheres in them. Universals, particulars, inherence and nonexistence are also ontologically distinct and irreducible world constituents; in contrast to the first three categories, they can be substrata only of abstract properties (*dharma*), but not of further ontologically founded entities, including the universal 'existence' – that is, they can function as logical subjects (*dharmin*) only.

(I) The category of substance (*dravya*) comprises nine items. The first four are (1–4) the four elements, earth, water, fire and wind, which exist in the form of eternal atoms and impermanent aggregates. The fifth element, (5) 'ether' (*ākāśa*), functions primarily as the eternal substratum of sound; it is inferred by elimination from the very existence of the quality sound, which requires a substantial support. Because sound can arise everywhere, 'ether' is considered as one and omnipresent. In such qualities, including eternity, 'ether' resembles time, space and the individual souls or selves. (6) Time (*kāla*) is conceived as a timeless, static and inactive substance responsible for our notions of relative position in time and the qualities of temporal remoteness and proximity in limited and noneternal substances. Similarly, (7) space (*diś*) accounts for our notions of relative spatial position and remoteness and proximity in space. The ubiquitous (8) selves (*ātman*) are restricted to individual bodies as the places of their experiences and activities only because their atom-sized and eternal (9) 'internal organs' (*manas*) are connected with a body. However, the self may have originally been considered as having limited dimension, that is, as being contained within the body, and thus capable of motion and physical activity.

The impermanent substances, the objects of everyday experience, are wholes (*avayavin*) consisting of a single element each, with the possible admixture of further elements. These wholes constitute something new over and above their parts (*avayava*), a claim contested especially by the Buddhists. According to the classical theory of causality, the smallest whole is constituted by two conjoined atoms; the first visible whole is the sun mote or triad, composed of three dyads. All further substances are produced by various numbers of larger, visible parts.

(II) The qualities (*guṇa*) are unrepeatable quality individuals, particularizations in time and space of abstract qualities such as colour or flavour. They are ontologically distinct from the substances in which they inhere, but dependent on them as their substrata. Caused in the whole substance by the qualities of its parts, they are destroyed with its destruction. Some qualities inhere in only one substance, such as temperature, colour, flavour and smell, the 'special qualities' of the physical elements. They accumulate in the eternal atoms of wind, fire, water and earth, where they too are eternal: wind possesses only (tepid) temperature, fire (hot) temperature and (bright white) colour, and so on. Other qualities inhere in more than one substance simultaneously, for example, the 'common qualities' conjunction and separation, important factors in causation, and number (above one). The list of seventeen qualities in the *Vaiśeṣikasūtra* further enumerates the 'common qualities' dimension (ranging from atomic size to large size to infinite size, that is, ubiquity), separateness, and remoteness and proximity (in space and time). Further 'special qualities', namely of the self, are cognition, pleasure and pain, desire and aversion, and effort, all impermanent. It is by effort that the omnipresent self, incapable of movement itself, initiates mechanistically conceived psychological and physical processes. To these seventeen seven more are added by Praśastapāda's time: weight, fluidity, viscosity, disposition (comprising momentum, elasticity, and impressions responsible for recollection left in the self by cognitions), merit (*dharma*) and demerit (*adharma*), and sound, the 'special quality' of 'ether'.

It is not observed that, for example, colours possess further colours. Moreover, if they did, this would result in an infinite regress. Motion, on the other hand, is only observed with corporeal things. Therefore, all qualities are devoid of further qualities or motions.

(III) The five items in the category of motion (*karman*) go back to a classification of human actions: throwing upwards and downwards, bending and stretching, and going. Subsequently all other types of motion, inhering in atoms, the 'internal organs' and impermanent substances, are subsumed under 'going'; motion itself is momentary and inheres in only one substance at a time. It plays an essential role in the atomistic-mechanistic world view of Vaiśeṣika, for example, in causation, to effect the conjunction between substances to produce new wholes (see CAUSATION, INDIAN THEORIES OF §5), and in the mechanistic explanation of natural processes, macrocosmic (for example, meteorological) and microcosmic (for example, digestion, birth and death, cognition), often effected by 'the invisible' (*adṛṣṭa*), a force also at work in the ritual and ethical context (see §7) and later identified with merit and demerit inhering in the self. A complete chapter of the *Vaiśeṣikasūtra* is devoted to mechanics in the broadest sense, although a science of mechanics, as in ancient Greece, did not evolve.

Like qualities, motions are ontologically separate from, but dependent on, supporting substances; they are also devoid of qualities or further motions.

5 Ontology: the younger categories

(IV) Universals (*sāmānya*, literally 'commonness', 'sameness'/'similarity') inhere in substances, qualities and motions; they are the hypostasized generic properties responsible for the connection of various entities with the same concept or designation and for their conception as belonging to the same group. Contrary to qualities, they are one, eternal and repeatable; for example, the one universal 'cow-ness', characterized as having horns, a dewlap, a tail, and so on, resides fully and simultaneously in every cow alive and is unaffected by the demise of an individual cow. Although dependent on substances, qualities and motions as their substrata, universals provide them with their generic character and identity. The highest universal is 'being-ness' or existence, which is common to substances, and so on; the lower or specific universals (*sāmānyaviśeṣa*), such as 'substance-ness', 'colour-ness' and 'hot-ness', effect not only a notion of recurrence and inclusion of their substrata in one class, but also of their exclusion from entities belonging to other classes. Special attention is devoted to the differentiation of real universals from mere abstract properties (*dharma*); by Udayana's time, criteria have been developed to discern real from unreal universals (see UNIVERSALS, INDIAN THEORIES OF §2).

(V) The elusive category particularity (*viśeṣa*) or ultimate particularity (*antyaviśeṣa*), as clarified by Halbfass (1992), comprises, according to Praśastapāda, the 'factors of irreducible individual identity'. These particularities assert timeless, unchangeable generic and numeric identity for permanent entities, notably the individual atoms, selves and 'internal organs'; they allow accomplished Yogis to discern individual atoms of earth with their special powers of perception, for example. Particularities also inhere in the unitary substances 'ether', time and space. For Candramati, they alone possess particularity, inasmuch as their generic identity cannot be asserted by specific universals: there are no other entities in their class to be included.

(VI) Inherence (*samavāya*, literally 'concourse') is the unitary eternal entity responsible for the connection of distinct entities which are in a relationship of support and supported and cannot exist separately. It causes the notion that something is 'here', that is, resides in something else; for example, a product or whole, such as a cow, inheres in its causes or parts, such as horns, dewlap, tail, and so on. The entities belonging to different categories are joined by way of this dependent residence to form the actual complex things of this world. At the base are the substances; due to inherence the universals existence, substanceness and, for example, cow-ness reside in a substance, as do its qualities, such as white colour, and motions, that is to say going. White colour and going are again related to existence and their respective generic characters by inherence.

The ontology of classical Nyāya closely resembles that of Vaiśeṣika. This is due to their similar background regarding philosophy of nature (see §3). The historically later chapters of the *Nyāyasūtra* basically presuppose and assert classical Vaiśeṣika ontology in their discussions of the means and (soteriologically relevant) objects of valid cognition. The Vaiśeṣika categoriology, however, was fully adopted and further developed starting with Uddyotakara only. The lasting points of difference are mainly of a scholastic nature; a major one concerns the mode of colour change in fired pots. According to Vaiśeṣika, the fire destroys the pot up to its atoms, which lose their original dark colour due to the heat; subsequently the heat causes a new colour in them, and thanks to 'the invisible' a similar pot is built up again, with a new reddish colour. Nyāya, on the other hand, allows tiny interstices in the structure of the pot into which the fire can intrude; its heat then causes a colour change of the *whole* pot, which remains structurally intact and the same throughout the process. The independently minded thinker Bhāsarvajña argued for revisions of the categories, but without lasting impact. In his innovative *Padārthatattvanirūpaṇa* (Examination of the True Nature/Reality of the Categories), the sixteenth-century Navya-Naiyāyika Raghunātha Śiromaṇi eliminates 'ether', time and space, for example, as separate categories by ascribing their roles to God, and introduces new categories such as the moment and potency.

6 Epistemology, logic and dialectics

The very composition of the *Nyāyasūtra* demonstrates the traditionally central interest of Nyāya in these areas. Among the sixteen categories of debate in Nyāya, the means or instruments of valid cognition (*pramāṇa*) occupy the first place. The larger number of *pramāṇas* current at the time is reduced to four: (1) perception (*pratyakṣa*), (2) inference (*anumāna*), (3) analogy or comparison (*upamāna*), and (4) verbal testimony (*śabda*). In Vaiśeṣika, the *pramāṇas* are treated under the category of quality because cognition is a 'special quality' of the self. Cognition is divided into knowledge and nescience; knowledge includes perception and inference as *pramāṇas*, as well as recollection and the intuitional cognition of omniscient seers. Analogy and verbal testimony are subsumed under inference. Both schools distinguish between, for example, perception as a means and the resulting knowledge (*pramā*); in the controversy about the intrinsic or extrinsic validity of the resulting knowledge they adopt the latter position. They further hold that the *pramāṇas*, although of different natures and modes of functioning, can converge on the same object, contrary to the view that their objects are exclusive (see EPISTEMOLOGY, INDIAN SCHOOLS OF §2; KNOWLEDGE, INDIAN VIEWS OF §3).

(1) *Perception* (as *pramā*) arises from a contact between self, sense, 'internal organ' (*manas*) and object (= perception as *pramāṇa*). The atom-sized, swiftly moving 'internal organ' serves as the regulating link between the omnipresent self and the elementary-materially conceived senses (see §2); this explains the denial of the simultaneity of different sense perceptions and cognitions in general. The senses either move out to their objects, as do the visual rays, or are approached by them. A differentiation into six types of contact was necessitated by the introduction of Vaiśeṣika categoriology to account for the perception of, say, colour, which as a quality cannot be the substratum of a further quality conjunction (see SENSE PERCEPTION, INDIAN VIEWS OF).

Large substances that possess colour are perceptible by vision and touch as something over and above their qualities. Some thinkers even maintained that their perception without any qualities is sometimes possible. Generally they appear with other substances, qualities and motion as their qualificands; due to the perception of their specific universals they appear qualified as similar to others of their class. At first, only the 'special qualities' of the self were assumed to be perceptible by a specific contact between the 'internal organ' and the self; from them its existence had to be inferred. However, several thinkers also claimed its self-perception through this contact. The other perceptible qualities and motion are perceived only when inhering in perceptible substances; this perception is further dependent on perception of their specific universals, whereas the perception of universals, lacking further universals, merely follows that of their substrata. Inherence is only inferable in Vaiśeṣika, whereas in Nyāya it is perceived as qualifying its relata, like nonexistence.

Unlike DIGNĀGA, certain Naiyāyikas (the Ācāryas, commentators on the *Nyāyavārttika*) maintained that perception can be conceptual, that is, that language/concepts in the form of impressions may be part of its causal complex and may influence its content. In doing so, they gave up the realistic principle, defended by the Vyākhyātṛs (commentators on the *Nyāyabhāṣya*), that the external and internal objects of perception have to be equivalent.

(2) *Inference* depends on perception and is threefold: (a) 'as before', (b) 'as the rest' and (c) 'observed from similarity'. The *Nyāyasūtra* provides no further explanations here, and all the commentaries seem unreliable. Albrecht Wezler (1969) has argued convincingly that parallel passages in early Buddhist texts preserve the appropriate examples: (a) refers to recognition by some special mark, (b) to inductive generalization and (c) to analogical reasoning. Vātsyāyana provides two alternative explanations for each type, none of which fits the *sūtra*'s terminology smoothly. For instance, (b) is explained as inference either from effect to cause or by elimination.

Perhaps the original intention of the *sūtra* was lost because inference was just one among many topics in manuals of debate (see §3) and numerous attempts to characterize it were current; for example, the *Vaiśeṣikasūtra* refers to four situations in which entities can function as sound reasons or signs to infer others: A is connected (to B), A is related by inherence (to B), A is related by inherence to the same thing (as B), and A is in contradiction (to B). As a *pramāṇa*, inference appears in the *Nyāyasūtra* in a category different from the members of proof. Only after VASUBANDHU merged inference and proof did the former become central in Indian philosophy. Subsequently, the two are distinguished in Nyāya and Vaiśeṣika only in

terms of purpose, as 'inference for oneself' and 'inference for another'. The old notions of inference are largely forgotten, and the structure of proof becomes basically that of inference, dominated from Praśastapāda and Uddyotakara onwards by the concept of three characteristics (trairūpya) of a valid reason and refined by Trilocana's concept of an essential relation between probans and probandum (see INFERENCE, INDIAN THEORIES OF §§4–6).

The members of proof are proposition, reason, illustration (by similar or dissimilar examples), application and conclusion. For example:

> Sound is impermanent,
>
> because it is produced,
>
> like a pot (which is produced and impermanent).
>
> Sound is like that (that is, produced).
>
> Therefore, it is impermanent.

A dissimilar example would be the self, which is not produced, and is permanent.

For Nyāya, there are twenty-four types of sophistries with which to attack such an argument unfairly, and twenty-two ways of losing a wrangle ('points of defeat'), of which the use of fallacious reasons is most important philosophically. Fallacious reasons appear also as a separate category, which consists of the deviating or inconclusive reason, the reason contradicting a tenet, the reason which is the same as the original issue, the reason which is the same as the probandum, and the reason which has passed the proper time (for enunciation). The *Vaiśeṣikasūtra* also mentions two fallacious reasons ('unestablished non-statements of a reason'), the unreal/untrue and the doubtful. Subsequently, all of them are reinterpreted, sometimes drastically, and refined within the framework of *trairūpya*. The fallacious reasons of Vaiśeṣika are equated with the first two of Nyāya (in reverse order), and Praśastapāda adds a third type, the reason which does not lead to any decision; it subsumes the too specific reason, a subtype of the Nyāya inconclusive reason. The last two items in Nyāya, in their updated forms, are adopted also in later Vaiśeṣika.

(3) By *analogy* one knows the connection of a certain designation with an object. Analogy as *pramāṇa* is hardly ever used in philosophical discussion; it is employed very narrowly and should not be confused with cognition of similarity, which is obtained by perception and inference.

(4) *Verbal testimony* is defined as instruction by a reliable person and includes everyday linguistic communication and scriptures. Correct reasoning cannot be in conflict with the Vedic scriptures; yet their argumentative corroboration, even validation, is proclaimed to be the central task of Nyāya. In

practice, however, Nyāya is more concerned with the nature of articulated sound *per se*, its duration, and the relationship between words and their referents. On all these issues Nyāya held its own views and strongly opposed not only Buddhists, but also Mīmāṃsakas and Sāṅkhyas (see TESTIMONY IN INDIAN PHILOSOPHY).

7 Soteriology and ethics

Both schools claim that knowledge of their categories leads to release (*apavarga*). In Nyāya, Vātsyāyana narrowed this knowledge to adequate understanding of the twelve soteriologically relevant objects of valid cognition; appearing as a separate category, they indicate the more harmonious integration of soteriology in early Nyāya than in Vaiśeṣika (see §§2–3). The *Nyāyasūtra* proclaims that with the absence of wrong understanding (which absence is caused by adequate understanding of the categories), the three faults (*doṣa*) – craving, aversion and delusion – disappear, and subsequently the linguistic, mental and physical activity instigated by them ceases; the cessation of activity means that a result of activity will not arise and thus not effect a new life for it to be experienced by the acting subject. Consequently – suffering being found nowhere but in life – no suffering will occur; release, which is defined as final and complete liberation from suffering, is attained. According to the *Vaiśeṣikasūtra*, liberation (*mokṣa*) technically consists in the absence of all conjunctions concerning the self and involving it in pleasure and pain, and in the nonmanifestation of a new body for it. In liberation, all 'special qualities' of the self vanish. This idea of liberation evoked strong criticism, especially from Vedāntists, who compared it to the undesirable state of an unconscious stone.

Although the faults or moral defilements (*kleśa*) may be natural to the self, release is possible, just as atoms of earth can lose their natural black colour when a pot is fired (see §5). Furthermore, because the faults are conditioned by wishful expectative thinking relating back to previous experience, their naturalness is doubtful, and they can be wiped out by elimination of this conditioning through adequate understanding. Adequate understanding is initiated by a preceptor and attained by contemplation and yogic exercises repeatedly practised in quiet secluded spots, accompanied by perfection of the self with the help of general and specific rules of restraint (*yama, niyama*). The grasp on knowledge has to be trained incessantly; here friendly debate with knowledgeable disciples, teachers, fellow students and others striving for salvation is recommended. Even wrangle and dispute involving mere criticism of the other party, the other

two types of debate, can serve to protect and strengthen the ascertainment of the true nature of things. Unlike the *Nyāyasūtra*, the *Vaiśeṣikasūtra* proclaims that orthodox, ritual-dominated merit (*dharma*) accomplishes uplift in subsequent lives and liberation. The elusive sixth chapter treats orthodox ethical and ritual conduct, specifying means that effect a certain purpose or result which is called 'the invisible' (*adṛṣṭa*; see §4) and that are conducive to uplift. However, in contrast to the initial proclamation, the activity of merit and demerit is stated as the cause of the self's involvement in rebirth, which highlights the complex and problematic integration of soteriology and ethics. The notion of a supreme god, whose function within the atomistic-mechanistic worldview of Vaiśeṣika is mainly regulative, is found first in Praśastapāda's work.

See also: HINDU PHILOSOPHY; ONTOLOGY IN INDIAN PHILOSOPHY

References and further reading

Bhaduri, S. (1947) *Studies in Nyāya-Vaiśeṣika Metaphysics*, Bhandarkar Oriental Series 5, Poona: Bhandarkar Oriental Research Institute. (Surveys and explicates basic issues regarding the category of substance – the doctrine of elements, time and space, atomism and causality.)

Bronkhorst, J. (ed.) (1994) *Proceedings of the Panel on Early Vaiśeṣika, Hong Kong, Asiatische Studien/ Études Asiatiques* 48 (2). (Wide-ranging collection of essays by specialists on various aspects and problems of early Vaiśeṣika.)

* Candramati (early 6th century) *Treatise on the Ten Categories*, trans. H. Ui, *The Vaiśeshika Philosophy according to the Daśapadārtha-Śāstra*, ed. F.W. Thomas, London: Royal Asiatic Society, 1917; repr. Chowkhamba Sanskrit Studies 22, Varanasi: The Chowkhamba Sanskrit Series Office, 1962. (A study of Vaiśeṣika and Nyāya doctrines as reported in early Buddhist literature is prefixed to an annotated translation of Candramati's treatise on the ten categories; also contains the Chinese text.)

Chemparathy, G. (1983) *L'autorité du Veda selon les Nyāya-Vaiśeṣikas*, Conférences et travaux 2, Louvain-la-Neuve: Centre d'histoire des religions. (Examines the attitude especially of Nyāya towards the Vedic scriptures and socio-religious orthodoxy.)

Faddegon, B. (1918) *The Vaiçeṣika-System, Described with the Help of the Oldest Texts*, Verhandelingen der Koninklijke Akademie van Wetenschappen te Amsterdam, Afdeeling Letterkunde, Nieuwe Reeks XVIII 2, Amsterdam: Johannes Müller. (The most comprehensive classic on all aspects of Vaiśeṣika;

contains copious translations from *Vaiśeṣikasūtra*, detailed discussions of the *Padārthadharmasaṅgraha* and important extracts from Śrīdhara's *Nyāyakandalī*. Although written before the discovery of Candrānanda's commentary, it is still a valuable and thoughtful exposition.)

Frauwallner, E. (1955) 'Candramati und sein *Daśapadārthaśāstra*', in O. Spies (ed.) *Studia Indologica*, Bonner Orientalische Studien, Neue Serie 3, Bonn: Selbstverlag des Orientalischen Seminars der Universität Bonn, 65–85; repr. in G. Oberhammer and E. Steinkellner (eds) *Kleine Schriften*, Wiesbaden: Franz Steiner, 1982, 202–22. (Evaluates Candramati's innovative treatise and places it in its historical context.)

* —— (1956) *Geschichte der indischen Philosophie* (History of Indian Philosophy), vol. 2, Reihe Wort und Antwort 6/II, Salzburg: Otto Müller Verlag, 15–250. (A most valuable reconstruction of the origins and development of Vaiśeṣika, with an exposition of the earliest philosophy of nature in the Nyāya school; also a clear, detailed and reliable presentation of the classical Vaiśeṣika system, including the first stages of scholasticism.)

Guha, D.C. (1968) *Navya Nyāya System of Logic*, Delhi: Motilal Banarsidass, 2nd rev. edn, 1979. (Explains and exemplifies the basic terminology and techniques of Navya-Nyāya philosophical analysis.)

Halbfass, W. (1991) *Tradition and Reflection: Explorations in Indian Thought*, Albany, NY: State University of New York Press. (Chapter 9, 'Competing Causalities: Karma, Vedic Rituals, and the Natural World', explores the concept of *adṛṣṭa* and its ambiguous position between philosophy of nature and ethics in its historical setting.)

* —— (1992) *On Being and What There Is: Classical Vaiśeṣika and the History of Indian Ontology*, Albany, NY: State University of New York Press. (Clearly and fascinatingly written philosophical inquiry into the main issues of Vaiśeṣika ontology; insightful and extensively documented. Contains translations of key passages on Vaiśeṣika ontology.)

Hattori, M. (1972) 'Praśastapāda and Dignāga: A Note on the Development of the Vaiśeṣika Theory of *Anumāna*', *Wiener Zeitschrift für die Kunde Südasiens* 16: 169– 80. (On the relationship of Praśastapāda's theory of inference and fallacious reasons to early Buddhist logic.)

* Houben, J.E.M. (1994) 'Liberation and Natural Philosophy in Early Vaiśeṣika: Some Methodological Problems', in J. Bronkhorst (ed.) *Proceedings of the Panel on Early Vaiśeṣika, Hong Kong, Asiatische Studien/Études Asiatiques* 48 (2): 711–48. (Reviews the controversial standpoints on the original orientation of Vaiśeṣika and argues for a new methodological approach to the problem.)

Isaacson, H. (1993) 'Yogic perception (*yogipratyakṣa*) in early Vaiśeṣika', *Studien zur Indologie und Iranistik* 18: 139–60. (Shows the development of the theory of yogic perception within *Vaiśeṣikasūtra* up to Praśastapāda.)

* Jayanta Bhaṭṭa (late 9th century) *Nyāyamañjarī*, trans. J.V. Bhattacharyya, *Jayanta Bhaṭṭa's Nyāya-Mañjarī [The Compendium of Indian Speculative Logic]*, vol. 1, Delhi: Motilal Banarsidass, 1978. (Being an English translation of a Bengali translation of the Sanskrit original, this is often more of a vague paraphrase than an accurate translation.)

Joshi, L.V. (1986) *A Critical Study of the Pratyakṣa Pariccheda of Bhāsarvajña's Nyāyabhūṣaṇa*, Research Work Publication Series 22, Ahmedabad: School of Languages, Gujarat University. (A detailed annotated paraphrase of the section on perception in one of the most interesting Nyāya texts; Bhāsarvajña takes up the most important theories of his time and discusses them in an independently minded manner.)

Matilal, B.K. (1986) *Perception: An Essay on Classical Indian Theories of Knowledge*, Oxford: Clarendon Press. (Wide-ranging collection of analytically and comparatively orientated essays on the means of valid cognition in general, the distinction between knowledge and illusion, and the relationship of perception to the external world; special emphasis is put on Nyāya views.)

—— (1990) *Logic, Language and Reality: Indian Philosophy and Contemporary Issues*, Delhi: Motilal Banarsidass, esp. chaps 1–2. (Chapter 1 examines basic issues of early and classical Nyāya, such as the categories of debate, the definition of inference, and fallacious reasons, and chapter 2 discusses topics such as empty terms, universal concomitance in inference, and the role of definition in Navya-Nyāya. The author endeavours to reassess these and other issues in the setting of contemporary Western philosophy.)

Mesquita, R. (1995) 'Der *Apavarga*-Begriff bei Śrīdhara: Eine vedāntische Erlösungslehre?' (Śrīdhara's Concept of *Apavarga*: A Vedāntic Theory of Release?), in M. Juntunen, W.L. Smith and C. Suneson (eds) *Sauhṛdyamaṅgalam: Studies in Honour of Siegfried Lienhard on his 70th Birthday*, Stockholm: The Assocation of Oriental Studies, 215–58. (Detailed examination of Śrīdhara's exceptional position in Nyāya-Vaiśeṣika regarding the nature of the liberated self.)

Narain, H. (1976) *Evolution of the Nyāya-Vaiśeṣika Categoriology*, vol. 1, *Early Nyāya-Vaiśeṣika*

Categoriology, Varanasi: Bharati Prakashan. (Starting from discussions of the concept of category in both schools, the book examines the possible sources of the categories and attempts to reconstruct their early development; written with a comparative perspective.)

Nenninger, C. (1992) *Aus gutem Grund: Praśastapādas anumāna-Lehre und die drei Bedingungen des logischen Grundes* (On Good Grounds: Praśastapāda's Theory of *Anumāna* and the Three Conditions for Logical Grounds), Philosophia Indica: Einsichten–Ansichten 1, Reinbek: Dr Inge Wezler. (Translation and analytical study of the section on inference in the *Padārthadharmasaṅgraha*.)

* *Nyāyasūtra* (*c*.400 AD), trans. G. Jha, *The Nyāya-Sūtras of Gautama with the Bhāṣya of Vātsyāyana and the Vārtika of Uddyotakara*, Indian Thought 4–11, 1912–19; repr. Delhi: Motilal Banarsidass, 4 vols, 1984. (Complete translation together with the first preserved commentary and its subcommentary; contains profuse notes from further commentaries. However, the translation of the basic text is heavily influenced by the commentaries.)

Oberhammer, G. (1963) 'Ein Beitrag zu den Vāda-Traditionen Indiens' (A Contribution on the Indian Vāda Traditions), *Wiener Zeitschrift für die Kunde Süd- und Südostasiens* 7: 63–103. (On the background of Nyāya within the larger tradition of debate.)

—— (1984) *Wahrheit und Transzendenz: Ein Beitrag zur Spiritualität des Nyāya* (Truth and Transcendence: A Contribution on Nyāya Spirituality), österreichische Akademie der Wissenschaften, phil.-hist. Klasse, Sitzungsberichte 424, Veröffentlichungen der Kommission für Sprachen und Kulturen Südasiens 18, Vienna: Verlag der österreichischen Akademie der Wissenschaften. (The only monograph dedicated exclusively to soteriology as well as meditative and yogic practices in Nyāya; it utilizes Vātsyāyana's Nyāyabhāṣya and Bhāsarvajña's Nyāyabhūṣaṇa.)

—— (1991) *Terminologie der frühen philosophischen Scholastik in Indien: Ein Begriffswörterbuch zur altindischen Dialektik, Erkenntnislehre und Methodologie* (Terminology of the Early Indian Philosophical Scholastics: A Technical Dictionary of Ancient Indian Dialectics, Epistemology and Methodology), vol. 1, *A–I*, österreichische Akademie der Wissenschaften, phil.-hist. Klasse, Denkschriften 223, Beiträge zur Kultur- und Geistesgeschichte Asiens 9, Vienna: Verlag der österreichischen Akademie der Wissenschaften. (Alphabetically arranged articles on the technical terms of dialectics, epistemology and methodology, mainly in works up

to the sixth century; the articles study the terms from the philological-historical point of view.)

Oberhammer, G., Prets, E. and Prandstetter, J. (1996) *Terminologie der frühen philosophischen Scholastik in Indien: Ein Begriffswörterbuch zur altindischen Dialektik, Erkenntnislehre und Methodologie* (Terminology of the Early Indian Philosophical Scholastics: A Technical Dictionary of Ancient Indian Dialectics, Epistemology and Methodology), vol. 2, *U–Pū*, österreichische Akademie der Wissenschaften, phil.-hist. Klasse, Denkschriften 248, Beiträge zur Kultur- und Geistesgeschichte Asiens 17, Vienna: Verlag der österreichischen Akademie der Wissenschaften. (See Oberhammer 1991.)

Perry, B.M. (1997) 'Early Nyāya and Hindu Orthodoxy: *ānvīkṣikī* and *adhikāra*', in E. Franco and K. Preisendanz (eds) *Beyond Orientalism: The Work of Wilhelm Halbfass and its Impact on Indian and Cross-Cultural Studies*, Poznań Studies in the Philosophy of the Sciences and the Humanities 59, Amsterdam/Atlanta, GA: Editions Rodopi, 449–70. (Study of the four basic Nyāya commentaries on the self-understanding of Nyāya with regard to Vedic orthodoxy and on the relationship between reasoning and orthodox religious authority; also addresses the issue of who is qualified to study Nyāya.)

Potter, K.H. (ed.) (1977) *Encyclopedia of Indian Philosophies*, vol. 2, *Indian Metaphysics and Epistemology: The Tradition of Nyāya-Vaiśeṣika up to Gaṅgeśa*, Princeton, NJ: Princeton University Press, and Delhi: Motilal Banarsidass. (Introductory survey and detailed summaries of individual works intended primarily for philosophers.)

Potter, K.H. and Bhattacharyya, S. (eds) (1993) *Encyclopedia of Indian Philosophies*, vol. 6, *Indian Philosophical Analysis: Nyāya-Vaiśeṣika from Gaṅgeśa to Raghunātha Śiromaṇi*, Princeton, NJ: Princeton University Press, and Delhi: Motilal Banarsidass. (Introductory survey and detailed summaries of individual works intended primarily for philosophers.)

* Praśastāpada (early 6th century) *Padārthadharmasaṅgraha* (Compendium of Properties of the Categories), trans. G. Jha, *Padārthadharmasaṅgraha of Praśastapāda, with the Nyāyakandalī of Śrīdhara, Pandit*, new series, 25–37, 1903–15; repr. Chaukhambha Oriental Studies 4, Varanasi/New Delhi: Chaukhambha Orientalia, 1982. (A fundamental Vaiśeṣika text.)

Preisendanz, K. (1989) 'On *ātmendriyamanorthasannikarṣa* and the Nyāya-Vaiśeṣika Theory of Vision', *Berliner Indologische Studien* 4/5: 141–213. (Discusses contact between self, senses, 'internal organ' and object as part of the definition of perception;

also contains a study of Nyāya-Vaiśeṣika optics in comparison with ancient Greek optics.)

* Raghunātha Śiromaṇi (15th–16th century) *Padārthatattvanirūpaṇa* (Examination of the True Nature/Reality of the Categories), trans. K.H. Potter, *The Padārthatattvanirūpaṇam of Raghunātha Śiromaṇi*, Harvard Yenching Studies Series 17, Cambridge, MA: Harvard University Press, 1957. (Translation of a Navya-Nyāya attempt to revise radically the traditional Vaiśeṣika categories.)

Ramanujam, P.S. (1979) *A Study of Vaiśeṣika Philosophy with Special Reference to Vyomaśivācārya*, University of Mysore Other Publication 68, Mysore: University of Mysore. (A clear and reliable paraphrase of large portions of the *Vyomavatī*.)

Schmithausen, L. (1965) *Maṇḍanamiśra's Vibhramaviveka, mit einer Studie zur Entwicklung der indischen Irrtumslehre* (Maṇḍanamiśra's *Vibhramaviveka*, with a Study of the Development of the Indian Theory of Error), österreichische Akademie der Wissenschaften, phil.-hist. Klasse, Sitzungsberichte 247, 1, Veröffentlichungen der Kommission für Sprachen und Kulturen Südasiens 2, Vienna: Verlag der österreichischen Akademie der Wissenschaften. (Hidden as an appendix is the most remarkable study of theories of error in classical Indian philosophy. Of special importance to Nyāya studies is the reconstruction of the respective positions of the Ācārya and Vyākhyātṛ schools, and of the relationship between error and conceptual construction.)

Shastri, D.N. (1964) *Critique of Indian Realism*, Agra: Agra University; repr. as *The Philosophy of Nyāya-Vaiśeṣika and its Conflict with the Buddhist Dignāga School*, Delhi: Bharatiya Vidya Prakashan, 1976. (Exceptionally lively presentation of the major ontological and epistemological issues in the controversy between Nyāya-Vaiśeṣika realism and its Buddhist opponents.)

* Thakur, A.L. (1969) '*adṛṣṭa* and *dharma* in the Vaiśeṣika Philosophy', *Ṛtam* 1 (1): 51–8. (Critical examination of some key passages in *Vaiśeṣikasūtra* to demonstrate the original purely scientific orientation of Vaiśeṣika.)

* *Vaiśeṣikasūtra* (*c.* 2nd–3rd century AD), trans. and ed. N. Sinha, *The Vaiśeṣika Sûtras of Kaṇāda with the Commentary of Śaṅkara Miśra and Extracts from the Gloss of Jayanârâyana together with Notes from the Commentary of Chandrakânta and an Introduction by the Translator*, Allahabad: Panini Office, 1911; repr. Sacred Books of the Hindus 20, Delhi: S.N. Publications, 1986. (Translation of the fifteenth-century commentary *Vaiśeṣikasūtra-Upaskāra*, including the *sūtra*-text transmitted in it;

the translation of the *sūtras* follows the interpretation of this rather late commentary by Śaṅkara Miśra.)

* *Vaiśeṣikasūtra* (*c.* 2nd–3rd century AD), trans. M. Nozawa, 'The Vaiśeṣikasūtra with Candrānanda's Commentary (1)', *Numazu College of Technology Research Annual* 27: 97–116, 1992. (A translation of the first two chapters with parallel Sanskrit materials. Candrānanda's commentary contains a more original version of the *sūtra*-text than Śaṅkara Miśra's, and the interpretation, although clearly post-Praśastapādan, reflects an earlier stage of the system.)

Vattanky, J. (1993) *Development of Nyāya Theism*, New Delhi: Intercultural Publications. (Historical exposition of the Nyāya-Vaiśeṣika arguments for the existence of God and of the controversy with Buddhist philosophers.)

Viśvanātha Pañcānana (17th century) *Bhāṣāpariccheda* and auto-commentary *Siddhāntamuktāvalī*, trans. Mādhavānanda, *Bhāṣā-Pariccheda with Siddhānta-Muktāvalī by Viśvanātha Nyāya-Pañcānana*, Calcutta: Advaita Ashrama, 1954. (Translation of the most popular syncretistic manual.)

Wada, T. (1990) *Invariable Concomitance in Navya-Nyāya*, Sri Garib Dass Oriental Series 101, Delhi: Sri Satguru Publications. (A clear introduction to basic Navya-Nyāya concepts, with translations and explanations of important passages on the invariable concomitance between probans and probandum in inference.)

* Wezler, A. (1969) 'Die "dreifache" Schlussfolgerung in *Nyāyasūtra* 1.1.5' (The 'Threefold' Inference in *Nyāyasūtra* 1.1.5), *Indo-Iranian Journal* 11: 190–211. (Clarification of the most probable original meaning of the *Nyāyasūtra*'s definition of inference, by comparison with early Buddhist texts.)

—— (1982) 'Remarks on the Definition of "*yoga*" in the *Vaiśeṣikasūtra*', in L.A. Hercus *et al.* (eds) *Indological and Buddhist Studies: Volume in Honour of Professor J.W. de Jong on his Sixtieth Birthday*, Canberra: Faculty of Asian Studies, 643–86. (Argues that the sections on yoga, liberation and yogic perception were not part of the original *Vaiśeṣikasūtra*, but half-hearted concessions to contemporary philosophical tendencies.)

ELI FRANCO
KARIN PREISENDANZ

NYGREN, ANDERS (1890–1978)

Nygren hoped to recover the uniqueness of Christianity from the impurities introduced by the attempts of nineteenth-century liberal theology to free it from metaphysical speculation and confessional dogmatism. He aimed to do this by grounding all religion in an analytic philosophy of religion which would enable him to stress the objective character of Christian theology in contrast to the arbitrariness of confessional theology. He achieved international influence by his claim in Agape and Eros *(1930–6) that the uniqueness of Christianity is love in the sense of* agape, *as opposed to Platonic* eros.

Like many of his theological contemporaries in Sweden, Nygren sought to show the legitimacy of theology as a university subject. While a professor at Lund (1924–48), he argued that theology could withstand positivistic criticism of the sort made by Axel HÄGERSTRÖM (§5), whose attack on Hegelian-inspired perspectives sought to include theology in its anti-metaphysical cleansing of Swedish philosophy. Nygren, like Hägerström, accepted Kant's criticism of a rational theology based on the traditional proofs of God's existence, but rejected Kant's reduction of religion to ethics (see KANT, I. §11). Like SCHLEIER-MACHER (§7), he insisted that religion is a distinctive perspective, as are the perspectives of reason, practice and ascetic value. But Nygren does not base religion on a specific religious experience, which would make it primarily subjective. Rather, religions are an obvious historical fact. Nygren viewed philosophy in a Kantian fashion, as a critical study of the necessary conditions of meaning. Theology as a university subject could be justified as a historical critical study of the meaning of Christianity, and so could be utterly objective, intersubjective and testable (unlike confessional theology, which rests on revelation alone, as does the neo-orthodoxy of Barth and Brunner).

By the time of Nygren's last major work, *Meaning and Method* (1972), philosophy had taken a linguistic turn, with which he felt at home. Drawing upon Wittgenstein's *Philosophical Investigations*, he was able to develop his philosophy of religion in its idiom. He stressed context as crucial to the meaning of language, and held that philosophy could clarify the differences and relations between basic contexts of meaning. He also added what he called 'the context of contexts', consisting of four great questions which in *Agape and Eros* he had called 'fundamental motifs'. He claimed that these larger contexts are simply given in human life, and summarized them as the question of truth, which is institutionalized as science; the question of good and evil, and right and wrong, institutionalized as law and ethical traditions; the question of the beautiful, institutionalized in art; and the question of the eternal, institutionalized as religion.

Nygren argued that philosophy of religion is the specification of the fundamental presuppositions that concern human encounters with the eternal; this for him is not an abstraction, such as timelessness, but that which breaks into time and enables us to see that life is not subject merely to the conditions of finitude. He did not perform this task, but indicated four elements in the existential confrontation with the eternal, which occur wherever there is religion: an unveiling, a disquieting judgment, a reconciliation, and a vital fellowship. These elements are merely formal and are specified only from a knowledge of the content of actual religions, but they enable one to specify the logical place of religion in relation to other fundamental perspectives, and to clarify confusions in religion that result from mixing contexts.

Nygren maintained that the task of theology is the study of concrete religions. He called his method 'motif research' and supposed it applicable to all historical research. One could discover the basic notion around which all the historical phenomena revolved, and which provided the context of meaning for those phenomena. The answer each religion gives to the fundamental question of the eternal is its motif. For Judaism it is law, for Christianity it is *agape* and for Hellenic civilization it is *eros*.

Nygren contrasted the distinctive Christian conception of love, which he called *agape*, with the Platonic notion, which he called *eros* (see LOVE §2). All *eros* is egocentric and acquisitive, whereas *agape* springs wholly from within and takes no account of worth. The former is human, the latter divine. Nygren claimed that, as fundamental motifs, these should not be mixed, but that historically they had been, above all by Augustine. Only with the Reformation was the original New Testament notion of *agape* restored. However, this thesis has been countered, and Nygren's characterization of both *agape* and *eros* challenged (Burnaby 1938; D'Arcy 1954; Markus 1955).

List of works

Nygren, A. (1930–6) *Agape and Eros*, London: Society for Promoting Christian Knowledge. (Contrasts Christian and human love.)

—— (1949) *Commentary on Romans*, Philadelphia, PA: Muhlenberg. (A contribution to a recovery of Martin Luther's teachings.)

—— (1972) *Meaning and Method*, Philadelphia, PA: Fortress. (A systematic account of Nygren's integration of theology and philosophy of religion.)

References and further reading

* Burnaby, J. (1938) *Amor Dei*, London: Hodder & Stoughton. (A careful defence of Augustine against Nygren.)
* D'Arcy, M.C. (1954) *The Mind and Heart of Love*, London: Faber & Faber, 2nd edn. (A Roman Catholic response to Nygren's view of *agape* and *eros*.)
Hall, T. (1978) *Anders Nygren*, Waco, TX: Word. (A general introduction.)
Kegley, C.W. (ed.) (1970) *The Philosophy and Theology of Anders Nygren*, Carbondale, IL: Southern Illinois University Press. (A collection of essays.)
* Markus, R.A. (1955) 'The Dialectics of Eros in Plato's *Symposium*', *Downside Review* 233: 219–30. (A criticism of Nygren's characterization of *eros*.)
* Wittgenstein, L. (1953) *Philosophical Investigations*, ed. G.E.M. Anscombe and R. Rhees, trans. G.E.M. Anscombe, Oxford: Blackwell. (Wittgenstein's influential account of language.)

DIOGENES ALLEN

O

OAKESHOTT, MICHAEL JOSEPH (1901–90)

Although Michael Oakeshott was in his own time a lone figure in a philosophical world dominated by Oxford analysis, he has come to be recognized as the most notable British political philosopher of the century. He is best known for his view that political activity is neither purely empirical nor the application of ideas, but 'the pursuit of intimations'. His image of culture as a conversation between different kinds of understanding has been widely accepted. Oakeshott first became celebrated in attacking what he called 'rationalism' in the Cambridge Journal *(which he edited) in 1947. Oakeshott's rationalist is a restless political meddler who believes that politics is putting ideas into effect. The fullest statement of his political philosophy is* On Human Conduct *(1975a), in which the modern state is understood as a tension between civil and enterprise association. Exploring the idea of a civil association is perhaps Oakeshott's most notable contribution to political philosophy.*

1. Modes of experience
2. Epistemology
3. Political philosophy

1 Modes of experience

Michael Oakeshott was born at Chelsford, Kent, and attended St George's School, Harpenden. He studied history at Gonville and Caius College, Cambridge, and became a fellow after two years spent visiting German universities and as a schoolmaster. During the Second World War he served in the British army. In 1952 he succeeded Harold Laski as professor of political science at the London School of Economics, a post from which he retired in 1969.

The early Oakeshott was confidently classified as an idealist on the basis of *Experience and its Modes* (1933) and some contemporaries early on were tempted to pigeonhole and ignore him. Susan Stebbing reviewing the work in *Mind* thought that it merely reworked Bradley. A.J. Ayer said of Oakeshott's conservatism that 'it's all in Burke'. One reviewer as late as *On Human Conduct* (1975a) merely assimilated him to Wittgenstein. All of this was to

miss a highly original philosophical intelligence which explored the idea of the state more deeply than any of his contemporaries.

In *The Voice of Poetry in the Conversation of Mankind* (1959) Oakeshott provided the best short synoptic view of his philosophy, and also launched a famous image: human life is an endless conversation between different 'voices'. Practice, science, history and poetry are voices, while philosophy is 'the impulse to study the quality and style of each voice', and to reflect upon the relationship of one voice to another. The philosopher's reflections, however, make no specific contribution to this conversation, for only those with a specific conceptual point of view have anything to contribute. Philosophy is in particular distinct from practice, and can make no direct contribution to it, though Oakeshott occasionally allows that it may have such a virtue as 'hindering irrelevance'.

In *Experience and its Modes*, however, Oakeshott had appeared to give philosophy a rather grander role: it was the pursuit of 'what is ultimately satisfactory in experience'. The modes, by contrast, were forms of experience limited or 'arrested' by their logical dependence upon constitutive assumptions. Practice, for example, is experience understood in terms of desire and frustration – *sub specie voluntatis*. Science cultivates a mechanical world understood in terms of quantity. History is the world understood in terms of its pastness. Philosophy explores these conditionalities in the search for a concrete understanding of experience as released from the abstract or fragmentary character of the modes. It is both what is ultimately satisfactory in experience, and also recognized as a somewhat perverse enterprise: most of the time, men understandably prefer 'the empty kisses of abstraction'.

Oakeshott is evidently hard to classify. A consistent allegiance in his work is to a Platonic conception of philosophy as exploring the conditionalities of experience in order to discover its postulates – but Oakeshott's philosopher has no timeless realm to contemplate. Again, he seems to reveal the grand vision of the philosophical vocation found in Hegel, yet he combines this vision with an underlabouring insistence on philosophy's irrelevance to the world which links him to British empiricism, especially Hobbes. What is certainly clear is that he took philosophy to be the activity of thinking through the conditions of some human activity, purging it of contingency and merging its conclusions and its presuppositions in an ideal character revealing the logic of our understanding. His intellectual life consisted in successive inquiries of this kind – the first published in *Experience and its Modes*, a second in *The Voice of Poetry in the Conversation of Mankind* (where the fundamentals are revisited in order to accommodate art to the system of modes) and finally and most magisterially in the first two essays of *On Human Conduct*. Let us first, however, consider this same intellectual exercise performed on a smaller scale in essays written around 1946. They are to be found in *Religion, Politics and the Moral Life* (1993a).

2 Epistemology

The basic error about political philosophy, he argued in 'The Concept of a Philosophy of Politics', was to think that it consisted merely in the *application* of some already established philosophy to the field of politics. Oakeshott's objection to this procedure is that 'application' is altogether too mechanical a process to have any place in philosophy. Oakeshott denied that philosophy could provide anything with foundations – one of the doctrines which has led Rorty and others to assimilate him to modern forms of pragmatism (see PRAGMATISM). Nor did it provide criteria of action, for practice could never achieve the coherence of a philosophical concept.

Oakeshott's ontology is sceptical without being in any way solipsistic. The world is composed of images, or 'intelligibles'. A thing is what it is imagined to be, but might be any number of other things. Concepts such as 'thing' or 'fact' are merely verdicts or judgments about some object of experience which always appears to the understanding in one specific guise or other, never as any kind of basic datum. Oakeshott frequently reverts to the doctrine of the *Meno* in which understanding always begins with something already in some degree understood, and moves on to other understandings, without ever achieving finality. Although he contrasts practical skill with rationalist notions of technology, Oakeshott rejects any notion of a basic level of common sense (frequently identified with practice) to which all controversies can be assimilated. The aim of *Experience and its Modes* is to show the impossibility of assimilating one mode to another, and drawing the conclusion that irrelevance, or *ignoratio elenchi*, is the most crippling form of error. In *The Voice of Poetry* he complains that the voice of practice is becoming a bore in the modern world because it is becoming strident and tries to dominate the conversation. Part

of the reason for this is that practice and science can seem to be mutually assimilable because they have some names in common – such as 'fact'.

History also suffered from the kind of uncritical monism which took historical facts to be the same kind of logical entity as facts in science and practice. A major thread in Oakeshott's career was his lifelong devotion to thinking out the minimal epistemological conditions of historical understanding. One effect was to banish the idea of cause from the field. He recognized, of course, that historians often affirmed causal relationships, but he interpreted this as a rhetoric of emphasis within a process in which the aim was to compose the circumstantial understanding available from the records so as to answer to the question: what happened? Only this could provide the intelligibility allowing us to understand why it happened. Such intelligibility was the most we might expect from history, but it was also the only manner in which human life itself might be explained.

3 Political philosophy

In his last major work, Oakeshott typically started all over again. *On Human Conduct* begins with a long essay on theorizing human conduct. Whereas nature may be understood in terms of process, the human world is self-conscious and procedural. The basic confusion of the social sciences has been a failure to clarify the distinction between, as it were, a wink and a blink.

The 'engagement' of understanding is, he tells us, a continuous, self-moved, critical enterprise of theorizing. It emerges out of 'misty intimations of intelligibility'. We distinguish 'goings on' in terms of some characteristic; identification is specification in terms of an ideal character composed of characteristics. At this point in Oakeshott's phenomemology of understanding a more coherent system of thought, which he calls a 'conditional platform of understanding' has emerged: every 'going on' is what it is in respect of being understood in terms of an ideal character specified as a composition of characteristics. WITTGENSTEIN took a similar view in construing ideas in terms of 'family resemblances'. A theorist may, however, treat an identity not as a verdict to be accepted, but as an invitation to make such an identity more intelligible, and this can only be done by seeking to understand it in terms of its conditionality.

The voices and modes of Oakeshott's earlier formulations have here given way to a more pluralistic scheme. The theorizer may 'fish' for the understandings available from these conditional platforms of understanding. Yet the irony of all theorizing, Oakeshott remarks, is its propensity to generate, not an understanding, but a not-yet-understood. Thinking thus leads the theorizer towards higher platforms of understanding concerned with exploring the postulates of that activity itself.

Turning to human conduct, Oakeshott finds that it is a set of 'goings on' which exhibit intelligence. We necessarily act in terms of some specific practice, and a practice is a language of self-disclosure. Inseparable from action in the moral dimension is what Oakeshott calls 'self-enactment' in which conduct reveals the self to itself and to others.

In the second essay, Oakeshott analyses the state, though the word itself is kept at bay (see STATE, THE). Feeling that the modern vocabulary of politics had been seriously corrupted, he reinstates Latin terms (such as *civitas*, *lex* and *respublica*) as technicalities. The task is to distinguish the 'civil condition'. It certainly is not to be found in those transactions of reciprocal desiring which belong to the social rather than the civil world. A second 'categorially distinct mode of association' is revealed in 'agents related in the joint pursuit of some imagined and wished-for common satisfaction' (1975a: 112): what Oakeshott called 'enterprise association'. The state as an enterprise association is a view almost irresistibly invoked by the familiar question: what is the end or purpose of the state? But enterprises are voluntary, while the state is compulsory.

There does remain, however, a distinct form of association corresponding to the civil condition. It is 'relationship in terms of the conditions of a practice'. The *cives* of a civil association relate to one another in nothing else but a recognition of the authority of rules, in respect of which they are all equal. They are thus not the comrades of an enterprise association, but much more like the speakers of a language, whose intelligibility derives from conforming to its rules. This is a formal relationship in that the rules do not specify any particular conduct; they are merely 'adverbial qualifications' of whatever a member might choose to do. But although formal, these rules constitute a practice which is moral in the basic sense of not being instrumental to the enjoyment of specific satisfactions.

Here then is an analysis of the forms of human association so intricate that Oakeshott created a complex vocabulary and style in which to express it. It leaves any attempt at synopsis far behind.

See also: POLITICAL PHILOSOPHY, HISTORY OF

List of works

Oakeshott, M.J. (1933) *Experience and its Modes*, Cambridge: Cambridge University Press. (A lucid and witty account of Oakeshott's sceptical idealism.)

—— (1939) *The Social and Political Doctrines of Contemporary Europe*, Cambridge: Cambridge University Press. (An anthology of writings on the doctrines current in the 1930s.)

—— (1959) *The Voice of Poetry in the Conversation of Mankind*, London: Bowes & Bowes. (A short essay on aesthetics which recapitulates his entire philosophical position.)

—— (1962) *Rationalism in Politics*, London: Methuen; expanded edn, ed. T. Fuller, Indianapolis, IN: Liberty Press, 1991. (Oakeshott's final and most systematic account of political philosophy.)

—— (1975a) *On Human Conduct*, Oxford: Clarendon Press. (Oakeshott's last major work of political philosophy, exploring the relation between civil and enterprise association.)

—— (1975b) *Hobbes on Civil Association*, Oxford: Blackwell. (Collects Oakeshott's essays on Hobbes, and notably the magisterial introduction to *Leviathan*.)

—— (1983) *On History and Other Essays*, Oxford: Blackwell. (Essays elaborating a complete account of the logic of historical inquiry.)

—— (1993a) *Religion, Politics and the Moral Life*, ed. T. Fuller, London: Yale University Press. (Notable for revealing the overriding concern with religion of the early Oakeshott.)

—— (1993b) *Morality and Politics in Modern Europe: The Harvard Lectures*, ed. S.R. Letwin, London: Yale University Press. (A short and lively account of modern European politics in lectures given at Harvard in 1958.)

—— (1996) *The Politics of Faith and the Politics of Scepticism*, ed. T. Fuller, London: Yale University Press. (A previously unpublished manuscript dealing in a philosophical manner with the way Oakeshott understood politics around 1950.)

Norman, J. (ed.) (1993) *The Achievement of Michael Oakeshott*, London: Duckworth. (Contains a full bibliography of Oakeshott's works by John Liddington.)

References and further reading

Greenleaf, W.H. (1966) *Oakeshott's Philosophical Politics*, London: Longmans. (An early attempt to bring Oakeshott's politics to a focus.)

Franco, P. (1990) *The Political Philosophy of Michael Oakeshott*, London: Yale University Press. (A full-length study of Oakeshott and his context.)

Grant, R. (1990) *Thinkers of Our Time: Oakeshott*, London: Claridge Press. (An excellent short account with some attention to Oakeshott's life and circumstances.)

KENNETH MINOGUE

OBJECTIVISM AND SUBJECTIVISM IN ISLAMIC THEOLOGY *see* ASH'ARIYYA AND MU'TAZILA

OBJECTIVITY

Objectivity is one of the central concepts of metaphysics. Philosophers distinguish between objectivity and agreement: 'Ice-cream tastes nice' is not objective merely because there is widespread agreement that it is true. But if objectivity is not mere agreement, what is it? We often think that some sorts of claim are less objective than others, so that a different metaphysical account is required of each. For example, ethical claims are often held to be less objective than claims about the shapes of middle-sized physical objects: 'Murder is wrong' is held to be less objective than 'The table is square'. Philosophers disagree about how to capture intuitive differences in objectivity. Those known as noncognitivists say that ethical claims are not, strictly speaking, even apt to be true or false; they do not record facts but, rather, express some desire or inclination on the part of the speaker. Others, dubbed subjectivists, say that ethical statements are in some sense about human desires or inclinations. Unlike the non-cognitivist, the subjectivist views ethical claims as truth-apt, but as being true in virtue of facts about human desires or inclinations. Some philosophers, referred to as antirealists, disagree with both non-cognitivism and subjectivism, and attempt to find different ways of denying objectivity. Quietists, on the other hand, think that there are no interesting ways of distinguishing discourses in point of objective status.

1 **Non-cognitivism and subjectivism**
2 **Anti-realist views of objectivity**
3 **Objectivity of meaning and quietism**

1 Non-cognitivism and subjectivism

Intuitively, an ethical claim such as 'It is right to help those in distress' is less objective than a claim such as 'The table is square'. What does this intuition amount to? Non-cognitivists, such as Ayer (1936), Blackburn

(1984) and Gibbard (1990), focus on the semantic function of the two claims. 'The table is square' has the function of asserting that a fact obtains in the world. If that fact obtains – if the table is square – then the claim is true; if not, it is false. Thus 'The table is square' is apt to be true or false: it is truth-apt. On the other hand, the non-cognitivist views 'It is right to help those in distress' as having a different semantic function: despite appearances, its function does not consist in asserting that a fact obtains in the world. It is not truth-apt; rather, it expresses an inclination, desire, or some other non-cognitive attitude of the speaker, in the same way that 'Hurrah!' or 'Boo!' merely expresses a favourable or unfavourable attitude. This is why some versions of non-cognitivism are called 'expressivism'. Ethical claims are less objective than claims like 'The table is square' since the latter are genuine truth-apt assertions, whereas the former are not. Non-cognitivists have viewed ethical claims as not objective in this sense for various reasons: because of widespread disagreement over moral matters, because moral facts seem 'queer' or 'odd', and because of the normative character of moral discourse.

There are problems with this way of capturing differences in objective status. Consider the inference:

1 If lying is wrong, then getting little brother to lie is wrong.
2 Lying is wrong.

3 Getting little brother to lie is wrong.

According to non-cognitivism, 'Lying is wrong' and 'Getting little brother to lie is wrong' are not truth-apt. But the inference is intuitively *valid*. And to say that an inference is valid is to say that the truth of the premises guarantees the truth of the conclusion. How can non-cognitivism explain the validity of the inference, given that it denies that (2) and (3) are even apt to be true? Relatedly, the non-cognitivist has a difficulty with (1). What sense can be made of a conditional whose antecedent and consequent are not truth-apt? Non-cognitivism has had difficulty in finding satisfactory answers to these questions (Hale 1993).

Subjectivists take a different tack. They admit that 'It is right to help those in distress' is truth-apt, that its sincere utterance makes a genuine assertion. They thus avoid the sort of difficulty outlined above. But if an ethical claim genuinely asserts that a fact obtains, what sort of fact is it? According to the subjectivist, it is simply a fact about the person making the claim: when I say 'It is right to help those in distress' I am asserting that I desire to help them. Ethical claims are truth-apt, but the facts they assert to exist are facts about us, our desires, inclinations or subjective states. When I say 'It is right to help those in distress' I literally *mean* 'I desire to help those in distress'. This contrasts with claims like 'The table is square' which, though truth-apt, are not analysable in terms of facts about human subjectivity. In this sense, 'The table is square' is the more objective.

Subjectivism has difficulty in accounting for moral disagreement. If Jones says 'It is right to help those in distress' and Smith says 'It is wrong to help those in distress', they are disagreeing with each other, indeed contradicting one another. But if Jones means 'I (Jones) desire to help the unfortunate', whereas Smith means 'I (Smith) do not desire to help the unfortunate', there is no contradiction. So in what sense do they disagree?

Subjectivism may try to deal with this by focusing on a wider range of desires than those possessed by the individual who utters the statement. 'It is right to help those in distress' literally means 'Most people desire to help the unfortunate', so that its content is spelled out in terms of intersubjective agreement in desires. But this also faces problems. If it were true, it would be a contradiction to say that helping the unfortunate is right even though most people do not desire to do it. But it is not a contradiction, so even this wider subjectivist analysis must be flawed.

2 Anti-realist views of objectivity

Suppose we admit that two types of claim are truth-apt and yet do not have an anthropocentric subject matter. Do we have to view them as equally objective? Anti-realists, such as Wright (1986, 1992) and Dummett (1978), think not. They try to show how differences in objectivity can be captured, without adopting either non-cognitivism or subjectivism. How can we distinguish between 'It is right to help those in distress' and 'The table is square' if we allow that both are truth-apt, and that neither is susceptible to a subjectivist analysis? One way would be to develop an analogue of the distinction between primary and secondary qualities, the locus classicus for which is Locke (1689) (see PRIMARY–SECONDARY DISTINCTION; SECONDARY QUALITIES). The standard example of a secondary quality is colour, while shape is usually held to be primary. What is involved in the claim that redness, for example, is a secondary quality? The idea is that there is a close relationship between facts about certain of our subjective states and statements like 'The mailbox is red'. In order to explain this relationship, we need to explain the notion of a best judgment. A judgment that an object is red is best when it is made in conditions that are optimally good for appraising whether or not the

mailbox is red. These conditions could be specified very roughly as those that obtain out of doors, in the shade, at lunch time on a lightly overcast summer afternoon. To say that redness is a secondary quality is to say that our best judgments concerning the redness of objects determine the extension of the concept red. The extension of a concept is the class of things to which that concept can correctly be applied. So our best judgments about whether objects are red *determine* which class of objects the concept red can properly be applied to. In contrast, a primary quality like squareness is one whose extension is determined independently of facts about best judgments concerning squareness. Best judgments in this case merely detect an independently determined extension.

This way of saying how 'The mailbox is red' is less objective than 'The table is square' is different from the subjectivist analysis. To say that redness is secondary is not to say that 'The mailbox is red' literally means that 'If conditions were best, we would judge that the mailbox is red'. The claim is the weaker one, that our best judgments determine whether the mailbox falls in the extension of red. The proposal that redness is a secondary quality can therefore avoid the problems associated with subjectivism. And since it does not deny that 'The mailbox is red' is truth-apt, it avoids the problems associated with non-cognitivism. One way, then, to claim that ethical claims are less objective than claims like 'The table is square' is to argue that ethical qualities such as right, wrong, good and bad are secondary rather than primary.

According to the anti-realist, there can be more than one way of saying that one type of claim is less objective than another. Even if we cannot show that ethical qualities are secondary, there might be other ways of contrasting ethical claims with different claims. One way concerns what Wright (1986) calls 'objectivity of truth'. This notion of objectivity features prominently in Dummett's discussions of realism. To say that a class of statements exhibits objectivity of truth is to say that '[they] may be fully intelligible to us even though resolving their truth-values may defeat our cognitive powers (even when idealized)' (Wright 1986: 5). Their truth might be 'evidence-transcendent': they are determinately either true or false, even if we are in principle incapable of citing evidence for or against them. Take Goldbach's Conjecture (that every even number greater than two is the sum of two primes), or some claim about past happenings in some far distant galaxy. We understand these claims, but we are in principle incapable of resolving their truth-values. This gives us one way of claiming that mathematical or cosmological claims are more objective than claims about morals or comedy. There is little temptation to think that claims about the moral status of an action, or about the comic quality of a joke, may in principle transcend our best cognitive efforts. There are no difficulties akin to those affecting non-cognitivism and subjectivism: there is no denial of truth-aptitude, nor an assignment of an anthropocentric subject matter.

3 Objectivity of meaning and quietism

The main danger for the anti-realist story about objectivity comes from Wittgenstein's rule-following considerations (RFC). According to Wright, the RFC endanger the objectivity of meaning. This is the view that 'the meaning of a statement is a real constraint, to which we are bound ... by contract, and to which verdicts about its truth-value may objectively conform, quite independently of our considered opinion on the matter' (Wright 1986: 5). The meaning of a statement imposes requirements on what counts as correct use of the statement, which determine what uses are correct and incorrect independently of any opinions we may subsequently form. The problem is that if the RFC destroy the idea that meanings are objective in this sense, they thereby threaten the various ways in which anti-realists attempt to draw comparisons concerning objectivity. For example, Wright believes that objectivity of truth implies objectivity of meaning. If the RFC force us to reject objectivity of meaning, they also force us to reject objectivity of truth. And if no discourses possess objectivity of truth, appealing to failure of objectivity of truth will be useless for drawing comparisons between discourses. Likewise, since the truth of any statement is a function of its meaning together with facts about the world, rejection of objectivity of meaning may entail that all qualities are secondary. The possibility of appealing to the primary–secondary distinction in order to draw a contrast will be endangered. In short, the RFC seem to threaten us with quietism about objectivity: the view that no principled, metaphysically interesting contrasts concerning objectivity can be drawn.

Anti-realists try to find ways of avoiding quietism, while retaining their interpretation of the RFC (Wright 1992: Ch. 6). Note that some philosophers, such as McDowell (1995), think that there is a different way in which quietism about objectivity can open up. McDowell does not view the RFC as threatening the objectivity of meaning. So the relevance of the primary–secondary distinction and evidence-transcendent truth is not threatened in the direct manner envisaged in the previous paragraph. The distinctions the anti-realist wishes to draw can still be drawn: instead, what the RFC threaten is the idea that there is any interesting metaphysical *point* to

be made by appealing to the distinctions in the first place. For example, it might be argued that the thought that the anti-realist primary–secondary distinction is of metaphysical relevance depends upon a conception of detecting or tracking facts that the RFC display to be untenable.

See also: PROJECTIVISM; REALISM AND ANTIREALISM

References and Further Reading

* Ayer, A.J. (1936) *Language, Truth and Logic*, London: Gollancz. (Mentioned in §1 above. Chapter 6 contains a classic statement of non-cognitivism about ethics.)
* Blackburn, S. (1984) *Spreading the Word*, Oxford: Oxford University Press. (Mentioned in §1 above. Chapters 5 and 6 develop a modern version of non-cognitivism.)
  Boghossian, P. (1989) 'The Rule-Following Considerations', *Mind* 98 (392): 507–49. (Comprehensive survey of the literature on the rule-following considerations.)
* Dummett, M. (1978) *Truth and Other Enigmas*, London: Duckworth. (Mentioned in §2 above. Influential anti-realist book which contains much discussion about the objectivity of truth.)
* Gibbard, A. (1990) *Wise Choices, Apt Feelings*, Cambridge, MA: Harvard University Press. (Mentioned in §1 above. Highly sophisticated development of non-cognitivism.)
* Hale, B. (1993) 'Can there be a logic of attitudes?', in J. Haldane and C. Wright (eds) *Reality, Representation and Projection*, Oxford: Oxford University Press. (Mentioned in §1 above. Excellent survey of the difficulties faced by non-cognitivism.)
  Hume, D. (1739–40) *A Treatise on Human Nature*, ed. P.H. Nidditch, Oxford: Clarendon Press, 1968. (Book III contains the classic statement of subjectivism in ethics.)
  Leiter, B. (ed.) (1997) *Objectivity in Law and Morals*, Cambridge: Cambridge University Press. (Collection of articles on the nature and role of objectivity in law and morality.)
* Locke, J. (1689) *An Essay Concerning Human Understanding*, ed. P.H. Nidditch, Oxford: Oxford University Press, 1975. (Bk 1, ch 8 contains the historical precursor of the primary–secondary quality distinction mentioned in §2 above.)
* McDowell, J. (1995) *Mind and World*, Oxford: Oxford University Press. (Mentioned in §3 above. Statement of quietism about objectivity.)
  Smith, M. (1994) *The Moral Problem*, Oxford: Blackwell. (Excellent study of the problems surrounding the objectivity of morals.)

* Wright, C. (1986) *Realism, Meaning, and Truth*, Oxford: Blackwell. (Mentioned in §§2 and 3. Develops anti-realist views on objectivity. The introduction provides an excellent survey: probably the best place to start a study of objectivity.)

* —— (1992) *Truth and Objectivity*, Cambridge, MA: Harvard University Press. (Mentioned in §§2 and 3. Further development of anti-realism. Chapter 6 contains a useful discussion of quietism.)

ALEXANDER MILLER

OBJECTUAL INTERPRETATION OF QUANTIFIERS *see* QUANTIFIERS, SUBSTITUTIONAL AND OBJECTUAL

OBLIGATION, POLITICAL

The problem of political obligation has been one of the central concerns of political philosophy throughout the history of the subject. Political obligations are the moral obligations of citizens to support and comply with the requirements of their political authorities; and the problem of political obligation is that of understanding why (or if) citizens in various kinds of states are bound by such obligations. Most theorists conservatively assume that typical citizens in reasonably just states are in fact bound by these obligations. They take the problem to be that of advancing an account of the ground(s) or justification(s) of political obligation that is consistent with affirming widespread obligations. Other theorists, however, anarchists prominent among them, do not accept the conservative assumption, leaving open the possibility that the best theory of political obligation may entail that few, if any, citizens in actual states have political obligations.

Much of the modern debate about political obligation consists of attempts either to defend or to move beyond the alleged defects of voluntarist theories. Voluntarists maintain that only our own voluntary acts (such as freely consenting to the authority of our governments) can bind us to obedience. Because actual political societies appear not to be voluntary associations, however, voluntarism seems unable to satisfy conservative theoretical ambitions. Some individualists turn as a result to nonvoluntarist theories of political obligation, attempting to ground obligations in the receipt by citizens of the benefits governments supply or in the moral quality of their political institutions.

Others reject individualism altogether, defending communitarian theories that base our political obligations in our social and political roles or identities. Individualist anarchists reject instead the conservative ambitions of such theories, embracing a voluntarism which entails that most citizens simply have no political obligations.

1   **The problem**
2   **Communitarian theories**
3   **Voluntarist theories**
4   **Nonvoluntarist theories**
5   **Anarchist theories**

1   The problem

The problem of political obligation has been central to political philosophy from the earliest recorded philosophical texts to the most recent. While the actual term 'political obligation' is of relatively recent vintage, arguments as old as those of Plato's early dialogue, *Crito* (*c.*395–87 BC), are clearly intended to address some version of the problem. Political obligations, as these are commonly understood, are the moral obligations (or duties) of citizens to support their countries, governments or political and legal institutions. They are usually taken to include at least the obligation to obey the laws of the land (or the just laws) and are often thought to include also further obligations of loyalty and 'good citizenship'.

The problem of political obligation, then, is that of understanding the force and nature of these moral bonds and, most importantly, of understanding when (or if) and for what reasons (if any) the members of various kinds of states are subject to them. Peoples' political obligations constitute the core of the moral relationship that exists between them and their polities, and they are thus closely related to such corresponding concepts as the legitimacy or *de jure* authority of the state (see AUTHORITY §4; LEGITIMACY). The question here is not: under what institutional requirements, backed by force, do we stand? Rather, political philosophers ask whether in addition to (or conceivably because of) the threat of institutional coercion, blind political habits and emotional grounds for obedience, there are also strong *moral* reasons for supporting and complying with the demands of our laws, governments or states.

The problem of political obligation has usually been understood conservatively. So understood, it is the problem of finding a sound justification for our intuitive conviction that most citizens (or at least those in certain familiar kinds of states) do in fact have political obligations. Conservative theorists will thus be centrally concerned with providing a suitably 'general' account of political obligation, one that shows why all citizens of good states have the obligations we suppose they have. But the problem can also be understood without any conservative commitments, so that an account's lack of generality is not necessarily a defect. On this understanding, the theorist's job is simply to give as full as possible an account of political obligation, without any special concern for justifying our pre-theoretical beliefs about the subject. Thus, an anarchist theory (which denied the existence of any political obligations) might on this latter understanding still constitute a successful (that is, valid, nondefective) theory of political obligation.

Theories of political obligation can be (roughly) divided into four groups, the most basic division being that between 'communitarian' and 'individualist' theories. Communitarians typically maintain that our very identities are constituted in part by our roles (such as 'membership') in political society and that our political obligations are tied conceptually to, and follow trivially from, these roles. Individualists maintain, by contrast, that we should not in this way think of ourselves as essentially political beings; instead, our political obligations rest not on our institutional roles, but on contingent relations between political associations and ourselves (such as our consent to them or our receipt of benefits from them).

Individualist theories of political obligation can be further divided into two classes. 'Voluntarists' ground people's political obligations in their personal performance of politically significant voluntary acts, such as promises or contracts to obey, consent to authority, or free acceptance of benefits from a political scheme. 'Nonvoluntarist' (individualist) theories hold that no such voluntary performance is necessary for political obligation. Simple nonvoluntary receipt of benefits may bind us, for instance, or the moral qualities of a government may bring it under more general moral duties that require us to give it our support.

The fourth group consists of the anarchists. 'Anarchist' theories deny altogether the existence of political obligations. While the inspiration for an anarchist view can itself be either individualist or communitarian, anarchism rejects the conservative assumptions of the standard theories in both categories.

None of these four approaches to the problem of political obligation is new. Indeed, three of them are suggested in various passages in Plato's *Crito* (see PLATO §6). There, Socrates argues first that he must obey the state's commands because it has made him what he is (50d–e), suggesting a communitarian derivation of obligation from his politically-constituted

identity. But he later contends as well (in a more individualist fashion) both that his obligations stem from a tacit promise to obey (51e–53a) and that the care and benefits provided for him by the state bind him to obedience (51c–e) (suggesting, respectively, voluntarist and nonvoluntarist positions).

2 Communitarian theories

Drawing their inspiration from Plato, Aristotle, Hegel and Wittgenstein, communitarians argue that our plans and purposes, our values, and thus essential aspects of our very identities, are given us by the roles we play within linguistic, social and political communities (see COMMUNITY AND COMMUNITARIANISM). It is as a result misleading to think (as individualists do) of our moral relation to the state as somehow optional or contingent. Citizen and state are not like unrelated contractors in economic negotiations, as voluntarists seem to maintain. Nor do our political obligations rest on externally derived moral duties, as nonvoluntarists claim. Rather we have obligations to obey the rules of our communities because this is part of what it means to be members of those communities. Who we are in our social contexts tells us what obligations we have. To ask for any further explanation of political obligation would be to ask the unintelligible question: why should our lives be regulated by what makes us what we are (Green 1882). The proper account of political obligation looks to justifications that are internal to our practices, not external to them.

Communitarians whose sympathies are Wittgensteinian typically advance some version of a conceptual argument: that political obligation is conceptually tied to membership in a particular political society, and that membership is not voluntary, optional or contingent upon external justifiability (Pitkin 1965–6; Horton 1992). Comparisons are often drawn between political obligations and family obligations (which are similarly nonvoluntary) or obligations to friends and colleagues (which we often 'acquire' rather than choose, and which we continue to have even when we do not want them). Lest we think these analogies appeal only to nonliberal theorists, it should be noted that they have motivated at least one well-known political liberal to offer an account of political obligation as an 'associative' or 'communal' obligation (Dworkin 1986).

Communitarians whose sympathies are more Aristotelian or Hegelian tend to modify or add to these conceptual arguments. Political community, they argue, is essential to human flourishing and the development of human moral capacities, such as agency or autonomy or self-conscious valuation. As such, not only are our political communities owed obedience and support (as long as they encourage this development); we have also an obligation to belong to and facilitate political communities (Taylor 1979). On this view, because our political relations contribute essentially to our identities as moral agents and autonomous choosers, these relations cannot themselves be thought of as freely chosen or as dependent on moral principles that bind us independent of our political roles. While feminist political philosophy has not focused centrally on the problem of political obligation, most feminist accounts are also broadly communitarian or 'contextual' in character (Hirschmann 1992).

3 Voluntarist theories

Individualist theorists deny that we are essentially political beings, that our political obligations are a simple function of our identities as socially constituted persons (Green 1988). The political realm is a contingent, nonessential aspect of human life (even if it is also a quite typical feature of it), and our unchosen social and political roles cannot simply be assumed justifiably to define our moral responsibilities. This denial of the communitarian's 'political naturalism' is most strongly stated (or assumed) by voluntarists. The classical individualist theories of political obligation were mostly voluntarist in character, and nearly every voluntarist theory prior to the twentieth century was some variant of a consent or contract theory of political obligation (see CONSENT; CONTRACTARIANISM §5). The terms of the modern debate about political consent were set most clearly by Locke (see LOCKE, J. §10). According to Lockean consent theory, political obligations are grounded in the personal consent of individual members to the authority of their government or political society. This consent can be either express (as in direct agreements or contracts to obey, oaths of allegiance, and so on) or tacit (indirectly given by other behaviour that signifies consent). But voluntary, intentional consent of some sort is necessary for political obligation; government without popular consent is tyranny (Locke 1690). Consent theories tend to focus on tacit (implicit, indirect) consent, given the apparent paucity of express consenters in modern political communities. Favourite candidates for acts of tacit consent on which our political obligations might rest include continuing to reside in a state one is free to leave, freely taking benefits from the state, voting in democratic elections and accepting adult membership in a state.

The intuitive appeal of consent theory (in its respect for each person's free choices) is considerable and its history is long and distinguished. But the theory has throughout that history been plagued by fundamental complaints that it is not in fact applicable to real political life. Real political societies are not voluntary associations and real citizens seldom give even tacit consent. Indeed, all of the acts alleged to constitute tacit consent to government are typically performed without any intention to consent to government authority at all; and they are often performed unfreely, simply because of the high cost of alternatives, such as emigration (Hume 1739–40). But if morally binding consent must be intentional and voluntary, such facts seem to force us to the conclusion that few citizens of actual states count as even tacit consenters and that consent theory cannot adequately account for the political obligations we believe these citizens to have (Simmons 1979).

Consent theorists have responded by specifying further conditions that must be satisfied if 'government by consent' is to be achieved (Beran 1987) and by insisting that genuine, binding consent is only given by full involvement in the political life of a participatory democracy (Pateman 1979). These responses, of course, involve to a certain extent giving up conservative ambitions in thinking about political obligation. But a more conservative move within the voluntarist camp has been to surrender instead the idea of consent as the paradigm ground of political obligation. Thus, fairness theories of political obligation maintain that our obligations are owed as reciprocation for benefits accepted from the workings of our cooperative legal and political institutions (Hart 1955). Consent to these institutions is not necessary for being obligated to support them and abide by their rules. Rather, it is enough that we freely accept the benefits that flow from the cooperative sacrifices of others; for to do so while refusing to do our own parts in the scheme would be to take unfair advantage of those who cooperated in good faith.

Fairness theories, however, have also been subjected to steady contemporary criticism. One prominent early proponent of a fairness account has since rejected it (for reasons followed by many others), arguing that citizens in actual political societies seldom freely accept the benefits their societies provide, but instead merely receive them without real choice (RAWLS, J. §1). And others have challenged the portrayal of modern political communities as large-scale cooperative schemes, sufficiently like small-scale cooperative enterprises to give rise to similar obligations of fairness (Simmons 1979). As a result of these criticisms, many individualist theorists have concluded that voluntarist accounts of political obligation are unpromising, and they have turned instead to nonvoluntarist theories.

4 Nonvoluntarist theories

The distance from voluntarist to nonvoluntarist (individualist) theories of political obligation can seem at first glance quite small. There are, for instance, nonvoluntarist versions of the fairness theory, according to which it is not our free acceptance of the benefits of government that grounds our obligations, but rather our (possibly nonvoluntary) receipt of certain cooperatively produced goods that are of great importance to both individuals and societies (such as the benefits of law enforcement and national defence) (Klosko 1992). And there are also nonvoluntarist gratitude theories, which view political obligation as a special case of the obligation to reciprocate in an appropriately grateful fashion for benefits conferred on us by others (Walker 1988). Such nonvoluntarist benefit (or reciprocation) theories obviously have much in common with voluntarist fairness theory. But the theoretical distance of such accounts from voluntarism is in fact considerable. For political obligations, instead of resting on what individuals choose to do (as in voluntarism), are now taken to rest on what merely happens to those individuals and on the virtues of the institutional arrangements under which they live. This is to locate the moral heart of political relationships in a quite different area than that identified by the voluntarist.

The distance from voluntarism is similarly deceptive in the case of hypothetical contractarian accounts of political obligation. Our obligations, on this approach, are determined not by our personal consent to (or contracts with) our political authorities, but by whether we (or some suitably described, more rational or more neutral version of us) would have agreed to be subject to such authorities in an initial choice situation (Rawls 1971; Pitkin 1965–6). Hypothetical contractarianism, because it centrally utilizes the idea of contract or consent, may at first seem to be just a development of or a variation on voluntarist consent theory (and its advocates often present it as such). In fact, however, hypothetical theories are no longer concentrating on individual choice or on specific transactions between citizen and state, but instead on the quality of the political institutions in question. Hypothetical contractarians ask whether our laws or governments are sufficiently just or good to have been consented to in advance by rational parties, in an initial specification of their terms of social cooperation. What matters here is not choice or individual history, but the nature and quality of government (see CONTRACTARIANISM §5).

This emphasis on quality of government is also present in utilitarian theories of political obligation, despite their constant opposition to contractarian views. According to utilitarians, our political obligations are based in the (direct or indirect) utility of support for and compliance with government (Hare 1976). Because obedience generally promotes social happiness, it is typically obligatory. But, of course, obedience only promotes social happiness if the specific laws or government in question are well-framed, utility-producing devices; our political obligations are thus derived reasonably directly from determinations of governmental quality.

The well-known contemporary objections to utilitarian moral theory (Rawls 1971) are only one reason why critics have found unconvincing the utilitarian account of political obligation. Like all nonvoluntarist (and communitarian) theories, utilitarians accept birth and benefaction within certain kinds of political communities as sufficient to justify political bonds. Critics worry that this misses the transactional, bilateral character of legitimate cooperative relationships, which in political cases should involve citizen and state jointly committing themselves to acceptable arrangements.

5 Anarchist theories

Anarchism comes in many forms (see ANARCHISM). Variants range from communist to libertarian (from Karl Marx to Lysander Spooner). Some anarchists deny the very possibility of a legitimate state, while others deny only the legitimacy of existing states. Some urge the destruction of existing states, others only selective disobedience to them. But all forms of anarchism are united in rejecting the conservative assumption that most citizens have political obligations.

It is illuminating to recall that much of the force of communitarian, nonvoluntarist fairness and voluntarist fairness theories of political obligation derives from the perceived failure of consent theory. Consent theory has been attacked as inapplicable to real political societies and alternative theories have been preferred for their superior ability to explain our obligations. But it is important to see that this attack rests squarely on a conservative approach to the problem of political obligation. If the conservative assumption is abandoned, consent theory no longer appears defective. Rather, it can be taken to specify the true grounds of political obligation, grounds that are simply not satisfied in actual or possible states. Voluntarist anarchism thus re-emerges as an interesting theoretical possibility.

Classical anarchism (of both communitarian and individualist varieties) recommended the abolition of the state. Late twentieth-century philosophical anarchism merely denies the existence of (widespread) political obligation, usually on voluntarist grounds, without making any revolutionary practical recommendations. Some philosophical anarchists have argued on a priori grounds that the authority of the state is inconsistent with individual autonomy (Wolff 1970). Others have argued only that existing states fail to satisfy the voluntarist requirements for political obligation (Simmons 1979). Both forms, however, have been attacked for failing to appreciate the overall force of multiple contributing grounds for political obligation (Gans 1992).

See also: CIVIL DISOBEDIENCE

References and further reading

All of the below involve detailed and sometimes subtle argument, but all are accessible also to readers without formal training in philosohy.

* Beran, H. (1987) *The Consent Theory of Political Obligation*, London: Croom Helm. (The most complete contemporary defence of consent theory.)
* Dworkin, R. (1986) *Law's Empire*, Cambridge, MA: Harvard University Press. (Chapter 6 offers a defence of communal obligations.)
* Gans, C. (1992) *Philosophical Anarchism and Political Disobedience*, Cambridge: Cambridge University Press. (Attack on philosophical anarchism.)
* Green, L. (1988) *The Authority of the State*, Oxford: Oxford University Press. (Good general discussion of problems of authority and obligation.)
* Green, T.H. (1882) *Lectures on the Principles of Political Obligation*, Ann Arbor, MI: University of Michigan Press, 1967. (Classic statement of a communitarian approach to political obligation.)
* Hare, R.M. (1976) 'Political Obligation', in T. Honderich (ed.) *Social Ends and Political Means*, London: Routledge & Kegan Paul. (Utilitarian account of political obligation.)
* Hart, H.L.A. (1955) 'Are There Any Natural Rights?', *Philosophical Review* 64 (2): 175–91. (First clear statement of the fairness account of political obligation.)
* Hirschmann, N. (1992) *Rethinking Obligation*, Ithaca, NY: Cornell University Press. (A feminist critique and reorientation of political obligation theory.)
* Horton, J. (1992) *Political Obligation*, Atlantic Highlands, NJ: Humanities Press. (The most thorough recent discussion of all aspects of the problem; comprehensive bibliography.)
* Hume, D. (1739–40) *A Treatise on Human Nature*, ed. P.H. Nidditch, Oxford: Oxford University Press, 2nd edn, 1978. (Influential critique of consent theory and a defence of broadly utilitarian view is given in book III, part II, chapters VII–X.)
* Klosko, G. (1992) *The Principle of Fairness and Political Obligation*, Lanham, MD: Rowman & Littlefield. (A nonvoluntarist fairness theory.)
* Locke, J. (1690) *The Second Treatise of Government*, in *Two Treatises of Government*, ed. P. Laslett, Cambridge: Cambridge University Press, 1960. (Classic statement of the consent theory of political obligation, centred in chapters 7 and 8.)
* Pateman, C. (1979) *The Problem of Political Obligation*, Berkeley, CA: University of California Press. (Discusses the history of the problem and defends a Rousseauian approach.)
* Pitkin, H. (1965–6) 'Obligation and Consent, I and II', *American Political Science Review*, 59 (4): 990–9 and 60 (1): 39–52. (Defends both a Wittgensteinian, communitarian approach and a version of hypothetical contractarianism.)
* Plato (*c.*395–87 BC) *Crito*, in *Plato: The Collected Dialogues*, ed. E. Hamilton and H. Cairns, Princeton, NJ: Princeton University Press, 1961. (The first recorded discussion of the problem of political obligation.)
* Rawls, J. (1971) *A Theory of Justice*, Cambridge, MA: Harvard University Press. (The most important hypothetical contractarian account of political obligation is given in chapter 6.)
* Simmons, A.J. (1979) *Moral Principles and Political Obligations*, Princeton, NJ: Princeton University Press. (Discusses individualist theories of political obligation and defends philosophical anarchism.)
* Taylor, C. (1979) 'Atomism', in A. Kontos (ed.) *Powers, Possessions, and Freedom*, Toronto, Ont.: University of Toronto Press. (Defends a Hegelian approach and an 'obligation to belong'.)
* Walker, A.D.M. (1988) 'Political Obligation and the Argument from Gratitude', *Philosophy and Public Affairs* 17 (3): 191–211. (Develops a gratitude theory of political obligation.)
* Wolff, R.P. (1970) *In Defense of Anarchism*, New York: Harper & Row. (A defence of an a priori version of philosophical anarchism.)

A. JOHN SIMMONS

OBSERVATION

Observation is of undeniable importance in the empirical sciences. As the source of information from the world itself, observation has the role of both motivating and testing theories. Playing this role requires more than just opening our eyes and letting nature act upon us. It requires a careful attention to the information conveyed from the world so that an observation is meaningful. Scientific observation, in other words, is more than a physical act of sensation; it must be an epistemic act as well, with sufficient meaning and credibility to contribute to knowledge. A report of an observation, therefore, must be more than a 'Yes, I see'. It must describe just what is seen, 'I see that _____'.

This obligation to make observation relevant to theory suggests that there is an essential influence of background theories on the observations themselves. The theories we believe or wish to test tell us which observations to make. And describing the results of observations, that is, bringing out their informational content, will always be done in the language of the conceptual and theoretical system already in place. For these reasons, observation is said to be indelibly theory-laden. And the influence of background beliefs is even greater in cases of indirect observation where machines, like microscopes and particle detectors, are used to produce images of the objects of observation. Here, the reliability of the machines, and hence the credibility of the observation, must be based on a theoretical understanding of the interactions that are the links in the chain of information.

The influence of theory on observation is often seen as a threat to the objectivity of the process of testing and verification of theories, and hence science in general. If theories are allowed to, indeed required to, select their own evidence and then to give meaning and credibility to the observations, the testing process seems to be unavoidably circular and self-serving. Observation that is theory-laden would guarantee success. But a look at the history of science shows that it does not. There are plenty of cases of observations that are used to disconfirm theories or at least undermine the theorist's confidence. Perhaps there is a kind of observation that is not influenced by scientific theory and can serve as a common, objective source of information to put theories to a rigorous and meaningful test. Or perhaps all scientific observation does bear the influence of background scientific theories, but not necessarily of the theory the observation is being used to test. This independence between the theories that support an observation and the theory for which the observation serves as evidence can break the circle in the process of testing and perhaps restore objectivity.

1   The role of observation

Empirical sciences, whether they are natural sciences like biology, geology and astronomy, or social sciences like psychology and anthropology, make claims that are contingent on what is going on in the world. Non-empirical enterprises like mathematics and logic aspire to what must be true of the world and to what things are possible in the world. But the goal of science is between these two extremes; it is to describe what is in fact true of the world and what does in fact happen. This requires some contact with the actual world and some information from the particular objects of interest themselves. This is the role of observation.

Observations in science are essential both to stimulate the formation of theories and to regulate the testing of theories. In the role as stimulus, observation of perplexing or surprising events will prompt questions of why these things happen, and thereby lead to theoretical explanations. Recurring phenomena call for an understanding of the principles of organization and unification, the theories, to make sense of the observations. And the observation of similarities among phenomena, as Newton noticed similarities in the events of a falling apple and the orbit of the moon, suggest the formation of a unifying theoretical account. In these ways and more, observation can initiate and guide the preparation of theory.

A proposed theory, a hypothesis, can then be tested by being used to make predictions of what will be observed under specified conditions. Actually doing the observations is then an essential part of testing and verifying the theory. Various models of this process of testing and confirmation have been proposed and advocated, differing in the nature of the relation between theory and observation (see CONFIRMATION THEORY). These models are all alike though in that they require some relation, some contact between theory and observation.

The importance of observation in science is of course because of the supposition that it is the source of information from the world itself – unlike theory, that begins as information from the minds of scientists. Observation is intersubjective, public and accessible to anyone willing to have a look. This is the reason to expect that observation will provide a source of agreement, a common ground of information to arbitrate disagreements between differing theoretical accounts. Observation must be the source of facts, if anything is, and must provide the objective foundations of science, if anything can.

Whether observation can fulfill of these weighty expectations is itself an issue of disagreement among scientists and philosophers. Understanding the role of observation in science and its potential to be objective or foundational requires a look at the details of what observation must be like in order to contribute to scientific knowledge, and the details of what it is in fact like in the activities of actual science. The questions to ask are these: can observation be a source of agreement to decide between differing theories? Does it in fact play this role in science? And is observation a source of objective information about the world?

2 Informational content

To play the role as stimulus and evidence for scientific theories, observations must fulfil some basic, informational requirements. To serve as evidence, that is, to be a meaningful influence on a theory, an observation must be *of* something that is relevant to the theory. Scientific observation must be informative in the sense of being an observation *that* something is the case. It must be more than just a physical act of sensation; it must be an epistemic act with sufficient meaning and credibility to contribute to knowledge. Credibility is achieved only with some assurance that the observation has been done with care and precision, and in conditions that are conducive to accuracy. And a meaningful observation must be one described in a language that is relevant to the theoretical knowledge it is meant to challenge, change or re-enforce.

An effective way to attend to the informational content of an observation and to its epistemic status is to focus on observation reports rather than on the physical act of perception. The useful question to ask of an observational contact with the world is not simply, 'do you see it?', but the more revealing, 'what do you see?' or 'do you see that this is that?' Answers to these questions, that require more than a nod, give the full description of the observation. These observation reports are the most basic empirical data in science. Even if the report is private, a report to oneself, a useful observation must be presented in an informational form, observing, for example, that the sky is blue, because undescribed sensations can have no impact on theory. Undescribed sensations cannot serve as evidence in science. They neither motivate nor test theories.

This emphasis on language motivates positivists to attempt a neat dichotomy between the observational and theoretical vocabularies of science (see LOGICAL POSITIVISM §4). Whether or not this sort of distinction can be made, and whether it has any significance for the structure of scientific knowledge, will be discussed in §6, below. The analysis of observation language, though, rather than simply the physical act

of observation, accurately acknowledges that observation in science is more than simply opening one's eyes and having a look. It is an important and careful activity whose epistemic value depends on what is observed and in what way. And these are assessable only of a meaningfully described observation, one with assertive informational content.

3 Theory-laden observation

The informational requirements as described above lead directly to the concern that observation in science is essentially theory-laden. Observation that is relevant to background knowledge will necessarily bear an influence from background knowledge. If this is true, that observation is influenced by theory, then observation loses its natural innocence. The activity of observation is not a passive acceptance of ready-made information (in the sense of ready-described and ready-justified) given by the objects of interest.

There are three distinct ways that theories can influence observations and that what we see can be dependent on what we think.

For one, background knowledge and the theories we have in mind are the source of authority in deciding what observations to make. Gathering data in science is neither comprehensive nor random, and it is a theoretical understanding of the world that directs our attention to what is important to observe and measure. This is not to suggest that advocates of theories seek out and report only the observations they are confident will reflect favourably on their theory. There is a difference between selecting the important tests and selecting rigged tests, and while the persuasion of theory can determine which observations to perform, it cannot determine how they will turn out. Only the act of observing can do that.

Another way to think of the theoretical impact in selecting observations is to note that what we observe of the world is always just a small sample of the whole thing, and it is important to be sure it is a representative sample. To be representative a sample must be relevantly diverse, and issues of relevance must always be settled under the influence of some theoretical understanding or other. Testing the effects of some drug, for example, may require observations of people of various ages, weights, medical histories, and so on. But the sample does not have to be representative of different hair colours or preferences in flavours of ice cream, because our understanding of physiology does not regard these as relevant to the effects of drugs. Thus a good sample is one that has been done in light of current background knowledge.

A second influence that theories can have on observation is in assessing the credibility and reliability of the observation report. Scientific observations are acceptable only if they are carefully done. Conditions must be correct, in order to reduce the chances of distortion, and the propriety of conditions is often prescribed by theory. This is particularly apparent in the case of machine-aided observations (see §7). A microscope, for example, is an acceptable tool in science because there is good reason to think that the image produced is an accurate view of the specimen. The good reason is based in theories of optics describing how the microscope works. This theoretical support is rarely explicit in the use of microscopes or the claims of microscopic observation, but it is a source of credibility that must be available in the scientific community. Scientists do not accept the images produced by just any machine, only those they know to be reliable. And even when no machines complicate the observation, the pragmatics of acceptability of observation reports are still leveraged by theory and background knowledge. If an observation report threatens a well-entrenched theory, it is common to look first for a mistake in the observation. This use of theory to edit observation is simply the manifestation of the high standards expected of scientific evidence.

The third aspect of complicity between background knowledge and observation is in giving meaning to the evidence. An observation must be of something that is relevant to theory and so it must be described in a language that makes contact with theory. The observation must be fitted into the system of theoretical concepts. The necessary promotion from a merely physical act of sensation to an epistemic act of observation takes place under the authority of the theories in our background knowledge. To a physicist, for example, the streaks in a cloud chamber are indicative of the passage of subatomic particles. The streaks mean particles, and it is only at this informative level that the observation functions as evidence, useful for making an impact on theory. And it is only under the influence of theory that the description as particle tracks is possible.

Taken together, these three ways in which theories guide observations lead to the notion of 'theory-laden observation' (see DUHEM, P.M.M.; HANSON, N.R.). The claim is that this is an essential aspect of science and scientific evidence, and not simply a lazy or suspicious way that science gets done by conniving scientists. To say that observation is theory-laden is to focus Kant's more general claim, that experience without concepts is blind, on the case of science.

4 Using theory-laden observation

Theory-laden observation has serious implications for scientific method and the role of objectivity in science. If all observation bears the imprint of some theory or other, then the results of observation are not pure information from the objects in the world themselves, nor will they necessarily be data that are shared and of universal agreement among scientists. Persons with different theoretical backgrounds may well judge different observations as important and credible, and because of this, hold their theories to different standards. They may even give different meanings to the same perceptual event, and thus draw different conclusions from seemingly the same tests. This poses an immediate threat to objectivity in the testing of theories. If observations cannot provide a common standard against which to test competing theories, those theories may be incommensurable, leaving us with no reasonable way to rate one more likely to be true than the other (see INCOMMENSURABILITY; UNDERDETERMINATION).

It would be a mistake to think that theory-laden observation is a guarantee that empirical testing will always come out positive and in support of the theories being tested. The history of science is full of examples in which observations went against theory. An interesting case is the solar neutrino problem. According to theory, the sun, like all other stars, is fuelled by nuclear reactions occurring at its core, reactions that produce neutrinos. The neutrinos ought to be detectable on the earth. The observation of neutrinos is enormously complicated and indirect, and it is profoundly influenced by theory. Nonetheless, the results of observations have been bad news for the theory being tested, the claim of nuclear reactions in the sun. Not nearly as many neutrinos as predicted have been observed. Thus, complicity between theory and observation does not necessarily compromise the testing process in the sense of guaranteeing a supportive outcome.

It is important to confront the threat to objectivity in the light of the details of each particular case of observation in science. A general analysis of the nature of observation and evidence may be enough to show that there is some theory complicity in scientific observation, but beyond that we should ask specifically which theories are involved in any particular case. Perhaps the theories that influence an observation are independent of the particular theory the observation is meant to test. In such a case, there is no circularity in the testing process and hence no threat to objectivity. A look at specific cases might also show that the requisite conceptual ingredient in observation does not rely on the theories that we take to be the currency of science but only on some specifically perceptual background knowledge. If the background knowledge is simply common sense, then the worry about theory-ladening is of little concern to science. Observation in this case can provide data of common consent, useful for settling issues of dispute between competing theories.

Studying actual cases of observation in science can also show whether theories supply a tacit influence over observations, or if observers and those who make use of observation reports are aware of the theoretical contribution in an explicit interpretation of perception. If there is this awareness, the conceptual or theoretical influences can perhaps be abstracted away to reveal a perceptual core. The question will then become whether or not these purely perceptual data have sufficient informational content to be useful as scientific evidence.

5   Indirect observation

Many observations in science are physically indirect in the sense that the observer does not interact immediately with the object itself. Intermediate interactions are required to convey information of the object to an observer. The most obvious cases of indirect observation involve tools that enhance our powers of perception, from a simple magnifier, to a compound telescope, to an enormous bubble chamber. Using such machines, scientists report the observation of objects such as the moons of Jupiter, alpha particles, or even events in the universe just seconds after the Big Bang. There are also cases of indirect observation that do not involve instruments, cases in which the object of observation has left a natural imprint on what can be directly perceived. In this sense, fossils are an image of life in the past, and striations in bedrock show the movement of glaciers (see GEOLOGY, PHILOSOPHY OF §1).

All of these cases of indirect observation have in common that the information from the object of interest is mediated by a more-or-less lengthy causal chain from object to scientist. The multiple interactions can impose a physical influence on indirect observation, much as theoretical complicity adds a conceptual influence. And there is an obvious correlation between the two in that more physical complication in an observation is likely to require more theory to keep track of the flow of information.

The image produced in an indirect observation may, in some cases, not even resemble the object that is allegedly observed. Audible clicks of a Geiger counter could be the final stage in the observation of a beta-decay event or the passage of a cosmic ray. The length of a column of mercury in a thermometer allows us to observe the temperature of some other object. But this may be stretching the concept of observation too thin, having come so far from the original expectation of a source of manifest and intersubjective information from the objects themselves. Such highly indirect observation that demands overt interpretation draws the question: do these events even count as being observation?

Answering this sort of question is complicated by the realization that indirectness of observation is a matter of degree, depending on the length and complication of the chain of interactions from the object of observation to the final image. This realization clarifies the important questions to ask of indirect observation. Is the degree of physical removal of the object epistemically significant in the sense that a longer journey makes the information less reliable and makes the event somehow less of an observation? Is there a cut-off, a way to mark an indirect link between observer and specimen as too long or too complicated to count as an observation?

6   Observability

A distinction between what can and what cannot be observed is crucial to an empiricist philosophy of science. Observability is epistemically significant insofar as observation is the foundation of testing and verification of scientific claims (see DEMARCATION PROBLEM §5). The theme of empiricism is that scientists are justified in believing that what they claim about observables is true, but not justified in what they claim about unobservables. There is no denying that the stuff of the world behaves *as if* it is composed of atoms, but that is no reason to believe that it really *is* composed of atoms (see FICTIONALISM; SCIENTIFIC REALISM AND ANTIREALISM §3). Only by observing can we have reason to believe, and so only of what is observable can we hope to have justified belief.

Empiricism incurs an obligation to supply the criteria for distinguishing between observables and unobservables. This might seem as easy as opening our eyes and seeing what we can see, but observability cannot be decided on the basis of observation, since what is observable is not always observed. Furthermore, what has not been observed is not necessarily unobservable. In fact, anything that is worth looking for has the status of being unobserved but observable. Planets around distant stars, for example, are worth looking for because, being relevantly similar to the planets we see in our solar system (for example, being large and solid), they are observable, though none has been observed. The famous Michelson–Morley experiment to measure the earth's motion through the electromagnetic ether was definitive in its results only by considering the ether to be in some indirect way observable. Since it was observable but not observed, the conclusion was that the ether simply did not exist. Had it been judged to be unobservable there would have been no surprise at the null results. In all cases there will be some antecedent conceptual reason to think that an object is observable, in at least an indirect way, and hence worth looking for.

Observability is not an intrinsic feature of the object or event in question. It is a relational property, observable-to-us, and so it is subject to change if the human capacity to perceive or to go places in the universe to have a look changes. This underscores the fact that observability is intended to have *epistemic*, not *ontological* significance. The empiricist is not claiming that what is unobservable does not exist. Rather, what is unobservable is such that we have no justification in claiming that it exists or that it does not. Justification can of course change, as observability can change.

Any significant distinction between what counts as observable and what does not must acknowledge the complication of the act of observation itself. Observability cannot be merely a function of the perceptual limitations of human observers, since observation must be more than merely a physical perceptual event; it must be an informative epistemic event. Nor can observability depend on being independent of theory if all observation is to some degree influenced by the observer's theoretical background.

There is a potential confusion in this issue of observability, as to whether it applies to the entities of science or to the language of science. It is in the best interest of empiricism to focus on the observability of the entities themselves rather than on the language, since how we describe something will always be influenced by our conceptual and theoretical background, but whether or not we see something is just a fact of our perceptual prowess. A child may not be able to describe the planet Venus as a planet or as Venus in particular, but they can surely see it when directed to the proper location in the sky. This strategy of deciding observability of things, independent of their description in language, threatens the informational requirements of observation. Undescribed observations cannot function as evidence and cannot contribute to scientific knowledge. That is why children and others who lack sufficient training in the conceptual background of scientists cannot step right up and do science, no matter how good their eyesight. Noting the need for informative observation, the issue of observability is going to have to involve some aspects of language and its theoretical associations.

Drawing a distinction between observables and unobservables is further complicated by the cases of indirect observation. It would be difficult to argue that any intermediate instrumentation whatsoever disqualifies an image from being a genuine observation, since viewing the world through a pane of glass or eye-glasses is surely observing the world. But there is little difference between this and using a magnifying glass, and so if what can be seen through a window is observable then so is what can be seen through a magnifier. And this begins a continuum of indirectness with no clear break between what ought to count as observable and what ought not. If the single lens of a magnifying glass enhances our powers of observation and expands the domain of what is observable, then why not the same for a microscope or a telescope, both of which are just a series of magnifiers stacked together? Why not an electron microscope, which does with electrons just as an optical microscope does with light? And so on. The challenge is to draw a line between what counts as observation and what does not in a way that is not arbitrary and that bears the epistemic significance required of empiricism.

7   Reliable observation

One can acknowledge that there is no sharp boundary between what is observable and what is not, yet still maintain that observability is of great epistemic importance. There are clear cases, after all, of things that we can observe, that the sky is blue for example, and equally clear cases of things that we cannot, that the 'up' quark has an electric charge of $+2 \backslash 3$. The colour of the sky is clearly observable, while the electric charge of a quark is not. And we have a higher level of justification for claims about the colour of the sky than we do for claims about the charge of a quark, precisely because of the difference in their observability. Similarly, in cases of machine-assisted observation such as a cloud chamber, there is a clear sense in which we observe the streaks in the chamber and from these we infer the presence of particles and subatomic events. The features of the streaks are more immediate to our perception, and for this reason, claims about the streaks are more reliable than are claims about the particles. Thus, observability, though not a sharp demarcation, is nonetheless significant in evaluating the justification for scientific claims.

At this point it may be advisable to consult science itself to understand differences of observability and their significance to the status of scientific entities and statements. This does not mean simply adopting the language of science and counting as observable whatever scientists say they observe. It requires an understanding of each scientific case of observation to see what, according to the scientific description, is going on. Science can provide a description of the causal chain and the flow of information from a putative object of observation to the observer, and can in each case reveal which theories are involved in giving meaning and credibility to the observation. A scientific account of the physical indirectness of an observation will detail not only the length of the interaction chain, but the reliability of the passage of information through each link. Understanding the interactions themselves shows that in each case there is some information that can and some information that cannot be conveyed. The physics of quarks, for example, indicates that while such properties as electric charge and mass can be discovered through interaction with a quark, the colour (not the normal visual colour but the specifically quantum-chromo-dynamical property given the whimsical name 'colour') can not. There is no interaction that reveals quark colour, and so this property is unobservable in principle, where it is a principle of science, not, philosophy. No amount of indirectness can sanction a claim to observe the colour of a quark.

The scientific account will also reveal the theoretical influence on an observation. Consulting science on the matter of observability will show exactly which theories are required to describe the physical indirectness of an observation and to give meaning to what is seen. This allows an assessment of the reliability of the theoretical support as well as its independence from the theories the observation is being used to test.

Given the complication of the issue of observability, and the need to consult the science of each case, the central question must be revised to be amenable to degrees of observability and to the specifics of each case. Of a scientific entity or some information in the world, it is not productive to ask simply whether it is observable or not. Better, more useful, to ask for the whole story, namely, how is it observed, or how is the information acquired? With the details explicit, the epistemic status of the information can be evaluated.

See also: EXPERIMENT; INFORMATION THEORY; MEASUREMENT, THEORY OF; THEORIES, SCIENTIFIC; THEORY AND OBSERVATION IN SOCIAL SCIENCES

References and further reading

Bogen, J. and Woodward, J. (1983) 'Saving the Phenomena', *Philosophical Review* 97: 302–52. (Introduces a distinction between data and phenomena that emphasizes that observation concerns data as evidence for claiming about phenomena, while phenomena are the proper object of explanation.)

Fodor, J. (1984) 'Observation Reconsidered', *Philosophy of Science* 51: 23–43. (Readable and relevant to the material of §§3, 5; arguing that observation is not theory-laden in any important way.)

Fraassen, B. van (1980) *The Scientific Image*, Oxford: Oxford University Press. (An empiricist account of the distinction between observable and unobservable entities.)

Hanson, N.R. (1958) *Patterns of Discovery*, Cambridge: Cambridge University Press; repr. 1961. (The origin of the phrase 'theory-laden observation'.)

Hacking, I. (1983) *Representing and Intervening*, Cambridge: Cambridge University Press. (Chapter 10, 'Observation' and chapter 11, 'Microscopes', discuss the role of theories in observation, in particular the role of optical theories in the use of microscopes.)

Kosso, P. (1992) *Reading the Book of Nature*, Cambridge: Cambridge University Press. (Chapter 6 gives a clear overview of observation in science, and chapter 9 makes the case for independence between a theory being tested and the theories that influence observation.)

Kuhn, T. (1962) *The Structure of Scientific Revolutions*, Chicago, IL: University of Chicago Press; 2nd edn, 1970. (An extremely influential book that includes the influence of theory on observation and the implications for incommensurability.)

Maxwell, G. (1962) 'The Ontological Status of Theoretical Entities', in H. Feigl and G. Maxwell (eds) *Minnesota Studies in the Philosophy of Science*, vol. 3, Minneapolis, MN: University of Minnesota Press. (Relevant to §5 in that it describes the continuum of indirectness of observation.)

Shapere, D. (1982) 'The Concept of Observation in Science and Philosophy', *Philosophy of Science* 49: 485–525. (Using science to describe observation as the flow of information.)

Woodward, J. (1989) 'Data and Phenomena', *Synthèse* 79: 393–472. (A detailed elaboration on Bogen and Woodward 1983.)

PETER KOSSO

OBSERVATION AND THEORY IN THE SOCIAL SCIENCES

see THEORY AND OBSERVATION IN SOCIAL SCIENCES

OCCASIONALISM

Occasionalism is often thought of primarily as a rather desperate solution to the problem of mind–body interaction. Mind and body, it maintains, do not in fact causally affect each other at all; rather, it is God who causes bodily movements to occur 'on the occasion of' appropriate mental states (for example, volitions), and who causes mental states, such as sensations, on the occasion of the corresponding bodily states (for example, sensory stimulation).

This characterization, while correct so far as it goes, is seriously incomplete. Occasionalists have seen the lack of real causal influence between mind and body as merely a special case of the more general truth that no two created beings ever causally affect each other. The one and only 'true cause' is God, with created beings serving as the occasions for his causal and creative activity, but never as causes in their own right. (The one possible exception to this is that created agents may themselves bring about their own acts of will; this is necessary if they are to be in any sense free agents.) Occasionalism has always been held primarily for religious reasons, in order to give God the honour due to him as the Lord and ruler of the universe. It has never, however, been a majority view among philosophical theists.

1   Medieval occasionalism
2   Early modern occasionalism
3   The case for occasionalism
4   Occasionalism and immaterialism

1   Medieval occasionalism

The first thinker clearly to articulate an occasionalist position was the Muslim theologian AL-GHAZALI. He wrote in defence of orthodox Islam against the philosophers AL-FARABI (§2) and IBN SINA (§5), both of whom propounded emanationist systems based on a combination of Aristotelianism and Neoplatonism (see CREATION AND CONSERVATION, RELIGIOUS DOCTRINE OF §3; ARISTOTELIANISM IN ISLAMIC PHILOSOPHY §2; NEOPLATONISM IN ISLAMIC PHILOSOPHY §§2–3). One of al-Ghazali's fundamental objections to the emanationist scheme was that it was necessitarian and denied God the freedom due to him as creator and as the author of miracles. (For al-Ghazali, as for other orthodox Sunnis, human freedom was not a major concern.) Over against this, he affirmed the teachings of orthodox Ash'arite theology, according to which all natural beings are completely inert and the true and sole agent in nature is God (see ASH'ARIYYA AND MU'TAZILA). Thus, there is no necessity in nature itself which could constrain or limit God's omnipotent will. Unlike the Ash'arites, however, al-Ghazali presents a philosophical argument for this position. The only form of necessity he recognizes is logical necessity, and he has little difficulty in showing that causes do not logically necessitate their effects. The relation between what we take to be causes and effects is merely one of correlation and is purely contingent; the one real, productive cause of all things is God. In addition to this philosophical argument based on a critique of causality, al-Ghazali appeals directly to the theological dogma of God's absolute omnipotence. Indeed, al-Ghazali's vision of God is such that God is virtually the only true existent: 'There is no other being *with* Him, for Him to be greater than it.... [N]one has being save through His Face – so that His Face alone is' (quoted in Fakhry 1958: 72).

Al-Ghazali's rejection of philosophy was disputed by IBN RUSHD, but his views became widely accepted throughout Sunni Islam. His occasionalism was sharply criticized and rejected by both MAIMONIDES (§4) and Aquinas, and never enjoyed wide support during the Christian Middle Ages. It was, however, embraced by the late medieval Ockhamist philosophers Pierre D'AILLY and Gabriel BIEL.

2   Early modern occasionalism

Occasionalism in modern philosophy took its 'occasion' from the problems over causality that arose in Descartes' philosophy (see DESCARTES, R. §§8, 11, 13). (Not only the problem of mind–body interaction, however; causal interaction among bodies was also problematic for Descartes.) Descartes himself had tendencies towards occasionalism, and this view was adopted by the Cartesian philosophers Louis de LA FORGE and Géraud de CORDEMOY. Arnold GEULINCX may have been the first to state an important principle that is also found, in modified form, as a premise in arguments concerning causation given by Malebranche and Hume. The principle states that something cannot be done unless there is knowledge of how it is done; more specifically, people do not do what they do not know how to do. This quickly disposes of the contention that the mind causes bodily movements; in order for the mind to do this, we should have to know how to control the physiological processes involved in making such movements – the firing of neurons, for instance. Clearly, however, we do not know this. The principle also excludes causal efficacy for corporeal bodies, since these bodies obviously lack knowledge of how their supposed effects are produced.

Nicolas MALEBRANCHE (§4) was clearly the most significant of the modern occasionalists. Basing his argument on the supposed impossibility of mind—body interaction, he writes that 'There is no real relation between one body and another, between one mind and another. In a word, no created thing can act upon another by an activity which is its own' (1688: 4.11). He argues, like Geulincx, that in order for our minds to be able to move our bodies we should have to understand, in full anatomical detail, how this is done. He also argues that God's causality pre-empts, as it were, any possible causality among creatures. No creature can exist unless God, by 'continuous creation', wills that it should exist. But in willing that a chair (for example) should exist, God must will that it exist in some particular place, in some particular state of motion or rest, and so on. Clearly, no created power (assuming there to be such) can cause the chair to be at rest or in motion unless God wills that it be so. But if God does will the chair to move, then necessarily it moves; there is nothing left to be done by any created agent. Thus, 'God communicates His power to created beings only because He has made their modifications the occasional causes...which determine the activity of His volitions in consequence of the general laws which He has prescribed to Himself' (1688: 7.10).

Occasionalism did not persist for long as a widely accepted view. But the influence of Malebranche was considerable, and is still felt today through Hume, many of whose sceptical arguments concerning causation derive from Malebranche.

3 The case for occasionalism

Is occasionalism simply a historical curiosity, or does it have the potential to become a viable position for present-day theists? Leaving aside Geulincx's far-from-evident principle, there are two principal arguments for occasionalism, based respectively on the critique of natural causality and on the pre-emptive causality of God. The argument from the critique of natural causality proceeds as we have already seen in al-Ghazali and Malebranche. Various criticisms are employed (many familiar to us through Hume) to argue that causality as we experience it in nature is not the necessary, genuinely productive relationship that we ordinarily take it to be. Natural causation having thus been disposed of, God is invoked as the 'true cause' for whose efficacious acts the various states of created beings are mere occasions. This argument, however, is dialectically weak. The occasionalist begins (as we all must) from our ordinary intuitions about causality developed through our ordinary, everyday causal interactions with the world. These intuitions are then undermined through the critique of causality. But then the occasionalist invokes those

very same intuitions in order to point to God as the truly efficacious and productive cause of all that occurs; causation by God, however, is not subjected to the kind of critical analysis that has been applied to natural causation. Clearly, this procedure is inconsistent. If the critique of causality is as effective as occasionalists think, then (as Hume rightly saw) divine causation is, if anything, worse off than natural causation in consequence.

In view of this, the main burden of support for occasionalism needs to be borne by the argument for the pre-emptive causality of God, also employed by both al-Ghazali and Malebranche. (The argument of Malebranche based on continuous creation is a special case of this.) Classical theists are in agreement that God's causal activity must be seen as universal and pervasive throughout the created world. To suppose that there is some part of created reality in which God's activity is not involved is just to make that part of the creation independent of God, which detracts from divine dignity. Any attempt to circumvent this problem by designating different aspects of causation which pertain respectively to God and to creatures runs up against the complaint that the aspect assigned to creatures is removed from the sphere of God's activity, thus diminishing the honour due to God. Medieval Aristotelians tried to meet this challenge by the theory of dual causation, which claims to give full value both to the divine 'first cause' and to creaturely 'second causes'. This theory was spelled out in their doctrines of divine conservation and divine concurrence with creaturely action, but no detailed consensus was arrived at (see CREATION AND CONSERVATION, RELIGIOUS DOCTRINE OF §5). Contemporary philosophical theology has barely begun to address the issue, so it could fairly be urged that on this point occasionalism presents theistic philosophy with a challenge it has not yet met.

4 Occasionalism and immaterialism

Whether this argument provides effective support for occasionalism depends on whether occasionalism is itself a tenable view. It can be argued on both epistemological and metaphysical grounds that the material substance posited by occasionalists is redundant and should be eliminated, leading to a Berkeleyan immaterialism (see BERKELEY, G. §§3, 6–7). Epistemologically, occasionalism holds that material substances make no causal contribution towards our perceptions of objects. Occasionalists hold, to be sure, that light waves (for example) travel from observed bodies to our eyes, that nerve impulses connect the eyes with the brain, and that consequent to this we experience visual images. But there is no

real causal connection between any two of these
stages; in particular, the visual images are not
produced by the brain (or even by the immaterial
mind), but rather by God 'on the occasion' of the
brain's being in an appropriate state. This means,
however, that we have no direct evidence for the
existence of the supposed intermediate stages in the
process, and it is hard to avoid Berkeley's conclusion
that it would be simpler for God to omit them.

A similar conclusion can be reached through
metaphysical considerations. Occasionalism holds
that created substances make no active causal
contribution to subsequent states of the world. But
then the occasionalist is faced with the question of
whether created substances are endowed with causal
powers at all. If they are, then God must somehow
intervene to prevent the powers from being exercised –
and indeed, the provision to created things of powers
that are never exercised and are not intended by God
to be exercised would seem highly unreasonable. So
the occasionalist must deny that created beings
possess causal powers. But what, if anything, might
created substances consist in, if they lack such powers
entirely?

Apparently the occasionalist answer is that while
created substances lack active powers they do possess
some passive powers; hence al-Ghazali's view of
material beings as inert, and Malebranche's willingness to attribute movability and impenetrability
(but not active power) to material objects. So as
Freddoso suggests, 'God would supply all the active
causal power in nature, while material substances
would receive and channel God's causal influence as
patients' (1988: 111). The difficulty with this is that
the active/passive distinction, as we make it, cannot
give occasionalism what it needs here. We do have
some grip on the difference between an object's acting
on another or being acted upon by another. (In many
cases this would coincide with the direction of energy
transfer.) But the very same molecular structure
which makes a billiard ball impenetrable by another
billiard ball also enables it, under appropriate
conditions, to propel the other billiard ball in a
desired direction. The active/passive distinction just
does not cut deep enough to play the role it is cast in
by occasionalism. But if material substances have
neither active nor passive powers, then it is difficult to
see the point of their existing – indeed, it is difficult to
see what could be meant by claiming that they exist.

The correct conclusion would seem to be that the
logic of occasionalism leads to Berkeleyan immaterialism, and that it is in this form, if any, that it may be
able to survive as a viable contemporary option. A
more attractive option, though slightly more remote
from classical occasionalism, can perhaps be found in

certain anti-realist interpretations of natural science
(see SCIENTIFIC REALISM AND ANTIREALISM).
Though diverging from the letter of both occasionalism and Berkeleyanism, these anti-realist views are
akin to them in spirit in their desire to uphold science
as an empirical enterprise while avoiding the mechanistic materialism which threatens on a realistic
interpretation of scientific theories.

See also: CAUSALITY AND NECESSITY IN ISLAMIC
THOUGHT; EDWARDS, J. §3; MIRACLES; RELIGION
AND SCIENCE

References and further reading

Berkeley, G. (1710, 1713) *A Treatise Concerning the Principles of Human Knowledge* and *Three Dialogues between Hylas and Philonous*, La Salle, IL: Open Court, 1986. (The basic texts for Berkeley's 'immaterialism'.)
Creery, W.E. (ed.) (1991) *George Berkeley: Critical Assessments*, London: Routledge & Kegan Paul. (Important collection of recent discussions of Berkeley's philosophy.)
* Fakhry, M. (1958) *Islamic Occasionalism and its Critique by Averroes and Aquinas*, London: Allen & Unwin. (Sets out al-Ghazali's occasionalism in its historical context, and develops the Thomistic answer to occasionalism.)
* Freddoso, A.J. (1988) 'Medieval Aristotelianism and the Case against Secondary Causation in Nature', in T.V. Morris (ed.) *Divine and Human Action: Essays in the Metaphysics of Theism*, Ithaca, NY: Cornell University Press, 74–118. (A penetrating study of the metaphysical aspects of occasional-ism.)
al-Ghazali (1095) *al-Ghazali's Tahafut al-falasifah: The Incoherence of the Philosophers*, trans. S.A. Kamali, Lahore: Pakistan Philosophical Congress, 1963. (Problem 17 is the basic source for al-Ghazali's occasionalism.)
McCann, H.J. and Kvanvig, J.L. (1991) 'The Occa-sionalist Proselytizer: A Modified Catechism', *Philosophical Perspectives* 5: 587–615. (A contem-porary defence of occasionalism; argues that occasionalism does not deprive laws of nature of their explanatory force.)
* Malebranche, N. (1688) *Dialogues on Metaphysics and On Religion*, trans. M. Ginsberg, London: Allen & Unwin, 1923. (An excellent introduction to Male-branche's occasionalism.)
—— (1674–5) *The Search after Truth and Elucidations of the Search after Truth*, trans. T.M. Lennon and P.J. Olscamp, Columbus, OH: Ohio State University

Press, 1980. (The basic source for the philosophy of Malebranche.)

Nadler, S. (ed.) (1993) *Causation in Early Modern Philosophy: Cartesianism, Occasionalism, and Pre-established Harmony*, University Park, PA: Pennsylvania State University Press. (Several of the articles discuss early modern occasionalism.)

WILLIAM HASKER

OCKHAM, WILLIAM OF

see WILLIAM OF OCKHAM

OGYŪ SORAI (1666–1728)

Ogyū Sorai (1666–1728) was one of the greatest, most erudite and most Sinocentric kogaku, *or 'Ancient Learning', philosophers of Tokugawa Japan. Sorai's call for a return to the most ancient philosophical classics of the Chinese tradition, the Six Classics, voiced the logical conclusion of* kogaku *tendencies. However, Sorai's ideas also inspired* kokugaku, *or 'National Learning', a literary movement advocating a return to the ancient writings of Japan which most purely expressed the Japanese soul prior to its distortion by Chinese philosophy.*

Sorai was born in Edo (now Tokyo), the shogun's capital. From 1679–90 Sorai's father, a *samurai*-physician who served the shogunate, was exiled to rural Kazusa (now in Chiba Prefecture) for reasons which are still unclear. In exile, Sorai's father supervised his son's study of the neo-Confucianism of ZHU XI, a post-Buddhist, metaphysical form of ancient Confucianism (see NEO-CONFUCIAN PHILOSOPHY). After returning to Edo, Sorai gained attention for his thorough grasp of Zhu Xi's teachings. From 1696 to 1709 he served Yanagisawa Yoshiyasu, grand chamberlain to the Shogun Tsunayoshi (1646–1709), as a scholar. Sorai's ideas informed the decision of Tsunayoshi's government in the 1703 'forty-seven *rōnin*' incident. He argued that the *rōnin* were praiseworthy for fulfilling a private morality, that of duty to their lord, but they also had broken public law by assassinating their lord's enemy, one of the shogun's officials. Rather than humiliate them with inflicted punishment, Sorai advised that the *rōnin* be allowed to commit ritual suicide (see BUSHI PHILOSOPHY §3).

After Tsunayoshi's death in 1709, Sorai became a private scholar. His first publication, a Sino-Japanese dictionary entitled *Yakubun sentei* (Expedients for Translating Chinese), earned him modest fame in 1711. His next work, the *Ken'en zuihitsu* (Reed Garden Miscellany), published in 1714, attacked the *kogaku* ideas of Itō Jinsai's *Gomō jigi* (The Meanings of Terms in the *Analects* and the *Mengzi*) from a neo-Confucian perspective. Sorai's attacks on Itō Jinsai are odd because earlier Sorai had written him expressing admiration for his *Gomō jigi*. Itō Jinsai never replied, leading to speculation that Sorai wrote the *Ken'en zuihitsu* out of resentment (see ITŌ JINSAI).

By 1717, Sorai had rejected neo-Confucianism in favor of his own brand of *kogaku* (ancient learning) thought. His masterworks, the *Bendō* (Discerning the Meaning of the Way) and *Bemmei* (Discerning the Meanings of Philosophical Terms), called for a revival of the ancient Chinese philosophy of the Six Classics. They also attacked both Itō Jinsai's revival of the ancient teachings of Confucius and Zhu Xi's neo-Confucianism for indulging in fanciful subjectivism rather than objective study of ancient philosophical language (see ZHU XI).

Sorai boasted that his philosophy would revive the Way of the ancient sage-kings (see CONFUCIAN PHILOSOPHY, CHINESE). That Way embodied the foundations of civilization, including the rites, music, penal laws and institutions of government. In Sorai's view, the sages earned their status because they invented the Way *ex nihilo*. Sorai thus denied the neo-Confucian claim that the Way existed both in the natural world and in human nature. He believed that there remained only one task for humanity, to follow the ancient Way reverently: neither rulers nor philosophers were to tamper with or deviate from it.

Unlike Zhu Xi, who claimed that sagehood was attainable via investigating things, Sorai alleged that it was impossible for men to become sages. While neo-Confucians insisted that human nature was universally good, Sorai denied that there was any moral value inherent in it. Rather, people were just born with various capacities and talents which could be realized by faithfully following the Way of the sages. When everyone perfected their talents, stability would reign.

While Confucius taught that *jin* (*ren* in Chinese), or humaneness, was a virtue that everyone should embody (see CONFUCIAN PHILOSOPHY, CHINESE §5), Sorai interpreted *jin* as the virtue of the great sages which enabled them to provide stability for the world through their Way. Religiously, Sorai insisted that people believe without question in ghosts and spirits, because the ancient sages made such belief part of their Way. Neo-Confucians, however, interpreted ghosts and spirits as the activities of *yin* and *yang*, thus defusing many superstitions about them (see YIN–YANG).

During his final years, Sorai provided the Shogun Yoshimune (1684–1751) with solutions for the social and economic ills plaguing the state. His *Taiheisaku* (Plan for an Age of Great Peace) and *Seidan* (Discourses on Political Economy) advised that urban-based *samurai* be relocated in rural areas away from the vices of the pleasure quarters. Sorai thought that the shogunate could thus provide for stability by creating, like the ancient sages, institutions which would rightly order human and natural resources.

See also: BUSHI PHILOSOPHY; CHINESE CLASSICS; CONFUCIAN PHILOSOPHY, CHINESE; CONFUCIAN PHILOSOPHY, JAPANESE; ITŌ JINSAI; NEO-CONFUCIAN PHILOSOPHY; ZHU XI

List of works

Ogyū Sorai (1666–1728) *Ogyū Sorai zenshū* (Complete Works), ed. Yoshikawa Kōjirō and Maruyama Masao, Tokyo: Misuzu shobō, 1974, 20 vols. (The definitive edition of Sorai's Complete Works.)

—— (1714) *Ken'en zuihitsu* (Reed Garden Miscellany), in Yoshikawa Kōjirō and Maruyama Masao (eds) *Ogyū Sorai zenshū* (Complete Works), Tokyo: Misuzu shobō, 1974, vol. 5. (The work in which Ogyū attacked the work of Itō Jinsai.)

—— (1717) *Bendō* (Discerning the Meaning of the Way), in Yoshikawa Kōjirō *et al.* (eds) *Ogyū Sorai*, Nihon shisō taikei vol. 36, Tokyo: Iwanami shoten; trans. O. Lidin, *Ogyū Sorai: Distinguishing the Way (Bendō)*, Tokyo: Monumenta Nipponica Monographs, 1970. (Lidin's edition is the only English translation of the Bendō.)

—— (1717) *Bemmei* (Discerning the Meanings of Philosophical Terms), in Yoshikawa Kōjirō *et al.* (eds) *Ogyū Sorai*, Nihon shisō taikei vol. 36, Tokyo: Iwanami shoten. (Calls for a revival of the ancient Chinese philosophy of the Six Classics.)

—— (1727) *Taiheisaku* (Plan for an Age of Great Peace), in Yoshikawa Kōjirō *et al.* (eds) *Ogyū Sorai*, Nihon shisō taikei vol. 36, Tokyo: Iwanami shoten. (Work on political economy.)

—— (1727) *Seidan* (Discourses on Political Economy), in Yoshikawa Kōjirō *et al.* (eds) *Ogyū Sorai*, Nihon shisō taikei vol. 36, Tokyo: Iwanami shoten. (Work on political economy.)

—— (*c.*1717) *Gakusoku* (Instructions for Students), in Yoshikawa Kōjirō and Maruyama Masao (eds) *Ogyū Sorai zenshū* (Complete Works), Tokyo: Misuzu shobō, 1974, vol. 1; trans. R. Minear in 'Ogyū Sorai's Instructions of Students: A Translation and Commentary', *Harvard Journal of Asiatic Studies* 36, 1976: 5–81. (The only translation of Sorai's *Gakusoku* in English. Accompanied by a lengthy, thoughtful essay.)

References and further reading

de Bary, W.T. and Bloom, I. (eds) (1979) *Principle and Practicality: Essays in Neo-Confucianism and Practical Learning*, New York: Columbia University Press. (An anthology including sophisticated essays, many pertaining to Sorai, by leading Japanese and American scholars.)

Bellah, R.N. (1978) 'Baigan and Sorai: Continuities and Discontinuities in Eighteenth-Century Japanese Thought', in Tetsuo Najita and I. Scheiner (eds) *Japanese Thought in the Tokugawa Period, 1600–1868*, Chicago, IL: University of Chicago Press. (Reveals how Sorai and Baigan represent antithetical poles in eighteenth-century Japanese thought.)

Bitō Masahide (1978) 'Ogyū Sorai and the Distinguishing Features of Japanese Confucianism', in Tetsuo Najita and I. Scheiner (eds) *Japanese Thought in the Tokugawa Period, 1600–1868*, Chicago, IL: University of Chicago Press. (Discusses the distinctively Japanese elements in Sorai's understanding of the Chinese notion of heaven.)

Imanaka Kanshi (1966) *Soraigaku kisoteki kenkyū* (A Basic Study of Sorai's Thought), Tokyo: Yoshikawa kōbunkan. (A major, post-Maruyama monograph on Sorai. Traces most of Sorai's ideas to Chinese sources.)

Lidin, O. (1973) *The Life of Ogyū Sorai*, Lund: Studentlitteratur. (The only biography of Sorai in English.)

Maruyama Masao (1974) *Studies in the Intellectual History of Tokugawa Japan*, trans. Mikiso Hane, Princeton, NJ: Princeton University Press. (An English translation of a seminal, though somewhat dated, work written in the early 1940s.)

McEwan, J. (1962) *The Political Writings of Ogyū Sorai*, Cambridge: Cambridge University Press. (Features numerous translations from Sorai's *Seidan* and *Taiheisaku*.)

Sakai Naoki (1992) *Voices of the Past: The Status of Language in Eighteenth-Century Japanese Discourse*, Ithaca, NY: Cornell University Press. (Argues that from the late seventeenth century, Japanese discourse began reconceptualizing the world in new and diverse ways, all of which had political consequences.)

Yamashita, S.H. (1984) 'Nature and Artifice in the Writings of Ogyū Sorai', in P. Nosco (ed.) *Confucianism and Tokugawa Culture*, Princeton, NJ: Princeton University Press. (Criticizes Maruyama's claim that Sorai's philosophy broke with the naturalistic thought of Zhu Xi.)

—— (1994) *Master Sorai's Responsals: An Annotated Translation of Sorai sensei tōmonsho*, Honolulu, HI: University of Hawaii Press. (A brief translation and study of Sorai's political philosophy.)

Yoshikawa Kōjirō (1983) *Jinsai, Sorai, Norinaga: Three Classical Philologists in Mid-Tokugawa Japan*, Tokyo: Tōhō gakkai. (Includes an English translation of Yoshikawa's seminal 'Sorai gakuan' (An Introductory Study of Sorai).)

Yoshikawa Kōjirō, Maruyama Masao, Nishida Taichirō and Tsuji Tatsuya (eds) (1973) *Ogyū Sorai*, Nihon shisō taikei vol. 36, Tokyo: Iwanami shoten. (Contains extensively annotated Japanese texts, in *kambun* and *bungo*, of Sorai's main works, the *Bendō, Bemmei, Gakusoku, Seidan, Taiheisaku* and selections from the *Sorai shū*, plus analytic essays by Yoshikawa, Tsuji and Maruyama.)

JOHN ALLEN TUCKER

OKEN, LORENZ (1779–1851)

In the early nineteenth century, Oken was one of several German scientists who developed views about the metaphysical presuppositions of science, promoted by Kant and especially by Schelling in order to forge links between their scientific investigations and the prevailing Romantic style of thought. Oken's particular concern was with biology, where he introduced bold taxonomic principles drawing on analogies with mathematical polarities and with our sensory and emotional capacities.

Lorenz Oken, or Okenfuss, was born in Bolsbach, in the Baden region of southern Germany, on 1 August 1779. His academic talents were recognized early, the local pastor and a neighbouring Franciscan Gymnasium providing the foundations of a classical education. Before graduating in 1804 from Freiburg University with a medical degree, he had become an enthusiastic supporter of the metaphysical speculations associated with *Naturphilosophie*, a movement endorsed by the early German Romantic thinkers which sought to uncover the general presuppositions of science, and had published an outline of his intended contributions (see NATURPHILOSOPHIE). In 1807 he was called on Goethe's recommendation to a chair of medicine at Jena University. His *Lehrbuch des Systems der Naturphilosophie* (Textbook of Systematic Philosophy of Nature) was published shortly after his arrival. He remained at Jena, becoming Professor of

Philosophy in 1812, but was dismissed in 1819 following his allegedly subversive political activities as editor of *Isis*, a periodical he founded in 1817 with the aim of providing comprehensive information about scientific and other matters to the general reader. The periodical was largely written by Oken himself and it rapidly became widely read, partly for the outspoken liberal politics it promoted. He subsequently held teaching posts in medicine and physiology at several universities, and was instrumental in founding the influential *Gesellschaft Deutscher Naturforscher und Ärzte* (German Society for Scientists and Doctors) in 1822. He ended his career as Rector of Zürich University and died in Zürich on 11 August 1851.

Like other post-Kantian thinkers, Oken believed that the structures in terms of which we understand the natural world are supplied, not by that world, but by the mind. KANT himself had initiated investigations of the metaphysical foundations of science which were intended to reveal these structures, and Oken's contemporaries, such as Hegel and Schelling, responded with their own versions of a philosophy of nature (see HEGEL, G.W. §7; SCHELLING, F.W. §1). In Oken's writings we find little of the logical analysis that these philosophers employed in describing these mental structures; instead, his abstract and generalized language conveyed in a philosophical idiom the Romantic conviction that imagination and feeling should play their part in scientific understanding. Thus, he took the applicability of mathematics to nature as a foundation for ideas about the spiritual and material, the eternal and the temporal, which also found expression in contemporary German Romantic poetry and art. For if nature is constructed by the self, though in opposition to the self, then as a whole it corresponds to mathematical infinity, because the self constructs it as unlimited in space, time and scope. And the origin of nature (conceptually, if not historically) corresponds to zero because the self constructs nature as originating from nothing, albeit with infinite potential. These constructs of an infinite nature and a primeval nothing are in polar opposition to each other, and the interaction between them generates our constructions and understandings of nature, just as the interaction between our conceptions of zero and infinity generates our constructions and understandings of natural numbers. In common with philosophers writing in the Romantic idiom of irony, contradiction and unrestrained feeling, Oken subjected language to enormous pressure. The resulting syntactical intensity mystified his readers but it was integral to the fervour of his thought, including his thought about nature.

In the physical sciences, his thinking was close to

that of Schelling. Indeed, the two men were in contact during the first decade of the nineteenth century, when Oken was developing his philosophy of nature. Both understood optical, electrical and magnetic phenomena in terms of polarities of light and darkness, attraction and repulsion, these polarities being manifestations of an abstract dialectic of productivity and product. Oken's tone when writing of these matters was one of enthusiastic endorsement rather than critical consideration, and his aphoristic style encouraged him to affirm rather than defend his conclusions. He did not, therefore, provide the elucidation of the difficulties of this philosophy that his contemporaries might have sought or that modern readers might require.

The biological and medical sciences were, he found, fruitful fields in which to apply the concepts and analogies suggested by his philosophy. They were, too, the sciences in which his expertise was recognized, for he was renowned as a meticulous descriptive anatomist. But the conventionality of his practical science stands in sharp contrast to the boldness of his theoretical speculations. So, for example, in taxonomy he used the idea of a single series of increasingly complex organisms, beginning with primal organisms, or 'Ur-thiere', and ending with human beings. Just as the comparable sequence of natural numbers displays patterns which are repeated within segments of the sequence, so Oken sought repeating patterns within his taxonomic series. In his earliest writings he had used the language of sensory and emotional capacities, often metaphorically, to describe these patterns, and he found imaginative ways of providing evidence of their applicability. However, if such patterns were not produced by perceptions of nature but by conceptions of our minds, it is not surprising that he was sometimes casual in confirming the details they implied.

Oken has a place in the history of biology and medicine for his experimental contributions to comparative anatomy, and for some of his taxonomic ideas which are said to anticipate certain modern views. His aim of bringing a Romantic style of thinking into his science led him to explore *Naturphilosophie*, and, in the history of philosophy, his significance is bound up with that of the distinctive coupling of speculative science with idealistic metaphysics. Certainly, Oken's philosophy served a need among his contemporaries, but it was his pedagogic and investigative skills, rather than his philosophical acumen, that earned their admiration.

See also: ROMANTICISM, GERMAN

List of works

Oken, L. (1804) *Uebersicht des Grundriss des Systems der Naturphilosophie* (Survey of a Plan for Systematic Philosophy of Nature), Frankfurt am Main: P.W. Eicheberg. (A brief outline of Oken's characteristic approach to philosophy of nature.)
—— (1805) *Die Zeugung* (Reproduction), Bamberg and Wirzburg: J.A. Goebhardt. (A speculative physiological essay on the generation of organisms from primordial 'infusoria'.)
—— (1808) *Erste Ideen zur Theorie des Lichts, der Finsterniss, der Farben and der Wärme* (Preliminary Ideas Towards a Theory of Light, Darkness, Colour and Heat), Jena: Friedrich Frommann. (Explores the anti-Newtonian implications of Oken's philosophy of nature for a rapidly changing part of physics.)
—— (1809–11) *Lehrbuch des Systems der Naturphilosophie* (Textbook of Systematic Philosophy of Nature), Jena: Friedrich Frommann, 3 vols; 2nd edn, 1831; 3rd edn, Zürich, F. Schulthess, 1843; trans. A. Tulk, *Elements of Physiophilosophy*, London, Ray Society, 1847. (A widely-read exposition of Oken's metaphysical philosophy of nature.)
—— (1813–26) *Lehrbuch der Naturgeschichte* (Textbook of Natural History), Leipzig and Jena: C.H. Reclam, 5 vols. (A treatise encompassing experimental findings in zoology, biology and mineralogy within Oken's philosophy of nature.)
—— (1833–41) *Allgemeine Naturgeschichte für alle Stände* (General Natural History for all Circumstances), Stuttgart: Hoffman, 13 vols. (Oken's final and most comprehensive study of natural history.)

References and further reading

Ecker, A. (1880) *Lorenz Oken. Eine biographische Skizze*, Stuttgart; trans. A. Tulk, *Lorenz Oken: A Biographical Sketch*, London: Kegan Paul, Trench & Co., 1883. (A flattering portrait by the son of one of Oken's colleagues; contains only meagre information about Oken's philosophy.)
Gould, S.J. (1984) 'The Rule of Five', *Natural History* 93 (10): 14–23. (Explains Oken's numerical system for explaining natural order, comparing it with other pre-Darwinian systems.)
Mullen, P.C. (1977) 'The Romantic as Scientist: Lorenz Oken', *Studies in Romanticism* 16: 381–99. (A recent account of Oken's life with some details about his philosophical ideas.)

BARRY GOWER

OLIVECRONA, KARL
(1897–1980)

Olivecrona was a Swedish jurist of the 'realist' school, and from 1933 Professor of Procedural Law in the University of Lund. He regards law as a body of 'independent imperatives' effective in bringing about certain patterns of behaviour in society. The reality of law is psychological and behavioural, not dependent on some metaphysical world of norms.

Olivecrona's theory is non-voluntarist: there is no individual or group 'lawmaker' whose will constitutes law. Legal rules are not strictly imperatives. Yet in setting patterns of behaviour they have an expressive and emotive function and are regarded by the addressees as if they were imperatives.

Many independent imperatives have a performative form: they purport to create ideal power-relations, rights, duties and the like, and only indirectly to command action or abstention in a physical sense. Such performatives prompt beliefs in valid law and rights, but these beliefs do not (cannot) refer to any fact. Yet they have social functions. They direct human conduct, facilitate concise law-making, and even convey some vague information, for example, that the 'owner' of an estate in the usual course of things has a kind of control over it. The most important function of criminal law is to promote the conviction that crime leads to punishment (see LEGAL CONCEPTS §4).

Olivecrona in his later work pursued the history of ideas about rights and related concepts. In this, he contributed to understanding the crucial role of the idea of *suum* in the natural law theories of, among others, GROTIUS and PUFENDORF. This idea is at the heart of ideas both of property and of personal rights to non-interference by others.

Olivecrona was a disciple of Axel HÄGERSTRÖM (§4), according to whom all knowledge concerns reality in time and space and the concept of value is inconsistent with reality; hence 'binding' law is an illusion. He has been grouped with Alf ROSS and Vilhelm Lundstedt as a 'Scandinavian realist' (see LEGAL REALISM §1), their 'realism' descending from Hägerström's anti-idealist materialism. Their work wrestles with significant problems concerning normative concepts such as 'right' and 'duty'. If these do not have material counterparts, but function in essentially action-guiding ways, what theory of language and of reality properly captures their sense? If philosophy peels off the air of magic and mystery surrounding them, can they continue to guide action effectively?

Olivecrona's work deserves credit for its clarity in posing the fundamental problems of legal philosophy. He gave a precise and comprehensive reconstruction of the conceptual apparatus of law consistent with his anti-metaphysical framework (see LEGAL POSITIVISM §5). Yet such a reconstructionism can be criticized as too remote from the internal point of view of lawyers and inadequate to capture legal reasoning and legal thought in the context of justification (see LEGAL REASONING AND INTERPRETATION). If juristic opinions are merely emotive and expressive, how can they be discussed intersubjectively? How can lawyers honestly fulfil their beneficial social functions (rightly recognized by Olivecrona) if they regard the 'valid law' as mere illusion?

See also: LAW, PHILOSOPHY OF

List of works

Olivecrona, K. (1939) *Law as Fact*, Copenhagen: Einar Munksgaard. (Basic 'realist' statement, flatly denying the existence of any 'world of norms'.)
—— (1951) 'Realism and Idealism: Some Reflections on the Cardinal Point in Legal Philosophy', *New York University Law Review* 26: 120–31.
—— (1971) *Law as Fact*, London: Stevens, 2nd edn. (Totally revised work, drawing much more on modern linguistic-analytical theory, especially that of J.L. Austin.)

References and further reading

Arnholm, C.J. (1962) 'Olivecrona on Legal Rights: Reflections on the Concept of Rights', *Scandinavian Studies in Law* 6: 11–33. (Explanation and critique of Olivecrona's views, drawing attention to the difference between his views and those of US realists.)
Bjarup, J. (1978) *Skandinavischer Realismus* (Scandinavian Realism), Freiburg/Munich: Alber. (Critical introduction to the works of Hägerström, Lundstedt, Olivecrona and Ross.)
Lewis, J.U. (1970) 'Karl Olivecrona: "Factual Realism" and the Reasons for Obeying a Law', *University of British Columbia Law Review* 5: 281–305.
MacCormack, G.D. (1970) 'Scandinavian Realism', *Juridical Review* 82: 33–54. (Interesting critique of the psychologism to be found in Olivecrona and in Alf Ross.)
Ruiter, D.W.P. (1993) *Institutional Legal Facts*, Dordrecht: Kluwer. (Chapter 1, on 'Legal Validity',

criticizes and presents an alternative to Olivecrona's performative-based account of validity.)

ALEKSANDER PECZENIK

OLIVI, PETER JOHN (1247/8–98)

Condemned repeatedly by religious authorities, Peter John Olivi is one of scholasticism's most original and colourful figures. Although better known for his involvement in social and political debates within the Franciscan order, Olivi also took up the leading epistemological and metaphysical concerns of his day. His outright scorn for Aristotle and cautious rapport with Augustine combine to produce an exciting, insightful body of philosophical work.

Olivi studied in Paris without becoming a master of theology and spent much of his adult life teaching at various Franciscan houses in southern France. Although he produced a wide-ranging body of work, most of his philosophical views are contained in his question–commentary on the second book of Peter Lombard's *Sentences* (see LOMBARD, P.) This lengthy treatise takes up a wide range of philosophical problems such as the nature of matter, form, substance, quantity, the soul, causation, motion and the problems of universals and individuation. Although imbued with the Aristotelian terminology and perspectives of his contemporaries, Olivi feels free to reject this influence when it suits him. He characteristically remarks of Aristotle, 'his authority and that of any infidel and idolator is nothing to me – especially as regards matters that belong to the Christian faith or are very near to it' (*Quaestiones in secundum librum Sententiarum* q.16 ad 6).

Many of Olivi's most interesting and influential arguments concern human volition and cognition. His views on these topics are often strikingly similar to those of his Franciscan successors John DUNS SCOTUS and WILLIAM OF OCKHAM. Olivi opposes any account from which it would follow that our will is constrained in its choices or determined to select one alternative over another. By his standards, human freedom requires that persons be able, at the same time at which they choose one thing, to choose instead its opposite; in other words that 'someone does one thing in such a way that at the same time he could have done the other while ceasing from the first – and vice versa' (*Quaestiones* q.57 ad 4). Olivi thinks that if free will is to be preserved, this counterfactual must hold not just until the moment of decision, but also at the moment of decision itself. To explain this difficult claim – that at the same time at which I did one thing I could have done the other – Olivi invokes the notion of natural priority (*Quaestiones* q.57 ad 10). Even though it seems as if I could not choose to cross the street at the very moment that I choose not to cross the street, I have an ability to choose otherwise which is naturally prior to but temporally simultaneous with the choice that I do make.

Olivi needs to make these subtle conceptual distinctions in order to reject any passivity or determinism on the part of will. In particular he wants to deny that the will is determined to choose in accordance with intellect's counsel. Intellect's role in decision-making is to present to the will various alternatives, presenting them as good in various respects. The will's own freedom, he holds, is a completely sufficient cause for its choosing one of those alternatives over another. Hence 'if one is asked why [a volition] ceases... it is fully sufficient to reply by saying that it was completely and sufficiently able to cease' (*Quaestiones* q.57 ad 5). Olivi claims that demanding any further explanation leads to the destruction of free will.

It is a peculiar feature of Olivi's thought that he sees a close connection between taking the will to be passive (and hence not free) and taking the cognitive powers to be passive. He says that it is the doctrine of the passivity of cognition that 'above all things moves many to believe that our will is totally passive' (*Quaestiones* q.58 ad 14). Olivi doesn't explain why anyone would link these two issues, but his concern on this point leads him to append to his discussion of will an extended attack on the standard medieval Aristotelian theory of human cognition. His central claim is that the human cognitive powers (intellect and senses) are not passive. To maintain this claim, Olivi reverses the usual causal order. We do not cognize in virtue of *receiving* external impressions; rather, our cognitive powers somehow reach out directly to their objects in the world. While Olivi rejects the ancient account in which vision takes place through a physical extromission, he allows what he calls a 'virtual extension' of the cognitive powers to the external world (*Quaestiones* q.26).

Although Olivi discusses the notion of virtual extension at length, it is never quite clear what he has in mind. However, the motivation for this position is clear enough. In part, he wants to reject any sort of passivity on the part of our cognitive powers. Further impetus comes from his claim that 'no body can directly move the soul's sensory powers, and much less the intellectual ones' (*Quodlibeta* I.4). In place of a direct causal connection, Olivi postulates an obscurely explained 'natural link' (*colligantia naturalis*) between mind and body (*Quaestiones* q.111). In the standard scholastic account, on the other hand, external objects produce forms (known as sensible and intelligible species) in our cognitive faculties. Olivi denies not only that these species are produced by external objects, but also that such species occur at all: there is no internal representation of objects in the external world beyond the act of cognition itself. This view became common in the fourteenth century (in the works of Ockham, for example), but Olivi seems to have been the first to hold it. His most interesting arguments are epistemological. If there were such species, he says, we 'would be diverted from seeing the object rather than led toward seeing it' (*Quaestiones* q.74). On this basis he raises sceptical problems concerning our knowledge of the external world. His theory of virtual extension, in contrast, allows a direct realist account of cognition.

Olivi's rejection of sensible and intelligible species was condemned by the Franciscan authorities, along with many of his other views. It seems clear that these philosophical claims drew ecclesiastical condemnation primarily because of his involvement in the controversial Franciscan spiritual movement. In any case, all of Olivi's writings were twice condemned and ordered to be burned. For this reason, at least, his work received less philosophical attention than it deserves. Enough of his writings have survived, however, so that this neglect need not persist.

See also: AUGUSTINIANISM; GERARD OF ODO; WILLIAM OF OCKHAM

List of works

There are no published translations of Olivi's philosophical works.

Olivi, Peter John (*c.*1282) *Quaestiones in secundum librum Sententiarum* (Questions on the Second Book of the *Sentences*), Bibliotheca Franciscana Scholastica 4–6, ed. B. Jansen, Quaracchi: Collegii S. Bonaventurae, 1922–6, 3 vols. (This edition contains Olivi's most important philosophical writings. it should be distinguished from his unedited *Sentences* commentary (1287–8).)

—— (*c.*1285) *Quaestiones logicales* (Logical Questions), ed. S. Brown, *Traditio* 42, 1986: 335–88. (A fairly technical set of questions on reference and the relation between species and genus.)

—— (*c.*1285) *Tractatus de verbo* (Treatise on the Mental Word), ed. R. Pasnau in *Essays in Honor of Fr. Gedeon Gál*, St Bonaventure, NY: Franciscan Institute Press, 1997. (Edits the philosophically

interesting beginning of Olivi's commentary on the Gospel of St John.)

—— (*c.*1287?) *Quodlibeta*, Venice, 1509. (There are no surviving manuscripts of these quodlibetal questions, making this early edition invaluable. Unfortunately, it has never been reprinted, and existing copies are very rare.)

References and further reading

Bérubé, C. (1976) 'Olivi, critique de Bonaventure et d'Henri de Gand' (Olivi's Critique of Bonaventure and Henry of Ghent), in *Studies Honoring Ignatius Charles Brady*, St Bonaventure, NY: Franciscan Institute. (Discusses Olivi's interesting and ambivalent treatment of the Augustinian theory of divine illumination.)

Bettoni, E. (1959) *Le dottrine filosofiche di Pier di Giovanni Olivi* (The Philosophical Doctrine of Peter John Olivi), Milan: Società Editrice 'Vita e Pensiero'. (A general survey of Olivi's philosophy.)

Burr, D. (1971) 'Petrus Ioannis Olivi and the Philosophers', *Franciscan Studies* 31: 41–71. (Studies Olivi's antipathy to non-Christian philosophy.)

—— (1976) 'The Persecution of Peter Olivi', *Transactions of the American Philosophical Society* 66: 3–98. (The most detailed study of Olivi's life.)

—— (1989) *Olivi and Franciscan Poverty: The Origins of the Usus Pauper Controversy*, Philadelphia, PA: University of Pennsylvania Press. (Up-to-date biographical details, and a thorough discussion of Olivi's role in controversies within the Franciscan order.)

Dumont, S. (1995) 'The Origin of Scotus's Theory of Synchronic Dependency', *Modern Schoolman* 72: 149–67. (Establishes that Scotus' libertarian theory of will has its origins in Olivi. Comments by S. MacDonald question the significance of the Olivi/Scotus position.)

Gieben, S. (1968) 'Bibliographia Oliviana (1885–1967)', *Collectanea Franciscana* 38: 167–95. (A very thorough guide.)

Jansen, B. (1921) *Die Erkenntnislehre Olivis* (Olivi's Epistemology), Berlin: Dümmlers. (The most complete discussion of Olivi's epistemology and philosophy of mind.)

Pacetti, D. (1954) 'Introduzione', in *Quaestiones quatuor de domina*, Quaracchi: Collegii S. Bonaventurae. (Catalogues Olivi's work, giving its printed and manuscript sources.)

Pasnau, R. (1997) *Theories of Cognition in the Later Middle Ages*, Cambridge: Cambridge University Press. (Discusses at length Olivi's novel views on mental representation and cognitive activity.)

Putallaz, F.-X. (1991) *La connaissance de soi au XIIIᵉ*

siècle. De Matthieu d'Aquasparta à Thierry de Freiberg (Self-knowledge in the Thirteenth Century: Matthew of Aquasparta and Dietrich of Freiberg), Paris: Vrin. (The chapter on Olivi ranges widely over his theories about the soul and knowledge.)

Schneider, T. (1973) *Die Einheit des Menschen* (The Unity of Human Beings), Beiträge zur Geschicte der Philosophie und Theologie des Mittelalters, NF 8, Münster: Aschendorff. (A study of events leading up to the Council of Vienna in 1312, which declared it heretical to deny that the intellective soul, *per se* and essentially, is the form of the body. Schneider devotes a chapter to Olivi's views, which were at the centre of the controversy.)

Simoncioli, F. (1956) *Il problema della libertà umana in Pietro di Giovanni Olivi e Pietro de Trabibus* (The Problem of Human Freedom in Peter John Olivi and Peter of Trabes), Milan: Società Editrice 'Vita e Pensiero'. (Contains some useful texts as well as a discussion of Olivi on free will.)

ROBERT PASNAU

OMAN, JOHN WOOD (1860–1939)

A central theme of John Wood Oman's writings is the possibility and actuality of knowledge that is not gained through science. He rejects as too simplistic the mechanistic view of the world. His belief in God rests not on the arguments of natural theology, but on the force and content of religious experience. The source of religion is to be found in our sense of the supernatural, from which stems also our moral dependence on God.

Born in the Orkney Islands in 1860, John Wood Oman was educated at the universities of Edinburgh and Heidelberg and served as a pastor in northern England for seventeen years. He then taught for a further twenty-eight years at the seminary of the English Presbyterian Church at Westminster College, Cambridge. He translated Friedrich Schleiermacher's *Lectures to Cultured Despisers of Religion* into English, and his emphasis on the centrality of religious experience was influenced by Schleiermacher's theology (see SCHLEIERMACHER, F. §7). He died in 1939.

Oman held religion to be an actual experience of an actual environment. It involves awareness of the holy, a direct sense or feeling of the supernatural. It also involves awareness of the sacred and a valuation of the supernatural as possessing absolute worth (see RELIGIOUS EXPERIENCE §1). The distinction between natural and supernatural is coextensive with the distinction between relative value and absolute value. None the less, Oman held, religion's core is not this sense or its accompanying valuation, but their object; its emphasis is not on experiences or feelings, but on what elicits them.

In *The Natural and the Supernatural* (1931), Oman finds the source of religion in a sense of the supernatural. The supernatural, he says, is a kind of environment with its own sanctions. Experience of this environment provides humans with a degree of transcendence of their natural environment. Contact with any environment includes perception of meaning, and perception of meaning typically involves interpretation as well as recognition. Hence there are differences in how the actual environment is conceived, and consequent differences in how it is experienced.

In primitive religion, the supernatural is conceived animistically. In polytheism, it is thought of as distinct divinities each ruling over a part of nature. In cosmic pantheism, it is viewed as an organic whole with integrally related parts. In idealistic pantheism, it is thought of as a spiritual whole without matter. Thus contacting animistic spirits, placating nature's rulers, finding unity with the cosmos, and escaping illusion, are seen as means of salvation in these religions. Different notions of salvation correlate with diverse conceptions of the supernatural.

In monotheism, the supernatural is conceived as a personal God. Priestly, legalistic religions divide the world into the secular and the sacred; prophetic religions find the supernatural through the natural. Those who follow priestly religions seek the supernatural through ceremonies, and those who embrace prophetic religions see their life as worship and their duties as God's commands. For priestly religions, daily awareness of one's mundane life contains a sense of abiding purpose, and the sense of the supernatural includes an awareness of something of unconditional worth that lays an absolute claim upon our devotion and obedience. Refusal to worship and obey divides one from the supernatural environment in which one's true hope lies.

For all of its diversity, Oman contends, religion has two main branches: 'pantheism and absorption into the One…monotheism and victory over the many' (1931: 407). The former focuses on escaping from the world, the latter endeavours to create a better world. Oman views prophetic monotheism, as manifested in the Old Testament prophets and in the teachings of Jesus, as the highest religion.

In *Grace and Personality* (1919), Oman discusses an issue fundamental to prophetic religion:

The essential quality of a moral person is moral independence and an ideal person would be of absolute moral independence. But the essential quality of a religious person is to depend on God; and he must be as absolutely dependent as a moral person must be absolutely independent.

(1919: 58)

For prophetic religions, every good is given by divine courtesy and none is due to human effort. From the moral point of view, nothing that is morally good can be deterministically produced. Oman suggests that grace involves God's giving us sufficient insight to see that what God wills is coextensive with what realizes our humanity; grace thus is not coercive but persuasive. Morality is not an arbitrary law, externally imposed, but a pattern for realizing our nature as persons.

Oman emphasized the importance of religious and moral experience in theology and philosophy of religion while also insisting on consistency and coherence. He was interested in religious traditions other than his own, and willing to learn from them. He did not suppose that this required that he reject his own tradition, think all experience equal, embrace relativism, or abandon efforts at rational assessments of religious doctrines.

List of works

Oman, J.W. (1902) *Vision and Authority*, London: Hodder & Stoughton. (An inquiry into the nature and object of Churchly authority.)

—— (1906) *The Problem of Faith and Freedom in the Last Two Centuries*, New York: A.J. Armstrong & Son. (Historical and critical discussion of faith and freedom in Anglo-European history over two centuries.)

—— (1919) *Grace and Personality*, Cambridge: Cambridge University Press. (A discussion of human freedom and responsibility, and divine sovereignty and grace.)

—— (1931) *The Natural and the Supernatural*, Cambridge: Cambridge University Press. (Offers an account of the relations between the natural and the supernatural with reference to the history of religions.)

References and further reading

Bevons, S.B. (1992) *John Oman and his Doctrine of God*, Cambridge: Cambridge University Press. (Discussion of Oman's particular monotheistic emphases.)

Elliot-Binns, J.E. (1956) *English Thought 1860–1900: The Theological Aspect*, London: Longmans, Green & Company. (Discusses the historical, philosophical, theological and social setting of English theology in the indicated period.)

Healey, F.G. (1965) *Religion and Reality: The Theology of John Oman*, Edinburgh: Oliver & Boyd. (General discussion of Oman's theological perspective.)

Horton, W.M. *Contemporary English Theology*, London: SCM Press. (Treats pre- and post-First-World-War English theology from a perceptive American perspective.)

Langford, T. (1969) *In Search of Foundations: English Theology 1900–1920*, Nashville, TN: Abington Press. (Presentation of English theological thought in its cultural and philosophical context; good bibliography.)

Mozley, J.K. (1951) *Some Tendencies in British Theology*, London: SPCK. (Discussion of British theology from *Lux Mundi* (1889) to the thought of Oman.)

KEITH E. YANDELL

OMNIPOTENCE

Traditional theism understands God to be the greatest being possible. According to the traditional conception, God possesses certain great-making properties or perfections, including necessary existence, omniscience, perfect goodness, and omnipotence. Philosophical reflection upon the notion of omnipotence raises many puzzles and apparent paradoxes. Could an omnipotent agent create a stone so massive that that agent could not move it? It might seem that however this question is answered, it turns out that, paradoxically, an omnipotent agent is not truly all-powerful. Could such an agent have the power to create or overturn necessary truths of logic and mathematics? Could an agent of this kind bring about or alter the past? Is the notion of an omnipotent agent other than God an intelligible one? Could two omnipotent agents exist at the same time? If there are states of affairs which an omnipotent agent is powerless to bring about, then how is the notion of omnipotence to be intelligibly defined? Yet if the notion of omnipotence is unintelligible, then traditional theism must be false. Another obstacle to traditional theism arises if it is impossible for God to be both perfectly good, and omnipotent. If an omnipotent God is powerless to do evil, then how can God be omnipotent?

1   **What omnipotence means**
2   **The paradox of the stone**

1 What omnipotence means

The intelligibility of the divine attributes, considered individually and in combination, is a central concern among philosophers of religion. Among the attributes of the God of traditional theism is omnipotence. Some philosophers have tried to understand omnipotence in terms of the power to perform some suitably comprehensive set of tasks. Examples of tasks are to create a stone too massive for oneself to lift, to do evil, or to make oneself non-omnipotent. Experience has proved, however, that such an approach to the analysis of omnipotence is fruitless. More promising is the effort of some philosophers (such as Rosenkrantz and Hoffman 1980a, Flint and Freddoso 1983, and Wierenga 1989) to analyse omnipotence in terms of the power to bring about a suitably defined set of states of affairs (where a state of affairs is a propositional entity, which either obtains or fails to obtain).

Two senses of 'omnipotence' come to mind. First, there is the notion of having it within one's power to bring about any state of affairs whatsoever, including impossible and necessary states of affairs. Descartes, in the *Meditations* (1641), appears to have had a notion close to this one. But, as Aquinas in his *Summa theologiae* (1266–73) and Maimonides in his *Guide for the Perplexed* (c.1190) recognized, it is not possible for an agent to bring about an impossible state of affairs (for example, there being a colourless red object), since if it were, it would be possible for an impossible state of affairs to obtain, which is a manifest contradiction. Nor is it possible for an agent to bring about a necessary state of affairs (for example, any red object's being coloured). If it is possible for an agent, a, to bring about a necessary state of affairs, s, then possibly, (1) a brings about s, and (2) if a had not acted, then s would not have obtained. But a necessary state of affairs obtains whether or not anyone acts, so (2) is false. Therefore, it is not possible for an agent to bring about a necessary state of affairs. The first sense of omnipotence is consequently unintelligible.

A second sense of 'omnipotence' is that of maximal power. In this sense, the overall power of an omnipotent being could not be exceeded by any being. It does not follow that a being with maximal power can bring about every state of affairs, since doing so is impossible. Nor does it follow that a being with maximal power can bring about everything that any other being can bring about. From the fact that a can bring about s, and b cannot, it does not follow that a is overall more powerful than b, for it might be that b can bring about some thing or things that a cannot. This is the only sense of omnipotence that may be coherent. Thus, if a putative analysis of the concept of omnipotence is offered in defence of its intelligibility, then it should be an attempt to analyse the concept of maximal power.

Power is not the same thing as ability. Power is ability plus opportunity. A being who had maximal ability but was prevented by circumstances from exercising it would not be omnipotent. Necessarily, nothing prevents an omnipotent being from exercising its powers when it wills to do so.

Some have thought that there could be two (or more) omnipotent agents, a_1 and a_2, at the same time, t. If this were possible, then it could happen that at t, a_1 strives to move a button (while remaining omnipotent), and at t, a_2 strives to keep that button still (while remaining omnipotent). In a case of this kind, the button would be unaffected (as to its motion or rest) by either one of them. Thus, in such a case, a_1 would at t lack the power to move the button, and a_2 would at t lack the power to keep the button still. Since it is absurd to suppose that an omnipotent being lacks the power to move a button or the power to keep it still, neither a_1 nor a_2 is omnipotent. Hence, there could not be two omnipotent beings at the same time.

Could there be a contingently omnipotent being? This seems possible on first thought, but the following argument seems to show the opposite. A being cannot have any perfection unless it has every perfection. This, together with the assumptions that a contingently omnipotent being has a perfection, and that an essentially omnipotent being has a perfection (namely essential omnipotence) which a contingently omnipotent being lacks, implies that contingent omnipotence is impossible.

In addition, assuming that traditional theism is true, God has necessary existence and is essentially omnipotent. Since there could not be more than one omnipotent being, it follows that there could not be a contingently omnipotent being (see NECESSARY BEING).

However, the first argument against the possibility of contingent omnipotence is incorrect. For example, a perfect triangle need not have the perfections of omniscience or omnipotence. Thus, it is false that a being cannot have a perfection unless it has every perfection.

The second argument against the possibility of contingent omnipotence presupposes traditional theism. But in analysing omnipotence, it is preferable to remain neutral about whether theism is true or false. In that case, omnipotence will not be assumed to be attributable only to the God of traditional theism or only to an essentially omnipotent being.

2 The paradox of the stone

One challenge to the coherence of the notion of omnipotence is based on the so-called paradox or riddle of the stone. Can an omnipotent agent, a, bring it about that there is a stone of some mass, m, which a cannot move? If the answer is 'yes', then there is a state of affairs that a cannot bring about, namely (i) that a stone of mass m moves. On the other hand, if the answer is 'no', then there is a different state of affairs that a cannot bring about, namely (ii) that there is a stone of mass m, which a cannot move. Thus, it might appear that omnipotence is paradoxical. But the appearance of paradox can be overcome if either (i) or (ii) is impossible, for, as has been seen, an omnipotent agent need not be able to bring about an impossible state of affairs. If, on the other hand, both (i) and (ii) are possible, then it is possible for some omnipotent agent to bring it about that both (i) and (ii) obtain, though at different times, and so there is a second solution to the paradox.

The first solution comes into play when there is an *essentially* omnipotent agent, a_1. The state of affairs of a_1's being not omnipotent is impossible. Therefore, a_1 cannot bring it about that a_1 is not omnipotent. Since, necessarily, an omnipotent agent can move any stone, no matter how massive, state of affairs (ii) is impossible.

The second solution presupposes the only other alternative: that there is a *contingently* omnipotent agent, a_2. In this case, a_2's being non-omnipotent is a possible state of affairs; and presumably, it *is* possible for a_2 to bring it about that a_2 is non-omnipotent. So a_2 can create and move a stone of mass m when omnipotent, and *then* bring it about that a_2 is not omnipotent and is unable to move that stone of mass m. Thus, a_2 is able to bring about both (i) and (ii), but only if they obtain at different times.

3 Things that an omnipotent agent is powerless to do

At this point, it might be thought that an analysis of omnipotence could be simply stated as the power to bring it about that any contingent state of affairs obtains. However, the following contingent states of affairs show that this simple analysis fails:

(a) A stone rolled.
(b) A stone rolls at t (where t is a past time).
(c) Socrates walks for the first time.
(d) The Nile floods an odd number of times less than four.

(e) A ball rolls and no omnipotent agent ever exists.
(f) Jones freely decides to walk.

(a) is a past state of affairs. Since it is impossible for any agent to have power over the past (this is the so-called 'necessity of the past'), no agent, not even an omnipotent one, can bring about (a). Similarly, although (b) can be brought about prior to t, the necessity of the past implies that even an omnipotent agent cannot bring about (b) after t. In the case of (c), prior to Socrates' first walk, an omnipotent agent can bring about (c). But once Socrates has walked, even an omnipotent agent cannot bring about (c). With respect to (d), before the Nile's third flooding, an omnipotent agent can bring about (d), whereas after the Nile's third flooding, even an omnipotent agent is powerless to bring about (d). (e) presents a special problem. While it is clear that (e) could not be brought about by an omnipotent agent, some philosophers (such as Hoffman and Rosenkrantz 1988) argue that it is possible for a non-omnipotent agent to bring about (e) by rolling a ball when, in fact, no omnipotent agent ever exists. (Recall that a maximally powerful being need not be able to bring about every state of affairs that any other being can.) Finally, an omnipotent agent other than Jones cannot bring about (f) if the libertarian theory of free will is correct, but apparently a non-omnipotent agent – namely Jones – can bring about (f).

Thus, an adequate analysis of omnipotence should not require an omnipotent agent to have the power to bring about (a), (b), (c), (d), (e) or (f), assuming in the case of (f) that libertarianism is correct. Given the seemingly wide disparity among contingent states of affairs (a)–(f), it might be conjectured that there is no analysis of omnipotence that can deal adequately with all of them while capturing the intuitive scope of power involved in omnipotence. Yet the following observations set the stage for just such an analysis.

For an adequate analysis of omnipotence, identifying some distinctive features of (a)–(f) might enable one to state an analysis of this kind. First, as (a) is not possibly brought about by any agent, an omnipotent agent should not be required to have the power to bring about a state of affairs unless it is possible that some agent brings about that state of affairs. Second, although (b) and (c) are possibly brought about by some agent, they are not repeatable – in other words, it is not possible that they obtain, then fail to obtain, and then obtain once more. (Note that the conditions that do not require an omnipotent agent to be able to bring about (a) and (b) also do not require that agent to be able to bring about impossible or necessary states of affairs.) Third, while (d) is repeatable, it is not unrestrictedly repeatable – it cannot obtain, then fail to obtain, then obtain again, and so forth throughout all of time. Fourth, even if (e) is unrestrictedly repeatable, it is a complex state of affairs, namely a conjunctive state of affairs, whose second conjunct is not repeatable. Reflection on the nature of repeatability and its relation to the power to bring about states of affairs leads to the conclusion that an omnipotent agent ought not to be required to have the power to bring about either a state of affairs which is not unrestrictedly repeatable or a conjunctive state of affairs one of whose conjuncts is not unrestrictedly repeatable. Finally, although (f) is unrestrictedly repeatable, (f) is identifiable with or analysable as a conjunctive state of affairs having three conjuncts, whose second conjunct is not possibly brought about by anyone. The conjunctive state of affairs in question can be informally expressed as follows: (I) Jones decides to walk, and (II) there is no *antecedent* sufficient causal condition of Jones' deciding to walk, and (III) there is no concurrent sufficient causal condition of Jones' deciding to walk. Because, as we have explained, it is impossible for an agent to have power over the past, the state of affairs which is the second conjunct of this conjunctive state of affairs is not possibly brought about by anyone. Hence, an omnipotent being should not be required to have the power to bring about a state of affairs which is identifiable with or analysable as a conjunctive state of affairs one of whose conjuncts is not possibly brought about by anyone.

4 An analysis of omnipotence

Based on insights gleaned from the preceding discussion, omnipotence can be analysed in three steps as follows (where '$=_{df.}$' means 'is defined as'):

Step 1. The period of time t is a sufficient interval for $s =_{df.} s$ is a state of affairs such that: it is possible that s obtains at a time-period which has the duration of t.

Step 2. A state of affairs s is unrestrictedly repeatable $=_{df.} s$ is possibly such that: $(\forall n)(\exists t_1)(\exists t_2)(\exists t_3)\dots(\exists t_n)(t_1 < t_2 < t_3 < \dots < t_n$ are periods of time which are *sufficient intervals* for s, & s obtains at t_1, s does not obtain at t_2, s obtains at $t_3,\dots$, s obtains at $t_n \equiv n$ is odd).

In the preceding definition, n ranges over all natural numbers, and $t_1,\dots,t_n$ are non-overlapping. Also, it is assumed for the purposes of this definition that either it is possible that time has no beginning, or it is possible that time has no end.

Step 3. (D1) x is omnipotent at $t =_{df.} (\forall s)$ (it is possible for some agent to bring about $s \rightarrow$ at t, x has it within his power to bring about s).

In (D1), x ranges over agents, and s over states of affairs which satisfy the following condition:

(C1) (Ci) s is unrestrictedly repeatable, and of the form 'in n minutes, p', & (p is a complex state of affairs $\rightarrow$ each of the components of p is unrestrictedly repeatable & possibly brought about by someone), or (Cii) p is of the form 'q forever after', where q is a state of affairs which satisfies (Ci).

Two technical explanations concerning (C1) are in order. First, n ranges over real numbers, and p is not itself equivalent to a state of affairs of the form 'in n minutes, r', where n is not equal to zero. Second, by a *complex* state of affairs is meant a state of affairs which is either constructible out of other states of affairs by use of the logical apparatus of first-order logic enriched with whatever modalities one chooses to employ, or else analysable (in the sense of a philosophical analysis) into a state of affairs which is so constructible. Accordingly, a *component* or *part* of a complex state of affairs s is one of those states of affairs out of which s, or an analysis of s, is constructed.

Happily, (D1) does not require an omnipotent agent to be able to bring about impossible or necessary states of affairs, or states of affairs such as (a)–(f). Moreover, (D1) does not imply that an omnipotent agent lacks any powers which an agent of this kind ought to possess. This is because an agent's bringing about a state of affairs can always be 'cashed out' in terms of that agent's bringing about an unrestrictedly repeatable state of affairs which satisfies the antecedent of the definiens of (D1). In other words, necessarily, for any state of affairs s, if an agent a brings about s, then either s is an unrestrictedly repeatable state of affairs which satisfies the antecedent of the definiens of (D1), or if not, then a brings about s by bringing about q, where q is an unrestrictedly repeatable state of affairs which satisfies the antecedent of the definiens of (D1). For example, an omnipotent agent can bring about the state of affairs 'that in one minute, Socrates walks for the first time' by bringing about the state of affairs 'that in one minute, Socrates walks', when this walk is Socrates' first. And while the former state of affairs is a non-repeatable one which (D1) does not require an omnipotent agent to be able to bring about, the latter state of affairs is an unrestrictedly repeatable state of affairs which (D1) does require an omnipotent agent to be able to bring about.

5 On the compatibility of God's omnipotence and perfect goodness

Some philosophers have thought that omnipotence is incompatible with certain other attributes. In particular, it has been argued that traditional theism, which posits a necessary, essentially omnipotent, essentially omniscient and essentially perfectly good deity, is faced with this problem. The charge has been that such a deity lacks the power to bring about evil, while non-omnipotent (and morally imperfect) beings such as ourselves possess this power. The exact form of the problem varies depending on what exactly the relation between God and evil is supposed to be. Suppose that if God exists, then this is a best possible world. Then if God exists, there could not be an evil unless it is necessary for some greater good, and any state of affairs containing evil incompatible with there being a maximally good world is impossible. Such a state of affairs could not be brought about by any agent whatsoever. In that case, any evil that any person brings about (moral evil) or that occurs in nature (natural evil) is necessary for some greater good. Assume that God exists and that, for instance, some person, S, brings it about than an evil, e, exists. Then, given our assumptions, since S's bringing it about that e exists is necessary for some greater good, it is compatible with God's perfect goodness that God brings it about that S brings it about that e exists. On the other hand, if God exists and some or all evil is metaphysically incompatible with this being a maximally good world, then neither God nor anybody else has the power to bring about that evil. The main idea here is that if God's nature places moral restrictions on the nature of the universe and on what God can bring about, then it also places parallel restrictions on what any other agents can bring about. So, for example, if there being suffering in the universe is necessary for this being a maximally good world, then God cannot create a (maximally good) world without the presence of suffering of the appropriate sort (see EVIL, PROBLEM OF).

Other theists, for example, Alvin Plantinga, do not hold that God's existence implies the existence of a maximally good world, but do hold that God seeks to create as good a world as God can (see Plantinga 1974). They allow that there may be evil that is unnecessary for any greater good that outweighs it. An evil of this sort involves free decisions of agents other than God which God does not prevent but which these other agents can prevent. Plantinga argues that God does no wrong in permitting an evil of this kind because God is powerless to bring about a crucial good – the existence of free human agents – without there being such an evil. Alternatively, it might be argued that God does no wrong in this sort of case because God does not know how to do better, since such knowledge is impossible. However, as an omnipotent God is *not* required to have power over free decisions of agents other than God, it can be seen

that on these views, God's omnipotence and perfect goodness can be logically reconciled to the extent indicated along the lines taken above in discussing the view that God's existence requires a maximally good world. Of course, nothing that has been said here decides the issue of how much, if any, evil is compatible with the existence of the traditional God.

See also: FREEDOM, DIVINE; GOD, CONCEPTS OF; GOODNESS, PERFECT §§2–3; MONOTHEISM; PROCESS THEISM

References and further reading

* Aquinas, T. (1266–73) *Summa theologica*, Chicago, IL: Great Books, Encyclopedia Britannica, 1952, vol. 1. (A readily available complete edition with a useful bibliography; see particularly Ia, 25, 3.)
* Descartes, R. (1641) *Meditations on First Philosophy*, trans. J. Cottingham, R. Stoothoff and D. Murdoch, in *The Philosophical Writings of Descartes*, vol. 2, Cambridge: Cambridge University Press, 1984. (The standard edition; see particularly meditation 1.)
* Flint, T. and Freddoso, A. (1983) 'Maximal Power', in A. Freddoso (ed.) *The Existence and Nature of God*, Notre Dame, IN: University of Notre Dame Press, 81–113. (An attempt to analyse omnipotence.)
  Hoffman, J. (1979) 'Can God Do Evil?', *Southern Journal of Philosophy* 17 (2): 213–20. (Discusses the question of the coherence of divine omnipotence and perfect goodness.)
* Hoffman, J. and Rosenkrantz, G. (1988) 'Omnipotence Redux', *Philosophy and Phenomenological Research* 49 (2): 283–301. (Critically surveys several analyses of omnipotence in the recent literature.)
* Maimonides (c.1190) *Guide for the Perplexed*, trans. M. Friedlander, London: George Routledge & Sons, 1904. (See part I, chapter 15. This edition is readily available in paperback published by Dover Books.)
  Pike, N. (1969) 'Omnipotence and God's Ability to Sin', *American Philosophical Quarterly* 6 (3): 208–16. (Argues that divine omnipotence and perfect goodness are incompatible.)
* Plantinga, A. (1974) *God, Freedom, and Evil*, New York: Harper & Row. (Important free-will defence of theism against the problem of evil.)
* Rosenkrantz, G. and Hoffman, J. (1980a) 'What an Omnipotent Agent Can Do', *International Journal for Philosophy of Religion* 11 (1): 1–19. (The original version of the analysis of omnipotence presented in the text above.)
—— (1980b) 'The Omnipotence Paradox, Modality,

and Time', *Southern Journal of Philosophy* 18 (4): 473–9. (Discusses the problem of the stone; contains a useful bibliography concerning this issue.)

* Wierenga, E. (1989) *The Nature of God*, Ithaca, NY: Cornell University Press. (Wide-ranging discussion of recent work on omnipotence with a defence of the author's analysis; see chapter 1.)

JOSHUA HOFFMAN
GARY ROSENKRANTZ

OMNIPRESENCE

Western Scripture and religious experience find God present everywhere. Western thinkers make sense of this as their concepts of God dictate. Pantheists hold that God's being everywhere is every bit of matter's being a part or an aspect of God. Panentheists say that as God is the soul of the universe, God's being everywhere is his enlivening the whole universe as souls enliven bodies. But most theists reject these views, as most think that if God is perfect, he cannot be, be made of, or be embodied in a flawed and material universe. Most theists think God intrinsically spaceless, that is, able to exist even if no space exists. Still, theists argue that God's knowledge of and power over creation make him present within it without occupying space or being embodied in matter. Some add that God is present in space not just by power and knowledge but in his very being. These try to explain a spaceless God's presence in space by likening it to the presence of a universal attribute like hardness. Hardness is not spread over hard surfaces, occupying them by having parts of itself in parts of them. Each part of a hard surface is hard. So all of hardness is in each part of a hard surface. So too, theists say, God is not spread out over space, filling parts of it with parts of himself. Rather, all of God is wholly present at each point in space and in each spatial thing.

1   Introduction
2   Omnipresence and embodiment
3   Omnipresence and divine spatiality
4   The omnipresence of a spaceless God

1   Introduction

Western Scripture vividly states that God is present everywhere. The Psalmist asks:

Where can I go from your Spirit?
Where can I flee from your presence?
If I go up to the heavens, you are there;
If I make my bed in the depths, you are there.

If I rise on the wings of the dawn, if I settle on the far side of the sea,
even there your hand will guide me, your right hand will hold me fast.

(Psalms 139: 7–10)

Theists fill out the concept of God mainly by drawing inferences from God's being perfect (see GOD, CONCEPTS OF §§2–6). Such thinking also backs the claim that God is omnipresent: a God from whose presence one could escape would be less perfect than a God inescapable.

If time and space are really one, God is omnipresent in time as in space. But most have thought of omnipresence only in relation to space, so this entry treats only space. We are present in each volume of space which includes us: the space of this room, and also this galaxy. But we are primarily present only in places we fill (I am in the galaxy because my body fills a place which is in the galaxy) and immediately present only to places directly next to our places. So if God is perfectly present to every place, he either fills or is next to each place. If nothing can exclude God, God fills not just places but the things which occupy them.

2   Omnipresence and embodiment

Pantheism is the doctrine that all material things compose or manifest one thing, which is God (see PANTHEISM). If all matter is part or an aspect of God, then God is wherever any material object is, that is, wherever God has a part or aspect. But the whole of God is not where any one part of God is, and God is not literally everywhere if there are true vacua, though he permeates all space if (say) some part of God is present in each volume of space, however small. Treatments of omnipresence should distinguish its nature (what it is to be omnipresent), cause (what makes God omnipresent) and manner (the kind of presence God has everywhere). For pantheism, then, God's omnipresence (if any) is the way space contains God; it rests on God's having every object as a part or aspect, and God is present as material objects are: parts of God in parts of a location, and the whole of God in the whole. SPINOZA (§§2–4) (if a pantheist) is an exception, claiming that though all extension is an attribute of God, and all bodies modes of God, God has no parts or at least is indivisible (*Ethics* I, props 12–13).

For Stoic panentheists, 'God' named the spirit whose body is the cosmos, and also the living cosmos that spirit enlivens. So Stoics thought that God permeates the cosmos as a soul permeates its body, sustaining the cosmos as soul sustains body. The Stoic world-soul was a fiery material stuff. So Stoics held that the stuff of God occupies space and shares spaces with all other material stuffs, which are not parts of God quite as the cosmos' fiery parts are. The Stoic theory of mixture allowed this, claiming that all ingredients of a mixture are present in each place the mixture occupies. For Stoicism, the cosmos existed amid a surrounding vacuum, and so though omnipresent in the cosmos, God was not literally present in every place. For Stoics, a finite space circumscribes God: the cosmos' dimensions are God's. To Stoics, then, God's omnipresence in the cosmos is the way he enlivens it; it rests on the world's embodying God, and God is in the world as soul in body (see STOICISM §§3–5).

One's account of omnipresence depends largely on whether one holds that:

(UB)   the universe is God's body.

Why accept (UB)? If one finds pure physicalism a persuasive metaphysic, (UB) gives God a place within it. It surely is at least easier to understand the claim that God acts if God has some sort of body; this makes his actions more like those of persons we know. The Stoics thought that only material things *can* act. TERTULLIAN agreed, and inferred that God is a body (*Against Praxeas*, ch. 7); the Stoics inferred that God must be not just material but the most perfect material thing, the cosmos (see GOD, CONCEPTS OF §3). Swinburne argues that embodiment comes in degrees, and that the way God knows and acts in the universe embodies him in it to some extent. That is one's body, Swinburne reasons, which one can control or move directly as a 'basic action', and about whose states one knows immediately (1993: 104–6). Hartshorne (1964: 200) makes the same case. Sarot (1992) argues that God has emotions which require having a body. Some feminists (for example, McFague 1987: 69–77) argue that its ethical and spiritual consequences favour (UB).

None of this is compelling. Bodiless agency, mental life and feelings are conceivable; recent philosophy of mind helps by stressing the *functional* cores of our concepts of thought, action and emotion (Alston 1989: 64–80). Further, we make God more conceivable only by moulding our idea of God more in our own image. Some degree of this is inevitable, but it is wise to minimize it if ANSELM OF CANTERBURY (§4) is right that God's greatness puts him beyond our full conceptual grasp (*Proslogion*, ch. 15). If Swinburne and Hartshorne offer more than argument by analogy, they premise that necessarily, if *x* can move *y* directly or know about *y* immediately, then *x* is embodied in *y*. This is false if telekinesis and telepathy are logically possible. For it is not plausible that while

a telepath reads my thoughts or a telekinetic moves my limbs, my body houses two persons. Finally, ethical and spiritual intuitions differ greatly, and so are frail grounds for metaphysical conclusions.

Why has mainstream Western theism so wholly rejected divine embodiment? If God is the most perfect possible being, God cannot exist only as embodied in part of the universe. For if he did, a being greater than him would be possible, namely one with just his knowledge and power, but the whole universe as a body. But even (UB) renders God physically finite if (as physicists now believe) the universe is finite. If he is physically finite, God has a surpassable value and importance; were he/the universe bigger, he might well be better.

If (UB) is true, the universe is all living matter; it is one large animal. PLATO (§16) was willing to say this (*Timaeus*, 30b–c), but few wish to follow him. Again, the universe includes many items whose inclusion in God seems beneath God's dignity. If the universe is God's body, flaws in the universe are flaws in God's body. If my body is flawed, *I* am flawed; we say that *I* have a bad back, not merely that my body has one. Thus flaws in the universe are flaws in God; and if there is in fact a problem of natural evil, the universe is flawed (see EVIL, PROBLEM OF §§1, 6). Again, if part of my body is ill, *I* am ill. But then when parts of God's body are ill, as when humans have colds, God himself is sick. Being able to be ill, however, is an imperfection.

We can damage material things. If these are parts of God's body, then we can damage God, since to damage parts of someone's body is to damage that person. We can also literally push God (or parts of God) around. Such divine vulnerability seems unbecoming. It is why the Christian doctrine of the Incarnation shocked the Greeks and provoked Chalcedonian Christology as an antidote (see INCARNATION AND CHRISTOLOGY §1).

If (UB) is true, then either necessarily God exists only if embodied, or God has a body only contingently. On the first alternative, God exists contingently (Swinburne), or the universe exists necessarily (Hartshorne); both claims are highly debatable. If God exists only if embodied, the universe *is* God; it constitutes him. But if the universe is God, it would still be God if it contained one atom less. If so, it would still be God without yet another atom, and so on, to the eventual conclusion that a universe consisting of a single atom would still be God. But a single atom is certainly destructible; hence, God is possibly destructible, and so destructible now. The universe can be caused to exist; it is quite possible that the Big Bang had a cause. So if God does not exist save as embodied in a universe, God can be caused to exist – and cannot have created the universe *ex nihilo*. Further, if we are parts of God, our freedom is a lack of divine self-control, another imperfection in God.

Finally, many scientists and philosophers think there can be other universes, not spatially or temporally connected with ours (see COSMOLOGY §3). Suppose that there is a second universe. Then if God is our universe, he cannot have made the other. His bringing it to be, an act in our time and space, would connect that universe to ours, and so the two would not be spatiotemporally discrete after all. Nor can God have both universes as bodies. If God's thoughts in one universe are spatiotemporally connected to his thoughts in the other, then God's thoughts connect the universes, making one of what we supposed were two. But one being cannot have two spatiotemporally unconnected lifelong streams of thought. So if there can be two universes and God must be embodied, there can be a universe God did not make, and there is a possible contingent object, a second universe, that God cannot create. Further, if a universe can embody a God, then if there can be two universes, arguably there can be a second God.

The view that God can exist unembodied but is contingently embodied may escape some of the difficulties raised. But its price may be emptying (UB) of most of its content: what does (UB) mean if the objections above do not apply, and how does it differ from traditional unembodied theism?

3 Omnipresence and divine spatiality

Many rabbis called God the universe's place (*makom*). St Paul said of God 'in him we live and move and have our being' (Acts 17: 27–8). Picking up this theme, Anselm declaimed to God that 'You are not in space...but all things are in you. For you are not contained by anything but rather you contain all else' (*Proslogion*, ch. 19). For Anselm, then, God's omnipresence is his way to contain all spatial things; Anselm *may* take this containment spatially (Leftow 1989).

For the Cambridge Platonist MORE (§5), all substance, as such, is extended, and infinite space is in fact God's infinite extension. Bradwardine and Oresme had moved this way in the fourteenth century; Spinoza too took infinite extension to be a divine attribute (*Ethics* I, prop. 15, proof). NEWTON (who read More) held that God is not space, but is present everywhere, and by being everywhere makes space exist. For Newton, God, by being spatial, establishes space: space is absolute in the sense of not being reducible to *creatures'* spatial relations, but reduces to or depends on God's spatiality. For BERKELEY (§§6–7), to be is to be perceived by God, and so all

space is divine perceptual space, a space 'within God's mind'. Newton was not a Berkeleyan divine phenomenalist, but his claim that infinite space is God's *sensorium* also seems to make all space God's perceptual space.

For these thinkers, even if God is immaterial, he is spatially extended or space is somehow literally in God. God's omnipresence is the way God spatially includes space and creatures; it rests on God's being, or being the foundation of, space, and God is present as space is. For all save Berkeley, the whole of God is not present at any point or to any creature.

4 The omnipresence of a spaceless God

In the West, Platonism first took God to be immaterial and intrinsically spaceless (that is, able to exist even if no space exists). So Platonism first discussed a spaceless God's presence in space. PLOTINUS (§§3–5), whose views were most important historically, took being in to be a variety of depending on. Spatially contained objects depend on their containers. So for Plotinus, spatial containment is one kind of being in. But it is not the only kind (*Enneads* VI, 4, 2). Plotinus held that soul is not in body but body in soul, and God is not in the world, but the world in God. For God to be omnipresent, he thought, is for God to 'contain' space and the world, that is, for the whole universe to depend on God. The availability since Plotinus of non-spatial uses of 'in' and 'contain' cautions us in reading the apparently spatial language of later treatments of omnipresence.

Plotinus thought God present everywhere as a whole, because each part of space causally depends on the whole of God. He took God to be whole in the whole of space and whole in each part of space, rather than having parts occupying parts of space. Plotinus noted that even if an object controlled or conserved has parts, its conserver need not have parts, for the whole controlling power is related as a whole to each part of the controlled object, rather than part by part. He used analogies to suggest that being whole in the whole and in each part is conceivable even apart from his causal account of being in. Light seems to be everywhere without being divided into parts; the sound of a spoken word seems to be present as a whole in an entire area and also in each part of that area, since in each part one can hear the whole sound. Plotinus also argued that an immaterial soul is present as a whole in its whole body and in each part of its body, claiming that only this can explain how the soul feels pain in all parts of the body. For Plotinus, then, to be omnipresent is to contain the universe; God's omnipresence rests on God's causal relation to the universe; and God's presence is causal, not spatial, and not by parts.

AUGUSTINE (§§7–8) brought Plotinus' views into Christian thought, taking over Plotinus' general account of omnipresence, his argument about the soul's presence in the body, and his analogies of light and sound. Again, like Plotinus, Augustine models God's presence on that of abstract entities. The whole of a universal such as blueness is present at each point in a blue surface; so, too, the whole of God is at each point of space. Making a blue area larger does not make it bluer; being bluer is a matter of intensity. So, too, God's presence varies intensively, not extensively. As wholly present in any space or thing, God need not be more present in a large area than in a small, but God is more present in a saint than in a sinner. A universal such as blueness is in space without having parts covering parts of space (the parts of a blue surface are parts of the surface but not of blueness); so, too, God. Blueness does not have as dimensions (limits of its spatial extent) the spatial dimensions of its location(s). For wherever it is located, blueness is whole (each point in a blue surface is fully blue) and yet also present as a whole outside that place (at other places, or outside space altogether); again, the same is true of God. The abstract-entity comparison suggests that an immaterial God can fill a place without being contained by it, excluding other things from it, or being intrinsically spatial or physical. Perfect-being theology finds presence as a whole everywhere a more perfect way to be present, making God more fully present at each place.

Augustine took God's creating and sustaining all things to provide a further sense (like Plotinus') in which he is present in them; Aquinas made the Aristotelian roots of this thinking plain (*Summa theologiae* Ia, 8, 1). Aristotle insists that agents move only by direct contact with what they move (*Physics* VII, 2). Aquinas (among others) reads this as implying that a 'contact of power' links any immaterial agent and its effects (*Summa theologiae* Ia, 8, 2 *ad*. 1; 52, 1). If two things touch (that is, are in contact), they are in some sense at the same place. On the doctrine of divine simplicity AQUINAS (§9) and other medieval thinkers shared, God is identical to God's power (*Summa contra gentiles* II, 8). So if God's power is in some way at the place of its effects, so is God. Later medieval philosophers (such as WILLIAM OF OCKHAM §9) increasingly questioned the doctrine of contact action. If action at a distance is possible, God's acting at a place does not entail that he is in any way present there. But a more basic point is that 'contact of power' seems just a metaphor. Whether or not things can act at a distance, immaterial things in no way literally touch material things.

Aquinas inherited from Lombard's *Sentences* (I, d. 37) the formula that God is in all things by power, presence and essence. Aquinas took God's indwelling by presence to be his having full, immediate knowledge of all things, and so took God's knowledge of spatial things to provide yet another sense in which God is present to them (*Summa theologiae* Ia, 8, 3). Perhaps Aquinas' thought is that if all things are present to God's knowledge, then as 'present to' is a symmetric relation, it follows that God's knowledge is present to all things, and given divine simplicity, God is identical to God's knowledge (*Summa contra gentiles* I, 45).

For Augustine and Anselm (*Monologion*, chaps 13–14), God is omnipresent because and in the sense that he creates and rules all. For Karl Barth, God rules all because he is omnipresent: 'all divine sovereignty...is based on the fact that for God nothing exists which is...not near' (1957: 461). For Aquinas, God is omnipresent because and in the sense that he knows all things immediately. For Newton, God knows because he is present:

> The *sensorium* of animals (is) that place to which the sensitive substance is present and into which the sensible images of things are carried...that there they may be perceived by their immediate presence to that substance...there is a Being, incorporeal...intelligent, omnipresent, who in infinite space, as (if) in his *sensorium*, sees the things themselves...and comprehends them wholly by their immediate presence to himself.
> (*Optics*, query 28; appended to Leibniz and Clarke [1717] 1956)

If God's omnipresence has some truly spatial meaning, it has an independent content which lets it explain other divine attributes. If it has none, the doctrine of omnipresence reduces to a metaphor for God's omniscience and creatorhood. This reduction may not be what Scriptural authors intended. Jeremiah declaims:

> 'Can anyone hide in secret places so that I cannot see him?' declares the Lord.
> 'Do I not fill heaven and earth?' declares the Lord.
> (Jeremiah 23: 24)

The suggestion seems to be that God's knowledge rests on his omnipresence, not vice versa. Again, the religious (and even more the mystical) sense of God's presence seems to be not just that God knows us or creates us, but that God is in some sense here with us. So something closer to literal spatial location seems needed. Spaceless-God accounts do not provide it, save by the abstract-entity analogy.

See also: CREATION AND CONSERVATION, RELIGIOUS DOCTRINE OF §5; OCCASIONALISM

References and further reading

* Alston, W. (1989) *Divine Nature and Human Language*, Ithaca, NY: Cornell University Press. (Important work on the concept of a bodiless God's action in the world. Clear and careful.)
* Anselm (1076) *Monologion*, in J. Hopkins and H. Richardson (eds and trans) *Anselm of Canterbury*, Toronto, Ont.: Mellen, 1974, vol. 1. (Explores God's relation to space at length.)
* —— (1077–8) *Proslogion*, in. J. Hopkins and H. Richardson (eds and trans) *Anselm of Canterbury*, Toronto, Ont.: Mellen, 1974, vol. 1. (Stresses God's 'containing' space.)
* Aquinas, T. (1259–65) *Summa contra gentiles*, trans. A. Pegis (bk 1) and J. Anderson (bk 2), Notre Dame, IN: University of Notre Dame Press, 1975. (Clear, careful statement of classical theism.)
* —— (1266–73) *Summa theologiae*, New York: Benziger Brothers, 1948. (Book 1, question 8 treats God's relation to space.)
* Aristotle (mid 4th century BC) *Physics*, trans. R. Hardie and R. Gaye, in R. McKeon (ed.) *The Basic Works of Aristotle*, New York: Random House, 1941. (Gives the view of causal agency supposed in many treatments of omnipresence.)
Augustine (417) 'Letter 187', in *Letters 165–203*, trans. W. Parsons, The Fathers of the Church, vol. 30, ed. J. DeFerrari, New York: Fathers of the Church, Inc., 1955. (His most thorough treatment of God's relation to space.)
* Barth, K. (1957) *Church Dogmatics* II: 1, ed. and trans. G.W. Bromiley and T.F. Torrance, Edinburgh: T. & T. Clark. (Treats central divine attributes including omnipresence. Rambling but interesting.)
Brom, L. van den (1993) *Divine Presence in the World*, Kampen: Kok Pharos. (Idiosyncratic argument for a spatial God; wide in scope.)
* Hartshorne, C. (1964) *Man's Vision of God*, Hamden, CT: Archon. (Freewheeling case for and depiction of an embodied God.)
Jantzen, G. (1984) *God's World, God's Body*, Philadelphia, PA: Westminster. (Clear exposition and defence of the claim that the universe is God's body.)
Koyré, A. (1957) *From the Closed World to the Infinite Universe*, Baltimore, MD: Johns Hopkins Press. (Valuable study of interaction between views of divine omnipresence and developing views of space.)
* Leftow, B. (1989) 'Anselm on Omnipresence', *The New Scholasticism* 63 (3): 326–57. (Reads Anselm's talk of God containing the world spatially.)
* Leibniz, G.W. and Clarke, S. (1717) *The Leibniz–Clarke Correspondence*, ed. H.G. Alexander, Manchester: Manchester University Press, 1956. (Includes relevant extracts from Newton.)
* McFague, S. (1987) *Models of God*, Philadelphia, PA: Fortress. (Examines the ethical and spiritual advantages of taking the universe to be God's body.)
* Plato (c.366–360 BC) *Timaeus*, trans. B. Jowett, in E. Hamilton and H. Cairns (eds) *Collected Dialogues of Plato*, Princeton, NJ: Princeton University Press, 1961. (His cosmology, depicting the material world as ensouled and alive.)
* Plotinus (c.250–66) *Enneads* VI, trans. A.H. Armstrong, Cambridge, MA: Loeb Classical Library, Harvard University Press, 1988. (Seminal early treatment of spaceless beings' presence in space.)
* Sarot, M. (1992) *God, Possibility and Corporeality*, Kampen: Kok Pharos. (Case for divine embodiment, with encyclopedic references to literature.)
* Spinoza, B. (1676) *Ethics*, in E. Curley (trans.) *The Collected Works of Spinoza*, Princeton, NJ: Princeton University Press, 1985, vol. 1. (Book 1 gives his theory of a spatial God.)
* Swinburne, R. (1993) *The Coherence of Theism*, revised edn, New York: Oxford University Press. (Clear treatment of many issues in philosophical theology; discusses omnipresence, disembodied agency and partial divine embodiment.)
* Tertullian (c.213) *Against Praxeas*, in A. Roberts and J. Donaldson (eds) *The Ante-Nicene Fathers*, Peabody, MA: Hendrickson, 1994, vol. 3. (Second-century Christian polemic; treats God as embodied.)
Wainwright, W. (1987) 'God's World, God's Body', in T. Morris (ed.) *The Concept of God*, New York: Oxford University Press, 72–87. (Fine, clear discussion of pros and cons of divine embodiment.)

BRIAN LEFTOW

OMNISCIENCE

The concept of omniscience has received great attention in the history of Western philosophy, principally because of its connections with the Western religious tradition, which views God as perfect in all respects, including as a knower. Omniscience has often been understood as knowledge of all true propositions, and though several objections to any simple propositional account of omniscience have been offered, many philosophers continue to endorse such an analysis. Advocates of divine omniscience have discussed many problems connected with both the extent of omniscience and the relation between this property and other alleged divine attributes. Three such issues are: Can an omniscient being properly be viewed as immutable? Would an omniscient being have knowledge of the future, and is such knowledge consistent with our future actions' being genuinely free? And should omniscience be thought of as including middle knowledge? That is, would an omniscient being know (but have no control over) what other free beings would in fact freely do if placed in various different situations?

1 **Omniscience and perfection**
2 **The analysis of omniscience**
3 **Omniscience, foreknowledge and freedom**
4 **Omniscience and middle knowledge**

1 Omniscience and perfection

The concept of omniscience, though of considerable philosophical interest in itself, has attracted enormous attention throughout the history of philosophy primarily because of its theological connections. Most Western theists have embraced a picture of God as a being perfect in all respects, and this commitment has naturally led philosophers in this tradition to investigate the notion of noetic perfection. Such perfection is plausibly thought to entail omniscience – knowledge of everything. Hence the view that God is omniscient has been commonplace in Western monotheism.

Of course, to endorse this claim of divine omniscience is to open the door to several obvious questions. How exactly is omniscience to be understood? Of what is an omniscient being knowledgeable? And are there not reasons (related to time and human freedom) to suspect that omniscience might be a more limited perfection than one might initially have thought?

2 The analysis of omniscience

At first glance, the concept of omniscience, unlike many other divine attributes, would seem to be open to a very simple and direct analysis: a being is omniscient if and only if it knows all true propositions. Many philosophers would contend that such an analysis is indeed fully adequate. Still, questions have been raised.

Some, following Aquinas, have denied that perfect knowledge is properly thought of as propositional in structure. Our need to carve up our acquaintance with reality via discrete, complex propositions, it is argued,

is a sign of our imperfection. A truly perfect knower would have no need for propositional knowledge, but instead would possess a simple and immediate intuitive awareness of reality. Many of the advocates of this position see it as flowing from the notion of divine simplicity, an attribute which has received renewed attention in recent years (see SIMPLICITY, DIVINE). Most philosophers, though, are reluctant to ascribe absolute simplicity to God; not coincidentally, perhaps, the view that God's knowledge is wholly non-propositional is also a minority view.

However, the analysis of omniscience offered above can also be questioned even by those who view divine knowledge as propositional. Assuming that God knows all true propositions, one might argue, his knowledge would still be imperfect if he knows *only* propositions. Three types of knowledge which supposedly go beyond the propositional are of particular interest here.

The first is *de re* knowledge, knowledge of things rather than knowledge of propositions. *De re* knowledge often appears to be present when the corresponding propositional, or *de dicto*, belief is not. For example, if JoAnn mistakenly believes that my pet iguana Willard is an alligator, then she might know *de re* of my pet iguana that he is green, even though the *de dicto* belief that my pet iguana is green is one that she rejects. Though the distinction between *de re* knowledge and propositional knowledge seems reasonable, this distinction may not require any emendation of the analysis of omniscience, since it is not clear that a being who knows all true propositions (including such truths as that Willard is an iguana) would be lacking any *de re* knowledge.

A second and similar objection to the propositional analysis of omniscience focuses on *de se* knowledge, knowledge of oneself. Such knowledge, one might contend, can be present even in the absence of the corresponding *de dicto* knowledge. If Anastasia, hospitalized with amnesia and unaware of her name, reads an old newspaper account of her early life, she may well know *of herself* that she is in hospital, even though she does not believe that Anastasia is in hospital. Furthermore, one might question whether anyone distinct from Anastasia *could* possess the exact *de se* knowledge she has. Some defenders of the propositional analysis attempt to deal with this *de se* objection in a manner similar to the *de re* one: complete propositional knowledge, they argue, rules out any absence of knowledge which is held *de se*. Such responses call upon us to view Anastasia's *de se* knowledge as knowledge of a special type of proposition (perhaps involving her individual essence or haecceity), one which someone distinct from Anastasia could know, and one which anyone who knows all true propositions would know. Since many would question the existence of such special propositions, though, this type of response is quite controversial (for further discussion, see Wierenga 1989).

The third objection to the propositional analysis suggests that there is a distinctive qualitative dimension to certain kinds of knowledge which is ignored by that analysis. For example, even the most exhaustive propositional knowledge about chocolate leaves out a crucial element in a complete knowledge of chocolate – namely, knowing what chocolate tastes like. A being who knew all true propositions about chocolate, but who lacked actual acquaintance with its taste, could not be said to have perfect knowledge. Various responses to this objection are available. Some defenders of the propositional analysis flatly deny that experience of the sort suggested is required for one's knowledge of chocolate to be complete; others agree that we would expect a perfect being to possess such qualitative awareness, but deny that it should be thought of as knowledge in anything more than an analogical sense.

Though the three objections discussed here pose significant problems for the propositional analysis, problems sufficient to have led some philosophers to complicate or abandon it, none is clearly decisive, and many advocates of the propositional view remain. Whatever one's verdict on this matter, though, one who embraces the belief that God is omniscient faces many difficult questions concerning both the scope of omniscience and the compatibility of divine omniscience with other attributes commonly ascribed to God.

One such question is how a God who has perfect knowledge of our ever-changing world could himself be utterly immutable. Since immutability itself is often viewed as a perfection, and since it seems to be entailed by two other attributes (simplicity and eternity) frequently deemed essential to a perfect being, many theists are strongly inclined to view God as unchanging (see IMMUTABILITY). Yet complete knowledge seems to require change on the part of the knower whenever there is change on the part of that which is known. In the face of this objection, some theists have abandoned the view that God is utterly immutable; they suggest that so long as God is stable in his powers, constant in his providential care for his creatures, resolute in his intentions, and so on, we need not be concerned by trivial changes in his noetic activity. Other theists have denied that the argument forces us to jettison immutability. For example, advocates of divine eternity have maintained that God's eternal perspective would allow him (in a sense) simultaneously to view events that are not simultaneous from our perspective; hence, his knowledge of

all such events need imply no change in him (see ETERNITY). Though fraught with the potential for (and, as critics see it, the actuality of) paradox, this view has been developed with ingenuity by several writers (see especially Stump and Kretzmann 1981).

In addition to the question concerning immutability, two other significant issues connected with omniscience have received much critical attention. First, does an omniscient being know what we *will* freely do in the future circumstances which will in fact obtain? Second, does an omniscient being know what we *would* freely do were other circumstances to obtain?

3   Omniscience, foreknowledge and freedom

If God is all-knowing, it seems reasonable to assume that he knows not only what did happen and what is happening, but also what will happen. But how could comprehensive divine foreknowledge be compatible with the contingency of what is foreknown? In particular, how could our actions be free, be such that we could have done otherwise, if an infallible God knew in advance what we would do? This question has vexed some of the greatest minds in Western history, from the Greek tragedians (especially Sophocles) to such Christian luminaries as AUGUSTINE (§§6, 10), AQUINAS and Jonathan EDWARDS (§2); in contemporary philosophy of religion, it remains perhaps the most-discussed problem connected with the attribute of omniscience.

Though the problem has been explicated in many different ways, perhaps its strongest form can be presented as follows. Suppose God knows that I will perform a certain action tomorrow – for example:

(1)   God knows that I will go horseback riding tomorrow.

Clearly, this cannot be knowledge that God has recently acquired; if his omniscience is (so to speak) a stable feature, it must be knowledge he has always possessed. So:

(2)   God knew last year that I will go riding tomorrow.

But (2) tells us about what was true in the past, and we generally think that what happened in the past is necessary – not, perhaps, logically necessary, but necessary in the sense of being fixed, settled and beyond anyone's control. In this sense of necessity (which is variously called temporal necessity, accidental necessity and necessity *per accidens*), it follows from (2) that:

(3)   It is necessary that God knew that I will go riding tomorrow.

Of course, no one can know something which is false. Indeed, in the case of God, traditional theists insist that God cannot so much as believe something which is false. So from (3) it follows that:

(4) If God knew that I will go riding tomorrow, then I will go riding tomorrow.

Now, (3) tells us that a certain truth is beyond anyone's control, while (4) spells out a logical consequence of that truth. But surely what follows logically from something which is necessary must itself be necessary in that same sense. If (3) and (4) are beyond dispute, then, it follows that we are also saddled with:

(5) It is necessary that I will go riding tomorrow.

And since what I do by necessity is not something over which I hold the reins of power, it follows that my act of riding tomorrow is beyond my control, and hence will not be a free action. As this argument form could evidently be unharnessed from our equine example, the conclusion to which we are led is that no action can be free if God possesses foreknowledge.

Responses to this argument are many and varied; virtually no step is beyond dispute. Some have reacted by accepting the conclusion that foreknowledge rules out freedom and consequently rejecting the claim that our actions are free. Others who embrace the incompatibilist conclusion (the thesis that foreknowledge and freedom are incompatible) react in the opposite way: instead of denying freedom, they deny foreknowledge, and so deny that a premise such as (1) is ever true of a free action. Rather than denying that God is omniscient, many such incompatibilists suggest that omniscience does not require foreknowledge. Just as omnipotence does not entail the power to do what cannot be done (see OMNIPOTENCE §§1–3), so, they argue, omniscience does not include the power to know what cannot be known; since foreknowledge of free actions has been shown by this argument to be impossible, we ought not expect an omniscient being to have such foreknowledge (see Hasker 1989). Other incompatibilists, especially those favourably disposed towards the notion of divine eternity, criticize the argument's blatantly putting God in the temporal realm. No divine cognitive activity, they insist, takes place in time, and hence the use of ordinary tensed propositions to refer to such activity is out of place. For such incompatibilists, (1) and especially (2) ought to be rejected.

Compatibilist rejoinders (that is, responses by those who see foreknowledge and freedom as compatible) come in two basic forms. The first of these is to deny that (3) follows from (2). Many facts about the past – those commonly called hard facts about the past – are exclusively about the past, and these do have the kind of necessity at issue in this discussion. But (2) is not exclusively about the past; it is about the future as much as it is about the past, and hence qualifies as only a soft fact about the past. Unlike hard facts about the past, soft facts need not be seen as necessary; hence, (3) does not follow from (2), and the argument dissolves.

This type of response, which draws its inspiration from William of Ockham, is often referred to as the Ockhamist response. An amazing amount of literature on this position has been generated and a large number of variations on it proposed. Various ways of understanding the notion of temporal or accidental necessity have been offered, and numerous means (often of great technical complexity) of distinguishing hard from soft facts have been formulated (see Plantinga 1986). Some commentators have even suggested that the hard/soft distinction may be too coarse for the problem at hand: even if (2) turned out to be a soft fact about the past, it might well have a hard 'core' – such as the fact that God *believed* last year that I will ride tomorrow – which is sufficient for an analogue of the incompatibilist argument to succeed.

The second basic form of compatibilist response is to deny that (5) follows from (3) and (4). More generally, such a response denies that accidental necessity is closed under entailment or logical implication; that is, it suggests that an accidentally necessary proposition can entail a proposition that is not accidentally necessary. Such a response, which was suggested by the sixteenth-century Spanish theologian Luis de MOLINA (§§1–3) and has come to be known as the Molinist response, seems most plausible when accidental necessity is understood as applying to those truths which are beyond our ability to cause to be false (see MOLINISM). So understood, (3) seems clearly true (at least as long as we grant that we lack causal power over the past), as does (4), but (5) does not clearly follow. If we already knew that I had no power to cause my *not* riding tomorrow, the inference might be uncontroversial; but, of course, my causal impotence with regard to the future is what the argument is trying to prove and hence can hardly be assumed in this context.

It has been suggested that whether an Ockhamist or a Molinist response to the argument is more appropriate depends upon how accidental necessity is analysed. Under some interpretations of necessity (ones which equate the accidentally necessary with that which I cannot cause to be false), (3) will follow from (2), but (5) will not follow from (3) and (4). Under other interpretations (ones which equate the accidentally necessary with that which would be true no matter what I might do), (5) will be derivable from (3) and (4), but (3) will not follow from (2). On this view, the incompatibilist argument derives whatever plausibility it has from equivocation.

4 Omniscience and middle knowledge

Closely related to the issues discussed in the preceding section is the question of middle knowledge. Molinists have claimed that between God's natural knowledge (of necessary truths not under his control) and his free knowledge (of contingent truths under his control) is a third category of divine knowledge called middle knowledge – knowledge of contingent truths not under God's control. The most significant components of middle knowledge, according to Molinists, are the counterfactuals of creaturely freedom. These are conditional statements specifying, for any creature God might create and any situation in which that creature might be placed and left free, what it would freely do if placed in that situation. Molinists insist that, while there are truths of this sort, God would have no control over them because such control would conflict with creatures' being free in the full-fledged libertarian sense.

As Molinists see it, counterfactuals of creaturely freedom help us to understand how it is that God knows the future. Prior to any creative decision on his part, God knows via middle knowledge how any set of creatures he might create would freely respond to any creative action he might perform. Using this knowledge, God can decide which beings he will create in which situations. Given this decision, he can know immediately what free actions will in fact be performed. Assuming that all other facts about the future result either from necessary truths or from other divine decisions (for example, regarding which causal laws to establish and when, if ever, to intervene in their normal operations), it follows that God's foreknowledge would be not only complete, but also in no sense dependent upon his observing or being affected by that which he foreknew.

If God possesses middle knowledge, though, its value to him far exceeds its ability to produce foreknowledge. For central to the tradition is the claim that God not only knows what will happen, but directs the course of events; he is a sovereign, provident deity, not an all-knowing but passive witness to earthly occurrences. Middle knowledge gives God the means to exercise such providence in a very strong sense, for it allows him a clear way to incorporate even the free actions of his creatures in a complete and specific providential plan.

The advantages middle knowledge would offer in constructing a coherent picture of an omniscient God are widely, though not universally, acknowledged. Also recognized is the fact that there is a strong *prima facie* case for thinking that an omniscient being would know the sort of truths which compose middle knowledge. On the surface, it surely looks as though counterfactuals of the sort at issue – such as 'If I were to go to the doctor tomorrow, the nurse would take my blood pressure' – have a truth value, one which we often know and upon which we base our actions. Even when we do not know whether such a conditional is true or false, our natural assumption is that there is a fact of the matter here, a fact which we would like to know and which any omniscient being would have to know.

Despite its theoretical fecundity and initial plausibility, middle knowledge has been the subject of enormous controversy, and several powerful arguments have been marshalled against it. Some critics, following the Thomistic attack initiated by Molina's contemporary BÁÑEZ, have charged that the Molinist position is founded on a view of freedom which is metaphysically and theologically misguided. God's sovereignty, they have contended, would be compromised were he powerless in the face of contingent truths about his creatures. A careful analysis of the notion of freedom, they suggest, allows us to see the counterfactuals in question as subject to divine control.

A more common line of attack among contemporary philosophers of religion grants Molinism its libertarian picture of freedom, but insists that this picture requires us to deny the possibility of true counterfactuals of creaturely freedom. For what, it is asked, could ground such a truth? If the action in question is truly free, no element of the situation could necessitate its performance; nor, in many cases, will there be any activity in the past, present or future of the actual world which can be seen as grounding the counterfactual, for most such conditionals will refer to creatures and/or situations which are never actual. There are truths, such critics grant, about what creatures *might* do if placed in certain circumstances, and perhaps even truths about what they *probably* would do, but truths of this sort fall far short of providing God with the kind of foreknowledge and providential control championed by the Molinist. While some critics view the apparent failure of Molinism with regret, others see it as a cause for celebration; a God who needs and is willing to take risks in interacting with his creatures is actually preferable, they suggest, to the all-controlling, manipulative God of the Molinists.

Molinists have offered thoughtful responses to such critics. Abandoning the libertarian picture of freedom, they have argued, is philosophically indefensible and theologically dangerous, in so far as it would render God ultimately responsible for evil. Some Molinists have responded to the grounding objection by questioning either the meaning or the truth of the claim that all propositions need grounds; others have suggested that counterfactuals of creaturely freedom do indeed have grounds, though (as with propositions about the past or the future, or about what is metaphysically possible) we might not find such grounds at the present time or in the actual world. Finally, Molinists have charged that the risk-taking, playing-the-odds picture embraced by some of their critics gives us a God who is little more than 'the bookie than which none greater can be conceived', a deity far inferior to that required by the Western religious tradition.

See also: GOD, CONCEPTS OF; PROVIDENCE §§3–4

References and further reading

Adams, M. (1967) 'Is the Existence of God a "Hard" Fact?', *Philosophical Review* 76 (October): 492–503. (A response to the Pike article cited below; offers a version of the Ockhamist position noted in §3.)

Alston, W. (1986) 'Does God Have Beliefs?', *Religious Studies* 22 (3–4): 287–306. (A clear, accessible discussion of the non-propositional picture of divine knowledge noted in §2 and the implications of such a picture for problems connected to immutability and foreknowledge.)

Fischer, J. (1983) 'Freedom and Foreknowledge', *Philosophical Review* 92 (January): 67–79. (Prominent attack on the type of Ockhamism defended by Adams in the essay noted above.)

Flint, T.P. (1990) 'Hasker's *God, Time and Knowledge*', *Philosophical Studies* 60 (1): 103–15. (An attempt to respond to the anti-Molinist argument offered in the Hasker book listed below.)

Freddoso, A. (1988) 'Introduction', in A. Freddoso (trans. and ed.) *On Divine Foreknowledge: Part IV of the Concordia*, Ithaca, NY: Cornell University Press, 1–81. (Excellent detailed presentation of the Molinist positions described in §3 and §4, along with summaries of and responses to major criticisms of Molinism.)

* Hasker, W. (1989) *God, Time and Knowledge*, Ithaca, NY: Cornell University Press. (Challenging and sophisticated arguments against Molinism, along with a defence of the notion of a risk-taking God noted in §4.)

Kretzmann, N. (1966) 'Omniscience and immutability', *The Journal of Philosophy* 63 (14): 409–21. (Influential presentation of the argument mentioned in §2 for the incompatibility of omniscience and immutability.)

Pike, N. (1965) 'Divine Omniscience and Voluntary Action', *Philosophical Review* 74 (1): 27–46. (Much-discussed version of the argument for freedom's incompatibility with divine omniscience.)

* Plantinga, A. (1986) 'On Ockham's Way Out', *Faith and Philosophy* 3 (3): 235–69. (Careful and sophisticated discussion of the Ockhamist position discussed in §3.)

* Stump, E. and Kretzmann, N. (1981) 'Eternity', *The Journal of Philosophy* 78 (8): 429-58. (Controversial but intriguing defence of the oft-maligned thesis of divine eternity.)

—— (1985) 'Absolute Simplicity', *Faith and Philosophy* 2 (4): 353–82. (The pre-eminent contemporary articulation of and argument for the claim that simplicity ought to be included among the divine attributes.)

* Wierenga, E. (1989) *The Nature of God*, Ithaca, NY: Cornell University Press. (Technical but very rewarding examination of most of the issues discussed in this entry.)

THOMAS P. FLINT

ONTOLOGICAL ARGUMENT
see GOD, ARGUMENTS FOR THE EXISTENCE OF

ONTOLOGICAL COMMITMENT

A person may believe in the existence of God, or numbers or ghosts. Such beliefs may be asserted, perhaps in a theory. Assertions of the existence of specific entities or kinds of entities are the intuitive source of the notion of ontological commitment, for it is natural to think of a person who makes such an assertion as being 'committed' to an 'ontology' that includes such entities. So ontological commitment appears to be a relation that holds between persons or existence assertions (including theories), on the one hand, and specific entities or kinds of entities (or ontologies), on the other.

Ontological commitment is thus a very rich notion – one in which logical, metaphysical, linguistic and epistemic elements are intermingled. The main philosophical problem concerning commitment is whether there is a precise criterion for detecting commitments in accordance with intuition. It once seemed extremely important to find a criterion, for it promised to serve as a vital tool in the comparative assessment of theories. Many different criteria have been proposed and a variety of problems have beset these efforts. W.V. Quine has been the central figure in the discussion and we will consider two of his formulations below.

Many important philosophical topics are closely connected with ontological commitment. These include: the nature of theories and their interpretation; interpretations of quantification; the nature of kinds; the question of the existence of merely possible entities; extensionality and intensionality; the general question of the nature of modality; and the significance of Occam's razor.

1 **Fundamental problems**
2 **Problems of detail**
3 **Two further problems**
4 **Translation and triviality**

1 Fundamental problems

The intuitive source of the notion of ontological commitment is people asserting things to exist. It may thus be thought of as a *binary relation* between persons or assertions of existence and the entities or kinds of entities they assert to exist. The main philosophical problem concerning commitment is whether there is a precise criterion for detecting commitments in accordance with intuition. Anyone who seeks a criterion of commitment must first decide what sorts of entities may properly stand in the positions of the relation. Unfortunately there are at least *five* significant candidates for occupying its first position: persons; acts of uttering (or inscribing); utterances (or inscriptions), that is, the actual 'tokens' produced; sentences uttered (or inscribed), that is, the 'types' of which tokens are produced; and propositions (which on some accounts are often expressed on occasions of utterance or inscription). And there is a similarly diverse range of candidates for the second relatum. So there is a daunting array of seemingly different ways to see commitment as a binary relation.

An encouraging thought about this proliferation is that it may not ultimately matter which approach one takes because, given any plausible choice, the relation may be thought of as holding *derivatively* between pairs of the unchosen sorts in a more or less natural way. It may also be that moving to a ternary (and so on) treatment would help absorb some of the complexity, but commitment is typically viewed as a binary relation, and we will follow that precedent here.

Another difficulty is that our intuitive talk of commitment is crucially ambiguous. Sometimes we

speak as if a person who says there are whales is (thereby) committed to the existence of mammals, sometimes not. So, there is a sense of commitment that 'tracks entailments' and one that does not. Both senses are surely legitimate, but we should decide which we are discussing at the outset. If we distinguish thus between '*prima facie*' and 'all-in' commitment, then it is fair to say that the discussion provoked by W.V. QUINE mainly concerns the former. This is not surprising given his famous antipathy to essential properties and analytic truth, as well as his explicit claims that the notion of commitment belongs to the 'theory of reference' (and not to the 'theory of meaning'). But we will see that some of Quine's formulations can seem more suitable for assessing all-in commitment than *prima facie*.

Quine's stated criteria are sometimes meant to reveal commitment to *specific* entities, sometimes to *kinds* of entities. We will focus on the latter. Here are two representative examples:

> (1) to say that a given existential quantification presupposes objects of a given kind is to say simply that the open sentence which follows the quantifier is true of some objects of that kind and none not of that kind.
>
> (Quine 1953a: 131)
>
> (2) entities of a given sort are assumed by a theory if and only if some of them must be counted among the values of the variables in order that the statements affirmed in the theory be true.
>
> (Quine 1953b: 103)

There is a serious problem of interpretation for any criterion intended to apply to theories. (This includes (1), for Quine's mention of open sentences following quantifiers reveals that he is thinking of certain sorts of formal theory.) The problem is that we use 'theory' in at least three different ways. First, we attribute 'informal theories' to people on the basis of their natural-language claims. Then we 'represent' these informal theories formally. Here the canonical notion is that of an (axiomatic) first-order theory along with an 'interpretation', which consists of a non-empty domain (the 'range' of quantifiable variables) plus an assignment of 'extensions' based on that domain to the nonlogical symbols of the theory. Note that we have already spoken of the purely syntactic component as a 'theory', but we also regard the syntax plus the extensional semantics as an 'interpreted theory'. So an unqualified use of 'theory' could mean any of three different things.

Now it seems almost nonsensical to think of a

purely syntactic object (such as an uninterpreted sentence or theory) as ontologically committed to anything (except perhaps the syntactic elements that comprise it). Unfortunately this is the most literal construal of (1). Another construal makes the interpreted theory (or sentence, and so on) bear the commitment. This makes much better sense, but it may not make for a much better criterion. What (1) does under this understanding is, in effect, to define a certain metalinguistic relation term, 'presupposes' (see PRESUPPOSITION). The relation this term expresses is evidently ternary – it relates interpreted closed sentences, objects (from the domain) and (somehow) *kinds*. The definition utilizes the notions of a formula with one free variable, the satisfaction relation (understood as relating objects and formulas – Quine's 'true of'), objects and (somehow) kinds. So (1) offers a new piece of terminology in the metatheory of interpreted first-order theories, enhanced by whatever is needed to talk about kinds in whatever way is intended. To this extent it is harmless enough, but it is not clear what it has to do with intuitive commitment. Notice that on its basis we may distinguish two sorts of objects in the domain of a theory: those that are of kinds 'presupposed' by at least one existential sentence; and, as may occur, those that are not. But any theory with both sorts of entities is already committed to all of them in a far more basic way since they are all essential components of that theory. No theory without them is the same theory.

It may therefore seem best to view (1) as directed to the case of informal theories, and the same may be said of (2). The intuitive idea is perhaps that the 'ontology' of an interpreted formal theory is 'transparent': It simply consists of the members of its domain of interpretation (or a readily distinguishable subset of them). So one might hope to reduce the hazy question of the commitments of informal theories to the transparent case of their formal representatives. But if the commitments of a given informal theory are unclear, then it would seem that the choice of its formal representative must also be unclear. So it appears that any criterion conceived in this way cannot work: to apply it we must first find a representing theory, but we cannot do this unless we already know the informal commitments.

The search for a criterion to apply to *theories* may thus seem fated to produce either near nonsense, triviality or practical futility, depending on what is meant by 'theory'. This would not be welcomed by Quine, especially since the original idea was to find a neutral means for assessing something not always clearly in view. It was to help us compare theories, sometimes with something like Occam's razor in

mind. (Of course there may be a criterion for informal theories that makes no similar appeal to formal representatives.)

2   Problems of detail

We now consider some problems that arise from the details of (1) and (2). A serious defect of (1) is that it offers no means of assessing informal theories that make false existence claims. Since there are no unicorns, there is no interpreted theory the domain of which contains unicorns, and so there is none with unicorns available to satisfy relevant open sentences.

(2) offers an improvement over (1) in just this respect. For it may be seen as ruling that there *must* be some unicorns in the domain of *any* interpreted theory that would be a suitable representative of the informal theory, and there may be a way of understanding this that makes no intuitive commitment to unicorns.

Now let us return to the matter of whales and mammals. It is clear that if the informal claim that there are whales receives a suitable (interpreted) first-order formulation, then a relevant open sentence will be true of some mammals and not true of any non-mammals. So (1) finds the informal theory committed to mammals as well as to whales. Whether (2) has the same consequence evidently depends on whether whales *must* be mammals, not (as in (1)) on whether they actually are mammals. So a philosopher who accepts (2) and, like Quine, denies that any entities have any non-trivial essential (or necessary) properties may claim that the distinction between *prima facie* and all-in commitment is a distinction without a difference (see ESSENTIALISM).

But this means there is a further difficulty in trying to evaluate Quine's formulations in the style of (2): they yield different results depending on the background philosophical views of the person applying them. When Quine applies (2) to an informal theory of whales, he concludes that it is not committed to mammals. But when an essentialist applies it, the conclusion is the opposite.

Formulations such as (1) and (2) reveal the influence (and importance) of a period that featured intense work in the areas of extensional formal semantics and the axiomatization of both scientific and philosophical theories. Such criteria are fairly characterized as seeing existential quantification as the source (and signal) of ontological commitment. They may be seen as differing elaborations of the theme expressed in Quine's famous slogan, 'To *be* is to be a value of a variable' (1939). Quine would later adopt a somewhat different perspective on the matter, the perspective of 'ontological relativity', which we will mention below. But there remain two very general criticisms of efforts in the quantificational spirit that merit separate discussion.

3 Two further problems

For a time the influence of Tarskian formal semantics was so great that it must have been difficult to imagine that any essentially different treatment of quantification could be defensible. But there is a coherent alternative called the substitutional interpretation. On this interpretation the semantics of a first-order language includes a non-empty set of terms of that language called the 'substitution class'. An existential quantification is counted true if and only if there is a member of the substitution class such that the result of removing the quantifier and replacing all resulting free occurrences of its variable by that member is true. So the truth-conditions for the quantifiers make no appeal to a domain of (potentially) extra-linguistic entities. Depending on how truth-values are assigned to atomic sentences – and one possibility is by sheer stipulation – a given substitutionally interpreted theory may have no intuitive ontological commitment beyond the constituents of the language itself, the truth-values, and perhaps some simple sets (including functions) of these entities.

The usefulness of substitutional quantification for representing informal theories may be debated (see QUANTIFIERS, SUBSTITUTIONAL AND OBJECTUAL). One may ask whether the concept of truth embodied in a given substitutional theory appropriately matches the one implicit in a given informal theory. If the intuitive verdict is that the informal theory has non-trivial extra-linguistic commitment, then a substitutional theory lacking such commitment will be metaphysically inadequate (though it might get the truth-values right). But there remains the simple fact that the substitutional interpretation is perfectly coherent. From this it appears to follow that the mere assertion of an existential sentence does not provide a sufficient condition for non-trivial ontological commitment. So an adequate criterion of commitment should not presuppose that it does. The very existence and coherence of the substitutional interpretation thus creates a real difficulty for 'quantificational' criteria in the spirit of (1) or (2).

It has often been claimed, for one reason or another, that commitment is an 'intensional' notion (see INTENSIONAL ENTITIES §1). The main reason why (2) improves upon (1) is that it contains the word 'must'. But this suggests that the improvement is gained only at what Quine must see as great cost, namely, by exploiting the notion of *necessity*, which belongs to the theory of meaning. For it is natural to interpret the condition stated in (2) as meaning that it is necessary that if the statements affirmed in the theory are true, then objects of the required sort are values of its variables.

Others have found intensionality not in an appeal to necessity but in the (claimed) 'referential opacity' of the commitment relation itself, that is, in the resistance of its second position both to the substitution of coreferential expressions and to existential generalization. Commitment to Twain does not entail commitment to Clemens; nor does commitment to unicorns (*or* horses) entail there being entities to which one is committed. (Note that a plausible claim of opacity can only be made concerning *prima facie* commitment.)

Here is a further (but related) reason to suspect intensionality. Suppose we try to state a criterion in which the condition expresses a binary relation between persons or theories (and so on) and something else. What are the plausible candidates for the second relatum? Consider first the theory that simply says there are horses. Well, there *are* horses, but the theory is not committed to any of them (either individually or collectively). One natural thought is that the second relatum is the property (or kind), being a horse. Accordingly, to say that the theory is committed to horses would mean that it cannot be true unless the property is instantiated. But properties are intensional entities. (In the case of commitment to specific entities, 'possible objects', including *merely* possible objects, are natural candidates analogous to properties.) There are other possibilities, but it has been argued that any adequate relational treatment must be intensional.

Yet another approach sees theories not as linguistic or quasi-linguistic entities, whether formal or informal, but rather as propositions (or sets of propositions). Then a theory is committed to, say, unicorns if it entails the proposition that unicorns exist. This approach is intensional because propositions are intensional entities. (It also appeals to entailment, which is usually (though not universally) thought to rest on necessity.)

So the suspicion of intensionality may arise for a number of reasons. But the intensionality always seems to flow from one of two somewhat related sources. The first is the classical problem of explaining how we can either assert or deny the existence of things that in fact do not exist. The other is that we are treating *prima facie* rather than all-in commitment. The (claimed) intensionality of commitment is not in itself disturbing, but it was vexing for Quine because of his general aversion to the intensional.

4 Translation and triviality

The possibility that an adequate criterion of commitment would somehow be 'trivial' arose in §1. Remarkably enough, it also surfaced in Quine in the wake of his important doctrines of 'ontological relativity' and the 'inscrutability of reference'. Details of these positions cannot be discussed here, but their effect on the matter of a criterion should be mentioned.

The key effect is to cast the question of a criterion as one concerning *translation*. Theories are stated in languages. An ontological criterion must also be stated in a language. For our purposes, the language of a criterion may be viewed as a technically enhanced version of an appropriate fragment of English. Call such a language E^*. Now it seems clear that if the question whether a theory T is committed to entities of kind K can be settled at all, then it can be settled as follows: simply translate the assertions (or theorems) of T into E^* and see whether the results include 'There exist objects of kind K' (where 'There exist' is understood referentially).

For reasons flowing from the aforementioned doctrines, there is a sense in which Quine does not regard this as 'settling' the question of T's ontology, because he thinks 'There exist objects of kind K', in E^*, is itself ontologically indeterminate. But he also thinks that this is an indeterminacy that cannot be removed and should not be lamented.

Any such 'translational' criterion can easily seem trivial. For either we already know the commitments of T, and so have no need for it, or else we do not, and so cannot apply it. Yet it seems perfectly natural and correct independently of the Quinean doctrines and, in particular, independently of their implication that it does not settle the question of a theory's commitment.

See also: FREE LOGICS, PHILOSOPHICAL ISSUES IN; LOGICAL AND MATHEMATICAL TERMS, GLOSSARY OF; ONTOLOGY

References and further reading

The following items all involve complex argumentation and at least some technicality. Many contain valuable further references.

Cartwright, R.L. (1954) 'Ontology and the Theory of Meaning', *Philosophy of Science* 21: 316–25. (The classic statement of the idea that ontological commitment involves the notion of necessity, as discussed in §3.)

Dunn, J.M. and Belnap, N.D. (1968) 'The Substitution Interpretation of the Quantifiers', *Noûs* 2:

179–85. (A discussion and technical presentation of substitutional semantics, as discussed in §3.)

Jubien, M. (1972) 'The Intensionality of Ontological Commitment', *Noûs* 6: 378–87. (Argues that any adequate criterion of commitment that treats the notion as a relation must be intensional, as mentioned in §3.)

Kripke, S.A. (1976) 'Is there a Problem about Substitutional Quantification?', in G. Evans and J. McDowell (eds) *Truth and Meaning*, Oxford: Clarendon Press, 325–419. (Argues that attempts to see substitutional quantification as covertly carrying the commitments of referential quantification are incorrect. Very detailed and technical in places. See the present §3.)

Marcus, R.B. (1972) 'Quantification and Ontology', *Noûs* 6: 240–50; repr. in *Modalities*, Oxford and New York: Oxford University Press, 1993, 75–87. (A classic statement of the ontological neutrality of substitutional quantification, as discussed in §3.)

—— (1978) 'Nominalism and the Substitutional Quantifier', *Monist* 61: 351–62; repr. in *Modalities*, Oxford and New York: Oxford University Press, 1993, 111–24. (Explores the congeniality of substitutional quantification for various forms of nominalism.)

* Quine, W.V. (1939) 'A Logistical Approach to the Ontological Problem', presented at the fifth International Congress for the Unity of Science, Cambridge, MA; repr. in *The Ways of Paradox and Other Essays*, New York: Random House, 1966, 64–9. (An early discussion of naming, reference and ontology. The source of 'To *be* is to be a value of a variable' mentioned in §2.)

* —— (1953a) 'Notes on the Theory of Reference', in *From a Logical Point of View*, Cambridge, MA and London: Harvard University Press, 1961, 130–8. (The source of criterion (1), discussed in §§1–3, and of an explicit claim that commitment belongs to the theory of reference.)

* —— (1953b) 'Logic and the Reification of Universals', in *From a Logical Point of View*, Cambridge, MA and London: Harvard University Press, 1961, 102–29. (The source of criterion (2), discussed in the present §§1–3. Contains an explicit claim of the need for a criterion of commitment.)

—— (1968) 'Ontological Relativity', *Journal of Philosophy* 65: 185–212; repr. in *Ontological Relativity and Other Essays*, New York and London: Columbia University Press, 1969, 26–68. (An early statement of the doctrine of ontological relativity and related matters, as mentioned in §4.)

—— (1981) 'Things and Their Place in Theories', in *Theories and Things*, Cambridge, MA and London: Belknap Press, 1–23. (More on ontological relativity, including the idea that the question of the ontology of a theory is fundamentally a question concerning translation. See the present §4.)

Scheffler, I. and Chomsky, N. (1958–9) 'What is Said to Be', *Proceedings of the Aristotelian Society* 69: 215–24. (The classic statement of the idea that the commitment context is referentially opaque; discussed in §3.)

Schwartz, R. (1993) 'On "What is Said to Be"', *Synthese* 94: 43–54. (A contemporary attempt to capture a concept of commitment using only extensional resources. See the present §§3, 4.)

MICHAEL JUBIEN

ONTOLOGY

The word 'ontology' is used to refer to philosophical investigation of existence, or being. Such investigation may be directed towards the concept of being, asking what 'being' means, or what it is for something to exist; it may also (or instead) be concerned with the question 'what exists?', or 'what general sorts of thing are there?' It is common to speak of a philosopher's ontology, meaning the kinds of thing they take to exist, or the ontology of a theory, meaning the things that would have to exist for that theory to be true.

1   **Existence and being**
2   **What is there?**
3   **Ontological commitment**

1   Existence and being

Since so many central debates of philosophy concern what types of things exist, scrutiny of the arguments used in them was bound to lead to investigation of the concept of existence and its logic. The most famous case of this kind is the Ontological Argument for the existence of God , and one of the most famous moves in the ensuing debate is Kant's claim that existence is not a property or predicate of existing things: 'cats exist' clearly tells us something, but it does not tell us of things which, in addition to being furry, feline and fleet of foot, have the further property of existence (see GOD, ARGUMENTS FOR THE EXISTENCE OF §§2–3; EXISTENCE).

This point, with which modern logic agrees, may teach us to formulate 'cats exist' as 'there are things which are cats' – in which it doesn't even look as if existence is functioning as a predicate. But many will think that this does not take us very far. It does not tell us how to describe the difference between a world in which cats exist and one in which they do not – other than by repeating the formula 'there are cats'; it will not advance our understanding of what it is for something to exist. Nor will it touch the somewhat dizzying question 'why does anything exist, rather than nothing?'.

Some philosophers, however, have taken an interest in existence or 'being' (as it tends to appear in their works or in the English translations), not because it appears as part of so many philosophical claims but because they take it for the central concept of philosophy. The most prominent examples are, in antiquity, PARMENIDES, and in the twentieth century Martin HEIDEGGER.

2   What is there?

In its characteristically philosophical form, this is not a question of detail (for example, are there mammoths?) but about the most general *kinds* of thing: are there universals, or only particulars? – is there mind or spirit, or is there only matter? – is there anything that exists without being in space and time? Thus the debate on the first of these questions between Platonists and nominalists, or on the second between idealists and materialists, might in each case be described as a difference of opinion about the correct ontology. So might the conflict over whether values are objective aspects of reality, or rather 'in the eye of the beholder', a matter of how we react to things rather than the things themselves (see EMOTIVISM; PROJECTIVISM).

The questions 'What kinds of thing *ultimately* exist?' or '…*really* exist?' or '…exist *in themselves*?' are even more characteristically philosophical forms of the general ontological question. To understand what usually lies behind these additional terms one needs a grasp of (1) the concept of a *reduction* and (2) the distinction between appearances and things-in-themselves.

Reduction. Berkeley famously claimed that material objects were just collections of 'ideas' (see BERKELEY, G. §3). He did not mean that there were no chairs or tables, but that such things did not have a material, non-mental component; what really existed was all mental. There are spirits and their ideas, and we speak of chairs and so on when the latter occur in familiar, stable groupings. In modern terminology, he was claiming that material objects can be *reduced to* ideas. There are other common examples. In political discourse we often speak of what a particular state has done – but without having to suppose that there are such things as states distinct from the individual people who compose them. A once-popular thesis about the nature of mind was that there is nothing but bodies and their behaviour, and that words apparently naming mental states and happenings are just convenient ways of indicating types of behaviour (see BEHAVIOURISM, ANALYTIC; REDUCTIONISM IN THE PHILOSOPHY OF MIND).

Things-in-themselves. We may distinguish between the way a thing appears, which will depend partly on the faculties and situation of whoever is perceiving it, and the way it is, independently of how anyone perceives it. The latter is the thing-in-itself. The terminology was made instantly famous by Kant, arguing that space and time (and therefore everything in space or time) were merely the way in which a non-spatiotemporal reality, things-in-themselves, appeared to humans (see KANT §5).

3   Ontological commitment

The notion of ontological commitment has come to prominence in the second half of the twentieth century, mainly through the work of Quine (see QUINE, W.V. §5). On Quine's view the right guide to what exists is science, so that our best guide to what exists is our best current scientific theory: what exists is what acceptance of that theory commits us to.

But what is that? How do we determine what existents the acceptance of a given theory commits us to? Quine proposes a criterion, often summarized in the famous slogan 'to be is to be the value of a variable'. We are to see what types of thing are quantified over when the theory is stated in canonical form with predicate calculus as the underlying logic; the theory's ontological commitment is precisely to things of those types. This line of thought has given rise to much discussion (see ONTOLOGICAL COMMITMENT).

See also: ABSTRACT OBJECTS; BEING; IDEALISM; ONTOLOGY IN INDIAN PHILOSOPHY; REALISM AND ANTIREALISM; UNIVERSALS; VALUE, ONTOLOGICAL STATUS OF

References and further reading

Heidegger, M. (1953) *An Introduction to Metaphysics*, trans. R. Manheim, New Haven, CT: Yale University Press, 1959. (Heidegger's understanding of being. Readers new to Heidegger may not find this as introductory as the title had led them to hope.)

Kant, I. (1781, 1787) *Critique of Pure Reason*, trans. N. Kemp Smith, London: Macmillan, 1929. (For the famous passage about existence not being a predicate, A598/B626–A601/B629; for the distinction between appearances and things-in-themselves a good example is A45/B62–A46/B63.)

Nozick, R. (1981) *Philosophical Explanations*, Oxford: Oxford University Press. (Chapter 2, 'Why is there something rather than nothing?' is at times a little bewildering, but good fun – for the more experienced reader.)

Quine, W.V. (1948) 'On What There is', in *From a Logical Point of View*, Cambridge, MA: Harvard University Press, 1953. (Classic paper on existence and ontological commitment. First published in the *Review of Metaphysics*.)

Williams, C.J.F. (1981) *What is Existence?*, Oxford: Clarendon Press. (Extensive discussion of all the issues arising out of the 'logic and language' – rather than the 'deep metaphysics' approach to existence.)

EDWARD CRAIG

ONTOLOGY IN INDIAN PHILOSOPHY

All Indian philosophical traditions are deeply engaged with ontology, the study of being, since clarity about the nature of reality is at the heart of three intimately connected goals: knowledge, proper conduct and liberation from the continued suffering that is part of all human existence. The formulation of a list of ontological categories, a classification of reality by division into several fundamental objective kinds, however, is less widespread. There is little room for a doctrine of distinct, if related, ontological categories in a philosophical school that takes reality as one, even less if that one lies beyond description. If the phenomenal world is but illusory appearance, as, for example, in the Vedānta of Śaṅkara, then a determination of kinds of entities does not recommend itself as a means to adequate analysis of the world. Even the Sāṅkhya tradition's realism reduces the world to an evolution from two fundamental entities, spirit and matter. Categories make sense within the context of a pluralistic realism, an analysis of the world that finds it to be composed of a multiplicity of real entities. Such a view is found to some extent in Jaina philosophy, but is primarily defended and developed in the Nyāya-Vaiśeṣika school.

The Nyāya-Vaiśeṣika categories are seven: substance, quality, motion, universal, particular, inherence and not-being. While all are understood as real entities and objects of knowledge, substance is most fundamental as each of the others in some way depends on substance. Substances are nine: earth, water, fire, air, ether, time, space, self and mind. The first four are atomic: they may combine to form macroscopic substance, such as a clay pot, but in incomposite form they are indestructible atoms, as are the last two. Ether, time and space, likewise indestructible, are unitary and pervade all. In its irreducible parts, all substance is eternal; every composite whole is a destructible substance.

A relation of containment, called inherence, structures the categories. The qualities, actions and universals by which we might characterize a pot inhere in it. They are distinct entities from the pot, yet cannot exist apart from their underlying substrate. Composite substances like a pot are also contained in their parts by inherence, but the smallest parts, eternal substances, exist independently as receptacles that contain nothing. A whole, greater than the sum of its parts, is said to inhere in the parts while the parts are the inherence cause of the whole.

Eternal substance, the ultimate substrate of all, is a bare particular. An entity that is nothing but a receptacle for other entities, it furnishes criteria for separability and individuality, but cannot be defined in itself apart from others. This aspect of the concept of substance leads later Nyāya-Vaiśeṣika into extensive analysis of relations and negation.

1 **Categories**
2 **Relations**
3 **Substance**
4 **Qualities and their inherence in substance**
5 **Action**
6 **Universal and particularity**
7 **Inherence**
8 **Parallels to the relation of inherence**
9 **Later developments to inherence and relations**
10 **Nonexistence or absence**
11 **The nature of the self**

1 Categories

While ontological speculation lies at the heart of all schools of classical Indian thought, a great portion of the tradition is not conducive to a doctrine of ontological categories. Categories provide a means to analyse the world according to the distinct kinds of entities that are the ingredients of all reality. The tradition growing out of the philosophical treatment of the Vedas in the Upaniṣads, in which all questions of ontology press towards the transcendent and the being of the phenomenal world is doubted and rejected as an illusion, ought to have limited use for such a tool. The arguments of Buddhist thinkers taking all phenomena as the only existence, a flux with no underlying reality, also leave no place for a classification of discrete kinds of realities. A theory of categories develops not in an idealism or nominalism, but presupposes some kind of pluralistic realism.

The most extensive system of ontological categories in classical Indian thought was worked out over the course of several hundred years by the Nyāya-Vaiśeṣika school. Traditionally this begins with the *Vaiśeṣikasūtra* of the legendary Kāṇāda, followed by the commentary of VĀTSYĀYANA (fifth century AD) and the work of Praśastapāda (sixth century). The resulting most widely accepted list contains seven categories, the first three of which each comprise a standard list of members, as follows: (1) substance, which includes earth, water, fire, air, ether, time, space, mind and self; (2) quality, which includes colour, taste, smell, touch, number, measure, separateness, conjunction, disjunction, priority, posteriority, cognitions, pleasure, pain, desire, aversion, volition, gravity, liquidity, viscidity, disposition, merit, demerit and sound; (3) action, which includes throwing upwards, throwing downwards, contraction, expansion and going; (4) universal; (5) particularity; (6) inherence; (7) absence or nonexistence.

This list was appropriated in part by other schools, notably Jaina thinkers, who took substance as an all-inclusive category that is further subdivided and concurred to an extent with Vaiśeṣika in positing real, individual souls. The Jaina tradition could be viewed as an expansion of Sāṅkhya dualism: in addition to conscious but formless reality and nonconscious material reality, it recognizes a nonconscious but formless reality (see JAINA PHILOSOPHY §1; SĀṄKHYA §2). This is a doctrine of substance, classifying three kinds of permanent realities, and not a doctrine classifying appearances that are nothing in themselves, but are derivative manifestations of a transcendent reality. In addition to conscious reality, souls, and nonconscious matter, atoms and their aggregations, there are four kinds of nonconscious yet immaterial substance, each a medium for change. These are the media of motion, rest, space and time. All reality is identified with substance, which is seen as unifying permanence and impermanence. This all-inclusive category of substance is designed to explain how an entity can remain a real, self-same individual throughout change. Mīmāṃsā also makes use of the notion of substance. In general, however, where categories appear in Indian thought outside the Nyāya-Vaiśeṣika tradition, they are ancillary tools, not the root of ontology. Such is the view of Vedāntin compendia of philosophy – short works that classify and summarize other schools – in considering Nyāya-Vaiśeṣika early and primitive, containing useful instruments for analysis but no insight into truth.

In the philosophical vocabulary of European languages, 'category' is a derivative of the Greek word first appropriated for philosophical jargon by ARISTOTLE (§7). *Kategoria*, from the verb *kategorein*, literally 'to speak in the marketplace', entered the language of jurisprudence meaning 'to accuse', that is, to say something about someone. Aristotle adopted it for a classification of the different ways to say things about other things, a classification of kinds of predicates. A philosophical claim lies behind Aristotle's method. If language is thought reflecting what there is, then the structure of language is the key to the structure of reality. The Indian term for 'category', *padārtha*, the object or meaning (*artha*) of a word (*pada*), suggests a related notion. Though it is not in the Vaiśeṣika texts, some Indian grammarians drew a connection between the first three categories, substance, quality and action, and the distinction between noun, adjective and verb. Certain Vaiśeṣika arguments do rely explicitly on word meaning, claiming that words could have no meaning if universals were not real entities.

All seven categories are all mentioned in the *Vaiśeṣikasūtra*, although the word we translate as 'category', *padārtha*, occurs only once, in a disputed verse where it designates the first six. The term does not become clearly established until Praśastapāda's commentary on the *Vaiśeṣikasūtra*, the *Padārthadharmasaṅgraha* (Compendium of Properties of the Categories). The categories are not only the meaning or object of words; they represent a classification of all being, a definitive listing of the various kinds of things that exist. Each category represents a distinct kind of entity.

The reality of each category rests on three aspects: individual unity, causality and independence. (1) Whatever is a real entity is a separate individual, knowable as such, even if it cannot exist apart from something else. (2) Each category of thing is known as a cause: substance causes substance, quality quality, action action, universal and particularity cause cognition, particularity in an ultimate sense causes the individuality of eternal substances, and inherence causes subsistence in. (3) Most individual realities are dependent on or contained in something else, with the chain of dependence going back to independent eternal substances.

This does not yet give much clue as to what each category is. That task requires patience, since each category, while separate, is largely defined through relations to other categories.

2   Relations

Despite the emphasis on the particularity (*viśeṣa*) of the individual, the source of the name Vaiśeṣika, none of the categories can be adequately grasped without reference to others. Śrīdhara (tenth century) writes that the categories 'become objects and properties with reference to one another' (*Nyāyakandalī*, comment to III.1). In Vaiśeṣika all relations obtain between two entities. Most significant to understanding the structure of the categories is the relation called inherence. Itself a category, inherence informs the nature of all categories. There are two central aspects to its definition. It is a permanent relation, in contrast to the relations of conjunction and disjunction. The conjunction of two objects – two pebbles in contact, say – can soon be dissolved. Inherence, on the other hand, is a relation that persists until one or both of the relata are destroyed. Furthermore, inherence is explained by the metaphor of containment. In an inherence relation, one of the individuals is always contained by the other, which is its container. The contained is said to inhere in the container.

The relation of contained to container is the primary example of a relation of superstratum to substrate. (It is not, however, the only one. Other relations, including conjunction when one object is on top of another, are also of this general sort; see §9.) Common synonyms for the term 'substrate' (*ādhāra*) include 'locus' (*adhikaraṇa*) and 'abode' (*āśraya*).

3   Substance

The realism of the entire Nyāya-Vaiśeṣika system is rooted in the category of substance (*dravya*). It is the one category that comprises a plurality of independently existing individuals. Some of the others are dependent on substance as their substrate (quality, motion, ultimate particularity), some are dependent on cognition (universal, particularity), and inherence is a relation of other categories. Unlike a number of the categories, for which a variety of terms have been attempted as translations, *dravya* has been rendered virtually without exception as 'substance', from the Latin translation for the first of Aristotle's categories. Beyond its technical usage in Vaiśeṣika, *dravya* can mean in Sanskrit any thing or object, a material or ingredient, thus medicine, also wealth or money, or, more broadly, any object of possession.

Substance is the basic stuff of which all things material and immaterial are made; it is the ultimate possessor. The inherence relation of containment manifests the ontological priority of substance. Qualities, actions, universals and particularities exist only as contained in something else. Substance is also self-productive, meaning that only substances can cause the existence of other substances. Conversely, substances can be contained only in other substances. When a substance comes into being, it is produced from the unification of previously existing substances, as when two clay halves are joined to form a pot. The pot is said to inhere in the halves; the parts contain the whole. The parts of a substance can of course be contained in simpler parts, but because this chain of containment cannot continue *ad infinitum*, there must be simplest substances. Since a substance exists as contained by being produced from other substances and the simplest atoms are contained in nothing simpler, the latter are eternal. Composite substances are dependent and transient, ultimate atoms independent and permanent.

Since impermanent substances arise through the physical union of prior substances, only material substances can become and pass away. Physical substances have an eternal form as well: atoms of earth, water, fire and air are many and indestructible. The material atoms are, in a sense, contained in something other, although this is not considered inherence. Ether, space and time are three substances that are said to be one, not many, eternal, all-pervasive and a receptacle for corporeal things. The soul or self (*ātman*), of which there are many, is immaterial and therefore eternal. Mind, countless atoms of which populate the world, is distinct from soul. It is understood as an unconscious instrument that transmits perception to the soul. Since this occurs through contact and mind possesses action (motion), it is said to be material, although it never combines to produce composite substances as the other physical substances do; it is material but not 'tangible'. Mind possesses qualities, such as number, dimension and separateness, which are attributed to both material and immaterial substances, but Praśastapāda also gives it priority and posteriority, which are elsewhere said to inhere only in material substances, as well as ability, which is otherwise thought to inhere only in immaterial substances.

Not only mind, but the other kinds of substance are distinguished from one another by the qualities that can inhere in them. Consciousness and other mental attributes are not identical to soul, but are qualities that the soul can possess. The physical substances together with ether are distinguished in that each is the receptacle for a particular kind of quality, associated with a particular sense. Earth is the substrate for smell, water for taste and natural fluidity, fire for colour, air for touch, and ether for sound. Where a quality is associated with a specific substance, it is the mark (*lakṣaṇa*) of that substance. The mark is a cognitive mark, allowing us to recognize substances, but is not an essence (*svarūpa*) identical with the nature of the substance (see §9).

Although ultimate, eternal substances are the only truly independent individuals, all instances of every category are interpreted as real, separate entities, even if dependent. Even nonexistences are entities, though having no positive nature of their own. Caused

substances are wholes, born with the conjunction of the substances that make up their parts. (The parts, not the conjunction, are interpreted as the cause of the whole; see §7.) Despite the dependence on its parts, the whole is no less an entity unto itself than are its parts, the parts of its parts, or the ultimate atoms. Just as every quality or action in a substance is logically separable and unique, and therefore a real entity, so too are composite substances real individuals.

Against the traditions that hold the phenomenal world to be an illusory manifestation of a nondual transcendent reality, Vaiśeṣika ontology sides with theories of causality called *asatkāryavāda*, which deny the pre-existence of an effect in its cause (see CAUSATION, INDIAN THEORIES OF §§1, 5). Each caused thing is a new thing. In this, there is agreement with the Buddhist schools, the major philosophical opponents of the classical Nyāya-Vaiśeṣika thinkers. They clash where the Buddhists assign the novelty of all effects to the momentariness of all existence, while a system of ontological categories like the Vaiśeṣika system is a means to justify permanent identity of individual entities through time (see MOMENTARINESS, BUDDHIST DOCTRINE OF). Substances, taken as substrates of qualities and other categories, permit an explanation of how a thing can remain one identical individual while undergoing change. A rock rolls down a hill, but is the same rock; the motion inheres in the rock but is not identical to it. A soul can acquire knowledge it did not always have or experience coming and passing pleasures and pains, all while remaining the same individual.

Nevertheless, the permanence of individuals must be qualified. Nothing exists if not in a substance, and this substrate of all that really exists exists either as an atom or as a unity composed of atoms. The atoms are uncreated and indestructible, but any change in the composition of a caused substance produces a new substance. If a clay pot is chipped, or even if a few molecules are brushed from its surface, the substance that was the original pot is destroyed as surely as if smashed with a sledgehammer.

This is reflected in the Vaiśeṣika treatment of particularity or individuality. Individuality is the category designating what distinguishes individuals as separate entities. It inheres in substance, yet does not inhere in any composite substance such as 'this sherd'. A pure and simple individuality can reside only in an ultimate substance, an atom. It is not needed to verify the separate existence of a composite substance, or a quality or action, because the individuality of a whole and of an attribute is demonstrated by containment in a substrate, and therefore by the relation of inherence. At the lowest level, however, a substance can inhere in nothing. Here, indeed, individuality is an indispensable concept. For atoms and other eternal substances are the necessary building blocks of the individuality of all other things. As the ultimate abodes of individuality, the atoms must be distinct from all they contain. Therefore, no attribute of an atom can serve to show what it is as distinct from the next atom. As ultimate, the atoms are a plurality of indistinguishables, unable to be distinguished by themselves, but only by the necessary inherence of individualities.

The attempt to identify substance leads Nyāya-Vaiśeṣika into a dilemma. Pure independence is what it is to be real. An individual quality or an action is one because it is in a substance; substances that are whole are one, because the parts they are in are substances; the smallest parts, the atomic substances, are one because they are independent from all else. As has been seen, this adds up to the ontological priority of eternal substances, given that to be is to be a separable individual. But by the same token it becomes very difficult to state what a given atom is – it cannot be identified with any of its predicates, for it is their substrate and an individual distinct from them – and therefore difficult to say how the given atom is in itself distinct from the next given atom. What is the substance apart from what it has? There seems to be no way to say, and yet there must be if knowledge as distinct from error is knowledge of the real. Consequently some thinkers in the Nyāya-Vaiśeṣika tradition are led to posit obscure ways of directly perceiving a substance apart from whatever inheres in it. The cow barely visible in the shadows at night yet distinctly a cow is said to be a perception of the substance by itself, because its attributes, specifically its true colour, are not perceived. Such arguments, unsurprisingly, were ridiculed by rival schools. In the same vein, Srīdhara affirms that yogins of developed skill directly intuit individual atoms. If the positive determination of individuals as separate is tenuous at best, one is left with distinguishing entities negatively by reference to relations with other individuals. As Nyāya-Vaiśeṣika thought develops, negative relations take a place of increasing importance (see §10).

4 Qualities and their inherence in substance

Quality (*guṇa*) and action or motion (*karman*) are the two categories in addition to substance that are considered objects (*artha*). Praśastapāda also expresses this by saying that 'beingness' applies to all categories, but 'being' as a general term only to substance, quality and motion, while the remaining three have 'self-being', their being in themselves

(*svabhāva*; at Praśastapāda's time, nonexistence was not yet an acknowledged category).

Like actions, qualities exist as individual realities, not independently but inhering in substances. Some are causes of other qualities and each contains the universal 'qualityness'. The number of qualities specifically listed varies slightly in different texts. Praśastapāda lists those occurring in material substances as colour, taste, smell, touch, priority, posteriority, gravity, fluidity, viscidity and speed. Ten qualities inhere in immaterial substances only: intellect, pleasure, pain, desire, aversion, effort, virtue, vice, ability and sound. Those remaining occur in both: number, dimension, separateness, conjunction and disjunction.

A number of the qualities are commonly called aids to perception. Though not identical to substance or the essence of substance, the qualities allow us to distinguish substances as separate kinds and as separate individuals (see §§3, 9). Qualities (as well as actions) have another important function with respect to the discernment of individual entities: they allow us to identify real and enduring individuals. Substances can change with respect to quality or action and yet remain the same substance. This was a central aspect of Aristotle's categories: substance provided a means to explain stability within change. The degree to which the Vaiśeṣika categories provide this is, however, in comparison with Aristotle, severely limited. The restrictions on identity through change are evident in the ways qualities act as causes and appear as effects.

Certain qualities are uncaused. These are the qualities that are 'marks', such as the smell of earth, which are coeval with permanent substance. Caused qualities are produced in one of five ways: by antecedents like qualities, conjunction, disjunction, action or by 'cooking' (*pācaka*), which is defined as hot touch or contact with fire. Action causes the qualities of conjunction, disjunction and speed. Conjunction and disjunction are among the several qualities (along with number and separateness when greater than one) that are relations and are therefore said to inhere in more than one substance at a time, thus not actually distinguishing individuals. Disjunction is said to cause only sound and secondary disjunction.

Of the three remaining causal modes, conjunction in two forms accounts for identity of changing substance. A conjunction is the contact of substances, without those substances thereby forming one (although conjunction occurs wherever a composite substance is produced). As a cause of qualities, conjunction other than cooking (cooking being conjunction of fire with another substance) is primarily associated with the immaterial qualities, that is to say, the attributes of soul. Understanding, pleasure, pain and other mental qualities can come to be contained in the soul or leave the soul without altering the real identity of the individual soul.

Cooking is in fact a specific kind of conjunction. Praśastapāda does not give a list of qualities caused by cooking, as he does for the other species of qualitative cause. Yet it seems clear that cooking is efficacious wherever a material substance undergoes change of quality without being destroyed. Praśastapāda mentions cooking as a cause explicitly only in connection with one substance, earth. Whether other substances can undergo qualitative change by hot touch is left ambiguous. Also, while a change in the odour or taste of earth is mentioned as a possible effect of cooking, colour is the most frequent example. Thus, a clay jar fired is the same substance as the greenware, though its colour has been changed.

'Cooking' may strike the reader as odd, yet it has a crucial explanatory function in the categories. Each quality is one entity, just as much as each substance is one. Containment in the substance, however, guarantees the unity of the quality. Whenever there is a change in the underlying substance, a new and distinct quality is born, and, apart from the few instances of 'cooking', any change in quality is a change in underlying substance (see §6).

5 Action

Action (karman, also translated 'motion'), the third category and the last recognized as an 'object', is significant in the causal mechanism of conjunctions and disjunctions, two qualities that, in turn, are central in the explanation of qualitative change. The actions are attributes that exist only momentarily and only in material substances. Divided into five kinds – throwing upwards, throwing downwards, contraction, expansion and motion (gamana, also translated 'going') – actions may arise from gravity, fluidity, conjunction or effort. The first three qualities productive of actions all reside in material substances. The quality of effort, volitional dispositions of the soul, establishes the link of action with consciousness. The category nevertheless does not overlap fully with a usual notion of agency, being always rooted in material reality. Thus all action occurs as some kind of physical motion. The divisions within this category were always a subject of debate even within the Nyāya-Vaiśeṣika tradition. If all actions are movements of material substances, then why not take the first four simply as various instances of the fifth, motion? Each of the two pairs of opposites is, unlike motion, associated with a definite direction. It was

also asserted that these directed actions may be produced by conscious effort, unlike motion, which may occur in the absence of consciousness. Thus the kinds of action serve to distinguish intentionally caused movement from blind events.

Just as the list of actions was disputed, so too was the status of action as a category distinct from quality (notably by Raghunātha in the sixteenth century). In fact the category of action furnishes the basis for the changing object. Although not all qualities are permanent or coeval with their substrates (some change while the underlying substance retains identity), all are nevertheless static. In the firing of a clay jar, one colour replaces another. When conjunction, a quality closely associated with actions, occurs, it is one unitary object that inheres in two substances. Action, on the other hand, is dynamic, and, while inhering in substances just like qualities, is momentary. Unlike qualities, which can produce other qualities, an action never produces another action. So in a chain reaction of ricocheting balls, to take an example, a conjunction of two substances produces an action, which terminates when the next contact is made, which conjunction in turn produces another action, and so forth.

6 Universal and particularity

The universal (sāmānya) and particularity (viśeṣa, also translated 'individuator' or 'describer') inhere in other entities and allow us to group and distinguish them. A quality is distinguished in name from a universal by the addition of an abstract suffix to designate the universal. 'Red' is a quality, but 'redness' is a universal. The strict separation of qualities and motions from the substances that contain them makes universals indispensable. Qualities and actions are individual – the red contained in one substance is by its inherence a separate thing from the red contained in another – and consequently qualities (as well as actions and substances) cannot be grouped or related in virtue of what they are in themselves. It is another side of the dilemma with substance: it is something other than its attributes, yet it is not possible to state what it is other than its attributes.

This dilemma is the threat of nominalism, and to some extent the two categories of universal and particularity ward off nominalistic objections to the realism of the categories. Such objections arose in the extensive debates with Buddhist thinkers, who argued that all universals were mental constructs at most (see NOMINALISM, BUDDHIST DOCTRINE OF). The Buddhist claim in fact does not appear incompatible with the ambiguous assertion of the Vaiśeṣikasūtra that both universal and particularity are 'with regard to the understanding' (*buddhyapekṣa*). Later commentaries said that the universal is the cause of the cognition of inclusion, and the particularity the cause of the cognition of difference, while insisting that these categories, like the others, are real in themselves, not a mental product.

The universal may be defined as that which inheres in a plurality of objects and brings about the idea of itself in any one. The universal pervades all its objects, having the same form in all in which it inheres. In this it is distinct from qualities. Thus the blue of a blue substance is one individual, coextensive with and momentarily posterior to its underlying substrate. (The quality is produced momentarily after the substance is produced, since it is caused by the substance; to make it simultaneous would risk rendering the quality and substance identical.) It inheres in only one thing, and is itself the locus of inherence. The universal blueness, however, as opposed to the quality blue, inheres as one in the many distinct and individual qualities that are all correctly called blue. The inclusiveness of the universal is said to distinguish it from its substrate. Thus, for example, substanceness is not identical with substance, since the latter is known by exclusion, by reference to what it is not. A further conclusion drawn is the eternality of universals, since, as independent from their substrates, universals are not produced by their substrates and so do not go out of existence with the destruction of the substrate.

Unlike the quality that it is in, nothing is in the universal. Since it is not a locus of inherence, the universal (like the particularity and the category of inherence) is not an object. Even with the commitment to the reality of universals, there is a sense in which they do not exist. One reason for this is a regress problem. The most general of universals, being, inheres in all objects, that is to say in all substances, qualities and actions. If 'being' were to inhere in universals as well, and universals could therefore be substrates of inherence, then 'being' itself would be an object, requiring a yet more general kind of 'being' to inhere in it, and so forth *ad infinitum*.

Universals not only allow us to include, but also to distinguish. 'Blueness' makes it possible to group all blue entities as one in respect of colour, but it also distinguishes from other colours. For this reason the universals are divided into 'higher' and 'lower'. Of the higher there is only one, 'being', since it is the only universal that is purely inclusive, all objects being its substrates. All other universals allow discrimination, and so cause both the cognition of inclusion as well as the cognition of particularity. All universals more specific than 'being' are therefore called 'particular universals' (*sāmānyaviśeṣa*). Any cognition that

involves inclusion due to similarity of form, however, is properly called a universal, not a particularity.

Particularities, the cause of the cognition of distinction, like universals inhere eternally in substrates without themselves being inhered in. Unlike universals, however, each particularity inheres in only one substrate. Since they are eternal, and since they have only one substrate, that substrate can only be an eternal substance: atoms, ether, time, space, soul or mind. The atomic substances are characterized by nothing in themselves that allows their discrimination, and therefore particularity is ascribed as the cause of knowing atoms to be distinct, a distinction perceptible to the yogin alone.

Despite the seemingly unclear ontological status of universal and particularity, they are crucial concepts in the Vaiśeṣika system of categories. As has been seen, there is nothing about a substance itself, which is presented as a bare receptacle, a harbour for attributes, to allow us to say what the substances, the foundations of reality, are in themselves. This function falls largely to these categories, and is defended on the grounds that, apart from the reality of universals, there would be no unity of individuals, and consequently no object denoted by words, which would entail the vacuity of all categories.

7 Inherence

Inherence, perhaps the least accessible of the categories, is nevertheless essential both to the organization of the Nyāya-Vaiśeṣika categories and to the ontological priority of substance. This category represents a special kind of relation. It is the permanent and indissoluble connection of two entities which are knowably distinct. The relation of inherence also indicates an order of dependence, being a relation of container to contained. In virtue of the permanence and the order, inherence is distinguished from the other kinds of relation, the pair 'conjunction' and 'disjunction', which are classified as qualities.

The categories could be (and to a large extent are by the eleventh-century philosopher UDAYANA) defined simply in terms of inherence relations. Substance can inhere in substance, and is inhered in by qualities, actions and universals. Eternal substances are distinguished because they are also inhered in by a particularity. Qualities inhere in substances and have qualityness inhering in them; actions inhere in one substance at a time and have actionness inhering in them. Universals inhere in a plurality of entities but have nothing inhering in them. Likewise, nothing inheres in particularities, which, however, inhere in only a single substance. The relation inherence itself inheres in nothing and has nothing inhering in it.

In the order of inherence relations among the categories, the contained provides unity and identity, the container the reality of the single individual entity. Universals are not themselves objects, but are contained in objects of all sorts, actions, qualities and substances; actions and qualities are objects, but always contained in substances; substances, if contained at all, are contained in another substance. The nesting of contained and container comes to an end with the atomic, eternal substances.

The category of substance provides the foundation for the Nyāya-Vaiśeṣika quest for permanence and self-sameness, the continuity underlying all change. A quality must be a quality of something, an action must have an agent, and a word, to have meaning, must refer to something.

The inherence of substance in substance is always a whole–part relation, the whole inhering in the parts. As the whole is itself a unitary substance, the relation implies that the whole is something more than the aggregate of its parts. In support of this contention, the inherence of substance in substance is considered a special case of causality. The whole inheres in the parts and the parts are the inherence cause of the whole. The cloth inheres in the threads and the threads are the inherence cause of the cloth. The inherence of cloth in threads is not the same as the conjunction of the woven threads, on the grounds that conjunction, a temporary relation, occurs when action joins two previously separately existing substances, whereas the cloth, as contained, cannot exist separately from the threads. Thus, an aggregate of material substances does not make the whole aggregate one substance, but the inherence of the whole in the parts does. The clay pot is one substance, a whole that inheres in its parts, other substances, ultimately earth atoms; but two pots touching remain a distinct pair. A living organism is one substance made of innumerable substances, yet remains distinct from the ground it stands on. Classical Vaiśeṣika says little beyond distinguishing inherence from conjunction to maintain that wholes are other than aggregates. Other contentions make the distinction difficult to uphold, as the slightest change in a composite substance, brushing a few molecules off the pot surface, transforms it into an entirely different whole, an utterly new substance. Inherence, while rendering substances the foundation of a pluralistic realism as the containers that are not contained, also obscures what the individual unity of the substances consists in.

8 Parallels to the relation of inherence

It is instructive to compare the relation of inherence with a partial analogue in Aristotle's *Categories*. The analysis of predication shows for Aristotle a relation of containment that points to an ultimate substratum. A universal term, such as 'horse', can act both as subject and predicate in a sentence. But 'this horse', the term denoting an individual animal, can function only as subject. Grammatically, it is an ultimate subject of predication, and indicates a substance. Entities, which are denoted with words, may be said of something, present in something, both said of and present in, or neither said of nor present in. The term 'this horse' is an example of the last, and therefore indicates a substance, which, in the strictest sense, can neither be said of nor is present in anything else.

A tool for analysis, these relations do not constitute separate categories for Aristotle, unlike the Vaiśeṣika category of inherence. Moreover, in early Nyāya-Vaiśeṣika there is nothing analogous to the Aristotelian 'said of' relation. The difference is revealing for understanding the structure and organization of the Vaiśeṣika categories. Members of the Aristotelian category 'quality' (of which Aristotle gives no definitive listing) can be both 'said of' and 'present in', although not in the same sense. In the universal statement 'Roses are red', the quality 'red' is said of the subject 'rose' and the quality is real (for other red substances exist) even though the red rose in my vase withers and turns brown. But it may also be said that the rose in my hand is red in the sense that red is 'present in' it, meaning a particular red, a red that is no longer when a petal falls. Aristotle asserts the universality of qualities along with their dependence on ontologically fundamental substance: red exists without this red thing, but not without red things; and this red does not exist apart from this red thing.

The manner in which a quality may be conceived as present in a substance in Aristotle is analogous to the Vaiśeṣika understanding of qualities, which are in all cases individual and coextensive with the substances in which they inhere. Thus the Vaiśeṣika literature goes to lengths to defend the reality of a colour such as 'variegated'. Where a composite material substance does not have one single shade throughout (the fabric of a Hawaiian shirt, for example), its colour must nevertheless be one. The quality is one not by being what it is, but by being contained. Consequently any change in quality – with the exception of the cases distinguished as qualitative change due to 'cooking' (see §4) – is due to an underlying change in the containing substance. In Aristotle, where one petal falls the rose still is, although altered, and that particular red is no more; in Vaiśeṣika, both the substance itself and its qualities have been succeeded by new entities.

Therefore it might be said that in the Vaiśeṣika categories the identity of form is a separate consideration from the unity of an individual. This also marks a telling difference from Aristotelian ontology, where the individual substance is not only one as a substrate, but is one because it is a 'this', an essence. (Although some of the Vaiśeṣika substances are distinguished by qualities peculiar to that kind, this 'mark' is never the equivalent of the Greek notion of essence.) Nothing in classical Vaiśeṣika is analogous to the Aristotelian notion of a quality being said of, not present in, a substance. Vaiśeṣika does acknowledge a real unity of form to qualities of different individuals. This must be explicable by means of the inherence relation, and thus the universals, such as substanceness, qualityness, redness, are recognized as a distinct category. These too are present by containment. Redness inheres, not in substances, but in the reds, which in turn inhere in substances. When a person smells the rose, inhaling pollen in the process, the original composite substance has been destroyed and replaced by a new one, yet we will continue, correctly, to call it a rose.

9 Later developments to inherence and relations

Where Aristotle grounded the individuality of substances in an essence, which led him to wrestle in the *Metaphysics* with maintaining the ontological priority of substance to form, the Nyāya-Vaiśeṣika categories were careful to keep substance separate from quality and universal. This led to another philosophical difficulty, the difficulty of saying what a substance in itself is, to give content to the assertion that a substance apart from all other categories has a *svarūpa*, a nature in itself. We have seen this in a couple of respects. It is difficult to justify the distinction of a whole from an aggregate. And the ultimate substances are reduced to bare particulars, atoms, which in themselves cannot be distinguished, requiring the introduction of particularity as a category. The term *svarūpa*, self-nature, was often connected more closely with the discussion of universals as they qualify substances, not the substances in themselves.

Navya-Nyāya, in the Nyāya-Vaiśeṣika tradition the 'new' school inspired by Udayana and beginning with GAṄGEŚA (fourteenth century), significantly expands the analysis of relations, in general associating relations more intimately with the relata. Thus inherence was traditionally asserted to be one, on the grounds that it is always the same relation, a permanent relation of contained to container. This item of doctrine becomes a matter of debate, with some asserting that inherences are many and equal in number to the pairs of entities related by inherence.

The kinds of relation were also rethought. In the earlier period, relations were explained primarily by inherence, a separate category, as well as conjunction and disjunction, which are qualities. Navya-Nyāya, holding that the individual may also be related to other entities by its own nature, locates some relations not in separate categories, but in the individuals. This *svarūpasambandha* ('self-linking connector', 'peculiar relation') comes to have many varieties, but is especially important as the relation between a particular universal, that is, a universal less abstract than 'being' that therefore distinguishes what it qualifies from other things, and the entity the universal qualifies. For Praśastapāda, short of yogic knowledge of a substance as its very self, the knowledge of substances and other individuals is had by perception of an individual's own nature (*svarūpa*), which is the perception of a particular universal (*sāmānyaviśeṣa*) inhering in the individual. In Navya-Nyāya, the universal form, while still of a different category from the individual it qualifies, is more closely associated with the individual by making the relation of redness to red and of Bobness to Bob not inherence but *svarūpasambandha*. The form is still separate, but its relation to the individual is located in the individual itself, no longer in a third category. In the face of ultimate substances, bare and seemingly indefinable particulars, the particular relation marks an attempt to make definition possible by a more elaborate mechanism of specifying a substrate's relation to other entities.

The other major use of the *svarūpasambandha* relation is in explaining negations, in the relation of a substrate to something nonexistent, as in the proposition 'There is no pot on the mat'. This relation involves the final category.

10 Nonexistence or absence

The seventh category is of later origin than the first six. Discussed in the *Vaiśeṣikasūtra*, although not classified as a category, it is given little attention by Praśastapāda. It is acknowledged as a separate category by later writers and accepted without question in the subsequent Navya-Nyāya tradition. With the acceptance of nonexistence as a category, the structure of the categories is threefold. Substance, quality and action are all *satta*, reality, the name of the highest universal, and are all designated objects. The first three as well as universal, particularity and inherence are all designated *bhāva*, real, existing or present, in distinction to the seventh, *abhāva*, nonexistence or absence. Analysis of negation comes to be a central concern of Navya-Nyāya, including such questions as whether an absence is perceptible and whether the absence of an absence is positive or negative, that is, whether it is itself an absence. The basic division of nonexistence or absence was into four: prior absence is the nonexistence of an entity before it has been produced, posterior absence is its nonexistence after destruction, absolute absence is its nonexistence at all times and mutual absence is the nonexistence of one thing in another, such as the mutual absence of fire in water. The assertion of a mutual absence is equivalent to an assertion of nonidentity.

Any assertion of nonexistence is taken as an implicit reference to some positive entity, called the *pratiyogi* (counterpositive), which could be present in a substrate. Ultimate atomic substances appeared in themselves to be bare receptacles. Even with the addition of particular relations grounded in the individual substrate, to say something about an entity in itself is to say something about its relation to something else. Consequently a negative statement demands that the absence be a distinct entity, even though having no *svarūpa*, no nature of its own. 'There is no pot on the mat' is an assertion that, like any other assertion about the mat, places the mat in relation to something other, namely an absence (see NEGATIVE FACTS IN CLASSICAL INDIAN PHILOSOPHY).

11 The nature of the self

A theory of categories is intended to lay out the structure of reality, affording knowledge of what is. For philosophy in India, a person seeks knowledge of what is, not to satisfy human curiosity, but to fulfil the highest possible goal, commonly described as liberation of the soul. Traditionally, philosophical knowledge is one means to that end. The realism of the categories yields at the same time an account of that highest state of soul.

Part of that account, much disputed by other schools of thought, is the reality of soul (rejected by the Buddhists) and the plurality of individual souls (rejected by most other major schools). While material substances are defined and their existence is inferred by their attributes, it is still argued that perception of material substances themselves as distinct from all inhering qualities is possible. The establishment of the soul is more problematic, because it is asserted from the outset that the soul is an imperceptible substance. Therefore it is knowable only by inference. The existence of the self is inferred primarily from perception and agency. There must be a perceiver to whom the perception belongs, an agent who acts. Beyond this argument, the soul is inferred on the basis of the understanding of the nature of qualities: since no quality is independent – all exist only inhering in a substance that can contain them –

and since we perceive certain qualities that are not encountered in material substances, namely, cognition, pleasure, pain and so forth, the self must exist as their substrate. There are no marks of soul in the sense that smell is the mark of earth. Certain qualities can exist in soul alone – pleasure, cognition and others – and all can also be absent. No qualities are coeval with soul. More clearly than for any other substance, soul is a container, not identifiable with and separate from any of its contents. To seek out and grasp the structure of reality is therefore to grasp the self. Liberation is 'the subsistence of the self in its own pristine condition, marked by the cessation of all the specific qualities pertaining to it' (Śrīdhara, *Nyāyakandalī*, to *Padārthadharmasaṅgraha* VI, x; trans. G. Jha, 1915). Paradoxically, the simple picture drawn of the soul epitomizes the entire system of categories in its intricate complexity.

See also: CATEGORIES; MATTER, INDIAN CONCEPTIONS OF §2; NYĀYA-VAIŚEṢIKA; ONTOLOGY; UNIVERSALS, INDIAN THEORIES OF

References and further reading

Faddegon, B. (1918) *The Vaicesika System*, Amsterdam: Akademie van Wetenschappen. (An early descriptive survey with summaries and translations of some texts.)

Halbfass, W. (1992) *On Being and What there Is*, Albany, NY: State University of New York Press. (An excellent, informed, very readable account of classical Vaiśeṣika.)

Ingalls, D. (1951) *Materials for the Study of Navya-Nyāya Logic*, Boston, MA: Harvard University Press. (Inevitably technical, but a good brief introduction to Navya-Nyāya.)

Matilal, B.K. (1977) *Nyāya-Vaiśeṣika*, vol. 6.2 of *A History of Indian Literature*, ed. J. Gonda, Wiesbaden: Harrassowitz. (A good scholarly survey.)

Nyāyasūtra (c.400 AD), trans. G. Jha, *Gautama's Nyāyasūtras with Vātsyāyana Bhāṣya*, Poona Oriental Series 59, Poona: Oriental Book Agency, 1939. (One of the foundational works in the Nyāya-Vaiśeṣika tradition; for further reference, Potter 1977, and Potter and Bhattacharyya 1993 are excellent sources.)

Potter, K.H. (ed.) (1977) *Encyclopedia of Indian Philosophies*, vol. 2, *Indian Metaphysics and Epistemology: The Tradition of Nyāya-Vaiśeṣika up to Gaṅgeśa*, Princeton, NJ: Princeton University Press. (A good scholarly survey.)

Potter, K.H. and Bhattacharyya, S. (eds) (1993) *Encyclopedia of Indian Philosophies*, vol. 6, *Indian Philosophical Analysis: Nyāya-Vaiśeṣika from Gaṅg-*

eśa to Raghunātha Śiromaṇi, Princeton, NJ: Princeton University Press. (Similar in structure to Potter 1977, covering a later period.)
* Praśastāpada (6th century) Padārthadharmasaṅgraha (Compendium of Properties of the Categories), trans. G. Jha, Padārthadharmasaṅgraha of Praśastapāda, with the Nyāyakandalī of Śrīdhara, Chaukhambha Oriental Series 4, Varanasi: Chaukhambha Orientalia, 1915. (One of the foundational works in the Nyāya-Vaiśeṣika tradition; for further reference, Potter 1977, and Potter and Bhattacharyya 1993 are excellent sources.)
* Vaiśeṣikasūtra (c. 2nd–3rd century AD), trans. and ed. N. Sinha, The Vaiśeṣika Sûtras of Kaṇâda with the Commentary of Śaṅkara Miśra, Sacred Books of the Hindus 6, Allahabad: Pāṇini Office, 1911. (One of the foundational works in the Nyāya-Vaiśeṣika tradition; for further reference, Potter 1977, and Potter and Bhattacharyya 1993 are excellent sources.)

DAVID AMBUEL

OPACITY see INDIRECT DISCOURSE; INTENSIONAL LOGICS; MODAL LOGIC, PHILOSOPHICAL ISSUES IN; PROPOSITIONAL ATTITUDE STATEMENTS; SEMANTICS, POSSIBLE WORLDS

OPERA, AESTHETICS OF

Opera, which may be defined as a dramatic action set in large part to music, is an inherently unstable art form, more so than any other. It has been characteristic of its practitioners and critics to call it periodically to order, in idioms which vary but carry much the same message: the music exists to further the drama. This has often been taken to be a matter of settling the priority of two elements: music and text. But in fact three are involved: music, text and plot (or action).

Opera began very abruptly in Northern Italy at the end of the sixteenth century, partly as the result of discussions about its possibility. To begin with, familiar Greek myths were employed, set in the vernacular, with simple accompaniments so that every word could be heard. This led to pre-eminence for the singers and for spectacle. After each wave of excess – vocal prowess, dance interludes, stilted plots and texts, then once

again, in the nineteenth century, empty display, and later gargantuan orchestras – there was a movement of revolt. Philosophers rarely took part in these aesthetic disputes, most of them being uninterested in music, and possibly more relevantly, being uninterested in any subject which can only be studied in historical terms. But it is fruitless to think about opera apart from its manifestations; every great operatic composer makes his own treaty between the potentially warring elements, Wagner being the most passionate propagandist for his own conception. In the twentieth century the aesthetics of opera have become pluralistic, as has, to an unprecedented degree, the form itself. The perpetual danger is that opera should degenerate into entertainment, and it is always the same message that recalls it to its original function – one which most spectators and listeners are happy to ignore: opera is a form of drama.

1 **The constituents of opera, and a promising beginning**
2 **Aesthetics and history**
3 **Mozart: sublime complexity**
4 **The trauma of Wagner**
5 **Aesthetic pluralism**

1 **The constituents of opera, and a promising beginning**

An opera is a drama which is in large part sung and is accompanied by an orchestra. Hence one can see that it is not an art form in which the elements are likely to remain in a stable relationship. The history of theorizing about opera, which naturally runs alongside the history of opera itself, is one of constant complaint and propaganda for a return to the ideals of the founders of the form – though as musical and other means develop, it is taken for granted that they will be realized in different idioms.

Although drama with musical accompaniment was no new thing when the theorists of opera were holding their debates in Florence towards the end of the sixteenth century, it had never been discussed in a systematic way. The Florentine theorists wished to return to something approaching the original performance-conditions of Greek tragedy; they were typical of Renaissance propagandists, both in seeking a validation for their theories by claiming that they were a return to antiquity and in having only a vague idea of what that would be. The Camerata, as they called themselves, were in fact concerned to bring a new art form into existence in the light of the possibilities of staging large-scale spectacles at North Italian courts – an art form in which actors with fine singing voices could perform versions of classical myths with whatever instrumental forces happened to be available. It may well be the only major kind of art for which an agenda has been worked out in advance of any actual examples.

As a notoriously liquid language, Italian possessed an in-built possibility of lyricism which was lavishly exploited by the first great master of opera, Monteverdi (1567–1643), whose *Orfeo* got the form off to a remarkably impressive start. It is sparsely accompanied, so that every word can be clearly understood. The elements of opera – singing, orchestral music, text and drama – are in the accord that the Camerata had promulgated. Most of Monteverdi's subsequent operas are lost, but his last two, dating from the early 1640s, survive; though they are both different from *Orfeo*, and from one another, they maintain the principles and thus the balance which he had exemplified from the beginning. But having begun as a court entertainment, opera rapidly became one that appealed to the masses. It would be absurd to maintain that its popularity led to its decline. That would probably have occurred in any case, but what took over were an ever-greater lavishness in stage spectacle, longer and less relevant dance interludes, and a tendency on the part of the vocal soloists to demonstrate their often prodigious technique. Within a century of its birth, opera had already become decadent.

2 Aesthetics and history

The aesthetics of any art form, if they are to serve any useful purpose, are necessarily closely linked to the form's history; this is especially the case with the performing arts. The great manifestos which punctuate opera's history have all been devoted to the same task: that of recalling opera to the high ideals with which it began, and analysing the factors which have led to its departure from them. How large, for example, can the orchestra become without rendering the words that the singers are producing incomprehensible or even inaudible? How can one hope to understand a singer who produces an elaborate sequence of notes on a single syllable? The old tug of war between pleasure and instruction is nowhere more acute than in opera, instruction favouring simplicity of means, pleasure various kinds of display. Many of opera's greatest practitioners and all its leading theorists have been people who conceived of it as playing an important role in society, and of performances of significant works as serving to unite the audience in a celebration of shared communal values. But the temptations to indulge in one or another mode of virtuosity have repeatedly proved too strong.

A more deep-seated reason for the instability of opera lies in its relationship with the purely instrumental music of its time. For its earliest practitioners this was hardly a problem, since instrumental music as such was not yet a going concern. There is nothing in Monteverdi's operas that we can recognize as large-scale musical organization. Music remains subordinate to drama to a degree which ears familiar with Mozart or Wagner can find frustrating. But, in the eighteenth century, before purely instrumental music was fully under way as an autonomous art, composers of opera were developing the aria, in which a character who was previously getting through a lot of musical prose, as it may be termed, takes their time to explore an emotion at greater length, to a melody which is appropriate to that emotion. The effect of this was to hold up the action, so that opera tended, in its second century, to become increasingly static.

This stalemate could not be broken until instrumental music became much more diverse in its modes of organization than it had been before the birth of sonata form, in the latter part of the eighteenth century. However much discussion of opera there might have been, it could not attain an adequate degree of detail and sophistication until music itself had advanced beyond a dependence on dance forms and counterpoint. For debate about the relationship between text, drama and music depends on what are envisaged as the possibilities of music. The expression of conflicting emotions only becomes feasible when contrasting themes are brought into relationship with one another and their conflicts are resolved in terms of more or less large-scale harmonic organization. That is what happened in the sonatas, symphonies and chamber works of Haydn and Mozart, and what therefore enabled Mozart to write his operatic masterpieces, which dwarf all those that preceded him. By contrast Gluck (1714–87), the co-author of the Preface to his opera *Alceste*, one of the most famous of all insistences on the primacy of drama, gives the impression of advance in his 'reform operas' only by returning, in his own way, to a pre-Handelian simplicity. He made a virtue of necessity by avoiding all musical elaboration, thus conveying a unique sense of directness and dramatic relevance.

3 Mozart: sublime complexity

Mozart (1756–91) is the only great composer who is equally distinguished in operatic and instrumental works. His greatness in each fed that in the other. He had no need to theorize about opera, because he was able to take over into his operas the procedures that he employed above all in his sublime series of piano concertos. In his mature operatic masterpieces the glories, above all, are the huge ensembles. Though, strictly speaking, they are not in sonata form, they give the listener the firmest sense of a musical argument which underpins and indeed absorbs into itself the text and action, creating a seamless whole.

It is perhaps these works, more than any others, which led Joseph Kerman, in his influential *Opera as Drama* (1956), to claim that, in relation to opera, music serves the same function that poetry serves in poetic drama; above all in Shakespeare. That cannot be quite right. If one wishes, one can read libretti by themselves (not recommended). But one cannot read Shakespeare's plays without the poetry. The most one can do along those lines is paraphrase it. Shakespeare does his thinking in the language which he commits to paper. But in opera, even when the librettist and the composer are the same person, there are the words and there is the music, and one can admire or deplore the setting of the former to the latter. What precisely follows from this it is hard to say. Certainly the effect in the finest of operas is one of indissolubility. But there remains a crucial difference between the intensification of effect which music can achieve, and the absolutely singular effect of poetic drama. That is one reason why there is so much more criticism of poetic drama than of opera. Mozart's *Don Giovanni* is perhaps as complex a figure as Shakespeare's *Hamlet*, but though there are vast amounts of commentary on both these characters, that on Hamlet will always far outstrip that on the Don. Poetry seems to challenge us to explain its implications, since if it is as great as Shakespeare's we will never complete the task. Music, at least when it functions as it does in Mozart's operas, deepens a meaning which the text and action provide, and can add ambiguities and complexities, but within more circumscribed limits, it seems. Thus even in the case of a work as fascinating in its levels of operation as *Così fan tutte*, there is always the text to refer to, and the text is rather straightforward. In one way, the music itself provides most of the criticism of the drama that we need, at the same time as it creates it.

4 The trauma of Wagner

As with nearly all supreme creative figures, Mozart was both an inspiration and a depressant to his successors. In the presence of his works, discussion of the aesthetics of opera seems superfluous. But once more, degeneration set in, and once more in Italy, the home of opera. The writers of so-called *bel canto* opera were largely unconcerned with theory, and in any case the culture industry of which they were a part gave them no time for anything but the composition of their next work. But it was the dominance of singers which again led to drama yielding to music.

Meanwhile, in Paris, the demand for lavish spectacle reached a new pitch of vulgarity, perfectly catered for by the white elephants of Meyerbeer (1791–1864). 'Effects without causes' was Wagner's description of his operas. It is Wagner (1813–83) who provided the next set of fundamental arguments about the nature and function of opera. Having himself set off on a course which was internationally influenced, with Meyerbeer as one of the contributors to his development, he was led by a series of historical events (many of which were unconnected with his art) to think with a depth and sustained energy about opera which has no parallel in the history of any of the arts, and which has set the agenda for operatic aesthetics ever since.

Wagner's dissatisfaction with opera was part of a wider revulsion from the whole society in which he lived. As a participant in the Dresden uprising of 1848–9 he was impelled both to think through the whole set of relations between politics and art, and to develop the concept of a total work of art, which would mirror the reintegration of man and society, and without which he could see only misery ahead. He saw in myth the fundamental truths about the human condition, but it was myth reinterpreted from a psychological standpoint. This could only be realized by the writing of libretti (he always wrote his own) of a complexity and density previously unknown, and the relegation to a subordinate place of music, which would nevertheless possess a degree of sophistication comparable to that of Beethoven's instrumental works. The aim was something far more ambitious than any operatic composer, indeed any artist, had entertained before: the transformation of consciousness by overwhelming communal experience.

The enormous body of theorizing which Wagner produced after the failure of the uprising is characterized by generalizations of Hegelian proportions, and expressed in language no less forbidding. But when he was introduced to the writings of Schopenhauer in 1854, he revised his views about the importance of music in relationship to the other elements of music drama, moving to a position where he saw it as the main conveyor of the drama. His celebrated later statement, that his dramas were 'deeds of music made manifest', sums up his new position. There has been an enormous amount of debate about the connections between Wagner's theories and his practice, but the overwhelming force of the latter and the ambitiousness of the former have guaranteed that his views and his art have been a major focus of aesthetic discussion, and not only of opera. Operatic theory and practice have been polarized, for the last 140 years, into pro- and anti-Wagnerian positions. The most strenuous objectors have been of two kinds: those who feel that his claims for art, and for music drama in particular, are preposterously inflated, and who have therefore advocated a return to some kind of pre-Wagnerian aesthetic (Stravinsky being the most articulate case); the second group have seen opera as an instrument of social change only on the condition that it stresses its own artificiality and leads its spectators to think about issues in a highly conscious way. Pre-eminent among this school have been the Marxists Brecht and Weill.

5 Aesthetic pluralism

Few general conclusions can be drawn from studying the history of opera and its commentators. Each operatic composer of genius has worked out the relationship between text, drama and music in his own way. Since operas which possess a fine text but contain no distinguished music do not survive, and some operas survive which possess a wretched plot and text but magnificent music, it is often claimed that opera is fundamentally a musical, not a dramatic form. The fact that one can enjoy an opera while having only a vague idea of what is being sung or what the action is seems to point in the same direction. These claims leave open the view that the operas which matter most are those in which drama is articulated by music, and that those in which only the music counts are less artistically significant.

Operas are popular for different reasons, and many opera lovers, or fans, are more interested in hearing superb voices show off than in anything else. The distinction between entertainment and art seems to be more laxly applied here than in the case of most other art forms. The battle for opera as a serious form, which ranks at its best with the greatest art forms, is one that is constantly having to be re-fought; it can be no coincidence that it is always conducted in terms of opera as drama.

See also: MUSIC, AESTHETICS OF; PERFORMING ART §§1–3

References and further reading

Donington, R. (1991) *Opera and its Symbols*, New Haven, CT: Yale University Press. (A highly original history of opera and its aesthetics in terms of recurring symbols.)

Goldmann, A. and Sprinchorn, E. (eds) (1964) *Wagner on Music and Drama*, New York: E.P. Dutton. (An excellent selection of Wagner's prose, unfortunately in terrible translation; but no other is available.)

* Kerman, J. (1956) *Opera as Drama*, New York: Oxford University Press, 2nd edn, 1989. (The most

influential account of opera to have been published this century.)

Kivy, P. (1988) *Osmin's Rage: Philosophical Reflections on Opera, Drama and Text*, Princeton, NJ: Princeton University Press. (An historical account of opera from Monteverdi to Mozart, substituting for 'opera as drama' a notion of 'drama made music'.)

Strunk, O. (ed.) (1950) *Source Readings in Music History*, New York: W.W. Norton. (Contains all the seminal texts of the history of operatic aesthetics up to the end of the nineteenth century, except for inadequate representation of Wagner.)

Williams, B. (1992) 'The Nature of Opera', in *The New Grove Dictionary of Opera*, London: Macmillan, vol. 3. (A brilliant short account of the basic issues in operatic aesthetics and practice.)

MICHAEL TANNER

OPERATIONALISM

'Operationalism', coined by the physicist Percy W. Bridgman (1927), has come to designate a loosely connected body of similar but conflicting views about how scientific theories or concepts are connected to reality or observation via various measurement and other procedures. Examples of an operation would be the procedure of laying a standard yardstick along the edge of a surface to measure length or using psychometric tests to measure sexual orientation. In the 1920–50s different versions of operationalism were produced by, amongst others: Bridgman, who was concerned with the ontology of basic units in physics; behaviourists such as E.C. Tolman, S.S. Stevens, who were concerned with the measurement of intervening variables or hypothetical constructs not accessible to direct observation, as well as B.F. Skinner, who sought to eliminate such nonobservables; and positivistic philosophers of science who were analysing the meaning of terms in scientific language. Conflation of their different operationalist philosophies has led to a great deal of nonsense about operational definition, methodology of observation and experiment, and the meaning of scientific concepts. Operationalist doctrines were most influential in the social sciences, and today the primary legacy is the practice of operationally defining abstract social science concepts as measurable variables.

1   Bridgman
2   Logical positivism
3   Behaviourisms
4   The operationalist legacy

1 Bridgman

Nineteenth-century physics extended the scope of Newtonian mechanics to include radiant heat, sound, electricity and magnetism, and so on, by modelling these phenomena as waves through a rarefied fluid-like ether. The 1887 Michelson–Morely interferometer experiments failed to detect a suitable ether, thereby laying the basis for the replacement of Newtonian mechanics by relativity theory. P.W. BRIDGMAN viewed the Einsteinian revolution as challenging the assumptions on which classical experimental physics was based, and thus saw special relativity theory as calling into question all absolute physical principles and the existence of absolute physical matter. What, then, could be the subject matter experimental physics studied? Perceiving Einstein as having built relativistic physics out of various basic or elementary operations such as were used to measure relative simultaneity, he concluded that these basic operations not only connected theory to experiment but themselves were what experimental science studied. The heart of Bridgman's operationalism thus was an ontological view about the basic constituents of empirical reality. When he said, 'we mean by any concept nothing more than a set of operations; the concept is synonymous with the corresponding set of operations' he was making the claim that concepts ultimately referred to constituent basic operations and nothing more. He thus rejected the idea that there were any *things* which the basic measurement procedures measured. In later works he embraced the incipient subjectivism of this position.

Bridgman insisted that each operation defines a separate concept, by which he meant that the referents of a given concept were precisely the mix of operations used in the specific operational definition. Critics charged that concepts like *temperature* admit of different measurement procedures, and so it was a mistake to equate the *meaning* of temperature with any particular procedure for measuring temperature. The extension of the term 'temperature' encompasses things measured by different procedures, but extension is not the sense of 'meaning' in Bridgman's dictum that the meaning of a concept is the set of operations; for his position denied the existence of things which could be the extension of a concept. Bridgman readily acknowledged that there could be connections among operationally defined concepts, and that terms like 'temperature' encompassed such connected operationally defined concepts. The basis of these connections was theory. For example, the various distinct concepts lumped under the rubric 'length' are 'connected' by the Lorentz transformation group from relativity theory – a kind

of 'fusion' of concepts (see RELATIVITY THEORY, PHILOSOPHICAL SIGNIFICANCE OF §1). Not all concepts in theories were definable by operations of physical measurement or experimental manipulation and design, and Bridgman allowed that 'paper and pencil' operations could be used to operationally define them.

For Bridgman operational analysis was a means for explicating and validating scientific concepts by disassembling theories and determining what was objective (rooted in basic operations). Non-objective theory content led to pseudo-problems. However, operational definition was not intended by Bridgman to be constitutive of concepts, a formula for doing science, the meaning link between formal and factual propositions, or a means of eliminating subjectivity from scientific knowledge. He increasingly found positivistic and behaviourist 'operationalist' philosophies that attempted to do so uncongenial. Although he had extended exchanges with operationalists like Stevens and Skinner, these eventually led to total estrangement.

2 Logical positivism

Logical positivists, too, focused on the implications of the Einsteinian revolution: where Newtonian mechanics went wrong was postulation of the fictitious ether, which, referring to nothing, was said to be an empty or meaningless concept. Utilizing resources of the new symbolic logic they sought to develop a precise language for doing science in which concepts referring to fictitious entities were precluded. Things were ontologically real precisely if statements about them could be verified. In their reconstructed language for science, vocabulary terms were divided into the *logical*, the *observational* and the *theoretical*. Logical portions of language were reduced to symbolic logic and hence were tautological. Observational terms referred to directly experienceable things and so observation-language assertions were epistemically and ontologically non-problematic. Unrestricted introduction of theoretical terms led to the postulation of fictitious entities. To avoid this, legitimate theoretical terms had to be suitably defined by a 'dictionary' of 'correspondence rules' that gave observational content to theoretical assertions. Until correspondence rules are added, the only meanings theoretical terms have are those 'implicitly defined' by the formal connections in theoretical laws (see THEORIES, SCIENTIFIC §§1–2).

Initially the correspondence rules were required to be *explicit definitions* that reduced theoretical terms to abbreviations for complex observable conditions according to Schlick's dictum that the meaning of a statement is its method of verification (see MEANING AND VERIFICATION §2). Explicit definitions are stipulative definitions, hence analytic truths. Positivists assimilated Bridgman's dicta that the meaning of a concept is its corresponding set of operations and that each operational procedure is identified with a distinct concept to explicit definition since basic operations could be described using observation terms. Such conflation fundamentally distorts Bridgman's position. Positivistic operational definitions are describing procedures for measuring the very physical things Bridgman denied, and operational definitions are being put forward both as a method for doing science and as connecting the formal to the factual.

Later positivists came to see that some terms in theoretical physics could not be identified with observable conditions. Taking an increasingly realist position on theoretical terms they became concerned that, say, temperature could be measured via different operational procedures, so they loosened restrictions on admissible theoretical terms by admitting a plurality of *reduction sentences* which were operational procedures *partially defining* the terms by specifying observable meaning relative to a specific experimental context. Different operational definitions of the same term allowed for different procedures and contexts. Reduction sentences assert contingent relations between apparatus, theoretical entities, and their observable manifestation as the output of detectors or measuring devices. They are empirically true or false, and thus do not specify meaning analytically like stipulative explicit definitions. What connects the various correspondence rules partially defining 'temperature' is the contingent fact that all these temperature procedures are measuring the same physical *thing*.

Positivists continued to conflate their position with Bridgman's, now likening operational definitions to reduction sentences – which led them to criticize Bridgman's view that each operational procedure defined a distinct concept. They also criticized Bridgman for his growing emphasis on the subjectivity he saw growing out of the denial of any absolute physical reality and his view that the objectivity of science rested in what scientists *do* when they operationalize.

Later the positivists came to see that some terms (such as the Ψ function in quantum mechanics) could not be individually defined even by reduction sentences. This led to the weaker requirement that theoretical terms did not have to be individually operationally defined so long as they occurred essentially in the theory and the theory itself had observable consequences specified by an *interpretive system* of correspondence rules linking the theoretical

and observational components. Positivists were never able satisfactorily to specify requirements for interpretive systems that demarcated scientific from nonscientific systems. Trading on earlier conflations, in moving to interpretive systems some positivists saw themselves as rejecting Bridgman's operationalism.

3 Behaviourisms

Although 'operationalism' was introduced to psychology around 1930, S.S. Stevens brought it to prominence. He argued that scientific disputes are rooted in disagreements over the application of concepts. Since the application of concepts is rooted in concrete operations, agreement on the operations that should be associated with a concept would eliminate previously unresolvable disagreements. If there are disagreements in the application of a concept these can be resolved in an 'operational regress' in which applicability is settled by iterated appeal to less problematic concepts.

Operations consist in gross physical behaviours (say, laying a yardstick along a surface) and a result (number at the point of edge congruence). *Denoting* is the most fundamental behaviour on which all operations depend. *Results* are the outcomes of discrimination, which 'is the fundamental operation of all science'. Science thus depends on observer characteristics and so psychology becomes 'the propaedeutic science', providing data on which operational procedures depend. But psychology *qua* science itself must be operationalist.

Although operations rest in scientists' discriminatory capabilities, Stevens rejected any notion of a sensory given or subjective basis for science. Operations *are* behaviours and the basic operation is 'to react discriminatively'. Science thus is 'public'. Measurement scales are constructed out of complexes of operations which determine their arithmetical properties.

Around 1933–4, Stevens encountered Bridgman's operationalism and logical positivism, and in subsequent writings allied his independently developed 'operationalist' philosophy with their positions despite substantive disagreements over their reliance on subjective experience or the sensory given. It is unclear whether Stevens subscribed to the view that concepts are synonymous with their associated operations, but he was unsympathetic towards what he understood to be positivism's 'linguistic operationalism'.

E.C. Tolman pioneered an 'operationalist' approach to mental phenomena in the 1920s, although he did not adopt the term until 1936. Mentalistic concepts required external criteria of application.

Behaviour is a complex function of stimulus conditions, hereditary makeup, past training and appetite or aversion. *Intervening variables* represent an organism's readiness to respond to stimuli and are to be operationally defined by means of standard experiments. One measures independent and dependent variables. Intervening variables are specified by holding all but one independent variable constant then determining the curve expressing the functional relationship between the selected independent and the dependent variable. Intervening variables thus required defining experiments. As Carnap was making the switch from explicit definitions to reduction sentences, Tolman spent some time in Vienna (1933–4), and his characterizations increasingly resembled Carnap's hypothetical constructs defined by reduction sentences. Whereas positivists viewed the operations linguistically, Tolman continued to construe them psychologically.

Stevens' articulation of the operationalist position provided focus for discussions of methodological issues surrounding behaviourism. Clark Hull (1940) had been an early advocate of the geometric method in psychology and quickly allied himself with axiomatic themes in positivism. Although he made little contribution to operationalism himself, his student Spence collaborated with the positivist Gustav Bergmann to produce a positivistic explicit definition version of operationalism (1941). B.F. Skinner was an early advocate of an explicit definition version of operationalism which held that since explicit definitions rendered theoretical terms (including intervening variables) eliminable, there was no justification for allowing theoretical terms in science. Hempel (1958) presents the positivistic rejoinder, stressing the importance of systematization and integration which theoretical terms allow.

Criticisms charged that operationalism was trivial or was a minor part of science, needlessly proliferated concepts, ultimately leaves psychological concepts undefined, and makes experimental error meaningless since there is no standard against which operations can be validated. The last charge was rebutted later by development of evaluative notions such as concurrent and construct validity.

4 The operationalist legacy

Although positivism had limited influence in the development of operationalist philosophies, it was an active focus of comparison and dissemination for disparate operationalist views. Scientific practice in psychology and sociology became increasingly behaviourist and operationalist in a manner that minimized fundamental differences. It became commonplace that theoretical terms should be operationally defined, but what that demanded became increasingly unclear.

MacCorquodale and Meehl (1948) crystallized issues when they construed intervening variables as those definable by explicit definitions and hypothetical constructs as those only definable via reduction sentences. Today it is commonplace that operational definitions are required when 'remote' quantitative variables are invoked. Yet exactly what operational definitions come to remains unresolved due to the conflations noted above. Disputes over the adequacy of operational definitions are frequently dismissed as 'mere semantic disputes' – a move appropriate only for stipulative explicit definitions – when they turn on whether the operational definitions correctly capture empirical connections between hypothetical-construct theoretical terms and various observable states of independent and dependent variables.

Nevertheless operational definitions remain an adequacy requirement for social science research.

See also: BEHAVIOURISM IN THE SOCIAL SCIENCES; BEHAVIOURISM, ANALYTIC; LOGICAL POSITIVISM; SCIENTIFIC METHOD

References and further reading

* Bergmann, G. and Spence, K.W. (1941) 'Operationalism and Theory in Psychology', *Psychological Review* 48: 1–14; repr. in M.H. Marx (ed.) *Psychological Theory: Contemporary Readings*, New York: Macmillan, 1951. (Presents an explicit definition positivistic version of operationalism.)
* Bridgman, P.W. (1927) *The Logic of Modern Physics*, New York: Macmillan. (Original statement of his operationalism.)
—— (1936) *The Nature of Physical Theory*, Princeton, NJ: Princeton University Press; repr. *Philosophical Writings of Percy Williams Bridgman*, New York: Arno Press, 1980. (In this work Bridgman pursues the subjectivist tendencies in his operationalism.)
—— (1950) *Reflections of a Physicist*, New York: Philosophical Library; 2nd edn, 1955; repr. Arno Press, New York, 1980. (The 2nd edition of 1955 contains ten papers additional to the original of 1950. Contains reprints of nearly all his philosophical and nontechnical papers on operationalism.)
Carnap, R. (1936–7) 'Testability and Meaning', *Philosophy of Science* 3: 420–66, 4: 1–40. (Classic positivistic criticism of explicit definition operationalization and articulation of reduction sentences approach.)
—— (1956) 'Methodological Character of Theoretical Concepts', in H. Feigl and M. Scriven (eds)

Minnesota Studies in the Philosophy of Science, Minneapolis, MN: University of Minnesota Press, vol. 1, 33–76. (Positivistic interpretative system account of operationalization which has extended discussion of operationalizing psychological concepts.)

Chronbach, L. and Meehl, P.H. (1955) 'Construct Validity in Psychological Tests', *Psychological Bulletin* 52: 281–302. (Classic articulation of validity notions for evaluating operational definitions.)

Hardcastle, G. (1995) 'S.S. Stevens' Philosophy of Science', *Philosophy of Science* 62: 404–24. (Assesses relations of Steven's operationalism to other behaviourisms and positivism.)

Hempel, C.G.(1952) *Fundamentals of Concept Formation in Empirical Science*, Chicago, IL: University of Chicago Press. (Positivistic account of operationalization that criticizes reduction sentence approach and introduces interpretative sentences.)

* —— (1958) 'The Theoretician's Dilemma', in H. Feigl, M. Scriven and G. Maxwell (eds) *Minnesota Studies in the Philosophy of Science*, Minneapolis, MN: University of Minnesota Press, vol. 2, 37–98; repr. *Aspects of Scientific Explanation and Other Essays in the Philosophy of Science*, New York: Free Press, 1965. (Positivistic rejoinder to Skinner on necessity of theoretical terms.)

* Hull, C.L. *et al.* (1940) *Mathematico-Deductive Theory of Rote Learning: A Study in Scientific Methodology*, New Haven, CT: Yale University Press. (Unsuccessful attempt to do psychology the positivistic way using symbolic logic.)

Israel, H. and Goldstein, B. (1944) 'Operationalism in Psychology', *Psychological Review* 51: 177–88. (Scathing attack on operationalism that prompts Boring to organize the 1945 'Symposium on Operationalism'.)

Koch, S. (ed.) (1959) 'Epilogue', *Psychology: A Study of a Science*, New York: McGraw-Hill, vol. 3, 729–88. (One of his many critical attacks on behaviourist operationalisms.)

* MacCorquodale, K. and Meehl, P.E. (1948) 'Hypothetical Constructs and Intervening Variables', *Psychological Review* 55: 95–107; repr. in H. Feigl and W. Sellars (eds) *Readings in the Philosophy of Science*, New York: Appleton-Century-Crofts, 1953. (Classic differentiation of intervening variables and hypothetical constructs on the basis of operational definition form.)

Moyer, A.E. (1991) 'P.W. Bridgman's Operational Perspective on Physics', *Studies in the History and Philosophy of Science* 22: 237–58, 373–97. (Historical account. 'Part I: Origins and Development' and 'Part II: Refinements, Publications, and Receptions'.)

Rogers, T.B. (1989) 'Operationalism in Psychology: A Discussion of Contextual Antecedents and an Historical Interpretation of its Longevity', *Journal of the History of the Behavioral Sciences* 23: 139–53. (Historical account.)

Schlick, M. (1936) 'Meaning and Verification', *Philosophical Review* 45: 339–69; repr. in H. Feigl and W. Sellars (eds) *Readings in Philosophical Analysis*, New York: Appleton-Century-Crofts, 1949. (Argues the meaning of a statement is its method of verification.)

Skinner, B.F. (1961) *Cumulative Record*, New York: Appleton-Century-Crofts. (Enlarged edition that contains reprintings of his papers detailing his operationalism and rejection of theories.)

Smith, L.D. (1986) *Behaviorism and Logical Positivism: A Reassessment of the Alliance*, Stanford, CA: Stanford University Press. (Comprehensive history arguing that behaviourist operationalism has minimal debts to positivism.)

Stevens, S.S. (1935) 'The Operational Basis of Psychology', *American Journal of Psychology* 47: 323–30. (Programmatic statement of his 'operationism'.)

—— (1935) 'The Operational Definition of Psychological Concepts', *Psychological Review* 42: 517–26. (Basic statement of his 'operationalism'.)

—— (1936) 'Psychology: The Propaedeutic Science', *Philosophy of Science* 3: 90–103. (Stevens 'fast-moving' summary of the operationalist point of view written for philosophers of science.)

—— (1939) 'Psychology and the Science of Science', *Psychological Bulletin* 36: 221–63. (An influential review article.)

Suppe, F. (1977) 'The Search for Philosophic Understanding of Scientific Theories', in F. Suppe (ed.) *The Structure of Scientific Theories*, Urbana, IL: University of Illinois Press, 2nd edn, 3–243. (Contains a comprehensive discussion of positivistic views on theories; pages 17–27 contains a detailed discussion of their changing operationalist views.)

Tolman, E.C. (1932) *Purposive Behavior in Animals and Men*, New York: Century. (Introduces intervening variables method but does not call it operationalist.)

—— (1966) *Behavior and Psychological Man: Essays in Motivation and Learning*, Berkeley, CA: University of California Press. (Reprinting of many of his papers on operationalism and behaviourism.)

Waters, R.H. and Pennington, A. (1938) 'Operationalism in Psychology', *Psychological Review* 45: 414–23. (Ambivalent critique raising the measurement error problem.)

Walter, M.L. (1992) *Science and Cultural Crisis: An Intellectual Biography of Percy Williams Bridgman*

(1882–1961), Stanford, CA: Stanford University Press. (Part III is a comprehensive account of Bridgman's operationalism and his interactions with positivists and behaviourists.)

FREDERICK SUPPE

OPERATORS, MODAL

see MODAL OPERATORS

OPTICS

Optics as physics concerned with the manipulation and study of light and, more recently, the general study of electromagnetic radiation, has a history back to ancient Egypt, and systematic study to classical Greece. But physics has proved better able to manipulate light than to explain its fundamental nature.

'Geometrical optics' treats light as a bundle of discrete rays, tracing their rectilinear paths reflected from surfaces and refracted through transparent media. 'Physical optics' treats light as a wave. It explains the dispersion of white light into spectral colours, the bands and colour patterns of diffraction phenomena, and aspects of the absorption and scattering of light. Characterizing the way in which the physical aspects of light become the perceptual aspects of shape and colour joins physics, physiology and philosophy in the perennial question of the correspondence of our perceptions to the physical world itself.

A modern view of light describes it in terms of massless particulate photons. This 'quantum optics' treats the absorption and emission of light by matter, providing precise knowledge of matter's inner structure, and the technology of lasers. Philosophically, quantum optics has led to the fundamental question: what is light? What is this natural entity which is created and destroyed in a particle-like way and yet propagates through space – and lenses, holes and slits – in a wave-like way? Experiments in which individual photons interfere with themselves make it hard to think of them as having unique paths. Experiments involving the correlation of photon properties threaten attempts to describe photons as having individual properties and interacting only locally.

1   **History**
2   **Classical optics**
3   **Vision**
4   **Light and relativity theory**
5   **Light and quantum mechanics**

1   History

Optical technology goes back at least three millennia. Mirrors made of polished copper and bronze were in use in ancient Egypt. The earliest known theories of light were held by the Greeks, who recognized the rectilinear propagation of light and stated the law of reflection. Lens combinations, in the form of the refracting telescope and microscope, were developed in the sixteenth century, and used notably by Galileo (see GALILEI, G. §2). But the historical debate about light relevant to current discussions of its nature began in the late seventeenth century.

Isaac Newton was the chief champion of the corpuscular account of light, holding that the different colours of light he saw in his dispersal of white light by means of a prism were associated with different corpuscles (see NEWTON, I. §2). His view stood against the undulatory view championed by Christiaan Huygens.

In Huygens' view, light was solely the result of rapidly (but finitely) propagating longitudinal undulations in ethereal matter, undulations which slowed down in denser media (in contrast to Newton's more rapidly moving corpuscles). Huygens was able to derive the laws of reflection and refraction, to explain the double refraction of certain crystals, and to recognize in it a manifestation of a kind of double character to light itself, a 'two-sidedness' as Newton described it, the phenomenon we now call polarization. The wave model was much improved by Thomas Young and Augustin Fresnel in the early nineteenth century. They introduced the revolutionary idea that ethereal undulations could interfere negatively as well as positively, thereby accounting for the diffraction patterns (bands of light and dark) arising from obstacles and apertures.

The peculiar two-sidedness of light remained a problem until Young's suggestion that ethereal undulations were transverse to the ray direction. Polarization was then simply a manifestation of the undulations of the ether in perpendicular directions.

This largely qualitative model of light propagation was rendered firmly quantitative by the work of James Clerk MAXWELL in the mid-nineteenth century. Maxwell's concern was with the nature of electrical and magnetic phenomena, and he was able to distill the essence of these phenomena into a very small set of mathematical expressions (see ELECTRODYNAMICS). From these equations, Maxwell was able to show that an electromagnetic disturbance could propagate as a transverse wave, with a speed determined by basic, and independently measurable, electric and magnetic properties of the medium. When Maxwell substituted known values of these properties into his velocity expression, the number he obtained was the same as that empirically determined (by Fizeau and Foucault) for the speed of light, roughly 186,000 miles per second. Light appeared to be precisely an electromagnetic disturbance propagated in the form of transverse waves through the ether.

Mathematically, with Maxwell's equations, the modern model of physical optics is complete. But conceptually, a great step had yet to be taken. For though Maxwell's mathematical analysis did not require any physical model of the ether, he remained firmly in the grip of it as a material underpinning. Yet as much as he was unable to imagine an electromagnetic undulation without an underlying undulatory medium, Maxwell nonetheless recognized the electromagnetic field itself as a repository of energy. In a vision with roots in the ideas of Michael Faraday, Maxwell saw the space surrounding electrified and magnetic bodies as suffused with energy. Rather than electromagnetic energy flowing through conductors with the flow of current, it was seen as flowing around and into them from the surrounding immaterial field. This view of the electromagnetic field as an autonomous entity, and light as an undulation in the field itself, is the field theory of physical optics (see FIELD THEORY, CLASSICAL).

2 Classical optics

These two views of light – the remnants of the corpuscular model in ray or geometrical optics and the electromagnetic wave model in physical optics – together define what is called classical optics. Almost all the optical phenomena comprising the world of visual experience, and the many ubiquitous optical apparatus which enhance this world, are generally understood in terms of classical optics.

Geometrical optics traces the rectilinear paths of light reflected from surfaces and refracted through transparent media in an optical system. Such a system, besides mirrors and lenses, may contain prisms, apertures, beamsplitters, gratings, filters, polarizers, diffusers, even fibre bundles. Each ray from an object point is traced through the system to a single point on an image plane. All these points make up the geometrical image of the object as formed by the system.

Where the wave character of light becomes important is in the realm of physical optics. Physical optics treats the entire spectrum of electromagnetic radiation, from radio waves of kilometre wavelengths, through microwaves, infrared, visible and ultraviolet light, to X-rays and finally gamma rays at a thousand-millionth of a millimetre. Though vastly different processes are involved in the emission and absorption of electromagnetic radiation over this range, its propagation through space – and through lenses, holes and slits – is treated in a perfectly unified way by Maxwell's equations and their interpretation; descriptive of an autonomous, energy-containing, yet immaterial field. Polarization, interference, diffraction, are all variations on the basic field-wave property of superposition: the linear combination of the perpendicularly oriented transverse components of multiple waves. Together with aspects of the absorption and scattering of light, they fully account for the shapes and colours we perceive in the world. How our visual universe is created from the processes of physical optics is another matter, however.

3 Vision

Our eyes are highly complex compound lens systems with electrochemical receptors. Place these eyes in the world of physical optics and one does have the means for accounting for virtually all the visual appearance of the world, though it is surprising how many and various are the physico-optical properties of objects that contribute to our perception of them. Still, though the image of the world on our retinas must contain all the information required for seeing, the relationship between that information and the content of our visual field is far from straightforward.

The resolution of detail permitted by our lens–receptor system, understood passively as a camera, is far less than what we actually resolve perceptually. We have blind spots and blood-vessel shadows on our retinas, chromatic aberration and scattering in our lenses, quivering and drifting induced by eyeball musculature, yet we see no vestiges of these in our perceptual world. Clearly, much visual processing goes on in the brain. Unfortunately, the further one moves from the visual receptors themselves and into the activity of the visual cortex of the brain, the less certain our understanding is.

The intimate involvement of the brain in seeing inevitably raises the philosophical issue of the correspondence of the visual field and the real world. Is, for instance, colour a genuine physical property, a combination of physical properties, or supervenient on some set of physical properties? An objectivist would answer the question in the affirmative. A subjectivist might counter that colours are only properties of physical objects in the sense of being dispositions of those objects to affect us visually in the way they do. As our understanding of neurophysiology increases, this debate becomes ever more subtle (see COLOUR, THEORIES OF).

4 Light and relativity theory

Nineteenth-century concerns with the anomalous physical properties of the luminiferous ether, and generations of efforts to detect it, were swept aside conceptually in the early twentieth century by Albert Einstein's special theory of relativity (see EINSTEIN, A. §2). (Michelson and Morley's interferometer experiment in 1887, popularly regarded as definitive, established any velocity of the earth with respect to an ether at less than 4,700 metres per second. Results from the 1980s limit this to 0.05 metres per second. Manipulation of light continues to have its own dynamic, independent of conceptual revolutions.) In Einstein's theory, the velocity of light is completely independent of the relative velocity of the source or any observer. (This assumption of Einstein's, in turn, has now been tested for relative velocities more than 90 per cent of light speed.) In a spatial analogy, this invariant velocity is like a far object that remains always at the same distance, no matter how one moves.

Conceptually, this anomalous property of light falls right out of the modern formulation of Einstein's theory as a spacetime theory (see SPACETIME §2). The intrinsic geometry of nature is four-dimensional, and our experience of it is as three-dimensional space and one-dimensional time, thus our notion of simultaneity and our determinations of velocity, are a function of our relation to this intrinsic geometry, our state of motion. In this formulation, light has a special place, traversing a special set of intrinsic straightest paths in (generally curved) spacetime. It is our locally-variable velocity determinations that produce the universal invariant velocity of light (see RELATIVITY THEORY, PHILOSOPHICAL SIGNIFICANCE OF §§1–2). Its invariance is enshrined in our current choice of world standards: the velocity of light was in 1983 set at its best measured value of 299,792,458 metres per second and the international standard of length was adjusted accordingly. All measured distances must now be thought of as light seconds.

5 Light and quantum mechanics

Einstein is closely associated with the other great twentieth-century revolution in our understanding of light, the quantum or (as it is now called) photon theory (see EINSTEIN, A. §4). In proposing that light is transmitted by free quanta that retain their particulate character as they travel through space, Einstein joined Max PLANCK in imagining that the exchange of energy between radiation and matter could take place only discontinuously, in energy quanta related to the frequency of the radiation.

The myriad interference effects that wave optics explained so readily were to be accounted for by inter-quanta interactions. Niels Bohr's treatment of the spectrum of the hydrogen atom added a crucial third component to this early quantum theory. In Bohr's treatment, atomic electron orbits of only certain energies were allowed. The frequency of radiation emitted and absorbed by the atom reflected the transitions between these discrete electron energy states, with the energy–frequency relation that of Planck.

Bohr's central idea has led to the vast field of modern spectroscopy, in which the emission and absorption of radiation by matter is analysed for astoundingly precise knowledge of molecular, atomic, nuclear and subnuclear structure. (The laser – a coherent, tightly focused beam of light created by the stimulated de-excitation of a population of atoms all excited to precisely the same state – has been one product, and essential tool, of modern spectroscopy.)

But the problem Einstein confronted with his hopes for an inter-quanta interaction theory of light interference now looms larger than ever. For it is now possible to manipulate experimentally single photons of light, and interference effects persist. The classic experiment involves placing a half-silvered mirror, or other beamsplitter, downstream from a light source, creating dual optical paths. (A half-silvered mirror is one in which the metallic coating is too thin to be opaque, so light will be both reflected and transmitted through it.) The presence of single photons is confirmed by correlating detection events in each path: perfect anticorrelation is unambiguous evidence for single photons. Yet when path detectors are replaced by mirrors, and the paths recombined, an interference pattern of individual photon impacts gradually accumulates. This occurs even when (effectively) the choice of mirrors or detectors is made after the light passes through the beamsplitter. It seems difficult to say, prior to the downstream choice of detectors or mirrors, that the light followed a single path (detectors) or both paths (mirrors). Yet surely any sense of unique energetic history would require that circumstance to be decided at the beamsplitter.

Another classic experiment is based on yet another proposal made by Einstein (see EINSTEIN, A. §5) and developed by John Bell in the 1960s (see BELL'S THEOREM). The proposal has to do with multi-component quantum systems, spatially separated after being prepared in such a way that the properties of the individual components are tightly correlated. The results from the separate detections of component properties are predicted to display correlations that are inconsistent with the two-fold view that the properties established at preparation are retained throughout the individual path histories, and that the measured values reflect only local interactions with the detectors. The experiment involves the preparation from a single light source of pairs of photons with correlated polarizations. Travelling different optical paths, the streams of photons display individual randomly oriented polarizations, which nevertheless upon coincident comparison exhibit the unusual correlations. It seems difficult in this case to maintain the view that the photons can indeed be prepared with determinate properties and then causally separated.

In these experiments the interpretive problems of light merge with the general interpretive problems of the quantum theory (see QUANTUM MECHANICS, INTERPRETATION OF). Our great sophistication in manipulating light places it at the experimental centre of this most profound contemporary controversy.

References and further reading

Hardin, C.L. (1988) *Color for Philosophers*, Indianapolis, IN: Hackett Publishing Company. (A good source for the discussion of §3.)

Hecht, E. and Zajac, A. (1974) *Optics*, Reading, MA: Addison-Wesley. (A good undergraduate text, accessibly written. Strong on manipulations of all kinds, from Maxwellian electrodynamics in §2 to lasers in §5.)

Ronchi, V. (1939) *Storia della luce*, Bologna: Zanicelli; trans. and revised by V. Barocas, *The Nature of Light: An Historical Survey*, Cambridge, MA: Harvard University Press, 1970. (The standard historical survey through the eighteenth century.)

Zajonc, A. (1993) *Catching the Light: The Entwined History of Light and Mind*, New York: Bantam. (An unusual history, with quantum optics (§5) through 1991, written by a physicist.)

ROGER JONES

ORDINAL LOGICS

By an ordinal logic is meant any uniform effective means of associating a logic (that is, an effectively generated formal system) with each effective ordinal representation. This notion was first introduced and studied by Alan Turing in 1939 as a means to overcome the incompleteness of sufficiently strong consistent formal systems, established by Kurt Gödel in 1931.

The first ordinal logic to consider, in view of Gödel's results, would be that obtained by iterating into the constructive transfinite the process of adjoining to each system the formal statement expressing its consistency. For that ordinal logic, Turing obtained a completeness result for the class of true statements of the form that all natural numbers have a given effectively decidable property. However, he also showed that any ordinal logic (such as this) which is strictly increasing with increasing ordinal representation cannot have the property of invariance: in general, different representations of the same ordinal will have different sets of theorems attached to them. This makes the choice of representation a crucial one, and without a clear rationale as to how that is to be made, the notion of ordinal logic becomes problematic for its intended use.

Research on ordinal logics lapsed until the late 1950s, when it was taken up again for more systematic development. Besides leading to improvements of Turing's results in various respects (both positive and negative), the newer research turned to restrictions of ordinal logics by an autonomy (or 'boot-strap') condition which limits the choice of ordinal representations admitted, by requiring their recognition as such in advance.

1 **Incompleteness, consistency statements and reflection principles**
2 **Ordinal logics; Turing's results**
3 **Subsequent work**
4 **Autonomous progressions of theories and reflective concepts of proof**

1 Incompleteness, consistency statements and reflection principles

The point of departure for the study of ordinal logics is Kurt Gödel's second incompleteness theorem, also referred to as the theorem on unprovability of consistency (see GÖDEL'S THEOREMS). With each effectively generated formal system S containing a modicum of arithmetic is associated the arithmetical statement Con_S of consistency of S. If S is consistent then Con_S is not provable in S, and so the system S' obtained by adjoining Con_S as an axiom to S is stronger than S. It may, in fact, happen that S' is inconsistent, but if S satisfies a condition slightly stronger than consistency (to be described below) so also does S'. Let C be the class of effectively generated formal systems satisfying this strengthened consistency condition. Thus by beginning with any system S_0 in C and forming, in succession, $S_1 = S'_0$, $S_2 = S'_1, \ldots$, we obtain more and more complete systems in C. As will be explained in §2, this procedure can also be extended into the transfinite, since the union of any effectively generated sequence of systems in C is again in C. In this section, matters concerning formal systems and extension principles such as those of Gödelian type will be explained as needed to make these notions precise. Certain preliminaries from recursion theory and arithmetical definability theory are necessary for this purpose (see COMPUTABILITY THEORY; RECURSION-THEORETIC HIERARCHIES).

The variables $x, y, z, \ldots$ are here taken to range over the set $N = \{0, 1, 2, \ldots\}$ of natural numbers. For $P(x)$ a property of natural numbers, $\{x : P(x)\}$ denotes the set of all x in N for which $P(x)$ holds. The class $\sum_1^0$ in the arithmetic hierarchy consists of all sets of the form $\{x : \exists y R(x, y)\}$ where R is primitive recursive; $\sum_1^0$ is coextensive with the class of recursively enumerable (RE) sets, i.e. those which are effectively generated according to Church's thesis. There is a uniform $\sum_1^0$ enumeration $W_e = \{x : y T(e, x, y)\}$ of all $\sum_1^0$ sets for $e = 0, 1, 2, \ldots$, where T is a suitable primitive recursive relation; e is said to be an *index* of an effectively generated set W if $W = W_e$. The only other classes in the arithmetic hierarchy to which reference will be made below are the $\prod_1^0$ sets $\{x : \forall R(x, y)\}$ and the $\prod_2^0$ sets $\{x : \forall y \exists z R(x, y, z)\}$. (See RECURSION-THEORETIC HIERARCHIES for more information about the $\prod$ and $\sum$ classifications.)

For simplicity, on the formal side we shall deal only with systems whose language is that of first order (or elementary) number theory. Primitive recursive relations may be taken as basic, or defined (by a method due to Gödel) in terms of the operations of addition and multiplication. Either way, we can then speak of formulas in $\sum_1^0$, $\prod_1^0$ and $\prod_2^0$ form (among others). All notions of truth and definability are referred to the standard model, in which the variables are taken to range over N and the basic operations and relations receive their intended interpretation.

To carry notions of effectiveness over to the syntactic side, one uses the association with each formula A of its Gödel number, denoted $\#A$. Then the above enumeration of $\sum_1^0$ sets induces an enumeration of sets of formulas, $S[e] = \{A : \#A \in W_e\}$; a set S of formulas is said to be effectively generated (or RE) if $S = S[e]$ for some e, and in that case e is called an *index* or *presentation* of S. Effective operations on such sets are explained in terms of operations on their indices. Moreover, effective sequences $S_n (n \in N)$ of RE sets of formulas can be considered as given by (an index f of) a total recursive function $\{f\}$ with $S_n = S[\{f\}(n)]$ for each n. Associated effectively with each such f is an index of $\cup_n S_n$ as an RE set.

Gödel's incompleteness theorems apply to effectively generated extensions of a formal system containing a modicum of arithmetic. Most familiar for the latter purpose is the system PA of Peano Arithmetic (Peano's axioms in first-order form), though much weaker systems suffice. Thus in the following, only RE sets S of formulas will be considered for which S includes PA. Then A is provable from S if A is a consequence of S by means of the axioms and rules of the first-order predicate calculus with identity. For simplicity, we assume that the non-logical axioms of S are given as closed formulas, that is, sentences. S is *consistent* if it does not prove the sentence $0 \neq 0$, and is *1–consistent* if each $\sum_1^0$ sentence provable in S is true. S is called ω-*consistent* if there is *no* formula $A(x)$ for which we have both $\exists x A(x)$ and $\neg A(\bar{n})$ provable in S for each n. (The notion of ω-consistency was introduced by Gödel in 1931 to show that if G is the sentence which expresses of itself that it is not provable in S then $\neg G$ is not provable in S; it was observed later that 1-consistency suffices for this conclusion.) Finally, S is said to be *true* if each sentence of S is true. Note that truth implies ω-consistency which implies 1-consistency which, in turn, implies consistency. We write $S_1 \subseteq S_2$ if every A provable in S_1 is provable in S_2, and $S_1 \equiv S_2$ if $S_1 \subseteq S_2$ and $S_2 \subseteq S_1$. S_2 is said to be stronger than S_1 if $S_1 \subseteq S_2$ but some A is provable in S_2 which is not provable in S_1.

With each index or presentation e of an effectively generated system S is associated a $\sum_1^0$ formula $Prov_S(x)$ which expresses that x is the number of a formula provable from S. Then the $\prod_1^0$ sentence $Cons = \neg Prov_S(\#A_0)$, where A_0 is $(0 \neq 0)$, formally expresses the consistency of S. (To be more precise, we should write $Prov_e(x)$ and Con_e for these formulas, for each index e of S.) According to Gödel's second incompleteness theorem, if S is consistent (and includes PA) then S does not prove Con_S. By hypothesis, Con_S is true in this case, but it may be that $S' = S \cup \{Con_S\}$ is inconsistent; however, if S is 1-consistent then so also is S'.

For familiar systems S, we come to accept their consistency by informally recognizing that each axiom of S is true, hence that each sentence A provable from S is true. The formal statement of the latter recognition can be given in the language of arithmetic without the truth predicate, simply as

$(*) Prov_S(\#A) \rightarrow A$

For, by Tarski's truth criterion (see TARSKI'S DEFINITION OF TRUTH), we have $Tr(A) \leftrightarrow A$. The collection of all statements of the form (*) is called the *(local) reflection principle* (Rfn_S) for S. Note that the instance $Prov_S(\#A_0) \rightarrow A_0$, with A_0 as above, is equivalent to $\neg Prov_S(\#A_0)$, that is, to Con_S. In other words, the consistency of S is a consequence of Rfn_S. As with the addition of Con_S to S, 1-consistency is preserved under the expansion of S by all instances of Rfn_S for which A is in $\prod_2^0$ form. However, we must assume a stronger hypothesis for the full extension, namely: if S is true so also is $S \cup Rfn_S$. In the following, we shall be concerned with the extensions of systems given by $S' = S \cup \{Con_S\}$ and $S' = S \cup Rfn_S$, among others. In each of these cases, an index of S' is found effectively from one for S.

2 Ordinal logics; Turing's results

Passages from S to S' for effectively generated S, such as described in the preceding section, can be iterated effectively into the transfinite by using closure under effective unions at limit stages. For this one needs a notion of a system of recursive (or 'constructive') ordinal notations. The first such system was introduced in 1936 by Alonzo Church and Stephen C. Kleene using representations of ordinals by certain terms in Church's lambda calculus (see LAMBDA CALCULUS). Several variants of this system were subsequently introduced which are all equivalent in the sense that the same ordinals are represented by the different systems. One of these was given by Kleene (1938) in more current recursion-theoretic terms as a subset O of N together with a partial ordering relation $<_O$ between elements of O and a map $a \mapsto |a|$ from O into the ordinals, with the property that if $a <_O b$ then $|a| < |b|$. This representation is not in general unique, that is, the same ordinal α may have many $a \in O$ with $|a| = \alpha$ (if there are any such $a \in O$ at all). The relation $<_O$ is tree-like in the sense that for each $b \in O$, $\{a : a <_O b\}$ is linearly ordered by $<_O$.

The system O is also equipped with: (i) a unique element 0_O with $|0_O| = 0$, (ii) a recursive operation sc_O from O to O such that for $a' = sc_O(a)$, $|a'| = |a| + 1$ and (iii) a recursive operation $\lim_O$ from indices of recursive increasing sequences of members of O to O, such that whenever $\{f\}(n) = a_n$ is in O and $a_n <_O a_{n+1}$ for all n then $|\lim_O(f)| = \lim_n |a_n|$. Finally, O is the least set satisfying the recursive closure conditions (i) – (iii). An ordinal α is said to be recursive if $\alpha = |a|$ for some $a \in O$; in a sense, these are the effectively countable ordinals. The least non-recursive ordinal is denoted ω_1^{CK}, i.e. the least effectively uncountable ordinal (in the sense of Church and Kleene).

Turing's notion of ordinal logic in his seminal 1939 paper was framed in terms of the lambda calculus; moreover, his notion of a logic was idiosyncratic in that he only considered sets of $\prod_2^0$ formulas. Basically, for Turing, an ordinal logic is any effective association of a logic in his sense with each constructive ordinal notation. The following is an adaptation of Turing's notions to the more current recursion-theoretic framework together with the treatment of logics as formal systems in the sense of §1, which respects all of his results.

Thus, by an *ordinal logic* is meant any partial recursive E which associates with each $a \in O$ an index $E(a)$ of an effectively generated formal system S_a, so that $S_a = S[E(a)]$. In the rest of this section S_a is assumed to be a set of sentences in the language of arithmetic with $PA \subseteq S_a$. The logic given by E is denoted by $\langle S_a^E \rangle_{a \in O}$, and the superscript '$E$' is suppressed when there is no ambiguity. An ordinal logic is said to be *invariant* (*up through* α) if for all a, $b \in O$ with $|a| = |b|$ and $|b| \leq \alpha$ we have $S_a \equiv S_b$; it is said to be *increasing* (*strictly increasing, up through* α) if whenever $a <_O b$ then $S_a \subseteq S_b$ (S_b is stronger than S_a, for $|b| \leq \alpha$). The ordinal logic is said to be *continuous* if whenever f represents an increasing sequence in O, then $S_{\lim_O(f)} = \cup_n S_{\{f\}(n)}$. Finally, it is said to be *complete* for a class T of sentences if for each A in T there exists $a \in O$ with A provable in S_a.

Of special interest are ordinal logics obtained in the following way. We suppose given a partial recursive function (called a *succession principle*) which associates with each index of an effectively generated system S an index of a system S' extending S. Then given any initially specified system S_0 containing PA, one can construct an ordinal logic $\langle S_a \rangle_{a \in O}$ such that:

(i) $S_{0_O} = S_0$, (ii) $S_{sc_O(a)} = S'_a$ for each $a \in O$, and (iii) the ordinal logic is continuous. Then given any notion of correctness $\mathcal{C}$ of systems which applies to S_0 and which is closed under the operation $S \mapsto S'$ and under effective unions, each S_a will belong to $\mathcal{C}$. This holds for the collection $\mathcal{C}$ of 1-consistent systems when $S' = S \cup \{Con_S\}$ and for the collection of true systems when $S' = S \cup Rfn_S$. An ordinal logic constructed satisfying (i) – (iii) is said to be based on the succession principle $S \mapsto S'$; it is strictly increasing if S' is always stronger than S, for S in $\mathcal{C}$.

For the ordinal logic based on the succession principle $S' = S \cup Rfn_S$, Turing obtained completeness for the class T of true $\prod_1^0$ sentences. He asked whether one can obtain completeness for the class of true $\prod_2^0$ sentences; this was answered in the negative by Feferman in 1962 (see §3). In any case, Turing's $\prod_1^0$ completeness result is disappointing (as he himself thought) due to the following general result which is obtained: an ordinal logic cannot be strictly increasing and invariant. Thus a true $\prod_1^0$ sentence provable in some S_a need not be provable in an S_b with $|b| = |a|$, and so the completeness result is sensitive to which ordinal notations are used.

Closer inspection of Turing's arguments revealed the following. First of all, his completeness result for true $\prod_1^0$ sentences already holds for the ordinal logic based on the succession principle $S' = S \cup \{Con_S\}$. For this, one associates with each primitive recursive predicate $R(x)$ a number a_R such that a_R is in O just in case $\forall x R(x)$ is true, and is such that $|a_R| = \omega + 1$

141

and S_{a_R} proves $\forall x R(x)$ when that holds. The notation a_R is not 'natural', unlike our usual notation for $\omega + 1$; it is simply fabricated to do this job. Similarly, an ordinal logic can't be strictly increasing and invariant up through $\omega + 1$; this is best possible for continuous ordinal logics, since one has unique notations in O for the natural numbers, hence invariance up through ω.

The original aim for ordinal logics was to obtain an association of effective formal systems S_α with ordinals α in such a way that $S_{\alpha+1} = S'_\alpha$ and $S_\alpha = \cup_{\beta < \alpha} S_\beta$ for limit α. The definition of ordinal logics as assignments $a \mapsto S_a^E$ for $a \in O$ was necessitated in order to make the association effective. Unless one has some canonical way of associating with each recursive ordinal α an $a \in O$ with $|a| = \alpha$, the notion of ordinal logic is problematic for its original purpose.

3 Subsequent work

Turing did no further work on ordinal logics after 1939, and the subject went into limbo until it was taken up again in the late 1950s by Georg Kreisel and by Feferman. Part of Feferman's work (1962) consisted in recasting Turing's work from the lambda calculus in ordinary recursion-theoretic terms and in sharpening his results, essentially as described in the preceding section. Finally, attention was restricted to continuous ordinal logics based on a given effective succession principle $S \mapsto S'$; these were called *transfinite recursive progressions of axiomatic theories*. The new work in 1962 was for a recursive progression based on the so-called *uniform reflection principle for a logic S* (RFN_S) which consists of all sentences of the form

$$(**) \forall x Prov_S(\#A(\overline{x})) \rightarrow \forall x A(x)$$

where for each n, $\overline{n}$ is the numeral denoting n. Thus (RFN_S) for $A(x)$ expresses that if S proves $A(\overline{n})$ for each n then $\forall x A(x)$ is true, and so it is a kind of formalized ω-rule. The main result of the author's 1962 work was that for the recursive progression based on the uniform reflection principle, we have completeness for *all* true arithmetical sentences. Moreover, one obtains completeness along suitable paths P through O (i.e. where P is a subset of O linearly ordered by $<_O$ which contains a representative for each recursive ordinal). Namely, it was shown that there is a path P through O (and recursive in O) such that for each true arithmetical sentence A, there exists $a \in P$ with A provable in S_a. Now this completeness result is sensitive to the choice of path because of Turing's non-invariance result, and so the crucial question to be raised is: *what is a natural path*

P through O? As of the time of writing, there is still no convincing answer to this question. Familiar natural systems of ordinal representation all close off at a recursive ordinal. One feature of these is that they are defined inductively; furthermore, sets generated by arithmetical inductive definitions are in the class $\prod_1^1$ in the analytic hierarchy (as is the set O). (See RECURSION-THEORETIC HIERARCHIES for more information about the analytic hierarchy.) It was shown by Feferman and Spector in 1962 that $\prod_1^1$ paths through O exist, but that if P is any such path then $\cup_{a \in P} S_a$ is incomplete for true $\prod_1^0$ sentences. Hence if the answer to the question about natural paths requires them to be inductively defined, one will have a very strong incompleteness result for recursive progressions restricted to natural ordinal notations.

4 Autonomous progressions of theories and reflective concepts of proof

In order to characterize informal concepts of proof embodying some kind of stepwise reflective character such as that of *finitist proof* or *predicative proof*, Georg Kreisel suggested in 1958 the use of certain ordinal logics restricted by an *autonomy* (or 'bootstrap') condition. The restriction consists in allowing one to advance to an S_a for $a \in O$ only if it has been proved in some previously accepted $S_b (b <_O a$ that a is in O. Formally, this requires an extension of the language of arithmetic to admit predicates expressing well-foundedness in one way or another. Not so incidentally, imposition of the autonomy condition partially circumvents the problem of which ordinal notations are to be used in an ordinal logic. However, the purposes are substantially different, since autonomous progressions are incomplete for true $\prod_1^0$ sentences and break off at a recursive ordinal.

For the concept of predicative provability in analysis, Kreisel proposed consideration of an autonomous progression of ramified analytic systems. In 1964, Kurt Schütte and Feferman independently obtained a characterization of the least non-predicatively provable ordinal under this proposal. In a 1991 article, Feferman introduced a notion of *reflective closure* of a system S which does not require any of the (problematic) machinery of ordinal logics and showed that the reflective closure of PA has exactly the same arithmetical consequences as the autonomous progression of ramified systems. It is proposed there that the reflective closure of a system S contains everything one ought to accept if one has accepted the basic notions and principles of S.

See also: LOGICAL AND MATHEMATICAL TERMS, GLOSSARY OF

References and further reading

Davis, M. (ed.) (1965) *The Undecidable: Basic Papers on Undecidable Propositions, Unsolvable Problems and Computable Functions*, Hewlett, NY: Raven Press. (Includes a reprinting of Turing's 1939 paper on ordinal logics, among other fundamental papers by Gödel, Church, Kleene, Turing and Post.)

* Feferman, S. (1962) 'Transfinite Recursive Progressions of Axiomatic Theories', *Journal of Symbolic Logic* 27: 259–316. (Re-examination, technical improvement and extension of Turing's work on ordinal logics as described in §3.)

* —— (1964) 'Systems of Predicative Analysis', *Journal of Symbolic Logic* 29: 1–30. (Use of autonomous progressions of theories for the characterization of predicate provability in analysis, referred to in §4.)

—— (1988) 'Turing in the Land of O(z)', in R. Herken (ed.) *The Universal Turing Machine: A Half-Century Survey*, Oxford: Oxford University Press, 113–47. (A readable account of how Turing came to work on ordinal logics, together with a semi-technical exposition of his basic results and of subsequent work.)

* —— (1991) 'Reflecting on Incompleteness', *Journal of Symbolic Logic* 56: 1–49. (Introduces the concept of reflective closure and shows its equivalence with the autonomous progression for predicative provability; referred to in §4.)

* Feferman, S. and Spector, C. (1962) 'Incompleteness Along Paths in Progressions of Theories', *Journal of Symbolic Logic* 27: 383–90. (The incompleteness results described in §3.)

* Gödel, K. (1931) 'Über formal unentscheidbare Sätze der *Principia Mathematica* und verwandter Systeme I', *Monatshefte für Mathematik und Physik* 38: 173–98; trans. 'On Formally Undecidable Propositions of *Principia Mathematica* and Related Systems', in J. van Heijenoort (ed.) *From Frege to Gödel: A Source Book in Mathematical Logic, 1879–1931*, Cambridge, MA: Harvard University Press, 1967, 592–617. (Gödel's fundamental paper on incompleteness of sufficiently strong formal systems; reprinted in the original and in English translation in Gödel 1986.)

—— (1986) *Collected Works*, vol. 1, *Publications 1929–1936*, ed. S. Feferman, J.W. Dawson Jr, S.C. Kleene, G.H. Moore, R.M. Solovay, and J. van Heijenoort, New York and Oxford: Oxford University Press.

Hodges, A. (1993) *Alan Turing: The Enigma*, London: Burnett Books; New York: Simon & Schuster. (A very readable, absorbing and informative biography of Turing with a description of all his work.)

* Kleene, S.C. (1938) 'On Notation for Ordinal Numbers', *Journal of Symbolic Logic* 3: 150–5. (Kleene's system *O* of recursive ordinal notations described in §2.)

* Kreisel, G. (1960) 'Ordinal Logics and the Characterization of Informal Concepts of Proof', *Proceedings of the International Congress of Mathematicians, 14–21 August 1958*, Cambridge: Cambridge University Press, 289–99. (Proposed the use of autonomous ordinal logics for the characterization of finitist proof and suggested a similar use for predicative proof; referred to in §4.)

—— (1970) 'Principles of Proof and Ordinals Implicit in Given Concepts', in J. Myhill, R.E. Vesley and A. Kino (eds) *Intuitionism and Proof Theory*, Amsterdam: North Holland, 489–516. (Discussion of the work on autonomous ordinal logics for finitist and predicative provability.)

* Turing, A.M. (1939) 'Systems of Logic Based on Ordinals', *Proceedings of the London Mathematical Society*, series 2, 45: 161–228; repr. in M. Davis (ed.) *The Undecidable*, Hewlett, NY: Raven Press, 1965, 155–222. (Turing's fundamental paper on ordinal logics whose notions and results are described in §2.)

SOLOMON FEFERMAN

ORDINARY LANGUAGE PHILOSOPHY

Ordinary language philosophy is a method of doing philosophy, rather than a set of doctrines. It is diverse in its methods and attitudes. It belongs to the general category of analytic philosophy, which has as its principal goal the analysis of concepts rather than the construction of a metaphysical system or the articulation of insights about the human condition. The method is to use features of certain words in ordinary or non-philosophical contexts as an aid to doing philosophy. The uses in non-philosophical contexts are taken to be paradigmatic; it is in them that meaning lives and moves and has its being. All ordinary language philosophers agree that classical philosophy suffered from an inadequate methodology that accounts for the lack of progress. But proponents of the method do not agree about whether philosophical problems are solved or dissolved; that is, they do not agree about whether philosophical problems are genuine problems for which there are solutions or whether they are merely pseudo-problems, which can at best be diagnosed.

1   The justification of the method

Ordinary language philosophy flourished between 1940 and 1965. It was practised most vigorously at the University of Oxford although it had distinguished practitioners in places as remote from each other as Nebraska in the USA and Adelaide in Australia. There was no comparable movement in Europe, although the most famous philosopher associated with ordinary language philosophy, Ludwig Wittgenstein, was born and brought up in Austria. Ordinary language philosophy evolved out of logical positivism. Although these two shared a negative opinion of traditional philosophy and promoted the virtues of clarity and precision, their differences are more striking. While logical positivism was scientistic and anti-metaphysical, ordinary language philosophy is anti-scientistic and neutral about metaphysics. It is anti-scientistic because it holds that science is a technical discipline that logically depends upon nontechnical concepts. The argument for this position is that science depends upon technical terms; every technical term must be defined either in words that have ordinary meanings or in other technical terms. If the latter, then these terms themselves must eventually be defined in words that have ordinary meanings since technical terms inherently require an explication in ideas that are already understood. Hence all science depends upon a pre-theoretical understanding of the world. As J.L. AUSTIN said, ordinary language is not the last word, but it is the first ([1961] 1970: 185). Ordinary language philosophy is neutral about metaphysics: some practitioners think that metaphysics can be done and others think that it cannot. There is a similar split over whether such traditional conflicts as realism versus nominalism and free will versus determinism have a resolution.

Behind ordinary language philosophy lies an idea that goes back to Socrates, namely that since language is the expression of thought, studying language is a good way to study the concepts that people have. In order to understand what a cause is, or what truth or knowledge is, it makes sense to look at how people use the words 'cause', 'truth' and 'knowledge'. This requires looking closely at situations in which such words can be and are used, and when they cannot be and are not, in order to understand the scope and limits of the concepts they express. Such studies invite the question of the general conditions under which the concepts apply; and that connects the method with traditional philosophical concerns. A presupposition of the method is the anti-Cartesian belief that a person's mental life is not transparent and that people do not have direct access to their own concepts.

Proponents of the method also believed that most philosophically interesting concepts are more complex and rich than usually depicted and that the surest, if not the only, way to uncover these features is to study the actual deployment of them in a variety of linguistic contexts. One of the great failings of other types of philosophy is therefore supposed to be oversimplification. Austin quipped that oversimplification was not so much the occupational hazard of philosophers as it was their occupation. He thought that philosophers concentrated on one or two favoured uses of a word, when the word itself had a much more complex meaning, which was best revealed by investigating the full spectrum of its uses. Austin resisted the idea that there should be one or two categories into which every kind of object should fit. 'Why, if there are nineteen of any thing, is it not philosophy?' he asked. There is another philosophical reason for studying ordinary language. Philosophers care to keep separate things separate. This requires an adequate set of distinctions. Austin believed that ordinary language contained many more distinctions than a philosopher could think up sitting in an armchair, both because ordinary language had to function efficiently for people in a vast array of situations and also because it had evolved over a very long period of time. For the most part, useful distinctions would survive; useless ones would disappear. Wittgenstein thought that one of the big problems with classical philosophy was that philosophical language did not do any real work: 'philosophical problems arise when language *goes on holiday*' (1953: §38; original emphasis).

This helps to explain why Austin wrote a paper about 'Three Ways of Spilling Ink' ([1961] 1979). Although the choice of spilling ink was intended to be playful and deflating, a wry allusion to the philosophical enterprise itself, it had a serious purpose. The three ways – deliberately, intentionally and on purpose – are three dimensions that are relevant to the issue of assigning responsibility for an action, clearly a philosophical topic; but previous philosophers had not differentiated between them. Through a series of clever examples, Austin illustrated that there are subtle but important differences between acting deliberately, intentionally and on purpose. There is one further reason why Austin chose to study ways of spilling ink: he wanted a non-momentous, not previously studied action in order to avoid the distortions that come from preconceptions. The distinctions operating within ordinary language are not polluted by philosophical prejudices.

2   Paradigm case arguments

One of the most intriguing and seemingly powerful tactics devised by ordinary language philosophers is the 'paradigm case argument'. Such arguments were typically deployed to refute scepticism, either in general or with respect to specific items, to show that in (at least some of) speech, some determinate knowledge is presupposed. For example, in order to be able to doubt either that people have hands or that something specific is a hand, the word 'hand' must have a meaning; and this meaning is or can be taught by pointing to something and saying that it is a hand. In such a situation, there is no room for doubting that that thing is a hand since it is paradigmatically the kind of situation in which the word is defined. Consequently, the ability to doubt that there are hands presupposes that one knows or did know that something is or was a hand. Thus is scepticism refuted. Variations on this argument were developed to prove that human beings know that they have free will, that the past is real, that some things are red, and that induction and deduction are cogent ways of reasoning. Wittgenstein's remark, 'It is part of the grammar of the word "chair" that *this* is what we call "to sit on a chair"' (1958: 24; original emphasis), has sometimes been taken as at least hinting at the strategy of paradigm case arguments.

However, there are general objections to paradigm case arguments. Even if there are situations in which people say 'This is a hand (or red)' in a paradigmatic case of hand-naming (or red-attributing), it does not follow that the intended object of reference is a hand (or red). If the speaker is being deceived by a Cartesian demon or is the subject of a neurosurgeon's experiment, then what the speaker says may be false, and they may have no way of knowing that it is false. From the fact that a person believes that they are viewing an object under ideal conditions, it does not follow that they are.

Another objection is that the arguments seem to be too strong in the sense that they can be applied to prove that certain things exist that we do not believe exist. For example, one way to explain the meaning of the word 'witch', which historically may actually have been used, would have been to point to some woman, probably an old, poor, friendless and unattractive one, and to say 'That is a witch'. For that community of speakers, that woman would have been a paradigm case of a witch. But very few people today would want to hold that she was in fact a witch. Although proponents of paradigm case arguments wanted to restrict the words that could be taught by paradigm examples, it is dubious that they discovered a principled way of doing this.

3   Criticisms

Ordinary language philosophy tended to offend the unconverted. It often gave the impression of being trite or vacuous; of being concerned merely with verbal issues or semantics. Explicit treatments of how many ways there were to spill ink, or the difference between shooting a donkey accidentally or by mistake did not endear critics, who thought the examples highlighted the triviality of the enterprise and demeaned the profession of philosophy. One philosopher complained, 'I don't care how truck drivers talk', and another that he did not care how Oxford dons talked. This covers the spectrum of one dimension of criticism.

A more general objection is that ordinary language philosophy talks only about words and not things; it seems to glory in verbal disputes and questions of semantics. Austin would have disagreed:

> one thing needs specially emphasizing to counter misunderstandings. When we examine what we should say when, what words we should use in what situations, we are looking again not *merely* at words... but also at the realities we use the words to talk about: we are using a sharpened awareness of words to sharpen our perception of, though not as the final arbiter of, the phenomena. For this reason, I think it might be better to use, for this way of doing philosophy, ... 'linguistic phenomenology', only that is rather a mouthful.
>
> ([1961] 1970: 182; original emphasis)

Another complaint targeted the Oxonian ideal that philosophers should speak clearly and precisely; it was summarized in the slogan 'Clarity is not enough'. But the ordinary language philosophers never said it was. Clarity was one ideal, preached as a reaction against the German and British idealism of the nineteenth century; not the only one.

The two strongest criticisms were that neither the methodology of ordinary language philosophy nor its results were systematic. These criticisms are independent. One could have a systematic way of studying ordinary language, which would yield the result that ordinary concepts lack the kind of structure that is typically counted as systematized knowledge. And one could hold that systematic results are obtainable using a non-systematic procedure. It is not easy to evaluate these criticisms, and ordinary language philosophers did not agree about the proper response.

4 Systematic methodology and results

Far from being moved by the charges that they did not have a systematic methodology and did not seek systematic results, Wittgenstein and other ordinary language philosophers, including O.K. Bouwsma (1965), would have vaunted them. They thought that one of the chief pitfalls of philosophy was the belief in and desire for systematization, a defect attributable to the desire to make philosophy a science. Wittgenstein always held that philosophy is not like science; it is either higher or lower. Unlike science, which always aims at change in the name of progress, ordinary language and the thinking that it expresses are fine as they are and do not need improvement: 'Philosophy may in no way interfere with the actual use of language, it can in the end only describe it. For it cannot give it any foundation either. It leaves everything as it is' (1953: §124). Behind this idea is the belief, shared by Wittgenstein and G.E. Moore, that ordinary language is the expression of a common sense view of the world that cannot be wrong in its basic components.

Other ordinary language philosophers would deny that they apply no systematic method. Austin adumbrated a methodology explicitly in several essays, notably 'A Plea for Excuses' ([1961] 1970), and the method was refined by Avrum Stroll (1973). In any case, it may be unfair to require a strict methodology of ordinary language philosophy since the idea that scientists proceed according to a strict methodology is dubious.

Even if there were no systematic methodology, that would not preclude an orderly investigation of a phenomenon; one dictated by the phenomenon itself. P.F. STRAWSON treated the foundations of logic in an orderly way, in the course of arguing that the project of formal logic to codify inferences in general must fail because 'ordinary language has no exact logic'. Although Strawson does not employ a systematic methodology in a technical sense, he is not averse to systematic results. In *Individuals* (1959), he presents what he takes to be the general conceptual scheme by which humans conceive all of reality.

Neither proceeding with a fixed methodology nor proceeding systematically determines whether one's results will be systematic. Stroll used a systematic methodology to study the concept of surfaces (1988); and one of his central results is that there is no one concept of surface, but many, which sometimes intermingle. This result is part of a broader claim that humans categorize the world in a piecemeal fashion. Thus Stroll would deny the fairness of the claim that ordinary language philosophy has no methodology and would hold that the application of his method reveals that there is no single, neat system that humans use to think about surfaces. And yet Stroll does not eschew generalization. He formulates theorems, as general as the subject allows, about various concepts of surfaces, each of which has limited applications.

The most lasting results of ordinary language philosophy have been in the philosophy of language. While there is a difference between ordinary language philosophy, which tries to solve philosophical problems by studying bits of linguistic usage, and the philosophy of language, which tries to give a general account of what language is and how it functions, interest in one is often accompanied by interest in the other. Austin and GRICE devised powerful theories of speech acts and conversation, respectively, complete with technical vocabularies (see SPEECH ACTS). John Searle and Zeno Vendler, who were trained by these philosophers and practised ordinary language philosophy early in their careers, have also produced lasting work in the philosophy of language.

At the opposite end from searching for systematic results is the practice of deconstruction. Although it is usually associated with continental philosophy, a good case can be made for applying the term to some ordinary language philosophy. Deconstruction is the tactic of showing that some philosophical distinction is hopelessly flawed, usually because the characterizations of the terms are incoherent. In *Sense and Sensibilia* (1962), Austin showed that the distinction material/immaterial was bogus and led to mistakes. In *Surfaces*, Stroll showed how the apparently proper distinction direct/indirect does not have general application. In particular, this distinction almost never makes sense in application to perception, and its misapplication has led to serious mistakes in the theory of perception.

A renewed interest in metaphysics, partially attributable to Strawson's book *Individuals*, the development of powerful logical theories that could be used to describe natural languages, and a renewed interest in scientific treatments of the mind contributed to the decline of ordinary language philosophy in the late 1960s. The techniques and insights of ordinary language philosophy were no longer conspicuous in philosophy during the 1990s, but some of them had been incorporated into it.

See also: ORDINARY LANGUAGE PHILOSOPHY, SCHOOL OF

References and further reading

* Austin, J.L. (1961) *Philosophical Papers*, ed. J.O. Urmson and G.J. Warnock, London: Oxford

University Press, 2nd edn, 1970, 3rd edn, 1979. (Collected essays of the most prominent Oxford practitioner of ordinary language philosophy.)

* —— (1962) *Sense and Sensibilia*, New York: Oxford University Press; repr. 1979. (An attack on some standard philosophical treatments of perception in the spirit of ordinary language philosophy.)

Bouwsma, O.K. (1965) *Philosophical Essays*, Lincoln, NE: University of Nebraska Press; repr. 1982. (A collection of Bouwsma's distinctive way of doing philosophy.)

Caton, C. (ed.) (1963) *Philosophy and Ordinary Language*, Urbana, IL: University of Illinois Press. (Classic essays in ordinary language philosophy.)

Donnellan, K.S. (1967) 'Paradigm-Case Arguments', in *The Encyclopedia of Philosophy*, ed. P. Edwards, New York: Macmillan, vol. 6, 39–44. (Includes a good bibliography.)

Flew, A. (ed.) (1965) *Logic and Language* (first and second series), Garden City, NY: Anchor Books; repr. Oxford: Blackwell, first series, 1978; second series, 1973. (Classic essays in ordinary language philosophy.)

—— (ed.) (1966) *Essays in Conceptual Analysis*, London: Macmillan. (Standard examples of ordinary language philosophy.)

Grice, H.P. (1958) 'Postwar Oxford Philosophy', repr. in *Studies in the Way of Words*, Cambridge, MA: Harvard University Press, 1989. (A defence of the method of ordinary language philosophy.)

Martinich, A.P. (1991) 'Analytic Phenomenological Deconstruction', in *Certainty and Surface in Epistemology and Philosophical Method*, ed. A.P. Martinich and M. White, Lewiston, NY: Mellen, 165–84. (Relates ordinary language philosophy to late twentieth-century continental philosophy.)

Ryle, G. (1971) *Collected Papers*, London: Hutchinson, 2 vols. (Ryle's essays range more broadly than ordinary language analysis.)

* Strawson, P.F. (1952) *Introduction to Logical Theory*, London: Methuen. (An ordinary language analysis of the foundations of logic.)

* —— (1959) *Individuals: An Essay in Descriptive Metaphysics*, London: Methuen; new edn, London: Routledge, 1990. (A descriptive metaphysics by an ordinary language philosopher.)

* Stroll, A. (1973) 'Linguistic Clusters and the Problem of Universals', *Dialectica* 27: 219–59. (The most complete and cogent statement of the method of ordinary language analysis.)

* —— (1988) *Surfaces*, Minneapolis, MN: University of Minnesota Press. (A powerful application of the method to an issue relevant to both metaphysics and epistemology.)

—— (1994) *Moore and Wittgenstein on Certainty*, New York: Oxford University Press. (Explores the connection between ordinary language and common sense beliefs.)

* Wittgenstein, L. (1953) *Philosophical Investigations*, Oxford: Blackwell, 2nd edn, 1958; repr. 1973. (The most famous work of ordinary language philosophy.)

* —— (1958) *The Blue and Brown Books*, Oxford: Blackwell. (A work in which Wittgenstein seems to hint at the strategy of paradigm case arguments.)

A.P. MARTINICH

ORDINARY LANGUAGE PHILOSOPHY, SCHOOL OF

The label 'ordinary language philosophy' was more often used by the enemies than by the alleged practitioners of what it was intended to designate. It was supposed to identify a certain kind of philosophy that flourished, mainly in Britain and therein mainly in Oxford, for twenty years or so, roughly after 1945. Its enemies found it convenient to group the objects of their hostility under a single name, while the practitioners thus aimed at were more conscious of divergences among themselves, and of the actual paucity of shared philosophical doctrine; they might have admitted to being a 'group' perhaps, but scarcely a 'school'. The sharp hostility which this group aroused was of two quite different sorts. On the one hand, among certain (usually older) philosophers and more commonly among the serious-minded public, it was labelled as philistine, subversive, parochial and even deliberately trivial; on the other hand, some philosophers (for instance, Russell, Popper and Ayer), while ready enough to concede the importance in philosophy of language, saw a concern with ordinary language in particular as a silly aberration, or even as a perversion and betrayal of modern work in the subject.

How, then, did 'ordinary language' come in? It was partly a matter of style. Those taken to belong to the school were consciously hostile to the lofty, loose rhetoric of old-fashioned idealism; also to the 'deep' paradoxes and mystery-mongering of their continental contemporaries; but also to any kind of academic jargon and neologism, to technical terms and aspirations to 'scientific' professionalism. They preferred to use, not necessarily without wit or elegance, ordinary language. (Here G.E. Moore was an important predecessor.) Besides style, however, there were also relevant doctrines, though less generally shared. Wittgenstein, perhaps the most revered philosopher of the period, went so far as to suggest that philosophical problems in general actually consisted in, or arose from, distortions and misunderstandings of ordinary language, a 'clear view' of which would accomplish their dissolution; many agreed that there was some truth in this, though probably not the whole truth. Then it was widely held that ordinary language was inevitably fundamental to all our intellectual endeavours– it must be what one starts from, supplying the familiar background and terms in which technical sophistications have to be introduced and understood; it was therefore not to be neglected or carelessly handled. Again it was urged, notably by J.L. Austin, that our inherited everyday language is, at least in many areas, a long-evolved, complex and subtle instrument, careful scrutiny of which could be expected to be at least a helpful beginning in the pursuit of philosophical clarity. It was probably this modest claim– overstated and even caricatured by its detractors– which was most frequently supposed to be the credo of ordinary language philosophers. It was important that Russell – like, indeed, Wittgenstein when composing his Tractatus Logico-Philosophicus *(1922) – firmly believed, on the contrary, that ordinary language was the mere primitive, confused and confusing surface beneath which theorists were to seek the proper forms of both language and logic.*

1 **The 'ordinary language' label**
2 **General character of the 'school'.**
3 **Philosophical tenets**
4 **Later developments**

1 The 'ordinary language' label

It is not at all easy to discern the historical origin of the label 'ordinary language'. Other philosophical schools do not present this difficulty; pragmatists, for instance, or logical positivists consciously, even proudly, identified themselves as such. But being an ordinary language philosopher seems always to have been something of which one was accused, rather than something which one claimed. The philosophers so designated were a roughly recognizable group, but they would certainly have objected to the suggestion that they formed a 'school'. That suggestion seems to have originated among those seeking to set up a convenient target to attack; those attacked would mostly not have claimed the label for themselves, and indeed would probably have objected, not disingenuously, that it was unclear to them what it was supposed to mean. We must first ask what this group (rather than school) comprised, and why it was regarded in some quarters with such remarkable hostility.

After anticipatory stirrings in the pre-war years, the philosophical 'tendency' in question flourished

from 1945 for roughly the next twenty years, being confined almost wholly to the sphere of philosophy in English, and within that sphere chiefly, if only through weight of numbers, to philosophy in Oxford. 'Oxford philosophy' was, in fact, an alternative label which had some currency at the time. Here the position of Wittgenstein is a perturbing factor. Among 'Oxford philosophers' he was, well before the publication of *Philosophical Investigations* in 1953, the most esteemed and influential of contemporaries; on the other hand he lived and worked, somewhat reclusively, in Cambridge rather than Oxford, and also (less trivially) himself regarded Oxford as 'a philosophical desert', the meagre fruits of which were to him utterly distasteful. The explanation of this odd state of affairs is partly that Wittgenstein was temperamentally incapable of attachment to any group of which he was not the acknowledged leader; and partly that, while 'Oxford philosophy' was certainly closely akin in substance to Wittgenstein's later work, its characteristic cool, ironic urbanity of manner was odious to him, wholly lacking in the *Sturm und Drang* which really serious philosophizing entailed. Thus it came about that, while Wittgenstein was always conspicuous among those arraigned as 'ordinary language philosophers', he himself would furiously have disclaimed any kinship with the other targets of that critical fire.

Why did ordinary language philosophy incur such hostility? There were two quite distinct reasons. The first, put succinctly, was that in certain quarters it was confusedly regarded as a species of, or a descendant of, logical positivism (see LOGICAL POSITIVISM). Old-fashioned philosophers, and many high-minded members of the general reading public, had of course been outraged – as it was intended that they should be – by the brisk dismissiveness of, for example, A.J. Ayer's *Language, Truth and Logic* of 1936; and it was easily though wrongly supposed for many years thereafter that 'young' or 'modern' English-language philosophers were all more or less of the same deplorable party – iconoclastic, sceptical, irreverent, subversive of true seriousness – all logical positivists. More significant, however, was the hostility of some leading figures from well within the professional circles of philosophy itself: Russell perhaps most conspicuously, but also, for example, Popper and, perhaps less vehemently, Ayer. This will be explored further in §3 below; but the basic charge here was that 'Oxford' or 'ordinary language' philosophy was an aberrant, trivializing perversion of good philosophical practice, substituting, in place of honest theorizing and argument, pedantic scrutiny of intrinsically uninteresting detail. The target-figure here seems to have been a most unlikely-looking amalgam of

Wittgenstein and J.L. Austin – the former cast as the heresiarch, perhaps, the latter as the pedant. The most furious onslaught was made, with Russell's blessing, in Ernest Gellner's *Words and Things* (1959).

2 General character of the 'school'

To a more than trivial extent, membership of the group in question was a matter of style. There was a conscious hostility to the lofty, rather loose rhetorical manner of, for example, its idealist predecessors; this did not preclude – as the writings of, say, Gilbert Ryle sufficiently illustrate – elegance and wit, but it ruled out eloquence and uplift. (Here, once more, Wittgenstein is a perturbing factor. Though his presence broods, so to speak, over the group, the style of his own writings is absolutely idiosyncratic, personal to himself, seemingly owing nothing to any predecessor, and unlike that of any contemporaries, even of his own disciples.) There was an even more emphatic distaste for the riddle-spinning, paradox-delighting 'deep' discourse of most contemporary continental philosophers, with whom, indeed, any kind of academic communication was neither sought nor, probably, practicable. (In this particular distaste there was, I think, an element of moral disapproval; it was felt that the weird, mind-boggling pronouncements of some continental sages were not only unprofitable but largely bogus – an intellectual fraud.) So far, the doggedly plain-man manner of G.E. Moore was a significant influence; nor, so far, does the 'ordinary language' style much diverge from that of logical positivism (see MOORE, G.E. §3). There is, however, a further point to be made. It was characteristic of logical positivism that, while certainly hostile to philosophical uplift and eloquence, it regarded mathematics and the physical sciences with special reverence; and this tended in philosophical writings towards a liking for the highly regimented handling of batteries of specially introduced technical terminology. This too the 'ordinary language' school typically avoided. This was not a matter of dogma: Austin, for example, was entirely happy to employ invented technical terms in his work in the philosophy of language when he felt a clear need for them; it was rather that members of the group did not particularly like philosophical technicality or neologism, suspecting that it was usually unnecessary and often did more harm than good. A large part of the reason for applying the 'ordinary language' label was that it was in entirely – and deliberately – ordinary language that those so identified almost always wrote and debated.

A point of more philosophical substance was that members of the 'ordinary language' group were unfriendly, at the very least, towards the idea of philosophical 'theories'. In practice this took the form of a deliberate abstention from the pursuit of generality, of wide-ranging explanations or justifications, of purportedly systematic examination of whole families of concepts; as Bernard Williams has observed, in the relevant period, '"Piecemeal" was a term of praise.' Limited issues were to be addressed strictly one at a time, particular concepts brought, as it were, individually under the microscope, and each thoroughly dealt with before going on to another. It was often remarked that the typical 'Oxford' philosopher of the post-war years recorded his researches in discrete papers and articles rather than in whole books; and it is worth noting that as early as 1933 the periodical *Analysis* was launched with the specific aim of promoting and publishing papers far shorter, far more tightly circumscribed in intention than the usual offerings to established philosophical journals.

Diverse motives were at work here. In the case of Wittgenstein himself and his closest followers, theory was rejected as being fundamentally out of place in, inappropriate to, philosophy; it was held that the problems of philosophy were essentially not the sort of perplexities for which theory-construction could offer any solution – even, perhaps, that to talk of 'solution' was itself to put the case in false terms. This must be further considered in what follows. For Austin, however, and probably for many others, the preference for 'piecemeal' working was a simpler matter of prudently limited ambition, of not biting off more than one could analytically chew. It was felt – in this following Moore – that much traditional philosophy had come to grief through the attempt to settle far too much far too quickly; impatient to get to the great work of theory-construction, philosophers had too often simply neglected or hastily over-simplified or carelessly misrepresented the relevant detail, with the inevitable consequence that the theories turned out to be chimerical and often laughably fragile. It was not that theory was held to be intrinsically out of place; it was simply that, in the current state of philosophical affairs, it was premature and over-ambitious. What was felt to be needed at the time was patient spadework – walking, even plodding if necessary, before trying to run. It was probably in this respect that the ordinary language group was most clearly not to be identified with logical positivism; for the latter, after all, was itself a highly ambitious theory, and fundamentally a theory of meaning, which was indeed supposed capable of settling, rigorously and in fairly short order, almost everything. The first chapter of *Language, Truth and Logic* is entitled 'The Elimination of Metaphysics'; the last is entitled 'Solutions of Outstanding Philosophical Disputes'. It was Austin in particular who regarded such sweeping claims as not only injudicious and unjustified, but as rather disreputable.

3 Philosophical tenets

In dealing more directly with the distinctive philosophical tenets of the ordinary language group, one must begin with the later views of Wittgenstein – not, as has been noted in §1 above, because he would have claimed or conceivably tolerated classification as a member of that group, but because first, he was a pervasive, even dominant influence on those who were its members, and second, in his later work 'ordinary' language was accorded a particularly clear and fundamental place.

The story, briefly, is this. In the early work that issued in the *Tractatus Logico-Philosophicus* of 1922, Wittgenstein had sought – then following quite closely lines laid down by Russell – to work out and exhibit the essence of all language, its really fundamental character and mode of working; and this he found in the fundamental relation, on which all meaning depended, between what he called elementary propositions and atomic facts, a relation which he called 'picturing'. But of course the propositions that occur in the actual use of language are, he held, never themselves elementary propositions. So what are they? The answer seemed to lie ready to hand: they are – they could only be – truth-functional compounds of elementary propositions, constructions, in accordance with the principles of Russellian logic, from the necessary though nearly undetectable basic material. It was, of course, to be not only admitted but emphatically affirmed, that languages in their ordinary use do not look at all like this; no one, if asked simply to observe a language and describe it, would arrive at anything resembling this description. But the reason for this was held to be that the surface of language, its easily-visible features, were radically confusing and misleading as to its essential character; the theorist must seek to find, beneath or behind mere surface vagueness and superfluities, the essential structure that – according to theory – must be there (see RUSSELL, B. §9; Wittgenstein, L.J.J. §§3–5).

Briefly, over the next ten years or so, Wittgenstein came to two conclusions: first, that the theory of the *Tractatus* was not in fact the rigorous unveiling of fundamental truth from behind misleading surface phenomena, but was rather the perverse foisting upon the real world of artificial and fantastic theoretical preconceptions; and second, crucially, that this was the general character of philosophical theorizing, and the genesis of all philosophical problems and perplexities. 'Philosophical theories are a product of the imagination, and they offer us simple, but seemingly profound pictures, which blind us to the actual complexities of language. The new philosophy is an organized resistance to this enchantment, and its method is always to bring us back to the linguistic phenomena, with which we are perfectly familiar, but which we cannot keep in focus when we philosophize in the old way' (Pears 1971: 16). Or in Wittgenstein's own words: 'What *we* do is to bring words back from their metaphysical to their everyday usage'; and again: 'We must do away with all *explanation*, and description alone must take its place' (1953: §116, 109). This is 'ordinary language' philosophy in the fairly strong and precise sense that it holds that a clear view, a plain description, an uncorrupted grasp of ordinary language will exorcize, so to speak, philosophical perplexity, which arises when familiar concepts are, at the supposed behest of 'theory', crudely mishandled: 'the idea is that in philosophy to theorize is to falsify, and the facts about language are offered as a corrective' (Pears 1971: 38). This thesis is very close to that of Wittgenstein's near-contemporary, Gilbert Ryle, as set out in his 'Systematically Misleading Expressions' of 1932 and developed in his later description of philosophy as, essentially, the rectification of 'category mistakes' (see RYLE, G. §1). Almost all members of the ordinary language group accepted the thesis, more or less fervently, as an illuminating contribution to the handling of some of the problems of philosophy, though few would have ventured to maintain, as Wittgenstein at least appeared to do, that every philosophical problem had this linguistic origin and was amenable to this linguistic treatment. Austin in particular was always explicitly opposed to any suggestion that 'philosophical' problems were of any single sort, or that any simple strategy or method would be appropriate to every case.

A different point may be made by reference again to Ryle. In discussing what he calls the 'very misleading phrase "ordinary language",' he says, 'I do think that a philosopher's arguments, when couched in technical terms, tend either to elude one or in fact to go agley. It's much easier to catch a philosopher out, including oneself, if he is not talking in technical terms with which you are unfamiliar, and the most important thing about a philosopher's arguments is that it should be as easy as possible for other people, and especially for himself, to catch him out if he can be caught out' (Magee 1971: 111). This fairly modest idea, which surely owes a good deal to the practice, if not to any stated doctrine, of G.E. Moore, was very widely accepted. It would not have been held that there was no place in philosophy, ever, for invented technical terminology, but it certainly was held that such terminology should always be regarded warily, even with suspicion. Even, for instance, the fairly harmless-looking term of art 'sense-datum' was held to be a potentially damaging stumbling-block in the philosophy of perception (see Austin's *Sense and Sensibilia* (1962)).

A rather different, but again not particularly controversial tenet was that 'acquiring the use of technical vocabularies can only take place against a background of ordinary language...ordinary language is the basis on which technical language is erected to begin with' (Caton 1963: ix). Roughly, technical terms are defined, some no doubt in other technical terms, but ultimately in non-technical, everyday terms. Unless we are clear and careful in our handling of those terms, hoped-for technical refinements will be liable to lapse into confusion.

One should bring in here a related but, for a time, far more ambitious thesis, which became known in the literature as 'the paradigm case argument'. This was the claim that in the general interests of lucidity one should not only accurately describe the ordinary use of expressions; one can also appeal to the fact that an expression has an ordinary use as a cogent argument in itself. If an expression is in established, ordinary use, then its meaning will be settled (and learned) by reference to the standard or paradigm cases in which it is applied by speakers of the language; and if it really is in ordinary use, there must be such cases. But this general truism may seem to have highly important implications. The verb 'know', for example, is in common use; we can all recognize 'paradigmatic' cases in which a person would be said to know something. If so, that is what knowledge is, and in those cases there is knowledge. One need say no more in refutation of scepticism. Or consider the case of denial of freedom of the will. It will not – cannot – be denied that there are paradigmatic, 'meaning-illustrating' circumstances in which people are ordinarily said to do things freely, of their own free will. If so, that is what free will is, and there *is* free will. To deny that there is free will, while conceding, as of course one must, that certain instances actually occur which are standard examples of what 'acting freely' ordinarily means, is not merely to take up a position which no sensible person would accept: it is to propound a thesis which could not be true, which seems indeed self-contradictory.

One can see why this form of argument was, for a time, highly appealing. It was, in the preferred style of the period, satisfactorily deflationary. It was both simple and, at least, plausible. It seemed that ordinary language, at this point at least, could do real philosophical work. Nevertheless, though the paradigm case argument was accorded much powder and shot by such vehement critics as Ernest Gellner (1959: 30–7), it probably never had many wholehearted

supporters. It was not only that it seemed altogether too quick, even slick, uncomfortably suggestive of some philosophical sleight-of-hand. It had more serious deficiencies. In many cases it seems not really to engage with the problem at issue. In the case of free will, for example, even if it were taken as establishing that there are – must be – 'paradigmatic' instances of persons acting freely, perhaps not much is achieved, for the perplexed philosopher is probably not inclined to deny that that is so; his worry is that he cannot see how it could be so, given other things that we wish to preserve, such as scientific principles; and on that the quick argument sheds no light at all. But no doubt the most serious deficiency was always that the quick inference from 'ordinary use' to the existence of actual instances was highly insecure. That the use of an expression is current and well-established in the language does not show that such use is, in all or even any respects, justified and legitimate. There was at one time, and no doubt still is, a meaning and ordinary use for the words 'witch' and 'leprechaun', but we are not obliged to conclude that there are or were witches or leprechauns. The reality of miracles is not deducible from the currency in English of the word 'miracle'.

Less ambitious and less controversial was the view, associated particularly with J.L. Austin, that ordinary language can sometimes be a valuable philosophical resource (see AUSTIN, J.L. §2). At least in areas of general, perennial human concern – in perception, for example, or human action and behaviour – natural languages will be found to have evolved highly complex and often subtle (though familiar) vocabularies and idioms, so devised as to mark genuine distinctions that have been found to be of importance. If so, then it will surely be prudent for philosophical discussion in such areas at least to begin with careful and comprehensive scrutiny of the relevant 'ordinary' vocabulary, the distinctions and connections found there being probably 'more sound...and more subtle, at least in all ordinary and reasonably practical matters, than any that you or I are likely to think up in our armchairs of an afternoon – the most favoured alternative method' (Austin 1960: 182).

It was probably this view of Austin's which was most commonly taken to be the central characteristic credo of the ordinary language group, and not wholly unfairly – it was a view very widely accepted both in theory and practice. Critics, however, too often fanned the flames of their hostility by grossly overstating the claim that was being put forward. It was suggested that Austin was peddling a comprehensive panacea for all philosophical ills – suggesting that exhaustive examination of ordinary language would be, for the resolution of every philosophical problem, the only fruitful and necessary procedure. But this was a crude caricature. Austin was always insistent that the problems assembled under the name 'philosophy' were of very many quite different sorts, needing quite different treatments. What he said, and many agreed with him, was that, in suitable cases, scrutiny of the resources of ordinary language would probably be one good way to begin.

Finally, however, it may be that what most firmly united the members of this 'school' or group was the simple belief that ordinary everyday language was interesting, deserving of attention, worth investigating. A famous illustration of this would be the contrast between Russell's article 'On Denoting' of 1905 and Strawson's 'On Referring' of 1950. Both address the same issue – certain problems raised by the use of so-called definite descriptions, such as 'the author of *Ulysses*'. But whereas Russell glances rather perfunctorily at what he took here to be the muddled primitive practices of ordinary language and hurries on to the construction of his own Theory of Descriptions, Strawson finds our own everyday practices of referring to things both interesting and important, and indeed such that, if accurately described, they reveal as unnecessary the revisionary formlization which Russell attempted. There is a somewhat similar contrast between Ayer's *The Foundations of Empirical Knowledge* (1940) and Austin's *Sense and Sensibilia*. Ayer's real interest is in epistemology and the theory called phenomenalism; 'what we say' in the field of perception seems to him fairly trivial (see AYER, A.J. §3). Austin, by contrast, finds our everyday language on perceptual matters to be quite rich, complex and subtle, and again (he perhaps hints) such that, if we accurately describe it, we may in the end see no need for the invention of new terminology or the continuation of theories. I would mention here also A.R. White's *Modal Thinking* (1975), a book which deliberately eschews the technicalities and problems of formal modal logic in favour of detailed examination of the use and interconnections of such everyday expressions as 'possible', 'can' and 'may'.

4   Later developments

It was perhaps inevitable that the philosophical 'frame of mind' described here should in time not so much wither away as evolve into something different. Essentially, what proved unstable in the ordinary language outlook was the rejection of theory, the deliberate abstention from generalization in favour of the 'piecemeal', case-by-case scrutiny of discrete particulars. The desire to generalize, to unify, to understand, to find patterns and connections and

system seems too profoundly characteristic of philosophy to be long suppressed. Furthermore, the question came increasingly to be raised: why should it be suppressed? It had been held, notably by Austin and in practice by many others, that generalization and theory-construction was dangerously over-ambitious and premature; but surely it could not be premature for ever; and ambition need not be wholly renounced. Wittgenstein, indeed, had gone further. He had rejected all theory, all 'explanation', as not merely premature but as radically misconceived and inappropriate to philosophy, but that depended on his own view of what philosophical problems are and what philosophy is – a view which, as remarked above, was never very widely accepted as the whole truth. Thus philosophers came increasingly to ask (perhaps some had never really ceased to ask): is small-scale piecemeal description really enough? Why should one not try to explain, to interconnect, to paint a general picture? Why, in short, should one not have a theory? Such a progression seems particularly clear in the work of P.F. Strawson (see STRAWSON, P.F. §§2–8). We have, in 'On Referring', the careful delineation of part of the use of everyday language, its use in referring to individual items. But this led on, in *Individuals* (1959), to the theory that a certain class of items – substantial spatiotemporal individuals – provides the basic targets of reference and subjects of predication. And in due course the further questions of why that should be so and whether it might have been otherwise led into the quite self-consciously quasi-Kantian theorizing of *The Bounds of Sense* (1966). But that is merely one good example of what occurred very generally – namely, from about 1960 onwards, a massive resurgence of the readiness to theorize, to seek not merely to observe but to understand, not merely to describe but to explain. The work of the 'ordinary language school' will perhaps have been justified if the products of this resurgence are found to be less crude, less obscure, less hastily fabricated, and less fragile than have been all too many philosophical theories of the past.

See also: ORDINARY LANGUAGE PHILOSOPHY

References and further reading

* Austin, J.L. (1962) *Sense and Sensibilia*, Oxford: Clarendon Press. (Austin uses an analysis of our ordinary language of perception to criticize the 'sense-datum' theory of Ayer (1940).)
* —— (1960) *Philosophical Papers*, Oxford: Oxford University Press, 3rd edn, 1979. (The paper 'A Plea for Excuses' (pages 175–204) offers unusually explicit 'ordinary language' doctrine.)

* Ayer, A.J. (1936) *Language, Truth and Logic*, London: Gollancz. (A brief and brilliant exposition of logical positivism.)

* —— *Foundations of Empirical Knowledge*, London: Macmillan. (The main target of Austin's *Sense and Sensibilia*.)

* Caton, C.E. (ed.) (1963) *Philosophy and Ordinary Language*, Urbana, IL: University of Illinois. (Contains a number of representative articles, including 'Ordinary Language' by Ryle, and Strawson's 'On Referring'. It also has a good bibliography.)

Flew, A. (ed.) (1965) *Logic and Language*, New York: Doubleday. (A useful collection in one volume of two anthologies of representative papers, originally published by Blackwell in 1951 and 1953.)

* Gellner, E. (1959) *Words and Things*, London: Gollancz. (A fiercely polemical, even intemperate attack on 'linguistic philosophy'. Russell's strongly supportive introduction is historically interesting.)

* Magee, B. (ed.) (1971) *Modern British Philosophy*, London: Secker & Warburg. (A series of dialogues both with and about contemporary philosophers, originally done for radio; clear and useful, and with a valuable appendix of suggested reading.)

—— (ed.) (1978) *Men of Ideas*, London: BBC. (A collection of conversations, originally televised, that with Bernard Williams (pages 134–49) being particularly relevant and useful.)

Passmore, J. (1957) *A Hundred Years of Philosophy*, London: Duckworth. (Contains an instructive chapter on 'Wittgenstein and Ordinary Language Philosophy' (pages 425–58).)

* Pears, D. (1971) *Wittgenstein*, London: Collins, Modern Masters series. (An admirable brief account.)

* Russell, B. (1905) 'On Denoting', *Mind* new series 14: 479–93; repr. in B. Russell, *Logic and Knowledge*, London: Allen & Unwin, 1956, 41–56. (Contains Russell's 'theory of descriptions', initially regarded as a classic piece of linguistic analysis, but later the target of Strawson (1950).)

—— (1959) *My Philosophical Development*, London: Routledge, 1993. (The chapter, 'Some replies to criticism' is fiercely critical of 'ordinary language philosophy'.)

* Ryle, G. (1971) *Collected Papers 2*, London: Hutchinson. ('Systematically Misleading Expressions' (1932), referred to in §3, is on pages 39–62. See also 'Categories', 170–84.)

* Strawson, P.F. (1950) 'On Referring', *Mind* new series 59; repr. in P.F. Strawson, *Logico-Linguistic Papers*, London: Methuen, 1971, 1–27. (Famous ordinary-language critique of Russell (1905).)

* —— (1959) *Individuals*, London: Methuen. (Strawson here moves beyond the analysis of ordinary language to 'descriptive metaphysics'.)

* —— (1966) *The Bounds of Sense*, London: Methuen. (A critical discussion of Kant's masterpiece. The connections between Strawson's works above are usefully discussed in B. Magee, *Modern British Philosophy*, 117–24.)

Urmson, J.O. (1956) *Philosophical Analysis*, Oxford: Clarendon Press. (Part III, 'The Beginnings of Contemporary Philosophy' is relevant; the book is also one of Russell's targets in *My Philosophical Development*.)

* White, A.R. (1975) *Modal Thinking*, Oxford, Blackwell. (An unusually single-minded example of the 'ordinary language' method at work.)

* Wittgenstein, L.J.J. (1922) *Tractatus Logico-Philosophicus*, London: Routledge & Kegan Paul, 1961. (A new translation from the German of this desperately difficult work.)

* —— (1953) *Philosophical Investigations*, Oxford: Blackwell. (Not an easy work, but essential reading.)

GEOFFREY WARNOCK

ORESME, NICOLE (*c.*1325–82)

Nicole Oresme, a French thinker active in the third quarter of the fourteenth century, occupies an important position in late medieval natural philosophy. He was especially notable for his mathematical approach, in which he represented the intensities of qualities and of speeds by geometrical straight lines, which allowed them to be 'plotted' in principle against both distance and time. He held that the shapes of the resulting graphs would then have explanatory force in the manner of ancient atomism, but, like the latter, his doctrine had a weak empirical basis. His graphical representations of speed have been compared to those later given by Galileo, but there are no grounds for positing influence. He was prominent in developing a particular mathematical language of ratios, which had earlier been used by Thomas Bradwardine to propose a 'law' relating speeds to forces and resistances, and Oresme likewise applied the language to cosmological and physical questions. He was a firm opponent of much of astrology and of magic, and to this end he employed both naturalistic and sceptical arguments. He gave many strong arguments in favour of a daily rotation of the earth, but finally concluded that it was at rest: his gambit had primarily a sceptical and fideistic purpose.

1   Life

Originating from Normandy, Oresme was educated at the University of Paris, where in 1348 he entered the College of Navarre (a royal foundation), and in 1356 became master of its theological class and hence Grand Master of the whole college. Soon afterwards he came into close contact with the royal court, and was in a more or less formal sense a tutor to the Dauphin, who in 1364 ascended the throne as Charles V. Oresme's association with the court remained through a variety of ecclesiastical appointments, culminating in that of the bishopric of Lisieux in 1377.

Oresme's writings are grounded in traditional Aristotelian scholasticism, but informed by an acute mathematical consciousness and coloured to an extent by incipient humanistic currents. The result is an elegant and urbane scepticism, which is nevertheless powered by a strong desire for scientific knowledge and, although Oresme's works cover a wide range of philosophical topics, his main importance lies in issues affecting cosmology and natural philosophy.

2   Mathematics and mathematical physics

Oresme was capable of seeing the world in strongly geometrical terms, to such an extent that he has often been compared with DESCARTES and his famous claim that his physics was nothing but geometry. Oresme, however, was not so strongly reductionist, and his geometrical picture is richer and more complicated. A central idea was that qualities could be represented at any point by straight lines erected perpendicularly to the subject that they informed (in the case of a linear or two-dimensional subject), proportional in length to the intensity of the quality. In the case of a solid subject, this would ideally have given rise to a four-dimensional configuration for each of its qualities, but because the space available to him was dimensionally limited Oresme conceived it as being conflated by superposition into three dimensions. Oresme then maintained that the shape of the configuration would have explanatory power, so that, for example, a quality that displayed a saw-like 'graph' would be especially pungent. Oresme was very excited by the potential explanatory capabilities of his 'imagination', and explicitly compared his doctrine to ancient atomism (see ATOMISM, ANCIENT). Nevertheless, it must be admitted that the empirical basis was weak: Oresme did not specify how the differing intensities of qualities should physically be measured, and rather mutedly admitted that 'the ratio of intensities is not so properly nor so easily attained by the senses as the ratio of extensions' (*De configurationibus*).

By Oresme's time there was a growing tendency, especially through the influence of the so-called Oxford Calculators, to treat speeds by analogy with qualities (see OXFORD CALCULATORS). Within the Aristotelian tradition, motions and their speeds were essentially holistic, with the focus being on the whole motion of the whole body from its beginning to its end. Using Oresme's mathematizing approach, this gave rise to a view of the speed of a body's motion as a sort of five-dimensional object, with three spatial dimensions (those of the subject), one temporal dimension and one dimension of intensity of speed. If we focus on the motion of a point, this reduces the dimensions to two, with intensity of speed being plotted against time. This allows for comparison of different speeds: for instance, a speed whose intensity increases uniformly through time can, by equation of areas, be shown to be equivalent to a uniform speed with the intensity that the non-uniform speed had at half-time. This is close to an essential theorem of Galileo in his *Two New Sciences*, and even the diagrams are reminiscent of each other (see GALILEI, GALILEO). This has given rise to much discussion of the possible influences of fourteenth-century discussions on later mechanics. The issue is still open, but probably actual influence did not extend much beyond the idea (obvious to us, but not always so) of representing instantaneous velocities or intensities of speeds by straight lines proportional in length to their magnitudes.

Problems of measure did not end with the representation of physical quantities by straight lines: these themselves had to be measured, and in the Middle Ages in this context the language of ratios (not usually regarded as being themselves numbers or fractions) was especially important. This rested on the intuition that a meaningful numerical expression of the quantity of a straight line could only be given (assuming that one did not regard the line as being made up of a certain number of points) by comparison with another line. Sometimes this was achieved tacitly by the assumption of one straight line to act as unit, but in most theoretical discussions two or more lines were explicitly brought into play, so that we could give an expression of the mutual measure of A to B by saying, for instance, that they were as 19 to 13. This was unproblematic for rational ratios, but not when it was a question of expressing the ratio of two incommensurable quantities. In Book V of the

Elements, Euclid had given a sophisticated criterion (usually ascribed to EUDOXUS) for equality between ratios in general (see MECHANICS, ARISTOTELIAN), but this was often misunderstood and little used in the Middle Ages, and in any case did not give a quantitative expression of the size of the measure.

A more interesting development came from the musical tradition, and depended on a peculiarity of mathematical language. This tradition depended heavily on ratios, and allowed for their combination so that, for instance, combining the ratios of 7:5 and 5:4 gave rise to the ratio of 7:4. This was often regarded as addition, whereas we should be more inclined to think in terms of the multiplication of the corresponding fractions. Nevertheless the addition view gave rise to a perfectly coherent theory, which easily led by extension to the multiplication and division of ratios by numbers, and in turn to the possibility of numerical expressions of the sizes of at least some irrational ratios. There are some hints of this in Robert GROSSETESTE, but in the early fourteenth century Thomas BRADWARDINE developed the theory more explicitly, showing for instance how the ratio of the diagonal of a square to its side, which we should say was as $\sqrt{2}:1$, could be numerically expressed or 'denominated' as 'half of the double ratio'. Bradwardine did not provide much systematic development of the pure mathematical theory of denominating ratios, but this task was undertaken by Oresme in his *Algorismus proportionum* (Algorism of Ratios) and *De proportionibus proportionum* (On Ratios of Ratios). He clearly showed how ratios partook of the nature of continuous quantity and could be multiplied by any fraction, but also that there were still probably irrational ratios that were not commensurable with any rational ratio, and hence were not susceptible of denomination by the new techniques.

Bradwardine made use of his language of ratios to give expression to a new law of motion, which has sometimes been regarded as radically anti-Aristotelian. In fact, given the addition view of the composition of ratios, it could (at the time) be regarded as a perfectly natural interpretation of ARISTOTLE and his commentator, Averroes (see IBN RUSHD). The law was adopted by Oresme, who expressed it as: 'Speed follows the ratio of the power of the mover to the thing moved, or its resistance' (*De proportionibus proportionum*). It is thus syntactically very simple but, if translated into modern mathematical language, it demands the use of a logarithmic or exponential function, which does violence to the context of its origin. Oresme, who with his very systematic approach to ratios could focus clearly on ratios between ratios, was concerned

to show that, given any two unknown ratios (rational or irrational), it was probable that they were incommensurable with each other and, if so, then given any two speeds, it was probable that they were incommensurable with each other. This result was a major feature in his attacks on many aspects of contemporary astrology.

3 Astrology and magic; naturalism and scepticism

Oresme was a prominent opponent of both astrology and magic, and some of his criticisms were clearly intended for the ears of members of the French royal court. To this end one of his anti-astrological tracts was written in French, and although like all contemporary Western scholars, Oresme's customary literary language was Latin, he was also a pioneer in writing philosophical treatises (including some Aristotelian translations) in the vernacular. With the possible exception of his *Questio contra divinatores horoscopios* (Question Against Horoscopic Divinators), Oresme did not deny the reality of astrological influences, but he did contest the ability of men to make predictions from them except in the most general of ways, and he warned against the moral dangers of attempting to do so. One of his most sophisticated, although possibly least effective, arguments was that from the probable incommensurability of motions noted above. If some of the heavenly motions were incommensurable with each other, then the planets could never return simultaneously to exactly the same positions, and so any precise occurrence of a Great Year, implying a cyclical universe, was impossible. Oresme concluded his most developed treatise on the subject, the *De commensurabilitate vel incommensurabilitate motuum celestium* (On the Commensurability or Incommensurability of the Heavenly Motions) with a dream in which Apollo presided over a debate between Arithmetic and Geometry as to whether there is such incommensurability, but the dream vanished before Apollo was able to pronounce a definitive judgement. Thus, although Oresme had argued for the probability of incommensurability, he emphasised that even here there is no certainty.

Oresme morally condemned magic if it were indeed employing evil demons, but was also keen to show that many effects often accounted magical were in fact produced naturalistically. Ironically, astrology had often been used to give such explanations, but Oresme necessarily employed a variety of other strategies. Among these were appeals to perceptual errors, trickery and the large effects of small causes, but especially notable was the configuration doctrine discussed above, which could in principle account for a host of occult virtues and happenings that were otherwise inexplicable. Puzzlingly, however, Oresme makes little if any appeal to this doctrine in a group of works later than the *Tractatus de configurationibus qualitatum et motuum* (Treatise on Configurations of Qualities and Motions) and assigned by manuscript evidence to 1370. This has led some scholars to contest the dating, but perhaps more plausibly we should see it as evidence of an almost playfully sceptical tendency, revealed especially in Oresme's later work: to elaborate in considerable detail an elegant and imaginative schema, but to conclude that in the end it may be no more than imaginary. A particularly renowned example of this (together with other examples less well-known) occurs in his *Livre du ciel et du monde* (Book on the Heavens and the World) of 1377. In the course of his commmentary on the French translation of Aristotle's *On the Heavens* which he presents there, Oresme questions the standard view of a stationary Earth and presents very strong arguments in favour of its diurnal rotation, before famously concluding that:

> Everyone holds and I believe that [the heaven] is thus moved and not the Earth, 'for God has established the orb of the Earth, which shall not be moved', notwithstanding the reasons to the contrary, for they are persuasions that do not conclude evidently. But considering all that has been said, one could believe that the Earth is thus moved and not the heaven, and the contrary is not evident; and yet at first glance this seems as much or more against natural reason as all or many of the articles of our faith. And so what I have said in this way for diversion can be valuable for confuting and reproving those who would impugn our faith with reasonings.
>
> (*Livre du ciel et du monde*)

In this way, an enlightened but sceptical scientific attitude buttressed religious fideism.

See also: BRADWARDINE, T.; GALILEO, G.; MECHANICS, ARISTOTELIAN; NATURAL PHILOSOPHY, MEDIEVAL

List of works

Oresme, Nicole (1351–5?) *Algorismus proportionum* (Algorism of Ratios), ed. M. Curtze, *Der Algorismus Proportionum des Nicolaus Oresme*, Berlin: S. Calvary & Co., 1868. (Latin text of the mathematical work on the algorithm of ratios. An English translation of Part I can be found in E. Grant, 'Part I of Nicole Oresme's *Algorismus proportionum*', *Isis* 56, 1965: 327–41, reprinted in E. Grant, *Studies in Medieval Science and Natural Philosophy*, London: Variorum Reprints, 1981.)

—— (1351–5?) *De proportionibus proportionum* (On Ratios of Ratios), ed. E. Grant, *De proportionibus proportionum and Ad pauca respicientes*, Madison, WI: University of Wisconsin Press, 1966. (Latin text and English translation of a treatise concerning ratios and motions.)

—— (1351–5?) *Ad pauca respicientes* (To Those Who Reflect On a Few Things), ed. E. Grant, *De proportionibus proportionum and Ad pauca respicientes*, Madison, WI: University of Wisconsin Press, 1966. (Latin text and English translation of a treatise concerning celestial motions and the question of the Great Year.)

—— (1351–5?) *De commensurabilitate vel incommensurabilitate motuum celestium* (On the Commensurability or Incommensurability of the Heavenly Motions), ed. E. Grant, *Nicole Oresme and the Kinematics of Circular Motion: Tractatus de commensurabilitate vel incommensurabilitate motuum celi*, Madison, WI: University of Wisconsin Press, 1971. (Latin text and English translation of Oresme's most mature work on the question of the commensurability or incommensurability of the heavenly motions.)

—— (1351–5?) *Quaestiones super Geometriam Euclidis* (Questions on Euclid's *Geometry*), ed. H.L.L. Busard, Leiden: Brill, 1961. (Latin text and English paraphrase of questions loosely related to Euclid's *Elements*.)

—— (1351–5?) *Tractatus de configurationibus qualitatum et motuum* (Treatise on Configurations of Qualities and Motions), ed. M. Clagett, *Nicole Oresme and the Medieval Geometry of Qualities and Motions: A Treatise on the Uniformity and Difformity of Intensities known as Tractatus de configurationibus qualitatum et motuum*, Madison, WI: University of Wisconsin Press, 1968. (Contains Latin text and English translation of Oresme's principal work on his doctrine of configurations. Clagett also suggests a provisional chronological ordering of Oresme's writings.)

—— (1360?) *Livre de divinacions* (Book on Divinations), ed. G.W. Coopland, *Nicole Oresme and the Astrologers: A Study of his Livre de Divinacions*, Liverpool: Liverpool University Press, 1952. (Contains French text and English translation of one of Oresme's anti-astrological works as well as the Latin text of another earlier work.)

—— (1370?) *Questio contra divinatores horoscopios* (Question Against Horoscopic Divinators), ed. S. Caroti, *Archives d'histoire doctrinale et littéraire du moyen age* 43, 1976: 201–310. (Edition of Latin text of an anti-astrological question, the first part of a four-part work, probably to be dated to 1370.)

—— (1370?) *De causis mirabilium* (On the Marvels of Nature), ed. B. Hansen, *Nicole Oresme and the Marvels of Nature: A Study of his De causis mirabilium with Critical Edition, Translation and Commentary*, Toronto, Ont.: Pontifical Institute of Mediaeval Studies, 1985. (Edition of the second part of the four-part work just noted. It concentrates on naturalistic explanations of marvellous effects: the title is not Oresme's own.)

—— (1372–4) *Le Livre de Politiques d'Aristote* (The Book on the *Politics* of Aristotle), ed. A.D. Menut, *Transactions of the American Philosophical Society*, new series 60, Part 6, Philadelphia: American Philosophical Society, 1970. (French translation with commentary on Aristotle's *Politics*.)

—— (1377) *Le livre du ciel et du monde* (Book on the Heavens and the World), ed. A.D. Menut and A.J. Denomy, Madison, WI: University of Wisconsin Press. (Edition and English translation of Oresme's French translation of and commentary on Aristotle's *On the Heavens*.)

References and further reading

Babbitt, S.M. (1985) *Oresme's Livre de Politiques and the France of Charles V, Transactions of the American Philosophical Society* 75, Part 1, Philadelphia: American Philosophical Society. (Study of Oresme's commentary on Aristotle's *Politics* in its historical context.)

Caroti, S. (1979) 'La Critica contro l'Astrologia di Nicole Oresme e la sua Influenza nel Medioevo e nel Rinascimento' (Nicole Oresme's Criticism of Astrology and its Influence in the Middle Ages and Renaissance), *Atti della Accademi Nazionale, Classe di Scienze Morali* 238: 543–685. (Thorough study of Oresme's anti-astrological writings and their influence.)

—— (1984) '*Mirabilia*, Scetticismo, e Filosofia della Natura nei *Quodlibeta* di Nicole Oresme' (Marvels, Scepticism and Philosophy of Nature in Nicole Oresme's *Quodlibets*), *Annali dell'Istituto e Museo di Storia della Scienza di Firenze* 9: 3–20. (Oresme's attempts to naturalise apparently magical phenomena; sees signs of the influence of the *De configuationibus* in the works dated 1370.)

—— (1993) 'Oresme on Motion (*Questiones super Physicam* III, 1–7)', *Vivarium* 31: 8–36. (Oresme's conception of the ontological status of motion as being that of a mode or condition of the thing moved.)

Durand, D.B. (1941) 'Nicole Oresme and the Mediaeval Origins of Modern Science', *Speculum* 16:

167–85. (Classic early discussion of Oresme's place in the development of science.)

Grant, E. (1962) 'Late Medieval Thought, Copernicus, and the Scientific Revolution', *Journal of the History of Ideas* 23: 197–220. (A still very useful study, which contrasts Oresme and Copernicus on the motion of the Earth.)

—— (1981) *Studies in Medieval Science and Natural Philosophy*, London: Variorum Reprints. (Several of the chapters relate to Oresme.)

—— (1993) 'Jean Buridan and Nicole Oresme on Natural Knowledge', *Vivarium* 31: 84–105. (The differing positions of Buridan and Oresme on the status of natural philosophy *vis-à-vis* theology.)

Menut, A.D. (1966) 'A Provisional Bibliography of Oresme's Writings', *Mediaeval Studies* 28: 279–99. (A supplementary note can be found in *Mediaeval Studies* 31, 1969: 346–7.)

Molland, A.G. (1974) 'Nicole Oresme and Scientific Progress', *Miscellanea Mediaevalia* 9: 206–20. (Oresme's ambivalent attitude to the possibility of making progress in natural philosophy.)

Quillet, J. (ed.) (1990) *Autour de Nicole Oresme* (Concerning Nicole Oresme), Paris: Vrin. (Useful collection of essays, including P. Souffrin on instantaneous velocity, S. Caroti on the philosophy of nature in the 1370 collection, M. Lejbowicz on the anti-astrological writings and J. Quillet on happiness.)

Souffrin, P. and Segonds, A.P. (eds) (1988) *Nicolas Oresme: Tradition et Innovation chez un Intellectuel du XIV Siècle* (Nicole Oresme: Tradition and Innovation in a Fourteenth-Century Intellectual), Padua: Programma e 1+1, and Paris: Les Belles Lettres. (Collection of essays, including E. Grant on knowledge and truth, H. Hugonnard-Roche on argumentation, J. Meusnier on probabilism, G. Molland on holism and mathematical science, J.D. North on physics and cosmology and A.P. Youschkevitch on mathematics.)

Sylla, E.D. (1984) 'Compounding Ratios: Bradwardine, Oresme and the First Edition of Newton's *Principia*', in E. Mendelsohn (ed.) *Transformation and Tradition in the Sciences*, Cambridge: Cambridge University Press, 11–43. (Oresme's work on ratios as part of a continuing tradition.)

GEORGE MOLLAND

ORGANON *see* ARISTOTLE

ORIENTALISM AND ISLAMIC PHILOSOPHY

Orientalism is the concept that there is something very special and different about the thought of those living in the East, which can be discovered through the methods of scholarship current in the West. It is a reflection of the relationship of imperial and intellectual domination of a West which feels it is superior to an 'inferior' East. This often results in an understanding of Islamic philosophy which sees the latter as essentially unoriginal, derivative and of only historical interest. While orientalists have produced interesting and important work, most fail to appreciate the independent status of the material which they analyse.

1　The notion of Orientalism
2　Orientalism as a political doctrine
3　The Orientalist approach to Islam
4　Orientalism and Islamic philosophy

1　The notion of Orientalism

Orientalism is the branch of scholarship that uses traditional Western methods as a means of understanding and gathering knowledge pertaining to the Orient. The term was also used by Edward Said (1978) to elucidate his own challenge to the validity of such methods.

On the one hand, Orientalism has given us much of what we know about the Oriental world at large. Late nineteenth-century authors are especially worthy of consideration for their contributions to an understanding of foreign cultures and peoples. On the other hand, however, several problems arise from the attitudes and methods used in traditional Orientalist discourse, which in turn has had an impact – often negative – upon Western consciousness. This influences and distorts the framework through which the West approaches the Orient in general and Islam in particular.

The Orient encompasses a far greater area than simply that of the Arabs and the Muslim community; exotic images from India, China, Japan and Korea are conjured up in the minds of Western people when they think of the Orient. However, Orientalism has had a particular impact on the study and understanding of Islamic philosophy. Many scholars' understanding of Islamic philosophy is, 'that Islamic civilization as we know it would simply not have existed without the Greek heritage' (Rosenthal 1975: 14).

2　Orientalism as a political doctrine

Orientalism has several different but interrelated meanings. In its general sense, it describes the way in which the West looks at the Orient in order to understand it within the context of Western experience. More specifically, Orientalism is a categorical approach by Western scholars as an attempt to form a collective body of knowledge about the Orient. Included in this enterprise is the study of Eastern philosophies, history, religion, culture, language and social structures. To understand the effect of Orientalism on Islamic philosophy, however, we need first to understand it as a political doctrine; from its inception, Orientalism was primarily political and secondarily cultural and philosophical.

Orientalism as a system of the knowledge began in the late seventeenth century, reaching its zenith in the late nineteenth and early twentieth centuries. During this period Britain and France, and later the USA, were involved in the struggle for Western domination. This Anglo–French–American experience was essentially imperialistic. Implicit in the Orientalist attitude, therefore, is the belief that the Orient had passed its golden age as the West was being 'born', and was thus in decline. This view of the Orient as backward and barbaric led to interpretations which resembled more closely what scholars wished to believe, rather than what actually was the case. In philosophy, this attitude led to the belief that the entire system of Islamic philosophy was based upon the Greek inheritance; this in turn led to the belief that Islamic philosophers were not good Muslims, as philosophy and religion apparently could not be reconciled.

Along with this attitude, Orientalism also played an active role in advancing Western interests in the East. The pursuit of knowledge of the Orient was often not an end in itself. The study of Islamic philosophy merely confirmed many Western scholars in their belief of the superiority of their own culture.

3　The Orientalist approach to Islam

From the beginning, Orientalists have viewed Islam in two ways. First, as it had borrowed liberally from Abrahamic (Judaeo-Christian) traditions, Islam was considered to be a crude parody of Christianity. Second, Islam was looked upon as an alien menace which historically had enormous military and political success throughout the world, and consequently was a threat to Western civilization.

In Orientalism, Islam first had to be placed within the realm of Western understanding with respect to Christian concepts rather than regarded on its own terms. One way of accomplishing this was to make analogies between Christian religions and Islam. The obvious parallel is the one which some Orientalists draw between Muhammad and Christ. Since Christ is central to the Christian faith, Westerners assumed that Muhammad holds the same place in Islam. This misconception helped to popularize the use of the name 'Mohammedanism', a term highly offensive to Muslims. The Christ analogy also served to reinforce the notion that Muhammad was nothing more than an 'impostor' and a pale version of the Christian Messiah.

Islam also provided a provocation to the West in another respect. From the time of the Arab conquests in the seventh century to the ascendancy of the Ottoman Empire, Islam itself posed a formidable challenge to the Christian world. Islamic empires – Arab, Ottoman or those in Spain and North Africa – had quite effectively challenged and, at least for short periods of time, dominated Christian Europe.

4 Orientalism and Islamic philosophy

The first wave of Muslim conquest in AD 632–4 secured for the Arab Muslims the strongly Hellenized territories of Syria and Egypt along with the western part of the Sassanian Persian empire. At first the new conquerors may have been suspicious about the culture of classical antiquity, as both religion and language separated the Arab Muslims from the vanquished peoples. However, the former overcame their anxiety remarkably quickly and began instead a cultural conquest and assimilation of ancient knowledge.

Philosophers such as IBN SINA, AL-KINDI, AL-FARABI and IBN RUSHD all interpreted the Islamic inheritance of classical philosophy and attempted an assimilation of it into mainstream Islam in their writings (see ARISTOTELIANISM IN ISLAMIC PHILOS-OPHY; NEOPLATONISM IN ISLAMIC PHILOSOPHY; PLA-TONISM IN ISLAMIC PHILOSOPHY). The classification of the sciences, in encyclopedic proportions, was carried out by the likes of al-Khwarizmi in his *Mafatih al-'ulum*, and by a group of scholars in the ninth and tenth centuries who called themselves the 'Brethren of Purity' (Ikhwan al-Safa'). The attitude of these and other philosophers was one of acceptance and the transferring of intellectual history, rather than an adoption of so-called 'foreign' ideas. Many of these ideas were foreign indeed, as we do not see any mention of them in the Qur'an and earlier traditional works, but the underlying theme was the gaining and spread of knowledge, *'ilm*. Gaining of knowledge is obligatory according to the tradition of Muhammad, the prophet of Islam, who said: 'Seeking knowledge (*'ilm*) is obligatory upon all Muslims, men and women.'

This approach is clearly brought out in the epistles of the Ikhwan al-Safa' (see IKHWAN AL-SAFA'). During a lengthy debate in these epistles, between humans and animals in the court of the king of the *jinn*, examples from history are given in which the conquering nations took over, translated into their language and made their own the knowledge of vanquished peoples. Solomon is cited as a classic example:

> Our sciences and the sciences of all the nations are [acquired] one from the other. If this was not the case, from where did the Persians get astrology, astronomy and observatories? Did not they take it from the Indians? If it was not for Solomon, where did the Israelites get the sciences.... He took it from the kings of all nations when he conquered their territories and transformed them to He-brew...

(Rasa'il Ikhwan al-Safa' 2: 288)

This transcendental open-mindedness has been misrepresented many times by Western scholars, who are more interested in finding something new in the Islamic sciences than in attempting to under-stand the transmission of the corpus of human knowledge from one people to another. The Orien-talist outlook mentioned above appears clearly when scholars such as Walzer and Rosenthal expend much effort in finding faults within the Islamic philosophi-cal system, rather than using their impressive abilities to develop a better understanding of the amalgama-tion and legacy that has been left by the Islamic philosophers. In Walzer's important work, *Greek into Arabic* (Walzer 1962), the attitude is that everything the Arab philosophers had to say was 'borrowed' from the Greeks. Even when we are not able to find the source, according to Walzer, it can be assumed safely that the original Greek source is no longer extant.

This imaginary dichotomy between philosophy and theology, as assumed by the Orientalists, has led to a severe crippling of the understanding of the achieve-ments of the Islamic philosophers. This attitude itself has its roots in the initial reaction to the impact of Greek philosophy upon Christianity. Orientalist scholars assume that the Muslims felt exactly the same as the early Christians did about the conflict between philosophy and theology. Of course there were debates between Islamic philosophers and theologians, but in the Arab and Islamic milieu the attitude was rather different from that in the Christian world; in the former, the philosophers were simply taking what they assumed was their legitimate inheritance from the corpus of human knowledge.

In conclusion, these notions about the Orient

eventually 'created' the Orient. The 'Orient' (East) is, in fact, only East from an European perspective: it is a relative, not absolute, term. More precisely, the 'Orient' is whatever the Orientalists say it is: it is a series of abstractions based upon Western-generated ideas rather than upon Oriental realities. Islamic philosophy needs to be studied as more than just a reflection of Greek ideas; it needs to be considered as an area of thought which came into contact with a variety of different cultures, and which developed out of these and out of a meditation on the Islamic sciences themselves into an independent and original form of philosophical thought.

See also: GREEK PHILOSOPHY: IMPACT ON ISLAMIC PHILOSOPHY; ILLUMINATIONIST PHILOSOPHY; ISLAM, CONCEPT OF PHILOSOPHY IN; ISLAMIC PHILOSOPHY, MODERN; ISLAMIC THEOLOGY; MYSTICAL PHILOSOPHY IN ISLAM

References and further reading

Corbin, H. (1993) *History of Islamic Philosophy*, trans. L. Sherrard, London: Kegan Paul International. (One of the very few approaches to Islamic philosophy which is not especially orientalist.)

* Ikhwan al-Safa' (1956) *Rasa'il Ikhwan al-Safa'* (Epistles of the Brethren of Purity), Cairo. (The letters of the Brethren of Purity, which provide evidence of their 'humanistic' views.)

Jalal al-Azm, S. (1982) 'Orientalism and Orientalism in Reverse', *Khamsin* 8: 5–27. (Interesting description of how some Islamic writers go in for Orientalism in reverse, arguing that only Muslims can understand Islamic culture.)

Leaman, O. (1996) 'Orientalism and Islamic Philosophy', in S.H. Nasr and O. Leaman (eds) *History of Islamic Philosophy*, London: Routledge, 1143–8. (A critique of persistent Orientalist attitudes to the study of Islamic philosophy.)

* Rosenthal, F. (1975) *The Classical Heritage in Islam*, London: Routledge & Kegan Paul. (Useful account of the links between the classical world and Islam.)

* Said, E. (1978) *Orientalism*, London: Routledge & Kegan Paul. (A key work on the subject of Orientalism by the writer who really started the controversy.)

* Walzer, R. (1962) *Greek into Arabic*, Oxford: Cassirer. (Excellent on the links between Greek culture and Islamic philosophy.)

UBAI NOORUDDIN

ORIGEN (*c.*185–*c.*254)

An ascetic Christian, prodigious scholar and dedicated teacher, Origen devoted his life to exploring God's revelation. Much of his work takes the form of commentaries on Scripture. He argued that Scripture has three levels: the literal, the moral and the spiritual. The literal level veils the others, and we need God's help to find the divine mysteries behind the veil. His commentaries directly or indirectly influenced the practice of exegesis throughout the patristic period and the Middle Ages.

Origen used his spiritual exegesis, as well as arguments, concepts and models drawn from philosophy, to tackle the theological problems of his day: the compatibility of providence and freedom, the relation of the Father, Son and Holy Spirit to each other and to rational creatures, the problem of evil, and the origin and destiny of the soul. He is famous – or infamous – for arguing that the souls of angels, demons and human beings enjoyed a previous heavenly existence, but that they sinned and fell. God created the world to punish and remedy their faults.

1 **Life and works**
2 **Revelation**
3 **Theology**
4 **Rational creatures**

1 Life and works

Origen was born to Christian parents in Alexandria. When he was seventeen, his father was martyred in the persecutions of Septimius Severus. Origen, the oldest child, supported his family by teaching grammar. Shortly afterwards, Bishop Demetrius asked Origen to take charge of the catechetical school in Alexandria. In that time of persecution, such a charge meant preparing catechumens not only for baptism, but for martyrdom as well. Accordingly, in addition to teaching, Origen tended to the martyrs at their trials and in prison, and even accompanied them to their executions. He himself lived an ascetic life, sleeping and eating very little, devoting himself to teaching, study and pastoral work with an uncompromising intensity.

He studied philosophy in Alexandria, perhaps with Ammonius Saccas, who taught PLOTINUS. He read widely in Greek philosophy, but also studied Jewish writers, in particular PHILO OF ALEXANDRIA, and was conversant with rabbinical traditions. In Alexandria, he founded his own school of advanced study. However, at some time between AD 230 and 233, Origen fell from Demetrius' good graces and was banished from the church of Alexandria. Origen then moved to Palestine, where he enjoyed strong support from the bishops, and founded another school of advanced study. When the persecution of Christians resumed under the Emperor Decius, Origen was arrested, imprisoned and tortured. When the persecutions ended, he was released. He died shortly thereafter.

Origen wrote a prodigious number of works, some scholarly, some polemical, but all with the pastoral aim of helping Christians to avoid error and deepen their knowledge of moral and spiritual truth. In *Kata Kelsou* (Against Celsus; known in its Latin translation as *Contra Celsum*), he defends Christianity against charges of irrationality levelled by the pagan philosopher CELSUS. Origen's *Peri archōn* (On First Principles) is the first work of Christian systematic theology; however, acutely aware of his own fallibility, he proposes the elements of his system very tentatively. Origen also preached and wrote commentaries on nearly every book of Scripture, although most of these works have not survived and some exist only in Latin translations. It is impossible to overestimate the importance of these commentaries, whose methodology and content had a profound influence on Basil of Caesarea, Gregory Nazianzen and Gregory of Nyssa in the East, and on Jerome and Ambrose in the West (see PATRISTIC PHILOSOPHY). Through these writers, Origen influenced the practice of exegesis throughout the Middle Ages.

2 Revelation

In Origen's view, Christians can come to understand moral and spiritual truths through study of Scripture. The Holy Spirit revealed these truths to the apostles and prophets, who recorded them in their writings for the benefit of the faithful. However, to express these truths plainly would risk allowing the enemies of the Church to ridicule them. Consequently, the authors veiled these truths in narratives and legal ordinances which constitute the literal level of Scripture. To find the spiritual level, Origen uses typological and allegorical exegesis. Typological exegesis, practised before Origen by Justin and Irenaeus as well as by the authors of the New Testament, interprets passages in the Old Testament as foreshadowing something in the gospel, whether historical or spiritual. Allegorical interpretation, practised before Origen by PHILO OF ALEXANDRIA, understands every detail of Scripture to have a moral or spiritual significance.

Finding the spiritual meaning of Scripture requires more than philological skill. As Origen sees it, one must first lead the spiritual life, a life of devotion to Christ in prayerful and diligent study of the Scriptures. As one becomes more like Christ and partici-

pates in him, one becomes worthy to be taught the mysteries of the spiritual gospel hidden by the literal gospel. Christ himself must lift the veil from the letter. Origen supposes that Jews, Gnostics and literalists misread the Scriptures because they do not listen to Christ's explanation, available inwardly to those who lead the spiritual life. In his commentaries and homilies, Origen often prays for Christ's help, or asks his listeners to pray for him, so that Christ might lift yet more of the veil from the letter. This process will continue in the next life, where Christ will teach the blessed, face to face, more and more of the spiritual mysteries (see REVELATION).

3 Theology

The prophets and apostles taught in plain terms only a small part of the spiritual gospel, including the most important truths: that God is one and the creator of the world; that his Son took a human body without resigning his divinity, and that he suffered, died and rose from the dead; that the Holy Spirit inspired the saints of both Testaments; that the rational soul is free and will be rewarded or punished according to its deserts. The apostles left the explanation and clarification of these truths to others who have received the gift of wisdom from the Holy Spirit. Origen's theology consists largely of what he takes to be this explanation and clarification. Acutely aware of the immensity of this task and of his own limitations, Origen often presents his views tentatively. With equal intensity and humility, he combs the Scriptures to investigate the relationship among the persons of the Trinity, God's motives in creation; the incarnation and resurrection, and the origin and destiny of human beings, angels and demons. For these investigations, Origen borrows concepts, models and arguments from various philosophical schools, including the Stoic, Peripatetic and, in particular, the Platonic schools (see NEOPLATONISM; PLATONISM, EARLY AND MIDDLE). Though he finds philosophical tools and speculations useful in the service of Christianity, he warns his students to give their allegiance to God and not to any philosophical school. Too often, giving allegiance to one school means closing one's mind to other ways of thinking.

In Origen's theology, God is a Trinity of three beings or hypostases: the Father, the Son and the Holy Spirit, coeternal, incorporeal and uncreated. Each of these three beings has its own attributes and role to play in the created world and in the life of the Trinity itself. The Father is absolutely simple, immutable and impassible. He receives nothing from any source, but is himself the source of all being and all goodness. The Son, begotten by the Father, bears the titles Wisdom, Word, Truth and Life, which characterize him as he is in himself, and about one hundred further titles which characterize his relationship to the created world, such as Redeemer, Good Shepherd and High Priest. The Holy Spirit sanctifies rational creatures, conferring spiritual gifts on them. The Spirit receives being and goodness from the Father, and wisdom and intelligence from the Son.

Origen's admirers and detractors alike express worries about his subordination of the Son and Holy Spirit to the Father. Only the Father is God in his own right; the Son and Holy Spirit merely participate in his Godhead, as they participate in his being and goodness. However, Origen never asserts that the Son and Holy Spirit are God or good to a lesser degree than the Father, only that they receive their Godhead and goodness from him.

The Father creates the world and everything in it *ex nihilo*, not from pre-existent matter. Origen sometimes proposes that the Father creates not just one world but a succession of worlds, though that series itself has a beginning in time. His denial of the eternity of this series makes him vulnerable to the criticism that God was idle before the creation. However, to think God idle is both inconceivable and impious. God so overflows with goodness and creative power that it is impossible for him not to exercise this power and to manifest his goodness. Recalling the verse from Psalms 104 (103), 'In Wisdom hast thou made them all', Origen speculates that in addition to the temporal creation, there is also an eternal creation: The Father eternally creates in the Son, whose chief title is Wisdom, the plans and patterns of the temporal world as an expression of his power and goodness. In the Son, then, exist the genera and species of all things, and perhaps the patterns for individuals as well. The Son, therefore, provides the link between the One and the many (see TRINITY).

4 Rational creatures

Origen develops much of his thought about rational creatures by reflection on the problem of evil and the goodness of God (see EVIL, PROBLEM OF). He was impressed by the great inequalities of life: inequalities of power, privilege and opportunity, of flourishing and suffering. Why are some rational creatures angels, some demons and others human beings? Why are some human beings born into power and privilege and others not? Why are some Christians martyred for their beliefs? The Gnostics claim, Origen writes, that some souls are by nature good, others evil, and still others indifferent, and one's lot in life depends on the nature of one's soul. Otherwise one's lot would be a matter of blind luck (see GNOSTICISM). Origen rejects this Gnostic view. God's providence governs every individual's life, so the inequalities of life cannot be due to luck. Moreover, because he is good and just, God would not introduce inequality arbitrarily and, therefore, unjustly.

Origen proposes that rational creatures enjoyed a pre-existent life, united to God in heavenly contemplation. God created them entirely equal and sinless. However, because they were rational, their actions were up to them; and because God created them out of nothing, they were mutable. Although Christ's human soul retained its innocence, other souls – perhaps all others – fell from their original union with God. Origen sometimes suggests that they grew satiated and lost interest in their contemplation of God. God responded to their fall by creating the world and assigning the fallen creatures a place in it according to their deserts. Those who distanced themselves from God the least became angels; those who distanced themselves the most became demons; and those whose fall was neither great nor small became human beings.

Human life, then, is God's punishment for sins committed in the pre-existence. The particular circumstances in which human beings find themselves – their advantages and disadvantages – are assigned to them according to their deserts. However, Origen finds God's punishment remedial as well as retributive. God is a doctor who sends us bitter medicine only to cure us. Origen also likens God to a loving tutor whose discipline aims at teaching the pupil a lesson. He puts us to the test because he wants us to face the secrets of our hearts: it is only through temptation that we see what we are really like. If we do not learn our lessons in this lifetime, then God does not abandon us, but continues the plan for our salvation into our next life (see SALVATION).

From Paul's teaching that, at the end, God will be all in all, Origen formulates his account of the *apocatastasis*, or restoration, when rational creatures regain the purity of their original state and God fills their minds. In *Peri archōn*, Origen suggests that the *apocatastasis* will be universal, so that all rational creatures, even the Devil, will eventually turn to God. However, he has no settled view on this subject. In a letter to friends in Alexandria, he explicitly denies that the Devil will be saved, and his homilies on Jeremiah suggest that some human beings too will suffer eternal punishment.

See also: PATRISTIC PHILOSOPHY; REVELATION; TRINITY

List of works

Origen (*c.*185–*c.*254) Works, in *Origenes werke*, Die Griechischen Christlichen Schriftsteller des ersten drei Jahrhunderte, Berlin: Akademie Verlag, 1899–1913. (Editions of the works of Origen, including all the individual works cited below.)

—— (218–38) *Ōrigenous tōn eis to kata Iōannēn* (Commentary on the Gospel according to John), ed. E. Preuschen in *Origenes werke*, Leipzig: Hinrichs, 1903; trans. R.E. Heine, Washington, DC: Catholic University of America Press, 1989. (Meticulous effort to uncover the spiritual meaning of the most profound and complex gospel. An important source for Origen's theology of the Trinity and exegetical methodology.)

—— (220–30) *Peri archōn* (On First Principles; in Latin, *De principiis*), ed. P. Koetschau in *Origenes werke*, Leipzig: Hinrichs, 1913; trans. G.W. Butterworth, *On First Principles*, New York: Harper & Row, 1966. (A systematic treatment of God, rational creatures and their return to God. The original Greek manuscript survives only in fragments; the Latin translation, *De principiis*, is complete.)

—— (233) *Peri euchēs* (On Prayer), ed. P. Koetschau in *Origenes werke*, Leipzig: Hinrichs, 1899; trans. J.E.L. Oulton in *Alexandrian Christianity*, London: SCM Press, 1954. (A discussion of prayer and its role in Christian life; contains an interpretation of the Lord's Prayer.)

—— (235) *Eis marturion protrepticos* (Exhortation to Martyrdom), ed. P. Koetschau in *Origenes werke*, Leipzig: Hinrichs, 1899; trans. H. Chadwick in *Alexandrian Christianity*, London: SCM Press, 1954. (Intended to encourage, strengthen and instruct Christians awaiting martyrdom.)

—— (241–44) Homilies on Jeremiah, ed. E. Klosterman, *Jeremiahomilien*, in *Origenes werke*, Leipzig: Hinrichs, 1901. (Homilies exposing Jeremiah, containing attacks against adversaries of Christianity and discussions of resurrection and punishment in the afterlife.)

—— (248) *Kata Kelsou* (Against Celsus; in Latin, *Contra Celsus*), ed. P. Koetschau in *Origenes werke*, Leipzig: Hinrichs, 1899; trans. H. Chadwick, Cambridge: Cambridge University Press, 1965. (A defence of Christianity against pagan attacks, together with counterattacks against paganism.)

References and further reading

Clark, E.A. (1992) *The Origenist Controversy: The Cultural Construction of an Early Christian Debate*, Princeton: Princeton University Press. (Thorough discussion of the controversies over Origenist thought in the late fourth and early fifth centuries.)

Crouzel, H. (1989) *Origen*, trans. A.S. Worrall, San Francisco: Harper & Row. (An exploration of select aspects of Origen's thought.)

Daniélou, J. (1955) *Origen*, trans. W. Mitchell, London: Sheed & Ward. (Useful and readable introduction to Origen's thought.)

Harl, M. (1958) *Origène et la fonction révélatrice du Verbe Incarné* (Origen and the Revelatory Role of the Incarnate Word), Paris: Patristica Sorbonensia, Éditions du Seuil. (Thorough discussion of the incarnate Christ's role as revealer of God.)

JEFFREY HAUSE

ORIGINAL SIN *see* SIN

ORPHISM

Orphism, a speculative trend within Greek religion, claimed the mythical singer Orpheus as founder and prophet. In changing forms, it is in evidence from the 6th century BC to the end of antiquity. Hexameter poems were attributed to Orpheus, especially a theogony about the origin of gods, world and mankind, and sectarian groups led an 'Orphic life', practising mystery cults supposedly founded by Orpheus. The main goal was salvation of the soul from evil, traced to 'ancient guilt', with a view to a blessed existence after death; this usually included the doctrine of transmigration

Myths about Orpheus, son of the Muse Calliope and a Thracian called Oiagros, are in evidence from the sixth century BC and current in the fifth. Orpheus, a lyre-player and singer, is said to have taken part in the expedition of the Argonauts. He enchants even animals with his music. He descends to the netherworld to get back his wife Eurydice, an attempt that fails. Although torn to pieces by Thracian bacchants, his severed head continues to sing and to give oracles.

A theogony is attributed to Orpheus, the key document of which is a fragmentary papyrus book, unearthed at Derveni in 1962, containing quotations and allegorical commentary on Orpheus' text (see Most and Laks 1997). The theogony begins with 'Night', from which a series of 'kings' of gods springs: Uranos (Heaven), Cronos and Zeus. Zeus, after a strange incident of 'swallowing' a 'phallus (?)', brings forth the other gods from himself and proceeds methodically to establish the world. Then, by incest with his 'Mother', he begets a further offspring, Persephone, leading towards the creation of mankind.

The Derveni text ends here. Plato alludes to Orpheus' theogony, which comes to a stop 'in the sixth generation' (Dionysus as the father of man?). He attests that, according to the teachings of Orphics (*Orphikoi*), the soul is incarcerated in the body during this life to be punished for certain unspeakable crimes. The corresponding myth is traceable through much-debated allusions in older texts, but becomes explicit in later sources: mankind rose from the soot of the Titans, burnt by the lightning of Zeus after they had treacherously killed and eaten the child Dionysus (also called Zagreus), son of Persephone and Zeus; hence the sufferings, the warning against falling back into the 'old Titanic nature', and the yearning to get rid of the 'unlawful forefathers', 'to reach the end of the cycle, and to take breath from evil'. The means towards this are ritual purifications and the adoption of a 'pure' life, the 'Orphic life', characterized above all by vegetarianism. There are special myths about the judgment of the dead and punishments or blissful existence in the netherworld, and a belief in transmigration, with repeated chances of personal guilt and atonement in successive lives. Transmigration, together with certain taboos, constitutes an overlap with PYTHAGOREANISM (§3). This makes it impossible to decide exactly what role Orphic literature and teaching played in the emergence of the concept of a personal 'soul', or *psychē* (see PSYCHĒ), independent of the body and antithetical to it, before Plato's philosophical restatement of this theory (see PLATO §§10–13).

Other evidence is the gold lamellae found in tombs of southern Italy, Thessaly, Lesbos and Crete (see Pugliese Carratelli 1993 for a partial translation of the evidence). Dated from the late fifth to the second century BC, these bear instructions for the dead on how to pursue their way towards bliss in the beyond. The texts differ in length and in specific details, but still form an interlocking whole. As they refer to 'bacchants and initiates' (Hipponion, southern Italy) and to the 'release' wrought by Bacchios, that is, Dionysus (Pelinna, Thessaly), they clearly presuppose rites of Dionysiac or 'Bacchic' mysteries, spread by travelling initiation priests. The initiate may proclaim his identity as 'son of Earth and starry Heaven'; there is the prospect of Elysian life, after drinking from the 'lake of memory'; there also occurs the declaration 'you have become god instead of a human'; in addition, there are suggestive but enigmatic formulae such as 'kid I fell into the milk'. The reference to transmigration is opaque, and that to

Orpheus is not explicit, but Orphism remains the most probable context.

Orphics, in connection with Dionysus and with dualistic speculation about 'soul–body' and 'life–death–life', also are attested at Olbia in the fifth century BC. Instructions for practical mysteries are found in an Egyptian papyrus text from the third century BC (see Kern 1963: fr. 31).

In Hellenistic times, the theogony of Orpheus went through various conflicting versions and expansions. Oriental influence can be discerned in the striking predilection for grotesque mixtures of images. 'Unageing Time' (*Chronos ageraos*), for example, appears in the form of a three-headed snake, with the heads of a bull, a god and a lion. The main text had 'Time' (Chronos) for the primeval god, hatching an 'Egg' from which the world was fashioned. The Egg then broke in half to release a mysterious god of light, Phanes, also called Erikepaios (an unexplained name) and identified with Dionysus. At a later stage, Zeus swallowed Phanes and everything else in order to recreate the whole of the world from himself; here one can trace Stoic concepts and terms about the 'sympathy' of the universe (see POSIDONIUS §5). This theogony became a reference text for Neoplatonic philosophers until the end of paganism, from Porphyry to Proclus and Damascius. A revelation of polytheism more serious than those of Homer and Hesiod, it was adapted to Platonic ontology by allegorical interpretation. There is also a collection of 'Hymns of Orpheus', stemming probably from a sectarian community in Asia Minor, which testifies to the ongoing practice of Orphic cults in the imperial age (see Quandt 1952).

By contrast, long before, in the third century BC, a 'Testament of Orpheus' had been fabricated. Reflecting contacts with Judaism, it sets out to counter the Orphic theogony. In it, Orpheus revokes polytheism and proclaims the one god, creator of the universe. This was used by both Jews and Christians to rebuke paganism (see Riedweg 1993 for a detailed discussion).

References and further reading

Borgeaud, Ph. (ed.) (1991) *Orphisme et Orphée*, Geneva: Droz. (Takes account of recent discoveries.)

Brisson, L. (1995) *Orphée et l'Orphisme dans l'Antiquité Gréco-Romaine*, Aldershot: Variorum. (Scholarly articles on special problems.)

Derveni Papyrus, as 'Der Orphische Papyrus von Derveni', *Zeitschrift für Papyrologie und Epigraphik* 47 (1982), appendix 1–12. (Preliminary edition of the Derveni Papyrus.)

* Kern, O. (ed.) *Orphicorum Fragmenta*, Berlin: Weidmann, 2nd edn, 1982. (Collection of fragments, outdated but not yet replaced; fragment 31 is the Egyptian papyrus text.)

* Most, G.W. and Laks, A. (eds) (1997) *Studies on the Derveni Papyrus*, Oxford: Clarendon Press. (Additions to the text, English translation, interpretative studies.)

  Nilsson, M.P. (1952) 'Early Orphism and Kindred Religious Movements', in Nilsson, *Opuscula Selecta*, Lund: Gleerup, vol. 2, 628–83. (A solid survey of earlier work.)

* Pugliese Carratelli, G. (ed.) (1993) *Le lamine d'oro 'Orfiche'*, Milan: Scheiwiller. (Texts of the gold plates; still incomplete.)

* Quandt, G. (1952) *Orphei Hymni* (Hymns of Orpheus), Berlin: Weidmann. (Standard edition of the Greek text.)

* Riedweg, C. (ed.) (1993) *Jüdisch-hellenistische Imitation eines orphischen Hieros Logos* (Jewish-Hellenistic Imitation of a 'Sacred Discourse' of Orpheus), Tübingen: Narr. (Contains the Testament of Orpheus.)

  West, M.L. (1983) *The Orphic Poems*, Oxford: Clarendon Press. (Concentrates mainly on the Derveni theogony and further Orphic theogonies, including the evidence from Olbia.)

WALTER BURKERT

ORTEGA Y GASSET, JOSÉ
(1883–1955)

The Spanish philosopher Ortega borrowed themes from early twentieth-century German philosophy and applied them with new breadth and urgency to his own context. Calling his philosophy 'vital reason' or 'ratiovitalism', he employed it initially to deal with the problem of Spanish decadence and later with European cultural issues, such as abstract art and the mass revolt against
· *moral and intellectual excellence. Vital reason is more a method for coping with concrete historical problems than a system of universal principles. But the more disciplined the method became, the deeper Ortega delved into Western history to solve the theoretical and practical dilemmas facing the twentieth century.*

1 Life
2 Relations between reason and life
3 Works

1 Life

Typifying liberal Spanish philosophers of the late nineteenth and early twentieth centuries, José Ortega y Gasset philosophized in order to reverse Spain's historical decline. Born into two publishing families, he achieved eminence as a philosopher-journalist, an educator, and in 1931 as a politician. Postdoctoral studies in Germany acquainted him with Neo-Kantian philosophers of culture Georg Simmel and Hermann Cohen (see NEO-KANTIANISM). From Cohen's follower Paul Natorp, Ortega learned of Husserl's phenomenology, which he introduced into Spain in 1913 in newspaper articles, three years after obtaining the Chair in Metaphysics at the University of Madrid (see HUSSERL, E.; PHENOMENOLOGICAL MOVEMENT). His first book, *Meditaciones del Quijote* (Meditations on Quixote) (1914), employs phenomenological descriptions in essays on the salvation of Spanish culture by means of Cervantes' insights. Among journals Ortega founded, the most distinguished, *Revista de Occidente* (Review of the West), begun in 1924, informed Spaniards of innovations in philosophy, anthropology, physics and art. Ortega phenomenologically analysed avant-garde art in his renowned *La deshumanización del arte* (The Dehumanization of Art) (1925). He sensed significant progress being made in saving Spanish civilization through rigorous concepts.

Yet the following eleven years offered little cause for optimism. In 1929, intervention in university affairs by the dictator Miguel Primo de Rivera prompted Ortega to resign his Chair. Renting theatres, he offered a Bergson-style public course, *¿Qué es filosofia?* (What Is Philosophy?) (1929–30), in which he unveiled his mature principles of human existence. In 1930 Ortega's best-known book appeared, *La rebelión de las masas* (The Revolt of the Masses), launching a philosophical attack on an over-egalitarian age for aggrandizing mediocrities such as Primo and Mussolini. During the Second Spanish Republic (1931–6), Ortega founded a party of intellectuals. While an elected Member of the Spanish Parliament, he deplored extremism of right and left, only to abandon politics himself in 1932 and leave the country in 1936, before civil war erupted.

In 1945 he returned to Franco's Spain, but the hostility of Church and State drove him to lecture abroad whenever possible in his final years. In his richest, most rigorous work, the posthumous *La idea de principio en Leibniz y la evolución de la teoria deductiva* (The Idea of Principle in Leibniz and the Evolution of Deductive Theory) (1946–50), he rebuts hostile clerics. To Spain and Spanish America he bequeathed an elegant and precise philosophical vocabulary, along with a number of outstanding students, notably Xavier Zubiri and Juan David García Bacca.

2 Relations between reason and life

The problem of the relationship between reason and life lies at the root of Ortega's thinking. Both terms vary in meaning as his method of 'vital reason' matures, the variations stemming from his dialogues with contemporaries. He corresponded with the older philosopher Miguel de UNAMUNO, who, with KIERKEGAARD and Liberal Protestant theologians, conceived authentic existence as the struggle between reason and life: life affirms immortality after death; reason denies it. But Ortega dodged religious issues to concentrate on the philosophy of culture. In Georg SIMMEL he found an opposition posited between life as process and life as cultural principle, with authentic culture a synthesis of both. Hence in *El tema de nuestro tiempo* (The Modern Theme) (1923), Ortega wrote, 'Life should be cultured, but culture must be vital'. Simmel's notion of life as process, a continual becoming, drew Ortega close to NIETZSCHE, BERGSON and the Darwinists (see VITALISM). Yet Ortega found a more fruitful idea in Cohen, who held that, to be oneself, it is necessary to use logic, such as the induction and deduction employed in mathematical physics. Ortega embraced the conception of life as a search for identity, but qualified Cohen's emphasis on scientific logic: for Ortega, the problem of personal identity stands in the foreground, and the solution of physico-mathematical logic only at midground. Therefore, from 1910, Ortega's point of departure became the idea of life as a problem of self-authentication, but without Cohen's faith in the constructs of scientific reason as a solution to it.

Ironically, it was Cohen's fervent follower Natorp who drew Ortega's attention to other forms of reasoning, by alerting him to the strengths and weaknesses of Husserlian phenomenology. Before 1907, Husserl had stressed the cognitive value of the direct contemplation of essences called 'intuition' (*Anschauung*): I can 'intuit' an apple, the colour red, a circle, a mythical fruit. From 1907 on, however, Husserl stressed that 'pure' intuition requires self-conscious reflection, and Natorp argued that reflection is a mental construct, mediating between mind and object and thereby preventing the pure intuition of essences. Natorp's objection would recur from 1914 to 1950 in all Ortega's discussions of Husserl. However, Ortega incorporated into his own thought a modified version of the unmediated intuition of the pre-1907 Husserl. 'Vital reason' is most concisely formulated in the phrase, 'I am myself and my circumstance'; according to Ortega, I am a self-aware interaction with my concrete surroundings, a repertory of possibilities which my intuitive reason helps me realize. The word 'circumstance', as employed in 1914, also connotes Ortega's homeland. So, unlike Unamuno, who perceives an irreconcilable clash between reason and life, Ortega applies Husserlian intuitive reason to resolve problems of national life or 'circumstance'.

Ortega's thinking on life and reason deepened in 1929. Reading the work of Husserl's student Heidegger in 1928 helped Ortega to organize his earlier philosophy into the four principles first formulated in *What Is Philosophy?*: (1) my life is the 'radical reality', the framework in which all other realities (including reason) appear; (2) my life is a self-conscious problem of individual realization; (3) my problem amounts to deciding among specific possibilities for self-authentication; (4) the plurality of these possibilities defines my freedom in life; their quantitative finiteness, my limitation. But, rejecting Heidegger's ontological jargon, the mature Ortega adopted the life-centred lexicon of Wilhelm DILTHEY, whose philosophy of history Ortega read thoroughly in 1928. Thus emerged the last step in the evolution of 'vital reason', its absorption of what Dilthey called 'historical reason'. Ortega's third basic principle defines life as decision among possibilities, but what determines the decision, according to Dilthey, is a generational worldview (*Weltanschauung*), a system of subrational beliefs. Narrating the beliefs guiding great decisions can solve cultural problems.

What, therefore, is 'vital reason' as method? First, the posing of a current philosophical problem; second, phenomenological reduction of the problem; finally, narration of historical causes of the problem so as to solve it in practice. The structure of Ortega's most concise book illustrates this – *Historia como sistema* (History as System) (1935). Here he poses the problem of the loss of faith in scientific reason, because it is felt to be incapable of defining human being. How then should one reorient humankind in the universe? Phenomenological reduction prescribes the suspension of historical forejudgments, ascent to universals, descent from universals to essences, and description of essences. So Ortega suspends the historical forejudgments, received from the natural sciences, that humans have a nature, a changeless substance knowable with scientific logic. He also dismisses ideas of humans as body or psyche, since he regards such ideas as naturalistic. Instead, he finds that the 'radical reality' of each human being is precisely the life of that individual, and he describes that existence by enumerating its main aspects: its self-consciously problematic quality, the capacity for making decisions from among possibilities, and the limitations on these possibilities. Since historical reason can explain the decision-making, history is the discipline which will orient human beings in the universe by narratively clarifying their beliefs, defining them and instructing them in past errors to avoid such errors in the future. In proof, Ortega narrates the history of the West, in which belief in God gave way to belief in nature (whose study is natural science), and once scientism faltered, there arose belief in nothing but disillusionment, the science of which is history.

3 Works

Ortega's production exceeds the dozen volumes of over 500 pages each in the *Alianza* edition of his *Obras Completas*. Like Simmel and Max Scheler he addresses a vast thematic spectrum; let us summarize, first, his most translated work, *The Revolt of the Masses*, and, second, his *Leibniz* book, the one most deserving of philosophical attention.

Like all his major writings, *The Revolt of the Masses* begins with the posing of a current issue: Why do the masses demand space in cultural sites once reserved for the moral and intellectual elite? Ortega dismisses as historical forejudgments all political and economic explanations. Instead, he accepts what for him is a self-evident universal: an idea of society as dynamic interaction between moral and intellectual minorities and multitudes. Out of these two pure human types – elites and masses – Ortega derives a definition of the then-current mass type: a hybrid, it combines the great potential of the elite with the inertia of the mass type of bygone eras. Though powerful, the masses of the 1930s create nothing and even rebel against the elite, which does in fact create. The revolt evinces cultural strengths – the rise in the quality of life, the adventure of living in a dangerous era, the growth of personal possibilities – but even greater weaknesses – mass aggressiveness in public affairs, opposition to liberalism, obliviousness to history, overspecialization, excessive reliance on the state, and historical demoralization. Ortega proposes as a panacea the formation of a 'United States of Europe'.

From 1946 to 1950, he penned his Leibniz book in response to intellectually rebellious 'mass-men' – Spanish and Mexican Neo-Thomists who wrongheadedly criticize his mental style as metaphorical, overly dependent on sensory evidence and lacking stable principles. In 1946, on the tercentennial of Leibniz's birth, he posed a central problem: why, after formulating many philosophical principles, did Leibniz treat them so lightly? The implication was that the

playful Ortega was in some way akin to the rigorous Leibniz, and this conclusion emerges along with the corollary that Ortega's foes themselves lack rigour and principles. Using 'historical reason', he shows that ARISTOTLE, the father of Neo-Thomism, displayed excessive dependence on the senses, inexactness and inconsistency in handling principles. Ortega divides all philosophers into the disciplined, principled variety, based on intuition and not the senses (Plato, Descartes, Leibniz, Husserl, Dilthey and Ortega) and the less 'principled' type (Aristotle, the Stoics, the Schoolmen, Kierkegaard, Ortega's rivals Unamuno and Heidegger, and his detractors, the Neo-Thomists). 'Aristotelians' tend towards sombreness, anguish, inimical to genuine philosophy, while the Presocratics and Plato likened philosophizing to riddle-solving or participating in sports and games. This attitude, Ortega feels, confirms his distinction between rational ideas and subrational beliefs; humans act upon ideas or mere theories without ultimate seriousness, while beliefs act upon humans and are taken seriously. Therefore Ortega's apparent non-seriousness, like Leibniz's, does not negate his discipline. He confesses early opposition to Unamuno's tragic sense of life, the clash between reason and life, by speaking of a 'sportive and festive sense of existence', which implied an intellectual sportsman's endeavour to harmonize life and reason. 'Vital reason' is no more deficient in principles than the philosophies of Plato, Husserl and Dilthey. Ortega, one of the twentieth century's greatest essayists, deserves recognition as a brilliant transitional philosopher, bridging Husserl's phenomenology and Heidegger's ontology of existence with his own four principles.

See also: SPAIN, PHILOSOPHY IN

List of works

Ortega y Gasset, J. (1914) *Meditaciones del Quijote*, Madrid: Residencia de Estudiantes; trans. E. Rugg and D. Marín, *Meditations on Quixote*, New York, 1961. (Ortega's first book, intended to be one of a series of ten – not completed. It contains Ortega's ideas on 'radical reality', and the seminal phrase 'I am myself and my circumstances'.)

—— (1923) *El tema de nuestro tiempo*, Madrid: Calpe; trans. J. Cleugh, *The Modern Theme*, New York, 1933; repr. 1961. (Ortega's exposition of perspectivism and vitalism.)

—— (1925) *La deshumanización del arte e ideas sobre la novela*, Madrid: Revista de Occidente; trans. H. Weyl, *The Dehumanization of Art: Ideas on the Novel*, Princeton, NJ, 1948. (Ortega's best-known works of aesthetics, combining an appraisal of the state of art in the early twentieth-century Europe with a characteristically energetic exposition of how aesthetic experience functions.)

—— (1929–30) *¿Qué es filosofía?*, Madrid: Revista de Occidente, 1958; trans. M. Adams, *What Is Philosophy?*, New York, 1960. (A course of eleven lectures given by Ortega in 1929, of note because closure of the university meant that the last ten were given in a theatre. A good example of Ortega as a communicator.)

—— (1930) *La rebelión de las masas*, Madrid: Revista de Occidente; trans. A. Kerrigan, *The Revolt of the Masses*, Notre Dame, IN, 1986. (Radically elitist analysis of the threat posed to society, culture and democracy by the masses.)

—— (1935) *Historia como sistema y Concordia y libertad*, Madrid: Revista de Occidente; trans. H. Weyl and W. Atkinson as 'History as System', in *Philosophy and History*, Oxford, 1941; also as *History as a System and Other Essays toward a Philosophy of History*, Greenwood, CN, 1961. (Ortega formally conceptualizes the idea of historical reason as narrative reason.)

—— (1946–83) *Obras Completas* (Complete Works), Madrid: Revista de Occidente; vols 1 and 2, 1946; vols 3–6, 1947; vol. 7, 1961; vols 8 and 9, 1962; vols 10 and 11, 1969; vols 1–11 repr. and vol. 12, Madrid: Alianza Editorial, 1983. (Standard edition of the author's complete works.)

—— (1947–50) *La idea del principio en Leibniz y la evolución de la teoría deductiva*, Madrid: Revista de Occidente; trans. M. Adams, *The Idea of Principle in Leibniz and the Evolution of Deductive Theory*, New York, 1971. (Essay in which Ortega contrasts philosophers according to principle, and focuses his own playful style of 'vital reason', or 'reason from life's point of view'.)

References and further reading

Cerezo Galán, P. (1984) *La voluntad de aventura. Aproximación crítica al pensamiento de Ortega*, Barcelona: Ariel. (Insightful on Ortega's early reactions to Husserl and Heidegger.)

Donoso, A. and Raley, H.C. (1986) *José Ortega y Gasset: A Bibliography of Secondary Sources*, Bowling Green, OH: Philosophy Documentation Center. (The most complete bibliography of research about Ortega, alphabetized by authors and themes.)

Orringer, N.R. (1984) 'La crítica de Ortega a Aristóteles y sus fuentes', *Cuadernos Salmantinos de Filosofía* (Salamanca) 11: 557–98; repr. in M. Durán, *Ortega, hoy*, Veracruz, 1985, 173–224.

(Contributor's detailed source study of Ortega's *Leibniz* book.)

—— (1984) 'Ortega y Gasset's Critique of Method', *Comparative Criticism* 6: 135–54. (Presents the arguments of §2 above.)

Ouimette, V. (1982) *José Ortega y Gasset*, Boston, MA: Twayne. (Concise biography and brief but clear synthesis of Ortega's philosophy.)

N. ORRINGER

OSWALD, JAMES (1703–93)

James Oswald, Scottish theological writer, used the philosophy of 'common sense' to try to found religious and moral conviction on principles that were impervious to scepticism. In a long running controversy over Church discipline, he defended the right of individual parishes to choose their ministers, seeing the prevailing system of patronage as favouring the advocates of a fashionable kind of civility that was too tolerant of scepticism and intellectual innovation, and too indifferent to the Church's traditional concerns with public and private morality. Though never part of the Aberdeen philosophical community, Oswald corresponded with Reid, and late in life collaborated with him in charitable work for the sons of clergy.

James Oswald was born at Dunnet in Caithness, where he succeeded his father as parish minister in 1726. He moved to Methven, Perthshire, in 1750, ministering there till 1783. He was Moderator of the General Assembly of the Church of Scotland in 1765, when he was awarded an honorary doctorate at Glasgow. As early as 1732, reporting to the Caithness Presbytery on a colleague's conduct, Oswald cited 'the common sense of mankind' to determine the binding character of promises. In *Submission and Obedience* (1753) he used the same authority to justify seeing the institutions of government as part of the divine plan for the world, arguing that the Church's mission could only be accomplished on the assumption that it too operated according to comparable principles of good order and government. From these derive obligations to duty, both civil and religious, which are 'obvious to the Understanding of Men'. This is reminiscent of George Turnbull's contention in his *Philosophical Enquiry* (1726, published 1731) that whatever is fit and binding in individuals' relations with one another and with God can be known by common sense (see TURNBULL, G.). Turnbull and Oswald were products of the same divinity school at Edinburgh; they also shared a view of miracles as law-governed events.

'Common sense', meaning a direct deliverance of our common human reason or cognitive faculty, was cited by Oswald to justify practices the abandonment of which would undo social institutions, affront conscience or undermine religion. He subsequently extended it to cover all beliefs a challenge to which could be considered destructive of sense or sanity. Wherever the self-evidence of common-sense judgments was impugned, some form of incoherence (social or intellectual) would ensue. The commonest way of seeming to impugn them was to allow that they needed, or were even capable of, reasoned justification. On the contrary, they were held to constitute the primary truths which all reasoned justification must already assume (see Common sense school).

Oswald was unperturbed at the diversity of principles to which he accorded common-sense status, and in *An Appeal to Common Sense* (1766–72) resisted any attempt to give a precise analysis of this status or rest it on more formal criteria. The thread holding his primary truths together is that they had virtually all been targets of Hume's scepticism (see HUME, D.). Oswald commended Hume for seeing they are beyond the scope of reasoning, but he equated this too narrowly with strict demonstration, and argued against Hume that neither custom nor sentiment, both of which he considered highly fallible resources and the roots of bigotry and folly, could account for the transparent certainty of these unreasoned truths. Some degree of mental maturity, intelligent observation, even repeated experience, may be necessary to our initial appreciation of them, but thereafter their 'self'-evidence exceeds any other evidence we could cite for them. Oswald also criticized Francis Hutcheson and Henry Home for placing moral perception in feeling rather than cognitive judgment, but he agreed that moral training proceeds more by engaging the heart than the intellect (see HUTCHESON, F.; HOME, H. (LORD KAMES)).

Oswald's primary truths fluctuate between the particular and the universal. They include beliefs with regard to our own existence and continued identity; the existence, identity and relative placings of objects around us and their motions, powers and causal operations expressed in the laws of nature; the existence of other sentient life with powers of action and traits of character; mathematical axioms; the being and providence of God; the real distinction between vice and virtue and its enforcement through punishment and reward; and the existence of obligations to God, others and ourselves. These are topics too central to this life and the next to be left to the rarified argumentation of the learned, and Oswald supposed it inherently ridiculous that the intelligent multitude should remain in suspense on them. A certain amount of unacknowledged chauvinism entered into Oswald's characterization of this multitude, whom he tended to see reflected in the persons of property and judgment who formed the mainstay of the Church of Scotland.

The laws of nature, for Oswald, are not formal, mathematical laws, but such relatively nebulous principles as that bodies sink by virtue of their weight, or that fire has the power to consume combustible materials. He means that the gravity of bodies and the power of fire are too much facts of life to be subject to caveats of inductive logic. In arguing that God's existence is evident to common sense, he wishes to avoid the metaphysical nicety of a priori demonstration and the inductive hazards of argument by analogy. To detect design, even on a limited scale, in inanimate nature is no different in principle from recognizing it among animals and humans, which in turn is no different (notwithstanding Hume's argument to the contrary) from actually experiencing the powers of things in their manifestation; and once Oswald has reached this point he develops his argument beyond the strict requirements of common sense philosophy, into a general theodicy.

Oswald's *Appeal* was sympathetically received in *The Monthly Review*, and by the Dissenter William Enfield in a tract directed to Joseph Priestley (see PRIESTLEY, J.). Philip Skelton commended Oswald's argumentative skill but thought he undervalued revelation. Favourable notices in *Göttingische Anzeigen* led to a German translation (1774), but the popularity of Oswald's work was shortlived. Priestley (1774) condemned his declamatory rhetoric, his restricted understanding of 'reason', and his dogmatic use of 'common sense' as an arbitrary block to legitimate enquiry. The translator of Claude Buffier's *First Truths* (1780) (see BUFFIER, C.) thought Oswald grossly over-extended the scope of common sense, and that he failed to see how often he was describing what were implicitly reasoned judgments.

See also: ENLIGHTENMENT, SCOTTISH

List of Works

Oswald, J. (1753) *Some Thoughts Relating to that Submission and Obedience Due to the Authority and Decisions of the Supreme Judicature of the Church. Communicated in Two Letters from One Clergyman to Another*, Edinburgh: Wright. (Issued anonymously.)

—— (1766) *A Sermon, Preached at the Opening of the General Assembly of the Church of Scotland, May 22. 1766: To which are annexed, Letters on Some*

Points of Importance Contained in the Sermon, Edinburgh: Kincaid and Bell.

—— (1766–72) *An Appeal to Common Sense in behalf of Religion,* vol. 1, Edinburgh: Kincaid and Bell; vol. 2, Edinburgh: Kincaid and Creech; German translation by F.E. Wilmsen, *Appelation an den gemeinen Menschenverstand zum Vortheil der Religion,* Leipzig: 1774, 2 vols. (Issued anonymously.)

—— (1767) *Letters concerning the Present State of the Church of Scotland, and the Consequent Danger to Religion and Learning, from the Arbitrary and Unconstitutional Exercise of the Law of Patronage,* Edinburgh: Gray. (Issued anonymously.)

—— (1770) *The Divine Efficacy of the Gospel Dispensation: A Sermon Preached before the Society in Scotland for Propagating Christian Knowledge,* Edinburgh: Kincaid and Bell.

—— (1774) *Six Sermons on the General Judgment,* Edinburgh: Gray.

—— (1791) *Hypocrisy Detestable and Dangerous: Four Sermons,* Glasgow: Duncan and Chapman. (Issued anonymously.)

References and further reading

* Anon. (1780) *'Preface' to First Truths, and the Origin of our Opinions, Explained: With an Enquiry into the Sentiments of Modern Philosophers relative to our Primary Ideas of Things: Translated from the French of Père Buffier,* to which is prefixed a *Detection of the Plagiarism, Concealment, and Ingratitude of the Doctors Reid, Beattie, and Oswald,* London: Johnson.

Ardley, G. (1980) *The Common Sense Philosophy of James Oswald,* Aberdeen: Aberdeen University Press. (A polemical, somewhat partisan exposition of Oswald's *Appeal to Common Sense.*)

Cooper, J. (1948) *James Oswald (1703–93) and the Application of the Common Sense Philosophy to Religion,* unpublished dissertation, University of Edinburgh. (A slightly sentimentalized intellectual biography, offering a convenient survey of Oswald's principal writings, and original research on his early career.)

* Enfield, W. (1770) 'A Second Letter to the Reverend Dr Priestley', appended to *Remarks on Several Late Publications Relative to the Dissenters: In a Letter to Dr Priestley,* London: Bladon. (Issued anonymously.)

Kuehn, M. (1987) *Scottish Common Sense in Germany, 1768–1800,* Kingston, Ont., and Montreal: McGill-Queen's University Press, ch. 3. (Examines the reception of Oswald's philosophy.)

Laurie, H. (1902) *Scottish Philosophy in its National Development,* Glasgow: Maclehose, ch. 9. (Includes a hostile appraisal of Oswald's work.)

* Priestley, J. (1774) *An Examination of Dr Reid's Inquiry into the Human Mind on the Principles of Common Sense, Dr Beattie's Essay on the Nature and Immutability of Truth, and Dr Oswald's Appeal to Common Sense in behalf of Religion,* London: Johnson; repr. New York: Garland Publishing, 1978.

Sher, R.B. (1985) *Church and University in the Scottish Enlightenment,* Edinburgh: Edinburgh University Press. (Discusses Oswald's role in Church politics.)

Skelton, P. (1784) 'Some thoughts on Common Sense, Intended for the More Intelligent Reader' in *Works,* vol. 6, Dublin: privately published.

* Turnbull, G. (1731) *A Philosophical Enquiry Concerning the Connexion Betwixt the Doctrines and Miracles of Jesus Christ,* London: Willock. (Published under the pseudonym Philanthropos.)

M.A. STEWART

OTHER MINDS

It has traditionally been thought that the problem of other minds is epistemological: how is it that we know other people have thoughts, experiences and emotions? After all, we have no direct knowledge that this is so. We observe their behaviour and their bodies, not their thoughts, experiences and emotions. The task is seen as being to uncover the justification for our belief in other minds. It has also been thought that there is a conceptual problem: how can we manage to have any conception of mental states other than our own? It is noteworthy that there is as yet no standard view on either of these problems. One answer to the traditional (epistemological) problem has been the analogical inference to other minds, appealing to the many similarities existing between ourselves and others. This answer, though it is no longer in general favour among philosophers, still has its defenders. Probably the favoured solution is to view other minds as logically on a par with the unobservable, theoretical entities of science. That other people have experiences, like us, is seen as the best explanation of their behaviour.

1 **What generates the two problems of other minds?**
2 **Who has the epistemological problem?**
3 **The analogical inference to other minds**
4 **Other minds as theoretical entities**
5 **Criteria and other minds**
6 **Private language and other minds**

1   What generates the two problems of other minds?

The epistemological problem arises from two facts. We lack direct knowledge of the mental states of other people. We have such knowledge of at least some of our own mental states. Put the two claims together and we have the traditional problem of other minds. The relevant asymmetry, between our own case and that of others, turns on the question of direct knowledge, not observation. Being able to observe the mental states of others would not enable us to avoid the problem. What would be needed would be the ability to observe those mental states as the mental states of others. They would have to come labelled. The situation would only then be symmetrical. We would have the direct knowledge we lack.

The same asymmetry generates the conceptual problem. How can we have the concept of other people's experiences given that we have direct knowledge only of our own experiences, labelled as our own? Once again, the problem is not that we cannot observe the pains of others. What would be needed would be observing such pains as, indeed, the pains of others.

There has been comparatively little discussion of the conceptual problem, and no more will be said here about the conceptual problem of other minds, other than to note that solving it would not, other than controversially at best, remove the epistemological problem. That problem will be hereinafter the one to be discussed.

2   Who has the epistemological problem?

The heroic way of avoiding the problem of other minds is to deny that the claimed asymmetry, between ourselves and others, holds. Some have done so by insisting that we have direct knowledge of the mental states of others, though this has generally been seen as implausible. However, there seems to be an important strand of thinking within feminist theory that would endorse this rejection of our asymmetry (see FEMINISM AND PSYCHOANALYSIS). Similarly, continental European philosophy has commonly taken the view that other people are needed for us to acquire our own sense of ourselves as persons (see ALTERITY AND IDENTITY, POSTMODERN THEORIES OF). So our sense of others goes before our sense of self. That would seem to demand some capacity to know about others before one knows about oneself. The asymmetry would, presumably, be reversed, and the problem of other minds give way to the problem of our own minds.

Given that the asymmetry is accepted, and thus the traditional understanding of the problem of other

minds, it has been almost a commonplace to believe that only a traditional dualist view of the mind produces a difficult problem of other minds (see DUALISM). Though generally theories of mind accept the asymmetry, not all are thought to have a difficult problem. Behaviourism (see BEHAVIOURISM, ANALYTIC) is a theory of mind that either is thought to have no problem at all, or, if it does, nevertheless has no difficulty in solving the problem. There is no special problem about knowing about the behaviour and behavioural dispositions of another.

Functionalism is another theory of mind that is thought not to have a difficult problem. Mental states are viewed as internal states of the organism, regulating its responses to its surroundings. The various mental states are differentiated by their various roles, and they have no other features relevant to their being the mental states they are (see FUNCTIONALISM). It is then claimed to be straightforward, faced with the behaviour of others, to infer that such internal states exist, in the appropriate relations to the behaviour. Eliminative materialists have been seen as not having any problem. If there are no minds, then there are no other minds, therefore there is no problem of other minds (see ELIMINATIVISM).

However, it has been argued that all theories of mind leave the other minds problem intact, and difficult. Theories of mind are, indeed, theories of mind, all minds, one's own and others. Given that they are to be true of all minds, including other minds, they cannot, it has been argued, be used to show that there are, indeed, other minds. It is unacceptable to argue that, say, functionalism is true, and then use this to solve the other minds problem, since it cannot be known to be true, to hold of minds in general, unless it holds of other minds. How could that be known without the other minds problem having been, somehow, solved?

In conjunction with this line of argument, it has been pointed out that a theory of mind, embracing all minds, needs to embrace its propounder's mind as well as other minds. So a crucial part of the evidence (generally implicit) for a theory of mind will be that the theory fits the propounder's experience. That is the only way direct evidence in its favour can be obtained. So the propounder's experience is crucial. It has been argued that there is no escaping dependence on that experience and, as we shall see, any such dependence has been seen to be a fatal weakness, whenever it exists, in any would-be justification for belief in other minds.

3   The analogical inference to other minds

The traditional solution to the problem of other

minds has been the analogical inference to other minds. Other people behave like me in similar circumstances and have the same physico-chemical composition. When I burn myself it hurts and I cry out and wince. When other people are burned they cry out and wince. I can thus infer that they are in pain too. More generally, others are very like me. I know I have beliefs, experiences and emotions. So I am entitled, given how like me they are, to infer that other people also have beliefs, experiences and emotions.

This traditional analogical inference to other minds is now generally incorporated in a hypothetic inference (scientific inference, inference to the best explanation) to other minds. That there are alternative hypotheses about others which have to be ruled out requires that the argument take the form of a hypothetic inference (see INFERENCE TO THE BEST EXPLANATION). But the appeal to one's own case, and to similarities, remains crucial in this analogical/hypothetic inference.

That, indeed, one's own case is crucial, gives rise to the classical, continuing objection to the analogical inference to other minds, that it is a generalization from one case. Such generalizations are almost invariably unsound. Though there have been attempts to put the analogical inference to other minds in a form that avoids this objection, it is generally accepted that such attempts have not succeeded.

However, its supporters argue that, even so, the analogical/hypothetic inference remains a sound inference, despite its dependence on one case. More than one case is needed where what is at issue is the question of a causal link between events. Where it can be known from one case that there is such a causal link, that one case will then be enough. It is claimed that the relevant causal link, involving mental states, can be known to hold from one's own case. Though it has traditionally been insisted that the relevant causal link is between mental states and behaviour, it has been urged that the relevant causal link needs to be between brain states and mental states if the analogical/hypothetic inference is to be defensible.

The other classical objection to the analogical inference to other minds has been that its conclusion was impossible to check, not just in fact, but in principle. This feature no longer seems to be seen as having any epistemological relevance.

4   Other minds as theoretical entities

This is probably, among Anglo-American philosophers, the favoured solution to the problem of other minds. The justification is in the form of a hypothetic inference. That others have mental states is hypothesized to account for how they behave. However, one proceeds purely from the outside. No evidence gathered from one's own case is used to support this hypothesis. The one case objection thought widely to be fatal to the analogical inference is, crucially, avoided, so it is widely believed.

It is generally considered that treating other minds in this way, as theoretical entities, will succeed if one has a functionalist (or some such) view of the mind. The two seem made for each other. However, the argument in §1, that no theory of mind has an advantage over any other in supporting belief in other minds would, if successful, apply to this particular attempt to avoid dependence on one's own case.

It has been argued, conversely, that unless one enlists the help of a functionalist (or some such) theory of the mind, treating other minds as theoretical entities will not succeed. A traditional view of mental states, allowing that they have intrinsic content – in particular, phenomenal properties, such as the hurtfulness of pain (see QUALIA) – cannot be supported by this method. Treating the mental states of others as theoretical entities, it is argued, will not provide those states with the needed intrinsic properties. That content can only be filled in by an appeal to one's own case.

5   Criteria and other minds

Treating other minds as theoretical entities, though an alternative to the analogical inference, takes the form of a hypothetic inference. Criterialists, by contrast, have sought to avoid the one case problem by eschewing any form of inference. They have insisted that the link between behaviour and mental states is neither entailment (as in behaviourism) nor an inductive inference. The link is claimed to be conceptual and such links are characterized as criterial. Behaviour is a criterion for the presence of mental states. It has been claimed by some that such a non-inferential connection is required if we are to have any concept of the experiences of others.

An example of such a claimed non-inferential link would be the claim that itching is conceptually linked to scratching, not merely contingently correlated. Our concept of itching is that it disposes one to scratch. It is further claimed that scratching is, thereby, evidence of itching, given that itching disposes one to scratch.

That there are such conceptual links has been widely argued and widely denied. That, if there are, they would provide a sufficient basis for belief in the mental states of other people has been, if anything, even more vigorously contested. The thrust of the attack on the use of criteria to support belief in other minds seems to be that such conceptual links fail to bridge the gap between observed behaviour and the unobserved inner states to which they are conceptually linked. If there is no entailment directly from the one to the other, and there is no appeal to some form of inductive inference, it is argued that we are left with the gap. The gap cannot be crossed by *fiat*, as it were.

One way of understanding what has been called the attitudinal approach to other minds, is to see it as going beyond other uses of criteria in insisting that our conception of other human figures is that they are souls, have experiences. That is how we perceive them. It is as immediate as that, preceding any belief. This criterial view seems, however, to inherit the criterial gap. However we conceive of reality, our conceptions might be mistaken. There are attitudes to things and people which, though more immediate and deeper than inferential belief, are, nevertheless, mistaken (racist and sexist attitudes might be given as instances).

6 Private language and other minds

It has been widely accepted that language is a public phenomenon. Some have insisted that it is essentially public. One way of understanding this claim is classically associated with Wittgenstein. A language that is necessarily private, that is, such that only one person can understand it, is (logically) impossible (see PRIVATE LANGUAGE ARGUMENT).

The connection with the problem of other minds has been controversial. However, it seems clear that the connection exists in the reason given for the impossibility of such a private language. That reason bears directly on the analogical inference to other minds.

A necessarily private language is claimed to be impossible because a language has to be, in principle, subject to checking by someone other than an individual user of the language. Generally, a user of the analogical inference to other minds is in breach of this principle. They have insisted that each of us knows what psychological terms mean (at any rate, some of them) from our own case and only from our own case. Their usage would not then be, in principle, one that could be checked for consistency. Functionalists, by contrast, make no such claim, and it should be noted that the connection from private language to other minds depends on the use of terms whose meaning would be private in the relevant sense. The connection is not directly to any particular argument to other minds.

The argument that a check is needed (in principle, so Robinson Crusoe is not in trouble) has generally been that, in its absence, no distinction can be made between its seeming to the language user that their usage is consistent, and its being so. They have only their impression to go on. The issue has been vigorously contested.

That a private language is impossible has not generally been used explicitly as an argument for other minds. Nor could it be. After all, it is only in principle that a language is to be checkable by other people. An important, though indirect role, however, could be seen as its supporting the criterialist insistence on the need for a conceptual connection between inner states and publicly observable states (see CRITERIA).

See also: MIND, CHILD'S THEORY OF

References and further reading

These are all non-technical and manageable with reasonable effort.

Buford, T.O. (ed.) (1970) *Essays on Other Minds*, Chicago, IL: University of Illinois Press. (A useful, varied collection, including some classical items, particularly two by N. Malcolm expounding Wittgenstein.)

Hill, C.S. (1991) *Sensations: a Defense of Type Materialism*, New York: Cambridge University Press. (Chapter 9, 'Knowledge of other minds', discusses the conceptual problem of other minds, and also defends a version of the analogical inference to other minds.)

Hyslop, A. (1994) *Other Minds*, Dordrecht: Kluwer. (An extended defence of the analytical/hypothetic inference to other minds.)

McDowell, J. (1982) 'Criteria, Defeasibility, and Knowledge', *Proceedings of the British Academy*, 68: 455–79. (Hostile to criteria but exploring the issues at a fundamental level.)

McGinn, C. (1984) 'What is the Problem of Other Minds?', *Proceedings of the Aristotelian Society*, supplementary vol. 58: 119–37. (A discussion of the conceptual problem of other minds.)

Pargetter, R. (1984) 'The Scientific Inference to Other Minds', *Australasian Journal of Philosophy* 62: 158–63. (A good (favourable) account of other minds as theoretical entities.)

* Wittgenstein, L. (1953) *Philosophical Investigations*, Oxford: Blackwell. (The classical source for criterialism and private language.)

ALEC HYSLOP

OTTO, RUDOLF (1869–1937)

Rudolf Otto, an early and leading student of religious experience, was a devout Christian thinker (part theologian, part philosopher, part phenomenologist of religious experience) who was strongly influenced by the philosophy of Immanuel Kant. He held that numinous experience – experience of the uncanny that is strongest and most important in cases in which it seems to its subject to be experience of God – is unique in kind. Such experience of God, he held, occurred in both Semitic and South Asian monotheistic traditions. Recognizing the intellectual or doctrinal content of numinous experience, but influenced by Kant's thesis that knowledge-giving concepts cannot refer beyond possible objects of sensory experience, Otto tried to remain faithful to both numinous experience and Kantian philosophy by talking about 'ideograms' that express the content of numinous experience but, allegedly at least, are not concepts.

Rudolf Otto was born into a devout Lutheran family in Peine, Hanover. Between 1888 and 1891 he studied theology in Erlangen, Göttingen and Bavaria. In 1891 he returned to Göttingen, where he became acquainted with Ritschlian theology. He received his licentiate in theology there for a study entitled 'Spirit and Word According to Luther', and was appointed a *Privatdozent* in 1899. He became Professor of Systematic Theology in 1904, a post which he also held in Breslau (1914–17), and in Marburg from 1917 until his retirement in 1929. He travelled widely in Egypt, Palestine, Greece, North Africa, India and the Far East. He learned Sanskrit and was an early figure in the effort to make South Asian and Indian thought accessible to a European audience. Otto was a pioneer in the history and phenomenology of religion, and the author of profound studies of mysticism, Śaṅkara, Meister Eckhart, India's religions and the kingdom of God. The present entry will focus on his view of religious language and his account of numinous experience.

Otto, influenced by Kant, denied that concepts apply to God. But he also asserted the fundamental importance of doctrines about God and contended that it is possible for human beings to experience God. Kant had claimed that no concept could apply, in such a way as to produce knowledge of anything, to anything that cannot somehow be sensed. The application of concepts beyond the range of objects of possible sensory experiences, he held, yields no knowledge. Since God is not a candidate for being literally sensed, the concept 'God' can have no knowledge-providing application. Otto, working in Kant's shadow, proposed to substitute 'numinous

ideograms' for concepts. God is inaccessible to reason, but, Otto held, can be felt in numinous experience, where one is encountered by God. This enables one to form an ideogram of God. Otto's examples of ideograms are 'the Void' and 'the Wholly Other', and he wrote that the necessity for ideogramic expression and the ineffability of the numinous experience 'teaches us the independence of the positive content of the experience from the implications of its overt positive expression' ([1917] 1923: 34). His acceptance of a Kantian perspective, his contention that numinous experience is incapable of full conceptualization, his view that God has a conceptually accessible aspect and a conceptually inaccessible aspect, and his attraction to negative theology blended together to yield talk about ideograms. None of this led Otto to conceive of God as irrational or to say that contradictions can be true of God. None the less, the force of 'ideogram' is suspiciously like that of 'concept', applied to something that is not an object of possible sense experience.

Otto is most famous for his emphasis on numinous experience, which ranges from a vague sense of the uncanny to explicit putative experiences of God. These latter, stronger versions of numinous experience form our primary grounds for thinking that there is a God. They are, Otto believed, genuine encounters with God, the powerful content of which leaves no doubt as to the reality of the experience's object. To have a numinous experience is to experience (at least apparently) a being who is majestic, awesome, living, holy and overwhelming, in whose presence one realizes one's unholiness, dependence and comparative insignificance. What is most important for Otto is the being that is experienced; one's reactions to it are but corollaries to the being's own attributes. Further, the object of numinous experience possesses ultimate and unsurpassable worth. A human being is passive, not active, in such experiences. Otto believed that such experiences guarantee their own veridicality, needing no help from natural theology or philosophical argument.

Kant claimed that moral experience is not reducible to any other sort of experience, and that morality has an indefeasible validity all its own. Otto agreed about morality and made the same claim regarding religion and numinous experience. Thus he stressed that numinous experiences, while in some ways resembling other experiences, are none the less unique in their content. Further, they are inexplicable in natural terms. Hence religion has a genuine object and theology a distinct subject matter (see RELIGIOUS EXPERIENCE).

However, it is not clear that even if numinous experience is indeed unique in kind that this yields veridicality; on one popular view of secondary qualities, each is unique in type and secondary qualities are mind-dependent. Nor is it clear that numinous experience is not veridical even if it is not unique in content. But be that as it may, Otto's emphasis on the centrality of numinous experience in monotheistic traditions has had a strong influence on the philosophy and phenomenology of religion.

List of works

Otto, R. (1907) *Naturalismus und Religion*, Tübingen: Mohr; trans. J.A. Thomson and M.H. Thomson, *Naturalism and Religion*, London: Williams & Norgate, 1907. (Here Otto endeavours to keep what seems right in naturalism without eliminating religion.)

—— (1909) *Kantisch-Fries'sche Religionsphilosophie*, Tübingen: Mohr; trans. E.B. Dicker, *The Philosophy of Religion Based on Fries and Kant*, London: Williams & Norgate, 1931. (Otto's philosophy of religion discussed in terms of the perspectives that most influenced it.)

—— (1917) *Das Heilige*, Munich: Beck, 25th edn, 1936; trans. J.W. Harvey, *The Idea of the Holy*, Oxford: Oxford University Press, 1923. (Otto's *magnum opus*, in which he develops his account of numinous experience.)

—— (1926) *West-Östliche Mystik*, Gotha: Klotz; trans. B.L. Bracey and R.C. Payne, *Mysticism East and West*, New York: Macmillan, 1932. (Interesting and controversial comparison of Śaṅkara and Eckhart.)

—— (1930) *India's Religion of Grace and Christianity Compared*, trans. F.H. Foster, London: SCM Press. (Argues that Hindu monotheism includes a theology of divine grace.)

—— (1931) *Religious Essays*, trans. B. Lunn, London: Oxford University Press. (Essays supplementary to *The Idea of the Holy*.)

—— (1938) *The Kingdom of God and the Son of Man*, Grand Rapids, MI: Zondervan Press. (Otto's interpretation of the kingdom of God.)

References and further reading

Almond, P.C. (1984) *Rudolph Otto: An Introduction to His Philosophical Theology*, Chapel Hill, NC: University of North Carolina Press. (Good, accessible discussion of Otto's thought and influence.)

Davidson, R.F. (1947) *Rudolph Otto's Interpretation of Religion*, Princeton, NJ: Princeton University Press. (Discussion of Otto's notion of the numinous as religiously central.)

Yandell, K.E. (1971) *Basic Issues in the Philosophy of Religion*, Boston, MA: Allyn & Bacon. (Discusses Otto's account of religious experience; see chapter two.)

KEITH E. YANDELL

OVERTON, RICHARD
(d. *circa* 1665)

Overton was one of the leading figures of the radical Leveller movement in England in the 1640s. He fought for the equality of all men before the law and for complete religious and political toleration, often by appealing to notions such as the social contract and the natural law. In metaphysics he denied that the soul is a separate immaterial and immortal substance, arguing that immortality is not achieved until the resurrection. His views on the soul may have influenced Milton.

Overton's dates are unknown. An Englishman, he may have spent some time in the Netherlands and appears to have matriculated in Queens' College, Cambridge in 1631. He was most active from the early 1640s to the mid-1650s, and was arrested and imprisoned several times for political reasons. He probably died in the mid-1660s.

In numerous pamphlets, some of which were published under the pseudonym 'Martin Marpriest', Overton expressed his political views about religious toleration, democratic republicanism, the importance and dignity of the individual's property, and the equality of all men before the law. Often this was done in a vivid humorous and satirical style. While Overton appealed to notions such as the social contract and the natural law, he did not present any detailed philosophical analysis of these concepts. His most important pamphlets include: *The Araignement of Mr. Persecution* (1645) which contains his ideas on toleration; *A Remonstrance of Many Thousand Citizens* (1646a) which calls for the abandonment of monarchy, arguing that all power rests with the people; *An Arrow against all Tyrants* (1646b) which emphasizes the political rights of the individual; and *An Appeale from the Degenerate Representative Body of the Commons of England Assembled at Westminster* (1647) which upholds the principles of 'right reason' that in some circumstances justify a direct appeal to the people. Also important are his editorials for the weekly newspaper *The Moderate* (1648–9). It has been argued that Overton played an important role in the development of seventeenth-century 'possessive individualism' according to which the individual is naturally the owner of their own person. However, the nature of Overton's individualism is still a matter of dispute among scholars.

Overton's most philosophical work is *Mans Mortalitie* (1643) (a revised version of the book first appeared in 1655 under the title *Man wholly Mortal*). Overton's denial of an immaterial and immortal soul, and his view that all hope for a future life is in the resurrection, link his work to doctrines in early Christian thought. Some of Overton's arguments are similar to those of POMPONAZZI in *On the Immortality of the Soul* (1516). Other influences include Socinianism, George Wither's introduction and translation of Nemesis' *The Nature of Man* (1636), and Henry Woolnor's *The True Originall of the Soule* (1642) (see SOCINIANISM).

According to Overton, the belief in an immortal soul is a 'heathenish invention' which later made its way into Christian dogma. He attempts to argue for his position both through an interpretation of the Bible and through philosophical reasoning. His arguments are very much couched in scholastic terminology, for example, 'form and matter' and 'potentiality and actuality'. To a large extent, his strategy consists in pointing out absurdities in the immortalist position.

Overton's main philosophical argument against the natural immortality of the soul is based on his view that what is called 'the soul' is not an immaterial substance: since man is wholly a compound material being, he cannot be intrinsically indestructable or immortal. As in his political writings, Overton in *Mans Mortalitie* emphasizes the rationality of man, but for him, rationality does not entail immateriality. Rather, he argues that rationality is a function of man's material being. The difference between man and beast is said to be only a matter of degree. Man is an animal whose (physical) parts are endowed with several faculties which make him a 'living Rationall Creature'. All of man's faculties depend on the body and are thus mortal: this is true of faculties which men have in common with beasts as well as of those which are distinctive of man (that is, reason, consideration, science and so on). The faculties exist in the human body as accidents exist in a subject. It is only through the body that the faculties constitute a unitary human self; their 'unite substance' is in the body. If it were possible for man's faculties to exist independently of the body, we would have to assume as many souls as there are faculties. Thus we would be led to the absurd conclusion that each faculty constitutes a separate soul and that there is no unitary self to which the various faculties belong.

Overton infers from the essential physical nature of man that (1) man is not by nature indestructible or immortal and that (2) man's immortality is a gift of God received at the resurrection. Thus, Overton does not deny immortality altogether, but he makes the afterlife dependent on the resurrection. While he rejects the notion of an immaterial human soul, it is not clear that his 'materialism' extends universally. What he says about the soul is at least consistent with the view that there are non-human immaterial spirits (for example, angels). But he assigns to God a material dwelling-place in subscribing to the belief that the sun is the seat of divinity.

Mans Mortalitie aroused considerable controversy. It was attacked as heretical in the House of Commons in 1644, and it came under attack in print by Guy Holland in *The Prerogative of Man* (1645), Alexander Ross in *The Philosophicall Touchstone* (1645), Thomas Edwards in *Gangraena* (1646), and several others. On the positive side, Overton's views on the soul are sometimes said to have influenced Milton; but the matter is controversial.

See also: SOUL, NATURE AND IMMORTALITY OF THE

List of works

Overton, R. (1643) *Mans Mortalitie*; ed. H. Fisch, Liverpool: Liverpool University Press, 1968. (A reprint of the 1643 edition, with textual notes and a brief introduction by the editor. The most impotant differences between this and the revised 1655 edition are noted.)

—— (1645) *The Araignement of Mr. Persecution*; repr. in W. Haller *Tracts on Liberty in the Puritan Revolution 1638–1647*, vol. 3, New York: Columbia University Press, 1934. (Argues against religious uniformity.)

—— (1646a) *A Remonstrance of Many Thousand Citizens*; repr. in W. Haller *Tracts on Liberty in the Puritan Revolution 1638–1647*, vol. 3, New York: Columbia University Press, 1934. (Expresses Overton's republicanism; defends the equality of all men before the law.)

—— (1646b) *An Arrow against all Tyrants*; repr. with prefatory note, University of Exeter: The Rota, 1976. (Written in the form of a letter to 'Henry Martin, a Member of the House of Commons'; attempts to justify men's natural rights.)

—— (1647a) *An Appeale from the Degenerate Representative Body of the Commons of England Assembled at Westminster*, London. (Addressed to the New Model Army which is 'now the only formal and visible head that is left unto the people'. Argues that a direct appeal to the people can be justified in some circumstances.)

—— (1647b) *The Commoners Complaint*; repr. in W. Haller *Tracts on Liberty in the Puritan Revolution*

1638–1647, vol. 3, New York: Columbia University Press, 1934. (Recounts the misfortunes of Overton and his wife in order to illustrate the suppression of 'the just rights and freedoms of the Commons of England'.)

References and further reading

Burns, N.T. (1972) *Christian Mortalism from Tyndale to Milton*, Cambridge, MA: Harvard University Press. (Contains a chapter 'Overton, Milton and Hobbes'.)

* Edwards, T. (1646) *Gangraena, or, A Catalogue and Discovery of many of the Errours, Heresies, Blasphemies and pernicious Practices of the Sectaries of this Time*; repr. with intro., The University of Exeter: The Rota, 1977. (A polemic against the Levellers and Overton's mortalism.)
Frank, J. (1955) *The Levellers. A History of the Writings of Three Seventeenth-Century Social Democrats: John Lilburne, Richard Overton, William Walwyn*, Cambridge, MA: Harvard University Press. (Discusses Overton's political pamphlets.)
Gimelfarb-Brack, M. (1979) *Liberté, égalité, fraternité, justice! La vie et l'oeuvre de Richard Overton, Niveleur*, Berne: Lang. (The only monograph devoted to Overton, with a detailed biographical account and a good bibliography.)
* Holland, G. (1645) *The Prerogative of Man: Or, his Soules Immortality*, Oxford. (A critique of Overton's *Mans Mortalitie*, rejecting both Overton's interpretation of the Bible and his philosophical reasoning. According to Holland, the article of the resurrection 'proves nothing against the perpetuity of the Soule'.)
Macpherson, C.B. (1962) *The Political Theory of Possessive Individualism. Hobbes to Locke*, Oxford: Clarendon Press. (Chapter III.4 deals with Overton as a 'possessive individualist'.)
* Pomponazzi, P. (1516) *De immortalitate animae*, trans. W.H. Hay, II as *On the Immortality of the Soul*, in E. Cassirer, P.O. Kristeller and J.H. Randall, Jr (eds) *The Renaissance Philosophy of Man*, Chicago, IL: University of Chicago Press, 1948. (A reliable English translation of Pomponanzzi's best known treatise, by which Overton may have been influenced.)
* Ross, A. (1645) *The Philosophicall Touch-Stone*, London. (Attempts to prove 'the immortality of mans soule briefly, but sufficiently'. Overton's arguments are described as 'the weak Fortifications of a late Amsterdam Ingeneer, patronizing the Soules Mortality'.)
Watner, C. (1980) '"Come what, come will": Richard Overton, Libertarian Leveller', *The Journal of Libertarian Studies* 4: 405–32. (On Overton's pamphleteering career and the libertarian aspects of the Leveller movement.)
* Wither, G. (1636) *The Nature of Man. A learned and useful Tract, written in Greek by Nemesius, . . . Englished by Geo. Wither*. (Nemesius, Bishop of Emesa, wrote *De natura hominis* in c. 400. Wither's introduction bears resemblances to Overton's views.)
* Woolnor, H. (1641) *The True Originall of the Soule*, London. (Argues that the soul is produced 'neither by creation nor by propagation', but by a 'certain meane way between both'. The soul consists of 'matter of a higher kind'.)
Wootton, D. (1991) 'Leveller Democracy and the Puritan Revolution', in *The Cambridge History of Political Thought 1450–1700*, ed. J.H. Burns and M. Goldie, Cambridge: Cambridge University Press, 412–42. (A general discussion of the Leveller movement, with references to Overton and to Edwards' *Gangraena*.)

UDO THIEL

OWEN, GWILYM ELLIS LANE (1922–82)

G.E.L. Owen led the reorientation in ancient philosophy that began in the 1950s in Britain and North America. He approached the texts with a profound knowledge of classical scholarship, but also as an analytic philosopher, understanding them as conceptual investigations of live philosophical interest. Concerned primarily with the logic of argumentation, philosophy of science and metaphysics, he wrote influential articles on Parmenides, Plato and Aristotle. Equally important were his classes at Oxford (1953–66), at Harvard (1966–73) and finally at Cambridge, in which he constantly developed and tested his ideas and methods.

1 Logic and metaphysics in Plato and Parmenides
2 Dialectic, physics and metaphysics in Aristotle

1 Logic and metaphysics in Plato and Parmenides

After an interruption for war service, G.E.L. Owen completed his BA at Corpus Christi College, Oxford, and stayed on for the new graduate degree of B.Phil., which he took in 1950, the second year it was awarded. His B.Phil. thesis, written under the supervision of Gilbert RYLE, was a bold and far-reaching study of logic and metaphysics in the 'later dialogues' (as under his influence these particular works came to be called) of PLATO: *Parmenides, Theaetetus, Sophist, Statesman* and *Philebus*; in it he laid the groundwork for the series of remarkable graduate seminars on Plato that he later gave at Oxford, Harvard and Cambridge. It led to his first article, 'The Place of the *Timaeus* in Plato's Dialogues' (1953), in which he set himself the task of overturning the scholarly consensus in regarding the *Timaeus* as the culmination of Plato's work in metaphysics. Timaeus majestically portrays the construction of the physical world by a god looking to separated Platonic Forms as models ('paradigms') of the qualities and substances to be imposed upon the transient 'flux' of physical reality. This seemed to Owen to rest on metaphysical theses, familiar from such 'middle-period' dialogues as *Phaedo* and *Republic*, that the more sophisticated 'later' dialogues had overthrown. So it was rather in the logical explorations of the 'later' dialogues that the high point of Platonic metaphysics was reached. In Owen's view, philosophically well-motivated ambitions had led Plato in the middle dialogues to linguistic and conceptual abuses in postulating the 'being', 'unity' and 'stability' of Forms and describing the character of physical objects as multiplicities that 'become' or 'appear' but 'are' not anything. Disturbed by the resulting logical difficulties and paradoxes, he undertook in the 'later' dialogues a careful examination of the logic of these and related concepts. He discovered that kind of philosophical analysis to be inherently rewarding, and hoped thereby to replace the earlier theory of Forms with a conceptually more adequate version. This early work of Owen's was carried forward later in brilliant papers on the analysis of being and not-being in the *Sophist* and on the antinomies about unity developed at length in the *Parmenides*. His work on the logical and metaphysical analyses of the 'later' dialogues fundamentally altered, and deepened, the study of these works – even if his arguments did not win most scholars over to dating the *Timaeus* early, close to the *Republic*.

Owen was the first University Lecturer at Oxford, and subsequently the first Professor, appointed specifically for Ancient Philosophy (1953); later he went to Harvard to establish a graduate programme there in Classics and Philosophy. He did massive research for his year-long lecture-courses at Oxford, attended also by graduate students, on the Presocratics. Only his interpretations of PARMENIDES and ZENO OF ELEA were ever published. For Owen, Parmenides was a 'philosophical pioneer of the first water', not the cosmologist in the tradition of ANAXIMANDER that conventional scholarship saw. He stood self-consciously aside from that tradition, using independent deductions to work out the characteristics that, by force of logic, reality must possess. He argued that anything that can be thought of or spoken about must 'be' or 'exist', and that what 'is not' or 'does not exist' is literally unthinkable. Since change, differentiation and plurality of any kind would logically require the being of what 'is not', reality must be a single, timeless, spatially continuous, internally undifferentiated, unchanging entity. Reality as it appears to us, and as the earlier cosmologists represented it, is essentially diverse and changing. But Parmenides' 'much-contested proof' reveals how seductive conventions of human thought are which, despite their logical appearance, rest on logically unacceptable foundations.

2 Dialectic, physics and metaphysics in Aristotle

More than half of Owen's published papers, and a similar proportion of his teaching, dealt with ARISTOTLE. Here again, he was primarily interested in the logic of arguments. In a reversal of Werner Jaeger's then-dominant picture of Aristotle's philosophical development, Owen showed that Aristotle's early work in logic had led him while still a member of Plato's Academy to reject Plato's theory of Forms. Only much later did independent study lead to a sort of 'Platonism' in his metaphysical thought. Central to Owen's work on Aristotle was his account of the role of 'dialectic', presented in '*Tithenai ta phainomena*' (1961): this title refers to the process of 'setting down' the phenomena needing to be sorted out in order to reach a general theory in some area of inquiry. As Owen noticed, even in a subject like physics the 'phenomena' for Aristotle are mostly not results of observation, but certain opinions *about* what is observed: matters of common or customary opinion, or ordinary linguistic usage, or the views of the 'wise' – respected philosophers or other experts. A 'dialectical' inquiry works through these 'phenomena' so as to discover and then resolve tensions among them by making appropriate distinctions: the 'true' theory is the one that can claim maximum support from the phenomena once so reconstructed. For Owen, such 'dialectical' reasoning was a paradigm of good philosophical method. He examined it in several contexts in Aristotle's *Physics*, especially the theories of time and motion, and at several stages of Aristotle's engagement with 'first philosophy', or metaphysics.

Owen's students, and others who came under his influence in formative years, spearheaded a wide expansion of work on ancient philosophy. Their research includes logic, metaphysics and philosophy of science, but also ethics, political philosophy, philosophy of mind and other fields, and it extends into the post-Classical periods of Hellenistic, Roman and later ancient philosophy.

List of works

Owen's unpublished seminar notes and papers are deposited in the Classics Faculty Library, University of Cambridge.

Owen, G.E.L. (1986) *Logic, Science and Dialectic*, ed. M.C. Nussbaum, London: Duckworth. (A collection of all Owen's published scholarly papers, with the exception of six book reviews and one commentary.)

References and further reading

Schofield, M. and Nussbaum, M.C. (1982) *Language and Logos*, Cambridge: Cambridge University Press. (Studies in ancient Greek philosophy by fifteen scholars, former students and others indebted to the stimulus of discussion with him, presented to Owen on his sixtieth birthday.)

JOHN M. COOPER

OXFORD CALCULATORS

'Oxford Calculators' is a modern label for a group of thinkers at Oxford in the mid-fourteenth century, whose approach to problems was noticed in the immediately succeeding centuries because of their tendency to solve by 'calculations' all sorts of problems previously addressed by other methods. If for example the question was, what must a monk do to obey the precept of his abbot to pray night and day, a 'calculator' might immediately rephrase the question to ask whether there is a minimum time spent in prayer that would be sufficient to fulfil the abbot's precept, or a maximum time spent that would be insufficient to fulfil the precept. Or, if grace was supposed to be both what enables a Christian to act meritoriously and a reward for having so acted, then a calculator might ask whether the degree of grace correlated with a meritorious act occurs at the moment of the meritorious act, before the act when the decision to act is being made, or after the act when the reward of increased grace is given. If a body was hot at one end but cold at the other, then a calculator might ask not whether it is to be labelled hot or cold, but how hot it is as a whole. Finally, if it was asked whether a heavy body acts as a whole or as the sum of its parts, then a calculator might take the case of a long thin rod falling through a tunnel pierced through the centre of the earth and attempt to calculate how the rod's velocity would decrease as parts of the rod passed the center of the cosmos, if it acted as the sum of its parts.

Of these four questions, the last two were asked by Richard Swineshead, a mid-fourteenth century fellow of Merton College, Oxford, whose Liber calculationum *(Book of Calculations) led to his being given the name 'Calculator'. By association with Richard Swineshead, other Oxford masters including Thomas Bradwardine, Richard Kilvington, William Heytesbury, Roger Swineshead and John Dumbleton have been labelled the 'Oxford Calculators'. Their work contains a distinctive combination of logical and quantitative techniques, which results from the fact that it was often utilized in disputations on sophismata (*de sophismatibus*). This same group of thinkers, with emphasis on their mathematical rather than logical work, has been called the 'Merton School', because many but not all of the Calculators were associated with Merton College, Oxford. Besides calculatory works, the same authors wrote works in which calculatory techniques are not so prominent, including commentaries on Aristotle, mathematical compendia and commentaries on Peter Lombard's* Sentences.

1 **Richard Swineshead's** *Liber calculationum*
2 **Calculations and disputations on sophismata**
3 **Calculations and measures of motion**
4 **Calculations and logic**
5 *De incipit et desinit*; **maxima and minima**
6 **Calculations and natural philosophy**
7 **Calculations and theology**

1 Richard Swineshead's *Liber calculationum*

The central book of the Oxford calculatory tradition, the *Liber calculationum* (Book of Calculations) focuses on applications of mathematical techniques to natural philosophical problems (Murdoch and Sylla 1976). Of the sixteen treatises of the *Liber calculationum*, the first four deal with the intension and remission of forms or the increase and decrease of qualities such as heat or whiteness. First, the issue of the intension and remission of forms is raised in the abstract. Should the degree of heat, for instance, be measured by nearness to the maximum degree of heat or by the distance from zero degree (Clagett 1950)? Second, questions concerning the intension and remission of forms are raised concerning a body nonuniformly qualified with heat or some other quality. Should it be said to be as hot as its maximum degree or as hot as its mean degree? Third, how should one characterize the combined degree of an element having two unequal qualities, such as heat and moisture: is the combined degree as intense as the mean between its degree of heat and its degree of moisture or is it, for example, only as intense as the more remiss quality? Swineshead concludes that such an element is as intense as the geometric mean between its two qualities, so that if one quality is in the second degree and the other in the eighth, then the element as a whole should be said to be in the fourth degree.

Having debated and determined such questions about the measures of qualities, the *Liber calculationum* turns next to measurements of quantities of bodies, first to degrees of density or rarity and then to measures of velocity of augmentation and diminution. Treatise VII deals with the problem of reaction. If a hot body heats the cold body next to it, will the cold body simultaneously react and cool the hot body? If, for action to occur, the agent must have more power than what it acts on, how can each of the two neighbouring bodies have sufficient power to act on the other at the same time? Treatise VIII consequently asks directly how the power of an agent should be measured. Is it, for instance, by its intensity, so that a body hot in the fourth degree would have a power in the fourth degree? Or does power depend on the 'multitude of form', taken to depend not only upon the intensity and extension of the form, but also upon the density of the matter in which it inheres? Also, how is the 'difficulty of action' to be measured? Is it by the ratio between the power of the agent and the resistance or is it, as Swineshead concludes, simply by the power of the agent acting to its utmost?

Treatise X deals with maxima and minima and Treatise XI with the problem, mentioned at the start of this article, of a thin rod moving through the centre of the earth (Hoskin and Molland 1966). Treatises XII and XIII deal with illumination and the action of light sources. Treatises XIV and XV deal with problems of quantifying local motion with respect to its causes, first explaining in the abstract how velocity varies when the ratio of force to resistance varies, assuming the truth of Thomas Bradwardine's dynamical function (see BRADWARDINE, T.), and second in the concrete, assuming that resistance is encountered by an agent as it moves through a medium of varying resistance. Finally, Treatise XVI of the *Liber calculationum* deals with the rates at which a body takes on the maximum degree of a quality; as, for instance, a heating agent warms a body next to it, first assimilating the parts of the body nearest to the agent and then parts farther away.

As can be seen from this brief survey of the contents of the *Liber calculationum*, the Oxford 'calculations' in their core manifestation concerned every technique that had been developed up to that time for introducing quantification into natural philosophy, plus some new ones (see NATURAL PHILOSOPHY, MEDIEVAL). The intension and remission of forms was a type of quantification previously most highly developed in determining the degrees of compound medicines. Measurements of illumination had been developed within the science of optics or perspective and possibly also in astrology, where each planet was supposed to exert an influence on earth depending upon its position in the heavens. Ways of relating forces, resistances and velocities of local motion had received a thorough treatment in Thomas Bradwardine's *De proportionibus velocitatum in motibus* (On the Ratios of Velocities in Motion), completed in 1328. The 'calculator' focused his attention only on physical questions, but the theory of intension and remission of forms had been and continued to be applied by others to the intension and remission of charity or grace in the human soul, and calculations could also be applied in theology.

2 Calculations and disputations on sophismata

What gave 'calculations' their distinctive style was the fact that they were connected not only to natural philosophy or theology, but also to the disputations on sophismata (*de sophismatibus*) prominent at Oxford in this period (Sylla 1982). As exercises occurring at the culmination of the undergraduate curriculum, disputations on sophismata were devoted to the explication of propositions that are at first glance counterintuitive, such as 'Infinite are finite' (*Infinita sunt finita*) or 'Socrates is whiter than Plato begins to be white'. In an oral disputation on a sophisma, students or masters competed against each other in proposing and arguing for and against possible resolutions. In an earlier period, disputations *de sophismatibus* called upon the disputants to use especially what they knew of logical or grammatical theory. As time went on, natural philosophy and mathematics were also called upon, thus resulting in the so-called calculations.

What disputations *de sophismatibus* were like in earlier fourteenth-century Oxford, before calculations became prominent, can be seen in Richard Kilvington's *Sophismata*, which includes the sophisma mentioned above, 'Socrates is whiter than Plato begins to be white' (Kretzmann and Kretzmann 1990) (see KILVINGTON, R.). Assuming the case that Socrates has some degree of whiteness and that Plato begins to intensify in whiteness starting from zero, the sophisma sentence seems to apply, but not without problems. Suppose that the comparative term 'whiter' is taken to be measured by the ratio of the more intense quality to the less intense, so that if Socrates is white in the second degree and Plato in the first degree, then Socrates will be said to be twice as white as Plato. If Plato has zero whiteness at $t0$ and subsequently begins to intensify in whiteness, then when one considers the ratio between the whiteness of Socrates and that of Plato, it will get larger towards the beginning of Plato's intensification, tending to infinity as Plato's whiteness tends to zero. It seems to follow that immediately after Plato begins to intensify in whiteness, Socrates will be infinitely whiter than Plato, but this seems to be contradictory, it might be argued, because Socrates is only finitely white. Is something wrong with the analysis? Confronted with such sophismata, Oxford scholars concluded that it might be useful to study systematically how any and all things should be quantified.

William Heytesbury's *Sophismata* and *Regulae solvendi sophismata* (Rules for Solving Sophismata) exemplify the forms that Oxford disputations on sophismata took after the introduction of calculations (Wilson 1956). HEYTESBURY divides his rules for solving sophismata according to set techniques, referred to by historians as 'analytical languages' or 'conceptual algorithms' (Murdoch 1969, 1975). There are purely logical techniques, such as ways of solving 'insolubilia', or self-falsifying propositions, such as 'I am telling a lie'. Other techniques analyze sophismata in terms of first and last instants, maxima and minima, and measures of motion in the categories of local motion, alteration, and augmentation and diminution. The same sophisma sentence could be analysed on different occasions applied to different hypothetical situations ('cases') and using different analytical languages. Thus the sophisma sentence 'Socrates is whiter than Plato begins to be white' might be analysed by considering that motion of alteration is a so-called successive entity extrinsically limited at its beginning and its end; there is no first instant of alteration but only a last instant before the alteration begins, and no last instant of alteration but only the first instant at which the final degree has been induced.

On another occasion the same sophisma sentence could be analyzed using the language of maxima and minima, pointing out that as Plato moves from zero whiteness the intension of whiteness increases continuously, so that there is no minimum degree of whiteness gained, but rather smaller and smaller degrees *ad infinitum* down to zero. When the implication was drawn from the case that if relative intensities are measured by the ratio they have to each other, then Socrates will be infinitely whiter than Plato immediately after he begins to be white, then the sophisma sentence could be analyzed using distinctions about senses of the words 'immediate' and 'infinite'. Sometimes 'infinite' is used to mean a 'potential infinite', and sometimes an 'actual infinite'. Thus the integers are potentially infinite because, given any integer, one can find a higher integer; but

the integers are not actually infinite because there is no single infinite number. Heytesbury's *Sophismata* demonstrates in practice the many rules that he lays out in the *Regulae solvendi sophismata*.

3 Calculations and measures of motion

The Oxford Calculators' belief in the potential power of mathematics to solve problems of sophismata seems to have been inspired by the success of Thomas Bradwardine's *De proportionibus velocitatum in motibus* (Crosby 1955) (see BRADWARDINE, T.). Bradwardine had shown how neatly the Euclidian theory of ratios could be used to clarify the relations of forces, resistances and velocities in motions as discussed with less success in Aristotle's *Physics*. Bradwardine's function, relating forces, resistances and velocities, was said to measure motion with respect to its cause (*tanquam penes causam*), while measures of the distances traversed or intensities or sizes gained were said to be measures with respect to effect (*tanquam penes effectum*). Discussions of alternative ways of measuring local motion, alteration, and augmentation and diminution *tanquam penes effectum* are common in the works of the Oxford Calculators.

4 Calculations and logic

These mathematical considerations were introduced into a context that had already been highly developed through the application of the new logic, especially the theories of supposition and syncategoremata (see LANGUAGE, MEDIEVAL THEORIES OF; LOGIC, MEDIEVAL). The problematic meaning of a sophisma could be shown to result from a confusion of compounded and divided senses, as in the sentence 'Something white can be black'. The word 'infinite' was said to have a syncategorematic sense, corresponding to the potential infinite, as well as a categorematic sense, corresponding to the actual infinite. The sophisma sentence 'Infinite are finite' was explained by saying that when 'infinite' appears at the beginning of a sentence, it is to be taken syncategorematically. There is not one thing that is infinite, but many things which together are infinite. In this way the calculators could conclude that there is no one infinite number, but all the numbers together are infinite, meaning something like the modern statement that the set of all integers is infinite.

5 *De incipit et desinit*; maxima and minima

Walter BURLEY, in his work on first and last instants and in his works on intension and remission of forms, had developed techniques that were also used as analytical languages by the later Calculators. As described above, the technique of first and last instants or of analyzing the use of the verbs 'it begins' and 'it ceases' (*incipit et desinit*), distinguished whether a permanent form (such as whiteness) or a successive entity (such as the motion of traversing a distance) has a first instant of being or a last instant of non-being. Using the analytical language of maxima and minima, it might be asked whether there is a maximum weight that Socrates can carry or a minimum weight too heavy for him. Again, propositions or sophismata would be analyzed using supposition theory to see which alternative was the correct one.

6 Calculations and natural philosophy

After their development, the techniques of the Oxford Calculators were also applied not only to solving explicitly labelled sophismata, but also to dealing with the normal questions of natural philosophy (see NATURAL PHILOSOPHY, MEDIEVAL). Roger Swineshead, author of the *Obligationes* and *Insolubilia* (and thought to be a distinct person from Richard Swineshead, despite a confusion of names in the manuscripts), made such an application in his *De motibus naturalibus* (On Natural Motions), alternating sections dealing with motion in the categories of place, quality and quantity with sections explicitly devoted to measures of motion, often proposing sophismata that could be developed using these measures. Thus Roger Swineshead proposed that a body which gains a degree uniformly throughout is altered indivisibly more than a body which in the end is non-uniformly qualified with the given degree as the minimum uniform degree that does not qualify it.

Calculatory techniques were also used by John Dumbleton, author of a large *Summa logicae et philosophiae naturalis* (Summa of Logic and Natural Philosophy) which combined calculation with something resembling a commentary on the natural works of Aristotle. Thus the techniques of the Oxford Calculators were seen as useful in the ordinary business of natural philosophy, although they gained their special flavor by frequent use in disputations *de sophismatibus*.

7 Calculations and theology

Shortly after they were put to use in the disputations *de sophismatibus*, the techniques of the Oxford Calculators became very popular at Paris and elsewhere, often in combination with the nominalistic analyses associated with WILLIAM OF OCKHAM. Bachelors of theology commenting on Peter Lom-

bard's *Sentences* frequently used calculatory techniques to address theological problems. In many cases, calculatory techniques indeed helped to resolve technical questions such as those concerned with degrees of grace or with first and last instants (for example, whether there is a first instant of salvation or a last instant of sinfulness). While some commentators applied the calculatory techniques wherever possible, others deplored the invasion of such quibbling technicalities into sacred subjects (Murdoch 1978).

See also: NATURAL PHILOSOPHY, MEDIEVAL

References and further reading

* Clagett, M. (1950) 'Richard Swineshead and Late Medieval Physics', *Osiris* 9: 131–61. (An analysis especially of the first treatise of the *Liber calculationum*.)
—— (1959) *The Science of Mechanics in the Middle Ages*, Madison WI: University of Wisconsin Press. (Text, translations and commentaries. Provides the context, within medieval mechanics, of the work of the Oxford Calculators.)
* Crosby, H.L. (ed. and trans.) (1955) *Thomas of Bradwardine: His Tractatus de proportionibus*, Madison, WI: University of Wisconsin Press. (The treatise that most inspired the mathematical side of the Calculators' work.)
Gilbert, N. (1976) 'Richard de Bury and the "Quires of Yesterday's Sophisms"' in E.P. Mahoney (ed.) *Philosophy and Humanism: Renaissance Essays in Honor of Paul Oskar Kristeller*, New York: Columbia University Press. (Describes the impact of the Oxford calculations at Paris and some of the negative reaction engendered there.)
* Hoskin, M. and Molland, A.G. (1966) 'Swineshead on Falling Bodies: An Example of Fourteenth Century Physics', *British Journal for the History of Science* 3: 150–82. (Edition of Treatise XI of Swineshead's *Calculationes* dealing with motion of a rod through the centre of the earth.)
* Kretzmann, N. and Kretzmann, B. (1990) *The Sophismata of Richard Kilvington*, Oxford: Oxford University Press and Cambridge: Cambridge University Press. (Best place to start for an understanding of how sophismata were solved in practice.)
Lewis, C. (1980) *The Merton Tradition and Kinematics in Late Sixteenth and Early Seventeenth Century Italy*, Padua: Antenore. (Investigates the extent of the Calculators' influence in Italy.)
Longeway, J. (1984) *William Heytesbury On Maxima and Minima: Chapter 5 of Rules for Solving Sophismata, with an anonymous fourteenth-century*

discussion, Dordrecht: Reidel. (Contains an English translation of Heytesbury on maxima and minima, plus the Latin text of the anonymous discussion.)

Maier, A. (1952) *An der Grenze von Scholastik und Naturwissenschaft* (On the Border between Scholasticism and Natural Science), 2nd edn, Rome: Edizioni di Storia e Letteratura. (See III.1. 'Die Calculationes des 14. Jahrhunderts'.)

—— (1966) *Die Vorläufer Galileis im 14. Jahrhundert* (The Precursors of Galileo in the Fourteenth Century), 2nd edn, Rome: Edizioni di Storia e Letteratura. (See especially, 'Der Funktionsbegriff in der Physik des 14. Jahrhundert' (The Concept of Function in the Physics of the Fourteenth Century), 81–110.)

Molland, A.G. (1968) 'The Geometrical Background to the "Merton School"', *British Journal for the History of Science* 4: 108–25. (Explains background of Bradwardine's function.)

* Murdoch, J.E. (1969) 'Mathesis in Philosophiam Scholasticam Introducta: The Rise and Development of the Application of Mathematics in Fourteenth-Century Philosophy and Theology', in *Actes du Quatrième Congrès International de Philosophie Médiévale*, Montreal, Que.: Institut d'Études Médiévales, 215–54. (How quantification entered medieval natural philosophy.)

* —— (1975) 'From Social into Intellectual Factors: An Aspect of the Unitary Character of Medieval Learning', in J.E. Murdoch and E.D. Sylla (eds) *The Cultural Context of Medieval Learning*, Dordrecht: Reidel, 271–339. (Describes in some detail the conceptual algorithms or analytical languages used throughout much of fourteenth-century philosophy and theology.)

* —— (1978) *Subtilitates Anglicanae in Fourteenth-Century Paris: John Mirecourt and Peter Ceffons*, New York: New York Academy of Sciences. (Describes the vogue for Oxford calculatory ideas in Parisian theology.)

* Murdoch, J.E. and Sylla, E.D. (1976) 'Swineshead (Swyneshed, Suicet, etc.), Richard', in C.C. Gillispie (ed.) *Dictionary of Scientific Biography*, vol. 13, New York: Charles Scribner's Sons, 184–213. (Extended description of the *Book of Calculations*, treatise by treatise.)

Sylla, E. (1971) 'Medieval Quantifications of Qualities: The "Merton School"', *Archive for the History of the Exact Sciences* 8: 9–39. (Describes the ways that the Calculators quantified qualities as contrasted with Nicole Oresme.)

—— (1973) 'Medieval Concepts of the Latitude of Forms: The "Oxford Calculators"', *Archives d'histoire doctrinale et littéraire du moyen age* 40: 223–83. (The work of the Calculators as related to latitudes, degrees of quality and intension of forms.)

* —— (1982) 'The Oxford Calculators', in N. Kretzmann, A. Kenny and J. Pinborg (eds) *The Cambridge History of Later Medieval Philosophy*, Cambridge: Cambridge University Press, 540–63. (Addresses especially the connection of the work of the calculators to Oxford undergraduate disputations on sophismata.)

—— (1986) 'Galileo and the Oxford *Calculatores*: Analytical Languages and the Mean-Speed Theorem for Accelerated Motion', in W.A. Wallace (ed.) *Reinterpreting Galileo*, Washington, DC: Catholic University of America Press, 53–108. (Addresses the question of whether Galileo used the work of the Oxford Calculators, and especially the Merton mean-speed theorem, in his kinematics.)

—— (1987) 'The Oxford Calculators in Context', *Science in Context* 1: 257–79. (How the work of the Calculators was related to the academic milieu in which it was carried out.)

—— (1991) *The Oxford Calculators and the Mathematics of Motion, 1320–1350*, New York: Garland. (Ph.D. dissertation, Harvard University, 1970; contains chapters on the physics of motion in the categories of quality and place, on measurement by proportionalities and latitudes, and on the wider calculatory tradition, as well as extensive outlines in Latin of several key calculatory works.)

Weisheipl, J.A. (1959) 'The Place of John Dumbleton in the Merton School', *Isis* 50: 439–54. (How Dumbleton's *Summa* relates to the work of the other Calculators.)

—— (1968) 'Ockham and Some Mertonians', *Mediaeval Studies* 30: 163–213. (Overview of the work of the Calculators in comparison to Ockham.)

—— (1969) 'Repertorium Mertonense', *Mediaeval Studies* 331: 174–224. (Most thorough available catalogue of works, with manuscript locations, of the Oxford Calculators.)

* Wilson, C. (1956) *William Heytesbury: Medieval Logic and the Rise of Mathematical Physics*, Madison, WI: University of Wisconsin Press. (Decribes the contents of Heytesbury's *Rules for Solving Sophismata* and related works.)

EDITH DUDLEY SYLLA

P

PAINE, THOMAS (1737–1809)

Thomas Paine, born in Norfolk, England, spent his early years as an undistinguished artisan and later excise officer. In 1774 he emigrated to America and settled in Philadelphia where he became a journalist and essayist. His Common Sense *(1776) and sixteen essays on* The Crisis *(1776–83) were stunning examples of political propaganda and theorizing. In the late 1780s, in Europe, Paine wrote* The Rights of Man *(1791–2) and attacked the English political system. During the French Revolution he was a Girondin in the French Convention and wrote* The Age of Reason *(1794, 1796), savagely criticizing Christianity. He died in New York in 1809, an important figure in the sweep of the revolutionary politics in America, England, and France at the end of the eighteenth century.*

1 Background and republican political theorizing
2 Propaganda against England
3 Role in the French Revolution

1 Background and republican political theorizing

Thomas Paine was born on 29 January 1737 in Thetford, in Norfolk, England, where he spent the first thirty-seven years of his life, a poor, unsuccessful, and unknown artisan. In desperation he emigrated to America in 1774 and rapidly received recognition as an intellectual leader of the American Revolution.

The juxtaposition of Paine's early career and later fame has attracted wide attention. In periods of conservative stability Paine has been reviled as an extreme radical on the fringes of the American Revolution, a demagogic drunkard not fit to be associated with the Founding Fathers of the United States. In periods of ferment commentators have hailed Paine as an authentic democrat of the people, whose thought and practice can be a model for the left.

Paine's natural talents and the more open social structure of America obviously contributed to the astonishing improvement in his fortunes by the mid-1770s. But the colonial uprising was mainly middle-class in its orientation, led by the political gentry. In this social milieu Paine was something of an outsider. His background and personality made him unpre-

dictable and never fully acceptable. He himself was never at ease in the upper reaches of the society he was helping to create, although he gloried in the recognition and status he had achieved.

Paine's success was to some extent a product of his marginal status. He had a shrewd understanding of the actual political world and was zealously committed to government by and for the masses. But he was no more an erudite thinker than the other American founders, nor were his political notions unconventional in their context. None the less, he had the rare gift – always presumed to be the produce of his working life – of being able to write for the populace. Paine understood what the people wanted or needed to hear better than any of the other Founding Fathers. All of his tracts from the seventies to the nineties hit the nerve of popular debate while simultaneously advancing the democratic ideas that the Americans had taken from John LOCKE and the English 'Commonwealthmen'.

Paine was interested in applied science and absorbed popular expressions of Newtonian physics (see NEWTON, I.). A series of laws governed the natural world. They were open to the understanding of all and could be put to work for human benefit. Paine was a 'rationalist' in an era termed the American Enlightenment, believing that fundamental truths could be arrived at by careful investigation and reflection on experience. Thus, he rejected Christianity, as depending on unreasonable beliefs (for example, the Virgin birth), and delighted in pointing out inconsistencies in the Bible. Instead, the harmonies of the natural world led one to conclude that a benevolent Deity had created an ordered cosmos. This 'clockwork' God did not, however, intervene directly in human life but had imprinted humankind with moral impulses that enabled people to achieve happiness on earth once they had rationally considered their own best interests.

This set of metaphysical and moral beliefs led to a grasp of political life that was indebted to Locke and crucial to Paine's philosophical politics. The creator allocated 'natural rights' to all people – or at least all men – equally. Differences in station were justified only because of variations in talent, industry, and frugality. In the order of things men should be provided with equal opportunities and an equal voice in determining how society should be governed.

Society was the natural outcome of the human condition – the relationships that derived from human beings living together, raising their young, and co-operating in common endeavour. These joint implicit responsibilities embodied the social contract. On the other side, government was a negative instrument only necessary to the extent that matters went awry; its powers were limited and, in the natural course of things, largely unnecessary.

What had gone wrong in America to impel the nation's leaders to revolution? Paine and others like him embraced the views of some dissenters in England earlier in the eighteenth century. These Commonwealthmen had developed a critique of English society that supposed the monetary power of the Crown to have destroyed balanced government. The Commonwealthmen looked back to a time of imagined civic virtue and forward to a restoration of the natural scheme of governance.

At the end of the eighteenth century, Paine popularized and extended this view in America, leavening it with Lockean individualism. This was the 'republicanism' of the colonies, which combined a constellation of historical, political, and philosophical ideas. The opponents of the Commonwealthmen, Paine said, had triumphed in England, corrupted its society, and wished to place a yoke of tyranny on the colonies. Paine, in contrast, urged the liberty of individual conscience, religious toleration, resistance to tyrants, and reform of the legislature. He denounced hereditary political institutions and desired to lodge power with 'the people', no matter how restrictedly they were defined.

2 Propaganda against England

Paine elaborated these views in the 1770s as the most inflammatory and didactic exhorter of the Revolutionary forces. *Common Sense* (1776) presented a justification for the Revolution, and the first *Crisis* paper (1776) is sometimes credited with keeping the Revolutionary army intact during the early fighting. In the 1780s Paine joined the Federalists in supporting a new constitution. He believed that a powerful central authority would promote the commercial and territorial expansion he desired, and he saw the Federalists as safeguarding *laissez-faire* economics in a democratic empire.

When Paine returned to Europe in the late 1780s, however, he focused again on theorizing about revolution, especially the one occurring in France and its potential for human liberation. At the same time he hoped to change the contours of English politics. Although first welcomed by men like Edmund BURKE, who had sympathized with the American colonies, Paine became disgusted with the possibilities for renewal of the English system. *The Rights of Man* (1791–2) explicitly attacked Burke's ideas and defended the French Revolution. Paine was contemptuous of the claims of tradition and custom that led to commitment to a hereditary monarchy. The book's praise of French politics also signalled a break with the increasingly conservative American Federalists who came to fear the radicalism of the Continent.

The Rights of Man additionally suggested ways in which a republic could effect the rudiments of a welfare state, and hinted at the potential for redistributive economic justice. This concern was later fleshed out in *Agrarian Justice* (1797). But even in 1792 Paine had gone too far for English authorities and was indicted for sedition. He fled to Paris in September. The events of the 1790s and his writings in that decade have ever after made him a hero to the English left.

3 Role in the French Revolution

In France Paine combined the political theorizing and revolutionary action that were characteristic of his career. But when the Girondins lost control of the Convention and the French Terror began, Paine was endangered. Isolated by his ignorance of the language, he refused to alter his now conservative ideas and was taken to the prison where he assumed he would be put to death. In 1794, however, he was released and lived quietly with the American Ambassador to France, James Monroe.

In *The Age of Reason* (1794), written during this time in France, Paine returned to his religious concerns. He articulated the premises of Enlightenment Deism (see DEISM) but also bitterly assaulted Christianity and its biblical basis. Too conservative in France, his religious views proved too hostile to established institutions when he returned to America in 1802. He was vilified in many quarters as a representative of the Anti-Christ and lived out his last years in penury and public disgrace.

See also: AMERICAN PHILOSOPHY IN THE 18TH AND 19TH CENTURIES; FRANKLIN, B.; JEFFERSON, T.

List of works

Paine, T. (1947) *Complete Writings of Thomas Paine*, ed. P.S. Foner, New York: Library of America, 2 vols. (*Four Letters on Interesting Subjects* (1776) and *Old Truths and Established Facts: Being an Answer to a Very New Pamphlet Indeed* (1792), both probably written by Paine, are not included.)

References and further reading

Ayer, A.J. (1988) *Thomas Paine*, Chicago, IL: University of Chicago Press. (Notable because the author was a famous twentieth-century philosophical and humanist writer.)

Claeys, G. (1989) *Thomas Paine: Social and Political Thought*, London: Routledge. (Concentrating on *The Rights of Man*, this study places the tract in the context of Paine's earlier writings and evolving thoughts.)

Fast, H. (1943) *Citizen Tom Paine*, New York: Grove Atlantic. (A novel with an excellent psychological characterization.)

Foner, E. (1976) *Tom Paine and Revolutionary America*, Oxford: Oxford University Press. (Excellent study.)

BRUCE KUKLICK

PAKṢILASVĀMIN

see VĀTSYĀYANA

PALEY, WILLIAM (1743–1805)

William Paley, theologian and moral philosopher, expressed and codified the views and arguments of orthodox Christianity and the conservative moral and political thought of eighteenth-century England. Paley says that his works form a unified system based on natural religion. Like others during this period, Paley thought that reason alone, unaided by revelation, would establish many Christian theses. He is confident that a scientific understanding of nature will support the claim that God is the author of nature. Paley belongs to the anti-deist tradition that holds that revelation supplements natural religion. The most important revelation is God's assurance of an afterlife in which the virtuous are rewarded and the vicious are punished. Natural and revealed religion, in turn, provide the foundation for morality. God's will determines what is right and his power to reward and punish us in the afterlife provide the moral sanctions. On the whole, Paley is concerned with sustaining Christian faith, and ensuring that people known what their duties are and do them.

1 Life and writings
2 Theological and apologetical writings
3 Ethical and political writings

1 Life and writings

Paley was born in Peterborough, England. He entered Christ's College Cambridge in 1759 and graduated in 1763 with highest distinction. After teaching for a few years in a small school, he returned to Cambridge where he taught moral philosophy, divinity and Greek testament for nine years. His lectures were noted for their clarity and lucid organization. He left Cambridge when he married, obtaining the first of various positions in the Church of England, the highest as archdeacon of Carlisle.

Paley wrote four books. In the first, *The Principles of Moral and Political Philosophy* (1785), he defends theological utilitarianism. In his *Horae Paulinae: Or The Truth of the Scripture History of St Paul Evinced* (1790), he defends the authenticity of the New Testament writings, in particular the scriptural history of St Paul. In *A View of the Evidences of Christianity* (1794), he defends revelation and argues for the veracity of Christian miracles. In *Natural Theology* (1802), his best known work today, Paley develops a detailed statement of the argument from design. Except for his *Horae Pauline*, his writings enjoyed a huge success and went through numerous reprintings. His *Principles* was adopted as a textbook at Cambridge in 1786 and his *Evidences* in 1822, and both were used as textbooks in England and the United States until well into the mid-1800s. His portrait hangs in Christ's College along with those of Milton and Darwin. His works, however, have by and large faded into obscurity.

2 Theological and apologetical writings

Paley addresses his *Natural Theology* to Christian readers with the hope that it may help to sustain their belief in God in times of doubt and that they may come to see the world as a 'temple' and life as 'an act of adoration'. The argument of the *Natural Theology* has two parts. In both parts he defends the argument from design against some traditional objections (see GOD, ARGUMENTS FOR THE EXISTENCE OF). First, Paley wants to establish that there are strong rational grounds for belief in the existence of God. He argues that the natural order, like a watch, was clearly designed for a purpose. As in the case of the watch, we should infer that the universe had an intelligent creator. Because each example alone is sufficient to support the conclusion that there is an intelligent author of nature, Paley says that by enumerating examples he is adding to the proof. He offers many detailed examples to support the claim that the various parts of nature are like machines exhibiting design and purpose. Most of his examples are from anatomy, and his favourite is the eye. Its intricate structure parallels that of a telescope and both obviously serve a purpose. Paley considers but dismisses a number of alternative explanations for the purposefulness of the natural world. For example, he argues that nature's intricate structure is so striking that it could not be a product of the chance coming together of atoms.

Second, Paley argues that a scientific understanding of nature helps to establish the traditional attributes of a Christian God. God is a person, since, as a contriver, he must have a mind. The fact that nature exhibits a uniform plan suggests his unity, although Paley acknowledges that this only shows a 'unity of counsel'. As cause of nature, God's power and intelligence must be adequate to their effect, yet the terms 'omniscient' and 'omnipotent', he admits, are only convenient superlatives. Paley devotes considerable effort to attempting to establish God's benevolence, arguing that the contrivances of nature are beneficial and that it is 'a happy world after all'. In addition, God gave us and other animals the capacity to experience pleasure, even though, he assumed, pleasure is biologically unnecessary. But Paley concedes that natural religion cannot by itself solve the problem of evil (see EVIL, PROBLEM OF).

Paley addresses the credibility of christian revelation in his *Evidences*. He assumes that God chose to reveal his will to the early Christians by performing miracles. The credibility of revelation thus turns on whether there are good reasons for believing that these miracles occurred. But David Hume (1777) had argued that it is contrary to experience that miracles should be true, but consistent with experience that testimony should be false (see HUME, D. §2; MIRACLES). So there are two issues: should we believe in the occurrence of miracles, and is the testimony of the witnesses credible? Paley takes up these issues one by one. What tells against miracles, Hume thought, is the fact that the laws of nature work uniformly. Paley counters that if we have independent proof that there is a God who created the universe – including the laws of nature – for special purposes, it is not improbable that God may have occasionally intervened in the natural order. In response to Hume's charge that the witnesses to miracles are not credible, Paley replies that the suffering of the early converts demonstrates their sincerity. Both Christian and non-Christian sources attest to their ordeals. Moreover, the New Testament writings are authentic, neither forged nor altered during their transmission. Further support for their authenticity is given in *Horae Paulinae*. The many undesigned coincidences between the Acts of the Apostles and Paul's letters, Paley argues, show that neither is fraudulent. In the *Evidences* Paley also responds to Hume's complaint that the miracle stories of various religions undermine each other's credibility, arguing that those of other religions may be dismissed on a number of grounds, including delusion and exaggeration.

3 Ethical and political writings

Paley insists that natural and revealed religion are the true foundation for morality, chastising those moralists who decline to bring in scriptural authorities. He also complains that most earlier theorists did not pay sufficient attention to working out what in specific instances our duties are, and getting people to do them. The key elements of Paley's theory are summed up in his three-part definition of virtue: 'the doing of good to mankind, in obedience to the will of God, and for the sake of everlasting happiness' (1785: 47). Paley is a theological voluntarist: God's will ultimately determines what is right (see VOLUNTARISM). Since God is benevolent and wills our happiness, the rule we should use in deciding what to do is the utility principle. Right actions are those which promote the general happiness. Although we are basically self-interested creatures, God's power to reward and punish us in an afterlife make it in our interest to promote the happiness of others. Paley thinks that moral obligation is an unproblematic notion. It is like the obligation of a soldier to obey his officer or a servant his master, namely, being 'urged by a violent motive resulting from the command of another' (1785: 66). As Paley acknowledges, the only difference between prudential and moral obligation on this view is that the sanctions attaching to prudence are confined to this world whereas moral sanctions look to the 'world to come' (1785: 71).

Most of the *Principles* consists in a detailed discussion of our duties to God, others and ourselves. The last section contains his political theory. In most cases Paley defends the status quo. He does not use the utility principle as a tool of reform as did the later utilitarians. He argues that it is consistent with God's will that people own property and that the positive law of each country should regulate its distribution. He also argues that inequalities in wealth are advantageous to society, increasing productivity, and hence the general happiness. Like other utilitarians, Paley objects to the social contract theory. He traces the origin of government to paternal authority and the need for strong leaders in times of war. Citizens continue to obey out of habit and self-interest. The reason people ought to obey government is that God wills the general happiness and civil society promotes that end. In his discussion of more topical issues, Paley, as might be expected, defends the status quo;

even so, throughout his adult life he vehemently opposed the slave trade and actively sought to end it.

See also: DEISM; PROVIDENCE; UTILITARIANISM

List of works

There is no modern edition of Paley's works, but his works are readily available in many libraries. Selections from his *Natural Theology* are to be found in numerous introductory philosophy textbooks and in anthologies of classical readings in philosophy of religion.

Paley, W. (1785) *The Principles of Moral and Political Philosophy*, Dublin: Exshaw, White. (Based on lectures Paley gave while teaching at Cambridge, its success is said to have moved Bentham to publish his *Introduction to the Principles of Morals and Legislation*. The opening sections contain his objections to the moral sense theory and a defence of theological utilitarianism. The rest of the book consists in a detailed discussion of our particular duties to God, others and ourselves, as well as Paley's political theory.)

—— (1790) *Horae Paulinae: Or The Truth of the Scripture History of St Paul, Evinced by a Comparison of the Epistles which bear his Name with the Acts of the Apostles, and with one another*, London and Dublin. (This is a work in Christian apologetics and is the least philosophically interesting of Paley's writings. He defends the authenticity of both the Acts of the Apostles and Paul's thirteen letters.)

—— (1794) *A View of the Evidences of Christianity. In three parts*, London and Dublin. (A work in Christian apologetics, Paley defends the credibility of Christian miracles and so Christian revelation against Hume's objections. He thinks this task is important because revelation is our only assurance of an afterlife in which the good are rewarded and the evil are punished.)

—— (1802) *Natural Theology: Or, Evidences of the Existence and Attributes of the Deity, collected from the Appearances of Nature*, London: Faulder and Philadelphia, PA: John Morgan. (The most widely read of Paley's works, it contains a detailed reststatment of the argument from design. Although Hume's *Dialogues on Natural Religion* (1779) consists in a sustained and devastating attack on the argument from design, Paley does not reply to these objections.)

References and further reading

Barker, E. (1948) 'Paley and His Political Philosophy',

in *Traditions of Civility*, Cambridge: Cambridge University Press. (A sympathetic discussion of Paley's political theory.)

Clark, M. (1974) *Paley*, Toronto, Ont.: University of Toronto Press. (A general introduction to Paley's thought with a detailed biography.)

* Hume, D. (1777) 'Of Miracles', in *An Enquiry Concerning Human Understanding*, ed. L.A. Selby-Bigge, revised P.H. Nidditch, Oxford: Clarendon Press, 1988. (Argues that the power of testimony to establish the credibility of miracles and thereby to establish the authority of a religious system.)

LeMahieu, D. (1976) *The Mind of William Paley*, Lincoln, NE: University of Nebraska Press. (A general, thematic study of Paley's theology and philosophy.)

Raphael, D. (1991) *British Moralists: 1650–1800*, Indianapolis, IN: Hackett Publishing Company, vol. 2. (Contains selections of the works of many of the British Moralists of the seventeenth and eighteenth centuries. Includes a short selection of some of the theoretically more interesting parts of Paley's moral theory.)

Schneewind, J. (1977) 'The Early Utilitarians', in *Sidgwick's Ethics and Victorian Moral Philosophy*, Oxford: Clarendon Press. (A clear summary of Paley's utilitarianism which places it in the context of other utilitarian writers of the period.)

—— (1990) *Moral Philosophy from Montaigne to Kant*, Cambridge: Cambridge University Press, vol. 2. (Contains selections of the works of many seventeenth- and eighteenth-century moral philosophers from both sides of the British Channel. In addition to an informative general introduction, each individual selection has a separate introduction, annotation and bibliography. Contains a slightly more comprehensive selection of the theoretically interesting parts of Paley's moral theory, including his objections to the moral sense theory and his account of rights.)

CHARLOTTE R. BROWN

PANAETIUS (*c.*185–*c.*110 BC)

Panaetius, a Greek philosopher from Rhodes, brought new vitality to Stoicism in the second century BC by shifting the focus of its ethical theory from the idealized sage to the practical problems of ordinary people. Working a century after Chrysippus had systematized Stoicism, Panaetius is often labelled the founder of 'Middle Stoicism' for defending new and generally more moderate positions on several issues. Because none of his writings survive, his influence is hard to gauge precisely and easily underrated. But his impact, especially in Rome where he was closely associated with many in the ruling elite, was profound. His emphasis on public service and the obligations imposed by power and high station probably helped shape the ideology of Roman imperialism. Through Cicero, whose writings preserve many of his ideas, he had lasting influence, especially on early modern moral and political thought.

1   Life and works
2   Practical ethics

1   Life and works

Panaetius, the eldest son of an eminent family on the commercially important Greek island of Rhodes, studied at the great library in Pergamum before coming to Athens in the 150s BC. There he studied under Diogenes of Babylon, the leading Stoic of the time. Visiting Rome in the 140s BC, he stimulated intense interest in Greek philosophy in general and Stoicism in particular among the so-called 'Scipionic circle' – a loose-knit group of politically conservative but culturally philhellenic nobles centred on Scipio Aemilianus (then the dominant figure in Rome) and idealized in Cicero's dialogue *On the Republic*. He accompanied Scipio as an informal advisor on a major diplomatic tour of Egypt, Asia Minor and Greece in 140–138 BC, then returned to Athens. Around 130 BC he succeeded Antipater of Tarsus as head of the Stoic school in Athens and taught there until his death about twenty years later. The most notable of his numerous students was POSIDONIUS.

Famously learned, Panaetius wrote on geography, astronomy, musical theory and philology as well as philosophical subjects. But none of his books survives, and while extant works by many other writers are indebted to his work, a shortage of explicit citations makes it impossible to reconstruct his thought in detail. We are best informed about his treatise *On Duty*, which CICERO (§2) followed closely in writing *On Duties* (see §2). Other works included *On Providence* (used by Cicero in *On the Nature of the Gods*), *On Equanimity* (a major source for essays on the same theme by SENECA and PLUTARCH), a work on enduring pain and another on government. Living at a time of renewed interest in earlier philosophy, Panaetius especially admired Aristotle (probably for his lost dialogues and not the extant treatises) and above all Plato, whom he styled 'the Homer of philosophers' and quoted often. He also discussed the life and thought of Socrates and his companions, and

the authenticity of dialogues ascribed to Plato and others.

Panaetius arrived in Athens when the Stoic system elaborated by Chrysippus and his successors faced acute criticism from rival schools of philosophy, and, although his most original and influential work was in ethics, he proposed modifying Stoic positions in other areas as well. He joined Academic sceptics in marshalling arguments against the validity of divination, which earlier Stoics had considered a reliable science and an important sign of providence; against astrology, for example, he cited the remoteness of the stars, diversity in the lives and characters of twins, and the manifest influence of heredity and environment. In cosmology, he vigorously defended the Stoic conception of the cosmos as directed by an immanent providential deity but abandoned the two closely related doctrines of cosmic conflagrations and eternal recurrence (whereby the universe is periodically reduced to undifferentiated fire, then regenerated identically in an everlasting cycle) (see STOICISM §5) in favour of the Aristotelian thesis that the cosmos is everlasting. In philosophy of mind, he simplified the Stoic model of the soul by restricting it to cognitive and appetitive functions. He also argued that inherited psychic traits show that the human soul is mortal, on the ground that inheritance entails birth and anything born must die.

2   Practical ethics

Panaetius' most enduring legacy is in ethics, where he significantly broadened the appeal of Stoicism by formulating a theory of obligation rich in implications for all social ranks and especially for the conduct of public affairs. Although his writings are lost, much of his theory survives in Cicero's *On Duties*, which was closely modelled on his own treatise *On Duty*. There Panaetius focused on two questions: what actions does virtue require, and what actions are advantageous? (Cicero chides him for neglecting what to do when the two conflict, but then justifies the omission by arguing that conflicts are illusory because transgressing virtue is never really advantageous.) Downplaying the gap between doing what is right and doing it from perfectly virtuous motives – encapsulated in the Stoic distinction between 'duties' or 'appropriate acts' (*kathēkonta*) and 'correct acts' (*katorthēmata*) (see STOICISM §§15–16) – Panaetius emphasized practical precepts over abstract principles, and, in order to help people of imperfect character make 'progress' toward virtue, he constructed systematic rules of conduct for the proper pursuit and use of things that Stoicism maintained have only instrumental value, such as wealth, power and prestige.

Panaetius based his proposals on the Stoic account of moral development through a natural process called 'familiarization' or 'affiliation' (*oikeiōsis*) (see HIEROCLES; STOICISM §14). But he refined this theory by tracing all four cardinal virtues back to infant roots: wisdom to an innate desire for knowledge, justice to the social impulses inherent in rationality, courage to an impetus to excel, and temperance to an instinct for self-preservation. Accordingly he reformulated the Stoic acount of the human good – originally defined as 'living virtuously' and standardly explicated as 'living in agreement with nature' – as 'living by our naturally given propensities'. This richer picture of human nature served in part to answer charges that the Stoic ideal of virtue was neither natural nor attainable: by ascribing 'seeds' of virtue to everyone, Panaetius highlighted the continuity between normal human tendencies and the perfect virtue of a sage. But his account also justified assigning greater moral worth to ordinary people and their actions; and in his treatment of the several virtues he paid little attention to how a sage would behave and a great deal to what everyone else should do.

In charting the duties associated with each virtue, Panaetius gave new prominence to positive obligations involving the wellbeing of society and its members. Justice, for instance, he extended to include not only prohibitions against causing harm to others but also duties to avert or remedy harm through generosity and public service; and courage, which earlier Stoics had associated primarily with scorning danger and enduring pain, he analysed as a species of 'magnanimity' (literally 'greatness of soul'), which he argued finds its finest expression in constructive civil leadership, not military triumph. A similar emphasis on effective action over purity of motives appears in his account of temperance, where he shifted the focus from personal to social welfare by introducing a highly original analysis of 'propriety' (*prepon*, Latin *decorum*). Exploiting analogies with the theatre, he classified duties under four kinds of 'roles' (Latin *personae*): some duties apply universally because imposed by (1) human nature, but many vary individually because imposed by (2) individual capacities and temperament, (3) station and circumstance, or (4) our own deliberate choice. One aim of this schema was to guide deliberation by articulating the variables affecting what different people should do. But since propriety is achieved by balancing the obligations imposed by one's several roles, the schema also gave new weight to social and ethical diversity and showed more clearly how to achieve moral 'progress'.

Panaetius' account of propriety reflects his rejection of the asceticism and iconoclasm early Stoics had adopted from the Cynics. But his concessions to the more humane values of civility and urbanity also marked a major expansion of the scope of obligation and gave Stoic ethics a new and distinctly political orientation. While focused on personal conduct, his ethical theory articulates a paradigm of public service that imposes substantial social and political obligations on people of talent, wealth and influence, but reduces demands on those less favoured by birth or fortune. The result is a model of paternalism which Cicero and others exploited in order to justify the aristocratic institutions of Rome. Panaetius, whose life spanned the period when the formerly autonomous Greek states were reduced to Roman provinces, thus provided Romans with a framework for justifying imperialism in general, and Roman rule in particular, as a relation of mutual advantage that could foster peace, prosperity and political stability.

See also: ARETĒ; EUDAIMONIA

References and further reading

Alesse, F. (1994) *Panezio di Rodi e la tradizione stoica* (Panaetius of Rhodes and the Stoic Tradition), Naples: Bibliopolis. (Meticulous study of Panaetius' innovations in ethics, psychology and cosmology.)

* Cicero, M.T. (late 44 BC) *On Duties* (*De officiis*), trans. M. Griffin and E.M. Atkins, Cambridge: Cambridge University Press, 1991. (The first two thirds of this work are based directly on Panaetius' lost treatise *On Duty*; the remainder purports to complete his unfinished work.)

Dawson, D. (1992) *Cities of the Gods: Communist Utopias in Greek Thought*, Oxford: Oxford University Press. (Chapter 5 argues that Panaetius dramatically shifted Stoic political and social thought in conservative directions.)

Gill, C. (1988) 'Panaetius on the Virtue of Being Yourself', in A. Bulloch, E.S. Gruen, A.A. Long and A.F. Stewart (eds) *Images and Ideologies: Self-Definition in the Hellenistic World*, Berkeley, CA: University of California Press, 330–53. (Clear general account of Panaetius' major innovations in ethics.)

* Panaetius (*c.*185–*c.*110 BC) Fragments, in *Panaetii Rhodii Fragmenta* (Fragments of Panaetius of Rhodes), ed. M. van Straaten, Leiden: Brill, 3rd edn, 1962. (Standard collection of Greek and Latin texts on Panaetius' life and thought; excludes substantial material not explicitly ascribed to him but reasonably believed to derive from his work.)

STEPHEN A. WHITE

PAN-AFRICANISM

Pan-Africanism covers a wide range of intellectual positions which share the assumption of some common cultural or political projects for both Africans and people of African descent. The political project is the unification of all Africans into a single African state, sometimes thought of as providing a homeland for the return of those in the African diaspora. More vaguely, many self-identified pan-Africanists have aimed to pursue projects of solidarity – some political, some literary or artistic – in Africa or the African diaspora. The Pan-Africanist movement was founded in the nineteenth century by intellectuals of African descent in the Caribbean and North America, who saw themselves as belonging to a single negro race. As a result the Africa of pan-Africanism has sometimes been limited to those regions of sub-Saharan Africa largely inhabited by darker-skinned peoples, thus excluding those lighter-skinned north Africans, most of whom speak Arabic as a first language.

In the twentieth century this racialized understanding of African identity has been challenged by many of the African intellectuals who took over the movement's leadership in the period after the Second World War. Founders of the Organization of African Unity, such as Gamal Abdel Nasser of Egypt and Kwame Nkrumah of Ghana had a notion of Africa that was continental. However, the movement's intellectual roots lie firmly in the racial understanding of Africa in the thought of the African-American and Afro-Caribbean intellectuals who founded it.

Pan-Africanism began as a movement in the diaspora among the descendants of the slave populations of the New World and spread to Africa itself. As a result the forms of solidarity it articulated aimed to challenge anti-black racism on two fronts: racial domination in the diaspora and racialized colonial domination in the African continent. The movement's fissures have occurred where these two clearly distinguishable projects have pulled it in different directions.

1 First formulations: W.E.B. Du Bois
2 Nineteenth-century origins
3 The pan-African congresses and the Garvey movement
4 George Padmore
5 Legacy

1 First formulations: W.E.B. Du Bois

The term *pan-Africanism* was coined around the time of the first pan-African congress in London in 1900. However, the idea of a form of solidarity of the negro race appeared in the nineteenth century. Like eastern European pan-slavism and the forms of nationalism that created modern Germany and Italy, these early forms of solidarity reflected a philosophical tradition derived from HERDER in which peoples were the central participants in the creation of world history, expressed themselves in literature and folk culture and sought political expression in nation-states. The first black intellectual to produce a fully theorized account was W.E.B. Du Bois (1868–1963) in his paper 'The Conservation of Races' (1897) which was the second occasional paper to be published by the American Negro Academy and made use of the term *pan-negroism*. Du Bois studied with William JAMES as an undergraduate at Harvard and went on to do graduate work at the University of Berlin. He was, therefore, familiar with the intellectual traditions of modern European nationalism and their philosophical underpinnings.

In 'The Conservation of Races' (1897) Du Bois argued that 'the history of the world is the history, not of individuals, but of groups, not of nations, but of races' (1897: 76). (He mentions Slavs, Teutons and the Romance race, indicating that, like so many other Western intellectuals of his day, he thought of real nations as races.) He argued that the differences between races were 'spiritual, psychical differences – undoubtedly based on the physical, but infinitely transcending them' (1897: 77). Also, he insisted (in a manner reminiscent of Herder) that each race was 'striving, each in its own way, to develop for civilization its particular message' (1897: 78).

The problem for pan-negroism thus framed was how negro people were to deliver their message. Du Bois was clear that African-Americans (whom he called the 'advance guard of the negro people' (1897: 79)) were to play the leading role in that task. He thought so because, although their ancestors had arrived in the New World as slaves, some like himself had been exposed to the best education and the highest forms of knowledge.

2 Nineteenth-century origins

Although Du Bois's formulation owed much to the intellectual ferment of European nationalism, it also had roots in the thought of a number of earlier African-American thinkers, whose work is best understood in the context of the broad nineteenth-century history of anti-slavery, or *abolitionist* thought. The focus of attention for all the major black thinkers in the New World in the early nineteenth century was the abolition of slavery and the slave trade. As it was widely believed that racial antagonism between blacks and whites was inevitable (a common view explicitly held by US presidents Jefferson and Lincoln) one major preoccupation of some abolitionists was to find territories that could be inhabited by freed blacks. The colony of Sierra Leone was created in the late eighteenth century by UK abolitionists as a home for freed blacks and the black poor of the UK. The American Colonization Society played a similar role in the creation of Liberia in the 1820s. Other schemes were proposed to colonize parts of Latin America, the Caribbean and the US western frontier.

All of these schemes presupposed that Africans and their descendants in the New World belonged naturally together in a political community separated from other peoples. There were significant voices raised in protest against this assumption, notably that of the American ex-slave and abolitionist Frederick Douglass. They were joined by many others after the USA formally recognized the citizenship of people of African descent in the post-Civil War amendments to the US constitution. In the first half of the nineteenth century the majority view among white and black intellectuals was that a home was needed for the negroes if they were to be free.

Perhaps the three most important black intellectual ancestors of pan-Africanism were Martin R. Delany (1812–85), Alexander Crummell (1822–98) and Edward Wilmot Blyden (1832–1912). Martin Delany was born in southern USA, but his family moved to Pennsylvania during his youth. He began a medical education at Harvard, but was forced to leave by the refusal of white students to work alongside him. Delany's contributions to the prehistory of pan-Africanism began with a sense of a profound connection with Africa. He was proud that he was a 'full-blooded negro' and he named his children after Toussaint L'Ouverture, the black leader of the Haitian revolution, Ramses after the Egyptian Pharaoh and Alexandre Dumas after the French novelist who had some African ancestry. Delany was also a powerful voice for black emigration from the USA. He argued in *The Condition, Elevation, Emigration and Destiny of the Colored People of the United States* (1852) that only in a country without white people could black people flourish. In that early work, Delany refrained from making the obvious suggestion that blacks should travel to Africa. This was not because he was against the idea but because he and other leaders of the re-emigration movement believed that most African-Americans, convinced by anti-negro propaganda, were likely to see Africa as inhospitable. In his *Official Report of the Niger Valley Exploration Party* (1861), written after he had been to Africa, he wrote of the continent as 'our fatherland' and argued that its regeneration required the development of a 'national character'. He proposed the formula, 'Africa for the African race and black men to rule them'

(Geiss 1974: 165), which is one of the earliest formulations of a pan-Africanist principle.

Alexander Crummell was born in New York and educated in the UK at Cambridge University, the first African-American to attend. He was also an ordained Anglican clergyman and the first African-American intellectual to spend a significant amount of time in Liberia. When Delany visited that country in 1859, he met Crummell who had been there by then for two decades. In *The Future of Africa: Being Addresses* (1862), a collection of essays and lectures written while he was in Liberia, Crummell developed a vision of Africa as the motherland of the negro race. In 'The English Language in Liberia' (1860a), based on a lecture given on Liberian independence day, he argued that African-Americans exiled in slavery to the New World, by divine providence had been given 'at least this one item of compensation, namely, the possession of the Anglo-Saxon tongue'. Similarly he argued for the providential nature of the transmission of Christianity to negro slaves, believing that it was the duty of 'free coloured men' in the USA to work for the Christianization of their ancestral continent. In the essay 'The Relations and Duties of Free Colored Men in America to Africa' (1860b), he expressed with great clarity the underlying racial basis of his understanding of negro identity, defining a race as 'a compact, homogeneous population of one blood ancestry and lineage' and arguing that each race had certain 'determinate proclivities' which manifested themselves in the behaviour of its members. Crummell, with Blyden, was one of the founders of Liberia College, later the University of Liberia. Unlike Blyden he did not become a permanent resident of Liberia. He returned rather to the USA where he continued to argue for the importance of an engagement with Africa on the part of blacks in the African diaspora. Crummell was the leading spirit in the foundation of the American Negro Academy and was present at the meeting at which Du Bois first read 'The Conservation of Races' (1897). He was a significant influence on Du Bois, who included an essay about Crummell in his influential publication *The Souls of Black Folk* (1903).

Edward Wilmot Blyden was born in the West Indies. He travelled to Liberia in 1850 under the auspices of the American Colonization Society. He became a citizen of that country for the rest of his life. Like Crummell, he was a priest. Blyden was a polyglot scholar whose essays included quotations in the original languages from ALIGHIERI, DANTE, Virgil and Saint-Hilaire. He studied Arabic in order to teach it at Liberia College and later became the Liberian ambassador to Queen Victoria. In *Christianity, Islam and the Negro Race* (1887), first delivered as a lecture to the American Colonization Society in 1883, he too expressed the conviction that underlies Du Bois's first explicit formulation of pan-Africanism: 'Among the conclusions to which study and research are conducting philosophers, none is clearer than this – that each of the races of mankind has a specific character and specific work' (1887: 94).

Both Blyden and Crummell had little respect for the traditional cultures of Africa. They shared the conviction that the task of Christianized blacks of the diaspora owed a responsibility towards the conversion of their African cousins. Blyden argued that one could not deduce from Africa's 'state of barbarism' any innate deficiency in the negro. He observed that 'there is not a single mental or moral deficiency now existing among Africans – not a single practice now indulged in by them – to which we cannot find a parallel in the past history of Europe' (1887: 58). He was convinced that the negro race had an intrinsic affinity with religion and that the diffusion of Islam in west Africa had laid the groundwork for conversion to Christianity.

3   The pan-African congresses and the Garvey movement

If the intellectual ancestry of pan-Africanism is in the work of Du Bois, Delany, Crummell and Blyden, its institutional history begins with Sylvester Williams, a London barrister born in Trinidad. In 1897 he planned to bring together the 'African race' around the world. In July 1900, after a preliminary conference in 1899, such a gathering took place in London. There were four African representatives – one each from Ethiopia, Sierra Leone, Liberia and the Gold Coast colony – and around twelve from the USA, including Du Bois; eleven representatives came from the West Indies and five from London.

The conference opened with the aim of allowing black people to discuss the condition of the black race around the world. In 1921 Du Bois and others organized a second congress which met in three sessions in London, Brussels and Paris. This time there were representatives from Francophone and Lusophone Africa. A final declaration was issued which insisted on the equality of the races, the diffusion of democracy and the development of political institutions in the colonies. It also urged the return of negroes to their own countries and attention under the rubric of the League of Nations both to race relations in the industrialized world (the 'negro problem') and the condition of workers in the colonies. A third congress occurred in London in 1923 and continued in Lisbon. This second stage of the congress was more an opportunity for Du Bois to talk

to some people from the Portuguese colonies on his way from London to Liberia where he was the official representative of the USA to preside over the installation of the Liberian president.

The Pan-African Congress movement disappeared until the fifth congress in Manchester in 1945 at which the continent took on a key role, as opposed to the diaspora. From there Du Bois's contribution was overshadowed by Kwame Nkrumah, who was to be Ghana's first prime minister. Du Bois was the only significant African-American present.

During the period between the First and Second World Wars when the Pan-African Congress movement was most active, sentiment received a substantial practical boost from the growth of the Garvey movement led by Marcus Garvey. He was a Jamaican immigrant to the USA, who developed his Universal Negro Improvement Association into the largest black movement in the African diaspora. The slogan of the movement was 'Back to Africa' and Garvey planned a shipping line for the purpose, although relatively few members of the organization actually left the New World for the Old.

Garvey's commitment to racial pride and to the celebration of black historical achievement and his concern to link the diaspora to the continent make him an important figure in the movement's history.

4   George Padmore

George Padmore (1902–59), a West Indian-born intellectual played an important role in planning the congress in 1945. Born Malcolm Nurse, Padmore was a Trinidadian who spent time in the USA studying at Columbia University and Fisk, a black university which Du Bois also attended. Padmore worked for the Communist Party as an organizer among students at Howard University, the black university in Washington, DC. Later he spent time in Germany and Russia, where he became the head of the Negro Bureau of the Red International of Labour Unions in 1930. In the next few years he worked for communist organizations in Austria and Germany, moving to London in 1935. From then until his death in 1959 he was the leading theorist of pan-Africanism and a close friend and adviser of Kwame Nkrumah. His *Pan-Africanism or Communism? The Coming Struggle for Africa* (1956) is probably the most important statement of his position.

5   Legacy

In the period after the Second World War African intellectuals were preoccupied with the question of independence. Once independence was attained, pan-

Africanism became an ideology through which relations among the newly independent states could be thought about. Pan-Africanist rhetoric continues to be important in the language of the Organization of African Unity founded in 1963. In that same period, black intellectuals in North America were taken up with questions of civil rights. There were always resonances between these two projects – Du Bois was involved in both throughout his long life and died a citizen of Ghana. African diplomats sought to get civil rights questions raised in the forum of the United Nations, but pan-Africanism took philosophical form in the period leading up to Padmore's work. Its major theoretical works are those of Padmore and Du Bois.

References and further reading

* Blyden, E.W. (1887) *Christianity, Islam and the Negro Race*, repr. Edinburgh: Edinburgh University Press, 1967. (Blyden's major work.)

Brotz, H. (1994) *African-American Social and Political Thought*, New York: Basic Books. (Contains significant excerpts from the works of all the major figures of the movements, with annotations and brief biographies.)

Clarke, J.H. (1974) *Marcus Garvey and the Vision of Africa*, New York: Vintage. (A spirited biography of Garvey.)

* Crummell, A. (1860a) 'The English Language in Liberia', in *The Future of Africa: Being Addresses*, repr. Detroit, MI: Negro History Press, 1969. (A lecture given on the occasion of Liberian independence day.)

* —— (1860b) 'The Relations and Duties of Free Colored Men in America to Africa', in *The Future of Africa: Being Addresses*, repr. Detroit, MI: Negro History Press, 1969: 215–81. (Written from Liberia in the form of a letter to an African-American correspondent.)

* —— (1862) *The Future of Africa: Being Addresses*, repr. Detroit, MI: Negro History Press, 1969. (A collection of Crummell's major writings from Liberia.)

* Delany, M.R. (1852) *The Condition, Elevation, Emigration and Destiny of the Colored People of the United States*, repr. in *Search for a Place: Black Separatism and Africa, 1860*, Ann Arbor, MI: University of Michigan Press, 1969; Salem, NH: Ayer, 1988. (Delany's first defence of African-American emigration.)

* —— (1861) *Official Report of the Niger Valley Exploration Party*, repr. in *Search for a Place: Black Separatism and Africa, 1860*, Ann Arbor, MI: University of Michigan Press, 1969. (The report Delany wrote urging emigration to Africa after a visit there.)

* Du Bois, W.E.B. (1897) 'The Conservation Of Races', repr. in S. Foner (ed.) *W.E.B. Du Bois Speaks. Speeches and Addresses 1890–1919*, New York: Pathfinders Press, 1970: 73–85. (A key early statement of Du Bois's racial vision.)

* —— (1940) *Dusk of Dawn: An Essay Toward an Autobiography of a Race Concept*, repr. Millwood, NY: Kraus-Thomson Organization Limited, 1975. (An historical reflection on Du Bois's changing understanding of race, published in his seventy-third year.)

* —— (1903) *The Souls of Black Folk*, repr. New York: Penguin, 1996. (Du Bois's major statement on US black culture.)

Garvey, M. (1923–6) *Philosophy and Opinions of Marcus Garvey*, repr. New York: Atheneum, 2 vols, 1992. (A compilation of Garvey's writings exploring many of the issues central to pan-Africanism.)

* Geiss, I. (1974) *The Pan-African Movement: A History of Pan-Africanism in America, Europe and Africa*, New York: Africana Publishing Company; London: Methuen. (A solid scholarly survey of key figures in the movement and of its antecedents.)

Hooker, J.R. (1967) *Black Revolutionary: George Padmore's Path from Communism to Pan-Africanism*, New York: Praeger.

Lynch, H.R. (1967) *Edward Wilmot Blyden: Pan-Negro Patriot 1832–1912*, London: Oxford University Press. (A fine biography of Blyden.)

Moses, W.J. (1978) *The Golden Age of Black Nationalism: 1850–1925*, Hamden, CT: Archon Books. (An elegant cultural history exploring the life and work of figures such as Crummell, Blyden, Delany and Du Bois.)

Padmore, G. (1953) *The Gold Coast Revolution: the Struggle of an African People from Slavery to Freedom*, London: D. Dobson.

* —— (1956) *Pan-Africanism or Communism? The Coming Struggle for Africa*, repr. Garden City, NY: Doubleday, 1971. (Padmore's major theoretical statement of pan-Africanist principle.)

K. ANTHONY APPIAH

PANENTHEISM *see* GOD,

CONCEPTS OF

PANPSYCHISM

Panpsychism is the thesis that physical nature is composed of individuals each of which is to some degree sentient. It is somewhat akin to hylozoism, but in place of the thesis of the pervasiveness of life in nature substitutes the pervasiveness of sentience, experience or, in a broad sense, consciousness. There are two distinct grounds on which panpsychism has been based. Some see it as the best explanation of the emergence of consciousness in the universe to say that it is, in fact, universally present, and that the high-level consciousness of humans and animals is the product of special patterns of that low-level consciousness or feeling which is universally present. The other ground on which panpsychism is argued for is that ordinary knowledge of the physical world is only of its structure and sensory effects on us, and that the most likely inner content which fills out this structure and produces these experiences is a system of patterns of sentient experience of a low level.

1   **The nature of panpsychism**
2   **Arguments for panpsychism**
3   **Consciousness in panpsychism**

1   The nature of panpsychism

Through prejudice and misunderstanding, panpsychism is often thought a somewhat fanciful doctrine; thus commentators often try to save some admired master from association with it. Consequently, an uncontroversial list of panpsychists is problematic. Especially debated is the case of Spinoza, and there is some argument too over Whitehead, though certainly many process philosophers working in the Whitehead and Hartshorne tradition are panpsychists. Other thinkers either committed, or strongly inclined, to panpsychism include Gustav FECHNER, R.H. LOTZE, Friedrich Paulsen (d.1908) William JAMES, Josiah ROYCE, C.H. Waddington (d.1975) and Charles Hartshorne. LEIBNIZ, SCHOPENHAUER and BERGSON advanced positions akin to panpsychism.

Panpsychism is expressed somewhat variously in virtue of differing usages of such words as 'consciousness', 'sentience', 'feeling' and 'experience'. Here we shall use the word 'consciousness' taken in a very broad sense. (Readers may mentally substitute 'sentience', if they prefer, provided they do not understand this purely behaviourally.) Any individual such that there is a truth *as to what it is like to be it* (in general or at some particular moment) is conscious, and its consciousness is what that truth concerns. I may have limited power to grasp what it is like to be

you, but I cannot seriously doubt that there is something there to be right or wrong about, as sensible people think also true about animals (except perhaps the very simplest). But if I try to imagine what it is like to be this table here, everyone will agree that there is nothing there to be imagined.

The point is not that one's conscious states must be like something, must have a character; that is true of everything. But things do divide, in common opinion, into those such that there is and those such that there is not *something that it is like to be them* (though this expression is only an idiomatic pointer to something it requires a certain sophisticated obtuseness to be unable to identify).

The paradigm panpsychist maintains that each of the ultimate units of the physical world (whether particles, events or even mutually influencing fields) out of which all other physical things are made, are conscious in this sense. Of course, they are not self conscious, or thoughtful, but each has some dumb feeling of its own existence and of its exchange of influence with other things. It does not follow, they will rightly insist, that every physical thing is conscious. Many things, such as sticks and stones, made of these ultimate units are not so. Thus while a stone will be composed of conscious units without itself being conscious, a waking human brain will both itself be conscious and be composed of what is conscious, perhaps at two levels (for example, the neurons in the brain may be individually conscious and also made up, like everything else, of ultimate physical units which are so). Hence panpsychism, as such, leaves open the question as to which individuals above the minimal scale are sentient and which not, though particular systems of panpsychism may have their own suggestions as to how this can be decided. (Some think an element of behavioural spontaneity is its chief external mark.)

2   Arguments for panpsychism

The first argument for panpsychism is that it can ground the best account of how something so apparently novel as consciousness could have arisen within a physical world whose development has otherwise been simply a re-arrangement of the homogeneous. One theory based on this argument is that the experience of those non-ultimate units in nature which are conscious are literally composed of the experiences of their ultimate parts. Thus my experience consists in the experiences of my neurons (and those of the experiences of their ultimate parts) which unite in a way in which the experiences of the parts of non-conscious things do not. Thus nothing essentially novel has come into the universe with human or animal consciousness, only new solidifications of the consciousness (sometimes called 'mind dust') already pervasive in the universe.

This is not a very satisfactory view. For consciousness seems to exist only in distinct individual units or 'centres', and it seems doubtful that these can combine to make more comprehensive ones. Even if this is not in principle impossible (and some panpsychists have reasons for thinking it possible in principle), introspection of our own consciousness hardly suggests that any of its components have a distinct sense of their own being.

However, there are various ways in which the theory may be made more promising. Perhaps it is a law of mental nature that when conscious individuals form a system of a certain type, that system becomes conscious in its own right so that its behaviour is due to a combination of the mental states of its parts and its mental state as a whole, without the latter strictly being composed of the former. If so, the emergence of high-level consciousness like ours is due to laws concerning the 'charge' of consciousness associated with matter in general rather than the result of its purely physical character, and thereby seems more intelligible.

The panpsychism we have considered so far implies no particular view of the nature of physical reality. It simply holds that each ultimate unit of the physical world has a certain 'charge' of sentience, which is additional to its physical characteristics, and that in certain circumstances more complex units of nature receive their own individual 'charge' of sentience too.

The second argument for panpsychism favours the different conclusion that consciousness is the real 'stuff' of the physical universe (though this may be further reinforced by the first argument). It starts with the claim that, metaphysics apart, we only know the structure of physical things as such (and of the physical world in general) and their sensory effects on centres of consciousness like ourselves – identified as the consciousness pertaining to certain complex physical things similarly specified – not the content in which that structure is realized concretely. Thus our knowledge of physical reality, so far as it goes beyond characterizations of things simply as the cause of certain sensations in ourselves, is rather like the kind of knowledge of a piece of music which someone born deaf might have from a musical education based entirely on the study of musical scores, such as could lead them to play (perhaps somewhat lifelessly) compositions on the piano without having any idea of the specific quality of heard sound in general or of the particular sounds currently being produced.

It being acknowledged that (metaphysics apart) we only know the structure of physical reality (or only

the structure and the experiences it produces in us), a speculative mind will wonder whether its qualitative nature must remain entirely unknown. They will reflect that there is one kind of thing, after all, of which we do know the inherent quality, namely our own consciousness and, by inference, also the consciousness of other humans and to a limited extent animals. In short, we know the generic nature of consciousness and a good deal about the specific forms it can take. Moreover, we are incapable even of conceiving in any genuinely full way any thing more than a mere abstract structure (needing to be embodied in something more concrete to exist) which is not a form or a content of consciousness. (This is an essentially idealist claim which cannot be examined here: see IDEALISM §2.) Could this be because what we call the generic essence of consciousness is in fact the generic essence of all possible fully concrete reality? If so, the reality which produces 'perceptual' experiences in us, and the structure of which science (and less precisely, common sense) aspires to formulate and control, must somehow be composed of consciousness. This is at least a hypothesis worth exploring as the only alternative to saying that matter is unknowable in its inner essence, and as likely also to cast light on the mind–body or mind–brain relationship.

3   Consciousness in panpsychism

But how can consciousness have that kind of structure? The simplest hypothesis is that there are innumerable interacting centres of consciousness which are the inner being of nature's ultimate physical units; that there are definite lines of possible influence between them, either connecting them immediately or through 'intervening' ones; and that the 'geometry' of these lines is more or less adequately represented by what we conceive of as their spatial or spatiotemporal relations (or those of complexes including them), while a description of any particular physical process is thus a purely structural account – supplemented by an indication of how it is liable to affect our own perceptual experiences – of the way in which these possible influences have become actual.

However, there are various alternative paths which an attempt to understand the world panpsychistically may take. In particular, there are alternative accounts of how the over-all or dominant consciousness of a human being (such as is calling itself 'I' when one speaks) or animal fits into the scheme. The hypothesis just described suggests that the laws which govern the interaction of such a dominant centre of consciousness with the lower-level centres of consciousness which constitute its body, and via that with other things, are distinct from those which govern those interactions between lower-level centres of consciousness which constitute more 'purely physical' processes both within its body and in nature at large. This has a certain kinship to dualism since, though mind and matter are ultimately the same kind of 'stuff', fresh laws of interaction apply where centres of consciousness of a higher level than those present throughout nature come into operation (see DUALISM §5). Also it is likely to conceive the spatial location of such a dominant centre of consciousness as more diffuse than that of the physical units corresponding to the centres which it dominates. (In principle, it can recognize wholes other than animals with a similarly dominant consciousness diffusely existing within them.)

However, other forms of panpsychism try to fit our consciousness into a world of interacting centres of consciousness whose structural description remains solely that of universal physics. These have some kinship with 'double aspect' conceptions of mind and brain. Various further versions of panpsychism are possible too, all sharing the claimed advantage of conceiving the mind–brain relation as a relation between things which are of the same generic kind. Actually, panpsychists have tended to develop their theories on the basis of an event or process ontology rather than that of individual continuants which endure through a certain length of time, so that for them the natural world in its inner being consists of innumerable streams of interacting experience rather than of interacting sentient continuants. Panpsychism is also sometimes associated with some form of absolute idealism according to which all things are included in one all-embracing consciousness in a manner which displays itself as their containment in a single spatiotemporal system.

References and further reading

Hartshorne, C. (1950) 'Panpsychism' in V. Ferm (ed.) *A History of Philosophical Systems*, New York: Philosophical Library, 442–53. (A clear statement of Hartshorne's panpsychism.)
—— (1962) *The Logic of Perfection*, La Salle, IL: Open Court. (Chapters 7 and 8 offer a statement of Hartshorne's process philosophy, including his panpsychism – what he prefers to call his 'psychicalism'.)
James, W. (1890) 'The Mind-Stuff Theory', in *The Principles of Psychology*, vol. 1, ch. 4, London: Macmillan; Cambridge, MA: Harvard University Press, 1981. (Critical examination of the view that animal and human consciousness is a totality composed of little bits of sentience pervasive in the natural world.)
—— (1911) 'Novelty and Causation: The Perceptual View', in *Some Problems of Philosophy*, ch. 13, New York: Longmans, Green & Co. (This appears as ch. 9 in the scholarly Harvard University Press edition of 1979. A late work of James in which he seems finally to adopt the panpsychism with which he had toyed throughout his life.)
Nagel, T. (1974) 'Panpsychism', *Philosophical Review* 53 (October); repr. in *Mortal Questions*, Cambridge: Cambridge University Press, 1979. (An influential philosopher who sees some point in panpsychism, even if he does not endorse it.)
Paulsen, F. (1892) *Introduction to Philosophy*, 2nd US edn, trans. F. Thilly, intro. W. James, New York: Holt & Company, 1930. (A fascinating discussion of a range of philosophical problems, many of which the author thinks are best solved by the view that the inner essence of what appears to us as physical is pervasively mental.)
Royce, J. (1892) *The Spirit of Modern Philosophy*, New York: W.S. Norton & Co., 1967. (In chapter 12 Royce distinguishes between the world of description and the world of acquaintance. The second, which is mental, is the inner essence of the former, which is the world as viewed by science.)
Sprigge, T.L.S. (1983) *The Vindication of Absolute Idealism*, Edinburgh: Edinburgh University Press. (The first half of this book provides a defence of panpsychism.)
Whitehead, A.N. (1929) *Process and Reality*, corrected edn, New York: Free Press, 1978. (The main statement of Whitehead's process philosophy which many, but not all readers, understand as committed to panpsychism.)

T.L.S. SPRIGGE

PAN-SLAVISM

In B.H. Sumner's words: 'Since Pan-Slavism was in general not so much an organized policy, or even a creed, but rather an attitude of mind and feeling, it was at the time correspondingly difficult to gauge its power, just as it is now to analyse its different elements' (Sumner 1937). Logically and philosophically weak, and in fact usually deficient in any kind of intellectual structure, this identification with, preference for, and emphasis on the Slavs has, nevertheless, been a presence in European (and to a much lesser extent world) history ever since its emergence in early nineteenth century.

1   Origins

While modern Pan-Slavism had some interesting predecessors, such as the seventeenth-century Croat and Roman Catholic priest Juraj Križanić who spent many years in Russia and advocated Slav unity under the Muscovite tsar, its own emergence should be dated from the first part of the nineteenth century. It was produced by two related intellectual and cultural phenomena: the new Romantic ideology centred on organicism and, increasingly, historicism; and the establishment of modern philology. The first provided the fundamental worldview for at least the early stages of Pan-Slavism; the second pinpointed the object of allegiance and devotion, the organism to which one belonged, namely Slavdom as attested by the use of a Slav language. Some pioneers of new thought, notably HERDER, not only provided the necessary framework for Pan-Slavism, but also themselves dealt favourably with the Slavs. Ironically, that new thought, although many-sided, rich, and eventually as extensive as Western civilization itself, could also be regarded as most especially German.

2   Pan-Slavism in Central and Eastern Europe

Very much in the spirit of the age, Pan-Slav ideas eventually influenced Slav intellectuals wherever they could be found, including the small and isolated Sorbian communities in Saxony. Even the briefest account must mention developments in four large areas: the Czech and Slovak territories of the Habsburg Empire; Illyrian or South Slav lands (the latter being another crucial linguistic designation, although in fact it omitted Bulgaria), both inside the Habsburg state as in the cases of the Croats and the Slovenes, and outside it as in the case of most of the Serbs; divided Poland; and Russia.

In this climate of ill-defined hopes and dreams nationalism took hold of two young Lutheran Slovaks who may be regarded as the fathers of early Pan-Slavism, Jan Kollár (1793–1852) and Pavel Josef Šafařík (1795–1861). Kollár became its first poet, Šafařík its first scholar. Kollár's inspiration came directly from his student years at the University of Jena, 1817–19, and represented both a faithful reproduction of the new German Romantic nationalism and its transformation into a Slav one, in opposition to the German. The two pioneers were followed by numerous other enthusiasts including the indefatigable writer Ludevít Stúr (1815–56) and the historian Frantisek Palacký (1798–1876), who 'construed Czech history as a struggle between the peace-loving, naturally democratic Slavs and the bellicose and aristocratic Germans' (Kohn 1953: 24). Different kinds of Slavs constituted almost half of the population of the Habsburg Empire, and Slav issues were bound to be prominent in its politics, especially in the age of nationalism. The revolutionary years of 1848 and 1849 witnessed such developments as a revolution in Prague, as well as in Vienna and in Budapest, an abortive Pan-Slav congress in Prague, and Croat support of the Habsburgs in their war against the Hungarians. The settlement of 1867 transformed the state into a dual entity, Austrian-German and Hungarian, increasing Slav dissatisfaction and also suggesting further change into a triune body, the Slavs finally becoming equal to the two dominant nationalities. But other possibilities were pre-empted by the First World War and the resulting collapse of the Habsburg Empire. That war, of course, was significantly related, both in its immediate origins and in its more fundamental causes, to Slav, even Pan-Slav, issues.

Backward in terms of education and participation in general European culture, in fact many of them oriented for centuries more towards Istanbul than towards Vienna, the South Slavs too began to be affected by Pan-Slavism. Ljudevit Gaj (1809–72) was the moving spirit of this Illyrism, later Yugoslavism (South Slavism). A Croat, educated in Graz and Budapest, influenced by Kollár and active especially in Zagreb, Gaj produced a *Short Outline of Croat-Slovene Orthography* which did much to establish the modern unified Serbo-Croatian literary language, which the author used to publish the first Croatian newspaper and even to create the Croatian national anthem. Croat-centred Yugoslavism was further developed by the Roman Catholic bishop Josip Juraj Strossmayer (1815–1905) and other Zagreb intellectuals. But other South Slavs were less responsive. The Serbs, following Vuk Stefanović Karadžić (1787–1867), writer and language reformer, and other pioneers, stressed their own nationalism and looked at contemporary Serbia as the Piedmont of the South Slavs, who were to be brought together in the great Serbia of the future. Even the representatives of the small Slovene people, animated by their poet France Prešeren (1800–49), emphasized Slovene cultural distinctiveness and considered themselves loyal Austro-Slavs. As to the Bulgarian awakening, promoted especially by Iurii Hutsa (1802–39), better known after his change of name as Iurii Ivanovich Venelin, it consisted mainly in a certain emancipation from the Greek ecclesiastical and intellectual domination and a bid for a mighty Bulgaria sponsored by Russia.

Whereas South Slavs, and some other Slavs as well, can be described as 'awakening' in the first decades of the nineteenth century, Poland was then experiencing a literary and intellectual renaissance of world significance. The disparity makes all comparisons inadequate. Such thinkers as Stanislaw Staszic (1755–1826), Josef Marie Hoene-Wroński (1778–1853), August CIESZKOWSKI (1814–94), Bronislaw Trentowski (1808–69) and the historian Joachim Lelewel (1786–1861), together with such great writers and poets as Adam Mickiewicz (1789–1855), Juljusz Slowacki (1809–49) and Zygmunt Krasiński (1812–59), focused explosively their Slav, and indeed Pan-Slav, themes on the historic and contemporary tragedy of Poland and in particular on its relations with Russia. Suggested remedies ranged from wise leadership of Slavdom by the Russian tsar to hopes for a revolutionary and democratic Russia united with a similar Poland, and to still more unreal messianic and apocalyptic visions – often accompanied by some of the most brilliant denunciations and criticisms of Russia and the Russians ever made. Moreover, Polish messianic thought easily burst the boundaries of Slavdom, presenting Poland as the redeemer of the world, 'Christ of the nations'.

3 Pan-Slavism in Russia

In contrast to Habsburg Slavs or Poles, Russians (or at least Great Russians, not to prejudge the complex and evolving issues of Ukrainian and Belorussian nationalisms) did not live in a state dominated by other nationalities. Nor was the Russian Empire a marginal Balkan principality. Indeed Russia stood out as the only Slav world power, the beacon of expectation and hope for many non-Russian as well as Russian Pan-Slavs. Yet, in spite of its impressively advantageous position, Russian Pan-Slavism both in its nature and its historical role bore a striking resemblance to its counterparts west and south of the Russian borders. Derived from German Romanticism, 'Slav' themes were ably developed by a number of Russian intellectuals, meshing well with a certain sympathy for the Slavs (not the Poles, however), in particular as against Turkey and later the Germanic empires, present in the broader Russian public. Yet Pan-Slav intentions were usually at cross-purposes with government policy, and Russian Pan-Slavism remained characteristically a matter of sentiment – and at times a bugbear to ill-informed foreigners – but not an effective force.

The Slavophiles, who constructed the most comprehensive and the most creative Russian Romantic ideology, are of special interest for the 'Slav' theme (see SLAVOPHILISM). The leading members of the group, all of them landlords and gentlemen-scholars of broad culture and many intellectual interests, included Aleksei Stepanovich Khomiakov (1804–60), who applied himself to everything from theology and world history to medicine and technical inventions, Ivan Vasil'evich Kireevskii (1806–56) who has been called the philosopher of the movement, his brother Pëtr Vasil'evich Kireevskii (1808–56) who collected folk songs and left very little behind him in writing, Konstantin Sergeevich Aksakov (1817–60), a specialist in Russian history and language, his brother Ivan Sergeevich Aksakov (1823–86), later prominent as a publicist and a Pan-Slav, and Iurii Fëdorovich Samarin (1819–76), who was to have a significant part in the emancipation of the serfs and wrote especially on certain religious and philosophical topics, on the problem of the borderlands of the empire, and on the issue of reform in Russia. This informal group, gathering in the salons and homes of Moscow, flourished in the 1840s and 1850s until the death of the Kireevskii brothers in 1856 and of Khomiakov and Konstantin Aksakov in 1860.

Slavophilism expressed a fundamental vision of integration, peace and harmony among human beings. On the religious plane it produced Khomiakov's concept of *sobornost'*, an association in love, freedom, and truth of believers, which Khomiakov considered the essence of Orthodoxy. Historically, so the Slavophiles asserted, a similar harmonious integration of individuals could be found in the social life of the Slavs, notably in the peasant commune – described as a 'moral choir' by Konstantin Aksakov – and in such other ancient Russian institutions as the *zemskii sobor* (a kind of Muscovite estates general to advise the tsar). Again, the family represented the principle of integration in love, and the same spirit could pervade other associations of human beings. As against love, freedom and cooperation stood the world of rationalism, necessity and compulsion. It too existed on many planes, from the religious and metaphysical to that of everyday life. Thus it manifested itself in the Roman Catholic Church – which had chosen rationalism and authority in preference to love and freedom and had seceded from Orthodox Christendom – and, through the Catholic Church, in Protestantism and in the entire civilization of the West. Moreover, Peter the Great introduced the principles of rationalism, legalism, and compulsion into Russia, where they proceeded to destroy or stunt the harmonious native development and to seduce the educated public (see ENLIGHTENMENT, RUSSIAN §1). The Russian future lay in a return to native principles, in overcoming the Western disease. After being cured, Russia would take its message of harmony and salvation to the discordant and dying West. The all-embracing Slavophile dichotomy represented – as pointed out by F. Stepun and others – the basic romantic contrast between the romantic ideal and the Age of Reason. As to Russian Pan-Slavism, the Slavophiles should be considered its important predecessors rather than its fully-fledged adherents. The Slavs never occupied a central position in their teaching, and in fact had only a minor and superficial connection with Khomiakov's theology and none at all with Ivan Kireevskii's philosophy. Yet other members of the group, and even the same Khomiakov, developed popular 'Slav' themes in prose and poetry, glorifying their imaginary ancestors and brothers, and providing one of the most decisive and far-reaching criticisms of the West available. There was a certain logic to Ivan Aksakov's becoming, later in the century, a leader of a genuine Pan-Slav movement. (Professor S. Lukashevich even suggested that he did so after he concluded that a titanic war between the Slavs and the Germans would shake Russia to its very depths and thus bring about the return to the old Russian spirit and principles and the end of the 'Western', Petrine period of Russian history – a crucially important transformation, unaccounted for in the original Slavophile theory.)

'Slav' and even Pan-Slav ideas were also propounded by certain adherents to the government ideology which came to be known as Official Nationality, such as Professors Mikhail Petrovich Pogodin (1800–75) and Stepan Petrovich Shevyrev (1806–64), although never by Tsar Nicholas I himself or his immediate assistants. Other enthusiasts included two great literary figures, the poet Fëdor Ivanovich Tiutchev (1803–73) and, later, the novelist Fëdor Mikhailovich DOSTOEVSKII (1821–81), as well as a number of lesser writers. Russian Pan-Slavism even acquired a remarkable supporter on the extreme left: Mikhail Aleksandrovich BAKUNIN (1814–76), 'founder of nihilism and apostle of anarchy', who believed in the great revolutionary potential of the Slavs and participated in the Pan-Slav congress in Prague in 1848 and some other revolutionary events of those years.

The Russian Pan-Slav movement of the second half of the nineteenth century is usually traced to the Moscow Slav Benevolent Committee founded in January 1858 and to its later sections or more autonomous organizations in such cities as St Petersburg, Kiev and Odessa. The committees devoted themselves to cultural and philanthropic enterprises such as scholarships for Balkan students in Russia and some financial aid to schools and churches in the Orthodox parts of the Ottoman and Habsburg Empires. They also served as a fulcrum for Pan-Slav thought, with special emphasis on the Russian language as the obvious common language for the Pan-Slav world. A Pan-Slav congress was held in Moscow in 1867, with eighty-one Slav guests from abroad, but it produced no tangible results, the question of Poland remaining the most intractable divisive issue. Russian Pan-Slavism experienced a great revival during the Balkan Wars of the late 1870s as thousands of Russian volunteers flocked to fight for the Bulgarians and the Serbs against the Turks before Russia itself joined the fray. But if the Treaty of San Stefano of 1878 could be considered the high point for Russian Slav sentiments and Pan-Slavism, its remaking that same year at the Congress of Berlin came as a sharp disappointment. Slav and Pan-Slav sentiments also rose occasionally later in connection with major events in the Balkans. The First World War itself became inevitable when Russia came to the aid of Serbia against Austria-Hungary. Bulgaria, however, chose to fight on the opposite side, Habsburg Slavs provided manpower for the Habsburg armies, although some of them went over to the Russians, while Poland remained a problem for the Russian Empire until its dying day.

Together with world politics, the intellectual climate also changed. Whereas Pan-Slavism stemmed from Romanticism and developed for decades within the Romantic framework, in the second half of the nineteenth century it came to be influenced and even dominated by new trends of thought: 'realistic' (as in *realpolitik*), pragmatic and at the same time scientistic, that is, applying (or rather misapplying) scientific categories to human society and history. Danilevskii's *Rossiia i Evropa*, published in the periodical press from 1869 and as a book first in 1871, and frequently referred to as the Bible of Pan-Slavism, may be considered the epitome of the new approach. An able natural scientist, Nikolai Iakovlevich Danilevskii (1822–85) concluded that universal history and culture were delusions and that the only reality consisted in the existence and evolution of entirely separate linguistic-ethnographic entities. He discovered about a dozen such entities as well as some peoples who did not properly belong to history, because they offered either nothing or only destruction. Five laws were basic to the historical process: (1) language identified race or family of peoples; (2) for its particular civilization to develop that entity had to have political independence; (3) the basic principles of each entity were unique and could not be transmitted to another cultural-historical type; (4) to obtain the full richness of development each entity should be a federation of states and not absorbed by one of them; (5) as in the case of perennial monocarpic plants the period of growth of these cultural-historical types was indefinite, but the florescence and fruition of each occurred briefly and only once. The next step in history was to be the replacement of the Romano-Germanic, or European, by the Slav type, led, of course, by Russia – for in the visions of Ivan Aksakov and other Pan-Slavs a titanic war loomed on the horizon. Once successful, the Slavs could well institute the first society harmoniously synthesizing all four main aspects of human activity: the religious, the cultural, the political and the socioeconomic (it is especially in this last respect that the earlier cultural-historical types had proven so far deficient). In the meantime only Slav success mattered, not chimeras of universal civilization, universal standards or humanity itself.

4 Historical character and significance

At least so far Pan-Slavism has proven abortive as it failed in its expressed aim of uniting the Slavs, let alone of inaugurating a new Slav age of European and world history. The fortuitous circumstance that all Slavs found themselves, after the Second World War, within the confines of the Soviet Union or its East European satellites was but a vicious travesty of the Pan-Slav ideal, because that ideal could not even be expressed in the new regime, except in a highly circumscribed manner and in subservience to quite different beliefs of the new rulers. Nor did communist unity survive.

Reasons for the failure of Pan-Slavism are not difficult to find. A destabilizing and destructive doctrine, it had to challenge continuously the establishment, or rather establishments. Hence Austro-Slavism, which reflected both the restrictions on Pan-Slavism in the Habsburg state and the willingness of many Slavs to accommodate themselves to these restrictions at the expense of broader Pan-Slav vistas. In Russia the Pan-Slavs never captured the government and could only very occasionally provide valuable support for it or throw significant obstacles in its path. Old religions were often at cross purposes with Pan-Slavism. Thus the Russian emphasis on Orthodoxy or the Polish on Roman Catholicism frequently alienated and even antagonized Slavs who adhered to other creeds. Moreover, Pan-Slavism proved to be only one of the secular beliefs in modern European history, and not the most powerful one. Its overwhelming rival has been nationalism. The two are remarkably similar in their irrationality, romantic origins, linguistic emphasis and organicism. However, Romantic nationalism demands allegiance to the so-to-speak primary, 'national' group, while Pan-Slavism and its counterparts direct it to the larger, secondary group, 'tribal', more broadly ethnic or 'racial'. And it is to the primary group that the allegiance has been

going. Thus Bulgaria fought a whole series of wars with Serbia; Ukrainian nationalism rose in opposition to Poland and Russia; Russian–Polish relations hardly need comment; even more telling may be the collapse of Yugoslavia (not Pan-Slav, to be sure, but nevertheless a secondary formation, for it aimed to bring at least the South Slavs together) in Croatian and Serbian massacres.

See also: SOUTH SLAVS, PHILOSOPHY OF

References and further reading

* Danilevskii, N. Ia. (1869) *Rossiia i Evropa* (Russia and Europe), New York: Johnson Reprint Corporation, 1966. (The so-called Bible of Pan-Slavism.)

Fadner, F. (1961) *Seventy Years of Pan-Slavism in Russia, Karazin to Danilevskii, 1800–1870*, Washington, DC: Georgetown University Press. (A good antidote for those readers who might imagine that this entry exhausts the subject.)

Kohn, H. (1953) *Pan-Slavism: Its History and Ideology*, Notre Dame, IN: University of Notre Dame Press. (Provides a rich and varied picture. Professor Kohn also published several other books related to the topic of this article.)

Petrovich, M.H. (1956) *The Emergence of Russian Panslavism, 1856–1870*, New York: Columbia University Press. (Professor Petrovich wrote with a certain lustre as well as with a marvellous sense of humour.)

Riasanovsky, N.V. (1952) *Russia and the West in the Teaching of the Slavophiles: A Study of Romantic Ideology*, Cambridge, MA: Harvard University Press. (Contains a useful bibliography.)

—— (1959) *Nicholas I and Official Nationality in Russia, 1825–1855*, Berkeley and Los Angeles, CA: University of California Press.

—— (1992) *The Emergence of Romanticism*, New York and Oxford: Oxford University Press.

Sumner, B.H. (1937) *Russia and the Balkans, 1870–1880*, Oxford: Clarendon Press. (Some crucial problems presented by a primarily diplomatic, rather than intellectual, historian.)

Walicki, A. (1982) *Philosophy and Romantic Nationalism: The Case of Poland*, Oxford: Oxford University Press. (An excellent study. Other relevant books by Professor Walicki are also very highly recommended.)

NICHOLAS V. RIASANOVSKY

PANTHEISM

Pantheism contrasts with monotheism (there is one God), polytheism (there are many gods), deism (God created the world in such a way that it is capable of existing and operating on its own, which God then allows it to do) and panentheism (in God there is a primordial and unchanging nature, and a consequent nature that changes and develops). Etymologically, pantheism is the view that Deity and Cosmos are identical. Theologically, it embraces divine immanence while rejecting divine transcendence. If atheism is the denial that anything is divine, pantheism is not atheism; if atheism is the claim that there is no Creator, Providence, transcendent Deity, or personal God, pantheism is atheistic.

Spinoza, perhaps the paradigm figure for pantheism, was described by some as 'a God-intoxicated man' and by others as an atheist. On his account, only God or Nature exists, a single, necessarily existing substance whose modes and qualities exhaust reality. Conceivable equally properly as physical or as mental, God or Nature is no proper object of worship, creates nothing, grants freedom to none, hears no prayer, and does not act in history. Personal immortality, on Spinoza's view, not only does not occur, but is logically impossible. It is one thing to value nature so highly that one calls it a divinity, another to believe in God in any monotheistic sense.

This much said, it must be admitted that 'pantheism' is not easy to define precisely. As conceived here, pantheism need not be a variety of materialism, and if it is materialistic it includes a high view of the worth of matter. Yet 'pantheism' has served as a term of abuse, and as another term for 'atheism' and 'materialism' and 'deism', terms bearing quite different senses.

1   **God and world**
2   **Varieties of pantheism**
3   **Two routes to pantheism**
4   **Spinoza: God or Nature**
5   **Consequences**

1   God and world

Within a pantheistic perspective, God is not conceived as transcending the universe and so is not thought of as Creator or Providence, cause of the world though distinct from it, an agent who affects history, or a comprehending hearer of prayer and receiver of worship. There is nothing not part of the world on which the world might depend. Monotheism means by 'world', roughly, 'whatever exists besides God' and this makes possible its claim that the world depends for its existence on God while God exists indepen-

dently. Pantheism means by 'world' simply 'all there is' with nothing left over, and hence rejects any Creator/creature distinction. From a monotheistic standpoint, this is atheism, however valuable the pantheist may conceive everything, or each thing, to be (see ATHEISM §1).

Nor, in contrast with polytheism, does pantheism view nature as coming under the control of various beings, each with limited capacities and knowledge. Polytheistic deities are gods and goddesses of limited capacities, but they are typically conceived as possessing a transcendence of nature incompatible with pantheism. Further, pantheism is a radical type of monism, holding both that there is, strictly, only one thing, however many and diverse its interlocking elements, and one fundamental kind of thing (see MONISM). Thus not only the distinction between Creator and creation, in which the former transcends the latter, but such distinctions as soul and body, concrete and abstract, and immaterial and material, seen as identifications of kinds of things such that anything belonging to one kind cannot belong to the other, are rejected.

2   Varieties of pantheism

Historical views often identified as pantheistic include Hesiod's *Theogony* and Stoicism, with its doctrine that God is a rational spirit who, shapeless himself, makes himself into all things, and its view of God as the tension or tendency to coherence that holds together the various sorts of things that there are, each sort itself defined in terms of its degree of internal tension or coherence (see HESIOD; STOICISM §§3–5). XENOPHANES (§3) arguably viewed the cosmos as a living, conscious, divine unity. The Upaniṣads (800 BC and later) contain passages in which Brahman is represented as claiming identity with all sorts of things. The pantheistic and polytheistic tendencies expressed in the Upaniṣads are countered by other passages that offer a more monotheistic view and a tendency in Hinduism to henotheism. Advaita Vedānta Hinduism, represented classically by ŚAṄKARA, holds that there exists only qualityless Brahman, a view similar to Schelling's (see SCHELLING, F.W.J. VON §2; VEDĀNTA). Johannes Scottus ERIUGENA (§3) held that anything exists only in so far as it participates in the essence of God, but he also insisted that no term applicable to creatures can be predicated of God. FICHTE (§§6–7) thought of the world as the material through which the Ego achieves its moral work, and identified the divine with a moral order that is composed of Ego and world. Giordano BRUNO (§5) held God to be distinct from finite individuals only by including them within God's being, and followed Hermetic writings in making the unity of the All in the One a basic theme of his own thought (see HERMETISM). MEISTER ECKHART, BOEHME and HEGEL (§§3–5) are not infrequently read pantheistically. Benedict de Spinoza's philosophy is a particularly fully developed and influential version of pantheism (see SPINOZA, B. DE §§2–4).

3 Two routes to pantheism

One might arrive at a pantheistic view of things by first believing that a self-conscious ontologically independent being exists, and then coming to think that if B depends for its very existence on A then B is part of A or B is in some other manner not a distinct being from A. Then one would have started as a monotheist and ended as a pantheist. This process will be helped along if one also thinks that if B depends for its very existence on A, then for any quality Q that B has, B has Q only because A causes B to have Q. Monotheism plus determinism plus the view that dependence rules out distinctness will yield pantheism. This is one route.

A different possible route goes in the opposite direction, as it were. If one believes that everything that exists depends every moment for its existence on something else, that everything that exists is valuable by virtue of simply existing, and that dependence rules out distinctness, then one will presumably conclude that there exists but one organic thing and (at least if one believes that valuable parts guarantee a valuable whole or else that the whole itself is valuable just by virtue of its existing) that this one thing is valuable. If one thinks very highly of its value, one may express one's view by saying that it is divine, using 'divine' in some such sense as 'possesses the highest possible value'. It is perhaps in this attitude that pantheism contrasts with atheism, in so far as there is a contrast.

4 Spinoza: God or Nature

Either route will leave one in the position of thinking that there is one whole composed of intimately related and interdependent parts. One rather precise way of putting this doctrine was developed by Spinoza. Spinoza's complex views, classically expressed in his *Ethics* (1677) come to something like the following. *God or Nature* is the only thing that exists. It is a substance – a possessor of states and properties and not itself a state or property. It has logically necessary existence, and each item that exists that is not identical to God or Nature is a mode or state of it, or a characteristic of it. Causal connections are properly understand as matters of, or at least as

somehow isomorphic with, logical entailments. God or Nature is described as 'cause of itself', but this is not intended literally. It is Spinoza's way, not of saying that God or Nature both does not exist (so that its existence can be caused) and does exist (in order to do the causing), but that it is logically impossible that God or Nature should not exist or should depend for existence on anything.

Spinoza thinks that fatalism is true – any true proposition is necessarily true and any false proposition is necessarily false. Thus nothing that does exist could possibly have failed to exist, and nothing that does not exist could possibly have existed. Thus, while Leibniz and a great many other philosophers have talked about and thought in terms of possible worlds, believing that there is an infinite number of ways things might have been, for Spinoza there is not a multiplicity of possible worlds. There is exactly one way that things might have been, and that is the way things are; possibility is necessarily coextensive with actuality. Any characteristic that any state of God or Nature has is one that it could not possibly not have had, and any characteristic that any state of God or Nature lacks is one that it could not possibly not have lacked. Hence true natural science should be conceived of as analogous to the geometrician Euclid's *Elements*, which itself is conceived of as consisting of necessarily true axioms and necessarily true theorems that necessarily follow from the axioms. True physics is a fully developed deductive (every axiomatic truth is included and every derivable theorem has been derived) system whose axioms are necessarily true, and physical reality is isomorphic with true physics. Psychology, the science of mental states, is also a fully developed deductive system whose axioms are necessarily true.

God or Nature can be conceived under the attribute of extension, as what exactly corresponds to the true physics. God or Nature can also be conceived under the attribute of thought, as what exactly corresponds to the true psychology. Each way of conceiving it is entirely correct and leaves nothing out, save the fact that there is another equally exhaustive way of correctly describing and explaining things. Along with the various attributes and their corresponding theories, there is a set of notions – substance, attribute, mode, cause, finite, infinite, and the like – that are involved in one's conceiving anything under any attribute, and thus that are in principle core concepts in any theory.

Indeed, Spinoza thinks that while we are able to conceive of only two attributes of God or Nature, there is an infinite number of attributes, to each of which in principle corresponds an exhaustive description of everything and an explanation of everything it is logically possible to explain, and each of which has its own core concept that plays within it the same role that extension and thought play in the theories they are central to. While 'being a body' and 'being a mind', then, are kind-defining features for Spinoza, he denies that they define ontologically incompatible kinds. Rather, he holds, they define exhaustive accounts of things, neither of which can be translated into the other, and each of which gives an account of the same thing as the other; necessarily connotatively incommensurate, they are necessarily denotatively identical. The resulting view is neither materialism, which would require that the true physics be the whole story, nor idealism, which would require that the true psychology be the whole story.

5   Consequences

Several consequences follow from a pantheistic perspective:

(1) *Regarding freedom.* A person is *categorically free* regarding an action if and only if, under prevailing conditions, they have the power both to perform and to refrain from performing it, and, whichever they do, they do not make false a law of logic or of nature, or some truth about the past. No one can possess categorical freedom if pantheism is true. This consequence is especially clear for Spinoza's version; his epigram is that freedom is only ignorance of causes. Human freedom presupposes logically possible alternatives to what is done, and according to Spinoza there are none. Divine freedom is a matter of none of the characteristics of God or Nature following from any essence but God or Nature's own (see FREEDOM, DIVINE §§1–2). What is valued for humans is an understanding of the nature of things, joined with equanimity in accepting truths as necessary truths. In other varieties of pantheism, too, possessing freedom requires a separateness and autonomy hard to reconcile with pantheistic metaphysics. A categorically free agent is independent in the sense that they can so act as to determine some of their own properties in a manner not already determined by the situations and properties of other things. The unity that pantheism posits arises from everything depending for its existence and its properties on the existence and properties of other things (or on everything else depending for its existence and properties on one thing). States of a substance, parts of an organism, are not categorically free agents, even if the substance or organism is all-encompassing.

(2) *Regarding immortality.* Another consequence concerns individual immortality. In Spinoza's version, individual survival is logically impossible. Martha's body is a state or mode of God or Nature conceived

under the attribute of extension. It is identical to what can also be described as Martha's mind or soul, which is the same mode as Martha's body, though now considered under the attribute of thought. Martha's body ultimately dies and disintegrates; hence it necessarily dies and disintegrates. Since Martha's mind or soul is identical to Martha's body, Martha's mind or soul ceases to exist when Martha's body ceases to exist. Spinozistic 'immortality' is a matter of what Martha knew corresponding to a part of what God or Nature conceived under the attribute of thought knows, and of Martha's material remains being composed of physical stuff that is part of what makes up God or Nature conceived under the attribute of extension. Spinoza is thus committed to the problematic view that necessarily, and hence either eternally or everlastingly, true propositions can entail propositions that specify particular temporal limitations, such as 'Martha exists from the date of her birth to the date of her death, neither before the one nor after the other'. 'The one substance there is necessarily exists' must, regarding its finite modes, entail propositions having the form 'Mode M exists only for a while'.

Even in pantheism's non-Spinozistic varieties, individual persons are conceived as so related to both other persons and to things that the very existential dependence and causal interaction that constitutes or yields their unity (that makes things *pan*theistic) militates against any ontologically deep individuality at any time. The at least potential separateness of a person from their body and natural environment, of the sort that doctrines of individual survival typically presuppose, is inconsistent with a pantheistic conception of things (see SOUL, NATURE AND IMMORTALITY OF THE §2).

(3) *Regarding error and evil.* It is Spinoza's view that all error is simply confusion; what is false is self-contradictory and thus, he believes, cannot be thought. The closest, then, it is possible to come to error is that one only confusedly understands the truth. There can be no such thing as false belief. Similarly, there is no room for genuine evil. What is, necessarily is, and the distinctions we make between good and evil have no purchase on a world in which it is logically impossible that anything be different.

Even if there are logically contingent truths, if everything is thought of as divine there is pressure to deny that anyone actually believes erroneously or that anything is genuinely evil (intellectual error itself may be seen as one variety of evil). Admittedly, dependence and lack of clarity are not perfections, but a pantheist can claim that they (in contrast to error and evil) are inevitable concomitants of being less than the whole. Thus while God or Nature cannot be evil, and

God or Nature is all there is, a mode may seem defective considered by itself, but were it considered in the full context of its necessary existence as part of a system of modes and hence as part of God or Nature, its apparent defectiveness would vanish. Neither can there be sin, and so there can be no need for divine forgiveness (see Evil §3).

Spinoza's statement of pantheism allows one to see what it entails. *Mutatis mutandis*, similar conclusions regarding freedom, personal immortality, and error and evil are likely to follow from other versions of pantheism.

See also: Deism; God, concepts of

References and further reading

Flint, R. (1877) *Theism*, Edinburgh and London: William Blackwood & Sons. (Baird Lecture for 1876; polytheism, pantheism and theism are compared in chapter 2.)

—— (1879) *Anti-Theistic Theories*, Edinburgh and London: William Blackwood & Sons. (Baird Lecture for 1877, with discussion of the history and content of pantheism in chapters 9 and 10; see also the appendices.)

Orr, J. (1897) *The Christian View of God and the World*, New York: Charles Scribner's Sons. (The Kerr Lectures for 1890–1; critical of pantheism, with discussion of its nature and history.)

* Spinoza, B. de (1677) *Ethics Demonstrated in Geometrical Order and Divided into Five Parts*, trans. E. Curley, *The Collected Works of Spinoza*, vol. 1, Princeton, NJ: Princeton University Press, 1985. (Spinoza's *magnum opus* in metaphysics and epistemology.)

Thomas, G.F. (1965) *Religious Philosophies of the West*, New York: Charles Scribner's Sons. (A critical analysis of religious thinkers from Plato to Tillich; see chapter 7.)

—— (1970) *Philosophy and Religious Belief*, New York: Charles Scribner's Sons. (A systematic sequel to the historically ordered previous volume; see chapter 4.)

KEITH E. YANDELL

PARACELSUS (PHILIPPUS AUREOLUS THEOPHRASTUS BOMBASTUS VON HOHENHEIM) (1493–1541)

Paracelsus (pseudonym of Theophrastus Bombastus von Hohenheim) was an itinerant Swiss surgeon and physician who formulated a new philosophy of medicine based on a combination of chemistry, Neoplatonism and the occult, all within a Christian framework. His works, usually in German rather than Latin, were mostly published after his death. His importance for medical practice lay in his insistence on observation and experiment, and his use of chemical methods for preparing drugs. He rejected Galen's explanation of disease as an imbalance of humours, along with the traditional doctrine of the four elements. He saw the human being as a microcosm that reflected the structure and elements of the macrocosm, thus presenting a unified view of human beings and a universe in which everything was interconnected and full of vital powers. Paracelsian chemical medicine was very popular in the late sixteenth and seventeenth centuries, largely due to its presentation as part of a general theory.

1 Life and works
2 Microcosm and macrocosm
3 Medicine and chemistry
4 Influence

1 Life and works

Theophrastus Bombastus von Hohenheim (sometimes given the additional names Philippus Aureolus) was born in Einsiedeln, a small Swiss town near Zürich. His pseudonym, Paracelsus, first recorded in 1529, may mean 'greater than Celsus' (a Roman medical writer). When his father, a medical doctor interested in alchemy, moved to Villach in Austria in 1502, Paracelsus came into contact with mining technology and the study of metals. He worked as an apprentice in the mines near Schwaz, but otherwise little is known of his education. He may have studied with Johannes Trithemius (1462–1516), author of many works on magic. He probably studied medicine at the University of Ferrara (1513–16), though there is no documentary evidence that he received a degree. Although medical training had a practical component, the focus was academic, involving study of standard Latin translations of Hippocrates (see Hippocratic medicine), Galen and Avicenna (see Galen; Ibn Sina). He then worked as an army surgeon during his travels across Europe from 1517 to

1524. Surgery was primarily a practical discipline, and much of the surgical literature was in the vernacular. The relationship between academically trained physicians and surgeons was an uneasy one, and Paracelsus persistently complained that he was recognized as a surgeon, not as a physician. From 1524 to 1525 Paracelsus was in Salzburg, but had to leave in a hurry, possibly because of involvement in a peasant rebellion. Subsequently he visited a number of spas, and developed an interest in the minerals found in spa waters. In 1526 he was in Strasbourg where he made some useful contacts leading to his appointment (March 1527) as municipal physician in Basle. This post carried with it the right to lecture, and led to a major clash with the university, which had not been consulted. Paracelsus announced that he was not going to teach the works of Hippocrates and Galen, and he burned the Canon of Avicenna in public. Furthermore, he gave his lectures in Swiss-German, not Latin. After verbally attacking a magistrate for not giving him full support in a case brought for non-payment of fees (a frequent problem), he was forced to flee from Basle early in 1528. He now began a second set of journeys in Switzerland, Austria, Bohemia and Southern Germany, which are much better documented than his earlier journeys. In 1529, he visited Nuremberg where he studied and wrote on syphilis. He gave a very accurate description of the disease, but his recommendations for treatment were highly controversial. In 1533 he spent time in the mining areas of Appenzell, studying the diseases of miners, and giving the first written account of an occupational disease. He also continued his studies of spa waters. He claimed that he effected many marvellous medical cures, but seems never to have had much financial success. He was invited to Salzburg by the bishop, but died there in 1541, leaving few possessions.

Paracelsus was a prolific writer, though few of his works were published during his lifetime. Those that were, tended to be about prophecy and astrological forecasts. A few works require special mention. In his *Paragranum* (1529–30), he argued that medicine should be based on the four pillars of natural philosophy, astronomy, alchemy and virtue, by which he meant the individual powers of doctors, patients, herbs and metals. In his *Volumen medicinae paramirum* (c.1520) and his *Opus paramirum* (1531) he discussed basic medical doctrines. His main work on surgery, *Grosse Wundarznei*, was written in 1536 and printed immediately. His greatest and most comprehensive work, *Astronomia Magna*, was written 1537–8 and published in 1571. The first collected edition of his works dates from 1589–91, and was followed by other editions and by Latin translations.

His works were widely diffused during the seventeenth century.

2 Microcosm and macrocosm

Paracelsus attacked medical orthodoxy in the name of Christian philosophy. He set out to find a new basis for medicine, and indeed for the study of the whole human being, by reverting to the ancient wisdom of Neoplatonism, enriched by elements from Hermeticism (or Hermetism), alchemy, astrology and magic. His favourite contemporary source was Marsilio FICINO (§2). He presented the resulting mixture in a biblical framework, emphasizing the necessity of Christian faith for those who sought the power of controlling natural forces, especially in healing the sick. He also emphasized the old doctrine of the two Books, the Book of Nature and the Book of Revelation (namely, the Bible), from both of which humans learn to read.

Paracelsus' central doctrine concerned the relationship between the greater world, the macrocosm, and the lesser world, the microcosm, or human being. The elements making up the human being are those found in the macrocosm, and their structural relations are the same. In particular, the human reflects physical reality through the corporeal body which is perishable, living or spiritual reality through the astral body which gives life but is also perishable, and purely spiritual reality through the immortal soul which will take on an eternal body. Conversely, just as the human being is alive, so the macrocosm is permeated by life, and even metals grow. Furthermore, the entire universe is characterized by an elaborate series of correspondences. Plants and minerals contain powers or virtues which capture those of celestial bodies, and these powers in turn relate to states of the human body.

These doctrines have both epistemological and practical implications. Because the human being reflects the macrocosm, knowledge of external objects can be reached through knowledge of internal states and relations, particularly those involving the astral body. Knowledge is also bound up with power. Although human beings are endowed with wisdom, and hence are not governed by the stars, knowledge of the stars is particularly important in practice. Astrology enables us to know the powers, relations and influences of celestial bodies, and natural magic shows us how to control them.

Paracelsus' natural philosophy included a new doctrine of elements. He rejected the traditional four elements of earth, air, fire and water, accepting them only as visible composites. In their place he proposed sulphur and mercury, both found in Arabic alchemical sources, and salt, which he added himself. These elements should not be confused with the composites we normally call sulphur, salt and mercury. As an element, sulphur represents a principle of organization, mercury a principle of activity, and salt a principle directing matter towards a solid state. Nor should they be thought of as basic particles, for they have different qualities in different objects.

3   Medicine and chemistry

Paracelsus' rejection of the traditional four elements had a direct effect on his medical theory. Traditional medicine explained illness in terms of the four humours or bodily fluids to which the four elements gave rise: blood, phlegm, choler (or red or yellow bile) and black bile (or melancholy). Illness was taken to be a lack of balance between the four humours, a balance restored through diet and herbal medicine. Emotions, too, were linked to the four humours, and people were sanguine, phlegmatic, choleric or melancholic according to which humour predominated. These internal, mechanistic explanations were dismissed by Paracelsus. For him, diseases are distinct from one another, and are often related to chemical imbalances in specific organs that result from an interaction with external agents. These agents could be minerals, or they could be 'astral poisons' transmitted by the air. Astral influences were particularly important in explaining mental illness. Diseases are combated through the plants and metals whose 'signatures' show them to have the appropriate virtues or powers. There is always a precise correspondence between a disease and its antidote (see MEDICINE, PHILOSOPHY OF; HIPPOCRATIC MEDICINE).

Paracelsus brought his practical experience to bear on the problem of treating diseases. Through his studies of alchemy and mining he had learned much about metals, and metallurgical techniques. He developed new laboratory methods, such as the concentration of alcohol by freezing. He used chemical techniques to derive extracts from traditional herbs, but more importantly he employed such substances as mercury, arsenic and antimony in his treatments. Unfortunately, while his observations of diseases were remarkably exact, it is unlikely that his ability to cure them surpassed that of traditional practitioners.

Paracelsus' real achievement was his unified approach to chemistry which brought together alchemical, metallurgical and pharmaceutical techniques. Indeed, he came to see the whole world and its creation in terms of chemical transformation and separation.

4   Influence

From the 1550s onwards, as his works were edited and translated, Paracelsus' reputation began to grow. Paracelsian doctors were appointed to various European courts. Van HELMONT was influenced by him, and NEWTON possessed a major edition of his works. At the same time, his philosophy was attacked by such figures as MERSENNE and GASSENDI, and there were disputes, often complex and bitter, between Galenists and Paracelsians in faculties of medicine.

Paracelsianism is particularly significant for the history of modern science. In the words of Charles Webster, 'the first major confrontation of the Scientific Revolution was between Paracelsus and Galen, rather than between Copernicus and Ptolemy' (1982: 3–4). The reasons for Paracelsus' popularity had to do with his presentation of a mystical, vitalistic philosophy of nature within a Christian framework. The continued attention paid to Paracelsus, and to Neoplatonism and the occult in general, show that a non-mechanistic, non-quantitative, non-mathematical approach still made sense, even to those who, like Newton, were responsible for advances in the new science.

See also: ALCHEMY §5; HERMETISM; HIPPOCRATIC MEDICINE; MEDICINE, PHILOSOPHY OF; RELIGION AND SCIENCE

List of works

Paracelsus (c.1520–1541a) *The hermetic and alchemical writings of Aureolus Philippus Theophrastus Bombast*, trans. A.E. Waite, London: J. Elliott, 1894; repr. Berkeley, CA: Shambhala and New York: Random House, 1976. (Good translations of selected works on alchemy and hermetic medicine.)

—— (c.1520–1541b) *Sämtliche Werke. I. Abteilung. Medizinische, naturwissenschaftliche und philosophische Schriften* (Collected Works. Division I: Writings on Medicine, Natural Science and Philosophy), ed. K. Sudhoff, vols 6–9, Munich: O.W. Barth; vols 1–5, 10–14, Munich and Berlin: R. Oldenburg, 1922–33. (Standard critical edition.)

—— (c.1520–1541c) *Sämtliche Werke. II. Abteilung. Die theologischen und religionswissenschaftlichen Schriften* (Collected Works. Division II: Writings on Theology and Religion), vol. 1, ed. W. Matthiessen, Munich: O.W. Barth, 1923; vols 2–7 and supplementary volume, ed. K. Goldammer *et al.*, Wiesbaden: Franz Steiner, 1955–73. (Standard critical edition.)

—— (c.1520) *Volumen medicinae paramirum*, trans. K.F. Leidecker, *Bulletin of the History of Medicine,* supplementary vol. 11, Baltimore, MD: Johns Hopkins University Press, 1949. (Discussion of basic medical doctrines. The original text is found in *Sämtliche Werke. I. Abteilung*, vol. 1.)

—— (1529–30) *Paragranum*, in K. Sudhoff (ed.) *Sämtliche Werke. I. Abteilung. Medizinische, naturwissenschaftliche und philosophische Schriften*, vol. 8, Munich: O.W. Barth, 1922–33. (Argues that medicine should be based on the individual powers of doctors, patients, herbs and metals.)

—— (1531) *Opus paramirum*, in K. Sudhoff (ed.) *Sämtliche Werke. I. Abteilung. Medizinische, naturwissenschaftliche und philosophische Schriften*, vol. 9, Munich: O.W. Barth, 1922–33. (Discussion of basic medical doctrines.)

—— (1536) *Grosse Wundarznei*, in K. Sudhoff (ed.) *Sämtliche Werke. I. Abteilung. Medizinische, naturwissenschaftliche und philosophische Schriften*, vol. 10, Munich and Berlin: R. Oldenburg, 1922–33. (Paracelsus' major work on surgery.)

—— (1571) *Astronomia Magna*, in K. Sudhoff (ed.) *Sämtliche Werke. I. Abteilung. Medizinische, naturwissenschaftliche und philosophische Schriften*, vol. 12, Munich and Berlin: R. Oldenburg, 1922–33. (Paracelsus' most comprehensive work. Although written in 1537–8, *Astronomia Magna* was only published posthumously.)

—— (1951) *Selected Writings*, ed. J. Jacobi, trans. N. Guterman, New York: Pantheon; 2nd edn, 1958. (A thematically organized series of translations based on the critical edition; useful glossary and bibliography.)

References and further reading

Allers, R. (1944) 'Microcosmus from Anaximandros to Paracelsus', *Traditio* 2: 319–407. (Scholarly study of a key notion.)

Debus, A.G. (1977) *The Chemical Philosophy: Paracelsian Science and Medicine in the Sixteenth and Seventeenth Centuries*, New York: Science History Publications. (A standard two-volume work on Paracelsus and his influence.)

—— (1978) *Man and Nature in the Renaissance*, Cambridge: Cambridge University Press. (A good short introduction to Renaissance science and medicine, with full bibliography.)

—— (1991) *The French Paracelsians: The Chemical Challenge to Medical and Scientific Tradition in Early Modern France*, Cambridge: Cambridge University Press. (About the influence of Paracelsus.)

Pagel, W. (1982) *Paracelsus: An Introduction to Philosophical Medicine in the Era of the Renaissance*, revised 2nd edn, Basle and New York: Karger. (The standard account of Paracelsus' life and works.)

—— (1985) *Religion and Neoplatonism in Renaissance Medicine*, London: Variorum. (A collection of papers most of which are devoted to Paracelsus.)

Siraisi, N.G. (1990) *Medieval and Early Renaissance Medicine: An Introduction to Knowledge and Practice*, Chicago, IL, and London: University of Chicago Press. (Very readable, full of fascinating details and illustrations.)

Vickers, B. (1984) 'Introduction', in *Occult and scientific mentalities in the Renaissance*, Cambridge: Cambridge University Press, 1–55. (Places Paracelsus in context.)

* Webster, C. (1982) *From Paracelsus to Newton: Magic and the Making of Modern Science*, Cambridge: Cambridge University Press. (Referred to in §4. A readable, short discussion of the relation between occult studies and early modern science.)

E.J. ASHWORTH

PARACONSISTENT LOGIC

A logic is paraconsistent if it does not validate the principle that from a pair of contradictory sentences, A and ~A, everything follows, as most orthodox logics do. If a theory has a paraconsistent underlying logic, it may be inconsistent without being trivial (that is, entailing everything). Sustained work in formal paraconsistent logics started in the early 1960s. A major motivating thought was that there are important naturally occurring inconsistent but non-trivial theories. Some logicians have gone further and claimed that some of these theories may be true. By the mid-1970s, details of the semantics and proof-theories of many paraconsistent logics were well understood. More recent research has focused on the applications of these logics and on their philosophical underpinnings and implications.

The idea that a contradiction implies everything (*ex contradictione quodlibet* – ECQ) has always been a contentious one in logic. Despite this, formal paraconsistent logics, which do not validate ECQ, are creatures of the twentieth century. The earliest ones were constructed in Russia by N.A. Vasil'ev *c*.1912 – an Aristotelian logic – and I.E. Orlov in 1929 – a relevance logic (see Anderson, Belnap and Dunn 1992). However, these had no impact at the time.

Work on formal paraconsistent logics did not begin in earnest until after the Second World War. Since then they have been proposed independently by many logicians, the earliest notable ones being S. Jaśkowski (in Poland) in 1948, F.G. Asenjo (Argentina) *c.*1954, N.C.A. da Costa (Brazil) *c.*1958 and T.J. Smiley (the UK) in 1959. Work on relevance logic by A.R. Anderson and N.D. Belnap (in the USA) also started in the late 1950s (see RELEVANCE LOGIC AND ENTAILMENT), and the specifically paraconsistent aspects of relevance logic were developed by R. Routley and others (in Australia) in the late 1960s and 1970s. (Note that a paraconsistent logic need not be relevant.) Since then, work on formal paraconsistent logic has continued apace in many places, but most notably in Brazil (under the leadership of da Costa) and Australia. (Some of the original work is rather difficult to come by or of a rather preliminary nature. The best access points in the literature are: Jaśkowski (1969); Asenjo (1966); da Costa (1974); Anderson and Belnap (1975); and Routley (1977).)

A major motivation behind the construction of formal paraconsistent logics has always been the idea that in many contexts we may have information that is inconsistent, but from which we want to draw conclusions in a controlled way. (The term 'paraconsistent' was coined by M. Quesada at the third Latin American Symposium on Mathematical Logic in 1976, to indicate just this.) Examples that are frequently appealed to are: evidence provided by different witnesses, constitutions and other legal documents, various scientific theories, numerous philosophical theories, and information in a computer database. In such contexts, even though the data are incorrect, if we are stuck with them (as we may well be), then the logic had better be paraconsistent. Moreover, inconsistent scientific theories, even if they are not correct, may still be useful, or good approximations to the truth.

Some paraconsistent logicians have claimed that inconsistent theories may actually be true (see, for example, Priest 1987). The view that some contradictions or contradictory theories are true is called 'dialeth(e)ism' – from 'dialetheia' (a term coined by Priest and Routley in 1982), which means a true statement of the form $A \& \sim A$. The most commonly cited examples of dialetheias are the paradoxes of self-reference, such as Russell's and the liar paradox (see PARADOXES OF SET AND PROPERTY; SEMANTIC PARADOXES AND THEORIES OF TRUTH). The failure to obtain consensus on any consistent account of the paradoxes gives this suggestion its appeal. Other suggested examples of dialetheias include: statements about objects on the borderline of some vague predicate; moral dilemmas; and dialectical contradictions in the tradition of Hegel and Marx.

Some approaches to paraconsistent logic, such as Smiley's, obtain a suitable inference relation by starting with the classical one and filtering out ECQ

and other undesirables. Such logics typically give up the transitivity of entailment. A more common approach is to specify a notion of entailment semantically, defined in terms of truth-preservation over a class of interpretations. For this approach, it is necessary to have a mechanism whereby contradictory sentences may simultaneously hold in an interpretation. For this reason, one may think of paraconsistent logic as a kind of dual of intuitionist logic (see INTUITIONISM), the former violating the law of non-contradiction, the latter violating the law of the excluded middle. (Though it is quite possible to have a paraconsistent logic in which $\sim (A \& \sim A)$ is semantically valid.) Paraconsistent logics of this kind characteristically invalidate the Disjunctive Syllogism (DS): $A \vee B$ and $\sim A$ entail B. For both premises may be true in virtue of the properties of A, while B is not.

Various techniques have been proposed to achieve the required end. Jaśkowski's is to interpret 'true' as 'true in some possible world or other'. Da Costa's is to give up the truth-functionality of negation, so that if A is true, $\sim A$ may be either true or false. Routley's is to treat negation as an intensional operator, so that $\sim A$ is true at a world w if A is false at some associated world, w^*. Asenjo's suggestion (which can also be harnessed in the semantics of relevance logics) is to allow sentences to take a non-classical truth value, which may be thought of as *both true and false*, and which is a fixed point for negation.

By the mid-1970s the semantics and proof theories of many paraconsistent logics were well developed. More recently, much work has gone into their applications, both technical and philosophical. The technical applications all involve the investigation of inconsistent theories. Notable results in this area include a proof that naïve set theory with (an unrestricted comprehension axiom and) a suitable underlying paraconsistent logic is non-trivial (Brady 1989), and a proof (by R. Meyer) that there is a (consistent!) arithmetic that can prove its own non-triviality. The techniques involved in the latter involve the construction of models of full first-order arithmetic, many of which are finite (see Meyer and Mortensen 1984). It is also possible to construct non-trivial theories that contain both self-reference and epistemic operators, and that are semantically closed, in the sense of Tarski (see Priest 1991a).

The philosophical applications are more diffuse. Traditionally, consistency was thought to be the cornerstone of many important philosophical notions (for example, truth, rationality), but the viability of paraconsistent logic throws down a challenge to any such claim. In the light of this, a reappraisal both of such notions and of the significance of results that turn on consistency, for example, Gödel's incompleteness theorems, is called for and is in train.

Many would be prepared to concede the possibility of a limited use for paraconsistent logic, for example, as an inference engine for a computational database. The major criticism as far as this goes is that a paraconsistent logic is too weak to permit useful inference. In particular, a number of writers have argued that the DS is essential to most practical inference. In the author's opinion, this sort of objection carries little weight. For a start, the logical resources of the programming language PROLOG are validated in most paraconsistent logics when suitably interpreted. More generally, most paraconsistent logicians have been prepared to accept the usability of principles such as the DS in consistent ('normal'?) contexts. This idea has motivated the construction of formal non-monotonic logics in which the DS is a default inference (see Batens 1989; Priest 1991b).

Much of the criticism of paraconsistent logic has fallen on dialetheism. One of the chief general criticisms is that the paraconsistent semantics for negation fails to capture (true) negation, but this is difficult to make stick for the many-valued semantics. Some have argued that if contradictions are not to be rejected as logically unacceptable then logic is ruined as an instrument of rational criticism, but this objection trades on a confusion of what is possible according to formal logic and what is rationally possible. A third important general criticism is that if one is to accept A one must rationally reject $\sim A$. However, dialetheism aside, there are situations where we seem to have little rational option but to accept a contradiction (for example, the paradox of the preface). Most of the application-specific criticisms have tried to undercut a dialetheic solution to the self-referential paradoxes by arguing that paraconsistent solutions to these collapse into triviality – or, at least, fail to do so only by *ad hoc* manoeuvres of a kind that make consistent purported solutions so unsatisfactory. To date, such arguments have not hit the mark squarely. (On much of the above, see Smiley and Priest (1993).)

The possibility of violations of the law of non-contradiction was widely canvassed by pre-Aristotelian philosophers. Aristotle attacked this possibility in *Metaphysics* (1005b8–1009a5). His arguments are distinctly dubious, as was shown by Łukasiewicz (1971), but his authority has determined subsequent orthodoxy. Only a few (notably Hegel) have challenged it. Even fewer have produced a sustained defence of the law. The technical viability of paraconsistent logic and dialetheism therefore raises a challenge to contemporary philosophy of no little significance.

See also: LOGICAL AND MATHEMATICAL TERMS, GLOSSARY OF

References and further reading

* Anderson, A.R. and Belnap, N.D. (1975) *Entailment*, vol. 1, Princeton, NJ: Princeton University Press. (A summary of the early work on relevance logic.)
* Anderson, A.R., Belnap, N.D. and Dunn, J.M. (1992) *Entailment*, vol. 2, Princeton, NJ: Princeton University Press. (Includes references to Vasil'ev and Orlov.)
* Asenjo, F.G. (1966) 'A Calculus of Antinomies', *Notre Dame Journal of Formal Logic* 7: 103–6. (A report of Asenjo's early work on paraconsistent logic.)
* Batens, D. (1989) 'Dynamic Dialectical Logics', in G. Priest, R. Routley and J. Norman (eds) *Paraconsistent Logic*, Munich: Philosophia, ch. 6. (The first non-monotonic paraconsistent logic.)
* Brady, R.T. (1989) 'The Non-Triviality of Dialectical Set Theory', in G. Priest, R. Routley and J. Norman (eds) *Paraconsistent Logic*, Munich: Philosophia, ch. 16. (Includes a proof that naïve set theory with a suitable underlying paraconsistent logic is non-trivial.)
* Costa, N.C.A. da (1974) 'On the Theory of Inconsistent Formal Systems', *Notre Dame Journal of Formal Logic* 15: 497–510. (A report of da Costa's early work on paraconsistent logic.)
* Jaśkowski, S. (1969) 'Propositional Calculus for Contradictory Deductive Systems', *Studia Logica* 24: 143–57. (An English translation of the earliest influential paper on paraconsistent logic.)
* Łukasiewicz, J. (1971) 'The Law of Contradiction in Aristotle', *Review of Metaphysics* 24: 485–509. (An English translation of Łukasiewicz's critique of Aristotle, on the law of non-contradiction.)
* Meyer, R.K. and Mortensen, C. (1984) 'Inconsistent Models for Relevant Arithmetics', *Journal of Symbolic Logic* 49: 917–29. (On models of inconsistent arithmetics.)
* Priest, G. (1987) *In Contradiction*, The Hague: Kluwer. (A detailed defence of dialetheism.)
—— (1989) 'Dialectic and Dialetheic', *Science and Society* 53: 388– 415. (A discussion of Hegel, Marx and dialetheism.)
* —— (1991a) 'Intensional Paradoxes', *Notre Dame Journal of Formal Logic* 32: 193–211. (The construction of non-trivial theories containing both self-reference and epistemic operators.)
* —— (1991b) 'Minimally Inconsistent LP', *Studia Logica* 50: 321–31. (Consistency as a default assumption.)
—— (1984) 'Paraconsistent Logic', in D. Gabbay and F. Guenthner (eds) *Handbook of Philosophical*

Logic, vol. 2, Dordrecht: Reidel, 2nd edn, forthcoming. (The best reference work on paraconsistent logic currently available. It has a thorough overview of the technical aspects, with some philosophical comment and references to the literature.)

Priest, G., Routley, R. and Norman, J. (eds) (1989) *Paraconsistent Logic: Essays on the Inconsistent*, Munich: Philosophia. (This standard reference work includes many interesting papers, a bibliography up to the mid-1980s and editorial essays which go into the topics discussed here at much greater length.)

* Routley, R. (1977) 'Ultralogic as Universal?', *Relevance Logic Newsletter* 2: 50–90, 138–75; repr. as an appendix in *Exploring Meinong's Jungle, and Beyond*, Canberra: Research School of Social Sciences, Australian National University, 1980. (A statement of Routley's earlier views on paraconsistency.)

* Smiley, T.J. (1959) 'Entailment and Deducibility', *Proceedings of the Aristotelian Society* 59: 233–54. (The earliest filter paraconsistent logic.)

* Smiley, T.J. and Priest, G. (1993) 'Can Contradictions be True?', *Proceedings of the Aristotelian Society*, supplementary vol. 67: 17–54. (A debate concerning a number of objections to dialetheism.)

GRAHAM PRIEST

PARADIGMS *see* KUHN, THOMAS (§4)

PARADOXES, EPISTEMIC

The four primary epistemic paradoxes are the lottery, preface, knowability, and surprise examination paradoxes. The lottery paradox begins by imagining a fair lottery with a thousand tickets in it. Each ticket is so unlikely to win that we are justified in believing that it will lose. So we can infer that no ticket will win. Yet we know that some ticket will win. In the preface paradox, authors are justified in believing everything in their books. Some preface their book by claiming that, given human frailty, they are sure that errors remain. But then they justifiably believe both that everything in the book is true, and that something in it is false.

The knowability paradox results from accepting that some truths are not known, and that any truth is knowable. Since the first claim is a truth, it must be knowable. From these claims it follows that it is possible that there is some particular truth that is known to be true and known not to be true.

The final paradox concerns an announcement of a surprise test next week. A Friday test, since it can be predicted on Thursday evening, will not be a surprise yet, if the test cannot be on Friday, it cannot be on Thursday either. For if it has not been given by Wednesday night, and it cannot be a surprise on Friday, it will not be a surprise on Thursday. Similar reasoning rules out all other days of the week as well; hence, no surprise test can occur next week. On Wednesday, the teacher gives a test, and the students are taken completely by surprise.

1 **Lottery and preface paradoxes**
2 **Knowability paradox**
3 **The surprise examination paradox**

1 Lottery and preface paradoxes

The lottery paradox – first developed in Kyburg (1961) – and the preface paradox – originally formulated in Makinson (1965) – have a similar structure, although some (for example, Pollock (1986)) hold that they have different solutions. Each hinges on a conflict between a rule of acceptance, a condition on the transfer of warrant, and an axiom about warrant.

Rule of acceptance: There is some threshold short of certainty where acceptance of a claim is warranted or justified.

Transfer condition: A set of warranted claims is closed under deduction. That is, a set of warranted claims includes all the deductive consequences of that set.

Warrant axiom: It is not possible to be warranted in believing p and, for the same time and the same individual, be warranted in believing not p.

One standard approach is to find some fault with the transfer condition. Denials of the transfer condition sometimes result from explicit consideration of these paradoxes, sometimes from more general considerations within the theory of knowledge. For example, Kyburg addresses the lottery paradox explicitly and holds that it relies on the faulty conjunction principle, the principle according to which a person is warranted in believing a conjunction $p\&q$ if they are warranted in believing p and warranted in believing q. In this way, outright contradictions are thought to be avoidable in the set of warranted beliefs for a person at a time, while still allowing that the set can be inconsistent, that is, be such as to deductively imply a contradiction. Other epistemologists (for example, Nozick (1981)) develop general theories of knowledge to answer the Gettier problem in which the transfer condition is abandoned (see GETTIER PROBLEMS; DEDUCTIVE CLOSURE PRINCIPLE).

To accept such a solution may require abandoning a coherence theory of justification, for a commonly proposed minimal condition for coherence is logical consistency. If this approach is the best available for solving these paradoxes, the paradoxes will have taught us that coherence theories of justification must be abandoned (see KNOWLEDGE AND JUSTIFICATION, COHERENCE THEORY OF §3).

A point of importance concerning those who abandon the transfer condition explicitly to solve the paradoxes is that abandoning the conjunction principle alone will not do the trick: the paradoxes can be generated without employing any conjunction principle. In the lottery paradox, one can infer from individual premises that each particular ticket will lose, together with the knowledge of exactly how many tickets there are in the lottery, that no ticket will win. This claim can be deduced without using the conjunction principle, yet contradicts the knowledge that some ticket will win, thereby violating the warrant axiom according to which contradictory warranted claims are impossible.

Moreover, a fully satisfactory solution to these paradoxes that denies the deductive closure condition would need to offer an alternative principle in its place. For it is obvious that some of our beliefs are warranted precisely because we deduce them from other things we know.

A different approach is to question the rule of acceptance. There are two approaches that could be taken here. The first is simply to succumb to the paradox, granting that no acceptance is ever warranted when a claim is less than certain. This solution, however, seems unduly restrictive. For the small chance of illusion, hallucination and other types of misperception indicate that our ordinary perceptual beliefs are less than certain.

Alternatively, one may be suspicious of the idea of acceptance or belief, on Bayesian grounds. Bayesian epistemology arises within the context of an application of a subjective interpretation of probability theory to epistemological issues, and begins by noting that we believe some things more strongly than others (we believe that $2 + 2 = 4$, and that there is at present no life on Mars, but we are much more confident of the first than the second) (see PROBABILITY THEORY AND EPISTEMOLOGY). So, perhaps, the concept of belief in ordinary language is a coarse-grained way of talking about certain mental states that, strictly speaking, only come in degrees. Once such a viewpoint is accepted, two lines emerge as to how to treat the ordinary concept of belief. First, one might hold that there is no such thing as belief *simpliciter*, but rather there are only *degrees of belief*, and hence that the acceptance condition is ill-formed since it is formulated using the concept of belief *simpliciter*. Another alternative is to think that there is some way of understanding the ordinary concept of belief in terms of degrees of belief, using the lottery and preface paradoxes to show that such a definition cannot proceed in terms of some threshold of degree of belief above which the ordinary concept of belief applies (Kaplan 1981). The task for this kind of Bayesian view is to give an account of the ordinary concept of belief which, in conjunction with the transfer condition, does not violate the warrant axiom. In either case, the Bayesian approach gives some reason to be suspicious of the acceptance condition, and thereby suggests that the paradoxes might best be dealt with by abandoning or altering that condition.

2 Knowability paradox

The knowability paradox derives from work by Fitch (1963) on value concepts. The paradox depends on two claims:

(1) Everything is knowable – that is, for all propositions p, if p is true, then it is possible that it is known (by someone at some time) that p is true.

(2) Some things are not known – that is, there exists some proposition p, such that p is true, and it is not known that p is true.

We then substitute an instance of (2) – a claim of the form 'q is true and it is not known that q is true' – as the value for p in the first claim. Since we are committed to the truth of this instance of (2), the antecedent of (1) is true when this instance of (2) is the value for p in (1). We thus deduce that it is possible that a certain conjunction is known, namely that q is true and that it is not known that q is true. Since to know a conjunction is to know that each of its conjuncts is true, we can infer that it is possible that it is known that q is true and that it is known that it is not known that q is true. However, since knowledge implies truth, the latter piece of knowledge implies that it is not known that q is true. So we thereby deduce that it is possible that it is both known and not known that q is true.

The crucial features of this argument are the distribution principle (that is, that knowledge of a conjunction implies knowledge of each of the conjuncts) and the factive character of knowledge (that is, that knowing p implies p). The remainder of the argument relies on no principles of inference beyond those of first-order quantification theory with modal operators. So the paradox has much broader implications than merely those concerning knowledge. Fitch (1963), for example, used the paradox to argue that verificationism, the thesis that all truths are knowable, entails a very silly form of verificationism according to which all truths are known (see MEANING AND VERIFICATION §6). The broader implications of the paradox, almost completely unaddressed in the literature, concern versions of antirealism according to which truth is an epistemic notion (for example, truth is empirical confirmation in the long run, or verification by an ideal scientific community, or what is warrantedly assertible, and so on). Such antirealisms fall within the scope of the paradox, for these epistemic notions distribute over conjunction every bit as much as knowledge does, and their theory of truth makes these epistemic notions factives. So, the paradox can be formulated in terms of the claims that some truths are not justified or verified in this special antirealist way, and that all truths are epistemic in the favoured antirealist way.

The paradox could be resolved in a way that retains both claims (1) and (2) above if knowledge fails to distribute over conjunction. The paradox requires moving from knowledge of a conjunction to knowledge of each of the conjuncts, that is, from K(A&B) to K(A) & K(B). Some theories of knowledge deny such a principle (for example, Nozick (1981)); however, these denials are not supported by independent argument but are rather only implications of the general theory. Because of this feature, the denial can easily appear to be a defect of the theory rather than a virtue. In any case, denying the principle requires a further explanation of the difference between cases where such distribution is acceptable and those where it is not, for it is clear that one can come to know, for example, that the George owns a car by learning that George owns a car and a truck.

3 The surprise examination paradox

The surprise examination paradox first appeared in print in D.J. O'Connor (1948). It originated earlier when a Swedish mathematician, Lennart Ekbom, discussed at Ostermalms College a difficulty he had noticed with an announcement by the Swedish Broadcasting Company during the Second World War. The announcement said that a civil-defence exercise was to be held during a particular week. No one was to know in advance which particular day of the week the exercise would be conducted. Ekbom noticed that the unexpectedness of the exercise was problematic, which forms the core of the surprise examination paradox. This paradox appears in many guises and under many names, including among others the 'prediction' and 'hangman' paradoxes. All have essentially the same form as that represented by the surprise examination.

Sceptical approaches to this paradox deny that the announcement of a surprise examination warrants any beliefs about the future. Thus, Quine (1953) maintains that even a surprise examination announced only one day in advance would not be paradoxical, for such an examination would be a surprise as long as one could not know in advance that the examination would be given tomorrow.

Non-sceptical approaches to the paradox grant that one can know on the basis of the announcement that an examination will take place. For such approaches, an examination given the last day of the week would thereby not be a surprise, contrary to the Quinean approach above. Such approaches, in order to resolve the paradox, must find something wrong with the announcement itself (Shaw 1958; Kaplan and Montague 1960) or with the inferences by the students (Meltzer 1964), for the paradox ends by having an examination occur that surprises the students. A standard approach following the first line is to show that the teacher's statement is self-referentially incoherent, as in the Liar paradox where 'This statement is false' is incoherent. For example, the announcement might mean or imply 'There will be a surprise examination next week, and there being no surprise examination is deducible from this entire statement'.

Such approaches have been rejected for violating a coherence requirement on the announcement (Bosch 1972), according to which it is plainly obvious that the announcement is coherent and hence that any adequate resolution of the paradox must locate an error in the students' reasoning.

More recent discussion has focused on different varieties of the paradox, and whether formal approaches to the paradox suffice to resolve it. In spite of being originally castigated as 'rather frivolous' (O'Connor 1948), this paradox has attracted by far the most attention of the epistemic paradoxes (nearly one hundred articles have been written on it, compared to only a handful for the others). Moreover, hardly anything uncontroversial is to be found regarding the paradox, including how to interpret the announcement, how to resolve the paradox, whether there is one or several paradoxes involved, whether the paradox is simply a variant of other well-known paradoxes, and what conditions a proper resolution of the paradox must satisfy. Some would hold that it is the deepest of the paradoxes; in any case, the attention it has received shows that it is far from frivolous.

See also: EPISTEMIC LOGIC; SCEPTICISM

References and further reading

Binkley, R. (1968) 'The Surprise Examination in Modal Logic', *Journal of Philosophy* 65: 127–36. (Develops a sceptical approach to the paradox interpreted as involving modal operators.)

* Bosch, J. (1972) 'The Examination Paradox and Formal Prediction', *Logique et Analyse* 15: 505–25. (Argues that the paradox must find a flaw in the students' reasoning rather than in the announcement itself.)

Edgington, D. (1985) 'The paradox of Knowability', *Mind* 95: 557–68. (Attempts to develop a variation of verificationism immune to the knowability paradox.)

* Fitch, F. (1963) 'A Logical Analysis of Some Value Concepts', *The Journal of Symbolic Logic* 28 (1963): 135–42. (The original source for the central argument of the knowability paradox.)

* Kaplan, M. (1981) 'A Bayesian Theory of Acceptance', *The Journal of Philosophy* 78: 305–30. (Develops an account of acceptance in terms of degrees of belief that avoids the lottery paradox.)

* Kaplan, D. and Montague, R. (1960) 'A Paradox Regained', *Notre Dame Journal of Formal Logic* 1: 79–90. (Searches for a truly paradoxical reading of the announcement in the surprise examination paradox, and finds one that makes the announcement analogous to a 'liar' statement.)

* Kyburg, H. (1961) *'Conjunctivitis', Probability and the Logic of Rational Belief*, Middletown, CT: Wesleyan University Press. (The original source of the lottery paradox.)

* Makinson, D.C. (1965) 'The Paradox of the Preface', *Analysis* 25: 205–7. (The original source of the preface paradox.)

* Meltzer, B. (1964) 'The Third Possibility', *Mind* 73: 430–3. (Argues that the students' reasoning is at fault for assuming the law of excluded middle.)

* Nozick, R. (1981) *Philosophical Explanations*, Cambridge, MA: Harvard University Press. (A view on which knowledge is not closed under deduction, and knowledge does not distribute over conjunction.)

* O'Connor, D.J. (1948) 'Pragmatic Paradoxes', *Mind* 57: 358–9. (The original published version of the surprise examination paradox.)

* Pollock, J. (1986) 'The Paradox of the Preface', *Philosophy of Science* 53: 246–58. (Presents a solution to the preface paradox that arises out of artificial intelligence work on defeasible reasoning.)

* Quine, W.V. (1953) 'On a So-Called Paradox', *Mind* 62: 65–7. (Argues that the announcement could be coherent even if given only one day in advance, thereby proposing a sceptical solution to the surprise examination paradox.)

* Shaw, R. (1958) 'The Paradox of the Unexpected Examination', *Mind* 67: 382–4. (Claims that the solution to the paradox is found in distinguishing two readings of the announcement, only one of which can be used to deduce that no such examination can be given and which is self-referentially incoherent.)

Williamson, T. (1993) 'Verificationism and Non-Distributive Knowledge', *Australasian Journal of Philosophy* 71: 78–86. (Argues that knowledge must distribute over conjunction.)

JONATHAN L. KVANVIG

PARADOXES OF SET AND PROPERTY

Emerging around 1900, the paradoxes of set and property have greatly influenced logic and generated a vast literature. A distinction due to Ramsey in 1926 separates them into two categories: the logical paradoxes and the semantic paradoxes. The logical paradoxes use notions such as set or cardinal number, while the semantic paradoxes employ semantic concepts such as truth or definability. Both often involve self-reference.

The best known logical paradox is Russell's paradox concerning the set S of all sets x such that x is not a member of x. Russell's paradox asks: is S a member of itself? A moment's reflection shows that S is a member of itself if and only if S is not a member of itself – a contradiction.

Russell found this paradox by analysing the paradox of the largest cardinal. The set U of all sets has the largest cardinal number, since every set is a subset of U. But there is a cardinal number greater than that of any given set M, namely the cardinal of the power set, or set of all subsets, of M. Thus the cardinal of the power set of U is greater than that of U, a contradiction. (The paradox of the largest ordinal, discussed below, is similar in structure.)

Among the semantic paradoxes, the best known is the liar paradox, found by the ancient Greeks. A man says that he is lying. Is what he says true or false? Again, either conclusion leads to its opposite. Although this paradox was debated in medieval Europe, its modern interest stems from Russell, who placed it in the context of a whole series of paradoxes, including his own.

1 General comments

Etymologically, a paradox is something 'against' ('para') '[common] opinion' ('dox'). Nowadays it means a claim that seems absurd but has an argument to sustain it. A paradox appears 'paradoxical' when one is uncertain which premise to abandon.

The paradoxes about sets involve the principle of comprehension, which states that, for any concept, there is a class of all those objects for which the concept is true. (We use the terms 'class' and 'set' interchangeably, thus allowing each author discussed below to keep his own terminology.) Historically, the paradoxes about sets are related to the traditional antinomies of the infinite (as expressed, for example, by Galileo), to Zeno's paradoxes and to Kant's antinomies (see §4 below).

2 Burali-Forti: how not to discover a paradox

The paradox of the largest ordinal, often called Burali-Forti's paradox, is as follows. The set of all ordinals is well-ordered and so has an ordinal number, Ω, which is the largest ordinal. But for any ordinal α, there is a larger ordinal $\alpha + 1$. Hence $\Omega + 1$ is larger than Ω, a contradiction.

The early history of this paradox is a comedy of errors. In 1897 Cesare Burali-Forti *almost* discovered it. He failed to do so because he misunderstood Cantor's definition that a linearly ordered set is 'well-ordered' if (a) it contains a first element, (b) every element with a successor has an immediate successor and (c) every set of elements with a successor has an immediate successor. Accidentally omitting (c) from the definition, Burali-Forti introduced a new notion of 'perfectly ordered class' and gave for such classes an argument close to the paradox. But the conclusion he drew was that the order types of such classes are not linearly ordered. He did not think he had

discovered a paradox, since nothing that he wrote challenged previous results. Later that year, he realized that he had misconstrued Cantor's definition, but saw no contradiction between his work and Cantor's, since his concerned perfectly ordered classes, not ordinals. For five years, there was no discussion in print about Burali-Forti's article. (This has often been mistakenly denied, as when van Heijenoort stated that Burali-Forti's article 'immediately aroused the interest of the mathematical world' (1967: 104).)

In 1902, after Louis Couturat alerted him to Burali-Forti's work, Russell asserted (wrongly) in print that Burali-Forti claimed that the ordinals are not linearly ordered. Here was the beginning of a genuine paradox, for Russell applied Burali-Forti's argument to the ordinals. Russell's solution was to claim that the class of all ordinals has no ordinal since it is not well-ordered. (Later he rejected this solution.)

In 1903 Russell gave the first clear statement of the paradox of the largest ordinal in his book *The Principles of Mathematics*. Thus Russell was the key figure in its emergence. Alonzo Church erroneously claimed that 'it was through Burali-Forti's paper that there first came to general attention the threat to the foundations of mathematics that is constituted by the antinomies' (1971: 235). It was not Burali-Forti but Russell who first pointed out this threat in print.

3 Cantor: side-stepping the paradoxes

In 1883 CANTOR had introduced infinite ordinal numbers (see SET THEORY; CANTOR'S THEOREM). He distinguished sharply between finite ordinals, infinite ordinals and what he called the 'absolutely infinite', which included the set of all ordinals. In 1897, when Hilbert asked whether every set can be well-ordered, Cantor answered yes. Cantor's argument indirectly included the paradox of the largest ordinal and explicitly relied on the absolutely infinite. Yet he did not regard this as paradoxical, since he had previously made the relevant distinction between the infinite and the absolutely infinite. (E.H. Moore independently found this ordinal paradox and wrote about it to Cantor in an unpublished letter of 1898.)

Replying to Hilbert, Cantor made the notion of the absolutely infinite more precise. In print two years earlier, he had defined a set as a 'gathering together' of distinct objects. Now he called a set 'completed' if it is possible, without contradiction, to think of all its members as gathered together into a whole; any other set, such as that of all ordinals, was 'absolutely infinite'. In his Paris lecture of 1900, Hilbert affirmed that each of Cantor's infinite cardinal numbers is consistent, but denied that there exists a set of all cardinals. Nevertheless, Hilbert gave no indication that set theory was threatened.

In 1899 Cantor communicated to Dedekind the proof that every set can be well-ordered (see Cantor 1991). Once more, the paradox of the largest ordinal was involved when Cantor showed, as part of the proof, that the collection of all ordinals is absolutely infinite. Now Cantor distinguished between what he called consistent collections and inconsistent collections; only the former were sets. (A 'consistent' collection was what he had earlier called 'completed'.) Writing to Hilbert shortly afterwards, Cantor saw Dedekind's foundation as threatened, since Dedekind assumed that every well-defined collection was consistent. Cantor had pointed out to Dedekind that the collection of everything thinkable, which Dedekind had used to prove the existence of an infinite set, was inconsistent.

4   Russell: the paradoxes emerge

The paradoxes were not discussed in print until 1903, when they appeared in Russell's *Principles of Mathematics*. But Russell had found the paradox of the largest cardinal before he learned of Burali-Forti's article or of Cantor's unpublished thoughts on the subject. Russell's own paradox emerged in May 1901 from simplifying his paradox of the largest cardinal.

But the roots of Russell's paradox go much deeper. In 1896 he had rejected Cantor's infinite ordinals as 'impossible and self-contradictory'. During that period Russell proposed various antinomies in the spirit of Kant and Hegel, including the 'contradiction of relativity'. In 1898 he characterized mathematics as follows:

> One pervading contradiction occurs almost ... universally. This is the contradiction of a difference between two terms, without a difference in the conceptions applicable to them. I shall call it the contradiction of relativity. This, with addition and the manifold, appear to define the realm of Mathematics.
>
> (1898: 166)

By 1899, Russell was no longer an idealist but a Platonist. Although he ceased propounding antinomies in the style of Kant, he proposed one that originated with Leibniz. 'Mathematical ideas', he wrote in his 1899–1900 draft of the *Principles*, 'are almost all infected with one great contradiction. This is the contradiction of infinity. All antinomies, ... so far as they are valid at all, will be found reducible to the antinomy of infinite number' (1900: 70).

What was this antinomy of infinite number? In 1899 Russell gave it the following form, while distinguishing between

> (a) all numbers, (b) the greatest number, (c) the last number. Observe that (b) ... means the number applying to the greatest collection. All three are commonly called infinite number, and imply an antinomy, since their being can be both proved and disproved. (a) the most fundamental: There are many numbers, therefore there is a number of numbers. If this be N, $N + 1$ is also a number, therefore there is no number of numbers.
>
> (1899: 265)

Russell's antinomy of infinite number has the same formal structure as the paradox of the largest cardinal, which he formulated only in late 1900. That paradox can be stated in the following way: the class of all cardinal numbers has a cardinal number; but there is another class which has a larger cardinal number (by Cantor's theorem, the set of subsets of a set with cardinal N has a cardinal larger than N); hence there is no cardinal number of the class of all cardinal numbers. Likewise, the antinomy of infinite number has the same formal structure as his later paradox of the largest ordinal.

In November 1900 Russell redrafted part of the *Principles*. The following passage from that draft manuscript contains the earliest version of his paradox of the largest cardinal, which is closely connected with the antinomy of infinite number.

> There is a certain difficulty in regard to the number of numbers, or the number of individuals or of classes. Numbers, individuals, and classes, each form a perfectly definite class, and ... every class must have a number. Now the number of individuals must be the absolute maximum of numbers, since every other class is a proper part of this one.... But Cantor has given two proofs ... that there is no greatest number.

Soon Russell informed Couturat that Cantor's proofs were erroneous when applied to the class of all classes. Couturat doubted the existence of that class. But Russell vigorously defended it: 'If you grant that there is a contradiction in this concept, then the infinite always remains contradictory' (Moore and Garcia-diego 1981: 327).

In May 1901 Russell discovered his paradox by applying Cantor's proof that there is no greatest cardinal to the class of all classes. During that month he wrote the earliest surviving manuscript containing his paradox. It was not expressed in terms of classes but of predicates:

> We saw that some predicates can be predicated of

themselves. Consider now those... of which this is not the case.... But there is no predicate which attaches to all of them and to no other terms. For this predicate will either be predicable or not predicable of itself.

(1993: 195)

Either case implies the opposite, hence a contradiction. Thus there is no predicate predicable of all and only those predicates not predicable of themselves. Russell concluded that the principle of comprehension was false. A year later, he wrote to Frege about it. While Frege saw that the paradox for predicates did not arise in his system, he was devastated by the class form of Russell's paradox. Frege abandoned the principle of comprehension, which seemed to him the only possible logical foundation for arithmetic.

In 1903 Russell published Russell's paradox, together with the paradoxes of the largest cardinal and the largest ordinal, in the *Principles*. By that date, one or more of these three paradoxes was also known to Dedekind and Hilbert (thanks to Cantor), to Husserl (thanks to Zermelo; see §5 below), to Peano (thanks to Russell) and to E.H. Moore (independently, in a letter to Cantor), but none of them published such a result. Russell's and Frege's reactions to the paradoxes, which they treated as a major challenge, stand in striking contrast to the early reactions of the others mentioned.

Russell's book also generalized his paradox: if R is a relation, suppose there is some w such that, for any x, x has the relation R to w if and only if x does not have the relation R to x; substituting w for x leads to a contradiction; hence there is no such w (1903: 102). (Russell's paradox results from substituting membership for R.) Later Quine expressed Russell's generalization as follows: nothing can have a relation to all and only those things that do not have it to themselves.

At the end of this book Russell tentatively presented his earliest version of the theory of types as a solution to the paradoxes. Then 'x is a member of x' was meaningless, since if x is a member of u, then x and u had to belong to different types (see §7 below).

5 Hilbert, Bernstein and Grelling: German reaction to the paradoxes

Cantor was not alone in recognizing, before paradoxes were published, that there is no set of all sets. In his 1890 book on the algebra of logic, Ernst Schröder rejected such a universal set, arguing that it leads to a contradiction. Reviewing Schröder's book, Edmund Husserl rejected both Schröder's argument and his conclusion, since both resulted from a failure to distinguish between being a member of a set and being a subset. In 1902 Ernst Zermelo informed Husserl that Schröder was correct in his conclusion, although mistaken in his argument. Zermelo showed that a set which contains each of its subsets as a member is self-contradictory. He did so by stating Russell's paradox, which he had found by 1900, before Russell. Zermelo concluded that there is no set of all sets.

In 1903 Hilbert wrote to Frege that Zermelo had discovered Russell's paradox three years earlier, after Hilbert had informed Zermelo of other paradoxes which Hilbert had found a year before that. (In an 1899 letter to Frege, Hilbert had observed that there is no set of all cardinal numbers, but gave no hint that this was a threatening discovery.) Influenced by Frege rather than Russell, Hilbert first published on the paradoxes in 1905. He rejected the principle of comprehension, regarding it as the source of the paradoxes. These showed that traditional logic did not satisfy the demands of set theory; they would be solved only by an axiomatic development of logic. That year he devoted a long series of lectures to the problem without coming to a solution. Although one often reads that he did not concern himself with logic during the next decade, in fact he repeatedly lectured on the paradoxes. He only reached a solution in 1917 when he adopted Russell's theory of types (see §7 below).

In Germany the first published discussion about the paradox of the largest ordinal occurred in 1905. Felix Bernstein used this paradox while attempting to refute Zermelo's proof (1904) that every set can be well-ordered, arguing that there is indeed a set W of all ordinals (Moore 1982: chap. 2). But in France, Jacques Hadamard rejected Bernstein's argument: 'It is the very existence of the set W that generates a contradiction.... One has the right to form a set only with previously existing objects, and it is easily seen that the definition of W presupposes the opposite' (Hadamard in Moore and Garciadiego 1981: 339).

Several neo-Friesian philosophers commented on the paradoxes, including Alexander Rüstow (1910), in his book on the liar paradox, and Gerhard Hessenberg (1906), who found the notion of set unclear. Hessenberg argued that Russell's paradox was not dangerous for mathematicians, since they did not use a universal set, but that the paradox of the largest ordinal was dangerous.

In 1908 the neo-Friesian philosophers Kurt Grelling and Leonard Nelson discussed those paradoxes, including the predicate form of Russell's paradox. Grelling formulated a related paradox, later called Grelling's paradox: a word is called autological if it applies to itself, and otherwise is called heterological. Thus 'short' is autological and 'long' is heterological. Now 'heterological' is either autological or heterological. But either possibility leads to the opposite.

6 Berry, König and Richard: paradoxes of definability

The first paradoxes of definability emerged during 1904–5 from three distinct sources. Richard's paradox, due to Jules Richard, was the first to be published. Conceived as a response to Hadamard's comments on the paradox of the largest ordinal (see §5 above), but directed at the continuum of real numbers, Richard's paradox was the following: consider in decimal form all the real numbers that can be defined by a finite number of words. These numbers form a denumerable set E, whose members are $a_1, a_2, a_3, \ldots$. We define a real number N not in E by letting the nth decimal place of N be one more than the nth place of a_n unless the nth place is 8 or 9 (in which case the nth place of N is 1). Since N differs from the nth place of a_n for each n, then N is not in E. But N is defined by a finite number of words and so is in E, a contradiction.

In 1906 Henri Poincaré stressed the importance of Richard's paradox, and found in it a single explanation for all the paradoxes: objects defined by a vicious circle must be avoided. In Richard's paradox, there is a vicious circle since N is defined by using E but is itself in E. If one restricted E to those numbers defined without reference to E, there would be no contradiction. Yet Poincaré viewed the actual infinite, which he rejected, as being equally the source of the paradoxes.

Although it was the first definability paradox to be published, Richard's was not the first to be discovered. That honour goes to George Berry of Oxford University. In December 1904 Berry sent Russell the following paradox: consider the least ordinal not definable in a finite number of words; this ordinal is itself defined in a finite number of words, a contradiction.

This paradox, which Russell published in 1906 in response to Poincaré's comments on Richard's paradox, is known by the name he gave it: the paradox of the least indefinable ordinal. At that time Russell modified this paradox to give one that did not involve the actual infinite and that he called Berry's paradox, although Berry did not formulate it: the least integer not nameable in fewer than nineteen syllables. But this integer has just been named in eighteen syllables, a contradiction.

A fourth paradox of definability, called the Zermelo–König paradox, was found in 1905 by Julius König, who published it not as a paradox but to refute Zermelo's claim that the continuum of real numbers can be well-ordered. König observed that the set of real numbers which are definable in a finite number of words is denumerable. Since the continuum is not denumerable, there are real numbers x which cannot be defined in a finite number of words. If the continuum can be well-ordered, then there is a least such x, a contradiction. Hence the continuum cannot be well-ordered.

Once Richard's paradox was seen to be similar to König's result, it became clear that they concerned definability and had nothing to do with well-ordering the continuum.

7 Russell: solving the paradoxes by type theory

In 1905 Russell discussed three kinds of solutions to the paradoxes: zigzag theories, theories of limitation of size, and no-classes theories. In a zigzag theory, a property $\phi(x)$ determines the class of all x satisfying $\phi(x)$ when $\phi(x)$ is sufficiently simple; the difficulty with such a theory, Russell noted, was in specifying what made $\phi(x)$ sufficiently simple. A theory of limitation of size, such as that of Cantor or later Zermelo, would state that a property $\phi(x)$ determines the class of all x satisfying $\phi(x)$ if the class is 'limited' in size; the difficulty here was to specify how large an ordinal exists. Finally, a no-classes theory would dispense with assuming the existence of classes and operate directly with properties; although such a theory would preserve classical analysis and geometry, it was unclear how much set theory would survive.

Russell also gave a general form to all paradoxes about classes: suppose that there is a property ϕ and a function f such that if ϕ is satisfied by all members of the class u, then $f(u)$ satisfies ϕ and is not a member of u; the assumption that there is a class w of all x satisfying ϕ and that $f(w)$ exists leads to the contradiction that $f(w)$ has and does not have the property ϕ. In Russell's paradox, ϕ is 'x is not a member of x' and $f(u)$ is u; in the paradox of the largest ordinal, ϕ is 'x is an ordinal' and $f(u)$ is the ordinal number of u.

In the *Principles* (1903) Russell had tentatively presented his earliest version of the theory of types as a solution to the paradoxes. But during 1903 Russell became dissatisfied with his theory of types, and in 1904 adopted a zigzag theory. In 1905 and 1906 he preferred a no-classes theory. But the boundaries between his different theories were fuzzy. In 1906 he stressed that his no-classes theory contained types and was close to his 1902 theory of types.

The emergence of definability paradoxes coincided with a shift in Russell's views. Earlier, he had primarily investigated paradoxes involving classes. In 1906 he was increasingly occupied with the liar paradox. In that context he formulated the vicious circle principle, which any proposed solution to the paradoxes must satisfy: whatever involves a bound variable must not be a possible value of that variable. While accepting Poincaré's analysis that vicious circles caused the paradoxes, Russell vigorously rejected Poincaré's claim that the actual infinite caused them too.

In 1908 Russell published his *ramified* theory of types, which included much of the no-classes theory. Whereas in 1900 Russell had vigorously defended the class of all classes, his theory of types explicitly rejected it (as well as the notions of all propositions, all relations, all definitions and all ordinals). The heart of the theory was the distinction between orders and types, where orders concerned definitions, and the central assumption was his dubious axiom of reducibility, which was used to solve the semantic paradoxes.

Russell's theory was not well received at first, and was rejected by Poincaré in part because of the axiom of reducibility. The *simple* theory of types, which dispensed with this axiom and with definability, was due to Leon Chwistek and Ramsey in the 1920s (see THEORY OF TYPES). In the simple theory, there was no concern with the semantic paradoxes, which could not even be formulated in it.

8 Zermelo: solving the paradoxes by axiomatizing set theory

In 1908 ZERMELO published his axioms for set theory, without reformulating logic or mentioning the semantic paradoxes. To understand Zermelo's motivation, we must consider two articles he published that year in the same journal, finished within two weeks of each other, and which referred to each other. The second article contained his axiomatization, while the first defended his theorem that every set can be well-ordered. The first also gave a new proof of his theorem, based explicitly on axioms from his second article. The two articles form a single unity, revealing that his axiomatization was motivated as much by a concern to secure his theorem as by the need to solve the paradoxes (see Moore 1978).

The key to Zermelo's axiomatization was his axiom of separation, which restricted the principle of comprehension to subsets of any previously existing set. To preserve set theory, he included axioms which generated sets from previously existing sets, especially the power set and union axioms (see SET THEORY, DIFFERENT SYSTEMS OF).

But Zermelo's approach seemed arbitrary until he introduced the cumulative type hierarchy of sets in 1930. This hierarchy began with the empty set as the lowest level, and any level S was followed by a next level, the power set of S. The levels were indexed by ordinals, and when the index was a limit ordinal, the level was the union of all previous levels. The hierarchy of levels was cumulative since a member of any level belonged to all following levels, by contrast with Russell's types, which were disjoint.

Today Zermelo's hierarchy, as embodied in the Zermelo–Fraenkel axioms formulated in first-order logic, is generally accepted by mathematicians as the proper solution to the logical paradoxes. Among philosophers, the semantic paradoxes still lack such a generally accepted solution.

9 Brouwer, Weyl and Skolem: attacking set theory with paradoxes

Opponents of set theory repeatedly used the paradoxes as a weapon against it. This began with Poincaré in 1906 and continued with Brouwer in 1907 (see INTUITIONISM). Both saw intuition as central, the axiomatization of logic as suspect, and the natural numbers as fundamental. Both engaged in later attacks on axiomatization and set theory. A decade later Hermann WEYL continued the attack on analysis and set theory, using Grelling's and Richard's paradoxes.

In 1923 Thoralf Skolem used a different paradox to argue that set-theoretic concepts are relative, not absolute. Skolem's paradox states that there is a countable model for axiomatic set theory, although there exist uncountable sets. The solution distinguishes between levels. There exists some set M which is uncountable within the model, where there is no function mapping M onto the natural numbers; but outside the model there is such a function, and so, from outside, all the sets in the model are seen as countable.

10 Zermelo, von Neumann and Gödel: turning paradoxes into theorems

From a mathematical perspective, what is most striking is how paradoxes have repeatedly been turned into theorems. We consider four examples.

For Zermelo, Russell's paradox became the theorem of his axiomatic set theory that there is no set of all sets (1908).

For von NEUMANN, the paradox of the largest ordinal became the theorem of his axiomatic set theory (1925) that every set can be well-ordered. The proof was based on the axiom that every proper class (and no set) can be mapped one-to-one onto the class of all sets. Thus proper classes, which were 'too big' to be sets, were rehabilitated by no longer being considered to be contradictory, as they had been for Cantor and Zermelo. In effect, von Neumann made precise Cantor's distinction between consistent and inconsistent collections.

Gödel's incompleteness theorem, which states that any sufficiently rich formal system contains propositions that cannot be proved or refuted in the system (see GÖDEL'S THEOREMS), was obtained, in part, by applying Richard's paradox to the notion of provability (1931).

Finally, Tarski's theorem on the indefinability of truth (1933) had a close connection with the liar paradox. Tarski saw the universality of natural languages as the source of the semantic paradoxes, since this universality allows truth to be defined in such languages (see TARSKI'S DEFINITION OF TRUTH).

See also: LOGICAL AND MATHEMATICAL TERMS, GLOSSARY OF; SEMANTIC PARADOXES AND THEORIES OF TRUTH

References and further reading

Benthem, J.F. van (1978) 'Four Paradoxes', *Journal of Philosophical Logic* 7: 49–72. (Analyses the interrelations between the paradox of the largest cardinal, Russell's paradox, Curry's paradox about self-reference without negation, and Löb's version of the liar paradox.)

Beth, E.W. (1964) *The Foundations of Mathematics*, Amsterdam: North Holland. (Part 6 has an older, but still useful, summary of the paradoxes.)

* Cantor, G. (1991) *Briefe* (Letters), ed. H. Meschkowski and W. Nilson, Berlin: Springer. (Includes Cantor's 1899 letters to Dedekind and 1897–1900 letters to Hilbert relating to the paradoxes.)

* Church, A. (1971) 'Logic, History of, IV: Modern Logic', in *Encyclopaedia Britannica* vol. 14: 231–7. (A general discussion, including the paradoxes.)

Fraenkel, A.A., Bar-Hillel, Y. and Levy, A. (1973) *Foundations of Set Theory*, Amsterdam: North Holland. (A careful analysis of the various solutions of the logical paradoxes, including axiomatic set theory, the theory of types, and metamathematics.)

Garciadiego, A. (1985) 'The Emergence of the Non-Logical Paradoxes of the Theory of Sets, 1903–1908', *Historia Mathematica* 12: 337–51. (The early history of the semantic paradoxes.)

* Grelling, K. and Nelson, L. (1908) 'Bemerkungen zu den Paradoxieen von Russell und Burali-Forti' (Remarks on the Paradoxes of Russell and Burali-Forti), *Abhandlungen der Fries'schen Schule*, new series, 2 (3): 301–34. (Grelling's paradox.)

* Heijenoort, J. van (ed.) (1967) *From Frege to Gödel: A Source Book in Mathematical Logic, 1879–1931*, Cambridge, MA: Harvard University Press. (Translates relevant articles by Burali-Forti, Gödel, König, Richard, von Neumann and Zermelo. Includes Russell's 1902 letter announcing his paradox to Frege and mentioning that he had previously sent the paradox to Peano but received no reply.)

* Hessenberg, G. (1906) *Grundbegriffe der Mengenlehre* (Fundamental Concepts of Set Theory), Göttingen: Vandenhoeck & Ruprecht. (The earliest textbook of set theory.)

Hughes, P. and Brecht, G. (1975) *Vicious Circles and Infinity: A Panoply of Paradoxes*, Garden City, NY: Doubleday. (A popular anthology of many paradoxes.)

* Moore, G.H. (1978) 'The Origins of Zermelo's Axiomatization of Set Theory', *Journal of Philosophical Logic* 7: 307–29. (The role of the axiom of choice and the paradoxes in axiomatization.)

* —— (1982) *Zermelo's Axiom of Choice: Its Origins, Development, and Influence*, New York: Springer. (The second chapter indicates how the paradoxes were intertwined with Zermelo's proof that every set can be well-ordered.)

—— (1988) 'The Roots of Russell's Paradox', *Russell: The Journal of the Bertrand Russell Archives*, new series, 8: 146–56. (The connection between Russell's paradox and his antinomy of infinite number.)

* Moore, G.H. and Garciadiego, A. (1981) 'Burali-Forti's Paradox: A Reappraisal of its Origins', *Historia Mathematica* 8: 319–50. (Detailed historical treatment of this paradox.)

Peckhaus, V. (1990) *Hilbertprogramm und kritische Philosophie: das Göttinger Modell interdisziplinarer Zusammenheit zwischen Mathematik und Philosophie* (Hilbert's Programme and Critical Philosophy), Göttingen: Vandenhoeck & Ruprecht. (Includes reaction to the paradoxes by the neo-Friesian school.)

Rang, B. and Thomas, W. (1981) 'Zermelo's Discovery of the "Russell Paradox"', *Historia Mathematica* 8: 15–22. (How Zermelo found Russell's paradox, prior to Russell, and discussed it with Husserl.)

* Russell, B.A.W. (1898) 'An Analysis of Mathematical Reasoning, Being an Inquiry into the Subject Matter, the Fundamental Conceptions, and the Necessary Postulates of Mathematics', in *The Collected Papers of Bertrand Russell*, vol. 2, *Philosophical Papers 1896–99*, ed. N. Griffin and A.C. Lewis, London: Routledge, 1990, 155–242. (Includes the contradiction of relativity.)

—— (1899) 'The Fundamental Ideas and Axioms of

Mathematics', in *The Collected Papers of Bertrand Russell*, vol. 2, *Philosophical Papers 1896–99*, ed. N. Griffin and A.C. Lewis, London: Routledge, 1990, 261–305. (Includes the antinomy of infinite number.)

* —— (1903) *The Principles of Mathematics*, Cambridge: Cambridge University Press; 2nd edn, London: Allen & Unwin, 1937; repr. London: Routledge, 1992. (First publication of Russell's paradox, the paradox of the largest cardinal and the paradox of the largest ordinal.)

—— (1906) 'Les paradoxes de la logique', *Revue de métaphysique et de morale* 14: 627–50; trans. 'On "Insolubilia" and their Solution by Symbolic Logic', in *Essays in Analysis*, ed. D. Lackey, London: Allen & Unwin, 1973. (Analysis of the paradoxes, including the semantic ones.)

* —— (1993) *The Collected Papers of Bertrand Russell*, vol. 3, *Toward the 'Principles of Mathematics' 1900–02*, ed. G.H. Moore, London and New York: Routledge. (See 'The Principles of Mathematics (Draft of 1899–1900)' (3–180) on the antinomy of infinite number; and 'Part I of the *Principles*, Draft of 1901' (181–208) for the earliest extant version of Russell's paradox.)

* Rüstow, A. (1910) *Der Lügner* (The Liar), Leipzig: Teubner. (The liar paradox.)

* Zermelo, E. (1904) 'Beweis, daß jede Menge wohlgeordnet werden kann', *Mathematische Annalen* 59: 514–16; trans. S. Bauer-Mengelberg, 'Proof that Every Set can be Well-Ordered', in J. van Heijenoort (ed.) *From Frege to Gödel: A Source Book in Mathematical Logic, 1879–1931*, Cambridge, MA: Harvard University Press, 1967, 139–41. (Zermelo's proof of the well-ordering theorem.)

GREGORY H. MOORE

PARANORMAL PHENOMENA

The term 'paranormal phenomena' refers to the class of anomalous events studied within the field of parapsychology. Parapsychology's principal areas of investigation are extrasensory perception (ESP), psychokinesis (PK), and cases suggesting that personal consciousness survives the death of one's body. ESP phenomena are apparent instances of anomalous transfer of information. They divide into telepathy, clairvoyance and precognition. PK phenomena are forms, roughly speaking, of apparent mind-over-matter. Survival research deals primarily with cases of ostensible reincarnation and mediumship (or 'channelling').

The data of parapsychology raise a number of deep philosophical issues. Cases suggesting survival challenge materialist theories of the mind, and (according to some) provide good evidence for Cartesian dualism. ESP and PK challenge assumptions about the nature and temporal direction of causal relations, and also suggest the intimidating possibility that we have direct access to and influence on the thoughts and bodily states of others.

1 **Varieties of paranormal phenomena**
2 **The challenge to materialism**
3 **Problems of causality**

1 Varieties of paranormal phenomena

Paranormal phenomena, the phenomena investigated in parapsychology, are often called 'psi' phenomena. The term 'psi', an abbreviation for 'psychic', is considered by many to be more theoretically neutral than 'paranormal', 'psychic' or 'parapsychological': it seems to avoid issues about what should count as normal, and appears not to beg the question as to whether the phenomena under consideration fall naturally within the domain of psychology or whether they are explainable in physical terms.

Although the boundaries of parapsychology are not rigidly defined, it is clear that the field is concerned with anomalous phenomena falling into three principal areas of investigation. The first is the evidence for extrasensory perception (ESP). The study of ESP focuses on two sorts of phenomena in particular. 'Telepathy' is the influence of one person's mental states on those of another, other than by the usual or known means, and 'clairvoyance' is the similarly anomalous influence of a physical state of affairs on a person's mental states. For example, it would be a case of telepathy if a person's thoughts were directly caused by someone at a remote location thinking about something similar. It would be clairvoyance if a person's thoughts about a plane crash were directly caused by a distant plane crash. Although popular treatments of ESP suggest that telepathy and clairvoyance are types of anomalous knowledge (of remote states of affairs), philosophers and parapsychologists have long recognized that the evidence for ESP often suggests nothing more than anomalous types of causal interaction, without any sort of robust cognition deserving to be called 'knowledge'. For example, suppose that a burning house in another city caused one to have nothing more than – possibly incongruous – thoughts about fire or burning houses. If that occurs without the subject knowing that the house (or some house) is burning, it would be a manifestation of what C.D.

Broad (1962) called 'clairvoyant interaction' rather than 'clairvoyant cognition'.

The second area of parapsychological investigation is psychokinesis (PK), often called 'mind-over-matter'. The study of PK concerns the apparent ability to produce physical effects independently of familiar or recognized sorts of intermediate causal links. These effects include the ostensible movement of remote objects, materializations (the apparently instantaneous production of matter), and apports (the apparently instantaneous relocation of an object). In cases of so-called 'macro-PK', as in poltergeist disturbances and mediumistic phenomena such as table levitations, the effects are produced on objects visible to the naked eye. By contrast, present-day laboratory investigations of PK study what is called 'micro-PK', the production of statistically significant nonrandom behaviour in normally random microscopic processes such as radioactive decay and thermal noise.

Although cases of apparent precognition should be classified as types of telepathy or clairvoyance, they raise distinctive issues about causality. That is because they suggest that an event (such as a plane crash) can causally influence an *earlier* state of affairs (say, a precognitive dream of the plane crash) (see CAUSATION §7; TIME TRAVEL §1). Of course, that interpretation would be resisted by those who are opposed to backward causation. In that case, if apparent precognitions cannot be explained away as mere coincidences or in terms of normal or familiar processes, two options remain. First, one could explain precognition as a form of unconscious inference based on contemporaneous information acquired by ESP. For example, the precognizer might have learned through ESP about the *present* state of the plane or mental state(s) of the passengers or crew, and that information might have surfaced to conscious awareness in a dream or premonition. Second, one might interpret precognition as a type of PK, as telepathic influence, or both, by which the precognizer brings about the events apparently precognized.

The third area of parapsychological investigation deals with evidence suggesting the survival of personal consciousness following bodily death. Survival research focuses on cases of ostensible reincarnation and mental mediumship (that is, 'channelling' of information from an apparently deceased communicator). The evidence for survival consists primarily of anomalous knowledge of two sorts. First, some individuals demonstrate knowledge of facts or information which they presumably had no normal opportunity to acquire, and which concerns obscure or intimate details of some deceased person's life. Second, some individuals display skills or abilities –

for example, speaking a language or playing a musical instrument – which they had no normal opportunity to acquire or develop, but which were associated with a deceased person either apparently communicating through a medium or apparently reincarnating in (or possessing) the person displaying the anomalous skills or abilities.

2 The challenge to materialism

Popular writings (and some philosophical works) on parapsychology often assert that the existence of paranormal phenomena would be evidence against materialist theories of the mental, and in favour of dualism (see DUALISM; MATERIALISM IN THE PHILOSOPHY OF MIND). But that claim is somewhat contentious and in need of clarification.

It is important to note that there are at least two major forms of dualism. The first is Cartesian (or substance) dualism, according to which nature consists of two distinct kinds of stuff: mental (which is unextended and thinking) and physical (which is extended and unthinking). A somewhat weaker form of dualism is a level-of-description dualism, according to which nature may be described by means of either mentalistic or physicalistic vocabularies that are not entirely inter-translatable. For example, partisans of this weaker form of dualism might assert that nature consists of only physical stuff, but that the physical sciences have significant descriptive or explanatory limitations – say, in connection with the domain of mental states. (And that position can assume various forms. See, for example, ANOMALOUS MONISM; EPIPHENOMENALISM). Or, one could argue that nature is not inherently either mental or physical, but that different aspects of nature can be characterized relative to different vocabularies, or at different levels of description (see NEUTRAL MONISM). Proponents of these two sorts of position could be thought of as substance-monists but level-of-description dualists. They illustrate how one can hold that mental phenomena generally are not adequately described or explained in physical terms, without claiming that the mind is a distinct kind of substance or thing. One might even say that 'the mind' is merely a general term for the class of mental events (or a certain aspect of what persons and some other organisms do), just as 'the weather' is a general term for the class of meteorological events (or a certain aspect of planetary phenomena).

Now initially, at least, it would appear that the phenomena of ESP and PK present no more of a threat to materialist theories of the mental than do everyday cognitive phenomena such as memory and volition. In fact, one can (at least hope to) handle the former just as many (at least hope to) handle the latter. The strategies would be the same in both cases. For example, one might concede that we cannot now specify the physical mechanisms underlying psychological phenomena generally, but then argue that somewhere down the road, a more sophisticated physical science will accommodate all such currently intractable phenomena. Or, one might attempt to specify underlying mechanisms or processes for the mental phenomena in question (for example, as many have tried in the case of memory and as some parapsychologists have attempted for at least certain psi phenomena). There are also many others who contend that mental phenomena generally cannot be explained with respect to underlying physical mechanisms or processes. One would think that from their perspective, the existence of ESP and PK pose problems of explanation no deeper than those posed by normal mental processes. Psi phenomena would be inexplicable in physical terms, but not in virtue of any of their features that are distinctively paranormal. As far as the physical sciences are concerned, they would be as intractable as the phenomena of memory and volition, and for the same reasons. Hence, although the forms of ESP and PK might support a level-of-description dualism, it would not be in virtue of their paranormality.

Some might argue that out-of-body experiences (OBEs) would support a stronger, Cartesian dualism. For example, suppose that a subject reports on a state of affairs visible only from the spot allegedly visited while ostensibly out of the body (there is some experimental and anecdotal evidence for this). And suppose that at the time of the experience, physical perturbations are detected at the spot where one's perceptual perspective seems to be, even though there is no object visibly occupying that position (there is preliminary experimental evidence for this as well). Would that show that the mind is a thing that can leave and function physically apart from the body? In principle, one could argue instead that OBEs are nothing but imagery-rich clairvoyance, and that the physical disturbances can be explained as a form of accompanying PK.

Probably the only sort of parapsychological evidence that could clearly help support Cartesian dualism would be the evidence for survival. If it could be shown conclusively that consciousness survives the death and decomposition of the body, we might decide that this state of incorporeal existence can only be explained in terms of a mental substance. On the other hand, evidence of survival might equally be used to argue for a form of idealism, or a pluralistic worldview with an inventory of substance-kinds of at least three.

3 Problems of causality

Some might think that the phenomena of ESP and PK pose problems about causality because they would be examples of action-at-a-distance. But in fact, that issue worries few scientists and philosophers. Most would reject the claim that all causality is by physical contact (as in, billiard-ball causality), and some would, in any case, hold out hope for specifying the as yet undiscovered physical processes that allegedly fill in the apparent spatial causal gaps.

The most vexing problems about causality posed by the evidence concerns temporal direction. We have already noted that apparent precognition suggests that precognized events cause (earlier) precognitive experiences (although other explanatory options remain). In recent years, additional *prima facie* evidence for retro-causation has been provided by some provocative micro-PK experiments, designed and originally conducted by physicist Helmut Schmidt, and later replicated in other laboratories. These are experiments using pre-recorded random targets.

The general structure of such an experiment is as follows. Suppose that on day one a binary random number generator (that is, an electronic coin-flipper) is automatically activated (in the absence of anyone present) to record sequences of heads and tails onto audio cassettes, heads in the right channel and tails in the left. Suppose twenty such cassettes are recorded, and suppose also that a duplicate record of heads and tails is simultaneously produced on paper punch tape for the purpose of a permanent record. Then on day two, half of the cassettes are randomly selected to be test tapes, leaving the other cassettes designated as control tapes. At this point no one knows the contents of any of the tapes. On day three, the ten test tapes are played back to a subject who thinks he is taking a normal PK test with spontaneously generated targets. A computer counts the numbers of heads and tails (with a duplicate record once again being made on punch tape), and it turns out that the test tapes contain a statistically significant excess of heads over tails (and also that the effect size is similar to that demonstrated by subjects when all targets are being generated in real time). Then the control tapes are examined for the first time, and it turns out that they contain only chance levels of heads and tails (and also that both they and the test tapes match the punch-tape record for day one). But the only difference between the test and control tapes is that the test tapes were played for a subject making a PK effort. So it appears that the subject's effort on day three biased the random generator on day one to produce an excess of heads only for the test tapes (whose selection as test tapes, recall, was not decided until later). In some follow-up experiments, it appeared that repeated playback of the pre-recorded targets to the subject (without the subject's knowing this) seemed to increase the hit rate and improve overall PK scores. Schmidt called this an 'addition effect'.

Once again, other explanatory options remain, even if one rules out explanations in terms of normal or familiar processes. For example, some have suggested that the results of these experiments could be explained in terms of clockwise (and presumably unconscious) psychic functioning, apparently on the part of the experimenter. Although some regard this sort of apparent 'super-psi' as antecedently incredible in its scope and refinement, others argue that it is not substantially different from what has been documented anecdotally (especially in the best poltergeist cases and cases of physical mediumship).

What many find most unsettling about the evidence for ESP and PK is that if these phenomena occur, then presumably they do not occur only in the lab, or when parapsychologists set out to look for them. They might be occurring surreptitiously or inconspicuously much of the time in everyday contexts and even in normal scientific research. In fact, reliable evidence for ESP and PK seems to force us to entertain seriously a 'magical' worldview usually associated only with so-called primitive cultures, and according to which we have direct and intimate access to and influence on the thoughts and bodily states of others.

See also: EXPERIMENT; PARAPSYCHOLOGY; REINCARNATION

References and further reading

Almeder, R. (1992) *Death and Personal Survival: The Evidence for Life After Death*, Lanham, MD: Rowman & Littlefield. (A useful presentation and sympathetic evaluation of the evidence for postmortem survival. Its critiques of sceptical dismissals of the evidence are especially good.)

Braude, S.E. (1979) *ESP and Psychokinesis: A Philosophical Examination*, Philadelphia, PA: Temple University Press. (Gives an overview of some of the best experimental evidence in parapsychology and considers its philosophical implications. Also examines related theoretical issues in the philosophy of mind, and contains additional chapters on synchronicity and the meaning of 'paranormal'.)

—— (1986) *The Limits of Influence: Psychokinesis and the Philosophy of Science*, New York & London: Routledge & Kegan Paul; revised edn, Lanham, MD: University Press of America, 1997. (A presentation, defence and philosophical assessment of the evidence for large-scale psychokinesis (PK), focusing on nineteenth- and twentieth-century cases of physical mediumship. Also contains detailed examinations of apparitions and precognition, including a discussion of retro-causation.)

—— (1987) 'Psi and Our Picture of the World', *Inquiry* 30: 277–94. (An overview of the implications of the evidence of parapsychology for prevailing scientific theories, the debate between dualists and monists, and traditional views of causality.)

—— (1992) 'Survival or Super-Psi?' and 'Reply to Stevenson', *Journal of Scientific Exploration* 6: 127–44, 151–6. (An examination of the difficulties in distinguishing evidence of postmortem survival from evidence of psychic functioning among the living. Argues that the latter hypothesis is more interesting, subtle and plausible than its critics usually suppose.)

* Broad, C.D. (1962) *Lectures on Psychical Research*, London: Routledge & Kegan Paul. (A classic, careful, comprehensive and philosophically penetrating examination of both experimental and anecdotal evidence, marred only by extended discussion of some now-discredited card-guessing tests. Excellent discussions of apparitions, mediumship and out-of-body experiences.)

Penelhum, T. (1970) *Survival and Disembodied Existence*, London: Routledge & Kegan Paul. (A study of some difficulties in making sense of the notion of bodiless existence and personal identity.)

Scriven, M. (1976) 'Explanations of the Supernatural', in S.C. Thakur (ed.) *Philosophy and Psychical Research*, New York: Humanities, 181–94. (Useful discussion of the constantly shifting and slippery meaning of the terms 'supernatural' and 'materialism', as well as the obstacles to rejecting psi phenomena in virtue of their *prima facie* incompatibility with received science.)

STEPHEN E. BRAUDE

PARAPSYCHOLOGY

Tales of dreams that come true, 'mind over matter' and other such oddities are both familiar and old. Parapsychology investigates such things, attempting to use scientific and, especially, experimental methods to investigate whether and in what circumstances humans can glean information without using ordinary perceptual means (that is, by extrasensory perception or ESP) or can alter the physical environment simply by willing it (that is, by psychokinesis). Such phenomena, if they exist, are often grouped under the heading psi(-phenomena).

It is sometimes claimed that parapsychology presents a challenge to physicalism. However, ostensible psi-phenomena are known through their physical effects and are studied within parapsychology by ordinary scientific methods. In fact, models intended to explain psi-phenomena by known physical processes have been seriously discussed within parapsychology. In any case, parapsychology alone could not show that psi-phenomena have no physical explanation; that is a judgment for physics itself. More important, physicalism is a very broad doctrine that should not simply be equated with the requirement that everything be explained within physics. It is very unclear what we would gain by denying that psi-phenomena are physical.

1 Origins and method
2 Parapsychology and physicalism
3 Conclusion

1 Origins and method

Parapsychology has its roots in nineteenth-century investigations of spiritualism. Although parapsychologists still occasionally study spontaneous phenomena such as hauntings and individual so-called 'gifted' subjects who appear to have strong psychic abilities, the dominant tone of the field in the twentieth century was set by the American researcher Joseph B. Rhine, who opened his laboratory at Duke University in 1930. Rhine is responsible for such terms as 'extrasensory perception' (ESP) and 'psychokinesis'. He believed that the best way to investigate parapsychological phenomena was by the rigorous use of statistical methods, and he typically worked with ordinary subjects in experiments that involved simple choices among clearly distinguishable targets (for example, cards with a limited number of distinct symbols). He also emphasized questions about the psychological correlates of psychic ability and the factors that might inhibit or facilitate it. Rhine's work became the model for most parapsychological research thereafter.

The flavour of parapsychological research can be gleaned from an important example: the so-called *ganzfeld* (from the German for 'whole field') studies. In these experiments, the subject is put into a state of relaxation and mild sensory deprivation – a state that is hypothesized to be conducive to psi. Then an experimenter in a separate room concentrates on one of four randomly selected pictures. Finally, a second experimenter, who does not know which picture was viewed, shows copies of all four to the subject, who is

asked to choose the one he thinks was the target. By chance, subjects should be right 25% of the time. The actual success rate is closer to 33%. This is a large effect by social science standards. If you could find a casino with these sorts of odds, you would win $130 for every $100 you bet. Across the many *ganzfeld* studies that have been performed up to the writing of this entry, it has been estimated that the observed effect would occur by chance roughly one time in a billion.

2 Parapsychology and physicalism

Clearly there are different sorts of questions one could ask about such experiments. Some have to do with the design of the experiment. Particularly important will be questions about procedures for preventing fraud and, more generally, what we might term 'sensory leakage' – cues detectable by the familiar five senses. Other questions have to do with statistical analysis, replication and randomization. Questions about randomization are particularly subtle and are the subject of some ongoing debate, but even some of parapsychology's harsher critics agree that there is no simple way to dismiss the *ganzfeld* experiments. However, beyond these methodological issues are questions about just how results of this sort ought to be interpreted assuming they stand up to scrutiny. In particular, do they undermine physicalism?

Rhine (1954), writing before the *ganzfeld* experiments, believed that the answer is yes. On the basis of his own work, he believed that psi-phenomena are not subject to shielding, do not diminish with distance and, in fact, cannot be explained by appeal to normal physical mechanisms. He speculated that, instead, they involve some sort of non-physical 'psi energy' that displays its effects by being converted into ordinary physical energy. Rhine welcomed this conclusion because he saw physicalism and what he took to be its attendant determinism as a threat to freedom and responsibility (see DETERMINISM AND INDETERMINISM; DUALISM; MATERIALISM IN THE PHILOSOPHY OF MIND).

It is hard to see how Rhine's hypothesis of 'psi energy' could address his own concerns. It may be that freedom and responsibility require deliberation and other intentional phenomena to have a certain autonomy from the non-psychological (see FREE WILL). This might argue against reductionism or eliminativism. But the connection between this claim and the existence of some supposedly non-physical means of propagating information or influence – 'psi energy' – is obscure at best. How would the ability to move things or know things with the help of 'psi energy' add to one's moral freedom? Indeed, what would it have to do with deliberation and choice at all? Moreover, it is not at all clear how Rhine's hypothesis would render psi non-physical. Positing a new form of energy as part of the explanation for manifestly physical effects would seem to be a proposal for an addendum to physics itself.

In fact, nothing in the results of parapsychology provides clear reasons to think that parapsychological phenomena, if genuine, violate normal physical principles. This is not least because physicists have not given any sustained attention to the question of how such things might be explained. Here it is worth remembering that the history of science provides numerous examples of phenomena (magnetism, for instance) that once were thought beyond the pale of physics but which are now understood as unquestionably physical. But there is a more general point: the mere fact that we do not have an explanation of a phenomenon in terms of fundamental physics has never really been taken as a reason to count the phenomenon as non-physical. For example, thermodynamic phenomena counted as physical before statistical mechanics attempted to provide micro-accounts of such things as temperature and entropy (see THERMODYNAMICS). Physics may never have much to say about economics, but by itself this hardly shows that physicalism is false, since physicalism is a much broader doctrine than reductionism and kindred notions (see REDUCTION, PROBLEMS OF; REDUCTIONISM IN THE PHILOSOPHY OF MIND).

It might be thought that such examples fail to do justice to the worry. Whatever the details of a microscopic account of thermodynamic phenomena, the universality of the principles of thermodynamics makes it virtually impossible to imagine what could be meant by classing them as non-physical. And while economics may group things in ways that that make reduction to physics implausible (try to give a physical definition of 'money') nothing in economics suggests any obvious conflict with physics. Psi-phenomena seem very different. They seem anomalous, and anomalous in a particular way: they look essentially like action at a distance – information or influence travels we know not how from one point to another. That is the sort of thing for which we expect a mechanism or medium and which we also expect to satisfy a variety of physical principles such as conservation laws.

Suppose we found a replicable psi-phenomenon for which no mechanism was forthcoming and which persistently refused to mesh smoothly with the laws of physics. What then?

Our sense that such things as ESP and psychokinesis ought to involve a mechanism or medium is presumably part of a larger sense that they ought to be explainable, and that a satisfactory explanation would posit some process connecting the distant events. As it turns out, however, nature is not innocent of apparently unmediated connections. Within quantum mechanics there are strong correlations among distant events that seem to defy explanation by appeal to any reasonable mechanism (see BELL'S THEOREM). While it must be stressed that these phenomena do not permit the sending of signals, they should at least caution us not to put too much stock in our intuition that all connections must be explained by appeal to a mediating process. It is debatable whether these quantum mechanical connections are *explained* in quantum theory – or anywhere else – at all. Still, there is a difference. Quantum mechanics is a fundamental theory and at that level we might expect explanation or perhaps even intuitive intelligibility to come to an end. Parapsychology deals with the macroscopic level, and that is not where we expect to bump up against the limits of explanation.

It is not clear how much weight to give such intuitions about the macroscopic. Once again, quantum mechanics is instructive. Given the fundamental laws of quantum mechanics, it is deeply puzzling that measurements, which are macroscopic events, actually have results at all (see QUANTUM MEASUREMENT PROBLEM). Needless to say, attempts to solve the problem, whether by conceptual innovation or physical speculation, continue, but there is no guarantee that they will produce satisfactory results.

We might characterize physicalism in terms of some idealized final physics. If brute exceptions to the principles of that ideal physics had to be carved out to accommodate parapsychological phenomena, then it might be held that physicalism, construed as a doctrine about the hegemony of physics, was false. This would mean that principles and laws of physics would lack the sort of universality sometimes claimed for them, and it would mean that natural phenomena are less unified than we might have hoped.

However, just such things have already been argued by some philosophers of science on grounds quite independent of parapsychology. It has been argued that physics has no special rule in enumerating the kinds of things there are nor in generating the laws they obey (see Dupre 1993). It has been argued that the laws of physics themselves do not fit together in any smooth way. And it has been argued that the very idea of physical laws as features of nature rather than just features of the models we use is deeply suspect (see LAWS, NATURAL).

We have been asking whether parapsychological phenomena might conflict with physicalism. The answer is a resounding 'Perhaps'. But suppose, hypothetically, that the answer is 'Yes'. What then? Are such doctrines as Cartesian dualism (see DUAL-ISM) forced upon us? Must we regard parapsychological phenomena as supernatural? Have we discovered the limits of science itself?

The only sensible answer to each of these questions is 'No!' Nature may well be highly variegated, but positing a non-spatial mental substance is as uninformative in light of parapsychology as it is without it. Parapsychological phenomena are peculiar if genuine, but their manifestations are changes in the physical make-up or the belief states of natural things, including such things as ourselves. As it stands, the very existence of psi remains controversial and so any claims about psi, as well as any claims based on it, remain answerable to checking by means that rely ultimately on the familiar five senses. If, in some improbable future, psychic phenomena became so common and so robust that we could rely on them as we rely on more familiar means of gaining knowledge or altering the landscape, this would mean that there are more ways of coming to know and change the world than we had previously thought, but it is hard to see how this would demonstrate any limitations on science; if anything, it would augment its resources.

3 Conclusion

A healthy scepticism about parapsychological claims is perfectly reasonable. Psi-phenomena would, indeed, violate various common-sense expectations and parapsychology is a field in which fraud and wishful thinking have been special problems. Furthermore, there is something odd about a field whose subject matter is largely defined negatively. At the same time, the best of parapsychological research applies the same standards that hold in the rest of science. Psi-phenomena *could* precipitate a scientific revolution, but so might any number of other things. As things stand, the results are modest and the implications unclear. For now the appropriate response would seem to be to wait and see.

See also: PARANORMAL PHENOMENA

References and further reading

Bem, D.J. and Honorton, C. (1984) 'Does Psi Exist? Replicable Evidence for an Anomalous Process of Information Transfer', *Psychological Bulletin* 115: 4–19. (Honorton developed the ganzfeld technique. Following Bem and Honorton's article is a critique by psychologist Ray Hyman and a reply by Bem.)

Broughton, R.S. (1991) *Parapsychology: The Con-troversial Science*, New York: Ballentine Books. (An introduction to parapsychology intended for a general audience.)

Cartwright, N. (1983) *How the Laws of Physics Lie*, Oxford: Oxford University Press. (Cartwright argues that laws in physics are neither as important for explanation nor as unified as has often been argued.)

* Dupre, J. (1993) *The Disorder of Things: Metaphysical Foundations of the Disunity of Science*, Cambridge, MA: Harvard University Press. (A defence of what the author refers to as 'ontological pluralism', including an extensive critique of reductionism and, more generally, of the view that physics has a special primacy among the sciences.)

Edge, H.L., Morris, R.L., Palmer, J. and Rush, J.H. (1986) *Foundations of Parapsycholgy: Exploring the Boundaries of Human Capability*, Boston, MA, London and Henley: Routledge & Kegan Paul. (The authors are all active researchers in parapsychology. The essays deal with historical, methodological and experimental issues.)

Flew, A. (ed.) (1987) *Readings in the Philosophical Problems of Parapsychology*, Buffalo, NY: Prometheus Books. (A useful collection of classic and recent articles on parapsychology. The essay by Irving Thalberg, 'Are Paranormal Events Non-Physical?', is a useful discussion of parapsychology and physicalism.)

Kurtz, P. (ed.) (1985) *A Skeptic's Handbook of Parapsychology*, Buffalo, NY: Prometheus Books. (As the title suggests, a collection of articles mostly sceptical in tone, though with a few essays by partisans of psi.)

* Rhine, J.B. (1954) 'The Science of Non-Physical Nature', *Journal of Philosophy* 51: 801–10. (Rhine offers his reasons for believing that psi-phenomena cannot be understood within the framework of physics. Excerpts from this essay are reprinted in Flew (1984).)

Teller, P. (1984) 'A Poor Man's Guide to Supervenience and Determination', *The Southern Journal of Philosophy*, Spindell conference supplement 22: 137–62. (A review of the literature on supervenience, which is an important concept in certain versions of non-reductive materialism. Teller goes on to argue that materialism is such a general thesis that it is virtually a necessary truth.)

ALLEN STAIRS

PARETO PRINCIPLE

A social state is said to be Pareto-efficient when there is no feasible alternative to it in which at least one individual is better off while no individual is worse off. The Pareto principle tells us to move from Pareto-inefficient to Pareto-efficient states. Suppose a large basket of fruit is shared among a group in some way or another – one apple, two peaches, a dozen cherries each, for instance. If the fruit can be exchanged so that at least some people get more enjoyment from what they have, and no one gets less, the Pareto principle instructs us to do so; indeed, it instructs us to carry on exchanging until no more improvements of this kind are possible.

The Pareto principle gets its name from the Italian economist Vilfredo Pareto (1848–1923), who showed that when a competitive market reaches an equilibrium, the outcome is Pareto-efficient, or a 'Pareto-optimum' (Pareto 1906). Pareto believed that valid interpersonal comparisons of utility are impossible, and so rejected the utilitarian view that a society is efficient when it maximizes aggregate utility. But each person could judge whether they were better off in state S1 or state S2, and so Pareto concluded that if everyone preferred S2 social welfare must be greater in S2, whereas if some preferred S1 and some S2, no such judgment could be made.

The Pareto principle has a weaker and a stronger form. The weaker holds that we should choose S2 in preference to S1 when everybody judges that they are better off in S2; the stronger holds that we should choose S2 when nobody judges that S1 is better, and at least one person judges that S2 is better. The weaker version requires that everyone gain if the change is to be a Pareto improvement; the stronger version requires only that some should gain and nobody lose.

For many economists the Pareto principle seems to be self-evidently rational. How can we settle for a state of affairs when there is a feasible alternative that improves the position of some but worsens that of no one? The problem is rather that, seen as a criterion of efficiency, the principle is still too weak. In the real world there are likely to be many Pareto-efficient states to choose between, but here the principle gives us no guidance. If in moving from S1 to S2 many badly-off people gain but a few well-off people lose, we might think there is a gain in overall efficiency. But we cannot make such a judgment using the original Pareto principle alone (see ECONOMICS AND ETHICS §3).

Philosophers have been less certain that the principle is a requirement of practical rationality.

Two kinds of questions have been raised. Suppose that S1 represents a state of affairs that is distributively just by some criterion – for instance, each person enjoys an equal level of welfare. If in S2 some people are better off than in S1 but the criterion of justice is violated – welfare levels are no longer equal – it may not be irrational to choose Pareto-inefficient S1 over Pareto-efficient S2.

Second, Sen (1982) has argued that the Pareto principle may conflict with the liberal principle that each person should decide matters falling in their private domain, such as which position they sleep in. If people have strong 'meddlesome preferences' – that is, they are deeply concerned about what goes on in other people's personal domains – there will be cases in which the Pareto principle selects a social state that the liberal principle would exclude. This issue has now generated a substantial body of literature suggesting different ways of avoiding Sen's paradox.

References and further reading

Buchanan, A. (1985) *Ethics, Efficiency, and the Market*, Oxford: Clarendon Press, ch. 1. (A critical defence of the Paretian notion of efficiency.)

Cohen, G.A. (1995) 'The Pareto Argument for Inequality', *Social Philosophy and Policy* 12 (1): 160–85. (Attacks Rawls' use of the Pareto principle to justify economic inequalities.)

Little, I.M.D. (1957) *A Critique of Welfare Economics*, Oxford: Oxford University Press, 2nd edn, chaps 6–7. (A critical review of welfare economists' attempts to extend the Pareto principle.)

* Pareto, V. (1906) *Manual of Political Economy*, trans. A.S. Schwier, London: Macmillan, 1972. (The original source of the Pareto principle.)

Rawls, J. (1971) *A Theory of Justice*, Cambridge, MA: Harvard University Press, §§12–13. (Rawls invokes the Paretian criterion of efficiency, and argues that the difference principle gives us a way of choosing between the many possible Pareto-efficient social distributions on the grounds of justice.)

* Sen. A. (1982) *Choice, Welfare and Measurement*, Oxford: Blackwell, chaps 13–14. ('The Impossibility of a Paretian Liberal' contains the original statement of Sen's argument. 'Liberty, Unanimity and Rights' develops it through a review of the literature provoked by the first article.)

DAVID MILLER

PARMENIDES (early to mid 5th century BC)

Parmenides of Elea, a revolutionary and enigmatic Greek philosophical poet, was the earliest defender of Eleatic metaphysics. He argued for the essential homogeneity and changelessness of being, rejecting as spurious the world's apparent variation over space and time. His one poem, whose first half largely survives, opens with the allegory of an intellectual journey by which Parmenides has succeeded in standing back from the empirical world. He learns, from the mouth of an unnamed goddess, a dramatically new perspective on being. The goddess's disquisition, which fills the remainder of the poem, is divided into two parts; the Way of Truth and the Way of Seeming.

The Way of Truth is the earliest known passage of sustained argument in Western philosophy. First a purportedly exhaustive choice is offered between two 'paths' – that of being, and that of not-being. Next the not-being path is closed off: the predicate expression '... is not' could never be supplied with a subject, since only that-which-is can be spoken of and thought of. Nor, on pain of self-contradiction, can a third path be entertained, one which would conflate being with not-being – despite the fact that just such a path is implicit in the ordinary human acceptance of an empirical world bearing a variety of shifting predicates. All references, open or covert, to not-being must be outlawed. Only '... is' (or perhaps '... is...') can be coherently said of anything.

The next move is to seek the characteristics of that-which-is. The total exclusion of not-being leaves us with something radically unlike the empirical world. It must lack generation, destruction, change, distinct parts, movement and an asymmetric shape, all of which would require some not-being to occur. That-which-is must, in short, be a changeless and undifferentiated sphere.

In the second part of the poem the goddess offers a cosmology – a physical explanation of the very world which the first half of the poem has banished as incoherent. This is based on a pair of ultimate principles or elements, the one light and fiery, the other heavy and dark. It is presented as conveying the 'opinions of mortals'. It is deceitful, but the goddess nevertheless recommends learning it, 'so that no opinion of mortals may outstrip you'.

The motive for the radical split between the two halves of the poem has been much debated in modern times. In antiquity the Way of Truth was taken by some as a challenge to the notion of change, which physics must answer, by others as the statement of a profound metaphysical truth, while the Way of Seeming was widely treated as in some sense Parmenides' own bona fide physical system.

1 Life and work

Parmenides lived and taught and, if the ancient tradition is reliable, framed legislation at Elea (modern Velia), a Greek city in southern Italy. His most eminent pupil was ZENO OF ELEA, author of the celebrated motion paradoxes. Plato in his *Parmenides* describes a visit by Parmenides and Zeno to Athens, usually thought to be around 450 BC, when he says Parmenides was aged about 65, Zeno about 40. He implies that Parmenides' work had been published a good deal earlier, since Zeno had defended it against its critics in his youth, perhaps around 470 BC. It could in fact have appeared as early as the 490s. In any case, the visit Plato describes is probably fictional, and the chronological details are open to suspicion (see SOCRATIC DIALOGUES §1). The only completely safe chronological assertion is that Parmenides wrote before Zeno, Anaxagoras and Empedocles.

About 150 lines survive from his poem, which was his sole published work. Most of these (around 107) belong to its first part, the proem plus the Way of Truth, which appears largely complete. The second part, the Way of Seeming, must originally have been at least as long. The numbered ordering of the fragments, established by editors, seems mainly reliable, but the original position of a few (especially fragments 3 and 5) remains controversial.

The language, which constantly exploits echoes of Homeric epic, is opaque and densely metaphorical. It will be impossible in what follows to do justice to many important questions of nuance. A further complication is that Parmenides is compelled to borrow for his arguments the very language of negation, change and differentiation which his conclusions will ultimately outlaw.

The Way of Truth is methodically argued. Although the opening describes Parmenides' journey to a goddess who undertakes his enlightenment, this symbolizes less a religious revelation or appeal to mere authority than his own hard-won arrival at a god's-eye view, his intellectual odyssey of distancing himself from the familiar temporal world: he travels to the gates at which the paths of night and day meet, a mythically inspired vantage point which erases the alternation of night and day, together, we may suppose, with all the associated temporal and spatial distinctions. When the goddess proceeds to enlighten him, it is with a coordinated set of arguments. Her most favoured form of argument starts from the conclusion: *c*, because *b*, because *a*.

2   The three paths

An initial choice offered is between two paths. Later a third path, although not even represented as a formal possibility, has to be mentioned and blocked off because despite its incoherence it is the route which ordinary people actually try to take.

The first two paths are: '(It) is' (*esti*) and '(It) is not' (*ouk esti*). It turns out that you can only coherently say the former, and this in the later moves will radically restrict what can be truly said of that-which-is. But what is the status of this 'is'? In particular, does it have a subject and/or a predicate?

Unlike English 'is', its Greek equivalent *esti* can constitute a grammatically complete sentence, '(It) is', even when as here no explicit subject is supplied. At this initial stage, when we are still finding out what restrictions must be imposed on the character of whatever 'is', the failure to specify any subject term, even 'it' or 'something', looks deliberate. What, if anything, can stand as the subject of 'is' must not be in any way prejudged.

The Greek use of 'be' does not fall neatly into a complete or existential use ('*x* is') and an incomplete or copulative one ('*x* is *y*'). To be is, primarily, to be *something*, but this may be specified ('*x* is red', '*x* is a book') or left unspecified ('*x* is'). To a Greek ear these are not distinct senses; they also tend to shade into the so-called 'veridical' use, where 'being' means 'being the case', since the 'being' in question is viewed as once again copulative, *x*'s being *y*. It has long been disputed whether Parmenides' use of 'be' is existential, copulative, veridical or one 'fused' out of these. While some kind of fused usage looks likeliest, no confusion need arise from thinking of his poem as primarily an inquiry into what there is. At least, his description of that-which-is as ungenerated, continuous, immobile etc. suggests an object rather than (as on a narrowly veridical reading) a truth – indeed, an object which directly and successfully competes with the phenomenal world for the status of what-there-is.

There are few uncontroversial points of interpretation, but the opening argument can be paraphrased, with explanatory glosses, along the following lines.

There are two conceivable paths [that is, ways forward]: *to say '...is', and to say '...is not'* [these are actually presented as '...necessarily is' and '...necessarily is not'; contingency is assumed to involve an illicit conflation of being with not-being, and is therefore held over as a third path, see below]. *But saying '...is not' is not a way forward that you could ever actually explore* [that is, '...is not' is a predicate which can never be successfully supplied with a subject, by either (a) thinking of the subject or (b) naming it]. *This is because (a) you could not know that-which-is-not* [that is, you could not know what it is, since that-which-is-not is nothing; therefore you could not pick it out in thought as a subject], *(b) nor could you speak of it* [the nonexistent is not available for referring to]. *Besides, anything that you can speak of and think of* [that is, pick out as a subject term] *must be* [and is therefore automatically debarred from serving as subject of '...is not']. *This is because it is, at least, possible for it to be* [being conceivable, it at least *could* exist], *whereas for a 'nothing' to be is impossible* [there could never exist a non-existent thing]. *In short, '...is not' is a path that you could never travel* [an expression with no application] (frs 2, 6.1–3).

Likewise you can discount a third path, 'the one wandered by know-nothing two-headed mortals' [when they place their trust in the senses and accept a world of contingency, change and diversity]. *They 'consider being and not-being the same and not the same'* [since phenomenal things possess predicates only in certain respects, at certain times, etc., every case of being is also a case of not being; this is self-contradictory – see rule 2 in §3 – and/or entails the now outlawed not-being]. *It is a back-turning path. Do not out of habit follow it, relying on your senses, but judge by reason my refutation* [of it] (frs 6.4–9, 7).

3   The description of that-which-is

What follows is a journey down the one path that remains negotiable, the path of '...is' (fr. 8.1–49). Now that the inquiry has been focused exclusively on that-which-is, the goddess is ready to tell Parmenides *what* it is, and proceeds to enumerate its predicates. These, or perhaps the ensuing arguments for them, she calls the 'signposts' along the route.

On this path there are many signposts that it is [1] *unborn and unperishing,* [2] *a unique whole,* [3] *unshaken* [= unmoved], [4] *perfect/complete/balanced* [the text is disputed here, but §8 will tend to favour *atalanton*, 'balanced'] (fr. 8.2–4).

She immediately adds, '*Nor was it once, nor will it be, since it is now, one, continuous.*' It is controversial whether this is a fifth item on the list of signposts and, if so, where it is proved. It may be safer to regard it as her parenthetical justification of the preceding present tense '...it *is* unborn' etc., explaining that for an altogether undifferentiated entity a past and future cannot be distinguished from its present. It has been held that the move introduces the notion of timeless being. On another interpretation, 'now' signals that it still occupies time, but with the *passage* of time abolished – possibly foreshadowing the later notion of eternity. (On time, see also §7.)

Analogous to the question of time is that of space. Some would take the goddess's description of that-which-is to make it an altogether non-spatial entity, others a space occupier albeit without spatial distinctions. Is it an entity as innocent of spatio-temporal being as, say, the number 2, or something which occupies space and time but is nevertheless not subject to spatial and temporal distinctions? The following analysis will favour the latter, which not only is the more straightforward reading of the text but also allows the individual arguments to work better (especially those for predicates 3 and 4).

The favourite objection to a literal spatial reading has been that that-which-is will then prove to be a finite sphere, in which case it will have to be surrounded by vacuum or not-being, in contravention of Parmenides' own ban. However, this difficulty arises only given the starting assumption that space is infinite. That assumption became standard in Ionian philosophy (see ANAXIMANDER §2; MELISSUS §3), but is much less evident in the western Greek tradition to which Parmenides belongs: EMPEDOCLES, like Plato and Aristotle later, regarded the universe as a finite sphere bounded by the heaven, with no space, empty or otherwise, beyond it. The very notion of space as a self-subsistent entity with its own dimensions, slow to emerge in ancient thought, was probably unknown to Parmenides. Provided Parmenides' sphere is envisaged from within, like the familiar world with its apparently spherical sky, not from outside like an orange, the supposition of space beyond need not impose itself. Arguably, his spherical being is a radical redescription of our own spherical world, in which no feature beyond the shape itself survives.

At fragment 8.6–49 the goddess defends in turn each of the predicates of that-which-is. The arguments lean on two implicit rules.

Rule 1: no proposition is true if it implies that, for any *x*, '*x* is not' is, was or will be true. This draws directly on the preceding argument (see §2).

Rule 2: there are no half-truths (that is, no proposition is both true and false; no question can be answered 'Yes and no'). This may sound innocuous, but is used lethally to outlaw all qualified truths and ensure that nothing can possess a given predicate

in one way (at one time, in one respect, etc.) but not in another, as is required by the variable world believed in by two-headed mortals. One might think that even in that world temporally or otherwise qualified propositions would obey rule 2, for example, that 'My egg is warm at 9 am' and 'My egg is not warm at 2 pm' could both be true without qualification. But Parmenides would insist that the unqualified proposition 'My egg is warm' is another which must obey the rule, and not come out true in a way, false in a way.

The arguments proceed as follows.

4 The denial of generation and destruction

It cannot [taken as a whole] have had a beginning, since (a) that would have been from previous not-being [rule 1], *and (b) there could have been nothing, prior to its generation, to make it come into being precisely when it did, rather than sooner* [a celebrated anticipation of the Principle of Sufficient Reason] (fr. 8.6–10).

Likewise it must be totally or not at all [rule 2; that is, it cannot be generated piecemeal]: *no additional bits can come into being, since that too would be from previous not-being* [rule 1] (fr. 8.11–14).

Thus both generation and [by parity of reasoning] *destruction are excluded* [In both wholesale and piecemeal destruction something comes not to be, contravening rule 1. But there is no obvious analogue to (b) above, the Principle of Sufficient Reason: in that-which-is there might well, for all we know at this stage of the argument, be sufficient reason for destruction to occur later rather than sooner, for example, progressive decay.] (fr. 8.13–21).

5 Continuity

It is also indivisible [or perhaps 'undivided']. *This is because it is completely homogeneous, its continuity not disrupted by varying degrees of being* [This would entail corresponding degrees of not-being, contrary to rule 1. Since it cannot to any extent not-be at one point what it is at another, there is nothing true of any individual part to distinguish it from any other part. So talk of 'parts' becomes empty.] (fr. 8.22–5).

6 Immobility

'*Motionless, in the limits of mighty bonds', (a) 'it is unstarting and unstopping'* [it neither starts off nor comes to a halt], *because coming-to-be and perishing have already been refuted* [and starting is the coming-to-be of motion, stopping is the perishing of motion]. *And (b) it stays just where it is, held by Necessity 'in the bonds of a limit which imprisons it all round'* [that is, that-which-is, taken as a whole, does not move anywhere, because it entirely fills its own spatial boundary, leaving itself no room to move]. [And it must have this boundary] *'because it is not fitting for that-which-is to be incomplete'* [absence of a definite boundary being a form of incompleteness]. *This in turn is because 'it is not lacking: if it were, it would lack everything'* [and therefore not exist at all; by rule 2, it cannot be both lacking and not lacking] (fr. 8.26–33).

This argument is often read as one against change in general; but the language strongly suggests that motion is the target. (Nothing in it specifically excludes the perpetual rotational movement of a sphere, but would this be conceivable in an entity with no distinct parts (see §5)?) Its 'boundary' argument works better for motion than for other forms of change. Parmenides' general objection to change may be located not here but in his arguments against generation (see §4), where the denial of piecemeal generation could well include that of new properties.

7 Monism

So far the goddess has defended predicates 1, 2 and 3 (see §3). The next lines, fragment 8.34–41, are difficult and controversial. They appear to interrupt the sequence of arguments, with the proof of predicate 4 not beginning till line 42. Some regard them as somehow part of that proof, others as a summary of results so far, yet others as a digression against empiricism. A still likelier explanation is that before she can embark on her final proof, concerning the shape of that-which-is, the goddess must pause to establish formally its *singularity*. She has already demonstrated that it itself forms an undivided whole, but she must still show that neither (a) thought, nor (b) time, nor (c) the plural objects of the phenomenal world, can be anything over and above it. The following paraphrase suggests how.

(a) *Thinking is identical with that which prompts thought* [that is, its object, being]. *'For in what has been said* [that is, the preceding arguments] *you will not find thinking separate from being'* [It has been seen that thought and being always go together, since not-being is unthinkable. There are no grounds for distinguishing the thinking subject from the object thought. Thinking is being and being is thinking. See also fragment 3 (of uncertain location) – *'For to think and to be are the same'* – which has often been given other, somewhat strained, translations to avoid this admittedly very difficult notion.] (fr. 8.34–8).

(b) *'Neither is there, nor will there be, time* [for the reading of the text, see Coxon (1986)] *over and above being, since Fate has bound it down to be the whole* [hence spatially all-inclusive, so that there can be no external measure of time] *and unmoved* [so that there can be no internal measure of time].*'*

(c) *'Therefore* [since that-which-is is all-inclusive and motionless] *it* [that-which-is itself] *has been named all the things which mortals have posited, believing them to be real' and to undergo changes of all kinds* [That is, when ordinary people talk about empirical objects, properties etc. they are speaking, not (impossibly) of nothing, but of that-which-is, even if they are radically misdescribing it. So the fact that ordinary talk is about something does not mean that there is something over and above that-which-is for it to be about.] (fr. 8.38–41).

Whether or not posterity was right to proclaim Parmenides the champion of the One against the Many, he was undoubtedly a monist. But MONISM as such was not new. All his major forerunners, from Thales to Heraclitus, had believed everything to be ultimately analysable as manifestations of one thing, namely a single underlying stuff. Parmenides was the first *eliminative* monist. Everything is still one, but in a way which, instead of accounting for plurality, eliminates it.

8 Symmetry

'But since there is an outermost limit [see §6], *it is bounded on all sides, like the mass of a well-rounded ball, being equally balanced on all sides from the centre* [that is, it is spherical in shape; many interpreters make it resemble a sphere in some other way than shape, for example, in perfection or uniformity, which risks underplaying this geometrically precise description, and makes the grounds which follow less apposite]. *For it must not be bigger or smaller here than there* [it cannot be asymmetrical, as it would have to be if not a sphere]. *For there is no not-being to prevent it reaching the same distance'* [if it were cut off short in one direction, that would mean its not-being beyond that point, in contravention of rule 1], *nor are there degrees of being* [it cannot be asymmetrical by thinning out in places], *because it is, as a whole, 'immune'* [to depletion], *having precisely equal being throughout, up to its limits* (fr. 8.42–9).

This ends the Way of Truth. Can the goddess really be telling Parmenides that that-which-is is literally spherical, without jeopardizing its partlessness? In a sphere you can distinguish hemispheres, segments and other parts. True, but at least the sphere is the one solid that you *can* think of as a whole without distinguishing parts (contrast, for example, a cube, which must be thought of with eight corners etc.). And the upshot of the poem so far, with its attack on human perspectives, has been to persuade Parmenides not to try to enforce any such distinctions. See also fragment 4 (of uncertain location): *'Gaze in thought equally upon absent things as firmly present. For thought will not split off that-which-is from clinging to that-which-is, scattered or gathered everyhow everywhere in the world.'*

9 The Way of Seeming

The goddess now turns to the 'opinions of mortals', and sets out, unargued, an analysis of the phenomenal world in terms of the combination of two opposite 'forms' or elements, one light and fiery, the other heavy and dark. The surviving fragments are scanty, but the cosmology includes the following: a role for a creative goddess, a detailed description of the heavens as a set of concentric bands, an embryology and a physiology of human thought.

The Way of Seeming has been promised by the goddess from the outset: *'You must find out everything – both the unshaken heart of well-rounded truth, and the opinions of mortals. In them there is no true trust, but you must learn them too anyway...'* (fr. 1.28–31). At its opening she calls it 'deceitful', if also 'plausible'. She adds that Parmenides must learn it *'so that no opinion of mortals may outstrip [or overtake] you'* (fr. 8.61), apparently meaning that the cosmology will be the best of its kind, able to compete successfully with those already offered by others. And there can be no doubt that this part of the poem is, for whatever reason, making an original contribution to cosmology. It even incorporates two major astronomical discoveries: that the Morning Star is identical to the Evening Star, and that the moon's light comes from the sun. But if all cosmology is false, what is the point of even entering such a contest?

Where Parmenides' major predecessors had been material monists, Parmenides offers his own distinctively dualist scheme. So his analogous move from one entity in the Way of Truth to two in the Way of Seeming is anything but casual. Indeed, the arithmetical point is precisely what the goddess emphasizes: mortals *'have made up their minds to name two forms, of which they should not name one'* (fr. 8.53–4). This, although sometimes taken to mean that they should not name *so much as* one, or even not *merely* one, is most easily read as saying that precisely one out of the two is a mistake. That itself, if correct, might be understood as purely numerical: any total of two is one too many. Or it can be taken specifically: one of these two forms is identical with that-which-is, but the other should not have been added – in which case it becomes tempting (and Aristotle among others was tempted) to assimilate the illicit second element to what in the Way of Truth was called not-being. As to which element is which, it is usually the fiery element

that is assumed to correspond to that-which-is, although Popper (1992) has advocated the dark heavy one, in which the fiery one produces the mere semblance of change, just as the moon, in reality solidly spherical, was known by Parmenides to appear to wax and wane through the play of light on it.

The question remains how the cosmology relates to the Way of Truth. Some have held that it itself contains a measure of truth, others on the contrary that it is there to expose the patent falsity of any departure from strict monism. Of these, the former sits ill with the goddess's contrast between mortal opinions and truth, while the latter conflicts with the fact that the cosmology, rather than being *patently* false, is highly 'plausible'. A more attractive possibility is that she wants to show how surprisingly similar the deceptive empirical world is to the stark Way of Truth. The whole range of cosmic phenomena can be generated by allowing the intrusion of just one additional item – by starting out with two instead of one. This hypothesis makes good sense of the often noticed fact that the cosmological descriptions in the Way of Seeming pointedly echo the language of the Way of Truth. For example, the description of the *'encircling heaven'* as *'bound down by Necessity to hold the limits of the stars'* (fr. 10) recalls that of that-which-is as held motionless by Necessity in the bonds of a limit (see §6).

Thus interpreted, the Way of Seeming does not pretend to vindicate phenomena, but it does tackle the biggest headache faced by any convert of Parmenides: how can human experience have got things quite so catastrophically wrong? The answer is that the step from appearance to reality is much smaller than it may initially look.

This admittedly still does not begin to explain how the error of mortals ever occurred. If Parmenides is right, there are no separate thinking subjects. All thought is that-which-is thinking itself. How it could find room to misconceive itself is a question on which Parmenides leaves us to puzzle.

10 Influence

Parmenides marks a watershed in Presocratic philosophy. In the next generation he remained the senior voice of Eleaticism, perceived as champion of the One against the Many. His One was defended by ZENO OF ELEA and MELISSUS, while those who wished to vindicate cosmic plurality and change felt obliged to respond to his challenge. Empedocles, ANAXAGORAS (§2), LEUCIPPUS and DEMOCRITUS framed their theories in terms which conceded as much as possible to his rejections of literal generation and annihilation and of division. On the other hand, in this they were swayed less by Parmenides' own primary argument, the inadmissibility of '...is not', which won few converts, than by an older and less controversial premise, the impossibility of generation *ex nihilo*.

PLATO (§16), in his *Sophist*, did take up puzzles raised by Parmenides' rejection of not-being. But it was in recognition of Parmenides' rigorous methodology, not his doctrines, that in his later work Plato expressed a degree of allegiance to the Eleatic tradition, letting Parmenides or an unnamed follower of his eclipse Socrates as principal speaker in three major dialogues.

Plato's own declared veneration of Parmenides is exceeded by that of the Neoplatonists, who treat his 'one being' as an integral part of their own metaphysical hierarchy. Among his modern admirers, perhaps the most prominent is HEIDEGGER, for whom Parmenides was the last great thinker before the 'forgetting of being' which has blighted the subsequent history of metaphysics.

See also: BEING; MELISSUS; PRESOCRATIC PHILOSOPHY

References and further reading

There are good English translations of all or most of Parmenides in Austin (1986), Barnes (1979, 1986), Coxon (1986), Gallop (1984), Guthrie (1962–78), Hussey (1972) and Kirk, Raven and Schofield (1983). With Parmenides more than most writers, any translation is an interpretation, and it is prudent always to compare two or more.

Austin, S. (1986) *Parmenides. Being, Bounds, and Logic*, New Haven, CT: Yale University Press. (In-depth study of Parmenides' logic.)

Barnes, J. (1979) *The Presocratic Philosophers*, London: Routledge & Kegan Paul, chaps 9–11. (An unconventional but exhilarating analysis)

—— (1987) *Early Greek Philosophy*, Harmondsworth: Penguin. (Chapter 9 is a translation of Parmenides' fragments, complete with the contexts in which they are preserved.)

* Coxon, A.H. (1986) *The Fragments of Parmenides*, Assen: Van Gorcum. (An important edition, informative on the text and secondary tradition)

Furley, D. (1973) 'Notes on Parmenides', in E.N. Lee, A.P.D. Mourelatos and R. Rorty (eds) *Exegesis and Argument*, Assen: Van Gorcum, 1–15; repr. in D. Furley, *Cosmic Problems*, Cambridge: Cambridge University Press, 1989, 27–37. (Incisive commentary on a series of crucial passages.)

Furth, M. (1968) 'Elements of Eleatic Ontology', *Journal of the History of Philosophy* 6: 111–32; repr.

in A.P.D. Mourelatos, *The Pre-Socratics*, Garden City, NY: Doubleday, 1989, 241–70. (Classic exposition of the 'fused' sense of 'be' in Parmenides.)

Gallop, D. (1984) *Parmenides of Elea*, Toronto, Ont.: University of Toronto Press. (Contains text, translation and notes; a basic and clear exposition, founded principally on the interpretation of Owen (1960).)

Guthrie, W.K.C. (1962–78) *A History of Greek Philosophy*, Cambridge: Cambridge University Press, 6 vols. (The most detailed and comprehensive English-language history of early Greek thought; the treatment of Parmenides, in volume 2 pages 1–80, is a helpful guide to the scholarship.)

* Heidegger, M. (1954) 'Moira (Parmenides VIII, 34–41)', in *Early Greek Thinking*, San Francisco, CA: Harper & Row, 1975, 79–101. (Heidegger's interpretation and appreciation of Parmenides on the relation of thought to being, in English translation.)

Hussey, E. (1972) *The Presocratics*, London: Duckworth. (Chapter 5 contains a lucid short account of Parmenides.)

Kahn, C.H. (1969) 'The Thesis of Parmenides', *Review of Metaphysics* 22: 700–24. (Leading exposition of the 'veridical' sense of 'be' in Parmenides.)

—— (1988) ' Being In Parmenides and Plato', *La Parola del Passato* 43: 237–61. (Further refines Kahn's 1969 interpretation.)

Kirk, G.S., Raven, J.E. and Schofield, M. (1983) *The Presocratic Philosophers*, Cambridge: Cambridge University Press, 2nd edn. (A valuable survey of Presocratic philosophy, including texts and translations; Parmenides occupies chapter 8.)

Long, A.A. (1963) 'The Principles Of Parmenides' Cosmogony', *Phronesis* 8: 90–107; repr. in R.E. Allen and D.J. Furley (eds), *Studies in Presocratic Philosophy*, London: Routledge & Kegan Paul, 1975, vol. 2, 82–101. (Important study of the Way of Seeming.)

Mackenzie, M.M. (1982) 'Parmenides' Dilemma', *Phronesis* 27: 1–12. (One of the most philosophically interesting discussions of Parmenides.)

Mourelatos, A.P.D. (1970) *The Route of Parmenides*, New Haven, CT: Yale University Press. (A subtle overall reading of Parmenides, sensitive to his place in the poetic as well as the philosophical tradition.)

Owen, G.E.L. (1960) 'Eleatic Questions', *Classical Quarterly* 10: 84–102; repr. in R.E. Allen and D.J. Furley (eds), *Studies in Presocratic Philosophy*, London: Routledge & Kegan Paul, 1975, vol. 2, 48–81; repr. in G.E.L. Owen, *Logic, Science and Dialectic*, London: Duckworth, 1986, 3–26. (The seminal modern study of Parmenides as philosopher.)

* Parmenides (early to mid 5th century BC) Fragments, in H. Diels and W. Kranz (eds) *Die Fragmente der Vorsokratiker*, Berlin: Weidemann, 6th edn, 1952, vol. 1, 217–46. (The standard collection of the ancient sources; includes Greek texts with translations in German.)

* Popper, K.R. (1992) 'How the Moon Might Shed Some of her Light Upon the Two Ways of Parmenides', *Classical Quarterly* 42: 12–19. (Radical proposal concerning the relation between the two halves of the poem.)

Reinhardt, K. (1916) 'The Relation Between the Two Parts of Parmenides' Poem', trans. in A.P.D. Mourelatos, *The Pre-Socratics*, Garden City, NY: Doubleday, 293–311. (Classic study of the problem.)

Seidel, G.S. (1964) *Martin Heidegger and the Pre-Socratics*, Lincoln, NE: University of Nebraska Press. (Explains the fundamental importance of Parmenides to Heidegger's conception of metaphysics.)

Sorabji, R. (1983) *Time, Creation and the Continuum*, London: Duckworth. (Chapter 8 deals with Parmenides' treatment of time.)

Stokes, M.C. (1971) *One and Many in Presocratic Philosophy*, Washington, DC: Center for Hellenic Studies. (Locates Parmenides in a historical context.)

DAVID SEDLEY

PARTICULARS

Particulars are to be understood by contrasting them with universals, that term being used to comprise both properties and relations. Often the term 'individuals' is used interchangeably with 'particulars', though some restrict the term 'individuals' to those particulars whose existence has more than momentary duration.

It is sometimes taken as a distinctive feature of particulars that they cannot be in more than one place at a time, whereas universals are capable of being wholly present in more than one place at a given time: if you have a white thing here and a white thing there, then you have two particulars but only one property. This way of distinguishing between particulars and universals may help us to focus on apt paradigm cases of each, but arguably this does not get us to the heart of the matter. On the one hand, some think it is possible, at least in principle, for a magician, or Pythagoras, or a time traveller, or a subatomic particle to be in two places at

once, even though each is a particular. On the other hand, some think that there are properties which could not possibly be manifested in two different places at the same time, and yet which nonetheless are universals: think, for instance, of the divine property of absolute perfection, or of the conjunction of all intrinsic properties of a Leibnizian monad (or possible world); or of Judas' property of simply being Judas.

Particulars are things which have properties and which stand in relations – particulars 'instantiate' properties and relations. By itself, however, this does not distinguish particulars from universals since universals, too, are naturally thought to have properties and to stand in relations. What distinguishes particulars is the fact that, while a particular instantiates properties and relations, nothing instantiates a particular. Universals both 'have' (properties and relations) and are 'had'; particulars 'have' but are not 'had'. Since a particular is not instantiated by another thing, it is sometimes said to exist 'in itself', whereas a universal exists 'in' something else. For this reason, the term 'particular' is related to the term 'substance', which is traditionally used to mean something capable of independent existence.

1   **What is at stake**
2   **Bare particulars**
3   **Bundles of properties**
4   **Properties particularized**
5   **Particulars as aggregates**
6   **The state of the art**

1   What is at stake

In some of his dialogues, Plato seems to assume that nothing is real, knowable or of value unless it is permanent (see PLATO §15). The particular things we experience through the senses are all impermanent; so Plato infers that these particulars are unreal, unknowable and of no value. The things which are real, knowable and of value are the moral, political, aesthetic and mathematical ideals which individual people, social groups and works of art may aspire towards but never really embody perfectly – the Forms.

In an ancient Buddhist text, the existence of common-sense particulars is called into question (Horner 1963: 34–8; Eliot 1910: 668–72). Suppose, for example, that you reach out and touch something, saying 'This is a chariot'. The ancient sage calls attention to the fact that what you are touching is, more strictly, a wheel, and more strictly still, a hub, spoke or rim, and of course only the surface of that. So there is really no such thing as a chariot; and the same goes for other particulars, including persons. A person is like a flame, or an eddy in a river – there is nothing which persists through the passage of time. Particulars are only shadows cast by quirks of Indo-European syntax, with no more substantiality than the 'It' in 'It is raining'.

In contrast, for Descartes there is nothing more certain than the existence of the self: his philosophy rests on the famous inference 'I think, therefore I am'. Western liberal democracies place great store, at least in theory, on the importance of the individual. In the arts, a conception of individual artistic genius has held us in a tight grip. And modern mathematical logic rests heavily on names and variables which are interpreted as picking out individuals from a domain of discourse. In a great many ways, individuals, or particulars, are central to our thinking, not only about this world of impermanence but also about the timeless truths of mathematics. Many philosophers are therefore diametrically opposed to the Platonic or Buddhist deflation of particulars.

2 Bare particulars

Aristotle agreed with Plato that knowledge – science – is concerned with things which are necessary and hence permanent. Yet for Aristotle this did not exclude knowledge of particulars. Admittedly, each particular is subject to generation and corruption; nonetheless, each particular does have certain essential properties in virtue of which it belongs to a species and genus. And although individuals are transient, species are permanent. Individuals can be subjects of knowledge, thanks to their possession of essential properties (see ARISTOTLE §§14–15).

Aristotelian essentialism is often disavowed by philosophers but, arguably, essentialist assumptions are pervasive in our thinking at both a common-sense and a philosophical level. The essentialist holds that each particular has certain properties which it cannot lose except by ceasing to exist, and which it could not have lacked from the start except by never having come into being. The contrary doctrine is sometimes called the doctrine of 'bare particulars' – that particulars do not have essential properties. Although essentialism is regularly disparaged by philosophers, so is the contrary doctrine of bare particulars. The rejection of both together would require a radical elimination of the very idea of any but merely verbal necessities or possibilities, as in Quine (1953).

3 Bundles of properties

Consider a particular which has several essential properties and several accidental properties. There is room to consider a theory which identifies the particular with the collection of essential properties, and there is room to consider a theory which identifies the particular with the collection of all its properties. On consideration, however, it can be seen that a particular cannot be identified with any collection which includes an accidental property. An accidental property is something which, by definition, the particular could have lacked. But the bundle of properties which includes that accidental property would not have been the bundle that it is if it had not included that property.

Consider, therefore, the theory which identifies a particular with the collection of its essential properties. An objection can be raised if we show that there can be several particulars which share exactly the same essential properties. Certainly Aristotle thought that different members of the same species share the very same essential properties. For Aristotle, therefore, what distinguishes particulars of the same species is not their 'form', but the 'matter' on which this form is impressed.

Hence if we are to identify a particular with a collection of essential properties, we must suppose that distinct particulars cannot ever share exactly the same essential properties. Each particular must have some property which no other particular could have. This is what is called an individual essence. One way of thinking of an individual essence is by construing it to be an unshareable conjunction of severally-shareable properties as, for example, Leibniz's monads. An alternative would be to suppose that for each particular there is a simple essential property called a 'haecceity' (from Latin, meaning 'thisness') which that particular alone possesses and which nothing else could have had either instead of or as well as it. This notion was articulated by the Islamic philosopher Avicenna (see IBN SINA §4), and was taken up by some of the scholastic philosophers in Europe, such as Duns Scotus in the thirteenth century, but has been roundly denounced by many since that time.

4 Properties particularized

There is thus a line of argument which leads from the stereotypically empiricist idea that a thing is a bundle of properties to the distinctly non-empiricist doctrine of haecceities or individual essences. An empiricist can avoid inconsistency by particularizing properties.

For the sake of illustration, suppose coldness to be a typical property of a thing. According to some philosophers, then, the coldness of one block of ice is one thing, and the coldness of another block of ice is quite another thing. It is not just that the second block of ice is a second instance of a cold thing but, rather, the coldness of the second block of ice is a second instance of coldness. Whenever something is cold, there exists something which we may call its coldness: this may be called a 'property instance' or (following D.C. Williams) a 'trope'. According to the trope theory, a particular can be taken to be a 'bundle of properties' provided we take each of these properties to be an abstract particular.

The trope theory is a contender for, but has not attracted, majority support. Some of the Scholastic nominalists, like Ockham, can be read as having articulated such a view, and the view has been revived by a series of philosophers in the twentieth century: a classic exploration is found in Nelson Goodman's *The Structure of Appearance* (1951) (see NOMINALISM §§2, 4).

5 Particulars as aggregates

Emergentism is the doctrine that something new emerges or comes into being when materials come together and take the form of something with a kind of unity and persistence across time, as for instance a living being. Such a thing is constituted by a plurality of parts, but is something distinct from just the aggregate of those parts.

The distinction between a thing and the aggregate of its parts can be drawn by reference to their logical independence: you could have had either one without the other. Consider a particular ship, say the ship of Theseus. This ship is constituted by planks of wood. But the planks could have existed without ever constituting a ship; and the ship could have been constituted by different planks. Hence the ship is not the same thing as the aggregate of the planks which constitute it.

This conception of an individual as something other than just the aggregate of its parts has been bedevilled by a puzzle, famously described by Hobbes (Molesworth 1837–45 (4): 135; the example traces back to Plutarch's 'Life of Theseus' §§22–3). Suppose that, over time, worn planks on the ship of Theseus are replaced by new ones, and a working ship is maintained in continuous existence; meanwhile, the worn planks which are taken away are gradually reassembled in just the way they were arranged in the original ship. One principle leads us to say that the working ship with new planks is the ship of Theseus; another principle leads us to say that the reassembled ship with worn planks is the ship of Theseus. Yet an individual ship cannot be in two places at once: which of them is the ship of Theseus? This ship puzzle can be paralleled by puzzles of personal identity across time (see PERSONAL IDENTITY).

Objections of this sort have been raised against the theory that there are particulars which have parts, but

which are not just the aggregates of those parts (the contrary theory takes all particulars to be just the aggregates of their parts). Goodman and Quine (1947) have been very influential in promoting the idea that particulars are best understood through the theory of the part–whole relation, or mereology (see MEREOLOGY). Furthermore, according to Goodman, Quine and others, an individual which persists through some interval of time has distinct parts existing at each distinct time in that interval. Among the things which exist at one time is a timeslice which exists only at that time; among the things which exist at another time is a different timeslice; the thing which exists across several distinct times is just an aggregate of distinct timeslices.

Hobbes' puzzle question, 'Which is the ship of Theseus?', is then diagnosed as turning upon a merely verbal vagueness. There are two distinct aggregates which are broadly ship-shape, and it is mere semantic indeterminacy which makes us unsure as to which of them should be called 'the ship of Theseus'. Similar reasoning applies equally to persons.

6 The state of the art

Strawson (1959) draws a distinction between 'revisionary' and 'descriptive' metaphysics. In revisionary metaphysics, a theory is advanced to replace our ordinary language and thinking. In descriptive metaphysics, a description is given of the deepest presuppositions of our existing theories. Using these criteria, the broadly Aristotelian theory does seem to qualify as a relatively descriptive theory, by contrast with Plato's more revisionary claims that particulars are unreal, unknowable and of no value. The Aristotelian theory is also more descriptive than theories which deny that particulars have essential properties, theories which take particulars to be bundles of tropes and theories which treat all particulars as merely the aggregates of the spatial and temporal parts out of which they are constituted. The more revisionary theories may be right; but the more conservative theories still have a lot of life left in them. The time is not ripe for a consensus to emerge on the nature of particulars.

See also: IDENTITY; SUBSTANCE; UNIVERSALS

References and further reading

Adams, R.H. (1979) 'Primitive Thisness and Primitive Identity', *Journal of Philosophy* 76: 5–26. (A difficult but seminal article on particulars as irreducible to shareable properties.)

Armstrong, D.M. (1980) 'Identity Through Time', in

P. van Inwagen (ed.) *Time and Cause*, Dordrecht: Reidel, 67–78. (An accessible defence of particulars as aggregates of timeslices, as discussed above in §5.)

—— (1989) *Universals: An Opinionated Introduction*, Boulder, CO, San Francisco, CA and London: Westview Press. (An introductory exposition of a late twentieth century resuscitation of a roughly Aristotelian theory distinguishing particulars from universals.)

Campbell, K. (1989) *Abstract Particulars*, Oxford: Blackwell. (An accessible defence of properties particularized, as discussed in above in §4. Useful for further references.)

* Eliot, C.W. (ed.) (1910) *Sacred Writings*, vol. 2, in *The Harvard Classics*, New York: Collier, vol. 45. (Contains source material translated from the Milindapañha and from the Visuddhimagga, mentioned in §1 above.)

* Goodman, N. (1951) *The Structure of Appearance*, Cambridge, MA: Harvard University Press. (A difficult but important landmark on particulars as bundles of properties or as aggregates of timeslices, and of properties particularized, and of other ways of construing particulars.)

* Goodman, N. and Quine, W.V. (1947) 'Steps Toward a Constructive Nominalism', *Journal of Symbolic Logic* 12: 105–22. (A difficult but important work defending nominalism, and also laying the groundwork for mereology or the theory of aggregates, relevant to §5 above.)

* Horner, I.B. (ed. and trans.) (1963) *Milinda's Questions, Sacred Texts of the Buddhists*, Oxford, Pali Text Society, vol. 22. (Source material on the Buddhists' treatment of persisting individuals as mere aggregates of momentary things in 'Questions of King Milinda and Nāgasena' mentioned above in §1.)

Lewis, D.K. (1976) 'Survival and Identity', in A.O. Rorty (ed.) *The Identities of Persons*, Berkeley, CA: University of California Press, 17–40. (A difficult but clear exposition of a theory of persons as aggregates of timeslices.)

* Molesworth, W. (ed.) (1837–45) *Elements of Philosophy*, vol. 4 of *The English Works of Thomas Hobbes of Malmesbury*, London: J. Bohn. (Part 2, chapter 2: 135 contains a famous passage on the ship of Theseus, mentioned in §5 above.)

Parfit, D. (1984) *Reasons and Persons*, Oxford: Clarendon Press. (An accessible and entertaining exposition of a theory of persons as aggregates of timeslices, and of supposed consequences that this might have for moral theory.)

* Quine, W.V. (1953) 'Three Grades of Modal Involvement', *Proceedings of the XI International Congress of Philosophy* 14: 65–81; repr. in *The Ways of Paradox and Other Essays*, New York: Random House, 1966, 155–74. (A classic attack on Aristotelian or any other sort of essentialism,)

* Strawson, P.F. (1959) *Individuals: An Essay in Descriptive Metaphysics*, London: Methuen. (A transcendental justification of a roughly Kantian sort, for a common-sense theory of individuals as irreducible to properties.)

* Williams, D.C. (1966) *The Principles of Empirical Realism*, Springfield, IL: Charles Thomas. (A classic defence of a theory of properties particularized.)

JOHN BIGELOW

PARTIINOST'

Partiinost' (Russian for partyness, often translated as party-mindedness, partisanship or party spirit) was long the controlling principle of Soviet Marxism. Though commonly identified with thought control, partiinost' originally signified social analysis of thought joined with moral judgment, an ancient combination that can work against the powers that be as well as for them. Lenin's version changed from revolt to thought control after his party came to power in 1917, but especially after Stalin's 'revolution from above' twelve years later. In 1950 Stalin began a restriction of partiinost' by declaring 'science' separate from 'ideology'. Such reform accelerated after his death in 1953, but slowed down from the mid-1960s to the late 1980s. Then a new burst of reform set off the collapse of the Soviet system and of partiinost', though the problems that engendered it – the entanglement of group interests and claims of truth – persist.

The self-serving nature of group beliefs has often been exposed. Xenophanes on divinity ('If oxen could paint, their gods would be oxen'), Thrasymachus on justice ('the interest of the stronger') and Thomas More on 'a conspiracy of the rich, who pursue their own aggrandizement under the name of the commonwealth', are famous examples. Hobbes distinguished between ideas that involve interests – such as justice – and ideas that 'cross no man's ambition, profit, or lust', such as the sum of angles in a triangle. He added however: 'If [that sum] had been ... contrary to the interest of men that have dominion ... it would have been, if not disputed, yet by the burning of all books of geometry, suppressed, as far as he whom it concerned was able.' Thus his sociology of ideas included a bellicose determinism: a ruling party is compelled to suppress thought that threatens its interests. He had seen parties or 'factions' bring civil war; the only remedy was for the sovereign to suppress them.

'Party' has not always meant factiousness. Shakespeare imagined the War of the Roses brought to an end by those who 'dare maintain the party of the truth', and the philosophers of the Enlightenment have been praised as 'the party of humanity'. The emergence of modern parties, as special-interest groups engaged in routine contests for power, made identification of a party with the interests of humanity seem threadbare rhetoric, hardly concealing the sordid realities of partisan self-seeking. That may be one reason why *Das Kommunistische Manifest* (*The Communist Manifesto*) of 1848 declared that 'the Communists do not form a separate party opposed to other working-class parties'.

MARX and ENGELS were political isolates without a significant party, not only in 1848 but through most of their lives, in part because they admired the scholar who seeks all-human truth rather than the 'party man' who serves special interests. Belief in disinterested inquiry mingles in Marx's writing with insistence that ideology is unavoidable when class interests are entangled with claims of reason. Only the proletarian overthrow of class rule will bring the end of class bias in ideas. In march towards truth the manifesto of 1848 says that Communists do not 'form a separate party', but they are 'the most advanced and resolute section...of the proletariat, [who] have over the great mass...the advantage of clearly understanding the line of march, the conditions and the ultimate general results of the proletarian movement'. Thus Marx in 1848 laid out a rationalization of *partiinost'* for Communist Party-states of the twentieth century.

But that *is* a rationalization, which ignores contrary elements in Marx's thought and in its uses, both for liberal pluralism by Marxists in Germany and for one-party tyranny by Marxists in Russia or in China and other 'underdeveloped' places. Liberal pluralism has emerged mostly in 'developed' lands, often through protracted experience of civil war, while Hobbesian choices between civil war and autocracy have attended the spread of party politics to places perceived as 'backward', in acute need of drastic 'development'.

In nineteenth-century Russia talk of *grazhdanstvennost'*, citizenship, as something to be created through organized struggle, foreshadowed *partiinost'*. Chernyshevskii opened 'Antropologicheskii printsip v filosofii' (The Anthropological Principle in Philosophy) (1860) with a declaration that 'every philosopher has been a representative of one of the political parties struggling in his time for predominance over the society to which the philosopher has belonged'.

Even P.L. LAVROV, the Russian radical who exalted the 'critically thinking individual', enjoined such a thinker to serve 'the people' through a party, 'to devote his energies to this party and to be guided by its advice'. 'Party' here signified commitment to a dream of an ideal system, which provoked splits as readily as organizations among fellow dreamers. Party discipline, often preached, was an additional impetus to splitting. Trotsky's famous warning against Lenin's version of such discipline – that it would replace the working class by the Party, the Party by the Central Committee, the Central Committee by the dictator – could come true only with the accession to state power (see LENIN, V.; TROTSKY, L.).

In 1895, when Lenin first used the word *partiinost'*, Russia was an autocracy without political parties. He was criticizing a fellow Marxist for showing the inevitability of capitalism but not its evil, though objectivity requires condemnation along with explanation. 'Materialism includes, so to speak, *partiinost'*, obliging one in any judgment of an occurrence to take directly and openly the viewpoint of a definite social group'. Like Chernyshevskii and Lavrov, Lenin was pointing to a fellowship of belief rather than a concrete political organization, and that was still his usage in *Materializm i empiriokrititsizm* (Materialism and Empiriocriticism) (1909). By that time a Marxist party had been formed, and had split into Bolsheviks and Mensheviks, but Lenin's book assigned all philosophers to two 'parties' of a much broader kind: idealists and materialists, who had been serving the interests of rulers and ruled, of faith and science, since ancient times.

With that crude class analysis of philosophical schools Lenin justified the expulsion from the Bolshevik organization of comrades who rejected the dialectical materialism that he had learned from PLEKHANOV, a Menshevik in party affiliation. Lunacharskii, one of the expelled Bolsheviks, challenged Lenin to acknowledge his break with a rule laid down by Bebel, a German Marxist leader:

> ...'We have no dogma and therefore cannot have heretics'. Let us grant that Bebel was mistaken, that both heresy and its condemnation are a possible phenomenon in Social Democracy. But don't we have the right to expect that in our Party free thought will have at least the same guarantees as are given to it by the Catholic Church, which prides itself on its intolerance?

(Joravsky 1961: 39)

Lenin ignored that demand for precision and due process; *partiinost'* was casually invoked, never carefully analysed, even after 1917, when his party won power and suppressed rival parties.

At first the Central Committee limited its efforts to control intellectual life. Its ideological bureaucracy correlated ideas with the interests of social classes rather than parties in the literal sense, and did not try to enforce strict uniformity on thinkers. Such laxity was assailed in a 'discussion' following Stalin's complaint, in 1929, that 'theorists' were not adequately serving 'practicians', whose 'chief' (*vozhd'*) he was. Henceforth he would be 'chief' of 'theorists' as well, philosophers included. 'The basic lesson of the philosophical discussion', as an ideological official (Kol'man) explained to mathematicians, was to end 'all efforts of any theory, of any scholarly discipline, to conceive itself as an autonomous, independent discipline... isolated from Party guidance'.

Philosophy became commentary on speeches of Stalin or decrees of the Central Committee, while ideological bureaucrats complained that the commentary was timid and unoriginal, and that it was subversive to limit *partiinost'* by attempting careful distinctions between science and ideology. The 'primacy of practice' required philosophers to dig up quotes from 'the classics of Marxism-Leninism' showing that the changing intuitions of Party leaders were justified by theory as well as practice. In short, an anti-intellectual, authoritarian pragmatism was the heart of Stalinist *partiinost'*. One of its effects was an ironic inversion of the social analysis of thought compacted with moral judgment, which had once been the meaningful core of the concept. Ferocious attacks on individualistic thinkers regenerated admiration of the type, while servants of 'the people's party' came to be regarded as immoral lickspittles, saying nothing of substance.

The stultifying effects on intellectual life, including the creative expertise demanded by practical leaders, brought Stalin to call a retreat. In 1950 he announced that 'no science [*nauka*] can develop and prosper without the clash of opinions, without freedom of criticism', a 'generally recognized rule that has been ignored and violated in the worst way'. Of course he blamed 'petty despots' in charge of particular disciplines, not the Central Committee or the concept of *partiinost'*, but he opened the way to restriction of the concept by declaring that 'science' or 'scholarship' (*nauka*) was not part of ideology. Efforts to spell out such restriction were feeble until Khrushchev began 'de-Stalinization' after Stalin's death in 1953. Even then Soviet philosophers were much more timid than their Polish and Yugoslav comrades. Kolakowski was especially forceful in showing the absurdities of 'institutional Marxism', which insisted that the intuitions of Party chiefs were infallible products of a scientific ideology.

The ouster of Khrushchev in 1964 checked further

debate until the late 1980s, when another reformist party chief, Gorbachev, began a campaign for 'openness' and 'restructuring'. That led so swiftly to systemic collapse that serious discussion of *partiinost'* hardly began. It became instantly extinct, remembered only to be denounced or renounced by the minority of Russian thinkers still sympathetic to Marxism in some form. Serious inquiry in the sociology of knowledge, including the complex interdependence of group interests and claims of truth, is barely beginning to address the record of *partiinost'*, whether in Russia or in other Communist countries.

See also: IDEOLOGY; MARXIST PHILOSOPHY, RUSSIAN AND SOVIET

References and further reading

Chernyshevskii, N.G. (1860) 'Antropologicheskii printsip v filosofii' (The Anthropological Principle in Philosophy), *Sovremennik*. Republished many times, for instance, in *Polnoe sobranie sochinenii*, vol. 7. (Major article by the founding father of Russian populism.)

* Hobbes, T. (1651) *Leviathan*, ed. R. Tuck, Cambridge: Cambridge University Press, 1991. (See especially chapters 11 and 22.)

Joravsky, D. (1961) *Soviet Marxism and Natural Science 1917–1932*, New York: Columbia University Press and London: Routledge. (See especially 'Lenin and the Partyness of Philosophy' and 'The Great Break, 1929–1932'.)

—— (1983) 'The Stalinist Mentality and the Higher Learning', in *Slavic Review*, 575–600. (The bizarre patterns of *partiinost'* in various scholarly disciplines.)

Kolakowski, L. (1964) *Der Mensch ohne Alternative: von der Möglichkeit und Unmöglichkeit Marxist zu sein* (Man Without Alternative: On the Possibility and the Impossibilty of Being Marxist), Munich: Piper. (Exposé of the absurdities in *partiinost'*, by the eminent Polish philosopher.)

Kol'man, E. (1931) *Na bor'bu za materialisticheskuiu dialektiku v matematike* (In Struggle for Materialist Dialectics in Mathematics), Moscow: Gos. nauch.-tekh. izd. (An ideological official on *partiinost'*. At the end of a long life he 'repented'.)

Lavrov, P.L. (1884) 'Sotsial'naia revoliutsiia i zadachi nravstvennosti' (Social Revolution and the Tasks of Morality), in *Vestnik narodnoi voli*; repr. in *Filosofiia i sotsiologiia* (Philosophy and Sociology), Moscow: Mysl' 1965.

Lenin, V.I. (1909) *Materializm i èmpiriokrititsizm*, in *Polnoe sobranie sochinenii*, Moscow: Gospolitizdat, 1958–69, 5th edn, vol. 18; *Materialism and Empiri-*

ocriticism, in *Collected Works*, Moscow: Progress and London: Lawrence & Wishart, 4th English edn, vol.14. (Also, see *Partiinost'* in the subject index of the collection.)

Marx, K. and Engels, F. (1848) *Das Kommunistische Manifest*, trans. *The Communist Manifesto*, in D. Fernbach (ed.) *The Revolutions of 1848*, Harmondsworth: Penguin, 1973, 62–98.

Stalin, I.V. (1950) 'Marksizm i voprosy iazykoznaniia' (Marxism and Questions of Linguistics) in *Sochineniia* (Works), vol. 3, Stanford: Hoover Institute, 1967; trans. *Marxism and Linguistics*, New York, International Publishers, 1951. (The 1950 declaration on freedom of criticism, widely translated.)

DAVID JORAVSKY

PARTISANSHIP *see* PARTIINOST'

PASCAL, BLAISE (1623–62)

Blaise Pascal was a mathematical prodigy who numbered among his early achievements an essay on conic sections and the invention of a calculating machine. In his early twenties he engaged in the vigorous European debate about the vacuum, undertaking, or causing to be undertaken, a series of experiments which helped to refute the traditional view that nature abhors a vacuum and setting out clearly the methodology of the new science. In 1646 he came under the influence of Jansenism; this he seems to have rejected for a short time in the early 1650s, but he then underwent a profound spiritual experience which transformed his life and drew him into close association with leading Jansenists, with whom he collaborated in producing the polemical Lettres provinciales *(1656–7). At the same time he planned to write an apology for the Christian religion, but ill-health so affected his final years that this only survives in the fragmentary form of the* Pensées *(1670). He made significant contributions to mathematics, especially in the fields of geometry, number theory and probability theory, and he also helped to describe the 'esprit géométrique' which characterized the new science of the 1650s. He argued that geometry was superior to logic in that it could provide not only demonstrative procedures but also axioms from which to work; and he set down appropriate rules of argument. His religious writings were published shortly after his death; many attempts have been made to reconstruct the apology which they encapsulate. It seems most likely that this would have fallen into two parts, the first setting out the wretchedness of humans without God, the second demonstrating the truth of Christianity and the felicity of the religious life. Humans are portrayed in Augustinian terms as corrupt, vapid creatures, prey to their passions and the delusions of imagination; but they are also shown to possess greatness through their reason and self-awareness, which can bring them to recognize that Christianity alone has represented their predicament accurately, and that they should turn to religion, even if initially they lack the instinctive faith which is the hallmark of the saved. In the 'wager' fragment, Pascal employs his mathematical insights to revivify an old apologetic argument (that it is wiser to bet on God existing rather than on his not existing) and to link it to an existential imperative (that we all are obliged to choose between these alternatives). The adroit interplay between scepticism, rationalism and faith of the first part is succeeded by a second part which argues the veracity of Christianity from Biblical interpretation, prophecies and miracles. Pascal concedes that this cannot carry absolute conviction; but he insists that the rejection of such arguments is caused not by man's rational powers but by his corrupt passions. Pascal's* Pensées *are written for the most part in terse aphoristic form; he aspired to a style that was so accessible that the reader would believe he was experiencing as his own the thoughts that he read. Although Pascal said at the end of his life that he considered his mathematical pursuits a quite separate enterprise from his religious writings, a common epistemology can be found in both, together with a scientific outlook which Pascal saw as superior to the philosophical alternatives of his day.*

1   Early life and mathematical works
2   The debate over the vacuum
3   Pascal and Jansenism
4   Works posthumously published
5   Mathematical philosophy
6   Theology and the human condition

1   Early life and mathematical works

Blaise Pascal was born in Clermont in Auvergne, the son of a government official who was also an enthusiast for the new mathematical learning. With his family, he moved to Paris in 1631, and stayed there until 1638, when his father was forced to flee because of his public opposition to an aspect of Richelieu's fiscal policy. Blaise was educated privately by his father, who wanted him to be fully conversant with Greek and Latin before introducing him to mathematics: but his prodigy son worked out for himself the principles of geometry as far as the thirty-second proposition of Book I of Euclid at the age of twelve. It was also during this Parisian period that he was able to attend the mathematical academy of Father Marin MERSENNE who was actively engaged both in European scientific and philosophical circles and in the religious controversy surrounding the new scientific ideas, as Pascal himself was also to become engaged. It is unclear how well-grounded Pascal was in the classics and in traditional Aristotelian logic and physics, and whether his unconventional education contributed to the originality that he showed in his later career.

After his father had been pardoned by Cardinal de Richelieu for his dissent and given the office of royal tax commissioner for the province of Haute Normandie, Pascal went with him to Rouen in 1640; in the same year his first mathematical publication, the *Essai pour les Coniques* (Essay on conical sections), appeared. Two years later he invented a calculating machine, which he had originally conceived to help his father with his tax work; this remarkable achievement was far in advance of the industrial skills required to produce it, although various versions were made and demonstrated to scientific colleagues, prominent politicians and members of the aristocracy.

2 The debate over the vacuum

Between 1646 and 1648, Pascal became embroiled in the fierce European debate concerning the existence of the vacuum. Torricelli's experiment with a barometer, which involved placing a tube of mercury upside down in a bowl of mercury, had been made public in France by Mersenne in 1644, and had given rise to many competing interpretations. Nearly all of these had recourse to the notion of atmospheric pressure as an explanation, and there was general agreement that the space at the top of the tube contained some kind of rarefied and invisible matter, which was consistent with the Aristotelian adage *natura abhorret vacuum*. In 1647, Pascal published his *Expériences nouvelles touchant le vide* (Experiments on the vacuum); this was the summary of a series of experiments he conducted with Pierre Petit, using variously sized and shaped tubes and different liquids. Through them he was able to determine the quantity of water and mercury that could be supported by air pressure and the size a siphon had to be in order to function. He also set out in this summary the reasons why there was no rarefied and invisible matter occupying the space above the column of liquid supported in the barometer, but did not feel able yet to affirm the existence of a vacuum. He was challenged in his conclusions by Father Étienne Noel, the Jesuit Rector of the Collège de Clermont in Paris and a proponent

of traditional Aristotelian physics; Pascal set out in his reply what are now taken to be the basic principles governing the application of scientific judgment and method. At the same time, he wrote to his brother-in-law Florin Périer to ask him to undertake the experiment of carrying a barometer up a mountain (the Puy-de-Dôme), the results of which showed that the level in the column of mercury varied with height. Pascal confirmed this himself on a church tower in Paris, and published the findings in 1648 in his *Récit de la grande expérience de l'équilibre des liqueurs* (Account of the great experiment on equilibrium in liquids); he concluded that experiment, not authority, governed physics, that his experiments had shown that nature has no horror of a vacuum, and that air pressure accounts for all the effects associated with said imaginary horror. These experimental writings played an important role in discrediting Aristotelian and scholastic scientific ideas (see ARISTOTLE; ARISTOTELIANISM, MEDIEVAL; ARISTOTELIANISM, RENAISSANCE).

3 Pascal and Jansenism

Pascal's father suffered an accident in 1646, which brought him into contact with a priest sympathetic to the ideas of Cornelis Jansen (1585–1638), the bishop of Ypres. Pascal also encountered Jansenist ideas on grace and piety, and was deeply affected by them, as were other members of his family. After her father's death in 1651, Blaise's sister Jacqueline became a nun at the convent at Port-Royal, which was the centre of Jansenist doctrine and religious practice in France (see PORT-ROYAL). Pascal opposed her vocation strongly, and indeed for two years thereafter led a life very different from hers, consorting with free-thinkers, gamblers and libertines of fashionable Parisian society; but on the night of 23 November 1654 he underwent a profound spiritual experience which altered his life irrevocably.

This 'nuit de feu' was such that Pascal sewed the record that he made of it at the time of the event itself as a permanent memento into his clothes, where it was found at his death. The document records an experience of conversion; not an intellectual experience, but one which persuaded Pascal of the superiority of instinctive belief. (This conviction was strengthened two years later, when his niece was cured miraculously at Port-Royal of an apparently incurable fistula.) As a result of his experience, Pascal went to Port-Royal-des-Champs for a two-week retreat in 1655. There he met Isaac Le Maistre de Saci, a Jansenist theologian, with whom he had a debate, an account of which was published in 1720 as *Entretien avec M. de Saci* (A conversation with M. de

Saci). This debate indicates not only that Pascal had conceived of an apology of the Christian religion in terms which would speak most powerfully to the very libertines and gamblers of the Parisian society which he had just forsaken, but also that he felt that one of the most powerful voices with which he had to contend was that of Michel de MONTAIGNE, the gentleman philosopher who had championed the cause of scepticism in the later sixteenth century. It is also clear that he felt the need to reassure those who had been shaken in their faith by new scientific developments, especially those in astronomy. Among Pascal's immediate sources of inspiration was Antoine ARNAULD, the leading Jansenist theologian and philosopher, who was at that time on the point of being condemned by the Sorbonne for his religious views. Together with Arnauld and Pierre Nicole, another prominent Jansenist, Pascal composed the *Lettres provinciales* (Provincial letters), a series of eighteen letters published in 1656–7. These constitute a scathing attack on the moral and theological views of the Jesuits, who were the most vociferous opponents of both Arnauld and Jansenism. In this debate the Jesuits were somewhat unfairly represented as a religious faction which engaged in deliberate deception for political ends and sacrificed doctrine to morals, and the Jansenists were for their part depicted as crypto-Calvinists whose interpretation of St Augustine was both erroneous and heretical. Pascal and his co-authors tried vigorously to rebut the charge of heresy levelled at Jansen's writings while still acknowledging the authority of the Church that as Roman Catholics they were bound to accept. As it transpired, the debate was won *de facto* by the Jesuits; the *Lettres provinciales* were placed on the Index of Forbidden Books in 1657, and the Jansenist movement itself was condemned by the Pope shortly after. But the wit of the letters and their dazzling display of satire and irony have ensured that the judgment of posterity has been accorded to Pascal's side, at least in literary terms. For all that, the school at Port-Royal was closed in 1661, and the remaining *solitaires* and nuns were forced to sign a document to mark their submission to the Roman Catholic Church; this prompted Pascal to write the *Écrit sur la signature du formulaire* (Tract on the signing of the formulary), urging Port-Royalists not to sign. In it he reiterated the defence of Jansenism which is found in the *Lettres provinciales*, distinguishing between fact and faith or law in matters of religion. Councils, Fathers of the Church and popes are infallible on matters of faith, but not on matters of fact, and Pascal contends that the identification of Jansenism with heresy is a matter of fact, not law. The *Écrit* was never published because Nicole and Arnauld contradicted Pascal's

advice. After a stormy altercation with them, Pascal renounced all further engagement in religious controversy. Instead he devoted his final months of life to the poor of the part of Paris in which he lived, not only making over all his worldly goods to them, but also organizing what was in effect the world's first omnibus service, which carried passengers from one part of Paris to another for a fixed fare. Throughout his short life, he had never enjoyed long periods of good health; he died on 19 August 1662 after a protracted and painful illness, and his final days were marked by his own deep piety and his desire to fulfil his religious duties to the last.

4 Works posthumously published

Although Pascal was well known to the European scientific community in his lifetime, few of his works were published. His last foray into the world of mathematics – the solution to a set of problems concerning the nature of the cycloid – was in fact circulated anonymously as a competition in 1658, although its author was sufficiently well-known for the Dutch mathematician and physicist Christiaan Huyghens (1629–95) to write to Pascal about it in the following year. After Pascal's death some mathematicians (including Leibniz) had access to his scientific papers, but these did not all appear in print until much later. Pascal's religious writings, however, were posthumously edited by his family and friends; the *Pensées* and other short works appeared in 1670, and the *Entretien avec M. de Saci* in 1728. The original edition of the *Pensées* was both an abridgment and a reworking of Pascal's papers, only part of which had been put in order by him; since the mid-nineteenth century various attempts have been made to reconstruct the manuscript as it was left by Pascal, culminating in Louis Lafuma's edition of 1952 which is now taken to be standard. More recently still Pol Ernst has been able not only to reconstruct the pages which were cut up by Pascal himself when he decided to arrange the fragments into thematic groups, but also to establish the date of composition of the major part of the project (1656–8). This recent scholarship has permitted a (somewhat conjectural) chronological ordering of the *Pensées* to be published and has opened up new possibilities for their interpretation.

5 Mathematical philosophy

Pascal himself said in a letter to Pierre Fermat written in 1660 that he felt that his religious writings had little connection with his scientific and mathematical work. His outlook, however, was deeply influenced by what he conceived to be a new way of looking at the world inspired by geometry, and most commentators would agree that all his writings are impregnated with it. He himself made strictly mathematical contributions to number theory, geometry and probability theory, but he also involved himself in the wider polemic about the status of science in his day. In his letter to Father Noel, he set out the prerequisites of sound scientific methodology, laid down the rules for making affirmative or negative scientific judgments (through axioms and apodictic demonstration), and for establishing or disproving hypotheses about the physical world, which in his view could never be more than provisional. In the same letter, Pascal referred to the rival claims of authority (in this case, the authority of Aristotle) and scientific demonstration; this topic is more fully developed in the *Préface sur le traité du vide* (Preface to a treatise on the vacuum) (1651?), in which Pascal shows that experiment and correct reasoning should govern the sciences, and that authority and historical example have no place in them. His view of science is very much a progressive one; as more and more experiments are undertaken with more sophisticated instruments, previously accepted hypotheses are supplanted by newer ones. Thus the hypothesis of occult qualities or powers, which was postulated to explain what lies beyond sensory perception, and the Aristotelian distinction between act and potency, should be replaced if experimentation can show that they are inadequate according to Pascal's rules. Natural causation and phenomena are unchanging; human attempts to understand them are relative to the historical moment at which the attempts are made. In a striking image, Pascal refers to the successive generations of scientists as a single person in a perpetual state of existence and development. Thus, when we disagree with scientists of the past, we are not contradicting them, since by applying the principle of charity we would have to agree that we would have understood the world in their way had we lived in their times with their resources; and it follows also that they would have agreed with us today for the same reasons. (It is worth noting that Pascal is willing to believe that past scientists acted and wrote in good faith, whereas he refused to concede that his Jesuit opponents did so.)

De l'Esprit géométrique et de l'art de persuader (On the spirit of geometry and the art of persuasion) (1657–8?) is a yet more sophisticated presentation of the new scientific outlook. Pascal begins by conceding that definitions in geometry are nominal and not real, and that what are taken for axioms are intuitive perceptions which can neither be demonstrated nor reasonably be doubted. The four terms which he identifies in this way are number, space, movement and time. All share the property of being infinitely divisible and infinitely extensible. This insight is counter-intuitive to those who conceive knowledge as finite but, unless it can be grasped, then the geometric spirit itself cannot be comprehended. Pascal is not claiming that man's capacity for knowledge is unlimited; merely that the immediate information of his senses and his reason have to be transcended if scientific advances are to be made. Geometry emerges from this as superior to logic, in that it can both provide axioms and engage in demonstration, whereas logic can only do the latter.

The second part of the work is devoted to the thorny problem of persuasion; here the will comes into question as the path through which human assent to a given argument is to be obtained. Even here, however, a method or a set of rules are supplied for the correct conduct of an argument. Terms must be given clear definitions, axioms must be incontrovertible and must all be explicit, and conclusions should be checked by substituting definitions for the terms used. Pascal's discussion of scientific method is therefore distinct from Bacon's negative use of induction although, like Bacon, he conceives of science in evolutionary terms; nor does it evince Descartes' greater reliance on the resources of human reason; it harnesses the arguments of the sceptics, but escapes from their epistemological dilemma by positing intuitive truths which do not come to us from the exercise of our intellect (see BACON, F. §§2–6; DESCARTES, R. §§2–3).

6 Theology and the human condition

In 1658, Pascal gave an account of his planned apology for the Christian religion to his friends at Port-Royal, which is probably the reason for his cutting up his sheets of reflections and notes and arranging them into bundles. It is far from certain, however, that all the fragments which survive were written as part of this one project, or that the project was anything like complete and fixed in Pascal's mind. Not only are sections of the text in dialogue, with none of the voices clearly identified, it also seems likely that the grammatical first person who appears in a number of other fragments does not refer in all cases to Pascal himself. Such interpretative problems have not deterred past editors from partial or total reconstructions of the apology. The Lafuma edition, which is less interventionist, begins with a section devoted to the proposed organization of the work, which makes its general character clear. In the first part, the human condition was to be described, and shown to be wretched; in the second, human felicity with God and the truth of the Christian religion were to be demonstrated. In a series of sections entitled 'vanity', 'misery', 'ennui', 'causes of effects', 'greatness', 'contradictions', 'distraction', 'philosophers', Pascal sets out a description in implicitly Augustinian terms of human experience of the world. The arbitrariness and injustice of human political institutions, the vapidity of human pastimes, the false notions of social hierarchy, and the wilful flight of humans from confronting the primordial questions of their existence are all memorably expressed, often in terse aphoristic form. Notable is the very low assessment of the moral nature of humanity, whose self is said to be hateful. Pascal then turns to the paradox that in the human's very wretchedness there lie the seeds of greatness. Although the passions and imagination pervert and oppress them, humans also possess reason and self-awareness, and even can attain to certain knowledge about their environment through their intuitive grasp of geometric axioms. Such intuition, which Pascal sites in the heart, is also where true faith in God is to be found; the function of his apology is to persuade his reader rationally that the Christian religion is true because its description of the human condition is accurate, but it cannot do more than predispose the reader to receive the gratuitous divine gift of faith. In this sense it is a superfluous enterprise; and although in his *Écrits sur la Grâce* (Writings on grace) (1657–8?) he tries to come to terms with the Tridentine proposition that the just are able of themselves to obey the Commandments, Pascal seems to concede the inefficacy of instilling rational conviction alone at various points in the *Pensées*.

As he does elsewhere, Pascal here sets up powerful binary oppositions between philosophies and exploits their reciprocal failings and strengths. Scepticism is modest in its claims, yet impotent and negative; dogmatism (roughly, rationalistic neo-Stoicism) is presumptuous and yet has some purchase on the real world. Philosophy is therefore incapable both of knowing humanity and of taking action. Pascal finds a way beyond this impasse by exploiting his insight about the infinitely great and the infinitely small in a novel manner: humans are everything with respect to nothing, and nothing with respect to everything (God and the cosmos). They are also imbued with a desperate desire for certainty, and cannot suspend their judgment indefinitely, because they are subject to an existential imperative: 'you must take on the bet, for you are in the game' (Pascal 1670: 550 [L418]). This is the context of the famous wager argument, which had been used before Pascal by other apologists. Either God exists, or he does not: if human life is vain and wretched (as Pascal believes he has demonstrated), humans have nothing to lose by betting on the next life (that is submitting to the

Christian religion), for they have lost nothing in the case of God's nonexistence, and gained everything if he does exist. Some have seen this argument as purely rhetorical; others have accused it of being a case of *petitio principii* (the worthlessness of life is presupposed in the conclusion that we have nothing to lose in sacrificing the allegedly vain pleasures of this world); yet others see in it an ingenious example of decision theory *avant la lettre*. Whatever interpretation is given to it, it can be seen to be particularly apposite to the potential constituency of libertines and gamblers whom Pascal was intending to address.

Pascal's apology is therefore not simply fideistic, postulating the two truths of faith and reason; it employs both faith and reason, as well as doubt, to achieve certainty. As one *pensée* has it 'one must doubt in the right way, assert in the right way, and submit in the right way' (1670: 523 [L170]). Descartes tried to demonstrate too much, and relied on his *cogito* to gain knowledge of an infinite and hence incomprehensible God; Montaigne doubted too much, and did not agonize enough about his passive acceptance of ignorance and hedonism; only Pascal (and his mentor St Augustine) used reason to affirm, to negate and to recognize its own limitations appropriately. In the second part of his apology, Pascal planned to use arguments from Biblical history, prophecies, miracles, and above all else the interpretation of Holy Writ to present the case for the truth of Christianity; but he conceded that such proofs were not absolutely convincing, although they were sufficient to secure the consent of those who read them free from the perverting effects of their own corrupt passions.

In the *Pensées*, as in the *Esprit géométrique*, Pascal is at pains to stress the importance of style. The great art, which he identified in Epictetus, in Montaigne's essays as well as in his own writings, was to write in such a way that those reading would think that they could have written the text themselves. As he shrewdly put it: 'it is not in Montaigne, but in me that I find all that I find in his text' (1670: 591 [L689]). Knowledge has to be made desirable, and also to be made accessible; the writer is its undetectable mediator; truth, as he had asseverated in the letter to Father Noel, is itself not a historical or personal phenomenon. The fortunes of his own writings do not seem to bear this out. In the late seventeenth century, he was the champion of those who embraced Augustine's gloomy vision of corrupt human nature; in the eighteenth century, he was reviled for the same reason by moralists of a more optimistic bent; in the twentieth century he was caused to doubt the existence of God in the early part, a Kierkegaardian existentialist in the middle, and is now appreciated as a rhetorician and precursor of probability theory. The sustained interest shown in his work is a testament to its linguistic brilliance, its brevity and its clear vision of an epistemology embracing both the seen and the unseen, the intuited and the perceived, and the natural and the supernatural, all grounded in an impressively coherent outlook derived from his particular conception of geometry.

See also: DECISION AND GAME THEORY

List of works

Pascal, B. (1963) *Oeuvres complètes* (Complete works), ed. L. Lafuma, Paris: Seuil. (The standard edition which includes the correspondence.)

—— (1640) *Essai pour les Coniques* (Essay on conical sections). (Published as a poster.)

—— (1647) *Expériences nouvelles touchant le vide* (Experiments on the vacuum), Paris: Margat.

—— (1648) *Récit de la grande expérience de l'équilibre des liqueurs* (Account of the great experiment on equilibrium in liquids), Paris: Savreux.

—— (1651?) *Préface sur le traité du vide* (Preface to a treatise on the vacuum). (Unpublished manuscript.)

—— (1656–7) *Lettres provinciales*, trans. A.J. Krailsheimer as *The Provincial Letters*, Harmondsworth: Penguin, 1967; trans. T. M'Crie *et al.* in *The Provincial Letters: Pensées: Scientific Treatises*, Chicago, IL and London: Encyclopaedia Britannica, 1990. (The French first editions of the various letters are without imprint: both translations are good.)

—— (1657–8?) *De l'Esprit géométrique et de l'art de persuader* (On the spirit of geometry and the art of persuasion).

—— (1657–8?) *Écrits sur la Grâce* (Writings on grace).

—— (1661) *Écrit sur la signature du formulaire* (Tract on the signing of the formulary). (Unpublished manuscript.)

—— (1670) *Pensées*, Paris: Port-Royal; seconde copie repr. ed. P. Sellier, Paris: Mercure de France, 1991; trans. A.J. Krailsheimer, Harmondsworth: Penguin, 1995.

—— (1728) *Entretien avec M. de Saci* (A conversation with M. de Saci), in P. Desmolets (ed.) *Continuation des Mémoires de littérature et d'histoire*, Paris: Tronchai.

—— (1990) *The Provincial Letters: Pensées: Scientific Treatises*, trans. T. M'Crie *et al.*, Chicago, IL and London: Encyclopaedia Britannica.

—— (1992) *Discours sur la religion et sur quelques autres sujets* (A Discourse on religion and other subjects), ed. E. Martineau, Paris: Fayard/Colin.

(An edition based on the supposed chronological composition of the *Pensées*.)

References and further reading

Carraud, V. (1992) *Pascal et la philosophie* (Pascal and philosophy), Paris: PUF. (Comprehensive, accessible and orthodox account.)

Davidson, H.M. (1979) *The origins of certainty: means and meaning in Pascal's Pensées*, Chicago, IL and London: University of Chicago Press. (Relates Pascal to developments in seventeenth-century epistemology.)

Descotes, D. (1993) *L'argumentation chez Pascal* (Argumentation in Pascal), Paris: PUF. (Highly technical account of Pascal's logic, using nonstandard notation.)

* Ernst, P. (1990) *Géologie et stratigraphie des Pensées de Pascal* (Geology and stratigraphy of the Pensees of Pascal), Paris: Thesis of the University of Paris IV, 4 vols. (Mentioned in §4 above.)

Goldmann, L. (1959) *Le dieu caché. Études sur la vision tragique dans les Pensées de Pascal et dans le théâtre de Racine*, Paris: Gallimard; trans. P. Thody as *The hidden God: a study of tragic vision in the Pensées of Pascal and the tragedies of Racine*, London, Routledge & Kegan Paul, 1964. (A Marxist reading of Pascal, relating him to the worldview of his class.)

Hacking, I. (1975) *The emergence of probability: a philosophical study of early ideas about probability, induction and statistical inference*, Cambridge: Cambridge University Press. (Contains the claim that the wager argument is an early example of decision theory.)

Krailsheimer, A. (1980) *Pascal*, Oxford: Past Masters. (A good general introduction.)

McKenna, A. (1990) *De Pascal à Voltaire* (From Pascal to Voltaire), Oxford: Voltaire Foundation, 2 vols. (Thorough study of the early reception of Pascal, and of the influences on his thought.)

Marin, L. (1975) *La critique du discours: sur la logique de Port-Royal et les Pensées de Pascal* (The critique of discourse: on the Logic of Port-Royal and the *Pensées* of Pascal), Paris: Minuit. (A thought-provoking account of Jansenist philosophy.)

Mesnard, J. (1967) *Pascal*, Paris: Hatier. (A very good introduction in French.)

—— (1976) *Les Pensées de Pascal* (The *Pensées* of Pascal), Paris: Société d'édition d'énseignement supérieur. (Good nontechnical account of the religious and literary aspects of the *Pensées*.)

Mesnard, J. *et al.* (eds) (1979) *Méthodes chez Pascal* (Methods in Pascal), Paris: PUF. (Contains good papers on all aspects of Pascal's writing.)

Metzer, S.E. (1967) *Discourses of the fall: a study of Pascal's Pensées*, Berkeley, CA: University of California Press. (Good on religious aspects of Pascal's thought.)

Parish, R. (1989) *Pascal's Lettres provinciales: a study in polemic*, Oxford: Oxford University Press. (Best available account of the *Lettres provinciales*.)

Sellier, P. (1970) *Pascal et saint Augustin* (Pascal and St Augustine), Paris: Colin. (Excellent study of Pascal's debt to Saint Augustine.)

Thirouin, L. (1991) *Le hasard et ses régles: le modèle du jeu dans la pensée de Pascal* (Chance and its rules: the model of gambling and play in Pascal's thought), Paris: Vrin. (Very good on the relationship of Pascal's thought to mathematics.)

IAN MACLEAN

PASSMORE, JOHN ARTHUR (1914–)

John Passmore was born in New South Wales and studied at the University of Sydney. He taught there before moving to Otago in New Zealand and then to the Australian National University. He is perhaps best known for A Hundred Years of Philosophy *which has been widely recognized as a major feat of philosophical scholarship. He has contributed widely to topics in the history of philosophy, philosophy of education, philosophy of science and philosophy of the environment. He is one of the pioneers of what has come to be called applied philosophy.*

Passmore was born in Manly, New South Wales. He was an early student of the influential Scottish-born philosopher John Anderson at the University of Sydney. He taught at Sydney before going to the Chair of Philosophy at the University of Otago in 1950. In 1955 he moved to the Institute of Advanced Studies at the Australian National University where he was Reader and then Professor of Philosophy. He has held a number of senior visiting appointments in universities outside Australia and was Tanner Lecturer at Cambridge University in 1980.

For much of his career Passmore was something of a lone voice in Australian philosophy. His interests were more historical and applied than was usual in Australia in the 1950s and 1960s; indeed his work was probably better known during this period in Britain and America than in Australia. This changed with an increase in interest in the history of philosophy and especially in the contributions philosophers can make to issues of general concern that started in the 1970s,

and many of his writings, particularly those on the philosophy of the environment, have become a focal point of discussion in Australia as well as overseas. He has an unusual ability to write argumentatively rigorous and philosophically sophisticated prose that readers not professionally involved in philosophy find challenging but not intimidating. In consequence his influence has extended well beyond philosophy departments. He has played an important role in showing the world at large how philosophers of an essentially analytical bent can make major contributions on subjects of general concern. He must be regarded as one of the pioneers of applied philosophy.

Passmore's best known book, especially among professional philosophers, is *A Hundred Years of Philosophy*, first published in 1957. It is widely recognized as a remarkable work of scholarship that displays an encyclopedic knowledge of the major philosophical movements of the preceding one hundred years combined with an intimidating understanding of their historical origins. It established his reputation in the history of philosophy. It has been a goldmine for teachers and students of philosophy, and a major first port of call for non-philosophers.

It is, however, his writings on the philosophy of the environment that have been the most influential in the sense of setting the agenda (see ENVIRONMENTAL ETHICS; GREEN POLITICAL PHILOSOPHY). In *Man's Responsibility for Nature* he argues that we need as a matter of urgency to change our attitudes to nature, that we cannot go on living, as we have been, as predators on the biosphere. At the same time he argues vigorously against the view that we should see our present predicament as a sign that we should abandon the Western scientific and rationalist tradition and embrace some form of irrationalism or mysticism. The book is both an important contribution to environmental philosophy and an attack on the scientific irrationalism that is prevalent in some sections of the environment movement. In particular, he argues that the view that it is the Western tradition *per se* that is responsible for our present predicament is based on a misreading of and a selective attention to the complex historical facts. Rather, Passmore argues, we should use the tools that this tradition has provided us with to find our way out of our present predicament. A distinctive feature of the argument of the book, and indeed of much of Passmore's work, is the way it is set within a historical setting. He seeks to tell us how we got to where we are before telling us what we should do about it.

In *Philosophical Reasoning* a number of distinctive styles of reasoning in philosophy are identified and subjected to critical scrutiny. The book was published in the early 1960s, a time during which it was commonly claimed that these distinctive styles of argument, recently uncovered, served to dissolve many traditional philosophical problems. The enthusiasm with which philosophers embrace a new style of argumentation is not always matched by their readiness to examine its credentials, and this book played an important, if sobering, role.

See also: AUSTRALIA, PHILOSOPHY IN

List of works

Passmore, J.A. (1951) *Ralph Cudworth*, Cambridge: Cambridge University Press.

—— (1952) *Hume's Intentions*, Cambridge: Cambridge University Press.

—— (1957) *A Hundred Years of Philosophy*, London: Duckworth.

—— (1961) *Philosophical Reasoning*, London: Duckworth.

—— (1970) *The Perfectibility of Man*, London: Duckworth.

—— (1974) *Man's Responsibility for Nature*, London: Duckworth.

—— (1985) *Recent Philosophers*, London: Duckworth.

—— (1991) *Serious Art*, London: Duckworth.

References and further reading

Brown, R. and Rollins, C.D. (1969) *Contemporary Philosophy in Australia*, London: Allen & Unwin. (Articles on sundry philosophical topics by Australians, with an introduction by Alan Donagan on the state of Australian philosophy and its background.)

FRANK JACKSON

PATAÑJALI (*c.* 2nd century BC)

The grammarian Patañjali lived in the second century BC, before the appearance of the classical systems of Indian philosophy. The aspects of his thought that we would call philosophical are concerned primarily with questions of meaning and meaning-bearers in language.

1 Patañjali and philosophy
2 The linguistic units that have meaning
3 Do phonemes have meaning?
4 The meaning of a word

1 Patañjali and philosophy

Patañjali is the author of the *Mahābhāṣya* (Great Commentary), which comments on Pāṇini's famous grammar called *Aṣṭādhyāyī* (*c.* fourth century BC) and on Kātyāyana's *Vārttikas*; the latter have only survived as part of the *Mahābhāṣya* (Great Commentary) (*c.* second century BC). Patañjali is one of the few authors of early India whose approximate date is probably known. He lived around the middle of the second century BC in the north of India during the incursions into the country of the Graeco-Bactrian king Menander, to which he refers. This early date is confirmed by the absence of influence from the classical systems of Indian philosophy on his thought, with the possible exception of Sarvāstivāda Buddhism.

The *Mahābhāṣya* is not primarily a philosophical treatise. It addresses some philosophical questions in its introduction (whose title is *Paspaśāhnika*) while commenting upon certain grammatical rules (*sūtra*) of Pāṇini. Interestingly, Patañjali (who often sides in this respect with Kātyāyana) does not always share Pāṇini's point of view.

2 The linguistic units that have meaning

Rule 1.2.45 of Pāṇini's grammar states that 'what is meaningful, but is not verbal root or affix, is nominal stem' (*arthavad adhātur apratyayaḥ prātipadikam*). If we use the term 'stem' to refer to both verbal roots and nominal stems, this *sūtra* makes clear that for Pāṇini only stems and affixes really have meaning. Combinations of stems and affixes, that is, words and sentences, have at best meanings that are derived from those of the constituent stems and affixes. For Patañjali the situation is the exact opposite of this: words and sentences, not stems and affixes, are meaningful. This is clear from his discussion of rule 1.2.45 where he observes that this *sūtra* would assign the designation 'nominal stem' (*prātipadika*) to words and sentences. This contingency is avoided with the help of some far-fetched and unconvincing arguments. Next Patañjali turns to the question of how stems and affixes can be thought to have meaning, which he considers problematic, unlike Pāṇini. In Patañjali's opinion the nominal stem *vṛkṣa* on its own expresses no meaning. Cardona (1967–8) delineates the following solution offered by Patañjali: the method of concurrent occurrence of meaning and linguistic unit (*anvaya*) and absence of these two (*vyatireka*) shows that *vṛkṣa*, which is the common part of *vṛkṣas*, or 'one tree' and *vṛkṣau*, or 'two trees', must have the meaning, 'tree'. In this way, Patañjali derives the meaning of the stem *vṛkṣa* from the 'real' meanings 'one tree' and 'two trees'. The pair *pacati*, 'he cooks' and *paṭhati*, 'he recites', he similarly points out (*sūtra*1.3.1) allows us to assign a meaning to the common part -*ati*. Speaking generally, the meanings of stems and affixes are derived from the meanings of complete words.

Patañjali's deviation from Pāṇini is most easily explained by the hypothesis that he was influenced by the Sarvāstivāda Buddhists, who had reified phonemes and words (and perhaps sentences), but not stems and affixes, into existing 'real' elements (*dharma*). This is confirmed by the fact that Patañjali, too, accepts phonemes and words, but not stems and affixes, as independently (and eternally) existing entities. In connection with these independently existing phonemes and words, Patañjali uses several times the expression *sphoṭa*, which plays a major role in the discussions of later grammarians. Unlike them, Patañjali does not look upon the *sphoṭa* as a meaning-bearer, according to Joshi (1967). He speaks, for example, of the *sphoṭa* of individual phonemes. This *sphoṭa* is different from the sound (*dhvani*) which manifests it. The word or phoneme (*śabda*) is the *sphoṭa* and the sound is a property of the word or phoneme. If one person speaks slowly, another quickly, the *sphoṭa* is the same, only the manifesting sound is different (see LANGUAGE, INDIAN THEORIES OF §§1, 3).

3 Do phonemes have meaning?

Although reticent with regard to the meaningfulness of stems and affixes, Patañjali pays great attention in his second chapter (*āhnika*) to the question of whether individual phonemes have meaning. He argues that certain stems and affixes consist of just one phoneme. The verbal root *i*, for example, means 'go'. Certain words which are identical but for one phoneme, express different meanings: *kūpa* means 'well', *sūpa* 'soup', *yūpa* 'sacrificial post'. Also, the removal of one phoneme can change the meaning: *vṛkṣa* means 'tree', *ṛkṣa* 'bear'. Finally, if phonemes had no meaning, collections of phonemes could have no meaning either; one hundred blind people cannot see more than what one blind person can see. Patañjali subsequently rejects these arguments. Sounds normally have no meaning, because they can be modified, elided, or change position in a grammatical derivation. Since only collections of phonemes have meaning, nothing can be concluded from sets of similar words like *kūpa*, *sūpa* and *yūpa*, nor indeed from the pair *vṛkṣa* and *ṛkṣa*. Collections of phonemes can have features which the constituent phonemes do not possess: a chariot, too, can perform functions which its parts cannot.

4 The meaning of a word

What is the meaning of a word according to Patañjali? In the second *āhnika* four kinds of words are distinguished according to what they refer to: words that refer to a genus (*jātiśabda*), those that refer to a quality (*guṇaśabda*), those that refer to an action (*kriyā śabda*) and arbitrary proper nouns (*yadṛcchā śabda*). The first three of these clearly designate nouns, adjectives and verbs respectively. But in the first *āhnika* Patañjali enumerates (twice over) the following four classes of words: nominal words (*nāman*), verbs (*ākhyāta*), preverbs (*upasarga*) and particles (*nipāta*). This enumeration is taken from Yāska's *Nirukta* (*c.* third century BC [1967: I.1]), where the meanings of these different types of words are elaborately discussed. Nominal words (nouns and adjectives), for example, are there described as 'having *entity* as their predominant notion' (*sattvapradhāna*), verbs as 'having *being* as their predominant notion' (*bhāvapradhāna*) (Kahrs 1986: 117). Patañjali was probably aware of the meanings assigned to words there.

Elsewhere (especially in *sūtra* 1.2.64) Patañjali distinguishes two possible meanings of words: the form (*ākṛti*) or the individual object (*dravya*). The former of these two positions is associated with the name of Vājapyāyana. Vyāḍi, on the other hand, held that words denote individual objects. Here, it seems, the discussion concerns itself with nouns primarily. In fact, there is reason to believe that for Patañjali 'form' (*ākṛti*) and 'genus' (*jāti*) were synonyms. Patañjali himself held that both form and individual object constitute the meaning of words.

See also: MEANING, INDIAN THEORIES OF §§1–2

List of works

Patañjali (*c.* 2nd century BC) *(Vyākaraṇa-)Mahāb-hāṣya*, ed. F. Kielhorn, 1880–5, 3 vols; 3rd edn, ed. K.V. Abhyankar, Poona: Bhandarkar Oriental Research Institute, 1972. (Comments on Pāṇini's *Aṣṭādhyāyī*.)

—— (*c.* 2nd century BC) *Mahābhāṣya*, trans. S.D. Joshi and J.A.F. Roodbergen, Poona, 1968. (Eleven volumes have appeared between 1968 and 1990. They continue to be published.)

References and further reading

Bronkhorst, J. (1987) *Three Problems Pertaining to the Mahābhāṣya*, Poona: Bhandarkar Oriental Research Institute. (Especially chapter 3, 'The Ma-

hābhāṣya and the development of Indian philosophy'.)

* Cardona, G. (1967–8) '*Anvaya* and *vyatireka* in Indian grammar', *Adyar Library Bulletin* 31–2: 313–52. (Discusses the use of this pair of conceptual tools.)
—— (1980) *Pāṇini: a Survey of Research*, Delhi: Motilal Banarsidass. (A full bibliographical breakdown of editions and translations of the *Mahābhāṣya*.)
* Joshi, S.D. (1967) *The Sphoṭanirṇaya of Kauṇḍa Bhaṭṭa*, Poona: University of Poona. (The introduction contains a discussion of Patañjali's views on the nature of words.)
* Kahrs, E. (ed.) (1986) 'Durga on *bhāva*', in *Kalyàamitrārāgaṇam: Essays in Honour of Nils Simonsson*, Oslo: Norwegian University Press, 115–44. (Discusses the possible interpretations of *sattvapradhāna* and *bhāvapradhāna*.)
* Pāṇini (*c.* 4th century BC) *Aṣṭādhyāyī*, ed. and trans. O. Böhtlingk, Leipzig, 1887; repr. Hildesheim and New York: Georg Olms, 1977. (Pāṇini's famous grammar book.)
* Yāska (*c.* 3rd century) *Nirukta*, ed. and trans. L. Sarup, Delhi: Motilal Banarsidass, 1967. (The meanings of different types of words are discussed in detail.)

JOHANNES BRONKHORST

PATERNALISM

Restriction of people's liberty of action is paternalistic when it is imposed for the good of those whose liberty is restricted and against their will. The argument in favour of paternalism is that, if one can prevent people from harming themselves, there is no reason not to do so. Versions of the ethical creed of liberalism tend to oppose paternalism. One argument is that as a practical matter the policy of permitting paternalism tends to do more harm than good in the long run, or at least less good than a strict refusal to countenance paternalism would achieve. Another argument appeals to a right of autonomy which paternalism is held to violate whether or not its consequences on the whole are undesirable. Paternalist advocacy can be 'hard' or 'soft'; soft paternalism is the doctrine that paternalism can only be justifiable when the individual action that is being restricted was not chosen in a substantially voluntary way.

1   The concept of paternalism
2   Utilitarianism for and against paternalism
3   The right to autonomy; hard and soft paternalism

1   The concept of paternalism

One behaves paternalistically if one treats an adult as though one were a parent dealing with a child. One's behaviour shows concern for the welfare of the person and a presumption that one's judgment about what will promote it is superior. The paradigm of paternalism, and the focus of most philosophical discussion of it, is restriction of people's liberty against their will for their own good.

Whether a restriction of liberty is paternalistic or not depends on its rationale. If most people want a law requiring that they wear seat-belts when riding in cars for their own protection, and we enact a law in order to cater to this desire, enforcing this policy restricts people's liberty, but not against their will. In its application to the minority who do not want to be under this requirement, the law is still not paternalistic – though it may be unfair – if its rationale is administrative convenience and not the aim of restricting people's freedom against their will for their own good.

2   Utilitarianism for and against paternalism

The case for paternalism is simple. If we can prevent people from harming themselves, why not do it? According to act utilitarianism, one ought always to do whatever would produce the most good (utility) for people (and perhaps other sentient creatures) (see UTILITARIANISM). Whenever restricting someone's liberty to prevent harm to that very person is the utility-maximizing act, then act utilitarianism requires us to do it. Utilitarianism imposes stricter requirements of benevolence than most people accept (see HELP AND BENEFICENCE). One might hold that the better the cost-to-benefit ratio of a paternalistic act, the more obligatory the performance of the act. Or one might hold that so long as a paternalist imposition would do more good than harm, it is permissible even if not morally required.

In *On Liberty* (1859), a classic statement of a liberal utilitarian antipaternalism, John Stuart Mill does not dispute the theoretical possibility that in particular circumstances restricting someone's liberty for their own good might be the best thing to do from a utilitarian standpoint. Mill nevertheless proposes a liberty principle, which asserts that in modern societies the liberty of a sane and cognitively competent adult should never be restricted except to prevent harm to other persons who do not consent to this involvement (see MILL, J.S. §12).

Among its several implications, Mill's liberty principle forbids paternalistic restriction of liberty. Mill argues that we should adhere to this principle because in the long run, as a practical matter, rigid adherence to this rule would better promote utility than any alternative policy including the more flexible rule that forbids paternalism except in those particular situations in which paternalism happens to be utility-maximizing. Given that humans, including the humans who would administer any paternalist rule, are imperfectly rational, imperfectly well-informed, and not always disposed to be moral, the attempt by society to follow the liberty principle would produce more human happiness than any other course.

Mill's pragmatic defence of the liberty principle appeals to the likelihood that individuals will know their own interests better than those who are tempted to impose paternalistically on them, so such restriction will often be misguided. He also sketches a broad account of human nature and of what is needed to promote human fulfilment. According to Mill, humans vary in their natures. Given this diversity, no one or a few modes of life will be suitable for everyone. Moreover, our individual natures are not transparent to ourselves. One must learn about one's own individual nature in order to develop a reasonable plan of life. This process of individual self-discovery requires wide freedom to try out different modes of life and to observe the results of other people's experiments in living. As we learn about the possibilities inherent in our nature, we come to value some above others, and work to mould our characters so as to conform to a self-chosen ideal. In short, Mill believes we need to develop our individuality to have a good chance of happiness, and to develop individuality we need wide individual freedom.

Leaving aside the merits of Mill's bold psychological speculation, one notes that his argument from the need for individuality to a rule against paternalism is incomplete. Even if we need wide freedom to develop our individual natures, it might well be best if people are stopped from the most disastrous and stupid self-harming activities.

A second criticism of Mill's argument is that, even if his claim that refraining from paternalistic imposition would maximize utility in the long run were correct, it might still be morally desirable to embrace some paternalism to achieve fair distribution of utility. A strict no-paternalism policy will tend to produce good outcomes for prudent individuals who are skilled at making and executing personal decisions and less good outcomes for individuals whose prudential skills are poor. On the average the imprudent bad choosers will be living worse lives. Even if strict no-paternalism happened to be utility-maximizing, instituting some paternalism might be better for worse-off persons, and required by fairness

norms, especially if one thinks that imprudence is often nonblameworthy.

3 The right to autonomy; hard and soft paternalism

A more direct argument for the rejection of paternalism would dispense with utilitarian calculations and simply posit a moral right to live one's own life as one chooses so long as one does not thereby harm others in wrongful ways. On this view each individual has a right to autonomy, a right to govern their own life. Neither other individuals nor society as a whole has the authority to restrict an individual's liberty so long as the person's conduct is at worst self-harming and does not violate the rights of others.

The right to autonomy just described is stronger than a right against paternalistic imposition, because restriction of someone's liberty of action is paternalistic only if done for the sake of the individual who is coerced (or others who consent voluntarily to share involvement in the activity), and one might restrict an individual's liberty when it is conceded that the individual is not wrongfully harming others, in circumstances such that restricting the person's liberty would benefit others.

The right to autonomy as so far characterized is little more than a slogan pending further clarification of what its components might mean. One idea that calls for clarification is the idea that I have the right to act according to my own choices in self-affecting matters. But some restriction of people's choices does not seem to involve any overriding of their considered judgment and will. If Gertrude drinks a cup of poison, thinking it is harmless wine, she does not choose to bring about her death voluntarily. If Ulysses is driven temporarily insane by the Sirens' song, restricting his liberty for his own good is not really done against his will, because the will that chooses on the basis of insane impulse is not his authentic will. The ideal of voluntary choice encompasses many disparate disabilities. The more one chooses voluntarily, the more one is not choosing in ignorance of material matters of fact, not choosing on the basis of an error in reasoning, not choosing under conditions that tend to cloud judgment, not choosing under threat of coercion or duress, not insane or lacking basic cognitive capacities, and so on. Writers have distinguished 'hard' and 'soft' advocacy of paternalism. Soft paternalism is the doctrine that paternalism can only be justifiable when the individual choice that is restricted fails to be substantially voluntary – to meet a threshold level of voluntariness. The hard paternalist position holds that paternalism can be justifiable even if the individual action that is restricted is substantially voluntarily chosen.

One might interpret the right of autonomy as prohibiting paternalistic restriction of liberty only if the individual choice that is restricted is substantially voluntary. Or one might adopt a sliding scale: the more voluntary the choice, the stronger the moral presumption against the legitimacy of paternalism. Other views are possible – for example, one might hold that the legitimacy of paternalism depends both on the degree of voluntariness of the choice that is to be restricted and on the severity and danger of self-harm which the chosen conduct threatens to bring about.

See also: CONFUCIAN PHILOSOPHY, CHINESE §5; CONSENT; FREEDOM AND LIBERTY; LAW AND RITUAL IN CHINESE PHILOSOPHY; LIBERALISM; RESPECT FOR PERSONS

References and further reading

Buchanan, A.E. and Brock, D. (1989) *Deciding for Others: The Ethics of Surrogate Decision Making*, Cambridge: Cambridge University Press, esp. 29–47. (Wide-ranging discussion of the treatment of the incompetent.)

Dworkin, G. (1972) 'Paternalism', *Monist* 56: 64–84. (Criticizes Mill on paternalism.)

Feinberg, J. (1986) *The Moral Limits of the Criminal Law*, vol. 2, *Harm to Self*, Oxford: Oxford University Press. (Most comprehensive recent treatment of the issue of paternalistic restriction of liberty.)

Hill, T.E., Jr (1991) 'Autonomy and Benevolent Lies', in *Autonomy and Self-Respect*, Cambridge: Cambridge University Press, 25–42. (Argues that some types of paternalistic manipulation violate autonomy and human dignity.)

* Mill, J.S. (1859) *On Liberty*, Indianapolis, IN: Hackett Publishing Company, 1978. (Classic statement of a liberal utilitarian argument against paternalism in the context of a broad defence of individual freedom.)

Nozick, R. (1974) *Anarchy, State and Utopia*, New York: Basic Books. (Rejects paternalism by arguing for libertarian individual rights.)

Parfit, D. (1984) *Reasons and Persons*, Oxford: Oxford University Press, esp. 307–21. (Discusses issues of personal identity as they bear on the question of the rationality of caring now about the wellbeing of future stages of oneself, or of what one takes to be oneself.)

RICHARD J. ARNESON

PATOČKA, JAN (1907–77)

*Patočka was a Czech philosopher, one of the last pupils of Husserl. From the mid 1930s he developed his own approach to philosophical problems of the life-world (*Lebenswelt*), its structures and human activities in it. After 1945 he expanded this theme to incorporate other phenomenological problems (movement, freedom, aesthetics). He also paid much attention to the history of philosophy since antiquity, particularly to Comenius. After 1972, when the Communist system deprived him of his academic position, he elaborated his philosophical concept of History in his 'Heretical Essays'. He was one of the authors of the political manifesto of the Czechoslovak political opposition, Charter 77, and his name became a symbol of moral resistance against totalitarian power.*

Patočka (born in Turnov, died in Prague) was a leading Czech philosopher of the twentieth century. After studying in Prague, Paris, Berlin and Freiburg, where he was a pupil of Husserl and Heidegger, he was awarded a Chair at Prague's Charles University as a result of his work *The life-world as a philosophical problem*. At this time he was secretary of the Czech–German group 'Cercle philosophique de Prague', and helped with the preparation of the International Philsophical Congress in Prague in 1934. During the Nazi occupation of Czechoslovakia (1939–45) universities were closed, and Patočka taught at a grammar school. After the war he returned to his university post but was dismissed for political reasons in 1949. He could, however, carry on his scientific work at the Academy of Sciences. At the time of the 'Prague Spring' (1968) he was reinstated at the University, but had to leave again in 1972. Subsequently, he organized illegal lectures and seminars, joined an opposition movement against the Communist regime and was co-author of the political manifesto, Charter 77. When he suddenly died after a series of police interrogations, his name became a symbol of moral resistance against totalitarian power, and of the fight for human rights.

Patočka follows the humanistic tradition of Czech thinking which starts with the founder of the Czech Reformation, Jan HUS, and his predecessors; he demands that philosophy should lead us from daily banality to full humanity. The philosopher is defined as one who has broken through the cycle of demand and consumption, who has elevated themselves above the world towards permanent values. Patočka links this mission of philosophy with an analysis of the crisis of modern rationality as described by Husserl. He seeks a way out of this crisis in the adherence to the life-world. This is the elementary world of humans, the pre-reflexive and prescientific world, but a world in which we can find the sense of our existence. Patočka does not understand this world in the sense of Husserl's transcendental subjectivity, but emphasizes its existential, ontological dimension, its autonomy and non-reducibility; he calls his approach 'asubjective phenomenology'. Humans control this world (and are controlled by it) by three different kinds of movement. First, the movement of acceptance, 'taking root', that is finding one's place in the world. Second, the movement of defence, the labour which keeps humans going in the world and secures their basic needs. Third, the movement of truth, transcendence, which humans use to step over matters given to them directly and with which they reach the world as a whole. Patočka was alone for a long time in developing the problems of the life-world. Only from the end of the 1950s were these problems dealt with more frequently in phenomenological writing. The international philosophical public first saw the fundamentals of Patočka's work in the 1976 French translation of his *The life-world as a philosophical problem*.

Another of Patočka's contributions to phenomenological problems concerns the philosophy of history. Husserl himself only touched on the question of history in his *Crisis in the European Sciences*, where he understands the problem of history in a narrow sense as the problem of the *notion* of the life-world. He does not take this problem as far as a concrete human life in the world, in society and in history (see HUSSERL, E. §12). Patočka attempted to do that in his work *Heretical Essays on the Philosophy of History*, written in the early 1970s at a time when he was not allowed to publish in his home country. This book, which outlined the foundations for Patočka's political activities, was therefore distributed illegally. (A French translation appeared in 1981, with a prologue by Ricoeur and an epilogue by Jakobson.) According to Patočka, history starts when people realize the problems of their hitherto matter-of-course life, when the meaning of their life as understood until then is shattered and they discover the possibility of a free life. This happened first in the Greek *polis*, origin of politics, history and philosophy, whose inter-relationship became the legacy of European people. The loss of the previous purpose of life was the beginning of a search for a deeper, freer and more demanding purpose, but not for the final purpose – history is not something conclusive. This is why one cannot take the attitude of a disinterested spectator towards history; each has to feel responsible for it. From this follows the need to influence general matters and at the same time to 'look after one's soul'. Care for the soul is unthinkable without care for the commune.

Human activity is a prerequisite for the movement of history.

Throughout his life, Patočka also studied the history of philosophy, understanding it as a stimulus for live philosophizing. In this spirit he wrote studies of Socrates, Plato, Aristotle and numerous works on COMENIUS. It is mainly to Patočka's credit that Comenius ceased to be seen as just a brilliant educator: Patočka proved that Comenius's ideas on education were based on an original philosophical concept, so that his outstanding position in the history of European philosophy has also to be recognized.

See also: CZECH REPUBLIC, PHILOSOPHY IN

List of works

Patočka, J. (1936) *Le monde naturel comme un problème philosophique* (The life-world as a philosophical problem), trans. J. Daněk, Amsterdam: Martinus Nijhoff, 1976. (The translation which first brought Patočka's fundamental ideas to an international audience.)

—— (1976–7) 'Wars of the 20th Century and the 20th Century as War', *Telos* 30: 116–26. (The closing chapter of the book 'Heretical Essays on the Philosophy of History'.)

—— (1977) 'The Husserlian Doctrine of Eidetic Intuition and its Recent Critics', in F. Elliston and P. McCormick (eds) *Husserl, Exposition and appraisals*, Notre Dame, IN, and London: University of Notre Dame Press, 150–9. (An interpretation of one of the central notions of Husserl's philosophy.)

—— (1987–92) *Ausgewählte Schriften* (Selected Writings), Stuttgart: Klein-Cotta, 5 vols. (The most important works of Patočka in German translation, including writings on culture, philosophy of history, phenomenology and Czech issues.)

References and further reading

Bloss, S., Stróżewski, W. and Zumr, J. (eds) (1995) *Intentionalität, Werte, Kunst – Husserl, Ingarden, Patočka* (Intentionality, Values, Art – Husserl, Ingarden, Patočka), Prague: Filosofia. (Essays on the three phenomenologists by German, Polish and Czech authors in both English and German.)

Horak, P. and Zumr, J. (eds) (1992) *La Responsabilité/ Responsibility*, Entretiens de Prague, Institut International de Philosophie, 1990, Prague: L'Institut de Philosophie de l'Academie Tchecoslovaque des Sciences. (A session in honour of Patočka, with the texts of lectures delivered by R. Klibansky, P.

Ricoeur and L. Hejdánek, and a bibliography of translations of Patočka's writings into European languages.)

Kohak, E. (1989) *Jan Patočka: Philosophy and Selected Writings*, Chicago, IL: University of Chicago Press. (A study with English translations of some important works by Patočka.)

Tassin, E. and Richir, M. (eds) (1992) *Jan Patočka, philosophie, phénoménologie, politique* (Philosophy, phenomenology, politics), Grenoble: Jérôme Milou. (Essays in French on Patočka by French, German and Czech authors.)

Translated by G.R.F. Bursa

JOSEF ZUMR

PATRISTIC PHILOSOPHY

*Early Christian writers used terminology and ideas drawn from Graeco-Roman philosophical literature in their theological writings, and some early Christians also engaged in more formal philosophical reflection. The term 'patristic philosophy' covers all of these activities by the 'fathers' (*patres*) of the Church. The literature of nascent Christianity thus contains many concepts drawn from Graeco-Roman philosophy, and this early use of classical ideas by prominent Christians provided an authoritative sanction for subsequent philosophical discussion and elaboration.*

Early Christians were drawn to philosophy for many reasons. Philosophy held a pre-eminent place in the culture of the late Hellenistic and Roman world. Its schools provided training in logical rigour, systematic accounts of the cosmos and directions on how to lead a good and happy life. While philosophical movements of the period, such as Neoplatonism or Stoicism, varied widely in their doctrines, most presented accounts of reality that included some representation of the divine. These rationally articulated accounts established the theological and ethical discourse of Graeco-Roman culture. As such, philosophy had a natural appeal to Hellenistic Jewish and early Christian thinkers. It provided a ready language in which to refine ideas about the God of the ancient Hebrew scriptures, and to elaborate the trinitarian God of Christianity. It also helped to bring conceptual coherence to the ideas found in the scriptures of both religions. Finally, it provided the common intellectual discourse that those communities required in order to present their central tenets to the majority culture of the Roman empire.

To a considerable extent, the notion of 'philosophy' suggested to the ancients a way of life as much as an intellectual discipline. This too drew Christians to the

teachings of the philosophers. While there were doctrines and prescriptions of behaviour specific to the major schools, philosophers in general tended to advocate an ethically reflective and usually rather ascetic life, one which conjoined intellectual with moral discipline. This ethical austerity was prized by early Christians as an allied phenomenon within Graeco-Roman culture to which they could appeal in debates about the character of their new movement. The tacit validation that philosophy offered to the Christian movement was thus multifaceted, and, while it was sometimes thought to be associated with unacceptable aspects of pagan religious culture, philosophy provided some educated Christians with a subtle social warrant for their new life and beliefs.

It should be noted that ancient Christianity was itself a complex movement. Like Graeco-Roman philosophy, Christianity included a broad spectrum of beliefs and practices. Thus those early Christians who developed their beliefs with reference to philosophy endorsed a wide range of metaphysical and ethical doctrines, ranging from materialism to extreme transcendentalism, from asceticism to spiritual libertinism. Yet, while diversity is evident, it is also true that the Christian movement came to develop a rough set of central beliefs and some early forms of community organization associated with those beliefs. This incipient 'orthodoxy' came to value some sorts of philosophy, especially Platonism, which seemed best suited to its theological agenda. This tacit alliance with Platonism was fraught with ambiguity and uncertainty, and it was never a reciprocal relationship. Nonetheless, in the second and third centuries a type of Christian philosophical theology emerged which owed much to the Platonic school and became increasingly dominant among orthodox Christian authors. It was this trajectory that defined the character of patristic philosophy.

Early Christian thought had its origins in Hellenistic Judaism, and its initial character was defined by the dominant patterns of that tradition. This early phase extended through the first half of the second century AD, as Christianity began to define its distinctive themes associated with the nature and historical mission of Jesus Christ. Throughout the second century, Christianity became increasingly a movement made up of gentile converts; some of these new members had educations that had included philosophy and a few were even trained as philosophers. Thus Christian thought began to show increased contact with the Graeco-Roman philosophical schools, a trend no doubt reinforced by the critical need for Christians – as a proscribed religious minority – to defend their theology, ritual practices and ethics in the face of cultural and legal hostility.

This so-called 'age of the apologists' lasted through-out the second and third centuries, until Christianity began to enjoy toleration early in the fourth century. However, it would be a mistake to consider Christian philosophical thought in that period as primarily directed towards the surrounding pagan society. In many respects philosophy, as the intellectual discourse of Graeco-Roman culture, offered gentile Christians a means to clarify, articulate and assimilate the tenets of their new faith. This process of intellectual appropriation appears to have been of considerable personal importance to many Graeco-Roman converts. Christian philosophical theology helped them to recover ideas familiar from their school training and to find unfamiliar concepts defended with the rigour much prized within Graeco-Roman culture.

After Christianity became a licit religion in the fourth century, philosophical activity among Christians expanded. The task of theological self-articulation became increasingly significant as Christianity grew in the fourth and fifth centuries towards majority status within the Empire, with imperial support. In this later period the range and sophistication of Christian thought increased significantly, due in part to the influence of pagan Neoplatonism, a movement that included a number of the finest philosophers active since the classical period of Plato and Aristotle. Later patristic philosophy had a defining influence upon medieval Christian thought through such figures as Augustine and Dionysius the pseudo-Areopagite, estab-lishing both the conceptual foundations and the authoritative warrant for the scholasticism of the Latin West and Greek East.

1   **Influences**
2   **Beginnings of Christian thought**
3   **Early Christian Platonism**
4   **Origen**
5–6 **Later patristic philosophy**

1   Influences

Judaism in the time of Jesus of Nazareth was the heir of centuries of reflection on the unique existence of God, some of which was partly conditioned by Greek philosophical speculation. The book of Proverbs in the Old Testament emphasizes the one God who is the source of all wisdom and who produced the world (Proverbs 3: 19; 8: 22–31). Here wisdom begins to appear in a hypostatized role, as a quasi-independent power which serves to instantiate and express the hidden purposes of God (Proverbs 8: 1–31). Wisdom is the first product of God, and as such is a mediator between God and humanity. In the *Wisdom of Solomon*, an intertestamental work written between

100 BC and AD 50, wisdom (*sophia*) is presented as a distinct power that orders the cosmos and reveals the moral structure that conforms to that divine produc-tion. Wisdom is praised for her power and exalted as the source of prophecy and human sanctity. These texts indicate a characteristic aspect of Hellenistic Jewish theology: exaltation of a single, universal God in cosmological and ethical terms combined with discussion of a secondary principle that serves as an instrument of divine production and moral revelation.

PHILO OF ALEXANDRIA, the pre-eminent Jewish philosopher of the period, was preoccupied with the articulation of biblical theology in terms of Greek philosophy. His treatises, written in Greek, had a defining influence on early Christian philosophy, both in method and content. The works of Philo present philosophical interpretations of the Hebrew Bible, which he read in a Greek translation (the Septuagint), using strategies of allegorical exegesis. His philo-sophical sources are characteristic of the Hellenistic period, a mixture of Stoic, Peripatetic, Pythagorean and Platonic conceptions in which the transcendent-alism of the Pythagoreans and Platonists was predominant (see PLATONISM, EARLY AND MIDDLE; PERIPATETICS; PYTHAGOREANISM; STOICISM). For Philo, the patriarchs, especially Moses, were philoso-phers; it was to Moses that God revealed the transcendent archetypes upon which creation was based. These paradigms – understood as Platonic forms – constituted both the inherent patterns of order within the cosmos and the transcendent powers which generated it. Collectively, they were described as the Logos or divine Word, the 'place' of the forms. Philo used numerous ways to express this notion of an intermediate level of reality; sometimes the Logos seems to be only an aspect of God, in his role of relating to his products, but at other times the Logos seems to be a secondary entity that emerges from God and is used as an instrument to structure the cosmos. Other names or figures are also used, such as Wisdom (as we have seen), Goodness or Sovereignty; each represents an independent aspect of the divine nature. These 'principles' or 'powers', however understood ontologically, function to mediate between the pri-mordial aspect of God and the cosmos that emerged from him.

One aspect of Philo's portrayal of God bears particular mention: his unwillingness at times to attribute descriptive terms to God, particularly those that suggest direct divine interaction with the cosmos. Here Philo seems not only to be building upon traditional Hebraic reluctance to employ a proper name for God, but also to be drawing upon Pythag-orean and Platonic theology, which proscribed ascribing predicates to the 'One' or the 'Good'.

Powers such as Logos or Sophia appear as the pre-eminent representations of the hidden and unsearchable divine nature, the self-revelation of God in metaphysical terms. But He Who Is, the God of Exodus, remained hidden in his august transcendence. This model of philosophical theology, with its interplay between a largely ineffable God and intermediate divine representations, would have a major effect on subsequent Christian thought, suggesting a philosophical approach to reflecting on the nature of Christ (see God, CONCEPTS OF).

The use of philosophical discourse in Hellenistic Jewish thought was part of a natural strategy of cultural association, drawing Judaism into discussion with ideas that were well-established within its host society. But it represents as well an internal development away from more archaic anthropomorphic conceptions of God, a development common to the Mediterranean religions of the age. Philo's use of Graeco-Roman philosophy is an important instance of this anti-anthropomorphism. God is a remote divine being who, if he can be described at all, can be approximated by metaphysical terms such as 'One', 'Good' or 'Monad'. It was God's Logos or Sophia that acted as a demiurge to craft the cosmos and now controls the world according to God's good purposes.

2 Beginnings of Christian thought

Some of this thinking seems to have influenced the earliest Christian writers of the New Testament, especially Paul and John. Although there is no firm consensus among scholars on the precise details of this relation, some patterns are evident. In Romans 1: 19–21, creation is understood to be an act of divine revelation, universal in its scope. The one God must, for Paul, be more than the guardian of an individual people, but also the source and judge of all humanity (Romans 3). The one God directs all things providentially for the good. This idea of a single God whose universal revelation is creation can also be found in speeches attributed to Paul in Acts (14 and 17).

It is in explaining the nature of Jesus Christ that the letters attributed to Paul clearly evince aspects of Hellenistic Jewish wisdom theology. Colossians 1: 15–23 presents a pre-existent cosmic power who is the image of the invisible God and the entity first born from God. This being is the creative power, by whom all things came into being, whether earthly or heavenly. The cosmic Christ is thus ontologically central: 'all things were created by him, and for him, and he is before all things, and by him all things consist' (Colossians 1: 16–17). In Paul's theology it is this power that manifested itself in Jesus of Nazareth, who died on the cross in order to reconcile a fallen

world to himself and thus to God. The exact import of such Pauline passages is difficult to assess, since their conceptual background can only be approximately recovered. The same is true of the splendid prologue to the Gospel of St John. Similar prepositional language is used there to indicate the causal and ontological significance of a unique entity. The Word or Logos was *with* God in the beginning and serves as the power *through* which all things were made. As such, the Logos is the principle of life and light, and a power manifested historically in the human person of Jesus of Nazareth. This iteration of a cosmic mediator in Pauline and Johannine texts became the basis of subsequent Christian ontology, although these interpretations would differ significantly.

In the early second century, we find evidence of a developing consensus among Christian authors about God's metaphysical properties. Ignatius, the early second-century bishop of Antioch, writes about Christ as a timeless, invisible, intangible, and impassible being who shed these characteristics in order to become human (*Epistle to Polycarp* 3: 2). In the mid-century *Apology* of Aristides, God is presented in philosophical terms as the unmoved mover, the ruler of the universe and an eternal being without beginning or end. As such, he is understood to be ungenerated, immutable, free from need or defect, immobile and exempt from partition or division. These metaphysical epithets were commonplace among pagan philosophers of the period, and their adoption by early Christian apologists suggests a common theological discourse to which the new movement was making explicit appeal (see God, CONCEPTS OF).

The effort to articulate a first principle which was transcendent of the cosmos led many Graeco-Roman thinkers, particularly Pythagoreans and Platonists, to reject the ascription of many characteristics, such as mutability or mobility, to the deity. This 'negative theology' came sometimes to regard all predication to be inadequate, so that even notions such as perfection or immateriality seemed too restrictive (see NEGATIVE THEOLOGY). This tendency – mediated through Jewish thought – is also to be found in second-century Christian thinkers, especially some loosely classed as 'gnostics', who believed that they possessed a special, higher knowledge (*gnosis*) of the ineffable God beyond the divinity revealed in the sacred scriptures (see GNOSTICISM). An example is Basilides, a gnostic teacher of the mid-second century, who adopted a line of thinking whose roots go back at least as far as Plato's Academy. He held that the first principle could not be described by analogy with anything within the cosmos, but was best thought of as 'without being'. This completely transcendent power cannot be understood from the perspective of the universe; indeed, even calling it 'ineffable' is suspect. Similar views are common among other second- and third-century gnostic Christian authors. Their theology usually contrasted a hidden first principle, to whom special access is required, with lesser but misguided divine powers, whose presence is more easily attested.

However, this transcendentalism was not the whole story in early Christian thought. Some Christians were influenced by more materialistic Roman philosophical schools, and their thinking was sharply opposed to the strongly transcendentalist tendencies of the gnostics. Perhaps the best example is TERTULLIAN, a Roman jurist who converted to Christianity and campaigned vigorously for an understanding of the scriptures which was corporealistic, along the lines of Stoicism and Roman medical theory. For Tertullian, God was a spirit *sui generis*, a being understood in an attenuated materialist way, as a force which was invisible but nonetheless part of the cosmos. Similarly, the human soul was a corporeal entity, transmitted in the act of conception and immortal only through divine intervention. Such thinking was constructed in opposition to the developing transcendentalism of the early Christian Platonists, and it underscores the fact that the scriptural record could well have been read through a very different philosophical prism. But, as it happened, Tertullian's materialistic theology became a dead end, as the affinity of Platonism and Christianity was successfully argued by Christian philosophers in the second century.

3 Early Christian Platonism

By the latter half of the second century AD, Christianity had become largely a gentile movement, with a complex political and cultural relationship to the Roman Empire. Philosophical reflection was an important component in the developing self-articulation of the movement. A good example is the second-century *Apology* of Athenagoras of Athens, who wrote eloquently to the Stoic Emperor MARCUS AURELIUS in defence of Christianity, arguing that in rejecting the pagan gods Christians were not atheists, but believers in a single first principle. This cultural polemic is supported by his philosophical treatise *On the Resurrection of the Dead*. Here he addresses the composite nature of the human person, and argues that the unity of body and soul must be restored after death through resurrection of the body if human beings are to fulfil the eternal destiny intended by their divine creator. These arguments have an Aristotelian flavour, indicating a sophisticated and flexible

use of philosophical sources. Similarly the three books entitled *Ad Autolycum* by Theophilos of Antioch, written about AD 181, contain arguments cast in philosophical terms. Written by a Christian convert to a pagan friend, these treatises argue for the uncreated nature of God, who is immutable but creates through his Logos. This Word exists both within God and also as the external expression of God through which he expressed himself in the act of creation.

The most important of these early apologists was Justin Martyr, who was executed *circa* AD 165. Justin was trained as a philosopher, having tried the Stoic, Peripatetic, Pythagorean and Platonic schools before converting to Christianity. His extant writings include two *Apologies* and a *Dialogue with Trypho the Jew*. Justin spent time as an itinerant Christian philosopher and even wore the philosopher's cloak (*pallium*) before settling in Rome, where he founded a school. Justin's approach to Graeco-Roman philosophical and religious culture was complex. In his view, the ancient Greek thinkers had access to the Old Testament and learned from it. Moreover, the divine Logos, the Wisdom of God, was the rational foundation of both the universe and the human soul, so that a natural knowledge of God was accessible to pagan philosophers. For Justin, all who think and act according to reason do so by participating in the Logos. Abraham and SOCRATES were Christians in anticipation of Christ, the incarnate Logos. Justin thus used philosophy to present a broad defence of Christianity, one that not only employed specific arguments in defence of scriptural conceptions, but also discovered a wide-ranging historical scheme to conjoin both the Hebraic and Hellenic cultures within Christianity.

The central locus of Christian philosophical activity in the second century was Alexandria, a major cultural centre of the Empire. There we find a Christian school, a succession of Christian teachers and pupils whose activities seem to parallel that of pagan philosophers. CLEMENT OF ALEXANDRIA is the first of the Alexandrian Christian teachers about whom much is known, although he himself refers to several earlier figures, especially Pantaenus, a former Stoic. Clement was probably a convert; he was born in mid-century and died around AD 215.

His principal work, the *Stromateis* (Miscellanies), is a compendium of ethical and theological observations on a wide range of topics. Clement's goal seems to have been the presentation of a broadly educated, cultured form of Christianity. Its adepts would be Christian gnostics; unlike others who claimed that name, they would be both members of the developing orthodox movement and truly enlightened thinkers. Their life was described by Clement in ethical terms drawn from Stoic, Platonic and Aristotelian literature, characterized by an effort to approximate the stability and impassibility of God's own being. Pagan philosophy was significant in Clement's view since it represented a parallel phenomenon, the result of the illumination of the Greeks by the divine Logos. This notion of the natural knowledge of God allowed Christians like Clement to treat philosophy as an anticipation of Christianity, a path to a common fund of knowledge completed by the revelations found in the Jewish and Christian scriptures.

In reading scripture, Clement owed much to Philo's allegorical method of exegesis. Through the latter, Clement was able to discover the gnostic, or deeper, meaning of texts whose origins and character seemed remote from cultured Graeco-Roman sensibilities. This more advanced reading, grounded in philosophy, separated the simple believer from the mature or gnostic Christian, whose wisdom was enriched by this joint foundation in natural and revealed truth. Clement's capacious model of Christian wisdom, with its compatibilist understanding of the Graeco-Roman and Hebraic traditions, helped to establish an enduring Christian approach to philosophy and, more generally, to the classical heritage.

Clement's Logos theology had another feature which followed Philo's thought, namely his emphasis on the unknowability of God. This 'negative' theology was, as we have seen, an important theological strategy in the period. The concept of a primordial but uncharacterizable godhead revealed through a lower power or aspect was widely accepted by Pythagoreans, Platonists and many heterodox Christian gnostics. But Clement, like Philo before him, put this negative theology to a positive use. The ultimate God was understood as beyond finite description, having no conceptually adequate predicates; but God was not thereby cut off from the world, nor was the cosmos at the mercy of ignorant or malevolent intermediate powers. For Clement, this hidden God, alluded to by the philosophers, was made manifest in his Word, the Logos, the transcendent power which produced the world and then became present in the person of Jesus of Nazareth. It is this fine balance between the hidden and the apparent that characterizes Clement's theology, setting his views into sharp contrast both with heterodox gnosticism and with more affirmative or literalist approaches to theology within early Christianity. This difference, between apophatic theology (the theology of *apophasis* or denial) and kataphatic theology (that of *kataphasis* or assertion) thus came to the surface within orthodox Christianity through the catechetical school at Alexandria.

4 Origen

The greatest theologian in the era before Christianity's legitimation in the fourth century was ORIGEN of Alexandria, a product of the Alexandrian Christian school. Origen was born into a Christian family about AD 185; his father was martyred, a fate which Origen himself also suffered, dying subsequent to torture in the Decian persecution around AD 254–5. An intense reader of scripture from his youth, Origen studied both in Christian schools and in the pagan philosophical school of Ammonius Saccas, the teacher of PLOTINUS. Origen's many writings encompass apologetics (for example, *Contra Celsum* (Against Celsus)), biblical commentary and systematic treatises (*De principiis* (On First Principles)). Much has been lost, although the substantial works that remain give ample evidence of vast scriptural erudition combined with a bold command of contemporary Platonic thought. Origen may fairly be said to be the most innovative Christian thinker of the pre-Nicene era, the most brilliant and important Christian intellectual before Augustine.

Unlike Clement, Origen generally avoided negative theology, perhaps because of its popularity among the heterodox gnostic thinkers whom he opposed. His theology focused upon the self-diffusion of God, a single divinity that produced a finite and intelligible image. This image – the Word – is the collective world of the Platonic intelligibles and the foundation of the lower, created cosmos. The Word is eternally generated by the Father, so that God is eternally productive of his perfect image. As such, the Logos appears to hold an intermediate status in the structure of reality, the link between God and the cosmos. Matter was also attributed by Origen to God, who was thus the only foundation of reality.

Origen also made human freedom central. Souls were seen as rational beings created with free choice. On Origen's Platonic exegesis of Genesis, souls that turned away from God descended to lower levels of reality. Freedom of choice produced psychic precipitation, the falling of rational souls into their present corporeal state. This primordial loss of perfection resulted in a cosmic system of distinct worlds. Each degree of reality was attuned to the level of the soul's descent. Souls only slightly separated from God could continue to engage in everlasting contemplation; Origen identified these with the stars. Others were entombed in human bodies and are subject to death. The demons are souls who chose the most extreme removal from God. Thus the cosmos was the direct manifestation of a fundamentally moral phenomenon; reality is the expression of the ethical disposition of its inhabitants. No other Christian philosopher in the patristic period linked moral freedom so directly with ontology.

Since evil is, in this theory, the direct result of the soul's choice, the natural evils of our world and mortality itself are epiphenomena of moral evil (see EVIL, PROBLEM OF). Death is thus punitive, and suffering educative. The cosmos is a vast penal colony designed for the rehabilitation of souls. Origen seems moreover to have held that all souls would eventually be successfully reformed. This universalism presents cosmic history as a providential process which will eventuate in a restoration of perfection, 'that God may be all in all'. Whether this reformation of souls precludes for Origen an additional, subsequent misuse of freedom is unclear. One corollary of Origen's universalism, that the devil would be saved, was not lost on his contemporaries; it contributed to the controversy which surrounded Origen's thought throughout late antiquity.

5 Later patristic philosophy: Gregory of Nyssa, Marius Victorinus, Ambrose

In AD 313, the imperial Edict of Milan initiated a new era of religious legitimacy for Christianity; shortly thereafter, the great ecumenical Council of Nicaea (AD 324–5) began the process of defining orthodoxy with imperial support. Christian philosophy was influenced by both events. No longer was there a need for political polemics in defence of the faith, although the effort to present Christianity to educated pagans continued unabated. Now, internal efforts to define and explain the doctrines of orthodoxy came to the fore.

These developments are particularly evident in the works of three Cappadocian bishops, Gregory Nazianzen (circa AD 330–90), Basil of Caesarea and Gregory of Nyssa (circa AD 330–90). Of these, the most philosophically acute was Gregory of Nyssa, whose theology is much influenced by Origen and by post-Plotinian Platonism (see NEOPLATONISM). Unlike Origen, Gregory did not ground his thought exclusively on a model of free will and psychic precipitation. Rather, divine creation is the dominant image and the soul but a creature conditioned by God's providential intention. That eternal plan involved materiality and the body. Thus the fall constituted a desecration of human nature, but it did not generate the mingling of soul with body. The misery of human life can be overcome only by restoration of our original state through God's intervention, through Christ. Philosophy can guide the soul to recognition of its condition, but the soul can be saved only by God's activity. Philosophy alone can never be sufficient for salvation.

Gregory's thought put a renewed emphasis on the conceptual transcendence of God, so that the divine Father was presented along Plotinian lines as being beyond all predicative descriptions. In Gregory's case, this view was based upon a sharp recognition of divine infinity. The created soul has, as its future course, the eternal process of the contemplation of God's infinitude; unification of the human soul with the one God can never be wholly consummated.

Gregory of Nyssa and the other Cappadocians are evidence of a great emergence of Christian Platonism in the Greek world of the late fourth century. This same post-Nicene flowering of philosophical theology also occurred in the western portions of the Empire. Here the influence of the Greek philosophical schools was somewhat less direct, in part because of linguistic difficulties, but it was still felt. MARIUS VICTORINUS was a Roman rhetorician much influenced by the works of the Plotinian school; he translated some of these into Latin and wrote treatises with a pronounced Neoplatonic influence in defence of Nicene orthodoxy. For Victorinus, Platonism seemed a conceptual resource and philosophical ally of Christian orthodoxy. This is also true to an extent of Ambrose, the great fourth-century bishop of Milan, who was concerned not only with re-drafting Christian theology in a Platonic idiom accessible to cultured pagans, but also with presenting Christian asceticism and theology as a successful rival to Platonic philosophy. His strategy had internal resonance within Christianity as well, allowing orthodoxy to assert its superiority to Arianism, Manicheism and other forms of Christianity (see MANICHEISM). His greatest success was the conversion (from Manicheism) of the North African rhetorician Augustine, whom he baptized in AD 387. It was the preaching of Ambrose, together with his treatises, that led Augustine to study 'the books of the Platonists' which Marius Victorinus had translated. This proved a spiritually volatile mixture, sending Augustine into an orthodox Christian trajectory and a life of asceticism.

6 Later patristic philosophy: Augustine, Boethius, Pseudo-Dionysius

Like Gregory of Nyssa and Ambrose, AUGUSTINE was determined to construct a coherent Christian theology which could stand as a compelling alternative to the still active and prestigious pagan tradition. It is well to remember that Julian the Apostate, the recidivist emperor who sought to restore a paganism through the revitalization of polytheistic cult and Neoplatonic theology, ruled during Augustine's youth (AD 361–3). Augustine's thought might well be considered as a fresh response to the same set of desiderata as had moved Gregory and Ambrose: problems internal to Christianity and external ideas which were hostile to orthodoxy. Perhaps because he read little Greek and had an informal philosophical education, Augustine's thought is less a Christianized Platonism than it is a systematic development of Christian theology, using Platonic epistemology and metaphysics. Often Augustine seems intent on answering classical philosophical questions in novel, Christian ways.

Nowhere is this clearer than in the *Confessiones* (Confessions), where Augustine carefully asserts his own personal success at Plotinian contemplation in the vision at Ostia, only to conclude that pagan philosophy, while providing the soul with epistemic access to God, was inadequate as a means of assuring continuing salvific association with God. Augustine presents this theme as an autobiographical refutation both of Manichean materialism, now confounded by the soul's transcendental vision through contemplation, and Platonism, found wanting in its prideful over-estimation of the soul's natural proximity to the eternal and the divine. These opponents are the background to the brilliantly original account of memory and time in Books X and XI of the *Confessiones*, where the phenomenology of the fallen, embodied, and temporally constrained soul is explored. This account of the human soul constructing a lapsarian self and so constituting time as the medium of its collective anxiety and loss had a decided impact on the development of the introspective consciousness of the West and on the framing of a philosophical account of Genesis.

Throughout the vast corpus of his later writings, Augustine frequently makes use of philosophical notions, usually in contexts whose primary focus is theological. In the *De civitate Dei* (City of God), however, he returns to the question of the value of philosophy, especially Platonism. In this sustained argument, he makes plain his admiration for the intellectual utility of philosophy, while rejecting the philosophers' pretence to salvific efficacy and excoriating their continuing acceptance of polytheistic cult. It is interesting to note that Augustine views Platonism as a natural approximation to Christianity, achieved through reason but without the benefit of revelation. Yet the Platonists were, in the end, spiritually incoherent, accepting a first principle, the Good or One, while countenancing polytheistic worship.

While Augustine was in many respects a *sui generis* thinker with a penchant for original reflection on philosophical topics, there were other Christian thinkers in late antiquity whose works were more clearly bound by philosophical conventions.

BOETHIUS is an outstanding example. An active member of the Roman senatorial circle during the Ostrogothic period in Italy, Boethius undertook the revival of technical philosophy at a time of its marked decline in the western provinces. He translated and commented on some of Aristotle's logical works, and wrote a series of five theological treatises on the Christological debates of his time. Most important for medieval and renaissance readers, he completed the *De consolatione philosophiae* (Consolation of Philosophy), a protreptical work on the value of the philosophic life, while a political prisoner before his execution. In most respects, Boethius was a conventional Christian Platonist, although the Christian element can be found only in his theological works (see PLATONISM, MEDIEVAL). His efforts to articulate and defend the congruity of divine foreknowledge and human freedom were critical to later medieval scholasticism, as were his commentaries on Aristotle. His pupil Cassiodorus continued aspects of the encyclopedic legacy of Boethius, concentrating his efforts on articulating the seven traditional liberal arts (grammar, dialectic, rhetoric, arithmetic, geometry, music and astronomy). He also wrote a treatise on the soul, arguing that it is transcendent of materiality, but distinct from God in its capacity for evil. As is the case with his teacher Boethius, Cassiodorus is significant primarily for his role in transmitting classical philosophy to the medieval age (see ENCYCLOPEDISTS).

At about the same time (early sixth century) in the Greek East there surfaced a collection of treatises under the name of Dionysius the Areopagite (St Paul's Athenian convert in Acts 17). The identity of the actual author has been the subject of extended speculation and remains undetermined, although the works came to be accepted as genuine in both the Byzantine East and later in the Carolingian West (see PSEUDO-DIONYSIUS). These treatises represent the high-water mark of compatibilism between Christianity and late Platonism. They centre on the absolute predicative transcendence of God. The soul must grasp the total darkness of divinity as well as the vast manifestation of its hidden nature in the cosmos that emerged from it. The whole of reality is a theophany, an expression of the One who cannot be known *per se*. The levels of reality that are manifest to us constitute grades of being, each part of a pattern of divine self-presentation and return. The concept of God, while undefinable, is not privative or nugatory but can be partially understood as characterizing the source of reality.

This theology represents a Christian redaction of the pagan Platonism of the fifth century. While assuredly Christian in its theological terminology, its basic ontology is intelligible only when read against the metaphysics of the pagan Neoplatonists. This was one possible line for Christian intellectual development. However, there were others who resisted such assimilation. Chief among them was John PHILOPONUS, who was active in the Greek East during the first half of the sixth century. Philoponus was sharply opposed to pagan Neoplatonism, especially that of PROCLUS. He criticized Aristotelian and Neoplatonic claims about the eternity of the cosmos, and favoured a model of temporal creation. Even if the world were beginningless, it must be seen as a contingent system that depended for its existence upon a transcendent source. In his view, the eternalism of the pagan cosmologists occluded this central metaphysical point (see ETERNITY OF THE WORLD, MEDIEVAL VIEWS OF). Moreover, the commitment of many pagan Platonists to a theory of necessary cosmic emanation from the One further confused the issue. In consequence, Philoponus attempted to clarify the fundamental ontological dependence of a contingent cosmos upon its divine creator. He is a representative of a vigorous Christian philosophical movement in late antiquity which sought to sharpen the lines of conceptual demarcation between Christianity and pagan Platonism, while using common methods of philosophical argumentation to achieve that end.

The closing of the pagan Platonic academy in Athens was ordered by the Emperor Justinian in 529. Subsequently philosophy continued in a variety of Christian philosophical schools, each committed to different, rival theologies, including monophysites, Chalcedonians and Nestorians. It was on this foundation that later Byzantine Christian philosophy and early Islamic philosophy were able to develop, transmitting the thought of both the classical and the patristic traditions into the medieval period.

See also: AUGUSTINE; BOETHIUS, A.M.S.; BYZANTINE PHILOSOPHY; CLEMENT OF ALEXANDRIA; ENCYCLOPEDISTS; GNOSTICISM; HELLENISTIC PHILOSOPHY; MANICHEISM; MARIUS VICTORINUS; NEOPLATONISM; ORIGEN; PELAGIANISM; PLATONISM, EARLY AND MIDDLE; TERTULLIAN, Q.S.F.

References and further reading

Armstrong, A.H. (ed.) (1966) *The Cambridge History of Later Greek and Early Medieval Philosophy*, Cambridge: Cambridge University Press. (The major review of philosophy in late antiquity.)

* Augustine (397–401) *De civitate Dei* (The City of God), trans. J. O'Meara, Harmondsworth: Penguin, 1972. (Influential work of Augustine.)

* —— (413–27) *Confessiones* (Confessions), trans. R.S. Pine-Coffin, Harmondsworth: Penguin, 1961; trans. H. Chadwick, Oxford: Oxford University Press, 1991. (Influential work of Augustine.)

Chadwick, H. (1981) *Boethius: The Consolations of Music, Logic, Theology and Philosophy*, Oxford: Clarendon Press. (A study of Boethius and his age.)

Hadot, P. (1995) *Philosophy as a Way of Life: Spiritual Exercises from Socrates to Foucault*, trans. M. Chase, Oxford: Blackwell, 1995. (Essays on ancient philosophy as a spiritual discipline.)

* Origen (220–30) *Peri archōn (De principiis)* (On First Principles), ed. P. Koetschau, Leipzig: Hinrichs; trans. G.W. Butterworth, *On First Principles*, New York: Harper & Row, 1966. (Edition and translation of Origen's work.)

* —— (220–30) *Contra Celsum* (Against Celsus), ed. P. Koetschau in *Origenes werke*, Leipzig: Hinrichs; trans. H. Chadwick, Cambridge: Cambridge University Press, 1965. (Edition and translation of Origen's work.)

Osborne, E. (1993) *The Emergence of Christian Theology*, Cambridge: Cambridge University Press. (Examines pre-Nicene Christian thought.)

Pelikan, J. (1993) *Christianity and Classical Culture: The Metamorphosis of Natural Theology in the Christian Encounter with Hellenism*, New Haven, CT: Yale University Press. (A study of Cappadocian natural theology.)

* Quasten, J. (1950–60) *Patrology*, Utrecht/Antwerp: Spectrum Publishers. (Comprehensive review of early Christian literature.)

Rist, J.M. (1994) *Augustine: Ancient Thought Baptized*, Cambridge: Cambridge University Press. (Augustine's thought reviewed in reference to later classical philosophy.)

Stead, C. (1994) *Philosophy in Christian Antiquity*, Cambridge: Cambridge University Press. (A short study of later pagan and early Christian thought.)

Wolfson, H.A. (1956) *The Philosophy Of The Church Fathers*, Cambridge, MA: Harvard University Press. (Dated, but comprehensive.)

JOHN PETER KENNEY

PATRIZI DA CHERSO, FRANCESCO (1529–97)

Francesco Patrizi was an Italian humanist and anti-Aristotelian who took up a newly-founded chair of Platonic philosophy at Ferrara in 1578, the first such chair in Europe. Through his various writings he contributed to poetic theory, rhetoric, and historiography, as well as to military history and hydraulics. His two most influential works were his Discussiones Peripateticae *(1581) and his* Nova de universis philosophia *(New Philosophy of Universes) (1591). Patrizi cast doubt on the authenticity of many of the works attributed to Aristotle, and argued that Aristotle's philosophy was incompatible with Christianity. He believed it should be replaced with his own synthesis of Platonism, Neoplatonism, and Hermeticism (or Hermetism). Patrizi saw light as the basic metaphysical principle, and interpreted the universe in terms of the diffusion of light* (lumen) *from God, the primary light* (prima lux). *His most influential doctrine concerned space, which he argued to be infinite, three-dimensional, and distinct from the bodies it contained.*

1 Life and works
2 Anti-Aristotelianism
3 Light-metaphysics
4 Philosophy of nature

1 Life and works

Francesco Patrizi (Franciscus Patritius) was born in Cherso, near Trieste. He studied in Venice and Ingolstadt, before going to Padua where he studied and taught private pupils for a number of years (1547–54). It was at this leading Aristotelian institution that he was introduced to Marsilio Ficino's *Theologia platonica* (Platonic Theology) (see FICINO §3), and became a Platonist. He spent some years away from the university, serving as secretary and administrator to various Venetian noblemen, and travelling extensively in France, Spain and Cyprus (where he perfected his knowledge of Greek). His return to the academic world marked the belated institutional recognition of Platonic philosophy. Shortly after Francesco de'Vieri (Verino) had begun teaching Platonic philosophy at Pisa in 1576, Patrizi took up a newly-founded chair of Platonic philosophy at Ferrara in 1578. In 1592 he was called to Rome by Pope Clement VIII and became professor of Platonic philosophy at the Sapienza. He still held this post at his death, despite ecclesiastical censure of his writings by the Roman Congregation of the Index, which ordered changes in his *Nova de universis philosophia* (New Philosophy of Universes).

Patrizi's humanist and literary interests are shown in his works on poetry, rhetoric and history. He wrote poetry himself, one of his earliest writings was a discourse on types of poetic inspiration (*Discorso della diversità dei furori poetici*) (1553), and he later entered into a dispute with the poet Torquato Tasso about poetics. In his *Della poetica* (1586) he attacked

the Aristotelian theory of poetry as mere imitation, and appealed to the marvellous as an aesthetic category (see ARISTOTLE §29). The poet, who is 'maker of the marvellous', operates on the soul, putting it in tune with cosmic harmony. His views about the relationship between words and things also appear in his earlier work on rhetoric (*Della retorica*) (1562), where he claimed that search for rhetorical ornamentation had corrupted the original Adamic language which gave direct access to things (see LANGUAGE, RENAISSANCE PHILOSOPHY OF §2). In his work on history (*Della historia*) (1560), which had a great influence on later historiography, he attacked Ciceronian orthodoxy (see CICERO §2). He wanted to separate history from rhetoric, seeing it as an autonomous discipline with its own intellectual justification based on a grasp of causes and effects.

His other works included discussions of love, unpublished during his lifetime, in which he blended Neoplatonism with a naturalistic materialism. In another vein entirely, he wrote on military history, and was also the author of treatises on hydraulics, stemming from the conflict between Ferrara and Bologna over the silting of the river Po. Surviving correspondence shows his links with various intellectual circles.

His two most important works were the *Discussiones peripateticae* (*Discussionum peripateticarum tomi quattuor*) where we find his main attack on Aristotelianism, and the *Nova de universis philosophia* which presents his light-metaphysics and his philosophy of nature.

2 Anti-Aristotelianism

The prime source for Patrizi's attack on Aristotle is his *Discussiones peripateticae* published at Basle in 1581, though the first volume had been issued separately at Venice in 1571. This volume contained a biography of Aristotle which highlighted his personal shortcomings, such as stealing the ideas of his predecessors, and a history of Peripatetic philosophy. The three additional books discussed Aristotle's sources, the discord between Plato and Aristotle, and the defects of particular Aristotelian doctrines. Patrizi cast doubt on the authenticity of many of the works attributed to Aristotle, and he foreshadowed modern commentators by arguing that Aristotle's *Metaphysics* was a series of fragmentary treatments of diverse topics rather than an integrated whole (see ARISTOTLE §11).

Patrizi's main philosophical quarrel with Aristotle was that his philosophy was incompatible with Christianity, especially with respect to the providence and omnipotence of God. In his Dedicatory Epistle to

Nova de universis philosophia, he blamed the study of Aristotle for the fact that 'Common men laugh indiscriminately at Philosophers with this saying, which is now a commonplace: this man is a philosopher, he does not believe in God' (Henry 1979: 559–60). The remedy for this situation was to be found in Patrizi's own philosophical synthesis of Platonism, Neoplatonism and Hermeticism (also known as Hermetism).

In order to understand Patrizi's synthesis, we must recognize his belief, taken from Ficino (see FICINO, M. §2), in an ancient theology (*prisca theologia*) handed down to sixteenth-century thinkers by a long and continuous tradition which began with Moses or even Noah, and which had the work of PLATO as its ancient culmination. Both Plato himself, whom Patrizi presented as a genuinely systematic thinker, and the various works of the Hermetic tradition, were fitted into a Neoplatonic framework (see NEOPLATONISM).

Patrizi's attachment to non-Aristotelian sources is shown by his textual work. He translated John Philoponus' commentary on Aristotle's *Metaphysics* (1583) (see PHILOPONUS §2) and Proclus' *Elements of Theology and Physics* (1583) (see PROCLUS §§2, 4, 9). One of the works he appended to his *Nova de universis philosophia* was his Latin translation of the *Theology of Aristotle*, a ninth-century Arabic compilation of extracts from PLOTINUS (§4) which Patrizi described as 'the mystic philosophy of the Egyptians dictated by Plato and taken down by Aristotle'. He also added an edition and Latin translations of the Greek *Corpus Hermeticum* and some other Hermetica, including the Latin *Asclepius*, all probably dating from between AD 100 and 300, as well as the Chaldean Oracles, a work of the second century AD, which he attributed to Zoroaster (see CHALDAEAN ORACLES). Contemporaries such as Teodoro Angelucci in his *Exercitationes* (1585) were already beginning to cast doubt on the historicity of the *Corpus Hermeticum*, when viewed as the work of the mythical Egyptian sage, Hermes Trismegistus, and as part of the *prisca theologia* handed on by Orpheus to the ancient Greeks, but Patrizi insisted on its authenticity and importance. In his Dedicatory Epistle he wrote: 'Surely Hermes' little book on piety and philosophy contains more philosophy than all of Aristotle's work' (Henry 1979: 553). He also claimed that Hermes was a little earlier than Moses, and had spoken more clearly of the Trinity (see HERMETISM).

3   Light-metaphysics

Patrizi's main philosophical work, *Nova de universis philosophia* (Ferrara, 1591; Venice, 1593), is divided into four parts. Part One is called 'Panaugia' (all-

splendour), a word borrowed from Philo Judaeus (see PHILO OF ALEXANDRIA). In the Platonic tradition, light had always been seen as a symbol of goodness and as the closest analogy to God in the physical world, and had early been turned into a metaphysical or ontological principle. Patrizi presented God as the primary light (*prima lux*), who produces light (*lumen*), first in his Son, then in all other incorporeal creatures. Finally, God produces all corporeal creatures via the diffusion of light in space. The roots of Patrizi's view can be found, not just in PLOTINUS and Proclus, but also in the medieval Jewish philosopher IBN GABIROL and the Christian Robert GROSSETESTE (§3) (see ILLUMINATION).

Part Two is called 'Panarchia' (all-principle) and discusses the first principles that stem from God, who is One but who is also called the One-all. The highest principles are unity, essence, life and intelligence. The four lowest principles are nature, quality (see FICINO, M. §3), form and body. The intermediate principle is soul, which is midway between spirit and matter. In his discussion of this hierarchy of being, Patrizi was mainly concerned with the higher principles and the nature of God.

Part Three is called 'Pampsychia' (all-soul), and discusses all types of soul, from the irrational souls of plants to the world soul which animates the entire cosmos.

The fourth part is called 'Pancosmia' (all-world), and it is here that we find Patrizi's views on mathematics and natural science.

4   Philosophy of nature

Patrizi's view of space, which he called a 'corporeal incorporeal', is fundamental to his philosophy of nature. Space has to be corporeal because it is extended or three-dimensional; it has to be incorporeal because it lacks both resistance and density, and can serve as a container for fully corporeal things. A similar analysis can be applied to light, which Patrizi also called a 'corporeal incorporeal'; both space and light can then be seen as borderline entities between the realms of matter and spirit. Indeed, the analysis can be extended to soul, which also falls between the realms of matter and spirit (see §3), because soul is diffused throughout the physical world without itself being a physical thing.

Patrizi argued that space is prior to ordinary corporeal objects both metaphysically and temporally, and that it is a condition of the existence of other things. He was clearly influenced here by Plato's *Timaeus* (see PLATO §16), but his presentation was strengthened by his systematic, principled, rejection of Aristotle's conclusions about place. ARISTOTLE was confused because he had no notion of an incorporeal corporeal and did not see that what distinguishes space from body is not merely dimensionality but resistance.

Patrizi's theory of space led him to new views of the void. Most notably, he called for an actually infinite void outside the physical world. Betraying some confusion (since an infinite space will have no centre), he added that it must be round, with the rotating earth as its centre. He also accepted an inter-particulate void, made of the naturally existing spaces between corpuscular bodies. Finally, like Telesio, he took stock arguments about the possibility of a naturally occurring intra-mundane void or vacuum, and used them against Aristotle's denial of such a vacuum. He included reference to empirical data such as the operation of bellows and water clocks and what happens to closed containers of frozen water, but no actual experiment seems to have been involved. Theoretical reasoning predominated, and he did not really go beyond knowledge already available from ancient and Arabic sources. Both here and in his general discussion of space, Patrizi can be seen as preparing the way for modern science, but his role should not be overemphasized.

Another part of Patrizi's philosophy of nature involved replacing Aristotle's four basic qualities, hot, cold, wet and dry, with the four principles space, light (*lumen*), heat and *fluor* (fluidity, flux), which combine to form a hierarchy of mixed bodies. Particularly important here is the claim that *fluor* offers resistance to *lumen*. A corollary of this list of basic principles which were not hard or solid, was Patrizi's claim that the heavens were fluid, and that the heavenly bodies were not fixed in hard, solid spheres as had commonly been thought. It is important to note that while Patrizi's contemporary Tycho Brahe had astronomical arguments for the same view, Patrizi's arguments were basically metaphysical.

A cautious assessment is also appropriate when one considers Patrizi's praise of mathematics, especially geometry, for this seems more closely linked with his belief in an intelligible world and ideal forms than with any belief that mathematics could provide a tool for developing philosophy or for explaining the physical world.

Patrizi seems to have been more influential than the other so-called philosophers of nature, BRUNO, CAMPANELLA and TELESIO, and he was widely read in the seventeenth century. His theory of light was attacked by MERSENNE (§3), while his views on space may have been handed on to NEWTON (§4) through the Cambridge Platonist, Henry MORE (§5), as well as GASSENDI (§4).

See also: HERMETISM; NEOPLATONISM; PLATONISM, RENAISSANCE; TELESIO, B.

List of works

Patrizi da Cherso, F. (1553) *Discorso della diversità dei furori poetici* (Discourse on Types of Poetic Inspiration), Venice: G. Griffio. (Included in a volume with a series of other works, starting with *La città felice*.)
—— (1560) *Della historia* (On History), Venice: A. Arrivabene.
—— (1562) *Della retorica* (On Rhetoric), Venice: F. Senese.
—— (1529–97) *L'amorosa filosofia* (The Philosophy of Love), ed. J.C. Nelson, Florence: Istituto Nazionale di Studi sul Rinascimento, 1963.
—— (1581) *Discussionum peripateticarum tomi quattuor (Peripatetic Discussions in Four Books)*, Basle. (On the limits of Aristotelianism as a basis for Christian theology.)
—— (1586) *Della poetica* (On the Art of Poetry), ed. D. Aguzzi Barbagli, Florence: Istituto Nazionale di Studi sul Rinascimento, 1969–71, 3 vols.
—— (1591) *Nova de universis philosophia* (New Philosophy of Universes), Ferrara. (The Venice 1593 edition was published after Patrizi had been criticized by the Congregation of the Index.)
—— (1970) *Emendatio in libros suos Novae philosophiae* (Amendments to the Books on the New Philosophy), in P.O. Kristeller (ed.) *Rinascimento* 10: 215–18.
—— (1975) *Lettere ed opuscoli inediti* (Unpublished Letters and Short Works), ed. D. Aguzzi Barbagli, Florence: Istituto Nazionale di Studi sul Rinascimento. (The opuscula include a dialogue on love, a discussion of the order of Plato's dialogues, and works on hydraulics.)

References and further reading

Antonaci, A. (1984) *Ricerche sul neoplatonismo del Rinascimento: Francesco Patrizi da Cherso* (Investigations of Neoplatonism in the Renaissance), Galatina (Lecce): Salentina. (About the *Discussiones* and their background.)
* Henry, J. (1979) 'Francesco Patrizi da Cherso's concept of space and its later influence', *Annals of Science* 36: 549–75. (Referred to in §2. A detailed discussion of Patrizi's role in the development of concepts of void space and an infinite universe.)
Kristeller, P.O. (1964) *Eight Philosophers of the Italian Renaissance*, Stanford, CA: Stanford University Press. (Contains a readable introduction to Patrizi's thought.)

Purnell, F. (1976) 'Francesco Patrizi and the critics of Hermes Trismegistus', *Journal of Medieval and Renaissance Studies* 6: 155–78. (Patrizi's response to criticisms of the Hermetic writings.)

Schmitt, C.B. (1967) 'Experimental Evidence for and against a Void: The Sixteenth-Century Arguments', *Isis* 63: 352–66; repr. in C.B. Schmitt, *Studies in Renaissance Philosophy and Science*, London: Variorum, 1981. (Useful material on Patrizi's philosophy of nature.)

Wilmott, M.J. (1985) '"Aristoteles exotericus, acroamaticus, mysticus": two interpretations of the typological classification of the "Corpus Aristotelicum" by Francesco Patrizi da Cherso', *Nouvelles de la république des lettres* 2: 67–95. (Patrizi's re-evaluation of Aristotle's texts.)

E.J. ASHWORTH

PAUL OF VENICE
(1369/72–1429)

Like other teachers in fifteenth-century Italian universities, Paul of Venice focused on logic and natural philosophy in an undergraduate programme directed toward the education of medical students. Despite Paul's theological training and important position in the order of Augustinian friars, nearly all his works are non-theological. His prolific writings popularized the achievements of Oxford logic and Parisian physics in a framework derived from Aristotle and Averroes. As a philosopher he is best known for his Averroist position on the human soul, and for his moderate realism with respect to universals.

Paul of Venice (Paolo Nicoletti Veneto, born Udine 1369/1372, died Padua 1429) was active in three spheres. As an Augustinian friar, he served as Provincial of his Order. As a diplomat, he served as an ambassador of the Venetian Republic to Germany, Hungary and Poland. His most important career, however, was as a university teacher and author of textbooks. He taught briefly at various Italian universities, but his most constant association was with the University of Padua. He studied at the Augustinian *studium* in Padua both before and after his theological studies in Oxford (1390–3), and he taught at the University itself for many years. His academic concerns are reflected in the nature and number of his writings.

By far the most popular of all his works was the early *Logica parva*, which survives in over eighty manuscripts and was still being printed at the end of the sixteenth century. It shows the clear influence of his stay in England, for it takes the form of the textbooks then in use at Oxford and Cambridge. It begins with a tract called *Summule*, which summarizes standard medieval material on terms, propositions and arguments, and then offers a series of short treatments of supposition theory, consequences, the proof of terms, obligations and insolubles (see LOGIC, MEDIEVAL). Paul uses sophismata, or puzzle-cases, to illuminate logical points, a standard technique in English logic texts. One of his less popular logic texts, the *Sophismata*, is entirely devoted to such puzzles, and they also form a large part of his *Logica magna*. The latter work, immensely long, was little read in Paul's time, but in the twentieth century a good deal of attention has been paid to it because it summarizes much of the logical work of the second half of the fourteenth century. Here as elsewhere, Paul often copied his sources word for word, and his own contribution was largely limited to modifying or expanding the views of others. Thus his solution to the problem of insolubles, which differs from the one he gives in the *Logica parva*, is a modification of Roger Swyneshed's solution (see LANGUAGE, MEDIEVAL THEORIES OF; OXFORD CALCULATORS).

The most popular of Paul's logic works after the *Logica parva* is a commentary on Aristotle's *Posterior Analytics* which, as a discussion of scientific reasoning, supplements his equally popular *Summa philosophie naturalis* (Summa of Natural Philosophy). Each of these works survives in over fifty manuscripts and a number of printed editions. The *Summa* begins with a discussion of physics, and ends with short treatises on the soul and on metaphysics. In the latter, Paul uses material on the latitudes of forms drawn from the Oxford Calculators and the Parisian John of Ripa to explain the hierarchy of being. He argued that, contrary to the traditional theological view, God is not properly regarded as the measure of creatures since he is infinitely distant from them. Instead, finite things are ordered in the hierarchy of being in accordance with their distance from the bottom of the hierarchy, the zero grade of being.

One of Paul's chief philosophical concerns was the nature of universals, an issue he discussed in various places, including the *Summa philosophie naturalis*. His intention was to reconcile the 'modern' view, that knowledge begins with the cognition of singulars, with a realist view of universals that he saw as more consonant with ARISTOTLE and Averroes (see IBN RUSHD). He argued that universals have real existence independent of the work of the intellect, but that their existence apart from singular things is only potential. His realist view of universals affected his attitude to Aristotle's categories, which he saw as reflecting the ontological structure of reality, and it is noteworthy that a large part of the discussion of metaphysics in the *Summa* is devoted to the categories (see UNIVERSALS).

Another of Paul's concerns in the *Summa* was the nature of the human soul. He adopted the Averroist thesis that the possible intellect is one for all human beings, but argued that this one soul was individuated by becoming the substantial form of individual human beings. As a result, my knowledge can indeed be different from your knowledge. Only in his later commentary on Aristotle's *De anima* (the *Scriptum super libros De anima*) did Paul worry about the compatibility of what he took to be the correct interpretation of Aristotle and Averroes with Christian doctrine. This commentary also reveals that Paul had changed his mind about the agent intellect. In the *Summa* he argued that it was the same as the possible intellect, but now he argued that it was to be identified with God. A further feature of Paul's Averroism was his acceptance of the thesis that the sensitive soul which we have in common with animals and the intellective soul which characterizes human beings are two separate souls (see AVERROISM).

The tension in Paul's works between the positions of Aristotle and Averroes and the rather different results of fourteenth-century Oxford and Paris is well illustrated by his changing position on impetus theory. In his *Summa*, he gave an account of projectile motion in terms of the impetus the projected object receives from its projector, a doctrine that he took largely from the Parisians John BURIDAN and ALBERT OF SAXONY. In his commentary on Aristotle's *Physics*, which was written in 1409, he reverted to the Aristotelian view that natural motion depends on the continued activity of a mover (see NATURAL PHILOSOPHY, MEDIEVAL). Despite Paul's often-changing opinions and his frequent lack of originality, his work was very influential in Italy during much of the fifteenth and sixteenth centuries.

See also: ARISTOTELIANISM, MEDIEVAL; ARISTOTELIANISM, RENAISSANCE; AVERROISM; LOGIC, MEDIEVAL; NATURAL PHILOSOPHY, MEDIEVAL

List of works

Note: a number of Paul's works, including the *Scriptum super libros De anima* and the *Sophismata*, are not available in any modern edition; see Bottin (1983) for a list of early printed editions.

Paul of Venice [Paulus Venetus] (1395–6) *Logica parva*, trans. A.R. Perreiah, Munich, Vienna: Philosophia Verlag, 1984. (Translation and thematic analysis of Paul's most popular logical work; unreliable on the historical background.)

—— (1397–8) *Logica magna*, ed. and trans. in a series of volumes, Oxford: Oxford University Press for the British Academy, 1978–. (Several volumes, some without much scholarly apparatus, have appeared so far.)

—— (1397–8) *Logica magna (Tractatus de suppositionibus)*, ed. and trans. A.R. Perreiah, St Bonaventure, NY: The Franciscan Institute, 1971. (Contains part of Paul's discussion of supposition theory: the omissions are not indicated.)

—— (1408) *Summa philosophie naturalis* (Summa of Natural Philosophy), Hildesheim: Georg Olms, 1974. (Facsimile reprint of 1503 edition; difficult to read. A summary of natural philosophy, including *On the Soul* and *Metaphysics*.)

References and further reading

Bottin, F. (1983) 'Logica e filosofia naturale nelle opere di Paolo Veneto' (Logic and Natural Philosophy in the Works of Paul of Venice), in A. Poppi (ed.) *Scienza e Filosofia all'Università di Padova nel Quattrocento*, Trieste: Lint, 85–124. (A useful discussion of major themes; gives an accurate list of Paul's works and their early printed editions.)

Conti, A. (1990) *Johannes Sharpe: Quaestio super Universalia*, Florence: Olschki. (Contains a partial edition of Paul's Question on universals, together with discussion and references.)

—— (1996) *Esistenza e Verità: Forme e Strutture del Reale in Paolo Veneto e nel Pensiero Filosofico del Tardo Medioevo* (Existence and Truth: Forms and Structures of Reality in Paul of Venice and the Philosophical Thought of the Late Middle Ages), Rome: Instituto Storico Italiano per il Medio Evo. (The first full study of Paul's metaphysics, with special emphasis on being and existence, universals and singulars, and problems of individuation.)

Olivieri, L. (ed.) (1983) *Aristotelismo Veneto e Scienza Moderna* (Venetian Aristotelianism and Modern Science), Padua: Antenore. (Contains articles on different aspects of Paul's work.)

Perreiah, A.R. (1986) *Paul of Venice: A Bibliographical Guide*, Bowling Green, OH: Philosophy Documentation Center. (A bibliography of manuscripts only; also includes a biography of Paul and a contentious discussion of the authorship of the *Logica magna*.)

E.J. ASHWORTH

PAULUS VENETUS *see* PAUL OF VENICE

PEACE *see* WAR AND PEACE, PHILOSOPHY OF

PECHAM, JOHN (*c.*1230–92)

John Pecham, an English Franciscan, taught at Paris and Oxford, and died as Archbishop of Canterbury. His philosophical career represents a concentrated effort to defend the traditional views of Augustine and Anselm (among other theologians) against what was perceived as a growing tendency toward heterodox Aristotelianism, exemplified in such doctrines as the eternity of the world, a single intellect for all humankind and a divinity that had no knowledge of individual beings.

Born in Patcham in Sussex, England, Pecham was educated at the Benedictine monastery at Lewes and joined the Franciscans at Oxford during the 1250s. After continuing his education at Oxford, he was sent to Paris in the 1260s to complete his theological studies and in 1270 became regent master in Paris in the Franciscan chair of theology. Sometime after 1271 he returned to Oxford, where he became the Franciscan regent master of theology. He held that position until 1275, when he was elected minister provincial of the Franciscans in England, and in 1277 he was appointed lecturer to the papal curia. In 1279 he was named Archbishop of Canterbury, an office he held until his death.

As a student in the late 1260s, Pecham had undoubtedly heard the sermons of BONAVENTURE, who had alerted his listeners to the growing threat of unorthodox Aristotelianism. If Pecham was not directly involved in compiling the list of thirteen errors condemned in 1270 by Etienne Tempier, Bishop of Paris, he certainly would have agreed that the condemned propositions were erroneous. Together with William de la Mare, Pecham was one of the first Franciscans to oppose Thomas AQUINAS, whose opinions were viewed as compromising Christian doctrine and too deferential to ARISTOTLE and Averroes (see IBN RUSHD). This tendency continued in the followers of Pecham, namely MATTHEW OF AQUASPARTA, Roger MARSTON, Bartholomew of Bologna, William of Falagar and, later, VITAL DU FOUR.

A true follower of Bonaventure, Pecham shows a fundamental allegiance to AUGUSTINE while accommodating the philosophy of Aristotle where possible. In the critically edited texts of the surviving works, Pecham shows little interest in logic or metaphysics. His writings reveal a preoccupation with the theory of knowledge, philosophical psychology, natural philosophy and science. In his theory of knowledge, Pecham supported Augustinian divine illumination with regard to first principles, claiming that the human intellect needed the 'eternal reasons' for the certitude of intellectual and moral first principles, although not for their contents (see AUGUSTINIAN-ISM). In contract to Aquinas, Pecham held that the human (as well as the angelic and divine) intellect had a direct knowledge of singulars. According to Aquinas' interpretation of the Aristotelian thesis that the senses know the singular and the intellect the universal, the intellect must reflect on phantasms, products of the imagination, which receives its images from the senses, and then abstract the universal from the phantasms. In response, Pecham argues that the intellect abstracts either knowingly or unknowingly. If knowingly, then it had direct knowledge of the singular in the first place; if unknowingly, then how can it be called intellectual knowledge at all?

In addition to a set of disputed questions on the soul (*Quaestiones de anima*), Pecham also wrote a treatise on the soul (*Tractatus de anima*). In the former, he dismisses traducianism, which would have the human soul come from the divine substance, or from the bodies of the parents, or develop from a sensitive soul. Nor were all human souls created at the beginning of time, as Origen had held. Rather, each soul is created directly by God and infused into the body. Pecham vigorously defends the immortality of the soul, claiming that this can be demonstrated by seven irrefutable arguments (see SOUL, NATURE AND IMMORTALITY OF THE). At the same time, he is opposed to multiple souls in the human being. There is only one (intellective) human soul, which, however, encapsulates the vegetative and sensitive functions as grades of a single intellectual 'form'. He strenuously attacks as heretical Averroes' denial that each human being had its own rational soul. Such an opinion jeopardized immortality and rendered the statement 'I understand' impossible, as Aquinas had pointed out.

The powers of the soul, though multiple, are not really distinct from one another or from the soul. The vegetative grade of the form is distinguished into nutritive, augmentative and generative. The sensitive grade has motive and apprehensive powers, the latter being distinguished into external (the five senses) and internal powers, the latter including the 'common sense', the imagination, the estimative (determining what is friendly or hostile) and the memory. The intellectual soul likewise has apprehensive and motive powers, the apprehensive being the agent intellect, the 'possible' intellect and the intellectual memory. The rational appetite or will comprises concupiscible and irascible powers whereby it seeks the good and flees the harmful, powers which it shares with the sensitive grade. Freedom is not a separate power of the will; nevertheless, the will is so free that it can withhold consent in the face of the dictates of the (practical) intellect. This virtual containment of the various powers in the one intellectual soul anticipates, it would seem, the formal distinction of DUNS SCOTUS.

In natural philosophy, Pecham opposes Aquinas on several issues. In Aristotle's view, every composite substance was made up of matter and form. Aquinas had held that prime matter, as the basis for substantial change, was pure potentiality. Pecham held that it was a positive identity, essentially and really distinct, so that by his divine power God could create prime matter distinct from any form whatever (*Quodlibeta quatuor* IV q.1). Aquinas likewise had held that there was but one substantial form in the human being uniting the soul to the body. Pecham responded with his theory of multiple grades, vegetative and sensitive, which persisted as (substantial) components of the human composite (*Quodlibeta quatuor* IV q.25). Thus the bodily, vegetative and sensitive 'forms' are not successively 'corrupted out' by the advent of the higher forms, as Aquinas would have it, but remain as grades of the higher form. Pecham may have been the first to introduce the grades theory as a refinement of 'tri-animism' or the plurality of substantial forms. While his treatise on this subject is apparently lost (Douie 1952: 280 n. 2), the salient points of his theory undoubtedly survive in his faithful disciple Roger Marston's *Quodlibet* II q. 22 (see NATURAL PHILOSOPHY, MEDIEVAL). Pecham likewise rejected Aquinas' view on the eternity of the world. The latter held that although *de facto* the world was created in time and there is nothing theologically or philosophically repugnant to the world's being created from all eternity (Brady 1974; Bukowski 1979). Like Bonaventure, Pecham believed that creation from all eternity was fundamentally contradictory (see ETERNITY OF THE WORLD, MEDIEVAL VIEWS OF).

Pecham wrote a treatise on optics as well as a textbook on optics, the *Perspectiva communis*, and also a treatise on the spheres, a set of four disputed questions on the stars and a tract on mystical numbers (*De numeris misticis*). In addition he wrote numerous treatises on Franciscan spirituality (Brady 1974; Teetaert 1933) including a tract on evangelical poverty. Much of Pecham's work survives only in manuscripts, namely a considerable number of disputed questions and his commentary on the *Sentences* of Peter LOMBARD, the last three books of which appear to have been lost. A comprehensive assessment of his thought must await the critical edition of these works.

See also: ARISTOTELIANISM, MEDIEVAL; AUGUSTINIANISM; BONAVENTURE; ETERNITY OF THE WORLD, MEDIEVAL VIEWS OF; SOUL, NATURE AND IMMORTALITY OF THE

List of works

Pecham, J. (1269–73) *De numeris misticis* (On Mystical Numbers), ed. B. Hughes, *Archivum Franciscanum Historicum* 78, 1985: 3–28, 333–83. (Edition of Pecham's tract on mystical numbers.)

— (1277–9) *Perspectiva communis*, ed. D. Lindberg, *John Pecham and the Science of Optics*, Madison, WI: University of Wisconsin Press, 1970. (Includes brief biographical sketch in English and extensive bibliography.)

—— (1269–73) *Quaestio disputata 'De aeternitate mundi'* (A Disputed Question on the Eternity of the World), ed. O. Argerami, *Patristica et Mediaevalia* 1, 1975: 82–100. (Edition of Pecham's disputed question on eternity.)

—— (1269–73) *Quaestiones de aeternitate mundi* (Questions on the Eternity of the World), ed. I. Brady, 'John Pecham and the Background of Aquinas's *De aeternitate mundi*', in *St. Thomas Aquinas (1274–1974): Commemorative Studies*, Toronto, Ont.: Pontifical Institute of Mediaeval Studies, vol. 2, 11–71; ed. and trans. V. Potter, New York: Fordham University Press, 1993. (Further questions on the eternity of the world.)

—— (1269–73) *Quaestiones de anima* (Questions on the Soul), ed. H. Spettmann, Beiträge zur Geschichte der Philosophie und Theologie des Mittelalters 19, 5, 1918. (Also includes *Quaestiones de beatitudine corporis et animae* and *Quaestiones de anima* excerpted from Pecham's commentary on Book 1 of Lombard's *Sentences*.)

—— (1269–73) *Quodlibeta quatuor* (Four Quodlibets), ed. G. Etzkorn and F. Delorme, Bibliotheca Franciscana Scholastica Medii Aevi XXV, Grottaferrata: Collegio S. Bonaventura, 1989. (Includes copious cross-references to parallel treatment in Pecham and near contemporaries.)

—— (1269–73) *Summa de esse et essentia* (Summa on Existence and Essence), ed. F. Delorme, Rome: Studi Franciscani, 1928. (Edition of this metaphysical treatise.)

—— (1269–73) *Tractatus de anima* (Treatise on the Soul), ed. G. Melani, Studi Francescani, vol. 1, Florence: Edizioni Studi Francescani, 1948. (The immortality and powers of the soul.)

—— (1269–73) *Tractatus de perspectiva* (Treatise on Optics), ed. D. Lindberg, St Bonaventure, NY: Franciscan Institute Publications, 1972. (Edition of treatise on optics.)

—— (1279–92) *Registrum epistolarum Fratris Ioannis Peckham* (Register of Letters of Brother John Pecham), ed. C.T. Martin, 3 vols. in Rerum Britannicarum Scriptores, London, 1788. (Edition of Pecham's collected correspondence.)

References and further reading

* Brady, I. (1974a) 'Jean de Pecham', *Dictionnaire de Spiritualité* 8: 645–9. (Concentrates on Pecham's spiritual writings.)

—— (1974b) 'John Pecham and the Background of Aquinas's De aeternitate mundi', *St. Thomas Aquinas (1274–1974): Commemorative Studies*, vol. 2: Toronto, Ont.: Pontifical Institute of Mediaeval Studies, 11–71. (Study plus text of Pecham's *Disputed Questions on the Eternity of the World*.)

* Bukowski, T. (1979) 'J. Pecham, T. Aquinas et al. on the Eternity of the World', *Recherches de Théologie Ancienne et Médiévale* 46: 216–21. (Disputes Brady's claim that Aquinas directed his *De aeternitate* treatise against Pecham.)

Callebaut, A. (1925) 'Jean Peckham O.F.M. et l'augustinisme', *Archivum Franciscanum Historicum* 18: 441–72. (Pecham's place in Augustinian thought.)

Crowley, T. (1951) 'John Peckham O.F.M. Archbishop of Canterbury: Versus the New Aristotelianism', *Bulletin of the John Rylands Library* 33: 242–55. (On Pecham's role as an opponent of Aquinas and his followers.)

Doucet, V. (1933) 'Notulae bibliographicae de quibusdam operibus Fr. Ioannis Pecham, O.F.M.', *Antonianum* 8: 307–28, 425–59. (Best study of Pecham's works and manuscripts.)

* Douie, D. (1952) *Archbishop Pecham*, Oxford: Clarendon Press. (Focuses on Pecham's career as archbishop.)

Ehrle, F. (1889) 'J. Peckham über den Kampf des Augustinismus und Aristotelismus in der zweiten Hälfte des 13. Jahrhunderts' (J. Pecham and the Debate over Augustinianism and Aristotelianism in the Second Half of the Thirteenth Century), *Zeitschrift für katholische Theologie* 13: 172–93. (Discusses Pecham's own role in the debate.)

Etzkorn, G. (1989) 'John Pecham, O.F.M.: A Career of Controversy', in E.B. King *et al.* (eds) *Monks, Nuns, and Friars in Mediaeval Society*, Sewanee, TN: The Press of the University of the South, 71–82. (Pecham opposing the secular masters and Aquinas.)

Lindberg, D. (1965) 'The "Perspectiva Communis" of John Pecham: Its Influence, Sources and Content', *Archives Internationales d'Histoire des Sciences* 18: 37–53.

—— (1968) 'Bacon, Witelo, and Pecham, the Problem of Influence', *XII Congres Internationale d'Histoire des Sciences* 111-A: 103–7. (Article discussing Pecham's influence.)

Spettmann, H. (1919) 'Die Psychologie des Johannes Pecham', Beiträge zur Geschichte der Philosophie und Theologie des Mittelalters 20: 1–102. (On Pecham's epistemology.)

* Teetaert, A. (1933) 'Pecham, Jean', *Dictionnaire de Théologie Catholique* 12: 100–14. (In French; most comprehensive and thorough.)

Wielockx, R. (1985) 'Jean de Pecham', *Catholicisme* X: 1005–7. (Short survey.)

GIRARD J. ETZKORN

PECKHAM, JOHN *see* PECHAM, JOHN

PEIRCE, CHARLES SANDERS (1839–1914)

Peirce was an American philosopher, probably best known as the founder of pragmatism and for his influence upon later pragmatists such as William James and John Dewey. Personal and professional difficulties interfered with his attempts to publish a statement of his overall philosophical position, but, as the texts have become more accessible, it has become clear that he was a much more wide-ranging and important thinker than his popular reputation suggests.

He claimed that his pragmatism was the philosophical outlook of an experimentalist, of someone with experience of laboratory work. His account of science was vigorously anti-Cartesian: Descartes was criticized for requiring an unreal 'pretend' doubt, and for adopting an individualist approach to knowledge which was at odds with scientific practice. 'Inquiry' is a cooperative activity, whereby fallible investigators progress towards the truth, replacing real doubts by settled beliefs which may subsequently be revised. In 'The Fixation of Belief' (1877), he compared different methods for carrying out inquiries, arguing that only the 'method of science' can be self-consciously adopted. This method makes the 'realist' assumption that there are real objects, existing independently of us, whose nature will be discovered if we investigate them for long enough and well enough.

Peirce's 'pragmatist principle' was a rule for clarifying concepts and hypotheses that guide scientific investigations. In the spirit of laboratory practice, we can completely clarify the content of a hypothesis by listing the experiential consequences we would expect our actions to have if it were true: if an object is fragile, and we were to drop it, we would probably see it break. If this is correct, propositions of a priori metaphysics are meaningless. Peirce applied his principle to explain truth in terms of the eventual agreement of responsible inquirers: a proposition is true if it would be accepted eventually by anyone who inquired into it. His detailed investigations of inductive reasoning and statistical inference attempted to explain how this convergence of opinion was achieved.

Taken together with his important contributions to formal logic and the foundations of mathematics, this verificationism encouraged early readers to interpret Peirce's work as an anticipation of twentieth-century logical positivism. The interpretation is supported by the fact that he tried to ground his logic in a systematic account of meaning and reference. Much of his most original work concerned semiotic, the general theory of signs, which provided a novel framework for understanding of language, thought and all other kinds of representation. Peirce hoped to show that his views about science, truth and pragmatism were all consequences of his semiotic. Doubts about the positivistic reading emerge, however, when we note his insistence that pragmatism could be plausible only to someone who accepted a distinctive form of metaphysical realism. And his later attempts to defend his views of science and meaning bring to the surface views which would be unacceptable to an anti-metaphysical empiricist.

From the beginning, Peirce was a systematic philosopher whose work on logic was an attempt to correct and develop Kant's philosophical vision. When his views were set out in systematic order, positions came to the surface which, he held, were required by his work on logic. These include the theory of categories which had long provided the foundations for his work on signs: all elements of reality, thought and experience can be classified into simple monadic phenomena, dyadic relations and triadic relations. Peirce called these Firstness, Secondness and Thirdness. He also spoke of them as quality, reaction and mediation, and he insisted that the error of various forms of empiricism and nominalism was the denial that mediation (or Thirdness) was an irreducible element of our experience. Peirce's 'synechism' insisted on the importance for philosophy and science of hypotheses involving continuity, which he identified as 'ultimate mediation'. This

emphasis upon continuities in thought and nature was supposed to ground his realism. Furthermore, his epistemological work came to focus increasingly upon the requirements for rational self-control, for our ability to control our inquiries in accordance with norms whose validity we can acknowledge. This required a theory of norms which would explain our attachment to the search for truth and fill out the details of that concept. After 1900, Peirce began to develop such an account, claiming that logic must be grounded in ethics and aesthetics.

Although pragmatism eliminated a priori speculation about the nature of reality, it need not rule out metaphysics that uses the scientific method. From the 1880s, Peirce looked for a system of scientific metaphysics that would fill important gaps in his defence of the method of science. This led to the development of an evolutionary cosmology, an account of how the world of existent objects and scientific laws evolved out of a chaos of possibilities through an evolutionary process. His 'tychism' insisted that chance was an ineliminable component of reality, but he argued that the universe was becoming more governed by laws or habits through time. Rejecting both physicalism and dualism, he defended what he called a form of 'Objective Idealism': matter was said to be a form of 'effete mind'.

1 Life and works

Peirce's father, Benjamin Peirce, was one of the most respected American mathematicians of the nineteenth century. As well as holding chairs in mathematics and astronomy at Harvard, he was instrumental in establishing the American Academy of Arts and Sciences and served as Superintendent of the United States Coast Survey. Charles, whose remarkable intellectual abilities were soon recognized, was brought up in Cambridge, Massachusetts, in a house often visited by the leading philosophical and scientific figures of the time. Indulged and encouraged, his abilities were evident even in his most youthful writings. His undergraduate career at Harvard (1855–9) was undistinguished, but he was subsequently the first student to graduate *summa cum laude* in chemistry from the University's new Lawrence Scientific School.

By the late 1860s, Peirce's future looked bright. From 1861 he had worked as an aide to the Coast Survey. He lectured on logic at Harvard several times between 1865 and 1869. By 1867, his first important series of philosophical papers was appearing and he was elected to the American Academy of Arts and Sciences. In 1872 he founded a 'Metaphysical Club' where he discussed philosophical issues with kindred spirits, including William JAMES, Chauncey Wright, Francis Abbot, and Oliver Wendell Holmes Jr. Although some friends already feared that Peirce's independence of mind and his difficult and wild personality would prove obstacles to academic success, his future seemed assured when, in 1879, he obtained a lectureship in logic in the new Graduate School at Johns Hopkins University. At Johns Hopkins, Peirce and a small group of talented students made important contributions to the logic of relations and the theory of probabilistic reasoning, and (independently of Frege) Peirce and his student O.H. Mitchell introduced quantifiers into logic (see PREDICATE CALCULUS).

In the mid-1880s Peirce's professional life fell apart. His post at Johns Hopkins was suddenly terminated due to his personal irregularities, and his unreliability soon led to the end of his employment with the Coast Survey. Retreating to rural Pennsylvania, Peirce built a house where he lived with his second wife, often in desperate poverty, until his death in 1914. He was not wholly cut off from the academic world. His friend William James arranged for him to give occasional series of lectures in Cambridge, Massachusetts – although he faced the widespread suspicion that he would be a bad moral influence upon the young students of Harvard. He continued to publish and he wrote many reviews for *The Nation*; and he produced eighty-thousand manuscript pages which are a major source for scholars trying to understand his later philosophical position. In 1903 he entered into an important correspondence with Victoria Lady Welby, an English scholar whose work in 'Significs' suggested a common interest with Peirce the semiotician. Lady Welby introduced Peirce's work to I.A. Richards and C.K. Ogden, whose account of them, *The Meaning of Meaning*, helped bring them to the attention of the wider philosophical community.

A finished statement of Peirce's philosophical system was never completed, but his published writings and manuscripts are extensive and range widely. During the late 1860s, a series of papers appeared, in the *Journal of Speculative Philosophy* and elsewhere, which summarized his early ideas on cognition, inference, logic, signs and the theory of categories. Attempts to incorporate this material into a textbook on logic in the early 1870s were thwarted, in part because of intractable problems about reference. However, material intended for this text surfaced, in a less systematic form, in Peirce's most famous series of papers, *Illustrations of the Logic of Science*, which appeared in the *Popular Science Monthly* in 1877–9. This included his best-known papers, 'The Fixation of Belief' and 'How to Make Our Ideas Clear', the standard source for his pragmatism. The most important work from the early 1880s was in formal logic, and *Studies in Logic*, a book of essays by Peirce and his students at Johns Hopkins, contained the Peircean version of the logic of quantification – which provided the key to solving his problems about reference.

The second half of the 1880s saw Peirce's interest turn to metaphysics and the revision of his theory of categories. An important series of five papers on metaphysical topics appeared in *The Monist* in 1891–3. Several attempts to collect his earlier papers in book form and to write a logic text survive from the following decade, including the important *Grand Logic* of 1893. Constantly seeking funding to support various grandiose publishing ventures, Peirce made a very useful application to the Carnegie Foundation for support to write thirty-six 'memoirs' summing up his philosophical position in 1902. Although unsuccessful, the surviving drafts of the application cast invaluable light upon the structure of his thought. Also useful are lectures delivered at or around Harvard during this period. A fascinating series dealing with logical and metaphysical topics was given to the Cambridge Conferences in 1898 and has been published as *Reasoning and the Logic of Things*. After William James had made pragmatism famous, Peirce devoted much energy to displaying the superiority of his version of the doctrine, and he valuably seized the opportunity when invited to lecture on pragmatism at Harvard in 1903. He returned to the task of proving pragmatism in an incomplete series of papers published in *The Monist* a few years later. And it was around this time, in 1908, that he offered his 'Neglected Argument for the Reality of God': his view of God was somewhat pantheist, and he shared his father's view of scientific research as an attempt to read God's 'great poem', holding that scientific observation was a kind of religious experience.

2   Inquiry and the fixation of belief

In his writings from the 1860s and 1870s, Peirce explicitly questioned Cartesian assumptions about cognition. The papers in the *Journal of Speculative*

Philosophy challenged the claim that we have introspective knowledge of our own mental states and disputed the foundationalist view that we have 'intuitive' knowledge – knowledge which is not logically dependent on prior opinions. The influence of the common-sense tradition emerges when Peirce criticizes Descartes's use of the method of doubt. Cartesian doubt is impossible: it will be 'mere self-deception and not real doubt'. Peirce enjoins us not to pretend to doubt in philosophy what we do not doubt in our hearts. Cartesians find the ultimate test of certainty in the individual consciousness, while Peirce urges us to follow the successful sciences in trusting to the critical conversation of a community of inquirers. And philosophy should follow the sciences in trusting the 'multitude and variety of its arguments rather to the conclusiveness of any one'. Our experience of the growth of knowledge suggests that although we are fallible, we can make progress as members of a community of investigators. Descartes and his followers have provided no reason for us not to emulate this in philosophy. Peirce's work on logic and epistemology attempted to vindicate this fallibilist but optimistic view of scientific inquiry. In the 1860s, he tried to do this by arguing that all thoughts are signs and all mental action is inference, and then explaining the grounds of our trust in the forms of reasoning that are used in science. We shall focus here on the arguments he employed in the following decade.

In 'The Fixation of Belief' (1877), Peirce is concerned with 'guiding principles of reasoning'. These are propositions which formulate rules of inference: an inference is good if its guiding principle is true. Habits of reasoning express such guiding principles and almost any proposition could express one: to the proposition that all humans are mortal corresponds the rule that on hearing of the humanity of someone, their mortality may be inferred. However, Peirce is concerned with the special class of logical rules, of propositions that are 'absolutely essential as guiding principles' and he tells us that these are 'necessarily taken for granted in asking whether a certain conclusion follows from certain premises'. The papers in the *Illustrations of the Logic of Science* attempt to draw out facts and principles which 'are deduced from the assumptions which are involved in the logical question', and which we must 'already know before we can have any clear conception of reasoning at all'. He is hunting for the presuppositions of inquiry and with the fundamental norms which govern our participation in it.

The paper begins by characterizing inquiry which, we are told, starts with the posing of a question, with a real doubt, and concludes with the settled accep-

tance of an answer to the question, with belief. Both belief and doubt are characterized in a functionalist manner: beliefs are settled states which 'guide our desires and shape our actions'; doubt is an unsettled state whose only effect on action is to provoke inquiry directed at its elimination. A genuine doubt is required to motivate inquiry (contrary to Cartesian doctrine) and once the doubt has been eliminated, inquiry comes to an end: 'the sole object of inquiry is the settlement of opinion'. Since to believe something is always to believe it to be true, it is empty to say that our aim in inquiry is to arrive at the truth.

What methods should we use in order to settle opinions or fix beliefs? Peirce considers four: three prove unsatisfactory and the method of science is endorsed. It is the only method which is consistent with the presuppositions of inquiry, so the norms it provides are 'absolutely essential'. Were we to adopt the method of tenacity, we would seize on any answer to our question, doing all that was required to ignore or resist anything that might persuade us to abandon it. The 'social impulse' prevents us from making this our method: our certainty will inevitably be disturbed when we encounter people who hold other opinions and it is inevitable that we will do so. Proponents of the method of authority would allow a monarch or religious leader to choose an answer for an entire community and would control sources of available information to prevent our certainties being shaken. But this too will fail: no one could control opinions on *every* question, and we would eventually face problems through encountering people who are not subject to our chosen authority. The failure of these methods shows that we cannot live with a method which ignores the social dimension of inquiry or one that allows the correctness of an answer to be determined by the will of some individual. The a priori method meets these conditions: we are to accept the answer to our question which is 'agreeable to reason', the answer which seems most plausible. But this fails because the correctness of an answer remains a subjective matter: the method would be likely to make truth a matter of fashion.

The method of science introduces objectivity. It requires us to carry out inquiries in accordance with norms which reflect the following fundamental hypothesis:

There are real things, whose characters are entirely independent of our opinions about them; those realities affect our sense according to regular laws, and, though our sensations are as different as our relations to the objects, yet, by taking advantage of the laws of perception, we can ascertain by reasoning how things really are; and any man, if he have sufficient experience and reason enough about it, will be led to the one true conclusion.

(1992–4: 120)

Peirce's arguments in favour of this method are rather unclear, but he strongly suggests that it alone is in harmony with 'the logical question'. It is the only method 'which presents any distinction of a right and wrong way'.

The feeling which gives rise to any method of fixing belief is a dissatisfaction at two repugnant propositions. But here already is a vague concession that there is some *one* thing to which a proposition should conform. Nobody, therefore, can really doubt that there are realities...

(1992–4: 120)

But Peirce also insists that everyone uses this method about 'a great many things', abandoning it only when unsure how to do so, and points to the triumphs of the scientific tradition as further recommendation. However the method of science has so far been formulated sketchily, and we should now examine Peirce's attempts to fill in some of the details.

3 Pragmatism

Although Peirce did not use the word in print until more than twenty years later, 'How to Make Our Ideas Clear' (1878a) introduces the rule for achieving complete clarity about the contents of concepts, propositions and hypotheses which was later called 'pragmatism'. The rule helps us to carry out scientific investigations in a responsible, self-controlled manner, but Peirce's principle also has important applications within logic and philosophy. First, it is used to clarify concepts like reality and probability, which are fundamental to his understanding of the method of science. Second, its account of the meaning of propositions helps to explain how the method of science can indeed show anyone 'the one true conclusion' to an investigation. And third, it is needed to demonstrate that there are no important propositions – and none on which science depends – whose truth values cannot be established using the method of science. Peirce must show, for example, that all 'ontological metaphysics' is 'gibberish' (see MEANING AND VERIFICATION).

Peirce contrasts three grades of clarity in our apprehension of a concept or proposition. I possess the first when I unthinkingly apply the concept in my experience, and the second involves possession of an abstract definition. For example, we can define reality as 'that which is not whatever we happen to think it', but is unaffected by what we may think of it. These notions of clarity, familiar from rationalists' talk of 'clear and distinct ideas', can appear sufficient only in the light of a discredited logic and philosophy. The third 'pragmatist' grade, Peirce later stressed, accords with experimentalist approaches to inquiry and laboratory experience. His formulation of his method for achieving this third grade of clarity is:

Consider what effects, which might conceivably have practical bearing, we conceive the object of our conception to have. Then our conception of those effects is the whole of our conception of the object.

(1992–4: 132)

His examples, and his later formulations, clarify this obscure statement. For example:

To say that a body is heavy simply means that, in the absence of opposing force, it will fall. This (neglecting certain specifications of how it will fall, etc., which exist in the mind of the physicist who uses the word) is evidently the whole conception of weight.

(1992–4: 133)

From the proposition that the body is heavy, I can derive conditional propositions predicting the experiential results of different actions: if I reduce the force acting to support the heavy body, it will fall. Pragmatism holds that I can provide a *complete* clarification of a concept by listing such conditional propositions: they tell me what effects my actions will have if the concept applies to a specified object. As Peirce insisted, this is an 'experimentalist's' view of the content of propositions.

'How to Make Our Ideas Clear' uses the principle to clarify the concept of reality. Listing different methods for investigating the velocity of light, Peirce notes that, while users of each may initially produce different results, 'as each perfects his method and his processes, the results will move steadily together towards a destined centre'. It is typical of scientific inquiry that 'no modification of the point of view taken, no selection of other facts for study, no natural bent of mind even, can enable a man to escape the predestinate opinion'. Peirce's clarification of the concept of reality is thus: 'The opinion which is fated to be ultimately agreed to by all who investigate is what we mean by the truth, and the object represented in this opinion is the real'. Truth is defined by reference to long-run convergence of opinion among responsible inquirers: it is not independent of 'thought in general' but it is independent of what any individual may think at any particular time.

Another important application of Peirce's principle

273

is his account of probability, presented in the third paper of the series, 'The Doctrine of Chances' (1878b) (see PROBABILITY, INTERPRETATIONS OF). Urging that we clarify the idea of probability by examining 'what real and sensible difference there is between one degree of probability and another', he follows Locke in identifying probability as a property of inferences. Deductively valid arguments are those which belong 'to a genus of arguments all constructed in the same way, and such that, when their premises are real facts, their conclusions are so also. If the argument is demonstrative, then this is always so; if it is only probable, then it is for the most part so' (1992–4: 146). The probability of a mode of argument is thus 'the proportion of cases in which it carries truth with it'. A probability statement formulates a guiding principle for such an inference. If the probability of a tossed coin landing with heads uppermost is 0.48, then a claim is made about inferences from the premise that this coin was fairly tossed to the conclusion that it lands with heads uppermost: in the long run, such inferences will be successful around 48 per cent of the time. Pragmatism supports a frequency account of probability.

> As we go on drawing inference after inference of the given kind, during the first ten or hundred cases the ratio of successes may be expected to show considerable fluctuations; but when we come to the thousands and millions, these fluctuations become less and less; and if we continue for long enough, the ratio will approximate towards a fixed limit.
>
> (1992–4: 146)

4 Induction and the method of science

So far, the method of science has been defined in terms of its underlying presupposition: for any question that we investigate, there is a correct answer which we are fated to reach if we carry out our investigations long enough and well enough. A more detailed account is needed of the scientific method and of how this convergence in opinion is to be secured. What inferences and methods should we employ, and how do they lead us to the truth?

Like other nineteenth-century thinkers, Peirce emphasized the self-correcting character of inductive reasoning: in the long run, error is sure to be eliminated and whatever survives testing will be the truth. Peirce's development of this idea exploited an analysis of statistical sampling ('quantitative induction') which attempted to establish that successive sampling of a population is guaranteed eventually to discover the proportion of the population having a particular character. This was supplemented by the

claim that all inductive inference can be modelled on statistical sampling.

Suppose we wish to know the proportion of white beans in large bag of beans. Drawing out a handful, we find that 75 per cent of these beans are white. An inductive argument would then tentatively conclude that 75 per cent of the beans in the whole bag were white. So long as the handful is sufficiently large, and the beans in the bag are evenly distributed, the probability is high that the proportion of white beans in the bag as a whole is fairly close to 75 per cent. Moreover, if it is not, further sampling will arrive at a figure that is more accurate than the original one. The mathematical details of Peirce's approach need not delay us, although we should note that this is in harmony with his pragmatist clarification of the concept of probability: if the probability of a bean drawn from the bag being white is 0.75, then as we draw more and more handfuls, we expect to find that 75 per cent of those that we draw are indeed white.

But quantitative induction forms only a small part of scientific inference. The experimental testing of theories involves an apparently different form of inference which is referred to as 'hypothesis' in Peirce's earlier writings, and later as 'qualitative induction'. But Peirce's pragmatism reveals an analogy between quantitative and qualitative induction. For pragmatism holds that there is nothing to the content of a hypothesis apart from a set of conditional predictions, expectations about the experiential consequences we should expect our actions to have were the theory to be true. We are not in a position to test every one of those conditional predictions, although we can see that, if all were confirmed, the hypothesis would be true. When a hypothesis is tested empirically, then, we sample those predictions, and we infer from the success of the sample to the reliability of the 'population' of predictions forming the content of the hypothesis. The probability calculus is not applicable in these cases, of course, but as long as the pragmatist principle clarifies the full meaning of the hypothesis, the parallel cannot be denied.

There is an important difference between quantitative and qualitative induction. When subsequent sampling conflicts with my estimate that 75 per cent of the beans are white, it does so by introducing a revised estimate of the proportion: eventually, continued sampling will arrive at the correct figure. When evidence conflicts with a hypothesis in the course of qualitative induction, it does not introduce a replacement hypothesis. We depend upon our ability to think of promising hypotheses and to choose the right ones for empirical test. These matters are addressed in Peirce's account of 'abduction'. Much of the logic of abduction investigates methodological rules to be followed in deciding which hypotheses to test: we should prefer those that can be tested economically and whose falsity would be quickly exposed; we should also favour those that seem simple, cohere with our metaphysical views, or appeal to explanatory mechanisms similar to those that have been successful elsewhere in science. Many of these matters concern the economics of research: we plan our investigations in order to maximize progress and minimize expenditure of time, money and effort.

5 Abduction and critical common-sensism

More fundamental than this 'economics of research', however, is the 'primary abduction' on which all scientific activity depends, the presupposition or hope that we have a capacity for guessing right. We have a 'natural instinct for the truth': 'the human mind is akin to the truth in the sense that in a finite number of guesses it will light upon the correct hypothesis' (1931–58: 7, 139). Unless we can be confident that we shall think of a good hypothesis fairly soon, the motivation to carry out scientific research would weaken. Of course, this provides no reason for believing that the primary abduction offers, at best, grounds for hoping that it is correct. The history of science helps by showing that 'it has seldom been necessary to try more than two or three hypotheses made by clear genius before the right one was found'.

Peirce's account of the growth of scientific knowledge involves one further complexity. When first introduced, a hypothesis offers a vague picture which is incomplete and incorrect in many of its details: at best, we hope that some precise revision of it can be defended. Inductive testing will guide us in making revisions, in rejecting some adjustments and developing others:

> The familiar kinetical theory of gases illustrates this well. It began with a number of spheres almost infinitesimally small occasionally colliding. It was afterward so modified that the forces between the spheres, instead of merely separating them, were mainly attractive, that the molecules were not spheres, but systems, and that the part of space within which their motions are free is appreciably less than the entire volume of the gas. There was no new hypothetical element in these modifications.
>
> (1931–58: 7, 135–6)

This background to abduction will also contain beliefs and inferences drawn from common sense. Such beliefs and inferences are 'acritical': they cannot be subjected to critical evaluation and when asked to defend them we can say only 'everything counts for them and nothing counts against them'. This slowly evolving body of opinions is indubitable and can almost be seen as instinctive. It is certain largely because common-sense beliefs are invariably vague: any proposed precise version of them would be fallible, but its defeat would not demonstrate that another way of making them precise cannot be found. General ideas drawn from analytical mechanics provide a common-sense framework against which research in physics develops, and the assumptions about beliefs, desires and meanings reflected in decision theory and microeconomics articulate the common-sense background to the social and human sciences. Peirce's 'critical common-sensism' emphasizes the role of such instinctive certainties in grounding our policy of reflective critical inquiry. We should try to doubt such inferences and propositions in order to satisfy ourselves that they are indeed part of common sense, but, of course, we should not deceive ourselves into thinking that they are indeed dubitable on disreputable Cartesian grounds.

Although common-sense beliefs and vague theoretical pictures are hard to criticize, Peirce described himself as a 'contrite fallibilist': we are aware that most of our theories require revision and we anticipate that any of them might have to be abandoned (see FALLIBILISM). We look on them as currently accepted opinions, acknowledging that accepting them now is the best means to eventual progress towards the truth. In Peirce's later writings, he expresses this fallibilism by denying that we should ever *believe* our current scientific results, and arguing that pure scientific research should be divorced from any concern with the useful applications which its results may have. Ironically, the method of science does not provide a means to the short-term fixation of belief.

Belief, according to Peirce, must result from instinct or sentiment, from the action of common sense, and he was scathing about those who trust theoretical reflection in connection with 'vital' matters. When facing important moral decisions or agonizing over the existence of God, we should spurn reflective deliberation, trusting instead our moral and religious sentiments, the instinctive manifestations of common-sense wisdom.

6 Architectonic and self-control

From around 1900, Peirce insisted that his work in logic and epistemology should be embedded in a systematic framework: a proof of pragmatism and a defence of induction were required, and his search for these led to the attempt to ground logic in aesthetics and ethics and to his development of phenomenology as a fundamental branch of philosophy. Why was he dissatisfied with his earlier defence of his views?

First (a minor point), he came to deny that we could establish that something is true by showing that it is a presupposition of inquiry: at best, that warrants our *hoping* that it is true. Hence his views risk refutation through a demonstration that what scientists hope to be true is not in fact so. Second, his pragmatism claimed that all scientific propositions can be fully elucidated using the pragmatic principle: there is nothing to their content apart from conditional predictions. Scientific work is shaped by explanatory ideals which guide us in establishing a *system* of knowledge. If concepts, such as continuity, which have a role in setting these ideals cannot be elucidated using the pragmatist principle, then Peirce's pragmatism would be on shaky ground. He needed to show that such concepts were consistent with pragmatism – a conclusion his hero Kant would have denied. Moreover, he aspired to an argument for pragmatism which would convince even those who antecedently believed that they understood concepts that it would rule out of court. A particular threat concerned Peirce's realism. He wished to take natural necessity seriously, and to claim that pragmatism was committed to the objectivity of 'would-bes' – to statements about what *would* occur in various possible situations (see §9 below). However, it is commonly assumed that the kind of verificationism that his position represents cannot make sense of the objectivity of 'would-bes'. Many were convinced by Hume and others that verificationism required nominalism.

Finally, his argument for the superiority of the method of science claimed that the 'social impulse' acted against methods such as tenacity and authority. If this is a *psychological* claim about human inquirers, it is hard to see how it establishes the *normative* claim that only the method of science ought to be employed. Moreover, we have noted that since the method of science only promises to settle belief stably in the long run, requiring us to identify our interests with those of the wider community, we are required to use a different method (trusting to instinct) when we try to settle vital questions. So, it seems, we do use an alternative method much of the time. Or if we use the method of science, confident that we can trust its results in connection with everyday matters, there is a question about the right with which we do so. And why is it rational for us to devote our lives to the cooperative pursuit of long-run stable settlement of beliefs? How can the search for the truth about reality be a good goal for us to adopt? It seems that Peirce must embed his views in a general theory of rationality, in a general theory of how we can order our lives in a self-controlled manner. Otherwise, his

defence of the method of science begs too many questions.

By the late 1890s, Peirce was emphasizing that philosophy should have an architectonic character. It should be systematic and guided by a plan of the structure of knowledge as a whole. Thus he relied upon an explicit classification of the sciences, especially the philosophical sciences which can be schematized thus:

(1) Mathematics
(2) Phenomenology (or 'Phaneroscopy')
(3) Normative science:
    (a) Aesthetics
    (b) Ethics
    (c) Logic:
        (i) Speculative grammar
        (ii) Critic
        (iii) Methodeutic
(4) Metaphysics

Mathematics, our 'practice of necessary reasoning', needs no foundations, but provides techniques used by phenomenology to obtain a theory of categories from reflection upon all that appears to us in any way. Using these categories, the first two normative sciences provide an account of the rationality of ends: they identify what it is possible to admire unconditionally, and what it is possible to adopt as an unconditional end for conduct. Logic then investigates the norms governing inquiries: the first branch provides a systematic account of sign interpretation and reference; the second classifies arguments and explains their validity; and the third states and defends the methodological principles that guide inquiries. Peirce's theory of truth is defended within his logic. Metaphysics develops a general scientific account of 'the most general features of reality and real objects'. Together, these philosophical sciences explain the possibility of rational, self-controlled inquiry.

7 Categories, phenomenology and normative science

Throughout his career, Peirce's philosophical ideas depended upon a system of categories, a set of universal conceptions which could be used to classify anything that could be experienced, thought about or imagined (see CATEGORIES). Growing out of his criticisms of Kant's theory of categories during the 1860s, the system was subject to considerable development and refinement until the final decade of his life and had a fundamental role in grounding his other philosophical views. Although his terminology varied, he most commonly referred to these categories as 'Firstness', 'Secondness' and 'Thirdness'. It is easiest to understand them by following Peirce himself in seeing how they are reflected in the logical forms of a 'perfectly exact, systematic and analytic language in which all reasoning could be expressed and be reduced to formal rules'. Such a language might contain expressions like '... is red' which express properties of a single subject as well as relational expressions such as the two place '... is taller than...' and the three place '...gives...to...'. Peirce insisted that an adequate language would contain expressions of all these three kinds, and also that it need contain no expressions for relations between four or more objects. Concepts or phenomena are classified as forms of Firstness, Secondness and Thirdness according to whether they are expressed by general expressions which take one, two or three subjects. Firstness is what it is independently of anything else, Secondness involves what is in relation to something else, and Thirdness is manifested when something mediates between two others.

Peirce's important 1867 paper 'On a New List of Categories' contained the first published version of the theory. It appeared before Peirce had worked much on the logic of relations and made no use of the terminology of Firstness, Secondness and Thirdness. However it was self-consciously Kantian in defending a system of categories by discussing what was required to reduce the manifold of sense to the unity of a proposition: Peirce spoke of reducing the manifold of Substance to the unity of Being. We do so, he urged, by ascribing a quality to the substance, by classifying it or describing it. But how can we do that? Since 'we know a quality only by means of its contrast or similarity with another', we can ascribe qualities to things only because we can make relational judgments of similarity and difference. And we can make judgments of similarity only because we can carry out 'comparisons': we can interpret one object as a representation of another. So making sense of things by ascribing qualities to them depends upon our ability to make relational judgments and to work with the three-place relation of representation. All three categories are required for even the simplest kind of judgment. Peirce soon came to reject the assumption that quality (monadic characteristics) had a special role in unifying the manifold: the logic of relations led to the overthrow of Aristotelian logic and taught that relational judgments were just as fundamental as these simple monadic ones. Although this led to a reformulation of his theory of categories, he continued to use the argument of this early paper.

He claimed that it embodied his 'one contribution to philosophy'.

With the development of the logic of relations, Peirce exploited his 'remarkable theorem' that it was impossible to define triadic relations in terms of simpler ones, whereas it was always possible to provide such definitions for relations with four or more relata. Within standard systems of the logic of relations, this does not hold: it is possible to reduce triadic relations to dyadic ones. However, recent scholarship suggests that Peirce's claim holds for his own systems of logic and that, for the purposes of constructing a system of categories, the Peircean systems are more perspicuous than those encountered in standard logic texts. Since this argument uses mathematics to defend the categories and mathematics was the foundational discipline without Peirce's architectonic structure, Peirce's continued reliance upon this argument is not surprising.

However, from the late 1880s new quasi-empirical arguments were introduced, culminating after 1900 in a phenomenological defence of them. 'A Guess at the Riddle' (1887–8) traced the 'triad' through logic and semiotics, in metaphysics, psychology, physiology and biology, and in physics and theology, thereby producing a 'long list' of categories. This investigation culminated in the development of Peirce's evolutionary metaphysics (see §10 below). Although not intended as a proof of the theory of categories, it was relevant to establishing a doctrine fundamental to Peirce's realism: Thirdness is found in the physical and biological realms as well as among mental and linguistic phenomena.

From 1903, Peirce undertook to defend his categories by looking 'directly upon the universal phenomenon, that is upon all that in any way appears, whether as fact or as fiction'. With the aid of special analytical techniques, his search again discovered the three fundamental categories, Firstness, Secondness and Thirdness. Since he remained convinced by the early 'logical' arguments, there is a question of why this further defence was required. The answer lies in Peirce's architectonic, his account of how the philosophical sciences all hang together. If the categories are to be used in logic and the other normative sciences, they must be defended in a more fundamental discipline. Since formal logic is a branch of mathematics, this may not seem problematic, but the logical argument for the categories required Peirce to show that a particular mathematical formalism could indeed be used as a system of formal logic: formal logic is, after all, a branch of *applied* mathematics. By showing that a formalism which incorporates the categories is adequate to describe 'all that in any way appears, whether as fact or as fiction', Peirce can be confident in relying upon his categories when he turns to the study of our attempts to discover the facts in logic.

Peirce's work in normative science seeks a theoretical account of what we can admire unconditionally (aesthetics), adopt as an ultimate end (ethics), or adopt as a fundamental goal for inquiry (logic). Thought experiments are employed: we consider different possible objects of experiments or imagine living with a particular aim in various counterfactual circumstances. In each case, the good consists in a manifold of phenomena each with their own qualitative character of Firstness, but standing in dyadic relations, reacting against each other. But this Secondness is mediated: the whole exhibits a coherence or unity which we can apprehend. Beauty, goodness and truth involve a kind of organic unity which excites our admiration, motivates our conduct and satisfies our inquiries. The method of science ensures progress towards a coherent body of opinions which brings our actions and experiences into harmony.

8 Signs and interpretations

Peirce's semiotic provides a wholly general theory of meaning and representation. An important move in his critique of the Cartesian conception of mind during the 1860s was that all thoughts and experiences are signs. In later years, he used these semiotic conceptions to develop a sophisticated account of language – particularly of the language used by a 'scientific intelligence'. His philosophical account of science and mathematics focused upon the role of science interpretation in both, and important problems in the ontology of mathematics were answered by reference to the special character of the signs or representations used within that discipline. And the grounds of logic or deductive validity were traced to features of meaning and the sign relation. It is not surprising that Peirce described logic as 'only another name for *semiotic*, the quasi-necessary or formal doctrine of signs'. There are few of Peirce's writings that are not concerned with questions of meaning and signification.

His work exploits the fundamental insight that signification is a form of Thirdness. The sign relation is irreducibly triadic, and the third element in this relation is interpretation. A name denotes an object or a sentence stands for a state of affairs by virtue of being interpreted in subsequent thought, speech or action as doing so. The interpretant, which is itself a sign with the same object, thus mediates between the original sign and its object. Thus my understanding of a report that an animal before me is a cat can be

variously manifested in my explicitly thinking or saying that this is what the utterance means, in my inferring that the animal probably likes milk, in my offering it cat food, or in my showing surprise when in suddenly barks. Unless the sign has the capacity to produce such interpretant thoughts (the meaning of which in turn depends upon how they are interpreted) it would have no significance. Since a thought too is a sign, the content of a thought (or any other mental event) is determined by how it is interpreted and developed in subsequent thought. In general, the content of a thought or utterance depends upon its effects.

Much of Peirce's writings about signs was directed at constructing a classification of types of signs: he sought an exhaustive classification of signs, objects and interpretants. One motivation for this was Peirce's desire to defend the pragmatist principle by showing that it would enable us to be reflectively aware of all those features of how a sign should be interpreted that were relevant to our scientific purposes. He argued that the 'ultimate logical interpretant' of a sign was a habit of expectation which could be fully described by application of the pragmatist principle. Some of the classifications are of more general interest, offering important insights into thought, language and other forms of representation. And his writings on signs contain valuable contributions to the understanding of mental phenomena such as emotions, sensory experiences and religious experience as well as interesting discussions of proper names, vagueness, conditionals, modality, quantification, force and content and other live issues in the philosophy of language.

The question of how we are guided in arriving at interpretations of signs introduces the best known of Peirce's classifications, that between icon, index and symbol. Roughly, interpretation of an iconic sign is grounded in a resemblance between the sign and its object, interpretation of an index exploits a 'real existential relation' between the two, and we can defend our interpretation of a symbol by reference to an established practice of so interpreting it. Photographs and maps are icons, signposts and pointing fingers are indices, and it is easy to see that natural language has a strong symbolic component. The utterance of a symbolic sign is always a *replica* of the symbol (a token of the type), and its interpretation appeals to the interpretations offered of other replicas or tokens. Peirce denied that there were 'pure' icons or indices. Maps and signposts are 'hypo-icons' and 'hypo-indices', having a strong conventional component. The rules governing the use of maps do not fix the interpretation of particular features of the map unaided: they rather guide us in how to use it as an icon. Similarly, although we are able to understand pointing fingers only because we are masters of the practice of doing so, the rules of this practice do not explicitly lay down what a particular finger is pointing at. Rather, they guide us in how to interpret the finger as a conventional index.

This classification exploits Peirce's system of categories. Interpretation of an index depends upon a dyadic existential relation between sign and object: it exploits properties the sign would lack if its object did not exist. When we understand a symbol, we appeal to triadic features of the sign, such as how its replicas have been interpreted in the past. And an understanding of icons exploits common features of sign and object which each could have, even if the other had not existed. In his 1885 paper, 'On the Algebra of Logic: a Contribution to the Philosophy of Notation', Peirce announced that an adequate language for descriptive or scientific purposes must contain signs of all three kinds. Indeed, any proposition must have symbolic, iconic and indexical components. Indices such as names, demonstrative expressions, pronouns and quantifier expressions are required if the proposition is to speak of any external things at all: the universe of discourse must be specified indexically. Symbols are the only general signs, and generality is essential to reasoning: we must be able to recognize that premises and conclusions contain tokens of the same word or phrase type, replicas of the same symbol.

The value of iconic signs is that we can exploit their similarity with their objects, learning more about the latter by noting features of the icon. We can make discoveries about the terrain by making measurements on a map, or learn more about a building by examining a photograph. A proposition provides a sort of diagram of a state of affairs, mirroring its logical structure. Inference exploits this abstract resemblance: we learn more about the world by making substitutions in propositions in the light of other information that is to hand and observing the result of our 'experiment'. This is clearest when we think of formal logic, which, like all of mathematics, constructs iconic representations of the structure of propositions and arguments which enable us to investigate the validity of arguments. Unless descriptive propositions were icons and shared abstract structural properties with their objects, Peirce argued, we could make no sense of how reasoning can provide us with new knowledge. The formal character of reasoning shows that we interpret propositions as icons. So any language is a device for constructing conventional, logical diagrams which are tied down to concrete, existing things through the use of indices.

After 1900, Peirce sought a proof for his pragma-

tism. He needed to show that no aspect of the meaning of a proposition, nothing relevant to its cognitive functioning, was omitted when we clarify it using the pragmatist principle. One strategy was to develop his theory of signs and show that interpreting a proposition in the light of pragmatism produced its most explicit ('ultimate') logical interpretant. Another strategy was to construct a complete classification of argument forms and to show that we needed no information missed by a pragmatist elucidation in order to employ a proposition in reflective, controlled argument. An important tool here was the system of existential graphs (see LOGIC MACHINES AND DIAGRAMS). A system of formal logic analogous to later natural deduction systems, the graphs promised 'moving pictures of thought' which would exhibit the structure of all possible forms of argument. As well as a complete system of propositional and predicate calculus, the graphs promised an account of sophisticated reasonings involving modality, continuity and abstraction. If all reasoning is reflected in the system of existential graphs, and if the pragmatic principle is true for all concepts whose conceptual role is modelled within them, then the pragmatist is vindicated. Unfortunately there is little evidence that Peirce completed the graphs to his satisfaction.

9 Realism

Peirce described himself as a realist, rejecting nominalism and epistemic idealism as the source of most philosophical ills (see NOMINALISM; REALISM AND ANTIREALISM). This can be surprising because pragmatism is often understood as an antirealist, verificationist doctrine.

It is useful to distinguish three different themes in his realism. The first is a response to the problem of universals. Peirce argues that it is a mistake to understand realism about 'generals' or universals as a claim about the existence of a particular realm of curious abstract objects. Realists are committed to the objectivity of propositions concerning whether this or that object is a horse; they are not committed to the existence of horseness as a special particular. This view was most clearly expressed in an 1870 review of a new edition of Berkeley's works where Peirce distinguishes two conceptions of reality, nominalist and realist. They differ in how they develop the uncontroversial claim that the real is 'that which is not whatever we happen to think it, but is unaffected by what we may think of it'. Nominalists note that our thoughts are caused by sensations which are, in turn, caused by something outside the mind, and identify the real with these efficient causes of our sensations and thoughts. This picture of reality, which is closely allied to the representative theory of perception and the correspondence theory of truth, makes problematic the question of whether anything in reality corresponds to general conceptions such as 'horse' or 'man' and encourages the sort of mistrust of our conceptual interpretation of sensory input that makes Cartesian strategies attractive. Peirce favours the realist conception which notes that 'to every question there is a true answer, a final conclusion, to which the opinion of every man is constantly gravitating'. Reality is the 'final cause' of inquiry, the answer to a question that we are 'fated' to reach if we inquire long enough and well enough.

This view of reality is reminiscent of Kant's 'empirical realism', and encourages realism about generals because it is objective whether (for example) Pegasus was a horse. The account of reality obtained from the pragmatist principle supports this form of 'realism'. However, since truth is explained in terms of the convergence of opinion, there is no conceptual gap between truth and what efficient, responsible inquirers would agree upon. The position thus appears to be in tension with the realist view that truth is not determined by what we take it to be. Moreover, a realist will presumably hold that there are many truths which inquiry will never uncover, all trace of them having been lost. In the 1870s, Peirce suggested that this was a verbal matter of whether a diamond which was created and destroyed without being exposed to any sort of test was hard, but he later insisted that this was a mistake which his realism enabled him to avoid.

A second theme in Peirce's realism responded to this difficulty. Peirce's realism became more extreme in the 1880s when he defended objective modalities. Natural laws manifest real, natural necessity and there are facts concerning 'would-bes' – subjunctive conditionals concern what *would* occur in various counterfactual (but real) possibilities (see Laws, natural; Counterfactuals). The conditionals employed when we clarify a concept using the pragmatist principle are expressed in the subjunctive mood: they concern what would happen (or what would have happened) had certain actions been carried out. So in later work, Peirce's frequency theory of probability is transformed into a propensity view: the probability of an argument is the proportion of cases in which it *would* transmit truth from premises to conclusion.

Returning in 1906 to the example of the diamond which is destroyed before being tested for hardness, Peirce noted that science teaches that diamonds have in common a molecular structure which accounts for their hardness. We know that if it had been tested, it would have proved hard. The hardness of individual diamonds is not ontologically prior to the fact that diamonds (in general) are hard. This form of realism is connected to the reality of Thirdness. Since we directly experience Thirdness, we are directly aware of necessity or mediation. Peirce's synechism turns the question of realism into the question whether there is real continuity, real mediation.

The third theme reflects Peirce's answer to problems about reference which he faced during the 1870s: we directly perceive external things, referring to them demonstratively in perceptual judgments (see Reference). This allows for the possibility of reference to external objects (including theoretical entities) while being aware that some questions about their character have answers which will never be discovered by us. The irreducibility of Secondness is relevant here: we are aware of external things as reacting against us, as 'other'; and this is reflected in the fact that reference to external things is fundamentally indexical, involving demonstrative expressions in perceptual judgments. Theoretical entities are known to exist because they too possess Secondness – they react with other existing things.

10 Scientific metaphysics and evolutionary cosmology

In *The Monist* (1891–3), Peirce published a series of five papers which fit poorly with the anti-metaphysical flavour of his pragmatist writings. Developing themes that he had been exploring since 1883–4, they contained an evolutionary cosmology, which, he suggested, involved a form of objective idealism, and they argued, against Darwin, that this process of evolution should be seen as, in a sense, purposive: 'agapastic' evolution was driven by evolutionary love, and the universe is a vast mind perfecting itself through time (see Idealism). Some commentators, like Thomas Goudge (1950), attributed this work to a philosophical split personality: the naturalistic, tough-minded, anti-metaphysical pragmatist betrayed a taste for transcendental speculation which could not be reconciled with the rest of his work. Peirce himself was clearly sensitive to the need to show that the different elements of his philosophical vision formed a unity. His cosmology attempted to understand the most general features of our view of the world using the method of science. Metaphysics was empirical, differing from the special sciences only in its generality and in its avoidance of sophisticated experiment: its data was drawn from everyday facts whose very familiarity is likely to hide them from our notice.

He also insisted that his metaphysics was required by his work on logic and the method of science: self-controlled reasoning, employing the scientific method, was possible only if a Peircean metaphysics is possible too. In 'The Fixation of Belief', Peirce sought presuppositions of inquiry. He soon saw that showing that something was a presupposition of inquiry (or of a particular inquiry) did not establish its truth: at best, we are warranted in *hoping* that it is true. We must hope that there is a reality, independent of us, of which we can obtain knowledge, that the questions we investigate have answers, that we possess the freedom needed for logical self-control, that we can tell the difference between a good argument and a bad one, that we have the instincts posited in the 'primary abduction' and so on. We must look to metaphysics for the account of mind and reality that explains the truth of these hopes or regulative ideas. If no such account is possible, rational self-control is an illusion.

According to Peirce, the fundamental rule of logic is: 'Don't block the road of inquiry.' We should never assume that any question lacks an answer or that any regularity lacks an explanation: we should always hope that an explanation is to be found. This led him, in 1883 and later, to set himself the task of explaining the fact that there are general laws. Nominalists take there to be brute regularities which have no explanation, and physical atomism appears to require this nominalistic picture. If all law and regularity can be explained, nominalism must be rejected and Peirce is committed to the rejection of metaphysical or physical atomism. Peirce's answer is to construct an evolutionary metaphysics which traces the evolution of law out of pure possibility (of Thirdness out of Firstness). And this evolutionary story enjoins that the universe contains pure chance (Peirce's 'tychism'): a generalizing tendency reinforces chance regularities and the universe becomes steadily more regular and ordered. Just as we acquire more and more habits as our hypotheses are confirmed and habits of expectation are reinforced, so the universe itself becomes more and more 'hidebound with habits' (see DETERMINISM AND INDETERMINISM).

The analogy just offered is important for understanding Peirce's evolutionary story: our ideas of inference, purpose and the growth of knowledge – ideas linked to the practice of sign interpretation – provide the model we must use in making sense of the physical world. Problems of interaction show that we require a monistic system of metaphysics, and physicalism can make no sense of consciousness and other mental phenomena. Hence Peirce's view that the entire universe is a vast mind: laws are analogous to habits, and the ways in which laws determine events have to be understood by appeal to teleology and final causation. Physical events differ from ordinary mental events in being less flexible, being more 'hidebound with habits'. We arrive at a form of idealism which,

although it does not make reality depend upon the contents of human minds or on its being known, still holds that our fundamental explanatory categories are those most familiar from ordinary psychological explanation. The evolution of law is not the mechanical and meaningless process described by Darwin. Peirce's evolution is 'agapastic': evolutionary love is manifested in the ways in which the universe becomes steadily more perfect. Against this background, it is no surprise that in 1908 Peirce published a 'Neglected Argument for the Reality of God'. He believed that the Universe was a vast mind, and that even those who explicitly defend atheism are likely to have a natural belief in this pantheistic god. It is manifested in a confidence that the Universe is steadily becoming more perfect, and in our sense that through contributing to science we contribute to 'the process of creation', to the growing rationality of the Universe.

See also: DOUBT; EMPIRICISM; HEGELIANISM §5; INDUCTION, EPISTEMIC ISSUES IN; LOGIC IN THE 19TH CENTURY; PRAGMATISM §1; SCEPTICISM; SCIENCE, 19TH CENTURY PHILOSOPHY OF; SCIENTIFIC REALISM AND ANTIREALISM; SEMIOTICS; TRUTH, PRAGMATIC THEORY OF §1

List of works

Although Peirce published extensively, he did not publish any major philosophical treatises summarizing his position. The following list samples some of the more important pieces, but inevitably it omits much that is significant: any list of 'major works', particularly after 1890, will be controversial and arbitrary. This material is all readily available in the first two collections, listed below.

Peirce, C.S. (1931–58) *Collected Papers of Charles Sanders Peirce*, ed. C. Hartshorne and P. Weiss (vols 1–6) and A. Burks (vols 7–8), Cambridge, MA: Harvard University Press, 8 vols. (A selection of papers and excerpts from manuscripts which was responsible for introducing Peirce's work to a wide audience. Since the material is organized thematically rather than chronologically and the texts are not all reliable, this edition is being superseded by *The Writings of Charles S. Peirce*.)

—— (1982–) *The Writings of Charles S. Peirce: A Chronological Edition*, ed. M. Fisch, C. Kloesel, E. Moore, N. Houser *et al.*, Bloomington, IN: Indiana University Press. (A reliable and extensive selection of Peirce's published and unpublished writings, organized chronologically, and expected to run to thirty volumes. An indispensable tool for research, it is probably less useful for the new reader. The introductions to the different volumes provide an invaluable intellectual biography of Peirce.)

—— (1992–4) *The Essential Peirce*, ed. N. Houser, and C. Kloesel, Bloomington, IN: Indiana University Press. (An excellent two-volume selection which contains reliable texts of all of Peirce's most important published and unpublished works.)

—— (1867) 'On a New List of Categories', *Proceedings of the American Academy of Arts and Sciences* 7: 287–98. (A classic but difficult paper, containing the first published statement of Peirce's theory of categories. Reprinted as chap. 1, vol. 1 of Houser and Kloesel (eds) *The Essential Peirce*.)

The first three of the following papers contain an attack on Cartesian approaches to philosophy, introduce Peirce's claim that all thought is in signs, and develop an account of truth and cognition on this basis. They are reprinted as chapters 2 to 4 of Houser and Kloesel (eds) *The Essential Peirce*.

—— (1868a) 'Questions Concerning Certain Faculties Claimed for Man', *Journal of Speculative Philosophy* 2: 103–14; (Challenges the Cartesian assumption that we can trust introspection as a source of information about the mind and denies that there are any 'intuitions', first premises for reasoning which are not shaped by earlier thoughts.)

—— (1868b) 'Some Consequences of Four Incapacities' *Journal of Speculative Philosophy* 2: 140–57; (The first published statement of Peirce's semiotic – his claim that all thought is in signs – and his ideas about reality.)

—— (1868c) 'On a New List of Categories', in Houser and Kloesel (eds) *The Essential Peirce*, Bloomington, IN: Indiana University Press, 1–10. (The first statement of Peirce's post-Kantian categorial scheme.)

—— (1869) 'Grounds of Validity of the Laws of Logic: Further Consequences of Four Incapacities', *Journal of Speculative Philosophy* 2: 193–208. (Draws out the implications of the two previous papers for the explanation of the validity of inductive and deductive reasoning.)

—— (1870) 'Fraser's *The Works of George Berkeley*', *North American Review* 113: 449–72. (A lengthy review which contains important discussions of realism versus nominalism (Houser and Kloesel (eds)) and Peirce's conception of truth. Chapter 5 of this series of six papers is based on Peirce's attempt to write a logic text during the early 1870s. Although they are readable and extremely influential, the role of Peirce's theories of signs and categories is not made explicit. Available in chapters 7 to 12 of Houser and Kloesel (eds).)

—— (1877) 'The Fixation of Belief', *Popular Science Monthly* 12: 1–15. (Classic statement of Peirce's theory of inquiry, defending the method of science as a method for replacing doubt by settled belief.)

—— (1878a) 'How to Make Our Ideas Clear', *Popular Science Monthly* 12: 286–302. (Introduces the pragmatist principle for clarifying concepts and ideas and uses it to explain the meaning of Reality.)

—— (1878b) 'The Doctrine of Chances', *Popular Science Monthly* 12: 604–15 (Uses the pragmatist principle to clarify our understanding of statements of probability.)

—— (1878c) 'The Probability of Induction', *Popular Science Monthly* 12: 705–18. (Develops his view of probability and links it to an account of the success of inductive reasoning.)

—— (1878d) 'The Order of Nature', *Popular Science Monthly* 13: 203–17. (Attacks Mill's defence of inductive reasoning and argues that the success of science requires that human beings possess 'innate ideas': due to natural selection, they are predisposed to arrive at the correct theories of the world.)

—— (1878e) 'Deduction, Induction and Hypothesis', *Popular Science Monthly* 13: 470–82. (A formal and historical classification of the kinds of reasoning used in science.)

—— (1887–8) 'A Guess at the Riddle', manuscript, 1887–8. (This manuscript elaborates Peirce's system of categories through showing how they are manifested in different fields of knowledge. Chapter 19 of Houser and Kloesel (eds).)

Although occasionally hard and obscure, the first five of the following papers present the metaphysical system which Peirce had been developing throughout the 1880s. Reprinted as chapters 21 to 25 of Houser and Klousel (eds).

—— (1891) 'The Architecture of Theories', *The Monist* 1: 161–76. (Discusses the proper approach to developing a system of metaphysics and describes the fundamental concepts to be used. His evolutionary cosmology is sketched and the importance of chance and continuity for an adequate philosophical system is emphasized.)

—— (1892a) 'The Doctrine of Necessity Examined', *The Monist* 2: 321–37. (Criticizes the most common arguments for determinism and defends his 'tychism', the doctrine that the universe must contain absolute chance.)

—— (1892b) 'The Law of Mind', *The Monist* 2: 533–59. (Introduces Peirce's 'synechism', the use of the idea of continuity in philosophy. The paper discusses the mathematical analysis of continuity as well as emphasizing its importance for understanding the mind.)

—— (1892c) 'Man's Glassy Essence', *The Monist* 3: 1–22. (Applies Peirce's theory of categories and his synechism to the understanding of matter and the relations between mind and body: contains the suggestion that 'matter is effete mind'.)

—— (1892d) 'Evolutionary Love', *The Monist* 3: 176–200. (Discusses the mechanisms of evolution, finally defending 'agapism', the doctrine that love is operative in the evolution of the universe.)

—— (1898) *Reasoning and the Logic of Things*, ed. K.L. Ketner, Cambridge, MA: Harvard University Press. (An important series of lectures which provides a useful introduction to Peirce's work in logic and philosophy. As well as an important discussion of theory and practice, they contain clear introductions to some of his logical theories and a useful discussion of causation and continuity. Hilary Putnam's valuable introduction contains useful information about Peirce's work on the mathematics of continuity.)

—— (1903) *Pragmatism*, in *Collected Papers of Charles Sanders Peirce*, ed. C. Hartshorne and P. Weiss (vols 1–6), Cambridge, MA: Harvard University Press, 1931–58, vol. 5, 13–131. (Lectures to Harvard University philosophy department, which attempt to state and defend Peirce's pragmatism. They elaborate his views on phenomenology and the categories; logic, ethics and aesthetics as normative sciences; abduction and perceptual judgments; and realism. An important, though sometimes obscure source.)

The first three of the following papers were part of an uncompleted series intended to 'prove' pragmatism. Manuscript drafts of later papers in the series survive.

—— (1905a) 'What Pragmatism Is', *The Monist* 15: 161–81. (Clarifies Peirce's pragmatism, relating it to laboratory practice and christening it 'pragmaticism' to distinguish it from William James' position.)

—— (1905b) 'Issues of Pragmaticism', *The Monist* 15: 481–99. (Contains important discussions of Peirce's mature realism and his critical common-sensism.)

—— (1906) 'Prolegomena to an Apology for Pragmaticism', *The Monist* 16: 492–546. (An introduction to Peirce's 'existential graphs', a system of formal logic which is to have a fundamental role in the unfinished proof of pragmatism.)

—— (1908) 'A Neglected Argument for the Reality of God', *Hibbert Journal* 7: 90–112. (An interesting argument for God's reality which is intended to fit Peirce's account of the method of science.)

Eisele, C. (ed.) (1976) *The New Elements of Mathematics*, The Hague: Mouton. (A five-volume anthology of Peirce's contributions to mathematics and mathematical logic.)

Hardwick, C. (ed.) (1977) *Semiotic and Significs*, Bloomington, IN: Indiana University Press. (This contains Peirce's correspondence with Lady Welby and is an important source for his work on signs.)

References and further reading

The secondary literature on Peirce is now enormous and the list below omits much that is interesting and important. The most important source of journal articles is the quarterly *Transactions of the Charles S. Peirce Society*.

Brent, J. (1993) *Charles Sanders Peirce: A Life*, Bloomington, IN: Indiana University Press. (A fascinating study of Peirce's career and of his troubled personal life.)

Burch, R. (1991) *A Peircean Reduction Thesis*, Lubbock, TX: Texas Tech University Press. (An important study which develops Peirce's formal logic and his use of it to defend his categories.)

Colapietro, V. (1989) *Peirce's Approach to the Self*, Buffalo, NY: State University of New York Press. (Discusses Peirce's philosophy of mind and subjectivity from a perspective that takes his semiotic very seriously.)

Fisch, M. (1986) *Peirce, Semiotic and Pragmatism*, Bloomington, IN: Indiana University Press. (A collection of papers dealing with biographical and philosophical matters by a distinguished scholar whose influence on the development of Peirce studies has been unparalleled.)

* Goudge, T. (1950) *The Thought of C.S. Peirce*, Toronto: University of Toronto Press. (Influential early monograph which argued that the tough-minded, naturalistic, empiricist aspect of Peirce's work could not be reconciled with the speculative, 'transcendental' side of his character.)

Hausman, C. (1993) *Charles S. Peirce's Evolutionary Philosophy*, Cambridge: Cambridge University Press. (This book emphasizes the systematic structure of Peirce's work, studying his pragmatism, his theory of categories and his account of continuity and places special emphasis upon his metaphysical writings.)

Hookway, C. (1985) *Peirce*, London: Routledge & Kegan Paul. (A general account of Peirce's work which develops the interpretations offered in this entry.)

Misak, C. (1991) *Truth and the End of Inquiry*, Oxford: Oxford University Press. (A book which concentrates on Peirce's theory of inquiry and defends a Peircean conception of truth.)

Murphey, M. (1961) *The Development of Peirce's Philosophy*, Cambridge, MA: Harvard University Press; reprinted 1993, Indianapolis, IN: Hackett Publishing Company. (Influential and important book which established the importance of studying the development of Peirce's work, claiming that he defended four distinct systems.)

* Ogden, C.K. and Richards, I.A. (1923) *The Meaning of Meaning*, London: Kegan Paul. (Influential discussion of meaning and literature containing an appendix on Peirce's work in semiotic.)

Rescher, N. (1978) *Peirce's Philosophy of Science*, Notre Dame, IN: University of Notre Dame Press. (Guide to Peirce's philosophy of science placing interesting emphasis upon his ideas about the economics of research.)

Robin, R. (ed.) (1967) *Annotated Catalogue of the Papers of Charles S. Peirce*, Amherst, MA: University of Massachusetts Press. (An essential guide to Peirce's many important manuscripts in the Houghton Library at Harvard.)

Skagestad, P. (1981) *The Road of Inquiry*, New York: Columbia University Press. (Argues for the relevance of Peirce's philosophy of science for current debates over realism.)

* Welby, V. (1903) *What is Meaning?*, London: Macmillan. (Contains some of Welby's work in 'Significs' and reviewed by Peirce in *The Nation*.)

CHRISTOPHER HOOKWAY

PELACANI DA PARMA, BIAGIO *see* BLASIUS OF PARMA

PELAGIANISM

Pelagius, a Christian layman, was active around AD 400. The thesis chiefly associated with his name is that (i) human beings have it in their own power to avoid sin and achieve righteousness. Critics objected that this derogates from human dependence on the grace of God. Pelagius did not deny that the power to avoid sin is itself a gift of God, an enabling *grace; but he was understood to deny the need for* cooperative *grace, divine aid in using the power rightly, or at least to assert that (ii) such aid is a reward for human effort, and so not an act of grace. Later thinkers who held that God's aid, though not a reward, goes only to those who do make an effort, were accused of believing that (iii) there is no need of* prevenient *grace in causing the effort in the first place. So Pelagianism is a tendency to magnify human powers: its defenders saw it as a (frightening) challenge to humans, its detractors as an insult to God. It was hard without Pelagianism to find a place for free will, or with it for original sin.*

1　**Pelagius**
2　**The reaction**
3　**Massilians**
4　**Ockhamists**
5　**Grace and free will**

1　Pelagius

Pelagius lived from around 360 to after 418, came from Britain, moved to Rome as a young man, and was later active in Palestine. Rome in the Christianized empire of the 380s had become an administrative backwater (the Western capital having moved to Milan) in which families with glorious names cultivated the memory of their pagan past. Even so, Christian adherence was beginning to be prudent and fashionable; and Pelagius, finding that the new religion often sat lightly on these people, formed – or more likely joined – a puritan group which propagated Christianity as a complete change of life. He insisted that each time you confront a choice you have the possibility of making the right one; and (a stronger claim) that you have the possibility of making the right choice always – the possibility of perfection, sinlessness. The bonds of habit do not excuse. God has fashioned commandments that are suitable to our condition. No one should complain 'like insolent and incompetent servants, "It's too much, it's too difficult, we're only human, there's a limit to what a person can cope with"' (*Ad Demetriadem* 16).

This power to act aright comes by God's grace, that is, as a favour, and in particular through Christ, who 'delivered us from the wrath of judgment by remitting sins, and by his teaching and example' (*Expositiones*, on 1 Thessalonians 1: 10). Human perfection is not an immunity to sin, let alone the antinomian licence to do anything whatever blamelessly; on the contrary, one must keep 'running' (*Ad Demetriadem* 27). Under pressure from critics, Pelagius was willing to 'denounce anyone who believes or says that the grace of God by which "Christ came into this world to save sinners" [1 Timothy 1: 15] is not necessary in each hour, in each moment, in each act that we do' (reported in Augustine, *De gratia Christi* 2.2). But right action is always possible; as he said in a phrase gently mocked by Augustine, 'We are unable to be unable to be unsinners' (*De natura*, quoted in Augustine, *De natura et gratia* 49.57).

2 The reaction

Neither in this nor his other opinions was Pelagius conscious of innovation, but he came under attack from two redoubtable controversialists, Jerome (c.342–420) and AUGUSTINE (§§6, 13). Jerome, unfairly equating sinlessness with Stoic 'apathy' – emancipation from appetites such as hunger – accused (perhaps counter-accused) him of being tainted with the views of the earlier Church Father Origen, who had lately come under suspicion of heresy. By this time Jerome and Pelagius were neighbours in Palestine, where Pelagius had fled before the impending sack of Rome by the Visigoths in 410. Passing through Carthage in his flight, Pelagius had left there a colleague, Coelestius, whose views on baptism came to Augustine's ears along the African coast at Hippo. Pelagius in Palestine was accused of heresy in 415, but acquitted. The Africans appealed, and in 418 an imperial rescript banned the expression of support for Pelagians and exiled their leaders from Rome, whose bishop Zosimus, after wavering, issued a (lost) ecumenical letter of condemnation. From that time Pelagianism has been a heresy.

The nature of a heresy is defined by the decrees of the Church, not the opinions of its supposed adherents. The Pelagian heresy consists mainly of two parts, both of which Augustine attempted (in his voluminous extant writings on the affair) to fasten on the members of Pelagius' circle and to refute: restriction of the scope of grace, and denial of original sin. On grace, a council held at Carthage in 418 condemned three graded errors: that God's grace is of no avail in aiding people not to sin; that it gives such aid but only by instructing and is not the means of having the motive and the strength not to sin; and that it aids obedience to God's law but only by making obedience easier (Denzinger and Schoenmetzer 1967: 225–7). On original sin the same council declared it heretical to deny either that Adam's sin is transmitted to his progeny or that infants who die unbaptized will suffer in hell (Denzinger and Schoenmetzer: 223–4). Pelagians had argued that since only avoidable deeds are sinful, infants must be sinless and their baptism cannot be for the remission of sins.

3 Massilians

Under these blows the Pelagian movement lost impetus. But in Augustine's last years a moderated form of it arose which even after his death continued to trouble his follower Prosper of Aquitaine (c.390–c.463). People were saying, Prosper anxiously reported to Augustine, that 'all effort is abolished, all virtues destroyed, if God's arrangements precede [in the old sense, 'prevent'] human wills, and under the name of predestination a kind of fatal necessity is introduced' (Epistula 225.3). Pelagius had held that predestination 'is the same as foreknowledge' (Expositiones, on Romans 8: 29). But if it is causative, 'preventing' the will, how can the will be free? A number of monastic communities felt the same way, especially in southern Gaul. According to John Cassian of Marseilles (Massilia): 'We acknowledge that human efforts cannot secure it [perfection] by themselves without the aid of God; on the other hand we insist that only people who work and sweat receive God's mercy and grace' (De institutis 12.14) Even if one cannot succeed without help, one must be able to try on one's own: anything else would impose fatalism. It was left to later centuries to worry over Augustine's unsatisfactory response to this problem; meanwhile the defiance of these 'Massilians' was eventually condemned at a council at Orange in 529.

4 Ockhamists

In western Christian controversy, accusations of Pelagianism have never died out; but we must now skip to the fourteenth century. William of Ockham wrote: 'As to Pelagius' error, I say that his view was that everyone has the power, from what is purely natural to him, to avoid every sin, actual and original, and to merit eternal life as his due [de condigno]' (Dubitationes addititie AA-BB; Leff 1975: 494 n.208). Ockham is applying a distinction foreign to Pelagius' lifetime, between 'condign' and 'congruous' merit. You merit something de condigno when it is your due, de congruo when it is merely fitting or 'meet' (article 13 of the 39 Articles of the Church of England) (see SANCTIFICATION §2). He ascribes to Pelagius the view that human beings before grace already have the power to earn salvation. The ascription is unhistorical, but Pelagius does seem committed, as the Massilians also were committed, to the weaker thesis that fallen human nature suffices to make God's cooperative aid a fitting reward for good human effort; to 'do what is in you' is a 'congruous merit'. This was Ockham's own position (in his language); so that it is not surprising that an attack on him and others by his Oxford contemporary Thomas BRADWARDINE (§3) should have been entitled De causa Dei contra Pelagium. Ockham's special contribution had been to maintain that even the fittingness of reward for good effort depends on God's valuing the effort; God might have preferred a will such as Satan's (see WILLIAM OF OCKHAM §10). Nevertheless, grace is a response; even if not subsequent to the good will in time, it is conditional on it, and thus not prevenient in the sense demanded by the council of Orange. Bradwardine (and Luther, who later concurred) had reason for his label.

5 Grace and free will

During the sixteenth and seventeenth centuries interest in Pelagianism was kept alive by the perceived difficulty for its opponents of reconciling grace with free will. Erasmus, unfriendly to Augustine, defended free will against LUTHER. According to Calvin, every champion of free will is an enemy of prevenient grace, and so guilty of the Massilian error which was now called semi-Pelagianism. But two ways out were sought by others. The heretical Roman Catholic bishop Jansen, rabid Augustinian, argued that spontaneity is enough for freedom: fallen man is subject to 'the necessity of sinning' (1640, 'De statu naturae lapsae' 3.11), but free will is compatible with necessity because everything is in our power which 'happens when we will' (1640, 'De gratia' 6.5 264a B). Arminius, inspirer of the breakaway Remonstrant movement among Dutch Calvinists, preferred a solution that had meanwhile been urged by Spanish Jesuits, notably in Molina's brilliant *Concordia*: although free will excludes necessity, causes – even divine ones – do not necessitate, so that prevenient grace is not 'irresistible' (1629: 4.122b; 1825 (I): 600) even when 'efficacious' (see MOLINA, L. DE §§1–3). What had turned out to be the major conceptual tangle in the Pelagian question was thereafter bequeathed, without its identification of God's will as first cause, to the attention of secular philosophy.

See also: GRACE; JUSTIFICATION, RELIGIOUS; PREDESTINATION; SIN §2

References and further reading

Abercrombie, N. (1936) *The Origins of Jansenism*, Oxford: Clarendon. (Surveys orthodox anti-Pelagianism in the Roman Catholic tradition, and includes valuable summaries of Molina's *Concordia* and Jansen's *Augustinus*.)

* Arminius (Harmens, J.) (1629) *Declarationes*, in *Opera theologica*, Louvain; trans. J. Nichols, *The Works of James Arminius*, London: Longman, 1825. (Rejected strict Calvinism.)

* Augustine (418) *De gratia Christi et de peccato originali* (On the Grace of Christ and on Original Sin), Corpus Scriptorum Ecclesiasticorum Latinorum, vol. 42, Vienna: Tempsky, 1866–. (Contains excerpts from Pelagius' treatise on free will, *De libero arbitrio* (*c*.415); a translation can be found in Schaff (1886–9).)

* —— (413–15) *De natura et gratia* (On Nature and Grace), Corpus Scriptorum Ecclesiasticorum Latinorum, vol. 60, Vienna: Tempsky, 1866–. (Contains excerpts from Pelagius' treatise on nature, *De natura* (414); a translation can be found in Schaff (1886–9).)

—— (429–30) *Opus imperfectum* (Work Unfinished), Patrologiae Cursus Completus, series Latina, vol. 45, ed. J.P. Migne, Paris, 1844–55. (Contains long excerpts from the treatise *Ad Florum* (To Florus, *c*.426) by Pelagius' follower Julian of Eclanum.)

Bonner, G.I. (1987) *God's Decree and Man's Destiny*, London: Variorum. (Chapter 11 is valuable on Pelagianism in Pelagius' day.)

* Bradwardine, T. (*c*.1344) *De causa Dei contra Pelagium*, ed. H. Savile, London, 1618. (Attack on Ockham.)

* Cassian, J. (*c*.415) *De institutis* (On Modes of Life), Corpus Scriptorum Ecclesiasticorum Latinorum, vol. 17, Vienna: Tempsky, 1866–; trans. E.C.S. Gibson, in P. Schaff and H. Wace (eds) *A Select Library of the Nicene and Post-Nicene Fathers of the Christian Church*, series 2, Oxford: Parker, and New York: The Christian Literature Co., 1890–1900, vol. 11. (A source of what was later called semi-Pelagianism.)

* Denzinger, H. and Schoenmetzer, A. (1967) *Enchiridion symbolorum, definitionum et declarationum de rebus fidei et morum* (Handbook on the Creeds, etc.), 34th edn, Barcelona, Freiburg im Breisgau, Rome, New York: Herder; an earlier edn trans. R.J. Deferrari, *The Sources of Catholic Dogma*, St Louis, MO and London: Herder, 1957. (Contains all the Roman Catholic condemnations of Pelagianism.)

Evans, R.F. (1968) *Pelagius: Inquiries and Reappraisals*, London: A. & C. Black. (A careful examination of the evidence for Pelagius' place in the thought of his time.)

Ferguson, J. (1957) *Pelagius: an Historical and Theological Study*, Cambridge: Heffer. (Remains the most readable attempt at a full appraisal.)

* Jansen, C.O. (1640) *Augustinus*, Rouen: Berthelin, 1652. (Magisterial exposition of Augustine on grace, containing the first serious history of the Pelagian heresy.)

Leff, G. (1957) *Bradwardine and the Pelagians: A Study of his 'De Causa Dei' and its Opponents*, Cambridge: Cambridge University Press. (An account of the Ockhamists.)

* —— (1975) *William of Ockham: The Metamorphosis of Scholastic Discourse*, Manchester: Manchester University Press, and Totowa, NJ: Rowman & Littlefield. (Useful for references to Ockham's opinions.)

* Molina, L. de (1588) *Liberi arbitrii cum gratiae donis, divina praescientia, providentia, praedestinatione et reprobatione concordia* (Concord of Free Will with Grace, etc.), ed. J. Rabeneck, Madrid: Society of Jesus, 1953. (Elaborate and undervalued examination of problems surrounding free will.)

Passmore, J. (1970) *The Perfectibility of Man*, London: Duckworth. (Chapter 5 comments on the perennial tension between Pelagianism and Augustinianism in Christianity.)

* Pelagius (406–9) *Expositiones xiii epistularum Pauli*, ed. A. Souter, *Pelagius' Expositions of Thirteen Epistles of St Paul*, Texts and Studies 9, part 2, Cambridge: Cambridge University Press, 1926; partly trans. T.S. de Bruyn, *Pelagius' Commentary on St Paul's Epistle to the Romans*, Oxford: Oxford University Press, 1993. (Anonymous, but certainly by Pelagius, though so much corrupted in transmission that his comments on theologically sensitive matters are often hard to recover.)

* —— (413) *Ad Demetriadem*, Patrologiae Cursus Completus, series Latina, vol. 30: 15–45, ed. J.P. Migne, Paris, 1844–55; also vol. 33, 1099–1120. (Besides this letter to Demetrias and the *Expositiones* above, a varying number of other surviving letters and short treatises have been attributed to Pelagius. See also Augustine above.)

* Prosper of Aquitaine (*c.*428) no. 225 of Augustine's *Epistulae*, Corpus Scriptorum Ecclesiasticorum Latinorum, vol. 57, Vienna: Tempsky, 1866–; trans. P. de Letter, in J. Quasten *et al.* (eds), *Ancient Christian Writers: the Works of the Fathers in Translation*, vol. 32, Westminster, MD: Newman Press, and London: Longmans, Green & Co., 1946–. (Champion of Augustinianism.)

Rees, B.R. (1988) *Pelagius: A Reluctant Heretic*, Woodbridge: Boydell Press. (Embodies recent scholarship.)

Rupp, E.G. and Watson, P.S. (eds) (1969) *Luther and Erasmus: Free Will and Salvation*, in J. Baillie, J.T. McNeill and H.P. van Dusen (eds) Library of Christian Classics, London: SCM Press, and Philadelphia, PA: Westminster Press, 1953–. (A translation by A.N. Marlow and B. Drewery of Erasmus' *De libero arbitrio* (On Free Will) and Luther's *De servo arbitrio* (On the Bondage of the Will), with introduction.)

Schaff, P. (ed.) (1886–9) *A Select Library of the Nicene and Post-Nicene Fathers of the Christian Church*, series 1, repr. Edinburgh: T. & T. Clark; Grand Rapids, MI: Eerdmans, 1971–80, vol. 5. (Contains translations of the works by Augustine cited above.)

* William of Ockham (*c.*1340) 'Dubitationes addititie', appendix to *Super iv libros sententiarum reportatio*, in Gregg (ed.) *Opera plurima*, vol. 4. (A small part of Ockham's grand philosophical construction.)

CHRISTOPHER KIRWAN

PELAGIUS *see* PELAGIANISM

PERCEPTION

Sense perception is the use of our senses to acquire information about the world around us and to become acquainted with objects, events, and their features. Traditionally, there are taken to be five senses: sight, touch, hearing, smell and taste.

Philosophical debate about perception is ancient. Much debate focuses on the contrast between appearance and reality. We can misperceive objects and be misled about their nature, as well as perceive them to be the way that they are: you could misperceive the shape of the page before you, for example. Also, on occasion, it may seem to us as if we are perceiving, when we do not perceive at all, but only suffer hallucinations.

Illusions and hallucinations present problems for a theory of knowledge: if our senses can mislead us, how are we to know that things are as they appear, unless we already know that our senses are presenting things as they are? But the concern in the study of perception is primarily to explain how we can both perceive and misperceive how things are in the world around us. Some philosophers have answered this by supposing that our perception of material objects is mediated by an awareness of mind-dependent entities or qualities: typically called sense-data, ideas or impressions. These intermediaries allegedly act as surrogates or representatives for external objects: when they represent aright, we perceive; when they mislead, we misperceive.

An alternative is to suppose that perceiving is analogous to belief or judgment: just as judgment or belief can be true or false, so states of being appeared to may be correct or incorrect. This approach seeks to avoid intermediary objects between the perceiver and the external objects of perception, while still taking proper account of the possibility of illusion and hallucination. Both responses contrast with that of philosophers who deny that illusions and hallucinations have anything to tell us about the nature of perceiving proper, and hold to a form of naïve, or direct, realism.

The account of perception one favours has a bearing on one's views of other aspects of the mind and world: the nature and existence of secondary qualities, such as colours and tastes; the possibility of giving an account of the mind as part of a purely physical, natural world; how one should answer scepticism concerning our knowledge of the external world.

1   Perception, objects, appearance and illusion

We perceive objects, features of objects, and events: I can see a lilac bush, notice the texture of a piece of velvet, hear an explosion. We can also perceive facts, that things are a certain way: I may see that there are three empty coffee cups in my office, or smell that the milk has gone off. When we perceive things, they appear a certain way to us and we come to acquire knowledge concerning them, but one can also perceive facts without perceiving any object in particular: scanning the horizon you might see that there is nothing at all in your vicinity; you have perceived that something is the case, but there is no object that you have seen.

Objects can vary in their appearance: how something looks to you depends on the point of view from which you see it; how things appear to you depends on the conditions under which you perceive, for example whether the lighting is good; and they depend on your powers of perception, for example how much you can smell or taste may depend on whether you have a cold. The same object may appear differently to different observers. Furthermore, you may not only perceive different aspects of an object from others, you may misperceive it, or suffer an illusion concerning it.

One misperceives something where one does perceive it, but it appears differently to one from how it really is. Misperceptions occur in different ways: one might mistake a clump of grass for a rabbit; in odd lighting the walls of a room may look peach, even when they are really off-white; one may be subject to illusions due to disease. Other examples of illusion happen in normal conditions of perception to all perceivers. Here is one example, common in psychology text books, called the Ponzo illusion:

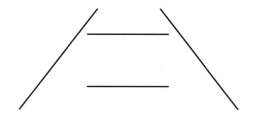

The two horizontal lines are in fact the same length, even though the top one looks longer. Psychologists and neuroscientists are adept at causing other illusions as well: in one alarming example, subjects are made to feel as if their noses are growing back into their heads.

It is also possible to bring about hallucinations. These are cases in which it seems to subjects as if they are really seeing or feeling something, when in fact they are seeing nothing at all. They are most commonly caused by psychological disturbance, but it is also possible to bring them about through appropriate stimulation of the brain: apparent sightings of lights, called phosphenes, arise from stimulation of the visual cortex.

Philosophers tend to draw the same conclusion from all these of kinds of example: it is possible for things to seem a certain way to you, even if they are not that way. Just as one cannot determine from the object of perception how things appear to a perceiver, so one cannot determine from how things appear to a perceiver what the object of perception is, or even whether there is such an object. This implies that an account of perception involves two distinct tasks: on the one hand, it needs to explain what perceptual experience is, the state of mind when things sensorily appear a certain way to one; on the other, it needs to explain what it is for such an experience to be a genuine perception of some object, as opposed to a mere illusion or hallucination.

Under what conditions is a perceptual experience the perception of a given object? One might think that how things appear must match the object in some respect, but there seems to be no particular respect in which I must perceive correctly in order to perceive an object: one can misperceive the colour, shape, location, taste, smell or texture of things. Even if how things appear to me matches perfectly the scene before me, I do not necessarily perceive the scene: if a scientist has induced a visual hallucination in me as of an orange, merely placing an orange in front of my blindfolded eyes will not thereby make me see it. In response to such examples of veridical hallucination, some philosophers have suggested that one can perceive an object only if it causes one's perception of it. This condition is not sufficient by itself to distinguish veridical hallucinations from perceptions: the orange before my blindfolded eyes may be resting on the switch of the machine inducing the hallucination. Various attempts have been made to refine the causal condition in order to give a complete account of the difference between hallucination and perception, but none as yet seems entirely satisfactory in explaining our ability to discern a difference between the two.

The basic task for any theory of perceptual experience is to explain the following. In perceiving, things appear to you a certain way. For example, when you see a red patch on the wall in front of you, it can look to you as if there is a red patch there. In such a case, where you perceive things to be the way that they are, a case of veridical perception, a description of what your experience is like – that is, of how things appear to you – is also a true description of what you can see. In this case, it seems as if a description of your experience is also a description of the things in the world which you can perceive. However, you could have an experience just the same for you even if you were having an illusion, and not seeing something red, or a hallucination and not seeing anything at all. In either case, you would be inclined to give the same description of your experience as in the veridical case, but in neither would the description be true of what was before you in the world, since no red patch would be there. So, how can it be correct to describe your experience in terms of objects in the world, when the description can be true when applied to your experience, but false when applied to the world? This is the question which lies behind the so-called argument from illusion, and different theories of perception answer it in different ways.

2 Sense-datum theories of perception

Some philosophers claim that we are not aware, or anyway not immediately aware, of objects in the world around us, but only of things which depend on the mind for their existence and nature. Suppose that there is no red patch on the wall before me, but that a neuroscientist has so affected my brain that it looks to me as if there is a red patch before me. One might think that it could only appear to me as if some red thing was before me, if there actually was something red of which I was aware. Since the neuroscientist can give me the hallucination just by affecting my brain in the right way, it seems as if bringing about the experience was sufficient for there to be such a red patch for me to be aware of. At least in the case of hallucination, I would be aware of an entity which depended for its existence on my awareness of it;

philosophers have used the term sense-datum, for such entities (see SENSE-DATA).

The hallucination could be just the same for me as the experience I would have were I actually looking at a physical red patch on the wall. And the neuroscientist could be bringing this about by stimulating my visual cortex in just the way it would be stimulated if I was looking at the wall. So, it may seem plausible to suppose that my hallucination is of the same sort as the experience I would have were I genuinely perceiving. If the hallucinatory experience is of a kind which involves being aware of a sense-datum, then even in the case of veridical perception I will be aware of such a mind-dependent entity. Hence we arrive at the sense-datum theory of experience: that we are aware of mind-dependent entities in all perceptual experience.

One criticism of this line of thought is that it involves a form of fallacious reasoning. If I believe that there are fifteen elephants in the next room, it does not follow that there are fifteen elephants in the next room which I believe to be there – after all, my belief may be false – so it would be a mistake to accept the latter claim on the basis of the former. Critics suggest that in the above claim, when one moves from the uncontroversial claim that it looks to me as if there is a red patch before me, to the conclusion that there is a red patch which looks to be before me, just such a mistake in reasoning has been made. However defenders of sense-datum theories of perception would agree that the claim does not follow simply as a matter of logic. Rather, they claim that we can only offer an adequate explanation of what experience is like, if we accept that the latter claim is true when the former is.

How good an explanation of what experience is like does this offer? The theory is committed to claiming that when things appear a certain way to you, then some sense-datum actually is that way. Suppose it seems to you as if there is a rabbit in the field before one, is one then aware of some mind-dependent bunny? In order to resist this conclusion, the sense-datum theorist needs to restrict the range of qualities which can strictly be apparent to us; namely to only those which sense-data might plausibly be thought to have. In the case of vision, this has traditionally been restricted to colour, shape and size (there is some dispute over whether visual data are located in a two-dimensional or a three-dimensional visual space). Hence, it could not strictly look (in the relevant sense) as if a rabbit was before one, only as if something rabbit-shaped were there.

If appearances are to be accounted for solely in terms of mind-dependent entities, what connection holds between experience and the objects of perception, such as the rabbit? Representative theories of perception typically hold that material objects are the indirect or mediate objects of perception in virtue of reliably causing our experiences of sense-data. I can perceive the rabbit in front of me, because the visual experience of something rabbit-shaped is caused by the rabbit. One traditional objection to representative theories of perception is that they lead to scepticism concerning the external world (see SCEPTICISM). In response, some philosophers adopt an alternative view of the connection between objects of perception and experience, taking physical objects to be no more than constructions out of mind-dependent entities or experiences (see PHENOMENALISM; IDEALISM §2). Few philosophers find this position acceptable. Must a sense-datum theorist choose between scepticism and idealism? One may deny that representative theories of perception introduce any special sceptical problems. Whether this is so or not, depends on whether sense-data should be thought of as cutting us off from the external world, as a veil of perception, rather than providing us with our only access to the world.

Are the metaphysical implications of the sense-datum theory acceptable? It requires us to accept that in addition to such familiar things as rocks and chairs, and discoveries such as black holes and neutrinos, there are mind-dependent objects which come into and go out of existence as each person has an experience. Philosophers have complained that such entities must be inherently mysterious and that we can discern no readily agreed method of determining when one has the same or a different sense-datum. Furthermore, their existence would rule out explaining how the mind comes to be part of a purely physical, natural world (see MATERIALISM IN THE PHILOSOPHY OF MIND).

Some philosophers have thought that these worries would be lessened if we eliminated inner objects of awareness, and appealed instead simply to ways in which one senses. According to this view, when one senses a red patch, one should not suppose that there has to be some object, a patch which one senses, but rather that one senses redly or in a red manner. One might compare this to singing a lullaby: we need not suppose that there is some thing which the singer sings, rather that they have sung in a certain, quieting manner. Where the sense-datum theory posits inner objects and qualities in order to explain the character of perceptual experience, this adverbial theory of experience appeals just to the manners or qualities of experiencing, sometimes called qualia, subjective qualities or sensational properties of experience (see MENTAL STATES, ADVERBIAL THEORY OF).

Critics of the adverbial theories have pointed out that we make a distinction between on the one hand

sensing a red square and green triangle, and on the other sensing a green square and a red triangle. It is difficult to explain this difference without appealing to the idea that an object is both square and red in the one case, and square and green in the other. There seems to be no sense in which a state of mind, or a sensing, could literally be square or round.

There is a further objection to be made from how we describe our experiences which applies to both adverbial and sense-datum theories. Various philosophers have denied that introspection of one's visual experience reveals the mind-independent objects which one perceives, and the features which one perceives them to have. Our experience of the world is diaphanous or transparent: introspection of it takes one through to the objects and features in the world, much as in staring at a pane of glass head on, one's attention is taken through to what lies beyond it.

The objection has two aspects to it. On the one hand, there is a negative claim that no introspective evidence can be found for the existence of mind dependent objects or qualities. Since such things are introduced as just that of which one is aware, one might expect that if there are such things, they should just be obvious through introspection. It is not evident that this negative claim is correct: opponents have claimed that evidence for them is provided by the example of after-images; or in the way that a nearer object can fill up more of one's field of view than a more distant object, even though both look the same size; or in our awareness of the fact that we are seeing the shape of an object rather than feeling it. Whether such examples really do demonstrate the existence of subjective qualities is a matter of further dispute, but the other element of the transparency objection can be made without having to settle that matter. It points out a positive element of the character of experience, as revealed through introspection, namely that mind-independent objects of perception are there in your experience. An account of experience which appeals solely to sense-data and qualia would not predict that these mind-independent elements should be part of our experience.

One reply to this is to deny that perceptual experiences really do have this diaphanous character. So, it has been suggested that we describe an experience as of a cube merely in order to indicate the typical cause of such experiences. But this suggestion is implausible. We do sometimes pick out experiences indirectly by reference to their typical cause, as when we call a certain distinctive pain a nettle sting. In this case it does not seem as if the term nettle should be applied directly to a description of what the pain is like. But one may claim that visual experience is not like that, the description of experience as of something red, or square, or hard involves applying those terms directly to what one senses.

The objection is more pressing against adverbial theories than sense-datum theories. We describe our visual and tactual experiences in terms of shape properties. As noted above, a sense-datum theorist will dispute whether we also have to describe our experiences in terms of other qualities which could only be the properties of material objects. However, even if the objection is not decisive, it has been influential as a motivation for an alternative account of perceptual experience.

3 Intentional theories of perception

If it can seem to me that there is a red patch on the wall in front of me, when nothing physical is there, and the patch in question seems to be a part of the objective world external to me, then perhaps it can seem to me as if something is so, without anything actually having to be that way. We are all familiar with the fact that one may think that something is the case, when it is not so, as when one believes England will win the World Cup at cricket, and one may think about something, even if it does not really exist, as when small children hope that Santa Claus will visit their house that night. An intentional theory of perception claims that the case of perceptual experience is parallel to these examples: perceptual experience is intentional, and allows for incorrectness in its content, and non-existence of its objects in just the way that beliefs and judgments may do so (see INTENTIONALITY).

When it appears to one as if there is a red patch before one, one's experience represents the world as containing such a patch. If there is no patch there, how one's experience represents the world to be is incorrect, and one's experience is illusory. If the object of one's experience is non-existent, like Santa Claus, then one's experience is a hallucination and not the perception of anything. For the intentional approach, experience is ascribed a representational content which may be correct or incorrect; the experience is veridical, or illusory depending on the correctness of this content. What the experience is like for the subject, as revealed through reflection on it, is to be explained by that representational content. It is important to note that the intentional theory does not introduce the representational content of experience as an object of awareness, in the way that a sense-datum theory introduces sense-data as objects of awareness. Rather, the intentional theory claims that, in the case of perceiving, the objects of awareness are the mind-independent objects that

one perceives, and which one's experience represents to be present. In the case of hallucination, there are no objects of awareness, but the character of experience is just the same as that in the case of perception: in both cases it is to be explained by the representational content that the experience has. So the intentional theory offers an account not of the objects of awareness, but rather the mode in which we can be aware of objects in the world.

How like belief could experience be? One view is that we can identify experience with the acquiring of beliefs, or with dispositions to acquire belief. A problem for this suggestion is that one can disbelieve one's senses. Those familiar with the Ponzo illusion do not believe that the top line is longer, but it still looks longer. A belief theory of experience may respond to this example by claiming that you are still disposed to believe that the top line is longer, it is just that other beliefs you have prevent you forming that belief. But this response is not really satisfactory: when you look at the illusion, you then have an experience which could have led to the belief in question; no mere disposition to acquire a belief can be identified with an occurrent state of mind which interacts with one's other mental states.

This suggests that experiencing is not believing, but one might still claim that both states have the same representational content. That claim has also been denied. For the conditions needed for thinking something may be different from the conditions for having certain kinds of experience: it seems conceivable that we can have the same experiences as infant humans or as other animals, but they cannot share the same thoughts as us; our beliefs are expressible linguistically, and rest on sophisticated conceptual abilities which neither infants nor other animals need have. One may also claim that the character of experience is too rich to be encompassed by any one set of categories, or set of concepts that one can bring to bear on it. For these, and related reasons, some philosophers have claimed that the content of experience is different from that of thought or belief in not being purely conceptual: experience has a non-conceptual content as well (see CONTENT, NON-CONCEPTUAL).

Is this sufficient to explain the character of experience, and the differences between experiencing things to be a certain way and merely believing or thinking them to be that way? Many philosophers have thought not. They have insisted that there must be some form of non-representational quality to experience in addition to any representational content it may have (see QUALIA). The issue here returns us to the first part of the transparency objection to sense-datum theories: it is an open question whether there are evidently subjective, or qualitative aspects of experience other than how the world is presented to us. If one accepts that there are, then there is more agreement than one might initially have supposed between traditional sense-datum theories, which supplement awareness of sense-data with interpretation, and alternatively intentional theories, which supplement representational content with subjective qualities.

4 Naïve realism and disjunctive theories of appearance

Sense-datum theories of perception appeal to illusions and hallucinations in arguing for the existence of inner objects of perception, and intentional theories of perception appeal to illusions to justify the view that experience is representational. But there is a strand of philosophical criticism which denies that one can draw any conclusion about perception from cases of illusion and hallucination. One motive for such criticism is an endorsement of a certain kind of naïve, or direct, realism concerning perception.

Defenders of sense-datum theories claim that the best account of experience commits one to thinking that one can sense a quality only if there actually is an instance of that quality which one senses – the argument from illusion then leads them to suppose that such qualities must be mind-dependent; defenders of intentional theories claim that the best account of experience commits one to thinking that experience is directed at, or of, mind-independent objects – the example of illusion leads them to claim that one's experience merely represents these things. A naïve realist might endorse both the initial claim of the sense-datum theorist and that of the intentional theorist, while trying to resist their conclusions: on this view, when one perceives, one is aware of some mind-independent objects and their features, and such objects and features must actually be there for one to have such an experience. This cannot be true of cases where there is no appropriate physical object of perception, as in hallucination, so the naïve realist must claim that the account applies only to cases of perception. Hence they must deny that the state of mind one is in when one perceives something is of a sort which could have occurred even were one having an illusion or hallucination. They must claim that when it appears to one as if there is a red patch there, then either there is a red patch which is apparent to one, or it is merely as if there were such a red patch apparent to one: nothing more need be in common between the situations, such as an inner object of which one is aware, or a representational content. The view, which we can call a disjunctive theory of

appearances, claims that perceptual experience does not form a common kind of state across perception, illusion and hallucination.

The view has been thought objectionable for a number of reasons. First, as all sides agree, for any perception one has, one could have a matching illusion or hallucination which one could not distinguish from the perception. According to the disjunctive view, there is a genuine difference here, but how can there be a difference in the conscious state of mind which the subject is unable to detect? The disjunctive view is committed to claiming that we can be misled about the kind of conscious state we are in; indeed one might sum up the view as claiming that illusions and hallucinations mislead one not only about objects in the world, but about themselves as well.

Second, the same brain activity as can bring about perceptions can bring about hallucinations. Furthermore, any physical outcome a case of perceiving can produce, for example kicking a ball, could equally well be caused by a matching hallucination. So the disjunctive view must claim that there is a real difference between experience which is a perceiving and one which is a hallucination even though there is no causal difference between them. But many philosophers claim that there can only be a real difference between things where they differ in their causal powers. It remains a matter of dispute whether the consequences of the view are unacceptable or the objections without answer – a similar set of arguments attends debates about the nature of content and thought (see CONTENT: WIDE AND NARROW).

See also: BODILY SENSATIONS; EMPIRICISM §3; PERCEPTION, EPISTEMIC ISSUES IN; SECONDARY QUALITIES; VISION

References and further reading

Austin, J.L. (1962) *Sense and Sensibilia*, Oxford: Clarendon Press. (Posthumously published lectures on perception which contain a scathing attack on the argument from illusion and sense-data. Hugely influential in its time, and aspects of it continue to be significant.)

Burnyeat, M. (1979) 'Conflicting Appearances', *Proceedings of the British Academy*, 65: 69–111. (A provocative discussion of the argument from illusion from ancient Greek debate to early twentieth-century discussions of sense-data.)

Crane, T. (ed.) (1992) *The Contents of Experience*, Cambridge: Cambridge University Press. (Various useful articles some defending intentional theories of perception, some forms of subjectivism. The introduction to the collection is also a useful survey of the topic.)

Cornman, J. (1975) *Perception, Common Sense and Science*, New Haven, CT: Yale University Press. (A very comprehensive presentation of the debate and its implications for metaphysics and theory of knowledge.)

Dancy, J. (ed.) (1988) *Perceptual Knowledge*, Oxford: Oxford University Press. (A collection of papers on knowledge and perception, which reprints some of the most important papers on perception in recent years. In particular: P.F. Strawson, 'Perception and its Objects', is a good introduction to the subject; D.M. Armstrong, 'Perception and Belief', presents a belief-analysis of perception while F. Dretske, 'Sensation and Perception', attacks Armstrong, and introduces the idea of perception containing 'analogue information'; H.P. Grice, 'The Causal Theory of Perception' defends the causal theory of object perception, and David Lewis, 'Veridical Hallucination and Prosthetic Vision' offers an account of what it is to see the scene before one, rather than to see an object, in terms which refine the causal theory; Paul Snowdon, 'Perception, Vision and Causation' presents a disjunctive theory of appearances as a part of an attack on Grice's causal theory; John McDowell, 'Criteria, Defeasibility and Knowledge' presents a disjunctive theory of appearance as a general account of perception.)

Gibson, J.J. (1966) *The Senses considered as Perceptual Systems*, London: Allen & Unwin. (Controversial psychologist, defender of ecological or direct theory of perception and critic of the role of representation in psychological theories, still influential among some philosophers.)

Grice, H.P. (1962) 'Some Remarks about the Senses', in R. Butler (ed.) *Analytic Philosophy*, 1st Series, Oxford: Blackwell, 133-53. (A good discussion of the differences between the senses.)

Harman, G. (1989) 'The Intrinsic Quality of Experience', in J. Tomberlin (ed.) *Philosophical Perspectives 4: Action Theory and Philosophy of Mind*, Atascadero, CA: Ridgeview, 31–52. (Defends an intentional theory of perception, using the transparency argument, denies that there are any non-representational features of experience, and criticizes Peacocke's arguments in Peacocke (1983).)

Jackson, F. (1977) *Perception: A Representative Theory*, Cambridge: Cambridge University Press. (A very clear and vigorous defence of a sense-datum theory of experience; contains very useful criticisms of belief-analyses in ch. 2 and adverbial theories in ch. 3; as well as responses to objections from scepticism to representative theories of perception in ch. 5.)

Marr, D. (1982) *Vision*, New York: W.H. Freeman. (Presents a general cognitive psychological view of vision, equally influential among psychologists and philosophers.)

O'Shaughnessy, B. (1989) 'The Sense of Touch', *Australasian Journal of Philosophy* 67: 37–58. (Interesting discussion of the sense of touch and the contrasts between touch and sight.)

Peacocke, C.A.B. (1983) *Sense and Content*, Oxford: Clarendon Press, ch. 1. (Defends the view that experience has both representational content and certain non-representational features which Peacocke calls sensational properties.)

—— (1992) *A Study of Concepts*, Cambridge, MA: MIT Press, ch. 3. (Develops a sophisticated variant of the intentional theory involving types of non-conceptual content variously labelled, 'scenario content' and 'proto-propositional content'; modifies the views presented in Peacocke (1983).)

Perkins, M. (1983) *Sensing the World*, Indianapolis, IN: Hackett Publishing Co. (Defends an account of the representative theory of perception somewhat like Jackson's, except its form is closer to that of an adverbialist theory rather than a sense-datum one. Separate chapters discuss each sense modality in turn.)

Searle, J. (1983) *Intentionality*, Cambridge: Cambridge University Press, ch. 2. (A defence of an intentional theory of perception which criticizes both sense-datum theories and Austin's views.)

Swartz, R. (ed.) (1965) *Perceiving, Sensing and Knowing*, Berkeley, CA: California University Press. (A large collection of articles and extracts from books on perception, now almost entirely out of date: a useful source for early- and mid-twentieth-century views on perception.)

Yolton, J. (1984) *Perceptual Acquaintance from Descartes to Reid*, Minneapolis, MN: Minnesota University Press. (A discussion of the history of philosophy of perception which questions the popular attribution of representative theories of perception to various early modern philosophers, including Descartes and Locke.)

M.G.F. MARTIN

PERCEPTION, EPISTEMIC ISSUES IN

We learn about the world through our five senses: by seeing, hearing, smelling, tasting and feeling. Sense perception is a primary means by which we acquire knowledge of contingent matters of fact. We can also acquire such knowledge by, for instance, conscious reasoning and through the written and spoken testimony of others; but knowledge so acquired is derivative, in that it must be based, ultimately, on knowledge arrived at in more primary ways, such as by sense perception.

We can perceive something without acquiring any knowledge about it; for knowledge requires belief, and we can perceive something without having any beliefs about it. Viewing any but the most simple visual scenes we see many things we form no beliefs about. However, when we perceive something, we are acquainted with it by its sensorially appearing (looking, sounding, smelling and so on) some way to us. For we see something if and only if it looks some way to us, hear something if and only if it sounds some way to us, and so on. When, based on how they appear, we form true beliefs about things we perceive, the beliefs sometimes count as knowledge.

Often the way something appears is the way it is. The red, round tomato looks red and round; the sour milk tastes sour. But the senses are fallible. Sometimes the way something appears is different from the way it is. Appearances can fail to match reality, as happens to various extents in cases of illusion. There are, for instance, optical illusions (straight sticks look bent at the water line) and psychological ones (despite being exactly the same length, the Müller-Lyer arrows drawings look different in length). In such cases, looks are misleading.

The ever-present logical possibility of illusion makes beliefs acquired by perception fallible: there is no absolute guarantee that they are true. But that does not prevent them from sometimes counting as knowledge – albeit fallible knowledge. Recognitional abilities enable us to obtain knowledge about things from how they perceptually appear. Sense perception thus acquaints us with things in a way that contributes to positioning us to acquire knowledge about them. The central epistemic issues about sense perception concern its role in so positioning us.

1　Perceptual knowledge is perceiving-that
2　The primary–secondary perceiving-that distinction
3　Primary perceiving-that and sense experience
4　Perceiving-that and the interaction of beliefs
5　Perceptual knowledge is fallible

1　Perceptual knowledge is perceiving-that

Sense perception plays at least some role in the acquisition of virtually all our empirical knowledge. Are there any cases of factual knowledge that deserve the label 'perceptual knowledge'? Sensorially perceiving that P is a way of knowing that P (in part) by perceiving, and for this reason is fairly standardly

taken to deserve that label. Thus it is held that one has visual knowledge that P if and only if one sees that P, auditory knowledge that P if and only if one hears that P, and so on: one might see that the light has turned green; hear that the piano is out of tune; smell that the milk is sour; taste that there is garlic in the food; or one might feel the tomato is over-ripe.

We speak of seeing-whether, seeing-when, seeing-where, seeing-how, seeing-who and seeing-which. These all involve seeing-that. For example, one sees whether there is a chair in the room if and only if one sees that there is a chair in the room or one sees that there is not a chair in the room. One sees where the corkscrew is if one sees, for instance, that it is on the table; and one sees who is at the door if one sees that it is Tom. (These claims generalize to the other senses.)

When one sees, hears, smells, tastes or feels that P, one believes that P, and P is true. What distinguishes these ways of perceiving that P is the perceptual means by which the belief is acquired or sustained – whether it is by seeing and so on – and the perceptual means of acquisition of at least some of the evidence on which the belief is based.

2　The primary–secondary perceiving-that distinction

It is possible for one to perceive that A is (has/would) F by perceiving that B is G, when A is distinct from B and/or F is distinct from G. One might, for instance, hear that the alarm clock is ringing by hearing that a ringing sound is coming from the bedroom; smell that the toast is burning by smelling that a burnt odour is coming from the toaster; taste that the wine is from southeastern Australia by tasting that it has such-and-such a taste; or see that the branch would support one's weight by seeing that it has a certain thickness. In such cases, perceiving that B is G is part of the constitutive means by which one perceives that A is F: the way one perceives that A is F, how one perceives that A is F is, in part, by perceiving that B is G. Moreover, that B is G – something one perceives to be the case – is part of the evidence on which one's belief that A is F is based.

Fred Dretske (1995) has drawn a useful technical distinction between primary and secondary cases of perceiving-that A is (has/would) F. One secondarily perceives that A is F if and only if one perceives that A is F by perceiving that B is G, where A is distinct from B and/or F is distinct from G; one primarily perceives that A is F if and only if one perceives that A is F, but not secondarily.

A striking feature of secondarily perceiving that A is F is that it does not require perceiving A. One might see that the fuel tank is empty by seeing that the gauge reads empty, and thus without seeing the fuel tank itself. In contrast, when one primarily perceives that A is F, one does so at least partly by means of perceiving A; moreover, one must perceive of A that it is A and F. This condition is met in all cases of perceiving that A is F – whether primarily or secondarily – partly by perceiving A. If one sees the car is touching the kerb (in part) by seeing the car, then one sees of it that it is a car and touching the kerb.

3   Primary perceiving-that and sense experience

A related distinction can be drawn between primary and secondary appears-as-if states. Some A *primarily appears* to one as if it is A and F if and only if it appears to one as if it is A and F, but not by appearing to one as if it is B and G, for any B distinct from A or any F distinct from G. A secondarily appears to one as if it is A and F if and only if it appears to one as if it is A and F, but not in a primary way. When one secondarily perceives that A is F partly by means of A's appearing to one as if it is A and F, A secondarily appears to one as if it is A and F. When one primarily perceives that A is F, A primarily appears to one as if it is A and F. Thus, if one primarily hears that a sound is coming from the left, then a sound coming from the left sounds to one as if it is a sound and coming from the left.

G.N. Vesey (1971) labels appears-as-if states 'epistemic appearances'. Like beliefs, such states have propositional contents and involve the exercise of concepts. However, as Frank Jackson (1977) argues, they are not beliefs or even inclinations to believe. One Müller-Lyer arrow may visually look to me as if it is longer than the other without my believing the one is longer than the other, or even being inclined to so believe. Familiar with the illusion, I may be certain they are of the same length.

Roderick Chisholm (1957) labels the use of sensory-appearance words in such locutions as 'A appears (looks/sounds, and so on) as if it is F' and 'It appears as if A is F' their 'epistemic use'. He has distinguished such uses from their phenomenal use, their use in locutions of the form 'A appears —— to S', where what fills in the blank are terms for sensory properties – properties such as redness, squareness, loudness, saltiness, putridness, and the like – or terms for properties wholly composed of sensory properties. (He also distinguishes their use in locutions such as 'A looks like an F to S', labelling it the 'comparative use'.) The phenomenal use of an appearance verb is not equivalent to its epistemic use or any restricted range of its epistemic use. For while A cannot appear to one as if it is F unless one has the concept of F, A can phenomenally appear F to one without one's having the concept.

When A primarily appears to one as if it is A and F, A phenomenally appears F to one. Thus, one is in an epistemic appearance state only if one is undergoing a sense experience. But how else, exactly, epistemic appearances relate to sense experiences is an empirical question that bears on such issues as the functional architecture of our minds, and whether naturalistic accounts of intentionality and sensory consciousness are possible – issues that go to the heart of the mind–body problem. On one currently leading proposal – developed by Dretske, Alvin Goldman, Christopher Peacocke and others – which promises to integrate with current information-processing psychological models of percepts and concepts, sense experiences have a kind of non-conceptual representational content, and states such as epistemic appearances conceptually utilize aspects of their contents. On this picture, sense experiences by which we perceive (rather than hallucinate) discriminate certain sorts of environmental states of affairs within the range of our sense organs. We acquire perceptual recognitional concepts – either through a combination of our genetic endowment and normal processes of maturation or through perception-based learning – and in the process come to undergo epistemic appearances that discriminate states of affairs partly by means of their discrimination by our sense experiences. In acquiring perceptual recognitional abilities, we thus build on our endowed perceptual discriminative capacities in a way that enables us to acquire knowledge about things we perceive from how they phenomenally appear to us.

4   Perceiving-that and the interaction of beliefs

When one perceives that A is F by perceiving that B is G, one believes that A is F, believes that B is G, and the first belief state is based, in part, on the second. The basing relation involves causal dependence: the basing belief must contribute to causing the other belief or, if the believer already possesses that belief, to causally sustaining it.

Secondary perceiving-that does not require that the perceiver should consciously infer that A is F from the fact that B is G. Such conscious inferences are atypical – people in the process of acquiring perceptual recognitional abilities by learning make them (think of learning to read) – but once the abilities are fully acquired, the belief that A is F is typically formed without the mediation of conscious inference. Indeed, one can see that A is F by seeing that B is G without either consciously thinking that A is F or that B is G. Such conscious thought episodes are usually absent in cases of perceiving-that.

As Dretske (1995) notes, to perceive that A is F by

perceiving that *B* is *G*, *B*'s being *G* must indicate, in the circumstances in question, that *A* is *F*. The one must indicate the other in the way in which, in certain circumstances, that there is smoke indicates that there is fire. The nature of indication remains a topic of discussion. But on one view if, in certain circumstances *C*, *Q* indicates that *P*, then, it is at least highly probable that if *C* and *Q*, then *P*.

Philosophers are divided over whether in cases of secondary perceiving-that, one must know that *B*'s being *G* indicates (in the circumstances) that *A* is *F*; and even over whether one must be justified in believing that, that is, believe it for reasons that would justify one in believing it. Proponents of strong internalism maintain that in cases of secondarily perceiving that *A* is *F*, one's reasons for believing that *A* is *F* must include that *B*'s now being *G* indicates that *A* is *F*, and that this must itself be held for reasons that suffice for one to know it. Proponents of weak internalism require only that it be held for reasons that suffice for one to be justified in believing it. Proponents of externalism maintain that even the requirement that the perceiver should be justified in believing the relevant indication relation holds grossly over-intellectualizes perceptual knowledge. Externalists charge that internalists conflate the issue of whether people know with whether they know that they do, and/or whether they are justified in believing or claiming that they do. Beliefs that count as perceptual knowledge, they maintain, are warranted by the reliability of their source. Internalists counter that this unacceptably makes perceptual knowledge a matter of luck (see INTERNALISM AND EXTERNALISM IN EPISTEMOLOGY).

Nevertheless, to perceive that *A* is *F* by perceiving that *B* is *G*, the perceiver must regard *B*'s being *G* as indicating, in the circumstances, that *A* is *F*. That *B*'s being *G* so indicates that *A* is *F* is a theoretical hypothesis about the relationship between *B*'s being *G* and *A*'s being *F*. Since secondary perceiving-that requires a background belief in such a hypothesis, secondary perceiving-that is theory-ladened.

Natural indication plays a role in primary perceiving-that as well. To primarily perceive that *A* is *F*, its basically appearing to one as if *A* is *F* must indicate, in the circumstances, that *A* is *F*. It is controversial, however, whether to primarily perceive that *A* is *F*, one must believe that its appearing to one as if *A* is *F* indicates, in the circumstances, that *A* is *F*. Internalists maintain that such a belief is required and must be at least justified. Externalists typically deny that even such a belief is required; the requirement, they maintain, over-intellectualizes primary perceiving-that. If such a belief is required, perceivers who lack beliefs about how things appear to them could not be

perceivers-that. Thus, animals and very young children (who lack the concept of experience) would never perceive that anything is the case. (That is not to deny they ever perceive anything. Perceiving things does not require perceiving-that.)

Even if there is no such belief requirement on primary perceiving-that, primary perceiving-that is, nevertheless, in a sense, theory-ladened: it is dependent on background beliefs. Whether one would, in any situation, believe that *A* is *F* will depend, at least to some extent, on what else one would believe in that situation. As Wilfred Sellars (1968) argues, every mode of belief-acquisition involves, to some extent, the interaction of beliefs (see SELLARS, W. §3).

5 Perceptual knowledge is fallible

Proponents of sense-data theory maintain that when *A* is a kind of sense datum, and *F* is a sensory property, its primarily appearing to one as if *A* is *F* provides one with conclusive reason to believe that *A* is *F*. Sense data cannot be hallucinated, and cannot appear to have sensory properties they lack. Thus, in such cases, if it primarily appears to one as if *A* is *F*, then *A* is *F*. There is no appearance–reality gap here. Sense data are essential components of sense experiences; the way they appear is an aspect of the experience itself. To have a colour-experience, for instance, is just to immediately see or visually sense a coloured visual sense datum. (This is an act-object theory of sense experience.) Sense data are, on these grounds, claimed to be essentially private: only you can perceive yours and only I can perceive mine.

Some sense-data theorists defend an empiricist thesis according to which such primary epistemic appearance states provide an infallible foundation for all empirical knowledge (see FOUNDATIONALISM §1; EMPIRICISM §4). Introspection affords an infallible way of knowing whether it primarily looks to one as if *A* is *F* (see INTROSPECTION §§1–3). One can know a priori that if it primarily looks to one as if *A* is *F*, then *A* is *F*. So, relying only on introspection and a priori reasoning, one can know both what it is that primarily appears to one to be the case, and that it is the case. Such theorists acknowledge that on this indirect realist view, there is a logical gap between states of one's sense data having sensory qualities and extra-experiential states of affairs involving material objects and physical events. In response to the charge that their view renders the physical world itself unknowable – hidden behind a veil of sensory appearance – they hold that beliefs about such extra-experiential matters can be arrived at by theorizing about the causal factors responsible for our perceiving sense data.

There are two main lines of argument for the existence of sense data. One is the argument from illusion, demonstrated as follows:

(P1) If something looks F to one, then one sees something F

(P2) In cases of illusion, something looks F, but nothing physical that one sees is F

(C) Therefore, in cases of illusion, one sees something nonphysical

The argument is standardly supplemented by an appeal to a continuity-of-experience principle to the effect that since our non-illusory experiences are phenomenologically like our illusory ones, if we see nonphysical things when undergoing illusory experiences, we do so also when undergoing non-illusory ones. This principle has been plausibly challenged by J.L. Austin (1962) (see AUSTIN, J.L. §2). But to focus on the argument from illusion itself, it is valid only if 'see' is used relationally throughout – used in such a way that if S sees X, then there is an X such that S sees it. For the phenomenal use of 'see' has no existential import. (A victim of delirium tremens may phenomenally see a pink elephant, even though there is no pink elephant that they see.) If 'see' is used phenomenally in (P1), the premise is unobjectionable; but the argument is invalid. However, if 'see' is used relationally, then (P1) renders the argument question-begging.

The second line of defence is that nothing physical could be a primary bearer of sensory properties. No compelling case for this has been made, however. According to secondary-quality views of sensory properties, they are dispositions to appear phenomenally in certain ways; for example, redness is the disposition to look red. According to primary-quality views, sensory properties are experience-independent properties; on one version, they are the physical bases for dispositions to appear phenomenally in certain ways; so, for instance, the basis for a physical surface's disposition to look red might be its having a certain sort of disposition to affect light (for example, a certain sort of spectral reflectance distribution). Both sorts of theories admit of many non-equivalent versions (see SECONDARY QUALITIES §1; COLOUR, THEORIES OF §3). A secondary-quality theory need not apply that there are sense data. And if any primary-quality theory of sensory properties is correct, then the second line of defence of sense data theory fails.

The first and foremost problem with sense-data theory is that there is no good reason to believe that there are any sense data, and compelling reason to believe there are none. Philosophers in the Wittgensteinian tradition have challenged the very coherence of the notion of an essentially private entity. (Some of the literature on Wittgenstein's argument against the possibility of an essentially private language bears on this.) But even if the notion is coherent, the problems for sense-data theory remain legion. Sense data are wholly immaterial. So, unless physics cannot be trusted, they lack causal powers. How, then, do sense experiences influence epistemic appearances? If sense experiences are partly constitutive of epistemic appearances rather than causes of them, such aspects of epistemic appearances could exert no causal influence on beliefs. How, then, could we form beliefs about our sense data?

Intuitive support for sense-data theory comes from the fact that we speak of seeing such things as red after-images. When we see a red after-image, there is nothing physical that we see that is red. But in these cases we see something red only in the phenomenal sense, not in the relational sense. Seeing a red after-image just consists in having a certain sort of visual experience – as of, say, a red circle – acquired in a certain way. Experiences are states or events, and thus are not themselves coloured. Moreover, while we relationally perceive by having sense experiences, we do not perceive sense experiences themselves.

Coloured areas, sounds, odours and tastes, which are among the usual candidates for sense data, arguably meet some of the conditions which sense-data theorists maintain they meet. For example, they play a primary role in perceiving material objects. We can say that a subject basically perceives A by undergoing a sense experience E if and only if the subject perceives A by undergoing E, but not by perceiving something else B by undergoing E. Arguably, sounds are basically heard, odours basically smelled, tastes basically tasted; and, if 'colour' is used in an extended sense to include brightness properties (for example, glaring, glowing and so on) as well as chromatic colours (red, green and so on) and achromatic colours (white, black, and shades of grey), what are basically seen are coloured surfaces and volumes.

As David Sanford (1976) and others argue, coloured surfaces and the rest are, however, not sense data. They are publicly observable: you and I can both see the brown surface of the table top, hear the loud sound of the gunshot, or smell the putrid odour of the cheese behind the refrigerator. The brown volume of the Coca-Cola can be photographed; sounds can be recorded. Sounds and odours travel in physical space: objects emit, produce or give off sounds and odours. On a direct realist view, coloured surfaces and the rest are not constituents of sense experiences; rather, they are in physical space before our sense organs and among the causes of our sense experiences.

Coloured surfaces and the rest are, moreover, arguably the primary bearer of sensory properties. A material object is loud only if the sound of it is loud, putrid only if the odour of it is putrid, red only if some surface or volume of it is red. On a secondary-quality theory, they are the primary bearers of the relevant dispositions; on a primary-quality theory, they possess physical bases for the dispositions.

The thesis that coloured surfaces and the rest are basically perceived and primary bearers of sensory properties offers no support to infallible foundationalism. We can have illusory experiences of them and even hallucinate them. A sufferer of delirium tremens might hallucinate the pink surface of an elephant, a sufferer of command-hallucinations the sound of a voice issuing commands. According to intentional theories of sense experience, the first has a visual experience as of a pink surface, the second an auditory experience as of sounds. These experiences have contents. But nothing pink is seen; no sound is heard.

See also: FALLIBILISM; SENSE-DATA

References and further reading

Alston, W. (1986) 'Internalism and externalism in epistemology', in *Epistemic Justification*, Ithaca, NY: Cornell University Press, 185–226. (Careful treatment of the varieties of internalism and externalism.)

Armstrong, D.M. (1973) *Belief, Truth and Knowledge*, Cambridge: Cambridge University Press. (Offers a causal, reliabilist account of perceptual knowledge.)

* Austin, J.L. (1962) *Sense and Sensibilia*, London: Oxford University Press. (Criticizes A.J. Ayer's sense-data theory.)

Ayer, A.J. (1940) *The Foundations of Empirical Knowledge*, London: Macmillan. (Defends an empiricist theory of the foundations of empirical knowledge which postulates sense-data.)

* Chisholm, R.M. (1957) *Perceiving: A Philosophical Study*, Ithaca, NY: Cornell University Press. (Examines the role of epistemic justification in perceptual knowledge; distinguishes the epistemic, comparative and phenomenal uses of appearance words; and attempts to say how sense experiences must be related to objects we perceive by having them.)

Crane, T. (ed.) (1994) *The Contents of Experience: Essays on Perception*, Cambridge: Cambridge University Press. (Contains an essay on the adverbial theory of sense experience – the theory that sense experiences are ways of being sensorially appeared to; an essay on the disjunctive theory of sense experience – a theory according to which there is no experiential state common to perception and hallucination – and contains several essays on the intentional theory.)

Dancy, J. (ed.) (1988) *Perceptual Knowledge*, Oxford: Oxford University Press. (Contains several seminal papers on epistemic issues in perception.)

Dretske, F.I. (1969) *Seeing and Knowing*, London: Routledge & Kegan Paul, Chicago, IL: University of Chicago Press. (Examines the relational use of 'see'; defends the view that seeing things does not require seeing-that; offers an analysis of seeing things, an analysis of seeing-that, and distinguishes primary from secondary perceiving-that.)

—— (1980) *Knowledge and the Flow of Information*, Cambridge, MA: MIT Press/Bradford Books. (Offers an information-theoretic account of the contents of percepts and of concepts, and of perceiving things.)

—— (1995) 'Perceptual Knowledge', in J. Dancy and E. Sosa (eds) *A Companion to Epistemology*, Oxford: Blackwell. (Contains the account of the distinction between primary and secondary knowledge presented in §2 above which, along with §4, relies heavily on this essay.)

Goldman, A. (1976) 'Perceptual Knowledge and Discrimination', *Journal of Philosophy* 73 (20): 771–91. (Offers an analysis of perceptual knowledge as involving discriminative capacities, and argues that perceptual knowledge has a pragmatic, contextual dimension. What counts as adequate evidence in a typical country setting to see of something that it is a barn may fail to be adequate evidence if one is in 'phoney barn country', an area peppered with papier mâché barn facsimiles.)

Grice, H.P. (1961) 'The Causal Theory of Perception', *Proceedings of the Aristotelian Society* supplementary vol. 35: 121–68. (Account of perceiving things in terms of causal relations between sense experiences and what is perceived; argues that looks-as-if states are always involved in perception, even though we do not typically use 'looks as if' locutions in such situations since they pragmatically imply doubt-and-denial conditions.)

Hilbert, D. (1987) *Color and Color Perception*, Stanford, CA: Centre for the Study of Language and Information, Stanford University. (Defends a primary-quality theory of colour, according to which surfaces colours are spectral reflectance distributions.)

* Jackson, F. (1977) *Perception: A Representative Theory*, Cambridge: Cambridge University Press. (Sophisticated defence of sense-data theory, arguing that only visual sense data could be the primary bearers of colour.)

Jackson, F. and Pargatter, R. (1987) 'An Objectivist's Guide to Subjectivism About Color', *Revue Internationale de Philosophie* 160: 127–41. (Defence of a primary-quality theory of colours as the physical bases of dispositions to look coloured.)

Johnson, M. (1992) 'How to Speak of Colors', *Philosophical Studies* 68: 221–63. (Defends a dispositional theory of colour.)

Lewis, D. (1980) 'Veridical Hallucination and Prosthetic Vision', *Australasian Journal of Philosophy* 58: 239–49. (Analyses the capacity to see in terms of a wide pattern of counterfactual dependence between possible scenes before one's eyes and matching visual experiences.)

McDowell, J. (1994) *Mind and World*, Cambridge, MA: Harvard University Press. (Contains a chapter in which it is argued that coherentism is false since experiences can rationally constrain beliefs, and a chapter in which it is argued that experiences have only conceptual content.)

McLaughlin, B.P. (1984) 'Perception, Causation, and Supervenience', *Midwest Studies in Philosophy* 9: 569–91. (Distinguishes basic from non-basic perception of things using the by-relation as in §5 above; argues that sounds, odours, tastes and coloured surfaces are physical; and argues that since non-basic perception has a pragmatic dimension, the problem of what kind of causal connection pairs perceived objects with sense experiences by which they are perceived should be restricted to basic perception.)

Moore, G.E. (1922) 'The Nature and Reality of Objects of Perception', in *Philosophical Studies*, London: Routledge & Kegan Paul, 1960, 31–86. (Contains an early version of sense-data theory.)

Peacocke, C. (1992) 'Scenarios, Concepts, and Perception', in T. Crane (ed.) *The Contents of Experience: Essays on Perception*, Cambridge, Cambridge University Press, 1994, 105–35. (Develops several related notions of non-conceptual contents of visual experiences.)

Perkins, M. (1984) *Sensing the World*, London: Routledge & Kegan Paul. (Contains a detailed, empirically well-informed discussion of sounds, odours, tastes and coloured surfaces; argues that we are directly sensorially conscious of such things as the colours of surfaces, the loudness of sounds, the saltiness of tastes and the putridness of odours.)

Pitcher, G. (1971) *A Theory of Perception*, Princeton, NJ: Princeton University Press. (Offers a doxastic theory of sense experience according to which sense experiences are suppressed inclinations to believe.)

Price, H.H. (1954) *Perception*, London: Methuen. (Defends sense-data theory.)

* Sanford, D. (1976) 'The Primary Objects of Perception', *Mind* 85: 189–208. (Argues that sounds are primary objects of hearing, odours are primary objects of smelling, tastes are primary objects of taste, coloured expanses are primary objects of seeing, and that theses primary objects of perception are physical existents.)

* Sellars, W. (1968) *Science and Metaphysics*, London: Routledge & Kegan Paul. (Contains seminal essays on epistemic issues in perception. See especially 'Empiricism and the Philosophy of Mind', which contains a discussion of the Myth of the Given.)

Strawson, P.F. (1974) 'Causation in Perception', in *Freedom and Resentment and Other Essays*, London: Methuen, 76–89. (Discusses the role of causation in the notion of perception, and presents an intentional theory of sense experience.)

Urmson, J.O. (1968) 'The objects of the five sense', *Proceedings of the British Academy* 54: 117–31. (Argues that sounds and odours are not sense data, but also argues that nothing in vision plays a role analogous to the roles played by sounds in hearing and by odours in smelling.)

* Vesey, G.N.A. (1971) *Perception*, London: Macmillan. (Introduces the term 'epistemic appearance', and discusses the phenomenal and relational uses of perception verbs.)

BRIAN P. McLAUGHLIN

PERCEPTION, INDIAN VIEWS OF *see* SENSE PERCEPTION, INDIAN VIEWS OF

PERFECT-BEING THEOLOGY *see* GOODNESS, PERFECT

PERFECTION *see* GOODNESS, PERFECT

PERFECTIONISM

Perfectionism is a moral theory according to which certain states or activities of human beings, such as knowledge, achievement and artistic creation, are good apart from any pleasure or happiness they bring, and what is morally right is what most promotes these human 'excellences' or 'perfections'. Some versions of perfectionism hold that the good consists, at bottom, in the development of properties central to human nature, so that if knowledge and achievement are good, it is because they realize aspects of human nature. With or without this view, perfectionisms can differ about what in particular is good, for example, about the relative merits of knowing and doing. The most plausible versions of perfectionism affirm both self-regarding duties to seek the excellences in one's own life and other-regarding duties to promote them in other people. Some critics argue that the latter duties, when applied to political questions, are hostile to liberty and equality, but certain versions of perfectionism endorse liberty and equality. Perfectionist ideas can also figure in a pluralist morality where they are weighed against other, competing moral ideas.

1 **Broad versus narrow perfectionism**
2 **Theoretical and practical perfections**
3 **Perfectionism and other-regarding duties**
4 **Perfectionism and politics**
5 **Perfectionism in pluralism**

1 Broad versus narrow perfectionism

Despite being ignored by English-speaking philosophers for much of the twentieth century, perfectionism is one of the leading moralities of the Western tradition. It is wholly or in part the morality of, among others, Plato, Aristotle, Aquinas, Leibniz, Hegel, Marx, Nietzsche, Brentano, T.H. Green, F.H. Bradley, G.E. Moore and W.D. Ross.

Defined broadly, perfectionism is a teleological morality with an objective theory of the human good (see GOOD, THEORIES OF THE; TELEOGICAL ETHICS; WELFARE). As a teleological morality, it is centred on claims about the good and characterizes right action in terms of the good, for example, as that which will result in the most good possible (see RIGHT AND GOOD). Its structure, therefore, is similar to that of utilitarianism (see UTILITARIANISM). But whereas utilitarians traditionally characterize the good subjectively, as consisting in pleasure, the fulfilment of desires, or 'happiness', perfectionists value states or activities of humans other than happiness (see HAPPINESS; HEDONISM). They hold that, for example, knowledge, achievement, and aesthetic appreciation are good apart from any pleasure or satisfaction they bring. Their presence in a life makes that life better independently of how much they are wanted or enjoyed, and their absence impoverishes it even if it is not a source of regret.

Defined more narrowly, perfectionism is based on an objective theory of a special kind. It holds that the good consists at bottom in developing one's 'nature', or realizing a 'true self' (see HUMAN NATURE §1): certain properties are central to one's identity, and one's good consists in developing these properties to a high degree. In some versions of this narrower perfectionism the relevant identity belongs to one as an individual, but more commonly it is shared with all human beings, so that, for example, the properties distinctive of or essential to humans determine the human good. If knowledge and achievement are good, on this view, it is because they realize aspects of human nature.

Narrow perfectionism has often been accompanied by dubious non-moral views, for example, that developing human nature is each human's 'function' or purpose, or that premises about human nature entail conclusions about the good. But it is best considered apart from these views, as making only the moral claim that a being's good is determined by its nature. If this claim can be sustained, narrow perfectionism has two attractive features. Its central ideal of developing human nature is intuitively appealing in itself, or at least has been found so by philosophers from Aristotle to Marx and Nietzsche. And this ideal offers to unify what might otherwise be an unordered list of objective goods. But narrow perfectionism faces serious objections. It must provide a more precise definition of human nature that both retains the intrinsic appeal of the narrow ideal and includes only properties that in themselves seem worth developing. This dual test is not passed by the commonest definitions of human nature, since humans have both distinctive properties (such as killing things for fun) and essential properties (such as occupying space) that do not seem morally valuable. Indeed, many contemporary philosophers doubt whether, especially given the findings of evolutionary biology, any true theory of human nature can ground plausible claims about value (see EVOLUTION AND ETHICS). If they are right, narrow perfectionism is no longer a viable option. The most plausible morality of this kind is not a narrow but a merely broad perfectionism, one that makes objective claims about the good without grounding them in human nature.

2 Theoretical and practical perfections

Different versions of perfectionism can differ in their particular claims about the good. (Among narrow perfectionisms, these differences rest on deeper disagreements about human nature.) Some perfectionists, notably Plato, Aristotle and Aquinas, take the highest human good to be the development of theoretical reason, found especially in the contemplation of knowledge. Others value most, or only certain, practical excellences of acting on the world. Marx equates the human good with productive labour, especially in cooperation with others, while Nietzsche values large-scale, world-transforming creativity. A third view, found in Bradley, values theoretical and practical perfections equally and characterizes them in parallel ways. On this view the best knowledge is explanatorily integrated, with general principles explaining more particular known truths. The greatest practical goods involve a similar integration, with many subordinate ends achieved as means to a single overarching end. This grants perfectionist value to any life that is highly unified, and to particular activities that are complex and difficult.

More specific perfectionist claims find intrinsic goodness in political activity, either by government leaders or democratic participants; in love, friendship and other interpersonal relations; and in the creation or appreciation of artistic beauty. There can also be intrinsic perfectionist evils, such as false belief and failure. A more difficult question is whether moral virtue should be a perfectionist good and vice a perfectionist evil. This connects to the larger issue of how perfectionism accounts for other-regarding duties.

3 Perfectionism and other-regarding duties

Perfectionism gives a central place to self-regarding duties. Whereas some philosophers confine moral evaluation to acts that affect other people, perfectionists affirm moral duties to seek goods such as knowledge and achievement in one's own life. To be a complete morality, however, perfectionism must also capture other-regarding duties such as the duties not to kill, to relieve starvation, and so on.

Some perfectionists attempt this within a formal structure that is egoistic, so each human's ultimate duty is only to seek their own perfection. They do so by claiming that virtuous action, including the exercise of other-regarding virtues such as justice and beneficence, is part of the agent's good (see EGOISM AND ALTRUISM §4; VIRTUE ETHICS; VIRTUES AND VICES §3). But this egoistic account of other-regarding duties is problematic. In a merely broad perfectionism, one can simply add virtue to a list of objective goods. But especially if virtue is given special weight against other goods, it is hard to see how the resulting morality differs significantly from a non-perfectionist one that simply tells agents to act justly and beneficently without tying this to claims about their good. Some egoistic perfectionists try to derive the goodness of virtue within narrow perfectionism. Thus, some argue that human nature consists in rationality, and that exercising rationality requires acting virtuously. But if there is a sense of rationality

in which rationality is plausibly part of human nature, for example, is plausibly essential to humans, this rationality does not seem specially tied to virtuous action. It can be exercised not only in just and beneficent acts but equally in ones that ignore others' needs (such as philosophizing while others starve) or positively hurt them.

A more promising approach is to give perfectionism a universalistic structure, so each human's ultimate duty is to promote the greatest perfection of all, with others' good counting as much as one's own (see UNIVERSALISM IN ETHICS). This yields other-regarding duties, though on a distinctive basis: the reason we ought to relieve starvation and not kill is to promote others' excellence. And, given a universalistic structure, perfectionism can go on to treat virtue as good. It can hold, as Brentano, Moore and Ross have done, that whenever something is good, loving it for itself, that is, desiring, pursuing, or taking pleasure in it for itself, is also good. Then desiring and pursuing the objective good of others, which for perfectionists constitutes virtue, is itself an objective good. This account of virtue is an attractive addition to broad perfectionism, but it presupposes that each agent should already care about the perfection of all. Given a structure that already grounds other-regarding duties, perfectionism can add that fulfilling these duties virtuously promotes one aspect of the agent's good. It is harder for it, while remaining distinctively perfectionist, to derive other-regarding duties from a concern only with the agent's perfection.

4 Perfectionism and politics

Applied to political questions, perfectionism uses the same teleological standard as for evaluating acts by individuals: the best government, leader or law is the one that most promotes perfection. Though this is a classical view of politics, some critics worry that it threatens the values of liberty and equality (see EQUALITY; FREEDOM AND LIBERTY). Will a state committed to objective goods not force citizens into activities it deems valuable, thereby violating individual liberty? Instead of distributing resources equally, will it not concentrate them on a small elite with the greatest talents for excellence? Some perfectionisms, for example, those of Plato, Aristotle and Nietzsche, substantiate these worries, but others, notably Marx's and Green's, endorse liberty and equality. They do so because of specific features of their structure and theories of value.

Perfectionism can most simply value liberty by making the free choice of one's life-activities itself an objective good (see AUTONOMY, ETHICAL). This perfectionist valuing of choice lies behind the classical liberalisms of Wilhelm von Humboldt and J.S. Mill. In addition, perfectionism can hold, as Green did, that the value of any activity depends crucially on the attitude with which it is done, and that state coercion not only cannot produce good attitudes but is likely to discourage them. These arguments leave room for non-coercive state action to promote perfection, such as subsidizing good activities or in other ways encouraging them.

Some perfectionisms are anti-egalitarian because of their structure. Thus, Nietzsche makes the goal of individual and state action the greatest perfection, not of all, but of the few best individuals. The most attractive perfectionisms, however, give equal weight to gains in perfection by all people. And they will support roughly equal distributions of resources if they can make the following empirical claims: that people's overall talents for perfection do not differ immensely, and that many highly valuable perfections require only modest resources. Some theories of the good, such as Plato's and Aristotle's, make these empirical claims unlikely, but others, such as Green's, support them. If perfection is largely a matter of people's attitudes, then many inexpensive activities can have value, and each person has many chances to have some worthwhile talent. There is further support for equality if the perfections of different people enhance each other. If each person's development requires a similar development for others, as Marx held, then all will do best in a society where all have the resources for excellence. In short, though some versions of perfectionism do deny liberty and equality, others, arguably the most plausible, endorse them.

5 Perfectionism in pluralism

Perfectionist ideas can figure not only in a pure morality but also in a pluralist one where they are weighed against competing ideas about, for example, utility or rights (see MORAL PLURALISM). One possibility is a teleological pluralism with a duty to promote not only perfectionist goods but also utilitarian ones such as pleasure. J.S. Mill's theory, with its distinction between higher and lower pleasures, fits this mixed teleological pattern (see MILL, J.S. §9). Another pluralist morality combines a teleological duty to promote what is good with non-teleological duties about killing, truth-telling and the like, as Ross's theory does. In these pluralist contexts perfectionist ideas make a distinctive contribution, grounding both self-regarding and other-regarding duties to pursue objective goods such as knowledge and achievement. The central perfectionist thought is that these states are good independently of any connection with happiness and that a prime moral duty is to promote them in oneself and in others.

See also: ARETĒ; CONSEQUENTIALISM; EUDAIMONIA; SELF-REALIZATION

References and further reading

Aristotle (*c*. mid 4th century BC) *Nicomachean Ethics*, trans. with notes by T. Irwin, Indianapolis: Hackett Publishing Company, 1985. (Immensely influential version of narrow perfectionism.)

Attfield, R. (1987) *A Theory of Value and Obligation*, London: Croom Helm. (Narrow perfectionism extended beyond humans to all living organisms.)

Hurka, T. (1993) *Perfectionism*, New York: Oxford University Press. (Survey of narrow and broad perfectionism.)

Marx, K. (1844) *Economic and Philosophical Manuscripts*, in K. Marx and F. Engels, *Collected Works*, vol. 3, New York: International Publishers, 1975. (Outlines human perfection as productive, cooperative activity.)

Moore, G.E. (1903) *Principia Ethica*, Cambridge: Cambridge University Press, ch. 6. (Expounds an elaborate objective theory of the good.)

Nietzsche, F. (1886) *Jenseits von Gut und Böse*, trans. W. Kaufmann, *Beyond Good and Evil*, New York: Vintage Books, 1966. (Brazenly anti-egalitarian perfectionism.)

Rawls, J. (1971) *A Theory of Justice*, Cambridge, MA: Harvard University Press, section 50. (Contains a liberal-egalitarian critique of perfectionism.)

Raz, J. (1986) *The Morality of Freedom*, Oxford: Clarendon Press. (Perfectionism in political philosophy, with autonomy as a central value.)

THOMAS HURKA

PERFORMATIVES

There are certain things one can do just by saying what one is doing. This is possible if one uses a verb that names the very sort of act one is performing. Thus one can thank someone by saying 'Thank you', fire someone by saying 'You're fired' and apologize by saying 'I apologize'. These are examples of 'explicit performative utterances', statements in form but not in fact. Or so thought their discoverer, J.L. Austin, who contrasted them with 'constatives'. Their distinctive self-referential character might suggest that their force requires special explanation, but it is arguable that performativity can be explained by the general theory of speech acts.

In *How to Do Things with Words* (1962), J.L. Austin challenges the common philosophical assumption that indicative sentences are necessarily devices for making statements. Just as nonindicative sentences are marked grammatically for nonassertive use (interrogative sentences for asking questions and imperative sentences for requesting or ordering), certain *indicative* sentences are also so marked. Austin's paradigm is any sentence beginning with 'I' followed by an illocutionary verb (see SPEECH ACTS §1), such as 'promise', 'apologize' or 'request', in the simple present tense and active voice. One can make a promise by uttering the words 'I promise to go', but not by uttering 'I promised to go' or 'She promises to go'. The first-person plural can be performative too, as in 'We apologize...', and so can the second-person passive, as in 'You're fired'. The word 'hereby' may be used before the performative verb to indicate that the utterance in which it occurs is the vehicle of the performance of the act in question.

Austin contended that these 'explicit performative utterances' are, unlike 'constatives' (statements, predictions, hypotheses, and so on), neither true nor false. In saying 'I promise to go' one is making a promise, not stating that one is making it. A performative promise is not, and does not involve, the statement that one is promising. It is an act of a distinctive sort, the very sort (promising) named by the performative verb. And, according to Austin, making explicit what one is doing is not describing what one is doing or stating that one is doing it.

Now it is also possible to promise without doing so explicitly, without using the performative verb, and this raises the question of whether there is a theoretically important difference between promising explicitly and doing it inexplicitly. A superficial difference is that in uttering the words 'I promise to go' the speaker is saying that he is promising to go and that this, what he is saying, is assessable as true or false. It is true just in case he is doing what he is doing – that is, promising to go. In general, in making an explicit performative utterance the speaker is saying what he is doing – and is thereby doing it. Does this mean that performativity requires a theoretically special explanation?

One suggestion is that performativity is a matter of linguistic meaning. Perhaps there is a special semantic property of performativity, so that it is part of the meaning of words like 'promise', 'apologize' and 'request' that one can perform an act of that very sort by uttering a performative sentence containing that verb. One problem with this suggestion is that it implausibly entails that such verbs are systematically ambiguous. For a performative sentence can be used literally but nonperformatively – for example, to report some habitual act. For instance, one might say 'I apologize...' to describe typical situations in which one apologizes. Moreover, it seems that even if verbs like 'promise', 'apologize' and 'request' were never used performatively, they would still mean just what they mean in fact. Imagine a community of users of a language just like English in which there is no practice of using such verbs performatively. When people there perform acts of the relevant sorts, they always do so, just as we sometimes do, without using performative verbs, such as making promises by saying 'I will definitely...', giving apologies by saying 'I'm sorry', and issuing requests by using imperative sentences. In this hypothetical community the verbs 'promise', 'apologize' and 'request' would seem to have the same meanings that they in fact have in English, applying, respectively, to acts of promising, apologizing and requesting. The only relevant difference would be that such acts are not performed by means of the performative form. It seems, then, that in our community, where they are sometimes performed in this way, performativity is not a matter of meaning.

It might be suggested that a special sort of convention is required for uses of the performative form to count as promises, apologies, requests, and so on. Explaining this by appealing to convention is gratuitous, however, for performativity is but a special case of a more general phenomenon. There are all sorts of other forms of words which are standardly used to perform speech acts of types not predictable from their semantic content, such as 'It would be nice if you...' to request, 'Why don't you...?' to advise, 'Do you know...?' to ask for information, 'I'm sorry' to apologize, and 'I wouldn't do that' to warn. In particular, there are hedged and embedded performatives, such as 'I can assure you...', 'I must inform you...', 'I would like to invite you...', and 'I am pleased to be able to offer you...', utterances to which the alleged conventions for simple performative forms could not apply. Could such conventions be suitably generalized? The variety of linguistic forms standardly used for the indirect performance of such speech acts seems too open-ended to be explained by any convention (or set of conventions) that is supposed to specify just those linguistic forms whose utterance counts as the performance of an act of the relevant sort.

An alternative explanation is needed. In general, speech acts are acts of communication, whose success in that regard requires the audience to identify the speaker's intention (see SPEECH ACTS §2). As Bach and Harnish (1979) have argued, what is special about the use of standardized forms of words, such as those illustrated above, is not that they provide the precedent for any conventions. Rather, the precedent provided by standardization serves to streamline the inference required on the part of the audience.

Convention seems relevant to performativity only in certain institutional contexts, where a specific form of words is designated, and often required, for the performance of an act of a certain sort. This is true of those performative utterances involved in, for example, adjourning a meeting, sentencing a criminal, or christening a ship. However, ordinary performative utterances are not bound to particular institutional situations. Like most speech acts, they are acts of communication and succeed not by conformity to convention but by recognition of intention (see COMMUNICATION AND INTENTION).

See also: AUSTIN, J.L.; SEARLE, J.R.; SPEECH ACTS

References and further reading

* Austin, J.L. (1962) *How to Do Things with Words*, Cambridge, MA: Harvard University Press. (Formulates the distinction between performative and constative utterances and proposes a convention-based account of their successful felicitous performance.)
* Bach, K. and Harnish, R.M. (1979) *Linguistic Communication and Speech Acts*, Cambridge, MA: MIT Press. (Chapter 10 argues that performativity can be explained inferentially, without appealing to any special meanings or conventions connected with performative verbs.)
—— (1992) 'How Performatives Really Work', *Linguistics and Philosophy* 15: 93–110. (Critically examines Searle's conventionalist approach and defends the inferentialist account.)
Recanati, F. (1987) *Meaning and Force: The Pragmatics of Performative Utterances*, Cambridge: Cambridge University Press. (Surveys the literature on performatives and presents an inferentialist account of how they work.)
Searle, J.R. (1989) 'How Performatives Work', *Linguistics and Philosophy* 12: 535–58. (Critically examines the inferentialist approach and defends a conventionalist account.)

KENT BACH

PERFORMING ART *see* ART, PERFORMING

PERIPATETICS

The title 'Peripatetics' designates followers of the philosophical tradition founded by Aristotle: at first those who continued his inquiries, and in the Roman period those who interpreted and commented on his writings. The distinctive Peripatetic tradition was eventually absorbed into Neoplatonism. The adjective 'Peripatetic' is often used as an equivalent of 'Aristotelian'. Peripatetic doctrines were marked by a rejection of the extreme views characteristic of Stoicism.

'Peripatetic' was the name applied to the Aristotelian tradition in philosophy, the name allegedly deriving from a habit of walking about (*peripatein*) while teaching but more probably from teaching in a colonnade or *peripatos*. The independent history of the tradition in antiquity falls into three principal phases. In the sixty years after the death of ARISTOTLE in 322 BC, his followers, and especially the heads of the school (see THEOPHRASTUS; STRATO), continued his philosophical and scientific inquiries into a wide variety of topics. The school was not concerned to recommend a way of life – or perhaps saw the pursuit of disinterested theoretical inquiry as itself a way of life. Its failure to provide the moral guidance that other contemporary schools were offering (see EPICUREANISM; HELLENISTIC PHILOSOPHY; STOICISM) may have contributed to its subsequent decline; and from the middle of the third to the middle of the first century BC there were few Peripatetics of importance – Critolaus, who accompanied CARNEADES §1 on the embassy to Rome in 155 BC, is the chief exception – and interest in Aristotle took the form of summary accounts of his doctrines (like that preserved for us by Diogenes Laertius), often reflecting later preoccupations.

This type of interest was continued, but on a more informed basis, by scholars such as Arius Didymus and Nicolaus of Damascus after the event which is commonly thought to have begun the third phase of the Peripatetic tradition, Andronicus of Rhodes' revival, in the mid-first century BC, of direct study of the 'esoteric' or previously unpublished treatises which we possess today. We need not believe the story, in Plutarch and Strabo, that these texts had been hidden in a cellar in Asia Minor until the first century BC. But with Andronicus there began a sequence of commentaries which extended from Andronicus himself to the end of a distinctive Peripatetic tradition and even beyond. There was a corresponding decline of interest in the 'exoteric' or published works, now lost to us.

The commentators concentrated on the aspects of Aristotle's treatises which are 'philosophical' in a modern sense, neglecting the biological, rhetorical and political writings. Important figures were Andronicus' pupil Boethus, Aspasius, whose commentary on the *Nicomachean Ethics* is the earliest of the commentaries we possess except through later reports, and above all, ALEXANDER OF APHRODISIAS. The commentators sought to reconcile discrepancies between different Aristotelian texts and thus furthered the construction of Aristotelianism as a distinctive system of doctrine. After Alexander those who undertook the study of Aristotelian texts and produced commentaries on them were, with the exception of Themistius, Neoplatonists who regarded Aristotle's philosophy as an introduction to that of Plato (see ARISTOTLE COMMENTATORS; NEOPLATONISM §2).

In philosophical doctrine the distinctive feature of the Peripatetic tradition is moderation. In metaphysics members of the school advocated a this-worldly realism which rejected both Platonic transcendent Forms and Stoic nominalism. In physics and theology a recurring theme is that the universe – regarded with Aristotle as everlasting – is a system in which the same degree of organization cannot be expected at every level. In ethics, although individual formulations varied, Peripatetics followed Aristotle himself both in advocating moderation with regard to the emotions (*metriopatheia*) rather than the Stoic rejection of them (*apatheia*), and in regarding external goods as having some influence on human happiness even though virtue itself was much more important.

See also: ARISTOTLE §30

References and further reading

For works by individual Peripatetics, see CARNEADES, DIOGENES LAERTIUS, PLUTARCH, STRATO and THEOPHRASTUS. For Aspasius and Themistius, see ARISTOTLE COMMENTATORS.

Barnes, J. (1997) 'Roman Aristotle', in J. Barnes and M. Griffin (eds) *Philosophia Togata II: Plato and Aristotle at Rome*, Oxford: Clarendon Press, 1–69. (Important challenge to the long-standing consensus that Andronicus produced the first edition of the Aristotelian corpus as we know it.)

Gottschalk, H.B. (1987) 'Aristotelian Philosophy in the Roman World', in H. Temporini and W. Haase (eds) *Aufstieg und Niedergang der römischen Welt*, Berlin: de Gruyter, II 36: 2, 1079–1174. (A detailed and clear account of the Peripatetic tradition from Andronicus to the generation before Alexander of Aphrodisias.)

Moraux, P. (1973–) *Der Aristotelismus bei den Griechen (Aristotelianism among the Greeks)*, Berlin: de Gruyter, 3 vols. (The definitive treatment of the Peripatetic tradition in the Roman period. Volume 2 was published in 1984, volume 3 is forthcoming.)

Sharples, R.W. (1997, forthcoming) 'The Peripatetic School', in D.J. Furley (ed.) Routledge History of Philosophy, vol. 2, *Aristotle to Augustine*, London: Routledge. (A general account of the history of the school, with bibliography.)

Wehrli, F. (1969–78) *Die Schule des Aristoteles (The Aristotelian School)*, Basle: Schwabe, 2nd edn. (Collected fragments and testimonia of Peripatetics of the Hellenistic period, with German commentary.)

R.W. SHARPLES

PERLOCUTIONARY ACT

see PRAGMATICS (§§2, 13); SPEECH ACTS

PERSIAN PHILOSOPHY

see AL-'AMIRI, ABU'L HASAN MUHAMMAD IBN YUSUF; AL-DAWANI, JALAL AL-DIN; AL-GHAZALI, ABU HAMID; IBN MISKAWAYH, AHMAD IBN MUHAMMAD; MIR DAMAD, MUHAMMAD BAQIR; MULLA SADRA (SADR AL-DIN MUHAMMAD AL-SHIRAZI); AL-RAZI, FAKHR AL-DIN; AL-SABZAWARI, AL-HAJJ MULLA HADI; AL-SIJISTANI, ABU SULAYMAN MUHAMMAD; AL-SUHRAWARDI, SHIHAB AL-DIN YAHYA; AL-TUSI, KHWAJAH NASIR

PERSONAL IDENTITY

What is it to be the same person today as one was in the past, or will be in the future? How are we to describe cases in which (as we might put it) one person becomes two? What, if anything, do the answers to such questions show about the rationality of the importance we

attach to personal identity? Is identity really the justifier of the special concern which we have for ourselves in the future? These are the concerns of this entry.

In order to answer the question about the persistence-conditions of persons we must indulge in some thought experiments. Only thus can we tease apart the strands that compose our concept of personal identity, and thereby come to appreciate the relative importance of each strand. There are plausible arguments against attempts to see the relation of personal identity as constitutively determined by the physical relations of same body, or same brain. I can survive with a new body, and a new brain. But it does not follow; nor is it true, that a person's identity over time can be analysed exclusively in terms of psychological relations (relations of memory, belief, character, and so on). To the contrary, the most plausible view appears to be a mixed view, according to which personal identity has to be understood in terms of both physical and psychological relations. This is the view which can be extracted from our core (that is, minimally controversial) set of common-sense beliefs about personal identity.

The possibility of the fission of persons – the possibility that, for example, a person's brain hemispheres might be divided and transplanted into two new bodies – shows that the mixed view has to incorporate a non-branching or uniqueness clause in its analysis. The concept of personal identity, contrary to what we might first be inclined to believe, is an extrinsic concept (that is, whether a given person exists can depend upon the existence of another, causally unrelated, person).

Some philosophers have recently tried to forge an important connection between theories of personal identity and value theory (ethics and rationality). The possibility of such a connection had not previously been investigated in any detail. It has been argued that, on the correct theory of personal identity, it is not identity that matters but the preservation of psychological relations such as memory and character. These relations can hold between one earlier person and two or more later persons. They can also hold to varying degrees (for example, I can acquire a more or less different character over a period of years). This view of what matters has implications for certain theories of punishment. A now reformed criminal may deserve less or no punishment for the crimes of their earlier criminal self. Discussions of personal identity have also provided a new perspective on the debate between utilitarianism and its critics.

1   Criteria of personal identity

What is it to be a person? What is it for a person at one time to be identical to some person at a later time? Although the two questions are obviously related, my concern in this entry will be with the second question. (For more on the first question, see PERSONS; MIND, BUNDLE THEORY OF.) However, I assume this much about what it is to be a person: a person is a rational and self-conscious being, with a (more or less) unified mental life. There are indeed cases (multiple personality, split-brain patients, and so on) in which the apparent lack of mental unity casts doubt on whether a single person occupies a given body (see SPLIT BRAINS). But such cases are exceptional. A normal person is a mentally unified individual. The central question of personal identity is the question of what distinguishes the sorts of changes we mentally unified individuals can survive from the sorts of changes which constitute our death.

On one very familiar view (associated with Plato, Descartes and the Christian tradition) a person can survive bodily death. Bodily death is not the sort of change which constitutes personal death. On this view, a person is an immaterial (that is, non-spatial) soul, only contingently attached to a physical body (see SOUL, NATURE AND IMMORTALITY OF THE; SOUL IN ISLAMIC PHILOSOPHY). This view has few philosophical adherents today. It is fraught with metaphysical and epistemological difficulties. (For example: how can an immaterial soul interact with the material world? How can I know that you have a soul?) In what follows I simply assume, without further argument, that our continued existence is not the continued existence of an immaterial soul.

I do not have to deny that in some possible worlds, there are persons who are immaterial souls; but ours is not such a world. And our concern here is with the conditions for the identity over time of actual (human) persons. Once we have given up the immaterialist view of ourselves, we can say the following. A person is a psychophysical entity, which is essentially physically embodied. That is a person (a typical adult human, for example) consists of a biological organism (a human body), with a control centre (the brain) that supports their mental life. Persons are essentially mental, and essentially physically embodied. But this is not the end of puzzles about personal identity; it is just the beginning.

When we judge that a friend before us now is identical to the friend we saw yesterday, we typically make this judgment of personal identity under optimal conditions. In such a case, our friend today is physically continuous with our friend yesterday (they possess the very same brain and body). And our friend today is also psychologically continuous with our friend yesterday (they possess the very same beliefs, character, desires, memories, and so on, with only very slight changes). In this case, our identity judgment is true in virtue of the obtaining of both physical and psychological continuities. The puzzle of personal identity is: which continuity (if any) is the more important or central to our concept of personal identity? Evidently, reflection on the paradigm case just described will not help us to answer that question. We need to consider thought experiments where the continuities come apart.

There are three broad accounts or criteria of personal identity over time: the physical criterion, the psychological criterion, and the mixed criterion. These criteria do not purport just to offer quite general ways of telling or of finding out who is who. They also purport to specify what the identity of persons over time consists in: what it is to be the same person over time. According to the physical criterion, the identity of a person over time consists in the obtaining of some relation of physical continuity (typically either bodily continuity or brain continuity). On this view, to be the same person is to be the same living biological object (whether body or brain).

According to the psychological criterion, the identity of a person over time consists in the obtaining of relations of psychological continuity (overlapping memory chains, or memory together with the retention of other psychological features such as well-entrenched beliefs, character, basic desires, and so on). The psychological criterion splits into a narrow version and a wide version. According to the narrow version, the cause of the psychological continuity must be normal (that is, the continued existence of one's brain) if it is to preserve personal identity; according to the wide version, any cause will suffice (normal or abnormal). (See Parfit 1984 ch. 10 for more on this distinction.) Sub-versions of the wide and narrow versions differ over the question of whether any one psychological relation is privileged with respect to identity preservation. (For example, John Locke thought that memory was such a privileged relation.)

Each of the physical and psychological criteria divides into many different versions. The distinctive claim of the mixed criterion is that no version of either the physical or psychological criterion is correct. The best account of a person's identity over time will make reference to both physical and psychological continuities.

I now want to examine in more detail different versions of the physical and psychological criteria. My conclusion will be that all familiar versions of

these criteria are open to objection, and that we should accept the mixed criterion. The mixed criterion best captures our core (that is, minimally controversial) beliefs about personal identity.

We can begin with the physical criterion. As noted, this criterion divides into two criteria: the bodily criterion and the brain criterion.

2 Physical criteria

Physical criteria: the bodily criterion. According to the bodily criterion, person A at time t_1 is identical to person B at t_2 if and only if A and B have the same body (that is, they are bodily continuous). Note that A and B can truly be said to have the same body, even though the body at the later time has no matter in common with the body at the earlier time (see CONTINUANTS). In such a case, however, the replacement of matter must be gradual, and the new matter must be functionally absorbed into the living body. This is how it is in the life of a normal human being.

The bodily criterion accords with most of our ordinary judgments of personal identity. However, there appear to be logically possible cases in which the deliverances of the bodily criterion conflict with our considered judgments. The particular case I have in mind is that of brain transplantation. Such transplants are, of course, technologically impossible at present; but that is hardly relevant. The speculations of philosophers are not confined to what is technologically possible.

Sydney Shoemaker was the first to introduce such cases into the philosophical literature. He wrote:

It is now possible to transplant certain organs...it is at least conceivable...that a human body could continue to function normally if its brain were replaced by one taken from another human body....Two men, a Mr. Brown and a Mr. Robinson, had been operated on for brain tumors, and brain extractions had been performed on both of them. At the end of the operations, however, the assistant inadvertently put Brown's brain in Robinson's head, and Robinson's brain in Brown's head. One of these men immediately dies, but the other, the one with Robinson's head and Brown's brain, eventually regains consciousness. Let us call the latter 'Brownson'....When asked his name he automatically replies 'Brown'. He recognizes Brown's wife and family ..., and is able to describe in detail events in Brown's life ... of Robinson's life he evidences no knowledge at all.

(Shoemaker 1963: 23–4)

We can suppose, in addition, that Brown and Robinson are physically very similar, and that their bodies are equally suited for the realization of particular dispositions or abilities (for example, playing the piano, or hang-gliding).

The description of this case which commands almost universal assent is that Brown is the same person as Brownson. Virtually no one thinks that the correct description is: Robinson acquires a new brain. Receiving a new skull and a new body seems to be just a limiting case of receiving a new heart, new lungs, new legs, and so on. If Brown is the same person as Brownson, and yet Brownson's body is not the same body as Brown's body, then it follows that the bodily criterion is false.

Physical criteria: the brain criterion. In the light of this example, it would be natural for a defender of the physical criterion to move to the brain criterion: A at t_1 is the same person as B at t_2 if and only if A and B possess the same brain. But is this a plausible criterion of personal identity? I think not. The following scenario is conceivable. Imagine that robotics and brain science have advanced to such a stage that it is possible to construct a silicon brain which supports the very same kind of mental life as that supported by a flesh-and-blood human brain. Imagine also that parts of a human brain (say, a cancerous part) can be replaced by silicon chips which subserve the very same mental functions as the damaged brain tissue.

Suppose that the whole of my brain gradually becomes cancerous. As soon as the surgeons detect a cancerous part, they replace it with silicon chips. My mental life continues as before – the same beliefs, memories, character, and so on, are preserved. Eventually, the surgeons replace all my biological brain with a silicon brain. Since my mental life, and physical appearance and abilities, are unaffected by this replacement, we have no hesitation in judging that I have survived the operation. The procedure preserves personal identity. But is this judgment of personal identity consistent with the brain criterion? The answer to this question depends on whether my (later) silicon brain is deemed to be identical to my (earlier) human brain.

It is plausible to suppose that, if an object (such as a heart, brain or liver) is biological, then that very object is essentially biological. That is, for example, my flesh-and-blood brain could not have been anything but a biological entity. This essentialist thesis is consistent with the view that the function of any given biological object (a human heart, for example) could, in principle, be carried out by a non-biological object (a mechanical pump, say). Hence, I am happy to concede that my later silicon brain is indeed a brain; but it is not remotely plausible to think that it is the same brain as my earlier human brain. Rather, the effect of all the tissue removals and bionic insertions

in my skull is to destroy one brain and replace it with another.

Our brain example shows that the sort of matter or stuff with which we replace an object's removed parts can affect the overall identity of that object, even if continuity of form or function is preserved. My (earlier) human brain is not identical to my (later) silicon brain. Yet I survived the operation. Hence, the brain criterion is false.

However, there is a deeper worry about the tenability of the brain criterion. Why did we move to the brain criterion, in response to counterexamples to the bodily criterion? Was it because the human brain is a three-pound pinkish-grey spongy organ that occupies human skulls? No, we moved to the brain criterion because of what the human brain does, namely, supports directly our mental life. It is surely because of its mind-supporting function that we are inclined to single out the brain as the seat of personal identity. Consequently, we should not see our identity over time as tied necessarily to the continued existence of the human brain we presently have. What matters most is that our stream of mental life continues to be supported by some physical object, not that it continues to be supported by the very same biological organ.

3   Psychological and mixed criteria

I take the bionic brain example to undermine not just the brain criterion, but also the narrow version of the psychological criterion – I survive with a bionic brain, yet the cause of my psychological continuity is abnormal. Hence, it might be thought, the combined effect of these conclusions is to push us towards the wide version of the psychological criterion. Indeed some readers may have wondered why I made no appeal in the first place to examples such as Bernard Williams's brain-state transfer device or Derek Parfit's teletransporter in order to establish the wide version of the psychological criterion.

What are these examples? First, Williams describes a device which can wipe a brain clean, while recording all the information stored in the brain. This machine can then reprogramme another clean brain. The machine can thus preserve psychological continuity in the absence of any physical continuity. Second, Parfit has made much use of the *Star Trek* fantasy of teletransportation. In this scenario, a physical and psychological blueprint is made of a person. The person is then painlessly destroyed. The blueprint is transmitted to another location where, out of different matter, an exact physical and psychological replica of the original person is made.

Some philosophers have claimed that, in both these

examples, the original person is identical to the later person, and so concluded that physical continuity is not necessary for personal identity over time. Other philosophers have taken the opposite view, and concluded that physical continuity is necessary for personal identity over time. But these are judgments in which theory is being allowed to dictate intuitions. In truth, there simply is no general agreement about whether the original is the same person as the replica, in cases in which there is psychological continuity but no physical continuity.

Further, there appears to be a decisive objection to the wide version of the psychological criterion – the criterion which holds that personal identity over time consists in psychological continuity, however that continuity is caused. (A defender of the wide version would agree with my verdicts about the counter-examples to the body and brain criteria, and would also regard the normal operation of the brain-state transfer device and the teletransporter as identity-preserving.) Imagine that I step into the teletransporter booth. My psychophysical blueprint is constructed, and sent to another location, where a replica is created. Unfortunately, the machine malfunctions and fails to destroy me. I step out of the booth, intrinsically no different from when I went in. In this case, we have no hestitation in judging that I continue to exist in the same body, and therefore that the replica is not me. But both me-later and my replica stand to me-earlier in the relation of psychological continuity. If the cause of that continuity is deemed to be irrelevant to personal identity, as in the wide version of the psychological criterion, then it ought to be the case that both later candidates have an equal claim to be me. Yet, as we have seen, we strongly believe that I am identical to the later person who is physically and psychologically continuous with me. Consequently, the wide version of the psychological criterion cannot be correct.

I conclude that the best account of personal identity over time is provided by the mixed criterion. We have seen that neither continuity of body nor brain (nor, by extension, the continuity of any other human organ) is a necessary condition for personal identity over time. But we should not conclude from this that psychological continuity, whatever its cause, is sufficient for personal identity over time. As just noted, that thesis does not accord with our intuitions. The most consistent and plausible view that can be recovered from our core set of common-sense judgments appears to be the following: psychological continuity is necessary for personal identity over time; a sufficient condition of personal identity over time is not psychological continuity with any cause, but psychological continuity with a cause that is either

normal or continuous with the normal cause (this is why I continue to exist with a bionic brain). One might well ask: why do we have just this concept of personal identity and not some other (such as the wide version of the psychological criterion)? Here, as with other conceptual analyses, there may be no non-trivial answer to this question.

Our discussion thus far has made a certain simplification. The counterexample to the wide version of the psychological criterion exploited the fact that relations of psychological continuity are not logically one-one. In that example, one of the streams of psychological continuity did not have a normal cause. However, it is logically possible for a person at one time to be psychologically continuous with two or more later persons, even when both streams of psychological continuity have their normal cause (that is, the continued existence of the brain hemispheres). But the relation of identity is logically one-one: I cannot be identical to two distinct people. It seems, therefore, that the sufficient condition for personal identity endorsed in the previous paragraph will have to be modified, unless either such branching is impossible or the possibility of branching can be redescribed so that it does not conflict with our sufficient condition. The problem raised by the possibility of branching continuities is known as the problem of fission.

4 Fission of persons

As we have seen, much work in personal identity has made use of various thought experiments or imaginary scenarios. The method of thought experiments in personal identity has recently been subject to criticism. It has been claimed that we should not take our intuitions about thought experiments as guides to philosophical truth, since such intuitions may be prejudiced and unreliable. These criticisms are, I think, misplaced. For one thing, such criticisms ignore the frequent and legitimate use of thought experiments in virtually all traditional areas of philosophy (for example, in theories of knowledge and in ethics). Why is their use in discussions of personal identity singled out for criticism? Second, and more important, thought experiments can be useful in understanding the structure of a concept and the relative importance of its different strands, provided that there is general agreement about the best description of the thought-experiment. There is such general agreement about the counterexamples to the body and brain criteria. Some philosophers have tried to gain mileage from thought experiments in the absence of such general agreement – for example, the case of teletransportation discussed above. But it would be unwarranted to infer from the existence of such abuses that thought experiments can never perform any useful function in discussions of personal identity (see THOUGHT EXPERIMENTS).

One thought experiment which has been much discussed in recent years, and which does not fall into the teletransporter category of thought experiments, is that of the fission or division of persons. This thought experiment is interesting because it shows us something about the nature or metaphysics of personal identity, about what it is to be the same person over time.

Fission is a situation in which one thing splits into two (or more) things. Fission does occur in nature (amoebae, for example). Fission of persons, of course, does not occur – but it might. We can devise a thought experiment to flesh out this possibility. Consider a person, Arnold. Like us, Arnold has a mental life that is crucially dependent upon the normal functioning of his brain. Arnold also has a property which most of us do not have, but might have done: each of his brain hemispheres support the very same mental functions. If one of Arnold's hemispheres developed a tumour, that hemisphere could simply be removed and Arnold's mental life would be unaffected.

Suppose that Arnold's body develops cancer. The surgeons cannot save his body, but they can remove Arnold's brain and transplant both hemispheres into two brainless bodies, cloned from Arnold's body many years ago. Arnold agrees to this and the operation is successfully carried out. The fission of Arnold has taken place. We now have two people – call them Lefty and Righty – both of whom are psychologically continuous with Arnold (same character, beliefs, apparent memories of a common past, and so on). They are also physically similar to Arnold, and each contain a hemisphere from Arnold's brain. There is both physical and psychological continuity linking Arnold with Lefty and with Righty. Suppose also that Lefty and Righty are in different rooms in the hospital, and exercise no causal influence on each other. How should this case be described – who is who? A number of responses have been suggested, which we shall examine in turn.

(1) 'The case is not really possible, so we can say nothing about it and learn nothing from it.' This view is implausible. Hemisphere transplants may be technologically impossible; but they are surely not logically impossible. Indeed, hemisphere transplants, like other organ transplants, appear to be nomologically possible (that is, consistent with the laws of nature). If so, such transplants are also logically possible. Response (1) is not a serious contender.

(2) 'Arnold has survived the operation, and is one or the other of Lefty or Righty.' Immediately after fission, Lefty and Righty are physically and psychologically indistinguishable. Both stand in the same psychological and physical relations to Arnold. They both believe that they are Arnold. According to response (2), one is right and the other wrong.

Response (2) is implausible for two reasons. First, since Lefty and Righty are symmetrically related to Arnold in respect of physical and psychological continuities, the claim that, for example, Arnold is Lefty, can only be sustained on something like the Cartesian view of persons. If we think of the person as an immaterial ego that typically underlies streams of psychological life, we can suppose that Arnold's ego pops into the left-hand stream of consciousness, leaving the right-hand stream ego-less or with a new ego. As noted at the beginning of §1, this view of persons is bizarre. The postulation of such an ego is idle, and conflicts with both science and common sense.

Second, the metaphysical absurdity of the Cartesian view has an epistemic counterpart. According to response (2), when Arnold divides, he survives in one of the two streams. So either Arnold is Lefty or Arnold is Righty. But how can we know which? From the third-person point of view, we have no reason to make one identification rather than the other. Nor is appeal to the first-person perspective of any help: both Lefty and Righty take themselves to be Arnold. Nothing in either stream of consciousness will reveal to its bearer that it is Arnold. So if, for example, Arnold is Lefty, this truth will be absolutely unknowable. There may be no incoherence in the idea of unknowable truths, but we should be suspicious of any theory of personal identity which implies that truths about who is who can be, in principle, unknowable. For these reasons, we should reject response (2).

(3) 'Arnold survives fission as both Lefty and Righty.' There are three ways in which we can understand this response. According to the first way, Lefty and Righty are sub-personal components of a single person, Arnold. According to the second way, Arnold is identical to both Lefty and Righty (hence, Lefty is Righty). According to the third way, Lefty and Righty together compose Arnold (so that two persons are parts of one larger person, just as Scotland and England are parts of one larger country).

These views are hard to believe. It seems plain common sense that Lefty and Righty are both persons (not sub-personal entities), and that they are numerically distinct. Lefty and Righty both satisfy the normal physical and psychological criteria for personhood. They qualify as persons. And they are two. They may be exactly alike immediately after fission, but exact similarity does not imply numerical identity. (Two red billiard balls may be exactly similar, yet numerically distinct.) Further, they will soon begin to differ, mentally and physically, so that it would be intolerable to regard them as anything but distinct persons.

According to the remaining version of response (3), Arnold exists after fission composed of Lefty and Righty, now regarded as persons in their own right. This is sheer madness. The postulation of Arnold's existence in this circumstance (in addition to that of Lefty and Righty) does no work whatsoever. It is completely idle. Second, can we really make any sense of the idea that one person might be composed of two separate persons? That one person might be composed of two bodies and two minds? To be a single person is to possess a unified mental life. (This is why we are sometimes reluctant to regard a split-brain patient as constituting a single person.) Yet, supposedly, after fission Arnold is permanently composed of two unconnected spheres of consciousness. How could they possibly constitute a single person? If Lefty believes that Clinton will win the next election, and Righty believes that he will not, does Arnold believe that Clinton will both win and lose the next election? Such problems multiply. It seems that all ways of understanding response (3) skewer our concept of a person to such an extent that they cannot be taken seriously.

5   Fission of persons (cont.)

(4) 'The case of Arnold's fission has been misdescribed. Lefty and Righty exist prior to fission, but only become spatially separate after fission.' This theory also has different versions. Some philosophers think that only Lefty and Righty occupy the pre-fission body, and that the name Arnold is ambiguous. Others think that three people (Arnold, Lefty and Righty) occupy the pre-fission body, but that only Lefty and Righty survive fission. The differences between these versions of the theory will not concern us.

This theory is very strange. It involves a tremendous distortion of our concept of a person to suppose that more than one person occupies the pre-fission body. Surely to one body and a unified mind, there corresponds only one person? However, the strangeness of response (4) may depend on one's general metaphysics. In particular, the degree of strangeness may depend on whether we accept a three- or four-dimensional view of continuants such as persons.

On the three-dimensional view of persons, persons are wholly present at all times at which they exist (much as a universal, such as redness, is said to be wholly present in each of its instantiations). On this view, persons are extended only in space, not in time, and have no temporal parts. On the four-dimensional view of persons, persons are four-dimensional entities spread out in space and time. Persons have temporal parts as well as spatial parts. Hence, at any given time, say 1993, only a part of me is in existence, just as only a part of me exists in the spatial region demarcated by my left foot. (See TIME for more on the contrast between three- and four-dimensional views.)

On the three-dimensional view of persons, response (4) is not just strange but barely intelligible. Consider a time just prior to fission. On this view, two wholly present persons (entities of the same kind) occupy exactly the same space at the same time. This ought to be as hard to understand as the claim that there are two instantiations of redness in some uniformly coloured red billiard ball. On the four-dimensional view, however, Lefty and Righty are distinct persons who, prior to fission, share a common temporal part. It ought to be no more remarkable for two persons to share a common temporal part than for two persons (Siamese twins) to share a common spatial part.

Suppose, for present purposes, that we accept the four-dimensional view. Response (4) is still counter-intuitive. It is implausible to hold that two persons (Lefty and Righty) share a common temporal segment in the absence of any psychological disunity. We should be loath to give up the principle that to each psychologically unified temporal segment there corresponds just one person. Second, there is the problem of how we are to account for the coherence and unity of the I-thoughts associated with the locus of reflective mental life that occupies the pre-fission body. How can there be such unity if two persons occupy that body? These objections to response (4) may not be decisive, but they do show that the multiple occupancy view is problematic, and we should avoid it if we can.

(5) 'What's the problem? When Arnold divides into Lefty and Righty, Arnold ceases to exist (one thing cannot be two). Lefty and Righty then come into existence, and are numerically distinct, though initially very similar, persons.' This is the response I favour. When Arnold divides, there are two equally good candidates for identity with him. Since they are equally good, and since one thing cannot be two things, Arnold is identical to neither. And since there is no one else with whom we could plausibly identify Arnold, Arnold no longer exists. This response respects the logic of identity, and does not violate our concept of a person by supposing that one (post-fission) person is composed of two persons or that more than one person occupies the pre-fission body. This is a victory for common sense!

Indeed it is so. But it is important to realize that, in embracing response (5), we are committing ourselves to a quite particular conception of the identity over time of persons. On this view, Arnold is not Lefty. Why is this true? The reason given is not: because Arnold and Lefty do not have the same body, or because Arnold and Lefty do not have the same (whole) brain. (These would anyway be bad reasons – see §1.) The reason is that one thing cannot be two. Arnold is not Lefty because Righty also exists. Whether Arnold continues to exist depends upon whether he has one continuer or two. Since Lefty and Righty are causally isolated from each other, this implies that the identity over time of a person can be determined by extrinsic factors. Theories that allow for such extrinsicness are sometimes called best-candidate theories of personal identity. According to these theories, B at t_2 is the same person as A at t_1 if and only if there is no better or equally good candidate at t_2 for identity with A at t_1. If there are two equally good candidates, neither is A.

Are such theories, and hence response (5), acceptable? Some philosophers have thought not, but for bad reasons. It has been thought that best-candidate theories violate the widely accepted thesis that identity sentences are, if true, necessarily true and, if false, necessarily false. Is not the upshot of response (5) precisely that Arnold is not Lefty, but that had Righty not existed (had the surgeon accidently dropped the right hemisphere, for example), Arnold would have been Lefty? Here we have to be careful. The widely accepted thesis is that identity sentences containing only rigid singular terms (that is, terms which do not shift their reference across possible worlds) are, if true, necessarily true and, if false, necessarily false. We can read the term Lefty as rigid or as non-rigid. If it is non-rigid (perhaps abbreviating the definite description 'the person who happens to occupy the left-hand branch'), then it is true that, had Righty not existed, Arnold would have been Lefty. But this result is consistent with the necessity of identity and distinctness. If Lefty is rigid, then the best-candidate theorist, if he is to respect the necessity of identity, must deny that Arnold would have been Lefty if Righty had not existed. If Righty had not existed, Arnold would then have occupied the left-hand branch, but that person (namely, Arnold) is not Lefty. Lefty doesn't exist in the nearest world in which Righty does not exist, though an exact duplicate of Lefty – twin Lefty – exists there.

Best-candidate theories do not violate the necessity of identity. However, they do have consequences that might be thought objectionable. Consider again the world in which Arnold divides into Lefty and Righty. According to the best-candidate theory, Lefty can truly say, 'Thank goodness Righty exists, otherwise I wouldn't have existed'. Given that Lefty and Righty exert no causal influence on each other, such dependency is apt to seem mysterious.

These consequences are not objectionable. They simply illustrate the fact that properties like being occupied by Lefty (where Lefty is understood to be rigid) are extrinsic properties of bodies. That is, whether the left-hand body has the property of being occupied by Lefty, rather than by Twin Lefty, is fixed by an extrinsic factor (namely, the existence or non-existence of Righty). But this is not counter-intuitive. The property being occupied by Lefty is not a causal property of a body. In contrast with properties of shape and weight, and so on, this identity-involving property does not contribute to the causal powers of any body in which it inheres. (The causal powers of the left-hand body are unaffected by whether Lefty or Twin Lefty is the occupant.) It is typical of a non-causal property that its possession by an object may depend upon what happens to other objects which exercise no causal influence on it. For example, the property of being a widow is not a causal property and, unsurprisingly, whether a woman is a widow may depend upon what happens to someone who, at the relevant time, exercises no causal influence on her. Response (5) teaches us that identity-involving properties (like being occupied by Lefty) are also extrinsic. This is not a counter-example, merely a consequence.

The best-candidate theory provides the most satisfying response to the case of fission. It also reveals something important about our concept of personal identity: its structure is that of an extrinsic concept. This result may be surprising, but it is not objectionable. If we combine this result with the central claim of the last section, we arrive at the following modified sufficient condition for personal identity over time: A at t_1 is identical to B at t_2 if A stands to B in the relation of psychological continuity with a cause that is either normal or continuous with the normal cause, and there is no better or equally good candidate at t_2 for identity with A at t_1.

6 Value theory

In this final section, I investigate the implications (if any) of the metaphysics of personal identity for value theory. A contemporary philosopher, Derek Parfit, is the most well-known advocate of such implications: he argues that the most plausible metaphysics of persons yields radical conclusions for ethics and rationality (value theory).

It has, of course, long been acknowledged that there is a link between theories of persons and value theory. For example, a religious person's belief that we are immaterial souls will obviously bear on their view of the morality of abortion and euthanasia. However, in this case, the value of persons is not called into question; what is in question is simply the extension of the concept person. The intent of Parfit's project is far more subversive: it is to undermine the significance we currently attach to personal identity and distinctness. Whether or not it is ultimately successful, it is important to recognize the form or shape of this project.

The central feature of Parfit's value theory is the thesis that personal identity is not, in itself, an important relation. It is various psychological relations which matter, relations which are concomitants of personal identity in the normal case (but not, for example, in the case of fission). According to this theory, it would be irrational of me strongly to prefer my own continued existence to death by fission.

I will be concerned with arguments for the thesis that personal identity is not what matters. This thesis has two strands. One strand is that personal identity over time is unimportant; the other strand is that personal identity at a time is unimportant. (These are the diachronic and synchronic strands, respectively.) The thesis that the identity of a person over time is unimportant has been taken to undermine the self-interest theory of rationality, and has implications for the tenability of trans-temporal moral notions such as compensation, responsibility and personal commitment. The thesis that the identity and distinctness of persons at a time is unimportant has been thought to lend support to utilitarianism.

The thesis that personal identity over time is unimportant implies that pure self-interested concern is irrational. That is, it is irrational for me to be especially concerned about the fate of some future person just because that person is me. It follows that the self-interest theory of rationality is false. According to this theory, which has dominated so much thinking about rationality (see RATIONALITY, PRACTICAL) there is only one future person that it is supremely rational for me to benefit: the future person identical to me. Since the self-interest theory places immense weight on a relation which has no rational significance, this theory cannot be correct.

Further, if we do not believe that personal identity over time is important, this may change our attitude to punishment, compensation and commitment. Consider a case where there are only weak psychological connections between different stages of the same life. (For example, a one-time criminal may now be completely reformed, with a new and more respectable set of desires and beliefs.) On the present view, the grounds are thereby diminished for holding the later self responsible for the crimes of the earlier self, or for compensating the later self for burdens imposed on the earlier self, or for regarding earlier commitments as binding on the later self. The truth that the earlier person is the later person is too superficial or unimportant to support the opposite view.

The thesis that the identity and distinctness of persons at a time is unimportant has been taken to imply that the fact of the 'separateness of persons' is not 'deep', and that less weight should be assigned to distributive principles. The synchronic thesis thus supports (in part) the utilitarian doctrine that no weight should be assigned to distributive principles: we should simply aim to maximize the net sum of benefits over burdens, whatever their distribution (see UTILITARIANISM).

These are radical claims. They are all underwritten by the thesis that personal identity is not what matters. What are the arguments for this thesis? I shall discuss one argument for the diachronic thesis (the argument from fission), and one argument for the synchronic thesis (the argument from reductionism).

Recall our earlier discussion of fission. I argued that the most plausible description of fission is that the pre-fission person is numerically distinct from the post-fission offshoots. This constitutes the first premise of the argument from fission (which I will present in the first person): (1) I am not identical to either of my fission products. The second premise is this: (2) fission is not as bad as ordinary death. This premise is taken to imply a third: (3) my relation to my offshoots contains what matters. The first and third premises jointly imply that personal identity is not what matters.

This is an interesting argument, which has had many adherents in recent years. But there is a problem with it. The problem concerns the move from the second to the third premise. The second premise is certainly true: the prospect of fission is not as bad as that of ordinary death. What grounds this premise, and what exhausts its true content, is simply that presented with a choice between those two options, virtually everyone would choose fission. Such a choice is both explicable and reasonable: after fission, unlike after ordinary death, there will be people who can complete many of my projects, look after my family, and so on. However, if the third premise is grounded in the second, the claim that my relation to my offshoots contains what matters merely reflects the innocuous truth that fission is preferable to ordinary death. This robs the argument of any radical import. Its conclusion does nothing to undermine the rationality of self-interest, or the rationality of strongly preferring continued existence to both fission and ordinary death. (This argument is not improved if it is merely asserted that fission is just as good as ordinary survival. What is the argument for this claim?)

What of the argument from reductionism? Reductionism is the view that a description of reality which refers to bodies and experiences, but omits reference to persons, can be complete. It would leave nothing out (see PERSONS §3). The argument from reductionism attempts to show that, if reductionism is true, the fact of the separateness of persons (the fact that you and I are distinct persons, for example) is not deep or significant, and hence less weight should be assigned to distributive principles.

The argument can be presented as follows. Suppose that reductionism is true: reality can be completely described without reference to persons. If such a complete and impersonal description is possible, how can the boundaries between persons be important? Failing an answer to this question, the argument from reductionism concludes that the boundaries between persons are not morally significant.

The validity of this argument turns on the truth of the general principle that if reality can be completely described without referring to Fs, then the boundaries between Fs cannot be of any importance. Both the interpretation and plausibility of this principle are unclear. A more definite worry is that reasons may be presented for dissatisfaction with the argument's premise, reductionism about persons. (In particular: can our mental life really be completely described in impersonal or identity-neutral terms?) Unless those objections can be met, we should reject the argument from reductionism.

The central arguments for the thesis that identity is not what matters are both open to dispute. The failure of these arguments emphasizes how difficult it is to undermine the importance I attach to the fact that such-and-such a person tomorrow is me, and to the fact that you are not me. Unless other arguments are forthcoming, we can continue reasonably to believe that personal identity is important, and to endorse the traditional views in ethics and rationality which that belief supports.

See also: ALTERITY AND IDENTITY, POSTMODERN THEORIES OF; CONSCIOUSNESS §1; MORALITY AND IDENTITY; REINCARNATION §§4–6; SUBJECT, POSTMODERN CRITIQUE OF

References and further reading

* Descartes, R. (1641) *Meditations*, trans. E.S. Haldane and G.R.T. Ross, Cambridge: Cambridge University Press, 1969. (Famous argument for the distinctness of mind and body, and for the immateriality of the soul.)

Garrett, B.J. (1990) 'Personal Identity and Extrinsicness', *Philosophical Studies* 59: 177–94.

—— (1992) 'Persons and Values', *Philosophical Quarterly* 42: 337–45. (These articles expand on the material in §§2 and 3.)

Hume, D. (1739) *A Treatise of Human Nature*, ed. L.A. Selby-Bigge, Oxford: Clarendon Press, 1978, 251–63. (Classic statement of a sceptical position about the unity of personal identity.)

Lewis, D. (1976) 'Survival and Identity', in A.O. Rorty (ed.) *The Identities of Persons*, Los Angeles: University of California Press. (Lewis defends the multiple occupancy thesis criticized in §3.)

* Locke, J. (1690) *An Essay Concerning Human Understanding*, ed. J. Yolton, London: Dent, 1961, bk II ch. xxvii. (A subtle discussion of persons, thinking substances, and consciousness. Locke is a defender of a memory version of the Psychological Criterion of personal identity (see §1).)

Noonan, H. (1989) *Personal Identity*, London: Routledge & Kegan Paul. (First-rate historical and contemporary survey.)

Nozick, R. (1981) *Philosophical Explanations*, Cambridge, MA: Harvard University Press, ch. 2. (Exciting discussion of the 'best-candidate' theory.)

* Parfit, D. (1984) *Reasons and Persons*, Oxford: Oxford University Press, Part 3. (An excellent introduction to many of the themes of this entry.)

* Shoemaker, S. (1963) *Self-Knowledge and Self-Identity*, Ithaca, NY: Cornell University Press. (Influential discussion of issues concerning criteria of personal identity over time.)

Unger, P. (1992) *Persons, Consciousness and Value*, New York: Oxford University Press. (Thorough and imaginative contemporary discussion. Defence of the physical criterion of personal identity.)

Wiggins, D. (1980) *Sameness and Substance*, Oxford: Blackwell, ch. 6. (Contains doubts about the possibility of the fission of persons.)

* Williams, B. (1973) 'The Self and the Future', in Williams, B. (ed.) *Problems of the Self*, Cambridge: Cambridge University Press. (Discussion of one famous thought experiment which seems to support the psychological criterion when described in one way, and to support the physical criterion when described in another way.)

BRIAN GARRETT

PERSONALISM

Personalism is the thesis that only persons (self-conscious agents) and their states and characteristics exist, and that reality consists of a society of interacting persons. Typically, a personalist will hold that finite persons depend for their existence and continuance on God, who is the Supreme Person, having intelligence and volition. Personalists are usually idealists in metaphysics and construct their theories of knowledge by inference from the data of self-awareness. They tend to be nonutilitarian in ethics and to place ultimate value in the person as a free, self-conscious, moral agent, rather than in either mental states or in apersonal states of affairs. Typically, holding that a good God will not allow what has intrinsic value to lose existence, they believe in personal survival of death.

The term 'personalism', even as a term for philosophical systems, has myriad uses. There is said to be, for example, atheistic personalism (as in the case of McTaggart, famous for embracing both atheism and the immortality of the soul), absolute idealistic personalism (Hegel, Royce, Calkins), and theistic personalism (Bowne, Brightman, Bertocci). Leibniz and Berkeley are seen as early personalists; both were theists and idealists. Kant, while not strictly a personalist, was influential in personalism's history. In particular, B.P. Bowne (1847–1910) borrowed freely from Kant, while refusing to accept a Kantian transcendentalism in which our basic concepts or categories apply in a knowledge-giving way only to appearances and not to reality. R.H. Lotze made personality and value central to his worldview, and was a European precursor of American personalism.

1   Criteria for personalism
2   The personalist worldview
3   Idealism and theism
4   Howison and Brightman

1   Criteria for personalism

Some negative criteria may be helpful. Presumably one is ruled out as a serious candidate for being a personalist if one supposes that persons are made up out of some more ultimate constituents on which they depend, or if one supposes that something else has as great value as or greater value than self-conscious agents, or if one supposes that there is neither a Supreme Person nor any other person who exists independently of nonpersons. Presumably, again, a personalist does not think that persons have proper parts – that persons can themselves be components of other persons. To put things positively, for the personalist, persons are simple (noncomposite), of

an intrinsic worth not equalled by nonpersons, and at least one of their number is ontologically ultimate.

Kant, Berkeley, Lotze and Bergson were major philosophical influences on Borden Parker BOWNE (1847–1910), the principal founder of an American school of philosophy standardly called 'personalism'. This is the central sense of the term, at least in so far as it is applied to American philosophy. Bowne's philosophy is idealistic, theistic and (of course) personalistic. He finds in human self-consciousness, and especially religious and moral experience, clues to the nature of things. In his view, beginning with direct awareness is not only the safest, but the only proper method in epistemology and the only route to a correct metaphysic. Persons are self-conscious agents. In the self-awareness of persons lies the basis of knowledge and the proximate source of continuity through change, a personal God being the ultimate source of all finite being:

> Now when we consider our life at all critically, we come upon two facts. First, we have thoughts and feelings and volitions which are inalienably our own. We also have a measure of self-control, or the power of self-direction. Here, then, we find in our experience a certain selfhood and a relative independence. This fact constitutes our personality. The second fact is that we cannot regard ourselves as self-sufficient and independent in any absolute sense. And a further fact is that we cannot interpret our life without admitting both of these facts.
>
> (Bowne 1908: 280–1)

2   The personalist worldview

Personalism, beginning with these facts, develops a worldview that begins with immediate, self-conscious experience and interprets not only the life of the individual but the world at large in personalistic terms. This involves the claim that the basic categories or fundamental concepts of our thought should be understood in terms applicable to persons and their experiences.

The notions of substance, unity, identity and change find their home in personal unity and identity. Each person, aware of themselves as having fleeting experiences and as existing throughout those experiences, is acquainted with a self-conscious intelligence that experiences change and hence endures. What unifies our experiences at any time is that all are states belonging to a single mind, and what provides experiential continuity over time is that mind's continued existence as a subject of experience. Our self-awareness, then, gives us knowledge of our status as mental substances or selves; memory plus self-awareness grants us knowledge of our own identity and continuity.

The notions of contingency, dependence and freedom receive similar treatment. Each person is aware of thinking and acting, affecting their environment and guiding much of the course of their thought and conduct; they are also aware of things that intrude themselves on their attention, impede their will, and externally aid or thwart their wellbeing. Thus there is consciousness both of a degree of independence, in which one somewhat transcends one's environment, and a degree of dependence, in which one's life and wellbeing are dependent on what one encounters. We are aware of being able to act freely within a large but not unlimited framework. This experiential complexity is an accurate clue to our existence as distinct but dependent creatures, individuals who are finite responsible agents.

The category of causality also receives personalistic analysis in connection with Bowne's idealism. This view, in part inherited from BERKELEY (§§3, 6–8), consists in holding that there are no mind-independent extended things; what ordinary perception consists in, and what science's laws range over, is human experiences with perceptual contents. There are then, in Bowne's view, no physical objects, only perceptual experiences, and science does not require the existence of mind-independent things. In addition, our perceptual experiences succeed one another, but nothing in our awareness of them informs us that a preceding perceptual experience brings about or produces its successor; causality, in so far as perception reveals it or science discusses it, is but a matter of sequential regularities. Science records perceptual regularities but does not recount genuine causal connections.

None of this is intended to dismiss science or to deny its achievements. Bowne here echoes Berkeley's view that, in effect, while it is clear that the laws of physics are true, it is not at all clear that what they are true of is mind-independent. The equations of basic physics presumably are correct; what they range over is not a matter for science to decide. Direct awareness, however, does decide it, and what they are true of is perceptual experiences. Whatever the merits of this view of science, it was neither Berkeley's nor Bowne's intention to reject scientific data. Bowne was quite content to accept evolutionary theory, and viewed it (in an idealist version) as telling us much about the process by which God brought about finite persons in an environment suitable for moral growth and religious awareness.

None the less, the fact that science is possible is, suggests Bowne, highly significant. It is not logically impossible that our experiences should be random

and our attempts to make sense of our perceptual environment – to predict, understand, explore and exploit it – regularly fail. That our perceptual environment is composed of experiences with perceptual contents rather than extended mind-independent objects in no way precludes this unfortunate scenario as a live option; the perceptual world might have been simply incoherent. Since we do not produce our perceptual experiences, we do not cause their orderliness.

The concepts of space and time also receive personalistic treatment. If all there is to what we refer to as extended physical objects is the contents of our perceptual experiences, then we have no reasons to suppose that space itself has mind-independent existence. Space is nothing beyond relationships between human experiences with perceptual content. Since the mind itself is not identical to its perceptual experiences or reducible to the contents of those experiences, minds are not in space.

More surprising, perhaps, is Bowne's contention that the mind itself is not in time. Time, too, he claims, is but a relationship between human experiences (perceptual or not), and since the mind is what *has* experiences, it is not included in relationships that hold only among its experiences. Hence it is not in time. (Presumably Kant's views particularly influenced Bowne here.)

3 Idealism and theism

In the case of each of the basic concepts discussed above, Bowne contends, we find no reason to suppose that their role in knowledge resides in ranging over things that are neither minds nor mind-dependent. Neither do we find reason to think that what they apply to in knowledge-giving ways is something less or other than what is actually there to be known.

The possibility of science, Bowne holds, requires explanation. So does our existence as enduring individuals. Further, our existence, not only as selves, but as agents who partially transcend their environments also requires explanation.

Bowne contends that the only causation we experience is the exercise of our own powers as agents; here, he holds, we are aware of something being brought about or produced by something else, not merely of one kind of thing temporally following some thing of another kind in a way typical of members of those kinds. Since we have experiences that we did not cause that reflect opinions we do not hold, values we do not accept, or plans we did not make, and since we generally represent others as aiding or opposing us, and agreeing or disagreeing with us, it is most reasonable to ascribe these to minds like ourselves. The idealist's ground for believing in minds other than one's own is that experiences one has but did not cause are to be explained by one's mind being affected by another mind – mental telepathy (or its close cousin).

Further, if we stick to what our experience suggests, then we will explain the existence of mental substances which enjoy continuity of existence and regularity in sense perception by a mind whose effects these things are – a God who has created us as real but limited agents. In this way, among others, Bowne's idealism and his monotheism mesh. Berkeley had suggested that those perceptual contents that we refer to as providing our natural environment are best viewed on the analogy of a divine language – as experiences that God causes and which manifest a constant structure that renders our experience manageable, that is, as a case of sustained benevolent mental telepathy (or its close cousin). Bowne follows Berkeley's example.

Similarly, we will explain the existence of finite minds by the creative action of an infinite mind whose existence does not itself need explanation, and as we find that our actions, in so far as they are rational, stem from our purposes, we may take it that this mind intended to produce creatures such as ourselves. Thus we are led to believe in a personal God possessed of intelligence and will and (since it is good that persons be created) moral goodness. Theism provides a single explanation that traces each of these facts to the same source. Of course, it is logically possible that these inferences may have led us to false conclusions, but they are eminently reasonable inferences – more so than any competitors; and we have no good reason to think the conclusions in question to be false.

Since, Bowne argues, no mind is or can be a part of any other mind – necessarily each is distinct from every other – the notion of a single cosmic mind of which each finite mind is a piece or a partial manifestation is incoherent. Further, our independence, limited though real, argues against any such view, as do the facts that we have false beliefs and perform wrong actions. So we may dismiss any notion of a 'world mind' of which we are modes.

Similarly, since we plainly are aware of our own existence and experiences, we may dismiss any suggestion that our self-awareness is somehow illusory; for that matter, illusions too require self-conscious subjects. Hence we may also dismiss any notion of there being a qualityless reality underlying the one we experience, and the view that what exists is utterly unlike what we experience.

At this point, personalism's metaphysics links up with its ethics. Persons as self-conscious agents possessed of freedom have inherent worth; they themselves – not certain of their more pleasant or more contemplative states – are the locus of ultimate value. Since there is a morally good God who will not allow intrinsic personal worth to be destroyed, there is individual immortality.

4 Howison and Brightman

George Holmes Howison (1834–1916) was another American personalist. A philosopher and mathematician, he graduated from Marietta College (Ohio) and taught mathematics at Washington University (St Louis), where he joined the St Louis Philosophical Society. He also taught philosophy at the Massachusetts Institute of Technology, Harvard Divinity School, and the Concord School of Philosophy, moving in 1884 to the University of California to organize a philosophy department there.

In sharp contrast to Bowne, Howison thought that a person who depended for existence on God could not be a free moral agent. Hence he posited self-determining persons, each of whom seeks in their own way to fulfil themselves as an individual. Persons are not created and have no beginning to their existence. In so far as one seeks fulfilment properly, one does so in ways that do not infringe on others doing likewise. God, on his account, serves as an example of the moral ideal – a sort of Aristotelian final cause rather than an efficient cause, a standard of perfection but not a creator. Howison views evolution not as having produced a society of interacting minds each seeking fulfilment, but as the product of that seeking.

Bowne's successor at Boston University was another personalist, Edgar Sheffield Brightman (1884–1953). A student of Bowne's, he taught at Nebraska Wesleyan University (1912–15), Wesleyan University (1915–1919), and in 1919 at Boston University, where in 1925 he became the first Borden Parker Bowne Professor of Philosophy. Perhaps his best-known suggestion is that the divine nature contains a 'given' which God's will neither created nor approves. This, Brightman held, is the primary source of evil. God is constantly gaining control over the given, and thus growing as a person, but complete victory is not in sight. While distinctive, this perspective is typical of neither monotheism nor personalism. Bowne's own approach to evil appealed to human freedom and the conditions under which the growth of finite minds to moral maturity is possible.

Personalism as a school has not achieved the fame or influence of pragmatism (another American philosophical perspective). It is most accurately seen as a type of theistic idealism that does not purport to offer a new philosophical perspective. In its articulation by

Bowne, and later Brightman and Bertocci (Brightman's successor at Boston), its philosophical perspective is at least as clear and cogent as its contemporary competitors.

See also: IDEALISM

References and further reading

Bertocci, P. (1952) *An Introduction to the Philosophy of Religion*, New York: Prentice Hall. (An introductory study by Brightman's successor that focuses on the teleological argument.)

—— (1970) *The Person God Is*, London: Allen & Unwin. (A defence of monotheism.)

* Bowne, B.P. (1908) *Personalism*, Boston, MA: Houghton Mifflin. (A popular presentation of the personalist viewpoint, based on the N.W. Harris Lectures of 1907 at Northwestern University; see the entry on Bowne for a list of his works.)

Brightman, E.S. (1940) *A Philosophy of Religion*, New York: Prentice Hall. (An introductory discussion by Bowne's successor of most of the issues in philosophy of religion.)

Cunningham, G.W. (1953) *The Idealistic Argument in Recent British and American Philosophy*, Century; Westport, CT: Greenwood Press, 1969. (Discusses a century of Anglo-American idealist thought (1808–1910) in expository and critical terms; includes a chapter on Bowne.)

Deats, P. and Robb, C. (eds) (1986) *The Boston Personalist Tradition in Philosophy, Social Ethics, and Theology*, Macon, GA: Mercer University Press. (Discussion of personalism's roots, trunk and branches by thinkers associated with the tradition.)

Flewelling, R.T. (1915) *Personalism and the Problems of Philosophy*, New York: Methodist Book Concern. (A sympathetic discussion of personalism that concentrates on Bowne's position, which it sets in philosophical context.)

Howison, G.H. (1934) *George Holmes Howison, Philosopher and Teacher*, ed. J.W. Buckingham and G.W. Stratton, Berkeley, CA: University of California Press. (Collection of Howison's works.)

KEITH E. YANDELL

PERSONS

We are all persons. But what are persons? This question is central to philosophy and virtually every major philosopher has offered an answer to it. For two thousand years many philosophers in the Western tradition believed that we were immaterial souls or Egos, only contingently attached to our bodies. The most well-known advocates of this view were Plato and Descartes. Few philosophers accept this view now, largely because it is thought to face a number of intractable metaphysical and epistemological problems (for example: how can an immaterial soul or mind interact with the material world? How can I know that you have a soul?). The recoil from Cartesianism has been in three different directions. One direction (the animalist) emphasizes the fact that persons are human beings, evolved animals of a certain sort. A second direction (the reductionist) is represented by David Hume: the self or person is not a Cartesian entity, it is a 'bundle of perceptions'. Finally, there is a theory of persons influenced by the views of John Locke, according to which persons are neither essentially animals nor reducible to their bodies or experiences.

1   **What is a person?**
2   **Persons and human beings**
3   **Reductionism**

1   What is a person?

We can all tell persons apart from other kinds of thing, such as kangaroos, mountain ranges and billiard tables. We are also very good at re-identifying the same person at different times. These are cognitive skills we all possess and exercise effortlessly all the time. So we all know that Madonna is a person but the Empire State Building is not, and the 1990 Governor of Arkansas is the same person as the 1997 US President. But can we say anything at a general or abstract level about the grounds of these uncontroversial truths?

Whatever else might be required to be a person, it seems clear that a person is a mental being. A person is the type of entity that possesses a mind. (The mind does not have always to be conscious: a sleeping or comatose person is still a person.) We can be more specific. Not just any mental being is a person. My cat is a mental being – it can feel pain or hunger, for example – yet it is not a person. So a person is (at least) a being that possesses a particular sort of mind. A person does not just have sensations of pain and pleasure, but also intentional, world-directed, mental states like belief, desire, fear and hope.

Indeed, persons possess a range of particularly sophisticated mental states, including self-reflective mental states. I am capable of having not just the belief that it is raining but also beliefs about myself. These are not just beliefs about someone who happens to be me (as when I think 'the person born on such-and-such a day is Scottish', referring to myself but forgetting that *I* am that person). They are fully self-conscious beliefs about myself, the sort of beliefs I have when I say 'I remember that it snowed last Christmas' or 'I intend to holiday in Fiji when this term is over'. Persons are self-conscious mental beings. This observation is confirmed when we reflect on how much of what matters in our mental life and social interactions presupposes the self-consciousness of ourselves and others.

This view of persons was expounded clearly by John Locke in the seventeenth century (see LOCKE, J. §8). Locke wrote that a person is 'a thinking, intelligent being, that has reason and reflection, and can consider itself as itself, the same thinking thing, in different times and places' (1689, 2 (27): 9). In this definition, Locke specifies some of the elements that comprise our concept of self-consciousness. In particular, he cites thinking, intelligence, reason, reflection and the ability to engage in tensed first-person judgements. These features he holds to be constitutive of our concept of a person. We now have the more abstract and general account we were seeking of why Madonna is a person and the Empire State Building is not. In addition, we also have a more abstract and general account of the grounds for our ordinary judgements of personal identity over time. On this view, the reason why the 1990 Governor of Arkansas is the same person as the 1997 US President is because a single stream of consciousness (continuity of character, beliefs intentions and so on) uniquely links the 1990 Governor with the 1997 President (see PERSONAL IDENTITY §1).

An important feature of Locke's account is that his definition of a person in no way presupposes the answer to a more traditional question: namely, to what ontological category do persons belong? That is, are persons immaterial (non-spatial) souls only contingently attached to their bodies (as Plato and Descartes believed)? Are persons wholly material beings? If so, are persons necessarily animals of a certain sort, or might there be robot persons? On Locke's view, these questions cannot be answered simply by examination of our concept of a person. Reflection on what it is to be a person cannot alone decide the question of whether we are immaterial souls, animals or bionic beings. In order to decide that question we need to investigate ourselves empirically, albeit in a fairly undemanding way. On the strongest version of Locke's view, not only is it not true a priori that all persons are animals, it is not necessary either. If all persons are human beings, this is just a contingent truth.

2 Persons and human beings

We must be clear about what is and what is not controversial in Locke's view. It is not controversial that the features Locke cited (reason, reflection and so on) are central to our concept of a person. What has seemed controversial to some is the stronger claim that truths about the ontological status of persons (for example, that all persons are animals) are contingent. This stronger claim is denied by animalists. They hold that all persons *must* be animals. They do not hold that all persons have to be human beings – chimpanzees and dolphins, for example, could qualify as persons if their behaviour revealed a suitably impressive mental life.

This move away from the Lockean position is apt to seem unpersuasive. To start with, animalists can hardly be presenting their definition as an a priori conceptual truth. People who believe in the actual existence of non-animal persons (God, angels, souls and so on), or people who believe in the possibility of robot persons, do not appear to be committing any conceptual error. Further, the truth that I am a human being (or, more generally, an animal) seems resolutely a posteriori. Animalists must therefore conceive of their definition as a necessary a posteriori truth. And its source must lie in the further supposed truth that animality is a necessary a posteriori constraint on possession of the mental life which is characteristic of persons. But what reason do we have to believe this? As far as I can see, we have none.

More tellingly, the most plausible description of certain thought experiments counts against the animalist position. I can make perfectly good sense of the possibility that I might gradually become an entirely bionic being. My various bodily and brain parts may gradually be replaced by functionally identical bionic parts. Provided that the changes preserve my continuing mental life, abilities and appearance, we would have little hesitation in saying that I survived a process of total replacement. Yet, at the end of the process, I am not an animal of any sort. Consequently, it cannot be true that all persons must be animals. Hence, we have good reason to think that the truth that all persons are animals is merely contingent. In addition, we also have good reason to think that the relation between a person and the human being they share their matter with is not that of numerical identity. If I can survive the destruction of the human being with whom I am presently spatially coincident, I cannot be identical to that human being. The Lockean view has been vindicated.

3 Reductionism

The issue of reductionism is perhaps the most complex topic that any theory of persons must address. In order to assess reductionism, we must be clear about what the position involves, what reasons there are to believe in it, and what arguments there are against it. Reductionism is an ontological view of persons. We can begin to understand the view by contrasting it with two different ontological views of persons. One view is Cartesian: persons are immaterial substances which are only contingently linked to their bodies (see DESCARTES, R. §8; DUALISM). The other view, which we might call the Intermediate view, holds that persons are psychophysical substances, which are necessarily embodied. This is a version of the Lockean view defended in the previous section.

Unlike defenders of the latter views, the reductionist holds that the ontological status of persons is secondary or derivative. The primary elements of our ontology are mental states (pains, 'thinkings', 'rememberings' and so on) and physical bodies. Reductionism has received expression in a number of ways. The most common is that a person is nothing 'over and above' their body and mental life. Alternatively, facts about persons and personal identity are 'verbal'. It is a verbal issue whether we choose to call two people at different times 'the same person', just as it is a verbal decision whether to call seasickness 'pain'. However, these suggestions are rather vague, and need to be sharpened. The key thought is that we can completely describe all mental and physical events impersonally, without reference to persons. The experiences that make up a person's life, on this view, are not essentially events in the life of a person, any more than the bricks that make up a house are essentially parts of a house.

Thus understood, why should we believe in reductionism about persons? One reason is that reductionism has been thought to be the only serious alternative to Cartesianism. But as we have seen, this overlooks the possibility of the Intermediate view. It is worth emphasizing that there is no instability in the Intermediate view. This view implies that no reductive account of persons is available. This would be problematic only if all genuine concepts and relations must admit of reductive analyses. That condition is simply a dogma.

It might be thought that another reason favouring reductionism is Hume's famous remark about the unencounterability of the subject in introspective experience. Hume wrote that 'when I enter most intimately into what I call *myself*, I always stumble on some particular perception or other, of heat or cold, light or shade, love or hatred, pain or pleasure. I never

catch myself at any time without a perception, and never can observe anything but the perception' (Hume 1739 (1976): 252). However, Hume's failure to encounter himself in experience is a fact about the phenomenology of inner reflection. It does not imply that the self does not exist or that we can completely describe all mental life without reference to persons.

Reductionism thus lacks any compelling motivation. In addition, the view faces a number of difficulties. First, reductionists have a problem explaining why we find it so hard to make anything of the idea of an unowned or subjectless experience. A particular toothache, for example, has to be *had* by someone. Experiences require subjects. But there is a deeper problem for the reductionist. The mental life of a human being does not, of course, simply consist in experiences of pleasure and pain. The mental life of a normal human includes mental states with complex contents, for example, intending to visit grandmother next month, or remembering how Alice Springs looked at dawn last year. The contents of these mental states appear to presuppose personal identity. I can only be said to remember, from the inside, *my own* experiences; I can intend only that *I* do such-and-such. But in that case there seems to be no prospect of a complete and impersonal description of these mental states – personal identity is built into them.

The standard manoeuvre in the face of this objection is to invoke the concept of, for example, quasi-memory. This concept is stipulated to be like ordinary memory in all relevant respects, except that quasi-memory does not presuppose personal identity. I can quasi-remember, from the inside, someone else's experiences. For example, as the result of a brain-graft, I may come to have a quasi-memory of standing in front of the Taj Mahal (even though I know that I have never been to India). Since quasi-memory does not presuppose personal identity, the reductionist can re-describe the psychological life of a person without using terms, such as memory and intention, which presuppose personal identity.

The crucial question is whether the notion of quasi-memory can serve the reductionist's purposes. Is the concept of quasi-memory intelligible independently of the concept of memory? Is the content of a quasi-memory really identity-neutral? Quasi-memories are *illusions* of memory; so the content of a quasi-memory is not identity-neutral, it is merely illusory in respect of its identity-involving content. This parallels what we are inclined to say about the contents of perceptual illusions. Consequently, despite its ingenuity, the retreat to quasi-memory cannot stave off a fundamental objection to reductionism (McDowell 1993: §6). These objections to reductionism, only gestured at here, are powerful. The onus is upon the reductionist to reply to them.

See also: MIND, BUNDLE THEORY OF; REDUCTIONISM IN THE PHILOSOPHY OF MIND

References and further reading

Cassam, Q. (1992) 'Reductionism and First-Person Thinking', in D. Charles and K. Lennon (eds) *Reduction, Explanation, and Realism*, Oxford: Clarendon Press. (Another useful critique of reductionism.)

—— (1993) 'Parfit on Persons', *Proceedings of the Aristotelian Society* 1993 (1): 17–37. (Useful critique of reductionism.)

Evans, G. (1982) *The Varieties of Reference*, Oxford: Oxford University Press. (Groundwork for the discussion in Section 6 of McDowell. 6.6 and 7.5 are especially relevant.)

Garrett, B.J. (1990) 'Persons and Human Beings', *Logos* 11: 47–56. (More detailed discussion of the issues raised in §2 and §3 above.)

—— (1991) 'Personal Identity and Reductionism', *Philosophy and Phenomenological Research* 51 (2): 361–73. (As with the 1990 article, a more detailed examination of the issues discussed in §2 and §3.)

* Hume, D. (1739) *A Treatise of Human Nature*, ed. L.A. Selby-Bigge, Oxford: Clarendon Press, 1978. (Classic statement of the 'bundle theory' of the self outlined above in §3.)

* Locke, J. (1689) *An Essay Concerning Human Understanding*, ed. J. Yolton, London: Dent, 1961. (A subtle discussion of persons, thinking substances, and consciousness. Book II, chapter 27 contains the relevant passages, as cited in §1 above.)

* McDowell, J.H. (1993) 'Reductionism and the First Person', in J. Dancy (ed.) *Reading Parfit*, Oxford: Blackwell. (A sophisticated attack on reductionism.)

BRIAN GARRETT

PERSONS, RESPECT FOR

see RESPECT FOR PERSONS

PETER OF AILLY *see* AILLY, PIERRE D'

PETER OF AUVERGNE (d. 1304)

Peter of Auvergne, a thirteenth-century Parisian master, wrote extensively on logic, natural philosophy and theology. His thought progresses from modism in logic to an independent synthesis of Aristotelian philosophy along the lines begun by Thomas Aquinas, culminating in a theology reconciling the ideas of his teachers Henry of Ghent and Godfrey of Fontaines. His reputation has been based largely on his association with Aquinas, but recent investigations have shown the independence of his thought.

Peter of Auvergne was a secular master at the University of Paris in the thirteenth century. He was born at Crocq (Crocy) in south-central France, appointed rector of the university on 7 March 1275, awarded the bishopric of Clermont on 21 January 1302, and died 25 September 1304.

Peter's many works allow us to witness his intellectual development. He is credited with writing commentaries on all of Aristotle's works, but some of these have been lost and some surviving works are of doubtful attribution. His earliest commentaries, on the *logica vetus* (old logic), are typical of modistic logic, characterized by a confidence that grammatical analysis can reveal a link between reality, signification and understanding (see LANGUAGE, MEDIEVAL THEORIES OF; LOGIC, MEDIEVAL). His early commentaries are influenced also by the recent assimilation of the *Posterior Analytics*, which motivated the attempt to establish an Aristotelian science based upon universal and necessary propositions. Peter was an early practitioner of the question–commentary in the Faculty of Arts at Paris, although he combines older traditions of textual analysis with his promotion of the modistic programme. The *Posterior Analytics* commentary attributed to him shows a considerable degree of complexity, as do the undoubtedly authentic *Sophismata*. Peter's logical works influenced Simon of Faversham, Durandus of Auvergne and Radulphus BRITO.

As a young Master of Arts at Paris, Peter was appointed rector of the university to help settle the conflict between the followers of SIGER OF BRABANT and those of Alberic of Rheims, which indicates his conciliatory personality as well as his considerable reputation among his contemporaries. His fame was sufficiently great to motivate the false attribution to him of works by Albert the Great, Thomas Aquinas, an anonymous imitator (the Anonymus Matritensis) and, following the condemnation at Oxford in 1270, works by Siger of Brabant.

However, Peter's greatest fame comes from his association with Thomas AQUINAS. The extent of their personal contact is not known, but Peter was one of the earliest influenced by Aquinas' natural philosophy and theology and, most importantly, he completed Aquinas' unfinished commentary on Aristotle's *On the Heavens*. His work was also adapted to complete Aquinas on the *Meteora* and the *Politics*. Five other works of his have been printed among the works of Aquinas. Nonetheless, much modern scholarship has been devoted to showing that Peter frequently disagreed with Aquinas.

Many commentaries on natural philosophy belong to Peter's next stage of development and, if all are authentic, Peter mastered the works of Aristotle to an extent unparalleled since Albert the Great. These works, like medieval commentaries on the *Parva naturalia* in general, have not yet attracted much investigation. The commentary on the *Physics* once attributed to Siger of Brabant, now plausibly attributed to Peter by William Dunphy (1953), belongs to this period; it addresses incipiently many themes of Peter's later *Quodlibets* (see NATURAL PHILOSOPHY, MEDIEVAL).

Peter's commentary on the *Metaphysics* shows an author concerned not merely with understanding Aristotle's text, but also with formulating an Aristotelian metaphysics which accommodates theology as well as explaining the world. Because several Peters from Auvergne flourished at the same period, doubts have been raised about whether the author of the *Metaphysics* commentary is the same as the logician of the 1270s and the theologian of the *Quodlibets*, but scholars now generally accept the single attribution. It may be noted that both the commentaries on the *Metaphysics* and on Porphyry's *Isagōgē* attributed to Peter use the unusual expression 'determination of matter' (*signatio materiae*) in discussing individuation; and *Metaphysics* V q. 32 argues in exactly the same way as does the commentary on the *Categories* q. 50, that identity is a purely mind-dependent relation.

Peter's commentary on the *Ethics* is typical of its milieu; it often follows Aquinas, although in question–commentary form. His writings on the *Politics* (a question–commentary and a literal commentary adapted to complete Aquinas' commentary) influenced later writers, particularly his views that a virtuous multitude has a right to rule and that laws should serve the many rather than the elite few.

Peter came late to theology, not becoming a master of theology until the end of the 1290s. His theology has been seen as part of a continuing evolution away from the ideas of Thomas Aquinas, because of the influence of his teachers HENRY OF GHENT and GODFREY OF FONTAINES; Peter occasionally refuses to take sides in conflicts between the ideas of these two masters. Peter holds that theology is a separate science; he accepts Godfrey's criticism of the view of that theology is a science subalternate to the science of happiness. As a theologian, Peter revises his theory of individuation, accepting Godfrey's view that form is the principle of individuation. Following the impetus of Bishop Tempier's condemnation of 1277, which criticized limitations of God, Peter emphasizes the distinction between God's absolute power and God's ordained power, and insists that God in his absolute power can do anything which does not involve a contradiction; but he holds that the creation of an actual infinity of things involves such a contradiction. Peter defends moderate Aristotelian positions against threats posed by the ideas of Averroes (see IBN RUSHD), such as divine ignorance of particular things or an eternal world, although Peter (like Aquinas) accepts the possibility of an eternal world with its concomitant infinity of souls (see AVERROISM). At times Peter subscribes to Neoplatonism, in particular the positing of an emanation from the First Cause and a hierarchy of being (see PLATONISM, MEDIEVAL).

Only a few questions from Peter's commentary on the *Sentences* seem to have survived. Polemical comments in the *Sentences* commentary by John Quidort (see JOHN OF PARIS) suggest that Peter held that immaterial beings (such as God and angels) produce effects directly by the intellect, rather than via the will, and that many powers of the soul result from divine illumination (Muller 1961).

Peter of Auvergne's long career shows us a thirteenth-century Parisian master of more than ordinary productivity and influence. In outline, his thought progresses from modism in logic to an independent Aristotelian synthesis along the lines begun by Aquinas, culminating in a theology reconciling the ideas of his famous teachers. However, our complete assessment of his contribution is still clouded by uncertain attributions and unedited texts.

See also: AQUINAS, T.; ARISTOTELIANISM, MEDIEVAL; LOGIC, MEDIEVAL

List of works

Peter of Auvergne (c. 1270s) *Sophismata*. (Sophisma III is edited and discussed in S. Ebbesen (1988) 'Concrete Accidental Terms: Late 13th Century Debates about Problems Relating to Such Terms as "album"', in N. Kretzmann (ed.) *Meaning and Inference in Medieval Philosophy: Studies in Memory of Jan Pinborg*, Dordrecht: Reidel.)

—— (c. 1275) *Quaestiones super Praedicamentis* (Questions on the Categories), ed. R. Andrews, 'Petrus de Alvernia: Quaestiones super Praedicamentis. An Edition', *Cahiers de l'institut du moyen-âge grec et latin* 55, 1987: 3–84. (Edition of Peter's questions on Aristotle's *Categories*.)

—— (c. 1275) *Quaestiones super librum Perihermenias* (Questions on *De interpretatione*). (An edition of q. 12 is to be found in S. Ebbesen (1986) 'Termini accidentales concreti: Texts from the Late Thirteenth Century', *Cahiers de l'Institut du Moyen-âge grec et latin* 53: 37–150.)

—— (1277–83) *Quaestiones super librum Ethicorum* (Questions on Aristotle's *Nicomachean Ethics*). (An edition of what survives of this commentary is in A.J. Celano, 'Peter of Auvergne's Questions on Books I and II of the *Ethica Nicomachea*: A Study and Critical Edition', *Mediaeval Studies* 48, 1986: 1–110.)

—— (c. 1280s) *Quaestiones in Metaphysicam* (Questions on the *Metaphysics*). (An edition of ten *quaestiones* appears in A. Monahan, 'Peter of Auvergne's *Quaestiones in Metaphysicam*', in J.R. O'Donnell (ed.) *Nine Mediaeval Thinkers*, Studies and Texts 1, Toronto, Ont.: Pontifical Institute of Mediaeval Studies, 1955. An edition of *Quaestiones* V q. 18 is to be found in S. Ebbesen, '*Termini accidentales concreti: Texts from the Late Thirteenth Century*', *Cahiers de l'institut du moyen-âge grec et latin* 53, 1986: 37–150. An edition of *Quaestiones* XII qq. 6a–d is to be found in W. Dunphy, 'The 'Quinque viae' and Some Parisian Professors of Philosophy', in *St. Thomas Aquinas 1274–1974: Commemorative Studies*, Toronto, Ont.: Pontifical Institute of Mediaeval Studies, 1974, vol. II.)

—— (1296–1300) *Quodlibeta*. (Published editions include Quodlibet I q. 21 (1296) and Quodlibet V qq. 9–10 (1300), G. Cannizzo, 'I 'Quodlibeta' di Pietro d'Auvergne', *Rivista di Filosofia neo-scolastica* 56, 1964–5: 486–500, 605–48, and 57: 67–89; Quodlibet II q. 5 (1297), E. Hocedez, 'Une question inédite de Pierre d'Auvergne sur l'individuation', *Revue néo-scolastique de philosophie* 36, 1934: 335–86.)

—— (before 1304) Quaestiones super librum Posteriorum (Questions on the *Posterior Analytics*), selections edited in S. Ebbesen and J. Pinborg, 'Studies in the Logical Writings Attributed to Boethius de Dacia', 1970, and J. Pinborg, 'A New MS of the Questions on the *Posteriora Analytica* Attributed to Petrus de Alvernia (Clm. 8005) with the Transcription of Some Questions Related to Problems of Meaning', *Cahiers de l'institut du moyen-âge grec et latin* 3, 1973: 1–54; 10: 48–62.

(Edition of questions 23–6 and 31–3, possibly by Peter of Auvergne, of unestablished date.)

—— (before 1304) Quaestiones super librum Physicorum (Questions on the *Physics*). (An edition of Books I–IV of a work formerly attributed to Siger of Brabant but now believed to be Peter of Auvergne's Questions on the *Physics*, can be found in P. Delhaye (ed.) *Siger de Brabant 'Questions sur la Physique d'Aristote'*, Les Philosophes Belges XV, Louvain: Institut superieur de philosophie, 1941.)

References and further reading

* Dunphy, W. (1953) 'The Similarities Between Certain Questions of Peter of Auvergne's *Commentary on the Metaphysics* and the Anonymous *Commentary on the Physics* Attributed to Siger of Brabant', *Mediaeval Studies* 15: 159–68. (Parallel passages suggest that the *Physics* commentary may be by Peter of Auvergne.)

Hocedez, E. (1930) 'La théologie de Pierre d'Auvergne' (The Theology of Peter of Auvergne), *Gregorianum* 11: 526–55. (Analysis of the theological material of the *Quodlibets*.)

—— (1933) 'La vie et les oeuvres de Pierre d'Auvergne' (The Life and Works of Peter of Auvergne), *Gregorianum* 14: 3–36. (Biography and list of works.)

—— (1935) 'La philosophie des Quodlibets de Pierre d'Auvergne' (The Philosophy of the Quodlibets of Peter of Auvergne), in A. Long *et al.* (eds) *Aus der Geisteswelt des Mittelalters. Studien und Texte Martin Grabmann zur Vollendung des 60. Lebensjahres von Freunden und Schülern gewidmet*, Beiträge zur Geschichte der Philosophie des Mittelalters Suppl. 3.2, Munich: Aschendorff. (Philosophical aspects of the *Quodlibets*.)

Lohr, C.H. (1972) 'Medieval Latin Aristotle Commentaries, Authors: Narcissus-Richardus', *Traditio* 28: 334–46. (Lists manuscripts of Aristotelian commentaries.)

* Muller, J.-P. (ed.) (1961) *Jean de Paris (Quidort) O.P. 'Commentaire sur les 'Sentences'*, Rome: Herder. (Passages in Quidort's *Commentary on the Sentences* may give hints about the doctrines of Peter of Auvergne's lost *Commentary on the Sentences*.)

Roensch, F.J. (1964) *Early Thomistic School*, Dubuque, IA: The Priory Press, 92–8. (Summary of life and works.)

White, K. (1990) 'St. Thomas Aquinas and the Prologue to Peter of Auvergne's *Quaestiones super De sensu et sensato*', *Documenti e studi* I (2): 427–56.

(Influence of Aquinas on Peter's Questions on Aristotle's *On the Senses*.)

ROBERT ANDREWS

PETER OF SPAIN (*c*.1205–77)

For hundreds of years, a number of works in philosophical psychology, medicine and logic have been attributed to a single thirteenth-century author known as Peter of Spain. According to the latest research, however, there were actually two authors of that name. One, who later became Pope John XXI, wrote on medicine and on the soul. In his writings on the soul, this Peter argued for an independent material form that prepared the body for the soul, its substantial form, and he took an Augustinian view of God's role in illuminating the intellect in ordinary cognition. The second Peter of Spain was a Spanish Dominican who wrote the logical works. He is chiefly known for his Tractatus, *an influential textbook of logic written before 1250, expounding both traditional topics and the theory of supposition, concerning reference in sentential contexts.*

The first Peter was born in Lisbon around 1205, of noble parentage. He completed the liberal arts course at Paris in the 1220s and then studied medicine, probably in southern France, becoming a professor of medicine at Siena in 1245. Peter wrote his medical works, including the famous *Thesaurus pauperum* (A Treasury for the Poor) and his treatises on the soul in the 1240s and 1250s, as well as an exposition of the works of PSEUDO-DIONYSUS. From 1250 Peter lived mostly in Lisbon, enjoying various preferments. In 1272 he became physician to Pope Gregory X, and in 1273 Archbishop of Brage and Cardinal of Frascati. He was elected pope in 1276. As Pope John XXI, he issued two Bulls in 1277 to Etienne Tempier, the Bishop of Paris, ordering the examination of teaching at the University of Paris. Tempier's condemnation of 219 heretical propositions in theology and natural philosophy emphasized the absolute power of God, contributing to the general fourteenth-century stance that the laws of nature are contingent on God's will and reflect no strict impossibilities (see ARISTOTELIANISM, MEDIEVAL). In May 1277 the roof of the pope's private study collapsed and he died of his injuries.

In his treatises on the soul, Peter reveals himself a conservative Augustinian of the stamp of Robert GROSSETESTE. Pursuing the question why the soul, a unity in itself and the form of the body, should give rise to many organs, he points out that the soul has many powers, and needs different organs to realize these powers in matter. Thus there are sense organs for the sensitive power, muscles for the power of self-movement and so on. He identifies two agent intellects, one within the individual human soul, which abstracts forms as they occur in nature from sensible particulars, and the other God himself, who must illuminate the abstracted form in the soul to impart scientific knowledge. Scientific knowledge presupposes a cognition of the form prior to its realization in the material world, from which we can see why things that have the form must be as they are if they are to realize the form in matter. Thus the soul can understand itself only by understanding its powers as prior to their material implementation in the body, so that it can see what shape the body must take to be the body of such a form. Just as the eyes need light to see, so the intellect needs God's illumination to make natural objects intelligible to it. The soul's intellectual powers are not a product of natural processes, but of God himself, while other powers could be produced purely naturally (see SOUL, NATURE AND IMMORTALITY OF THE).

The second Peter was most noted for his *Tractatus*, summarizing the logic of his time in twelve tracts, concerning not only the traditional Aristotelian topics but also the theory of supposition, a logical doctrine first developed in the twelfth century (see LANGUAGE, MEDIEVAL THEORIES OF; LOGIC, MEDIEVAL). Peter claims that the signification of a term belongs to it considered in abstraction from the term's occurrence in a particular proposition. Thus, the term 'man' always signifies the universal *man*. However, an occurrence of this term may 'supposit' for different things in different sentences, for instance, for a specified or unspecified individual, or several individuals, as in 'a man is running' 'that man is running' and 'all men are running'. For though the 'natural supposition' of a term is always the same – namely, all past, present and future individuals that fall under the term's signification – its 'accidental supposition' varies with context. Peter assumed that a term, all by itself, has a natural capacity to refer rooted in its signification, and that its use in a sentence may restrict that natural supposition in various ways but in no way accounts for it. All this coordinates well with realism, which explains how universals could be conceived independently of reference to individuals, and takes reference to individuals to depend on a prior grasp of universals (see REALISM AND ANTIREALISM; UNIVERSALS). In his *Syncategoremata* (On Syncategorematic Words), Peter insists that the copula has no function other than joining the predicate and subject terms, which each have their own signification and reference independently of their sentential context. Peter's views on these matters are at odds with those of WILLIAM OF SHERWOOD, whose characteristically English approach is more friendly to nominalism (see NOMINALISM). His *Tractatus* and *Syncategoremata* were written in the 1230s in southern France, at Toulouse or Montpellier, from which the earliest medieval commentaries on these works stem, including those of Robert Anglicus and William Arnaldi.

See also: AUGUSTINIANISM; LANGUAGE, MEDIEVAL THEORIES OF; LOGIC, MEDIEVAL; UNIVERSALS

List of works

Peter of Spain [Pope John XXI] (before 1258) *Expositio libri De anima, De morte et vida, et De causis longitudinis et brevitatis vitae* (Explanation of [Aristotle's] *On the Soul, On Death and Life* and *On the Length and Brevity of Life*), ed. M. Alonso, *Obras filosóficas*, vol. 3, Madrid: Instituto de Filosofico 'Luis Vives', 1952. (Brief commentaries on Aristotle's works.)

—— (before 1258) *In De anima* (Commentary on [Aristotle's] *On the Soul*), ed. M. Alonso, *Obras filosóficas*, vol. 2, Madrid: Instituto de Filosofico 'Luis Vives', 1944. (A more extended commentary on Aristotle's *On the Soul*.)

—— (before 1258) *Scientia libri De anima* (The Science of the Book *On the Soul*), ed. M. Alonso, *Obras filosóficas*, vol. 1, Madrid: Instituto de Filosofico 'Luis Vives', 1941. (An exposition of Peter's own views on the soul, closely informed by his study of medicine.)

—— (before 1258) *Expositio super libros de Beato Dionisio* (Exposition of the Books of the Blessed Dionysius the Areopagite), ed. M. Alonso, *Exposiao sobre os livros do Beato Dionisio Areopagita*, Lisbon: Instituto de alta cultura, 1957. (A theological work, expositing some Neoplatonic mystical treatises bearing on our knowledge of God which were, at the time, semi-canonical because of their attribution to Dionysius the Areopagite, who was supposed to have been converted by St Paul.)

—— (1272) *Thesaurus pauperum* (A Treasury for the Poor), Antwerp: T. Martin, 1947. (A brief medical handbook for poor students who could not afford the more massive volumes from which its information is extracted.)

Peter of Spain [writer on logic] (*c.*1230) *Tractatus* (Treatises), ed. L.M. De Rijk, Assen: Van Gorcum, 1972; trans. J.P. Mullally, *The Summulae Logicales of Peter of Spain*, Notre Dame, IN: Notre Dame University Press, 1945; trans. F.P. Dineen, *Language in Dispute*, Philadelphia, PA: Benjamins, 1990;

selections translated in N. Kretzmann and E. Stump, *The Cambridge Translations of Medieval Philosophical Texts: Volume One: Logic and the Philosophy of Language*, Cambridge: Cambridge University Press, 1988. (De Rijk's introduction is important. The translations in Kretzmann and Stump are the best.)

—— (*c.*1230) *Syncategoremata* (On Syncategorematic Words), ed. L.M. De Rijk, trans. J. Spruyt, Leiden: Brill, 1992; trans. J.P. Mullaly, *Peter of Spain: Tractatus Syncategorematum and Selected Anonymous Treatises*, Milwaukee, WI: Marquette University Press, 1964. (Concerns words which do not themselves have signification, but alter the meanings of terms with signification in the sentences in which they occur.)

—— (*c.*1230) *Tractatus exponibilium* (Treatise on Exponible Propositions), ed. and trans. J. Spruyt, *Peter of Spain on Composition and Negation*, Nijmegen: Ingenium, 1990. (Part of the *Syncategoremata*. Concerns sentences with a misleading grammatical form, usually involving a concealed negation.)

References and further reading

De Libera, A. (1982) 'The Oxford and Paris traditions in Logic', in N. Kretzmann, A. Kenny and J. Pinborg (eds) *The Cambridge History of Later Medieval Philosophy*, Cambridge: Cambridge University Press. (Places Peter's logical work in the context of his time.)

d'Ors, A. (1997) 'Petrus Hispanus O.P., Auctor Summularum', *Vivarium* 25: 21–71. (Presents the evidence that there were in fact two writers known as Peter of Spain.)

Longeway, J. (1992) 'Peter of Spain', in J. Hackett (ed.) *Dictionary of Literary Biography*, vol. 115, *Medieval Philosophers*, Detroit: Bruccoli Clark Layman. (Contains a full bibliography.)

JOHN L. LONGEWAY

PETRARCA, FRANCESCO (1304–74)

With Dante and Boccaccio, Petrarca (known as Petrarch) made the fourteenth century the most memorable in Italian literature. He was also the first great humanist of the Italian Renaissance. He brilliantly and self-consciously exemplified humanism's classical, rhetorical, literary, and historical interests; with him the movement came of age. He was a proponent not only of classical Rome ('What else is history,' he once asked, 'than the praise of Rome?'), but also of contemporary Rome, constantly calling for the popes at Avignon to return to their proper See and urging restoration of Rome as the seat of the Empire, even if that meant supporting the visionary Roman revolutionary Cola di Rienzo. He came to see himself also as a moral philosopher. His ethical interests were closely tied to his cultural interests and personal situation as a lay moralist (though technically he was a cleric). His outlook and method differed from that of contemporary Aristotelians, whom he attacked on a broad cultural front, sounding many of the themes that would become common in subsequent conflicts between humanism and scholasticism in the Renaissance.

1   **Life and poetry**
2   **Ethical writings**
3   **Humanist culture**

1   Life and poetry

Petrarca, known in the English world as Petrarch, was born in Arezzo. The son of a Florentine exile, he left Tuscany with his family in 1312 to become part of the sizeable Italian colony around the papal court of Avignon in Provence, where his father found employment as a notary (see HUMANISM, RENAISSANCE §1). In 1316, young Francesco was sent to study law at the University of Montpellier and then, in 1320, to the University of Bologna. Petrarca did not want to be a lawyer, and when his father died in 1326 he returned home to live off his inheritance. Around 1330, as his inheritance ran out, Petrarca decided upon a clerical career. He only took minor orders, but the ecclesiastical benefices he accumulated allowed him to live a comfortable life. In 1337 he had a son, Giovanni, and in 1343 a daughter, Francesca, who proved to be a great comfort to him in his old age.

About 1337, after returning from his first visit to Rome, Petrarca had finally had his fill of Avignon and purchased a country home in nearby Vaucluse. He enjoyed his rural retreat immensely, and it was there that he began many of his most important projects. Nonetheless, in 1341, he left Vaucluse for a wider stage: Petrarca had arranged a ceremony for himself in Rome, at which he would be crowned poet laureate. (He believed it to be the first such event since antiquity, but in fact Albertino Mussato had been crowned poet laureate at Padua in 1315.) Wanting the sanction of major political authority, he arranged to have himself 'examined' by King Robert of Naples before proceeding on to the elaborate coronation

ceremony in Rome. He also made sure that the Roman authorities conferred upon him all the rights and privileges of a university master in the two disciplines of poetry and history. He then went to Parma to enjoy the patronage of its lord, Azzo da Correggio. He returned to Vaucluse in the spring of 1342.

For the next decade Petrarca frequently returned to Italy for lengthy stays, and in the summer of 1353 finally settled there. To the dismay of his Florentine friends, he accepted the hospitality of the Visconti tyrants of Milan. He continued to travel, once even to Prague on a Visconti embassy, but he maintained his residence in Milan until 1362, when he decided that he preferred to live in Venice. The Republic provided him with the Palazzo Molin on the Riva degli Schiavoni in return for the bequest of his books, which the Venetians (vainly) hoped to make the core of a public library. In the agreement, doubtless in accordance with Petrarca's desires, the Venetian Senate called him a 'moral philosopher'. In 1368, however, Petrarca changed residence yet again, this time moving to Padua and the protection of its tyrant Francesco da Carrara. He died in his country home at Arquà near Padua.

Petrarca had earned the laurel crown in Rome as a Latin poet. Early in his career, he wrote metrical letters (eventually published as the *Epistolae Metricae*); he also wrote Latin eclogues (collected as the *Bucolicum Carmen*) and composed *Africa*, the first Latin epic written since antiquity. Over his career Petrarca wrote more poetry in Latin than in Italian (he referred to his Italian poems as 'mere trifles' in later life), but in the high Renaissance Petrarca's Latin style no longer found favour: the Europe-wide movement of 'Petrarchism' exclusively involved the imitation of his vernacular poetry. Most of Petrarca's surviving Italian poems were the work of his maturity, and Petrarca was refining his major collection of Italian poems (the *Canzoniere* or *Rime Sparse*) until his death. Today his Italian poems are the only part of his writings widely admired in the original.

Although he wrote sonnets on other themes (including the grand patriotic hymn 'Italia mia'), the vast majority of Petrarca's Italian lyrics concern his love of Laura. He first saw her in Avignon on 6 April 1327, and although she rejected him, Laura remained the abiding love of his life. Inspired by her, Petrarca composed (in the vernacular) the collection of *Trionfi* (*Triumphs*), which began with the *Triumphus Cupidinus* (Triumph of Love) in the 1330s. The *Triumphus Pudicitiae* (Triumph of Chastity) (written in the 1340s) celebrated Laura's honour and purity, which Petrarca saw as elevating him as well. After Laura died, he wrote the *Triumphus Mortis* (Triumph of

Death) and subsequently the *Triumphus Famae* (Triumph of Fame), *Triumphus Temporis* (Triumph of Time) and *Triumphus Eternitatis* (Triumph of Eternity), finishing the collection with the hope of seeing Laura forever in heaven.

2 Ethical writings

At his coronation as poet laureate, Petrarca had made sure that he was also recognized as a historian. He had in fact begun in 1337 a series of biographies of classical, predominately Roman, heroes, called *De Viris Illustribus* (On Illustrious Men). But by the time of his move to Venice in 1362, he wished also to be considered a moral philosopher. One of his first efforts as a moral philosopher was the unwieldy *Rerum Memorandarum Libri* (Books on Matters that Ought to be Remembered), begun about 1343 and never completed. Scholars have deduced that it was supposed to be a work on the four cardinal virtues (prudence, justice, courage and temperance) and perhaps the corresponding vices. In fact it is a compilation of examples and anecdotes illustrating the different aspects of prudence.

Far more successful and interesting is the dialogue *Secretum* (The Secret), first written in the 1340s, when Petrarca was undergoing a mid-life crisis, and subsequently revised. Petrarca has St Augustine examine why he, Petrarca, was suffering from depression (called by the name of one of the deadly sins, *accidia*). With his youth behind him and death waiting just over the horizon, Petrarca still could not shake free of earthly desires, most specifically, of his love of Laura and his desire for fame. The Augustine of the dialogue is quite unhistorical. He is a voluntarist who blames Petrarca's problems on insufficient will power (though towards the end he tells Petrarca to call on God to make good the failings of his will). The dialogue ends with Petrarca understanding better his predicament, but not really having overcome it. Petrarca was in fact a great admirer of AUGUSTINE as the master psychologist of the *Confessiones* (Confessions).

No less personal was the treatise *De Vita Solitaria* (On the Solitary Life), begun at Vaucluse in 1346. This work has strong religious overtones, but was in fact a lengthy defence of Petrarca's very secular and comfortable life away from the madding crowd and free of commitments that might limit his freedom to write and study. The next year, after visiting his brother Gherardo, a monk at the Carthusian monastery of Montrieux, he more legitimately made many of the same arguments in a paean to monastic life which he entitled *De Otio Religioso* (On Religious Leisure).

His most 'professional' and largest work as a moral philosopher was the *De Remediis Utriusque Fortunae* (*On the Remedies of Good and Bad Fortune*). Inspired by the Stoic ideal of the wise man who does not let the vagaries of fortune affect his inner peace, Petrarca started on his *Remedies* about 1354 and finished in 1366. Though cast in the form of a dialogue, *Remedies* was in essence a recipe book for a life of moderation. If you enjoyed anything, Petrarca told you why you should not be too elated by it. For instance, he explained that the enjoyment of wrestling was senseless for the spectator and insane for the participant. He also offered advice to encourage people who were facing misfortunes: for example, he argued that those who had been blinded were at least spared the many painful sights that life visits upon us. In all, he detailed 122 kinds of good fortune and 132 of bad fortune and their remedies. If some of his remedies strike us as ineffective, it is at least clear that he was striving to be practical and of genuine use to ordinary people.

In his ethical pronouncements Petrarca tended to favour Stoic formulas, but operationally, in his own life, he lived as an Aristotelian, desiring an adequate supply of worldly goods, friends, leisure, moderate pleasures, and the support of the powerful so that he could satisfy to the fullest his creative and intellectual impulses. Nonetheless, he was generally unsympathetic to ARISTOTLE, while usually speaking well of PLATO. On the authority of Augustine, he believed that Plato's doctrines harmonized well with Christianity. He especially attacked as opponents of Christianity Aristotle's Arab commentator Averroes (see IBN RUSHD) and contemporary Aristotelians who agreed with Averroes.

These tendencies stand out in one of his last works, the invective *De Sui Ipsius et Multorum Ignorantia* (On His Own Ignorance and That of Many Others), started in 1367 and completed in 1371. Four Venetians favouring the Aristotelian scientific tradition had pronounced Petrarca a good man but an ignorant one, after discovering at a dinner party in 1366 that he could not answer certain questions in zoology. In response, Petrarca said he would not take account of the classical eloquence for which he was famed, but which his critics disdained; he feigned Socratic ignorance for his own self and attacked as inane the vaunted scientific knowledge of his critics, avowed the superiority of Christian faith over any philosophical wisdom, and while asserting Plato's superiority over Aristotle, confessed that his philosophical guides were the eloquent Latin authors CICERO and SENECA.

3 Humanist culture

As the intellectual weakness of this invective reveals, Petrarca's stance was more cultural than philosophical. In contrast with the legal, scientific and philosophical bias of contemporary learned culture, he proposed a learning dominated by rhetorical, literary, historical and classicist interests. His largest body of writing is his letters, which, inspired by his discovery of Cicero's *Familiar Letters* at Verona in 1345, he gathered, revised and published in several different collections. The first collection was his *Epistolae Familiares* (*Familiar Letters*); then came his *Rerum senilium libri* (*Books of Matters of Old Age*); he brought together some polemical letters in a collection called *Liber sine nomine* (Book Without Name); and finally there are various letters of his that he never incorporated into any collection. Addressed to prelates, secular rulers, friends and enemies, Petrarca's letters spread the new culture of humanism as effectively as any of his writings. Since he did not merely study his favourite authors, but conversed with them as well, he even addressed some letters to Cicero and other worthies of antiquity. He also cultivated the other most preferred humanist rhetorical genre, the oration, several times making speeches on behalf of the Visconti (see HUMANISM, RENAISSANCE §2).

In sum, apart from his vernacular poetry, Petrarca left to posterity not so much a philosophy as a classicizing language, a set of literary genres, a constellation of literary and historical interests, and a body of newly discovered classical texts which gave emerging Renaissance humanism self-awareness and a cultural agenda. He also gave Renaissance humanism its first hero.

See also: ALIGHIERI, DANTE; HUMANISM, RENAISSANCE §§2, 4

List of works

Petrarca, F. [Petrarch] (1304–74) *Opere latine* (Works in Latin), ed. A. Bufano, Turin: Unione tipografico-editrice torinese, 1975, 2 vols. (Excellent anthology; includes original text with facing Italian translation for the Latin.)

—— (1304–74) *Canzoniere* or *Rime Sparse*, trans. R.M. Durling, *Petrarch's Lyric Poems: The Rime Sparse and Other Lyrics*, Cambridge, MA: Harvard University Press, 1976. (English translation of Petrarca's vernacular poetry.)

—— (begun 1330s) *Trionfi*, in F. Neri *et al.* (eds) *Rime, Trionfi e poesie latine*, Milan and Naples: Ricciardi, 1948; trans. E.H. Wilkins, *The Triumphs of Petrarch*, Chicago, IL: University of Chicago Press, 1962. (One of Petrarca's major collections of vernacular poetry. The Neri anthology includes the original text; Wilkins is an English translation.)

—— (begun 1337) *De Viris Illustribus* (On Illustrious Men), ed. G. Martellotti, Florence: Sansoni, 1964. (Modern critical edition of Petrarca's series of biographies of classical, predominately Roman, heroes.)

—— (begun 1340s) *Africa*, trans. T.G. Bergin and A.S. Wilson, New Haven, CT, and London: Yale University Press, 1977. (English translation of the first Latin epic since antiquity. The poem is now more valued for historical than literary reasons; Petrarca did not publish it in his lifetime.)

—— (begun 1340s) *Petrarch's Bucolicum Carmen*, trans. T.G. Bergin, New Haven, CT, and London: Yale University Press, 1974. (English translation of Petrarca's Latin eclogues.)

—— (begun 1340s) *Secretum*, in D. Martellotti *et al.* (eds) *Prose*, Milan and Naples: Ricciardi, 1955; trans. W.H. Draper, *Petrarch's Secret*, London: Chatto & Windus, 1901. (Dialogue with Augustine, in which the saint takes a voluntarist approach to solving Petrarca's mid-life anxieties; first written in the 1340s but subsequently revised. Martellotti gives the original text with facing Italian translation of the Latin; Draper is a translation into English.)

—— (begun c.1343) *Rerum Memorandarum Libri* (Books on Matters that Ought to be Remembered), ed. G. Billanovich, Florence: Sansoni, 1943. (Modern critical edition of one of Petrarca's first works of moral philosophy; it was never finished. A compilation of examples and anecdotes illustrating different aspects of prudence.)

—— (after 1345) *Epistolae Familiares*, ed. V. Rossi and U. Bosco, Florence: Sansoni, 1933–42, 4 vols; trans. A.S. Bernardo, *Letters on Familiar Matters*, vol. 1, Albany, NY: State University of New York Press, vol. 2, Baltimore, MD: Johns Hopkins University Press, 1975–82. (Petrarca's first collection of letters. Rossi and Bosco is a modern critical edition; Bernardo a translation into English.)

—— (after 1345) *Rerum senilium libri* (Books of Matters of Old Age), in *Opera Omnia*, Ridgewood, NJ: Gregg Press, 1965, vol. 2, 812–1070; trans. A.S. Bernardo *et al.*, *Letters of Old Age*, Baltimore, MD: Johns Hopkins University Press, 1975–82, 2 vols. (Petrarca's second collection of letters. The Gregg Press *Opera* is a reprint of the three-volume Basle edition of 1554; Bernardo provides an English translation.)

—— (after 1345) *Liber sine nomine* (Book Without Name), ed. P. Piur, *Petrarcas 'Buch ohne Name' und die päpstliche Kurie, ein Beitrag zur Geistes-*

geschichte der Frührenaissance, Halle: Niemayer, 1925. (Collection of Petrarca's polemical letters.)

—— (begun 1346) *De Vita Solitaria* (On the Solitary Life), in D. Martellotti *et al.* (eds) *Prose*, Milan and Naples: Ricciardi, 1955. (A lengthy defence of Petrarca's comfortable life of study and writing at Vaucluse. Original text with facing Italian translation of the Latin.)

—— (*c.*1354–66) *De Remediis Utriusque Fortunae*, in *Opera Omnia*, Ridgewood, NJ: Gregg Press, 1965, vol. 1, 1–254; trans. C.H. Rawski, *Petrarch's Remedies for Fortune Fair and Foul*, Indianopolis, IN: Indiana University Press, 1991, 5 vols. (Inspired by Stoic ideals, Petrarca's largest work as a moral philosopher; attempts to offer practical help for ordinary people. The Gregg Press *Opera* is a reprint of the three-volume Basle edition of 1554; the translation includes bibliographical references, indexes and a commentary by Rawski.)

—— (1371) *De Sui Ipsius et Multorum Ignorantia*, trans. H. Nachod, *On His Own Ignorance and That of Many Others*, in E. Cassirer *et al.* (eds) *The Renaissance Philosophy of Man*, Chicago, IL: University of Chicago Press, 1948. (Begun in 1367 and completed in 1371. Polemical attack on medieval definitions of scientific knowledge and defence of the superiority of the Christian faith over philosophical wisdom; Petrarca asserts Plato's superiority over Aristotle, and acknowledges his philosophical debt to Cicero and Seneca.)

References and further reading

Billanovich, G. (1951) 'Petrarch and the Textual Tradition of Livy', *Journal of the Warburg and Courtauld Institutes* 14: 137–208. (Important for Petrarca's classical scholarship.)

Foster, K. (1984) *Petrarch: Poet and Humanist*, Edinburgh: Edinburgh University Press. (Good on Petrarca's poetry.)

Kristeller, P.O. (1964) *Eight Philosophers of the Italian Renaissance*, Stanford, CA: Stanford University Press, ch. 1. (The first chapter treats Petrarca's philosophical ideas.)

—— (1983) '*Petrarcas Stellung in der Geschichte der Gelehrsamkeit*' (Petrarca's Place in the History of Learning), in K.W. Hempfer and E. Straub (eds) *Italien in Humanismus und Renaissance: Festschrift für Erich Loos um 70 Geburtstag*, Wiesbaden: Steiner. (A synthesis of much useful material.)

Mann, N. (1984) *Petrarch*, Oxford: Oxford University Press. (An elegant appreciation.)

Nolhac, P. de (1907) *Pétrarque et l'humanisme*, Paris: Librairie Champion, 2nd edn, 2 vols. (Old but important.)

Rico, F. (1974) *Vida u obra de Petrarca: I. Lectura del Secretum* (Life and Work of Petrarca. Vol. 1: Reading the *Secretum*), Padua: Antenore. (A fundamental study.)

Wilkins, E.H. (1961) *Life of Petrarch*, Chicago, IL: University of Chicago Press. (The best biography in English by a master of Petrarchan scholarship.)

JOHN MONFASANI

PETRARCH *see* PETRARCA, FRANCESCO

PETRAŻYCKI, LEON (1867–1931)

Leon Petrażycki was a strikingly original philosopher of law whose theoretical system ranged over moral and legal philosophy, theory of science, psychology and sociology. The aim of his philosophy of law is 'Legal Policy', that is, social engineering through law directed at the 'social ideal of love'.

A Polish nobleman, born in the county of Vitebsk (in present-day Belarus), Petrażycki was educated at the Russian high school in Vitebsk and studied medicine and law at the Russian Imperial University in Kiev. From 1890 to 1906, he held a scholarship in Berlin, and from 1898 to 1917 was Professor in History of Legal Philosophy at St Petersburg University. From 1919 to 1931 he held a chair in sociology at the University of Warsaw. He published in German, Russian and Polish.

Petrażycki's ontology is materialist in a broad sense. Values do not exist. Material objects and psychical phenomena do exist objectively, yet causality is an axiom of theoretical reason. His epistemology is moderately realist: science employs empirical observation, induction and deduction, to construct an analogue of reality. Practical reason is founded on the social postulate of love. His methodology demands that theories be neither 'jumping' (too wide: saying about a whole class what is true only for part of it) nor 'lame' (too narrow: saying of part alone what is true of the whole).

His psychology is based on a new classification of psychical phenomena. Beyond feeling, knowing and willing, there exist 'impulsions'. They are passive-active: for example, feeling hunger, one strives for food. Moral impulsions consist of the 'feeling' of one's duty together with an active readiness to do it. Legal impulsions are the only phenomena around which to build an adequate legal theory. So sound legal theory is psychological. Studying law is studying legal impulsions. These are imperatively attributive, that is, concerning one's own duties intertwined with another's rights or vice versa. These are studied by introspection in one's own case, only analogically in others'.

Law is explained in evolutionary terms. A person whose rights are not respected retaliates. The legal psyche is thus aggressive (while the moral psyche, lacking the element of rights, is peaceful). Legal rules and legal concepts adapt themselves unconsciously to achieving unity among legal impulsions of different people. Positive law, and also the law of illegal organizations, laws of games, and so on, are to be studied subject to the same criteria of theoretical adequacy. The impulsions of positive law are attached to intersubjectively cognizable 'normative facts', in the case of 'official law' such as legislation or custom. Legal rules are projections of shared legal impulsions. Doctrinal law makes law more uniform and better adapted to its pacific social function.

Petrażycki accounted for the evolution of law comprehensively since Roman times, and anticipated later theories in many fields, for example, in relation to post-decisional dissonance, the cognitive role of language, and the hypothetico-deductive method in science. Yet legal institutions cannot be fully described in individualistic-psychological terms, and lame theories, not being false, are in many cases better than none at all.

See also: LAW, PHILOSOPHY OF; WRÓBLEWSKI, J.

List of works

Petrażycki, L. (1955) *Law and Morality*, trans. H.W. Babb, 20th Century Legal Philosophy Series, vol. 7, Cambridge, MA: Harvard University Press. (This is the only version available in English of Petrażycki's work; it gives an account of all his main ideas.)

References and further reading

Olivecrona, K. (1948) 'Is a Sociological Explanation of Law Possible?', *Theoria* 14: 167–207. (Petrażycki's theory is taken as a significant attempt to elaborate a non-voluntaristic concept of law in socio-psychological terms.)

Timasheff, N.S. (1947) 'Petrażycki's Philosophy of Law', in P. Sayre (ed.) *Interpretations of Modern Legal Philosophies: Essays in Honour of Roscoe Pound*, Cambridge, MA: Harvard University Press,
748–69. (A spirited attempt to reconcile Petrażycki's work to the philosophical concerns of the post-war world.)

ALEKSANDER PECZENIK

PHENOMENALISM

On its most common interpretation, phenomenalism maintains that statements asserting the existence of physical objects are equivalent in meaning to statements describing sensations. More specifically, the phenomenalist claims that to say that a physical object exists is to say that someone would have certain sequences of sensations were they to have certain others. For example, to say that there is something round and red behind me might be to say, in part, that if I were to have the visual, tactile and kinaesthetic (movement) sensations of turning my head I would seem to see something round and red. If I were to have the sensations of seeming to reach out and touch that thing, those sensations would be followed by the familiar tactile sensations associated with touching something round.

Rather than talk about the meanings of statements, phenomenalists might hold that the fact that something red and round exists just is the fact that a subject would have certain sequences of sensations following certain others. The phenomenalist's primary motivation is a desire to avoid scepticism with respect to the physical world. Because many philosophers tied the meaningfulness of statements to their being potentially verifiable, some phenomenalists further argued that it is only by reducing claims about the physical world to claims about possible sensations that we can preserve the very intelligibility of talk about the physical world.

There are very few contemporary philosophers who embrace phenomenalism. Many reject the foundationalist epistemological framework which makes it so difficult to avoid scepticism without phenomenalism. But the historical rejection of the view had more to do with the difficulty of carrying out the promised programme of translation.

1 **Why phenomenalism?**
2 **Criticisms**
3 **Responses**

1 Why phenomenalism?

Philosophers who embraced phenomenalism typically did so in the attempt to defeat scepticism with respect to the physical world. On one historically prominent and intuitively plausible model of our perceptual relations to the physical world, physical objects are different from, but causally responsible for, sensations which allow us to know those objects. Our sensations are the end product of a long causal chain that (we believe) involves our sense organs and ultimately our brain states. In veridical experience, our sensations in some sense represent the objects we take to be their cause. In illusion and hallucinatory experiences, our sensations fail to represent their external causes (see PERCEPTION).

This view of perception and the closely related view of the nature of our knowledge of physical objects are grist for the sceptic's mill. It seems easy enough to establish that the subjective, fleeting sensations that cause us to believe in the existence of physical objects never guarantee the truth of what we believe. The representative realist takes sensations to be the *effects* of physical objects, effects that could, in principle, be produced some other way (by artificially stimulating the relevant region of the brain, for example). But if our only access to the physical world is through sensations, then how could we ever establish sensations as a reliable indicator of the existence of physical objects? The most common way we have of establishing one thing as a sign of something else is to establish a correlation between the two in past experience. But we could never correlate a sensation with a physical object different from a sensation if all we have to go on ultimately are sensations. We can establish connections between sensations, but never between sensations and their alleged causes.

The phenomenalist seeks to rescue common sense from the sceptical implications of representative realism. The root of scepticism lies in a mistaken conception of the physical world, the phenomenalist argues. We must avoid the sceptic's attempt to drive a wedge between sensations and objects, by finding a conceptual link between the existence of physical objects and the occurrence of sensations. But we must do so without making the existence of physical objects depend on the occurrence of any *actual* sensations. It seems obvious that the very concept of a physical object is the concept of an object whose existence is independent of minds and their actual experiences. The table I see now can continue to exist even if I leave the room and there is no-one else around to perceive it. If the concept of a physical object is the concept of something that can exist even when it is unsensed, we cannot identify physical objects with sensations. But, the phenomenalist argues, that does not prevent us from analysing the meaning of physical-object statements into more complex statements describing sensations. We should view statements asserting the existence of physical objects as equivalent in meaning to statements describing

'possible' sensations. More precisely we should take physical object statements to be making conditional assertions about the sensations someone *would* have *were* that person to have certain other sensations. Subjunctive (counterfactual) conditionals of this sort are made true by connections between sensations, and there seems to be no insurmountable difficulty in establishing correlations between past sensations of the sort necessary to establish causal connections between patterns of sensations (assuming, of course, that we will be able to deal with other sceptical problems concerning knowledge of the past and induction) (see COUNTERFACTUAL CONDITIONALS).

Phenomenalism is compatible with a number of different views about the nature both of sensations and of the selves that have sensations. Many of the historically important phenomenalists were sense-datum theorists who analysed a visual sensation, for example, in terms of a subject's being directly aware of a two-dimensional object existing outside of physical space and exemplifying phenomenal colour and shape (see SENSE-DATA). But there is nothing to stop a phenomenalist from embracing a so-called adverbial or appearing theory which identifies sensations with the mind's exemplifying certain non-relational properties (see MENTAL STATES, ADVERBIAL THEORY OF). Just as phenomenalists may disagree among themselves over the nature of sensations, so too they may disagree over the analysis of that which has sensations. A phenomenalist can take the subject of sensations to be a mind of the sort posited by Berkeley, or can attempt to reduce subjects themselves to 'bundles' of actual and possible sensations (see MIND, BUNDLE THEORY OF).

Because early statements of phenomenalism were often not clear, it is difficult to make any definite claims about the historical origins of the view. There are certainly passages in which the idealist, Berkeley, seemed to suggest the conditional analysis of physical objects in trying to explain how his view that only minds and ideas (which include sensations) exist is compatible with common sense. In one passage he seems to argue that the story of a creation that takes place before the existence of finite minds should be understood in terms of truths about what finite minds would have experienced had they existed ([1713] 1954: 100). A more promising candidate for being the first phenomenalist might be John Stuart Mill (1865). Mill identified physical objects with the 'permanent possibility of sensations' and explained this in terms of the sensations one would have under certain conditions (see MILL, J.S. §6).

2 Criticisms

For their enterprise to be successful, it is necessary that phenomenalists actually produce plausible 'translations' of statements about the physical world into statements employing purely 'phenomenal' language – that is, statements referring to nothing other than minds and their sensations. Any reference to physical objects will 'contaminate' the subjunctive conditionals employed by the phenomenalist and will defeat the whole purpose of the analysis which is to reduce fully talk about the physical world to allegedly less problematic talk about sensations. Historically, the most influential objections to phenomenalism focused on the alleged impossibility of plausibly completing a phenomenalistic analysis. The clearest of these objections was advanced by Roderick Chisholm (1948) and has become known as 'the argument from perceptual relativity'. The phenomenalist, C.I. LEWIS, argued (1946) that part of what it means to claim that there is a doorknob in front of me and to the left is that if I were to seem to see the doorknob and seem to be initiating a certain grasping motion, then in all probability the feeling of contacting a doorknob would follow. CHISHOLM points out that if the conditional really were part of what the existence of a doorknob involved, then it would be impossible for the doorknob to be there without the conditional being true. But it is easy to imagine a situation in which, though the doorknob is there, I would not be able to have any tactile sensations of it. My hand might be anaesthetized; then, even though the doorknob is there, I would not feel anything upon seeming to reach out to touch it. The proposition that there is a doorknob there does not entail anything about what sensations I would have were I to have others, because the sensations I would have always depend on facts about the internal and external *physical* conditions of perception (facts about the lighting conditions, sense organs, and so on). We cannot, however, revise the conditionals we employ in a phenomenalistic analysis to make reference to standard or normal physical conditions of perception (the argument goes) without referring to the physical world and thus defeating the goal of providing an analysis that refers to nothing other than connections between sensations.

Another closely related objection to phenomenalism argues that contingent subjunctive conditionals of the sort employed by phenomenalists in their analyses presuppose *lawful* regularities between sensations. But again, because sensations are always causally dependent on physical conditions, there simply are no lawful regularities involving sensations alone.

The above objections are often presented by philosophers sympathetic to the general philosophical framework presupposed by phenomenalists. Certainly many contemporary philosophers reject many of the assumptions that motivated phenomenalists. Thus, for example, many contemporary epistemologists reject the kind of foundationalism that led phenomenalists to worry that a resolution of sceptical problems was impossible if we separate physical objects from sensations. A good many of these epistemologists embrace some version of externalism which allows one to know facts about the physical world simply by having one's beliefs caused in the appropriate way (see INTERNALISM AND EXTERNALISM IN EPISTEMOLOGY). Still other contemporary philosophers reject the conception of philosophical analysis as an attempt to specify necessary and sufficient conditions for the truth of propositions. Again, many of these will accept an externalist or causal theory of *meaning* which makes the meaning of expressions largely an empirical question inaccessible to a priori analysis. Such views of meaning will either reject, or significantly reinterpret, the verifiability criterion of meaning that drove so many phenomenalists (see MEANING AND VERIFICATION).

3 Responses

It is impossible in this context to evaluate challenges to the phenomenalist's basic philosophical presuppositions. But is there any response that the phenomenalist might make to the argument from perceptual relativity? The key to such a response would seem to involve 'protecting' the antecedents of the subjunctive conditionals employed by the phenomenalist. That something round is before me now entails only that if I were to seem to reach out and grasp the object *under certain conditions*, I would seem to feel something round. The phenomenalist's critics claim that one cannot specify the relevant conditions without introducing reference to the physical world, thereby defeating the whole purpose of the analysis. But is that true? A phenomenalist might argue that one can introduce into one's phenomenalistic analysis a clause about normal or standard conditions whose purpose is to *denote* those conditions (*whatever* they are) that normally (defined statistically) accompany certain sequences of sensations. The normal conditions clause might include reference to other facts about what sensations would follow others, facts about 'things-in-themselves' (construed as entities whose intrinsic nature will always remain a complete mystery), facts about the intentions of a God and so on. While the introduction of such a clause would move one away from 'pure' versions of phenomenalism by allowing into one's analysis expressions that might denote things other than minds and sensations, it might be argued that the modification is epistemically harmless, for we are always justified in believing, other things being equal, that conditions are normal, that is to say that conditions are as they usually are.

Once one modifies the analysis this much, however, it is not altogether clear why one should not move all the way to a version of what might be called a causal theory of objects, one that resembles classical phenomenalism much more than representative realism. On this 'phenomenalistic' causal theory, to assert the existence of a physical object is simply to assert the existence of a thing (whatever its intrinsic character might be) that has the power to produce certain sensations and that would produce certain patterns of sensations following an initial sequence of sensations *when conditions are normal*. This 'causal' theory looks a great deal like phenomenalism – indeed it may be another natural way of construing Mill's reference to physical objects as the permanent possibilities of sensations. Unlike traditional phenomenalism, however, this theory might have an easier time analysing physical-object statements which assert only the existence of something (somewhere, sometime) having certain physical characteristics. Such statements are a real problem for traditional phenomenalism, for when the physical-object statement fails to describe a physical object in relation to potential perceivers of those objects, it is not clear whose sensations we can plausibly refer to in our subjunctive conditionals. Notice, however, that the kind of causal theory sketched above faces identical problems to classical phenomenalism when it comes to specifying *subjunctively* the relevant powers to produce sensations. If this is right, there may not be as huge a gap as was historically supposed between phenomenalism and at least some causal theories of the physical world.

See also: EMPIRICISM; IDEALISM; PERCEPTION, EPISTEMIC ISSUES IN

References and further reading

Ayer, A.J. (1936) *Language, Truth and Logic*, New York: Dover, 2nd edn, 1946. (Contains a vigorous defence of logical positivism and a phenomenalistic analysis of physical-object propositions in terms of actual and possible sense-data.)

* Berkeley, G. (1713) *Three Dialogues Between Hylas and Philonous*, ed. C.M. Turbayne, Indianapolis, IN: Bobbs-Merrill, 1954. (Attacks representative realism and defends the view that physical objects can be reduced to 'ideas' – where 'ideas' include sensations. There are passages in which he seems to defend the phenomenalistic view that one should

appeal to counterfactuals describing possible sensations in the analysis of physical objects.)

* Chisholm, R. (1948) 'The Problem of Empiricism', *Journal of Philosophy* 45 (1948): 412–17. (Contains what is probably the single most influential objection to phenomenalism, presented in a remarkably clear and straightforward manner.)

Firth, R. (1950) 'Radical Empiricism and Perceptual Relativity', *Philosophical Review* 59 (1950): 164–83, 319–31. (A vigorous defence of phenomenalism against the argument from perceptual relativity. Firth's defence rests on certain general considerations about meaning, and the article, while clearly written, will be accessible only to those with a strong philosophical background.)

* Lewis, C.I. (1946) *An Analysis of Knowledge and Valuation*, La Salle, IL: Open Court. (Despite his reservations about the word, Lewis in this book presents what I take to be the most sophisticated and detailed defence of phenomenalism. The book is accessible to relatively unsophisticated philosophy students provided that they are willing to spend some time studying it.)

* Mill, J.S. (1865) *An Examination of Sir William Hamilton's Philosophy*, London: Longmans, Green, 1889. (Mill's identification of physical objects with the permanent possibility of sensations and his explication of what he means using subjunctive conditionals describing sensations makes him a good candidate for one of the earliest phenomenalists.)

RICHARD FUMERTON

PHENOMENOLOGICAL MOVEMENT

The phenomenological movement is a century-old international movement in philosophy that has penetrated most of the cultural disciplines, especially psychiatry and sociology. It began in Germany with the early work of Edmund Husserl, and spread to the rest of Europe, the Americas and Asia. In contrast with a school, a movement does not have a body of doctrine to which all participants agree; rather, there is a broad approach that tends to be shared. The phenomenological approach has at least four components.

First, phenomenologists tend to oppose naturalism. Naturalism includes behaviourism in psychology and positivism in social sciences and philosophy, and is a worldview based on the methods of the natural sciences. In contrast, phenomenologists tend to focus on the socio-historical or cultural lifeworld and to oppose all kinds of reductionism. Second, they tend to oppose speculative thinking and preoccupation with language, urging instead knowledge based on 'intuiting' or the 'seeing' of the matters themselves that thought is about. Third, they urge a technique of reflecting on processes within conscious life (or human existence) that emphasizes how such processes are directed at (or 'intentive to') objects and, correlatively, upon these objects as they present themselves or, in other words, as they are intended to. And fourth, phenomenologists tend to use analysis or explication as well as the seeing of the matters reflected upon to produce descriptions or interpretations both in particular and in universal or 'eidetic' terms. In addition, phenomenologists also tend to debate the feasibility of Husserl's procedure of transcendental epoché or 'bracketing' and the project of transcendental first philosophy it serves, most phenomenology not being transcendental.

Beyond these widely shared components of method, phenomenologists tend to belong to one or another of four intercommunicating and sometimes overlapping tendencies. These tendencies are 'realistic phenomenology', which emphasizes the seeing and describing of universal essences; 'constitutive phenomenology', which emphasizes accounting for objects in terms of the consciousness of them; 'existential phenomenology', which emphasizes aspects of human existence within the world; and 'hermeneutical phenomenology', which emphasizes the role of interpretation in all spheres of life. All tendencies go back to the early work of Husserl, but the existential and hermeneutical tendencies are also deeply influenced by the early work of Martin Heidegger. Other leading figures are Nicolai Hartmann, Roman Ingarden, Adolf Reinach and Max Scheler in realistic phenomenology, Dorion Cairns, Aron Gurwitsch and Alfred Schutz in constitutive phenomenology, Hannah Arendt, Jean-Paul Sartre, Maurice Merleau-Ponty, and Simone de Beauvoir in existential phenomenology, and Hans-Georg Gadamer and Paul Ricoeur in hermeneutical phenomenology.

1 **Matrix and origins**
2 **Realistic phenomenology**
3 **Constitutive phenomenology**
4 **Existential phenomenology**
5 **Hermeneutical phenomenology**
6 **Prospects**

1 Matrix and origins

Phenomenology began in the reflections of Edmund HUSSERL during the mid-1890s, but some find forerunners as far back as PLATO and Aristotle. There are immediate anticipations in the work of four figures, not all of whom influenced all phenomenol-

ogists. In *Essai sur les données immediates de la conscience* (Time and Free Will) (1889), Henri BERGSON offered a concrete and qualitative description of conscious life with an emphasis on how it flows and how abiding geometrized objects are constructed. He did not influence Husserl, but sits in the background for Roman INGARDEN, Kitarō NISHIDA and French phenomenology. In *Psychologie vom empirischen Standpunkt* (Psychology from an Empirical Standpoint) (1874), Husserl's teacher Franz BRENTANO urged the priority of a descriptive over an explanatory psychology of psychical phenomena, which he distinguished from physical phenomena by their *Intentionalität* (intentionality) or directedness at immanent contents. Husserl eventually opposed his teacher's immanentism, denying that physical objects have an 'inexistence' in intentional acts; developed a richer classification of mental phenomena; and came to call his work phenomenology rather than descriptive psychology.

Wilhelm DILTHEY similarly called for a descriptive psychology, held that it would be fundamental among the human sciences (*Geisteswissenschaften*), and described the construction of the historical world in such sciences. Husserl's interest in these matters took some time to be recognized; the debt Martin HEIDEGGER owed to Dilthey has been more easily appreciated. Finally, in *Principles of Psychology* (1890) William JAMES was also concerned to describe what he called the stream of thought, including believing and willing, and his distinction between 'the object of thought' and 'the topic of thought' resembles that between 'the object as it is intended' and 'the object that is intended'. James was read by Husserl and some later phenomenologists.

After studying mathematics and astronomy at Leipzig, pursuing mathematics at Berlin, and hearing Brentano lecture at Vienna, Husserl took his doctorate in mathematics at Vienna under Leo Königsberger. He then habilitated under Brentano's disciple Carl Stumpf at Halle in 1887 and taught there as *Privatdozent* until 1901, when he became an Extraordinarius at Göttingen. He became Ordinarius at Freiburg in 1916, retired in 1928 and died in 1938.

Husserl's Berlin teacher in mathematics, Carl Weierstraß, encouraged the quest for absolutely secure foundations within mathematics, but Husserl went beyond mathematics to seek grounds for all the sciences. His first work, *Philosophie der Arithmetik* (1891), attempted to account for the concept of number by relating it, in the manner of Brentano's psychology, to the mental operation of counting. This work in descriptive psychology was soon contested by Gottlob FREGE as being psychologistic – psychologism being the doctrine, prominently defended by

John Stuart MILL and his followers in Germany, that empirical psychology is the fundamental philosophical discipline and that because concepts and propositions are mental contents, logic is a branch of psychology and logical laws are empirical psychological laws. The myth later arose that Frege helped Husserl overcome his psychologism, but close study by J.N. Mohanty, Karl Schuhmann and others of correspondence and minor writings has shown that Husserl took this step in 1894 for other reasons.

Early in his second major work, *Logische Untersuchungen* (Logical Investigations) (1900–1) – the work that actually launched the phenomenological movement – Husserl contended that logic is not fundamentally an art based on the facts of mental life, but instead fundamentally contains 'pure logic' as a theoretical science of ideal logical forms that are not themselves parts of conscious life. Later in this work he then reflected on the correlative psychical processes in which logical forms are intended, provoking accusations of a relapse into psychologism from those for whom any reference to conscious processes is anathema. What Husserl's less extreme anti-psychologism forbade was in fact the reduction of logical structures to real intentional processes.

The key doctrine in the latter part of the *Investigations* proposes that just as there can be fulfilment of empty intentions of sensuous objects, for example, when we see or hear the same matters as had merely been conceived of previously, there can also be fulfilment of empty categorial intentions by categorial intuition, that is, a non-sensuous seeing of how predication takes form. Propositional truth is accomplished when a formerly empty predicative judgment is brought into coincidence with a predicatively formed state of affairs. Husserl could then call for a return '*zu den Sachen selbst*', best rendered as 'to the matters themselves', that is to say, a return from the blind manipulation of symbols to an insightful approach to the corresponding states of affairs, which include the matters themselves of concern to formal logic. This injunction was soon generalized beyond the theory of logic, formal ontology and the theory of parts and wholes to regions of all sorts; the phenomenological movement then ensued.

The four successively emerging, intercommunicating and sometimes overlapping tendencies within the phenomenological movement thus far all stem from the so-called 'descriptive' phenomenology of the first edition of the *Logical Investigations*.

2 Realistic phenomenology

Immediately after the publication of the *Logical Investigations*, Johannes Daubert persuaded a group of fellow students of Theodore Lipps at Munich to abandon Lipps' psychologism and accept the *Logical Investigations* as their philosophical bible. Many of these students, including Adolf REINACH, soon went to Husserl at Göttingen. The phrase 'phenomenological movement' first arose in this group, and realistic phenomenology became a distinct tendency within it only when Husserl developed the so-called 'transcendental turn' that its members did not accept. Daubert published nothing in his lifetime. Alexander Pfänder's *Phänomenologie des Wollens* (Phenomenology of Willing) (1900) is retrospectively seen as the earliest major document of realistic phenomenology, and he and Reinach, as well as Max SCHELER and Moritz Geiger, led the first generation of realistic phenomenologists. In 1913, together with Husserl, they began editing the *Jahrbuch für Philosophie und phänomenologische Forschung*, the quasi-official organ of the movement. The second generation includes Theodor Celms, Hedwig Conrad-Martius, Dietrich von Hildebrand, Roman Ingarden, Aurel Kolnai, Edith Stein and Kurt Stavenhagen.

In order to gain a systematic body of a priori knowledge on a wide range of matters, this first tendency emphasizes Husserl's eidetic method. Eidetic method involves suspending belief in any actual facts with which one begins, feigning variations of the matter at issue, and then grasping the invariant or universal essence that the facts, fantasies and any 'thought experiments' exemplify or instantiate. Since there is always already a vague and tacit acquaintance with essences, eidetic method is a procedure of clarification and description: a method of discovery, not invention. Terms and relations of possibility, compossibility, necessity and contingency by virtue of which facts are intelligible are thus disclosed. Husserl importantly distinguished formalizing universalization, which yields formal ontology, from generalizing universalization, which yields taxonomies. Mistakes in employing this method – its use in accounting for itself included – can be made, but are also in principle discoverable and corrigible by means of it.

The realistic phenomenologists maintained a metaphysical realism of universals and particulars. Geiger contributed to aesthetics and the a priori foundations of geometry. In *Der Formalismus in der Ethik und die materiale Wertethik* (Formalism in Ethics and Non-Formal Ethics of Values) (1913, 1916) Scheler objected to Kant's ethical formalism and advocated a value-realism in ethics. Reinach analysed accusing, commanding, promising, questioning and other social speech acts in *Die apriorischen Grundlagen des bürgerlichen Rechts* ('The Apriori Foundation of the Civil Law') (1913), thereby contributing to the philosophy of law as well as the human sciences.

Conrad-Martius and Stavenhagen contributed to the philosophy of religion, and Stein is now recognized not only for reflections on empathy and the human sciences, but also, through lectures from around 1930 collected posthumously under the title *Die Frau* (1959), for contributions to feminism. HARTMANN showed the influence of Husserl and Scheler in his rejection of Neo-Kantianism and his central reliance on eidetic method in *Grundzüge einer Metaphysik der Erkenntnis* (Outline of a Metaphysics of Knowledge) (1921) and *Ethik* (1925). Ingarden, chiefly known for *Das literarische Kunstwerk* (The Literary Work of Art) (1931), carried realistic phenomenology to Poland. Gustav SHPET introduced phenomenology into Russia.

Herbert Spiegelberg, a student of Pfänder, later wrote the monumental *The Phenomenological Movement* (1960) as well as descriptively oriented studies; more recently, Karl Schuhmann has functioned as the historian of realistic phenomenology. Barry Smith and David Woodruff Smith lead the efforts to connect current Anglo-American analytical philosophy not only with Brentano and related Austrian philosophy, but also with realistic phenomenology.

3 Constitutive phenomenology

The founding text of constitutive phenomenology is the first book of Husserl's *Ideen zu einer reinen Phänomenologie und phänomenologischen Philosophie* (Ideas Pertaining to a Pure Phenomenology and to a Phenomenological Philosophy) (1913). Posthumous works have made it clear that Husserl's transcendental constitutive phenomenology began by 1906 and is broader than the books published in his lifetime seem to show. Even during his lifetime he recognized in 'Nachwort zu meinen Ideen...' (Postscript to my Ideas...) (1930) a 'constitutive phenomenology of the natural attitude', also called a 'mundane' or 'worldly' phenomenology, that amounts chiefly to phenomenological psychology. Much in the realistic, existential and hermeneutical tendencies can be seen as convergent with this mundane constitutive phenomenology. Nevertheless, the aim of most constitutive phenomenology is transcendental.

Constitutive phenomenology emphasizes processes within conscious life as they are intentive of objects, but it also reflects correlatively on the objects as intended in such processes. Constitutive phenomenology is specified by its concern with constitution. To analyse the 'constitution' of a matter is definitely not to distinguish the components of which it is composed, but rather to describe the syntheses of intentive processes in conscious life with which it correlates as an intentional object. The expression

was taken from Kantianism, but is not confined to operations of conceptually structuring objects. There is pre-predicative experience in which objects are constituted as perceived, valued, willed and so on, but not yet formed into states of affairs.

Between *Logical Investigations* and *Ideas I*, Husserl published 'Philosophie als strenge Wissenschaft' (1911). It shows how his concern had broadened from the formal sciences of logic and mathematics to include the natural as well as the human or cultural sciences. Thus what he seeks in *Ideas I* are subjective conditions for the possibility of science of all kinds. His transcendentalism, however, differs from those of Kant and others in so far as he holds that the conscious life in which the world and worldly sciences could be subjectively grounded is itself the object of reflective observation, eidetic intuition and description.

The opening part of *Ideas I* is devoted to eidetic method. It has unfortunately led to confusion between the eidetic and the transcendental methods, between going from 'facts' to 'essences' and going from conscious life in the world to conscious life as transcendental. Conscious life in its non-worldly or transcendental status is the same life that is originally encountered in the 'natural' or naively world-accepting attitude of the zoological and cultural sciences as well as in everyday life; but if the world is not to be grounded in part of itself, part of this worldly or natural (and realistic) attitude needs to be reduced to a transcendentally reflective attitude, and the conscious life, then reflectively thematized, needs to have its 'being in the world' placed in suspense. This is accomplished through transcendental phenomenological bracketing or 'epoché', a species of suspended judgment focused on the spatial, temporal and causal relations of conscious life with the rest of the world. In this attitude the world can be seen as an object intended to by non-worldly conscious life that, in the technical signification of the word, 'constitutes' it. 'Constitution' refers to the ways in which types of objects correlate with types of conscious processes. Husserl went on then to assert that conscious life has a more fundamental being than its being in the world, which not even all other transcendental phenomenologists accept.

In its middle parts *Ideas I* describes the natural attitude and transcendental epoché, offering detailed analyses of the parallel structures of the 'noema' or object as it is intended to and the 'noesis' or intentive conscious process in which objects are constituted. It also discusses how conscious life has an inner time in which each conscious process is 'protentive' to later and 'retrotentive' to earlier processes; how there is an 'I' who can engage in the processes strictly called acts;

how sensuous 'stuff' is formed in perception; and how objects have characteristics as believed in, valued and willed, as well as modes of appearance and manners of givenness, including clarity and distinctness in recollection and imagination as well as in perception and 'eideation'.

The last part of *Ideas I* is devoted to rational justification. The theory of reason is the culmination of transcendental phenomenology. Justification for Husserl comes from the seeing, intuiting or 'evidencing' of the matters themselves. There is adequate and inadequate evidence, and apodictic and assertoric evidence, and such can directly and indirectly justify not only believing, but also valuing and willing; there is then epistemological, axiological and practical reason.

The second book of Husserl's *Ideas*, chiefly composed in 1912–15 and devoted to the natural and human sciences, was also worked on by his assistants Edith Stein and Ludwig Landgrebe; although it was not published until 1952, it was known in manuscript to Martin Heidegger before *Sein und Zeit* (Being and Time) (1927) and to Maurice Merleau-Ponty before *Phénoménologie de la perception* (Phenomenology of Perception) (1945). Husserl returned to the formal sciences in 'Formale und transzendentale Logik' (Formal and Transcendental Logic) (1929).

At Freiburg during the 1920s and in retirement until his death in 1938, Husserl went beyond the 'static phenomenology' that uses eidetic method to disclose types of possible objects and consciousness. 'Genetic phenomenology', as he termed it, seeks to elucidate how active syntheses have origins in passive syntheses, a search that emphasizes time in individual life but also extends into history, intersubjectivity, the genesis of the lifeworld, and the teleology of conscious life in what he more broadly calls 'generative phenomenology'. These are all central issues in the later Husserl and in the background of his last work, *Die Krisis der europäischen Wissenschaften und die transzendentale Phänomenologie* (The Crisis of European Sciences and Transcendental Phenomenology) (1936).

Husserl's thought was eclipsed in Germany during the Nazi period, but continued to be developed after the Second World War by a number of figures, three of whom can be mentioned. First, in *Théorie du champ de la conscience* (The Field of Consciousness) (1957), Aron Gurwitsch draws upon Gestalt psychology to revise Husserl's accounts of the 'I' and attention, denying the need for the former as organizer and asserting the inherent organization of the field of consciousness into theme, thematic field, and margin. Second, in *Collected Papers* (1962–96), Alfred Schutz reflects from the standpoint of the 'constitutive phenomenology of the natural attitude' on the everyday common-sense constitution of the socio-cultural lifeworld and on how the cultural sciences – economics and sociology in particular – can know aspects of it. And, third, in *Zur Kritik der hermeneutischen Vernunft* (The Critique of Hermeneutical Reason) (1972), Thomas Seebohm returns to the traditional methodical hermeneutics as interpretation and critique of texts and traces that was pursued in Friedrich Schleiermacher, Augustus Boeckh and Wilhelm Dilthey, and seeks a transcendental phenomenological grounding for it.

It has been easy on the basis of the publications of his lifetime to caricature the mature Husserl as a modern-day (but nonrepresentationalist) Cartesian for whom disembodied and situationless intellects reflect upon the forms of their own thinking and have great difficulties knowing and interacting with one another. Closer study shows, however, that places for philosophy of the cultural as well as the natural sciences, for value theory and ethics, and for embodiment, empathy and communal life are sketched in those very same publications, although only developed in lectures and manuscripts, many of which have been published posthumously in *Husserliana* (see PHENOMENOLOGY, EPISTEMIC ISSUES IN).

4 Existential phenomenology

Existential phenomenology is not structured by the complex concern for reason and the theory of science so prominent in constitutive phenomenology. Existential phenomenology draws ultimately upon the mundane reflective-descriptive spirit of the *Logical Investigations* as well upon the intensified interest in the 1920s and 1930s in NIETZSCHE and KIERKEGAARD, the latter urging a new signification for the word 'existence'. The immediate occasion, however, is a misconstrual of Martin Heidegger's *Being and Time*. This incomplete masterpiece is actually not devoted to human existence but rather 'fundamental ontology'.

The old word 'ontology' had been revived by Husserl to name eidetic accounts of objects and their regions; realistic phenomenologists continue that usage, and Husserl investigates the regional ontologies of nature, body, psyche and culture in *Ideas II*. Attempting to radicalize constitutive phenomenology, Heidegger's work is 'ontology' because it explicates the Being of beings (*Sein der Seienden*) and 'fundamental' because it seeks grounds beyond the mundane regional ontologies recognized by Husserl. The work contains an 'existential analytic' of human being or 'Dasein', not for a philosophical anthropology but as a means to this fundamental ontology.

Dasein – also translated as 'existence' or, in the early French translations of Henri Corbin, *réalité humaine* – is the being where the world is disclosed and the being whose mode of being is to understand Being, to bring it and related matters to light through seeing rather than constructing, and to find words for such matters. Dasein, Heidegger says, is being-in-the-world. This is not the world referred to in the positive sciences that Husserl emphasized even in *Die Krisis*, but rather the world as a set of everyday concerns and purposes, the world in which equipment is used and talk goes on. Dasein finds itself thrown into a situation not of its choosing; it is concerned with the future; it is for the most part distracted; and, deep down, it is anxious before its most extreme possibility – its own nothingness. But Dasein can heed the call of its own inmost possibility to live authentically and resolutely. Such terms were also used by Heidegger to support National Socialism during the 1930s, but they disappeared from his writing after the war, when he completed his turning (*Kehre*) from the oblique approach through Dasein to the direct thinking of Being.

Being was always Heidegger's central issue. The third division of Part I of *Sein und Zeit* was to have gone beyond Dasein to show how the meaning of Being is time, but that division was not written, which made it even easier to construe the analytic of Dasein as philosophical anthropology, a construal that Heidegger emphatically challenged in his *Brief über den 'Humanismus'* ('Letter on Humanism') (1947).

Hannah ARENDT was influenced by Karl JASPERS as well as Heidegger during the 1920s, and is thus arguably the first existential phenomenologist, even though her contributions to political theory and problems of ethnicity, such as *The Origins of Totalitarianism* (1951), only appeared after the war. It is also arguable that existential phenomenology appears in Japan with Miki Kiyoshi's *Pasukaru niokeru Ningen no Kenkyu* (A Study of Man in Pascal) (1926) and Kuki Shuzou's *Iki no Kouzou* (The Structure of Iki) (1930). Chiefly, however, the existential tendency developed in France during the 1930s. The early Emmanuel LEVINAS interpreted Husserl and Heidegger together and helped introduce phenomenology into France and overall has more in common with the existential than with the other tendencies. Gabriel MARCEL reflected upon fidelity, having, hope, promising and so on; opposed intellectualism and 'objectivity'; and emphasized the embodiment, finitude, sensuousness and situatedness of existence in the world. His chief interest, however, independently paralleling Heidegger, is in Being as the ground of existence. Like Arendt, Sartre and Beauvoir, Marcel was not a professional academic and often wrote for general audiences.

The background influences on phenomenology in France in the 1930s also included Scheler, the rediscovered early and humanistic MARX, and especially HEGEL as presented by Jean Wahl and Alexandre KOJÉVE, who both argued for extensive convergencies between the phenomenologies of Hegel and Husserl. The issues of finitude, freedom, history, negation and individual and group conflict became prominent for Beauvoir, Merleau-Ponty and Sartre, who led the classic period of French phenomenology.

Jean-Paul SARTRE studied Husserl and began to write on the ego, imagination and emotion in the mid-1930s, soon also studying Scheler and Heidegger. His *L'être et le néant* (Being and Nothingness) appeared in 1943. Sartre's approach relies on reflection upon, and eidetic description of, types of intentionality and objects as they present themselves, and he produced concrete analyses of many matters, for instance, historicity, authenticity, situation and especially individual freedom, which, for him, is the source of meaning and value. Human reality is what it has chosen to be, for existence precedes essence. In later work Sartre's emphasis on freely choosing individuals declined, he became doubtful about phenomenology's ability to explain historical conditioning, and turned to the writings of Marx.

Maurice MERLEAU-PONTY did pursue an academic career and chiefly wrote for fellow academics. He found many insights in science – especially cultural or human science, psychology in particular – but, like other existential phenomenologists, he opposed objectification and categorization and emphasized the ambiguous, concrete, contingent and particular. Against the early Sartre, he considered human freedom to be limited by its situation. In his main work, *Phenomenology of Perception*, he was concerned not with pure consciousness, but rather with human existence as embodied perception (or behaviour) in the world, and with how what is perceived has, for subjects, inherent structures of the sort described in Gestalt psychology and Aron Gurwitsch's work (see GESTALT PSYCHOLOGY). While the body can be objectified in science, it is originally lived as subjective, and art, language, the other, politics, sexuality, space and so on, are to be analysed in relation to it. Merleau-Ponty died having composed only part of his body-focused ontology.

Simone de BEAUVOIR, often too closely associated philosophically with Sartre, is the third leading French existential phenomenologist. She likens existential conversion, a suspending of will in order to grasp the conditions of one's life, to Husserl's transcendental epoché; appreciates Heidegger's concern with the future, but finds change rather than being-toward-death central; and accepts from Merleau-Ponty that the human body is historical, denying, however, that a woman is her reproductive or sex-object body. For her, phenomenology is centrally concerned with friendship, as her autobiography and letters show, and also with age, class, ethnicity, gender, oppression and liberation. Beauvoir inspired the second wave of feminism with *Le deuxième sexe* (The Second Sex) (1949), opposing the myth by which categories defined in contrast with male categories are imposed on women; analysing the lived experience of meaning in feminine being-in-the-world; and urging that females are not born but become women (see FEMINISM).

Existential phenomenology spread widely from France. It was also extended to the human sciences, beginning with work in The Netherlands and Flanders during the 1950s, and has been represented in the United States by Maurice Natanson and in a structural version by Bernhard Waldenfels in Germany. It was eventually eclipsed by structuralism in France, but became central to the vast expansion of phenomenology in the United States that began in the 1960s – where the relevance of existential phenomenology for new problematics, such as feminism, is increasingly recognized (see EXISTENTIALISM; EXISTENTIALIST ETHICS; EXISTENTIALIST THEOLOGY).

5 Hermeneutical phenomenology

According to the *Logical Investigations*, perception, recollection, imagination and so on have a sense or meaning prior to expressions in propositional form, and some consider this insight an anticipation of hermeneutical phenomenology. This fourth tendency also begins – and without the 'existential' interpretation – in Heidegger's *Being and Time*. Traditional hermeneutics was chiefly interpretation of texts, but now all experience is seen as being affected by language and interpretation. Heidegger interprets 'phenomenology' as the *logos* of the *phainomenon*, these words being construed, respectively, as what makes matters manifest and what is made manifest, the latter including undisclosed as well as disclosed aspects. The phenomena of authenticity, death, care and above all Being itself are thus interpretable. Dasein always already has some understanding of Being that can be refined through philosophical interpretation, although the truth thus won conceals as well as reveals. The analysis of Dasein that so influenced existential phenomenology is actually a hermeneutics of Dasein that seeks to bring out hidden aspects. This includes self-interpretations, which refer back to earlier generations and are thus historical.

The hermeneutical approach, especially to texts, continues in Heidegger's later work, although the word hermeneutics does not.

The first phenomenological interpretation beyond Heidegger is Hans-Georg Gadamer's *Platons dialektische Ethik* (Plato's Dialectical Ethics) (1931) (see GADAMER, H.-G.). It accepts Heidegger's notion of revealing and concealing truth as well as his focus on the active participant in life rather than the scientific observer. Its emphasis on the ethical aspects of the openness of one interlocutor to another is continued in his quite influential *Wahrheit und Methode* (Truth and Method) (1960). Not exclusively focused on texts, this is a 'philosophical hermeneutics' that is concerned with the general theory of understanding, that defends tradition and authority against Enlightenment attacks, and that is urged for use in law, literature and theology. It remains phenomenological in its use of Husserl's notion of intentionality and theory of perception to oppose naturalism and relativism. Interpretations even of the unthought in a text seek to be fulfilled by the matters themselves referred to by the text.

Paul RICOEUR studied Marcel and Jaspers as well as Husserl and Heidegger while interned as a prisoner of war. In 1950 he published the translation of Husserl's *Ideen I*, which he began in the camp; he subsequently played a central role in advancing French Husserl scholarship and regularly contended that his own evolving position was compatible with Husserl's original inspiration, whereby meaning is transcendent of conscious life. The first expression of his own thought converged with realistic phenomenology in employing eidetic method to analyse the voluntary and involuntary (he had also studied Pfänder's work). His concerns then with freedom, the other and evil converged with existential phenomenology, and, finally, he has focused on understanding as requiring texts or text-like structures and he thus joined hermeneutical phenomenology. He interprets not only religious symbols, for example, of the creation, but also the unconscious of psychoanalysis in works such as *Le conflit des interprétations* (The Conflict of Interpretations) (1969a). More recent work interprets metaphor, time, narrative, the 'same' or 'self' and the other.

Gadamer and Ricoeur have promoted hermeneutical phenomenology quite actively and this tendency has been strong in the United States. Calvin O. Schrag has contributed to the philosophy of language in *Experience and Being* (1969), Don Ihde to the philosophy of technology in *Technics and Praxis* (1979), Graeme Nicholson to the philosophy of perception in *Seeing and Reading* (1984), and then there is Patrick Heelan's *Space-Perception and the*

Philosophy of Science (1983) and Joseph J. Kockelmans' *Ideas for a Hermeneutic Phenomenology of Natural Science* (1993). Other philosophical work has been done in aesthetics, ethics, history, language, law, literature, politics and religion. Hermeneutical phenomenology has extensively influenced not only the philosophy of the human sciences but the human sciences themselves.

Lest the debates within the movement and the structure of this essay give the impression that phenomenology went off in four separate ways, it must be emphasized that hermeneutical phenomenology draws nearly as much on existential and constitutive phenomenology as on the early Heidegger; that, while highly original, existential phenomenology is conscious of its central inspiration in Husserl and Scheler as well as Heidegger; that there has been from the outset extensive mutual borrowing as well as criticism between constitutive and realistic phenomenology; and that, by virtue of his effort reflectively to analyse and describe the matters themselves of conscious life and what is, in manifold ways, intended in it, Husserl is, as Ricoeur has said, not the whole of phenomenology, but he is 'more or less its centre' (see HERMENEUTICS).

6 Prospects

The phenomenological movement began with Husserl's *Logical Investigations*. History has shown that Wilhelm Dilthey was correct to proclaim this work 'epochal'. Besides the tendencies sketched above, a shifting geographical focus can be noted. This focus was in Germany until 1933, then shifted to France until about 1960; after that, while inspiration came from both Germany and France, the largest part of phenomenologists have come from the United States. Other enduring national traditions of phenomenology began in Japan, Russia and Spain before the First World War; arose in Australia, Czechoslovakia, Hungary, Italy, Korea, The Netherlands and Flanders, Poland and Yugoslavia, as well as the United States and France between the wars; and emerged after the Second World War in Canada, China, Great Britain, India, Portugal, Scandinavia and South Africa. By the 1980s, genuinely international (and not just transatlantic) conferences and other forms of collaboration were intensifying; now that generations-deep underground tendencies have begun surfacing after the end of the Cold War, it is all the more likely that this trend will continue. It may turn out that the German, French and American periods of the phenomenological movement began to be succeeded in the early 1990s by an international period in which there are many centres.

As a century-old, world-wide, still growing and increasingly multidisciplinary movement, phenomenology is arguably the central movement in twentieth-century philosophy, and its vitality and momentum should carry it far into the twenty-first century.

See also: PHENOMENOLOGY IN LATIN AMERICA; PHENOMENOLOGY OF RELIGION

References and further reading

Arendt, H. (1951) *The Origins of Totalitarianism*, New York: Harcourt Brace Jovanovich; 2nd edn, enlarged, 1958. (A mature work in which history and ethnicity are emphasized as aspects of communal human existence.)

* Beauvoir, S. de (1949) *Le deuxième sexe*, Paris: Gallimard; trans. H.M. Parshley, *The Second Sex*, New York: Knopf, 1953. (The founding text for the second stage of feminism, which emphasizes not just formal equality but gender-specific cultural attitudes that need to be reconciled.)

Becker, O. (1923) 'Beiträge zur phänomenologischen Begründung der Geometrie und ihrer physikalischen Anwendungen' (Contributions to the phenomenological grounding of geometry and its applications in physics), *Jahrbuch für Philosophie und phänomenologische Forschung 7*. (As the title indicates, deals with geometry and its applications.)

* Bergson, H.-L. (1889) *Essai sur les données immediates de la conscience*, Paris: Alcan; trans. F.L. Pogson, *Time and Free Will*, London: Macmillan, 1910. (Anticipates the phenomenological focus on inner time, the time of the stream of conscious life, in contrast with the time coupled with space in which trees grow.)

* Brentano, F. (1874) *Psychologie vom empirischen Standpunkt*, ed. O. Kraus, Hamburg: Felix Meiner; trans. A.C. Rancurello, D.B. Terrell and L.L. McAlister and ed. L.L. McAlister, *Psychology from an Empirical Standpoint*, London, Routledge, 1969; 2nd edn, 1995. (Fundamental text of the descriptive psychology from which phenomenology arose through the rejection of immanentism.)

Caputo, J. (1987) *Radical Hermeneutics*, Bloomington, IN: Indiana University Press. (Example of recent hermeneutical phenomenology.)

Derrida, J. (1990) *Le probléme de la génèse dans la philosophie de Husserl* (The problem of genesis in Husserl's philosophy), Paris: Presses Universitaires de France. (Beginning of this author's challenging interpretations of Husserl.)

* Dilthey, W. (1985–) *Selected Works*, ed. R.A. Makkreel and F. Rodi, Princeton, NJ: Princeton University Press, 6 vols. (Central author in relation to

whose work phenomenologists reflect on the cultural sciences.)

Embree, L. *et al.* (1996) *The Encyclopedia of Phenomenology*, Dordrecht: Kluwer. (Reviews the whole movement and can be used to approach particular figures, national traditions, and tendencies in it.)

* Gadamer, H.-G. (1931) 'Platos dialektische Ethik: Phänomenologische Interpretationen sum Philebos', in *Platos dialektische Ethik*, Hamburg: Felix Meiner, 1968; trans. *Plato's Dialectical Ethics*, New Haven, CT: Yale University, 1991. (Arguably the first document of hermeneutical phenomenology beyond Heidegger.)

* —— (1960) *Wahrheit und Methode*, Tübingen: J.C.B. Mohr; trans. *Truth and Method*, London: Sheed & Ward, 1975. (This author's masterpiece.)

* Gurwitsch, A. (1957) *The Field of Consciousness*. Pittsburgh, PA: Duquesne University Press, 1964; trans. M. Butor, *Théorie du champ de la conscience*, Bruges and Paris: Desclée de Brouwer. (Creative development of constitutive phenomenology incorporating descriptive results from Gestalt psychology.)

* Hartmann, N. (1921) *Grundzüge einer Metaphysik der Erkenntnis* (Outline of a Metaphysics of Knowledge), Berlin: de Gruyter. (Metaphysical development from Husserl and realistic phenomenology.)

* —— (1925) *Ethik*, Berlin: de Gruyter; trans. S. Coit, *Ethics*, London: Allen & Unwin, 1932. (Major contribution to phenomenological ethics.)

* Heelan, P. (1983) *Space-Perception and the Philosophy of Science*, Berkeley, CA: University of California Press. (Recent hermeneutical contribution.)

* Heidegger, M. (1927) 'Sein und Zeit', *Jahrbuch für Phänomenologie und phänomenologische Forschung* 8; trans. J. Macquarrie and E. Robinson, *Being and Time*, London: SCM Press, 1962. (Incomplete masterpiece of second most important figure in phenomenology and source of hermeneutical as well as existential phenomenology.)

* —— (1947) *Platons Lehre von der Wahrheit. Mit einem Brief über den 'Humanismus'*, Bern: Francke; trans. F.A. Capuzzo and J.G. Gray, 'Letter on Humanism', in M. Heidegger, *Basic Writings*, ed. D.F. Krell, New York: Harper & Row, 1986, 193–242. (Text in which Heidegger rejects existential interpretation of *Sein und Zeit*.)

* Husserl, E. (1891) *Philosophie der Arithmetik*, ed. L. Eley, The Hague: Martinus Nijhoff, 1970. (Attempts to account for the concept of number by relating it to the mental operation of counting.)

* —— (1900–1) *Logische Untersuchungen*, Halle: Max Niemeyer; trans. J.N. Findlay, *Logical Investigations*, London: Routledge & Kegan Paul, 1970. (Epoch-making source of the phenomenological movement in which the reflective-descriptive approach was radicalized and extended beyond the original epistemology of logic and mathematics.)

* —— (1911) 'Philosophie als strenge Wissenschaft', *Logos* 1 (1910–11) 289–341; trans. as 'Philosophy as rigorous science', in *Husserl: Shorter Works*, ed. P. McCormick and F.A. Elliston, Notre Dame, IN: University of Notre Dame Press, 1981, 166–97. (Shows how Husserl's concern broadened from logic and mathematics to include the natural sciences.)

* —— (1913) *Ideen zu einer reinen Phänomenologie und phänomenologischen Philosophie, Erstes Buch*, in *Husserliana* vol. 3, ed. W. Biemel, The Hague: Martinus Nijhoff, 1976; trans. F. Kersten, *Ideas pertaining to a Pure Phenomenology and to a Phenomenological Philosophy, First Book*, The Hague: Martinus Nijhoff, 1983. (Founding text of Husserl's mature constitutive phenomenology.)

* —— (1913) *Ideen zu einer reinen Phänomenologie und phänomenologischen Philosophie, Zweites Buch*, in *Husserliana* vol. 4, ed. M. Biemel, The Hague: Martinus Nijhoff, 1952; trans. R. Rojcewicz and A. Schuwer, *Ideas Pertaining to a Pure Phenomenology and to a Phenomenological Philosophy, Second Book*, The Hague: Martinus Nijhoff, 1989. (Shows Husserl's theory of the lived body and interest in the cultural as well as the natural sciences.)

* —— (1929) 'Formale und transzendentale Logik: Versuch einer Kritik der logischen Vernunft', *Jahrbuch für Philosophie und phänomenologische-Forschung*, 10: v–xii; 1–298; trans. D. Cairns, *Formal and Transcendental Logic*, The Hague: Martinus Nijhoff, 1969. (Husserl's mature philosphy of logic and mathematics.)

* —— (1930) 'Nachwort zu meinen Ideen...' ; trans. as 'Author's Preface to the English edition of *Ideas*', in *Husserl: Shorter Works*, ed. P. McCormick and F.A. Elliston, Notre Dame, IN: University of Notre Dame Press, 1981, 43–53. (Recognizes a 'mundane' or 'worldly' phenomenology, that amounts chiefly to phenomenological psychology.)

* —— (1931) Cartesianische Meditationen, in *Husserliana* vol. 1, ed. S. Strasser, The Hague: Martinus Nijhoff, 1960; trans. G. Pfeiffer and E. Levinas, *Méditations Cartésiennes*, Paris: Vrin, 1931; trans. D. Cairns, *Cartesian Meditations*, The Hague: Martinus Nijhoff, 1960. (Short, long available, but quite difficult atttempt by Husserl to summarize his position.)

* —— (1936) *Die Krisis der europäischen Wissenschaften und die transzendentale Phänomenologie*, in

Husserliana vol. 4, ed. W. Biemel, The Hague: Martinus Nijhoff, 1954; trans. D. Carr, *The Crisis of European Sciences and Transcendental Phenomenology*, Evanston, IL: Northwestern University Press, 1972. (Husserl's last work, this text shows an historically oriented approach to natural science, emphasizes the lifeworld, and the relation of psychology to other cultural sciences with transcendental phenomenology.)

* Ihde, D. (1979) *Technics and Praxis*, Dordrecht: Reidel. (The beginning of this author's rich phenomenological philosophy of technology.)

* Ingarden, R.W. (1931) *Das literarische Kunstwerk*, Tübingen: Max Niemeyer; trans. G.G. Grabowicz, *The Literary Work of Art*, Evanston, IL: Northwestern University Press, 1973. (Major contribution to phenomenological aesthetics.)

* James, W. (1890) *Principles of Psychology*, New York: Henry Holt. (Anticipation of phenomenology recognized by Husserl, Gurwitsch, Schutz and others.)

* Kuki, S. (1930) *Iki no Kouzou* (The structure of Iki), Tokyo: Iwanami-shoten. (Arguably an early contribution to existential phenomenology.)

* Kockelmans, J.J. (1993) *Ideas for a Hermeneutic Phenomenology of Natural Science*, Dordrecht: Kluwer. (Culminating contribution to hermeneutical phenomenology.)

* Merleau-Ponty, M. (1945) *Phénoménologie de la perception*, Paris: Gallimard; trans. C. Smith, *Phenomenology of Perception*, London: Routledge & Kegan Paul, 1962. (Major text of this author and of existential phenomenology.)

* Miki, K. (1926) *Pasukaru niokeru Ningen no Kenkyu* (A study of man in Pascal), Tokyo: Iwanami-shoten. (Probably the first manifestation of existential phenomenology, but long unrecognized in the West.)

Mohanty, J.N. (1982) *Husserl and Frege,* Bloomington, IN: Indiana University Press. (Studies connections between these two tradition founders and dispels myth that Husserl overcame his psychologism under Frege's influence.)

* —— (1989) *Transcendental Phenomenology: An Analytic Account*, Oxford: Blackwell. (Excellent recent presentation.)

Mulligan, K. (ed.) (1987) *Speech Act and Sachverhalt: Reinach and the Foundations of Realist Phenomenology*, The Hague: Martinus Nijhoff. (As the title indicates, discusses the foundations of realist phenomenology.)

* Nicholson, G. (1984) *Seeing and Reading*, Atlantic Highlands, NJ: Humanities Press International. (Hermeneutical phenomenology of perception.)

* Pfänder, A. (1900) *Phänomenologie des Wollens*, Leipzig: Johann Ambrosius Barth; trans. H. Spiegelberg, in *Phenomenology of Willing and Motivation*, Evanston, IL: Northwestern University Press, 1967. (Important early text of realistic phenomenology.)

* Reinach, A. (1913) 'Die apriorischen Grundlagen des bürgerlichen Rechts', in *Sämtliche Werke*, ed. K. Schuhmann and B. Smith; trans. 'The Apriori Foundation of the Civil Law', *Alethia* (1982) 3: 1–142. (As the title indicates, deals with the apriori foundations of civil law.)

* Ricoeur, P. (1969a) *Le conflit des interprétations. Essais d'herméneutique*, Paris: Seuil; ed. D. Ihde; trans. W. Domingo et al., *The Conflict of Interpretations: Essays in Hermeneutics*, Evanston, IL: Northwestern University Press, 1974. (Mature expression of author's hermeneutical phenomenology.)

—— (1969b) *Hermeneutics and the Human Sciences*, New York: Cambridge University Press. (Hermeneutical phenomenology of human or cultural sciences.)

* Sartre, J.-P. (1943) *L'être et le néant*, Paris: Gallimard; trans. H.E. Barnes, *Being and Nothingness*, New York: Philosophical Library, 1956. (Major source of existential phenomenological ontology.)

* Scheler, M. (1913, 1916) *Der Formalismus in der Ethik und die Materiale Wertethik*, Bern: A. Francke; trans. M.S. Frings and R.L. Funk, *Formalism in Ethics and Non-Formal Ethics of Values*, Evanston, IL: Northwestern University Press, 1973. (Major ethical position from standpoint of realistic phenomenology.)

* Schrag, C.O. (1969) *Experience and Being*, Evanston, IL: Northwestern University Press. (Early expression of hermeneutical phenomenology in United States.)

* Schutz, A. (1962–96) *Collected Papers*, Dordrecht: Kluwer Academic Publishers. (Highly influential source for constitutive phenomenology of the natural attitude and phenomenology of the social type of natural sciences.)

* Seebohm, T. (1972) *Zur Kritik der hermeneutischen Vernunft* (The Critique of Hermeneutical Reason), Bonn: Bouvier. (Transcendental phenomenological grounding of the method of the historical human sciences.)

Sokolowski, R. (1974) *Husserlian Meditations*, Evanston, IL: Northwestern University Press. (Fine example of Husserlian research.)

* Spiegelberg, H. (1982) *The Phenomenological Movement*, 3rd edn, revised and enlarged with the collaboration of K. Schuhmann, The Hague: Kluwer Academic Publishers. (Classic study only superceded by Embree's 1996 Encyclopedia.)

* Stein, E. (1959) *Die Frau, Ihre Aufgabe nach Natur und Gnade*, Louvain: E. Nauwelaerts; trans. F.M. Oben, *Essays on Women*, in *Collected Works* vol. 2, Washington, DC: ICS Publications, 1987. (Late recognized inception of phenomenological investigations of gender.)

LESTER EMBREE

PHENOMENOLOGY

see ARENDT, HANNAH; BEAUVOIR, SIMONE DE; BRENTANO, FRANZ CLEMENS; CATTANEO, CARLO; GADAMER, HANS-GEORG; HARTMANN, NICOLAI; HEIDEGGER, MARTIN; HUSSERL, EDMUND; INGARDEN, ROMAN WITOLD; MERLEAU-PONTY, MAURICE; PHENOMENALISM; PHENOMENOLOGICAL MOVEMENT; PHENOMENOLOGY, EPISTEMIC ISSUES IN; PHENOMENOLOGY IN LATIN AMERICA; PHENOMENOLOGY OF RELIGION; RICOEUR, PAUL; SCHELER, MAX FERDINAND; SARTRE, JEAN-PAUL; SHPET, GUSTAV GUSTAVOVICH

PHENOMENOLOGY, EPISTEMIC ISSUES IN

Phenomenology is not a unified doctrine. Its main proponents – Husserl, Heidegger, Sartre and Merleau-Ponty – interpret it differently. However, it is possible to present a broad characterization of what they share. Phenomenology is a method of philosophical investigation which results in a radical ontological revision of Cartesian Dualism. It has implications for epistemology: the claim is that, when the foundations of empirical knowledge in perception and action are properly characterized, traditional forms of scepticism and standard attempts to justify knowledge are undermined.

Phenomenological method purports to be descriptive and presuppositionless. First one adopts a reflective attitude towards one's experience of the world by putting aside assumptions about the world's existence and character. Second, one seeks to describe particular, concrete phenomena. Phenomena are not contents of the mind; they all involve an experiencing subject and an experienced object. Phenomenological description aims to make explicit essential features implicit in the 'lived-world' – the world as we act in it prior to any theorizing about it. The phenomenological method reveals that practical knowledge is prior to propositional knowledge – knowing that arises from knowing how.

The key thesis of phenomenology, drawn from Brentano, is that consciousness is intentional, that is, directed onto objects. Phenomenologists interpret this to mean that subjects and objects are essentially interrelated, a fact which any adequate account of subjects and objects must preserve. Phenomenological accounts of subjects emphasize action and the body; accounts of objects emphasize the significance they have for us.

The aim to be presuppositionless involves scrutinizing scientific and philosophical theories (Galileo, Locke and Kant are especially challenged). Phenomenology launches a radical critique of modern philosophy as overinfluenced by the findings of the natural sciences. In particular, epistemology has adopted from science its characterization of the basic data of experience.

The influence of phenomenology on the analytic tradition has been negligible. The influence on the Continental tradition has been greater. The phenomenological critique of modern science and philosophy has influenced postmodern thought which interprets the modernist worldview as having the status of master narrative rather than truth. Postmodern thought also criticizes the positive phenomenological claim that there are essential features of the lived-world.

1 Phenomenological reduction
2 Presuppositionless description
3 Uncovering essence
4 Phenomenological ontology

1 Phenomenological reduction

The first phenomenological move is the phenomenological reduction, also called by HUSSERL 'bracketing' or 'the epoché'. The move involves distancing oneself from one's everyday 'immersion' in the ordinary practical activities of life, adopting a reflective standpoint upon one's experience of the world. This is taken to be the necessary standpoint from which to engage in genuine philosophical enquiry, one which phenomenologists criticize other philosophers for failing to adopt. The philosophical standpoint is radically different from the 'natural' attitude of common sense and of scientific enquiry.

The crucial difference is that, in the natural attitude, one assumes unquestioningly that the world exists. The philosophical attitude, in contrast, puts aside – brackets – this assumption.

The philosophical standpoint after the reduction is differently characterized by transcendental phenomenology (Husserl) and existential phenomenology (Heidegger, Sartre, Merleau-Ponty) (see PHENOMENOLOGICAL MOVEMENT). Husserl believed that it was a 'transcendental' standpoint, 'outside' the natural world. Existential phenomenologists believed that such a standpoint is neither attainable nor necessary. The human standpoint is essentially *in* the world. The reduction is only partial: one cannot put aside all one's existential assumptions at the same time. However reflective, the philosopher still takes for granted the existence of the armchair.

This first phenomenological move can appear puzzling: What is this reflective standpoint? Why is it essential for philosophical investigation? How can one put aside one's belief that the world exists? It is important to note, however, that there are clear similarities between phenomenological reduction and certain familiar, traditional moves made in articulating scepticism about the external world. The sceptic, in challenging the claim that we can know that the external world exists, is clearly requiring us to suspend our everyday judgment that it does (see SCEPTICISM).

The point of the phenomenological reduction is to bring to our attention the realm of phenomena, the 'lived-world', the world as we experience it. What exactly are phenomena? What is normally wanted in response to this question is an account of how phenomena relate to objects in the external world: are they real features of these objects or are they merely features of experiencing subjects? It is important to see that this question is supposed to have been ruled out by the phenomenological reduction. We are no longer assuming that there *is* an external world. Of course, following the reduction, there still *appears* to be a world. One aim of phenomenology is to explore how the world appears with a view to finding the experiential basis for, and meaning of, our belief that the world exists independently of our experience of it. Phenomena are our experiences of the world; we must, at this stage, remain neutral concerning the ontological status of that 'world'.

2 Presuppositionless description

The second phenomenological move is to describe phenomena without presuppositions. This is a difficult instruction to follow. Description normally has some purpose; what is the phenomenological purpose? One central phenomenological purpose is to

expose and avoid certain philosophical presuppositions. One such presupposition involves the notion of sensation which has had a central role in philosophy since Descartes, and in particular the idea that sensations are the basic atoms of experience. This thesis, it is claimed, has blinded philosophers to the true character of experience; phenomenological description can avoid this theoretical assumption.

The first phenomenological discovery, following the reduction, is that 'nothing has changed'. The world of objects does not disappear or dissolve into an airy realm of mere contents of consciousness. Nor does one's experience transform into bare colour patches, uninterpreted sounds and so on. To characterize experience in this way is a 'mistake' which traditional epistemology has made.

A natural objection to raise at this stage is that no-one claims that uninterpreted sense data are what we are conscious of: they are rather to be construed as the unconscious building blocks of conscious experience. The phenomenological reply to that criticism is to ask what, if not conscious experience, is the basis for the philosophical belief in sensations?

The diagnosis is as follows: modern philosophy has taken its account of the physical world from physics which focuses exclusively on the primary qualities of objects. Philosophers, notably Locke, set themselves the task of reconciling this account of the physical world with human experience (see LOCKE, J. §2). The thesis is that objects as construed by physics have powers to affect experiencing subjects. The notion of sensation as the basic data of perception is derived, not from experience, but from scientific findings, in particular scientific accounts of human sense organs: given what our sense organs are like, this is what the basic sensory data *must* be like. Sensations are theoretical entities of psychology. Philosophical accounts of perception and empirical knowledge, empiricist and rationalist alike, have endorsed this same notion of sensation.

The phenomenological criticisms of these philosophical theses are, first, that while theoretical entities may have a place in the natural sciences, they have no legitimate place in philosophical enquiry. Physics offers a highly abstract conception of objects. This has been extremely successful in making predictions about the world and facilitating manipulations of it; but philosophy and science have different aims. Philosophy should not take scientific realism for granted. The thesis that objects are properly defined in terms of their primary properties is another philosophical thesis which phenomenological description should not presuppose. Second, sensations are theoretical entities of a school of psychology which fails on its own terms to give an adequate account of perception. But, even if the notion of sensation had been a successful one in scientific psychology, that would be no reason for philosophy to adopt it. It is not just the notion of sensation but also the psychologists' conception of the mind as having contents which is challenged by phenomenology. This conception of the mind is another assumption which phenomenological description needs to avoid. Third, the notion of sensation has given rise to problems in epistemology which are insoluble because that very notion of sensation as mental contents caused by external objects always allows the sceptical challenge to be put, since there is no way of testing the causal claim. That the relation between experience and objects is a causal, contingent one is another presupposition which phenomenological description is to avoid. Moreover, even if knowledge of the external world could be justified by being shown to be based on sensations, this would not justify *our* claims to knowledge since sensations are not the basic data of our perceptions. Nothing in the phenomena supports this notion of sensation.

According to phenomenology, the philosophical thesis that sensations are the basic units of experience is not only false; it is indicative of a misconception of the philosophical enterprise. It is not the task of philosophy to seek to reconcile the findings of science with experience, but to explore the experiential basis of beliefs, including scientific ones. Phenomenological description aims to reveal, not the constitutive parts – the 'atoms' – of a phenomenon, but the greater whole, the 'synthesis' which makes it the phenomenon it is. Careful scrutiny from the reflective standpoint, can reveal this 'synthesis' because all its details are 'implicit' in the phenomenon. In the natural attitude, one notices only the explicit features.

How does one set about phenomenological description? First one selects a philosophically significant topic, a 'theme', for example, perceiving physical objects. Next, one selects a phenomenon – for example, seeing a table. What is implicit in this phenomenon? What are the surrounding features which make it the phenomenon it is? Vision is explicitly involved. Vision and other senses are implicitly involved: if we see something as a table, we have a range of expectations concerning how it would appear from other angles, to the touch, to hearing, and so on. Support for the claim that these expectations are implicit in the phenomenon lies in the fact that we would be surprised if they were not realized in the appropriate circumstances. If we explore these expectations further, we find that implicit in seeing the table are certain motor skills: we could move around the table, bump into it and so on. Also involved in perceiving the table is that one

knows what sorts of uses tables are put to, which typically involves having engaged in those practices. The significance of the table as something to be sat at, worked on or eaten from is implicit in seeing it and refers back to practices of sitting, working and eating. These are all features of the perceiving subject.

Phenomenological description also reveals implicit features of the object perceived, the wider 'synthesis' surrounding the way the table is involved in this phenomenon. The table appears as figure against a ground. The background contributes to the phenomenon – one would miss it if it were not there; but it is not the focus of one's attention. The table presents itself as a unified object, persisting unchanging as one walks around it. The table looks heavy, smooth, dusty, bare, uncluttered – colours and shapes are not the only visible features. The table appears as an artefact, manufactured from raw materials by someone using other artefacts; it was made for someone's use, in a certain sort of social setting. These are the sorts of features which phenomenological description reveals.

3 Uncovering essence

Such descriptions of specific 'concrete' phenomena, it is claimed, bring to light the richness and variety of the lived-world in contrast to the abstractions in terms of which scientific theory represents the world. The philosophical significance is twofold. First, such descriptions, it is claimed, have a critical role: they show that the theoretical presuppositions which were originally set aside are false: the descriptions serve as counterexamples to any philosophical theory which endorses the presuppositions. Second, they have a positive role: by describing particular phenomena, one can uncover essences, essential features of the lived-world.

One essential feature of phenomena is the intentionality of consciousness: consciousness is directed upon objects (see INTENTIONALITY). The phenomenological interpretation of this, what attention to the phenomena reveals, is that the relation between consciousness and its objects is an internal one. As such, it is not amenable to causal explanation. All consciousness is essentially consciousness of objects and all objects are essentially, if not explicitly, objects of consciousness. Idealist and realist claims to the contrary ignore this essential feature implicit in all phenomena.

An essential feature of perception is that it presupposes practical skills. All perceptual knowledge essentially depends on knowing how. Propositional knowledge is always 'situated' in practice. Philosophical accounts of the foundations of knowledge have often ignored this essentially practical foundation.

An essential feature of objects is their practical significance for us: they resist or assist our efforts to use them and live with them. Objects of theoretical knowledge are essentially also objects of our concern. Philosophical accounts of the character of objects in the external world have ignored this essential basis of theory in practice. Further, objects of the lived-world are not discrete entities, standing in causal, mechanical, contingent relations; they have internal relations with each other. Objects are essentially parts of complex wholes.

This move from description to essence looks problematic since it appears to involve a move from particular claims to universal and necessary ones. Phenomenologists differ in the way they purport to uncover essences. For transcendental phenomenology, essences can be detected only from the reflective standpoint, the standpoint of the transcendental ego. Essences have their origin in the transcendental ego: experience is structured as it is because the ego is structured as it is. Husserl believed that transcendental phenomenology leads to transcendental idealism (see IDEALISM §§3, 7). For existential phenomenology, there is no such transcendental ego, no transcendental grounding of the essential features of experience. The reflecting subject, the subject that is practising phenomenology and finding essential features of the lived world, is still an existential subject, living in the world.

As a test for what is essential, Husserl uses the criterion that we cannot imagine it otherwise. So, for example, we cannot imagine a perception of a physical object which did not involve 'horizons', expectations concerning other possible perceptions of it; we cannot imagine believing that a solid physical object exists without also knowing that there are possible circumstances – waking from a dream, its fading into thin air – which would show that belief to be false.

MERLEAU-PONTY looks for essential features of the perception of objects in natural capacities which are temporally prior to perceiving objects. He appeals to psychological data (drawn especially from Gestalt psychology) concerning, for example, the way babies focus their eyes on objects of interest and comfort while quite unable to focus on other less significant objects in their visual field (see GESTALT PSYCHOLOGY). Such examples, he claims, show that natural responses to significant surroundings are temporally prior to the perception of objects. From this temporal priority, Merleau-Ponty believes, follows a logical priority: there are necessary prerequisites of learning or perceiving, features implicit in experience without which we would not have the experience we do.

Husserl and Merleau-Ponty believed that, by uncovering essences, phenomenology could avert the

'crisis' threatened by the prevalence of positivism. HEIDEGGER and SARTRE introduce an explicitly moral dimension into the search for essences. Both believe that one can reveal essences by stripping away all that is inauthentic in one's dealings with the world. For Sartre, the search will reveal that all essence is dependent on human interests, human projections of non-being onto the world of Being; for Heidegger the end point of the search will be that Being will simply reveal itself as that with which we are 'primordially' connected (see BEING §4). Analytic philosophers have problems with that 'Being'. A sympathetic reading of these phenomenologists would be that they are seeking to characterize, not a state which philosophical enquiry enables one to achieve, but rather the process of philosophical enquiry. One may never reach the point at which all one's beliefs are true, all one's values as they ought to be. There may be no sense to attach to such a possibility, nothing which would count as recognizing it to obtain. One can, none the less, strive against false beliefs and bogus values. On this reading, Heidegger and Sartre may appear misguided in their attempts to say the unsayable; but we can see them as putting forward recognizable philosophical ideals.

4 Phenomenological ontology

Phenomenology shares with Cartesian dualism the belief that subjects and objects are radically different kinds of thing. They are not, however, logically distinct, nor are they the kinds of thing Descartes took them to be (see DESCARTES, R. §8). Subjects are essentially situated in the world, and the world of objects is essentially our home. Philosophical accounts of conscious subjects and objects in the world must never lose sight of this essential interrelatedness. The transcendental ego might seem to constitute an exception to this; but the claim of transcendental phenomenology is that the transcendental standpoint is just one standpoint which the ego can take and, from that standpoint, it can reflect upon itself as an empirical ego essentially situated in the world.

The phenomenological account of the conscious subject is of a viewpoint on the world, an 'openness' to the world. Further, since perceiving the world essentially involves acting in and on the world, the conscious subject is essentially an active and, so, embodied subject. Our bodies are not mechanisms in which consciousness happens to reside; they are the possessors of habits and skills without which action – and therefore perception – would not be possible. All phenomenologists emphasize the importance of the body, but Merleau-Ponty produces the most systematic account. Bodily skills and habits – what he terms 'bodily intentionality' – are in many respects exercized 'pre-consciously': conscious attention to habitual engagement with one's familiar surroundings can, notoriously, disrupt performance. Subjectivity is essentially bodily. The subject of consciousness depends on the 'body-subject'. The body, with its skills and habits, cannot operate except on appropriate instruments, in a suitable habitat, in a world of objects amenable to its skills – miming is a special art.

The phenomenological account of objects is that they present themselves as objects of our gaze, to be wondered at. We perceive them, not as bearers of purely factual primary and secondary properties, but as having all manner of significance, ambiguities and indeterminacies. Sartre writes with approval that Husserl has restored to objects their horrors and their charm. For phenomenology, these – usually deemed at best tertiary properties of objects – are the properties which make them possible objects for us, that without which we could never have discovered their primary and secondary properties.

Underlying the perceptual properties of objects are their practicality: they are, in Heidegger's terms, 'ready-to-hand' prior to being 'present-at-hand'. As such, they presuppose wider wholes which give the specific instruments a meaningful context. Ultimately, the context is the whole world, and it is a communal world – an essential backdrop for all subjects.

In summary, subjects are essentially bodily, with skills and habits which require instruments and habitats to develop and come into play. The intentionality of consciousness depends on bodily intentionality. Objects compel, invite or resist our actions. Our ability to view them with a neutral scientific gaze involves our ignoring the very features which enable them to be objects for us.

Modern philosophy, empiricist and rationalist, it is claimed, has ignored these fundamental interactions which are presupposed by any propositional knowledge of the world. Deprived of this practical underpinning, propositional knowledge is open to sceptical challenge in a way in which practical knowledge, knowing how to do things, is not. Any notion of a pure conscious subject or an independently existing object is the result of a process of abstraction from the lived-world. To proceed to worry about how the one can interact with or have knowledge of the other is to forget the starting point in practice from which the process of abstraction proceeds, a starting point which, according to phenomenology, is implicit in all phenomena and can be read off from them from a suitably reflective standpoint.

A natural objection to raise against phenomenology is that it gives an account only of intentional objects, objects of consciousness, and not of 'real' objects in the external world. The phenomenological rejoinder to this is firstly, that intentional objects are not to be construed as mental contents, inner effects or representations of an external world. Second, phenomenology would press the objector to articulate the distinction between intentional and 'real' object. Phenomenology explores the basis in experience of claims concerning the existence of 'real' objects; any account of 'real' objects which does not so relate them to objects of experience is strictly nonsense. On the phenomenological account of our relations with the external world, we find that our experience is mostly just as it should be to support our claims that the world exists and that we know that it does.

See also: Brentano, F.C.; Consciousness; Introspection, psychology of; Knowledge, tacit; Perception, epistemic issues in

References and further reading

Brentano, F. (1874) *Psychologie vom empirischen Standpunkt*, trans. A.C. Rancurello, D.B. Terrell and L.L.McAlister as *Psychology from an Empirical Standpoint*, London: Routledge & Kegan Paul, 1973. (Complex discussion of psychology. This translation is reliable and readable.)

Cooper, D.E. (1996) *Heidegger*, London: The Claridge Press. (Short and highly readable introduction to the work of Heidegger. Chapter 3 is especially relevant.)

Dreyfus, H.L. (1979) *What Computers Can't Do: The Limits of Artificial Intelligence*, New York: Harper & Row. (Phenomenological critique of artificial intelligence.)

—— (1982) *Husserl, Intentionality and Cognitive Science*, Cambridge, MA: MIT Press. (Applications of phenomenology to recent developments in philosophy.)

—— (1991) *Being-in-the-World: A Commentary on Heidegger's 'Being and Time', Division I*, Cambridge, MA: MIT Press. (Clear and helpful commentary.)

Hammond, M., Howarth, J. and Keat, R. (1991) *Understanding Phenomenology*, Oxford: Blackwell. (Clear and readable introduction to phenomenology through analyses of writings by Husserl, Merleau-Ponty and Sartre.)

Heidegger, M. (1927) *Sein und Zeit*, trans. J. Macquarrie and E. Robinson as *Being and Time*, Oxford: Blackwell, 1962. (Difficult and often obscure. The translation is conscientious, with helpful notes and index.)

—— (1993) *Basic Writings*, trans. D. Farrell Krell, London: Routledge. (Selection of Heidegger's works from 1927 until his death. The later works promise a depth which is challenging if hard to fathom. Contains a general introduction, and brief introductions to each section.)

Husserl, E. (1931) *Cartesianische Meditationem*, trans. D. Cairns as *Cartesian Meditations*, The Hague: Martinus Nijhoff, 1977. (Short but demanding text outlining the phenomenological method, with many technicalities and few examples. The translation is mainly faithful, with many notes.)

—— (1936) *Die Krisis der europäischen Wissenschaften und die transzendentale Phänomenologie*, trans. D. Carr as *The Crisis of European Sciences and Transcendental Phenomenology*, Evanston, IL: Northwestern University Press, 1970. (A longer and more readable work than *Cartesian Meditations*. The translation contains a helpful introduction and notes.)

Langer, M.M. (1989) *Merleau-Ponty's 'Phenomenology of Perception': A Guide and Commentary*, London: Macmillan. (Detailed exposition of Merleau-Ponty's text.)

Merleau-Ponty, M. (1945) *Phénoménologie de la Perception*, trans. C. Smith as *Phenomenology of Perception*, London: Routledge & Kegan Paul, 1981. (Combines detailed criticism with engaging description. The translation replaces a detailed and useful table of contents with an index.)

Sartre, J.-P. (1943) *L'Être et le Néant*, trans. H. Barnes as *Being and Nothingness*, London: Methuen, 1958. (Combines at times tortuous argument with flowing and peceptive descriptions. This translation has been criticized for inaccuracies, but the introduction by Mary Warnock is helpful as, in parts, is the Key to Special Terminology.)

JANE HOWARTH

PHENOMENOLOGY IN LATIN AMERICA

The Latin American struggle against the positivism of the nineteenth century was the primordial endeavour of the founders of Latin American thought, such as José Enrique Rodó (1872–1917), José Vasconcelos (1882–1959), Alejandro Korn (1860–1936), Carlos Vaz Ferreira (1871–1958), Alejandro Deústua (1849–1945), Enrique Molina (1871–1956) and Antonio Caso (1883–1946). These thinkers fought to win their philosophical freedom in a battle against continuing such European currents as Neo-Kantianism and the existential-phenomenological movement, on the one hand and on the other, developing a philosophy that was purely Latin American.

In all of this the influence of the Spanish philosopher José Ortega y Gasset (1883–1955) was fundamental. Ortega y Gasset was mainly interested in the problems of history and culture. His famous apothegm, 'I am myself and my circumstance' (1947: 322), was the justification for a phenomenological movement axiological in nature, as well as being the point of departure for the affirmation of Latin American circumstance.

Few have cultivated the Husserlian style of phenomenology in Latin America outside the classroom. Latin American thinkers have preferred to apply the phenomenological method to the different fields of knowledge. In particular, those dealing with socio-cultural aspects, literary criticism, socio-economic structures and juridical axiology. In all works related to axiology the thought of the philosophers Nicolai Hartmann (1882–1950) and Max Scheler (1874–1928) were enormously influential.

Many of those originally inclined towards phenomenology drifted from the 1970s onwards, towards analytic philosophy, philosophy of science and logical neopositivism.

1   **Phenomenology and literature**
2   **Relevant thinkers: Argentina**
3   **Relevant thinkers: Brazil**
4   **Relevant thinkers: Colombia, Costa Rica, Chile**
5   **Relevant thinkers: Mexico**
6   **Relevant thinkers: Peru, Puerto Rico, Uruguay, Venezuela**

1   Phenomenology and literature

Theoretical Latin American writers in the field of literary criticism are interested especially in the ontology of the literary work. This interest, which includes the task of discovering and/or constructing Latin American subjectivity and identity in relation to their specific and differing surroundings, focuses on the basic principles of phenomenological epistemology. They base their own epistemology on the epistemological thinking of early Husserl. This phase of the philosophy of HUSSERL (§3), also known as neorealism, states that reality can be grasped in the essences as revealed in consciousness.

Particularly important is the application to literature of the Husserlian formula the mutual implication of subject and object and his notion of transcendental subjectivity. Graciela Maturo (1928–), for example, uses these ideas to achieve her goal of explaining (and to construct by explanation) the peculiarity of Latin American subjectivity. This critical approach to Latin American literature is justified because, as in other countries, especially France, Spain, Germany and Italy, the literary work of art is used to reveal aesthetic, ethical or metaphysical philosophical intuitions and preoccupations. Maturo makes this point in her writings and the phenomenological method helps her to describe the literary phenomenon on a particularly interesting continent. In doing so, she joins other writers and thinkers who have tried to accomplish the construction of a Latin American identity, which is separate from, although influenced by Europe (see MARGINALITY; CULTURAL IDENTITY).

2 Relevant thinkers: Argentina

Carlos Astrada (1894–1970) was professor at the University of La Plata and Buenos Aires. His background was in Neo-Kantianism under the teachings of Scheler, Husserl and Heidegger in Freiburg (see NEO-KANTIANISM). He first oriented his work towards existential phenomenology (1936), but later returned to Kant and moved on to Marx, then Hegel (1967). Astrada interpreted authentic existential freedom more as social liberty than as individual freedom. He contributed interesting works in the area of phenomenology.

Arturo Cambours Ocampo applied the phenomenological method to literary creation in his book, *Lenguaje y creación: notas para una fenomenología del estilo literario* (Language and Creation: Notes Towards a Phenomenology of Literary Style) (1970). He showed the usefulness of the phenomenological method for studying the language of literature in *Literatura y estilo: notas para una estética del escritor y su experiencia fenomenólogica* (Literature and Style: Notes Towards an Aesthetic of the Writer and their Phenomenological Experience) (1985). His aim was to establish the aesthetics upon which the literary style is founded.

Raúl Castagnino is a literary critic with a phenomenological orientation. He is a member of the phenomenological movement which is literary in nature and has many followers in Latin America and elsewhere. He became known especially for *El análisis literario: introducción metodológica a una estilística integral* (Literary Analysis: Methodological introduction to an Integral Stylistics) (1953).

Carlos Cossio (1903–) was mostly preoccupied with the philosophy of law. He managed to achieve an original synthesis between phenomenology and existentialism, asserting that the object of law is human behaviour: the norms of behaviour were not themselves laws.

Juan Luis Guerrero (1899–1957) forged his academic career as professor of ethics at the University of Buenos Aires and of aesthetics at the University of La Plata. Influenced by Max Scheler, Guerrero's conception was centred around the gnoseological aspect of individual subjectivity, on the ethics of the human personality and on aesthetics.

J.A. Madile's primary interest was the phenomenol‌ogcial nature of the epistemological problem. The influence of Nicolai Hartmann is clearly evident in his work.

Graciela Maturo (1928–) followed a current of thought which was also intensively cultivated in Europe to apply her phenomenologcial knowledge and reflections in the field of literature. She considered phenomenology the best methodology and the most appropriate approach to unravel the elements characteristic of Latin American literature and literary criticism, as she states in *Fenomenología, creación y crítica: sujeto y mundo en la novela latinoamericana* (Phenomenology, Creation, and Criticism: Subject and World in the Latin American novel) (1989). She also discusses the interaction of Latin American versus European identities. In *Imagen y expresión: hermenéutica y teoría literaria desde America Latina* (Image and Expression: Hermeneutics and Literary Theory from Latin America) (1991), several authors contribute to the influence of phenomenological-existentialist hermeneutics, principally cultivated in France.

3 Relevant thinkers: Brazil

Creso Coimbra was interested in Latin American identity. He applied phenomenology to the problems of culture in his work *Fenomenología da cultura brasileira* (Phenomenology of Brazilian Culture) (1972).

Julio Fragata was a follower of Husserl and attempted to establish a Husserlian phenomenology as the basis of all philosophical enterprise, as illustrated in *A fenomenologia de Husserl como fundamento da filosofia* (The Phenomenology of Husserl as the Foundation of Philosophy) (1959). Subsequently in *Problemas da fenomenologia do Husserl* (Problems in the Phenomenology of Husserl) (1962), he analysed the contrast between the early and later works of Husserl.

Alfredo Naffah Neto (1947–) witnessed both state terrorism and the work of the country's death squads. He successfully applied the phenomenological method to the historical situation of the last dictatorships of Brazil (1985).

4 Relevant thinkers: Colombia, Costa Rica, Chile

In Colombia Danilo Cruz Vélez was interested in the

problems of the philosophy of culture and philosophical anthropology. The influence of Scheler and Heidegger were in evidence in his central thesis (1970) which focused on the concept of philosophy as a perpetual beginning, without any presuppositions.

In Costa Rica Helio Gallardo (1942–) was involved with the trend of searching for a philosophy deeply rooted in Latin American social problems. He implemented phenomenological analysis to understand those problems. On the occasion of the quincentenary of the encounter of cultures in the Americas, he wrote *500 años: fenomenología del mestizo: violencia y resistencia* (500 Years: Phenomenology of the Mestizo: Violence and Resistance) (1993).

In Chile Mario Ciudad was influenced by Henri-Louis Bergson, as was the entire first generation of the opponents of logical neopositivism. His work, *Bergson y Husserl: diversidad en la coincidencia* (Bergson and Husserl: Diversity in Coincidence) (1960) showed an interest in the phenomenology of Husserl and tried to find points of coincidence with the philosophy of life of Bergson.

5 Relevant thinkers: Mexico

Antonio Caso (1883–1946) became well known through a series of lectures in which he refuted the wave of positivism at that time. He introduced new philosophical currents, emphasizing the philosophy of Bergson and Husserl. The latter enabled him to broaden the idea of positivism. He worked on the development of his own thought inspired by his intuitions with respect to essence and existence. His distinctiveness derived from his pluralist concept of reality and his interpretation of philosophy as a kind of synthesis of reflections about nature and culture. For Caso, philosophy is an integratory superscience in which existence and thought are concordant.

Carmen Cecilia Hernández de Ragoña utilized phenomenological methods in *Fenomenología histórica de las religiones* (Historical Phenomenology of Religions) (1975) to analyse other fields, cultivating especially the phenomenology of religion.

Samuel Ramos (1897–1959), a disciple of Antonio Caso, was influenced by Ortega y Gasset and Scheler. He was concerned with humanity generally, starting with the Mexican (1934). He attempted the affirmation of freedom with personality by overcoming the conditioning imposed by the circumstances of civilization.

Arturo Rivas Saínz applied the phenomenological method to the poetic phenomenon with clarity, insight and a great command of metaphysical intuition (1950).

6 Relevant thinkers: Peru, Puerto Rico, Uruguay, Venezuela

Peruvian, Francisco Miró Quesada Cantuarias (1918–) wrote extensively in the areas of the phenomenology of logic and the philosophy of science (1941), both of which he deemed rigorous enough to resolve the problems of humankind. He never abandoned his preoccupation with humanity's problems in the ethical-political sphere. His compatriot José Tamayo Herrera was interested in mythopoetic activity – the ability to create myths. His ideas feature in *Fenomenología de la creación poética* (Phenomenology of the Poetic Creation) (1963).

In Puerto Rico, Charles Rosario, with a focus on poetry and philosophy, applied his knowledge of phenomenological philosophy to contemporary Puerto Rican society (1965). From 1898 there was a convergence of two contrasting points of view which have remained unresolved. These are the Puerto Rican's identity with Spanish and Anglo-Saxon cultures, both of which are based on the economic and political power of the USA and the need to reaffirm a distinct Puerto Rican cultural identity through literature and thought. Rosario uses the phenomenological method which describes the social, moral, literary and other phenomena to explain the traumatic change from an agricultural society to an industrial one. The change produced a crisis for Puerto Ricans in the perception of their own identity, especially in comparison with other Latin American countries.

In Uruguay Homero Altesor in his book, *Fenomenología del cuerpo: anatomía filosófica* (Phenomenology of the Body: Philosophical Anatomy) (1986) applied phenomenology to the analysis of the different parts of the human body as a function of the total harmony of humankind.

Juan Llambías de Azevedo (1907–1972) based juridical axiology on the phenomenology of Scheler and Hartmann, as well as Husserl, to establish the reality of rights as an objective value independent from any subjective judgment. Llambías de Azevedo (1940) explained a prolix phenomenology of the acts of conscience that allow the constitution of the object of the law. The investigation of the essence of the object of the law drew him, after Nicolai Hartmann, towards identifying an aporetics of law. The most important aspect of this aporetic was the relationship between the content of law and values. In addition to any subjective dimension of the judgment of values Llambías de Azevedo rejected any relativism with respect to the subjective dimension of it. Following Scheler, he submits that the supreme value is the person, who is the ultimate foundation of the law and of the values of justice and equality.

In Venezuela Ernesto Mayz Vallenilla (1925–) wrote several works interpreting and expounding the works of Dilthey, Husserl and Heidegger (1956; 1960). His thesis was based on the conception of temporality which starts from nothingness. His thought is within the tradition of the propounding of Americanist thought. The main part of his work has compared and contrasted Heidegger and Marx.

See also: EXISTENTIALIST THOUGHT IN LATIN AMERICA; PHENOMENOLOGICAL MOVEMENT

References and further reading

* Altesor, H. (1986) *Fenomenología del cuerpo: anatomía filosófica* (Phenomenology of the Body: Philosophical Anatomy), Montevideo: Imprenta Mimeográfica Pesce. (Phenomenology applied to different parts of the human body.)
* Astrada, C. (1936) *Idealismo fenomenológico y metafísica existencial* (Phenomenological Idealism and Existential Metaphysics), Buenos Aires: Imprenta de la Universidad. (Existential phenomenology.)
* —— (1967) *Fenomenología y praxis* (Phenomenology and Praxis), Buenos Aires: Ediciones Siglo Veinte. (Astrada discusses the practice of phenomenology.)
Barreto, O. (1992) 'Fenomenología de la religiosidad mapuche' (Phenomenology of Mapuche Religiosity), *Documentario Patagónico* (Patagonian Documentary), Buenos Aires: Centro Salesiano de Estudios 'San Juan Bosco'. (A series from the Salesian Historical Archive of northern Patagonia.)
Bormida, M. (1976) *Etnología y fenomenología: ideas acerca de una hermenéutica del extrañamiento* (Ethnology and Phenomenology: Ideas About the Hermeneutics of Estrangement), Buenos Aires: Ediciones Cervantes. (Part of the trend of affirmation of Hispanic US thought.)
* Cambours Ocampo, A. (1970) *Lenguaje y creación: notas para una fenomenología del estilo literario* (Language and Creation: Notes Towards a Phenomenology of Literary Style), Buenos Aires: Ediciones Cervantes. (An application of phenomenology to literary creation.)
* —— (1985) *Literatura y estilo: notas para una estética del escritor y su experiencia fenomenólogica* (Literature and Style: Notes Towards an Aesthetic of the Writer and their Phenomenological Experience), Buenos Aires: Ediciones Marymar. (The text includes a bibliography of critical texts.)
Caso, A. (1933) *El concepto de la historia universal y la filosofía de los valores* (The Concept of Universal History and the Philosophy of Values), Mexico: Ediciones Botas. (The writer introduces new philosophical currents.)
—— (1934) *La filosofía de Husserl* (The Philosophy of Husserl), Mexico: Imprenta Mundial. (A discussion of the phenomenologist.)
—— (1941) *Positivismo, neopositivismo y fenomenología* (Positivism, Neopositivism and Phenomenology), Mexico: Centro de Estudios Filosóficos de la Facultad de Filosofía y Letras. (The author broadens the idea of positivism, developing ideas inspired by his intuitions with respect to essence and existence.)
* Castagnino, R.H. (1953) *El análisis literario: introducción metodológica a una estilística integral* (Literary Analysis: Methodological introduction to an Integral Stylistics), Buenos Aires: Editorial Nova. (A stylistic analysis from a phenomenological perspective.)
* Ciudad, M. (1960) *Bergson y Husserl: diversidad en la coincidencia* (Bergson and Husserl: Diversity in Coincidence), Santiago de Chile: Anales de la Universidad de Chile. (The author compares the two philosophers.)
* Coimbra, C. (1972) *Fenomenología da cultura brasileira* (Phenomenology of Brazilian Culture), São Paulo: LISA. (Phenomenology applied to Brazilian cultural problems.)
* Cruz Vélez, D. (1970) *Filosofía sin supuestos: de Husserl a Heidegger* (Philosophy without Presuppositions: from Husserl to Heidegger), Buenos Aires: Editorial Sudamericana. (Influenced by Scheler and Heidegger.)
* Fragata, J. (1959) *A fenomenologia de Husserl como fundamento da filosfia* (The Phenomenology of Husserl as the Foundation of Philosophy), Braga: Livraria Cruz. (An attempt to establish Husserlian phenomenology as the basis of philosophy.)
* —— (1962) *Problemas da fenomenologia do Husserl* (Problems in the Phenomenology of Husserl), Braga: Livraria Cruz. (Compares early and later works of Husserl.)
* Gallardo, H. (1993) *500 años: fenomenología del mestizo: violencia y resistencia* (500 Years: Phenomenolgy of the Mestizo: Violence and Resistance), San José: Editorial Departamento Ecuménico de Investigaciones. (A search for a philosophy rooted in Latin American social problems.)
* Hernández de Ragoña, C.C. (1975) *Fenomenología histórica de las religiones* (Historical Phenomenology of Religions), Mexico: Editorial Jus. (Interesting analysis of the phenomenology of religion.)
* Llambías de Azevedo, J. (1940) *Eidética y aporética del derecho: prolegómenos a la filosofía del derecho* (Eidetics and Aporetics of Law: Prolegomena to the Philosophy of Law), Buenos Aires: Espasa-

Calpe. (Juridical axiology based on the phenomenology of Scheler and Hartmann.)

* Maturo, G. (1989) *Fenomenología, creación y crítica: sujeto y mundo en la novela latinoamericana* (Phenomenology, Creation and Criticism: Subject and World in the Latin American novel), Buenos Aires: F. García Cambeiro. (Phenomenology applied to Latin American literature and literary criticism.)

* —— (1991) *Imagen y expresión: hermeneútica y teoría literaria desde America Latina* (Image and Expression: Hermeneutics and Literary Theory from Latin America), Buenos Aires: F. Garcia Cambeiro. (A literary theoretical approach to hermeneutics.)

* Mayz Vallenilla, E. (1956) *Fenomenología del conocimiento: el problema de la constitución del objeto en la filosofía de Husserl* (Phenomenology of Knowledge: the Problem of the Composition of the Object in the Philosophy of Husserl), Caracas: Facultad de Humanidades y Educación, Universidad Central de Venezuela. (Examines the works of Husserl.)

* —— (1960) *Ontología del conocimiento* (Towards a New Humanism), Caracas: Facultad de Humanidades y Educación, Universidad Central de Venezuela. (A new approach to humanism.)

Millas, J. (1956) 'Ortega y la responsibilidad de la inteligencia' (Ortega and the Responsibility of Intelligence), Serie Negra, *Filosofía* 2, Santiago: Anales de la Universidad de Chile. (A discussion of Ortega y Gasset's work.)

* Miró Quesada Cantuarias, F. (1941) *Sentido del movimiento fenomenológico* (The Meaning of the Phenomenological Movement), Lima: Librería e imprenta D. Miranda. (A comprehensive study that includes the phenomenology of Husserl, Nicolai Hartmann and Heidegger.)

* Naffah Neto, A. (1985) *Poder, vida e morte em situação de tortura: esboço de uma fenomenologia do terror* (Power, Life and Death in a Situation of Torture: Draft of a Phenomenology of Terror), São Paulo: Hucitec. (Phenomenology applied to the historical situation of Brazil.)

* Ortega y Gasset, J. (1947) *Meditaciones del Quijote: Obras Completas*, vol. 1, Madrid: Revista de Occidente, 6th edn, 1963, trans. E. Rugg and D. Marín, *Meditations on Quixote*, New York: W.W. Norton, 1961. (An example of a work by one of the founders of phenomenology.)

* Ramos, S. (1934) *El perfil del hombre y la cultura en México*, Mexico: Imprenta Mundial, trans. P.G. Earle, intro. T.B. Irving, *Profile of Man and Culture in Mexico*, Austin, TX: University of Texas Press, 1962. (Discusses humanity, beginning with the Mexican.)

* Rivas Sáinz, A. (1950) *Fenomenología de lo poético: notas de asedio* (Phenomenology of the Poetic: Notes of Siege), Mexico: Tezontle. (Phenomenology of poetics.)

* Rosario, C. (1965) *Primer encuentro* (Phenomenology of Everyday Life: Puerto Rico becomes a Mass Society), San Juan: Ateneo Puertorriqueño. (Phenomenology is used to explain the change from an agricultural to an industrial society.)

* Tamayo Herrera, J. (1963) *Fenomenología de la creación poética* (Phenomenology of the Poetic Creation), Lima: Empresa Editora América. (Phenomenology applied to the ability to create myths.)

MARÍA TERESA BERTELLONI

PHENOMENOLOGY OF RELIGION

The phenomenology of religion is a descriptive approach to the philosophy of religion. Instead of debating whether certain religious beliefs are true, it asks the question 'What is religion?' It seeks to deepen our understanding of the religious life by asking what (if anything) the phenomena we normally take to be religious have in common that distinguishes them from art, ethics, magic or science. Since the search for what is common presupposes difference and brings to light an astonishing array of divergent beliefs and practices, the quest for the essence of religion unfolds quite naturally into questions of typology 'What are the most illuminating ways of classifying religious differences?'

Sometimes the phenomenology of religion is motivated by a desire for quasi-scientific objectivity, combined with at least a soft scepticism about metaphysical speculation; if we cannot decisively resolve the metaphysical mysteries of life, people with this approach argue, at least we can give an unbiased description of those interpretations of the world we normally designate religious. At other times the phenomenology of religion has a more existential orientation: whether or not our arguments can settle questions about the ultimate shape of being, we have to choose our own mode of being-in-the-world; and if we are to decide intelligently whether or not to be religious, we need to be as clear as we can about what it means to be religious – ineluctable uncertainty may make faith something of a leap, but the leap need not be blind.

1 **Descriptive philosophy of religion**
2 **Scientific and existential phenomenology of religion**
3 **The sacred**

1 Descriptive philosophy of religion

Typically, the philosophy of religion is a normative enterprise, reflecting on the truth of religious beliefs. Thus proofs of the existence (and nature) of God are offered in the attempt to establish the truth of various theistic claims, while the existence of evil is offered as evidence against such claims. Both sides of this argument attempt to show that the other's arguments do not decisively establish the conclusion put forth, and the discussion often turns from the question of truth to the question of rationality. If God's existence cannot be decisively proved or disproved, is it rational to believe in God? But this, too, is a normative question.

By contrast, the phenomenology of religion brackets or temporarily sets aside such questions as to whether we are obliged or permitted or forbidden by the standards of truth and rationality to hold various religious beliefs. Instead, its point of departure is the fact that religion is an observable phenomenon of human life, and its task is to help us better understand what religion is by giving descriptive analyses of that aspect of human experience. In this regard it strongly resembles the philosophy of science and the philosophy of art, the tasks of which are neither to praise nor to bury science and art, but to give us deeper insight into the structures and functions of these widespread human activities. In all three cases, the observability of the phenomena is no guarantee of agreement when it comes to descriptive analysis.

By asking the question 'What is religion?', the phenomenology of religion expands the subject matter of the philosophy of religion in two ways. First, since religion is as much a matter of practice as of belief, it abandons the assumption that the philosophy of religion is primarily concerned with locating religious belief on some hierarchical scale of cognitive acts inspired by Plato's divided line. Instead, it focuses attention on religion as a language game that is a fully fledged form of life or mode of being-in-the-world.

Second, in seeking the essence, the common nature, or at least the family resemblances of a wide variety of phenomena usually taken to be religious, it requires a multicultural approach not usually found in the normative philosophy of religion, which often restricts itself to issues arising out of Jewish and Christian monotheism. Data for philosophical reflection emerge from work in comparative religion or the history of religions, such as Frazer's *The Golden Bough* or Eliade's *Patterns in Comparative Religion*.

As the search for the essence or common core of religion encounters divergences, numerous and often sharp, among religious beliefs and practices, a new task arises: typology. Now the question 'What is religion?' is supplemented by the question 'What differences among religious phenomena are most fundamental, and what kinds of classification are most illuminating?' It often turns out that historically distinct traditions, such as Judaism, Christianity, Islam, Hinduism, Buddhism, Daoism and so forth, can be replaced for such purposes by categories that cut across these traditions. Among these categories are Eliade's distinction of cosmos from history, James' distinction of once-born from twice-born and Bergson's distinction of static/closed from dynamic/open (see ELIADE, M. §2; BERGSON, H.-L. §8.)

2 Scientific and existential phenomenology of religion

Historically speaking, the phenomenology of religion is a post-Kantian affair, and one strand has Kant himself and Husserl as its mentors. From KANT (§8) comes scepticism regarding metaphysical disputes about the way the world really is, along with the notion that we can nevertheless set forth the basic structures of our experience of the world. By making the phenomenal rather than the noumenal our subject matter, we can retain the goal of a philosophy that is scientific in the sense of giving us objective knowledge about something. Husserl's ideal of philosophy as rigorous science seeks to preserve this moment in Kant from lapsing into naturalism or psychologism. At the same time, his accounts of transcending the natural attitude by moving from fact to essence and by bracketing questions about the reality of the world as distinct from the mode of its givenness in experience (the *epoche*) seek to give methodological rigour to the descriptive tasks of postmetaphysical philosophy (see HUSSERL, E.).

A quite different motivation underlies the existential orientation in the phenomenology of religion. This strand presupposes both the hermeneutical and the existential turns phenomenology was to take away from Husserl's conception of a rigorously scientific philosophy; and it replaces Kant and Husserl with Heidegger and Kierkegaard as mentors for the phenomenology of religion. The hermeneutical critique, building on the late work of Husserl, becomes fully explicit in HEIDEGGER (§§2–3) and GADAMER (§§3–4). All our cognitions are interpretations whose own possibility presupposes our immersion in language, in culture and in history in such ways that the ideal of a purely scientific understanding, free from all particular perspectives and presuppositions, is a chimera. No phenomenology can have as its goal the preservation of scientific objectivism in a postmetaphysical context.

What then can the goal be? It is at this point that

KIERKEGAARD (§§4–6) is able to provide an existential answer. Not only does reflection always emerge from within the concrete situatedness of human existence; it has as its goal the clarification of the possibilities that confront us so that we can choose responsibly what kind of lives to live, especially since we must choose without the epistemic guarantees we would like.

As a descriptive approach to the philosophy of religion, the phenomenology of religion is more than just an alternative to the normative mode. It is always, at least implicitly, a critique of the latter. In its scientific mode, it extends the Kantian judgment that theoretical reason cannot settle metaphysical disputes to reason in all its modes, and views traditional philosophy of religion as engaging in speculation that is unwarranted because undecidable. While the existential mode often shares this view, its critique grows primarily out of its appreciation of Pascal's distinction between the God of the philosophers and the God of Abraham, Isaac and Jacob. It fears that the debates over natural theology too quickly become a theoretician's luxury in a realm of abstraction that loses touch both with the living God and with the concrete concerns and inescapable choices of existing individuals.

Both kinds of phenomenology of religion assume a kind of Socratic ignorance, a denial that we can attain final certainty about ultimate reality; and both place the Socratic question 'What is religion?' in this context. Sharing the Socratic preoccupation with the question about the way we should live, the existential mode transforms the objective question 'What is religion?' into the subjective question 'What would it mean to be religious as distinct from being irreligious?'

These two modes of phenomenology of religion are ideal types. Some important descriptions of the religious experience proceed with hardly a pause for methodological reflection; others proceed on the basis of historical, psychological, sociological or even literary self-understandings; still others, with clear philosophical intent, describe their project in ways that do not correspond exactly to these descriptions of the scientific and existential modes. But these tendencies can be perceived, in varying degrees, across a vast body of literature, all of which can be read as contributing to this philosophical project. We read descriptions of the religious life phenomenologically, whatever their genre, when we look for meanings (or essences) rather than facts; when we view these meanings as living, as what happens rather than what happened; and, if we move to the existential mode, when we consider these meanings as live options, as possibilities for our own existence.

3   The sacred

Phenomenology is a kind of empiricism; it addresses itself to the modes of our experience. But this does not keep it from making the world (the object of experience) its theme in various ways. Similarly, the phenomenology of religion is not compelled to focus on the subjective side of religion (for example, faith) as distinct from its objective side (for example, God). Indeed, if anything, the tendency has been to focus precisely on the 'object' of religious experience.

However, this is doubly problematic. First, the concept of God or gods is not appropriate for such religious 'objects' as the Buddha nature, which is at once the being of all things and *anatta*, no-self or no-substance; the *mana* of the Melanesians, and its many dynamistic correlates; or even the spirits of animistic religion. Second, even in contexts that speak freely about God, the claim is widespread that the highest experience of God or Brahman or the Buddha nature and so forth is beyond the structure of subject–object experience. Hence the quotation marks when speaking of the 'object' of religion.

The terms 'sacred' and 'holy' have come to serve as the generic names for the 'object' of religion. The ways in which these notions are spelled out provide the first answer to the question 'What is religion?' or 'What is the common feature in virtue of which we call this very diverse set of phenomena religious?' Two classic accounts highlight possibilities for both convergence and divergence.

Geerardus van der Leeuw gives a triadic structure to his classic work *Religion in Essence and Manifestation: A Study in Phenomenology* (1933): the object of religion, the subject of religion, and object and subject in their reciprocal operation. The object of religion, which he calls the sacred, is above all else power. But this power is not just any agency. Van der Leeuw stresses its remoteness. However frequently one encounters it, it never becomes usual or familiar, but remains a *'highly exceptional* and *extremely dangerous "Other"'* ([1933] 1963 (1): 24). Accordingly, encounters with the sacred are accompanied by amazement, fear, and especially awe.

Van der Leeuw stresses that in its 'primitive' – that is, dynamistic and animistic – forms, this notion of sacred power lacks two features that often accompany it in the religions of the world's 'high' civilizations. The first of these is a principle of unity in terms of which it is possible to think of the universe as an ordered and integrated cosmos. The second is a moral link between power and something like justice so that 'the ground of the world may be trusted' ([1933] 1963 (1): 31). In its generic sense, then, the sacred power 'remains merely dynamic, and not in the slightest degree ethical or "spiritual"' ([1933] 1963 (1): 28).

Rudolf Otto's earlier study, *The Idea of the Holy* (1917), challenges this latter claim. Seeking to elaborate on what SCHLEIERMACHER (§7) called the feeling of absolute dependence, he defines the holy or the numinous as the *mysterium tremendum et fascinans* (overwhelming and fascinating mystery). To speak of the holy as mysterious is to focus explicitly on that in the 'object' of religion which is non-rational or ineffable in the sense of exceeding our conceptual apprehension. To call it the *mysterium tremendum* is to accentuate the awe-fulness of the holy, its ability to evoke fear and dread. This is the aspect of the sacred that allows it to be designated the 'Wholly Other'. Finally, to describe it as *fascinans* is to find it to be 'uniquely attractive and *fascinating*' ([1917] 1958: 31). If the wrath of God is an expression of tremendousness, the mercy of God is an expression of the fascinating aspect of the holy. We are naturally ambivalent before the holy, drawn to it and repelled by it at the same time (see OTTO, R.).

But for Otto, this complex 'object' of experience is not just a matter of power but also of value. Before the numinous I experience not only the limits of my power but also the limits of my worth. The notions of sin and defilement that emerge go beyond the notions of guilt and remorse derived from morality, just as holiness is not reducible to goodness; however, the value categories of religion are intimately related to those of morality. Over against van der Leeuw, Otto leaves us with two important and probably inter-related questions: Is the dialectical tension between attraction and repulsion generic to religion, or only a feature of some species? And is there an essential link between religion and morality, or is the supreme and unique value of the holy a specific rather than a generic feature of religion?

One approach to this latter question involves the sharp distinction between religion and magic. If the sacred is a matter of value-free power, then it entails no normative restraints against making it a means to human ends. The only barriers are technical, and the sacred power is on a par with atomic power: can we figure out safe and reliable procedures for putting this power at our own disposal? On Otto's view that the holy is a category of value, we should say at this point that we are no longer dealing with religion but with magic. On van der Leeuw's view, by contrast, we should speak here of instrumental religion, recognizing that phenomena we normally designate as religious sometimes have this means–end structure constrained by no values but our own purposes.

See also: EXISTENTIALIST THEOLOGY; MYSTICISM, NATURE OF; RELIGIOUS EXPERIENCE

References and further reading

Bergson, H.-L. (1932) *Les Deux Sources de la morale et de la religion*, Paris: F. Alcan; trans. R.A. Audra and C. Brereton, *The Two Sources of Morality and Religion*, Garden City, NY: Doubleday & Company, 1935. (A dyadic typology.)

Eliade, M. (1949) *Le mythe de l'éternel retour: archétypes et répétition*, Paris: Gallimard; trans. W.R. Trask, *The Myth of the Eternal Return*, Princeton, NJ: Princeton University Press, 1954. (A dyadic typology.)

* —— (1949) *Traité d'histoire des religions*, Paris: Payot; trans. R. Sheed, *Patterns in Comparative Religion*, New York: New American Library, 1958. (A rich, thematic study of a wide variety of phenomena.)

* Frazer, Sir J.G. (1922) *The Golden Bough: A Study in Magic and Religion*, New York: Macmillan, abridged edn, 1960. (An encyclopedic source of materials.)

James, W. (1902) *The Varieties of Religious Experience*, Cambridge, MA: Harvard University Press, 1985. (A classic study that includes a dyadic typology along with studies of conversion, saintliness and mysticism.)

* Leeuw, G. van der (1933) *Phänomenologie der Religion*, Tübingen: J.C.B. Mohr (Paul Siebeck); trans. J.E. Turner, *Religion in Essence and Manifestation: A Study in Phenomenology*, New York: Harper & Row, 1963. (First major study to call itself a phenomenology of religion.)

* Otto, R. (1917) *Das Heilige*, Gotha: L. Klotz; trans. J.W. Harvey, *The Idea of the Holy*, New York: Oxford University Press, 1958. (Classic source of descriptions of the holy as 'Wholly Other' and as *mysterium tremendum et fascinans.*)

Ricoeur, P. (1960) *La symbolique du mal*, Paris, Aubier; trans. E. Buchanan, *The Symbolism of Evil*, New York: Harper & Row, 1967. (Rich study of the symbolic and mythological dimensions of religion, with a fourfold typology.)

Westphal, M. (1984) *God, Guilt, and Death: An Existential Phenomenology of Religion*, Bloomington, IN: Indiana University Press. (A comprehensive, introductory study that includes discussion of methodology and the essence of religion along with a triadic typology.)

MEROLD WESTPHAL

PHILIP THE CHANCELLOR (1160/85–1236)

Philip occupies a pivotal place in the development of medieval philosophy. He is among the very first in the Latin West to have a fairly complete picture of both the newly available natural philosophy and metaphysics of Aristotle and the work of the great Muslim thinkers, Avicenna and Averroes. His Summa de bono, *composed sometime between 1225 and 1236, shows the broadening of philosophical interests and the growth of philosophical sophistication that accompanied reflection on these new materials. Philip's* Summa *had a major impact on subsequent thirteenth-century thinkers, particularly Albert the Great, whose own* Summa de bono *is closely modelled on that of Philip.*

Philip the Chancellor (Philippus Cancellarius) studied at Paris and became Master of Theology there. He was named chancellor of Notre Dame in 1217 and held that position until his death. As the chancellor, Philip was charged with supervising teaching at the University of Paris, and in that capacity he was a key player in several of the university's formative crises. In addition to *Summa de bono*, his works include various (unpublished) *quaestiones*, some four hundred sermons (still unpublished), a homiletics manual on the Psalms and some highly regarded poetry.

Philip's *Summa de bono* is a massive summary of theological and philosophical matters, roughly similar in size to Peter Lombard's *Sentences* and William of Auxerre's *Summa aurea*. However, although Philip's project is in the tradition of these earlier works, it is strikingly different. He takes the notion of the good (*bonum*) as the point of departure and organizing principle for his *Summa*. After a brief introductory discussion which includes three questions on the metaphysics of goodness and four on the highest good and the way created good flows from it, he devotes the entire work to created goods. He offers no extended treatment of God, the Trinity, Incarnation or the sacraments, topics that dominate Lombard's *Sentences* (see LOMBARD, P.)

The main parts of Philip's *Summa* correspond roughly to the divisions marked by his theoretical classification of the main kinds of created good. The first part is devoted to the good creatures possess by virtue of their nature (*bonum naturae*). Under this heading he discusses the nature of purely intellectual creatures (angels), purely corporeal natures (things created on the first five days of creation), and creatures composed of both intellectual and corporeal natures (human beings). The short second part is devoted to the good possessed by actions by virtue of their type (*bonum in genere*). The third and last part deals with the good that belongs to a creature because of a perfection it has by virtue of both its own nature and activity and the activity of God. Philip calls this the good associated with grace (*bonum gratiae*) and includes under it the topics of grace and virtue. In this third part of *Summa de bono*, Philip gives only passing attention to questions having to do with grace, devoting most of it (roughly half the entire *Summa*) to a detailed treatment of the theological and moral virtues. This part of the *Summa* significantly advances the project, begun by WILLIAM OF AUXERRE, of elaborating a comprehensive, systematic moral theory.

Philip's classification of created goods identifies two other sorts of created good which do not figure in the plan of the *Summa*: the good that belongs to an action because of features of it less general than its type – namely, its end and circumstances (*bonum a fine, bonum a circumstantia*) – and the good associated with a perfection that is a pure gift of God – namely, glory (*bonum gloriae*). It is unclear whether Philip intended to include discussions of these goods and, hence, whether he left the *Summa* unfinished. *Summa de bono* is best known for its opening questions, which may constitute the first systematic treatise on the transcendentals. In his prologue, Philip proposes to begin the *Summa* with an inquiry into the relation of good (bonum) to being, one and true (*ens, unum, verum*) because these are the most general principles and because ignorance of the nature of principles can lead one to shipwreck in matters of faith. Philip's position in these questions is seminal. Drawing on suggestions from the newly available Muslim tradition of commentary on Aristotle and reflecting a new, sophisticated familiarity with the concepts of Aristotelian metaphysics, Philip's account centres around the thesis that the transcendentals are extensionally equivalent, although they are intensionally or conceptually distinct. The exposition and defence of this thesis is the defining characteristic of the thirteenth-century discussion of the transcendentals, which includes the work of ALEXANDER OF HALES, ALBERT THE GREAT, AQUINAS and BONAVENTURE.

See also: ALBERT THE GREAT; ARISTOTELIANISM, MEDIEVAL; WILLIAM OF AUXERRE

List of works

Philip the Chancellor (1225–36) *Summa de bono*, ed. N. Wicki, *Philippi Cancellarii Summa de bono*, Berne: Francke. (The traditional dating of *Summa de bono* places it in the period from 1228 to 1236, but Wicki argues for an earlier date, 1225–8.)

References and further reading

MacDonald, S. (1992) 'Goodness as Transcendental: The Early Thirteenth-Century Recovery of an Aristotelian Idea', *Topoi* 11: 173–86. (An examination of *Summa de bono*'s opening questions on the metaphysics of goodness and their place in the development of thirteenth-century thought.)

Wicki, N. (1985) *Philippi Cancellarii Summa de bono* vol. 1, Berne: Francke, especially ch. 1, 'Vie de Philippe le Chancelier' and ch. 3, 'Données de la tradition manuscrite et problèmes d'histoire littéraire'. (Succinct, authoritative account of Philip's life and work and a useful survey of the important secondary literature.)

SCOTT MacDONALD

PHILO JUDAEUS *see* PHILO OF ALEXANDRIA

PHILO OF ALEXANDRIA (*c.*15 BC–*c.* AD 50)

Philo of Alexandria is the leading representative of Hellenistic-Jewish thought. Despite an unwavering loyalty to the religious and cultural traditions of his Jewish community, he was also strongly attracted to Greek philosophy, in which he received a thorough training. His copious writings – in Greek – are primarily exegetical, expounding the books of Moses. This reflects his apologetic strategy of presenting the Jewish lawgiver Moses as the sage and philosopher par excellence, *recipient of divine inspiration, but not at the expense of his human rational faculties. In his commentaries Philo makes extensive use of the allegorical method earlier developed by the Stoics. Of contemporary philosophical movements, Philo is most strongly attracted to Platonism. His method is basically eclectic, but with a clear rationale focused on the figure of Moses.*

Philo's thought is strongly theocentric. God is conceived in terms of being. God's essence is unreachable for human knowledge (negative theology), but his existence should be patent to all (natural theology). Knowledge of God is attained through his powers and, above all, through his Logos *('Word' or 'Reason'), by means of which he stands in relation to what comes after him. In his doctrine of creation Philo leans heavily on Platonist conceptions drawn from reflection on Plato's* Timaeus. *The conception of a creation* ex nihilo

('from nothing') is not yet consciously worked out. Philo's doctrine of human nature favours the two anthropological texts in Genesis 1–2, interpreting creation 'according to the image' in relation to the human intellect. With regard to ethics, both Stoic concepts and peculiarly Jewish themes emerge in Philo's beliefs. Ethical ideals are prominent in the allegorical interpretation of the biblical patriarchs.

Philo's influence was almost totally confined to the Christian tradition, which preserved his writings. He was unknown to medieval Jewish thinkers such as Maimonides.

1   Life and works
2   Philosophical position
3   Epistemology
4   Theology
5   Doctrine of creation
6   Doctrine of human nature, ethics
7   Influence

1   Life and works

The thought of Philo of Alexandria is very much the product of his combined Alexandrian and Jewish background. Biographical details are very scarce, but we know that he was born into a prominent and extremely wealthy Jewish family (Josephus, *Antiquities* XVIII 258). In AD 39 he was chosen as leader of a delegation that sailed to Rome to protest to the emperor Gaius Caligula against the pogrom suffered by the Jewish community of Alexandria at the hands of the local populace. The interview with the emperor went badly, but did not cost him his life (see the unintentionally hilarious report in *Embassy to Gaius* 349–67). This incident is often connected with a passage at the beginning of *On the Special Laws*, where Philo complains that involvement in political affairs distracts him from more serious pursuits, and looks back wistfully to the time when he could fully devote himself to the life of philosophy.

From his writings it is apparent that Philo received a thorough training in Greek philosophy, although we have no idea from whom he received it (it has been suggested he may have had house tutors). His knowledge of the Platonic and Stoic traditions is especially thorough. His writings thus provide important, although imprecise, information on contemporary philosophical developments in Alexandria. Philo's extensive use of Plato's *Timaeus* and other dialogues reflects the beginnings of the Middle Platonist movement associated especially with the figure of Eudorus (see PLATONISM, EARLY AND MIDDLE §1). He is also the first writer to cite the so-called 'ten modes' of the Neo-Pyrrhonist AENESI-

357

DEMUS, who was active in Alexandria a generation before his birth.

Philo was a prolific writer, and the majority of his works appear to have survived. These amount to exactly fifty treatises in all. They can best be divided into three separate groups:

(1) There are five purely *philosophical* treatises, discussing subjects such as the eternity of the cosmos, divine providence, and the rationality of animals. These offer much valuable material on Greek philosophy, and it is only occasionally possible to discern that their author was Jewish.
(2) In addition there are four *historical/apologetic* works, in which Philo defends Judaism against contemporary attacks.
(3) The remaining forty-one works are all *commentaries* on the books of Moses.

These are best sub-divided into four categories:

(a) Two books on the life of Moses, introducing the writer of the holy books to a broad public, both Jewish and Greek.
(b) Ten books on the Exposition of the law, first describing the creation of the world (Genesis 1–3) and the lives of the patriarchs Abraham and Joseph, then expounding the Decalogue, the Special Laws and other subjects related to Mosaic legislation.
(c) The Allegorical commentary in twenty-one books, giving an astonishingly complex running commentary on Genesis 2–17, in which the chief exegetical method used is allegorization of the text.
(d) Eight books of Questions and answers on Genesis and Exodus, in which questions are posed on most verses of the biblical text, and both literal and allegorical answers are given in a consecutive but formally unconnected way.

The great majority of Philo's writings thus concentrate on the five books of Moses (or Pentateuch), which he read in the Greek translation of the Septuagint. The direction of Philo's loyalties is very clear. He wishes to defend the cultural and religious heritage of his people in their minority position in Alexandrian society. His chief apologetic strategy is to focus in on the figure of the great sage Moses, exploiting the considerable prestige accorded to barbarian sages such as Zoroaster and the Egyptian priests in contemporary Greek philosophy. Moses is the great sage and paradigm for righteous and holy living. His writings, if appropriately read, are an inexhaustible fount of wisdom.

It may seem, however, that Philo is facing an impossible task. Only a few passages in the Pentateuch, such as the creation account and the stories of Moses on the mountain, offer much scope for philosophical elucidation. His solution is to exploit the method of allegorical interpretation, invented and developed by earlier Greek philosophers (including Stoics) in order to defend the authority of Homer. Like Homer, Moses allegorized: that is to say, he said one thing but meant another. The meaning behind his words has to be uncovered. Moses tells the story of the patriarch Abraham (and Philo would never deny that this progenitor of the Jewish race existed), but the deeper meaning of the text reveals the story of the human soul on the path to perfection and felicity (see §6). Philo is one of the great masters of the allegorical method. In practice it gives him the scope he needs to introduce Greek philosophical doctrines and so develop his own philosophical views by means of a presentation of Mosaic thought.

2 Philosophical position

Understandably, Philo shows no loyalty to any particular school of Greek philosophy. None can match the prestige enjoyed by the school of Moses. From this viewpoint Philo's method may be considered thoroughly eclectic, but with a clear rationale. It is apparent from his commentaries, however, that his philosophical sympathies lie with Platonism. He is particularly attracted to the revival of transcendentalism undertaken in the Middle Platonist movement. Stoic doctrines are found especially in the area of ethics (see §6). Other themes reflect the influence of Jewish thought, and so offer interesting contrasts with ideas in Greek philosophy.

3 Epistemology

Philo makes no attempt to present a systematic theory of knowledge, but there is at least one epistemological question that he cannot avoid: How was it possible for Moses to attain the pinnacle of human wisdom? Moses is regarded as a prophet, exalted beyond other human beings. Philo distinguishes between two types of prophecy, both of which have antecedents in Greek reflection on the subject. In the first kind, which enables the prophet to predict the future, the prophet is empowered to 'stand outside' himself and through divine possession become an instrument of the divine voice speaking through him. This may be called *ecstatic* prophecy. In the second type the prophet is also inspired by God, but remains in full possession of his rational abilities, which allows his mind to contemplate the nature of reality in its fullness. This may be termed *noetic* prophecy. The prophet is one who 'through virtue rather than birth has advanced to the service of the truly Existent, . . . since he has within him a noetic sun and shadowless beams of light, which give him the clear apprehension of things invisible to sense but perceptible to the mind' (*On the Special Laws* 4.192). Philo's Platonist assumptions emerge clearly here, even if the term 'apprehension' (*katalēpsis*) has a Stoic background. It is above all this second type of prophecy, exemplified by Moses' vision of the *paradeigma* (a Platonic technical term) of the tabernacle and its contents on Mount Sinai (*Exodus* 25: 9), that enables him to be the sage *par excellence* and the author of the sacred books.

4 Theology

As a result of his Jewish background Philo's thought is resolutely theocentric. God is conceptualized primarily in terms of true being. The link to Platonism is apparent, but for Philo the source is above all God's words to Moses in *Exodus* 3:14, 'I am he who IS'. It is typical of Philo that he alternates speaking of God in personal and impersonal terms: that is, between 'he who is' and 'that which is'.

Crucial to Philo's theology is the distinction between God's *existence* and his *essence*. Through observation and experience of the natural world and particularly of their own intellectual powers, human beings can without any difficulty conclude that God exists and that he is creator of the universe. However, gaining knowledge of God's essence is beyond the reach of human conceptual abilities. Not even the great Moses, although he made many requests, was granted this privilege. God is unknowable in his essence, and thus also unnameable, uncircumscribable and unutterable: that is, there is no name or description that can give accurate expression to his essential nature. Philo thus has a negative and a positive theology, rather similar to what one finds in the Middle Platonist handbook of ALCINOUS.

God is thus utterly transcendent. At the same time, however, he stands in close relation to the cosmos as its creator and provident maintainer (see §5). Philo argues that the two chief names for God refer to his powers (*dynameis*). The name *theos* (God) indicates his creative power (from the root *tithēmi*, 'I set in place'); the name *kyrios* (Lord) indicates his ruling power. More famously the figure of God's Logos (usually rendered 'Word', but 'Reason' is better) is invoked in order to explain God's relation to what is other than him. Philo's Logos doctrine is complex and certainly not always philosophically consistent. This is due to its double origin in both Jewish thought (especially the 'and God said' in Genesis 1) and Greek thought (especially STOICISM (§3)) (see LOGOS). The Logos has an immanent aspect, indicating the divine

presence in the created realm. It also has a transcendent aspect, and is sometimes identified with the intelligible world. The chief difficulty posed by Philo's doctrine of the Logos is the following. Sometimes Philo speaks of the Logos as if it were simply an aspect of the divine nature, namely that aspect which is accessible to human thought precisely because it is related (in a model/image relation) to that which follows it. At other times the Logos is treated as a *hypostasis*, that is, a self-subsistent theological entity that is at least to some degree independent of God himself. As a Jew, however, Philo refuses to accept the Platonist solution of a hierarchy of divine principles at different ontological levels (see NEOPLATONISM §3).

5 Doctrine of creation

A second pillar of Philo's thought is the doctrine of creation. Philo is utterly convinced that visible material reality has been created by God, and has nothing but scorn for the minority opinion that it was the result of chance or spontaneous development. Furthermore, because God has created the universe, he will also take care of it through the action of divine providence. Philo agrees with Plato against the Stoics that, although the universe had a beginning, it will not be subject to total destruction. This, he argues, was already Moses' view, as shown by Genesis 8: 22 (see *On the Indestructibility of the Cosmos* 1–19).

In his treatise *On the Creation of the Cosmos According to Moses*, Philo presents his views on creation in greater detail. The cosmos was created in six days. This does not mean that God needed a length of time in which to complete his work. In fact, everything came into being simultaneously, because time commenced with the cosmos itself. The details of Philo's interpretation are strongly influenced by contemporary interpretations of Plato's *Timaeus*. Remarkably, the first day of creation is taken to describe the creation of the intelligible cosmos, which serves as model for the visible cosmos and is equated with the Logos (see §4). If one would wish to summarize the doctrine of creation, Philo writes, 'one might say that the noetic cosmos [of day one] is none other than the Logos of God while he [that is God] is engaged in his creative task' (*On the Creation of the Cosmos* 24). It is noteworthy that Philo does not dissociate God from the creative task and attribute it solely to his Logos, because this would surely endanger the conviction of a unique God.

Philo is less than clear on the origin and ontological status of matter, and especially on the question whether it is created by God or has an independent existence before creation. He does not discuss the question in his commentary on the creation account (Genesis 1: 2 is taken to refer to the intelligible world), and elsewhere he appears to vacillate. It is safest to conclude that he remains prisoner of the axiom almost universally present in Greek philosophy that nothing can come out of nothing, and so is unable to face the full consequences of a doctrine of creation *ex nihilo* such as was developed in early Christian thought (in reaction to Gnosticism).

Philo's cosmology follows the dominant Platonic-Aristotelian model. The cosmos is a work of great beauty and order, produced by a good and gracious creator. It is not autonomous, and certainly should not be worshipped. This was the mistake made – in terms of Philo's allegorical scheme – by the Chaldaeans, whom Abraham left behind in his search for the true God (*On the Life of Abraham* 68–71).

6 Doctrine of human nature, ethics

Philo's doctrine of human nature, the third pillar of his thought, is based primarily on the two texts in the creation account, Genesis 1: 26–27 and 2: 7, both of which are interpreted in terms of the Greek philosophical ideal of human reason. In the former text human beings, male and female, are created 'according to the image (*eikōn*) of God', which is taken to mean that they resemble God not in terms of the body or the lower soul with its passions, but through the rational soul or the mind, which is also their immortal part. In the latter text the human body is 'inbreathed' by God's spirit (*pneuma*). This creative act is also taken to refer to the formation of the human rational faculty. Following basically Platonist lines, Philo regards the human goal (*telos*) as 'assimilation (*homoiōsis*) unto God'. This can be accomplished because of the human image relation to God: that is, it can be accomplished through the powers of the intellect. It is in gaining knowledge of God that humans become like God. This was the nature of Moses' paradigmatic quest. What might seem to be the ultimate goal, however, the knowledge of God's essence, is unreachable, because then assimilation would become identity, which is impossible on account of the gulf separating creator and creature (an instructive contrast can be drawn with Plotinus' doctrine of the union with the One; see PLOTINUS §3).

In the formulation of his ethical ideals Philo extracts much from Stoicism, but places it in a basically Platonist framework. The journey of the soul involves various stages. It begins with the struggle against the passions resulting from association with the body. As learners advance, they develop the exercise of reason and embark on the path of the virtues. The goal to be attained is the life of perfection, the life lived by the wise person (*sophos*). The wise person is characterized by a freedom from all passion (*apatheia*), not in the sense of having no emotions whatsoever, but because irrational passions have been converted into rational emotional states (*eupatheiai*). However, the ideal of the wise person as represented by Moses is lofty and seldom attained. For many the patriarchs are more accessible symbols of the level a human being can attain. They represent three aspects of the quest for perfection. Abraham is the learner, Isaac is the man with natural aptitude for the quest, Jacob is the practiser who never yields in his struggle to reach the goal. The quest for perfection and the ideal of the wise person is the fourth and final pillar of Philo's thought.

Philo's ethics are not entirely Greek. In his treatment of the virtues Jewish themes can be detected. Philo is more positive towards the feelings of repentance and pity than we find in Greek ethics, and tends to regard piety as the greatest of the virtues. Foreign to Greek philosophical thought also is his emphasis on the nothingness (*oudeneia*) of human beings before God's face, a theme which anticipates the role of humility in Christian ethics.

7 Influence

Philo's influence on the course of philosophical thought was limited to the Christian tradition. The church fathers preserved his works because his method of using Greek philosophical themes to explain scripture appealed to them. Attempts by Wolfson (1947, 1968) and others to demonstrate Philo's influence on later Platonist thought have not been successful. Medieval Jewish philosophers did not know Philo, and Jewish interest in him did not revive until the sixteenth century. From the viewpoint of the history of ideas Philo is interesting above all because in his writings the traditions of Greek philosophy and Judaeo-Christian thought converge for the first time.

List of works

The names of Philo's fifty treatises cannot be included here (but see the sub-division given in §1). A list with the conventional English and Latin titles can be found at the beginning of Loeb Classical Library edition. The chronology of individual writings cannot be determined with any certainty.

Philo (20–50 AD) *Philo*, trans. F.H. Colson and G.H. Whitaker, Loeb Classical Library, Cambridge, MA: Harvard University Press and London: Heinemann, 1929–62, 10 vols, plus 2 suppl. vols, trans. R. Marcus. (The standard English translation, with Greek text; badly in need of revision.)

—— (20–50 AD) *The Works of Philo Complete and Unabridged*, London: Bohn's Classical Library, 1854–5; reprint trans. C.D. Yonge, Peabody, MA: Hendrickson, 1993. (A single volume edition with modern numbering; unreliable and incomplete.)

—— (20–50 AD) *On Providence*, vols I and II in M. Hadas Lebel (ed.) *Les Œuvres de Philon d'Alexandrie*, vol. 35, *De providentia I et II*, Paris: Les Éditions du Cerf, 1973. (Survives only in Armenian; not included in the Loeb Classical Library edition.)

—— (20–50 AD) *On Animals*, ed. A. Terian, *Philonis Alexandrini de Animalibus: The Armenian Text with an Introduction, Translation and Commentary*, Chico, CA: Scholars Press, 1981. (Survives only in Armenian; not included in the Loeb Classical Library edition.)

—— (20–50 AD) *The Contemplative Life*, trans. D. Winston, *Philo of Alexandria: The Contemplative Life, The Giants and Selections*, New York and Toronto, Ont.: Paulist Press, 1981. (The best anthology of Philo's writings, containing many of his more interesting philosophical passages.)

—— (20–50 AD) *The Giants*, trans. D. Winston, *Philo of Alexandria: The Contemplative Life, The Giants and Selections*, New York and Toronto, Ont.: Paulist Press, 1981. (The best anthology of Philo's writings, containing many of his more interesting philosophical passages.)

References and further reading

Baer, R.A. (1970) *Philo's Use of the Categories Male and Female*, Leiden: Brill. (Important work on the male–female relation in the interpretation of the creation account and the doctrine of human nature.)

Dillon, J.M. (1977) *The Middle Platonists: 80 B.C. to A.D. 220*, London: Duckworth, 139–81. (Excellent on Philo's Platonism.)

Mansfeld, J. (1988) 'Philosophy in the Service of Scripture: Philo's Exegetical Strategies', in J.M. Dillon and A.A. Long (eds) *The Question of 'Eclecticism'*, Berkeley, CA: University of California Press, 70–102. (On Philo's rationale in using philosophical ideas.)

Radice, R. and Runia D.T. (1988) *Philo of Alexandria: An Annotated Bibliography 1937–1986*, Leiden: Brill. (Comprehensive and heavily indexed guide to the scholarly literature, continued yearly in the journal *The Studia Philonica Annual*.)

Runia, D.T. (1986) *Philo of Alexandria and the Timaeus of Plato*, Leiden: Brill. (Standard treatment of Philo's extensive exploitation of Plato's cosmological dialogue.)

—— (1990) *Exegesis and Philosophy: Studies on Philo of Alexandria*, London: Variorum. (Collection of studies on exegetical method and philosophical content.)

—— (1993) *Philo in Early Christian Literature*, Assen: Van Gorcum and Minneapolis, MN: Fortress. (On Philo's reception and preservation in the Christian tradition.)

Tobin, T.H. (1983) *The Creation of Man: Philo and the History of Interpretation*, Washington, DC: Catholic Biblical Association of America. (Strong on Platonist background; emphasizes the differing traditions used by Philo.)

Winston, D. (1985) *Logos and Mystical Theology in Philo of Alexandria*, Cincinatti, IL: Hebrew Union College Press. (Best compact introduction to Philo's theology.)

—— (1990) 'Judaism and Hellenism: Hidden Tensions in Philo's Thought', *The Studia Philonica Annual* 2: 1–19. (Important observations on Philo's theory of prophecy and ethics.)

* Wolfson, H.A. (1947) *Philo, Foundations of Religious Philosophy in Judaism, Christianity and Islam*, Cambridge, MA: Harvard University Press, 4th edn, 1968, 2 vols. (Magnificent synthesis, but too systematic and too Jewish a view of Philo.)

DAVID T. RUNIA

PHILO OF LARISSA
(*c.*159–*c.*83 BC)

Philo, head of the Academy from 110 to 88 BC, likened philosophy to medicine. No doubt he was a conscientious therapist himself; but we know little enough about his methods and practices. For most of his life he seems to have been a happy sceptic, and an unremarkable one. But towards the end of his career he introduced – or was deemed to have introduced – startling innovations into the Academy: in particular, by rejecting or modifying the reigning definition of knowledge he was able to separate himself from the scepticism of his school and to rewrite its history.

1 Life and thought
2 Epistemology

1 Life and thought

Philo came from Larissa in Thessaly. As a boy he was taught philosophy by a certain Callicles, a friend of

CARNEADES; so that by the time he moved to Athens – perhaps in 134 BC – he was already acquainted with Academic philosophy (see ACADEMY). For some years he continued his studies with Clitomachus, whom he eventually succeeded as scholarch in 110 BC. He remained in office for two decades. Then, in 88 BC, during the turmoil of the Mithridatic War, he left Athens and travelled to Rome. He resumed his teaching, impressing CICERO and Cicero's friends. Some five years later he died.

Our evidence for Philo's thought is meagre. The most substantial text develops a parallel between philosophy and medicine. Doctors must first persuade their patients to accept their own treatment and to reject the advice of rival practitioners; then they must eliminate the causes of disease and implant the causes of health; next they must examine the nature of health, which is the goal of their art; fourth, they must produce comprehensive prescriptions for diet and regimen; and finally – for life is brief and patients are busy – they must prepare a summary brochure on 'healthcare for all'.

So it is also with philosophers. First, a protreptic discourse commending virtue and refuting its detractors; then the elimination of false opinions, which infect the organs of the soul, and the introduction of true opinions; third, an account of the ultimate aim of philosophizing, namely 'happiness' (see EUDAIMONIA); then practical prescriptions, comprising an ethics and a political philosophy; and finally handbooks for the hurried.

The conception of philosophy as mental therapy was neither unique to Philo nor original to him, but his is the most expansive version of the thing which any ancient text presents. We know little about the particular forms which his therapy took: one notice indicates that he did not altogether abjure the soft pleasures of the Epicureans; another informs us that he taught rhetoric (but perhaps separately from philosophy); otherwise the chief points of interest lie in epistemology.

2 Epistemology

For most of his career Philo of Larissa appeared as an unexceptional philosopher. He continued the Academic technique of arguing 'on both sides' (see CARNEADES §1); and he professed some form of scepticism. In short, 'he enhanced the teachings of Clitomachus' (Numenius, in Eusebius, *Preparation for the Gospel* XIV 9.1) without adding anything new to them. And then, near the end of his life, he produced work which scandalized his old colleagues, who could hardly believe that it came from his pen.

The innovation is depicted by Cicero as sudden and shocking, and dated to Philo's Roman period. Other texts hint at a gradual realization rather than a flash of enlightenment – and to some extent Philo seems to have been anticipated by Carneades' pupil Metrodorus. However that may be, the scandalous innovation appears to have had two aspects, one of them philosophical, the other historical.

Philo urged that

> as far as the Stoic criterion, i.e. apprehensive appearance (*phantasia katalēptikē*), is concerned, things are inapprehensible; but as far as the nature of the things themselves is concerned, they are apprehensible.
> (Sextus Empiricus, *Outlines of Pyrrhonism* I 235)

If things are apprehensible in themselves but not according to the Stoic criterion, then presumably the Stoic criterion is false: it must constitute, or be based upon, a mistaken conception of what knowledge is. And Cicero reports that Philo 'weakens and destroys' the Stoic account of apprehension. In particular, he denied the crucial element in the Stoic account, namely the claim that an apprehensive appearance must be such that it *could not* have come from any source other than the source it in fact came from (*Academics* II 18) (see STOICISM §12).

We are not told why Philo rejected this claim: no philosophical arguments on the matter have survived. But we do know one result of his having done so: scepticism could now be avoided – for the Academic arguments for scepticism had fastened upon the very clause which Philo decided to reject (see ARCESILAUS §2; CARNEADES §4).

Looking out of my window I receive an appearance of a magpie on the lawn. I thereby know that there is a magpie on the lawn provided that the appearance is an apprehensive appearance. According to the standard definition, the appearance will only be apprehensive if it *could not* have been caused by anything other than a magpie on the lawn. But surely it *could* have been caused by any number of other things – by a jay on the lawn or by an ingenious hologram. And something like this seems to hold not only of my magpie but of all appearances: hence scepticism. But once we reject the requirement that an apprehensive appearance *could not* have been otherwise caused, the sceptical argument collapses. Knowledge does not require that the magpie appearance *could not* have been caused by a jay – but only that it *was not* caused by a jay. Since the appearance was *in fact* appropriately caused, it is apprehensive; and I thereby know that there is a magpie on the lawn.

Such, or so it seems, was the philosophical aspect of Philo's innovation. It would be silly to shower praise on him, for we do not know why he rejected the standard account of knowledge, or what he offered in its place, or how he replied to the objections which his innovation excited. But his innovation was admirable: the requirement that apprehensive appearances *could not* have been otherwise caused is implausibly strong.

Philo was now able to look afresh at the history of the 'sceptical' Academy. Arcesilaus and Carneades, he saw, had not really been attacking *knowledge* or arguing for *scepticism*; rather, they had been attacking a false conception of what knowledge was. Perhaps they themselves supposed that they were attacking the very citadel of knowledge; but in point of fact they were tilting at an antiquated windmill. Hence the 'sceptical' Academy had never been sceptical: its heroes had never cast any doubt on the possibility of knowledge.

No need, therefore, to speak of an Old and a New Academy. The dogmatism of Plato's original school had presupposed the sane, Philonian, account of knowledge – an account which the Peripatetics had inherited; and the 'New' Academics had implicitly countenanced Platonic dogmatism. Hence Philo 'denied that there were two Academies' (Cicero, *Academics* I 13).

Philo's innovations were roughly greeted. Some Academicians maintained that his abandonment of the standard definition of knowledge was folly – and self-destructive folly to boot, inasmuch as he would now be dragged back to the very scepticism which he had hoped to escape (see ANTIOCHUS §2). Others accused Philo of misunderstanding the achievement of the New Academy and of betraying his heritage. The controversy was heated; but we learn no details. Nor does Philo seem to have had much effect. After him, it is true, sceptical Platonists were hard to find, but there is no reason to believe that this was due to the arguments of Philo.

References and further reading

Barnes, J. (1989) 'Antiochus of Ascalon', in M. Griffin and J. Barnes (eds) *Philosophia Togata I: Essays on Philosophy and Roman Society*, Oxford: Clarendon Press. (Includes an account of Philo's innovations.)

* Cicero, M.T. (early 45 BC) *Academics*, trans. H. Rackham, Loeb Classical Library, Cambridge, MA: Harvard University Press and London: Heinemann, 1933. (The primary source for Philo's dispute with Antiochus.)

Mette, H.-J. (1986/7) 'Philon von Larisa und Antiochus von Askalon', *Lustrum* 28/9: 9–63. (Collects the ancient testimonies on Philo.)

Tarrant, H. (1985) *Scepticism or Platonism? The Philosophy of the Fourth Academy*, Cambridge: Cambridge University Press. (An account of the philosophical orientation of Philo's Academy.)

JONATHAN BARNES

PHILO THE DIALECTICIAN (late 4th–early 3rd centuries BC)

A member of the Dialectical school, Philo was a Greek philosopher whose claim to fame is twofold. First, he maintained that one proposition implies another if and only if either the former is false or the latter is true, however irrelevant the two propositions may be to one another. Second, he maintained that some things are necessarily prevented from happening and are nevertheless possible: the water around them prevents shells at the bottom of the ocean from ever being actually perceived; nevertheless, such things are perceptible. As often happened with Dialecticians' ideas, these ideas of Philo elicited (and perhaps were meant to elicit) notoriety rather than agreement.

1 Life, works and reputation
2 What follows from what?
3 Possibility

1 Life, works and reputation

Philo's birthplace is unknown: the belief that it was Megara is a misconception based on the further misconception that he belonged to the MEGARIAN SCHOOL. In fact, Philo was a Dialectician (see DIALECTICAL SCHOOL). He was a pupil of the eminent Dialectician DIODORUS CRONUS at the same time as ZENO OF CITIUM. In spite of his great admiration for both Diodorus and Philo, Zeno left to found the Stoic School (see STOICISM). Philo stayed. He wrote a no longer extant dialogue called the *Menexenus*; its characters included the five daughters of Diodorus, who were themselves all Dialecticians. He also wrote *On Meanings* (or perhaps *On Sign-Inferences*) and *On Forms of Argument*; these works too have been lost, as have the works which the prominent Stoic CHRYSIPPUS wrote in reply. Philo had the Dialectician's characteristic interest in paradoxes, and his name is associated with many of them. The only topics on which we have any details of his views are implication and modality.

2 What follows from what?

Hellenistic logicians generally, and rightly, agreed that no falsehood ever follows from a truth: for example, if it is daylight but I am not talking, then 'I am talking' does not follow from 'It is day'. In consequence, a necessary condition for one proposition to follow from another is that either the former is true or the latter is false. Then, as now, logicians agreed that this condition is necessary; then, as now, logicians disagreed over what other conditions are necessary (see DIODORUS CRONUS §3). Philo's contribution was to maintain that there are no other necessary conditions, and that this condition is therefore not only necessary but also sufficient. In short, according to Philo, one proposition follows from another when and only when either the former is true or the latter is false.

Already in antiquity, this definition was known to have some bizarre consequences. One is that whenever it is day but I am not talking, the proposition 'I am talking' does not follow from the proposition 'It is day'; it does however follow on all other occasions; that is, it follows throughout the night, and it follows also whenever I am talking in the daytime. Thus one proposition can follow from another even though the pair are, to all appearances, entirely irrelevant to one another. Another bizarre consequence known to antiquity is that 'It is day' follows from 'It is night' during the daytime, but not otherwise. Thus even where two propositions are relevant to one another in such a way that each evidently implies the other's falsehood, one of them will also imply the other's truth.

In modern times, people have sometimes given Philonian accounts of conditionals: a conditional is true, on such an account, if and only if either the antecedent is false or the consequent is true. No modern logician however has given such an account of when an argument is valid. Philo did. Like other Hellenistic logicians, he will have meant his definition of 'following from' to apply simultaneously both to the relation between consequent and antecedent in a true conditional and to the relation between conclusion and premises in a valid argument. According to all Hellenistic logicians, the conditional 'If it is day, it is night' is true if and only if the argument 'It is day; so it is night' is valid; and hence, according to Philo, that argument is valid throughout the night and invalid during the day.

It is not known why Philo adopted so strange an idea. His idea is however fairly easily inferred from a couple of assumptions which were widely current among Hellenistic logicians. One of those assumptions runs: validity is only one among several features which our reasonings should possess. That the conclusion follows from the premises is one thing; that the premises are acknowledged as true is another; that the conclusion is not already acknowledged as true is a third; and so on. The other assumption runs:

each of these features contributes in a different way to turning our reasonings into decent proofs; and the distinctive contribution of validity is to ensure that we will not reach false conclusions unless we have started from false premises. This distinctive contribution has been made if the conclusion follows from the premises in the manner defined by Philo. Hence why should not Philo's definition of 'following from' be an adequate definition of validity?

3 Possibility

Diodorus Cronus defined the possible as that which either is or will be true (see DIODORUS CRONUS §4). Philo devised examples which, if acceptable, refute Diodorus' definition. The examples ascribed to Philo have a common pattern. A typical example runs: a log in mid-Atlantic is not and never will be burning; this is because the log is 'necessarily prevented' from burning by the water that surrounds it; nevertheless, the log can burn; this is because the subject *log* is 'appropriate' to the predicate *burns*, and because 'the bare appropriateness of the subject' to a predicate is enough to make it, 'in itself and as far as its own nature is concerned', capable of having the predicate. Now only if things are possible does it make sense to talk about preventing them: thus since asbestos cannot burn, we need not immerse asbestos in the Atlantic, or take any other precautions, to prevent it from burning. Hence we cannot easily dismiss Philo's examples of possibilities that neither are nor ever will be actual. The very fact that they are prevented from happening indicates, we might say, that they are genuine possibilities.

It is not only Diodorus' definition that Philo's examples threaten. These examples threaten also the more widely accepted thesis that a thing cannot do what it necessarily does not do. For according to Philo's examples, things can act in ways in which they are necessarily prevented from acting; and yet it seems that they necessarily do not do what they are necessarily prevented from doing.

Perhaps Philo's purpose in devising his examples was simply to embarrass the consensus equating the impossible with the necessarily false. Later sources however tell us that, besides his examples, Philo also gave a definition of possibility. According to Philoponus: Philo says that the possible is that which is actualized or can be actualized, even though it never is actualized; as when we say that the shell at the bottom of the ocean is perceptible (*On Aristotle's Prior Analytics* 169).

And according to Boethius, Philo gave systematic definitions of a range of modal concepts:

Philo says that the possible is that which, by the intrinsic nature of the proposition, would receive truth, as when I say that today I will reread the *Bucolics* of Theocritus: this, if nothing external prevents it, can in itself be truly asserted. This very same Philo defines the necessary in the same way, as that which, since it is true in itself, never could be receptive of falsehood. The non-necessary moreover he defines as that which in itself could receive falsehood: and the impossible as that which in accordance with its intrinsic nature never could receive truth.

(De Interpretatione II 234)

The definition in Philoponus moves around too tight a circle to be illuminating. Less unhelpful are the definitions in Boethius. The definitions of the necessary and the non-necessary are not circular at all. Moreover, the clauses about 'intrinsic nature' mean that even the definitions of the possible and the impossible are not as tightly circular as the definition in Philoponus. Nevertheless, these definitions leave something to be desired. Where our subject is *log* and our predicate is *burns*, we have some independent understanding of talk about the subject's 'nature', and its 'appropriateness' to the predicate; but where our 'subject' is the proposition *I will today reread the Bucolics of Theocritus* and our 'predicate' is *true*, such talk is hardly comprehensible save as a long-winded way of saying that the proposition is possible. It is therefore difficult to avoid the suspicion that these definitions were devised not by Philo himself, but by later scholars drawing on his examples of unrealized possibilities. This suspicion is confirmed by the way that the definitions in Boethius invoke as unproblematic the equivalence between the impossible and the necessarily false that Philo's own treatment of his examples had apparently undermined.

See also: CONSEQUENCE, CONCEPTIONS OF; LOGIC, ANCIENT §5; MODAL LOGIC; MODAL LOGIC, PHILOSOPHICAL ISSUES IN

References and further reading

Döring, K. (1972) *Die Megariker* (The Megarics), Amsterdam: Grüner. (Collection of ancient sources, together with some German commentary.)

Giannantoni, G. (1990) *Socratis et Socraticorum Reliquiae* (The Fragments of Socrates and the Socratics), Naples: Bibliopolis. (Volume 1 pages 414–37 contains a complete collection of the ancient evidence about Philo.)

Kneale, W. and Kneale, M. (1962) *The Development of Logic*, Oxford: Clarendon Press. (Chapter 3, sections 1, 2 and 3, discusses Philo.)

Long, A.A. and Sedley, D.N. (1987) *The Hellenistic Philosophers*, Cambridge: Cambridge University Press. (Contains some of the main sources, together with English commentaries and translations.)

NICHOLAS DENYER

PHILODEMUS (*c.*110–*c.*40 BC)

Philodemus of Gadara, a Greek epigrammatic poet, was also an influential Epicurean philosopher. Scrolls containing many of his works, buried by the eruption of Vesuvius in AD 79, have been partially recovered and deciphered. Their themes include epistemology, theology, ethics, philosophical history, poetics, rhetoric and music. He energetically defends Epicureanism against other philosophies, and his own interpretation of Epicureanism against rival factions. Although not a notably original thinker, Philodemus became highly regarded in educated Roman circles.

Philodemus was born in Gadara, southeast of the Sea of Galilee, and died in Italy. He studied at Athens under Zeno of Sidon, then head of the Epicurean school, to whom he retained a lifelong loyalty. Moving to Italy probably in the 70s, he became a friend and philosophical adviser to L. Calpurnius Piso Caesoninus, the father-in-law of Julius Caesar. He seems to have spent some of his life at Herculaneum, probably in his patron's villa, where an Epicurean library consisting largely of his works was excavated in the 1750s. He was known and highly respected by CICERO, and seems to have numbered the poets Virgil and Horace among his circle.

Before the recovery of his philosophical library, Philodemus was known mainly as the author of some elegant epigrams preserved in the Palatine Anthology. Most of them are on the theme of love, but among the others are an invitation to a celebration in honour of Epicurus' birthday, poems about modest feasts and a prayer for a safe journey. The carbonized papyrus scrolls containing his philosophical treatises, because of the adverse physical conditions in which they survived, all lack at least their opening part, and most of them are altogether very poorly preserved. It has nevertheless been possible to gain from them considerable insight into Philodemus' working methods and attitudes to philosophical history and orthodoxy, and his views on the liberal arts. While some of his works may be independent compositions, others, such as *On Signs* and *On Frankness*, are little more than his own transcripts of the lectures he had heard from Zeno in Athens.

Philodemus' wide interest in rhetoric, music and poetry, although at first sight surprising in an Epicurean, is probably not untypical of the school in his day. With regard to rhetoric, he cites chapter and verse from his Epicurean authorities to attack as heterodox the austere rival wing of the school which regarded all rhetoric as philosophically unacceptable. In *On Music*, he criticizes the belief that music influences character: being irrational, it cannot influence the morally all-important rational soul, and it gains its educational power only when combined with language. His *On Poems*, as well as being a major source on Hellenistic poetics, is of particular interest for its development of the thesis that only the combination of word and thought can make a poem a good one. *On the Good King According to Homer* carries a covert political message for Philodemus' Roman audience, praising the mild Homeric king Alcinous as a just ruler who brings prosperity.

Later Philodemus turned to such ethical themes as death and anger, as well as to more practical topics like household management. His *On Frankness* is a work of especial interest, exploring its topic in the specifically Epicurean context of teacher–pupil relationships, with special emphasis on the therapeutic aspect of Epicurean philosophy as medicine for the soul. In *On Anger*, Philodemus seeks a middle position between the Stoic aim of eradicating passion and the Peripatetic ideal of 'moderate emotion': some anger is natural and inevitable, but it should always be controlled by reason to the greatest possible extent (see PERIPATETICS; STOICISM §19).

On Signs is an epistemological treatise, recording debates between Epicureans (including Zeno of Sidon) and critics who are probably Stoics. The Epicurean method of inference based on similarity, whose main species are (1) induction and (2) analogical reasoning from the visible to the invisible, is defended as both sound and scientifically fundamental (see EPICUREANISM §7). Two other works, *On the Gods* and *On Piety*, explore the nature of divinity and defend Epicurus' theology against critics who considered it impious. Philodemus' reverence for his Epicurean authorities finds a more concrete embodiment in his biographical studies of early Epicureans through their collected correspondence. He also gained some recognition for his historical work *Compendium of the Philosophers*, from which his histories of two schools, the Academy and the Stoa, partially survive among the papyri.

There is little evidence that Philodemus was interested in physics. His main fields were ethics, theology and the liberal arts. He may be read as on the one hand a school loyalist, deeply concerned with Epicurean traditions and their correct interpretation, and on the other hand an ambassador mediating these traditions to a largely Roman audience.

List of works

Few of Philodemus' treatises are at present available in usable English translations, although much valuable work has been done since 1970 on improving the Greek texts. The following are the more important or accessible among them. They cannot be individually dated, but were probably written in the order given below. Further editions of Philodemus' works will be found in the series *La scuola di Epicuro*, general editor M. Gigante, Naples: Bibliopolis, and English translations in the forthcoming series D. Blank, R. Janko, and D. Obbink (eds) *Philodemus' Aesthetic Works*, Oxford: Oxford University Press.

Philodemus (*c*.80–40 BC) *Rhetorica*, in 7 or more books, in H.M. Hubbell 'The Rhetorica of Philodemus', *Transactions of the Connecticut Academy of Arts and Sciences* 23 (1920): 243–382; Books I–II trans. D. Blank, Oxford: Oxford University Press, forthcoming. (The former is not a translation but an exegetical paraphrase)

—— (*c*.80–40 BC) *On Piety*, ed. D. Obbink, *Philodemus on Piety Part I*, Oxford: Oxford University Press, 1996. (Epicurean views about piety; exposition of erroneous beliefs; includes text and translation of the philosophical part.)

—— (*c*.80–40 BC) *On the Good King According to Homer*, ed. T. Dorandi, *Filodemo. Il buon re secondo Omero*, Naples: Bibliopolis, 1982. (Text, Italian translation and commentary; how to derive a benefit from the poetry of Homer.)

—— (*c*.80–40 BC) *History of the Academy*, ed. T. Dorandi, *Filodemo. Storia dei filosofi. Platone e l'Academia*, Naples: Bibliopolis, 1991. (Text, Italian translation and commentary; about Academics from Plato to Aristus.)

—— (*c*.80–40 BC) *On Anger*, ed. G. Indelli, *Filodemo. L'ira*, Naples: Bibliopolis, 1988. (Text, Italian translation and notes; on the Epicurean view of anger and how to deal with this passion.)

—— (*c*.80–40 BC) *On Frankness*, ed. A. Olivieri, *Philodemi peri parrēsias libellus*, Leipzig: Teubner, 1914; trans. D. Kanstan, D. Clay, C. Glad., J. Thorn and J. Ware, Atlanta, GA: Scholars Press, 1998. (The former is Greek text only; the latter includes an emended version of Olivieri's text, with facing translation, introduction and notes.)

—— (*c*.80–40 BC) *On Signs*, P. De Lacy and E. De Lacy, *Philodemus, On Methods of Inference*, Naples:

Bibliopolis, 2nd edn, 1978. (Text, English translation and notes; on Epicurean scientific method.)

References and further reading

Annas, J. (1989) 'Epicurean Emotions', *Greek, Roman and Byzantine Studies* 30: 145–64. (Exposition of Philodemus' *On Anger*.)

Asmis, E. (1990) 'Philodemus' Epicureanism', in W. Haase (ed.) *Aufstieg und Niedergang der römischen Welt*, Berlin and New York: de Gruyter, II 36: 4, 2369–2406. (Useful survey article.)

Erler, M. (1994) 'Epikur; Die Schule Epikurs; Lukrez' (Epicurus; The School of Epicurus; Lucretius), in H. Flashar (ed.), *Die Philosophie der Antike, Band 4: Die Hellenistische Philosophie*, Basle: Schwabe, 289–362. (Informative about Philodemus, with extensive bibliography.)

Gigante, M. (1983) *Ricerche Filodemee* (Research on Philodemus), Naples: Macchiaroli, 2nd edn. (Pioneering essays on Philodemus.)

—— (1990) *Filodemo in Italia*, Florence: Le Monnier; trans. D. Obbink, *Philodemus in Italy. The Books from Herculaneum*, Ann Arbor, MI: University of Michigan Press, 1995.(Historical evaluation of Philodemus.)

Nussbaum, M. (1994) *The Therapy of Desire*, Princeton, NJ: Princeton University Press. (Makes extensive use of Philodemus' *On Anger* and *On Frankness* in reconstructing Epicurean moral therapy.)

Obbink, D. (ed.) (1995) *Philodemus and Poetry*, Oxford: Oxford University Press. (Important collection of essays, with extensive bibliography.)

Sedley, D. (1989) 'Philosophical Allegiance in the Greco-Roman World', in M.T. Griffin and J. Barnes (eds) *Philosophia Togata. Essays on Philosophy and Roman Society*, Oxford: Clarendon Press, 97–119. (Examines Philodemus' attitude to his school's scriptures.)

MICHAEL ERLER

PHILOLAUS (*c.*470–380/9 BC)

The Greek philosopher Philolaus of Croton, a contemporary of Democritus and Socrates, was a preeminent Pythagorean. His book counts as the first written treatise in the history of Pythagoreanism. Surviving in fragments, it constitutes an important source for our knowledge of fifth-century Pythagoreanism and supplements the picture given by Aristotle of Pythagorean doctrine.

Like earlier Presocratics Philolaus sought to furnish a comprehensive cosmology. Arguing from logical propositions, he posited two pre-existing principles: 'unlimited things' and 'limiting things'. United by harmony these two principles account for the formation of the cosmos and its phenomena. Since Philolaus also invokes number as an all-powerful explanatory concept, it is likely that he associated his first principles and the things originating from them with numbers. The emphasis on harmony and number accords with early Pythagoreanism.

Philolaus also wrote on musical theory and astronomy. A noteworthy feature of his astronomy is the displacement of the earth from the centre of the cosmos by fire, pictured as the 'hearth' of the universe. The fragments further attest Philolaus' interest in embryology, the causes of diseases, and physiology combined with psychological functions.

It was not unusual for early Greek philosophers to treat such a wide variety of topics. The distinctive elements of the thought of Philolaus are the logical arguments evinced in the fragments and the epistemological role of number for understanding the structure of reality.

1   Life
2   First principles
3   Cosmogony and number
4   Astronomy
5   Miscellanea

1   Life

It is generally believed that Philolaus was a native of Croton in southern Italy where Pythagoras had established a community of disciples, although Philolaus would have been too young to have known the master himself. He is also associated with Tarentum and Thebes, cities he is likely to have sought out after the anti-Pythagorean revolts in Croton around 450 BC. That he spent time in Thebes is certain from a report in Plato's *Phaedo* (61d) stating that Philolaus lectured in that city. This must have occurred before 399 BC, the dramatic date of the *Phaedo*. Plato himself, during his travels to Sicily around 388 BC, may have met Philolaus, but this remains speculative.

Ancient sources relate that Philolaus published three books of Pythagoras which Plato sought to buy at great expense. Although these books have been shown to belong to later pseudo-Pythagorean literature, the story at least indicates that Philolaus contributed to the dissemination of Pythagorean ideas and that Plato was interested in Philolaus. Indeed, Plato was charged in antiquity with having copied his *Timaeus* from a book by Philolaus. Bearing the standard Presocratic title, *On Nature*, Philolaus' text represents the first attested written work of PYTHAGOREANISM. With Philolaus, Pythagoreanism passes from an oral to a written tradition. A core of the fragments that survive from Philolaus' book have been established as genuine. These, as well as the testimonies of other ancient authors about Philolaus, form the basis for reconstructing his philosophy.

1 First principles

The Presocratic tradition in Greek philosophy, for all its diversity, has in common the central quest to understand, explain and, if possible define the essential nature (*physis*) of the world. Philolaus emerges from that tradition. The very beginning of his book sets out clearly the object of his philosophical concern: 'The nature in the cosmos was joined together from unlimiteds and limiters, both the whole cosmos and everything in it' (fr. 1). Like other Presocratics Philolaus seeks to explain the nature that makes up this world-order, and from the outset he states his explanatory principles: unlimiteds and limiters (the Greek literally translates as 'unlimited and limiting things'). The existence of both is justified on logical grounds: since the cosmos cannot be composed solely of limiters nor solely of unlimiteds, it must therefore be composed of both, as is evidenced by the phenomena of the world (fr. 2). If all things were wholly limited or wholly unlimited, the multiplicity and diversity that characterizes the world would be non-existent. (Here and in fragment 6, where the principles are said to be 'neither alike nor related', Philolaus may be polemicizing against the Eleatic arguments of PARMENIDES (§§4–8) and MELISSUS (§§2–4), who by postulating a single, uniform and eternally stable being denied all plurality, diversity and change.) Moreover, the possibility of human knowledge depends upon the existence of *both* principles, for 'there will not at all be anything that knows if all things were unlimited' (fr. 3).

Because Philolaus does not supply examples for 'unlimiteds and limiters', scholars have conjectured empty spaces and atoms, the even (or unlimited) and odd (or limited) elements of number or material components and their defining shapes, but none of these hypotheses receives unqualified support from the fragments. Possibly Philolaus never intended to define these principles more narrowly, given the epistemological scepticism he expresses at the beginning of fragment 6:

> The being of things, being eternal, and nature itself admit of divine and not human knowledge except

that none of the things that exist and are known by us could have come to be if the being of the things from which the cosmos is composed did not already exist, [the being] of both limiters and unlimiteds.

The eternal and essential nature of things, including that of limiters and unlimiteds, ultimately lies beyond human understanding. Limiters and unlimiteds as universal, pre-existing principles have at this pre-cosmic stage an indefinable, abstract quality. But when they are joined in the actual process of forming the cosmos and the things in it, their manifest operation renders them in some sense concrete and knowable. On the best evidence of the fragments, the unlimited and limiting principles and the things composed of them become known through number.

3 Cosmogony and number

'The cosmos is one' (fr. 17). Limiters and unlimiteds alone, however, do not suffice to account for the unity of the universe. As opposing principles they need to be joined in order to produce a cosmos, a term that in Greek expresses beauty, order and structure. In a continuation of fragment 6, Philolaus reveals what links the unlimited and limiting principles:

> But since these principles pre-existed and were neither alike nor related it would have been impossible for them to be ordered (*kosmēthēnai*), if harmony (*harmonia*), in whatever way it came to be, had not come upon them. Now like things and related things did not require in addition any harmony, but things unlike and not related . . . such things must be closely linked by harmony, if they are going to be contained in an order (*en kosmōi*).

With the introduction of *harmonia* (literally, a 'fitting together'), Philolaus evidences a continuity with those Presocratics who emphasized a bonding force in the universe (see EMPEDOCLES §3; HERACLITUS §3), and especially with the Pythagoreans for whom *harmonia* was a central tenet (see PYTHAGOREANISM §2). Philolaus is not concerned with fathoming the origin of harmony but simply postulates it as necessary to explain the manifest coherence of things.

While the cosmological significance of harmony as an ordering force is implied throughout fragment 6, its specific application to the generation of the cosmos is made in the next fragment: 'The first thing fitted together, the One, in the middle of the sphere is called the hearth' (fr. 7). In Philolaus' astronomy (see §4) the universe is conceived of as a sphere (the uniform nature of a sphere in which the notions of 'up' and 'down' are relative is stressed in fragment 17). For the concept of a spherical cosmos Philolaus may have been indebted to Parmenides. But breaking with the geocentric view of the Presocratics Philolaus locates in the middle of the sphere the element of fire, here called the hearth (in Greek domestic and religious culture the burning hearth occupied the centre of households and temples). As the centre of a sphere was considered its 'origin', so fire functions as the origin of the cosmos, which develops from the centre outwards. The primacy of fire (which also figures significantly in the philosophy of Heraclitus and Hippasus the Pythagorean), its status as the 'first thing' in the cosmos, finds a telling correspondence in Philolaus' biology, according to which our bodies at the embryonic stage are solely constituted out of the 'hot'. It was common in Greek thought, especially among medical writers with whom Philolaus shows some acquaintance, to make analogies between the life of humans (or animals) and the larger cosmic organism; in Philolaus, the heat or fire that has such a definitive role in biological generation is likewise the primary element in the formation of the cosmos, the starting point of all generation.

As the central fire is itself a result of harmony, it must then also be a compound of unlimited and limiting things, but the extant fragments again do not specify what these are. The product, however, is clearly a unity, described as 'the One'. Of the different interpretations concerning the One in fragment 7, the view taken in this entry is that it refers to the number one. In fragment 4 Philolaus states emphatically that 'all things that are known have number; for it is impossible for anything whatsoever to be understood or known without it'. With this assertion Philolaus places himself squarely in the Pythagorean tradition of number philosophy, although it remains questionable whether he equated things with numbers as some Pythagoreans apparently did. Without question, however, number plays a crucial epistemological role for Philolaus: things can only be understood by means of number. Philolaus breaks down number into 'two proper kinds, odd and even, and third from a mixture of both of these, even-odd' (fr. 5); of the two proper kinds there are 'many forms, which each thing itself signifies'. This means that individual things in the world are signified by the many forms of number, which are the even and odd natural numbers, while it is implied that there are not many forms of the 'even-odd'; possibly only one. That form of the even-odd would be the One, since the Pythagoreans considered the One to be both odd and even in so far as it originates the number series that must consist of both odd and even numbers. It fits Philolaus' system that he should assign the number one to the 'first thing

fitted together'. For things to 'have number' means that they can be known by their mathematical structure. The central fire, a harmonization of limiters and unlimiteds, is thus comprehended by a number that is itself a mixture of unlimited and limited – in numerical terms, of even and odd (the Pythagoreans put even on a par with unlimited and odd with limit). Just as the One stands at the beginning of the number series, so the central fire is the starting point for the development of the universe that, taken as a whole, will also be one (fr. 17), while the constituent bodies of the universe are signified by the numbers deriving from the One. In assigning the One to the central fire Philolaus intimates from the outset the close connection between things and their informing numbers that will remain a permanent feature of the cosmos.

The surviving fragments do not explain how the cosmogonical process continued, but a clue may be taken from passages in Aristotle that appear to be based partly on Philolaus' book. Aristotle reports that immediately after the construction of the Pythagorean One, the unlimited is drawn in and limited by the limit. From this and other Aristotelian accounts the picture emerges of the cosmos as a living organism that breathes in various unlimited stuffs from 'outside the heaven', the locale of all that is infinite. The particular unlimiteds are time, breath and the void (emptiness). Their interaction with the One, which is here given a limiting function, produces an orderly world where bodies (and numbers, spatially conceived) are separated by the interjection of empty space (see DEMOCRITUS §2) and time is divided into measurable units. Some of this information probably derives from other Pythagorean sources, but that Philolaus subscribed to the general concept of a breathing universe originating from the One is suggested again by his embryology: the living animal, being hot, immediately upon birth draws in cold air from the outside and discharges it again, thus starting the regulated process of respiration (A27). This is paralleled on the cosmic level where the central fire (the hot) draws in and imposes limits on breath (the cold) or the void, which are unlimiteds from outside the universe.

4 Astronomy

The most striking feature of Philolaus' astronomy, as noted in §3, is the location of fire in the centre of the spherical cosmos. It is the hearth of the universe (this is not the sun, which is but one of the orbiting planets – heliocentrism first appears with Aristarchus in the third century BC). Philolaus' departure from the usual geocentric world-view of the Greeks appears to be motivated by Homer's description of Tartarus 'as far below Hades as heaven is from earth' (*Iliad* VIII 16). Although Homer does not associate Tartarus with fire, the ancient Pythagorean idea of a fire in the middle of the earth as well as the volcanic fires of southern Italy would have led Philolaus to postulate a sole central fire, identified with the Tartarus of Greek myth (hence also called the 'prison' or 'defence tower of Zeus' in the Philolaic-Pythagorean tradition). The central fire forms the natural counterpart to the fiery envelope that surrounds the spherical universe at its uppermost boundary (A16). In between and revolving around the central fire, apparently at decreasing velocities, are ten astronomical bodies in the following order: counter-earth; earth; moon; sun; the five planets (in no specified order); and the fixed stars. The counter-earth was not simply introduced, as Aristotle charges, to bring the number of all the planets up to the perfect Pythagorean ten. Rather, Philolaus seems to have posited it as a kind of earth in reverse, the world of the dead, and identified it, again according to the Homeric model, with the invisible Hades of Greek myth. Because it could not be seen, he theorized that the earth in its orbit rotates only once on its axis (this itself was to prove a fruitful idea in the history of astronomy), thus keeping its inhabited side turned away from the centre and rendering the counter-earth invisible. There are also indications that Philolaus shared the belief that the earth moved in an inclined orbit (ellipsis) to account for the different altitudes of the sun and the change of seasons. Other astronomical theories held by Philolaus deal with the periodic destruction of the earth, or parts of it, by fire and water (A18), the nature of the sun (which is like a glass reflecting the light and heat of the central fire) (A19) and the inhabitants of the moon (A20).

Philolaus' astronomy thus combines elements of inventive theorizing based on myth (the central fire, the counter-earth) with empirical data concerning celestial phenomena (night and day, the four seasons, etc.) to yield an orderly cosmos. Obviously, his astronomy must be appreciated within the context of the fifth century BC in which the progressive thought of the day was an amalgam of elementary scientific observations, philosophical preconceptions and mythological remnants.

5 Miscellanea

The discovery, attributed to Pythagoras, that the concordant intervals that make musical harmony possible could be expressed by certain numerical ratios, found a cosmic application in Pythagoreanism: 'the whole universe is harmony and number' (see PYTHAGOREANISM §2). It is not surprising, therefore,

that Philolaus, after describing the cosmic role of *harmonia* (fr. 6), constructs a diatonic scale to account for 'the size of harmony', incorporating the basic Pythagorean ratios of octave (2 : 1), the fifth (3 : 2) and the fourth (4 : 3) (fr. 6a). One significance of Philolaus' musical theory is that it may lie at the basis of Plato's account of the ratios comprising the structure of the world-soul (*Timaeus* 34b).

Philolaus also called the human soul a harmony (A23). Some scholars have argued that this isolated testimony is based on an inference from Plato's *Phaedo*, where the soul as a harmony of opposites is presented as a Pythagorean teaching, and is therefore spurious. But in the light of the pre-eminent role that Philolaus assigns to harmony, it is reasonable to assume that he would have brought this universally important concept to bear on any particular discussion of the soul.

Further interests of Philolaus concerned biology and medicine, but it is not known to what extent he wrote about these topics. Of his views on embryology and disease we have a single report (A27). Philolaus believed that the embryo is innately hot, because both sperm and the womb in which it is deposited are hot. Immediately at birth, 'the hot' inhales cold air from the outside and emits it again 'like a debt'; the process of respiration is presented as necessary for the cooling of the body. Diseases originate from bile, blood, and phlegm.

Philolaus posited four physiological principles, classified as follows:

The head is the seat of intellect, the heart of life and sensation, the navel of rooting and first growth, the genitals of the sowing of seed and generation. The brain is the origin of man, the heart the origin of animals, the navel the origin of plants, the genitals the origin of all (living things). For all things both flourish and grow from seed.

(fr. 13)

By locating intellect in the head, Philolaus differs from those Presocratics who associated thinking with the heart (for example, Empedocles). Another noteworthy detail is that Philolaus distinguishes between thought and sensation; this distinction was to be developed and clarified by Plato, who in the *Timaeus* also located psychic functions in different parts of the body. Overall, Philolaus' fourfold division of faculties, neatly applied in a hierarchical fashion to humans, animals, plants and all organisms, manifests the Pythagorean, and generally Presocratic, impulse to detect the order and structure by which the multiplicity of the world's phenomena can be comprehended.

See also: Archytas; Neo-Pythagoreanism; Presocratic philosophy

References and further reading

Huffman, C.A. (1993) *Philolaus of Croton: Pythagorean and Presocratic*, Cambridge: Cambridge University Press. (Contains all the authentic as well as the spurious fragments and testimonia, with English translations, commentaries and readable interpretative essays; also includes a comprehensive bibliography. Argues that the One in fragment 7 does not refer to number but rather to a paradigmatic unity as found in much of Presocratic thought.)

Kahn, C.H. (1974) 'Pythagorean Philosophy before Plato', in A.P.D. Mourelatos (ed.) *The Presocratics*, Garden City, New York: Doubleday. (A useful introductory essay that emphasizes Philolaus as a primary source for our knowledge of early Pythagoreanism.)

Kingsley, P. (1995) *Ancient Philosophy, Mystery and Magic: Empedocles and Pythagorean Tradition*, Oxford: Oxford University Press. (An important book which throws new light on the study of Pythagoreanism; includes two chapters exploring the mythical background to Philolaus' notion of the central fire.)

* Philolaus (*c.*470–380s BC) Fragments, in H. Diels and W. Kranz (eds) *Die Fragmente der Vorsokratiker* (Fragments of the Presocratics), Berlin: Weidmann, 6th edn, 1951, vol. 1, 398–419.(The standard collection of the ancient sources both fragments and testimonia, the latter designated by 'A'; includes Greek texts with translations in German.)

Schibli, H.S. (1996) 'On "The One" in Philolaus, Fragment 7', *Classical Quarterly* 46.1: 114–30. (Argues on the basis mainly of Aristotle that Philolaus' 'One' is best understood as number.)

HERMANN S. SCHIBLI

PHILOPONUS (*c.* AD 490–*c.*570)

John Philoponus, also known as John the Grammarian or John of Alexandria, was a Christian philosopher, scientist and theologian. Philoponus' life and work are closely connected to the city of Alexandria and its famous Neoplatonic school. In the sixth century, this traditional centre of pagan Greek learning became increasingly insular, located as it was at the heart of an almost entirely Christian community. The intense philosophical incompatibilities between pagan and Christian beliefs come to the surface in Philoponus' work.

His œuvre comprised at least forty items on such diverse subjects such as grammar, logic, mathematics, physics, psychology, cosmology, astronomy, theology and church politics; even medical treatises have been attributed to him. A substantial body of his work has come down to us, but some treatises are known only indirectly through quotations or translations. Philoponus' fame rests predominantly on the fact that he initiated the liberation of natural philosophy from the straitjacket of Aristotelianism, through his non-polemical commentaries on Aristotle as well as his theological treatises deserve to be appreciated in their own right.

Philoponus' intellectual career began as a pupil of the Neoplatonic philosopher Ammonius, son of Hermeas, who had been taught by Proclus and was head of the school at Alexandria. Some of his commentaries profess to be based on Ammonius' lectures, but others give more room to Philoponus' own ideas. Eventually, he transformed the usual format of apologetic commentary into open criticism of fundamental Aristotelian-Neoplatonic doctrines, most prominently the tenet of the eternity of the world. This renegade approach to philosophical tradition, as well as the conclusions of his arguments, antagonized Philoponus' pagan colleagues; they may have compelled him to abandon his philosophical career. Philoponus devoted the second half of his life to influencing the theological debates of his time; the orthodox clergy condemned him posthumously as a heretic, because of his Aristotelian interpretation of the trinitarian dogma, which led him to enunciate three separate godheads (tritheism).

The style of Philoponus' writing is often circuitous and rarely entertaining. However, he combines an almost pedantic rigour of argument and exposition with a remarkable freedom of spirit, which allows him to cast off the fetters of authority, be they philosophical or theological. Although his mode of thinking betrays a strong Aristotelian influence, it also displays a certain doctrinal affinity to Plato, stripped of the ballast of Neoplatonic interpretation. His works were translated into Arabic, Latin and Syriac, and he influenced later thinkers such as Bonaventure, Gersonides, Buridan, Oresme and Galileo.

1–2 The grammarian and commentator
3 The critic
4 The theologian
5 Influence

1 The grammarian and commentator

In order to appreciate the magnitude of Philoponus' achievement as a philosopher, one has to consider briefly the background. One common way for philosophers in late antiquity to develop and communicate their ideas was the composition of commentaries on classical philosophical authors such as Plato and Aristotle. Generations of commentaries were written from the time of Alexander of Aphrodisias (early third century AD) to the seventh century and later, forming a massive tradition. Many of these works evolved out of the school practice of the Neoplatonists (see NEOPLATONISM §1) and conformed to several requirements: (1) the commentaries consisted of an extremely detailed oral exegesis of a philosophical text, designed for the benefit of students; (2) not uncommonly, pupils were responsible for taking verbatim notes of their teachers' instruction, thus turning the lecture into a book; (3) each commentary constituted a step within a substantial curriculum of philosophical training which began with Aristotle and aimed at progressing towards Plato – a commentator was expected to demonstrate the agreement between Plato and Aristotle, indeed, to show forth the harmony among all ancient philosophers including Homer; and (4) philosophy in this way was viewed as education as much as pagan religious exercise by which human beings could perfect their intellect and character with a view to 'becoming godlike as far as possible'.

After a basic education in grammar Philoponus, who was probably born into a Christian family, embarked on this curriculum. As a pupil of AMMONIUS, SON OF HERMEAS, he assumed responsibility for writing down the lectures of the school's ailing head: the commentaries on Aristotle's *On Generation and Corruption*, *On the Soul*, *Prior Analytics* and *Posterior Analytics* explicitly state in their titles that they are 'based on Ammonius' seminars'. The commentaries on the *Categories*, the *Physics* and the *Meteorology* do not make such claims, which suggests, in conjunction with other evidence, that Philoponus was teaching these courses himself. Presumably succeeded Ammonius at some point, although he never held the chair of philosophy but remained *grammatikos*, professor of philology. After the death of Ammonius, the school's leadership seems to have passed into the hands of the mathematician Eutocius and then on to the philosopher Olympiodorus, who was pagan.

In many ways, Philoponus' commentary on the *Categories* may be regarded as typical of its kind. The exegesis of Aristotle's text is prefaced by a general clarification of matters of interest to the student reading philosophy for the first time. Beginners were first instructed in Aristotle's logical works, arranged according to the principle of increasing complexity: the *Categories*, dealing with simple utterances, were followed by the *De interpretatione* (on propositions), the *Prior Analytics* (on syllogisms) and the *Posterior Analytics* (on proof). Discussing the problem of the subject matter (*skopós*) of the *Categories* (see ARISTOTLE §7), Philoponus says that the *Categories* are about simple utterances (*phōnai*) signifying simple things (*pragmata*) by means of simple concepts.

As opposed to the Stoics, Neoplatonists followed Alexander of Aphrodisias in regarding logic not as a separate philosophical discipline but as philosophy's tool, its *Organon*. In their commentaries on the *Prior Analytics*, both Philoponus and Ammonius attempt to reconcile the two positions.

The contemporary Athenian Neoplatonist SIMPLICIUS, who spent much time repudiating Philoponian ideas, doubted Philoponus' competence as a logician, and modern scholars tend to agree with him. Historians of logic, however, acknowledge that Philoponus was the first to render a satisfactory definition of the syllogism which states that the major premise includes the predicate term of the conclusion, the minor premise the subject term (*On Aristotle's Prior Analytics* 67). In Philoponus, one also encounters for the first time the schematic diagram facilitating the construction of valid syllogisms, later termed by the schoolmen *pons asinorum* (*On Aristotle's Prior Analytics* 274).

The commentary on Aristotle's *On the Soul* is perhaps the earliest commentary to contain passages in which Philoponus abandons proper exegesis in order to modify or criticize Aristotelian doctrine, a tendency even more conspicuous in the *Physics* commentary, which can be dated to 517. It is convenient to distinguish between two kinds of criticism: substantial modification of Aristotelian ideas on the one hand, outright rejection on the other. Philoponus' commentary *On the Soul* presents a good example of the first kind of criticism. In *On the Soul* (II 7) Aristotle understood light as incorporeal and described its appearance as an instantaneous transition from the potentiality (*dýnamis*) of a medium to be transparent to the actuality (*enérgeia*) of transparency. The description fails to account both for the laws of optics and for the phenomenon that the region below the moon is warmed by the light of a celestial body, the sun. Philoponus proceeds to interpret the term *enérgeia* not as an actual state but as an 'incorporeal activity' which is capable of warming bodies, just as the soul is in the case of animals. Due to this shift of terminology, light is now understood as dynamic. It is possible to trace Philoponus' further development of the idea: in the *Meteorology* commentary, which belongs to a stage when Philoponus had already abandoned the assumption of an immutable celestial element (*aithēr*), he argues that light and heat may be best explained as consequences of the nature of the sun, which is fire. Heat is generated when the rays emanating from the sun are refracted and warm the air through friction.

2 The grammarian and commentator (cont.)

Philoponus' commentary *On Aristotle's Physics* contains an array of examples of innovative and critical commentary. One of his most celebrated achievements is the theory of impetus, which is commonly regarded as a decisive step from an Aristotelian dynamics towards a modern theory based on the notion of inertia. Concepts akin to impetus theory appear in earlier writers such as Hipparchus and Synesius, but Philoponus never mentions them. As far as one can tell from the text (*On Aristotle's Physics* 639–42), his point of departure is an unsatisfactory Aristotelian answer to a problem that was to puzzle scientists for centuries: why does, for example, an arrow continue to fly after it has left the bowstring? Since Aristotle supposed that (1) whenever there is motion there must be something which imparts the motion, and (2) mover and moved must be in contact, he was led to conclude that the air displaced in front of the projectile somehow rushes round it and pushes from behind, thus propelling the projectile along. This theory was still in vogue among Aristotelians of the sixteenth century, despite the fact that a thousand years earlier Philoponus had demolished it. He proposed instead that a projectile moves on account of a kinetic force impressed on it by the mover, which exhausts itself in the course of the movement. Philoponus compares this 'incorporeal motive *enérgeia*', as he calls it, to the activity earlier attributed to colour and light.

Once projectile motion was understood in terms of an impetus in this way, it became possible to reassess the role of the medium: far from being responsible for the continuation of a projectile's motion, it in fact impedes it (*On Aristotle's Physics* 681). Against Aristotle Philoponus concludes that there is in fact nothing to prevent one from imagining motion taking place through a void. As regards the natural motion of bodies falling through a medium, Aristotle's verdict that the speed is proportional to the weight of the moving bodies and indirectly proportional to the density of the medium is disproved by an experiment similar to that which Galileo was to carry out centuries later (*On Aristotle's Physics* 682–4).

Philoponus' impetus theory ties in with wider criticisms of Aristotelian principles of physics. Aristotle had dismissed the notion of a void as an incoherent logical impossibility. Philoponus concedes that in nature empty spaces never become actual, but he insists that a clear conception of the void is not only coherent but also necessary if one wants to explain movement in a plenum (the place-swapping of bodies presupposes that there is empty space to be filled; *On Aristotle's Physics* 693–4) or such phenomena as the force of the vacuum (571–2). Philoponus' elaborate defence of the void (675–94) is closely related to his conceptions of place and space (*On Aristotle's Physics* 557–85). Aristotle defined the place of a body as the inner surface of the body that contains it (*Physics* IV 4); Philoponus replies that place ought to be conceived as the three-dimensional extension equal to the determinate size of the body, that is, its volume. Likewise, space is indeterminate pure three-dimensional extension devoid of body. It is not infinite, however, but coextensive with the size of the universe.

Philoponus' discussion of matter dovetails well with this conception of space. In the commentary *On Aristotle's Physics* (687–8) he argues in a vein similar to Aristotle in *Metaphysics* (VII 3). In abstracting all qualities from body Aristotle arrived at prime matter, which the Neoplatonists later defined as incorporeal and formless. Philoponus, in contrast, arrives at something he calls 'corporeal extension', which is a composite of prime matter and indeterminate quantity and must not be confused with space. His argument here may still be regarded as elaboration on Aristotle. However, in book XI of the polemical treatise against Proclus (see §2), he rejects the Aristotelian-Neoplatonic conception of prime matter and lets the most fundamental level of his ontology be constituted by 'the three-dimensional', indeterminate corporeal extension. In this he claims to be following the Stoics; this lowest ontological level is reminiscent of the Cartesian *res extensa*, although Descartes would not permit the distinction between space and corporeal extension (see STOICISM §3; DESCARTES, R. §11).

In order to rebuff the likely objection that the three-dimensional cannot be the most fundamental level of being because extension, belonging to the category of quantity, is an *accident* and requires the assumption of an underlying *subject*, Philoponus argues that extension is in fact an essential and inseparable differentia of the three-dimensional, just like heat in fire or whiteness in snow. Thus quantity is constitutive of body as such, which amounts to a promotion of quantity to the category of substance. There are indications that Philoponus would have modified Aristotle's scheme of the *Categories* if he had revised his early commentary on that treatise.

The incomplete commentary on the *Meteorology* may well be the last commentary Philoponus wrote on Aristotle. It is worth noting how the lectures are presented, with an air of aloofness and, at times, deliberate vagueness. In several places, especially when he has to comment on the nature and movement of the heavens, Philoponus breaks off and refers the student to previously published work: what Philoponus *really* has to say about the text seems no longer appropriate for the classroom. He has successfully shaken off the weight of Aristotle's and anyone else's authority, and far from demonstrating the harmony among philosophers he himself contributes to their dissent. The commentator has turned into a critic.

3   The critic

In the fifth century, the Athenian Neoplatonist Proclus wrote a defence of the pagan Greek belief in the eternity of the world. His aim was to show that Christian creationism was intellectually untenable. Eighteen arguments were loosely grouped around the myth of Plato's *Timaeus*, which, according to Proclus, was consistent with an eternalist reading.

In 529, when the Emperor Justinian suppressed pagan philosophy in Athens, Philoponus published a reply entitled *On the Eternity of the World against Proclus*. The book is something like an anti-commentary to the Proclean arguments. Combing through the text Philoponus repudiates literally every single point made by Proclus. Although his efforts are evidently motivated by faith, he keeps Biblical theology out of his polemic, attempting to refute Proclus solely within the framework of Platonism. The *Timaeus* is read as a genuine account of creation, and a fresh analysis of the processes of generation and corruption even renders viable an idea which Greek philosophers never allowed: creation out of nothing. Even if it were true that creation out of nothing never occurs in nature, Philoponus argues, God is surely more powerful a creator than nature and therefore capable of it.

Philoponus' battle against eternalism may be divided into three different stages. The first, the work against Proclus, is followed by a second and even more provocative publication, *On the Eternity of the World against Aristotle*. This work was published *c.*530–4 and involved a close scrutiny of the first chapters of Aristotle's *On the Heavens* (on the theory of aether) and the eighth book of the *Physics* (on the eternity of motion and time). The third stage is represented by one, perhaps two non-polemical treatises in which arguments against eternity and for creation were arranged in systematic order.

Like the polemic against Proclus, that against Aristotle is mainly devoted to removing obstacles for the creationist. If Aristotle were right about the existence of an immutable fifth element (*aithēr*) in the celestial region, and if he were right about motion and

time being eternal, any belief in creation would surely be unwarranted. Philoponus succeeds in pointing to numerous contradictions, inconsistencies, fallacies and improbable assumptions in Aristotle's philosophy of nature. Dissecting the text in an unprecedented way, he consistently refutes Aristotle's arguments and so paves the way for demonstrative arguments for non-eternity. One such argument (fr. 132) reported by Simplicius (*On Aristotle's Physics* 1178.7–1179.26) relies on three premises: (1) if the existence of something requires the pre-existence of something else, then it will not come to be without the prior existence of the other; (2) an infinite number cannot exist in actuality, nor be traversed in counting, nor be increased; and (3) something cannot come into being if its existence requires the pre-existence of an infinite number of other things, one arising out of the other. From these not un-Aristotelian premises, Philoponus deduces that the conception of a temporally infinite universe, understood as a successive causal chain, is impossible. Furthermore, given that the spheres have different periods of revolution, the assumption of their motion being eternal would lead to infinity being increased, even multiplied, which Aristotle thought absurd.

The non-polemical treatises exploit, among others, Aristotle's argument that an infinite *dýnamis* cannot reside in a finite body (*Physics* VIII 10); Philoponus infers that since the universe is finite, it cannot have the *dýnamis* to exist for an infinite time. As in the case of the theory of light, this argument involves a shift of meaning. In the context of Aristotle's prime mover argument, *dýnamis* meant 'kinetic force'; Philoponus, however, uses the word in the sense of 'existential capacity' or 'fitness'.

By the end of the 530s Philoponus seems to have stopped producing philosophical works; for reasons on which one can only speculate, his career as a philosopher was over.

4   The theologian

Since there is no evidence that John Philoponus belonged to a clerical order, it is difficult to picture his professional life as a theologian. He published his theological treatises under the same name as before, *Iōánnēs grammatikós*, but it seems hard to imagine him as a professor of grammar. Likewise, his nickname *philóponos* (lover of work) is probably best interpreted as an acknowledgement of his literary productivity, not as an indication of his status as one of the Christian brethren in Egypt who called themselves by that name.

Perhaps some fifteen years after his attack on Aristotle, Philoponus published the Creation story,

On the Creation of the World (*De opificio mundi*), his only theological work extant in Greek. While discussing the biblical text Philoponus frequently refers to philosophers such as Aristotle, Plato and Ptolemy as well as to Basil the Great, whose own treatise on the Creation served as his inspiration (see CREATION AND CONSERVATION, RELIGIOUS DOCTRINE OF). The treatise has received some attention from historians of science, because Philoponus suggests at one point (I 12) that the movement of the heavens could be explained by a 'motive force' impressed on the celestial bodies by God at the time of creation. Philoponus had discussed impetus theory for the first time in the context of forced motion (see §2); now he applies the theory to the universe at large. Significantly, Philoponus compares the rotation imparted to the celestial bodies to the rectilinear movements of the elements as well as to the movements of animals: they are all brought about by the creator's divine impetus. Due to this suggestion Philoponus is often credited with having envisaged, for the first time, a unified dynamic theory, striving to give the same kind of explanation for phenomena which Aristotle had to explain by various different principles.

Judging from the fragmentary evidence, Philoponus' later theological treatises are characterized by a curious mixture of Christian piety and Aristotelian philosophy. On the eve of the fifth Council (Constantinople 553), Philoponus stepped forward as a partisan of monophysite Christology which, in the course of the century, had become increasingly influential in the eastern part of the empire. The monophysites, who emphasized the divinity of Christ, were scandalized by the conjunction of Christological formulas enunciated at the Council of Chalcedon in 451. There Christ was confessed to be: (1) consubstantial (*homooúsios*) with the Father; (2) consubstantial with humans; (3) one person and one *hypóstasis* ('existence'); and (4) 'discernible in two natures', a phrase referring to the '*unitatem personae in utraque natura intelligendam*' endorsed by the Bishop of Rome and familiar to theologians of the Latin West. Although propositions (1), (2) and (3) were no longer controversial, proposition (4) could be read as an unholy concession to those who regarded Jesus merely as a divinely inspired man. In addition, how could it be sensible to predicate two entirely different natures of a single entity?

In the *Arbiter* Philoponus takes the view that the phrase 'in two natures' ought to be abandoned. His main strategy is to argue that in this context the meaning of the terms 'nature' and '*hypóstasis*' is virtually identical. 'Nature' has two senses, one general, one particular – we can speak of the nature of man in general or of the nature of this individual man. When one speaks of the unification of two natures in Christ, the reference cannot be to the universal natures of godhead and manhood (otherwise it would be true to say that the Father and the Spirit have also become man, since the universal nature of 'godhead' applies to them as it does to the Son). Hence, the reference must be to the particular nature of the Logos and the particular nature of Jesus the man. But 'particular nature' is virtually the same as *hypóstasis*, which Philoponus uses also as a synonym of 'person' and 'individual'. Since it is agreed that Christ is one person and *hypóstasis*, he must consequently be of one nature, albeit a complex one which combines and preserves the properties of both god and man: 'one composite nature' (*mía phýsis sýnthetos*).

Besides monophysitism Philoponus' name is associated with the precarious doctrine of tritheism. However, there is an important difference: whereas monophysitism was a reputable and powerful movement among Eastern theologians, tritheism is merely a hostile label attached to those who were not afraid to render the mystery of the Trinity intelligible by drawing some clear distinctions. Already in the *Arbiter* it became clear that Philoponus associated with the term *hypóstasis* something like 'primary substance' in the Aristotelian sense (see above). The fragments of the very late treatise *On the Trinity* confirm this: since *hypostasis* is certainly not an accident of divinity, it must be the case that the three *hypostases* of the Trinity are three divine substances with distinct properties. Only on this assumption, too, is it reasonable to speak of consubstantiality: if there were only *one* divine substance, what could it mean to say that it is consubstantial with itself? When the Cappadocians spoke of the Trinity as 'one substance (*ousia*), three *hypostases*', they were not, Philoponus argues, enunciating a fourth primary substance, but using 'substance' in the secondary, abstract sense. In accordance with Aristotle Philoponus goes on to claim that universals exist only in the human mind, thus reducing monotheism apparently to a mere concept. In order to refute any reminiscences of pagan polytheism Philoponus points out that, unlike the gods of the pagans, the three divinities of the Trinity are all of the same divine nature (in the universal sense).

Philoponus had followers, but this kind of trinitarian philosophy was unacceptable to anyone not committed to Aristotle's ontology. And so, the so-called tritheists faced immediate and severe criticism; Philoponus himself was condemned (posthumously) by the Council of Constantinople in 680/1. It is often stated that Philoponus was one of the first thinkers to reconcile Aristotelian philosophy with Christianity;

his contemporaries probably took a different view. Pagan philosophers certainly abhorred the way in which Philoponus used Christianity as a vantage point from which to disturb the harmony of the wise, and Christian theologians could not but castigate his dubious attempt at comprehending a spiritual mystery by making it conform to Aristotle.

5 Influence

In addition to inciting the disapproval of his contemporaries, both pagan and Christian, Philoponus' immediate influence may have been considerable among fellow monophysites in Egypt, but his condemnation as a heretic in 681 made the further proliferation of his theological ideas impossible. Likewise, his arch enemy Simplicius, also a pupil of Ammonius, son of Hermeas, submitted Philoponus' anti-eternalism almost immediately to thundering polemic which resounded through the centuries with the effect that later thinkers like Thomas AQUINAS and Zabarella underestimated Philoponus in general. Although his work was studied by the Arabs, who referred to him as Yahya an-Nahwi or Yahya al-'Asqalani, they too tended to side with Aristotle. However, the arguments against eternity eventually persuaded BONAVENTURE and GERSONIDES, and impetus theory was reaffirmed by BURIDAN and his pupil ORESME. In the sixteenth century, the first editions and numerous translations (into Latin) of Philoponus' commentaries and the treatise against Proclus began to appear in print. In particular his criticism of Aristotle in *On Aristotle's Physics* was widely discussed and persuaded such diverse thinkers as Giovanni PICO DELLA MIRANDOLA and, for different reasons, Galileo GALILEI.

See also: ARISTOTLE COMMENTATORS

List of works

John Philoponus (*c.*510–15) *On Words with Different Meanings in Virtue of a Difference of Accent* (*De vocabulis quae diversum significatum exhibent secundum differentiam accentus*), ed. L.W. Daly, American Philosophical Society Memoirs 151, Philadelphia, PA: American Philosophical Society, 1983. (A philosophically unimportant work on Greek homonyms.)

—— (*c.*510–15) *On Aristotle's On Generation and Corruption*, ed. H. Vitelli, *Commentaria in Aristotelem Graeca* XIV 2, Berlin: Reimer, 1897. (A commentary based on Ammonius' seminars containing virtually no criticism of Aristotle.)

—— (*c.*510–15) *On Aristotle's On the Soul*, ed. M. Hayduck, *Commentaria in Aristotelem Graeca* XV, Berlin: Reimer, 1897. (Probably the ideas are substantially Ammonius'. The authenticity of book III is disputed, because a Latin version attributed to Philoponus differs from the text transmitted in Greek (see Verbeke 1966).)

—— (*c.*512–17) *On Aristotle's Categories*, ed. A. Busse, *Commentaria in Aristotelem Graeca* XIII 1, Berlin: Reimer, 1898. (A *Categories* commentary typical of the school of Ammonius.)

—— (*c.*512–17) *On Aristotle's Prior Analytics*, ed. M. Wallies, *Commentaria in Aristotelem Graeca* XIII 2, Berlin: Reimer, 1905. (Purports to be based on Ammonius' seminars.)

—— (*c.*515–20) *On Aristotle's Posterior Analytics*, ed. M. Wallies, *Commentaria in Aristotelem Graeca* XIII 3, Berlin: Reimer, 1909. (Also purporting to be based on Ammonius, but there are signs of a later revision.)

—— (517) *On Aristotle's Physics*, ed. H. Vitelli, *Commentaria in Aristotelem Graeca* XVI– XVII, Berlin: Reimer, 1887–88; trans. A.R. Lacey, *Philoponus, On Aristotle's Physics 2*, London: Duckworth, 1993; trans. M. Edwards, *Philoponus, On Aristotle's Physics 3*, London: Duckworth, 1994; trans. P. Lettinck, *Philoponus, On Aristotle's Physics 5 to 8*, London: Duckworth, 1994. (This work represents the starting point for Philoponus' independent intellectual development; it includes important digressions on the notions of "place" and "void".)

—— (*c.*520–40) *On the Use and Construction of the Astrolabe*, ed. H. Hase, Bonn: E. Weber, 1839, and *Rheinisches Museum für Philologie* 6: 127–71, 1839; repr. and trans. A.P. Segonds, *Jean Philopon, traité de l'astrolabe*, Paris: Librairie Alain Brieux, 1981; trans. H.W. Green in R.T. Gunther (ed.) *The Astrolabes of the World*, Oxford: Holland Press, 1932, 2 vols; repr. London: Holland Press, 1976, 61–81. (The oldest extant Greek treatise on the astrolabe.)

—— (529) *On the Eternity of the World against Proclus* (*De aeternitate mundi contra Proclum*), ed. H. Rabe, Leipzig: B.G. Teubner, 1899. (Philoponus' first major polemical treatise.)

—— (*c.*530–4) *On the Eternity of the World against Aristotle* (*De aeternitate mundi contra Aristotelem*), trans. C. Wildberg, *Philoponus, Against Aristotle on the Eternity of the World*, London: Duckworth, 1987. (Not extant, this work consists of reconstructed fragments.)

—— (*c.*530–5) *On Aristotle's Meteorology*, ed. M. Hayduck, *Commentaria in Aristotelem Graeca* XIV 1, Berlin: Reimer, 1901. (This set of classroom

lectures exemplifies how open criticism of Aristotle could at the same time be signalled and suspended.)
—— (*c.*530–5) *On the Contingency of the World* (*De contingentia mundi*), trans. S. Pines, 'An Arabic summary of a lost work of John Philoponus', *Israel Oriental Studies* 2 (1972): 320–52; for similar excerpts in Simplicius, see D. Furley and C. Wildberg, *Philoponus, Corollaries on Place and Void with Simplicius, Against Philoponus on the Eternity of the World*, London: Duckworth, 1991, 95–141. (A short, non-polemical anti-eternalist treatise.)
—— (*c.*530–40) *On Nicomachus' Introduction to Arithmetic*, ed. R. Hoche, parts I/II, Wesel: Bagel, 1864, 1865, part III, Berlin: Calvary, 1867. (The only mathematical work attributed to Philoponus.)
—— (*c.*546–9) *On the Creation of the World* (*De opificio mundi*), ed. W. Reichardt, Leipzig: Teubner, 1897. (The date of composition originally proposed by the editor appears more likely now than the frequently suggested 557–60.)
—— (*c.*552) *Arbiter (Diaetetes)*, trans. A. Šanda, *Opuscula monophysitica Ioannis Philoponi*, Beirut: Typographia Catholica PP.Soc.Jesu, 1930; extracts trans. W. Böhm, *Johannes Philoponos, Grammatikos von Alexandrien*, Munich, Paderborn and Vienna: Schöningh , 1967, 414–29. (A philosophical justification of monophysitism; not extant in Greek, the former is Syriac text with Latin translation, the latter a German translation.)
—— (567) *On the Trinity* (*De trinitate*), trans. A. Van Roey, 'Les fragments trithéites de Jean Philopon', *Orientalia Lovaniensia Periodica* 11 (1980): 135–63. (The main source for a reconstruction of Philoponus' trinitarian doctrine; not extant so Syriac fragments with Latin translation.)

References and further reading

Haas, F.A.J. de (1996) *John Philoponus on Matter. Towards a Metaphysics of Creation*, Leiden: Brill. (Offers a lucid discussion of Philoponus' conception of matter, its roots in the whole Neoplatonic-Aristotelian tradition, and its significance for Philoponus' doctrine of creation.)
Hainthaler, T. (1990) 'Johannes Philoponus, Philosoph und Theolog in Alexandria' (John Philoponus, Alexandrian Philosopher and Theologian), in A. Grillmeier (ed.) *Jesus der Christus im Glauben der Kirche, Band 2/4: Die Kirche von Alexandrien mit Nubien und Äthiopien nach 451*, Freiburg, Basle and Vienna: Herder, 109–49. (Particularly valuable as a survey of Philoponus' theological ideas.)
Lee, T.-S. (1984) *Die griechische Tradition der aristotelischen Syllogistik in der Spätantike* (The Greek Tradition of Aristotelian Syllogistic in Late

Antiquity), Göttingen: Vandenhoeck & Ruprecht. (A comparative evaluation of Alexander's, Ammonius' and Philoponus' commentaries on the *Prior Analytics*.)
Sambursky, S. (1962) *The Physical World of Late Antiquity*, London: Routledge & Kegan Paul, 154–75. (Standard work on late ancient theories concerning space, time, matter and mechanics.)
Scholten, C. (1996) *Antike Naturphilosophie und christliche Kosmologie in der Schrift De opificio mundi des Johannes Philoponos* (Ancient Philosophy of Nature and Christian Cosmology in John Philoponus' Treatise De opificio mundi), Berlin: de Gruyter. (A careful analysis of the natural philosophy behind key concepts employed in Philoponus' commentary on the Biblical Creation story.)
Sorabji, R.R.K. (1983) *Time, Creation and the Continuum*, London: Duckworth. (Pages 193–231 contain a lucid discussion of Philoponus' anti-eternalist infinity arguments.)
—— (ed.) (1987) *Philoponus and the Rejection of Aristotelian Science*, London: Duckworth. (A collection of twelve articles on Philoponus' physical theories, his theology and historical influence; extensive bibliography.)
Verbeke, G. (ed.) (1966) *Jean Philopon, Commentaire sur le de anima d'Aristote, traduction de Guillaume de Moerbeke* (John Philoponus, Commentary on Aristotle's *On the Soul*, translated by William of Moerbeke), *Corpus Latinum Commentariorum in Aristotelem Graecorum* III, Paris: Éditions Béatrice-Nauwelaerts; parts thereof trans. W. Charlton, *Philoponus, On Aristotle on the Intellect (de Anima 3.4–8)*, London: Duckworth, 1991. (This Latin commentary differs substantially from the Greek commentary *On the Soul*.)
Verbeke, G. (1985) 'Levels of Human Thinking in Philoponus', in C. Laga, J.A. Munitz and L. van Rompay (eds) *After Chalcedon: Studies in Theology and Church History*, Leuven: Peeters, 451–70.
Verrycken, K. (1990) 'The Development of Philoponus' Thought and its Chronology', in R.R.K. Sorabji (ed.) *Aristotle Transformed*, London: Duckworth, 233–74. (A clear exposition of the main ideas that mark Philoponus' intellectual development; the whole volume is an excellent guide to philosophy in late antiquity, with extensive bibliography.)
Wildberg, C. (1988) *John Philoponus' Criticism of Aristotle's Theory of Aether*, Berlin: de Gruyter. (An analysis of books I–V of *On the Eternity of the World Against Aristotle*.)
Wolff, M. (1971) *Fallgesetz und Massebegriff* (The Law of Falling Bodies and the Concept of Mass),

Berlin: de Gruyter. (A discussion of Philoponus' dynamics and theory of matter.)

CHRISTIAN WILDBERG

'PHILOSOPHY OF X'
see UNDER X

'PHILOSOPHY OF LIFE'
see LEBENSPHILOSOPHIE

PHLOGISTON *see* CHEMISTRY, PHILOSOPHICAL ASPECTS OF (§2)

PHOTOGRAPHY, AESTHETICS OF

Claims that photography is aesthetically different from and, in many versions of the argument, inferior to the arts of painting and drawing have taken various forms: that photography is a mechanical process and therefore not an artistic medium; that it is severely limited in its capacity to express the thoughts and emotions of the artist; that its inability to register more than an instantaneous 'slice' of events restricts its representational capacity; that it is not a representational medium at all. Some of these arguments are thoroughly mistaken, while others have an interesting core of truth that will emerge only after some clarification. Central to this clarification is an account of the precise sense in which photography is mechanical, and an explication of our intuition that a photograph puts us 'in touch with' its subject in a way that a painting or drawing cannot. Both these ideas need to be separated from the mistaken view that it is the nature of photography to provide images that are superlatively faithful to the objects they represent. Throughout this entry we shall consider only the case of photographs of a relatively unmanipulated kind, ignoring darkroom techniques that blur the distinction between photography and painting.

1   The supposed limitations of photography
2   Photography as mechanism

1   The supposed limitations of photography

Photography and the traditional forms of image-making – painting and drawing – differ in important ways. Intuitively, a painting can be 'of' something that does not exist (though this idea is hard to make precise in an acceptable way); a photograph can only be of something that actually transmitted light into the mechanism. A photograph can depict more than the artist intended to depict, such as when magnification displays evidence of a crime; a painting records what the artist thought the scene looked like, and the grain of discriminability is set by the artist's own visual acuity and manual skill. Certain kinds of subject seem to have more force or cause more offence when represented photographically; a photograph of martyrdom would be difficult to appreciate aesthetically, whatever its compositional merits. It has not, however, been easy to explain these judgments within a unified theory of the nature and limitations of photography.

One kind of argument for the artistic inferiority of photography depends on claims about the limitations of what photography can convey – limitations which favour the particular, the instantaneous and the visible or surface features of things over the general, the progressive and the hidden aspects, and especially over the underlying emotional and motivational themes. Most of these arguments apply also to painting, an art against which they are rarely directed. It is true that painting can explicitly present a narrative by placing noncontemporaneous events within the same frame, while a photograph of the 'pure' or unmanipulated kind cannot. But even paintings that confine themselves to the depiction of a single moment can draw on beliefs and traditions external to the work to provide narrative force. Photographs can also achieve narrative status by appeal to such sources. It has also been argued that the 'mechanical' nature of the photographic method does not allow significant scope for expressive or intentional qualities. In exactly what sense photography is mechanical is a question we shall examine in detail later on, but any acceptable explication of that notion will surely have to accommodate the fact that some photographs do express beliefs, evaluations and emotions through the evident choices the photographer has made concerning such things as lighting, depth of field, exposure and subject. It may be true that there are fewer choices to be made in determining the visible appearance of a photograph than in determining the visible appearance of a painting, where every brush stroke is, in principle, a matter of independent decision. It does not follow that photography is a less expressive medium than painting. Sometimes the restrictions that an artistic form imposes on its practitioners give a special significance to the choices they are able to make within the constraints imposed. Arguments to the effect that photography is, by its nature, artistically limited are most charitably understood as reactions against the excessively ambitious claims sometimes made on behalf of photography: that it makes representational painting redundant, that it has an unrivalled capacity for documentation, or that it represents the world to us in an undistorted and uninterpreted form.

The claim that photography faithfully reproduces appearance, in the sense that photographs of things are or can be superlative likenesses of them, needs to be distinguished from another thesis with which it is sometimes confused: that photography mechanically reproduces the appearances of things. Both these claims have been used to advance a further claim: that photography gives us access to things in the real world rather than providing, as painting does, mere representations of those things. Let us call these claims the likeness thesis, the mechanicity thesis and the reality thesis respectively. Critics of the reality thesis have attacked both the mechanicity thesis and the likeness thesis. Against the likeness thesis I believe they have been successful, having shown that there is nothing about photography as a medium that makes its products essentially more faithful than painting to visible appearances. Against the mechanicity thesis, however, the critics have been less successful, their efforts having been directed against its naive and implausible versions. But while the mechanicity thesis stands, it provides little support for the reality thesis, as we shall see.

2 Photography as mechanism

Claims that photography is a mechanical medium are common; clear expositions of the thesis are rare. Perhaps the clearest has been offered by Kendall Walton (1984) .Compare a painting and a photograph of a rose. In both cases there is a dependence between the appearance of the rose and the appearance of the picture; if the rose had been different in various ways, the picture would have been different, and so, correspondingly, would the viewer's experience of looking at the picture. But there is a difference between the painting and the photograph: the patterns of dependence that hold in the case of the painting hold in virtue of facts about the painter's mental state. If the rose had had more petals, the painting would have shown more – but only because the painter would have mentally registered the greater number and incorporated it into the painting. In testing for dependence in the case of painting, if we vary the appearance of the rose, but hold fixed the painter's beliefs about its appearance, the appearance of the painting does not vary. Things are different

with the photograph; holding fixed the photographer's mental state leaves the dependence between scene and photograph intact. Had the rose had more petals, the photograph would have shown more, regardless of whether the photographer noticed their number. A hallucinating painter will paint what they think is there; a photograph will show what is there. Photography is mechanical in that the relevant counterfactuals are independent, in the sense just described, of mental states. Here we shall concentrate on this version of the claim that photography is mechanical.

Having explicated the mechanicity thesis, let us now make the reality thesis comparably plausible and precise. Some versions of the reality thesis seem to assert obvious falsehoods. André Bazin's claim (1967) that 'the photographic image is the object itself' is hard to reconcile with the fact that the Washington Monument and a photograph of it are utterly distinct and possibly very distant from each other in space and time. A better explication is provided once again by Kendall Walton, according to whom photographs are 'transparent': seeing a photograph of X is a case of *really seeing* X, just as seeing X through a window or through a telescope and seeing X's reflection in a mirror are such cases. On the other hand, seeing a painting or drawing of X is not a case of seeing X. Photographs are 'aids to vision', whereas 'handmade' images are ways of representing. Roger Scruton (1981) has likened photography to the artful arrangement of a frame around a street scene; what we see inside the frame may be pleasing, but it is not a representation. It is the same, he says, with the photograph. Scruton is best understood as asserting, not that the photograph of the street is, or contains, the street, but that seeing the photograph is a way of seeing the street. This way of understanding the reality thesis does not require the photograph to be identified with or even overlap with its subject; we may see someone in a mirror without having to suppose that the mirror is part of the person. Nor does it require spatiotemporal proximity between photograph and subject; we now see stars that ceased to exist millions of years ago. It is this version of the reality thesis which I shall consider. I shall call it the transparency thesis.

Let us see how, on Walton's construal, the mechanicity thesis supports the transparency thesis. Recall that the patterns of dependence holding between the rose and the photograph of the rose hold also between the rose and my experience of seeing the photograph of the rose, and that these dependencies hold independently of the beliefs of the photographer. Let us say that in that case my experience of the photograph is 'mechanically dependent' on the state of the rose. By contrast, my experience of looking at the painting of the rose is 'intentionally dependent' on the state of the rose; if we imagine the appearance of the rose to vary but hold fixed the painter's mental states, my visual experience of seeing the painting does not vary. Now consider the case where I directly see a rose in front of my eyes, through a window, through a lens or in a mirror. All these are cases of mechanical dependence; they are also cases of genuinely seeing the rose. Seeing the photograph of the rose shares this mechanical dependence, but seeing the painting of one does not. So seeing the photograph of the rose is to count as genuinely seeing the rose, but seeing the painting is not.

This nexus of views about the mechanicity and transparency of photography has the advantage of not denying certain facts about photography which are sometimes cited in favour of the view that there is not, after all, any principled difference between photography and other representational media like painting: for example, that people typically choose the subject, location and lighting conditions of the photographs they take, and that these choices can all be made with more or less skill, aesthetic sensibility and expressive effect. While true, these considerations are largely irrelevant to the thesis that photographs are mechanical and transparent. When we look at something with the naked eye, how it looks to us depends on lighting conditions and on spatial relations between the viewer and the object viewed, and we can choose to look at this rather than at that. None of this impugns the claim that seeing things with the naked eye is in a certain sense a mechanical process: that when we look in a certain direction it is not up to us or to anyone else to decide what we see; what we see is determined 'mechanically' by what is in front of our eyes and not by decisions or preferences. Nor is it an objection to the claims of mechanicity and transparency that photographs do not always look very much like – and never look exactly like – the things they are photographs of. A photograph may grossly distort the appearance of a man by being created with the help of a distorting lens. But you can look at a man through a distorting lens, thereby seeing him in a grossly distorted way: you are still seeing the man. Nor need the advocate of mechanicity and transparency deny that skills are exercised in the production of photographs, and that photographs so produced may exhibit these skills.

Does the mechanicity of photography provide a convincing argument for its transparency? Imagine two indiscernible clocks, A and B, where mechanical connection ensures that the time told by the hands of A causally determines the time told by those of B. If I

am looking at clock B, then it is true of my current visual state that, if the hands of A told a different time, my current visual awareness of B would have been correspondingly different. And these counterfactuals, we may assume, are independent of the intentions of agents in the sense described above. But my seeing B is not also a case of my seeing A. So mechanicity is not sufficient for transparency.

Walton grants the insufficiency of mechanicity for transparency; there might, he concedes, be a machine which examines objects and churns out linguistic descriptions of them in such a way that there is mechanical dependency between the object and the descriptions produced; but reading the descriptions would not be a case of seeing, or of perceiving in any way, the thing described. What stops reading the description from being a case of seeing the object described is, Walton claims, the lack of relevant similarities between the experience of reading and the experience of seeing the object itself. Here we are close to the assertion that mechanicity and likeness (in some relevant respect) jointly constitute a sufficient condition for transparency. But that is not so: the experience of seeing clock B from our earlier example is, in every relevant respect, very much like the experience of seeing clock A, but seeing clock B is not a case of seeing clock A. This is not to say that the transparency thesis is false, but merely that it is not supported by the mechanicity thesis.

See also: FILM, AESTHETICS OF; SEMIOTICS

References and further reading

Batkin, N. (1991) 'Paul Strand's Photographs in *Camera Work*', *Midwest Studies in Philosophy* 16, ed. P. French, T. Uehling and H. Wettstein, Notre Dame, IN: Notre Dame University Press, 1991. (Combines philosophical analysis of photographic representation with critical reflection on an important moment in the history of photography.)

* Bazin, A. (1967) 'The Ontology of the Photographic Image', in *What is Cinema?*, vol. 1, Berkeley, CA, and Los Angeles, CA: University of California Press. A translation of selected essays from *Qu-est-ce que le cinéma?* 4 vols, 1958–65, Paris: Éditions du Cerf. (Advocates a version of the reality thesis.)

Currie, G. (1991) 'Photography, Painting and Perception', *Journal of Aesthetics and Art Criticism* 49: 23–9. (Argues that the mechanicity thesis does not support the reality thesis.)

* Scruton, R. (1981) 'Photography and Representation', *Critical Inquiry* 7: 577–603. Reprinted in *The Aesthetic Understanding*, New York: Methuen,

1983. (Argues that photography is a representationally and expressively impoverished form.)

Snyder, J. and Allen, N.W. (1976) 'Photography, Vision and Representation', *Critical Inquiry* 2: 143–69. (Argues against both the likeness thesis and the mechanicity thesis, without distinguishing between them very clearly.)

* Walton, K. (1984) 'Transparent Pictures. On the Nature of Photographic Realism', *Critical Inquiry* 11: 246–77. (Argues that the mechanicity thesis supports the reality thesis, while importantly clarifying both.)

GREGORY CURRIE

PHYSICALISM *see* MATERIALISM

IN THE PHILOSOPHY OF MIND

PHYSIS AND NOMOS

In the fifth and fourth centuries BC a vigorous debate arose in Greece centred on the terms physis *(nature)* and nomos *(law or custom). It became the first ethical debate in Western philosophy. Is justice simply a matter of obeying the laws, or does it have some basis in nature? If the laws conflict with my natural needs and desires, why should I submit to them? Is society itself 'natural', and what difference might the answer make to our evaluation of it? Both* nomos *and* physis *had their supporters, while some tried to dissolve the antithesis altogether.*

Physis has two principal meanings. It can refer to the cosmic order as a whole, or to the prime constituent(s) of that order: in these contexts it can often be translated as 'reality'. It can also refer to the intrinsic characteristics of a thing, especially a living thing, or to the thing's growth towards these characteristics. This dynamic aspect of *physis* can seem to give it a prescriptive as well as a descriptive force: it is *good* that things grow towards their mature state and achieving it constitutes their flourishing.

Nomos (plural: *nomoi*) can signify both the unwritten customs and the written laws of a society, and sometimes also an unwritten universal law of divine origin. Even when it refers to a custom, its force is always prescriptive: it indicates not merely a practice, but what the majority accepts as the right practice. However, increasing travel and historical researches heightened awareness of how particular *nomoi* differ between cultures and over time, and the consequent sense of their transience prompted growing speculation about their authority.

The debate was entered by playwrights, orators and historians as well as philosophers. In Sophocles' *Antigone* (450–60), the particular laws of the state are opposed to the universal ordinances (*nomima*) of the gods. Normally, however, the contrast was between the *nomoi* of a particular state and the perceived requirements of human nature – a theme so common that sliding from what is right in law to what is right by nature and vice versa became a standard debating move (see Aristotle, *Sophistical Refutations* 173a7–16). One leading supporter of *physis* was ANTIPHON, who argued that the claims of the laws are generally antithetical to those of human nature, and that the individual's interests will be best served by following the latter when legal punishment can be avoided, especially given the inevitability of nature's reprisals if flouted, compared to the uncertain outcome of a broken law.

Amongst other champions of *physis*, CALLICLES in Plato's *Gorgias* makes a radical distinction between conventional justice and 'natural justice'. It is a 'law of nature' that the naturally superior should seize political control; they should also freely indulge their physical desires. Such behaviour is only termed unjust and intemperate by a convention of the weak majority. The notion of a 'law of nature' also occurs in Thucydides' Melian dialogue (V 105.1–3), where the Athenians claim that it is simply an empirical fact that the superior power can do what it wishes; considerations of justice are only relevant among equals. THRASYMACHUS, however, in Plato *Republic* I, holds that justice is the invention of those in power: they make the laws in their own interests and call obedience to these laws 'justice'. The prudent will on the contrary further their own interests, acting unjustly where necessary. This position is stated in terms of the *nomos/physis* debate at *Republic* 359c.

Underlying all these differing positions is a view of humanity as naturally in conflict. The same premise, however, was also employed by supporters of *nomos*, such as Critias and PROTAGORAS (§§2–3). Both argue that without *nomos* life would be chaotic, brutish and short: humans cannot survive unless they live in societies, and societies cannot exist without an agreed moral code. Protagoras, however, seems to offset people's natural aggression with their innate capacity to absorb social training. DEMOCRITUS (§5) further advocates that people internalize the *nomoi* of society so that these become the *nomos* of the soul.

Protagoras' position has links with the social contract theories prevalent during this period (see, for example, the celebrated position put forward by

Glaucon in Plato's *Republic* 358e–359b). In Plato's *Crito*, Socrates argues that each citizen, by freely electing to remain in their city and receive the benefits of its protection, has made an implicit contract to abide by its *nomoi*. Perhaps the strongest defence of *nomos*, however, comes with Plato and Aristotle, who in different ways seek to dissolve the *nomos/physis* antithesis by claiming that receptivity to *nomoi* is an essential aspect of human *physis*.

The debate had important political implications. Each term was used to serve both oligarchic and democratic causes. Traditionally *physis* had been employed by aristocrats to support the notion of a superior class naturally fitted to rule, but by the late fifth century BC appeals to *physis* were also being used to question the social hierarchy. Antiphon claimed that there was no natural distinction between the high- and low-born, or between Greek and non-Greek, and in the mid fourth century Alcidamas attacked as unnatural the institution of slavery. But the defenders of these social distinctions also appealed to *physis*, as Aristotle does regarding slavery in *Politics* book I.

The liberal deployment of *physis* was associated with the democratic belief that human excellence (see ARETĒ) could be taught through immersion in the *nomoi* of the state, rather than being acquired through aristocratic inheritance. The supremacy of written *nomoi* was also upheld by democratic supporters, while oligarchs increasingly claimed backing from the controversial unwritten *nomoi*.

Issues of epistemology and language were also embraced. Democritus claimed that sensible properties exist only by convention, while in Plato's *Cratylus* it is considered whether there is a 'natural name' for each thing, or whether this too is a matter of *nomos* (see LANGUAGE, ANCIENT PHILOSOPHY OF). Nor were the gods above scrutiny: a fragment of the lost play *Sisyphus* (possibly by Critias) argues that the gods are a political invention to promote social control.

The debate raises tough philosophical problems. Is the derivation of an ethical prescription from appeals to nature legitimate? (See NATURALISM IN ETHICS.) Some scholars hold that the teleological connotations of *physis* make such a derivation at least plausible. Again, can human nature even be distinguished from *nomos*, either conceptually or in practice?

Despite such difficulties, the debate initiated an important tradition in ethical and political thought which required that perceived human needs and desires at least be taken into consideration, even if they are ultimately to be transcended.

References and further reading

Classen, C.J. (ed.) (1976) *Sophistik*, Darmstadt: Wissenschaftliche Buchgesellschaft. (A useful collection of German and English articles.)

Guthrie, W.K.C. (1969) *A History of Greek Philosophy*, vol. 3, Cambridge: Cambridge University Press; part of vol. 3 repr. as *The Sophists*, Cambridge: Cambridge University Press, 1971. (A thoughtful and scholarly exploration; see especially pages 55–134.)

Heinimann, F. (1945) *Nomos und Physis*, Basle: Reinhardt. (A classic study in German which places the debate in its intellectual and historical context.)

Kerferd, G.B. (1981) *The Sophistic Movement*, Cambridge: Cambridge University Press. (Clear and stimulating; the *nomos/physis* debate is discussed particularly in chapter 10.)

McKirahan, R.D. (1994) *Philosophy Before Socrates*, Indianapolis, IN: Hackett. (A helpful collection of translated texts with a lucid commentary; for the *nomos/physis* debate see chapter 19.)

ANGELA HOBBS

PHYSICS, PHILOSOPHY OF

see BELL'S THEOREM; BOHR, NIELS; BOYLE, ROBERT; BRADWARDINE, THOMAS; EINSTEIN, ALBERT; ELECTRODYNAMICS; EXPERIMENT; FIELD THEORY, CLASSICAL; FIELD THEORY, QUANTUM; GALILEI, GALILEO; GENERAL RELATIVITY, PHILOSOPHICAL RESPONSES TO; MACH, ERNST; MATTER; MAXWELL, JAMES CLERK; MEASUREMENT, THEORY OF; MECHANICS, ARISTOTELIAN; MECHANICS, CLASSICAL; NEWTON, ISAAC; OXFORD CALCULATORS; QUANTUM MEASUREMENT PROBLEM; QUANTUM MECHANICS, INTERPRETATION OF; REDUCTION, PROBLEMS OF; RELATIVITY THEORY,

PIAGET, JEAN (1896–1980)

The Swiss psychologist Jean Piaget was the founder of the field we now call cognitive development. His own term for the discipline was 'genetic epistemology', reflecting his deep philosophical concerns. Among Piaget's most enduring contributions were his remarkably robust and surprising observations of children. Time after time, in a strikingly wide variety of domains, and at every age from birth to adolescence, he discovered that children understood the world in very different ways from adults.

But Piaget was really only interested in children because he thought they exemplified basic epistemological processes. By studying children we could discover how biological organisms acquire knowledge of the world around them. The principles of genetic epistemology could then be applied to other creatures, from molluscs to physicists. Piaget's other enduring legacy is the idea that apparently foundational kinds of knowledge were neither given innately nor directly derived from experience. Rather, knowledge was constructed as a result of the complex interplay between organisms and their environment. Piaget saw this view as an alternative to both classical rationalism and empiricism.

1 The stages of development
2 The mechanisms of development
3 Piaget's influence
4 After Piaget

1 The stages of development

Piaget described development as a series of wide-ranging stages. At each stage children had quite different basic logical and representational capacities, which underpinned all their behaviour. Infants initially arrived in the world with nothing but motor reflexes and sensory systems. During infancy they elaborated these basic capacities into complex contingent instructions for behaviour, which related actions and sensations. Piaget called these 'sensorimotor schemas'. Infants could make substantial progress even within this apparently limited framework. They learned a great deal about objects, space, action and causality. Nevertheless, there were, quite literally, no representations of the world in infancy, and no conception of a world independent of the

infant's experience. There were only instructions for action.

Piaget defended this position with examples of apparently peculiar and irrational behaviour in infancy. One set of examples involved infants' attempts to obtain interesting objects. Six month-old infants behaved as if objects that disappeared under a cloth no longer existed. If they were in the midst of reaching for an object and it was hidden under a cloth, they would give up their attempt to get it. Later, they learned that pulling the cloth would make the object reappear. But if the object was hidden under one cloth and then under another they would continue to search under the original cloth. Similarly, 9-month-olds who learned to pull a blanket towards them to get an object on top of the blanket would continue to do so even when the object was placed to one side of the blanket.

Children only developed the capacity to represent the external world symbolically at about 18 months. This new kind of representation was reflected in the development of language, pretend play and deferred imitation. These symbolic representations also allowed children to understand that there was a world independent of their experience of it. And they enabled children to solve problems 'in their heads', without actually having to act on the world.

These representations, however, initially had little logical or causal structure. They were 'pre-operational'. As a result preschool children were unable to perform even simple logical and causal reasoning. When they were asked to explain natural phenomena they resorted to animistic explanations, or to explanations in terms of their own desires, and they might reverse cause and effect. For example, a 3-year-old child who was asked why it got dark at night might reply that it got dark because we need to sleep or because you could not see then. Similarly, preschool children were unable to understand even simple logical principles such as the law of transitivity. If they were told that stick *A* was longer than stick *B* and stick *B* than stick *C*, they might still deny that *A* was longer than *C*. Finally, these very young children showed little understanding of hierarchical relationships, such as class-inclusion. If you showed them an array of four red flowers and two white ones, they would report that there were more red flowers than flowers.

At about 6, children did begin to use causal and logical reasoning. These kinds of reasoning were, however, initially closely tied to the perceptual appearances of objects. They were 'concrete operational'. The most famous examples of this involved 'conservation'. In a conservation task the properties of objects remain the same in spite of transformations of the object's appearance. In a classic experiment, Piaget showed children a tall, thin glass of water, poured the water into a short, wide glass and asked children whether there was the same amount of water, more, or less. Seven-year-olds consistently said that there was less water in the short glass, even after the water was poured back and forth from glass to glass. The children were unable to use information about relations among objects and transformations of objects to override perceptual information about the features of objects.

Piaget thought concrete operations were reflected in the child's understanding of psychological states as well as physical objects. Just as school-age children were unable to coordinate different perceptual appearances, they were unable to coordinate their own experiences and those of others (see MIND, CHILD'S THEORY OF). They were 'egocentric'. If 7-year-olds were shown a complex scene from one perspective, they could not project how the scene would look to another person at a different viewpoint. Similarly, in moral reasoning children calculated harm by looking at the actual amount of damage that was caused, without considering intention or motivation (see MORAL DEVELOPMENT). Only at adolescence, in the stage of formal operations, did children become able to use logical and scientific reasoning in a way that was fully abstracted from the details of their own experience.

2 The mechanisms of development

Piaget rejected both the classical developmental mechanisms of nativist views, such as maturation, and those of empiricist views, such as association or reinforcement. Moreover, he also rejected, or at least underplayed, the influence of language and social interaction. Instead he proposed three very general mechanisms of development, all involving an interaction between the knowledge the child had already developed and new information from the outside world. Piaget called his overall view of development 'constructivism'.

Assimilation. The child adapted and interpreted information from the world to fit his existing schemas. The manifestations of assimilation ran from a newborn who generalized his sucking reflex from a nipple to a rattle, to a preschool child who used blocks as dolls in her pretend play, to a school-age child in a conservation task who simply misreported counter-evidence to his claims about the water.

Accommodation. The opposite effect took place: the child was forced to adapt his schemas to fit new information from the world. Again these effects could vary from an infant who had to change his style of

sucking to accommodate the unyielding rattle, to a preschool child who imitated her mother's phone conversation in an initially uncomprehending way, to a child in a conservation task who at least temporarily admitted that the same water was in both glasses.

Equilibration. This really represented a kind of balance between assimilation and accommodation. When the child's representations and the evidence from the world matched, the process of accommodation and assimilation would end and the child could at least temporarily settle on a particular kind of representation. Piaget saw cognitive development as a highly dynamic process, constantly balancing representations that had already been constructed with new input from the outside world.

Moreover, the child's active attempts to interact with the world were the basic motor driving this dynamic process. Assimilation and accommodation could work only if the child were engaged with the world, usually by physically acting on it. Piaget sometimes illustrated the mechanisms with the biological example of an animal literally assimilating part of its environment by eating it, and literally accommodating the food by physically changing its body as a result.

3 Piaget's influence

Much of Piaget's most significant work was produced in the 1920s and 1930s in Geneva. But Piaget, like the Gestalt psychologists, remained largely unknown in the United States during the long reign of behaviourism (see BEHAVIOURISM, METHODOLOGICAL AND SCIENTIFIC; GESTALT PSYCHOLOGY). However, a few Piagetians, like Gestaltists, came to America after the war, and kept the tradition alive in small enclaves in liberal arts colleges. In the 1960s Piaget was rediscovered in the United States and fully translated into English. His rediscovery was itself both a consequence and a cause of the 'cognitive revolution' in psychology. Piaget was one shining example of how you could construct an account of the mind that was mentalistic, but that also emphasized the biological foundations of psychology. Unlike earlier psychologists such as Brentano and Wundt, but like Chomsky and the early computationalists, he detached the idea of mentalistic explanation from phenomenology (see MIND, COMPUTATIONAL THEORIES OF; UNCONSCIOUS MENTAL STATES).

Moreover, Piaget's work led to the recognition that developmental questions were of broad interest and importance in psychology (until the 1960s much developmental psychology was located in home economics departments). Piaget also had a strong influence on education, particularly on 'progressive' educational theory and practice.

4 After Piaget

Where does the theory stand now? Most of Piaget's actual observations, often based only on pen and paper notes of a few children, have held up remarkably well. On the other hand, new techniques have given us a much broader additional database. Most often, the new data suggest that children are more competent and sophisticated in their under-standing of the world than Piaget supposed. These new observations have led most cognitive develop-mentalists to reject the details of Piagetian theory (see COGNITION, INFANT; COGNITIVE DEVELOPMENT).

In particular, the idea of broad-ranging stages of development has come under increasing attack. Instead, cognitive development appears to be quite specific to particular domains of knowledge. For example, the infant who fails to understand object permanence may show a sophisticated and clearly representational understanding of object movement or of human action. The same child who gives an animistic or pre-causal explanation of the fact that it gets dark at night will give an entirely accurate causal account of how their tricycle works. The preschool child who is egocentric in Piaget's experiments can tell you that someone on the other side of a screen from them will not be able to see what they themselves see. Even newborn infants show a rich understanding of some domains.

Similarly, it appears that Piaget overestimated the importance of action in cognitive development, particularly in infancy. Very young infants show signs of reasoning and learning about objects, well before they can act on them. On the other hand, Piaget probably underestimated the importance of social interaction and language in cognitive development. Much of the new research suggests that children are extremely sensitive to social information and are tuned in to the social world from an early age. More generally, Piaget's account of assimilation and accom-modation as the basic mechanisms of 'constructivism' now seems too vague.

Some developmentalists have seen these problems as a reason for rejecting not only the detailed theory but the project of 'constructivism' – of a middle way between classical nativism and empiricism – alto-gether. Many have returned to one version or another of the classical philosophical alternatives. Modularity theories, for example, are a variant of classical rationalism (see MODULARITY OF MIND). Connec-tionist or dynamic systems theories, or some version of social constructivism, are a variant of classical empiricism (see CONNECTIONISM; EMPIRICISM). How-ever, most developmentalists would probably prefer to revise Piaget's general view of development rather than to replace it. Perhaps the clearest contemporary theoretical legacy of Piaget is the idea that cognitive development is the result of the same mechanisms that lead to theory change in science (see SCIENTIFIC METHOD; KUHN, T.). Testing or confirming the theory by experiment might be a modern version of assimilation, while revising the theory in the light of counter-evidence would be more like accommodation. Piaget's most enduring legacy of all, however, was the idea that the grand questions of 'genetic epistemol-ogy', questions that date back to Socrates, could be answered by paying attention to the small details of the daily lives of our children.

List of works

Piaget, J. (1926) *The Language and Thought of the Child*, London: Kegan Paul, Trench, Trubner & Co; New York: Harcourt Brace.

—— (1929) *The Child's Conception of the World*, London: Kegan Paul, Trench, Trubner & Co; New York: Harcourt, Brace.

—— (1930) *The Child's Conception of Physical Causality*, London: Kegan Paul, Trench, Trubner & Co.

—— (1948) *The Moral Judgement of the Child*, trans. M. Gabain, Glencoe, IL: Free Press.

—— (1952) *The Child's Conception of Number*, trans. C. Gattegno and F.M. Hodgson, London: Routle-dge & Kegan Paul.

Piaget, J. *et al.* (1952) *Judgment and Reasoning in the Child*, New York: Humanities Press.

Piaget, J. (1952) *The Origins of Intelligence in Children*, trans. M. Cook, New York: International Universities Press.

—— (1954) *The Construction of Reality in the Child*, trans. M. Cook, New York: Basic Books.

Piaget, J. and Inhelder, B. (1956) *The Child's Concep-tion of Space*, trans. F.J. Langdon and J.L. Lunzer, London: Routledge & Kegan Paul.

Piaget, J. (1957) *Logic and Psychology*, with an introduction on Piaget's logic by W. Mays, New York: Basic Books.

Piaget, J., Inhelder, B. and Szeminska, A. (1960) *The Child's Conception of Geometry*, trans. E.A. Lunzer, London: Routledge & Kegan Paul.

Piaget, J. (1962) *Play, Dreams, and Imitation in Childhood*, trans. C. Gattegno and F.M. Hodgson, New York: Norton.

References and further reading

Flavell, J. (1968) *The Developmental Psychology of Jean Piaget*, Princeton, NJ: Van Nostrand. (One of the first and still the best account of Piaget's psychological theory. Piaget himself has a Kantian style that can be very rough-going. Flavell is the best way to get a clear sense of the general view.)

Flavell, J., Miller, P. and Miller, S. (1993) *Cognitive Development*, Englewood Cliffs, NJ: Prentice Hall, 3rd edn. (A contemporary account of cognitive development post-Piaget, written at a quite introductory level.)

ALISON GOPNIK

PICO DELLA MIRANDOLA, GIOVANNI (1463–94)

Giovanni Pico della Mirandola, today the best known of Renaissance philosophers, was a child prodigy and gentleman scholar who studied humanities, Aristotelianism and Platonism with the greatest teachers of his day. He claimed to have mastered, by the age of twenty-four, all known theological systems, Christian and non-Christian, from Moses to his own time. He was the first important Christian student of the Jewish mystical theology known as Kabbalah. The purpose of Pico's philosophical and theological studies was to produce a grand synthesis of religious wisdom which would both deepen understanding of Christian truth and also serve as an apologetic weapon against non-Christians. This was the project outlined in Pico's most famous work, De dignitate hominis *(On the Dignity of Man) (1486), and further illuminated by his* Conclusiones *(1486) and* Apologia *(1487). As part of this larger project, Pico planned to write a concord of Plato and Aristotle, of which only a fragment, the treatise* De ente et uno *(On Being and the One) (1491), was ever finished. Although he proposed to found a new theological school based on an esoteric reading of all theologies past and present, he did not believe that these theologies were the same in substance, differing only in expression. He insisted on the differences between Platonism and Christianity, while holding that every major theological tradition did contain some elements of truth.*

In addition to other, non-philosophical works, Pico wrote the Commento *(1486), a commentary on a Neoplatonic poem that in effect constituted a critique of Marsilio Ficino's most famous work, the dialogue* De amore *(On Love) (1469). He criticized Ficino as too literary and defended the use of precise technical language in philosophy. Pico used Neoplatonic metaphysics to rediscover the 'secret mysteries' of pagan theology (though he sometimes criticized the reliability of the Neoplatonists as guides to Plato's thought) and offered a fresh interpretation of the metaphysics of love based on his own reading of Platonic sources, seeing human erotic love as a psychological process distinct from cosmic love.*

1   **Life and works**
2   **The theory of love**
3   **The Roman disputation**
4   **The concord of Plato and Aristotle**

1   Life and works

Giovanni Pico della Mirandola was born in the small north Italian principality of Mirandola in 1463. Though he eventually succeeded an older brother as Count of Mirandola and Concordia, he was originally intended by his parents for an ecclesiastical career. With this end in view he was sent in 1477 to the University of Bologna to study canon law. In 1479 he left Bologna without taking his degree and went to Ferrara, where he studied with the famous humanist schoolmaster Battista Guarino. By 1480 he was in Padua hearing lectures on Aristotelian philosophy and studying privately with the Jewish Averroist Elijah Delmedigo (see AVERROISM, JEWISH). He also at this time formed a lasting friendship with the great Venetian scholar and humanist Ermolao Barbaro. Barbaro tried to interest Pico in his own project of freeing Aristotle from the 'corrupt' interpretations of medieval Arabic and Latin commentators with the help of Aristotle's ancient Greek commentators. In 1482 Pico wrote to Marsilio FICINO asking for a copy of his recent *Theologia platonica* (Platonic Theology) (1474). He evidently found the work interesting, for in 1484 he came to Florence to sit at Ficino's feet and master the new Platonic sources that Ficino was making available to the Latin world. In 1485 Pico went to Paris to study medieval scholastic philosophy, returning to Florence a year later, where he began to study Hebrew and Arabic with the Jewish Kabbalist Flavio Mithridates. After a scandalous episode in which he attempted to abduct the wife of an Aretine tax official, Pico settled in Perugia where he continued his Hebrew and Kabbalist studies under the tutelage of several Jewish teachers.

Pico's education thus exposed him to practically every sort of philosophical subculture that high Renaissance Europe could offer: humanism, Paduan Averroism, the theological traditions of the great religious orders (particularly Thomism), and the more esoteric traditions of Florentine Neoplatonism and medieval Jewish Kabbalah. Pico mastered each of these traditions without himself being mastered by any of them. Despite his enviable knowledge of Greek, Arabic and Hebrew, and his ability to write elegant humanist Latin, Pico never endorsed the shallow humanist tendency to dismiss scholastic philosophy because of its neglect of good Latinity and its unconcern with the study of Greek philosophy in the original. In a famous letter to Ermolao Barbaro (1485), Pico praised the great medieval philosophers and defended the right of philosophers to use their own precise technical language. Pico was equally discriminating in his use of Ficinian Platonism. As he wrote in another letter to Barbaro (echoing Cicero), he came to his studies with Ficino 'not as a deserter' from Aristotle 'but as a spy' (*explorator*). His own doctrines, though clearly indebted to Ficino as well as to ancient Neoplatonists, were at the same time distinctive, and Pico did not hesitate to criticize even the most authoritative ancient sources, such as PLOTINUS and PROCLUS, when he believed that they had misread Plato (see PLATONISM, RENAISSANCE).

Pico's career as a philosophical writer began in 1486, when he composed the original draft of his *Commento sopra una canzona de amore composta da Girolamo Benivieni secondo la mente e opinione de' Platonici* (Commentary on a poem about love composed by Girolamo Benivieni, according to the understanding and opinion of the Platonists), known as the *Commento* for short. This work contained extracts from three other works, never published and now presumably lost: a commentary on Plato's *Symposium*, a poetic theology (a reconstruction of 'ancient theology' based on his reading of the pagan myths) and a treatise on love. In 1486 Pico also conceived the idea of holding a great public disputation (or 'council' as he referred to it) in Rome in which he would reveal a new theological system based on a profound study of all philosophies and theologies past and present. In aid of this project he published the *Conclusiones*, a list of 900 theses drawn from Christian, Jewish, Muslim, Platonic, Aristotelian, Hermetist, Orphic, Zoroastrian, Kabbalist and other sources. He announced that he would defend his theses publicly early in 1487, and summoned to the disputation the Pope, the College of Cardinals, and all philosophers and theologians in Italy, offering to pay the travelling costs of any challengers. He also composed, in December 1486, the so-called *De dignitate hominis* (*Oration on the Dignity of Man*) which was intended as an introductory speech to open the 'council'. This was to become Pico's most famous work.

On 20 February 1487 Pope Innocent VIII, at the instigation of some theologians at his court, ordered Pico's disputation suspended and appointed a commission of inquiry which in due course condemned thirteen of Pico's theses. Pico responded by publishing his *Apologia* in defence of the condemned theses. In a bull dated 4 August 1487 but not (it seems) published until November, Innocent finally condemned all 900 theses *en bloc* and ordered Pico arrested for heresy. By this time Pico had escaped to France, where he was detained by the French king at the Pope's request. The philosopher was eventually allowed to return to Florence (1488) to live under the protection of Lorenzo de' Medici, who had intervened on his behalf with the Pope. Apart from brief visits to Ferrara, Pico spent the last six years of his life at Lorenzo's 'court', attempting to carry forward his project of making a concord of all theologies. In 1489 he published *Heptaplus de opere sex dierum Geneseos* (*On the Sevenfold Narration of the Six Days of Genesis*), an attempt to turn the first chapter of Genesis into a textbook of Greek cosmology through the liberal use of allegory. The short tract *De ente et uno* (*On Being and the One*) was completed in 1491; it was part of a much longer work demonstrating the concord of Plato and Aristotle which was left unfinished at Pico's death in 1494 and is now lost. After the death of Lorenzo de' Medici, Pico came briefly under the influence of the religious reformer Savonarola (see SCEPTICISM, RENAISSANCE §3), and it is to this part of his life that Pico's biblical commentaries and shorter religious and devotional writings belong. Pico also composed a long tract against astrology, an exposition of Kabbalah and a number of letters and poems. Here we shall be concerned only with the philosophical portion of Pico's literary production.

2 The theory of love

Pico's independence as a thinker and his synthetic abilities are well illustrated by his first major work of philosophy, the *Commento*. This was a philosophical commentary in the manner of Dante's *Convivio* on some verses by Pico's friend, Girolamo Benivieni, a gentleman-poet who like Pico had been a disciple of Ficino. Benivieni had composed a *canzone*, 'Amor dalle cui', in emulation of the famous *canzone* 'Donna me prega' written about 1285 by Guido Cavalcanti (whose descendent, Giovanni Cavalcanti, happened to be Ficino's 'Platonic lover'). Guido Cavalcanti's poem had interpreted the phenomena of human love using the Aristotelian psychology and physics just then coming into vogue in Florence; Benivieni, two centuries later, tried to use Ficino's new Platonic metaphysics to describe divine love. His *canzone* was in fact based on five chapters (II.5, 7; V.4; VI.4, 7) of Ficino's most popular work, *De amore* (*On Love*)

(1469) (see FICINO, M. §4). Pico's *Commento* on the poem had two chief aims. One aim was to rediscover the 'secret mysteries' of pagan theology using Neoplatonic metaphysics as a key: in the manner of Proclus and Pletho, Pico argued for identifying pagan divinities with various metaphysical entities and principles (Venus for example with Beauty itself, Uranus with God, Neptune with Mind, Vulcan with the Demiurge of the *Timaeus*, and so forth). Pico's second aim was to supplement and correct Ficino's account of the metaphysics of love with a fresh interpretation based on Pico's own reading of Platonic sources. The original draft of the *Commento*, indeed, was in essence a sharp and often personal critique of *De amore*. (In the draft finally published in 1519, the attacks on Ficino were edited out by mutual friends.)

Pico criticized Ficino on numerous points, both methodological and doctrinal. Pico found Ficino's approach too literary, faulting it for its failure to define terms and employ precise scholastic terminology. Doctrinally, Pico insisted against Ficino that the contemplative intellect while in the body does not enjoy union with God himself, but only with the First Mind, the highest unity in the Plotinian hypostasis of *nous* (see PLOTINUS §3). Moreover, while Ficino had built his conception of Platonic love on the metaphysical identity of *philia* and *eros*, friendship and love, Pico asserts that the *eros* of which Plato spoke in the *Symposium* is a special sort of metaphysical power, distinct from friendship, from God's love for his creatures and from other unitive powers in the cosmos (see LOVE). In the same way, Pico argues for a sharp distinction, both metaphysical and moral, between physical and intellectual love, against Ficino's view that the two 'Venuses' formed a continuum, a unified system of cosmic dynamics. Against Ficino, again, Pico adopts an anti-Plotinian definition of Beauty, seeing it as a visual or intelligible harmony rather than an emanation from an Idea of Beauty belonging to *nous*. Finally, Pico rejects Ficino's attempt to integrate human love into a cosmic cycle of divine creative love descending from God down to creatures and linked back to God by the desire of creation for its creator. Pico, instead, sees love as a psychological process distinct from cosmic love. Divine love is a desire excited by intelligible beauty, and Pico assimilates the excitation of divine love in the rational soul to the process of cognition. In this way Pico transforms Aristotle's analysis of cognition in *On the Soul* (see ARISTOTLE §17), as well as elements taken from PLOTINUS and Avicenna (see IBN SINA), into an esoteric key to the speech of Diotima in the *Symposium*.

Despite the vehemence of Pico's disagreements with Ficino, one may not assume that the *Commento* represents Pico's considered views on any question. As the subtitle indicates, the work is intended as a kind of thought experiment or mental game. 'According to the understanding and opinion of the Platonists' means 'what a Platonist would or ought to say about love', not necessarily what Pico himself believed. This is a broadly Averroist approach to Plato in that Pico distinguishes explicitly between 'Christian truth' and Platonic 'understanding and opinion', and it was designed, like much of Pico's work, to infuriate his teacher Ficino. The aim of Ficino's scholarly and philosophical work was always to show the harmony of Plato with Christianity; his chief opponents were Aristotelian Averroists who in Ficino's view were deepening the divide between religion and philosophy (see AVERROISM). Pico's *Commento* insists at numerous points on the differences between Platonism and Christianity. He asserts that the Platonists believed in the eternal recurrence of the cosmos; in the preexistence of the soul; in the possibility of embodied souls having direct knowledge of God; in the existence of intermediate creators between God the Supreme Creator and the cosmos. All of these doctrines since the twelfth century had subjected Platonists to charges of unorthodoxy. But since Pico in the *Commento* was writing under the persona of a Platonist, we are not licensed to assume that he had necessarily, at this stage of his career, embraced unorthodox beliefs, nor that his thought went through a development from an early Platonism to a mature Aristotelianism. Where Pico speaks *in propria persona* his works display great internal consistency.

3 The Roman disputation

Within a month of circulating the first draft of his *Commento*, indeed, Pico had published his own 900 theses and had begun drafting an oration meant to introduce them to the learned world. The oration is in effect an apology for a layman's devoting himself to theology and an answer to critics of Pico's proposed disputation. It belongs to the genre of the academic prolusion, a speech meant to introduce a university course of lectures or a formal disputation. Like most academic prolusions, it is divided into two parts, the first part praising the subject-matter, the second offering an overview of the material to be covered. Pico praises his subject-matter, theology, arguing that human beings fulfil the highest potentialities of their nature by contemplating divine things. Humans have a protean nature which permits them to live like beasts or angels, but they have a moral duty to live the highest kind of life of that they can. In order to achieve an angelic life of contemplation and love of the divine, one must pass through the stages of mystical education as set forth by PSEUDO-DIONYSIUS the Areopagite: purification, illumination, perfection. Following Byzantine tradition, Pico assimilates these stages to the four parts of philosophy, arranged hierarchically from the lowest (moral philosophy and dialectic), through natural philosophy, to the highest (metaphysics or theology) (see BYZANTINE PHILOSOPHY). Using allegory he then proceeds to find these same stages in a variety of theological traditions, including the Mosaic, Pauline, Platonic, Zoroastrian and Pythagorean. Like Plato, Pico believes that the illumination acquired at the apex of metaphysical consciousness will bring order and peace to the individual soul and unity among all rational beings who share this highest form of consciousness (see ILLUMINATION).

Pico's speech was given the title *On the Dignity of Man* by its sixteenth-century editors, and this has led to much misleading commentary on the part of modern scholars. The posthumous title seems to have been derived from the first few pages of the text, where Pico states (in the form of a myth) that the excellence of the human being does not derive from its central place in the Great Chain of Being (as Ficino had maintained), but precisely from its ability to choose its own place in the order of nature. Themselves standing outside the order of nature, human beings can shape their own essence; they can degrade themselves to live like beasts, or can raise themselves to the angelic order. Modern interpreters have seen this passage as embodying a distinctively Renaissance anthropology or even as the forerunner of more modern conceptions of human nature. It has been implausibly maintained that Pico's conception of the human being – placed in the centre of the world as an observer but outside the hierarchy of fixed essences – anticipates Descartes' theory of mind; or that Pico's description of the plasticity of human nature and the impact of moral choices upon metaphysical dignity can be linked to the existentialist doctrine that existence precedes essence. It should nevertheless be recognized that, despite its modern ring, much of Pico's anthropology is derivative from Boethius and Greek patristic sources, particularly from the Platonisms of Gregory of Nyssa (see PATRISTIC PHILOSOPHY) and ORIGEN. Pico chose not to advertise his debt, probably because the orthodoxy of both Gregory and Origen was suspect. In any case, Pico's account of the 'chameleon' nature of human beings very likely represents an attempt to understand in a Christian sense the Pythagorean and Platonic doctrines of palingenesis or the transmigration of souls. Pico's statement that humans stand outside the triple hierarchy of being, occupying (as he says in the

Heptaplus) a 'fourth world', may not amount to more than a dramatic restatement of the familiar twelfth-century doctrine of the human being as a microcosm of the universe.

The second part of the *Oration* explains why Pico wanted to defend so many theses from so broad a range of sources both Christian and non-Christian. Disputations in theology faculties of the period typically involved a few dozen theses, mostly from Christian authorities. In Italy theological disputation was normally confined to licensed members of religious orders. So Pico's performance, though not unprecedented, was highly unusual for a layman who lacked a university degree. Pico argued that the method and aims of his inquiry required him to cover a vast field. Theologians who belonged to developed school traditions could confine themselves to the clarification of details. But he was proposing to found a new theological school altogether, and a school based on an esoteric reading of all theologies past and present. He could not therefore be expected to limit himself to a few points of disputation. The same procedure, he observed, was followed by Aristotle, who always began a new inquiry by reviewing all previous opinions. Pico went on to give a *tour d'horizon* of the 900 theses, trying especially to show why the Latin and Arabic theological traditions ought to be enriched by the study of ancient theologies such as Platonism, Hermeticism, Zoroastrianism, Orphism and Kabbalism (see FICINO, M. §2). Pico took particular pride in his efforts to study Kabbalah from a Christian perspective; in the revival of 'ancient theology' this was one area where he had clearly moved beyond the work of Ficino. Pico assured his audience that, rightly understood, this esoteric theological tradition handed down from the time of Moses would only strengthen Christian efforts to convert the Jews.

Pico's published *Conclusiones* and his *Apologia* cast further light on his goals as a philosopher and theologian. Pico's aim is not to show that all theologies agreed in all respects. He was not an eclectic of the ancient type who believed that all philosophers agreed in substance, disagreeing only about words. He held that every major theological tradition contained elements of truth and that these elements could be combined into a grand synthesis that was at the same time compatible with orthodox Christianity. Like NICHOLAS OF CUSA, he believed that the understanding previous theologians had of the sources of their own theological traditions was not necessarily correct. In fact his aim was to construct a new theology using material from existing historical theologies as building blocks. His new theology would be superior to existing theologies because it would give a richer understanding of Christian truths. This is not to imply that Pico was interested in directly challenging Christian dogmas. But he did wish (like many humanists) to move Christian theological speculation beyond the narrow circle of traditional authorities represented by Aristotle, the Bible and the *Sentences* of Peter LOMBARD. Situating Christian theology in the spectrum of world theologies would show both the superiority of Christian truth and the presence of Christian truths in all religions. Pico's ecumenism is therefore a militant ecumenism. At the same time, Pico hoped that recovering the esoteric truths of other religious traditions would make the mysteries of Christianity more intelligible.

Pico's concordism might then be read as a kind of Thomistic project to incorporate non-Christian wisdom into a Christian speculative framework. But there is a critical difference between Thomas Aquinas and Pico which is best grasped by noting what is left out of Pico's theology. Pico has no ecclesiology, no soteriology in the traditional sense, and no doctrine of grace. Instead, Pico emphasizes the radical freedom of human beings in this life to achieve angelic levels of illumination and moral dignity through the exercise of powers belonging to human nature *qua* human. The neglect of grace is typical of the humanist theologies of the period, and reflects the widespread contempt for the Church's practice of reinforcing its wealth and position by marketing spiritual favours. That Pico attempted to propagate his new theology among the highest authorities in Christendom thus becomes a highly significant fact. It suggests that he shared some of the aims, if not the strategies, of the Protestant reformers of the next generation. It implies that the theological movement started by Ficino and Pico was not the esoteric and politically quietist movement it is sometimes represented as being, but had transformative aims as radical as those of Girolamo Savonarola and Martin Luther.

4 The concord of Plato and Aristotle

After Pico's first brash attempt to convert the Roman church to his new theology had failed, he devoted his energies to working out two pieces of his larger concordist project: the concord of Christianity and Kabbalism and the concord of Plato and Aristotle. The former task was taken up first, in *Heptaplus de opere sex dierum Geneseos* (*On the Sevenfold Narration of the Six Days of Genesis*). Here Pico, like the Platonists of the twelfth century, attempted to use a non-Christian theology as a key to the creation stories in the first chapter of Genesis (see CHARTRES, SCHOOL OF). Unlike the hexaemeral treatises of the earlier Platonists, however, Pico maintained that Genesis 1

was an esoteric text. Moses had deliberately implanted in it secret cosmological doctrines that might be abstracted by an interpreter learned in Kabbalist lore. Pico's stated purpose in wresting cosmological mysteries from the Bible was to show that Moses knew what the best philosophers knew. He could in this way show that there was no gap between reason and revelation. But whatever Pico's stated aims, his view of Genesis had radical implications. To employ a modern parallel, it is as though a contemporary exegete of the Bible should maintain that there was not only no conflict between Genesis and evolutionary biology, but that Moses had intentionally concealed evolutionary teachings under the guise of Genesis' account of creation. This radical claim, combined with Pico's circular hermeneutical method, in effect turns the literal sense of Genesis into a myth and subordinates traditional Christian teachings to the teachings of philosophers and non-Christian theologians.

Of Pico's other project of his last years, the concord of Plato and Aristotle, we have only the short tractate *On Being and the One*. The purpose of this work was to criticize one of the cardinal theological doctrines of Ficino and the ancient Neoplatonists, namely the radical transcendence of the One 'beyond being'. On this issue Ficino followed Plotinus and Proclus, who had in turn based themselves on a particular reading of Plato's *Parmenides* (see PLATO). The Neoplatonists regarded that dialogue as an esoteric work containing the most sublime mysteries of Platonic theology. Against Ficino, Pico maintained that *esse ipsum* (being itself) and the One were 'convertible' or identical in extension, and that both were distinct from *ens* (participated being). This conception was borrowed from Thomas AQUINAS; Pico's originality lay in claiming that it was shared by both Plato and Aristotle. To argue the point, Pico was obliged to challenge two assumptions that had gone largely unexamined for a millennium. The first, characteristic of ancient Neoplatonists but found also among Greek patristic and Byzantine interpreters, as well as Latin theologians such as AUGUSTINE, was that Plato was superior to Aristotle in theology (see ARISTOTELIANISM, MEDIEVAL; PLATONISM, MEDIEVAL). Pico maintained that Aristotle was Plato's equal as a theologian. In effect he includes Aristotle among the ancient theologians. The second assumption was that the Neoplatonists were reliable guides to the thought of Plato. This too Pico denied. Pico revived the Academic sceptical interpretation of the *Parmenides*, which regarded the dialogue as an eristic work, a dialectical exercise containing no positive doctrines. Unlike the Academic sceptics, however, Pico did not interpret all the dialogues of Plato this way. While in his view the *Parmenides* was a purely eristic work, other dialogues of Plato, particularly the *Sophist* and *Philebus*, could be used to recover Plato's own views on metaphysical questions and to correct the false readings of the *platonici*.

Pico's interpretation of Plato thus represents a step towards the modern distinction between Plato and the Neoplatonists, even if his view of the authentic Plato is very different from that of modern scholarship. His exegetical project is very much a Renaissance project in its attempt to distinguish the original source from later glosses and to privilege the former over the latter. Pico's concordism also reflects the situation of Renaissance philosophy in another respect. In the central Middle Ages, philosophical study in the universities had been carefully regulated by official curricula, textbooks and university statutes. Theology was even more closely controlled. By the fifteenth century, thanks largely to the humanist movement, philosophers were being introduced to an ever-widening range of philosophical and theological opinion, often in far less regulated circumstances. The bewildering variety of intellectual choices and the greater freedom of study (if not of expression) posed a major challenge to philosophers of the later fifteenth and sixteenth centuries. Some philosophers responded by embracing scepticism; others by advocating fideism (see SCEPTICISM, RENAISSANCE); still others – ultimately the most influential group – by exploring new methodologies for adjudicating between incommensurable systems of thought. Pico's concordism represents a fourth alternative. If many of Pico's hermeneutical techniques, especially allegory, now seem little more than primitive forms of secondary elaboration, the dream of a great theological system that would reconcile in itself trans-historical and trans-cultural truths taken from all forms of religious wisdom was one that would have a considerable fortune down to the present day.

See also: ARISTOTELIANISM, RENAISSANCE; FICINO, M.; HERMETISM; KABBALAH; PLATONISM, RENAISSANCE

List of works

Pico della Mirandola, G. (1463–94) *Opera omnia* (Collected Works), Basle: Heinrich Petri, 1572; repr. Turin: Bottega d'Erasmo, 1971. (Volume two of the 1971 edition contains photo-reprints of all works of Pico not contained in the original 1572 edition.)

—— (1485) 'Letter to Ermolao Barbaro (3 June 1485)', Latin text in *Opera omnia*, Turin: Bottega d'Erasmo, 1971, 351–8; trans. Q. Breen, 'Giovanni Pico della Mirandola on the conflict of philosophy and rhetoric', *Journal of the History of Ideas* 13 (1952): 325–426. (Referred to in §1. Pico defends technical scholastic terminology against humanist critics. The second letter to Barbaro mentioned in §1 can be found in volume 1, page 368, of the 1557 *Opera omnia* (printed in Basle; repr. Hildesheim: Olms, 1969).)

—— (1486) *Commento*, in E. Garin (ed.) *De dignitate hominis, Heptaplus, De ente et uno e scritti vari*, Florence: Vallecchi, 1942; trans. S. Jayne, *Commentary on a Canzone of Benivieni*, New York: Lang, 1984. (Pico's version of Platonic love; discussed in §2. Jayne's English translation has a useful introduction and textual improvements.)

—— (1486) *Conclusiones sive theses DCCCC* (Nine Hundred Conclusions or Theses), ed. B. Kieszkowski, Geneva: Droz, 1973. (Referred to in §§1 and 3. A list of theses for debate which summarizes Pico's concordist philosophy.)

—— (1486) *De dignitate hominis*, in E. Garin (ed.) *De dignitate hominis, Heptaplus, De ente et uno e scritti vari*, Florence: Vallecchi, 1942; trans. C.G. Wallis, P.J.W. Miller and D. Carmichael, *Pico della Mirandola: On the Dignity of Man, On Being and the One, Heptaplus*, Indianapolis, IN, and New York: Library of Liberal Arts, 1965; ed. E. Garin, *La cultura filosofica del Rinascimento italiano*, Florence: Sansoni, 1961, 231–40; trans. E.L. Forbes, *On the Dignity of Man*, in E. Cassirer, P.O. Kristeller and J.H. Randall (eds) *The Renaissance Philosophy of Man*, Chicago, IL, and London: University of Chicago Press, 1948. (Referred to in §§1 and 3. An overview of Pico's concordism. Garin 1961 gives the original version of the text.)

—— (1487) *Apologia*, in *Opera omnia*, Turin: Bottega d'Erasmo, 1971, vol. 1, 114–240. (Referred to in §3. Pico defends himself against the charge of heresy.)

—— (1489) *Heptaplus de opere sex dierum Geneseos* (On the Sevenfold Narration of the Six Days of Genesis), in E. Garin (ed.) *De dignitate hominis, Heptaplus, De ente et uno e scritti vari*, Florence: Vallecchi, 1942; trans. C.G. Wallis, P.J.W. Miller and D. Carmichael, *Pico della Mirandola: On the Dignity of Man, On Being and the One, Heptaplus*, Indianapolis, IN, and New York: Library of Liberal Arts, 1965. (Referred to in §§1 and 4. Harmonizes Christianity and Kabbalah on the interpretation of Genesis.)

—— (1491) *De ente et uno*, in E. Garin (ed.) *De dignitate hominis, Heptaplus, De ente et uno e scritti vari*, Florence: Vallecchi, 1942; trans. C.G. Wallis, P.J.W. Miller and D. Carmichael, *Pico della Mirandola: On the Dignity of Man, On Being and the One, Heptaplus*, Indianapolis, IN, and New York: Library of Liberal Arts, 1965. (Referred to in

§§1 and 4. Harmonizes Plato and Aristotle on the nature of God.)

References and further reading

Allen, M.J.B. (1986) 'The Second Ficino–Pico Controversy: Parmenidean Poetry, Eristic and the One', in G.C. Garfagnini (ed.) *Marsilio Ficino e il ritorno di Platone: Studi e documenti*, Florence: Olschki, 417–55; repr. in M.J.B. Allen, *Plato's Third Eye: Studies in Marsilio Ficino's Metaphysics and its Sources*, London: Variorum, 1995. (Pico and Ficino's encounter over the interpretation of the *Parmenides*; see §4.)

Aranci, G., De Marco, P. and Verdon, T. (1994) 'Teologie a Firenze nell'età di Giovanni Pico della Mirandola' (Theologies in Florence during the Age of Giovanni Pico della Mirandola), special issue of *Homo vivens* 5 (2). (Recent work on Pico from the quincentenary celebrations.)

Craven, W.G. (1981) *Giovanni Pico della Mirandola, Symbol of His Age: Modern Interpretations of a Renaissance Philosopher*, Geneva: Droz. (Useful antidote to the secondary literature; better on destruction than reconstruction.)

Di Napoli, G. (1965) *Giovanni Pico della Mirandola e la problematica dottrinale del suo tempo* (Giovanni Pico della Mirandola and the Doctrinal Issues of His Time), Rome: Desclé. (Pico's relationship to late Quattrocento scholasticism.)

* Ficino, M. (1469) *De amore*, trans. S. Jayne, *Commentary on Plato's Symposium On Love*, Dallas, TX: Spring Books, 1985. (Referred to in §2. Gives a useful introduction describing the influence of *De amore* on Renaissance literature.)

* —— (1474) *Theologia platonica de immortalitate animae* (Platonic Theology, On the Immortality of the Soul), ed. and trans. R. Marcel, *Théologie platonicienne de l'immortalité des âmes*, Paris: Les Belles Lettres, 1964–79, 3 vols. (Referred to in §1. Edition of the Latin text with a French translation.)

Garin, E. (1937) *Giovanni Pico della Mirandola, Vita e dottrina* (Life and Doctrines), Florence: Le Monnier. (Standard account of Pico's life; interpretation of works now largely superseded.)

Lubac, H. de (1974) *Pic de la Mirandole: Études et discussions* (Studies and Discussions), Paris: Aubier Montaigne. (Pico and his patristic sources.)

Reinhardt, H. (1991) *Freiheit zu Gott: Der Grundgedanke des Systematikers Giovanni Pico della Mirandola* (Freedom towards God: The Basic Thought of the Systematic Thinker Giovanni Pico della Mirandola), Weinheim: VCH Acta humaniora. (Pico as forerunner of Vatican II.)

Roulier, F. (1989) *Jean Pic de Mirandole (1463–1494), humaniste, philosophe et théologien* (Humanist, Philosopher and Theologian), Geneva: Slatkine. (Comprehensive monograph on Pico.)

Viti, P. (ed.) (1994) *Pico, Poliziano, e l'umanesimo di fine Quattrocento* (Pico, Poliziano and Humanism at the End of the 15th Century), Florence: Olschki. (Contains important new biographical material on Pico.)

Wirszubski, C. (1989) *Pico della Mirandola's Encounter with Jewish Mysticism*, Cambridge, MA: Harvard University Press. (Pico and Kabbalism.)

JAMES HANKINS

PIETISM

'Pietism' refers to a Protestant reform movement, arising in the late 1600s in Lutheran Germany, which turned away from contests over theological and dogmatic identity in Protestant confessionalism and urged renewed attention to questions of personal piety and devotion. As such, it has only the most tenuous historical connections to the Christocentric piety of the devotio moderna *or the northern humanist piety of Erasmus or Zwingli. It found its first major voice in P.J. Spener and A.H. Francke, and established its principal centres of influence at the state university at Halle in 1691 and the Moravian community at Herrnhut in 1722. Pietism found followers and allies in the European Reformed churches, in the Church of England (especially through the example of John and Charles Wesley and through the Moravian exile community in England), and in Britain's English-speaking colonies. In the colonies, pietism not only found Lutheran and Reformed colonial hosts, but also saw in New England Puritanism a movement of similar aspirations. Pietism's impact on the spirituality of western Europe and America was clearly felt in the eighteenth-century Protestant Awakenings, and continues to have an influence in the shape of Anglo-American evangelicalism.*

1 Definition
2 History
3 Continuing influence

1 Definition

Pietism may be defined very broadly as a reawakening in western Europe (and Europe's American colonies) of the most intense and aggressive forms of devotional Christianity from about 1650 to 1750. In this broad sense, it can include Jansenism in Roman Catholic France, the Non-Jurors, the eighteenth-century Moravians, and the English and American Methodists who followed John and Charles Wesley. But in its most specific use, the term 'pietism' was first used in 1674 to refer to the followers of the German Lutheran spiritual reformer Philip Jakob Spener, and it is from this particular movement within Lutheranism that 'pietism' is generally understood to derive its historical identity.

Pietism can be characterized as a Christian and Protestant movement which located the essence of Christianity more in the quality of an individual's personal feeling of relationship to God than in a rational assent to the various forms of Christian theology or in submission to any Christian rites of identity, such as baptism or the Eucharist. It stands apart from its medieval, mystical and humanist predecessors in its biblicism, its persistently Protestant forms, and the extraordinary energies it devoted to promoting popular awakenings and evangelism. Similarly, pietism's preoccupation with 'personalizing' Christian belief was never a matter of total withdrawal from conventional Christian forms, but rather a matter of emphasis in the priority and use of those forms, since not even the most radical pietist groups completely repudiated the Christian sacraments or questioned the validity of organized churches. But the pietists did subordinate these considerations to those of personal devotion to God. This allowed them to take a remarkably tolerant and irenic stance towards questions of confessional debate within Protestantism, since such questions had little significance for the pietists except in so far as they promoted the individual's personal devotion to God.

But irenicism across confessional boundaries stopped short when pietists addressed the boundary between those who had experienced a renewed dedication of their spiritual lives to God and those who either had not or did not care to do so. Pietists drew a deep antithetical line between those who had experienced a 'new birth' or 'second birth' (*Wiedergeburt*) and those with a purely 'notional' Christianity, who had never experienced contrition and repentance. On the one hand, this drove them to proselytization and missionary programmes among nominal Christian and non-Christian populations in Europe, America and Asia, but on the other, it drove them to place so much distance between 'notional' Christianity and their own personal practice that many pietists came close to a demand for moral perfection. In the case of John Wesley, perfection was actually promoted as an attainable goal (see SANCTIFICATION §3).

2 History

The foundations for pietism lie in the first wave of Protestantism, which cultivated a strong sense of personal Christian spirituality alongside its concern with revising Catholic dogma. Much of that devotionalism was submerged, however, during the waves of religious warfare that swept over Europe as a result of the Reformation, and lasted, with intermissions, until 1648. The need clearly to identify who Protestantism's friends and enemies were fostered a century of theological system-building and confession-writing (*Verconfessionalisierung*) in Germany. But by the end of the Thirty Years' War, with the German lands devastated by the marauding criss-cross of Protestant and Catholic armies, no absolute victor had emerged to legitimize any of the Protestant confessions, and many Lutherans felt betrayed by the failure of their state churches and princes to deliver either Protestant triumph or reform of public life. After 1680, these anxieties were heightened by a renewed Catholic determination to undo the Westphalian compromises of 1648 within Catholic-ruled domains.

Spener was pastor and senior of the ministerium in Frankfurt. He became convinced that the state Lutheran churches had failed the German people and had descended into theological irrelevance and doctrinal trivia. Disgusted, he published *Pia Desideria: or, Heartfelt Desires for a God-Pleasing Improvement of the True Protestant Church* (1675) as his blast against the prevailing lifelessness of the Lutheran churches, and in it he set out six proposals for reviving the German churches:

(1) rededicate the energies of the churches to the study of the Bible as the object of devotional meditation and spirituality;
(2) break down the wall of separation between clergy and laity;
(3) emphasize practical, rather than theological or intellectual, Christianity, in terms of service and worship;
(4) abandon religious argument and controversy with other churches or sects;
(5) reorganize the training of future ministers in the German universities so as to stress the formation of spiritual lives rather than doctrine;
(6) revitalize preaching with view to promoting the people's edification.

In 1686, Spener was appointed official preacher to the court of the Duke of Saxony. There, he met and influenced a young lecturer at the Saxon university at Leipzig, August Hermann Francke. As a theological student, Francke acknowledged that he had grasped confessional Lutheranism 'only in my reason and in my thought' and it was not until he had experienced repentance (*Bußkampf*) that 'all sadness and unrest of my heart was taken away at once, and I was immediately overwhelmed as with a stream of joy so that with full joy I praised and gave honor to God who had shown me such great grace.' Francke 'arose a completely different person' and became Spener's friend and disciple, and when in 1691 the Elector Frederick William III of Prussia promoted the *Ritterakademie* at Halle to the rank of university, Francke was appointed a professor and quickly turned Halle into an engine of pietist recruitment and evangelism. Still another centre of pietist energy sprang up in 1722 under the leadership of Nikolaus Ludwig Graf von Zinzendorf. Zinzendorf was the eldest son of a noble Saxon family, but his parents (and especially the grandmother who was mostly responsible for his upbringing) had been greatly influenced by Spener. His estates at Berthelsdorf lay directly across the track of Moravian Protestant refugees, fleeing forced conversion by the Jesuits under imperial Habsburg rule. Zinzendorf, hearing of the plight of these refugees, turned Berthelsdorf into a refuge for the Moravians and helped organize a community there named 'Herrnhut' ('the Lord watches over'), with a view to turning the entire effort into an experiment in organized pietism.

Spener's criticism of the state Lutheran churches in Germany made the pietists an object of suspicion for Lutheran confessionalists. The use of field meetings, and the encouragement of 'children's testimony' (testimony to religious experience by children in public adult meetings) among Silesian pietists disturbed Lutheran leaders, and the pietists' absorption in personal piety led to charges of indifference to, and even outright departure from, the Lutheran confessional standards. In 1734, Zinzendorf himself was charged with straying from the letter of Lutheran theology; in 1736, he was banished from Saxony. The resurgence of Catholic attempts to impose religious uniformity in France and the Austrian domains also provided an opportunity for Catholic authorities to abrogate tacit agreements with Lutheran minorities in their lands, and in November 1731, the pietist Lutherans of Salzburg were expelled by the archbishop and began a march across Europe that ended only when Prussia opened its doors to approximately 20,000 of the exiles.

Zinzendorf, borrowing money from sympathetic Dutch bankers, moved across Protestant Europe to promote local pietist movements in Württemburg (where he alternately dominated and antagonized F.C. Oetinger and J.A. Bengel) and Switzerland (where the major pietist converts among the state Reformed clergy were Samuel Schumacher and Samuel Lutz in

Berne). He was also able to carry the Moravian example abroad, founding new *Herrnhuts* at Marienborn and Herrnhaag in 1736 and 1738, gaining official recognition for the Moravians in England, sponsoring Moravian missions to the West Indies, and planting a Moravian colony in British North America. It was in Georgia that a party of Moravian immigrants confronted the young John Wesley, then an emissary of the Church of England, and when Wesley returned to London in 1738, it was in a Moravian society-meeting in London's Aldersgate Street that he experienced the vivid personal conversion that led to the founding of Methodism.

Pietism also found already existing allies among the English-speaking Puritans in the British colonies of New England. Spener had drawn significant encouragement from the writings of the English Puritans Lewis Bayly, John Bunyan and Richard Baxter, and the expatriate William Ames wielded great influence on the Dutch pietists Willem Brackel and Abraham Hellenbroeck. Although by the early 1700s much of Puritanism's fervour had settled back on its lees in Britain and New England, the American Puritan minister Cotton Mather insisted in 1717 that 'the *American Puritanism*' was 'so much of a Peece with the Frederician Pietism, that if it were possible... to be transferr'd unto our Friends in the lower *Saxony*, it would find some Acceptance' (Lovelace 1979: 33). The Puritan philosopher-theologian Jonathan EDWARDS (§1), whose reading list included most of the prominent German pietist titles, was moved by the example of the New Jersey Dutch pietist T.J. Freylinghuysen, the Methodist George Whitefield, and the Scots-Irish pietist Gilbert Tennent to promote (and then write a series of sympathetic rationalizations for) the colonial religious revivals known as the 'Great Awakening' (1739–44). By the time of the deaths of Edwards in 1758 and Zinzendorf in 1760, pietism had taken up residence in all of the confessional Protestant churches of Europe, and had established missions or colonies in Greenland, Scandinavia, Egypt, Ceylon and the Caribbean.

3 Continuing influence

Many accounts of pietist history suggest a communal harmony that many of the pietists actually lacked: Zinzendorf could be tyrannical and bullying, and the resentment of Francke's successor at Halle, Gotthilf August, at Zinzendorf's high-handedness led to a cooling of relations between Halle and Herrnhut. Wesley, similarly, was dictatorial and self-centred, breaking ties over personal and theological issues with his talented associate Whitefield and with his Welsh disciples Howell Harris and Daniel Rowland. As a result, pietism never achieved any measure of hegemony within any major Protestant confessional grouping in the 1700s. Only among separatist movements such as the United Brethren and the Methodists did pietism become the dominant form of theological identity, and even then, by the time the Methodists separated from the Church of England after Wesley's death, the movement had become an expression of an idiosyncratic Wesleyanism rather than the larger spirit of pietism.

Part of that failure was due to the ferocious resistance offered to pietism by confessional theologians. Lutheran confessionalists were concerned that the pietist preoccupation with personal experience would obscure the forensic status of justification, which according to Lutheran dogma was established not by the individual's repentance, but by the death of Jesus Christ (see JUSTIFICATION, RELIGIOUS §4). Calvinist theologians, even those in New England otherwise inclined to sympathize with them, were troubled by the pietists' willingness to redefine the atonement of Christ in general terms in order to heighten the possibility of repentance and redemption for all, which appeared in Calvinist eyes to diminish the actual worth of the atonement as a real means of redemption (see ATONEMENT §4). Wesley in particular repudiated the moderate Calvinism of the Church of England's Thirty-Nine Articles of Religion for an evangelicalized Arminianism which converted the free-will rationalism of Jacobus Arminius into an engine for freely chosen and freely demanded conversion. And, as in the example of both Halle and the Methodists, the high demands of pietism for Christian conduct could easily yield to legalistic requirements for conformity to mere behavioural codes.

However, many other criticisms of the pietists as ascetic, anti-cultural or anti-intellectual have less justification. Except for the Moravians, pietist movements were open associations with little inclination towards communal withdrawal from the world. Francke, the most talented organizer among the pietist leaders, created one of the largest public charities in Europe with the Halle Orphanage in 1695, and his example was imitated (though on a lesser scale) by both Wesley and Whitefield. The musical culture of the Moravians, even in their colonial settlements, was of a very high order, and pietist hymnody, especially from Charles Wesley and Gerhard Tersteegen, has been absorbed into the Church music of many of their confessional critics. If the pietists were, at first appearance, hostile to any learning that lacked personal piety, they also shared a basic similarity with the Enlightenment in their refusal to accept the testimony of past authority for truth and the demand that truth be grounded in demonstration and experience. The pietist revolt against formalism would be re-echoed in the Christian Romantics, especially in Friedrich SCHLEIERMACHER (§§1, 7) (who has been rightly called the executor of pietism's last will and testament) and Søren KIERKEGAARD (§4). The pietist influence mediated in America by the 'Great Awakening' had a long-term influence in American pragmatic philosophy and has been the dominant force in the shaping of modern American and British evangelicalism.

References and further reading

Beyreuther, E. (1978) *Geschichte des Pietismus* (History of Pietism), Stuttgart: Steinkopf. (General history and critique of pietism.)

Erb, P.C. (ed.) (1983) *Pietists: Selected Writings*, New York: Paulist Press. (Anthology of major pietist writings, including excerpts from Spener, Francke, Tersteegen and Zinzendorf, with introduction.)

Heppe, H. (1879) *Geschichte des Pietismus und der Mystick in der Reformiter Kirche der Niederlande* (History of Pietism and Mysticism in the Dutch Reformed Church), Leiden: Brill. (History of pietist influence on Dutch Calvinism.)

* Lovelace, R.F. (1979) *The American Pietism of Cotton Mather: Origins of American Evangelicalism*, Grand Rapids, MI: Eerdmans. (Stresses the connections between American Puritanism and Continental pietism.)

Nagy, P. (1976) 'Pragmatism and American Pietism', *Transactions of the Charles Sanders Peirce Society* 12 (1): 165–81. (Connects the concentration of pietism upon the active and therapeutic influence of religion with the shape of American pragmatism.)

Rack, H.D. (1989) *Reasonable Enthusiast: John Wesley and the Rise of Methodism*, London: Epworth. (Intellectual biography of Wesley, with detailed treatment of his interaction with the Moravians.)

* Spener, P.J. (1675) *Pia Desideria: or Heartfelt Desires for a God-Pleasing Improvement of the True Protestant Church*, trans. T.G. Tappert, Philadelphia, PA: Fortress, 1964. (Standard English edition of this work, with introduction.)

Stoeffler, F.E. (ed.) (1976) *Continental Pietism and Early American Christianity*, Grand Rapids, MI: Eerdmans. (Essays on the influence of pietism on various early American religious communities, including German Lutheran, Dutch Reformed and Moravians.)

—— (1965) *The Rise of Evangelical Pietism*, Leiden: Brill. (Surveys the background to the rise of pietism and concludes with a survey of Spener.)

Ward, W.R. (1992) *The Protestant Evangelical*

Awakening, Cambridge: Cambridge University Press. (Overview of eighteenth-century evangelical revivals in Central Europe and America, with special attention to the role played by pietism and especially by Zinzendorf.)

ALLEN C. GUELZO

PISAREV, D. *see* RUSSIAN MATERIALISM: 'THE 1860S'

PLANCK, MAX KARL ERNST LUDWIG (1858–1947)

Planck was a German theoretical physicist and leader of the German physics community in the first half of the twentieth century. Famous for his introduction of the quantum hypothesis in physics, Planck was also a prolific writer on popular-scientific and philosophical topics. Even more so than his younger contemporary Albert Einstein, Planck was well-known in his day for his defence of a realist conception of science and his explicit criticism of the positivism of Ernst Mach and the Vienna Circle.

Max Planck was born in Kiel and after 1867 moved with his family to Munich. Planck studied physics with Philipp von Jolly at Munich and with Herman von HELMHOLTZ and Gustav Kirchhoff at Berlin, taking his doctorate in Munich in 1879. After working as a *Privatdozent* in Munich, Planck was named *Außerordentlicher Professor* in Kiel in 1885. Most of his career was lived in Berlin, where he was called as Kirchhoff's successor in 1889, being named *Ordentlicher Professor* in 1892. During his Berlin years, Planck became perhaps the most influential figure in the German physics community, serving, among other roles, as secretary of the Prussian Academy of Sciences from 1912 until 1938 and as President of the Kaiser-Wilhelm-Gesellschaft from 1930 to 1935 and again briefly after the Second World War, before it was renamed the Max-Planck-Gesellschaft in his honour in 1946. Among Planck's students in Berlin was Moritz SCHLICK, who completed a dissertation under Planck in 1904. From 1914 until 1933, Albert EINSTEIN was one of his closest colleagues; Erwin Schrödinger was his successor. After retirement in 1928, Planck continued to be quite active, writing especially on broader popular and philosophical topics, and struggling after 1933 to preserve some of the dignity and integrity of German physics under Hitler. Planck was a political conservative and a defender of the highest ideals of German culture. For all of Planck's prominence, his life was dogged by tragedy, including the death of his first wife Marie, in 1909, the deaths of his twin daughters Grete and Emma, in childbirth in 1917 and 1919, the death of his elder son Karl, from war wounds in 1918, the destruction by bombing in 1944 of his home in Berlin-Grünewald, along with all of the personal papers and possessions it contained, and the execution of his younger son Erwin, in 1945, for complicity in the plot to assassinate Hitler.

Planck's early work concerned primarily thermodynamics and efforts to clarify the concept of entropy – this in the tradition of Rudolf Clausius and the mechanical theory of heat. One early controversy involved his defence of the mechanical worldview against energeticist critics of atomism and mechanism, including Wilhelm Ostwald and Georg Helm; another involved his defence of the second law of thermodynamics as a deterministic law against Ludwig Boltzmann's statistical interpretation of the entropy law (see THERMODYNAMICS). Planck's most famous contribution to physics, for which he earned the Nobel Prize in 1918, was his introduction of the quantum hypothesis. The idea of the quantum first appeared in the formula for the frequency distribution of the energy of black-body radiation as a function of temperature that Planck derived late in 1900. The Planck formula contained two constants. One is the constant, h, later recognized as representing the quantum of action and named the Planck constant. Planck originally thought that it was only the exchange of energy between matter and radiation that was quantized. Einstein first proposed in 1905 that free radiant energy itself exists in a quantized form as photons. Planck's analysis of how the second constant, k, the Boltzmann constant, entered the derivation of the distribution formula yielded a theoretical determination of the value of Avogadro's number and hence confirmation of the atomistic hypothesis. Planck was an early and enthusiastic supporter of the theory of relativity (see RELATIVITY THEORY, PHILOSOPHICAL SIGNIFICANCE OF), but to the end of his life remained sceptical of the Copenhagen interpretation of quantum mechanics associated with Niels BOHR and Werner HEISENBERG (see QUANTUM MECHANICS, INTERPRETATION OF).

Planck's commitment to atomism led him into a well-known debate with Ernst MACH over realism and positivism (Planck 1909, 1910; Mach 1910) (see SCIENTIFIC REALISM AND ANTIREALISM; LOGICAL POSITIVISM). In his lecture, 'Die Einheit des physikalischen Weltbildes' (1909), Planck argued against

Mach that 'however little we know about their more specific properties, the atoms are no more and no less real than the heavenly bodies', adding that what sustained the 'great masters' of natural science – Copernicus, Kepler, Newton, Huygens and Faraday – in their struggles against 'received opinion' and 'higher authorities' was not the 'economical point of view' but their 'rock-solid...belief in the reality of their world picture'. With the rise of the Vienna Circle and logical empiricism in the later 1920s (see VIENNA CIRCLE), Planck returned to this theme. It was sufficiently important for him to make it the focus of his first major address to the Kaiser-Wilhelm-Gesellschaft after being named its President. *Positivismus und reale Außenwelt* (1930) represents Planck's most thoroughgoing critique of positivism. According to Planck, when positivism is carried to its logical conclusion, it 'denies the concept and the necessity of an objective physics, that is to say, one independent of the individuality of the researcher'. An objective physics is achieved only through a 'step into the metaphysical', with the hypothesis 'that our experiences do not themselves constitute the physical world, that they instead only give us information about another world that stands behind them and is independent of us, in other words, that a real external world exists.'

List of works

Planck, M. (1909) 'Die Einheit des physikalischen Weltbildes' ('The Unity of the Physical World Picture'), *Physikalische Zeitschrift* 10: 62–75; repr. *Die Einheit des physikalischen Weltbildes*, Leipzig: S. Hirzel; repr. in Planck 1949, 28–51; trans. in Planck 1925, 1–41. (Planck's first critique of Machian positivism.)

—— (1910) 'Zur Machschen Theorie der physikalischen Erkenntnis. Eine Erwiderung' ('On Mach's Theory of Physical Knowledge: A Reply'), *Physikalische Zeitschrift* 11: 1,186–90. (Planck's rejoiner to Mach's reply.)

—— (1920) *Die Entstehung und bisherige Entwicklung der Quantentheorie*, Leipzig: J.A. Barth; trans. H.T. Clarke and L. Silberstein, *The Origin and Development of the Quantum Theory*, Oxford: Clarendon Press, 1922. (Nobel Prize address.)

—— (1925) *A Survey of Physics: A Collection of Lectures and Essays*, trans. R. Jones and D.H. Williams, London: Methuen; repr. *A Survey of Physical Theory*, New York: Dover, 1960. (An early collection of Planck's popular and philosophical essays in English translation.)

—— (1930) *Positivismus und reale Außenwelt* (Positivism and the Real External World), Leipzig:

Akademische Verlagsgesellschaft; repr. in Planck 1949, 228–45; trans. in Planck 1932, 64–106. (Planck's mature critique of positivism.)

—— (1932) *Where Is Science Going?*, trans. J. Murphy, New York: W.W. Norton; repr. Woodbridge, CT: Ox Bow Press, 1981. (A second collection of Planck's popular and philosophical writings in translation.)

—— (1936) *The Philosophy of Physics*, trans. H.W. Johnston, New York: W.W. Norton. (The third and final English-language collection of Planck's popular and philosophical essays.)

—— (1948) *Wissenschaftliche Selbstbiographie*, Leipzig: J.A. Barth; repr. with additional documents bearing upon its origin, Halle/Saale: Deutsche Akademie der Naturforscher Leopoldina, 1990; trans. F. Gaynor, *Scientific Autobiography*, New York: Philosophical Library, 1949; repr. New York: Greenwood Press, 1968. (Planck's scientific autobiography.)

—— (1949) *Vorträge und Erinnerungen* (Lectures and Reminiscences), Stuttgart: S. Hirzel, 5th edn; 10th edn, Darmstadt: Wissenschaftliche Buchgesellschaft, 1965. (The most complete collection of Planck's popular and philosophical writings. Contains an expanded version of *Wege zur physikalischen Erkenntnis* (Paths to Physical Knowledge), Leipzig: S. Hirzel, 1944.)

—— (1958) *Physikalische Abhandlungen und Vorträge. Aus Anlaß seines 100. Geburtstages (23. April 1958)* (Physical Papers and Lectures. On the Occasion of His 100th Birthday), Braunschweig: Friedrich Vieweg und Sohn. (Planck's collected scientific papers.)

References and further reading

Heilbron, J.L. (1986) *The Dilemmas of an Upright Man: Max Planck as Spokesman for German Science*, Berkeley, CA: University of California Press. (Definitive recent biography focusing on the personal and institutional setting of Planck's work.)

Hermann, A. (1973) *Max Planck in Selbstzeugnissen und Bilddokumenten* (Max Planck in His Own Words and Photographic Records), Reinbeck: Rowohlt. (An accessible biographical collection.)

Kangro, H. (1976) *Early History of Planck's Radiation Law*, London: Taylor & Francis. (A detailed study of Planck's derivation of the energy distribution law for black-body radiation.)

Klein, M.J. (1962) 'Max Planck and the Beginnings of the Quantum Theory', *Archive for History of Exact Sciences* 1: 459–79. (Klein's three papers constitute one of the definitive studies of Planck's work on the radiation law.)

—— (1963) 'Planck, Entropy, and Quanta, 1901–1906', *The Natural Philosopher* 1: 83–108. (See 1962.)

—— (1966) 'Thermodynamics and Quanta in Planck's Work', *Physics Today* 19 (11): 23–32. (See 1962.)

Kretzschmar, H. (1967) *Max Planck als Philosoph* (Max Planck as a Philosopher), Munich and Basel: Ernst Reinhardt. (The most recent extended study of Planck's philosophy, informative even though it goes too far out of its way to dispute materialist, Marxist-Leninist interpretations of Planck's philosophy.)

Kuhn, T.S. (1978) *Black-body Theory and the Quantum Discontinuity 1894–1912*, Oxford: Clarendon Press. (Along with Kangro and Klein, the other major historical study of Planck's work on the quantum hypothesis.)

Lowood, H. (1977) *Max Planck: A Bibliography of His Non-technical Writings*, Berkeley, CA: Office for the History of Science and Technology, University of California. (Quite detailed and comprehensive.)

* Mach, E. (1910) 'Die Leitgedanken meiner naturwissenschaftlichen Erkenntnislehre und ihre Aufnahme durch die Zeitgenossen' (The Main Principles of My Theory of Scientific Knowledge and its Reception by My Contemporaries), *Physikalische Zeitschrift* 11: 599–606. (Mach's reply to Planck's criticism in 'Die Einheit des physikalischen Weltbildes'.)

Vogel, H. (1961) *Zum philosophischen Wirken Max Plancks. Seine Kritik am Positivismus* (On the Philosophical Work of Max Planck: His Critique of Positivism), Berlin: Akademie-Verlag. (A helpful study even though it attempts to impose a materialist, Marxist-Leninist interpretation on Planck's philosophy.)

DON HOWARD

PLATFORM SUTRA

The Platform Sutra *is the single most important work of early Chinese Chan Buddhism, perhaps of the entire Chan/Sŏn/Zen tradition. It purports to contain the teachings of the Sixth Patriarch Huineng (638–713), whom it celebrates as an illiterate but enlightened sage. The centrepiece is an exchange of verses attributed to Shenxiu (606?–706) and Huineng, generally taken to represent, respectively, a gradual or progressive self-cultivation leading to perfect enlightenment and a sudden or subitist style of practice in which enlightenment is attained all at once. The* Platform Sutra *was actually composed around 780, more than a century after the events it describes. Its reportage is demonstrably inaccurate and its traditional interpretation problematic, but this does not alter the profound mythopoeic importance of the text.*

The events described in the *Platform Sutra* supposedly took place at the Chan community led by Hongren (601–74), described here as the Fifth Patriarch. Needing a successor, he instructed his students each to compose and submit a verse describing their understanding of Buddhism. The only one to do so was Shenxiu, depicted here as the earnest and well-educated but as yet unenlightened senior student of the community, who after much consternation wrote the following:

> The body is the *bodhi* tree.
> The mind is like a bright mirror's stand.
> At all times we must strive to polish it
> and must not let dust collect.

Hongren praised this verse in public and instructed his students to recite and practice according to it, but in private he told Shenxiu that it was insufficient. Shortly thereafter, Huineng, who was working in the rice threshing room, heard Shenxiu's verse being recited by an acolyte. He immediately understood that its author was still unenlightened and offered his own response:

> *Bodhi* originally has no tree.
> The bright mirror also has no stand.
> Fundamentally there is not a single thing.
> Where could dust arise?

Hongren rejected this verse in public, but in private he bestowed both a final teaching and the status of Sixth Patriarch on Huineng, gave the still unordained layman his robe and bowl as proof of the transmission, and told him to leave the monastery. Huineng spent the next sixteen years living with hunters in the mountains before he presented himself at a Buddhist temple, was recognized as the Sixth Patriarch, and received ordination as a Buddhist monk.

It is the dust-polishing of the first verse that has been interpreted since at least the time of Zongmi (780–841) onward as an expression of gradualism, while the negations contained in the second verse are taken as evidence of subitism. The third line of the second verse, in fact, has been described by the modern Zen popularizer D.T. Suzuki as 'a bomb thrown into the camp of Shen-hsiu [Shenxiu] and his predecessors' (Suzuki 1949: 22). However, these interpretations, the religious identity of the Northern and Southern schools and the nature of the relationship between them are habitually misunderstood in popular writings on Chan.

First, note that there is no explicit reference to gradual improvement in 'Shenxiu's' verse; in fact, Shenxiu and his followers taught a doctrine of the constant and perfect practice of the *bodhisattva*. In the Chinese Buddhist context of the eighth century and beyond, gradualism was considered too elementary, limited by the dualistic conceptualization of enlightenment as a goal that should be reached through progressive effort. In fact, the historical Shenxiu's teachings are expressed in dualistic terms, but they are not gradualistic. Second, where is the subitism of 'Huineng's' verse? This verse cannot stand by itself, but is dependent on the first. If the original author of these verses understood Shenxiu's teachings, then the intent would have been to suggest that Huineng's were similar in content but more advanced in that they went beyond conceptual or dualistic positions. This explanation of the meaning of the two verses is supported by the following details: (1) Shenxiu and Huineng were never at Hongren's side at the same time, so that the story is fictional; (2) the famous third line above is not contained in the earliest version of the text (from Dunhuang), which actually attributes two slightly different verses to Huineng; and (3) the terms used in both verses – including the third line cited here – were derived from Northern school sources (McRae 1986: 1–6, 235–38.) The doctrines of the *Platform Sutra* are similar to those of the Oxhead school of early Chan, which made extensive use of a thesis–antithesis–synthesis form of doctrinal exposition.

Nevertheless, the populist image of Huineng as illiterate sage was profoundly important to the development of Chinese Chan, in that it provided a framework by which to emphasize the primacy of the actual experience of enlightenment over all other factors. By recognizing Huineng as Sixth Patriarch, the Chan tradition showed that – in theory, at least – it would not hesitate to recognize someone so déclassé as an illiterate woodcutter from the far south. Thus, in a fashion akin to the legendary acceptance of Shun as sage emperor, every subsequent selection of a successor by any teacher within Chan – no matter how well-placed the candidate might be in social, political, or economic terms – could similarly be ascribed to purely religious factors. The paradoxical impact of the Huineng story was thus strong ideological support for the developing lineage schema of Chan, in which masters were identified within specific networks of patriarchal relationship.

In addition, from the advent of the *Platform Sutra* the Chan school maintained a consistent preference for sudden over gradual, as well as an equal reluctance to use dualistic doctrinal formulations in teaching. This combination resulted in the development of a new type of religious practice: encounter dialogue, the sometimes spontaneous repartee between master and student that formed the new locus of spiritual cultivation. Huineng had exemplified an intuitive style of teaching that responded to the needs of individual students, and this image was transformed with time into the more dynamic persona of monks such as LINJI (d. 866 or 867), who forced his students through their spiritual paces with shouts and fists. The texts of later periods of Chan are stylistically quite different from the *Platform Sutra*, which thus marked the end of early Chan even as it helped lay the groundwork for later developments.

See also: BUDDHIST PHILOSOPHY, CHINESE; LINJI; SELF-CULTIVATION IN CHINESE PHILOSOPHY; ZONGMI

References and further reading

* McRae, J.R. (1986) *The Northern School and the Formation of Early Ch'an Buddhism*, Honolulu, HI: University of Hawaii Press. (A reappraisal of early Chan, including the *Platform Sutra*.)
* Suzuki, D.T. (1949) *The Zen Doctrine of No-mind*, London: Rider. (A largely outmoded but widely known interpretation of Chan.)
Yampolsky, P.B. (ed. and trans.) (1967) *The Platform Sutra of the Sixth Patriarch*, New York: Columbia University Press. (The most widely used translation of the Dunhuang text, with a long introduction on the history of the text.)

JOHN R. McRAE

PLATO (427–347 BC)

Plato was an Athenian Greek of aristocratic family, active as a philosopher in the first half of the fourth century BC. He was a devoted follower of Socrates, as his writings make abundantly plain. Nearly all are philosophical dialogues – often works of dazzling literary sophistication – in which Socrates takes centre stage. Socrates is usually a charismatic figure who outshines a whole succession of lesser interlocutors, from sophists, politicians and generals to docile teenagers. The most powerfully realistic fictions among the dialogues, such as Protagoras *and* Symposium, *recreate a lost world of exuberant intellectual self-confidence in an Athens not yet torn apart by civil strife or reduced by defeat in the Peloponnesian War.*

Some of Plato's earliest writings were evidently composed in an attempt to defend Socrates and his philosophical mission against the misunderstanding and prejudice which – in the view of his friends – had brought about his prosecution and death. Most notable of these are Apology, *which purports to reproduce the speeches Socrates gave at his trial, and* Gorgias, *a long and impassioned debate over the choice between a philosophical and a political life. Several early dialogues pit Socrates against practitioners of rival disciplines, whether rhetoric (as in* Gorgias*) or sophistic education (*Protagoras*) or expertise in religion (*Euthyphro*), and were clearly designed as invitations to philosophy as well as warnings against the pretensions of the alternatives. Apologetic and protreptic concerns are seldom entirely absent from any Platonic dialogue in which Socrates is protagonist, but in others among the early works the emphasis falls more heavily upon his ethical philosophy in its own right. For example,* Laches *(on courage) and* Charmides *(on moderation) explore these topics in characteristic Socratic style, relying mostly on his method of elenchus (refutation), although Plato seems by no means committed to a Socratic intellectualist analysis of the virtues as forms of knowledge. That analysis is in fact examined in these dialogues (as also, for example, in* Hippias Minor*).*

In dialogues of Plato's middle period like Meno, Symposium *and* Phaedo *a rather different Socrates is presented. He gives voice to positive positions on a much wider range of topics: not just ethics, but metaphysics and epistemology and psychology too. And he is portrayed as recommending a new and constructive instrument of inquiry borrowed from mathematics, the method of hypothesis. While there are continuities between Plato's early and middle period versions of Socrates, it is clear that an evolution has occurred. Plato is no longer a Socratic, not even a critical and original Socratic: he has turned Socrates into a Platonist.*

The two major theories that make up Platonism are the theory of Forms and the doctrine of the immortality of the soul. The notion of a Form is articulated with the aid of conceptual resources drawn from Eleatic philosophy. The ultimate object of a philosopher's search for knowledge is a kind of being that is quite unlike the familiar objects of the phenomenal world: something eternal and changeless, eminently and exclusively whatever – beautiful or just or equal – it is, not qualified in time or place or relation or respect. An account of the Form of Beautiful will explain what it is for something to be beautiful, and indeed other things are caused to be beautiful by their participation in the Beautiful. The middle period dialogues never put forward any proof of the existence of Forms. The theory is usually presented as a basic assumption to which the interlocutors agree to subscribe. Plato seems to treat it as a very general high-level hypothesis which provides the framework within which other questions can be explored, including the immortality of the soul. According to Phaedo, *such a hypothesis will only stand if its consequences are consistent with other relevant truths; according to* Republic *its validity must ultimately be assured by its coherence with the unhypothetical first principle constituted by specification of the Good.*

The Pythagorean doctrine of the immortality of the soul, by contrast, is something for which Plato presents explicit proofs whenever he introduces it into discussion. It presupposes the dualist idea that soul and body are intrinsically distinct substances, which coexist during our life, but separate again at death. Its first appearance is in Meno, *where it is invoked in explanation of how we acquire a priori knowledge of mathematical truths. Socrates is represented as insisting that nobody imparts such truths to us as information: we work them out for ourselves, by recollecting them from within, where they must have lain untapped as latent memory throughout our lives. But innate forgotten knowledge presupposes a time before the soul entered the body, when it was in full conscious possession of truth.* Phaedo *holds out the promise that the souls of philosophers who devote their lives to the pursuit of wisdom will upon death be wholly freed from the constraints and contaminations of the body, and achieve pure knowledge of the Forms once again.*

Republic, *Plato's greatest work, also belongs to this major constructive period of his philosophizing. It gives the epistemology and metaphysics of Forms a key role in political philosophy. The ideally just city (or some approximation to it), and the communist institutions which control the life of its elite governing class, could only become a practical possibility if philosophers were to acquire political power or rulers to engage sincerely and adequately in philosophy. This is because a philosopher-ruler whose emotions have been properly trained and disciplined by Plato's reforming educational programme, and whose mind has been prepared for abstract thought about Forms by rigorous and comprehensive study of mathematics, is the only person with the knowledge and virtue necessary for producing harmony in society. Understanding of Forms, and above all of the Good, keystone of the system of Forms, is thus the essential prerequisite of political order.*

It remains disputed how far Plato's vision of a good society ruled by philosopher-statesmen (of both sexes) was ever really conceived as a blueprint for practical implementation. Much of his writing suggests a deep pessimism about the prospects for human happiness. The most potent image in Republic *is the analogy of the cave, which depicts ordinary humanity as so shackled by illusions several times removed from the illumination of truth that only radical moral and intellectual conversion could redeem us. And its theory of the human psyche is no less dark: the opposing desires of reason, emotion and appetite render it all too liable to the internal conflict which constitutes moral disease.*

While Republic *is for modern readers the central text in Plato's œuvre, throughout much of antiquity and the medieval period* Timaeus *was the dialogue by which he was best known. In this late work Plato offers an account of the creation of an ordered universe by a divine craftsman, who invests pre-existing matter with every form of life and intelligence by the application of harmonious mathematical ratios. This is claimed to be only a 'likely story', the best explanation we can infer for phenomena which have none of the unchangeable permanence of the Forms. None the less* Timaeus *is the only work among post-*Republic *dialogues, apart from a highly-charged myth in* Phaedrus, *in which Plato was again to communicate the comprehensive vision expressed in the Platonism of the middle period dialogues.*

Many of these dialogues are however remarkable contributions to philosophy, and none more so than the self-critical Parmenides. *Here the mature Parmenides is represented as mounting a powerful set of challenges to the logical coherence of the theory of Forms. He urges not abandonment of the theory, but much harder work in the practice of dialectical argument if the challenges are to be met. Other pioneering explorations were in epistemology (*Theaetetus*) and philosophical logic (*Sophist*).* Theaetetus *mounts a powerful attack on Protagoras' relativist theory of truth, before grappling with puzzles about false belief and problems with the perennially attractive idea that knowledge is a complex built out of unknowable simples.* Sophist *engages with the Parmenidean paradox that what is not cannot be spoken or thought about. It forges fundamental distinctions between identity and predication and between subject and predicate in its attempt to rescue meaningful discourse from the absurdities of the paradox.*

In his sixties Plato made two visits to the court of Dionysius II in Sicily, apparently with some hopes of exercising a beneficial influence on the young despot. Both attempts were abysmal failures. But they did not deter Plato from writing extensively on politics in his last years. Statesman *explores the practical knowledge the expert statesman must command. It was followed by the longest, even if not the liveliest, work he ever wrote, the twelve books of* Laws, *perhaps still unfinished at his death.*

1 Life

Evidence about Plato's life is *prima facie* plentiful. As well as several ancient biographies, notably that contained in book III of Diogenes Laertius' *Lives of the Philosophers*, we possess a collection of thirteen letters which purport to have been written by Plato. Unfortunately the biographies present what has been aptly characterized as 'a medley of anecdotes, reverential, malicious, or frivolous, but always piquant'. As for the letters, no scholar thinks them all authentic, and some judge that none are.

From the biographies it is safe enough to accept some salient points. Plato was born of an aristocratic Athenian family. He was brother to Glaucon and Adimantus, Socrates' main interlocutors in the *Republic*; his relatives included Critias and Charmides, members of the bloody junta which seized power in Athens at the end of the Peloponnesian War. He became one of the followers of Socrates, after whose execution he withdrew with others among them to the neighbouring city of Megara. His travels included a visit to the court of Dionysius in Sicily. On returning from Sicily to Athens he began teaching in a gymnasium outside the city, called the Academy.

The *Seventh Letter*, longest and most interesting of the collection of letters, gives a good deal of probably trustworthy information, whether or not it was written by Plato himself. It begins with an account of his growing disenchantment with Athenian politics in early manhood and of his decision against a political career. This is prefatory to a sketch of the visit to Dionysius in Syracuse, which is followed by an elaborate self-justifying explanation of why and how, despite his decision, Plato later became entangled in political intrigue in Sicily, once the young Dionysius II had succeeded to his father's throne. There were two separate visits to the younger Dionysius: one (*c.*366 BC) is represented as undertaken at the behest of Dion, nephew of Dionysius I, in the hope of converting him into a philosopher-ruler; the other (*c.*360 BC) was according to the author an attempt to mediate between Dionysius and Dion, now in exile and out of favour. Both ventures were humiliating failures.

Of more interest for the history of philosophy is Plato's activity in the ACADEMY. We should not conceive, as scholars once did, that he established a formal philosophical school, with its own property and institutional structures. Although he acquired a house and garden in the vicinity, where communal meals were probably taken, much of his philosophical teaching and conversation may well have been conducted in the public space of the gymnasium itself. Some sense of the Academy's distinctive style may be gleaned from evidence of the contemporaneous writings of the philosophical associates he attracted, notably his nephew SPEUSIPPUS, XENOCRATES, ARISTOTLE and the mathematician EUDOXUS. Discussion of Plato's metaphysical ideas figured prominently in these; but orthodoxy was not expected, to judge from their philosophical disagreements with him and with each other. Aristotle's early *Topics* suggests that an important role was played by formal disputation about philosophical theses.

From the educational programme of the *Republic* one might have guessed that Plato would have attached importance to the teaching of mathematics as a preparation for philosophy, but we have better evidence for his encouraging research in it. While he was not an original mathematician himself, good sources tell us that he formulated problems for others to solve: for example, what uniform motions will account for the apparent behaviour of the planets. Otherwise there is little reliable information on what was taught in the Academy: not much can be inferred from the burlesque of comic playwrights. Since almost certainly no fees were charged, most of those who came to listen to Plato (from all over the Greek world) must have been aristocrats. Some are known to have entered politics or to have advised princes, particularly on constitutional reform. But the Academy had no political mission of its own. Indeed the rhetorician Isocrates, head of a rival school and admittedly not an unbiased witness, dismissed the abstract disciplines favoured by the Academy for their uselessness in the real world.

2 Writings

Thrasyllus, astrologer to the emperor Tiberius, is the unlikely source of the arrangement of Platonic writings adopted in the manuscript tradition which preserves them. For his edition of Plato he grouped them into tetralogies, reminiscent of the trilogies produced in Athenian tragic theatre. These were organized according to an architectonic scheme constructed on principles that are now only partially apparent, but certainly had nothing to do with chronology of composition. His arrangement began with a quartet 'designed to show what the life of the philosopher is like' (Diogenes Laertius, III 57): *Euthyphro*, or 'On Piety', classified as a 'peirastic' or elenctic dialogue (see SOCRATES §§3–4), which is a species of one of his two main genres, the dialogue of inquiry; *Apology*, *Crito* and *Phaedo* are all regarded as specimens of exposition, his other main genre, or more specifically as specimens of ethics. These four works are all concerned in one way or another with the trial and death of Socrates.

There followed a group consisting of *Cratylus*, or 'On the Correctness of Names', *Theaetetus*, or 'On Knowledge', *Sophist* and *Politicus* (often anglicized as *Statesman*). Plato himself indicates that the last three of this set are to be read together. They contain some of his most mature and challenging work in epistemology, metaphysics and philosophical methodology. In this they resemble *Parmenides*, with its famous critique of the theory of Forms, the first of the next tetralogy, which was completed by three major dialogues all reckoned 'ethical' by Thrasyllus: *Philebus*, an examination of pleasure, *Symposium* and *Phaedrus*, both brilliant literary divertissements which explore the nature of love.

A much slighter quartet came next: two dialogues entitled *Alcibiades*, plus *Hipparchus* and *Rivals*. None of these, with the disputed exception of the first *Alcibiades*, is thought by modern scholarship to be authentic Plato. They were followed by *Theages*, a short piece now generally reckoned spurious, *Charmides*, *Laches*, *Lysis*. These three works are generally regarded by modern scholars as Socratic dialogues: that is, designed to exhibit the distinctive method and ethical preoccupations of the historical Socrates, at least as Plato understood him, not to develop Plato's own philosophy. Thrasyllus would agree with the latter point, since he made them dialogues of inquiry: *Laches* and *Lysis* 'maieutic', in which the character 'Socrates' attempts as intellectual midwife to assist his interlocutors to articulate and work out their own ideas on courage and friendship respectively; *Charmides* elenctic, with the interlocutors Charmides and Critias and their attempts to say what moderation is put to the test of cross-examination, something Thrasyllus interestingly distinguished from philosophical midwifery.

The next group consisted of *Euthydemus*, *Protagoras*, *Gorgias*, *Meno*, important works in which modern scholarship finds analysis and further elaboration by Plato of the Socratic conception of virtue. The first three present a Socrates in argumentative conflict with sophists of different sorts (see SOPH-

ISTS), so it is understandable that under the general heading 'competitive' Thrasyllus characterized *Euthydemus* and *Gorgias* as dialogues of refutation, and *Protagoras* as a dialogue of display – presumably because Protagoras and Socrates are each portrayed as intent on showing off their debating skills. *Meno*, on the other hand, is labelled an elenctic work. It was followed by the seventh tetralogy: *Hippias Major* and *Hippias Minor*, two very different dialogues (of refutation, according to Thrasyllus), both featuring the sophist of that name; *Ion*, a curious piece on poetic performance; and *Menexenus*, a still more curious parody of a funeral oration, put in the mouth of Pericles' mistress Aspasia.

For the last two tetralogies Thrasyllus reserved some of Plato's major writings. The eighth contained the very brief (and conceivably spurious) *Clitophon*, in which a minor character from the *Republic* plays variations on themes in the *Republic*, the second dialogue in the group, and generally regarded nowadays as Plato's greatest work. This quartet was completed by *Timaeus* and its unfinished sequel *Critias*, no doubt because these dialogues represent themselves as pursuing further the discussions of the *Republic*. The pre-Copernican mathematical cosmology of *Timaeus* no longer attracts readers as it did throughout antiquity, and particularly in the Middle Ages, when the dialogue was for a period the only part of Plato's *œuvre* known to the Latin West. Finally, the ninth tetralogy began with the short *Minos*, a spurious dialogue taking up issues in the massive *Laws*, Plato's longest and probably latest work, which was put next in the group. Then followed *Epinomis*, an appendix to *Laws* already attributed to one of Plato's pupils in antiquity (Philip of Opous, according to a report in Diogenes Laertius, III 37). Last were placed the *Letters*, briefly discussed above.

3   Authenticity and chronology

Thrasyllus rejected from the canon a variety of minor pieces, some of which still survive through the manuscript tradition. Modern judgment concurs with the ancient verdict against them. It also questions or rejects some he thought genuinely Platonic. But we can be fairly sure that we still possess everything Plato wrote for publication.

Attempting to determine the authenticity or inauthenticity of ancient writings is a hazardous business. Egregious historical errors or anachronisms suffice to condemn a work, but except perhaps for the *Eighth Letter*, this criterion gets no purchase on the Platonic corpus. Stylistic analysis of various kinds can show a piece of writing to be untypical of an author's *œuvre*, without thereby demonstrating its inauthenti-

city: *Parmenides* is a notable example of this. Most of Plato's major dialogues are in fact attested as his by Aristotle. The difficult cases are short pieces such as *Theages* and *Clitophon*, and, most interestingly, three more extended works: the *Seventh Letter*, *Alcibiades I* and *Hippias Major*. Opinion remains divided on them. Some scholars detect crude or sometimes brilliant pastiche of Plato's style; a parasitic relationship with undoubtedly genuine dialogues; a philosophical crassness or a misunderstanding of Platonic positions which betrays the forger's hand. Yet why should Plato not for some particular purpose recapitulate or elaborate things he has said elsewhere? And perhaps he did sometimes write more coarsely or didactically or long-windedly than usual. Such assessments are inevitably matters of judgment, on which intelligent and informed readers will legitimately differ.

Prospects for an absolute chronology of Plato's writings are dim. There are no more than two or three references to datable contemporaneous events in the entire corpus (leaving aside the *Letters*). Relative chronology is another matter. Some dialogues refer back to others. A number of instances have been mentioned already, but we can add a clear reminiscence of *Meno* in *Phaedo* (72e–73b), and of *Parmenides* in both *Theaetetus* (183e–184a) and *Sophist* (217c). According to one ancient tradition *Laws* was unfinished at Plato's death, and Aristotle informs us that it was written after *Republic* (*Politics* 1264b24–7), to which it appears to allude (see, for example, *Laws* 739a–e). Attempts have sometimes been made to find evidence, whether internal or external, for the existence of early versions of works we possess in different form (see for example Thesleff 1982). One example is the suggestion that Aristophanes' comedy *Ecclesiazousae* or *Assembly of Women* (388 BC) was parodying an early version of book V of *Republic*. But while the idea that Plato may have revised some of his writings is plausible, concrete instances in which such revision is plainly the best explanation of the phenomena are hard to find. Even if they were not, it is unlikely that the consequences for relative chronology would be clear.

For over a century hopes for a general relative chronology of Plato's writings have been pinned on the practice of stylistic analysis. This was pioneered by Lewis Campbell in his edition of *Sophist* and *Politicus*, published in 1867. His great achievement was to isolate a group of dialogues which have in common a number of features (added to by subsequent investigators) that set them apart from all the rest. *Timaeus*, *Critias*, *Sophist*, *Politicus*, *Philebus* and *Laws* turn out to share among other things a common technical vocabulary; a preference for certain particles, conjunctions, adverbs and other qualifiers over alternatives favoured in other dialogues; distinctive prose rhythms; and the deliberate attempt to avoid the combination of a vowel at the end of one word followed by another vowel at the beginning of the next. Since there are good independent reasons for taking *Laws* to be Plato's last work, Campbell's sextet is very likely the product of his latest phase of philosophical activity. Application of the same stylistic tests to the Platonic corpus as a whole, notably by Constantin Ritter (1888), established *Republic*, *Theaetetus* and *Phaedrus* as dialogues which show significantly more of the features most strongly represented in the late sextet than any others. There is general agreement that they must be among the works whose composition immediately precedes that of the *Laws* group, always allowing that *Republic* must have taken several years to finish, and that parts of it may have been written earlier and subsequently revised. *Parmenides* is ordinarily included with these three, although mostly on non-stylistic grounds.

Since Campbell's time there have been repeated attempts by stylometrists to divide the remaining dialogues into groups, and to establish sequences within groups. The heyday of this activity was in the late nineteenth and early twentieth centuries. Since the 1950s there has been a revival in stylistic study, with the use of increasingly sophisticated statistical techniques and the resources of the computer and the database. Secure results have proved elusive. Most scholars would be happy to date *Phaedo*, *Symposium* and *Cratylus* to a middle period of Plato's literary and philosophical work which may be regarded as achieving its culmination in *Republic*. But while this dating is sometimes supported by appeal to stylistic evidence, that evidence is in truth indecisive: the hypothesis of a middle period group of dialogues really rests on their philosophical affinities with *Republic* and their general literary character. The same can be said *mutatis mutandis* of attempts to identify a group assigned to Plato's early period.

The cohesiveness of Campbell's late group has not gone unchallenged. For example, in 1953 G.E.L. Owen mounted what for a while seemed to some a successful attack on his dating of *Timaeus* and *Critias*, on the ground that these dialogues belong philosophically in Plato's middle period. Broadly speaking, however, stylistic studies have helped to establish an agreed chronological framework within which most debates about philosophical interpretation now take place. This is not to say however that there is unanimity either about the way Plato's thought developed or about the importance of the notion of development for understanding his philosophical project or projects in the dialogues.

4 The Platonic dialogue

Who invented the philosophical dialogue, and what literary models might have inspired the invention, are not matters on which we have solid information. We do know that several of Socrates' followers composed what Aristotle calls *Sōkratikoi logoi*, discourses portraying Socrates in fictitious conversations (see SOCRATIC DIALOGUES). The only examples which survive intact besides Plato's are by XENOPHON, probably not one of the earliest practitioners of the genre.

One major reason for the production of this literature was the desire to defend Socrates against the charges of irreligion and corrupting young people made at his trial and subsequently in Athenian pamphleteering, as well as the implicit charge of guilt by association with a succession of oligarchic politicians. Thus his devotion to the unstable and treacherous Alcibiades was variously portrayed in, for example, the first of the *Alcibiades* dialogues ascribed to Plato and the now fragmentary *Alcibiades* of Aeschines of Sphettos, but both emphasized the gulf between Alcibiades' self-conceit and resistance to education and Socrates' disinterested concern for his moral wellbeing. The same general purpose informed the publication of versions of Socrates' speech (his 'apology') before the court by Plato, Xenophon and perhaps others. Writing designed to clear Socrates' name was doubtless a particular feature of the decade or so following 399 BC, although it clearly went on long after that, as in Xenophon's *Memorabilia* (see XENOPHON §2). After starting in a rather different vein *Gorgias* turns into Plato's longest and angriest dialogue of this kind. Socrates is made to present himself as the only true politician in Athens, since he is the one person who can give a truly rational account of his conduct towards others and accordingly command the requisite political skill, which is to make the citizens good. But he foresees no chance of acquittal by a court of jurors seeking only gratification from their leaders.

Placing Socrates in opposition to Alcibiades is a way of defending him. Arranging a confrontation between a sophist (Protagoras or Hippias) or a rhetorician (Gorgias) or a religious expert (Euthyphro) or a Homeric recitalist (Ion) and Socrates is a way of exposing their intellectual pretensions, and in most cases their moral shallowness, while celebrating his wit, irony and penetration and permitting his distinctive ethical positions and ethical method to unfold before the reader's eyes. The elenchus (see SOCRATES §§3–4) is by no means the only mode of argument Socrates is represented as using in these fictional encounters. Plato particularly enjoys allowing him to exploit the various rhetorical forms favoured by his interlocutors. But it is easy to see why the dialogue must have seemed to Plato the ideal instrument not only for commemorating like Xenophon Socrates' style of conversation, but more importantly for exhibiting the logical structure and dynamic of the elenchus, and its power in Socrates' hands to demolish the characteristic intellectual postures of those against whom it is deployed.

In these dialogues of confrontation Socrates seldom succeeds in humbling his interlocutors into a frank recognition that they do not know what they thought they knew: the official purpose – simultaneously intellectual and moral – of the elenchus. It would not have been convincing to have him begin to convert historical figures with well-known intellectual positions. The main thing registered by their fictional counterparts is a sense of being manipulated into self-contradiction. In any case, the constructive response to the extraordinary figure of Socrates which Plato really wants to elicit is that of the reader. We have to suppose that, as conversion to philosophy was for Plato scarcely distinguishable from his response to Socrates (devotion to the man, surrender to the spell of his charisma, strenuous intellectual engagement with his thought and the questions he was constantly pursuing), so he conceived that the point of writing philosophy must be to make Socrates charismatic for his readers – to move us to similar devotion and enterprise. In short, the dialogues constitute simultaneously an invitation to philosophy and a critique of its intellectual rivals.

Whatever Plato's other accomplishments or failures as a writer and thinker, one project in which he unquestionably succeeds is in creating a Socrates who gets under the reader's skin (see SOCRATES §7). Plato has a genius for portrayal of character: the 'arrogant self-effacement' of Socrates' persona; the irony at once sincere and insincere; the intellectual slipperiness in service of moral paradox; the nobility of the martyr who loses everything but saves his own soul, and of the hero who stands firm on the battlefield or in face of threats by the authorities; relentless rationality and almost impregnable self-control somehow cohabiting with susceptibility to beautiful young men and their erotic charm. Also important is the ingenious variety of perspectives from which we see Socrates talking and interacting with others. Sometimes he is made to speak to us direct (for example, *Apology*, *Gorgias*). Sometimes Plato invites us to share complicity in a knowing narrative Socrates tells of his own performance (as in *Charmides*, *Protagoras*). Sometimes someone else is represented as recalling an unforgettably emotional occasion when Socrates dominated a whole roomful of people, as in the most powerfully

dramatic dialogues of all, *Phaedo* and *Symposium*. Here we have the illusion that Socrates somehow remains himself even though the ideas advanced in them must go beyond anything that the historical Socrates (or at any rate the agnostic Socrates of *Apology*) would have claimed about the soul and its immortality or about the good and the beautiful.

5 The problem of writing

It might seem strange that an original philosopher of Plato's power and stature should be content, outside the *Letters* if some of them are by him, never to talk directly to the reader, but only through the medium of narrative or dramatic fiction, even granted the pleasure he plainly takes in exhibiting his mastery of that medium. This will become less mysterious if we reflect further on Socrates and Socratic questioning. At any rate by the time of the *Meno*, Plato was wanting to suggest that the elenchus presupposes that understanding is not something one person can transmit in any straightforward way to another, but something which has to be worked out for oneself and recovered from within by recollection. The suggestion is made by means of an example from mathematics, where it is transparently true that seeing the answer to a problem is something that nobody else can do for us, even if Socrates' questions can prompt us to it. The moral we are to draw is that in pressing his interlocutors on what they say they believe, Socrates is merely an intellectual midwife assisting them to articulate for themselves a more coherent and deeply considered set of views, which will ideally constitute the truth.

The Platonic dialogue can be interpreted as an attempt to create a relationship between author and reader analogous to that between Socrates and his interlocutors. Given that that relationship is to be construed in the way indicated in *Meno*, the point of a dialogue will be like that of the elenchus: not to teach readers the truth (it is strictly speaking unteachable), but to provoke and guide them into working at discovering it for themselves. Most of the dialogues of Campbell's late sextet are admittedly more didactic than one would expect on this view of the dialogue, and it is significant that except in *Philebus* Socrates is no longer the main speaker. Yet even here use of the dialogue form can be taken as symbolizing that responsibility for an active philosophical engagement with what Plato has written rests with the reader, as the difficulty and in some cases the methodological preoccupations of most of these works confirms.

In a much discussed passage at the end of *Phaedrus* (275–8), Socrates is made to speak of the limitations of the written word. It can answer no questions, it cannot choose its readers, it gets misunderstood with no means of correcting misunderstanding. Its one worthwhile function is to remind those who know of what they know. By contrast with this dead discourse live speech can defend itself, and will be uttered or not as appropriate to the potential audience. The only serious use of words is achieved when speech, not writing, is employed by dialecticians to sow seeds of knowledge in the soul of the learner. If they commit their thoughts to writing they do so as play (*paidia*). The *Seventh Letter* (341–2) makes related remarks about the writing of philosophy; and at various points in, for example, *Republic*, *Timaeus* and *Laws*, the discussions in which the interlocutors are engaged are described as play, not to be taken seriously.

Interpreters have often taken these written remarks about writing with the utmost seriousness. In particular the Tübingen school of Platonic scholarship has connected them with references, especially in Aristotle, to unwritten doctrines of Plato. They have proposed that the fundamental principles of his philosophy are not worked out in the dialogues at all, but were reserved for oral discussions in the Academy, and have to be reconstructed by us from evidence about the unwritten doctrines. But this evidence is suspect where voluble and elusive when apparently more reliable. There are two star exhibits. First, according to the fourth century BC music theorist Aristoxenus, Aristotle used to tell of how when Plato lectured on the good he surprised and disappointed his listeners by talking mostly about mathematics (*Harmonics II*, 30.16–31.3). Second, at one point in the *Physics* (209b13–6) Aristotle refers to Plato's 'so-called unwritten teachings'; and the Aristotelian commentators report that Aristotle and other members of the Academy elsewhere wrote more about them. Plato's key idea was taken to be the postulation of the One and the great and the small, or 'indefinite dyad' as principles of all things, including Forms. In his *Metaphysics* (I.6) Aristotle seems to imply that in this theory the Forms were construed in some sense as numbers. It remains obscure and a subject of inconclusive scholarly debate how far the theory was worked out, and what weight we should attach to it in comparison to the metaphysical explorations of the dialogues of Plato's middle and late periods (see for example Ross 1951, Gaiser 1968, Guthrie 1978, Gaiser 1980, Burnyeat 1987).

The general issue of how far we can ascribe to Plato things said by interlocutors (principally Socrates) in his dialogues is something which exercises many readers. The position taken in this entry will be that no single or simple view of the matter is tenable: sometimes, for example, Plato uses the dialogue form to work through a problem which is vexing him;

sometimes to recommend a set of ideas to us; sometimes to play teasingly with ideas or positions or methodologies without implying much in the way of commitment; and frequently to suggest to us ways we should or should not ourselves try to philosophize. As for the Tübingen school, we may agree with them that when it introduces the Form of the Good the *Republic* itself indicates that readers are being offered only conjectures and images, not the thorough dialectical discussion necessary for proper understanding. But the notions of seriousness and play are less straightforward than they allow. Playing with ideas – that is, trying them out and developing them to see what might work and what will not – is the way new insights in philosophy and science are often discovered. When we meet it in Plato's dialogues it usually seems fun without being frivolous. Nor should we forget that the Platonic dialogue represents itself as a spoken conversation. It seems hard to resist the thought that we are thereby invited to treat his dialogues not as writing so much as an attempt to transcend the limitations of writing. Perhaps the idea is that they can achieve the success of living speech if treated not as texts to be interpreted (despite Plato's irresistible urge to produce texts devised precisely to elicit attempts at interpretation), but as stimuli to questions we must put principally to ourselves, or as seeds which may one day grow into philosophy in our souls.

6 Early works

There is widespread scholarly agreement that the following are among Plato's earliest writings: *Apology*, *Crito*, *Ion*, *Hippias Minor*, *Laches* and *Charmides*. *Apology*, as we have noted, best fits into the context of the decade following Socrates' death, and so does *Crito*, which explores the question why he did not try to escape from the condemned cell; the others are all short treatments of questions to do with virtue and knowledge, or in the case of *Ion*, with expertise (*technē*), and all are relatively simple in literary structure. The brief *Euthyphro* and the much longer *Protagoras* and *Gorgias* (with which *Menexenus* is often associated) are usually seen as having many affinities with these, and so are put at least fairly early, although here anticipations of the style or content of the mature middle-period dialogues have also been detected. The connections in thought between *Lysis*, *Euthydemus* and *Hippias Major* and middle-period Plato may be argued to be stronger still, even though there remain clear similarities with the dialogues generally accepted as early. We do not know whether Plato wrote or published anything before Socrates' death; *Menexenus* cannot be earlier than 386 BC, *Ion* might be datable to around 394–391 BC, but otherwise we can only guess.

All those listed above fall under the commonly used description 'Socratic dialogues', because they are seen as preoccupied with the thought of the historical Socrates as Plato understood him, in contrast with writings of the middle period, where 'Socrates' often seems to become a vehicle for exploring a more wide-ranging set of ideas (see SOCRATES §2). In the Socratic dialogues discussion is confined almost exclusively to ethical questions, or problems about the scope and credentials of expertise: metaphysics and epistemology and speculation about the nature and powers of the soul are for the most part notable by their absence. Use of the elenchus is prominent in them as it is not, for example, in *Republic* (apart from book I, sometimes regarded as an early work subsequently reused as a preface to the main body of the dialogue). The hypothesis that philosophizing in this style was the hallmark of the historical Socrates is broadly consistent with what we are given to understand about him by Xenophon, Aristotle and Plato's *Apology* – which is usually thought to be particularly authoritative evidence, whether or not it is a faithful representation of what Socrates really said at his trial.

How historical the historical Socrates of the hypothesis actually is we shall never know. The conjecture that many of the Socratic dialogues are early works is likewise only a guess, which gets no secure support from stylometric evidence. None the less the story of Plato's literary and philosophical development to which it points makes such excellent sense that it has effectively driven all rival theories from the field. The placing of individual dialogues within that story remains a matter for controversy; and doubts persist over how far interpretation of Plato is illuminated or obstructed by acceptance of any developmental pattern. With these provisos, the account which follows assumes the existence of a group of early Socratic dialogues in the sense explained.

The convenience of the description 'Socratic dialogues' should not generate the expectation of a single literary or philosophical enterprise in these writings. It conceals considerable variety, for example as between works devoted to articulating and defending the philosophical life and works which problematize Socratic thought as much as they exhibit its attractions. This distinction is not an exhaustive one, but provides useful categories for thinking about some of the key productions of Plato's early period.

7 Apologetic writings

Moral, or indeed existential, choice, to use an anachronistic expression, is the insistent focus of *Apology*. God has appointed Socrates, as he represents it to his judges, to live the philosophical life, putting himself and others under constant examination. The consistency of his commitment to this mission requires him now to face death rather than abandon his practice of philosophy, as he supposes for the sake of argument the court might require him to do. For confronted with the choice between disobeying God (that is, giving up philosophy) and disobeying human dictate (that is, refusing to do so), he can only take the latter option. What governs his choice is justice:

> It is a mistake to think that a man worth anything at all should make petty calculations about the risk of living or dying. There is only one thing for him to consider when he acts: whether he is doing right or wrong, whether he is doing what a good man or a bad man would do.
>
> (*Apology* 28b)

Whether death is or is not a bad thing Socrates says he does not know. He does know that behaving wrongly and disobeying one's moral superior – whether divine or human – is bad and shameful. The demands of justice, as his conscience (or 'divine sign') interpreted them, had earlier led him to choose the life of a private citizen, conversing only with individuals, rather than the political life: for justice and survival in politics are incompatible. When he did carry out the public obligations of a citizen and temporarily held office, justice again compelled him to choose the dangerous and unpopular course of resisting a proposal that was politically expedient but contrary to the law. As for those with whom he talked philosophy, they too faced a choice: whether to make their main concern possessions and the body, or virtue and the soul; that is, what belongs to oneself, or oneself. And now the judges too must choose and determine what is just as their oath requires of them.

Crito and *Gorgias* continue the theme in different ways. *Crito* has often been found difficult to reconcile with *Apology* when it argues on various grounds (paternalistic and quasi-contractual) that citizens must always obey the law, unless they can persuade it that it is in the wrong. Hence, since the law requires that Socrates submit to the punishment prescribed by the court, he must accept the sentence of death pronounced on him. The higher authority of divine command stressed in *Apology* seems to have been forgotten. Once again, however, the whole argument turns on appeal to justice and to the choices it dictates: we must heed the truth about it, not what popular opinion says; we must decide whether or not we believe the radical Socratic proposition that retaliation against injury or injustice is never right (see SOCRATES §4). *Gorgias*, one of the longest of all the dialogues, ranges over a wide territory, but at its heart is the presentation of a choice. Socrates addresses CALLICLES, in whose rhetoric Nietzsche saw an anticipation of his ideal of the superman:

> You see that the subject of our arguments – and on what subject should a person of even small intelligence be more serious? – is this: what kind of life should we live? The life which you are now urging upon me, behaving as a *man* should: speaking in the assembly and practising rhetoric and engaging in politics in your present style? Or the life of philosophy?
>
> (*Gorgias* 500c)

The dialogue devotes enormous energy to arguing that only philosophy, not rhetoric, can equip us with a true expertise which will give us real power, that is power to achieve what we want: the real not the apparent good. Only philosophy can articulate a rational and reliable conception of happiness – which turns out to depend on justice.

8 *Laches* and *Charmides*

Contrast the works outlined in §7 with *Laches* and *Charmides*, which were very likely conceived as a pair, the one an inquiry into courage, the other into *sōphrosynē* or moderation. Both engage in fairly elaborate scene setting quite absent from *Crito* and *Gorgias*. In both there is concern with the relation between theory and practice, which is worked out more emphatically in *Laches*, more elusively in *Charmides*. For example, in *Laches* Socrates is portrayed both as master of argument about courage, and as an exemplar of the virtue in action – literally by reference to his conduct in the retreat from Delium early in the Peloponnesian War, metaphorically by his persistence in dialectic, to which his observations on the need for perseverance in inquiry draw attention.

A particularly interesting feature of these dialogues is their play with duality. Socrates confronts a *pair* of main interlocutors who clearly fulfil complementary roles. We hear first the views of the more sympathetic members of the two pairs: the general Laches, whom Socrates identifies as his partner in argument, and the young aristocrat Charmides, to whom he is attracted. Each displays behavioural traits associated with the virtue under discussion, and each initially offers a definition in behavioural terms, later revised in favour of a dispositional analysis: courage is construed as a

sort of endurance of soul, *sōphrosynē* as modesty. After these accounts are subjected to elenchus and refuted, the other members of the pairs propose intellectualist definitions: according to Nicias (also a general), courage is knowledge of what inspires fear or confidence, while Critias identifies *sōphrosynē* with self-knowledge.

Broad hints are given that the real author of these latter definitions is Socrates himself; and in *Protagoras* he is made to press Protagoras into accepting the same definition of courage. There are also hints that, as understood by their proponents here, this intellectualism is no more than sophistic cleverness, and that neither possesses the virtue he claims to understand. Both are refuted by further Socratic elenchus, and in each case the argument points to the difficulty of achieving an intellectualist account which is not effectively a definition of virtue in general as the simple knowledge of good and bad. *Laches* explicitly raises the methodological issue of whether one should try to investigate the parts of virtue in order to understand the whole or vice versa (here there are clear connections with the main argument of *Protagoras*).

Aristotle was in no doubt that Socrates 'thought all the virtues were forms of knowledge' (*Eudemian Ethics* 1216b6); and many moves in the early dialogues depend on the assumption that if you know what is good you will *be* good (see SOCRATES §5). But *Laches* and *Charmides* present this Socratic belief as problematical. Not only is there the problem of specifying a unique content for the knowledge with which any particular virtue is to be identified. There is also the difficulty that any purely intellectual specification of what a virtue is makes no reference to the dispositions Charmides and Laches mention and (like Socrates) exemplify. In raising this difficulty Plato is already adumbrating the need for a more complex moral psychology than Socrates', if only to do justice to how Socrates *lived*. If the viewpoints of Laches and Nicias are combined we are not far from the account of courage in *Republic*, as the virtue of the spirited part of the soul, which 'preserves through pains and pleasures the injunctions of reason concerning what is and is not fearful' (442b).

9 Other dialogues of inquiry

In *Protagoras* it is Socrates himself who works out and defends the theory that knowledge is sufficient for virtuous action and that different virtues are different forms of that knowledge (see ARETĒ). He does not here play the role of critic of the theory, nor are there other interlocutors who might suggest alternative perceptions: indeed Protagoras, as partner not adversary in the key argument, is represented as accepting the key premise that (as he puts it) 'wisdom and knowledge are the most powerful forces governing human affairs' (352c–d). It would be a mistake to think that Plato found one and the same view problematic when he wrote *Laches* and *Charmides* but unproblematic when he wrote *Protagoras*, and to construct a chronological hypothesis to cope with the contradiction. *Protagoras* is simply a different sort of dialogue: it displays Socratic dialectic at work from a stance of some detachment, without raising questions about it. *Protagoras* is an entirely different kind of work from *Gorgias*, too: the one all urbane sparring, the latter a deadly serious confrontation between philosophy and political ambition. *Gorgias* unquestionably attacks hedonism, *Protagoras* argues for it, to obtain a suitable premise for defending the intellectualist paradox that nobody does wrong willingly, but leaves Socrates' own commitment to the premise at best ambiguous (see SOCRATES §6). Incommensurabilities of this kind make it unwise to attempt a relative chronology of the two dialogues on the basis of apparent incompatibilities in the positions of their two Socrates.

Space does not permit discussion of *Ion*, or of *Hippias Minor*, in which Socrates is made to tease us with the paradox – derived from his equation of virtue and knowledge – that someone who *did* do wrong knowingly and intentionally would be better than someone who did it unintentionally through ignorance. Interpretation of *Euthyphro* remains irredeemably controversial. Its logical ingenuity is admired, and the dialogue is celebrated for its invention of one of the great philosophical questions about religion: either we should do right because god tells us to do so, which robs us of moral autonomy, or because it is right god tells us to do it, which makes the will of god morally redundant.

Something more needs to be said about *Lysis* and *Euthydemus* (which share a key minor character in Ctesippus, and are heavy with the same highly charged erotic atmosphere) and *Hippias Major*. They all present Socrates engaging in extended question and answer sessions, although only in *Hippias* is this an elenchus with real bite: in the other dialogues his principal interlocutors are boys with no considered positions of their own inviting refutation. All end in total failure to achieve positive results. All make great formal play with dualities of various kinds. Unusually ingenious literary devices characterize the three works, ranging from the introduction of an *alter ego* for Socrates in *Hippias* to disruption of the argument of the main dialogue by its 'framing' dialogue in *Euthydemus*, at a point where the discussion is clearly either anticipating or recalling the central books of

Republic. All seem to be principally preoccupied with dialectical method (admittedly a concern in every dialogue). Thus *Hippias* is a study in definitional procedure, applied to the case of the fine or beautiful, *Lysis* a study in thesis and antithesis paralleled in Plato's œuvre only by *Parmenides*, and *Euthydemus* an exhibition of the contrast between 'eristic', that is, purely combative sophistical argument, demonstrated by the brothers Euthydemus and Dionysodorus, and no less playful philosophical questioning that similarly but differently ties itself in knots. It is the sole member of the trio which could be said with much conviction to engage – once more quizzically – with the thought of the historical Socrates about knowledge and virtue. But its introduction of ideas from *Republic* makes it hard to rank among the early writings of Plato. Similarly, in *Lysis* and *Hippias Major* there are echoes or pre-echoes of the theory of Forms and some of the causal questions associated with it. We may conclude that these ingenious philosophical exercises – 'gymnastic' pieces, to use the vocabulary of *Parmenides* – might well belong to Plato's middle period.

10   The introduction of Platonism

Needless to say, no explicit Platonic directive survives encouraging us to read *Meno*, *Symposium* and *Phaedo* together. But there are compelling reasons for believing that Plato conceived them as a group in which *Meno* and *Symposium* prepare the way for *Phaedo*. In brief, in *Meno* Plato introduces his readers to the non-Socratic theory of the immortality of the soul and a new hypothetical method of inquiry, while *Symposium* presents for the first time the non-Socratic idea of a Platonic Form, in the context of a notion of philosophy as desire for wisdom. It is only in *Phaedo* that all these new ideas are welded together into a single complex theory incorporating epistemology, psychology, metaphysics and methodology, and constituting the distinctive philosophical position known to the world as Platonism.

Meno and *Symposium* share two features which indicate Plato's intention that they should be seen as a pair, performing the same kind of introductory functions, despite enormous differences for example in dialogue form, scale and literary complexity. First, both are heavily and specifically foreshadowed in *Protagoras*, which should accordingly be reckoned one of the latest of Plato's early writings. At the end of *Protagoras* (361c) Socrates is made to say that he would like to follow up the inconclusive conversation of the dialogue with another attempt to define what virtue is, and to consider again whether or not it can be taught. This is exactly the task undertaken in

Meno. Similarly, not only are all the *dramatis personae* of *Symposium* except Aristophanes already assembled in *Protagoras*, but at one point Socrates is represented as offering the company some marginally relevant advice on how to conduct a drinking party – which corresponds exactly to what happens at the party in *Symposium* (347c–348a).

Second, both *Meno* and *Symposium* are exceedingly careful not to make Socrates himself a committed proponent either of the immortality of the soul or of the theory of Forms. These doctrines are ascribed respectively to 'priests and priestesses' (*Meno*) and to one priestess, Diotima, in particular (*Symposium*); in *Meno* Socrates says he will not vouch for the truth of the doctrine of immortality, in *Symposium* he records Diotima's doubts as to whether he is capable of initiation into the mysteries (a metaphor also used of mathematics in *Meno*) which culminate in a vision of the Form of the Beautiful. In *Symposium* these warning signs are reinforced by the extraordinary form of the dialogue: the sequence of conversations and speeches it purports to record are nested inside a Chinese box of framing conversations, represented as occurring some years later and with participants who confess to inexact memory of what they heard.

Phaedo for its part presupposes *Meno* and *Symposium*. At 72e–73b *Meno*'s argument for the immortality of the soul is explicitly recalled, while the Form of Beauty is regularly mentioned at the head of the lists of the 'much talked about' Forms which *Phaedo* introduces from time to time (for example, 75c, 77a, 100b). It is as though Plato relies upon our memory of the much fuller characterization of what it is to be a Form supplied in *Symposium*. Unlike *Meno* and *Symposium*, *Phaedo* represents Socrates himself as committed to Platonist positions, but takes advantage of the dramatic context – a discussion with friends as he waits for the hemlock to take effect – and makes him claim prophetic knowledge for himself like a dying swan (84e–85b). The suggestion is presumably that Platonism is a natural development of Socrates' philosophy even if it goes far beyond ideas about knowledge and virtue and the imperatives of the philosophical life to which he is restricted in the early dialogues.

11   *Meno*

Meno is a dialogue of the simplest form and structure. It consists of a conversation between Socrates and Meno, a young Thessalian nobleman under the spell of the rhetorician Gorgias, interrupted only by a passage in which Socrates quizzes Meno's slave, and then later by a brief intervention in the proceedings on the part of Anytus, Meno's host and one of Socrates' accusers at his trial. The dialogue divides into three sections: an unsuccessful attempt to define what virtue is, which makes the formal requirements of a good definition its chief focus; a demonstration in the face of Meno's doubts that successful inquiry is none the less possible in principle; and an investigation into the secondary question of whether virtue can be taught, pursued initially by use of a method of hypothesis borrowed from mathematics. Although the ethical subject matter of the discussion is thoroughly Socratic, the character and extent of its preoccupation with methodology and (in the second section) epistemology and psychology are not. Nor is *Meno*'s use of mathematical procedures to cast light on philosophical method; this is not confined to the third section. Definitions of the mathematical notion of shape are used in the first section to illustrate for example the principle that a definition should be couched in terms that the interlocutor agrees are already known. And the demonstration of an elenchus with a positive outcome which occupies the second is achieved with a geometrical example.

It looks as though Plato has come to see in the analogy with mathematics hope for more constructive results in philosophy than the Socratic elenchus generally achieved in earlier dialogues. This is a moral which the second and third sections of *Meno* make particularly inviting to draw. In the second Socrates is represented as setting Meno's untutored slave boy a geometrical problem (to determine the length of the side of a square twice the size of a given square) and scrutinizing his answers by the usual elenctic method. The boy begins by thinking he has the answer. After a couple of mistaken attempts at it he is persuaded of his ignorance. So far so Socratic. But then with the help of a further construction he works out the right answer, and so achieves true opinion, which it is suggested could be converted into knowledge if he were to go through the exercise often. The tacit implication is that if elenchus can reach a successful outcome in mathematics, it ought to be capable of it in ethics too.

None the less direct engagement with the original problem of what virtue is is abandoned, and the discussion turns to the issue of its teachability, and to the method of hypothesis. Here the idea is that instead of investigating the truth of proposition p directly 'you hit upon another proposition h ('the hypothesis'), such that p is true if and only if h is true, and then investigate the truth of h, undertaking to determine what would follow (quite apart from p) if h were true and, alternatively, if it were false' (Gregory Vlastos' formulation (1991)). After illustrating this procedure with an exceedingly obscure geometrical example, Socrates makes a lucid application of it to the ethical problem before them, and offers the Socratic thesis that virtue is knowledge as the hypothesis from which the teachability of virtue can be derived. The subsequent examination of this hypothesis comes to conclusions commentators have found frustratingly ambiguous. But the survival and development of the hypothetical method in *Phaedo* and *Republic* are enough to show Plato's conviction of its philosophical potential.

The slave boy episode is originally introduced by Socrates as a proof of something much more than the possibility of successful inquiry. The suggestion is that the best explanation of that possibility is provided by the doctrine of the immortality of the soul, a Pythagorean belief which makes the first of its many appearances in Plato's dialogues in *Meno* (see Psychē; Pythagoras §2; Pythagoreanism §3). More specifically, the idea as Socrates presents it is that the soul pre-exists the body, in a condition involving conscious possession of knowledge. On entry into the body it forgets what it knows, although it retains it as latent memory. Discovery of the sort of a priori knowledge characteristic of mathematics and (as Plato supposes) ethics is a matter of recollecting latent memory. This is just what happens to the slave boy: Socrates does not impart knowledge to him; he works it out for himself by recovering it from within. Once again, although the Socrates of *Meno* does not in the end subscribe to belief in learning as recollection of innate knowledge, it is embraced without equivocation in *Phaedo*, as also in the later *Phaedrus*. But *what* exactly is recollected? *Phaedo* will say: knowledge of Forms. *Meno* by contrast offers no clues. The introduction of the theory of Forms is reserved for *Symposium*.

12 *Symposium*

Symposium has the widest appeal of all Plato's writings. No work of ancient Greek prose fiction can match its compulsive readability. Plato moves through a rich variety of registers, from knockabout comedy and literary parody to passages of disturbing fantasy or visionary elevation, culminating in a multiply paradoxical declaration of love for Socrates put in the mouth of a drunken Alcibiades. Love (*erōs*) is the theme of the succession of *encōmia* or eulogies delivered at the drinking party (*symposion*) hosted by the playwright Agathon: not sublimated 'Platonic' love between the sexes, but the homoerotic passion of a mature man for a younger or indeed a teenager. This continues until Aristophanes (one of the guests) and Socrates broaden and transform the discussion. Socrates' speech, which is a sort of anti-eulogy,

develops a general theory of desire and its relation to beauty, and it is in this context that the idea of an eternal and changeless Form makes its first unequivocal appearance in Plato's *œuvre*. Thus Plato first declares himself a metaphysician not in a work devoted to philosophical argument, but in a highly rhetorical piece of writing, albeit one in which fashionable models of rhetoric are subverted.

Love and beauty are first connected in some of the earlier *encōmia*, and notably in Agathon's claim that among the gods 'Love is the happiest of them all, for he is the most beautiful and best' (195a). This thesis is subjected to elenchus by Socrates in the one argumentative section of the dialogue. Agathon is obliged to accept that love and desire are necessarily love and desire *for something*, namely, something they are in need of. Following his concession Socrates argues that beauty is not what love possesses but precisely the thing it is in need of. This argument constitutes the key move in the philosophy of the dialogue, which Plato elaborates in various ways through the medium of Diotima, the probably fictitious priestess from whom Socrates is made to claim he learned the art of love in which he has earlier (177d) claimed expertise. First she tells a myth representing Love as the offspring of poverty and resource, and so – according to her interpretation – occupying the dissatisfied intermediate position between ignorance and wisdom which characterizes philosophy: hence presumably the explanation of Socrates' claim to be an expert in love, since the pursuit of wisdom turns out to be the truest expression of love. Then she spells out the theoretical basis for this intellectualist construction of what love is. The theory has rightly been said to combine 'a psychology that is strictly or loosely Socratic with a metaphysics that is wholly Platonic' (Price 1995).

This psychology holds that a person who desires something wants not so much the beautiful as the good, or more precisely happiness conceived as permanent possession of the good. Love is a particular species of desire, which occurs when perception of beauty makes us want to reproduce. (Socrates is made to express bafflement at this point: presumably an authorial device for indicating that Diotima's line of thought is now moving beyond anything Plato considered strictly Socratic.) Diotima goes on to explain that reproduction is the way mortal animals pursue immortality, interpreted in its turn in terms of the longing for permanent possession of good with which she has just identified desire. Other animals and many humans are content with physical reproduction, but humans are capable of *mental* creation when inspired by a beautiful body, and still more by a beautiful soul or personality. This is how the activities of poets and legislators and the virtuous are to be understood.

Perhaps Plato thought these ideas, although no longer Socratic, provided a convincing explanation of the drive which powered Socrates' philosophical activity in general, and made him spend so much time with beautiful young men in particular. However that may be, in what follows he has Diotima speak of greater mysteries which 'I do not know whether you [that is, Socrates] would be able to approach'. These are the subject of a lyrical account of how a true lover moves step by step from preoccupation with the beauty of a single beloved, to appreciating that there is one and the same beauty in all bodies and so loving them all, and then to seeing and loving beauty in souls or personalities and all manner of mental creations, until he 'turns to the great sea of beauty, and gazing upon this gives birth to many gloriously beautiful ideas and theories, in unstinting love of wisdom [that is, philosophy]' (210d). The final moment of illumination arrives when the philosopher-lover grasps the Beautiful itself, an experience described as the fulfilment of all earlier exertions. Unlike other manifestations of beauty the Form of the Beautiful is something eternal, whose beauty is not qualified in place or time or relation or respect. It is just the one sort of thing it is, all on its own, whereas other things that are subject to change and decay are beautiful by participation in the Form. Only someone who has looked upon it will be capable of giving birth not to images of virtue (presumably the ideas and theories mentioned a little earlier), but to virtue itself, and so achieving immortality so far as any human can.

It is striking that the doctrine of the immortality of the soul forms no part of Diotima's argument. If we assume the scholarly consensus that *Symposium* postdates *Meno*, this poses something of a puzzle. One solution might be to suppose that, although *Meno* presents the doctrine, Plato is himself not yet wholly convinced of its truth, and so gives it no role in his account of the desire for immortality in *Symposium*. This solution might claim support from the fact that *Phaedo* takes upon itself the task of arguing the case for the immortality of the soul much more strenuously than in *Meno*, and in particular offers a much more careful and elaborate version of the argument from recollection. Additionally or alternatively, we may note that when Plato presents the doctrine of the immortality of the soul in the dialogues, he always treats it as something requiring explicit proof, unlike the theory of Forms, which generally figures as a hypothesis recommending itself by its explanatory power or its ability to meet the requirements of Plato's epistemology. Since Diotima's discourse is not constructed as argument but as the explication of an idea, it is not the sort of context which would readily accommodate the kind of demonstration Plato apparently thought imperative for discussion of the immortality of the soul.

13 *Phaedo*

The departure point for *Phaedo*'s consideration of the fate of the soul after death is very close to that idea of love as desire for wisdom which Diotima offers at the start of her speech in *Symposium*. For Socrates starts with the pursuit of wisdom, which he claims is really a preparation for death. This is because it consists of an attempt to escape the restrictions of the body so far as is possible, and to purify the soul from preoccupation with the senses and physical desires so that it can think about truth, and in particular about the Forms, which are accessible not to sense perception but only to thought. Pure knowledge of anything would actually require complete freedom from the body. So given that death is the separation of soul from body, the wisdom philosophers desire will be attainable in full only when they are dead. Hence for a philosopher death is no evil to be feared, but something for which the whole of life has been a training. The unbearably powerful death scene at the end of the dialogue presents Socrates as someone whose serenity and cheerfulness at the end bear witness to the truth of this valuation.

Symposium implied that a long process of intellectual and emotional reorientation was required if someone was to achieve a grasp of the Form of Beauty. *Phaedo* has sometimes been thought to take a different view: interpreters may read its argument about recollecting Forms as concerned with the general activity of concept formation in which we all engage early in life. In fact the passage restricts recollection of Forms to philosophers, and suggests that the knowledge they recover is not the basic ability to deploy concepts (which Plato seems in this period to think a function of sense experience), but hard-won philosophical understanding of what it is to be beautiful or good or just. The interlocutors voice the fear that once Socrates is dead there will be nobody left in possession of that knowledge; and the claim that pure knowledge of Forms is possible only after death coheres with the *Symposium* account very well, implying as it does that the path to philosophical enlightenment is not just long but a journey which cannot be completed in this life.

The proposal that the soul continues to exist apart from the body after death is immediately challenged by Socrates' interlocutors. Much of the rest of *Phaedo* is taken up with a sequence of arguments defending that proposal and the further contention that the soul is immortal, pre-existing the body and surviving its demise for ever. The longest and most ambitious of these arguments is the last of the set. It consists in an application of the method of hypothesis, which is explained again in a more elaborate version than that presented in *Meno*. The hypothesis chosen is the theory of Forms, or rather the idea that Forms function as explanations or causes of phenomena: beautiful things are beautiful by virtue of the Beautiful, large things large by virtue of the Large, and so on. Socrates is made to represent his reliance on this apparently uninformative or 'safe and simple' notion of causation as a position he has arrived at only after earlier intellectual disappointments: first with the inadequacies of Presocratic material causes, then with the failure of Anaxagoras' promise of a teleological explanation of why things are as they are (see ANAXAGORAS §4).

He soon goes on to argue however that the hypothesis can be used to generate a more sophisticated model of causation. Instead of proposing merely that (for example) hot things are hot by virtue of the Hot, we may legitimately venture the more specific explanation: 'Hot things are hot by virtue of fire', provided that it is true that wherever fire exists, it always heats things in its vicinity, being itself hot and never cold. After elaborating this point Socrates is ready to apply the model to the case of life and soul. By parity of reasoning, we may assert that living things are alive not just in virtue of life, but in virtue of soul, given that wherever soul exists it makes things it occupies alive, being itself alive and never dead. From this assertion there appears to follow the conclusion whose derivation is the object of the exercise: if soul is always alive and never dead, it must be immortal (that is, incapable of death) and so imperishable.

Phaedo, like *Republic*, ends with a sombre myth of last judgment and reincarnation, designed primarily to drive home the moral implications of Plato's distinctive version of soul–body dualism. It reminds us of the Pythagorean origins of the doctrine of the immortality of the soul. Yet the Platonism of *Phaedo* owes a great deal also to the metaphysics of PARMENIDES. Both here and in *Symposium* the characterization of Forms as simple eternal beings, accessible only to thought, not the senses, and the contrast both dialogues make with the changing and contradictory world of phenomena, are couched in terms borrowed from Parmenides and the Eleatic tradition which he inaugurated. Platonism can accordingly be seen as the product of an attempt to understand a fundamentally Socratic conception of philosophy and the philosophical life in the light of reflection on these two powerful Presocratic tradi-

tions of thought, using the new methodological resources made available by geometry.

14 *Republic*

Republic is misleadingly titled. The Greek name of the dialogue is *Politeia*, which is the standard word for constitution or ordering of the political structure: 'political order' would give a better sense of what Plato has in mind. There is a further and deeper complication. Once you start reading the dialogue you find that it is primarily an inquiry into justice, conceived as a virtue or moral excellence of individual persons. The philosophical task it undertakes is the project of showing that justice so conceived is in the best interests of the just person, even if it brings nothing ordinarily recognizable as happiness or success, or indeed (as with the sentence of death passed on Socrates) quite the opposite. Thus *Republic* carries forward the thinking about justice begun in early dialogues such as *Apology*, *Crito* and *Gorgias*. Why, then, the title's suggestion that it is a work of political rather than moral philosophy?

One way of answering this question is to attend to the formal structure of *Republic*. After book I, an inconclusive Socratic dialogue which none the less introduces, particularly in the conversation with THRASYMACHUS, many of the themes pursued in the rest of the work, the interlocutors agree to take an indirect approach to the problem of individual justice: they will consider the nature of justice and injustice in the *polis*, that is the (city-)state, in the hope that it will provide an illuminating analogy. Books II–IV spell out the class structure required in a 'good city'. It is suggested that in such a state political justice consists in the social harmony achieved when each class (economic, military, governing) performs its own and only its own function. This model is then applied to the individual soul (see PSYCHĒ). Justice and happiness for an individual are secured when each of the parts of the soul (appetite, emotion, reason) performs the role it should in mutual harmony. In working out the idea of psychic harmony, Plato formulates a conception of the complexity of psychological motivation, and of the structure of mental conflict, which leaves the simplicities of Socratic intellectualism far behind, and one which has reminded interpreters of Freudian theory, particularly in books VIII–IX. Here he examines different forms of *un*just political order (notably oligarchy, democracy and tyranny) and corresponding conditions of order, or rather increasing *dis*order, in the soul.

Political theory therefore plays a large part in the argument of the dialogue, even though the ultimate focus is the moral health of the soul, as is confirmed by the conclusion of book IX. Socrates suggests that it may not matter whether we can actually establish a truly just political order, provided we use the idea of it as a paradigm for founding a just city within our own selves.

This account of *Republic* omits the central books V–VII. These explore the notion of political order much further than is necessary for the purposes of inquiry into individual justice. This is where Plato develops the notion of a communistic governing class, involving the recruitment of talented women as well as men, the abolition of the family, and institution of a centrally controlled eugenic breeding programme. And it is where, in order to meet the problem of how the idea of the just city he has been elaborating might ever be put into practice, he has Socrates introduce philosopher-rulers:

> Unless either philosophers rule in our cities or those whom we now call rulers and potentates engage genuinely and adequately in philosophy, and political power and philosophy coincide, there is no end, my dear Glaucon, to troubles for our cities, nor I think for the human race.
>
> (*Republic* 473c–d)

What Plato perhaps has most in mind when he makes Socrates speak of 'troubles' is as well as civil war the corruption he sees in all existing societies. As he acknowledges, this makes the emergence of an upright philosopher-ruler an improbability – and incidentally leaves highly questionable the prospects of anyone but a Socrates developing moral order within the soul when society without is infected with moral disorder.

Here we touch on another broadly political preoccupation of *Republic*, worked out at various places in the dialogue. It offers among other things a radical critique of Greek cultural norms. This is highlighted in the censorship of HOMER proposed in books II and III, and in the onslaught on the poets, particularly the dramatists, in book X, and in their expulsion from the ideal city. But these are only the more memorable episodes in a systematic attack on Greek beliefs about gods, heroes and the departed, on the ethical assumptions underlying music, dance and gymnastics (see MIMĒSIS), and again erotic courtship, and on medical and judicial practice. *Republic* substitutes its own austere state educational programme, initially focused on the training of the emotions, but subsequently (in books VI and VII) on mathematics and philosophy. Plato sees no hope for society or the human race without a wholesale reorientation, fostered by an absolute political authority, of all the ideals on which we set our hearts and minds.

Republic itself is written in such a way as to require the reader to be continually broadening perspectives on the huge range of concerns it embraces, from the banalities of its opening conversation between Socrates and the aged Cephalus to its Platonist explication of the very notion of philosophy in the epistemology and metaphysics of books V–VII. At the apex of the whole work Plato sets his presentation of the Form of the Good, as the ultimate goal of the understanding that philosophy pursues by use of the hypothetical method. The dialogue offers a symbol of its own progress in the potent symbol of the cave. We are like prisoners chained underground, who can see only shadows of images flickering on the wall. What we need is release from our mental shackles, and a conversion which will enable us gradually to clamber out into the world above and the sunlight. For then, by a sequence of painful reorientations, we may be able to grasp the Good and understand how it explains all that there is.

15 Critical dialogues

Parmenides is that rare phenomenon in philosophy: a self-critique. Plato here makes his own theory of Forms the subject of a penetrating scrutiny which today continues to command admiration for its ingenuity and insight. *Theaetetus* (datable to soon after 369 BC) also reverts to Plato's critical manner. It applies an enriched variant of the Socratic elenchus to a sequence of attempts to define knowledge. The confidence of *Phaedo* and *Republic* that Platonist philosophers are in possession of knowledge and can articulate what it consists in is nowhere in evidence, except in a rhetorical digression from the main argument. Methodological preoccupations are dominant in both works. *Parmenides* suggests that to defend the Forms against its critique, one would need to be much more practised in argument than is their proponent in this dialogue (a young Socrates fictively encountering a 65-year old Parmenides and a middle-aged Zeno). And it sets out a specimen of the sort of exercise required, running to many pages of purely abstract reasoning modelled partly on the paradoxes of ZENO OF ELEA , partly on Parmenides' deductions in the Way of Truth (see PARMENIDES §§3–8). *Theaetetus* likewise presents itself, initially more or less explicitly, later implicitly, as a model of how to go about testing a theory without sophistry and with due sympathy. While the conclusions achieved by this 'midwifery' – as Socrates here calls it – are as devastatingly negative as in the early dialogues, we learn much more philosophy along the way. Many readers find *Theaetetus* the most consistently rewarding of all the dialogues.

A sketch of the principal concerns of the two dialogues will bring out their radical character. *Parmenides* raises two main questions about Forms. First, are there Forms corresponding to every kind of predicate? Not just *one* and *large*, or *beautiful* and *just*, familiar from the middle period dialogues, but *man* and *fire*, or even *hair* and *dirt*? Socrates is represented as unclear about the issue. Second, the idea that other things we call for example 'large' or 'just' are related to the Form in question by participation is examined in a succession of arguments which seek to show that, however Forms or the participation relation are construed, logical absurdities of one kind or another result. The most intriguing of these has been known since Aristotle as the Third Man: if large things are large in virtue of something distinct from them, namely the Form of Large, then the Large itself and the other large things will be large in virtue of *another* Form of Large – and so *ad infinitum*.

Theaetetus devotes much of its space to considering the proposal that knowledge is nothing but sense perception, or rather to developing and examining two theories with which that proposal is taken to be equivalent: the view of PROTAGORAS (§3) that truth is relative, since 'man is the measure of all things', and that of Heraclitus that everything is in flux, here considered primarily in application to the nature of sense perception. The dialogue is home to some of Plato's most memorable arguments and analogies. For example, Protagoreanism is attacked by the brilliant (although perhaps flawed) self-refutation argument: if man is the measure of *all* things, then the doctrine of the relativity of truth is itself true only in so far as it is believed to be true; but since people in general believe it to be false, it must be false. The next section of *Theaetetus* worries about the coherence of the concept of false belief. Here the soul is compared to a wax tablet, with false belief construed as a mismatch between current perceptions and those inscribed on the tablet, or again to an aviary, where false belief is an unsuccessful attempt to catch the right bird (that is, piece of knowledge). In the final section the interlocutors explore the suggestion that knowledge must involve the sort of complexity that can be expressed in a *logos* or statement. Socrates' 'dream' that such knowledge must be built out of unknowable simples fascinated WITTGENSTEIN (§5), who saw in it an anticipation of the theory of his *Tractatus*.

Are we to infer that in opening or reopening questions of this kind Plato indicates that he is himself in a real quandary about knowledge and the Forms? Or is his main target philosophical complacency in his readers, as needing to be reminded that no position is worth much if it cannot be defended in strenuous argument? Certainly in the other two dialogues grouped here with *Parmenides* and *Theaetetus* the theory of Forms is again in evidence, presented as a view the author is commending to the reader's intellectual sympathies. *Cratylus* is a work whose closest philosophical connections are with *Theaetetus*, although its relative date among the dialogues is disputed. It is a pioneering debate between rival theories of what makes a word for a thing the right word for it: convention, or as Cratylus holds, a natural appropriateness – sound somehow mirroring essence (see LANGUAGE, ANCIENT PHILOSOPHY OF §2). Underlying Cratylus' position is an obscurely motivated commitment to the truth of Heracliteanism (see CRATYLUS). For present purposes what is of interest is the final page of the dialogue, which takes the theory of Forms as premise for an argument showing that the idea of an absolutely universal Heraclitean flux is unsustainable. As for *Phaedrus*, it contains one of the most elevated passages of prose about the Forms that Plato ever wrote.

The context is an exemplary rhetorical exercise in which *Symposium*'s treatment of the philosophical lover's attraction to beauty is reworked in the light of *Republic*'s tripartition of the soul. Subsequently Plato has Socrates dismiss the speech as 'play', useful only for the methodological morals about rhetorical procedure we happen to be able to derive from it – together with a preceding denunciation of love by Socrates, capping one by his interlocutor Phaedrus – if we are dialecticians. This comment has led some readers to conjecture that Phaedrus accordingly marks Plato's formal leave-taking of the theory of Forms: in retrospect he sees it more as rhetoric than as philosophy or dialectic, which will henceforward confine itself to something apparently less inspiring – the patient, thorough, comprehensive study of similarities and differences. Yet Phaedrus is pre-eminently a dialogue written not to disclose its author's mind, but to make demands on the sophisticated reader's. Perhaps Socrates' great speech on the philosophical lover is 'play' not absolutely, but only relative to the controlling and unifying preoccupation of the dialogue, which is to work through a fresh examination of rhetoric, going beyond Gorgias in explaining how it can be a genuine form of expertise, based on knowledge of truth and variously geared to the various psychological types to which oratory addresses itself. We might speculate that Plato writes the speech as he does precisely because he thinks or hopes many of his readers will be of a type persuadable to the philosophical life by its vision of the soul's desire for the Beautiful.

16 Later dialogues

The theory of Forms also figures prominently in *Timaeus*. *Timaeus* is Plato's one venture into physical theory, and appropriately has in the Italian Greek Timaeus someone other than Socrates as main speaker. It is presented as an introduction to the story of Atlantis, allegedly an island power defeated by the prehistoric Athenians, and mentioned only by Plato among classical Greek authors. The conflict between Atlantis and Athens was to be the subject of *Critias*, conceived as a dialogue that would demonstrate the political philosophy of *Republic* in practice. But *Critias* was never completed, so *Timaeus* stands as an independent work.

The argument of *Timaeus* is based on the premise that the universe is not eternal but created – although debate has raged from antiquity onwards whether this means created in time, or timelessly dependent on a first cause. From the order and beauty of the universe Plato infers a good creator or craftsman (*dēmiourgos*), working on pre-existing materials (with their own random but necessary motions) from an eternal blueprint encoding life and intelligence: namely, the Form of Animal. The greater part of *Timaeus* consists in an account of how first the universe (conceived of as a living creature), then humans are designed from the blueprint for the best. Much use is made of mathematical models, for example for the movements of the heavenly bodies and the atomistic construction of the four elements. The account is presented as inevitably only a 'likely story', incapable of the irrefutable truths of metaphysics.

There is no more austere or profound work of metaphysics in Plato's *œuvre* than *Sophist*. Like many of the post-*Republic* dialogues it is 'professional' philosophy, probably written primarily for Plato's students and associates in the Academy. The style of *Sophist* and the remaining works to be discussed is syntactically tortuous and overloaded with abstraction and periphrasis; they are altogether lacking in literary graces or dramatic properties which might commend them to a wider readership. *Sophist*'s main speaker is a stranger from Elea, symbolizing the Parmenidean provenance of the problem at the heart of the long central section of the dialogue: how is it possible to speak of what is not (see PARMENIDES §2)? This puzzle is applied for example both to the unreality of images and to falsehood, understood as what is not the case. The solution Plato offers required some revolutionary moves in philosophical logic, such as the explicit differentiation of identity from predication, and the idea that subject and predicate play different roles in the syntax of the sentence. These innovations and their bearing on analysis of the verb 'to be' have made *Sophist* the subject of some of the most challenging writing on Plato in the twentieth century.

The companion dialogue *Politicus* or *Statesman* addresses more squarely than *Republic* did the practical as distinct from the theoretical knowledge of the ideal statesman. Its contribution to this topic consists of three major claims. First is the rejection of the sovereignty of law. Plato has nothing against law as a convenient but imprecise rule of thumb in the hands of an expert statesman, provided it does not prevent him using his expertise. Making law sovereign, on the other hand, would be like preferring strict adherence to a handbook of navigation or a medical textbook to the judgment of the expert seafarer or doctor. If you have no such expert available, a constitution based on adherence to law is better than lawlessness, but that is not saying much. What law cannot do that expert rulers can and must is judge the *kairos*: discern the right and the wrong 'moment' to undertake a great enterprise of state. This proposition follows from the second of Plato's key claims, which is represented as one true of all practical arts: real expertise consists not of measuring larger and smaller, but in determining the norm between excess and defect – a notion which we ordinarily think more Aristotelian than Platonic (see ARISTOTLE §22), although it recurs in a different guise in *Philebus*. Finally, Plato thinks we shall only get our thinking straight on this as on any matter if we find the right – usually homely – model. *Statesman* makes the statesman a sort of weaver. There are two strands to the analogy. First, like weaving statesmanship calls upon many subordinate skills. Its job is not to be doing things itself, but to control all the subordinate functions of government, and by its concern for the laws and every other aspect of the city weave all together. Second, the opposing temperaments of the citizens are what most need weaving together if civil strife is to be avoided, and (as in *Republic*) expert rulers will use education and eugenics to that end.

Statesman shares themes with both *Philebus* and *Laws*. *Philebus* is the one late dialogue in which Socrates is principal speaker, as befits its ethical topic: the question whether pleasure or understanding is the good, or at least the more important ingredient in the good life. After so much insistence in middle-period dialogues on the Form as a unity distinct from the plurality of the phenomena, it comes as a shock to find Socrates stressing at the outset that there is no merit in reiterating that pleasure or understanding is a unity. The skill resides in being able to determine what and how many forms of understanding and pleasure there are. What *Philebus* goes on to offer next is a model for thinking about how any complex structure is produced, whether a piece of music or the universe itself. It requires an intelligent cause creating a mixture by imposing limit and proportion on something indeterminate. This requirement already indicates the main lines of the answer to our problem, at any rate, if it is accepted that pleasure is intrinsically indeterminate. Clearly intelligence and understanding will be shaping forces in the good life, but pleasures are only admissible if suitably controlled. At the adjudication at the end of the dialogue, this is just the result we get. The majority of the many forms of pleasure defined and examined in the course of the dialogue are rejected. They do not satisfy the criteria of measure and proportion which are the marks of the good.

17 Laws

The vast *Laws* is in its way the most extraordinary of all Plato's later writings, not for its inspiration (which flags) but for its evidence of tireless fascination with things political. Its relation to *Republic* and *Statesman* has been much debated. What is clear is that Plato is legislating – through the last eight of its twelve long books – for a second best to the ideal state and ideal statesman of *Republic*, with greater zeal than *Statesman* might have led one to expect. Is this because he has lost faith in those ideals, which still seemed alive in *Statesman* at least as ideals? That view is in danger of overlooking *Republic*'s own indication that it would be wrong to expect in practice anything but an approximation of the ideal.

Philosophers do not often read *Laws*. But book X presents Plato's natural theology, as the background to laws dealing with atheists. And perhaps the most interesting proposal in the dialogue concerns the very idea of legislation. It is the notion of a 'prelude' to a law, which is the attempt the legislator should make to *persuade* citizens of the necessity of the prescriptions of the law itself. Here is a theme which relates interestingly to conceptions of reason, necessity and persuasion found in several other dialogues, notably *Republic* and *Timaeus*.

18 Plato's influence

Plato's influence pervades much of subsequent Western literature and thought. Aristotle was among those who came to listen to him in the 'school' he founded in the Academy; and a great deal of Aristotle's work is conceived in explicit or implicit response to Plato. Other philosophical traditions flourished after Aristotle's time in the last centuries BC, and the Academy of the period read Plato through sceptical spectacles (see ARCESILAUS). But from the first century AD onwards Platonism in various forms, often syncretistic, became the dominant philosophy of the Roman Empire (see PLATONISM, EARLY AND MIDDLE), especially with the rise of Neoplatonism in late antiquity (see NEOPLATONISM). Some of the Fathers of the early Greek Church articulated their theologies in Platonist terms; and through Augustine in particular Plato shaped, for example, the Western Church's conception of time and eternity (see PATRISTIC PHILOSOPHY). A Neoplatonist version of him prevailed among the Arabs (see PLATONISM IN ISLAMIC PHILOSOPHY).

With the translation of Plato into Latin in the high Middle Ages (see PLATONISM, MEDIEVAL) and the revival of Greek studies in the Renaissance, Platonism (again in a Neoplatonic guise) once more gripped the minds of learned thinkers in the West, for example at the Medici court in fifteenth century Florence (see PLATONISM, RENAISSANCE). But none of the great philosophers of the modern era has been a Platonist, even if Plato was an important presence in the thought of a Leibniz or a Hegel or a Russell. Probably he has never been studied more intensively than in the late twentieth century. Thanks to the availability of cheap translations in every major language and to his position as the first great philosopher in the Western canon, he figures in most introductory courses offered every year to tens of thousands of students throughout the developed world.

List of works

Plato (390s–347 BC) *Platonis Opera*, ed. J. Burnet, Oxford: Clarendon Press, 1900–7, 5 vols. (The classic Oxford Classical Texts edition of the Greek text of all Plato's works, including those frequently regarded as spurious or dubious; follows the Thrasyllan organization of the corpus adopted in the manuscript tradition.)

—— (390s–347 BC) *Platonis Opera*, vol. 1, *Euthyphro, Apologia Socratis, Crito, Phaedo, Cratylus, Theaetetus, Sophistes, Politicus*, ed. E.A. Duke, W.F. Hicken, W.S.M. Nicoll, D.B. Robinson and J.C.G. Strachan, Oxford: Clarendon Press, 1995. (The first volume of a new Oxford Classical Text, designed to replace Burnet's 1900–7 edition.)

—— (390s–347 BC) *The Collected Dialogues of Plato including the Letters*, ed. E. Hamilton and H. Cairns, Princeton, NJ: Princeton University Press, 1961. (Useful one-volume collection of translations by various hands; excludes a few of the dialogues generally regarded as spurious.)

—— (390s–347 BC) *Plato: Complete Works*, ed. J.M. Cooper, Indianapolis, IN: Hackett, 1997. (The most complete one-volume collection, with translations by various hands; includes *Spuria* and *Dubia*, introductions and bibliography; many dialogues are also available separately in paperback editions.)

Any chronological order for Plato's writings is speculative. That given below reflects the view of Plato taken in this entry. The list includes all the works generally agreed to be authentic, and one or two that may be inauthentic.

c.395–387 BC

—— *Ion*, trans. and ed. T.J. Saunders, in *Plato: Early Socratic Dialogues*, Harmondsworth: Penguin, 1987. (Includes bibliography.)

—— *Hippias Minor*, trans. R. Waterfield, in T.J. Saunders (ed.) *Plato: Early Socratic Dialogues*, Harmondsworth: Penguin, 1987. (Includes bibliography.)

—— *Crito*, ed. J. Burnet, in *Plato's Euthyphro, Apology of Socrates, and Crito*, Oxford: Clarendon Press, 1924; trans. R.E. Allen, *Socrates and Legal Obligation*, Minneapolis, MN: University of Minnesota Press, 1970. (The former contains notes on the Greek text, the latter notes and essays.)

—— *Apology*, ed. J. Burnet, in *Plato's Euthyphro, Apology of Socrates, and Crito*, Oxford: Clarendon Press, 1924; trans. R.E. Allen, *Socrates and Legal Obligation*, Minneapolis, MN: University of Minnesota Press, 1970. (The former contains notes on the Greek text, the latter notes and essays.)

—— *Gorgias*, ed. E.R. Dodds, *Plato Gorgias*, Oxford: Clarendon Press, 1959; trans. T.H. Irwin, *Plato: Gorgias*, Oxford: Clarendon Press, 2nd edn, 1995; trans. R. Waterfield, *Plato Gorgias*, Oxford and New York: Oxford University Press, 1994. (A major work of scholarship, Dodds includes introduction, summaries and full commentary on the Greek text; Irwin and Waterfield include bibliographies.)

c.386–380 BC

—— *Menexenus*, trans. and ed. R.G. Bury, in *Plato: Timaeus, Critias, Cleitophon, Menexenus, Epistles*, Loeb Classical Library, Cambridge, MA: Harvard University Press and London: Heinemann, 1929. (Greek text with facing English translation.)

—— *Euthyphro*, ed. J. Burnet, in *Plato's Euthyphro, Apology of Socrates, and Crito*, Oxford: Clarendon Press, 1924; trans. R.E. Allen, *Plato's 'Euthyphro' and the Earlier Theory of Forms*, London: Routledge & Kegan Paul, 1970. (The former contains notes on the Greek text, the latter commentary and essays.)

—— *Laches*, trans. I. Lane, in T.J. Saunders (ed.)

Plato: Early Socratic Dialogues, Harmondsworth: Penguin, 1987. (Includes bibliography.)

—— *Charmides*, trans. D. Watt, in T.J. Saunders (ed.) *Plato: Early Socratic Dialogues*, Harmondsworth: Penguin, 1987. (Includes bibliography.)

—— *Protagoras*, trans. B. Jowett, revised M. Ostwald, *Plato Protagoras*, Indianapolis, IN: Bobbs-Merrill, 1956; trans. C.C.W. Taylor, *Plato: Protagoras*, Oxford: Clarendon Press, 2nd edn, 1991. (Ostwald includes a classic essay by G. Vlastos as introduction; Taylor includes notes and bibliography.)

—— *Meno*, ed. R.S. Bluck, *Plato's Meno*, Cambridge: Cambridge University Press; ed. and trans. R.W. Sharples, *Plato: Meno*, Warminster: Aris & Phillips, 1985; trans. J.M. Day, *Plato's Meno in Focus*, London and New York: Routledge, 1994. (Bluck includes introduction and commentary on the Greek text; Sharples includes notes and bibliography; Day has both introduction and bibliography as well as essays by various hands.)

—— *Symposium*, ed. R.G. Bury, *The Symposium of Plato*, Cambridge: Cambridge University Press, 2nd edn, 1932; ed. K.J. Dover, *Plato: Symposium*, Cambridge: Cambridge University Press, 1980; trans. A. Nehamas and P. Woodruff, *Plato: Symposium*, Indianapolis, IN: Hackett, 1989; trans. R. Waterfield, *Plato Symposium*, Oxford and New York: Oxford University Press, 1994. (Both Bury and Dover include introductions and notes on the Greek text; also Nehamas and Woodruff, and Waterfield, include introduction and bibliography.)

—— *Phaedo*, ed. C.J. Rowe, *Plato: Phaedo*, Cambridge: Cambridge University Press, 1995; trans. R. Hackforth, *Plato's Phaedo*, Cambridge: Cambridge University Press, 1955; trans. D. Gallop, *Plato Phaedo*, Oxford and New York: Oxford University Press, 1993. (Rowe includes introduction, notes on the Greek text and bibliography; Hackforth offers commentary; Gallop includes notes and bibliography.)

c.380–367 BC

—— *Hippias Major*, ed. D. Tarrant, *The Hippias Major attributed to Plato*, Cambridge: Cambridge University Press, 1928; trans. P. Woodruff, *Plato: Hippias Major*, Oxford: Blackwell, 1982. (The former offers Greek text with introduction and commentary; the latter includes introduction, essays and bibliography.)

—— *Republic*, ed. J. Adam, revised. D.A. Rees, *The Republic of Plato*, Cambridge: Cambridge University Press, 1963, 2 vols; trans. P. Shorey, *Plato:*

Republic, Loeb Classical Library, Cambridge, MA: Harvard University Press and London: Heinemann, 1930, 2 vols; trans. A.D. Lindsay, revised T.H. Irwin, *Plato: Republic*, London: Dent, 1992. (Adam includes Greek text with notes; the Loeb edition has Greek text with facing English version; Lindsay includes introduction and bibliography.)

—— *Cratylus*, ed. L. Méridier, *Platon: Cratyle*, Budé series, Paris: Les Belles Lettres, 3rd edn, 1961; trans. H.N. Fowler, in *Plato: Cratylus, Parmenides, Greater Hippias, Lesser Hippias*, Loeb Classical Library, Cambridge, MA: Harvard University Press and London: Heinemann, 1926. (Méridier offers Greek text with facing French translation, introduction and notes; Fowler has Greek text with facing English translation.)

—— *Euthydemus*, ed. E.H. Gifford, *The Euthydemus of Plato*, Oxford: Clarendon Press, 1905; trans. R.K. Sprague, *Plato, Euthydemus*, Indianapolis, IN: Bobbs-Merrill, 1985; trans. R. Waterfield, in T.J. Saunders (ed.) *Plato: Early Socratic Dialogues*, Harmondsworth: Penguin, 1987. (Gifford includes Greek text with notes; Sprague and Waterfield both include bibliographies.)

—— *Lysis*, trans. D. Bolotin, *Plato's Dialogue on Friendship*, Ithaca, NY: Cornell University Press, 1979; trans. D. Watt, in T.J. Saunders (ed.) *Plato: Early Socratic Dialogues*, Harmondsworth: Penguin, 1987. (Both include bibliographies.)

—— *Parmenides*, trans. F.M. Cornford, *Plato and Parmenides*, London: Routledge & Kegan Paul, 1939; trans. M.L. Gill and P. Ryan, *Plato: Parmenides*, Indianapolis, IN: Hackett, 1996. (Cornford supplies a running commentary; Gill and Ryan include substantial introductory essay and bibliography.)

—— *Theaetetus*, ed. L. Campbell, *The Theaetetus of Plato*, Oxford: Clarendon Press, 1883; trans. J.H. McDowell, *Plato: Theaetetus*, Oxford: Clarendon Press, 1973; trans. M.J. Levett, revised M. Burnyeat, *The Theaetetus of Plato*, Indianapolis, IN: Hackett, 1990. (Campbell includes Greek text and notes; Burnyeat includes bibliography and book-length introductory essay of classic status.)

c.366–360 BC

—— *Phaedrus*, ed. and trans. C.J. Rowe, *Plato: Phaedrus*, Warminster: Aris & Phillips, 1986; trans. A. Nehamas and P. Woodruff, *Plato: Phaedrus*, Indianapolis, IN: Hackett, 1995. (Both includes bibliographies; the latter also includes an introduction.)

—— *Timaeus*, ed. A. Rivaud, *Platon: Timée, Critias*, Budé series, Paris: Les Belles Lettres, 1925; trans. F.M. Cornford, *Plato's Cosmology*, London: Routledge & Kegan Paul, 1937. (The former has Greek text with facing French translation, introduction and notes; the latter includes commentary of classic status.)

—— *Critias*, ed. C. Gill, *Plato: The Atlantis Story*, Bristol: Bristol Classical Press, 1980; trans. H.D.P. Lee, *Plato: Timaeus and Critias*, Harmondsworth: Penguin, 1971. (Gill includes introduction and commentary.)

—— *Sophist*, ed. L. Campbell, *The Sophistes and Politicus of Plato*, Oxford: Clarendon, 1867; trans. F.M. Cornford, *Plato's Theory of Knowledge*, London: Routledge & Kegan Paul, 1935; trans. N.P. White, *Plato: The Sophist*, Indianapolis, IN: Hackett, 1993. (Campbell's is the classic edition, especially for the introduction on Plato's late style, and includes notes on the Greek text; White includes introduction and bibliography, Cornford a running commentary.)

—— *Statesman (Politicus)*, ed. L. Campbell, *The Sophistes and Politicus of Plato*, Oxford: Clarendon Press, 1867; trans. J.B. Skemp, *Plato: The Statesman*, London: Routledge & Kegan Paul, 1952; ed. and trans. C.J. Rowe, *Plato: Statesman*, Warminster: Aris & Phillips, 1995. (Campbell's is the classic edition, especially for the introduction on Plato's late style; Skemp offers a substantial introduction; Rowe includes bibliography and notes.)

c.360–347 BC

—— *Philebus*, ed. R.G. Bury, *The Philebus of Plato*, Cambridge: Cambridge University Press, 1897; trans. R. Hackforth, *Plato's Examination of Pleasure*, Cambridge: Cambridge University Press, 1945; trans. J.C.B. Gosling, *Plato: Philebus*, Oxford: Clarendon Press, 1975; trans. D. Frede, *Plato: Philebus*, Indianapolis, IN: Hackett, 1993. (Bury offers notes on the Greek text, Hackforth a commentary, Gosling and Frede include substantial introductions and bibliography.)

—— *Seventh Letter*, ed. R.S. Bluck, *Plato's Seventh and Eighth Letters*, Cambridge: Cambridge University Press, 1947; trans. W. Hamilton, *Plato: Phaedrus and Letters VII and VIII*, Harmondsworth: Penguin, 1973. (Bluck includes Greek text with notes.)

—— *Laws*, ed. E.B. England, *The Laws of Plato*, Manchester: Manchester University Press, 1921, 2 vols; trans. T.J. Saunders, *Plato: Laws*, Harmondsworth: Penguin, 1970. (England includes Greek text with notes; Saunders includes introduction, summaries and bibliography.)

References and further reading

Allen, R.E. (1965) *Studies in Plato's Metaphysics*, London: Routledge & Kegan Paul. (A collection of mostly seminal essays by various hands.)

* Aristoxenus (late 4th century BC) *Harmonics*, trans H.S. Macran, *The Harmonics of Aristoxenus*, Oxford: Clarendon Press, 1902. (Contains Greek text and English translation, with introduction and notes.)

Brandwood, L. (1990) *The Chronology of Plato's Dialogues*, Cambridge: Cambridge University Press. (A sober critical history of the stylometric study of Plato, including assessments of the work of Campbell and Ritter.)

Burnyeat, M.F. (1987) 'Platonism and mathematics: a prelude to discussion', in A. Graeser (ed.) *Mathematics and Metaphysics in Aristotle*, Bern and Stuttgart: Paul Haupt Verlag, 213–40. (A challenging re-evaluation of Plato's treatment of the epistemological and ontological status of mathematics, including a new approach to the 'unwritten doctrines'.)

* Campbell, L. (1867) *The Sophistes and Politicus of Plato*, Oxford: Clarendon Press. (Includes a pioneering introductory essay on Plato's late style.)

* Diogenes Laertius (*c*. early 3rd century AD) *Lives of the Philosophers*, trans. R.D. Hicks, *Diogenes Laertius: Lives of Eminent Philosophers*, Loeb Classical Library, Cambridge, MA: Harvard University Press and London: Heinemann, 1925, 2 vols. (Greek text with facing English translation; book III contains Diogenes' life of Plato.)

Friedländer, P. (1958, 1964, 1969) *Plato*, trans. H. Meyerhoff, London: Routledge & Kegan Paul, 3 vols. (An account of the dialogues particularly recommended for its treatment of the philosophical significance of their literary characteristics.)

* Gaiser, K. (1968) *Platon's ungeschriebene Lehre* (Plato's Unwritten Teaching), Stuttgart: Ernst Klett, 2nd edn. (An authoritative statement of the Tübingen interpretation of Plato.)

* —— (1980) 'Plato's enigmatic Lecture "On The Good"', *Phronesis* 25: 5–37. (A lucid restatement in English of the Tübingen interpretation.)

Grote, G. (1867) *Plato and the Other Companions of Sokrates*, London: John Murray, 2nd edn, 3 vols. (An unrivalled account of the dialogues by the greatest nineteenth-century Plato scholar.)

Grube, G. (1980) *Plato's Thought*, London: Athlone Press. (Accessible introductory account of Plato's

thought, with new introduction and bibliography by D. Zeyl.)

* Guthrie, W.K.C. (1975, 1978) *A History of Greek Philosophy*, vol. 4, *Plato, The Man and his Dialogues: Earlier Period*, vol. 5, *The Later Plato and the Academy*, Cambridge: Cambridge University Press. (The Plato volumes of the most detailed and comprehensive English-language account of Greek philosophy; indispensable for bibliography and general orientation; volume 5 includes an assessment of the Tübingen school's interpretation of Plato.)

Irwin, T.H. (1995) *Plato's Ethics*, Oxford: Oxford University Press. (A major philosophical study.)

Kahn, C.H. (1996) *Plato and The Socratic Dialogue*, Cambridge: Cambridge University Press. (An important study questioning developmental assumptions in standard accounts of the chronology of the dialogues.)

Kraut, R. (1992) *The Cambridge Companion to Plato*, Cambridge: Cambridge University Press. (Useful collection of essays by different authors on many aspects of Plato's work; includes extensive bibliography.)

* Owen, G.E.L. (1953) 'The Place of the *Timaeus* in Plato's Dialogues', *Classical Quarterly* 3: 79–95; repr. in R.E. Allen, *Studies in Plato's Metaphysics*, London: Routledge & Kegan Paul, 1965, 313–38; repr. in G.E.L. Owen, *Logic, Science and Dialectic*, London: Duckworth, 1986, 65–84. (Controversial attempt to interpret *Timaeus* as a middle-period dialogue.)

* Price, A.W. (1995) *Mental Conflict*, London: Routledge. (An exploration of the theories of mind devised by Greek philosophers to account for psychological conflict.)

Popper, K.R. (1966) *The Open Society and its Enemies*, vol. 1, *The Spell of Plato*, London: Routledge & Kegan Paul, 5th edn. (The most influential work on Plato in the twentieth century; attacks Plato's political thought as totalitarian.)

* Ritter, C. (1888) *Untersuchungen über Platon: die Echtheit und Chronologie der Platonischen Schriften* (Researches into Plato: The Authenticity and Chronology of the Platonic Writings), Stuttgart: Kohlhammer. (The best example of a sustained use of stylistic criteria to determine questions of chronology and authenticity.)

* Ross, W.D. (1951) *Plato's Theory of Ideas*, Oxford: Clarendon Press. (Particularly valuable for its review of the evidence for Plato's 'unwritten doctrines'.)

Scott, D. (1995) *Recollection and Experience: Plato's Theory of Learning and its Successors*, Cambridge: Cambridge University Press. (Important for its exegesis of Platonic 'recollection' and of the philosophical tradition it inaugurated.)

* Thesleff, H. (1982) *Studies in Platonic Chronology*, Helsinki: Societas Scientiarum Fennica. (Speculations premised on the assumption that many dialogues are revisions of earlier versions.)

Vlastos, G. (1981) *Platonic Studies*, Princeton, NJ: Princeton University Press, 2nd edn. (Penetrating essays by a leading scholar.)

* Vlastos, G. (1991) *Socrates: Ironist and Moral Philosopher*, Cambridge: Cambridge University Press. (A study of the Socrates of the early dialogues.)

MALCOLM SCHOFIELD

PLATONISM, EARLY AND MIDDLE

Platonism is the body of doctrine developed in the school founded by Plato, both before and (especially) after his death in 347 BC. The first phase, usually known as 'Early Platonism' or the 'Early Academy', ran until the 260s BC, and is represented above all by the work of Plato's first three successors, Speusippus, Xenocrates and Polemo. After an interval of nearly two centuries during which the Academy became anti-doctrinal in tendency, doctrinal Platonism re-emerged in the early first century BC with Antiochus, whose school the 'Old Academy' claimed to be a revival of authentic Platonism, although its self-presentation was largely in the terminology forged by the Stoics. The phase from Antiochus to Numenius is conventionally known as Middle Platonism, and prepared the ground for the emergence of Neoplatonism in the work of Plotinus. Its leading figures are Antiochus, Eudorus, Plutarch of Chaeronea, Atticus, Alcinous, Albinus, Calvenus Taurus and Numenius. Its influence is also visible in major contemporary thinkers like the Jewish exegete Philo of Alexandria and the doctor Galen.

Like Neoplatonism, Early and Middle Platonism were founded on a very close reading of the text of Plato, especially the Timaeus*, often facilitated by commentaries, and further supplemented by knowledge of his 'unwritten doctrines'. However, Early and Middle Platonists did not develop nearly so elaborate a metaphysics as the Neoplatonists, and there was a much greater concentration on ethics. Most Middle Platonists regarded Aristotle as an ally, and incorporated significant parts of his thought into Platonism, especially in ethics and logic. Some were Neo-Pythagorean in tendency, and most claimed in some sense to be able to trace Platonic thought back to Pythagoras.*

The Platonists developed the dualism of the One (an active, defining principle) and the Indefinite Dyad (an indeterminate, material principle), bequeathed by Plato, especially through his oral teachings. These eventually emerged as, respectively, God and matter, supplemented by the Platonic Forms, which Middle Platonists typically identified with God's thoughts. The world-soul was distinguished from the demiurge or creator, who was in turn either distinguished from or collapsed into the primary divinity, a supreme intellect. Some, notably Plutarch, postulated in addition a counterbalancing evil world-soul. As regards the human soul, Plato's division of it into a rational plus two irrational parts was maintained, along with his doctrine of transmigration. There was also an increasing focus on the intermediary role played by daemons in the functioning of the world.

*In ethics, most Middle Platonists came to effect an assimilation between Plato's and Aristotle's views. All agreed with Plato and Aristotle, against the Stoics, that as well as moral there are also non-moral goods, such as health and wealth. While there was a consensus that the latter are not necessary for happiness, some, notably Antiochus, defended the view that non-moral goods are indispensable, at least to supreme happiness. In addition, Aristotle's doctrine that virtue lies in a 'mean' became a central feature of Platonist ethics. As for the 'goal' or 'end' (*telos*) of life, this came from the first century BC onwards, perhaps starting with Eudorus, to be specified by Platonists as 'likeness to God'. Finally, the issue of determinism was, in the wake of Hellenistic philosophy, recognized as important by Middle Platonists, who defended the existence of free will.*

Platonism never developed its own logic, but adopted Peripatetic logic, including both syllogistic and the theory of categories, both of which, it was claimed, had been anticipated by Plato.

1 **Historical outline**
2 **Plato's legacy**
3 **Early Platonist metaphysics**
4 **Middle Platonist metaphysics**
5 **Psychology**
6 **Theology**
7 **Daemons**
8 **Ethics**
9 **Logic**

1 Historical outline

PLATO was succeeded in the headship of the Academy (see ACADEMY) by his nephew SPEUSIPPUS, whose most distinctive contributions to Platonism were developments of Plato's 'unwritten doctrines', based on a mathematicizing metaphysics. Speusippus' own successor, Xenocrates, did much more to further the formalization of Plato's thought into a system. He was succeeded in turn by Polemo, whose own contributions were mainly in ethics (see Ariston of Chios §2), although he is said still to have maintained the Platonic system as a whole: Polemo's contemporary Crantor was the first Platonic commentator. Soon after Polemo's death, the Academy became the sceptical 'New Academy', and remained so for nearly two centuries. Only in the early first century BC was a serious attempt made, by Antiochus of Ascalon, to recreate doctrinal Platonism under the title 'Old Academy', although his version was perceived as uncomfortably close to Stoicism. Antiochus, like most Middle Platonists in his wake (the main exceptions being Eudorus and Atticus), regarded Aristotle as himself a Platonist, whose ideas could, with some caution, be incorporated into Platonism.

Antiochus strongly rejected the claim of the sceptical Academics to be true to the Platonic tradition, although some later Platonists, notably Plutarch of Chaeronea, were prepared to accept the contribution of the New Academy to the overall development of Platonism, and to use the arguments of the New Academy (as, indeed, was Antiochus himself on occasion) to combat the Stoics. It was perhaps around this time that a tradition grew up which held that the New Academics had 'dogmatized in secret', using scepticism merely as a device for confounding their opponents, particularly the Stoics, and revealing positive Platonic doctrines to trusted disciples after years of initiation. In general, however, the scepticism of the New Academy came to be regarded as an aberration in Platonism.

The Athenian 'Academy' does not seem to have survived into the later part of the first century BC (we hear of only two other heads, the first of whom was Antiochus' brother, Aristus). Thereafter there was no central Platonic school, and the centre of activity in Platonism shifted for a while to Alexandria, where we find the shadowy figure of Eudorus propounding a more transcendental, Pythagorean-influenced Platonism. He apparently wrote a commentary on Plato's *Timaeus*, as well as a critical one on Aristotle's *Categories*. He also seems to have written on the first principles of the Pythagoreans, expounding his own doctrine in the process. Perhaps close in date to Eudorus is the anonymous commentator on Plato's *Theaetetus*, part of whose commentary survives on papyrus.

The next known representative of Platonism, in the early first century AD, is the emperor Tiberius' court philosopher Thrasyllus, who came from Alexandria, and produced what was to become the definitive edition of Plato's works (see Plato §§2–3). In addition, something can be learnt of contemporary Platonism from the works of the Jewish philosopher Philo of Alexandria. The scene then moves back to Athens, in the latter half of the first century, with Plutarch's teacher Ammonius, who was prominent in civic life there. Plutarch himself did not continue Ammonius' school – it is doubtful whether anyone did – but set up a circle of his own in his home town Chaeronea.

Plutarch is an interesting mixture of influences. On the one hand he supported an almost Persian degree of dualism in his interpretation of Plato, which involves, among other things, a literal interpretation of Plato's creation myth of the *Timaeus*, and belief in an independent, irrational world-soul. On the other he fostered a hospitality to the tradition of the New Academy, which sets him at odds with the tradition of both Antiochus and Eudorus, although this did not make him a sceptic to any serious extent. In ethics, Plutarch inclined to Aristotelian moderation rather than Stoic asceticism.

In the next generation, we find in Athens Calvenus Taurus from Beirut, who ran a school of much the same simple nature as that of Ammonius (although we cannot judge whether he is in a strict sense Ammonius' successor). Taurus was, like Plutarch, Aristotelian in his ethics, but he did not share Plutarch's views on the temporal creation of the world. He was perhaps succeeded in Athens by Atticus, who may also be the first incumbent of the Chair of Platonic Philosophy which the emperor Marcus Aurelius (§1) set up in Athens in AD 176. Atticus, however, agreed with Plutarch, against Taurus, on the question of the temporal creation of the world, and showed, in the one (polemical) work of his of which we have any fragments, a strong aversion to the Aristotelian tradition, with a corresponding hospitality to the Stoics. We know of a pupil of his, Harpocration of Argos, who seems, however, also to be influenced by the Neo-Pythagorean tradition emanating from Numenius.

Neo-Pythagoreanism is a significant force in Middle Platonism (see Neo-Pythagoreanism). Although most of its adherents wished to be regarded as a distinct sect, it seems more accurate to regard it as a phenomenon emanating from the Early Academy, and specifically from the tendency of Speusippus and Xenocrates to project their versions of Platonism back onto Pythagoras. Perhaps its most substantial figures are Moderatus of Gades, who repudiated the Platonists and claimed to be restoring the true doctrines of Pythagoras, and Numenius of Apamea (Syria), the 'grandfather' of much of Neoplatonism, noted for his knowledge of, and hospitality towards, oriental philosophical and religious systems, including Judaism. Plotinus seems more influenced by Numenius than by any other Middle Platonist.

Other influential Platonists of the second century included Gaius and his pupil Albinus, the teacher of GALEN. We also have two important handbooks of Platonism of the time: one, the *Didaskalikos* or 'Manual of Platonism' by ALCINOUS (whom scholars long wrongly identified with Albinus), the other, *On Plato and his Doctrine*, composed by the distinguished north African rhetorician APULEIUS of Madaura. Both are invaluable summaries of Platonic doctrine of the early centuries AD.

2 Plato's legacy

Plato bequeathed to his successors not so much a well-rounded and coherent philosophical system as an immensely fertile and provocative series of problems. Certainly there were distinctive doctrines that one can identify as Platonic – the theory of Forms or the doctrine of the (tri)partition of the soul – but even these, when examined, are seen to be fluid and open-ended. There was also a persistent tradition about 'unwritten doctrines' of Plato's, in particular, the derivation of everything from just two principles, the 'One' and the 'Indefinite Dyad'. Such views are better seen as working hypotheses, to be taken up and developed at will by his successors.

Plato's immediate successors were not obedient disciples, but independent thinkers who, to para-phrase the words of the most independent of them, Aristotle, 'loved Plato, but loved truth more'. Nor, so far as we can see, did Plato demand or encourage unquestioning acceptance of his beliefs. The whole rationale of composing dialogues rather than formal treatises, as well as the process of dialectic, indicates the opposite. It is in fact a profound mystery how Plato presented, or 'published', the dialogues, and what relation they were meant to have to the on-going work of the school. In the case of at least one dialogue, the *Timaeus*, one of the most influential in later times, and in view of the controversy that sprang up immediately after Plato's death as to its correct interpretation, it would seem that the master himself declined to give an authoritative exegesis of it. If, among Plato's own pupils, Aristotle could maintain that Plato taught the temporal creation of the world (*On the Heaven* I 12, II 2) while Speusippus and Xenocrates could deny this, claiming that Plato only presented such a scenario 'for instructional purposes', it cannot be the case that Plato himself made his intentions clear.

If then the dialogues are not the sole repository of Platonic doctrine, what is? There is, in fact, consider-able secondary evidence as to the views entertained by

Plato on certain basic questions. A good deal of this is preserved only in late authorities, such as the commentators on Aristotle (particularly Alexander and Simplicius) – although such information is sometimes explicitly referred back to contemporaries of Plato, such as Hermodorus. The greatest single source is however Aristotle himself, and Aristotle had been an associate of Plato's for twenty years. It has been claimed that Aristotle's reports of Platonic doctrines not present in Plato's dialogues are based on repeated misunderstandings of the content of the dialogues (Cherniss 1945); this view is too extreme, but we must always remember that Aristotle, although he doubtless knew what he was talking about in each instance, is nearly always giving a polemical and allusive, rather than a scholarly and systematic, account of what he knows. Nevertheless, by looking at his evidence with a properly critical eye, one can deduce a body of doctrine which is, in broad outline at least, coherent and reasonable, and fits in well with the developments attributed to Speusippus and Xenocrates.

3 Early Platonist metaphysics

To begin with first principles, it seems clear that Plato, in his later years at least, had become increasingly attracted by the philosophical possibilities of Pythag-oreanism: that is to say, the postulation of a math-ematical model for the world (see PYTHAGOREANISM §2). Mathematics seems to have been a discipline much worked on in the Academy, and the insights derived from this (amplified by the researches of his mathematician colleagues such as EUDOXUS, Me-naechmus and Theaetetus) drove Plato progressively to certain general conclusions. He arrived at a system which involved a pair of opposed first principles, and a triple division of levels of being, the latter doctrine giving a vital central and mediating role to the soul, both world-soul and individual soul. Reflections of these basic doctrines can be seen in such mature dialogues as the *Republic*, *Philebus*, *Timaeus* and *Laws*, but they can not be deduced from the dialogues alone.

As first principles Plato established the One and the Indefinite Dyad. The One is an active principle, imposing 'limit' (*peras*) on the limitlessness (*apeiron*) of the opposite principle. The Dyad is regarded as a sort of duality (also termed by Plato 'the great-and-small'), infinitely extensible or divisible, being simul-taneously infinitely large and infinitely small. The influence of the Dyad is to be seen all through nature in the phenomena of continuous magnitudes, and in excess and defect which have continually to be checked by the imposition of the correct measure.

This process has an ethical aspect also, since, anticipating a well-known doctrine of Aristotle, the virtues are to be seen as correct measures ('means') between extremes of excess and deficiency on a continuum (see §8).

The Indefinite Dyad is primarily the basic unlimitedness or 'otherness' on which the One acts, but it is also the irrational aspect of the soul, and again the substrate of the physical world, corresponding to Plato's 'receptacle' of becoming. Plato notoriously does not have a doctrine of 'matter' (*hylē*) as such, in the Aristotelian sense, but he does address the question of the nature of such 'substratum' as there may be to the action of the various active principles in his system, namely God, the Forms and the soul. He addresses this particularly in the *Timaeus*. For him, the 'receptacle' (*hypodochē*) or 'place' (*chōra*), introduces into the Forms, as they are projected forth from the intelligible realm through the mediation of soul, an element of indefinite multiplicity and imperfection which it is beyond the power of God to overcome completely.

By acting upon the Dyad, 'limiting' it, the One generates the Form-numbers. At this point, however, the evidence becomes confused. It seems that Plato came finally to view the Forms as numbers, or mathematical entities of some sort. A special importance is attached by him, as it was by the Pythagoreans, to the 'primal numbers', one, two, three and four, and their sum total, ten (the decad). The first four numbers seem to be in some way inherent in the One, and come to actuality in the process of the initial limitation of the Dyad. In *Metaphysics* XIII 7, Aristotle attacks the Platonist doctrine of Form-numbers, which seems to describe a process whereby numbers are generated by, first, the Dyad producing the number two, by doubling the One, and then producing other numbers by adding to two and to each successive number either the One or itself. The whole process remains obscure however, as perhaps it was in Plato's own mind. From this action of the primal numbers upon the Dyad, and its reaction on them, all other Form-numbers are generated.

These numbers are what the Platonic Forms have become. But how many of them are there? The numbers up to ten certainly hold some sort of distinctively basic position, but the multiplicity of physical phenomena requires that the basic numbers combine with each other in some way to produce compound numbers, which can stand as the formulas for physical phenomena. There must, in fact, be a hierarchy among the Forms. Within the decad, the first four numbers (the *tetraktys*) came to play a major part in Plato's cosmology, as they did in those of his successors. They are the principles providing the link between the absolute unity of the One and the three-dimensional physical multiplicity around us. These four also have a geometrical aspect, although how that is linked to their essential nature is not clear in Plato (in Speusippus' system, certainly, the geometricals are a separate level of being). None the less, one is also the point, two the line, three the plane and four the solid – the last two being triangle and pyramid respectively. (For early Platonist innovations on this scheme, see SPEUSIPPUS §2; XENOCRATES §2.)

4 Middle Platonist metaphysics

Middle Platonists were always in the position of oscillating between the poles of attraction constituted by Stoicism and Peripateticism (see STOICISM; PERIPATETICS), although they added to the mixture of these influences a strong commitment to a transcendent supreme principle, and a non-material, intelligible world apart from this one, which stands as a paradigm for it. Provided that one accepted this basic position, a fairly wide range of views on ethical, physical and logical questions was acceptable, there being no central body or institution to prescribe any strict degree of orthodoxy.

By the first century BC Platonism had established a system of three principles: God, matter and the system of Forms. The fact that the Forms were viewed as the contents of God's mind does not seem to have conflicted with their status as an independent principle, the paradigmatic cause of the world. This was presumably on the ground that the object of God's thought was also an objective reality, true being.

Throughout the Middle Platonist period, a dominant theme is the nature and activity of the supreme principle, or God. Some later Platonists preserved the opposition of the Old Academy of Monad, or One, and Dyad, although they varied the relationship that they postulated between the two: Antiochus seems simply to have accepted the Stoic pair of an active and a passive principle (the Platonic Forms being subordinated to the Stoic *logos* or cosmic 'reason' (see STOICISM §§3, 5; LOGOS §1), but Eudorus, while re-establishing the Academic and Pythagorean Monad and Dyad, placed above them both a supreme One, possibly drawing some inspiration here from the metaphysical scheme of Plato's *Philebus*. Plutarch returned to the basic duality, but he and his follower Atticus granted the Dyad rather more independence than would be traditional for Platonism, because of their commitment to a pre-cosmic 'evil', or disorderly principle. As for the Forms, Plutarch and Atticus saw them as thoughts of God, although Atticus was accused by Porphyry later of maintaining that they are outside the divine intellect, which probably only means that he wished to assert their objective reality.

For Alcinous and Apuleius, God is dominant and matter simply passive, not even attaining to actuality, while the Forms are, once again, God's thoughts. In the Neo-Pythagoreanism of Numenius, however, a radical dualism seems to be asserting itself, although partially held in check by the influence of mainstream Platonism. Since it was from Numenius more than from any other variety of Platonism that Plotinus derived his inspiration, this tendency to dualism later persisted within his thought.

It is important also to notice the remarkable system propounded by the Neo-Pythagorean Moderatus of Gades at the end of the first century AD, since it seems to anticipate to some extent Plotinus' system of *hypostases*. According to Porphyry, Moderatus attributed to Plato a system according to which 'the first One is above being and all essence, while the second One – which is the 'truly existent' and the object of intellection – is the Forms; the third, which is the realm of the soul, participates in the One and the Forms, while the lowest nature, that which comes after it, that of the sense-world, does not even participate, but receives order by reflection from those others'. Moderatus sees an appropriate level of matter manifesting itself at each of these levels.

5 Psychology

In early Platonist metaphysics, it may be only at the level of soul that the four basic numbers assume their geometrical aspect. The composition of the soul in the *Timaeus* is certainly intimately bound up with the doctrine of the four dimensions (see §3) and the relations of proportion between them. From the soul, the four dimensions are projected upon matter, in the form of combinations of basic triangles, to form the four elements, fire, air, water and earth. Thus an uncompromisingly mathematical model of the universe is laid down.

The doctrine of the soul is a central feature of Plato's system, but it is not without its obscurities. The form which the Form-numbers take on in the soul, and the manner in which they are projected upon matter, are problems to which one can find no satisfactory answer in surviving documents. These problems relate primarily to the world-soul, but the individual soul is of the same composition, although its relation to the world-soul is obscured by figurative language in the *Timaeus* (41d). (For one development of Plato's account, see XENOCRATES §2.) In the individual soul, if we may believe Aristotle (*On the Soul* I 2), the four dimensions of point, line, plane and solid correspond to four levels of cognition: intuitive knowledge (*nous*); scientific knowledge (*epistēmē*); opinion (*doxa*); and sense-perception (*aisthēsis*). This fourfold division seems to be alluded to in Plato (*Laws* X, 894a), and the Line simile of the *Republic* (VI, 509d–) may in some ways adumbrate it.

The questions of the survival of the individual soul, and of its periodic reincarnation, are not settled definitively in early Platonism. Plato certainly argues for the immortality of the soul, but does this include the two lower, irrational elements of the soul, its 'spirited' and 'appetitive' parts? These are called 'mortal' in the *Timaeus*, but the *Phaedrus* suggests on the contrary that they too might be immortal. Again, is the process of transmigration into animals to be taken seriously, as a passage in the *Phaedrus* (249b) might suggest, or can human souls only pass into other human bodies? These questions were answered variously by later Platonists. The soul is certainly the linch-pin of the universe for Plato, mediating as it does between the intelligible and sensible realms of existence, and containing in itself the elements or principles of both.

Speusippus and Xenocrates are reported to have considered the entire tripartite soul immortal, but no details of their arguments are reported. The most developed Middle Platonist descendant of their view is in chapter 25 of Alcinous' *Didaskalikos*. The discarnate soul has three parts: the 'discriminative' or 'cognitive', the 'impulsive' or 'dispositional', and the 'appropriative'. These seem to be three irreducible aspects of the soul, when viewed in dissociation from specific bodily organs. Only during incarnation do they become respectively the 'rational' (or 'calculating'), the 'spirited' and the 'appetitive' parts, harnessed to the requirements of incarnate life.

6 Theology

Part of the process of tidying up loose ends in Plato's thought which seems to have taken place in the Early Academy involved distinguishing between the Good of the *Republic* (and perhaps the 'Monad' from the 'unwritten doctrines') and the creator or 'demiurge' of the *Timaeus*. The latter could not straightforwardly be regarded as a supreme deity, since he turns to another entity, the paradigm, or 'essential living being', which is not of his making. There are thus the conditions here for a distinction between a primary and secondary God, the first totally transcendent, and no more than the ultimate condition of all being (in something of the same way as Aristotle's 'unmoved mover'), the second an active creator.

How this matter was handled in the Early Academic period is less than clear, however. Both

Speusippus and Xenocrates recognized hierarchies of being, but they do not seem to have made this particular contrast. Middle Platonism does come to recognize besides the first principles two intermediate and mediating entities which are to some extent in competition with one another: namely, the demiurge and the world-soul. If the *Timaeus* was not taken as literally creationist, the demiurge could properly disappear, and blend into the supreme divine intellect, becoming its active, causative aspect. This is the path followed in Philo of Alexandria's *On the Creation of the World* and Alcinous' *Didaskalikos* (ch. 10). For others, however, the demiurge comes to be seen as a subordinate God, sometimes, as by Atticus (fr. 8), assimilated to the Stoic *logos*, but sometimes, as by Numenius (frs 15 and 16), presented as a distinct creator-God, subordinate to a supreme, static, self-contemplating entity, derived from the Good of the *Republic*. As for the world-soul, it starts out as the entity whose creation by the demiurge is described in the *Timaeus*, but traces appear, in such thinkers as Philo and Plutarch, of a rather more august figure, which almost seems to reflect the Speusippean principle of multiplicity, a figure not positively evil, but simply responsible for multiplicity, and thus for all creation. In Philo this figure appears as *sophia*, or God's 'wisdom', an entity interchangeable with the Dyad. Elsewhere, as in Alcinous' *Didaskalikos* (chaps 10 and 14) and in Plutarch's *On the Creation of Soul in the Timaeus*, the world-soul is depicted as an irrational entity, requiring 'awakening' by God, who is the demiurgic intellect.

7 Daemons

The question of daemons, or intermediate beings, is something which Plato leaves vague, but was of considerable importance for his successors. Plato's chief exposition of the role of daemons occurs in *Symposium* (202e), where they are presented as messengers or intermediaries between gods and humans, hence themselves less than perfectly divine. Daemons of similar status occur in the myth in Plato's *Statesman*, assisting the god in his administration of the world (271d–e), and the so-called 'young gods' of the *Timaeus* (who are at least partially to be identified with the planetary and star-gods) perform similar tasks for the demiurge.

In time two theories emerged on the nature of daemons, one 'static', the other 'dynamic'. Both these theories recognize a place for 'evil' daemons, either as retributive agents of God, or as souls undergoing punishment in the universe who are filled with malice towards human beings. Xenocrates is the earliest Platonist who seems to have developed a theory of daemons: he held the 'static' view – which he expressed in geometrical terms – that they are a distinct and permanent level of being. His daemons sound like permanent fixtures in the universe, although the question of their relationship with disembodied souls is unclear in the evidence available to us. The later, alternative theory, represented by such figures as Plutarch and Apuleius, is a 'dynamic' one according to which daemons are in fact souls, on their way either up or down the scale of being towards complete purification, and thus divinization, in the sun, or conversely towards renewed embodiment on the earth (see PLUTARCH OF CHAERONEA §5).

The Middle Platonist cosmos was in fact filled with subordinate, intermediate beings, chiefly daemons, but also in later times with such entities as heroes and angels. Heroes and angels, the latter possibly non-Hellenic in origin (they are found in the Chaldaean Oracles, frs 137–8; see CHALDAEAN ORACLES), were certainly accepted by Neoplatonic times into the Platonic universe. Heroes are more respectable, but the distinction between them and daemons in the Middle Platonic period is not quite clear. The Stoic Posidonius wrote a treatise *On Heroes and Daemons*, but it is lost. One distinction might be that heroes are souls formerly embodied, but this distinction assumes a permanent class of unembodied souls, which is only acceptable on the 'static' theory. Whatever the differences in detail, however, it is common ground for all Platonists that between God and humans there must be a host of intermediaries, in order that God may not be contaminated or disturbed by too close an involvement with matter.

8 Ethics

Many of the main concerns of later Platonist ethics already appeared in the Early Academy. Definitions of happiness were produced by Speusippus, Xenocrates and Polemo. Polemo's formula, 'life in accordance with nature', made him an important forerunner of Stoicism (see STOICISM §17). At the very beginning of the Middle Platonist era, Polemo's definition of happiness, now identified formally as the 'end' or 'goal' (*telos*) of life, was revived by Antiochus. When we turn to Alexandrian Platonism, however, in the person of Eudorus, we find that the Antiochian definition, influenced as it is by Stoic thought, had been abandoned in favour of a more spiritual, perhaps more truly Platonic, ideal of 'likeness of God' (*homoiōsis theōi*), derived from a famous passage of Plato's *Theaetetus* (176b), and from the *Timaeus* (90a–d). This formula remained the distinctive Platonic definition of the *telos* ever afterward.

A second key issue was whether virtue is sufficient

for happiness. Polemo championed the view that, although virtue is sufficient for happiness, there are also non-moral goods. This goes back to Plato, and especially to his distinction in *Laws* I, 631b–c, between higher, or 'divine' goods – that is, goods of the soul, the virtues – and lower or 'human' goods – that is, goods of the body such as health or beauty, and external goods such as good fame or wealth. This passage was constantly cited in later Platonist debate. By Antiochus' time the battle lines had already been clearly drawn between the Peripatetics and the Stoics, and Platonists had to make their choice. Antiochus, although Stoicizing in so much else, sided here with the Peripatetics and the Early Academy in declaring that for complete happiness all three classes of good were required in some measure: goods of the body and external goods as well as the virtues. In this he was opposed by Eudorus, who sided with the Stoics, declaring that the two inferior classes of good could not count as an integral part of happiness, or the *telos*. This was not the end of the argument however. All through the period the two alternatives secured adherents: Plutarch and Taurus agreed with Antiochus and the Peripatos, Alcinous and Atticus with the Stoa.

A frequent further feature of Middle Platonist ethics, well represented in Apuleius and Alcinous, is the incorporation of the Aristotelian definition of virtue as based on a 'mean' (see ARISTOTLE §22). There are in fact sufficient indications that Plato (see especially *Statesman* 283e–285b) had regarded the virtues as intermediate states between the two extremes of 'too much' and 'too little', with justice (symbolized by the Pythagorean *tetraktys* (see §3)) as the force holding the universe together – a metaphysical concept as well as an ethical one.

A question with considerable consequences for ethics, although it was seen rather as a part of physics, is that of free will and necessity, with which is intertwined that of God's providence. Before Epicurus and the Stoics (Chrysippus in particular) had stated the problem of determinism in its starkest form (see EPICUREANISM §12; STOICISM §§20–1), the question had not, it seems, been one of great urgency. Plato presents it only in mythical form (*Republic* X, especially 617d–619a, *Phaedrus*), but he does, like ARISTOTLE (§20), maintain a belief in personal freedom of choice. Aristotle treats the suggestion that there is no such thing as freedom of choice as a mere sophistic paradox (*Nicomachean Ethics* III). Xenocrates did write an essay on fate (*heimarmenē*), but its contents are unknown. For the Middle Platonists, the problem of free will and necessity could not be dismissed so easily, and they found little help in Plato or Aristotle, although they did make appeal to key passages of both. Philo of Alexandria, in his *On Providence*, gives us the first defence of the Platonist position, which asserts both freedom of the will and the existence of providence with more vigour than logical force. Plutarch also touches on the theme repeatedly, although his most serious discussions of the subject have not survived: the essay *On Fate* surviving under his name is certainly not by him, though it is of great interest for Middle Platonic theory. Alcinous and Apuleius both contribute short discussions of the topic. In general, however, the Middle Platonists, while producing many scholastic formulations, fail to solve the problem, and bequeathed it in all its complexity to Plotinus.

9 Logic

In the area of logic, we must distinguish between what we can discern of genuinely Early Academic logic and what ultimately became accepted in the Platonic school, the latter being nothing less than Aristotelian logic in its entirety and including developments by Aristotle's pupils Theophrastus and Eudemus. The evidence points to Plato's having bequeathed to the Academy the system of division (*diairesis*), as first outlined in the *Phaedrus* (265d–), a system which acquired also a cosmogonic aspect. It is the soul's business to bring order out of chaos by making the right 'divisions', hitting the right means and harmonies. There is no evidence that Plato himself developed anything as elaborate as the Aristotelian syllogistic and system of categories, although Aristotle's 'ten categories' could be seen as little more than an elaboration of the two basic categories of 'absolute' (that is, substance) and 'relative' adopted by the Early Academy. Plato himself seems to have distinguished the basic categories of 'absolute' (*kath' hauto*) and 'other-relative' (*pros hetera*), the latter subdivided into 'opposite-relative' (*pros enantia*) and 'relative' proper (*pros ti*), which in its turn was divided into 'definite' and 'indefinite'. This much was reported by Plato's own pupil Hermodorus (quoted by Simplicius, *On Aristotle's Physics* 247.30–; Hermodorus, fr. 7), undoubtedly representing the practice of the Academy in his day, not the evidence of the dialogues.

In the field of logic, the primary achievement of the Middle Platonic period was to appropriate Aristotelian logic, together with the developments attributable to Theophrastus and Eudemus, for Platonism. Theophrastus and Eudemus had developed the system of hypothetical syllogisms which had been more or less ignored by Aristotle. They distinguished between 'pure' and 'mixed' hypotheticals, the latter being those adopted later by the Stoics (although the

Stoics seem to have been the first to develop a logic of propositions rather than terms) (see LOGIC, ANCIENT). In so far, then, as the Middle Platonists borrowed from Stoic logic (which they also did), they doubtless felt justified in this by finding it largely prefigured in Theophrastus. We find this synthesis exhibited in Alcinous' *Didaskalikos* (ch. 6), as well as in Apuleius' *De interpretatione* and Galen's *Introduction to Logic*. In the *Didaskalikos*, both categorical and hypothetical syllogisms are discerned in Plato's dialogues, particularly *Parmenides*. Plato is further credited there with knowledge of the ten Aristotelian categories, which Alcinous discerns once again in the *Parmenides*, while Plutarch (*On the Creation of Soul* 1023e) sees them operating in *Timaeus* (37a–b). The anonymous commentator on Plato's *Theaetetus*, who finds the categories in the *Theaetetus*, also makes extensive use of Aristotle's *Topics* as a handbook for the analysis of Platonic arguments.

Along with this tendency towards synthesis, however, there existed a tradition within the anti-Aristotelian wing of Platonism (Eudorus, Lucius, Nicostratus and Atticus), criticizing Aristotle's *Categories* (although not, it seems, the rest of his syllogistic). The anti-Aristotelians challenged Aristotle's originality (he was accused of stealing the idea of the ten categories from the Pythagorean Archytas), his completeness and the validity of some of his distinctions. Also, taking him to be making a division of reality rather than of language, they asserted that his distinctions were suitable to the sensible world but not to the intelligible.

Despite all this activity, it cannot be said that the Middle Platonists added much that is valuable to the science of logic. There are a few lost works of Plutarch, such as *A Reply to Chrysippus on the First Consequent*, *A Lecture on the Ten Categories*, *A Discourse on Hypothesis*, and *On Tautology*, which sound interesting, but there is little reason to suppose, on the basis of Plutarch's surviving works, that they contributed much of basic importance (see further PLUTARCH OF CHAERONEA §6).

See also: CALCIDIUS; CELSUS; GALEN; NEOPLATONISM §1

References and further reading

Editions of texts and fragments for individuals in the Platonic tradition – Alcinous, Antiochus, Apuleius, Calcidius, Celsus, Galen, Numenius, Philo of Alexandria, Plato, Plutarch of Chaeronea, Speusippus and Xenocrates – can be found in the entries under their names. Some others are included in the following list.

* Albinus (mid 2nd century AD) *Prologue*, ed. O. Nüsser, *Albins Prolog und die Dialogtheorie des Platonismus*, Stuttgart: Teubner, 1991. (A study of Albinus within the context of Platonist school instruction.)
* Anon. (*c.*50 BC–AD 150) *On Plato's Theaetetus*, ed. G. Bastianini and D. Sedley, *Corpus dei papiri filosofici*, part 3, Florence: Olschki, 1995, 227–562. (Partially preserved on papyrus, the earliest surviving commentary on Plato.)
* Atticus (early 2nd century AD) Fragments, in E. des Places (ed.), *Atticus, Fragments*, Paris: Les Belles Lettres, 1977. (The standard collection, with French translation and notes.)
* Calvenus Taurus (mid 2nd century AD) Fragments, in M.-L. Lakmann (ed.) *Der Platoniker Tauros in der Darstellung des Aulus Gellius* (The Platonist Tauro as presented by Aulus Gellius), Leiden and New York: Brill, 1994. (Full discussion of all references to Taurus' teaching activities.)
* Cherniss, H. (1945) *The Riddle of the Early Academy*, Berkeley and Los Angeles, CA: University of California Press. (Includes useful material on early Platonist metaphysics; over-sceptical about the 'unwritten doctrines' of Plato.)
* Crantor (early 3rd century BC) Fragments in H.-J. Mette (ed.) 'Zwei Akademiker heute: Krantor von Soloi und Arkesilaos von Pitane' (Two Academics in Contemporary Scholarship: Crantor of Solus and Arcesilaus of Pitane), *Lustrum* 26 (1984): 7–94. (With German commentary.)
Deitz, L. (1987) 'Bibliographie du platonisme impérial antérieur à Plotin' (Bibliography of imperial Platonism before Plotinus), in W. Haase (ed.) *Aufstieg und Niedergang der römischen Welt*, Berlin and New York: de Gruyter, II 36: 1, 124–82. (The fullest Middle Platonist bibliography currently available.)
Dillon, J. (1977), *The Middle Platonists*, London: Duckworth. (A full introduction to Middle Platonism; has much on Early Platonism also.)
Dodds, E.R. (1928) 'The Parmenides of Plato and the Origin of the Neoplatonic One', *Classical Quarterly* 22: 129–42. (Seminal contribution on Moderatus.)
Dörrie, H. and Baltes, M. (1987–96), *Der Platonismus in der Antike (Platonism in Antiquity)*, Stuttgart and Bad Cannstatt: Frommann-Holzboog, vols 1–4. (Monumental selection of sources with rich commentary.)
Gersh, S. (1986) *Middle Platonism and Neoplatonism, The Latin Tradition*, Notre Dame, IN: University of Notre Dame Press. (Useful accounts of Antiochus, Apuleius and Calcidius.)
Glucker, J. (1978) *Antiochus and the Late Academy*,

Göttingen: Vandenhoeck & Ruprecht. (Important rewriting of the history of the Platonic 'school'.)

* Harpocration (*c.* AD 175) ed. J. Dillon, 'Harpocration's *Commentary on Plato*: Fragments of a Middle Platonic Commentary', *California Studies in Classical Antiquity* 4 (1974): 125–46; repr. in J. Dillon (ed.) *The Golden Chain*, Aldershot: Variorum, 1990. (Collection of fragments, with translation and commentary.)

* Hermodorus (mid 4th century BC) Fragments, in M. Isnardi Parente (ed.) *Senocrate – Ermodoro, frammenti*, Naples: Bibliopolis, 1981. (Fragments with Italian translation and notes.)

Krämer, H.-J. (1967) *Der Ursprung der Geistmetaphysik* (The Origin of the Metaphysics of Mind), Amsterdam: Grüner. (Stimulating but speculative; good on Xenocrates.)

Merki, H. (1952) *Homoiōsis Theōi: Von der Platonischen Angleichung an Gott zu Gottähnlichkeit bei Gregor von Nyssa* (Likeness to God: From the Platonic Assimilation to God to Likeness to God in Gregory of Nyssa), Freiburg: Paulusverlag. (The only full-length study of the Platonist *telos*.)

Moraux, P. (1973, 1984) *Der Aristotelismus bei den Griechen* (Greek Aristotelianism), vols 1–2, Berlin and New York: de Gruyter. (Important on the Aristotelian elements in Middle Platonism.)

* Plato (mid 4th century BC) Unwritten Doctrines in K. Gaiser, *Platons ungeschriebene Lehre* (Plato's Unwritten Doctrine), Stuttgart: Klett, 1963. (The testimonia are collected at the end of the volume.)

* —— (*c.*366–360 BC) *Timaeus*, trans. F.M. Cornford, *Plato's Cosmology*, London: Routledge & Kegan Paul, 1933. (Plato's hugely influential work on cosmology.)

* Polemo (late 4th–early 3rd century BC) Fragments, ed. M. Gigante, 'Polemonis Academici Fragmenta', *Rendiconti dell'Accademia Archeologica di Napoli* 51 (1976): 91–144. (Fragments in Greek and Latin only.)

Tarrant, H. (1993) *Thrasyllan Platonism*, Ithaca, NY, and London: Cornell University Press. (A reconstruction of Thrasyllus' contribution to the Platonist tradition.)

Whittaker, J. (1987) 'Platonic Philosophy in the Early Centuries of the Empire', in W. Haase (ed.) *Aufstieg und Niedergang der römischen Welt*, Berlin and New York: de Gruyter, II 36: 1, 81–123. (A most useful survey, but somewhat concentrated on Alcinous.)

Zintzen, C. (ed.) (1981) *Der Mittelplatonismus* (Middle Platonism), Darmstadt: Wissenschaftliche Buchgesellschaft. (Reprints a number of classic papers on Middle Platonism.)

JOHN DILLON

PLATONISM IN ISLAMIC PHILOSOPHY

Plato seems to have been more an icon and an inspiration than an authentic source for Islamic philosophers. So far as is known, the only works available to them in Arabic translation were the Laws, *the* Sophist, *the* Timaeus *and the* Republic. *His name was often invoked as a sage and an exemplar of that wisdom available to humankind among the Greeks before the revelation of the Qur'an. This in itself could represent a kind of affront to orthodox Islam, which tended to view the human situation before the Qur'an's 'coming down' as one of pervasive ignorance (*jahaliyya*). However, the rise of humanist culture in Baghdad during the ninth and tenth centuries AD, which involved Syriac Christian translators, presupposed a gradual acceptance of Greek wisdom in which Plato figured paradigmatically, even though far fewer of his works were made available in translation than those of Aristotle.*

Plato's influence on Islamic philosophy can be observed most clearly in ethics and political philosophy, given the works available to Islamic thinkers. However, his role lay more in creating an environment hospitable to philosophical reflection than in contributing to the formation of specific philosophical doctrines (where the influence of Aristotle was stronger) (see ARISTOTELIANISM IN ISLAMIC PHILOSOPHY). He was referred to as 'the sublime and divine Plato', no doubt because his writings seemed to lead one more directly than any other Greek philosopher to reflect on human actions in the light of transcendent goals. At this level of inspiration, collections of sayings attributed to Plato, notably on the adverse relation of knowledge to wealth and power, helped to set a stage on which philosophy could play a propaedeutic role for Muslims seeking truth as they followed the 'straight path' laid out in the Qur'an. At the same time 'philosophy' so practised could present itself as an encompassing way of life, so competing with observant Islam. Here a discussion inspired by Plato regarding the relative weight of logic and grammar is relevant, since Arabic had tended to legislate semantic conflicts by recourse to grammar, while Greek philosophical texts (themselves originating in another language) extolled logic as a norm for rational discourse, transcending the peculiarities of a single tongue and the grammar proper to it. This potential conflict came to the fore in considering the qualities required for a just ruler of a Muslim polity, specifically regarding the relative merits of 'prophecy' (the generic Islamic term for the deliverances of revelation) and philosophical reason.

The *locus classicus* for such considerations is Plato's *Republic*, which offered an ideal paradigm for a just ruler that was adopted in lieu of Aristotle's more legislative treatment in the *Politics* – the only text of Aristotle's not translated into Arabic. Al-Farabi's treatise on the 'perfect state' (*al-Madina al-fadila* (The Virtuous City)) presents a didactic Neoplatonic version of Plato's *Republic*, one in which 'the Good' is transmuted into 'the First' in such manner that the ordering proper to cosmos and the microcosmic ideal polity emanates from the ever-fruitful One (see AL-FARABI §§2, 4). Al-Farabi states unequivocally that philosophical reason outstrips prophecy as a requisite for the wise and just ruler, but the pattern established in his treatise was able to be adapted by those who weighed their relative merits otherwise. What was severely contested, however, was the relevance of Plato's ideal scenario (or its adaptation by al-Farabi) to the actual ruling of an Islamic polity. Rulers themselves took issue with it, speaking from experience, as did intellectuals (such as AL-'AMIRI) who assimilated Plato's lofty philosophical ideals to Sufi ascetic practices. For such as these, Plato's dictum that philosophers are prevented from attaining wisdom by the mores of the city in which they live spoke more directly to their experience.

Plato's teaching on the human soul as 'an incorporeal substance that moves the body' seemed to offer a philosophical teaching conducive to Islam, even though Ibn Sina's way of adopting this teaching would put 'philosophy' in conflict with Qur'anic faith in resurrection of the body (see IBN SINA §6; AL-GHAZALI §3). Ethical thinkers like IBN MISKAWAYH adopted Plato's tripartite division of the soul, however, in elaborating an ethical teaching relating Islam to a wider humanist culture, relying on extant sayings which quoted Plato: 'whoever rules his reason is called wise; whoever rules his anger is called courageous; and whoever rules his passion is called temperate.' The influence of sayings of this sort would permit a wise ruler like Ibn al-'Amid to say that he considered himself a 'member of the following [*shi'a*] of Plato, Socrates and Aristotle'. In this manner, Plato contributed an anthropology to Islamic thought which could be used to elaborate the 'straight path' of the Qur'an as well as bring it into contact with a wider humanist civilization.

See also: ARISTOTELIANISM IN ISLAMIC PHILOSOPHY; AL-FARABI; GREEK PHILOSOPHY: IMPACT ON ISLAMIC PHILOSOPHY; NEOPLATONISM; PLATO; PLATONISM, EARLY AND MIDDLE

References and further reading

Alon, I. (1991) *Socrates in Medieval Arabic Literature*, Leiden: Brill. (Interesting account of the different ways in which the figure of Socrates was used in the history of Islamic philosophy.)

Badawi, 'A. (1968) *La transmission de la philosophie grecque au monde arabe* (The Transmission of Greek Philosophy in the Arab World), Paris: Vrin. (Detail of texts of Plato available to Arabs.)

* al-Farabi (*c.*870–950) *al-Madina al-fadila* (The Virtuous City), trans. R. Walzer, *Al-Farabi on the Perfect State*, Oxford: Clarendon Press, 1985. (Transmutation of Plato's *Republic*.)

Kraemer, J. (1979) 'Alfarabi's *Virtuous City* and Maimonides' Foundations of the Law', in M. Kister, S. Pines and S. Shaked (eds) *Studia Orientalia Memoriae D.H. Baneth Dedicata*, Jerusalem: Magnes. (Analysis of al-Farabi's transmutation of the *Republic*.)

—— (1986a) *Humanism in the Renaissance of Islam*, Leiden: Brill. (Describes the cultural revival in Baghdad during the Buyid age.)

—— (1986b) *Philosophy in the Renaissance of Islam*, Leiden: Brill. (Abu Sulayman al-Sijistani and his philosophical environment.)

* Ibn Miskawayh (940–1030) *Tadhib al-akhlaq* (Cultivation of Morals), ed. C. Zurayk, Beirut, 1967; trans. C. Zurayk, *The Refinement of Character*, Beirut, 1968. (A summary of Ibn Miskawayh's ethical system.)

Peters, F. (1996) 'The Greek and Syriac Background', in S.H. Nasr and O. Leaman (eds) *History of Islamic Philosophy*, London: Routledge, ch. 3, 40–51. (Discussion of some of the important features of Greek and Syriac culture as sources of Islamic philosophy.)

Rosenthal, F. (1940) 'On the Knowledge of Plato's Philosophy in the Islamic World', *Islamic Culture* 14: 398–402. (Traces some key sayings of Plato.)

—— (1975) *The Classical Heritage in Islam*, trans. E. and J. Marmorstein, London: Routledge. (A rich description of Plato's heritage in the Islamic world.)

Walzer, R. (1960) 'Aflatun', in *Encyclopedia of Islam*, Leiden: Brill, vol. 1: 234–5. (Survey of Platonic texts available to Arabs.)

—— (1962) 'Platonism in Islamic Philosophy', in *Greek into Arabic: Essays in Islamic Philosophy*, Columbia, SC: University of South Carolina Press. (Reprint of lecture detailing four aspects of Plato's influence.)

DAVID BURRELL

PLATONISM, MEDIEVAL

Medieval Platonism includes the medieval biographical tradition, the transmission of the dialogues, a general outlook spanning commitment to extramental ideas, intellectualism in cognition, emphasis on self-knowledge as the source of philosophizing, and employment of the dialogue form. Platonism permeated the philosophy of the Church Fathers, the writings of Anselm and Abelard, the twelfth-century renaissance, the Italian Renaissance and the northern renaissance. Indeed the mathematical treatment of nature, which inspired the birth of modern science in the works of Kepler and Galileo, stems in part from late medieval Pythagorean Platonism.

*The term 'Platonism' is of seventeenth-century origin. Medieval authors spoke not of Platonism but rather of Plato and of Platonists (*platonici*), applying the term 'Platonist' to an extreme extramental realism about universals, or a commitment to the extramental existence of the Ideas. Thus John of Salisbury characterized Bernard of Chartres as 'the foremost Platonist of our time' in regard to his theory of ideas. For Aquinas, Platonists hold an overly intellectualist account of human knowledge, ignoring the mediation of the senses. In general, medieval writers agreed with Cassiodorus' maxim, Plato theologus, Aristoteles logicus. Plato was primarily a theologian, an expert on the divine, eternal, immaterial and intelligible realm, a classifier of the orders of angelic and demonic beings, whereas Aristotle was primarily a logician and classifier of the forms of argument.*

Medieval Platonism combines elements drawn from Middle Platonism and Neoplatonism. It generally assumes a dualistic opposition of the divine and temporal worlds, with the sensible world patterned on unchanging immaterial forms, often expressed as numbers. It also affirms the soul's immortality and direct knowledge of intelligible truths, combined with a suspicion of the mortal body and a distrust of the evidence of the senses. Neoplatonists sympathized with Porphyry's aim (in his lost De harmonia Platonis et Aristotelis*) of harmonizing Plato with Aristotle. A Platonic outlook (largely inspired by the* Timaeus*) dominates the early Middle Ages from the sixth to twelfth centuries, whereas the thirteenth and fourteenth centuries, the age of scholasticism, witnessed an explosion in the knowledge of Aristotelian texts, often transmitted through Arabic intermediaries. The new interest in Aristotle was such that, although the* Timaeus *was widely lectured on during the twelfth and early thirteenth centuries, by 1255 it was no longer required reading at the University of Paris. Interest in Plato re-emerged in the Italian Renaissance with the availability of genuine works of Plato, Plotinus and*

Proclus. Nevertheless, through Pseudo-Dionysius in particular, Platonism reverberates in many thirteenth-century authors, especially in theology.

1   **Platonism and Christianity**
2   **The sources of medieval Platonism**
3   **Platonism in the debates about universals**
4   **Twelfth-century Platonism**
5   **Platonism in the thirteenth century**

1   Platonism and Christianity

Platonism's medieval popularity is related to its overall religious outlook. The early Christian Fathers, especially CLEMENT OF ALEXANDRIA, ORIGEN, Gregory of Nyssa, Basil, Ambrose and AUGUSTINE, regarded Platonism as closer to Christianity than other ancient pagan philosophies, and readily grasped it as the vehicle for articulating the Christian message (see PATRISTIC PHILOSOPHY). Plato was praised for anticipating Christianity by recognizing the existence of a unique, transcendent, benevolent deity who freely created the world. Plato also taught the doctrine of a created immortal, rational human soul, made in the image of God (*Theaetetus* 176b), and even prescribed a way of salvation. Plato was also an expert on the nature of the divine intelligences. ERIUGENA, for example, thought of Plato as one who taught the nature of the world soul and of angels (*Periphyseon* III.732d). Indeed some, such as Peter ABELARD and JOHN OF SALISBURY, even discovered hints of the Trinity in Plato (Abelard, *Theologia Christiana* I.68; John of Salisbury, *Policraticus* VII.5).

Augustine's Platonism was hugely influential on medieval philosophy, and Book VIII of his *De civitate Dei* (City of God) is a convenient source book of ancient philosophical ideas. Augustine portrays Platonism as a systematic philosophy focused on unity, truth and goodness. In his early *De vera religione* (On True Religion), Augustine claimed one need only change a few words to see how closely Plato resembled Christianity (*De vera religione* IV.7), and in *De civitate Dei*, Plato is portrayed as the philosopher closest to Christianity; for example, Plato had defined philosophy as the love of God (VIII.11). According to the *Confessiones*, Augustine's conversion to Christianity had been influenced by his reading 'books of the Platonists' (*libri platonicorum*), most likely Marius Victorinus' translations of PLOTINUS and PORPHYRY. These texts convinced Augustine that truth was incorporeal and that God was eternal, unchanging and the cause of all things, paralleling truths revealed in St Paul's epistles. Augustine was deeply influenced by the Christian Neoplatonism of Victorinus: *Confessiones* VII.11 reproduces Victorinus's doctrine of the various levels of reality (see MARIUS VICTORINUS). Also according to Augustine, Plato's understanding of God as true being mirrored the Biblical definition of God as 'I Am Who Am' (Exodus 3:14).

Among the most important Augustinian texts for medieval readers were the *De genesi ad litteram* (Literal Commentary on Genesis) and *De doctrina Christiana* (On Christian Doctrine) which provided the medieval world with a semiotics and scriptural hermeneutics, influencing Cassiodorus, Rhabanus Maurus, HUGH OF ST VICTOR, Peter LOMBARD, BONAVENTURE, GROSSETESTE and ERASMUS. *De doctrina Christiana* offered a formidable scriptural justification for Christian appropriation of pagan thought: just as the Jews fleeing captivity had borne off the spoils of the Egyptians, so too the Christians could make use of the pagan heritage to teach morality and religion. The work reiterates Ambrose's claim that Plato's wisdom came directly from the Prophet Jeremiah. Augustine later recognized that Plato lived about a century after Jeremiah, but he continued to entertain the notion that Plato could have learned about the Bible from contact with holy men in Egypt, and medieval philosophers, including Abelard and FICINO, carried on this tradition. However, the Christian Fathers often suspected Plato because of his commitment to the soul's pre-existence and transmigration, his polytheism and his silence on the incarnation (interpreted as an innocent ignorance by Petrarch and Ficino).

Platonism persisted in theological discussions on the nature of the divinity. Neoplatonic writers from Eriugena to NICHOLAS OF CUSA thought of God as both beyond being (*superessentialis*) and yet the form of all created beings (*forma omnium*). Eriugena calls God the 'form of forms' (*forma formarum*); for THIERRY OF CHARTRES, God is 'the form of being' (*forma essendi*). Following the condemnations of Amaury of Bène and DAVID OF DINANT in 1210, neo-Aristotelian philosophers criticized these formulations as leading to pantheism. Thus AQUINAS developed his distinction between the divine being and the individual being of each thing. However, both MEISTER ECKHART and Nicholas of Cusa later reapplied the formula *forma omnium* to God.

Aside from theology and cosmology, Platonism was evident in medieval epistemology, ethics and social and political thought. The Platonic emphasis on certain knowledge over opinion, on intellectual knowledge as opposed to the unreliable offerings of the senses, entered into the Middle Ages through Augustine. The Platonic doctrine of recollection continued in the Augustinian form of illuminationism (for example, in Bonaventure), whereby the mind is said to know by being illuminated from within (either by a natural or a divine light or by a combination of both) (see AUGUSTINIANISM). Plotinus' identification of evil with privation and non-being was repeated by Augustine and Aquinas. In the medieval period, Platonism in mathematics, the view that mathematical entities (such as numbers and classes) exist separately in their own right, took the form of a defence of the reality of universals as real things (*res*) against the nominalist position that universals were merely words (*voces*) (see BURIDAN, J.; UNIVERSALS).

2 The sources of medieval Platonism

Until the fifteenth century, the only Platonic texts available in the Latin west were part of the *Timaeus* (17a–53b) and, from the mid-twelfth century, the *Meno* and *Phaedo*. Medieval Platonism was largely indirect, filtered through the writings of the Christian Fathers, especially Augustine. Gregory of Nyssa's Platonism influenced Eriugena. Aspects of Platonism (for example, the theory of ideas) were also transmitted through Latin writers including CICERO, SENECA, Martianus Capella, Aulus Gellius, Macrobius, BOETHIUS, Cassiodorus and Isidore (see ENCYCLOPEDISTS, MEDIEVAL). Medieval discussions of Platonic ideas were based not on Platonic dialogues (for example, Aquinas shows no evidence of having read the *Meno*), but primarily on Augustine's discussion of ideas in his *De diversis quaestionibus LXXXIII* (On Eighty-Three Different Questions), Question 46, which itself drew on Cicero's *Academics* I.19. For Augustine, the Platonic Ideas (*ideae*) were really divine paradigms in the mind of God. Augustine distinguished the divine ideas from the *logoi* or *rationes* of things, created forms which guaranteed the continuity of the species through time, a version of the Stoic seminal reasons discussed chiefly in his *De genesi ad litteram*. Similarly, medieval people learned of Platonic arguments for the immortality of the soul from Cicero's *Tusculan Disputations*.

The *Timaeus* was the only Platonic dialogue widely circulating through the whole medieval period, available in the fourth-century Latin translation of CALCIDIUS. Cicero's earlier translation (*De universo*) was almost unknown in the early Middle Ages (although Augustine expressly cites it in *De civitate Dei* XIII.16). Also in wide circulation in the Middle Ages was Calcidius' extensive, eclectic *Commentary on the Timaeus*, mingling elements of Middle Platonism (inspired by NUMENIUS) and Porphyrian Neoplatonism. It popularized a Middle Platonist view of Plato for the Middle Ages, in which the cosmos is constructed from three principles: God (*deus*), form (*exemplum*) and matter (*silva*). The first principle,

God, is the Supreme Good, cause of all and end of all, beyond substance and nature and above all intellect. God is also characterized as free will and as providence. The second principle is matter, understood as neither sensible nor intelligible, lacking all form. The divine mind informs matter as soul vivifies body. The third principle is form, the intelligible world of the Ideas, understood as God's thoughts. The world soul, understood as made by God, is a kind of second mind. Calcidius was frequently glossed in the twelfth century in particular; of interest to medieval writers was his discussion of the four elements and his number speculation. Interest in numbers was justified by Scripture, and buttressed by Augustine in *De musica* and by Boethius' *De arithmetica*, and by other texts that communicated Pythagorean Platonism to the West (for example, Martianus Capella's *De nuptiis Philologiae et Mercurii* (The Marriage of Philology and Mercury)). Calcidius' *Commentary* includes references to the argument in *Phaedrus* that the soul is self-moving, the comparison in *Theaetetus* of the mind with a wax tablet and the *Republic*'s comparison of the Form of the Good with the sun.

Macrobius' *Commentarius in somnium Scipionis* (Commentary on the Dream of Scipio) was another influential source of Porphyrian Neoplatonism, especially important for twelfth-century philosophers such as WILLIAM OF CONCHES. Macrobius focuses on the final section of Cicero's *On the Republic*, his version of Plato's *Republic*, which is known as 'Scipio's Dream' (*somnium Scipionis*). Here a dream is recounted which is reminiscent of the Myth of Er, providing an account of the destiny of human souls emphasizing the need to live a life of virtue and hold the body in contempt. Macrobius' allegorical interpretation offers a typically Neoplatonic cosmology including the three hypostases, One, Mind and Soul. The account of the world soul includes a discussion of the nature of the self-mover. Macrobius gives an account of the procession of the soul from God down through the Homeric 'golden chain' of beings (see ENCYCLOPEDISTS, MEDIEVAL §3). Martianus Capella's fourth-century allegorical compendium of the Liberal Arts, the *De nuptiis Philologiae et Mercurii*, also conveyed Platonic sentiments (see ENCYCLOPEDISTS, MEDIEVAL §4), as did Cassiodorus' *Institutiones* (Institutions) and Isidore of Seville's *Etymologiae* (Etymologies) (see ENCYCLOPEDISTS, MEDIEVAL §§6–7). These works were influential from the ninth century to the twelfth century in particular.

The most influential work of BOETHIUS was his *De consolatione philosophiae* (Consolation of Philosophy), which transmitted a Stoicized Platonism to the medieval world. This work presents the Platonic view that the soul can become forgetful of itself through immersion in the affairs of the body, but that it can recover its essential rational nature and attain to the vision of God. Several poems in the *De consolatione philosophiae* transmit in condensed form a Platonic cosmology, especially III metrum 9, '*O qui perpetua mundum ratione gubernas*' (You, who in perpetual order, govern the universe), which was widely commented on from the ninth century onwards (for example, by Remigius of Auxerre).

Also from the ninth century, medieval authors were exposed to another blend of Platonism deriving from PROCLUS and emphasizing the transcendence of the divine, to the extent that the divine is better described as non-being than as being. These Christian texts, purporting to be written by Dionysius, St Paul's convert at Athens, and thus as ancient and authentic as the Gospels themselves, were in reality pious forgeries produced by a sixth-century Christian follower of Proclus. Pseudo-Dionysius' *De divinis nominibus* (The Divine Names) examines scriptural and philosophical appellations for the divine and argues that they all fail to fully express the nature of the highest being, who is nameless and beyond all names. Names are really processions from the divinity and do not reach the divinity itself. Negations, in fact, express the nature of the divine more accurately than affirmations. This theme is expressed even more radically in the *De mystica theologia* (Mystical Theology), which had enormous influence on the later medieval mystical tradition, transmitting to the Latin West the Platonism of the *Parmenides* in the form of negative theology. Pseudo-Dionysius had an enormous influence on ALBERT THE GREAT, AQUINAS, BONAVENTURE and GROSSETESTE among others, particularly through his concept of the self-diffusion of the good (*bonum diffusivum sui*), his principle that all things have being through being one, and his notion that the being of all things is the 'above being' of the divinity (*esse omnium est superesse divinitatis*) (see PSEUDO-DIONYSIUS).

Both Boethius and Pseudo-Dionysius contributed to the development of medieval Platonism by continuing to emphasize the primacy, transcendence and unspeakability of the one, good God. Pseudo-Dionysius, however, following Proclus, formalized the system of hierarchical levels postulated to exist between the divine One and the formless nothing, chiefly in two books: *De coelesti hierarchia* (The Celestial Hierarchy) and *De ecclesiastica hierarchia* (The Ecclesiastical Hierarchy). Influenced by Pseudo-Dionysius' Proclean formulations, medieval Platonists thought of reality as a series of ontological levels which proceed from the One right down to the nebulous realm of formless matter.

Johannes Scottus ERIUGENA, an Irishman who

resided at the Carolingian court, produced in the ninth century the first synthesis of the Platonism of Augustine and Pseudo-Dionysius. Eriugena's Platonism is indirect, through Greek Christian Platonists, Basil and Gregory of Nyssa as well as Pseudo-Dionysius. Though aware of the theological differences between the Augustinian and Dionysian traditions, he regarded them as different expressions of the one truth. Eriugena's dialogue *Periphyseon* (On the Division of Nature) developed a Neoplatonic cosmological system which synthesized Dionysian and Augustinian Platonism. All things proceed from and return to the One in an eternal cosmic cycle (*exitus–reditus*), which is at the same time God's self-articulation. The spatio-temporal world which appears solid and corporeal is really an incorporeal world of qualities which emanates from the primordial causes, which are eternal but created ideas in the mind of God. Eriugena boldly identifies Augustine's primary causes with Pseudo-Dionysius' divine willings, thus synthesizing eastern and western interpretations of the Platonic ideas.

All things must return to their source, and the divine ideas will be reunited in God. Human souls are originally one with the One, but in their outgoing they become shrouded in appearances, generating the corporeal body. Each will also return to be one in the Logos, though each soul will remain at the level dictated by the level of its intellectual contemplation. Eriugena follows Gregory of Nyssa in claiming that corporeal body is merely an illusion produced by the commingling of incorporeal qualities, and that the division of the sexes is a consequence of the Fall. The unformed matter from which God creates is really God's own hidden, transcendent nature. Although Eriugena refers to the world soul (*Periphyseon* I.476c), drawing on Macrobius and Virgil, it does not play a significant part in his system but perhaps is to be identified with the Holy Spirit, as in later twelfth-century Platonism.

3 Platonism in the debates about universals

The medieval debate over the ontological status of universals (signified by general terms such as 'animal' or 'man') re-enacts the dispute between PLATO and ARISTOTLE over the nature of forms. This problem emerges in Porphyry's *Isagōgē* (Introduction) where, introducing Aristotle's *Categories*, he raises a number of questions while commenting on Aristotle's *De interpretatione (Peri hermeneias)* I 16a 3–18, including whether universals had real existence or were only creations in the mind; if they were real, whether they were corporeal or incorporeal; and if incorporeal, whether they existed apart from sensible things or

were contained in them (see PORPHYRY). BOETHIUS, in his commentaries on Porphyry, suggested an answer to the question which attempted to reconcile Plato with Aristotle. For Boethius, following Aristotle, a universal is by its nature predicable of many things, and hence is not an individual and cannot be a sensible substance. However, neither is it a merely empty category since it is indeed the thought of something. The species is the result of the mind's abstracting from what is given in the senses. The universal is in itself immaterial, but it subsists in material beings and does not exist apart from things, as Plato thought (see UNIVERSALS).

Medieval interpretations of Boethius led to the dispute between nominalism (identified with Roscelin of Compiègne) and realism (identified with William of Champeaux and Bernard of Chartres). William of Champeaux, a teacher at the Cathedral School of Notre-Dame in Paris, known chiefly through his student and critic Peter Abelard, was an extreme realist. According to John of Salisbury, Bernard of Chartres was also a Platonist about universals, holding that aside from the ideas in God there were created forms (*formae nativae*) that existed apart from God and from the mind (Dutton 1991: 70–96). According to Abelard, WILLIAM OF CHAMPEAUX held the view that a universal exists in common in each of the instances; thus man exists identically in Socrates and in Plato. In order to be identical in each instance, it must be identical in itself and to a thing existing apart. Roscelin, on the other hand, maintained that universals were mere names, utterances, 'vocal breath' (*flatus vocis*) as Anselm termed them (see ROSCELIN OF COMPIÈGNE).

Peter ABELARD, who had been taught by both Roscelin and William, attempted to mediate between these extremes, especially in his *Logica ingredientibus* (Logic for Beginners). Abelard, who regarded Plato as the 'greatest of philosophers' (*maximus philosophorum*), held a modified Platonism about universals, whereby the universals are held to be forms existing in the mind of God (*conceptio Dei*). He ridiculed the nominalist position that species were merely words, but he was also critical of the view that species were things. Species were predicated of things, and only words, not things, can be predicated of things. The problem is to decide what ontological status these *predicamenta* (substantial categories) have. For Abelard, a thing is always concrete and individual. When several things, such as humans, share a common nature, what they share is 'being human' (*esse hominem*). This is not itself a thing but neither is it merely a name; it is a concept founded in the thing but not existing in the same mode as the thing. Abelard's interest is in the meaning which is expressed by a proposition, the *dictum* (what is said), which is neither identical with the words nor with the thing but is something intermediate.

4 Twelfth-century Platonism

In the eleventh century, Platonism, mediated through Augustine's works, is evident in ANSELM, most notably in the *Monologion* and particularly in this work's acceptance of the existence of the forms and the self-existent highest good. The twelfth century saw a Platonic renaissance, centred mainly in the cathedral schools of Chartres and St Victor (see CHARTRES, SCHOOL OF; HUGH OF ST VICTOR), and was characterized by cosmological speculation inspired by the *Timaeus*, combined with Boethius, Macrobius and Martianus Capella. The challenge was to produce a complete scientific picture in conformity with Genesis from the fragment of Plato's natural philosophy which was known.

From Philo and the Middle Platonists onwards, the parallels between Plato's cosmology in the *Timaeus* and the account of creation in Genesis provided the opportunity for Platonic commentaries on the work of the six days (the *Hexaemera*). *Timaeus* 41c was interpreted as teaching that the world is created by the will of God who is 'Father of all'. ABELARD deduced from the *Timaeus* that God – the most perfect being – had created the most perfect world, a doctrine which was revived by LEIBNIZ in the seventeenth century. For twelfth-century authors, Plato's literary method of exposition was similar to Christian parable; Plato taught using fables and symbols (*integumenta*, or 'coverings') which the commentator must interpret.

Using Calcidius' commentary on the *Timaeus* (see §2), twelfth-century Platonists developed an account of the world in terms of the four elements and in terms of complex number symbolism. Among commentators on the *Timaeus*, perhaps the most Platonic were Bernard of Chartres, Thierry of Chartres and William of Conches. These writers stress the relation between macrocosm and microcosm, and harmony between the divine and created spheres. WILLIAM OF CONCHES, who probably taught at Chartres, is the most important of the twelfth-century Platonists, and his *Timaeus* commentary is the most extensive medieval commentary on that dialogue. For William, the *Timaeus* is a unified theological work displaying the beneficence of the creator. He also commented on Boethius' *De consolatione philosophiae* and on Macrobius, as well as composing two systematic works, *Philosophia mundi* and a revised version entitled the *Dragmaticon*, set in the form of a dialogue between the Duke of Normandy and the Philosopher. Many Pythagorean

elements and much number symbolism was associated with the articulation of cosmology in the twelfth century. THIERRY OF CHARTRES in his *De sex dierum operibus* (Concerning the Works of the Six Days) sees creation as an articulation of unity into plurality, following the suggestion of CALCIDIUS.

William, also following Calcidius, sees the *Timaeus* as a work of natural justice showing how God creates and governs the world. God has established an unvarying natural law which is discoverable at the heart of things. For him, God creates the intellectual realm and allows other causes (such as stars) to govern the lower world, thus proposing a doctrine of mediated creation at variance with Augustine's single-act view (see NATURAL PHILOSOPHY, MEDIEVAL). The Chartres school followed Bernard of Chartres in positing a level of created forms between God and sensible reality, influenced by Eriugena's primordial causes and Augustine's seminal reasons (see §2). Seeking to reconcile Plato and Aristotle, as John of Salisbury reports, Bernard of Chartres posited intermediaries between God and created things. These native forms (*formae nativae*) link the eternal archetypes to passive matter (*hyle*) (see CHARTRES, SCHOOL OF).

William's account of creation discusses the role of the four elements in detail. Like others (for example, Adelard of Bath), William saw himself as expanding on the teaching of Plato: 'It is not my intention to expound here the words of Plato, but to set down here the view of natural scientists [*physici*] concerning substances; but even if I have not expounded Plato's words, I have said all that he said about elements, and more' (*Dragmaticon*, quoted in Dronke 1988: 309). He attempts to define the elements and addresses the question as to whether they are perceptible by the senses and corporeal and whether the division of matter ends with these indivisibles (atoms). William takes the view that the four elements are corporeal, unchanging substances which, however, are only found in combination. The elements then are corporeal but are actually grasped by intellect since they are too small to be perceived by the senses on their own. Though they are unchangeable, they are created. God first made the four elements from nothing and then everything else out of the four elements, except the soul of man, which God made directly.

A major challenge to Christianizing Plato's cosmology was to interpret the role played by the Platonic Demiurge (see PLATO §16). Christian Platonists were initially quick to identify the Demiurge with the Logos, the Second Person of the Trinity. This allowed them to make a further identification between the Holy Spirit and the world soul (*anima mundi*), which in the *Timaeus* enlivens the material cosmos. William of Conches initially, in his commentary on Macrobius, quite boldly identified the world soul of the *Timaeus* with the Holy Spirit, as Abelard was alleged to have done. The Council of Sens had condemned the identification, attributing it to Abelard. William then appears to have grown more cautious, simply offering a number of different views in his *Philosophia* Book One (the world soul is the Holy Spirit, or a natural force implanted in things by God, or a certain incorporeal substance in bodies) and making no reference to the world soul in his *Dragmaticon*.

Bernard Silvestris, in his partly versified, allegorical account of the creation, the *Cosmographia*, makes use of many Platonic ideas from the *Timaeus*, including that of a world soul personified as Endelichia (who also appears in Martianus Capella and Cicero), but in a manner quite different from William of Conches. Bernard has a world of ideas (Noys) and a domain of unformed matter (personified as Silva – Calcidius' term for 'matter'). Gradually Noys imposes order on Silva until the whole world has been made. The sensible world imitates the intelligible; man is a microcosm of the macrocosm. Bernard also saw Plato as beginning with two principles: *unitas et diversum*, unity and diversity (see BERNARD OF TOURS). William of Conches explicitly connects Plato with Pythagoras, and argues that since number possesses the highest perfection, nothing can exist without number. Another Platonic cosmology in versified form was Alan of Lille's *De planctu naturae* (The Lament of Nature), a dialogue between the poet and Nature, which was influenced by Bernard Silvestris.

5 Platonism in the thirteenth century

Thirteenth-century knowledge of Plato drew on the usual sources in Augustine and Latin writers, but also gained new insights into Plato from criticisms contained in the rediscovered works of Aristotle and his Arabic commentators, especially Averroes (see IBN RUSHD). Rather stiff literal translations of the *Meno* and *Phaedo* were produced by Henricus Aristippus in the 1150s; although listed in the library of the Sorbonne after 1271, these texts were not much studied and had little influence. Similarly, William of Moerbeke's translation of part of the *Parmenides* with Proclus' commentary also had little influence until popularized by Nicholas of Cusa. Moerbeke also translated Proclus' *Elements of Theology* which was available to Thomas Aquinas. Moerbeke's follower, the Flemish encyclopedist Henry Bate, was one of the first to be able to discern the difference between Plato's own texts and the later Platonism of Proclus.

In general, however, Platonism in the thirteenth century survived mainly in the universities' theology faculties, as the arts faculty syllabuses were gradually reorganized to accommodate the new Aristotelianism.

One of the most influential texts for thirteenth-century philosophers was the *Sentences* of Peter LOMBARD. Lombard stated that Plato had three principles to explain the cosmos: matter, forms and the divine artificer, whereas Aristotle had only two: matter and species. This passage was regularly commented on to clarify whether Plato and Aristotle accepted the doctrine of creation, and whether they thought that creation was compatible with the beginninglessness of the world (as Aquinas held). In his commentary on the *Sentences*, ALBERT THE GREAT acknowledged that Plato had posited a world of forms that existed independently of the mind of God. Albert's outlook was strongly influenced by Neoplatonism and no doubt helped to shape the Platonism in the thought of his student, Thomas Aquinas.

Though AQUINAS is the great exponent of the new Aristotelianism, adopting Aristotle's criticisms of the univocal understanding of the good in Plato and other criticisms of the existence of the Ideas, yet he remains quite Platonic in other domains, for example, in his account of participation (how created things participate in being and receive the gift of *esse* from the divine being) which was strongly influenced by Pseudo-Dionysius. Aquinas sides with Aristotle against Platonism, which he sees as a doctrine that overstressed the mind's intellectual capacities, claiming that humans could know immaterial forms directly without mediation of the senses. In *Summa contra gentiles* I.13.10, in his discussion of the argument for the existence of God from motion, Aquinas explicitly discusses the difference between the Platonic and Aristotelian conceptions of the nature of motion, drawing on *Phaedrus* 245c. His source, however, is not directly Plato but more probably the tradition stemming from Calcidius and Macrobius.

Robert GROSSETESTE translated and commented on Pseudo-Dionysius. His *De luce* (On Light) offers a typically Neoplatonic cosmology and metaphysics of light. Grosseteste's account of the soul weds Aristotelian naturalism with a Neoplatonic account of the higher principles of intellect and reason.

Platonism in the thirteenth century is often associated with members of the Franciscan order and with a mathematical approach to the understanding of nature. RICHARD RUFUS OF CORNWALL defended Plato's theory of ideas against Aristotle's criticisms, and Bonaventure's *Itinerarium mentis in Deum* (Journey of the Mind to God) is thoroughly Platonic (see BONAVENTURE). Bonaventure accepted a form of Augustinian illuminationism, a Christianized version of Platonic recollection (see AUGUSTINIANISM). For Bonaventure, sensible things are traces of divine things. In typically Platonic terms, Bonaventure's sixth step in the mind's advancement towards God refers to the Good beyond being.

The later thirteenth century saw a re-emergence of an Averroist Platonism, particularly with regard to the knowledge of separate substances. SIGER OF BRABANT, for example, took a more Platonic line than Aquinas had done in arguing for the soul's direct knowledge of separate intelligible substances. Henry of Ghent's doctrine of the separate being of essences (*esse essentiae*) was also considered Platonist (see HENRY OF GHENT). Meister Eckhart held Neoplatonic, Proclean-inspired theories of the nature of the soul, and his affirmation of an uncreated part of the soul parallels the doctrine of the undescended part of the soul in pagan Neoplatonism (see NEOPLATONISM). The German Dominican writers DIETRICH OF FREIBERG and Berthold of Moosburg are more openly favourable to Plato and Proclus, with Berthold writing a commentary on Proclus' *Elements of Theology*.

NICHOLAS OF CUSA appears to have introduced William of Moerbeke's Latin translation of the *Parmenides* to a medieval audience, and he was also familiar with Proclus' *Commentary on the Parmenides*. Nicholas developed a strongly Neoplatonic account of the nature of the divine being who so transcends and reconciles all oppositions as to be called the 'coincidence of opposites' (*coincidentia oppositorum*), echoing Eriugena's view of God as 'the opposite of opposites' (*oppositio oppositorum*). Drawing on the twelfth-century hermetic text *The Book of the Twenty-Four Philosophers*, Nicholas represents God as an infinite sphere whose centre is everywhere and whose circumference is nowhere. Elsewhere, for example in *De li non aliud* (On the Not-Other), he develops the immanence and transcendence of God. In *De docta ignorantia* (On Learned Ignorance), Nicholas expresses the Platonic view that forms or notions exist separately from the things of which they are the forms, rejecting Aristotle's criticisms as shallow misunderstandings. Here Nicholas follows Eriugena and Thierry of Chartres in calling God 'form of all' (*forma omnium*), 'form of being' (*forma essendi*) and 'form of forms' (*forma formarum*). For Nicholas, all forms exist as one in God but 'contractedly' in created things.

See also: ARISTOTELIANISM, MEDIEVAL; AVERROISM; CHARTRES, SCHOOL OF; GILBERT OF POITIERS; GROSSETESTE, R.; MEDIEVAL PHILOSOPHY; NEOPLATONISM; PLATONISM IN ISLAMIC PHILOSOPHY; PLATONISM, EARLY AND MIDDLE; PLATONISM, RENAISSANCE; PSEUDO-DIONYSIUS

References and further reading

Aertsen, J. (1992) 'The Platonic Tendency of Thomism and the Foundations of Aquinas' Philosophy', *Medioevo* 18: 53–70. (A recent critical assessment of the impact of Platonism on Thomas.)

* Alain of Lille (*c.*1120–1203) *De planctu naturae* (The Lament of Nature), ed. N. Häring, *Studi Medievali* ser. 3, 19, 1978: 797–879. (Critical edition of Latin text only.)

* Augustine (401–14) *De Genesi ad litteram* (The Literal Commentary on Genesis), trans. J. Taylor, New York: Newman Press, 1982, 2 vols. (First full-length English translation of this hugely influential commentary on Genesis. An indispensable sourcebook of Augustinian ideas on creation, the seminal principles and the nature of man.)

* —— (413–27) *De civitate Dei* (The City of God), trans. H. Bettenson, Harmondsworth: Penguin, 1984. (English translation of Augustine's mature discussion of the Christian goal of creating a heavenly kingdom in the light of the difficulties of the earthly kingdom of the Roman Empire.)

Beierwaltes, W. (ed.) (1969) *Platonismus in der Philosophie des Mittelalters* (Platonism in Medieval Philosophy), Darmstadt: Wissenschaftliche Buchgesellschaft. (A collection of important articles in German on the influence of Platonism in the Middle Ages, including the ground-breaking 1916 article by Clemens Baeumker, 'Der Platonismus im Mittelalter'.)

—— (1990) 'Eriugena's Platonism', *Hermathena* 149: 53–72. (Authoritative article seeking to define Eriugena's Platonism, arguing that Eriugena's Platonism is indirect, transmitted through theological authorities.)

Bernard of Chartres (*c.*1110–*c.*1125) *Glosae super Platonem* (Glosses on Plato), ed. P.E. Dutton, *The Glosae super Platonem of Bernard of Chartres*, Toronto, Ont.: Pontifical Institute of Medieval Studies, 1991. (Contains critical text of the commentary on *Timaeus* with an excellent introduction in English on the nature of the commentary, with a discussion of Bernard's concept of native forms (*formae nativae*).)

Chenu, M.-D. (1968) *Nature, Man and Society in the Twelfth Century*, trans. J. Taylor and L.K. Little, Chicago: University of Chicago Press. (Scholarly but readable account of the twelfth-century renaissance.)

Cherniss, H.F. (1930) *The Platonism of Gregory of Nyssa*, Berkeley, CA: University of California Press.

(The standard account of the Platonism of the Cappadocian Father who strongly influenced the formation of Christian Platonism.)

Copenhaver, B.P. and Schmitt, C.B. (1992) 'Platonism', in B.P. Copenhaver (ed.) *Renaissance Philosophy*, Oxford: Oxford University Press, 127–95. (Excellent survey of the nature of Platonism in the Renaissance.)

Dronke, P. (1974) *Fabula: Explorations into the Uses of Myth in Medieval Platonism*, Leiden: Brill. (Good discussion of medieval understanding of Platonic allegory, the world soul and the cosmic egg.)

* —— (ed.) (1988) *A History of Twelfth-Century Western Philosophy*, Cambridge: Cambridge University Press. (Indispensable. Contains detailed accounts of philosophical developments in the twelfth century, especially the chapters 'The Platonic Inheritance' by T. Gregory, 'Philosophy, Cosmology and the Twelfth-century Renaissance' by W. Wetherbee and 'Thierry of Chartres' by Dronke.)

* Dutton, P.E. (1984) 'The Uncovering of the *Glosae super Platonem* of Bernard of Chartres', *Medieval Studies* 46: 192–221. (Discusses Dutton's reasons for attributing the twelfth-century commentary on the *Timaeus* to Bernard of Chartres.)

* Eriugena, Johannes Scottus (*c.*867) *Periphyseon* (On the Division of Nature), trans. I.-P. Sheldon-Williams, revised by J.J. O'Meara, Montreal: Bellarmin; Washington, DC: Dumbarton Oaks, 1987. (Complete English translation of the *Periphyseon*.)

Garin, E. (1955) 'Ricerche sulle traduzioni di Platone nella prima metà del sec. XV' (Research on the Platonic Tradition in the First Half of the Fifteenth Century), in *Medioevo e Rinascimento: Studi in onore di Bruno Nardi*, Florence. (Garin is the classic source for the study of the influence of Plato in the late medieval and Renaissance period.)

—— (1958) *Studi sul platonismo medievale* (Studies in Medieval Platonism), Florence: Le Monnier. (Important scholarly research on Platonism.)

Gersh, S. (1986) *Middle Platonism and Neoplatonism: The Latin Tradition*, Notre Dame, IN: University of Notre Dame Press, 2 vols. (Well-documented, authoritative survey of the Latin Platonic tradition including Cicero, Apuleius, Calcidius, Macrobius, Martianus Capella and Boethius.)

Gibson, M. (1969) 'The Study of the *Timaeus* in the Eleventh and Twelfth Centuries', *Pensiamento* 25: 183–94. (Useful critical discussion on the influence of Calcidius on twelfth-century writers.)

Gregory, T. (1955) *Anima Mundi* (World Soul),

Florence. (Definitive study in Italian of the medieval tradition of the world soul.)

—— (1958) *Platonismo medievale: studi e ricerchi* (Medieval Platonism: Studies and Research), Rome: Instituto Storico Italiano per il Medio Evo. (One of the most important scholarly studies of medieval Platonism.)

—— (1974) 'Abélard et Platon' (Abelard and Plato), in E.M. Buytaert (ed.) *Peter Abelard*, Louvain. (A study of Abelard's Platonism.)

Hankins, J. (1990) *Platonism in the Italian Renaissance*, Leiden: Brill, 2 vols. (Well-documented, up-to-date critical study of Renaissance Platonism.)

Haren, M. (1992) *Medieval Thought: The Western Intellectual Tradition from Antiquity to the Thirteenth Century*, 2nd edn, London: Macmillan. (Excellent, extremely readable survey of medieval intellectual history.)

Henle, R.J. (1956) *St. Thomas Aquinas and Platonism*, The Hague: Nijhoff. (Collects together with useful comments Thomas' references to Plato throughout his works. Texts are given in Latin only.)

Klibansky, R. (1982) *The Continuity of the Platonic Tradition during the Middle Ages*, London: The Warburg Institute; Millwood, NY: Kraus International Publications. (Re-issue of 1939 edition with supplementary chapters. The classic study on the transmission of Platonism in the Middle Ages focusing on the knowledge of the original texts and the history of their translation.)

Knowles, D. (1988) *The Evolution of Medieval Thought*, 2nd edn, London: Longman. (Reliable historical survey of medieval thought.)

Little, A. (1950) *The Platonic Heritage of Thomism*, Dublin: Golden Eagle Press. (Survey of Platonic influence on Thomas.)

Macrobius (probably *c.*430) *Commentary on the Dream of Scipio*, trans. W.H. Stahl, New York: Columbia University Press, 1952. (Edition with introduction and notes. Extremely important source of Platonic ideas, especially from ninth to the twelfth centuries.)

Martianus Capella (perhaps *c.*470) *De nuptiis Philologiae et Mercurii* (The Marriage of Philology and Mercury), trans. W. H. Stahl, R. Johnson and E.L. Burge in *Martianus Capella and the Seven Liberal Arts*, vol. 2, New York: Columbia University Press, 1977. (Complete English translation of this sprawling commentary on all aspects of knowledge, divided into the seven liberal arts. The section on 'Dialectic' is an important compendium of philosophical ideas from diverse sources.)

McEvoy, J. (1982) *The Philosophy of Robert Grosseteste*, Oxford: Clarendon Press. (Comprehensive study of the philosophy of Grosseteste, emphasising the continuity between his scientific and theological interests, with an excellent discussion of light metaphysics.)

Nicholas of Cusa (1440) *De doctora ignorantia* (On Learned Ignorance), ed. and trans. J. Hopkins, *Nicholas of Cusa on Learned Ignorance: A Translation and Appraisal of De Docta Ignorantia*, 2nd edn, Minneapolis, MN: Banning, 1985. (English translation with commentary of an important fifteenth-century text which develops a negative theological approach.)

Southern, R.W. (1970) 'Humanism and the School of Chartres', in R.W. Southern (ed.) *Medieval Humanism and Other Studies*, Oxford: Blackwell, 61–85. (The classical account of twelfth-century humanism, revised in Southern (1979).)

—— (1979) *Platonism, Scholastic Method and the School of Chartres*, Reading: University of Reading. (Important study which updates and revises Southern's earlier account of twelfth-century humanism, taking issue with the traditional view of a Chartres 'school'.)

—— (1982) 'The Schools of Paris and the School of Chartres', in R.L. Benson, G. Constable and C.D. Lanham (eds), *Renaissance and Renewal in the Twelfth Century*, Cambridge, MA: Harvard University Press, 113–37. (Critical reconsideration of the extent of the so-called School of Chartres.)

Spade, P.V. (ed.) (1994) *Five Texts on the Medieval Problem of Universals: Porphyry, Boethius, Abelard, Duns Scotus, Ockham*, Indianapolis, IN: Hackett. (An excellent selection of the key texts in the medieval debate on universals.)

Steel, C. (1990) 'Plato latinus', in J. Hamesse and M. Fattori (eds) *Rencontres de cultures dans la philosophie médiévale. Traductions et traducteurs de l'antiquité tardive au XIVe siècle. Actes du Colloque international de Cassino*, Louvain-La-Neuve: Institut d'Études Médiévales, 301–16. (Up-to-date, authoritative survey of the Latin tradition of Plato.)

Wetherbee, W. (1972) *Platonism and Poetry in the Twelfth Century*, Princeton, NJ: Princeton University Press. (Excellent on intellectual and literary background to twelfth-century poetry, especially Alain de Lille.)

William of Conches (c.1130) *Glosae super Platonem* (Commentaries on Plato), ed. E. Jeauneau, Paris: Vrin, 1965. (William's glosses on the *Timaeus*.)

DERMOT MORAN

PLATONISM, RENAISSANCE

Though it never successfully challenged the dominance of Aristotelian school philosophy, the revival of Plato and Platonism was an important phenomenon in the philosophical life of the Renaissance and contributed much to the new, more pluralistic philosophical climate of the fifteenth and sixteenth centuries. Medieval philosophers had had access only to a few works by Plato himself, and, while the indirect influence of the Platonic tradition was pervasive, few if any Western medieval philosophers identified themselves as Platonists. In the Renaissance, by contrast, Western thinkers had access to the complete corpus of Plato's works as well as to the works of Plotinus and many late ancient Platonists; there was also a small but influential group of thinkers who identified themselves as Christian Platonists. In the fifteenth century, the most important of these were to be found in the circles of Cardinal Bessarion (1403–72) in Rome and of Marsilio Ficino (1433–99) in Florence. Platonic themes were also central to the philosophies of Nicholas of Cusa (1401–64) and Giovanni Pico della Mirandola (1463–94), the two most powerful and original thinkers of the Quattrocento. While the dominant interpretation of the Platonic dialogues throughout the Renaissance remained Neoplatonic, there was also a minority tradition that revived the sceptical interpretation of the dialogues that had been characteristic of the early Hellenistic Academy.

In the sixteenth century Platonism became a kind of 'countercultural' phenomenon, and Plato came to be an important authority for scientists and cosmologists who wished to challenge the Aristotelian mainstream: men like Copernicus, Giordano Bruno, Francesco Patrizi and Galileo. Nevertheless, the Platonic dialogues were rarely taught in the humanistic schools of fifteenth-century Italy. Plato was first established as an important school author in the sixteenth century, first at the University of Paris and later in German universities. In Italy chairs of Platonic philosophy began to be established for the first time in the 1570s. Though the hegemony of Aristotelianism was in the end broken by the new philosophy of the seventeenth century, Plato's authority did much to loosen the grip of Aristotle on the teaching of natural philosophy in the universities of late Renaissance Europe.

1   **The revival of Plato**
2   **Renaissance anti-Platonism**
3   **Cardinal Bessarion and the Roman academy**
4   **The Platonism of the Florentine school**
5   **Plato in humanist schools and in universities**
6   **Plato and the new cosmologies**

1 The revival of Plato

'More men praise Aristotle; greater men, Plato.' So wrote Petrarch (see PETRARCA, F. §2) around 1368 in the invective *De sui ipsius et multorum ignorantia* (*On His Own Ignorance and That of Many Others*) (completed in 1371). Petrarch's opinion came to be representative of the humanist movement in general during the Renaissance (see HUMANISM, RENAISSANCE). The humanists deplored the extent to which Aristotle dominated the philosophical curricula of contemporary universities. They knew from their classical reading that the ancients, both pagan and Christian, had considered Plato to be the greatest of philosophers. They also knew that the Byzantines, their schoolmasters in matters Greek, had regarded the study of Aristotle's writings as propaedeutic to that of the 'higher', more sublime philosophy of Plato. The neglect of Plato thus became for humanists a standard part of their polemic against scholasticism's narrowness as an educational programme. The humanists, like their idol CICERO, wished to see the educated elites of Renaissance Italy introduced to the full range of ancient philosophy. Hence the humanist project to restore the educational values of classical antiquity brought about the revival of Platonic studies in the early Renaissance.

The study of Plato had not been entirely neglected in the Middle Ages (see PLATONISM, MEDIEVAL). Medieval readers had inherited from antiquity two partial versions of the *Timaeus* made, respectively, by Cicero and CALCIDIUS, and Calcidius' rendering, accompanied by his commentary, had been among the most widely-studied texts of the twelfth century. Henricus Aristippus in the mid-twelfth century had translated the *Phaedo* and the *Meno*, and around 1280 Aquinas' translator, the Dominican William of Moerbeke, translated Proclus' commentary on the *Parmenides*, which included much of Plato's text in the lemmata. Much was also known indirectly of Plato's writings via the Latin philosophical tradition, especially Cicero, Apuleius, Macrobius and Augustine, as well as through Avicenna and other Arabic philosophers. The Latin Aristotle, too, was important for the medieval knowledge of Plato; the arguments of the *platonici* in favour of metaphysical realism frequently cited by scholastic philosophers came mostly from this source.

Still, the Italian humanists in the course of a single century did far more to make Plato available in Latin than ten centuries of Western medieval scholarship had done. Leonardo Bruni (see ARISTOTELIANISM, RENAISSANCE §7; HUMANISM, RENAISSANCE §§5, 7), Uberto Decembrio and Cencio de'Rustici, all pupils of the émigré Greek Manuel Chrysoloras (d. 1415), translated among them some ten dialogues, including the *Gorgias*, *Crito*, *Phaedo*, *Apology* and *Republic*. In the following generation the *Republic* was translated twice more, by Uberto Decembrio's son Pier Candido and by the Sicilian Antonio Cassarino. The Milanese humanist Francesco Filelfo translated the *Euthyphro* and some of the *Letters*, while in Rome the papal secretary Rinuccio Aretino rendered the *Crito*, *Euthyphro* and *Axiochus*. GEORGE OF TREBIZOND, a humanist and papal secretary from Venetian Crete, turned the *Laws*, *Epinomis* and *Parmenides* into Latin. In 1462 Pietro Balbi, a protégé of Nicholas of Cusa and Bessarion, translated Proclus' *Platonic Theology*. In Florence, Lorenzo Lippi da Colle, a neo-Latin poet and protégé of Piero de'Medici, translated the *Ion*. The translation activity of the humanists culminated in the work of Marsilio FICINO, who in 1484 published the first complete Latin version of Plato's works and in 1496 published a series of annotations and commentaries on the major dialogues. Ficino also published in Latin the complete works of PLOTINUS and a number of works by minor ancient and Byzantine Platonists. So while in 1400 the Latin world possessed only two complete and two partial versions of the Platonic dialogues and a developed commentary tradition only on the *Timaeus*, by the end of the fifteenth century it had available in Latin all thirty-six dialogues of the Thrasyllan canon, the pseudo-Platonic *Definitions* and *Halcyon*, three of the six *Spuria*, and a large and sophisticated body of ancient and modern commentaries and other aids to the study of Plato's texts.

The progress of Platonic studies continued in the sixteenth century. Ficino's *Platonis opera* in Latin was revised three times (1532, 1557 and 1592) and there were two fresh Latin versions of the complete works, those of Janus Cornarius (1561) and Jean de Serre (1578). The *editio princeps* of Plato in Greek, edited by Marcus Musurus, was published by Aldus in 1513. It was followed by the major recensions of Simon Grynaeus (1534), Marcus Hopper (1556) and Henri Estienne (1578). The latter edition remained standard until the early nineteenth century. The trickle of vernacular translations of Plato that began in the fifteenth century turned into a flood in the sixteenth, though the first complete edition of Plato's works in a vernacular language was Dardi Bembo's Italian version published in 1601.

Renaissance scholarship on the text of Plato was not always accompanied by an understanding of Platonic thought. Before the time of Bessarion and Ficino humanist translators commonly had a very imperfect grasp of the philosophical arguments and doctrines they were endeavouring to translate. Since they were eager for Plato to be accepted in the

Christian world, it was common for them to bowdlerize (especially passages alluding to homosexuality) and Christianize (especially references to polytheism). After the middle of the Quattrocento, however, Renaissance humanist scholars and Platonists largely accepted the guidance of the ancient Neoplatonic tradition in interpreting the works of Plato. Thanks largely to Cardinal Bessarion's *In calumniatorem Platonis* (Against Plato's Calumniator) (1469) and Ficino's commentaries on Plato, Neoplatonic interpretations of Plato dominated the later Renaissance and continued to find followers in the early modern period, down to Thomas Taylor and Samuel Taylor Coleridge in the later eighteenth century. Despite the dominance of the Neoplatonic Plato, however, there was from the beginning of the Renaissance a minority tradition of interpreting Plato. In antiquity itself the theological Plato of the Neoplatonists had been balanced by the sceptical Plato of the New Academy. In Cicero and in Augustine's *Contra Academicos* (Against the Academics) Renaissance humanists met another Plato, a Plato without positive doctrines of his own, an ironic and playful doubter who liked to disguise his own opinions while presenting all points of view in inconclusive dialogues. One can find traces of this sceptical Plato in many Renaissance writers, from Petrarch (see PETRARCA, F.) and Leonardo Bruni in the early Renaissance to MELANCHTHON, Nizolius, RAMUS and MONTAIGNE in the sixteenth century. Yet only rarely do those who view Plato as a sceptic work out their interpretation in detailed readings of the dialogues themselves. The most famous, indeed almost the only example of this, is Giovanni Pico della Mirandola's reading of the *Parmenides* as a dialectical display, an interpretation which explicitly challenged Ficino's theological reading (see PICO DELLA MIRANDOLA, G. §2).

In the sixteenth century Renaissance interpreters of Plato began to move away from these traditional alternatives. Although the credit for distinguishing between Plato's original doctrine and that of his Neoplatonic interpreters is often given to Friedrich SCHLEIERMACHER in his 1804 edition of Plato, in fact the distinction has a long prehistory in Renaissance and early modern scholarship, going back to Jean de Serre's introduction to the Stephanus edition (1578) of Plato. The Protestant reformers were highly suspicious of rationalistic theologies in general and attempts to combine pagan philosophy with Christianity in particular. They were as hostile to Ficino's attempt to base Christian theology on Plato as they were to the Aristotelian theology of the scholastics. Protestant scholars who wanted to save Plato from the Florentine Platonists declared either that he should be

read purely as literature, laying aside his theological views, or, like Jean de Serre, that his true philosophy needed to be cleansed of 'les gloses des Platoniciens'. Although de Serre's own attempt to reconstruct Plato's original philosophical views was not impressive, the principle he enunciated allowed later interpreters such as Isaac Vossius, LEIBNIZ, and Jakob Brucker (author of the first critical history of philosophy), to shake off the Neoplatonic interpretation of Plato.

2 Renaissance anti-Platonism

The virulence of the opposition to the Platonic revival explains much about the character of that revival and about the approaches to Plato characteristic of Renaissance Platonists. Though Aristotle had been successfully domesticated in European universities during the thirteenth century (see ARISTOTELIANISM, MEDIEVAL §4), this circumstance did little to smooth the path for Plato in the fifteenth. The attempt to revive the Platonic texts during the early Renaissance was opposed by a number of authoritative figures such as the Dominican reformer Cardinal Giovanni Dominici, St Antoninus (the Archbishop of Florence), Pope Paul II and the famous preacher Girolamo Savonarola. Scholastic opponents of Plato in the sixteenth and seventeenth centuries repeated the same criticisms over and over again. But criticism of Plato was not confined to scholastics. A number of humanists and patrons of the humanities also had reservations about renewing the study of Plato. Indeed, Plato's chief critic in the fifteenth century was GEORGE OF TREBIZOND, a humanist and papal secretary, whose *Comparatio philosophorum Aristotelis et Platonis* (Comparison of the Philosophers Aristotle and Plato) (1458; printed in 1523 as *Comparationes philosophorum Aristotelis et Platonis*) constituted a compendium of Renaissance anti-Platonism. Trebizond's arguments presented a real challenge to the Platonic revival. The humanist movement had battened on the promise that the recovery of antiquity would mean the recovery of sound moral doctrine and brilliant examples of virtue. Plato represented a threat to this humanist project on several fronts.

The criticisms may be reduced to three. The first was the charge that Plato's teaching was unsystematic and therefore pedagogically useless. Critics complained that his doctrine was too obscure, being hidden under the personae of interlocutors who contradicted each other. Socratic dialogue was considered far more difficult to follow than the Ciceronian dialogues popular among the humanists. At the same time Plato, unlike Aristotle, had neither divided his works systematically by subject matter nor adapted them to the understanding of beginners. As a result, it was difficult for teachers to lecture on Plato's writings in the painstaking, line-by-line fashion employed in Renaissance schools and universities, and it was difficult for students to memorize and retain his doctrine. The second and more serious set of charges focused on the moral deficiencies of the dialogues. Most notorious were the passages in Book V of the *Republic* where Plato has Socrates advocate a system of common ownership of women, children and goods; abortion; female military service; and other doctrines. Criticism of Platonic communism had a long history, from Aristotle himself to Lactantius, Jerome and Gratian's *Decretum* (the most popular medieval textbook of church law), and the doctrine had been routinely condemned in the Middle Ages, first by canon lawyers and later by scholastic commentators on *Politics* II. In the Renaissance, however, humanists through their translations gave direct access to the text of Plato and so revived the storm of disapprobation. Plato's critics declared that any philosopher who promoted such doctrines should not be read in schools. Other passages caused different kinds of trouble. Dialogues such as the *Lysis*, *Charmides* and *Symposium*, depicting scenes of homosexual gallantry, caused grave offence. It was difficult to understand why Plato had spent the first two books of the *Laws* arguing for the value of drunkenness in moral education. And in the *Laws* as in other dialogues Plato gave unequivocal approval to the worship of the gods of the Greek Pantheon – gods whom the Fathers of the Church had identified as demons. Plato even admitted that Socrates had lived his life in obedience to a demon.

This leads to the third group of charges against Plato: that his theological views were incompatible with Christian truth. The humanists, quoting a famous passage in Augustine's *De civitate Dei* (The City of God), had argued that Plato's belief in individual immortality and creation made his theology closer to Christianity than Aristotle's (see Augustine §8). Plato's critics replied that, whatever his merits as a theologian, they were outweighed by his defects. They attacked his heterodox views on the pre-existence and transmigration of souls. They noted that, even if Plato had believed in creation, he had not believed in creation *ex nihilo*; in the *Timaeus* it seemed that the 'receptacle' (or 'prime matter', as it was called by Renaissance interpreters) was already in being at the moment of creation. Other critics believed that the subordinationist architecture of Plato's intelligible cosmos (as explicated by later Platonists) had encouraged the Arian heresies of the fourth century and was therefore dangerous. Though there were

similar theological problems with the reception of Aristotle, Plato's critics pointed out that, in the case of Aristotle, it was possible to separate the unorthodox parts from the useful parts. If his *Metaphysics* and On the Soul were dangerous, they could be omitted or read only after suitable formation. The student could benefit from the Organon or *On Generation and Corruption*, where logic and physical questions were dealt with (it seemed) in isolation from theology. But in the case of Plato, this could not be done. The immortality proofs of the *Phaedo* and *Meno* were mixed up hopelessly with the doctrine of pre-existence. The myth of creation in the *Timaeus* was inseparable from passages that appeared to posit the eternity of unformed matter. The refutation of atheism in *Laws* X was advanced in support of a system of polytheistic cultus. Socrates' description of the ascent to the form of Beauty in the *Symposium* is made among the drunkenness and disordered passions of a pagan dining party.

The advocates of Plato did their best to protect him. As has been noted, many humanist translators bowdlerized obscure or unorthodox passages in their translations. Pier Candido Decembrio employed an elaborate system of arguments, prefaces, glosses and chapter headings in his translation of the *Republic* to give the impression that the work was a systematic treatise on politics and not the welter of obscure and multidirectional argument it appeared to be at first sight. Later Quattrocento interpreters of Plato had more sophisticated ways of defending Plato. The pagan Platonists of late antiquity, in rivalry with Christian theologians of the time, had converted the Neoplatonism of Plotinus into a systematic theology and had developed elaborate hermeneutical methods designed to educe this theology from the dialogues of Plato. The hermeneutics of the later Platonists, especially Proclus, were taken over by Bessarion and Ficino and applied anew to Plato's works. The technique of allegory was particularly useful in dealing with offensive or heterodox passages. Certainly, any fifteenth-century reader who had wanted to understand the dialogues of Plato in depth would naturally have resorted to the late ancient commentators on Plato simply because they were among the few available guides to his thought. But the recovery of the Neoplatonic interpretation of Plato was also driven by the need to protect him from the criticism of contemporaries.

3 Cardinal Bessarion and the Roman academy

The interest of the popes and the papal court in Plato goes back to the very beginnings of the Platonic revival, when Bruni dedicated his translation of the

Phaedo to Innocent VII in 1405. A fair proportion of the early humanist translations of Plato can be associated with Roman cardinals or with the papal court, and about a quarter of the approximately 350 manuscripts containing these versions are of Roman provenance. The correspondence of Roman humanists in the first half of the Quattrocento is filled with references to the opinions and sayings of Plato. In this period, the interest of the Roman curia in Plato, reflecting its devotion to humanist ideals, was mostly literary, moralistic and apologetic. From Cicero, Seneca and other Latin sources the Romans had become curious about the figure of Socrates as a model of virtuous conduct. They were delighted to find confirmation of Christian truths in Plato's eschatological myths and in his proofs of the immortality of the soul. They were attracted by Plato's ability to place his literary skill at the service of moral and religious lessons.

With the Council of Ferrara/Florence in 1438-9, however, there was a decisive shift in interest towards Plato's cosmology, his mathematical physics and particularly his psychology and theology. There were two principal reasons for what might be called the 'metaphysical turn' in the reception of Plato. The first was the presence at the Council of the Greek philosopher Gemistos (who later changed his name, rather mysteriously, to Pletho). The Council of Ferrara/Florence had been called in an attempt to put an end to the schism between the Greek and Latin churches, and Pletho, among the most learned men of the Greek world, had been taken along by the Greek delegation as a theological adviser. Though Pletho was later accused of paganism by the conservative cleric George Scholarios (later to become the Orthodox Patriarch Gennadios) as well as by the equally conservative Roman convert, George of Trebizond, it is unclear whether he was really a pagan or rather an extreme syncretist who combined Orthodox Christianity with other forms of religious wisdom, including Platonism. Platonism, which Pletho referred to as 'the Hellenic theology', was in any case not to be identified with the 'vulgar' ancient polytheism of myth and cult, but was an esoteric religious wisdom known to the better minds among the ancient pagans. The key to understanding this hidden wisdom for Pletho was the *Platonic Theology* of Proclus, which Pletho saw as a kind of *summa* or systematic treatment of the Platonic dialogues. Pletho believed himself to have prophetic powers and predicted that within a short time Christianity and Islam would disappear, to be replaced by a new, purified Hellenic theology based on Plato.

The paganizing and prophetic sides of Pletho's thought, however, remained hidden at the time of the Council. During the Council Pletho attracted attention chiefly for his lectures, later published under the title *De differentiis Platonis et Aristotelis* (On the Differences between Plato and Aristotle) (1439). These were attended by many Westerners, who thus received their first initiation into the Neoplatonic interpretation of Plato. They were intended to illustrate two main themes: the superiority of Plato to Aristotle in terms of their relative compatibility with Christianity, and the basic concord of Plato with Aristotle.

These themes had considerable resonance at the Council. The council's purpose was to reconcile the theology of the Latins, whose speculative development was based largely on Aristotelian logic and natural science, with the theology of the Greeks, heavily indebted to the form of late Platonism associated with Pseudo-Dionysius the Areopagite. To the Byzantine cleric Bessarion (who in 1439 was created a cardinal of the Roman church) Platonism seemed to offer a formula for reconciling the two traditions. Ancient Platonists had believed that there existed beyond the multiplicity of ordinary sense-experience radical unities in the cosmos, and that these unities were cognizable only in a heightened state of awareness called *noesis*. Since language was based on sense-experience, it was inadequate for representing the radical unities of the divine realm. The discursive reasoning and dogmatic definitions of the Latins were thus inappropriate tools for theology. Platonism, regarding dogmas, liturgical forms and creeds as inadequate approximations or symbols of inexpressible truths, could thus provide the basis for a theology of concord between Greeks and Latins. Both Greek and Latin creeds could be true, even if they seemed opposed from the viewpoint of discursive reasoning. Bessarion used this conception to convince the Greeks that they were not abandoning Orthodoxy by acceding to Latin liturgical practices and Latin formulations of the creed. The belief that a theology of concord could be built upon Platonic foundations proved a durable one. It was responsible for much of Platonism's popularity in the dawning age of religious controversy, while Aristotelian theologies were frequently blamed for rigidity and dogmatism. Platonic concordism was an important element in the philosophical development of Nicholas of Cusa, whose famous treatise *De docta ignorantia* (*On Learned Ignorance*) (1440) grew out of reflection on the theological issues of the Council.

Following the Council there arose a dispute among the intellectuals of the émigré Greek colony in Rome whose headquarters was Bessarion's palace library or 'academy'. The dispute lasted for thirty years. At issue was whether Platonism or Aristotelianism formed a better speculative framework for Christian theology. Behind this issue lay the even more charged question of whether and how the Byzantine theological tradition might be integrated with the Latin. This 'Plato–Aristotle Controversy', as it is called, culminated in George of Trebizond's *Comparatio philosophorum Aristotelis et Platonis* (1458) and Bessarion's reply, *In calumniatorem Platonis* (drafted 1459, printed 1469). The aim of George's work was to show the total incompatibility of Plato (and by implication, the 'corrupt' traditions of Byzantine theology) with the 'pure' Aristotelian theologies of the Latin church. Bessarion's *In calumniatorem* in Books I, III and IV consisted of a point-by-point refutation of George's *Comparatio*, while Book V sought to discredit George by attacking his translation of Plato's *Laws*. Book II provided a summary of Platonic theology, based on the Greek Church Fathers and on late ancient Platonists, particularly Proclus. In addition to introducing the Latin West to the late ancient and Byzantine view of Plato's theology, Bessarion's work made clear for the first time to Western scholars the degree to which the theological tradition of ancient Greek Christianity had been indebted to Platonism. The publication of his *In calumniatorem* coincided with the beginnings of the Renaissance revival of the Greek Fathers, and the latter did much to increase the popularity of Platonism in the later fifteenth and sixteenth century.

4   The Platonism of the Florentine school

Florentine humanists had been interested in Plato from the late fourteenth century, when Coluccio Salutati had acquired copies of Calcidius and of Henricus Aristippus' translation of the *Phaedo*. The interest continued in the early fifteenth century with Leonardo Bruni (see ARISTOTELIANISM, RENAISSANCE §7; HUMANISM, RENAISSANCE §§5, 7), who dedicated two of his seven translations of Plato to Cosimo de'Medici, the great banker, politician and patron of arts and letters. The Medici over several generations played a key role in the revival of Plato in Florence. Cosimo de'Medici is said to have heard Pletho's lectures during the Council of Florence, and it was probably from Pletho that Cosimo purchased the manuscript of Plato's dialogues he later gave to Marsilio FICINO to serve as a basis for his translation. In 1462 Cosimo gave Ficino a house in Florence and a farm in the countryside near his own villa of Careggi. Cosimo's grandson, Lorenzo 'the Magnificent', continued to support Ficino by acquiring several benefices for him and paying the printing costs of some of his scholarly works. Ficino had other patrons besides the Medici, and the Medici supported

philosophers of many other schools besides Ficinian Platonism, but by the early sixteenth century the Medici had acquired a reputation for special devotion to Plato. In 1513, the *editio princeps* of Plato's works in Greek was dedicated to the Medici pope, Leo X, whose father Lorenzo had received the dedication of Ficino's Latin translation of Plato thirty years earlier.

Ficino and Cristoforo Landino were the two central figures in the Florentine school of Platonism. Landino was a professor of rhetoric and Latin literature at the University of Florence who gave Platonizing interpretations of various literary works, most famously Virgil's *Aeneid* and Dante's *Divina Commedia* (Divine Comedy). Landino also composed the *Disputationes Camaldulenses* (Camaldulensian Disputations) (1472), a brilliant depiction of Lorenzo's entourage engaged in philosophical discussions about the immortality of the soul. These dialogues show better than any other source the character of Florentine Platonism during the 1470s. Marsilio Ficino, one of the greatest scholars of the century, was only briefly a professor at the University; he kept instead a private *gymnasium* or *academy* where he educated numerous members of the Florentine elite. He also gave public lectures on Plato and Plotinus and maintained a large philosophical correspondence. He translated all the works of Plato and Plotinus in addition to those of a number of other ancient Neoplatonists, and wrote a major work amassing arguments to prove the immortality of the soul. Besides Ficino, Landino and their pupils, it is hard to find other important intellectuals in the Florence of Lorenzo de'Medici who were deeply influenced by Platonism. Johannes Argyropoulos, while lecturing at the University of Florence, introduced Platonic elements into his explications of Aristotle. Angelo Poliziano came briefly under Ficino's spell during the mid-1470s, when he produced his Platonizing *Stanze per la giostra* (Stanzas for the Tournament) and an unfinished translation of the *Charmides*. The astronomer Lorenzo Bonincontri, the humanist Bartolomeo Scala and the philosopher Giovanni PICO DELLA MIRANDOLA all made eclectic use of Ficinian Neoplatonism. Most important of all, from the point of view of spreading interest in Platonism, was Lorenzo de'Medici himself, whose Italian poetry frequently contained themes, images and conceits borrowed from Ficino's writings.

While the chief theme of Bessarion's Platonism was the integration of Greek and Latin theological traditions, Ficino's Platonism was broader and more polymorphous in its interests. Ficino considered his main role to be that of a theological reformer. He wanted to restore Platonism to its ancient function as the handmaid of Christian theology, replacing the failed Aristotelian syntheses of Christianity and Aristotle that had characterized the medieval period. His chief concern as a philosopher was establishing a rational basis for the doctrine of the immortality of the soul, the key issue separating 'secularizing' from 'Christianizing' Aristotelians in Italian universities of the Renaissance. But Ficino and his followers were also interested in using the truths of Platonism to explore many other subjects, including astrology, magic, medicine, literary theory, musical theory and the theory of love.

With the fall of the Medici in 1494 and the coming of Savonarola, Ficinian Platonism was temporarily eclipsed, and many of his followers became Savonarolans. In the sixteenth century, interest in Ficino's work revived and his Platonism exerted a broad cultural influence. Especially popular was Ficino's 'philosophy of love', which provided European poets in the Petrarchan tradition with a new repertory of conceits and images. It is nevertheless difficult to find professional philosophers who could be called Ficinian Platonists. In Florence, Francesco Cattani da Diacceto continued Ficino's work during the first Medici Restoration, but disagreed with him on many points, preferring the concordism of Pico. Later in the century Francesco de'Vieri the Younger attempted another revival of Ficinian Platonism. In Rome, Ficino's most important epigone was the Augustinian Giles of Viterbo, a preacher and theologian of the papal court whose theology is thought to have influenced the programmes of Michelangelo's decoration of the Sistine Chapel ceiling and Raphael's frescos in the papal *Stanze*. The definition of the immortality of the soul as an official Catholic dogma by the Fifth Lateran Council (1512–7) may be partly credited to Giles' influence and to that of Ficino's former pupil, Pope Leo X. Ficino's studies of magic and the occult were appropriated by figures as diverse as Symphorien Champier, AGRIPPA VON NETTESHEIM, PARACELSUS and Giordano BRUNO. Ficino's belief in an 'ancient theology' (see FICINO, M. §2) remained influential, even after the *Corpus Hermeticum* was exposed as a forgery by the Protestant scholar Isaac Casaubon in the early seventeenth century. Finally, Ficino's contention that Plato's philosophy was more compatible with Christian theology than Aristotle's continued to find numerous champions among both humanists and scholastics for more than a century.

5 Plato in humanist schools and in universities

Despite the intellectual energies expended on the Platonic revival of the fifteenth century, it was a long time before the dialogues of Plato were included regularly in the curricula of Renaissance schools and universities. Manuel Chrysoloras, the Byzantine émigré who taught the first generation of Italian humanists to learn Greek, seems to have read the *Gorgias* and the *Republic* privately with some of his pupils. There is some evidence that the famous humanist schoolmasters Guarino Veronese and Gasparino Barzizza used Chrysoloras' Latin translation of the *Republic* in private tutorials with certain students. George of Trebizond reports having heard lectures on the *Gorgias* in the school of another famous schoolmaster, Vittorino da Feltre, presumably in the 1420s, and the Byzantine Theodore Gaza, who had been an assistant to Vittorino, lectured on the same text at the University of Ferrara in 1446. In Battista Guarino's educational tract, *De ordine docendi et studendi* (A Plan of Teaching and Study) (1456) – a work said to capture the educational practice of Guarino Veronese – the reading of Plato and Aristotle is recommended as the crown of a long programme of humanistic studies, but it is not known how often, if ever, the full programme was carried out. In 1459 another Byzantine, Johannes Argyropoulos, is said to have lectured privately in Florence on Plato's *Meno*. Ficino gave public lectures on Plato's *Philebus*, Plotinus' *Enneads*, and no doubt other texts as well, but these lectures were probably not part of any school or university course of study.

In the 1490s the study of Plato spread to Northern Europe with the lectures of Paulus Niavis (Paul Schneevogel) on the pseudo-Platonic *Epistulae* (Letters) and *Erastes* (in Ficino's translations) at the University of Leipzig. From the first decade of the sixteenth century until the 1580s there was considerable interest in Plato among humanistically inclined masters at the University of Paris and particularly at the Collège Royale. A number of famous French classical scholars such as Jérôme Aleander, Denys Lambin, Adrien Turnèbe and Marc-Antoine Muret are known to have lectured on a wide variety of texts. Most of these texts were chosen from among shorter and easier dialogues of interest to students of literature, such as the *Crito*, *Apology*, *Hipparchus*, *Minos*, *Theages*, *Euthyphro*, *Cratylus*, Book I of the *Republic*, Socrates' speech from the *Symposium*, and the pseudo-Platonic *Epistulae*. Turnèbe was rather more ambitious, giving courses on the *Timaeus* and *Phaedo*, among other texts. Petrus Ramus used Plato as a stick with which to beat Aristotle in his famous anti-Peripatetic lectures, and encouraged the study of Plato by making his own translation of the pseudo-Platonic *Epistulae*. It was in part Ramus' influence that led to a renewed interest in Plato in German *gymnasia* of the late sixteenth century. The reformer and humanist Johannes Sturm had lectured on the

Gorgias in Strasbourg as early as the 1540s, but in the 1580s and 1590s there were schools in Cologne, Nuremberg, Rostock and Strasbourg where students could study the *Apology, Gorgias, Theaetetus, Phaedrus* and *Republic*.

With the exception of Ficino's lectures almost all of this study took place in humanist schools or as a result of university lecture courses given by humanists. The emphasis was mostly on grammar and on providing general moral and cultural formation. Scholastic philosophers for a long time did not lecture on Plato nor make him the subject of their professional attentions; Pico's proposal to defend Platonic theses in 1487, had it taken place, would have been the first known instance of a scholastic disputation involving Platonic texts (see PICO DELLA MIRANDOLA, G. §1). This began to change at the end of the fifteenth century when in 1497 Niccolò Leonico Tomeo (1456–1531) was appointed to lecture on the Greek text of Aristotle and Plato at the University of Padua. The philosopher and magician Henricus Cornelius AGRIPPA VON NETTESHEIM (1486–1535), too, is known to have lectured on the *Symposium*, either at Pavia or Turin, in the second decade of the sixteenth century. Yet it was only in the 1570s that professional philosophers began to teach Plato in the universities with any regularity. Special chairs for the teaching of Platonic philosophy were established in several Italian universities. Most important was the chair set up at Pisa by the Medici grand dukes, who saw themselves as continuing the historic commitment of the Medici to Platonic philosophy. The chair was occupied for half a century by four professors, Francesco de'Vieri the Younger (appointed 1576), Jacopo Mazzoni (1588–97), Carlo Tommasi da Cortona (*c.*1597–1606), and Cosimo Boscagli (d. 1621). Francesco PATRIZI DA CHERSO (1529–97), the greatest expert on Plato of the late Renaissance, was for thirteen years (1578–92) the occupant of a special chair of Platonic philosophy at the University of Ferrara; in 1592 he moved to the Sapienza in Rome where he taught Plato until his death. There was also an unsuccessful attempt to establish a chair in Platonic philosophy at the University of Bologna. All the 'Platonic professors' were serious students of Plato's philosophy who lectured extensively on the text of Plato in Latin, the *Timaeus, Republic* and *Phaedo* being special favourites.

6 Plato and the new cosmologies

The introduction of Plato into the philosophy faculties of Italian universities was one of several signals that the hegemony of Aristotelian philosophy was weakening. The Plato chairs were founded in the belief that

his philosophy was more compatible with Christianity than Aristotle's; Patrizi promised Pope Gregory XIV that replacing Aristotle with Plato in the universities would purify Catholic theology and put an end to the Protestant schism. Claims such as these revived the interest of philosophers in comparing Plato and Aristotle. There was already by the middle of the sixteenth century a flourishing literature on this topic. A spectrum of opinion emerged, ranging from Francesco Patrizi's view, in his *Discussiones peripateticae* (Peripatetic Discussions) (1581), that Plato was superior at all points to Aristotle, to the opposite view, maintained by Aristotelian scholastics such as Girolamo Borro (one of Galileo's teachers) in his *De peripatetica docendi atque discendi methodo* (On the Peripatetic Method of Teaching and Learning) (1584). Somewhere in the middle were Francesco de'Vieri the Younger and Jacopo Mazzoni, who, following what had by then become the traditional Florentine position, argued for the concord of Plato and Aristotle and for the harmony of both philosophers with Christian theology.

The search for a more adequate philosophical basis for Christian theology led ultimately to the new science and philosophy of the seventeenth century, and Renaissance Platonism had a significant role to play in this development. The 'new cosmologists' of the late sixteenth century frequently invoked Plato as a counter-authority when attacking Aristotelian science – even men such as TELESIO, CAMPANELLA and GALILEO, who otherwise made little use of Platonism in their science. Sometimes Galileo, when trying to conceal the shameful novelty of his science, would pretend to be reviving a lost, pre-Aristotelian cosmology – an apologetic strategy that recalls Ficino's belief in an 'ancient theology'. There were in fact some striking similarities between the new science and Platonic science, the latter reconstructed (sometimes tendentiously) from the *Timaeus* and other dialogues. Already in the 1540s COPERNICUS had been encouraged by the symbolic role of the sun in Platonic metaphysics (as mediated by Ficino's *De sole*) to embrace the heliocentric hypothesis. Heliocentrism remained linked to Neoplatonism as late as the time of BRUNO and KEPLER. In the late sixteenth century other elements of Platonic science appealed. Plato was credited with a simplified elemental theory which by excluding quintessence undermined the physical basis of the two-sphere universe. The light-metaphysics of Patrizi and Bruno, an inheritance from Proclus and the pseudo-Dionysius, has been considered a forerunner of Galileo's distinction between primary and secondary qualities. Giordano Bruno's belief in infinite worlds was taken from Proclus via Nicholas of Cusa. Proclus was also an important source for Patrizi's rather different, more mathematical argument for the infinity of the cosmos. The new cosmologists moreover professed to find in the *Timaeus* authority for their non-Aristotelian concepts of gravity, time and space, as well as for the 'mathematization of the cosmos' that begins with the generation of Patrizi and Galileo. Though it was ultimately the new science of Galileo and NEWTON that put an end to the dominance of Aristotelian science, the 'countercultural' influence of Plato was important in loosening the allegiance of Renaissance natural science to its medieval past.

See also: FICINO, M.; HUMANISM, RENAISSANCE; PATRIZI DA CHERSO, F.; PICO DELLA MIRANDOLA, G.; PLATO; PLATONISM, EARLY AND MIDDLE; PLATONISM IN ISLAMIC PHILOSOPHY; PLATONISM, MEDIEVAL

References and further reading

* Bessarion (1469) *In calumniatorem Platonis* (Against Plato's Calumniator), in L. Mohler (ed.) *Kardinal Bessarion als Theologe, Humanist und Staatsmann*, vol. 2, Paderborn and Berlin: Schoningh, 1923–42; repr. Aalen: Scientia, 1967. (Referred to in §§1–3. Cardinal Bessarion's defence of Plato against the criticisms of George of Trebizond.)

Copenhaver, B.P. and Schmitt, C.B. (1992) *Renaissance Philosophy*, Oxford: Oxford University Press. (A clear and reliable introductory textbook.)

* George of Trebizond (1458) *Comparationes philosophorum Aristotelis et Platonis* (Comparisons of the Philosophers Aristotle and Plato), Venice: Iacobus Pentius, 1523; repr. Frankfurt am Main: Minerva, 1965. (George's famous attack on Plato; referred to in §§2–3. The manuscript version of this work (published in 1458) was entitled *Comparatio philosophorum Aristotelis et Platonis*.)

Hankins, J. (1990) *Plato in the Italian Renaissance*, London, Leiden and Copenhagen: Brill, 2 vols. (A detailed account of the reception of Plato in the fifteenth century.)

Kraye, J. (1993) 'The Philosophy of the Italian Renaissance', in G.H.R. Parkinson (ed.) *Routledge History of Philosophy, volume IV: The Renaissance and Seventeenth-century Rationalism*, London and New York: Routledge, 16–69, esp. 26–37. (A short, accessible overview with full bibliographies.)

Kristeller, P.O. (1956) *Studies in Renaissance Thought and Letters*, Rome: Edizioni di Storia e Letteratura. (Important for the context of Ficino and for the later influence of Ficinian Platonism.)

—— (1964) *Eight Philosophers of the Italian Renaissance*, Stanford, CA: Stanford University Press. (A readable introduction to the philosophy of Ficino, Pico, Bruno and Patrizi among others.)

—— (1979) *Renaissance Thought and Its Sources*, New York: Columbia University Press. (Contains a masterly overview of key themes in Renaissance philosophy with special attention to Platonism.)

* Landino, C. (1472) *Disputationes Camaldulenses* (Camaldulensian Disputations), ed. P. Lohe, Florence: Sansoni, 1980. (Referred to in §4. Imaginary conversations on Platonic themes between Lorenzo de'Medici and members of his circle.)

* Nicholas of Cusa (1440) *De docta ignorantia*, ed. E. Hoffmann and R. Klibansky, Leipzig: Meiner, 1932; trans. J. Hopkins, *Nicholas of Cusa on Learned Ignorance: A Translation and Appraisal of De Docta Ignorantia*, Minneapolis, MN: Arthur J. Banning Press, 2nd edn, 1985. (Referred to in §4. Platonic paradoxes about the knowledge of God.)

* Patrizi da Cherso, F. (1581) *Discussionum peripateticarum tomi quattuor* (Peripatetic Discussions in Four Books), Basle. (Referred to in §6. On the limits of Aristotelianism as a basis for Christian theology.)

* Petrarca, F. [Petrarch] (1371) *Le Traité 'De sui ipsius et multorum ignorantia'*, ed. L.M. Capelli, Paris: Honoré Champion, 1906; trans. H. Nachod, *On His Own Ignorance and That of Many Others*, in E. Cassirer *et al.* (eds) *The Renaissance Philosophy of Man*, Chicago, IL: University of Chicago Press, 1948. (Critique of scholastic Aristotelianism and pioneer text of humanist Platonism; referred to in §1.)

* Pletho [Georgios Gemistos] (1439) *De differentiis Platonis et Aristotelis* (On the Differences between Plato and Aristotle), ed. B. Lagarde, 'Le *De differentiis* de Pléthon d'après l'autographe de la Marcienne', in *Byzantion* 43 (1973): 312–43; trans. C. Montague, in C.M. Woodhouse, *Gemistus Plethon: The Last of the Hellenes*, Oxford: Clarendon Press, 1986, ch. 11. (Referred to in §3. Argues for the superiority of Plato to Aristotle.)

Schmitt, C.B. (1976) 'L'introduction de la philosophie platonicienne dans l'enseignement des universités à la Renaissance' (The Introduction of Platonic Philosophy in the Teaching of Renaissance Universities), in *Platon et Aristote à la Renaissance*, Paris: Vrin, 93–104. (Collects evidence for the study of Plato in Italian universities of the late Renaissance.)

Yates, F.A. (1964) *Giordano Bruno and the Hermetic Tradition*, London: Routledge & Kegan Paul. (Classic work on the impact of the Ficinian magical tradition upon the development of modern science.)

JAMES HANKINS

PLEASURE

From Plato and beyond, pleasure has been thought to be a basic, and sometimes the only basic, reason for doing anything. Since there are many forms that pleasure can take and many individual views of what pleasure consists in, much attention has been given to how pleasures may be distinguished, what their motivational and moral significance might be, and whether there may not be some objective determination of them, whether some may be good or bad, or some better as pleasures than others.

But first there is the question of what pleasure is. It has been variously thought to be a state of mind like distress only of the opposite polarity; merely the absence or cessation of or freedom from pain; a kind of quiescence like contentment; or the experiencing of bodily sensations which, unlike sensations of pain, one does not want to stop. We also identify and class together particular sources of pleasure and call them pleasures of the table, company, sex, conversation, solitude, competition, contemplation or athletic pleasures. In this sense there may be some pleasures which we do not enjoy. But most generally pleasure is what we feel and take when we do enjoy something. This raises the questions of what is encompassed by 'something', what it is to enjoy anything, and the extent to which theories of pleasure can accommodate both our passivity and activity in pleasure. The most influential theories have been those of Plato, Aristotle and empiricists such as Hume and Bentham.

1 Logically proper objects of enjoyment
2 Theories of pleasure
3 Morally proper objects of enjoyment
4 The content of enjoyment

1 Logically proper objects of enjoyment

Elizabeth Anscombe observes that there is both enjoyment of substances: activities themselves, or things, or happenings, or existence itself; and enjoyment of facts: that one made the visit, that one is talking to the wittiest person in the room, that the sun is shining again. Both kinds may be illusory, the apparent fact not a fact, the activity not actually occurring, which calls for qualification in terms of what one thinks to be so as possibly opposed to what is so. The significance of these distinctions is that it may be true that I am enjoying what I take to be the fact that I am having a holiday while it is false that I am enjoying the holiday itself; and the first may be true even though I am mistaken in thinking that I am having a holiday: I may be on call and about to be summoned.

This gives us one interpretation of the distinction between true and false pleasures: my holiday would be truly pleasant if it is true both that I am enjoying the holiday and the fact that I am having a holiday and it is true that I am having a holiday. If any one of these is false it might reasonably be thought that my holiday could not be truly pleasant. But this is not the only interpretation of this distinction.

2 Theories of pleasure

Plato thought that pleasure is the replenishment or filling of a natural lack (for example, *Republic* IX) or, better, in a move to include something more active, the perception of the replenishment of a natural lack (*Philebus*). So eating is a pleasure if one is hungry and one is attending to and enjoying eating as satisfying one's hunger. What one enjoys is always some process which one perceives as restoring a deficiency that has occurred and one has become aware of. Pleasure is not caused by these processes or the perception of them; they are the pleasures in question. So according to this theory the proper object of enjoyment is a process which is perceived to restore the body's silence or remove the clamour of the mind.

This raises the question of how natural lacks may be identified. Even if it is true that one lacks what one desires, it does not follow that all lacks so identified are natural. And while this theory may accommodate plausibly bodily desires and pleasures it seems not easily to deal with intellectual ones, though the examples of curiosity and the pleasures of education may lessen these doubts. Posing greater difficulties are the pleasures of anticipation and memory, and aesthetic pleasures. These are undoubtedly pleasures but only in a strained sense do they imply lacks. Plato was aware of these problems, and partly because of them came in the *Philebus* to see that there was no theory that covered all pleasures.

Freud's theory of pleasure can be regarded as a mirror image of Plato's. Both are homoeostatic theories in that pleasure is the return to rest, though Freud sees that not in replenishment but in discharge of affect at the point where the person's interest is invested.

Aristotle in *Nicomachean Ethics* appears to offer two theories: pleasure is the unimpeded activity of a natural faculty (VII); pleasure completes an activity by supervening upon it 'as the bloom of youth does on those in the flower of their age' (X). Whether or not these are two theories, at least they agree in that the proper object of enjoyment is not a process as Plato thought, but an activity. Aristotle's distinction is that a process is not complete until it reaches its end whereas an activity has no end in this sense and is complete in itself. One cannot enjoy convalescing because one is not yet well, though one can enjoy such health as one has at any one time. As we might say, activities concern our purposes rather than our ends. If we purpose to be calm and reasonable we do not cease our activity because it has been once successful, whereas our end of being in Cambridge in the spring is extinguished once it is achieved. Pleasure is in achievement, completion, perfection, whether the achievement is continuous or episodic.

G.E.L. Owen has argued that there are two theories but they are about different things. In book VII Aristotle is concerned with the objects of enjoyment; in book X he has moved to the question of what enjoying contributes to the enjoyed activity, in the realization, perhaps, of the need to embrace our passivity. He answers that pleasure is a perfection added to an activity which is already complete in itself. It seems on this view, however, that Aristotle has two sometimes incompatible determinations of the proper object of enjoyment: the unimpeded activity itself, perfect as the prime of youth is perfect; and the perfection of that activity, the bloom on the cheek of those in the prime of youth. It is as if one is in the first case enjoying the unimpeded listening to a Schubert sonata and in the second enjoying the perfection of one's listening. The second may be part of one's enjoyment of the first but it need not be. Perhaps the solution is that one's enjoyment enhances one's listening and the more exquisite one's enjoyment the more perfect one's listening. In that case Owen's two theories do not remain distinct and neither, as a good consequence, does our activity and passivity in pleasure.

Henry Sidgwick in *The Methods of Ethics* written towards the end of the nineteenth century observed that Aristotle's theory in one form or another was still current. His interpretation of it is that every normal sense perception or rational activity has its corresponding pleasure and that the most perfect, the exercise of an unimpaired capacity on the best object, is the most pleasant. The pleasure follows the activity immediately giving it a kind of finish like the bloom of youth.

Empiricist theories of pleasure have three characteristics: first, pleasures are quantifiable; second, pleasures either are bodily sensations (see BODILY SENSATIONS) localized like those that occur when one warms one's hands before a fire or nonlocalized like the physical wellbeing after exercise, or are qualities or impressions of such sensations; and third, there is an extensional relation between the pleasure and its object which may or may not be a part of its cause. It is a serious question whether any empiricist from Locke and Hume through Bentham and John Stuart Mill to the pioneers in psychological theory are consistent empiricists about pleasure.

Pleasure comes in amounts which can be increased or decreased and calculated or measured and quantitatively compared. Bentham distinguishes five variables which are involved in determining the total amount of pleasure given by a particular experience: intensity, duration, fecundity (possibilities of further pleasures), purity (absence of mixture with pain) and extent. This requires that pleasures be identifiable occurrences like sensations, or an immediately recognizable quality of such occurrences, which have the right kind of properties for quantification.

So pleasures are caused by other occurrences and the relation between the pleasure experienced and the object of it is quite contingent (or extensional). I may be enjoying the wine I am savouring but why I am enjoying it may have nothing to do with the wine itself. I may have been conditioned or otherwise caused to enjoy whatever is put in front of me. Even when the wine itself is the occasion of my enjoyment of it, it could have been otherwise. That is, empiricist theories of pleasure, while being able to accommodate talk of objects of enjoyment, do not determine what those objects are. There are in theory no proper objects and there is no activity in our enjoyment, only process.

3 Morally proper objects of enjoyment

For classical utilitarian and hedonistic theories (see HEDONISM; UTILITARIANISM) the only morally proper object is pleasure and the absence of pain. But such singularity at the highest level requires quotidian diversity. The most common way of dealing with the question of whether some objects of enjoyment are morally better than others is to distinguish between higher and lower pleasures. For example, John Stuart Mill in the second chapter of *Utilitarianism* writes that some kinds of pleasures are more desirable and more valuable than others and so differ in quality as well as in quantity. 'It is better to be a human being dissatisfied than a pig satisfied; better to be Socrates dissatisfied than a fool satisfied.' He follows Plato who says (*Republic* IX) that the greatest pleasures are those associated with the exercise of our highest faculties (reason) and that apart from their intensity mental pleasures are preferable to any amount of physical pleasure.

Clearly this is tendentious for all that it might appeal to us. Those competent to judge between pleasures doubtless must have experience of them but there would appear to be no place for the idea of expertise in comparative judgments of them. A better test would be whether the pursuit of a particular pleasure is self-defeating.

Aristotle's approach looks more promising. Pleasures, being so closely associated with the activities to which they add perfection, can be compared and judged by evaluating the activities themselves, which one does by considering the lives in which they naturally occur. The bad man's pleasures are not the good man's pleasures since the good man chooses not to live the kind of life the bad man enjoys. Julia Annas argues that Aristotle must therefore reject hedonism and any form of utilitarianism that includes hedonism as a part because for him pleasure is not a single end specifiable independently of different chosen activities and the lives they partly constitute. This yields another interpretation of the distinction between true and false pleasures: true pleasures are those of a good life and false pleasures are not. This shifts the question to what a good life is, but that question has a clearer focus.

4   The content of enjoyment

This question does not concern the objects of enjoyment but what it is to enjoy anything. Empiricist theories construe enjoyment as the having of bodily sensations or episodes like sensations: thrills, transports, raptures or convulsions; the list is Gilbert Ryle's. It is Ryle's argument that this construal of pleasure, though natural to the pioneers in psychological theory, is seriously mistaken. Their programme, he believed, was to construct a dynamic theory of human conduct in which such things as wantings and likings are processes, the mental counterparts to the pressures and attractions of mechanical theory. Psychic motions could be calculated if the durations and intensities of pleasures and desires were measurable and construed on the model of the parallelogram of forces.

But, he argues, pleasure or enjoyment are not processes of any sort. My enjoyment of a game, for example, is not some occurrence that accompanies the game itself, that could distract my attention from the game, that can occur by itself without the game, be described as processes are, as fast or slow, as having some location within the body image, as being, indeed, pleasant or not! These absurdities flow from the mistaken thought that the role of the concept of pleasure is the precise counterpart of the concept of pain. Ryle shows that pleasure is not a sensation as pain mostly is and so not an affective process. There are ways of construing pleasure and pain that will keep them as counterparts, but that will succeed only in making both pleasure and pain not sensations themselves but attitudes to sensations; and there are

ways of keeping pains as sensations and not attitudes to sensations, but then they would no longer be counterparts of pleasures. Are there sensations of pleasure rather than pleasurable sensations of warmth, touch, motion, and the like? There seem to be some obvious examples but if there are they are hardly representative of everything that we enjoy and we should do better to avoid misleading assimilations entirely.

This returns us to the necessity of thinking of pleasure as something we take, to our being active and not merely passive in enjoyment. The activity need not be vigorous and may be merely the activity of the imagination or of paying attention or of attending finely to what is happening or to what we are engaged in doing. There are resonances here with Aristotle, and Ryle comes close. He speaks of our liking and disliking as special qualities of the interest we have in an activity, and of that interest itself as a special quality of the activity in question.

This does not imply that we do not feel anything when we enjoy something, only that our feeling enjoyment is not usefully interpreted as being something like a bodily sensation, localised or not. Neither does it follow that we cannot compare our pleasures and discuss their merits and demerits, or contrast them with our pains and miseries. We do, but not by counting and calculating. Contemporary calculations of welfare functions have little to do with pleasure as here reviewed. Unless we take pleasure in what we do and experience, we should get none; but if we feel nothing, it is not pleasure that we take.

References and further reading

* Annas, J. (1980) 'Aristotle on Pleasure and Goodness', in A. Oksenberg Rorty (ed.) *Essays on Aristotle's Ethics*, Berkeley and Los Angeles, CA: University of California Press, 285–99. (A very good collection of essays on Aristotle's views on a number of related topics.)
* Anscombe, G.E.M. (1967) 'On the Grammar of "enjoy"', repr. in *The Collected Philosophical Papers of G.E.M. Anscombe*, vol. 2, Oxford: Blackwell, 1981, 94–100. (Intricate argument but no technicality.)
* Aristotle (*c.* mid 4th century) *The Ethics of Aristotle*, trans. J.A.K. Thomson, Harmondsworth: Penguin, 1955. (A classic of Western philosophy.)
* Bentham, J. (1789) *An Introduction to the Principles of Morals and Legislation*, ed. J.H. Burns and H.L.A. Hart, repr. London: The Athlone Press, 1980, esp. ch. V. (A classic text.)
  Freud, S. (1920) *Beyond the Pleasure Principle*; repr. in *The Standard Edition of the Complete Psychological*

Works of Sigmund Freud, trans. and ed. J. Strachey, London: Hogarth Press, vol. 18. (Characteristically inventive and contentious.)

Gibbs, B. (1986) 'Higher and Lower Pleasures', *Philosophy* 61: 31–59. (A readable and erudite discussion of the subject.)

Gosling, J.C.B. (1975) *Plato, Philebus*, Oxford: Clarendon Press. (The principal commentary on the dialogue.)

Gosling, J.C.B. and Taylor, C.C.W. (eds) (1982) *The Greeks on Pleasure*, Oxford: Clarendon Press. (A scholarly and informative discussion of an immense topic.)

Hume, D. (1739–40) *A Treatise on Human Nature*, ed. L.A. Selby-Bigge, Oxford: Clarendon Press, 1888, esp. Book I, part IV, section II; Book II, part I, section I; Book III, part I, sections I and II. (A classic text.)

Mill, J.S. (1861) *Utilitarianism, repr. in Collected Works*, vol. X, Toronto, Ont: University of Toronto Press. (A classic text.)

* Owen, G.E.L. (1972) 'Aristotelian Pleasures', *Proceedings of the Aristotelian Society*, 1972: 135–52. (A challenging interpretation.)

* Plato (*c.*380–367 BC) *Republic*, trans. H.D.P. Lee, Harmondsworth: Penguin, 1955. (A classic of Western philosophy.)

* Ryle, G. (1954) 'Pleasure', in *Dilemmas*, Cambridge: Cambridge University Press, 54–67. (An entertaining, deflationary, essay.)

* Sidgwick, H. (1874) *The Methods of Ethics*, London: Macmillan, 1962, esp. Bk II, ch. VI. (A classic text.)

GRAEME MARSHALL

PLEKHANOV, GEORGII VALENTINOVICH (1857–1918)

Known as 'the Father of Russian Marxism', Plekhanov was the chief popularizer and interpreter of Marxism in Russia in the 1880s. His interest in the philosophical aspects of Marxism made him influential outside as well as inside Russia. He was a prolific writer, and dealt with several aspects of Marxist thought.

Plekhanov was an important figure in the Russian revolutionary movement. He was a founder member of the Russian Social Democratic Party, and a leading figure in its Menshevik wing after it split into Bolsheviks and Mensheviks in 1903. As a politician, Plekhanov was constantly involved in polemics with political and ideological opponents. Most of his theoretical works are to some degree polemical, and it was the conflicts among Russian revolutionary groups

that shaped Plekhanov's interpretation of Marx's thought.

A basic feature of this interpretation was that Russia's historical development was like that of Western European countries, and would pass through a capitalist phase before progressing to socialism. Accordingly, Plekhanov gave prominence to those of Marx's writings which could be presented in a deterministic way. Plekhanov insisted that Marxism was a materialist doctrine (as opposed to an idealist one) and as such recognized the primacy of matter in all spheres of existence.

Plekhanov was in many ways an innovator, being the writer who first coined the term 'dialectical materialism', and who drew attention to the Hegelian origins of Marx's system. His writings were quickly translated into several European languages. His interpretation of Marxism was much admired by Lenin, and was to form the basis of the official ideology of the Soviet Union. The conception of Marxism that Plekhanov propounded continues to exercise a profound influence on conceptions of Marxism throughout the world.

1–2 Life
3 Plekhanov's Marxism
4 Significance and evaluation of Plekhanov's work

1 Life

Georgii Valentinovich Plekhanov was born in 1857 in the village of Gudalovka in the Tambov province in central Russia. His family belonged to the minor land-owning nobility. From 1868 Plekhanov attended the military academy in Voronezh, and with the intention of following a military career, in 1874 he enrolled in the St Petersburg Mining Institute.

It was while studying in St Petersburg that Plekhanov first came into contact with representatives of the Russian revolutionary movement, including S.M. Stepniak-Kravchinskii, P.B. Akselrod and L.G. Deich, who belonged to the group 'Land and Liberty'.

The members of Land and Liberty held that the function of revolutionaries was to articulate and strive to achieve the concrete aspirations of the common people. They believed that they should avoid projecting onto the people the desires of the educated intelligentsia. The term to describe a revolutionary of this kind was 'Narodnik' (Populist). In the 1870s Russian revolutionaries inspired by BAKUNIN, LAVROV or MARX all considered themselves to be 'Narodniki'. The slogan which Plekhanov held best to embody the Narodnik principle was: 'The liberation of the workers is the task of the workers themselves'. These were the opening words of the

First International's constitution, and had been written by Marx.

In the 1870s there were three main currents of opinion in the Russian revolutionary movement: (1) the followers of Bakunin, who believed that life in the village communities had made the Russian peasants natural communists, and that it only required agitation by the revolutionaries to stir them into rebellion against the state; (2) the followers of Lavrov did not agree that Russian peasants were socialists by nature, and thought that they ought to be educated by the intelligentsia, to bring them up to the same level of consciousness as the intellectual elite in society; (3) the disciples of Tkachëv, by way of contrast, were of the opinion that there was no need to prepare the common people in any way for revolution; it was simply a matter of seizing control of the state by a well-organized conspiracy, and then using the state machinery to change society in a way beneficial to the common people.

At the start of his revolutionary career Plekhanov became a Bakuninist. As such, he was hostile to the state, and thought that the only worthwhile change would be a social one that would come from below. Like most Russian revolutionaries of the period Plekhanov considered political activity a waste of effort. He believed that Marx was in agreement with Bakunin on this point, since he understood Marx to have argued on this that the economic and social base brought about changes in the political superstructure and not the other way round.

In December 1876 Plekhanov organized and took part in Russia's first revolutionary demonstration, held at the Kazan Cathedral in St Petersburg. Several participants were arrested, but Plekhanov himself escaped, and began his life as a professional revolutionary. The following year he went abroad, spending several months in Paris, where he met Lavrov, and in Berlin, where he made contact with the German Social Democrats.

On his return to Russia in 1877 Plekhanov conducted revolutionary agitation in Saratov, recruiting local workers and students to Land and Liberty. After a brush with the police, he returned to the capital and joined the editorial board of the journal *Zemlia i volia* (Land and Liberty), to which he contributed the article 'The Law of the Economic Development of Society and the Tasks of Socialism in Russia'. In it he argued that since the communal system of agriculture was still prevalent in Russia, socialism might be established there directly, without the necessity for capitalist development to run its course.

Consistent with the belief that social change came from the economic base, Land and Liberty maintained that terrorism was incapable of bringing about social transformation, but that it might be used as a reprisal against the authorities. This position began to change following the wave of popular sympathy aroused by the trial and acquittal of Vera Zasulich in 1878 for her assassination attempt on the governor of St Petersburg. This gave an impetus to the use of terror as a political weapon. In 1879 Land and Liberty split to give rise to two new organizations: 'People's Will', which favoured the use of terror, and 'Black Repartition' led by Plekhanov, which adhered to Narodnik principles and eschewed any type of political action.

In order to avoid arrest, Plekhanov left Russia in 1880, expecting to be able to return shortly. In fact he remained in exile for thirty-seven years, until the Revolution of 1917. In Paris Plekhanov translated 'The Communist Manifesto' into Russian as one of a series of socialist works to be published by himself in association with Lavrov. Marx and Engels supplied a foreword in which they admitted the possibility that the peasant commune might be the basis for communist development in Russia. By 1881, however, Plekhanov had come to the conclusion that Russia had now embarked on the path of capitalist development, and that all other paths were now closed to it. Plekhanov considered his change of view to be an adoption of Marxism, but it was a viewpoint out of step with Marx's own thinking.

2 Life (cont.)

Plekhanov's Black Repartition group was overshadowed by People's Will, especially after the latter group organized the assassination of Alexander II in 1881. In 1883 Plekhanov launched a new group, the 'Liberation of Labour', which, he claimed, espoused the doctrines of Marx and Engels. He elaborated the new group's standpoint in a work entitled *Sotsializm i politicheskaia bor'ba* (*Socialism and the Political Struggle*), published in October 1883. The book admitted that Black Repartition had been wrong to reject political action, but condemned People's Will for having gone too far in the opposite direction, and adopting the Blanquist tactics of Tkachëv. The Liberation of Labour, Plekhanov argued, was the optimum synthesis of the two extremes represented by Black Repartition and People's Will.

Lev Tikhomirov replied to Plekhanov's book on behalf of People's Will, pointing out that his organization's standpoint and tactics had been grossly misrepresented by Plekhanov. In response Plekhanov published the book *Nashi raznoglasiia* (*Our Differences*) (1884). This argued that the adherents of People's Will subscribed to a quasi-Slavophile notion that Russian development was unlike that of Western Europe, and that Russia could avoid a capitalist stage. This quasi-Slavophile doctrine Plekhanov dubbed 'Narodism', changing completely the usage of the term. He traced the origins of this Narodism to Herzen and Chernyshevskii, claiming that everyone who believed that Russia might avoid capitalist development belonged to the Narodnik current. This presentation of Russian intellectual history was hotly contested at the time, especially by those Plekhanov classed as Narodniks, but it later gained wide acceptance.

In the late 1880s Plekhanov studied Hegel's philosophy, and made use of this in his polemical essay against Tikhomirov, 'Novyi zashchitnik samoderzhaviia' (A New Champion of Autocracy) (1889) and the article 'Zu Hegel's sechzigstena' (On the Sixtieth Anniversary of Hegel's Death) published in German in 1891. In this latter work Plekhanov first gave currency to the term 'dialectical materialism' to characterize Marx's philosophical method. Plekhanov elaborated the concept of 'dialectical materialism' at length in *K voprosu o razvitii monisticheskogo vzgliada na istoriiu* (The Development of the Monist View of History) (1895), in which he drew on his studies of classical German Philosophy and French materialism of the eighteenth century. Plekhanov believed that Marx's dialectical materialism was a synthesis of elements taken from both of these schools – metaphysical materialism and dialectical idealism (see DIALECTICAL MATERIALISM §§1–2).

In this work Plekhanov also accused his Narodnik opponents of 'subjectivism', which he traced back to Lavrov's *Istoricheskie pis'ma* (Historical Letters) (1870). He tried to find writings by Marx which would also condemn 'subjectivism', and interpreted Marx's contributions to *The Holy Family* (1845) in this light.

At the turn of the century Plekhanov and the other members of Liberation of Labour became involved in a polemic with a new generation of social democrats in Russia, who believed that the efforts of revolutionaries should be devoted less to abstract theorizing and more to catering for the concrete needs of the workers' movement. Plekhanov labelled social democrats of this type 'Economists', and enlisted Lenin's help in a campaign to discredit them.

At the Second Congress of the Russian Social Democratic Labour Party in 1903 Plekhanov supported Lenin and the Bolsheviks against the Menshevik wing. By the end of the year, however, he had changed affiliations and sided with the Mensheviks. In later years he was constantly to vacillate between the two wings of the party. In the years following the 1905 Revolution, when a 'Liquidationist' current appeared within Menshevism arguing that in the new conditions there was no longer any need for an underground party organization, Plekhanov joined with the Bolsheviks in denouncing this as heresy. Between 1907 and 1910 he also cooperated with Lenin in a campaign against the current of Russian socialist philosophy represented by Aleksandr BOGDANOV, his main publication in this respect being the series of open letters with the general title 'Materialismus Militans'.

Plekhanov's accord with the Bolsheviks was destroyed after the outbreak of the First World War. Whereas the left wing of Russian Social Democracy condemned the war, Plekhanov became an ardent advocate of an Entente victory over the Germans. He maintained this position even after he returned to Petrograd in April 1917, contributing pro-war articles to the Menshevik newspaper *Edinstvo* (Unity).

The main theoretical work written by Plekhanov after *The Development of the Monist View of History* was *Osnovnye voprosy marksizma* (Fundamental Questions of Marxism), which appeared in 1908. This, however, mainly restated ideas which had been formulated in earlier writings. In 1909 the Moscow publishing house Mir commissioned Plekhanov to write a history of Russian social thought in the nineteenth century. This project became Plekhanov's main literary endeavour for the rest of his life. When he died, on 30 May 1918, however, only three out of a projected seven volumes had been completed.

3 Plekhanov's Marxism

Plekhanov became an extremely influential interpreter of Marx's ideas because he wrote at an early and crucial stage in their propagation. He was attracted to the scheme of historical determinism associated with Marx's name in the early 1880s when both Marx and Engels were still alive, and when relatively few of Marx's works had been published (see MARX, K. §8).

Moreover, Marx died in 1883 without leaving behind him a completed system. Originally he had intended to deduce the categories of political economy in the same manner as Hegel had deduced the categories of philosophy, and in doing so show that the world market was contained in the concept of capital. The reasoning was that when capital – externalized human social nature – became a world system and reached its point of culmination, it would collapse and give way to socialism. By the 1870s, however, Marx had come to realize that the circulation and reproduction of capital would not of itself erode existing economic and social structures. In studying the economic processes in Russia he formed the opinion that capitalist development might be forestalled there and socialism established on the basis of the peasant commune.

Although Plekhanov was well aware of Marx's views on the possibilities of Russian development, he did not try to amplify or propagate them. Instead, he attributed to Marx the doctrine that all countries passed through the same historical stages, and that capitalist development would necessarily take place in Russia.

Plekhanov was not a dispassionate student of Marx's ideas. He approached them as a polemicist, emphasizing some aspects of Marx's work and ignoring others as the stance he took in a given polemic required. The kind of philosophical questions Plekhanov took up were invariably those which had a bearing on the factional disputes in which he was involved.

The dispute on the efficacy of political action impelled Plekhanov to examine the relationship between historical determinism and the freedom of human action. This was to be a recurrent theme in his writings. Plekhanov argued that freedom and necessity were interconnected 'dialectically', that they formed the kind of unity, a freedom–necessity, that Schelling had proposed in his philosophy of identity (see SCHELLING, F.W.J. §2). He also compared the interrelationship between freedom and necessity to Spinoza's Substance, which led him to define Marxism as a variety of Spinoza's philosophy. Plekhanov also claimed that the freedom–necessity relationship had been satisfactorily formulated by Hegel when he stated that freedom implied knowledge of the laws of nature and submission to them. The primacy given to necessity in this formulation allowed Plekhanov to assert that the course of history was determined, not by human volition, but by the material productive forces.

In keeping with this conception of human history Plekhanov repeatedly stressed that human nature was not a constant, but an eternally changing product of the historical process. He claimed that Schelling, Hegel and Marx had all subscribed to this view. He was only able to find a single (ambiguous) passage in Marx to support this contention.

Plekhanov emphasized that 'dialectics' as he understood it differed substantially from simple evolution. He quoted Hegel to the effect that in both nature and human history transformations of quantitative into qualitative differences took place not gradually, but by 'leaps'. These leaps Plekhanov considered to be characteristic of the dialectical method that Marx and Engels had taken over from Hegel. In fact, in the passage cited Hegel was concerned to show that creation and destruction ought to be accounted for in terms of the development of the Concept, and that in changes from quantity to quality and *vice versa* the element of unpredictability – the 'cunning of the Concept' – operated at even the most basic levels of existence. Hegel's actual argument was lost on Plekhanov, who had only a superficial understanding of Hegel's system.

Plekhanov drew a firm distinction between idealist and materialist philosophies, asserting that only the latter were compatible with Marxism. He rejected any suggestion that human knowledge of the material world was conditioned in some way by the constitution of the human mind. He insisted that things-in-themselves were material objects and these directly or indirectly acted on the human senses to produce sensations. Materialism, as Plekhanov understood it, recognized the material nature of things, while idealism denied this materiality. This was an argument taken up by Lenin in his book *Materializm i émpiriokrititzism* (*Materialism and Empiriocriticism*) (1909) (see LENIN, V.I. §1). The implication was that Marx's philosophical conceptions were derived from the eighteenth-century French materialist tradition rather than from the line of inquiry that Kant had initiated and to which Fichte, Schelling and Hegel had, in their turn, contributed.

4 Significance and evaluation of Plekhanov's work

Plekhanov was able to achieve prominence as an authority on the philosophical foundations of Marx's thought because by the end of the nineteenth century knowledge of the intellectual context in which Marx had grown up had become extremely rare. As a result, his standing was high not only in Russia, but also throughout Europe. It was largely in the interpretation given to them by Plekhanov that Marx's ideas were received by the wider public. This is indicated by the fact that Plekhanov's term 'dialectical materialism' as a synonym for 'Marxism' gained general currency.

Dialectical materialism, as Plekhanov had elaborated it, formed the philosophical foundation for the official ideology of the Soviet state. In this form it was widely propagated throughout the world, and was the presentation in which most people were introduced to Marx's thought. Even the influential Marxist philosopher Georg LUKÁCS took Plekhanov's interpretation of Marxism as the starting point for his own conception of Marx's ideas. Lukács regarded Plekhanov and Engels as commentators on Marx of approximately equally high stature.

Plekhanov came to Marx's system when that system was incomplete and was in the process of modification by its author. It therefore lacked an obvious internal cohesion. Plekhanov exacerbated this situation by preserving the historical determinist aspect which Marx had rejected, and refusing to recognize, as Marx had done, human social nature as the driving force behind the historical process. As a result, Plekhanov propounded a 'Marxism' that was internally inconsistent and contained the almost mystical implication that somehow 'matter' would, in the course of human history, create a socialist society by 'leaps'.

Moreover, Plekhanov's insistence for polemical reasons on interpreting Marx's disagreements with the Bauer brothers in 1844–5 as a campaign against 'subjectivism' gave a misleading impression of the character of Marx's system and how it had emerged. Marx was in fact concerned to combat the common perception that philosophical abstractions had an existence apart from the concrete material they generalized. This was the sense in which he considered himself a 'materialist'. The attempt to eliminate abstractions and other forms of 'reflection' linked Marx to the main current of German philosophy. Plekhanov classed the latter as 'idealist' and would not countenance any debt by Marx to it.

The polemical tactic of assigning all previous Russian socialist currents to the category of Narodism distorted the intellectual history of Russia. It gave the impression that Narodism and Marxism were two distinct phases in the development of Russian socialist thought, and that Narodism was characterized by 'subjectivism', a Slavophile belief in Russia's unique-ness, and a conviction that capitalism could not take root in Russia. Narodism in this sense was a creation of Plekhanov's, but because it formed an integral part of Soviet ideology, it was incorporated into Soviet historical writing.

See also: MARXIST PHILOSOPHY, RUSSIAN AND SOVIET §§1–2

List of works

Plekhanov, G.V. (1923–7) *Sochineniia* (Works), ed. D. Riazanov, Moscow: Gosizdat, 24 vols. (The fullest edition.)
—— (1956–8) *G.V. Plekhanov: Izbrannye filosofskie proizvedeniia*, Moscow: Gosizdat, 5 vols; trans. B. Trifonov, *G. Plekhanov: Selected Philosophical Works*, Moscow: Progress, 1974–81, 5 vols. (This edition contains most of Plekhanov's main theoretical writings.)
—— (1883) *Sotsializm i politicheskaia bor'ba*, Geneva: Tipografiia gruppy 'Osvobozhdenie Truda'; *Socialism and the Political Struggle*, in *Selected Philosophical Works*, Moscow: Progress, 1974–81, vol. 1, 49–106.
—— (1884) *Nashi raznoglasiia*, Geneva: Tipografiia gruppy 'Osvobozhdenie Truda'; *Our Differences*, in *Selected Philosophical Works*, Moscow: Progress, 1974–81, vol. 1, 107–352.
—— (1895) *K voprosu o razvitii monisticheskogo vzgliada na istoriiu*, St Petersburg: Skorokhodova; *The Development of the Monist View of History*, in *Selected Philosophical Works*, Moscow: Progress, 1974–81, vol. 1, 480–737.
—— (1908) *Osnovnye voprosy marksizma*, St Petersburg: Slovo; *Fundamental Questions of Marxism*, in *Selected Philosophical Works*, Moscow: Progress, 1974–81, vol. 3, 117–83.
—— (1910) 'Materialismus Militans' in *Ot oborony k napadeniiu* (From Defence to Attack), St Petersburg; *Selected Philosophical Works*, Moscow: Progress, 1974–81, vol. 3, 188–283. (A series of open letters against the current of Russian socialist philosophy represented by Aleksandr Bogdanov.)
—— (1914–16) *Istoriia russkoi obshchestvennoi mysli* (History of Russian Social Thought), trans. M. Niqueux and M. Godot, *Histoire de la pensée sociale russe*, preface by J. Scherrer, Paris: Institut d'Études Slaves, 1984. (The 1984 edition is a translation into French of Plekhanov's 'Introduction' to this unfinished work.)

References and further reading

Baron, S. (1962) 'Between Marx and Lenin: George Plekhanov', in L. Labedz (ed.) *Revisionism: Essays on the History of Marxist Ideas*, London: Allen & Unwin. (This short biographical essay concentrates more on Plekhanov's political views than his philosophical ideas.)
—— (1963) *Plekhanov: The Father of Russian Marxism*, Stanford, CA: Stanford University Press. (The fullest biography of Plekhanov in English. Baron describes Plekhanov as 'one of the most sensitive and creative of Marx's disciples', perhaps not appreciating the extent to which Plekhanov distorted Marx's system.)
Kolakowski, L. (1978) *Main Currents of Marxism*, Oxford: Oxford University Press, vol. 2, ch. 14. (A perceptive analysis of Plekhanov's philosophical development.)
Walicki, A. (1969) *The Controversy over Capitalism: Studies in the Social Philosophy of the Russian Populists*, Oxford: Clarendon Press. (First published in 1965 as an introduction to a Polish collection of 'Narodnik' writings on social philosophy. This collection was an expanded version of a previously published Soviet work of the same type. Walicki's essay elaborates on the Soviet interpretation, originating with Plekhanov, that the 'subjectivist'

Narodnik doctrines gave way to the 'objectivist' Marxist current.)

—— (1980) *A History of Russian Thought from the Enlightenment to Marxism*, Oxford: Clarendon Press. (This repeats the version first advanced in the 1965 introductory essay.)

JAMES D. WHITE

PLOTINUS (AD 204/5–70)

Plotinus was the founder of Neoplatonism, the dominant philosophical movement of the Graeco-Roman world in late antiquity, and the most significant thinker of the movement. He is sometimes described as the last great pagan philosopher. His writings, the so called Enneads, *are preserved as whole. While an earnest follower of Plato, he reveals other philosophical influences as well, in particular those of Aristotle and Stoicism. Plotinus developed a metaphysics of intelligible causes of the sensible world and the human soul. The ultimate cause of everything is 'the One' or 'the Good'. It is absolutely simple and cannot be grasped by thought or given any positive determination. The One has as its external act the universal mind or 'Intellect'. The Intellect's thoughts are the Platonic Forms, the eternal and unchanging paradigms of which sensible things are imperfect images. This thinking of the forms is Intellect's internal activity. Its external act is a level of cosmic soul, which produces the sensible realm and gives life to the embodied organisms in it. Soul is thus the lowest intelligible cause that immediately is immediately in contact with the sensible realm. Plotinus, however, insists that the soul retains its intelligible character such as nonspatiality and unchangeability through its dealings with the sensible. Thus he is an ardent soul-body dualist. Human beings stand on the border between the realms: through their bodily life they belong to the sensible, but the human soul has its roots in the intelligible realm. Plotinus sees philosophy as the vehicle of the soul's return to its intelligible roots. While standing firmly in the tradition of Greek rationalism and being a philosopher of unusual abilities himself, Plotinus shares some of the spirit of the religious salvation movements characteristic of his epoch.*

1   Life and writings

We possess a fairly reliable account of Plotinus' life and writings by PORPHYRY, his student and editor. Porphyry composed a biography, *On the Life of Plotinus and the Order of his Books*, which prefaced his posthumous edition of Plotinus' writings. At the age of twenty eight Plotinus began his philosophical studies in Alexandria under a certain Ammonius (often called Ammonius Saccas, and not to be confused with Ammonius the teacher of PLUTARCH OF CHAERONEA (§1) or with AMMONIUS, SON OF HERMEAS) and studied with him for several years. After making a futile attempt at a journey to the East in order to acquaint himself with the philosophy of Persia and India, he settled in Rome at the age of forty. He established a school in Rome and stayed there except during his final illness.

The extant corpus of Plotinus' writings is one of the largest we have of any ancient philosopher, and we probably possess everything he wrote. His works are treatises, written in Greek, that grew out of discussions in his school, and vary greatly in length and scope. Porphyry arranged the treatises according to subject matter into six 'enneads' – six sets of nine treatises. In order to arrive at this division he had to split some treatises. Conventionally, references to the *Enneads* are often given only in numbers: 'V 3(49).2, 14–16', for instance, means '5th Ennead, 3rd treatise (which is number 49 on Porphyry's chronological list of Plotinus' writings), chapter 2, lines 14 to 16'.

2   General characteristics

Plotinus' thought grows out of a tradition of so-called Middle Platonism (see PLATONISM, EARLY AND MIDDLE), which developed during the first two centuries AD. The Middle Platonists interpreted Plato dogmatically: that is, unlike the Academic sceptics, they took Plato to hold definite views. Their interests lie primarily in metaphysics and psychology, broadly understood. Even if they show obvious influence from other schools of thought – many Aristotelian and Stoic notions had become a part of the language of philosophy itself – Middle Platonists believe that the fundamental philosophical truths are to be found in Plato. Plotinus shares these general characteristics.

It is sometimes said that Plotinus is a system builder who never reveals his whole system in an organized way, and that the system must be inferred from bits and pieces here and there in his writings. Another common dictum is that every one of his treatises presupposes all the rest and the whole system. There is something to these claims. However, even if behind Plotinus' writings there lies a more organized comprehensive view than meets the eye, his mind is not that of the rigid system builder. His philosophical genius rather consists in the exceptional sensitivity and depth of thought with which he addresses difficulties inherent in the Platonic tradition.

3   The One and the hierarchy of principles

Plotinus works with a fundamental dichotomy between the intelligible (*to noēton*) and the sensible (*to aisthēton*). The intelligible world is the realm of the real (in the sense of existing independently, being by virtue of itself), and it is unchanging and non-spatial. The sensible world, by contrast, is an unreal, changeable image of the intelligible, expressed in spatial extension. Within both these realms there are further divisions, so that the result is a hierarchical ontology. At the apex of the hierarchy is the One (also referred to as the Good), then, in descending order, are Intellect and Soul (see NOUS; PSYCHĒ). These three levels, the One, Intellect and Soul, are often called *hypostases* and their names are customarily capitalized. Particular souls – of people, animals and the soul of the sensible world itself – also belong to the intelligible order but are in close contact with the sensible realm. The hierarchy continues in the sensible world, where organisms, forms in matter (that is, sensible qualities), inanimate bodies and matter constitute the main stages. As is evident from the non-spatial nature of the intelligible world, such terms as 'hierarchy', 'above' and 'below' in the present context are not to be understood spatially but as indicating ontological priority.

The One, Intellect, Soul, and, with certain qualifications to be explained below, matter too, are explanatory postulates of the kind the Greek philosophers called principles (*archai*) (see ARCHĒ). Plotinus takes a strong realist position with regard to his principles: not only do they exist, they are more real, exist in some fuller sense, than that which they were meant to explain. Inorganic bodies, organisms and their functions, and human consciousness are phenomena to be accounted for in terms of the principles.

Considerations such as the following help explain the plurality of stages in the Plotinian hierarchy. Once a distinction has been made between what is to be accounted for and a principle that explains it, questions may arise about the principle itself: the principle itself may turn out to have features that stand in need of an explanation. A further principle must then be assumed to account for the first one. The process of seeking further principles continues until a principle that needs no further explanation is reached, a principle about which no further questions can be asked. For Plotinus this ultimate principle is the One.

Plotinus generally holds that the principles themselves must have the features they explain. For instance Soul, which is the principle of life, is itself alive. Moreover, the principles ideally have these features in such a way that it is pointless to ask why they have them. The principle possesses in and of itself what other things possess as a derived and contingent feature and hence one that requires explanation. Plotinus frequently expresses this by saying of a principle that it is such and such in itself (*en heautōi*), whereas other things have the same feature as in another (*en allōi*).

Unity is a central concept in Plotinus' doctrine: each stage of the hierarchy has a characteristic kind of unity, with the One as the absolutely simple ultimate principle which is the cause of all other unity that there is, and thereby, the cause of everything else whatsoever. To be is to be one thing, to be unified, and the more unified something is the more of a being it is. The most striking feature of the world of everyday experience is in fact the unity of it as a whole and of individual objects, especially living things, in it. The organization, regularity and beauty that are evident in the world of everyday experience, all of which may be said to express its unity, cannot be explained in terms of its constituent parts. The latter are what is unified and their unity is an imposed feature which must come from elsewhere. The unity revealed in the sensible world is in Plotinus' view far from perfect but it gives the sensible world the reality it has. The same may be said of our experiences of ourselves: introspection will show that the human soul has a more perfect kind of unity than anything pertaining to the body, although even the soul does not have unity of itself (IV 2(4).2; IV 7(2).6–7). Thus, the world of everyday experience, both the external world and our mental life, point beyond themselves to a higher level of reality which is its principle.

This process of going upwards from everyday phenomena obviously draws on Plato's dialectic as described for instance in the *Symposium* and the *Republic*. There are many instances of such a procedure in the *Enneads*, the most famous being Plotinus' first treatise, *On Beauty* (I.6911)), where he builds on Diotima's speech in the *Symposium*. This treatise has been influential in art, especially during the Renaissance. The ascent from the beauty of corporeal things to the Beautiful itself is, as one would expect, interpreted in terms of the Plotinian hierarchy and general doctrine of intellectual ascent (see §6). There is a noteworthy deviation from Plato's views of the arts as expressed in the *Republic* in that for Plotinus art does not imitate nature but operates parallel with nature (I 6.3; V 8(31).1). Thus, the artist uses the intelligible world directly and gives it an expression in the sensible world.

Ignoring the intermediate stages for the moment, the self-sufficiency of the principles with regard to the features they explain, together with the claim that whatever else there is presupposes unity, leads to the highest principle, the One, which is both absolutely simple and unique (V 4(7).1). The doctrine of the One, even if adumbrated by the tradition before Plotinus, is probably his most significant innovation. Some of his Middle Platonist predecessors believed in a simple first principle, but like Aristotle they thought that this simple principle was an intellect of some sort. In Plotinus' view, by contrast, Intellect involves plurality: there is plurality in thought because there is at least a conceptual distinction between the thought and its object, and what is thought is in any case varied (see, for example, V 3(49).10).

The One is unique and involves no variation or limitation. From this it follows that the One cannot be given any positive characterization. It cannot be grasped by thought or known in its true nature since any thought of it distorts in so far as the thought is bound to be composite (V 5(32).6; VI 9(9).4). It would even be inappropriate to say of the One that it is, or that it is one inasmuch as such expressions indicate something unified rather than the absolutely simple nature that gives unity to whatever is unified (VI 9.5). Nevertheless, it is possible to approach the One and even become one with it in a kind of non-cognitive union, a 'vision' which defies all description (VI 9.8–11). It is as a result of this doctrine of a union with the ultimate principle, a union which transcends conceptualization, that Plotinus has been called a mystic. Without wishing to deny the significance of this union with the One, it must be said that it does not play a major role in his writings. In spite of the fact that the One is ineffable, Plotinus manages to say a great deal about it. This is however not a real inconsistency: the ineffability of the One is the thesis that one cannot predicate anything of it since any predication would imply the One's composition. This does not mean one cannot talk about its relations to other things and in general about its role in the ontology.

Even if there are precedents in Plotinus' tradition for a supreme formal principle, most of his predecessors would postulate in addition other ultimate principles. In Plotinus everything derives from the One, even if the lower levels in the hierarchy function in fact as principles of multiplicity. In this sense Plotinus is an ardent monist.

4 Intellect, Soul and the sensible world

The divine Intellect, the stage after the One, is also the realm of the (Platonic) Forms and of the real or primary being. The identification of the realm of the Forms with primary being is straightforward: by definition each Form is eminently and of itself that which it causes in others. But this primary being is also the universal Intellect: the Forms exist as the thoughts of Intellect, whose thinking of the Forms is described as self-thought, and its knowledge of them as a kind of self-knowledge (see especially V 5, V 8(31) and V 3). Of several arguments Plotinus advances for the claim that the Forms are internal to the Intellect, the philosophically most interesting one is an argument to the effect that if the Forms are outside the Intellect, its knowledge of them must be acquired; but the Forms are the standards of judgment and if the Intellect does not possess these standards previously it will lack the necessary means of recognizing the impression of each Form for what it is. So, if the Intellect does not essentially contain the Forms as its thoughts, its knowledge becomes problematic: an unacceptable conclusion since it is agreed that the universal divine Intellect has supreme knowledge. Plotinus' identification of primary being with a divine Intellect implies that there is a level of reality where knowledge and being, epistemology and ontology, coincide. This Plotinus takes to be a necessary condition of the possibility of knowledge.

As mentioned above, Intellect is characterized by a greater unity than the sensible world. This is first of all brought out by the fact that Intellect is non-spatial and non-temporal and hence free from the dispersion that has to do with space and time. Second, the part–whole relations in Intellect are such that not only does the whole, which is more than the sum of its parts, contain its parts, the whole is also implicit in each of the parts (see, for example, VI 2(43).20). Third, there is no real distinction between subject and attribute at the level of Intellect. Instead Plotinus posits intellectual substance and its activity (energeia), which is identical with the substance. Much of this doctrine about the relationships between items on the level of Intellect is founded on interpretations and suggestions in Plato's late dialogues. Plotinus takes the five 'greatest kinds' of the Sophist – being, sameness, difference, motion and rest – as the highest genera of his ontology. Each of these is distinct, but nevertheless presupposes and is interwoven with all the others. As a whole they constitute the Intellect or the intelligible substance. Particular Forms are generated from them.

The integrity of Intellect implies that Intellect's thought is different from ordinary discursive thought:

Intellect grasps its objects and all their relations in an atemporal intuition of the whole, employing neither inferences nor words; the vehicles of its thought are the very things themselves, the prototypes and causes of which all other things, whether natural phenomena or lower modes of human thought, are inferior manifestations.

Soul is the level below Intellect. On account of the multiplicity of its functions, Soul is in some ways the most complex of the Plotinian *hypostases* and conceptually the least unified one. The historical sources of Plotinus' notion of Soul are primarily Plato's dialogues, above all the *Timaeus*, but Plotinus' psychology also reveals strong Aristotelian and Stoic influences.

Plotinus makes certain distinctions within the psychic realm. There is the *hypostasis* Soul, which remains in the intelligible realm, and there are the World-Soul and the souls of individuals, where the latter two are on the same level (IV 3(27).1–8). Within the two latter types of soul, Plotinus further distinguishes between a higher and a lower soul, corresponding to a distinction between soul which operates directly through a body and soul which does not (this distinction coincides with the distinction between rational and non-rational soul). Soul is the intelligible level which is responsible for the sensible world. The lower soul, sometimes referred to as nature (*physis*), produces matter itself, inorganic bodies and ordinary living things, including the sensible cosmos itself, which according Plotinus is a supreme organism (IV 4(28).33).

Plotinus holds that all souls are one, that all souls are identical with the *hypostasis* Soul (and by implication with one another). The Neoplatonists after Porphyry rejected this doctrine but Plotinus maintains it consistently and attaches considerable importance to it (IV 9(8); VI 4 (22).4; IV 3.1–8). Such a doctrine seems to be implied by the combination of two Plotinian doctrines that we have just mentioned: the Soul's membership of the intelligible realm (or the realm of real being) and the integrity of that realm.

It has been mentioned that Intellect is outside space and time. In *On Eternity and Time*, Plotinus states his views on time. The treatise contains interesting and powerful criticisms of the views of Aristotle, the Stoics and the Epicureans. As is often the case, Plotinus' own views are a development of Plato's *Timaeus*. He defines eternity as 'the life which belongs to that which exists and is in being, all together and full, completely without extension or interval' (III 7 (45).3, 36–8) and time as 'the life of soul in the movement of passage from one mode of life to another' (III 7.11, 43–5). Thus, time comes in at the level of Soul as the 'image of eternity'. This means that Soul, in producing the sensible world, unfolds in successive stages what at the level above is present all together and without temporal interval.

Certain difficulties arise precisely on account of Soul's close relationship with the sensible. In the first place, how can Soul cause, administer and ensoul the extended sensible world without thereby coming to share in its extended nature? How can Soul operate in different parts of extension without being divisible into spatially distinct parts itself? If it is divided, its intelligible status will be lost or at least seriously threatened. This difficulty is increased by the fact that according to common and deeply ingrained opinion Soul is present in the bodies it ensouls. Plotinus was deeply disturbed by these and other puzzles having to do with Soul's relationship with the sensible realm as is demonstrated by the fact that he returns to the questions repeatedly. Despite brave attempts, it is questionable whether he succeeds in giving a satisfactory account of them.

One solution Plotinus frequently suggests and argues for, mainly from facts about the unity of consciousness in sensation, is that the Soul is present as a whole at every point of the body it ensouls. In this way it can be at different places without being divided. Its being present as a whole in different parts of space shows its different ontological status from that of bodies which have numerically distinct spatial parts (see, for example, IV 2 (4).2). Another account, however, presents Soul as not present in body at all, but rather the reverse – body as present in Soul. Body is in Soul in the same way that bodies may be said to be in light or in heat: they thereby become illuminated or warm without (in Plotinus' view) dividing or affecting the source of light or heat in any way. Similarly, bodies become ensouled, alive, by virtue of the presence of Soul. These ideas are explored in VI 4 (22) and 5 (23) (constituting a single treatise), which contain what is perhaps Plotinus' subtlest account of the relation between the sensible and the intelligible. Here he attempts to explain the apparent presence of the intelligible in the sensible in terms of its having effects in the sensible without being locally present there.

At the bottom of the Plotinian hierarchy lies matter. Plotinian matter is like the One in that it permits no positive characterization, but this is for exactly the opposite reasons. The One is, one might say, so full, so perfect, that it eludes any positive description. Matter, on the contrary, is such on account of its utter privation, or lack of being: it is sheer potentiality. Matter in Plotinus' system is the receptacle of immanent bodily forms, such as colours, shapes and sizes. Physical objects, bodies, are composites of matter and such immanent forms (VI

3(44).15). Matter itself is not subject to change but underlies change: as Forms come and go matter remains unaffected (III 6(26)). It is as such imperceptible, but reason convinces us of its existence as a purely negatively characterized substrate of forms. As what underlies the forms of bodies, it might be tempting to identify matter with space or with mass. Plotinus nevertheless rejects this, maintaining that the three-dimensionality of space presupposes local determination and that mass contains form, whereas matter is totally indeterminate and without form (II 4(12).8–12). Nevertheless, matter is the principle of spatial extension in that the dispersion characteristic of space is due to matter. Matter is an explanatory principle in the sense that it is necessary for explaining plurality, although it is not a principle of being in Plotinus' sense.

In the treatise I 8(51), Plotinus discusses at length questions concerning evil, a topic also brought up in many other treatises. The intelligible world is perfect and totally self-sufficient. While the sensible world is not, it is a reflection of the former and contains nothing which does not have its origins there. It is therefore puzzling how evil can arise. Plotinus argues that evil as such does exist and he identifies it with matter, understood as lack of all form, or non-being. This is absolute evil. Other things are evil in a relative way in so far as they have a share in matter.

5 Causation and critique of Aristotle

In the preceding account of the Plotinian principles mention has been made of the relationships between the *hypostases*. It remains, however, to address this topic generally. Plotinus inherits from Plato two ways of describing the relationship: the language of participation and the language of model (*paradeigma*), imitation and image (*eikōn*, *eidōlon*). A lower level participates in a higher one, and thereby comes to have the character of the latter, or it imitates the higher to the same effect. Both these ways of describing the relation see it from the viewpoint of the effect. Plotinus and the other Neoplatonists have in addition ways of describing the relation in terms of the causal agency of the higher level. This is what is commonly called emanation, although Plotinus' language is quite varied here. He often simply uses expressions such as 'to make' (*poiein*) and 'to proceed' (*proienai*) for the activity of a higher realm. He also frequently uses the analogies of the sun and the light it radiates, fire and heat and the like, to illustrate how a higher *hypostasis* generates a lower, and occasionally he uses the metaphors originating in language about water (for example, 'to flow out'). He is well aware of the fact that these are metaphors that must

not be understood too literally. The term 'emanation' may mislead in so far as it suggests that the cause spreads itself out. Plotinus, on the contrary, consistently maintains that the cause always remains unaffected and loses nothing by giving away.

In Plotinus there is sometimes an explicit and often an implicit distinction drawn between 'internal' and 'external activity' (*energeia*) (see, for example, V 3.12; V 4(7).2). This distinction runs through every Plotinian cause down to Soul and is crucial for an understanding of causation in the system. Keeping in mind what has been said about the identity of a substance with its activity, the internal activity will be the same as the thing itself. In terms of the light analogy the internal act is analogous to whatever the source of light, considered in itself and as a source of light, is doing. The external act is this same entity considered as operating in something else, causing the brightness on the wall for instance.

The matter is more complicated still: there is not only a process from the cause, but also a reversion (*epistrophē*) of the produced towards its source without which the external act is incomplete. Since there is no pre-existent material principle, a recipient of form, what becomes informed must come from the informing cause. Thus, the outgoing aspect of a given level in the hierarchy functions as a material principle for the level below, the returning aspect as the informing of that material principle. Thus, reversion is equivalent to imitation. The product is an image or expression of the original, an effect, which nevertheless is not cut off from its cause, because the effect depends on the activity of the cause.

All activity except the internal activity of the One is a form of thinking or contemplation (*theōria*) (III 8(30)). (Even the One's activity appears to be mental activity of a sort, although it is not 'thinking' (see, for example, V 4(7).2; VI 8(39).16.) This holds even of the activity of the lower phase of the World Soul, nature, which creates the sensible forms in matter: all action (*praxis*) and production (*poiēsis*) have contemplation as their goal; production is the result of weak or imperfect thinking. We may visualize the system as a hierarchy where each stratum has an external activity, which in an attempt to grasp in thought its source creates an image of it, revealing it as more 'unfolded', less unified. So in a way the same items exist on every level: the One is everything there is, but in such a unified form that no distinctions are to be found. Likewise, Intellect and Soul, and finally the physical world contain everything there is. Only at the very lowest levels, that of matter and immanent sensible forms, is there no generation, which is another way of saying that we have reached the bottom.

Plotinus wrote some treatises on technical philosophical subjects such as potentiality and actuality (II 5(25)) and substance and quality (II 6(17)). The treatise on matter (II 4(12)) may also be said to belong to this group. The most extensive among such treatises, however, is VI 1(42)–3(44), which Porphyry gave the title 'On the Kinds of Being'. In VI 1 Plotinus critically discusses Aristotle's *Categories* (see ARISTOTLE §7; CATEGORIES §1), which he takes to be about the genera of being and, more briefly, the so-called Stoic categories (see STOICISM §6). He presents in VI 2 his own account of the genera of intelligible being, which for him is the only real being, and in VI 3 a revised version of Aristotle's categories doctrine is offered as an account to hold for sensible things. Plotinus' criticisms of Aristotle's category doctrine are founded on the assumption that it is about the genera of being. His main critical points are: (1) Aristotle's *Categories* fail to give a place to intelligible beings and hence cannot present a universal doctrine of the genera of being – it cannot be supposed to hold for both sensibles and intelligibles since there is no common genus for both and no discourse covering both at once; (2) each of the categories described by Aristotle fails to be one genus.

6 Human beings

A noteworthy feature of Plotinus' psychology is his use of Aristotelian machinery to defend what is unmistakably Platonic dualism. For instance he uses the Aristotelian distinctions between rational, perceptive and vegetative soul much more than the tripartition of Plato's *Republic* (see PSYCHĒ). He employs the Aristotelian notions of power (*dynamis*) and act (*energeia*), and sense perception is described very much in Aristotelian terms as the reception of the form (*eidos*) of the object perceived (see ARISTOTLE §18). However, he never slavishly follows Aristotle and the reader should be prepared for some modifications even where Plotinus sounds most Aristotelian.

Plotinus identifies human beings with their higher soul, reason. The soul, being essentially a member of the intelligible realm, is distinct from the body and survives it. It has a counterpart in Intellect which Plotinus sometimes describes as the real human being and real self. As a result of communion with the body and through it with the sensible world, we may also identify ourselves with the body and the sensible. Thus, human beings stand on the border between two worlds, the sensible and the intelligible, and may incline towards and identify themselves with either one. For those who choose the intelligible life, philosophy (dialectic) is the tool of purification and ascent. As noted previously, however, it is possible to

ascend beyond the level of philosophy and arrive at a mystical reunion with the source of all, the One. In contrast with the post-Porphyrian Neoplatonists, who maintained theurgy as an alternative, Plotinus stands firmly with classical Greek rationalism in holding that philosophical training and contemplation are the means by which we can ascend to the intelligible realm.

Plotinus' account of sense perception is an interesting example of how he can be original while relying on tradition. Sense perception is the soul's recognition of something in the external sensible world. The soul alone only knows intelligibles and not sensibles. If it is to come to know an external physical object it must somehow appropriate that object. On the other hand, action of a lower level on a higher is generally ruled out and a genuine affection of the soul is impossible because the soul is not subject to change. Plotinus proposes as a solution that what is affected from the outside is an ensouled sense organ, not the soul itself. The affection of the sense organ is not the perception itself however, but something like a mere preconceptual sensation. The perception properly speaking belongs to the soul. It is a judgment (*krisis*) or reception of the form of the external object without its matter. This judgment does not constitute a genuine change in the soul for it is an actualization of a power already present. In formulating this problem Plotinus' dualism becomes sharper, and in some respects closer to Cartesian dualism, than anything found in Plato or previous ancient thinkers. Plotinus contrasts sense perception as a form of cognition with Intellect's thought, which is the paradigm and source of all other forms of cognition. Sense perception is in fact a mode of thought but it is obscure. This is because the senses do not grasp the 'things themselves', the thoughts on the level of Intellect, but mere images. Since they are images they also fail to reveal the grounds of their being and necessary connections.

As the preceding account may suggest, Plotinus sees the goal of human life in the soul's liberation from the body and from concerns with the sensible realm and identification with the unchanging intelligible world. This is in outline the doctrine of Plato's middle dialogues. There are noteworthy elaborations, however. Plato holds that the soul's ability to know the Forms shows its kinship with them (*Phaedo* 79c–e). Plotinus agrees and presents a doctrine about the nature of this kinship which is left unclear in Plato. For as we have seen the whole realm of Forms is for Plotinus the thought of Intellect. The human soul has a counterpart in Intellect, a partial mind which in fact is the true self and is that on which the soul depends. This has two interesting consequences for the doctrine of spiritual ascent: (1) the soul's ascent may be correctly described as the search after oneself and, if successful, as true self-knowledge, as fully becoming what one essentially is; (2) on account of Plotinus' doctrine about the interconnectedness of Intellect as a whole, gaining this self-knowledge and self-identity would also involve gaining knowledge of the realm of Forms as a whole.

Plotinus' views on classical Greek ethical topics such as virtues (see ARETĒ) and happiness (see EUDAIMONIA) are determined by his general position that intellectual life is the true life and proper goal of human beings. He devotes one treatise, I 2(19), to the virtues. The suggestion in Plato's *Theaetetus* (176a–b) that the virtues assimilate us with the divine is central to his views on them, and serves as his point of departure. The question arises how to reconcile this doctrine with the doctrine of the four cardinal virtues in the *Republic*. Plotinus distinguishes between political virtues, purgative virtues and the paradigms of the virtues at the level of Intellect. These form a hierarchy of virtues. The function of the political virtues (the lowest grade) is to give order to the desires. It is not clear, however, how these can be said to assimilate us to god (Intellect), for the divine does not have any desires that must be ordered and hence cannot possess the political virtues. Plotinus' answer is that although god does not possess the political virtues, there is something in god answering to them and from which they are derived. Furthermore, the similarity that holds between an image and the original is not reciprocal. Thus, the political virtues may be images of something belonging to the divine without the divine possessing the political virtues.

There are two treatises dealing with happiness or wellbeing: I 4(46) and I 5(36). In the former treatise Plotinus rests his own position on Platonic and Aristotelian doctrines, while criticizing the Epicureans and Stoics. He rejects the view that happiness consists at all in pleasure, a sensation of a particular sort: one can be happy without being aware of it. He also rejects the Stoic account of happiness as rational life. His own position is that happiness applies to life as such, not to a certain sort of life. There is a supremely perfect and self-sufficient life, that of the Intellect, upon which every other sort of life depends. Happiness pertains primarily to this perfect life that is in need of no external good. Since all other kinds of life are reflections of this one, all living beings are capable of at least a reflection of happiness according to the kind of life they have. Human beings are capable however of attaining the perfect kind of life, that of Intellect. In the latter treatise Plotinus holds with the Stoics that none of the so-called 'external evils' can deprive a happy person of their happiness and that

none of the so-called 'goods' pertaining to the sensible world are necessary for human happiness (see STOICISM §§15–17). In I 5 he argues that the length of a person's life is not relevant to happiness. This is because happiness, consisting in a good life, is the life of Intellect and this life is not dispersed in time but is in eternity, which here means outside time.

7 Influence

Plotinus is one of the most influential of ancient philosophers. He shaped the outlook of the later pagan Neoplatonic tradition, including such thinkers as Porphyry and PROCLUS, and he left clear traces in Christian thinkers such as Gregory of Nyssa (see PATRISTIC PHILOSOPHY §5), AUGUSTINE and BOETHIUS. Since all these were extremely influential in their own right, Plotinus has had great indirect impact. He clearly played a significant role in preparing for medieval philosophical theology. A forged extract from the *Enneads* was known in the Islamic world as the *Theology of Aristotle*. The supposed Aristotelian origin of this text helped the fusion of Aristotelianism and Neoplatonism that characterizes much of Arabic philosophy. Neoplatonism saw a revival in Europe during the Renaissance. A Latin translation of the *Enneads* by Marsilio FICINO first appeared in 1492 and gained wide distribution. Plotinus exerted considerable direct influence on many sixteenth-and seventeenth-century intellectuals. Even if the popularity of Neoplatonism and Plotinus receded in the seventeenth century, many individual thinkers since have read and been influenced by Plotinus, for instance BERKELEY, SCHELLING and BERGSON.

See also: NEOPLATONISM

List of works

Plotinus (*c.*AD 205–66) *Enneads*, trans. A.H. Armstrong, Loeb Classical Library, Cambridge, MA: Harvard University Press and London: Heinemann, 1966–88. (Based on the authoritative editions of P. Henry and H.-R. Schwyzer, with minor modifications; Greek text with English translation.)

References and further reading

Armstrong, A.H. (1940) *The Architecture of the Intelligible Universe in the Philosophy of Plotinus*, Cambridge: Cambridge University Press. (A classic study.)

Atkinson, M. (1983) *Plotinus: Ennead V.1 On the*

Three Principal Hypostases, Oxford: Oxford University Press. (Very valuable commentary on a central treatise; abundant in references.)

Blumenthal, H.J. (1971) *Plotinus' Psychology*, The Hague: Martinus Nijhoff. (A detailed pioneering work.)

—— (1987) 'Plotinus in the Light of Twenty Years' Scholarship, 1951–1971', in W. Haase (ed.) *Aufstieg und Niedergang der römischen Welt*, Berlin and New York: de Gruyter, II 36. (Good bibliography.)

Bussanich, J. (1988) *Philosophia Antiqua*, vol. 49, *The One and its Relation to Intellect in Plotinus: A Commentary on Selected Texts*, Leiden: Brill. (Treats a central and important aspect of Plotinus' thought.)

Corrigan, K. and O'Cleirigh, P. (1987) 'The Course of Plotinian Scholarship from 1971 to 1986', in W. Haase (ed.) *Aufstieg und Niedergang der römischen Welt*, Berlin and New York: de Gruyter, II 1. (Good bibliography.)

Emilsson, E.K. (1988) *Plotinus on Sense-Perception: A Philosophical Study*, Cambridge: Cambridge University Press. (Analytic approach to Plotinus' philosophy of mind.)

Gerson, L.P. (1996) *Plotinus*, London: Routledge. (Extensive philosophical discussion of most aspects of Plotinus' thought.)

Lloyd, A.C. (1990) *The Anatomy of Neoplatonism*, Oxford: Oxford University Press. (A philosophically penetrating study, rewarding even if not an easy read.)

O'Meara, D.J. (1993) *Plotinus: An Introduction to the Enneads*, Oxford: Oxford University Press. (Highly recommendable introduction to Plotinus; contains a good bibliography.)

Rist, J.M. (1967) *Plotinus: The Road to Reality*, Cambridge: Cambridge University Press. (Essays on various Plotinian topics.)

Schroeder, F.M. (1992) *Form and Transformation: A study in the Philosophy of Plotinus*, Montreal: McGill University Press. (Contains several sensitively written essays on special topics.)

EYJÓLFUR KJALAR EMILSSON

PLURALISM

'Pluralism' is a broad term, applicable to any doctrine which maintains that there are ultimately many things, or many kinds of thing; in both these senses it is opposed to 'monism'. Its commonest use in late twentieth-century philosophy is to describe views which recognize many sets of equally correct beliefs or evaluative standards; and in this sense it is akin to 'relativism'. Societies are sometimes called 'pluralistic', meaning that they incorporate a variety of ways of life, moral standards and religions; one who sees this not as undesirable confusion but a proper state of things, espouses pluralism.

The principle famously known as Ockham's Razor – that we should posit no more entities than our purposes demand – expresses a disinclination to ontological pluralism, though not of course a promise that we can always dispense with it (see OCKHAM, W. §2; DURANDUS OF ST POURÇAIN). Kant believed such a disinclination to be a basic trait of human reason, which naturally seeks as much unity as possible in its view of reality (see KANT §8). A similar evaluation emerges in Leibniz's view that God's creation contains a maximum of individual variety falling under a minimum of general laws.

Ironically, Kant's own philosophy sowed the seeds of pluralism in another sense, at least equally important and conceptually rather more difficult: that there may be many ways of interpreting the world and reacting to it, very different from each other yet equally justified. Kant did not himself take that view; but by making the world we experience something that we construct, and which therefore depends on the nature of our own mental workings, he invited the thought that at other times, or in other cultures, others might construct it differently.

At one level, Hegel accepted the invitation, declaring the forms of human thought and experience to be historically variable. But this was no true pluralism, since he held the variation to be progressive, and progressing towards the point at which consciousness will see things as they really are. So later ways of thinking, though still inadequate, are less inadequate than earlier ones, and Hegel's friendliness to pluralism is only provisional – behind it lies a firm commitment to the view that ultimately there is just one true way to see reality.

Monotheists are almost certain to be unfriendly to pluralism, since they will typically hold that there is a uniquely true set of beliefs and a uniquely right set of moral standards – those of the deity – so that any *de facto* pluralism is just an effect of human incapacity. Hence significant support for any thoroughgoing pluralism acquired real momentum only in the nineteenth century as thinkers, following the lead of D.F. STRAUSS and FEUERBACH, began to view God as a projection of the human mind, or to abandon theism altogether. Nietzsche's 'perspectivalism' – truth exists only as truth from a particular perspective, and the Truth (capital T) does not exist at all – is one of its products (see NIETZSCHE, F. §4).

That conclusion was certainly connected with Nietzsche's view that belief and the closely related concept of truth are in fact instruments for advancing the believer's purposes ('Truth is that kind of error without which a species cannot live'); and a variant of this view is central to the pragmatism of William JAMES. It leads very naturally to pluralism. For we are quite familiar with the idea that different individuals or groups may have different purposes and needs, as may the same individual or group at different times and in different circumstances. So if responsiveness to needs and purposes is what validates belief and/or determines truth, these may differ as well. Then we find ourselves with a plurality of truths, and a resulting tendency to hold that 'true', when properly used, must really mean 'true *for* S' (some person or group) and that where the relevant values of S differ, two 'truths' are not necessarily commensurable with each other (see RELATIVISM).

One should distinguish between a true pluralism and the toleration of minority opinions or codes of behaviour. Toleration of deviant opinion is quite compatible with believing that there is just one set of truths. Non-interference can still be argued for on the grounds that the existence of certain false opinions and certain forms of bad behaviour are lesser evils than what would be needed to suppress them; or, as J.S. MILL (1859) argued, because we may be more likely to light on the truth if a variety of opinions are represented in our debates – a view one might call *methodological* pluralism. However, in going on to praise individuality as an essential component of human well-being, and to argue the case for allowing a private sphere immune from legal and social pressure, Mill was advocating a limited but genuine pluralism of life-styles. A concern of liberal political theory has been to understand the arrangements needed to permit and support such pluralism while maintaining a stable society.

This is no purely theoretical exercise, for there are also social and political influences favouring certain types of pluralism. Many societies are now culturally and religiously diverse; and 'postcolonial' attitudes make for a far more egalitarian and less judgmental approach to other peoples' practices and beliefs. Sustaining such an attitude, where different cultures find themselves in close contact with each other, indeed for many purposes intermingled, is not without its problems; and it is not clear how far religious believers can sincerely regard other religions in so tolerant a way without in effect giving up their own.

See also: ANTHROPOLOGY, PHILOSOPHY OF; CITIZENSHIP; MONISM; MULTICULTURALISM; POSTMODERNISM; PRAGMATISM; RELATIVISM; RELIGIOUS PLURALISM; TOLERATION

References and further reading

James, W. (1904) 'Humanism and Truth', *Mind* 13 (October): 457–75; repr. in *Pragmatism* and *The Meaning of Truth*, ed. A.J. Ayer, Cambridge, MA: Harvard University Press, 1978. (Readable statement of the pragmatic view of the nature of truth, from which a pluralism naturally emerges.)

* Mill, J.S. (1859) *On Liberty*, London: Dent, 1972. (See chapter 2 for what is called above 'methodological pluralism', chapter 3 for something more like pluralism proper: the value of individuality.)

Nietzsche, F. (1883–8) *The Will to Power*, trans. W. Kaufmann and R.J. Hollingdale, New York: Vintage, 1968. (Sections 553–69 exemplify the pluralistic 'perspectivalism' widely found in Nietzsche's writings.)

Rawls, J. (1993) *Political Liberalism*, New York: Columbia University Press. (Argues for principles and a polity which citizens may reasonably endorse in spite of having diverse or pluralist substantive values.)

EDWARD CRAIG

PLURALISM, COGNITIVE
see COGNITIVE PLURALISM

PLURALISM, MORAL
see MORAL PLURALISM

PLURALISM, RELIGOUS
see RELIGIOUS PLURALISM

PLUTARCH OF CHAERONEA (*c.* AD 45–*c.*120)

The Greek biographer and philosopher Plutarch of Chaeronea is the greatest Greek literary figure of the first century AD. He is properly called Plutarch of Chaeronea, to distinguish him from the minor fourth-century AD Platonist Plutarch of Athens. His fame rests not so much on his contributions to philosophy as on those to history and biography. Indeed, despite the survival of a large body of philosophical and semi-philosophical writings known under the collective title Moralia, *most of his more technical philosophical treatises have perished. Nevertheless, his importance for our understanding of the development of Middle Platonism is great. Plutarch is a reasonably orthodox Platonist (in so far as that expression has any meaning), although his Platonism has some distinctive features. Against Antiochus, he accepts the sceptical New Academy as part of the Platonic tradition, but he also exhibits a degree of cosmic dualism (postulating a pre-cosmic evil soul) which goes rather beyond the Platonist norm. It is misleading, however, to oppose him to a supposed tradition of 'school-Platonism'.*

*As the ethical 'end' or 'goal' (*telos*), he adopts the normal later Platonist one of 'likeness to god'. In ethics, as in logic, he tends to favour Aristotelianism rather than Stoicism (advocating, for example, moderation of the passions rather than their extirpation, and appropriating as authentically Platonic the Aristotelian categories and syllogistic). A tendency to favour New Academic scepticism seems indicated in the titles of some of his lost works, but is not very evident in the surviving ones.*

As first principles, he postulates a pair consisting of God – who is one, the Good, and really existent – and the Platonic-Pythagorean Indefinite Dyad, which is a principle of multiplicity, and ultimately material. As secondary principles, he seems to adopt a logos, *or active reason-principle of god, although the evidence for this is not copious, and a world-soul, which is essentially irrational but desirous of 'impregnation' with reason by the* logos. *There is also in the universe, however, an active principle of disorder, which can never be entirely mastered by the divinity. A hint of Persian dualism seems to enter here into Plutarch's thought. Such a system is derivable above all from his essay* On Isis and Osiris, *which may not be entirely typical. Other distinctive features include a tendency to triadic divisions of the universe, a developed demonology, and an interesting combination of Aristotelian and Stoic logics.*

1   **Life and works**
2   **Ethics**
3   **Metaphysics – first principles**
4   **Psychology**
5   **Daemonology**
6   **Logic and epistemology**

1   Life and works

Plutarch of Chaeronea is the dominant figure in Platonism, and in Greek literature as a whole, in the latter part of the first century AD, and the first quarter

of the second (see PLATONISM, EARLY AND MIDDLE). Born probably around AD 45 (he presents himself as a beginning student of philosophy in Athens in AD 66/7), he lived until at least AD 119, when he is reported to have been appointed Procurator of Achaea (presumably a largely honorary post) by the emperor Hadrian. He came from the small town of Chaeronea in Boeotia, where his family had been prominent for many generations, and this connection remained important to him throughout his life, as also did his connection with Delphi, where he was elected in later life a priest of Apollo. In Athens he studied under a Platonist named Ammonius (not to be confused with AMMONIUS, SON OF HERMEAS), of Egyptian origin, who became a prominent citizen of Athens, and to whom Plutarch seems to have owed a degree of cosmic dualism which colours his Platonism. In later life, after undertaking some travel, notably to Rome, he settled down in Chaeronea, presiding over a 'mini-Academy' of his friends and relations, and taking an active part in local politics, including those of Delphi. Most of his dialogues are set in either Chaeronea or Delphi.

A vast body of work by Plutarch has come down to us, much of it, however, non-philosophical – most notably his 'parallel lives' of famous Greeks and Romans – although philosophical reflections may be found anywhere in his work. On the other hand, many of his more technical philosophical works, some with tantalizing titles, are lost (discarded, no doubt, in favour of Neoplatonist treatments of the same subjects, making a full evaluation of his philosophical position more difficult. He was, however, a regular (one hesitates to say 'orthodox') Platonist. It would be wrong to regard him as a maverick, or an 'eclectic'.

His chief surviving works of philosophical interest are the following: *On Isis and Osiris, On the E at Delphi, On the Oracles at Delphi, On the Obsolescence of Oracles, Is Virtue Teachable?, On Moral Virtue, On Delays in Divine Punishment, On the Daemon of Socrates, On the Face in the Moon, Problems in Plato, On the Creation of the Soul in the Timaeus.* Interesting things are said elsewhere, scattered, for example, through the biographies, in the nine books of *Table Talk*, or in the many other essays which, although Plutarch would have considered them 'philosophical', we would tend to regard as merely 'literary'. We also have a number of treatises of a polemical nature, directed against other schools, notably the Stoics and the Epicureans. Against the Stoics are: *On the Contradictions of the Stoics* and *On Common Conceptions [koinai ennoiai], against the Stoics*; and against the Epicureans: *That one cannot live happily following Epicurus, Against Colotes* (Colotes had attacked the implicit scepticism of Plato and others) and *The Doctrine 'Live in Obscurity'* [*lathe biōsas*, the basic Epicurean injunction].

This is a vast corpus, and certain variations of doctrine undoubtedly emerge, but basically Plutarch can be seen as a consistent Platonist, well within the parameters of what might be considered 'orthodoxy' – bearing in mind that there was no canon of orthodoxy, and that a wide latitude of doctrine was acceptable within the tradition.

2 Ethics

As regards the 'end' or 'goal' (*telos*) of life, for Plutarch, as for all later Platonists after Antiochus, the supreme object of human endeavour is 'likeness to god' (as opposed to the Stoic 'conformity to nature', adopted by Antiochus (see PLATONISM, EARLY AND MIDDLE §8). This is achieved through the exercise of the virtues, but particularly through the acquisition of theoretical wisdom (*sophia*), rather than practical wisdom. We find this well expressed in a passage of the dialogue *On Delays in Divine Punishment* (550d), where Plutarch himself is the speaker. Here, in fact, the *telos* of conformity to nature is artfully subsumed under the 'higher' one of likeness to god by the statement that 'Nature kindled vision in us', so that the soul should come to a knowledge of god.

On the subject of virtue and happiness, Plutarch inclines on the whole to the more 'broad-minded' ethical position of Antiochus, as against the Stoic-Pythagorean asceticism (see NEO-PYTHAGOREANISM) observable in such figures as Eudorus and PHILO OF ALEXANDRIA. Significantly, his terminology in this area is Aristotelian rather than Stoic. In his essay *On Moral Virtue* we have a useful statement of his ethical theory. It takes the form of an attack on the Stoic position that the soul is unitary, and that there is no such thing as a distinct irrational part. Moral virtue is to be distinguished from theoretical virtue, in that it has emotion (*pathos*) as its subject matter and reason as its form, reason acting to harmonize the essentially disorderly passions, and thus producing a set of virtues as 'means'. This is really Peripatetic theory (see ARISTOTLE §22) overlaid with Pythagorean influences.

Peripatetic too is Plutarch's position that all three types of good – spiritual, bodily and external – make their contribution to happiness (*On Common Conceptions* 1060c–), aligning him once again with Antiochus against Eudorus. In this passage he attacks Chrysippus for not admitting bodily and external goods as an essential component of happiness, although nature commends them to us (see STOICISM §§15–16).

3 Metaphysics – first principles

Plutarch's view of the supreme principle, or God, is just what one would expect of a Platonist: God is real being (*to ontōs on*), eternal, unchanging, non-composite, one (*On the E at Delphi* 392e). He knows all things and directs all things (*On Isis and Osiris* 351d, 382b), thus exercising providence (*pronoia*). He is also 'the object of striving for all nature' (*On the Face of the Moon* 944e), and thus is aligned with the Aristotelian prime mover (see ARISTOTLE §16). To this 'Monad' is opposed an 'Indefinite Dyad', as 'the element underlying all formlessness and disorder' (*On the Obsolescence of Oracles* 428f; *On Isis and Osiris* 369c). This is not simply matter, but a more actively disorderly principle which acts on matter, in opposition to the Monad, to produce the differentiation and multiplicity of beings. It is this principle which Plutarch sees as active in the pre-cosmic chaos described in Plato's *Timaeus*. The interaction of these two primal forces generates, first, number (and so the system of Forms) and then the physical world. In Plutarch's emphasis on the Dyad (and on the existence of an 'evil' world-soul) there is discernible an element of dualism which is more than Platonic, although its derivation is unknown (see also his comparison of Monad and Dyad with Ormuzd and Ahriman the warring supreme divinities of Zoroastrian religion, at *On Isis and Osiris* 369e).

The first principle creates, and relates to, the world through suitable intermediaries, primary among which is the *logos* (cosmic 'reason') (see LOGOS §1). Originally a Stoic concept, *logos* appears in a Platonist context already in the thought of PHILO OF ALEXANDRIA. It has been doubted whether Plutarch really maintained a *logos* doctrine, but the evidence that he did seems sufficient. In a passage of *On Isis and Osiris* (373a–b), for example, two aspects, or moments, of the god Osiris are distinguished as his soul and his body. His soul is 'eternal and indestructible', whereas his body is repeatedly torn asunder by Typhon (the Indefinite Dyad) and is constantly being reassembled by Isis (the world-soul). The 'body' of Osiris, as it turns out, is the *logos* in its immanent aspect, in matter, whereas his soul is the transcendent *logos*, as the sum total (and organizing principle) of the Forms in the mind of god.

As for the status of the Forms as thoughts of God (the standard Middle Platonic view), we may refer to the passage in the essay *On Delays in Divine Punishment* mentioned in §2, where we see God himself, as the totality of the Forms, presented as the model (*paradeigma*) for the physical world, and for mankind in particular. This seems based on an interpretation of Plato's *Timaeus*, according to which god (as the creator or 'demiurge') is his own *paradeigma* (instead of looking to it as something external). Unfortunately, we lack Plutarch's essays *Where are the Forms?* and *How does Matter Participate in the Forms? It Makes the Primary Bodies*, but we can derive some idea of their contents both from this passage and from the title of the latter essay. Presumably what Plutarch means by 'it makes the primary bodies' is that matter (with which Plutarch has no hesitation in identifying Plato's 'receptacle' in *Timaeus*), on being 'irradiated' by form, constitutes the basic triangles of which the four elements are composed.

Besides the general theory of Forms, Plutarch produces in *On the Obsolescence of Oracles* a remarkable doctrine connecting the five 'greatest kinds' of Plato's *Sophist* with the basic constituents of the physical world, namely, the four elements plus the physical world as a whole. He is here taking the five basic molecules described by Plato in the *Timaeus* (53c–56c) – of which the cube represents earth, the pyramid fire, the octahedron air and the eikosihedron water – and relating them respectively to rest, motion, identity and difference, while the dodecahedron, which represents the physical world as a whole, corresponds to being. Whether this is an original contribution of Plutarch's is not clear, but it anticipates interestingly the use of the 'greatest genera' by Plotinus as a set of 'categories' for the intelligible world (see PLOTINUS §4).

The celebrated 'dualism' of Plutarch comes out in his description of the Forms as 'seized by the element of disorder and confusion which comes down from the region above' (*On Isis and Osiris* 373a). This seems to imply not just the rather negative unruly material principle of the *Timaeus*, but a positive force, a 'maleficent soul', which has at some stage itself already broken away from the intelligible realm. We seem thus to be brought close to Gnostic beliefs, but Plutarch claims the authority of Plato for this. In *Laws* (X 896d), Plato seems, at least, to postulate, in opposition to the beneficent world-soul, another 'of the opposite capacity', which is responsible for all irrational motion in the universe. Anything which is soul is also alive and self-moving, so that a considerable step has been taken beyond the inanimate principle of 'otherness' or 'necessity' postulated in the *Timaeus*.

4 Psychology

This 'negative' or 'evil' principle in the universe, however, must be distinguished from the world-soul proper, which, although essentially irrational, is a 'positive' force, in the sense that it strives for ordering (or in mythical terms, 'impregnation') by the *logos*.

Plutarch's position on this, however, is somewhat complex. In *On Isis and Osiris*, Isis is equated with the 'receptacle' of the *Timaeus* and with matter, as well as with wisdom, and takes on very much the same role as does wisdom in the earlier system of the Platonizing Jew Philo of Alexandria, suggesting a tendency in Alexandrian Platonism (if we may connect Plutarch with that through Ammonius) to identify at least the positive aspect of matter with the world-soul, and to connect them both with the Pythagorean/Early Academic Dyad, which is not properly an 'evil' principle, as is the 'Seth-Typhon' figure in Plutarch's system. This amalgam produces an entity which is on the one hand 'fallen' and imperfect (although filled with longing for perfection), on the other the cause of our creation and the vehicle by which we can come to know God. In his treatise *On the Creation of the Soul in the Timaeus*, Plutarch presents us with the remarkable image of a 'slumbering soul', which is periodically roused to rationality by the 'better element' (the *logos*). This seems to be inspired by a non-literal interpretation of the myth of Plato's *Statesman*, since it becomes plain from what follows (1027a) that the process of arousal is actually not periodic but continuous. We have therefore an essentially irrational world-soul, completely interwoven with a rational soul or *logos*, thus maintaining a constant cosmic tension.

The belief in an eternal, independent irrational soul naturally has consequences for Plutarch's views on the composition both of the world-soul and of the individual soul, as described, in particular, in the *Timaeus*. Indeed, Plutarch devotes to this question a whole treatise, *On the Creation of the Soul in the Timaeus*, constituting a detailed exposition of his views, in the form of an extended commentary on the *Timaeus*. The specific problem concerns what we are to understand by 'the substance which is divisible about bodies' in the description of the elements of the soul. Plutarch criticizes his Platonist predecessors, such as XENOCRATES §2 and Crantor, for not recognizing that this 'divisible substance' must in fact be the irrational 'disorderly' soul that animates the pre-cosmic chaos (*On the Creation of the Soul* 1014b). So this disorderly element which Plato calls 'necessity' (*Timaeus* 48a, 56c, 68e) cannot be taken as something characterless, such as matter, but must be an active principle, the disorderly or 'maleficent' soul. We must distinguish, he argues, between matter, as described in *Timaeus* (50e), which is bereft of all quality and power of its own, and this refractory element in the universe, which has distinct powers and qualities. He adduces Plato (*Philebus* 24a and *Statesman* 273b) to fortify his position – which depends, however, on the premise of the unity of Plato's thought.

A noteworthy doctrine of Plutarch's is his strong distinction between the human soul and the human mind. Of course, such a distinction had always been present in some form in philosophic speculation, and perhaps most notably in Aristotle's *On Soul*, but Plutarch seems to give it a special twist. In *On the Face in the Moon*, we find the assertion that mind is just as distinct from soul as soul is from body. We may note here, apart from the unequivocal tripartition of the human being, a notion of three terms and two conjunctions – body and soul producing the irrational soul (*to alogon*), soul and mind producing the reason (*logos*). The rational soul, then, as our centre of consciousness, is not to be seen as mind in its pure state, but rather as consisting in the conjunction of pure mind with something lower and essentially irrational. This doctrine takes on a further twist in *On the Daemon of Socrates*, where we find the mind presented as in a way *external* to the body, presiding over it as its 'daemon', while different individuals have very different relations to their highest element, some allowing it to float freely 'above' them, others dragging it down into contamination with bodily concerns. This owes something, perhaps, to Aristotle's *On the Soul* III 5, but also to Plato's *Timaeus*. The latter (90a) refers to 'the most authoritative element of our soul' as a daemon, which God has given to each one of us, and which raises us up from earth towards our kindred in the heavens. Nevertheless, Plutarch's doctrine is interestingly distinctive, finding analogues in certain treatises of the *Corpus Hermeticum*, Treatises I and X in particular.

This threefold division of the individual has its equivalent on the cosmic level, in the form of a threefold division of the universe, such as we find in *On the Face in the Moon*, where Plutarch bases his theory on one of Xenocrates' concerning the combination of three 'densities' or 'tunings' of matter with the elements fire, air and earth respectively. Plutarch also proposed another, more complex, theory, which can be found in *On the Daemon of Socrates*. Here, the Monad, mind and nature (which could be taken as the irrational soul) are presented as three 'links' holding together four levels of being. How seriously Plutarch took, or means us to take, these constructions is uncertain, but they do serve as evidence for the existence of interesting lines of speculation. In particular, the identification in the latter passage of the highest principle as a Monad superior to a mind finds something of a parallel in the theological chapter 10 of the *Didaskalikos* of ALCINOUS.

5 Daemonology

The more transcendent the supreme deity becomes,

the more he stands in need of other beings to mediate between him and the material world, over which, in Platonism, he always exercises a general supervision (*pronoia*). The *logos* fulfils this function, but Plutarch, like all other Platonists, also postulates a daemonic level of being, and his theorizing about these entities is more elaborate than is found elsewhere. For Plutarch, both god's transcendence and his providential care for the world must be preserved, and the universe can tolerate no sharp divisions or sudden transitions. The basic inspiration for this concept of daemons in linking together the incompatible extremes of the universe is a famous passage in Plato's *Symposium* (202e), but the details were obviously worked out further by his follower Xenocrates, who is a major source for Plutarch.

In the dialogue *On the Obsolescence of Oracles*, for example, we find a geometrical elaboration of the basic Platonic doctrine attributed to Xenocrates, and commended by the speaker, according to which daemons are compared to isosceles triangles, median between the equilateral of the gods and the scalene, representing humanity. Earlier Plutarch's adoption of Xenocrates' tripartition of the world in *On the Face in the Moon* was noted. Here the moon, which served there as the focus of the median realm, and as the proper place of souls (and indeed as the symbol of the world-soul), is now made to serve also as the proper place of daemons, which is suitable to their mediating status.

Plutarch, like Xenocrates, recognizes the existence of both 'good' and 'evil' daemons, and in this connection we must distinguish a complexity, and possible incoherence, in his account of them. According to one view, daemons are souls in the process of either ascent from or descent into incarnation; according to another, they are permanent members of a spiritual hierarchy. Plutarch seems to entertain, at various points, both what one might term a 'static' and a 'dynamic' theory of daemons. A good statement of the latter view occurs in *On the Obsolescence of Oracles*, which describes a constant process of transmutation of human souls into daemons and 'heroes' (a distinct category in later Platonism), and even occasionally (as in the case of Heracles) into gods. There may well be a degree of incoherence in Plutarch's theory. It is really not clear whether some souls remain permanently disembodied (to constitute either good or evil daemons), or whether all are subject to the process of ascent and descent.

It remains to speak of the personal or guardian daemon, the most notable example of which, for later Platonists, was the 'daemon' of Socrates. In Plutarch's essay *On the Daemon of Socrates*, we find a vivid description of how the guardian daemon can assist an individual. These guardians are, it seems, all souls who have been through incarnation themselves, and have now earned their release from the cycle of rebirth; they are not souls that have never suffered incarnation. Only noble souls are qualified to serve as guardians.

In connection with his theory of the guardian daemon, Plutarch indulges in some interesting speculations about the mode of contact between the daemonic and the human mind, and between mind and matter in general (*On the Daemon of Socrates* 588f–589b). This is a problem which had not bothered Platonists, from Plato onwards, as much as it should have, and Plutarch does not really address the true difficulties (he simply speaks with wonder of the 'slight impulse' by which the mind sets the bones and sinews in motion), but at least he raises the question. Only Plotinus, later, really tries to address the problem of the mode of interaction between the material and the immaterial (for example, in *Enneads* III 6(26).1–5).

6 Logic and epistemology

Technical logic was not among Plutarch's more vital concerns, and there is in his extant works not much to indicate which system he followed, although there is no reason to think that it differed much from that set out somewhat later in Alcinous' *Didaskalikos* (ch. 6), which is itself a basic account of Middle Platonic logic. Plutarch did compose a *Lecture on the Ten Categories*, now lost, of which one would gladly have known the contents. Did he remain true to Aristotle, or did he, perhaps, adopt some of the Pythagoreanizing 'corrections' introduced by Eudorus, such as the placing of quality before quantity? We also find in the extant list of Plutarch's works two other treatises whose titles sound logical, *A Reply to Chrysippus on the First Consequent* and *On Tautology*, as well as some works on rhetoric, which was counted as a part of logic. Apart from revealing a tendency to attack the Stoics, which is what we should expect from Plutarch, these titles do not tell us very much.

That Plutarch regarded Plato as being already in possession of the so-called Aristotelian logic is indicated in *On the Creation of the Soul*, which is a commentary on *Timaeus* 37a–b, a passage in which most of the Aristotelian categories might be discerned, if viewed with the eye of an adherent. Sceptics might object to the equating of the examination of identity and difference with quantity and quality, and the equating of a thing's *existence* in a certain sense with its *activity*. A loyal Platonist could, however, argue that any distinguishing of a thing from other things must involve a statement of its quality and

quantity (as indeed Aristotle himself notes in the *Categories* (11a15)), and that, on Plato's own principle, as laid down in the *Sophist* (248c), existence means acting and being acted upon. Furthermore, the Aristotelian categories 'being-in-a-position' and 'having' can conceivably be viewed as latent in the latter part of the passage. Plato, then, in Plutarch's view, knows the categories, but is not concerned with enumerating them anywhere as baldly as did his famous pupil. On the basis of these categories, Plutarch declares, Plato constructs his epistemology, according to which the soul, when operating on the level of sense-perception, produces opinions which are fine and true, and when operating on the level of pure reason, intelligence and knowledge. These true opinions and beliefs, a Platonist would claim, are naturally expressed in syllogistic form. Alcinous, in *Didaskalikos* ch. 6, discerns various syllogisms in the first and second hypotheses of the *Parmenides*. Plutarch would doubtless have agreed with him, but we lack any evidence on this. In another passage, however, from the polemical treatise *Against Colotes* (1115d–), Plutarch appears to identify Plato's discussion of non-being as 'otherness' in the *Sophist* (255a–258e, especially 257b) as providing a stimulus to both Aristotelian and Stoic logic. Aristotle and the Stoics, the argument runs, seized on the concepts of 'not-being' and 'otherness' discussed in the *Sophist*, divested them of their metaphysical implications, and constructed purely logical systems out of them.

In projecting the Aristotelian and Stoic logical systems back into Plato, Plutarch is in agreement, as has been said, with what we find in Alcinous, and also among other near-contemporaries, such as APULEIUS and GALEN. There is no sign in his extant works of the disposition to attack Aristotelian logic, in particular the categories, that is evident in Eudorus before him, or in his own follower Atticus. On the other hand we do find, in *On the E at Delphi*, an interesting commendation of the Stoic hypothetical syllogism as the basic component of human reasoning, as stated by Plutarch's friend Theon. He seems to rank it as superior to the Aristotelian, but this may simply be a consequence of the context, which concerns the elucidation of the Delphic E, here interpreted as 'if' (*ei*).

List of works

Plutarch (late 1st–early 2nd century AD) *Lives*, ed. B. Perrin *et al.*, Loeb Classical Library, Cambridge, MA: Harvard University Press and London: Heinemann, 1914–26, 11 vols. (Greek text with facing translation: comparative pairs of biographies of major figures from Greek and Roman history.)

—— (late 1st–early 2nd century AD) *Moralia*, ed. F.C. Babbitt *et al.*, Loeb Classical Library, Cambridge, MA: Harvard University Press and London: Heinemann, 1927–76, 16 vols. (Greek text with facing translation: essays, speeches and treatises on a wide range of issues, largely philosophical. Of particular importance are volumes 5, 7 and 12–13.)

References and further reading

* Alcinous (*c.* 2nd century AD) *Didaskalikos tōn Platōnos dogmatōn*, in J. Dillon (ed.) *Alcinous, The Handbook of Platonism*, Oxford: Clarendon Press, 1993. (English translation, with introduction and philosophical commentary.)

Babut, D. (1969) *Plutarque et le stoicisme*, Paris: Presses Universitaires de France. (Very useful on Plutarch's relation to Stoicism.)

Brenk, F.E. (1977) *In Mist Apparelled: Religious Themes in Plutarch's Moralia and Lives*, Leiden: Brill. (A good discussion, particularly on daemonology.)

—— (1987) 'The Religious Spirit of Plutarch', in W. Haase (ed.) *Aufstieg und Niedergang der römischen Welt*, Berlin and New York: de Gruyter, II 36: 1, 248–349. (Updating of previous work.)

Dillon, J. (1977) *The Middle Platonists*, London: Duckworth. (Chapter 4 is an introductory account of Plutarch.)

Froidefond, C. (1987) 'Plutarque et le Platonisme', in W. Haase (ed.) *Aufstieg und Niedergang der römischen Welt*, Berlin and New York: de Gruyter, II 36: 1, 184–233. (A good survey, but, disputably, sees *On Isis and Osiris* as the culminating expression of Plutarch's metaphysics.)

Jones, R.M. (1916) *The Platonism of Plutarch*, Menasha, WI: Banta; repr. New York: Garland, 1980. (Oversimplified and out of date, but still of some value.)

* Plato (*c.*366–360 BC) *Timaeus*, trans. F.M. Cornford, *Plato's Cosmology*, London: Routledge & Kegan Paul, 1937. (Plato's hugely influential work on cosmology.)

Thévenaz, P. (1938) *L'Ame du monde, le devenir, et la matière chez Plutarque* (World-Soul, Generation and Matter in Plutarch), Paris: Les Belles Lettres. (Includes a translation of the first part of the *On the Creation of the Soul*.)

Ziegler, K. (1951), 'Plutarchos von Chaironeia', in Pauly-Wissowa (ed.) *Realencyclopädie der Klassischen Altertumswissenschaft*, 21: 1, cols 636–962. (An excellent general survey; also published separately.)

JOHN DILLON

PNEUMA

Pneuma, *'spirit'*, *derives from the Greek verb* pneo, *which indicates blowing or breathing. Since breathing is necessary for life and consciousness,* pneuma *came to denote not only wind and breath but various vital functions, including sensation and thought, and was understood by some philosophers as a cosmological principle. It became especially important in Stoicism, which explained the world in terms of matter and the rational structure exhibited in all its forms; this is established by rhythmical variations in the* tonos *or 'tension' of the* pneuma.

In Hebrew tradition, where Greek was used, pneuma *stood for life, consciousness, and for invisible conscious agents, angels or demons. In Christian thought it denotes divine inspiration, in particular the Holy Spirit acknowledged as a divine Person. At John 4:24 it is used, unusually, to describe God himself.*

1 **Early Greek philosophy and medicine**
2 **The Stoics**
3 **Jewish and Christian thought**

1 Early Greek philosophy and medicine

ANAXIMENES (§1), the third in the traditional list of philosophers, regarded air as the basic substance of the universe, which it penetrated and controlled like breath in the human body; it was thus divine, or the source of divinity. Other forms of matter derive from it by condensation (wind, water, earth) or rarefaction (fire). In most accounts it is named as air, *aēr*, but *pneuma* is once found, and is a likely alternative.

DIOGENES OF APOLLONIA (§§2–3) also regarded air as the universal source, an imperishable and intelligent divine being which prescribes the orderly structure of the world: 'All things see and hear and have intelligence from this same (thing)'. It constitutes the soul (see PSYCHĒ) of all living creatures; and an elaborate description of the veins in the human body probably served to show how it was distributed. Theophrastus summarizes Diogenes' views of sensation and emotion; apparently the air within us assumes various qualities which it transmits to the brain. There is no explicit reference to *pneuma*; but in fragment 4 'men and other animals live by the air which they breathe' (*anapneonta*).

Meanwhile EMPEDOCLES (§6) had also taught that air is diffused through the body (fr. 100), but without giving it a primary role in sensation; rather, each of the four elements is perceived by the corresponding element within us (fr. 109); but these are mixed together in the blood, so that consciousness resides in the heart (fr. 105). Thereafter physicians centred on the island of Cos continued to regard the brain as the central directive organ, while the Sicilian school located it in the heart, from which *pneuma* proceeds along with the blood.

PLATO uses *pneuma* to denote both wind and breath. At *Theaetetus* 152b people's differing perceptions of the same wind (*pneuma*) as warm and cold are used to illustrate the subjectivity of sense perception. At *Phaedo* 70a, 77e, the theory of a breath-soul is gently derided. The physiology of the *Timaeus* probably reflects the teaching of the Sicilian school conveyed by Plato's contemporary Philistion, particularly in the description of diseases; 82e refers to noxious *pneuma* in the veins; 78–9 discusses the physics of respiration, and choking sensations are mentioned at 84e and 91e, but there is no general attempt to connect *pneuma* with consciousness or muscular control.

Sicilian influence can also be found in Aristotle's contemporary Diocles of Carystus and in ARISTOTLE himself. Both distinguish two species of *pneuma*: the air which is breathed in and regulates the temperature of the body, and a psychic *pneuma* regarded as the seat of vital warmth which resides in the heart, once again identified as the seat of consciousness (see STRATO §5).

2 The Stoics

The Stoics gave the concept of *pneuma* its most comprehensive development (see STOICISM §3). It was described as a blend of air and fire, the two active elements; but an alternative theory conceived of it as the substance underlying the four elements, although its fineness and rapid movement are still emphasized. *Pneuma* varies in its *tonos* or intensity; and rhythmical variations of *tonos* can exhibit structural organization and thus express reason itself, as we now know the human voice does. Rationality is thus present at various levels; in the consistency of physical substances, in the self-preservation of plants and animals and in human reason, itself identified as a physical system, the 'directive principle', *hēgemonikon*, located in the heart, assuming the old theory of the arteries as air-channels by which pneumatic messages are accepted and delivered. Sight as well as hearing was explained by impulses of *pneuma*.

Human reason itself is a lower analogue of the cosmic reason which penetrates every level of being such that the cosmos is compared to a living organism whose parts exhibit orderly coherence. In its physical aspect that reason is described as 'constructive fire' which generates the four elements and the orderly structure of the world, and persists when this structure is resolved back into it in a universal conflagration, from which a new and similar world will evolve. In contrast, the human reason can survive death, but not persist indefinitely.

The Stoics acknowledged the traditional Greek cults, sometimes identifying the cosmic reason ('intelligent *pneuma*') with Zeus and explaining the other gods as physical elements (for example, Hera as air, *aēr*) (see STOICISM §5). Since the world existed for the benefit of rational creatures, especially mankind, some later Stoics conceived Zeus in theistic terms as kindly and protective. Less perceptive critics, including many Christians, caricatured the Stoics as mere pantheists who identified God with the material universe.

Among medical writers Erasistratus distinguished between the vital *pneuma* centred in the heart and the psychic *pneuma* residing in the brain. A similar doctrine was taught by GALEN, who is otherwise critical of Erasistratus. Neither kind of *pneuma* is identified with the soul; the psychic *pneuma* is its primary instrument. (For the Pneumist school of medicine see HELLENISTIC MEDICAL EPISTEMOLOGY §1.)

3 Jewish and Christian thought

Stoic influence appears in the biblical book of Wisdom (7: 22), which represents the divine wisdom as a distinct personality endowed with intelligent spirit (*pneuma noeron*). In PHILO OF ALEXANDRIA (§4) Platonic ideas predominate, and the Logos assumes more importance; in *Creation* 1.24 it is identified with the 'intelligible world' (see LOGOS §2). *Pneuma* however reproduces two distinct words employed in Israelite tradition; *ruach* is a god-given life-giving principle which assumes personal characteristics only when located in a human body; *nephesh* denotes this principle as personalized. Philo used *pneuma* to denote both wind and breath, which (1) permeates the whole body, (2) is despatched through the windpipe for speaking, (3) is the material of the *hēgemonikon*, (4) is identified with divine inspiration conveying truth and knowledge. Philo does not, like the Stoics, use *pneuma* to denote God himself, although at *Giants* 27 it is given comparable epithets.

Pneuma is freely used in the New Testament, usually with little philosophical reference; but St Paul introduces a triad of 'spirit, soul and body' (1 *Thessalonians* 5: 23), perhaps a modification of the Platonic intellect, soul, body, suggested by the use of *pneuma* for *ruach*. Valentinians and other Gnostics used this Pauline triad in a doctrine of three classes of people: the Gnostic elect, ordinary Christians and pagans, all of whom had appropriate destinies. Other Gnostics (Sethians and Basilides) used *pneuma* to denote a principle intermediate between light and darkness, or between the highest reality and gross matter.

New Testament usage includes the commonplace 'wind' and 'breath', the latter also regarded as a life-giving force surrendered at death. Its use by St John (4: 24) to denote God himself is unusual; but it commonly denotes discarnate personal agents, both beneficent and malign, as well as the human personality or its various moods and affections, including divine inspirations, which are called, or originate from, the 'Holy Spirit' (or 'Spirit of God'), seen in the divine presence manifested in Jesus and present derivatively in his disciples and the Church at large. The Holy Spirit is linked with God and Christ in a trinitarian confession, at first informally (2 Corinthians 13: 14, *c.* AD 55), but soon in a credal formula (Matthew 28: 19, perhaps *c.* AD 100, but recalling established usage).

The Apologists and other second-century Christians adopted this trinitarian confession, but gave the Spirit little philosophical consideration, while emphasizing the divine Logos, as in Philo's Platonism, as God's intermediary. *Pneuma* however sometimes denotes the divine element in Christ, who is 'God according to the (his?) *pneuma*'. ORIGEN (§3) carefully discusses all three divine Persons and distinguishes their functions, once confining the Spirit's influence to the Church, whereas the Logos instructs all rational beings in obedience to the Father. This strongly hierarchical Trinity slightly resembles the triadic theology developing in Platonic circles; Eusebius could quote Numenius with approval. But the terminology is quite different; and in PLOTINUS (§4) the third hypostasis, Soul, corresponds, if at all, with the Christian Logos; and *pneuma* is used, *inter alia*, for a principle which unites Soul with matter.

The Creed of Nicaea (AD 325), gave the Spirit only formal recognition; but a revival of Origenistic ideas soon encouraged a more concrete presentation: and *c.* AD 360 a controversy led to recognition of the full and equal divinity of the three divine Persons. Thereafter the Spirit's distinctive impact was recognized in devotional literature more than in the Church's formal theology.

See also: QI

References and further reading

Bauer, W. (1957) *A Greek-English Lexicon of the New Testament*, trans. W.F. Arndt and F.W. Gingrich, Chicago, IL: University of Chicago Press, *pneuma* (*pneuma*), 680–5; repr. 1979, 674–8. (Good brief analysis with some notes on non-Christian usage; requires some knowledge of Greek.)

Burton, E.W. (1918) *Spirit, Soul and Flesh*, Chicago, IL: University of Chicago Press. (Useful source book from Aeschylus to the New Testament; Greek texts with English translations.)

Kittel, G.F. (ed.) (1968) *Theological Dictionary of the New Testament*, *pneuma* (*pneuma*) and *pneumatikos*, Grand Rapids, MI: Eerdmans, vol. 6, 334–451. (Full scale survey, including *pneuma* in the Greek world, besides biblical and Gnostic usage; English translation from the German.)

Sandbach, F.H. (1975) *The Stoics*, London: Chatto & Windus. (Well written introductory account; consult the index entry *pneuma*.)

Verbeke, G. (1974) *Pneuma*, in Ritter, J., *Historisches Wörterbuch der Philosophie*, Basle: Schwabe, vol. 3, Geist, II, cols 157–62. (Authoritative brief study in German.)

CHRISTOPHER STEAD

POETRY

Though poetry today seems a relatively marginal topic in philosophy, it was crucial for philosophy's own initial self-definition. In ancient Greece, poetry was revered as the authoritative expression of sacred myth and traditional wisdom. With Socrates and Plato, philosophy began by distinguishing itself from poetry as a new, superior form of knowledge which could provide better guidance for life and even superior pleasure. Just as the sophists were attacked for relativism and deception, so were poets stridently criticized for irrationality and falsehood. For Plato, not only did poetry stem from and appeal to the emotional, unreasoning aspects of human nature; it was also far removed from truth, being only an imitation of our world of appearances which itself was but an imitation of the real world of ideas or forms. He therefore insisted that poets be banished from his ideal state because they threatened its proper governance by reason and philosophy.

Subsequent philosophy of poetry has been devoted to overcoming Plato's condemnatory theory, while tending to confirm philosophy's superiority. This task, begun by Aristotle, was for a long time pursued primarily under Plato's general model of poetry (and indeed all art) as imitation or mimesis. *The main strategy here was to argue that what poetry imitates or represents is more than mere superficial appearance, but rather general essences or the ideas themselves. For such theories, poetry's relation to truth is crucial. Other theories were later developed that preferred to define and justify poetry in terms of formal properties or expression, or its distinctively beneficial effects on its audience. These strategies became increasingly influential from the time of Romanticism, but can be traced back to more ancient sources.*

The vast majority of theories follow Plato in treating poetry as a distinct domain, separate from and subordinate to philosophy. But since Romanticism, some have argued for the essential unity of these two enterprises. Great philosophy is here seen as the poetic creation of new ways of thinking and new forms of language, while the role of poetry as uniting and gathering things together so that the truth and presence of being shines forth.

1   **The attack on poetry**
2   **Defence of poetry as imitation**
3   **Artefact theories**
4   **Expression theories**
5   **Use theories**
6   **The unity of poetry and philosophy**

1   The attack on poetry

As Plato remarked, 'There is an ancient quarrel between philosophy and poetry.' Philosophy developed in Athens, largely through a struggle for intellectual supremacy fought between the sophists and the artists. Poetry was the prime artistic enemy since it best expressed the sacred wisdom of tradition and lacked the banausic character of plastic art. Socrates and Plato aggressively defined philosophy in sharp contrast to poetry, claiming that it provided superior wisdom and more sublime joys of contemplation. The critique of poetry that attacked its irrationality and ignorance reached its virulent peak in Book X of Plato's *Republic*, but can already be found in earlier Socratic dialogues such as *Ion* and *Apology*. Poets (and their rhapsodes or performers, of which Ion is one) do not really know how and of what they speak; they have no genuinely teachable knowledge or skill, but must rely on the divine madness of inspiration, with which they in turn infect and mislead their audiences. Poets not only lack the knowledge to explain their compositions, but they have no real specialist knowledge of the topics or arts they describe; and they mislead the public by suggesting that they are wise men (*sophoi*) and have such knowledge. Philosophy, in contrast, is said to provide not only a superior kind of truth, but, as we see in the *Symposium*, greater beauty and higher pleasures of desire. If poetry affords a view of beautiful objects, philosophy offers the rapt contemplation of the more perfect forms on which these beauties are based, culminating in the vision of the form of Beauty itself.

Plato's *Republic* paradoxically affirms poetry's importance and its dangerous lack of value. Books II and III assign poetry a central role, though closely censored and controlled, in the education of the state's guardians (censorship being essentially limited to impieties and falsehoods about the gods and to the imitation of weak behaviour and low characters). But Book X banishes all poetry from the state except for 'hymns to the gods and praises of famous men'.

Plato offers many arguments here. Since poetry is merely a representation of the appearance of the objects in our world, which is itself a world of appearances that imitates the real world of ideal forms, poetry is metaphysically inferior – a mere appearance of an appearance. For similar reasons, it is also epistemologically inferior. As an imitation of an imitation, poetry is 'thrice removed from the truth', and its teachings are therefore unreliable and misleading, far worse than the opinions of artisans, let alone the knowledge of philosophers which reaches the forms themselves. Poetry is also psychologically suspect because, in appealing to the senses and emotions rather than to 'the calculating and rational principle in the soul', it is based on and stimulates 'an inferior part of the soul'.

This intimate link to our lower nature of senses and passions provides Plato with his most damning argument against poetry: its insidious moral corruption. Poetry perverts the soul by strengthening its lower part and undermining its rule by reason – feeding 'the passions instead of drying them up, she lets them rule'. Since it is neither easy nor amusing to imitate calm wisdom, poetry relies on a display of strong emotions that noble people would be loath to display in reality but that they assume can be safely enjoyed when fictionally represented in another (for example, indulging one's pity for another's imagined grief and fear). But, Plato argues, since reason's guard is lowered while sentiment is raised, 'the contagion must pass from others to themselves'. Here we find a theory of poetry's irrational contagion that is psychologically more subtle than that offered in *Ion*. We also find the spur to Aristotle's defence of poetry through the idea of catharsis.

2   Defence of poetry as imitation

While Aristotle's *Poetics* defines poetry as imitation, thus distinguishing it from mere writing in verse, his account of imitation is broader and more positive than Plato's. He insists on imitation's cognitive value and rejects the Platonic metaphysics that located general forms in a transcendental world of ideas. By their very nature, humans imitate more than all other animals and learn first through imitation. The pleasures of imitation or representation are essentially cognitive. Since we are pleased by representations of things that in themselves would displease us (for example, corpses and hated animals), such pleasure must come from the recognition or inference of the thing represented. For 'the act of learning is not only most pleasant to philosophers' but to others as well, even if they achieve less of it. Here we already see a recurrent pattern in Aristotle in which the defence of poetry none the less implies and reinforces the superiority of philosophy.

Aristotle thought that poetry's imitations diverged according to the poet's natural dispositions. 'Noble actions of noble heroes' were represented in tragedy and epic, while 'Comedy is an imitation of baser men'. Epic differs from tragedy in having narrative (rather than dramatic) form, a single meter, and no limit in length of action. Aristotle devotes most attention to tragedy, arguing that it is the higher form, since it is more concentrated, effective and unified. Its analysis in terms of six parts (most important of which are plot and character) initiates the formalist approach to poetry, which we shall consider later.

Despite its different modes, poetic imitation was united, for Aristotle, in representing general, essential truths (based on 'the laws of probability or necessity') rather than mere superficial appearances or concrete particularities. 'Poetry, therefore, is more philosophical and more significant than history, for poetry is more concerned with the universal, and history more with the individual.' Such praise may answer Plato's critique of imitation, but only by implicitly affirming philosophy's superiority. In any case, the idea of poetry as imitation of general truths was influentially revived in the eighteenth century by Samuel JOHNSON and applied to painting by Joshua Reynolds. Aristotle offers yet another way of defending imitation: in tragedy, as in portrait painting, representations should be ameliorative, making their noble subjects look 'better than they are'. Tragedy, moreover, is specifically defended against the charge that it corrupts the soul by inspiring passions of pity and fear. To protect the soul from their harmful lurking influence, such passions need to be exorcized through poetic arousal and harmlessly poetic, cathartic discharge.

The Neoplatonist Plotinus offered a strategy that could accept Plato's transcendental metaphysics and still affirm the value of poetry as imitation (see PLOTINUS §3). The poet, he argued, is able to circumvent the sensual objects of material nature so as to imitate 'the Ideas from which Nature itself derives'. Employing this strategy, later thinkers could argue that poetry was one of our highest achievements and forms of truth. The idea that poetry could represent transcendent ideas was maintained by

Italian Neoplatonists in the sixteenth century and played a central role in the German Romanticism of Novalis and F.W.J. SCHELLING, for whom 'poetry is a representation of the absolute' (1859); the English poet Shelley similarly theorized that the 'poet participates in the eternal, the infinite, and the one' (1824).

Like his colleague Schelling, Hegel saw art's function as one of representing ideas (see HEGEL, G.W.F. §8); he therefore claimed poetry's superiority to all the other arts, on the grounds that it was better suited to represent ideas and ideality since it relied less on material media. 'Poetry is...the universal art of the mind', which 'is not fettered...to an externally sensuous material' (1835–8). But such praise, like Aristotle's, still subordinated poetry to the higher value of philosophy, which is altogether free of sensuous shape.

3 Artefact theories

Perhaps Aristotle's most successful defence of poetry was not to redeem the value of *mimesis*, but to suggest a very different way of conceiving poetry – as a formal artefact that can be appreciated in terms of its own composition and not simply by what it represents. His *Poetics* is mostly an analysis of the form of tragedy in terms of its six parts (plot, character, diction, thought, spectacle and melody), showing how they should function to constitute the work as an effective, unified whole. Here Aristotle introduces his influential notion of organic unity, which requires that the object have 'a proper magnitude' and 'a proper arrangement of the component elements'. The plot (the most important part) must be so tightly unified that 'if any one part is transposed or removed, the whole will be disordered and disturbed'.

Aristotle's conception of poetry as a rational activity of constructing objects (a making or *poiesis* involving knowledge and 'true reasoning') serves to counter Plato's attack on poetry as irrational inspiration that contaminates the soul and corrupts action. But it also serves to minimize poetry's ethical import and render it inferior to *praxis* or action. While poetry's making has its end outside itself and its maker (its end and value being in the object made), action has its end both in itself and in its agent, who is affected by how they act, though not allegedly by what they make (*Nicomachean Ethics* VI).

Aristotle's view of poetry as 'making' later developed into the idea that the poet does not so much imitate nature as create a separate imaginative world. Adumbrated in Sidney's 'An Apology for Poetry' (1583) and in some works of the Italian renaissance, this view achieved considerable influence and elaboration in the movements of Romanticism and 'art for art's sake', which, in seeing poetry as a second creation, tended to regard it as an end in itself and to deify its creator. The early Romantic Karl Philip Moritz (1788) insisted that a poem (or any authentic work of art) creates a coherent world of its own and has its entire value and purpose in itself. This idea of poetry's intrinsic order and value (and its external purposelessness) was reinforced by Kant's account of the purposeful purposelessness of beauty and by Edgar Allen Poe's advocacy of the 'poem written solely for the poem's sake', a notion that inspired theorists of 'art for art's sake' (1850). Their position is expressed in A.C. Bradley's claim that the nature of 'poetry is to be not a part, nor yet a copy, of the real world... but to be a world by itself, independent, complete, autonomous' (1909).

Though it may distance itself from Romanticism, poetic theory of the twentieth century has mostly shared the view of poetry as a well-organized formal object to be examined and valued on its own linguistic terms. In continental theory, this approach is reflected both in the formalist and structuralist schools, while in Anglo-American criticism it is seen in T.S. Eliot's early objectivism and in the New Critical views he inspired. In aesthetics it is best represented by Monroe Beardsley's principles of independence and autonomy, which assert that literary works are individual, self-sufficient entities whose meaning and value are independent of the works' genesis and reception (Beardsley 1973). Poetry's gain in autonomy as 'object' seems, here again, to be paid for by isolating it from the real world of practice.

4 Expression theories

Another influential theory of poetry conceives it as the expression of the poet's mind and feelings. Such expression theories can be traced back to Longinus, who, in defining sublimity, emphasized the poet's greatness of soul and 'vehement and inspired passion' (*On the Sublime*). But in modern times they begin with Giambattista Vico (see VICO, G. §4), who linked poetry with myth, religion and language itself as the primal, creative way in which human imaginative thought gives form, meaning and expression to the reality and experience it encounters (Vico 1744). The idea of poetry as the natural expression of our formative, organic and synthetic imagination is developed by Coleridge and endorsed by Shelley, who defines poetry as 'the expression of the imagination connate with the origin of man' (1824). Croce's theory of art as formative intuition-expression also emerges from this line of thought, while other expressionist theories instead emphasize the expression of emotions (see CROCE, B. §2; ARTISTIC

EXPRESSION §4). Thus Wordsworth (1800) and Mill (1833) respectively define poetry as 'the spontaneous overflow of powerful feelings' and 'feeling, confessing itself, to itself, in moments of solitude'. In contrast to Mill's suggestion of the privacy of poetic expression, Tolstoy (1896) advocated that art should not merely express but communicate emotion to the audience. I.A. Richards (1924) likewise stresses the importance of poetry's effect on the readers' emotions and attitudes, though not on their intellectual beliefs. By viewing poetry as 'emotive language', he sought to free it from the demand on referential language that it be assessed in terms of literal or scientific truth, and so to free it from condemnation as absurd falsehood.

5 Use theories

Another group of theories defines poetry by its characteristic uses. If Aristotle helped define tragedy by its cathartic effect, Horace more widely and influentially defined poetry's aims as pleasure and useful instruction, which could be optimally combined. This idea, elaborated by Sidney and Samuel Johnson (who thought it the writer's duty to better the world), is endorsed in some form by many modern humanists. Differences, however, typically arise both as to the nature of this pleasure (for example, how sensual, formal or cognitive it is) and as to the kind of edification poetry offers (for example, didactic presentation of alleged truths or merely an educational sensitizing of emotions). Matthew Arnold (1881) assigned poetry the necessary function of providing a consoling, meaningful interpretation of life, after science had destroyed the consolation of religion. Many other uses have been given to poetry, though Sartre (1948) defines it in contrast to prose by its non-utility. T.S. Eliot (1933), who increasingly emphasized poetry's functions of pleasure, edification, the expansion and refinement of language and (through it) of feeling and thought, also came to realize that poetry was a social product, whose functions and very forms change over history as a result of changing social factors and needs. This raises the doubt, voiced most loudly by analytic aestheticians, such as Morris Weitz (1955), that an open genre like poetry cannot be defined in terms of any permanent essence or function. Perhaps it is then best explained not by ahistorical definition but by rich historical narrative.

6 The unity of poetry and philosophy

While most follow Plato in viewing poetry as distinct from philosophy, several important Romantic and post-Romantic thinkers have advocated their synthesis or fundamental unity. The basic strategy is to construe poetry very broadly as the basic expression of our formative, synthetic imagination and then to argue that all creative philosophical work involves such imaginative construction in presenting a unifying vision of the world. Thus Hegel (as a young Romantic, before he developed his mature philosophy) affirmed that the philosopher needs as much aesthetic power as the poet, and Coleridge insisted that one cannot be 'a great poet without being at the same time a profound philosopher' (1817). As Schlegel defined the Romantic programme, 'poetry and philosophy should be made one' in a continuing effort to shape the world creatively through integrative imaginative interpretation (Schelgel 1797–1800).

With his striking view of the world as an artistic text created by imaginative interpretation, Friedrich NIETZSCHE too identifies the philosopher with the poet, since both try to reinterpret and so reshape the world in accordance with their will and values. Late Heidegger (1971) links poetry with philosophy in a different way. Real philosophy or thinking is poetic not because it wilfully reinterprets the world in a novel representation, but because it respectfully and concretely unveils or illuminates the world's obscured truth of being. Poetry is 'the saying of the unconcealedness of what is'. Moreover, since truth's revelation depends on the creation of 'a clearing' or world where it can occur and be seen, poetry founds truth by gathering objects together into a world and providing a sense of that world's unity. Here, as in earlier Romantic theories, poetry is broadly conceived as a formative force common to all art and not merely poetry in the standard sense. Heidegger calls this narrower genre 'poesy' and regards it as privileged since it exists in language, the medium of truth which identifies and links beings. The strategy of seeing poetry as philosophy by seeing the latter in terms of language and insisting on the essentially poetic nature of language can be traced back through the Romantics to Vico.

The contemporary American philosophers Richard RORTY (1989) and Stanley Cavell (1988) are among those who advocate a unity of philosophy and poetry. Rorty's glorification of the philosopher as 'strong poet' is basically Nietzschean, but, to safeguard liberal democracy, he insists that the philosopher's wilful, radically innovative poetic reconstructions be confined to the private sphere of self-creation. Cavell, more in the tradition of English Romanticism, thinks poetry and philosophy can redeem each other and the world, through a heightened recognition and celebration of ordinary experience. Recognizing their Romantic roots, these contemporaries turn to poetry as a model because they think that conceiving philosophy under the scientific model has made it increasingly technical, but of extremely limited value for what they see as its central tasks of interpreting our lives and perfecting ourselves.

See also: LESSING, G.E. §2; STRUCTURALISM IN LITERARY THEORY §3

References and further reading

Abrams, M.H. (1953) *The Mirror and The Lamp: Romantic Theory and the Critical Tradition*, New York: Oxford University Press. (An excellent study of the varieties of poetic theory under the fourfold classification of theories into imitative, pragmatic, expressive and objective, similar to the one employed here. Useful bibliography.)

Adams, H. (ed.) (1992) *Critical Theory Since Plato*, New York: Harcourt Brace, 2nd edn. (A compendious anthology of aesthetic writings from most of the major figures in Western thought, prefaced by very brief but helpful introductions and bibliographies.)

* Aristotle (c. mid 4th century BC) *Nicomachean Ethics*, trans. and notes T. Irwin, Indianapolis, IN: Hackett Publishing Company, 1985. (Aristotle's ethical theory.)

* —— (c. mid 4th century BC) *Poetics*, trans. R. Janko, Indianapolis, IN: Hackett Publishing Company, 1987. (Aristotle's famous examination of the nature of poetry and tragedy; referred to in §3 above.)

* Arnold, M. (1881) *The English Poets*, London: Ward. (Its 'Introduction' expresses Arnold's view discussed in §5.)

* Beardsley, M. (1973) *The Possibility of Criticism*, Detroit, MI: Wayne State University Press, 1973. (A clear and accessible expression of the philosophy of New Criticism.)

* Bradley, A.C. (1909) *Oxford Lectures on Poetry*, London: Macmillan. (Contains Bradley's famous lecture 'Poetry for Poetry's Sake'.)

* Cavell, S. (1988) *In Quest of the Ordinary*, Chicago, IL: University of Chicago Press. (A case for the importance of uniting philosophy and literature for the recognition of the ordinary.)

* Coleridge, S.T. (1817) *Biographia Literaria*, Princeton, NJ: Princeton University Press, 1983. (A well-edited edition of this richly suggestive but often difficult work.)

* Croce, B. (1909) *Aesthetic*, trans. D. Ainslie, London: Macmillan, 1922. (The first volume of Croce's Philosophy of Spirit; selections in Adams (1992).)

* Eliot, T.S. (1933) *The Use of Poetry and the Use of Criticism*, London: Faber & Faber, 1964. (A very readable mix of English literary history and theory based on Eliot's Norton lectures at Harvard.)

* Hegel, G.W.F. (1835–8) *The Philosophy of Fine Art*, trans. F.P.B. Osmaston, London: G. Bell & Sons, 1920. (A difficult four-volume work, with a very useful introduction.)

* Heidegger, M. (1971) *Poetry, Language, Thought*, trans. A. Hofstadter, New York: Harper & Row. (A collection of several later essays by Heidegger on the relations of poetry and language to philosophy.)

* Johnson, S. (1759) *Rasselas*, ed. J.P. Hardy, Oxford: Oxford University Press, 1988; also in A.T. Hazen (ed.) *The Works of Samuel Johnson*, New Haven, CT: Yale University Press, 1958. (Johnson's novel parallels Voltaire's *Candide*, musing on human malevolence and vanity. Selections in Adams (1992).)

Lacoue-Labarthe, P. and Nancy, J.-L. (1988) *The Literary Absolute*, New York: State University of New York Press. (A study of the German Romantic theories of Schlegel, Schelling and Novalis.)

* Longinus (1st century AD) *On the Sublime*, trans. W.R. Roberts, *Longinus on the Sublime*, Cambridge: Cambridge University Press, 1899. (Longinus' account of the sublime, primarily in relation to literature. Reprinted in Adams (1992).)

* Moritz, K.P. (1788) 'Über die bildende Nachahmung des Schoenen', in J. von Hans (ed.) *Schriften zur Ästhetik und Poetik*, Tübingen: M. Niemeyer, 1962. (Hailed by many as the first important formulation of the aesthetics of Romanticism.)

* Mill, J.S. (1833) 'What is Poetry?', *Monthly Repository* January 1833; also in H. Adams (ed.) *Critical Theory Since Plato*, New York: Harcourt Brace, 2nd edn, 1992. (First part of the essay later published as 'Thoughts on Poetry and its Varieties' – an early attempt by Mill to provide a theory of poetry and art, strongly influenced by Thomas Carlyle.)

* Nietzsche, F. (1873) 'On Truth and Lies in a Nonmoral Sense', in D. Brazeale (ed. and trans.) *Philosophy and Truth: Selections from Nietzsche's Notebooks of the Early 1870s*, Atlantic Highlands, NJ: Humanities Press, 1979. (Selections in Adams (1992).)

* Plato (c.395–387 BC) *Apology*, trans. H. Tredennic, Harmondsworth: Penguin, 1954; reprinted in Plato, *The Collected Dialogues including Letters*, ed. E. Hamilton and H. Cairns, Oxford: Oxford University Press, 1975. (Plato's account of the trial of Socrates.)

* —— (c.395–387 BC) *Ion*, trans T.J. Saunders, Harmondsworth: Penguin, 1987. (A short, accessible dialogue dealing with expertise and poetic performance. This edition includes a bibliography.)

* —— (c.386–380 BC) *The Symposium of Plato*, ed. R.G. Bury, Cambridge: Cambridge University Press, 2nd edn, 1932; trans. A. Nehamas and P. Woodruff, *Plato: Symposium*, Indianapolis, IN: Hackett, 1989. (Plato's most widely read dialogue, set in a drinking party hosted by the playwright Agathon and dealing with themes of love and beauty.)

* —— (c.380–367 BC) *Republic*, trans. P. Shorey, Cambridge, MA: Loeb Classical Library, Harvard University Press, 1930. (Plato's greatest work, an inquiry into justice and the ideal political order.)

Plotinus (c.AD 250) *Enneads*, trans. S. MacKenna, revised by B.S. Page, London: Faber & Faber, 1956. (Plotinus' applies his Platonic concept of the hierarchy of phenomena to the realm of the aesthetic, building on Diotima's speech in the *Symposium*. See especially *Enneads* 5.8.)

* Poe, E.A. (1850) 'The Poetic Principle', in H. Adams (ed.) *Critical Theory Since Plato*, New York: Harcourt Brace, 2nd edn, 1992. (Edgar Allen Poe's thesis on the nature of poetry.)

* Richards, I.A. (1924) *Principles of Literary Criticism*, London: Routledge. (A very influential work for the New Criticism.)

* Rorty, R. (1989) *Contingency, Irony and Solidarity*, Cambridge: Cambridge University Press. (Rorty's account of the philosopher as strong poet.)

* Sartre, J.-P. (1948) *What is Literature?*, trans. D. Caute, New York: The Philosophical Library, 1949. (Draws an interesting distinction between poetry and prose literature in terms of its disengagement from utility.)

* Schelling, F.W.J. (1859) *The Philosophy of Art*, trans. D.W. Stott, Minneapolis, MN: University of Minnesota Press, 1989. (Presents a highly complex and systematic theory of Romantic, idealist aesthetics that was influential in German Romanticism.)

* Schlegel, F. (1797–1800) 'Lyceum Fragments and Athenaeum Fragments', in E. Behler and H. Eichner (eds) *Kritische Schriften und Fragmente*, 1988. (A brief selection can be found in Adams (1992).)

* Shelley, P.B. (1824) 'A Defence of Poetry', in J. Shawcross (ed.) *Literary and Philosophical Criticism*, 1909. (Classic text of English Romanticism in which Shelley makes exalted claims about the importance of poetry and the stature of poets; reprinted in Adams (1992).)

Shusterman, R.M. (1992) *Pragmatist Aesthetics*, Oxford: Blackwell. (Contains an expanded account of the philosophical strategy of compartmentalizing poetry, discussed in §§1–3, as well as a critical account of Rorty's theory of the strong poet.)

—— (1997) *Practicing Philosophy: Pragmatism and*

the *Practical Life*, London: Routledge. (Examines the resurgence of the idea of philosophy as a poetics of life in twentieth-century philosophy, while also noting some of its pre-Romantic roots.)

* Sidney, Sir P. (1583) *An Apology for Poetry*, in L. Soens (ed.) *Sir Philip Sidney's Defence of Poesy*, Lincoln, NB: University of Nebraska Press, 1970. (A stirring defence of poetry's value and of its impunity from falsehood, since it does not truly assert propositions; reprinted in Adams (1992).)

* Tolstoi, L. (1896) *What is Art?*, trans. A. Maude, New York: Bobbs-Merrill, 1962. (An extremely important formulation of the expression-communication theory of art; selections in Adams (1992).)

* Vico, G. (1744) *The New Science*, trans. T.G. Bergin and M.H. Fisch, Ithaca, NY: Cornell University Press, 1968. (A very rich, influential work and perhaps the first to argue that language and thought are essentially poetic.)

* Weitz, M. (1955) 'The Role of Theory in Aesthetics', *Journal of Aesthetics and Art Criticism* 16: 27–55. (An influential analytic essay on the problem of defining art and its genres.)

Wordsworth, W. (1800) 'Preface to Second Edition of the Lyrical Ballads', in *The Prose Works of William Wordsworth*, Oxford: Clarendon Press, 1974. (An influential classic of English Romantic criticism that provides the essential theory of Wordsworth's poetry; reprinted in Adams (1992).)

RICHARD M. SHUSTERMAN

POINCARÉ, JULES HENRI (1854–1912)

Although primarily a mathematician, Henri Poincaré wrote and lectured extensively on astronomy, theoretical physics, philosophy of science and philosophy of mathematics at the turn of the century. In philosophy, Poincaré is famous for the conventionalist thesis that we may choose either Euclidean or non-Euclidean geometry in physics, claiming that space is neither Euclidean nor non-Euclidean and that geometry is neither true nor false. However, Poincaré's conventionalism was not global, as some have claimed. Poincaré held that only geometry and perhaps a few principles of mechanics are conventional, and argued that science does discover truth, despite a conventional element.

Poincaré followed new developments in mathematics and physics closely and was involved in discussion of the foundations of mathematics and in the development of the theory of relativity. He was an important transi-

tional figure in both of these areas, sometimes seeming ahead of his time and sometimes seeming very traditional. Perhaps because of the breadth of his views or because of the way in which philosophers focused on issues or small pieces of his work rather than on accurate history, interpretations of Poincaré vary greatly. Frequently cited by the logical positivists as a precursor, and widely discussed in the philosophy of science and the philosophy of mathematics, Poincaré's writings have had a strong impact on English-language philosophy.

1 **Life and work**
2 **General philosophy of science**
3 **Geometric conventionalism**
4 **Semantic conventionalism**
5 **Philosophy of mathematics**

1 Life and work

Henri Poincaré was born on 29 April 1854 in Nancy, France. His father was a physician and his cousin Raymond became president of the Third Republic during the First World War. Poincaré received his education at the Lycée of Nancy, and at the École Polytechnique and the École des Mines in Paris. He worked briefly as an engineer before obtaining his doctorate in mathematics in 1879, and after teaching for a short time at the University of Caen, in 1881 became a professor at the University of Paris, where he taught mathematical physics until his death on 17 July 1912. His mathematical work was extremely wide-ranging, and he is considered to be the last person able to make major contributions in all areas of mathematics. He also made important contributions to astronomy and theoretical physics, as well as to philosophy of science and philosophy of mathematics.

Poincaré's early mathematical work was in function theory, and before the age of thirty he became famous for his discovery of automorphic functions of one complex variable ('Fuchsian' functions). Poincaré's description of his discovery while entering a bus is quoted widely in discussions of scientific discovery: 'At the moment when I put my foot on the step the idea came to me, without anything in my former thoughts seeming to have paved the way for it, that the transformations I had used to define the Fuchsian functions were identical with those of non-Euclidean geometry' ([1908, 1913b] 1982: 387–8).

Poincaré was awarded first prize for a contribution to a competition on the n-body problem, leading to his celebrated work in celestial mechanics (*Œuvres*, vols 7, 8). It was in this context that Poincaré proved his recurrence theorem that was influential in the development of chaos theory (see CHAOS THEORY). He then worked in algebra and number theory, and eventually founded algebraic topology, a combinatorial theory of n-dimensional figures (*Œuvres*, vol. 6). Poincaré's lectures in mathematical physics at the University of Paris discussed a wide range of problems in turn-of-the-century physics, which he recognized to be a period of transition or even crisis (*Œuvres*, vols 9, 10). He also developed his conventionalism, claiming that there is no true metric geometry of space and that the choice of Euclidean or non-Euclidean geometry in physics is a matter of convenience (see SPACE §3; GEOMETRY, PHILOSOPHICAL ISSUES IN). There has been controversy over whether or not his contribution to the theory of relativity can be said to have anticipated Einstein's theory. Near the end of his life Poincaré became involved in discussion over the foundations of mathematics and developed an original solution to the semantic and set-theoretical paradoxes (see PARADOXES OF SET AND PROPERTY §9).

Poincaré published over 500 scientific papers and over thirty books. He was elected to the Académie des Sciences, the Légion d'Honneur and the Académie Française in France, as well as numerous foreign scientific and philosophical societies, and was awarded many prizes and honours. Interpreted as a total radical conventionalist, as an ultra-traditionalist or as inconsistent, Poincaré has been the source of continual discussion and comment by philosophers.

2 General philosophy of science

In 1890s France Poincaré had to face a popular climate decidedly hostile to science. While French philosophers turned away from Comte's positivism and Taine's materialist determinism towards the idealism of Henri Bergson, Poincaré became a popularizer of science and defended it against the attacks in vogue in the popular press, such as Tolstoi's argument that science is useless because it cannot tell us how to live, and the charge that science is 'bankrupt'. On the other hand, the long success of experimental science and the overturning of principles that were once held to be certain led Poincaré to think that rationalism was dead. The hypothetical method is the central feature of Poincaré's philosophy of science, and he considered it to be a middle ground between the dogmatic claims of the rationalist old guard and the contemporary anti-science views. A large motivation for his philosophical views seems to have been his desire to prove that science is cumulative and that the efforts of scientists in the past had not 'been sterile and vain', despite the great changes that

were coming about in physics and mathematics ([1905, 1913b] 1982: 280).

Poincaré distinguished three kinds of hypothesis: 'natural', 'indifferent' and 'real generalizations'. Natural hypotheses are first principles that are assumed a priori to be true. 'Indifferent hypotheses' is Poincaré's name for 'mechanical models' and refers to the nineteenth-century British tradition (of Faraday and Maxwell) of making a representation in a physical sense that provides a mechanical explanation of unobserved processes. Following a traditional form of usage (not one which Poincaré employed, however) we can refer to 'real generalizations' as fundamental laws, which should be contrasted with phenomenological laws that are taken directly from experience (see LAWS, NATURAL §1).

Poincaré is often read as an instrumentalist, one who holds that sciences should aim at giving an account of what is observable, not at explaining phenomena in terms of unobservable entities and processes (see SCIENTIFIC REALISM AND ANTIREALISM §1). Poincaré's view that the (metric) geometry of space is a matter of convention is often thought to be part of an instrumental view of all theoretical entities in science including space. However, Poincaré insisted that scientific theory is (or can be) true. In fact, Poincaré was involved in a dispute with Duhem over whether or not fundamental laws carry a truth-value. DUHEM claimed that fundamental laws are neither true nor false because they are always approximate, a view that Poincaré rejected. Furthermore, while Poincaré explicitly denies the existence of atoms in *Science and Hypothesis* (1902a), arguing that the atomic hypothesis was useful but not the only possible explanation for chemical and other phenomena, he accepted their reality after he learned of the work of Perrin (Nye 1976), which shows that Poincaré had no general injunction against theoretical entities. In at least one case, Poincaré also accepted the refutation of a fundamental principle of physics, what he calls a 'natural hypothesis', by empirical theory. When he accepted the quantum theory as presented in the first Solvay conference in 1911, Poincaré gave up the hypothesis of continuity (McCormmach 1967).

3 Geometric conventionalism

Poincaré argued that we have no intuition of distance and therefore no a priori method of choosing an external standard to define distance. Furthermore, Poincaré argued that there is no spatial feature by which an external standard can be determined empirically and, therefore, alternative metrics are possible. Since statements about geometry cannot be determined a priori and cannot be determined empirically, they have a special status as conventions. Poincaré's geometric conventionalism has often been analysed in the context of later discussions of space-time theories. The most widely promulgated argument for conventionalism is epistemological, and Poincaré's conventionalism has been thought by most interpreters to be based on an epistemological argument.

Poincaré presented two arguments that have been interpreted as defending conventionalism with epistemological arguments. In his famous parable of what measurement would be like in a non-Euclidean world, he introduces temperature as a 'distorting influence' on our measuring devices, which was taken to be an argument that one can always introduce a new hypothesis to account for data that contradicts one's theory. In other words, it has often been thought that Poincaré was using a version of the Duhem–Quine thesis (see UNDERDETERMINATION §3) to defend conventionalism. However, the parable was part of an argument to prove that a non-Euclidean world is imaginable. Since a conventionalist must refute a priori arguments that space is Euclidean (such as Kant's), this argument plays an important role in the debate over conventionalism, but it may not be the whole story. Another of Poincaré's arguments that has been interpreted as epistemological concerns the definitions of primitive terms in physics. Lobatchevskii proposed using astronomical measurements to decide between Euclidean and non-Euclidean geometry. In a passage that has been the subject of much controversy, Poincaré argued that the most such measurements can tell us is what ratios obtain between certain physical objects, in this case light rays. If one takes light rays to be straight lines, one is committed to a particular metric geometry by the results of empirical testing, but one could associate straight lines with some other physical object.

The problem with the epistemological interpretation of Poincaré's geometric conventionalism is that Duhemian underdetermination arguments establish his thesis too well. If we interpret Poincaré as using such an argument to defend his thesis of the conventionality of metric, it becomes difficult to understand how he could use such arguments in the case of metric only. If Poincaré did not deny the truth of physics in general, conventionality of metric cannot simply be a special case of a global underdetermination of theory by evidence.

An alternative defence of conventionalism bases geometric conventionalism on a fully relational theory of space. Poincaré went even further than current Einsteinian theories in rejecting Newtonian absolute space and held a purely relational view: there is no physical space and all of mechanics should be described in terms of the relations of physical objects (see SPACE §§2–3). These relations between physical objects are expressed in geometric terms but, according to Poincaré, any metric properties expressed in these relations are artifacts of our description. He thought that pure relationalism is empirically confirmed and that even acceleration and rotation can be treated as relative motions. Poincaré's physics is very programmatic, despite the fact that he followed developments in theoretical physics very closely and himself developed ideas for a theory of relativity that was close to that of Lorentz (Darrigol 1995). However, neither the special theory of relativity nor the general theory of relativity are relational in a sense that will support the conventionality of metric since relationalist theories of space cannot account for all spatial features without adding enough structure to determine a congruence standard (see RELATIVITY THEORY, PHILOSOPHICAL SIGNIFICANCE OF).

Given that arguments for relationalism fail, one may agree with Sklar that the only way left to argue for conventionalism is the global underdetermination argument (Sklar 1974). While the epistemological interpretation of conventionalism provides a strong defence, it is not compatible with Poincaré's general views. The misrepresentation of Poincaré's philosophical views has made him look inconsistent, and inconsistency is arguably worse than holding a view that has been disconfirmed by empirical theory, which is all that is implied by interpreting Poincaré as basing his conventionalism on a relational theory of space.

4 Semantic conventionalism

The idea that conventionalism can be defended by changing the explicit definitions of terms has led to a semantic interpretation of Poincaré's views, especially his claim that Euclidean and non-Euclidean geometries are translatable. Poincaré often says that geometry is the language of physics and that we can translate a physical theory that uses Euclidean geometry into one that uses non-Euclidean geometry in much the same way as we might translate a French text on physics into German (Stump 1991: 640). Poincaré's claim that Euclidean and non-Euclidean geometries are translatable has generally been thought to be based on his introduction of a model to prove the consistency of Lobachevskian geometry and to be equivalent to a claim that Euclidean and non-Euclidean geometries are logically isomorphic axiomatic systems, but this interpretation is anachronistic because Poincaré never developed a formal conception of scientific theories. Interpreting conventionalism as part of a general semantic theory leads to the charge that it is trivial (trivial semantic conventionalism). For example, we could defend

Poincaré's claim that physical bodies can be described as if they were in a strongly curved Lobachevskian space if we were to redefine 'rigidity' and postulate universal forces as distorting influences, but Poincaré specifically rejected such arguments when he distanced himself from É. LE ROY's interpretation of his conventionalism. Poincaré clearly intends his conventionalism to be more than a trivial change in notation.

Poincaré's translation thesis has a mathematical rather than a meta-mathematical basis. The mathematical basis of Poincaré's translation thesis is that the underlying manifolds of Euclidean and Lobachevskian geometries are homeomorphic (topologically equivalent). Assuming as Poincaré did that metric relations are not factual, it follows that we can rewrite a physical theory using Euclidean or Lobachevskian geometry to express the same facts. Because of his desire to prove that science is cumulative, Poincaré wrongly predicted that Euclidean geometry will always remain the preferred geometry in physics. He felt he could do so because his conventionalism would allow him to be able to rewrite in a Euclidean framework any experiment that seems to prove that the world is Lobachevskian.

5 Philosophy of mathematics

In the last years of his life, Poincaré became involved in discussions over the foundations of mathematics (1908). Concerning pure geometry, Poincaré holds the formalist-sounding views that we have no preaxiomatic understanding of geometric primitives, that rigour demands that we eliminate all appeals to intuition in geometry, and that pure (metric) geometry is neither true nor false. However, he takes quite a traditional position on arithmetic, holding that the axioms of arithmetic are synthetic a priori truths, that the notion of whole number is irreducible, and that we have a special intuitive knowledge of the fundamental principles of arithmetic – mathematical induction and the continuum. Poincaré takes an anti-Kantian view in geometry, since he accepts the consistency of non-Euclidean geometries and denies that we have any intuition of geometry, but in arithmetic Poincaré explicitly defends Kant's view that a special intuition of number is necessary against the claim of the logicists that arithmetic can be reduced to logic (see KANT, I. §5; LOGICISM). (Despite his explicit defence of Kant, Poincaré's idea of arithmetical intuition cannot be the same as Kant's, since he had argued earlier that we have no intuition of time, as well as no intuition of space.)

Poincaré criticized Russell's logicist programme by arguing that it is impossible to remove intuition from arithmetic. He argued that any proof of the principle of mathematical induction must rely on principles that cannot be purely logical, a critique of logicism that turned out to be correct. He also correctly predicted that it would be impossible to prove that arithmetic is consistent if one followed Hilbert's point of view in defining numbers by a system of axioms. His criticism of Hilbert and of Peano's axiomatization of arithmetic as not leading to true definitions of numbers may seem surprising, since Poincaré had praised Hilbert's work on geometry in a long review and even had adopted some of Hilbert's methods (Poincaré 1902b, 1904) (see HILBERT'S PROGRAMME AND FORMALISM §2).

Although Poincaré became involved in disputes over the foundations of mathematics mostly as a critic, he also developed a positive solution to the semantic and set-theoretical paradoxes in his discussion of impredicative definitions, which make use of a set of which the object to be defined is a member. He was one of the first to discuss a vicious circle principle and argued that the paradoxes can be solved if viciously circular impredicative definitions are not allowed. It is generally acknowledged that Poincaré's philosophy of mathematics is broadly speaking intuitionistic (see INTUITIONISM §1). Besides his support of a Kantian view of arithmetic, Poincaré rejected the actual infinities of a realist interpretation of set theory. However, Folina (1992) has argued persuasively that Poincaré staked out a position between classical Platonism and intuitionism in the philosophy of mathematics by arguing that Poincaré's conception of the continuum is more classical than intuitionist.

See also: CONVENTIONALISM; LOGIC IN THE 19TH CENTURY

List of works

Poincaré, H. (1902a) *La Science et L'Hypothése*; Paris: Flammarion, 1968. (Philosophical discussions of mathematics and physics, notably including his views on the continuum and geometric conventionalism.)

—— (1902b) 'Les Fondements de la Géométrie', *Bulletin des Sciences mathématiques*, 2nd series, 26: 249–72; repr. *Œuvres*, 1915–56, vol. 11, 92–113. (A review of Hilbert's *Foundations of Geometry* and a development of topological ideas.)

—— (1904) *Rapport sur les Travaux de M. Hilbert, professeur à l'Université de Goettingen, Présentés au troisième du prix Lobatchefsky*, Kasan: Imperial University Press. (A longer version of 1902b.)

—— (1905) *La Valeur de la Science*; Paris:

Flammarion, 1970. (Philosophical discussions of mathematics and physics, notably including views on the number of dimensions of space and a clarification of his conventionalism.)

—— (1908) *Science et Methode*; Paris: Flammarion, 1920. (Philosophical discussions of mathematics and physics, notably including a discussion of logicism and of the set-theoretical paradoxes.)

—— (1913a) *Derniéres Pensées*; Paris: Flammarion, 1963. (Posthumous collection of philosophical and popular scientific writings. Covers the infinite, ether theories, quantum theory, dimensions, and the axioms of geometry.)

—— (1913b) *The Foundations of Science: Science and Hypothesis, The Value of Science, Science and Method*; Washington, DC: University Press of America, 1982. (Single volume-edition of his collected philosophical and popular scientific papers. Contains translations of 1902a, 1905 and 1908.)

—— (1913c) *Mathematics and Science: Last Essays*; New York: Dover, 1963. (Translation of 1913a.)

—— (1916–56) *Œuvres*, Paris: Gauthier-Villars. (Collected mathematical and scientific writings.)

References and further reading

* Darrigol, O. (1995) 'Henri Poincaré's Criticism of Fin de Siècle Electrodynamics', *Studies in History and Philosophy of Modern Physics* 26: 1–44. (See §3.)

* Folina, J. (1992) *Poincaré and the Philosophy of Mathematics*, London: Macmillan. (A study of Poincaré's philosophy of mathematics.)

Friedman, M. (1983) *Foundations of Space-Time Theories: Relativistic Physics and Philosophy of Science*, Princeton, NJ: Princeton University Press. (A study of spacetime theories, including criticism of conventionalism.)

Giedymin, J. (1982) *Science and Convention: Essays on Henri Poincaré's Philosophy of Science and the Conventionalist Tradition*, Oxford: Pergamon Press. (A collection of papers on conventionalism, with an especially useful chapter on the controversy over Poincaré's contribution to the theory of relativity.)

—— (1991) 'Geometrical and Physical Conventionalism of Henri Poincaré in Epistemological Formulation', *Studies in History and Philosophy of Science* 22: 1–22. (A defence of the epistemological interpretation of Poincaré's conventionalism.)

Greffe, J.L., Heinzmann, G. and Lorenz, K. (eds) (1996) *Henri Poincaré: Science et philosophie, Science and Philosophy, Wissenschaft und Philosophie, International Congress Nancy, France 1994*, Paris: A. Blanchard, and Berlin: Akademie Verlag.

(A large collection of current work on Poincaré, stemming from the 1994 Poincaré Congress.)

Grünbaum, A. (1968) *Geometry and Chronometry in Philosophical Perspective*, Minneapolis, MN: University of Minnesota Press. (Classic non-epistemological defence of spacetime conventionalism.)

Hadamard, J.S. (1922) The Early Scientific Work of Henri Poincaré, *Rice Institute Pamphlet* IX: 111–83. (See 1933.)

—— (1933) The Later Scientific Work of Henri Poincaré, *Rice Institute Pamphlet* XX: 1–86. (Extensive analysis of Poincaré's scientific work.)

Heinzmann, G. (1996) 'Actes du Congrès Henri Poincaré 1994', *Philosophia Scientiae* 1 (2–4). (Three special issues of the journal, containing work stemming from the 1994 Poincaré Congress.)

Holton, G. (1974) *The Thematic Origins of Scientific Thought: Kepler to Einstein*, Cambridge, MA: Harvard University Press. (Contrasts the scientific styles of Poincaré and Einstein.)

* McCormmach, R. (1967) 'Henri Poincaré and the Quantum Theory', *Isis* 58: 37–55. (Study of Poincaré's acceptance of the early quantum theory.)

Miller, A.I. (1984) *Imagery in Scientific Thought: Creating 20th Century Physics*, Boston, MA: Birkhäuser. (Study of scientific creativity, with Poincaré and Einstein as the main examples.)

Mooij, J.J.A. (1966) *La Philosophie des Mathematiques de Henri Poincaré*, Paris: Gauthier-Villars. (The classic study of Poincaré's philosophy of mathematics.)

* Nye, M.J. (1976) 'The Nineteenth-Century Atomic Debates and the Dilemma of an "Indifferent Hypothesis"', *Studies in the History and Philosophy of Science* 7: 245–68. (Includes a study of Poincaré's acceptance of the existence of atoms.)

Pap, A. (1946, 1968) *The A Priori in Physical Theory*, New York: Russell & Russell. (An influential interpretation of Poincaré's conventionalism as a linguistic theory of the a priori.)

Reichenbach, H. (1928) *Philosophie der Raum-Zeit-Lehre*, Berlin and Leipzig: de Gruyter; trans. M. Reichenbach, *The Philosophy of Space and Time*, New York: Dover, 1957. (Classic statement of the epistemological argument for geometric conventionalism.)

Rey, A. (1907) *La Théorie de la physique chez les physiciens contemporains*, Paris: Alcan. (A classic study of Poincaré's geometric conventionalism.)

Rougier, L.A.P. (1920) *La Philosophie géométrique de Henri Poincaré*, Paris: Alcan. (A classic study of Poincaré's geometric conventionalism.)

* Sklar, L. (1974) *Space, Time, and Spacetime*, Berkeley, CA: University of California Press. (A classic

presentation of spacetime theories, including criticism of conventionalism as in §3.)

Stump, D.J. (1989) 'Henri Poincaré's Philosophy of Science', *Studies in History and Philosophy of Science* 20: 335–63. (Elaboration of the material in §§2 and 3 above.)

* —— (1991) 'Poincaré's Thesis of the Translatability of Euclidean and non-Euclidean Geometries', *Nous* 25: 639–57. (Elaboration of the material in §4 above)

Torretti, R. (1978, 1984) *Philosophy of Geometry from Riemann to Poincaré*, Dordrecht: Reidel. (Detailed presentation of the development of geometry, including an interpretation of Poincaré's conventionalism.)

DAVID J. STUMP

POINSOT, JOHN *see* JOHN OF ST THOMAS

POLAND, PHILOSOPHY IN

Philosophy in Poland has developed largely along the same lines as its Western European counterpart. Yet it also has many aspects which are peculiar to itself. Historically, the founding of the University of Cracow in 1364 marks the formal beginning of Polish philosophy as an academic discipline: prior to this, philosophy was taught at numerous smaller schools, and many Poles were educated abroad, which accounts for the early influence of Western scholars and literature.

In the medieval period, philosophy in Poland followed four chronologically successive currents of thought: the via moderna, which attached itself to the nominalism of Ockham and his disciples; the via communis, which sought to find a compromise between the old ways and these new ideas; the via antiqua, which marked a return to earlier philosophical trends; and a period of early humanism. The thought of Aristotle became dominant during the fifteenth century, as was the case at practically all universities of Central and Western Europe, and although this prevailed until the eighteenth century, philosophy did not remain stagnant – variations were numerous (including Protestant Aristotelianism). The prominence of political thought in the sixteenth century reflects the fact that Poland developed a new constitutional order at this time, the 'democracy of nobles' (the nobility accounted for about ten per cent of the total population). Nicholas Copernicus, prominent in modern astronomy and

natural science, played a fundamental role in the development of philosophy during this period.

The eighteenth-century Polish Enlightenment was shaped mainly by the clergy and hence was initially Christian in outlook. A more radical Enlightenment programme was propagated at a later stage. The following century saw the loss of Polish independence, and Polish thinkers were more prominent in exile than in their own country. At home, this coincided with a period of Romanticism and mystical philosophy ('Messianism'), with influences of Kant and particularly of Hegel. The end of the nineteenth century saw a variety of old and new philosophical orientations, ranging from medieval thought to positivism and Marxism, while 1895 saw the beginning of the Lwów School of philosophy which was to become prominent in the twentieth century.

After Polish independence in 1918, logic and methodology flourished under the influence of the Lwów School. However, elements of a variety of other Western schools of thought were also present, including that of British analytical philosophy. After the Second World War, administrative strictures were imposed in order to give prominence to Marxism. A certain liberalization took place after 1956, but its effects were dampened by a highly intrusive censorship. Despite this, philosophy in Poland continued to build upon the pre-Communist trends of Thomism and phenomenology, and to incorporate the new modes of thought emerging in the West. Since 1989–90, Marxism has lost its politico-administrative supports and censorship has disappeared, so that contemporary philosophy in Poland is entering a new phase of development.

1   The medieval period
2   The modern period
3   The nineteenth and twentieth centuries
4   Contemporary Polish philosophy

1   The medieval period

Between the tenth and fifteenth centuries, philosophy in Poland developed in a manner akin to its Western European counterpart. It shared the same religious and metaphysical base, the same scholarly resources and the same school structure. Close contact was maintained with Western scholars, and so the influences on the development of philosophy were similar, facilitated by the widespread use of Latin. Nevertheless, Polish philosophy at this time also had its own defined peculiarities, especially in the fields of Practicism (and an accompanying interest in socio-political problems and in 'devotio moderna' – Mateusz z Krakowa (d. 1410), Jakub z Paradyża (d. *c.*1464) and others), an almost-universally accepted

Concordism, an exceptional flourishing of Buridanism and a methodological emphasis on the separation of philosophy from theology (see BURIDAN, J.). Conciliarism was also prevalent. Several other disciplines flourished in Poland at this time, including law (which developed a *jus gentium* long before Grotius), science (in which Copernicus was educated) and historico-philological thought which gave birth to Polish humanism.

Poland's conversion to Christianity in 966 marked the beginning of the culture which bred this philosophy and learning. Schools possessing libraries with philosophical works were founded during the tenth to twelfth centuries, in conjunction with cathedrals and religious houses, and scholarly literature was imported from abroad. The first Polish chronicles were written by Gall. Anonim in the eleventh to twelfth centuries, and by the beginning of the fourteenth century, schools in Poland numbered in excess of 100. The liberal arts were widely taught and many Poles were sent abroad to be educated, studying in Paris, Bologna, Montpelier and Padua.

Scholars of international stature emerged during the twelfth and thirteenth centuries, including Wincenty Kadłubek (d. 1223), the chronicler, lawyer and philosopher; Marcin Polak (d. 1278–9), author of the famous papal and imperial chronicles; Peregryn z Opola (d. after 1333), whose sermons were disseminated throughout Europe; and Witelo (d. *c.*1290), whose philosophy, while concerned with anthropology, optics, demonology and the metaphysics of light, remained under Platonic and Neoplatonic influences while drawing from Chalcidius, Avicenna (see IBN SINA), Alhazen (see IBN HAZM) and Algazel (see AL-GHAZALI), among others. In the first half of the fourteenth century, many other philosophers and theologians with Polish connections received widespread recognition in ethics, anthropology, physics, metaphysics and logic. All came under the decisive influence of Aristotle and all assigned a subordinate role to philosophy in relation to theology.

The foundation of the University of Cracow by King Casimir the Great in 1364 marked the watershed in the history of medieval philosophy in Poland. Following its reform under the royal Jagiełło family (Jadwiga and Władysław) in 1400, the University became an important European centre of learning, and by the beginning of the fifteenth century, the so-called *via moderna* (associated with the nominalism of William of OCKHAM and his followers) developed dynamically there (see NOMINALISM. By the second half of that century, the search for compromise between *the via antiqua* and the *via moderna* gave birth to the so-called *via communis* (the 'common path'), following the rules of Concordism. Precursors

of that path include Pihotr Wysz (d. 1414), a distinguished philosopher whose commentaries on the works of Aristotle have recently been rediscovered.

Among those who favoured the *via communis* position were the Cracow lawyers Stanisław z Skarbimierza (d. 1431) and Paweł z Włodkowic (d. after 1434). The latter's doctrines on just war theory and on political and religious freedom were a novelty in Europe and influenced subsequent Polish toleration during the period of the religious wars in the sixteenth and seventeenth centuries. Other advocates of the *via communis* include the two most important Polish philosophers of the first half of the fifteenth century, Paweł z Worczyna (d. *c.*1430) and Benedykt Hesse (d. 1456). Paweł's work in ethics is characterized by Practicism, while Hesse's commentaries on the works of Aristotle maintain a spirit of Buridanism modified by the influence of Londorius. The new physics developed by Hesse departs from Aristotle and introduces new concepts into natural science, such as the theory of impulse. In his great commentary on the Gospel of Matthew, Hesse addresses problems of ethics, asceticism, law and economics, resolving them in a spirit of pragmatism and practicality.

The second half of the fifteenth century also saw a brief revival of Neoplatonism, Thomism, Scotism, Averroism and Augustinianism. By the end of the century, however, explicit humanistic tendencies began to appear; among its chief advocates was the most famous of Polish scholars, Nicholas COPERNICUS.

2 The modern period

Owing to lively contacts with Italian centres of learning, the beginnings of Renaissance humanism were evident in Poland as early as the first half of the fifteenth century (see HUMANISM, RENAISSANCE). Early humanism was characterized primarily by its literary character. The writings of Aristotle continued to be the basic texts in philosophical education in Poland. From the beginning of the sixteenth century, however, a renewed interest in ancient texts became widespread, and teaching and commentaries on Aristotle began to change noticeably. At the University of Cracow, Renaissance Aristotelianism prevailed under the influence of Jan Schilling (d. 1518) and Grzegorz za Stawiszyna (d. 1540) who both sought to explain Aristotle using Aristotle himself rather than scholastic commentary.

Humanism brought a philosophical method different from that of scholasticism, based on a broad range of ancient texts. Philosophy was now primarily regarded as an instrument for perfecting individuals as citizens and thus for perfecting society. The works of ERASMUS of Rotterdam played a significant role in this process. However, the eclecticism of Renaissance philosophy became prevalent at the University of Cracow from the end of the second half of the sixteenth century (this model also dominated in the first fifty years of the influential Zamość Academy from its foundation in 1595). The curriculum began to incorporate a broader spectrum of ancient writings, including Plato, the Stoics, the Neoplatonists and St Augustine. CICERO was especially popular.

While particular emphasis was placed on practical disciplines, the most interesting results were achieved in logic. In his *Commentariorum Artis Dialecticae* (1563), for example, Jakub Górski (d. 1585) examines Stoic dialectics in conjunction with Aristotle's logic, closely connecting logic and rhetoric. He discusses proofs with the help of probability arguments, limiting the discussion, however, to the most well-established proofs. Adam Burski (d. 1611) offers a rich anthology of ancient texts from the history of logic in his *Dialectica Ciceronis* (1604). It expounds on ancient dialectics, comparing and contrasting the logic of the Stoics with that of Aristotle.

The spirit of the Reformation, both positive and negative, prevailed in the extensive social and political writings which started in the 1540s. These were characterized by the fusing of religious and the political ideas. Republican and democratic currents of thought were decisively dominant, and the ideology of an absolute monarchy had few or no representatives in sixteenth-century Poland. Of the numerous political writers at this time, two expressed their views in the context of broader philosophical theories. Andrzej Frycz Modrzewski (d. circa 1572) was the author of the foundational work *De Republica Emendanda* (1551–4) which contained proposals for the reform of social customs, the law, the church, education and the army. Although a proponent of strong monarchy, he subordinated royal power to the rule of law, advocating that the king should be chosen by representatives of all classes. He proposed the creation of a criminal code which was to be binding on all and stressed the values of Christianity, while striving for union between Protestantism and Roman Catholicism. The resulting united Polish Church he envisaged as dependent on the king and on an ecumenical council which would exercise supreme power. Modrzewski's works were translated into several languages. In contrast to this his contemporary, Stanisław Orzechowski (d. 1566), identified Polish national traditions with Catholicism and stressed the importance of the clergy and the superiority of their way of life, thus inaugurating the Counter-Reformation in Polish political writing.

Poland was not unaffected by the rebirth of Thomism (and, to a lesser extent, Scotist philosophy) throughout Europe in the second half of the sixteenth century which was closely connected to the post-Tridentine reform movement in the Roman Catholic Church. At the turn of the seventeenth century, the Dominican and the Jesuit models of Thomistic philosophy as a commentary on Aristotle had become prevalent all over Europe. The former model, cultivated at the University of Cracow and the Zamość Academy, stressed the necessity of remaining faithful to the teachings of Thomas Aquinas, while the latter followed SUÁREZ in emphasizing the need to update them, and was endorsed at the Jesuit-run Vilnius Academy. The Franciscans, meanwhile, philosophized in the spirit of John DUNS SCOTUS.

A new dimension was added with the advent of Protestant Aristotelianism – Protestants did not have their own university in Poland, although they operated five schools where the level and range of philosophy taught was not fundamentally different from their university counterparts. (The Czech philosopher COMENIUS taught at one such school in Leszno from 1628 to 1656.) Political philosophy in the seventeenth century generally followed the republican-democratic trends of the previous century. However, absolute monarchy was advocated in some quarters.

The first half of the eighteenth century saw a continuation of the Scholastic Aristotelianism of the Dominicans and opposition to modern theories by figures such as Jerzy Gengel (d. 1730) and Adam Malczewski (d. 1754). By mid-century, however, characteristic perspectives of Enlightenment philosophy (the so-called *philosophia reccentiorum*) had penetrated Poland, primarily from Germany and Italy. This connected certain threads of Aristotelian philosophy with selections from Descartes, Gassendi, Locke, Newton and Leibniz. Epistemological and methodological concerns were primarily taken up in logic, limiting and sometimes even eliminating formal logic. Questions about world view (*Weltanschauung*) were prominent in metaphysics, while the teaching of natural law developed in ethics (see NATURAL LAW). The duty of taking part in social and political life was emphasized, as well as the essential role of Christianity in forming an authentic moral culture. Aristotelian philosophy of nature was limited or even abandoned in favour of the modern natural sciences. As the evolution and development of the Polish Enlightenment was carried out by the Catholic clergy, especially the religious orders and to a lesser extent the Protestant clergy, the typical anti-religious tendencies did not feature initially. By the end of the century, however, French and English influences had seeped through to inspire a more radical Enlightenment programme of rationalism, empiricism and naturalism (see ENLIGHTENMENT, CONTINENTAL).

3 The nineteenth and twentieth centuries

Until 1830, influences of the French Enlightenment, German Kantianism and the Scottish philosophy of 'common sense' continued to be the main traits identifiable in Polish philosophy (see NEO-KANTIANISM; COMMON SENSE SCHOOL). Precursors of the Messianic philosophy which would dominate between the uprisings of November 1830 and January 1863 also appeared, marked by certain supra-national traits connected with Romanticism and post-Kantian German Idealism (see GERMAN IDEALISM; ROMANTICISM, GERMAN). These also possessed certain national characteristics that were part of Poland's religious and cultural traditions, and especially of its political and social situation as a nation deprived of statehood and sovereignty. General features of this Messianism include spiritualism, a highly personalized notion of the relationship between God and humans, and an orientation towards action and change – especially moral transformation of the person and the nation.

Most prominent at the time were Józef Maria Hoene-Wroński (d. 1854), who propounded a decidedly rationalistic philosophy, and August CIESZKOWSKI (d. 1894) who represented the non-rationalistic side. Both systems, which had Neoplatonist orientations, were richer than Hegelianism by virtue of their theories of action and the future. This was also the period of the so-called 'Catholic Philosophy' which, in Poland, often came closer to fideism and either was subject to Hegelianism or opposed to it. (Outside Poland, this philosophy came to be connected to neo-scholasticism.) Jewish philosophy developed in Poland during this period, influenced by Enlightenment rationalism and German Idealism. Its most prominent representatives included Mendel Lewin Satanower and Nachman KROCHMAL.

Positivism (as well as variations on Neo-Kantianism which came close to positivism) became widespread after 1863. This occurred not just as a result of the influence of COMTE, J.S. MILL, SPENCER and Bain, as well as scientism and Darwin's theory of evolution (see DARWIN, C.): a domestic pre-positivistic tradition with roots in both the eighteenth century and Poland's politico-social conditions also entered the picture. Representatives of positivism during this period include Michał Wiszniewski (d. 1865) who also sympathized with the Scottish school (though he was not without Kantian influences). An English translation of his *Charaktery rozumów ludzkich* (Sketches and Characters or the Natural History of Human

Intellects) was published in London in 1853. Within a broader understanding of positivism, Polish contributions are evident in the fields of scholarly research on mediumism (Investigations of problems concerning hypnosis and parapsychology – Julian Ochorowicz, d. 1935) and the methodology of medicine (Władysław Biegański, d. 1919). Representatives of other philosophical orientations of the late nineteenth and early twentieth centuries include Henryk Struve (d. 1912), an eclectic post-Hegelian scholar, and Wincenty Lutosławski (d. 1954), a proponent of the 'national philosophy' who was influential not so much for his spiritualistic metaphysics as his *Origin and Growth of Plato's Logic* (1897), a work on the chronology of Plato's corpus.

A new era of development began in Polish philosophy at the end of the eighteenth century, largely due to the 1895 appointment of Kazimierz TWARDOWSKI to the chair of philosophy at the University of Lwów, and to the establishment of the first specialized philosophical journal in Poland, *Przegląd Filozoficzny*, in Warsaw in 1897–8. The Lwów School (subsequently called the Lwów–Warsaw School) founded by Twardowski emphasized the use of detailed analysis, clear and precise philosophizing and inspired research in logic and methodology. (Notwithstanding certain common figures, one should distinguish the Lwów–Warsaw School of Philosophy from the Warsaw School of logic – which arose after 1918 – and the Warsaw School of mathematics.)

Many of Twardowski's students became prominent in their own right in the fields of philosophy, logic and psychology. Leopold Blaustein (d. 1944) was the author of many original works on descriptive psychology and was a pioneer in psychology pertaining to film and radio. Kazimierz AJDUKIEWICZ (d. 1963) produced important results in theory of language and logical analysis of the theoretical problems of cognition. His works, especially those published in *Erkenntnis* and in the Polish *Studia Philosophica* (along with Tarski's famous 1933 paper 'Pojęcie prawdy w językach nauk dedukcyjnych' – translated as 'The Concept of Truth in the Languages of the Deductive Sciences') influenced the development of the Vienna Circle and gave birth to logical semantics (see TARSKI, A.; VIENNA CIRCLE). Czeżowski (d. 1981), another student of Twardowski, turned from formal logic to general theory of science and treated logic as learning in the general form of a science. Admitting various forms of immediate knowledge, he was a probabilist in terms of evaluating knowledge in relation to reality. Zawirski (d. 1948) also became prominent: he produced the book *L'évolution de la notion du temps* as well as various works in the philosophy of physics, multivalent and intuitionist logic and was a founder of causal logic (see POLISH LOGIC).

Other philosophical orientations were evident in interwar Poland. Empirical-critical thought was promoted by thinkers such as Władysław Heinrich (d. 1957), Narcyz Łubnicki (d. 1988) and Bolesław J. Gawecki (d. 1984). Joachim Metallman (d. c.1942) was primarily interested in epistemology and methodology of the natural sciences. Leon Chwistek (d. 1944) pursued formal logic, searching for the logical system most compatible with nominalism which could simultaneously serve as a basis for metaphysics. He was also an artist and art theoretician. Władysław Tatarkiewicz (d. 1980) was distinguished in the history of philosophy, the history of aesthetics and art history. The style of philosophizing in his works on axiology is evocative of G.E. MOORE and similar authors in analytic philosophy (see AXIOLOGY).

Benedykt Bornstein occupies a unique position in this era through his metaphysical speculation, connected as it was with logic and mathematics (known as geometric logic or 'topologic'). He linked pan-rationalism with accentuation of the foundational role of intellectual intuition. His last publications include *Geometric Logic* (1939), *Teoria absolutu. Metafizyka jako nauka ścisła* (*The Theory of the Absolute. Metaphysics as Science*) (1948). Roman INGARDEN (d. 1970) promoted an objectivist version of phenomenology, thereby providing an alternative to the Lwów–Warsaw School and to minimalist analytical-positivist thought.

Notwithstanding the presence of several active representatives, Thomism in Poland before the Second World War possessed an eclectic and derivative character compared to Thomism abroad. The dominant influence came from the Louvain School, from whence came the founder and first rector of the Catholic University of Lublin (KUL), Idzi Radziszewski. Two important initiatives deserve note. First, the international project 'Corpus Philosophorum Medii Aevii' was founded at this time by Konstanty Michalski (d. 1947), a distinguished historian of philosophy and pioneer of the Thomistic philosophy of history. Second, on the occasion of the third Polish Philosophical Congress in Cracow in 1936, the project of the renewal of Thomistic philosophy and theology was formulated by what came to be known as the 'Cracow Circle'. This group of four opted to employ contemporary tools of logic. Their initiative was a novelty, even beyond Polish Thomism, and their aims were in part accepted at KUL after 1945.

Despite the loss of many promising academics and students during the Second World War, philosophy in Poland has been significantly active since that time. Having strengthened its political position, the ruling communist party sought to subordinate the whole culture to its Marxist ideology. However, despite many pressures and restrictions, the Communists never quite succeeded in eliminating non-Marxist orientations in Polish intellectual life. The traditions of the Lwów–Warsaw School continued in logic and in the methodology of the sciences. The objectivist phenomenology of Ingarden continued, at least in aesthetics and art theory, while at KUL, the Lublin School of existential Thomism developed. Polish thought passed through periods of Stalinism, Marxism, the Solidarity phase of 1980–1 and into the final breakthrough of 1989–90, which ended the domination of the Communist party.

4 Contemporary Polish philosophy

At the present time, philosophy in Poland represents a wide range of schools and perspectives. Phenomenology, Thomism, various schools of positivism and post-positivism, Marxism and the philosophy of dialogue (encounter) are all represented. The influences of Augustinianism, Hegelianism, hermeneutics and process philosophy can also be noted (see HERMENEUTICS; PROCESS PHILOSOPHY).

Phenomenology owes its position in Poland especially to Roman Ingarden, who continued to teach and whose thought flourished in Cracow after the Second World War. Notables among his students include Władysław Stróżewski, who connected phenomenology first with existential Thomism and later with certain elements of Platonism and Hegelianism in a 'dialectical phenomenology', and Józef Tischner who, in the end, departed far from the thought of his mentor. In phenomenological circles one also finds Karol Wojtyła (later Pope John Paul II), whose personalism combines the philosophy of being in the existentialist Thomistic spirit with the philosophy of subject in the spirit of classical phenomenology.

The primary centre of Thomistic philosophy is at the Faculty of Philosophy at KUL, and this philosophical orientation also prevails in the Faculty of Christian Philosophy at the Academy of Catholic Theology in Warsaw (Mieczysław A. Krąpiec, Stefan Swieżawski, Mieczysław Gogacz). Existential Thomism, borrowing from Gilson and Maritain while emphasizing the importance of the theory of being, supplies the intellectual framework, with the more traditional school of Thomism declining in prominence in recent years. At the Pontifical Academy of Theology (PAT) in Cracow, the philosophy of dialogue has been promulgated, while Andrzej Nowicki formulated a Marxist version of the philosophy of encounter ('inkontrologia'). PAT, under the banner of philosophy in science, fosters a programme of interdisciplinary research (based upon identification and resolution of philosophical problems in the context of particular sciences) employing ideas from Platonism and from process philosophy. Since the death of Izydora Dąmbska in 1983, the Lwów–Warsaw School has been less prominent than in former years.

Marxism in Poland, although primitive, doctrinaire and Stalinist after the Second World War, later differentiated itself into various orientations. These have included humanist (invoking the young Marx), scientific (appealing to Engels), moderate, Leninist/revisionist, open Marxism (invoking modern scientific methodology and certain post-positivistic trends), and those who promoted a programme of eclectic 'universalism'. 'Individualistic' philosophers include Andrzej Grzegorczyk (a logician whose philosophy connects elements of scientism, existentialism and a Christian world view) and Jerzy Szymura (who defended a version of Hegelianism close to that of Bradley). Prominent Poles living abroad include Józef M. Bocheński (d. 1995) (following a Thomistic period, he later identified himself as an analytical philosopher who cherished the Aristotelian tradition), and Leszek Kołakowski who has changed from Marxist to critic of Marxism and whose current views can be characterized as a post-Hegelian, post-Marxist historicism and sociologism with a positivistic version of rationalism.

See also: ARISTOTELIANISM IN THE 17TH CENTURY; ENLIGHTENMENT, CONTINENTAL; ENLIGHTENMENT, JEWISH; HUMANISM, RENAISSANCE; KROCHMAL, N.; MARXIST PHILOSOPHY, RUSSIAN AND SOVIET; THOMISM

References and further reading

Birkenmajer, A. (1972) 'Histoire de sciences et de l'enseignement en Pologne', *Studia Copernicana* 4 (X): 819. (A history of the sciences and of general education in Poland.)

* Bornstein, B. (1939) *Geometric Logic*, Warsaw: Wolna Wszechina Polska. (Mentioned in §3 above. An interesting parallel between the structure of space and the structure of thought.)

* —— (1948) *Teoria absolutu. Metafizyka jako nauka ścisła* (The theory of the absolute. Metaphysics as science), Łódź: Łódzkie Towarzystwo Naukowe. (An attempt to treat geometric structure of space as a representation of the structure of being; mentioned in §3 above.)

Chudy, W. (1990) 'Filozofia polska po II wojnie światowej' (Polish philosophy after the Second World War), *Studia Philosophiae Christianae* 26

(1): 129–41. (Survey of Polish philosophy in the period 1945–90.)

Czerkawski, J. (1992) *Humanizm i scholastyka* (Humanism and scholasticism), Lublin: RW KUL. (Studies in the history of philosophical culture in Poland in the sixteenth and seventeenth centuries.)

Domański, J., Szczucki, L., Ogonowski, Z. (eds) (1978–9) *700 lat myśli polskiej* (Seven-hundred years of Polish thought), 5 vols, Warsaw: PWN. (Includes a selection of classical texts and essays by Polish scholars from the thirteenth to the nineteenth centuries, excepting the eighteenth.)

—— (1989) *Zarys dziejów filozofii w Polsce; wieki XIII–XVII* (A short history of philosophy in Poland, 13th–17th centuries), Warsaw: PWN. (This work contains an extensive bibliography of classical texts and essays by contemporary scholars.)

Gogacz, M. (1978) 'Tomizm w polskich środowiskach uniwersyteckich XX wieku' (Thomism in Polish university circles in the 20th century), in *Studia z dziejów myśli świetego Tomasza z Akwinu*, Lublin: TN KUL, 335–50. (Survey of twentieth-century Thomist philosophy in Polish academia.)

Hinz, H., Sikora, A. (eds) (1964) *Polska myśl filozoficzna. Oświecenie. Romantyzm* (Polish philosophical thought: The Enlightenment and Romanticism), Warsaw: PWN. (An anthology of writings by eighteenth- and nineteenth-century Polish philosophers, with a bibliography of their works.)

Jordan, Z.J. (1963) *Philosophy and Ideology*, Dodrecht: Martinus Nijhoff. (Traces the development of philosophy and marxism in Poland since the Second World War.)

Kadler, A. (ed.) (1955, 1960, 1971) *Bibliografia filozofii polskiej* (Bibliography of Polish philosophy), 3 vols, Warsaw: PWN. (Vol. 1 (1750–1830); Vol. 2 (1831–64); Vol. 3 (1865–95). More volumes in preparation. Contains valuable bibliographic material for the student interested in more advanced study.)

Kuksewicz, Z. (ed.) (1975–88) *Dzieje filozofii średniowiecznej w Polsce* (History of medieval philosophy in Poland), 10 vols, Wrocław: Ossolineum. (Six authors describe medieval Polish logic, methodology of science, philosophy of being, philosophy of nature, philosophy of man – theory of soul, epistemology, moral philosophy, beginnings of humanism in Poland, beginnings of social sciences – and methodological principles.)

* Lutosławski, W. (1897) *Origin and Growth of Plato's Logic*, London: Longmans, Green. (Famous work on the chronology of Plato's corpus. Mentioned in §3 above.)

* Modrzewski, A.F. (1551) *De Republica Emendanda*,

Cracow. (Contained proposals for extensive social reform. Mentioned in §2 above.)

Ogonowski, Z. (1992) *Filozofia polityczna w Polsce w XVII wieku i tradycje demokracji europejskiej* (Political philosophy in Poland in the 17th century and the traditions of European democracy), Warsaw: PAN. (An anthology of texts by seventeenth-century Polish philosophers.)

Skolimowski, H. (1967) *Polish Analytical Philosophy*, London and New York: Routledge & Kegan Paul. (Review of the main features.)

Stępień, A.B. (1966) 'Fenomenologia w Polsce (w powojennym dwudziestoleciu)', *Studia Philosophiae Christianae* 2 (1): 29–47. (Phenomenology in Poland in the twenty years after the Second World War.)

—— (1968) 'La filosofia tomastica nella Polonia contemporanea', *Sapienza* 1968: 509–28. (Survey of Thomistic philosophy in Poland, written during the 1960s.)

—— (1975) 'La filosofia nella Polonia contemporanea', *Rivista di Filosofia Neo-scolastica* 67: 288–99. (Review of philosophy in contemporary Poland.)

Szaniawski, K. (ed.) (1988) *The Vienna Circle and the Lvov-Warsaw School*, Dodrecht: Kluwer Academic Publishers. (Vol. 28 in the Nijhoff International Philosophy series. Not for the beginner.)

Szczucki, L. (ed.) (1978) Nauczanie filozofii w Polsce w XV–XVIII wieku (Teaching philosophy in Poland in the 15th–18th centuries), Wrocław: Ossolineum. (A selection of writings about the teaching of philosophy in Cracow, Zamość, Gdansk and Torun.)

Wielgus, S. (1990) *Obca literatura biblijna w Średnio-wiecznej Polsce* (Foreign biblical literature in medieval Poland), Lublin: Redakcja Wydawnictw KUL. (A collection of foreign, Western biblical writings which were present in medieval Polish schools and in the University of Cracow in the fifteenth century.)

—— (1991) 'Die Theorie des Menschen in den Werken Krakauer Theologen aus der zweiten Hälfte des XV Jahrhunderts' in B. Mojsisch and O. Pluta (eds) *Historia Philosophiae Medii Aevi*, vol. 1, Amsterdam and Philadelphia, PA: B.R. Grüner, 1047–64. (An exposition of the philosophical theory of man, based on the main Polish biblical commentaries written in the second half of the fifteenth century.)

—— (1992) *Średniowieczna łacińskojęzyczna biblistyka polska* (Polish medieval biblical science in Latin), Lublin: Redakcja Wydawnictw KUL. (Reviews the scientific production of medieval Polish scientists who were taking up theology and philosophy.)

—— (1995) 'Średniowieczna filozofia w Polsce (Polish medieval philosophy)', in *Z badań nad średniowiec-zem*, Lublin: Redakcja Wydawnictw KUL. (A brief history of medieval Polish philosophy with a very extensive bibliography of Polish medieval texts and essays by contemporary scholars.)

* Wiszniewski, M. (1837) *Charaktery rozumów ludzkich* (*Sketches and characters or: The natural history of human intellects*), Cracow, 1842. (Mentioned in §3 above. The translation was published by Saunders & Otley in London (1853) under the pseudonym James Whitecross.)

Woleński, J. (1989) *Logic and Philosophy in the Lvov-Warsaw School*, Dodrecht: Kluwer Academic Publishers. (This is the English version of the first extensive monograph on the Lwów–Warsaw School.)

* Zawirski (1936) *L'évolution de la notion du temps*, Cracow: PAU. (Mentioned in §3 above. An outline of the history of various conceptions of time, with analytical and critical commentaries.)

JAN CZERKAWSKI
ANTONI B. STĘPIEŃ
STANISŁAW WIELGUS

POLANYI, MICHAEL (1891–1976)

Michael Polanyi was almost unique among philosophers in not only fully acknowledging but in arguing from the tacit dimensions of our knowledge which concern the many things which we know but cannot state nor even identify. He argued that our knowledge is a tacit, personal integration of subsidiary clues into a focal whole, and he elaborated this structure of knowing into a corresponding ontology and cosmology of a world of comprehensive entities and actions which are integrations of lower levels into higher ones. Polanyi used these accounts of knowing and being to argue against the 'critical' demands for impersonal, wholly objective and fully explicit knowledge, against reductionist attempts to explain higher levels in terms of lower ones, and to defend the freedom of scientific research and a free society generally.

1   Life
2   Tacit integration
3   Applications

1   Life

Michael Polanyi was born in Budapest into a distinguished Jewish family. He trained as a doctor but was primarily interested in research in chemistry. He was also active in support of liberal movements in

Hungary but was sceptical of socialism. Opposed to the Bolshevik government in 1919 and distrusted by the Horthy regime which overthrew it, he left Budapest in 1919 and pursued a career in chemistry in Germany. In 1933 he emigrated to England and became Professor of Physical Chemistry at the University of Manchester. He made several visits to the Soviet Union, where a meeting in 1935 with Bukharin alerted him to Marxist proposals for the central planning of scientific research. He was already writing on economics and trying to articulate his ideas of a free society.

In 1948 he gave up his distinguished career in chemistry and was appointed to a non-teaching chair in Social Science in order to prepare his Gifford Lectures for 1951–2, which later became *Personal Knowledge* (1958), his most important book. In 1959 he became a Senior Research Fellow at Merton College, Oxford. Linguistic analysis, which was prevalent there, gave little support to his style of philosophy, but he attracted more attention in the USA, where he gave several series of lectures, published as *The Tacit Dimension* (1966) and *Meaning* (1975).

His philosophical work, in content and style, was never merely academic. Replete with examples, especially from natural science, it always addressed itself beyond purely philosophical questions to the social and political problems of the twentieth century. Every one of his books begins with some aspect of our present discontents, works back to their presuppositions, articulates a constructive alternative, and then indicates the new directions which thought, science and society should take.

2 Tacit integration

Polanyi is best known for his statement from *The Tacit Dimension*, 'We know more than we can tell' (1966: 4). From *Personal Knowledge* onwards, he gives many examples of such tacit knowledge. But his unique contribution to philosophy is his account of knowing as a tacit integration of subsidiary clues into a focal whole. Whereas phenomenology stresses that consciousness is intentional in that it is always consciousness of something, Polanyi shows that mind has a double intentionality: A attends from B to C (see INTENTIONALITY; PHENOMENOLOGICAL MOVEMENT). We attend *from* the subsidiary clues and to the focal whole. For example, a blind man using a stick does not pay attention to the impact of his stick upon his hand, but to the tip of the stick and what that tells him about what it touches. The sensations in the palm of his hand are subsidiary clues which he integrates into a focal awareness of the path and obstacles in

front of him. If we switch our attention to the subsidiary clues, then sooner or later we shall lose sight of the focal object to which we were attending. We attend from words to their meanings, and by repeatedly pronouncing a word we forget what it means. We can regain its meaning only by using it. This relation of subsidiary details and clues to the focal whole is a functional one. We use the clues or details to apprehend or perform the focal whole. Subsidiary awareness is therefore more than merely subconscious or fringe awareness. Furthermore, what we attend to can itself become a subsidiary clue used in attending to something else, as when learning to play the piano we first attend to our fingers, and then from them to the music to be played.

Polanyi shows that these integrations pervade all our knowledge, and not just perception. They control our use of language, which can never be rendered exact and precise. Because we always attend from some set of subsidiary clues, we can never make our knowledge wholly focal. Therefore we can never make it wholly explicit and articulate, nor subject it to a complete critical scrutiny. It must always rest upon the tacit and therefore acritical foundations of personal judgment and commitment. The objectivist ideal of a fully tested, detached, impersonal and 'objective' knowledge cannot be met. But knowledge is 'personal' and not 'subjective'. It is attention away from ourselves to a world that anchors our commitments. Reality outruns our conceptions of it and shows itself in ways that we cannot anticipate (see TACIT KNOWLEDGE).

We use as subsidiary clues details of the object known, its context and ourselves. The object known is itself a comprehensive entity, or complex performance, in which details on a lower level are integrated by the principles of operation of the next higher level which determine the boundary conditions left open by the operational principles of the lower level. In attending from its subsidiary details, we re-perform, as it were, its own internal integration. Our own bodies are primarily what we use and so attend *from*, in knowing and acting within the world. We indwell them. Likewise, by extension, we indwell the objects that we know. As the blind man incorporates his stick into his body by indwelling it, so we incorporate our acquired knowledge, ideas and frameworks into our minds by indwelling them. Polanyi bridges the Cartesian gap between the self and an 'external world' with the indwelling of tacit integration (see DUALISM).

Polanyi described his philosophy as a 'post-critical' and 'fiduciary' one, which aims to enable us explicitly to hold beliefs which we know might be false. As against the 'critical' attempt to apply the method of doubt and to reject whatever cannot be proved, it seeks to articulate the ultimate beliefs which are presupposed by our proximate ones and practices. The premises of science, for example, are embodied and tacitly known in the practice of scientific research. From results which we already accept as true and methods which we already hold to be valid we can try to articulate the principles and beliefs which they presuppose. We cannot start with the latter and use them to justify the former (see MERLEAU-PONTY, M.).

3 Applications

Polanyi applied his account of tacit integration in knowing and being to many topics, such as the relation between language and meaning, the structure of a work of art, the refutation of various reductionisms, the relation of body and mind, the nature of discovery, and the role of tradition in conveying tacit knowledge. His distinctive philosophy of science emphasizes the roles of the personal factors of belief, passionate engagement, imagination and authority, as against supposedly exact and impersonal observations and procedures, and denies the conventional distinction between 'discovery' and 'justification'. For what science aims at is truth, and not just trivial truths, but scientifically valuable ones. No random generation of problems and hypotheses can guide it, only the trained but tacit sense of the scientist for what is significant, probable and discoverable by himself with the means at his disposal. For example, it is a matter of judgment as to whether discrepant observations can be ignored as inevitable error, left to be cleared up later, or taken to require a revision of current theory (see SCIENTIFIC METHOD).

In his political and economic theory Polanyi argued that 'objectivist' assumptions have undermined our ability to uphold our personal commitments to intangible ideals. Totalitarian systems, such as Marxism, take advantage of this to discredit moral ideals and freedom, and disguise, in supposedly objective predictions of the future course of history, their own calls for centralized power to attempt a total renewal of society. Scepticism is no longer sufficient to combat destructive ideologies. A free society is one that is dedicated to transcendent ideals such as truth, justice and charity and not one that is 'open' to all ideologies. Its freedom is principally the 'positive' one to serve those ideals. But science, the economy and other activities of human life cannot be centrally planned. They manifest the spontaneous order of the mutual adjustment of individual elements.

Polanyi argued against the dichotomy of fact and value. The activities of life and mind have their own internal standards. To know them, we must grasp and apply those standards and recognize relevant entities and events as 'achievements', realizations of those standards, which cannot be neutrally described nor be apprehended by detached observation.

List of works

Polanyi, M. (1940) *The Contempt of Freedom*, London: Watts; repr. New York: Arno Press, 1975. (Four essays on the Soviet economy, the Marxist threat to science, and collectivist planning.)

—— (1945) *Full Employment and Free Trade*, Cambridge: Cambridge University Press; 2nd edn, 1948. (Polanyi's exposition of Keynes' theory.)

—— (1946) *Science, Faith and Society*, London: Oxford University Press; 2nd edn, with new preface, Chicago, IL: University of Chicago Press, 1964. (Science, as self-dedication in faith to the discovery of truth, provides a model for a free society.)

—— (1951) *The Logic of Liberty*, London: Routledge. (Ten papers on freedom in science, the economy and society, and the logical impossibility of central planning.)

—— (1958) *Personal Knowledge*, London: Routledge. (Polanyo's *magnum opus*, expounding and elaborating his central ideas on the personal, tacit and fiduciary roots of knowledge.)

—— (1959) *The Study of Man*, London: Routledge. (An elaboration of Polanyi's account of man as a responsible knower and agent.)

—— (1966) *The Tacit Dimension*, London: Routledge. (The structure of tacit integration and its implications.)

—— (1969) *Knowing and Being*, ed. M. Grene, London: Routledge. (Fourteen articles elaborating various aspects of Polanyi's philosophy.)

Polanyi, M. and Prosch, H. (1975) *Meaning*, Chicago, IL: University of Chicago Press. (Polanyi's final statement of his philosophy, focusing on the notion of meaning, in perception, language, art, myth, religion and society.)

Polanyi, M. (1996) *Society, Economic, Philosophy: Selected Papers by Michael Polanyi*, ed. R.T. Allen, New Brunswick, NJ: Transaction Publishers. (Twenty-five of Polanyi's articles not reprinted in his books, with full bibliography and summaries of all the articles not selected.)

References and further reading

Allen, R.T. (1990) *Polanyi*, London: Claridge Press. (A general introduction).

—— (1992) *Transcendence and Immanence in the*

Philosophy of Michael Polanyi and Christian Theism, Lewiston, NY: Mellen for Rutherford House (Edinburgh). (Explores the theological applications of Polanyi's philosophy.)

Crewdson, J. (1994) *Christian Doctrine in the Light of Michael Polanyi's Theory of Personal Knowledge: A Personalist Theology*, Lewiston, NY: Mellen. (A theological development of Polanyi's philosophy.)

Gelwick, R. (1977) *The Way of Discovery*, New York: Oxford University Press. (A general introduction.)

Langford, T. and Poteat, W. (eds) (1968) *Intellect and Hope*, Durham, NC: Duke University Press. (Studies of particular aspects of Polanyi's work. Includes a bibliography up to 1967.)

Poteat, W. (1985) *Polanyian Meditations*, Durham, NC: Duke University Press. (Applications and elaborations of Polanyi's epistemology.)

Prosch, H. (1986) *Michael Polanyi: A Critical Exposition*, New York: State University of New York Press. (A more advanced introduction.)

Sanders, A.F. (1988) *Michael Polanyi's Post-Critical Epistemology: A Reconstruction of Some Aspects of 'Tacit Knowing'*, Amsterdam: Rodolfi. (Compares Polanyi with other contemporary philosophers.)

Scott, D. (1985) *Everyman Revived*, Lewes: The Book Guild. (A more informal introduction.)

R.T. ALLEN

POLISH LOGIC

The term 'Polish logic' was coined by McCall to signal the important contributions to modern logic by logicians from Poland between the wars. There were several centres of research, of which the Warsaw school, which grew out of the earlier Lwów–Warsaw philosophical movement, was the most significant. Its development was closely connected with the Warsaw school of mathematics, which gave it its characteristic mathematical bent.

Polish logic took as its point of departure the main trends in logical research of the time and it has influenced both subsequent logical research and subsequent work in the Western analytic tradition of philosophy. Its chief contributions were: (1) an enrichment of existing logical theory (including work on Boolean algebras, the sentential calculus, set theory, the theory of types); (2) new logical theories (for example, Leśniewski's systems, Łukasiewicz's many-valued logics, Tarski's theory of truth, theory of the consequence operation and the calculus of systems); (3) new methods and tools as well as improvements of existing methods (for example, the matrix method of constructing sentential calculi, axiomatizability of logical matrices, algebraic and topological interpretations of deductive systems, permutation models for set theory, the application of quantifier elimination to decidability and definability problems); and (4) the application of formal methods to the study of the history of logic, resulting in a new understanding of the logics of Aristotle, the Stoics and the medievals.

1 **Historical introduction**
2 **Łukasiewicz: sentential calculi and history of logic**
3 **Leśniewski: foundations of mathematics**
4 **Tarski: semantics and metamathematics**
5 **Other work**
6 **Post-war developments**
7 **Polish notation**

1 Historical introduction

In 1918, after 120 years of subjugation by foreign powers, Poland reappeared on the map of Europe as a free and independent nation-state. In 1939 the outbreak of the Second World War reversed these brief gains, bringing down the curtain on the Second Republic and inflicting massive damage on its economy, culture and learning. The main centres of logic research between these dates were Cracow, Lwów, Poznan, Wilno and, most importantly, Warsaw. The Warsaw school of logic, founded by Łukasiewicz and Leśniewski, began as an intellectual offshoot of the Lwów–Warsaw philosophical movement, but quickly eclipsed it in both quantity and quality of research.

The development of the Warsaw school of logic was closely connected with that of the Warsaw school of mathematics. In 1918 one could already speak of Warsaw as a fairly strong centre of research in set theory and topology under the direction of Janiszewski, Mazurkiewicz and Sierpiński. The two schools shared organizational structures, swapped directors and collaborated on many academic initiatives. This accelerated the development of both schools and deepened their research in key areas. In later years Kuratowski, Lindenbaum, Tarski and finally Mostowski made significant contributions to both schools.

2 Łukasiewicz: sentential calculi and history of logic

Łukasiewicz's more philosophical research culminated in his study of the principle of contradiction in Aristotle (1910), which was an important influence on the development of logic in Poland. After his discovery of a 'non-Aristotelian' many-valued logic (1918–20; see ŁUKASIEWICZ, J. §3), he turned to the study of the logic of propositions – in particular, to the sentential calculus, which he believed to be the simplest deductive discipline central to all scientific reasoning, and around which he built a research programme which served as a focus for research work on propositional logics throughout Poland (see Łukasiewicz 1941).

Łukasiewicz's programme can be seen as divided into two periods. The first, up to 1930, is characterized by conceptual and foundational achievements (see Łukasiewicz and Tarski 1930; Łukasiewicz 1929).

Notable among the conceptual achievements are a definition of a recursive grammar for propositional languages (including propositional quantifiers); the now famous bracket-free notation known as Polish notation; a precise definition of the syntactic operations of substitution and replacement; a new axiom system for classical propositional logic together with a new completeness proof for this system; formulations of several systems of many-valued logic (see MANY-VALUED LOGICS, PHILOSOPHICAL ISSUES IN); a rigorous distinction between considerations of syntax and proof theory, on the one hand, and metalogical and semantic considerations on the other; and the invention of the matrix method of constructing sentential calculi.

Among the foundational achievements are various technical results in the search for single-sentence axiomatizations (notably by Tarski), Wajsberg's discovery of a criterion for finite axiomatizability, Lindenbaum's theorem on the existence of adequate matrices for arbitrary systems of propositional logic closed under substitution, and pioneering studies of partial calculi (for example, the pure implicational and the pure equivalential fragments of classical sentential logic) and of sentential calculi extended by propositional quantifiers and variable functors of higher order.

The second period, from 1931 on, is characterized by the expansion of the programme to cover a greater number of propositional calculi, and its enrichment with new methods drawn from algebra and topology.

Noteworthy results of this period include a complete algebraic semantics for Lewis' S5 (see Wajsberg 1933), Jaśkowski's invention – independently of Gentzen – of the idea of a system of natural deduction (see Jaśkowski 1934; NATURAL DEDUCTION, TABLEAU AND SEQUENT SYSTEMS §1), a complete algebraic semantics for intuitionistic logic (Jaśkowski 1936), a topological interpretation of certain sentential calculi, notably the intuitionist variant (Tarski 1956), and a proof of the separability of the intuitionist connectives (Wajsberg 1938).

Still, a great deal of research in this period continued to be devoted to finite logical matrices.

Wajsberg (1935), Sobociński (1936) and Słupecki (1939a) worked on solutions to the axiomatizability problem for many-valued logics. Słupecki (1939b) found a criterion for functional completeness of finite algebras.

Łukasiewicz also founded a programme of historical research whose goals were both a thorough exegesis and an analytical reconstruction of ancient and medieval logic. The source of this programme was his own book on Aristotle (1910), which distinguished ontological, logical and psychological formulations of the principle of contradiction. Łukasiewicz himself traced the historical roots of propositional logic to Stoic dialectic and countered prevailing views of the Middle Ages by shedding new light on the importance of the achievements of Petrus Hispanus and Duns Scotus (1934); he provided an axiomatic reformulation of Aristotle's syllogistic (1929, 1939, 1951; LOGIC, ANCIENT §7). In the course of these investigations, Łukasiewicz introduced a new formal idea: the concept of a 'rejection system' – a Hilbert-type system for disproving rather than proving formulas – which he intended as a syntactic counterpart to the semantic device of refutation. This idea was subsequently elaborated by Słupecki (1949).

Under Łukasiewicz's influence a number of scholars outside Warsaw undertook related research. In Wilno, Czeżowski (1936) studied the treatment of modal sentences in Aristotle and Korcik (1937) provided an interpretation of some of Aristotle's writings in terms of a theory of the conversion of assertoric sentences. Bocheński (1938) wrote a history of the treatment of modal sentences in ancient and medieval times. In Poznan, Jordan (1937) studied the use of the axiomatic method from Plato and Eudoxus to Euclid's *Elements*. In Cracow, Salamucha analysed Saint Thomas' *ex motu* proof of the existence of God (1934), showed that William of Ockham had anticipated large parts of classical propositional calculus (1935) and wrote a scholarly treatise on medieval antinomies (1937).

Łukasiewicz's programme revealed that ancient and medieval logicians had considered 'formal' problems similar in character to some of the problems addressed by contemporary formal logic. This prompted a new interest in the subject and eventually led to a critical re-evaluation of large parts of the history of logic (see Scholz 1931; Łukasiewicz 1951; Mates 1953; Bocheński 1951, 1956; Kotarbiński 1957).

3 Leśniewski: foundations of mathematics

The main goal of LEŚNIEWSKI was to provide a foundation for mathematics that would yield a real understanding of the antinomies and not simply avoid them. He did not accept the principles and assumptions of Cantorian set theory, regarding them as artificial and counterintuitive. He found the notion of an empty set an affront to reason. He was suspicious of *Principia Mathematica* on the grounds that its formalism was careless, ambiguous and did not pay sufficient attention to the use/mention distinction. He was an uncompromising critic of formalism for formalism's sake, and sought to ground mathematics in extensionalism, constructive nominalism and two-valued logic, insisting that only these principles would assure that it expressed meaningful, true sentences about the real world. He was, in the words of Tarski, the first person to become fully aware that a language which contains its own semantics and within which the usual logical laws hold must inevitably fall prey to liar-type paradoxes and hence be inconsistent.

The cornerstones of Leśniewski's work are *Mereology* (1927–31, outlined in 1916), *Ontology* (1920), his theory of semantic categories (1929) and *Protothetic* (1929) (see Leśniewski 1992). The notion of a semantic category, due originally to Husserl, plays a role in Leśniewski's construction of formal theories similar to that played by the notion of type in *Principia Mathematica*. Ajdukiewicz later reformulated the theory of semantic categories in the form of a calculus (see AJDUKIEWICZ, K. §5; Ajdukiewicz 1978, article 7).

Constructive nominalism had important metalogical consequences for Leśniewski, confronting him with problems of how to describe a system, its language, axioms and rules (especially rules of definition). Notoriously, he clung to the belief that at any particular moment a logical system contains only as many theorems as have been proved up to that point in time. This led him to an extreme constructivism in the theory of definitions. Definitions in his system were 'creative', that is, after introducing definitions of new terms, the system was, in his sense, stronger than before. His definitions can thus not be regarded as mere abbreviational conveniences.

Tarski, in his 1924 doctoral dissertation under Leśniewski, investigated a fragment of *Protothetic* which might be called the second-order propositional calculus. He showed that in this system all sentential functors can be defined in terms of the equivalence connective and universal quantifier; and that one can prove counterparts to all the basic metalogical laws for classical propositional calculus. These results supported Leśniewski's conviction that metatheoretical considerations outside the system were dispensable.

Mereology influenced Tarski in his papers on solid geometry and Boolean algebras, and also found application in Woodger and Tarski's work on the axiomatic foundations of biology (see Woodger 1937). Sobociński (1934) published successive simplifications of the axiom system for *Ontology*. Kotarbiński's philosophy of reism, and his classic *Elements* (1929), owe much to the ideas of Leśniewski.

Leśniewski's influence spread chiefly through lectures and seminars. He was unquestionably one of the founding fathers of logic in Poland between the wars. Only after the Second World War, through some of his students' publications and a monograph by Luschei (1962), did the wider community take an interest in his achievements (see Srzednicki, Rickey and Czelakowski 1984). Some notes from his Warsaw lectures were collected and published in 1988.

4 Tarski: semantics and metamathematics

The role of TARSKI in the development of Polish logic was in every way exceptional. Up to 1939 he published about sixty research papers covering various aspects of logic, set theory, measure theory (including the famous Banach–Tarski theorem on the 'paradoxical' decomposition of the sphere), axiomatic and structural aspects of Boolean algebras, truth theory and other areas of semantics (see Tarski 1956).

Tarski's contributions in pure logic were outstanding, and his work in formal or 'scientific' semantics and metamathematics helped shape Polish logic. His signal achievement was to establish that, for languages with specifiable structure, semantic notions such as satisfiability, truth, consequence and definability could be treated mathematically, and that this was fruitful (see TARSKI'S DEFINITION OF TRUTH; CONSEQUENCE, CONCEPTIONS OF; MODEL THEORY).

A metamathematical theme was present in Polish logic from the early 1920s, beginning with Ajdukiewicz (1921). Tarski's efforts allowed investigations of the sentential calculi to be carried out within an explicitly metamathematical framework. Tarski generalized this framework to a mathematical theory of two primitive concepts (sentence and consequence) which he called 'the methodology of the deductive sciences'. Within this theory he was able to provide a conceptual apparatus for investigating deductive systems. (Lindenbaum contributed much to this work, including the widely known Lindenbaum maximality lemma.) Tarski later enlarged his metamathematics to encompass the calculus of systems and the concepts of ω-consistency and ω-completeness. These contributions were of a foundational nature, explicitly concerned with metatheory *per se*, and consciously framed in a meta-metalanguage. (See Tarski 1956.)

One of Tarski's best-known discoveries is the 1930 theorem on the eliminability of quantifiers for the theory of real closed fields, together with its consequences for the decidability of the arithmetic of real numbers and elementary geometry, and the definability of sets of reals. To this category also belongs Tarski and Mostowski's work of the late 1930s on the decidability of the theory of well-orderings.

A recurring motif in Tarski's work was the idea of algebraization. He believed that by abstracting an algebraic calculus from a theory, the tools developed for the theory could be extended to other disciplines. This idea exerted a far-reaching influence on the subsequent course of logical investigations in Poland and elsewhere.

Largely through Tarski's work on truth, Polish logic also influenced philosophy. He spoke out against allowing one's repertoire of methods to be constrained by philosophical 'isms' such as formalism, logicism, constructivism or intuitionism (though his own scientism was exempt), and urged free use of all the resources of set theory, including transfinite techniques. He never accepted Wittgenstein's thesis that there is only one language of philosophical and scientific discourse, and persuaded some members of the Vienna Circle (most notably Carnap) to set it aside as well (see Tarski 1992).

5 Other work

Four recurring themes characterized the work of the Warsaw set theorists: (1) the axiom of choice, its equivalents and various weakenings, and its role within and beyond set theory; (2) the continuum hypothesis, its role in mathematics and its relation to the axiom of choice; (3) the problem of the independence of the axiom of choice from other principles of set theory; and (4) the arithmetic of cardinal and ordinal numbers (see AXIOM OF CHOICE; SET THEORY).

Sierpiński's paper (1918) was the first major contribution to (1). He argued that before an informed decision could be made concerning whether to adopt the axiom of choice, one should first investigate its deductive strength. In 1924, Tarski discovered that several statements in the arithmetic of infinite cardinals were equivalent to the axiom of choice and also systematized the theory of finite sets and showed that it was necessary to assume the axiom of choice to prove the equivalence of various definitions of finiteness (see Tarski 1986: vol. 1, 39–48, 65–117). Lindenbaum was the first to pose the question 'What is the logical relation between the continuum hypothesis and the axiom of choice?'. These and related results were summarized in a 1926 paper by Lindenbaum and Tarski (see Tarski 1986:

vol. 1, 171–204), where the two authors famously stated, without proof, that the generalized continuum hypothesis implies the axiom of choice (188, theorem 94). In 1934, Sierpiński published a compendium of principles known to be consequences of the generalized continuum hypothesis, but it was not until 1947 that he was able to supply the missing proof (1976: 485–8).

In 1938 Mostowski investigated the independence of definitions of finiteness in a system of type theory by means of the method of relativization of quantifiers (see Mostowski 1979: vol. 2, 18–67). During the years 1935–8 he and Lindenbaum also refined and extended Fraenkel's permutation models to investigate the independence of the axiom of choice from the ordering principle and various weaker forms of the axiom (vol. 1, 290–338; vol. 2, 70–4).

In Cracow, Sleszyński published a survey of the development of formal logic from Aristotle to Russell and Whitehead. Especially valuable is his treatment of nineteenth-century mathematical logic (1925–9). W. Wilkosz wrote textbooks on modern set theory and axiomatic foundations of number theories.

Chwistek developed a system for the foundation of logic and mathematics. Starting from several improvements of the ramified theory of types (see THEORY OF TYPES), he arrived at a purely constructivist theory without the axioms of reducibility and extensionality and without impredicative definitions (1924–5). Later, with his pupils J. Herzberg and W. Hetper, he outlined a formal theory of expressions called 'rational metamathematics' (1935). Chwistek's work in logic was strongly influenced by his philosophical beliefs, which set him apart from the mainstream of Polish logic (1961–3).

Pepis (1937, 1938) investigated the decision problem for the predicate calculus; more specifically, he dealt with the problem of reducing the question of the satisfiability of a logical formula from the general case to that of a formula having a special normal form.

6 Post-war developments

The Second World War caused the deaths of many logicians, including Lindenbaum and his wife J. Hosiasson-Lindenbaum (who worked on inductive logic), Herzberg, Hetper, Pepis, Salamucha, Z. Schmierer and Wajsberg. Others were forced to emigrate: Bocheński, H. Hiż, Jordan, Łukasiewicz, H. Mehlberg, Sobociński and Tarski. Manuscripts were lost or destroyed, among them Łukasiewicz's manuscript for a book on syllogistic, Mostowski's notes on the proof of quantifier elimination for well-orderings, and Leśniewski's *Nachlaß*. Galley proofs of a new journal, *Collectanea Logica*, were destroyed in 1939 and the journal never appeared.

Post-war Polish logic picked up where pre-war work had left off. In mathematical logic and the foundations of mathematics, the main figure was Mostowski (1979), whose contributions were wide-ranging, along with A. Grzegorczyk, A. Erenfeucht, J. Łoś, C. Ryll-Nardzewski and R. Suszko. Łoś is best known for his 1954 notion of categoricity-in-power, his 1955 lemma on ultraproducts and generally for his work on model theory (parts of which were carried out in collaboration with Suszko). Ryll-Nardzewski contributed to model theory (omitting types and ω-categoricity) and arithmetic (showing first-order Peano arithmetic is not finitely axiomatizable). Together, Łoś and Ryll-Nardzewski shed light on the logical importance of Tychonoff's compactness theorem and the prime ideal theorem. Joint papers by Grzegorczyk, Mostowski and Ryll-Nardzewski (see Mostowski 1979: vol. 1, 371–89; vol. 2, 427–31) are important for our understanding of natural numbers and ω-logic. Mostowski's expository essays and surveys have influenced the wider philosophical community (see Mostowski 1952, 1955, 1965).

Tarski's ideas of the algebraization of logic and of metamathematics were elaborated in numerous papers by Rasiowa and Sikorski and culminated in a classic work, *The Mathematics of Metamathematics* (1963).

In 1958 Łoś and Suszko proposed applying Tarski's theory of the consequence operation to investigations of abstract sentential calculi. This became a research paradigm of post-war Polish logic, drawing on concepts and tools from contemporary model theory and universal algebra. Its principal contributors were J. Czelakowski, W. Dziobak, W.A. Pogorzelski, T. Prucnal, Suszko, P. Wojtylak, R. Wójcicki and A. Wroński. Wójcicki (1987) summarizes the most important results of this programme.

The following logical journals were established in Poland after the Second World War: *Studia Logica* (in 1953), *Bulletin of the Section of Logic* (in 1972), *Reports on Mathematical Logic* (in 1973) and *Logic and Logical Philosophy* (in 1993). An account of post-war Polish logic can be found in Wójcicki (1997) and that of the foundations of mathematics in Marek (1977).

7 Polish notation

In Polish logical notation all operators are placed before the variables over which they have scope.

Np	Negation ($\neg$)
Kpq	Conjunction ($\wedge$)
Apq	Weak or inclusive disjunction ($\vee$)
Jpq	Strong or exclusive disjunction, or non-equivalence ($\not\equiv$)
Cpq	Conditional ($\rightarrow$)
Epq	Biconditional ($\leftrightarrow$)
Dpq	Sheffer stroke or non-conjunction ($\mid$)
Πpq	Universal quantification ($\forall$) (of q with respect to the sentential variable p)
Σpq	Existential quantification ($\exists$) (of q with respect to the sentential variable p)
ΠxFx	Universal quantification (of Fx with respect to the individual variable x)
ΣxFx	Existential quantification (of Fx with respect to the individual variable x)

Because we know for each operator whether it is one-place or two-place, we know how many of the following letters fall within its scope. So parentheses are not required to avoid ambiguity or to show association. For example, $p \rightarrow (q \rightarrow r)$ is written $CpCqr$ and $(p \rightarrow q) \rightarrow r$ is $CCpqr$; and

$$((p \wedge q) \rightarrow \neg r) \rightarrow (r \rightarrow (\neg p \vee \neg q))$$

is $CCKpqNrCrANpNq$.

The parenthesis-free notation, later called Polish notation, was invented by Łukasiewicz in 1924 and published (1929) in application to the sentential calculus, the sentential calculus with quantifiers and Aristotle's syllogistic. (See also Łukasiewicz and Tarski 1930: 39, note 2; 54–.) The notation is very convenient in theoretical considerations; sometimes it is also used in textbooks (see, for example, Prior 1955).

See also: LOGICAL AND MATHEMATICAL TERMS, GLOSSARY OF

References and further reading

* Ajdukiewicz, K. (1921) *Z metodologii nauk dedukcyjnych*, Lwów: Nakładem Polskiego Towarzystwa Filozoficznego; trans. J. Giedymin, 'From the Methodology of Deductive Sciences', *Studia Logica* 19: 9–46, 1966. (Referred to in §4.)
* —— (1978) *The Scientific-World Perspective and other Essays 1931–1963*, ed. J. Giedymin, Dordrecht: Reidel. (Twenty-two papers in English translation with an introduction by the editor comparing

Ajdukiewicz's radical conventionalism to the conventionalism of Poincaré and LeRoy; referred to in §3.)

* Bocheński, I.M. (1938) *Z historii zdań modalnych* (From the History of Modal Sentences), Lwów: Wydawnictwo OO. Domnikanów. (Referred to in §2.)

* —— (1951) *Ancient Formal Logic*, Amsterdam: North Holland. (Referred to in §2.)

* —— (1956) *Formale Logik*, Freiburg and Munich: Alber; trans. I. Thomas, *A History of Formal Logic*, Notre Dame, IN: University of Notre Dame Press, 1961; repr. New York: Chelsea, 1970. (Referred to in §2.)

* Chwistek, L. (1924–5) 'The Theory of Constructive Types (Principles of Logic and Mathematics)', *Annales de la Société Polonaise de Mathématique* 2: 9–48, 3: 91–141. (Referred to in §5.)

* —— (1935) *Granice nauki: zarys logiki i metodologii nauk ścisłych*, Warsaw and Lwów: Książnica Atlas; revised edn trans. H.C. Brodie and A.P. Coleman, *The Limits of Science: Outline of Logic and of the Methodology of the Exact Sciences*, London: Routledge & Kegan Paul, 1948. (Referred to in §5.)

* —— (1961–3) *Pisma filozoficzne i logiczne* (Philosophical and Logical Writings), ed. K. Pasenkiewicz, Warsaw: PWN, 2 vols. (Almost all of Chwistek's works written in Polish: in volume 1, his philosophical, methodological and aesthetic writings; in volume 2, his logical and mathematical ones (together with *Granice nauki*). Referred to in §5.)

* Czeżowski, T. (1936) 'Arystotelesa teoria zdań modalnych' (Aristotle's Theory of Modal Propositions), *Przegląd Filozoficzny* 39 (3): 232–41. (Referred to in §2.)

* Jaśkowski, S. (1934) *On the Rules of Supposition in Formal Logic*, Warsaw: Nakładem Seminarium Filozoficznego Wydziału Matematyczno-Przyrodniczego Uniwersytetu Warszawskiego; repr. with notational changes in S. McCall (ed.) *Polish Logic 1920–1939*, Oxford: Clarendon Press, 1967. (Referred to in §2.)

* —— (1936) 'Recherches sur le système de la logique intuitioniste', in *Actes du Congrès International de Philosophie Scientifique, Paris 1935*, vol. 6, *Actualités Scientifiques et Industrielles*, Paris: Hermann, 58–61; trans. in S. McCall (ed.) *Polish Logic 1920–1939*, Oxford: Clarendon Press, 1967. (Referred to in §2. For a detailed elaboration of Jaśkowski's semantics for intuitionist logic see Surma (1971).)

* Jordan, Z. (1937) *O matematycznych podstawach systemu Platona: z historii racjonalizmu* (Mathematical Foundations of Plato's System: On the History of Rationalism), with a French summary, Poznan: Nakładem Poznańskiego Towarzystwa Przyjaciół Nauk. (Referred to in §2.)

—— (1945) *The Development of Mathematical Logic and of Logical Positivism in Poland Between the Two Wars*, Oxford: Oxford University Press; partly repr. in S. McCall (ed.) *Polish Logic 1920–1939*, Oxford: Clarendon Press, 1967, 346–406. (Succinct and readable, but without technical details; lacks historical perspective.)

* Korcik, A. (1937) *Teoria konwersji zdań asertorycznych u Arystotelesa w świetle teorii dedukcji: studium historyczno-krytyczne* (The Theory of Conversion of Assertoric Propositions in Aristotle in the Light of the Theory of Deduction: Critical and Historical Study), Wilno: Wydawnictwo Studiów Teologicznych. (Referred to in §2.)

* Kotarbiński, T. (1929) *Elementy teorii poznania, logiki formalnej i metodologii nauk* (Elements of the Theory of Knowledge, Formal Logic and the Methodology of Sciences), Lwów: Ossolineum; 2nd revised edn, Warsaw: PWN, 1961; 2nd edn trans. O. Wojtasiewicz, *Gnosiology: The Scientific Approach to the Theory of Knowledge*, Oxford: Pergamon Press, and Wrocław: Ossolineum, 1966. (Referred to in §3.)

* —— (1957) *Wykłady z dziejów logiki* (Lectures on the History of Logic), Wrocław and Łódź: Ossolineum; 2nd edn, Warsaw: PWN, 1985. (Referred to in §2.)

* Leśniewski, S. (1988) *S. Leśniewski's Lecture Notes in Logic*, ed. J.T.J. Srzednicki and Z. Stachniak, Dordrecht: Kluwer. (Notes from lectures and seminars given by Leśniewski in the period 1919–39. They cover topics ranging from his own systems to Peano arithmetic and Whitehead's theory of events. Referred to in §3.)

* —— (1992) *Collected Works*, ed. S.J. Surma, J.T. Srzednicki and D.I. Barnet, with an annotated bibliography by V.F. Rickey, Warsaw: PWN, and Dordrecht: Kluwer, 2 vols. (English translation of all Leśniewski's published works. Flawed in some respects; see a review in *History and Philosophy of Logic* 15: 227–35, 1994.)

* Łukasiewicz, J. (1910) *O zasadzie sprzeczności u Arystotelesa: studyum krytyczne* (On the Principle of Contradiction in Aristotle: A Critical Study), Cracow: Polska Akademia Umiejętności; 2nd edn with an introduction and notes by J. Woleński, Warsaw: PWN, 1987. (Referred to in §2.)

* —— (1929) *Elementy logiki matematycznej*, ed. M. Presburger, Warsaw: PWN; 2nd revised and abridged edn, ed. J. Słupecki, Warsaw: PWN; trans. *Elements of Mathematical Logic*, Oxford: Pergamon Press, and New York: Macmillan, 1963. (Referred to in §2.)

* —— (1934) 'Z historii logiki zdań', *Przegląd Filozoficzny* 37: 417–37; German trans. by the author, 'Zur Geschichte der Aussagenlogik', *Erkenntnis* 5: 111–31, 1935; trans. On the History of the Logic of Propositions, in *Selected Works*, ed. L. Borkowski, Amsterdam: North Holland, 1970; and in S. McCall (ed.) *Polish Logic 1920–1939*, Oxford: Clarendon Press, 1967. (According to H. Scholz, the most interesting thirty pages ever written on the history of logic. Referred to in §2.)

* —— (1939) 'O sylogistyce Arystotelesa' (On Aristotle's Syllogistic), *Sprawozdania Polskiej Akademii Umiejętności* 44: 220–7. (Referred to in §2.)

* —— (1941) 'Die Logik und das Grundlagenproblem', *Les entretiens de Zürich sur les fondements et la méthode de sciences mathématiques, 6–9 décembre 1938*, 82–100; trans. 'Logic and the Problem of the Foundations of Mathematics', in *Selected Works*, ed. L. Borkowski, Amsterdam: North Holland, 1970. (Referred to in §2.)

* —— (1951) *Aristotle's Syllogistic from the Standpoint of Modern Formal Logic*, Oxford: Oxford University Press; 2nd enlarged edn, 1957. (Referred to in §2.)

—— (1970) *Selected Works*, ed. L. Borkowski, Amsterdam: North Holland. (Anthology of all important papers from the entire creative work of Łukasiewicz.)

* Łukasiewicz, J. and Tarski, A. (1930) 'Untersuchungen über den Aussagenkalkül', *Comptes Rendus des Séances de la Société des Sciences et des Lettres de Varsovie* (Classe 3) 23: 30–50; trans. 'Investigations into the Sentential Calculus', in J. Łukasiewicz, *Selected Works*, ed. L. Borkowski, Amsterdam: North Holland, 1970; and in A. Tarski, *Logic, Semantics, Metamathematics: Papers from 1923 to 1938*, trans. and ed. J.H. Woodger, Oxford: Clarendon Press, 1956. (Referred to in §2.)

* Luschei, E.C. (1962) *The Logical Systems of Leśniewski*, Amsterdam: North Holland. (The only book which describes the whole of Leśniewski's scientific achievements; includes a large chapter on terminological explanations and directives. An invaluable and unique guide for those who want to read the originals, but it is not a systematic exposition of Leśniewski's systems. Referred to in §3.)

* Marek, W. (1977) 'The Foundations of Mathematics in Poland after World War II', in R.O. Gandy and J.M.E. Hyland (eds) *Logic Colloquium '76*, Amsterdam: North Holland, 129–38. (Referred to in §6.)

* Mates, B. (1953) *Stoic Logic*, Berkeley and Los Angeles, CA: University of California Press. (Referred to in §2.)

McCall, S. (ed.) (1967) *Polish Logic 1920–1939*, Oxford: Clarendon Press. (Classic anthology of papers by Ajdukiewicz, Chwistek, Jaśkowski, Leśniewski, Łukasiewicz, Słupecki and Wajsberg, with notes by Kotarbiński on the development of formal logic in Poland in the years 1900–39; includes part of Jordan (1945).)

* Mostowski, A. (1952) *Sentences Undecidable in Formalized Arithmetic: An Exposition of the Theory of Kurt Gödel*, Amsterdam: North Holland. (Referred to in §6.)

* —— (1965) 'Thirty Years of Foundational Studies: Lectures on the Development of Mathematical Logic and the Study of the Foundations of Mathematics in 1930–1964', *Acta Philosophica Fennica* 17: 1–180; repr. New York: Barnes & Noble, 1966; and in *Foundational Studies, vol. 1*, Amsterdam: North Holland, 1979. (History of mathematical logic from Gödel to P.J. Cohen, written from a Polish point of view; referred to in §6.)

* —— (1979) *Foundational Studies*, Amsterdam: North Holland, 2 vols. (An anthology of the most important of Mostowski's works from 1937–76; includes a complete bibliography and five essays summarizing his work on decidability, recursion and hierarchy theory, set theory, model theory, logical calculi and arithmetic. Volume 1 may be of interest for its survey and expository papers. Referred to in §§5–6.)

* Mostowski, A. *et al.* (1955) 'The Present State of Investigations on the Foundations of Mathematics', *Rozprawy Matematyczne (Dissertationes Mathematicae)* 9: 1–48. (Referred to in §6.)

Pearce, D. and Woleński, J. (eds) (1988) *Logischer Rationalismus: Schriften der Lemberg–Warschauer Schule* (Logical Rationalism: Writings of the Lwów–Warsaw School), Frankfurt: Athenaeum. (Shorter papers, in German, by Ajdukiewicz, J. Hosiasson-Lindenbaum, M. Kokoszyńska, Kotarbiński, Łukasiewicz and Tarski.)

* Pepis, J. (1937) *O zagadnieniu rozstrzygalności w zakresie węższego rachunku funkcyjnego* (On the Decision Problem in the Domain of the Restricted Functional Calculus), with a German summary, Lwów: Archiwum Towarzystwa Naukowego we Lwowie, §3, vol. 7, fasc. 8, 1–172 ([465]–[616]). (Referred to in §5.)

* —— (1938) 'Untersuchungen über das Entscheidungsproblem der mathematischen Logik' (Investigations into the Decision Problem of Mathematical Logic), *Fundamenta Mathematicae* 30: 257–348. (Referred to in §5.)

* Prior, A. (1955) *Formal Logic*, Oxford: Clarendon Press; 2nd edn with corrections, 1962. (An example of the use of Polish notation in a textbook.)

* Rasiowa, H. and Sikorski, R. (1963) *The Mathematics of Metamathematics*, Warsaw: PWN. (Referred to in §6.)

* Salamucha, J. (1934) 'Dowód "ex motu" na istnienie Boga: analiza logiczna argumentacji św. Tomasza z Akwinu', *Collectanea Theologica* 15: 53–92; trans. 'The Proof *ex motu* for the Existence of God: Logical Analysis of St. Thomas' Arguments', *The New Scholasticism* 32: 334–72, 1958. (Referred to in §2.)

* —— (1935) 'Logika zdań u Wilhelma Ockhama' (Propositional Logic in William of Ockham), *Przegląd Filozoficzny* 38 (3): 208–39. (Referred to in §2.)

* —— (1937) 'Pojawienie się zagadnień antynomialnych na gruncie logiki średniowiecznej' (The Appearance of the Problem of Antinomies in Medieval Logic), *Przegląd Filozoficzny* 40 (1): 68–89, 40 (3): 320–43. (Referred to in §2.)

* Scholz, H. (1931) *Geschichte der Logik*, Berlin; repr. as *Abriß der Geschichte der Logik*, Freiburg: Alber, 1959; trans. K.F. Leidecker, *Concise History of Logic*, New York: Philosophical Library, 1961. (Referred to in §2.)

* Sierpiński, W. (1918) 'L' axiome de M. Zermelo et son rôle dans théorie des ensembles et l'analyse' (Zermelo's Axiom and its Role in Set Theory and Analysis), *Bulletin de l'Académie des Sciences de Cracovie, Classe des Sciences Mathématiques*, série A, 97–152; repr. in *Oeuvres Choisies*, vol. 2, *Théorie des Ensembles et ses Applications, Travaux des Années 1908–1929*, Warsaw: PWN–Editions Scientifiques de Pologne, 1975. (Referred to in §5.)

* —— (1934) *Hypothèse du Continu* (The Continuum Hypothesis), Monografie Matematyczne, vol. 4, Warsaw: Grasiński. (Referred to in §5.)

* —— (1976) *Oeuvres Choisies* (Selected Works), vol. 3, *Théorie des Ensembles et ses Applications, Travaux des Années 1930–1966* (Set Theory and its Applications: Papers from 1930 to 1966), Warsaw: PWN–Editions Scientifiques de Pologne. (Referred to in §5.)

* Sleszyński, J. (1925–9) *Teoria dowodu. Podług wykładów uniwersyteckich Prof. Dr Jana Sleszyńskiego opracował S.K. Zaremba* (The Theory of Proof. Edited by S.K. Zaremba from the University Lectures of Professor Dr. Jan Sleszyński), Cracow: Nakładem Kółka Matematyczno-Fizycznego Uczniów Uniwersytetu Jagiellońskiego, 2 vols. (Referred to in §5.)

* Słupecki, J. (1939a) 'Dowód aksjomatyzowalności pełnych systemów wielowartościowych rachunku zdań', *Comptes Rendus des Séances de la Société des Sciences et des Lettres de Varsovie* (Classe 3) 32: 110–28; trans. 'A Proof of the Axiomatizability of Full Systems of Many-Valued Sentential Calculus', *Studia Logica* 29: 155–68, 1971. (Referred to in §2.)

* —— (1939b) 'Kryterium pełności wielowartościowych systemów logiki zdań', *Comptes Rendus des Séances de la Société des Sciences et des Lettres de Varsovie* (Classe 3) 32: 102–9; trans. 'A Criterion of Fullness for Many-Valued Systems of Propositional Logic', *Studia Logica* 30: 153–7, 1972. (Referred to in §2.)

* —— (1949) 'On Aristotelian Syllogistic', *Studia Philosophica* (Poznań) 4: 275–300. (Referred to in §2.)

* Sobociński, B. (1934) 'O kolejnych uproszczeniach aksjomatyki "ontologii" prof. S. Leśniewskiego', in *Fragmenty Filozoficzne. Księga Pamiątkowa ku Uczczeniu Piętnastolecia Pracy Nauczycielskiej w Uniwersytecie Warszawskim Profesora Tadeusza Kotarbińskiego*, Warsaw: Nakładem Uczniów, 144–60; trans. 'Successive Simplifications of the Axiom-System of Leśniewski's Ontology', in S. McCall (ed.) *Polish Logic 1920–1939*, Oxford: Clarendon Press, 1967. (Referred to in §3.)

* —— (1936) 'Aksjomatyzacja pewnych wielowartościowych systemów teorii dedukcji' (Axiomatization of Certain Many-Valued Systems of the Theory of Deduction), *Roczniki Prac Naukowych Zrzeszenia Asystentów Uniwersytetu Józefa Piłsudskiego w Warszawie* 1: 399–419. (Referred to in §2.)

* Srzednicki, J.T.J., Rickey, V.F. and Czelakowski, J. (eds) (1984) *Leśniewski's Systems: Ontology and Mereology*, The Hague: Martinus Nijhoff, and Wrocław: Ossolineum. (Twelve representative papers on ontology and mereology by Leśniewski's pupils, Z. Kruszewski, C. Lejewski, J. Słupecki, B. Sobociński; and their pupils, J. Canty, R. Clay and B. Iwanuś. Referred to in §3.)

Surma, S.J. (1971) 'Jaśkowski's Matrix Criterion for the Intuitionistic Propositional Calculus', *Universitas Iagiellonica Acta Scientiarum Litterarumque*, vol. 265, *Schedae Logicae* 6: 21–54. (See Jaśkowski 1936.)

—— (1977) 'On the Work and Influence of Stanisław Leśniewski', in R.O. Gandy and J.M.E. Hyland (eds) *Logic Colloquium '76*, Amsterdam: North Holland, 191–220. (A biography and annotated bibliography of Leśniewski, with an outline of his logical systems.)

—— (1979) 'On the Origin and Subsequent Application of the Concept of Lindenbaum Algebra', in L.J. Cohen, J. Łoś, H. Pfeiffer and K.-H. Podewski (eds) *Logic, Methodology and Philosophy of Science*, Amsterdam: North Holland, vol. 6, 719–34. (Rather technical exposition of the subject described in the title, with a full bibliography of Lindenbaum's works.)

—— (1987) 'The Logical Work of Mordchaj Wajsberg', in J. Srzednicki (ed.) *Initiatives in Logic*, Dordrecht: Martinus Nijhoff, 101–15. (An account of Wajsberg's life and his logical research.)

Szumilewicz-Lachman, I. and Cohen, R.S. (ed.) (1994) *Zygmunt Zawirski: His Life and Work. With Selected Writings on Time, Logic and Methodology of Science*, trans. F. Lachman, Dordrecht: Kluwer. (Valuable especially for Zawirski's two papers, 'The Genesis and Development of Intuitionistic Logic' and 'The Evolution of the Notion of Time'; also includes essays by Szumilewicz-Lachman on the Lwów–Warsaw school and the Vienna Circle.)

* Tarski, A. (1956) *Logic, Semantics, Metamathematics: Papers from 1923 to 1938*, trans. and ed. J.H. Woodger, Oxford: Clarendon Press; repr. and ed. J. Corcoran, Indianapolis, IN: Hackett Publishing Company, 2nd edn, 1983. (Referred to in §§2, 4. For a careful presentation of the content of the book see the review by W.A. Pogorzelski and S.J. Surma, *Journal of Symbolic Logic* 34 (1): 99–106, 1969.)

* —— (1986) *The Collected Papers*, ed. S.R. Givant and R.N. McKenzie, Basle: Birkhäuser, 4 vols. (Reprints of all of Tarski's writings excluding his books; unfortunately original pagination has not been kept.)

* —— (1992) 'Alfred Tarski: Drei Briefe an Otto Neurath', ed. R. Haller, trans. J. Tarski, *Grazer Philosophische Studien* 43: 1–32. (Referred to in §4.)

* Wajsberg, M. (1933) 'Ein erweiterter Klassenkalkül', *Monatshefte für Mathematik und Physik* 40: 113–26; trans. 'An Extended Class Calculus', in *Logical Works*, ed. S.J. Surma, Wrocław: Ossolineum, 1977. (Referred to in §2.)

* —— (1935) 'Beiträge zum Metaaussagenkalkül I', *Monatshefte für Mathematik und Physik* 42: 221–42; trans. 'Contributions to the Meta-Calculus of Propositions', in *Logical Works*, ed. S.J. Surma, Wrocław: Ossolineum, 1977. (Referred to in §2.)

* —— (1938) 'Untersuchungen über den Aussagenkalkül von A. Heyting', *Wiadomości Matematyczne* 46: 45–101; trans. 'On A. Heyting's Propositional Calculus', in *Logical Works*, ed. S.J. Surma, Wrocław: Ossolineum, 1977. (Referred to in §2.)

* Wójcicki, R. (1987) *Theory of Sentential Calculi. An Introduction*, Dordrecht: Reidel. (Referred to in §6.)

* —— (1997) 'The Postwar Panorama of Logic in Poland', in M.L. dalla Chiara *et al.* (eds) *Logic and Scientific Methods*, Dordrecht: Kluwer, 497–508. (Referred to in §6.)

Woleński, J. (1989) *Logic and Philosophy in the Lvov–Warsaw School*, Dordrecht: Kluwer. (An authoritative and comprehensive treatise with an excellent bibliography.)

* Woodger, J.H. (1937) *The Axiomatic Method in Biology*, with appendix by A. Tarski, Cambridge: Cambridge University Press, and New York: Macmillan. (Referred to in §3.)

JAN ZYGMUNT

POLITICAL PHILOSOPHY

Political philosophy can be defined as philosophical reflection on how best to arrange our collective life – our political institutions and our social practices, such as our economic system and our pattern of family life. (Sometimes a distinction is made between *political* and *social* philosophy, but I shall use 'political philosophy' in a broad sense to include both.) Political philosophers seek to establish basic principles that will, for instance, justify a particular form of state, show that individuals have certain inalienable rights, or tell us how a society's material resources should be shared among its members. This usually involves analysing and interpreting ideas like freedom, justice, authority and democracy and then applying them in a critical way to the social and political institutions that currently exist. Some political philosophers have tried primarily to justify the prevailing arrangements of their society; others have painted pictures of an ideal state or an ideal social world that is very different from anything we have so far experienced (see UTOPIANISM).

Political philosophy has been practised for as long as human beings have regarded their collective arrangements not as immutable and part of the natural order but as potentially open to change, and therefore as standing in need of philosophical justification. It can be found in many different cultures, and has taken a wide variety of forms. There are two reasons for this diversity. First, the methods and approaches used by political philosophers reflect the general philosophical tendencies of their epoch. Developments in epistemology and ethics, for instance, alter the assumptions on which political philosophy can proceed. But second, the political philosopher's agenda is largely set by the pressing political issues of the day. In medieval Europe, for instance, the proper relationship between Church and State became a central issue in political philosophy; in the early modern period the main argument was between defenders of absolutism and those who sought to justify a limited, constitutional state. In the nineteenth century, the social question – the question of how an industrial society should organize its economy and its welfare system – came to the fore.

When we study the history of political philosophy, therefore, we find that alongside some perennial questions – how can one person ever justifiably claim the authority to govern another person, for instance? – there are some big changes: in the issues addressed, in the language used to address them, and in the underlying premises on which the political philosopher rests his or her argument. (For the development of the Western tradition of political philosophy, see POLITICAL PHILOSOPHY, HISTORY OF; for other traditions, see POLITICAL PHILOSOPHY IN CLASSICAL ISLAM; POLITICAL PHILOSOPHY, INDIAN; AFRICAN PHILOSOPHY, ANGLOPHONE; MARXISM, CHINESE; BUSHI PHILOSOPHY; SHŌTOKU CONSTITUTION; SUNZI; MARXIST THOUGHT IN LATIN AMERICA.)

One question that immediately arises is whether the principles that political philosophers establish are to be regarded as having universal validity, or whether they should be seen as expressing the assumptions and the values of a particular political community. This question about the scope and status of political philosophy has been fiercely debated in recent years (see POLITICAL PHILOSOPHY, NATURE OF). It is closely connected to a question about human nature (see HUMAN NATURE). In order to justify a set of collective arrangements, a political philosophy must say something about the nature of human beings, about their needs, their capacities, about whether they are mainly selfish or mainly altruistic, and so forth. But can we discover common traits in human beings everywhere, or are people's characters predominantly shaped by the particular culture they belong to?

If we examine the main works of political philosophy in past centuries, they can be divided roughly into two categories. On the one hand there are those produced by philosophers elaborating general philosophical systems, whose political philosophy flows out of and forms an integral part of those systems. Leading philosophers who have made substantial contributions to political thought include PLATO, ARISTOTLE, AUGUSTINE, AQUINAS, HOBBES, LOCKE, HUME, HEGEL and J.S. MILL. On the other hand there are social and political thinkers whose contribution to philosophy as a whole has had little lasting significance, but who have made influential contributions to political philosophy specifically. In this category we may include CICERO, MARSILIUS OF PADUA, MACHIAVELLI, GROTIUS, ROUSSEAU, BENTHAM, FICHTE and MARX. Two important figures whose work reflects non-Western influences are IBN KHALDHUN and KAUṬILYA. Among the most important twentieth-century political thinkers are ARENDT, BERLIN, DEWEY, FOUCAULT, GANDHI, GRAMSCI, HABERMAS, HAYEK, OAKESHOTT, RAWLS, SARTRE and TAYLOR.

Political institutions and ideologies

What are the issues that, historically and today, have most exercised political philosophers? To begin with, there is a set of questions about how political institutions should be arranged. Today we would think of this as an enquiry into the best form of state, though we should note that the state itself is a particular kind of political arrangement of relatively recent origin – for most of their history human beings have not been governed by states (see STATE, THE). Since all states claim AUTHORITY over their subjects, two fundamental issues are the very meaning of authority, and the criteria by which we can judge forms of political rule legitimate (see LEGITIMACY; CONTRACTARIANISM; GENERAL WILL; POWER; TRADITION AND TRADITIONALISM). Connected to this is the issue of whether individual subjects have a moral obligation to obey the laws of their state (see OBLIGATION, POLITICAL), and of the circumstances under which politically-inspired disobedience is justifiable (see CIVIL DISOBEDIENCE; REVOLUTION). Next there is a series of questions about the form that the state should take: whether authority should be absolute or constitutionally limited (see ABSOLUTISM; CONSTITUTIONALISM); whether its structure should be unitary or federal (see FEDERALISM AND CONFEDERALISM); whether it should be democratically controlled, and if so by what means (see DEMOCRACY; REPRESENTATION, POLITICAL). Finally here there is the question of whether any general limits can be set to the authority of the state – whether there are areas of individual freedom or privacy that the state must never invade on any pretext (see LAW, LIMITS OF; FREEDOM OF SPEECH; COERCION; PROPERTY; SLAVERY), and whether there are subjects such as religious doctrine on which the state must adopt a strictly neutral posture (see NEUTRALITY, POLITICAL; TOLERATION).

Beyond the question of how the state itself should be constituted lies the question of the general principles that should guide its decisions. What values should inform economic and social policy for instance? Part of the political philosopher's task is to examine ideas that are often appealed to in political argument but whose meaning remains obscure, so that they can be used by politicians from rival camps to justify radically contrasting policies. Political philosophers try to give a clear and coherent account of notions such as EQUALITY, FREEDOM and LIBERTY, JUSTICE, NEEDS AND INTERESTS, PUBLIC INTEREST, RIGHTS and WELFARE. And they also try to determine whether these ideas are consistent with, or conflict with, one another – whether, for instance, equality and liberty are competing values, or whether a society might be both free and equal at once.

Further questions arise about the principles that should guide one state in its dealings with other states. May states legitimately pursue what they regard as their national interests, or are they bound to recognize ethical obligations towards one another (see DEVELOPMENT ETHICS)? More widely, should we be seeking a cosmopolitan alternative under which principles of justice would be applied at global level? (see INTERNATIONAL RELATIONS, PHILOSOPHY OF; JUSTICE, INTERNATIONAL). When, if ever, are states justified in going to war with each other? (See WAR AND PEACE, PHILOSOPHY OF.)

Over about the last two centuries, political debate has most often been conducted within the general frameworks supplied by rival ideologies. We can think of an ideology as a set of beliefs about the social and political world which simultaneously makes sense of what is going on, and guides our practical responses to it (see IDEOLOGY). Ideologies are often rather loosely structured, so that two people who are both conservatives, say, may reach quite different conclusions about some concrete issue of policy. Nevertheless they seem to be indispensable as simplifying devices for thinking about a political world of ever-increasing complexity.

No political philosopher can break free entirely from the grip of ideology, but political philosophy must involve a more critical scrutiny of the intellectual links that hold ideologies together, and a bringing to light of the unstated assumptions that underpin them. The most influential of these ideologies have been LIBERALISM, CONSERVATISM, SOCIALISM, nationalism (see NATION AND NATIONALISM; EURASIAN MOVEMENT; PAN-SLAVISM; ZIONISM; PAN-AFRICAN-ISM) and Marxism (see MARXISM, WESTERN; MARX-IST PHILOSOPHY, RUSSIAN AND SOVIET; MARXISM, CHINESE). Other ideologies are of lesser political significance, either because they have drawn fewer adherents or because they have been influential over a shorter period of time: these include ANARCHISM, COMMUNISM, FASCISM, LIBERTARIANISM, REPUBLICANISM, SOCIAL DEMOCRACY and TOTALI-TARIANISM.

Contemporary political philosophy

The last quarter of the twentieth century has seen a powerful revival of political philosophy, which in Western societies at least has mostly been conducted within a broadly liberal framework. Other ideologies have been outflanked: Marxism has gone into a rapid decline, and conservatism and socialism have survived only by taking on board large portions of liberalism.

Some have claimed that the main rival to liberalism is now communitarianism (see COMMUNITY AND COM-MUNITARIANISM); however on closer inspection the so-called liberal–communitarian debate can be seen to be less a debate about liberalism itself than about the precise status and form that a liberal political philosophy should take – whether, for example, it should claim universal validity, or should present itself simply as an interpretation of the political culture of the Western liberal democracies. The vitality of political philosophy is not to be explained by the emergence of a new ideological revival to liberalism, but by the fact that a new set of political issues has arisen whose resolution will stretch the intellectual resources of liberalism to the limit.

What are these issues? The first is the issue of social justice, which in one form or another has dominated political philosophy for much of the century. Most of the many liberal theories of justice on offer have had a broadly egalitarian flavour, demanding at least the partial offsetting of the economic and social inequal-ities thrown up by an unfettered market economy (see MARKET, ETHICS OF THE; JUSTICE; RAWLS, J.; DWORKIN, R.; though for dissenting views see HAYEK, F.A. VON; NOZICK, R.). These theories rested on the assumption that social and economic policy could be pursued largely within the borders of a self-contained political community, sheltered from the world market. This assumption has become increasingly questionable, and it presents liberals with the following dilemma: if the pursuit of social justice is integral to liberalism, how can this be now be reconciled with individual freedoms to move, communicate, work, and trade across state boundaries?

The second issue is posed by feminism, and especially the feminist challenge to the conventional liberal distinction between public and private spheres (see FEMINIST POLITICAL PHILOSOPHY). In many respects feminism and liberalism are natural allies, but when feminists argue for fundamental changes in the way men and women conduct their personal relationships, or advocate affirmative action policies for employment that seems to contravene firmly-entrenched liberal principles of desert and merit, they pose major challenges to liberal political philosophy (see DESERT AND MERIT).

Third, there is a set of issues arising from what we might call the new politics of cultural identity. Many groups in contemporary societies now demand that political institutions should be altered to reflect and express their distinctive cultures; these include, on the one hand, nationalist groups asserting that political boundaries should be redrawn to give them a greater measure of self-determination, and on the other cultural minorities whose complaint is that public institutions fail to show equal respect for those attributes that distinguish them from the majority (for instance their language or religion) (see NATION AND NATIONALISM; MULTICULTURALISM; POSTCOLONIALISM). These demands once again collide with long-established liberal beliefs that the state should be culturally neutral, that citizens should receive equal treatment under the law, and that rights belong to individuals, not groups (see CITIZENSHIP; AFFIRMATIVE ACTION; DISCRIMINATION). It remains to be seen whether liberalism is sufficiently flexible to incorporate such demands.

Finally, liberalism is challenged by the environmental movement, whose adherents claim that liberal political principles cannot successfully address urgent environmental concerns, and more fundamentally that the liberal image of the self-sufficient, self-directing individual is at odds with the ecological picture of humanity's subordinate place in the system of nature as a whole (see GREEN POLITICAL PHILOSOPHY; ENVIRONMENTAL ETHICS). Liberalism, it is said, is too firmly wedded to the market economy and to consumption as the means of achieving personal well-being, to be able to embrace the radical policies needed to avoid environmental disaster.

None of these problems is capable of easy solution, and we can say with some confidence that political philosophy will continue to flourish even in a world in which the sharp ideological divisions of the mid-twentieth century no longer exist. We may also expect a renewal of non-Western traditions of political philosophy as free intellectual enquiry revives in those countries where for half a century or more it has been suppressed by the state. Political questions that have concerned philosophers for two millennia or more will be tackled using new languages and new techniques, while the ever-accelerating pace of technological and social change will generate new problems whose solution we can barely begin to anticipate.

See also: ALIENATION; CIVIL SOCIETY; CONSENT; CORRUPTION; CRITICAL THEORY; CULTURE; ECONOMICS AND ETHICS; EVOLUTION AND ETHICS; HISTORICISM; LIBERALISM, RUSSIAN; PARETO PRINCIPLE; POPULATION AND ETHICS; POSTMODERNISM AND POLITICAL PHILOSOPHY; VIOLENCE; WORK, PHILOSOPHY OF; PARTIINOST'; ANTI-SEMITISM; RELIGION AND POLITICAL PHILOSOPHY; FAMILY, ETHICS AND THE; PATERNALISM; RACE, THEORIES OF; SOVEREIGNTY; CULTURAL IDENTITY; LAW, PHILOSOPHY OF

Further reading

Goodin, R. and Pettit, P. (1993) *A Companion to Contemporary Political Philosophy*, Oxford: Blackwell. (A comprehensive guide to current thinking in political philosophy, this book focuses especially on normative issues.)

Hampsher-Monk, I.W. (1992) *A History of Modern Political Thought, Major Political Thinkers from Hobbes to Marx*, Oxford: Blackwell. (Contextualized studies of the political theories of Hobbes, Locke, Hume, Rousseau, The Federalist, Burke, Bentham, Mill, Hegel and Marx.)

Kymlicka, W. (1990) *Contemporary Political Philosophy*, Oxford: Oxford University Press. (Each chapter covers a major school of contemporary political thought.)

Wolff, J. (1996) *An Introduction to Political Philosophy*, Oxford: Oxford University Press. (An accessible general introduction which discusses the arguments of both historical and contemporary political philosophers.)

DAVID MILLER

POLITICAL PHILOSOPHY, AFRICAN *see* AFRICAN PHILOSOPHY, ANGLOPHONE

POLITICAL PHILOSOPHY, HISTORY OF

The history of political philosophy attempts to yield a connected account of past speculation on the character of human association at its most inclusive level. 'History' or 'philosophy' may be stressed depending on whether the organizing principle is the temporal sequence or conceptual framework of political thought. Anglophone work has increasingly been organized around distinctive political 'languages' defined by specific vocabularies, syntaxes and problems, for example, classical republicanism, Roman law, natural law, utilitarianism. Chronologically it has been usual to observe divisions between ancient, medieval, Renaissance, early modern and modern periods of study.

Ancient Greece is the source of the earliest political reflection, with a continuous history in the West. Here reflection on the nature and proper organization of political community stimulated inquiry into the difference between nature and convention, the public and the

domestic realm, the distinctive character of political rule, the relationship between political life and philosophy, the identity of justice, and the taxonomy of state-forms – as well as a more sociological investigation of the stability and decline of political regimes.

Greek political vocabulary was adapted to existing Roman republican practice (by Polybius and Cicero for example), which soon gave way to an imperial constitution stressing peace, order and unity. Rome thus generated two contrasting political ideals – that of the virtuous active republican citizen, and that of the unified empire governed by Roman law. Together with questions about the causes of its own rise and decline, Rome thus provided political values and historical material for subsequent philosophical and historical reflection.

Christianity undermined the pagan autonomy of politics in the name of a higher, transcendent ideal. However, it adapted much of Greek rationalism and the political vocabulary of classical culture in elaborating a creed and an institutional form. In turn it lent legitimacy to imperial and royal officeholders of Rome and barbarian successor-kingdoms.

Medieval political philosophy was characteristically preoccupied with the relationship between pope and king, church and regnum, but philosophy as a discipline was subordinated to theology. This was challenged by the rediscovery of Aristotle's self-sufficiently secular political ideal, a challenge met for a while by Aquinas' synthesis. However, the autonomy of secular politics was continually reasserted by a sequence of writers – Bartolus of Sassoferrato, Marsilius of Padua, Bruni and Machiavelli – who revived and reformulated classical republicanism using both Roman law and new Renaissance techniques and insights.

The Reformation, although initially politically quiescent, gave rise to new conflicts between secular and sacred rule. In particular, radical claims about the responsibility of all believers for their own salvation fed through in various ways into more individualistic political philosophies. In early modern Europe, using the strikingly new (and originally Catholic) vocabulary of natural right, Hugo Grotius aspired to provide a common secular basis for a shared political morality, on the basis of individual rights derived from a universal right of self-preservation. This was widely explored by seventeenth and eighteenth century thinkers, notably Hobbes and Locke, and culminated politically in the American and French Revolutions. In the aftermath of the French Revolution, language of natural rights was rejected both by conservative thinkers, such as Burke, and by a new, utilitarian radicalism largely forged by Bentham.

Attempts to grasp the political character of economic transformations and Empire in early modern Europe resulted in a growing engagement with the essentially historical character of politics, the dynamic of which republican discourse was particularly well suited to exploring. Avoiding the loss of liberty which the acquisition of Empire had seemed to entail in Rome involved rethinking possible patterns of politico-economic development, providing a new definition of liberty which stressed personal and economic over political freedom, and proposing that impersonal institutional devices could replace virtuous motives in guaranteeing political liberty and stability. Such possibilities were explored by Montesquieu and Constant in France, Hume and Smith in Britain and 'Publius' (Madison, Hamilton and Jay) in America. They were rejected outright by Rousseau, for whom only the active citizen could guarantee rights, civic or civil.

The French Revolution was not only an event in which political philosophy played an important if hotly contested role; it also, like the rise and fall of Rome, provided a central topic for subsequent political reflection. The character of modernity, the nature of revolution, the relationship of political ideas to political action, the strength or weakness of rationalism as an informing principle, the viability and desirability of the Revolutionary ideals of liberty, equality and fraternity, all became topics of philosophical speculation by post-Revolutionary thinkers such as Constant, Cabet, de Tocqueville, Burke, de Maistre, Saint-Simon, Owen and Coleridge, as well as a later generation including Comte, Carlyle and Marx.

In contrast to his predecessors' use of Lockean psychology and the conditioning effects of experience and association to understand the processes of socio-economic change, Kant's postulation of the transcendent self initiated a new vocabulary of idealism. This culminated in Hegel's attempt to show how philosophical and historical (including political) change could be understood as the development and realization of a trans-historical consciousness or Geist, seeking to overcome internal tensions through a process of projection and transcendence.

The notion that human self-understanding and practices are to be understood historically immensely influenced subsequent political thinking, being central to the ideas of Marx, Nietzsche and Freud (as well as shaping many of J.S. Mill's modifications of classical utilitarianism). All three of the former owed insights to Hegel's claims about the crucial and emblematic character of the master–slave struggle. However, while for Hegel and Marx the slave's insights represent the transition to a higher form of consciousness – mediated in Marx's case by a class revolution – for Nietzsche (despairingly) and Freud (resignedly) repression was a constitutive and self-perpetuating feature of modern politics.

While nineteenth century political thought was preoccupied with the historical conditioning of political sensibilities, Freud's discovery of the unconscious was accompanied by the emergence of a mass, irrationalist politics, characteristic of the twentieth century, and more suited to sociological than philosophical analysis. Nevertheless rationalist political theory, deriving from utilitarianism, and frequently drawing on (and contributing to) economic thought, remains the dominant accent in contemporary political philosophy.

1 **Nature of the subject**
2 **Ancient: Greek**
3 **Ancient: Roman**
4 **Medieval**
5 **Renaissance**
6 **The Reformation**
7 **Scepticism and toleration**
8 **Early modern natural rights theory**
9 **The political language of a modern commercial society**
10 **Response to the French Revolution**
11 **Idealism and Marxism**

1 Nature of the subject

At its broadest the history of political philosophy encompasses all recoverable philosophical reflection on the nature of politics. However, if more than a merely chronological presentation, it must give some account of the relationships obtaining over time between political philosophies. Such an account may emphasize the philosophical or the historical character of those relationships. Two extreme positions may be identified. At one extreme the history of political philosophy is conceived of as a series of attempts to articulate essentially timeless and universal truths about the character of human political association; the relationship between past political philosophers is understood as a shared and highly abstract trans-historical conversation. The other extreme stresses the constitutive character of contingent historico-political circumstance on the formulation of political philosophy, and hence upon its history. For these scholars the relationship between past political philosophers will be much mediated by their contemporaries' and predecessors' less philosophical works – sermons, tracts, polemic and the more symbolic forms expressed in ceremonial and institutional frameworks.

During the last thirty years the history of political philosophy, certainly in the Anglophone world, has been revolutionized by the second – historical – approach. This has affected content as well as methodology and has paralleled more general doubts

about the possibility of characterizing philosophy as an activity abstracted from other social activities. The revolution involved rejecting the notions that 'ideas' could be identified as appropriate units of diachronic historical investigation (Skinner 1988), and that philosophically abstract political writings could, in themselves, comprise a history (Pocock 1971). More constructively, the revolution claimed that works of political philosophy were best – indeed perhaps only – to be fully understood, either individually or as part of a history, by relating them to their immediate linguistic and controversial context. The history of political philosophy was now to be understood as an account of linguistic and controversial innovation undertaken within relatively stable and discrete political languages – those of republicanism, natural jurisprudence or utility, for example.

While the historians of political philosophy address essentially historical questions, political philosophers have increasingly also used readings of the history of political philosophy to frame philosophical arguments. These have particularly focused on the identity and supposed political and philosophical legacy of the Enlightenment (see FOUCAULT, M.; HABERMAS, J.; MACINTYRE, A.; HISTORICISM).

2 Ancient: Greek

The history of political philosophy normally begins with the Greeks. Although philosophical reflection on politics was conducted in many early cultures, for example in China and ancient Mesopotamia, and although in some cases the texts produced (such as the Jewish Old Testament) subsequently influenced Western political thought, a continuous tradition of treating political questions at a high level of philosophical abstraction began in Greece of the fifth century BC.

Presocratics and Sophists: physis and nomos. The progress of Greek science, in seeking to provide agentless explanations of natural phenomena, created a bifurcated language of impersonal, natural laws contrasted with the conventional laws or rules governing human society (see PHYSIS AND NOMOS). In the rapidly changing, commercial, and increasingly egalitarian, society of fifth-century Athens this linguistic polarity was soon deployed in philosophical disagreements over the proper character of human political institutions. At least some of the Sophists – a heterogeneous group of professional teachers – taught that human laws were mere conventions and that nature sanctioned only prudential limits on self-interest (see SOPHISTS). For Ancient Greeks virtue was an instrumental quality or skill that brought success – and success was a sufficient sign of virtue. In a democratic city-state, this was the art of persuasion, political or forensic oratory. But could mere success, regardless of means or content, count as virtue?

Socrates and Plato. Against these naturalistic, and in some cases morally opportunistic, arguments emerged the figure of Socrates. Although himself seen as a Sophist by moral conservatives and charged at his trial with 'making the weaker argument appear the stronger', Socrates, while a rationalist critic of conventional moral pieties (see *Euthyphro* and book I of the *Republic*), aspired to a transcendent political morality, and a metaphysical identity of the self which could be harmed only by moral turpitude. His acceptance of the death sentence, while believing it to have been wrongfully imposed, and his refusal to accept an offer of escape from friends, demonstrated his strong sense of political obligation, stemming from a contractual account of the relationship between state and citizen (see SOCRATES).

This is the intellectual setting of the *Republic* in which Socrates' pupil – Plato, using his master's persona to develop his own ideas – invokes the transcendent world of the Forms to rebut Thrasymachus' claim that justice is merely whatever serves the self-interest of 'the strongest' (see THRASYMACHUS). While the particular institutional recommendations of the *Republic*, – equality of women, abolition of the family, communism – have clearly been marginal issues in Western political philosophy until relatively recently, the work identified what would become major and recurrent themes: the bearing of epistemology on political reality, cognitive and moral preeminence as a claim to privileged rule, the relationship between social class structure and individual psychology, the political role of education and the political dimensions of the processes of social change. Plato's appeal to a rational, if veiled, truth, and his conception of the bad or imperfect as the corruption or privation of the true or good, proved congenial to the construction of a Christian philosophy.

Aristotle. Aristotle's championship of man's political nature also locates him in the Greek debate about the rival claims of nature and convention (see ARISTOTLE). For Aristotle, nature, while not transcendent, was not simply empirically given, but involved a *telos*, an end or purpose which all natural entities possessed. For freemen, this included the achievement of civic life in a *polis* (a Greek city-state). Cultures – such as that of the Persians – which did not support such communities were unnatural and their inhabitants inferior. Nature was not only everywhere goal-directed, but internally complex and composed of diverse relations of rule and subordination. The *polis* for Aristotle was a complex entity comprising various subordinate forms of association (notably the

family and the village) and containing a corresponding diversity of forms of rule. That form of association and rule which he identified as distinctively political obtained peculiarly and uniquely amongst equals (unlike most moderns Aristotle identified equality as a condition, not a presupposition, of political status). Apart from philosophical speculation itself, living in the *polis* allowed the citizen the fullest exercise and highest development of their faculties.

The categories Aristotle identified in his *Politics* provided an enduring vocabulary for political analysis down at least to the emergence of modern political science in the nineteenth century. He devoted sustained attention to the concept of citizenship and produced a sixfold classification of constitutions – monarchy, tyranny, aristocracy, oligarchy, democracy, ochlocracy – according to whether rule was by the one, the few rich or the many poor, and whether it was conducted in the interests of the rulers themselves or the whole people. He also explored the social conditions which might render these types stable and the characteristics of mixed regimes, preferring – as most practicable – a hybrid aristocracy-democracy, or 'polity'. Although Aristotle's political writings were lost to Europe until their recovery in the thirteenth century, his work – together with Greek and Roman practice – was the source of a major European political tradition, republicanism.

Plato and Aristotle, like most Greeks of the classical period, saw the polis as the essential environment for the life of the fulfilled individual, and saw no unavoidable conflict between its demands and the proper aspirations of the individual.

Hellenistic schools. The aspiration to unite the languages of nature and citizenship was severely stressed by the breakdown of the city-state and the emergence of Macedonian and subsequently Roman imperialism. In the absence of a political structure in which to locate them, political categories in Hellenistic culture either disappeared from the analysis of man's nature – which stressed either the individual's natural sensations (see EPICUREANISM) or the withdrawal from social obligation (see CYNICS) – or else they were projected onto a larger canvas, the cosmos itself, in which a shared rationality was claimed to generate universal citizenship and universal subjection to 'natural law' (see NATURAL LAW; STOICISM).

3 Ancient: Roman

Although the Greek observer Polybius applied Aristotelian categories to Roman history and gave an influential account of the dynamics of constitutional change, Roman republican political practice long predated theoretical reflection about it.

It was only with the imminent collapse of the republic that a theoretical synthesis of indigenous practice with Greek political language, influenced by Stoicism, was provided by Cicero, in his *On the Republic* and *Laws*. The text of the former was lost in late antiquity, but a number of important passages survived in quotation, including the definition of justice ('that which gives to every man his due') and of a commonwealth ('the people's affair; and the people is not every group of men, associated in any manner, but is the coming together of a considerable number of men who are united by a common agreement about law and rights and by the desire to participate in mutual advantages') (Cicero, *On the Republic*: 129). In the *Laws*, he gave clear expression to the idea of a universal natural law transcending the positive laws of particular states. Cicero's *Duties* became a hugely influential handbook of practical political morality while his work on rhetoric included a suggestive account of the passage of humans from a condition of nature into one of political society (see CICERO).

The establishment of a post-republican order under Augustus heralded a literary glorification of republican history and austere personal morality (see the work of Livy and Virgil), accompanied in practice by a consolidation of the various republican powers into the office of the princeps. The slide into imperial absolutism evoked Plutarch's use of biography as a form of political reflection (*Lives of the Emperors*) and Tacitus' influential essay on the oratorical political implications of the loss of public debate (*Dialogue on Oratory*) as well as a eulogy of the simple, virtuous and free Germans living outside the Empire (*Germania*).

Roman republicanism and law. Rome bequeathed to the West two potent political vocabularies and evaluative associations: one – going back to Aristotle – based on the active life of austere republican virtue and participatory citizenship (at least for the economically independent); and another – quintessentially Roman – based on a unified and authoritarian imperial system, essentially juridical and administrative. The judgment of the former on the latter was negative in the extreme; empire destroyed *virtù*, even civic and political life itself. On the other hand, the peace and prosperity normally prevailing under the unified Empire passed on another set of ideals. Roman law provided a vital political and jurisprudential resource for succeeding societies and political thinkers as well as comprising a mine of historical evidence. The sources were the compilations of the sixth century Emperor Justinian (collectively known as the *Corpus Iuris Civilis*). While these compilations had little directly to say about politics, and were neither systematically integrated nor metaphysically grounded, they were a rich source of examples and maxims, applied politically down to the late eighteenth century (see ROMAN LAW).

The incorporation of Christianity into the tradition of political theory both joined Judaic tradition with that of the Graeco-Romans and created a new language with a new agenda, and an authoritative, if hardly unequivocal, text (the Bible). The early Christians, expecting Christ's return, expressed an active contempt for earthly matters. Later recognition that this return was not imminent forced Christian thinkers to address the question of the Church's relationship to secular authorities – a question that became more complicated when the Roman Empire became Christianized.

Although the language of apostolic Christianity was thus originally separated from politics, it was, from early on, suffused with Greek philosophical influences. With the conversion of Constantine (AD 312) and the granting of toleration, however, and even more with Theodosius' adoption of Christianity as the public religion of the Empire (AD 393), Christian religious thought, Greek philosophy and Roman political thought and institutions were drawn together. Despite attempts by, for example, Tertullian, to reject Greek canons of rationality ('I believe because it is absurd'), and by Donatus and others to create a purified Church membership in, but independent of, the secular realm, the ideal that emerged was of the Church as a secular catholic body, including sinners and saints, committed to articulating a single and philosophically coherent orthodox creed (Nicaea), and establishing a *modus vivendi* with Christian secular powers. More threatening to Christian autonomy was the widespread tendency, particularly identified with EUSEBIUS and Prudentius, and shared by AUGUSTINE in his early writings, to endow the Roman adoption of Christianity, and therefore Roman political institutions themselves, with providential and even eschatolological significance – to blend the universal Church and the universal empire, as images of the heavenly society, and even to see it as an intimation of the second coming of Christ.

The sack of Rome by its Gothic mercenaries under Alaric (AD 410) seemed to impugn not only this implicit Christian philosophy of history, but the power of the Christian God and the historical status of Christianity itself. Augustine's *The City of God* was composed to repudiate such implications, to distinguish both the Christian Church from Roman politics, and the idealized Heavenly City of the elect from the secular Church on Earth. As the title suggests, Augustine self-consciously drew on Graeco-Roman political language, systematically subverting its secular meaning and projecting it on to a

Christian, transcendent realm. This rhetorical strategy had already been used by Augustine's teacher Ambrose, who gave a Christian meaning to the Ciceronian dictum that the foundation of justice was good faith, and applied Cicero's image of the body politic to the body of Christ as his church. Yet while Ambrose tended to continue to identify Christian emperors with Christian purposes, Augustine's most celebrated move was to repeat Cicero's definition of justice – 'which gives to every man what is his due' – and to argue that since the secular realm distracts man from union with his God, the secular city, even when Christian, can never be truly just.

Augustine applied to politics a Christianized Platonism already explored by PLOTINUS in order to avoid the dualist heresy of MANICHEISM (of which he had at one time been a devotee). Christian Platonism could account for evil, not (heretically) as a countervailing cosmic force, but simply as a privation of good, brought about by humans' own wrongful ordering of priorities. Since the Fall humans were congenitally incapable of correct evaluation of things without the intervention of divine grace. Political institutions and the peace they could bring were of value, but only to deal with outward and secular conflict; they were incapable of reaching men's souls. Man was sociable by nature and political through sin.

In 494 AD an authoritative statement of the relationship between Church and polity was provided by Pope Gelasius I, who articulated the doctrine of the two swords, spiritual (*auctoritas sacrata pontificum*) and secular (*regalis potestas*). Emperors were to submit to the Church's teachings on religious issues, clerics were to obey the laws. The emperor was to wield the secular sword at the command of the Church. This went beyond the Pauline injunction to leave to Caesar that which was Caesar's, and assumed a deeper identity between 'Christian' and 'Roman' and a division of labour – spiritual and political – amongst Roman Christians in pursuit of a shared end.

4 Medieval

The supervention of the Germanic kingdoms on an already fragmented Roman Empire and the subsequent centuries of only sporadic order did not terminate Roman political discourse or the periodic aspiration to reinstitute the universal Christianized Roman Empire. It did result, however, in the temporary loss of important works which might have sustained it (Aristotle's *Politics*; Cicero's *On the Republic*; Justinian's *Corpus*), and it did largely end systematic political philosophy. For many centuries the known 'texts' of political philosophy have been largely the practices, oaths, institutions and proclamations of political actors, and as we have come to recognize linguistic acts we have, conversely, also recognized the textual qualities of acts.

While kingship was a characteristically Germanic institution, marginalized – at least in philosophical treatises – by the republican traditions of Greece and (republican) Rome, it became enmeshed in the language and concepts of Roman law, Christianity and universal empire, almost as soon as it appeared. The persistence of a diversity of rulers within Christendom, and the existence of a Church claiming universal spiritual jurisdiction, provided the parameters within which this language had to be redefined. Despite the subsequent myths of elective councils and of constitutional and popular kingship, early Germanic kings, especially those who seemed capable of restoring a Holy Roman Empire, often continued to claim, or had bestowed upon them, Roman imperial authority. Sometimes the language of imperial kingship itself was ascribed to the Church: Isidore of Seville saw the existence of a universal church as the body of Christ the King as nevertheless quite compatible with the existence of a diversity of secular kingdoms. The rulers of such kingdoms were, however, all to be thought of as providentially appointed, and were obliged to pursue Christian ends; where they did not, they were seen as just instruments of God's wrath.

Philosophy, in medieval education, was in the service of and subordinated to theology. It attempted to establish coherence by synthesizing the deliverances of eminent authorities on disputed questions. The most striking achievement of this kind lay in the work of Thomas AQUINAS. He synthesized not only much of the elaborate and diverse Christian tradition but also sought to incorporate into it the potentially threatening naturalistic political philosophy of Aristotle, newly recovered from the world of Arabic scholarship and translated by William of Moerbeke. Aquinas' agreement with Aristotle's claim that man had a natural end or *telos* in political or social life – however qualified by the further end in God to which only the Church could minister – marked a different and much more congenial view of the relationship between politics and Christian belief, and between man's natural and religious ends, than Augustine's. For Aquinas, 'grace does not abolish nature but perfects it'. Aquinas offered an influential account of a nesting hierarchy of laws governing the world – eternal, divine, natural and human – and of the kind of reason governing each and their method of promulgation. Such a hierarchy held the potential, present in all juristic thought, for a critical appraisal of positive law, yet Aquinas, while expressing a prudentially grounded preference for a limited monarchy, tended, like many medieval thinkers, to look to local positive law in defining legitimate political institutions.

Within the language – and the practice – of law, a major tension existed between the Roman law doctrine locating the law in the will of the prince and both natural-jurisprudential and Germanic customary doctrine which implied the duty of the prince to legislate according to pre-existing universal, natural or customary standards, a tension which influenced much of the language of sovereignty and constitutionalism (see ROMAN LAW; COMMON LAW). This was expressed in two contrasting medieval beliefs about the source of political authority, which (to simplify) might be seen as ascending from the people or as descending from God (Ullman 1966). The fourteenth-century Jurist Bartolus of Sassoferrato and his pupil Baldus elaborated a justification of the popular source of sovereignty in city-states. Natural reason, whether through custom or the active consent of citizens, was, according to them, adequate to create an autonomous and self-sufficient commonwealth. Each thinker applied the Roman law terminology of corporations to both city-states and kingdoms. Political entities could thus be conceived of as *personae fictae*, with a continuous identity, distinct from the natural persons comprising them or their ruler. An even more strikingly methodologically individualist – even anarchistic – position was advanced by the nominalist WILLIAM OF OCKHAM.

Another language, deriving not from Roman law but from Germanic custom – the language of community – provided a variant of the view that power ascended. Medieval communities of various kinds were customary collectivities without necessarily being legally *personae*. Thus there was another language through which the idea of a collective unity could be articulated. Here, and in certain feudal structures, we find the origins of the idea of political representation.

The Church was also a collective entity, on one description a *corpus mysticum* identified with the body of Christ. Yet just as the kingdom had a transcendent identity as well as a physical one, so the Church needed a legal and political identity as well as a religious one. Conciliarist thinkers, notably NICHOLAS OF CUSA, developed a view of the Church as superior to the pope and capable of representation through its council. Some, such as Pierre d'AILLY and Jean GERSON, drew a parallel between the secular model of the mixed constitution – king, aristocracy and *demos* or people – and the structure of the Church, comprising pope, cardinals and council. (See Black 1970.)

5 Renaissance

From the end of the eleventh century, the emergence and growth of self-governing cities in northern Italy, their internal political relations, and their antagonistic relationship with the Holy Roman Emperor (who claimed allegiance from many of them), created two important needs: first, for the production of impressive and persuasive diplomatic and other kinds of ceremonial, public and commercial documents; second, for a language capable of articulating resistance to imperial authority. The first was met by the development of a sophisticated class of scribes, the *dictamini*, who applied their knowledge of classical rhetoric and literature increasingly to the development of distinctive civic genres – model orations, city chronicles and political advice books. The second was more problematic. Both Catholicism and Roman law, drawing on Rome's imperial rather than republican legacy, emphasized the importance of political unity: the lowest regions of Dante's *Inferno* were reserved for those who had destroyed the sources of either religious or political unity – Judas Iscariot, Brutus and Cassius. It was one of the ideological triumphs of the civic republican Renaissance to convert Brutus into a hero.

Both MARSILIUS OF PADUA and BARTOLUS OF SASSOFERRATO used scholastic and juristic resources to elaborate *de facto* legitimations of the autonomy of city-states from both imperial and papal authority. Bartolus spelled out the claim that free cities were 'princes to themselves', and that this meant that they were free both to assign jurisdictions and to establish forms of internal government without higher approval (Skinner 1978). Marsilius' strikingly modernistic (and heretical) view not only presented the 'whole body of the people', legislating through their representatives, as the source of law, but subordinated ecclesiastical authority to that law. In this notion of disparate, individually omnicompetent political entities lay the origin of the conception of a world of states which supervened on the aspirant universality of Christendom. Marsilius and Bartolus both derived their views from a republican argument, although the autonomy of states was also consistent with a Roman law defence of the absolute ruler, now thought of as *imperator in regno suo*.

However, there was a language available to, and increasingly being recovered by, both the *dictatores* and the humanist scholars of classical literature which praised, indeed glorified, the active political life in the free polity. Although initially the *dictatores* focused purely on classical rhetorical technique and style, and humanists were uninterested in or even repelled by the political life of the Ancients, by the fourteenth century both were employing ancient models to revive classical republicanism. This celebrated the liberty secured by active citizenship and explored *topoi* – founding, location, laws, institutions, political culture and social order – which affected the freedom and survival of the republic, thereby reviving interest in the secular causal processes at work in historico-political change.

The culmination of this development was the writing of Niccolò Machiavelli. Appropriating in particularly innovative ways the characteristic genres of the new civil science – the advice book (*The Prince, The Art of War*), the classical textual commentary (*Discourses on ... Livy*), the civic history (*History of Florence*) – Machiavelli repudiated not only Christian homiletics but many Ciceronian values (see MACHIA-VELLI, N.).

The major polarity in Machiavelli's analysis was between *virtù* – the energy and capacity to act effectively in the political realm – and *fortuna* – the personification of those unpredictable secular forces which control human affairs. Political action comprised the imposition of order (form) on an inchoate political nature (matter). In so presenting politics, Machiavelli scandalously presented man performing a divine role. In *The Prince* Machiavelli pays particular attention to the extreme situation of a ruler seeking power where there is either no pre-existing order, or one inimical to his rule, thus highlighting the role of and qualities comprising *virtù* in the absence of assistance from custom, divine grace or nature. Such extreme but politically paradigmatic circumstances required, he claimed, absolute political autonomy and an opportunistic subordination of moral norms, whether Christian or classical, to the requirements of political survival.

In the *Discourses* Machiavelli turned his attention to the problems of republican regimes. His focus on Roman history provoked a deeper analysis of the secular processes, the interplay between historical circumstance, laws, military experience and social structure which shaped the characters of the citizens and the survival of the state. This analysis was to prove immensely influential for later republicanism, both as ideology and as an emergent secular historico-sociological analysis.

6   The Reformation

While Machiavelli considered religion only as a factor in political sociology, the Protestant Reformation reinvigorated both religious ideals and religious jurisdiction as a source of political argument. Underlying Luther's rejection of indulgences, outward forms and the jurisdictional authority claimed by the Church, lay a more fundamental theological question – that of man's free will in gaining salvation (see LUTHER, M.). This was made explicit in his exchange with the Christian humanist ERASMUS. Luther argued that humankind were saved through faith (not works) bestowed by God (not individual human will, however trained or disciplined). This theology not only undermined – as intended – the sacramental and clerical efficacy of the Church, it changed its identity from a catholic and secular administrative structure into a *congregatio fidelis*, with purely admonitory power. At the same time Luther distinguished sharply between man's spiritual and worldly existence. For secular purposes man possessed free will, and political obedience was required, not only to curb sin and for the purposes of natural peace, but because even tyrants represent God's will in the world and may not be actively resisted. German peasants in revolt blasphemed by 'making Christian freedom a physical thing' (Oakley 1991: 173). It was the mistake of the Anabaptists' 'radical reformation' to erode Luther's distinction between the spirit and the world, which led them to believe they could, by acts of political will, provoke moral and religious reformations.

Perhaps the most difficult problem for Reformation thinkers to articulate remained the question of resistance where the magistrate opposed the reformation required by God. Luther himself after 1530 acknowledged that where the constituted authority itself allowed an active right of resistance (for example, in canon and civil law), it was not sinful to resist if magistrates – even the emperor – acted outside the law. Two distinct arguments emerged. One was constitutional, and sought to legitimate resistance by identifying officeholders other than the emperor (or, later, the French or Spanish king) as 'powers that be [which] are ordained of God' who might exercise a right – indeed a duty – of resistance consistent with St Paul's authoritative injunction to obey established power (Hotman, Beza, Mornay). This could be done either by federalizing relations within the Empire, or dignifying what Calvinists called 'inferior magistrates' – variously identified with provincial or civic officials and buttressed by classical allusions to Spartan ephors and Roman tribunes. The other more radical argument licensed the resistance even of private individuals. According to it the failure of rulers to operate within the laws defining their office effectively reduced them to the status of private individuals against whose actions other individuals and collectivities possessed – under canon, civil, and even natural law – a right of active defence.

Reformation discourse was also radicalized by the language of covenant theology. Calvin presented holy history as a series of covenants between God and his people. Reformation churches were formed through covenants among their members, who had a duty to God to maintain the terms on which the community was instituted. The theory thus provided a radical individualist and contractual basis for political authority, obedience and resistance, which was, however, utterly theological in origin. The initial separation between world and spirit was thus overcome in the political language of the Reformation, which had on the one hand incorporated a secular theory of resistance to government and, on the other, formulated an individualistic account of the source of political authority in voluntary agreement.

Calvinist constitutional resistance theory was further elaborated in France by the minority Huguenots, anxious to appeal to a wider constituency against the emergence of an absolutism increasingly inclined to impose Catholic orthodoxy (Salmon 1987; Kelly 1970) and above all in the Spanish Netherlands, where the successful Dutch Revolt occasioned a massive pamphlet literature elaborating a language of civic independence, the true significance of which is only just coming to be acknowledged (Van Gelderen 1993).

7 Scepticism and toleration

From these contexts, too, emerged a range of arguments in favour of religious toleration (see TOLERATION). Some of these appealed to the essential similarity of all religions and the unimportance of dogma. Others deployed sceptical arguments, claiming that it was wrong to coerce other people over matters in which rational certainty was unattainable. Meanwhile, Michael de L'Hopital and Jean Bodin forwarded *politique* arguments which held that, whether truth in religious questions was attainable or not, toleration should be practised as a condition of civil peace.

One major consequence of internal religious war, in France, the Low Countries and – as is increasingly being recognized – Germany, as well as later in England, was a revival of ancient Stoicism (see LIPSIUS, J.; MONTAIGNE, M.E. DE; STOICISM). This fuelled both an inner perseverance and constancy in the face of adversity and political acceptance of *de facto* powers. A growing moral agnosticism led politically to a renewed, sceptically-based insistence on the need to accept the established faith and political order. In this context there appeared too a controversial new political term: 'reason of state' – the 'knowledge by which ... stable rule over people may be founded, preserved and extended ... when such actions cannot be considered in the light of normal rules' (Botero in Burke 1991: 480).

Both the term 'state' and a vocabulary in which its imperatives could be presented as autonomous and irresistible were now available. They were first assembled by Jean BODIN, who used legal terminology to define sovereignty rather than inquiring into the constitutional practice of particular regimes or assembling it from distinct powers as, even in imperial Roman law, it always had been. Eschewing Roman law as a historically parochial phenomenon, Bodin sought to understand sovereignty analytically as a necessary feature of the state – 'an absolute and perpetual power over citizens and subjects' (see SOVEREIGNTY). All office in the state is held at the sovereign's pleasure. Moreover, the sovereign not only enforces the law, but makes it (without consultation if it pleases), and stands above it, bound only by the objective conditions that determine its own survival – a rule of succession, conformity to natural law and the law of God.

From this basis Bodin proceeded to analyse the natural and historical circumstances affecting the successful establishment of states. In thus admitting natural and historical considerations only as factors affecting success or failure in instituting an abstractly defined conception of state, Bodin cut through both the competing languages of legal constitutionalism and naturalism, while not quite closing the door to interpretations of God's purposes.

Annexing a Bodinian conception of sovereignty to a strict interpretation of the divine ordination of political power expressed in God's grant to Adam yielded the socially reverberant language of patriarchalism associated with Sir Robert FILMER, Locke's famous protagonist. The historico-philosophical (as opposed to sociological) interest of Filmer lay perhaps less in his patriarchalism than in the objections he was able to pose to the radical contract theory emerging amongst the Levellers and other participants in the English Civil War – objections that Locke later sought with some ingenuity to overcome. Filmer's counterargument drew upon theories of long standing – amongst Catholics, as he gleefully pointed out in *Patriarcha* – which grounded political power in a voluntary contract of individuals and derived from this principles both of resistance and of private property.

8 Early modern natural rights theory

Several Catholic publicists of the Reformation period had argued for constitutional limitations on political power, which was conceived to emanate from, and in some ultimate sense remain in, the community. John MAJOR followed Gerson in articulating an unlimited subjective conception of 'right' as free disposal, drawing the corollary that kings can have no such right over their people. However, it was the Spanish neo-Thomists who began to elaborate the most distinctive and far-reaching natural rights language to combat a range of opponents, including Lutherans, Machiavellians, conciliarists and Catholic apologists of Iberian imperialism in America.

The revival of Thomism was an attempt to counter the heretical (Lutheran) view that humans were incapable of knowing God's law, and that dominion was founded only on (inscrutable – and therefore unquestionable) grace. Dominicans and Jesuits reasserted Aquinas' hierarchy of law, with NATURAL LAW as both a specification of divine and eternal law and a practicable criterion of the legitimacy of human, positive laws. Stretching Aquinas, they also claimed natural law was imprinted in, and even a habit of, the mind, available to all humans independent of revelation (see MOLINA, L. DE; SOTO, D. DE; SUÁREZ, F.). This enabled them to establish the legitimacy of secular institutions (and indeed that of the Church, as a historical entity with a tradition of doctrinal interpretation) by deriving them directly under natural law. This same argument also refuted the claims of Machiavelli, curiously allied to those of Luther, concerning the irresistibility of reason of state.

Although human community was natural, and although natural law was available to men in what became known as the 'natural condition', in which men were free and independent, political society was a voluntary human creation. Although the concept of the 'social contract' was not yet theoretically elaborated, and although Suárez emphasized the pre-existence of community to avoid already notorious difficulties involved in constituting it from individuals through contract, the notion of consent or agreement to the establishment of political rule – as one condition of its legitimacy – is clearly present (see VITORIA, F. DE).

One important application of neo-Thomism had been the claim made on behalf of King Ferdinand of Spain that American Indians – being evidently incapable of political society – must lack natural reason and so be natural slaves who might justifiably be captured and deprived of their possessions. This position was attacked from the 1530s onwards by members of the school of Salamanca using similar neo-Thomist language. Vitoria and Las Casas in particular cited the, by then, undoubted empirical evidence of Aztec and Inca capacity for civilized life, demonstrating that Indians had indeed used their natural reason to construct political institutions. They could not therefore be slaves, and their property and authority was legitimated under natural law.

This vocabulary of a state of nature, natural law

and the establishment of political authority by a contract alienating natural rights was transformed from an identifiably Catholic position into the foremost language of the modernizing and Protestant communities of Europe within the space of a generation, largely by the Dutchman Hugo GROTIUS. Writing initially in the context of international legal controversy, where neither sceptical acceptance of positive authority nor appeal to shared values was productive, Grotius performed a series of moves which subsequent generations regarded as constitutive of modern natural law theory. First, following the Jesuits, he located the source of natural law in the will of the agent. Second, following ancient and revived stoicism, he made self-preservation the primary natural right: self-defence and a right of acquisition followed as consequences of this. Third, he emphasized the potentially naturalistic grounds of such a theory, which would hold even if (scandalously contrary to his own professed belief) there were no God. Perhaps even more importantly, he adopted a systematic and deductive mode of argument which self-consciously modelled itself on mathematics.

Immediately picked up by Selden and Hobbes in England, by Samuel Pufendorf in Germany and at the Swedish court, and by John Locke, working in England and The Netherlands (and aided by the popularizing work of the Frenchman Jean Barbeyrac), within two generations this enterprise had gained a huge pre-eminence in political-philosophical discourse. Taken literally, the idea of a comprehensive, aboriginal, subjective natural right assumed that legitimate political authority must have emerged through some consensual transfer of right from the individual. This might lead either to a historical search for plausible relics of such a contract in customary law (see SELDEN, J.) or to its identification with specific events – such as Magna Carta or practices such as the coronation oath. Alternatively, philosophers might try to reconstruct the terms of such a grant of authority a priori, on the grounds of what would have been reasonable or – in the case of most thinkers including Locke who retained a natural law constraint – legitimate to agree to. Some thinkers made the grant of right virtually unconditional, binding and irrevocable, establishing as it did the power to punish, which they tied logically or effectively to obligation; others saw it as highly conditional and revocable. Some, like Hobbes, considered there to be two contracts – a contract of union constituting society and a contract of subjection or government between the resulting society and its rulers (HOBBES, T. §7). Others denied the latter (see ROUSSEAU, J.-J.) or the former (as had Vitoria and the Jesuits), or conflated the two (Hobbes). At its most radical, the criterion of natural right became a continuing condition of governmental legitimacy, and the failure to respect it presumptive grounds for resistance (as, for example, wuth the Levellers, Locke and Paine).

Hobbes' masterpiece, *Leviathan*, inserted a Bodinian idea of sovereignty into a synthesis of the language of natural right and contract, materialistic psychology and naturalistic epistemology. His sustained deductive argument, supposedly modelled on geometry, established a model for political philosophy which has lasted, and increased in fascination, until the present day.

A major issue for the new natural rights language, which played a central role in the increasingly commercial and imperial states of Europe, was that of the origin and moral limits of private property rights. A divine sanction for property rights was a logical casualty of the new secular basis of modern natural rights theory, and it was implausible to attach them directly to the natural condition. Arguing against the Royalist Robert Filmer, who identified all authority – political and economic – with the patriarchal monarch or male household head, John Locke distinguished the different occasions and mechanisms by which political and property rights emerged – a collective act of trust and individual labour, respectively. In so doing he gave a philosophical justification of some main aspects of the modern state, combining as it did centralized political authority with dispersed economic rights.

9   The political language of a modern commercial society

Hobbes, despite the fascination of his ideas, was widely repudiated for the atheism confidently supposed to underlie his egoism, naturalism and materialism. The powerful new view of natural right as unconstrained and subjective was seen to license a threateningly egoistic psychology – despite attempts to mollify it by ascriptions of natural sociability to humans (as in Pufendorf). Such worries were reinforced by the increasingly commercial character of society, analysis of which was a major preoccupation for eighteenth century thinkers. Bernard Mandeville's claim that the 'private vices' of individuals aggregatively produced 'public benefits' still seemed to offer – as he may have intended – only the alternatives of austerity or hypocrisy (see MANDEVILLE, B.). His opponents sought to diffuse this opposition either by asserting an innate moral disposition or moral sense (see MORAL SENSE THEORIES; HUTCHESON, F.), or by constructing some convincing account of how moral dispositions emerged from more primitive psycholo-

gical traits, such as sympathy (see HUME, D.) or sociability (see SMITH, A.).

The growing preoccupation with the social processes by which the moral sentiments – or more generally the 'opinion' on which politics was increasingly seen to rest – were constructed, transmitted and sustained revealed a tension in political philosophy between moral philosophy or natural jurisprudence and historical sociology. A republican tradition deriving ultimately from Machiavelli's speculations on the decline of Rome, but reinterpreted by Harrington and his English followers, and by Montesquieu in France, provided a helpful vocabulary in which to treat patterns of secular historical change. Yet while this republican language was a rich resource in theorizing long-term and impersonal socio-economic processes, it was preoccupied with decline and initially suspicious of wealth, commerce and refinement as destructive of the public virtue required in the commonwealth.

The emergence of a political theory built around a programme of 'politeness' in seventeenth century France and in Britain at the start of the eighteenth century by Shaftesbury, by Addison and Steele in their journal *The Spectator* and by Francis Hutcheson was one of a series of attempts to accommodate the polity's presumed need for political virtue with the development of a wider commercial society. The ultimate achievement of Adam Smith and David Hume was to explain how the progress of commerce, by encouraging rational patterns of thought, wider social interaction and refined appetites, led to the decline of irrational 'enthusiasms' – party political or religious – and encouraged the emergence of a polite society supportive of liberal, moderate politics (see ENTHUSIASM). Like Montesquieu they came to reject the simple contrast between the liberty of republics and the servility of monarchies, and described modern, commercial monarchies as supportive of a new kind of private liberty resting on structural features rather than on individual qualities. Both thinkers, however, recognized the precariousness of this balance, Smith pointing to the debilitating effects produced by the division of labour, and Hume to the danger of regimes bankrupting their economies through succumbing to the temptation offered by the new institutions of public credit. In general this analysis drew attention to the vital role of opinion in sustaining, or undermining, political rule, a preoccupation wholly in keeping with the undoubted fact of increasing popular political mobilization. Hume's programme for a more complaisant politics involved the deployment of sceptical and consequentalist arguments to displace opinions derived from metaphysical notions of right in favour of sober understandings of interest.

Belief in right was, nevertheless, the motivating force behind two modern Revolutions in America and France. While Locke, Blackstone and English common law maxims ('no taxation without representation') were invoked to justify resistance to English tyranny, American publicists increasingly drew on Montesquieu and Hume in seeking to establish a constitutional settlement in their new, extensive and federal republic. *The Federalist Papers* composed by 'Publius' (Jay, Madison and Hamilton) sought to adapt republican vocabulary to persuade a wide political public that the proposed constitution provided for a central government powerful enough to replace the defective Articles of Confederation, while leaving enough power to the states to assuage the worries of those who believed that republican liberty could not survive in large polities. Through its popular, yet state-by-state, ratification the American constitution comprised an uneasy tension between popular and constitutional sovereignty. The restraint of power, something of an eighteenth-century Anglophone preoccupation, was achieved in America through its division – between centre and periphery, between different government institutions (legislature, executive, judiciary) and through the staggering of elections over time.

In France, the preoccupation with 'opinion' took a much more didactic form through the activities of the *philosophes* particularly in the assembling and publication – principally by Denis Diderot and Jean d'Alembert – of *L'Encyclopédie*, a self-conscious attempt to reform the terminology and preoccupations of scientific, cultural and political language. Much influenced by a reading of Lockean psychology and politics, but with strong materialist and agnostic strands, the *philosophe* movement conducted an elitist rather than a democratic intellectual guerrilla war in (and later from outside) the territory of French absolutist sovereignty. However, it was the anti-*philosophe* Jean-Jacques Rousseau who produced the most arresting political philosophy, synthesizing French absolutism and his native Genevan republicanism.

Rousseau fundamentally challenged the growing accommodation of inherited political languages to commercial modernity so evident in the writings of Hume, Montesquieu and Smith, and later 'Publius' and the *philosophes*. His *Discourses*, especially that on the *Origins of Inequality*, while recognizing the essentially sociohistorical sources of morality, asserted an intimate connection between the development of commercial civilization and that of dependency, inequality and loss of self. For him there

was hardly space – conceptual or historical – for an account of a society advanced enough to be civil and moral without yet being divided and corrupt. In *Du contrat social* (The Social Contract), however, he sought to present this possibility in the language of contract theory. Central to his argument was the absolute, yet inalienable, quality of sovereignty established by the contract constituting society and retained by the citizens in their collective identity as a sovereign body independent of government. Rousseau claimed thereby to have solved the paradox of political freedom, for despite subjection to a common sovereign, each as legislator 'remains as free as before'.

Rousseau's attempts to ensure constitutionality – through observation of due formal processes, the subjection of all to universally phrased laws and his insistence both that the sovereign body could never be represented, and that it might sometimes fail to express the legitimizing, but noumenous, 'general will' – were widely ignored by his followers during the Revolution, reaching their most ironic expression in Robespierre's claim to embody the latter in his person.

The French Revolution – like the rise and fall of Rome before it – defined a matrix of problems and linguistic perspectives for political thinkers of the succeeding centuries. These included the conception of sovereignty as popular will and the consequent dangers of popular mobilization, the identity and significance of the Revolution within world historical processes and the relationship between philosophical doctrine and politico-historical outcomes.

10 Response to the French Revolution

The dominant language of the Revolution was that of modern, secular, natural rights, which interpreted such rights as inherent properties of individuals, and which attempted to deduce the legitimacy of particular institutional arrangements from these abstract ethical principles. While this model of political philosophizing remains very much alive today (see RAWLS, J.) its implication in the violence of the Revolution led to strong philosophical reactions.

Both features of natural rights were attacked by Edmund BURKE, whose response has had an enduring appeal in the Anglophone and German-speaking worlds. *Reflections on the Revolution in France* stressed the inadequacy of human reason to comprehend the function and utility of many social institutions, beliefs and practices which have been built up over time through adaptation to local circumstance. Drawing on sceptical epistemology and common law jurisprudence, Burke privileged the collective knowledge embodied in customs and institutions over individual claims to knowledge, particularly those that derived from analytical or deductive reasoning. The Revolution was thus, at the level of ideas, an outbreak of irrational secular 'enthusiasm', parallel to religious movements of the past. Moreover its particular content – natural right – licensed the intrusion into politics of all human agents whether suitably educated or not. Important responses to Burke included those of Tom Paine, William Godwin and Mary Wollstonecraft, who, while rhetorically defending natural rights against Burke's attack, used a republican vocabulary of virtue both to open discussion of the political significance of the private arena and to establish a political role for women.

In France the aftermath of the Revolution produced attempts to divert the language of republican liberty from its ancient austere and civic-activist roots, to which Benjamin Constant famously sought to add an understanding of modern, commercial liberty. Alexis de Tocqueville, too, in *De la démocratie en Amérique* (Democracy in America), provided a socio-historical analysis both of the *ancien régime* and of what he took to be the paradigm of emerging modern society. Meanwhile the rationalist, social-engineering aspect of the Enlightenment might be said to have lived on in the industrial utopianism of Fourier, Saint-Simon and his followers including Comte (see UTOPIANISM; SAINT-SIMON, C.-H. DE R.; COMTE, A.).

While the language of radical natural rights declined in the nineteenth century (later to be revived in the era of international charters and organizations) a new radical language – that of secular utilitarianism – was being consciously forged at this time by Jeremy Bentham and would be elaborated and promulgated by his many reforming disciples (see BENTHAM, J.; UTILITARIANISM). While general appeals to utility had been common in earlier epochs, particularly in CICERO and his followers, Bentham proposed something much more precise; namely, that the aggregate quanta of anticipated pleasure and pain should be the sole criterion of public policy. He also laid out exhaustively the dimensions by which the necessary calculations might be attempted. Resolutely dismissive of metaphysics – including inalienable natural rights (which he viewed as 'nonsense on stilts') – Bentham's initial work was in jurisprudence, applying positivist criteria to Blackstone's *Commentaries on the Laws of England*, but he gradually arrived at the view that only a democratic franchise could ensure the political will to implement the utilitarian legal code he sought. Influential in British and French nineteenth-century social reforms and in a variety of liberal nationalist movements from Greece to South America, Bentham's version of utilitarianism nevertheless ran into philosophical difficulties, from which John Stuart Mill, the son of Bentham's collaborator James Mill, sought to rescue it.

Mill's reformulations involved acknowledging a qualitative dimension of pleasure, limiting utility's potential for eroding moral rules – especially justice – by developing, in all but name, a distinction between rule- and act-utility, and placing the utilitarian assessment of political phenomena and institutions within an historical, developmental schema. In this way – and by a famous defence of the liberty needed to innovate – he sought to increase, as well as use, the 'good qualities' present in society, and to secure 'utility in the largest sense, grounded on the permanent interests of a man as a progressive being'. This extension of utilitarian language nevertheless diminished its original programmatic policy appeal, as well as its original distance from the ideal-regarding criteria to which Mill's successors, the 'New Liberals', increasingly turned.

11 Idealism and Marxism

Late nineteenth-century liberals in Britain (such as T.H. Green, Bernard Bosanquet and F.H. Bradley) and in Italy (Benedetto Croce) appealed to a revived idealist language which, following Kant, had developed through to mid-century in Germany, but, with a few significant exceptions (such as Coleridge) had not exported well (see IDEALISM). This language rejected the Lockean premise of an essentially passive mind, and instead emphasized, in varying degrees, the agency of the mind in organizing experience, and the essentially ideational character of reality. Powerfully articulated by KANT, the social and political implications of this were spelled out most fully by HEGEL, who sought to synthesize history and philosophy – time being, he claimed, the dimension in which thought articulates itself through a series of projections which it does not initially recognize as its own product. In the social sphere of right (objective mind), Hegel sought to show that the essentially legal categories of right such as property, contract and punishment – no less than the institutions of the family, civil society and ultimately the state itself – are not obstacles to individual freedom. Instead they are logically necessary corollaries of the very idea of a free will which come into historical existence as these different aspects of consciousness separate themselves out. Working to an agenda set very much by the French Revolution, Hegel defined freedom as the historical movement of will from mere potential and contingency towards its differentiated concrete embodiment in institutions. Attempts, such as those of the

Jacobins, to appeal directly to abstract standards – 'the revolutionary will' – therefore courted a destructive anarchy. For Hegel the will finds emancipation when it recognizes the differentiated structures of the modern state as its own product. Another, only questionably political, view would be taken by Nietzsche for whom self-creativity required the individual will to power to overcome all 'given' contexts, natural or historical; failure to do so would reinforce a 'slave' mentality of subjection (see NIETZSCHE, F.).

Hegel's development from the *Phenomenology* to the elements of the *Encyclopedia of the Social Sciences* including the *Philosophy of Right*, represents an increasingly abstract – although always historicized – account of what was, in his initial writings, a deeply socially embedded history of consciousness. The political legacy of his philosophy was extremely ambiguous, since the claim that historical progress represents the working out of reason in the world could be read either as an endorsement of the status quo or as an exhortation to subject it to rational criticism. However, since Hegel's conception of reason was supposed to be inscrutable to those acting on its behalf, the former reading is the more plausible.

Largely for political reasons, the battle over Hegel's legacy was fought in terms of the philosophy of religion. A series of commentators – David Strauss, Ludwig Feuerbach and the young Karl Marx – sought to interpret religion, which Hegel had described as 'truth in a veil', as a representation of the rationality or irrationality of the life of its own society. While FEUERBACH saw Christianity as mystified anthropology and the incarnation of Christ as an allegory of the religious form assumed by humanism, he was unable to explain why humanism should have taken this form in the first place. In the early writings of Marx he argued that the sources of religion, as an alienated form of consciousness, could be traced to social deformations of man's essentially creative nature, which Marx located in the economy. Marx interpreted Hegel's historical schema of the alienation of mind from its own intellectual products as a mystified account of the alienation of humanity from its own material products. This entailed in turn a series of alienations – from creative activity (experienced as drudgery), from other humans (experienced as material factors or competitors), from nature (experienced as something to be subjected) and from men's own philosophical identity or 'species being' (as collective creators) (see ALIENATION).

The consequence of this alienated activity was a structure of alienated and alienating institutions, the primary political feature of which was the class dominance of those effectively controlling the means of subsistence. The state – on Hegel's account the 'presupposition of civil society' – was shown instead to be a product of civil society, and thus dependent on the balance of class power. In the words of the *Communist Manifesto*: 'the executive of the modern state is but a committee for managing the common affairs of the whole bourgeoisie'.

Although Marx arrived at his revolutionary position through an internal critique of idealism, and such language persisted in his writings, his actual analysis of historical processes, and of the particular form of society then prevailing, owed much to the Scottish historical sociologists and the political economy spawned by Smith's *The Wealth of Nations*. The conception of social evolution through stages characterized as different 'modes of subsistence', and the notion of the social production of ideas and institutions intrinsic to and functional for each stage, was vital to his historiography. Equally the development, from Smith to Ricardo (interpreted by Marx as a development in objective economic circumstance), of a terminology for analysing the creation and distribution of value, was vital to his critical economics and to his projections about pauperization, shifts in social structure, demand failure and the falling rate of profit, which he claimed would immobilize capitalism as a means of deploying resources and generating wealth.

The young Marx had criticized capitalism for denying the human essence – what he viewed as a collective rational creativity. The mature Marx self-consciously eschewed metaphysical ideals. His socialism was scientific in the sense of claiming to rest on an objective analysis, whereby competition amongst capitalists would gradually increase the division of labour and reduce the labour factor of production, simultaneously diminishing profits (which on Marx's analysis ordinarily represented surplus value created by labour), reducing demand and swelling the ranks of the unemployed and unskilled workers. Revolution would occur when profit rates were too low to generate investment despite the huge productive potential developed by capitalism. Production would have then to be organized socially – which only the dispossessed workers would be willing to do.

Classical Marxism retreated under the combination of theoretical developments in economics – principally marginalist analysis – and political developments in early twentieth-century western Europe, especially the advent of social democracy. Its Leninist version, which sought to apply Marxism to newly industrialising states as vulnerable points in capitalism conceived of as an international system, survived as an ideology of Soviet imperialism in eastern Europe and anti-imperialist movements elsewhere, but largely ceased to generate serious philosophical work (see MARXISM, CHINESE; MARXIST PHILOSOPHY, RUSSIAN AND SOVIET; MARXIST THOUGHT IN LATIN AMERICA; MARXISM, WESTERN). Varieties of Marxism continued to inspire political analysis, however, notably that associated with the Frankfurt School (see CRITICAL THEORY; FRANKFURT SCHOOL).

Most of the major languages of political theory have similarly survived to the present, albeit in changed or often hybrid form. Thus Rawls' synthesis of utilitarian and Kantian perspectives is enmeshed in a debate with a variety of communitarian approaches with debts to revived Aristotelian or republican language, and with secularized versions of natural rights language and contractarian theory (see Gauthier 1986; CONTRACTARIANISM). Wholly new challenges to these adaptations of traditional languages are to be found in the voices of feminist theorists who have offered strikingly unfamiliar and rewarding perspectives on what were thought to be well understood historical texts, as well as a different agenda for contemporary political philosophy.

See also: AL-AFGHANI; BUSHI PHILOSOPHY; GANDHI, M.K.; GUANZI; HUAINANZI; JIA YI; KUMAZAWA BANZAN; MARSILIUS OF PADUA; MARXISM, CHINESE; POLITICAL PHILOSOPHY, INDIAN; POLITICAL PHILOSOPHY IN CLASSICAL ISLAM; SHŌTOKU CONSTITUTION; SUNZI; WILLIAM OF OCKHAM; YI YULGOK; ZIONISM

References and further reading

* Black, A.J. (1970) *Monarchy and Community: Political Ideas in the Later Conciliar Controversy 1430–1450*, Cambridge: Cambridge University Press.
* Burke, P. (1991) 'Tacitism, Scepticism, and Reason of State', in J. Burns and M. Goldie (eds) *The Cambridge History of Political Thought 1450–1700*, Cambridge: Cambridge University Press.
  Burns, J. (ed.) (1988) *The Cambridge History of Political Thought, c.350–1450*, Cambridge: Cambridge University Press.
  Burns, J. and Goldie, M. (eds) (1991) *The Cambridge History of Political Thought, 1450–1700*, Cambridge: Cambridge University Press. (A collection of essays by individual authors, with an extensive bibliography.)
* Cicero (54–51 BC) *De republica* (On the Republic), trans. G.H. Sabine and S.B. Smith, *On the Commonwealth*, Columbus, OH: Ohio State University Press, 1929.
* Gauthier, D. (1986) *Morals by Agreement*, Oxford: Clarendon Press.

  Hampsher-Monk, I.W. (1992) *A History of Modern Political Thought, Major Political Thinkers from Hobbes to Marx*, Oxford: Blackwell. (Contextualized studies of the political theories of Hobbes, Locke, Hume, Rousseau, The Federalist, Burke, Bentham, Mill, Hegel and Marx.)
* Hobbes, T. (1651) *Leviathan*, ed. R. Tuck, Cambridge: Cambridge University Press, 1991.
* Kelly, D.R. (1970) *Foundations of Modern Historical Scholarship: Language, Law and History in the French Renaissance*, New York: Columbia University Press.
* Machiavelli, N. (1531) *Discorsi sopra la prima deca di Tito Livio*, trans. L. Ricci, 'Discourses on the First Ten Books of Titus Livy', in *The Prince and The Discourses*, New York: Modern Library, 1950.
* —— (1532) *Il principe*, trans. L. Ricci, 'The Prince', in *The Prince and The Discourses*, New York: Modern Library, 1950.
* Oakley, F. (1991) 'Christian Obedience and Authority, 1520–1550', in J. Burns and M. Goldie (eds) *The Cambridge History of Political Thought 1450–1700*, Cambridge: Cambridge University Press.
  Plamenatz, J. (1993) *Man and Society*, ed. R. Wokler, Harlow: Longman, 3 vols. (Revised text of a classic study with historical contextual material excised from the original edition reinserted by Wokler.)
* Pocock, J.G.A. (1971) 'Languages and Their Implications', in *Politics, Language and Time*, New York: Atheneum Press.
  —— (1975) *The Machiavellian Moment*, Princeton, NJ: Princeton University Press. (The development of the language of republicanism from Aristotle to the American Frontier, chiefly in Italy and England from the sixteenth to eighteenth centuries.)
  Pocock, J.G.A., Schochet, G.J. and Schwoerer, L.G. (eds) (1993) *The Varieties of British Political Thought 1500–1800*, Cambridge: Cambridge University Press, in association with the Folger Institute, Washington, DC.
* Salmon, J.H.M. (1987) *Renaissance and Revolt*, Cambridge: Cambridge University Press.
  Skinner, Q. (1978) *The Foundations of Modern Political Thought*, Cambridge: Cambridge University Press, 2 vols. (The political languages of the Renaissance and Reformation.)
* —— (1988) 'Meaning and Understanding in the History of Ideas', in J. Tully (ed.) *Meaning and Context: Quentin Skinner and his Critics*, Cambridge: Polity Press.
* Ullman, W. (1966) *Principles of Government and Politics in the Middle Ages*, London: Methuen.
* Van Gelderen, M. (1993) *The Dutch Revolt*, Cambridge: Cambridge University Press.

Wolin, S. (1960) *Politics and Vision*, Boston, MA: Little, Brown. (Idiosyncratic but insightful.)

IAIN HAMPSHER-MONK

POLITICAL PHILOSOPHY IN CLASSICAL ISLAM

Political philosophy in Islam is the application of Greek political theorizing upon an understanding of Muhammad's revelation as legislative in intent. In lieu of Aristotle's Politics, *unknown in medieval Islam, Plato's political philosophy assumed the primary role in an explanation of the nature and purpose of the Islamic state. Al-Farabi conceived of the prophet as a latter day philosopher-king, Ibn Bajja and Ibn Tufayl took their cue from Socrates' fate and cautioned the philosopher against the possibility of successfully engaging in a philosophical mission to the vulgar masses, and Ibn Rushd presented philosophy as a duty enjoined by the law upon those able to philosophize.*

1 Background
2 al-Farabi
3 Ibn Bajja and Ibn Tufayl
4 Ibn Rushd

1 Background

Two principal facts have formed political philosophy in Islam: first, the revelation of Muhammad, and second, the absence of Aristotle's *Politics*, whether by intention or historical circumstance, from the canon of texts translated from Greek and Syriac in ninth-century Baghdad (see GREEK PHILOSOPHY: IMPACT ON ISLAMIC PHILOSOPHY §2). Muhammad's revelation is of course foundational for Islam itself. From the vantage point of political theorizing, however, the revelation accounts for the perceived divinity of the state (the caliphate) which Muhammad is taken to have founded. It further accounts for the state's legal basis, with the state established on and grounded in obedience to a set of divine injunctions and sanctions. Muhammad's revelation, then, was perceived by political philosophers in Islam as providing an opportunity to understand and clarify the nature of the perfect state here and now, not in some distant future when human nature might be transformed. For Islamic political philosophers, the divine law (*shari'a*) revealed to Muhammad was a necessary and sufficient condition for bringing about human felicity.

The second fact noted above, the absence of Aristotle's *Politics* from the Arabic philosophical

corpus, is of capital importance in understanding Islamic political philosophy. As late as the sixth century AH (twelfth century AD), this work was apparently unavailable (see Rosenthal's introduction to *Averroes' Commentary on Plato's Republic* (1969: 22)). The absence of the *Politics* meant that Plato and Platonic political philosophy, as found in the *Republic* and the *Laws*, became paradigmatic (see PLATONISM IN ISLAMIC PHILOSOPHY). The implications of this are enormous, for Aristotle's critique of Platonic political philosophy from the standpoint of his own non-idealist philosophical anthropology was not to become part of the tradition of political philosophy in Islam. Instead, what we find in the Islamic political philosophers are variations on standard Platonic themes, pre-eminently the notion of the prophet as an analogue to the Platonic philosopher-king, the ambiguous role of philosophy in the practical political sphere, and the deep division between an elite and the vulgar masses (see PLATO §14). These themes are especially prominent in the founder of political philosophy in Islam, al-Farabi, and it is to him that one must first turn.

2 al-Farabi

For AL-FARABI (§4), 'the idea of the philosopher, supreme ruler, prince, legislator, and Imam is but a single idea. No matter which one of these words you take, if you proceed to look at what each of them signifies among the majority of those who speak our language, you will find that they all finally agree by signifying one and the same idea' (*Tahsil al-sa'ada*: 43–4). These remarks, not anomalous in the Farabian corpus, indicate the convergence, indeed identity, of theoretical and practical concerns. These dual concerns, reminiscent of the Platonic notion of the philosopher-king, are together present in the Farabian notion of the prophet. For al-Farabi, the Prophet (Muhammad) is to be understood as a divinely inspired legislator, offering a perfect way of life and a community in which to flourish.

The successors to the Prophet – caliphs and imams – preserve this original beneficence by so ruling that each group of believers is offered a measure of truth commensurate with its particular capacity to comprehend it. This latter stratification of the social and political framework is again reminiscent of Plato and his division of the perfect state into intellectually disparate groups. For al-Farabi, the relevant division is between those who are able to ground their belief philosophically and those who are not, these latter being the 'simple' believers. Religion is an imitation of philosophy in this scheme, the former presenting the truth in a non-theoretical, non-abstract way, in pictorial terms replete with parables and stories. Viewed thus, al-Farabi's political teaching may well be seen as interpreting the historical state founded by Muhammad along the lines of Platonic utopian theorizing. However, such Platonically-inspired intellectual elitism is offered not as a blueprint for political reform in a distant future, but rather as a fair description of Muhammad's constitution and the state he founded. In its own way, Farabian political philosophy is a defence of Islam.

3 Ibn Bajja and Ibn Tufayl

In turning to IBN BAJJA and IBN TUFAYL, one turns not only from East to West, from Baghdad to Andalusia, but one also notes a marked change of emphasis away from that aspect of al-Farabi's political Platonism which identified the prophet with a philosopher-king who rules a state founded on and governed by a divine law. For Ibn Bajja and Ibn Tufayl, philosophy (theoretical insight) and practical politics do not mix. They are quite incommensurable. As Leaman puts it: 'ibn Bajja's problem is how the philosopher in the imperfect state should relate to society' (Leaman 1980: 110). The emphasis here must be upon the notion of 'the imperfect state'. Courtiers both, Ibn Bajja and Ibn Tufayl must have taken a hard look at the political scene around them and drawn the relevant (pessimistic) conclusions.

In his *Tadbir al-mutawahhid* (The Governance of the Solitary), Ibn Bajja addresses himself to the *nawabit* (weeds) in imperfect societies. These *nawabit* are the nonconformists in the societies they inhabit. They do not share the common goals and aspirations. Simply put, they are the philosophers in an imperfect world, and for Ibn Bajja the focus is how best to secure their happiness and safety. Ibn Bajja's 'realism' leads him to fasten upon that strand of the Platonic political philosophical tradition which is the underside of al-Farabi's political Platonism, the non-utopian strand. The problem for the philosopher in the midst of an imperfect society is to achieve happiness while avoiding dirty hands, not befouling himself (and philosophy) with the hopes and desires of the masses. The *nawabit* dwell amongst people, but do not find perfection in their midst. Thus they must live in isolation, dissociating themselves from 'those whose end is corporeal [and] those whose end is the spirituality that is adulterated with corporeality' (*Tadbir al-mutawahhid*: 78). The background here is no less Platonic for its being non-utopian and apolitical. For Plato, Athens and her citizenry stand guilty by their execution of So-CRATES, the philosopher. The lesson to be drawn is clear for Ibn Bajja as he forcefully denies any easy

commensurability between philosophy and politics, between theory and practice in imperfect societies. For Ibn Bajja, the *nawabit* exist in spite of the society they inhabit (as in *Republic* VI 496d–e), and thus owe it nothing.

Ibn Tufayl's allegorical tale, *Hayy ibn Yaqzan* (The Living Son of the Vigilant), is not at odds with the 'realism' of his predecessor Ibn Bajja. Indeed, the story may well be read as a vivid elaboration of the latter's thought about the incommensurability of philosophy and politics in an imperfect world and the resulting isolation which the philosopher must seek if he is ever to achieve felicity. The whole thrust of Ibn Tufayl's allegory is the lesson that Hayy, the protagonist, finally learns painfully, that the philosopher will be unable to communicate successfully the deepest truths (the illuminative mysteries) as discovered by himself to mankind at large. Hayy's strenuous efforts to instruct, born of compassion for and inexperience of humanity, are shown to be useless as even the best among men 'recoiled in horror from his ideas and closed their minds.... [And] the more he taught, the more repugnance they felt' (*Hayy ibn Yaqzan*: 150). Worse, Hayy comes to realize that not only are his pedagogical efforts nugatory, but they are also counterproductive, for they tend to undercut the very beliefs which the simple (non-philosophical) believers hold. The tale ends with Hayy, dispirited, returning to the isolated island whence he came.

Plato's pessimism about the possible transformation of the empirical realm is manifest in the works and teachings of Ibn Bajja and Ibn Tufayl. The philosopher-king, the prophet, has no greater a foothold among his contemporaries than did Abraham amongst the idolaters or Socrates amongst the Athenians. The mass of mankind cannot become philosophers, and to attempt such a transformation is both dangerous for the philosopher and bad public policy. Both Ibn Bajja and Ibn Tufayl may be understood as cautioning would-be prophets (philosophers) of the perils inherent in their mission. Correlatively, they can be read as urging a rather conservative (traditional) status quo political agenda, in which stability and order prevail and are grounded in a punctilious observance of the law (*Hayy ibn Yaqzan*: 153–4). If society cannot be remade from the ground up, then perhaps no innovation whatever should be tolerated, lest anarchy and antinomianism prevail.

4 Ibn Rushd

IBN RUSHD (Averroes) wrote commentaries on both Plato's *Republic* and Aristotle's *Nicomachean Ethics*. For Ibn Rushd, the *Nicomachean Ethics* provides the theoretical substructure for the practical sciences, while the *Republic* (in lieu of Aristotle's *Politics*) provides the practical, political foundations for the attainment of human felicity, the goal of the practical sciences. So conceived, Plato's *Republic* provides a kind of blueprint for the best political order. In this framework, Ibn Rushd resuscitates the Farabian emphasis on the active role the philosopher should play in the political arena. Though he is aware of the precarious position of the philosopher, this activist focus should be understood in contrast to that of his Andalusian predecessors, Ibn Bajja and Ibn Tufayl, and their focus upon the necessity for the philosopher to maintain an apolitical stand.

Ibn Rushd thus shares with al-Farabi the view that philosophy has political implications. He underscores this dramatically by grounding the very study of philosophy in the law. The first question of his famous *Fasl al-maqal* (Decisive Treatise on the Connection between Religion and Philosophy) is: 'What is the attitude of the law to philosophy?' Ibn Rushd's answer is that the law commands the study of philosophy for those capable of it. There is thus a duty to philosophize. It should be noted, however, that the study of philosophy is no idle enterprise for Ibn Rushd, for given the legal injunction upon those capable of studying philosophy, a practical political obligation follows. The law revealed by the Prophet is a divine law, given to insure the well being of the entire community. If then the law enjoins philosophy, the philosopher is obliged to 'use' his wisdom for the benefit of all, in just the same way that the Farabian prophet (or Platonic philosopher-king) uses his wisdom, in a manner commensurate with the audience in question. Inasmuch as only the philosopher has an insight into the truth in a 'straight', undiluted way, without mediation of the senses, only he can interpret the law in an appropriate manner. Only the philosopher can allegorize when necessary, for only he knows the grounds upon which the allegory resides.

In his own way, Ibn Rushd provides an important defence of philosophy in a society governed by lawyers and judges like himself. Lest politics and political philosophy be handed over to those who (merely) apply the law, Ibn Rushd argues forcefully for a practical political philosophy which probes the foundations and guiding principles of the law. This, then, is arguably the greatest achievement of political philosophy in Islam, to conceive of a society grounded in obedience to a divine law as itself the manifestation of a coherent and theoretically defensible structure.

See also: AL-FARABI; GREEK PHILOSOPHY: IMPACT ON ISLAMIC PHILOSOPHY; IBN BAJJA; IBN RUSHD; IBN TUFAYL; LAW, ISLAM PHILOSOPHY OF; PLATONISM IN ISLAMIC PHILOSOPHY; POLITICAL PHILOSOPHY, HISTORY OF; POLITICAL PHILOSOPHY, NATURE OF

References and further reading

Butterworth, C.E. (ed.) (1992) *The Political Aspects of Islamic Philosophy*, Cambridge, MA: Harvard University Press. (An up-to-date collection of essays on, among others, al-Kindi, al-Razi, al-Farabi, Ibn Sina, Ibn Bajja, Ibn Tufayl and Ibn Rushd.)

Daiber, H. (1996) 'Political Philosophy', in S.H. Nasr and O. Leaman (eds) *History of Islamic Philosophy*, London: Routledge, ch. 50, 841–85. (Account of some of the main political thinkers from the classical period.)

* al-Farabi (*c.*870–950) *Tahsil al-sa'ada* (The Attainment of Happiness), trans. M. Mahdi, *Al-Farabi's Philosophy of Plato and Aristotle*, Ithaca, NY: Cornell University Press, 1962. (Translation, with introduction and notes, of *Tahsil al-sa'ada* and the précis of the philosophy of Plato and Aristotle.)

Frank, D. (1996) 'Ethics', in S.H. Nasr and O. Leaman (eds) *History of Islamic Philosophy*, London: Routledge, ch. 55, 959–68. (The ethics of the classical period, with particular reference to their links with society.)

Galston, M. (1990) *Politics and Excellence: The Political Philosophy of Al-Farabi*, Princeton, NJ: Princeton University Press. (Al-Farabi's political philosophy against the backdrop of the Greek philosophical tradition.)

* Ibn Rushd (*c.*1174) Commentary on Plato's *Republic*, ed. and trans. E.I.J. Rosenthal, *Averroes' Commentary on Plato's Republic*, Cambridge: Cambridge University Press, 1969; trans. R. Lerner, *Averroes on Plato's Republic*, Ithaca, NY: Cornell University Press, 1974. (Rosenthal is an edition of extant Hebrew text, with introduction, translation and notes. Lerner is a translation with introduction and notes, in part critical of Rosenthal.)

* Ibn Tufayl (before 1185) *Hayy ibn Yaqzan* (The Living Son of the Vigilant), trans. L.E. Goodman, *Ibn Tufayl's Hayy ibn Yaqzan*, Los Angeles, CA: Gee Tee Bee, 1983. (A felicitous translation of the tale, with introduction and notes.)

* Leaman, O. (1980) 'Ibn Bajja on Society and Philosophy', *Der Islam* 57 (1): 109–19. (Ibn Bajja's political philosophy.)

—— (1988) *Averroes and His Philosophy*, 2nd edn, Richmond: Curzon. (A recent study of Ibn Rushd's metaphysics, practical philosophy, and theory of language and truth.)

* Lerner, R. and Mahdi, M. (eds) (1963) *Medieval*

Political Philosophy: A Sourcebook, Ithaca, NY: Cornell University Press. (Important collection of primary texts in translation, including al-Farabi's *al-Siyasa al-madaniyya* (The Political Regime) and *Tahsil al-sa'ada*, Ibn Bajja's *Tadbir al-mutawahhid*, Ibn Tufayl's *Hayy ibn Yaqzan* and Ibn Rushd's *Fasl al-maqal*.)

Mahdi, M. (1991) 'Philosophy and Political Thought: Reflections and Comparisons', *Arabic Sciences and Philosophy* 1: 9–29. (A fine overview of the nature of political philosophy in Islam.)

Rosenthal, E.I.J. (1962) *Political Thought in Medieval Islam*, Cambridge: Cambridge University Press. (The most comprehensive account in English. Part II is entitled 'The Platonic Legacy'.)

DANIEL H. FRANK

POLITICAL PHILOSOPHY, INDIAN

While Western political theory has been framed as the struggle between the state and the individual, Indian political philosophy has been more concerned with issues of self-liberation, morality and leadership. Until recently, with the advent of institutionalized or syndicated Hinduism, Indian society made a softer distinction between state and religion. Classical Indian political theory, as with Kauṭilya, centred on axioms on how to maintain and expand power. Kauṭilya argued that reason, the edicts of the king, and his own rules of governance, the Arthaśāstra, *were as important for decision-making as the ancient religious treatises, which defined social structure and one's duty to family, caste and God. With the exception of the* Arthaśāstra, *politics was expressed through the ability not so much to govern as to define social and moral responsibility, what one could or could not do and who could oversee these rules.*

Like all civilizations, India had periods of rule by accumulators of capital and traders, warriors and kings, and Brahmans and monks; there were also revolts by peasants. Still, philosophy was in the hands of the Brahmans, the priestly class. This philosophy was primarily not about artha *(economic gain) or* kāma *(pleasure), but about* dharma *(virtue) and* mokṣa *(liberation from the material world). The attainment of salvation, of release from the bonds of karma, was far more important than the relationship between the individual and the sovereign, as was the case in Western political philosophy.*

1 Historical background
2 Temporal dimensions
3 The Indian episteme
4 *Varṇa*
5 Structure, history and the cycle
6 Postcolonial discourses

1 Historical background

While the European Enlightenment was considered the end of Church power and the beginning of secular power, of humanism and liberalism, there was no similar Enlightenment in India. This is not to say that there was no tension between king and Brahman, between state and religious authorities; indeed, Nicholas Dirks (1987) writes that the central conundrum in Indian history has been who should rule: the Brahman or the *kṣatriya* (warrior)? KAUṬILYA focused more on coercive power and less on interpretive power. In contrast, the Buddha, committed to interpretive power, remained silent when questioned whether the *ātman* (the individual soul) and Brahman (the Cosmic Consciousness) exist. Understanding that a positive response would reify the self, returning its control to the Brahmanical class, he opened up the self and consciousness to more liminal spaces. Furthermore, recognizing that official state power was largely circumscribed by priestly power, he focused less on royal power and more on the spiritual community (*saṅgha*) and on right livelihood as a way of social transformation.

Thus, instead of the search for a perfect society, of the linear march and inevitable victory of democracy and progress, the regulation and liberation of the self has been far more important. It is this self and its emancipation from personal and social history that has been the centre of Indian philosophy. Indian political thought, however, should not be seen as fundamentally despotic, with authoritarianism the rule. Indeed, P.R. Sarkar (1987) makes the controversial claim that democracy first originated with the Licchivis of Vaiśālī, a clan that flourished over 2,500 years ago. They developed a written constitution, abolished the monarchy and, through elections, formed an executive body.

However, while in Western political theory the assumption of man as evil led to the system of federalism, to checks and balances of power, in India neither evil nor good was assumed. *Vidyā* (introversion, leading to enlightenment or good) and *avidyā* (extroversion, leading to degeneration or evil) remain in constant struggle, both simultaneously present. Evil was explained as ignorance, as *māyā*, not as an embodied force. The ideal leader is the one who can lift the veil of untruth, transcend this duality (or at

521

least minimize *avidyā*) and thus become the moral and spiritual leader. In contrast, Islamic political theory has been saddled with the problem of reattaining the perfect state achieved during the time of the Prophet (see POLITICAL PHILOSOPHY IN CLASSICAL ISLAM). India did not have such a historical event; only Rāma Rājya, the mythical kingdom of Rāma, where food was abundant and all lived in peace, had utopian connotations. But it was only in the twentieth century that this imagined polity became a political platform, largely in response to the utopias of Marxism, liberalism and Islam. Still, for Indians it is not so much a secular state that is desired (one that is amoral, efficient and fair) but a pluralistic state that does not take sides with religions, thereby enabling authentic cultural plurality.

2 Temporal dimensions

Whereas Western political philosophy creates a division between the religious and the secular, between Church and State, Indian (and Chinese) philosophy, based less on monotheistic, highly structured religions, and more on direct intuitive experiences of the mysterious, has found this to be unnecessary. A different temporal orientation is also taken. Instead of a linear movement from ancient, to classical or feudal, to modern (scientific, rational, nation-state-oriented), or from religious, to philosophical, to scientific, as with Auguste COMTE, there is a complex historical cycle with different temporal levels. At one level, there is the cosmic time of the stars and gods; at another level, there is the fourfold structure of student, householder, active citizen, and renunciate; at the societal level, there is the rise and fall of society, a process which involves the degeneration of righteousness from the golden, to the silver, to the copper and then to the iron. In the iron age, the *avatār*, or redeemer, brings all back to *dharma* and the golden era (*satya-yuga*) begins again, but with the silver around the corner. This was the promise of Kṛṣṇa to be reborn whenever virtue declines. At the level of the individual, Indian philosophy is the story of karma, of endless births, with escape only possible through enlightenment (see KARMA AND REBIRTH, INDIAN CONCEPTIONS OF). Instead of utopia pulling society forward, 'eupsychias' (ideal places of the mind) have been more prevalent. However, even as the self has been central, history has been dynastic, consisting of epics and myths, of ages and episodes, not of the workers' struggle, as recent Marxist Indian philosophers have argued; structure has been far more important than agency.

Traditional Indian historiography has framed the past as Hindu (Vedic), Muslim and Modern (British rule and then Independence). However, unlike the Western scheme there is no pretence that prior eras are stepping stones to the present, no overarching theory of scientific progress. This is not to deny the reformist urges throughout Indian history, and particularly the efforts of Raja Rammohun Roy (see BRAHMO SAMAJ) and AUROBINDO GHOSE, but rather to argue that moral philosophy has been more central than the massive social engineering of Marxism or the amoral market mechanisms of liberal capitalism. Even when utopia has been imagined, such as Rāma Rājya, it has been done with the past in mind, not with the pull of the future.

3 The Indian episteme

Indian political theory should not and cannot be divorced from the Indian episteme, the boundaries of knowledge that contextualize what is knowable. The liberation of the self is the centrepiece of this system. Doing so frees one from karma and helps one to live in *dharma* and achieve *mokṣa*. Truth is considered not so much as accuracy or fidelity to the empirical but as therapy, as that which reduces suffering. In this sense, classical Indian philosophy is postmodern, with reality consisting of many levels and different traditions and philosophies touching these levels – true epistemological pluralism. Truth is thus 'both/and' instead of 'true and false'. This means that contradictions are tolerated. Moreover, there are many ways of knowing the world: devotion, reason, sense-inference, authority and intuition (see KNOWLEDGE, INDIAN VIEWS OF). The physical universe and the mental universe are considered symmetrical: as above, so below; as inside, so outside. Individual and cosmos, body and mind, self and society are linked together. Politics and religion are thus not separated but linked. There is a holistic unity of discourse, with truth ultimately residing in the individual, even though Brahmans and rulers have attempted to have authority vested in caste and state. Philosophical systems are also grand, touching every level of existence from bathing to political economy, world order and cosmic meaning. Order and elegance are as important as accuracy in the Indian episteme. This episteme itself is not questioned, but is the given in Indian philosophy.

Unlike other epistemes, which undergo dramatic shifts, the Indian episteme is additive. New discourses are added, changing the episteme and Indianizing the new discourse. Modernity, of course, is threatening to force the classical pluralism of Tantra, Vedānta, Buddhism and Islam to fit into the straitjacket of nationalism, of one people, one guru or one god. This has led to a politics of structured religion, to the creation of a 'Hinduism', a religion linked to national identity. In this realist model, it is the state and its functionaries that are most important. Reality is not moral or spiritual, but about capturing power so as to ensure that the identity of and material gains for one's community or nation are maximized. The self is no longer devoted to selfless service (*sevā*), but to maximizing wealth and power. In this self, the Other is to be feared: the Other is the enemy, not to be embraced, as Gandhi argued, but used for personal gain. However, while in the short run Hindu nationalism may become hegemonic, its exclusionary tactics will most likely self-destruct. It will 'other' itself. In the long run, the ecology of cultures and traditions that is India will soften modernity's univocal claims, making it but one view among many.

4 Varṇa

The 'Other' has generally been more those of a different class than those of a different religion, since Indian religious and philosophical traditions are syncretic and universal. It is *varṇa* (social division; literally 'colour') that both orders society and creates structural problems for social justice and transformation. While *varṇa* for Orientalists is an all-encompassing social structure, others have argued that Indian society is no different from other historical societies, where agency has existed at times with individuals, at times with religious authorities, at times with traders and at times with the military. Caste is one category, but not the final category of analysis. Defenders of caste have argued that it is one among many ways of ordering the world – of engaging in politics. Politics is about the negotiation of power and meanings. While modernizers want to rid India of caste, they forget its relationship to order, with caste basically creating a permanent underclass, as in other societies. For the political theorist Rajni Kothari (1970), more important than *varṇa* is *jhat*, the myriad associations, relationships and lineages that are perceived as caste.

For GANDHI, the task was to make everyone into *śūdras* (peasants) to create a society with equal distribution. His was a devastating critique of modernity and instrumental rationality, not of technology, as commonly thought. For Gandhi, self-reliance is the road and the goal. One cannot distinguish between ends and means. This counters the classical position of the *Bhagavad Gītā*, where, in certain situations, violence is allowed, especially since at the level of the Absolute, victim and victor are united in destiny.

The legacies of Gandhi are many. Two are critical: self-reliance rather than instrumental rationality – that is, humans should work together to build small-scale communities – and nonviolence. In conflicts, it is nonviolence that is victorious since it touches the heart of the oppressor, thereby transforming the oppressor. Indeed, for Gandhi, history itself is the march from violence to nonviolence, from barbarism to civilization.

5 Structure, history and the cycle

The work of P.R. Sarkar (1921–90) is an alternative to the critical traditionalism of Gandhi and the reforming efforts of Aurobindo. Sarkar attempts to develop a political theory that has structure (historical patterns), agency (the role of individuals and leadership) and superagency (the role of divine intervention). For Sarkar, there are four types of power: the economic, or *vaiśyan*, the coercive/protective, or *kṣatriyan*, the normative/ideological, or Brahman, and the chaotic/disruptive, or *śūdra*. Sarkar derives these from the classical Indian social system of *varṇa*, but reinterprets them not as biological caste categories but as evolutionary, psychosocial paradigms.

These four types of power are related to four historical ages: the age of workers, the age of warriors, the age of intellectuals and the age of capitalists. At the end of the capitalist era, there is a workers' revolution; this leads to a centralization of power, from which evolves an age of warriors, in which there is a centralized polity. Each age has it own contradictions, and by denying the other forms of power, each era naturally leads to the next. These are not ideal types, nor is Sarkar's cycle a defence of current modernity, as with the historian Buddha Prakash, who argues (1958) that the current age is the Golden Era – rather than an *avatār*, independence and industrialism have awakened India after centuries of oppressive sleep.

Sarkar does not intend to end the cycle of history – it is not societal perfection he seeks – but he hopes to minimize the exploitation in each era through the development of a new type of leader, the *sadvipra*, one with a complete and pure mind. The *sadvipra* exists in a context not of state or individual, but of *samāj*, or family: a selfless family on a collective journey through life. Through such leadership, Sarkar envisages a new society committed to gender coordination, self-reliant cooperative economies, and *pramā*, a dynamic balance between physical, mental and spiritual potentials.

However, unlike classical political philosophy, where the sage exists *outside* traditional constructs of power (being neither Brahman nor *kṣatriya*), in Sarkar's model, this new type of power – protective, service-based, innovative and interpretive – is placed at the centre of the wheel. Like Aurobindo with his yogocracy and Gandhi with his *satyāgrahī*, Sarkar develops the ideal of a modern yogi. This, however, is not the religionization of politics but its spiritualization, the aim that Aurobindo and Gandhi struggled to achieve.

But for Aurobindo, history is not structural but idealistic, a process in which the Godhead enters individuals and communities. Thus, following Hegel, nationalism becomes part of the manifestation of the soul, of the divine drama. It becomes an extraordinary event that represents the will of Consciousness in creating a better human condition. For Aurobindo, God works not only through *avatārs* such as Kṛṣṇa, but also through nationalistic and other movements as well.

6 Postcolonial discourses

More recent Indian political theory has been concerned with creating a post-colonial self, with ridding India of the intimate enemy of the British history. This is not a history of dynasties or of large meta-narratives, but a history of the subaltern, of women, of the epistemologically oppressed, as developed by writers such as Ashis Nandy, Ranajit Guha, Vandana Shiva and Gayatri Spivak. This rewriting of India has been a search for a historically grounded India not overlaid with spiritual essences, for a politics of individuals and communities struggling to create a new self, an often localized identity that has meaning in its own mythological, cultural and economic context. Development, science and instrumental rationality are criticized as violent, disempowering of communities and dangerous to the environment.

Borrowing from postmodernist critiques of the construction of identity, the categories of 'Hinduism', 'caste', 'Mother India' and 'nation' are questioned. The politics of how these discourses are used by state power further to regulate, militarize and homogenize society are deconstructed with the intention of rescuing the plurality of truth that has typified Indian philosophy.

See also: DUTY AND VIRTUE, INDIAN CONCEPTIONS OF; POLITICAL PHILOSOPHY, HISTORY OF; POLITICAL PHILOSOPHY, NATURE OF; POSTCOLONIALISM

References and further reading

Copley, A. (1993) 'Indian Secularism Reconsidered: from Gandhi to Ayodhya', *Contemporary South Asia* 2 (1): 47–65. (Criticism of the new syndicated Hinduism.)

Dhawan, G. (1957) *The Political Philosophy of Mahatma Gandhi*, Ahmedabad: Navajivan Publishing House. (Excellent summary of Gandhi's life and thoughts; easy to follow.)

* Dirks, N. (1987) *The Hollow Crown*, Cambridge: Cambridge University Press. (Difficult but rewarding. Explores power, culture and kingship in Indian history.)

El-Affendi, A. (1991) *Who Needs An Islamic State?*, London: Grey Seal Books. (Excellent analysis of Islamic political theory; easy to follow.)

Guha, R. and Spivak, G.C. (1988) *Selected Subaltern Studies*, New York: Oxford University Press. (Difficult but novel approach to politics and history.)

Inayatullah, S. (1997) 'Prabhat Rainjan Sarkar: Agency, Structure and Transcendence', in J. Galtung and S. Inayatullah (eds) *Macrohistory and Macrohistorians*, Westport, CT: Praeger, 132–40. (An easy introduction to Sarkar's thought – comparisons to other grand thinkers such as Ibn Khaldun, Karl Marx and Herbert Spencer are made.)

—— (1997) *Situating Sarkar: Historical, Structural and Poststructural Inquiries*, Singapore: Ananda Marga Publications. (Explores Sarkar's political and social thought. Uses a critical Foucauldian analysis, also comparative essays on diverse thinkers such as Ssu-Ma Ch'ien, Montesquieu, Aurobindo and Gandhi.)

Inden, R. (1986) 'Orientalist Constructions of India', *Modern Asian Studies* 20 (3): 401–46. (Breakthrough article on the construction of the text of India.)

* Kauṭilya (c.320 BC) *Arthaśāstra*, ed. and trans. T.N. Ramaswamy, *Essentials of Indian Statecraft: Kauṭilya's Arthashastra for Contemporary Readers*, London: Asia Publishing House, 1962. (An abridged version that is easier to get through than the original.)

* Kothari, R. (1970) *Caste In Indian Politics*, New Delhi: Orient Longman. (Traditional but useful political-science approach to caste.)

Murty, K.S. (ed.) (1967) *Readings in Indian History, Philosophy and Politics*, London: Allen & Unwin. (Short essays by Aurobindo, Nehru, Kosambi, Majumdar, Panikkar, Munshi, Murti and others. Covers Marxist, idealistic, theistic, humanistic and other renderings of Indian political philosophy; an essential and easy read.)

Nandy, A. (1967) *Traditions, Tyranny and Utopias*, New Delhi: Oxford University Press. (Brilliant, difficult, but very important book that touches on politics, culture and history.)

* Prakash, B. (1958) 'The Hindu Philosophy of History', *Journal of the History of Ideas* 16 (4):

494–505. (Novel rendering of Indian political history that mixes the classical and the modern.)

Said, E. (1979) *Orientalism*, New York: Vintage Books. (The classic work on how the Orient has been fabricated by the West; skilfully written.)

Sardar, Z. (ed.) (1997) *South Asia: Fifty Years On*, special issue of *Futures* 29 (10). (Essays on the future of south Asia by leading south Asian thinkers.)

* Sarkar, P.R. (1987) *PROUT in a Nutshell*, trans. V. Avadhuta, Calcutta: Ananda Marga Publications, 16 vols. (Creative polemic, not technical, but written as *sūtras* rather than analysis. PROUT is Progressive Utilization Theory, an alternative global model of political economy, which Sarkar claims will succeed communism and capitalism.)

Shiva, V. (1988) 'Reductionist Science as Epistemological Violence', in A. Nandy (ed.) *Science, Hegemony and Violence: A Requiem for Modernity*, Delhi: Oxford University Press, 232–57. (Brilliant chapter by a leading environmental and feminist writer; difficult for those not accustomed to poststructural sensibilities.)

Thapar, R. (1966) *A History of India*, vol. 1, Baltimore, MD: Penguin. (Classical study of Indian history.)

Varma, V.P. (1960) *The Political Philosophy of Sri Aurobindo*, New York: Asia Publishing House. (Excellent explanation of the grand neo-Hegelian system of Aurobindo.)

—— (1974) *Studies in Hindu Political Thought and its Metaphysical Foundations*, Delhi: Motilal Banarsidass. (Located in the Indian episteme, a useful and thorough approach.)

SOHAIL INAYATULLAH

POLITICAL PHILOSOPHY, NATURE OF

Political philosophy developed as a central aspect of philosophy generally in the world of ancient Greece, and the writings of Plato and Aristotle made a basic and still important contribution to the subject. Central to political philosophy has been a concern with the justification or criticism of general political arrangements such as democracy, oligarchy or kingship, and with the ways in which the sovereignty of the state is to be understood; with the relationship between individual and the political order, and the nature of the individual's obligation to that order; with the coherence and identity of the political order from the point of view of the nation and groups within the nation,

and with the role of culture, language and race as aspects of this; with the basis of different general political ideologies and standpoints such as conservatism, socialism and liberalism; and with the nature of the basic concepts such as state, individual, rights, community and justice in terms of which we understand and argue about politics. Because it is concerned with the justification and criticism of existing and possible forms of political organization a good deal of political philosophy is normative; it seeks to provide grounds for one particular conception of the right and the good in politics. In consequence many current controversies in political philosophy are methodological; they have to do with how (if at all) normative judgments about politics can be justified.

1 Universalism in political philosophy
2 The critique of political philosophy
3 The communitarian response

1 Universalism in political philosophy

A central question in the history of political philosophy has been the concept of the political itself, and therefore the range of actions which can and should be subject to law and coercive interference. Political philosophers have tried several argumentative strategies in their attempts to provide a solution. One such strategy, which has taken many different forms, has been to invoke a conception of human nature (see HUMAN NATURE). If we could reach a good understanding of human nature and basic human needs, desires and purposes, we could then devise the appropriate set of political arrangements which would best meet them. Sometimes such conceptions of human nature have in turn been set against much wider philosophical theories about the place of human nature in the cosmos (as for example in Plato, Augustine and Aquinas); sometimes in relation to God specifically, as the creator who endowed persons with the nature they have (as for example in the writings of Calvin or, in a more limited way, Locke); sometimes in a view of the place of human beings in the natural order (as for example in Hobbes, or Aristotle via his writings on the relationship between man and the biological order); or in an account of how human needs and powers develop in history (as in Hegel and Marx). Equally, some conceptions of human nature as a basis for political organization have been much more limited and empirical in form (as for example in the utilitarian writings of Bentham, who took as a fact of life the propensity of human beings to seek pleasure and avoid pain). Despite all of these differences, we may find a similar strategy being adopted; namely, that in order to justify a particular set of political arrangements we have to understand the basic needs, drives, desires, interests and purposes of human beings and then argue from these to a proper understanding of the appropriate nature and role of politics in human life.

It follows from this view that the claims of political philosophy are both universal and foundationalist. They are universal in that most political philosophers have assumed that their claims about human nature and the concomitant understanding of politics, society and the individual are quite general in scope and not restricted to an understanding of human nature in the context of a particular culture and society. They are foundationalist in the sense that a conception of the good political order is taken to rest upon an objectively true account of human nature. In addition, political philosophy has frequently been regarded as teleological in character, directed towards goals set by the nature of what it is to be human and the kind of political organization which will fulfil human nature as we understand it.

2   The critique of political philosophy

This conception of political philosophy has met with fierce criticism during the twentieth century, to the extent that in the middle years of the century political philosophy as a normative discipline was regarded as dead. There were various reasons for this. One central reason has to do with the claimed relationship between philosophical prescriptions about the good society and its political form, and the basis for such judgments in accounts of human nature. Following the lead of David HUME, many empiricist philosophers have argued that there is a logical gap between any account of human nature and the evaluative and prescriptive consequences which are thought to derive from this (see FACT/VALUE DISTINCTION). On this view there cannot be anything in the conclusion of a valid argument which is not present in the premises. If a theory of human nature is supposed to be empirically grounded, that is to say testable or verifiable by empirical investigation, then such a set of empirical propositions about human nature cannot support evaluative conclusions about political organization. (This is sometimes known as the is/ought gap.) This claim has frequently gone alongside the claim that the theories of human nature with which political philosophers have operated have not been strictly empirical but rather have been constructed with a strong evaluative dimension built into them – that, for example, some human needs or human purposes have higher moral priority over others. On this view, the reasons why political philosophers have thought that their theories of human nature have

supported evaluative conclusions is that the theories themselves have contained ineliminable evaluative elements. The upshot is that theories of human nature cannot provide a secure foundation for political philosophy, because either they are empirical theories which will not support normative conclusions or they are themselves normative and stand in need of justification.

This objection to the strategies followed by normative political philosophers has been reinforced by a growing sense of the subjectivity of values. Sometimes this is taken as a sociological observation – that it is as a matter of fact that the modern world is marked by the view that moral values are matters of subjective preference. If this is so neither normative political philosophy nor the normative understanding of human nature with which political philosophers have worked can be given an objective foundation. Moral judgments, whether they apply to theories of human nature encompassing accounts of human needs and purposes and the priorities between them, or directly to the nature and scope of politics, are matters of subjective preference.

Equally, attempts have been made by philosophers such as the logical positivists who flourished in the 1930s to provide an elaborate justification for understanding moral judgments in a subjective and emotive way (see LOGICAL POSITIVISM; EMOTIVISM). The positivists argued that apart from the truths of logic and mathematics, which are tautologies (that is to say, hold by definition), the only meaningful statements are those which are in principle empirically verifiable, as for example the propositions of natural science and everyday empirical observations. This led them to the view that moral judgments, including those made about the nature of politics, have no cognitive content, convey no information. Rather they embody or evince the emotional attitudes of those who make the judgments. In this sense moral judgments are irredeemably subjective.

In the same vein it was argued that political philosophers, particularly utilitarians such as Bentham and J.S. Mill, had committed what G.E. Moore called the naturalistic fallacy when they attempted to give normative conceptions such as good and bad an empirical definition in terms of pleasure and pain (see MOORE, G.E. §1). These conceptions are not extensionally equivalent because it is always possible to say 'this is pleasant, but is it good?', a question which would make no sense if the words denoted the same thing. Again, this would mean that it is impossible to give an empirical basis to normative reasoning about politics.

These philosophical arguments about the limitation of empirical justification for normative conclusions reinforced the idea that normative judgments are subjective. If this is so then the project of normative political philosophy has to be abandoned. There can be no foundationalist or universalist basis for political judgments. If political philosophy has a role at all it is very modest and involves conceptual analysis – that is to say, clarification of the concepts that might be used in empirical political science with a view to purging such concepts of evaluative, and therefore subjective, overtones.

3 The communitarian response

Over the past thirty years, however, there has been a vigorous resurrection of political philosophy. How have political philosophers felt able to engage in a discipline which had looked nothing more than a pseudodiscipline, merely recording the consequences of the moral predilections of the theorists themselves?

Several factors have contributed to the revival. It has not proved possible to produce a watertight account of the principle of verifiability central to positivism, whose aim was to provide a clear criterion in terms of which the empirical and the non-empirical could be demarcated. Partly because of this, and partly under the influence of Wittgenstein's later writing, there has been much more attention paid to the meaning that terms have in particular contexts (including the moral and political), than to any attempt to impose some kind of antecedent standard of meaningfulness on language. This has freed political philosophy to consider, for example, the meaning which a term such as 'justice' might have in different discourses, contexts and communities, rather than trying to establish its meaning a priori (see, for instance, Walzer 1983).

Those who wish to link analysis in political philosophy to the interpretation of the communities and networks within which values and principle have their meaning have come to be called, in one contemporary usage of the term, 'communitarians' (see COMMUNITY AND COMMUNITARIANISM). This approach to political philosophy does not aim to justify values and principles in some foundationalist or universalistic sense, but rather to interpret (in a way that goes beyond surface description) the values which animate a particular society, or specific communities or discourses within it. It side-steps the problem of justification posed by the positivists and others who regard values as subjective. It eschews the idea of providing some kind of universalistic foundation for political values, rooted, for example, in a theory of human nature. It takes communities and the social meanings embodied in communities and other ways of life as basic and seeks to interpret them.

Another reason for the revival was that the underlabourer role to which positivism consigned political philosophy – providing central definitions of political concepts to be used in empirical political analysis – proved impossible. The evaluative component of political terms is not a peripheral and detachable feature, but is central to the meanings which these terms have in particular discourses, ideologies and communities. This perception is linked to the idea that basic social and political concepts are essentially contestable (Gallie 1956). This is the view that such concepts cannot be given some wholly neutral, value-free, experiential definition; rather, their meaning is bound to different ways in which different discourses and communities construe human purposes, human interests and human flourishing.

Recognizing this may lead us to two alternative conclusions. The first limits political philosophy to description and interpretation. Given that political concepts are essentially contestable, and that they are contested because their meaning is relative to a particular discourse or ideology, then all that political philosophy can do is describe the role which the concept plays in one discourse and explain how its meaning differs in others (see IDEOLOGY §4). On the other hand, if a political philosopher wishes to do more than trace how a political concept relates to a wider network of beliefs and values, and instead wishes to offer some basic justification for using that concept in a particular way, then that must involve privileging one way of thinking about human interests and purposes over another. This would take the subject back to its more traditional form, that is reflecting on human purposes and the nature of human flourishing and endorsing a set of political values which would facilitate this.

The problem here is how to ground a normative theory of politics in circumstances where people disagree about their conceptions of the good. In so far as this dilemma has been solved in contemporary political philosophy it has been in one of two ways. The first has been to put, as John RAWLS (§4) argues: 'the Right before the Good' (Rawls 1971). That is to say, we can recognize that citizens differ about what they take to be good in human life, but nevertheless they have an interest in the justice of the political framework within which they pursue their own diverse goals. One can argue that it is possible to produce a compelling account of the rules of justice within a diverse society by making some rather minimal assumptions about certain basic human goods which all people are assumed to want more rather than less of, whatever else they may think is good in life; and then to invoke some general principles of rationality to decide upon rules governing the distribution of such 'primary goods'. Theories of this kind aim to justify a political order by reasoning on the basis of slight assumptions about human goods, while recognizing the pervasive nature of moral diversity in relation to more specific human goals and purposes.

The other main approach to the problem of justification has been to emphasize the idea of dialogue in politics, and to explore the conditions for free and rational dialogue about basic political precepts. Here again is recognition of the problem of philosophical justification of principles in a situation of moral diversity, and the response is to ask under what conditions rational and noncoercive dialogues about political goals could take place. Examples of this sort of approach are to be found in the work of Ackerman (1980) and HABERMAS (1987).

Contemporary political philosophy does not have a settled nature. Following the challenge of positivism, it has become much more reflective about methodology, but as the different approaches of communitarians and foundationalists illustrate, there are still profound differences about the scope and ambition of political philosophy. Is it to be engaged in justification or interpretation? Is it concerned with universal values or the values of particular communities? Are the problems of moral diversity to be resolved by invoking minimal assumptions about human nature and applying formal modes of reasoning to these, or by grappling with this diversity as it manifests itself in the different interpretations of values in a particular society?

See also: POLITICAL PHILOSOPHY, HISTORY OF

References and further reading

* Ackerman, B. (1980) *Social Justice in the Liberal State*, New Haven, CT: Yale University Press. (A book which seeks to produce an argument in favour of liberal political arrangements while making use of minimalist moral assumptions by utilizing neutral dialogue.)

Barry, B. (1965) *Political Argument*, London Routledge & Kegan Paul. (A classical text in post-war political philosophy. An excellent example of conceptual analysis. Important also in its contrast between 'want regarding' and 'ideal-regarding' political philosophies.)

—— (1973) *The Liberal Theory of Justice*, Oxford: Clarendon Press. (A systematic analysis of J. Rawls' *Theory of Justice* in both its methodological and substantive aspects.)

Berlin, I. (1958) *Four Essays on Liberty*, Oxford: Oxford University Press, 1969. (A contemporary classic adumbrating the distinction between negative and positive liberty.)

* Gallie, W.B. (1956) 'Essentially Contested Concepts', *Proceedings of the Aristotelian Society* 56. (A classic piece of analysis which shows that there cannot be a purely neutral analysis of political concepts.)

Galston, W. (1991) *Liberal Purposes*, Cambridge: Cambridge University Press. (A book from within the American Liberal tradition which shows that Liberalism has to draw upon some conception of the virtues.)

Gewirth, A. (1978) *Reason and Morality*, Chicago, IL: University of Chicago Press. (Probably the most thorough going defence of rights within the context of moral pluralism.)

* Habermas, J. (1987) *The Philosophical Discourse of Modernity*, Cambridge: Polity Press. (One of Habermas' many books which provides background to the points made in this entry.)

Kymlicka, W. (1989) *Liberalism, Community, and Culture*, Oxford: Clarendon Press. (Looks at the relationship between liberalism and 'thicker' ideas about community and culture.)

Plant, R. (1991) *Modern Political Thought*, Oxford: Blackwell. (An overview of many aspects of post-war political thought.)

Rawls, J. (1971) *A Theory of Justice*, Cambridge, MA: Harvard University Press. (*The* classic text of post-war political philosophy in which the strategy of putting the 'Right' before the 'Good' is developed in a very sophisticated way.)

—— (1993) *Political Liberalism*, New York: Columbia University Press. (Considers how public deliberation about constitutional arrangements should be conducted in a liberal society.)

Rorty, R. (1989) *Contingency, Irony, and Solidarity*, Cambridge: Cambridge University Press. (Develops ideas drawn from Wittgenstein and continental philosophy into a 'postmodern' approach to political philosophy.)

* Walzer, M. (1983) *Spheres of Justice: A Defence of Pluralism and Equality*, New York: Basic Books; London and Oxford: Blackwell. (A challenging book which rejects the idea that there can be 'thin' moral conceptions which can be drawn upon to underpin principles to govern society.)

RAYMOND PLANT

POLITICAL THEOLOGY
see THEOLOGY, POLITICAL

POMPONATIUS, PETRUS
see POMPONAZZI, PIETRO

POMPONAZZI, PIETRO (1462–1525)

Pietro Pomponazzi was the leading Aristotelian philosopher in the first quarter of the sixteenth century. His treatise De immortalitate animae *(On the Immortality of the Soul) (1516) argues that although faith teaches immortality, natural reason and Aristotelian principles cannot prove it. In* De incantationibus *(On Incantations) (first published in 1556), Pomponazzi attempts to demonstrate on rational grounds that all reported miraculous suspensions or reversals of natural laws can be explained by forces within nature itself. Separating faith and reason once again, Pomponazzi proclaims his belief in all canonical miracles of the Church. These arguments cast doubt on morality, for without an afterlife, humanity is deprived of rewards for virtue and punishment for evil; and nature itself appears to be governed by impersonal forces unconcerned with human affairs. However, morality is restored to the universe by the human powers of rational reflection which lead to the pursuit of virtue. Yet in* De fato *(On Fate) (first published in 1567), Pomponazzi challenges the very basis of his own ethical doctrine by arguing that all activity of insentient and sentient beings is directed to preordained ends by environmental factors. Unable to justify human freedom on rational grounds, he then seeks to re-establish it using arguments derived from Christian natural theology, thus reversing his usual separation of faith and reason.*

1　Life and works
2　Immortality
3　Miracles
4　Morality and freedom

1　Life and works

Pietro Pomponazzi (Petrus Pomponatius) was born in Mantua. His adult life was spent as a professor of natural philosophy at the Universities of Padua, Ferrara and Bologna, where he was admired by his students and paid well. Many of his unpublished lectures and questions survive because students, impressed by their intellectual rigour, copied and recopied them. Pomponazzi's most productive years were spent at the University of Bologna where he taught from 1511 until his death. During this period, he published the immortality treatises, *De immortali-* *tate animae* (*On the Immortality of the Soul*) (1516), *Apologia* (1518) and *Defensorium* (1519), and wrote but did not publish *De incantationibus* and *De fato* (each written in 1520 but published posthumously in 1556 and 1567 respectively).

2　Immortality

Pomponazzi's most famous work, the treatise *On the Immortality of the Soul* (1516), encloses the philosophic argument in a conventional fideistic shell. At the beginning and end of the treatise, he remarks that the doctrine of immortality must be accepted as revealed truth, certain and indubitable; all contrary arguments are false (see SOUL, NATURE AND IMMORTALITY OF THE §2). The philosophic core of the treatise, however, argues strongly for mortality on rational and Aristotelian grounds. The philosophic argument holds that only the intellect, the highest part of the soul, is capable of surviving the body. Proof of this survival must be found in an activity of the intellect that functions without bodily dependence. No such activity can be discovered, however, because the highest activity of the intellect, the attainment of universals in cognition, is always mediated by sense impressions. Thus even the highest power of intellection is always directly linked to and sustained by the sensitive powers which, in turn, are dependent on the vegetative power. All sources agree that the sensitive and vegetative powers weaken and perish, and hence the intellect, although immaterial in itself, must perish with them. The whole soul therefore dies with the body.

The philosophic doctrine of mortality thus stands in direct opposition to the religious doctrine of immortality. Is Pomponazzi proclaiming the simultaneous truth of two opposites? Some contemporary critics claimed that he asserted the notion of a 'double truth': the doctrine of immortality can be simultaneously true in theology and false in philosophy. However, there is no evidence to support such a claim. He held to only one truth but whether that was the truth of faith or philosophy is open to question. There is good reason to believe that Pomponazzi maintained the absolute truth of philosophy. In discussing the origin of the doctrine of immortality, he notes that religious lawmakers asserted immortality 'not caring for truth but only for righteousness'. Apparently, the truth the religious lawmakers 'do not care for' is the philosophic doctrine of mortality.

On Immortality provoked an immediate furore. Public attacks on Pomponazzi culminated in a warning by Pope Leo X demanding that he disavow the doctrine of mortality and bring his position in line with the decree of the Fifth Lateran Council (1513) which had declared the immortality of the soul to be a dogma of the Church. The intervention of Pomponazzi's powerful friends in the Church allowed him to continue teaching and to publish replies to his critics. The attacks were accompanied by a spate of books written against Pomponazzi, who wrote two works in his own defence. In his *Apologia* (1518) he replied to Gaspar Contarini and in *Defensorium* (1519) he answered Agostino NIFO (§1). Although more elaborate and diffuse than the original treatise, these works do not alter Pomponazzi's basic position. A full-scale attack came from the prominent Dominican theologian Bartolomeo de Spina. He alone charged Pomponazzi with heresy and demanded an Inquisitorial trial. His call went unheeded. Spina wrote two books against Pomponazzi but the first one, *Tutela veritatis de immortalitate* (The Whole Truth Concerning Immortality) (1519), is probably the more significant. Noting Pomponazzi's assertion that immortality is the invention of religious lawmakers, Spina concludes that Pomponazzi's attitude is not that of a believing Christian.

This issue continues to divide Pomponazzi's interpreters. If, as Pomponazzi always says, revelation proceeds from supernatural truths beyond rational discourse, it follows that reason cannot invalidate any proposition of faith. This fideism, many scholars argue, is certainly compatible with faith so there is no reason to doubt Pomponazzi's sincerity (see Kristeller 1964). Others have reached a different conclusion (see Pine 1986). Citing Pomponazzi's constant identification of philosophy with truth and religions with social convention, they argue that he stressed the importance of religions as a force producing social cohesion but lacking in speculative veracity. The association of truth with philosophy is particularly striking in his idealization of the philosopher as one who is isolated, derided and persecuted for his lonely struggle towards virtue and truth.

3 Miracles

Pomponazzi's investigation of miracles, *De incantationibus*, was written in 1520 but published posthumously in 1556. The decision to leave the work unpublished probably stemmed from Pomponazzi's concern for his own safety after the immortality controversy.

The philosophical discussion of miracles, proceeding by rational argument alone, is again enclosed in a fideistic shell, professing belief in all canonical miracles of the Church. Yet the philosophical discussion discovers natural causes, first for contemporary events deemed miracles, then for biblical miracles, and finally for the miracles specifically related to the founding of all religions. Thus Pomponazzi concludes with a natural basis for religion itself, which now becomes the effect of the workings of the Intelligences, divine impersonal forces moving the heavens, rather than the fiat of a personal deity.

Many supposedly miraculous cures and visions produced by magicians and divine messengers undoubtedly occurred, says Pomponazzi. Yet they all have perfectly natural explanations. Naturalistic accounts are also applied to biblical events, casting doubt on the miracles of Moses, Elisha and Christ. After the discussion of particular miracles, religion itself is depicted as a product of the Intelligences and subject to the eternal cycles of birth, growth and decay. At its birth, a religion is favoured by the Intelligences. It is at that point that the heavens, directed by the Intelligences, produce 'sons of God', men possessing the ability to command nature. But as the natural process develops, every religion grows weaker and eventually dies. Christianity itself is dying, having reached the end of its life cycle.

The doctrine of a universe without miracles, says Pomponazzi, cannot be spread to the vulgar. They must still believe that a providential God, angels and demons are the causes of 'miraculous events'. But the philosophical elite knows that these are 'fictions' designed to lead men to virtue (see MIRACLES).

4 Morality and freedom

Pomponazzi's conception of morality is based on the free choice of the individual. That choice is free only when the passions are subdued and reason is ascendant. Since only the philosophic elite is capable of dominating the passions, they alone are truly free. Through reason they understand that virtue is its own reward and vice its own punishment. The masses, ruled by their passions, are subject to environmental and planetary forces eliminating their freedom.

The centrality of the concept of freedom in Pomponazzi's thought is underlined by his insistence in the last book of *De fato* that freedom is a metaphysical necessity based on the Great Chain of Being. For that chain of being requires a nature differentiated both from the gods and from the lower forms of life, all of whose natures are fixed and hence without freedom of choice. The universe, he insists, requires a being whose nature is a product of free choice rather than a fixed essence. Human nature is created by individual choices rather than a divinely given essence. This theme, asserted in various forms throughout Pomponazzi's works, is in contradiction to the determinism he forcefully defends in the first book of *De fato*. Thus the battle between freedom and determinism is at the very core of Pomponazzi's thought and is never fully resolved.

The attack on freedom in Book 1 of *De fato* takes the form of a defence of Stoic determinism (see STOICISM §20). Every event, Pomponazzi argues, is directed by an external cause which guides its internal nature to a predetermined end. Although we deliberate over moral alternatives, our choices are already determined by natural forces directing our wills. Yet after subjecting the will to environmental determinants, Pomponazzi undertakes a new attempt to save human freedom within a framework of Christian theology. This represents a surprising reversal of method since all of Pomponazzi's previous works have insisted that theology is not a legitimate concern of the philosopher who always proceeds 'within natural limits'. By combining doctrines derived from Aquinas and Duns Scotus, Pomponazzi attempts to rescue the will from environmental determinants, although he recognizes that his solution is not entirely satisfactory (see FREE WILL §2).

When Pomponazzi moves from environmental determinants to the attributes of God, the problem is still more complicated. Pomponazzi discusses divine omniscience in the specific form of divine foreknowledge. Divine foreknowledge apparently precludes human freedom for if God infallibly knows all events before they occur, human deliberation about alternatives cannot affect the outcome. Any denial of this theological determinism implies that we can choose an alternative unknown to God. This impugns God's infallibility, as we would then have the power to falsify his knowledge. Here Pomponazzi draws on the Boethian–Thomistic solution which attempted to reconcile divine foreknowledge and human freedom by designating God's knowledge as 'timeless' (see OMNISCIENCE §§3–4). This timelessness is a total simultaneity in which all events are eternally present to God without succession. There is no future mode in God's eternal knowledge, for that would make divine knowledge indeterminate and possibly false. Pomponazzi qualifies this traditional view in an original way by asserting that God knows what is future to us in two ways: determinately and indeterminately. When any future event becomes past or present within the temporal flow, God knows this event as determinate. Such events are 'beyond their causes', with all their potentialities actualized so that God knows them determinately; they correspond to some settled actuality. This mode of divine foreknowledge Pomponazzi calls the future-as-present or future-as-past. Events which have not yet occurred within the temporal flow are designated the future-as-future. These events are by logic and nature unknown and unknowable. God's knowledge of them is uncertain in the sense that such an event is contingent. God's infallible foreknowledge is not destroyed by this contingent mode because he still possesses all temporal modes within his 'timeless' eternity. As God himself decides to prescind from the determinate modes of the future, he limits his future knowledge to pure contingency, thus allowing for the free operation of the human will. As unusual as this position is when compared to Pomponazzi's other teachings, it seems dictated by his recognition of the need to provide a metaphysical ground for ethics.

Pomponazzi's arguments are marked by the realization and admission of difficulty and paradox. His conclusions are attained only after the most complete elaboration of all possibilities. It is his tenacity in the face of complexity and honesty in the confrontation of difficulty that makes Pomponazzi, in Kristeller's words, 'one of the most difficult but also one of the most sympathetic and interesting of the philosophers of the Aristotelian school, of the Renaissance and of every age' (1983: 23).

See also: ARISTOTELIANISM, RENAISSANCE §5; CAJETAN §4; FICINO, M. §3

List of works

Pomponazzi, P. (before 1516) 'Pietro Pomponazzi: Utrum anima sit mortalis vel immortalis' (Whether the Soul is Mortal or Immortal), ed. W. Van Dooren, Naples: Nouvelles de la République des lettres, 1989. (A fine critical edition with an analysis of *Pomponatius in Libros de Anima* (Pomponazzi's commentary *On the Soul*). Set forth just before the *De immortalitate*, Pomponazzi here elaborated most major aspects of his theory which is developed more decisively in 1516.)

—— (1516) *De immortalitate animae*, trans. W.H. Hay II, *On the Immortality of the Soul*, in E. Cassirer, P.O. Kristeller and J.H. Randall, Jr (eds) *The Renaissance Philosophy of Man*, Chicago, IL: University of Chicago Press, 1948. (A reliable English translation of Pomponazzi's best known treatise. It provoked the immortality controversy, arguing for the philosophic doctrine of mortality while accepting immortality on faith alone. Excellent footnotes by Kristeller and a useful introductory essay by Randall.)

—— (1525) *Tractatus acutissimi, utilimi et mere peripatetici* (The Most Insightful, Useful and Fully Peripatetic Treatises), Venice. (The only collected edition; contains Pomponazzi's early works on physics, the three immortality treatises – *De immortalitate animae* (1516), *Apologia* (1518), *Defensorium Auctoris* (1519) – and the late work *De nutritione et augmentatione* (On Nutrition and Growth) (1521), which treats in part the problem of materialism in regard to the soul. With the notable exception of G. Zanier (1991), *De nutritione* has been neglected by Pomponazzi scholars.)

—— (1556) *De naturalium effectuum causis sive de incantationibus* (On the Natural Effects of Causes or on Incantations), Basle. (An attack on miracles which finds natural causes for all miracles and then reduces all religious miracles to the effect of heavenly forces.)

—— (1567) *De fato, de libero arbitrio, praedestinatione providentia dei libri V* (Five Books on Fate, Free Will, the Providence of God and Predestination), ed. R. Le May, *Libri quinque de fato, de libero arbitrio, de praedestinatione*, Lugano: Thesauris Mundi, 1957. (The most complex of Pomponazzi's published works. Beginning by arguing for Stoic determinism, the treatise then seeks to rescue free will, using arguments from Christian natural theology, and develops a novel theory of divine activity to rescue human freedom in light of divine foreknowledge and predestination. May provides an excellent critical edition of *De fato* with full references to all of Pomponazzi's sources, the manuscript literature and secondary sources.)

—— (1462–1525) *Studi su Pietro Pomponazzi* (Studies on Pietro Pomponazzi), ed. B. Nardi, Florence: Felice Le Monnier, 1965. (A very important collection of articles. Nardi traces Pomponazzi's evolving position on immortality, reason and revelation, resurrection and miracles, with very full quotations from Pomponazzi's unpublished lectures and questions. The classroom comments on religious doctrines are often more critical than in the published works.)

—— (1462–1525) *Corsi inediti dell' insegnamento padovano* (Unpublished Courses from the Paduan Teaching), ed. A. Poppi, Padua: Antenore, vol. 1, 1966; vol. 2, 1970. (Critical editions of Pomponazzi's lectures, demonstrating that Pomponazzi's basic position on immortality was developed around 1504. Other important issues (such as the *regressus* and universals) are discussed.)

References and further reading

Di Napoli, G. (1963) *L'immortalità dell'anima nel Rinascimento* (The Immortality of the Soul in the Renaissance), Turin. (A full discussion of the doctrine of immortality among the humanists, Platonists and Aristotelians of the Renaissance. A large portion of the book is devoted to Pomponazzi and the immortality controversy.)

Fiorentino, F. (1868) *Pietro Pomponazzi, Studi storici su la suola Bolognese e Padovana del secolo XVI con molti documenti inediti* (A Historical Study of the Bolognese and Paduan School of the Sixteenth Century with Many Unpublished Documents), Florence: Successori Le Monnier. (A classic study. Fiorentino was the first to emphasize Pomponazzi's defence of the rational doctrine of mortality as opposed to medieval arguments for the indemonstrability of immortality. Very complete on the historical background of the doctrine of immortality in ancient and medieval eras, with a clear analysis of Pomponazzi's theory of the soul, and a less successful attempt to analyse *De incantationibus* and *De fato*.)

* Kristeller, P.O. (1964) *Eight Philosophers of the Italian Renaissance*, Stanford, CA: Stanford University Press. (Referred to in §2. A series of essays on the major Italian philosophers of the Renaissance notable for its clarity and careful delineation of major ideas. The chapter on Pomponazzi presents a balanced and nicely articulated view of *De immortalitate animae*. The author argues for Pomponazzi's sincerity in regard to religion.)

* —— (1983) *Aristotelismo e sincretismo nel pensiero di Pomponazzi* (Aristotelianism and Syncretism in the Thought of Pomponazzi), Padua: Antenore. (Quoted in §4. A brief, brilliant essay showing the influence of Platonic, Neoplatonic and Stoic sources on Pomponazzi. Successfully demonstrates that Pomponazzi's epistemology is more empiricist that Aristotle's.)

* Pine, M.L. (1986) *Pietro Pomponazzi: Radical Philosopher of the Renaissance*, Padua: Antenore. (Referred to in §2. The only work attempting a full analysis of Pomponazzi's philosophy since Fiorentino (1868). A full discussion of the evolution of the doctrine of immortality is presented, as well as a complete analysis of the immortality controversy. *De incantationibus* and *De fato* are thoroughly examined. An attempt is made to find textual basis for the insincerity of Pomponazzi's assertions of Christian faith.)

Tavuzzi, M. (1995) 'Silvestro da Prierio and the Pomponazzi Affair', *Renaissance and Reformation*, new series, 19 (2): 47–61. (A fine discussion shedding new light on the role of Spina in the immortality controversy. Spina was clearly encouraged by Silvestro da Prierio, a high Papal official who was vehemently opposed to Pomponazzi and claimed he had been misrepresented in Pomponazzi's *Apologia*.)

Zanier, G. (1991) 'La biologia teoretica del pensiero pomponazziano' (Biological Theory in Pomponazzi's Thought), in D. Facca and G. Zanier, *Filosofia, Filologia, Biologia: Itinerai dell'Aristotelismo cin-*

quecentesco (Philosophy, Philology, Biology: Paths of 16th-Century Aristotelianism), Rome, 105–30. (The only work devoted to an analysis of major themes in the neglected *De nutritione et augmentatione* (1521). An interesting discussion taking full account of *De incantationibus* and *De fato*. The argument demonstrates that Pomponazzi still maintains mortality in this late work.)

MARTIN L. PINE

POPPER, KARL RAIMUND (1902–94)

Popper belongs to a generation of Central European émigré scholars that profoundly influenced thought in the English-speaking countries in this century. His greatest contributions are in philosophy of science and in political and social philosophy. Popper's 'falsificationism' reverses the usual view that accumulated experience leads to scientific hypotheses; rather, freely conjectured hypotheses precede, and are tested against, experience. The hypotheses that survive the testing process constitute current scientific knowledge. His general epistemology, 'critical rationalism', commends the Socratic method of posing questions and critically discussing the answers offered to them. He considers knowledge in the traditional sense of certainty, or in the modern sense of justified true belief, to be unobtainable.

After the Anschluss, *Popper was stimulated by the problem of why democracies had succumbed to totalitarianism and applied his critical rationalism to political philosophy. Since we have no infallible ways of getting or maintaining good government, Plato's question 'Who should rule?' is misdirected. To advocate the rule of the best, the wise or the just invites tyranny disguised under those principles. By contrast, a prudently constructed open society constructs institutions to ensure that any regime can be ousted without violence, no matter what higher ends it proclaims itself to be seeking. Couched in the form of extended critiques of Plato and Platonism as well as of Marx and Marxism, Popper's political philosophy has had considerable influence in post-war Europe, East and West.*

1 **Life and works**
2 **Theory of science**
3 **Later ideas**
4 **Democracy, society and individualism**

1 Life and works

Born in Vienna in 1902, the youngest child of a barrister, Karl Raimund Popper was educated at the University of Vienna, where he studied mathematics, music, psychology, physics and philosophy. He taught in secondary school between 1930 and 1936. Apprehension about Nazism persuaded him to emigrate in 1937, to become lecturer in philosophy at Canterbury University College, Christchurch, New Zealand. In January 1946 he became Reader in Logic and Scientific Method at the London School of Economics, was promoted to professor in 1949, and retired from full-time teaching in 1969. Among many honours, he was knighted in 1965, elected Fellow of the Royal Society in 1976, and made a Companion of Honour in 1982.

After a specialized start in the philosophy of science, Popper revealed himself as a philosopher of wide reach, making contributions across the spectrum from Presocratic studies to modern logic, from politics to probability, and from the mind–body problem to the interpretation of quantum theory. With all of his books in print, and translated into many languages, Popper's is one of the most discussed philosophies of the century. Yet, he insisted, his ideas are systematically misunderstood and misrepresented; this led him to devote uncommon energy to issues of interpretation and commentary on his own work.

Popper published three major works between 1935 and 1945. The first, *Logik der Forschung* (1935), his theory of science, appeared in English as *The Logic of Scientific Discovery* only in 1959. The second, *The Poverty of Historicism* (1957), first appeared in 1944–5 and extended his theory of science to history and society, severely criticizing the notion of historical laws. The third, *The Open Society and Its Enemies* (1945), is a two-volume treatise on the philosophy of history, politics and society.

Popper's other principal works consist of two collections of major papers, *Conjectures and Refutations* (1962), and *Objective Knowledge* (1972); a Library of Living Philosophers volume (1974) containing an intellectual autobiography and a set of replies to his critics, the former appearing separately as *Unended Quest* (1976); a collaboration with Sir John Eccles on a study of the mind–body problem, *The Self and Its Brain* (1977); *Die Beiden Grundprobleme der Erkenntnistheorie* (The Two Basic Problems of the Theory of Knowledge) (1979), the extant fragment of the book he was writing before *Logik der Forschung* superseded it; and the long-delayed *Postscript to the Logic of Scientific Discovery* (1982–3), much of which dates from the period 1955–7. Most of these books have seen multiple editions, involving sometimes minor and sometimes major changes. Throughout his career Popper also produced many original papers on diverse topics, and lectured all over the world. His manuscripts and correspondence fill some 450 archive cartons at the Hoover Institution, Stanford University.

2 Theory of science

Two problems structure Popper's theory of science: he calls them 'the problem of induction' and 'the problem of demarcation'. The problem of induction can be formulated: what relation holds between theoretical knowledge and experience? The problem of demarcation can be formulated: what distinguishes science from metaphysics as well as from logic and mathematics?

The received answers to these problems are: we get knowledge from experience by means of induction, that is, by inferring universal theories from accumulations of particular facts; and the inductive method demarcates science from metaphysics as well as from logic and mathematics. However, HUME showed that inductive inferences are invalid, hence the *problem* of induction: either we get knowledge from experience by invalid means (irrationalism) or we do not get any at all (scepticism); and induction collapses as a demarcation criterion (see DEMARCATION PROBLEM §1; INDUCTION, EPISTEMIC ISSUES IN).

In Part I of *The Logic of Scientific Discovery*, Popper's solutions to these two problems are set out and shown to converge: knowledge results when we accept statements describing experience that contradict and hence refute our hypotheses; thus a deductive rather than an inductive relation holds between theoretical knowledge and experience. Experience teaches us by correcting our errors. Only hypotheses *falsifiable* by experience should count as scientific. There is no need for the inductive leap that Hume thought illogical but unavoidable; and the Hobson's choice between irrationalism or scepticism is avoided. To the question, 'where do hypotheses come from, if not inductively from experience?', Popper answers, like Francis Bacon, that they come from our propensity to guess (see BACON, F. §6); in any case they cannot come from observation alone because there is no observation without hypotheses. Hypotheses are both logically and psychologically prior to observation. We are theorizing all the time in order to navigate in the world, and our encounters with negative evidence are the bumps that deliver information about the shape of reality.

The Logic of Scientific Discovery is dialectical in style, dealing with the traditional alternatives and the objections to each idea as it goes along. It is remarkable how frequently critics rediscover objections set out and answered in the book. The commonest objection is that, just as no amount of

experience will conclusively verify a statement, so no amount of experience will conclusively falsify it. To answer this objection Popper points to a logical asymmetry. A universal statement cannot be derived from or verified by singular statements, no matter how many are marshalled. It can, however, be contradicted by one singular statement. The logic of falsification is the issue; conclusiveness is a red herring. Another argument, to the effect that the force of falsifying evidence can always be evaded by *ad hoc* definition or simple refusal to countenance it, Popper finds insuperable. The way to proceed, he concludes, is to entrench falsifiability in a methodology.

For Popper, a methodology is a policy decision governing action and embodied in norms or 'methodological rules'. Our decisions concern which course of action will best foster our aims. Thus falsificationism is made into a supreme rule to the effect that the 'rules of scientific procedure must be designed in such a way that they do not protect any statement in science against falsification' ([1935] 1959: 54). The rule for causality is typical of the small number offered: 'we are not to abandon the search for universal laws and for a coherent theoretical system, nor ever to give up our attempts to explain causally any kind of event we can describe' ([1935] 1959: 61). A broad epistemological ambition is revealed when Popper generalizes: 'It might indeed be said that the majority of problems of theoretical philosophy, and the most interesting ones, can be reinterpreted...as problems of method' ([1935] 1959: 56) (see SCIENTIFIC METHOD §2).

Throughout *The Logic of Scientific Discovery*, Popper defines his position by debate and contrast with logical positivist positions regarding meaning, and with two traditional views regarding science, inductivism and the conventionalism of POINCARÉ and DUHEM (see CONVENTIONALISM §1; LOGICAL POSITIVISM §4). It is notable that, like the logical positivists, Popper expresses unbounded respect for science. Unlike them, he grants a constructive (historical) role to metaphysics in science, seen as directly descended from the earliest Greek speculations about the nature of the world. The demarcation between science and metaphysics is thus a matter for decision, not a discovery about the nature of things. Popper's attacks on central logical positivist contentions contributed to the demise of that movement.

Popper respects conventionalism as self-contained, defensible and most likely consistent. His objection is that it risks treating obsolete or floundering science as incontrovertible truth. Yet Popper is a conventionalist in one respect: methodology. As opposed to the 'methodological naturalism' of the logical positivists, who treat the demarcation between science and metaphysics as a difference existing in the nature of things, or rather, in the nature of language, Popper is a 'methodological conventionalist', proposing rules that embody choices or decisions – which are in turn governed by aims. His demarcation should be judged, Popper maintains, by whether it proves fruitful in furthering the aims of discovering new ideas and new problems.

Part II of *The Logic of Scientific Discovery* consists of chapters on theories, falsifiability, the empirical basis, testability, simplicity, probability, quantum theory and corroboration. Each is an expansion, development and defence of the ideas briefly stated in Part I and parries a particular cluster of critical objections. The chapters on probability and corroboration, for example, deal at length with the objections that the pervasive probability statements of modern science are not falsifiable, and that they measure the strength of our inductive evidence. The chapters endeavour to show how probability statements can be falsified in relevant ways, and how they are better interpreted as statements of frequencies rather than as measures of inductive support.

3 Later ideas

The English translation of *The Logic of Scientific Discovery* is palimpsestic: while translating it Popper intercalated comments, glosses, developments and corrections in new footnotes and appendices, as well as drafting a supplementary work, the three-volume *Postscript* of 1982–3. Opinion differs over whether all this is fully consistent. A case in point is 'The Aim of Science' section of the *Postscript*, published already in 1957, which argues that science aims at satisfactory explanations. It centres around a historical example (Galileo, Kepler, Newton), showing how each theory superseded and explained its predecessor. Satisfactory explanation, in addition to being testable, must fulfil other conditions, making it a rather stronger aim than falsifiability, one that may or may not be the same as the aim of science articulated at the end of *The Logic of Scientific Discovery*, of discovering 'new, deeper and more general problems'.

Certainly Popper acknowledges some changes of view. Since metaphysical dispute surrounded the concept of truth, he carefully avoided using it in *The Logic of Scientific Discovery*, making do with logical relations (implication, tautology, contradiction). Later, convinced by Tarski's work, he made free use of the concept of truth and of getting nearer to the truth (verisimilitude). Again, his criticisms of conventionalism in *The Logic of Scientific Discovery* were methodological. In later years they were also openly

metaphysical, as Popper espoused a robust realism and indeterminism (1982b, 1983b).

Throughout *The Logic of Scientific Discovery* there are Darwinian metaphors – the struggle for survival among theoretical systems, natural selection, fitness to survive – although, in the last pages of the book, the view that science is an instrument of biological adaptation is rejected. This Darwinian leitmotif became a controversial issue in Popper's later work: did evolutionary biology yield to the same methodological analysis as physics? Were the central ideas of DARWIN or of the modern synthesis falsifiable? To complicate matters, Popper changed his mind on this central question, viewing Darwinism as a historical hypothesis in *Objective Knowledge*, and as an unfalsifiable near tautology in *Unended Quest*. In contrast to his earlier view, Popper also began to advocate an evolutionary epistemology, that is, an attempt to explain the very existence of a truth-seeking science within the framework of natural selection, in effect to give a biological twist to Kant's problem, 'How is knowledge possible?' His second Herbert Spencer Lecture (1975) treats both endosomatic and exosomatic adaptations as forms of knowledge. Biological considerations also weigh heavily in Popper's part of *The Self and Its Brain*. Pitting himself against the reductionist materialism of most contemporary mind–body specialists, Popper there marshalled mainly indirect arguments for an interactive pluralism.

Reflections on biology seem to have been behind a bold new metaphysical initiative of 1967–8, especially the provocatively entitled 'Epistemology Without a Knowing Subject' (1972: ch. 3). Distinguishing the world of physical things from the world of mental things, Popper argued that objective knowledge is located in neither, but in 'World 3' – the world of humanly created objective contents of thought. Such intellectual products have an objective existence: theories, problems, problem-situations, theoretical situations and critical arguments have properties and logical interrelations that lack physical or mental analogues. Stored knowledge exists even if no living person retrieves it. Critics of World 3 find some of its consequences counterintuitive: for example, it contains not only all truths, but also all falsehoods, which thus have an equally objective 'existence'.

In the late 1940s Popper published a particularly forceful and elegant system of natural deduction that is of considerable interest, both intrinsically and because in it he views deductive logic as the *organon* of criticism (1947a, 1947b). He reports that while he has repaired some defects in it, he never brought it to completion. His technical attentions became focused on the theory of probability, to which he had already contributed in *The Logic of Scientific Discovery*. The result was a highly abstract axiomatic system that made no explicit assumptions about any logical relations among the elements on which probability is defined, and thereby established that probability is a genuine generalization of deducibility. The system is open to many new interpretations of probability statements. A particularly important one, superseding the frequency interpretation of *The Logic of Scientific Discovery*, views probabilities as measures of the 'propensities' of states of the world to develop one way rather than another. In the *Postscript* (1982a) and *A World of Propensities*, this view was developed into a striking new metaphysics (see PROBABILITY, INTER-PRETATIONS OF §4).

4 Democracy, society and individualism

In *Unended Quest*, Popper recounts how, as a politically conscious adolescent, he flirted with Communism. He was quickly disillusioned when he judged Communist actions irresponsible in leading to the deaths of some demonstrators. (Individual autonomy, responsibility, Socratic fallibilism and the obligation to reduce suffering are the keynotes of his scattered remarks about ethics.) In the 1920s he began a critique of Marx and Marxism, first tried out in a talk of 1935, 'The Poverty of Historicism'. 'Historicism' is Popper's name for the idea that there are inexorable laws of historical development: the demand that if natural science can predict eclipses then social science ought to be able to predict political revolutions. In a highly systematic way, Popper set out to show how both those who think the social sciences are not at all like the natural sciences (the 'anti-naturalists') and those who think the social sciences very like the natural sciences (the 'naturalists'), share the aim of predicting history. Both recommend the methodology of historicism, which he sees as impoverished and inclined to treat societies as wholes responding to the pressures of inchoate social forces (see HISTORICISM).

Instead, Popper recommends 'methodological individualism': rules to the effect that the behaviour and actions of collectives should be explained by the behaviour of human individuals acting appropriately to the logic of their social situation as best they can and as best they see it. Not only was the alternative unfruitful, he argued, but the best social explanations of Plato and Marx were individualist. What look like holistic phenomena are to be explained as the 'unintended consequences' of such individual actions reverberating through the social set-up (see HOLISM AND INDIVIDUALISM IN HISTORY AND SOCIAL SCIENCE §1).

According to methodological individualism, social

theories are tested not by historical predictions, which are little more than prophecies, Popper argues, but by attempts to invent institutions that correct social faults by social engineering. Man-made social institutions are hypotheses in action, he says. If we are to refute these hypotheses we need to avoid complicating matters with large-scale experiments, or too many at once, otherwise assessment will be impossible. For we must also reckon with the interference factor of 'the Oedipus effect', that is, the way in which a prediction about the future becomes an altering factor in the situation as human beings are aware of it, thus 'interfering' with the outcome.

The Open Society and Its Enemies was a 'truly unintended consequence' of an attempt to expand aspects of *The Poverty of Historicism* to satisfy puzzled friends. When it grew too large, Popper made it a separate work. On publication in 1945 it elevated him from academic obscurity to academic fame. He became a controversial and well-known public intellectual.

Described modestly as a 'critical introduction to the philosophy of politics and of history', *The Open Society* had become, in the seven years of its gestation, a major treatise on the intellectual and social ills of the time, offering an explanation of how totalitarianism had gained intellectual respectability and how purging post-war society of it would involve rethinking politics, education and social morality. Its title refers to two ideal-types used throughout. A closed society is one which takes a magical or tabooistic attitude to tradition and custom, which does not differentiate between nature and convention. An open society marks that difference and confronts its members with personal decisions and the opportunity to reflect rationally on them. Heraclitus, Aristotle and Hegel are briefly discussed, but the book's two intellectual anti-heroes are PLATO in volume 1 and MARX in volume 2.

The volume entitled 'The Spell of Plato' answers two questions: first, why Plato espoused totalitarian ideas and second, why students of Plato have whitewashed that fact and beautified him. The answer to the first question, a deeply sympathetic piece of writing, sketches a portrait of the young Plato contemplating with dismay the closed world of tribal Athens giving way to a more liberal and open society, with loss of social privilege and chaos arriving hand in hand. Popper insists on the brilliance of Plato's sociological analysis of the causes of change and of his proposals to arrest it and staunch the deterioration it brings. In answer to the second, Popper courts controversy by suggesting that Plato's intellectual followers, flattered by the role offered them, engaged in a long-running *trahison des clercs* by presenting as liberal and enlightened the doctrine of the philosopher king.

To expose the commitment of Plato and Platonists to totalitarianism, Popper had to clarify our ideals of a liberal and democratic social order and show how Plato indulges in persuasive definitions, while attempting to show that his totalitarian *Republic* is 'just'. (Popper also mounts a general attack on the idea that philosophy should seek out the essence of universal words such as justice, democracy and tyranny. He argues that natural science uses the methodology of nominalism, not of essentialism, and social science and philosophy would do well to follow suit.) Mindful of Plato's distaste for majority rule, as rule of the mob or rule of the worst, Popper carefully discusses tyranny, and concludes that the problem is not the question of what is popular, for certain kinds of tyrants are very popular and could easily be elected. So an open and liberal society is not to be identified with a popularly elected government. No more is it a matter of what is just, good or best, for none of these offers insurance against tyranny in their name. In line with his theory of science, and of knowledge generally, he proposes a *via negativa*. The issue is not what regime we want, but what to do about ones we do not want. The problem with tyranny is that the citizens have no peaceful way in which to rid themselves of it, should they want to. Popper proposes a now famous and generally endorsed criterion for democracy as that political system which permits the citizens to rid themselves of an unwanted government without the need to resort to violence. He exposes Plato's question, 'Who should rule?', and all similar discussions of sovereignty as subject to paradoxes because the question permits an inconsistency to develop between the statement designating the ruler (for example, the best or wisest should rule) and what the ruler commands (for example, the best or wisest may then tell us: obey the majority, or the powerful). Popper noticed that the question carries the authoritarian implication that whoever is so named is *entitled* to rule. He replaces them with the practical question 'how can we rid ourselves of bad governments without violence?', with its implication that rulers are on permanent parole. Popper's is a fundamentally pessimistic view that all governments are to one extent or the other incompetent and potentially criminal in their misbehaviour, and that only a political system which allows them to govern at the sufferance of citizens who can withdraw their support readily is one with more or less effective checks against abuse. Even so, the fallibility of our institutional hypotheses enjoin upon us an eternal vigilance.

The second volume, 'The High Tide of Prophecy,

Hegel and Marx', argues that the prophetic tendency in Heraclitus and Plato produced in Hegel a damaging incoherence and charlatanry, and in Marx a project for the scientific study of society that, despite noble emancipating aims, foundered, especially among the followers, on the confusion of prediction with unscientific historical prophecy and hence on a fundamental misconstruction of scientific method. The chapters on Marx are among the most penetrating commentaries ever written on him, and are both sympathetic in their appreciation and unremitting in their criticism. Although Popper clearly regards Plato as the deeper thinker, he argues that Marx has much to teach us about how moral and emancipatory impulses can go awry. Marxists and the radical experimenters of the Soviet Union are judged harshly, as are all forms of nationalism.

Appearing in 1945 just after the end of the war, a war that had forged an alliance with the Soviet Union, the book antagonized many powerful intellectual interest groups. Platonists were taken aback to be accused of being apologists for totalitarian tendencies in Plato (even though Popper was not the first to point these out) and Marxists were equally affronted. The aftermath was strange. Although Popper was at first widely read and indignantly denounced, it later became bad form among Marxists and classicists to mention him by name. Yet, to an extraordinary extent, in the following decades his work set the agenda for apologetic Platonists, Hegelians and Marxists. In many cases a book or article makes most sense when seen as covertly engaged in trying to confute some point Popper made in *The Open Society*.

As a teacher of philosophy, Popper displayed ambivalence: philosophical problems emerge from science (1962: ch. 2), so the best preparation was an education in a first-order subject, preferably scientific. In the classroom, he had the charisma of one possessed by intellectual problems, thinking about them all the time. In lecture or seminar he could be intellectually fierce and confrontational, in personal encounter sweet and encouraging. He regularly displayed an astonishingly quick intuitive grasp of the logic of any position presented to him, even from the most meagre of clues, and an eagerness to strengthen and elaborate on it before setting about criticizing it. He thus exemplified the values he advocated: intellectual seriousness, personal responsibility and disinterestedness, that is, doing justice to ideas regardless of their temporary embodiment. The failure of much critical commentary to meet these standards lies behind his complaint of misrepresentation. But there are also other reasons. If Popper is correct, not only is much in the traditional way of doing philosophy misdirected, but even the questions are wrongly put. Any attempt to map Popper's ideas into traditionally oriented discussions risks misrepresentation. The frequent practice of reconstructing Popper's philosophy timelessly, plucking materials from works published as far apart as fifty years, flies in the face of his emphasis on the structuring role of problems and problem-situations in all intellectual activity, particularly inquiry. To do justice to the originality and creativity of his work, scholarship needs in the first instance to respect its intellectual context of production.

See also: CARNAP, R.; DISCOVERY, LOGIC OF; EXPLANATION IN HISTORY AND SOCIAL SCIENCE; FALLIBILISM; INDUCTIVE INFERENCE; LAKATOS, I.; LIBERALISM; MEANING AND VERIFICATION; NATURAL DEDUCTION, TABLEAU AND SEQUENT SYSTEMS; SCIENTIFIC REALISM AND ANTIREALISM; VIENNA CIRCLE

List of works

Popper, K.R. (1935) *Logik der Forschung* (The Logic of Research), Vienna: Springer; trans. *The Logic of Scientific Discovery*, London: Hutchinson, 1959. (Crisp and incisive statement of his classic ideas on philosophy of science and of epistemology. The English translation contains additional material, as explained in §3.)

—— (1945) *The Open Society and Its Enemies*, London: Routledge. (A critical introduction to the philosophy of history and of politics that takes Plato, Hegel and Marx to task for their anti-democratic and anti-critical tendencies.)

—— (1947a) 'New Foundations for Logic', *Mind* 56: 193–235, with corrections in (1948) 57: 69–70. (A system of natural deduction.)

—— (1947b) 'Logic Without Assumptions', *Proceedings of the Aristotelian Society*, 48: 251–92. (Investigates the notion of deducibility and the foundations of logic in language.)

—— (1957) *The Poverty of Historicism*, London: Routledge. (States and rebuts the arguments for belief in inexorable laws of human destiny.)

—— (1962) *Conjectures and Refutations*, London: Routledge. (A wide-ranging collection of essays from the period 1940–62, including several that have become classics.)

—— (1972) *Objective Knowledge*, Oxford: Clarendon Press. (A collection of essays from 1948–72, many being extensions of and alterations to his original philosophy of science and epistemology.)

—— (1975) 'The Rationality of Scientific Revolutions', in R. Harré (ed.) *Problems of Scientific Revolutions*, Oxford: Clarendon Press, 72–101.

(Popper's answer to Kuhn's irrationalist view of scientific revolutions.)

—— (1976) *Unended Quest*, London: Fontana. (Intellectual autobiography; approachable and written with considerable verve.)

Popper, K.R. and Eccles, J.C. (1977) *The Self and Its Brain*, Berlin: Springer. (Joins a fellow Nobelist in proposing an evolutionist and interactionist model of the mind–body problem.)

Popper, K.R. (1979) *Die Beiden Grundprobleme der Erkenntnistheorie* (The Two Basic Problems of the Theory of Knowledge), Tübingen: Mohr. (All that survives of the book Popper was working on when he turned instead to The Logic of Scientific Discovery.)

—— (1982a) *Quantum Theory and the Schism in Physics*, London: Hutchinson. (Reflections on problems of the interpretation of quantum mechanics; part II of the *Postscript*.)

—— (1982b) *The Open Universe*, London: Hutchinson. (Statement of Popper's metaphysical indeterminism; part III of the *Postscript*.)

—— (1983) *Realism and the Aim of Science*, London: Hutchinson. (Long commentary on many of the issues originally discussed in The Logic of Scientific Discovery and their reception; part I of the Postscript.)

Popper, K.R. and Miller, D. (1983) 'A Proof of the Impossibility of Inductive Probability', *Nature* 302: 687–8. (Proof that evidence, far from supporting a hypothesis, undermines the statement of the evidence and hence the hypothesis itself.)

Popper, K.R. (1987) 'Why Probabilistic Support is Not Inductive', *Philosophical Transactions of the Royal Society of London*, A321: 569–91. (Restatement and elaboration of Popper and Miller (1983).)

—— (1990) *A World of Propensities*, Bristol: Thoemmes. (The propensity interpretation of probability statements developed as a full-blown metaphysics.)

—— (1992) *In Search of a Better World*, London: Routledge. (Speeches and address to general audiences.)

—— (1994a) *Knowledge and the Body–Mind Problem*, London: Routledge. (Essays from his last thirty years on the mind–body problem and other matters.)

—— (1994b) *The Myth of the Framework*, London: Routledge. (Essays from his last thirty years on the philosophy of physical and social science.)

Schilpp, P.A. (ed.) (1974) *The Philosophy of Karl Popper*, La Salle, IL: Open Court. (Two volumes, containing Popper's intellectual autobiography, 33 critical essays and 'Replies to My Critics', as well as a complete bibliography up 1973.)

Adorno, T.W. *et al.* (1976) *The Positivist Dispute in German Sociology*, London: Heinemann. (Contains Popper's 'The Logic of the Social Sciences' and 'Revolution or Reform?'.)

References and further reading

Ackermann, R. (1976) *The Philosophy of Karl Popper*, Amherst, MA: University of Massachusetts Press. (A review and positive evaluation of Popper's philosophy of science.)
—— (1993) *A Philosopher's Apprentice*, Amsterdam: Rodopi. (An idiosyncratic reminiscence of studying with Popper.)
Albert, H. (1985) *Treatise on Critical Reason*, Princeton, NJ: Princeton University Press. (Critical rationalism as expounded by a leading German Popperian.)
Andersson, G. (1994) *Kuhn's, Lakatos's, and Feyerabend's Criticism of Critical Rationalism*, Leiden: E.J. Brill. (Critical rationalism defended against its major critics.)
Bartley, W.W., III (1962) *The Retreat to Commitment*, New York: Knopf. (An influential attempt to improve upon Popper's critical rationalism.)
—— (1976–82) 'Critical Study: The Philosophy of Karl Popper: Parts I, II and III', *Philosophia* 6: 463–94; 7: 676–716; 12: 121–221. (A sympathetic critical essay on the Schilpp volume (1974).)
Berkson, W. and Wettersten, J. (1984) *Learning from Error*, La Salle, IL: Open Court. (An investigation into the origin of Popper's ideas in his early psychological researches.)
Bunge, M. (ed.) (1964) *The Critical Approach to Science and Philosophy*, New York: Free Press. (The first collection of essays discussing Popper's ideas.)
Burke, T.E. (1983) *The Philosophy of Popper*, Manchester: Manchester University Press. (Critical commentary on a few selected topics. Popper is said to have set the agenda in a number of fields. Wittgenstein gets the worse of some comparative discussions.)
Gellner, E. (1985) 'Positivism Against Hegelianism', in *Relativism and the Social Sciences*, Cambridge University Press. (A robust critical review of the metaphysical issues between Popper and his idealist critics.)
Hacohen, M.H. (1993) 'The Making of the Open Society: Karl Popper, Philosophy and Politics in Interwar Vienna', unpublished Ph.D. dissertation, Columbia University. (A lengthy attempt to relate Popper's work to the Viennese context.)
Hattiangadi, J.N. (1978–9) 'The Structure of Problems, Parts I and II', in *Philosophy of the Social Sciences*, vol. 8, 345–65; vol. 9, 49–76. (Argues that

solving problems is a sufficient aim for science and that the history of science is lines of debate.)
Jarvie, I.C. (1972) *Concepts and Society*, London: Routledge. (A Popperian philosophy of the social.)
Jarvie, I.C. and Shearmur, J. (eds) (1996–7) *Philosophy of the Social Sciences*, special issues, 26 (4) and 27 (1). (In celebration of the 50th anniversary of the publication of *The Open Society and its Enemies* containing eight papers on the origins, impact and contemporary relevance of Popper's great book.)
Johansson, I. (1975) *A Critique of Karl Popper's Methodology*, Stockholm: Akademiforlaget. (A vigorous assault on Popper's methodology.)
Leblanc, H. (1989) 'Popper's Formal Contributions to Probability Theory', in *Perspectives on Psychologism*, The Hague: Nijhoff, 341–67. (An important evaluation of Popper's technical contribution.)
Levinson, P. (ed.) (1982) *In Pursuit of Truth*, Atlantic Highlands, NJ: Humanities. (A second collective volume in Popper's honour.)
Magee, B. (1973) *Popper*, London: Fontana/Collins. (The first comprehensive exposition for the general reader.)
Miller, D. (1994) *Critical Rationalism: Restatement and Defence*, La Salle, IL: Open Court. (Sharp and forceful, including discussion of critical issues surrounding truth and probability.)
Munz, P. (1985) *Our Knowledge of the Growth of Knowledge*, London: Routledge. (Wittgenstein's theory of knowledge is criticized as relativist, Popper's evolutionary view is defended.)
O'Hear, A. (1980) *Karl Popper*, London: Routledge. (Critical account that treats Popper timelessly and within the received framework of academic philosophy and, unsurprisingly, vindicates Wittgenstein.)
—— (ed.) (1995) *Karl Popper: Philosophy and Problems*, Cambridge: Cambridge University Press. (Fifteen Royal Institute of Philosophy lectures that range widely over Popper's work.)
Pralong, S. and Jarvie, I.C. (eds) (1997) *Popper's Open Society After 50 Years*, London: Routledge. (The proceedings of a Prague conference originally organized by Ernest Gellner, to assess Popper's work in the context of the opening up of former Iron Curtain countries.)
Radnitzky, G. (1968) *Contemporary Schools of Metascience*, Goteborg: Akademiforlaget. (A survey of the field from a Popperian 'criticist' perspective.)
Schroeder-Heister, P. (1984) 'Popper's Theory of Deductive Inference and the Concept of a Logical Constant', *History and Philosophy of Logic* 5: 79–110. (Reconstructs Popper's ideas on logic so as to take account of criticism.)
Simkin, C. (1993) *Popper's Views on Natural and Social Science*, Leiden: Brill. (An accurate and

mildly critical account by a colleague from the New Zealand days.)

Stove, D. (1981) *Popper and After. Four Modern Irrationalists*, Oxford: Pergamon. (A scathing, if less than persuasive, attack.)

Wettersten, J. (1992) *The Roots of Critical Rationalism*, Amsterdam: Rodopi. (Argues that tensions in Popper's work and among his followers go back to the philosophical and psychological traditions he was attempting to reconcile.)

Williams, D.E. (1989) *Truth, Hope and Power: The Thought of Karl Popper*, Toronto, Ont.: University of Toronto Press. (An ambitious commentary that perhaps overreaches its grasp.)

Wisdom, J.O. (1952) *Foundations of Inference in Natural Science*, London: Methuen. (One of the earliest and best expositions of Popper's ideas in English.)

IAN C. JARVIE

POPULATION AND ETHICS

Ethical concern with population policies and with the issue of optimal population size is, generally speaking, a modern phenomenon. Although the first divine injunction of the Bible is 'be fertile and multiply', systematic theoretical interest in the normative aspects of demography has become associated largely with recent developments which have provided humanity with unprecedented control over population size, mainly through medical and economic means. Once the determination of the number of people in the world is no longer a natural given fact, but rather a matter of individual or social choice, it becomes subject to moral evaluation.

However, the extension of traditional ethical principles to issues of population policies is bedevilled by paradoxes. The principle of utility, the ideal of self-perfection, the idea of a contract as a basis for political legitimacy and social justice, the notion of natural or human rights, and the principle of respect for persons – all these presuppose the existence of human beings whose interests, welfare, rights and dignity are to be protected and promoted. But population policies deal with the creation of people and the decision concerning their number. They relate to the creation of the very conditions for the application of ethical principles.

1 'The population bomb'
2 Optimum population size
3 Means of implementation

1 'The population bomb'

The number of people now living is larger than the number who have ever lived in all past generations of humanity taken together. This striking fact of absolute numbers stands alongside a rate of growth which now doubles the population of the world every thirty-five years. Sharp awareness of the threat that these facts and trends present goes back to the early nineteenth century, primarily to the work of Thomas Malthus, who argued that the number of people multiplies in geometric progression while the resources which support their life can be expected to grow at most in arithmetic progression. The threat of overpopulation arising from this gap in rates of growth can be checked either by factors like death from starvation, illness and war, or by preventive measures such as controlling the number of births. Following Malthus, it is commonly believed that there is an ethical asymmetry between the two kinds of checks: the premature death of living people is morally worse than the non-creation of new people. Thus, a rise in life expectancy is generally considered a blessing, while an increase in births is treated as a menace. However, balancing world population is particularly problematic, since overpopulation is primarily due to the decrease in death rates rather than the increase in birth rates. Consequently, even if very restrictive population policies were implemented (such as zero population growth), many decades would pass before the number of births and the number of deaths balanced one other.

Concern with the danger of overpopulation is historically and analytically associated with two major normative issues, themselves interdependent: the just distribution of welfare across generations (usually referred to as the problem of savings); and responsibility for the environment (conservation). Thus, since the 1920s economists have attempted to fix optimum population size in economic terms, such as the highest income per capita across generations, and theories of justice (particularly since RAWLS) have tackled the population question through the principles of justice applied intergenerationally (see FUTURE GENERATIONS, OBLIGATIONS TO; JUSTICE). Meanwhile, environmentalists have argued over the last few decades that the number of people in the world should be limited in terms of the carrying capacity of the planet and respect for the integrity of the natural environment, either for the sake of future people ('shallow ecology') or for its own sake ('deep ecology') (see ENVIRONMENTAL ETHICS). However, one can take the opposite approach and rather than subordinate the issue of population to economic or ecological considerations, treat the existence and number of people as the foundation for both economic justice and environmental policies. Thus, for instance, one may take the existence of a growing population as a *given* fact which should dictate a new approach to the natural environment in which the wilderness will have a radically weakened status.

The metaphors of 'the population bomb' and 'population explosion' typically convey a morally negative evaluation of the increase in the number of human beings. However, beyond the empirical debate between the 'alarmist', neo-Malthusian view and its opponents who see no danger in population growth as such, a critical philosophical analysis of the issue raises the following questions. Is the size of world population an ethical issue at all? If it is, what are the normative criteria for determining the 'right' (or optimal) size? If such criteria can be formulated and justified, what are the ethical constraints in implementing suitable policies for the attainment of this size?

2 Optimum population size

The question of optimal population size touches upon the deepest problems concerning the nature of value: is value ascribed impersonally to 'the world', or only to actual human beings whose very existence is presupposed by any evaluation? The first view (impersonalism) treats the population issue as a function of a value or an end considered in abstraction. The ideal number of people is that which would promote that end to the maximal degree. This could be average or total utility, the foundation of a Kantian 'kingdom of ends', or the establishment of a Marxian classless society. The second view (commonly called 'person-affecting') holds that moral evaluation applies only to existing human beings and hence cannot serve to assess the value of any particular number of human beings, indeed not even of the very existence of humanity. According to this view, 'good' is always 'good *for*', and consequently one cannot say that to be born (or not to be born) is a morally good (or bad) thing. Increasing or reducing the number of future people cannot in the person-affecting view be considered morally desirable (or obligatory) since the interests of no particular people are promoted or rights of particular persons respected either by bringing them into the world or by preventing them from coming into existence.

The two views face difficult problems, which have been extensively discussed by Derek Parfit (1984). Take first utilitarianism, which has been the most popular version of impersonalism in the context of population questions (see UTILITARIANISM). Total utilitarianism leads to the so-called 'repugnant con-

clusion', according to which the world would be overcrowded with people whose extremely low quality of life is offset by their huge number, thus achieving the highest value of total utility. Average utility fares no better, since it recommends a policy which on the one hand would make it obligatory to bring a new child into the world whose happiness would be a little above the current average, and on the other hand would prohibit the addition of extra people whose standard of living would be even slightly below that enjoyed by present people. Negative utilitarianism, which aims at the overall reduction of pain rather than the promotion of happiness, could lead to the absurd ideal of total abstention from procreation.

Turning from these impersonal criteria to the person-affecting view, we are confronted by the problem of identity. We cannot say that population policies serve the interests or the welfare of future people since they themselves directly and indirectly affect the identity of those people. Thus, if we decide on a restrictive population policy, for example, by introducing family planning programmes, the people who are actually going to be born are not the same as those who would have been born had we abstained from interfering in people's reproductive choices. The idea of an optimal population size is therefore logically incoherent. On the one hand, there is the indeterminacy of an ideal based on the combination of two variables; namely, 'maximum happiness to maximum people', which has been shown traditionally to have no unique 'solution', as it can be achieved equally by raising the amount of happiness or by raising the number of people. On the other hand, there is the incommensurability of the respective value of two populations consisting of different individuals; namely, the problem of identity, in which case the person-affecting view makes it impossible to compare the value of the lives of alternative sets of people.

Other philosophers have noted the special difficulties incurred in applying contract theory to the issue of population. These derive from the problem of representation in Rawls' 'original position': who takes part in the initial contract? All possible people (but can these be even theoretically identified?)? All actual people (but their number is exactly the issue to be decided by the contract)? Representatives of each generation, or rather a representative of one particular generation, who does not know which generation it is? Contractors negotiating their coming into being, their very existence, is an idea which leads to interesting paradoxes that have been discussed primarily by John Rawls (1971) and his critics (see CONTRACTARIANISM §7).

Our intuitions concerning optimal population size are also indeterminate. Beyond some clear upper and lower limits of over- and underpopulation, we do not have any firm beliefs as to the right balance between the quantity and quality of human lives. Furthermore, our preferences concerning numbers are typically 'adaptive', that is to say they are themselves formed and affected by the size of population to which we belong. We thus tend to project our own preferences on our descendants, assuming (without justification) that they would not want to live in a more crowded environment than we did. From this welfarist perspective, optimal population size is a myth and the population issue lies in principle beyond the scope of ethics. Yet, we can be sure that future generations are going to have some basic needs and wants which will be hard to fulfil if the rate of population growth remains unchecked. This in most views provides a moral justification for control measures.

3 Means of implementation

Even if there are criteria for fixing a desired population size, all philosophers agree that there are constraints on their implementation. One fundamental problem belongs to distributive justice: how should the burden of achieving the demographic goal be distributed, both within the present generation and between generations? Unlike the abstract issue of optimal population size, which deals with future (possible) people, the implementation of population policies affects actual people and their interests. Thus, for instance, should the burden of curtailing growth fall on all classes equally (as in China where each family is allowed to have no more than one child) or proportionally to the actual (or desired) number of children in a family? Should poor families be compensated when reproductive restraint means that they have fewer working members (an acute problem in the Third World)? Should religious beliefs play a role in deciding differential criteria in the distribution of the burden of birth control? Furthermore, may rich nations make economic aid conditional upon the adoption of family planning programmes? These questions of distributive justice can be tackled in terms of the various theories of justice. But when raised on the intergenerational level they become elusive. The goal of a certain population size can be achieved either by an aggressive policy within, for example, two generations or by a milder one within four. The problem is that full equality in distribution of the burden would require a spread over an indefinite number of generations, which is absurd.

Population policies usually involve a gap between private rights and public interest, and hence require politically enforced coordination (so as to avoid free riders). This is Garrett Hardin's view of the *Tragedy of the Commons* (1968), in which overgrazing can be prevented (for the benefit of everybody) only by state interference. But procreation is usually considered a private matter in which the law should not interfere. Positive means, like enforcing sterilization or legally limiting the number of children, are usually considered immoral. But indirect incentives (positive or negative) through taxation, free birth control or education are acceptable. There is also wide agreement today that a rise in the standard of living, as well as an improvement in the status of women in society and in the family, are both desirable goals in themselves and effective means of restraining population growth.

References and further reading

Barry, B. (1977) 'Justice Between Generations', in P. Hacker and J. Raz (eds) *Law, Morality, and Society*, Oxford: Clarendon Press. (Deals with the problems of applying traditional theories of justice in the intergenerational sphere.)

Bayles, M. (1980) *Morality and Population Policy*, Tuscaloosa, AL: University of Alabama Press. (A comprehensive discussion of the ethics of population policies and their implementation.)

Dasgupta, P. (1987) 'The Ethical Foundation of Population Policies', in D. Gale Johnson and R.D. Lee (eds) *Population Growth and Economic Development*, Madison, WI: University of Wisconsin Press. (A sophisticated analysis by an economist of the issue of optimum population size.)

* Hardin, G. (1968) 'The Tragedy of the Commons', *Science* 162 (December): 1243–8. (A classic presentation of the problem of coordination in population policies.)

Hartmann, B. (1987) *Reproductive Rights and Wrongs: The Global Politics of Population Control and Contraceptive Choice*, New York: Harper & Row. (A feminist point of view of the subject.)

Heyd, D. (1992) *Genethics: Moral Issues in the Creation of People*, Berkeley, CA: University of California Press. (A radically person-affecting view; see in particular chapter 5.)

Narveson, J. (1967) 'Utilitarianism and New Generations', *Mind* 76 (1): 62–72. (The first modern discussion of the problems of applying utilitarian principles to population issues.)

Parfit, D. (1984) *Reasons and Persons*, Oxford: Clarendon Press. part IV. (Extensive discussion of the paradoxes of population; includes a critique of the person-affecting view.)

* Rawls, J. (1971) *A Theory of Justice*, Cambridge, MA.: Harvard University Press, sections 44–5. (The

application of the theory of justice to future generations, particularly in the issue of savings.)

Sikora, R.I. and Barry, B. (eds) (1979) *Obligations to Future Generations*, Philadelphia, PA: Temple University Press. (The best collection of essays on the subject.)

Singer, P. (1976) 'A Utilitarian Population Principle', in M. Bayles (ed.) *Ethics and Population*, Cambridge, MA: Schenkman. (A sophisticated person-affecting view.)

DAVID HEYD

POPULISM, RUSSIAN

see HERZEN, ALEKSANDR IVANOVICH; LAVROV, PËTR LAVROVICH; MIKHAILOVSKII, NIKOLAI KONSTANTINOVICH

PORNOGRAPHY

There are three main questions about pornography. (1) How is pornography to be defined? Some definitions include the contention that it is morally wrong, while others define it neutrally in terms of its content and function. (2) Why is it wrong? Some accounts see the moral wrong of pornography in its tendency to corrupt individuals or to have detrimental effects on the morality of society; other accounts declare pornography to be objectionable only in so far as it causes physical harm to those involved in its production, or offence to unwilling observers. (3) Should pornography be restricted by law? Controversy here centres around whether the law should be used to discourage immorality, and whether the importance of free speech and individual autonomy are such as to rule out legislating against pornography. Here, the pornography debate raises very general questions about law and about autonomy in liberal societies.

1   **What is pornography?**
2   **What is wrong with pornography?**
3   **What justifies legislating against pornography?**

1   What is pornography?

The question appears simple, but it admits of many conflicting answers. Etymologically, 'pornography' means the depiction of women as prostitutes, and although this may now appear an inappropriate definition, some feminists have appealed to it as part of an argument for the legal restriction of pornography. Thus Andrea Dworkin and Catharine MacKinnon (1988) have proposed that pornography be defined as 'the graphic, sexually explicit subordination of women whether in pictures or in words', and they go on to include within the definition representations in which women are presented dehumanized as sexual objects or commodities, or as whores by nature, or as experiencing sexual pleasure in being raped. The definition is contentious for a number of reasons. First, it seems unduly restrictive, since it excludes, for example, gay pornography and child pornography. Moreover, the definition is value-laden. In declaring that pornography definitionally involves the subordination of women, Dworkin and MacKinnon assume that it is morally wrong but this needs to be shown, not simply stated. For these reasons, some writers have proposed a 'neutral' definition of pornography, which aims to identify pornographic material by reference to its degree of sexual explicitness and to leave open the question whether such explicitness is morally objectionable or an appropriate object of legal restriction.

An example of this second approach is the 1979 *Report of the Committee on Obscenity and Film Censorship in England and Wales* ('The Williams Report'). The Report uses the term 'pornography' to refer to 'a book, verse, painting, photograph, film, or some such thing – what may in general be called a *representation*', and proposes that 'a pornographic representation is one that combines two features: it has a certain function or intention, to arouse its audience sexually, and also a certain content, explicit representations of sexual material (organs, postures, activity etc.). A work has to have both this function and this content to be a piece of pornography' (8.2). This definition simply refers to the function and content of representations and leaves questions of morality and of legal restriction to be addressed separately.

However, this definition has also been criticized on the grounds that it does not accurately reflect current usage. Thus, the 1986 Meese Commission in the United States declared that 'the appellation "pornography" is undoubtedly pejorative', and objected to the Williams definition because it did not reflect this fact. Similarly the US Johnson Commission (1970) declined to use the term at all in its legal recommendations, arguing that it appeared to have 'no legal significance and most often denoted subjective disapproval of material rather than its content or effect'.

There is, therefore, considerable controversy surrounding the definition of pornography: in ordinary usage it appears to be a pejorative term, which expresses subjective disapproval of sexually explicit material; but it is argued that to be useful in a legal context it must go beyond the merely subjective and make reference to content and function in a way which is, as far as possible, morally neutral.

2   What is wrong with pornography?

There is also considerable dispute about whether and why pornography is morally wrong, and about whether the nature of any wrongness is sufficient to justify legal restriction or prohibition. Some argue that pornography corrupts those who consume it. Indeed this claim is built into the current British law governing obscenity, which defines material as 'obscene' when it has a 'tendency to deprave and corrupt' those who are likely to read, see or hear it. A similar understanding of the wrong of pornography is implicit in the Dworkin-MacKinnon Ordinance, which construes pornography as a purveyor of sexist images of women and a corrupting influence on society. For them, pornography acts as a kind of moral poison in the societal water supply, and can serve to legitimize contemptuous attitudes towards women, and possibly even sexual violence against them.

In both cases the charge against obscene material generally, and pornographic material in particular, is that it is morally damaging, either to the individuals who consume it or to society in general.

Others, however, eschew reference to moral harm, either because they are sceptical about the very notion, or because they feel that it should not be appealed to in a legal context. Thus, the Williams Report deems pornography to be wrong only in so far as its production involves the infliction of physical harm, or if it causes offence to unwitting and unwilling observers. Moral wrongness is not, in itself, any part of the case against pornography. Indeed, as was noted above, the Williams Report defines pornography simply in terms of sexual explicitness and makes no reference to its moral status.

3   What justifies legislating against pornography?

Not surprisingly, the different definitions of pornography, coupled with different accounts of why it may be objectionable, yield different proposals for legal action. Those who believe that pornography may be restricted because it is morally damaging, either to the consumer or to society more generally, are often accused of paternalism (see PATERNALISM). This is a serious charge because an important guiding principle

of liberal democratic societies is that the state should be neutral between competing conceptions of the good. It should not attempt to impose on its citizens any particular, favoured understanding of the best way to live, nor should it prohibit or discourage actions simply on the grounds that they are believed to be morally undesirable (see LIBERALISM).

Connectedly, the principle of free speech is a very important one in liberal societies, and some have argued that restricting or suppressing pornography offends against that principle (see FREEDOM OF SPEECH). The importance of free speech is often explained by reference to individual autonomy: people can best become autonomous in societies where they are able to develop their own views and opinions, and that requires that they have access to a wide range of opinions and beliefs from which they themselves may choose (see AUTONOMY, ETHICAL).

However, both the argument from neutrality and the argument from free speech have been questioned, most notably by feminists who claim that the free availability of pornography is itself something which undermines the neutrality of the state and denies freedom of speech to certain groups. Thus, it has been suggested that pornography is akin to racist speech: just as racist speech may undermine the self-respect of black people or minority groups, so pornography undermines the self-respect of women and makes it difficult for them to develop autonomy.

This feminist critique of pornography also questions the individualist assumptions of liberal political philosophy. On this understanding, the justification for legislating against pornography is not the moral harm or offence which it causes to specific individuals, but rather the damage which is done to the self-esteem of women as a group.

See also: LAW, LIMITS OF; LIBERALISM; SEXUALITY, PHILOSOPHY OF

References and further reading

Dworkin, A. (1981) *Pornography: Men Possessing Women*, New York: Putnam. (The most influential statement of important feminist objections to pornography.)

* Dworkin, A. and MacKinnon, C. (1988) *Pornography and Civil Rights: A New Day for Women's Equality*, Minneapolis, MN: Organizing Against Pornography. (Contains a statement of the Model Ordinance governing pornography presented to the State of Minneapolis by Dworkin and MacKinnon.)

Dworkin, R. (1985) 'Do We Have a Right to Pornography?', in *A Matter of Principle*, Cambridge, MA: Harvard University Press. (A clearly written philosophical defence of the liberal commitment to free speech in the specific context of the pornography debate.)

Hawkins, G. and Zimring, F.E. (1988) *Pornography in a Free Society*, Cambridge: Cambridge University Press. (A comparative anaysis of three reports on pornography – the American Meese and Johnson Reports, and the British Williams Report.)

MacKinnon, C.A. (1994) *Only Words*, London: HarperCollins. (One of the most recent, and most controversial, statements of feminist objections to pornography.)

* Williams, B. *et al.* (1979) *Report of the Committee on Obscenity and Film Censorship* ('The Williams Report'), Cmnd 7772, London: Her Majesty's Stationery Office; abridged version repr. as B. Williams (ed.) *Obscenity and Film Censorship*, Cambridge: Cambridge University Press, 1981. (A British Report which appeals to John Stuart Mill's harm principle in its recommendations for changes to the laws governing obscenity and film censorship.)

SUSAN MENDUS

PORPHYRY (*c.*233–309 AD)

The late ancient philosopher Porphyry was one of the founders of Neoplatonism. He edited the teachings of Plotinus into the form in which they are now known, clarified them with insights of his own and established them in the thought of his time. But, in reaction to Plotinus, he also advanced the cause of Aristotle's philosophical logic. Indeed, Porphyry is responsible for the resurgence of interest in Aristotle, which continued to the Middle Ages and beyond. Because of Porphyry, later Greek philosophy recovered both its Platonic and its Aristotelian roots, and Neoplatonism aimed to combine inspired thought with academic precision.

He was a scholar of great learning, with interests ranging from literary criticism and history to religion. An example is his defence of vegetarianism, which anticipated the modern debate on ecological preservation. Humans and animals belong to the same family. Seeking to preserve life is a matter of extending philanthropy and respect to all living species, which are our natural siblings. Ideally we ought to display 'harmlessness' even towards plants, except that our bodies, being composite and mortal, need to consume something else for food. Thus we should be ever conscious of the destructive effect that our eating

habits and consumerism have on the creation of which we are part, and should try to keep to a simple lifestyle.

Porphyry's attention to logic, metaphysics and all other topics was driven by his firm belief that reason exercised by pure mind leads to the true essence of things, the One God. Intellectual activity detaches the soul from passions and confusions, and concentrates its activity on the real things. Porphyry attacked Christianity and Gnosticism because he thought they appealed to the irrational. Mysteries and rituals are fitted for those who are unable to practise inward contemplation. Salvation comes to those leading the life of the philosopher-priest.

1   **Life and philosophical conflicts**
2   **Language and metaphysics**
3   **Ethics**
4   **Literary theory**
5   **Influence**

1   Life and philosophical conflicts

Porphyry was born in the ancient Phoenician port of Tyre. His parents were Syrian and he was originally named after his father Malkhos ('king'). He spent many years expanding his general knowledge, and learning the languages (including Hebrew) and religions of the eastern Roman Empire. He then travelled to Athens, one of the two main centres of teaching in the Empire, and became a mature student of the eminent scholar Longinus. According to the vivid descriptions typical of the age, Longinus was a 'living library and walking museum' and the academic's critical attention to detail, clarity of style and erudition left their permanent mark on the keen student. Longinus renamed him 'Porphyry', which in Greek means 'purple', the royal dye for which Tyre was famous.

At the age of thirty, Porphyry went to join PLOTINUS in Rome. His first impression of him was ambivalent: Plotinus was original but could not express himself clearly – 'The seminars were like conversations' and 'The logical coherence of the argument was not made obvious'. Longinus disagreed with Plotinus over the contents of reality, the Platonic Forms. Longinus considered them distinct from the thoughts about them. Plotinus taught that they are identical with thoughts in God's intellect. 'On the third try' Porphyry came to 'understand with difficulty' Plotinus' position, was persuaded and 'tried to rouse in the master the ambition to organize his doctrines' (*Life of Plotinus* 18).

Five years later Porphyry moved away from Rome to Sicily. His own retrospective explanation was that he suffered from depression to the point of contemplating suicide. Recent studies, however, have linked his decision to crises in Plotinus' circle. On the one side, Plotinus' closest spokesman, Amelius, turned increasingly to theurgy as the means to enlightenment, and moved away to Apamea (Syria) (see IAMBLICHUS). On the other, Porphyry disagreed with Plotinus' denigration of Aristotle, especially of his categories of being. Porphyry had concluded that the chief enemy was the irrational appeal of Gnosticism and Christianity (see GNOSTICISM). Hellenic philosophies had to close ranks. During his stay in Sicily Porphyry composed a treatise on the 'harmony of Aristotle and Plato' and wrote the key works that marked the revival of Aristotelian studies. He wrote them in a teachable form, especially the *Introduction* (*Isagōgē*) to logic and a commentary *On Aristotle's Categories* in user-friendly question and answer format. He also wrote the unique philosophical study of vegetarianism, *On Abstinence from Animal Food* (it includes an invaluable history of arguments for and against). Equipped with his knowledge of textual criticism and languages, he published a critical appraisal of Christian doctrines and the Bible (not superseded until modern times), and proved a Zoroastrian book a forgery. Most importantly he kept in touch with Plotinus, who entrusted him with revising his teachings.

Porphyry returned to Rome much later (in the early 280s) – well after Plotinus' solitary death in AD 270 from leprosy. In this period he married, continued his sojourns, wrote commentaries on Plato and treatises on ethical, philological and historical topics, and added to his already considerable reputation as the most lucid and learned scholar. Clarity and concision are indeed Porphyry's traits. He attracted the interest of Iamblichus, who may have visited him. However, he soon disagreed vigorously with Iamblichus' fondness for the supra-rational and they parted company in the 290s. By AD 301 or 305 Porphyry had completed the grand task of editing and publishing Plotinus' teachings in the form in which they are now known – the six *Enneads*. These he prefaced, in the conventional scholastic manner, with the master's biography. Interestingly, Plotinus is presented as the paragon of the true philosopher, who reaches enlightenment through contemplation, not through theurgy, in contrast to Iamblichus. During this latter period Porphyry was invited to the court of the eastern Roman emperor, but may have returned to Rome where he died.

2 Language and metaphysics

For Porphyry, Aristotle and Plato agree once their domains are demarcated. How are they in 'harmony'?

Porphyry's treatise on this is lost but we can extrapolate from other works and fragments, mainly those on Aristotle's logic. First, Porphyry disagreed with Plotinus over the fundamental divisions of things, the categories (see ARISTOTLE §7; CATEGORIES §1). What do we categorize? Our ways of talking (words)? Our ways of thinking (concepts)? Things that exist (beings)? Furthermore, when we form statements and propositions, are the predicates we use, linguistic expressions, concepts, classes, or realities? As Porphyry tells us in the commentary *On Aristotle's Categories*, the Stoics, several Middle Platonists and Plotinus (politely left unnamed in Porphyry's attack) took Aristotle's theory of categories to be about real beings, and rejected it. Platonists could never accept that only individual, material things constitute the ultimate substance. The Platonic separable Forms are the 'truly real', and as Plotinus asserted the true categories should follow from the 'five most general kinds' in Plato's *Sophist* (see PLOTINUS §4). Porphyry, in contrast, saw an inherent validity in Aristotle's analysis. The categories are indeed valid when limited to the fields of logic and semantics. We base our accounts and phrases on individual concrete 'substances': for example, this or that human, animal, house; we talk of physical qualities, places, and so on. Abstracted universals are constructs of personal minds, but are not real universals, the Forms. Thus, Aristotle's categories do not impinge on what may or not be independently real. In our ordinary experience we live in a world of 'signifying sounds' (sēmantikai phōnai). These enable us to communicate the concepts we acquire about the objects we sense. The fundamental divisions of our immediate common experience refer to 'expressions signifying objects' (*On Aristotle's Categories* 58.3–6).

Second, how well we communicate depends on how precise our definitions are. In the *Introduction* to Aristotle's logic (in the *Categories* and *Topics*), Porphyry argued that only five 'signifying terms' cover the range of predicates we use: genus (general type), species (specific), difference (what distinguishes a family of species from the rest within a genus), property (what is characteristic of a species) and accident. Things are thus defined by their 'properties in the strict sense' (kyriōs idia): for example, a horse is what neighs, and conversely, what neighs is a horse. Indeed, a thing is a 'bundle' (athroismos) of properties (compare RUSSELL, B.A.W. §12). Porphyry made the scheme amenable to Platonists by interpreting difference and property (also genus and species) as potentialities for fulfilment, not actualities. Defining a human as a laughing animal refers only to the capacity, which is always present, not the act of laughing itself. This makes it possible to admit degrees of fulfilment: the 'more or less' approximation to the archetypal form.

Third, Porphyry supported the distinction between immanent and transcendent universals. This we see earlier in the Middle Platonist ALCINOUS. Universals in concrete things correspond to the forms as Aristotle saw them, that is, as compounds with matter. Universals that are separable from material manifestation correspond to the Platonic Forms (see PLATONISM, EARLY AND MIDDLE §4).

Fourth, Porphyry seems to have interpreted a key passage in Aristotle's *Metaphysics* (XII) in a way that supported the Neoplatonic One as the foundation of all existence (see PLOTINUS §3). Since Porphyry's commentary on the *Metaphysics* is lost, evidence may be reconstituted from references to him in a commentary on the *Categories* by Dexippus, a student of Iamblichus (see Hadot 1974). For Aristotle, the study of physical substances presupposes a pure, intelligible substance. For a Neoplatonist like Porphyry, Aristotle suggests a series of substances, from the physical to the incorporeal. The latter can be described only by analogy with things perceived by the senses. Furthermore, the intelligible substance gives coherence to the series of substances only because it has itself received unity from a pure One.

The 'harmonization' through demarcation seems to underlie Porphyry's extensive discussion of incorporeals and corporeals in his *Sentences Leading to the Intelligibles*. Although it is intended as a concise introduction to Plotinus, it contains fresh ideas anticipating modern distinctions of mind/body. Soul, intellect and the One are classed together as incorporeal. They lack spatial extension, location and volume. Without corporeality, the categories and relations of our ordinary language, big–small, in–out, here–there etc., lose their normal reference. So to locate such incorporeals we resort to paradoxical statements: for example, 'everywhere and nowhere'. Bodies are not 'zoo-cages' for minds, nor do souls 'fall down' to earth. Rather, incorporeal entities exercise their activity in a particular area, according to their 'disposition'. Incorporeals and bodies do not mix but form an asymmetrical 'assimilation' and 'union'. For Porphyry, this is the reason why our world of experience 'remains much distant' from reality (*Sentences* 35.30).

From another perspective, the Neoplatonic One emerges as the sole entity to possess its own foundation for existence. Everything else exists in relation to it. This, together with the telescoping of the metaphysical differences between soul and intellect may mean that Porphyry was a monist. On the other hand, in his *Sentences* we see a proliferation of elemental bodies of the soul. The controversial

anonymous *Commentary on the Parmenides*, attributed to Porphyry or a follower, reinforces the importance of the One, but also offers first evidence of the threefold structure, being–life–intellect, which will typify the complex metaphysics of Iamblichean Neoplatonism. It may simply be the case that Porphyry contracted or expanded metaphysical layers depending on the distinction he was examining.

Porphyry extended his polymathy to religion. He wrote on daemons and is the first to quote the CHALDAEAN ORACLES. Because these appear to be out of character for someone known for his rationalist attitude, it has been suggested that he was concerned with them in his earlier, pre-philosophical life. However, belief in the existence of such entities was commonplace in all strata of ancient society. What is more pertinent is his evaluation of such things. Judging from his attack on Iamblichus, Porphyry does not dismiss rituals and spirit-work but limits them to a purifying role (see §3). The divine cannot be reached in this way. Philosophical contemplation alone can activate the soul towards intellect and the One God.

3 Ethics

Porphyry treats ethics as applied metaphysics and epistemology. We garner his views from lines in the *Sentences* which refer to virtue, from the *Letter to Marcella* (Porphyry's wife) and from *On Abstinence*. In all three the goal of moral life is 'becoming like God'. In the first two he establishes that intellectual contemplation is the surest path to God. In the third he fleshes out how a rational, just life preserves things and does no harm to them.

The best example of his ethics is in the opening remarks of his *Letter to Marcella*, where he reminds his wife, 'you should put aside irrational distress, which is an emotion, and not be led by trivial judgments, but remember the divine words by which you were initiated into upright philosophy. For a steadfast attention to these words will habitually prove itself in action. It is deeds that give proof of our doctrines, and we must live by our faith to bear faithful witness to our teachings' (8.4–8).

The aim of ethics is to show the way of assimilating one's self to the true being, the Neoplatonic One. Since intellect is the level closest to the divine One, the path to God is philosophical. One must first reach the state of 'impassibility' (apatheia) (see STOICISM §9). The calm, rational mind separates from the passions that try to tear apart the unity of human life (on separation of soul, see PLATO §13). A person's living presence is not the body and therefore cannot be physically located. 'Surely, you must not think of my self as something that can be touched and be incidental to the senses: my true self is remote from the body, without colour and shape, not to be touched by the hands but grasped only by the mind' (*Letter to Marcella* 8.11–3).

For Porphyry, true priests are the 'wise', those philosophers who practise what they teach: 'Whoever practises wisdom practises knowledge of God, not by always praying and sacrificing, but by practising piety in the actions towards God... we must make ourselves pleasing to God, and consecrate our own disposition by making it similar to the immortal and blessed nature'. He also states: 'The wise soul joins with God and always beholds God and keeps his company.... It is not the utterance of the wise that is honourable to God, but deeds. A wise person honours God even silent.... The wise person, therefore, alone is a priest, alone is beloved by God, alone knows how to pray' (17.1–6, 16.7–17.2).

The philosopher respects all life as expressions of the One true being. Thus the philosopher-priest is a pacifist towards all types of life. There should be no killing, even for food, and certainly no killing of animals. Furthermore, we should regret that we have to eat other life forms, even plants (*On Abstinence* III 27).

Following Plotinus, Porphyry identified four kinds of virtue: civil life, purification, contemplation and exemplary. Each is fit for an appropriate grade of life: 'There is a difference between the virtues of the citizen; those of the one who attempts to rise to contemplation, and who, on this account, is said to be contemplative; those of the one who does contemplate perfectly; and finally those of the pure Intelligence, which is completely separated from soul' (*Sentences* 32). Each virtue befits a level of awareness:

> The objects (*skopoi*), differ with the kind of virtues. The object of the civil virtues is to moderate our passions to conform withthe activities of human nature. That of the purificatory virtues is to detach the soul completely from the passions. That of the contemplative virtues is to apply the soul to intellectual activities, even to the extent of no longer having to think of the need of freeing oneself from the passions.... The exemplary virtues reside within intelligence.
>
> (*Sentences* 32)

4 Literary theory

During his time with Longinus, Porphyry developed his skill for literary criticism – 'critic' (*kritikos*) was a title of professional recognition. What is the meaning of a literary account? How are we to understand it? Does it refer to concrete or symbolic events? The last question was the more problematic because it opens wide the field of interpretation and links literature to the representational arts. The question then arises whether the creation of an artist (*poiētēs*) reflects truth or somehow misleads. Put in a Platonic context, do artists (in literature, sculpture, drawing) use artistic images as representations and 'imitations' of intangible truths, or do they exercise their artistic 'licence' (*exousia*) without regard for truth, and so present distortions and falsehoods?

Porphyry showed his 'critical' skill both negatively (to prove that some Gnostic and Christian holy books were recent forgeries) and positively (notably the allegorizing of Homer's *Odyssey* and the Cave of Nymphs). Building on a tradition that can be traced to NUMENIUS (a second-century AD Platonist, who anticipated Plotinus and Iamblichus), Porphyry interpreted the Homeric hero as the human soul. The hero's journey is an allegory for the journey of the soul through life with the attendant travails and terrors: the process of psychological internalization. Poetic descriptions of the lands, dwellings and temples the hero visits, and of the people and wondrous creature he encounters, can be interpreted on many levels according to the Neoplatonic levels of knowledge and being.

Works of literature and art are not just for entertainment or purging the emotions. They may point to truths about knowledge and being, just as language mediates reality. Thus literary theory (and aesthetics) becomes part of the philosopher's purview.

5 Influence

As the editor and publicist of the *Enneads*, Porphyry ensured the dissemination of Plotinian thought. Although he expanded the emerging Neoplatonic metaphysics, in this he remained in his master's shadow. This Plotinian-Porphyrian theological Neoplatonism can be seen in AUGUSTINE and his followers in the Latin West.

Porphyry shone independently, however, in his work on Aristotle and logic. He is the pivotal figure among the ARISTOTLE COMMENTATORS, rescuing Aristotelian studies from total obscurity and securing their place in post-Plotinian philosophy. It is this new, broader Neoplatonism we find in BOETHIUS, and it is this which gave rise to medieval scholasticism and so-called Aristotelianism (see ARISTOTELIANISM, MEDIEVAL; ARISTOTELIANISM, RENAISSANCE). On the Greek side, both Porphyry and Aristotle became part of the Iamblichean Neoplatonism and were enshrined in the curriculum that lasted for centuries. In the Latin West, we may trace the influence of Porphyry's

Isagōgē both to autonomous logical theory (see, for example, the work of Shyreswood and WILLIAM OF OCKHAM), and to the debate on nominalism and realism (see ABELARD). We may also profitably reflect on Porphyry's contribution to the problem of sense and reference.

See also: NEOPLATONISM

List of works

Porphyry's works may be dated according to very broad eras of interest, the mainly Aristotelian, followed by the Platonic, then finally a work against Iamblichus (*Letter to Anebo*) and an edition of Plotinus' *Enneads*. Twenty or so of his eighty titles survive.

Porphyry (mid 3rd century AD) *Philosophy from the Chaldaean Oracles*, ed. G. Wolff, *De philosophia ex oraculis*, Berlin: Springer, 1856; repr. Hildesheim: Olms, 1962. (Greek text.)

—— (mid 3rd century AD) *On Aristotle's Categories*, trans. S. Strange, London: Duckworth, 1992. (English translation; for Greek text, see *Introduction (Isagōgē)*.)

—— (mid 3rd century AD) *Introduction (Isagōgē)* ed. A. Busse, *Isagoge et in Aristotelis categorias commentarium*, CAG 4.1, Berlin: Reimer, 1887; trans. E. Warren, *Porphyry the Phoenician: Isagōgē*, Toronto, Ont: Pontifical Institute of Medieval Studies, 1975. (English translation.)

—— (mid 3rd century AD) *Cave of the Nymphs in the Odyssey*, Arethusa Monographs 1, ed. L.G. Westerink, Buffalo, NY: State University of New York Press, 1969; trans. R. Lamberton, *Porphyry on the Cave of the Nymphs*, Barrytown, NY: Station Hill, 1983. (Greek text with English translation.)

—— (mid 3rd century AD) *The Homeric Questions*, ed. R. Schlunk, New York: P. Lang, 1993. (Greek text and translation.)

—— (mid 3rd century AD) *Against the Christians*, ed. A. von Harnack, *Porphyrius. Gegen die Christen*, Berlin: Reimer, 1916; trans. R.J. Hoffmann, *Porphyry Against the Christians: The Literary Remains*, Frome: Prometheus Trust, 1994. (The former is Greek text, the latter an English translation of the fragments.)

—— (late 3rd century AD) *Letter to Marcella*, ed. W. Pötcher, Leiden: Brill, 1969; trans. K. Wicker, *Porphyry the Philosopher, To Marcella*. (The former is Greek text and German translation, the latter an English translation.)

—— (late 3rd century AD) *History of Philosophy*, ed. E. des Places and A. Segonds, *Porphyre. Vie de Pythagore, – Lettre à Marcella, – frg. de l' Historie de la philosophie*. Paris: Les Belles Lettres, 1982. (Parallel Greek text and French translation.)

—— (late 3rd century AD) *On Abstinence from Animal Food*, ed. J. Bouffartigue and M. Pattilon, *Porphyre. De l'Abstinence*, Paris: Les Belles Lettres, 1977–94. (Parallel Greek text and French translation.)

—— (late 3rd century AD) *Sentences Leading to the Intelligibles*, ed. E. Lamberz, *Porphyrius Sententiae ad Intelligibilia*, Leipzig: Teubner, 1975; trans. K. Guthrie, *Launching-Points to the Realm of Mind*, Grand Rapids, MI: Phanes Press, 1988. (The former is Greek text; the latter is an English translation of an earlier edition.)

—— (late 3rd century AD) *Letter to Anebo*, ed. A.R. Sodano, *Porfirio. Lettera ad Anebo*, Naples: L'Arte Tipografica, 1958. (Greek text and Italian translation; 'Anebo' was Porphyry's pseudonym for Iamblichus, so the Letter usually appears with editions of Iamblichus' *On the Mysteries*.)

—— (mid to late 3rd century AD) *Select Works of Porphyry*, trans. T. Taylor, London, 1817; repr. Frome: Prometheus Trust, 1994. (Includes English translations and explanatory notes for *Abstinence from Animal Food*, *Cave of the Nymphs in the Odyssey* and *Auxiliaries to the Perception of Intelligible Natures*.)

—— (mid 3rd to early 4th century AD) *Fragmenta*, ed. A. Smith, Stuttgart and Leipzig: Teubner, 1993. (Collection of surviving Greek and Latin fragments of Porphyry's works on Aristotle, Plato, metaphysics, science, history, religion and literature.)

—— (early 4th century AD) *Life of Plotinus and The Enneads of Plotinus*, trans. A.H. Armstrong, Loeb Classical Library, Cambridge, MA: Harvard University Press and London: Heinemann, 1966. (Parallel Greek text and English translation.)

References and further reading

Brisson, L. (ed.) and Centre National Recherche Scientifique (1990–2) *Porphyre. La vie de Plotin* (Porphyry. The Life of Plotinus), Paris: Vrin. (Important articles on Porphyry in relation to Plotinus.)

Dombrowski, D. (1984) *The Philosophy of Vegetarianism*, Amherst, MA: University of Massachusetts Press. (Porphyry and the Platonic background on vegetarianism.)

Edwards, M.J. (1990) 'Porphyry and the Intelligible Triad', *Journal of Hellenic Studies* 110: 14–25. (On Porphyry's Neoplatonic metaphysics.)

Evangeliou, C. (1988) *Aristotle's Categories and Porphyry*, Leiden: Brill. (The logic and ontology of Porphyry's theory.)

Hadot, P. (1968) *Porphyre et Victorinus*, Paris: Études Augustiniennes. (Mainly on metaphysics and theology, and their relation to Christianity.)

* —— (1974) 'The Harmony of Plotinus and Aristotle according to Porphyry', in R. Sorabji (ed.) *Aristotle Transformed*, Ithaca, NY: Cornell University Press. (Further analysis on the harmony between Plato and Aristotle.)

Lamberton, R. (1986) *Homer the Theologian: Neoplatonist Allegorical Reading and the Growth of the Epic Tradition*, Berkeley and Los Angeles, CA: University of California Press. (Includes extensive study of Porphyry's literary criticism and theory of interpretation.)

Romano, F. (1985) *Porfirio di Tiro*, Catania: University of Catania. (Survey of Porphyry's philosophy.)

Smith, A. (1974) *Porphyry's Place in the Neoplatonic Tradition*. The Hague: Martinus Nijhoff. (Classic study of Porphyry in relation to Plotinus.)

—— (1987) 'Porphyrian Studies since 1913', in W. Haase (ed.) *Aufstieg und Niedergang der römischen Welt*, Berlin and New York: de Gruyter, II 36:2, 719–73. (Survey of scholarship on Porphyry.)

Sorabji, R. (ed.) (1990) *Aristotle Transformed*, Ithaca, NY: Cornell University Press. (Articles on Porphyry, Aristotle and logic.)

Spade, V. (ed.) (1994) *Five Texts on the Mediaeval Problem of Universals: Porphyry, Boethius, Abelard, Duns Scotus, Ockham*, Indianapolis, IN: Hackett Publishing Company. (Translated texts showing a development of Porphyry's thought.)

LUCAS SIORVANES

PORT-ROYAL

The reform of the abbey of Port-Royal-des-Champs in 1608 coincided with the vast movement of monastic reform which characterized the Counter-Reformation. In 1624 a second abbey was created, Port-Royal-de-Paris and, after some rivalry among spiritual leaders of the day, this was directed by Jean Duvergier de Hauranne, abbot of Saint-Cyran and one of the leaders of the parti dévot *hostile to Richelieu. In 1640 the abbot's friend Jansenius published the* Augustinus, *a résumé of Augustine's doctrine, of which five propositions on divine grace were condemned by the Vatican. Ecclesiastics in France were obliged to accept this condemnation, and the resistance of the nuns of Port-Royal brought about persecution, imprisonment and finally the destruction of the abbey in 1710. The intellectual history of the abbey extends far beyond*

theological quibblings, however. In 1626, Saint-Cyran defended Charron against the Jesuit Garasse and formed a firm alliance between the Pyrrhonism of Montaigne and the philosophy of Augustine. In the 1640s, Antoine Arnauld played an important role in the diffusion of Cartesianism, confirmed by the publication of the Logique de Port-Royal *(1662). The 1670 publication of Pascal's* Pensées *can be interpreted as a symptom of the rivalry between Descartes and Gassendi in contemporary apologetics and, in the following years, the polemics between Arnauld and Malebranche played an important role in the definition of Christian rationalism.*

1 **Rise and fall of Port-Royal**
2 **Intellectual life**

1 Rise and fall of Port-Royal

In June 1599, Jacqueline Arnauld was chosen as coadjutrix of the Cistercian abbey of Port-Royal-des-Champs, south of Paris near Versailles. On 5 July 1602, under the name of Mother Marie-Angélique de Sainte-Madeleine (Mother Angélique), she succeeded Jeanne de Boulehart as abbess. At that time, the crucial role that Port-Royal would play in the religious, political, philosophical and cultural world of seventeenth century Europe could not have been anticipated.

A sermon preached by a visiting friar in March 1608 was the occasion of the spiritual conversion of Mother Angélique and, with the advice of Cistercian abbots and a number of spiritual directors from various orders, she introduced the strict rules of the Cistercians into the abbey of Port-Royal. The reform of Port-Royal thus coincided with the vast movement of monastic reform which characterized the Counter-Reformation: Port-Royal soon gained a considerable reputation and the reform spread to other monasteries of the Cistercian order. In May 1625, the nuns of Port-Royal-des-Champs were transferred to the new abbey of Port-Royal in Paris and, in July 1627, the community was transferred from the jurisdiction of the Cistercian order to that of the archbishop of Paris. After the creation of the Institut du Saint-Sacrement in 1633, the community became the subject of intense rivalry among the leading spiritual directors in Paris: the Oratorians around Bérulle, Sébastien Zamet (Bishop of Langres), Octave de Bellagarde (Bishop of Sens), and Jean Duvergier de Hauranne (Abbot of Saint-Cyran). The latter became the spiritual director of Port-Royal in 1635. He was a friend of Cornelius Jansenius (Bishop of Ypres), and their spiritual ambitions were based on a return to the authority of AUGUSTINE, to positive theology, and on opposition to the influence of the Jesuits in France. This had political implications, in so far as Saint-Cyran could be said to belong to the 'parti dévot', strongly opposed to Richelieu's foreign policy of alliance with Protestant nations to resist the pressure of the Habsburgs in Spain and Austria. Jansenius' pamphlet *Mars gallicus* (1635) is an indication of the political resistance to official foreign policy and, on the 14 May 1638, Saint-Cyran was arrested and imprisoned in the dungeon of Vincennes. He was released only after the death of Richelieu in 1643, and died himself a few months later.

Nevertheless, by this time, the movement of spiritual reform at Port-Royal had gained considerable impetus. In January 1637 a well-known lawyer, Antoine Le Maistre, retired from the professional world to seek spiritual guidance at Port-Royal-de-Paris; his example was followed by others and, in mid-1638, these 'Solitaires' withdrew to Port-Royal-des-Champs, accompanied by the school ('Petites Ecoles') of Port-Royal, recently founded in Paris. The great work by Jansenius, *Augustinus* (1640), aimed to give a faithful résumé of Augustinian theology and revived old quarrels on the nature and power of divine grace. On 6 March 1642, the papal bull *In eminenti* condemned the work of Jansenius and in 1643 and 1644 Antoine ARNAULD produced his *De la Fréquente communion* and his defence of Jansenius. Port-Royal was henceforth to be known as the centre of 'Jansenist' (or, as Port-Royal theologians claim, 'Augustinian') theology. In 1649, Nicolas Cornet, 'syndic' of the Faculty of Theology of the Sorbonne, reduced Jansenius' doctrine to seven articles and submitted them to the Vatican for examination; five of them were condemned in the papal bull *Cum occasione*, published on 31 May 1653, and this condemnation was renewed in the bull *Ad sacram* on 16 October 1656. This same year, a condemnation of Jansenist theology was demanded of all ecclesiastics. The resistance of the nuns of Port-Royal drew political persecution on the abbey, since Mazarin sought to exploit the Jansenist quarrel in his negotiations with the Vatican.

The year 1655 was important in the development of public opinion concerning theological affairs. The occasion that sparked events was the refusal of communion to the duke of Liancourt, a friend of Port-Royal, by Charles Picoté, a vicar of Saint-Sulpice, on the grounds that the duke had provided accommodation in his house for Toussaint Desmares and Amable de Bourzeis, both notorious Jansenists. Antoine Arnauld wrote two lengthy letters in defence of the duke, which had little effect, but the theologian then asked Pascal to try his hand: from January 1656 onwards, the *Provincial Letters* were an immediate

success and contributed to the popular image of Jesuit casuistry and moral laxism (see PASCAL, B.). Moreover, despite the expulsion of Antoine Arnauld from the Sorbonne, the Jansenist cause seemed to be under divine protection when, in March 1656, Pascal's niece, Marguerite Périer, was miraculously cured of a dangerous eye infection. Debates on the 'miracle de la Sainte-Epine' led Pascal to develop the notion of historical testimony and thus embark on the project of an apology, of which the *Pensées* provides the unfinished sketch.

But political interests proved too strong for Port-Royal. First Mazarin, then King Louis XIV, were each determined to eliminate this source of potential resistance to monarchical power. The abbey was forbidden to receive new nuns, the boarding school for girls was suppressed as were the 'Petites Ecoles', and the 'Solitaires' were expelled. The abbey was thus condemned to die and, despite the 'Peace of the Church' (a respite from persecution between September 1668 and April 1679), the exile of Antoine Arnauld and Pierre Nicole and the tight control exercised by the archbishop of Paris brought an end to Port-Royal. The last nuns were dispersed in 1709, and the abbey was destroyed the following year.

In 1713, the papal bull *Unigenitus*, condemning 101 propositions extracted from the book of *Réflexions morales* (1693) by Pasquier Quesnel, created new conflicts that lasted throughout the eighteenth century. Jansenism now left the moral and theological field and began a Parliamentary and political career.

2 Intellectual life

Much has been said (by L. Goldmann, in particular) of the Parliamentary links of the Jansenists and this sociological characteristic has been interpreted in terms of a 'tragic' philosophy attributed to Pascal and to Racine. Objections have been formulated by J. Orcibal and J. Mesnard. Beyond the extreme fragility of Goldmann's interpretation of 'Jansenist' authors, suffice it to say that all religious orders recruited their members from the Parliamentary milieu: Port-Royal was no exception. Furthermore, Port-Royal had many connections with the *noblesse d'épée*, as can be seen from the list of nuns, of girls at the boarding-school and pupils at the Petites Ecoles. A full sociological analysis of the world of Port-Royal has yet to be completed; the financial history of the abbey would also reveal many secrets. The Parisian group of friends cannot suffice to characterize the community, since a vast network of friends of Port-Royal was established throughout the country, concentrated in particular in the dioceses of sympathetic bishops at such as those at Angers, Alet, Beauvais, Rouen,

Troyes, Châlons-sur-Marne, Montpellier and in Lorraine.

The intellectual history of the abbey is intricate. Many of the nuns themselves had considerable intellectual qualities and proved them in the archives which provided, in the following century, ample material for the historical defence of 'Jansenism'. Moreover, for the first time in Catholic theology, the resistance of the nuns to the demand for condemnation of Jansenius in 1656 was founded on the definition of the rights of the individual conscience: a major step towards the formulation, in the following century (and following the writing of Pierre BAYLE), of a doctrine of religious toleration.

Among the friends of Port-Royal, cultural activity was extremely important. Apart from the vast theological productions of Saint-Cyran and Antoine Arnauld, the pedagogical activity of the Petites Ecoles gave rise to a number of works by Claude Lancelot, as well as to the *Grammaire générale et raisonnée* (1660) and the *Art de penser* (or *Logique de Port-Royal*) (1662). Arnauld d'Andilly produced influential translations of Biblical history and Patristics; Isaac Le Maistre de Sacy produced an important translation of the Bible, which reflects the changing status of the layman in the Catholic church in the seventeenth century. Le Nain de Tillemont, a pupil of the Petites Ecoles, gained a great reputation as a historian. The influence of Jansenism on Racine, also a pupil at Port-Royal, has been much debated. Some critics discern an Augustinian influence in the works of Pascal, La Rochefoucauld, Nicole, Mme de La Fayette and Mme de Sévigné; La Fontaine was involved in the composition of a *Recueil de poésies chrétiennes et diverses* (1671), and the director of this volume, Brienne, was a close friend of Port-Royal and the probable author of the *Discours sur les passions de l'amour*. Augustinian moralism, which founded a portrait of human nature akin to that painted by HOBBES, was later to influence Bayle, LOCKE and MANDEVILLE. Conversations of friends of Port-Royal have been recorded in the *Recueil de choses diverses* (1670–1). Outside literature, Philippe de Champaigne and his nephew (and adopted son) Jean-Baptiste were among the foremost painters of the day: Philippe de Champaigne's portraits of the theologians and nuns of Port-Royal are outstanding.

In the field of philosophy, Port-Royal was first characterized by the intervention in 1626 of Saint-Cyran in defence of Charron, the disciple of MONTAIGNE, against the attack of the Jesuit Garasse. This can be interpreted as an alliance of Augustinian theology with Christian Pyrrhonism, and heralded the subsequent quarrels between rationalists and Pyrrho-nists after the publication of Descartes' *Discours de la méthode* (1637) (see DESCARTES, R. §3; PYRRHON-ISM). The introduction of Cartesianism into Port-Royal opened a new era, sometimes called the 'second Port-Royal', strongly influenced by the authority of Antoine Arnauld, author of the fourth set of *Objections* to Descartes' *Meditations*. Arnauld was indeed extremely favourable to the 'new philosophy' of Descartes, regarded as a much needed replacement for the Thomist Aristotelian defence of religious faith (see MEDIEVAL PHILOSOPHY). Charles Wallon de Beaupuis, a former pupil of Arnauld, was the director of the Petites Ecoles at Port-Royal. The duke of Luynes, a neighbour of the abbey in his château of Vaumurier, first translated into French Descartes' *Meditations* in 1647, the *Objections* being translated by Clerselier. Nicolas Fontaine gives an account of vivisection at Port-Royal, based on the Cartesian theory of animal-machines and, according to the testimony of his niece, Marguerite Périer, this was an aspect of Cartesian philosophy with which Pascal agreed. A manuscript of Louis Du Vaucel, published by G. Rodis-Lewis, testifies, however, that the adoption of Cartesianism was not unanimous at Port-Royal.

The publication of the *Logique de Port-Royal* (1662), with subsequent editions bringing a number of important additions, was a major event in the intellectual history of the seventeenth century. A first version was sent by Arnauld to Mme de Sablé in April 1660, and this copy may help to solve the vexed question of the role played by Nicole in the composition of the text. Furthermore, a note in the *Recueil de choses diverses* attributes a role in the composition to Le Bon, a teacher at the Petites Ecoles, who is supposed to have worked on notes by Descartes' disciple Clerselier. The work constitutes an attempt to present a synthesis of Augustinian, Cartesian and Pascalian thought, and exerted a strong influence on MALEBRANCHE and his recalcitrant Benedictine disciple, Robert DESGABETS and, indeed, on the whole context of debate around the 'new philosophy'. This debate was particularly lively at the Oratoire, where André Martin composed, under the pseudonym of Ambrosius Victor, a systematic comparison of passages extracted from Augustine and Descartes (1667), and from which Bernard Lamy suffered exile after a series of Cartesian lectures (1675). It may be added that, whereas Arnauld remained faithful to Cartesianism throughout his life, strongly denouncing the sceptical work of Pierre-Daniel HUET, Nicole seems to have been lukewarm: he composed a stringent criticism of Desgabets' attempts to provide a detailed Cartesian account of transubstantiation, and his sympathy for

Descartes' philosophy seems to have been limited to an adherence to the criterion of 'évidence'.

The publication of Pascal's *Pensées* (1670) was a new occasion for Cartesian thought to make itself felt in works emanating from Port-Royal. Recent critics interpret this edition as an attempt to disguise, by careful modifications of the text, a Gassendist critique of Descartes as Cartesian apologetics. Key terms in Pascal's vocabulary are marked by the influence of GASSENDI, and yet Arnauld, who directed the editorial committee, managed to produce an apology compatible with Cartesianism. The success of the work was immediate, and it exerted an influence on subsequent philosophers, in particular on Malebranche, Bayle, Locke and even HUME.

Antoine Arnauld's philosophical controversies with Malebranche in themselves constituted an important chapter of intellectual life at Port-Royal. The controversies began in 1680 when Arnauld came across a manuscript version of Malebranche's *Traité de la nature et de la grâce*: despite Arnauld's last-minute attempt to discourage Malebranche, the treatise was printed and the Jansenist theologian promptly attacked the Oratorian's so-called 'Epicureanism' (see EPICUREANISM). A debate on the nature of pleasure and happiness ensued, in which Pierre Bayle played an important role by publishing detailed analyses in the *Nouvelles de la république des lettres* and finally coming down strongly in favour of Malebranche. In 1683 Arnauld's critique of Malebranche's *Recherche de la vérité* appeared in *Des Vraies et des fausses idées* (1683), which was to involve the two philosophers in a long and intense debate on the nature of ideas. Originally regarded as friend of Port-Royal, Malebranche became a bitter enemy of the Port-Royal theologians, denouncing them in the ironic formula 'personnes de piété' (see ARNAULD, A. §3).

The paradoxically parallel influence of Epicurus, Montaigne and Augustine in seventeenth-century France put Port-Royal at the centre of debates on theological, ecclesiastical, moral, philosophical and literary questions. The Port-Royal theologians and their friends were quick to appeal to public opinion, and thus played a major part in the transformation of these debates from obscure, technical quibblings to major events in social and intellectual history.

See also: LOGIC IN THE 17TH AND 18TH CENTURIES; MORALISTES

References and further reading

* Arnauld, A. (1641) *IVes Objections aux Méditations philosophiques de Descartes*, in Descartes, R. *Méditations métaphysiques* (Metaphysical meditations), ed. F. Alquié, Paris: Garnier frères, 1967, vol. II: 632–704. (Arnauld's objections to Descartes' *Méditations*.)
* —— (1643) *De la Fréquente Communion, où les sentiments des Pères, des papes et des Conciles, touchant l'usage des Sacrements de Pénitence et d'Eucharistie, sont fidèlement exposez* (Of Frequent Communion), Paris. (First attack by Antoine Arnauld against 'laxist' morals of the Jesuits.)
* —— (1683) *Des vraies et des fausses idées contre ce qu'enseigne l'auteur de la Recherche de la verité* (Of true and false ideas), Cologne. (Arnauld's attack on Malebranche's epistemology.)
* Arnauld, A. and Lancelot, C. (1660) *Grammaire générale et raisonnée, contenant les fondements de l'art de parler expliquez d'une manière claire et naturelle* (General and analytical grammar), Paris. (Famous French grammar composed for the schools of Port-Royal.)
* Arnauld, A. and Nicole, P. (1662) *La Logique ou l'art de penser*, ed. P. Clair and F. Girbal, Paris: Vrin, 1981; trans as *Logic or the Art of Thinking*, ed. J. Vance Buroker, Cambridge: Cambridge University Press, 1996. (The 1981 French version is a good critical edition of this major seventeenth century text. The manuscript mentioned in the text is in the Bibliothèque Nationale f.fr. 19915)
* Bayle, P. (1684–8) *Nouvelles de la république des lettres*, Rotterdam. (Bayle's periodical work, consisting of book reviews; in 1685 he inserts an appendix to defend Malebranche against Arnauld.)
* Descartes, R. (1637) *Discours de la Méthode* (Discourse on method), ed. E. Gilson, Paris: Vrin, 1925. (Descartes famous discourse inaugurating a philosophical revolution against Aristotelian scholastic tradition.)
* —— (1680–5) *Discours sur les passions de l'amour* (Discourse on the passions of love), ed. G. Brunet, Paris, 1959. (Pseudo-Pascalian text, now attributed to Brienne by J. Mesnard.)
* Goldmann, L. (1955) *Le Dieu caché. Etude sur la vision tragique dans les Pensées de Pascal et dans le théâtre de Racine* (Study of the tragic vision in Pascal's Pensées and the plays of Racine), Paris: Gallimard. (Controversial sociological interpretation, relating the 'tragic' vision of these two authors to the social situation of Parliamentary circles in the seventeenth century.)
* Jansenius, C. (1635) *Alexandri Patricii Armacani, theologi, Mars Gallicus, seu de justitia armorum et foederum regis Galliae libri duo* (The French God of War), Louvain. (Pro-Spanish pamphlet against Richelieu's policy of protestant alliance.)
* —— (1640) *Cornelii Jansenii episcopi Iprensis*

Augustinus, Louvain. (Exposition of the doctrine of Saint Augustine.)

Lafond, J. (1977) *La Rochefoucauld. Augustinisme et littérature*, Paris: Klincksieck, 3rd edn, 1986. (Major study in the perspective suggested by P. Sellier.)

—— (ed.) (1992) *Les Moralistes du XVIIe siècle*, Paris: R. Laffont. (Excellent editions of major French moralists, including Pascal, La Rochefoucauld, La Bruyère and an excellent introduction on epigrammatic literature.)

Lafond, J. and Mesnard, J. (eds) (1984) *Images de La Rochefoucauld: Actes du Tricentenaire*, Paris: PUF. (Articles on the reception of La Rochefoucauld and on his relations with Port-Royal and the hôtel de Liancourt.)

* La Fontaine, J. de and Loménie de Brienne, H. de (eds) (1671) *Recueil de poésies chrétiennes et diverses* (Collection of Christian and diverse poetry), Paris. (Important collection for the definition of Port-Royal esthetics, prefaced by Nicole.)

Lesaulnier, J. (1992) *Port-Royal insolite: édition critique du Recueil de choses diverses*, Paris, Klincksieck. (Critical edition of conversations in 1670–1, between friends of Port-Royal in the circle of Jean Deslyons, who was often to be found at the hôtel de Liancourt.)

Lesaulnier, J. and McKenna, A.N. (eds) (1998) *Dictionnaire de Port-Royal au XVIIe siècle*, Paris: Universitas; Oxford: The Voltaire Foundation. (Bio-bibliographical dictionary of over 2,500 characters related to Port-Royal; the introduction examines Jansenist theology and the importance of Port-Royal in seventeenth-century culture; offers detailed chronology and exhaustive chronological bibliography.)

Malebranche, N. (1680) *Traité de la nature et de la grâce*, Amsterdam: Elzevier. (One of an important series of works in which the Oratorian Malebranche proposes an original alliance between Augustine's doctrine of grace and his own version of Cartesian rationalism. Bayle highlights the publication of this work as the turning point in relations between Malebranche and Port-Royal.)

Martin, A. [Ambrosius Victor] (1667) *Philosophia christiana*, Paris. (Collection of works in which the Oratorian Martin proposes an alliance of Saint Augustine and Descartes.)

McKenna, A.N. (1986) 'La composition de la *Logique* de Port-Royal', *Revue philosophique* 1986: 183–206. (Details of current hypotheses.)

—— (1990) *De Pascal à Voltaire: le rôle des Pensées de Pascal dans l'histoire des idées entre 1670 et 1734*, vols 276–7 of *Studies on Voltaire and the eighteenth century*, Oxford: Oxford University Press. (Lengthy study of Pascal's reception and influence on major philosophers and minor writers, including apologists and clandestine philosophers.)

Mesnard, J. (1965) *Pascal et les Roannez*, Paris: Desclée de Brouwer. (Detailed history of family relations, thus giving a clear picture of the Parisian circles within which Pascal moved.)

—— (1992) *La Culture du XVIIe siècle*, Paris: PUF. (Important collection of articles on all aspects of seventeenth-century literature.)

—— (1993) *Les Pensées de Pascal*, Paris: SEDES. (The best global commentary on the *Pensées*. Pages 309–30: refutation of Goldmann's interpretation of Pascal and Racine.)

Nadler, S. (1989) *Arnauld and the Cartesian Philosophy of Ideas*, Manchester: Manchester University Press. (Good study of Arnauld's philosophy which is readily comprehensible to the non-specialist.)

—— (1992) *Malebranche and Ideas*, New York and Oxford, Oxford University Press. (Good study of Malebranche's polemical debate with Arnauld.)

* Orcibal, J. (1947–8) *Les Origines du Jansénisme: 1, La Correspondance de Jansénius; 2–3, Jean Duvergier de Hauranne, abbé de Saint-Cyran et son temps*, Louvain-Paris. (Very detailed history of the career of Saint-Cyran and of his contacts in all social circles.)

* Pascal, B. (1964–) *Œuvres complètes*, ed. J. Mesnard, Paris: Desclée de Brouwer. (Monumental, critical edition of all Pascal's works, including a commentary relating his writing to spiritual traditions and contemporary debate. Four volumes published as of 1995.)

Pascal (1992), special edition of *XVIIe siècle* 177. (Recent research on Pascal's Pensées.)

* Quesnel, P. (1693) *Le Nouveau Testament en français avec des réflexions morales sur chaque verset, pour en rendre la Lecture plus utile et la Méditation plus aisée à ceux qui commencent à s'y appliquer* (New Testament in French with moral reflections on each verse), Paris: Pralard. (Commentary on the New Testament, from which were extracted 101 propositions condemned in the bull *Unigenitus*.)

Rodis-Lewis, G. (1950) 'Augustinisme et cartésianisme à Port-Royal' in *Descartes et le cartésianisme hollandais*, Paris and Amsterdam. (Important article showing controversy at Port-Royal over Cartesian philosophy and including the objections of Louis Du Vaucel.)

Sellier, P. (1970) *Pascal et saint Augustin*, Paris: Armand Colin. (Pioneer work on Pascal's theological thought, concluding that he was very well acquainted with Augustine's works.)

—— (1969) 'La Rochefoucauld, Pascal, saint Augustin', *Revue d'histoire littéraire de la France*

69: 551–75. (The first study to suggest a relation between La Rochefoucauld and Augustinian theology, a line of enquiry which has proved very useful.)

ANTONY McKENNA

POSIDONIUS (c.135–c.50 BC)

Posidonius of Apamea (Syria) was a Stoic philosopher and student of Panaetius. He taught in Rhodes. He combined a passion for detailed empirical research with a general commitment to the basic systematics of Stoic philosophy (which, however, he was willing to revise where necessary). As such he was probably the most 'scientific' of the Stoics. His wide-ranging investigations of all kinds of physical phenomena (especially in the areas of physical astronomy and meteorology) became particularly renowned, the best known case being his explanation of Atlantic tides as connected with the motions of the moon.

His most original philosophical contributions are to be located in the connected areas of psychology and ethics. Posidonius appears to have been committed to a slightly Platonizing version of Stoic psychology, according to which the passions are no longer regarded as a malfunctioning of the rational faculty, but as motions of the soul which take their origin in two separate irrational faculties (anger and appetite). This revised moral psychology is accompanied by some corresponding revisions in ethics such as the conception of moral education as the blunting of the motions of the irrational faculties.

1   **Life and writings**
2   **The Posidonian question**
3   **Logic**
4   **Physics**
5   **Ethics**
6   **Mathematics, geography and history**
7   **Influence**

1   Life and writings

Born in Apamea (Syria), Posidonius studied at Athens with the Stoics Antipater and PANAETIUS (that is, before 110 BC when the latter died). He settled in Rhodes where he founded a philosophical school of his own, and soon became one of the leading intellectual personalities of his time. He obtained Rhodian citizenship and held the highest political office (*prytanis*), Rhodes being at the time an independent ally of Rome. He represented Rhodes in an embassy to Rome where he negotiated with

Marius in 87/86 BC. Earlier he had travelled in the western Mediterranean visiting Etruria, southern Gaul (where he studied the habits of the Celts), Spain (where he observed Atlantic tides at Cadiz) and North Africa. Back in Rhodes he continued his philosophical activities. CICERO attended his lectures in 77 BC. Pompey visited him in 66 and 62 BC, on his way to and back from his campaign against Mithridates. In 51 BC Posidonius revisited Rome on a second embassy. He died soon after.

None of Posidonius' writings survive, so we are dependent on fragments (quotations) and testimonia provided by other ancient writers. More than forty titles of works are attested, the most important ones being: *Protreptics*; *Physical Theory* (consisting of at least eight books); *On the Cosmos* (at least two books); *Meteorologica* (at least seven books); *On the Ocean*; *On the Gods* (at least five books); *On Fate* (at least two books); *On Divination* (five books); *On the Soul*; *Ethical Theory*; *On Passions*; *On Duty* (at least two books); *On the Criterion*; *Against Zeno of Sidon*; and *Histories* (fifty-two books).

The belief that Posidonius also wrote separate commentaries on some of Plato's works (*Timaeus, Phaedrus, Parmenides*) has been rather persistent, but is based on an unwarranted inference from the relevant ancient testimonies.

2   The Posidonian question

Modern scholarly interest in Posidonius as a philosopher in his own right goes back to the first collection of fragments, edited by J. Bake in 1810. This collection triggered rather than settled the question to what extent Posidonian material, philosophical as well as doxographical, can be found in various ancient sources. In the nineteenth and twentieth centuries opinions on what might count as the Posidonian 'corpus' have differed widely. Under the influence of German *Quellenforschung* Posidonius was credited with the intellectual authorship of many ideas in such different authors as Cicero, Varro, Manilius, Vergil and SENECA, usually on arbitrary grounds and without any explicit ascription in the passages at issue. The various pictures of Posidonius to which this 'pan-Posidonianism' gave rise usually exhibited strongly metaphysical or even mystical features. In the course of the twentieth century more sceptical approaches have gradually prevailed, and the sound methodological principle that every assessment of Posidonius' thought should be based on explicitly attested evidence was at the basis of the edition of the fragments and testimonia by Edelstein and Kidd (1972). The rival edition by Theiler (1982) is still rather indebted to the German pan-Posidonianist tradition. The account which follows is based on attested fragments only; references are to the fragments (fr.) and testimonia (T) as numbered in the edition of Edelstein and Kidd.

3 Logic

Posidonius followed Stoic orthodoxy in dividing philosophy into three parts: physics, logic and ethics. He was more explicit than others, however, in stressing the interconnection of these parts, likening philosophy as a whole to a living being with physics as blood and flesh, logic as the bones and sinews, and ethics as the soul (frs 87, 88). What little is preserved of his works on the bones and sinews of philosophy does not suggest any major departures from mainstream Stoic logic, although Posidonius may have been the first Stoic to examine the logical basis of relational syllogisms, that is, syllogisms making use of relations like 'larger than' or 'equal to' (fr. 191).

4 Physics

Also in the area of physics – which Posidonius claimed to be primarily concerned with 'aetiology', or finding causes (fr. 18, T85) – he subscribed to the Stoic orthodoxy in many respects. Yet a typical feature of Posidonian physics was the way he extended his aetiological investigations to the smallest details of the whole range of physical phenomena (thus inviting a comparison with Aristotle; see also T85). Indeed his explanations of the size and distance of the sun, its settings and risings, the moon, solar and lunar eclipses, comets, halos, rainbow, thunder, hail and winds became particularly renowned in later antiquity. Yet he regarded these various physical phenomena as in one way or another interconnected by cosmic sympathy (*sympatheia*) – a feature, incidentally, which some scholars have taken to be the exclusive hallmark of Posidonian physics, but which is in fact firmly rooted in previous Stoic philosophy. Of particular interest in this respect is his theory of the tides in the ocean as being connected with the daily, monthly and annual motions of the moon (frs 138 and 214–20). The conception of cosmic *sympatheia*, together with the identification of the active principle of the cosmos with 'fate' (fr. 103), also provides the philosophical basis for the practice of divination, which Posidonius, unlike his teacher Panaetius, zealously defended (frs 106–13).

On the other hand Posidonius did not hesitate to propose revisions of early Stoic physics where he thought they were required. Thus he probably rejected the early Stoic claim that the void surrounding the cosmos was infinite, arguing instead that it was just large enough to be able to receive the cosmos during its periodic conflagrations (fr. 97a–b) (see STOICISM §5). A more important change concerned psychology, where Posidonius followed Stoic orthodoxy in defining the soul as a 'warm breath' (fr. 139) and in claiming that it does not have irrational *parts*, located in different bodily organs, but sided with PLATO (§14) and ARISTOTLE (§20, 22–3) against CHRYSIPPUS in maintaining that the soul has different *faculties* (frs 30–4, 142–6): a rational faculty, one irrational faculty responsible for anger and aggression, and yet another irrational faculty responsible for appetites (see PSYCHĒ).

5 Ethics

Posidonius made this moral psychology the basis of his theories concerning the nature of good and evil, the virtues and the end (frs 30, 38, 150a–b). He claimed that the origin of moral evil is not to be sought in the corrupting influence of external factors, as Chrysippus had thought, but in the emotional pull of the irrational faculties of the soul (frs 161, 169, 186). He accordingly rejected the Chrysippean conception of the passions as (false) judgments of the rational faculty of the soul (see STOICISM §19), arguing that it was unable to explain how emotions can arise and abate over time (fr. 165), that it would involve the counterintuitive consequence that animals and children, being irrational, do not have emotions (fr. 33), and that it left Chrysippus without a proper explanation of how emotions can arise in the first place (frs 34, 165). According to Posidonius, the passions are motions of one of the two irrational faculties of the soul (frs 151–2), a conception which he claims to be firmly rooted in common experience (fr. 156), supported by the language used by the ancient poets as well as by ancient practices (fr. 164, 50–2), and sanctioned by the authority of CLEANTHES (frs 32 and 166) and, possibly, ZENO OF CITIUM (T91, 93).

Each of the three psychic faculties of the soul has its own natural object (a revision of the early Stoic theory of *oikeiōsis* or natural appropriation; see STOICISM §14): the two irrational faculties strive after power and pleasure respectively, whereas the rational faculty naturally seeks the moral good (frs 158, 160). Each faculty accordingly has its proper virtue. Only the virtue of the rational faculty may be termed 'knowledge' and can be taught. The virtues of the irrational faculties (that is, their restraint) are irrational and have to be acquired through habituation (fr. 31). Moral education thus becomes a kind of therapy: the rational faculty is to be given predominance and the movements of the irrational faculties should be blunted by habituation and good practices (fr. 169. 106–17).

The end (*telos*) is defined as 'to live contemplating the truth and order of all things together and helping in organizing it, in no way being led by the irrational part of the soul' (fr. 186; the misleading 'part' here may not represent Posidonius' original wording). Posidonius appears to have regarded this definition as a clarification of the early Stoic definition of the end as 'living in accordance with nature' (fr. 185) (see STOICISM §17).

Apart from his revisions in moral psychology, Posidonius appears to have remained faithful to the main tenets of Stoic ethics, such as those concerning the self-sufficiency of virtue or the moral value of wealth and health.

6 Mathematics, geography and history

Most of Posidonius' contributions to what we would call the 'special sciences' are to be classed under philosophy (physics), with the exception of his work in mathematics and (at least part of) his work in history and geography. According to Posidonius mathematics (including astronomy) does not belong to philosophy at all, being crucially different from physics in so far as it is merely concerned with the quantitative aspects of phenomena and hence unsuitable for finding the essence of things, that is, for aetiology (fr. 18, T85). Indeed he remained faithful to this principle in using mathematical constructs and methods for descriptive rather than explanatory purposes, for example, to estimate the circumference of the earth (fr. 202) or to construct an orrery (T86). Nevertheless he also studied mathematics as a subject in its own right, defending the method and principles of Euclidean geometry against Epicurean criticisms in his 'Against Zeno of Sidon' (fr. 47).

His geographical works and his *Histories* (a continuation of Polybius' historical work, covering the period from 145 to *c.*86 BC) constituted a 'mixed bag' of simply descriptive passages – such as those dealing with the length of the 'isthmus' of Gaul (fr. 248) or with the revolt of mining slaves in Attica *c.*100 BC (fr. 262) – and more philosophical elements. As an example of the latter we may note the theory of geographical zones (*klimata*), which is supposed to explain some of the ethnological characteristics of the people inhabiting various parts of the world (frs 49 and 169, 85–95). These characteristics in their turn were thought to explain certain historical actions of those people (see also fr. 272 on the Cimbri). Moreover, there is a more general link between historiography and ethics in so far as history as a whole is presented as a process of gradual decline

caused by the preponderance of the irrational faculties of the soul (fr. 284).

7 Influence

Posidonius was highly esteemed in his own day, and his works were read and used by thinkers like Cicero. Yet the extent of his general philosophical influence is still a matter of debate and has certainly often been overestimated. Among later authors, such as Strabo, Cleomedes, and Alexander of Aphrodisias, he appears to have been primarily known for his detailed investigations in such special areas as meteorology and geography.

See also: CLEOMEDES; PANAETIUS; STOICISM §1

References and further reading

Bake, J. (1810) *Posidonii Rhodii Reliquiae Doctrinae*, Leiden: Haak. (The first collection of Posidonius' fragments.)

Dobson, J.F. (1918) 'The Posidonius Myth', *Classical Quarterly* 12: 179–95. (An influential critical assessment of 'pan-Posidonianism'.)

Edelstein, L. (1936) 'The Philosophical System of Posidonius', *American Journal of Philology* 57: 286–325. (A useful overview based on explicitly attested material only.)

Kidd, I.G. (1978) 'Philosophy and Science in Posidonius', *Antike und Abendland* 24: 7–15. (An investigation of Posidonius' conception of philosophy, mathematics and the liberal arts.)

* Kidd, I.G. (1988), *Posidonius II: The Commentary*, Cambridge: Cambridge University Press, 2 vols. (Rich commentary, full of further references, on Edelstein and Kidd (1972).)

Laffranque, M. (1964) *Poseidonios d'Apamée: essai de mise au point* (Posidonius of Apamea: an attempt at clarification), Paris: Presses Universitaires de France. (A good general introduction based on sound methodological principles; contains a useful overview of the history of Posidonian scholarship and of the Posidonian question.)

* Posidonius (*c.*135–50 BC) Fragments, in L. Edelstein and I.G Kidd (ed.) *Posidonius I: The Fragments*, Cambridge: Cambridge University Press, 1972; 2nd edn, 1989 (The modern standard edition of the fragments and testimonia.)

Reinhardt, K. (1921) *Posidonius*, Munich: Beck. (A study which has been influential and important in so far as it criticizes earlier pan-Posidonianist approaches, but which is itself too liberal in ascribing unattested material to Posidonius on the basis of the fuzzy notion of the 'innere Form'.)

Steinmetz, P. (1994) 'Poseidonios aus Apameia', in H. Flashar (ed.) *Die Philosophie der Antike, Band 4: Die Hellenistische Philosophie*, Basle: Schwabe, 670–705. (A clear general survey, rather indebted to Reinhardt's work, but useful for the bibliographical information it provides.)

* Theiler, W. (1982) *Poseidonios: Die Fragmente*, Berlin and New York: de Gruyter, 2 vols. (Is too liberal in including non-attested material and should therefore be used with caution; the commentary, however, may sometimes be useful.)

KEIMPE A. ALGRA

POSITIVISM *see* COMTE, ISIDORE-AUGUSTE-MARIE-FRANÇOIS-XAVIER; LEGAL POSITIVISM; LOGICAL POSITIVISM; POSITIVISM IN THE SOCIAL SCIENCES; POSITIVISM, RUSSIAN; POSITIVIST THOUGHT IN LATIN AMERICA

POSITIVISM IN THE SOCIAL SCIENCES

Positivism originated from separate movements in nineteenth-century social science and early twentieth-century philosophy. Key positivist ideas were that philosophy should be scientific, that metaphysical speculations are meaningless, that there is a universal and a priori scientific method, that a main function of philosophy is to analyse that method, that this basic scientific method is the same in both the natural and social sciences, that the various sciences should be reducible to physics, and that the theoretical parts of good science must be translatable into statements about observations. In the social sciences and the philosophy of the social sciences, positivism has supported the emphasis on quantitative data and precisely formulated theories, the doctrines of behaviourism, operationalism and methodological individualism, the doubts among philosophers that meaning and interpretation can be scientifically adequate, and an approach to the philosophy of social science that focuses on conceptual analysis rather than on the actual practice of social research. Influential criticisms have denied that scientific method is a priori or universal, that theories can or must be translatable into observational terms, and that
reduction to physics is the way to unify the sciences. These criticisms have undercut the motivations for behaviourism and methodological individualism in the social sciences. They have also led many to conclude, somewhat implausibly, that any standards of good social science are merely matters of rhetorical persuasion and social convention.

1   **Positivist doctrines**
2   **Influence on the philosophy and practice of the social sciences**
3   **Criticisms and contributions**

1   Positivist doctrines

In contemporary debates 'positivism' refers to a broad attitude about science and philosophy that has its origins in the social theories of Comte de SAINT-SIMON and Auguste COMTE and the philosophical doctrines of the logical positivists. The positivists often did not agree which doctrines were essential to their position or how those ideas should be interpreted, and the term 'positivism' has come to stand for a set of ideas that some positivists would not have fully endorsed. Though they advocated all the ideas discussed below in some form, this entry concentrates on the ideas currently associated with positivism, for it is those doctrines that have been most influential in debates about the social sciences.

Saint-Simon and Comte advanced three ideas typical of positivism: (1) that science is the highest form of knowledge and that philosophy thus must be scientific; (2) that there is one scientific method common to all the sciences; and (3) that metaphysical claims are pseudoscientific. The second of these ideas, frequently known as 'naturalism', is most directly relevant to the social sciences. It says that the social realm, as part of the natural world, can and must be studied by standard scientific methods. For Saint-Simon and Comte, this meant that laws governed the social world, and that the job of the social sciences was to identify those laws. They also believed that society should be run by an elite who could discern these laws and use them to solve social problems.

Subsequent positivists advocated these core ideas but with new interpretations and additions. The logical positivists shared the antimetaphysical sympathies of Comte and also wanted philosophy to be 'scientific'; they did not conceive of it as an empirical discipline. Instead they assimilated philosophy more to the model of logic, where the logician's task was to formulate the a priori rules of valid inference and explicate basic logical concepts. Philosophy became primarily clarifying and formulating the rules and concepts of good science, and the logical positivists were thus committed to the existence of a single, universal a priori scientific method (see LOGICAL POSITIVISM).

The logical positivists attacked metaphysics by bringing in the empiricist tradition (one foreign to Saint-Simon and Comte). They argued that sensory knowledge was the most certain and that any concept not directly about sensory experience should be 'translatable' into observational concepts. Those concepts that could not be so translated, primarily metaphysical concepts, were rejected as meaningless. This claim also led to a very specific and long-persuasive picture of science: science is divided into two parts – the observational and the theoretical – and theoretical terms must be definable in observational terms.

From these ideas the positivists drew several conclusions relevant to the social sciences. Since scientific knowledge came from applying an a priori logic of science, good social science must be value free (see VALUE JUDGMENTS IN SOCIAL SCIENCE §2). The logical positivists also thought that good science was unified science, and promoting the unity of the different sciences was one of their chief goals. By 'unity' they understood various things. They thought there was one scientific method common to all the sciences, including the social sciences. They also thought that the different sciences could and should be unified by being reduced to physics.

2 Influence on the philosophy and practice of the social sciences

Positivism strongly influenced both the practice of the social sciences and philosophical views about them. Naturalism, the view that good social science embodies the scientific method common to the natural sciences, is the dominant approach among practising social scientists (see NATURALISM IN SOCIAL SCIENCE §1). Operationalism, the idea that all theoretical terms must be specified by the operations that measure them, has been influential in the social sciences and is a variant of the positivist ideal of translating theoretical terms into empirical ones; the notion of revealed preference in economics – the idea that preferences of consumers should be identified with their observable consumption patterns – has similar roots (see OPERATIONALISM §2). Behaviourism in political science has similar origins, for again the idea is that only explanations based on directly observable factors are scientifically adequate.

One attempt to formulate the positivists' logic of science was Karl Popper's idea that good science is falsifiable and has undergone severe tests (1962). Many philosophers and social scientists have tried to use Popper's ideas to evaluate the social sciences. Popper himself argued that both Marxism and Freudian psychology were pseudoscientific because they were non-falsifiable. Similar doubts have been raised about economics, because economists often fail to reject their theories in the face of conflicting data (see POPPER, K.R.).

Positivist assumptions have also influenced the use of statistics in the social sciences. Much social research uses statistical methods to test hypotheses and implicitly treats statistical inference as a mechanical, purely logical process. Social research also often reports only correlations between variables, drawing no conclusions about causes. Both practices have positivist origins. The early developers of modern statistics were sympathetic to positivism, and interpreted their results as a concrete implementation of the positivists' a priori scientific method or logic of science. The refusal to draw causal conclusions comes in part from the positivist rejection of metaphysics, for many positivists thought causation an obscure metaphysical concept that should be rejected in favour of lawful regularities between observables. This emphasis on the observable also found a sympathetic ear among economists. Friedman's famous defence of economics against the charge that its models were highly unrealistic argued that only predictions count (1953); unrealistic theories did not matter if they predicted the observed data (see ECONOMICS, PHILOSOPHY OF §4).

Another influential idea was the positivists' notion that the various sciences should be unified by reducing them to physics. This was generally interpreted as the claim that the sciences form a hierarchy, with sociology reducible to psychology, psychology to biology, and biology to physics. These reductions were to show that the laws and theories of each science were derivable from or special cases of the science 'below' it. This positivist ideal fits well with the tradition in the social sciences known as methodological individualism, a doctrine asserting that all social phenomena must be explained as the outcome of individual behaviour. Methodological individualism remains the official philosophy of many economists, and philosophers have defended it as well. It is important to note, however, that much social science from the start rejected individualism for a holism that claimed macrosociological processes are essential to explanation; Comte, for example, advocated such a view (see HOLISM AND INDIVIDUALISM IN HISTORY AND SOCIAL SCIENCE).

Positivism also played a major role in numerous other debates in the philosophy of the social sciences. The idea of *Verstehen*, namely, that the social sciences rely on a special kind of intuitive insight to grasp the meanings of social phenomena, was roundly rejected by philosophers on the grounds that such a process could not be put in terms of observable data. Arguments that any social science dealing with meanings is scientifically inadequate also have positivist roots. Quine (1960), for example, argued that linguistic meaning is inherently indeterminate and thus scientifically suspect, because we cannot capture meanings in observational or physical terms (see QUINE, W.V. §2). Related doubts about a science of meaning turn on the fact that meanings involve intensionality – substituting terms with equivalent meanings does not always preserve the truth value of statements. This makes it difficult to turn social science theories into axiomatized formal systems, a requirement for good science again inherited from the positivists.

Finally, positivism has influenced in subtle ways how philosophers think philosophy of social science ought to be done. Relevant positivist assumptions include the following ideas: that philosophers should analyse scientific concepts; that such analyses ought to be roughly in the form of a definition or necessary and sufficient conditions; that the cognitive content of science can be fully and best expressed by identifying the formal structure of its theories; and that the epistemic evaluation of science requires reference only to the formal relation between data and hypothesis. These ideas still influence how philosophers practise the philosophy of social science. For example, the long debate over functional explanation in the social sciences has largely been framed in terms of finding the necessary and sufficient conditions for having a function or existing for a purpose (see FUNCTIONAL EXPLANATION §3). Much debate in philosophy of economics has been over what are the fundamental postulates of neoclassical economics, implicitly assuming that there is one theory to capture and that formalizing theories is the best way to understand a science. Current assessments of the social sciences also often ignore the social, psychological and historical factors that influence the social sciences as well as the empirical practices of social research; assessments are made instead by appeal to broad conceptual considerations about, for example, the nature of human agency ('free will') or the nature of mental phenomena ('having meaning'). This practice goes back to the positivists' emphasis on logical explication.

3 Criticisms and contributions

Positivism has, of course, been widely criticized. Perhaps most heavily criticized was the positivist claim that theories must be translatable into observa-

tional terms. This claim was criticized on several grounds: (1) the theory/observation distinction is difficult to draw in any sharp way, (2) attempts to translate theoretical terms into observational ones often presupposed theoretical terms in the process of describing the observational data; theoretical terms can be applied in indefinitely many ways to observations, and (3) even if the theory/observation distinction could be drawn, every scientific test involves background theoretical assumptions, thus showing that observational evidence has no absolute epistemic status. These criticisms also lead to doubts about the positivist notion of a unified science. If theoretical terms cannot and need not be reduced to observational ones, then it seems unlikely that the special sciences (biology, psychology, sociology, and so on) are reducible to physics or that they must be to be good science.

These criticisms certainly undercut positivist doctrines in the social sciences. Behaviourism and operationalism lose much of their motivation if good natural science is not translatable into purely observational terms. Methodological individualism likewise is much less plausible once the reductionist picture of scientific unity is rejected. In fact, a detailed literature has shown that precisely the same problems that prevent any reduction of the theoretical to the observational confront attempts to reduce the social to the individual.

The positivist search for an a priori universal scientific method was also criticized. Doubts about a universal scientific method came because the actual practice and history of science seems to show diverse methods across disciplines and historical periods. Doubts about the a priori status of scientific method resulted from the general philosophical attack, stemming from Quine's work, on foundationalism, which is roughly the idea that philosophy stands outside the sciences and can make a priori judgments about them. The holistic picture of theory evaluation mentioned above also suggested that abstract scientific methods far from exhaust the practice of science and that much substantive, domain-specific information is involved in their application.

These criticisms have many implications for the social sciences. Statistical inference is not a mechanical way to get at the truth from the data but instead depends on substantive background assumptions. Also, understanding and evaluating social science requires looking at a complex combination of practices and assumptions rather than focusing on formalized theories alone. Some social scientists and philosophers draw further and much more drastic conclusions. For example, it is widely claimed that the social sciences need not worry about being good science by natural science standards because there is no universal scientific method and because good science is only a matter of convention – good science is only a matter of what persuades or what powerful people in the scientific community accept. Many social scientists and philosophers now advocate these views and thus see naturalism as misguided.

These conclusion are hasty. It is true that at some level of description the different sciences use different methods. Yet it also true that the different specialities within the same science, for example, biochemistry and ecology within biology, also use different methods. To avoid the conclusion that there are as many methods as there are scientists, we might distinguish abstract from realized methods. Scientific virtues such as testability and objectivity are abstractions, ones that are embodied in different practices in different scientific domains. Differences in specific methods across time and place need not threaten naturalism if they result from adapting the same abstract scientific method to the specific circumstances of a given science. For example, the idea that a good test involves 'controls' for spurious influences is common to much good science, though how such control is achieved varies greatly from area to area. So there may be a broad core of scientific rationality that the social sciences can and must achieve, though its actual embodiments will no doubt depend on features specific to the social domain. Naturalism in this form remains a serious position.

It is likewise misguided to conclude from the demise of positivism alone that good science is merely a matter of what persuades, or a social construction. If methodological judgments are a not true a priori, they might none the less be empirically warranted. Good methods are those that effectively promote scientific goals such as truth. Thus we can grant the criticisms of positivism and yet still judge that some inquiries are better than others because experience shows they are better able to produce the truth. In short, the positivists' a priori universal method and an 'anything goes' approach are not the only two alternatives. However, if judgments about good science are both empirical and dependent on how scientific virtues are realized, philosophy of social science then must look carefully at the actual practice of social research and the distinction between philosophy and social science becomes blurred.

See also: Positivism, Russian

References and further reading

* Friedman, M. (1953) *Essays in Positive Economics*, Chicago, IL: University of Chicago Press. (Contains Friedman's instrumentalist defence of economics.)

Gordon, S. (1991) *The History and Philosophy of Social Science*, London: Routledge. (A broad survey that includes positivism's historical role in the social sciences.)

Hausman, D. (1992) *The Inexact and Separate Science of Economics*, Cambridge: Cambridge University Press. (A survey of issues in philosophy of economics with very clear discussions of positivism, Popper and post-positivist approaches to philosophy of science.)

Kincaid, H. (1996) *Philosophical Foundations of the Social Sciences: Analyzing Controversies in Social Research*, Cambridge: Cambridge University Press. (Discusses positivism and methodological individualism in the social sciences; defends the view of philosophy of social science suggested in §3.)

Laudan, L. (1987) 'Progress or rationality? The prospects for normative naturalism', *American Philosophical Quarterly* 24: 19–31. (Defends the idea mentioned in §3 that methodological judgments are empirical.)

McCloskey, D. (1985) *The Rhetoric of Economics*, Madison, WI: University of Wisconsin Press. (A sample of the literature arguing that the failure of positivism shows that judgements about good science are conventional.)

Passmore, J. (1957) *A Hundred Years of Philosophy*, Harmondsworth: Penguin. (Historical material on logical positivism.)

* Popper, K. (1962) *Conjecture and Refutations*, New York: Basic Books. (Outlines Popper's falsificationism and briefly applies it to Marx and Freud.)

* Quine, W. van O. (1960) *Word and Object*, Cambridge, MA: MIT Press. (Presents the arguments mentioned in §2 that there can be no science of interpretation.)

Suppe, F. (1977) *The Structure of Scientific Theories*, Urbana, IL: University of Illinois Press. (Surveys key criticisms of logical positivism.)

HAROLD KINCAID

POSITIVISM, RUSSIAN

Positivism in Russia was not a separate, well-defined philosophical school but, rather, a broad, multidisciplinary current of thought, characterized by a cult of 'positive science', commitment to scientific, empirical methods and rejection of the metaphysical tradition in philosophy. As a rule, Russian positivists sympathized with materialism, although distanced themselves from the metaphysical assumptions of materialist philosophy. Their philosophical aspirations were usually limited to the investigation of specific problems, but their optimistic belief in the power of science could push them in the direction of an all-embracing 'scientific philosophy'.

In accordance with the naturalistic evolutionism of the second half of the nineteenth century, scientific philosophy involved the conception of objective laws of development and biological and/or sociological relativism – both incompatible with the ethicist standpoint. Many Russian thinkers, especially the so-called 'subjective sociologists', tried to combine positivist scientism with ethicism, claiming an independent status for moral values. Their efforts, however, could be successful only at the expense of abandoning the scientific rigour demanded by consistent positivists. Hence their views were semi-positivist rather than positivist. Through undermining the arrogant self-confidence and monopolistic claims of the crude forms of positivistic scientism, they paved the way for the outspoken revolt against positivism at the end of the 1890s.

1   **Dogmatic and critical positivism**
2   **Positivism and psychology**
3   **Positivism and sociology**
4   **The revolt against positivism in social philosophy**

1   Dogmatic and critical positivism

The founder of positivism, Auguste COMTE, became known in Russia as early as the late 1840s. His critique of metaphysics and his conception of the three stages of human development (theological, metaphysical and positive) influenced Russian radicals of the 1860s, especially D. Pisarev (see RUSSIAN MATERIALISM: 'THE 1860S'), and Russian populists of the 1870s, especially Mikhailovskii (see LAVROV, P.L.; MIKHAILOVSKII, N.K.). For the latter Comte was more palatable than Herbert Spencer because he recognized the validity of a 'subjective method' in sociology and did not claim that a positivist approach to social philosophy was incompatible with value judgments.

The most consistent adherent of Comtian positivism in Russia was Grigory Vyrubov (1843–1913), active mostly in France, where he became a personal friend of Littré and a co-founder of *La Philosophie positive*, the chief organ of French positivism. His philosophical standpoint, expressed most clearly in his article 'Le certain et le probable, l'absolu et le relatif' (in the first volume of *La Philosophie positive*, 1867) is thoroughly dogmatic. Its basic proposition is that scientific knowledge can lay claim to absolute

truth and that the opposition between the absolute and the relative is in itself relative, because anything real that can be translated into the language of scientific laws can be called absolute. Following Comte, Vyrubov dismissed not only classical ontology but also epistemology, for which he proposed to substitute the methodology of individual sciences. Hence he was very hostile to any sign of a renewal of interest in Kantian criticism (see KANT, I. §4).

A different type of positivism was represented by Vladimir Lesevich (1837–1905). He accused Vyrubov of a naïve belief that all problems could be solved by science and postulated that positivism should concentrate on elaborating its own theory of knowledge. This required a rapprochement between positivists and Neo-Kantians. Positivism, Lesevich maintained, should become a '*critical* philosophy of reality'. To achieve this, positivists should learn from Kantian epistemological criticism without accepting the possibility of a priori knowledge.

Lesevich expounded these views in the 1870s. A decade later he drew near to the empiriocriticism of Ernst MACH and became the chief Russian representative of the 'second positivism', emphasizing the importance of epistemological reflection. On the other hand, he argued that epistemology should cease to exist as a distinct specialized discipline separated from science. In his book *What is a Scientific Philosophy?* (1891) he advocated the view that the task of 'scientific philosophy' was to make science 'philosophical', instead of just making philosophy 'scientific'.

In his theory of the social sciences Lesevich tried to mediate between positivism and the populist 'subjective method'. Lavrov and Mikhailovskii, he argued, were right in their criticism of Spencer's 'objectivist' approach to social evolution. Epistemological reflection shows that only the abstract sciences can make use of purely objective methods; the applied sciences are directed towards activity, and therefore have to solve problems of value judgments and value implementation. Many arguments for this line of reasoning were to be found, of course, in the works of the Neo-Kantians (see NEO-KANTIANISM, RUSSIAN §2).

2   Positivism and psychology

In the positivists' discussions on 'scientific philosophy' much attention was paid to psychology, which was often confused with epistemology. Vyrubov simply reduced epistemology to psychology, and even Lesevich was convinced that epistemology was largely based on psychological data.

The most extreme representative of positivistic

'psychologism' in the interpretation of the classical problems of philosophy was a professor at Moscow University, Matveii Troitskii (1835–99). His *Nemetskaia psikhologiia v tekushchem stoletii* (German Psychology of the Current Century), (2 volumes, 1867), was a vehement attack on the philosophical bias of German psychology, written from the point of view of English empirical, associationist psychology. His chief work, entitled *The Science of the Spirit* (2 volumes, 1882), was an attempt to provide a psychological interpretation of logic.

A more sophisticated version of psychologism was advocated by a liberal historian and philosopher, Konstantin Kavelin (1818–85). His main philosophical work, *Zadachi psikhologii* (The Tasks of Psychology) (1872), was a cautious defence of German Idealism, through interpreting it as a disguised form of psychological investigation which concentrated on the active side of the human psyche. In his theory of the relation between mind and body Kavelin represented a standpoint halfway between psychophysical parallelism and interactionism. This position did not satisfy either the materialists or the consistent idealists and spiritualists. The eminent physiologist Ivan Sechnov attacked *Zadachi psikhologii* for the treatment of psychic processes as autonomous phenomena, while the Slavophile Iurii Samarin (see SLAVOPHILISM) accused Kavelin of exaggerating the soul's dependence on the body and external environment.

Nikolai Grot (1852–99) was initially a more militant and consistent positivist. He studied under Troitskii and his first works – his master's thesis on the psychology of sense perception and his doctorate on the psychological interpretation of logic – displayed a consistently associationist standpoint. He also tried to justify 'naïve realism' in epistemology and deterministic evolutionism in the theory of mind.

In 1886 Grot was appointed professor at Moscow University and shortly afterwards became president of the Moscow Psychological Society. In 1889 he founded the journal *Problems of Philosophy and Psychology*. This gave him an influential position in academic philosophical circles in Russia. In the first issue of the journal he published a programmatic essay on the need of elaborating a distinctively Russian philosophical culture. His own philosophical position had by then undergone a substantial change: he turned away from positivism and openly declared his conversion to metaphysics. This new philosophy of 'monodualism' was to be a synthesis of monism and dualism and a resolution of ontological antinomies in the idea of God. But it was not a return to the speculative constructs of German Idealism: in his article 'What is Metaphysics?' (1900) Grot took care

to explain that he meant an inductive metaphysics, attempting to base itself on the data of inner experience and therefore closely linked to psychology. Towards the end of his life he tried to reconcile his new system with positivistic scientism. This was owing to his interest in the energetics of Wilhelm Ostwald, which revived his belief that natural sciences could provide a solution to metaphysical problems.

3 Positivism and sociology

The field in which Russian positivism made its most valuable contribution was sociology. The most philosophical among the positivist sociologists in Russia was Evgenii de Roberty (1843–1915), the follower of Comte, a friend of Vyrubov and a contributor to *La Philosophie positive*. He was one of the first representatives of self-conscious sociologism, that is, a point of view which maintains that social phenomena represent a specific property of organized matter, and therefore cannot be reduced to, or explained by, any wider class of better-known phenomena. Hence sociology should be a new fundamental discipline, completely independent of biology, psychology or economy. De Roberty developed this view in his major work in Russian, entitled *Sociology, Its Basic Task and Methodological Peculiarities* (1880).

Philosophical implications of this standpoint, elaborated mostly in de Roberty's works in French (such as *L'Inconnaissable*, 1889; *Sociologie d'action*, 1908; *Le Concept de la raison et les lois de l'univers*, 1912), included the view that an isolated individual cannot be a thinking being and therefore psychology ought to be based on sociology, and not vice versa. Another implication was the rejection of the classical definition of truth: objective truth, de Roberty argued, cannot exist, since truth is only a matter of collective experience; the difference between objective and subjective boils down to the difference between individual experience that has been totally dominated by collective experience, and individual experience that has been subjected to collective experience only to a minor extent. Finally, de Roberty's conception of the social roots of knowledge was linked to a philosophical interpretation of sociality as a specific and supreme form of energy – a 'supra-organic' energy, arising out of the interaction of many minds.

A different version of the Comtian tradition was represented in Russia by the outstanding historian of legal institutions, Maksim Kovalevskii (1851–1916). He saw himself as a supporter of Comte and, at the same time, a disciple of Marx (by whom he was befriended). In sociology he was a typical evolutionist, convinced of the uniformity and universal applicability of the basic laws of social development (see his *Sociology*, 2 volumes, 1910). He defined progress as the strengthening of the bonds of human solidarity – the constant expansion of the 'environment of peaceful coexistence', from tribal unity through national patriotism to the solidarity of the whole human race.

In his political views Kovalevskii was a moderate liberal. The liberal belief in universal laws of social progress was questioned by populist sociologists such as Lavrov and Mikhailovskii, who wanted Russia to develop differently from the West. As a rule, this course involved a departure from positivist scientism. The most positivistic among the populist theorists was the historian Nikolai Kareev (1850–1931). In his theoretical works, which include *Osnovnye voprosy filosofii istorii* (Fundamental Problems of the Philosophy of History) (1883) and *Etiudy sotsiologicheskie i filosofskie* (Sociological and Philosophical Studies) (1895) among others, he recognized four types of knowledge: numenological knowledge, being outside the scope of positive science; phenomenological knowledge, dealing with the phenomena themselves; nomological knowledge, determining the general laws; and deontological knowledge which justifies our ideals. He conceived of history as a phenomenological science, dealing with individual events; the task of sociology was to formulate general laws of historical development. The existence of such laws, however, did not exclude, in Kareev's view, the importance of individual choices; hence the need to supplement sociology by deontological, ethical knowledge. In this way Kareev tried to reconcile the positivist (and Marxist) conception of the objective laws of historical development with populist 'subjective sociology'.

4 The revolt against positivism in social philosophy

At the turn of the century Russian philosophy and social thought underwent a radical reorientation, known as the revolt against positivism. A peculiarly important role in this revolt was played by a group of thinkers (Pëtr Struve, Nikolai BERDIAEV, Sergei BULGAKOV and a few others) who wanted to oppose positivistic scientism (as leaving no place for moral ideals) and, at the same time, to resist populist 'subjectivism' (as containing an element of relativism and thus depriving moral ideals of objective validity). They realized this double task by embracing transcendental (Neo-Kantian) idealism, and soon developed it into transcendent (metaphysical) idealism; the final stage was an openly religious philosophy (see RUSSIAN RELIGIOUS-PHILOSOPHICAL RENAISSANCE §5).

Despite defining their main adversary as positiv-

ism, the thinkers in question did not engage in polemics against classical Western positivists and tended to ignore the adherents of positivism in Russia. Instead, they concentrated on the critique of Marxism, as interpreted by the theorists of the Second International. It was so because most of them were former Marxists and, more importantly, because the entire Russian intelligentsia saw the last word of the positive science of society in the 'scientific socialism' of Marx, and not in the theories of Comte or Spencer. In his populist phase, before becoming 'the Father of the Russian Marxism', Georgii PLEKHANOV defined Marxism in the Comtian fashion: as representing the 'positive stage' in the development of social theory. As a Marxist, he defended the position of a rigorously scientist objectivism, according to which ethical ideals must be derived from, and coincide with, the objective laws of historical necessity. Owing to this, the initial phase of the revolt against positivism in Russia took the form of a confrontation between deterministic Marxism and Kantian ethical idealism.

See also: POSITIVISM IN THE SOCIAL SCIENCES

References and further reading

Hecker, J.F. (1916) *Studies in History, Economics and Public Law, vol. 67, Russian Sociology, A Contribution to the History of Sociological Thought and Theory*, New York: Columbia University Press. (Detailed analysis of Kareev's social philosophy and sociology.)

Shkurinov, P.S. (1980) *Pozitivizm v Rossii xix veka* (Positivism in Russia in the Nineteenth Century), Moscow. (This relatively recent monograph on the philosophies of Russian positivism is the most comprehensive in Russian.)

Sorokin, P.A. (1928) *Contemporary Sociological Theories*, New York. (Detailed presentation of de Roberty's sociological theory.)

Walicki, A. (1980) *A History of Russian Thought from the Enlightenment to Marxism*, trans. H. Andrews-Rusiecka, Stanford, CA: Stanford University Press and Oxford: Clarendon Press. (General account in English.)

Zenkovsky, V. (1948–50) *Istoriia russkoi filosofii*, Paris: YMCA-Press, 2 vols; 2nd edn 1989; trans. G.L. Kline, *A History of Russian Philosophy*, London and New York: Routledge & Kegan Paul and Columbia University Press, 1953, ch. 12 and 25. (General account in English.)

ANDRZEJ WALICKI

POSITIVIST THOUGHT IN LATIN AMERICA

Between 1850 and the 1920s European positivism became a major intellectual movement in Latin America. It asserted that all knowledge came from experience; that scientific thinking was the model for philosophizing and that the search for first causes or ultimate reason typical of religion and metaphysics, was an obsolete mode of thinking. Positivism set out to discover the most general features of experience. Its tasks were to use them to explain and predict phenomena, to develop a social science that would furnish objective grounds for moral choice and to help create the best society possible.

In Latin America positivism became a social philosophy which represented a cogent alternative to romanticism, eclecticism, Catholicism and traditional Hispanic values. It offered the prospect of a secular society in which the knowledge gained from science and industry would bring the benefits of order and progress. It assumed that the social sciences had the power to improve the human condition and it demanded political action. Three main currents were in evidence: autochthonous positivism indigenous to the region and concerned with local social and political issues, social positivism derived from Auguste Comte and stressing the historical nature of social change, and evolutionary positivism influenced by Herbert Spencer and asserting the biological nature of society.

Autochthonous positivism emerged in the 1830s from the influx of liberal ideas which followed the wars of independence fought on the US continent by those wishing to gain freedom from Spain. Urging an intellectual revolution, swift social change and material progress, autochthonous positivism paved the way for European positivism proper. Social positivism appeared around the 1850s and argued for the necessity of educational reforms to solve the continent's problems. It required participation in political life and became a radical force in spite of opposition from supporters of the status quo. By the 1880s evolutionary positivism had steered the movement in a conservative direction in support of laissez-faire *policies, individualism and gradual change.*

1   European positivism

Also called naturalism, scientism and social Darwinism, European positivism was first defined by Saint Simon as the philosophic application of scientific methods to human affairs. Auguste COMTE systematically reshaped this insight into a method, a philosophy of science, a theory of development and a polity in *Cours de philosophie positive* (Course of Positive Philosophy) (1830–42).

Positive science does not acknowledge anything beyond the objective relations between phenomena given in experience. The method is to observe these relations and generalize them as coherent principles with which to explain reality. The scientific principles which result from these generalizations depend on the stage of development of the science. According to Comte's law of the three stages, the sciences, societies and the intellect pass through the mythical, metaphysical and positive stages, each representing a characteristic type of explanation of social structures and mental development. The sciences have progressed at different rates: the more general sciences, astronomy and physics, overcome the metaphysical stage earlier than the more specific sciences, such as chemistry or biology, which take longer. The last science to become positive was sociology. Its task was to solve the problems of attaining order and progress in society. In the *Système de politique positive* (System of Positive Philosophy) (1851–4) Comte describes the one society capable of achieving these goals, the sociocracy: a dictatorship of the proletariat and altruistic capitalists, under the moral tutelage of sociologist-priests of the Religion of Humanity.

In England, John Stuart MILL subscribed to positivism in early editions of *System of Logic* (1843) but recanted in *Auguste Comte and Positivism* (1865) because of the social and political implications of Comte's *Système de politique positive* (System of Positive Philosophy). Herbert SPENCER at first accepted Comte's stand on metaphysics and epistemology but eventually disagreed over the deeper nature of change in his essay *Reasons for Dissenting from the Philosophy of M. Auguste Comte* (1864). In *Social Statics* (1851) and later in *First Principles* (1862), Spencer developed an evolutionary principle that predated Darwin's formulation in 1859, which said that organisms are constantly challenged by the environment and other organisms. To survive they must adapt and pass on this adaptation to their offspring. This struggle for survival must produce stronger, more aggressive and cunning individuals, as only the fittest can survive. Like organisms, societies compete for limited resources. To survive they must adapt to internal or external changes. Complex societies which manage to survive, such as those in Europe, are the fittest. The struggle leaves no room for altruism, a lesson not to be lost on political economy, since only policies that stimulate individual competition but do not interfere with natural development, can increase a society's chances of survival.

2 Latin American positivism

In Latin America, European positivism gained widespread attention as a scientific philosophy that offered solutions to problems which overburdened the continent, such as lack of freedom, political anarchy, venality and economic chaos. Social positivists pointed to the continent's lack of development. Their solution was to reach the positive stage through lay education. It was to de-emphasize rhetoric and literature and teach mathematics and science instead of theology. The resultant effect would be better citizens free from superstition or dogma, motivated by altruism and competent to use the social sciences to reorganize society and develop industry. Evolutionary positivists diagnosed society as sick as a consequence of inferior racial mixtures. Their solutions were to improve the racial stock and stimulate economic growth through European human and capital migration, encourage individual independence and adopt a *laissez-faire* policy.

Both positivist camps justified their views with evidence gathered from the sciences. Furthermore both envisaged that the future result lay in a technological industrial society with a structure and wealth similar to that of the more civilized European nations. Another reason for the favourable reception of European positivism was the presence of an autochthonous variety. The ideas that had given rise to positivism in Europe had been discussed in Latin America before the wars of independence. These ideas incited a rejection of traditional Hispanic values and Catholic thought and fostered an appreciation of science and its potential for guiding reform. Autochthonous positivism has been portrayed as a parallel development, although could also be one of historical opportunism. Indeed, social or evolutionary positivists called select figures autochthonous positivists to capitalize on their prestige and legitimize positivist claims historically.

For details about the progress of positivism in Latin America, the historical circumstances of individual nations have to be taken into account. The most interesting are Argentina, Mexico, Brazil and Chile.

3 Argentina

In Argentina the first expression of a philosophy akin to positivism is found in the works of Domingo Sarmiento and Juan Bautista Alberdi (see ARGENTINA, PHILOSOPHY IN). Anticipating Spencer, Sarmiento (1845) pointed out the importance of ethnic and geographic factors in the formation of political character. For both philosophers humanity progresses from either a bucolic, or barbarian state to a complex urban culture, which is the road to civilization. Later in *Conflictos y armonías en las razas de América* (Conflict and Harmony Among the Races in America) (1883), Sarmiento adopted a racism justified by Spencerian evolutionism. He claimed that Latin America's lack of progress was due to racial inferiority deriving from the mixture of Indian, African and Mediterranean blood. He thought progress could only be made by improving the racial mixture through unrestricted immigration from northern European countries, such as Germany or Denmark. Alberdi's *Bases y puntos de partida para la organización política de la República Argentina* (Foundations and Points of Departure of the Political Organization of the Argentine Republic) (1852) foreshadowed arguments made by social positivists. In it he claimed that Argentina's social problems were the result of outdated ideas and traditions. He thought that reforms should be moral and educational and they should teach individuals self-reliance for self-rule. Alberdi joined Sarmiento's call for increased European immigration. They agreed that to govern was to populate, that is, to educate, improve and civilize. But in order to civilize through population a civilized population was needed in the form of European immigrants. Comtian positivism was introduced in 1872 into the Paraná Teachers College by Pedro Scalabrini and in 1910 at the National University of La Plata by J. Alfredo Ferreira. As positivism became so institutionalized, its influence was to prove long-lasting. It concerned itself mainly with scientific problems and educational improvements and voiced its proposals in journals, such as *La Escuela Positiva* (1894–9) and *El Positivismo: Órgano del Comité Positivista Argentino* (Positivism: Organ of the Argentine Positivist Committee) (1925–35), the latter the organ of the Comité Positivista Argentino.

Evolutionary positivism gained popularity among scientists at the University of Buenos Aires, such as psychiatrist José María Ramos y Mejía, palaeontologist Florentino Ameghino, sociologist Carlos Octavio Bunge and José Ingenieros, although they did not found a school. However, they did exercise considerable influence. An important exponent was Ingenieros, a psychiatrist by training who also distinguished himself in sociology and philosophy. In *Principios de psicología* (Principles of Psychology) (1911), Ingenieros begins as a committed evolutionist, but admitted the need for improvement because he felt inductivism neglected the speculative aspect of science. As a solution, in his book *Proposiciones relativas al porvenir de la filosofía* (Propositions About the Future of Philosophy) (1918), he proposed an experiential metaphysics that could generate future scientific hypotheses. Ingenieros also found evolutionary ethics unable to account for human ideals and in *Hacia una moral sin dogmas* (Towards a Moral Society Without Dogma) (1917) he pursued an idealism that can only be justified in evolutionary terms.

4 Mexico

As early as 1833 José María Luis Mora anticipated positivism by defining it as a practical attitude opposed to the theoretical and espoused by those who sought newer educational forms to replace the old colonial dogmatism (see MEXICO, PHILOSOPHY IN). In 'Revista política de las diversas administraciones que la República mexicana ha tenido hasta 1837' (Political Review of the Many Administrations the Republic has had Since 1837) (1837), Mora expressed dissatisfaction with the anarchy which followed independence and asserted that social progress would finally be made when Mexicans adopted a liberal attitude which guaranteed individual autonomy. The Mexican–American War (1845–8) and the French intervention (1863–7) reinforced this opinion and in 1867 President Benito Juárez called on Gabino Barreda, a student and follower of Comte, to reform education. The goal was an educated class that would lead the country out of economic stagnation and political chaos towards modernization and industrialization. Barreda believed that Mexico had undergone a political revolution and was ready for an intellectual one. This meant giving up Catholicism and liberalism as remnants of the theological and metaphysical stages for a new order akin to the positivist polity. According to Barreda, societies could progress only if they reached a consensus of opinion like that in the sciences. Thus, a scientific education was a necessary step towards progress.

Enactment of the public education law institutionalized Barreda's suggestions at the secondary level. A decade later a new class of intellectuals emerged who were trained along positivist lines. This generation, however, abandoned Comte for Spencer's evolutionism. They founded a political party, los Científicos, which advocated economic solutions and individual initiative over educational reforms. They supported the government in power from 1892–1910. The most interesting exponent of los Científicos was Justo Sierra. In *The Evolution of the Mexican People* (1900), Sierra uses the evolving organism analogy to argue that the cause of Mexico's illness was the sudden transition from a primitive to a militaristic society. The symptoms were revolutions and political atavisms. To restore health, what was needed was gradual evolutionary growth.

5 Brazil

Brazil's nineteenth-century intellectual development differed from the rest of Latin America (see BRAZIL, PHILOSOPHY IN). Colonized by Portugal, Brazil lacked universities and schools of philosophy. In 1821, without war or revolution, it became an independent monarchy. Social positivism was introduced by Luís Pereira Barreto and Benjamin Constant Botelho de Magalhães to science students around the 1870s at the Military School of Rio de Janeiro. Pereira Barreto eloquently listed in *As Três Filosofias* (Three Philosophies) (1874) the advantages of Comte's positivism and the need to liberate Brazil from religious dogma. Constant had become acquainted with Comte in 1857. He founded the Sociedade Positivista in 1871 and discussed positivism after 1873 in his science and mathematics lectures. Even the most orthodox aspects of social positivism were well received. Miguel Lemos and Raimundo Teixeira Mendes converted to Comte's Religion of Humanity. In 1881 they founded the Templo da Humanidade.

Evolutionary positivists formed a smaller yet influential group among lawyers at the Recife Law School. Its most important exponents were Tobias Barreto, author of *Estudos Alemães* (German Studies) (1882) and his students, Sílvio Romero and Clóvis Bevil qua, the latter one of the authors of Brazil's civil code. They criticized social positivists, particularly the orthodoxy, for suggesting abstract morality rather than concrete economic advances as remedies for Brazil's problems.

Antagonisms between social and evolutionary positivists worsened after 1888 when Constant led the overthrow of the monarchy. In shaping the new republican constitution, social positivists successfully argued for the separation of Church and state, the abolition of slavery and the establishment of a lay educational system. Even the national flag contained the positivist motto *Ordem e Progresso* (Order and Progress). Their more radical proposals, such as the establishment of a sociocracy and making the Cult of Humanity the official state religion, were blocked by evolutionists and liberals at the national level, although they remained part of certain state constitutions like that of Rio Grande do Sul.

6 Chile

Chile produced several social positivists, but scarcely any evolutionists. The earliest were José Victorino Lastarria and Francisco Bilbao, both students of Venezuelan humanist Andrés Bello while he resided in Chile. Lastarria came across Comte's ideas in 1868, although he had anticipated them in 'Investigaciones sobre la influencia social de la conquista y del sistema colonial de los Españoles en Chile' (Investigation into the Social Influence of the Conquest of Spanish Colonialism in Chile) (1844) in which he held that all historic movement was towards freedom and progress and that the colonial past, full of errors and dogmas, had to be overcome. Bilbao also blamed the colonial past and Catholicism in particular for Chile's lack of development. In *Iniciativa de la América: idea de un congreso federal de las repúblicas* (American Initiative: The Idea of a Federal Congress of Republics) (1856), he suggested the creation of a continental federation of republics which would allow equality, freedom of worship, universal education and would unify the continent under an international law.

As in Brazil, an orthodoxy appeared, led by brothers, Jorge and Juan Enrique Lagarrigue, who had read Comte's works in the 1870s. An eloquent writer, Juan Enrique applied a positivist analysis to issues of national and international peace, the role of women, socialism, the right to strike and the duty of the priesthood of Humanity to mediate between workers and patricians. He attacked parliamentary governments as bankrupt because they rested on metaphysical foundations. This stand clashed with less orthodox positivists such as jurist Valentín Letelier. Letelier had become acquainted with Comte at the same time as the Lagarrigue brothers and admired the positivist programme, but could not accept the religious dogma or the absolutism of the *Système de politique positive* (System of Positive Philosophy) (1851–4). This difference was most evident during the conflict in 1891 between an executive backed by conservatives and a liberal congress. Letelier sided with the congress on liberal grounds while the Lagarrigue brothers argued for a dictatorship of the executive to represent another step towards sociocracy.

7 Positivism elsewhere in Latin America

In other countries positivism was not as widespread. Uruguayan evolutionism was as much a reaction to an idealist and spiritualist philosophy as to political chaos and moral corruption. Positivists tried to improve the nation's morality as well as their material wealth through economic, political and educational reforms. In Cuba, a Spanish colony until 1898, there were no supporters of social positivism, but Spencer had an advocate in Enrique José Varona. Eugenio María de Hostos of Puerto Rico, also developed a sociology along evolutionist lines. Ecuadorean Juan Montalvo, Peruvian Manuel González Prada and José Martí, for example, found positivism a convenient framework in which to cast moral and political ideas without being committed to the doctrine.

8 The decline

Positivism declined towards the end of the nineteenth century. Intellectually it had become stifled and internal squabbles depleted its ranks. Politically it had shifted from being liberal and reformist to become conservative and inactive. Policies were too vague or impossible to implement, or else they were based on insubstantial empirical evidence. Los Científicos fell catastrophically during Mexico's revolution in 1910. Positivism was found to be philosophically inadequate. Alejandro Korn and Francisco Romero eroded its credibility in Argentina. In Uruguay, the philosophies of Carlos Vaz Ferreira and the literary works of José Enrique Rodó offered better alternatives. In Mexico, José Vasconcelos and Antonio Caso pointed to the doctrinal poverty of positivism. Eventually, vitalism, Marxism, existentialism, Platonism and a general return to classical philosophy offered more articulate views. By the 1920s positivism was a term of censure. However, its influence proved subtly pervasive as elements of the doctrine were evident in the views of its strongest detractors. As a legacy it left a trust in technological change and a belief in popular education and economic prosperity.

See also: ANTI-POSITIVIST THOUGHT IN LATIN AMERICA; POSITIVISM IN THE SOCIAL SCIENCES

References and further reading

* Alberdi, J.B. (1852) *Bases y puntos de partida para la organización política de la República Argentina* (Foundations and Points of Departure of the Political Organization of the Argentine Republic), Buenos Aires: Imprenta Argentina; repr. Buenos Aires: Depalma, 1964. (An argument for improving the political organization of Argentina through European immigration.)

Ardao, A. (1971) 'Assimilation and transformation of Positivism in Latin America', in R.L. Woodward (ed.) *Positivism in Latin America*, Lexington, MA: Heath, 11–16. (An excellent account of the different modes of positivist thought throughout Latin America.)

* Barreto, T. (1882) *Estudos Alemães* (German Studies), Recife: Typografia Central, 2nd edn, Rio de Janeiro: Laemmert, 1891, repr. Rio de Janeiro: Editora Record, 1991. (An exposition of European philosophy and evolutionism.)

* Bilbao, F. (1856) *Iniciativa de la América: idea de un congreso federal de las repúblicas* (American Initiative: The Idea of a Federal Congress of Republics), Paris: D'Aubusson y Kugelmann. (The author suggests the creation of a continental federation of republics to unify the continent under an international law.)

* Comte, A. (1830–42) *Cours de philosophie positive* (Course of Positive Philosophy), Paris: Bachelier, repr. in A. Comte, *Œuvres d'Auguste Comte*, Paris: Editions Anthropos, 1968, vols 1–6. (The main formulation of Comte's positivism, grounded in the study of the philosophy and history of science.)

* —— (1851–4) *Système de politique positive* (System of Positive Philosophy), Paris: Librarie Mathias, repr. in A. Comte, *Œuvres d'Auguste Comte*, Paris: Editions Anthropos, 1968, vols 7–10. (An attempt to ground science and progress on a religious and political system.)

Cruz C.J. (1964) *A History of Ideas in Brazil*, trans. S. Macedo, Berkeley, CA: University of California Press. (Good account of the development of positivism in Brazil.)

* Ingenieros, J. (1911) *Principios de psicología* (Principles of Psychology), Buenos Aires, repr. in *Obras Completas*, vol. 6, Buenos Aires: Elmer Editor, 1957. (An important reduction of psychology to evolutionary biology.)

* —— (1917) *Hacia una moral sin dogmas* (Towards a Moral Society Without Dogma), Buenos Aires: Losada, 1961. (An attempt to ground ethics on idealism and evolutionary theory.)

* —— (1918) *Proposiciones relativas al porvenir de la filosofía* (Propositions About the Future of Philosophy), Buenos Aires: Losada, 1960. (A programme to define philosophy along scientific positivist lines.)

Jaksić, I. (1989) *Academic Rebels in Chile*, Albany, NY: State University of New York Press. (An excellent treatment of academic philosophy in Chile.)

* Lastarria, J.V. (1844) 'Investigaciones sobre la influencia social de la conquista y del sistema colonial de los Españoles en Chile' (Investigation into the Social Influence of the Conquest of Spanish Colonialism in Chile), in *Discursos Académicos* (Academic Discourses), Santiago de Chile: Imprenta del Siglo, repr. in *Obras Completas de Don J.V. Lastarria*, vol. 7, Santiago de Chile: Imprenta Barcelona, 1906. (A negative assessment of the effects of Hispanic values in Chile.)

Martí, O.R. (1983a) 'Gabino Barreda and Moral Philosophy', *Aztlán* 14: 373–403. (A more detailed treatment of Barreda's positivism and moral philosophy.)

—— (1983b) 'Auguste Comte and the positivist utopias', in E.D.S. Sullivan (ed.) *The Utopian Vision*, San Diego, CA: San Diego State University Press. (A treatment of Comte's utopian views and its worldwide influence.)

—— (1989) 'Sarmiento y el positivismo' (Sarmiento and Positivism), *Cuadernos Americanos* (American Notebooks) 13: 142–54. (An examination of the claim that Sarmiento held views reflecting autochthonous positivism, published in a distinguished journal on Iberian and Iberoamerican culture, literature, philosophy, politics and the arts.)

* Mill, J.S. (1843) *System of Logic, Ratiocinative and Inductive*, London: J.W. Parker; repr. New York: Longmans, Green, 1961. (A logic text that endorses the positivist programme of reducing deductive to inductive logic.)

* —— (1865) *Auguste Comte and Positivism*, Ann Arbor, MI: Ann Arbor Paperbacks, 1973. (Mill's criticisms of Comte's philosophy.)

* Mora, J.M.L. (1837) 'Revista política de las diversas administraciones que la República mexicana ha tenido hasta 1837' (Political Review of the Many Administrations the Republic has had since 1837), in *Obras Sueltas*, Paris: Librería de Rosa, repr. Mexico: Porrúa, 1963. (A criticism of political developments in Mexico.)

Peel, J.D.Y. (ed.) (1972) *Herbert Spencer On Social Evolution*, Chicago, IL: University of Chicago Press. (A collection of Spencer's most important writings.)

* Pereira Barreto, L. (1874) *As Três Filosofias* (Three Philosophies), São Paulo, repr. in E. Spencer Macial de Barros (ed.) *Obras filosóficas*, São Paulo: Editorial Grijalbo, 1967. (An important exposition of positivism in Brazil.)

* *El Positivismo: Órgano del Comité Positivista Argentino* (Positivism: Organ of the Argentine Positivist Committee) (1925–35), Buenos Aires: Comité Positivista Argentino. (Argentinian journal which published articles with a Comtian positivist orientation.)

Revista Positiva, Filosófica, Literaria, Social y Política (Positivist, Philosophical, Literary, Social and

Political Review) (1901–14), Mexico. (Popular journal in its day.)

* Sarmiento, D.F. (1845) *Life in the Argentine Republic in the Days of the Tyrants; or, Civilization and Barbarism*, New York: Hafner, 1974. (An autochthonous positivist's classic in which he examines the social ills which affect Argentina.)

* —— (1883) *Conflictos y armonías en las razas de América* (Conflict and Harmony Among the Races in America), Buenos Aires: S. Ostwald. (An attempt to trace Latin American shortcomings to a mixture of inferior races.)

* Sierra, J. (1900) *The Political Evolution of the Mexican People*, Austin, TX: University of Texas Press. (A classic analysis of Mexican history by an important evolutionary positivist.)

* Spencer, H. (1851) *Social Statics*, London: John Chapman, repr. New York: Robert Schalkenbach Foundation, 1995. (An early formulation of sociology.)

* —— (1862) *First Principles*, London: Williams & Norgate, repr. in T.W. Hill (ed.), Westport, CN: Greenwood Press, 1976. (An important philosophical work that tries to structure philosophy along evolutionary principles.)

* —— (1864) *Reasons for Dissenting from the Philosophy of M. Auguste Comte and Other Essays*, Berkeley, CA: Glendessary Press, 1968. (Spencer's criticisms of Comte's philosophy.)

Woodward, R.L. (ed.) (1971) *Positivism in Latin America*, Lexington, MA: Heath. (An adequate anthology in English.)

Zea, L. (1981) *El Pensamiento Positivista Latinoamericano* (Latin American Positivist Thought), Caracas: Biblioteca Ayacucho. (The best collection of Latin American positivist writings.)

OSCAR R. MARTÍ

POSSIBLE WORLDS

The concept of Possible worlds arises most naturally in the study of possibility and necessity. It is relatively uncontroversial that grass might have been red, or (to put the point another way) that there is a possible world in which grass is red. Though we do not normally take such talk of possible worlds literally, doing so has a surprisingly large number of benefits. Possible worlds enable us to analyse and help us understand a wide range of problematic and difficult concepts. Modality and modal logic, counterfactuals, propositions and properties are just some of the concepts illuminated by possible worlds.

Yet, for all this, possible worlds may raise more problems than they solve. What kinds of things are possible worlds? Are they merely our creations or do they exist independently of us? Are they concrete objects, like the actual world, containing flesh and blood people living in alternative realities, or are they abstract objects, like numbers, unlocated in space and time and with no causal powers? Indeed, since possible worlds are not the kind of thing we can ever visit, how could we even know that such things exist? These are but some of the difficult questions which must be faced by anyone who wishes to use possible worlds.

1 Pros and cons
2 Extreme realism
3 Combinatorialism
4 Possible worlds as novels
5 Moderate realism

1 Pros and cons

Although known to Leibniz, it was not until the middle of the twentieth century that possible worlds came to occupy the attention of a significant number of philosophers and logicians (see LEIBNIZ, G.W. §3). While this was initially due to the discovery that possible worlds permitted the formulation of a model-theoretic semantics for modal logic, it gradually became clear that possible worlds could be used to shed light on many other notions which had been regarded as problematic: intensional logic, counterfactuals, propositions and properties are but some of the areas illuminated by possible worlds. Indeed, some have even argued that the existence of possible worlds is a tenet of our ordinary common-sense beliefs. It is uncontroversially true that there are many ways the world could have been – but what are these many ways but possible worlds under another name?

However, although possible worlds may provide solutions to old problems, they raise new difficulties of their own. Since possible worlds are not the kind of thing with which we can causally interact, how do we know that there are such things, and how have we come to possess the kind of modal knowledge we credit ourselves with? Then there is the problem of transworld identity: how one and the same object can exist at different possible worlds. The problem arises for the following reason: not only is it possible that there might have been people who were twelve feet tall, Quine himself might have been twelve feet tall. In possible worlds terms, this means that there is a possible world at which Quine is twelve feet tall, apparently making Quine exist in more than one world.

When it comes to questions about their metaphysical nature – what kinds of things possible worlds are – there is very little agreement. It is agreed that possible worlds must be capable of representing many different ways the world could have been, and there can be no possible worlds in which grass is both green and red; but whether possible worlds are abstract or concrete, whether they exist independently of us or are our own creation, whether they have structure or are simples – are all contentious issues.

2   Extreme realism

For the extreme realist, all possible worlds are on a par: there is no distinction in kind between the actual and the possible. All that marks off the actual world from the infinitely many merely possible worlds is that the actual world is the world we happen to inhabit. Just as the actual world contains flesh and blood human beings, so some merely possible worlds contain flesh and blood human beings. Just as the actual world is made up of concrete spatio-temporally extended objects, so other possible worlds are made up of concrete spatiotemporally extended objects.

At first sight it appears that the extreme realist must solve the problem of transworld identity by having one and the same object literally appearing in more than one world. But there is an ingenious alternative. Quine might exist at a possible world w not because he is a part of w, but because w contains some other person (call him 'Kwine') who *resembles* Quine. If Kwine and Quine share certain properties, if they lead similar lives and have similar parents then Kwine is said to be Quine's *counterpart*. It is possible for Quine to be twelve feet tall if there exists some world which contains a counterpart of Quine, and that counterpart is twelve feet tall.

Extreme modal realists use neither modal nor intensional concepts in their theory. Accordingly, they can use possible worlds to analyse non-circularly the concepts of necessity, of counterfactuals, of propositions and of properties. Since the number of different concepts taken as primitive is few, an advantage of this theory is that it is ideologically parsimonious.

Yet for all its strengths, extreme modal realism has few proponents. Although ideologically parsimonious, the theory is as ontologically unparsimonious as possible: for any kind of object there could be, be it a centaur, ghost or unicorn, there is some world which contains such an object. Moreover, the very idea that there is an infinite number of concrete possible worlds, all on an equal footing, simply defies belief. The view that there really are non-actual Centaurs, ghosts and unicorns goes against our strongly held common-sense beliefs.

3   Combinatorialism

The combinatorialist takes possible worlds as recombinations of the fundamental elements of the actual world. For any fundamental property F and any atomic object a, the combinatorialist maintains that it is possible that a instantiate F. *Any* collection of such states of affairs counts as a possible world.

The restriction to atomic objects and fundamental properties is needed to rule out impossible recombinations such as an object's being simultaneously both round and square, or red and green. It is a crucial part of the combinatorialist's idea that such a restriction succeed in ruling out all impossibilities. But there are reasons to think it does not. For there may be fundamental properties which are nevertheless mutually exclusive. For example, having a mass of one gram and having a mass of two grams may both be fundamental properties – but nothing can be simultaneously both one gram and two grams.

Not only are there recombinations which are not possible, there are possibilites which are not recombinations. For it is possible that there be things which do not actually exist, and possible that there have been different fundamental properties not instantiated in the actual world. Such possibilities cannot be constructed by recombining only actually existing objects and properties.

4   Possible worlds as novels

On this view, worlds are nothing more than consistent works of fiction which represent different possible states of affairs in the same way novels do. It is possible that grass is red if there is some consistent novel which contains the sentence 'grass is red', or some collection of sentences which entail that grass is red. Since novels can contain names for actually existing objects, any novel containing the sentence 'Quine is twelve feet tall' represents Quine as being twelve feet tall – thus dealing with the problem of transworld identity.

But though this theory neither inflates our ontology nor defies belief (there are few who doubt the existence of novels!), as it stands it simply fails to do justice to the facts of modality. For not any book can count as a possible world. For instance, any novel containing the two sentences 'Grass is red' and 'Grass is green' fails to represent a way in which the world *could* have been. We could avoid this problem by identifying possible worlds with those novels which *could have been true* – but there is a drawback. If the concept of possibility is being *used* in saying what possible worlds are, the concept of possibility cannot be analysed in terms of possible worlds on pain of circularity.

Not only are there novels which do not represent possible worlds, there are some possible worlds which are not represented by any novel. For there are infinitely many different lengths an object could be. Accordingly, there are an infinite number of different possible worlds. Yet there is only a finite number of novels. Moreover, there are merely possible worlds which contain as much complexity and detail as the actual world around us, yet we mortals have no hope of writing a novel describing such a world in such fine detail. Some possible worlds appear to elude our descriptive capabilities.

If we are to have any hope of reducing possible worlds to novels, then our novels cannot be the kinds of things we actually read or write. Instead, our novels must be identified with sets of sentences in some idealized abstract language, a language which, though not capable of being written or spoken, is capable of representing many more possible worlds. One way to implement this idea is to construct a language the terms and predicates of which are actual objects and properties and the sentences of which are set-theoretical constructions thereof. On this scheme, the ordered pair $\langle F, a \rangle$ is interpreted as saying that a is F. Possible worlds can then be identified with consistent sets of sentences.

Though such a powerful language enables one to represent an infinite number of different possibilities, it is still a moot point whether *all* the possible worlds can be represented. Moreover, the increase in power comes at a price. For possible worlds are now identified with mathematical objects: sets of ordered n-tuples. Unlike novels, the existence of mathematical objects *is* a contentious issue.

Finally, some fear that this theory does not provide an objective theory of modality. For sentences have the meanings they do in virtue of the way *we* interpret them: had there been no humans, there would have been no meaningful sentences. Accordingly, possible worlds owe their existence to us. This is difficult to square with the view that whether or not something is possible is a matter which is independent of human thoughts and beliefs. 'Possibly P' cannot be equivalent to 'There is a possible world in which P' if the former is objectively true but the latter holds only subjectively.

5 Moderate realism

Instead of taking possible worlds as sets of sentences, perhaps possible worlds should be constructed out of the *meanings* of sentences. Perhaps possible worlds should be taken as consistent sets of *propositions*.

Obviously, such entities must be understood as existing independently of our own thought and language if worlds are not to owe their existence to us. (Some variants of this theory replace propositions with *states of affairs* or *abstract properties*.)

This theory faces some familiar problems. As above, worlds are abstract. As above, since it is only those sets which *could* have been true which form the possible worlds, the theory cannot analyse possibility without circularity. Of yet greater concern is the fact that this theory takes the notion of proposition as primitive. Admitting such things as a new fundamental kind of object is ontologically costly, and some find the idea that there is an infinite number of abstract representations 'out there' every bit as ludicrous as extreme realism. Moreover, the notion of proposition had come under a lot of fire, and one of the more attractive features of possible worlds was that they promised to throw light upon these peculiar creatures. Yet how can this promise be fulfilled by a theory which itself takes this problematic notion as primitive?

See also: ABSTRACT OBJECTS; INTENSIONAL ENTITIES; INTENSIONAL LOGICS; MODAL LOGIC; MODAL LOGIC, PHILOSOPHICAL ISSUES IN

References and further reading

Armstrong, D.M. (1989) *A Combinatorial Theory of Possibility*, Cambridge: Cambridge University Press. (A defence of combinatorialism.)

Bricker, P. (1987) 'Reducing Possible Worlds to Language', *Philosophical Studies* 52: 331–55. (The author scrutinizes the position that possible worlds are novels but concludes that there are certain possibilities which lie forever beyond our descriptive resources.)

Lewis, D. (1986) *On the Plurality of Worlds*, Oxford: Blackwell. (An advanced, yet clear and thorough examination of the metaphysics of possible worlds. The author makes a surprisingly powerful case for extreme realism.)

Loux, M.J. (1979) *The Possible and the Actual*, Ithaca, NY: Cornell University Press. (A comprehensive collection of essays covering all theories of possible worlds.)

Plantinga, A. (1989) *The Nature of Necessity*, New York: Clarendon Press. (Aside from a careful and clear defence of moderate realism, this book includes an interesting discussion of essential properties and uses possible worlds to reassess medieval theological arguments for the existence of God.)

Rosen, G. (1990) 'Modal Fictionalism', *Mind* 99

(395): 327–54. (Rather than identifying each possible world with a fiction, Rosen suggests that we view the theory that there are possible worlds as itself a fiction.)

JOSEPH MELIA

POST, EMIL LEON (1897–1954)

Emil Post was a pioneer in the theory of computation, which investigates the solution of problems by algorithmic methods. An algorithmic method is a finite set of precisely defined elementary directions for solving a problem in a finite number of steps. More specifically, Post was interested in the existence of algorithmic decision procedures that eventually give a yes or no answer to a problem. For instance, in his dissertation, Post introduced the truth-table method for deciding whether or not a formula of propositional logic is a tautology.

Post developed a notion of 'canonical systems' which was intended to encompass any algorithmic procedure for symbol manipulation. Using this notion, Post partially anticipated, in unpublished work, the results of Gödel, Church and Turing in the 1930s. This showed that many problems in logic and mathematics are algorithmically unsolvable. Post's ideas influenced later research in logic, computer theory, formal language theory and other areas.

1 Life and early work
2 Canonical systems
3 Recursion theory
4 Other work

1 Life and early work

Emil Leon Post was born in Augustow, Poland. He emigrated with his family in 1904 to New York City, where he lived for the rest of his life. He received a BS from City College in 1917. As a graduate student in mathematics at Columbia University, he studied Whitehead and Russell's *Principia Mathematica* with Cassius J. Keyser. He wrote his dissertation under Keyser's guidance and received his Ph.D. in 1920. He received a postgraduate Proctor Fellowship to Princeton for 1920–1, where he studied with the geometer and postulate theorist Oswald Veblen. To this period can be dated the birth of many of his most important ideas. He taught mostly in New York City high schools until 1935, when he was appointed to the faculty of City College where he remained until his death. During his adult life, Post struggled constantly with manic-depressive illness. To a great extent, this accounts for the incomplete development of many of his ideas. But he also delayed publication while attempting to work out the most general possible results.

In his dissertation (published in 1921) Post carried out one of the first metamathematical studies of a system of logic. This was the propositional logic of *Principia Mathematica*. In addition to proving the completeness, consistency and decidability of this system, he showed that it is complete in a sense that is now called 'Post completeness', that is, the addition to the axiom set of any formula not provable from it produces an inconsistent system. (P. Bernays had proved completeness and consistency in his *Habilitationsschrift* of 1918, but only published these results in 1926.)

Post also showed, going beyond Sheffer (1913), that each truth-function can be defined by a combination of the negation ($\sim$) and disjunction ($\vee$) truth-functions of *Principia Mathematica*. In a later monograph (1941), he showed that a set of truth-functions is truth-functionally complete, as $\{\sim, \vee\}$ is, if and only if for each of five types of truth-function at least one member of the set does not belong to that type (see Pelletier and Martin 1990). At the end of his dissertation, Post also showed how to develop an *m*-valued propositional logic, as opposed to the traditional logic with its two values of True and False (see MANY-VALUED LOGICS).

2 Canonical systems

In his year as a Proctor Fellow at Princeton (1920–1), Post's main research was into 'generated sets' of strings on a finite alphabet, that is, inductively defined classes of strings. Post studied three categories of such 'canonical systems'. The systems he labelled 'canonical system *C*' are now known as 'Post production systems'. This laid the foundations for the field that is now called the theory of formal languages (see FORMAL LANGUAGES AND SYSTEMS). Each canonical system specifies a class of rule sets. These rule sets define languages, conceived as infinite sets of finite strings of characters on a finite alphabet. This approach is analogous to the specification of the class of recursive functions as those which result from a finite number of applications of a certain base group of number-theoretic functions. What is commonly called 'Church's thesis' is the proposition that the number-theoretic functions which can be computed by any means at all are exactly the ones that are the recursive functions. The converse is obvious (see CHURCH'S THESIS). Analogously, we can say that Post's thesis is that any finitely specifiable language is generated by the rules of some canonical system. He showed that any set of strings that can be generated using one of his canonical systems can be generated in either of the other two systems. Post was able to show that a decision procedure for his canonical systems furnishes a decision procedure for the first-order logic of *Principia Mathematica*. He sketched, but did not complete, a proof of the converse. This led him to conjecture that Hilbert's *Entscheidungsproblem*, that is, the decision problem for first-order logic, is unsolvable. This was more than ten years before Church's proof (1936) of its unsolvability (see CHURCH'S THEOREM AND THE DECISION PROBLEM).

3 Recursion theory

Post's canonical systems were later shown to be equivalent to other formulations of the class of computable procedures, such as lambda-definability, recursive functions and Turing machines. Using this equivalence, a set of formulas is called 'recursive' if there is a decision procedure for the set using any of the methods. It is called 'recursively enumerable' if there is a procedure using any of these methods which successively lists the elements of the set. Post's 'Recursively Enumerable Sets of Positive Integers and Their Decision Problems' (1944) is foundational for modern recursion theory. It was there that he first articulated the 'fundamental theorem' of recursion theory; that a set is recursive if and only if both the set and its complement are recursively enumerable.

In this paper, Post also shows that there is a recursively enumerable but undecidable set of positive integers for which the decision problem has the highest 'degree of unsolvability'. If there were a decision procedure for a set of this degree, there would also be a decision procedure for any other undecidable set. Post states the question, known as Post's Problem, of whether there are recursively enumerable but undecidable sets of positive integers which have lower than this maximum degree of unsolvability. The existence of sets of such lower degrees was shown independently in Muchnik (1956) and Friedberg (1957).

4 Other work

Post's methods gained the attention of mathematicians when he showed (1947) that there is no algorithmic method for solving the 'word problem of Thue' which dated from 1914. In this paper, he used the Turing machine formulation of computability. In the course of doing so, he provided a critique of details of Turing's paper. This is not surprising, since in 1936 he had independently formulated a notion of

computation very much like that of Turing (see TURING MACHINES).

In a diary entry Post wrote, 'I study Mathematics as a product of the human mind and not as absolute'. He believed that he was investigating a natural boundary between what he called the 'productive' and the 'creative' capacities of the human mind. For Post, the incompleteness of logical systems of proof showed that 'The logical process is essentially creative', that is, that the human capacity to know is not reducible to a system (see Appendix to Post 1965).

See also: COMPUTABILITY THEORY; LAMBDA CALCULUS

List of works

Post, E.L. (1993) *Solvability, Provability, Definability: The Collected Works of Emil L. Post*, ed. M. Davis, Basle: Birkhäuser. (This is a complete collection of work published in Post's lifetime, plus the posthumously published Post (1965). The editor's introduction is a comprehensive survey of Post's life and work.)

—— (1921) 'Introduction to a General Theory of Elementary Propositions', *American Journal of Mathematics* 43: 163–85; repr. in J. van Heijenoort (ed.) *From Frege to Gödel: A Source Book in Mathematics, 1879–1931*, Cambridge, MA: Harvard University Press, 1967, 264–83. (Post's dissertation; requires introductory knowledge of mathematical logic.)

—— (1936) 'Finite Combinatory Processes – Formulation I', *Journal of Symbolic Logic* 1: 103–5. (A conceptual account of the procedures now called Turing machines. Quite readable for anyone familiar with the latter.)

—— (1941) *The Two-Valued Iterative Systems of Mathematical Logic*, Annals of Mathematics Studies, No. 5, Princeton, NJ: Princeton University Press. (Difficult even for specialists; should be read after Pelletier and Martin (1990).)

—— (1944) 'Recursively Enumerable Sets of Positive Integers and Their Decision Problems', *Bulletin of the American Mathematical Society* 50: 284–316. (A beautiful paper; the most readable of Post's papers for anyone who has done an introductory mathematical logic course.)

—— (1947) 'Recursive Unsolvability of a Problem of Thue', *Journal of Symbolic Logic* 12: 1–11. (Specialized; requires familiarity with Turing machines.)

—— (1965) 'Absolutely Unsolvable Problems and Relatively Undecidable Propositions – Account of an Anticipation', in M. Davis (ed.) *The Undecidable*, Hewlett, NY: Raven, 1965, 338–433. (Post's own

account of the foundational significance of his canonical systems. A difficult but important paper.)
—— (1990) 'The Modern Paradoxes', ed. I. Grattan-Guinness, *History and Philosophy of Logic* 11: 85–91. (This essay on Russell's paradox is edited from Post's manuscripts and is not included in the *Collected Works* (1993).)

References and further reading

* Bernays, P. (1926) 'Axiomatische Untersuchung des Aussagenkalküls der *Principia Mathematica*' (Axiomatic Investigation of the Propositional Calculus of *Principia Mathematica*), *Mathematische Zeitschrift* 25: 305–20. (In addition to proving consistency and completeness of the propositional logic axioms of *Principia Mathematica*, about half of this article is devoted to independence proofs for those axioms.)
* Church, A. (1936) 'A Note on the *Entscheidungsproblem*', *Journal of Symbolic Logic* 1: 40–1, 101–2. (Church's classic article on the nonexistence of a decision procedure for first-order logic.)
  Davis, M. (ed.) (1965) *The Undecidable: Basic Papers on Undecidable Propositions, Unsolvable Problems and Computable Functions*, Hewlett, NY: Raven. (This important collection includes papers by Gödel, Church, Turing, Rosser and Kleene, besides papers by Post. Together these provide a comprehensive survey of the heroic age of computability theory.)
* Friedberg, R. (1957) 'Two Recursively Enumerable Sets of Incomparable Degrees of Unsolvability', *Proceedings of the National Academy of Sciences (USA)* 43: 236–8. (Independently of Muchnik (1956), Friedberg shows that there are degrees of recursive unsolvability. Uses the important priority method of proof.)
  Grattan-Guinness, I. (1990) 'The Manuscripts of Emil L. Post', *History and Philosophy of Logic* 11: 77–83. (Describes the collection of Post manuscripts kept at the American Philosophical Society in Philadelphia.)
* Muchnik, A.A. (1956) 'Nerazreshimost' problemy svodimosti teorri algoritmov' (On the Unsolvability of the Problem of Reducibility in the Theory of Algorithms), *Doklady Akademii Nauk SSSR* 108: 194–7. (Gives the positive answer to Post's Problem, that is, that there are degrees of reducibility for recursively enumerable, but non-recursive, sets.)
* Pelletier, F.J. and Martin, M.N. (1990) 'Post's Functional Completeness Theorem', *Notre Dame Journal of Formal Logic* 31: 462–75. (Gives an updated statement and proof of the main results of Post (1941).)
* Sheffer, H.M. (1913) 'A Set of Five Independent Postulates for Boolean Algebras, With Applications to Logical Constants', *Transactions of the American Mathematical Society* 14: 481–8. (Shows that the single 'Sheffer stroke' operator can be used to define the two basic propositional operators, '$\sim$' and '$\vee$', in the propositional logic of *Principia Mathematica*.)
* Whitehead, A.N. and Russell, B.A.W. (1910–13) *Principia Mathematica*, Cambridge: Cambridge University Press, 3 vols; 2nd edn, 1925–7. (Post carried out one of the first metamathematical studies of a system of logic on the propositional logic of *Principia Mathematica*.)

MICHAEL SCANLAN

POSTCOLONIAL PHILOSOPHY OF SCIENCE

Are there laws of nature that today's modern sciences are ill-designed to discover? Does the universal use of these modern sciences require their value-neutrality, or are their social values and interests an important cause of their universality? What resources for scientific knowledge can other cultures' science projects provide?

Such questions are raised by recent postcolonial global histories that focus analyses on the role of European expansion in the advance of modern science and in the decline of other cultures' science traditions. These accounts challenge philosophers to re-evaluate unsuspected strengths in other scientific traditions and identify modern science's borrowings from them. They also identify European cultural features that have, for better and worse, constituted modern sciences and their representations of nature and thus seek to develop more realistic and useful accounts of the values, interests, methods, universality, objectivity and rationality of science.

1 European values and interests of modern science
2 Universality, objectivity, methods, rationality

1 European values and interests of modern science

Since the 1960s, it has been clear that social values and interests do and must shape the fabric of scientific cultures, their practices and knowledge claims. The great explanatory power of science turns out to have been expanded by historically distinctive values and interests. By the 1980s, the widespread dissemination of postcolonial histories – ones that report the continual exchanges and interminglings between cultures 'from the beginning' – led to accounts of how different cultures' sciences advance and then decline within such global relations. One main focus has been on the cognitive effects on modern sciences of the two-way causal relations between European expansion and the development of modern sciences in Europe, and a second on the benefits of nourishing cultural diversity in the resources brought to explaining nature's regularities. Selin (1997) is a valuable resource for this second project.

Joseph Needham's comparative studies of Chinese and European sciences were an important precursor to the new postcolonial science studies (1969). From such a perspective, he argued that European sciences were indeed superior at explanation, but not for every valuable scientific project, or always for the reasons that historians and philosophers assumed. Moreover, some of their successes, not just their failures, were due to their cultural values and interests. For example, Christian values and interests shaped the conception of 'laws of nature', though Christian belief in the heavenly crystal spheres blocked the development of astronomy. Thus religious beliefs had both positive and negative effects on the growth of scientific knowledge.

Attempting to steer a more effective path than Needham did between the older internalist and externalist histories of science, the comparative science studies of Needham's intellectual heirs try to show how modern science's representations of nature are not culturally neutral: they make the European presuppositions characteristic of their societies. For example, what we know about nature is restricted largely to what the sponsors of modern science have wanted to know. This information is embedded in models, metaphors and narratives for nature's processes that they found culturally and politically congenial. It also both enriched and limited what could be detected by the culture's distinctive ways of organizing scientific work.

Thus scholars such as Blaut, Goonatilake, Hess, McClellan and many of the contributors to Petitjean *et al.* (1992) and Harding (1993) argue that the modern sciences have produced accounts mainly of those aspects of nature that permitted upper and rising classes of Europeans to multiply and thrive, especially through the advance of their military and other expansionist projects. Scientists answered questions about how to improve European land and sea travel, to identify economically useful resources in the colonies, to mine gold, silver and other ores, to manufacture and farm for the benefit of Europeans living in Europe, the Americas, Africa and Asia, to improve their health and occasionally that of the workers who produced profit for them, and to defend the Europeans against their enemies. Expansion turned the world into a laboratory for the sciences in Europe. Nature remains *for* those who own it and have the means of extracting its resources, they argue. Such sciences have not been designed to explain such things as how to preserve fragile environments and scarce resources.

Moreover, it is argued that even if modern sciences bore no such cultural fingerprints, their commitment to value-neutrality would itself mark them as culturally distinctive. Most cultures value not neutrality but their own values and interests and as such are culturally identifiable. Surprisingly, it turns out that abstractness and formality express distinctive cultural features, not the absence of any culture at all. Of course the cultural specificity of the neutrality ideal does not mark abstractness or formality as a defect, since most values and interests have the potential to enable us to 'see' nature in new ways. Instead, it raises questions about the conditions under which a commitment to neutrality advances the growth of knowledge.

2 Universality, objectivity, methods, rationality

Modern sciences are practised and admired around the world. Scientists come from every race, gender, class and culture, and the sciences' formal languages permit communication (and agreement) between all. Moreover, the laws of nature that modern science articulates predict how nature's forces will act on people indiscriminately, regardless of race, class, gender and culture. But such facts only support a weak claim to modern sciences' universality. The familiar 'strong universality' thesis argues that the uniqueness of the universality of scientific claims (the 'fact' that no other scientific traditions have produced universal claims) is the consequence of an internal, epistemological condition: methods that eliminate cultural fingerprints from scientific representations of nature's events and processes.

This uniqueness claim is challenged by postcolonial histories that show how the great explanatory power and appeal of modern sciences has been established in part as an empirical consequence of European expansion. Such accounts drive a wedge between the achievement of universality and the requirement of cultural neutrality. They suggest that other, culturally different, sciences could also generate empirically adequate laws of nature, ones that would be consistent with much of the evidence supporting the modern sciences' representations of nature. They argue that modern sciences are not necessarily the best for discovering all of the laws of nature; they have intrinsic metaphysical and epistemological limitations for, like all others, they are shaped by the cultural interests they represent, by local discursive resources, and by culturally-preferred forms of scientific work. They question that the sciences and technologies that have worked best to advance some groups in the Northern hemisphere will work best to advance the rest of the world's peoples, or, for that matter, to continue to sustain Northern elites.

Challenges to conventional conceptions of objectivity, method and rationality are also generated by these accounts – ones similar to those raised by gender theorists (see GENDER AND SCIENCE; FEMINIST EPISTEMOLOGY). Is the neutrality ideal that is so central to such concepts an obstacle to detecting the kinds of culture-wide values and interests in European sciences that are reported in the comparative studies? The postcolonial accounts started off thinking about modern sciences from the lives of people in cultures that have been disadvantaged by them. Are standpoint epistemologies thus required to explain the emergence of the postcolonial accounts in the first place, and to generate research methods capable of continuing to produce such more comprehensive and less distorted accounts? Should assessments of the rationality of modern sciences continue to be restricted to examining their technical, cognitive cores now that these are understood to be no longer separable from the cultural values and interests that permeate them?

Postcolonial science studies, emerging from both Northern and Southern science scholars, are part of the long tradition of criticism that has enabled the growth of knowledge. They challenge philosophers to consider an updated version of Thomas KUHN's famous question: should not single-stream histories of science be a source of phenomena to which theories of knowledge may legitimately be asked to apply?

See also: OBJECTIVITY; RATIONALITY AND CULTURAL RELATIVISM; SCIENTIFIC METHOD

References and further reading

Blaut, J.M. (1993) *The Colonizer's View of the World: Geographical Diffusionism and Eurocentric History*, New York: Guilford Press. (Shows historians' problems with Eurocentric histories, which are the ones assumed by the conventional histories of science upon which philosophies of science draw. Explores relationship between flourishing European cultures and decline of others.)

Goonatilake, S. (1984) *Aborted Discovery: Science and Creativity in the Third World*, London: Zed Press. (Effects of European expansion on Asian and European sciences.)

* Harding, S. (ed.) (1993) *The 'Racial' Economy of Science: Toward a Democratic Future*, Bloomington, IN: Indiana University Press. (Contributors analyse diverse contexts for thinking about how costs and benefits of modern sciences have not always been democratically distributed. Section on 'Objectivity, Method, and Nature: Value-Neutral?' draws out central philosophical implications of such undemocratic distributions.)

—— (1998) *Is Science Multicultural? Postcolonialism, Feminism and Epistemology*, Bloomington, IN: Indiana University Press. (Shows central challenges to conventional philosophies of science and epistemologies that are raised by two decades of multicultural, postcolonial and feminist science studies, and how many of these challenges are to be found also in post-Kuhnian, 'post positivist', philosophy of science.)

Hess, D. (1994) *Science and Technology in a Multicultural World: The Cultural Politics of Facts and Artifacts*, New York: Columbia University Press. (How scientific 'facts and artifacts' are culturally constructed in valuable ways for different cultures in the past and present. Challenges conventional assumptions about immunization of scientific facts from cultural influences.)

McClellan, J.E. (1992) *Colonialism and Science: Saint Domingue in the Old Regime*, Baltimore, MD: Johns Hopkins University Press. (The intimate relations between the development of modern sciences in France and the needs of slave holders through a study of the archives of an ambitious and distinguished French scientific institute in the Caribbean. Challenges conventional understandings of the epistemological–political 'innocence' of 'scientific problems'.)

* Needham, J. (1969) *The Grand Titration: Science and Society in East and West*, Toronto, Ont.: University of Toronto Press. (Comparisons and analyses of Chinese and Western sciences by the best-known (scientist–) historian of Chinese sciences. Identifies Eurocentric assessments of European and of Chinese sciences by leading histories of science – ones that philosophies of science assume.)

* Petitjean, P., Jami, C. and Moulin, A.M. (eds) (1992) *Science and Empires: Historical Studies about Scientific Development and European Expansion*, Dordrecht: Kluwer. (Forty papers of the more than 100 presented at a UNESCO 1990 conference in which scholars from around the world critically examined the relationship between the flourishing of empires – especially the 500 year old European one up through the late twentieth century – and of scientific and technological traditions. Contributors consistently challenge Eurocentric assump-

tions about the causes of the successes of European sciences and technologies.)

* Selin, H. (ed.) (1997) *Encyclopaedia of the History of Science, Technology, and Medicine in Non-Western Cultures*, Dordrecht: Kluwer. (Over 600 scholarly articles review the histories and accomplishments of non-European cultures' scientific and technological traditions. Includes many philosophically focused essays.)

SANDRA G. HARDING

POSTCOLONIALISM

The term 'postcolonialism' is sometimes spelled with a hyphen – post-colonial – and sometimes without. There is no strict general practice, but the hyphenated version is often used to refer to the condition of life after the end of colonialism while the non-hyphenated version denotes the theory that attempts to make sense of this condition. The term is regularly used to denote both colonialism and imperialism even though these refer to different historical realities.

Like postmodernism and poststructuralism, postcolonialism designates a critical practice that is highly eclectic and difficult to define. It involves a studied engagement with the experience of colonialism and its past and present effects at the levels of material culture and of representation. Postcolonialism often involves the discussion of experiences such as those of slavery, migration, suppression and resistance, difference, race, gender, place and analysis of the responses to the discourses of imperial Europe, such as history, philosophy, anthropology and linguistics. Since conditions under imperialism and colonialism proper are as much the subject of postcolonialism as those coming after the historical end of colonialism, postcolonialism allows for a wide range of applications and a constant interplay between the sense of a historical transition, a cultural location and an epochal condition. Postcolonialism is seen to pertain as much to conditions of existence in former colonies as to conditions in diaspora. Both are frequently linked to the continuing power and authority of the West in the global political, economic and symbolic spheres and the ways in which resistance to, appropriation of and negotiation with the West's order are prosecuted. However the term is construed, there is as much focus on the discourse and ideology of colonialism as on the material effects of colonial subjugation. Because it has its source in past and continuing oppression, postcolonialism furthermore has affinities with multicultural, feminist, and gay and lesbian studies.

1 **Seminal works**
2 **Problems with the term 'postcolonialism'**
3 **Colonial discourse analysis and the question of historiography**
4 **Diaspora, hybridity and identity**

1 Seminal works

It is generally agreed that the single most influential work to define the purview of the term was Edward W. Said's *Orientalism* published in 1978. Drawing on the work of Michel Foucault, Said's main thesis was that the Western academic discipline of Orientalism was strictly speaking a means by which the Orient was produced as a figment of the Western imagination for consumption in the West and also as a means of subserving the ultimate project of imperial domination. Said's main ideas have been both criticized and extrapolated across various disciplines, and it is mainly thanks to his book that what is known as colonial discourse analysis gained coherence. Among studies inspired by his work have been those by Gauri Viswanathan (1990), looking at the introduction of the paradigm of English studies in India and the degree to which it attempted to shape local attitudes to Empire; Patrick Brantlinger (1988), which looks at the forms of imperial ideology as perceivable in the literary writings of the period 1830–1914; Martin Bernal (1987; 1991), which through a careful analysis of the sources of Greek civilization sought to show not only that this was heavily indebted to the influence of a black Egyptian civilization, but also the degree to which the discipline of classical studies in the eighteenth century attempted to obscure this contribution in the dominant disciplinary paradigms that were in use; and Valentin Mudimbe (1988) which showed that the notion of African systems of knowledge had always been governed by a Western form of knowledge.

Another text which is thought to be seminal in the field of postcolonial studies is by Bill Ashcroft *et al.*, *The Empire Writes Back* (1989). This book was in many senses responsible for popularizing the term post-colonialism in literary studies, even though, as has been pointed out by Aijaz Ahmad (1995) among others, the term was first used by political scientists in the early 1970s to denote the condition of Third World political systems after decolonization. Before its publication much of what is described under the label of postcolonialism in literary studies was discussed under the rubric of contending terms such as 'New Literatures in English', 'International Literatures', 'Third World Literature' or 'Commonwealth Literature'. However, it was the notion of Commonwealth Literature that *The Empire Writes*

Back was most intent on displacing. The writers of the book were of the view that the term showed too close and uncomfortable a relationship to metropolitan Britain, and the term 'post-colonial' was seen as a means of transcending this relationship. Another influential thesis they advanced was that the literature coming out of former colonies had the express purpose of 'writing back' to the empire, and by a variety of textual strategies, of subverting the dominant categories of representation that had circulated from the imperial centre. In this impulse they sought to correct something for which Said's book had been heavily criticized, namely his complete silence on the voices of resistance and/or complicity that could easily be shown to have entered into a variety of relationships with Orientalist discourse. A third thesis of *The Empire Writes Back* was that postcolonial writing was also seriously contesting the domination of the English language by creating a variety of creolized and hybridized versions of the language. As a means of attending to this phenomenon, the authors proposed the term 'english' to designate this phenomenon; and even though their proposal for the use of this particular term was not readily taken up by other commentators on postcolonial writing, it is evident that the general note of resistance in their critical practice was taken up in numerous articles published in literary journals devoted to the field such as the *Journal of Commonwealth Literature, Callaloo, Wasafiri, Kunapipi* and *World Literature Written in English*, among others.

2 Problems with the term 'postcolonialism'

To gain a sense of the nature of some of the criticisms levelled against the term 'postcolonial', it is important to return to the question of its genesis. Though earlier it was noted it could be traced to the seminal publications of Said and Ashcroft *et al.*, such a perspective may obscure the complex and somewhat composite genealogy of the theoretical practices denoted by the term. These can fruitfully be linked to what one critic has noted as the 'wide-ranging retrospect taken in the 1980s on the exclusionary forms of reason and universality composed by a Western modernity complicit with imperial expansion and colonialist rule' (Parry 1997: 4). This major retrospective glance was itself filiated to the broader criticisms of Western philosophy formulated by Jacques DERRIDA and the subject of wide discussion in Western universities since the early 1970s. In this regard, the work of Michel FOUCAULT, as it described the discursive constitution of objects of knowledge in their insertion into hierarchies of power also proved influential and decisive. Behind all this, as has been

noted by Sherry Ortner (1984), was the emergence of a linguistic paradigm in the humanities and social sciences from the 1960s onwards. But most directly significant for postcolonialism was the gradual and increasingly important research done in the areas of feminist, multicultural, minority and gay and lesbian studies. The impulse they shared in common with postcolonial studies was the desire to contest the centrality and authority of distinctive systems of domination, together contributing to the deciphering of systems of representation designed to validate institutional subordination and silence the voice of competitors. Quite often, work of a thorough, interdisciplinary nature was pursued, such as that by Gayatri Spivak (1996) in her linking of Marxism, feminism and eclectic cultural criticism.

One of the key debates in postcolonialism is to what extent the term can be used to designate studies undertaken in a variety of different disciplines. Thus, postcolonialism is seen by some of its practitioners as the paradigmatic anti-hegemonic theoretical orientation, with colonialism taken to be the archetypal and most brutal expression of hegemony; any theoretical tendency that sees itself as anti-hegemonic is then easily taken to be affiliated to postcolonialism. For others, however, it is its productive circularity that calls the postcolonial object of study into being, while allowing unreflexive notions of nationhood, race and identity, and even of colonialism itself, to be deployed without attention to the specificities of each discipline.

Another debate relates to the unresolved temporal transcendence signalled in the first part of the word, when in fact there is evidence everywhere that colonialism has not been fully transcended. For Anne McClintock (1992) the central flaw in the term lies in its implicit links with Enlightenment notions of progress, since the 'post' marks nothing but the march of history without really attending to the difficulties involved in such an implicit filiation to Enlightenment notions of progress. Other terms such as 'neo-colonialism' are thought to succeed better in capturing the sense of the continuing but disguised influence of the imperial metropolis, especially as the latter is refracted through different forms of globalism in the control of the financial and primary-produce markets and in the dominant modes of information gathering and dissemination more generally. In spite of these criticisms, however, the term continues to be used widely, partly because there seems to be no clear rival to mark the distinctive field, and partly also because, as Kwame Anthony Appiah (1994: 240) puts it, the term is seen as an important 'space clearing gesture'. What is more important, perhaps, is to note that postcolonialism is symptomatic of the perception of continuing injustice in the global political economy, the victims of which are seen to be formerly colonized people as well as their diasporic descendants.

3 Colonial discourse analysis and the question of historiography

One of the areas that Said's work greatly inspired was the re-visiting of the era of colonialism in order to explore the links between knowledge and power. An important extension of his work, however, took the direction of showing that the colonial encounter affected both colonizer and colonized simultaneously, and that the formation of the colonizer's culture was heavily dependent upon the colonial encounter. The notion of an encounter between monolithic and radically opposed entities in history gave way to studies emphasizing the unstable nature of identity formation that affected both parties.

A major inflection of this kind of work has been the emphasis on a psychoanalysis of the colonial encounter and its effects. This view is most strongly associated with Homi Bhabha, whose *The Location of Culture* (1994) brings together a decade of essays devoted to this subject. This tendency was not really new in studies of colonialism. Notable studies psychoanalysing imperialism and colonialism had already been done for India by Ashis Nandy (1983) and for Africa by Franz Fanon (1952, 1961). The work of these writers was thought to be highly stimulating and to allow for very significant extrapolations to other geographical areas of the colonial encounter. Bhabha's main difference was in maintaining that resistance could be detected in the interstices of the unstable symbolic and discursive encounters between colonizer and colonized, and that the symbolic practices also revealed the unstable nature of colonial identity.

The nature of Bhabha's formulations is thought to have important implications for the study of colonialism. Of particular significance is the privileging of discourse in accounts of the colonial encounter and of resistance against it. Not only is this seen by mainstream historians as highly problematic in its avoidance of an engagement with the real and brutal processes of colonialism, it is also thought to privilege the reading practices of the critic themselves without paying adequate attention to the specific contours of relevant historical documents. Colonial discourse analysis may be said to have additional implications for the methodology of historical research and its writing. Notably, it regularly privileges metaphors and literary tropes and focuses on them as being of interpretive value in coming to terms with history.

Furthermore, such metaphors and tropes are also seen to be determinate of historical process and are taken to be succinct expressions of the main qualities of colonial ideology. This intense focus on literary figures then allows for a different historiographic practice from that practised by traditional historians; there is less attention to the broad range of archival materials such as journals, diaries, official reports and the like; less atention to the comparative analysis of such documents in the attempt to arrive at a hierarchy of their value as evidence; and much more attention to the enunciatory modalities of different literary tropes and their manifestation in different historical documents. The apparently a-historical nature of such forms of analyses has frequently been pointed out by historians; but it is also evident that there is a readiness on the part of some to attempt a fusion of the two forms of historical enquiry, in the hope that the strengths of both can be drawn upon for a fuller understanding of colonialism.

A less contentious new historiographic practice is that applied from the early 1980s by members of the Subaltern Studies group in India. Taking as their main point of disagreement the dominant Orientalist, nationalist and Marxist historiographies that had dominated historical accounts of India, they sought to challenge these and, in their place, to produce a 'history from below', that would attend to the processes of the formation of a critical consciousness within the Indian peasantry during the height of colonialism and its aftermath. The Subaltern Studies project drew inspiration from the work of Antonio GRAMSCI, especially from his concept of hegemony and the place of the subaltern in the formation of national consciousness. Despite producing a wide-ranging number of studies, the Subaltern Studies project could not be said to have formed a 'school' as such. None the less, it represents the most coherent attempt in postcolonial studies to seize the practice of writing history for the purpose of producing knowledge about people who had hitherto been absent from such history.

4 Diaspora, hybridity and identity

The question of diasporas is also an important dimension of postcolonial studies. What is generally taken to be the high point of modern imperialism took off from about 1830, and has fruitfully been related to the formation of a new world order after the abolition of slavery. Slavery itself had ensured that large numbers of Africans had been moved to the West Indies and America to work on plantations and to sustain the global industrial economy of the period. Indian indentured labour also featured prominently in this mass movement of peoples across various geographical locations.

That first phase of diaspora, marked mainly by slavery, was later succeeded by another, less coherent, phase. This second phase was especially pronounced from about the end of the decolonization period in the 1960s, when for various economic and other reasons a large number of Asians and Africans moved to Europe and America. The different phases of migration produced different relationships both to the countries of origin and to those of eventual sojourn. What is most significant, however, is that as generations of migrants settled in the West, an active diaspora consciousness began to be formed. Literature written by migrants is now an increasingly important part of postcolonial studies. Additionally, there have been serious attempts to discuss the complexities of cross-cultural existence and the ways in which this affects the individual psyche as well as the culture of the adopted country of residence. And in the United States, because the migrants who went there joined an already existing and active black population, the discussion of diaspora had to take account of a variety of often complex issues to do with identity.

Many of these issues have been steadily formulated by African-Americans themselves from as far back as the slavery period. W.E.B. Du Bois, author of *The Souls of Black Folk* (1903), formulates the notion of the split consciousness of black peoples, who continually have to see themselves in terms of the idea of an indigenous folk as well as in relation to their perception by the dominant categories of white America. And in a lecture series published as *Playing in the Dark* (1992), Toni Morrison revisits similar issues and asks what happens to the imagination of black authors who are conscious at some level of having to represent their own race to a race of readers that has always understood itself as universal, and has continually written minority races out of the account. The theme of identity formation for minority races has many resonances with Franz Fanon's ideas about the psychology of Africans under the brutal conditions imposed by French colonialism in Algeria. For others, the issue of identity in diaspora is seen more in the light of notions of hybridity, in which it is thought that the diasporic individual marries ideas from both country of origin and that of sojourn. The issues are vastly complicated as they are traced through different generations, and there are some who oppose the idea of hybridity, noting that it depends too much for its success on a concept of freedom which is ultimately class based. If postcolonialism seems to be a variable and problematic concept, to many its continuing use is sanctioned by the fact that there is

no clear alternative that is able to speak to the complexities of modern existence while simultaneously taking account of the historic configuration of colonialism in a cross-disciplinary and fertile way.

See also: POSTCOLONIAL PHILOSOPHY OF SCIENCE; RACE, THEORIES OF

References and further reading

Ahmad, A. (1992) *In Theory: Classes, Nations, Literatures*, London: Verso, 1–20. (Highly focused critique of postcolonialism from a Marxist perspective; immensely readable and absolutely essential.)

* —— (1995) 'The Politics of Literary Postcoloniality', *Race and Class* 36 (3). (Important discussion of some of the ideological underpinnings of postcolonialism; extends the discussion in §2.)

* Appiah, A.K. (1994) *In My Father's House: Africa in the Philosophy of Culture*, London: Methuen. (Important discussion of key concepts and problems in Pan-Africanist thinking in its unreflexive dependence on biological ideas of race.)

* Ashcroft, B., Griffiths, G. and Tiffin, H. (1989) *The Empire Writes Back: Theory and Practice in Post-Colonial Literatures*, London: Routledge. (Seminal introduction to literary postcolonialism; see §1.)

* —— (1995) *The Post-Colonial Studies Reader*, London: Routledge. (Comprehensive reader; divided into various topical sub sections, it contains many of the seminal essays in the field up to the date of its publication.)

* Bernal, M. (1987) *Black Athena*, vol. 1, London: Free Association Press. (Illuminating but controversial analysis of the discipline of classics, arguing for the influence of Black Egypt on Ancient Greece; see §1.)

* —— (1991) *Black Athena*, vol. 2, London: Free Association Press. (Continuation of the study of the black roots of Ancient Greek Civilization.)

* Bhabha, H. (1992) 'Postcolonial Criticism', in S. Greenblatt and G. Dunn (eds) *Redrawing the Boundaries: The Transformation of English and American Literary Studies*, New York: Modern Languages Association of America. (Expands on the idea of the productive eclecticism of postcolonialism in §2.)

* —— (1994) *The Location of Culture*, London: Routledge. (Seminal essays on the psychoanalyses of colonialism as noted in §3; very difficult for the beginner.)

* Brantlinger, P. (1988) *Rule of Darkness: British Rule Literature and Imperialism, 1830–1914*, Ithaca, NY: Cornell University Press. (Account of imperial ideology as perceivable in the work of certain

English writers; highly engaging and accessible; see §1.)

* Du Bois, W.E.B. (1903) 'The Souls of Black Folk', in H.L. Gates and N.Y. McKay (eds) *The Norton Anthology of African American Literature*, New York: Norton, 1997. (Seminal text of the literature of negro reconstruction and renaissance; fruitful links to be drawn with questions of diaspora and identity in postcolonial studies as noted in §4.)

* Fanon, F. (1952) *Black Skin, White Masks*, trans C.L. Markham, New York: Grove Press, 1967. (Seminal work in postcolonial theory dealing with the question of subjectivity under brutal colonial domination; engaging and stimulating; see §§3, 4.)

* —— (1961) *The Wretched of the Earth*, trans. C. Farrington, Harmondsworth: Penguin, 1967. (Another highly regarded work by Fanon; the essay entitled 'On National Culture' is especially interesting.)

Gates, H.L., Jr and McKay, N.Y. (1997) *The Norton Anthology of African American Literature*, New York: Norton. (Possibly the most important anthology of African American literature ever to be published.)

Guha, R. and Spivak, G.C. (1988) *Selected Subaltern Studies*, Oxford: Oxford University Press. (This special volume, containing a selection of papers by the Subaltern Studies group and with a foreword by Edward Said, gives a good indication of the range of the group's work.)

Kennedy, D. (1996) 'Imperial History and Post-Colonial Theory', *The Journal of Imperial and Commonwealth History* 24 (3): 345–63. (Represents a growing tendency by imperial historians to engage positively with aspects of colonial discourse analysis.)

Lefkowitz, M. (1996) *Not Out of Africa*, New York: Basic Books. (A point by point refutation of the central theses raised in Bernal's *Black Athena*.)

MacKenzie, J.M. (1995) *Orientalism: History, Theory and the Arts*, Manchester: Manchester University Press. (Delivers a sharp but measured critique of colonial discourse analysis and attempts to problematize the notion of Orientalism with a discussion of the fine arts and architecture in the imperial period.)

* McClintock, A. (1992) 'Pitfalls of the Term Post-Colonialism', in P. Williams and L. Chrisman (eds) *Colonial Discourse and Post-Colonial Theory*, New York: Harvester Wheatsheaf, 1993, 291–304. (Good discussion of the temporal implications of the postcolonialism; see §2.)

Morrison, T. (1992) *Playing in the Dark: Whiteness and the Literary Imagination*, London: Picador, 1993. (Exploration of the degree to which the predominantly white American literary canon has always depended upon a subliminal social engagement with blackness even when this is silenced; useful questions for identity formation in the diaspora as noted in §4.)

* Mudimbe, V.Y. (1988) *The Invention of Africa: Gnosis, Philosophy and the Order of Knowedge*, Bloomington, IN: Indiana University Press and London: James Currey. (Important contribution to the methodology of African studies, which argues that African systems of knowledge have so far been produced within an essentially Western epistemological framework; a bit difficult for the beginner; see §1.)

* Nandy, A. (1983) *The Intimate Enemy: Loss and Recovery of Self under Colonialism*, Delhi and Oxford: Oxford University Press. (Study of the effects of colonialism on modern Indian psyche and the ways to transcend these problems; see §3.)

O'Hanlon, R. (1988) 'Recovering the Subject: *Subaltern Studies* and Histories of Resistance in Colonial South Asia', *Modern Asian Studies* 22 (1): 189–224. (Very good overview of the work of the Subaltern Studies group; see§3.)

* Ortner, S.B. (1984) 'Theory in Anthropology since the Sixties', *Comparative Studies in Society and History* 26 (1): 126–66. (Discussion of the major alignments in theory in the social sciences and the humanities up to the early 1980s; see §2.)

* Parry, B. (1997) 'The Postcolonial: Conceptual Category or Chimera?', *The Yearbook of English Studies* 27: 3–21. (Good discussion of the composite provenance of postcolonialism raised in §2; this special number of YES is devoted to 'The Politics of Postcolonial Criticism'.)

Prakash, G. (1990) 'Writing Post-Orientalist Histories of the Third World: Perspectives from Indian Historiography', *Comparative Studies in Society and History* 32 (1): 383–408. (Extended discussion of Indian historiography and the place of the Subaltern Studies project outlined in §3.)

* Said, E.W. (1978) *Orientalism*, London: Chatto & Windus. (Seminal work taken to have inaugurated postcolonial studies; immensely readable; see §1.)

—— (1993) *Culture and Imperialism*, London: Chatto & Windus. (Continues what was started in *Orientalism* but this time focuses on the literary sphere; also immensely readable with an excellent bibliography.)

Sekyi-Otu, A. (1996) *Fanon's Dialectic of Experience*, Cambridge, MA: Harvard University Press. (An exciting and engaged analysis of Fanon's work, which attends both to his intellectual debts and to the creative potential inherent in his work; excellent as an introduction to Fanon's debts to classical Marxist theory.)

Slemon, S. (1994) 'The Scramble for Post-Colonialism', in B. Ashcroft, G. Griffiths and H. Tiffin (eds) *The Post-Colonial Studies Reader*, London: Routledge, 1995, 45–52. (Excellent overview of the applications of postcolonial theory; extends the account of the genealogy of the term raised in §3.)

* Spivak, G.C. (1996) *The Spivak Reader*, ed. D. Landry and G. MacLean, London: Routledge. (Contains all Spivak's seminal essays; her work is very useful for exploring the intersection between feminism, Marxism and deconstruction; particularly important is 'Can the Subaltern Speak?'; a bit difficult for the beginner; see §2.)

Thomas, N. (1994) *Colonialism's Culture: Anthropology, Travel and Government*, Cambridge: Polity Press. (Good discussion of the varying and differential practices of colonialism that challenges some of the central tenets in the work of Homi Bhabha and others raised in §2.)

* Viswanathan, G. (1990) *Masks of Conquest: Literary Studies and British Rule in India*, London: Faber & Faber. (Detailed discussion of the introduction of English literary studies into India and the ideological implications of this; see §1.)

Visweswaran, K. (1994) *Fictions of Feminist Ethnography*, Minneapolis, MN: Minnesota University Press. (Chapter 7 of this book offers a highly engaging discussion of notions of hybridity, contesting the term with a new one – hyphenation.)

Williams, P. and Chrisman, L. (1993) *Colonial Discourse and Post-Colonial Theory*, New York: Harvester Wheatsheaf. (Along with Ashcroft *et al.* (1995), a key teaching tool. Has an excellent general introduction pointing towards interesting areas of research in the field.)

Young, R. (1990) *White Mythologies: Writing History and the West*, London: Routledge. (Last three chapters offer stimulating discussion of the work of Edward Said, Homi Bhabha and Gayatri Spivak; significant for dealing with the question of the ideological implications of history writing in the West.)

ATO QUAYSON

POSTMODERN THEOLOGY

The term 'postmodernism' is loosely used to designate a wide variety of cultural phenomena from architecture through literature and literary theory to philosophy. The immediate background of philosophical postmodernism is the French structuralism of Saussure, Lévi-Strauss, Lacan and Barthes. But like existentialism, it has roots that go back to the critique by Kierkegaard and Nietzsche of certain strong knowledge claims in the work of Plato, Descartes and Hegel. If the quest for absolute knowledge is the quest for meanings that are completely clear and for truths that are completely certain, and philosophy takes this quest as its essential goal, then postmodernism replaces Nietzsche's announcement of the death of God with an announcement of the end of philosophy.

This need not be construed as the death of God in a different vocabulary. The question of postmodern theology is the question of the nature of a discourse about deity that would not be tied to the metaphysical assumptions postmodern philosophy finds untenable. One candidate is the negative theology tradition of Pseudo-Dionysius and Meister Eckhart. It combines a vigorous denial of absolute knowledge with a theological import that goes beyond the critical negations of postmodern philosophy. A second possibility, the a/ theology of Mark C. Taylor, seeks to find religious meaning beyond the simple opposition of theism and atheism, but without taking the mystical turn. Finally, Jean-Luc Marion seeks to free theological discourse from the horizon of all philosophical theories of being, including Heidegger's own postmodern analysis of being.

1   Key themes of postmodern philosophy
2   Postmodern theology as negative theology
3   Postmodern theology in a Nietzschean mode
4   Postmodern theology in a Kierkegaardian mode

1   Key themes of postmodern philosophy

The themes of philosophical postmodernism whose bearing on philosophical theology is most direct are Heidegger's 'destruction' of the history of ontology and Derrida's 'deconstruction' of the metaphysics of presence. Heidegger's destruction, originally announced in *Being and Time* (1927), becomes a critique of 'the onto-theo-logical constitution of metaphysics' in *Identity and Difference* (1957). His point of reference is Aristotle's attempt to unify being, which is said in many ways. At the categorial level, it is substance that plays the role of unifying first principle for all the *pros hen* equivocals. But how is the world of actual substances itself to be unified? By a highest substance, God, who is universal by being first. In other words, the whole realm of beings can only be understood fully with reference to the highest being by whom their being is ordered (see HEIDEGGER, M. §6).

Heidegger calls this confluence of the universality

of ontology with the primacy of theology 'onto-theology'. In a typically postmodern gesture, he treats this honoured principle, whose modern fulfilment he finds in Hegel, with undisguised disrespect. He remarks that in onto-theo-logy 'the deity can come into philosophy only insofar as philosophy, of its own accord and by its own nature, requires and determines that and how the deity enters into it' ([1957] 1969: 56). In other words, a tradition that stretches at least from Aristotle to Hegel uses God as a means to its own ends; anticipating the spirit of modern technology, it views even God as a resource in the service of its own will to power, the totalizing project of rendering the whole of being intelligible to human understanding. In transgressing this tradition, Heidegger invokes both a hermeneutics of finitude, which views such a project as hubris, and a hermeneutics of suspicion, which looks for hidden and disreputable motives beneath discourses generously decorated with piety.

Heidegger insists that his critique, so far from having its origin in atheism, can be seen as a form of religious protest. Echoing Pascal, he says of the god of philosophy as onto-theo-logy:

Man can neither pray nor sacrifice to this god. Before the *causa sui* man can neither fall to his knees in awe nor can he play music and dance before this god.

The god-less thinking which must abandon the god of philosophy, god as *causa sui*, is thus perhaps closer to the divine God. Here this means only: god-less thinking is more open to Him than onto-theo-logic would like to admit.

([1957] 1969: 72)

Heidegger develops this critique explicitly against the Hegelian holism that would attain absolute knowledge by developing an all-inclusive categorial scheme, the Logic, and an all-inclusive theory of actual beings, the Philosophies of Nature and of Spirit. Derrida has his own critique of Hegel, but in this context the deconstruction of the metaphysics of presence is best viewed as an assault on Cartesian foundationalism and its claim that, in a piecemeal manner and at the outset, we can achieve unambiguous meanings and final truths. It is just such meanings and truths that Derrida designates as presence, though the term 'immediacy' signifies much the same thing (see DERRIDA, J.).

What is present is both here and now, and Derrida's notion of presence has both spatial and temporal ramifications. To be fully present to the meanings and truths necessary for even piecemeal absolute knowledge is to have found the transcendental signified, a meaning or a truth so self-contained as to require no reference to anything outside itself in semantic space and so finished as to require no reference to any clarification or validation subsequent to this moment in time. Deconstruction is not so much the assertion that we never reach the transcendental signified as it is the continuous showing of the spatial differences and temporal deferrals that undermine claims of total clarity and final certainty.

Derrida (1968) invents the term *différance* to stand for this union of difference and deferral in the critique of logocentrism, which can be defined as the claim that absolute knowledge is possible, that either prior to all linguistic mediation (as in the work of Husserl) or subsequent to the essential completion of that mediation (as in the work of Hegel), human thought stands face to face with being. The spatial part of the argument derives largely from structuralism, while the temporal part is derived from Husserl's phenomenology of internal time consciousness for use, in typically *ad hominem* fashion, against Husserlian foundationalist claims of apodictic intuition.

For Heidegger and Derrida, as for Kierkegaard and Nietzsche, it is the temporal structure of human existence above all else that renders the transcendental signified a transcendental illusion for human thought. In this respect they are all Kantians, for whom it is foolish to claim the finality of eternity for human thought.

2 Postmodern theology as negative theology

The question of a postmodern theology that emerges is quite clear: what would a discourse look like that would still be theological but would vigilantly resist lapsing into metaphysics, which in this context signifies the confluence of onto-theo-logy, the metaphysics of presence, and logocentrism? Since Heidegger and Derrida are in agreement that we cannot just decide to leave metaphysics behind and be done with it, such a postmetaphysical theology will not be the triumphant freedom from all metaphysical tendencies, but the militant struggle against enslavement to them. Partly because of the mystical element in Heidegger's thought, and partly because the negative character of Derridean deconstruction has from the outset suggested affinities with negative theology, the tradition of mystical theology that has Pseudo-Dionysius and Meister Eckhart among its leading figures is easily viewed as a paradigm of postmetaphysical theology.

Derrida's answer to the question whether deconstruction is a kind of negative theology is an emphatic negative. Negative theology for Dionysius and Eckhart is part of the *via negativa*; it is a scepticism in the service of mysticism. In so far as deconstruction can be construed as a kind of scepticism, it serves no mystical project. It does not posit a 'superessential' deity, a God beyond being; it knows no nostalgia or hope for a pre- or postconceptual experience of pure presence to such a deity; and it does not address such a deity in the second person language ('you' or 'thou') of prayer or praise. Moreover, the mystical project, like its cousin, the logocentric project of Hegel, is committed to an overcoming of difference that betrays an allergic reaction to the very experience of otherness that deconstruction seeks to preserve.

Kevin Hart (1989) believes Derrida is right to reject the suggestion that deconstruction is a kind of negative theology. But he argues that negative theology is a deconstruction of positive theology, and in this way the paradigm of postmetaphysical theology. He agrees with Heidegger and Derrida that what the former calls the 'step back' out of meta-physics is an ongoing task. This means that negative theology will always be accompanied by positive theology, as it is in Dionysius and Eckhart.

But they have a distinctive account of the relation-ship between the two. For someone like Thomas Aquinas, positive theology is prior and negative theology is a supplemental check to see that our discourse is about God and not just our ideas of God. For Dionysius and Eckhart, negative theology is prior to all the statements of positive theology. At issue here is not the order of exposition, as if the question were what should go into Chapter One. The issue is whether the negative principle, the denial that our concepts could possibly be adequate to the divine reality, is the first principle of theology.

3 Postmodern theology in a Nietzschean mode

The 'postmodern a/theology' of Mark C. Taylor is not a negative theology of the sort just described. Like Derridean deconstruction, a major source of its inspiration, it lacks the nostalgia and hope that mysticism shares with the positive theologies of theism. It has a strong Nietzschean bent and describes deconstruction as the hermeneutics of the death of God. But it describes itself as between belief and unbelief, because its response to Nietzsche's an-nouncement is neither the joyous, atheistic acceptance of God's demise nor the angry or frightened, theistic rejection of it. This is not because it is indifferent to religious meaning, but because it finds both the simple affirmation and the simple denial of God's reality to be too deeply enmeshed in the metaphysical thinking from which postmodernism seeks to extri-cate itself.

Taylor begins his a/theology (1984) with a decon-structive critique of four concepts that have been central to Judaic and Christian religion: God, self, history and book. In relation to tradition, this is an anti-theological gesture, but it purports to be of religious significance by opening up new possibilities for religious imagination. The positive rethinking of the four deconstructed themes is not described as reconstruction but as nomad thought in order to signify that it neither has nor seeks any fixed points of reference. Life is wandering and erring, and thus a maze; but this a/theology seeks for signs of 'mazing grace', as Taylor puts it.

The path from Nietzsche to Derrida leads all but inevitably through Heidegger. So it is not surprising to find an important Heideggerian theme in Taylor's project, namely the attempt to find a mode of thought that is not enslaved to projects of mastery, control and domination. The task of a/theology is neither to get a handle on God, nor to find in God the key to our mastery of the world.

4 Postmodern theology in a Kierkegaardian mode

The postmetaphysical theology of Jean-Luc Marion owes no special debt to Kierkegaard; but it is written in a Kierkegaardian mode in the sense that it combines an uncompromising critique of the main-stream metaphysical traditions of the West with the desire to return to biblical religion. It points towards a dehellenized Christianity for those who still find themselves, or would like to find themselves, in the Church.

Marion (1982) stresses that the critique of meta-physics as onto-theo-logy is the critique of a certain kind of discourse. It does not entail either God's unreality or the absence of a divine character that is God's own, independent of our images and concepts of God. Its purpose is not to make the world safe for secularism, but to open the space for a new experience of God as love and as gift.

However, this space is to be found beyond the horizon of Being, and the Heideggerian notion that a critique of theology can represent a new openness to God is immediately supplemented with a critique of Heidegger. Marion affirms his identification of onto-theo-logy as the arrogant demand by philosophy that God enter its discourse on its terms and in its service. At least as strongly as Heidegger, he wants to free God from these constraints. But he insists that the 'step back' out of metaphysics is not a step back into Being. In other words, Heidegger's attempt to think Being is more nearly a continuation of the onto-theo-logical constitution of metaphysics than a decisive break with it. The move away from the Athens of Plato and Aristotle needs to be in the direction of the biblical Jerusalem rather than the pre-Socratic Magna Graecia.

The major premise of Marion's argument is the

distinction between an idol and an icon. It concerns the 'how' rather than the 'what' of perception, which means that one and the same object could be an idol for one observer and an icon for another. An object of religious significance is an idol when it satisfies our perception, fulfils our intentions, freezes our gaze and brings it to rest. We have arrived and need not go further. An object is an icon when our gaze finds it necessary to 'transpierce' it in search of what exceeds it, when the invisible remains invisible in its visibility, when what is presented opens an abyss that we can never finish probing. While the idol limits the divine to the measure of the human gaze, the icon signifies an openness to that which exceeds every human measure. This analysis can be transferred from the sensible to the intelligible realm. Concepts, too, can serve as idols, not by virtue of their content (their 'what') but by virtue of their use (their 'how'). Any theology that professes an adequation between its concepts and the divine reality is *ipso facto* idolatrous; this is the fatal flaw of onto-theo-logy.

Heidegger's thinking of Being breaks decisively with the Hegelian–Husserlian drive towards adequate concepts. But by making the human understanding of Being the horizon for any understanding of God, Heidegger also compels the divine to conform to the measure of human thought. After *Being and Time*, he understood the goal of philosophy to be to let things show themselves in and from themselves. Marion argues that the horizon of Being undermines this goal. The self-revelation of God as love and as gift shatters this and every horizon, for love and gift do not signify concepts that would be adequate to the divine reality and with which we might rest, but the excess of the divine reality to every attempt on our part to think it. For Marion, postmodern theology is the attempt to preserve this self-revelation from every philosophical theory of Being, modern or postmodern.

See also: FEMINIST THEOLOGY; NEGATIVE THEOLOGY; POSTMODERNISM; RELIGION AND EPISTEMOLOGY

References and further reading

Caputo, J.D. (1986) *The Mystical Element in Heidegger's Thought*, New York: Fordham University Press, 2nd revised edn. (Lucid study of the mystical side of the later Heidegger.)

Derrida, J. (1967) *La voix et le phénomène*, Paris: Presses Universitaires de France; trans. D. Allison, *Speech and Phenomena and Other Essays on Husserl's Theory of Signs*, Evanston, IL: Northwestern University Press, 1973. (Introduction to deconstruction as theory and practice through a detailed, deconstructive reading of Husserl.)

* —— (1968) 'Différance', in *Théorie d'ensemble*, coll. Tel Quel, Paris: Éditions du Seuil; trans. A. Bass, *Margins of Philosophy*, Chicago, IL: Chicago University Press, 1982. (Brief introduction to deconstruction, with a discussion of negative theology.)

—— (1987) 'Comment ne pas parler: Dénégations', in *Psyché: Inventions de l'autre*, Paris: Galilée; trans. H. Coward and T. Foshay, 'How to Avoid Speaking: Denials', in H. Coward and T. Foshay (eds) *Derrida and Negative Theology*, Albany, NY: State University of New York Press, 1992. (Key essay on negative theology.)

* Hart, K. (1989) *The Trespass of the Sign: Deconstruction, Theology and Philosophy*, Cambridge: Cambridge University Press. (Seminal study of postmodern theology as negative theology, with special reference to Heidegger and Derrida.)

* Heidegger, M. (1927) *Sein und Zeit, Jahrbuch für Philosophie und phänomenologische Forschung* 8: 1–438; trans. J. Macquarrie and E. Robinson, *Being and Time*, New York: Harper & Row, 1962. (Major initial attempt of Heidegger to work free from the history of ontology; see especially §§6 and 8 for the 'destruction' of the history of ontology.)

* —— (1957) *Identität und Differenz*, Pfullingen: Neske; trans. J. Stambaugh, *Identity and Difference*, New York: Harper & Row, 1969. (Important late Heideggerian account of the 'step back' from onto-theo-logical metaphysics.)

Lowe, W. (1993) *Theology and Difference: The Wound of Reason*, Bloomington, IN: Indiana University Press. (Derridean reflections on theology in relation to Karl Barth, among others.)

* Marion, J.-L. (1982) *Dieu sans l'être: Hors-texte*, Paris: Librairie Arthème Fayard; trans. T.A. Carlson, *God Without Being*, Chicago, IL: University of Chicago Press. (A classic postmodern theology with a sustained critique of Heidegger's ontology.)

* Taylor, M.C. (1984) *ERRING: A Postmodern a/ theology*, Chicago, IL: University of Chicago Press. (A search for religious meaning through the deconstruction of traditional concepts.)

MEROLD WESTPHAL

POSTMODERNISM

The term 'postmodernism' appears in a range of contexts, from academic essays to clothing advertisements in the New York Times. *Its meaning differs with context to such an extent that it seems to function like Lévi-Strauss' 'floating signifier' (Derrida 1982: 290): not so much to express a value as to hold open a space for that which exceeds expression. This broad capacity of the term 'postmodernism' testifies to the scope of the cultural changes it attempts to compass.*

Across a wide range of cultural activity there has been a sustained and multivalent challenge to various founding assumptions of Western European culture since at least the fifteenth century and in some cases since the fifth century BC: *assumptions about structure and identity, about transcendence and particularity, about the nature of time and space. From physics to philosophy, from politics to art, the description of the world has changed in ways that upset some basic beliefs of modernity. For example, phenomenology seeks to collapse the dualistic distinction between subject and object; relativity physics shifts descriptive emphasis from reality to measurement; the arts move away from realism; and consensus politics confronts totalitarianism and genocide. These and related cultural events belong to seismic changes in the way we register the world and communicate with each other.*

To grasp what is at stake in postmodernism it is necessary to think historically and broadly, in the kind of complex terms that inevitably involve multidisciplinary effort. This multilingual impetus, this bringing together of methods and ideas long segregated both in academic disciplines and in practical life, particularly characterizes postmodernism and largely accounts for such resistance as it generates.

Although diverse and eclectic, postmodernism can be recognized by two key assumptions. First, the assumption that there is no common denominator – in 'nature' or 'truth' or 'God' or 'the future' – that guarantees either the One-ness of the world or the possibility of neutral or objective thought. Second, the assumption that all human systems operate like language, being self-reflexive rather than referential systems – systems of differential function which are powerful but finite, and which construct and maintain meaning and value.

1 **Historical context**
2 **The role of language**
3 **Challenge to the bases of consensus and realism**

1 Historical context

'Postmodernism' is a historical term, indicating something that comes after modernity; so the defini-

tion of postmodernism varies depending on what is meant by 'modern'. When 'modern' refers to movements in the arts around the turn of the twentieth century – an efflorescence known as 'modernism' – then 'postmodern' refers to a fairly local phenomenon of the mid- to late-twentieth century (see MODERNISM). But when 'modern' is used in the historian's sense, to indicate what follows the medieval – that is, Renaissance culture and its sequels – then 'postmodern' refers to a more broadly distributed cultural phenomenon in European and US societies.

Given this latter use of the term 'modern', *postmodernism* is what follows and transforms that particular Renaissance (some would prefer to call it Enlightenment) modernity. It is in this broader sense of modernity that the term 'postmodernism' takes on its full meaning. Here it signals a revisionary shift in the system of values and practices that have been broadly codified in European life over several centuries. Confusion between these two historical meanings of the term 'modern' skews discussion of the crucial philosophical, political and social issues at stake in postmodernism.

Such confusion certainly is not relieved by the ahistorical contributions of recent French philosophy which has taken the demystification of Western metaphysics back to Plato. Known as post-structuralism, this philosophy has been crucial to theoretical discussion of postmodernism, but not identical with it; the historical horizon of post-structuralism occupies a period so vast that it practically ceases to allow for history at all, producing discussions that blot out awareness of postmodernity as a historical event. Luce IRIGARAY and Jacques DERRIDA, for example, take on the foundations of Western philosophy and do not limit their critiques specifically to modern European culture (see POST-STRUCTURALISM).

Modernity, defined from the vantage point of postmodernity, was a cultural epoch and 'episteme' (see §2) founded in a humanistic belief that the world is One. This belief, codified in centuries of realist art, representational politics and empirical science, is tantamount to the assertion that a common denominator can be found for all systems of belief and value: that the world is a unified field, explicable by a single explanatory system. As this belief developed through increasingly secular and materialistic practices it became less secure in its claims to universal applicability. After the Renaissance the 'totalizing' claim to universal applicability was increasingly transferred from divinity to infinity: especially the infinity of space and time as they were radically reconstructed by Renaissance art and science. Postmodernism is the condition of coping without these absolute common denominators, especially without the neutral and homogeneous media of time and space which are the quintessential, field-unifying media of modernity.

Postmodernism specifically challenges the European culture that took its direction from the Renaissance, developed through the seventeenth century and the Enlightenment, and remains a common discourse for most citizens of Western democratic societies. In philosophy, in the arts, in science, in political theory and in sociology, postmodernism challenges the entire culture of realism, representation, humanism and empiricism. Postmodern critique thus goes to the very foundation of personal, social and institutional definition. Its challenges to knowledge and institutions are felt particularly in universities.

2 The role of language

Already well under way in the nineteenth century, the critique of Enlightenment rationalism found its postmodern turning point in the spreading influence of Ferdinand de SAUSSURE, a Swiss teaching at Geneva whose lectures on linguistics (published in 1916 as *Cours de Linguistique Générale*) have become a keystone of postmodernism. Saussure's deceptively simple idea was that the linguistic sign acts reflexively, not referentially. The word, he said, functions not by pointing at the world, but by specifying an entire system of meaning and value in which each word has its function. (Technically, Saussure's word points to an idea, but that idea is itself linguistic; there is nothing prior to language.) To read or understand even the simplest linguistic sequence is to recognize difference; it is to perform an incalculably complex and continuous act of differentiation, which becomes more and more balanced and rich the more that linguistic sequence verges towards poetry or other complex usage.

In one way this is only common sense. Any speaker of more than one language knows the arbitrariness of the sign: what is 'dog' here, is 'chien' there. But the more languages one knows, the more obvious becomes the systemic value of any word, the more obvious the fact that it has no exact equivalent elsewhere, either in other languages or in the world. To take the simplest possible example, we understand the English word 'dog' not merely because conventionally we have associated it with a creature, but more complexly and largely because we differentiate it by composition and function from other words and functions (for example, from 'dot', 'log', 'bog', and from verbs, adverbs, conjunctions). What is being described in these rather dry terms is the language's capacity for poetry: its capacity as a living language to

provide its speakers with particular alphabets and lexicons of possibility, and to modify, even radically, the usages with which we constitute our worlds.

The postmodern moment, as DERRIDA says, is the moment 'when language invaded the universal problematic'; this is the moment when it becomes clear that everything operates by such codes, that everything behaves like language. Body language, garment language, the silent expression of gesture, the layout of a city or a fashion magazine or a university: all these are complex, coded systems of meaning and value in which we function simultaneously in several, even many, at once. Even in humdrum activities we are expert well beyond our conscious measures. Language thus conceived is a model of organization that is both powerful and finite.

For describing systems of value that work like language, the terms *episteme* and *discourse* have emerged as useful. *Episteme* suggests the systemic nature of all knowledge (one can speak of the Western episteme); and *discourse* suggests the systemic nature of all practices (moral, social, domestic, political, reproductive, economic, intellectual). These two terms at least help the mind to find the fulcrum that allows thought to run in directions different from those inspired by terms like 'reality' or 'nature' (see §3).

Postmodernism differs from deconstruction, with which it is sometimes confused. Deconstruction is a methodology with agendas similar to some of postmodernism but with a much more limited capability. Deconstruction is a negative movement by which an interpreter of a code or sign-system (for example a novel or a psychoanalysis) looks for what is *not* present rather than what is present – looks for the points of crisis and breakdown in a system or a rationalization rather than its more obvious positivities. This methodology has the initial value of opening interpretation to complex reading, but it soon gets lost in circularity; the negative quality of its questioning often limits the creativity of the response. It is almost as though deconstruction is riveted on what it has not got, operating on a kind of nostalgia for the referential view of language that postmodernism revises (see DECONSTRUCTION).

Postmodernism does not weep for referentiality. If the sign does not refer simply, but instead specifies a system of meaning and value, then interest lies in discovering what systems actually are in play and in seeing what different systems are capable of, whether they be literary texts, political movements or personal lives. This valence of postmodernism can be found not so much in the theoretical texts which have had such extensive recent attention, but in the creative work of artists and scientists who have in many cases anticipated the philosophical critiques of rationalism, and have gone well beyond them to locate their practical implications. Artists and film-makers like Magritte and Buñuel, postmodern novelists like Robbe-Grillet and Nabokov, post-Einsteinian scientists interested in quanta and chaos, feminists interested in new acts of personal and political attention, and architects who play with traditional conventions have explored the practical and material implications of postmodernism far more fully than have many of the more theoretical writers.

3 Challenge to the bases of consensus and representation

The view that all systems are self-contained and largely self-referential has a radical implication that either alarms or inspires – the implication that no system has any special purchase on Truth and, in fact, that it is impossible to establish a Truth. This implication goes beyond the recuperable relativism of the nineteenth century to unrecuperable difference in the twentieth. Where relative systems could still cohabit in the single world of modernity, postmodernity involves the recognition that, to a large extent, one's relative systems *construct* the world. In short, that the world is not One; that words like 'truth,' 'nature', 'reality' and even 'human' are weasel words because they imply, falsely, that an autonomous world of meaning and values exists, and that it *transcends* all finite and mutually exclusive human systems and somehow guarantees them. Postmodernism denies absolute status to any truth or nature or reality. The question always remains – what truth, which nature, whose reality?

While this post-structuralist critique of transcendence goes back to Plato, the postmodern version limits its ambit to the particular forms of transcendence made available in the Renaissance and Enlightenment. The discourse of modernity extends to infinity its neutral media of space and time and, in so doing, encourages us to forget finitude and to distribute our energy toward an infinite horizon. The discourse of postmodernity, on the other hand, treats time and space as dimensions of finite systems. This recognition of absolute and unmediateable finitude inspires reflexiveness because activity no longer can be referred to unchanging external absolutes. Such reflexiveness always remains experimental or improvisatory, and inaccessible to universal generalization.

The disappearance of transcendental reference creates four related crises: the crisis of 'the subject' (the irreducible individual, the one that is because it thinks or is conscious); the crisis of 'the object' (the 'things' – including the individual – that constitute a world that is single, not multiplied); the crisis of 'the sign' (the word that refers to the world thus constituted); and, consequently, the crisis of historicism (the temporal humanism that constitutes an uneasy unity in the world by formulating transcendence as The Future).

Postmodernism presents a new problematic of negotiation between finite systems of meaning and value where no transcendental reference is possible. This negotiation goes on all the time in complex ways but, in the discourse of modernity, neither philosophy, nor political science, nor indeed any science, nor even much art has attended to it. This new problematic is, in Craig Owens' words, 'how to conceive difference without opposition', and how to translate that problematic, as the Renaissance translated Christian humanism, into social and political terms.

Where modernity sought the single system, postmodernity plays with the elements of systems, combining them for limited agendas, using what is useful and leaving the rest, refusing responsibility for consistency within this or that totalized explanatory system. This 'bricolage' becomes a key value for postmodernism. What one wants to avoid at all costs is something without play, without slack, without the living capacity for movement; one wants play in the line, play in the structure, in the sense of flexibility and variability even to the point of reorganizing the structure.

By conceiving all particulars and practices as functions of systems rather than as semi-autonomous entities, postmodernism poses especially interesting problems for two agendas of modernity that are particularly valuable to twentieth-century social and political function: historicism and individualism. History as a single, universal system of human explanation depends upon a construction of temporality that belongs to humanism and the Renaissance; its very notion of temporality is a kind of single-point perspective in time. Postmodernism puts history in the interesting position of considering its own historicity. The individual subject, sometimes appearing as the Cartesian *cogito*, does not, despite alarms, entirely disappear in postmodernism into systemic function. But individual identity and agency do have new definitions and functions when all practice is conceived differentially and systemically rather than naturally. Whatever is individual about a life, its unique and unrepeatable poetry, comes not from some 'natural' essence but from its particular specification of the complex discourse it inhabits.

Given the extent of the reformation implied by postmodernism, it is not surprising to find a flutter of reaction against it, not all of it informed and much of it governed by a desire to rescue particular epistemic investments from devaluation. The emphasis on linguistic reflexiveness, on the power of a system of signs to constitute meaning and value, has been taken by some commentators as an expression of inward-looking narcissism, a flight from 'reality' and, even, a threat to morality and order: it is as if the social, political and epistemic problems to which postmodernism responds were created by it, rather than by the entire culture of modernity. Postmodernism does not spell the end of meaning and value, still less the end of humanist meaning and value, but it does spell the end of certain hegemonies, especially those vested in what Alain Robbe-Grillet calls 'habitual humanism'. In any case, Saussure's idea of the reflexivity, rather than the referentiality of language has by no means yet been fully explored.

The postmodern critique, amid clatter and confusion, is only just under way. There is no responsible way to anticipate its full implications or trajectory. One can see, however, that postmodernism offers both a new freedom and a new constraint. The emphasis on the constructed nature of all knowledge and projects means that, because they have been invented, they can be changed; there is, morally or socially speaking, no 'nature' of things. On the other hand, the fact that with our languages we inherit so much of our beliefs and values ready-made means that we are much less original and autonomous than modernity suggested, and we express agency more locally, more collectively and less heroically than modernity allowed.

See also: FOUCAULT, M.; PHENOMENOLOGY, EPISTEMIC ISSUES

References and further reading

* Derrida, J. (1966) 'La structure, le signe et le jeu dans le discours des sciences humains' ('Structure Sign and Play in the Discourse of the Human Sciences'), in *L'écriture et La Difference* (*Writing and Difference*), trans. A. Bass, Chicago, IL: University of Chicago Press, 1982. (A seminal essay based on Lévi-Strauss and Saussure; not for the beginner.)

Ermarth, E.D. (1992) *Sequel to History: Postmodernism and the Crisis of Representational Time*, Princeton, NJ: Princeton University Press. (Accessible interdisciplinary discussion of the main theoretical and historical issues of postmodernism; bibliography.)

Foucault, M. (1969) *L'Archaeologie du Savoir* (*The Archaeology of Knowledge*), trans. A.M. Sheridan Smith, New York: Pantheon; London: Tavistock, 1972. (Fairly accessible example of postmodern methodology from a key practitioner; English edition also includes the widely used 'Discourse on Language', Foucault's 1970 Inaugural Address at the College de France, originally published as 'L'ordre du discours', 1971.)

Harvey, D. (1992) *The Condition of Postmodernity: An Enquiry*, Oxford, Blackwell. (Sensible and wide-ranging cultural analysis.)

Hutcheon, L. (1989) *The Politics of Postmodernism*, London and New York: Routledge. (Thorough and intelligent introductory survey of discussion; bibliography.)

Lyotard, J.-F. (1979) *La condition postmoderne: rapport sur le savoir* (*The Postmodern Condition: A Report on Knowledge*), trans. G. Bennington and B. Massumi, Minneapolis, MN: University of Minnesota Press, 1984. (Standard, fairly accessible discussion of key issues.)

—— (1983) *Le Différend* (*The Differend: Phrases in Dispute*), trans. G. van den Abbeele, Minneapolis, MN: University of Minnesota Press, 1988. (Standard, fairly accessible discussion of key issues.)

Owens, C. (1983) 'The Discourse of Others: Feminists and Postmodernism', in H. Foster (ed.) *The Anti-Aesthetic: Essays on Postmodern Culture*, Port Townsend, WA: Bay Press, 57–82. (A good essay in a good collection on postmodernism and culture.)

Robbe-Grillet, A. (1958) 'La nature, l'humanisme, et la tragédie' ('Nature, Humanism and Tragedy'), in *For a New Novel: Essays on Fiction*, trans. R. Howard, Evanston, IL: Northwestern University Press, 1989. (Key essay in a useful collection; accessible, if hit-and-run, style)

Saussure, F. de (1916) *Cours de Linguistique Générale* (*Course in General Linguistics*), trans. W. Baskin, New York: McGraw-Hill, 1959. (Seminal lectures published from students' notes, c.1906–11.)

Tyler, S. (1987) *The Unspeakable: Discourse, Dialogue, and Rhetoric in the Postmodern World*, Madison, WN: University of Wisconsin Press. (Accessible interdisciplinary discussion of postmodernism and language.)

ELIZABETH DEEDS ERMARTH

POSTMODERNISM AND POLITICAL PHILOSOPHY

Just as there is much disagreement over both what is meant by 'postmodernism' and which thinkers fall under this rubric, so also is there disagreement over its implications for political philosophy. The claim of postmodernists that raises the most significant issues is that Western modernity's fundamental moral and political concepts function in such a way as to marginalize, denigrate and discipline 'others'; that is, categories of people who in some way are found not to measure up to prevailing criteria of rationality, normality and responsibility, and so on. The West's generally self-congratulatory attitude towards liberal democracy and its traditions obscures this dynamic. Postmodernism aims to disrupt this attitude, and its proponents typically see their efforts as crucial to a radicalization of democracy.

1 'Otherness' and critique
2 Radicalizing democracy

1 'Otherness' and critique

Postmodernism aims at exposing how, in modern, liberal democracies, the construction of political identity and the operationalization of basic values take place through the deployment of conceptual binaries such as we/them, responsible/irresponsible, rational/irrational, legitimate/illegitimate, normal/abnormal, and so on. Rather than focusing upon the first term of each pair, and thus encouraging a thoroughly affirmative image of the achievements of the West, postmodernists draw attention to the ways in which the boundary between the two terms is socially reproduced and policed. This process takes place within the general sway of what is seen as modernity's deep, but questionable, commitment to expanding our mastery of self, society and nature. This persistent commitment creates pressure for hardening boundaries, simultaneously fostering conformity among those who fall on the 'correct' side of the dividing lines, and marginalization and denigration for those on the 'wrong' side. The 'others' engendered by this dynamic may be racial, ethnic, sexual, national, or they may have no easily identifiable, external characteristics. They may simply not measure up in terms of some scale of normality. (Perhaps the classic postmodern critique in this vein is Foucault's *Discipline and Punish* (1977); see FOUCAULT, M.) Given these concerns, it is easy to see affinities between postmodernism and other contemporary political initiatives, such as multiculturalism and feminism (see FEMINIST POLITICAL PHILOSOPHY §6; MULTICULTURALISM).

Critics have often faulted postmodernists for the totalized quality of their critique. Both liberal democracies and far more authoritarian regimes are rendered into objects equally to be condemned: each creates and disciplines others, even if the precise mechanisms differ. This equation, critics have argued, robs political philosophy of any basis for making

crucial normative distinctions between types of regimes.

Proponents respond that this argument misses their point. They seek only to deepen the critique of democracy, by sensitizing its supporters to the problem of otherness. But exactly what political orientation follows from such a perspective? Although there is a fair amount of uncertainty here, it is possible to sketch several alternatives.

2 Radicalizing democracy

Perhaps the most directly engendered political orientation stemming from postmodernism would be the stance of ongoing, impertinent dissent in which the goal is to highlight continually various modes by which the cognitive machinery and institutions of existing democracy spawn otherness. This would be a type of anarchism whose substantive orientation is directly parasitic upon the qualities of the system it attacks. No alternative political vision is offered. At its best, this stance might have the salutary effect of continually bringing to light inconspicuous phenomena of injustice. At its worst, it might become a sort of automatic propensity to disrupt, unconcerned about deleterious side effects.

Although ongoing criticism is part of what an enhancement of democracy would imply for many postmodernists, it is usually seen, on its own, as being too limited. What more affirmative vision does postmodernism offer? Sometimes there is allusion to what might be called an 'other politics', radically divorced from the present. In this vein, DERRIDA has spoken of 'the future of another law... lying beyond the totality of this present' (1985: 298); similarly, Foucault (1980) offered the idea of 'a new form of right'. The meaning of such appeals remains problematic since they have not been elaborated in any detail. Critics suspect that such a 'politics of the ineffable' is a rather obvious strategy for those who begin with such totalized critiques (McCarthy 1991).

Another way of rethinking politics would be in terms of some reorientation of liberal democracy's spirit or institutions so as to make them more hospitable to otherness. One form this takes is a reconsideration of the prevailing understanding of democratic sovereignty and community as residing with 'the people', in whom final, unquestionable authority resides (see DEMOCRACY). This is a unifying, homogenizing concept that in fact has no reality in political processes and decisions, where, at most, segments of the population express their will. Postmodernists suggest that we reimagine democratic community in a more radically open way, as something never fully present, but rather always in essential relation to those who are absent from, or defeated or shunted aside in, any particular expression of political will. The bond of such a community would be acknowledged as a tenuous one, embodying as it does a more vivid realization of difference. It could be thought of as sustained by mutual 'agnostic respect', as Connolly (1991) has put it. In effect, this would mean that each individual or group would accept that the formation of its identity is always simultaneously the formation of that which it is *not* – its others. The resulting tension is inevitable; we thus do best to recognize and honour it as an existential condition. Ideally, democracy is the regime most congruent with this condition.

This sort of rethinking of the binary 'us/them' within a democratic community also has implications for how the external relations of polities are conceived. Postmodernism's broad questioning of the constitution and policing of fundamental political dichotomies strikes directly at the sharp internal/external distinction that is at the philosophical heart of the predominant, state-centred view of international politics. Postmodernism here would invite us to consider more critically the way the presence of a state boundary is allowed to discount radically possible obligations to others who are defined as part of what is external or foreign. All of the foregoing suggestions for rethinking democracy could be categorized as components of something like a new philosophical ethos for democracy; that is, a new sensibility towards political life. But how would this new attitude towards otherness take shape institutionally? What institutions would be more hospitable to otherness and yet constrain it where appropriate? There does not appear to be much agreement on answers to such questions.

Consider, for example, the liberal value of tolerance (see TOLERATION). Postmodernism would presumably urge one not just to tolerate otherness, but rather celebrate it to some degree. But what would this mean in specific cases? Would one be more tolerant than liberals of pornography or radical groups that preach racism, or less tolerant? If one opted for the latter alternative, on the grounds that to do otherwise would express hostility to women or racial minorities, would that not also constitute a kind of intensification and enhanced policing of the bonds of community, an us/them?

Similar perplexities arise over the issue of what is called the liberal neutrality of the state. This traditional and central value of liberal politics holds that the state ought to be largely neutral *vis-à-vis* various sorts of groups; it should avoid using law to enhance or impede their cultural flourishing (see LIBERALISM; NEUTRALITY, POLITICAL). Postmodernism would seem to be at odds with this value. The claim is that liberal states are not in fact ever able to be completely neutral; formal neutrality merely allows culturally hegemonic groups to dominate and marginalize less powerful ones. On this view, a fairer democratic state would then be one that fiscally and institutionally tried to maintain a better balance. Of course, as with toleration, specific proposals to implement such ideas generate new quandaries. If the state is to subsidize the cultural and organizational life of some groups to a far greater degree than now, what will the criteria be for who gets funds and who does not? Will the distinction supported/unsupported carry its own invidiousness; and will it be worse than the present liberal alternative? (See CITIZENSHIP §3).

See also: POSTMODERNISM

References and further reading

* Connolly, W. (1991) *Identity/Difference: Democratic Negotiations*, Ithaca, NY: Cornell University Press. (A careful attempt to engage a range of issues related to postmodernism and political philosophy.)

Critchley, S. (1992) 'A Question of Politics: The Future of Deconstruction', in *The Ethics of Deconstruction: Derrida and Levinas*, Oxford: Blackwell, 188–247. (An attempt to elucidate the idea of a postmodern democratic community.)

* Derrida, J. (1985) 'Racism's Last Word', trans. P. Kamuf, *Critical Inquiry* 12 (Autumn): 290–9. (Reflections on power and right from a postmodern perspective.)

* Foucault, M. (1977) *Discipline and Punish*, trans. A. Sheridan, New York: Random House. (A classic model of postmodern critique.)

* —— (1980) 'Two Lectures', in *Power/Knowledge: Selected Interviews and Other Writings, 1972–1977*, ed. C. Gordon and trans. C. Gordon et al., New York: Pantheon Books, 78–108. (Reflections on power and right from a postmodern perspective.)

Lyotard, J. and Thébaud, J.-L. (1985) *Just Gaming*, trans. W. Godzich, Minneapolis, MN: University of Minnesota Press. (An effort to articulate some postmodern criteria of fairness.)

* McCarthy, T. (1991) 'The Politics of the Ineffable: Derrida's Deconstructionism', in *Ideals and Illusions: On Reconstruction and Deconstruction in Contemporary Critical Theory*, Cambridge, MA: MIT Press. (Critique of a leading postmodern thinker.)

Taylor, C. (1984) 'Foucault on Freedom and Truth', *Political Theory* 12 (2): 152–83. (Critique of a leading postmodern thinker.)

White, S.K. (1991) *Political Theory and Postmodernism*, Cambridge: Cambridge University Press. (An overview of the controversy between postmodernists and their critics.)

Young, I. (1990) *Justice and the Politics of Difference*, Princeton, NJ: Princeton University Press. (An examination of the inadequacy of liberal approaches to justice for treating problems raised by radical critics such as postmodernists.)

STEPHEN K. WHITE

POSTMODERNISM, FRENCH CRITICS OF

French anti-postmodernism emerged with the generation of philosophers that came of age in the late 1970s and early 1980s and counts among its ranks some of the most visible and prolific young scholars in France. Unlike schools of thought such as phenomenology, existentialism or Marxism, French anti-postmodernism has no founding figure, central text or core doctrine; anti-postmodernism (a term seldom, if ever, used by the French) therefore is less a philosophical school than a characterization for a diverse group of thinkers who react against those trends that have dominated French intellectual life since the Second World War, especially Marxism, structuralism, existentialism and deconstruction. These trends, grouped together under the heading of 'postmodernism', are seen by anti-postmodernists as the last episodes in a failed intellectual adventure whose origins go back at least to the French Revolution.

Critical of nineteenth-century philosophy as having produced, on the one hand, totalizing, speculative philosophies such as those of Hegel and Marx, and, on the other hand, the anti-rationalism of Nietzsche and his postmodern scions, anti-postmodernists (or neo-moderns as the French prefer to say) represent a return to the concept of the individual and of history as the product of free human agency. Reaffirming the efficacy of public, rational discourse, they tend to be interested in political philosophy, taking democracy and its ideals as a model for raising and addressing philosophical issues. Pluralist in their outlook, they value the disciplinary structure of scholarly work; fields such as epistemology, theology, philosophy of science and the history of ideas which were neglected or marginalized by much postmodern thought have enjoyed renewed prestige and interest among the anti-postmodernists.

1 Historical background
2 Points of contention

1 Historical background

Several main currents shaped French philosophy during the last half of the twentieth century; the tradition of German philosophy has been most important of all. From the nineteenth century, Hegel, Marx and Nietzsche played particularly prominent roles as did the thought of Husserl, Freud and Heidegger from the twentieth century. In addition to these, the early twentieth-century Swiss linguist Ferdinand de Saussure is credited with providing the inspiration for the emergence of structuralism during the 1950s. The 1960s and 1970s in France produced a distinctive mélange of German and structuralist philosophy that is often referred to as post-structuralist or postmodern philosophy. Though both postmodernists and anti-postmodernists would agree on these influences and the general stages of development, they disagree on their nature and significance.

After the Second World War two philosophical traditions were particularly prominent in France. Thanks to Alexandre KOYRÉ and Alexandre KOJÈVE during the 1930s and to Jean Hyppolite, Maurice Merleau-ponty and others during the post-war years, Hegelianism displaced neo-Kantianism as the leading school of thought (see HEGELIANISM). In particular, Hegel's conception of an all-encompassing dialectical history became an important resource for philosophical and political reflection during these turbulent decades. Merleau-Ponty, Emmanuel LEVINAS and Jean-Paul SARTRE, among others, also introduced Husserl's phenomenology of consciousness and Heidegger's analysis of being and human existence to French thinkers. However, it was above all Sartre who, through his literary endeavours and political activism in addition to his philosophical works, popularized a synthesis of Marxism and existential phenomenology, an orientation that remained mainstream among the traditionally leftist French intelligentsia until the revolt of May 1968, after which its popularity waned. His existential Marxism was a humanism, that is, an ideology that envisaged an historical process of consciousness raising whereby individuals and humanity as a whole would be emancipated to their authentic mode of existence (see EXISTENTIALISM).

While existential Marxism became increasingly popular from the 1930s to the mid-1960s, beginning in the 1950s there was a second important intellectual development. Inspired by Saussure's linguistics, several disciplines developed the method of analysis and theory of meaning that came to be known as structuralism (see STRUCTURALISM). Among them were the anthropology of Claude LÉVI-STRAUSS, the psychoanalysis of Jacques LACAN, and the literary theory of Roland BARTHES. Of particular importance was the frame of reference for their analyses: they focused not on the 'lived experience' of an individual consciousness nor on the progressive emancipation of human nature, as did the existential Marxists, nor did they have a comprehensive ideology in the light of which the significance of a given historical phenomenon could be adduced. For structuralists, the meaning of a word or, more generally, a 'signifier' is determined not by the intentions of the individual but by its differential relation to the system of signifiers that constitutes a given language; meanings are therefore relative to a specific linguistic culture rather than a product of individual human consciousness or of a universal, eschatological system such as Hegel's. Therefore, in framing their investigations in terms of systemic structures and their instantiation in linguistic, social and psychological phenomena, the structuralists conceived of their method as scientific and objective in contradistinction to the subject-oriented, humanistic and ideological character of Hegelian, Marxist and phenomenological philosophies of consciousness.

Those philosophers educated in the 1950s and who emerged during the 1960s as dominant figures of postmodern philosophy were greatly influenced by structuralism in two particularly noteworthy respects. First, in privileging structure over process as well as the plurality of semiological systems over a universal system, they unequivocally rejected the cross-cultural and transhistorical philosophies of Marx and, especially, Hegel. Teleological history and its dialectical rationality came to be seen as an empty, neo-theological idealism divorced from facts. Second, and related to the first, the plurality of linguistic systems, and hence the plurality of possible meanings of a word or signifier, gave rise to a critique of the univocity of concepts. Above all, the concept of identity or of the self-identical subject so fundamental to philosophy since Descartes' *cogito* came to be seen as a substanceless fiction posited by the Western European philosophical tradition (see ALTERITY AND IDENTITY, POSTMODERN THEORIES OF). The structuralist critique of Hegelian history and its basis in subjectivity eventually led to the reconfiguration of Marxism in the structuralist philosophy of Louis ALTHUSSER, who coined the term *anti-humanism* to describe his Marxism in which individuals were conceived of as sites in a general system of production and in which history was conceived of as a process with no subject, that is, as having no underlying unity or direction.

Georges BATAILLE, Gilles DELEUZE and Pierre Klossowski were among those who introduced Nietzsche's thought to France in the late 1950s and 1960s; this, coupled with the later Heidegger's influential critique of technology and calculative reason, reinforced the anti-Hegelian elements of structuralism. Salient features of French Nietzscheanism were the critiques of identity, subjectivity and reason, the advocacy of the primordial status of language and the consequent centrality of 'questions of interpretation' in the place of 'questions of fact', and the rejection of progressivist or teleological conceptions of history. Discerning a complicity between the anthropocentrism of humanism and the metaphysics of modern philosophy inaugurated by Descartes and culminating in Kant and Hegel, postmodern philosophers influenced by Nietzsche – Heidegger, Jacques Lacan, Michel FOUCAULT, Gilles Deleuze, Jacques DERRIDA, among others – proclaimed, each in their own way, 'the death of man', that is, the end of metaphysical humanism, the collapse of which defines the postmodern condition. In this respect they all, in one manner or another, affirm along with NIETZSCHE an ontological nihilism. Despite significant differences among them, they all find in Hegel the culmination of foundationalist modern philosophy as well as its foundering, and they all accept the uncertain, perspectival and ontologically nihilistic character of the contemporary age. By 1979, when Jean-François Lyotard published *La Condition Postmoderne* (*The Postmodern Condition*, 1984) which popularized the philosophical sense of 'postmodernity' and after the traditionally progressivist left had suffered political collapse in the election of 1978, postmodernism – Derrida's deconstruction, Foucault's archaeo-genealogy and Deleuze's schizoanalysis, to name only the most prominent figures of postmodernism – had found a home in the leading universities and intellectual institutions of France (see DECONSTRUCTION; POSTMODERNISM; POST-STRUCTURALISM).

2 Points of contention

One of the most basic differences between postmodernists and anti-postmodernists is their divergent interpretations of history. Postmodernists hold that in some serious sense history and modernity have come to an end, be it with the collapse of Hegelianism, with the Nietzschean critique of metaphysics, or simply through exhaustion; their critiques and deconstructions are dedicated to driving home that the philosophical basis of progressive modernity has met its end. However, anti-postmodernists see postmodernism thereby as falling prey to a concept of historical necessity and therefore taking the collapse of speculative philosophy as determinative. Anti-postmodernists agree that the emancipatory project of Kant's Enlightenment and the subsequent absolutization of historical reason in Hegel and Marx were ill-fated. But they do not see this as the final or inevitable conclusion of modern philosophy or historical progress. Rather, what they see ending is postmodernism, which for them is not the deconstructive revelation of a Hegelian error but its continuation. Holding that postmodernism was too conditioned by the Enlightenment it sought to criticize, Luc Ferry proclaims that anti-postmodernists have grown beyond postmodernism and that 'for the first time no doubt in the history of humanity, we are living in a time when this critique [of Enlightenment reason] has reached the minimal threshold of maturity' (1995: 168).

If the metaphysics of the Enlightenment was a misadventure whose repercussions produced the terror of the French Revolution, the misology of Nietzsche and the postmodern critiques of subjectivity and reason, it nevertheless remains possible, according to anti-postmodernists, to discover other historical possibilities for thought and action than those that led to postmodernism. Accordingly, they are drawn to Alexis de TOCQUEVILLE rather than J.-J. Rousseau or Kant, to J.G. FICHTE rather than Hegel or Marx and to Benjamin CONSTANT rather than Nietzsche. Anti-postmodernists find in these and like thinkers not the death knell of history but indications of its infinitely open future horizon. For them, history is less the primary determinant (rational or otherwise) than it is a single, albeit important, element in human theoretical and practical endeavours.

A second and related basic issue at stake for anti-postmodernists also goes back to German Idealism. Although anti-postmodernists too are critical of the metaphysics of reason and its ideological excesses, they hold that the postmodern critique leads to a sterile nihilism. Vincent Descombes (1980: 182) sums up this complaint when he says for postmodernism there is:

no *original*, the model for the copy is itself a copy …no *facts*, only interpretations and any interpretation is itself the interpretation of an older interpretation; there is no *meaning proper* to words, only figurative meanings …no *authentic version* of a text, there are only translations; *no truth*, only pastiche and parody.

And as Luc Ferry claims, this anti-humanism cripples the individual and leads to authoritarianism, either by giving rise to a panoply of master thinkers (such as Hegel, Marx, Nietzsche, Heidegger, Foucault, Derrida) who produce hermetic systems of oracular discourse that admit of no falsification, or by elevating non-human things, such as the natural environment, to a point where humanity is rendered insignificant if not odious (see ECOLOGICAL PHILO-

SOPHY §1; NÆSS, A.). According to Ferry, the challenge of anti-postmodernism is to develop a non-metaphysical humanism, that is, a conception of rationality and the subject that leads neither to the ideological excesses of the post-Enlightenment, nor to their debasement in postmodernism.

The anti-postmodernist emphasis on the individual, reason and their vision of the future as open to determination by human spontaneity indicates that freedom and the belief in the efficacy of rational discourse are central to anti-postmodernist thought and also reveals its predominantly political orientation. Often identifying with the seventeenth-century 'quarrel of the ancients and the moderns' in which modern, scientifically oriented philosophy rejected the theological, aesthetical and moralizing thought of the Renaissance, anti-postmodernists tend to be concerned with that open space in which communal thought and activity are constituted and which is supported by democratic processes. In this regard, the communicative demands of cooperative political activity valued by anti-postmodernism is clearly at odds with the effacing of the distinction between fact and fiction wrought by structuralism and extended by the Nietzschean, postmodern critique of reason.

The anti-postmodern appeal to common sense has capitalized both on some of the extravagances of postmodernism and on its relatively esoteric character. However, although their concerns are substantive and their criticisms often illuminating, anti-postmodernists often indulge in characterizations; more importantly, anti-postmodernists have yet to address adequately issues raised by postmodernism that touch on the viability of a positive conception of anti-postmodernism. Among these are the constitution of the conscious subject, the nature of language and its relevance for discourse and knowledge, the manner in which the past bears upon and influences the future, and the possibility and value of a non-metaphysical rationality. Its ability to address these and related matters will determine whether anti-postmodernism signals the epochal shift many of its members claim is at hand, or whether it proves to be only the most recent reactionary philosophical tantrum.

See also: ALTERITY AND IDENTITY, POSTMODERN THEORIES OF; SUBJECT, POSTMODERN CRITIQUE OF THE.

References and further reading

* Descombes, V. (1980) *Modern French Philosophy*, trans. L. Scott-Fox and J.M. Harding, Cambridge: Cambridge University Press. (One of the earliest

and best overviews of French postmodern philosophy from an anti-postmodernist point of view.)

* Ferry, L. (1995) *The New Ecological Order*, trans. C. Volk, Chicago, IL: University of Chicago Press, 1995. (A clearly written extension of anti-postmodernist thought applied to ecological movements.)

Ferry, L. and Renaut, A. (1990) *French Philosophy of the Sixties: An Essay on Antihumanism*, trans. M. Schanckenberg, Amherst, MA: University of Massachusetts Press. (A call to arms by two leading anti-postmodernists.)

Lilla, M. (ed.) (1994) *New French Thought: Political Philosophy*, Princeton, NJ: Princeton University Press. (A representative selection of articles by anti-postmodernists focusing on political thought.)

* Lyotard, J.-F. (1979) *La Condition postmoderne: rapport sur le savoir*, Paris: Éditions de Minuit; trans. G. Bennington and B. Massumi, *The Postmodern Condition*, Minneapolis, MN: University of Minnesota Press, 1984. (A central text in postmodernism; somewhat challenging for the beginner.)

Nora, P., Gauchet, M. and Pomian, K. (eds) (1988) *Le Débat* 50 (May-August). (An important retrospective by one of the most important journals for anti-postmodernist thought; very clear for those who can read French.)

Pavel, T.G. (1989) 'The Present Debate: News From France', *Diacritics* 19 (1). (An excellent summary discussion of French philosophy in the 1980s.)

REGINALD LILLY

POST-STRUCTURALISM

Post-structuralism is a late-twentieth-century development in philosophy and literary theory, particularly associated with the work of Jacques Derrida and his followers. It originated as a reaction against structuralism, which first emerged in Ferdinand de Saussure's work on linguistics. By the 1950s structuralism had been adapted in anthropology (Lévi-Strauss), psychoanalysis (Lacan) and literary theory (Barthes), and there were hopes that it could provide the framework for rigorous accounts in all areas of the human sciences.

Although structuralism was never formulated as a philosophical theory in its own right, its implicit theoretical basis was a kind of Cartesianism, but without the emphasis on subjectivity. It aimed, like Descartes, at a logically rigorous system of knowledge based on sharp explicit definitions of fundamental concepts. The difference was that, for structuralism, the system itself was absolute, with no grounding in subjectivity. Post-structuralist critiques of structuralism typically challenge the assumption that systems are self-sufficient structures and question the possibility of the precise definitions on which systems of knowledge must be based.

Derrida carries out his critique of structuralist systems by the technique of deconstruction. This is the process of showing, through close textual and conceptual analysis, how definitions of fundamental concepts (for example, presence versus absence, true versus false) are undermined by the very effort to formulate and employ them. Derrida's approach has particularly influenced literary theory and criticism in the USA. In addition, Richard Rorty, developing themes from pragmatism and recent analytic philosophy, has put forward a distinctively American version of post-structuralism.

1   Structuralism
2   Post-structuralism: terminology
3   Two major post-structuralist theses
4   Derrida's critique of logocentrism
5   Post-structuralism and literary theory
6   Rorty's post-structuralist pragmatism

1   Structuralism

In his lectures on linguistics, Ferdinand de SAUSSURE proposed a view of language (*langue*) as a formal structure, defined by differences between systemic elements. According to Saussure, this structure is simultaneously present in and unites the two domains of thought and words. A given linguistic term (a sign) is the union of an idea or concept (the 'signified') and a physical word (the 'signifier'). A language is a complete system of such signs, which exists not as a separate substance but merely as the differentiating form that defines the specific structure of both signifiers (physical words) and signifieds (ideas). Saussure's view rejects the common-sense picture of the set of signifiers and the set of signifieds as independent givens, with the signifieds having meaning in their own right and the signifiers obtaining meaning entirely through their association with corresponding signifieds. Saussure denies this independence and instead maintains that signifiers and signifieds alike have meaning only in virtue of the formal structure (itself defined by differences between elements) that they share (see STRUCTURALISM IN LINGUISTICS).

Saussure's structuralist approach was very successful within linguistics, where it was applied and extended by, among others, Jakobson and Troubetzkoy. By the 1950s the approach had been adapted in anthropology (Lévi-Strauss), psychoanalysis (Lacan), and literary theory (Barthes); and there were hopes that it could provide the framework for rigorous accounts in all areas of the human sciences. Three distinguishing features of this framework were: (1) a rejection of all idealist views of concepts and meanings as derived from the activity of consciousness; (2) an understanding of concepts and meanings as, instead, grounded in the structural relations among the elements of abstract systems; (3) an explication of such structural relations solely in terms of bipolar differences (for example, real/unreal, temporal/non-temporal, present/absent, male/female).

2 Post-structuralism: terminology

Post-structuralism is obviously closely tied to structuralism, but commentators have characterized the relationship in a variety of mutually inconsistent ways. Some writers make no distinction between structuralism and post-structuralism, applying the single term 'structuralist' to the entire range of thinkers from Saussure through to Derrida. More commonly, post-structuralism is distinguished as a separate development, but there is disagreement as to whether it is primarily a reaction against structuralism or an extension of it (as the term *Neostrukturalismus*, commonly used by Manfred Frank and other German commentators, suggests). Apart from matters of definition, there is even disagreement as to whether major figures such as Barthes, Lacan and Foucault are structuralists or post-structuralists.

Michel Foucault's book, *Les mots et les choses* (translated under the title *The Order of Things*) is an instructive example. In one sense it is quintessentially structuralist. The book first uncovers the fundamental epistemic systems (which Foucault calls 'epistemes') that underlie and delimit the subjective thought of particular eras. It then goes on to show how the apparent ultimacy of subjectivity is itself just the product of one contingent episteme, that of modernity, which is even now disappearing (the famous 'death of man'). Nevertheless, Foucault's essentially historical viewpoint in the work demonstrates the limitation of structuralism: its inability to give any account of the transitions from one system of thought to another. Foucault seems to have seen from the beginning that structuralism cannot be historical, a fact that explains his constant insistence that he was not a structuralist, in spite of his obvious deployment of structuralist methods and concepts. So, although *Les mots et les choses* is a structuralist book, it at the same time makes clear the limits of structuralism and prepares the way for Foucault's later work on power and ethics which is distinctly post-structuralist (see

FOUCAULT, M.; POST-STRUCTURALISM AND THE SOCIAL SCIENCES).

Despite these ambiguities and disagreements, the concept of post-structuralism is useful, if not essential, for understanding philosophy in France during the latter part of the twentieth century. One fruitful approach is to think of post-structuralism as a philosophical reaction to the structuralism that was such a powerful force during the 1960s in linguistics, psychology and the social sciences. It was neither a simple rejection or extension of structuralism but a series of philosophical reflections on the structuralist programme and achievement.

3 Two major post-structuralist theses

Although structuralism was never formulated as a philosophical theory in its own right, its implicit theoretical basis was, as noted above, a kind of Cartesianism without the subject. (Hence, the association of structuralism with the notion of the 'death of the subject'.) Post-structuralist critiques of structuralism are typically based on two fundamental theses: (1) that no system can be autonomous (self-sufficient) in the way that structuralism requires; and (2) that the defining dichotomies on which structuralist systems are based express distinctions that do not hold up under careful scrutiny.

The first thesis is not understood so as to support the traditional idealist view that systematic structures are dependent on the constitutive activities of subjects. Post-structuralists retain structuralism's elimination of the subject from any role as a foundation of reality or of our knowledge of it. But, in opposition to structuralism, they also reject any logical foundation for a system of thought (in, for example, its internal coherence). For post-structuralists, there is no foundation of any sort that can guarantee the validity or stability of any system of thought.

The second thesis is the key to post-structuralism's denial of the internal coherence of systems. The logical structure of a system requires that the applications of its concepts be unambiguously defined. (In the formalism of elementary number theory, for example, there must be no question as to whether a given number is odd or even.) As a result, the possibility of a systematic structure depends on the possibility of drawing sharp distinctions between complementary concepts such as odd/even, charged/uncharged, living/non-living, male/female and so on. Post-structuralist philosophers have been particularly concerned with the fundamental dichotomies (or oppositions) underlying structuralist theories in the human sciences. Saussure's linguistics, for example, is based on the distinction of the signifier from the signified; Lévi-Strauss's anthropology of myths employs oppositions such as raw/cooked, sun/moon and so on. In each case, post-structuralists have argued that the dichotomy has no absolute status because the alternatives it offers are neither exclusive nor exhaustive.

4 Derrida's critique of logocentrism

This sort of critique was extended to philosophy, particularly by Jacques DERRIDA, who finds Western philosophical thought pervaded by a network of oppositions – appearance/reality, false/true, opinion/ knowledge, to cite just a few examples – that constitute what he calls the system of 'logocentrism'. This term derives from Derrida's conviction that at the root of Western philosophical thought is a fundamental distinction between speech (*logos*) and writing. Speech is privileged as the expression of what is immediate and present, the source, accordingly, of what is real, true and certain. Writing, on the other hand, is derogated as an inferior imitation of speech, the residue of speech that is no longer present and, therefore, the locus of appearance, deceptions and uncertainty. Plato's devaluation of writing in comparison with living dialogue is the most famous and influential example of this distinction. But Derrida finds the distinction pervading Western philosophy and regards it as not just a preference for one form of communication over another but the basis for the entire set of hierarchical oppositions that characterize philosophical thought. Speech offers presence, truth, reality, whereas writing, a derivative presentation employed in the absence of living speech, inevitably misleads us into accepting illusions.

Derrida's critiques of the speech/writing opposition – and of all the hierarchical oppositions that attend it – proceed by what he calls the method of 'deconstruction' (see DECONSTRUCTION). This is the process of showing, through close textual and conceptual analysis, how such oppositions are contradicted by the very effort to formulate and employ them. Consider, for example, the opposition between presence and absence, which plays a fundamental role in Husserl's phenomenology (and many other philosophical contexts). Husserl requires a sharp distinction between what is immediately present to consciousness (and therefore entirely certain) and what is outside of consciousness (and therefore uncertain). But once Husserl undertakes a close analysis of the immediately present, he discovers that it is not instantaneous but includes its own temporal extension. The 'present', as a concrete experiential unit, involves both memory of the just-immediately-past (retention, in Husserl's terminology) and anticipation of the immediate future (protention). Thus, the past and the future, both paradigms of what is absent (not present), turn out to be integral parts of the present. Husserl's own account of the presence/ absence opposition overturns it.

Deconstruction maintains that there is no stability in any of thought's fundamental oppositions. Their allegedly exclusive alternatives turn out to be inextricably connected; their implicit hierarchies perpetually reversible. As a result, there is an ineliminable gap between the intelligibility of a rational system and the reality it is trying to capture. Derrida expresses this gap through a variety of terms. He frequently speaks of *différance* (a deliberately misspelled homophone of the French *différence*) to emphasize, first, the difference between systematic structures and the objects (for example, experiences, events, texts) they try to make intelligible, and, second, the way in which efforts to make absolute distinctions are always deferred (another sense of the French *différer*) by the involvement of one polar opposite in the other. This latter phenomenon Derrida also discusses in terms of the 'trace' of its opposite always lingering at the heart of any polar term. He also employs the term 'dissemination' to refer to the way that objects of analysis slip through the conceptual net spread by any given system of intelligibility we devise for it.

5 Post-structuralism and literary theory

Thus far the discussion has focused on Derrida's deconstruction of the meaningful structures philosophers purport to find in reality and to express in their philosophical texts. But Derrida's approach is also readily applicable to literary texts (and the 'worlds' they create). This is because – like philosophical systems – poems, novels and other literary texts are typically thought to embody complete and coherent systems of meaning, which it is the task of literary criticism to extract. Although Derrida himself has dealt primarily with philosophical texts, his approach has been widely adopted by analysts of literature. (Of course, as should be expected, Derrida and his followers reject any sharp distinction between the philosophical and the literary.)

Traditional literary analysis has understood the meaning of a text as the expression of its author's mind; that is, as thoughts the author intended to convey in writing the text. The first stage of deconstructive criticism is the structuralist one of detaching meaning from authorial intention, locating it instead in the text itself as a linguistic structure. Roland Barthes, for example, showed how to analyse a text by Balzac entirely in terms of the formal codes it embodies, with no reference to what Balzac supposedly 'meant'. This structuralist move effects a 'death of the author' parallel to the anti-Cartesian 'death of the subject'. But the post-structuralists take the future step of denying a fixed meaning to even the autonomous text itself. It is not that a text lacks all meaning but that, on the contrary, it is the source of an endless proliferation of conflicting meanings. As deconstructionists delight in showing, any proposed privileged meaning of a text can be undermined by careful attention to the role in it of apparently marginal features. (For example, an orthodox Christian reading of Milton's *Paradise Lost* is deconstructed by a close study of certain details in its treatment of Satan.) There is no doubt, of course, that texts are often produced by authors trying to express what they think or feel. But what they write always goes beyond any authorial intention and in ways that can never be reduced to a coherent system of meaning.

The deconstructionist's point can also be understood as an undermining of the distinction between primary text and commentary. On the traditional view, a commentary is an effort to formulate as accurately as possible the content (meaning) of the text. To the extent that it is successful, a commentary expresses nothing more and nothing less than this meaning. But for deconstructionists the meaning in question does not exist, and the commentary must be understood as nothing more than a free elaboration of themes suggested, but not required, by the text. Unable to be a secondary reflection, the commentary becomes as much an independent creation as the text itself.

6   Rorty's post-structuralist pragmatism

Richard Rorty's work is far removed, in both antecedents and style, from that of continental post-structuralists (see RORTY, R.). His critique of Cartesianism, derived more from Dewey than from Heidegger, is aimed at twentieth-century analytic philosophy rather than the structuralist human sciences; and his urbanely lucid prose contrasts sharply with the wilfully playful convolutions of Derrida and his followers. None the less, Rorty's analyses lead him to a critique of traditional philosophy very similar to that of the post-structuralists.

The focal point of Rorty's critique is the project (called foundationalism) of providing a philosophical grounding for all knowledge. Modern foundationalism originates with Descartes, but Rorty sees it as also the *leitmotif* of Descartes' successors, through Hume and Kant down to the logical positivists. Like Derrida, Rorty attacks traditional systematic thought by calling into question some of its key distinctions.

Unlike Derrida, however, he does not carry out his attacks through close readings of classic texts but by deploying the results of recent analytic philosophy. He uses, for example, Quine's critique of the distinction between analytic and synthetic statements to argue that there are no foundational truths about the meaning of concepts. He appeals to Wilfrid Sellars's undermining of the distinction between theory and observation to reject empirical foundations of knowledge in interpretation-free sense data. He employs Donald Davidson's questioning of the distinction between the formal structure and the material content of a conceptual framework to reject Kantian attempts to ground knowledge in principles that define the framework of all possible thought.

In Rorty's view the upshot of these various critiques is to cut off every source of an ultimate philosophical foundation for our knowledge. Accordingly, he maintains, philosophy must give up its traditional claim to be the final court of appeal in disputes about truth. We have no alternative but to accept as true what we (the community of knowers) agree on. There is no appeal beyond the results of the 'conversation of mankind' so far as it has advanced to date. For us, there is no (upper-case) Truth justified by privileged insights and methods. There is only the mundane (lower-case) truth: what our interlocutors let us get away with saying.

It might seem that this rejection of foundationalism is a rejection of the entire tradition of Western philosophy since Plato. Rorty, however, distinguishes two styles of philosophy. First, there is *systematic philosophy*, the mainline of the Western tradition since Plato, which is defined by the foundationalist goal of ultimate justification. But, on the other hand, there is another enterprise, always marginal to the tradition, that Rorty calls *edifying philosophy*. Whereas systematic philosophers undertake elaborate and purportedly eternal constructions (which are always demolished by the next generation), edifying philosophers are content to shoot ironic barbs at the systematic thought of their day, exploding its pretensions and stimulating intriguing lines of counter-thought. The tradition of edifying thought can be traced back at least to the ancient Cynics and has been more recently represented by Kierkegaard, Nietzsche and the later Wittgenstein. Derrida's deconstructions are, on Rorty's view, a prime contemporary example of edifying philosophy.

Edifying philosophers, however, are philosophers only because they react against systematic philosophy. They do not differ from other sorts of cultural critics (novelists, literary theorists, social scientists) because of any distinctively philosophical method or viewpoint. If, in the wake of thinkers such as Derrida and

Rorty, systematic philosophy is abandoned, philosophy will be too. The triumph of post-structuralism would, for better or worse, be the end of philosophy as we have known it.

See also: POSTMODERNISM

References and further reading

Culler, J. (1982) *On Deconstruction: Theory and Criticism after Structuralism*, Ithaca, NY: Cornell University Press. (Excellent discussion of Derrida's views and of their impact on literary criticism.)

Dews, P. (1987) *Logics of Disintegration: Poststructuralist Thought and the Claims of Critical Theory*, London: Verso. (Analytic and critical essays on Derrida, Lacan, Foucault and Lyotard.)

* Foucault, M. (1966) *Les mots et les choses: une archéologie des sciences humaines*, Paris: Gallimard; trans. A. Sheridan, *The Order of Things*, New York: Random House, 1970. (A critical history of the origins of the modern social sciences.)

Frank, M. (1989) *What Is Neostructuralism?*, trans. S. Wilke and R. Gray, Minneapolis, MN: University of Minnesota Press. (A detailed study and critique of the movement.)

Rorty, R. (1989) *Contingency, Irony, and Solidarity*, Cambridge: Cambridge University Press. (A collection of essays that formulates Rorty's position and comments on the views of other post-structuralists.)

—— (1991) *Essays on Heidegger and Others*, Cambridge: Cambridge University Press. (Another collection of essays that formulates the author's position and comments on the views of other post-structuralists.)

Sturrock, J. (ed.) (1979) *Structuralism and Since*, Oxford: Oxford University Press. (A collection of introductory essays on the major figures.)

GARY GUTTING

POST-STRUCTURALISM IN THE SOCIAL SCIENCES

Structuralism was a twentieth-century approach in various social scientific disciplines (the 'human sciences') that promised to put them on a solid scientific basis. The origin and model of structuralism was Saussure's work in linguistics. Saussure's approach was later adapted in anthropology (by Lévi-Strauss), in psychoanalysis (by Lacan), and in literary theory (by Barthes). The core of structuralism was the treatment of distinctively human domains as formal structures in which meanings were constituted not by conscious subjects but by relations among the elements of a formal system.

Post-structuralism comprises a variety of reactions to structuralism, primarily by philosophers such as Derrida, Foucault, Deleuze, and Lyotard. The first stage of post-structuralist reflection on the social sciences, best represented by Foucault's discussion at the end of The Order of Things, *accepted the structuralist approach and drew from it the philosophical consequences for our understanding of the social sciences. A later stage (including Foucault's* Discipline and Punish *and Lyotard's writings from the 1970s on) sought to transform our conception of the human sciences through a critique of structuralist presuppositions. In this later stage, post-structuralists continued to accept structuralism's elimination of the conscious subject but maintained that human existence could not be adequately understood without taking account of non-structural causal factors such as power (Foucault) and desire (Lyotard). Foucault argued for the inextricable tie between our knowledge of society and society's power structures. Lyotard maintained that Lacan's structuralist version of psychoanalysis ignored the way that desire corresponds to a reality that escapes the boundaries of any formal structure. He also developed a political and ethical stance based on the fundamental value of a plurality of desires.*

1 Structuralism in the social sciences
2 Foucault's archaeology of structuralism
3 Foucault's genealogy of power
4 The unconscious and desire: from Lacan to Lyotard
5 Lyotard's politics of desire

1 Structuralism in the social sciences

Structuralism originated in Ferdinand de Saussure's linguistics, which treated language as a formal system. Saussure rejected the common, representationalist view of language as a set of physical objects (for example, sounds or marks) that have meaning only in the sense that they represent mental entities (ideas), which alone are intrinsically meaningful. On his picture, both signifiers (sounds or marks) and signifieds (ideas) have meaning simply in virtue of the formal structure that they share. This formal structure is the system of identities and differences that exist among linguistic elements (on one level, sounds; on another level, ideas). Saussure identified language (*langue*) with this formal structure (see SAUSSURE, F. DE).

Lévi-Strauss' cultural anthropology is a prime example of the extension of Saussure's view of language to the social sciences. He applies the basic approach of structural linguistics to anthropological phenomena such as kinship systems and myths. Lévi-Strauss describes such phenomena in terms of the signifier/signified distinction. Thus, for the case of kinship relations, the signifieds are the thought of a culture about family relationships (for example, about degrees of and respect due to such relationships, incest taboos), while the signifiers are the specific practices (customs, rituals, and so on) that 'express' these thoughts. As in the case of Saussurean linguistics, Lévi-Strauss' approach contrasts with a representationalist one. He does not, for example, see a society or culture as having certain ideas about kinship that are then implemented by practices corresponding to them (with the practices being material images of the society's self-understanding). Rather, both the ideas and the practices are specified by their shared formal structure, once again understood in terms of differences among elements within a system. We are, accordingly, able to understand a society's ideas and practices with no reference to the minds (thoughts or intentions) of subjects (see LÉVI-STRAUSS, C.).

2   Foucault's archaeology of structuralism

Foucault's *The Order of Things* supports the structuralist elimination of a central role for subjectivity (see FOUCAULT, M.). Using the term 'man' to denote subjectivity as the source and locus of mental representations of reality, he first argues that the category of 'man' was merely a contingent feature of modern (roughly, nineteenth-century) thought and as such has no essential role in accounts of human life and thought. In his concluding chapter, he further argues that the recent development of structuralist social sciences, particularly Lévi-Strauss' anthropology and Lacan's psychoanalysis, points the way to a mode of thought that does not rely on this category. Such sciences, he maintains, show how we could conceive of human reality without defining it in terms of its capacity for subjective representation. Foucault agrees that the modern social sciences – psychology and sociology, for example – are, like philosophy since Kant, based on the primacy of subjectivity. He even maintains that these 'sciences of man' solve the problem (which had frustrated philosophers since Kant) of how man could be both the constituting source of the world's meaning and, at the same time, just another natural object in the world.

In Foucault's view, the human sciences solve this problem by introducing the notion of the unconscious mind. Operating solely on the level of consciousness, philosophers could provide no coherent account of how man could be both an object within the world, fully describable in term of the fundamental categories (life, labour, and language) of the human sciences, and at the same time the transcendental subject that constitutes the world and all its objects. But, Foucault maintains, the paradox disappears once we think of the world, including man, as constituted by an unconscious mind that is not itself an object in the world. However, he further maintains that the standard modern social sciences merely describe the results of the operations of the unconscious mind; they are not able to give a direct account of the nature of the unconscious and of the conditions of its possibility. Such an account is provided only by the structuralist social sciences: Lacan's psychoanalysis and Lévi-Strauss' cultural anthropology.

According to Foucault, the key difference between ordinary human sciences and the structuralist sciences is that, unlike the former, the latter are able to explain consciousness and its representations of the world in terms of more fundamental principles. Specifically, Lacan and Lévi-Strauss provide a description of (respectively) psychological and cultural structures that are not themselves representational but that explain the functioning of conscious representations.

Foucault notes that in one sense these structuralist accounts provide a foundation for the modern human sciences by explaining their basic category of man. But he also notes that, in so doing, they destroy the centrality of this category. The deepest understanding of human reality is no longer in terms of the subject and its representations but in terms of unconscious structural systems. Because they thus undermine the fundamental category of the human sciences, Foucault labels these structuralist disciplines 'counter-sciences'.

3   Foucault's genealogy of power

Despite its strong structuralist sympathies, *The Order of Things* implicitly raises serious questions about structuralism that adumbrate Foucault's later post-structuralist viewpoint. The most serious issue concerns the status of Foucault's own methodology in the book. For all his praise of structuralism's surpassing modern thought and heralding the 'death of man', it is not at all clear that his own approach is structuralist. At root, this is because he writes as a historian, concerned with the temporal (diachronic) development of thought, while structuralist accounts can yield no more than synchronic time-slices of intellectual systems.

The Order of Things avoids this issue by restricting itself to questions about intellectual systems (*epistemes* in Foucault's terminology) at a given time. But, as he makes clear at several points (most notably in his Foreword to the English translation), there is ultimately no avoiding the essential historical question of the causes of transitions from one *episteme* to another. When Foucault subsequently takes up the causal question (particularly in *Discipline and Punish* and in volume one of *The History of Sexuality*), his approach becomes explicitly post-structuralist.

At the heart of Foucault's post-structuralism is his notion of power. He sees relations of power as the causal factors that lead from one *episteme* to another. Power as Foucault understands it has three key features, each of which puts it beyond the ordered systems of structuralism. First, power is productive. It not only expresses the repressive, exclusionary force of a system's constraints but also creates new domains of knowledge and practice. Second, power is not located in any single control-centre; it is dispersed throughout the social system in innumerable local seats of power. These seats interact with one another but do not form a unified system. Third, although it is intimately related to systems of knowledge, power is more than the play of signifiers and signifieds within such systems. It is ultimately the formative action of one body on another.

Foucault's explicit recognition of the relation of power to knowledge has important consequences for his understanding of the social sciences. These consequences are most explicitly developed by his study, in *Discipline and Punish*, of the connections between modern methods of social control (such as the prison) and the emergence of criminology and related social scientific disciplines.

Foucault presents *Discipline and Punish* as a genealogical history; that is, one that details the causal processes leading to significant changes in the history of thought. Genealogy concerns the connection between non-discursive practices and systems of discourse (bodies of knowledge). In this regard, Foucault's central claim is that there is an inextricable interrelation of knowledge (discourse) and power (expressed in non-discursive practices, in particular, the control of bodies).

In emphasizing the relation of knowledge and power, Foucault does not have in mind the standard Baconian idea, which sees knowledge as first existing as an autonomous achievement (pure science) that is later used as an instrument of action (technology). He maintains that knowledge simply does not exist in complete independence of power, that the deployment of knowledge and the deployment of power are simultaneous from the beginning. On the other hand, Foucault does not go so far as to identify knowledge with power; he does not, for example, make knowledge nothing more than an expression of social or political control. As he points out, if he thought there

was no difference between knowledge and power, he would not have had to take such pains to discover the precise ways in which they are related to one another.

Foucault's positive view is that systems of knowledge, although expressing objective (and perhaps even universally valid) truth in their own right, are none the less always more or less closely tied to the regimes of power that exist within a given society. Conversely, regimes of power necessarily give rise to bodies of knowledge about the objects they control (but this knowledge may – in its objectivity – go beyond and even ultimately threaten the system of domination from which it arises).

In *Discipline and Punish*, Foucault considers the specific case of the connection between modern social scientific disciplines and the disciplinary practices used to control human bodies in the modern period. His primary example is the relation of the practice of imprisonment to criminology and other social scientific disciplines that deal with crime and punishment (for example, social psychology). But he treats imprisonment in the context of modern disciplinary practices in general (as employed in schools, factories, the military, and so on); and he shows how the prison served as a model and centre of diffusion for this whole range of disciplinary practices. These practices form the matrix from which spring many of the most important modern social sciences. In the first volume of his *The History of Sexuality*, Foucault argues further that other modern human sciences – for example, psychoanalysis – are tied to modern mechanisms for controlling sexual behaviour.

4 The unconscious and desire: from Lacan to Lyotard

Just as Foucault argues the limitations of structuralist accounts of the social in the face of the reality of power, so Jean-François LYOTARD emphasizes the limits of structuralist psychology in the face of the reality of desire. In order to understand Lyotard's critique, it is necessary to place it in relation to the most important structuralist approach to psychology: Jacques Lacan's formulation of Freudian psychoanalysis.

The heart of Lacan's formulation is his claim that the unconscious mind has the structure of a language. Here he is understanding 'language' in Saussure's sense of a system of signs whose meanings are entirely defined by their roles in the system. As such, the unconscious has no essential connections to external objects and its desires (drives) refer to nothing beyond the semiological system from which they receive their meaning. Orthodox psychoanalysis (for example, Heinz Hartmann's ego psychology) regards the mature conscious ego and the 'objective' adult world to which it accommodates itself as the reality to which unconscious desires must be subordinated. Lacan, on the contrary, places this ego and its world in the domain of the 'Imaginary' and insists on its subordination to the 'Symbolic' (that is, the unconscious as an autonomous sign system). Lacan also allows for a domain of 'Reality', but he presents this as an unreachable limit of symbolic structures. Accordingly, desire is nothing more than a lack that can, in principle, never be fulfilled (see LACAN, J.).

In opposition to Lacan – and to many other structuralist and post-structuralist thinkers – Lyotard asserts the autonomy and primacy of the non-linguistic object. This is not to say that he revives the foundationalist claim (often associated with phenomenology) that the object is 'simply given' to the mind in an experience unformed by any linguistic categories. Lyotard agrees that there is no pre-linguistic experience. But, he maintains, it does not follow that the content of experience is exhausted by language. 'We can say that the tree is green, but this does not put the colour into the sentence' (1971: 52).

Lyotard expresses the independent reality of the object through his distinction between 'letter' and 'line'. By 'letter' Lyotard means a linguistic sign as understood by Saussure: an element in a system that has significance solely in virtue of its differences from other elements in a system. If, for example, a Magritte painting contains the written message, 'This is not a pipe', the letters used can have any physical shape at all (so long as those shapes allow us to distinguish a *t* from a *p*, and so on) and still convey the message. But, as lines in the painting, the precise shapes of the *p*, *t* and so on, are crucial. A thick red script will convey one aesthetic meaning, a thin green one another. For the *p* and *t* as letters, pre-linguistic content is irrelevant, but for them as lines it is crucial. For 'This is not a pipe' as read, there is no content irreducible to the linguistic system; but for 'This is not a pipe' as seen, there is. To use a parallel distinction of Lyotard's, the expression as discourse is not reducible to the expression as figure.

Given this account, Lyotard is able to reject Lacan's construal of desire as simply the lack of an object that can never be attained. Just as perception is fulfilled by an object with an intrinsic content that cannot be reduced to the linguistic structures of consciousness, so too desire can be fulfilled by an object irreducible to the linguistic structures of the unconscious. In this way, desire takes us beyond the boundaries of a purely structuralist understanding of the unconscious.

5 Lyotard's politics of desire

Lyotard's post-structuralist account of desire also has consequences for social and political thought. As Peter Dews (1987) has pointed out, psychological desire and political power must be thought of as necessary counterparts. Desire is precisely that which power constrains, and desire that which struggles against power. It should, therefore, be no surprise that desire is a fundamental category of Lyotard's social and political thought. Specifically, Lyotard tried to develop a 'libidinal politics': a theoretical and practical standpoint based on the fundamental value of the flourishing of a plurality of diverse desires. Lyotard, like Foucault, saw knowledge and power as essentially connected, and maintained that 'totalizing' theories (for example, Marxism) claiming universal validity are sources of totalitarian social structures that destroy the plurality of desires.

Lyotard pays particular attention to what he sees as the inevitable conflict between justice and truth. We continually – and properly – make judgments that particular situations or actions are unjust. But we are also inclined to think that these judgments themselves require justification through derivation from a general account of the nature of human society. We think, that is, that particular prescriptions regarding justice must be justified by the truth of general theoretical descriptions. Lyotard, however, maintains that this appeal to general truth is itself an instance of injustice. The general description presents a total picture of society that excludes all alternative views as false and rejects as unacceptable desires based on these views. But, according to Lyotard, such an exclusion is inconsistent with the fundamental value of maintaining a plurality of desires. He holds, accordingly, that we should be content with 'indeterminate' judgments about particular instances of justice and injustice and eschew 'determinate' judgments intended to justify indeterminate judgments. (A judgment is determinate or indeterminate depending on whether or not it is 'determined' by a general theoretical principle.)

Lyotard also formulates his view of justice in terms of his concept of the 'differend'. A differend is an incommensurability between different standpoints (language games, narratives – ultimately, desires). The sign of incommensurability is precisely the lack of any shared criteria for mediating the differences that define the differend. Lyotard holds that the goal of politics (and also of ethics and art) should be to produce and preserve differends; and, particularly, to protect them from the 'totalitarian terror' of exclusionary global truth-claims.

Lyotard's work is in many ways the most thorough and the most radical development of a post-structuralist view of society and politics. There is no doubt that his rejection of social and political theory takes us far beyond the framework of traditional discussions in philosophy and the social sciences. There will be continuing disagreement as to whether this rejection is a bracing liberation or a debilitating confusion.

See also: BARTHES, R.; POST-STRUCTURALISM; SEMIOTICS; STRUCTURALISM IN SOCIAL SCIENCE

References and further reading

* Dews, P. (1987) *Logics of Disintegration: Poststructuralist Thought and the Claims of Critical Theory*, London: Verso. (Includes analytic and critical essays on Lacan, Foucault, and Lyotard.)
* Foucault, M. (1966) *Les mots et les choses: une archéologie des sciences humaines*, Paris: Gallimard; trans. A. Sheridan, *The Order of Things*, New York: Random House, 1970. (A critical history of the origins of the modern social sciences.)
* —— (1975) *Surveiller et punir: naissance de la prison*, Paris: Gallimard; trans. A. Sheridan, *Discipline and Punish*, New York: Pantheon, 1977. (A geneological study of the modern prison and, more generally, of the disciplinary practices of modern society. The work introduces Foucault's influential views on knowledge and power.)
* —— (1976) *Histoire de la sexualité*, vol. 1: *la volonté de savoir*, Paris: Gallimard; trans. R. Hurley, *The History of Sexuality*, New York: Pantheon, 1978. (An introduction to a projected, but never completed, series of studies on aspects of modern sexuality.)
* Lyotard, J.-F. (1971) *Discours, Figure*, Paris: Klincksieck. (A radical deconstructive approach to aesthetics which criticizes the structuralist model for language and especially the Lacanian interpretation of Freud.)
  —— (1983) *Le Différend*, Paris: Les Éditions de Minuit; trans. G. Van Den Abbeele, *The Differend*, Minneapolis, MN: University of Minnesota Press, 1988. (Defines the political in terms of the fundamental 'differends' (disputes) which cannot be equitably resolved for lack of a universal rule of judgment applicable to all of the arguments.)
  Readings, B. (1991) *Introducing Lyotard*, London: Routledge. (A comprehensive survey of Lyotard's thought, emphasizing his work on art and politics.)

GARY GUTTING

POTENTIALITY, INDIAN THEORIES OF

Indian philosophers wrote a great deal about potential (śakti) and capacity (sāmarthya); both of these words may also be translated as 'power' or 'force'. The Sanskrit word śakti, like the English word 'potential', derives from a modal verb meaning 'to be able', so one might also see the study of potential as being the study of ability. The principal issue about which Indians debated was that of where exactly potential or ability is located. If, for example, it can be said that a person has a potential to compose a poetic masterpiece, then it can be asked where exactly that potential is located. Is it located entirely within the potential poet, or is it distributed somehow between the poet and the circumstances in which the person functions? If one says it is located entirely within the person, then it can be asked why they produce the masterpiece only at one specific time in their life instead of earlier or later. In other words, it seems that if circumstances were required to enable the person to realize their potential, then the potentiality would belong as much to external circumstances as to the person. This may not seem an interesting question in the abstract, but it became of interest to philosophers in particular contexts. It was generally agreed, for example, that nothing happens without a prior potential that becomes actualized. If this is so, then the question naturally arises, to what did the potential belong out of the actualization of which the universe 'happened'? Other questions that Indian philosophers debated were: To whom does the potential to become wise belong? How is the potential of a supposedly eternal language actualized to convey meaning? Attempting to answer such questions was a preoccupation of philosophers of every Indian school.

1　**God's potential to create**
2　**A complex being's potential to decompose**
3　**A person's potential for cultivating virtue**
4　**The potential of a sound to convey a meaning**

1　God's potential to create

Among the philosophical traditions in classical India, some were atheistic and others theistic. The issue of whether there existed a single creator for the entire universe was one that took on many dimensions as each side produced arguments and counter-arguments of increasing sophistication. Among the many dimensions that came up for discussion, one centred on the question of whether it made sense to say of a single creator that it had a potential (*śakti* or *sāmarthya*) to create, and if it did have such a potential, how that potential could be realized. If it could be shown that it made no sense to speak of a single creator having a potential to create something complex, argued the atheists, then the whole idea of creation through a single creator could be dismissed as unworthy of further consideration.

The principal strategy used by the atheists in questioning the creator's potential to create was to point out that those who spoke of a single creator, usually called the Supreme Lord (*parameśvara*) or some similar term, usually regarded the Lord as eternal. That is, the Lord was supposed never to have come into being (either from nothingness or from some other state of being) and was also supposed not to be liable to stop being. It was also generally accepted that nothing could be eternal unless it was also simple. That is, all eternal things were supposed to consist of exactly one part that was quite uniform in nature, so that the whole was not in any sense different from its unique part. Being indivisible, simple beings were generally supposed to be either omnipresent or infinitesimal. Those who posited the existence of a Supreme Lord usually argued that he uniformly pervades all of space at all times.

A question that naturally arises about an eternally simple ubiquitous being is how such a being is supposed to act. The way this question was pursued is illustrated by how it was approached by the Buddhist philosophers DHARMAKĪRTI (seventh century) and Śāntarakṣita (eighth century). They argued that action, as normally understood, involves undergoing some change of state. This change of state must be either a change in how the being in question is related to things outside itself, or a change in how parts within the being are related. The first kind of change, consisting of a change in relation to external things, normally involves some kind of motion, that is, a change in relative location over time. To a being that is everywhere all the time, however, motion is clearly impossible. This leaves internal change as the only remaining kind of change that a simple being might undergo. In the case of complex objects, internal changes of state are easily accounted for by referring to the gain or loss of parts, such as attributes, or to relational changes among the parts. It is, however, difficult to imagine just what kind of change of state is possible for a being that has only one part. And therefore it would appear that a simple being is not constituted in such a way as to have the potential for any kind of self-motivated action.

A second argument that atheists used in arguing against a supreme creator's potential to act in any way at all involved asking the question of where the supposed potential might reside. There appear to be two possibilities. It could be that the potential is contained entirely within the being that has it, or it could be that the potential lies outside the being. If it were argued that the potential to act is entirely resident within a being, then it could be asked what it is that triggers this potential into actuality. If the potential were self-activating, then it would have to be activating itself at all times, for otherwise it would require something outside itself to make it active at some times but inactive at others. But a potential that is perpetually active is not a potential at all; rather, it is an actuality. Even if one were to hold the view that the Supreme Lord is perpetually creating the universe, this would not explain why he creates the world slightly differently from one moment to the next, thereby giving the appearance of change to his creation. It is better, argued the atheists, to abandon the supposition that the potential to create is contained entirely with the Supreme Lord. This leaves the possibility that the Lord's potential to perform the action of creation comes from outside, just as an inanimate body's potential to be in motion comes from outside itself. In that case, argued the atheists, we should not be able to say that it is God who performs the action of creating the universe, but rather that it is that which is external to God that is performing the creative action, and that this external agent is merely using God as an instrument in the action being performed.

2 A complex being's potential to decompose

Whereas a simple being is not composed of parts and therefore lacks the potential to go out of existence through the process of decomposition, a complex or composite being is liable to decompose. It was agreed among classical Indian philosophers that complex objects are subject to destruction through decomposition. Where there was controversy was over the issue of how this decomposition comes about. In particular, there was controversy over whether the destruction of a complex thing requires a separate external cause to bring it about or whether complex things have an innate tendency to go out of existence spontaneously.

The position that complex things have an innate tendency to cease to exist was held by several Buddhist scholastics, such as VASUBANDHU (fourth or fifth century), Dharmakīrti, and Śāntarakṣita. Taking as their point of departure the Buddha's observation that all composite things are impermanent, the Buddhist scholastics grew increasingly committed to the view that all composite things are momentary, that is, that all complex beings perish in the very moment in which they arise (see MOMENTARINESS, BUDDHIST DOCTRINE OF).

Among the arguments that were used to defend this doctrine, one was based on an analysis of potentiality. Vasubandhu argued that if a given complex being were capable of remaining unchanged for two consecutive moments, then there would be no reason for it ever to undergo change. Suppose that a being had a certain set of properties in one moment and then had exactly the same set of properties in the subsequent moment. One might ask whether among those properties the potential to perish was to be found. If not, then the complex being would have no potential to perish and therefore would be eternal. But even if the potential to perish were among the properties of the complex being, the question would still remain of how that potential is actualized. If the potential is self-activating, then it must activate itself in each moment of its existence; but if the potential to perish is realized in each moment of a thing's existence, it follows that the thing exists for no more than one moment.

This conclusion that things perish in the very moment in which they arise is quite contrary to how things are experienced. In our experience of things, it seems that complex objects endure for a period of time and then go out of existence as a result of being acted upon by some destructive agent. A piece of wood, for example, continues to exist unchanged until it comes into contact with fire, which is the cause of the wood's destruction. One might ask why we should not take our experiences of these events at face value. In addressing this question, Vasubandhu points out that in fact we do not directly experience the destruction of the wood by the fire. What really happens is that we see the wood, then we see the fire, and then we no longer see the wood. It may be tempting to explain this sequence of events by saying that the presence of the fire causes the disappearance of the wood, but it would be a mistake to claim that one actually observes the causal process of destruction at work. Indeed, argues Vasubandhu, it is impossible to observe fire destroying a piece of wood; if the fire and the wood are observed to exist at the same time, then it is obvious that the existence of the fire is not a cause of the absence of the wood, for the simple reason that the wood is not absent. On the other hand, if the wood is present in one moment and absent in the next, fire existing where the wood used to be, then one might say that the wood was replaced by flame. Seeing one thing replaced by another, however, is not the same as seeing the subsequent thing destroy the former thing. After considering various other dimensions of this problem, Vasubandhu finally concludes that the problem of what causes the absence of a thing is one that arises only when one assumes that absence itself is an entity and therefore must have a cause. If, however, it is recognized that absence is not itself a thing, then it is clear that absence cannot have a cause, for only things have causes. Once it is recognized that there is no such thing as the cause of an absence, the question of how a potential cause of absence is actualized ceases to have any meaning.

3 A person's potential for cultivating virtue

The question of how a complex thing was supposed to become absent was not merely an issue for intellectual debate. An issue underlying this discussion was the question of whether certain vices, seen as responsible for keeping a person bound in the cycle of rebirth, required a special cause, such as human effort, to eliminate them. A representative account of the mechanism of karma and rebirth is that of Vasubandhu. According to his *Abhidharmakośa* (Treasury of Abhidharma), a decision to act in a particular way has several consequences, one of which is a predisposition to act in a similar way in the future. If, for example, one acts with the intention of injuring another, then making the decision to injure others will be that much easier to make in the future. An action, in other words, creates a latent predisposition, which in turn is a factor in creating a future action. A being who is caught in the round of rebirths is captured in that cycle as a result of various kinds of latent predisposition, the most important being the predisposition to pursue sensual pleasures, to dislike sources of displeasure, to have a tenacious belief in a permanent self, and to hold on to dogmas that legitimate one's choices of action. These predispositions are all regarded as potentials. Therefore, the question arises as to how their potentiality is activated. Moreover, each of these potentials can be seen as a complex thing that therefore has the potential to decompose. Here the question is whether the potential to degenerate requires an external cause. Does it take work to rid oneself of a bad habit?

Vasubandhu's response to this question is that it does not require special effort to rid oneself of a habit; rather, it takes work to keep the habit intact. It takes effort to keep oneself habituated to seeking pleasures and holding onto dogmas. What takes no effort is to let go of these habits. If one stops making the effort necessary to reinforce a bad habit, it will eventually dissipate through its own potential to perish. For this reason, most of the specific precepts of the spiritual life are negative in character: avoid killing, avoid theft, avoid sexuality, avoid lying and avoid intoxicants. Moreover, the most effective forms of meditation consist in simply noting what mental states are present and making no effort either to pursue them or avoid them. If simply noted but not acted upon, one's urge to kill or to make a scathing remark will perish by itself without creating a karma. By not creating a karma that reinforces the habit to act malevolently, one eventually becomes free of the malevolent habit and of the views necessary to justify acting on those habits.

Several schools of Hindu religious philosophy, and one strand of the Yogācāra school of Buddhism, asserted the view that every sentient being possesses a potential for wisdom. This wisdom was seen as something positive and not merely as the absence of vices and misconceptions, and therefore the potential to make one wise must also be seen as positive. As in other discussions of potentiality, a question that arose was how this potential for wisdom can be activated. One of the answers was that the potential is in fact activated at every moment; in other words, every sentient being is indeed wise in its truest nature. The apparent lack of wisdom in some beings, or lapses of wisdom in beings who are normally wise, can then be accounted for not as an actual lack of wisdom but as an occultation of actual wisdom. In other words, a being's innately radiant, blissful and virtuous nature is concealed by the darkness of a transitory episode of ignorance or vice. This position, of course, gives rise to the question of how the ignorance or vice comes into being and to whom it belongs if not to the innately wise mind itself. Śaṅkara's famous answer to this riddle was to reply that the question arises only from the perspective of ignorance, and since ignorance is ultimately illusory, there is not really a riddle here in need of an answer (see ŚAṄKARA).

4 The potential of a sound to convey a meaning

From the earliest times, Indian theorists of language were intrigued with the potential or power that language has to evoke images and emotional responses in the mind of the hearer. It was generally recognized, however, that this potential cannot reside entirely within the sounds themselves, since a person unfamiliar with a language will not have appropriate intellectual and emotional responses to the sounds heard. Grammarians and poeticians both observed that a verbal performance, such as a poem, only had its effect when it was heard by a cultivated intellect; generally speaking, the more learned and sophisticated the intellect of the hearer, the more richness the poem yielded. This was said to be true of all language, but was especially important for the religious poetry of the Vedas. A phrase of revealed Vedic poetry spoken in the context of a ritual performance was known as a *mantra*, and *mantras* were supposed to have a power not only to convey meanings, but to

influence physical events. The power of a *mantra* was said to be at its maximum when pronounced by a priest who had a perfect understanding of the Vedic Sanskrit language. This fact was enough to make Buddhist and Jaina philosophers question whether the power of language was a feature of the sounds themselves, as Brahmanical thinkers claimed. Buddhists and Jainas were also dubious about the claim that Sanskrit had a power greater than any other language to evoke meanings and emotions, arguing instead that whatever language the hearer knows most intimately is most meaningful to the hearer; this would suggest that the potential resides not in the sounds but in the community of people who know a language.

One further controversy debated by Indian theorists of language had to do with how the potential to convey meaning was located in a sentence, and what role the individual syllables played. Some argued that each syllable has its own independent potential and that the sentence's potential to convey meaning is the sum of the potentials of the syllables. Others argued that the sentence as a whole has a potential, and the function of the syllables is merely to make that potential fully realized for the hearer. According to this view, even if only the first syllable of a sentence is spoken, the sentence as a whole still has its full meaning-bearing potential, but the hearer receives only a partial glimpse into what that meaning might be.

See also: BHARTṚHARI; BUDDHIST PHILOSOPHY, INDIAN; GOD, INDIAN CONCEPTIONS OF; KARMA AND REBIRTH, INDIAN CONCEPTIONS OF; LANGUAGE, INDIAN THEORIES OF; PATAÑJALI

References and further reading

Ingalls, D.H.H. (1953) 'Saṃkara on the Question: Whose is *Avidyā*?', *Philosophy East and West* 3: 69–72. (A brief but intelligent exploration of the problem, mentioned in §3, of how an innately wise and blissful Brahman can be obscured by ignorance and to whom, given that Brahman is the essence of everything, this ignorance might belong.)

Jackson, R. (1993) *Is Enlightenment Possible?*, Ithaca, NY: Snow Lion. (Contains a discussion and translation of Dharmakīrti's arguments, mentioned in §1, concerning the possibility of divine action in general and God's potential to create the world in particular.)

Śāntarakṣita (eighth century) *Tattvasaṅgraha* (Grasping the Truths), trans. G. Jha, *The Tattvasaṅgraha of Shāntarakṣita with the commentary of Kamalashīla*, Delhi: Motilal Banarsidass, 1st edn, 1939; repr.

1986, 2 vols. (An extensive collection of arguments produced by Buddhist thinkers on topics debated between them and non-Buddhist opponents. Volume 1, chapters 1–7 contains Buddhist arguments against God, Brahman and other notions of single, eternal creators. Chapter 8 deals with the questions of perishability discussed in §2. Volume 2, chapter 29 deals with the question of the potential of a word to convey meaning, discussed in §4.)

* Vasubandhu (4th or 5th century) *Abhidharmakośa* (Treasury of Abhidharma), trans. L. de la Vallée Poussin, *L'Abhidharmakośa de Vasubandhu*, Brussels: Institut belge des hautes études chinoises, 1971 (reprint), 6 vols. (Best translation available of this Buddhist classic. Volume 3 contains chapter 4 of the original work, which deals with karma. Here are contained the arguments about the causes of a thing's disappearance discussed in §2. The discussion of virtue in §3 is based on chapters 4 and 5 of the original text, found respectively in volumes 3 and 4 of the translation.)

RICHARD P. HAYES

POTHIER, ROBERT JOSEPH (1699–1772)

Robert Joseph Pothier was one of the most influential of modern civilian jurists. At the end of a long period of rationalistic natural law thought, he produced a rational reconstruction of the civil law on the basis of which the transition from law as reason based on custom to law as product of the rational legislative will could be accomplished.

By his work in the systematization first of Roman law and subsequently of French customary law, Pothier cleared the way for the codification of French Law under Napoleon in the early nineteenth century. Born in Orléans of a family with a long tradition of service in the magistracy, he served most of his life as a magistrate in Orléans, becoming also a professor in the University of Orléans after publication of his first main work, which was a reconstitution of Justinian's *Digest* aimed at clarifying the underlying conceptual framework (see JUSTINIAN). This was the result of long and profound studies in Roman law (see ROMAN LAW §2). In each title he rearranged the materials, without further textual alteration, to reveal what he conceived to be the logical order underlying them.

Following upon this, he turned his attention to French law, which at that time was a patchwork, in the north based on various differing local customs according to different court districts, in the south on a partly modernized version of Justinianic civil law. He published a text on the customary law of Orléans, pointing out its variations from and similarities with other customs of different court jurisdictions in the north. Applying his rationalistic principles, Pothier then turned to a statement of the principles of law that in his view underlay both written and customary law in crucially important fields. His most notable contribution was his *Treatise on Obligations*, expounding general principles of contract-formation and contractual liability. This quickly achieved recognition inside and outside France, being translated into English in an American and a UK version in the early 1800s. It was followed by a series of works on more particular contracts, and then by work on matrimonial property and on marriage, interpreted as essentially a civil contractual obligation to which Church authorities also gave recognition, rather than as an essentially ecclesiastical or religiously-grounded institution.

In France, Pothier's influence was enormous, in that he provided a basis on which the compilers of a civil code could work when, in the circumstances of revolution, the idea of the rule of law was conceptualized as requiring abandonment of obscure customs expounded by judges, instead calling for their replacement with rationally ordered and duly published statutes (see RULE OF LAW (RECHTSSTAAT) §1). In the common law world, then also engaged in a prodigious effort of rationalization, his work was scarcely less influential, as the common law struggled to produce out of materials based on pre-modern forms of action a rational law of contract fit for an industrializing and commercializing society. Thus did natural law ideas, such as Pothier's, create a rational structure of legal concepts that more positivistic successors could adopt.

See also: LAW, PHILOSOPHY OF; LEGAL POSITIVISM; NATURAL LAW

List of works

Pothier, R.J. (1806) *A Treatise on the Law of Obligations or Contracts*, trans. W.D. Evans, London: Butterworth. (A well-known translation of the part of Pothier's work that was most influential in the English-speaking world, particularly in relation to the general theory of contracts.)

—— (1861) *Œuvres de Pothier*, ed. M. Bugnet, Paris: Cosse et Marchal, Henri Plon. (A complete set of Pothier's main writings annotated and correlated to the Civil Code and to current (1861) French legislation. A useful indicator of his influence on the Napoleonic Code.)

—— (1953) *A Treatise on the Contract of Letting and Hiring*, trans. G.A. Mulligan, Durban: Butterworths. (This is a more specialist work than (1806) above, but again gives insight into Pothier's theory of contracts.)

References and further reading

Smith, J.C. and Thomas, J.A.C. (1957) 'Pothier and the Three Dots', *Modern Law Review* 20: 38–49. (An essay on a problem of contemporary English law that reveals the historical influence of Pothier on the development of common law approaches to contract.)

NEIL MacCORMICK

POUND, ROSCOE (1870–1964)

Roscoe Pound was a legal thinker who exercised profound influence in the USA in the first half of the twentieth century. The approach he advocated, under the banner 'sociological jurisprudence', was to present law as essentially an instrument for the pursuit and reconciliation of human interests.

Long-term Dean of the leading law school, Harvard, Pound played a prominent role in defining the dominant approach to understanding and teaching law for twentieth-century Americans. To understand any body of law, he argued, one must understand what interests it serves, and must be careful to discriminate different types of interest. Some interests are individual, like the interest of each person in their own life and health; some are social, like the interests of a society in controlling the spread of infectious diseases; others are public, like the interest of the state in the health and fitness of citizens eligible for military service. The tasks of law-making and of judging are tasks of balancing and harmonizing actually or potentially conflicting interests, with a view to maximizing interest-satisfaction at the lowest possible cost in frustration of other interests. Hence law can be considered 'a continually more efficacious social engineering'.

Pound's is thus an optimistic as well as an instrumentalist view of law. His upbringing and education in Nebraska, his early training as a botanist and his work on the flora of Nebraska, followed by experience as legal practitioner and pro tem judge in his home state, no doubt contributed to the pro-

gressivism exhibited in the sociological jurisprudence he developed as a professor called back east to the Harvard Law School. His scientific training is doubtless also reflected in the care he took over working out a complete taxonomy of the interests he could detect as being served by the law. Significant here also is his typology of 'individual', 'social' and 'public' interests, and his attempt to map the connections and differences between them. Also important is his insistence that in a process of balancing, like must be compared with like, and interests should be brought within the same type before balancing can be properly carried out. Recognition of some interests as irreducibly social or irreducibly public marks off his theory from classical utilitarianism, to which he has obvious affinities. In trying to develop a distinctive 'jurisprudence of interests', he had predecessors such as the German jurist Rudolf von JHERING.

Pound engaged in polemics with 'American realism' (see LEGAL REALISM §2), arguing for what he saw as a rational approach to legal studies, rather than exaggerating law's indeterminacies, as he thought the realists did. His own theory suffered at the hands of sociologists and others who challenged his belief in the essential harmony of interests despite class and other divisions in society. His vast five-volume statement of his jurisprudence is so ponderous as to be nowadays little read; his shorter, more introductory, writings retain far greater interest and vitality. He is a significant figure among 'legal instrumentalists' in US intellectual history, but has little direct influence at present.

See also: LAW, PHILOSOPHY OF; LEGAL IDEALISM; PUBLIC INTEREST §5; SOCIAL THEORY AND LAW

List of works

Pound, R. (1922) *An Introduction to the Philosophy of Law*, New Haven, CT: Yale University Press. (Well-written statement of Pound's basic position, containing discussions of, for example, processes of legal argumentation, that retain contemporary relevance and remain much-quoted.)

—— (1942) *Social Control through Law*, New Haven, CT: Yale University Press. (Mature statement of Pound's conception of law as a kind of 'social engineering', controlling society with a view to maximal satisfaction of interests, acknowledging also the role of morals, religion and education.)

—— (1959) *Jurisprudence*, St Paul, MN: West Publishing Co., 5 vols. (Compendious account of the whole range of Pound's views on jurisprudential issues, including his exhaustive survey and taxonomy of interests; lacking the vitality of his earlier work.)

References and further reading

Setaro, F.C. (1942) *A Bibliography of the Writings of Roscoe Pound*, Cambridge, MA: Harvard University Press. (This is a comprehensive bibliography up to 1942, but Pound lived long and remained productive, hence Straight's bibliography was necessary to complete the job.)

Straight, G.A. (1960) *A Bibliography of the Writings of Roscoe Pound: 1940–1960*, Cambridge, MA: Havard Law School Library. (This, together with the Setaro bibliography, lists the whole vast corpus, of which only the more philosophically interesting works are noted above.)

Summers, R.S. (1982) *Instrumentalism and American Legal Theory*, Ithaca, NY and London: Cornell University Press. (Outstanding account by a leading US jurist of the various strands in the school of thought to which Pound belonged, providing a clear view of Pound's work in its context, and of his place in US thought.)

NEIL MacCORMICK

POWER

The general notion of power involves the capacity to produce or prevent change. In social and political philosophy, narrower conceptions of power specify the nature of these changes. Social power is the capacity to affect the interests of agents. Normative power is the capacity to affect their normative relations, such as their rights or duties.

There are long-standing conceptual disputes about the nature of power. Some emphasize the role of actual or potential conflicts of interest in defining power relations, others take legitimacy and consensus about norms as the basis. There is also a dispute, involving the nature of social explanation, about whether power must rest with agents or with social structures or forces of some kind. The lack of consensus on these matters raises the overarching question of whether the concept of power, which seems to function as a descriptive term, in some way involves evaluation.

1   Social power and interests
2   Normative powers
3   Problems of agency
4   Power and values

1   Social power and interests

In social and political theory, 'power' is sometimes used wherever causal language is appropriate. We may thus speak of the power of incentives in the labour market or the power of socialization in child development. This may prompt the thought that power is everywhere and beyond escape. (Michel Foucault sometimes makes such promiscuous use of the term; see, for example, Foucault 1980.) But to identify social power with causal power is to abandon a helpful concept, for there are theoretical and practical interests in distinguishing among the causal processes in social life.

Many views delimit social power by reference to a significant capacity to affect people's interests. (The question whether such power is better thought of as a resource or a relationship is somewhat artificial: it is both.) Hobbes (1651) said that power is one's 'present means to obtain some apparent future good', and thought the endless struggle for power an ineliminable part of human nature. The implicit reference to social conflict is made explicit in Max Weber's definition of power as: 'the probability that one actor within a social relationship will be in a position to carry out his own will despite resistance, regardless of the basis on which this probability rests' ([1922] 1968: 53).

What role do conflicts of interest have in power ascriptions? Steven Lukes (1974) has vigorously argued that since the most insidious and effective forms of power are those that affect people's conceptions of their interests, power is more than the capacity to influence overt decision making, and more than the capacity to control which issues reach the public agenda; it also includes the capacity to influence how people perceive their own interests. Thus, power may be present even in the face of apparent consensus. To identify such power, however, requires a view of interests that is objective in the sense that it is independent of the actual beliefs and desires of the subjects (see NEEDS AND INTERESTS).

Critics have wondered whether such a notion is very useful in descriptive and explanatory research (see §4). Perhaps a deeper worry, however, is whether 'objective interests' can be defined independently of power, for it seems natural to say that objective interests are those interests people would have if they were not constrained by power relations (Kernohan 1989). Moreover, both Weber's and Lukes' theories seem guided by the idea that power affects people to their detriment. Does this mean that justified acts of paternalistic control cannot be exercises of power? This suggests that although social power involves the capacity to affect the interests of people, it is to be identified less by its actual or intended ends than by its means, such as coercion or manipulation. While we may allow that such means are *prima facie* detrimental to people's interests, they need not be so when all things are considered.

2 Normative powers

Normative powers (for example, the power to promise or to command) involve the capacity to change normative relations: to create, extinguish or vary people's rights and duties. The relevant relations may be a matter of law, morality or social convention.

Some maintain that all normative powers may be reduced to powers to impose or remove duties which may in turn be reduced to direct or indirect threats of force. Each step of this reduction may be challenged – especially the second, which cannot account for the fact that people often recognize duties that they think neither will be nor should be enforced. Reductivist accounts, however, continue to be influential among sociologists who incline to a 'realistic' view of power.

The concept of normative power is important in legal philosophy, but some have also adopted it as the paradigm for political power in general. Hannah Arendt's quirky definition makes sense in this light: 'Power corresponds to the human ability not just to act but to act in concert. Power is never the property of an individual; it belongs to a group and remains in existence only so long as the group keeps together' (1970: 143). Her idea that power rests on accepted norms that constitute a group and that precede all instrumental reasoning about what the group should do is inspired by a particular account of what it is to be 'in power' (see ARENDT, H.). Similar thoughts underpin Talcott Parson's idea that power is a 'generalized medium of mobilizing commitments or obligation for effective collective action,' a 'generalized facility or resource' that rests on accepted norms of legitimacy (1967: 331). Focusing in these ways on norm-constituted capacities emphasizes consensus as opposed to conflict, which for Arendt is instead a matter of 'strength' or 'violence' and for Parsons 'force' or 'coercion'. It also assimilates political power to authority, which is one of the most important normative powers (see AUTHORITY).

Since normative power affects people's interests, it does fall under the general concept of social power. It is worth distinguishing, though, because of the way beliefs about legitimacy and norms mediate its effects. This partly explains why these theories make power relations seem less asymmetric than do Hobbesian or Weberian theories. To suppose that A has social power over B in respect of X often suggests that B does not have that same power over A in that same respect. But whether A and B mutually have the power to rule depends on the actual norms accepted in that society: these powers may be fully symmetrical.

3 Problems of agency

If power is a capacity to produce or prevent changes, in what does that capacity rest? Many assume that it must rest in individual or corporate agents. This is obvious in the case of normative power; but it is also implicit in the accounts of social power examined in §2, and explicit in Bertrand Russell's (1938) definition of power as 'the production of intended effects'. Even if one may exercise power unintentionally (for example, recklessly), only things with the capacity for agency can exercise power at all.

Others hold that social power rests in non-agential things called social 'structures' or 'forces'. For the Marxist philosopher, Nicos Poulantzas, individual agents are but the locations or 'bearers' of such forces, and power is 'the capacity of a social class to realize its specific objective interests' (1973: 104). This view has been criticized by Ralph Miliband (1969, 1970), who holds that political agents retain at least a relative autonomy from class structures. At bottom is a deep dispute about the cogency of determinist explanations for social change.

Michel Foucault's later writings suggest another non-agential view of power (Foucault 1978, 1980). First, he expands the relevant power structures to include realms of professional and scientific discourse. At its most extreme, this allows no distinction between claims to knowledge and bids for power. Second, such power creates agents: it is 'productive' and not merely 'repressive'. On this view, naming, classifying or diagnosing people, literally creates criminals, the insane, homosexuals, and so on (see FOUCAULT, M.).

It may be wondered whether this view is coherent. Whether or not the theory abstains from using the word 'knowledge' or claiming truth for itself, it none the less purports to have some sort of warrant which, on its own terms, must be understood as a bid for power. This is pragmatically self-defeating. Second, the productive thesis elides a distinction between the literal production of agents and the production of a sense of identity on the part of pre-existing agents. (So while, for example, homosexuals may not have been created in the nineteenth century, an emergent gay identity may have been.) But the general notion that social power may affect not only one's conception of one's interests, as Lukes says, but also one's conception of oneself as an agent capable of having interests, is an important deepening of that line of thought, and one independent of the more radical Nietzschean themes in Foucault's work.

4 Power and values

Power seems to function as a descriptive term. In certain limited contexts (for example, in bargaining theory or voting theory) it has proved possible to specify measures of power, and in the social sciences there are distinguished empirical studies of the bases of power. But in spite of this conceptual controversy persists, and not only over borderline cases, but also over what should be taken as paradigm cases of power. This may suggest that power is an 'essentially contested concept', disputes about which are fundamentally moral or political and which preclude resolution (see POLITICAL PHILOSOPHY, NATURE OF §3).

There are a number of sources of controversy here, and they need to be distinguished. First, referring as they do to causal capacities, power ascriptions inherit all the philosophical difficulties of causal language and, in particular, the difficulties of interpreting and evaluating counterfactual conditionals (see COUNTERFACTUALS; CAUSATION). Second, as we have seen, accounts of social power also inherit disputes about the nature of human agency and interests (see §2). Third, power ascriptions are shaped by the practical point or purpose in making them. One influential view, advanced by Lukes (1974) and by William E. Connolly (1974), is that power is ascribed to fix moral responsibility: those with power are those who should change things. This raises further questions: does responsibility require intentional action, or are recklessness or even just negligence enough?

This thesis must, however, be framed with care. First, even if there is a link between power and responsibility, it does not follow that to say 'A has power over B' is to make a moral judgment about A's blameworthiness, for A may have a justification or excuse for acting or failing to act. Second, lacking the power to change something may itself be an excusing factor, on the principle that ought implies can. If that is so, then it must be possible to make some power ascriptions independently of the relevant judgments about responsibility.

Moral values are not, in any case, the only way in which we might delimit the field. Power ascriptions are part of a larger social theory, so there are also theoretical values such as simplicity, fecundity, coherence, and so on, to be considered. Moreover, although views about the nature and importance of certain human interests also guide concept formation, this need not involve any moral appraisal or prescription. To say that money traders have great social power is to think certain effects more important than others because of their links to central human interests; but it is not directly to assign moral praise or blame. We should not confuse the plausible claim that all descriptions are value-laden, with the stronger and dubious claim that all descriptions are morally fraught.

References and further reading

* Arendt, H. (1970) 'On Violence', in *Crises of the Republic*, New York: Harcourt Brace. (Influenced by classical republican themes, this essay takes normative powers as the paradigm. See §2.)

Bachrach, P. and Baratz, M.S. (1962) 'The Two Faces of Power', *American Political Science Review* 56 (4): 947–52. (An important discussion of power as constituted by agenda-setting or background bias as well as by overt conflict.)

* Connolly, W.E. (1974) *The Terms of Political Discourse*, Lexington, MA.: D.C. Heath. (In particular, see pages 10–44 on essentially contested concepts, and pages 86–137 on power and responsibility. See §4.)

* Foucault, M. (1978) *The History of Sexuality*, vol. 1, *An Introduction*, trans. R. Hurley, New York: Vintage Books. (Pages 3–49 are particularly good on the 'repressive' hypothesis. See §3.)

* —— (1980) *Power/Knowledge: Selected Interviews and Other Writings, 1972–77*, ed. C. Gordon, New York: Pantheon Books. (Useful sampler. Power as ubiquitous in social life, with particular attention to its non-political and non-economic dimensions. See §§1, 3.)

Goldman, A. (1972) 'Toward a Theory of Social Power', *Philosophical Studies* 23: 221–68 (A detailed analysis of both individual and collective power in terms of getting what one wants.)

* Hobbes, T. (1651) *Leviathan*, ed. C.B. Macpherson, Harmondsworth: Penguin, 1968. (A conflict-based view of power based on an individualistic and egoistic moral psychology. See §1.)

* Kernohan, A. (1989) 'Social Power and Human Agency' *Journal of Philosophy* 86 (12): 712–25. (Argues that social power cannot be defined in terms of intentions, effects on interests or responsibility.)

* Lukes, S. (1974) *Power: A Radical View*, London: Macmillan. (One of the most influential, and controversial, accounts. See §§1, 4.)

* Miliband, R. (1969) *The State in Capitalist Society*, London: Weidenfeld & Nicolson. (A neo-Marxist study of forms of power in modern capitalism. See §3.)

* —— (1970) 'The Capitalist State: Reply to Nicos Poulantzas', *New Left Review* 59 (January–

February): 53–60. (A polemical reply to Poulant-zas' structural determinism. See §3.)

Morris, P. (1987) *Power: A Philosophical Analysis*, Manchester: Manchester University Press. (A good survey of the philosophical issues.)

* Parsons, T. (1967) *Sociological Theory and Modern Society*, New York: Free Press. (Essays defending and elaborating a consensus-based view of power. See §2.)

* Poulantzas, N. (1973) *Political Power and Social Classes*, trans. T. O'Hagan, London: New Left Books. (A structuralist-Marxist theory of political power in capitalist states. See §3.)

* Russell, B. (1938) *Power: A New Social Analysis*, London: Allen & Unwin, ch. 1. (Power as the key to social explanation. Surveys its forms, bases and the means of controlling it. See §3.)

Taylor, C. (1986) 'Foucault on Freedom and Truth,' in D. Couzens Hoy (ed.) *Foucault: A Critical Reader*, Oxford: Blackwell, 69–102. (An important critical discussion, in a useful collection.)

* Weber, M. (1922) *Economy and Society*, vol. 1., ed. G. Roth and C. Wittich, New York: Bedminster Press, 1968. (A major treatise on social and political economy, touching on a conflict-based view of power, related notions of authority and legitimacy, and important methodological issues. See §1.)

Wrong, D.H. (1979) *Power: Its Forms, Bases and Uses*, New York: Harper & Row. (An excellent survey from a sociological point of view.)

LESLIE GREEN

PRACTICAL ETHICS

see AGRICULTURAL ETHICS; ANIMALS AND ETHICS; APPLIED ETHICS; BIOETHICS; BUSINESS ETHICS; CIVIL DISOBEDIENCE; DEVELOPMENT ETHICS; ENGINEERING AND ETHICS; ENVIRONMENTAL ETHICS; FAMILY, ETHICS AND THE; GENETICS AND ETHICS; INFORMATION TECHNOLOGY AND ETHICS; JOURNALISM, ETHICS OF; LIFE AND DEATH; MARKET, ETHICS OF THE; MEDICAL ETHICS; NURSING ETHICS; POPULATION AND ETHICS; PORNOGRAPHY; PROFESSIONAL ETHICS; REPRODUCTION AND ETHICS; RESPONSIBILITIES OF SCIENTISTS AND INTELLECTUALS; SPORT AND ETHICS

PRACTICAL LEARNING SCHOOL *see* SIRHAK

PRACTICAL RATIONALITY
see RATIONALITY, PRACTICAL

PRACTICAL REASON AND ETHICS

Practical reason is reasoning which is used to guide action, and is contrasted with theoretical reason, which is used to guide thinking. Sometimes 'practical reason' refers to any way of working out what to do; more usually it refers to proper or authoritative, hence reasoned, ways of working out what to do.

On many accounts practical reasoning is solely instrumental: it identifies ways of reaching certain results or ends, but has nothing to say about which ends should be pursued or which types of action are good or bad, obligatory or forbidden. Instrumental reasoning is important not only for ethics and politics, but for all activities, for example, in working out how to travel to a given destination.

Other accounts of practical reason insist that it is more than instrumental reasoning: it is concerned not only with working out how to achieve given ends, but with identifying the ethically important ends of human activity, or the ethically important norms or principles for human lives, and provides the basis for all ethical judgment.

No account of objective ethical values can be established without showing how we can come to know them, that is, without showing that some form of ethical cognitivism is true. However, ethical cognitivism is not easy to establish. Either we must show that some sort of intuition or perception provides direct access to a realm of values; or we must show that practical reasoning provides less direct methods by which objective ethical claims can be established. So anybody who thinks that there are directly objective values, but doubts whether

613

we can intuit them directly, must view a plausible account of practical reason as fundamental to philosophical ethics.

1 Introduction

Most ethical positions or theories rely on one or more conceptions of practical reason, yet many fail to explicate, let alone to vindicate, the particular conceptions on which they rely. The only positions or theories which offer no account of practical reason are those which construe ethical claims either as noncognitive or as based directly on particular cognitions such as perceptions or intuitions that do not need to be linked to any reasoning process (see ANALYTIC ETHICS; EMOTIVISM; INTUITIONISM IN ETHICS; MORAL REALISM).

One pervasive disagreement among the proponents of various accounts of practical reason is between those who think that practical reasons should both justify and motivate action and those who think that they should justify, but need not motivate. The claim that reasons both justify and motivate is often labelled *internalism*, the thought being that anything that motivates (whether a desire, or a certain sort of belief, or some other internal state) must be internal to the agent who is motivated. The claim that reasons must justify but need not motivate is correspondingly termed *externalism* (see MORAL MOTIVATION §§1–2). Broadly speaking, internalists think that externalists fail to show how reason can be practical, since they do not adequately address the question of motivation, and externalists think that internalists lose sight of the fact that practical reason must be reasoned, since they build an account of the contingencies of motivation into their account of reason. There are many versions both of internalism and of externalism.

Accounts of practical reasoning can be grouped under two very general headings. Many accounts of practical reason are *end-oriented* (also known as *teleological* or *consequentialist*): they seek to show how reason can select action (also attitudes and policies) that will contribute to certain ends or results (see CONSEQUENTIALISM; TELEOLOGICAL ETHICS). Many proponents of end-oriented practical reasoning think that practical reason can do no more. Since no

objective account of the proper ends of human life can be found, we must settle for *subjective* accounts of human ends. We must agree with Hume that reason 'is, and ought only to be the slave of the passions' (Hume 1739–40: 415) (see RATIONALITY, PRACTICAL §1). However, there are other accounts of end-oriented practical reasoning which insist that reason can also identify certain *objective* ends, and so has the dual task of identifying the proper ends of action and guiding action towards those ends.

Yet other conceptions of practical reason do not view it as focused solely on ends and means to those ends. *Act-oriented* accounts of practical reason take it that action (also attitudes and policies) are guided by norms or principles, and that it is the task of practical reason to identify appropriate, reasoned norms and principles. Some norms and principles formulate very general ends, others point to quite specific acts: the Jesuit maxim 'For the greater glory of God' defines the end of an entire life; the homely advice 'Do not eat oysters unless there is a letter "r" in the name of the month' offers limited and specific advice. Although some norms and principles define ends, norm- and principle-guided reasoning cannot be assimilated to end-oriented reasoning, which sees all practical reasoning as bearing on a means-ends complex. Act-oriented reasoning sees it as bearing on practical propositions (norms, rules, principles) and as guiding action without reference either to supposed objective ends or to the subjective ends of any agents.

Many accounts of act-oriented reasoning see it as norm-based: they take it that the fundamental ethical orientations (norms, categories, commitments, beliefs, senses of identity: hereafter *norms*) accepted in a society or tradition, or in an individual's life, provide the fundamental premises for practical reasoning. On such accounts, practical reasoning is internal to societies: it appeals to the norms that constitute the bedrock of certain lives or ways of life, so cannot coherently be brought into question by those who live these lives.

Other critical accounts of act-oriented ethical reasoning object that uncritical appeal to accepted norms cannot provide acceptable premises for practical reasoning; arguing from accepted norms is quite arbitrary, hence quite unreasoned. Any conclusions reached in this way will be relative to the assumed norms, so can support no more than one or another version of ethical relativism (see MORAL RELATIVISM). Exponents of critical accounts of practical reason think that adequate act-oriented reasoning must offer reasons which do not presuppose any specific norms (or traditions, or identities), but rather must be public in the sense that they are relevant to an unrestricted audience, or, as Kant put it vividly in an early version of this thought, that they must 'address...the world at large' (1784: 57). The possibility of vindicating any critical, universal conception of act-oriented practical reason is questioned by proponents of other conceptions.

The search for a convincing account of practical reason raises issues fundamental not only to ethics and politics, but to a wide range of philosophical problems. They include the problem of seeing whether, and if so how, any account of practical reason can be vindicated without begging questions, the connection between practical and theoretical reason and the problem of showing how and how far various conceptions of practical reason can guide action, attitudes or policies.

2 End-oriented reasoning: reason is instrumental

Scepticism about the idea that reason has any objective ends of its own was put succinctly by Hume, who scoffed that "tis not contrary to reason to prefer the destruction of the whole world to the scratching of my finger' (1739–40: 416), insisted that "tis in vain to pretend, that morality is discover'd only by a deduction of reason' (457) and concluded that *ought* cannot be derived from *is* (469). If morality has no ends that are discovered by reason, then practical reason's only task is to show how the pursuit of the passions – of subjective ends – is to be organized effectively and efficiently. The central task of practical reason is the instrumental one of deploying our knowledge of causal relations to guide action: practical reason is simply an application of and derivative from aspects of theoretical reason; it needs no separate justification.

There is, however, a great deal to be said about the detailed operations of instrumental reasoning. In particular, if some metric can be found for the ends which are to be sought (for example, if there is a metric for the satisfaction of desires or preferences), and if the probabilities of achieving various ends can be quantified, then instrumental reasoning can be used to show which available actions maximize the satisfaction of preferences, and hence how given ends can be pursued efficiently. If this metric permits the desires or preferences of different persons to be measured using a common unit, practical reasoning may be able to guide social as well as individual decision-making and policy. Utilitarian ethical theory, game theory and a wide range of economic and social calculi have discussed numerous versions of subjective, end-oriented practical reasoning which are held to be appropriate for various contexts (see RATIONALITY, PRACTICAL; RATIONAL CHOICE THEORY; UTILITARIANISM.)

Merely instrumental accounts of practical reason have been criticized at least since Kant. The critics do not doubt that instrumental reasoning is a necessary aspect of practical reasoning, but they insist that it cannot be sufficient. All that it provides is an account of the use of empirical, and in particular causal, knowledge in pursuit of intrinsically arbitrary ends. Instrumental reasoners may show that it is necessary to break eggs if one wants to make an omelette, but they have nothing but preferences to cite as reasons for making or not making omelettes: all their conclusions are conditional on subjective ends. Instrumental reasoning in pursuit of individual preferences can support efficient egoism, or strategic thinking or certain limited and distinctively modern conceptions of prudence: but this is all it can do. (see MORAL MOTIVATION §§4–6; PRUDENCE §3).

Contemporary work on instrumental reasoning has addressed this criticism up to a point by insisting that practical reasoning requires not only that choices of action be instrumentally sound, but that they be based on well-ordered (for example, connected and transitive) preference-orderings. However, since these coherence conditions can be met by many different sets of preferences, the requirement of well-orderedness provides little further reasoned guidance. It does not add enough to an account of instrumental rationality to satisfy those who think that an account of practical reason should provide a more complete guide to reasoned choice, or to rebut the charge that instrumental reasoning gets no further than showing how intrinsically arbitrary (unreasoned) ends are to be pursued by rational means.

Some advocates of subjective end-oriented practical reasoning have held that desires and preferences, although subjective, provide an approximation to an objective account of the good. Some utilitarians, for example, have held that happiness is the sole good, that it is achieved by satisfying desires, and that therefore the optimal satisfaction of desires leading to maximal happiness produces the greatest good; they then claim that instrumental reasoning provides a sufficient account of practical reasoning for ethical as well as for egoistical, strategic and merely prudential purposes. Critics have countered that happiness is not the sole good, and moreover that it is not all of a sort, and cannot be aggregated, so that instrumental reasoning alone will not be enough to guide ethical choice. Others have objected that some sorts of happiness, such as happiness in the satisfaction of evil desires, or happiness produced by violating others' rights, does not contribute to the good at all, and conclude that instrumentally rational pursuit of happiness cannot be what ethics demands.

3 End-oriented reasoning: reason identifies objective ends

All of these difficulties would be resolved if reason could also identify objective ends. Instrumental reasoning is only one aspect of an older and more ambitious conception of end-oriented practical reasoning, which claims that reason both identifies the proper ends of action – the good – and can be used to steer action towards those ends. Such a position can be attributed to PLATO, on whose account reason not merely can know its proper object, the [Form of the] Good, but strives for the Good. Far from being inert, reason is intrinsically active, has its own desires and its own end. In this picture there is no gap between theoretical reason, which guides right cognition, and practical reason, which guides right action. Human knowledge and desire have a common focus on the Good; *nous* and *eros* are aspects of one capacity, and the remaining practical problem is to align human life as that capacity directs (see Frede and Striker 1996).

The metaphysical and epistemological claims needed to support this more traditional vision of practical reason are hugely ambitious. Yet despite the difficulty of justifying objective conceptions of end-oriented practical reason, it has been widely accepted in varied forms. Aristotle, for example, took issue with Plato's unitary conception of the Good, and insisted that there are many goods, but held that they include the Good for man, which constitutes the proper end for human action (see ARISTOTLE §§20–1; EUDAI-MONIA). He offers a complex account of supplementary patterns of practical reasoning which can be used to identify action that contributes to the good for man. These include the *doctrine of the mean*, which purportedly offers a nonmechanistic way of selecting 'intermediate' action, so avoiding unacceptable extremes, and the so-called *practical syllogism*, by which conclusions about action (or possibly actions themselves) are inferred from general principles and claims about particular situations (see Anscombe 1957). Many later Neoplatonist and Christian thinkers also combine the ideas that the Good can be known by reason and that it is the proper end of human life. Plato's teleological view of reason has been widely if tacitly shared by countless other writers who neither share his metaphysical position nor provide any alternative, but who speak of certain ends as 'reasonable' without much by way of explanation, and often with far less by way of defence than Plato offers.

Of course, knowing what the Good is – what the true ends of human life are – is never enough to guide action. The effective pursuit of these ends also requires the use of reason to calculate which of various available acts contributes to those ends most effectively, as well as to identify any actions, attitudes or policies that are components of those ends. However, by itself this calculating, predominantly instrumental, side of end-oriented practical reason, as discussed in §2, cannot guide action without assuming subjective ends.

4 Act-oriented reasoning: reason appeals to norms

Other accounts of practical reason hold that it must guide action without reference either to subjective ends (because its conclusions would then be conditional on something wholly arbitrary) or to objective ends (because there is none). An adequate account of practical reason must bear more directly on action, and more specifically on the practical propositions (norms, rules, principles) which agents follow or embody in their lives. Just as theoretical reasoning prescribes ways of moving between elements that have syntactic and semantic structure, so too must practical reasoning. The central problem in using any act-oriented conception of practical reason for ethical purposes is to show *why* some but not other norms or principles, and so some but not other types of action and ends, attitudes and policies, are either good or ethically required.

Many forms of act-oriented practical reasoning maintain that the basis for distinguishing certain types of action from others can be found in the categories, beliefs and norms that form the constitutive elements of a society or of a sense of identity. These constitutive norms cannot be brought into question by anyone for whom they constitute the horizons of life and thought, so can provide basic premises for reasoning about what is good or bad, required or forbidden.

Once some fundamental norms have been identified, practical reasoning can be extended both by instrumental reasoning and by analysing the logical connections and implications between different norms (for example, between requirements, prohibitions and permissions) and the structure of systems of norms. At its most formal this sort of analysis draws on deontic logic; less formal conceptual investigations of types and systems of rules have also been undertaken, particularly by philosophers of law (see DEONTIC LOGIC; LEGAL REASONING AND INTERPRETATION) (see Raz 1975; Schauer 1991). However, since act-oriented practical reasoning does not provide any metric for ends it cannot use the maximizing patterns of practical reasoning which some subjective forms of end-oriented reasoning favour.

Norm-based practical reasoning is uncontroversially part and parcel of daily life, but philosophical argument that it is the basis for all ethical reasoning is highly controversial. Arguments that all ethical reasoning appeals to norms can be found in the work of Hegel, in historicist, communitarian and relativist writing, and (in more individualistic forms) in work by Wittgensteinians and by Bernard Williams.

Hegel's view that there is no gap between *is* and *ought* expresses not the implausible thought that whatever is accepted is acceptable, that (contrary to Hume) *ought* can be generally be derived from *is*, but the more profound view that all thinking and action must grow not out of abstract theories and principles but out of the deep structures of our actual situations (Hegel's term is *Sittlichkeit*, often translated as *ethical life*) (see HEGEL, G.W.F. §8). The deep facts of our histories and lives are ones that we cannot 'go behind' and bring into question; rather they form the inescapable framework of our action, so constitute legitimate, indeed unavoidable, starting points for all practical, including ethical, reasoning.

Similar positions can be found in Wittgenstein and in certain Wittgensteinians. In Wittgenstein's assertion that 'there must be agreement ... in judgments' (1953: paragraph 242) and in the widespread view that certain issues are 'not a matter for decision' (see Winch 1972), we see further versions of the thought that certain categories and norms form inescapable frameworks for life and thought, and that those who live within them lack any external vantage point from which to question or undermine them (see WITTGENSTEINIAN ETHICS). More individualistic versions of the same approach can be found in Bernard Williams' contention (1976) that certain identity-constituting personal projects and commitments are part of the framework which reasoning must assume, so cannot query (see MORALITY AND IDENTITY §4).

Practical reasoning which appeals to constitutive norms, coupled with ordinary patterns of instrumental reasoning, has powerful means of guiding action at its disposal. Critics fear, however, that this power is bought too dearly. One alleged cost is that norm-based practical reasoning is supposedly conservative: it will always already have presupposed established (usually establishment) categories, norms, identities and commitments, and provides no vantage point from which they can be criticized. This criticism is rebutted by many proponents of norm-based reasoning who, like Hegel, point out that any constitutive norm, sense of identity or the like will be but part of a wider set of beliefs and norms, whose elements can be used to challenge, revise and renew one another (see MacIntyre 1981). Once norms and identities are seen in developmental, historical context there is no reason to suppose that practical reasoning that starts from those of a given place and time must be intrinsically conservative.

Perhaps a more worrying criticism of norm-based practical reasoning is that even if it is not intrinsically conservative, it is nevertheless unavoidably designed for those who have internalized a certain outlook and its categories and norms: it is insiders' reasoning. For outsiders, treating insiders' shared categories and norms, and the established practices and identities they support, as bedrock for practical reasoning lacks all justification, because it adopts arbitrary premises. Like instrumental reasoning, norm-based reasoning can at best reach conditional conclusions. Its advocates can only retort that there is no external vantage available from which these starting points can be rebutted or called into question.

5 Act-oriented reasoning: reason appeals to 'the world at large'

If act-oriented reasoning is to escape the confines and the criticisms which it incurs by treating socially specific categories and norms as the bedrock for ethical reasoning, then it must find some way of 'going behind' and criticizing these assumptions.

The classic version of a critical conception practical act-oriented reasoning was developed by Immanuel Kant, who held that reasoning should address 'the world at large' (that is, all reasoners) rather than the limited groups who share specific but intrinsically arbitrary norms and practices (see Kant 1784, 1786; O'Neill 1989 part I 1992). If practical reasoning is to meet this standard, its first requirement must be the rejection of any principles which cannot be adopted by all, regardless of their social background, their accepted categories and norms, their established practices, their senses of identity or their desires (see UNIVERSALISM IN ETHICS §§1–2, 5). Kant summarized this requirement in the words: 'Act only on that maxim through which you can at the same time will that it should be a universal law' ([1785] 1903: 421). He claims that this principle of practical reason provides the supreme principle of morality, and should be called the 'categorical imperative' because it is the only way of reasoning practically which does not introduce arbitrary assumptions, and so the only one that can reach unconditional, namely categorical, conclusions. The component norms of social traditions and senses of identity may be scrutinized using the categorical imperative; if they cannot be willed as universal laws they must be rejected as unreasoned.

Kant's attempt to vindicate this critical account of practical reasoning is based on the thought that anything which deserves to be called reasoning must be something that can be given or received, exchanged or followed, among the widest 'public', that is universally, and correspondingly that anything which invokes the norms and beliefs of limited groups, let alone the favoured projects of individual lives, calls for rather than provides reasons. The authority of reason is simply the requirement of living by fundamental principles that are fit for universal use (in other words, that are *lawlike*). Since we know no intrinsic sources of authoritative standards – we have no account of the objectively good – the only meagre authority with which we are left is the injunction to reject principles which cannot be principles for all.

Once this fundamental use of practical reason has been used to identify certain core ethical principles or rules, critical practical reasoning can be extended by some of the moves used by instrumental and norm-based practical reasoning. Kant insists that instrumental reasoning is indispensable (although he cannot reinstate the metric assumptions or maximizing calculi advocated by those who hinge reasoning on subjective ends). He speaks of instrumental reasoning as guided by the principle of the 'hypothetical imperative', since by itself it can only licence conditional conclusions. His full account of practical reasoning also relies on the transitions between different modalities of required action (for example, between claims about obligations, permissions and prohibitions) that are used in norm-based reasoning.

There are many passages in which Kant indicates that the principles of theoretical and practical reason are fundamentally the same (such as [1785] 1903: 391). However in his case this appears to be the result neither of the derivation of practical from theoretical reason (as in instrumental reasoning) nor of the fusion of theory and practice (as in Platonism) but because his vindication of reason unites practical and theoretical reason (see Neimann 1994; O'Neill 1989 part II, 1992; Velkely 1989).

Kant's vindication of practical reason is controversial, and its adequacy as a guide to action is even more so. Since Hegel criticized Kant, many commentators have concluded that this stripped-down conception of practical reason is simply not enough to guide action, or alternatively that it will guide it in the 'wrong' direction. Some object that virtually any principle can be universally adopted and that this account of practical reason is not robust enough to guide action; others object (with little plausibility) that the universality requirement makes rigidly uniform demands and leaves no room for the differentiation of action which human life requires. These classic (and incompatible) objections are respectively said to target empty 'formalism' and insensitive 'rigourism' (see Herman 1993; Hill 1992; O'Neill 1989 part II).

Kantian conceptions of practical reason have recently been taken up in two bodies of literature. Some writers have returned to Kant to look for more plausible interpretations of the procedures by which his conception of practical reason can guide action (see Herman 1993; Hill 1992; Korsgaard 1996; O'Neill 1989 part II) and to explicate his distinctive vindication of practical reason (see Neimann 1994; O'Neill 1989 part I, 1992; Velkely 1989). Others have offered a range of contemporary interpretations of the idea that the fundamental feature of practical reason is its capacity to be public (see Habermas 1995; Rawls 1993; McCarthy 1994).

6 Other aspects of practical reason

Few, if any, accounts of practical reason claim to offer a total guide for action (the exception may be certain utilitarian versions of subjective end-oriented reasoning, which supposedly reduce everything to calculation). Most insist that good practical reasoning must be linked with careful empirical reasoning, and that it will also need judgment to determine the specific way in which an end should be pursued or a norm or principle instantiated (see MORAL JUDGMENT). There is general acceptance of the point (emphasized by both Kant and Wittgenstein) that rules cannot provide instructions for their own application, and must be supplemented by judgment. Real life appeals to instrumental reasoning, to socially specific norms and to abstract principles are all inevitably indeterminate and must be augmented with judgment.

Reasoning practically is always a task rather than an automatic process, and there are therefore many ways in which it can fail. Some are cognitive failures (due, for example, to mistaken views about causal links or risks); others are closely linked to questions about motivation. Some central types of failure in practical reasoning have been the subject of extensive study (see AKRASIA; SELF-DECEPTION; SELF-CONTROL).

See also: EXAMPLES IN ETHICS; GOOD, THEORIES OF THE; MORAL EDUCATION; MORAL EXPERTISE

References and further reading

* Anscombe, G.E.M. (1957) 'On Practical Reasoning', in *Intention*, Oxford: Blackwell, 57–79; repr. in J. Raz (ed.) *Practical Reasoning*, Oxford: Oxford University Press, 1978, 33–45. (Discusses Aristotle's practical syllogism.)

Audi, R. (1989) *Practical Reasoning*, London: Routledge. (Useful and accessible survey of different conceptions and patterns of practical reasoning; discusses Aristotle, Hume and Kant.)

* Frede, M. and Striker, G. (eds) (1996) *Rationality in Greek Thought*, Oxford: Clarendon Press. (Scholarly papers on Greek views of reason.)

* Habermas, J. (1995) *Between Facts and Norms*, Cambridge, MA: MIT Press. (Extensive discussion of practical – including ethical – reasoning.)

* Herman, B. (1993) *The Practice of Moral Judgement*, Cambridge, MA: Harvard University Press. (Varied papers on Kantian approach to moral deliberation; discusses Williams' internalist criticism of the approach.)

* Hill, T.E., Jr (1992) *Dignity and Practical Reason*, Cambridge: Cambridge University Press. (Papers on Kant's account of practical reason and ethics.)

* Hume, D. (1739–40) *A Treatise of Human Nature*, ed. L.A. Selby-Bigge, revised by P.H. Nidditch, Oxford: Clarendon Press, 2nd edn, 1978. (Classic source for the view that there are no objective ends and that reason does not motivate but guides towards ends given by the passions.)

Kant, I. (1781/1787) *Critik der Reinen Vernunft*, trans. N. Kemp Smith, *Critique of Pure Reason*, London: Macmillan, 1973. (Kant's considerations on the vindication of reason are mainly to be found in the prefaces and in the final part, titled *The Doctrine of Method*.)

* —— (1784) *An Answer to the Question: 'What is Enlightenment?'*, trans. B. Nisbet, in H. Reiss (ed.) *Kant: Political Writings*, Cambridge: Cambridge University Press, 2nd edn, 1992, 54–60. (Famous short essay on political philosophy, including material on the vindication of reason.)

* —— (1785) *Grundlegung zur Metaphysik der Sitten*, in *Kants gesammelte Schriften*, ed. Königlichen Preußcxischen Akademie der Wissenschaften, Berlin: Reimer, vol. 4, 1903; trans. with notes by H.J. Paton, *Groundwork of the Metaphysics of Morals* (originally *The Moral Law*), London: Hutchinson, 1948; repr. New York: Harper & Row, 1964. (References made to this work in the entry give the page number from the 1903 Berlin Akademie volume; these page numbers are included in the Paton translation. Classic short account of critical ethical reasoning.)

* —— (1786) *What is Orientation in Thinking?*, trans. B. Nisbet, in H. Reiss (ed.) *Kant: Political Writings*, Cambridge: Cambridge University Press, 2nd edn, 1992, 237–49. (Short essay on thinking and philosophy of religion, including material on the vindication of reason.)

* Korsgaard, C. (1996) *Creating the Kingdom of Ends*, Cambridge: Cambridge University Press. (Papers on Kant's account of practical reason and ethics.)

* MacIntyre, A. (1981) *After Virtue: A Study In Moral Theory*, London: Duckworth. (An accessible defence of norm-based practical reasoning, and specifically of a Hegelianized reading of Aristotelian ethics. See ch. 5 for an account of deriving *ought* from *is*).

* McCarthy, T. (1994) 'Kantian Constructivism and Reconstructivism: Rawls and Habermas in Dialogue', *Ethics* 105: 44–63. (Compares conceptions of practical reason used in the later works of Rawls and Habermas.)

Nagel, T. (1970) *The Possibility of Altruism*, Princeton, NJ: Princeton University Press. (Important account of prudential and ethical reasoning.)

* Neimann, S. (1994) *The Unity of Reason: rereading Kant*, Oxford: Oxford University Press. (Argues for the unity of theoretical and of practical reason in Kant's philosophy).

* O'Neill, O. (1989) *Constructions of Reason: Explorations of Kant's Practical Philosophy*, Cambridge: Cambridge University Press. (Papers on Kant's vindication of reason and on patterns of ethical reasoning that start from the categorical imperative.)

* —— (1992) 'Vindicating Reason', in *Kant: A Cambridge Commentary*, Cambridge: Cambridge University Press. (On Kant's vindication of a critical conception of reason.)

* Rawls, J. (1993) *Political Liberalism*, New York: Columbia University Press. (Reformulation of his earlier political philosophy basing it on a conception of public reason.)

* Raz, J. (1975) *Practical Reason and Norms*, London: Hutchinson. (Careful account of conceptual links between different sorts of norms and systems of norms.)

* Schauer, F. (1991) *Playing by the Rules: A Philosophical Examination of Rule-Based Decision Making*, Oxford: Clarendon Press. (Conceptual investigation of types and systems of rules.)

* Velkeley, R. (1989) *Freedom and the End of Reason: On the Moral Foundation of Kant's Critical Philosophy*, Chicago, IL: University of Chicago Press. (Historically aware account of Kant's conception of reason and its vindication.)

* Williams, B. (1976) 'Persons, Character and Morality', in A.O. Rorty (ed.) *The Identities of Persons*, Berkeley, CA: University of California Press, 197–216; repr. in *Moral Luck: Philosophical Papers 1973–80*, Cambridge: Cambridge University Press, 1981, 1–19. (Argues that reasons for action must be internal to the agent's own life.)

* Winch, P. (1972) *Ethics and Action*, London: Routledge & Kegan Paul. (Deploys a Wittgensteinian conception of practical reason.)

* Wittgenstein, L.J.J. (1953) *Philosophical Investigations*, Oxford: Blackwell, 88, paragraph 242.

(This passage is usually read as a laconic formulation of the view that there are social limits to reason-giving.)

ONORA O'NEILL

PRACTICE see THEORY AND PRACTICE

PRAGMATIC THEORIES OF TRUTH see TRUTH, PRAGMATIC THEORY OF

PRAGMATICS

Analytic philosophers have made lasting contributions to the scientific study of language. Semantics (the study of meaning) and pragmatics (the study of language in use) are two important areas of linguistic research which owe their shape to the groundwork done by philosophers.

Although the two disciplines are now conceived of as complementary, the philosophical movements out of which they grew were very much in competition. In the middle of the twentieth century, there were two opposing 'camps' within the analytic philosophy of language. The first – 'ideal language philosophy', as it was then called – was that of the pioneers, Frege, Russell and the logical positivists. They were, first and foremost, logicians studying formal languages and, through these formal languages, 'language' in general. Work in this tradition (especially that of Frege, Russell, Carnap, Tarski and later Montague) gave rise to contemporary formal semantics, a very active discipline developed jointly by logicians, philosophers and grammarians. The other camp was that of so-called 'ordinary language philosophers', who thought important features of natural language were not revealed, but hidden, by the logical approach initiated by Frege and Russell. They advocated a more descriptive approach, and emphasized the 'pragmatic' nature of natural language as opposed to, for example, the 'language' of Principia Mathematica. Their own work (especially that of Austin, Strawson, Grice and the later Wittgenstein) gave rise to contemporary pragmatics, a discipline which (like formal semantics) has developed successfully within linguistics in the past thirty years.

From the general conception put forward by ordinary language philosophers, four areas or topics of research

emerged, which jointly constitute the core of pragmatics: speech acts; indexicality and context-sensitivity; non-truth-conditional aspects of meaning; and contextual implications. In the first half of this entry, we look at these topics from the point of view of ordinary language philosophy; the second half presents the contemporary picture. From the first point of view, pragmatics is seen as an alternative to the truth-conditional approach to meaning associated with ideal language philosophy (and successfully pursued within formal semantics). From the second point of view, pragmatics merely supplements that approach.

1 **Pragmatics and ordinary language philosophy**
2 **Speech acts**
3 **Contextual implications**
4 **Non-truth-conditional aspects of meaning**
5 **Indexicals**
6 **Levels of meaning**
7 **Open texture**
8 **The semantics/pragmatics distinction**
9 **Context and propositional attitudes**
10 **Presupposition**
11 **Interpretation and context-change**
12 **The strategic importance of conversational implicatures**
13 **Communicative intentions**
14 **The intentional-inferential model**
15 **Pragmatics and modularity**
16 **Cognitive science and contextualism**

1 Pragmatics and ordinary language philosophy

The linguistic investigations undertaken by ordinary language philosophers in what was to become 'pragmatics' had been notably anticipated by various researchers belonging to other traditions (phenomenologists like Marty or REINACH, linguists like Bally or Gardiner, psychologists like Bühler, or anthropologists like Malinowski). However, what influenced ordinary language philosophers most was the conception of language advocated by 'ideal language philosophers', against which they reacted strongly (see ORDINARY LANGUAGE PHILOSOPHY).

Central in the ideal language tradition had been the equation of, or at least the close connection between, the meaning of a sentence and its truth-conditions. This truth-conditional approach to meaning, perpetuated by contemporary formal semantics, is one of the things which ordinary language philosophers found quite unpalatable (see MEANING AND TRUTH). Their own emphasis was on the distinction between 'language' and 'speech' (Gardiner 1932) or, equivalently, between 'sentence' and 'statement' (Austin [1950] 1971; Strawson [1950] 1971). It is the sentence (a unit of 'language') which has meaning, according to ordinary language philosophers; whereas it is the statement made by uttering the sentence in a particular context which has truth-conditions. The sentence itself does not have truth-conditions. Truth can only be predicated of sentences indirectly, via the connections between the sentence and the 'speech act' it can be used to perform. Rather than equating the meaning of a sentence with its alleged truth-conditions, some philosophers in the pragmatic tradition have suggested equating it with its speech act 'potential' (which may include, as a proper part, a certain truth-conditional potential; see Alston 1964: 37–9).

Suppose that we posit abstract objects, namely 'propositions', which have their truth-conditions essentially. Then the point made by ordinary language philosophers can be put as follows: sentences do not express propositions *in vacuo*, but only in the context of a speech act. Given that the same sentence can be used to make different speech acts with different contents, the 'proposition' which is the content of the speech act must be distinguished from the linguistic meaning of the sentence *qua* unit of the language ('sentence meaning') (see PROPOSITIONS, SENTENCES AND STATEMENTS). It must also be distinguished from the contextually determined meaning of a particular utterance of the sentence ('utterance meaning'), for the latter includes much more than merely the propositional content of the speech act performed in uttering the sentence. Utterance meaning includes a rich 'non-truth-conditional' component: Besides the proposition it expresses, an utterance conveys indications concerning the type of speech act being performed, the attitudes of the speaker, the place of the utterance within the discourse, its presuppositions and so forth. Moreover there is a secondary layer of meaning which includes the 'contextual implications' of the speech act, and in particular what H.P. Grice called the 'conversational implicatures' of the utterance.

2 Speech acts

Speech act theory (see Austin 1975; Searle 1969) is concerned with communication: not communication in the narrow sense of transmission of information, but communication in a broader sense which includes the issuing of orders, the asking of questions, the making of apologies and promises, and so on. According to the theory, a speech act is more than merely the uttering of a grammatical sentence endowed with sense and reference. To speak is also to *do* something in a fairly strong sense: it is to perform what J.L. AUSTIN called an 'illocutionary

act'. In performing an illocutionary act, a speaker takes on a certain role and assigns a corresponding role to the hearer. By giving an order, speakers express the desire that their hearer follow a certain course of conduct and present themselves as having the requisite authority to oblige the hearer to follow the course of conduct in question, simply because it is their will. The social role taken on by the speaker who gives an order is embodied in the organizational notion of 'superior rank'. Austin stressed such institutional embodiments of illocutionary roles in order to show that language itself is a vast institution incorporating an array of conventional roles corresponding to the range of socially recognized illocutionary acts. From this point of view, assertion – the act of making a statement – is only one illocutionary act among many others.

Illocutionary acts have 'felicity conditions' (conditions which must be contextually satisfied for the illocutionary act to be successfully performed). Thus an assertion about an object 'presupposes' the existence of that object and is felicitous only if the object in question actually exists (Strawson [1950] 1971; Austin 1975). The study of felicity conditions is a central concern of speech act theory, along with the taxonomy of illocutionary acts. But the most central concern, perhaps, relates to the characterization of the very notion of an illocutionary act. Illocutionary acts are generally introduced ostensively, by examples, and they are distinguished both from the mere act of saying something ('locutionary act') and from the act of causing something to happen by saying something ('perlocutionary act', for example frightening, convincing and so on). The nature of the intermediate category of 'illocutionary acts' remains a matter of debate, however. The pioneers of speech act theory, Austin and SEARLE, advocated an institutional or conventional approach. In this framework the illocutionary acts performed in speech, like the acts that are performed in games (for example, 'winning a set' in tennis), are governed by rules and exist only against a background of conventions. But an alternative, 'intentionalist' view, originating from Grice [1957] 1989 and Strawson [1964] 1971, developed and is now the dominant trend in speech act theory (see §13) (see SPEECH ACTS).

3 Contextual implications

The notion of a contextual implication itself is a speech-act theoretic notion. If, besides the meaning or content of an utterance, there is another realm (namely that of the illocutionary act the utterance serves to perform), then along with the implications of what is said there will be a further set of implications derivable from the utterance (namely the implications of the illocutionary act itself). Some of these 'pragmatic' implications are fairly trivial. Thus, according to ordinary language philosophers, it is a rule of the language game of assertion that whoever asserts something believes what they say and has some evidence for it; even the liar, who does not obey this rule, has to pretend that they do if they want to participate in the game. This rule generates pragmatic implications: by asserting something and therefore engaging in the language game, the speaker 'implies' that they obey the rules of the game and, therefore, that they believe whatever they are asserting. The speaker cannot disavow these implications of their speech act without 'pragmatic contradiction'. A pragmatic contradiction is a conflict between what an utterance says and what it pragmatically implies. Thus Moore's famous paradoxical utterance, 'It is raining but I do not believe it', is not self-contradictory in the logical sense: the state of affairs it describes is logically possible (it might be raining without the speaker's knowing it). But the speaker's asserting that it rains implies that they believe it, and this contradicts the second part of the utterance. (The twin notions of pragmatic implication and pragmatic contradiction or 'pragmatic paradox' have been used to illuminate a variety of philosophical issues, including the nature of Descartes' *Cogito*.)

Less trivial are the contextual implications famously discussed by H.P. GRICE (1989). According to Grice, the speaker making an utterance does not merely imply that they respect the rules of the language game; among the pragmatic implications of the utterance, we find a number of additional assumptions contextually required in order to maintain the supposition that the rules of the game are being observed. Suppose that I am asked whether I will go out; I reply: 'It is raining'. As stated above, it is a rule of assertion that the assertor believes what they say and have some evidence for it. By virtue of this rule, my utterance implies that I believe that it is raining, and that I have some evidence for my assertion. Considered as an answer to a question, my utterance also implies that it provides the information requested by the addressee, for it is a rule of the Question-and-Answer game that the answerer must provide the requested piece of information. Now in order to maintain the supposition that the speaker's utterance actually provides the requested information, additional premises are needed: for example, the assumption that the speaker will not go out if it rains. In conjunction with this contextual assumption, the utterance implies that the speaker will not go out, thereby providing a negative answer to the question. In so far as they serve to

restore the utterance's conformity to the rules of the game, the conclusion that the speaker will not go out and the contextual assumption through which it is derived are further pragmatic implications of the utterance. Grice called them 'conversational implicatures'. Contrary to the more trivial pragmatic implications, they can be disavowed by the speaker without pragmatic contradiction (at least if there is another way of making the utterance compatible with the supposition that the rules of the game are being respected). This distinguishing feature of conversational implicatures is referred to as their 'cancellability'. Implicatures which are not disavowed are legitimately taken as part of what the utterance communicates. They constitute a second layer of meaning, additional to what is literally said (see §12) (see IMPLICATURE).

4 Non-truth-conditional aspects of meaning

Like pragmatic implications, non-truth-conditional aspects of meaning are easy to account for if speech is considered as a rule-governed activity (Stenius 1967). What is the meaning of, for example, the imperative mood? Arguably, the sentences 'You will go to the shop tomorrow at 8', 'Will you go to the shop tomorrow at 8?' and 'Go to the shop tomorrow at 8' describe the same (sort of) state of affairs. The difference between them is pragmatic rather than descriptive: it relates to the type of illocutionary act being performed by the utterance. Thus the imperative mood indicates that the speaker, in uttering the sentence, performs an illocutionary act of a 'directive' type. (Such an act is governed by the rule that if the speaker performs a directive act with content *P*, the addressee is to make it the case that *P*.) To account for this 'indication', which does not belong to the utterance's descriptive or propositional content, we can posit a rule or convention to the effect that the imperative mood is to be used only if one is performing a directive type of illocutionary act. This rule gives 'conditions of use' for the imperative mood. By virtue of this rule, a particular token of the imperative mood in an utterance **u** 'indicates' that a directive type of speech act is being performed by **u**. This (token-reflexive) indication conveyed by the token follows from the conditions of use that govern the type; these conditions of use constitute the linguistic meaning of the type (Recanati 1987: 15–7).

Pragmatic indications are a species of pragmatic implication: they are what the use of a particular expression pragmatically implies, by virtue of a certain condition of use conventionally associated with the expression. In contrast to more standard pragmatic implications, however, pragmatic indications are linguistically encoded, via the condition of use conventionally associated with the expression. Grice (1989) called such conventional pragmatic implications 'conventional implicatures', as opposed to 'conversational implicatures' (see IMPLICATURE §4). Whether they concern the type of the illocutionary act, as in the example I have given, or some other aspect of the context of utterance, pragmatic indications can always be accounted for in terms of conditions of use. They are 'use-conditional' aspects of meaning. Their exploration is one of the empirical tasks of semantics construed as the study of linguistic meaning under all its aspects (see §8 for an alternative construal of 'semantics').

5 Indexicals

Use-conditional meaning is not incompatible with descriptive content, in the sense that one and the same expression can be endowed with both. There are expressions which have a purely use-conditional meaning and do not contribute to truth-conditional content. Illocutionary markers like the imperative mood, or discourse particles such as 'well', 'still', 'after all', 'anyway', 'therefore', 'alas', 'oh' and so forth, fall into this category. Thus the following utterances have the same truth-conditional content, and are distinguished only by the pragmatic indications they respectively convey:

Well, Peter did not show up

Still, Peter did not show up

After all, Peter did not show up

Therefore, Peter did not show up

Alas, Peter did not show up

But there are also expressions which have a two-layered meaning. Indexicals are a case in point. A 'rule of use' is clearly associated with indexicals: thus 'I' is governed by a convention of use (it is to be used to refer to the speaker). By virtue of this conventional rule, a use **u** of 'I' token-reflexively indicates that it refers to the speaker of **u**. But **u** also contributes to the utterance's truth-conditional content. 'I' being a directly referential expression, its truth-conditional contribution (its 'content') is its actual referent, not the rule of use which contextually determines the referent (Kaplan 1989: 481–563; Recanati 1993).

Besides the horizontal distinction between truth-conditional and non-truth-conditional aspects of meaning, we see that there is a vertical distinction between two levels of meaning for indexical expressions (Strawson [1950] 1971; Kaplan 1989: 481–563). At the first level – corresponding to the linguistic meaning of the expression-type – we find the rule of

use conventionally associated with the expression. At the second level – corresponding to the context-dependent semantic value of the token – the rule of use determines the expression's 'content' (see DEMONSTRATIVES AND INDEXICALS).

6 Levels of meaning

The two distinctions we have made, between truth-conditional and non-truth-conditional aspects of meaning on the one hand, and between levels of meaning on the other hand, should not be conflated (as they often have been). Despite appearances, they are orthogonal to each other. In the same way as the truth-conditional content of an indexical sentence is context-dependent and, therefore, belongs to the second level of meaning, the pragmatic indications conveyed by an expression governed by a rule of use also are context-dependent and belong to the second level of meaning. In other words, a distinction must be made between the rule of use (first level of meaning) and the pragmatic indications it contextually generates, in the same way as we distinguish between the rule of use and the truth-conditional content it contextually determines.

That pragmatic indications, though conventional, are context-dependent is shown by examples like (1):

(1) The weather is nice, but I have a lot of work.

The conjunction 'but' is governed by a certain condition of use which distinguishes it from 'and'. According to Ducrot (1972: 128–9), 'but' is to be used only if the following conditions are contextually satisfied:

(i)   The first conjunct (P) supports a certain conclusion r;
(ii) The second conjuncts (Q) supports $not\text{-}r$;
(iii) Q is considered stronger than P, that is the whole utterance supports $not\text{-}r$.

Uttering (1) pragmatically implies that the conditions of use associated with 'but' are satisfied, that is that there is a conclusion r such that the first conjunct supports r and the second conjunct more strongly supports $not\text{-}r$. But the pragmatic implication conveyed by a particular utterance of (1) is much more specific. In context, the variable r is assigned a particular interpretation, for example 'we should go for a walk'. Example (1) therefore pragmatically implies something like the following: we should not go for a walk (because of all the work I have to do), despite the nice weather which suggests otherwise.

In so far as it is context-dependent and conveyed by the token, this pragmatic implication is to be located at the second level of meaning, alongside the content of indexicals. Even in a case where the pragmatic indication is fully conventional and not in need of contextual specification, it is conveyed by the token, not by the type. Thus a particular use **u** of the pronoun 'I' indicates that it (**u**) refers to the speaker of **u**. This token-reflexive indication is distinct from the rule of use, to the effect that for all x, if x is a token of 'I' it must be used to refer to the speaker of x.

The picture is further complicated by the Gricean distinction between what is literally said and what is non-literally or indirectly communicated. We end up with a three-fold distinction between the following layers of meaning:

First level. Rules of use ('character', in Kaplan's framework).

Second level. Truth-conditional content + pragmatic indications.

Third level. Conversational implicatures.

The need for a third level of meaning comes from the fact that the contextual process responsible for conversational implicatures (and non-conventional pragmatic implications in general) takes the second-level meaning of the utterance as input. When an expression is governed by a condition of use, using that expression pragmatically implies that the condition is satisfied. But conversational implicatures, in contrast to conventional implicatures, are not generated by virtue of a condition of use directly associated with a particular linguistic expression; they are normally generated by virtue of conversational norms that concern the content of utterances rather than the expressions which are used to convey that content. For example, a speaker should not say what he believes to be false (the 'maxim of quality' in Grice's terminology); as a result, saying that P pragmatically implies that the speaker believes that P. The generation of this pragmatic implication presupposes that the proposition expressed has been identified: from the fact that *the speaker has said that P*, together with the default assumption that the maxim of quality is respected, we can infer that *the speaker believes that P*. The implicature-generating process therefore deserves to be called a 'secondary pragmatic process' (Recanati 1993). There are three basic levels of meaning, with the context controlling the transition from the first to the second and from the second to the third. The proposition expressed by the utterance must first be contextually identified (primary pragmatic process) in order for the non-conventional pragmatic implications to be derived (secondary pragmatic process).

7 Open texture

For ordinary language philosophers, the truth-conditional or 'descriptive' content of an utterance is a property of the speech act, not a property of the sentence. A sentence only has truth-conditions in the context of a speech act. This is so not merely because of indexicality: the fact that the reference of some words depends on the context in a systematic way. Indexicality is only one form of context-dependence. There is another one, no less important, which affects the sense (the conditions of application) of words rather than their reference. According to Austin and Wittgenstein, words have clear conditions of application only against a background of 'normal circumstances' corresponding to the type of context in which the words were used in the past. There is no 'convention' to guide us as to whether or not a particular expression applies in some extraordinary situation. This is not because the meaning of the word is 'vague', but because the application of words ultimately depends on there being a sufficient similarity between the new situation of use and past situations. The relevant dimensions of similarity are not fixed once and for all; this is what generates 'open texture' (Waismann 1951). Ultimately, it is the context of utterance which determines which dimension of similarity is relevant, hence which conditions have to be satisfied for a given expression to apply (Travis 1975; 1981). It follows that the sense of ordinary descriptive words is context-dependent, like the reference of indexicals, though not quite in the same way. On this approach, which we may call 'contextualism', truth-conditions cannot be ascribed to sentence-types but only to utterances (Searle 1978; 1983).

Contextualism was a central tenet in the pragmatic conception of language developed by ordinary language philosophers (though some atypical ordinary language philosophers, like Grice, rejected it). This conception is, at bottom, a 'use theory of meaning'. Meaning is use, in the following sense: there is nothing more to meaning than use (Wittgenstein 1953). We are confronted with uses of words, and the meaning which those words acquire for us is only the sense we are able to *make* of those uses.

8 The semantics/pragmatics distinction

If much of contemporary pragmatics derives from the work of ordinary language philosophers, the name 'pragmatics' – contrasted with 'syntax' and 'semantics' – was coined by a philosopher in the ideal language tradition, Charles Morris (1938). The general conception associated with Morris' tripartite distinction has been very influential. On this conception (hereafter 'the traditional conception'), semantics and pragmatics are complementary studies: semantics deals with meaning understood as representational content, whereas pragmatics deals with use. This view, still influential today, is at odds with the more radical conception developed within ordinary language philosophy and sketched in the previous sections. (According to the latter view, meaning cannot be divorced from use; semantics *is* pragmatics.) However, as we shall see, the border between semantics and pragmatics has become much fuzzier as the traditional conception, with its sharp contrast between the two disciplines, was modified in order to account for indexicality, pragmatic indications and related phenomena.

The traditional conception is commonly glossed in two different ways, corresponding to two different distinctions. The first distinction is that between 'meaning' (that is, representational content) and 'force', to be found both in Frege and Austin. (Often the term 'sense' is used instead of 'meaning', and the distinction referred to as the 'sense-force distinction'. Some commentators insist on distinguishing the use of 'sense' as the complement of 'force' from the use of 'sense' as the complement of 'reference'; see SENSE AND REFERENCE.) An utterance (1) represents a certain state of affairs, and (2) serves to perform a certain speech act. The semantics/pragmatics distinction is often expressed in terms of this distinction: semantics deals with representational content and studies the relations between words and the world, while pragmatics studies the relations between words and their users. The second distinction is that between sentence meaning and utterance meaning. Semantics is supposed to deal with the linguistic meaning of sentence-types, while pragmatics is concerned with the total significance of an utterance of the sentence by a particular speaker in a particular context. The traditional conception is indifferently expressed in terms of either distinction because, according to the traditional conception, the conventional meaning of the sentence-type *is* its representational content.

The problem with the traditional conception is precisely that it rests on the equation of the meaning of a sentence with its representational content. This equation cannot be accepted, for two reasons:

(1) Indexical sentences represent a specific state of affairs only in context; their representational content depends on some feature of their context of use, hence it cannot be equated with the context-independent meaning of the sentence-type. Because the truth-conditions of indexical sentences depend on their use, some authors have argued that the study of truth-conditions for such sentences belongs to pragmatics

(Bar-Hillel 1954); it has even been suggested that pragmatics *is* the study of truth-conditions for indexical sentences (Montague 1968).

(2) As we have seen, there are use-conditional as well as truth-conditional aspects of the meaning of sentence-types. To account for them, it seems we must give up the purely truth-conditional conception of semantics and make room for a non-truth-conditional component within it. Alternatively, we can say that it is the business of 'pragmatics' to deal with some aspects of the linguistic meaning of sentence-types, namely those aspects which relate to use. Thus Gazdar (1979) defines pragmatics as 'semantics minus truth-conditions'.

Some philosophers have tried to defend the traditional conception by forcing use-conditional aspects of meaning into the mould of truth-conditional semantics. Take, for example, the imperative mood. One can use the pragmatic equivalence between the imperative 'Close the door!' and the 'explicit performative' 'I order you to close the door' (Austin 1975: 32) to support the claim that non-declarative sentences have a declarative paraphrase through which they can be given a truth-conditional analysis (Lewis 1970: 54–61). A number of similar attempts have been made to reduce use-conditional to truth-conditional aspects of meaning (for example, Davidson 1979). Despite these attempts, it is commonly acknowledged that not all aspects of linguistic meaning are truth-conditional. There are two components in the meaning of a sentence: a truth-conditional or descriptive component and a non-truth-conditional, pragmatic component. The pragmatic component of sentence meaning constrains the context of utterance: it is a 'procedural' component. As for the descriptive component of sentence meaning, it can no longer be equated with the truth-conditional content of the utterance (because of objection (1)), but it can still be construed as what *determines* that content with respect to a context of use.

This leaves us with two interpretations of the semantics/pragmatics distinction, both current in the contemporary literature. On one interpretation, dominant among philosophers, pragmatics deals with use – including use-conditional aspects of meaning (pragmatic indications, presuppositions and the like) – while semantics deals both with the descriptive component of sentence meaning and the truth-conditional content it determines (with respect to a context). The other interpretation, widespread among linguists, has it that semantics deals with conventional sentence meaning under all its aspects (including non-truth-conditional aspects), while pragmatics deals with use and the aspects of meaning which are contextual and use-dependent, that is, those that are conveyed by the utterance but cannot be ascribed to the sentence-type (Katz 1977: 13– 22). (This category of 'contextual meaning' is somewhat heterogeneous; it includes both the semantic values of context-sensitive expressions, which are constitutive of the proposition literally expressed by the utterance, and other aspects of meaning which are not 'literal', conversational implicatures, for example.)

9 Context and propositional attitudes

The descriptive component of sentence meaning can be equated with a function from contexts to propositions (Stalnaker 1970; Kaplan 1989: 481–563). The 'context' is often construed as a package of various situational factors relevant to determining the semantic values of the context-sensitive constituents of the sentence. (See §10 for an alternative construal.) Thus the place of utterance, the identity of the participants in the speech episode and the time of utterance are among the factors on which the proposition expressed by an indexical sentence depends. It would be a mistake, however, to hold that only such 'external' (that is, non-intentional) features of the situation of utterance have a role to play in the determination of what is said. In many cases, what the speaker 'has in mind' is the relevant factor. Thus 'John's book' can mean the book which John wrote, the book he bought, the book he is reading, and so forth. The sentence in which the expression occurs expresses a definite proposition only when a particular relation between John and a certain book has been contextually determined, but there is no 'rule' which enables the interpreter to determine the latter except that it must be the relation which the speaker 'has in mind'. (This is in contrast with the case of 'I': as Barwise and Perry (1983: 33) pointed out, the reference of 'I' is fixed by the rule that 'I' refers to the speaker, irrespective of the speaker's beliefs and intentions. Even if a speaker believes that they are Napoleon, their use of 'I' does not refer to Napoleon.) The same thing holds for demonstratives in general: contrary to the received opinion, the reference of a demonstrative is not the 'demonstrated' object, for there may be no accompanying demonstration; the reference, rather, is the object which the speaker has in mind and wishes to single out (Kaplan 1989: 565–614; Bach 1987).

It turns out that the context against which an utterance is interpreted includes factors like the intentions, expectations, beliefs and other propositional attitudes of the speaker and their audience. Especially important are the beliefs which are shared and 'mutually known' to be shared; they constitute a 'common ground' which can be exploited in discourse (see Stalnaker's 1974 paper 'Pragmatic Presuppositions' in Davis 1991; Clark 1992). This introduces the topic of 'presupposition' which is generally mentioned, along with speech acts, indexicals and implicatures, as one of the central issues in pragmatics.

10 Presupposition

There is a basic sense in which 'presupposing' is a pragmatic attitude towards a proposition: that of 'taking it for granted'. (One takes something for granted, for example, when one uses it as a hidden premise in an argument.) The 'context' is sometimes defined as a set of presuppositions in this sense, that is a set of propositions which are taken for granted at a given point in discourse (see Karttunen 1974, for example). Many authors think that in order to be part of the context, a proposition must be not only believed by the participants in the speech episode, but also believed to be believed, and so forth. Other authors find this 'mutual belief' requirement too strong (Smith 1982). Be that as it may, a more pressing question arises in connection with presuppositions. Beside the pragmatic notion of presupposition (where presupposing is something a *speech participant* does), is there also a purely semantic notion, where presupposing is something which a *sentence* does? For example, does the sentence 'John stopped teaching undergraduates' carry the presupposition that John used to teach undergraduates as part of its semantic, truth-conditional content?

The semantic notion of presupposition has been questioned on two grounds. First, it has been pointed out that presuppositions, like conversational implicatures, seem to be defeasible or cancellable. This might suggest that the basic, pragmatic sense is the only sense we can give to the notion of presupposition. *Sentences* do not have presuppositions; only the participants in a speech episode can presuppose something. This conclusion, however, seems too strong, for the conventional nature of presuppositions is manifest and well-documented. Arguably, what the defeasibility of presuppositions shows is not that presuppositions are non-conventional, but rather that they can be overridden if certain conditions are satisfied (Gazdar 1979).

More convincing is the claim that presuppositions, though part of the conventional meaning of the sentence, do not affect the truth-conditions of the utterance. Like pragmatic indications in general, the linguistic presuppositions associated with certain expressions (such as the verb 'stop' in the example above) can be construed as conditions of use or constraints on the context (see Stalnaker's 1974 paper

'Pragmatic Presuppositions' in Davis 1991). The linguistic presupposition encoded by the verb 'stop' is a certain constraint on the context, namely the requirement that it contain a speaker with a certain pragmatic attitude (the attitude of 'presupposing') towards a certain proposition, or (if the context is directly construed as a set of propositions) the requirement that it contain a certain proposition, namely the proposition that John used to teach undergraduates. An utterance of 'John stopped teaching undergraduates' is 'appropriate' only in a context in which this constraint is satisfied. The constraint in question belongs to the non-truth-conditional component of sentence meaning: it does not affect the (truth-conditional) 'content' of the utterance (see PRESUPPOSITION).

11 Interpretation and context-change

The rich, propositional notion of 'context' which features in discussions of presupposition is at the heart of contemporary pragmatics. As we have seen in connection with demonstratives and semantically indeterminate expressions, the context provides 'assumptions' concerning the speaker's intentions and expectations, which are used to determine the proposition expressed by the sentence. This process of determination is construed as fundamentally inferential and proposition-involving. (See §14 on the intentional-inferential approach.)

The propositional notion of context makes it possible to see the relation between context and content as two-way rather than one-way (Kamp 1985: 240). The proposition expressed, which depends on the context, itself changes the context. According to dynamic theories of discourse, the content of an assertion is normally fed into the context against which the next utterance will be interpreted (Karttunen 1974; Stalnaker 1978; Kamp 1985; Heim's 1988 paper 'On the Projection Problem for Presuppositions' in Davis 1991). The context of interpretation constantly changes – Stalnaker speaks of an 'ever-changing context' – because it evolves as discourse proceeds. Thus it is possible for the context to shift in the middle of an utterance. This possibility accounts for a number of puzzling facts, including the defeasibility of presuppositions (see DISCOURSE SEMANTICS).

If the proposition expressed by an utterance is normally fed into the context, the assumption that this proposition has been expressed *always* becomes part of the context as a result of the interpretation of the utterance. It is this assumption, together with the default assumption that the speaker respects the norms of conversation (plus various other assumptions included in the context), which make it possible to infer the conversational implicatures which enrich the overall meaning of the utterance. It follows that the contextual changes induced by an utterance by virtue of its expressing a certain proposition affect not only the interpretation of the utterances that follow, but equally the overall meaning of the very utterance responsible for the contextual change.

Another sort of context-change induced by an utterance has been described by David Lewis (1979). Sometimes the default assumption that the speaker respects the norms of conversation prevents the utterance from being interpreted with respect to the context at hand because, if it were so interpreted, it would violate the norms in question. This leads to a modification of the context in order to reach a more satisfactory interpretation. Thus if the utterance presupposes that P, and P is not part of the context at hand, it is introduced into the context in order to bring the utterance into conformity with the norms ('accommodation').

12 The strategic importance of conversational implicatures

If semantics and pragmatics both study the contextual determination of the proposition expressed (in so far as it depends both on the linguistic meaning of the sentence and the context), conversational implicatures fall within the sole domain of pragmatics, for they are not constrained by the linguistic meaning of the sentence in the way the proposition expressed is. Yet the theory of implicatures has important consequences for semantics. Thanks to Grice's theory, many intuitive aspects of meaning can be put into the 'pragmatic wastebasket' as implicatures, rather than treated as genuine data for semantics. Take, for example, the sentence 'P or Q'. It can receive an inclusive or an exclusive interpretation. Instead of saying that 'or' is ambiguous in English, we may consider it as unambiguously inclusive, and account for the exclusive reading by saying that in some contexts the utterance conversationally implicates that P and Q are not both true. When there is such a conversational implicature, the overall meaning of the utterance is clearly exclusive, even though what is strictly and literally said corresponds to the logical formula '$P \vee Q$'. It is here that the complementary character of semantics and pragmatics is particularly manifest. Semantics is simplified because a lot of data can be explained away as 'implicatures' rather than genuine aspects of the (literal) meaning of the utterance.

Grice's theory of implicatures has been extremely popular among semanticists precisely because it enables the theorist, when certain conditions are satisfied, to shift the burden of explanation from semantics to pragmatics. From this point of view, the most interesting notion is that of 'generalized' conversational implicatures (Grice 1989; Gazdar 1979; Levinson 1983). When a conversational implicature is generalized, that is generated by default, it tends to become intuitively indistinguishable from semantic content. Grice's theory has taught the semanticist not to take such 'semantic' intuitions at face value. Even if something seems to be part of the semantic content of an utterance, the possibility of accounting for it pragmatically must always be considered.

Grice's theory is important also because it has provided an influential argument against the contextualism professed by ordinary language philosophers. For example, Strawson had claimed that the truth-conditions of 'P and Q' in English are contextually variable: the notion of temporal succession, or that of causal connection, or a number of other suggestions concerning the connection between the first and the second conjunct can enter into the interpretation of 'P and Q', depending on the context (Strawson 1952: 81–2). 'They got married and had many children' means that they had children after getting married; 'Socrates drank the hemlock and died' means that he died as result of drinking the hemlock. Those aspects of the interpretation are very much context-sensitive; yet they affect the utterance's truth-conditions. The truth-conditions of 'P and Q', therefore, are not fixed by a rigid rule, but depend on the context. Against this view, Grice has argued that the truth-conditions of 'P and Q' *are* fixed and context independent. 'P and Q' is true if and only if P and Q are both true. Thus 'They got married and had many children' would be true, even if they had the children before getting married. Certainly the utterance conveys the suggestion that the children came after the marriage, but this suggestion is nothing other than a conversational implicature, according to Grice (see IMPLICATURE §6). It does not affect the utterance's semantic content – its literal truth-conditions. Grice criticized his fellow ordinary language philosophers for confusing the truth-conditions of an utterance with its total significance. Though controversial (Travis 1985), this argument has been very popular, and it has played a major role in the subsequent downfall of ordinary language philosophy.

13 Communicative intentions

The pioneers of pragmatics (Malinowski and Austin, for example) used to insist on the social dimension of language as opposed to its cognitive or representa-tional function. As pragmatics developed, however, it is the psychological dimension of language use that came to the forefront of discussions, in part as a result of Grice's work on meaning and communication.

Grice ([1957] 1989) defined a pragmatic notion of meaning: the notion of *someone* meaning something by a piece of behaviour (a gesture, an utterance and so forth). Grice's idea was that this pragmatic notion of meaning was basic and could be used to analyse the semantic notion, that is what it is for a linguistic *expression* to have meaning (see GRICE, H.P. §3). Strawson soon pointed out that Grice's pragmatic notion of meaning could also be used to characterize the elusive notion of an illocutionary act (Strawson [1964] 1971). In §2, the view that illocutionary acts are essentially conventional acts (like the acts which owe their existence to the rules of a particular game) was mentioned. This conventionalist approach was dominant in speech act theory until Strawson established a bridge between Grice's theory of meaning and Austin's theory of illocutionary acts. Illocutionary acts, in the new framework, can be analysed in terms of the utterly non-mysterious notion of a 'perlocu-tionary act'.

A perlocutionary act consists in bringing about certain effects by an utterance. For example, by saying to you 'It is raining', I bring it about that you believe that it is raining. Now, according to the suggested analysis, to perform the illocutionary act of asserting that it is raining is (in part) to make manifest to the addressee one's intention to bring it about, by this utterance, that the addressee believes that it is raining. An illocutionary act therefore involves the manifesta-tion of a corresponding perlocutionary intention. But there is a special twist which the suggested analysis inherits from Grice's original conception of meaning: the intention must be made manifest in a specially 'overt' manner. Not only must the speaker's intention to bring about a certain belief in the addressee be revealed by his utterance, but his intention to reveal it must also be revealed, and it must be revealed in the same overt manner. This characteristic (if puzzling) feature of overtness is often captured by considering the revealed intention itself as reflexive: a commu-nicative intention, that is the type of intention whose manifestation constitutes the performance of an illocutionary act, is the intention to achieve a certain perlocutionary effect (for example, bringing about a certain belief in the addressee) via the addressee's recognition of this intention. Also relevant to the characterization of overtness is the notion of 'mutual knowledge' (Lewis 1969; Schiffer 1972) which we have seen at work in the characterization of 'contexts' and 'presuppositions' (see §10) (see COMMUNICATION AND INTENTION; MEANING AND COMMUNICATION).

14   The intentional-inferential model

Even though the conventionalist approach to communication is still alive, the Grice-Strawson 'intentionalist' approach has gained wide currency in pragmatics. Typical in this respect are the neo-Gricean theories offered by Bach and Harnish (1979) and Sperber and Wilson (1986). They have put forward an inferential model of communication intended to supersede the 'code model' (or 'message model') that was inspired from Shannon and Weaver.

According to the code model, communication proceeds as follows: to communicate a certain content, the speaker encodes it into a sentence using the grammar of the language as a 'code' pairing contents and sentences (possibly with respect to a context of utterance); the interpreter, by virtue of their knowledge of the same grammar (and, perhaps, of the context), can decode the sentence and recover the intended content.

The alternative, inferential model of communication is very different. An utterance is seen as a meaningful action, one which provides interpreters with evidence concerning the agent's intentions. What distinguishes communicative acts from other meaningful actions is what can be inferred from the evidence: a communicative act is an act which provides evidence of a certain 'communicative intention' on the part of the speaker. In other words, the speaker's intention to communicate something is what explains their utterance, when considered as a piece of behaviour. From this point of view, the content of the communicative act – what is communicated – is the total content of the communicative intentions which can be inferred from it. Let us call this the utterance's communicative meaning, distinct from the literal or conventional meaning of the sentence (determined by the code, that is the grammar). Understanding is essentially an inferential process in this framework, and the conventional meaning of the sentence provides only part of the evidence used in determining the communicative meaning of the utterance.

15   Pragmatics and modularity

A characteristic feature of recent work in the Gricean tradition has been the explicit employment of concepts from (and the intention to contribute to) cognitive science. For example, Fodor's distinction between central thought processes and more specialized cognitive 'modules' has been found relevant to the characterization of the task of pragmatics (see MODULARITY). (See, for example, Kasher's papers in Davis 1991 and Tsohatzidis 1995.)

In the inferential framework, comprehension involves not only a specifically linguistic competence, namely knowledge of 'grammar', but also general intelligence (that is, world knowledge together with inferential abilities). Contextual assumptions of various sorts, including assumptions about the speaker's beliefs and expectations, play a crucial role not only in the inferential process which, according to Grice and his followers, underlies the generation of conversational implicatures, but also in the determination of the proposition literally expressed by the utterance (Carston 1988; Kempson 1988). Pragmatics, therefore, is concerned with the interaction between the language faculty and central thought processes in the task of linguistic comprehension (Sperber and Wilson 1986). It considers how the output of the linguistic module is centrally processed, that is processed against the interpreter's complete belief system.

The major difficulty here is the 'holistic' character of the belief system (Fodor 1983). How is the total cognitive background restricted so as to yield a 'context' of manageable size? Sperber and Wilson's 'relevance theory' addresses this crucial issue. Their view of pragmatics is grounded in a general theory of cognition as relevance-oriented. One of their central ideas is that the context in which an utterance is processed is not 'given' but 'constructed': it results from an active search driven by the overarching goal to maximize relevance.

Sperber and Wilson's claim that there is no special faculty or module corresponding to pragmatics (since pragmatics studies the interaction between general intelligence and linguistic modules) must be qualified. As Sperber himself stressed in various places (for example, Sperber 1994), there is one special capacity which communicators must possess and which, arguably, poor communicators (for example, autistic children) do not possess: the capacity to ascribe complex propositional attitudes, such as higher-order intentions. (As we have seen, understanding crucially involves a process of intention recognition, and the communicative intentions which must be recognized are complex, higher-order intentions.)

16   Cognitive science and contextualism

The intentional-inferential framework has been very influential in cognitive science. The Grice-Strawson interpretation of speech act theory has given rise to computational models of discourse where intention recognition plays a key role (see Grosz, Pollack and Sidner 1989; Cohen, Morgan and Pollack 1989). The idea that meaning is 'inferred' has also been taken very seriously. Many cognitive scientists believe that in interpretation the meaning of an utterance is arrived at by 'guesswork', rather than by decoding (Green 1989).

Typical in this respect are complex nominals (noun–noun compounds like 'finger cup' or adjective–noun compounds like 'philosophical kitchen'), which have received a good deal of attention. The semantic value which such expressions assume in context (unless they are idiomatic) is not predictable on a purely linguistic basis; it results from an act of 'sense creation'. Here again, what matters is what the speaker has in mind; the interpreter can only guess, using a variety of contextual clues. Such expressions whose sense is irreducibly contextual have been dubbed 'contextual expressions' (Clark 1992).

Contextual expressions are 'semantically indeterminate'. The extent of indeterminacy in language threatens the standard picture adhered to by most semanticists. According to that picture, 'what is said' is conventionally determined by the meaning of the sentence and the context. Then, and then only, is what the speaker really means 'inferred', if there is reason to think that what the speaker means is distinct from what is said (for example, if the speaker's literal contribution seems conversationally inappropriate and some further assumption is required in order to restore its conformity to conversational norms). As against this, both what is said and what is implied are seen as resulting from guesswork, because of semantic indeterminacy.

The fallback position for semanticists consists in holding that at least the meaning of the sentence-type is 'decoded' and can be read off the meanings of the constituents (as given in the lexicon) and the way they are put together. Decoding stops, and guesswork starts, only when we go from the meaning of the sentence to what the speaker means (this including both what is said and what is conversationally implied). But the fallback position itself has come under attack in the cognitive science literature. The very notion of the linguistic meaning of an expression-type has been questioned.

What is the linguistic meaning of a word? Is it possible to draw a line between 'pure' lexical knowledge and world knowledge? Arguably it is not (Langacker 1987: 154–66). For Langacker, the meaning of a word is a point of access into an essentially encyclopedic network. There is no distinction between 'dictionary' and 'encyclopedia'. A similar idea underlies Rumelhart's claim that interpretation is 'top down' from the bottom up (Rumelhart 1979). According to Rumelhart, what linguistic expressions do is evoke certain 'schemata' in memory. Those memorized schemata are part of our knowledge of the world. Interpretation, whether literal or non-literal,

consists in finding evoked schemata which fit the situation the speaker seems to be talking about.

Langacker and Rumelhart reject not only the dictionary/encyclopedia distinction but also the literal/non-literal distinction as traditionally conceived. They insist that the same cognitive processes are involved in literal and (for example) metaphorical interpretations (see Gibbs 1994; Recanati 1995). A psychologist, Douglas Hintzman, has gone even farther, questioning the most basic distinction: that between the meaning of an expression-type and the contextual meaning of the token. Hintzman has developed a multiple-trace memory model in which the cognitive experiences associated with past tokens of a word interact with the present experience involving a new token of the word to yield the contextual 'meaning' of the latter (Hintzman 1986). Hintzman's model does not appeal to the notion of the literal meaning of the word-type. Words, as expression-types, do not have 'meanings' over and above the collection of token-experiences with which they are associated. The only meaning that words have is that which emerges in context.

Rejecting the three distinctions above – literal/non-literal, dictionary/encyclopedia and type-meaning/token-meaning – amounts to rejecting the semantics/pragmatics distinction. The 'eliminativist' approach to linguistic meaning developed within cognitive science constitutes a return to contextualism, the radical conception of pragmatics associated with ordinary language philosophy (§7). Pragmatics absorbs semantics in a contextualist framework.

See also: STRAWSON, P.F.; WITTGENSTEIN, L.

References and further reading

* Alston, W. (1964) *Philosophy of Language*, Englewood Cliffs, NJ: Prentice Hall. (A textbook in the ordinary language tradition.)
* Austin, J.L. (1950) 'Truth', in *Philosophical Papers*, Oxford: Clarendon Press, 2nd edn, 1971. (Also includes 'Are There A Priori Concepts?' (1939) and 'Other Minds' (1946).)
* —— (1975) *How to Do Things with Words*, Oxford: Clarendon Press, 2nd edn. (Austin's lectures on speech act theory, delivered at Harvard University in 1955.)
* Bach, K. (1987) *Thought and Reference*, Oxford: Clarendon Press. (Discusses a number of pragmatic issues.)
* Bach, K. and Harnish, M. (1979) *Linguistic Communication and Speech Acts*, Cambridge, MA: MIT Press. (Speech act theory within an intentional-inferential framework.)

* Bar-Hillel, Y. (1954) 'Indexical Expressions', in *Aspects of Language*, Jerusalem: Magnes Press, 1970, 69–88. (Classic paper by a disciple of Carnap who was influenced by ordinary language philosophy. The 1970 collection also contains Bar-Hillel's pioneering papers on indexicality, context-dependence and pragmatic implication.)

* Barwise, J. and Perry, J. (1983) *Situations and Attitudes*, Cambridge, MA: MIT Press/Bradford Books. (A semantic theory which takes context-sensitivity seriously.)

* Bühler, K. (1990) *Theory of Language*, trans. D. Goodwin, Amsterdam: Benjamins. (Originally published in 1934, still worth studying.)

* Carston, R. (1988) 'Implicature, Explicature, and Truth-Theoretic Semantics', in R. Kempson (ed.) *Mental Representations: The Interface Between Language and Reality*, Cambridge: Cambridge University Press, 155–81. (On levels of meaning.)

* Clark, H. (1992) *Arenas of Language Use*, Chicago, IL: University of Chicago Press/Center for the Study of Language and Information. (An important collection of papers by a pragmatically-oriented psychologist, most of them written in collaboration. Part 1 concerns the context as 'common ground'; part 3 deals with 'sense creation'.)

* Cohen, P., Morgan, J.L. and Pollack, M. (eds) (1989) *Intentions in Communication*, Cambridge: MA: MIT Press. (Intention recognition and speech acts from a computational point of view.)

* Davidson, D. (1979) 'Moods and Performances', in A. Margalit (ed.) *Meaning and Use*, Dordrecht: Reidel, 1979, 9–20. (How to force pragmatic indications into the mould of truth-conditional semantics.)

* Davis, S. (ed.) (1991) *Pragmatics: A Reader*, New York: Oxford University Press. (A comprehensive collection, where many papers mentioned in this entry can be found. Includes, in particular, Harnish's 'Logical Form and Implicature' (1976), pages 316–64; Heim's 'On the Projection Problem for Presuppositions' (1988), pages 397–405; and Stalnaker's 'Pragmatic Presuppositions' (1974), pages 471–82.)

* Ducrot, O. (1972) *Dire et ne pas dire: principes de sémantique linguistique* (Saying and Not Saying: Principles of Linguistic Semantics), Paris: Hermann. (A speech-act theoretic approach to presupposition; contains insightful discussions of many pragmatic issues.)

* Fodor, J. (1983) *The Modularity of Mind*, Cambridge, MA: MIT Press/Bradford Books. (Distinguishes between input systems and central systems in the human mind.)

* Gardiner, A. (1932) *The Theory of Speech and Language*, Oxford: Clarendon Press. (A remarkable anticipation of speech act theory. Still worth reading.)

* Gazdar, G. (1979) *Pragmatics: Implicature, Presupposition and Logical Form*, New York: Academic Press. (Rigorous work in the formal-semantic tradition.)

* Gibbs, R. (1994) *The Poetics of Mind*, Cambridge: Cambridge University Press. (Argues that the same cognitive processes are at work in literal and non-literal communication.)

* Green, G. (1989) *Pragmatics and Natural Language Understanding*, Hillsdale, NJ: Erlbaum. (An introduction to pragmatics for cognitive scientists.)

* Grice, H.P. (1957) 'Meaning', in *Studies in the Way of Words*, Cambridge: Cambridge University Press, 1989, ch. 14. (Contains the William James Lectures and a collection of papers on the philosophy of language as well as his seminal article of 1957.)

* Grosz, B., Pollack, M. and Sidner, C. (1989) 'Discourse', in M. Posner (ed.) *Foundations of Cognitive Science*, Cambridge, MA: Bradford Books/MIT Press, 437–68. (A survey of computational pragmatics.)

* Hintzman, D. (1986) '"Schema Abstraction" in a Multiple-Trace Memory Model', *Psychological Review* 93 (4): 411–28. (An exemplar model of categorization which has deep implications for semantics and pragmatics.)

* Kamp, H. (1985) 'Context, Thought and Communication', *Proceedings of the Aristotelian Society* 85: 239–61. (An informal presentation of Discourse Representation Theory.)

* Kaplan, D. (1989) 'Demonstratives' and 'Afterthoughts', in J. Almog, H. Wettstein and J. Perry (eds) *Themes from Kaplan*, New York: Oxford University Press, 481–563, 565–614. ('Demonstratives' deals with the logic of indexicals, with 'Afterthoughts' providing further comments.)

* Karttunen, L. (1974) 'Presupposition and Linguistic Context', *Theoretical Linguistics* 1: 181–94. (The third in an important series of papers by Karttunen on presuppositions.)

* Katz, J. (1977) *Propositional Structure and Illocutionary Force*, New York: Crowell. (Semantics, pragmatics and speech act theory.)

* Kempson, R. (1988) 'Grammar and Conversational Principles', in F. Newmeyer (ed.) *Linguistics: The Cambridge Survey*, vol. 2, 139–63. (Redraws the boundary between semantics and pragmatics.)

* Langacker, R. (1987) *Foundations of Cognitive Grammar*, vol. 1, Stanford, CA: Stanford University Press. (A new paradigm, based on the rejection of traditional distinctions, such as syntax/semantics and semantics/pragmatics.)

* Levinson, S. (1983) *Pragmatics*, Cambridge: Cambridge University Press. (The standard textbook.)

* Lewis, D. (1969) *Convention*, Cambridge, MA: Harvard University Press. (Introduces the notion of 'common knowledge'.)

* —— (1970) 'General Semantics', *Synthèse* 22: 18–67. (Section 8 provides a truth-conditional treatment of non-declaratives.)

* —— (1979) 'Scorekeeping in a Language-Game', *Journal of Philosophical Logic* 8: 339–59. (On 'accommodation' and context-change.)

Malinowski, B. (1923) 'The Problem of Meaning in Primitive Languages', supplement to C. Ogden and I.A. Richards, *The Meaning of Meaning*, London: Routledge, 10th edn, 1949, 296–336. (Speech as a mode of social action.)

* Montague, R.M. (1968) 'Pragmatics', in R. Klibansky (ed.) *La Philosophie Contemporaine 1*, Florence: La Nuova Italia Editrice, 102–22. (A classic paper in formal semantics.)

* Morris, C. (1938) *Foundations of the Theory of Signs*, Chicago, IL: University of Chicago Press. (Introduces the famous trichotomy between syntax, semantics and pragmatics. See §8.)

* Recanati, F. (1987) *Meaning and Force: The Pragmatics of Performative Utterances*, Cambridge: Cambridge University Press. (A survey of pragmatics and speech act theory, with special attention to the debate between conventionalist and intentionalist approaches.)

* —— (1993) *Direct Reference: From Language to Thought*, Oxford: Blackwell. (The second part deals with the demarcation between semantics and pragmatics.)

* —— (1995) 'The alleged priority of literal interpretation', *Cognitive Science* 19: 207–32. (Criticizes Grice's sequential model of non-literal interpretation.)

* Rumelhart, D.E. (1979) 'Some problems with the notion of literal meaning', in A. Ortony (ed.) *Metaphor and Thought*, Cambridge: Cambridge University Press, 2nd edn, 1994, 71–82. (An iconoclastic paper. See §16.)

* Schiffer, S. (1972) *Meaning*, Oxford: Clarendon Press. (An important work in the Gricean tradition, introducing the notion of 'mutual knowledge'.)

* Searle, J. (1969) *Speech Acts*, Cambridge: Cambridge University Press. (A systematic theory of speech acts within a conventionalist framework.)

* —— (1978) 'Literal Meaning', in *Expression and Meaning*, Cambridge: Cambridge University Press, 1979, 117–36. (A collection of influential papers on speech act theory. 'Literal Meaning' generalizes context-sensitivity: words have conditions of satisfaction only against a background of assumptions and practices.)

* —— (1983) *Intentionality*, Cambridge: Cambridge University Press. (Chapters 5 and 6 bear on issues such as literal meaning, the 'background', and the role of speaker's intentions.)

* Smith, N. (ed.) (1982) *Mutual Knowledge*, London: Academic Press. (Contains an interesting debate between Clark and Carlson and Sperber and Wilson over mutual knowledge.)

* Sperber, D. (1994) 'Understanding Verbal Understanding', in J. Khalfa (ed.) *What is Intelligence?*, Cambridge: Cambridge University Press, 179–98. (The role of metarepresentations in communication.)

* Sperber, D. and Wilson, D. (1986) *Relevance: Communication and Cognition*, Oxford: Blackwell. (A cognitively oriented theory in the Gricean tradition. See §§14–15.)

* Stalnaker, R. (1970) 'Pragmatics', *Synthèse* 22: 272–89. (A lucid and original survey.)

* —— (1978) 'Assertion', in P. Cole (ed.) *Syntax and Semantics 9: Pragmatics*, New York: Academic Press, 1978, 315–22. (Sketches a theory of speech acts in terms of context-change.)

* Stenius, E. (1967) 'Mood and Language-Game', *Synthèse* 17: 254–74. (Language as a rule-governed activity. See §4.)

* Strawson, P.F. (1950) 'On Referring', in *Logico-Linguistic Papers*, London: Methuen, 1971, 1–27. (On presupposition and the sentence/statement distinction. The collections contains Strawson's most important papers in the philosophy of language.)

* —— (1952) *Introduction to Logical Theory*, London: Methuen. (Insists on the differences between natural and artificial languages.)

* —— (1964) 'Intention and Convention in Speech Acts', in *Logico-Linguistic Papers*, London: Methuen, 1971, 149–69. (A classic of speech act theory. See §13.)

* Travis, C. (1975) *Saying and Understanding*, Oxford: Blackwell. (Emphasizes the context-dependence of sense.)

* —— (1981) *The True and the False: the Domain of the Pragmatic*, Amsterdam: Benjamins. (A case for contextualism.)

* —— (1985) 'On What is Strictly Speaking True', *Canadian Journal of Philosophy* 15: 187–229. (Criticizes Grice's critique of contextualism.)

* Tsohatzidis, S.L. (ed.) (1995) *Foundations of Speech Act Theory: Philosophical and Linguistic Perspectives*, London: Routledge. (A new collection containing original papers on pragmatics and speech act theory.)

* Waismann, F. (1951) 'Verifiability', in A. Flew (ed.) *Logic and Language*, 1st series, Oxford: Blackwell, 17–44. (On 'open texture', by a disciple of Wittgenstein.)
* Wittgenstein, L. (1953) *Philosophical Investigations*, Oxford: Blackwell. (A pragmatic approach to language.)

FRANÇOIS RECANATI

PRAGMATISM

Pragmatism is a philosophical tradition founded by three American philosophers: Charles Sanders Peirce, William James and John Dewey. Starting from Alexander Bain's definition of belief as a rule or habit of action, Peirce argued that the function of inquiry is not to represent reality, but rather to enable us to act more effectively. He was critical of the 'copy theory' of knowledge which had dominated philosophy since the time of Descartes, and especially of the idea of immediate, intuitive self-knowledge. He was also a prophet of the linguistic turn, one of the first philosophers to say that the ability to use signs is essential to thought.

Peirce's use of Bain was extended by James, whose The Principles of Psychology *(1890) broke with the associationism of Locke and Hume. James went on, in* Pragmatism *(1907) to scandalize philosophers by saying that "'The true"... is only the expedient in our way of thinking'. James and Dewey both wanted to reconcile philosophy with Darwin by making human beings' pursuit of the true and the good continuous with the activities of the lower animals – cultural evolution with biological evolution. Dewey criticized the Cartesian notion of the self as a substance which existed prior to language and acculturation, and substituted an account of the self as a product of social practices (an account developed further by George Herbert Mead).*

Dewey, whose primary interests were in cultural, educational and political reform rather than in specifically philosophical problems (problems which he thought usually needed to be dissolved rather than solved), developed the implications of pragmatism for ethics and social philosophy. His ideas were central to American intellectual life throughout the first half of the twentieth century.

All three of the founding pragmatists combined a naturalistic, Darwinian view of human beings with a deep distrust of the problems which philosophy had inherited from Descartes, Hume and Kant. They hoped to save philosophy from metaphysical idealism, but also to save moral and religious ideals from empiricist or positivist scepticism. Their naturalism has been combined with an anti-foundationalist, holist account of meaning by Willard van Orman Quine, Hilary Putnam and Donald Davidson – philosophers of language who are often seen as belonging to the pragmatist tradition. That tradition also has affinities with the work of Thomas Kuhn and the later work of Ludwig Wittgenstein.

1 **Classical pragmatism**
2 **Pragmatism after the linguistic turn**
3 **Pragmatism as anti-representationalism**
4 **Pragmatism and humanity's self-image**

1 Classical pragmatism

Charles Sanders PEIRCE, William JAMES and John DEWEY – often referred to as the three 'classical pragmatists' – had very different philosophical concerns. Except for their shared opposition to the correspondence theory of truth, and to 'copy theories' of knowledge, their doctrines do not overlap extensively (see TRUTH, PRAGMATIC THEORY OF). Although each knew and respected the other two, they did not think of themselves as belonging to an organized, disciplined philosophical movement. Peirce thought of himself as a disciple of Kant, improving on Kant's doctrine of categories and his conception of logic. A practising mathematician and laboratory scientist, he was more interested in these areas of culture than were James or Dewey. James took neither Kant nor Hegel very seriously, but was far more interested in religion than either Peirce or Dewey. Dewey, deeply influenced by Hegel, was fiercely anti-Kantian. Education and politics, rather than science or religion, were at the centre of his thought.

Peirce was a brilliant, cryptic and prolific polymath, whose writings are very difficult to piece together into a coherent system. He is now best known as a pioneer in the theory of signs, and for work in logic and semantics contemporaneous with, and partially paralleling, that of Frege. Peirce's account of inquiry as a matter of practical problem-solving was complemented by his criticisms of the Cartesian (and empiricist) idea of 'immediate knowledge', and of the project of building knowledge on self-evident foundations (of either a rationalist or empiricist kind).

Peirce protested against James' appropriation of his ideas, for complex reasons to do with his obscure and idiosyncratic doctrine of 'Scotistic realism' – the reality of universals, considered as potentialities or dispositions. Peirce was more sympathetic to metaphysical idealism than James, and found James' version of pragmatism simplistic and reductionist. James himself, however, thought of pragmatism as a way of avoiding reductionism of all kinds, and as a counsel of tolerance. Particularly in his famous essay 'The Will to Believe' (1896), he attempted to reconcile science and religion by viewing both as instruments useful for distinct, non-conflicting purposes.

Although he viewed many metaphysical and theological disputes as, at best, exhibitions of the diversity of human temperament, James hoped to construct an alternative to the anti-religious, science-worshipping positivism of his day. He approvingly cited Giovanni Papini's description of pragmatism as 'like a corridor in a hotel. Innumerable chambers open out of it. In one you may find a man writing an atheistic volume; in the next someone on his knees praying for faith; in a third a chemist investigating a body's properties ... they all own the corridor, and all must pass through it'. His point was that attention to the implications of beliefs for practice offered the only way to communicate across divisions between temperaments, academic disciplines and philosophical schools.

Dewey, in his early period, tried to bring Hegel together with evangelical Christianity. Although references to Christianity almost disappear from his writings around 1900, in a 1903 essay on Emerson he still looked forward to the development of 'a philosophy which religion has no call to chide, and which knows its friendship with science and with art'. The anti-positivist strain in classical pragmatism was at least as strong as its anti-metaphysical strain, and so James and Dewey found themselves attacked simultaneously from the empiricist left and from the idealist right – by Bertrand RUSSELL as well as by F.H. BRADLEY. Both critics thought of the pragmatists as fuzzy and jejune thinkers. This sort of criticism was repeated later in the century by the disciples of CARNAP, most of whom dismissed the classical pragmatists as lacking in precision and argumentative rigour.

James wrote a few remarkable essays on ethics – notably 'The Moral Philosopher and the Moral Life' (1891), in which, echoing Mill's *Utilitarianism*, he says that every desire and need has a *prima facie* right to be fulfilled, and that only some competing desire or need can provide a reason to leave it unsatisfied. But neither James nor Peirce attempted any systematic discussion of moral or political philosophy. Dewey, however, wrote extensively in this area throughout his life – from *Outlines of a Critical Theory of Ethics* (1891) to *Human Nature and Conduct* (1922) and *Theory of Valuation* (1939).

Dewey urged that we make no sharp distinction between moral deliberation and proposals for change

in sociopolitical institutions, or in education (the last being a topic on which he wrote extensively, in books which had considerable impact on educational practice in many countries). He saw changes in individual attitudes, in public policies and in strategies of acculturation as three interlinked aspects of the gradual development of freer and more democratic communities, and of the better sort of human being who would develop within such communities. All of Dewey's books are permeated by the typically nine-teenth-century conviction that human history is the story of expanding human freedom and by the hope of substituting a less professionalized, more politically-oriented conception of the philosopher's task for the Platonic conception of the philosopher as 'spectator of time and eternity'.

In *Reconstruction in Philosophy* (1920) he wrote that 'under disguise of dealing with ultimate reality, philosophy has been occupied with the precious values embedded in social traditions... has sprung from a clash of social ends and from a conflict of inherited institutions with incompatible contemporary tendencies'. For him, the task of future philosophy was not to achieve new solutions to traditional problems, but to clarify 'men's ideas as to the social and moral strifes of their own day'. This conception of philosophy, which developed out of Hegel's and resembled Marx's (see HEGEL, G.W.F.; MARX, K.), isolated Dewey (particularly after the rise of analytic philosophy) from colleagues who thought of their discipline as the study of narrower and more precise questions – questions that had remained substantially unchanged throughout human history.

2 Pragmatism after the linguistic turn

Peirce was one of the first philosophers to emphasize the importance of signs. 'The word or the sign which man uses *is* the man himself,' he wrote, '... my language is the sum total of myself; for the man is the thought'. But, with the exception of C.I. LEWIS and Charles Morris, philosophers did not take Peirce's work on signs very seriously. Indeed, for decades Peirce remained largely unread: he had never published a philosophical book, and most of his articles were collected and republished only in the 1930s.

By that time philosophy in the English-speaking world was already in the process of being transformed by admirers of Frege, notably Carnap and Russell. These philosophers accomplished what Gustav Bergmann was to baptize 'the linguistic turn' in philosophy. They thought that it would be more fruitful, more likely to yield clear and convincing results, if philosophers were to discuss the structure of language rather than, as Locke and Kant had, the structure of the mind or of experience. The early analytic philosophers, however, accompanied this turn with a revival of the traditional empiricist idea that sense-perception provides foundations for empirical knowledge – an idea which, at the beginning of the century, the idealists and the classical pragmatists had united in rejecting. These philosophers also insisted on a strict distinction between conceptual questions (the analogue of Kant's 'transcendental' questions), now reinterpreted as questions about the meaning of linguistic expressions, and empirical questions of fact.

It was not until that distinction was questioned by Willard van Orman Quine in his groundbreaking 'Two Dogmas of Empiricism' (1951) that pragmatism was able once again to obtain a hearing (see QUINE, W.V. §8). James and Dewey had been viewed during the heyday of logical positivism as having prefigured the logical positivist's verifiability criterion of empirical meaningfulness, but as unfortunately lacking the powerful analytic tools which the new logic had made available. However, Quine's suggestion that empirical observation of linguistic behaviour could not detect a difference between necessary, analytic truths and contingent, synthetic, yet unquestioned truths helped revive the pragmatists' combination of holism, anti-foundationalism and naturalism.

That suggestion was reinforced by other publications which were roughly simultaneous with Quine's. In *Philosophical Investigations* (1953), Ludwig Wittgenstein mocked the idea that logic is both 'something sublime' and the essence of philosophy, an idea which the younger Wittgenstein had shared with Russell (see WITTGENSTEIN, L. §8). That book also reinvigorated the pragmatists' claim that most philosophical problems should be dissolved rather than solved. Wilfrid Sellars' 'Empiricism and the Philosophy of Mind' (1953) renewed both Peirce's assault on the idea of 'immediate experience' and his claim that the intentionality of the mental is derived from the intentionality of the linguistic, rather than conversely (see SELLARS, W.). In America, this article had the same devastating effect on the notion of 'sense-datum', and thus on the empiricist roots of logical positivism, that J.L. Austin's work was simultaneously having in Britain (see AUSTIN, J.L.). The work of Sellars and Austin conspired to deprive empiricism of the prestige which it had traditionally enjoyed in the Anglophone philosophical world.

Somewhat later, Thomas Kuhn's *The Structure of Scientific Revolutions* (1962) broke the grip of the positivist notion that natural science, because it offered paradigmatically rational methods and procedures, should be imitated by the rest of culture (see KUHN, T.S.). The effect of these various anti-empiricist and anti-positivist writings was to make many post-positivistic analytic philosophers sympathetic to Dewey's suspicions of the Cartesian-Kantian problematic of modern philosophy. Hilary PUTNAM, the best-known contemporary philosopher to identify himself as a pragmatist, has written appreciatively about all three classical pragmatists, praising their refusal to distinguish 'the world as it is in itself' from the world as it appears in the light of human needs and interests.

On Putnam's account, 'the heart of pragmatism ... was the insistence on the agent point of view. If we find that we must take a certain point of view, use a certain "conceptual system", when we are engaged in practical activity... then we must not simultaneously advance the claim that it is not really the way things are in themselves' (1987). Putnam holds that our moral judgments are no more and no less 'objective' than our scientific theories, and no more and no less rationally adopted. He agrees with Dewey that the positivists' attempt to separate 'fact' from 'value' is as hopeless as their pre-Quinean attempt to separate 'fact' from 'language'.

Putnam has also come to the defence of the most notorious and controversial of the classical pragmatists' doctrines: the so-called 'pragmatist theory of truth'. Peirce said 'the opinion which is fated to be ultimately agreed to by all who investigate is what we mean by the truth, and the object represented in this opinion is the real'. Putnam has revived this idea, arguing that even if we cannot follow Peirce in *defining* 'true' as 'idealized rational assertibility', the latter notion is, as a regulative ideal, inseparable from an understanding of the concept of truth. He has criticized the correspondence theory of truth by arguing that any such correspondence of a belief to reality can only be to reality under a particular description, and that no such description is ontologically or epistemologically privileged. Putnam follows Nelson GOODMAN in saying that 'there is no one Way the World Is'.

3 Pragmatism as anti-representationalism

Putnam is chary, however, of endorsing James' claim that '"The true"... is only the expedient in the way of our thinking, as "the right" is only the expedient in our way of behaving'. That formulation was attacked by James' contemporaries as at worst an invitation to self-deception, and at best a confusion of truth with justifiability. Dewey tried to avoid the controversy by ceasing to use the word 'truth', and speaking instead of 'warranted assertibility'. But this did not shield him from charges of confusion and inconsistency. Russell, reviewing Dewey, said that 'there is a profound instinct in me which is repelled by [Dewey's] instrumentalism: the instinct of contemplation, and of escape from one's own personality'. He and many other critics complained that pragmatism is unable to take account of the eternity and absoluteness of truth – of the fact that a sentence that contains no demonstratives is, if true, true in utter independence of changes in human needs or purposes. Putnam's treatment of truth is designed to avoid the appearance of relativism, and to escape such strictures as Russell's.

Despite its paradoxical air and its apparent relativism, however, James' claim does bring out pragmatism's strongest point: its refusal to countenance a discontinuity between human abilities and those of other animals. Pragmatists are committed to taking Darwin seriously. They grant that human beings are unique in the animal kingdom in having language, but they urge that language be understood as a tool rather than as a picture. A species' gradual development of language is as readily explicable in Darwinian terms as its gradual development of spears or pots, but it is harder to explain how a species could have acquired the ability to *represent* the universe – especially the universe as it really is (as opposed to how it is usefully described, relative to the particular needs of that species).

In a weak sense of 'represent', of course, an earthworm or a thermostat can be said to contain 'representations of the environment', since there are internal arrangements in both which are responsible for the reactions of each to certain stimuli. But it makes little sense to ask whether those representations are *accurate*. Philosophers who take epistemological scepticism seriously (as pragmatists do not) have employed a stronger sense of 'representation', one in which it does make sense to ask whether the way in which it best suits human purposes to describe the universe is an accurate representation of the universe as it is in itself (see SCEPTICISM).

The idea that knowledge is accurate representation and the idea that reality has an intrinsic nature are inseparable, and pragmatists reject both. In rejecting these ideas pragmatists are rejecting the problematic of realism and antirealism – the question of whether there is or is not a 'matter of fact' about, for example, mathematics or ethics, whether beliefs in these areas are attempts to correspond to reality. Whatever may be said about truth, pragmatists insist, we cannot make sense of the notion of 'correspondence', nor of that of 'accurate representation of the way things are in themselves' (see TRUTH, CORRESPONDENCE THEORY OF).

Donald DAVIDSON is the philosopher of language whose work is most reminiscent of the classical pragmatists' attempts to be faithful to Darwin.

Davidson has said that 'Beliefs are true or false, but they represent nothing. It is good to be rid of representations, and with them the correspondence theory of truth, for it is thinking that there are representations that engenders thoughts of relativism' (1989). He has argued that we need to get rid of what he calls 'the third dogma of empiricism', the distinction between the mind or language as organizing scheme, and something else (for example, the sensible manifold, the world) as organized content – the Kantian version of the dualism of subject and object (1974). In 'A Nice Derangement of Epitaphs' (1986), an attempt to radicalize and extend Quine's naturalistic approach to the study of linguistic behaviour, he has suggested that we 'erase the boundary between knowing a language and knowing our way about in the world generally', and that 'there is no such thing as a language, not if a language is anything like what many philosophers and linguists have supposed'.

Davidson does not wish to be called a pragmatist, however, since he equates pragmatism with unfeasible attempts to reduce truth to some form of assertibility, thereby making it an epistemic concept, rather than a merely semantic one. Unlike Peirce and Putnam, Davidson thinks that we should treat 'true' as a primitive term, and should neither attempt to revitalize the correspondence theory of truth nor replace it with a better theory of truth. Davidson's strategy is summed up in his recommendation that we not say 'that truth is correspondence, coherence, warranted assertibility, ideally justified assertibility, what is accepted in the conversation of the right people, what science will end up maintaining, what explains the convergence on single theories in science, or the success of our ordinary beliefs' (1990). We should, he says in the same article, not offer an analysis of the meaning of 'true', but rather confine ourselves to describing 'the ultimate source of both objectivity and communication', namely, 'the triangle that, by relating speaker, interpreter and the world determines the contents of thought and speech'. The trouble with the correspondence theory, on Davidson's view, is that it cuts out the 'interpreter' side of the triangle, and treats truth as relation of 'matching' between speaker and world.

If one follows Davidson's advice, one can give up the pragmatist theory of truth without giving up the Darwinian naturalism which that theory was a paradoxical-sounding attempt to articulate. Such naturalism, however, entails an abandonment of much of the problematic of contemporary philosophy. If truth is never the name of a relation ('corresponding', 'representing', 'getting right', 'fitting') which holds between sentences and non-sentences, there is no point in asking whether this relation holds for some true sentences (for example, perceptual reports or scientific theories) and not for others (for example, sentences about numbers or values). On this latter point, Putnam and Davidson are in agreement (see TRUTH, CORRESPONDENCE THEORY OF).

Michael DUMMETT has suggested, plausibly, that the problematic of realism and antirealism is at the heart of the Western philosophical tradition (see REALISM AND ANTIREALISM). If he is right, and if Davidson is right in thinking that we should now abandon that problematic, then James' and Dewey's suggestions about how to end the traditional and seemingly sterile quarrels between materialists and idealists, positivists and metaphysicians, theists and atheists, science-worshippers and poetry-worshippers look more promising. The heart of both men's pragmatism was not any particular doctrine about the nature of truth, of knowledge, or of value, but rather the hope that philosophy could renew itself by moving out from under traditional dualisms (subject–object, mind–world, theory–practice, morality–prudence) which recent science and recent social changes had, they believed, rendered obsolete.

The classical pragmatists saw themselves as responding to Darwin in the same way as the great philosophers of the seventeenth and eighteenth centuries had responded to Galileo and Newton. Philosophers such as Descartes, Locke and Kant attempted to accommodate old, precious, moral and spiritual aspirations to new scientific developments. James and Dewey thought that these attempts had been made obsolete by Darwin's new account of the origin of our species, and that fresh attempts were needed. If one reads Quine's and Davidson's naturalization of semantics as a continuation of philosophy's attempt to come to terms with Darwin, one can also read these two philosophers as continuing the larger enterprise which James and Dewey inaugurated.

4 Pragmatism and humanity's self-image

By stepping back from its relation to traditional empiricism on the one hand and to the linguistic turn on the other, one can put pragmatism in a larger context. Much twentieth-century philosophy has been devoted to a criticism of the view, shared by Plato and Aristotle, that a capacity to know things as they really are is central to being human. Philosophers influenced by Nietzsche – notably Heidegger, SARTRE and DERRIDA – have argued against the idea that cognition is the distinctively human capacity. Heidegger's treatment of inquiry as a species of coping, in his discussion of *Vorhandenheit* in *Being and Time* (1927), has much in common with Dewey's and Kuhn's attempts to see scientific progress as problem-solving

– as the overcoming of obstacles to the satisfaction of human needs, rather than as convergence towards a special, specifically cognitive, relation to reality. Both Dewey and Heidegger saw the Greek quest for certainty as debilitating. Neither granted the traditional assumption that, in addition to all the other needs human beings have, there is a need to know the truth (see HEIDEGGER, M.).

Heidegger's criticism of what he called 'onto-theology' – Western philosophy viewed as a series of attempts to find solace and support in the non-temporal – has much in common with Dewey's criticism of what he called 'intellectualism'. Both of these men saw the tradition which begins with Plato as a self-deceptive attempt to give the eternal priority over the temporal. So did BERGSON and WHITEHEAD, the founders of the tradition known as 'process philosophy', a tradition to which James (especially in his *Essays in Radical Empiricism*) made important contributions (see PROCESS PHILOSOPHY). This downgrading of the eternal is characteristic of a great deal of twentieth-century philosophy. It is found in James' criticisms of Bradley, in Putnam's criticism of Bernard Williams' claim that we can use an 'absolute conception of the world' as a regulative ideal of inquiry, in Heidegger's criticism of Husserl, and in Derrida's criticism of Heidegger.

Downgrading eternity means downgrading both the idea of truth as eternal and the assumption that knowledge of eternal truth is the distinctively human activity. From a Davidsonian, as from a Deweyan, point of view, the only point of the doctrine that truth is eternal is to contrast truth with justification (which is obviously neither eternal nor absolute, because it is relative to the composition of the audience to which justification is offered, and thus to historical circumstance). But that contrast can be formulated without treating 'truth' as the name of a goal to be reached, or of an object to be admired. Davidson's treatment of truth forbids us to think of inquiry as subject to a norm of acquiring true beliefs, in addition to the norm of providing adequate justification. There is no way to seek for truth apart from seeking for justification. Justification gets better as the community to which justification is offered becomes more sophisticated and complex, more aware of possible sources of evidence and more capable of dreaming up imaginative new hypotheses and proposals. So pragmatists place the capacity to create complex and imaginative communities at the centre of their image of humanity, superseding the ability to know. Dewey and Putnam agree that the aim of inquiry is what Putnam calls 'human flourishing' – the kind of human life which is possible in free, democratic, tolerant, egalitarian societies. These are the societies in which the arts and the sciences proliferate and progress, and within which idiosyncrasy is tolerated.

The obvious difference between James, Dewey and Putnam on the one hand and Nietzsche, Heidegger and Foucault on the other – between the two most prominent sections of the twentieth-century revolt against the Greek self-image of humanity – is that these three Europeans do not share the Americans' enthusiasm for, and optimism about, liberal-democratic society. Nietzsche's, and the early Heidegger's, insistence on the resolute authenticity of the lonely individual, and their exaltation of will as opposed to intellect, are equally foreign to Dewey and to Putnam (though they have some echoes in certain passages of James). Rather than replace intellect by will, in the manner of SCHOPENHAUER, pragmatists tend to replace knowledge by love, in the manner of Kierkegaard's contrast between Socrates and Christ (see KIERKEGAARD, S.A.).

For Dewey, the pragmatist who speculated most daringly, and developed the greatest historical self-consciousness, the glory of human beings is their ability to become citizens of a liberal-democratic society, of a community which constantly strives to see beyond its own limits – both with an eye to the inclusion of presently excluded or marginalized human beings and with respect to innovative intellectual and artistic initiatives. This is the capacity which most clearly sets us apart from other animals. It presupposes, of course, the capacity to use language, but for Dewey the point of having language, and therefore thought, was not to penetrate through the appearances to the true nature of reality, but rather to permit the social construction of new realities. For him, language was not a medium of representation, but a way of coordinating human activities so as to enlarge the range of human possibilities. These processes of coordination and enlargement, which make up cultural evolution, do not have a destined terminus called the Good or the True, any more than biological evolution has a destined terminus called The Ideal Life-Form. Dewey's imagery is always of proliferating novelty, rather than of convergence.

The naturalist strain in pragmatism, the attempt to come to terms with Darwin, is thus from a Deweyan point of view important mainly as a further strategy for shifting philosophers' attention from the problems of metaphysics and epistemology to the needs of democratic politics. Dewey once said that he agreed with Plato that politics was 'the science of the whole', a remark which summarized the following train of reasoning. Finding out what there is is a matter of finding out what descriptions of things will best fulfil our needs. Finding out what needs we should fulfil is a task for communal reflection about what human beings might become. Such cooperative inquiry into the possibilities of self-transcendence is best accomplished within a democratic society. So philosophers should stop asking about the nature of reality or of knowledge, and instead try to strengthen and improve the institutions of such societies by clarifying 'men's ideas as to the social and moral strifes of their own day'.

See also: DARWIN, C.; DOUBT; EMPIRICISM; LOGICAL POSITIVISM; PRAGMATISM IN ETHICS; SCIENTIFIC REALISM AND ANTIREALISM

References and further reading

Ayer, A.J. (1968) *The Origins of Pragmatism: Studies in the Philosophy of Charles Sanders Peirce and William James*, San Francisco, CA: Freeman, Cooper & Co. (A somewhat unsympathetic examination, by a disciple of Carnap, of selected aspects of classical pragmatism.)

Brandom, R. (1994) *Making It Explicit: Reasoning, Representing and Discursive Commitment*, Cambridge, MA: Harvard University Press, 1994. (Chapter 1 sketches the similarities between the pragmatist view of meaning and Wittgenstein's. Chapter 5 contains a strikingly original reinterpretation of the point of pragmatist theories of truth, and the formulation of a new theory along similar lines.)

* Davidson, D. (1986) 'A Nice Derangement of Epitaphs' in E. LePore (ed.) *Truth and Interpretation: Perspectives on the Philosophy of Donald Davidson*, Oxford: Blackwell, 433–46. (Attacks the idea that a language is a set of conventions, or something possessing an isolable structure. See the responses to this essay by Michael Dummett and Ian Hacking, in the same volume.)

* —— (1974) 'On the Very Idea of a Conceptual Scheme', repr. in *Inquiries into Truth and Interpretation*, Oxford: Oxford University Press, 1984. (Attacks 'the third, and perhaps last, dogma of empiricism: the distinction between scheme and content'.)

* —— (1989) 'The Myth of the Subjective' in M. Krausz (ed.) *Relativism: Interpretation and Confrontation*, Notre Dame, IN: University of Notre Dame Press, 159–72. (A criticism of the subject-object analysis of knowledge.)

* —— (1990) 'The Structure and Content of Truth', *Journal of Philosophy* 87: 279–28. (Argues that 'triangulation' between speaker, audience and world is required for intentionality.)

* Dewey, J. (1882–1953) *The Early Works, The Middle Works, The Later Works*, Carbondale, IL: Southern

Illinois University Press, 1969–90. (Dewey's view of the nature and function of philosophy is best summarized in *Reconstruction in Philosophy* (1920; vol. 12 of *The Middle Works*), his ethical views are most fully laid out in *Human Nature and Conduct* (1922; vol. 14 of *The Middle Works*) and his understanding of democracy in *The Public and Its Problems* (1927; vol. 2 of *The Later Works*).)

* —— (1903) 'Emerson – the Philosopher of Democracy', *The Middle Works*, vol. 3, 184–92. (This essay of 1909 describes Emerson as 'the first and as yet almost the only Christian of the Intellect'.)

Diggins, J.P. (1994) *The Promise of Pragmatism: Modernism and the Crisis of Knowledge and Authority*, Chicago, IL: University of Chicago Press. (A survey of uses of, and reactions to, the classical pragmatists' thought by twentieth-century social and cultural critics in the US.)

* James, W. (1890) *The Principles of Psychology*, Cambridge, MA: Harvard University Press, 1981. (James said that this thousand-page treatise, originally published in 1890, 'rejects both the associationist and the spiritualist theories [of mental functioning]'.)

* —— (1897) *The Will to Believe and Other Essays In Popular Philosophy*, Cambridge, MA: Harvard University Press, 1979. (The title essay (1896) defends the right to be religious in despite of science, and is James' best-known and most controversial publication. This volume also includes 'The Moral Philosopher and the Moral Life', which argues for 'the impossibility of an abstract system of ethics'.)

* —— (1907, 1909) *Pragmatism and The Meaning of Truth*, Cambridge, MA: Harvard University Press, 1979; reprint of two books in one volume. (*Pragmatism* (1907) is the classic statement of James' overall philosophical outlook. The essays collected in *The Meaning of Truth* (1909) – of which 'Humanism and Truth' and 'The Pragmatist Theory of Truth and its Misunderstanders' are the most incisive – defend his pragmatic theory of truth against its critics.)

* —— (1912) *Essays in Radical Empiricism*, Cambridge, MA: Harvard University Press, 1976. (Defends a kind of neutral monism, especially in the essays 'Does "Consciousness" Exist?' and 'A World of Pure Experience'.)

* Kuhn, T.S. (1962) *The Structure of Scientific Revolutions*, Chicago, IL: University of Chicago Press. (Initiated the reaction against the attempt to isolate a 'scientific method' which differentiated science from other areas of culture.)

Lewis, C.I. (1923) 'A Pragmatic Conception of the A Priori', *Journal of Philosophy* 20: 169–77. (A very influential article, which attempted to blend classical pragmatism with Kant. Lewis acted as intermediary between classical pragmatism and logical empiricism.)

Murphy, J.P. (1990) *Pragmatism: From Peirce to Davidson*, Boulder, CO: Westview Press. (An introductory textbook. Murphy sees Quine and Davidson as continuing the pragmatist tradition. Contains a substantial bibliography.)

Okrent, M. (1988) *Heidegger's Pragmatism*, Ithaca, NY, and London: Cornell University Press. (Part One of this book discusses sections 12–24 of *Being and Time*, in which Heidegger's anti-Cartesian arguments parallel those of the classical pragmatists.)

* Quine, W.V. (1951) 'Two Dogmas of Empiricism' in *From a Logical Point of View*, Cambridge, MA: Harvard University Press, 1953. (A groundbreaking essay which initiated the 'post-positivistic' period of analytic philosophy.)

* Peirce, C.S. (1934) *Pragmatism and Pragmaticism*, vol. 5 of *Collected Papers*, ed. C. Hartshorne and P. Weiss, Cambridge, MA: Harvard University Press. (See especially the anti-Cartesian polemic in 'Questions Concerning Certain Faculties Claimed for Man' (1868) and 'Some Consequences of Four Incapacities' (1868), and also the first explicit formulation of Peirce's pragmatism in 'How to Make our Ideas Clear' (1878). A new edition of Peirce's papers is now in preparation.)

Putnam, H. (1981) *Reason, Truth and History*, Cambridge: Cambridge University Press. (Chapter 8, 'The impact of science on modern conceptions of rationality', is an important statement of pragmatism's criticisms of logical empiricism.)

* —— (1987) *The Many Faces of Pragmatism*, La Salle, IL: Open Court, 83. (Collects essays in which Putnam offers pragmatist solutions of various problems.)

—— (1990) *Realism with a Human Face*, Cambridge, MA: Harvard University Press. (A collection of essays, replying to critics of pragmatism, and relating Putnam's own work to James', Dewey's, and Goodman's.)

—— (1992) *Renewing Philosophy*, Cambridge, MA: Harvard University Press. (Chapter 5, 'Bernard Williams and the absolute conception of the world' criticizes the notion of a description of reality which abstracts from human needs and interests.)

Rorty, R. (1991) *Objectivity, Relativism and Truth*, Cambridge: Cambridge University Press. (Part II of this book tries to fit Davidson's work into the pragmatist tradition by emphasizing his anti-representationalism.)

Saatkamp, H.J., Jr (ed.) (1995) *Rorty and the Pragmatists*, Nashville, TN: Vanderbilt University Press. (Includes five essays arguing that Rorty misreads and distorts both the classical pragmatists and Davidson, and Rorty's replies.)

Scheffler, I. (1974) *Four Pragmatists: A Critical Introduction to Peirce, James, Mead and Dewey*, London: Routledge & Kegan Paul. (Combines sympathetic presentation with detailed criticism.)

* Sellars, W. (1953) 'Empiricism and the Philosophy of Mind', in *Science, Perception and Reality*, London: Routledge & Kegan Paul, 1956. (Argues against the 'Myth of the Given' and for the claim that 'all awareness is a linguistic affair'.)

Smith, J.E. (1984) *Purpose and Thought: The Meaning of Pragmatism*, Chicago, IL: University of Chicago Press. (Emphasizes the classical pragmatists' anti-atomistic conceptions of the nature of experience.)

Thayer, H.S. (1968) *Meaning and Action: A Critical History of Pragmatism*, Indianapolis, IN: Bobbs-Merrill. (The most comprehensive history, containing material on C.I. Lewis, F.C.S. Schiller, G.H. Mead, and others, as well as on Peirce, James and Dewey.)

West, C. (1989) *The American Evasion of Philosophy: A Genealogy of Pragmatism*, Madison, WI: University of Wisconsin Press. (Puts pragmatism in the context of American intellectual life, with special reference to Emerson and to leftist politics.)

White, M.G. (1954) *Towards Reunion in Philosophy*, Cambridge, MA: Harvard University Press. (Treats pragmatism as a corrective to logical positivism.)

* Wittgenstein, L. (1953) *Philosophical Investigations*, Oxford: Blackwell. (Argues for a therapeutic approach to traditional philosophical problems, and against the Cartesian notion of immediate self-awareness.)

RICHARD RORTY

PRAGMATISM IN ETHICS

Two components of the pragmatist outlook shape its ethical philosophy. It rejects certainty as a legitimate intellectual goal; this generates a nondogmatic attitude to moral precepts and principles. It holds, secondly, that thought (even that exercised in scientific inquiry) is essentially goal-directed in a way that makes the refinement of the control we exercise over how we act (for example, in drawing conclusions) integral to achieving any cognitive goal such as that of truth. This makes it possible to treat scientific inquiry as a model of how we might respond to moral problems and the

reasonableness and impartiality required of a scientific inquirer as a paradigm of what may be expected in reaching moral judgments. This view of the nature of thought also inclines pragmatists to assess proposed solutions to moral conflicts in terms of consequences. But although human desires are taken as the raw material with which moral thinking must deal, it is not assumed that people's desires (what they take pleasure in) are fixed and can be used as a standard by which to assess consequences. Pragmatism is thus free to revert to a classical mode of thought (such as Aristotelianism) in which claims about human nature function as norms – a use which is made, for example, of the claim that humans are essentially social creatures.

1 **James: Fallibilism**
2 **Peirce: Reasonableness**
3 **Dewey: Consequentialism**
4 **Mead: Sociality**

1 James: Fallibilism

In 'Philosophical Conceptions and Practical Results' (1898), William JAMES drew the attention of the public to a distinctive philosophic outlook which C.S. Peirce had begun to articulate in published articles twenty years earlier. Pragmatism, as Peirce had come to label his doctrines, located truth and reality at the limit of an indefinitely prolonged process of inquiry and insisted that nothing on this side of that limit could be known with absolute certainty – an argument known as 'fallibilism' (see FALLIBILISM). Pragmatism had the effect of undermining any claim to absolute and final cognitive authority.

James had already applied this attitude to 'ethical science' in an address, 'The Moral Philosopher and the Moral Life' (1891). Here James insisted that, as in 'physical science', we should be ready to revise from day to day the basis on which we measure and compare various goods and ills; 'no philosophy of ethics is possible in the old-fashioned absolutist sense of the term' (1891: 208). Ethical science could not in James' view aspire to delineate 'any abstract moral "nature of things" existing antecedently to the concrete thinkers themselves' (193). Good and ill were brought into the world by the feelings and opinions of conscious beings (190–1); obligation arose through the claims such beings made on one another (194); and in the best world imaginable '*every* demand' would be 'gratified as soon as made' (202; original emphasis).

As this is clearly not possible in the world in which we live, the task is to 'satisfy at all times *as many demands as we can*' (205; original emphasis). This task is carried out, however imperfectly, by following custom and judging by what is conventionally recognized as good. But although in cases of conflict there is a presumption in favour of what any given society has discovered to be a viable relative equilibrium – discoveries indeed 'quite analogous to those of science' (205) – it was clear to James 'that there is nothing final in any actually given equilibrium of human ideals' (206). ''Rules are made for man, not man for rules'' (James quoting T.H. Green, 206) and 'the *highest* ethical life... consists at all times in the breaking of rules which have grown too narrow for the actual case' (209; original emphasis).

To anyone who believes ethical principles are independent of human desire, perhaps even independent of God's will, this position would appear very radical. James however moved to keep his position within prevailing attitudes concerning the importance of religion to morality by declaring that God's standing as a conscious being with extraordinary attributes gave his demands a special importance in the project of 'satisfying as many demands as we can'. Even unbelievers have to recognize how belief in God inclines a person to adopt a 'strenuous mood' towards the realization of ideals; 'in a merely human world without a God, the appeal to our moral energy falls short of its maximal stimulating power' (212). James moreover hedged his radical stance on two sides. Ethical scepticism was not to be regarded as 'being one possible fruit of ethical philosophizing' (184) (see MORAL SCEPTICISM). To give up the task of weaving conflicting demands into a more satisfactory system was to renounce moral philosophy. On the other hand it is incumbent on those who undertake philosophical reflection on moral principles not to apply a 'wayward personal standard' but to 'throw [their] own spontaneous ideals, even the dearest, impartially in with that total mass of ideals which are fairly to be judged' (199).

2 Peirce: Reasonableness

That we might impartially undertake the project of achieving 'ethical unity' – especially while acknowledging that the universe cannot be called upon to underwrite the hope that there is one correct outcome – is a notion that faces considerable resistance. It is particularly unappealing for anyone who holds that impartiality involves the kind of objectivity that consists in making thought conform to something antecedent to, and independent of, all thought and desire. The further suggestion that this project might have an intellectual standing comparable to that of natural science appears in this light (that of twentieth-century scientific realism) quite bizarre. In the nineteenth century, however, when it was not uncommon to regard the goal of natural scientists as

consisting in an ideal refinement of (human) scientific thought rather than in the conformity of thought to an independent object, these suggestions appeared less strange (see SCIENTIFIC REALISM AND ANTI-REALISM §1).

It was in the context of such an outlook that C.S. PEIRCE first formulated his views on truth and reality. In an 1871 review of an edition of the works of Berkeley, Peirce distinguished two accounts of 'the real'. The first was a 'thing out[side] of the mind which directly influences sensation, and through sensation thought'; the second was what would be represented in thought if we were to prolong indefinitely the process of removing from our thought any 'arbitrary, accidental element, dependent on the limitations in circumstances, power and bent of the individual; an[y] element of error, in short' (1958: 8.12). As Peirce's thought developed he gave considerable attention to the problem of explaining how experience should constrain this development without capitulating to the first of the above views.

It might have been interesting had Peirce considered what would be involved in refining desires or demands (individuals' perceptions of their interests) through a process of inquiry, and how this project should be constrained by experience. Peirce, however, devoted little attention to the place of ethics in relation to other intellectual endeavours until the final period of his life, by which time James had made Peirce's brainchild, pragmatism, a topic of widespread and lively controversy. In papers written after 1900 (see 1958: 1.573–677) Peirce placed the values and motives that should inform inquiry in the context of wider claims, 'The only desirable object which is quite satisfactory in itself without any ulterior reason for desiring it, is the reasonable itself' (1958: 8.140), and he speculated that 'there is an energizing reasonableness that shapes phenomena in some sense... and has moulded the reason of man into something like its own image' (1966: 291). Peirce also stressed that his own primary field of endeavour, logic, which he conceived broadly as including scientific methodology, was a 'normative science'. This meant that its principles were to guide the activity of deliberate thinking (especially that in natural science) in the way that ethical principles guided action. 'I regard Logic as the Ethics of the Intellect' (1966: 415); 'logic is only an application of morality', he wrote to Lady Welby in 1908–9 (1966: 406).

3 Dewey: Consequentialism

Peirce's conception of thought as a form of human conduct was, along with fallibilism, a central feature of the outlook of those who identified themselves as pragmatists during its initial period. This conception moreover functioned within a general view of mental activity as essentially goal-directed. In his *Principles of Psychology* (1890), James had taken '*the pursuance of future ends and the choice of means for their attainment [to be] the mark and criterion of the presence of mentality in a phenomenon*' (8; original emphasis) and treated a concept in general as 'really nothing but a teleological instrument' (482). During the 1890s, under the acknowledged influence of James, John DEWEY developed a position which he called 'instrumentalism' and which he was content to have identified as a form of pragmatism once there emerged a movement of that name.

Dewey's instrumentalism began with James' view, that representations (such as symbols, concepts and statements) should be treated as instruments and assessed relative to the purposes which they served, and developed from this a general account of problem-solving which characterized the aim of inquiry not in terms of discovering truth but in terms of unifying a discordant situation. The fullest version of this account is found in the sixth chapter of Dewey's *Logic: The Theory of Inquiry* (1938). This account of inquiry not only had the effect of insisting that theoretical questions be located in practical contexts, but was framed (some scholars believe primarily framed) with moral problems in mind. What James describes as the ideal resolution to a moral conflict, ('*Invent some manner* of realizing your own ideal which will also satisfy the alien demands' (1891: 205)) was for Dewey a better paradigm of the imperative of inquiry than 'Find out what is the case'.

It is important, however, to qualify this, for Dewey acknowledged to a greater extent than did James that the best resolution of a practical problem may lie in the modification of one's demands. Dewey stressed how much of moral education, as well as how much of the aim of moral reflection, consisted in making people mindful of the consequences of their conduct for themselves and for other people. The difference between 'reasonable and unreasonable desires and interests' (1939: 217) and that between the 'desirable' and the 'desired' (219) consists for Dewey in the extent to which a desire is informed by an understanding of the consequences of having it satisfied. Moral psychology commonly proceeds on the assumption that our desires are given and fixed, but 'nothing more contrary to common sense can be imagined than the notion that we are incapable of changing our desires and interests by means of learning what the consequence of acting upon them are' (218).

As a result of this outlook Dewey argued that moral thinking and thinking about values in general

is structured exhaustively by the relations of means-ends and means-consequences; and he moved to subvert the widely accepted distinctions between final and instrumental values and intrinsic and extrinsic goods (1938: 214). No means adopted to achieve an end is so completely extrinsic to the experience of the people who use it that its contribution to their lives may be ignored. Nothing is so valuable in and of itself that the consequences of realizing it (including especially the consequences of whatever means are adopted towards its realization) do not need to be carefully weighed. The doctrine that there are purely final ends was for Dewey a projection of the belief that there are desires which may be taken as original and unalterable.

The claim that nothing should be regarded as a final end was intended by Dewey to prevent any component or aspect of human life from being sought in isolation from its bearing on the rest of experience. The notion of a final end also applies, however, to global features of the totality of human endeavours. One pattern of choices of means to realize our natural impulses might require more cooperative activities and move us towards greater social dependence on one another; another might require more self-reliance and move us towards less integrated ways of living with one another. Either of these global outcomes might appeal to people as final ends or intrinsic values. Questions that may be framed when the notion of final end is used in this sense can be avoided only if Dewey has some basis for thinking that a complete working out of all the means available to pursue our partially thought-out impulses, together with a complete working out of the consequences of each of the means we might adopt, will leave us with precisely one global option. Dewey did not argue explicitly for this conclusion but at the same time he did not hesitate to endorse the value of shared experience (1925: 157), and the ideal of community, as supreme (1927: 325–50).

4 Mead: Sociality

Important aspects of Dewey's philosophy were undeniably shaped by his relationship with his friend and sometime colleague George Herbert MEAD. Mead developed a theory of the formation of the self and of rational thought which stressed the dependence of both on human sociality. What emerges in Mead's ethical writings is a more explicit acknowledgement than is made by Dewey that moral choices ultimately have to be assessed relative to a claim, at once factual and normative, about human nature. 'As human nature is essentially social in character, moral ends must be also social in their nature' (Mead 1934:

385). Dewey and Mead both wrote of the modification of desire as part of what was involved in developing a larger (broader) as opposed to a narrower self; 'the matter of selfishness is the setting-up of a narrow self over against a larger self' (1934: 388; compare Dewey and Tufts 1932: 302). But it was Mead who grounded the preference for the larger self in the claim about human nature. 'The escape from selfishness is not by the Kantian road of an emotional response to the abstract universal, but by the recognition of the genuinely social character of human nature' (1964: 220).

On this basis Dewey and Mead both identified themselves with movements for social reform, and Dewey achieved a degree of prominence in public life as a spokesman for a variety of causes on what was perceived as the left of American politics. As Dewey moved more into public life, logical positivism came to eclipse the influence of pragmatism in American universities. Positivism insinuated the view that truth and objectivity consist in the conformity of thought to an independent and antecedently existing reality (see LOGICAL POSITIVISM §1). Ethical scepticism became a live philosophic option and was promoted via the claim that statements expressing moral judgments could be nothing more than expressions of subjective feeling (see EMOTIVISM; MORAL SCEPTICISM §3). Even after the vogue for positivism waned, pragmatism remained unfashionable until about 1980 when it enjoyed a modest revival under the influence of Richard RORTY. 'Neo-pragmatism' has yet to define its position on matters of ethical theory, but its tendency to stress the values of individual and private, as opposed to communal and public, life suggests that its position is likely to represent a considerable departure at least from the pragmatism of Dewey and Mead.

See also: AXIOLOGY; PRAGMATISM

References and further reading

* Dewey, J. (1925) *Experience and Nature*, Chicago, IL, and London: Open Court; repr. in *John Dewey: The Later Works 1925–1953*, ed. J.A. Boydston, Carbondale, IL: Southern Illinois University Press, 1981–90, vol. 1. (A mature comprehensive statement of Dewey's philosophy.)

* —— (1927) *The Public and Its Problems*, New York: Holt; repr. in *John Dewey: The Later Works 1925–1953*, ed. J.A. Boydston, Carbondale, IL: Southern Illinois University Press, 1981–90, vol. 2. (The central text for Dewey's political theory.)

* —— (1938) *Logic: The Theory of Inquiry*, New York: Holt; repr. in *John Dewey: The Later Works 1925–1953*, ed. J.A. Boydston, Carbondale, IL: Southern Illinois University Press, 1981–90, vol. 12. (Dewey's attempt to develop a logical theory where thought is conceived of as constrained by the need to resolve some kind of difficulty.)

* —— (1939) 'The Theory of Valuation', in *Encyclopedia of Unified Science*, vol. II, Chicago, IL: University of Chicago Press; repr. in *John Dewey: The Later Works 1925–1953*, ed. J.A. Boydston, Carbondale, IL: Southern Illinois University Press, 1981–90, vol. 13. (A monograph arguing against emotivism and similar positivist trends.)

* Dewey, J. and Tufts, J. (1932) *Ethics*, New York: Holt; repr. in *John Dewey: The Later Works 1925–1953*, ed. J.A. Boydston, Carbondale, IL: Southern Illinois University Press, 1981–90, vol. 7. (A popular textbook which gives an account of the values of the moral life.)

Feffer, A. (1993) *Chicago Pragmatism and American Progressivism*, Ithaca, NY: Cornell University Press. (Places the thought of Dewey and Mead in its historical context.)

Gouinlock, J. (1972) *John Dewey's Philosophy of Value*, New York: Humanities Press. (Comprehensive philosophical background to Dewey's general ethical theory.)

* James, W. (1890) *The Principles of Psychology*, vol. 1, New York: Dover, 1950. (The basis of the philosophical psychology used by James, Dewey and Mead.)

* —— (1891) 'The Moral Philosopher and the Moral Life', in *The Will to Believe and Other Essays on Popular Philosophy*, New York: Dover, 1956, 184–215. (James' single most sustained treatment of ethics.)

* —— (1898) 'Philosophical Conceptions and Practical Results', *University Chronicle*, Berkeley, CA: University of California Press; repr. in *Collected Essays and Reviews*, ed. R.B. Perry, New York: Longmans, Green, 1920, 406–37. (The lecture in which James, in discussing and applying Peirce's ideas, launched pragmatism as a philosophical movement.)

Joas, H. (1985) *G.H. Mead: A Contemporary Reexamination of his Thought*, trans R. Meyer, Cambridge, MA: MIT Press, ch. 6. (Argues that Mead's interest in intersubjectivity led him to emphasize objectivity and universality more than Dewey did.)

* Mead, G.H. (1934) *Mind, Self and Society*, ed. C.W. Morris, Chicago, IL: University of Chicago Press. (A posthumous work on social psychology based on Mead's lectures including material on ethics.)

* —— (1964) *Selected Writings: George Herbert Mead*, ed. A.J. Reck, Chicago, IL: University of Chicago Press. (Articles published by Mead, including several on ethics and social policy.)

Myers, G.E. (1986) *William James: His Life and Thought*, New Haven, CT: Yale University Press, ch. 13. (Deals with morality and includes James' social views.)

* Peirce, C.S. (1958) *The Collected Papers of Charles Sanders Peirce*, ed. C. Harthorne and P. Weiss (1931–5, vols 1–6), revised by A.W. Burks (1958, vols 7–8), Cambridge, MA: Harvard University Press, vol. 8, paragraphs 7–38. (References as in this entry are standardly given by volume and paragraph number. This collection of Peirce's papers includes 'The Works of George Berkeley', his 1871 review of Berkeley.)

* —— (1966) *Charles S. Peirce: Selected Writings*, ed. P.P. Weiner, New York: Dover. (A representative selection of the Collected Papers with additional material such as correspondence with Lady Welby.)

J.E. TILES

PRAGUE SCHOOL *see*
Structuralism in linguistics (§2)

PRAISE AND BLAME

Praise and blame are philosophically interesting partly because, despite appearances, they are not simple opposites, but mainly because there are significant disagreements about whether, and when, they can be justified. The issue of justification connects praise and blame with some of philosophy's most central concerns: justice, desert and free will.

Disagreements about the justification of praise and blame tend to take two forms. In one the disagreement is about whether praise and blame can be justified without being deserved. Utilitarians, who argue that the rightness of praise and blame does not depend on desert, but on their contributing to the level of happiness, are opposed by those who believe that justice is of overriding value.

In its second form, the disagreement is about the essential requirements for deserving praise and blame. Among the conditions which have been proposed as essential are voluntariness (outlined originally by Aristotle), acting from the motive of duty (for praiseworthiness), and (usually in connection with blameworthiness) being free in a sense which is incompatible with determinism (the thesis that every event has a necessitating cause). Kant, who argued for both of the last two requirements, is a key figure in this debate.

1 The differences between praise and blame
2 Utilitarian versus desert theories of justified praise and blame
3 Kant
4 Determinism and free will

1 The differences between praise and blame

Blame is a more complex phenomenon than praise. While the term 'praise' simply describes the conveying of a positive evaluation, 'blame' has a responsibility-attributing sense which is as much a part of its meaning as its evaluative component (see RESPONSIBILITY).

Sometimes the responsibility-attributing sense predominates, as when a faulty carburettor is blamed for the malfunctioning of the car. But where persons are the objects, to blame is both to attribute responsibility and to censure. This does not mean that when inanimate things are blamed there is no element of evaluation: 'blame' always implies that something undesirable has occurred. But the extent to which blaming is an act of censure, as opposed (or in addition) to a judgment of responsibility is variable; whereas the extent to which praising is an act of commendation never varies, since it is just this.

Another difference is that while praise always consists in the voicing (either written or spoken) of approval, blame need not be voiced. One can blame oneself and others without saying so, because blame can consist in an attitude – for instance, the feeling of guilt which partly constitutes self-blame – or the silent passing of a judgment (as in 'She died without saying that she blamed him for the accident').

Because of these differences, blame (unlike criticism) can never simply be a negative version of praise. And although there is a considerable overlap in the constituency of objects which can be blamed and praised, there is not an exact coincidence either in the kinds of objects themselves, or the senses in which they can be blamed and praised.

2 Utilitarian versus desert theories of justified praise and blame

When philosophers disagree about the requirements for justified praising and blaming what concerns them is whether, and in what circumstances, these activities can be said to be morally right. And in considering this question they ignore some of the complexities mentioned above, to focus on those respects in which blame and praise *are* opposites – that is, to focus on blame as an act of censure and praise as an act of commendation.

There are broadly two kinds of dispute. The first is

between utilitarians, who hold that the rightness of praising and blaming is to be determined by the contribution such activities make to the maximization of overall wellbeing, and those who hold that praising and blaming can only be right when deserved (see JUSTICE; UTILITARIANISM). The second is over the question of what constitutes the deserving of blame and praise (see DESERT AND MERIT).

Utilitarianism regards the morality of praising and blaming, in the same way as it regards the morality of any act, in terms of the contribution these acts will make to the total level of happiness. So for the utilitarian praise and blame are morally justified if and only if they will help to increase overall happiness: they are seen as tools for encouraging beneficial (and discouraging harmful) behaviour. This means that the utilitarian could regard it as right to blame people for things they had not done, if this was the most effective way of maximizing happiness. In other words, from the utilitarian point of view it could be right to blame someone who was (as one might say) blameless.

This view is anathema to those who regard justice as a value which should not be sacrificed for other values. To justice-valuers, the rightness of praising and blaming is determined by desert. But what is it to deserve praise or blame? In the moral context, it requires first of all that the agent should have done something morally right or wrong. This is agreed on by all non-utilitarians. It is also agreed that the act for which the agent deserves to be praised or blamed needs to have been voluntary, a view which can be traced at least as far back as Aristotle, who, as paraphrased by Ross, held that 'praise and blame attach to voluntary actions', that is, 'actions done (1) not under compulsion and (2) with knowledge of the circumstances' (*Nicomachean Ethics*) (see ARISTOTLE §20; WILL, THE §1). The precise interpretation of each of these conditions of debate is a matter of debate, but for the purposes of this discussion, we can say that a voluntary act is one which has been performed knowingly and willingly.

3 Kant

But are knowledge and willingness enough? Kant (1785, 1788) held that praiseworthiness requires more: it also requires that the agent should be motivated by the thought of duty (see DUTY; KANTIAN ETHICS). This suggests an asymmetry between the motivational requirements for praiseworthiness and those for blameworthiness. We do not believe that blameworthy agents must be inspired to act wrongly by the very thought of wrong-doing, as Satan was in Milton's *Paradise Lost* ('Evil be thou my Good'). Although we

might regard such a motive as sufficient for blameworthiness, we do not regard it as necessary. It is considered enough, motivationally, for blameworthiness that agents were prepared to do what they knew to be wrong. But if Kant is right, it is not enough (motivationally) for praiseworthiness that they should merely have been prepared to do the right thing.

Many agree with Kant that praiseworthiness requires more than a willingness to do the right thing, but deny that praiseworthy acts must be motivated by the thought of duty, suggesting instead that such acts could have other admirable motives, such as sympathy, fellow-feeling, or a desire for justice. Kant would have agreed that these are admirable motives, but would have denied that they could be praiseworthy, because he held that praiseworthiness could be accorded only to actions which had moral worth and that such worth could not be based on any motives involving desires or other natural inclinations.

It has been argued that Kant's rejection of such motives as sources of moral worth is prompted by a concern for justice – a concern that something of such overriding value (as Kant thought moral worth to be) should not depend on the uneven and undeserved distribution of sympathetic and kindly inclinations, but should be available to all (see IMPARTIALITY). Kant's solution was to argue that the achievement of moral worth depends on the capacity to be moved by reason independently of desires and inclinations, a capacity which he appeared to think is possessed in equal measure by all adult human beings (apart from the insane) (see SELF-CONTROL). Kant held that this capacity is manifested when agents are moved to act solely by the thought of duty.

4 Determinism and free will

Kant also believed (1781/1787) that blameworthiness required the ability to be moved to action independently of desires and inclinations. Here his worry was causal determinism. He held (1788) that desires are causally determining and as such inimical to the freedom required for moral accountability, in particular the freedom to have acted otherwise. The thesis that causal determinism is incompatible with such accountability (known as 'incompatibilism'), has been endorsed by many philosophers who, like Kant, are motivated at least partly by the belief that accountability requires the ability to have acted otherwise (see FREE WILL). They argue as follows: if determinism is true, every event which has occurred, including the event of someone's acting, has had to occur; and since it would only be right to blame people for their actions if they could have acted otherwise, blame can never be justified. Kant, however, thought that blame could be justified, because he believed that the human capacity to be moved by reason (the same capacity he took to be the source of moral worth and which he thought enables us to act independently of our desires) in some way places us outside the causal order.

The latter belief has been subjected to much criticism, but many philosophers also reject the worry associated with determinism which led Kant to propose this as a solution. They argue that the essential requirement for moral accountability is simply the ability to act as one wants to, an ability which is not threatened by determinism.

But incompatibilists are not comforted by this, for they have another worry, which is often confused with the anxiety about the ability to have acted otherwise, but which is in fact separable from it. This is the belief that the desires, preferences and inclinations which cause our actions have themselves been caused by factors for which we could not possibly be responsible. And, the incompatibilist asks, if we are not responsible for the causes of our motivational states, how can we deserve to be held responsible (to be blamed) for their results? This consideration also partly underlies Kant's insistence that blameworthiness cannot depend on desires. But his response to this worry (1793) was to claim that we have the ability to choose our moral natures; that the way we are morally is ultimately up to us, where 'up to us' means 'not dependent on any feature for which we are not completely responsible'. (Here in its fullest form is Kant's belief that in virtue of our reason, we can somehow transcend our natural, desiring, emotional selves – see AUTONOMY, ETHICAL.)

The belief that we can desirelessly choose our natures (even our moral natures) has been dismissed as incoherent. But there is another model of freedom (known as 'agent-causation') which presents blameworthy agents as self-movers rather than self-choosers. The idea is that agents cause themselves to act in the light of their desires; they are not caused to act by their desires. This model too is thought to be problematic, but it is less easy to dismiss as incoherent. Both models are designed to meet the demand that there should be no contribution to an agent's actions for which the agent is not responsible.

The assumption that we cannot be morally responsible for our actions if we are not ultimately responsible for their causes (which motivates the above demand) has not received much direct attention. Those who find the assumption persuasive tend to treat it as something which does not require argument; those who do not find it persuasive tend either to ignore it, or to argue that our everyday practices of blame do not require justifications of this

ultimate kind. But it could be argued that the assumption requires a more focused investigation, to determine whether it is possible either to provide a justification for it or to demonstrate that it is not tenable.

See also: HONOUR; MORALITY AND EMOTIONS; SUPEREROGATION

References and further reading

* Aristotle (*c.* mid 4th century BC) *Nicomachean Ethics*, trans. with notes by W.D. Ross, Oxford: Oxford University Press, 1975, III 1. (Provides a discussion of praise and blame and an analysis of voluntary actions.)
* Kant, I. (1781/1787) *Critik der reinen Vernunft*, trans. N. Kemp Smith, *Critique of Pure Reason*, London: Macmillan, 1973, A528/B556–A558/B586. (Discusses the threat posed by causal determination to blameworthiness and the connection between reason and blame-deserving freedom.)
* —— (1785) *Grundlegung zur Metaphysik der Sitten*, trans. with notes by H.J. Paton, *Groundwork of the Metaphysics of Morals* (originally *The Moral Law*), London: Hutchinson, 1948; repr. New York: Harper & Row, 1964. (In the first chapter, Kant claims that moral worth belongs only to actions performed for the sake of duty. Ch. 2 touches on the connection between the human capacity for moral worth and the right of each human being to be treated with moral respect. In ch. 3, Kant argues for the connection between freedom, reason and morality.)
* —— (1788) *Critik der practischen Vernunft*, trans. L.W. Beck, *Critique of Practical Reason*, Indianapolis, IN: Bobbs-Merrill, 1956, 99. (A very clear statement of Kant's worry that determinism would make it impossible for agents to act otherwise.)
* —— (1793) *Die Religion innerhalb der Grenzen der blossen Vernunft*, trans. T.M. Greene and H.H. Hudson, *Religion Within the Limits of Reason Alone*, New York: Harper & Row, 1960, 40. (It is argued here that human beings can be held morally responsible for their actions only if they have freely chosen their moral natures.)
Klein, M. (1990) *Determinism, Blameworthiness and Deprivation*, Oxford: Oxford University Press. (Examines the free will/determinism debate and its relevance to blameworthiness. Appendix contains a commentary on an argument of Kant's which links morality and moral accountability with the existence of a desire-independent ability to act.)
—— (1990) 'Morality and Justice in Kant', *Ratio* 3 (1): 1–20. (A discussion of the connections between

Kant's views on moral motivation and his concern for justice.)

Sidgwick, H. (1874) *The Methods of Ethics*, London: Macmillan; 7th edn, 1907; 7th edn repr. 1963, 428. (Presents the utilitarian view of praise.)

Strawson, P.F. (1974) 'Freedom and Resentment', in *Freedom and Resentment and other Essays*, London: Methuen, 1–25. (Considered a classic, this is an extremely influential defence of the view that our everyday practices of moral appraisal do not require justifications which involve the falsity of determinism.)

Williams, B. (1962) 'The Idea of Equality', in P. Laslett and W.G. Runciman (eds) *Politics, Philosophy and Society*, vol. 2, Oxford: Blackwell; repr.in *Problems of the Self: Philosophical Papers 1956–72*, Cambridge: Cambridge University Press, 1973: 230–49. (Contains fascinating comments about the relationship between ideas of equality and moral worth in Kant's moral philosophy.)

—— (1971) 'Morality and the Emotions', in J. Casey (ed.) *Morality and Moral Reasoning*, London: Methuen, 1971; repr. in *Problems of the Self: Philosophical Papers 1956–72*, Cambridge: Cambridge University Press, 207–29. (Has inspired some of the discussion of Kant's belief that justice could only be achieved if moral worth were available to all.)

—— (1985) *Ethics and the Limits of Philosophy*, Cambridge, MA: Harvard University Press and London: Fontana, ch. 10. (Links the notion of blame which requires ultimate responsibility with what he calls 'the morality system' – a group of beliefs which he argues we would be better off without. Important, but not easy.)

—— (1989) 'Internal Reasons and the Obscurity of Blame', in *'Making Sense of Humanity' and other philosophical papers 1982–1993*, Cambridge: Cambridge University Press, 1995. (An interesting discussion of what Williams calls 'focused blame' and the way it works.)

MARTHA KLEIN

PRAMĀṆA *see* KNOWLEDGE, INDIAN VIEWS OF

PRATĪTYASAMUTPĀDA

see SUFFERING, BUDDHIST VIEWS OF ORIGINATION OF

PRAXEOLOGY

Praxeology belongs to the pragmatic tradition and thus emphasizes that concepts – and the world – must be understood through and elucidated in terms of human activities and practices. Praxeology is not a school but rather a movement, originating in Denmark and Norway in the 1960s and 1970s, with internal debates and disagreements. Praxeologists stress that good conceptual and ontological analyses proceed by (and are presented in the form of) careful analyses of particular examples or cases. They emphasize the situatedness of the philosopher in the world. The inspiration comes primarily from the early Heidegger and the later Wittgenstein.

The term 'praxeology' means here a systematic philosophical analysis and account (*logos*) of human activities and practices (praxis). Praxeology in this sense has also been labelled 'contextual pragmatics' and, in its more Wittgensteinian form, 'language game pragmatics' (see WITTGENSTEIN, L. §11). The 'praxiology' of Taduesz Kotarbiński (1965) and Lange (1963), which will not be treated here, is quite different, as it aims at a general scientific theory of efficient (rational) action; a similar idea is Ludwig von Mises' (1949) 'praxeology', a general theory of action in the form of a generalized political economy.

Praxeology started in Norway and Denmark and is still strongest in the Scandinavian philosophical community, though it has also had a considerable influence in the German speaking world. It began in the 1960s as a discursive, analytical practice in the circle around the Norwegian philosopher Jakob Meløe (1927–), which later, in the 1970s, came to be known as 'praxeology'.

The most important philosophical task according to Meløe and later praxeologists is careful description and elucidation of human activities in their concrete settings. 'The adequate *philosophers*', Meløe (1970: 20) says, 'are Wittgenstein, Heidegger and Austin, in that order'.

The praxeological movement is characterized by an integration of influences from various philosophical traditions, particularly phenomenology – stressing the life-world–pragmatism, hermeneutics and 'linguistic phenomenology' (see AUSTIN, J.L.; PHENOMENOLOGICAL MOVEMENT; PRAGMATISM). There exists, however, a variety of analytical orientations, covering fundamental ontology and pure conceptual analysis, as well as political–philosophical cultural critique.

Certain common convictions about the world and the best way of doing philosophy define what it is to be a praxeologist:

(1) human insights are primarily located in human activities (practices);

(2) human actions are of various, overlapping kinds;

(3) the articulation of these insights calls for careful description and further elaboration and analysis of cases of the activities in question.

The first point expresses the pragmatist's stance. The second is the expression of an anti-reductionist attitude: there are no final and universal schemes or action-types which apply to all possible human activities. What actions there are and how they are interrelated have to be brought to the fore through an analysis of particular cases.

Praxeology emphasizes the internal nature of the relation between an agent, the activity, the equipment and instruments, the material used or transformed and the context or 'landscape' in which the agent acts. From the point of view of praxeology an object *is* an object-as-used, an agent *is* a person-as-acting, the world *is* the world-as-we-act-and-live-in-it, and so forth. One source of inspiration here is Heidegger's discussion about tools (*Zeug*) in *Sein und Zeit* (Being and Time) (1927) (see HEIDEGGER, M. §3).

A knowing agent is seen as a constitutive element of an activity. Jakob Meløe says about somebody who is making shoes:

He sees what he needs to see to do what he does, he masters what he needs to master to do what he does, he knows what he needs to know to do what he does, etc. I abbreviate all this to: he *knows* what he is doing – and let it stand as an axiom that *the agent* knows what he is doing.

(1970: 23)

Furthermore, *in knowing this* agents also know *the world* they are acting in. Gunnar Skirbekk (1993: 153) calls the 'axiom' *the praxeological thesis*. This necessary and 'activity-constitutive' knowledge is to a large extent tacit (see KNOWLEDGE, TACIT).

Praxeology is anti-sceptical, and as part of that anti-solipsistic, in the sense that praxeologists take it as their starting point that on the whole we know what we do in our life-world and that one person's knowledge is also accessible to others. Jakob Meløe writes:

In a society with a complex division of work, we are all of us poor observers of the doings of most of our fellow men . . . . But also, there are no two jobs, or no two sets of practices, with no forms in common between them. And that is what makes our world one world.

(1970: 26)

The third point above expresses the praxeological method as well as the contextualist stance of praxeology. From the point of view of praxeology an activity is always situated in a context and cannot be understood as the kind of activity it is unless it is understood as an *activity-in-that-context*.

The method of praxeology is the exhibition of what is constitutive of or essential to a certain activity through a minute analysis of *examples*. This amounts to an exhibition of what is 'inherent' or necessarily presupposed in an activity. The goal is to *show* this rather than to prove it.

The particularistic and contextualistic nature of praxeology has led to vivid debates, especially in Norway and in Germany (Böhler *et al.* 1986; Skirbekk 1993), between praxeologists and representatives of transcendental and universal pragmatics (Apel, HABERMAS and their followers). Praxeology seems, for example, to make very strong, in some sense universal, hermeneutic claims about communication and knowledge.

Meløe's statement about what makes our world one world is a good example. Some praxeologists deny that any such universal 'theoretical claim' have been made at all. What seems to be a general presupposition is said to exist only as analytical *practice*. Some praxeologists, however, accept and stress the existence of universal presuppositions (Skirbekk 1993).

See also: HERMENEUTICS

References and further reading

* Böhler, D., Nordenstam, T. and Skirbekk, G. (eds) (1986) *Die Pragmatische Wende: Sprachspielpragmatik oder Transzendentalpragmatik?* (Pragmatic Change: Language Game Pragmatics or Transcendental Pragmatics?), Frankfurt am Main: Suhrkamp. (Focuses on the debate between contextualists and universalists. See also, in particular, the paper by Böhler and the comments to it.)

* Heidegger, M. (1927) *Sein und Zeit* (Being and Time), 7th edn, Tübingen: Max Niemeyer, 1953. (In particular the discussion about tools and understanding, §§12–34.)

* Kotarbiński, T. (1965) *Praxiology: An Introduction to the Sciences of Efficient Action*, Oxford: Pergamon Press and Warsaw: PWN–Polish Scientific Publishers.

* Lange, O. (1963) *Political Economy*, vol. 1, *General Problems*, Oxford: Pergamon Press and New York: Macmillan.

* Meløe, J. (1970) 'The Agent and his World', in G. Skirbekk (ed.) *Praxeology: An Anthology*, Oslo: Universitetsforlaget, 1983, 13–29. (The classic praxeological text).

—— (1988) 'The Two Landscapes of Northern Norway', *Inquiry* 31: 387–401. (Shows Meløe as a mature praxeologist with very instructive examples.)

* Mises, L. von (1949) *Human Action: A Treatise on Economics*, revised edn, New Haven, CT: Yale University Press, 1963.

Pahuus, M. (1983) 'On the Understanding of Tools and Articles for Use: A Comment on Jakob Meløe: The Agent and his World', in G. Skirbekk (ed.) *Praxeology: An Anthology*, Oslo: Universitetsforlaget, 1983, 30–7. (Showing the influence of Heidegger.)

Skirbekk, G. (ed.) (1983) *Praxeology: An Anthology*, Oslo: Universitetsforlaget. (The classical Scandinavian texts, also good as introductory reading.)

* —— (1993) *Rationality and Modernity: Essays in Philosophical Pragmatics*, Oslo: Scandinavian University Press and Oxford: Oxford University Press. (Especially 'Praxeological Reflections' and 'Contextual and Universal Pragmatics: Mutual Criticism of Praxeological and Transcendental Pragmatics'; good in bringing out the debate between contextualists and universalists.)

BENGT MOLANDER

PRAYER

The concept of prayer is now most commonly applied to any sort of communication which is addressed to God. That is, prayer is that activity in which believers take themselves to be speaking to God. One may ask God to do something (petitionary prayer), but that need not be the only sort of content that prayer may have. There are prayers in which one thanks God for something, and others in which one praises God and expresses one's adoration. A worshipper may also pray to express (or to make) a commitment to God, or to make a vow. Penitents pray to confess their sins, to express their repentance, and to ask for divine mercy and forgiveness. In general, any sort of speech-act which might be addressed by one human being to another could also be addressed to God, and thus be a prayer. Some such acts (such as, perhaps, commanding) might be thought inappropriate when addressed to God, but no doubt there can be inappropriate prayers. And some prayers may even be tentative and unsure about the existence of the addressee, prayers which might be thought of as beginning 'O God, if there is a God . . .'

Some writers, principally from within a tradition of mysticism, also apply the notion of prayer in a somewhat broader sense – in, for example, expressions like 'prayer of quiet' and 'prayer of union'. Here 'prayer' seems to mean any intentional state – worship, adoration, enjoyment of the divine presence and love, and so forth – which the worshipper believes to be associated with a genuine contact with the divine, regardless of whether it contains an element of communication addressed to God.

In the sense of a communication addressed to the divine, prayer seems to fit best with the theistic religions, which construe God as a person, or as something like a person. Here the addressee is taken to be someone who is an appropriate recipient of a communicative act. The fit seems rather more awkward in those religions which construe the divine reality in impersonal terms. With reference to prayer in the theistic religions, a principal topic of philosophical interest involves the omniscience and benevolence of God – if he knows all my needs and desires, why inform him of them through prayer? And will he not satisfy all my needs regardless of whether I pray? If divine benevolence is conditional on prayer, it seems less than perfect. A response to the first question is to point out that not all speech-acts need be construed as conveying information; a response to the second is to argue that our having to ask for things on behalf of ourselves and others might make for a better world than if this were not the case. Another issue is the way in which God responds to prayer. Some argue that God responds through miracles; others suggest that God, knowing our future prayers, providentially created a world that would satisfy them – thus prayer causally influences earlier events.

1   Prayer and divine omniscience
2   Prayer and divine benevolence
3   Prayer and the natural order of the world

1   Prayer and divine omniscience

The doctrine of divine omniscience, which is often a part of orthodox Christian theology, claims roughly that God knows every truth that is knowable. Most theologians have held that this includes all the truths about the future, including truths about the future acts of free creatures (see OMNISCIENCE). If God is omniscient in this way, then in prayer one does not inform God of something which he did not already know. Before one prays, God already knows what one wants, what one needs, what one will say in the prayer, what one will do, and so on. At this point, however, we must be careful. The divine foreknowledge may anticipate human action in the order of time, but it cannot substitute for that action, in the sense of making it irrelevant whether the action is actually done. For if the action were not done, then the divine knowledge would have been different from what it actually was. This applies to prayer as much as to anything else.

So perhaps God knows now that I will confess my sins tomorrow. But God knows this only if I will actually confess my sins tomorrow. If, when tomorrow comes, I do not confess, then God never knew that I would confess tomorrow. My action, so far from being made irrelevant by the foreknowledge, is instead essential to that foreknowledge.

It is true, however, that when in prayer I confess my sins, or express my desires and needs (or what I take to be my needs), and so on, I am not informing God of things which he did not already know. He already knew about those sins, he knew what I wanted, and what I thought I needed, and what I really needed. So there may be a problem about the point, the significance, of the practice of prayer in the light of the alleged omniscience of God.

Now it is true that the point of some human conversation is that of communicating information (or misinformation) to a hearer who did not previously know it. But that is certainly not the only point of speech within a purely human context. It is not even the only point of speech in the declarative, indicative mood. Students who respond to a teacher's classroom question are often not informing the teacher of something the teacher does not already know. Nor, in such cases, do the students even suppose that this is what they are doing. They are attempting to demonstrate or to exhibit their own knowledge of the subject matter, not to extend the teacher's grasp of that subject matter.

Closer to much religious praying, when I have wronged someone, and I apologize to that person for what I have done, the apology usually includes a statement of what was done. But the hearer is often already painfully aware of what was done, and I know that this is the case. I am not trying to make the hearer aware of what was done. But the apology involves my acknowledging what I did, and I do that by saying what I did. My statement has a point, though its point is not that of conveying new information. The point of the confession is that I 'own up' to what I did, that I acknowledge the responsibility for it. And that is a prerequisite for, or perhaps a part of, a sincere apology. In a similar way, when I congratulate someone on an achievement, I normally say what the achievement was. It is not that I think that the hearer is unaware of the achievement. But the congratulation loses much of its punch if it is not conversationally pegged to the item that gives rise to it.

The fact is that human speech, even within a purely human context, is extremely varied and flexible. If we are to take seriously the practice of prayer, then we need to allow for at least a similar degree of flexibility in the human address to God.

2 Prayer and divine benevolence

The concern about divine benevolence, in connection with prayer, arises primarily with reference to petitionary prayer, in which the worshipper asks God to do something. I ask God to do something for me, or for someone else, something which I presumably think will be good for the recipient. But we may think that if God is fully benevolent, then he already (and independently of my prayer) wants to do what is good for me and for the rest of the world. Furthermore, because of his omniscience, he already knows (independently of my prayer) what would be good for all of us. Is there any way, therefore, in which my prayer could be relevant to whether God does the thing for which I ask?

If there is any truth at all in the claims that God exists and loves his creation and knows what all of us need, then indeed there must be many good things which God does for us without our asking him. Many of the things which are in fact necessary for my life, health and happiness are things of which I am completely unaware. Even if I spent all of my time praying and did nothing else, I could not pray for all of those things. So it seems implausible to think that God does only those good things for which we pray. And there may also be things for which we pray, and which God does, but which he would have done for us anyway because he is good and he loves us.

There may, however, be another class of things. These are the things that it would be good for God to do for us *if we ask him*, and it would not be good for God to do them otherwise. These would be divine acts whose goodness was constituted, in whole or in part, by the fact that we have prayed for them. Or, to look at it from the other direction, they would be good because they were divine responses to human requests. If there are things which belong in this category, then our praying for them is not irrelevant to whether God does them.

There seem to be analogous things within purely human contexts. No doubt parents do many good things for their children, regardless of whether the children ask them – before, indeed, the children are mature enough to ask. But if the children are to grow into a genuinely personal relation with their parents, then some of the initiative must shift to the other side. Making a request of another person, and then acknowledging the response with thanks, is part (of course, it is only a part) of growing into actuality as a person oneself. Petitionary prayer seems to be based on the conviction that human beings are invited into an analogous sort of personal interaction with the divine person.

The difficulty regarding prayer and divine benevolence may be more severe when we think of praying for good things – healing, for example – for someone else. It may seem puzzling that a good thing which God might do for another person might depend in any way on *my* requesting it. Here too, we must remember that if there is anything at all to the theistic view of the world, then God must be doing many good things for each of us regardless of whether anyone prays for them. But it may also be the case that part of the divine purpose for the world – a good purpose – is that we should grow into a genuine community, a community of mutual love. That would be a community in which each of us does good things for the others, including the good of praying for the others, and each of us also receives with thanks this service from the others. It might be said that in such a community we all 'take in each other's washing'. Maybe in some deep way it is better that I do someone else's washing, and they do mine, than for each to do our own. If so, then there may be things which, in the end, it would be good for God to do for me if someone else asks for them, and not otherwise.

So far the relation of prayer to the divine benevolence has been discussed as it might appear to someone primarily concerned to understand this aspect of religious faith. But these concerns may also arise in a more polemical context, one in which these problems are incorporated into some special version of the problem of evil (see EVIL, PROBLEM OF §§1, 6). In that context, some alleged difficulty about prayer would function in an argument which was intended to cast doubt on the existence of God, or on the divine benevolence or power, and such like. Initially at least, cases of 'unanswered' prayer – cases in which we have prayed for good things, and those good things have not happened – seem to be the most plausible cases on which to focus. And it seems that there are many such cases. Think, for example, of all those who have prayed for peace while wars continue to abound. On reflection, however, we may well come to think that there is nothing special in this version of the problem of evil. We can readily think of many good things (or things, at least, which seem to us to be good) which God has evidently not done in the world. If that fact is really incompatible with the existence or goodness of God, then theism is already in terrible difficulty, and adding a few more cases of good things for which we have prayed will probably make little difference to the logic of the situation.

If, on the other hand, we can think of something which blunts the force of the general form of this problem, then probably the same sort of thing can be said about unanswered prayers. If, for example, it is relevant and useful to point out that we may be mistaken about what really would be good for us or for the world, then it would be equally relevant to observe that we may make similar mistakes when we pray for what we think is good. So the case of unanswered prayer probably does not generate a significantly different version of the problem of evil.

Curiously, however, the case of 'answered' prayer might be a more promising candidate for generating a special and distinctive variety of that problem. For we may think that, in some cases at least, the good thing that was done would not have been done without the prayer, and we may then construe that possibility as incompatible with divine benevolence. We might think, therefore, that we have discovered a special and curious fact about the world, that of good things done in response to prayers, which cannot be fitted into a more or less orthodox theistic view of the world.

There is, of course, a very large literature about the problem of evil, and it continues to be a live topic of controversy in the philosophy of religion. It is useful to keep in mind, when engaging in this controversy, the difference between a theodicy and a defence (see Hick 1966 and Plantinga 1967). Roughly, a theodicy is an attempt to explain, from a theistic point of view, why there is evil in the world, why God permits it, and so on. That is a relatively ambitious project, and one of the requirements for succeeding in it is that the explanations we give should be true – that is, that we correctly identify the divine intentions and purposes in allowing evil.

A defence, on the other hand, is more modest. Defenders attempt merely to refute some anti-theistic argument from evil by showing that it is invalid or that it has some false premise. Defenders may choose not to propose any positive explanation of their own as being the true account of evil. Perhaps they will not even claim to know any such account. They may instead content themselves with pointing out that there are some possible explanations which are compatible with the facts of the world. If there are possibilities of that sort, then the facts of the world (including the evils) are not logically incompatible with the existence and benevolence of God.

It was suggested above that there may be things which it would be good for God to do in response to a prayer, and not otherwise. If we construe that as the actual explanation for the phenomenon of answered prayer, then it would constitute a partial theodicy, a theodicy for that particular curious fact about the world. But the mere logical possibility of such things, even if there actually are no such things, could serve as the basis for a defence. That is, the fact that such cases are possible would show that cases of answered prayer are not by themselves incompatible with the benevolence of God. It does not seem, therefore, that prayer contributes any serious special element to the problem of evil. If we can find a satisfactory theodicy or defence as a response to the more general versions of the problem of evil, then that line of response will probably cover the case of prayer as well. And if there is no satisfactory theodicy or defence for the more general versions, then there will be plenty of trouble for theism regardless of what we say about prayer.

3 Prayer and the natural order of the world

The notion of God's doing something in the world has been prominent in the last few paragraphs, and that can hardly be avoided in discussions of petitionary prayer. For such prayers – 'Give us this day our daily bread', for example – characteristically ask God to do some more or less specific thing in the world. Perhaps the most purely 'spiritual' requests – 'Forgive us our sins', for example, or 'Receive us into the heavenly kingdom' – can be thought of as being divorced from the natural world and independent of what happens in it. But much petitionary prayer pretty clearly involves that world. There does not seem to be any plausible way of thinking about such prayer without also thinking about the possibility, or impossibility, of God's responding by way of some action in the natural world.

One such possible mode of divine response would be that of a miracle. Here a miracle will be construed as a direct and *de novo* causal or quasi-causal act of God which makes the natural world different from what it would have been, given only the other elements of the world and the ordinary causal laws and powers operative within it. This is close to the 'violation' concept which David Hume was trying to formalize in his celebrated definition, 'A miracle may be accurately defined, a transgression of a law of nature by a particular volition of the Deity, or by the interposition of some invisible agent' (1748, section X). Since Hume's time there has been a large amount of discussion of the possibility, actuality, significance, and so forth, of miracles in this sense (see, for example, Swinburne 1970). This topic is much too large to broach here, but it can be said that many participants in the practice of prayer consider this as one possible mode of divine response (see HUME, D. §2; MIRACLES).

Many theologians seem also to recognize another, non-miraculous, mode of response, which is sometimes called 'providential' (see, for example, Lewis 1947, Appendix B). The idea here is that the divine response to a petitionary prayer may consist of an event which happens in the 'ordinary' course of nature, through the operation of ordinary causes. So, for example, my recovery from an illness – prayed for by me and my friends – may happen by what seem to be the regular and ordinary effects of drugs, surgery, and so forth. But in what sense could the recovery then be a divine response to the prayer? Well, the course of the world may be thought to be determined by three sorts of factors – the laws of nature, the 'initial conditions' of the world, and the acts of free agents. (Some might want to include a fourth category, that of chance events. In this context, they can be handled in the same way as free acts.) Suppose we think also that God creates a world, in part, by creating laws of nature and initial conditions. He knows what future acts will take place in that world; in particular, he knows whether I and my friends will pray for my recovery from the illness. If then he arranges the laws of nature and the initial conditions in such a way that my recovery ensues, and if our prayers were a factor entering into the divine decision, then my recovery would be providential, and an answer to prayer, though it occurred in the ordinary way because of drugs and surgery.

This idea requires that we allow for the possibility of an event's playing a role in determining some previous event or state of affairs. So my prayer now is to be one of the factors that God considers in setting up the world 'in the beginning'. But this is probably not a special problem for prayer. For the most straightforward way of thinking about divine foreknowledge is to think that my action today determines something of what God knew yesterday and throughout all previous time. If I had done something different today then the divine knowledge would forever have been different – forever in the past as well as in the future.

Some prefer to resolve this problem by appealing to the idea that God is eternal, rather than, say, merely everlasting (see ETERNITY). And an eternal being is 'outside' time – for such a being there is no before or after. This, then, removes the 'fore' from the divine knowledge, and perhaps removes with it the feeling of a 'retrograde' causality in which my present act determines a previous state of knowledge in God. This appeal, of course, has its own difficulty; the idea of eternity is notoriously difficult to understand. But we have no guarantee that every truth is easy. Others (for example, Mavrodes 1984) prefer to accept the idea of temporally retrograde causality, or something like causality, in which future events play some role in shaping the world that comes before them. Perhaps the most interesting philosophical question in this connection is that of whether we can find any reason for a decisive rejection of this possibility.

See also: DEISM; PROCESS THEISM; PROVIDENCE; RELIGION AND SCIENCE

References and further reading

Hasker, W. (1989) *God, Time, and Knowledge*, Ithaca, NY: Cornell University Press. (Chapter 7 includes a critical discussion of the idea of temporally retrograde causality.)

* Hick, J. (1966) *Evil and the God of Love*, New York: Harper & Row. (This is an extensive discussion of several systems of theodicy.)

* Hume, D. (1748) *An Enquiry Concerning Human Understanding*, ed. L.A. Selby-Bigge and P.H. Nidditch, Oxford: Clarendon Press, 1975. (Section X is probably the most famous philosophical discussion of miracles in Western philosophy, and the focus of many subsequent discussions.)

* Lewis, C.S. (1947) *Miracles*, New York: Macmillan. (A general discussion of miracles. Appendix B discusses 'special providences' as distinct from miracles.)

—— (1964) *Letters to Malcolm*, New York: Harcourt, Brace & World. (Highly readable, but careful, discussions of many aspects of the practice of prayer.)

* Mavrodes, G.I. (1984) 'Is the Past Unpreventable?', *Faith and Philosophy* 1 (2): 131–45. (This is a further discussion and defence of the possibility of temporally retrograde causality.)

* Plantinga, A. (1967) *God and Other Minds*, Ithaca, NY: Cornell University Press. (Chapters 5 and 6 constitute a careful development of a free-will defence (not a theodicy) in connection with the problem of evil.)

Stump, E. (1979) 'Petitionary Prayer', *American Philosophical Quarterly* 16 (2): 81–91. (Largely a discussion of prayer and divine benevolence, with considerable reference to the early and medieval philosophical theologians.)

* Swinburne, R. (1970) *The Concept of Miracle*, London: Macmillan. (This is a defence of the possibility, and significance, of miracles in the Humean sense.)

St Teresa of Avila (1565) *The Autobiography of St. Teresa of Avila*, trans. E. Allison Peers, Garden City, NY: Image Books, 1960. (A fascinating mixture of autobiography, reflection and spiritual

advice and teaching by one of the great mystical writers.)

GEORGE I. MAVRODES

PRE-COLUMBIAN THOUGHT IN LATIN AMERICA *see* LATIN AMERICA, PRE-COLUMBIAN AND INDIGENOUS THOUGHT IN

PREDESTINATION

Predestination appears to be a religious or theological version of universal determinism, a version in which the final determining factor is the will or action of God. It is most often associated with the theological tradition of Calvinism, although some theologians outside the Calvinist tradition, or prior to it (for example, Augustine and Thomas Aquinas), profess similar doctrines. The idea of predestination also plays a role in some religions other than Christianity, perhaps most notably in Islam.

Sometimes the idea of predestination is formulated in a comparatively restricted way, being applied only to the manner in which the divine grace of salvation is said to be extended to some human beings and not to others. John Calvin, for example, writes:

> We call predestination God's eternal decree, by which he compacted with himself what he willed to become of each man. For all are not created in equal condition; rather, eternal life is foreordained for some, eternal damnation for others. Therefore, as any man has been created to one or the other of these ends, we speak of him as predestined to life or to death.

> (Institutes, *bk 3, ch. 21, sec. 5*)

At other times, however, the idea is applied more generally to the whole course of events in the world; whatever happens in the world is determined by the will of God. Philosophically, the most interesting aspects of the doctrine are not essentially linked with salvation. For instance, if God is the first cause of all that happens, how can people be said to have free will? One answer may be that people are free in so far as they act in accordance with their own motives and desires, even if these are determined by God. Another problem is that the doctrine seems to make God ultimately responsible for sin. A possible response here is to distinguish between actively causing something and passively allowing it to happen, and to say that God merely allows people to sin; it is then human agents who actively choose to sin and God is therefore not responsible.

1   **What is predestination?**
2   **Sources of the doctrine**
3   **Objections and emendations**

1   What is predestination?

The idea of predestination belongs to a group of theological ideas which are closely related (if, indeed, they are not practically identical). Among them are foreordination (which is often used merely as a stylistic variant of predestination), divine election (the divine choosing of some persons to receive the gift of salvation), divine providence, the divine governance of the world, divine decrees and divine sovereignty. Perhaps a little more distantly related is the idea of divine foreknowledge (a special case, presumably, of divine omniscience). Sometimes one of these ideas is defined in terms of some of the others. But all of them seem to be special theological concepts, and this method of definition is not very useful to someone who is trying to make an initial entry into this set of ideas.

CALVIN, however, in the passage quoted above, speaks of God as having 'compacted with himself what he willed to become of each man'. Similarly, the *Westminster Shorter Catechism* defines a divine decree as 'His eternal purpose according to the counsel of His will, whereby, for His own glory, He hath foreordained whatsoever comes to pass', a definition endorsed in the twentieth century by the prominent Calvinist theologian Louis Berkhof (1959: 102). Perhaps we can make a start, therefore, by thinking of predestination as something like a divine intention about how things should happen in the world. This intention belongs to eternity, or at least it predates the events to which it refers. Calvinist theologians usually add that this divine will is efficacious, in the sense that whatever is decreed, predestined, and so on, is certain to happen in just that way. This efficacy is sometimes said to be mediated through another divine act, the governance of the world.

Put in this way, the doctrine seems fairly straightforward, and makes a strong claim about the way in which the course of the world is related to the divine will. In response to an objection, however, many theologians introduce an important revision, which greatly weakens the idea. This revision will be considered in §3.

2   Sources of the doctrine

The doctrine of predestination appears to have four main sources:

(1) Certain biblical passages, most notably in the Pauline epistles, but also in some other places (Boettner (1948) cites all of these).

(2) Speculation based on rather general considerations about the divine nature and activity – God's creation of the world, his power, his majesty, and so on. A classic example is that of Thomas Aquinas, who argues that 'since every agent acts for an end, the ordering of effects towards that end extends as far as the causality of the first agent extends'. But God is the First Cause, whose causality encompasses that of all created agents. And so 'it necessarily follows that all things, inasmuch as they participate in existence, must likewise be subject to divine providence' (*Summa theologiae* Ia, q.22, a.2).

(3) Speculation and argument based on a different special attribute of God, namely his foreknowledge of all future events. 'Foreknowledge implies certainty, and certainty implies foreordination' (Boettner 1948: 44).

(4) Empirical observations of religiously significant facts about the world – for example, that various people, because of the circumstances of their birth, their culture, and such like, have vastly different opportunities for hearing and understanding the Christian message, that there is a great disparity in the responses of people who do hear that message, and so on (see, for example, Calvin's *Institutes*, bk 3, ch. 21, sec. 1).

The second and third of these lines of argument, especially, would seem to support the most general and extensive versions of predestination, if they support any at all.

3   Objections and emendations

From early on in the history of the Church – apparently, indeed, from at least the time of the writing of the Pauline epistles – various objections have been raised against the doctrine of predestination. These include:

(1) That it is inconsistent with other passages in the New Testament, such as those which suggest that all human beings will eventually be saved (Boettner (1948) cites and discusses some of these passages, as well as some of the other lines of objection).

(2) That it is incompatible with the justice and/or the

love of God, because it represents the divine choice and action as arbitrary and unfair.

(3) That it is incompatible with human moral responsibility, because it implies that there is no human free will (see FREE WILL).

(4) That it impugns the character of God, by making God morally responsible for sin (see OMNI-POTENCE §5).

One of the most serious difficulties which faces a person who considers these objections, and possible replies to them, is that of getting a clear idea of just how strong a claim is made by the doctrine of predestination. The idea of predestination has the 'feel' of a causal, or quasi-causal, notion. Initially at least, we tend to think that it is being used to provide a causal explanation of certain facts in the world. Why did this person receive the Gospel when that one did not? Ultimately, at least, it was divine predestina-tion, the divine decree, which had these results. Sometimes this sort of claim seems quite explicit:

An effect conceived in posse only raises [sic] into actuality by virtue of an efficient cause or causes. When God was looking forward from the point of view of His original infinite prescience, there was but one cause, Himself. If any other cause or agent is ever to arise, it must be by God's agency. If effects are embraced in God's infinite prescience, which these other agents are to produce, still, in willing these other agents into existence, with infinite prescience, God did virtually will into existence, or purpose, all the effects of which they were to be efficients.

(Dabney 1871 (1985): 212)

Often, as in this passage, the idea is developed by suggesting that God is the remote cause, the first cause, who determines all subsequent events by initiating a deterministic chain of causes and effects. This chain terminates in (in many cases) the actions of human agents, who are the proximate causes of events.

This sort of claim seems, of course, to generate immediately the third and fourth sort of objection mentioned above. With reference to free will, some writers (Luther seems to be a prominent example) seem content to accept the implication and to deny that there is any real free will. Others avail themselves of the idea sometimes called (in non-theological contexts) 'soft' determinism. They argue that God determines human acts by determining the motives, desires, and so forth, of human beings. Since humans then act in accord with their own desires and motives, they act 'freely', despite the fact that their acts are determined by a divine act from before the foundation of the world.

Perhaps the other objection, that this view makes God responsible for sin because it makes him the cause of each sinful act, seems more troublesome to proponents of predestination. There is a tendency for writers on this topic to put forward very strong and extensive claims about predestination, and to offer arguments which, if they are sound, support these very strong claims. But later, under the pressure of objections, they fall back on versions of the doctrine that seem to be radically revised and weakened.

An example of such a revised version appears in the *Westminster Confession of Faith* (1646), which says that:

God from all eternity did, by the most wise and holy counsel of his own will, freely and unchange-ably ordain whatsoever comes to pass; yet so, as thereby neither is God the author of sin; nor is violence offered to the will of the creatures; nor is the liberty or contingency of second causes taken away, but rather established.

(*Westminster Confession of Faith*, ch. 3)

This is evidently an attempt to address objections of the third and fourth types mentioned above. If we are to take it seriously, however, we may well be puzzled as to how we are now to understand the claim that God ordains all things. If God is not the author of sin, then it would seem that there are a great many events in the world of which God is not the author. And we may also wonder whether, if the world can have in it some sins of which God is not the author, it may not also have in it many other events of which God is not the author. Furthermore, what shall we say now of those arguments – from foreknowledge, for example – which would seem to include within the scope of the divine determination sins as well as anything else? If we take seriously the qualification that 'neither is God the author of sin', and so on, then what remains in our understanding of what divine foreordination amounts to?

In saying this, we may, on the other hand, be too careless and hasty in our understanding of the term 'author'. Could God be the cause of everything without being the author of everything? If so, then we could retain the *Westminster Confession* qualification while still accepting the arguments for God's universal causal responsibility. But in order to be relevant to the problem that is being addressed, authorship must be understood as generating moral responsibility for what one is the author of, while foreordination (or causality) without authorship must not generate such responsibility. What understanding of foreordination and authorship will satisfy these requirements?

One way of proceeding would be to construe foreordination as a very general sort of causal notion which includes at least two kinds of cause. One of them, authorship, is the sort that generates moral responsibility, and the other is the sort that does not. We have already mentioned two sorts of cause, remote and proximate. God was said to be the remote cause of everything, while (in many cases, at least) created agents were the more proximate causes. Unfortunately, however, this distinction does not have the right moral implications. Remote causes drain moral responsibility away from proximate causes. To construe authorship as proximate causality, and thus to say that God is not the proximate cause of sins, would have the opposite effect from that which the defender of predestination needs. The moral responsibility for sins would be transferred from the human agents to God, the remote cause.

A more promising strategy appeals to a different distinction. This is sometimes put as the difference between positive and negative causality, or between active and passive causality, or between causing something and merely allowing it to happen. This strategy is attractive because this distinction really does seem to have the required moral implications. The morality of doing an act yourself may be very different from that of merely allowing someone else to do a similar act, and actively causing something to happen may be morally different from merely allowing it to happen. So a nineteenth-century apologist for predestination says:

> To decree, is nothing more than to determine beforehand, or to foreordain; and, to resolve, or determine to do or permit anything, is to decree it in that sense.... That which is determined to be done, is decreed; and that which is determined to be permitted, is also decreed, when there is power to prevent it.... Now, in one or other of these ways, God 'has foreordained whatsoever comes to pass.' This, as you know, is the simple language of our catechism.
>
> (Smith 1854: 32–6)

And according to the Calvinist theologian Louis Berkhof, 'the decree respecting sin is not an efficient but a permissive decree, or a decree to permit, in distinction from a decree to produce, sin by divine efficiency' (1959: 108). Long before either of these, Thomas Aquinas had argued that reprobation (the predestination of some humans to damnation) was not the cause of the sinner's sin, although predestination was the cause of the elect's receiving grace. He says that predestination includes the will to confer grace, but of reprobation he says only that it 'includes the will to permit a person to fall into sin' (*Summa theologiae* Ia, q.23, a.3).

The crucial words in these accounts, of course, are 'permit', 'permitted', 'in one or other of these ways', and so on. What God permits may indeed be done by the free will of human beings, and perhaps it is then those human agents, and not God, who bear the moral responsibility for those acts. This really does undercut the objections that say that predestination makes God morally responsible for sin, or that it eliminates the free will of creatures.

But 'the simple language of our catechism' used what appear to be very strong notions – foreordination, predestination, divine election, and so on. One may be surprised to hear now that these apparently powerful claims about God can be satisfied merely by God's *allowing* other agents to act. At least, interpretations of this sort suggest that the doctrine of predestination may not be nearly as strong as it first appears, and that it is one which may be unusually prone to misapprehension.

See also: ETERNITY; FATALISM, INDIAN; GRACE; OMNISCIENCE; PROVIDENCE §§3–4; REPROBATION; SALVATION

References and further reading

* Aquinas, T. (1266–73) *Summa theologica*, trans. Fathers of the English Dominican Province, London: Burns, Oates & Washbourne., 1920. (This is an extensive and extremely influential piece of philosophical theology by one of the major figures in medieval philosophy and theology.)
* Berkhof, L. (1959) *Systematic Theology*, Grand Rapids, MI: Eerdmans, 4th edn. (A discussion of a standard range of theological topics by a significant American Calvinist theologian.)
* Boettner, L. (1948) *The Reformed Doctrine of Predestination*, Grand Rapids, MI: Eerdmans, 6th edn. (This is a very extensive and useful discussion of this topic by a strong defender of the Calvinist tradition.)
* Calvin, J. (1559) *Institutes of the Christian Religion*, trans. F.L. Battles, Philadelphia, PA: The Westminster Press, 1960. (This is the major theological work by one of the most prominent Protestant reformers of the sixteenth century.)
* Dabney, R.L. (1871) *Lectures in Systematic Theology*, Grand Rapids, MI: Baker Book House, 1985. (This was originally published as *Syllabus and Notes of the Course of Systematic and Polemic Theology Taught in Union Theological Seminary, Virginia*; the Baker volume is reprinted from the revised edition of 1878.)
* Smith, W.D. (1854) *What is Calvinism?*, Philadelphia, PA: Presbyterian Board of Publication. (This is a

highly polemical defence of Presbyterian Calvinism.)

* (1646) *Westminster Confession of Faith*, in P. Schaff (ed.) *The Creeds of Christendom*, New York: Harper & Brothers, 1919, vol. 3, 676–703. (A confessional statement which has been very widely used in Presbyterian churches; see page 604 for the quotation in §3.)
* (1648) *Westminster Shorter Catechism*, in P. Schaff (ed.) *The Creeds of Christendom*, New York: Harper & Brothers, 1919, vol. 3, 600–73. (The definition in §1 is from Question 7, on page 677.)

GEORGE I. MAVRODES

PREDICATE CALCULUS

The central feature of the 'predicate calculus' is a formal language designed to represent arguments involving generalizations. Aristotle had developed a formal logic of 'every', 'some' and 'no', but did not tackle the problem of combining these quantifiers (as they are now called) with relations, or with complex predicates, as in 'Everyone is F or G'. The Stoics had the beginnings of a sentential logic – the logic of the connectives 'and', 'or', 'if' and 'not' – which could later be adapted to deal also with complex predicates. The solution is not, however, a simple matter of pasting these two systems together. It involved four major steps. One was Boole's groundwork for a mathematical system of sentential logic by analogy with an algebra of truth and falsity. Another was De Morgan's move away from the traditional subject–predicate paradigm towards a relational one, so that relations of the form '_ loves _' could be treated naturally alongside predicates such as '_ is mortal'. The third was the invention by Peirce and Frege of the quantifier-and-variable notation. This solved the twin difficulties of adapting sentential logic to express complex predicates, as in $(\forall x)(Fx \lor Gx)$, and linking the quantifiers unambiguously to the right clauses in multiply general sentences, for example, '$(\forall x)(\exists y)x$ loves y' and '$(\exists y)(\forall x)x$ loves y' as alternative renderings of 'Everyone loves someone'. Finally there was Frege's break with the traditional semantics of quantified terms. Instead of treating 'every man' as the subject of 'Every man is mortal', he treats it as a second-level predicate governing the first-level predicate 'is mortal'. At one stroke this obviates the futile search for an entity answering to 'everyone' and provides the rationale for disambiguating multiply general sentences.

Frege and Peirce catered for quantification not merely over individuals but over properties, relations and functions of individuals, and Whitehead and Russell carried this further to cover quantification over relations of relations, and so on. These would now be called second-order or higher-order predicate calculi as opposed to the first-order predicate calculus – often simply called 'the' predicate calculus – with which this entry is primarily concerned.

One can give a mathematically precise characterization of the valid argument forms of the predicate calculus. That has become a kind of standard for demonstrating the logical validity of informal deductive arguments, and the semantics of the predicate calculus is the starting point for contemporary philosophy of language. Moreover, the analysis of argument that leads to and incorporates the predicate calculus is the most successful piece of philosophical analysis completed in modern times, and as such serves as a paradigm – for some to be emulated, for others to be avoided, but in one way or another central to the development of contemporary philosophy.

This entry concentrates on the central theme of the analysis of logical validity through an account of what it is for an argument 'form' of the predicate calculus to be valid.

1　**Language of the predicate calculus**
2　**Logically valid arguments and interpretations**
3　**Sentential logic**
4　**Expressive completeness**
5　**Truth and logical consequence**
6　**Formal deduction and decidability**

1　Language of the predicate calculus

The notation used here is that of the Hilbert school. A commonly used alternative, derived from Peano and Russell, employs $\sim$ for negation, & for conjunction, $\supset$ for the conditional, $\equiv$ for the biconditional and ( ) for the universal quantifier.

We build up the formulas of the predicate calculus from atomic formulas using the sentential connectives and quantifiers. To start with we need a stock of enough variables: $v_0, v_1, \ldots, v_n, \ldots$. The language may contain constant symbols and relation symbols. (One can also allow function symbols, which would be necessary, for example, for a standard treatment of arithmetic.) Let the constant symbols be $c_0, c_1, \ldots, c_n, \ldots$. Although the sentential connectives and quantifiers are often referred to as logical constants, in this entry, 'constant' always means a non-logical symbol serving as a name or potential name for an individual. Let the relation symbols be $R_0^n, R_1^n, \ldots, R_m^n, \ldots$. Those with a superscript of n are called n-placed and will be used for n-ary relations. One-placed or 'monadic' relation symbols may be called predicate symbols. It is convenient to bring the sentence letters of the sentential calculus (see §3) under this uniform notation by regarding them as zero-placed relation symbols. A 'term' is either a variable or a constant. (It will be assumed here that the language of the predicate calculus contains, as well as any non-logical relation symbols, the equality sign '=' used to denote the logical relation of identity. Some writers would call this 'predicate calculus with identity', keeping 'predicate calculus' for the version in which the equality sign is absent or in which identity is not given the special status of a logical relation.)

An 'atomic formula' is an expression either of the form $s = t$, where s and t are terms, or of the form $R^n v_1 v_2 \ldots v_n$, where $v_1, \ldots, v_n$ are terms, for some n. For example, $R^2 vc$ might be used for 'v is the daughter of Margaret Sanger', where R^2 stands for the daughter relation and c stands for Margaret Sanger. (Here and elsewhere we shall omit the official apparatus of subscripts for the sake of simplicity of exposition.)

The constants and relation symbols function here as schematic letters that may receive varying interpretations, but there is nothing to block fixing the interpretations of some of them in a definite way, which results in an interpreted language of a sort more closely related to ordinary language. The system with only schematic letters, those without a fixed interpretation, is known as the 'pure' predicate calculus, while systems with symbols that have fixed interpretations are known as 'applied' predicate calculi. Frege considered only applied predicate calculi without any schematic letters. Hilbert introduced and emphasized the importance of the device of schematic letters.

If ϕ and ψ are formulas, then so are those expressions formed as indicated using the sentential connectives: $\neg\phi$, $\phi \land \psi$, $\phi \lor \psi$, $\phi \to \psi$ and $\phi \leftrightarrow \psi$. If ϕ is a formula and x is a variable, then $(\forall x)\phi$ and $(\exists x)\phi$ are *quantified* formulas and the occurrence of ϕ is said to be the 'scope' of the quantifier. The symbols are formal counterparts of the English 'not', 'and', inclusive 'or', 'if...then', 'if and only if', 'for all', and 'there exists at least one', respectively. An occurrence of a variable x in a formula that is not in the scope of any quantifier over x (that is, a quantifier of the form $(\forall x)$ or $(\exists x)$) in the formula is said to be a 'free' occurrence, and a quantifier over the variable x in a formula is said to 'bind' every occurrence of x free in its scope. Such an occurrence (including the occurrence of x inside the quantifier itself) is then said to be 'bound' by the quantifier.

Some formulas are incomplete expressions, such as $R^2 vc$, which might be used for 'v is a daughter of Margaret Sanger', in which v is left free, while others are complete sentences and may be true or false on their own, such as $(\exists v)R^2 vc$, 'Margaret Sanger has a daughter' (literally, 'There exists v such that v is a daughter of Margaret Sanger'). That distinction can be made precise as follows: a variable 'occurs free' in a formula ϕ just if any of its occurrences in the formula is free. A 'sentence' is a formula in which no variable occurs free. Thus, while the sentential connectives may on occasion indeed connect sentences, they may also connect formulas that are not sentences.

2 Logically valid arguments and interpretations

An argument is 'valid' if it is impossible that the premises be true and the conclusion false. Validity is the central feature of good deductive arguments, for if an argument is valid and the premises true, it follows that the conclusion must also be true. Thus, valid arguments are exactly those suitable for what may be the paradigm application of deductive arguments: establishing the truth of the conclusion on the basis of the truth of the premises. The conclusion of a valid argument is said to be a 'tautological consequence' of the premises.

There are other desirable features for an argument to have: to establish the truth of its conclusion, the premises must be true; and to be part of an explanation of its conclusion, its premises must in some sense be better known or understood than the conclusion, and, in particular, the argument must not be circular. We do not discuss such secondary features further here. For the most part, they are only requisites of arguments employed for specific purposes, unlike validity, which is a condition for acceptability of any deductive argument. The notion of validity relies on a notion of possibility that is surely in need of further analysis (but see below).

There are arguments whose validity is not purely logical. For example, 'Caila is a female child, therefore Caila is a girl' is valid because a female child is necessarily a girl, although that fact does not appear in the argument. This argument has the 'form' '$F(c) \land C(c)$, therefore $G(c)$'. But so does 'Caligula was a famous caesar, therefore Caligula was a god', which is clearly not valid, since the premise is true and the conclusion false. In contrast, the argument 'Everyone is mortal, therefore Socrates is mortal' is itself valid and so is every other argument of the form '$(\forall x)M(x)$, therefore $M(s)$'. Here the validity of the argument does not depend on anything beyond its form, and in particular not on its subject matter: the reasons for its validity are 'topic neutral'. That has often been taken to be a criterion for something to be logical. (See Haack (1978) for a historical summary of views on what counts as logical, and Sher (1991) and Koslow (1992) for recent work on the subject.)

The primary business of logic is to characterize those arguments which are not only valid, but of a form such that every argument of that form is also valid; briefly, those which are 'logically valid'. It is obvious that logical validity depends on a prior notion of form (see LOGICAL FORM). The sentences of the pure predicate calculus are designed to serve as representatives of forms of sentences of natural language, and the notion that an argument is of a certain form can be made more precise using the idea of a 'natural-language interpretation'. For example, 'Caila is a female child, therefore Caila is a girl' is of the form '$F(c) \land C(c)$, therefore $G(c)$' under the interpretation that interprets 'c' as 'Caila', 'F' as 'is female', 'C' as 'is a child' and 'G' as 'is a girl'; but it is also of the form 'A, therefore B' under the interpretation that interprets 'A' as 'Caila is a female child' and 'B' as 'Caila is a girl'.

The same argument may have many forms. In general, a natural-language interpretation of an argument form must specify a name or definite description for each constant and a predicate for each predicate symbol. A predicate amounts to little more than a sentence with a single blank in it: '__ is female'. Each n-placed relation symbol will similarly be interpreted using an n-ary 'sentence form' – a sentence with n blanks in it. A binary relation symbol might be interpreted using, for example, '__ is spicier than __'. One needs some mechanism for specifying which term following a relation symbol corresponds to which blank in the sentence form that is its interpretation, but such details will be omitted here.

It follows from the stipulations above that an argument is logically valid if and only if it is of a form that yields a valid argument under all natural-language interpretations. Such a form will be called a valid argument form, and the problem of determining which arguments are logically valid thus amounts to that of determining which argument *forms* are valid.

It is tempting to suppose that an argument form is valid just in case it has no natural-language interpretation that yields an argument with true premises and a false conclusion. That would eliminate the troublesome notion of possibility from the basis of logic. Indeed, Carnap (1934) made proposals along closely related lines. Unfortunately, such a proposal does not serve as an adequate criterion for validity: as Tarski (1936) pointed out, it might be that our language happened not to be rich enough to give rise to the requisite variety of interpretations, and thus the validity of an argument could depend on the richness of parts of the language that were not used in the argument in question. It can in fact be shown that the language of arithmetic is rich enough to yield all the interpretations one could need for the predicate calculus presented here (see Kleene 1952 and Hasenjäger 1953), but it would be question-begging to assume it at the present stage.

3 Sentential logic

Since validity is defined in terms of whether or not the premises of an argument form can be true while the conclusion is not, it is first necessary to specify under what circumstances a sentence is true. We assume every sentence has a 'truth-value' of either T or F, where F is anything other than true – which may include, depending on one's view, not only false, but also meaningless, undefined and perhaps other possibilities. (Any sentence that is not true will be referred to, briefly though perhaps inaccurately, as false. For calculi allowing more than these two truth-values, see MANY-VALUED LOGICS.)

It is illuminating to begin with the simple case of 'sentential logic' (also called the propositional calculus); that fragment of the predicate calculus without variables, constants or quantifiers, and in which one only allows zero-placed relation symbols. According to the definitions given in §2, an atomic sentence is formed by such a symbol followed by zero terms. It thus amounts to no more than a single 'sentence letter'. It is possible to specify the form of some arguments in sentential logic. For example, 'Jane Austen and Charlotte Brontë were novelists, therefore Jane Austen was a novelist' has the form '$A \land B$, therefore A'. But many arguments cannot be formalized in sentential logic so as to be valid. For example, 'Everyone is mortal, therefore Hannah Arendt is mortal', has the form '$(\forall v)R^1(v)$, therefore $R^1(c)$', but this is not a form available in sentential logic. The only form available in sentential logic is the invalid 'A, therefore B'.

The truth-value of a sentence of sentential logic is determined by an assignment of truth-values to its constituent sentence letters, through the following inductive rules. The negation of a sentence is false if the sentence is true, and true if the sentence is false. The conjunction of two sentences is true if both are true, and false otherwise. The disjunction of two sentences is true if at least one is true, and false otherwise. A conditional $\phi \rightarrow \psi$ is true unless ϕ is true and ψ is false. A biconditional between two sentences is true if both sentences have the same truth-value and false otherwise. The idea of treating the truth-value of complex sentences as a function of the truth-values of their components (see COMPOSITIONALITY) – the idea of 'truth-functional' connectives – dates back to the

Stoics (see LOGIC, ANCIENT §5). The treatment of negation, conjunction and disjunction as truth-functional is scarcely controversial, but the same cannot be said of the truth-functional treatment of the conditional and biconditional (see COUNTER-FACTUAL CONDITIONALS; INDICATIVE CONDITIONALS).

The rules just given can be represented diagramatically in the following 'truth table':

ϕ	ψ	$\neg\phi$	$\phi\wedge\psi$	$\phi\vee\psi$	$\phi\to\psi$	$\phi\leftrightarrow\psi$
T	T	F	T	T	T	T
T	F	F	F	T	F	F
F	T	T	F	T	T	F
F	F	T	F	F	T	T

Let us use the table to compute the truth-value of $((A\leftrightarrow B)\wedge A)\to(\neg B)$, given values for A and B of T and F, respectively. The truth-value of $A\leftrightarrow B$, according to the table, is F. But then, applying the rule for $\wedge$ to that and the given value for A, the truth-value for $(A\leftrightarrow B)\wedge A$ is also F. Since the truth-value of B is F, that of $\neg B$ is T. Finally, applying the rule for $\to$ to the last two facts, the truth-value of the whole sentence is T. This computation is represented by the following line of a truth table.

A	B	$A\leftrightarrow B$	$\neg B$	$(A\leftrightarrow B)\wedge A$	$((A\leftrightarrow B)\wedge A)\to(\neg B)$
T	F	F	T	F	T

A sentence that is assigned the value T on every line of its truth table is known as a 'tautology', a term introduced by Wittgenstein, who emphasized the importance of the method of truth tables.

Suppose Γ is a finite set of sentences and ϕ a sentence of sentential logic. It is then possible to construct a truth table that lists the truth-values of ϕ and all the sentences in Γ under all possible combinations of truth assignments to the sentence letters they contain. Now, suppose there is no line of that truth table in which all the sentences in Γ receive the truth-value T and the sentence ϕ receives the value F. Then the corresponding argument form 'Γ, therefore ϕ' is valid. For consider an arbitrary natural-language interpretation. The argument it yields must be valid – if not it would have to be possible for the premises to be true and the conclusion false. But that is not possible, by hypothesis. On the other hand, suppose that there is a line of the table on which all the sentences in Γ are true and ϕ is false. Then the argument form is not valid. For choose a line of the table of the type just assumed to exist. Consider a natural-language interpretation of the argument form that interprets each sentence letter by 'Snow is black' if it is assigned F on the selected line of the table, and by 'Snow is white' if it is assigned T on the selected line. The argument yielded by the interpretation just

specified is one in which the premises are actually true and the conclusion is actually false. It is therefore not valid, and so the argument form is not valid.

This discussion demonstrates a remarkable fact: truth tables provide a precise criterion for whether or not an argument form in sentential logic is valid – it is valid just if there is no line of the table on which all the premises have value T and the conclusion has value F. (The troublesome notion of possibility has dropped out of the picture, since all that turned out to be relevant about possibility was the combinatorial list of possible ways for various simple sentences to be true or false.) Truth tables in fact constitute a mechanical decision procedure for whether an argument form of sentential logic is valid. For one can generate the table mechanically and then check it line by line.

Though truth tables provide a decision procedure in principle, it soon ceases to be a practically feasible one, since the number of lines of a truth table doubles with the addition of each sentence letter. The question of whether there is a more efficient procedure, in the sense that the difficulty of the computation grows as, for example, a polynomial function of the number of letters rather than an exponential one, is a version of perhaps the most important question in the theory of computational complexity (see Garey and Johnson 1979).

4 Expressive completeness

It might seem that the logic developed here is unduly limited in that it allows only five connectives. What about, for example, exclusive 'or', or the majority-of-three connective that holds among three sentences if and only if at least two of them are true? The 'expressive completeness theorem' for sentential logic shows that the limitation is only an apparent one: every truth-functional connective, specified by any truth table whatever, is definable using those already introduced.

The proof of 'expressive completeness' (often called functional completeness) can be illustrated using the majority-of-three connective as an example. The sentence formed by applying it to A, B and C has the same truth table as

$$(A\wedge B\wedge\neg C)\vee(A\wedge\neg B\wedge C)$$
$$\vee(\neg A\wedge B\wedge C)\vee(A\wedge B\wedge C),$$

a disjunction whose components correspond to the four possible ways in which the majority-of-three connective creates a true sentence, these being read off the lines of the truth table. This example is in 'disjunctive normal form', that is, a disjunction of conjunctions of sentence letters and their negations. One can alternatively express an arbitrary truth table by a sentence in 'conjunctive normal form', that is, a conjunction of disjunctions of sentence letters and their negations. (The majority-of-three connective becomes $(A \vee B) \wedge (B \vee C) \wedge (C \vee A)$.) Any truth table can similarly be expressed using only 'and', 'or' and 'not'.

It follows that any set of connectives that can be used to define 'and', 'or' and 'not' is expressively complete. It is an elementary exercise to show in this way that negation plus any one of $\vee$, $\wedge$ or $\rightarrow$ is expressively complete. The binary connective that forms a true sentence if and only if both components are false ('not or') is also expressively complete, as is the one that forms a false sentence if and only if both components are true ('not and'). These last facts were first published by Sheffer (1913), and expressively complete sets of connectives were classified by Post (1941) and Wernick (1942).

5 Truth and logical consequence

The next task is to extend the account of the truth-conditions of sentences to the full predicate calculus. The truth-value of an atomic sentence is determined by whether the objects denoted by the constants stand in the relation denoted by the relation symbol. This can be expressed mathematically by means of an 'interpretation function' that associates an object with each relevant constant symbol and a set of ordered n-tuples of objects with each relevant n-placed relation symbol. (Though natural-language interpretations and interpretation functions play similar roles – they fix how the constant and relation symbols are interpreted – they are not the same: a natural-language interpretation takes each symbol to a suitable item of natural language, while an interpretation function takes each symbol to a suitable set-theoretic object.) For example, the relation on persons specified by '_ is shorter than _' could be symbolized using R^2, which would then be taken by the corresponding interpretation function to the set S of all ordered pairs of persons in which the first person is shorter than the second. If c were to be interpreted as G.E. Moore and d as Kareem Jabbar, then R^2cd would take on the value T precisely because the ordered pair $\langle$G.E. Moore, Kareem Jabbar$\rangle$ is in the set S. The present method goes beyond that of natural-language interpretations in an important respect: an interpretation function can take a relation symbol to an arbitrary collection of ordered n-tuples, even though it might not be specifiable in ordinary language.

In an applied predicate calculus, one selects certain constant and relation symbols to stand for certain objects and sets of n-tuples, reserving the rest to function as schematic letters. One way of introducing integer arithmetic, for example, involves fixing symbols for zero, 'less than' and so on. One can then add to the axioms of a logical system special nonlogical axioms involving those symbols and even restrict the language to eliminate schematic letters.

The truth-value of a universally quantified sentence, say $(\forall v)R^2cv$ (which, on the above interpretation, reads 'G.E. Moore is shorter than everyone'), would be easy to characterize if every relevant object were the interpretation of some constant symbol. It would then be true if all the following sentences were: $R^2cc_0, R^2cc_1, R^2cc_2, \ldots$. But there is no reason to suppose that every relevant object has a name. Consider 'All ravens are black' – surely not every raven has a name. And certainly, no one language could name all the uncountably many real numbers. Nonetheless, each relevant object could be given a name, and so the following works. First, specify a non-empty set to be the domain of the quantifiers (persons, ravens, real numbers, . . .). Second, specify a new constant that has not been employed in any of the sentences under consideration. For our example, the domain is to be persons and the constant might be d. Then, continuing the example, $(\forall v)R^2cv$ is true if R^2cd is true no matter how the interpretation so far specified is expanded by interpreting the constant d as standing for a member of the domain.

It is now possible to give a precise definition of how the truth of sentences is determined. A 'language' (sometimes called a signature or similarity type) is a set of constant and relation symbols. (A language might better be called a vocabulary, but the terminology is standard.) A 'structure' (or 'interpretation') for a language $\mathcal{L}$ is an ordered pair with first member a non-empty collection – the 'universe' of the structure – and second member a suitable (in a sense defined immediately below) function with domain $\mathcal{L}$ – the 'interpretation function' of the structure. (The language is thus determined by the structure, being the domain of the interpretation function.) The interpretation function is required to map every constant symbol in $\mathcal{L}$ to a member of the universe, every sentence letter to a truth-value, every predicate symbol to a set, and every n-placed relation symbol, for n greater then 1, to a collection of ordered n-tuples of members of the universe.

When symbols with a fixed usage are in the language $\mathcal{L}$, one must require that the relevant objects be in the universe and that the interpretation function map such symbols to the correct objects and relations. We can avoid such complications by considering only languages that contain nothing but schematic letters.

Arithmetic, for example, is then considered in terms not of a particular language but of a particular structure, and the axioms of arithmetic, because they will be written using schematic letters, will have interpretations and interpretation functions in addition to the main one.

If $\mathfrak{A}$ and $\mathfrak{A}'$ are structures with the same universe such that the language of $\mathfrak{A}'$ includes the language $\mathcal{L}$ of $\mathfrak{A}$ and possibly some other symbols, and if the interpretation functions of the two structures agree on $\mathcal{L}$, then $\mathfrak{A}'$ is said to be an 'expansion' of $\mathfrak{A}$. When one structure is an expansion of another it differs only in that it may possibly expand the interpretation function to contain some additional symbols in its domain. Note that if d is some definite constant symbol not in $\mathcal{L}$, then for every member a of the universe of $\mathfrak{A}$ there is an expansion in which the interpretation of d is a.

The truth-value of a sentence in a structure is defined by the following conditions on all structures $\mathfrak{A}$ and sentences ϕ of the language of $\mathfrak{A}$:

(1)   (a) If ϕ is of the form $c_i = c_j$, then the truth-value of ϕ in $\mathfrak{A}$ is T if the interpretations of c_i and c_j in $\mathfrak{A}$ (that is, the values of the interpretation function on c_i and c_j) are the same, and the truth-value is F otherwise.

(b) If ϕ is a sentence letter, its value in $\mathfrak{A}$ is the truth-value to which it is mapped by the interpretation function.

(c) If ϕ is of the form $R^n c_1 \ldots c_n$ with $n > 0$, then the truth-value of ϕ in $\mathfrak{A}$ is T if the n-tuple formed from the interpretations of $c_1, \ldots, c_n$ (in that order) is a member of the interpretation of R^n (which, recall, is a set of n-tuples) and it is F otherwise.

(2)   If ϕ is a negation, conjunction, disjunction, conditional or biconditional, then its truth-value is determined from those of its constituents just as in sentential logic.

(3)   If ϕ is of the form $(\forall x)\psi$, $\mathcal{L}$ is the language of $\mathfrak{A}$ and $\mathcal{L}'$ is the language obtained from $\mathcal{L}$ by adding some definite constant symbol d not in $\mathcal{L}$, then the value of ϕ is T if the truth-value of the sentence $\psi(d)$ obtained from ψ by replacing every free occurrence of x by d is T in every expansion of $\mathfrak{A}$ to a structure for $\mathcal{L}'$. The truth-value is F otherwise.

(4)   If ϕ is of the form $(\exists x)\psi$, $\mathcal{L}$ is the language of $\mathfrak{A}$ and $\mathcal{L}'$ is the language obtained from $\mathcal{L}$ by adding some definite constant symbol d not in $\mathcal{L}$, then the value of ϕ is T if there is at least one expansion of $\mathfrak{A}$ to a structure for $\mathcal{L}'$, in which the truth-value of the sentence $\psi(d)$ obtained from

ψ by replacing every free occurrence of x by d is T. It is F otherwise.

It is now possible to define, as Tarski did (1936), logical consequence and logical truth for the predicate calculus in a way parallel to the definitions of tautological consequence and tautology given above. Let the language $\mathcal{L}$ contain only schematic letters. Let Γ be a set of sentences of $\mathcal{L}$ and ϕ a sentence of $\mathcal{L}$. Then ϕ is a 'logical consequence' of Γ if there is no structure for $\mathcal{L}$ in which every sentence in Γ has value T and ϕ has value F; and ϕ is a 'logical truth' if it receives value T in every structure for $\mathcal{L}$. As in the case of sentential logic, one can establish that an argument formalized in the predicate calculus is logically valid just if the formalization of the conclusion is a logical consequence of the formalizations of the premises. In this characterization of logical validity, the precise mathematical notion of a structure has replaced the troublesome notion of logical possibility.

For technical variants of the semantics presented here, including the idea of extending the language by giving the existing variables the role played here by the added constants, see Tarski (1936) and the textbooks by Mates (1965) and Tennant (1978). The customary semantics excludes the possibility of an empty universe or of constants that do not denote any individual, but both can be accommodated at the cost of some complication (see FREE LOGICS).

It is immediate from the definitions that in any structure, if c and d denote the same individual and ϕ is true, then so is the result of substituting d for any or all occurrences of c in ϕ. Likewise, relation symbols denoting the same set of ordered n-tuples, predicates denoting the same set, and sentences with the same truth-value, can all be substituted for one another without changing the truth-value. In short, the predicate calculus is 'extensional' through and through. Some natural-language forms are extensional, others not. Since 'Fibonacci' and 'Leonardo of Pisa' denote the same man and Fibonacci was a mathematician, it follows that Leonardo was a mathematician; but someone may know that Fibonacci was a mathematician without knowing that Leonardo was, so 'knows that' generates forms that are not extensional. The predicate calculus is not adequate to deal with such cases (see INTENSIONAL LOGICS), but even within the extensional sphere, there is no counterpart for the predicate calculus of the expressive completeness theorem for sentential logic. It will in general be true that for a given structure there will be relations on the structure not definable in the language of the structure, structures indistinguishable by any sentence, and more classes of structures for a language than there are sentences of the language.

As for the definability of quantifiers, many are indeed definable with the help of the equality sign, including 'there are n things such that' for each finite number n. But the quantifier 'for finitely many' cannot be defined in the first-order predicate calculus. It requires the resources of second-order predicate calculus, in which the quantifiers range over relations of objects as well as over individual objects (see SECOND- AND HIGHER-ORDER LOGICS).

6   Formal deduction and decidability

As an alternative to the semantic approach adopted above, the inferential role of the various logical constants can be specified by codifying a system of rules for deduction and proof. The idea goes back to Aristotle, though the first fully rigorous system is that of Frege (1879), with his insistence that there be absolutely no room for doubt or disagreement whether a putative proof is in accordance with the rules or not. Some have gone further and taken purely syntactic rules for the manipulation of the logical constants to be constitutive of their meanings, and systems of this sort have been used to introduce intuitionistic logic as well as the 'classical' logic expounded here (see INTUITIONISM; NATURAL DEDUCTION, TABLEAU AND SEQUENT SYSTEMS).

There are many varieties of deductive system (see FORMAL LANGUAGES AND SYSTEMS). The axiomatic variety is conceptually the simplest. A number of logical axioms are laid down, together with rules of inference of the form 'From $\phi_1, \ldots, \phi_n$ infer ψ' for suitably related ϕs and ψ. A common choice is to take the rule of *modus ponens*, 'From ϕ and $\phi \rightarrow \psi$ infer ψ', as the sole rule of inference, supplemented by numerous axioms to offset the absence of other rules. A formal deduction of a conclusion from a set of premises is defined as a finite sequence of sentences which ends with the conclusion and of which every member is either a logical axiom or a premise or else follows immediately from preceding members by a rule of inference. Formal proof is introduced as the limiting case of a deduction from the empty set of premises. A sentence is said to be 'deducible' from others in the system if there exists a formal deduction of it from them, and a sentence is a theorem if there exists a formal proof of it. Church (1956) gives a survey of axiomatic systems for sentential logic and for predicate logic. The latter generally invoke an extended deductive apparatus that covers formulas with free variables as well as sentences proper, but Quine (1955) presents an axiomatic system confined strictly to sentences.

Natural deduction systems include a more sophisticated kind of rule, designed to exploit assumptions –

propositions assumed for argument's sake and treated as extra premises for as long as they are wanted. Proof by *reductio ad absurdum* is a good informal illustration of the idea: wishing to prove ϕ, one supposes for argument's sake that it is false and tries to derive a contradiction, whereupon one discards the assumption and infers that ϕ must be true. The definition of formal deduction now has to keep track of the introduction and subsequent discharge (discarding) of assumptions; see, for example, Lemmon (1965). This complication is, however, offset by there being fewer or even no axioms, and by the comparative naturalness and brevity of deductions. (For this and some related kinds of deductive system see NATURAL DEDUCTION, TABLEAU AND SEQUENT SYSTEMS §1.)

To be adequate for its purpose, any deductive system must satisfy two conditions. It must be 'sound', in the sense that it does not license deductions whose conclusions do not follow logically from their premises. And it must be 'complete', that is, strong enough to ensure that every logical consequence of a set of sentences is deducible from them. When a system is both sound and complete, deducibility becomes equivalent to logical consequence and likewise theoremhood is equivalent to logical truth. Of the two conditions, completeness is nearly always much more difficult to establish. The first proof of the completeness of a deductive system for the predicate calculus was given by Gödel (1930; see also MODEL THEORY §4), while Henkin (1949) devised a novel method of proving completeness that has found applications far beyond its original one to the predicate calculus. Although second- and higher-order predicate calculi have significantly more expressive capacity than first-order, their great drawback is that there can never be a sound and complete deductive system for them (see SECOND- AND HIGHER-ORDER LOGICS §1). The dominant position of the first-order calculus is the result of its being rich enough to formalize a vast range of arguments from mathematics and elsewhere, yet simple enough for all its valid argument forms to be reducible to a few simple rules of inference.

If a sentence of the predicate calculus is a logical consequence of others, that fact can be shown by deriving it from them in a sound and complete deductive system. Although in practice this may require considerable ingenuity, in principle a machine can generate a list of successive finite sequences of sentences on which sooner or later the right one – by hypothesis there is a right one – will turn up. Nonetheless, the method of formal deduction does not provide a decision procedure for logical consequence. The fact that a deduction has not yet turned up means nothing. For there is in general no way of telling whether this is because no such deduction exists – that is, the conclusion in question is not a logical consequence of the premises – or whether it is merely that we have not tried hard or long enough. If we could find a counterexample – a structure in which the putative conclusion is false while the premises are true – that would indeed show that it is not a logical consequence of them. But the parallelism between truth tables and structures breaks down at this point. In sentential logic all one has to do is set out the relevant truth table and inspect its rows. There will, however, always be infinitely many relevant structures, not to mention structures with infinitely many objects. The analogue of setting out and inspecting the rows of a truth table thus involves infinitely many steps and cannot be carried out even in principle.

This strongly suggests the absence of a decision procedure for the predicate calculus, and Church has proved that none exists. However, positive results can be obtained in some restricted cases, the simplest and most important example being that there is a decision procedure for the monadic predicate calculus, that is, the fragment whose language includes predicate symbols but no n-placed relation symbols for $n > 1$. (See CHURCH'S THEOREM AND THE DECISION PROBLEM.) For further results of this sort, see Dreben and Goldfarb (1979). Many interesting questions concerning feasibility and quantificational logic arise (see Börger 1989).

See also: LOGICAL AND MATHEMATICAL TERMS, GLOSSARY OF

References and further reading

* Börger, E. (1989) *Computability, Complexity, Logic*, New York: North Holland. (A comparatively accessible treatment of the areas of research on the border between mathematical logic and computational complexity theory.)
* Carnap, R. (1934) *Logische Syntax der Sprache*, Vienna: Springer; trans. A. Smeaton, *Logical Syntax of Language*, London: Kegan Paul, 1937. (An influential discussion of the relation between ordinary language and the sort of formal language introduced here, the notions of logical truth and consequence and much else. Carnap (1935) discusses many of the same ideas in a less technical way.)
—— (1935) *Philosophy and Logical Syntax*, London: Kegan Paul, Trench, Trubner & Co. (A semi-popular account of Carnap's attitude towards philosophy. A clear and useful example of one important sort of impact the predicate calculus has had on philosophers for much of the twentieth century.)
—— (1942) *Introduction to Semantics*, Cambridge, MA: Harvard University Press. (An influential later discussion of the relation between ordinary language and the sort of formal language introduced here, the notions of logical truth and consequence, and much else.)
* Church, A. (1956) *Introduction to Mathematical Logic*, Princeton, NJ: Princeton University Press. (An influential, exceptionally rigorous introduction to the predicate calculus, with a wealth of historical information.)
* Dreben, B. and Goldfarb, W.D. (1979) *The Decision Problem: Solvable Classes of Quantificational Formulas*, Reading, MA: Addison-Wesley. (A detailed analysis of which fragments of the predicate calculus are simple enough have a decision procedure.)
* Frege, G. (1879) *Begriffsschrift, eine der arithmetischen nachgebildete Formelsprache des reinen Denkens*, Halle: Nebert; trans. '*Begriffsschrift*, a Formula Language, Modelled Upon That of Arithmetic, for Pure Thought', in J. van Heijenoort (ed.) *From Frege to Gödel: A Source Book in Mathematical Logic, 1879–1931*, Cambridge, MA: Harvard University Press, 1967, 1–82. (The classic source for the predicate calculus, in the form of second-order predicate calculus.)
* Garey, M.R. and Johnson, D.S. (1979) *Computers and Intractability: A Guide to the Theory of NP-Completeness*, San Francisco, CA: Freeman. (A very readable account of why truth tables are not a practical decision method, how the notion of a practical method can be characterized, and related problems of feasibility.)
* Gödel, K. (1930) 'Die Vollständigkeit der Axiome des logischen Funktionenkalküls', *Monatshefte für Mathematik und Physik* 37: 349–60; trans. 'The Completeness of the Axioms of the Functional Calculus of Logic', in J. van Heijenoort (ed.) *From Frege to Gödel: A Source Book in Mathematical Logic, 1879–1931*, Cambridge, MA: Harvard University Press, 1967, 582–91. (Cited in §5. The first proof of the completeness of an axiom system for the predicate calculus.)
* Haack, S. (1978) *Philosophy of Logics*, New York: Cambridge University Press. (A thorough and engaging synoptic account of many of the issues raised in this entry and of alternatives and generalizations of the logic introduced here.)
* Hasenjäger, G. (1953) 'Eine Bemerkung zu Henkins Beweis für die Vollständigkeit des Prädikatenkalküls der ersten Stufe', *Journal of Symbolic Logic* 18: 42–8. (Includes one of the first proofs that if a

sentence of the predicate calculus has a model, it has one with domain the natural numbers and in which all the predicates are definable in the language of arithmetic.)

* Henkin, L. (1949) 'The Completeness of the First-Order Functional Calculus', *Journal of Symbolic Logic* 14: 159–66. (Cited in §5.)

Hilbert, D. and Ackermann, W. (1928) *Grundzüge der theoretischen Logik*, Berlin: Springer, 2nd edn, 1938; trans. L.M. Hammond, G.G. Leckie and F. Steinhardt, *Principles of Mathematical Logic*, ed. R.E. Luce, New York: Chelsea, 1950. (A classic introduction to the predicate calculus, with a wealth of detail not available in later texts.)

* Kleene, S.C. (1952) *Introduction to Metamathematics*, Amsterdam: North Holland, and New York: Van Nostrand. (Perhaps the most influential modern text on the mathematics of the predicate calculus.)

* Koslow, A. (1992) *A Structuralist Theory of Logic*, New York: Cambridge University Press. (An insightful attempt to characterize what is logical in terms of an analysis of the consequence relation.)

* Lemmon, E.J. (1965) *Beginning Logic*, London: Nelson. (Cited in §5. An exceptionally user-friendly exposition of a natural deduction system for the predicate calculus.)

* Mates, B. (1965) *Elementary Logic*, New York: Oxford University Press. (Cited in §4.)

Peirce, C.S. (1931–58) *Collected Papers*, vol. 2, *Elements of Logic*, vol. 3, *Exact Logic*, ed. C. Hartshorne and P. Weiss, Cambridge, MA: Harvard University Press. (Peirce was one of the inventors of quantifiers, and he coined the term.)

* Post, E.L. (1941) *The Two-Valued Iterative Systems of Mathematical Logic*, Princeton, NJ: Princeton University Press. (Includes an analysis of complete sets of connectives for sentential logic.)

* Quine, W.V. (1940) *Mathematical Logic*, Cambridge, MA: Harvard University Press, 1955. (Cited in §5.)

* Sheffer, H.M. (1913) 'A Set of Five Independent Postulates for Boolean Algebras, With Application To Logical Constants', *Transactions of the American Mathematical Society* 14: 481–8. (The first publication of the fact that there is a single connective that is expressively complete for sentential logic.)

* Sher, G. (1991) *The Bounds of Logic: A Generalized Viewpoint*, Cambridge, MA: MIT Press. (A thorough working out of the Tarskian idea that what counts as logical should be characterized in terms of what can be characterized using semantics of the sort described in §4.)

Tarski, A. (1933) *Pojęcie prawdy w językach nauk dedukcyjnych*, Warsaw; trans. J.H. Woodger (1956), 'The Concept of Truth in Formalized Languages', in *Logic, Semantics, Metamathematics: Papers from 1923 to 1938*, ed. J. Corcoran, Indianapolis, IN: Hackett Publishing Company, 2nd edn, 1983, 152–278. (One of the most influential works of the century; includes the definition of truth presented here.)

* —— (1936) 'O pojęciu wynikania logicznego', *Przegląd Filozoficzny* 39: 58–68; trans. J.H. Woodger (1956), 'On the Concept of Logical Consequence', in *Logic, Semantics, Metamathematics: Papers from 1923 to 1938*, ed. J. Corcoran, Indianapolis, IN: Hackett Publishing Company, 2nd edn, 1983. (The definitive formulation of the semantic conception of consequence.)

* Tennant, N. (1978) *Natural Logic*, Edinburgh: Edinburgh University Press. (Cited in §4.)

* Wernick, W. (1942) 'Complete Sets of Logical Functions', *Transactions of the American Mathematical Society* 51: 117–32. (An analysis of the complete sets of connectives for sentential logic.)

Whitehead, A.N. and Russell, B.A.W. (1910) *Principia Mathematica*, vol. 1, Cambridge: Cambridge University Press; 2nd edn, 1925; repr. 1994. (This is the work that established that, in a suitable sense, all of classical mathematics can be formalized within the higher-order predicate calculus.)

SHAUGHAN LAVINE

PREDICATION

Some sentences have a very simple structure, consisting only of a part which serves to pick out a particular object and a part which says something about the object picked out. Expressions which can be used to say something about objects picked out are called predicates. Thus 'smokes' in 'Sam smokes' is a predicate. But 'predication' may refer either to the activity of predicating or to what is predicated. To understand either we need to know what predicates are and how they combine with other expressions.

Predicates, unlike proper names, can be negated. They combine with other expressions in ways described by categorial grammar: predicates are incomplete and are completed by other expressions, such as proper names. The word 'smokes' in 'Sam smokes' is called a monadic or 1-place predicate; predicates with two or more places are called relational predicates ('Sam loves Erna', '3 is between 2 and 4').

Since Frege it has been customary to hold that the incomplete or predicative parts of 'Sam smokes' and

'Sam is a smoker' are, respectively, 'smokes' and 'is a smoker' (see FREGE, G. §§2–4). According to an older view, the incomplete part of 'Sam is a smoker' is the copula 'is', which is completed by two complete expressions, 'Sam' and 'a smoker' ('a' can be ignored as an accident of English). Sometimes called 'the two name theory of predication', this view allows two types of name – proper names and common nouns.

Is predication merely a matter of words? Are mental acts or the senses of words essential to it? For Frege, names and predicates are correlated with ideal senses, and the sentential wholes to which they belong with ideal thoughts or propositions (see SENSE AND REFERENCE §2; Frege 1892a). The sense or meaning of a proper name is sometimes called an individual concept, that of a predicate a concept (Frege himself used neither 'concept' nor 'meaning' in this way). It has been held that to use a predicate is to perform a mental act of predicating and that to use a proper name is to perform a mental act of naming or referring. HUSSERL and others appeal to both senses and mental acts and conceive of the latter as tokenings of the former. The unity of thoughts and of thinkings, on these views, resembles but is prior to the unity of the sentence: predicative senses require non-predicative senses; predicatings require referrings or acts of quantifying over individuals.

Predication occurs in the context of a variety of mental acts and linguistic actions: I may wonder or ask whether Sam smokes. So to predicate is not always to judge or assert. To assert that if Sam smokes he will smell is not thereby to assert that Sam smokes, although it is to predicate this of him in the context of entertaining or supposing the thought that Sam smokes.

Frege and Husserl pointed out that to deny that Sam smokes is just to assert that he does not smoke. Denying and judging are not on a par because 'not' belongs within the sentence, its sense to that of the sentence. There is, it is true, the phenomenon of polemic negation, as when the third word of the following sentence is stressed: 'Wittgenstein was not German'. But this is a pragmatic phenomenon.

What is it that is predicated? Just as names designate things, so too predicates are said to stand in a semantic relation (reference, signification) to one or more of the following: properties (attributes); what Frege (in his own technical sense) called 'unsaturated concepts'; sets; and relations between objects and possible worlds (see SEMANTICS, POSSIBLE WORLDS §9). Thus predication may be held to involve saying of Sam that he falls under the sense of the predicate 'smokes', exemplifies the property of being a smoker, or belongs to the set of smokers – or some combination of these. The semantic values of predicates and other parts of a sentence are sometimes said to form states of affairs or situations – which may or may not obtain – or facts.

The foregoing contains five simplifications and questionable presuppositions. First, does predication only occur within sentences (thoughts, thinkings)? If a builder shouts 'Slab!' to his assistant is he not producing a non-elliptic predication? Second, we may wonder, with Wittgenstein (1968), to whom the preceding example is due, whether there is in fact any uniform type of semantic relation between predicates, on the one hand, and properties and their ilk, on the other hand.

Third, the apparent (surface, grammatical) forms of predicates can diverge in different ways from their logical (deep) forms. To say that Pierre is tall is not to predicate the monadic property of being tall of him but to predicate, of him and the average member of some reference class, the relational property of being taller than. Furthermore, if we accept the view (of Davidson; and of Parsons 1990) that many sentences involve quantification over events, then to say that Sam is smoking is to predicate of some event that it is an event of smoking and to predicate of it and Sam that Sam is the agent of it (see ADVERBS §1).

Fourth, according to Ramsey (1990) there is no essential distinction, in 'Socrates is wise', between its subject and monadic predicate because the sentence expresses the same proposition as 'Wisdom is a characteristic of Socrates'. So no fundamental classification between individuals and properties can be based upon such a distinction.

Finally, if we take seriously the claim that predicates are incomplete, then we should say that in 'Sam smokes' the predicate is not 'smokes' but '___ smokes', the gappy result of deleting the proper name from the sentence. Thus both 'Booth shot Lincoln' and 'Booth shot Booth' contain the predicate 'Booth shot ___'. But, as Geach indicates in his discussion of this example ('Quine on Classes and Properties', 1981: 222–5), the predicate here is not a physical part of the two sentences; it is a sentence pattern which 'Booth shot' helps to form. A related view is that such sentence patterns are abstract features of sentences, as melodies are of spoken sentences. But then we might wonder whether 'Booth ___' is not just as much a sentence pattern as 'Booth shot ___'.

See also: LOGICAL AND MATHEMATICAL TERMS, GLOSSARY OF; PROPER NAMES; PROPERTY THEORY; STRAWSON, P.F. §5

References and further reading

Frege, G. (1891) *Funktion und Begriff*, Jena: Pohle; trans. P.T. Geach, 'Function and Concept', in *Collected Papers on Mathematics, Logic and Philosophy*, ed. B. McGuinness, Oxford: Blackwell, 1984, 137–56. (Classic account of the role of functions in predication.)

* —— (1892a) 'Über Sinn und Bedeutung', *Zeitschrift für Philosophie und philosophische Kritik* 100: 25–50; trans. M. Black, 'On Sense and Meaning', in *Collected Papers on Mathematics, Logic and Philosophy*, ed. B. McGuinness, Oxford: Blackwell, 1984, 157–77. (The classic account of the sense and reference of sentences and their parts.)

—— (1892b) 'Über Begriff und Gegenstand', *Vierteljahrsschrift für wissenschaftliche Philosophie* 16: 192–205; trans. P.T. Geach, 'On Concept and Object', in *Collected Papers on Mathematics, Logic and Philosophy*, ed. B. McGuinness, Oxford: Blackwell, 1984, 182–94. (Classic account of what predicates and names signify.)

Geach, P.T. (1975) 'Names and Identity', in S. Guttenplan (ed.) *Mind and Language*, Oxford: Clarendon Press, 139–58. (Important treatment of the nature of predication, drawing on Frege.)

* —— (1981) *Logic Matters*, Oxford: Blackwell. (See 'History of the Corruptions of Logic' for a historical sketch of the relations between the two name theory and the theory fully worked out by Frege.)

* Parsons, T. (1990) *Events in the Semantics of English*, Cambridge MA: MIT Press. (Elegantly defends the controversial view that many sentences involve quantification over and predication of events and states.)

* Ramsey, F. (1990) 'Universals', in *Philosophical Papers*, ed. H. Mellor, Cambridge: Cambridge University Press, 8–30. (Stimulating, critical examination of some ways of distinguishing between subjects and predicates and between particulars and properties.)

Simons, P. (1981) 'Unsaturatedness', *Grazer Philosophische Studien*, 14: 73–95. (Surveys different types of unsaturatedness and incompleteness and their relations to the notions of function, functor and predication.)

* Wittgenstein, L. (1968) *Philosophical Investigations*, Oxford: Blackwell. (Includes discussion of a series of examples that throw doubt on the plausibility of many common assumptions about sentences and semantic relations.)

KEVIN MULLIGAN

PREDICTION IN THE SOCIAL SCIENCES *see* SOCIAL SCIENCES, PREDICTION IN

PREFACE PARADOX
see PARADOXES, EPISTEMIC

PRESCRIPTIVISM

Prescriptivism is a theory about moral statements. It claims that such statements contain an element of meaning which serves to prescribe or direct actions. The history of prescriptivism includes Socrates, Aristotle, Hume, Kant and Mill, and it has been influential also in recent times.

Moral statements also contain a factual or descriptive element. The descriptive element of morality differs between persons and cultures, but the prescriptive element remains constant.

Prescriptivism can allow for moral disagreement, and explain moral weakness. It can also explain better than other theories the rationality and objectivity of moral thinking.

1 Definition and history
2 Prescriptive and descriptive meaning
3 Prescriptivism defended

1 Definition and history

Prescriptivism is a meta-ethical theory about the meaning of moral statements which holds that, in addition to any factual or descriptive meaning they may have, there is a prescriptive element in their meaning which is irreducible to any factual equivalent, but serves to prescribe or direct actions (see ANALYTIC ETHICS §1; MORAL JUDGMENT §1).

The prescriptivity of moral statements has been recognized from the earliest times by philosophers, though it is only in the present century that thinkers have begun to develop a clear account of the relation between the descriptive and prescriptive elements in their meaning. Socrates was in part a prescriptivist, as is evident from the trouble he had in explaining how one could think something good, and yet not pursue it (see especially Plato's *Protagoras* (358) and *Gorgias* (467)) (see SOCRATES §6). Aristotle, who took up Socrates' problem about weakness of will, showed clearly, by his handling of it, a prescriptivist strand in his theory (*Nicomachean Ethics* 1145b23) (see

AKRASIA). *Phronēsis* or practical wisdom, which tells us what we ought to do, is described by him as *epitāktikē* or prescriptive (*Nicomachean Ethics* 1143a8) (see ARISTOTLE §23). The practical syllogisms which are the channel of this instruction all have prescriptive first premises (*Nicomachean Ethics* 1144a31, 1147a25; *On the Soul* 434a16; *On the Movement of Animals* 701a7); if they did not, they could not validly conclude in actions. He solved Socrates' problem in a way consistent with his prescriptivism (see Hare 1992a).

Hume also recognized the prescriptive element in the meaning of moral statements (see especially *A Treatise of Human Nature* (1739–40), where he wrongly claims that because of its lack of prescriptivity 'reason is perfectly inert') (see HUME, D. §4.8); but his settled theory was subjectivist rather than prescriptivist (the two kinds of theory are to this day often confused). He says that 'when you pronounce an action or character to be vicious, you mean nothing, but that from the constitution of your nature you have a feeling or sentiment of blame from the contemplation of it' (1739–40). Moral statements are for him reports rather than expressions of feelings or desires.

Kant rescued reason from inertia, and was clearly a prescriptivist; moral facts play no significant part in his ethical theory, the basic constituents of which are maxims, that is to say, prescriptions, originating in the will, and expressed often in the imperative (the German *soll* is equivalent to an imperative) (see KANTIAN ETHICS). Echoing the language of Hume about 'is' and 'ought', J.S. Mill avowedly declared himself a prescriptivist by calling moral statements 'imperatives' (1843) (see MILL, J.S. §11). But modern descriptivist opponents of prescriptivism, who often have a blind spot for prescriptivity, have seldom noticed these premonitions of modern prescriptivism.

In recent times many philosophers have held prescriptivist views of more or less considered kinds (such as Carnap 1935: 18; Ayer 1936, 1949; Stevenson 1944) (see AYER, A.J. §5; CARNAP, R. §3; STEVENSON, C.L.). These were all followers of emotivism, the view that moral statements get their meaning by expressing feelings or attitudes of approval or disapproval (see EMOTIVISM). But prescriptivists do not have to be emotivists; if they are concerned for the rationality of moral thinking they will not be. It is possible to hold, with Kant, that moral maxims originate in the rational will, which he says 'is nothing but practical reason' ([1785] 1903: 412), and that, though their main function is not to state facts, the adoption of them can be a rational process. A recent version of prescriptivism put forward by R.M. HARE has, following Kant, claimed objectivity, in a sense

carefully defined and distinguished from factuality, for moral statements (see Hare 1993).

2 Prescriptive and descriptive meaning

Prescriptive meaning is often likened generically to that of imperatives, which also prescribe actions; but careful ethical prescriptivists emphasize also the differences, as well as the similarities, between moral statements and imperatives. The chief of these differences is that moral statements also have, unlike imperatives, a descriptive or factual content. This is linked with another feature of moral statements, known in the jargon as universalizability: the feature that a moral statement about one situation must apply to any other situation similar in all its universal properties (that is, those which can be described without reference to the individuals involved). That moral statements are universalizable is acknowledged by most thinkers, whether or not they are prescriptivists (see UNIVERSALISM IN ETHICS).

If moral statements are universalizable in this way, they will inevitably acquire a descriptive function as part of their meaning; for someone who makes such a statement must think that the moral properties of the situation about which it is made supervene on its nonmoral properties (the reasons for making it) in accordance with a principle applying to all identically similar situations (see SUPERVENIENCE). Thus they will be taken to hold that there are facts that justify the statement, and it thus acquires a factual, descriptive content or meaning. However, since different people and cultures hold differing moral principles, this descriptive meaning (the truth conditions of the statement) may vary from one person or culture to another (see MORAL RELATIVISM). It is the prescriptive meaning which remains constant: whatever kinds of behaviour different people or cultures prescribe, they are all prescribing them for all similar cases. This, as we shall see, is what gives moral reasoning its grip.

The relation between the prescriptive and descriptive elements in the meaning of moral statements has been much misunderstood. The prescriptive meaning is the function all normative and evaluative statements have of guiding our actions. This shows up in the fact that someone who makes one about his own proposed actions but does not act accordingly exposes himself to a charge of speaking insincerely, as also does someone who makes one about other people's actions but does not will them (in the above broad sense) so to act.

The descriptive meaning is the standard or criterion or reason or principle in accordance with which the statement is made. For example, if I say,

'You ought not to say that, because it would be a lie,' I am applying the principle that one ought not to tell lies. The 'because'-clause does not merely repeat the 'ought'-statement; it adds a reason for it. A common mistake is to confuse the content of moral statements with the reasons for them. That this is a mistake is shown by the fact that different people might make the same moral statement for quite different reasons; they might disagree radically in their moral principles. They would then be giving the same prescription, but disagreeing in their reasons for it.

Likewise, two people who differ about a moral question, one saying, 'He ought,' and the other, 'He ought not,' are affirming and rejecting, respectively, the same moral statement; otherwise they would not be disagreeing. That is what is wrong with the kind of subjectivism mentioned above. The statement is the same because it contains the same universal prescription, which one of them accepts and the other rejects. The fact that they are disputing about the same statement, bound by the same logic, is what enables argument between them to begin, in order to seek a resolution of their dispute (see §3).

3 Prescriptivism defended

There are many confusions that have to be cleared up before we can understand the prescriptivist position. The first we have noticed already: prescriptivists hold that moral statements are expressions of volition (in a broad sense in which it covers Kant's rational will and Aristotle's *boulēsis* or rational desire). They do not hold that they are statements that the speaker in fact wills something. They are therefore not exposed to the charge that they make our duties depend on what we will, as if we could make something our duty by willing it. If that kind of subjectivism were correct, then if someone said that something was their duty they would mean that as a matter of fact they willed it; and if they really did will it, it would be impossible to refute them. Rather, prescriptivists hold that in making a moral statement we are expressing our rational will; and if someone else wills something different, the disagreement has to be resolved by reason, that is, by determining which prescription can be rationally willed in the light of all the nonmoral facts, and respecting the logical property of universalizability (see §2), which, as Kant again saw, affords a powerful weapon in moral argument.

Opponents of prescriptivism and in general of ethical internalism commonly object that it is possible for persons to make a moral statement but to have no disposition to act on it nor to desire others to act on it (see MORAL MOTIVATION §§1–3). They might be weak-willed persons or akratic, or satanists, who do

wrong acts just because they are wrong, or amoralists who do not accept moral statements as guides to action (see AKRASIA). Answers to these objections have been put forward by Hare (1992a, 1992b: 98, and 1981 respectively). They require careful distinctions between different senses in which one can think that something ought to be done, not all of which are prescriptive.

The prescriptive sense of words like 'ought' is their central but not their only sense, and the existence of other senses easily gives colour to objections of this sort. The fact that moral statements carry descriptive as well as prescriptive meaning also makes it easy for descriptivists, attending only to this descriptive meaning, to argue that the statements are purely descriptive, that is, that their meaning is determined by their truth conditions and by nothing else. Often such arguments are reinforced by appeals to the surface grammar of moral statements, which are commonly in the declarative or indicative mood (though 'ought'-statements are an exception). But the fact that such statements do have descriptive meaning, determined by truth conditions, alongside their prescriptive meaning is quite enough to explain such phenomena. These, however, do not show that they lack prescriptive meaning, nor that this is not central.

Moral words fall into two classes, according to how tightly the two parts of their meaning are tied to them. The distinction is sometimes made in terms of a contrast between 'thin' and 'thick' moral concepts. There are first the primarily prescriptive (or primarily evaluative) words like 'ought', 'wrong' and 'good', whose prescriptive meaning is more firmly attached to them than their descriptive. If someone starts making some of their moral judgments by entirely new standards (they have become a pacifist, say, or a vegetarian), they can still go on using those words, in the same senses, to express and apply the new standards.

By contrast there are other words, the secondarily prescriptive, whose prescriptive meaning is tied to them more loosely than their descriptive. If the standards encapsulated in these words are discarded, as in principle they can be, the words have to be discarded with them (see Hare 1963: 189, footnote).

A common move of descriptivists is to claim that there is no real difference in prescriptivity between prescriptive and descriptive speech acts, because either can be used to guide action. To say that a man has frequently beaten his first wife before their divorce may provide an incentive not to become his second; yet, it is claimed, the statement that he indulged in wife-beating is all the same descriptive. But a lady such as 'O' who liked to be beaten might not call him a bad husband (Réage 1954: 17). Thus 'wife-beater' is only contingently a pejorative term, but 'bad husband' is necessarily so. That is the difference between inherently and merely contingently action-guiding expressions. Only the former are genuinely prescriptive.

In spite of appearances, prescriptivism has the advantage over descriptivist theories when it comes to establishing the rationality and objectivity of moral thinking. Objectivity may be defined as acceptability to all rational thinkers. All forms of descriptivism have to rely on appeals either to generally accepted moral convictions, which may vary from one culture to another or to the meanings of words (especially secondarily prescriptive words) which encapsulate such culturally relative values. Only prescriptivists can rely solely on the logic of moral statements, which can be invariant between cultures; they can ask, as Kant did, what one can will to be a universal law, applicable whoever occupies whatever role in a situation. Faced with this question, rational thinkers will agree on the answer (see MORAL KNOWLEDGE §3). They will thus come to agree on principles giving the truth-conditions of moral statements – principles which are acceptable to all rational thinkers and depend solely on logic and the nonmoral facts. This is the only way to secure objective, culture-invariant, truth for moral statements (Hare 1993).

See also: LOGIC OF ETHICAL DISCOURSE

References and further reading

* Aristotle (*c.* mid 4th century BC) *Nicomachean Ethics*, trans. with notes by T. Irwin, Indianapolis, IN: Hackett Publishing Company, 1985. (Contains prescriptivist strands in his accounts of weakness of will, practical wisdom, and the practical syllogism.)
* —— (*c.* mid 4th century BC) *On the Soul*, trans. with notes by J.A. Smith, Oxford: Oxford University Press, 1931. (Discusses the prescriptive first premises of practical syllogism.)
* —— (*c.* mid 4th century BC) *On the Movement of Animals*, trans. A.S.L. Farquarson, Oxford: Oxford University Press, 1912. (Discusses the prescriptive first premises of practical syllogism.)
* Ayer, A.J. (1936) *Language, Truth and Logic*, London: Gollancz; 2nd edn, 1946, ch. 6. (Early and central discussion of emotivism.)
* —— (1949) 'On the analysis of moral judgments', *Horizon* 20; repr. in *Philosophical Essays*, London: Macmillan, 1965. (Important British advocate of emotivism.)
* Carnap, R. (1935) *Philosophy and Logical Syntax*, London: Routledge & Kegan Paul. (Early imperativist.)
Hare, R.M. (1952) *The Language of Morals*, Oxford: Oxford University Press.
* —— (1963) *Freedom and Reason*, Oxford: Oxford University Press.
* —— (1981) *Moral Thinking*, Oxford: Oxford University Press. (The last three items set out the author's prescriptivist position.)
* —— (1992a) 'Weakness of will', in L. Becker (ed.) *Encyclopedia of Ethics*, New York: Garland Publishing Company. (Includes discussion of moral weakness.)
* —— (1992b) *Essays on Religion and Education*, Oxford: Oxford University Press. (Includes papers on practical topics written from a prescriptivist point of view.)
* —— (1993) 'Objective Prescriptions', in E. Villanueva (ed.) *Naturalism and Normativity*, Atascadero, CA: Ridgeview; also published in A.P. Griffiths (ed.) *Ethics* (Royal Institute of Philosophy Lectures, 1992/3), Cambridge: Cambridge University Press. (On prescriptivism and truth in ethics.)
—— (1997) *Sorting Out Ethics*, Oxford: Oxford University Press. (Includes critical discussion of various ethical theories from a prescriptivist point of view.)
* Hume, D. (1739–40) *A Treatise of Human Nature*, ed. L.A. Selby-Bigge, revised by P.H. Nidditch, Oxford: Clarendon Press, 2nd edn, 1978, book 3, part I, section 1. (A classical attack on ethical realism.)
* Kant, I. (1785) *Grundlegung zur Metaphysik der Sitten*, in *Kants gesammelte Schriften*, ed. Königlichen Preußischen Akademie der Wissenschaften, Berlin: Reimer, vol. 4, 1903; trans. with notes by H.J. Paton, *Groundwork of the Metaphysics of Morals* (originally *The Moral Law*), London: Hutchinson, 1948; repr. New York: Harper & Row, 1964. (The reference made to this work in the entry gives the page number from the 1903 Berlin Akademie volume; the page number from the *original* German edition is 36. Both of these sets of page numbers are included in the margins of the Paton translation. This is the work of a prescriptivist who bases his ethics on 'rational maxims'.)
* Mill, J.S. (1843) 'The Logic of Practice or Art', in *System of Logic: Ratiocinative and Inductive*, London: Parker; repr. in *Collected Works of John Stuart Mill*, London: Routledge, vols 7 and 8, 1991, book 6, ch. 12. (Explains Mill's prescriptivism.)
* Plato (*c.*395–387 BC) *Gorgias*, trans. W.K.C. Guthrie, in E. Hamilton and H. Cairns (eds) *The Collected Dialogues including Letters*, Oxford: Oxford University Press, 1975. (Demonstrates prescriptivist elements in Socrates's thought.)

* —— (c.386–380 BC) *Protagoras*, trans. W.K.C. Guthrie, in E. Hamilton and H. Cairns (eds) *Plato, The Collected Dialogues including Letters*, Oxford: Oxford University Press, 1975. (Demonstrates prescriptivist elements in Socrates's thought.)

* Réage, P. (1954) *L'Histoire d'O*, Paris: Sceaux; cited in W. Young, *Eros Denied*, London: Weidenfeld, 1964, 241. (A well-known account of masochism.)

* Stevenson, C.L. (1944) *Ethics and Language*, New Haven, CT: Yale University Press. (The fullest exposition of emotivism.)

R.M. HARE

PRESOCRATIC PHILOSOPHY

The Presocratics were the first Western philosophers. The most celebrated are Thales, Anaximander, Pythagoras, Heraclitus, Parmenides, Zeno of Elea, Empedocles, Anaxagoras and Democritus. Active in Greece throughout the sixth and fifth centuries BC, they concentrated on cosmogony and cosmology – the tasks of explaining the world's origin and order, without recourse to mythology.

Socrates (469–399 BC) is perceived as marking a watershed in philosophy – a shift of focus from the origin and nature of the universe to human values. 'Presocratic' philosophy thus represents the era intellectually antecedent to Socrates, even though its exponents included contemporaries of his (some his juniors). Those thinkers contemporary with Socrates who shared his concentration on human values it is better not to call Presocratic (see SOPHISTS). No complete Presocratic text survives. We have only later writers' quotations ('fragments'), summaries (see DOXOGRAPHY), criticisms, and so on, from which to glimpse the originals.

A mythological construction of the world was already integral to the earliest poetry familiar to the Greeks (c.700 BC) (see HESIOD; HOMER). Philosophers' rationalizations of this picture concentrated initially on such questions as what the world's primeval stuff is, why the earth remains stable and, more generally, what made the world orderly. In time *kosmos* ('ordering'), came to mean 'world'. To explain cosmic order, biological, mechanical and even political models were developed. However, Presocratic philosophy was interested equally in the human soul and its destiny (see PSYCHĒ), and never altogether ignored human values. Another dominant issue was the possibility of human knowledge.

The main movements and phases were as follows.

The three sixth-century BC Milesian philosophers, starting with Thales, were monists: each posited a single primeval stuff – for example, water, air. These came to function not just as the world's originative stuff but also perhaps as its enduring substrate (see ARCHĒ; THALES §2; ANAXIMANDER §§2–3; ANAXIMENES; MONISM).

Pythagoreanism, although a secretive movement with cultic leanings, was highly influential throughout this era. Beyond a concern with the soul and survival, it promoted a mathematicizing approach to cosmology (see PYTHAGORAS §1; PYTHAGOREANISM §2; ORPHISM; PHILOLAUS §§2–3).

Heraclitus (c.540–480 BC) kept the formal focus on the cosmos and the soul, but his approach was largely governed by metaphysical concerns, especially the paradoxical interdependence of opposites (see HERACLITUS §3). Metaphysics and logic took centre stage soon after in the Eleatic movement, initiated by PARMENIDES and continued by ZENO OF ELEA and MELISSUS. Eleaticism was a radical critique of ordinary notions of being, defending instead a strict monism which outlawed all phenomenal distinctions and changes as illusory (see also GORGIAS §3).

The later fifth-century BC cosmologists sought to deflect this Eleatic critique. Most were pluralists, positing more than one underlying element. Their contributions culminated in the atomic system of DEMOCRITUS, which reduced all reality to atoms and void, conceding much to Eleaticism (see ATOMISM, ANCIENT; ANAXAGORAS; EMPEDOCLES; LEUCIPPUS)

Presocratic philosophy is often seen as materialistic. However, no philosopher before Leucippus and Democritus reduced life and intelligence to something inanimate. Previous Presocratics considered these ineliminably present in things – either as already intrinsic to the primordial stuff(s) or, in Anaxagoras' system, by virtue of an irreducible dualism of mind and matter.

See also: ALCMAEON; ANCIENT PHILOSOPHY; DIOGENES OF APOLLONIA; DOXOGRAPHY; EPICHARMUS; HIPPOCRATIC MEDICINE; NOUS; PHYSIS AND NOMOS; SOCRATES; XENOPHANES

References and further reading

Barnes, J. (1979) *The Presocratic Philosophers*, London: Routledge & Kegan Paul, chaps 9–11. (The most philosophically rewarding study of the Presocratics.)

—— (1987) *Early Greek Philosophy*, Harmondsworth: Penguin. (Translation of the main sources, embedded in the contexts in which they are preserved.)

Diels, H. and Kranz, W. (1952) *Die Fragmente der*

Vorsokratiker (Fragments of the Presocratics), Berlin: Weidemann, 6th edn, 3 vols. (The standard edition of the Presocratic philosophers and the Sophists; contains secondary testimonia, plus Greek texts of the fragments with translations in German.)

Furley, D.J. and Allen, R.E. (eds) (1975) *Studies in Presocratic Philosophy*, London: Routledge & Kegan Paul. (Two-volume collection of seminal papers.)

Guthrie, W.K.C. (1962–78) *A History of Greek Philosophy*, Cambridge: Cambridge University Press, 6 vols. (Volumes 1 and 2 are the most detailed and comprehensive English-language history of Presocratic thought.)

Hussey, E. (1972) *The Presocratics*, London: Duckworth. (Accessible introductory account.)

Kirk, G.S. (1960) 'Popper on Science and the Presocratics', *Mind* 69: 318–39, repr. in D.J. Furley and R.E. Allen (eds), *Studies in Presocratic Philosophy*, London: Routledge & Kegan Paul, 1975, vol. 1, 154–77. (Reply to an earlier version of Popper (1963).)

Kirk, G.S., Raven, J.E. and Schofield, M. (1983) *The Presocratic Philosophers*, Cambridge: Cambridge University Press, 2nd edn. (A valuable survey of Presocratic philosophy, including texts and translations.)

Long, A.A. (ed.) (forthcoming) *The Cambridge Companion to Early Greek Philosophy*, Cambridge: Cambridge University Press. (A series of essays on key philosophers and themes.)

McKirahan, R.D. (1994) *Philosophy before Socrates*, Indianapolis, IN: Hackett. (Comprehensive collection of sources in translation, with commentary.)

Mourelatos, A.P.D. (1974) *The Pre-Socratics*, Garden City, NY: Doubleday; repr. 1993. (Important collection of essays, with enlarged bibliography in the 1993 reprint.)

Popper, K.R. (1963) 'Back to the Presocratics', in *Conjectures and Refutations*, Routledge & Kegan Paul; repr. in D.J. Furley and R.E. Allen (eds), *Studies in Presocratic Philosophy*, London: Routledge & Kegan Paul, 1970, 1975, vol. 1, 130–53. (Tribute to the Presocratics for supposed anticipations of Popperian scientific method.)

DAVID SEDLEY

PRESUPPOSITION

There are various senses in which one statement may be said to 'presuppose' another, senses which are in permanent danger of being confused. Prominent among them are Strawsonian presupposition, a relation which obtains between statements when the falsity of one deprives the other of truth-value (for example, 'There was such a person as Kepler' is a Strawsonian presupposition of 'Kepler died in misery'); semantic presupposition, which obtains between a statement and a particular use of a sentence type, when the falsity of the statement means that that use will not after all constitute the making of a statement (for example, 'The name "Kepler" has a bearer' is a semantic presupposition of 'Kepler died in misery'); and pragmatic presupposition, a broader notion exemplified by the legitimate presumption that accepting or denying the statement 'Fred knows that the earth moves' means accepting 'The earth moves'.

1 Introduction
2 Strawsonian presupposition
3 Semantic presupposition
4 Pragmatic presupposition

1 Introduction

In most conversations a certain amount of knowledge is assumed by the parties. Conversing with people whom we know well, we can take it for granted that they know who we are and what we have recently been doing, along with much else. Ordinarily, 'presuppositions' are nothing other than these assumed parts of the conversational background.

The notions of presupposition which have been of greatest concern to linguists and philosophers, however, have been more narrowly defined (but see §4 below), typically being concerned with the way certain phrases or constructions indicate that the speaker is making a presupposition in the ordinary sense. So, if I affirm 'Wellington's victory at Waterloo was his greatest triumph', my form of words indicates that I am presupposing that Wellington was the victor at Waterloo and asserting that it was his greatest triumph. However, the commonly stressed opposition between presupposition and assertion is in some measure misleading. In asking 'Is Tony going to Salzburg again this summer?', I presuppose that he has been there before and inquire whether he intends to go there in the future; no assertion has been made.

This phenomenon may be closely related to another. If I affirm

(1)   All John's children are asleep,

I presuppose that John has children and assert that they are asleep. In affirming

(2) If all John's children are asleep, we should not leave the house,

I do not make the same assertion, but I do still presuppose that John has children. It is this that linguists have in mind when they speak of presuppositions being easily 'inherited': they are often (but not always) retained even when the clauses that convey them are sentically embedded so as to lose their own assertive force. Much of the work done by linguists on this topic has been concerned with identifying constructions in which presuppositions do not survive, and to explain why inheritance is blocked (see various authors collected in Davies 1991).

Philosophers writing on the subject, by contrast, have largely been concerned to elucidate the nature of presupposition: to explain what one thing's presupposing another really amounts to; and to specify the kinds of item between which the relation of presupposition obtains.

2 Strawsonian presupposition

The writer most responsible for bringing the notion of presupposition to the attention of philosophers is P.F. Strawson, from whose work (1) above is drawn. Commenting on the situation of somebody who makes an assertion by uttering (1), Strawson remarks that

> he will not normally, or properly, say this, unless he believes that John has children.... But suppose...John has no children. Then is it true or false that all John's children are asleep? Either answer would seem to be misleading. But we are not compelled to give either answer. We can, and normally should, say that, since John has no children, the question does not arise.
>
> (1952: 173–4)

Strawson is eventually led to advance the following general explanation: 'if [statement] S' is a necessary condition of the *truth or falsity* of [statement] S,... then S *presupposes* S'' (1952: 175; original emphasis). So the statement that John has children is a 'Strawsonian presupposition' of the statement that all John's children are asleep; for unless the former is true the latter is neither true nor false. Strawson's talk of a 'question [which] does not arise' is liable to mislead. If John has no children, then the question 'Is statement (1) true or false?' may be raised; but the correct answer will be that it is neither.

To understand the notion of Strawsonian presup-position properly, it is necessary to understand what exactly a statement is. Strawson distinguishes between declarative 'sentences' – linguistic types the use of which on various occasions of utterance enables people to say things – and the 'statements' thereby made. It is statements, not sentences, that are true or false. Should a presupposition fail, there will be a 'truth-value gap': a statement will qualify neither as true nor false. An analogous notion applies to other kinds of speech act. So a yes/no question Q may be said to presuppose a statement S if the truth of S is a necessary condition of Q's being answered by 'yes' or 'no' (see Strawson 1954).

The notion of Strawsonian presupposition has certainly found important philosophical application. In Strawson's own writings it forms the basis of a counter to Russell's suggestion that simple sentences involving 'definite descriptions' – that is, sentences of the form 'The F is G' – are not of subject–predicate form (see DESCRIPTIONS). Russell held that such a sentence is best analysed as an existential sentence, 'There is one and only one F, and it is G', whereby the statement that the F is G straightforwardly entails the existence of an F. Having attacked Russell's arguments in its favour, it was on precisely this score that Strawson tried to refute the theory itself: he insisted that the statement that the present king of France is bald presupposes (rather than entails) that there is a present king of France (see DESCRIPTIONS §4).

In assessing this suggestion, note that when contemplating statements which are neither true nor false, Strawson requires 'false' to bear a sense other than 'not true'. This means that, in the first place, the difference between Strawson and Russell is less than might at first have been supposed. Since Strawson accepts Russell's account of the conditions under which a statement made by uttering 'The F is G' will be true, he agrees *ipso facto* with his account of the conditions under which such a statement is not true. They differ only over the conditions for such a statement to be false, Strawson deeming such statements to be neither true nor false in circumstances where Russell would deem them straightforwardly false.

In the second place, however, we are driven to wonder what Strawson means by calling a statement 'false', given that it is not a synonym for 'not true'. It is reasonable to expect the attribution of falsity to a statement to be regulated by the principle that S is false just in case the negation of S is true, and this is a principle that Strawson's treatment respects; indeed, it seems that he takes this principle to be explanatory of the notion of falsity. But then it becomes crucial to have a test for identifying the negation of a statement, especially for natural languages, where the syntax does not necessarily make this obvious. Since Strawson's reluctance to classify 'The king of France is bald' as false when there is no king of France stems from a desire to reserve that attribution for the case in which there is a king of France and he is not bald, it is plain that Strawson regards the latter case as the proper negation of this statement. This, indeed, is what one might expect, given that Strawson is defending the view that 'The F is G' is a subject—predicate sentence. But the Russellian will want to draw a semantic distinction between 'It is not the case that the king of France is bald' and 'The king of France is not bald'. This suggests that the issue between them ultimately turns, not upon questions concerning presupposition, but upon the proper treatment of negation (and other logical modifiers) in natural languages.

3 Semantic presupposition

A rather different notion of presupposition is suggested by Frege: 'If anything is asserted, there is always an obvious presupposition that the simple or compound proper names used have a reference [*Bedeutung*]. If therefore one asserts "Kepler died in misery", there is a presupposition that the name "Kepler" designates something' (1892: 40). In order to see the difference between this notion of presupposition and Strawson's, it helps to make one assumption about statements; namely, that the same statement can be made in a variety of languages. Suppose, then, that there is a sequence of Chinese characters by the inscription of which it may be stated that Kepler died in misery. Such an inscription will certainly not contain the name 'Kepler', so it will not impede the making of that statement, should the English (or German) name 'Kepler' lack a reference. But in that case,

(3) The name 'Kepler' has a reference

plainly is not a Strawsonian presupposition of

(4) Kepler died in misery,

that is, of the statement made by uttering (4). For the latter statement could be made by inscribing the Chinese characters instead, and the statement thereby made could have a truth-value even if (3) were false. What does qualify as a Strawsonian presupposition of (4) is the following statement:

(5) There was such a person as Kepler.

We need, then, to distinguish the new notion of presupposition, exemplified by (4) and (3), from that exemplified by (4) and (5).

In explicating this new notion, it helps to invoke again Strawson's distinction between a (declarative) sentence type – which is the bearer of meaning – and the statement made when the sentence is uttered or used – which is the bearer of truth-value. For with that distinction in mind, we see that the new notion is not a relation between statements, but a relation between a sentence – as used (with a particular meaning) upon a particular occasion – and a statement. Thus, the sentence 'You are drunk' (as used on a particular occasion) presupposes that the speaker is addressing somebody, in the sense that if not, then the use of that sentence on a particular occasion will not constitute the making of a statement. Generally, then:

> A use of sentence σ in circumstance c presupposes statement S in so far as the truth of S is necessary for that use to qualify as the making of a statement.

When S and σ are so related, we may say that S is a 'semantic presupposition' of sentence σ, relative to c.

4 Pragmatic presupposition

Whatever the differences between them, Strawsonian and semantic presupposition are alike in depending upon the content of statements, or the meanings of sentence types. That is to say, they are alike in abstracting from the particular conversational purposes of the person uttering the sentence. In this respect they differ from another presupposition relation in which the actual speaker looms much larger. Following Stalnaker (1974), we might say that

> A statement S' is a 'pragmatic presupposition' of a statement S in so far as a hearer may reasonably infer that the speaker accepts S' either from their acceptance of S or from their denial of it.

One salient difference between this explication and the definition of a Strawsonian presupposition is that the notions of truth and falsity have been replaced by those of acceptance and denial (acceptance of the negation). Another is the introduction of the notion of a hearer's reasonable inference – reasonable, that is, by the lights of a well-run conversation.

Whether one statement is a pragmatic presupposition of another depends crucially, then, upon what constitutes a well-run conversation, a notion philosophers have tried to explicate by formulating general 'conversational maxims', such as the rule (R) that one's hearer may assume that one is making the logically strongest relevant statement compatible with one's beliefs. To illustrate this, and to show how a pragmatic presupposition might obtain even when a

Strawsonian presupposition does not, suppose that speakers are known to abide by (R), and consider the statements S: 'Fred knows that the earth moves' and S': 'The earth moves'. S' is not a Strawsonian presupposition of S: when S' is false, we may conclude simply that Fred's belief is not in fact knowledge and that S itself is straightforwardly false. All the same, a strong case can be made for the contention that S' is a pragmatic presupposition of S: I may reasonably infer that a speaker accepts S', should I hear them either accepting or denying S (see Stalnaker 1974). The case of accepting S presents no difficulty; and a denial of S amounts to an assertion of 'Fred doesn't know that the earth moves', an assertion which I may suppose that the speaker would not have made had they accepted the stronger statement 'The earth does not move'.

See also: DESCRIPTIONS; IMPLICATURE; LOGICAL AND MATHEMATICAL TERMS, GLOSSARY OF; PRAGMATICS

References and further reading

* Davies, S. (1991) *Pragmatics: A Reader*, New York: Oxford University Press. (Includes many papers showing the nature of contemporary work on presupposition by linguists, including articles on the problem of 'inheritance' mentioned in §1.)
* Frege, G. (1892) 'Über Sinn und Bedeutung', *Zeitschrift für Philosophie und philosophische Kritik* 100: 25–50; trans. 'On Sense and Meaning', in *Translations from the Philosophical Writings of Gottlob Frege*, trans. and ed. P.T. Geach and M. Black, Oxford: Blackwell, 3rd edn, 1980. (Introduces the notion of semantic presupposition. The page numbers of the original publication appear in the margins.)
* Stalnaker, R.C. (1974) 'Pragmatic Presupposition', repr. in S. Davies, *Pragmatics: A Reader*, New York: Oxford University Press, 1991.
  Strawson, P.F. (1950) 'On Referring', *Mind* 59: 320–44; repr. in *Logico-Linguistic Papers*, London: Methuen, 1971. (A classic paper, using presuppositional considerations to attempt to refute Russell's theory of descriptions. Note that the term 'presupposition' is not used in the paper; it is called 'implication in the special sense'.)
* —— (1952) *Introduction to Logical Theory*, London: Methuen. (Defines (Strawsonian) 'presupposition'.)
* —— (1954) 'A Reply to Mr. Sellars', *Philosophical Review* 63: 216–31. (Extends presupposition beyond the assertoric.)

IAN RUMFITT

PRICE, RICHARD (1723–91)

Richard Price was a Welsh dissenting minister who contributed widely to philosophy and public life in latter-eighteenth-century Britain. The leading British ethical rationalist of the period, Price did much to establish intuitionistic and deontological traditions in ethics. He put forward searching criticisms of alternative empiricist conceptions, arguing that they could not account for morality's necessity and that they lacked an adequate theory of moral agency. More constructively, he argued that, contrary to the empiricists, all knowledge depends on the contribution of reason, and that rationalistic moral knowledge is no more problematic in principle than ordinary empirical knowledge. He also articulated a normative ethics of integrity that stressed the duty diligently to search out moral truth and then to act on the truth as one sees it.

As a political philosopher, Price made fundamental contributions through his doctrine of liberty as self-determination. The moral duty individuals have to determine themselves by their best moral judgment, Price believed, ultimately grounds the values of political liberty, independence, and democracy as well. Price's radicalism on these scores earned him the famous opposition of Edmund Burke. Nor was Price's sponsorship of these ideas simply theoretical. He was an important friend of the American Revolution, and his pamphlets analysing and defending it were taken seriously by proponents and opponents alike.

Price also did important work on the mathematical theory of probability and in proposing and instituting various social and economic reforms and practices upon its basis. He was instrumental in making Thomas Bayes' ideas about probability accessible to the learned world, and in making use of these and other probabilistic theories in developing insurance, self-help, and other financial schemes.

1 Life and works
2 Meta-ethics
3 Normative ethics
4 Political philosophy

1 Life and works

Richard Price was born on 23 February 1723 at Tynton, Llangeinor, Glamorgan into a family that, on his father's side, had been involved in Welsh dissent for two generations. Much of Price's normative outlook can be understood against this background – his emphasis on piety, integrity, self-determination and freedom of conscience. Price's meta-ethics, on the other hand, was a reaction against Calvinist theological voluntarism of the sort represented by his dissenting minister father, Rice Price. As son Richard saw it, moral propositions claim by their very nature to represent an objective, necessary and non-arbitrary order. Voluntarism, whether secular or divine, must ultimately lead to moral scepticism (see MORAL SCEPTICISM; VOLUNTARISM). Consequently, Price believed that the moral core of religious dissent, to which he would be loyal throughout his life, could only be preserved by giving it a rationalist foundation. Together with articulating dissent's normative dimensions, this was Price's central philosophical project.

Price's great ethical work was *A Review of the Principal Questions and Difficulties in Morals* (1758). It is the repository of all his major ideas on ethics and the source of many of his political theories. The year *A Review* appeared, Price accepted a post at a Presbyterian church in Newington Green, near London. During the next fifteen years there, he published on an astonishing variety of topics. In 1764 and 1765 he edited Thomas Bayes' seminal writings on probability theory, publishing them in the *Transactions* of the Royal Society. *Four Dissertations*, a theological work, appeared in 1767. In 1770 and 1771 Price contributed three further papers to *Transactions*, one on astronomy and two on calculating life-expectancy and annuities, respectively. These last were incorporated into *Observations on Reversionary Payments* (1771), which established Price's considerable reputation in the field of insurance. It went through three editions, and part was expanded and published separately as *An Appeal to the Public on the Subject of the National Debt* in 1772.

Price's greatest fame, however, came from his political writings, beginning with *Observations on the Nature of Civil Liberty* (1776), a pamphlet that sketched his political philosophy and defended the American Revolution on its basis. Seven editions appeared during its first year of publication alone. Its major philosophical thesis was that states acquire legitimacy as trustees for consenting, self-determining moral agents, and have thereby a right to self-determination as representatives of their citizens. If, consequently, the American colonists wanted to govern themselves, that was both their right and duty. Price wrote several further works analysing and praising the American Revolution and one, *A Discourse on the Love of Our Country* (1789), celebrating the French Revolution, which drew Edmund Burke's ire in his *Reflections on the Revolution in France* (1790) (see BURKE, E.).

Throughout this period of extraordinary creativity and prominence, Price remained active in communities of dissent. He resigned his post at Newington Green in 1783, but continued an active participant there, as he did in St Thomas' Square, Hackney, to which he removed in 1787. His final sermon at Hackney came just months before his death.

2 Meta-ethics

Price advanced a rationalist meta-ethics along with a critique of the moral sense theories of Francis Hutcheson and David Hume, turning against them arguments Hutcheson had used to criticize secular and theological voluntarism (see HUME, D.; HUTCHESON, F.; MORAL SENSE THEORIES). Hutcheson (1725) had argued that moral good and evil are simple, irreducible ideas. Any reductionism, including voluntarism must fail, therefore, since it is one thing to say that I will suffer sanctions if I fail to act as commanded, but another to say that violation is morally wrong or evil and that sanctions will be deserved. Alternatively, if voluntarists hold that moral good consists in obeying authoritative commands, they then assume a background moral fact that can have no voluntarist explanation, namely, that these commands are ones that persons should obey.

Because he held an empiricist theory of ideas, Hutcheson concluded from this irreducibility that there is a distinctive moral sense which receives moral ideas. Price agreed that moral ideas are irreducible, but argued that attributing them to a contingent sense or sensibility makes them ultimately no less posited than if they were to depend on arbitrary command. According to Hutcheson, benevolence is morally good, not because it is intrinsically or necessarily warrants approbation, but because beings with our moral sense (including God) happen to approve it.

There are several different elements to the Pricean critique of empiricism. First, Price argued that moral judgments make an implicit claim to *objectivity*, while any empiricist account must understand them ultimately to concern subjective experience. Second, moral judgments attribute properties based on the *intrinsic nature* of their objects. Third, they attribute these properties *eternally* and *necessarily*. Fourth and finally, moral judgments attribute properties independently of any *arbitrary* standard. When we attribute viciousness to dishonesty, for example, we implicitly hold that, by its very nature, dishonesty has a property that depends not on any response we happen to have, standard we arbitrarily apply, or any other contingent feature.

What misled the empiricists, Price believed, was their general theory of ideas. Price insisted that reason is itself a source of ideas. Were it not, we would lack a whole host of concepts that cannot possibly come from experience alone. Following Ralph Cudworth (whose *Treatise on Eternal and Immutable Morality* appeared posthumously in 1731, after Hutcheson's

Inquiry), Price maintained that the notions of substance, duration, space, causation and necessity, among others, cannot come from sense experience, and so must be due to reason or the understanding (see CUDWORTH, R.). Nor should we doubt that reason is also the source of moral ideas. A rational basis for moral ideas, on the one hand, and any basis at all for the notions central to the science of nature, on the other, stand or fall together.

Price concluded that moral claims can be known by direct rational intuition. Some, the 'heads' of virtue, are self-evident. These are 'general principles', such as those enjoining veracity, fidelity, gratitude, justice and so on, that concern what it is right and wrong to do. Principles at this level of generality are bound to conflict in actual cases, however, and Price held that it is not self-evident what a person should do when they do. What is self-evident to reason is what moral considerations are relevant – what persons should and should not do, other things being equal.

Price's meta-ethics thus amounted to a metaphysical realism combined with a rational intuitionist epistemology (see REALISM AND ANTIREALISM). Moral propositions are like mathematical claims, Price thought. Their truth is determined by correspondence to facts about an objective, eternal, necessary order. And they are known through a rational perception of the same kind.

But how then is moral perception or knowledge related to motivation? One way this question arises is in connection with obligation, which Price's contemporaries tended to see as intrinsically tied to motive. Indeed some writers, rationalists *and* empiricists, maintained that obligation just is a motive, perhaps inescapable, perhaps distinctively moral. Price resisted this identification, holding that 'obligatory' is another name for the fundamental irreducible moral notion. Obligation consists in the eternal and immutable moral features of the objective situation in which persons find themselves, not on their motivational state. At the same time, Price held that the *perception* of irreducible moral features *is* linked to motivation and, indeed, that 'it is not conceivable' that a person who perceives that an action ought to be done 'can remain uninfluenced, or want a motive' (1758: 186). But if motivation is no part of the perceived ethical facts, and if the faculty of perception is the understanding (the same faculty involved in the motivationally inert perception of mathematical facts), what explains this necessary motivation? What makes it, as Hume put it, 'universally forcible and obligatory'?

Price's reply was a doctrine of rationally necessary affect and motive, of which this was but one example. The only alternative to believing that moral properties are objective, eternal and immutable is to hold that nothing has a nature that determines its moral properties. This would be true no less of God than of other beings. But we can hardly deny, Price argues, that God is good simply by virtue of his nature. And this commits us to the conclusion that goodness is an eternal, objective and immutable property of a being with such a nature. Moreover, there are other aspects of God's nature that would seem equally essential and not merely contingently true of him. For example, it hardly seems that it could be merely contingently true that God is pleased by virtue or by the perception of beauty generally, or that he is benevolent, or that he desires what is morally good and just for his creatures. But if we accept that affects and motives of these sorts are essential to God, Price argues, we should also believe that they are essential to rational nature, rather than deriving from some contingent or 'implanted' motive or sense. It follows that being moved by the perception of ethical facts is intrinsic to the understanding.

3 Normative ethics

Just as Price rejected empiricist metaethics, so also did he deny the proto-utilitarian, normative ethics it was frequently used to support. The 'heads of virtue' are various and distinct, and although benevolence is one of these, the others are not reducible to it. Piety, veracity, justice and the other 'heads' are self-evidently intrinsically morally relevant, regardless of their actual or usual consequences.

Price distinguished between the virtue of actions and the virtue of agents. The former concerns whether, all things considered, an action is objectively right, irrespective of the motives that actually led or will lead to it. An action manifests the agent's virtue, on the other hand, only if it is done from the proper motives. Most importantly, Price held, actions manifest agent-virtue only when the agent 'acts from a consciousness of rectitude and with a regard to it as his rule and end' (1758: 184). Behind this thesis lies Price's doctrine that genuine agency entails self-government, and that this involves a person guiding themselves by their convictions concerning what they should do. If moral virtue is a virtue of agents, therefore, it must include this element.

For Price, the virtuous agent is a person of integrity, concerned to determine what they should do and, having determined that, to act as they think they should. The first duty of moral agents is diligently to determine the virtuous act, to see under what self-evident general principles the alternatives before them fall, and carefully to judge what they should do, all things considered. God has made human beings so that moral truth is tolerably accessible to them if they will but use their understanding attentively. Having made a conscientious judgment, Price held, a moral agent should then follow their conscience 'steadily and faithfully', even if it should turn out to have been mistaken.

Price distinguishes between the abstract and practical virtue of actions. The abstract virtue of an act is its moral quality, considered independently of the agent's motives and beliefs, including those concerning what the agent should do. This is what moral agents attempt to determine in deliberation: 'What is the right thing to do owing to the objective features of my practical context?' Practical virtue, by contrast, depends on agents' beliefs about the alternatives confronting them, including, importantly, their beliefs concerning the abstract virtue of these alternatives. This analytical distinction grounds an important Pricean normative doctrine, namely, that when moral agents have seriously deliberated, what they then should do is what they think they should do. Practical virtue is thus not just a moral quality an action would have if the objective features of alternatives confronting them were as the agent believed. If the agent makes a serious judgment that they should do something, then they really should do it. To act otherwise would be to compromise their integrity.

Consequently, while Price's rational intuitionism stresses eternal and immutable moral qualities actions have owing to their objective, intrinsic nature, these concern only abstract virtue, which is, however, of the first importance in deliberation, as agents diligently seek to determine the abstract moral qualities of actions before them. But once deliberation is terminated and agents have formed considered beliefs, what they should then do is a matter of practical rather than abstract virtue. They should follow their conscientious judgment.

Coinciding in this normative doctrine are proto-Kantian theories of self-determining agency and character (see KANT, I.; KANTIAN ETHICS). Capacity to act on an independent judgment of what one ought to do is what makes a being a self-determining agent in the first place, and moral virtue consists in the excellent exercise of this capacity. Sometimes, indeed, Price seems to count any moral failure as a failure of agency, creating puzzles about how vice can ever be imputed to an agent.

4 Political philosophy

The idea that moral persons are autonomous and independent forms the basis of Price's political philosophy no less than of his ethics. He begins his *Observations on the Nature of Civil Liberty* with a discussion of four different kinds of liberty – physical liberty, moral liberty, religious liberty and civil liberty – arguing that the central idea running through them all is self-government. Physical and moral liberty are powers of self-determining agency, the latter, the power of following conscience. The third and fourth ideas, by contrast, are political rather than moral forms of liberty. A political order establishes religious liberty when each can exercise the form of religion they think best. And it establishes civil liberty when it is itself self-determining, governing itself 'without being subject to the impositions of any power' (1776: 3).

The central idea of Price's political philosophy is that the proper contrary of liberty is not hindrance, but slavery. A person is free when they can determine for themselves what they will do, and they are unfree when they are subject to arbitrary authority and control. The obstacles to moral liberty can be internal or external, political obstacles to 'liberty of the citizen' being primarily external. Citizens are unfree when they are subject to the will of others, most prominently, to the will of those who claim political authority over them. It is not enough for citizens to be free, moreover, that they face no actual obstacles to self-direction. Being subject to a master who can control at their pleasure is sufficient, even if the master chooses not to exercise control.

Price's central political tenet was thus a doctrine of the equal dignity of all persons as independent and autonomous. Legitimate political authority can derive only from the will of the people, therefore, and never once and for all but only continuously, subject to their continuing advice and consent. When numbers make direct democracy impossible, public officials function as representatives, their authority always deriving from and being answerable to, the will of the people. It follows also, Price argued, that a justified polity must ensure the equal liberty of all citizens. Citizens must be secured from threats to their liberty, whether posed by alien forces, by other citizens, or by government itself. Mastery by others deprives citizens, not just of valuable goods, but of their dignity as persons.

Price's enthusiasm for the American Revolution derived from his seeing it as the expression of these ideas. America provided the hope of a government rooted in equal dignity and so, Price thought, 'a new prospect in human affairs', 'beginning a new aera in the history of mankind' (1776–89: 17). To his American friends he recommended representative democracy, with legislators being frequently held to free elections, as well as a variety of measures designed to restrict entrenched power, including religious liberty and the abolition of primogeniture and all hereditary honours and titles. One thing that tempered his enthusiasm was the African slave trade (see SLAVERY) for which Price had nothing but scorn.

See also: EMPIRICISM; INTUITIONISM IN ETHICS; MORAL REALISM; RATIONALISM; UTILITARIANISM

List of works

Price, R. (1758) *A Review of the Principal Questions and Difficulties in Morals,* London: Millar; ed. D.D. Raphael, Oxford: Clarendon Press, 1974. (Price's major work in ethics. This edition has a useful introduction.)
—— (1764) 'An Essay towards solving a problem in the "Doctrine of Chances", by the late Rev. Mr. Bayes, F.R.S. communicated by Dr. Price, in a letter to John Canton, A.M., F.R.S.', *Philosophical transactions of the Royal Society* 1 (3): 370–418. (A presentation of what has come to be known as 'Bayes Theorem', which defines the relationship between the probability of a hypothesis given new evidence and the probabilities of this hypothesis independently of the evidence, the evidence on the condition of the hypothesis obtaining, and the evidence itself. This result has significant importance for the theories of probability and rational decision.)
—— (1765) "A Demonstration of the Second Rule in the Essay towards a solution of a problem in the Doctrine of Chances", *Philosophical Transactions of the Royal Society,* 1 (4): 296–325. (An improvement and development of the earlier paper.)
—— (1767) *Four Dissertations,* London: Cadell. (Price's theology.)
—— (1771) *Observations on Reversionary Payments,* London: Cadell and Davis. (Theoretical basis for life insurance.)
—— (1772) *An Appeal to the Public on Subject of the National Debt,* London: Cadell. (On public finance.)
—— (1776) *Observations on the Nature of Civil Liberty,* London: Cadell. (Price's major work of political philosophy.)
—— (1776–89) *Political Writings,* ed. D.O. Thomas, Cambridge: Cambridge University Press, 1992. (A fine selection of Price's political philosophical writings includes selections from *Observations on the Nature of Civil Liberty* and *Observations on the Importance of the American Revolution.*)
—— (1777) *Additional Observations on the Nature and Value of Civil Liberty and the War with America,* London: Cadell. (Further thoughts on politics and the American Revolution.)
—— (1778) *A Free Discussion of the Doctrines of*

Materialism and Philosophical Necessity, in a Correspondence between Dr. Price and Dr. Priestley, J. Johnson and T. Cadell, London. (Debate on free will and materialism.)
—— (1784) *Observations on the Importance of the American Revolution and the Means of Making it a Benefit to the World,* London: Cadell. (Price's analysis of the American Revolution.)
—— (1789) *A Discourse on the Love of Our Country,* London: Stafford and Cadell. (Includes Price's analysis of the French Revolution.)

References and further reading

Cudworth, R. (1731) *A Treatise on Eternal and Immutable Morality.* (A central rationalist work that much influenced Price.)
Hudson, W.D. (1970) *Reason and Right,* London: Macmillan. (A systematic discussion of Price's views in meta-ethics and normative ethics.)
Hutcheson, F. (1725) *An Inquiry into the Original of our Ideas of Beauty and Virtue; In Two Treatises,* London and Dublin: Darby. (A major empiricist work on which Price focused criticism.)
Thomas, D.O. (1977) *The Honest Mind: the Thought and Work of Richard Price,* Oxford: Clarendon Press. (The best introduction to Price's life and works – comprehensive and philosophically astute.)

STEPHEN DARWALL

PRICHARD, HAROLD ARTHUR (1871–1947)

One of the most influential Oxford philosophers of the twentieth century, Prichard was White's Professor of Moral Philosophy there from 1928 to 1937. His work combines epistemological realism and moral intuitionism. From 1906 onwards Prichard was active with the Oxford realists, who held, against idealists, that reality exists independently of mind, that knowledge is of reality, and that common-sense realism is correct. In ethics, he was the leader of the Oxford intuitionists who held, against utilitarianism, that common-sense morality is correct, its duties are known non-inferentially, and are an irreducible plurality of distinct kinds of act. His philosophical style displays concentration on specific problems, carefully using ordinary language to make precise distinctions in the absence of general theory. He influenced Oxford's next generation of Austin, Ryle, Hart and Berlin, who attended his classes and, occasionally, his 'philosophers' teas'.

1 Epistemological realism
2 Moral intuitionism

1 Epistemological realism

Early in this century philosophy in Oxford was dominated by the opposition between idealists, such as T.H. GREEN, F.H. BRADLEY and Bernard BOSANQUET, who held that mind constitutes reality, and the realists, such as J. Cook Wilson, H.W.B. Joseph, W.D. Ross and Prichard himself, who held that reality exists independently of mind (see IDEALISM). Prichard wrote his only book, *Kant's Theory of Knowledge* (1909), as a realist critique of Kant's transcendental analytic, and thereby developed the metaphysical and epistemological positions of the realist school. They are: (1) reality exists independently of mind; (2) if reality depends on mind then 'knowing is making', and mind makes reality. But (3) knowing is not making; knowing is being certain. Since we know when we know and know when we believe, as we show in choosing which word to use, it follows that knowledge is known in itself, while believing is known in relation to knowing (Urmson 1988).

Regarding perception, Prichard argues for a dualism of minds and objects and for common-sense realism. Prichard accuses Kant, and in other writings, Descartes, Locke, Berkeley, Hume and Russell, of wrongly hypostatizing 'appearances' when talking of how things themselves appear, thereby creating an intermediate entity variously called 'idea', 'representation', 'sensation', 'impression' or 'sense-datum'. These philosophers then quarrel over whether appearances copy reality or compose it. But they have given themselves an illusory problem.

2 Moral intuitionism

Prichard used the term 'intuitionist' to contrast his moral philosophy with that of the utilitarians. We can best approach his position by considering his greatest essay 'Does Moral Philosophy rest on a Mistake?' (1912). His affirmative response to this question is not modest, since the 'mistake' includes all moralists from Socrates to G.E. Moore. Their mistake is the assumption that there is something that all morally right actions have in common, from which their rightness can be inferred. According to Prichard, however, right actions possess no such quality. Thus moral knowledge is not inferential, but intuitive. One instance of this mistake is the belief that motives are the criterion of rightness. In discussing this view critically Prichard distinguishes two kinds of motive: 'moral', or acting from the conscientious desire to do what is right; and 'virtuous', or acting from an

intrinsically good desire, such as compassion. Whichever kind one invokes, however, Prichard denies that it provides a criterion of right action, since right actions are sometimes done from bad motives. Utilitarianism and other consequentialist theories of duty provide another instance of the mistake. Prichard rejects traditional utilitarianism because it reduces all duties to the single duty of maximizing happiness, whereas in fact duties are essentially plural. He likewise rejects Moore's 'ideal' utilitarianism, which postulates a fundamental duty of maximizing intrinsically good outcomes of any kind, because it wrongly implies that there is a fixed hierarchy of types of intrinsically good outcomes (see MOORE, G.E. §1). Thus Prichard rejects all consequentialist theories, and to the consequentialist claim that only consequences can resolve dilemmas rejoins that there is no single answer to dilemmas. Joseph, Prichard's fellow intuitionist, laments these conclusions, saying they 'leave moral duties in a heap' – as indeed they do (see CONSEQUENTIALISM; UTILITARIANISM).

Despite his many criticisms of previous moral theories, Prichard never doubted that there is moral knowledge. How is it possible? Prichard's critics usually answer for him, 'We know by intuition', and suggest, by rolling their eyes and other such body language, that intuition is rapid, unhearing and irrational. But more may be learned by attempting a new approach which connects Prichard's realism and his 'intuitionism'. As a realist, Prichard supported a common-sense realism which features common-sense knowledge of mind-independent objects. In morals, Prichard everywhere appeals to 'ordinary, unreflective morality'. Thus, the parallel claim is that the acts that are really right are the moral duties of ordinary morality. This realism of common-sense morality is composed of the kinds of actions connected with promising, truth-telling, helping the helpless, returning what one has borrowed, paying debts, returning kindnesses and so on. The suggestion is that although the different kinds of ordinary obligations have different structures, a child can be taught to recognize them. When young, obedience may require the threat of punishment, but later, Smith, who has borrowed Brown's electric drill, knows that he ought to return it because it is a loan and not a gift. From this basis, one can argue that intuition has a real object, namely the character of the kinds of moral action that are our ordinary obligations (see INTUITIONISM IN ETHICS §2).

Once Prichard's conception of intuitive moral knowledge is understood in this way, it becomes intelligible why he insists that before we know our duty we must consider an act's circumstances (for instance, when telling the truth about a wayward, dying son to a grieving mother) and its consequences (for instance, when a surgeon discusses a gory operation over dinner). But has Prichard not eliminated consequences as a criterion of rightness? Apparently only as the single criterion, for he insists that no moral theory omits consequences. This insistence causes him to raise the question 'What is the relationship between an action and its consequences?' Logically, he cannot identify an action with its consequences or motives. He first suggests that an action is 'setting oneself to effect a change' and later he decides that 'acting is willing'. Either way, Prichard clearly distinguishes 'motive' from 'intended consequences' and associates action with the latter. In turn, that permits him to argue that, depending on what will be taken for granted, we may include the intended consequences within the description of the act.

The remainder of Prichard's moral philosophy is remarkable in its subtlety, but also for working upon problems implicit in 'Does Moral Philosophy Rest on a Mistake?' Thus, in 'Duty and Interest' ([1928] 1949) Prichard considers whether the sense of duty is a sufficient motive or if duty must be motivated by desire, and thereby enters the internalist versus externalist debate. In his lectures on T.H. Green, he states that philosophers have mistakenly sought one moral justification of political obligation, whereas different political states have different problems, requiring different justifications. Other implications are developed in 'Duty And Ignorance Of Fact' ([1932] 1949). In asking if duty depends upon ignorance of facts, Prichard divides the question with regards to common morality. Which is correct: subjective duty, which depends upon knowledge of facts, or objective duty, which identifies duty with what is independent of mind? I cannot have a duty to help my distant, ailing aunt if I do not know of her plight but, equally, I have a duty to help the helpless. This problem deadened his capacity to finish 'a book on morals'. The essay 'The Obligation To Keep A Promise' ([c.1940] 1949) raises a problem akin to moral realism. First, however, Prichard is puzzled about the question 'What is promising?' 'I promised' is a statement that is either true or false. 'I promise' is not; it seems more like an action. But then promising, as doing, seems to create an obligation, an idea apparently foreign to Prichard's thought. J.L. Austin admired Prichard, and their exchange of letters on promising as doing attests to Prichard's influence on the formation of Austin's 'performative utterances' (see AUSTIN, J.L. §3; PERFORMATIVES).

See also: ORDINARY LANGUAGE PHILOSOPHY, SCHOOL OF

List of works

Prichard, H.A. (1906) 'Appearances and Reality', *Mind* 15: 223–9. (Prichard examines difficulties in two theories: 'we know things only as they appear to us, and not as they are in themselves' and 'we know only "phenomena" or "appearances"'. Since both theories deny realism, Prichard finds both unacceptable.)

—— (1907) 'A Criticism of the Psychologists' Treatment of Knowledge', *Mind* 16: 27–53. (Prichard writes, 'When...we perceive a chair or a tree, the direct object of the mind is the chair or tree, and not any mental modification referred to as a 'perception' or an image of it'.)

—— (1909) *Kant's Theory of Knowledge*, Oxford: Clarendon Press. (Prichard provides a common-sense realist criticism of Kant's Analytic. The argument is helpful to understanding Prichard's own theory of knowledge and should be considered by students of Kant.)

—— (1910) 'Philosophic Pre-Copernicanism: An Answer', *Mind* 19: 541–3. (Prichard defends naive realism against idealism: 'Study [of idealism] appears to resemble measles in that all students of philosophy must undergo an attack of it'.)

—— (1912) 'Does Moral Philosophy Rest on a Mistake?', in Pritchard 1949. (Prichard's richest work: it provides him with problems that he struggles with for the rest of his life.)

—— (1919) 'Professor John Cook Wilson', *Mind* 28: 297–318. (In Prichard's memoir of John Cook Wilson, he writes: 'To speak of him dispassionately as a philosopher is difficult for one who, like the present writer, enjoyed uninterrupted intercourse with him since he first became his pupil some five and twenty years ago'.)

—— (1928) 'Mr Bertrand Russell's *Outline of Philosophy*', *Mind* 37: 265–82. (A pugnacious attack on Russell's doctrines on knowledge and perception in *Outline of Philosophy*: 'I should like to ask Mr Russell...whether there really is a word of truth in this view from beginning to end'.)

—— (1949) *Moral Obligation, Essays And Lectures*, ed. and with a note by W.D. Ross, Oxford: Clarendon Press; revised and extended as *Moral Obligation and Duty and Interest, Essays and Lectures*, with intro. by J.O. Urmson, Oxford: Oxford University Press, 1968. (Contains all of Prichard's published moral writings, including 'Duty and Interest' (1928), 'Duty and Ignorance of Fact' (1932) and 'The Obligation to Keep a Promise' (c.1940).)

—— (1950) *Knowledge and Perception, Essays and Lectures*, ed. and with a preface by W.D. Ross,

Oxford: Clarendon Press. (A collection containing Prichard's most important nonmoral texts.)

References and further reading

Broad, C.D. (1950) 'Critical Notice, Moral Obligation: Essays and Lectures by H.A. Prichard', *Mind* 59: 55–6. (An insightful, sympathetic review by an able philosopher.)

Collingwood, R.G. (1939) 'Minute Philosophers', in *An Autobiography*, Oxford: Oxford University Press, ch. 3. (A biased account of the Oxford realists, but the book is well worth reading. Chapter 6, 'The Decay of Realism', is also relevant, since Collingwood had been a realist himself.)

Cook Wilson, J. (1929) *Statement and Inference, with other Philosophical Papers*, ed. A.S.L. Farquharson, Oxford: Clarendon Press, 2 vols; repr. 1969. (Writings of leader of Oxford realists, interesting in their own right, and containing letters to Prichard.)

Hornsby, J. (1980) *Actions*, London: Routledge & Kegan Paul. (Hornsby provides the most plausible interpretation of Prichard's account of action.)

Joseph, H.W.B. (1931) *Some Problems In Ethics*, Oxford: Oxford University Press. (A discussion of Prichardian themes by Prichard's fellow Oxford intuitionist and next-door neighbour.)

Mabbott, J.D. (1966) *An Introduction to Ethics*, London: Hutchinson University Library. (An easily read introduction to Prichard's type of moral philosophy.)

Passmore, J. (1957) 'Cook Wilson And Oxford Philosophy', in *A Hundred Years of Philosophy*, London: Gerald Duckworth, ch. 10. (Passmore's well-written history is the best introduction for the beginner.)

Price, H.H. (1947) 'Harold Arthur Prichard, 1871–1947', *Proceedings of the British Academy* 33: 331–50, Oxford: Oxford University Press. (Contains the best short account of Prichard's philosophy.)

Prior, A.N. (1951) 'The Virtue Of The Act And The Virtue Of The Agent', Philosophy, 26: 121–30. (Prior contends convincingly that Prichard's and Ross's struggle to decide the correctness of subjective or objective duty was argued by Price and others of the British Moralists.)

Ross, W.D. (1930) *The Right And The Good*, Oxford: Clarendon Press. (Ross professes 'my main obligation is to Professor H.A. Prichard', but also acknowledges his debt to G.E. Moore.)

—— (1939) *Foundations of Ethics*, Oxford: Clarendon Press. (Both of his books contain insightful and influential arguments on the Oxford intuitionist position.)

* Urmson, J. (1988) 'Prichard and Knowing', in J. Dancy, J. Moravcsik and C.C.W. Taylor (eds) *Human Agency: Language, Duty and Value*, Stanford, CA: Stanford University Press. (Contains the best discussion of Prichard's account of knowledge.)

Walsh, W.H. (1981) 'Kant's Critique of Pure Reason: Commentators in English, 1875–1945', *Journal of the History of Ideas* 42: 723–37. (Walsh does not praise Prichard as a Kant scholar, but recommends Prichard's *Kant's Theory of Knowledge* (1909) as impressive and as raising important questions regarding Kant's philosophy.)

JIM MacADAM

PRIESTLEY, JOSEPH (1733–1804)

A major figure of the British Enlightenment, Joseph Priestley is best known as a scientist and for his discovery of oxygen, though he was by profession a theologian, and also wrote on politics and education – more, indeed, than on science or metaphysics. His philosophical speculations were generally brought to support his theological arguments and were usually structured in a rhetorical rather than in a formal, systematic mode. He was a Unitarian in theology, an associationist, determinist and monist, with a curiously spiritualized materialism dependent, in part at least, on his scientific studies.

Joseph Priestley was born near Leeds, Yorkshire, England in 1733. He was self-educated in science and philosophy, reading on his own Locke's *Essay concerning Human Understanding* (1690) (see LOCKE, J.), Isaac Watts' *Logic: or the Right Use of Reason* (1725), and Willem Jacob Gravesande's Newtonian *Mathematical Elements of Natural Philosophy* (1720–1). At 19 he went to Daventry Academy to become a minister. Daventry's theological text was Philip Doddridge's *Course of Lectures on the Principle Subjects in Pneumatology, Ethics and Divinity* (printed 1763), from which Priestley learned of the CAMBRIDGE PLATONISTS and of the Newtonian physico-theologians. He also read, at Daventry, David Hartley's *Observations on Man, His Frame, His Duty, and His Expectations* (1749), a work of greatest influence on him, converting him to associationism and to the doctrine of philosophical necessity (determinism) (see HARTLEY, D.).

Initially failing as a dissenting minister, Priestley became a successful teacher of languages and *belles-lettres* at Warrington Academy. There also he began his scientific career, writing his *History and Present State of Electricity* (1767), to which were added experiments and observations of his own. In 1767 Priestley became a Unitarian minister in Leeds. There he commenced his career as a religious polemicist, wrote an *Essay on the First Principles of Government* (1768), from which Jeremy BENTHAM derived his utilitarianism, and continued his scientific work. For the *History and Present State of Discoveries relating to Vision, Light and Colours* (1772), he adopted some ideas of Rudjer Josef Boscovic, which he would subsequently use for his justification of materialism. He also wrote his first paper there, published in the *Philosophical Transactions* (1772) of the Royal Society of London, on the chemistry of gases.

He left Leeds in 1773, to become librarian and companion to Lord Shelburne. During this period he did the major part of his pneumatic chemistry and the major part of his formal metaphysical writing. Leaving Shelburne in 1780, he settled as a minister in Birmingham. There he spent much time defending his scientific and metaphyical ideas and continuing his religio-political attacks on Church establishment – to the point, finally, of inciting a riot which drove him from Birmingham to London in 1791 and then, in 1794, into exile in the USA. There he continued the activities of his Birmingham years, until he died at Northumberland, Pennsylvania in 1804.

Priestley's explicit attention to philosophical writing began with *An Examination of Dr. Reid's Inquiry ... On the Principles of Common Sense, &c.* (1775), attacking Scottish Common Sense Philosophy for its 'vain multiplication' (1775: 6) of separate, arbitrary, instinctive principles to explain perceptions (see COMMON SENSE SCHOOL; REID, T.). To disprove this naïve nativism, Priestley undertook an edition of selected parts of Hartley's *Observations on Man*, published as *Hartley's Theory of the Human Mind* (1775). Shorn of its specific references to religion and of the physiological doctrine of vibrations, this was, none the less, the avenue by which David Hartley's previously neglected *Observations on Man* was made known to the eighteenth and early nineteenth centuries.

Only in his first introductory essay to *Hartley's Theory of the Human Mind* does Priestley go beyond the *Observations on Man*, in which he was led into the most original of his metaphysical writing. In summarizing the physiological base suggested for associationism, Priestley asserted that Hartley's 'elementary' body mediating between mind and brain was unnecessary, and declared: 'I rather think that the whole of man is of some uniform composition, and that the property of perception...is the result of such an organical structure as that of the brain' (1775: xx).

This declaration provoked an outcry, prompting Priestley to write his *Disquisitions relating to Matter and Spirit* (1777). Into the *Disquisitions* Priestley poured the results of his thinking over the previous decades. 'Modern philosophical dualism' had no support from Scripture and led to the insolvable problem of interacting entities, matter and spirit, defined so that there was nothing in common between them. It also took no heed of recent discoveries in electricity, optics and chemistry. Far from being solid, inert and impenetrable, matter could be defined as a 'compages' of geometrical points, surrounded by spheres of alternating repulsive and attractive force.

With this publication no defence was sufficient to escape from accusations of materialist atheism, and that charge was enhanced by the publication of Priestley's *Doctrine of Philosophical Necessity Illustrated* (1777), in which he insisted that people's actions were determined by laws of nature. Priestley's arguments were ingenuous, emphasizing similarities between his doctrine and that of freewill: 'All the liberty...that I say a man has not, is that of doing several things when all the previous circumstances...are precisely the same' (1777: 7). None the less, the doctrine of philosophical necessity was representative of the relation of cause and effect, from which Priestley derived his arguments for the being of God, and he insisted that will is determined by motive, and motive by state of mind and view of things. When these remain the same, people will always make the same choice and determination.

Attacked for his views, Priestley responded – in such books as *A Free Discussion of the Doctrines of Materialism and Philosophical Necessity* (1778) – that nothing could be known of matter but its properties; that his monism could be called 'wholly spiritual' as easily as 'wholly material' (192); and that, by his description 'matter is...resolved into nothing but the *divine agency*, exerted according to certain rules' (250; original emphasis).

These proposals were too radical, and his anti-establishment persona too obvious, for Priestley's ideas to win any permanent acceptance in Britain. His achievements in all but science were soon forgotten, and Priestley has remained one of the neglected philosophical writers of his age.

List of works

Priestley, J. (1972) *The Theological and Miscellaneous Works of Joseph Priestley, LL.D. F.R.S. &c.*, ed. J.T. Rutt, New York: Kraus, 1972, 25 vols. (Contains all the philosophical works, but on the prefaces of the science books. Most of the latter, however, were reprinted separately by Kraus.)

References and further reading

Crook, R.E. (1966) *A Bibliography of Joseph Priestley 1733–1804*, London: Library Association.

Doddridge, P. (1763) *Course of Lectures on the Principle Subjects in Pneumatology, Ethics, and Divinity: with References to the most considerable Authors on each Subject*, ed. S. Clark, London: J.W. Clarke and R. Collins, W. Johnston, J. Richardson, S. Crowder and Co., T. Longman, B. Law, T. Field, and H. Payne and W. Cropley. (Doddridge may have given these lectures from the time of founding his Dissenting academy at Northampton in 1729. The lectures were used at Daventry Academy at least as late as 1775. They were printed for the first time in the edition cited here and were several times re-edited, with changes in the list of references, and republished (an early nineteenth-century American edition was published) but the edition of 1763 must be very like the form that Priestley used in 1750s.)

Gibbs, F.W. (1965) *Joseph Priestley: Adventurer in Science and Champion of Truth*, London: Nelson. (Standard full biography, but lacks complete documentation.)

* Hartley, D. (1749) *Observations on Man, His Frame, His Duty, and His Expectations*, London: Leake & Fredrick; repr. Hildesheim: Olms, 1967.

Schofield, R.E. (1997) *The Enlightenment of Joseph Priestley: A Study of His Life and Works from 1733 to 1773*, University Park, PA: Pennsylvania State University Press. (A detailed biography, but only of the first forty years of Priestley's life.)

Schofield, R.E. (1975) 'Priestley, Joseph', in *Dictionary of Scientific Biography* XI: 139–147, ed. C.C. Gillispie, New York: Scribner.

McEvoy, J.G. (1978–9) 'Joseph Priestley, "aerial philosopher"': Metaphysics and Methodology in Priestley's thought 1772–1781', *Ambix* XXV: 1–55, 93–116, 153–75; XXVI: 16–38. (A contrary view to that of Schofield.)

ROBERT E. SCHOFIELD

PRIMARY–SECONDARY DISTINCTION

The terminology of 'primary and secondary qualities' is taken from the writings of John Locke. It has come to express a position on the nature of sensory qualities – those which we attribute to physical objects as a result of the sensuous character of sensations they produce when they are perceived correctly by us. Since our senses can be differentiated from each other by the type of sensations they produce, sensory qualities are what Aristotle called 'proper sensibles' – those perceptible by one sense only. Colours, sounds, scents and tastes are always regarded as proper to their respective senses. What are the proper sensibles of touch, and whether there is similarly a single family of them, is a matter of controversy; but temperature at least is standardly regarded as proper to this sense. It is such sensory qualities that are candidates for being given the status of secondary qualities.

To regard sensory qualities as secondary is to hold that an object's possession of one is simply a matter of its being disposed to occasion a certain type of sensation when perceived; the object in itself possesses no sensuous character. Primary qualities, by contrast, are those which characterize the fundamental nature of the physical world as it is in itself. They are always taken to include geometrical attributes, and often some space-occupying feature; Locke's candidate for this latter was solidity. Although the terminology dates from the seventeenth century, this general doctrine goes back to the Greek atomists.

1   **Locke's account**
2   **The standard account**
3   **Reasons for the distinction**

1   Locke's account

Although the distinction between primary and secondary qualities is of ancient lineage, the terminology became current through the writings of John LOCKE, who was consciously drawing on the work of his older contemporary Robert BOYLE. Although a not unrelated distinction between primary and secondary attributes of matter is to be found in Medieval philosophy, when Boyle writes of 'secondary qualities, if I may so call them', he indicates that he took himself to be coining an expression to bear the sense that interests us. The distinction as it is drawn by Boyle and Locke is not one that centrally concerns the nature of sensory qualities or the relation between sensory states and physical reality, but rather the issue of what are fundamental and what are derivative attributes of material objects. This is clearly seen when one considers Locke's treatment of what are sometimes termed 'tertiary qualities' – such as a fire's power to melt wax. Such qualities are in fact termed 'secondary' by Locke; they differ from what are usually regarded as secondary qualities – that is, sensory qualities – only in that the latter are immediately and the former are mediately perceived. By 'secondary' Locke in fact means *derived, resultant* or *supervenient*.

In order best to understand this, we should bear in mind the hypothesis that Locke adopts as the most plausible account of the material world: namely, corpuscularianism, or what we would call atomism (although Boyle defines a corpuscle as a coalition of *minima naturalia* – which are the genuine atoms – so that a corpuscle is closer to our modern idea of a molecule) (see ATOMISM, ANCIENT). According to this view, everything material either is an atom – a small, naturally indivisible, solid body – or is a complex body consisting entirely of a number of such atoms. In any such complex body the constituent atoms will be arranged in a certain way, the technical term for such an arrangement being 'texture'. By 'quality' Locke means any feature of an object in virtue of which it has the power to affect another object. In virtue of the texture possessed by a complex object, as well as, perhaps, in virtue of the constituent atoms moving in relation to one another in the body (for example, vibrating), that object will possess certain powers – powers that no noncomplex, nontextured object could possess. All such powers are secondary qualities, since they derive from, or are secondary to, the arrangement and motion of the atoms constituting a complex body.

Thus there is no question for Locke as to whether a single atom may possess any secondary quality; such a thesis is analytically false. The only genuine question in this area concerns which of our ideas are excited by such derivative powers. It is an immediate consequence of this that no secondary quality is a universal or, as Boyle and Locke put it, 'catholic' attribute of matter, since they derive from particular, contingent configurations of atoms in complex bodies. By contrast, primary qualities are non-derivative, fundamental features of matter, and hence are possessed by everything material as such – even individual, simple atoms. ('Hence', because such writers regarded the idea that a quality could be underived and yet noncatholic – by having a bare, brute presence in some bodies but not in others – as a nonstarter. Primary qualities are fundamental in that they are essential attributes of matter as such.) Roundness, for example, can count as a primary quality even though not everything material is round, since it is but a determination of figure, which is possessed universally by body. Secondary qualities are immediately perceived when they are powers to occasion perceptual sensation in us, mediately perceived when they are powers to effect changes in other material objects, which latter changes alone we perceive.

One might object that the figure of a cricket ball ought to be a secondary quality since it results from an arrangement of the ball's constituent corpuscles. However, as far as the perception of the ball's shape is concerned, the cricket ball could just as well be a single, very large atom; the shape of the mass of configured atoms that is the ball is identical to the shape that a single atom may possess. We can see cricket balls and we cannot see individual atoms; however, the power of a cricket ball to appear round is not crucially dependent on the inner complexity of the ball, but simply on its size; atoms are simply too small to see. Another way of putting this introduces a second defining feature of the primary–secondary quality distinction: primary qualities excite ideas in us which *resemble* those qualities, whereas secondary qualities do not. With secondary qualities mediately perceived, this is obvious; we have no (pre-theoretical) idea of what it is in the fire that gives it the power to melt wax. Locke says that such qualities are generally agreed to be 'barely powers'. By this he of course does not mean that these powers are brute and ungrounded: they are grounded in the complex texture and perhaps motion of the object's constituent atoms. What he means is that they are barely powers as far as our ideas of them are concerned. Locke's view is that we are really not much better off when it comes to secondary qualities immediately perceived. Certain complex bodies have the power to excite various sensory states in us; it is in virtue of the texture and motion of an object's constituent atoms that it appears, for example, coloured or warm or scented to us. There is no colour or warmth or scent in objects distinct from the arrangement and perhaps motion of such objects' constituent atoms. So an object looks coloured because of such atomic facts; whereas, in contrast, a round object standardly looks round because it is round. This is all that Locke's muchcriticized notion of resemblance means.

2 The standard account

Primary and secondary qualities are usually not spoken of today as they were by Boyle and Locke, George BERKELEY being the principal instrument of change. In Berkeley we find two switches in terminology. First, the term 'secondary quality' is restricted to sensory qualities. Hence the central philosophical issue in this area becomes that of the relation between our senses and the nature of matter. Second, upholders of the primary–secondary quality distinction are said to hold that secondary qualities exist only in us – colours, scents and so on are merely sensations in the mind. 'Secondary' thus came to mean, or at least connote, 'in the mind' rather than 'derivative'. As an interpretation of Locke, this is half right and half wrong. For Locke, secondary qualities are certainly in bodies themselves. However, colours and so forth are merely in the mind. This is because colour, for example, is not a secondary quality for Locke; colour exists only in us, or in idea. When he wishes to advert to the corresponding secondary quality, he will use a phrase such as 'colour as it exists in bodies'. Because of all this, the precise meaning of 'secondary' is somewhat indeterminate in modern writings, although the general issue at stake is clear: do the sensuous features that we experience when we perceive physical objects inherently and irreducibly characterize the physical objects themselves? Does the world as it is in itself possess sensuous character?

3 Reasons for the distinction

Two sets of reasons exist for drawing our distinction: the first consists of reasons that are broadly empirical in nature, the second a priori. Under the first would fall even Locke's observation that secondary qualities can be altered by a merely mechanical process: for example, pounding certain substances changes their colour. How can this be unless such qualities are wholly subsumable under a merely mechanical account of the world? More recent discoveries concerning the precise nature of sensory perception allow a more detailed identification of such qualities with scientifically specifiable states of bodies. If, for example, an object's taste just is that in a body which gives rise under normal conditions to gustatory experiences when that body is placed in the mouth, and we discover that what thus causes such experiences is some chemical feature of that body, then taste must be identified, without remainder, with such a feature. By contrast, the best account available of why, for example, certain objects look round is that they are round.

A priori considerations must also be relevant, however, since roughly the same set of qualities have been given secondary status for over two thousand years. Certain qualities of bodies can be singled out a priori as being *sensory* in a distinctive sense. It is not just that such qualities are perceptible; but also that we must enjoy a particular kind of experience in order to cognize them. It suffices to know what a circle is to know that it is a figure, all the points in the boundary of which are equidistant from a single point. To grasp this, no particular kind of perceptual experience is necessary. In order, however, to understand what colours, scents and so forth are, we must enjoy perceptual experiences in the relevant sense modalities. Sensory qualities are sense-specific in that cognition of them requires the enjoyment of sensation that is definitive of a specific sense modality. The issue of whether sensory qualities are secondary or not is

the issue whether the very character of the sensation that we enjoy when we perceive a sensory quality is itself possessed by the object perceived. Is, say, the quale of redness which we experience when we see a red-looking object, inherently and irreducibly present in red objects, such that its presence by itself constitutes them as red?

Two distinct reasons may be offered for giving a negative answer to this. First, even if physical objects possessed such qualia, that fact would not constitute them having sensory qualities such as colours and scents. This is because it is possible that objects should possess such sensuous features in a manner that was irrelevant to the generation of perceptual experiences in us. Since, however, objects necessarily possess those sensory qualities they are discriminated as having by competent observers in normal circumstances, and since necessarily sensory qualities are the basis in objects of such discriminations, such a possibility shows that the possession by physical objects of such qualia does not logically suffice for possession of the respective sensory qualities: possession of such qualia does not *of itself* constitute the possession of any sensory quality. It remains, perhaps, a priori possible that such qualia should be contingently identifiable with sensory qualities – if they are indeed the physical basis of sensory discriminations; for a decision that this is in fact contingently false we need to turn to empirical considerations. Perhaps, however, certain high-level theoretical considerations, of a kind which seem to have motivated Locke, and which are not nicely categorized as either empirical or a priori, may count against even such a possibility: for example, the irremediably non-mechanical nature of such supposed physical qualia doubtless conflicts with an involvement in perceptual transactions with the physical world that perhaps must be at least partly mechanical in nature; certainly one of the seventeenth century's chief objection to the postulation of sensory qualities as 'real' was that they are ultimately unintelligible.

The second a priori consideration goes further and denies the very possibility of sensory qualia being merely physically realized. From the fact that sensory qualia determine sense modalities it is concluded that any such quale is an inherent feature of sensation. Nothing which is an inherent, qualitative characteristic of sensation could also be a feature of an insentient physical object, as sensory qualities are supposed to be. For example, for colour to be instantiated is for a sentient subject to be visually conscious is a certain manner. On this view there is as much chance of a mere physical object being sensuously coloured as there is of the pin that pricks you feeling pain.

Since the issue of secondary qualities concerns the nature of sensory qualities, whereas the issue of primary qualities concerns the fundamental nature of matter as material substance, philosophers can be and have been in substantial agreement over which qualities are secondary, while yet being in serious disagreement over the list of primary qualities. Although, perhaps, the issue of the secondary status of sensory qualities is amenable to a priori philosophical reflection, since the issue of primary qualities concerns nothing other than the fundamental concepts of physics, it is doubtless hubristic to expect any a priori settling of the question.

Finally, it is worth mentioning that the disjunction between primary and secondary qualities is not exhaustive – many qualities of physical objects are clearly neither physically fundamental nor sensory.

See also: QUALIA; SECONDARY QUALITIES

References and further reading

Alexander, P. (1985) *Ideas, Qualities and Corpuscles*, Cambridge: Cambridge University Press. (Detailed, scholarly treatment of the aspects of Locke's philosophy relevant to this topic.)

Boyle, R. (1666) *The Origin of Forms and Qualities According to the Corpuscular Philosophy*, repr. in *Selected Philosophical Papers of Robert Boyle*, ed. M.A. Stewart, Manchester: Manchester University Press, 1979. (Very readable account, and the source of Locke's ideas on this subject.)

Locke, J. (1689) *An Essay concerning Human Understanding*, ed. P.H. Nidditch, Oxford: Oxford University Press, 1975. (The most famous and influential traditional treatment of the subject.)

McGinn, C. (1983) *The Subjective View*, Oxford: Clarendon Press. (One of the best modern accounts of the issues.)

Sellars, W. (1963) 'Philosophy and the Scientific Image of Man', in *Science, Perception and Reality*, London: Routledge & Kegan Paul. (One of the most influential modern science-based accounts of the distinction.)

Smith, A.D. (1990) 'Of Primary and Secondary Qualities', *Philosophical Review* 99 (2): 221–54. (A recent account dealing with both historical and substantive issues concerning the distinction.)

A.D. SMITH

PRINCIPLE OF CHARITY
see CHARITY, PRINCIPLE OF

PRIOR, ARTHUR NORMAN (1914–69)

Prior is most often thought of as the creator of tense logic. (Tense logic examines operators such as 'It will be the case that' in the way that modal logic examines 'It must be the case that'.) But his first book was on ethics, and his views on metaphysical topics such as determinism, thinking, intentionality, change, events, the nature of time, existence, identity and truth are of central importance to philosophy. Using methods akin to Russell's in his Theory of Descriptions, he showed that times, events, facts, propositions and possible worlds were logical constructions. For example, we get rid of events by recognizing among other things that to say that the event of Caesar's crossing the Rubicon took place later than the event of Caesar's invading Britain is to say that it has been the case that both Caesar is crossing the Rubicon and it has been the case that Caesar is invading Britain. The title of the posthumous work, Worlds, Times and Selves (1977), indicates the breadth and depth of his thought. He is also fun to read. He died at the age of fifty-four, at the height of his powers.

1 **Life**
2 **Tense logic**
3 **Truth**
4 **Logical truth**
5 **Propositional attitudes and intentionality**
^ **Logic and ethics**

1 Life

Arthur Norman Prior was born in New Zealand. He entered the University of Otago in 1932, taking his BA in philosophy in 1935 and his MA in 1937. He studied under J.N. Findlay, working with him through Prantl's history of logic. Findlay made him an assistant lecturer in 1937, but after a year he left the university. The next eight years were spent in a wandering fashion, in Italy, France and Britain, in the New Zealand Air Force and as a freelance journalist. Prior's first marriage ended in 1943. Later that year he married Mary Wilkinson, and this marriage brought him great happiness and a collaborator in every aspect of his work. His writings, at first mostly theological but becoming increasingly philosophical, attracted notice, and in 1946 he succeeded Karl

Popper as lecturer at Canterbury University College at Christchurch in New Zealand, becoming professor in 1952. His first book, *Logic and the Basis of Ethics*, was published in 1949. By this time Prior's interests had become centred on logic, and in 1951 he submitted to his publishers a work which eventually saw the light as *Formal Logic* in 1955. In this, as in his subsequent works, he used the logical symbolism invented in Poland by Jan ŁUKASIEWICZ. Prior had close ties with Polish logicians, lecturing in Warsaw in 1961. He was John Locke Lecturer at Oxford University in 1956. In 1959 he returned to England to take up a chair at Manchester University. He also taught for periods in Chicago and Los Angeles. In 1966 he became a Fellow of Balliol College, Oxford. *Past, Present and Future* and *Papers on Time and Tense* were published in 1967 and 1968. Oxford gave him a Readership with effect from October 1969, but it was in that very month that his sudden death occurred, while he was on a visit to Norway. Various of his works were prepared for publication after his death, most notably *Objects of Thought* in 1971.

2 Tense logic

Prior became a player on the international philosophical scene with his delivery of the John Locke Lectures at Oxford in 1956, published in 1957 as *Time and Modality*. In these he explored analogies between the logic of necessity and possibility and the logic of past, present and future. He had earlier written an article on the Greek philosopher, DIODORUS CRONUS, who tried to reduce necessity to what is and always will be and possibility to what either is or at some time will be. This involved the use of tense operators, most importantly Pp and Fp, 'It has been the case that p' and 'It will be the case that p', having the same syntax as Lp and Mp, 'It is necessary that p' and 'It is possible that p'. Thus began a whole new branch of logic, 'tense logic', which for some years Prior developed single-handedly. *Past, Present and Future* and *Papers on Time and Tense* together traced the way the theory had grown and displayed the state of the art at that moment. As with all his logical work, systems were not created, proofs constructed or definitions given just for their own sake – for elegance or economy – but because philosophical issues were always being addressed. He believed that to regard tensed propositions as basic to the expression of facts about time was to give an affirmative answer to the metaphysical question whether or not, as it has become fashionable to say, 'time is tensed'. His article 'Thank Goodness That's Over' (1959) contains his best argument for this position. He found that different choices of axioms in tense logic could be used to characterize time as

unending, cyclical, discrete, continuous, and so on. The problem of determinism could also be given expression in formal terms, and philosophical views about ceasing to exist and coming into existence prompted modifications of tense-logical systems. Prior believed that propositions expressing facts about time in terms of relations between events or between events and times were reducible to propositions where time determinations were expressible by means of operators on sentences. This itself has implications for 'ontological' issues: we do not need to rank times or events as 'basic particulars'. Again, Prior's use of simple 'p' as opposed to 'Pp' or 'Fp' to represent present-tensed propositions led naturally to a 'redundancy theory' of the present, parallel in some ways to the redundancy theory of truth. It is raining now and it is true that it is raining if and only if it is raining (see TENSE AND TEMPORAL LOGIC; TRUTH, DEFLATIONARY THEORIES OF).

3 Truth

The use of tense operators, like that of modal operators, is a challenge to extensionalism: the material equivalence of p and q is not sufficient to guarantee that of Fp and Fq any more than that of Mp and Mq. Prior was uninhibited by extensionalist qualms, and equally uninhibited in his use of quantifiers to bind variables of categories other than that of names. He was accordingly happy to use quantificational formulas such as 'for every p' or 'for some q', following here the precedent of Łesniewski's 'Prototetic' (see ŁESNIEWSKI, S. §4). As well as the tense and modal operators, he made room for expressions like 'Robinson says that' or 'Jones thinks that' which form sentences out of sentences. The verbs of propositional attitude he described as predicates at one end and connectives at the other: to make 'said that' into a proposition I have to put something like 'Winnie-the-Pooh' in front of it and something like 'bees like honey' after it. Equipped in this way Prior is able to go ahead and paraphrase 'Jones believes whatever Robinson believes' by 'For every p, if Robinson believes that p, Jones believes that p'. He is thus able to give an analysis of 'true' in terms of quantifiers binding propositional variables. 'What Pooh said is true' means, roughly, 'For some p, Pooh said that p and p'. QUINE and Geach had frequently drawn attention to the analogies between the use of bound name-variables in quantificational formulas and the use of pronouns in natural languages. Since bound propositional variables correspond to sentences as bound name-variables do to names, Prior talks of them as 'prosentences'. This expression, first used by Prior in his article on the correspondence theory of truth in the Encyclopaedia of Philosophy edited by Paul Edwards, has since been used by Dorothy Grover and others to give the name 'prosentential theory of truth' to Prior's account of truth (see TRUTH, DEFLATIONARY THEORIES OF).

4 Logical truth

Prior had something to say not only about truth, but also about logical truth. He could make a profound point in a short paper apparently designed more as fun than as a serious contribution to philosophy. A perfect example of this is 'The Runabout Inference Ticket' (1960). Empiricists seek protection from the embarrassment caused them by our knowledge of logical truths by claiming that this sort of knowledge is due entirely to conventions of language. The necessary truth of propositions of the form 'If p, then either p or q' rests, on this view, on the fact that we have chosen to adopt conventions for the use of 'if' and 'or' which make it 'true by convention'. Prior described a new convention. We could introduce a word 'tonk' into our vocabulary. The conventions for using 'tonk' determine that from any proposition 'p' it is possible to infer a corresponding proposition 'p tonk q', and from 'p tonk q' it is possible to infer 'q'. Putting these together it would be legitimate on the basis of these conventions to infer any proposition from any other proposition. Every proposition of the form 'If p then q' would be a logical truth. Something has gone wrong: Prior leaves it to the reader to work out what that is.

5 Propositional attitudes and intentionality

When he died, Prior left a manuscript entitled *Objects of Thought*. The book has two parts, corresponding to the two senses of the phrase which is its title: 'What we think' and 'What we think of'. What we think are in a sense propositions, but Prior's understanding of 'proposition' is determined by his view, already described, of the syntax of sentences like 'Pooh thinks that bees like honey'. He regards propositions as 'logical constructions'. What this means is that sentences which have as their grammatical subjects expressions which seem to designate propositions mean no more than equivalent sentences in which no expression plays this role. Thus 'The proposition that Paris is in Scotland is false' means no more than 'It is not the case that Paris is in Scotland'. This is not saying of a strange object called a 'proposition' that it has the equally strange property of not being the case: it is saying something about Paris and Scotland. Similarly, in Prior's view, 'The proposition that Paris is the home of vice is believed by McTavish' does not

ascribe the property of being believed by McTavish to some proposition, but asserts that the property of being the home of vice in the eyes of McTavish belongs to Paris. The deep grammar of phrases like 'McTavish believes that' is the same as the surface grammar of 'in the eyes of McTavish': both belong to the category of adverbial phrases.

If what we think are in Prior's view logical constructions, what we think of are common-or-garden objects, rather than 'intentional' objects. One important consideration which led Frege and others to the view that in 'McTavish believes that Paris is the home of vice' the word 'Paris' designates an intentional object is that the sentence may change its truth-value if we substitute for 'Paris' another name of the same city. This supposed phenomenon was called by Quine 'referential opacity'. Prior, in 'Is the Concept of Referential Opacity Really Necessary?' (1963), maintained that the change of truth-value would occur only if the expression substituted for 'Paris' was a definite description, for example, 'the capital of France', and only then if the definite description had what Russell called 'secondary occurrence'. Substitution of names for names, when both are being used as names, does not, in Prior's view, lead in any case to change of truth-value. Nevertheless Prior is not an extensionalist, since he allows that substitution of coextensional predicates and materially equivalent propositions cannot always be made *salva veritate*. But Prior found difficulty in deciding when a name really was being used as a name, when McTavish's thought was directly about Paris, the city. Like Russell, he came to the view that few of our thoughts are directly about their objects. These are issues he debates in the second part of *Objects of Thought* (see PROPOSITIONAL ATTITUDE STATEMENTS).

6 Logic and ethics

Prior was at one time an editor of *The Journal of Symbolic Logic*, and his output in and contribution to the field of formal logic was considerable, though impossible to summarize in an entry of this length. At the same time, the early interest he showed in ethics was never extinguished. His work in this field, as in others, is notable for his learning in respect of the history of the subject, particularly, in this case, in the area of the seventeenth- and eighteenth-century British moralists. A good sample of his ability to put logic to work in the service of ethics is his essay 'The Autonomy of Ethics' (1960), reprinted in the collection, *Papers in Logic and Ethics* (1976a).

List of works

Prior, A.N. (1949) *Logic and the Basis of Ethics*, Oxford: Clarendon Press. (A logician's view of the so-called 'Naturalistic Fallacy' and its seventeenth- and eighteenth-century precursors.)

—— (1955) *Formal Logic*, Oxford: Clarendon Press. (A textbook providing an introduction to the propositional calculus, the predicate calculus, syllogistic and the logic of classes.)

—— (1957) *Time and Modality*, Oxford: Clarendon Press. (Prior's first attempt to apply the results of modal logic to a logic of tenses.)

—— (1959) 'Thank Goodness That's Over', *Philosophy* 34: 12–17; repr. in Prior, 1976a. (An argument for the indispensability of the 'A-series'.)

—— (1960) 'The Runabout Inference Ticket', *Analysis* 21: 38–9; repr. in Prior (1976a). (A *reductio ad absurdum* of the conventionalist account of logical truth.)

—— (1963) 'Is the Concept of Referential Opacity Really Necessary?', *Acta Philosophica Fennica* 16: 189–99. (This shows how distinctions of scope can provide an adequate explanation for failures of Leibniz's Law.)

—— (1967) *Past, Present and Future*, Oxford: Clarendon Press. (Together with the following volume, the main exposition of tense logic as Prior invented it.)

—— (1968) *Papers on Time and Tense*, Oxford: Clarendon Press. (With Prior (1967), the main exposition of tense logic.)

—— (1971) *Objects of Thought*, ed. P.T. Geach and A.J.P. Kenny, Oxford: Clarendon Press. (Prior's account of the nature of propositions and intentional objects.)

—— (1976a) *Papers in Logic and Ethics*, ed. P.T. Geach and A.J.P. Kenny, London: Duckworth. (A collection of Prior's most important papers not already contained in previous volumes. Includes 'The Autonomy of Ethics' 1960.)

—— (1976b) *The Logic of Propositions and Terms*, ed. P.T. Geach and A.J.P. Kenny, London: Duckworth. (Part of the original draft for the introduction to logic published earlier in part as *Formal Logic*.)

Prior, A.N. and Fine, K. (1977) *Worlds, Times and Selves*, London: Duckworth. (Further moves in the business of relativizing propositions to possible worlds, times and subjects of consciousness.)

References and further reading

Copeland, J. (ed.) (1996) *Logic and Reality: Essays in Applied Logic in Memory of Arthur Prior*, Oxford: Oxford University Press. (Proceedings of a conference held in New Zealand in 1992 to commemorate Prior's work.)

Grover, D. (1992) *A Prosentential Theory of Truth*, Princeton, NJ: Princeton University Press. (A development of Prior's ideas on Truth.)

Kenny, A.J.P. (1970) 'Arthur Norman Prior', *Proceedings of the British Academy* 56: 320–49. (Discussion of Prior's life and work.)

Williams, C.J.F. (1973) 'Prior and Ontology', *Ratio* 15: 291–302. (A critical notice of Objects of Thought.)

C.J.F. WILLIAMS

PRIVACY

The distinction between private and public is both central to much legal and political thought and subject to serious challenge on philosophical, practical and political grounds by critics of the status quo. Privacy – the state of being withdrawn from the world, free from public attention, interference or intrusion – is a cherished social value that is being offered ever more protection. Increasingly, laws require people to respect the privacy of others: privacy is recognized as a fundamental right in international documents and national constitutions, and recent customs and social norms forbid intrusions that were once accepted. The concept of privacy is also widely abused: it has been used to justify private racial discrimination and state neglect of domestic violence, as well as social abdication of general economic welfare through laissez-faire policies and the so-called privatization of social services. Critique of the public–private distinction is an important part of many critical theories, especially feminism and critical legal theory. These critics object that the public–private distinction is exaggerated, manipulable or incoherent.

1   Privacy as a social value
2   Public protection of privacy
3   Abuses of the public–private distinction
4   Critiques of the public–private distinction

1   Privacy as a social value

The origin of privacy is controversial. Some maintain that the public–private distinction originated with the Greeks and that '[s]uch delineations could not have been made in the theocracies of the ancient Near East because in such cultures god-as-ruler permeates everything and no notion of the private is possible' (Wiltshire 1989: 8–9). Others argue that up to the middle of the sixteenth century 'privacy... was neither possible nor desired' (Stone 1977: 6), and that it first arose a few hundred years ago, as household size reduced and as houses began to be built with corridors and private spaces. Although it is unlikely that either of these assertions is fully correct, it also seems clear that different periods in history are likely to have had somewhat different concepts of privacy, just as different cultures today have different concepts.

Privacy is central to liberal thought – as a right the state guarantees to protect from interference by others or by the state itself. In Western democratic societies, privacy is generally seen as a state of being or a right enjoyed by an individual. Privacy is considered basic to a free and open society and crucial for individual development. It facilitates spontaneity and insulates the individual from social pressure to conform. It contributes to autonomy, creativity, the capacity to form human relationships and the development of personal responsibility. For this reason, liberal political philosophies – J.S. Mill's *On Liberty* (1859) is a prime example – nearly always seek to draw a line between that part of human behaviour which is private, and therefore not subject to legal or social control, and that part which is of public concern (see LAW, LIMITS OF §4; LIBERALISM §§1–2).

Privacy is also extolled as essential to maintaining human relationships. Various collectivities, especially families, are sometimes said to require privacy or to be entitled to privacy. Unmarried heterosexual couples are often seen as deserving of a degree of privacy in order to be free to form a relationship. Lesbians, gay men and other sexual minorities have sought recognition of their relationships as alternative families entitled to privacy; sometimes this group-based approach has protected intimate relations more successfully than appeals to a notion of individual privacy.

2 Public protection of privacy

The concept of privacy as a legal right is of recent origin. In the USA it was introduced into the literature in 1890 by an influential law review article (Warren and Brandeis 1890). It received recognition as a constitutional right in the USA in 1965 in *Griswold* v. *Connecticut*, which established a privacy right for married couples to use birth control. This privacy right was found to attach to single people also and to protect an individual's access to abortion as well as to birth control (*Eisenstadt* v. *Baird* 1971; *Roe* v. *Wade* 1973). The right to privacy has also been recognized in major human rights documents such as the Universal Declaration of Human Rights.

Several competing state interests limit the protection given to privacy. Searches, seizures, involuntary blood and drug tests, and numerous other intrusions are allowed in the name of national security or crime detection. A major limitation upon privacy comes from competing rights, such as the freedom of speech and of the press (see FREEDOM OF SPEECH). In the USA, freedom of speech limits the protection given to 'public figures' against intrusions into privacy and limits defamation actions to cases in which the defamer acted 'maliciously' (*New York Times* v. *Sullivan* 1964). Freedom of the press has been found to override the interests of a rape victim to remain anonymous, even when the victim reasonably fears that the publication of their name would cause them to be targeted for further abuse and violence (*Florida Star* v. *BJF, US* 1989).

Computer technology has heightened concern regarding the protection of privacy by radically increasing the possibilities for gaining information about others. Large quantities of information about a person can now be collected, stored, processed and retrieved at relatively low cost. Data protection laws are being developed and refined in many countries to deal with these issues. Computer bulletin boards raise privacy issues that are just beginning to emerge. The widespread use of computers by children has facilitated access to them by adult child molesters who may pose as children and eventually set up a rendezvous.

3 Abuses of the public–private distinction

The public–private distinction has been improperly used to justify social policies that maintain power relations and leave defenceless people exposed to conditions that, if recognized as a public concern, should seem unacceptable. For example, exploitation and abuses of employees long went unchecked and legislative efforts to protect workers were overturned by courts on the basis of *laissez-faire* policies grounded in large part on the notion that private property should not be subject to public control. Even today labour unions in many countries are restricted on the basis of a public–private distinction: many aspects of the work environment and decisions related to these concerns are removed from collective bargaining because such issues are said to involve private management discretion that should not be meddled with by the public.

Racism and discriminatory decisions based on prejudice were until recently defended as a private prerogative, not to be interfered with by the state. Even as US courts began to protect the rights of African-Americans, the public–private distinction was used to limit review of racial discrimination to instances in which 'state action' could be found. 'Private' discrimination was not forbidden by the Constitution. Notions of privacy continue to limit the scope legislators give to employment discrimination laws, often exempting employers in small, more private-seeming establishments. The British Race Relations Act (1965), which forbids discrimination by anyone serving 'the public', was found not to protect against discrimination by a so-called private club that chose members 'by nomination and personal selection' (*Race Relations Board* v. *Charter and Others*, UK 1973).

The supposed privacy of the family has shielded brutality and abuse from public scrutiny and redress. In many areas of the world a special exemption to the rape laws withdraws protection from women who are married to the man who forces sexual intercourse upon them, no matter how brutally he does so. Many criminal and civil laws against physical assault have similar exemptions when the victim is the wife or the child of the perpetrator. Where the laws do forbid violence within the family, notions of family privacy nevertheless often limit the effectiveness of the enforcement of these laws.

Of course, there are those who would defend these uses of the public–private distinction as properly protective of private property, personal choice and family privacy. One reason that privacy needs to be protected, they could argue, is that individual cases arise in which the urge to intervene will be great, yet overall in the long run, non-intervention is to be preferred.

A second kind of abuse of the public–private distinction occurs when there is slippage between the descriptive claim that something is either public or private and the normative claim that it should be treated as public or private. This slippage leads to circular arguments and to efforts to foreclose discussion of the advantages and disadvantages of the policy advocated.

4 Critiques of the public–private distinction

What some critics see as an abuse of the public–private system distinction, others see as a problem inherent in the distinction itself. Since everything is socially conditioned, there is no sphere that is wholly private – there is a public dimension to private affairs and vice versa. Moreover, the line that is drawn between public and private does not reflect a natural distinction but an ideological purpose. It mystifies inequalities in society by treating them as irrelevant to political equality. Marx, for example, saw the division between the private individual and the public citizen as part of the alienation of mankind under capitalism.

The state was not the public bulwark against private oppression that liberal theorists supposed, but an agent of the ruling class.

Similar criticisms of *laissez-faire* capitalism were raised in the 1920s and 1930s by radical legal realists and others. The sphere of apparently free or private economic activity was dependent on legal rules created by the state, which thus structured and controlled power relations in society. Businessmen who called for an end to state regulation of the economy were inconsistent, because their own economic activity depended upon pro-business regulation.

The feminist critiques of the public–private distinction go further. Feminists point out that the public–private distinction is more than a distinction between the state and civil society, between the general interest and the particular interest, or between a person's public life as a citizen and private life as a self-regarding individual. It is also a distinction between men and women, between the public world of business and industry and the private, domestic world of the family. This gender association of private with women and public with men has important consequences for the role and status of women as well as for the particular meanings given to privacy (see FEMINIST POLITICAL PHILOSOPHY §§1, 7).

The legal realist critique of *laissez-faire* applies with equal force to arguments against state intervention in the family. The state structures domestic life through its family law provisions, as well as less noticeably through its policies regarding rape, employment discrimination, taxes, welfare benefits and childcare policies. Moreover, the public world of affairs – commerce, industry and so forth – is not separate from and opposed to the domestic world of the family; rather the two are inextricably interrelated (Olsen 1983). Carole Pateman has argued forcefully that the 'apparently impersonal, universal dichotomy between private and public' obscures the 'fact that patriarchalism is an essential, indeed constitutive, part of the theory and practice of liberalism' (Pateman 1983: 286)

Although many or most feminists might be said to accept privacy as such in that they, like others, appreciate solitude and would not want every aspect of their lives exposed to general public view, feminist criticism of the public–private distinction is more than just an objection to where the distinction is traditionally drawn and how it is used. Feminists challenge the way the line is drawn, the manner in which each term – public and private – is defined, and the basic dichotomous nature of the public–private distinction.

One way of understanding the gendered nature of privacy in Western thought is to consider that women are more closely associated with privacy but men are more assertive to claim a private realm for themselves. Women *are* privacy; they do not *have* privacy. Men as a group consider their interactions with women private, but as a group they also freely intrude upon the solitude of women, whether through street harassment or more gentle forms of imposition. This is a specific case of the general relationship between privacy and hierarchy. The hierarchically superior has privacy; the inferior does not. In order to have privacy, the inferior would have to exclude the superior in a way that is unnecessary for the superior.

References and further reading

Benn, S.I. and Gaus, G.F. (eds) (1983) *Public and Private in Social Life*, London: Croom Helm. (Collection of essays examining the public–private distinction in several contexts.)

Dallmeyer, D.G. (ed) (1993) 'The Public/Private Distinction and its Impact on Women', in part 2, *Reconceiving Reality: Women and International Law*, Studies in Transnational Legal Policy no. 25, American Society of International Law, 93–169. (Discussion of feminist critiques of the public–private distinction in the context of international law.)

Lacey, N. (1993) 'Theory into Practice? Pornography and the Public/Private Dichotomy', in J. Conaghan and A. Bottomley (eds) *Feminist Theory and Legal Strategy*, Blackwell, Oxford; and special issue of *Journal of Law and Society* 30 (93). (Contextualized feminist critique of the public–private distinction.)

* Mill, J.S. (1859) 'On the Limits to the Authority of Society over the Individual', ch. 4, *On Liberty*. (Classic liberal presentation of public–private distinction.)

* Olsen, F. (1983) 'The Family and the Market: A Study of Ideology and Legal Reform', *Harvard Law Review* 96: 1497–578. (Elaborate critique of the public–private dichotomy.)

—— (1993) 'Constitutional Law: Feminist Critiques of the Public/Private Dichotomy', *Constitutional Commentary* 10: 319–27. (Discussion of feminist critiques of the public–private distinction in the context of constitutional law.)

* Pateman, C. (1983) 'Feminist Critiques of the Public/Private Dichotomy', in S.I. Benn. and G.F. Gaus (eds) *Public and Private in Social Life*, London: Croom Helm. (Demonstrating the centrality of patriarchalism to liberalism in the context of feminist critique of the public–private dichotomy.)

—— (1988) *The Sexual Contract*, Stanford, CA: Stanford University Press. (Rich expansion and development of the argument expounded in Pateman (1983).)

Pennock, J.R. and Chapman, J.W. (eds) (1971) *Nomos XIII: Privacy* New York: New York University Press. (Classic, if dated, collection of essays on privacy.)

Schoeman, F. (ed) (1984) *Philosophical Dimensions of Privacy: An Anthology*, Cambridge: Cambridge University Press. (Collection of essays on privacy from a philosophical perspective.)

* Stone, L. (1977) *The Family, Sex and Marriage in England 1500–1800*. (Controversial history of family in England.)

Symposium (1982) 'The Public/Private Distinction', *University of Pennsylvania Law Review* 130: 1289–609. (Critiques and defences of the public–private distinction in the context of law.)

Wacks, R. (1993) *Privacy*, The International Library of Essays in Law and Legal Theory, Aldershot: Dartmouth Press, 2 vols. (Collection of essays on privacy from the legal perspective.)

* Warren, S. and Brandeis, L. (1890) 'The Right to Privacy', *Harvard Law Review* 4: 193. (Classic argument in favour of recognition of the common-law right to privacy.)

* Wiltshire, S.F. (1989) *Public and Private in Virgil's Aeneid*, Amherst, MA: University of Massachusetts Press. (Study of the classical origins of the public–private dichotomy.)

FRANCES OLSEN

PRIVATE AND PUBLIC

see PRIVACY

PRIVATE LANGUAGE ARGUMENT

Ludwig Wittgenstein argued against the possibility of a private language in his 1953 book Philosophical Investigations, *where the notion is outlined at §243: 'The words of this language are to refer to what can be known only to the speaker; to his immediate, private, sensations. So another cannot understand the language.' The idea attacked is thus of a language in principle incomprehensible to more than one person because the things which define its vocabulary are necessarily inaccessible to others; cases such as personal codes where the lack of common understanding could be remedied are hence irrelevant.*

Wittgenstein's attack, now known as the private language argument (although just one of many considerations he deploys on the topic), is important because the possibility of a private language is arguably an unformulated presupposition of standard theory of knowledge, metaphysics and philosophy of mind from Descartes to much of the cognitive science of the late twentieth century.

The essence of the argument is simple. It is that a language in principle unintelligible to anyone but its user would necessarily be unintelligible to the user also, because no meanings could be established for its signs. But, because of the difficulty of Wittgenstein's text and the tendency of philosophers to read into it their own concerns and assumptions, there has been extensive and fundamental disagreement over the details, significance and even intended conclusion of the argument. Some, thinking it obvious that sensations are private' have supposed that the argument is meant to show that we cannot talk about them; some that it commits Wittgenstein to behaviourism; some that the argument, self-defeatingly, condemns public discourse as well; some that its conclusion is that language is necessarily social in a strong sense, that is' not merely potentially but actually. Much of the secondary (especially the older) literature is devoted to disputes over these matters.

An account of the argument by the influential American philosopher Saul Kripke has spurred a semi-autonomous discussion of it. But Kripke's version involves significant departures from the original and relies on unargued assumptions of a kind Wittgenstein rejected in his own treatment of the topic.

1   **The significance of the argument**
2   **The nature of the argument**
3   **Related considerations**
4   **Kripke's Wittgenstein**

1   The significance of the argument

The idea that a language might be private is explicitly canvassed in the second of Bertrand Russell's lectures 'The Philosophy of Logical Atomism', and Wittgenstein's argument, though possibly directed against his own earlier views in *Philosophical Remarks*, may originate in the sustained criticism of Russell which informs much of his writing.

Immediately prior to the *Philosophical Investigations'* discussion of private language, Wittgenstein suggests that the existence of the rules governing the use of words and making communication possible depends on agreement in human behaviour. This agreement includes people's reacting in similar ways to similar training, and exemplifies contingent 'very general facts of nature' which make particular concepts and customs possible and useful. Thus, for instance, one can train most children to look at something by pointing at it (whereas dogs look only at one's hand), and this enables us to attach meaning to the gesture of pointing and derivatives like signposts. The immediate function of the private language argument is to show that the possibility of linguistic rules and concept formation in general depends upon the possibility of such agreement.

But it has a further, connected, function. Motivating Wittgenstein's discussions of both mathematics and psychology is hostility to metaphysical absolutes, to the idea that we can find the world as it really is in the sense that any other way of conceiving it must be wrong (compare Wittgenstein 1953: 230). Both numbers and sensations provide especially tempting cases for philosophers, who are inclined to imagine that these are objects which force their identities upon us, our classifications of them and the rules governing the uses of their names being dictated to us in advance by the phenomena themselves. Wittgenstein makes precisely analogous points in his treatment of the two cases. In both, the underlying confusion is about how the act of meaning determines the future application of a formula or name.

With numbers, one temptation is to confuse the mathematical sense of 'determine' in which, say, the formula $y = 2x$ determines the numerical value of y for a given value of x (in contrast with $y \neq 2x$, which does not) with a causal sense in which a certain training in mathematics determines that normal people will always write the same value for y given both the first formula and a value for x (in contrast with creatures for whom such training might produce a variety of outcomes). This confusion produces the illusion that the outcome of an actual properly conducted calculation is the inevitable result of the mathematical determining, as though the formula's meaning itself were shaping the course of events.

In the case of sensations, the parallel temptation is to suppose that their natures are self-intimating – I seem to feel what they are directly, so that I need only give a name to one of them and the rules for the subsequent use of that name will be fixed on the spot. Wittgenstein tries to show that this is an illusion, that even that apparently most self-intimating of all sensations, pain, derives its identity only from a sharable practice of expression, reaction and use of language. Now if, say, pain were to force its identity upon me in the way described, then the possibility of such a shared practice, which in turn depends upon those general background facts of nature, would be irrelevant to the concept of pain. That is, if the real nature of part of the world were revealed to me in a single mental act of naming, as the private linguist supposes, then all subsequent facts would necessarily be irrelevant and the name could be private. The private language argument concludes that they could not be irrelevant, that no names could be private, and that the notion of having the real nature of the world so revealed is confused.

Such confusions underlie a range of articulated philosophical ideas and theories, without themselves being so articulated. The argument thus attempts, not to refute any particular theory, but to remove the motivation for involvement in a range of seemingly independent tasks, problems and solutions. Here are some frequently cited examples.

A still very common idea, found in Locke, is that interpersonal spoken communication works by speakers' translation of their internal mental vocabularies into sounds followed by hearers' re-translation into their own internal vocabularies (see LOCKE, J. §5). Again, Descartes considered himself able to talk to himself about his experiences while claiming to be justified in saying that he does not know (or not until he has produced a reassuring philosophical argument) anything at all about an external world conceived as something independent of them. And he and others have thought: while I may be wrong in my judgments about the external world, I am infallibly correct if they are restricted to my sensations. Again, many philosophers have supposed there to be a problem of other minds, according to which I may reasonably doubt the legitimacy of applying, say, sensation-words to beings other than myself (see OTHER MINDS). In all such cases, the implication is that my language could in principle be private: for these problems and theories even to make sense, the ability to share must be irrelevant to meaning and it must be conceivable that I am confined to my own case. (This suggestion is controversial: the usual charge is that such philosophers are committed to supposing that there actually is a private language. But this is not obvious, and the argument would be just as significant if all they are committed to is the supposition that their presupposed internal language, for all the difference it would make to its usability for self-communing, could be private.) This is especially clear in the case of Descartes, who must hold it possible to identify one's experiences inwardly, that is, without using any resources supplied by one's embodiment in an independently existing world, such as the concepts acquired in a normal upbringing. How is this identification to be achieved? This is the question considered in the next section.

2 The nature of the argument

The private language argument is usually identified with §§256–71 of *Philosophical Investigations*, a tightly-knit discussion of sensations, with §258 being especially important. But this discussion cannot properly be detached from the earlier sections of the book, despite commentators having frequently done just this. As important as the already-noted connection with the lengthy prior discussion of rule-following is the treatment of ostensive definition.

The argument proper is preceded by a preliminary discussion (§§244–55) in which Wittgenstein distinguishes two senses of 'private' and argues that natural languages (English, for example) are private in neither. The question then arises, could anything be a private language? He approaches this question by considering how a private language might be arrived at. It cannot be reached via the actual language we speak, for that is not private, and the attempt to convert it by thought experiment into a private one by simply suspending all expression of sensation and imagining the speaker just to name a sensation, as it were in a vacuum, merely raises the question of what this is supposed to consist in and what it is for. But to give private language enthusiasts a run for their money, Wittgenstein imagines himself in the position of establishing a private language for the purpose of keeping a record of his sensations.

But he faces a serious impediment to discussing the matter at all: that doing so requires the mention of actions like ostensive definition, concentrating the attention, speaking, writing, remembering, believing, and so on, in the very process of suggesting that none of these can really be done in the circumstances under consideration. (This must be remembered in reading what follows, which in strictness should be constantly disfigured with scare quotes.)

He considers the idea that I simply *associate* a sign, say 'S', with a sensation by concentrating my attention on the sensation and saying 'S' to myself (the private analogue of ostensive definition), and points out that if this is to be a genuine definition it must establish a persisting connection between sign 'S' and that sensation: '"I impress [the connection] on myself" can only mean: this process brings it about that I remember the connection *right* in the future' (§258).

This single remark has caused much trouble. Many have thought 'I remember the connection *right*' means 'I use 'S' only when I have S.' This had the argument resting on scepticism concerning memory, and provoked the criticism that memory's fallibility is neither more nor less a problem for a private linguist than a public one, so that the argument threatens both or neither. Wittgenstein's defenders retorted that fallibility is no problem only where mistakes can be corrected; in the private case, there can be no checking of memories, hence no chance of correction, and consequently talk of correctness is inappropriate. The critics responded by arguing either that such checking is possible, or that correctness does not require checkability.

This interplay of criticism and defence characterizes much of the commentary on the argument. But it is beside the point. Both sides mistakenly assume the connection in question between 'S' and the sensation to be a connection of *truth*, so that remembering the connection right is a matter of making the judgment that I am experiencing S only in the presence of S. But the connection Wittgenstein says must be remembered is a connection of *meaning*. It can now be seen that the argument makes no appeal to the fallibility of memory.

Imagine I am a private linguist. I have a sensation, and make the mark 'S' at the same time, as one might in an ordinary case introduce a sign by ostensive definition. Now suppose that later, I use 'S' in judging that I am again experiencing the same sensation. What do I mean by 'S' on this second occasion?

It cannot be that I mean the sensation I am now experiencing, for this collapses the distinction between meaning and truth and removes the status of factual assertion from my judgment that I am experiencing S – it becomes at best a fresh ostensive definition. (Thus I cannot say informatively that my shirt is orange and with the same utterance explain what 'orange' means by exhibiting my shirt.)

Can it be rather that I mean the sensation I named 'S' on the previous occasion? That would presuppose that I had indeed succeeded in giving my sensation the name 'S', but this cannot just be assumed: for there to have been an ostensive definition of 'S', a technique for the use of 'S' must have been established, one which leads to my using 'S' in the same way as before. This, though, is just what is in question. What would using the sign in the same way be here? The same way as what? Wittgenstein's earlier discussion of ostensive definition showed that there can be such definitions only where a place for them is already prepared – just pointing and making noises does not establish what sort of thing is being pointed at, even in the public world, and as a private linguist I cannot even do that but at best can only concentrate my attention. 'S' must be the name of a *sensation*, and the fact that I have had a sensation and simultaneously inwardly muttered 'S' does not suffice to make 'S' the name of that sensation. (To name a sensation is to name a *kind*, but what kind? A sensation may be classified in indefinitely many ways: ache, sensation-in-leg, sensa-

tion-at-time-t, ...) And if one thinks a private linguist could remember the meaning of 'S' by remembering rightly the past correlation of 'S' with a certain kind of sensation, one presupposes what needs establishing: that there was such an independent correlation to be remembered. Fallibility of memory, even of memory of meaning, is neither here nor there: the point is that there has to be the right sort of occurrence in the first place to be a candidate for being remembered; and if there is not, no memory is going to create it. If, alternatively, we do not suppose that there is something to be remembered which is independent of the memory, then 'what seems right to me is right', that is, there is nothing to be right or wrong about. (These points are made in Wittgenstein 1953: 258–68.)

The conclusion is that it is impossible for a private linguist to establish and maintain a rule for the use of an expression, so that meaning is unobtainable in a private language. Only operating in a world independent of one's impressions of it, in which one's operations are thus in principle available for scrutiny, can provide the possibility of real correlations of signs with objects and consistency in the usage of those signs.

3 Related considerations

The argument as given is embedded in a collection of arguments, observations and reminders on the connected topics of the relations between expression and description of experiences, between mind and behaviour, and between self-knowledge and knowledge of others, concentrated mainly in §§243–315 of *Philosophical Investigations* but spreading into other sections and other works. This whole collection is sometimes referred to as the private language argument. But the question of private language is present in several of Wittgenstein's even apparently unrelated discussions, such as those of seeing-as (seeing a triangle as resting on its base, for example), and kinaesthesis, where the only available descriptions of the experiences involved which do justice to their contents make direct reference to a sharable world of public objects.

Central to his thought here is the belief that no one argument will suffice to eliminate the commitment to private language, for it is the result of various powerful illusions. One of these is the idea that one can study the nature of mental phenomena by introspection, as though this gave us direct and unmediated access to the truth-condition for, say, 'My neck is itching', a condition to which only I am privy (see INTROSPECTION, PSYCHOLOGY OF). In contrast, Wittgenstein argues, the nature of mental phenomena is grasped not by introspection but by examining 'language and the actions into which it is woven' (what he calls the 'language-game'), a publicly available practice of using words: with pain, this involves crying, complaining, comforting, administering analgesics and so on (*Philosophical Investigations*, §7).

Another source of the idea of a private language is that, where thoughts and sensations are concerned, there is in the normal first-person case no gap between truthfulness and truth. Philosophers are inclined to interpret this as a special epistemic authority about one's own mind, whose contents are hidden from others. Wittgenstein's treatment of this has been one of the most disputed parts of his discussion; he has been interpreted as suggesting that the lack of first-person uncertainty in utterances like 'My leg hurts' derives from their being not genuine reports of inner occurrences but sophisticated groaning. It is now a short (and often-taken) step to infer that this involves a commitment to supposing that there is nothing behind the outer behaviour, and thus to a form of behaviourism (see BEHAVIOURISM, ANALYTIC). Such oscillation between privacy and behaviourism, as though the former were the sole alternative to the implausibility of the latter, is typical of the bind philosophers get into in this area, so that they cannot see that the blocking of this route to private language involves the attempt to undermine assumptions common to both. These include such ideas as that witnessing a person's acts is being confronted with neutral behavioural data from which mentality must be inferred or constructed, and that dealing with other human beings is always a matter of hypothesis rather than of attitude and response. But Wittgenstein's view is that these ideas misconstrue the metaphorical inner/outer contrast; his rejection of this construal is not a denial of the reality of the inner.

4 Kripke's Wittgenstein

Saul Kripke's account of Wittgenstein's treatment of rules and private language has generated much second-order discussion of a kind notably different from that of Wittgenstein himself. This is often carried on without apparent concern for the question of whether Wittgenstein's own arguments are captured by Kripke's interpretation. Thus the phrase 'private language argument' has acquired a further sense in which it refers to the arguments as given by Kripke.

Kripke's interpretation resembles that given here in its emphasis on the dependence of the discussion of private language on that of rule-following. But Kripke (1982: 68) says, 'The impossibility of private language emerges as a corollary of his sceptical solution of his own paradox', one stated at *Philosophical Investigations* §201: 'No course of action could be determined by a rule, because every course of action can be made out to accord with the rule.' Apparently overlooking Wittgenstein's reference to this paradox as involving a misunderstanding, Kripke takes it to be a profound sceptical problem about meaning. He formulates this problem in two ways.

The first formulation is this: there is no fact in which someone's meaning something consists. The absence of this fact, in Kripke's view, leads Wittgenstein to abandon the explanation of the meanings of statements like 'Smith meant addition by 'plus'' in terms of truth-conditions; instead, they get explained in terms of assertibility-conditions, which involve actual (not merely potential) community agreement. (Hence the claim that this is a 'sceptical solution': Wittgenstein is supposed to concede to the sceptic the absence of truth-conditions for such statements.) This agreement, on Kripke's account, legitimizes the assertion that Smith meant addition by 'plus' despite there having been no fact of the matter, and it of course rules out the possibility of private language immediately (see PRIVATE STATES AND LANGUAGE §4). This first formulation, though, relies on the assumption that we have some idea of what a fact is, independent of a statement's being true; and one of the fundamental lessons of *Philosophical Investigations* is that there is no such idea to be had, that the only route to the identification of facts is via the (often not easily discerned) uses of the expressions in which those facts are stated. These uses give us the truth-conditions.

The other formulation of the problem is that there is no nexus between someone's meaning something and their subsequent behaviour, so that, for example, my grasp of the rule governing the use of 'plus' does not determine that I shall produce a unique answer for each of indefinitely many new additions in the future. The impression that something is missing here, though, is a result of just that kind of confusion about determination identified in §1 above.

Kripke's account is of great intrinsic interest, but despite the acuteness of some of its observations, as an interpretation of the private language argument it is thus deficient, especially because of his unargued reliance on ideas which Wittgenstein himself argued against. This has not deterred philosophers from using it, as Norman Malcolm's earlier account was used, as a way of avoiding direct confrontation with Wittgenstein's own text.

See also: CONSCIOUSNESS; CRITERIA; KRIPKE, S.A.; WITTGENSTEIN, L.

References and further reading

Because of the great difficulty of the subject matter, none of this material is straightforward, but none is technical.

Boghossian, P.A. (1989) 'The rule-following considerations', *Mind* 98 (392): 507–49. (A critical survey of the literature concerning the Kripkean version of Wittgenstein's arguments.)

Candlish, S. (1980) 'The real private language argument', *Philosophy* 55 (211): 85–94. (A fuller version of some of the points made in §2 of this entry.)

Canfield, J.V. (ed.) (1986) *The Philosophy of Wittgenstein*, vol. 9, *The Private Language Argument*, New York: Garland. (An extensive collection of papers exhibiting the variety of interpretations of the argument.)

—— (1986) *The Philosophy of Wittgenstein*, vol. 10, *Logical Necessity and Rules*, New York: Garland. (Contains some papers on the Kripke version.)

—— (1991) 'Private language, *Philosophical Investigations* §258 and environs', in R. Arrington and H.-J. Glock (eds) *Wittgenstein's Philosophical Investigations: Text and Context*, London and New York: Routledge, 120–37. (A discussion of some common assumptions about how the argument works.)

—— (1996) 'The Community View', *The Philosophical Review* 105 (4): 469–88. (A treatment of the issue of whether the private language argument requires language to be necessarily and actually, or merely potentially, social; examines both original texts and principal interpretations.)

Hacker, P.M.S. (1990) *Wittgenstein: Meaning and Mind, An Analytical Commentary on the Philosophical Investigations*, vol. 3, Oxford: Blackwell, 1–286. (Part of a massively detailed study of *Philosophical Investigations*; a good place to find out about textual sources, connections, ramifications, significance.)

Jones, O.R. (ed.) (1971) *The Private Language Argument*, London: Macmillan. (A collection of some of the earlier influential discussions of the argument. Also includes Wittgenstein 1968. Not much overlap with Canfield 1986.)

Kenny, A. (1973) *Wittgenstein*, London: Allen Lane: The Penguin Press, ch. 10. (One of the clearest accounts of the argument. Its version inspires, but differs from, that given in §2 above.)

* Kripke, S. (1982) *Wittgenstein on Rules and Private Language*, Oxford: Blackwell. (The final published version of Kripke's account.)

Malcolm, N. (1954) 'Wittgenstein's Philosophical Investigations', *The Philosophical Review* LXIII (4): 530–59. (Presents a highly influential early account of the private language argument.)

Winch, P. (1983) 'Facts and superfacts', *The Philosophical Quarterly* 33 (133): 398–404, repr. (slightly altered) in P. Winch *Trying to Make Sense*, Oxford: Blackwell, 54–63. (A clear and concise criticism of Kripke, from which some of the points in §4 above have been condensed.)

* Wittgenstein, L. (1953) *Philosophical Investigations*, Oxford: Blackwell, 3rd edn 1967. (The seminal text. Spare and difficult without being obscure or technical. The central material is found in §§243–315, but the earlier discussions of ostension in §§1–36 and rule-following, §§142–242, are also drawn upon in the argument. See also §§316–97, and pp. 220–4.)

—— (1968) 'Notes for lectures on "private experience" and "sense-data"', *The Philosophical Review* LXXVII: 275–320. (Also included in Jones 1971.)

—— (1975) *Philosophical Remarks*, Oxford: Blackwell. (A possible target of the private language argument.)

STEWART CANDLISH

PRIVATE STATES AND LANGUAGE

Something is 'private' if it can be known to one person only. Many have held that perceptions and bodily sensations are in this sense private, being knowable only by the person who experiences them. (You may know, it is often said, that we both call the same things 'green'; but whether they really look the same to me as they do to you, you have no means of telling.) Regarding the relation between private states and language two main questions have arisen:

(1) Could there be a 'private language', that is, a language in which a person communicates to themselves, or records for their own use, information about their own private states – this language being in principle incomprehensible to others, who do not know the nature of the events it is used to record. This question is primarily associated with Ludwig Wittgenstein.

(2) Can the nature of our private states affect the meaning of expressions in the public language, that is, the language we use for communicating with each other? Or must everything that affects the meaning of expressions in the public language be something which is itself public, and knowable in principle by anyone? Michael Dummett has argued that we must accept the second of these alternatives, and that this has far-reaching consequences in logic and metaphysics.

1 Epistemic privacy

The epistemically private is defined as whatever can in principle be known to one person only. The words 'in principle' are intended to exclude all cases in which something is in fact known to only one person, though it could be known to more. The only items that have generally been taken to be epistemically private in this very demanding sense are conscious mental states, primarily perceptual states and bodily sensations of a conscious subject, on the plausible grounds that nothing that a person can do can possibly give them a view of another's conscious states, but only of their bodily states and behaviour.

However, these grounds for taking such states to be epistemically private cannot by themselves decide the question whether there actually are any epistemically private items in the sense defined. Privacy, as we have seen, is defined in terms of what cannot be known to another, and from the fact that another cannot *experience* my headache it does not immediately follow that they cannot *know* what it is like. That must also depend on our understanding of knowledge, in particular on whether we can allow that what cannot be directly experienced by someone can nevertheless in some other way be known by them.

Discussion of this complex question is beyond the scope of this entry, in which it can only be remarked that some views of the nature of knowledge are not wholly unfavourable to the idea that the contents of another's consciousness may sometimes be known (see RELIABILISM; OTHER MINDS). Here it will be assumed that there are epistemically private states of the type commonly suggested.

We have spoken above of *two* questions concerning private states and language, and it is important to realize that, although related, they must be considered separately if clarity is to be achieved. To see this, the reader should consider the following. An impressive argument (discussed in §§2–3) for denying that private states can play any part in the semantics of the language that we speak with each other begins from the premise that the nature of one's private states is unknown to anyone else, and concludes that if it in any way affected the meanings of our words we would not know what any other person meant, and so could not speak this language with mutual understanding – which is then taken to be absurd. As it stands this argument clearly has no application whatever to the first question, the possibility of a private language. For a private language is understood to be one in which no other speaker is involved, so that the fact that one's private states are unknowable to others is entirely beside the point. To reach the analogous conclusion it would have to be said that private states are unknowable not just to others but to their owners as well, and this much stronger claim clearly requires further and altogether different argument. Conversely, we shall also see (§4) that it is possible to argue against the feasibility of a private language using a line of thought that may not apply to the question about the public language.

2 Acquisition and manifestation

Two arguments now frequently offered for the conclusion that private states can play no role in determining the meaning of any expressions of our (public) language are known as the acquisition and manifestation arguments. Each assumes that, in so far as there exists a language in which we communicate with each other, the expressions of that language must be used in the same sense or meaning by all of us. The acquisition argument then asks how this state of affairs could come about; the manifestation argument asks how we could tell that it obtained.

Suppose that there are expressions of this public language whose meaning depends on the nature of certain of the private states of competent speakers. (Plausible examples are colour words – it might well be thought that what I mean by 'red' depends at least in part on how certain things look to me – and words for sensations such as 'pain'.) Now consider the situation of language learners acquiring an understanding of one such expression. *Ex hypothesi* this means that they must come to use it in connection with private states of their own of the same kind as those already associated with it by competent speakers; but since these states, being private, are not accessible to the learners, how can they hit on the right meaning? Learning the language would call for an absurdly improbable series of lucky guesses.

The manifestation argument views the process from the other side: how are the teachers to tell that the learners have learnt their lesson correctly? How can the learners show that they have grasped ('manifest their grasp of') the right meaning? For to grasp the right meaning is to connect with the expression particular private states rather than others; and because they are private that is something which the teachers are in principle unable to check. We could never know, in the case of these expressions, what any other speaker means by them.

We should note that neither of these arguments

makes appeal to verificationism (see MEANING AND VERIFICATION) – both trade on the idea of what can be *known*, rather than of what is *meaningful*. The importance of this is not just that they avoid inheriting verificationism's weaknesses; it is also that otherwise they could not, without deep suspicion of circularity, be used to lead to a conclusion not altogether unlike verificationism – as they in fact have (see §5).

3 Responses to these arguments

One response, hinted at in §1, would be to deny that we have any states which are in principle unknowable to others. In view of the history of such sceptical debates this seems unlikely to lead to anything decisive.

A possible reply to the acquisition argument is as follows. Perhaps human beings naturally assume that others, when in broadly similar circumstances, experience inner states similar to those which they themselves experience. If that is so, and if the assumption is in most cases correct, then the problem posed by the acquisition argument can be answered. For since on this hypothesis the learner's private states resemble those of the teacher (when, for example, both are in the presence of the kind of object we call 'red') and are believed by both parties to do so, there is no difficulty in seeing how the learner can come to associate with the word 'red' private visual states which are of the same kind as those which the teacher associates with it.

But this does not settle the issue. For one thing, it makes no reply to the manifestation argument. For even if successful learning has occurred, how is anyone to tell? The teacher and the erstwhile learner have no way of knowing that they now mean the same. And if, as is often said, understanding someone is knowing what they mean, then they don't understand each other – contrary to the hypothesis that they are speaking a mutually intelligible language.

It is not obvious, however, that understanding someone does require knowledge of their meaning, if knowledge is taken to be more than confident true belief, as it nearly always is (see KNOWLEDGE, CONCEPT OF §2). For if your words express a certain thought, and I rightly and confidently believe that that is what they express, and so respond appropriately, it seems that everything we want of understanding has been achieved, and the additional demand for knowledge begins to look arbitrary.

Still the matter is not settled, for it may be replied that even if knowledge is not a necessary condition of understanding, nonetheless we *do* know what others mean by their words; therefore any theory which allows private states an essential role in semantics must be wrong, since it is committed to denying that we have such knowledge.

That commitment cannot be disowned, since it follows immediately from the definition of privacy, but it may be less damaging than it at first looks. Perhaps the claim to knowledge in this case, in so far as it implies the capacity to give good reasons for what we claim to know, is indeed dubious. Such a view is controversial, but certainly not obviously untenable. The idea that some of our most basic beliefs are produced by a psychological mechanism which is non-rational, in the sense that its operations are quite independent of any capacity we may have to *give reasons* for the beliefs it produces, has a reputable history (see for instance HUME, D.). To enable it to act successfully any animal, including ourselves and our ancestors, needs a reliable and rapid way of forming beliefs about its environment; so our basic belief-forming mechanisms cannot rest on reasoning, which is too slow and uncertain. And if a belief was not formed by reasoning there is little ground for thinking that it must nonetheless be certifiable, retrospectively, by rational argument, since it is not clear what additional practical benefit that would confer.

It is arguable, therefore, that the appeal to the threat of scepticism yields no decisive proof of the inadmissibility of private states in the semantics of public language.

4 The approach via rule-following

The question may also be viewed from another direction. Recent discussion of Wittgenstein's writings about rules (see MEANING AND RULE-FOLLOWING) has lead some (eminently Saul Kripke 1982) to suggest that the notion that two items are of the same kind can only have meaning against the background of a consensus in usage. This principle gives rise to the following argument.

Signs have meaning only because they are used in accordance with rules. So if anything plays an essential role in determining the meaning of a sign it must be capable of playing this role consistently, that is, in the same way on the various occasions on which the sign is used. Therefore private states can play an essential role only if it can be said that the same kind of private state was experienced on different occasions. But that, according to the above principle, can be so only if there is a communal practice with regard to these items among a number of speakers. And there can be no such communal practice – precisely because they are private. It follows that they play no part in the determination of meaning.

The 'consensus-principle', once accepted, instantly defeats the possibility of a private language, if that be understood as a language which of necessity only one person can speak. But that does not mean that it immediately dismisses private states from any position in the semantics of public languages. For if one can have true beliefs about another person's private states (as perhaps one can, so long as the hypothesis advanced at the beginning of §3 remains unrefuted) then there can be such a thing as agreement about these states, and even disagreement, at least where insincerity is suspected. And then if this is held not to satisfy the demand for communal practice, it needs to be explained why the consensus required should need to be based on mutual knowledge rather than just confident belief – no easy task, since it has not proved easy convincingly to establish *any* form of the consensus principle.

5   Further consequences

This question has not normally been pursued for its own sake, but rather for that of its alleged consequences. M.A.E. DUMMETT, having concluded that a speaker's grasp of the meaning of a sentence must consist in their potential for outward, publicly accessible behaviour, tentatively suggests a further conclusion: it must consist in the capacity to recognize whatever state of affairs it is that makes the sentence true, in other words to tell that it is true, if and when it is. We can grasp no meaning, and so have no grasp of truth, beyond what we can in principle recognize as true; and it is this which is held to define antirealism and require the abandonment, characteristic of intuitionist mathematics, of the law of excluded middle as a generally valid logical principle.

The response to this train of thought must depend on the answers to a number of questions. Is it clear that the recognition of the fact that the truth conditions of a sentence obtain is the only (publicly accessible) way to demonstrate ('manifest') understanding of it? Is it even clear that the act of recognizing that certain conditions obtain *is* in the required sense publicly accessible? This cannot just be assumed. Recognition is an intensional state, since one can recognize the fact that *p* without recognizing the fact that *q*, even if these two facts always obtain together; we are therefore lead into the difficulties connected with such states, in particular the question whether they can be captured in purely physical behaviour (see INTENSIONALITY; INTENTIONALITY §2).

But neither should it be assumed that problems about meaning and understanding are easily resolved, or Dummett's conclusions easily avoided, if we are allowed the contrary assumption, that private states may be given a role in semantics. For that it is still too unclear what kinds of private state there are, and what their role could be, and hence what difference it makes if we admit them.

See also: INTUITIONISTIC LOGIC AND ANTIREALISM; PRIVATE LANGUAGE ARGUMENT

References and further reading

All these items involve intricate argument but little or no technicality.

Craig, E.J. (1997) 'Meaning and Privacy', in *A Companion to the Philosophy of Language*, Oxford: Blackwell, 127–45. (Expansion of the material in this entry; also contains a section on the private language argument.)

Dummett, M.A.E. (1973) 'The Philosophical Basis of Intuitionistic Logic', in *Truth and Other Enigmas*, London: Duckworth, 1978, esp. 215–27. (Presents the arguments of §2 and suggests their connection with antirealism as discussed in §5.)

* Kripke, S.A. (1982) *Wittgenstein on Rules and Private Language*, Oxford: Blackwell. (Expounds the considerations leading to the 'consensus' principle as mentioned in §4. A particularly fine piece of writing.)

Wright, C.J.G. (1987) 'Introduction', to *Realism, Meaning and Truth*, Oxford: Blackwell, esp. 13–23. (Expounds and discusses the arguments from acquisition and manifestation and connects them with antirealism.)

EDWARD CRAIG

PROBABILITY, INTERPRETATIONS OF

The term 'probability' and its cognates occur frequently in both everyday and philosophical discourse. Unlike many other concepts, it is unprofitable to view 'probability' as having a unique meaning. Instead, there exist a number of distinct, albeit related, concepts, of which we here mention five: the classical or equiprobable view, the relative frequency view, the subjectivist or personalist view, the propensity view, and the logical probability view. None of these captures all of our legitimate uses of the term 'probability', which range from the clearly subjective, as in our assessment of the likelihood of one football team beating another, through the inferential, as when one set of sentences lends a degree of inductive support to another sentence, to the obviously objective, as in the physical chance of a radioactive atom decaying in the next minute. It is often said that what all these interpretations have in common is that they are all described by the same simple mathematical theory – 'the theory of probability' to be found in most elementary probability textbooks – and it has traditionally been the task of any interpretation to conform to that theory. But this saying does not hold up under closer examination, and it is better to consider each approach as dealing with a separate subject matter, the structure of which determines the structure of the appropriate calculus.

1   **The project**
2   **The formal theory**
3   **Relative frequency theories**
4   **Propensity theories**
5   **Subjective probabilities**
6   **Classical interpretations of probability**
7   **Logical interpretations and other approaches**

1   The project

The task of interpreting probability might be approached in three distinct ways. The first way is to see the project as one of providing an explicit definition of the term 'probability' or, more usually, of the predicate 'has a probability of value p'. The second is to provide operational content to this predicate; in other words, to provide a set of procedures by means of which various probability values can be measured or attributed. This second task may result only in the provision of sufficient conditions for attributing the predicate, and conversely a solution to the first task may be accomplished without the definition providing us with a way to measure probability values. At one time, when verificationism held sway, a failure to provide measurement criteria was considered fatal to a definition (see LOGICAL POSITIVISM §4; OPERATIONALISM), but we should keep separate these two tasks. The third approach is to provide an implicit definition of the predicate 'has a probability of value p' by means of an axiomatized theory of probability, followed by an interpretation or model for that theory. That is, because the concept of probability is often considered to be mysterious and inaccessible to observation in a way that the concept of, say, blue, is not, the best and perhaps the only way of providing content to the concept is by constructing a detailed theory of probability and providing a model within which the theory is true. This third project consists in putting structural constraints on possible interpretations of a probability function, and it will not ordinarily result in an explicit definition. It will also not usually assign specific values to outcomes, except

for certain extremal values, such as the certain or the impossible event.

2   The formal theory

The structure of elementary probability theory is often motivated by an appeal to familiar facts about relative frequencies. Suppose that a chance process, such as rolling a die, has N possible outcomes which form an outcome space $\Omega = \{1, 2, 3, 4, 5, 6\}$. By taking subsets of Ω, such as $\{2, 4, 6\}$, we have an event consisting in the die coming up even. Then take all possible subsets of Ω and this will form an algebra A of subsets of Ω, for example, a set of subsets of Ω closed under complementation ('negation') and union ('disjunction'). Let us say that an event E in A occurs if the elementary outcome, such as '2', is in E. Then we can define a probability function P over A by letting $P(E) = $ the number of times E occurs/the total number of repetitions of the chance process. This immediately gives us that

(1) $P(\Omega) = 1$

(2) $P(E) \geq 0$

(3)   If two events E and F are mutually exclusive, then $P(E \cup F) = P(E) + P(F)$.

For mathematical convenience, this elementary theory is usually extended by requiring countable additivity, wherein (3) is replaced by

(3′) $P(\cup_{i=1}^{\infty} E_i) \sum_{i=1}^{\infty} P(E_i)$ when the E_i are all mutually disjoint.

(The structure of A then needs to be more complex in ways that are inessential here.)

An important definition to add is that of conditional probability, $P(A \mid B)$, the probability of A given B, defined as $P(A \mid B) = P(A \cap B)/P(B)$. Two elements of A are *independent* if and only if $P(A \mid B) = P(A)$ or, equivalently, if $P(A \cap B = P(A) \times P(B)$.

This abstract calculus is now no longer tied to the particular interpretation with which we began, and the algebra can be one of propositions rather than events, an ontology preferable for logical or subjective interpretations. Different accounts of probability can now be compared to this axiomatic theory.

3   Relative frequency theories

Here the ontology is one of event types, and the probability is explicitly defined either as the actual finite relative frequency as in §2 above, or as the limit value of the relative frequency when the total number of repetitions goes to infinity. This gives the value of the probability as an empirical property of the sequence or reference class of outcomes which generates the frequency, rather than absolutely. A naïve finite frequency interpretation is clearly unsatisfactory. Suppose a die is rolled a finite number of times N. Then no outcome, say a '6', can have a probability value more fine-grained than on a scale 0, $1/N, 2/N, \ldots, 1$. Thus, after two throws, a '6' could only have a probability of 0, 0.5, or 1. This problem could be circumvented by requiring sufficiently many repetitions, where 'sufficiently many' would be a function of the number of possible outcomes and degree of precision required. A more standard remedy for this problem is to move to a limiting relative frequency interpretation, wherein the probability value is simply defined as the limit of m/N as $N \to \infty$, where m is the number of successes. This solves our first, definitional, task, but it produces a difficulty for the measurement project, for there is no guarantee that the value of the relative frequency after, say, 1,000 repetitions, will be the same as, or close to, the limiting value, because an unusual run of outcomes could occur initially. What one can do is appeal to the strong law of large numbers for binary valued outcomes, which asserts that if the repetitions of the experiment are independent and identically distributed (that is, the probability does not vary from repetition to repetition) then

for every $\varepsilon > 0$, with probability one $|m/N - p| > \varepsilon$ only finitely often.

This provides assurance that in the long run, the probability that the limiting frequency will differ from the 'true' value of p is zero, but at the cost of introducing a second order probability which in turn needs to be interpreted. As an additional requirement, Richard von Mises (1957) correctly insisted that limiting frequency values can only be drawn from random sequences of data. Thus, if our die gave us the sequence of outcomes 1, 2, 3, 4, 5, 6, 1, 2, 3, 4, 5, 6, ..., the limiting frequency of a '2' would be 1/6, but quite clearly on every $(6N+2)$nd throw ($N = 0, 1, 2, \ldots$) the probability of '2' would be 1, and would be 0 on any other throw. This highlights what is known as the problem of single-case probabilities – how do we transfer a probability value from a class to a single outcome? A standard answer is that the appropriate frequency for an outcome type is one drawn from a random sequence. Attempts to solve this single-case problem have led to complex and fascinating theories of randomness and statistical relevance, each of which is of philosophical interest in its own right (Sklar 1993).

4 Propensity theories

We have seen above that relative frequencies are defined relative to a class of outcomes. If we focus on the fact that outcomes can be produced by a fixed set of generating conditions, then it is reasonable to attribute probabilities to a system in a physical context, especially when the system producing the outcomes is irreducibly indeterministic. This gives us a chance disposition or *propensity* to produce a given outcome. For example, the probability of decay within the next minute is a physical property of a radioactive atom, just as is its atomic weight. This view, which seems to have originated with C.S. Peirce, and was resurrected by Karl Popper (see POPPER, K.R. §3), has been criticized as excessively metaphysical. This is an unfair criticism, for the propensity value can be measured empirically for a system with a fixed propensity by employing the strong law of large numbers, mentioned above, together with statistical estimation techniques, thus satisfying the operational criterion. Being a thoroughly ontological interpretation, propensity accounts do not provide an explicit reductionist definition of probability, for propensities are basic, often primitive, properties of the world. However, no satisfactory solution has yet been given for the third project of providing a propensity calculus. Nor, despite a number of efforts by Popper and others, has a satisfactory argument been provided that quantum probabilities are obviously propensities in any detailed sense (see CAUSATION; QUANTUM MECHANICS, INTERPRETATION OF; STATISTICS).

5 Subjective probabilities

In contrast to the objective interpretations just described, probability has always had a close relation with degrees of rational belief. Within this tradition, one can measure such degrees of belief operationally by means of betting behaviour. Here the elements to which the probabilities attribute values are propositions or sentences rather than events. By means of an ingenious operational process, known as the Dutch book method, within which the probability value is defined in terms of the lowest odds at which the gambler will accept a bet, one can show that plausible constraints on rational behaviour are satisfied if and only if axioms (1)–(3) and the definition of conditional probability of §2 hold. The subjective probability assignments are then said to be coherent. Thus we have satisfied the second and third criteria cited earlier, although it should be noted that different individuals can assign widely different values to a contingent proposition and both be coherent. De Finetti (1937), however, held that (3′) was not true for

703

subjective probabilities because placing an infinite number of bets makes no sense for human agents. The Dutch book method will give us what are called prior probabilities but, except for extremal values, these are not arrived at by an a priori process. Rather, they are the expression of an unarticulated amalgamation of background knowledge. Although there is some controversy over how best to revise beliefs in the light of empirical evidence, the traditional way to do this is via conditionalization, using Bayes' theorem. If H_j is a hypothesis (say that the die is fair), E is empirical evidence (say data from throws) and P_0 is our prior subjective probability assignment, then

$$P_1(H_j) = P_0(H_j \mid E) = P_0(E \mid H_j)P_0(H_j) / \sum_i P_0(E \mid H_i)P_0(H_i)$$

where $\{H_i\}$ is the set of hypotheses under consideration and P_1 is the new, posterior, probability assignment. Provided that the members of $\{H_i\}$ are distinct hypotheses (only one can be true at any time) and that $\sum_i P_0(H_i) = 1$ (the possibility that no member of $\{H_i\}$ is true is not entertained), $\sum_i P_0(E \mid H_i)P_0(H_i) = P_0(E)$, which gives $P_1(H_j) = P_0(H_j \mid E)P_0(H_j)/P_0(E)$.

The above gives us a normative theory of how agents should distribute their degrees of belief, but there has always been a divergence between this normative Bayesianism and individuals' actual degrees of belief. Investigations by psychologists and economists have revealed systematic differences from Bayesian prescriptions, even by agents well-versed in probabilistic reasoning.

6 Classical interpretations of probability

This approach allocates probability values by dividing the outcomes into equipossible cases, and then using a principle of indifference to give each equipossible case an equal probability. Thus, if one considers, on the basis of symmetry, that each side of a die is just as likely to come up as any other side, then the classical theory attributes a value of $1:6$ to each such outcome. This is not, contrary to many claims, always an a priori attribution, because it generally depends upon some specific empirical knowledge about symmetries of the system. The classical approach is unsatisfactory for a variety of reasons. First, it is limited to situations in which equipossible cases are available. Second, there are straightforward paradoxes associated with this approach, which allow different probability values to be attached to the same event. The simplest is one introduced by Bertrand. Suppose you have wine and water mixed, in a ratio somewhere between one

part of water to one of wine, and two parts water to one of wine. Using an indifference principle on the ratio water:wine, we have that the probability of the ratio lying between 1 and 1.5 is $1:2$. Now consider the ratio wine:water. This can lie between $1:2$ and 1, and the water:wine ratio of $1:5$ is a wine:water ratio of $2:3$. The indifference principle then says that the probability of this ratio lying between 1 and $2:3$ has a probability of $2:3$. This is contradictory.

7 Logical interpretations and other approaches

The logical approach takes propositions as the objects to which probabilities are ascribed, and interprets a conditional probability as a logical relation giving a degree of inductive support from the conditioning sentence to the conditioned. Thus, $P(H \mid E)$ is the degree of inductive support that the evidence statement E gives to the hypothesis H. To measure $P(H \mid E)$, Carnap (1945) considered state descriptions. In the simplest case, one lists all the individuals $a_1 \ldots a_n$ in a world and all the predicates $F_1 \ldots F_r$. Then a state description is an attribution of F_i or $\sim F_i$ to each individual a_j for all i and j, that is, a maximally consistent description of some possible world. If we now attribute, in an a priori way, a measure m on state descriptions (and this can be done in a number of ways), then the conditional logical probability is just $m(H \& E)/m(E)$. The principal drawback to using state descriptions is that learning from experience is impossible, simply because all predicates are logically independent and hence observing an instance of the property it represents gives no information about instances of any other. For this reason, Carnap switched to structure descriptions, within which individuals are indistinguishable. Interestingly, the differences between Maxwell–Boltzmann statistics, Bose–Einstein, and Fermi–Dirac statistics in physics are representable as differences that depend upon which states are physically possible. Because it is an empirical fact which particles satisfy which statistics, this sheds considerable doubt upon the whole enterprise of making a priori probability attributions.

There are now well-entrenched theories of comparative probability within which numerical values are not assigned, but one outcome is simply considered to be at least as probable as another. Alternatively, rather than assigning specific values to a proposition, intervals of probability can be assigned to mirror our uncertainty about the correct value via upper and lower probabilities. The connections between subjective probability and objective chance are now also the subject of much interest.

See also: CARNAP, R. §5; CONFIRMATION THEORY; DECISION AND GAME THEORY; FIELD THEORY, QUANTUM; INDUCTIVE INFERENCE; PROBABILITY THEORY AND EPISTEMOLOGY; RATIONAL BELIEFS; RATIONAL CHOICE THEORY; REICHENBACH, H. §3

References and further reading

* Carnap, R. (1945) 'On Inductive Probability', *Philosophy of Science* 12: 72–97. (An accessible introduction to logical probability by its primary advocate.)

Cohen, L.J. (1989) *An Introduction to the Philosophy of Probability and Induction*, Oxford: Clarendon Press. (Chapter 2 is a brief but useful critical survey of the interpretations discussed in this article.)

Feller, W. (1968) *An Introduction to Probability Theory and Its Applications*, New York: John Wiley & Sons. (Still the best introduction to the mathematical theory of probability. Volume 1 treats discrete outcome spaces; volume 2 (2nd edition 1971) deals with continuous outcome spaces.)

* Finetti, B. de (1937) 'Foresight: its Logical Laws, its Subjective Sources'; repr. in H. Kyburg and H. Smokler (eds) *Studies in Subjective Probability*, New York: John Wiley & Sons, 1964. (A classic source on subjective probability.)

Jeffrey, R. (1983) *The Logic of Decision*, Chicago, IL: University of Chicago Press, 2nd edn. (A systematic exposition of one variety of Bayesianism.)

Kahneman, D., Slovic, P. and Tversky, A. (eds) (1982) *Judgement under Uncertainty: Heuristics and Biases*, Cambridge: Cambridge University Press. (A collection of papers by psychologists describing how individuals reason probabilistically. See §5.)

Lewis, D. (1980) 'A Subjectivist's Guide to Objective Chance', in R. Jeffrey (ed.) *Studies in Inductive Logic and Probability*, vol. 2, Berkeley, CA: University of California Press. (Reprinted with important Postscripts in D. Lewis, *Philosophical Papers*, vol. 2, Oxford: Oxford University Press, 1986. This article details some connections between objective and subjective probabilities.)

* Mises, R. von (1957) *Probability, Statistics, and Truth*, New York: Dover, 2nd edn. (A nontechnical treatment of a relative frequency approach.)

Popper, K. (1974) 'Suppes's Criticisms of the Propensity Interpretation of Probability and Quantum Mechanics', in P.A. Schilpp (ed.) *The Philosophy of Karl Popper*, La Salle, IL: Open Court, 1,125–39. (A detailed treatment of a propensity theory. The article to which it is replying – P. Suppes, 'Popper's Analysis of Probability in Quantum Mechanics', 760–74 – should be read too.)

* Sklar, L. (1993) *Physics and Chance*, Cambridge:

Cambridge University Press. (Chapter 3 is a readable overview of probability, with a section – §4 – on randomness.)

PAUL HUMPHREYS

PROBABILITY THEORY AND EPISTEMOLOGY

The primary uses of probability in epistemology are to measure degrees of belief and to formulate conditions for rational belief and rational change of belief. The degree of belief a person has in a proposition A is a measure of their willingness to act on A to obtain satisfaction of their preferences. According to probabilistic epistemology, sometimes called 'Bayesian epistemology', an ideally rational person's degrees of belief satisfy the axioms of probability. For example, their degrees of belief in A and −A must sum to 1. The most important condition on changing degrees of belief given new evidence is called 'conditionalization'. According to this, upon acquiring evidence E a rational person will change their degree of belief assigned to A to the conditional probability of A given E. Roughly, this rule says that the change should be minimal while accommodating the new evidence. There are arguments, 'Dutch book arguments', that are claimed to demonstrate that failure to satisfy these conditions makes a person who acts on their degrees of belief liable to perform actions that necessarily frustrate their preferences. Radical Bayesian epistemologists claim that rationality is completely characterized by these conditions. A more moderate view is that Bayesian conditions should be supplemented by other conditions specifying rational degrees of belief.

Support for Bayesian epistemology comes from the fact that various aspects of scientific method can be grounded in satisfaction of Bayesian conditions. Further, it can be shown that there is a close connection between having true belief as an instrumental goal and satisfaction of the Bayesian conditions.

Some critics of Bayesian epistemology reject the probabilistic conditions on rationality as unrealistic. They say that people do not have precise degrees of belief and even if they did it would not be possible in general to satisfy the conditions. Some go further and reject the conditions themselves. Others claim that the conditions are much too weak to capture rationality and that in fact almost any reasoning can be characterized so as to satisfy them. The extent to which Bayesian epistemology contributes to traditional epistemological concerns of characterizing knowledge and methods for obtaining knowledge is controversial.

1   Degrees of belief and probability

We ordinarily make a tripartite distinction among believing Q, believing not-Q, and suspending belief with respect to Q. Advocates of subjective probability think that beliefs come in more finely graded degrees. They further claim that rationality requires that degrees of belief satisfy the probability calculus and change in accord with a rule called 'conditionalization'. The classic sources for this view, Ramsey (1931), de Finetti (1972) and Savage (1954), argued that beliefs failing to conform to the probability calculus lead to actions that frustrate the believer's goals and for that reason a rational person will attempt to bring their degrees of belief into line with the probability calculus (see RAMSEY, F.P. §2).

The degree to which someone believes that Q is manifested in their tendency to act on that belief. For example, if Arabella wants to get downtown by 5 p.m. and has a greater degree of belief that she will get downtown by 5 if she takes the train than if she takes the bus she will, other things being equal, take the train. One suggestion for measuring degrees of belief is in terms of the prices one is willing to pay for gambles. A simple gamble on Q is one in which $1 is paid if Q and nothing if not Q. Suppose that Arabella is willing to either buy or sell (in which case she is committed to pay the buyer of the gamble $1 if Q and nothing if not Q) a simple gamble on Q for x, where $0 \leqslant x \leqslant 1$. In this case x is the fair value of the gamble for Arabella and her degree of belief in Q is x. Advocates of subjective probability claim that an ideally rational person will assign degrees of belief to all propositions expressible in their language.

Nevertheless, measuring degrees of belief by willingness to pay for gambles is problematic. Experimental psychologists have accumulated evidence that seems to show that the value a person assigns to a gamble is dependent on how the gamble is described, on context, and is unstable (Kahneman, Slovic and Tversky 1982). Further, measuring degrees of belief in terms of gambles unrealistically assumes that the believer attaches no value (positive or negative) to gambling as such, that monetary gain corresponds to gains in utility, and that considering buying a gamble does not change one's degree of belief. These problems are not fatal since more sophisticated ways of measuring degrees of belief have been developed that do not depend on these assumptions. But even if there is a way of accurately measuring exact degrees of belief when they exist it is not plausible that we have exact degrees of belief in most propositions. Most people would be unwilling to assign a fair value to a gamble. Usually the amount we would be willing to pay for a gamble is less than the amount at which we would sell it. These considerations have led to proposals for representing degree of belief in terms of intervals or more complicated structures (Levi 1980). For the most part these complications will be ignored here.

Degrees of belief that conform to the probability calculus are called 'subjective probabilities' since they are relative to believers. To satisfy the probability calculus a function $P(A)$ (the probability of A) on a set of sentences (closed under negation and conjunction) must satisfy the consequences of the following axioms:

(1) $0 \leqslant P(A) \leqslant 1$

(2) $P(A) = 1$ if A is logically true

(3) $P(A \vee B) = P(A) + P(B) - P(A \& B)$

Degrees of belief that satisfy the probability calculus are said to be 'coherent'. Psychologists have accumulated evidence that shows that people's degrees of belief are typically not coherent. For example, subjects in experimental studies frequently assign a higher probability to a conjunction $Q \& R$ than they do to Q in violation of the probability calculus (Kahneman, Slovic and Tversky 1982) (see RATIONALITY OF BELIEF). The failure of beliefs to be coherent is not an objection to subjective probability since coherence is a normative notion. Advocates of subjective probability think coherence is a norm for degrees of belief in the way that logical consistency is a norm.

Among the more important arguments for the claim that rationality requires coherence is one based on 'the Dutch book' theorem. A Dutch book is a set of gambles such that one who takes the gambles suffers a net loss no matter what. For example, if someone has degrees of belief $P(Q) = 0.6$ and $P(-Q) = 0.6$ then they will exchange $.6 for a gamble on Q that pays $1 if Q and nothing otherwise, and $.6 for a gamble on $-Q$ which pays $1 if $-Q$ is true and nothing otherwise. They cannot win both, so no matter whether Q is true or false they will lose $.2. It can be proved that satisfaction of the probability calculus is necessary and sufficient for not being subject to this kind of Dutch book. This establishes that rationality requires coherence only if rationality requires immunity from Dutch books, which is not obvious.

2 Changing degrees of belief

Suppose that Arabella initially has degrees of belief $P(A)$, $P(B)$ and $P(A \& B)$ and that $P(A) \neq 0$ and then changes the degree of belief she assigns to A to $P'(A) = 1$. Conditionalization says that she rationally ought to change the degree of belief she assigns to B to $P'(B) = P(B|A)$. $P(B|A)$ is the *conditional probability* of B on A and is equal to $P(A \& B)/P(A)$. For example, if the initial degrees of belief are $P(M) = 0.5$, $P(W) = 0.4$, $P(U) = 0.1$ (M is the proposition that Colonel Mustard committed the crime, W is the proposition that Mrs. White did it, and U that Professor Plum did it), then when Holmes discovers that Colonel Mustard is innocent, conditionalization prescribes that his new degrees of belief should be $P'(W) = P(W|-M) = 0.8$ and $P'(U) = P(U|-M) = 0.2$. These changes seem reasonable since they involve the least change in degrees of belief required to accommodate the new information while maintaining coherence.

An important rule for calculating conditional probabilities is Bayes' theorem (after Thomas Bayes, who used it to calculate the probability that the stars are distributed randomly). Suppose that someone assigns degree of belief $P(H)$ (the prior probability of H) and conducts an experiment E with possible outcomes e and $-e$. Suppose also that they assign degrees of belief $P(e|H)$ and $P(e|-H)$. Then the conditional probability $P(H|e)$ is given by Bayes' theorem:

$$P(H|e) = \frac{P(H) \times P(e|H)}{P(H) \times P(e|H) + P(-H) \times P(e|-H)}$$

To apply Bayes' theorem one needs prior probabilities $P(H)$, $P(-H)$ and likelihoods $P(e|H)$, $P(e|-H)$. The likelihoods are usually thought of as deriving from statistical or theoretical information about probabilities. The prior probabilities are the believers' initial degrees of belief. Their status is controversial and has received much discussion some of which will be summarized later. As an example, suppose that a physician assigns the prior probability $P(D) = 0.3$ to the hypothesis that a patient has a certain disease. Suppose that there is a test for the disease with outcomes e and $-e$ such that $P(e|D) = 0.9$ and $P(e|-D) = 0.2$. If the test is conducted and yields result e then according to the rule of conditionalization the physician's new degree of belief $P'(D) = P(D|e)$, which by Bayes' theorem is 0.65.

Not all changes in degrees of belief are initiated by changes from an intermediate value to 1. Richard Jeffrey (1983) proposes a rule, 'Jeffrey Conditionalization' (JC), to accommodate such changes. If one changes the degree of belief assigned to A from $P(A)$ to $P'(A)$ then one should change the degree of belief assigned to B from $P(B)$ to

(JC) $P'(B) = P'(A) \times P(B|A) + P'(-A) \times P(B|-A)$

Conditionalization is the special case of JC in which $P'(A) = 1$ (and $P'(-A) = 0$). So, for example, if Arabella changes her degree of belief in M to 0.7, the degrees of belief she assigns to W and U should be 0.24 and 0.06. An analogue of Bayes' theorem can be derived to calculate how degrees of belief should change by JC.

A further suggested constraint on rational degrees of belief is a principle, called 'Reflection', that concerns attitudes towards future beliefs (van Fraassen 1984):

Reflection: $P_t(Q|P_{t+x}(Q) = b) = b$

According to Reflection, on the condition that a person assigns a degree of belief at time $t + x$ to Q of b they ought to assign a degree of belief at time t to Q of b. The principle expresses the idea that one should consider her future degrees of belief as being formed rationally on the basis of accurate evidence. Of course, if someone believes that for some reason the beliefs that she will have at $t + x$ are not formed rationally or accurately then it would seem that rationality may require departures from Reflection. For example, if one knew today that tomorrow one would be a subject in an hypnosis experiment and caused to believe that the earth is flat, that would provide no reason to believe today that the earth is flat.

David Lewis (1986) proposed another constraint on rational belief that connects beliefs about objective chances with degrees of belief.

(PP) $P_t(Q|ch_t(Q) = x \& E) = x$,

where $ch_t(Q)$ is the chance or objective probability at time t of Q. Objective probabilities are objective features of reality independent of our beliefs. There is controversy concerning how to construe objective probabilities. Among the proposals are that they are irreducible, that they are hypothetical frequencies (van Fraassen 1980), that they are actual frequencies, and that they are determined by the best fitting theory of the world (Lewis 1994) (see PROBABILITY, INTERPRETATIONS OF). In any case, PP says that the degree of belief one has at t in Q given the condition that the chance of Q at t is x and other admissible information E is itself x. To a first approximation E is admissible with respect to Q if E provides no information about how chance events at or after t will turn out. We apply PP when we assign a degree of belief of 0.5 to the event of the coin landing heads when flipped, given that we believe that the coin is fair. In situations where one does not know the objective chance of an event e

but assigns degrees of belief to exclusive and exhaustive hypothesis concerning that chance, PP can be used to provide the conditional degrees of belief of e given the various hypotheses. In the example of Bayes' theorem described above, the degrees of belief $P(e|D)$ and $P(e|-D)$ may derive from applications of PP. By linking objective chances and degrees of belief, PP grounds a Bayesian epistemology of objective chances. Exactly why PP should determine degrees of belief in chance events has not received much discussion.

There are Dutch book arguments for conditionalization, JC, and Reflection. The Dutch book argument for JC establishes that if a person places a value on conditional gambles (a conditional gamble is one that is in effect only if a condition is satisfied), and changes their degrees of belief in conformity with any rule other than JC, they will be susceptible to a Dutch book by a bookie who knows their rule.

The Bayesian principles of rationality concerning belief are part of a more general account of rationality connecting belief, preference and decisions called 'Bayesian decision theory'. In Bayesian decision theory decisions are seen as analogous to gambles in which the consequences of a decision depend on possible states of nature. The degree to which a decision-maker values a consequence c is its 'utility' $u(c)$. If we assume that a person has sufficiently many degrees of belief then utilities can be measured in terms of choices among gambles. If someone prefers c_1 to anything else and prefers anything else to c_n and is indifferent between a gamble in which they obtain c_1 with probability p, and c_n with probability $1 - p$ (according to their degrees of belief) then $u(c) = p$. The key principle of Bayesian decision theory is that one selects a decision from among the possible alternatives that maximizes expected utility. The expected utility of a decision is given by:

$$u(d) = \Sigma P(h_i) \times u(c_i).$$

The set $\{h_i\}$ is an exclusive and exhaustive set of states of nature, the $P(h_i)$ are the decision-maker's degrees of belief, and the $u(c_i)$ are the utilities the decision-maker assigns to the consequence c_i of their doing d when h_i obtains (see DECISION AND GAME THEORY).

The view that rationality requires that beliefs cohere, that they change by conditionalization, and that decisions obey the maximum expected utility rule form the core of 'Bayesian epistemology' (Reflection and PP are attractive additions but have not received as much discussion). Bayesian epistemology does not provide traditional analyses of knowledge or justification but it does describe ideals of synchronic and diachronic rationality. Some advocates think of it as

supplanting, and others as supplementing traditional epistemology.

One issue that arises within Bayesian epistemology involves the relationship between degrees of belief and other epistemological concepts. An issue that has received much discussion is acceptance. Epistemologists mean a number of different things by 'acceptance' although there seems to be agreement that someone who accepts a proposition is making a commitment to defend its reasonableness. Acceptance is usually thought of as rationally requiring closure under logical consequence and conjunction. If one accepts $h_1, \ldots, h_n$ then one rationally should accept every consequence of their conjunction. One proposal for connecting subjective probability and acceptance is rule R: one should accept h if $P(h) > r$ (where r is a threshold value close to 1). But this suggestion immediately leads to 'the lottery paradox'. Suppose that $r = 0.99$ and that a fair lottery has 1,000 tickets. The acceptance rule implies that one should accept each statement $-hk_i$ that says that ticket k_i will not win (since $P(-hk_i) = 0.999$). But one knows that one of the tickets will win, so one ends up accepting a contradictory statements. Various responses to the paradox have been proposed (see PARADOXES, EPISTEMIC §1).

3 Bayesian epistemology and scientific method

Support for the Bayesian approach to epistemology comes from the fact that various features of scientific method follow from Bayesian principles (Rosenkrantz 1977; Earman 1992) (see CONFIRMATION THEORY; INDUCTIVE INFERENCE; SCIENTIFIC METHOD). For example, a natural measure of the extent to which evidence e confirms hypothesis H is $P(H|e) - P(H)$. It is easy to see from Bayes' theorem that the greater the ratio $P(e|H)/P(e|-H)$ the more e confirms H. The conditional probabilities $P(e|H)$ and $P(e|-H)$ often measure how well the two hypotheses explain e. So Bayes' theorem endorses the principle that evidence confirms a hypothesis to the extent that the hypothesis outperforms its competitors in explaining the evidence. A related consequence of Bayes' theorem is that the greater the difference between $P(e|H)$ and $P(e|-H)$ the more the result of the test confirms one or the other hypothesis. In other words, the more severe the test the more the confirmation.

The Bayesian approach also rationally motivates experimentation. The uncertainty relative to an inquirer of a set of hypotheses $\{h_k\}$ is measured by the entropy of the probability distribution over the h_k; entropy $\{h_k\} = \Sigma P(h_k) \log P(h_k)$. Entropy is greatest when all the h_k are assigned equal probability and least when one of the hypotheses is assigned a probability of 1 and the rest 0. An inquirer would like to reduce the entropy of their probability distribution since that brings them closer to certainty. It is a consequence of the probability calculus that any experiment E that has an outcome e such that $P(e|h_i) \neq P(e|h_k)$ for $i \neq k$ has a positive expected value of reducing entropy. If E has outcomes which differentiate among the h_k and if outcomes of repetitions of E are independent given the h_k then it follows that the inquirer can expect that as they continue to experiment, the entropy will continue to decrease to its minimum; that is that they will eventually assign a probability of 1 to one of the hypotheses. Further, if the probabilities $P(e|h_k)$ reflect the actual frequencies that would be obtained on independent repetitions of E then it can be shown that they can expect to assign a probability of 1 to the true hypotheses.

While most epistemologists accept true belief as the goal of rational inquiry, this claim has recently been criticized as mistaken or unjustified (Stich 1992). An interesting by-product of the Bayesian theory of experimentation can also be used to provide a justification of the instrumental value of acquiring true belief (Loewer 1995).

4   Criticisms of Bayesian epistemology

There is little doubt that aspects of scientific method can be illuminated by the Bayesian framework. But it is much less clear either that Bayesian epistemology provides satisfactory answers to traditional epistemological questions or that the Bayesian account of rationality is cogent. The claim that the Bayesian account of rationality is correct has been challenged by attacking the arguments that rationality requires coherence and conditionalization and by attacking the relevance of the Bayesian account of rationality.

The Dutch book argument has been criticized by arguing that mere susceptibility to Dutch books does not make one irrational. A person who thinks that their beliefs are not coherent can refuse to buy or sell gambles and thus avoid Dutch books. The Dutch book argument for conditionalization is even less persuasive. The argument establishes only that someone who conforms to a rule for changing beliefs must conform to conditionalization to avoid Dutch books. But it is not clear that rationality requires that belief-change conforms to a rule. In fact, it seems that at least on some occasions we change our beliefs without conforming to any rule and that it is rational to do so. For example, when one learns of a new theory to which one had not previously assigned a degree of belief, it may be appropriate to reassess certain other degrees of belief. But it is hard to see how there could

be a plausible rule in this situation specifying how one should change those degrees of belief.

The most disturbing objection is that the Bayesian ideal is epistemically irrelevant to us because people have, at best, few exact degrees of belief. Further, it is practically impossible to make sure that one's degrees of belief are coherent or that they change by conditionalization. Bayesian epistemologists have attempted to deal with the first problem by changing their account to represent beliefs by sets of probability distributions. Coherence can be identified with a set of coherent degrees of belief. Whatever the plausibility of this suggestion for representing beliefs it makes the second problem even worse. This problem is that it will generally be impossible to determine whether an assignment of degrees to a collection of sentences is coherent. In fact there is no computationally effective method for achieving coherence in general since coherence requires assigning logically equivalent sentences the same degree, and never assigning a higher degree to A than to B if A logically implies B. There is no computationally effective method for determining in general whether or not A logically implies B.

The Bayesian response to these objections is to grant that, even if coherence and conditionalization are standards we cannot generally meet, they are ideals we should strive to approximate.

Whether or not conformity to Bayesian principles provides an epistemically valuable ideal, Bayesian epistemology is certainly incomplete as an account of rational belief. Specifically, there are at least three places at which it requires supplementation.

(1) If $P(A) = 0$, then $P(B|A)$ is undefined, so conditionalization on propositions with probability 0 is undefined. But it seems plausible that sometimes a rational person may change their degree of belief in a proposition from 0 to 1 (or an intermediate value). There are some suggestions in the literature for how to extend conditionalization to this case.

(2) There is no constraint on the conditions under which propositions can initiate conditionalization or Jeffrey conditionalization. For example, someone's beliefs can conform to Bayesianism even though they change their probabilities on the basis of unreliable hunches. Rationality apparently requires restrictions on the changes that can initiate changes. Empiricism suggests that the inputs should be restricted to reliable observations. However, it seems dogmatic to restrict all changes to those initiated by observations. Sometimes reflection on a problem or thinking up a new hypotheses initiates changes in degrees of belief in ways that are considered rational. Bayesians have yet to produce a compelling account of rationally legitimate belief-changes.

(3) Coherence does not preclude assigning a high degree of belief to the claim that the earth is flat or taking the observation of green emeralds observed before time t as evidence for all emeralds being 'grue' (that is, green if observed before t and blue otherwise). This has been called 'the problem of the priors' since subjective Bayesian puts no constraints on the prior probabilities $P(h_i)$ that enter as inputs into Bayes' theorem. Some Bayesians point to certain 'convergence theorems' to mitigate this problem (Savage 1954). According to one convergence theorem, even if experimenters begin with different probabilities concerning hypotheses $h_1, \ldots, h_n$ as long as these are nonzero and they agree on the likelihoods $P(e_k|h_i)$ of the outcomes e_k then, under very general conditions, repeated experimentation and conditionalization will result in the convergence of their degrees of belief concerning the h_i. However, this result is cold comfort since even approximate agreement may require an unrealistically large amount of experimentation. Also, there is nothing in subjective Bayesianism that requires agreement on the likelihoods on which the convergence results depend.

Some Bayesians have suggested principles or considerations that constrain rational probability distributions. One way of doing this invokes 'principles of indifference'. The simplest indifference principle says that if one has no definite knowledge concerning a set of exclusive hypotheses, one ought to assign them equal probabilities. For example, if one had no knowledge concerning whether a ball to be drawn from an urn was red, R, or not red, $-R$, then one ought to assign the two hypotheses a probability of 0.5. The trouble with this proposal is that the principle of indifference is very sensitive to exactly how the hypotheses are described. If the problem were described in terms of the hypotheses R, G (the ball is green), and B (the ball is blue) then the principle of indifference entails probabilities of a third for each hypothesis. More sophisticated indifference principles have been proposed (Jaynes 1968) that give unambiguous probability assignments in certain situations. But the situations in which these principles apply are highly idealized and, in any case, it is not at all clear why the probabilities they assign are more rational than alternatives.

Another approach to constraining rational probability distributions appeals to logical probability. The idea is that considerations of logic determine conditional probabilities $P(R|Q)$; the degree to which Q probabilifies R. This proposal has been developed for simple formal languages. Carnap (1950) introduced a number of such measures (see CARNAP, R. §5). For example, if a first-order language contains monadic predicates F and G and names $a, b, c, \ldots$ then one measure assigns equal probability to each 'state description' $Fa \& Ga \& Fb \& Gb \& \ldots$. One problem with this suggestion is that it precludes learning from experience since propositions concerning different individuals are probabilistically independent. A different suggestion assigns equal probability to each 'structure description' and then divides the probabilities equally among the state descriptions that satisfy the structure descriptions. The trouble with this idea is that it precludes assigning probabilities greater than 0 to generalizations. This can also be remedied (Hintikka 1966). However, no one has proposed a characterization of logical probability that is both applicable to ordinary beliefs and rationally compelling.

Another proposal for constraining rational probability distributions has received some discussion. It is that rational distributions are determined by consensus relative to a group (Lehrer and Wagner 1981). The idea is that a rational probability distribution relative to a group of 'experts' can be extracted by taking a weighted average – the weights representing group members' assessments of one another's reliabilities – of the degrees of belief of members of the group. This proposal has some awkward consequences. Specifically, all the members of the group can agree that two events are probabilistically independent, and yet the consensus distribution makes them dependent (Laddaga and Loewer 1985). The proposal is also too relativistic to represent rational priors. The problem of the priors is as unsolved today as it was when Bayes first proved his theorem.

See also: LEARNING; COMMON-SENSE REASONING, THEORIES OF

References and further reading

* Carnap, R. (1950) *Logical Foundations of Probability*, Chicago, IL: University of Chicago Press. (Classic presentation of the logical concept of probability.)
* Earman, J. (1992) *Bayes or Bust*, Cambridge, MA: MIT Press. (Excellent presentation of Bayesian inference in science.)
* Finetti, B. de (1972) *Probability, Induction, and Statistics*, New York: Wiley. (Classic presentation of the subjectivist concept of probability.)
* Fraassen, B. van (1980) *The Scientific Image*, Oxford: Oxford University Press. (Important work in the philosophy of science that argues for the view that scientists never have good reasons to believe claims about unobservables.)
* —— (1984) 'Belief and the Will', *Journal of Philosophy*

81 (5): 235–58. (Formulates and discusses the 'reflection principle' discussed in §2 above.)

* Hintikka, J. (1966) 'A Two Dimensional Continuum of Inductive Methods', in J. Hintikka and P. Suppes (eds) *Aspects of Inductive Logic*, Amsterdam: North Holland. (Extends the logical concept of probability to first order languages.)

* Jaynes, E.T. (1968) 'Prior Probabilities' I.E.E.E. *Transactions on Systems Science and Cybernetics* SSC-4: 227–44. (Sophisticated development of the principle of indifference for assigning prior probabilities.)

* Jeffrey, R. (1983) *The Logic of Decision*, New York: McGraw-Hill. (Excellent introduction to Bayesian Decision theory.)

* Kahneman, D., Slovic, P. and Tversky, A. (eds) (1982) *Judgement under Uncertainty: Heuristics and Biases*, Cambridge: Cambridge University Press. (Collection of articles concerning the psychology of probabilistic inference and decision reasoning.)

Kaplan, M. (1996) *Decision Theory as Philosophy*, New York: Cambridge University Press. (Discusses the role of acceptance in Bayesian epistemology.)

* Laddaga, R. and Loewer, B. (1985) 'Destroying the Consensus', *Synthèse* 62: 79–95. (Criticizes Lehrer's proposal for forming consensus degrees of belief.)

* Lehrer, K. and Wagner, C. (1981) *Rational Consensus in Science and Society*, Dordrecht: Reidel. (Develops an account of consensus degrees of belief.)

* Levi, I. (1980) *The Enterprise of Knowledge*, Cambridge, MA: MIT Press. (Develops a quasi-Bayesian account of inference and decision. Includes the idea of representing belief as sets of probability distributions.)

* Lewis, D. (1980) 'A Subjectivist's Guide to Objective Chance', in *Collected Papers*, New York: Oxford University Press, vol. 2, 1986. (Very significant article discussing the connection between subjective degrees of belief and objective probability.)

* —— (1994) 'Humean Supervenience Debugged', *Mind* 103: 473–90. (Follow up to Lewis' 1980 article.)

* Loewer, B. (1995) 'The Value of Truth', in E. Villanueva (ed.) *Rationality and Truth*, Atascadero, CA: Ridgeview Publishing Co. (Provides a Bayesian justification for the value of true belief.)

* Ramsey, F.P. (1931) 'Truth and Probability', in *Foundations of Mathematics and Other Essays*, London: Routledge & Kegan Paul. (Classic early presentation of subjective probability and utility.)

* Rosenkrantz, R. (1977) *Inference, Method, and Decision*, Boston, MA: Reidel. (The best overall introduction to Bayesian philosophy of science and approaches to statistics.)

* Savage, L.J. (1954) *Foundations of Statistics*, New York: Wiley. (Classic development of Bayesian foundations of statistics and decision theory.)

* Stich, S. (1992) *Fragmentation of Reason*, Cambridge, MA: MIT Press. (Poses formidable objections to epistemology and includes a criticism of the claim that truth is valuable.)

BARRY LOEWER

PROBLEM OF EVIL *see* EVIL, PROBLEM OF

PROCESS PHILOSOPHY

In the broad sense, the term 'process philosophy' refers to all worldviews holding that process or becoming is more fundamental than unchanging being. For example, an anthology titled Philosophers of Process *(1965) includes selections from Samuel Alexander, Henri Bergson, John Dewey, William James, Lloyd Morgan, Charles Peirce and Alfred North Whitehead, with an introduction by Charles Hartshorne. Some lists include Hegel and Heraclitus. The term has widely come to refer in particular, however, to the movement inaugurated by Whitehead and extended by Hartshorne. Here, process philosophy is treated in this narrower sense.*

Philosophy's central task, process philosophers hold, is to develop a metaphysical cosmology that is self-consistent and adequate to all experienced facts. To be adequate, it cannot be based solely on the natural sciences, but must give equal weight to aesthetic, ethical and religious intuitions. Philosophy's chief importance, in fact, derives from its integration of science and religion into a rational scheme of thought. This integration is impossible, however, unless exaggerations on both sides are overcome. On the side of science, the main exaggerations involve 'scientific materialism' and the 'sensationalist' doctrine of perception. On the side of religion, the chief exaggeration has been the idea of divine omnipotence. Process philosophy replaces these ideas with a 'panexperientialist' ontology, a doctrine of perception in which nonsensory 'prehension' is fundamental, and a doctrine of divine power as persuasive rather than coercive.

1 **Philosophy's central task**
2 **Two kinds of process**
3 **The mind–body problem**
4 **Perception and prehension**
5 **Reconciling science and religion**
6 **Developments in the movement**

1 Philosophy's central task

Process philosophy is based on the conviction that the central task of philosophy is to construct a cosmology in which all intuitions well-grounded in human experience can be reconciled. Whereas cosmologies were traditionally based on religious, ethical and aesthetic as well as scientific experiences, cosmology in the modern period has increasingly been based on science alone. Process philosophers find this modern cosmology, which can be called 'scientific materialism', inadequate to those human intuitions that are usually called aesthetic, ethical and religious and, more generally, to those 'commonsense' beliefs that we cannot help presupposing in practice – such as the belief that our thoughts and actions are not wholly determined by antecedent causes. Such beliefs, rather than being explained away, should provide the final criterion for philosophical thought. In enunciating this criterion, Whitehead (1929) and Hartshorne (1970) are adopting the pragmatic maxim of PEIRCE and JAMES that, if an idea cannot be lived in practice, it should not be affirmed in theory. The worldview of scientific materialism is also held to be inadequate for science itself. Although this is most obvious in biology and psychology (see §3 below), it is true even for physics (Whitehead 1925).

Part and parcel of philosophy's task is its role as 'the critic of abstractions'. Because of the tendency for overstatement, the abstractions from the more specialized disciplines usually need to be reformulated before they can be integrated into a self-consistent cosmology (Whitehead 1925). Because the abstractions of the physical sciences have recently been dominant, the primary critical task now is 'to challenge the half-truths constituting the scientific first principles' (Whitehead [1929] 1978: 10). At the root of these half-truths is usually the 'fallacy of misplaced concreteness', in which an abstraction from something, useful for particular purposes, is identified with the concrete thing itself. This fallacy lies behind scientific materialism, according to which everything, including human experience, is to be explained in terms of the locomotion of bits of matter devoid of spontaneity, internal process and intrinsic value (Whitehead 1925). The suggested alternative is to reconceive the basic units of the world as processes (see WHITEHEAD, A.N.).

2 Two kinds of process

Although 'process philosophy' (which Whitehead himself did not use) probably became the label for the school of thought he founded primarily because of the title of his main work, *Process and Reality* (1929),

the term is apt: 'The reality is the process' and 'an actual entity is a process' (Whitehead [1925] 1967: 72; [1929] 1978: 41). Whereas all process philosophies in the broad sense could agree with these statements, it is the particular interpretation given to them that constitutes the distinctiveness of Whiteheadian process philosophy. Central to this distinctiveness is the twofold idea that the actual units comprising the universe are momentary 'occasions of experience' involving two kinds of process.

Partly through the influence of quantum physics, Whitehead conceived of the most fundamental units of the world, the most fully actual entities, not as enduring individuals but as momentary events. Enduring individuals, such as electrons, molecules, and minds, are 'temporally ordered societies' of these momentary events. The idea that actual entities are events with both spatial and temporal extensiveness is indicated by calling them 'actual occasions' (Whitehead [1929] 1978: 77). Their temporal extensiveness means that they cannot exist at an 'instant' (understood as a durationless slice of time). Rather, they constitute, as Bergson had suggested, a more or less brief duration (from perhaps less than a billionth of a second in subatomic events to perhaps a tenth of a second at the level of human experience).

This idea paves the way for recognizing two kinds of process: a process within an actual occasion, called 'concrescence' (because it involves moving from potentiality to concreteness), and a process between actual occasions, called 'transition'. These two kinds of process involve the two basic kinds of causation: 'efficient causation expresses the transition from actual entity to actual entity; and final causation expresses the internal process whereby the actual entity becomes itself'. Through this distinction Whitehead seeks to fulfil a central task of philosophy: 'to exhibit final and efficient causes in their proper relation to each other' ([1929] 1978: 150, 84) . This proper relation is that every actual occasion begins by receiving efficient causation from prior actual occasions, completes itself by exercising final causation, understood as self-determination, and then exercises efficient causation upon following occasions. The temporal process involves a perpetual oscillation between efficient and final causation.

The two previous paragraphs provide two aspects of Whitehead's alternative to materialism's way of overcoming dualism in favour of a cosmology with only one type of actual entity. According to Cartesian dualism, minds were temporal but not spatial, while material bodies were spatially extended but essentially nontemporal (being able to exist at an instant). Whitehead's idea that all actual entities are spatio-temporal events overcomes that dualism. His idea that these events involve both concrescence and transition overcomes the further dualism between actual entities that can exert only efficient causation and those that can exercise self-determination. The central feature of Cartesianism, however, was the dualism between actual entities with experience and those without. This dualism is overcome through the rejection of 'vacuous actualities', meaning things that are fully actual and yet void of experience. This rejection is expressed positively by considering all actual occasions to be 'occasions of experience' (Whitehead [1929] 1978: 29, 167, 189). This doctrine means, with regard to the internal process of concrescence, that 'process is the becoming of experience' (Whitehead [1929] 1978: 166). The meaning is not that all actual entities are conscious – most are not – but that they have some degree of feeling.

Although 'panpsychism' is the customary name for philosophies of this sort, 'panexperientialism' is better for this particular version, partly because the term 'psyche', besides suggesting experience too sophisticated to attribute to atoms or even cells, also suggests that the ultimate units endure through time, rather than being momentary experiences. Another essential feature of process philosophy's version is that the 'pan', meaning 'all', does not refer to literally all things but only to all genuine individuals (see PANPSYCHISM §1). This distinction is central to process philosophy's solution to the mind–body problem.

3 The mind–body problem

Panexperientialists, like materialists, consider insoluble the problem of dualistic interaction: How could mind and brain cells, understood as actualities of ontologically different types, interact? Materialism seeks to avoid this problem by thinking of the mind as somehow identical with the brain. However, besides still having the problem of how conscious experience could arise out of insentient neurons, materialism is also hard-pressed to explain the apparent unity and freedom of our experience. The move by eliminative materialists, denying that there is any experience, unity or freedom to explain, rejects in theory what is inevitably presupposed in practice. Whiteheadian process philosophy suggests, on the basis of its panexperientialism, a 'nondualistic interactionism' meant to avoid the problems of both dualism and materialism. With dualism, it distinguishes (numerically) between mind and brain. The distinct reality of the mind, as a temporally ordered society of very high-level occasions of experience, provides a locus for the unity of our experience and its power to exercise self-determination. But by rejecting dualism's

assumption that the mind is ontologically different from the brain cells, panexperientialism removes the main obstacle to understanding how our experiences could interact with our brain cells. As Hartshorne puts it: 'cells can influence our human experiences because they have feelings that we can feel. To deal with the influences of human experiences upon cells, one turns this around. *We* have feelings that *cells* can feel' (1962: 229).

The freedom of bodily action has also been a problem for materialists, who may admit that they cannot help presupposing this freedom while claiming that the scientific worldview has no room for it. One of the assumptions behind this claim is that the behaviour of subatomic particles is fully specified by the laws of physics. A second is that all wholes, including human beings, are analogous to rocks and billiard balls, so that all vertical causation must run upward, from the most elementary parts to the whole. In process philosophy's panexperientialist ontology, by contrast, all actual entities are internally constituted by their relations to other occasions. This view allows for the emergence of higher-level actual occasions, so that spatiotemporal societies of actual entities can be of two basic types: besides aggregational societies, such as rocks, there is what Hartshorne (1972) calls the 'compound individual', in which a society with the requisite complexity gives rise to a 'dominant' member, which can then exercise downward causation on the rest of the society. This downward causation is possible, furthermore, because the 'laws' of nature are really its most widespread habits, and because atoms and subatomic particles are open to the particular influences of the environment in which they find themselves (Whitehead [1938] 1966: 154–5; [1933] 1967: 41).

4 Perception and prehension

Another distinctive feature of Whiteheadian process philosophy is its challenge to the 'sensationalist' theory of perception, according to which all knowledge of the world beyond the mind comes through sensory perception (see PERCEPTION, EPISTEMIC ISSUES IN). More fundamental than sensory perception, suggests Whitehead (1925), is a nonsensory mode of perception, called 'prehension', which may or may not be conscious. One example (which we call 'memory') occurs when an occasion of experience directly perceives occasions in its own past. Another instance is the mind's direct reception of influences from its brain (which sensory perception presupposes). This direct prehension of other actualities, through which we know of the existence of the 'external world', is also called 'perception in the mode of causal efficacy', because it provides the experiential basis, denied by Hume, for our idea of causation as real influence.

This idea of nonsensory prehension is central to process philosophy. It is implicit in the idea of panexperientialism: because sensory perception can be attributed only to organisms with sensory organs, the idea that all actual entities have experience presupposes a more primitive mode of perceptual experience that can be generalized to all individuals whatsoever. This idea is also presupposed in the acceptance of aesthetic, ethical and religious experiences as genuine apprehensions. It is crucial, thereby, to the task through which philosophy 'attains its chief importance,' that of fusing science and religion 'into one rational scheme of thought' (Whitehead [1929] 1978: 15).

5 Reconciling science and religion

One side of this task of reconciling science and religion involves what has been discussed above – the replacement of the materialistic worldview, with which science has recently been associated, with panexperientialism, which allows religious and moral experience as well as freedom to be taken seriously. The other side of the task involves overcoming exaggerations from the religious side that conflict with necessary assumptions of science. Here the main exaggeration involves the idea of divine power. Whitehead and Hartshorne do believe that a metaphysical description of reality points to the necessity of a supreme agent to which the name 'God' can meaningfully be applied. (Arguments for the existence of God are developed much more fully by Hartshorne (1941, 1962) than by Whitehead.) But they strongly reject the traditional doctrine of divine power, according to which God, having created the world *ex nihilo*, can interrupt its basic causal processes – a doctrine that, besides creating an insuperable problem of evil, also conflicts with the assumption of scientific naturalism that no such interruptions can occur. Their alternative proposal is that the power of God is persuasive, not coercive (Whitehead 1929, 1933; Hartshorne 1984).

6 Developments in the movement

Although Whitehead was one of the first philosophers to be included in 'The Library of Living Philosophers' (Schilpp 1941), his philosophy was largely ignored in the decades subsequent to its articulation in the 1920s and 1930s, partly because of the turn to anti-metaphysical forms of philosophy. Another factor was that, even within circles still interested in developing a naturalistic cosmology, Whitehead's panexperientialism and affirmation of God were felt to exceed the limits of a proper naturalism, which was largely equated with materialism (see MATERIALISM). The most prominent advocate of Whiteheadian process philosophy in the following decades, furthermore, was Hartshorne, whose focus on the idea of God, while creating interest in theological faculties, reinforced suspicions in philosophical circles. Around 1960, however, a spate of books on Whitehead's philosophy inaugurated a period of greater interest (Lawrence 1956; Leclerc 1958, 1961; Christian 1959; Lowe 1962; Sherburne 1961; Kline 1963). In 1971, a journal, *Process Studies*, was created for the purpose of furthering the study and development of process thinking. In 1991, a volume devoted to the philosophy of Hartshorne appeared in the 'Library of Living Philosophers' (Hahn 1991).

Whiteheadian process philosophy has exerted some influence in a number of branches of philosophy, such as the philosophies of science, education, and art. Its major influence thus far, however, has continued to be in the philosophy of religion (Cobb 1965, 1969; Frankenberry 1987; Griffin 1976, 1991; Ogden 1966), including discussions of the relation between science and religion in particular (Barbour 1966, 1990).

See also: PROCESS THEISM; PROCESSES

References and further reading

* Barbour, I. (1966) *Issues in Science and Religion*, Englewood Cliffs, NJ: Prentice Hall. (A widely used text written primarily from the perspective of process philosophy.)

* —— (1990) *Religion in an Age of Science*, San Francisco, CA: Harper & Row; London: SCM. (An updated replacement of the previous book, based on Gifford Lectures.)

* Browning, D. (1965) *Philosophers of Process*, New York: Random House. (Readable selection of writings of a number of 'process philosophers' in the broad sense.)

* Christian, W.A. (1959) *An Interpretation of Whitehead's Metaphysics*, New Haven, CT: Yale University Press. (Focusing on the idea of 'transcendence', this otherwise careful analysis is flawed by a misunderstanding of the 'perishing' of actual entities and thereby of the causal efficacy involved in 'transition'.)

* Cobb, J.B. (1965) *A Christian Natural Theology: Based on the Thought of Alfred North Whitehead*, Philadelphia, PA: Westminster. (This book, which has become a standard, provides one of the most

precise accounts of Whitehead's philosophy in the course of showing its relevance to religious issues.)

* —— (1969) *God and the World*, Philadelphia, PA: Westminster. (The first three chapters of this more popular presentation, based on a series of lectures, are especially recommended.)

* Frankenberry, N. (1987) *Religion and Radical Empiricism*, Albany, NY: State University of New York Press. (Places the relevance of Whitehead in the context of the radical empiricism of William James.)

* Griffin, D.R. (1976) *God, Power, and Evil: A Process Theodicy*, Philadelphia, PA: Westminster. (The first book-length treatment of theodicy from the perspective of Whiteheadian-Hartshornean philosophy.)

* —— (1991) *Evil Revisited: Responses and Reconsiderations*, Albany, NY: State University of New York Press. (Responses to critiques of previous book.)

—— (1997) *Unsnarling the World-Knot: Consciousness, Freedom, and the Mind-Body Problem*, Los Angeles, CA: University of California Press. (A lengthy treatment of the material in §3 above, developing the Whiteheadian position in relation to recent efforts by dualists and especially materialists.)

Griffin, D.R., Cobb, J.B., Ford, M.P., Gunter, P.A.Y. and Ochs, P. (1993) *Founders of Constructive Postmodern Philosophy: Peirce, James, Bergson, Whitehead, and Hartshorne*, Albany, NY: State University of New York Press. (Five original essays plus an introduction discussing the relevance of what these five philosophers have in common, such as panexperientialism, to current discussions.)

* Hahn, L.E. (ed.) (1991) *The Philosophy of Charles Hartshorne*, The Library of Living Philosophers vol. 20, La Salle, IL: Open Court. (Descriptive and critical essays about Hartshorne's philosophy with lengthy replies by Hartshorne plus an intellectual autobiography.)

Hartshorne, C. (1937) *Beyond Humanism: Essays in the New Philosophy of Nature*, Chicago, IL: Willet, Clark. (Collection of early essays arguing that nature is loveable in its parts and as a whole.)

* —— (1941) *Man's Vision of God and the Logic of Theism*, New York: Harper & Row. (Hartshorne's first attempt to apply the logic he had learned from C.I. Lewis and H.M. Sheffer to the philosophy of religion.)

* —— (1962) *The Logic of Perfection and Other Essays in Neoclassical Metaphysics*, La Salle, IL: Open Court. (The 'other essays' provide a very readable introduction to his philosophy of nature, freedom, and religion.)

* —— (1970) *Creative Synthesis and Philosophic Method*, La Salle, IL: Open Court. (The best survey of Hartshorne's philosophy.)

* —— (1972) *Whitehead's Philosophy: Selected Essays, 1935–1970*, Lincoln, NB: University of Nebraska Press. (Essays explaining the respects in which Hartshorne agrees and disagrees with Whitehead's version of process philosophy.)

* —— (1984) *Omnipotence and Other Theological Mistakes*, Albany, NY: State University of New York Press. (Dealing entirely with religious issues, this is the easiest of Hartshorne's books.)

* Kline, G.L. (ed.) (1963) *Alfred North Whitehead: Essays on His Philosophy*, Englewood Cliffs, NJ: Prentice Hall. (This still-helpful collection both reflected and helped spark the new interest in Whitehead's philosophy.)

* Lawrence, N. (1956) *Whitehead's Philosophical Development: A Critical History of the Background of Process and Reality*, Berkeley, CA: University of California Press. (A careful tracing of the development up to, but not including, Whitehead's *magnum opus*.)

* Leclerc, I. (1958) *Whitehead's Metaphysics: An Introductory Exposition*, New York: Macmillan. (Comparing the formative elements of Whitehead's system to Aristotle's four 'causes', this introduction is helpful except on efficient causation.)

* ——(ed.) (1961) *The Relevance of Whitehead: Philosophical Essays in Commemoration of the Centenary of the Birth of Alfred North Whitehead*, New York: Macmillan; London: Allen & Unwin. (A very good collection of essays by major commentators.)

* Lowe, V. (1962) *Understanding Whitehead*, Baltimore, MD: Johns Hopkins University Press. (In most respects still the best introduction.)

* Ogden, S.M. (1966) *The Reality of God and Other Essays*, New York: Harper & Row. (A philosophically rigorous but accessible explication and application of Hartshornean theism.)

* Schilpp, P.A. (1941) *The Philosophy of Alfred North Whitehead*, The Library of Living Philosophers vol. 3, New York: Tudor. (Descriptive and critical essays by many philosophers, including Lowe, Quine, R.W. Sellars, Hartshorne, Dewey and C.I. Lewis.)

* Sherburne, D.W. (1961) *A Whiteheadian Aesthetic: Some Implications of Whitehead's Metaphysical Speculation*, New Haven, CT: Yale University Press. (A vigorous and in some respects controversial account.)

* Whitehead, A.N. (1925) *Science and the Modern World*, New York: Free Press, 1967. (The first book of Whitehead's metaphysical period, it is essential

for understanding his alternative to scientific materialism.)

—— (1926) *Religion in the Making*, Cleveland, OH: World, 1960. (Whitehead's first application of his metaphysical vision to the philosophy of religion.)

* —— (1929) *Process and Reality: An Essay in Cosmology*, corrected edn, ed. D.R. Griffin and D.W. Sherburne, New York: Free Press, 1978. (His *magnum opus*, it contains both extremely illuminating and very difficult passages.)

* —— (1933) *Adventures of Ideas*, New York: Free Press, 1967. (Besides being one of Whitehead's most readable books, it provides the best insight into his overall position, including his philosophy of culture.)

* —— (1938) *Modes of Thought*, New York: Free Press, 1966. (His last and – along with *The Function of Reason* – his least technical book.)

DAVID RAY GRIFFIN

PROCESS THEISM

Process theism is a twentieth-century school of theological thought that offers a nonclassical understanding of the relationship between God and the world. Classical Christian theists maintain that God created the world out of nothing and that God not only can, but does, unilaterally intervene in earthly affairs. Process theists, in contrast, maintain that God and the basic material out of which the rest of reality is composed are coeternal. Moreover, process theists believe that all actual entities always possess some degree of self-determination. God, it is held, does present to every actual entity at every moment the best available course of action. And each entity does feel some compulsion to act in accordance with this divine lure. But process theists deny that God possesses the capacity to control unilaterally the activity of any entity. Thus, what occurs in relation to every aspect of reality involving a multiplicity of entities – for example, what happens in relation to every earthly state of affairs – is always a cooperative effort.

This understanding of the God–world relationship has significant theological implications. For instance, while classical Christians must attempt to explain why God does not unilaterally intervene more frequently to prevent horrific evils, process theists face no such challenge since the God of process thought cannot unilaterally control any earthly state of affairs. On the other hand, while most classical Christians maintain that God at times unilaterally intervenes in our world primarily because divine assistance has been requested,

process theists naturally deny that God can be petitioned efficaciously in this sense since they believe that God is already influencing all aspects of reality to the greatest possible extent. Moreover, while most Christian theists believe that God will at some point in time unilaterally bring our current form of existence to an end, process theists maintain that the same co-creative process now in place will continue indefinitely.

Not everyone finds the process characterization of the God–world relationship convincing or appealing. But few deny that process theism has become a significant force in modern American theology.

1   **Basic metaphysical tenets**
2–3 **Comparison with classical Christian theism**
4   **Critical discussion**

1 Basic metaphysical tenets

The basic metaphysical roots of process theism are found in the work of Alfred North WHITEHEAD (§4), with much of its explicit theological framework the result of the interpretation of Whitehead offered by Charles Hartshorne. While process theists differ among themselves on some issues, there is widespread agreement concerning the basic nature of reality.

Within the process metaphysic, the most fundamental constituents of reality are not 'things' or enduring substances. Rather, they are units of experience – usually called actual entities – that momentarily come into existence and then immediately perish. Each of these actual entities has a physical and mental component. As the entity comes into existence, the physical component takes account of (prehends) two things: its past – all that has gone before it; and God's initial aim – that which God sees as the best possibility open to it, given the concrete situation. The entity also automatically feels some impulse to act in accordance with God's initial aim. However, each actual entity has at least some power of self-determination, the function of its mental component. Thus, no actual entity is ever forced to do what God wants. It always has the power to choose its own subjective aim from among God's initial aim and all the real possibilities its past has made available. Once its decision is made, once the entity has unified the data from its perspective, it perishes as an experiencing subject and remains only as part of the past for all subsequent actual entities.

Some sets of actual entities, however, have a unity of their own. In these societies of entities, each entity still inherits its past from all other entities. But the inheritance from the past members of its own society is dominant. A subatomic particle such as an electron is a good example of a basic entity of this sort. There is no enduring substance that can be identified as an electron. But there are societies of 'electronic entities' in which each largely repeats the form of the previous entity in its society. In fact, the carry-over is so great that any given society of electrons appears to behave as if it were a single entity. Accordingly, basic societies or aggregates such as these are often called 'enduring individuals'.

Moreover, basic enduring individuals of a given type normally combine into more complex enduring individuals. Societies of subatomic particles form enduring atomic individuals, which themselves combine with other enduring atomic individuals to form enduring molecular individuals, which in turn combine with other molecular individuals. In the higher-order animal realm, for example, various societies of enduring cellular individuals combine to form enduring multicellular animal bodies with a central nervous system. In some of these enduring individuals, the enduring nervous system gives rise to what we label the enduring human mind or soul.

In short, in process thought the whole is truly greater than the sum of its parts. What we perceive phenomenally as enduring individuals – for example, humans, dogs, cats and trees – are not just bits of inanimate and animate matter in a certain configuration. Such enduring individuals are really 'societies of societies' of varying complexity – with some possessing a unity of experience (humans, dogs, cats) and others not (rocks, stars, books). Moreover, each society possessing a unity of experience retains to some extent its own autonomous power of self-determination even as it combines with other societies to create more complex societies (enduring individuals). The more complex an enduring individual of this type, the greater the influence of its mental pole, that is, the more actual options it has open to it and the more conscious it is of such options. This explains why humans behave in much more creative ways than dogs, which in turn behave in much more innovative ways than plants.

Within process thought, God is not an exception to this metaphysical order. But while there is disagreement over whether God is an enduring individual or an actual entity, God clearly occupies a unique position in the process system. Only God takes account of (prehends) all that happens in the world. God alone experiences all that every entity experiences. Thus, although each actual entity exists only momentarily, its past is not lost. All that has occurred exists everlastingly as a unified whole in God's consciousness. It is in this sense that the whole universe is included in, and penetrated by, God – that the world is God's body (see GOD, CONCEPTS OF §8).

God, however, also responds to what is experi-enced. God, in this capacity, is aware of all harmonized possibilities open to the world. It is on the basis of this knowledge that God continuously presents to every entity at every moment the optimum real possibilities open to it. Thus, while God is not an exception to the metaphysical rules which govern the process system, God is certainly the most significant individual within this system. God not only exerts more influence on the direction of the process than does any other enduring individual, God alone unifies this ontological process into a harmonized whole.

2 Comparison with classical Christian theism

Process theism is frequently compared to classical Christian theism by proponents and critics alike. Moreover, the two systems are in some ways similar. Proponents of both argue, in opposition to atheism or pure pantheism, for the existence of a God who is in some sense ontologically distinct from the rest of reality. Both believe that only a being who is morally perfect is worthy of worship. However, the differences between process theism and classical Christian theism are many and significant. The most crucial concerns God's power. Classical Christians have always held that God has the capacity to control everything (see OMNIPOTENCE §1). They differ significantly on the extent to which God actually exercises this power. In fact, some classical Christians believe God seldom chooses to intervene unilaterally. But even these theists – often called free-will theists – still uniformly agree that God *could* unilaterally control all aspects of reality. The fact that God often chooses not to do so is considered a self-imposed limitation.

However, within the process system the situation is quite different. Since all actual entities always possess some degree of self-determination, God could not unilaterally control any aspect of reality involving other entities, even if God so desired. In other words, within process thought, the fact that God never imposes the divine will on other entities is not a self-limitation. Rather, it is a metaphysical reality to which even God is subject. Persuasive power, as opposed to coercive power, is all that is available to God.

Another important difference surfaces in relation to the origin of our world. Classical Christian theists have normally held that the world is totally dependent on God in the sense that it was created *ex nihilo*. Although they differ considerably on the exact manner in which they believe this was accomplished, they maintain that there was once a time (logically speaking) when only God existed and that all else has been created, directly or indirectly, by divine decree (see CREATION AND CONSERVATION, RELIGIOUS DOC-TRINE OF).

Process theists, of course, do not agree. Since they believe that God cannot unilaterally control the activity of any other entity and that there has always existed a plurality of actual creative entities, they maintain that reality has always been the result of co-creative, interdependent activity. It is probably true, most process theists admit, that there was once a time when all actual entities other than God existed in a state of random, nonpurposeful activity. Moreover, the fact that we now have a vast array of highly complex, multistructured societies of actual entities is viewed as a tribute to the effectiveness of God's persuasive power. But God alone can guarantee nothing. God has always been dependent on the cooperation of all other self-determining entities to accomplish any creative goal.

Another fundamental classical Christian belief is that the world will reach a final and fixed state, a final *eschaton*. But process theists deny that there will ever be a time when the current process will stop. They deny, for example, that there can be a fixed state in which individuals experience eternal bliss or torment (see ESCHATOLOGY §1; FEMINIST THEOLOGY §2). The universe might at some point in time arrive at a state in which all actual entities are experiencing the maximum degree of harmonious, intense novelty, the highest good from the process perspective. But there could be no assurance that such a state would be long-lasting. A period of triviality or discord, the greatest evils, could quickly follow. What does in fact occur will always depend on the manner in which all other actual entities respond to God's influence.

Finally, many classical Christians have thought it important to maintain that God is omniscient in the sense that all that has occurred or will occur, including all that we will freely choose to do in the future, is open to the divine vision (see OMNISCIENCE). But process theists, not surprisingly, deny that God possesses such insight. God does know all that has occurred. However, since all reality is interdependent in the sense that what exists at every moment includes the self-determination of entities other than God, infallible knowledge of the future is impossible for any being, including God.

3 Comparison with classical Christian theism (cont.)

The significance of these doctrinal differences becomes most apparent when considered in relation to Christian practice.

Petitionary prayer. Both classical Christians and process theists acknowledge the importance and efficacy of prayer in which God is asked to respond to concerns. Those in both camps agree, for instance, that prayer of this type can affect the petitioner as well as any others who are aware of prayers being offered on their behalf. Some in both camps even believe that those who do not know that prayers are being offered for them may experience some direct effect (see PRAYER).

But for classical Christians the primary value of petitionary prayer lies in the fact that it sometimes initiates unilateral divine activity that would not occur if such activity were not freely requested. That is, such prayer is deemed important primarily because it is believed that certain states of affairs that God can and would like to bring about will occur only if divine assistance is sought. However, process theists naturally deny that petitionary prayer can ever be efficacious in this sense. Since process theists believe that all entities possess some power of self-determination, they naturally deny that a request for assistance can ever initiate *unilateral* intervention in earthly affairs. And since God is already doing all that is possible to persuade each entity at each moment to make the optimum choice, it can never be claimed that any activity on our part could induce God to become more involved than would otherwise have been the case.

Divine guidance. While it is important to note that both classical Christians and process theists share their thoughts and concerns with God in prayer, it is equally important to note that those in both camps also want God's perspective shared with them. That is, both classical Christians and process theists want to know God's will. Moreover, those in both camps believe that God not only can, but does, share the divine will with us (see PROVIDENCE).

However, classical Christians differ significantly from process theists on the question of how such knowledge is attained. While classical Christians believe that the divine perspective is something that God always desires to share with us, they hold that God at times does so only if such guidance is requested (only if it is consciously sought). On the other hand, process theists, as we have seen, believe that God always automatically presents to each of us at every moment the best available option. Furthermore, while most classical Christians believe that we can, at times, come to a fairly clear, *conscious* understanding of what God believes or how God would have us act if we are open to God and diligent in our search, process theists disagree. They believe that the manner in which the divine will is shared with all entities makes clear, conscious knowledge of that which God would have us do a very rare phenomenon.

Evil. All theists continue to face the following challenge: if God is omnipotent and perfectly good, why is there so much seemingly unnecessary pain and suffering in our world? Since classical Christians believe that God can unilaterally intervene in earthly affairs, they must maintain that God has decided to allow each instance of evil because such evil is either a necessary antecedent causal condition for the actualization of some creative goal (for example, God's desire that we learn patience) or an unavoidable by-product of some creative goal (for example, God's desire that we exercise freedom of choice). In short, classical Christians must maintain that God is powerful enough to rid the world of all evil, but possesses morally sufficient reasons for not doing so (see EVIL, PROBLEM OF).

Process theists, however, find this line of reasoning totally implausible. As they see it, a perfectly good being who could do more to rid the world of evil would surely do so. But the God of process theism, they are quick to point out, is not faced with this choice. God does deplore evil and is always attempting to persuade all other entities to help actualize the best possible states of affairs. For instance, God was horrified by the Holocaust and tried in every way possible to influence those responsible not to commit such atrocities. But since God cannot unilaterally control the self-determining activity of any other entity, God is never in a position to prevent any instance of evil such activity might produce. And therefore the fact that evil states of affairs arise (and sometimes even proliferate) does not count against God's goodness.

4 Critical discussion

Critics of process thought fall into three major categories. Some reject it because they believe its theological system to be incompatible with classical Christian doctrine. Pinnock (1987) has argued, for instance, that process theism must be rejected because process theists do not acknowledge the total transcendence of God, the full divinity of Jesus or the supernatural origin of Scripture. However, while this type of criticism may serve a useful function within the classical Christian system itself – namely, to dissuade those who may initially find the process system appealing – its value in the general debate over the adequacy of process thought is questionable. Critical contentions of this sort do make it clear that classical Christians differ from process theists on important points; but the reality of such differences is something process theists readily acknowledge.

Other critics argue that process theism must be rejected because some of its basic contentions are false or implausible. For example, Gruenler (1983) argues that the basic process metaphysic is incompatible with modern relativity theory. Others find the process explication of how the world as we know it came to be quite implausible. An even more common criticism of this type, though, is the contention by classical Christian theists that a being with the acknowledged limitations in power of the God of process theism is too weak to be considered worthy of worship.

In response to this latter claim, process theists maintain (as noted before) that a God who is worthy of worship must be perfectly good, but argue that only the God of process theism meets this requirement. The powerful, independent God of classical Christian theism, they grant, might be viewed as a convenient wish-fulfiller. But such a being cannot justifiably be viewed as a caring friend worthy of our loving respect. Moreover, they continue, given the amount of unnecessary evil in our world, only a God who could not do more to remove it can be considered morally praiseworthy (see GOODNESS, PERFECT).

Finally, some critics challenge the internal consistency of the process system. One of the most significant of these challenges centres around the question of whether the God of process theism would coerce (unilaterally control) other entities if this were possible (Basinger 1988). If process theists decide that God would do so, it then becomes difficult to see how they can justifiably maintain (as many do) that coercion is morally incompatible with divine perfection (as Ford 1978 says), or that persuasion is the greatest of all powers, the only power capable of worthwhile results (as Cobb 1976 says). On the other hand, if process theists maintain that God would not coerce even if possible, it then becomes difficult to understand how process theists can justifiably criticize the God of classical free-will theism for not coercing more often. Process theists, the critics in question allege, cannot have it both ways. In response, some process theists (for example, Griffin 1991) acknowledge that the God of process theism would coerce if possible, but deny that this is inconsistent with continuing to maintain that persuasive power, if properly understood, is morally superior to coercive power.

It is, of course, too early to assess the lasting impact of process thought. But this unique metaphysical system is clearly a significant force in American theology, and there is little reason to believe that it will not continue to offer an important alternative to classical Christian theism for some time to come.

See also: NATURAL THEOLOGY; POSTMODERN THEOLOGY; PROCESS PHILOSOPHY

References and further reading

* Basinger, D. (1988) *Divine Power in Process Theism: A Philosophical Critique*, Albany, NY: State University of New York Press. (An accessible challenge to the self-consistency of process thought.)
* Cobb, J.B., Jr (1969) *God and the World*, Philadelphia, PA: Westminster Press. (An introduction to process thought.)
  Cobb, J.B., Jr and Griffin, D.R. (1976) *Process Theology: An Introductory Exposition*, Philadelphia, PA: Westminster Press. (A very accessible introduction to process thought.)
* Ford, L. (1978) *The Lure of God*, Philadelphia, PA: Fortress Press. (An accessible, sympathetic explication of process thought.)
* Griffin, D.R. (1991) *Evil Revisited: Responses and Reconsiderations*, Albany, NY: State University of New York Press. (A rigorous philosophical defence of process thought.)
* Gruenler, R. (1983) *The Inexhaustible God*, Grand Rapids, MI: Baker Book House. (An accessible evangelical critique of process thought.)
  Hartshorne, C. (1948) *The Divine Relativity: A Social Conception of God*, New Haven, CT: Yale University Press. (A good introduction to Hartshorne's understanding of the interdependent relationship between God and the world.)
  Neville, R. (1980) *Creativity and God*, New York: Seabury Press. (A rigorous metaphysical critique of process thought.)
  Palin, D.A. (1994) *Probing the Foundations: A Study in Theistic Reconstruction*, Kampen: Kok Pharos. (An accessible introduction to, and defence of, process thought.)
* Pinnock, C. (1987) 'Between Classical and Process Theism', in R. Nash (ed.) *Process Theology*, Grand Rapids, MI: Baker Book House. (An accessible critique of process theism.)
  Whitehead, A.N. (1929) *Process and Reality*, New York: Macmillan. (Whitehead's most important work. Very difficult.)

DAVID BASINGER

PROCESSES

A process is a course of change with a direction and internal order, where one stage leads on to the next. Processes can be physical (such as atomic decay), biological (such as the growth of living things), artificial (such as building a house) and social (such as carrying out a criminal investigation). Much of what is said about processes can be said about sequences of events. The concept of event, however, suggests a separate occurrence, whereas that of a process suggests something which is ongoing. There are matters, such as development in organisms, where to see what is happening as part of a process has an advantage over thinking of it as an event. Causes are generally spoken of as events, but the more dynamic concept of causal processes may get nearer to expressing the transition between cause and effect. Moreover, to explain something as a stage in a process can take account not only of what has happened in the past, but of what might happen in the future. This may (but need not) involve purpose; with organisms it involves development through functionally interrelated activities. In some social processes there can be a practical, moral significance in seeing a situation as a stage in a process, since this can encourage us to look to a further stage where something constructive might be brought out of what could otherwise be seen as simply an untoward event or an unhappy situation.

1 General nature and types of processes
2 Causation in processes
3 Processes and events
4 Some metaphysical views

1 General nature and types of processes

Processes are systematic courses of change with an internal order and temporal direction. Their temporal direction consists in there being an absolute order in the stages by which they proceed. This need not imply that there is an absolute time apart from processes or events, and these might appear in a different order to observers in different frames of reference. But the order in which the stages of a process occur is irreversible. Most processes go towards completion at an end point, but this need not be so in all cases. There are also steady-state processes, periodic processes and staccato processes where the ongoing feature is one of sustaining a pattern.

A process has temporal parts. This is sometimes expressed by saying it 'perdures' – that is, it is not wholly present at any time. Substances which are wholly present at every time of their existence are said to 'endure'. Processes mostly involve physical movement. Some, however, have an internal order not reducible to the direction of any movements that may accompany them. For instance, an intellectual process of argument proceeds through the participants seeing that one statement follows from another, or that it should be abandoned because of critical considerations raised in the course of the argument. An argument need not reach a conclusion – it can be broken off and resumed.

While all processes have an internal order and a direction, there are different kinds which, besides intellectual processes, include natural, artificial and social ones. Natural processes follow laws, as with the chemical reactions which are involved in the metabolism of food. Biological natural processes are clearly irreversible – digested food cannot be turned back into parts of plants and animals. However, some physical processes are said to be reversible, as when a rotating wheel is 'put into reverse'. But here another process is set going whose stages run in the opposite direction, towards a state which is not identical to the originator of the process but is another of the same type.

Artificial processes are carried out teleologically by agents acting in natural conditions set by the available materials and the environment. Within these limits, the agents can sometimes vary the order in which what they do becomes a stage in a process. For instance, in constructing a house the foundations must be laid first and normally the walls built before the roof is put on. But the roof can be put on before the walls are built provided that there is a sufficient structure to support it. Natural processes can be interfered with through artificial processes, as in conducting experiments. The constituents of social processes are persons acting according to rules and conventions in environments set by natural and artificial processes. The upholding and administration of the Law is a collection of social processes with rules and conventions prescribing proper procedures (note that 'process' and 'procedure' have the same root). A legal trial is a social process – indeed 'process' is a technical term for legal proceedings.

Rules prescribe how certain social processes ought to be carried out. Customs and conventions show how a number of social processes are motivated by expectations as to how people are likely to behave according to the ways in which they have been socialized. The formal processes of law and government operate in a social environment sustained by these informal processes. Generalizations about social processes (and also some natural ones) are often statistical (see SOCIAL LAWS).

2 Causation in processes

Artificial and social processes involve teleological causation where agents act purposively, but depend on efficient causation for the results of their actions (see TELEOLOGY). Natural processes in accordance with laws are not thought to involve teleology, though this is controversial in the case of some biological processes. In considering these, there is a distinction between causation which is internal to the process and that which consists of action on it from outside. W.E. Johnson (1934) used the term 'immanent causation' for the systematic changes due to co-variable and coordinated functioning in the process taken as a whole, and 'transeunt causation' for the action of separate elements on one another. Science aims to discover efficient causation between the elements of a system (for instance, the chemical actions in the process of metabolism). But the concept of immanent causation may still be needed for describing its functioning as a whole. The nourishing of the body is carried out through a great number of mutually supporting processes – the beating of the heart circulates the blood, and the heart will fail to beat unless the blood supply reaches it. There are also feed-back processes which come into effect to restore imbalances (for instance in keeping the body temperature within limits). These have been given the name 'homeostasis'. They may not be teleological in the purposive sense, but are instances of immanent causation. Coordinated functioning in a changing system is the general character of what are called 'organic processes', as shown in the self-maintenance and development of living things.

3 Processes and events

Much of what is said philosophically about processes can also be said about events – for example, they have an internal order or direction, and an absolute order of before or after in their parts. What is pertinent here is how processes differ, if they do, from sequences of events. An event is an occurrence taken as a unit. It can be divided into temporal parts, each of which can then be taken as a shorter event. So the great storm in Britain in October 1989 can be taken as an event. It can be said that it was more severe at some times than at others, distinguishing its temporal parts as sub-events, such as the blowing of the gale from 1 a.m. to 1.15 a.m. It can then be said that the blowing of the gale at 1.10 a.m. caused the collapse of Mr Jones' chimney (another event). Causation is often said to be a relation between events. It can also be spoken of in terms of processes: as the gale went on blowing even more fiercely, it caused the waves to go on rising higher and to flood the sea front. The event-form gives a sequence of occurrences; the process-form suggests something was going on. In this respect, to speak in terms of causal processes may come nearer to a dynamic description of what was happening.

Events are often expressed by participles forming gerunds (sometimes called verb nominalizations), which are parts of verbs construed as nouns and prefaced by 'the' or 'a'. In the case of processes, the participle keeps its full verbal voice, perhaps in a continuous present. So in the phrase 'the striking of the clock woke me up', 'the striking of the clock' refers to an event, whereas in the phrase 'I woke up while the clock was striking', 'while the clock was striking' refers to a process.

4 Some metaphysical views

Some metaphysical views see reality as essentially in process – becoming, changing, passing away – or even claim that processes are all that exists. In that case there might be a philosophical description of the world expressed through verbs and adverbs. There would then be no things or persons, and this may raise a problem concerning agency. The subject of a proposition could be a dummy 'it'; 'Socrates is wise' would become 'It Socratizes wisely' or 'Socratizing wisely is going on'. Among the metaphysical religions, Buddhism has come nearest to such a view: in Buddhism there are no agents or substances, and the self is a stream of passing states. These are linked, however, in a causal process, or Karma (see BUDDHIST PHILOSOPHY IN INDIA §1; CAUSATION, INDIAN THEORIES OF).

A world of pure processes seems to need some structuring principle. The father of Western philosophies of process was HERACLITUS. His philosophy has come to us in cryptic sayings, notably that 'all things flow' (*panta rei*). Yet this flux contains a principle, the Logos, which structures the flux by tensions of opposing forces, never coming to rest in a stable equilibrium. The contrasting position was taken by PARMENIDES, who so pressed the assertions that what is, is, and what is not, is not, as to deny the reality of change. This aroused serious discussion through the arguments produced by ZENO OF ELEA. If everything not only is what it is, but is where it is, how does a moving body such as an arrow get from one position to another?

The problem of whether motion is a process of transition and not only occupancy of a succession of positions appears in a modern form in the so-called 'at–at' view given by Bertrand Russell. Motion is defined as *merely* (his italics) 'the occupation of different places at different times, subject to continuity' (1903: 473). Continuity here is density, and if space and time are dense continua this means that between any two positions or instants there will always be another. The 'at–at' view of motion states that a moving body will always be at the position appropriate to each instant. This, however, may not adequately meet Zeno's problem, which concerns motion as transition from one position to another. There is an analogous problem with the concept of change, defined as something having different proper-

ties at different times. This is perfectly true, but it loses the connotation of *changing* as being undergone by a subject.

The metaphysics of Aristotle contains a view of processes of becoming put in terms of the distinction between potentiality and actuality: things develop their potentiality towards full realization of their natures. This view of things as processes of becoming is circumscribed by his conception of a teleological development towards fixed essential natures. In spite of this limitation, Aristotle produced a subtle analytic treatment of the idea of a process of change. The word for this was *kinēsis*, as distinct from *metabolé* which was his general word for change. Our word 'kinetic' suggests movement, and *kinēsis* is best translated as 'process of change'. *Kinēsis* always contains a direction, a 'whence-whither' (*pothen poi*), but this need not be the direction of a movement in space; it can be the transition from one stage to another of a process of development. As a process of change *kinēsis* is continuous, though it may be broken off or interrupted.

Among other great philosophers, Hegel had a metaphysical system in which process played a central part (see HEGEL, G.W.F. §4). Notably, world history was said to develop in a dialectical pattern analogous to a process of thought, where each stage expressed a partial aspect of an ultimate idea of fully conscious rationality. Marx re-interpreted the dialectical process not as a movement towards rationality, but as a movement of social change, where oppositions and tensions arise through conflicts between classes, at particular stages of technological development. The end state is conceived not as ideal rationality, but as a form of society in which classes, and thereby the conflicts which had driven the dialectical process, would be abolished (see DIALECTICAL MATERIALISM). Views such as these have been castigated by Karl Popper (1957) as 'historicism', meaning by this that they impose a pattern on history. Nevertheless, such views have been constructive in encouraging the study of history as a complex of processes arising not only between individuals but out of relations between social institutions.

A philosophy of process which had a considerable influence in literature, for instance on Proust, was that of Bergson (see BERGSON, H.-L. §4). Bergson saw reality as an open-ended evolutionary process, 'creative', as producing new forms of life. The word 'life' is in place here, because Bergson thought of evolution as driven by a living force, *élan vital*. Biological evolution is an integral part of this, in which we ourselves are participants. It is a temporal process in a strong sense – indeed Bergson spoke of reality as *durée*, real duration, continually creative of what is new. This is contrasted with time as measured by intellectual devices which represent a moving and changing reality as if it were a succession of states arrested at successive instants. Bergson held that the intellect was committed to this 'cinematographical' approach, and therefore failed to capture the moving and changing reality. There is, however, another mental capacity – 'intuition', through which we have an immediate experience of this reality in our own consciousness.

The later philosophy of Whitehead gives a metaphysics of a pluralistic universe, whose constituents are 'processes of becoming' (see WHITEHEAD, A.N. §4). These are structured unities developing through their interrelations with each other. He used the generalized concept 'organism' for these unities. Their processes of becoming display reiterated patterns which can be given abstract formulations, especially through mathematics. Such intellectual formulations need not be considered distortions – Whitehead held that the world has a permanent basic structure which underlies them.

Whitehead's later philosophy is obscure, and it must be acknowledged that none of these metaphysical views, with the exception of that of Aristotle within his own terms, gives a precise critical discussion of what it is to be a process. Yet a number of matters such as growth, development, learning and producing creative work, are naturally thought of as processes, where understanding of what goes on at one stage is furthered by having regard to future as well as to past stages.

See also: CAUSATION; CHANGE; EVENTS; PROCESS PHILOSOPHY; PROCESS THEISM

References and further reading

Aristotle (*c.* mid 4th century BC) *Physics*, III–IV, trans. and ed. E.H. Hussey, Oxford, Clarendon Press, 1983. (The main source for *kinēsis*, referred to in §4 above.)

Bergson, H. (1907) *Évolution Créatrice* (Creative Evolution), trans. A. Mitchell, London: Macmillan, 1911. (The main source for the view outlined above in §4.)

Cannon, W.B. (1932) *The Wisdom of The Body*, Cambridge, MA, and London: Harvard University Press. (The original source for the concept of homeostasis mentioned in §2 above.)

Emmet, D. (1992) *The Passage of Nature*, London: Macmillan; Philadelphia, PA: Temple University. (A fuller treatment of the material in this entry.)

Hegel, G.W.F. (1832–45) *Lectures on the Philosophy of World History: Introduction: Reason in History*, trans. H.B. Nisbet, Cambridge: Cambridge University Press, 1975. (Especially relevant for the view of dialectical processes described in §4 above.)

Holz, H. and Wolf-Gazo, E. (eds) (1984) *Whitehead und der Prozeßbegriff: Whitehead and the Idea of Process*, Freiburg/Munich: Alber. (A collection of papers given to the First International Whitehead Symposium – English summaries of German and German of English papers.)

* Johnson, W.E. (1934) *Logic*, Cambridge: Cambridge University Press. (Pt III, ch. 6, outlines the view of immanent causation referred to above in §2.)

Munsat, S. (1969) 'What is a Process?', *American Philosophical Quarterly* 6 (1): 69–87. (Differs from the view expressed in this entry in holding that all processes have an end state and that natural processes proceed in a way analogous to following a rule.)

* Popper, K.R. (1957) *The Poverty of Historicism*, London: Routledge & Kegan Paul. (Popper's critique of theories of history, referred to in §4 above.)

Process Studies, School of Theology, Claremont, CA. (A journal largely concerned with views deriving from the later Whitehead. A number of articles are on the philosophy of religion.)

* Russell, B.A.W. (1903) *The Principles of Mathematics*, 2nd edn, London: Allen & Unwin, 1937. (Outlines the view of motion referred to in §4 above.)

Sellars, W. (1981) 'Naturalism and Process', *The Monist* 64 (1): 37–65. (This takes up a suggestion in vol. 1 of C.D. Broad's *An Examination of McTaggart's Philosophy* (Cambridge: Cambridge University Press, 1935) that there could be a view of the world solely in terms of processes.)

Whitehead, A.N. (1929) *Process and Reality*, ed. D.R. Griffiths and D.W. Shelbourne, New York: Free Press; London: Collier Macmillan, 1978. (Outlines the metaphysics of processes of becoming referred to in §4 above. Other important works by Whitehead include *Science and the Modern World* (1926), *Adventures of Ideas* (1933) and *Modes of Thought* (1938), all published by Cambridge University Press.)

DOROTHY EMMET

PROCLUS (*c.* AD 411–85)

The Greek Neoplatonist Proclus aimed to find a logical and metaphysical structure in which unity embraces but does not stifle diversity. He assumed the underlying unity of reality and of self, but was anxious to maintain the diversity of thought and existence. This led him to conceive of things as different species of one general whole, each part comprehending the rest but in its own specific, limited way. There are successive levels of awareness, thought and existence, ranging from that of ordinary experience, where we continuously have a passing understanding of the equally fleeting world, to that of ultimate unity, where we see the first principles and the total whole unqualified, as if by super-intuition. Reason, aided by imagination, and exercised by philosophy and science, elevates us towards that supreme state, which is at once the foundation of religious and of ethical values.

Proclus was interested in an integrated account of the nature of things. Asking questions about how and what we know, our perceptions and beliefs, prompts questions of the sort: what is the origin of knowledge? What is the nature of mind? Of the things we think and perceive? Of existence? For Proclus even questions about virtue, moral judgment and action, God, faith and salvation are all clarified by referring them to questions about their origins and nature. No subject escaped his attention, including the interpretation of poetic works by literary figures such as Homer, where Proclus saw language as a mediator to deeper truths. Philosophical inquiry leads to asking what order of reality substantiates things, whether in the field of mind, values, science or literature.

Proclus' system is complex, and he uses highly technical terms (most of which have their roots in Plato, Aristotle and Plotinus). But for him this is only appropriate to the richness of our conceptual world. We have complex and varied concepts about our surroundings and selves, not because humans necessarily have flamboyant fancies but because reality itself is complex. That we have glimpses of knowledge means that there is some unity between our mind and the objects of thought. Moreover, unity is essential to the identity of things, and without it they would be unintelligible, and conceptually unreal. The 'One' is a primitive absolute, and is fundamental to intelligibility and existence. Thinker, thoughts and realities are in some way one. Things are not disconnected but share layers of ever-increasing unity. Consequently questions about different kinds of being, knowledge, good, and so on, become questions about degrees.

Studying all this was not just a cerebral affair. To the Neoplatonist, understanding the scheme of things provided a guide on leading a good life and achieving what since Plato's days had been praised as the goal of human endeavour, 'true happiness' or eudaimonia.

1 Life

In his fifty-year career Proclus became the chief exponent of systematic Neoplatonism, the dominant philosophy of late antiquity. He was born in Byzantium, the capital of the eastern Roman Empire, but grew up in Lycia. The son of a successful advocate at the imperial court, he initially went to study law at Alexandria. However, while on a visit to Byzantium (associated with the foundation of a new university) he underwent a conversion to philosophy, which eventually led him to Athens at the age of nineteen. There Plutarch of Athens and Syrianus taught him Aristotle and Plato according to the Neoplatonic curriculum. He quickly rose to become the head of the prestigious Athenian School at the young age of twenty-five, until his death aged around seventy-five.

Proclus sought to practise what he taught. Biographical sketches and his poems reveal a man of passion. This he channelled into his academic work (teaching, seminars, writing), religious devotion and rigorous lifestyle (he was a vegetarian and abstemious). Friends, students and staff benefited regularly from his love and generosity, which compensated for his famous short temper and perfectionism. He was an inspiring figure and exercised his considerable authority politically both in and outside Athens. A proud defender of the 'Hellenic' values and religious multiformity, Proclus lived when Christianity became the state orthodoxy.

He was a prolific author, and we have evidence that he wrote more than forty titles. In keeping with the practice in the imperial Roman period, many of Proclus' treatises are extensive commentaries on classical greats. This does not mean they are not original: novel ideas and modifications or rejections of classical doctrines can be found in these commentaries, and in content there is little to distinguish them from monographs. For his general system the main sources are the *Commentary on Plato's Parmenides, Platonic Theology* (synonymous with metaphysics), the study manual *Elements of Theology*, and for additional detail, the *Commentary on Plato's Timaeus*.

2 Metaphysics

Proclus' overall metaphysical standpoint he shares

with his fellow Neoplatonists. He subscribes to realism, in that he accepts a reality independent of what we individuals think about it. But proper reality is not physical, because what we grasp with the five senses is episodic and often illusory. The things that exist are of the intellect – with the provision that such intellect and its ideas are not just personal but objective and universal (this can be traced to the revision of Aristotelian *nous* by the influential ALEXANDER OF APHRODISIAS (§2)).

In his response to the problem of unity/diversity Proclus wants to steer between conceiving things as disparate and lumping them into an undifferentiated heap. He employs a rule of mixture that originally belonged to the theory of material stuffs in ANAXAGORAS (§3), but which near Plotinus' time had been extended to the domain of intellect and concepts: 'Everything is in everything, in a manner proper to each.' If things (conceptual and material) are ultimately one, they cannot have sharp boundaries to distinguish them, but must extend in some way 'all within all'. Similarity (and dissimilarity) supersede strict identity and difference (*Platonic Theology* III 7 S and W, VI 347–50 Portus; *Elements of Theology* proposition 108).

This metaphysical reason combines with the exhaustion of possible logical options under a heading x (that is to say, x; x and not-x; not-x) to yield the chains of 'intermediaries' for which Proclus is well known. Any two polar (directly opposite) terms have one or more intermediary, which is more or less similar to either pole. Although threefold leitmotifs are pre-eminent (for examples see below on participation), in fact as many intermediaries can be inserted as required (see MANY-VALUED LOGICS). However Proclus does not accept that everything we can think merits a niche in reality: only those that do not depend on a particular mind (*Commentary on Plato's Parmenides* col. 1054, 895–7) but can already stand on their own 'foundation' (*hypostasis*) (henceforth, some of these 'hypostatic' terms are indicated by capitalization). The task of the philosopher is to discover the true ones.

To make sense of diversity we group things with a common characteristic. But this raises the questions what is the status of such characteristic and what is its relation to the group and parts? Proclus distinguishes three senses of 'whole', and recognizes the full implication of saying that a whole is the sum of parts plus the cause of its unity (see also Aristotle, *Metaphysics* 1041b, and, especially, Plato, *Theaetetus* 204–5). The essential whole is a 'monad', a singularity that cannot be analysed: it is a 'whole prior to the parts' (*Elements of Theology* propositions 67–9). The characteristic group-type in its pure state is such an unanalysed whole. It stands as a prototype that qualifies and embraces all possible specific forms of it. The many parts of the whole express the prototype but unequally, because they have it in different conditions (for example, light itself, the light of the sun, firelight, glow-worm light). An attribute can thus be regarded as a family, a series, headed by its own prototype (for example, the monad of life), followed by the multitude of diverse forms where the attribute is found (for example, life of animal, life of plant).

In Platonic philosophy the relation of a 'Form' to its material particulars was often described as 'participation', a sharing-in, because each particular cannot be said to possess the entire Form. For the late Neoplatonist, participation extends to relations between conceptual entities also, so Proclus talks in general of what is 'participated in' and its 'participant'. Participation created many problems, not least, how can the Form be shared out and still maintain its integrity? By the whole–part theorem, the whole in itself is indeed a single thing, and is exempt from direct distribution into parts: it is 'imparticipable'. Thus, we arrive at the threesome imparticipable–participated–participant. Because Proclus is dealing with a metaphysical order where the attribute is more perfect and real than its subject (which is defined, and thus perfected, by it), he further distinguishes between a participated attribute that is complete and reified in itself (called 'self-hypostasized'), and a participated that must be always within a participant to accomplish this (such attributes are called 'image' and 'trace'). Between the fully transcendent ('imparticipable') and the fully immanent stands the sovereign immanent. This intermediary is the linchpin of Proclus' account. It refers to objective realities (for example, cosmic bodies, certain universal forces and properties, spirits) that are within reach of our apprehension but independent of us.

The constant 'flow' from unity to plurality, Proclus calls 'procession'. It leaves the source 'remaining' undiminished. The thing that 'proceeds' has its character diluted and altered by the conditions it is found in (for example, Life itself becomes life of intellect, or life of plants). However, what 'descends' into plurality never severs its connection with its original, pure state, otherwise it would completely lose its definition (that is, the life of plant is still a life, not a plant-part). 'Reversion' is the tendency or movement to regain the lost pure definition (which is 'remaining' unaltered). These three are not discrete static states, but three distinguishable moments of a single dynamic process; practically everything undergoes all of them (with the One in a controversial position). For Proclus the three apply to every form, property or entity, not just to the conscious soul or cosmic strata of being (see PLOTINUS §3).

3 Levels

Things are composed of layers of qualities from corresponding degrees of reality. The various degrees are also modes because they modify any form, property or entity 'in the manner proper to each'. (This is the philosophical reason for the high number of peculiar adverbials in the vocabulary of Proclus and later Neoplatonists.) The grades are bunched into broad levels (in addition to unity), typically: real existence, life, intellect, soul, physicality and body. (Principal classical sources are Plato's *Sophist*, *Philebus*, *Parmenides*, *Timaeus*; see PLATO §§15–16.) Each level has its 'imparticipable monad', followed by the multitude that is participated in: for example, Intellect and intellects. Moving from one level to another involves a substantive change, a 'decrease' (*hyphesis*) or an 'elevation' (*anagōgē*). Properties accumulate successively: real existence has unity, life has real existence and unity, intellect has life, real existence, and unity, and so on. So the 'elevation' also brings an analytical reduction to first principles.

Proclus arranges the levels of being by degree of perfection (completion) and by generality (*Platonic Theology* III 20–6), which is an inversion of Aristotle's scheme of values. Soul is superior to body because it perfects it. Intellect perfects the soul, but is also more general because even animals have 'a trace of cognition'. Life is superior to intellect because it is more general (even plants have it) and there cannot be a lifeless intellect. Being is, likewise, superior again because even inanimates have it. The rule – first by dint of being more general, derives from Proclus' whole–part theorem (see also §6).

4 The One, the Good and the divine

The greatest unity, the 'One', transcends every possible attribution positive or negative, and so cannot be understood directly. It even transcends the very state of existence (see Plato, *Republic* 509b), so Proclus calls it 'not being' (*Elements of Theology* proposition 138), in the sense of prior to existent. This absolute metaphysical state coincides with that of value, since unqualified unity is the ultimate perfection (completion) desired by all. The One is identical to the Good and, as the supreme perfection, value and cause, is God. As fully imparticipable, God is transcendent, unknowable and ineffable. As the unity essential to everything that exists, the divine spark is immanent even in the lowliest material (see *Elements of Theology* proposition 145). However, Proclus

carefully distinguishes divinity proper from deification by participation (for example, a divine body). Properly divine are only the One and the 'self-hypostasized' unities (see the discussion on *henads* given below), and by extension those entities predicated by such a unity (*Elements of Theology* proposition 114). The unknowable, supra-rational divine can be approached intellectually by stripping away attributions (known in Christian theology as the apophatic way to God), or by analogy, inferring what the One is like by its known effects. Ultimately individuals can reach the One by placing their faith in it with their own immanent 'one' during theurgical and mystical acts (see CHALDAEAN ORACLES; IAMBLICHUS).

But such extreme transcendence is almost self-defeating. How can the One and Good relate at all to existence? Proclus rejected Iamblichus' two Ones (the fully transcendent and the causal). This still left the two fundamental problems (parallel to those faced, say, by modern big-bang cosmologists): How is existence produced from pre-existence? How does diversity arise from absolute simplicity? In answer to the first Proclus emphasizes the reified principles Limit and Unlimited (and Providence). In the second, he distinguishes the plurality of 'ones', the 'henads'.

The One is essentially a limit, for there is nothing else except it. This also means that the One has no boundary imposed upon it (by something else): it is unlimited in potency. Limit and the Unlimited become the starting points of the chain of causation that produces the levels of being. Limit supplies definition and discreteness, and the Unlimited the 'overflowing' capacity to exist in continuity. The third factor is the providential activity of the One, which reaches down to individual beings and perfects them with unity. Moreover, if the One is the prototype of oneness, then it must be the head of many participated 'ones', the 'henads'. A 'henad' is the very unity at the core of every existent, and there are as many henads as things that exist. Strictly the henads originate in the Limit, Unlimited and Providence, and so carry the seeds of differentiation at the root of the individual variety of things. Proclus distinguishes further the 'self-hypostasized henads' which belong to timeless or everlasting entities, the sort that tend to be worshipped as gods by diverse religions. The plain henads are the ones immanent in humans, animals, plants, minerals, and so on.

5 Intelligibles and soul

The highest level thought can reach is real existence, or pure being, the first broad category of the intelligibles. This is the object of thought (*noēton*) (the One is beyond thought). Here the contents of the One acquire their first layer of manifestation, in that they become 'really existent' and accessible to contemplation. Appropriately Proclus considers this to be the place of the universal pattern, the 'paradigm' (Plato, *Timaeus* 31a) and of eternity. Next he finds a middle intelligible level proper to pure Life, long before it is embodied in living beings. This stands for the capacity to multiply the contents of the whole. At the last intelligible level, the intellective (*noeron*), is Intellect itself (*nous*) (see NOUS). From here and above we conceive things directly, as by intuition. The Intellect's essence is 'pure mind' (as embodied in the god Cronos in Plato, *Cratylus* 396b), whose contents are made distinct by the power of Intellect, identified with Rhea (*Cratylus* 402) and the 'Goddess' of the Chaldaean Oracles. The active exercise of Intellect results in the creative conception of things (*poiētikon*) (Plato, *Timaeus* 28c; Aristotle, *On the Soul* 430a12). Creative Intellect is God the Maker (Plato, *Timaeus* 29d–30c), who gives determinate form to the physical world. The Creator is well distinguished from the One – in sharp contrast with Christian doctrine. Intellect has polar outlooks: one contemplates the higher intelligibles and has intellective ideas and forms; the other is involved in producing time, soul and the physical things of ordinary experience.

Soul is what makes a body alive and 'is a substance between the really existent and becoming' (*Commentary on Plato's Timaeus* III 254.13–17). In the Platonic tradition soul straddles two domains: one is intelligible and beyond the bound of time; the other is physical and constrained by body, space and time. Proclus thus defines the soul's essence as atemporal but its activity as operating in time, because it cannot actualize all of its contents at once but has to unroll them onto the passing time. He distinguishes the 'imparticipable monad' of soul, which lies 'above the (physical) world' (*hyperkosmios*) and is associated with no body. The traditional Platonic world-soul (what moves the cosmos in the determinate way measured by science), although just as singular, now becomes a participated soul, whose body is the whole corporeal universe.

6 Body, matter and the One

The qualities characteristic of a body are said to be its nature (*physis*). In living beings nature is the instinctive, non-rational aspect of life, which is inseparable from the functions of body. It can be distinguished from soul proper (which is purposeful and separable) and from pure body (which is itself passive). However such distinctions are not always needed and so nature is often grouped with soul or

body. An 'imparticipable' Nature is paradoxical (How can it be apart from a body?), which may explain why Proclus does not explicitly attribute to it the 'henads above and in the (physical) world' (*Platonic Theology* VI); although the link can be confirmed from diverse cross-references. Nature has the Necessity which determines physical behaviour. Indeed Nature's activity creates bodies directly, and seems also to be the monadic source of Body: there is no imparticipable body.

Body considered in itself is the last of things that exist in some sense. It is completely inert. Living beings move because of their vitality and inanimates according to their nature. For Proclus pure body is a quantity of a certain shape with three-dimensional extension. Matter, on the other hand, is not even a definite being, just the potential for something to be what it is.

At the low end of the metaphysical scale, entities become progressively less compound. There are living beings without a spark of intellect (plants), inanimates lack life, and matter lacks even determinate being. This is a result of the 'Proclean canon' that the more general and perfect the cause is, the further its extent of power. At the lower ranks, things receive attributes solely of the more general kind, not general *and* specific ones. Properties compound until the maximum number in the bundle is reached around the level of appearances that humans inhabit. From there, specific properties gradually diminish. So we arrive at simplicity in two different ways: in the superior sense is the One; in the inferior is matter.

For Proclus this makes matter one continuous, universal power, and a direct extension of the One's Unlimited (in contrast to Plotinus' bisection of matter into intelligible and sensible). Matter is indeed to a degree good and of value. Like the One, it is most obscure and formless: the One is prior to intelligible definition, and matter beyond its reach. This does not mean, however, that Proclus considered material objects a short-cut to the One. 'Reversion' to the One is an 'elevation' through levels of being in the maximal sense, those with perfected properties.

7 Evil?

Proclus rejects completely the existence of evil as something absolute. He cannot find it in any of the levels of being, not even in matter which 'is in some way good'. Everything, including matter, has its roots in the One, which is Good. If there were a source for evil (PLUTARCH OF CHAERONEA (§3) blamed an evil world-soul, Gnostics the Maker, and Christians the devil) it would have to be 'beyond even the total lack of existence... further than the nothingness of nonexistence' (*Commentary on Plato's Timaeus* I 374.14–17). What is commonly described as evil points to a relative weakness of the good: for example, when something is unnatural, or when it is bad for its purpose or deficient in some way (I 375, 381); in human actions, when the perpetrators are ignorant of what is best, and have a weak mind and soul (*On Evil* 50, 40–6).

Since evil is a parasitic and fictitious existence (*parhypostasis*) (*Platonic Theology* I 84–5), the only real choice open is the pursuit of the Good. This we fail to attain because of ignorance, inadequacies, selfish passions and a host of other restrictions. Freedom of action, therefore, means primarily to be free of such obstacles as inhibit or distort an individual's inherent desire to pursue the good.

8 Psychology

Psyche (usually translated as soul) is an alive, cognitive substance, as individual as the creature that has it. 'Mind' is a useful translation when contrasted with the perfect 'intellect' (*nous*), which stands above the partialities of soul. Every soul can cause spontaneous movement. The differences lie mainly in the way such movement is prompted and maintained by the soul's mental faculties. Animal *psyche* is simple. It is non-rational only, and concerned with sense-perception and appetites, although it still has a spark of intelligence. Human soul mixes rational and non-rational aspects (not parts because the soul itself is undivided). Thus, humans can lead a wide range of lives depending on how much they allow one aspect to control the other. Reflecting the complexity of its constitution, the human mind/soul has many faculties or 'powers'.

The non-rational side of the soul deals with input from the physical world. With sense-perception (*aisthesis*) the soul receives the sensible qualities of material objects through the sensory organs. The diverse impressions, 'affections', are first organized into a unified impression. Next, with its opinion-forming faculty (*doxa*), the soul produces basic beliefs from the sensory evidence and any judgment about the source of these sense-impressions. Finally it visualizes things internally with its image-making faculty (*phantasia*).

The rational side of the soul deals with the outpourings from the intellect. Using its highest faculty, called *logos* (a word with many meanings (see Logos), but in this context signifying reason, definition and modelling), the individual mind has access to the 'inexhaustible supply' of ideas and inspirations. But being particular, the human mind admits them fragmented (not as intellective wholes).

Soul has also its own concepts: '*psyche* was never a *tabula rasa* but is a tablet that has always been inscribed and is always writing itself and being written on by *nous*' (*Commentary on the First Book of Euclid's Elements* 16.8–10). Understanding is the result of the mental debate between successive arguments and propositions: that is, it is the result of 'discursive' reasoning. To compare the various concepts, the rational soul seems to employ its own imagination (*phantasia*), and sees representations of concepts as projections on the mind's screen from internal and external sources. By matching representations soul can complete or correct the impressions from the senses.

9 Soul and body

The individual soul, being particular, is incomplete and imperfect: it knows this and desires other things to complete it. Half-knowledge brings a sense of daring (*tolme*), which results in the soul's total descent into body (in contrast to Plotinus, who allowed a part to remain undescended). Once in the 'oyster shell' of the body it longs for proper completion and unification. From here the soul can be elevated, 'be saved', in three complementary ways, aided by the appropriate teachers and guiding spirits. With erotic love it strives to unite with the higher life (as in Plato's *Symposium*). With philosophical contemplation it reaches the intelligibles and speculates on the first principles. With theurgy (see Chaldaean Oracles; Iamblichus) it culminates in the leap of faith (*pistis*), which unites the soul's own 'one-henad' with the all-perfect One. The particular soul, through not knowing its place, can thus descend and ascend indefinitely through all the levels of thought and being (*Elements of Theology* proposition 206). This 'travel' is ontological when it involves the cycle of birth and death, and epistemological when the mind engages in lower or higher pursuits during a lifetime.

'Body' has several senses for Proclus. At its simplest it is pure space-extension, like a body of intangible light. Endowed with layers of qualities it becomes the physical body of our sensory experience. When soul descends into participation, it acquires a series of bodies, referred to as 'vehicles' (*ochemata*). Every participated soul has at first a tenuous, 'luminous' body-vehicle (for example, the world-soul has universal space). However, any soul that descends further into the physical domain acquires a further vehicle composed of the four elements, fire, air, water, earth. Finally, those that incarnate on earth (for example, humans) acquire their particular fleshly body. So soul-types suit their degree of participation in body (consistent with the overall metaphysics). The vehicles played an important part in religion. After death the soul is purified by shedding its non-rational nature and the associated elemental vehicle. It is left free to ascend with its luminous vehicle.

Since the essence of human life resides in an immortal soul, which is separable from the physical body, Proclus adheres to the Pythagorean-Platonic doctrine of transmigration of soul (see PLATO §11; PYTHAGORAS §2; PYTHAGOREANISM §3; PSYCHĒ). However, he does not believe that a soul can reincarnate backwards in the evolutionary scale towards full consciousness. References to reincarnations of humans in animals (Plato, *Timaeus* 42b–c), for Proclus, have sense if taken psychologically, not biologically: that is, a human can lead the life of a wolf (if unjust) or an ass (if gluttonous) but cannot be reincarnated as an actual wolf or ass.

10 Philosophy of science

Proclus' deep interest in the nature of reality includes the physical world and its scientific description by mathematics. He was familiar with practical and empirical science. In his main astronomical work, *Outline of Astronomical Hypotheses*, he describes the construction of a spherical astrolabe. He himself made some of the last reliable astronomical observations of antiquity (AD 475), and instilled this interest in AMMONIUS, SON OF HERMEAS and Heliodorus.

Proclus' theory of knowledge is linked to his metaphysics of graded being, so instead of the division into rationalism and empiricism he has degrees of knowledge dependent mainly on the level of consciousness and awareness of the thinker (and on the kind of being the object of thought is). The clearest kind of knowledge is reserved for the non-discursive contemplation proper to the intelligibles, where realities are perceived directly and complete, as by intuition. Knowledge of the physical world falls below this, for it combines discursive reasoning with sensory perception.

What arises from sensation is contingent and frequently confused. It is an opinion (*doxa*). Discursive reasoning (*dianoia*) uses concepts to define things, and to correct sensory evidence (as in the apparent smallness of the sun due to the distance from the observer). Scientific knowledge results from the reasoning activity of the soul, which matches sensory-derived opinions with concepts, according to positive criteria for truth: syllogistically demonstrable proof, and correspondence to (metaphysical) reality.

Proclus' applications of his theory of scientific knowledge are most evident in his philosophy of astronomy, and specifically in his rejection of Ptolemaic cosmology (in which he stands unique

until the Renaissance) (see PTOLEMY). Two remarkable examples can be summarized. Proclus rejects the precession: not the precession of the equinoxes as we now understand the phenomenon, but Ptolemy's interpretation of it as a movement of all the fixed stars. For Proclus, such stars cannot precess because it is in their nature to be fixed, and those who claim that their observations fit the hypotheses fall foul of the false–false–true Aristotelian syllogism (for instance, premises: dogs are blue, blue things bark; conclusion: dogs bark). He denies that the planets are moved by nested heavenly spheres (a doctrine that dominated European astronomy until the sixteenth century) because the arguments for them he finds to be conjectures, not necessary and demonstrable proofs, and because the celestial bodies are ontologically capable of moving by themselves in free space.

Proclus' philosophy of physics also marks a radical turn away from Aristotle on two key fronts: the elements of the physical world, and place as space. He rejects as *ad hoc* and superfluous Aristotle's fifth element for the heavens, the aether. The celestial bodies consist of the same (four) elements as the terrestrial. For instance, without a kind of fire the stars and the sun could not illuminate, and without a solid bit of earth-element they could not be opaque (as during eclipses). Employing his metaphysics of graded being, Proclus distinguishes the heavenly mode from the terrestrial: in the former, the elements are in their 'summits', for example, fire is purely illuminating, earth is purely tangible and opaque; in the latter, they are gross, for example, fire burns, earth is heavy. Furthermore, he develops a new account of the primary properties of the elements, which he derives from the size, shape and facility for motion of their particles.

The place a body occupies is not its boundary, as Aristotle stated. Proclus uniquely proposes that it must also be a kind of body, but without the mass that makes physical bodies resist each others' presence. It is three-dimensional space. By extension there is a cosmic space in which all the bodies of the universe are immersed. Space on its own, apart from the bodies that move in it, is like a body of light.

As to mathematics, Proclus rejects Aristotle's view that mathematical objects (numbers, points, lines, proportions and so on) are abstractions from physical things, and develops the Platonic argument that they exist independently of human experience, but without the inscrutability of Forms. Mathematicals have dimensions, occupy relative places, are many in number within each kind, and so share some of the features of physicality. They dwell in the mental essence of soul, but without dimension. Soul 'projects' them onto its imagination, as onto a screen, where they acquire their familiar dimensionality (*Commentary on the First Book of Euclid's Elements* 50–2). Thus mathematical knowledge is a mixture of reasoning and imagination. The mathematical study of bodies (mechanics, optics, astronomy) relies on holding particular images more than the study of shape in general (geometry). The study of numbers relies on it much less and therefore is closer to pure reasoning. Above all stands the study of rules and relations, of analysis and synthesis. Ultimately the objects of mathematics originate in the Limit–Unlimited of the One. Mathematics is a bridge between sensory perception and the most complete state of knowledge. Thus in education, mathematical study prepares the mind to apprehend the pure realities.

11 Influence

Through his students (for example, Ammonius) and writings, Proclus influenced later Greek philosophy at its two leading centres, Athens and Alexandria, until the end of antiquity in the seventh century. His metaphysical system was adopted by Pseudo-Dionysius the Areopagite for a Christian celestial hierarchy. In turn, this influenced both Byzantine thinkers (Maximus Confessor, John Damascene) and those of the Latin West (see ERIUGENA, J.S.; GROSSETESTE, R.). Islamic theologians of the tenth century, such as the Ikhwan al Safa', were inspired by Proclus' emanationism and theory of mathematicals (see IKHWAN AL SAFA'; NEOPLATONISM IN ISLAMIC PHILOSOPHY). Furthermore, Arab scholars produced a compilation of his *Elements of Theology* under an Aristotelian label. Thomas AQUINAS (§7) was the first to detect that Proclus was the author of the doctrines in all these works. Aquinas' friend William of Moerbeke rendered the first Latin translations of Proclus' main works. A new wave of Proclus' direct influence arrives in eleventh- to fifteenth-century Byzantium, and in Humanist Europe, notably with FICINO and NICHOLAS OF CUSA. From there, Proclus' philosophy and science can be found in KEPLER, the Cambridge Platonists (see CAMBRIDGE PLATONISM), SPINOZA, the English Romantics, COUSIN, and in various philosophers of idealism, culminating with Hegel (see IDEALISM; HEGEL, G.W.F.).

List of works

We cannot date Proclus' writings (many of which were based on lecture-courses) because he continued making additions after initial publication. The *Platonic Theology* seems to be his last major work. There are student's excerpts of the commentary on Plato's *Cratylus*, but commentaries on Plato's *Theaetetus*, *Philebus*, *Sophist*, *Phaedo*, *Phaedrus*, *Symposium* and on Aristotle's logic have not survived; on Plotinus there is only a tiny portion. In nineteenth-century London, Thomas Taylor, who influenced the Romantics, translated most of Proclus' works. However, the translations of modern, reliable editions of Greek texts are mainly in French or German (as are many of the studies).

Proclus (mid 5th century AD) *The Elements of Physics* or *On Motion*, ed. A. Ritzenfeld, *Institutio physica*, Leipzig: Teubner, 1912; trans. T. Taylor, 1831. (The former is a parallel Greek text and German translation, the latter an English translation; the text has no Neoplatonic theorems but is a short study manual on Aristotle's *Physics* books VI and VII and *On the Heavens* book I.)

—— (mid 5th century AD) *The Elements of Theology*, ed. and trans. E.R. Dodds, Oxford: Clarendon Press, 2nd edn, 1963; repr. 1992. (Systematic study manual of Proclus' Neoplatonism.)

—— (mid 5th century AD) *On Providence*, ed. D. Isaac, *Dix problèmes concernant la providence*, Paris: Les Belles Lettres, 1977; trans. T. Taylor, 1833; repr. Frome: Prometheus Trust, 1998. (Isaac has parallel Greek text and French translation; Taylor's English translation also includes *On Fate*, and *On Evil*.)

—— (mid 5th century AD) *On Fate*, ed. D. Isaac, *Providence, Fatalité, Liberté*, Paris: Les Belles Lettres, 1979. (Parallel Greek text and French translation.)

—— (mid 5th century AD) *On Evil*, ed. D. Isaac, *De l'existence du Mal*, Paris: Les Belles Lettres, 1982. (Parallel Greek text and French translation.)

—— (mid 5th century AD) *A Commentary on the First Book of Euclid's Elements*, ed. G. Friedlein, *In primum Euclidis elementorum librum commentarii*, Leipzig: Teubner, 1873; trans. G.R. Morrow, Princeton, NJ: Princeton University Press, 1970; repr. 1992. (Morrow is English translation of the 1873 text.)

—— (mid 5th century AD) *Commentary on Plato's Republic*, trans. A.J. Festugière, *Proclus Commentaire sur la République*, Paris: Vrin, 1970. (French translation.)

—— (mid 5th century AD) *Commentary on Plato's Timaeus*, ed. E. Diehl, *In Platonis Timaeum commentaria*, Leipzig: Teubner, 1903–6, 3 vols; repr. Amsterdam: Hakkert, 1965; trans. A.J. Festugière, *Proclus Commentaire sur le Timée*, Paris: Vrin, 1966–8, 5 vols; trans. T. Taylor, London, 1810; repr. Hastings: Chthonios Books, 1988; repr. Frome: Prometheus Trust, 1998. (Festugière provides a parallel Greek text and French translation; Taylor is a reprint of his 1810 English translation.)

—— (late 5th century AD) *Outline of the Astronomical Hypotheses*, ed. C. Manitius: *Hypotyposis astronomicarum positionum*, Leipzig: Teubner, 1909; repr. Stuttgart, 1974. (Parallel Greek text and German translation.)

—— (late 5th century AD) *Commentary on Plato's Alcibiades I*, trans. W.O. Neill, The Hague: Martinus Nijhoff, 1971; ed. A.Ph. Segonds, *Sur le premier Alcibiade de Platon*, Paris: Les Belles Lettres, 1985–6. (The former is an English translation, with commentary, the latter a parallel Greek text and French translation.)

—— (late 5th century AD) *Commentary on Plato's Parmenides*, ed. V. Cousin, *In Platonis Parmenidem*; Paris: Durand, 1864; repr. Hildersheim: Olms, 1961; trans. J.M. Dillon and G.R. Morrow, *Proclus' Commentary on Plato's Parmenides*, Princeton, NJ: Princeton University Press, 1987; repr. 1992. (Book 7 is preserved in a Latin rendering by W. Moerbeke, recovered by R. Klibansky and L. Labowsky, London 1953, published in a revised edition (ed.) C. Steel, *Commentaire sur le Parmenide de Platon*, 2 vols, Leuven: Leuven University Press, 1982–5; with introduction.)

—— (late 5th century AD) *Platonic Theology*, ed. H.D. Saffrey and L.G. Westerink, *Théologie platonicienne*, Paris: Les Belles Lettres, 1968–97; trans. T. Taylor, *The Platonic Theology in Six Books*, London, 1816; repr. New York: Selene Books, 1985–6. (The former is a parallel Greek text and French translation, the latter a reprint of Taylor's 1816 translation.)

References and further reading

Gersh, S. (1973) *Kinēsis Akinētos; A Study of Spiritual Motion in the Philosophy of Proclus*, Leiden: Brill. (Analysis of the central ideas of Proclus' metaphysics.)

Lloyd, A.C. (1967) 'Athenian and Alexandrian Neoplatonism', in A.H. Armstrong (ed.) *Cambridge History of Later Greek and Early Medieval Philosophy*, Cambridge: Cambridge University Press, 302–25. (A concise, excellent introduction to Proclus.)

—— (1990) *The Anatomy of Neoplatonism*, Oxford: Clarendon Press. (The logical structure of Proclus' metaphysics examined in depth; for the advanced reader.)

Saffrey, H.D. and Pépin, J. (eds) (1987) *Proclus: lecteur et interprète des anciens* (Proclus, Lecturer and Interpreter of the Ancients), Paris: CNRS. (Rich source for recent English, French and German articles on many aspects of Proclus' thought.)

Siorvanes, L. (1996) *Proclus: Neo-Platonic Philosophy and Science*, Edinburgh: Edinburgh University Press and New Haven, CT: Yale University Press. (Comprehensive account of Proclus, including analysis of his metaphysics and theory of knowledge, suitable for the newcomer.)

LUCAS SIORVANES

PRODICUS (*fl.* late 5th century BC)

Prodicus was a Greek Sophist from the island of Ceos; he was active in Athens. He served his city as ambassador and also became prominent as a professional educator. He taught natural philosophy, ethics, and of course rhetoric, but he is best known as an authority on correct language, specializing in fine verbal distinctions. Prodicus' greatest influence was due to his naturalistic interpretation of the traditional Greek gods; as a result, he later figured on the short list of famous atheists.

Prodicus came to Athens on public business as representative of his native Ceos, and seems to have settled there permanently as a professional teacher, earning large sums from his course of instruction. By 423 BC he was famous enough to be mocked by Aristophanes in his comedy the *Clouds*, together with Socrates, as a teacher of natural philosophy (*Clouds* 360–1; A5). The Platonic Socrates claims to have heard Prodicus lecture on language, although he could only afford the cheap, one-drachma course, not the deluxe course for fifty drachmas (Plato, *Cratylus* 384b). And Socrates says that he frequently sends students to Prodicus who do not seem apt to profit from associating with himself (Plato, *Theaetetus* 151b). Prodicus is cited in Plato's dialogues as an authority on 'the correctness of names'. Plato has made him a figure of fun by representing him as insisting upon fine distinctions between near synonyms such as 'pleasure' and 'enjoyment', 'wanting' and 'desiring' (see, for example, Plato, *Protagoras* 337a–c, 340a).

Prodicus was author of a book entitled *Hōrai* (Seasons) from which Xenophon (*Memorabilia* II 1.21–34) has extracted a long quotation or paraphrase known as the 'Choice of Heracles'. In this text two allegorical figures, women named Virtue and Vice, present Heracles with alternative paths to happiness, one of which is short and easy, while the other is long and arduous (Xenophon, *Memorabilia*, II. 1.21–34; fr.2). The rhetoric is picturesque, the morality is predictable, but the allegory became extremely influential.

The most interesting philosophical contribution of Prodicus was a naturalistic theory of the origin of religion (fr.5). According to Sextus Empiricus, Prodicus claimed that 'the ancients considered that sun, moon, rivers and springs, and generally all things beneficial for our lives, are gods because of their usefulness'. Other reports suggest that the development of agriculture played an important role in Prodicus' explanation, and that names like Demeter and Dionysus were said to reflect the invention of bread and wine. According to several authors, Prodicus denied the existence of the traditional Greek gods. If this is correct, his theory would be more anthropological than allegorical.

Prodicus' explanation of the origin of religion apparently presupposes a more general account of the evolution of human culture from primitive beginnings, when the life of mankind was like that of beasts. This account in turn belongs in a larger cosmological context: the attempt of Ionian natural philosophy to explain how the current world order developed from a more primitive state of affairs 'in the beginning'. The rise of human civilization is the final chapter in Presocratic cosmogony, as we find it more fully reproduced in later authors such as Lucretius.

Prodicus' explanation of Demeter and Dionysus as inventors of bread and wine is echoed in Euripides' *Bacchae* (274–85), where it is used to justify the worship of Dionysus. Since we do not have Prodicus' own words, it is difficult to know how far his theory is compatible with the allegorical practice by which later philosophers preserved respect for the civic cult by reinterpreting the traditional gods in more scientific terms. Like the evolutionary account, the allegorical interpretation is older than Prodicus. Thus Metrodorus of Lampsacus and other followers of Anaxagoras will identify Zeus with intelligence (*nous*), Athena with art or craft (*technē*), Achilles with the sun, Hector with the moon, and so on (A4 and 6). Diogenes of Apollonia is reported to have identified Zeus with cosmic intelligence in the form of air (see DIOGENES OF APOLLONIA §2). It was this type of allegory that became conventional (Apollo as the sun, Artemis as the moon, Athena as wisdom, and so on) and was later developed systematically by Stoicism. According to some scholars, Prodicus belongs in this tradition.

If the report of atheism is correct, however, Prodicus was concerned only to explain and not to justify the worship of the gods. The relevant parallel would be what we find in the *Sisyphus* fragment (fr.25 variously attributed to Euripides and to Critias), where the invention of the gods is described as the device introduced by a clever man in order to enforce morality. A similar cultural prehistory must lie behind the fragment 30 of Democritus (compare DEMOCRITUS §4), that claims that 'a few learned people raised their hands on high and called the Air "Zeus"'. Prodicus' theory was apparently more elaborate. He seems to have distinguished two stages in the development of religion. In the earlier stage human beings began to worship the forces of nature on which they depended: sun, rivers, springs, and things useful for life. In the next stage, moving from the state of nature, they deified cultural heroes and heroines who invented agriculture and useful arts: Demeter, Dionysus, Athena and the like were divinized mortals, like Heracles and Asclepius. On this view, Prodicus is the author of the theory of religion later known as Euhemerism, which claims that the gods were originally human beings who were deified because of their great achievements.

See also: SOPHISTS

References and further reading

Guthrie, W.K.C. (1969) *A History of Greek Philosophy*, vol. 3, Cambridge: Cambridge University Press; part of vol. 3 repr. as *The Sophists*, Cambridge: Cambridge University Press, 1971. (Full and scholarly account.)

Henrichs, A. (1975) 'Two Doxographical Notes: Democritus and Prodicus on Religion', *Harvard Studies in Classical Philology* 79: 93–123. (Discussion of key texts on Prodicus' theological thesis.)

—— (1984) 'The Sophists and Hellenistic Religion: Prodicus as the Spiritual Father of the Isis Aretologies', *Harvard Studies in Classical Philology* 88: 139–58. (Prodicus' theological thesis and its influence.)

Kerferd, G.B. (1981) *The Sophistic Movement*, Cambridge: Cambridge University Press. (A briefer, more personal interpretation than Guthrie (1969).)

* Plato (c.386–380 BC) *Protagoras*, trans. C.C.W. Taylor, Oxford: Oxford University Press, 2nd edn, 1991. (Shows Prodicus in conversation with Socrates, Protagoras and others. Includes a commentary; Prodicus appears in the gathering of famous Sophists.)

* Prodicus (fl. late 5th century BC) 'Fragments', in H. Diels and W. Kranz (eds) *Die Fragmente der Vorsokratiker* (Fragments of the Presocratics), Berlin: Weidmann, 6th edn, 1952, vol. 2, 380–. (The standard collection of the ancient sources in the original languages both fragments and testimonia, the latter designated with 'A'; includes Greek texts of the fragments with translation in German.)

Sprague, R.K. (ed.) (1972) *The Older Sophists*, Columbia, SC: University of South Carolina Press, 70–85. (Full English translation of the fragments and testimonia from Diels and Kranz (1952).)

* Xenophon (*c*.360 BC), *Memorabilia*, trans. E.C. Marchant, Loeb Classical Library, Cambridge, MA: Harvard University Press and London: Heinemann, 1923, II 1.21–34. (Greek text with English translation; Prodicus' 'Choice of Heracles' is at II 1.21–34.)

CHARLES H. KAHN

PROFESSIONAL ETHICS

Professional ethics is concerned with the values appropriate to certain kinds of occupational activity, such as medicine and law, which have been defined traditionally in terms of a body of knowledge and an ideal of service to the community; and in which individual professionals have a high degree of autonomy in their practice. The class of occupations aiming to achieve recognition as professions has increased to include, for example, nursing, while at the same time social and political developments have led to criticism of and challenge to the concepts of professions and professionalism. Problems in professional ethics include both regulation of the professional-client relationship and the role and status of professions in society. A central question for ethics is whether there are values or virtues specific to particular professions or whether the standards of ordinary morality are applicable.

1   **What is a profession?**
2   **Professional ethics: the problems**
3   **Theoretical approaches: external and internal**

1   What is a profession?

The term 'profession' is used in different senses. In a wide sense it simply means someone's occupation; in a narrower sense it refers to a certain kind of activity, one carrying with it a certain status and associated with a particular ethic. Traditionally a profession has been marked out by a body of knowledge, mastery of which (at least partly) regulated entrance to its ranks; and by an ideal of service (see Airaksinen 1994). Since the body of knowledge had the potential to confer power, money and status, professionals were expected to use their skills for the benefit of the community. Those groups which have long been secure in their recognition as professions, the so-called liberal or learned professions such as medicine, divinity and the

law, have also been characterized by a considerable degree of authority and autonomy in their practice. The epithet 'liberal' emphasized their suitability for the 'free man'; 'learned' brought out their relationship to a body of knowledge. The fact that professionals are said to 'practise' rather than 'work' is itself significant in reinforcing their autonomy and status. Along with the autonomy of the individual professional, professional bodies have also been accorded a significant degree of autonomy in controlling both access to the profession and professional conduct.

Eliot Freidson (1994) outlines the problems of defining 'profession' in terms of a number of characteristics or traits and considers instead a definition in terms of process, that is, how particular occupational groups gain professional status. He argues, however, that this covertly defines a profession as an occupation that has gained professional status. Freidson's view is that the concept of 'profession' is one that is tied to particular socio-cultural conditions, namely Anglo-American industrial nations which associate status with occupation, rather than with education, as is more common, he claims, in other European countries.

The traditional classification of professions has been subject to two contrasting trends: first, the attempt by some groups for recognition as professions or neo-professions; and second, challenge to the notion of professionalism either because of its conceptual inadequacy, as noted by Freidson, or on the grounds of its social consequences.

Nursing is a prominent example of an activity which has aimed at recognition as a profession, in its struggle to distance nurses from the image of handmaiden and to advance towards their acceptance as accountable professionals (see NURSING ETHICS); to discard the metaphor of loyalty and take up that of advocacy (see Winslow 1984). In such struggles, the concepts of professional autonomy and accountability play a part along with the identification of a body of knowledge.

Coinciding with a move on the part of some groups to become recognized as professions, there has been a challenge to the concepts of 'profession' and 'professionalism', and an attempt to replace the focus on the concept of profession with one of a set of competences, in other words, to concentrate on what people do and achieve rather than on their status. One reason for this has been that critical, reflective professionals, with autonomy over their practice, may be seen as a threat (see Williams 1996). A second reason is connected with the potential for professions to become self-serving elites (see Freidson 1994; Illich 1977). Yet a third is the increase in criticism if not litigiousness of more knowledgeable clients. Williams contrasts the professional approach and the competence-based approach in the following way: 'Competent workers are content to be described as such, and trainers do not try to push them any further, while reflective practitioners aspire to research their own practice and agencies' (Williams 1996: 8).

What is not in dispute between the two approaches is an attempt to distance what is required from incompetence. J.K. Davis (1991), for example, has argued that for professionals it would not be sufficient that a client was satisfied, if the professionals themselves felt that the service was below standard. For the professional, however, it is more than simply doing a competent job: a worker becomes a professional by professing reasons for doing their work in a certain way.

2 Professional ethics: the problems

Problems of professional ethics fall into two broad categories, but both arise essentially from professional power. The first is concerned with the professional-client relationship, while the second relates to the role of professions and professionals in society as a whole.

Although an ideal of service is supposed to provide a safeguard to promote the use of professional expertise to help rather than harm, specialist knowledge, to which professionals have access and clients do not, does give power to the professional, and the client is thus placed in a vulnerable position. One caveat however is that the paradigm of a relationship between two individuals is inadequate because it overlooks those professions which do not conform to this pattern, such as teaching, which may be but commonly is not done on a one-to-one basis (see Langan 1991).

The most thorough discussion of the professional-client relationship has taken place in relation to the medical profession, with regard both to the feasibility of applying traditional ethical theories to the problems of medical practice and to the development of a set of principles specific to the context of the relationship between health care professional and patient, as in Beauchamp and Childress' principles of biomedical ethics (1979) – autonomy, beneficence, nonmaleficence and justice. A question about the use of power in the medical context would be whether practitioners should use their expertise to decide, beneficently, what is in the patient's interest, or provide information to enable the patient to take an autonomous decision (see MEDICAL ETHICS §2).

The second category of problems is more concerned with the role and image of professionals in society. While it may be true that there has always been a tendency towards distrust of professionals,

this has been exacerbated by social and political developments (see Pellegrino 1991). The trend towards client autonomy, attempts by government to curb the independence and privilege of professionals, and media criticism have all had their effect. Darryl Koehn (1994) adds to this list the assault of academic disciplines such as sociology and philosophy. The sociological critique has suggested that professions, rather than being essentially moral enterprises, are in fact effective monopolistic institutions and that the professed commitment to ethical ideals, rather than conferring legitimacy on the profession, is nothing more than ideology. Ivan Illich has termed the mid-twentieth century the age of 'disabling' professions: far from using their knowledge to serve, they have become forms of control, claiming the authority to determine human needs. 'Homes are transformed into hygienic apartments where one cannot be born, cannot be sick and cannot die decently' (Illich 1977: 27).

Philosophers have taken issue with a self-derived ethic which permits professionals to be guided by standards other than those of ordinary morality. 'Problems in professional ethics typically arise when the values dominant within particular professions come into conflict with other values in the course of practice. Professionals are likely to perceive these values as dominant where others may not' (Goldman 1992: 1018). The possibility of self-derivation is linked with the autonomy of professional bodies in determining standards of practice. A self-derived ethic might take one of two forms. In one form it is associated with the idea that there are certain ways of behaving appropriate to different roles, which diverge from those suited to people who do not fill that role. For example, it might be argued that a lawyer is under an obligation, arising out of the lawyer's role, to achieve the best result for a client even if that conflicts with what they believe as a private individual.

> I remember a custody case for a most disagreeable man whose wife had left him with the children. I remember reducing her to floods of tears in the witness box and I felt very badly about it because I thought she was a very nice woman, which she was, and her husband was a shit. On professional grounds I knew I had done a really good job. But as a father of young children I really thought that the right result hadn't been achieved.
>
> (Quoted in Chadwick 1991)

It is possible to interpret this quotation in different ways. It might be seen either as a clash between professional standards and 'ordinary' morality, or as a conflict between two different moral viewpoints: the view that one's duty is to see justice done and the view that one's duty is to the client and the court.

The second form in which a self-derived ethic might find expression is in a code of professional conduct or code of ethics. The possession of a code of professional conduct has been pivotal in debates about what constitutes a profession. Such a code can fulfil a variety of functions (see Chadwick 1992): offering a public statement of ideals and values; providing a disciplinary mechanism for a professional body; reassuring the public that the profession upholds certain standards; and educating members of the profession to 'think like' others in the group (see Davis, M. 1991).

The standards incorporated in a code may be either higher or lower than the standards of ordinary morality. Professionals have traditionally been prevented from doing things which people in other spheres of activity are permitted to do, such as advertising. This arises out of the purported commitment to serve first the interests of clients, rather than their own profit. On the other hand this same commitment can act as a shield to protect professionals from the criticism that they do things which would be frowned on in terms of ordinary morality, such as lying to clients or physically hurting them in order to promote some further end identifiable as being in the client's interests (see Hayry and Hayry 1994).

Criticism of a self-derived professional ethic, whether in the form of role ethics or a code of conduct, is based on arguments that if an action is morally right it should be susceptible of justification by the same moral arguments that apply to the behaviour of any other member of society – professionals should not require special ethical norms to be determined by themselves. For it is not clear how such norms could be justified if not by common moral principles (see Goldman 1992).

If this point is accepted, however, there are arguments in favour of having, if not a self-derived ethic, at least an ethic specific to a given professional group, in order to promote consistency among practitioners rather than leaving moral judgment to the fallible individual alone. Even if it is acknowledged that the individual practitioner has autonomy in their practice, the requirements of accountability and a set of defined standards has the result that the practitioner may literally be called to 'give an account' of themselves and their practice in terms that their professional peers will recognize (see Holdsworth 1994). This arguably affords more protection than the absence of professionally defined norms but does not constitute an argument for dispensing with accountability to society as well.

Sociological and philosophical criticism have constituted aspects of a phenomenon which might be called the challenge to the ethics of trust in the professions (see TRUST). Traditionally the professional–client relationship has been regarded as a fiduciary one, in which the professional is worthy of trust and the client places trust in the professional. In the late 1980s and early 1990s, however, the ethics of trust was challenged. In the light of these challenges the question arises whether the appropriate response is to turn to an 'ethics of distrust' (see Pellegrino 1991). An ethic of distrust would proceed by attempting to regulate more closely the activities of professionals, by increased external monitoring and demands for accountability. According to one view this approach wins the day by default because the notion of an ethics of trust is not only difficult to sustain: it is actually incoherent.

Robert Veatch (1991) attacks what he sees as the three arguments supporting an ethic of trust: (1) that professionals serve the client's interest; (2) that professionals can present value-free facts to the client; and (3) that professionals should act on a set of virtues inherent in the profession. Veatch argues that modern professionals ought not to know what the client's interests really are – the most they can know is what the client's interests are in one particular area of life. Whereas medical professionals might be concerned primarily with promoting health, for example, health might not be the top priority for a patient (see Goldman 1992). Veatch also argues both that professionals cannot present value-free facts and that it is a serious mistake to think that any given profession is associated with one particular conception of virtue. For example, Talmudic and libertarian lawyers will be informed by different conceptions of the appropriate virtues.

A less pessimistic approach is to investigate the possibility of grounding trust in the professions anew. Koehn has argued that this is urgent because professions represent the mechanism chosen by Anglo-American morality for providing people with goods such as health and justice, and if professionals are not trustworthy, where are we to turn for help? For health and justice are not goods that are readily dispensed with. For Koehn, the challenge is to show not only that there are grounds for trust in the professions because they provide people with such goods, but also that they do not violate the requirements of ordinary morality.

3 Theoretical approaches: external and internal

How are the ethical questions to be addressed? The central issue seems to be the contrast between the external and internal perspectives. The external approach would be to take a normative theory, such as Kantianism or utilitarianism, and apply it to the issues arising in the professional–client encounter and the social role of professionals (see KANTIAN ETHICS; UTILITARIANISM). The alternative would be to examine whether, rather than applying such an external standard, there are values internal to particular professions. A feminist ethic of care could count as either external or internal according to how it was interpreted – whether, for example, an ethic of care provides a framework for addressing problems or whether it perceives care as a virtue inherent in certain professions (see Curzer 1993) (see FEMINIST ETHICS §1; NURSING ETHICS).

Providing an example of the application of an external theoretical framework, Richard Tur (1994) suggests that the standard conception of the lawyer's role arises from the political philosophy of liberalism with its neutrality concerning ideas of the good life, and is associated with the moral philosophy of utilitarianism (see LIBERALISM). The application of utilitarianism suggests both that the good lawyer is one who pursues the objectives of clients effectively, and that doing this under the adversarial system promotes the best interests of society as a whole. This is both because the adversarial system is justified in terms of facilitating the emergence of truth and because to allow individuals to pursue their own view of the good life will maximize social benefits.

The internal approach, on the other hand, might attempt to derive values internal to specific professions by examining the point of those professions. Rather than accepting them as Illich's 'dominant' professions that take it upon themselves to define human need, the question to ask is what pre-existing human need or value do and should they serve? This quest might take different forms. The identification of health and justice as goods that cannot readily be dispensed with, because they may be needed by vulnerable people, has been mentioned. Or there might be an argument for some intrinsic or 'transcendent' values embedded in a professional activity. In the case of law, Tur suggests innocence as an internal value that has implications for specific actions in practice – if innocence is non-negotiable then plea bargaining becomes unethical. Third, knowing the point of a practice such as a professional activity might point the way to virtues internal to the practice of that activity. The virtuous doctor and the virtuous lawyer will not need to apply an ethical theory such as engaging in a utilitarian calculation. As virtuous practitioners they will be able to see what is required in particular situations (see VIRTUE ETHICS; VIRTUES AND VICES).

On this view the virtues of a profession will be defined by reference to the meaning of the practice in question. This would facilitate an answer to the question, for example, of whether nursing ethics is distinct from medical ethics. The central issue that remains unresolved is whether the tension between a relativistic and a universalistic approach to professional ethics can be mediated by an appeal to the unity of the virtues in the moral life (see Meilander 1991) (see MORAL RELATIVISM; UNIVERSALISM IN ETHICS).

See also: APPLIED ETHICS; BUSINESS ETHICS; ENGINEERING AND ETHICS; JOURNALISM, ETHICS OF; MEDICAL ETHICS; RESPONSIBILITIES OF SCIENTISTS AND INTELLECTUALS; TECHNOLOGY AND ETHICS

References and further reading

* Airaksinen, T. (1994) 'Service and science in professional life', in R.F. Chadwick (ed.) *Ethics and the Professions*, Aldershot: Avebury, 1–3. (On issues concerning the human genome project.)

* Beauchamp, T.L. and Childress, J.F. (1979) *Principles of Biomedical Ethics*, New York: Oxford University Press; 4th edn, 1994. (Classic text on the four principles of biomedical ethics – autonomy, beneficence, nonmaleficence and justice.)

* Chadwick, R. (1991) 'Is There a Difference Between Standards and Ethics?', *Journal of Advances in Health and Nursing Care* 1: 75–89. (Discusses the difference between ethics and the standards defined by a profession.)

* —— (1992) 'The function of corporate codes of ethics', in *Business Ethics: Contributing to Business Success*, Sheffield: Sheffield Business School, 79–87. (Overview of the functions of codes.)

* Curzer, H.J. (1993) 'Is care a virtue for health care professionals?', *Journal of Medicine and Philosophy* 18 (1): 51–69. (A critique of care as a virtue.)

* Davis, J.K. (1991) 'Professions, Trades and the Obligation to Inform', *Journal of Applied Philosophy* 8 (2): 167–76. (Distinguishes between professionals and workers in trades.)

* Davis, M. (1991) 'Thinking Like an Engineer: the place of a Code of Ethics in the Practice of a Profession', *Philosophy and Public Affairs* 1 (20). (Analysis of a particular function of codes with reference to a specific example.)

* Freidson, E. (1994) *Professionalism Reborn: Theory, Prophecy and Policy*, Oxford: Polity Press. (On the concept of profession and the future of professionalism.)

* Goldman, A. (1992) 'Professional Ethics', in L.C. Becker (ed.) *Encyclopedia of Ethics*, Chicago, IL

and London: St James Press, 1018–20. (Introductory article.)

* Hayry, H. and Hayry, M. (1994) 'The Nature and Role of Professional Codes in Modern Society', in R.F. Chadwick (ed.) *Ethics and the Professions*, Aldershot: Avebury, 136–44. (Analysis of the role of codes.)

* Holdsworth, D. (1994) 'Accountability: the Obligation to Lay Oneself Open to Criticism', in R.F. Chadwick (ed.) *Ethics and the Professions*, Aldershot: Avebury, 58–87. (Analysis of the notion of accountability.)

* Illich, I. (1977) *Disabling Professions*, London: Marion Boyars. (A critique of professional authority.)

* Koehn, D. (1994) *The Ground of Professional Ethics*, London: Routledge. (Attempts to justify trust in the professions with reference to medicine, law and the ministry.)

* Langan, J. (1991) 'Professional Paradigms', in E.D. Pellegrino, *et al.* (eds) *Ethics, Trust, and the Professions: Philosophical and Cultural Aspects*, Washington, DC: Georgetown University Press, 221–35. (Points out the limitations of the paradigm of the professional–client relationship as one between two individuals.)

* Meilaender, G. (1991) 'Are There Virtues Inherent in a Profession?', in E.D. Pellegrino, *et al.* (eds) *Ethics, Trust, and the Professions: Philosophical and Cultural Aspects*, Washington, DC: Georgetown University Press, 139–55. (Compares views of professional ethics with reference to Oakeshott's forms of moral life.)

* Pellegrino, E.D. (1991) 'Trust and Distrust in Professional Ethics', in E.D. Pellegrino, *et al.* (eds) *Ethics, Trust, and the Professions: Philosophical and Cultural Aspects*, Washington, DC: Georgetown University Press, 69–85. (Explores the issues in the choice between an ethics of trust and an ethics of distrust in professional ethics.)

* Tur, R.H.S. (1994) 'Accountability and Lawyers', in R.F. Chadwick (ed.) *Ethics and the Professions*, Aldershot: Avebury, 58–87. (Contrasts external and internal values with reference to law.)

* Veatch, R. (1991) 'Is Trust of Professionals a Coherent Concept?', in E.D. Pellegrino, *et al.* (eds) *Ethics, Trust, and the Professions: Philosophical and Cultural Aspects*, Washington, DC: Georgetown University Press, 159–69. (Argues against an ethics of trust.)

* Williams, B. (1996) *Freedom on Probation: a case study of the Home Office enforced changes to the University education and training of probation officers*. (Considers the challenge to the notion of
professionalism with special reference to a specific case study.)

* Winslow, G. (1984) 'From Loyalty to Advocacy: A New Metaphor for Nursing', *Hastings Center Report* 14 (3): 32–40. (Discussion specifically relevant to professionalization of nursing.)

RUTH CHADWICK

PROFIAT DURAN *see* DURAN, PROFIAT

PROJECTIVISM

'Projectivism' is used of philosophies that agree with Hume that 'the mind has a great propensity to spread itself on the world', that what is in fact an aspect of our own experience or of our own mental organization is treated as a feature of the objective order of things. Such philosophies distinguish between nature as it really is, and nature as we experience it as being. The way we experience it as being is thought of as partly a reflection or projection of our own natures. The projectivist might take as a motto the saying that beauty lies in the eye of the beholder, and seeks to develop the idea and explore its implications.

The theme is a constant in the arguments of the Greek sceptics, and becomes almost orthodox in the modern era. In Hume it is not only beauty that lies in the eye (or mind) of the beholder, but also virtue, and causation. In Kant the entire spatio-temporal order is not read from nature, but read into it as a reflection of the organization of our minds. In the twentieth century it has been especially non-cognitive and expressivist theories of ethics that have adopted the metaphor, it being fairly easy to see how we might externalize or project various sentiments and attitudes onto their objects. But causation, probability, necessity, the stances we take towards each other as persons, even the temporal order of events and the simplicity of scientific theory have also been candidates for projective treatment.

1 Mechanisms
2 Consequences
3 A real debate?

1 Mechanisms

Projective theories recognize the role of our own natures in shaping the judgments we make. They also promise useful metaphysical economies, by seeing us as responding to a world with less in it than is needed if we think that to every judgment there corresponds an independent property of things. They may therefore be motivated in a number of ways. On the side of metaphysics we may have concerns that if the real world is conceived in some special way, we introduce mysterious properties with equally mysterious relations to other properties. Or, we may have epistemological worries about the ways we know of the independent properties. On the side of the subject we might want to recognize that the judgments in question have special relations to action or motivation or emotion, and we might find this inexplicable if we see ourselves as simply cognizing an independent order of facts. Projectivism is therefore best seen as an explanatory theory, and accepting a projective theory itself manifests the commitment that some aspect of the world is not as independent of us as we might think.

Within the broad characterization there are many different accounts of the mechanisms of projection, of the consequences of a projective theory and of the method whereby we should assess whether a projective theory is appropriate in one area or another. Perhaps the most simple and forthright combination of doctrines would be that the mechanism is one of displacing, or relocating, what is in fact a feature of our experience, and making it into a feature of the world. The consequence is that we make a mistake, erroneously treating the world as containing features that it does not really contain (an error theory). The appropriate method is then to sift through the evidence that such a displacement actually occurs, and to decide whether we can live with the thought that some area of our judgment is thoroughly entangled in error. A theory of this form is found in the treatment of colour by Cartesian philosophers such as MALEBRANCHE and ARNAULD. Colours are found only in the mind; the world itself is not coloured, but we naturally treat it as if it is. The answer to the question whether this makes God, who gives us this nature, a deceiver, is that it is good for us that we make the displacement, in the same way that it is good that we feel pains in our limbs: the mistake has a practical benefit. In more modern terms, colour vision is a useful adaptation to a world that is not coloured.

However, several features of this way of thinking may be questioned without departing from the projective model. We might deny that the mechanism is one of literal displacement. Perhaps the mind manages to make the world look as though some things have beauty, for example, without the really beautiful objects being in the mind itself; instead, some kind of pleasure or delight is objectified, it then appearing that there is a feature of things correlated with it. There would be no real or true bearer of beauty in the mental world but only the real, non-aesthetic properties of the object, the pleasure or delight that these arouse and the propensity we have to voice that pleasure by describing the object as beautiful. Theories of this tripartite kind are more commonly called projective in the contemporary idiom.

Historical examples include Spinoza's view that while everything is really necessary, we feel our own ignorance when faced with the course of events and voice it by describing events as contingent. There is Hume's view that the real object of perception is the regular pattern of events, although faced with this we 'make no scruple' of foretelling one event upon the occurrence of another, and voice this by describing them as causally connected. There is equally Hume's view that, faced with some features of character such as temperance and cheerfulness, the mind feels a pleasure which it voices by deeming those features virtues. When we do this we 'gild or stain' objects with the 'colours borrowed from internal sentiment', and thereby 'erect in a manner a new creation' (see HUME, D.). In Kant, apart from what is said about space and time, there is his attitude to the judgment of beauty – that it essentially voices a felt delight, not prompted by a literal perception of beauty (see KANT, I.).

In the twentieth century, F.P. RAMSEY and Bruno De Finetti held that talk of probabilities is a projection, not because events in the mental world are alone subject to probability, but because they saw such talk as voicing our degrees of confidence in response to observed frequencies of events. Also in Ramsey, to think of a regularity as a natural law is not to see it as somehow fixed by some special and mysterious locking device, but to give it a certain dignity as part of the system with which we meet the future. The emotive theory of ethics, designed to make a place for ethics despite its being neither empirical nor issuing in truths of logic, is a central example of the Humean approach (see EMOTIVISM). Other examples occur in the works of the later WITTGENSTEIN.

When something is described as nice, sublime, good or whatever, projective theories have traditionally found it important to locate the projected reaction, in the first instance, independently of describing it as 'whatever you feel'. If what you feel can only be identified as a tendency to make the judgment, then it is easy to think that no gain has been made. For if we are sincere, whenever we make a judgment we express a tendency to make the judgment. Seen this way there is an obligation on projectivists to identify the reaction in other terms: classic suggestions include a felt pleasure (lying behind judgments of beauty), a particular pressure on choice and action (behind ethical judgment), degrees of confidence (behind probabilities), willingness to rely on a regularity (behind seeing it as causal in nature) and so on.

2   Consequences

Each of the mechanisms outlined may suggest that some kind of error is involved. The stories bear some affinity to the familiar thought that an emotion may be incorrectly projected upon a thing, as when one nostalgically invests past events with an illusory glamour or perfection. However in the philosophical examples, it is not clear that we make any error when we project. We might think that we are deceived by our senses when we take the world as coloured, or by our passions when we take things to be beautiful, or by our degrees of confidence when we find events probable. But the alternative approach is that there is no question of error. All that is involved is a natural and desirable way of experiencing the world, and the fact that the categories involved have the projective explanation does not infect them with mistake. Discovering the mind-dependence of colours, for example, need not be presented as discovering that the world is not really coloured. It is just that the story behind the fact that it is coloured has its origin in the structure of our visual responses. To return to the analogy with the pain in the foot: it is not obviously an error to locate the pain in the foot (as it would be if the pain were really somewhere else, such as in the head).

If the metaphor of projection is dissociated from the idea of error, then it must be asked how much ordinary thought is compatible with the explanation. In ethics this question has proved especially controversial. To many writers it has seemed that the independent claim made on us by such things as moral obligation and duty becomes softened and lost if those categories are projections of attitudes or stances that we ourselves have taken up. The spectre arises that the explanation of the commitment in fact undermines it, so that there is a disharmony between ethics as it feels to the subject, and the philosophical appreciation of what it actually is. Others have argued that this is a mistake akin to worrying whether ethics is possible without God. There is no reason for the feeling of obligation to wane if it is revealed for what it is – a feeling – any more than there is reason for us to stop finding things funny when we recognize the subjective nature of that reaction. 'Quasi-realism' is a title invented to describe the attempt to reconcile

projective theories with the appearances of independent (and even demanding) fact in such areas.

One focus for the kind of debate that arises is the notion of knowledge. It is frequently thought that a projective theory should deny that there is real knowledge to be had in an area. Thus a common title for the position is 'noncognitivism', and many projectivists have been content to accept it. However, if projectivism about colour rejects the error theory, then it ought to be able to say not only that mail boxes in Britain are red, but that we know that they are. The force of saying this will be that there is no real possibility of an improved view of them, revealing that our original colour judgment was deficient – as it would be due to inadequate light, or a poor glimpse. Similarly in ethics, a projectivist may not only say that ingratitude is a vice, but that we know that ingratitude is a vice, again meaning that this judgment is secure enough for there to be no real chance of it being abandoned, whatever improvements in our moral sensibilities come about ('improvement' not meaning convergence on some antecedent truth, but simply better use of the virtues we already recognize: care, attention, imagination, sympathy). Once this is the landscape, it is hard to find simple ways of assessing projective theories.

3   A real debate?

Discontent may seize upon each of two dualisms, urging that projectivism magnifies the first, and the second is either underestimated or loses its identity as a distinct picture. The first is that of mind versus the world. In the case of colour, projectivism seems to depend upon this being a sharp division, with the issue being that of where the original place for colour is found – inside or outside, as it were. If projectivism in any area similarly depends upon separating how things are with one's mental life from how things are in the world, then it implies a highly controversial dualism, and may fall to a more unified picture of our lives in the world. This criticism may carry more weight in some areas than others. In the colour case, it may well be that proper attention to the way perception of colour, understood not as simply arousal of a sensation but as an engagement with the world, undermines the Cartesian story.

In the case of ethics, or modal judgment, or statements of law or probability, dualism does not seem to be the issue, since the non-representative nature of the basic responses is not a consequence of a split between mind and the world, but rather a consequence of distinguishing different aspects of the way we meet the world. This however introduces the second dualism, which is that of representation or description on one side, versus the reactions and responses that the projectivist needs to start with. Thus we have already touched on the apparent need for a projective theory to identify the reaction we project, at least initially, as something other than simply a judgment. But critics have frequently complained that the reactions cannot in fact be identified with the necessary precision without invoking the very vocabulary that needs to be avoided. For example, suppose we describe the state projected in making a positive ethical judgment as one of approval, the critic will say that approval is not a primitive feeling or sensation, but a highly complex state which is possible only to people already embedded in ethical practice. One reply is to say that we have enough grip of the primitive reactions (anger, guilt, willingness to succumb to pressure from others) in question to see our practices as based on them or developed out of them. Provided this rational reconstruction of the activity of moralizing is possible, a projectivist may grasp the nettle and put up with the apparent circularity: what is projected when we say that something is good may simply not be identifiable in any terms except those from the ethical family. Yet provided we can see how we got involved with this family, all may be well.

If the fundamental state of mind is not really one of making a judgment, then how can it properly acquire the trappings of judgment? A sharp form of this problem, originally aired by Frege, points to the numerous things we can do with judgments apart from voice them, and asks the projectivist to explain (see FREGE, G.). For example, if saying that feminism is a good thing voices an attitude to feminism, what is said by 'if feminism is a good thing, we should employ more women' or 'feminism might be a good thing, but I am not sure', where no attitude is voiced? Although this problem has been attacked head-on, it is still often felt that a 'Fregean abyss' separates judgments with content from the projectivist's ingredients. On the other hand, if the abyss can be crossed, then one might worry about the point of starting with a non-representative response in the first place. Here again the projectivist need not give in, for even if our basic responses are essentially intentional, purporting to represent properties of things, nevertheless there is scope for different theories of how they evolve to be that way, and the basic notion of the objectification of a response may well remain the central ingredient in any such explanation.

See also: RELATIVISM

References and further reading

Blackburn, S. (1993) *Essays in Quasi-Realism*, New York: Oxford University Press. (Chaps 5 and 6 locate some of the issues and introduce the task for a quasi-realist theory based on projectivism.)

Gibbard, A. (1990) *Wise Choices, Apt Feelings*, Cambridge, MA: Harvard University Press. (The most impressive overall theory of normative judgment yet to appear.)

Hume, D. (1748) *Enquiry Concerning the Principles of Morals*, ed. L.A. Selby-Bigge, Oxford: Clarendon Press, 1978. (Eminently readable, and the classic introduction of the metaphor of gilding and staining the world. See especially the first Appendix.)

Kant, I. (1790) *The Critique of Judgement*, trans. J.C. Meredith, London: Oxford University Press, 1927. (Not so eminently readable: a sustained effort to explain how the objective order reflects the categories imposed by the mind.)

Ramsey, F.P. (1927) 'Facts and Propositions', in *Foundations – Essays in Philosophy, Logic, Mathematics and Economics*, ed. D.H. Mellor, London: Routledge & Kegan Paul, 1978. (The first modern philosopher to develop the idea that the issue is not truth, but the nature of judgment.)

Stevenson, C.L. (1945) *Ethics and Language*, New Haven, CT: Yale University Press. (An old but classic investigation of emotivism as a theory of ethics.)

Wittgenstein, L. (1956) *Remarks on the Foundations of Mathematics*, Oxford: Blackwell. (A disjointed but deep and impressive attempt to loosen the grip of realism about mathematical truth and necessity.)

SIMON BLACKBURN

PROMISING

Promising is often seen as a social practice with specific rules, determining when a promise has been made and requiring that duly made promises be kept. Accordingly, many philosophers have sought to explain the obligation to keep a promise by appealing to a duty to abide by such rules, whether because of the social benefits of the practice or because fairness requires one to abide by it. Others see breaking a promise as a direct wrong to the person whose expectations are disappointed.

Since one can be obliged to keep a promise even when some other course of action would produce greater happiness (or better consequences as measured by some other standard), the obligation to keep a promise cannot be derived simply from the beneficial consequences of doing so (see CONSEQUENTIALISM). In order to explain this obligation, many philosophers have been drawn to the idea that promising is a social practice whose rules, including the rule that promises must in general be kept, we are bound to obey. They have, however, offered different accounts of why we are so bound.

Hume (1739–40) argued that promises depend on the existence of a convention, although his account differed from most modern ones in emphasizing the *virtue* of fidelity rather than a duty or obligation (see HUME, D. §4). Hume called fidelity (or more generally the virtue of justice, of which fidelity is a central component) an 'artificial' virtue because he thought that the moral approval that an instance of fidelity excites derives from the usefulness of the general pattern of which it is a part rather than from the consequences of that particular action (which may in fact lead to more harm than good).

Practice-based accounts of promises have sometimes been seen as a way of reconciling utilitarian and apparently nonutilitarian intuitions (see UTILITARIANISM). Rawls, for example, argued in 'Two Concepts of Rules' (1955) that (1) promise making, like a move in a game, is an action that presupposes the rules of a certain practice, and (2) while the practice as a whole can be given a utilitarian justification, actions within it can be justified only in ways that its rules specify (see RAWLS, J.). This means, in particular, that the fact that breaking a promise would produce more happiness than keeping it does not count as a justification for breaking it. Practice-based accounts typically involve two parts, corresponding to (1) and (2) above: an account of the social practice of promising and an explanation of the moral authority of this practice. The latter component need not, however, be utilitarian, and in *A Theory of Justice* (1971) Rawls himself offers a nonutilitarian account of this kind. The moral component in this account is the 'principle of fairness', which specifies that someone who voluntarily accepts the benefits of a just social practice is bound to do his or her part in turn, as the rules of that practice specify. It follows, assuming that the rules of the practice of promising are just, that those who help themselves to the benefits of this practice by using it to stabilize agreements are obliged to keep the promises they have made (except where those rules recognize justification for doing otherwise).

On this account, promising is taken to be a particular social institution, on a par with other institutions set up to provide and distribute various 'public goods'. All such institutions face the threat of 'free riding' by people who would like to get the benefits without bearing their share of the costs, and Rawls' appeal to the 'principle of fairness' construes breaking a promise as an instance of the more general wrong of 'free riding' in this way (see DECISION AND GAME THEORY).

But it is not obvious that the wrongs involved in breaking a promise, or making a deceitful promise, are of this general type. They seem more clearly to be wrongs *to* the person to whom the promise is made rather than to all those who contribute to keeping the institution going. Nor is it clear that promising is a social practice of this kind – one that, like a recycling scheme, is aimed at a certain social purpose, defined by certain (somewhat arbitrary) rules, and exists just in so far as the members of a certain group accept these rules as normative. When we try to decide, in a difficult case, whether someone has good reason for failing to fulfil a promise, it does not seem that we are addressing our minds to a kind of social fact, about what the rules of some particular practice are. Moreover, it seems that making a deceitful promise, or failing, without good reason, to keep a promise sincerely made, are wrongs of a kind that can also be committed in other ways without reference to promises or to any other 'practice'. There are many other ways to induce people to rely on us, thereby making it wrong to disappoint them.

This suggests that the wrongs involved in breaking a promise, or in making a deceitful one, belong to a broader class of wrongs having to do with our responsibility for the expectations we create. Practices of agreement-making, where they exist, are one mechanism for creating such expectations, but not the only one. A number of writers have offered 'expectation-based' accounts of promising along these lines. Difficulties faced by such accounts include the problem of explaining how promises can create expectations to begin with without appealing to a notion of obligation that does not arise from expectation, and the problem of explaining how promises can be binding in cases in which no expectation is in fact created (because, for example, the 'promise' that is offered is not believed).

There are obvious similarities between the idea of a promise and that of a legal contract, but there are also important differences. The law of contracts attempts to specify exactly the conditions that must be fulfilled in order for a valid contract to be made. As noted above, however, it is not clear that the morality of promises involves an informal institution with definite rules of this kind. The law of contracts, which deals chiefly with commercial transactions, is concerned primarily with questions of whether compensation is owed and how much, rather than with the obligation to specific performance. In the case of promises, however, our concern is almost wholly with the obligation to perform rather than with determining compensation.

See also: LOGIC OF ETHICAL DISCOURSE §3; TRUST; TRUTHFULNESS

References and further reading

Anscombe, G.E.M. (1978) 'Rules, Rights and Promises', in *Ethics, Religion and Politics, Collected Philosophical Papers*, vol. 3, Minneapolis, MN: University of Minnesota Press. (Argues that the reason someone has to rely on a promise depends on a prior notion of obligation.)

Atiyah, P.S. (1981) *Promises, Morals and the Law*, Oxford: Clarendon Press. (A study of the morality of promises from the point of view of an expert on the law of contracts.)

Cavell, S. (1979) *The Claim of Reason*, New York: Oxford University Press, ch. 9. (Critical discussion of Rawls' account of promising as a practice.)

Fried, C. (1981) *Contract as Promise*, Cambridge, MA: Harvard University Press. (An account of the law of contracts, seen as based on a prior moral idea of promises.)

* Hume, David (1739–40) *A Treatise of Human Nature*, ed. L.A. Selby-Bigge, Oxford: Clarendon Press, 1960, book 3, part II, sections 1, 2, 5. (Classic statement of the view that promises depend on a convention.)

MacCormick, N. (1972) 'Voluntary Obligations and Normative Powers I', *Proceedings of the Aristotelian Society*, supplementary volume 46: 59–78. (An account of promises based on expectation and reliance.)

* Rawls, J. (1955) 'Two Concepts of Rules', *Philosophical Review* 64: 3–32. (Argues that promising is an action defined by a social practice and is therefore governed by the rules of that practice.)

* —— (1971) *A Theory of Justice*, Cambridge, MA: Harvard University Press. (Defends, in §52, the principle of fairness as the basis of the obligation to keep a promise.)

Raz, J. (1972) 'Voluntary Obligations and Normative Powers II', *Proceedings of the Aristotelian Society*, supplementary volume 46: 79–101. (Criticizes MacCormick's view.)

Scanlon, T.M. (1990) 'Promises and Practices', *Philosophy & Public Affairs* 19: 199–226. (Criticizes the idea that promises depend on a social practice and defends an account based on expectation and reliance. Expands on points made in this entry.)

Searle, J. (1964) 'How to Derive "Ought" from "Is"', *Philosophical Review* 73: 43–58; repr. in W.D. Hudson (ed.) *The Is/Ought Question*, London: Macmillan, 1969. (A purported derivation of an 'ought' from an 'is' using the idea of promising as a social institution.)

T.M. SCANLON

PRONOUNS *see* ANAPHORA

PROOF THEORY

Proof theory is a branch of mathematical logic founded by David Hilbert around 1920 to pursue Hilbert's programme. The problems addressed by the programme had already been formulated, in some sense, at the turn of the century, for example, in Hilbert's famous address to the First International Congress of Mathematicians in Paris. They were closely connected to the set-theoretic foundations for analysis investigated by Cantor and Dedekind – in particular, to difficulties with the unrestricted notion of system or set; they were also related to the philosophical conflict with Kronecker on the very nature of mathematics. At that time, the central issue for Hilbert was the 'consistency of sets' in Cantor's sense. Hilbert suggested that the existence of consistent sets, for example, the set of real numbers, could be secured by proving the consistency of a suitable, characterizing axiom system, but indicated only vaguely how to give such proofs model-theoretically. Four years later, Hilbert departed radically from these indications and proposed a novel way of attacking the consistency problem for theories. This approach required, first of all, a strict formalization of mathematics together with logic; then, the syntactic configurations of the joint formalism would be considered as mathematical objects; finally, mathematical arguments would be used to show that contradictory formulas cannot be derived by the logical rules.

This two-pronged approach of developing substantial parts of mathematics in formal theories (set theory, second-order arithmetic, finite type theory and still others) and of proving their consistency (or the consistency of significant sub-theories) was sharpened in lectures beginning in 1917 and then pursued systematically in the 1920s by Hilbert and a group of collaborators including Paul Bernays, Wilhelm Ackermann and John von Neumann. In particular, the formalizability of analysis in a second-order theory was verified by Hilbert in those very early lectures. So it was possible to focus on the second prong, namely to establish the consistency of 'arithmetic' (second-order number theory and set theory) by elementary mathematical, 'finitist' means. This part of the task proved to be much more recalcitrant than expected, and only limited results were obtained. That the limitation was inevitable was explained in 1931 by Gödel's theorems; indeed, they refuted the attempt to establish consistency on a finitist basis – as soon as it was realized that finitist considerations could be carried out in a small fragment of first-order arithmetic. This led to the formulation of a general reductive programme.

Gentzen and Gödel made the first contributions to this programme by establishing the consistency of classical first-order arithmetic – Peano arithmetic (PA) – relative to intuitionistic arithmetic – Heyting arithmetic. In 1936 Gentzen proved the consistency of PA relative to a quantifier-free theory of arithmetic that included transfinite recursion up to the first epsilon number, ε_0; in his 1941 Yale lectures, Gödel proved the consistency of the same theory relative to a theory of computable functionals of finite type. These two fundamental theorems turned out to be most important for subsequent proof-theoretic work. Currently it is known how to analyse, in Gentzen's style, strong subsystems of second-order arithmetic and set theory. The first prong of proof-theoretic investigations, the actual formal development of parts of mathematics, has also been pursued – with a surprising result: the bulk of classical analysis can be developed in theories that are conservative over (fragments of) first-order arithmetic.

1 **Metamathematics**
2 **Hilbert's programme**
3 **Mathematical work**
4 **Logical tools**
5 **Reductive results**
6 **Outlook**

1 Metamathematics

Proof theory is a branch of mathematical logic founded by David Hilbert around 1920 to pursue his programme in the foundations of arithmetic (see HILBERT'S PROGRAMME AND FORMALISM). Consistency is the crucial logical notion connected with Hilbert's investigations. In traditional, Aristotelian logic it was viewed as a semantic notion: two or more statements are consistent if they are simultaneously true under some interpretation. In modern logic there is a syntactic definition that fits complex theories since Frege's *Begriffsschrift* (1879): a set of statements is consistent with respect to a logical calculus if no statement of the form $P \& \neg P$ is derivable from the statements by rules of the calculus. If these definitions are equivalent for a logic we have a significant fact, as the equivalence amounts to the completeness (and

soundness) of the logic's system of rules. The first such completeness theorem was obtained for sentential logic by Paul Bernays (1918) and, independently, by Emil Post (1921); the completeness of predicate logic was proved by Kurt Gödel in 1930. The crucial step in such proofs shows that *syntactic* consistency implies *semantic* consistency. The converse is established quite directly, but involves the notion of truth. Here we have located one central issue that has motivated proof-theoretic investigations: namely, to avoid the uncritical use of the broad concept of classical truth for infinite mathematical structures.

Cantor applied consistency in an informal way to sets. He distinguished, for example in a letter to Dedekind, a consistent from an inconsistent multiplicity: the latter is such 'that the assumption that all of its elements "are together" leads to a contradiction', whereas the elements of the former 'can be thought of without contradiction as "being together"'. Cantor had also conveyed these distinctions by letter to Hilbert in 1897. (See Purkert and Ilgauds (1987) for the text of the letters and Sieg (1990) for the wider historical context.) Hilbert pointed out, both implicitly (1900) and explicitly (1905), that Cantor had not given a rigorous criterion for distinguishing between consistent and inconsistent multiplicities. Hilbert suggested remedying the problem for analysis and giving the proof of the 'existence of the totality of real numbers or – in the terminology of G. Cantor – the proof of the fact that the system of real numbers is a consistent (complete) set' by establishing the consistency of an axiomatic characterization of the real numbers (1900). Indeed, he claimed that consistency could be established 'by a suitable modification of familiar methods'. Hilbert's own hints, partly in unpublished lecture notes, together with remarks by Bernays, make it plausible that he had a model-theoretic proof in mind. This problematic can be traced back to considerations in Dedekind's work (1888) as explicated carefully in his letter to Keferstein, where he asked of his notion 'simply infinite system', 'does such a system *exist* at all in the realms of our ideas? Without a logical proof of existence it would always remain doubtful whether the notion of such a system might not perhaps contain internal contradictions'. Clearly, Dedekind tried to establish consistency by exhibiting a suitable 'logical', that is, set-theoretic, model.

In 1904 Hilbert began to pursue a completely different strategy for giving consistency proofs. His new way of proceeding was still aimed at securing the existence of sets, but intended to exploit the formalizability of the theory at hand. Formalizations had to satisfy requirements stricter than those imposed on the structure of theories by the traditional (Euclidean) axiomatic-deductive method. The additional requirement was the regimentation of inferential steps in proofs: not only did axioms have to be given in advance, but the rules representing steps in mathematical arguments had to be taken from a predetermined list. To avoid a regression in the definition of proof and to achieve intersubjectivity at an absolutely minimal level, the rules had to be 'formal' or 'mechanical' and had to depend only on the syntactic form of statements. Thus, to exclude any ambiguity, a precise and effectively described language was also needed to formalize particular theories; the indications (Hilbert 1905) were very sketchy, however.

The general kind of requirements had been clear to Aristotle and were explicitly formulated by Leibniz; but only Frege, in his *Begriffsschrift*, presented – in addition to an expressively rich language with relations and quantifiers – an adequate logical calculus. Through the formalization of mathematical proofs Frege pursued a clear philosophical aim, namely to recognize the 'epistemological nature' of theorems. In the introduction to his *Grundgesetze der Arithmetik* (see FREGE, G.), he wrote: 'By insisting that the chains of inference do not have any gaps we succeed in bringing to light every axiom, assumption, hypothesis or whatever else you want to call it on which a proof rests; in this way we obtain a basis for judging the epistemological nature of the theorem.' An epistemological analysis of theorems was also aimed for by Hilbert in his work on the foundations of geometry, but done quite differently, relying on a more traditional axiomatic presentation and pushing forward genuinely metamathematical investigations. For the emerging proof-theoretic work the formal aspect Frege had emphasized would be exploited by Hilbert in a distinctively novel way.

Hilbert repeatedly gave courses on the foundations of mathematics in the period 1904 to 1917; the spirit of these lectures is captured in his Zurich talk 'Axiomatisches Denken' (1918). The mathematical development and philosophical clarification of a new consistency programme began to be given only in Hilbert's lectures on *Prinzipien der Mathematik* (Principles of Mathematics) presented in the winter term of 1917/1918. These lectures mark the beginning of the fruitful collaboration with Bernays, who supported Hilbert's preparation in essential ways and also wrote careful notes. The notes of these and later lectures are amazing documents, as one finds in them for the first time a detailed modern presentation of the syntax and informal semantics of predicate logic and of finite type theories. The 1917/1918 notes served as the basis for Hilbert and Ackermann's *Grundzüge der theoretischen Logik* (1928); indeed,

with minor exceptions the notes contain all the material presented in the book. In lectures during the summer term of 1920 and the winter term of 1921/1922, proof theory and the 'finitist consistency programme' emerged.

2 Hilbert's programme

For the purpose of the consistency programme, metamathematics was taken in Hilbert's 1921/1922 lectures to be included in, if not coextensive with, the part of mathematics acceptable to constructivists such as KRONECKER and Brouwer. The point of consistency proofs was no longer to guarantee the existence of sets, but to establish the instrumental usefulness of classical mathematical theories T – say, set theory – with respect to finitist mathematics. That focus rested on the observation that the statement formulating the consistency of T is equivalent to the reflection principle

$$Pr(a, `\sigma`) \Rightarrow \sigma.$$

Here, Pr is the finitist proof predicate for T, σ a finitistically meaningful statement, and 'σ' its translation into the language of T. A finitist consistency proof for T would thus ensure that T is a reliable instrument for the proof of finitist statements. Other important metamathematical issues were the completeness and decidability of theories.

The formalizability of mathematics was obviously crucial for this proof-theoretic approach, and the programmatic goal was seen as a way to circumvent some philosophical issues, for example, concerning the nature of infinite sets in the case of set theory. For these reasons Hilbert's philosophical position is (still) frequently equated with formalism in the sense of Frege's articles 'Über die Grundlagen der Geometrie' (1903, 1906; see FREGE, G.) and of Brouwer's inaugural address 'Intuitionism and Formalism' (1913). Such a view is not completely unsupported by some of Hilbert's polemical remarks during the 1920s, but on balance his philosophical views developed into a sophisticated instrumentalism, if that label is taken in Ernest Nagel's judicious sense (see Nagel 1961). Hilbert's is an instrumentalism emphasizing the contentual motivation of mathematical theories; that is perhaps most clearly expressed in the first chapter of Hilbert and Bernays (1934). A sustained philosophical analysis of proof-theoretic research in the context of broader issues in the philosophy of mathematics was provided by Bernays; his penetrating essays stretch over five decades (see Bernays 1976). Feferman (1988) and Sieg (1988) give complementary accounts; for altogether contrasting approaches, see Detlefsen (1986) and Simpson (1988).

The mathematical work is most remarkable for what it started, as it constitutes the beginnings of modern mathematical logic. Even before the work of Gödel and Gentzen it was rich in accomplishments: consider, as examples, Bernays' completeness proof for sentential logic; the partial solutions to the decision problem (Hilbert's *Entscheidungsproblem*) for predicate logic obtained by Behmann, Bernays, Schönfinkel and Herbrand; and the consistency proofs given by Ackermann, von Neumann and Herbrand. Taking for granted the broader conceptual clarifications and the focus on first-order logic, Herbrand's *'théorème fondamentale'* is perhaps the most significant result on purely logical grounds, but also because of its applicability in consistency proofs. Gödel pointed to its essence when he gave in a 1933 lecture the following formulation of Herbrand's theorem: 'If we take a theory which is constructive in the sense that each existence assertion made in the axioms is covered by a construction, and if we add to this theory the non-constructive notion of existence and all the logical rules concerning it, for example, the law of excluded middle, we shall never get into any contradiction' (see HERBRAND'S THEOREM).

The results obtained in the 1920s, including Herbrand's theorem, were disappointing when measured against the hopes and ambitions of the Hilbert school: Ackermann, von Neumann and Herbrand had established essentially the consistency of first-order arithmetic with a very restricted principle of induction (for quantifier-free formulas). Actual limits on finitist considerations for consistency proofs had been reached; that became clear in 1931 through Gödel's theorems and the realization that finitist proofs could be formalized in a weak fragment of number theory (see GÖDEL'S THEOREMS). Initially, Gödel did not share the view on the limits of finitist reasoning, as is clear from the final remarks in his 'Über formal unentscheidbare Sätze der *Principia Mathematica* und verwandter Systeme I' (On Formally Undecidable Propositions of *Principia Mathematica* and Related Systems) (1931) and contemporaneous correspondence with von Neumann and Herbrand. But by December 1933, when he lectured in Cambridge, Massachusetts, he had changed his position: having isolated a 'system A' – essentially a version of primitive recursive arithmetic (PRA) – he made the following claim: 'Now all the intuitionistic [that is, finitist] proofs complying with the requirements of the system A which have ever been constructed can easily be expressed in the system of classical analysis and even in the system of classical arithmetic, and there are reasons for believing that this will hold for any proof which one will ever be able to construct.'

The solvability of the *Entscheidungsproblem* had been made implausible by Gödel's results, but the actual proof of unsolvability had to wait until 1936 for a conceptual clarification of 'mechanical procedure' or 'algorithm'. Such a clarification was achieved mainly through the work of Church and Turing (see CHURCH'S THESIS; COMPUTABILITY THEORY). A precise notion of mechanical procedure was also needed to prove the incompleteness theorems for *general* 'formal' theories satisfying basic representability and derivability conditions; after all, Gödel had established limits only for (formalizations of) particular theories, such as the system of *Principia Mathematica* and then current axiomatic set theories. In his attempt to characterize a proper extension of the class of primitive recursive functions, Gödel introduced (in his Princeton lectures of 1934) the general recursive functions through an equational calculus (see COMPUTABILITY THEORY §2). The informal concept underlying Gödel's and also Church's approach – calculability of functions in a 'formal' calculus – was carefully analysed by Hilbert and Bernays (1939: supplement 2); they formulated recursiveness conditions for general deductive formalisms and showed that the number-theoretic functions whose values can be calculated in formalisms satisfying these conditions are exactly the general recursive ones.

The impact of the incompleteness theorems on Hilbert's programme was profound and yet limited. On the one hand, as remarked above, they pointed out definite limits of finitist considerations; on the other hand, they left open the possibility of modifying the programme to a *general reductive programme* that was no longer aiming for 'absolute' finitist consistency proofs, but rather for consistency proofs relative to 'appropriate' constructive theories. Before Gödel's results were known, Bernays (1930) had given a detailed and searching analysis of the philosophical aims of Hilbert's proof theory; in the *Postscriptum* published in 1976, Bernays expressed clearly what was lost due to the incompleteness theorems: the sharp distinction between what is intuitive and what is non-intuitive, a distinction that was basic for the proposed philosophical treatment of the problem of the infinite. Thus, it is this particular 'solution' to a philosophical problem that was shown to be impossible.

Work in proof theory continued with the explicit goal of achieving relative consistency proofs. Such work is in a venerable mathematical tradition, as the many examples of significant results show: for example, the consistency of non-Euclidean relative to Euclidean geometry; that of Euclidean geometry relative to analysis; the consistency of set theory with the axiom of choice relative to set theory without it; that of set theory with the negation of the axiom of choice relative to set theory. The mathematical significance of relative consistency proofs is often brought out by sharpening them to conservative extension results. Such results may ensure, for example, that the theories have the same class of provably total functions (see §6). However, the initial motivation for such arguments is most frequently philosophical: one wants to guarantee the coherence of the original theory on an epistemologically distinguished basis. One has to see the specific results that have been obtained in the pursuit of the general reductive programme from this perspective.

3 Mathematical work

The development of the general reductive programme is characterized by modifications of the two-pronged approach of Hilbert's original programme, namely (1) weakening the theories in which parts of mathematics are formalized, and (2) strengthening the theories in which the metamathematical considerations are carried out and, consequently, relative to which constructive consistency proofs can be given. The first modification reaches back to Weyl's *Das Kontinuum* (1918) and culminated in the 1970s, when it was realized that the classical results of mathematical analysis can be obtained in conservative extensions of first-order arithmetic. The second modification started with the work of Gödel and Gentzen in 1933, when they established independently the consistency of classical arithmetic relative to intuitionistic arithmetic; it led in the 1970s and 1980s to consistency proofs of subsystems of second-order arithmetic or, synonymously, subsystems of analysis relative to intuitionistic theories of constructive ordinals. Obviously, only a sketch of some main results can be attempted here.

Second-order arithmetic has been used for some time as a framework for the formal development of classical mathematical analysis; that is, the theory of the continuum set-theoretically described by Dedekind and Cantor. Because of this mathematical adequacy, second-order arithmetic and a variety of subsystems have been thoroughly investigated. The main set-theoretic principles for these systems are the comprehension axiom (CA)

$$(\exists X)(\forall y)(y \in X \Leftrightarrow S(y))$$

and the axiom of choice (AC) in the form

$$(\forall x)(\exists Y)S(x, Y) \Rightarrow (\exists Z)(\forall x)S(x, Z_x),$$

where S is in each case an arbitrary formula of the language and thus may contain set quantifiers; $y \in Z_x$ is defined to mean $\langle y, x \rangle \in Z$. These principles are impredicative, as the sets X and Z whose existence is postulated are in general characterized by reference to all sets of natural numbers. The induction principle is formulated either as a schema or as a second-order axiom

$$(\forall X)(0 \in X \,\&\, (\forall y)(y \in X \Rightarrow y' \in X)$$
$$\Rightarrow (\forall x)x \in X).$$

Theories are denoted by the name of their set-existence principle enclosed in parentheses; thus (CA) names full analysis. If ↾ follows its name, a theory uses the second-order axiom to formalize induction. Two general results are of interest, as they show that second-order arithmetic has a certain robustness: (CA) is proof-theoretically equivalent to Zermelo–Fraenkel set theory without the power-set axiom; (AC) is conservative over (CA) for Π_4^1-formulas and properly stronger, as there is a Π_2^1-instance of AC not provable in (CA). In the presence of full CA, the theories with the induction schema, respectively, the second-order axiom of induction are equivalent, but they can be of strikingly different strength, when the set-existence principles are restricted; for example, $(\Pi_\infty^0\text{-CA})$ ↾ is conservative over Peano arithmetic (PA), whereas $(\Pi_\infty^0\text{-CA})$ proves the consistency of PA.

In 1917/1918 Hilbert and Bernays used ramified type theory with the axiom of reducibility to develop analysis; the published presentation (1939: supplement 4) is based on this early work, but employs full second-order arithmetic as the formal framework. They encouraged developments with restricted means already in 1920, writing of Brouwer and Weyl:

> The positive and fruitful part of the investigations into the foundations of mathematics carried out by these two researchers fits into the mould of the axiomatic method and is exactly in the spirit of this method. For one investigates here, how a part of analysis can be delimited by a certain narrower system of assumptions.
>
> (1920: 34)

Subsystems of analysis are now mainly defined by restricting S in the set-existence schemata to particular classes of formulas. The set-theoretic demands can be reduced dramatically: Hilbert and Bernays' presentation (1939), for example, can be given quite readily in $(\Pi_1^1\text{-CA})$ ↾. Strictly mathematical work continued to accompany work on consistency proofs for subsystems; it had the aim of establishing the mathematical significance of subsystems and made use of work in the constructivist tradition.

By the mid-1970s, through final efforts of Feferman, Friedman and Takeuti, it was clear that classical analysis could be carried out in conservative extensions of number theory, for example, $(\Pi_\infty^0\text{-CA})$ ↾. In this context Friedman suggested pursuing a strategy familiar from investigations of the axiom of choice in set theory; namely, to establish the equivalence of certain set-existence principles with mathematical theorems. This theme is played with surprising variations in Friedman's and Simpson's work on subsystems and gave rise to the enterprise of 'reverse mathematics'. To mention just two, by now classic, examples: CA for arithmetic formulas is equivalent to the theorem that every bounded sequence of reals has a least upper bound and to König's lemma. Friedman introduced a second-order theory WKL_0 that extends primitive recursive arithmetic conservatively for Π_2^0-formulas; the theory is weak, but still provides a very good basis for developing parts of analysis and algebra. Simpson (1988) not only considers the development of mathematics in such a conservative extension of PRA a 'reductionist programme', but equates it with Hilbert's programme. One should recall, however, that Hilbert did not propose to redo all of mathematics in (a conservative extension of) PRA, but rather to justify – via finitist consistency proofs – the use of strong classical theories sufficient for the direct formalization of mathematical practice.

4 Logical tools

Hilbert's central idea for the metamathematical treatment of the consistency problem found its expression in what is known as the ε-calculus and the associated substitution method. Hilbert and Bernays (1939) present what was achieved in its terms; even Herbrand's (difficult) work was recast in terms of the ε-calculus. This tradition was kept up by Tait (1965) and more recently by Mints (1994). However, other logical tools turned out to be more useful for proof-theoretic investigations: Gentzen's sequent calculi (see NATURAL DEDUCTION, TABLEAU AND SEQUENT SYSTEMS §2) and Gödel's so-called *Dialectica* interpretation. In the latter, Gödel used computable functionals of finite type to obtain a reduction of intuitionistic arithmetic (HA); joining this reduction with the consistency of PA relative to HA, a consistency proof relative to the system of these functionals was obtained. Influenced by the considerations of Hilbert (1926), Gödel presented this work in a lecture at Yale in 1941, but published it only in 1958 (see GÖDEL'S THEOREMS). Spector (1962) gave a consistency proof for full classical analysis using bar recursive functionals of finite type; this proof prompted a searching analysis in the *Stanford Report on the Foundations of Analysis* (1963/1964).

Here the focus is on sequent calculi, as they have found the most extensive use and widest applicability.

In the form given to them by Tait (1968), they allow the proof of finite sets of formulas built up from literals (atomic formulas or negations of such), conjunction, disjunction, universal and existential quantification and – depending on the theory – infinitary conjunction and disjunction. Thus, for just first-order logic the basic logical symbols are '$\wedge$', '$\vee$', '$\exists$', '$\forall$' and the rules of the calculi include the following ones, where Γ is used as a syntactic variable ranging over finite sets of formulas, Γ, ϕ stands for the union of Γ and the singleton ϕ, and $a \in P(\Gamma)$ means that the parameter a occurs in one of the formulas in Γ:

$$\text{LA:} \qquad \Gamma, \varphi, \neg\varphi, \qquad \varphi \text{ atomic}$$

$$\wedge: \qquad \frac{\Gamma, \varphi_0 \quad \Gamma, \varphi_1}{\Gamma, \varphi_0 \wedge \varphi_1}$$

$$\vee_i: \qquad \frac{\Gamma, \varphi_i}{\Gamma, \varphi_0 \vee \varphi_1}, \qquad i = 0, 1$$

$$C: \qquad \frac{\Gamma, \varphi \quad \Gamma, \neg\varphi}{\Gamma}$$

$$\forall: \qquad \frac{\Gamma, \varphi a}{\Gamma, (\forall x)\varphi x} \qquad a \notin P(\Gamma)$$

$$\exists: \qquad \frac{\Gamma, \varphi t}{\Gamma, (\exists x)\varphi x}$$

The crucial claim established by Gentzen was his '*Hauptsatz*' or cut-elimination theorem: every derivation in the logical system using the cut rule C can be transformed into a cut-free or normal derivation. Inspecting the rules, one notices that the premises of all the rules (except for C) contain only subformulas of formulas in the conclusion. Consequently, a normal derivation of a sequent Γ contains only subformulas of elements in Γ. This is the crucial subformula property of normal derivations, providing a bound on the complexity of formulas that can occur in a proof of Γ. In Gentzen (1935) this metamathematical fact is established and used to obtain in a most perspicuous way the most far-reaching consistency result that had then been obtained, namely Herbrand's.

For full first-order number theory PA this treatment was extended by GENTZEN (1936) to a partial cut-elimination argument whose termination was established by quantifier-free transfinite induction up to the first epsilon number – $TI(\varepsilon_0)$. Gentzen showed (1943) that this induction schema for every ordinal α less than ε_0 can be established in PA; this is the first 'ordinal analysis' of a formal theory. In the

1950s Lorenzen and, much more extensively, Schütte used infinitary extensions of Gentzen's finitary systems; in particular for the treatment of PA they used the so-called ω-rule that allows one to infer $\Gamma, (\forall x)\phi x$ from the premises $\Gamma, \phi n$ for each natural number n (see NON-CONSTRUCTIVE RULES OF INFERENCE §1). Though derivations are now infinite, PA-derivations can be embedded into finitistically described ones and can be transformed effectively into cut-free derivations; the natural ordinal length of these derivations is bounded by ε_0. Schütte extended these methods to treat systems of ramified analysis RA_α (of order α) and obtained, in particular, ordinal bounds on the length of normal derivations in terms of the Veblen hierarchy of ordinal functions. This work was used in 1963 by Feferman and Schütte independently to characterize the ordinal Γ_0 of predicative analysis, that is, the first ordinal α such that $TI(\alpha)$ cannot be proved in RA_β for β less than α.

5 Reductive results

The mathematical work described in §3 was to a large extent inspired by the attempt to establish the significance of relative consistency proofs and/or to focus on manageable subsystems that might be a proper next target for such proofs. Most of the reductive results mentioned below can be established by the metamathematical tool of the sequent calculi, though some of the original proofs used different techniques.

The Gödel–Gentzen result for number theory can be extended to ramified analysis and also to obtain conservativeness for Π_2^0-formulas. This provides a relative consistency proof, as ramified systems with intuitionistic logic are certainly acceptable constructively (as long as the ordinals along which the systems are iterated are acceptable). In the early 1960s, partly through the study of predicativity, significant subsystems with S restricted to small classes of analytic formulas were isolated, among them $(\Sigma_1^1\text{-AC})$ and $(\Delta_1^1\text{-CA})$. Kreisel pointed out that

$$(\Sigma_1^1\text{-AC}) \supseteq (\Delta_1^1\text{-CA}).$$

Friedman showed that $(\Sigma_1^1\text{-AC})$ is conservative over $(\Delta_1^1\text{-CA})$ for Π_2^1-formulas; that the inclusion is proper was established later by Steel. Indeed, $(\Sigma_1^1\text{-AC})$ is conservative for Π_2^1-formulas over $(\Pi_0^1\text{-CA})_{<\varepsilon_0}$, a theory based on the transfinite iteration of the jump-operator and equivalent to ramified analysis of level less than ε_0. This result, due to Friedman, allowed the determination of the proof-theoretic ordinal of the systems, but it also showed – and this was quite unexpected – that these prima facie impredicative theories were predicative in the sense of Feferman and

Schütte. Feferman (1964) and Kreisel (1968) provide excellent summaries.

Friedman's theorem for $(\Sigma_1^1\text{-AC})$ turned out to be a special case of a general result: $(\Sigma_{n+1}^1\text{-AC})$ is conservative over $(\Pi_n^1\text{-CA})_{<\varepsilon_0}$ for formulas in F_n, where F_0 is Π_2^1, F_1 is Π_3^1, and F_n is Π_4^1 for $n > 1$ (see Friedman 1970). As just explained, the case $n = 0$ was of special interest for the study of predicativity; the case $n = 1$ is also to be placed in the context of foundational investigations. The most immediate context is provided by Feferman (1970), who relates the systems $(\Pi_1^1\text{-CA})_{<\varepsilon_0}$ to the classical theory for (less than ε_0 times iterated) classes defined by generalized inductive definitions. Well-known examples are the classes $\mathbf{O}$ of constructive ordinals and $\mathbf{W}$ of recursive well-founded trees. Between them, Friedman and Feferman reduced the subsystems $(\Sigma_2^1\text{-AC})$ and $(\Delta_2^1\text{-CA})$ to the classical theory of the tree classes $\mathbf{W}_\nu$ with index ν less than ε_0. Feferman (1977) gives a detailed survey of mathematical and proof-theoretic work, including these last results.

Kreisel had introduced intuitionistic theories of iterated inductive definitions in the *Stanford Report* (1963/4); these theories were viewed as codifying constructive principles that might be used in consistency proofs for subsystems of analysis. Feferman's and Friedman's work described above established connections between subsystems of analysis and classical theories of inductive definitions, making a crucial step towards answering the major problem posed by Kreisel (1968): reduce $(\Sigma_2^1\text{-AC})$ to a constructive theory of inductive definitions. That would provide, as Kreisel put it, 'a solution to Hilbert's problem for the subsystem of analysis...$(\Sigma_2^1\text{-AC})$'. The classical theories for classes defined by generalized inductive definitions are reducible to intuitionistic theories for accessible such classes. This allowed, in particular, a satisfactory solution of Kreisel's open problem, as $(\Sigma_2^1\text{-AC})$ was shown to be reducible to $(ID)_{<\varepsilon_0}(\mathbf{O})$, the intuitionistic theory of constructive number classes with index less than ε_0. These and many further results were obtained by Buchholz et al. (1981); in particular, the ordinal analysis of the subsystems at hand. This work was influenced by earlier considerations of Howard, Tait and Takeuti.

Subsystems of set theory, in particular of admissible set theory, were used by Jäger and Pohlers in the early 1980s to provide a unifying approach to the investigations and, it was hoped, an avenue for analysing even stronger systems than those corresponding to the subsystems mentioned above (see Jäger 1986). This has indeed been a successful strategy and reveals, in the work of Rathjen and others, a deep connection between large cardinals and the constructive ordinals needed for the proof-theoretic investigation of such systems. Rathjen (1995) succeeded in analysing $(\Pi_2^1\text{-CA})$; it seems that the techniques developed for this case might allow the treatment of full analysis. These proof-theoretic investigations can no longer be motivated by the concern of 'securing' mathematical practice: the systems that are investigated are much stronger than needed for practice; the constructive ordinals used in the metamathematical theory are obtained in analogy to large cardinals in set theory.

The systems WKL_0, $(\Pi_\infty^0\text{-CA})\restriction$ and $(\Pi_1^1\text{-CA})\restriction$ have been recognized as significant for the formalization of mathematical practice and are reducible to theories based on principles that are acceptable from constructive positions; after all, they are conservative for Π_2^0-formulas over PRA, HA and the intuitionistic theory for the finite constructive number classes $(\text{ID})_{<\omega}(\mathbf{O})$. This provides a coherent perspective bringing out the complementary character of mathematical and metamathematical work that ultimately aims at relating significant parts of mathematical practice to distinctive foundational positions. But there is no obvious answer to the question 'What is the mathematical significance of those subsystems, when taken as vehicles for the formal axiomatic study of ordinary mathematics?'; similarly there is no obvious answer to the question 'What is the philosophical significance of the corresponding systems PRA, HA and $(\text{ID})_{<\omega}(\mathbf{O})$, when taken as formal expressions of foundational positions?'. There is ample room for reflection on these questions; the work reported here and in the literature provides rich and crucial data (see Sieg 1990). For the philosophical reflection on the foundations of mathematics the investigations of subsystems of set theory provide additional, significant material: what are constructions that lead to 'accessible domains' and how is it that we recognize their associated laws?

6 Outlook

'Internal' mathematical and philosophical challenges of work in proof theory were sketched at the end of the previous section. However, the foundational goals of proof-theoretic investigations have been complemented over the last few decades by other important initiatives.

First, in the 1950s, Kreisel initiated work that was to exploit the gap between provability in particular formal theories and truth. That led, on the one hand, to 'global' characterizations of the provably total functions of theories and to related independence results. On the other hand, by attending 'locally' to mathematical details of proofs and by using proof-

theoretic techniques, it led to explicit computational information of mathematical significance. This seems to have come to fruition through work by Luckhardt (1989) and Kohlenbach (1995).

Second, methods and results of mathematical logic, but in particular of proof theory, have played an increasing role in computer science. Clearly, there has also been significant and stimulating influence in the other direction. Various (type) systems – for example, Martin-Löf's, Girard's system F, and Feferman's systems of explicit mathematics – have been used for the presentation of proofs and computations, but also for describing transformations on them.

Third, there is a direct connection to the general topic of theorem proving; investigations here, when focusing on automated proof search, might reflect back into proof theory by providing data for a 'structural theory of (mathematical) proofs'. Such a structural proof theory would go beyond the representation of proofs in formal theories and articulate search heuristics expressing leading mathematical ideas for particular parts of mathematics. Saunders Mac Lane suggested such an extension of proof-theoretic investigations in his Göttingen dissertation of 1934, but it has been pursued only recently through computer implementation of appropriate search procedures.

See also: HILBERT'S PROGRAMME AND FORMALISM; LOGICAL AND MATHEMATICAL TERMS, GLOSSARY OF

References and further reading

* Bernays, P. (1918) 'Beiträge zur axiomatischen Behandlung des Logik-Kalküls' (Contributions to the Axiomatic Treatment of the Logical Calculus), unpublished *Habilitationsschrift*, Göttingen University; published in much revised form, 'Axiomatische Untersuchung des Aussagen-Kalküls der *Principia Mathematica*' (Axiomatic Investigation of the Propositional Calculus of *Principia Mathematica*), *Mathematische Zeitschrift* 25: 305–20, 1926. (The first proof of the completeness of a calculus for sentential logic.)

* —— (1930) 'Die Philosophie der Mathematik und die Hilbertsche Beweistheorie' (Philosophy of Mathematics and Hilbert's Proof Theory), *Blätter für Deutsche Philosophie* 4: 326–67; repr. in *Abhandlungen zur Philosophie der Mathematik* (Essays on the Philosophy of Mathematics), Darmstadt: Wissenschaftliche Buchgesellschaft, 1976. (A searching analysis of the background for and the goals of Hilbert's proof theory.)

* —— (1976) *Abhandlungen zur Philosophie der Mathematik* (Essays on the Philosophy of Mathematics),

Darmstadt: Wissenschaftliche Buchgesellschaft. (Five decades of Bernays' essays.)

* Brouwer, L.E.J. (1913) 'Intuitionism and Formalism', *Bulletin of the American Mathematical Society* 20: 81–96; repr. in P. Benacerraf and H. Putnam (eds) *Philosophy of Mathematics: Selected Readings*, Cambridge: Cambridge University Press, 2nd edn, 1983, 77–89. (A formalism with which Hilbert's philosophical position is frequently equated.)

* Buchholz, W., Feferman, S., Pohlers, W. and Sieg, W. (1981) *Iterated Inductive Definitions and Subsystems of Analysis*, Berlin, Heidelberg and New York: Springer. (First proof-theoretic treatment of some impredicative subsystems of analysis.)

Davis, M. (ed.) (1965) *The Undecidable: Basic Papers on Undecidable Propositions, Unsolvable Problems and Computable Functions*, Hewlett, NY: Raven Press. (Anthology of the fundamental papers on the subject by Gödel, Church, Turing, Kleene, Rosser and Post.)

* Dedekind, R. (1888) *Was sind und was sollen die Zahlen?*, Braunschweig: Vieweg; trans. W.W. Beman (1901), 'The Nature and Meaning of Numbers', in *Essays on the Theory of Numbers*, New York: Dover, 1963. (*The* modern set-theoretic foundation of number theory.)

* Detlefsen, M. (1986) *Hilbert's Program: An Essay on Mathematical Instrumentalism*, Boston, MA, and Dordrecht: Reidel. (A contrasting approach to those of Feferman (1988) and Sieg (1988).)

* Feferman, S. (1964) 'Systems of Predicative Analysis', *Journal of Symbolic Logic* 29: 1–30. (An excellent summary of work described in §5.)

* —— (1970) 'Formal Theories for Transfinite Iterations of Generalized Inductive Definitions and Some Subsystems of Analysis', in J. Myhill, R.E. Vesley and A. Kino (eds) *Intuitionism and Proof Theory*, Amsterdam: North Holland. (See §5.)

* —— (1977) 'Theories of Finite Type Related to Mathematical Practice', in J. Barwise (ed.) *Handbook of Mathematical Logic*, Amsterdam: North Holland. (A detailed survey of proof-theoretic work.)

* —— (1988) 'Hilbert's Program Relativized: Proof-Theoretical and Foundational Reductions', *Journal of Symbolic Logic* 53: 364–84. (A philosophical analysis of proof-theoretic research.)

* Frege, G. (1879) *Begriffsschrift, eine der arithmetischen nachgebildete Formelsprache des reinen Denkens*, Halle: Nebert; trans. '*Begriffsschrift*, a Formula Language, Modelled Upon That of Arithmetic, for Pure Thought', in J. van Heijenoort (ed.) *From Frege to Gödel: A Source Book in Mathematical Logic, 1879–1931*, Cambridge, MA: Harvard University Press, 1967, 1–82. (This small booklet contains the most significant step from Aristotelian to modern logic.)

* Friedman, H. (1970) 'Iterated Inductive Definitions and Σ_2^1-AC', in J. Myhill, R.E. Vesley and A. Kino (eds) *Intuitionism and Proof Theory*, Amsterdam: North Holland. (See §5.)

* Gentzen, G. (1935) 'Untersuchungen über das logische Schließen', *Mathematische Zeitschrift* 39: 176–210, 405–565; repr. Darmstadt: Wissenschaftliche Buchgesellschaft, 1969; trans. 'Investigations into Logical Deduction', *American Philosophical Quarterly* 1: 288–306, 2: 204–18, 1964; repr. in *The Collected Papers of Gerhard Gentzen*, ed. M.E. Szabo, Amsterdam and London: North Holland, 1969, 68–131. (Gentzen's doctoral dissertation, including the calculi of natural deduction and sequents, and the consistency proof for arithmetic with quantifier-free complete induction.)

* —— (1936) 'Die Widerspruchsfreiheit der reinen Zahlentheorie', *Mathematische Annalen* 112: 493–565; repr. Darmstadt: Wissenschaftliche Buchgesellschaft, 1967; trans. 'The Consistency of Elementary Number Theory', in *The Collected Papers of Gerhard Gentzen*, ed. M.E. Szabo, Amsterdam and London: North Holland, 1969, 132–213. (See §4.)

* —— (1943) 'Beweisbarkeit und Unbeweisbarkeit von Anfangsfällen der transfiniten Induktion in der reinen Zahlentheorie', *Mathematische Annalen* 119 (1): 140–61; trans. 'Provability and Nonprovability of Restricted Transfinite Induction in Elementary Number Theory', in *The Collected Papers of Gerhard Gentzen*, ed. M.E. Szabo, Amsterdam and London: North Holland, 1969, 287–308. (The first 'ordinal analysis' of a formal theory; see §4.)

Gödel, K. (1986–95) *Kurt Gödel: Collected Works*, ed. S. Feferman *et al.*, New York and Oxford: Oxford University Press, 3 vols. (Includes all the individual papers mentioned in the text.)

* Hilbert, D. (1900) 'Über den Zahlbegriff' (On the Concept of Number), *Jahresbericht der Deutschen Mathematiker-Vereinigung* 8: 180–94; revised as appendix 6 of *Die Grundlagen der Geometrie*, Leipzig and Berlin: Teubner, 7th edn, 1930; trans. *The Foundations of Geometry*, Chicago, IL: Open Court, 2nd edn, 1971. (Hilbert's first paper addressing the foundations of arithmetic.)

* —— (1905) 'Über die Grundlagen der Logik und der Arithmetik', in A. Krazer (ed.) *Verhandlungen des dritten internationalen Mathematiker-Kongreßes in Heidelberg vom 8. bis 13. August 1904*, Leipzig: Teubner, 174–85; trans. 'On the Foundations of Logic and Arithmetic', in J. van Heijenoort (ed.) *From Frege to Gödel: A Source Book in Math-*

ematical Logic, 1879–1931, Cambridge, MA: Harvard University Press, 1967, 130–8. (Discusses the need for a greater formalization of proof theory.)

* —— (1918) 'Axiomatisches Denken' (Axiomatic Thinking), *Mathematische Annalen* 78: 405–15; repr. in *Gesammelte Abhandlungen*, vol. 3, Berlin: Springer, 1935. (Captures the spirit of Hilbert's lecture courses on the foundations of mathematics.)

* —— (1920) 'Probleme der mathematischen Logik' (Problems of Mathematical Logic), lecture notes available in the Hilbert Nachlaß at the University of Göttingen, 46 pages. (Lecture notes from the summer term of 1920, written by N. Schönfinkel and P. Bernays.)

* —— (1926) 'Über das Unendliche', *Mathematische Annalen* 95: 161–90; trans. 'On the Infinite', in P. Benacerraf and H. Putnam (eds) *Philosophy of Mathematics: Selected Readings*, Cambridge: Cambridge University Press, 2nd edn, 1983. (Fully developed formulation of the consistency programme and finitist standpoint; 'proof' of Cantor's continuum theorem.)

* Hilbert, D. and Ackermann, W. (1928) *Grundzüge der theoretischen Logik* (Principles of Theoretical Logic), Berlin: Springer, 2nd edn, 1938; trans. L.M. Hammond, G.G. Leckie and F. Steinhardt, *Principles of Mathematical Logic*, ed. R.E. Luce, New York: Chelsea, 1950. (Based on Hilbert's lectures in the winter term of 1917/1918.)

* Hilbert, D. and Bernays, P. (1934, 1939) *Grundlagen der Mathematik* (Foundations of Mathematics), Berlin: Springer, 2 vols; 2nd edn, 1968, 1970. (Classic work of mathematical logic; includes valuable statements of Hilbert's conception of the axiomatic method and finitary reasoning.)

* Jäger, G. (1986) *Theories for Admissible Sets: A Unifying Approach to Proof Theory*, Naples: Bibliopolis. (Uses subsystems of set theory to provide a unifying approach to the investigation of consistency proofs.)

* Kohlenbach, U. (1995) *Real Growth in Standard Parts of Analysis*, Habilitationsschrift, Frankfurt University. (Develops work initiated by Kreisel, exploiting the gap between provability and truth; see §6.)

* Kreisel, G. (ed.) (1963/4) *Stanford Report on the Foundations of Analysis*, unpublished seminar report, Stanford University. (Important papers (some published elsewhere) on subsystems of analysis that emerged from a seminar held at Stanford in the summer of 1963; the contributors are J. Harrison, W.A. Howard, G. Kreisel, R. Parikh and W.W. Tait.)

* —— (1968) 'A Survey of Proof Theory', *Journal of Symbolic Logic* 33: 321–88. (An excellent summary of work described in §5.)

* Luckhardt, H. (1989) 'Herbrand Analysen zweier Beweise des Satzes von Roth: Polynomiale Anzahlschranken' (Herbrand Analyses of Two Proofs of Roth's Theorem: Polynomial Bounds), *Journal of Symbolic Logic* 54: 234–63. (Develops work initiated by Kreisel, exploiting the gap between provability and truth; see §6.)

* Mints, G. (1994) 'Gentzen-Type Systems and Hilbert's Epsilon Substitution Method I', in D. Prawitz, B. Skyrms and D. Westerståhl (eds) *Proceedings of the Ninth International Conference, Uppsala, Sweden, 1991*, vol. 9, *Logic, Methodology and Philosophy of Science*, Amsterdam: North Holland. (Continues use of the ε-calculus used by Hilbert; see §4.)

* Nagel, E. (1961) *The Structure of Science – Problems in the Logic of Scientific Explanation*, New York: Harcourt Brace. (Hilbert's views developed into instrumentalism in Nagel's sense.)

* Post, E. (1921) 'Introduction to a General Theory of Elementary Propositions', *American Journal of Mathematics* 43: 163–85; repr. in J. van Heijenoort (ed.) *From Frege to Gödel: A Source Book in Mathematics, 1879–1931*, Cambridge, MA: Harvard University Press, 1967, 264–83. (Proves the completeness of a calculus for sentential logic.)

* Purkert, W. and Ilgauds, H.J. (1987) *Georg Cantor 1845–1918*, Basle: Birkhäuser. (A biography of Cantor that includes a number of very informative letters from Cantor to Hilbert from the late 1890s.)

* Rathjen, M. (1995) 'Recent Advances in Ordinal Analysis: $(\Pi_2^1\text{-CA})$ and Related Systems', *Bulletin of Symbolic Logic* 1: 468–85. (Analysis of $(\Pi_2^1\text{-CA})$.)

Schwichtenberg, H. (1977) 'Proof Theory: Some Applications of Cut-Elimination', in J. Barwise (ed.) *Handbook of Mathematical Logic*, Amsterdam: North Holland, 867–95. (An elegant presentation of the proof-theoretic analysis of elementary number theory, PA.)

* Sieg, W. (1988) 'Hilbert's Program Sixty Years Later', *Journal of Symbolic Logic* 53: 338–48. (A philosophical analysis of proof-theoretic research.)

* —— (1990) 'Relative Consistency and Accessible Domains', *Synthèse* 84: 259–97. (Provides a historical and philosophical perspective on current proof-theoretic work.)

* Simpson, S. (1988) 'Partial Realization of Hilbert's Program', *Journal of Symbolic Logic* 53: 349–63. (A contrasting approach to those of Feferman (1988) and Sieg (1988).)

* Spector, C. (1962) 'Provably Recursive Functionals of Analysis: A Consistency Proof of Analysis by an Extension of Principles Formulated in Current

Intuitionistic Mathematics', in *Recursive Function Theory*, Proceedings of Symposia of Pure Mathematics, Providence, RI: American Mathematical Society. (A consistency proof for full classical analysis.)

* Tait, W.W. (1965) 'The Substitution Method', *Journal of Symbolic Logic* 30: 175–92. (Continues use of the ε-calculus used by Hilbert; see §4.)

* —— (1968) 'Normal Derivability in Classical Logic', in J. Barwise (ed.) *The Syntax and Semantics of Infinitary Languages*, New York: Springer, 204–36. (Introduces and uses an elegant and technically convenient formulation of sequent calculi for the investigation of classical logic and subsystems of analysis.)

* Weyl, H. (1918) *Das Kontinuum: Kritische Untersuchungen über die Grundlagen der Analysis*, Leipzig: Veit; trans. T. Bole, *The Continuum: A Critical Examination of the Foundations of Analysis*, New York: Dover, 1994. (The first modification of Hilbert's original programme.)

WILFRIED SIEG

PROPER NAMES

The Roman general Julius Caesar was assassinated on 14 March 44 BC by conspirators led by Brutus and Cassius. It is a remarkable fact that, in so informing or reminding the reader, the proper names 'Julius Caesar', 'Brutus' and 'Cassius' are used to refer to three people each of whom has been dead for about two thousand years. Our eyes could not be used to see any of them, nor our voices to talk to them, yet we can refer to them with our words.

The central philosophical issue about proper names is how this sort of thing is possible: what exactly is the mechanism by which the user of a name succeeds in referring with the name to its bearer? As the example indicates, whatever the mechanism is, it must be something that can relate the use of a name to its bearer even after the bearer has ceased to exist.

In modern philosophy of language there are two main views about the nature of the mechanism. On one account, which originated with Frege, a use of a name expresses a conception or way of thinking of an object, and the name refers to whatever object fits, or best fits, that conception or way of thinking. Thus with 'Cassius', for example, I may associate the conception 'the conspirator whom Caesar suspected because of his size' (recalling a famous speech in Shakespeare's Julius Caesar*). Conception theories are usually called 'sense' theories, after Frege's term 'Sinn'. The other account is*

the 'historical chain' theory, due to Kripke and Geach. In Geach's words, 'for the use of a word as a proper name there must in the first instance be someone acquainted with the object named.... But... the use of a given name for a given object... can be handed on from one generation to another... Plato knew Socrates, and Aristotle knew Plato, and Theophrastus knew Aristotle, and so on in apostolic succession down to our own times. That is why we can legitimately use "Socrates" as a name the way we do' (1969–70: 288–9).

1 Sense theories: Introduction
2 Sense theories: Do names express senses?
3 Sense theories: Do senses determine reference?
4 Historical chains
5 Direct reference and Frege's puzzle

1 Sense theories: Introduction

The idea that names express reference-determining conceptions or 'senses' originated with Frege (1892). But Frege was led to it not by wondering about the mechanism of reference, but rather about the difference in 'cognitive value' between two true identity statements of the respective forms $a = a$ and $a = b$ (for example, 'Clark Kent is Clark Kent' and 'Clark Kent is Superman'). Statements of the former sort, he says, are a priori, while the latter 'often contain very valuable extensions of our knowledge and cannot always be established a priori' ([1892] 1980: 56). Frege takes this to show that the propositions expressed by $a = a$ and $a = b$ cannot be the same even when a and b are names of the same person. Yet if the names do corefer, there is no difference in the references of the constituents of $a = a$ and $a = b$; moreover, these two sentences are assembled in the same way. So either they cannot express different propositions, or else – and this is the inference Frege drew – what determines the proposition a sentence S expresses cannot just have to do with the structure of S and the *references* of its constituent words and phrases (see FREGE, G. §§3–4; SENSE AND REFERENCE §1).

Frege's proposal was that in addition to possessing a reference, any meaningful expression has a sense, the sense being a 'way of thinking' of the reference. The proposition a sentence expresses is determined by the senses of the words in it, not their references. Thus 'Clark Kent is Clark Kent' and 'Clark Kent is Superman' express different propositions because 'Clark Kent' and 'Superman' express different senses, senses which happen to be ways of thinking of the same reference. Taking the Superman fiction to be fact, the sense of 'Clark Kent' might be 'the mild-mannered reporter on *The Daily Planet* who has a crush on Lois Lane' while the sense of 'Superman' might be 'the blue-suited extraterrestrial who flies'. Here we specify different conceptions of the same individual in two definite descriptions (expressions of the form 'the so-and-so' – see DESCRIPTIONS). The proposition that Superman is Clark Kent therefore has the content that the blue-suited extraterrestrial who flies is the mild-mannered reporter on *The Daily Planet* who has a crush on Lois Lane, which may indeed be, in Frege's phrase, an extension of our knowledge.

It was Frege's view that in an ideal language each name would have a fixed sense and reference for everyone; in an ordinary natural language, there are names that fail to refer, and users may fail to agree on the sense of a name for a specific individual, which Frege thought of as deficiencies of natural language. In a modification of Frege's views, Searle (1958) allowed that a name may be associated with a whole range of descriptions, different users using different ranges; the bearer of the name need not satisfy all the conditions mentioned in the descriptions, only 'a sufficient number', an intentionally vague condition.

Sense theories along such lines as these have been called 'famous deeds' sense theories. Famous deeds sense theories appear to have been conclusively refuted by Kripke (1972, 1980). Kripke objects to such sense theories both as they respond to Frege's own puzzle about the difference between $a = a$ and $a = b$, and as they address our initial question about the mechanism of reference. Let us consider these two issues in turn.

2 Sense theories: Do names express senses?

According to Kripke, the propositions one expresses using names do not involve senses or ways of thinking expressed by the names, otherwise some such propositions would be both metaphysically necessary and a priori, which they are clearly not. For example, suppose the sense of 'Aristotle' is 'the pupil of Plato who tutored Alexander'. Then the sentence

(1)   Aristotle was a pupil of Plato

would express the proposition with the content

(2)   The pupil of Plato who tutored Alexander was a pupil of Plato.

But (2) is, in a certain sense, necessary, while (1) is not. There is no way things could have gone in which (a) a unique pupil of Plato who tutored Alexander exists and (b) that person was not a pupil of Plato. On the other hand, there are many ways things could have gone in which (a′) Aristotle exists but (b′) Aristotle was not a pupil of Plato (for example, he died young).

In other words, granted that there is such a person as Aristotle, he may be a pupil of Plato or he may not be. But granted that there is such a person as the pupil of Plato who tutored Alexander, it follows that he is a pupil of Plato.

This example brings out Kripke's famous distinction between 'rigid' and 'non-rigid' designators. In thinking about or describing other ways things could have gone (other possible worlds) we use a proper name such as 'Aristotle' consistently to denote the same person; this makes proper names rigid designators. But we use definite descriptions such as 'the pupil of Plato who tutored Alexander' differently. With respect to the actual world, this description picks out Aristotle; with respect to a possible world where someone else is the one and only pupil of Plato who tutored Alexander, the description picks out that other person, not Aristotle; and with respect to a possible world where either Plato or Alexander does not exist, the description fails to pick out anyone, even if Aristotle does exist. Hence such descriptions are non-rigid designators. Certain descriptions, such as 'the positive square root of 9', are as rigid as proper names, but this is on account of their subject matter, not their semantic role. It is because the typical famous deeds description is non-rigid that the contrast between pairs such as (1) and (2) *vis-à-vis* necessity and contingency arises (see REFERENCE §2).

Just as (1) and (2) differ in modal status, they differ epistemically: bracketing the question of existence, (2) is, in a limited sense, knowable a priori, while (1) is not. That is, granted that there was such a person as Aristotle, it is a further, empirical question whether he was a pupil of Plato (there may be a controversy among historians about this). But granted that there was such a person as the pupil of Plato who tutored Alexander, it is not a further question, *a fortiori* not an empirical one, whether he was a pupil of Plato.

The same objections arise to Searle's modified version of the sense theory. For example, no matter what range of descriptions we associate with a name, they will generate statements that are a priori in the manner of (2). If being ϕ logically implies being ϕ', then

(3)   The thing which is F-and-G or G-and-H is F' or G' or H'

is essentially the same as (2), just more complicated. But if the predicates F, G and H encapsulate famous deeds, the corresponding

(4) NN is F' or G' or H',

where 'NN' is the name with which 'the thing which is F or G or H' is associated, will be no more a priori than (1) (Kripke 1980).

3 Sense theories: Do senses determine reference?

Kripke (1972, 1980) demonstrates another flaw in famous deeds sense theories, namely, that they do not provide an adequate answer to the question about the mechanism of reference. This is because (1) the likely candidate for the sense of a name may pick out an object which is not in fact the name's bearer, or may fail to pick out anything, and (2) we can succeed in referring with a name even when we do not have a 'famous deeds' description associated with it.

Kripke illustrates (1) with two examples. If any description is associated with the name 'Gödel' it is 'the discoverer of the incompleteness of arithmetic'. Does this mean that 'Gödel' refers to that person? What if the theorem was actually proved by Schmidt, who died in strange circumstances, and Gödel got hold of Schmidt's work and represented it as his own? The very fact that we can understand this 'what if' shows that the reference of 'Gödel' is not fixed as whoever discovered the incompleteness of arithmetic. And though this example is fictional, there are similar actual cases: Peano's Axioms are not due to Peano; and Einstein was not the inventor of the atomic bomb (Kripke 1980). For a case where there are descriptions that do not pick out any object although the relevant name still refers, Kripke gives the example of the prophet Jonah, who really existed (according to the scholarly consensus), but whose career as described in the Bible is essentially fictitious. Again, the mere intelligibility of the claim 'Jonah was a historical person but everything uniquely identifying that the Bible says about him is fictitious' is enough to show that the reference of 'Jonah' is not fixed as the Hebrew prophet who was swallowed by a whale, or by any other condition, no matter how complicated or disjunctive, derived from the Book of Jonah.

As for (2), successful reference without associated (definite) descriptions, Kripke points out that most people can use the names 'Richard Feynman' and 'Murray Gell-Mann' to refer to those two people, but that, at best, all the typical person knows about either is that he is a famous physicist who won a Nobel Prize (this was before Feynman achieved popular fame for his role in the *Challenger* disaster inquiry). So we have difference in reference with no difference in associated descriptions; therefore associated descriptions are not at the heart of how proper name reference works.

Perhaps these examples only establish such a conclusion for descriptions that encapsulate famous deeds. Kripke considers some other approaches and concludes that they violate an important non-circularity condition: that candidate descriptions must not themselves embed the notion of reference in a way that cannot eventually be eliminated. For example, we might suggest that the reference of 'Socrates' is fixed as 'the man called "Socrates"'. Since 'called' just means 'referred to as', we do not explain how reference to Socrates is possible in this way: what we want to know is how Socrates *gets to be* the man referred to as 'Socrates'. So this goes nowhere as a proposal about the mechanism of reference, and Kripke plausibly argues that the same would be true for more complicated versions of the idea, for example, that 'Gödel' refers to the person to whom the proof of the incompleteness of arithmetic is commonly attributed. So these attempts at a non-famous-deeds description theory fail. However, in view of Kripke's critique of the famous deeds approach, it seems that if any sense theory is to work, it will have to be a non-famous-deeds account of some sort.

4 Historical chains

The main competing account of the mechanism of reference is the Geach–Kripke historical chain account, in which competence to refer with the name is transmitted across generations in the style adverted to in the quotation from Geach in this entry's prologue (1969–70). The historical chain account is sometimes called the 'causal' chain account, since it is held that the links in the chain are forged by transactions of a causal sort. In Kripke's own version, which he says is a 'picture' rather than a theory (1980: 97), a name is introduced into a community by some 'initial baptism' of an object with the name, and then the name is passed on from link to link, it being required at each step that the receiver of the name 'intend . . . to use it with the same reference as the [person] from whom he heard it' (1980: 96).

If we regard being told about, or otherwise hearing about, an object, as a way of becoming 'acquainted' with it, then the Geach–Kripke account instantiates an approach championed by Russell (1918), who made acquaintance with an object necessary for referring to it. However, Russell's notion of acquaintance was rather idiosyncratic: apart from my own sense-data, my self, universals and perhaps the present moment, I lack acquaintance with things, according to Russell. Since the ordinary names I use, ostensibly for other people and things, are not names of sense-data, Russell claimed that in a 'logical' sense, ordinary names are not 'proper' names. Rather, he suggested, they are definite descriptions in disguise (see RUSSELL, B.A.W. §9). For this reason, Kripke sometimes calls the view he opposes the 'Frege–Russell theory of names'. The point to bear in mind is that Frege and Russell had different accounts of how reference works (so there is no 'Frege–Russell theory of reference'), but because on Russell's account ordinary names do not really refer, the two philosophers end up saying similar-sounding things about such names.

Returning to Kripke's account of the mechanism of reference in terms of informational exchanges in which the intention to preserve reference is present, the obvious question is whether it is any improvement on circular description theories. After all, the notion of reference enters explicitly into Kripke's necessary condition for successful passing on of the name, and it also enters at the start of the chain, where some kind of demonstrative reference to the object being baptized is standardly made. To put the same question another way, if this account is explanatory, would there be anything wrong with a description theory which attributed to a name 'NN' and a user of the name U the sense 'the object at the start of the chain of reference-preserving links by which I came into mastery of this name', in which 'I' refers to U?

One problem with this version of a description theory is that no ordinary speaker of a natural language associates any such description with a proper name, since the description embodies a philosophical theory, and it is difficult to see how one could justify claiming that the association is 'implicit'. Here there is a contrast with Kripke's proposal, which only requires speakers to have the intention to preserve the reference of the new name they have just learned, and it is surely plausible that speakers do have such an intention. Still, there is some sense in which the fundamental nature of the mechanism of reference is left unexplained. For instance, what exactly is it about an actual baptismal service, or about parents announcing their choice of name, that causes a new 'common currency' (see Kaplan 1990) name to be added to the language? Or is the request for further explanation here a demand for a 'reductive' account of reference in terms of non-semantic notions (see REFERENCE §8), something perhaps impossible?

The causal chain picture is not without other difficulties, as Kripke mentions. For instance, straightforward application of the picture could lead to the conclusion that 'Santa Claus' is the name of a certain central European king, which seems wrong. Evans (1973) proposed a different causal account on which the 'causal source' of the information associated with the name determines whom it refers to, though in a possibly complex way. Evans observes that the reference of a name in a linguistic community can change over time if it was originally a name for x that was mistakenly but consistently misapplied to y: y would ultimately become the bearer of the name, being the dominant causal source of the information associated with it (unless, as Evans notes, younger

members of the community defer in their use of the name towards those for whom it was once a name for x). Evans subsequently elaborated his account (1982: ch. 11).

5 Direct reference and Frege's puzzle

A striking feature of the Geach–Kripke picture is that it leaves no role for sense to play as that which determines reference. The only candidate for the 'meaning' of a name is therefore the name's reference itself. A theory which claims that the meaning of a name is just its reference, pure and simple, is often called a 'direct reference' theory, 'direct' signifying that reference is not mediated via sense. Such theories trace their origins through Russell back to Mill (1843); more recently, the idea is prominent in the writings of Marcus on reference (1961), and has subsequently been developed and defended in a sustained form by Salmon (1986) and Soames (1994).

The main problem which direct reference theories face is the puzzle about the difference between $a = a$ and $a = b$. The general 'failure of substitutivity' puzzle is the puzzle of how it is possible for the meanings of two sentences to differ if the sentences have the same structure and their corresponding parts have the same meaning. For example,

(5) It is self-evident to any rational thinker that if Superman exists, then Superman = Superman

seems true and 'Superman' and 'Clark Kent' have the same reference. Therefore, according to direct reference theory, (5) should have the same meaning as

(6) It is self-evident to any rational thinker that if Superman exists, then Superman = Clark Kent.

But at first sight, (6) does not even have the same truth-value as (5), never mind the same meaning.

Failure of substitutivity is handled straightforwardly on a sense theory of names which allows that coreferential names can have different senses. The claim would be that (not merely the reference but) the sense of 'Superman' enters into the truth-condition of (5), while in (6) the sense of 'Clark Kent' is also involved. There are various mechanisms which might be invoked here, Frege's own being the simplest: in (5) and (6), according to Frege, the proper names refer to their *senses*, rather than to the person they normally refer to (see PROPOSITIONAL ATTITUDE STATEMENTS §1; SENSE AND REFERENCE §5). But the trouble with any explanation of substitutivity failure for proper names that invokes senses is that sense theories of proper names have been so thoroughly battered by Kripke.

Direct reference theory seems to have less to work

with to explain the semantic difference between (5) and (6). On perhaps the best known version of the theory, Salmon's, it is simply denied that there is a semantic difference between (5) and (6). The appearance that substitution changes truth-value in cases such as (5) and (6) is explained as being due to pragmatic effects (see PRAGMATICS). Apparently, the only alternative for a direct reference theorist is to identify some assumption in the argument that substitution of coreferring names ought not to change meaning and deny that assumption. This strategy produces a possible target. We suggested that what makes substitutivity failure puzzling is that sentences with the same structure whose corresponding parts have the same meaning should themselves have the same meaning. But this presupposes that the meaning of the entire sentence is wholly determined by the meaning of its parts and their manner of composition (see COMPOSITIONALITY). However, the notion of structure alluded to in the phrase 'manner of composition' is one which is sensitive only to syntactic categories of expression, not to the identity of expressions. There is another, more 'logical' notion of structure, on which use of a different word, even one with the same meaning, can disrupt structure (Putnam 1954). In this logical sense, the structure of 'if Superman exists, then Superman = Superman' is 'if Et then $t = t$', while 'if Superman exists, then Superman = Clark Kent' has the different structure 'if Et then $t = t^*$'. If we hold that substitution is acceptable only when it does not change logical structure, then from (5) we can infer merely

(7)   It is self-evident to any rational thinker that if Clark Kent exists, then Clark Kent = Clark Kent

which is presumably true if (5) is. Of course, this does not help with cases of substitutivity failure in which there is only one occurrence of the name being substituted ('Lois believes that Superman is an extraterrestrial'), but some direct reference theorists have tried to develop a more general notion of structure for these cases (Taschek 1995).

It is the handling of substitutivity puzzles that is the deciding issue between sense theories and direct reference theories of proper names. Sense theorists need to find a viable account of the senses of names and direct reference theorists need to find a persuasive account either of why substitutivity fails in cases such as (5), or else of why it gives such a convincing appearance of doing so.

See also: DE RE/DE DICTO; LOGICAL AND MATHEMATICAL TERMS, GLOSSARY OF; KRIPKE, S.A.

References and further reading

Burge, T. (1973) 'Reference and Proper Names', *Journal of Philosophy* 70: 425–39. (Argues that, semantically, proper names should be understood as certain kinds of predicate.)

Deutsch, H. (1989) 'On Direct Reference', in J. Almog, J. Perry and H.K. Wettstein (eds) *Themes from Kaplan*, Oxford and New York: Oxford University Press, 167–95. (Applies a Kaplan-style approach to context-dependence to proper names.)

Devitt, M. (1981) *Designation*, New York: Columbia University Press. (Develops a causal theory of reference using the 'language of thought' hypothesis.)

* Evans, G. (1973) 'The Causal Theory of Names', *Proceedings of the Aristotelian Society*, supplementary vol. 47: 187–208; repr. in *Collected Papers*, Oxford: Oxford University Press, 1985, 1–24. (A very accessible and insightful discussion of Kripke's account.)

—— (1979) 'Reference and Contingency', *The Monist* 62: 161–84; repr. in *Collected Papers*, Oxford: Oxford University Press, 1985, 178–213. (Discusses a category of proper name not considered in this article, which Evans calls 'descriptive' names. These are names whose reference is explicitly fixed by a definite description, and which figure in Kripke-style examples of the contingent a priori.)

* —— (1982) *The Varieties of Reference*, Oxford and New York: Oxford University Press. (Published after Evans' death; some parts are unfinished. As well as Evans' final thoughts on proper names, includes influential discussion on Frege, Russell and the notion of an 'object-dependent' thought.)

Forbes, G. (1990) 'The Indispensability of *Sinn*', *Philosophical Review* 99: 535–63. (Develops a non-famous-deeds sense theory of names and applies it to substitutivity failure.)

* Frege, G. (1892) 'Über Sinn und Bedeutung', *Zeitschrift für Philosophie und philosophische Kritik* 100: 25–50; trans. M. Black, 'On Sense and Reference', in *Translations from the Philosophical Writings of Gottlob Frege*, ed. P.T. Geach and M. Black, Oxford and New York: Blackwell, 3rd edn, 1980. (Widely regarded as the paper which inaugurated modern philosophy of language.)

* Geach, P.T. (1969–70) 'The Perils of Pauline', *Review of Metaphysics* 23: 287–300; repr. in *Logic Matters*, Berkeley, CA: University of California Press, 1972, 153–65. (States the historical chain view and discusses the use of names in intentional contexts.)

Jubien, M. (1993) *Ontology and the Fallacy of Reference*, Cambridge and New York: Cambridge University Press. (An unusual but interesting account of reference, based on 'revisionist' metaphysics.)

* Kaplan, D. (1990) 'Words', *Proceedings of the Aristotelian Society*, supplementary vol. 64: 93–117. (Includes an original and accessible discussion of how names should be individuated.)

* Kripke, S.A. (1972) 'Naming and Necessity', in D. Davidson and G. Harman (eds) *Semantics of Natural Language*, Dordrecht: Reidel, 252–355. (One of the most influential and widely discussed works in post-war philosophy.)

—— (1979) 'A Puzzle About Belief', in A. Margalit (ed.) *Meaning and Use*, Dordrecht: Reidel. (Develops two famous cases – the London/Londres case and the Paderewski case – in defence of the thesis that substitution puzzles do not necessarily tell against the principle of substitutivity.)

* —— (1980) *Naming and Necessity*, Oxford and New York: Blackwell. (The book version of Kripke (1972).)

* Marcus, R.B. (1961) 'Modalities and Intensional Languages', *Synthèse* 13: 303–22. (Includes an early statement of contemporary direct reference theory.)

* Mill, J.S. (1843) *A System of Logic*, London: Parker; repr. in *The Collected Works of John Stuart Mill*, ed. J.M. Robson, London: Routledge, 1996, vol. 7. (Draws a famous distinction between the denotation and the connotation of a word and defends a metalinguistic analysis of identity sentences.)

* Putnam, H. (1954) 'Synonymy and the Analysis of Belief Sentences', *Analysis* 14: 114–22. (Attacks compositionality assumptions in substitution puzzles.)

Recanati, F. (1993) *Direct Reference*, Oxford and New York: Blackwell. (Distinguishes a sense in which names are directly referential from two other semantically relevant senses in which they express modes of presentation. Also includes a good discussion of how 'what is said' by an utterance is determined.)

* Russell, B.A.W. (1918) 'The Philosophy of Logical Atomism', *The Monist* 28: 495–527; 29: 32–63, 190–222, 345–80; repr. in *Logic and Knowledge: Essays 1901–1950*, ed. R.C. Marsh, London: Routledge, 1992. (One of many possible sources of Russell's views, which changed throughout his long life. Lectures II and VI are the most germane to this entry.)

* Salmon, N. (1986) *Frege's Puzzle*, Cambridge, MA: MIT Press. (The most complete attempt by a direct reference theorist to account for the problem of (apparent) failure of substitutivity.)

* Searle, J. (1958) 'Proper Names', *Mind* 67: 166–73. (A significant elaboration of broadly Fregean themes.)

* Soames, S. (1994) 'Attitudes and Anaphora', in J.E. Tomberlin (ed.) *Philosophical Perspectives: 8 Logic and Language*, Atascadero, CA: Ridgeview, 251–72. (Within the context of direct reference theory, investigates the behaviour of anaphoric pronouns in propositional attitude ascriptions. Mostly non-technical, but rigorous.)

Strawson, P.F. (1959) *Individuals*, London: Methuen. (Chapter 6 includes an elaborated Fregean account that Kripke often uses as a stalking horse.)

* Taschek, W. (1995) 'Belief, Substitution, and Logical Structure', *Noûs* 29: 71–95. (Extends the approach of Putnam (1954) to account for a wider range of substitution puzzles.)

GRAEME FORBES

PROPERTIES *see* ABSTRACT OBJECTS; NATURAL KINDS; UNIVERSALS

PROPERTY

Most of the great philosophers have expressed views on property, its justification and limits, and especially on the justification of having private property; generally, one must understand these views against the background of the economic and social conditions of their times. Notable theories include first possession (roughly, 'whoever gets his or her hands on it justifiably owns it'), labour ('whoever made it deserves to own it'), utility and/or efficiency ('allowing people to own things is the most effective way of running society') and personality ('owning property is necessary for personal development').

Few thinkers now defend the first possession theory but all the other three have their contemporary supporters. Some philosophers combine two or more theories into multi-principled or 'pluralist' justifications of property ownership. Many express concern about wide gaps between rich and poor and argue for constraints on inequalities in property holdings.

1 Concept of property
2 History of theorizing about property
3 Systematic justifications of private property
4 Constraints on the distribution of property

1 Concept of property

The concept of property is understood in two main ways. First, it applies to material things such as tools, houses and land. Second, it applies to bundles of 'rights'. Most lawyers and philosophers stress the second understanding over the first. The first is too narrow to accommodate intangibles such as copyrights, patents and trademarks. Moreover, for purposes of legal and philosophical analysis the second understanding is more useful.

Here the word 'rights' covers many normative modalities (see RIGHTS §2). Following Hohfeld and Honoré, the package of rights called 'property' includes: claim rights to possess, use and receive income; powers to transfer, waive and exclude; a disability (a no-power) of others to force a sale; liberty rights to consume or destroy; and immunity from expropriation by the government. It is probably a vain enterprise to try to specify necessary and sufficient conditions for all and only those 'rights' that pertain to property rather than, say, to contract or tort. Yet it is a worthy undertaking to try to identify those 'rights' that seem most central to property or those rules that create such 'rights'.

The second understanding of property finds favour for many reasons. It applies to widely different cultures. It is useful in both legal and philosophical analysis. It can accommodate both 'will' and 'interest' theories of rights. It can capture both full ownership and limited property rights (such as easements), and both tangible and intangible property. It permits distinguishing among different sorts of property depending on the identity of the rightholder. Thus, a single person or a corporation has *private* property, a tribe has *communal* property and a government has *public* or *state* property.

This explanation of the concept of property is neutral with respect to which kinds of things can be the subject of property rights. Few would defend slavery, which is the most extreme form of property in the bodies or persons of others. More disputed are whether people can have property rights in the whole of their own bodies, in bodily parts for use in transplantation, in information, in cultural practices, in welfare payments or other forms of government largesse, or in seabed resources or objects in outer space.

The approach of Guido Calabresi and Douglas Melamed (1972) to the notion of property, which philosopher-economists and lawyer-economists often use, is not conceptually distinct from that of Hohfeld (1919) and Honoré (1961). For Calabresi and Melamed the basic idea is an 'entitlement'. An entitlement is, roughly, an interest that the law does or should protect. Decisions must be made as to which entitlements to protect and how to protect them. As to the latter decision, the law may use what Calabresi and Melamed call 'property rules', 'liability rules' and 'rules of inalienability'. These technical terms can be restated in Hohfeld's vocabulary. If a person's entitlement is protected by a property rule, then others have a disability (a no-power) with regard to obtaining the entitlement except at a price agreed to by its holder. If a person's entitlement is protected by a liability rule, then others have a disability with regard to obtaining or reducing the value of the entitlement unless they compensate its holder by an officially determined amount. If a person's entitlement is protected by a rule of inalienability, its holder has no power to transfer the entitlement to others. The real value of Calabresi and Melamed's approach rests in the light that it sheds on the integration of property and tort, on its application to pollution control, on its sensitivity to distributional as well as efficiency considerations, and on the choice between civil and criminal sanctions for violations of property rights.

2 History of theorizing about property

Many of the great philosophers have offered views on property. Plato actually expresses two different views (see PLATO §§14, 17). In the *Republic* he portrays an ideal society in which the rulers and auxiliaries have political power but almost no private property. Ordinary citizens possess private property, with limits on unequal distribution, but have almost no political power. In contrast, the *Laws* depicts a practical, second-best society. It favours individual private possession with underlying communal ownership. Regulations maintain a roughly equal distribution of property.

ARISTOTLE advocates private rather than communal ownership on grounds that relate to the smooth functioning of a society and its economy. His *Politics* fails, however, to show how property should, or can, be 'in a certain sense common, but, as a general rule, private'.

Locke, at least in the *Second Treatise*, offers a labour theory of property (see LOCKE, J. §10). The interpretation of his theory is disputed. It is unclear how much the theory rests on 'mixing' one's labour with unowned things, or on barring the idle from taking the benefit of the labourer's pains, and the extent to which the needs of others and restrictions on spoilage limit the acquisition of property by labour. It is also disputed whether Locke's theory is proto-capitalist or stems from some conception of natural law.

Hume and Bentham are the first important utilitarian theorists of property. For Hume, utility in the sense of common interest explains how private property arises (see HUME, D. §§4–5). It also justifies the general institution of private property and specific rules of property law. Bentham understands utility as the balance of pleasure over pain, and views property in terms of expectations (see BENTHAM, J. §2). The security of expectations, rather than equality in distribution, is for Bentham the weightier consideration in favour of private property. Nevertheless, Bentham is sharply critical of the English law of property of his day.

Kant and Hegel are also linked, although less closely and in more complicated ways than Hume and Bentham. For Kant, as for Locke, a form of private property can exist in the state of nature (see KANT, I. §10). But Kant has a social contract theory under which only society can give individual possession full normative significance as private property. Hegel regards Kantian private property as excessively individualistic and belonging to the domain of 'abstract right' (see HEGEL, G.W.F. §8). A more sophisticated form of property exists in 'civil society' – roughly, the social correlate of *laissez-faire* capitalism. Only in the 'state' does private property emerge fully transformed; private property, unequally distributed, still exists, but is subject to heavier state regulation in the organic interest of all citizens.

MARX dismisses Hegel's dialectical defence of private property as so much claptrap. Marx believes that capitalist production, not unequal distribution, is the more serious problem, because 'capitalism' distorts human relationships. In particular, private property under capitalism involves 'alienation' – that is, a separation of persons from nature, the products of their labour, other human beings and even themselves (see ALIENATION §4). *Pace* Marx, it is unclear that all forms of private property must involve alienation, or that alienation will be absent from the mature communist society that he envisages.

3 Systematic justifications of private property

First possession and entitlement. Attempts to justify the acquisition of property by being the first person to possess it have won few converts. The general difficulty is to show why first possession should support full ownership rather than limited rights of use. Specific difficulties include articulating which acts of possession count, explaining how long they must continue, and identifying the item or area possessed. Suppose that someone claims title to an acre of farmland by standing in one place for an hour. Why should that person not have to farm rather than

merely stand, to remain there for a year rather than just an hour, and to perform appropriate acts over the entire acre rather than only on an area two feet square? To many these difficulties have no ready solution. Still, those sympathetic to the rights of aboriginal peoples sometimes invoke first possession.

A related account is the libertarian entitlement theory of Robert NOZICK (1974). Nozick's position is hazy on which acts are appropriate acts of acquisition under his principle of justice in acquisition. The literature contains sharp attacks on his position. Among them are objections as to how any individual can, by unilateral action, impose moral duties on others to refrain from using certain resources, worries about inequalities of property holdings, and scepticism that anyone living today has morally valid property rights by transfer from some original acquirer. Nozick has not responded to these attacks. Other libertarian theories are either grounded in economics or based on strong conceptions of freedom and individual rights (see LIBERTARIANISM §3).

Labour. More promising are efforts to recast the labour theory in terms of the desert of the labourer. Lawrence Becker and Stephen Munzer offer somewhat different accounts of a labour–desert principle.

Becker (1977) holds that if a worker adds value to the lives of others in some morally permissible way and without being required to do so, that person deserves a fitting benefit. Property rights may be the most fitting benefit, and which benefit is 'most fitting' depends on purposes. However, Becker's theory leaves it unclear which purposes (for example, an attempt to gain property rights?) and whose purposes (the labourer's or those of other individuals?) are relevant. Also, he does not show why purpose should be the sole test of fittingness. Nevertheless, Becker rightly insists that losses inflicted by the labourer's work require some reduction in property rights or some offsetting compensation or taxation.

Munzer (1990) argues that if workers use their bodies to produce something or provide a service, then they have a prima facie claim to deserve property rights in the product or in wages. This claim is qualified by scarcity, by the needs and rights of others, and by some post-acquisition changes in situation. Restrictions on transfer may also apply. Moreover, since work is a social activity, a wage policy is in order that makes wages commensurate so far as possible with desert. The heavy qualifications that surround this version of the labour theory support moderate egalitarianism rather than the wide disparities in income and wealth that libertarian theories allow. Critics of Munzer's labour–desert principle have objected that its intellectual underpinnings are not sufficiently clear and that in both theory and practice no precise correlations exist between desert claims and property rights (see DESERT AND MERIT).

Utility and efficiency. Contemporary justifications of this sort owe a distant obligation to Hume and Bentham. These justifications often stress 'efficiency', which does not allow interpersonal comparison of individual preference satisfaction, over 'utility', which does allow them. Because of the invocation of efficiency, the most sophisticated advocates are frequently economists or academic lawyers influenced by economics rather than philosophers.

Utility and efficiency can, given some plausible assumptions about individuals' preferences, justify some public property as well as some rights of private property. They tend (again given certain assumptions about preferences) to justify moderate egalitarianism rather than highly unequal distributions of private property. However, more detailed information is needed to show how utility and efficiency can justify particular rules of property law or radical changes in existing property institutions. Perhaps the most influential theoretical result of applying efficiency to the law of nuisance bears the sobriquet 'Coase's Theorem' (Coase 1960). It holds that, under perfect competition and perfect information and with costless transactions, an efficient allocation of resources will result no matter what the decision of the courts concerning liability for damage.

Personality. Contrary to some reports, the personality theory of property did not die with Hegel and the British neo-Hegelians. The basic idea is that people need at least some private property in order to develop healthy character structures. The account of 'property for personhood' by Margaret Radin (1982) is probably the best known and most fully developed contemporary theory of this sort. She applies her theory to many practical legal problems, but some readers find the foundations of her account no clearer that those of Hegel. Her books also suggest that some things are so personal that they ought not to be property or 'commodities' at all.

Pluralist theories. The variety of possible justifications of property has suggested to some writers that the most plausible account of property is 'pluralist' – that is, contains two or more irreducible principles. Becker and Munzer explicitly embrace pluralist accounts. Other writers do so implicitly. Some critics dismiss such pluralism as eclectic. Other critics contend that if it is impossible to show that the principles never conflict, it is necessary to establish that conflict between principles is logically consistent and otherwise free from objection. Further, it may be harder to apply a pluralist theory rather than a unitary theory to practical problems. Still, those who favour a unitary theory – a theory with a single principle or at least a single supreme principle – must show how it can accommodate the complexity of considered moral judgments concerning property. For anyone who shares Proudhon's worry that property is theft, justification remains the key problem in the theory of property (see PROUDHON, P.-J.).

4 Constraints on the distribution of property

Justice and equality. The liberal tradition in political theory, stemming particularly from Mill, often tries to limit inequalities of property holdings (see MILL, J.S. §§11–12). The limitation can take the form of a side constraint or, in a pluralist theory, of a separate principle of justice and equality. Few philosophers argue for strictly equal holdings. More modest is the 'difference principle' of John Rawls (see RAWLS, J. §§1–2). Applied to property, this principle would hold that differences in holdings are justifiable only if they are to the greatest benefit of the least advantaged. A related view might concentrate on both the floor and the ceiling: Everyone should be ensured a minimum amount of property, and remaining inequalities, if any, should not undermine a fully human life for anyone in society.

Absence of exploitation. The radical tradition in political theory, traceable especially to Marx, stresses the need to eliminate exploitation and other differences in power that derive from unequal property holdings. Roughly, persons are exploited if others secure a benefit by using them as a tool or resource so as to cause them serious harm. Exploitation theory often concentrates as much on problems of economic production as it does on the real or imagined evils of unequal distributions of property. The 'critical legal studies movement', in some of its forms, objects to exploitation and differences in power as they relate to property (see CRITICAL LEGAL STUDIES). More rigorous accounts of exploitation come from the work of John E. Roemer (1982).

References and further reading

* Becker, L.C. (1977) *Property Rights: Philosophic Foundations*, London, Henley and Boston, MA: Routledge & Kegan Paul. (Admirably concise introduction.)
* Calabresi, G. and Melamed, A.D. (1972) 'Property rules, liability rules, and inalienability: one view of the cathedral', *Harvard Law Review* 85 (6): 1089–128. (Difficult but rewarding article.)
* Coase, R.H. (1960) 'The problem of social cost', *Journal of Law & Economics* 3 (1): 1–44. (See §3 of this entry.)
  Demsetz, H. (1967) 'Toward a theory of property

rights', *American Economic Review* 57 (2): 347–59. (Influential account of efficiency and the origins of property.)

* Harris, J.W. (1996) *Property and Justice*, Oxford: Clarendon Press. (Insightful study with many illustrations from English law.)

* Hohfeld, W.N. (1919) *Fundamental Legal Conceptions as Applied in Judicial Reasoning*, repr. West Port, CT: Greenwood Press, 1978. (Important but difficult reading.)

* Honoré, A.M. (1961) 'Ownership', in *Oxford Essays in Jurisprudence (First Series)*, ed. A.G. Guest, Oxford: Clarendon Press, 107–47. (Lucid, accessible and influential essay.)

Macpherson, C.B. (1962) *The Political Theory of Possessive Individualism: Hobbes to Locke*, Oxford: Clarendon Press. (Views Locke as a possessive individualist.)

* Munzer, S.R. (1990) *A Theory of Property*, Cambridge: Cambridge University Press. (A pluralist theory with detailed applications to corporations, bequests and government takings of private property.)

—— (1994) 'An uneasy case against property rights in body parts', *Social Philosophy & Policy* 11 (2): 259–86. (Discusses whether organs and other bodily parts should be the subject of property rights.)

* Nozick, R. (1974) *Anarchy, State, and Utopia*, New York: Basic Books, 150–82. (A lively and prominent libertarian account.)

Penner, J.E. (1996) 'The "Bundle of Rights" Picture of Property', *UCLA Law Review* 43 (3): 711–820. (Sustained criticism of the picture.)

—— (1997) *The Idea of Property in Law*, Oxford: Clarendon Press. (Emphasizes the centrality of exclusion, the social use of property and 'things' to the concept of property.)

* Radin, M.J. (1982) 'Property and personhood', *Stanford Law Review* 34 (5): 957–1015. (Uses Hegelian and non-Hegelian perspectives on persons to develop a communitarian theory of property.)

—— (1993) *Reinterpreting Property*, Chicago, IL, and London: University of Chicago Press. (Articles written between 1981 and 1992 that reveal a growing pragmatism.)

—— (1996) *Contested Commodities*, Cambridge, MA, and London: Harvard University Press. (Reworking of articles written between 1987 and 1995 that deal with 'commodification'.)

Reich, C. (1964) 'The new property', *Yale Law Journal* 73 (5): 733–87. (Perceptive treatment of government largess, property and liberty.)

* Roemer, J.E. (1982) *A General Theory of Exploitation and Class*, Cambridge, MA: Cambridge University Press. (Exploitation theory.)

Ryan, A. (1984) *Property and Political Theory*, Oxford: Blackwell. (Elegantly written historical survey.)

Tully, J. (1980) *A Discourse on Property: John Locke and his Adversaries*, Cambridge: Cambridge University Press. (Views Locke as a natural lawyer.)

Waldron, J. (1988) *The Right to Private Property*, Oxford: Clarendon Press. (A brilliantly argued study that includes insightful discussions of Locke, Proudhon and Hegel.)

STEPHEN R. MUNZER

PROPERTY THEORY

Traditionally, a property theory is a theory of abstract entities that can be predicated of things. A theory of properties in this sense is a theory of predication – just as a theory of classes or sets is a theory of membership. In a formal theory of predication, properties are taken to correspond to some (or all) one-place predicate expressions. In addition to properties, it is usually assumed that there are n-ary relations that correspond to some (or all) n-place predicate expressions (for $n \geqslant 2$). A theory of properties is then also a theory of relations.

In this entry we shall use the traditional labels 'realism' and 'conceptualism' as a convenient way to classify theories. In natural realism, where properties and relations are the physical, or natural, causal structures involved in the laws of nature, properties and relations correspond to only some predicate expressions, whereas in logical realism properties and relations are generally assumed to correspond to all predicate expressions.

Not all theories of predication take properties and relations to be the universals that predicates stand for in their role as predicates. The universals of conceptualism, for example, are unsaturated concepts in the sense of cognitive capacities that are exercised (saturated) in thought and speech. Properties and relations in the sense of intensional Platonic objects may still correspond to predicate expressions, as they do in conceptual intensional realism, but only indirectly as the intensional contents of the concepts that predicates stand for in their role as predicates. In that case, instead of properties and relations being what predicates stand for directly, they are what nominalized predicates denote as abstract singular terms. It is in this way that concepts – such as those that the predicate phrases 'is wise', 'is triangular' and 'is identical with' stand for – are distinguished from the properties and relations that are their intensional contents – such as those that are denoted by the abstract singular terms 'wisdom', 'triangularity' and 'identity', respectively. Once properties are represented by abstract singular terms, concepts can be predicated of them, and, in particular, a concept can be predicated of the property that is its intensional content. For example, the concept represented by 'is a property' can be predicated of the property denoted by the abstract noun phrase 'being a property', so that 'Being a property is a property' (or, 'The property of being a property is a property') becomes well-formed. In this way, however, we are confronted with Russell's paradox of (the property of) being a non-self-predicable property, which is the intensional content of the concept represented by 'is a non-self-predicable property'. That is, the property of being a non-self-predicable property both falls and does not fall under the concept of being a non-self-predicable property (and therefore both falls and does not fall under the concept of being self-predicable).

1　**Logical realism and conceptualism in second-order logic**
2　**Natural realism**
3　**Actualism and possibilism in modal logical realism**
4　**Nominalized predicates in property theories**
5　**Conceptual intensional realism**

1　Logical realism and conceptualism in second-order logic

FREGE (1879) was among the first to formalize a theory of properties and relations. His theory amounts to a version of standard second-order predicate logic (see SECOND- AND HIGHER-ORDER LOGICS). By 'standard' here is meant an axiomatic formulation that contains among its valid theses all instances of the full impredicative comprehension principle (CP), in which bound predicate variables may occur, so that a property or relation can be specified in terms of a totality to which it belongs. Formally, CP is described as follows:

$$(\exists F)(\forall x_1)\dots(\forall x_n)[F(x_1,\dots,x_n) \leftrightarrow \phi],$$

where F is an n-place predicate variable not occurring free in ϕ and $x_1,\dots,x_n$ are distinct individual variables.

By CP, every open formula ϕ containing n free individual variables is said to represent a property or relation, which, using the λ-abstraction operator (see LAMBDA CALCULUS), may also be represented by a λ-abstract, $[\lambda x_1 \dots x_n \phi]$, as a complex n-place predicate expression. (Here λ is an operator that binds n individual variables $x_1,\dots,x_n$, and when affixed to a

formula ϕ results in a complex predicate expression in which all of the occurrences of $x_1,\dots,x_n$ in ϕ are bound. For example, the complex predicate of being objects x and y such that

$$F(x,y) \rightarrow (\exists G)[G(x,y) \wedge G(y,x)]$$

can be represented by the

λ-abstract $\lambda xy(F(x,y) \rightarrow (\exists G)[G(x,y) \wedge G(y,x)])$.)

The λ-abstract is taken as a valid substituend of the bound n-place predicate variables in universal instantiation and to satisfy the principle of λ-conversion,

$$(\forall x_1)\dots(\forall x_n)([\lambda x_1 \dots x_n \phi](x_1,\dots,x_n) \leftrightarrow \phi).$$

Because every open formula constructed from atomic formulas in terms of the logical connectives – including quantifiers for individual and predicate variables – is assumed to represent a property or relation in such a theory, the theory is said to amount to a version of 'logical realism' (regarding the existence of universals).

Not every property theory or formal theory of predication will validate CP; that is, not every open formula need represent a property or relation in such a theory. In standard *predicative* second-order logic, for example, formulas containing bound predicate variables are not allowed to occur in the comprehension principle – a constraint that is supposed to restrict the assumption of properties to those that can be represented by first-order formulas where predicate quantifiers do not occur. No λ-abstract in which predicate quantifiers occur will be well-formed in such a theory, and the principle of universal instantiation for predicate quantifiers will be restricted to formulas that contain no bound predicate variables. Formulas with predicate quantifiers can be used to specify properties and relations in *ramified* predicative second-order logic – but only as values of predicate variables of a higher 'level' in the ramified hierarchy, so that no property or relation can be specified in terms of a totality encompassing that property or relation. (See Church 1956: §58.) The motivation for such a restriction is unclear, however, if properties and relations are assumed to exist independently of language and thought. In fact, a substitutional interpretation of predicate quantifiers, with predicate variables having only first-order formulas as their substituends, can be given for standard predicative second-order logic – and a similar related interpretation can be given for its ramification – so that the restriction is equivalent to a nominalistic theory of predication, according to which there are no universals – that is, no properties or relations – beyond the predicate expressions of first-order languages. (See Cocchiarella 1986: ch. 1; 1989: §3.)

In a constructive conceptualist theory of predication, where concepts are understood as the rule-following cognitive capacities underlying the use of predicate expressions, the intent of such a restriction on predicate quantifiers is to preclude the possibility of forming impredicative concepts, that is, concepts that presuppose or conceptually involve a totality to which they belong (such as the concept of a least upper bound of a class of real numbers that has upper bounds). The predicative logic of 'constructive conceptualism' can be formulated as a nonstandard predicative second-order logic in which not all predicate expressions – now including all λ-abstracts, even those in which bound predicate variables occur – are assumed to represent a predicative concept. Such a logic is 'free of existential presuppositions' regarding predicate expressions; and, in particular, no presumption is made independently of meaning postulates as to which predicate constants stand for predicative concepts and which do not. Such a predicative logic can also be ramified, so that concepts can be formed in terms of quantification over concepts formed at a prior 'stage' of the ramified hierarchy; but each 'stage' of the ramification differs from the 'levels' of ramification in standard ramified second-order logic in being 'free of existential presuppositions' regarding predicate expressions. Such a nonstandard predicative logic can also be seen as part of a pattern of conceptual development in which impredicative concept-formation becomes possible, that is, as leading to the validation of CP in a 'holistic' conceptualism – if, as seems warranted given the history of mathematics, a pattern of reflective abstraction in which an idealized transition to a limit is acknowledged to be conceptually possible. (See Cocchiarella 1986: ch. 2; 1989: §§7–8.)

The nonstandard predicative logic of constructive conceptualism, and, similarly, the impredicative logic of holistic conceptualism, will contain a property theory if it is assumed – in a framework of conceptual intensional realism, for example – that properties and relations are intensional objects and that most (if not all) concepts will have such an intensional object as their intensional content. As intensional objects, properties and relations will then be constituents of propositions as the intensional contents of sentences. But, as already noted, as intensional objects, properties and relations will be the objects that nominalized predicates denote as abstract singular terms (a topic we will return to in §4 below).

2 Natural realism

There is another conception of properties and relations for which it is inappropriate to construe them as intensional objects, and in particular as

constituents of propositions. On this alternative, properties and relations are components of states of affairs (which are part of the natural order, as opposed to propositions, which are part of the intensional order), and in that regard they are the physical, or natural, properties and relations involved in the laws of nature. Such physical or natural properties and relations may correspond to some of our concepts or predicate expressions, but in general not every concept or predicate expression will even purport to represent, still less have, such a natural property or relation corresponding to it. No comprehension principle will be valid when the predicate quantifier is taken to refer to a natural property or relation, accordingly, and any assumption that a formula represents a natural property or relation will always amount at best to an empirical hypothesis of an applied scientific theory.

Traditionally (as, for example, in Aristotle's theory), natural properties were said to exist only *in re*, that is, only in the concrete objects that have such properties, which means that

$$(\forall^N F)(\exists x_1)\ldots(\exists x_k)F(x_1,\ldots,x_k),$$

where '$\forall^N$' is a universal quantifier that refers to natural properties and relations when affixed to predicate variables, is valid in such a theory. For this reason, the theory may be called a 'moderate realism'. This thesis is too strong, however, if such a theory is to allow for physical or natural properties and relations – such as those of certain transuranic elements – that *could* be realized in our world as a matter of a natural or causal possibility, even though in fact they never are. In a *modal* moderate realism, the thesis is weakened to

$$(\forall^N F)\Diamond^c(\exists^e x_1)\ldots(\exists^e x_k)F(x_1,\ldots,x_k),$$

where '$\Diamond^c$' is a modal operator for a causal or natural possibility, and '$\exists^e$' is an existential quantifier that refers only to existing (concrete) objects when affixed to individual variables – and where individual variables and singular terms are otherwise 'free of such existential presuppositions'. The 'concept' of (concrete) existence, defined as

$$E!(x) =_{df} (\exists^e y)(x = y),$$

does not represent a natural property in such a theory – though an abstract property in the sense of an intensional object may be assumed as the intensional content of such a concept in conceptual intensional realism (which can be consistently combined with a natural realism in the general framework of 'conceptual realism'). (See FREE LOGICS for more on the logic of singular terms that are 'free of existential presuppositions'.)

3 Actualism and possibilism in modal logical realism

Existence is a property in 'modal logical realism', which is based on a logical or metaphysical notion of possibility and necessity (represented by '◇' and '□'; see MODAL LOGIC), and which can be either actualist or possibilist. In *possibilist* modal logical realism, individual variables bound by '∀' or '∃' have possible, as well as actual, objects as their values (and abstract objects as well if such are assumed), and the statement that 'Some things do not exist', formulated as $(\exists x)\neg E!(x)$, is well-formed and meaningful. Predicate variables bound by these quantifiers refer to properties that might apply to nonexisting, as well as existing, objects – though some properties, such as $[\lambda x\neg E(x)]$, apply only to nonexisting objects, whereas others, such as $[\lambda x E(x)]$, apply only to existing (concrete) objects.

In *actualism*, only the actualist quantifiers '∀ᵉ' and '∃ᵉ' are allowed, so that individual variables bound by these quantifiers have only actual (existing, concrete) objects as their values, and predicate variables bound by these quantifiers have only 'existence-entailing' (e-)properties and (e-)relations as their values – and hence

$$(\forall^e F)\Box[F(x_1,\ldots,x_n) \to E!(x_1) \wedge \ldots \wedge E!(x_n)]$$

is valid in actualism. Unlike the situation in possibilism, not every open formula or λ-abstract represents an e-property or e-relation, which means that the comprehension principle for actualist modal logical realism must be suitably restricted. (See Cocchiarella 1989: §10.)

4 Nominalized predicates in property theories

In addition to the question of which open formulas or λ-abstracts can be said to represent properties or relations (and can be valid substituends of quantified predicate variables), property theories also differ on the question of whether or not properties and relations have an individual (or 'objectual') as well as a predicable nature, and in particular on whether or not they can also have properties and be 'logical subjects' of predication the way objects in general are. In Frege's theory, for example, properties and relations are functions from objects to truth-values, where all functions, according to Frege, have an 'unsaturated' nature – a nature that categorially precludes them from being objects, all of which have a saturated nature. Even if predication is not explained in terms of functionality, however, properties and relations can still be construed as having an unsaturated nature that precludes them from being objects. In Wittgenstein's version of 'logical atomism' (see Wittgenstein 1922),

for example, and in natural realism as well, material or natural properties and relations are the nexuses (or modes of configuration) of states of affairs, and as such they cannot also be objects configured in states of affairs (see WITTGENSTEIN, L.; LOGICAL ATOMISM §1). Similarly, in conceptualism, predicable concepts, as rule-following cognitive structures underlying the use of predicate expressions, are unsaturated cognitive capacities whose exercise (or saturation) in thought and speech is what informs our speech and mental acts with a predicable nature – which means that concepts have only a predicable and not also an individual (or 'objectual') nature. This does not preclude the intensional content of concepts – which are also called properties and relations in the sense of the Platonist, rather than the Aristotelian, tradition – from being objects; namely, the abstract objects that nominalized predicates denote as abstract singular terms, as opposed to the unsaturated concepts that predicates stand for in their role as predicates. Frege held a view something like this in his version of logicism – except that, because of his commitment to an extensional logic, Frege took the objects denoted by abstract singular terms to be classes rather than intensional objects. The important point in all of these views is that even though the universals that predicate expressions stand for in a given formal theory of predication are not themselves objects (values of the individual variables), some (or all) of them may nevertheless have objects correlated with them as the denotata of the same predicate expressions nominalized as abstract singular terms.

The usual way of representing the nominalization of a simple or complex predicate expression as an abstract singular term is by simply deleting the parentheses and commas that are part of that expression's role as a predicate. Thus, whereas $F(x)$ and $R(x,y)$ are formulas in which F and R occur only as predicates, $G(F)$ and $G(R)$ are formulas in which they occur only as singular terms; and in $F(F)$ and $R(F,R)$, they occur first as predicates and then as singular terms. Similarly, where ϕ is a formula, $[\lambda x\phi]([\lambda x\phi])$ is a formula in which $[\lambda x\phi]$ occurs first as a predicate and then as a singular term. A stronger comprehension principle (CP_λ^*) can now be formulated in terms of identity,

$$(\exists F)([\lambda x_1\ldots x_n\phi] = F),$$

from which, by Leibniz's law (applied now even to abstract singular terms), CP is a consequence.

Bertrand Russell, like Frege, also maintained a version of logical realism; but, unlike Frege, Russell rejected the idea that properties and relations have an unsaturated nature that precludes them from being objects (even though he explained the unity of a proposition in terms of a relation occurring only as a relation and not also as an object). Unlike the situation for Frege, in other words, for Russell a nominalized predicate denotes the same property or relation as an abstract singular term that the predicate otherwise stands for in its role as a predicate. This difference is unimportant as far as Russell's paradox of predication is concerned, however, because the paradox, which can be derived from the following instance of CP (and hence from CP_λ^*) in which a nominalized predicate occurs as abstract singular terms,

$$(\exists F)(\forall x)[F(x) \leftrightarrow (\exists G)(x = G \land \neg G(x))],$$

applies to both Frege's and Russell's views of predicates and their nominalizations. Russell's way out of his paradox was the ramified theory of types, which involves grammatically categorizing predicate expressions not only in terms of the hierarchy of 'levels' of ramified second-order logic but also in terms of a 'vertical' hierarchy of orders in which predicates that take nominalized predicates as singular terms must always be of a higher order than the latter (see THEORY OF TYPES).

Later authors, such as L. Chwistek and F. Ramsey, noted that ramification into levels (of the 'horizontal' hierarchy) is not needed to avoid logical paradoxes such as Russell's, and that a simple theory of types suffices instead – though others, such as A. CHURCH, maintain that the ramified, 'horizontal' hierarchy is still needed for certain intensional or semantic paradoxes. R. Montague (1974) developed an intensional logic for natural language based on a version of simple type theory that was originally formulated by Church. Montague extended Church's theory by adding to it intension- and extension-forming operators (patterned after Frege's *Sinn/Bedeutung* distinction; see FREGE, G. §3), '^' and '˅', so that where ξ is a well-formed expression of the theory, $^\wedge\xi$ stands for the intension (or sense) of ξ, and $^\vee\xi$ stands for its extension (and hence $^{\vee\wedge}\xi = \xi$ is valid). Properties and relations of entities of types $t_1, \ldots, t_n$ are then taken as the intensions (or senses) of the classes of n-tuples of those types, and the predication of a property or relation (in intension) is defined as membership of the class that the property or relation has as its extension.

5 Conceptual intensional realism

There are other ways to avoid Russell's paradox besides type theory. One way is to return to standard second-order logic with nominalized predicates as abstract singular terms and restrict λ-abstracts so that only those that can be homogeneously (h-)stratified from an external (metalinguistic) point of view are well-formed. (An expression is 'h-stratified' if it is possible to assign natural numbers to the predicates and singular terms occurring in it so that singular terms flanking the identity sign, as well as all of the subject expressions of any predicate expression occurring in it, are assigned the same number, with the predicate itself assigned the successor of that number.) This amounts to restricting the comprehension principle CP_λ^* so that even though the above instance of CP for Russell's paradox is well-formed, it is not provable, because the λ-abstract

$$[\lambda x(\exists G)(x = G \land \neg G(x))]$$

is not h-stratified. The resulting system is equiconsistent with the simple theory of types.

Another way to avoid Russell's paradox in the context of second-order logic with nominalized predicates is to allow all λ-abstracts, h-stratified or not, to be well-formed and to retain the full comprehension principle CP_λ^*, but allow the first-order part of the logic to be free of existential presuppositions regarding singular terms. The principle of λ-conversion must then be qualified as follows,

$$[\lambda x_1 \ldots x_n \phi](a_1, \ldots, a_n) \leftrightarrow$$
$$(\exists x_1) \ldots (\exists x_n)(a_1 = x_1 \land \ldots \land a_n = x_n \land \phi),$$

where no x_i is free in any a_j, for all i, j such that $1 \leqslant i \leqslant j \leqslant n$. Then, even though

$$(\exists F)([\lambda x(\exists G)(x = G \land \neg G(x))] = F)$$

is provable as an instance of CP_λ^*, that is, even though $[\lambda x(\exists G)(x = G \land \neg G(x))]$ stands for a predicable concept in its role as a predicate, all that follows by the argument for Russell's paradox is that it cannot also denote an object in its role as an abstract singular term, because

$$\neg(\exists y)([\lambda x(\exists G)(x = G \land \neg G(x))] = y)$$

is also provable. In conceptual intensional realism, this result means that the attempt to 'object-ify' the content (in the sense at least of the truth-conditions) determined by the predicable concept represented by $[\lambda x(\exists G)(x = G \land \neg G(x))]$ as an intensional object (or property in the Platonist tradition) must fail. In a reconstruction of Frege's extensional theory, it means that there is no extension (class) corresponding to the property in question. This is not possible in a reconstruction of Russell's view, however, because for Russell every nominalized predicate denotes the same property that the predicate stands for. (See Russell 1903: §49.)

Finally, there are also strictly first-order property theories. Some are developed along the lines of Zermelo–Fraenkel set theory, with membership replaced by exemplification as a predication relation, and with the deletion at least of the axiom of extensionality (see Schock 1969), and sometimes also of the axiom of foundation (see Jubien 1989). (See SET THEORY, DIFFERENT SYSTEMS OF.) Some authors prefer to defer assuming specific axioms for predication and simply extend first-order logic to include nominalized predicates as abstract singular terms, leaving the choice open of how predication might be axiomatically developed as a relation regarding the denotata of such singular terms. (See Bealer and Mönnich 1989.) Others develop a first-order theory of properties based on assuming a similarity between revisionist theories of truth and predication as a first-order relation (see Turner 1987).

See also: LOGICAL AND MATHEMATICAL TERMS, GLOSSARY OF

References and further reading

Bealer, G. (1982) *Quality and Concept*, Oxford: Clarendon Press. (Accessible to readers with an intermediate-level knowledge of logic; presents a theory of properties, relations and propositions as a first-order intensional logic.)

* Bealer, G. and Mönnich, U. (1989) 'Property Theories', in D. Gabbay and F. Guenthner (eds) *Handbook of Philosophical Logic*, Dordrecht: Reidel, vol. 4, 133–251, 1994. (Argues for a first-order theory of properties, relations and propositions in which nominalized forms of complex predicates are included among the singular terms as 'intensional abstracts'.)

Chierchia, G. and Turner, R. (1988) 'Semantics and Property Theory', *Linguistics and Philosophy* 11: 261–302. (Develops a multi-sorted first-order theory of properties in which predication is analysed along the lines of a revisionist theory of truth.)

Chierchia, G., Partee, B. and Turner, R. (1989) *Properties, Types and Meaning*, vol. 1, Dordrecht: Kluwer. (This collection of papers is the result of a conference held in Amherst in 1986.)

* Church, A. (1956) *Introduction to Mathematical Logic*, Princeton, NJ: Princeton University Press. (An excellent text for the intermediate student; includes axiomatic and semantic formulations not only of propositional and first-order logic, but also of second-order logic, standard predicative and ramified second-order logic.)

* Cocchiarella, N.B. (1986) *Logical Investigations of Predication Theory and the Problem of Universals*, Naples: Bibliopolis. (Formal theories of predication are semantically associated in this book with theories of universals for nominalism, logical and natural realism, and constructive and holistic conceptualism. The first part of this book, which can be read by students with an intermediate-level knowledge of logic, deals with predication theories as second-order logics; the second part extends those theories to second-order logic with nominalized predicates as abstract singular terms.)

* —— (1989) 'Philosophical Perspectives on Formal Theories of Predication', in D. Gabbay and F. Guenthner (eds) *Handbook of Philosophical Logic*, vol. 4, Dordrecht: Reidel, 254–326. (Discusses in philosophical terms some of the formal theories of predication described in part 1 of Cocchiarella (1986).)

* Frege, G. (1879) *Begriffsschrift, eine der arithmetischen nachgebildete Formelsprache des reinen Denkens*, Halle: Nebert; trans. '*Begriffsschrift*, a Formula Language, Modelled Upon That of Arithmetic, for Pure Thought', in J. van Heijenoort (ed.) *From Frege to Gödel: A Source Book in Mathematical Logic, 1879–1931*, Cambridge, MA: Harvard University Press, 1967, 1–82. (Accessible to most students, although Frege's two-dimensional notation can be somewhat difficult at first; now recognized as a classic.)

—— (1952) *Translations from the Philosophical Writings of Gottlob Frege*, ed. P.T. Geach and M. Black, Oxford: Blackwell, 3rd edn, 1980. (The essays 'On Concept and Object' and 'Function and Concept' present a good exposition of Frege's view of properties (which he called 'concepts') and relations as unsaturated functions from objects to truth-values; widely accessible.)

* Jubien, M. (1989) 'On Properties and Property Theory', in G. Chierchia, B. Partee and R. Turner (eds) *Properties, Types and Meaning*, Dordrecht: Kluwer, vol. 1, 159–75. (A development of property theory as first-order theory based on a modified Zermelo–Fraenkel set theory.)

* Montague, R. (1974) *Formal Philosophy: Selected Papers of Richard Montague*, ed. R.H. Thomason, New Haven, CT: Yale University Press. (See especially the essays 'Universal Grammar' and 'The Proper Treatment of Quantification in Ordinary English' for a development of Montague's intensional logic along the Church–Frege lines. 'Pragmatics and Intensional Logic' includes a formulation of intensional logic along more traditional Russellian lines as a second-order modal logic.)

Parsons, C. (1971) 'A Plea for Substitutional Quantification', *Journal of Philosophy* 68 (8): 231–7. (Argues for a substitutional – as opposed to a referential – interpretation of predicate quantifiers for standard predicative second-order logic. Instead of having properties and relations as their values, bound predicate variables have only open formulas with no predicate quantifiers as their substituends.)

Parsons, T. (1977) 'Type Theory and Ordinary Language', in S. Davis and M. Mithun (eds) *Linguistics, Philosophy, and Montague Grammar*, Austin, TX: University of Texas Press, 127–51. (This paper illustrates what English would be like if it obeyed the rules of a theory of types.)

* Russell, B.A.W. (1903) *The Principles of Mathematics*, Cambridge: Cambridge University Press; 2nd edn, London: Allen & Unwin, 1937; repr. London: Routledge, 1992. (Includes an account of Russell's early view of properties, which Russell associated, but did not strictly identify, with propositional functions.)

* Schock, R. (1969) *New Foundations for Concept Theory*, Uppsala: Library of Theoria, no. 12. (A first-order theory of properties as intensional objects.)

* Turner, R. (1987) 'A Theory of Properties', *Journal of Symbolic Logic* 52: 455–72. (A first-order theory of properties based on an assumed similarity between predication and revisionist theories of truth.)

* Wittgenstein, L.J.J. (1922) *Tractatus Logico-Philosophicus*, trans. D.F. Pears and B.F. McGuinness, London: Routledge, 1961. (The properties and relations of this classic of logical atomism are the nexuses, or modes of configuration, of atomic states of affairs, and as such cannot themselves be configured as objects in states of affairs.)

NINO B. COCCHIARELLA

PROPHECY

Most people associate prophecy with prognostication. However, an understanding of philosophical theories of prophecy requires that we recognize the full range of functions that a prophet may serve: oracle, cognizer of the divine, moral and social critic, teacher, political leader, legislator, miracle-worker.

A recurring and fundamental issue, dating to ancient times, is whether prophecy is to be explained naturally or supernaturally. The Muslim philosopher al-Farabi and the Jewish philosopher Maimonides exemplify the naturalist orientation. They understood prophecy as an imaginative 'imitation' or translation of scientific and philosophical truths. Their accounts emphasize not only the intellectual but also the political, legislative and educational functions of prophecy. The Muslim al-Ghazali and the Christian Thomas Aquinas illustrate

the supernatural approach, albeit in greatly different ways.

The proposition that biblical prophetic experiences convey scientific and metaphysical knowledge was attacked in varied ways in the modern period. In religious traditions, prophets have been replaced as sources of religious knowledge by either mystics, or books and authoritative interpreters. However, theories of prophecy are linked to important issues about religious language, miracles, the nature of God, the ends of life, and the character of religion.

1 Functions of the prophet
2 Ancient theories: prophecy and veridical dreams
3–4 Medieval theories
5 Modern approaches
6 Prophecy in contemporary religion and philosophy of religion

1 Functions of the prophet

The term 'prophecy' immediately conjures up the ideas of 'prognostication' and 'divination'. However, most philosophical accounts of prophecy, particularly since medieval times, presuppose a far broader conception of the prophet's function. The Greek word *prophetes*, from which the English derives, denotes one who 'speaks for' a god, who imparts divine messages; and in religious traditions, these messages are of various kinds.

While biblical prophets foretell events in the future, religious traditions also imply that they possess divinely imparted knowledge about events in the distant past (for example, creation, or the history of the Jews). According to medieval philosophers, they also possess special knowledge of the structure and workings of the cosmos. Moreover, they bring a moral message. Prophets also perform miracles. Finally, of course, they experience the divine presence in visions, auditions or dreams (see, for example, Isaiah 6). These different functions of the prophet constitute the 'data' that philosophical theories of prophecy have sought to explain.

2 Ancient theories: prophecy and veridical dreams

Philosophical speculation about prophecy began with ancient theories about divination and veridical dreams. Democritus asserted that in dreams, 'images' (*eidōla*) – possibly originating from statues of gods – affect the soul and divulge the future. Aristotle, during an early Platonic stage of his thought, maintained that the soul has a capacity for divination by virtue of its godlike nature. Later, in *On Divination in Sleep* (one of the *Short Natural Treatises*), he maintained that prophecy does not come from a god, since it is not 'the best and the wisest' who experience veridical dreams, but rather the melancholic. Aristotle explored various naturalistic accounts of this phenomenon. Ironically, the notion that prophecy need not occur to the best and the wisest, which Aristotle cited to support naturalism, later became associated with the supernatural view that God can turn whomever he wants into a prophet. An Arabic recension of the *Short Natural Treatises* created the false impression that Aristotle had traced veridical dreams to a cosmic intellect. This misconception influenced later developments among Muslim and Jewish philosophers.

3 Medieval theories: Muslim philosophers

Medieval philosophers debated the extent to which God directly intervenes in the world. Prophecy was implicated in this general debate. Is prophecy divinely bestowed, or is it a natural human attainment? Is prophetic knowledge continuous with everyday or scientific cognition, or is it of a special kind? What faculties must one possess to attain prophecy? Is special preparation required? What is the significance of prophetic imagery? What is meant by divine speech? Philosophers' answers to these questions were anchored in their general metaphysical and epistemological theories; the theory of prophecy is a window into medieval epistemology, which in turn is rooted in medieval metaphysics.

A vital figure in the development of medieval theories of prophecy was the Arabic philosopher al-Farabi. Although discrepancies exist among his various writings and he does not always use the term 'prophecy' where one might expect it, the common understanding of al-Farabi as a 'Neoplatonized Aristotelian' may be summarized as follows (see AL-FARABI §2). Prophecy is attained by individuals of superior intellect by means of an 'emanation' from the 'active intellect'. This emanation flows first to the individual's passive (potential) intellect – thus actualizing the rational faculty – and then to the imaginative faculty. The imaginative faculty both receives and manipulates physical impressions. The prophet's (perfected) imagination frames, or represents, scientific and metaphysical truths in sensory images. This enables the prophet to convey aspects of these truths to the untutored masses. Imagination – in concert with the 'practical' intellect, which has also received the overflow – is associated as well with lawgiving and political skill. Al-Farabi's theory expresses his thesis that religion is an imaginative translation – or 'imitation'– of scientific and metaphysical truth. The fusion of philosophy, law and

politics in al-Farabi's thought is modelled after the philosopher-ruler of Plato's *Republic*. (In some places, we should note, al-Farabi calls the philosophical, nonimaginative reception of truth 'revelation' and ranks it above prophecy.) Veridical dreams and divination, as products of imagination, bear resemblance to prophecy.

While sharing al-Farabi's naturalism, Ibn Sina (Avicenna) held that the active intellect can impart genuine theoretical knowledge even of forms that the individual did not acquire by abstraction (see IBN SINA §§2–3, 5). Prophecy of this elevated type is due to a special 'intuition' or 'insight', and so Ibn Sina's theory is sometimes characterized as mystical. Reflecting, like al-Farabi, an emphasis on the prophet's political function, Ibn Sina believed that only prophets can create a bond between people, and he regarded the existence of prophetic lawgivers as a teleological provision of nature. He also developed a naturalistic account of how prophets work miracles: an excellent or noble soul may act upon physical matter, even as the soul acts upon one's body.

Against al-Farabi and Ibn Sina, other Muslim thinkers refused to see prophecy as naturally acquired. The Ash'arite AL-GHAZALI (§4) believed that God is the only true cause of events (see OCCASIONALISM §1). Hence God directly conveys prophetic knowledge: he imparts it to the angels, who pass it on to the prophet. Al-Ghazali regarded naturalistic philosophical approaches to prophecy as contrary to Islam, though he fell into various contradictions (for example, he recognized that the natural faculties of the soul play *some* role in prophecy). At points he also denied the political function of the prophet. Al-Ghazali believed that sciences are possible only by virtue of divine assistance, thereby significantly expanding the range of prophetic phenomena in accord with his metaphysics of divine causation.

4 Medieval theories: Jewish and Christian philosophers

Al-Farabi's theory of prophecy was adopted, with alterations and with the addition of motifs characteristic of Ibn Sina, by the Jewish philosopher Moses MAIMONIDES (§5) (*Guide to the Perplexed* II, chaps 32–48). Maimonides believed prophecy to be a natural process: 'an overflow' (emanation) from God through the intermediation of the active intellect towards the rational faculty and thence the imaginative faculty. (He allowed for a 'miraculous withholding' of prophecy from a qualified individual, but then again any natural process is subject to miracles.) The prophets' possession of imagination in combination with intellect sets them apart from philosophers, while their possessing philosophy in addition to imagination sets them off from soothsayers, diviners and statesmen. The prophecy of Moses is said by Maimonides to be an exception to his general account, but scholars have debated exactly where the difference lies.

Thus, Maimonides and al-Farabi take the object of prophetic knowledge to be natural science and metaphysics. While they recognize differing levels of prophecy, they require the prophet to have satisfied intellectual and not only moral prerequisites. Knowledge of the future depends on a combination of scientific knowledge and imagination. Both al-Farabi and Maimonides regard intellectual perfection, or perhaps intellectual-cum-political perfection, as the most noble end of human life; hence the highest type of prophet represents the most nearly perfect individual.

Maimonides adopts a striking method of biblical exegesis and a distinctive ontology of prophetic images. Prophetic language, as a product of imagination, is a figurative couching for scientific and religious claims and is utilized to communicate with the masses. Thus, Ezekiel's account of the chariot conveys for Maimonides the metaphysics of Neoplatonized Aristotelianism (*Guide to the Perplexed* III, chaps 1–8). The prophets' depiction of God in anthropomorphic terms likewise results from imagination (which Maimonides sometimes hints is needed even to facilitate the prophet's own apprehension). The 'sensory' objects in prophetic dreams and visions are products of imagination, not extramental existents.

Alexander Altmann (1978) has observed that, because Islamic and Jewish philosophers believed that every natural event, including scientific and philosophical cognition, results from a cosmic system of emanations tracing ultimately to God, naturalism about prophecy and providence was more religiously palatable to them than to thinkers whose metaphysics distinguishes sharply between divine activity and the natural order. Nevertheless, medieval critics found naturalism religiously unsatisfying and its accompanying figurative construal of biblical language exegetically implausible. Questions also arose about how, in the absence of direct divine aid, a prophet could predict events with the kind of detail that infuses biblical prophecies, especially in the case of predictions that entail knowledge of 'future contingents', the future free actions of human beings. In addition, the capacity of the prophet to acquire truths that reason cannot – for example, the belief in creation *ex nihilo* (*Guide to the Perplexed* II, ch. 25) – is hard to explain if prophetic knowledge issues naturally from normal philosophical and scientific reasoning. (However, a

naturalistic view might allow for a special direct or intuitive knowledge, as per Ibn Sina.)

Several Jewish philosophers before and after Maimonides, such as Judah Halevi and Hasdai Crescas are often thought to have adopted a supernatural view of prophecy. In truth, their theories are ambiguous. Isaac Abravanel's theory is perhaps a better example of a Jewish supernaturalist account of prophecy (see ISAAC ABRAVANEL §2).

Christian philosophical treatments of prophecy include Augustine's *De Genesi ad litteram* (The Literal Meaning of Genesis) XII and Aquinas' *Quaestiones disputatae de veritate* (Disputed Questions on Truth), q.12. Aquinas, as distinct from the naturalists, held that prophecy is a *donum Dei*, a pure gift of God. Prophecy results from unmerited grace, and God might even bestow it on someone who seems unfit. This supernatural account is qualified in several ways. For example, Aquinas recognizes naturalistic explanations of veridical dreams and pagan prophecies; also, when God bestows prophecy on the unfit, he does so by improving the individual's intellectual and imaginative faculties, whence prophecy ensues naturally. (God's activity seems to be further mediated by angelic activity.) Aquinas ignores the political function of prophecy so salient in Islamic accounts and in Maimonides' theory. Altmann (1978) has related Aquinas' theory to his rejection of much of Ibn Sina's ontology.

5 Modern approaches

In the modern period, the epistemic value of prophetic utterances came under varied attacks. Turning Maimonides' emphasis on imagination against him, Benedict de SPINOZA (§14) wrote that 'the prophets were endowed with unusually vivid imaginations, and not with unusually perfect minds'. Their scientific and philosophical beliefs merely reflected their own dispositions and prior opinions. Hence 'we are not at all bound to trust them in matters of intellect'. Spinoza's claims signalled the eclipse of the medieval position that prophecy delivers truth, as well as of its concomitant enterprise, the philosophical exegesis of Scripture (*Theologico-Political Treatise*: ch. 2).

The epistemological problem of authenticating prophecy had been well known to medieval philosophers, but subsequently the challenge to validate claims to revelation assumed a more antagonistic cast even on the part of believers. Thomas Hobbes attacked 'visions' as mere daydreams, and remarked famously that to say God has spoken to a person in a dream is 'no more than to say he dreamed that God spake to him'. In the absence of miracles, he said, we have no way to distinguish true revelation (1651: III, ch. 32). John LOCKE (§7), though himself a believer in divine revelation, held that 'firmness of persuasion is no proof that any proposition is from God' and insisted that a person must use reason 'to enable him to judge of his inspirations, whether they be of *divine* original or no' (1689: IV.xviii–xix).

Eminent thinkers, such as Isaac NEWTON (§7), accepted the truth of biblical prophecies, arguing that the fulfilment of some gave proof that the others will be fulfilled as well. Declarations that prophecies had been fulfilled were often impugned on the grounds that biblical prophecies were too obscure or ambiguous to be tested. Advancing a more general critique, David HUME (§2) concluded his classic argument against accepting reports of miracles by extending his distrust to reports of true prophecies: 'all prophecies [that is, true predictions not based on induction] are real miracles' (1748, 1751: sect. X).

With time, various theorists assimilated or reduced prophecy to such categories as ecstasy (an identification already made by the ancients), psychosis, poetic inspiration, hallucination, fabrication and demagoguery. Anthropologists viewed biblical prophecy as a phenomenon with cognates in many cultures, thereby diminishing any special claims of the prophets of the Bible and Qur'an. Even in theological circles, a distinction eventually emerged between the experience of (divine) presence and the experience of content. The content of a prophecy, on this account, represents a subjective, culturally conditioned human response to the experience of presence. Although the medieval view that the prophet exercises imagination also implied prophetic subjectivity, the modern approach implied a denigration of prophetic claims to objective truth and stressed the ethical response rather than the purely cognitive.

These varied challenges to traditional views often went along with deep admiration for the ethical thrust of prophetic religion, and theories respectful of prophecy continued to appear within theological frameworks. However, the overall contrast with medieval times is dramatic.

6 Prophecy in contemporary religion and philosophy of religion

It is sometimes said that prophecy differs from mysticism in its emphasis on God's word and communication of it. Assuming this distinction, we might say that, in the major religions, the role of prophets has been overshadowed by two things: at the one pole, mystics and, at the other, as Hobbes long ago noted, books and authoritative interpreters. Mystics and texts have thus become the primary medium of revelation. Prophecy also figures little in twentieth-century analytically oriented treatments of religion, though there has been some discussion of prophecy in connection with the alleged incompatibility of divine foreknowledge and human free will (see OMNISCIENCE §§3–4). Concepts connected to prophecy – revelation, mystical experience, miracles, the paranormal – are explored extensively by philosophers, but usually with scant or no reference to prophecy *per se*. All this is surprising in so far as the claims of traditional theism ultimately rest on the thesis that God communicates with human beings.

See also: CHALDAEAN ORACLES; ETERNITY; MYSTICISM, HISTORY OF; MYSTICISM, NATURE OF; PROVIDENCE; REVELATION

References and further reading

* Altmann, A. (1978) 'Maimonides and Thomas Aquinas: Natural or Divine Prophecy?', *AJS Review* 3: 1–19. (This article gives more detail about the material concerning ancient philosophy, Maimonides and Aquinas discussed in §§2–4.)
* Aquinas, T. (1256–9) *Disputed Questions on Truth*, Chicago, IL: Regnery, 1952. (Treats prophecy in the course of a discussion of predestination and foreknowledge.)
* Aristotle (384–322 BC) *Short Natural Treatises* (*Parva naturalia*), ed. W.D. Ross, Oxford: Oxford University Press, 1955. (*On Divination in Sleep* presents a critical account of prophecy as being divinely inspired.)
* Augustine (401–14) *De Genesi ad litteram*, trans. J.H. Taylor, *The Literal Meaning of Genesis*, New York: Newman Press, 2 vols, 1982. (Prophecy is discussed in Book XII, which is an influential account of different sorts of vision.)
  Davidson, H. (1992) *Alfarabi, Avicenna and Averroes on Intellect: Their Cosmologies, Theories of the Active Intellect, and Theories of the Human Intellect*, New York: Oxford University Press. (A thorough, insightful account. See the index to find items about prophecy.)
  al-Farabi (*c*.870–950) *Al-Farabi on the Perfect State: Abu Nasr al-Farabi's Mabadi' Ara Ahl al-Madina al-Fadila*, ed. and trans. R. Walzer, Oxford: Clarendon Press, 1985. (An edition of *The Principles of the Views of the Citizens of the Best State*. Relevant to §3, in conjunction with al-Farabi's *Aphorisms of the Statesman*.)
  al-Ghazali (1058–1111) *Mishkat al-Anwar* (The Niche of the Lights), trans. W.H.T. Gairdner, *Al-Ghazzali's Mishkat al-Anwar*, London: Asiatic Monographs Society, 19, 1924. (Described by Davidson

as an 'inadequate' edition; should be read together with Davidson (1992: 134–44).)

Heschel, A.J. (1962) *The Prophets*, New York: Harper & Row. (A two-volume study. In volume 2, Heschel attempts to reply to modern accounts of prophecy and develop his own account. Not highly rigorous, but engaging and suggestive. Relevant to §5.)

* Hobbes, T. (1651) *Leviathan*, ed. R. Tuck, Cambridge: Cambridge University Press, 1991. (Provides grounds for assessing claims of revelation; see III, ch. 32.)

Huby, P. (1979) 'The Paranormal in the Writings of Aristotle and his Circle', *Apeiron* 13 (1): 53–62. (Argues that Aristotle shifted from a supernatural to a naturalistic account of prophecy.)

* Hume, D. (1748, 1751) 'On Miracles', in *Enquiry Concerning the Human Understanding and Concerning the Principles of Morals*, ed. L.A. Selby-Bigge, Oxford: Clarendon Press, 2nd edn, 1972. (Section X is Hume's famous critique of miracles, which he extends to prophecy.)

Ibn Sina (first half of 11th century) *Kitab al-Najat*, trans. and ed. F. Rahman, *Avicenna's Psychology*, Westport, CT: Hyperion Press, 1952, esp. 32–8. (Partial translation of *The Book of Salvation*.)

* Locke, J. (1689) *An Essay Concerning Human Understanding*, ed. A. Fraser, Oxford: Oxford University Press, 1894; New York: Dover, 1959. (Locke emphasizes the role of reason in assessing revelation claims in Book IV.xviii–xix.)

Macy, J. (1985) 'Prophecy in al-Farabi and Maimonides: The Imaginative and Rational Faculties', in S. Pines and Y. Yovel (eds) *Maimonides and Philosophy*, Dordrecht: Martinus Nijhoff. (A fine analysis of comparisons and contrasts. Also contains a careful analysis of differences between four of al-Farabi's works on prophecy.)

Maimonides, M. (*c*.1190) *The Guide of the Perplexed*, trans. S. Pines, Chicago, IL: University of Chicago Press, 1963. (Maimonides' account of prophecy is in part II, chapters 32–48.)

Popkin, R. (1984) 'Predicting, Prophesying, Divining and Foretelling from Nostradamus to Hume', *History of European Ideas* 5 (2): 117–36. (An interesting analysis of how Hume undermined the enterprise of studying prophetic predictions.)

Rahman, F. (1958) *Prophecy in Islam*, Chicago, IL: University of Chicago Press. (Contains significant material, including extended quotations, on Islamic thinkers, especially al-Farabi, Ibn Sina and their 'orthodox' critics.)

Reines, A. (1970) *Maimonides and Abrabanel on Prophecy*, Cincinnati, OH: Hebrew Union College Press. (An arrangement and explanation of Isaac Abravanel's critical comments on Maimonides' *Guide*.)

* Spinoza, B. de (1670) *A Theologico-Political Treatise*, trans. R.H.M. Elwes, vol. 1 of *The Chief Works of Benedict de Spinoza*, New York: Dover, 1951. (See especially chapter 2.)

Stump, E. and Kretzmann, N. (1991) 'Prophecy, Past Truth, and Eternity', in J. Tomberlin (ed.) *Philosophical Perspectives 5: Philosophy of Religion*, Atascadero, CA: Ridgeview, 395–424. (A discussion, responding to David Widerker, of the special problem that prophetic foreknowledge poses for free will: whereas divine knowledge might be said to be 'outside time', that knowledge comes to be 'within time' once God has communicated his knowledge to a human prophet. This article suggests a reply.)

Wierenga, E. (1991) 'Prophecy, Freedom, and the Necessity of the Past', in J. Tomberlin (ed.) *Philosophical Perspectives 5: Philosophy of Religion*, Atascadero, CA: Ridgeview, 425–45, esp. 433–41. (Attempts to resolve the prophetic foreknowledge-versus-human free will problem described in the Stump–Kretzmann article.)

DAVID SHATZ

PROPOSITIONAL ATTITUDE STATEMENTS

Propositional attitude statements – statements about our beliefs, desires, hopes and fears – exhibit certain logical peculiarities. For example, in apparent violation of Leibniz's law of the indiscernibility of identicals, we cannot freely substitute expressions which designate the same object within such statements. According to Leibniz's law, every instance of the following scheme is valid:

a = b

*F(*a*)*

*Therefore, F(*b*)*

The validity of Leibniz's law seems beyond question. It says, in effect, that if an object has a certain property, then anything identical to that object also has that property. Valid instances abound. But consider the following apparently invalid instance:

(1) Hesperus is Phosphorus

(2) Hammurabi believed that Hesperus often rose in the evening

(3) Therefore, Hammurabi believed that 'Phosphorus' often rose in the evening.

If we take 'Hammurabi believed that... often rose in the evening' to serve as the predicate F and 'Hesperus' and 'Phosphorus' to be a and b respectively, this argument appears to be an instance of Leibniz's law. Yet (3) apparently fails to follow from (1) and (2). Hammurabi believed that Hesperus and Phosphorus were two heavenly bodies not one. And he believed that Hesperus did, but that Phosphorus did not rise in the evening.

We have derived a false conclusion from true premises and an apparently valid law. If that law is really valid, then our argument had better not be a genuine instance of the law. The tempting conclusion, widely accepted, is that we were wrong to construe propositional attitude statements as simple predications. We should not, that is, construe 'Hammurabi believed that... often rose in the evening' to be just a long predicate with the semantic function of attributing some property to the object commonly denoted by 'Hesperus' and 'Phosphorus'. But then the question arises: if attitude reports are not simple predications, what are they? Philosophers have disagreed sharply in their answers. Moreover, their disagreements are intimately connected to a wide range of deep issues about the nature of meaning and reference.

1　**Frege on attitude statements**
2　**Referential opacity**
3　**Innocence regained?**
4　**Structured complexes**
5　**Hidden indexicality**

1　Frege on attitude statements

Gottlob FREGE was among the first to offer systematic explanations of the form and content of propositional attitude statements (Frege 1892). Central to Frege's treatment of attitude statements is his distinction between sense and reference (see SENSE AND REFERENCE). Frege held that each significant linguistic expression plays two distinct but related semantic roles: it 'denotes' a reference and 'expresses' a sense. For example, the reference of a singular term like a proper name is typically some individual object. A sense, on the other hand, is a way of being given a reference. The sense of a proper name, for example, contains a condition, the unique satisfaction of which by an object *o* is necessary and sufficient to determine *o* as its reference. Perhaps the following captures the sense of 'Phosphorus':

o is Phosphorus just in case *o* is the last celestial object visible in the early morning sky just before sunrise.

The distinction between sense and reference holds not just for proper names but also for sentences. Frege took the reference of a complete declarative sentence to be its truth-value. A declarative sentence is thus a name of sorts – a name for a truth-value. So, for example, the reference of:

(4)　Phosphorus can often be seen in the evening sky

is the True, as Frege called it. On the other hand, the sense of a complete declarative sentence is supposed to be a thought, according to Frege. The sense of (4) is the thought that Phosphorus can often be seen in the evening sky.

Frege held that that two expressions may denote the same reference while expressing distinct senses. 'Hesperus' and 'Phosphorus' denote the same object, but differ in sense, from Frege's viewpoint. Something like the following satisfaction condition arguably captures the sense of 'Hesperus':

o is Hesperus just in case *o* is the first celestial object visible in the early evening sky after sunset.

Similarly, although sentence (4) and

(5)　Hesperus can often be seen in the evening sky

denote the same reference – namely, the True – they express different thoughts. For the thought that Phosphorus can often be seen in the evening sky is, according to Frege, distinct from the thought that Hesperus can often be seen in the evening sky. One indicator of their distinctness is the possibility that a rational cognizer can simultaneously believe the one, while disbelieving the other. Hammurabi was just such a cognizer.

It is worth enumerating three essential characteristics of Fregean thoughts. First, thoughts are the primary bearers of truth-conditions. The very identity of a thought is constituted by its having the truth-conditions that it has. Sentences, by contrast, have their truth-conditions only derivatively, by being associated with a thought, in virtue of the conventions of a language. Second, thoughts are composite structured entities. A thought is a whole, composed of constituent parts. The parts of thoughts are themselves senses. For example, the thought that Hesperus is often visible in the evening has the sense of 'Hesperus' as a constituent part. Third, thoughts are the objects of the propositional attitudes. To believe that Hesperus is often visible in the evening is to stand in a certain relation – the believing relation – to the thought that Hesperus is often visible in the evening. To wonder whether Hesperus is often visible in the evening is to stand in a different relation – the wondering relation – to that same thought.

Frege endorses a principle of compositionality for both sense and reference (see COMPOSITIONALITY).

He believes that both the reference and the sense of a complex expression are a function of the references and senses, respectively, of the constituent parts of that sentence (and the way those parts combine to form a whole). Two sentences which differ only by constituents which themselves have the same reference, should have the same truth-value. Similarly, two sentences which differ only by constituents which express the same sense, should themselves express the same thought. Now Frege is convinced that these compositionality principles are nowhere violated. But then the original quandary about attitude sentences remains.

Frege's way out is to say that despite our initial assessment 'Hesperus' as it occurs in (2) and 'Phosphorus' as it occurs in (3) do not share a reference. Call the sense and reference of a term as it occurs in direct discourse its 'customary' sense and reference. Frege claims that when an expression is embedded within a that-clause, it undergoes a shift in both its sense and its reference. In particular, he holds that obliquely occurring expressions, as he called them, denote not their customary referents, but their customary senses. Moreover, an obliquely occurring term denotes a new sense: what he calls its 'oblique' or 'indirect' sense. An indirect sense is a mode of presentation not of a term's customary reference, but of its customary sense. Thus in (2) 'Hesperus' refers not to the planet Venus but to the customary sense of 'Hesperus'. Similarly, in (3), 'Phosphorus' denotes the customary sense of 'Phosphorus'. Indeed, a whole sentence undergoes a shift in sense and reference when it is joined with 'that' to form a clause. The that-clause in (2), for example, does not denote a truth-value, but the thought customarily expressed by 'Hesperus often rose in the evening' when it stands on its own. It denotes, that is, the thought that Hesperus often rose in the evening. And (2) as a whole says that Hammurabi stands in the believing relation to that thought. Similarly, the that-clause in (3) denotes the thought that Phosphorus often rose in the evening. And (3) attributes to Hammurabi the property of believing that thought.

Clearly, if Frege is correct, the invalidity of our original argument does not, after all, violate Leibniz's law. Since the customary sense of 'Hesperus' is not identical to the customary sense of 'Phosphorus' our original argument turns out not to involve the substitution of co-referring terms.

2 Referential opacity

Philosophers have sometimes questioned the coherence of Fregean senses. W.V. Quine, for example, has argued that senses and related intensional notions are 'creatures of darkness' (Quine 1956). There is no saying, according to Quine, for arbitrary senses x and y, when x and y are the same sense and when they are two distinct senses (see QUINE, W.V. §8; RADICAL TRANSLATION AND RADICAL INTERPRETATION §§2–3). There can be no entities, he insists, where there are no determinate criteria of identity. But if senses go, so too must Frege's account of propositional attitude statements.

Quine endorses Frege's negative conclusion that obliquely occurring terms do not play their customary referential roles. He offers, however, a markedly different diagnosis of that failure. Like Frege, Quine believes that where reference happens substitutivity reigns – that is, Leibniz's law holds. But unlike Frege, Quine takes the failure of substitutivity within attitude statements at face value. And he concludes, in effect, that reference cannot be happening within the context of propositional attitude statements or that-clauses generally. That-clauses, he claims, are 'referentially opaque'. Embed a term which elsewhere functions referentially within such a clause and substitution is no longer permissible, not because reference shifts, but because the embedded term is stripped of its referential function. Quine suggests, in fact, that it is a mistake to speak of 'embedding' a referring expression within a that-clause at all. He suggests that an expression like 'believed that Hesperus often rose in the evening' functions rather like a primitive one-place predicate with no 'logically germane' constituent parts. In that case, sentences like (2) are misleadingly spelled. A more revealing spelling would treat this predicate as a single, though very long word somewhat like: 'believed-that-Hesperus-often-rose-in-the-evening'. The presence of the string 'Hesperus' in this very long word is merely an accident of orthography. It would be no more correct to regard 'Hesperus' as a grammatical constituent of this very long word, than it would be to regard the word 'cat' as grammatical constituent of the word 'cattle'.

Referential opacity explains another logical peculiarity of that-clauses, according to Quine. Consider the law of existential generalization:

$$F(a)$$

Therefore, $(\exists x)F(x)$

Informally, this scheme says that if a has F then there is something or other which has F. Existential generalization allows us to infer from the premise that 'John loves Mary' to the conclusion that 'John loves someone or other'. When we try to apply this evidently valid scheme within the context of a propositional attitude verb, we are led into apparent contradiction. Consider the following sentence:

(6)　The president suspects that someone is a spy.

As it stands, (6) is subject to two different readings. On one reading, (6) says that the president 'suspects true', as we might put it, a certain statement or proposition – the statement or proposition that spying sometimes happens. This reading has been variously called the '*de dicto*', 'notional', or 'referentially opaque' reading (see DE RE/DE DICTO). There is a second reading of (6) which attributes to the president not just the generalized suspicion that spying sometimes happens, but the state of being 'suspicious of' some person or other. We might paraphrase this reading of (6) by:

(6b)　The president suspects someone of being a spy

or by:

(6c)　There is someone whom the president suspects of being a spy.

This reading is variously called the '*de re*', 'relational', or 'referentially transparent' reading. The two readings are not generally equivalent. It is possible to suspect that spying happens even when one has no suspicions about any particular person. The ambiguity in sentences like (6) is sometimes traced to an ambiguity of quantifier scope. On the so-called *de dicto* or opaque reading of (6), the quantifier has narrow scope relative to 'believes'. On the so-called *de re* or transparent reading, the quantifier has wide scope relative to 'believes'. As a first pass, we might represent the *de dicto* reading by (6d) and the *de re* reading by (6e):

(6d)　The president suspects that $(\exists x)(x$ is a spy$)$

(6e)　$(\exists x)($The president suspects that x is a spy$)$.

Quine has argued that constructions like (6e), in which a quantifier sitting outside the scope of the attitude verb 'reaches in' to bind a variable that lies within the scope of that attitude verb, are deeply problematic. We cannot, he claims, 'quantify into' attitude contexts (Quine 1956). Or to put it in slightly different terms, propositional attitude verbs appear to block the interior reach of exterior quantifiers.

Suppose that the president has observed Stanley P. Young, a certain low-level White House aide, behaving in a rather furtive manner. He says with great conviction to the chief of White House security, 'Stanley P. Young is a spy.' That seems a sufficient basis for attributing to the president the belief that Stanley P. Young is a spy and thus a sufficient basis for taking this to be true:

(7)　The president believes that Stanley P. Young is a spy.

If we construe 'The president believes... is a spy' as a complex predicate, then from (7) and the law of Existential Generalization, we should be able to infer:

(8)　$(\exists x)($The president believes that x is a spy$)$.

There may be a number people whom the president believes to be spies. Stanley P. Young is one such person. 8′ below would also seem to follow:

8′　$(\exists x)(x =$ Stanley P. Young & the president believe that x is a spy$)$.

Now suppose that the president is subsequently introduced to one James Q. Money, a generous contributor to progressive causes and a man of stellar reputation. The president trusts Mr Money. When asked whether Money is a spy, the president denies even the possibility. That denial is grounds for inferring:

(9)　The president believes that James Q. Money is not a spy.

From (9) and Existential Generalization we can infer:

(10)　$(\exists x)($The president believes that x is not a spy$)$.

10′　$(\exists x)(x =$ James Q. Money & the president believe that x is not a spy$)$.

But unbeknownst to the president, James Q. Money leads a double life. He is none other than Stanley P. Young. Does the president believe or not believe James Q. Money, that is, Stanley P. Young, to be a spy? Intuition pulls in opposite directions. Since James Q. Money just is Stanley P. Young, we should, by Leibniz's law, be able to substitute 'Young' for 'Money' in 10′ without change of truth-value. Since this substitution happens outside the that-clause, it should be unaffected by the logical peculiarities of such clauses. Yet substitution yields:

10　$(\exists x)(x =$ Stanley P. Young & the president believe that x is not a spy$)$.

Examples 10 and 8′ are of dubious consistency. No one can both be and not be a spy. So how can anyone consistently both believe a person to be a spy and believe that very person not to be a spy?

The answer lies in referential opacity. Because (7) and (9) are opaque, they do not ascribe to the president incompatible relations to Money, that is, Young. Indeed, opaquely construed, the Quinean insists, neither (7) nor (9) relates the president to Money, that is, Young at all. Recall again the Quinean view that when opaque contexts are perspicuously spelled the illusion that they contain referring expressions as proper constituents will have been dispelled. Indeed, opacity renders quantified sentences like 10′ and 10 utterly nonsensical. For proper respelling reveals that there is no genuine occurrence of an interior variable for the exterior quantifier to bind. An analogy with quotation – which Quine takes to be the referentially opaque context *par excellence* – makes the reason clear. Consider:

(11) '*x* is a spy' is an open sentence.

Enclosing an expression within quotation marks seals that expression off from the reach of external quantifiers. The quantifier below does not bind the quoted variable:

(12) $(\exists x)$('*x* is a spy' is an open sentence).

What occurs within the quotation marks is really not a variable *in use*. It is rather a variable *being mentioned* (see Use/mention distinction and quotation). Similarly, though what occurs in 10′ and 10 bears a certain orthographic resemblance to a variable in use, it is not the real thing. For that reason we can no more quantify into propositional attitude contexts, Quine insists, than we can quantify into the context of quotation.

Quine's approach promises a way out of the threatened contradiction, but only by doing great violence to a number of potent intuitions. It seems frankly incredible that putatively referring terms embedded within a that-clause are mere grammatical illusions. Further, if propositional attitude statements lack logically germane constituents, there will be no accounting for certain systematic commonalities and differences among such statements. Compare and contrast, for example, (7) and (9) above with (13) and (14) below:

(13) The First Lady *doubts that* Young is a spy

(14) The vice-president *wonders whether* Young is a spy.

Example (13) seems to say that the First Lady doubts what the president believes, while (14) says that the vice-president has questions about what the First Lady and the president disagree about. Moreover, the president's belief, the First Lady's assurance and the vice-president's questions seem all to be about one and the same individual. Quine's approach abandons these intuitive judgments.

Quine is well aware of these costs. He believes, however, that we must pay the cost if we are to keep the creatures of darkness – Fregean senses and other intensional entities – at bay (see Intensional entities).

3 Innocence regained?

Donald Davidson has argued that if we could but regain our pre-Fregean semantic innocence:

> it would seem to us plainly incredible that the words 'The earth moves' uttered after the words 'Galileo said that' mean anything different, or refer to anything else, than is their wont when they come in other environments.
>
> (Davidson 1969: 172)

If Davidson is right then we can account for the logical peculiarities of attitude statements without positing Fregean reference shifts. Nor, if he is right, need we allow that otherwise referring terms are stripped of their referential functions when they occur in attitude contexts. Indeed, against Quine, Davidson holds that unless we have already been forced to introduce Fregean senses for other reasons, the peculiarities of attitude contexts provide no additional pressures to posit such entities. So if Davidson is right, Quine's drastic departures are not needed to keep intensions at bay.

Davidson defends what he calls a 'paratactic analysis' of the logical forms of indirect discourse, though his approach can be extended fairly directly to attitude ascriptions. Davidson's central claim is that a sentence like:

(15) Galileo said that the earth moves

is really a parataxis of two sentences. The first sentence of the parataxis in (15) ends with the word 'that'; the second starts with 'the earth'. By adding a bit of punctuation, we can represent (15) in a more perspicuous manner as:

(16) Galileo said that. The earth moves.

Call the first sentence the attribution sentence and the second the content sentence. In the attribution sentence of (16), the 'that' is a demonstrative pronoun which refers (on an occasion) to an utterance of the second sentence of (16).

Sentence (16) will be true, according to Davidson, just in case some utterance of Galileo's makes Galileo and the utterer of (16) 'samesayers'. Suppose that Galileo utters (17) and Smith utters (18):

(17) Eppur si muove.

(18) The earth moves.

In some sense, Galileo and Smith say the same thing. Moreover, if Smith utters (18) and Galileo utters (17) then 'the earth' in Smith's mouth and 'Eppur' in Galileo's mouth have the same reference.

Suppose that Smith wants to attribute Galileo's statement to Galileo. He can do so simply by saying the same thing as Galileo and then saying that he has just done so – as in the following scenario:

(19) Galileo: Eppur si muove.

(20) Smith: The earth moves. Galileo said that (too).

Here we have Galileo saying, in Italian, that the earth moves. We have Smith saying the same thing in English. And then we have Smith ascribing such a statement to Galileo. He does so by making a statement that turns himself and Galileo into samesayers (to use Davidson's phrase) and then stating that he has just done so. As matters stand, it remains unclear until Smith utters the second sentence of (20) just what the point of his initial utterance may be. But we can rectify that by reversing the order of the sentences as follows:

(21) Galileo said that. → The earth moves.

The arrow in (21) should be understood as a demonstration accompanying the demonstrative pronoun 'that'. The demonstrative refers to Smith's second utterance – the one by which Smith purports to turn himself and Galileo into samesayers. While Smith 'refers' to his own utterance, he implicitly 'quantifies over' Galileo's utterances. Smith says, in effect, that the demonstrated utterance of his and 'some utterance or other' of Galileo's make himself and Galileo samesayers.

Davidson's account yields a relatively straightforward explanation of the invalidity of inferences like the following:

(22) Galileo said that. → The earth moves.

(23) The earth is the third planet from the sun.

(24) Galileo said that. → The third planet from the sun moves.

There is no logical connection between the effect of substitution on the content sentence and the truth-values of the two attribution sentences. As Davidson puts it:

> There is no reason to predict, on grounds of form alone, any *particular* effect on the truth of [the attribution sentence] from a change in [the content sentence]. On the other hand, if the [content sentence] had been different in any way at all, [the attribution sentence] *might* have had a different truth-value, for the reference of the 'that' would have been changed.
>
> (Davidson 1969: 172)

Though Davidson's central idea is quite ingenious, there are both syntactic and semantic grounds for scepticism. For example, content clauses are not generally introduced by demonstratives. Neither

'whether' in 'Galileo wondered whether the earth moves' nor 'for...to' in 'I would prefer for you to leave' can plausibly be analysed as overt demonstratives. Moreover, demonstratives cannot in general be deleted, but the 'that' in '...said that...' can. Compare the following:

(25) Davidson saw that man over there.

(26) Davidson said that the paratactic analysis is true.

(27) ?Davidson saw man over there.

(28) Davidson said the paratactic analysis is true.

It is also difficult to see how to extend the paratactic analysis to *de re* ascriptions. Consider (29):

(29) Every philosopher believes that he is wise.

Example (29) says, in effect, that every philosopher has a high opinion of himself. But if we interpret (29) along Davidsonian lines as:

(30) Every philosopher believes that. He is wise.

we get something rather different.

Finally it is clear that we need to know more about the samesaying relation. If the paratactic analysis is to overcome the need to introduce Fregean senses and the like, then samesaying cannot just be a matter of expressing the same Fregean sense. Davidson owes us an account of samesaying which eschews senses and other intensional entities altogether. Davidson is fully aware of this debt and labours mightily to pay it (Davidson 1969).

4 Structured complexes

A class of theories which has recently gained favour with a number of philosophers is what might be called the structured complex approach (see INTENSIONAL LOGIC §5). Advocates of such theories maintain that attitude verbs express relations between agents and complex hierarchically structured entities of one sort or another. The core idea dates back to Carnap (1947). It has resurfaced, much modified, in Cresswell (1984), Segal (1989), Richard (1990), Higginbotham (1991) and Larson and Ludlow (1993). Different versions of this approach posit different structured complexes. Carnap posited hierarchically structured intensions. Others pair semantic values with something else: sometimes a sentence, sometimes a description of a sentence, sometimes a structured intension. Larson and Ludlow, for example, hold that that-clauses specify Interpreted Logical Forms (ILFs). An ILF is a kind of product of a phrase structure tree for a sentence and the sequence of semantic values for the semantically valued constituents of that sentence. On their approach, the sentence:

(31) Pierre admires London

will be associated with the ILF in Figure 1:

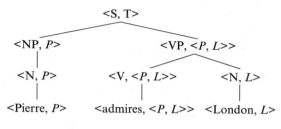

Figure 1

We need not worry about the exact formation rules that generate this ILF. The crucial point is that each node in this tree is labelled by a pair whose left member is either a lexical item (at the bottom-most nodes) or a phrase marker (at all other nodes) and whose right member is a semantic value. For example, the pair is the pair whose left member is the word 'Pierre' and whose right member is the reference of 'Pierre' (namely, Pierre himself). The pair > has left member 'admires' and a right member consisting of a pair whose members are Pierre and London. Such trees are intended to represent a sequence of semantic values and the order in which those semantic values are associated with the expressions whose values they are. Because lexical items (words themselves), and not just phrase makers, are constituents of ILFs, the following two sentences will have distinct ILFs:

(32) Hesperus rises in the evening.

(33) Phosphorus rises in the evening.

Nonetheless, (32) and (33) have, according to Larson and Ludlow, the same semantic content. That is, (32) and (33) have formally distinct but semantically equivalent ILFs. Armed with the notion of formally distinct but semantically equivalent ILFs, Larson and Ludlow are able to explain how it is possible for attitude statements like our original (2) and (3) to differ in truth-value. The thought is that an agent who stands in the believing relation to the ILF of 'Hesperus rises in the evening' need not *ipso facto* stand in the believing relation to the ILF of 'Phosphorus rises in the evening.' Yet one who believes that Hesperus rises believes the very same semantic content as one who believes that Phosphorus rises.

Notice that Larson and Ludlow walk the middle ground between Davidson and Frege. Their approach is ontologically conservative like Davidson's. For the structural descriptions and semantic values out of which ILFs are composed must already be introduced

in to our ontology to account for the semantic and syntactic character of sentences other than those about propositional attitudes. But their explanation of failures of substitutivity is analogous to Frege's own. They too appeal to the fact that, at least in attitude contexts, more is relevant to substitutivity than mere co-reference. That more is, however, not anything semantic. So we are not required, merely because of the peculiarities propositional attitude statements, to posit for each referring expression a second semantic role over and above its role of standing for a referent.

5   Hidden indexicality

Consider the following three theses:

(a) *The Direct Reference Thesis.* The sole semantic role of a proper name is to stand for its bearer.
(b) *Semantic Innocence.* A name plays the same semantic role when embedded within a that-clause as it plays when it occurs outside a that-clause.
(c) *The Fregean Intuition.* Propositional attitude statements which differ only by co-referring proper names may differ in truth-value.

Each of these theses has considerable independent plausibility. But they are not obviously consistent. Frege was moved to abandon both thesis (a) and (b) because he thought they could not be reconciled with (c) (see PROPER NAMES §5). More recently, Nathan Salmon (1986) has abandoned (c) out of a commitment to (a) and (b). He has insisted that it is merely a pragmatically generated illusion that sentences like (2) and (3) have different truth-values. He claims that strictly, literally speaking, one who believes that Hesperus rises *ipso facto* believes that Phosphorus rises. It is just that it is conversationally misleading to talk that way. That is because belief is not a two place relation between a believer and a proposition, but a three place relation between a believer, a proposition and what we might call a 'way of believing' that proposition. Propositions are never believed *simpliciter*, but always in some way or other, under some guise or other. Moreover, Salmon insists, a rational cognizer can believe a given proposition under one guise while failing to believe it under a different guise. But the crucial further point is that nothing in an attitude ascription semantically specifies the guise under which the proposition named by the that-clause is supposed to be believed. The guise simply does not enter into the strict literal truth-conditions of an attitude statement. Nonetheless, Salmon suggests, we can pragmatically suggest something about the guise, by using one expression rather than another semantically equivalent one in making an attribution. If we use 'Hesperus' we suggest something different about the guise than we would if were to use 'Phosphorus'. That is why it is pragmatically misleading to use 'Hesperus' and 'Phosphorus' interchangeably in making attitude ascriptions.

By contrast, hidden indexicalists insist on all of our principles, and offer a strategy, with several variants, for reconciling them (see Schiffer 1979; Crimmins and Perry 1989; Richard 1990; Crimmins 1992). Proponents of the hidden indexical approach generally agree with the view that belief is a three-place, rather than merely a two-place relation. They even agree that that-clauses which differ only by co-referring proper names must refer to the same (singular) proposition. But they insist that attitude ascriptions do not just pragmatically suggest information about the guise under which the specified proposition is believed. Information about the guise is part of what is strictly, literally said by an attitude ascription. That is why, against Salmon, the Fregean intuition is here to stay.

Yet, given the assumption of semantic innocence, how could that-clauses which differ only by corresponding co-referring proper names specify distinct ways of believing? The answer, according to the hidden indexicalist, is that there is more to an attitude statement than meets either the eye or the ear. Attitude reports contain hidden or unarticulated indexical constituents. These unarticulated constituents are not reflected in the surface grammatical structure of the sentence, but in a context of utterance they somehow refer to a way of believing. Consequently, attitude sentences, in context, manage to express propositions with more explicit constituents than they themselves have. Such sentences can be compared, the hidden indexicalist says, to sentences like the following in which one term of a relation is suppressed, but can be supplied, in context, by competent producers and consumers:

It is raining.	(Where?)
I am ready.	(For what?)
That is tall.	(For a what?)
Smith believes that p.	(How?)

When one utters, 'It is raining' on a certain occasion, one strictly, literally says that it is raining in a certain place – typically the place of utterance – even though no explicit constituent of one's utterance refers to that place. Just so, the hidden indexicalist maintains, when one utters a belief report on an occasion, one strictly, literally says that a certain proposition is believed in a certain way. And one does so even though no explicit constituent of one's utterances refers to the way of believing. Now the crucial further claim has to be that

although 'Hesperus' and 'Phosphorus' have the same semantic value and function innocently, even in that-clauses, nonetheless, exchanging one for the other can affect the way an unarticulated constituent gets hooked up to a reference as a function of context. And that can explain why they are not freely substitutable one for another.

Clearly, the hidden indexicalist owes us a detailed account of these matters. We need to be told what a way of believing is. We need to know how specified ways of believing vary as a function of facts about context and facts about articulated constituents. Fortunately, the best advocates of this approach have gone a long way towards answering such questions.

See also: DEMONSTRATIVES AND INDEXICALS; INDIRECT DISCOURSE; PROPOSITIONAL ATTITUDES

References and further reading

* Carnap, R. (1947) *Meaning and Necessity*, Chicago, IL: University of Chicago Press; enlarged 2nd edn, 1956. (Introduces the notion of an intensional isomorphism, the earliest version of the structured complex approach.)
* Cresswell, M. (1984) *Structured Meanings*, Cambridge, MA: MIT Press. (Argues for structured intensions as objects of propositional attitudes.)
* Crimmins, M. (1992) *Talk about Beliefs*, Cambridge, MA: MIT Press. (Defends a hidden indexical theory.)
* Crimmins, M. and Perry, J. (1989) 'The Prince and the Phone Booth: Reporting Puzzling Beliefs', *Journal of Philosophy* 60: 435–45. (Defends a hidden indexical theory.)
* Davidson, D. (1969) 'On Saying That', in D. Davidson and J. Hintikka (eds) *Words and Objections: Essays on the Work of W.V. Quine*, Dordrecht: Reidel, 158–74. (Articulates the paratactic analysis of indirect discourse.)
* —— (1967) 'Truth and Meaning', *Synthèse* 17: 304–23. (Articulates Davidson's broader semantic programme.)
* Devitt, M. (1996) *Coming to our Senses*, Cambridge: Cambridge University Press. (Defends a neo-Fregean account of attitude statements without positing Fregean senses; rejects hidden indexical approaches and direct reference.)
* Fodor, J. (1989) 'Substitution Arguments and the Individuation of Beliefs', in G. Boolos (ed.) *Method, Reasons, and Language*, Cambridge: Cambridge University Press. (Construes modes of presentations as expressions in the language of thought, while holding a referentialist semantics.)
* Frege, G. (1892) 'Über Sinn und Bedeutung' (On

Sense and Reference), *Zeitschrift für Philosophie und philisophische Kritik* 100: 25–50. (A seminal work of Frege's in which he argues for the distinction between the sense and reference of expressions and presents a number of important theses regarding the two notions. Translated as 'On Sense and Meaning' in P.T. Geach and M. Black (eds) *Translations from the Philosophical Writings of Gottlob Frege*, Oxford: Blackwell, 3rd edn, 1980.)

* Higginbotham, J. (1991) 'Belief and Logical Form', *Mind and Language* 6: 344–69. (Defends a version of the structured complex approach, drawing on the resources of contemporary syntactic theory. Relates this approach to Davidsonian extensional semantics.)
* Larson, R. and Ludlow, P. (1993) 'Interpreted Logical Forms', *Synthèse* 95: 305–57. (Articulates and defends the ILF approach.)
* Quine, W.V. (1956) 'Quantifiers and the Propositional Attitudes', repr. in *The Ways of Paradox and Other Essays*, Cambridge, MA: Harvard University Press, revised and enlarged edn, 1976. (This widely reprinted article contains Quine's argument against the permissibility of quantifying into opaque contexts.)
* —— (1960) *Word and Object*, Cambridge, MA: Harvard University Press. (Forcefully articulates Quine's disdain for intensions as 'creatures of darkness'.)
* Recanati, F. (1993) *Direct Reference*, Oxford: Blackwell. (A full-scale defence of the direct reference thesis which articulates yet another way to reconcile direct reference, innocence and the Fregean intuition.)
* Richard, M. (1990) *Propositional Attitudes: an Essay on Thoughts and How We Ascribe Them*, Cambridge: Cambridge University Press. (Argues that propositional attitude statements express relations to Russellian annotated matrices – a version of the structured complex approach; also defends the view that belief reports are indexical.)
* Salmon, N. (1986) *Frege's Puzzle*, Cambridge, MA: MIT Press. (Denies the Fregean intuition and defends innocence and direct reference.)
* Schiffer, S. (1979) 'Naming and Knowing', in P.A. French, T.E. Uehling, Jr and H.K. Wettstein (eds) *Contemporary Perspectives in the Philosophy of Language*, Minneapolis, MN: University of Minnesota Press. (First appearance of the hidden indexical approach.)
* Segal, G. (1989) 'A Preference for Sense and Reference', *Journal of Philosophy* 86: 73–89. (Another defence of a structured complex approach.)
* Soames, S. (1987) 'Direct Reference, Propositional Attitudes, and Semantic Content', *Philosophical Topics* 15: 47–87. (Denies the Fregean intuition, while defending innocence and direct reference.)

KENNETH A. TAYLOR

PROPOSITIONAL ATTITUDES

Examples of propositional attitudes include the belief that snow is white, the hope that Mt Rosea is twelve miles high, the desire that there should be snow at Christmas, the intention to go to the snow tomorrow, and the fear that one shall be killed in an avalanche. As these examples show, we can distinguish the kind of attitude – belief, desire, intention, fear and so on – from the content of the attitude – that snow is white, that there will be snow at Christmas, to go to the snow, and so forth. The term 'propositional attitudes' comes from Bertrand Russell and derives from the fact that we can think of the content of an attitude as the proposition the attitude is towards. It can be typically captured by a sentence prefixed by 'that', though sometimes at the cost of a certain linguistic awkwardness: it is more natural, for example, to talk of the intention to go to the snow rather than the intention that one go to the snow. The most frequently discussed kinds of propositional attitudes are belief, desire and intention, but there are countless others: hopes, fears, wishes, regrets, and so on.

Some sentences which contain the verbs of propositional attitude – believes, desires, intends, and so on – do not make ascriptions of propositional attitudes. For example: 'Wendy believes me', 'John fears this dog', and 'He intends no harm'. However, while these sentences are not, as they stand, ascriptions of propositional attitudes, it is arguable – though not all philosophers agree – that they can always be analysed as propositional attitude ascriptions. So, for example, Wendy believes me just in case there is some p such that Wendy believes that p because I tell her that p; John fears this dog just in case there is some X such that John fears that this dog will do X and so on.

Discussions of propositional attitudes typically focus on belief and desire, and, sometimes, intention, because of the central roles these attitudes play in the explanation of rational behaviour. For example: Mary's visit to the supermarket is explained by her desire to purchase some groceries, and her belief that she can purchase groceries at the supermarket; Bill's flicking the switch is explained by his desire to illuminate the room, and his belief that he can illuminate the room by flicking the switch; and so on. It is plausible – though not uncontroversial – to hold that rational behaviour can always be explained as the outcome of a suitable belief together with a suitable desire.

Some philosophers (examples are Grice and Schiffer) have used the propositional attitudes to explain facts about meaning. They hold that the meanings of sentences somehow derive from the contents of relevantly related beliefs and intentions. Roughly, what I mean by a sentence S is captured by the content of, say, the belief that I express by saying S.

One fundamental question which divides philosophers turns on the ontological status of the propositional attitudes and of their contents. It is clear that we make heavy use of propositional attitude ascriptions in explaining and interpreting the actions of ourselves and others. But should we think that in producing such ascriptions, we attempt to speak the truth – that is should we think that propositional attitude ascriptions are truth-apt – or should we see some other purpose, such as dramatic projection, in this usage? Or, even more radically, should we think that there is nothing but error and confusion – exposed by modern science and neurophysiology – in propositional attitude talk?

1 **Elementary distinctions**
2 **Propositional attitude states**
3 **Propositional attitude contents**
4 **Propositional attitude 'aboutness'**
5 **Defining propositional attitudes**
6 **Scepticism about propositional attitudes**

1 Elementary distinctions

Propositional attitude ascriptions standardly take the form 'X Fs that p', where 'X' denotes the subject of the attitude, 'F' is a verb of propositional attitude, and 'that p' gives the content of the attitude. So, for example, in the sentence 'John believes that snow is white', 'John' denotes the subject of the attitude, 'believes' is the verb of propositional attitude, and 'that snow is white' gives the content of the attitude.

Taking the form of these ascriptions at face value, it is natural to suggest that a propositional attitude ascription of the form 'X Fs that p' is true just in case X is in a propositional attitude state of type F – an F-state – which has the content that p. So, for example, 'John believes that snow is white' is true just in case John is in a belief-state which has the content that snow is white; 'Mary hopes that Sheila is happy' is true just in case Mary is in a hope-state which has the content that Sheila is happy; and so on. More generally, it is natural to divide a discussion of propositional attitudes into two parts: one part which focuses on the nature of propositional attitude states – the difference between hoping, fearing, believing, wishing, and so on – and one part which focuses on

propositional attitude contents – the difference between believing that snow is white, believing that snow is grey, believing that snow falls at night, and so forth.

It is plausible to think that belief and desire are the basic exemplars of two quite different kinds of attitudes, with characteristically different directions of fit. On the one hand, there are attitudes, like belief, which aim to fit the world – and, hence, which are important for theories of truth, impact of evidence, credence, and so on. And, on the other hand, there are attitudes, like desire, which aim to have the world fit them – and, hence, which are important for theories of value, virtue, wellbeing, and so on. Some philosophers think that all of the propositional attitudes can be explained in terms of beliefs and desires; they think that the apparent multiplicity of kinds of propositional attitudes is merely apparent – hope, for example, is a kind of desire about the future – and that direction of fit is the only fundamental dimension which needs to be considered in classifying the propositional attitudes.

2 Propositional attitude states

If beliefs, desires, intentions, and the like, are states of subjects, what kind of states are they? A plausible view is that they are functional states – states defined or determined or specified by their functional roles. According to functionalist theories, propositional attitude states are fully determined by their causal relations to one another, to perceptual inputs, and to behavioural outputs (see FUNCTIONALISM). So, for example, what makes a certain state a state of believing that there are *Cheerios* in the cupboard turns on its being typically caused by packets of *Cheerios*, or more precisely, on the role it plays in the processing of perceptual input – say, guessing the contents of that visually presented cardboard box in the cupboard; on the way it leads to other states – say, believing that there is cereal in the cupboard; and on the way it combines with hunger and desire to eat some cereal to produce behaviour that leads to eating.

There are, however, two different ways of thinking of functional states: as role states or as realizer states. Realizer states are first-order states that stand in the functional roles; they are the particular states which play the roles. Role states are second-order states: the state of being in, some first-order state playing a certain kind of functional role. So, in the case of belief, say, there is the first-order realizer state (the state which actually fills the belief role – the state which mediates between perceptual inputs and behavioural responses in the way distinctive of belief); and there is the second-order role state (the state of being in some state or other which realizes the belief role – the state of being in a state that mediates in the way distinctive of belief between perceptual inputs and behavioural outputs). Should we think of belief in particular and propositional attitudes in general as realizer states or as role states?

The obvious reason for holding that propositional attitude states are realizer states rather than role states is that the propositional attitudes are centrally involved in the causation of behaviour, and it is the realizer states but not the role states that are centrally involved in the causation of behaviour. It is, for instance, the particular internal state which fills the role we associate with believing that snow is white that causes the behaviour distinctive of this belief – for example, uttering the words 'Snow is white'.

There are, however, also considerations that point the other way, that favour holding, for example, that my belief that snow is white is the role state which is realized by some particular internal state of mine. In particular, it seems that taking propositional attitude states to be role states allows one to formulate psychological generalizations which one would miss if one took propositional attitudes to be realizer states. Consider, for example, the generalization: everyone who believes the world is going to end in ten minutes gets anxious. Suppose that there are actually M realizer states for the belief: $N_1, N_2, \ldots, N_M$. These states, we may suppose, each play the appropriate causally intermediate roles distinctive of the belief that the world is going to end in ten minutes in somewhat the way that transistors and valves, despite being very different, can both play the roles distinctive of amplification. If the belief state is identical with the realizer states, then the only way to generalize is to treat the realizer state as a disjunction $N_1 \lor N_2 \lor \ldots \lor N_M$. But this disjunction is ugly, and not suitable for the formulation of psychological law. The generalization can be saved by recasting it as one about role states, but then the only way the initial generalization can be a generalization about the belief that the world is going to end in ten minutes is if that belief is a role state. The general point is that the patterns we capture in psychological generalizations relate to role states, so the cost of holding that psychological states are realizer states is that psychological generalizations cease to relate psychological states.

Whether propositional attitude states are best thought of as role states or realizer states, it has seemed plausible to many philosophers that the realizer states are physical states of the brain – or, at any rate, states which supervene upon physical states of the brain (see MIND, IDENTITY THEORY OF; SUPERVENIENCE OF THE MENTAL). This is put

forward as a plausible scientific hypothesis. Only in the brain are there states of sufficient complexity to play the needed roles. It is, though, allowed as a logical possibility that there could have been other (perhaps even non-physical) realizer states which filled the same role.

Some philosophers, however, have worried about whether neural states could be the kinds of things which can be adverted to, even *inter alia*, in the explanation of rational action. The connections between neural states are merely causal, they argue – playing out the universal laws of physics, or of neuroscience – whereas the connections between states of propositional attitude are rational (and serve to rationalize behaviour). One belief makes another the rational one to have; what one believes and desires may make one action more rational than another; and so on (see REASONS AND CAUSES).

However, there are serious problems with this sort of objection. Would the cause of rationality be better served by having the attitudes occurring at random? And surely a decent account of the propositional attitudes places them in the physical world – they are not otherworldly mysteries – and given this, there seems little alternative to placing them in the brain: we know that the propositional attitudes play complex causal roles in the production of our behaviour, and only the brain has states capable of the needed complexity. Finally, it is unclear why one might suppose that functionally defined states cannot have the rationalizing properties which are alleged to vanish from the scientific picture (see Loar 1981 for further discussion).

3 Propositional attitude contents

The contents of propositional attitudes are propositions. That much is simply a matter of definition. But what are propositions? There are at least the following contenders: (1) collections of circumstances of evaluation, such as collections of possible worlds; (2) syntactic entities, such as interpreted sentences in natural language; (3) set-theoretic structures, such as Fregean thoughts (see FREGE §§3–4). Only some of the strengths and weaknesses of these different approaches can be examined here (see PROPOSITIONS, SENTENCES AND STATEMENTS).

(1) One important virtue of the theory that propositions are collections of possible worlds – that is, collections of complete ways that things could be (see SEMANTICS, POSSIBLE WORLDS) – is that it directly captures the intuition that propositions involve a sorting among ways that things could be. For example, in believing that snow is white, one believes that the actual complete way that things are is

among those complete ways that things could be in which snow is white; in desiring that snow falls at Christmas, one desires that the actual complete way that things are is among those in which snow falls at Christmas; and so on.

Perhaps the most important drawback of this theory is that its most plausible formulations seem to give the wrong results for attitudes with logically equivalent contents. For example, it entails that the belief that there are husbands is identical to the belief that there are wives. Because 'There are wives' is logically equivalent to 'There are husbands', the set of worlds where there are wives is one and the same as the set of worlds where there are husbands. Likewise, it makes the desire to prove that two and two are four identical to the desire to prove that arithmetic is not decidable, and the intention to draw an equiangular triangle identical to the intention to draw an equilateral triangle. As the objection is commonly put, the possible worlds theory delivers objects of the attitudes that are insufficiently fine grained – there are more distinct attitude contents than it allows.

In addition, there is a complication which needs to be addressed. Consider, for example, my belief that I am cold, or your belief that you are spilling sugar on the floor of the supermarket. These attitudes *de se* (about oneself), as they are called, need to be thought of as involving a sorting among ways that things might be centred on the subject – me, here and now, as it could be, rather than of complete ways things might be (see DEMONSTRATIVES AND INDEXICALS; CONTENT, INDEXICAL).

(2) One important virtue of the theory that propositions are syntactic entities – that is entities with sentence-like structure – is that it provides objects to discriminate between attitude contents which, as we have just seen, the possible worlds theory is unable to discriminate. For example, the sentence 'There are husbands' is distinct from the sentence 'There are wives'; and the theory can exploit this fact to distinguish the belief that there are husbands from the belief that there are wives. They are attitudes to different though equivalent sentences.

However, if the sentences are thought of as being in a natural language, this advantage is purchased at a price; it provides distinctions where it is plausible that there are none. Consider, for example, our practice of translating and interpreting those who speak different languages. Clearly, 'Snow is white' and 'La neige est blanche' are distinct sentences – but surely we are not thereby obliged to say that it is impossible for a monolingual French speaker to believe that snow is white? Consider, too, the belief that p, and the belief that p and p. There is at least some temptation to think that these are not distinct beliefs.

One response is to argue that the sentences in question do not belong to natural languages but rather to a language of thought – that is, to a neural system of information or information storage which is supposed to have syntactic structure, and that this is something we all share (and share with animals like dogs that lack public language but do seem to have propositional attitudes) (see LANGUAGE OF THOUGHT). One difficulty with this suggestion is that it seems wrong that a mere analysis of propositional attitudes will commit us to the existence of a language of thought, a substantive view about our neural natures. It seems to be an empirical question, for example, whether mental representation is language-like or map-like (see BELIEF §3), but the language of thought hypothesis commits us in advance to the former alternative.

(3) One important virtue of the theory that propositions are set-theoretic structures – that is entities whose basic structure is described by set theory (see SET THEORY) – is that it promises to cope with the difficulties mentioned above for the syntactic and possible worlds accounts. However, before we can see why this is so, we need to give some explanation of the theory.

Consider, for example, the sentence 'London is pretty'. A natural thought is that the proposition expressed by this sentence is somehow made up of the city of London (or some way of thinking about it) and the property of being pretty (or some way of thinking about the property of being pretty). More generally, the theory holds that propositions are composed from constituents which are somehow put together in an orderly (set-theoretic) fashion. The constituents in question include: individual objects (and perhaps modes of presentation thereof), which correspond to proper names and other singular terms; properties, which correspond to predicates; functions, which correspond to sentential operators (such as 'and' and 'possibly'), and so on.

This view has the resources to discriminate between the belief that there are husbands and the belief that there are wives, one of the examples that gave the possible worlds approach trouble. Roughly, the first has in its propositional object women and the property of being married to men, whereas the second has men and the property of being married to women. The view also has the resources to identify the propositions expressed by the sentences 'Snow is white' and 'La neige est blanche' and so allow that speakers of different languages can share beliefs, one of the examples that gave the sentential theory trouble. Although the words differ, the objects and properties they stand for are the same and hence the propositions thought of as constructed from them are the same. However, the theory in its typical form has to distinguish between the belief that p, and the belief that p and p – the propositional object of the second is special in involving the operation of conjunction – and this is not clearly desirable.

Another problem with set-theoretic approaches is that they involve various kinds of 'disreputable entities' – intensional properties, modes of presentation ('Fregean senses'), perhaps even set-theoretic functions – which many philosophers would like to exclude from their theories of the attitudes (see INTENSIONAL ENTITIES). They worry about how these entities can be tied to propositional attitudes, especially if these attitudes are thought of functionally. What causal role can intensional properties or sets, for instance, play? True, this is part of a hard question that arises for any account of the attitudes. We have been discussing competing views about what the objects of the attitudes are. But there is also the question as to how a given propositional attitude state gets attached to the proposition it is attached to; the question of what makes it true, for example, that a certain state is the belief that snow is white rather than that grass is green. We will set this important question aside except to remark that the set theoretic view of the nature of the attitudes is often thought to be especially ill placed to tackle it.

Plainly, there is much more to be said about each of the options discussed here (and about other options as well). The important point is that there are many dimensions to propositional content, and that it is far from easy to provide a theory which scores well on every dimension. A good theory of propositional content should have all of the following features:

(1) it should be naturalistically respectable – that is compatible with the outlook of natural science;
(2) it should capture the normative dimensions of propositional content;
(3) it should allow a fine-grained discrimination of the contents of propositional attitudes (logical equivalence is not sufficient for identity);
(4) it should not tie the possession of propositional attitudes too tightly to particular languages (for example, it should allow that the same attitudes can be had by creatures which do not share a language – and, indeed, that attitudes can be possessed by creatures which do not speak any language at all);
(5) it should make it clear how states which possess that kind of propositional content can play a role in the production of (rational) action.

4 Propositional attitude 'aboutness'

Many philosophers have been puzzled by the various ways and senses in which propositional attitudes can be about particular objects and kinds of objects (see INTENTIONALITY). Think, for example, of the beliefs which one might have about Aristotle, about Einstein, about President Clinton, about Zeus, about Mickey Mouse, about Meinong's round square, about gold, about phlogiston, about π, and about the greatest prime number. There are several different issues which can arise here.

One issue concerns the existence of the objects and kinds of objects which are the focus of the attitudes. There is a sense of 'about' in which one cannot have attitudes about an object (or kind of object) which does not exist – so that, for example, in this sense, one cannot have beliefs, hopes, fears, desires, and so on, about Zeus, the round square, the greatest prime number, Mickey Mouse and phlogiston, though one can have these attitudes about President Clinton and gold. (The cases of entirely past objects – Aristotle and Einstein – and numbers – π – raise other controversial questions about existence which cannot be taken up here.) This sense of 'about' is relational: the point parallels the impossibility of parking near the round square, shaking hands with Zeus, or adding three to the greatest prime number.

Another issue concerns the nature of the connection which obtains between subjects and those existent objects and kinds of objects which are the focus of given attitudes. If one is not appropriately connected to an object, then – in this sense – one cannot have attitudes about it. Suppose, for example, that by an extraordinary coincidence there is a planet somewhere in the universe whose history is exactly described by Tolkien's *Lord of the Rings*. Even though there is some sense in which Tolkien's work is true of this planet, nonetheless, the work is not about the planet (in the sense currently at issue). The reason is that the planet played no role at all in the causal history of the book. When, for example, one believes that Hawking is a genius, what makes it the case that one's belief is about Hawking is, very likely, at least in part, that there are chains of usage of the word 'Hawking' which are appropriately connected to that theoretical physicist. When I believe that that tree outside my window is shedding its leaves, what makes it a belief about that tree is, at least in part, the causal processes involving electromagnetic radiation passing between the tree and my retina which are involved in the formation of my belief. In general, it seems plausible to think that some kind of causal connection is required for these kinds of attitudes about particular objects.

However, while it is clearly correct to say that there is a sense in which the aboutness of propositional attitudes is a matter of standing in a relation, an appropriate causal connection on most views, it is also clear that there is another sense of 'about' which cannot be analysed in this way. In some sense we can have beliefs and desires about non-existent objects – for example, some people desire to find the fountain of youth, some believe that Meinong's round square is round, some hoped that Zeus would smite their enemies with a thunderbolt, and so on. It seems clear that those who, for example, hoped that Zeus would smite their enemies have a hope 'about' Zeus despite not standing in a relation, causal or otherwise, to Zeus.

How then should this final, non-relational, non-causal, sense of 'about' be analysed? Many alternatives present themselves. One might appeal to counterfactuals: attitudes 'about Zeus' are attitudes about something which does not exist, but which might have existed; attitudes 'about phlogiston' are attitudes about something which does not exist but which might have existed; and so on. One might hold that this sense of 'about' is only used in loose speech, and can be banished or paraphrased away in serious philosophical discourse: attitudes 'about Zeus' are really attitudes which focus on certain myths and stories; attitudes 'about phlogiston' are really attitudes about a false chemical theory; and so on. One might try various other options as well. The issue is too difficult to discuss adequately here: the important point is that there is at least a loose sense in which there is 'existentially neutral' content, that is, content which does not commit one to the existence in the actual world of the particular individuals and kinds to which the content does give apparent commitment.

There is also an important distinction between two different kinds of content: broad content and narrow content. Roughly speaking, narrow content is purely a matter of what goes on inside the head of a subject of propositional attitude states, whereas broad content is in part a matter of how things are in the world outside the head. More exactly, if two subjects are intrinsic duplicates who live under the same laws of nature and belong to the same kinds, then their attitudes are exactly alike in narrow content but may differ in broad content (see CONTENT: WIDE AND NARROW).

Once upon a time it was more or less taken for granted that the content of belief, for example, was narrow. How things are outside the head obviously affects whether your beliefs are true or false – your belief that London is pretty can only be true if London itself is pretty – but what you believe is a matter of how you are. But in fact the belief that London is pretty is a belief with broad content. I cannot believe that London, the capital city of England, is pretty unless I am appropriately causally connected to London, and that concerns how things are outside my head. Imagine that the universe is symmetrical, so that there is a region – call it Twin Earth – which is qualitatively identical to our own at all times. It will contain a city called 'London' and a twin of me. This twin will be an intrinsic duplicate of me and will produce the sentence 'London is pretty' as expressing what he believes. Nevertheless, his belief (and his sentence) will have a different content from mine. It will be about Twin London rather than about London, and will be true just if Twin London, rather than, London is pretty.

5 Defining propositional attitudes

The characterization of propositional attitudes in §2 was very rough, and leaves room for the thought that functionalism involves circularity of definition. We in effect identified the behaviour beliefs cause as behaviour that tends to realize desires, and this bit of inter-defining looks rather like circularity. However, the characterization can be improved in a way which makes it clear that this is not so – and, as an added bonus, also makes clear just what would be involved in the denial of the existence of propositional attitudes. The secret is to take the general account of the definition of theoretical terms provided by David Lewis and apply it to the propositional attitudes.

Roughly, the idea is to collect together a class of sentences involving the verbs of propositional attitude and treat this class as a simultaneous definition of the propositional attitudes. The same idea can be applied to other webs of theoretical terms. A very simple case is the definition of a wife as someone with a husband, and a husband as someone with a wife. We remove the air of circularity when we note that we could spell matters out as follows: x is a wife if there are two people, one male and one female, they are married to each other, and x is the female one. Consider, for a more complex example, the artworld and its denizens. Artists are producers of art works. Audiences are viewers or consumers of art works. Critics are critical assessors of art works. Galleries are places for the exhibition of art works. And art works are objects produced by artists for consumption by audiences, assessment by critics and display in galleries. Taken together, these sentences – or some more elaborate version thereof – can be taken to provide a simultaneous definition of the key terms: artist, audience, critic, gallery, artwork. And there is no (vicious) circularity involved because the other terms which feature in the various sentences – 'production', 'consumption', 'display', 'object', 'view', and so on –

are (assumed to be) independently understood. These terms in effect specify the key interconnections, and the definition of artist, work of art, and so on that is delivered amounts to saying that an artist is anyone who is appropriately interconnected.

The sentences which are collected together are either *prima facie* analytic truths – that is, conditionals and biconditionals which encode the inferential practices constitutive of possession of the concepts under analysis – or else claims involving the concepts to be analysed which are regarded as *prima facie* common knowledge by those, or most of those, who possess the concepts. Under the former account, there is no guarantee that the sentences will be immediately available to those who possess the concepts; however, it might be hoped that reasonable and reflective people can be brought to assent to them when the sentences are drawn to their attention. Under the latter account, there is no requirement that the sentences encode inferential practices constitutive of possession of the concepts under analysis: for all kinds of synthetic and a posteriori claims may be selected. However, the following constraint is to be observed: it should be commonly held to be a condition on attribution of possession of the concepts which are up for analysis to a subject that they do not reject, or fail to accept, too many of the chosen sentences.

On either account, one might doubt that there are sentences of the kind required by the analysis. So, for example, it might be said that it is notoriously difficult to provide exceptionless generalizations about the connections between beliefs, desires, intentions, actions, and so on. However, it is important to note that there is nothing in the account which requires that the platitudes in question must be couched as exceptionless generalisations. Indeed, a plausible thought is that most of the platitudes will instead make claims about what is normally the case – that is about what happens when all other things are equal, or when conditions are normal. So, for example, on either account, there are sentences like these: a system of beliefs and desires tends to cause behaviour that serves the subject's desires according to that subject's beliefs; beliefs typically change under the impact of sensory evidence; desires aim to have the world fit them; beliefs aim to fit the world, and so on.

The final point to note is that our definition tells us that the propositional attitudes are whatever it is that satisfies the chosen set of sentences and so stand in the specified relations. In the simplest case, there will be a unique natural collection of candidates for the propositional attitudes. In that case, the sentences provide an explicit definition of the propositional attitudes. But things may not be so simple: perhaps

there is nothing which satisfies the sentences exactly; and perhaps the only thing which satisfies the sentences is extremely unnatural, that is, gerrymandered. In these cases, we shall look for the best near-satisfier, where the criteria which guide our search are (1) considerations of naturalness; and (2) satisfaction of as many as possible of the more central platitudes. Put another way: application of a procedure which aims at achieving reflective equilibrium may lead to the rejection of some of the sentences, and perhaps to the elevation of further sentences to membership of the favoured class. Moreover, the procedure which aims at achieving reflective equilibrium is guided by judgments about (1) the naturalness of the resulting concept; and (2) the centrality or revisability of the sentences which are incorporated or rejected.

Of course, there is nothing in the account of this procedure which guarantees that there will be a point of reflective equilibrium: and, in the case in which there is no point of reflective equilibrium, we will need to give an error theory of the propositional attitudes – that is we will hold either that there were no coherent concepts characterized by our pre-reflective usage, or else that there simply is nothing to which our concepts apply.

6 Scepticism about propositional attitudes

There are various sceptical doubts which philosophers have had about propositional attitudes. Only some of these doubts will be mentioned here.

Some philosophers – W.V.O. Quine, Paul Churchland, Stephen Stich, for example – deny that there are any propositional attitudes – they deny that there are any beliefs, desires, intentions and the like. Sometimes, the source for this denial is philosophy of language (dislike of intensional contexts, and so on); other times, the source is metaphysics (failure to find a physical structure with which the states in question can be identified, for example). Sometimes, the view is that propositional attitudes are convenient fictions – useful instruments for making predictions of behaviour, but not suited to the business of serious science. On this view, talk of propositional attitudes has a second grade, merely instrumental, status, but there is no reason why we should not continue with it for purposes of prediction and explanation – a common comparison is with talk about the average family. Other philosophers argue that talk of propositional attitudes is intended as first grade scientific theorizing, but that it just happens to be seriously astray. On this view, talk of propositional attitudes is like talk of phlogiston: talk which sought to capture an important feature of reality and to be part of serious science, but failed (see ELIMINATIVISM).

Among philosophers who accept that there are propositional attitudes – that is, among those philosophers who accept that some propositional attitude ascriptions are strictly and literally true – there are philosophers who are sceptical of the relational analysis of those attitudes. Thus, some philosophers suppose that propositional attitudes should be given an adverbial analysis according to which, for example, one's belief that p is a matter of one's believing p-ly (see ADVERBIAL THEORY OF MENTAL STATES). They deny that the attitudes are relations to propositions. Sometimes, this denial is fuelled by worries about the candidate entities for those contents, the sets of worlds, structured set-theoretic entities, and the like we discussed earlier. Theorists who deny the relational view of the attitudes typically insist that a sentence like 'I believe that snow is white' is best written, from a logical point of view, as 'I snow-is-white believe', somewhat as 'I have a limp' is best written 'I limp'.

Yet other philosophers – Stephen Schiffer, for example – despair of the project of giving any philosophical account (theory, analysis) of propositional attitudes, while nonetheless supposing that our practice of making propositional attitude ascriptions is perfectly in order as it stands. The essence of their position is a denial of the need to give an account in anything like the traditional sense of the propositional attitudes (see QUIETISM).

Theorizing about propositional attitudes is a very difficult task. This brief summary only indicates a few of the controversial questions which such theorizing is bound to confront.

See also: ACTION; FOLK PSYCHOLOGY; INTENTION; DESIRE; PROPOSITIONAL ATTITUDE STATEMENTS; COMMUNICATION AND INTENTION

References and further reading

Braddon-Mitchell, D. and Jackson, F. (1996) *The Philosophy of Mind and Cognition*, Oxford: Blackwell. (Excellent, state-of-the-art textbook for philosophy of mind.)

* Churchland, P. (1981) 'Eliminative Materialism and the Propositional Attitudes', *Journal of Philosophy* 78: 67–90. (Well-known defence of a style of eliminativism about the propositional attitudes that sees propositional attitude talk as failed science.)

Davidson, D. (1968) 'On Saying That', *Synthèse* 19: 130–46. (Treatment of the contents of propositional attitude ascriptions in terms of sentences in English, but not as sentences of English.)

Fodor, J. (1975) *The Language Of Thought*, New York: Crowell (Defence of the hypothesis that there is a language of thought.)

Frege, G. (1917) 'Thoughts', in P. Geach (ed.) *Logical Investigations*, Oxford: Blackwell, 1977. (Famous defence of the view that the contents of propositional attitudes are abstract structured entities.)

* Grice, P. (1957) 'Meaning', *Philosophical Review* 66: 377–88. (A classic. Includes famous analysis of meaning in terms of propositional attitudes.)

Harman, G. (1972) *Thought*, Princeton, NJ: Princeton University Press. (Early, clear, exposition of a functionalist account of the mind and, in particular, the propositional attitudes.)

Kripke, S. (1982) *Wittgenstein on Rules and Private Language*, Oxford: Blackwell. (Classic text which deals, *inter alia*, with problems about the normativity of propositional attitude contents.)

* Lewis, D. (1970) 'How To Define Theoretical Terms', *Journal of Philosophy* 67: 427–46. (Masterly treatment of the definition of theoretical terms. Much better – but much harder – than the outline in §5!)

Lewis, D. (1994) 'Reduction of Mind', in S. Guttenplan (ed.) *A Companion to the Philosophy of Mind*, Oxford: Blackwell, 412–31. (Superb exposition of Lewis's philosophy of mind. Assumes some familiarity with the prior literature.)

* Loar, B. (1981) *Mind and Meaning*, Cambridge: Cambridge University Press. (Difficult, but very good, discussion of propositional attitudes, and their importance for philosophy of mind and philosophy of meaning.)

Pessin, A. (ed.) (1995) *The Twin Earth Chronicles*, London: Pergamon Press. (Collection of articles about Twin Earth, broad and narrow content, and so on. Good reading list.)

* Quine, W.V.O. (1960) *Word and Object*, Cambridge, MA: MIT Press and John Wiley. (Famous and elegant text which includes defence of a kind of eliminativism about propositional attitudes.)

Salmon, N. (1986) *Frege's Puzzle*, Cambridge, MA: MIT Press. (Defence of treatment of propositions as structured, set-theoretic entities.)

Salmon, N. and Soames, S. (eds) (1988) *Propositions and Attitudes*, Oxford: Oxford University Press. (Excellent collection of papers about the semantics of propositional attitude ascriptions. Good reading list.)

* Schiffer, S. (1972) *Meaning*, Oxford: Clarendon Press. (Defence of the view that propositional attitudes – in particular, belief and intention – are the key to meaning. Not easy going.)

* —— (1987) *Remnants of Meaning*, Cambridge, MA: MIT Press. (Retraction of the view that the propositional attitudes – in particular, belief and

intention – are the key to meaning, and of much else besides. Still not easy going.)

Stalnaker, R. (1984) *Inquiry*, Cambridge, MA: MIT Press. (Defence of the view that the contents of propositional attitudes are sets of possible worlds. Includes best available treatment of the objection that any such treatment makes the objects of the attitudes too coarse-grained.)

* Stich, S. (1983) *From Folk Psychology to Cognitive Science: The Case Against Belief*, Cambridge, MA: MIT Press. (Case for eliminativism about belief, and other propositional attitudes. Interesting, and reasonably accessible.)

GRAHAM OPPY

PROPOSITIONAL CALCULUS

see PREDICATE CALCULUS

PROPOSITIONS, SENTENCES AND STATEMENTS

A sentence is a string of words formed according to the syntactic rules of a language. But a sentence has semantic as well as syntactic properties: the words and the whole sentence have meaning. Philosophers have tended to focus on the semantic properties of indicative sentences, in particular on their being true or false. They have called the meanings of such sentences 'propositions', and have tied the notion of proposition to the truth-conditions of the associated sentence.

The term 'proposition' is sometimes assimilated to the sentence itself; sometimes to the linguistic meaning of a sentence; sometimes to 'what is said'; sometimes to the contents of beliefs or other 'propositional' attitudes. But however propositions are defined, they must have two features: the capacity to be true or false; and compositional structure (being composed of elements which determine their semantic properties).

One reason for distinguishing a sentence from 'what the sentence says' is that a sentence may be meaningless, and hence say nothing, yet still be a sentence. But perhaps the main reason is that two people, A and B, may utter the same sentence, for example, 'I am hot', and say the same thing in one sense but not in another. The sense in which they say the same thing is that they use the same words with the same linguistic 'meaning'. The sense in which they say something different is that they put the same words to different

'uses': A uses 'I' to refer to A, while B uses it to refer to B. Hence what A says may be true although what B says is false. If what is said can be true in one case and false in another, A and B have not made the same 'statement'. On the other hand, if B utters instead 'You are hot' when A utters 'I am hot', they put different sentences to the same use and make the same statement. On this view (see Strawson 1952), we must distinguish the 'sentence', the 'use' of the sentence, and the 'statement' made by using a sentence in a context of utterance. According to STRAWSON, it is not sentences but statements that are true or false.

Logicians usually abstract from the context of utterance of sentences in actual communication and talk of the propositions expressed as abstract entities. The main modern proponent of this conception is Frege. For Frege (1918), a proposition is a 'thought', which is both the cognitive meaning expressed by a sentence and the content of a propositional attitude such as belief or desire; thoughts are the 'senses' of sentences. Thoughts are distinguished according to the following principle: if it is possible rationally to believe that p and not to believe that q then the thought that p and the thought that q are distinct (see FREGE, G. §§3–4 ; SENSE AND REFERENCE §2).

Under a different, but related, conception, proposed by Carnap (1947), the proposition expressed by a sentence S is the set of possible worlds in which S is true (see SEMANTICS, POSSIBLE WORLDS §9–10). This view violates the compositional structure requirement, since such propositions are not grasped by grasping their components (see COMPOSITIONALITY). It also seems unable to differentiate between some distinct propositions. For example, there would only be one necessarily false proposition, since there is only one empty set of worlds, but intuitively there are many different necessarily false propositions.

An alternative view of propositions as entities is the (neo-)Russellian view that they are collections of actual entities making up 'facts' or 'states of affairs' (see FACTS §1). Thus the proposition expressed by 'Socrates is mortal' is the ordered pair ⟨Socrates, being mortal⟩, composed of the individual Socrates and the property of being mortal. Three questions for this view are: (1) Are the contents of false sentences negative facts, and are there such facts? (2) What is the criterion of identity for facts? (3) How can propositions as facts be the contents of propositional attitudes? The last of these can be seen as a version of the problem which led Frege to postulate senses: for the fact that $a = b$ must be the same fact as $a = a$, although someone who believes that $a = a$ does not thereby believe that $a = b$, and hence the propositions are not the same (see SENSE AND REFERENCE §1). Fregeans conclude that this

787

shows that we cannot dispense with the notion of sense. If Russellians deny this, they must complicate their account of facts or their account of propositional attitudes (see PROPOSITIONAL ATTITUDE STATEMENTS).

Whether one defines the intuitive notion of 'what is said' as a context-independent entity or by recourse to the notion of a statement or proposition expressed by an utterance in a particular context, one must say what it means for two sentences to express 'the same proposition' or make 'the same statement'. Both phrases rely on the notions of meaning and synonymy, criticized by Quine (1968; see QUINE, W.V. §8). But if we dispense altogether with propositions, statements or any other notion of the content of what is said, and choose instead to take sentences as truth bearers, we face two problems. The first is that sentences are unlikely candidates for the role of contents of propositional attitudes: if 'I believe I am stupid' introduces a relation between me and the English sentence 'I am stupid', it should be translated into German (say) as 'Ich glaube "I am stupid"', although the correct translation is 'Ich glaube daß ich dumm bin', which says nothing about any English sentence (Church 1950). The second problem is that, in spite of our ontological scruples about admitting propositions as entities, we still need such a notion to express the content of what is said or believed, and to account for the intentionality of thought in general. In that respect, however vague or ill-defined the notion of a proposition, it cannot be dispensed with.

See also: INTENSIONAL ENTITIES; LOGICAL AND MATHEMATICAL TERMS, GLOSSARY OF; MEANING

References and further reading

Blackburn, S. (1975) 'The Identity of Propositions', in S. Blackburn (ed.) *Meaning, Reference and Necessity*, Cambridge: Cambridge University Press. (A good statement of a deflationary alternative to the ontological conception of the problem.)

* Carnap, R. (1947) *Meaning and Necessity*, Chicago, IL: University of Chicago Press, 2nd edn, 1956. (The first modern formulation of the possible worlds account.)

Cartwright, R. (1962) 'Propositions', in R.J. Butler (ed.) *Analytical Philosophy, First Series*, Oxford: Blackwell, 81–103. (A classical discussion of the main issues.)

* Church, A. (1950) 'On Carnap's Analysis of Statements of Assertion and Belief', *Analysis* 10: 97–9. (States his translation argument against sentences as objects of belief.)

* Frege, G. (1918) 'Der Gedanke: eine logische Untersuchung', *Beiträge zur Philosophie des deutschen Idealismus* 1: 58–77; trans. P.T. Geach and R. Stoothoff, 'Thoughts', in *Collected Papers*, ed. B.F. McGuiness, Oxford: Blackwell, 1984, 351–72. (The classic statement of propositions as 'thoughts' or abstract entities.)

Geach, P.T. (1965) 'Assertion', *Philosophical Review* 74(4); repr. in *Logic Matters*, Oxford: Blackwell, 1968. (A criticism of the notion of statement.)

Nuchelmans, G. (1973) *Theories of the Proposition*, Amsterdam: North Holland. (The best historical account, although somewhat doxographic.)

* Quine, W.V. (1968) 'Propositional Objects', *Critica* 5: 3–22; repr. in *Ontological Relativity and Other Essays*, New York: Columbia University Press, 1969. (Includes a summary of Quine's misgivings about propositions as entities.)

Russell, B.A.W. (1918) 'The Philosophy of Logical Atomism', in *Logic and Knowledge: Essays 1901–1950*, ed. R.C. Marsh, London: Routledge, 1992. (Treats propositions as states of affairs in the world.)

Salmon, N. and Soames, S. (eds) (1988) *Propositions and Attitudes*, Oxford: Oxford University Press. (A good anthology on the semantics of propositional attitudes, focused on the Russellian view.)

Stalnaker, R. (1976) 'Propositions', in A.F. MacKay and D.D. Merrill (eds) *Issues in the Philosophy of Language*, New Haven, CT: Yale University Press, 79–92. (A good account of the possible worlds view.)

* Strawson, P.F. (1952) 'On Referring', *Mind* 59: 320–44; repr. in *Logico-Linguistic Papers*, London: Methuen, 1971. (Puts the classical arguments in favour of the notion of statement.)

PASCAL ENGEL

PROTAGORAS (*c*.490–*c*.420 BC)

Protagoras was the first and most eminent of the Greek Sophists. Active in Athens, he pioneered the role of professional educator, training ambitious young men for a public career and popularizing the new rationalist worldview that was introduced from Ionian natural philosophy. But unlike his contemporary Anaxagoras, Protagoras was sceptical of the dogmatic claims of the new science. His famous formula – 'Man is the measure of all things, of things that are, that they are, and of things that are not, that they are not' (fr. 1) – makes him the father of relativism and even, on some interpretations, of subjectivism. He was also considered the first theological agnostic: 'Concerning the gods, I am unable to know either that they exist or that they do not exist or what form they have' (fr.4). He was sometimes associated with the claim 'to make the weaker argument (logos) the stronger'.

1 Career
2 Teaching
3 Philosophical views

1 Career

Protagoras came from Abdera, the city of the atomist Democritus. As a professional educator, he visited Athens several times and was closely connected with the intellectual circle around the leading statesman Pericles. He is reported to have drawn up the laws for Thurii, a pan-Hellenic colony in southern Italy, founded on the site of Sybaris in 444 BC under Periclean leadership. His extraordinary prestige, as the wisest person and greatest teacher of his time, is brilliantly portrayed in the introductory scenes of Plato's dialogue *Protagoras* (see PLATO §9). Protagoras there declares that he is the first Greek openly to offer moral and political training on a professional basis.

Protagoras' agnosticism regarding the existence of the gods must have shocked many of his contemporaries. A widespread ancient tradition reports that he escaped from Athens after being condemned for impiety, and that he was subsequently drowned at sea. One version of the story claims that his books were publicly burned at Athens. Some scholars have doubted this report, on the grounds that in Plato's *Meno* (91e) Socrates says that Protagoras remained in good repute until the end of his life. On the whole, however, the ancient tradition is likely to be correct. If so, Protagoras was (like Anaxagoras) one of the first victims of the popular reaction against the rationalist Enlightenment, whose most famous victim was SOCRATES (§1).

2 Teaching

In Plato's *Protagoras*, Protagoras describes the content of his teaching as 'good judgment in administering the affairs of one's household and those of the city, so that one may be most capable of acting and speaking on public matters' (319a). He there declares that if any pupil is not satisfied with the requested fee (which was certainly high), he need only go to a temple to swear how much he thinks the training was worth, and pay no more. The primary appeal of his teaching was to ambitious young men from wealthy families, who hoped to gain an advantage for their political career from studying with him. In historical perspective, the Sophistic movement initiated by Protagoras can be seen as the beginning of higher education in Western culture. The Sophists were the first professors without a permanent school (see SOPHISTS).

Unlike some later Sophists who included the new natural philosophy in their curriculum, Protagoras seems to have focused his own training on practical concerns, and above all on eloquence and argument. He is credited with being the first to show that there can be an argument for and against every thesis (fr. 6a). Thus he is reported to have trained his students, like a modern debater, to argue both sides of every disputed question, and also to be able to praise and blame the same person (A20–1). We have in the *Dissoi logoi* (Twofold Arguments) an ancient collection of sample reasoning on opposite sides of issues concerning good and bad, just and unjust, whether virtue can be taught, and the like (see DISSOI LOGOI). The extant text of *Dissoi logoi* is estimated to postdate Protagoras, but manuals of this type probably represent a tradition of *antilogia* or contradictory argumentation going back to Protagoras. It was presumably because Protagoras was so celebrated as a master of argument and refutation that Plato has selected him as Socrates' opponent and victim in the duel of wits in the dialogue *Protagoras*.

Protagoras' teaching is associated with the claim 'to make the weaker argument the stronger'. This is easily given a hostile interpretation: to make a bad case seem good, and thus to deceive a gullible audience. Enemies of the Sophists like Aristophanes certainly took this view of the kind of training that Protagoras inaugurated, and they regarded the moral influence of the Sophists as nefarious. Protagoras himself, however, seems to have been a staunch defender of traditional morality. This is indicated not only by Plato's portrayal but also by his political role as legislator for Thurii. The contrast between *nomos* and *physis*, between conventional morality and the nature of things, was later used to undermine the authority of the moral tradition (see ANTIPHON; CALLICLES; PHYSIS AND NOMOS). If this contrast was used by Protagoras (as some scholars have supposed), it can only have functioned in favour of *nomos* and the customary moral tradition. For, as will be seen in §3, Protagoras denies the claims to absolute or objective knowledge associated with the notion of *physis*. For a relativist like Protagoras there is no knowledge of the nature of things except from a particular human perspective.

Protagoras was also a pioneer in the study of language and grammar. Two important grammatical observations are attributed to him: (1) the distinction of gender into masculine, feminine and neuter (A27), and (2) the distinction of discourse into prayer (or optative), question (interrogative), answer (indicative), and command (imperative) (A1, paragraph 53, where a more complex division is also ascribed to Protagoras). These grammatical distinctions were apparently developed in the context of critical comments on Homeric poetry in the name of *orthoepeia* or correctness of diction. Thus Protagoras is reported to have disapproved of the opening verses of the *Iliad* for using an imperative form ('Sing, muse, of the wrath of Achilles') rather than the optative, which would be more appropriate for a prayer (A29). And he seems also to have complained that Homer's word 'wrath' (*menis*) should be masculine rather than feminine (A28). Plato twice alludes to Protagoras as an expert on the correctness of names (*Cratylus* 391c) or the correctness of diction (*Phaedrus* 267c) and he presents Protagoras as claiming that skill in criticizing the poets constitutes a major part of education (*Protagoras* 338e). The complex concern with language that is characteristic of Sophist practice thus clearly begins with Protagoras, but our evidence is too meagre for an accurate appreciation of his personal contribution.

3 Philosophical views

Protagoras is famous for two quotations. The best known is from a book entitled *Truth*: 'Man is the measure of all things, of things that are, that they are, and of things that are not, that they are not' (fr.1). The other may be from a different work: 'Concerning the gods, I am unable to know either that they exist or that they do not exist or what form they have. For there are many obstacles to knowledge: the obscurity of the matter and the brevity of human life' (fr.4). There is at least a notional connection between these two doctrines, since the claims to dogmatic knowledge on the part of early poets and philosophers often invoke divine inspiration. Thus Parmenides, the most influential philosopher of the fifth century, presents his view as the revelation of a goddess. In rejecting any knowledge of the gods, Protagoras also rejects any claim to an absolute or god's-eye knowledge of the truth.

Protagoras' 'man-the-measure' formula was interpreted in two different ways: (1) the subjectivist interpretation takes the thesis to claim that whatever anyone believes is true; and (2) the relativist interpretation claims only that whatever anyone believes is true for the person who believes it. The subjectivist doctrine (1) is rather easy to refute. For if all beliefs are true, then the belief that the man-the-measure doctrine is false must also be true. So if anyone doubts the truth of the man-the-measure

thesis, the thesis itself must be false. This is the argument known as the *peritropē*, the claim that the thesis overturns itself. Plato in the *Theaetetus* interprets Protagoras' doctrine as the relativist thesis (2): that what anyone believes is true *for that person* (see RELATIVISM). Plato presents the *peritropē* argument as a refutation of this version also.

We do not know whether or not Protagoras applied his theory of truth to moral and political issues. Plato suggests that for Protagoras: 'whatever the city establishes as just, is just for that city as long as it judges so' (*Theaetetus* 177d). This form of cultural relativism, which combines the recognition of different moral codes with respect for established tradition, is likely to be historically correct for Protagoras, since we find a similar regard for *nomos* or custom, in the face of cultural diversity, defended by Protagoras' contemporary, the historian Herodotus. It would also be a convenient doctrine for an itinerant philosopher, who can thus endorse the established order in each society when travelling from city to city.

Other positions attributed to Protagoras may be connected with his relativist theory of truth. Thus it may have been a general reaction against dogmatic claims that led him to deny that the circle touches a straight line only at a single point, as is assumed in plane geometry (fr. 7). The paradoxical view that 'it is not possible to contradict someone', which was later defended by ANTISTHENES (§4), was originally ascribed to Protagoras. If all opinions are true, then two speakers who seem to disagree cannot really be contradicting one another: they must be talking about different things.

References and further reading

Burnyeat, M.F. (1976) 'Protagoras and Self-Refutation in Later Greek Philosophy' and 'Protagoras and Self-Refutation in Plato's *Theaetetus*', *Philosophical Review* 85: 44–69, 172–95. (A careful analysis of the man-the-measure thesis according to the subjectivist and relativist interpretations.)

Classen, C.J. (ed.) (1976) *Sophistik*, Darmstadt: Wissenschaftliche Buchgesellschaft. (An anthology which includes seven scholarly articles on Protagoras, three of them in English.)

Guthrie, W.K.C. (1969) *A History of Greek Philosophy*, vol. 3, Cambridge: Cambridge University Press; part of vol. 3 repr. as *The Sophists*, Cambridge: Cambridge University Press, 1971. (Full scholarly account.)

Kerferd, G.B. (1981) *The Sophistic Movement*, Cambridge: Cambridge University Press. (A briefer, more personal interpretation than Guthrie (1969).)

* Plato (*c.*386–380 BC) *Protagoras*, trans. C.C.W. Taylor,

Oxford: Oxford University Press, 2nd edn, 1991. (Dialogue showing Protagoras in debate with Socrates. A gathering of famous Sophists, where Socrates defeats Protagoras in a series of dialectical debates.)

* —— (*c*.370–367 BC) *Theaetetus*, trans. M.J. Levett, intro. M. Burnyeat, Indianapolis, IN: Hackett, 1990. (Contains a classic critique of Protagoras' relativism. Elaborate examination and refutation of Protagoras' thesis that man is the measure of what is.)

* —— (*c*.380–367 BC) *Cratylus*, trans. C.D.C. Reeve, in J. Cooper (ed.) *Plato, Complete Works*, Indianapolis, IN: Hackett Publishing Company, 1997. (Elaborate discussion on the correctness of names, whether conventional or natural; Protagoras is mentioned as having lectured on the topic.)

* —— (*c*.366–360 BC) *Phaedrus*, trans. A. Nehamas and P. Woodruff, in J.Cooper (ed.) *Plato, Complete Works*, Indianapolis, IN: Hackett, 1997. (In a long list of specialists on rhetoric, Protagoras is mentioned as having introduced refinements concerning correctness of diction.)

* Protagoras (*c*.490–*c*.420 BC) Fragments, in H. Diels and W. Kranz (eds) *Die Fragmente der Vorsokratiker* (Fragments of the Presocratics), Berlin: Weidmann, 7th edn, 1954, vol. 2, 253–71. (The standard collection of the ancient sources both fragments and testimonia, the latter designated with 'A'; includes Greek texts of the fragments with translations in German.)

Schiappa, E. (1991) *Protagoras and Logos, A Study in Greek Philosophy and Rhetoric*, Columbia, SC: University of South Carolina Press. (A rather speculative attempt at a systematic interpretation of Protagoras' thought.)

Sprague, R.K. (ed.) (1972) *The Older Sophists*, Columbia, SC: University of South Carolina Press, 3–28. (Full English translation of the fragments and testimonia from Diels and Kranz (1954).)

CHARLES H. KAHN

PROUDHON, PIERRE-JOSEPH (1809–65)

Pierre-Joseph Proudhon was a French social theorist, political activist and journalist. Claiming to be the first person to adopt the label 'anarchist', he developed a vision of a cooperative society conducting its affairs by just exchanges and without political authority. In his lifetime he exercised considerable influence over both militants and theorists of the European left, and he is remembered today as one of the greatest exponents of libertarian socialism. His last writings, though still strongly libertarian, advocated a federal state with minimal functions.

Proudhon was born in Besançon, in the French Jura, to a poor artisan family. He worked first as a printer, and was largely self-educated. At the age of thirty he won a fellowship from the local Academy and went to Paris, where he spent most of the rest of his life. During the 1840s his writings included *Qu'est-ce que la propriété?* (What is Property?) (1840), and *Système des contradictions économiques ou Philosophie de la Misère* (System of Economic Contradictions, or the Philosophy of Poverty) (1846), which laid the groundwork for his social and economic theory: the latter drew an acerbic reply (*The Poverty of Philosophy*) from Marx, who regarded Proudhon's views as those of a petit-bourgeois. By the time of the 1848 revolution he was prominent enough to win election to the Constituent Assembly, where, however, he was too isolated a figure to be effectual. After the advent of the Second Empire in 1851, Proudhon suffered periods both of imprisonment in France and exile in Belgium. During this period he wrote some of his most important books, notably his three-volume *De la justice dans la Révolution et dans l'Église* (On Justice in the Revolution and in the Church) (1858). Five years after Proudhon's death, many leaders of the Paris Commune, the most important socialist insurrection ever to take place in Western Europe, regarded themselves as his disciples. Russian anarchists, such as Tolstoi and Kropotkin, also acknowledged his influence.

Proudhon wrote in a muscular and impetuous style, often producing startling aphorisms, which on first glance may seem to be paradoxes. The two for which he is best known are 'property is theft' and 'God is evil'. Neither of these, however, can be taken at face value. With regard to the first aphorism, Proudhon believed that possession of a share in productive resources was immensely important: it was essential to the development of the (male) individual's inventive and productive powers. What he rejected as 'theft' was the existence of a property right which confirmed some people in their possession of resources, when others possessed none. Proudhon favoured a society in which possession of productive resources would be widely shared (in contrast to the collective ownership favoured by socialists such as Marx (see MARX, K. §12)). Producers would exchange their goods, not at a market price determined by the interaction between supply and demand, but at a price fixed by the average labour time required by the goods' production. Efficient producers would thus be rewarded.

791

The second famous aphorism, 'God is evil', also requires a context. Proudhon equates 'God' with ideas of fatality which exclude or downplay the idea of human agency. When he says, in *System of Economic Contradictions*, that 'the first duty of the free and intelligent man is to hunt the idea of God from his mind', he means that, to be free, people must abandon the idea that human circumstances are something other than a human construct. Part of unfreedom is the belief that the evolution of human society is the work of fate or providence and thus beyond the control of humans: this belief will vanish when there are no longer massive concentrations of economic and political power which remove decisions from the hands of ordinary people. Another part of unfreedom is the belief that one must obey authorities endowed with some special status which places them beyond the control of their subjects, an irrational belief which would not survive without religious support.

Independence – material and intellectual – was thus an important value for Proudhon. But he also stressed the interdependence arising from the complementarities in social life. The complementarity of different skills creates an incentive to reach agreement, as well as multiplying the power of human labour. The non-synchronized character of humans' needs makes possible the institution of credit: Proudhon's writings inspired some important practical reforms in the credit system. Interestingly, within the family unit, the principle of interdependence triumphed wholly over that of independence: Proudhon held rigid views about the sexual division of labour, and would have allowed women no role outside the household. Traditionalist aspects of Proudhon's thought have led some right-wing theorists to claim him for their own.

Proudhon's thinking reveals many influences: there are echoes of Fourier, Saint-Simon, Comte, British political economy, Hegel and Feuerbach. Rousseau (see ROUSSEAU, J.-J. §3), however, has a special importance for him, both positive and negative. What Proudhon shared with Rousseau was the idea that absolute personal independence could be reconciled with the social condition – that one can belong to a social order yet 'obey only oneself' (perhaps in the limited sense of obeying one's own reason). What he hated in Rousseau was the conclusion that this reconciliation could be achieved only in the state: it could best be achieved, Proudhon thought, in civil society, and in the reciprocity among groups of producers, characterized by mutual respect and complementarity of interest. Proudhon was a critic of political democracy, which he thought Rousseau had inspired: although he believed in the capacity of small groups to manage concrete affairs which they

could understand, he had no faith in the political discernment of the masses. When he came eventually to accept the need for government, he did so only on the condition that the primary units of government would be small communities constrained by immediate responsibility for their decisions: the radically decentralizing spirit of his earlier work is not abandoned.

See also: ANARCHISM §3; FREEDOM AND LIBERTY; PROPERTY; SOCIALISM

List of works

Proudhon, P.J. (1840) *Qu'est-ce que la propriété? ou Recherche sur le principe du droit et du gouvernement*, Paris: Brocard; trans. B. Tucker, *What is Property?*, New York: Dover, 1970. (The most accessible statement of his basic position.)

—— (1843) *De la création de l'ordre dans l'humanité, ou Principes d'organisation politique* (On the Creation of Human Order, or Principle of Political Organization), Paris: Prevot. (A systematic exposition of his views on religion, philosophy and political economy.)

—— (1846) *Système des contradictions économiques ou Philosophie de la misère*, Paris: Guillaumin; trans. B. Tucker, *System of Economic Contradictions, or the Philosophy of Poverty*, New York: Arno, 1972. (The fullest statement of his economic theory.)

—— (1851) *Idée générale de la Révolution au XIXe siècle*, Paris: Garnier; trans. J.B. Robinson, *General Idea of the Revolution in the Nineteenth Century*, London: Freedom Press, 1923. (Presents anarchism as the culmination of democratic principles.)

—— (1853) *Philosophie du progrès* (Philosophy of progress), Brussels: Lebègue. (Depicts history as the progress of freedom.)

—— (1858) *De la justice dans la Révolution et dans l'Église* (On justice in the Revolution and in the Church), Paris: Garnier, 3 vols. (The fullest statement of his ethical theory.)

—— (1861) *La guerre et la paix* (War and Peace), Paris: Dentu. (Calls for the replacement of war by industry as the basis of social organization.)

—— (1863) *Du principe fédératif et de la nécessité de reconstituer le parti de la Révolution*, Paris: Dentu; trans. R. Vernon, *The Principle of Federation*, Toronto, Ont.: University of Toronto Press, 1979. (Explains his acceptance of minimal government.)

—— (1865) *De la capacité politique des classes ouvrières* (On the Political Capacity of the Working Classes), Paris: Dentu. (Offers a programme for workers' self-emancipation.)

References and further reading

Hoffman, R.L. (1972) *Revolutionary Justice: The Social and Political Thought of P.-J. Proudhon*, Urbana, IL: University of Illinois Press. (Detailed exposition and commentary. Excellent bibliography.)

* Marx, K. (1847) 'The Poverty of Philosophy', in *Selected Writings*, ed. D. McLellan, Oxford: Oxford University Press, 1977. (A polemic against Proudhon's economic analysis.)

Noland, A. (1967) 'Proudhon and Rousseau', *Journal of the History of Ideas* 28: 33–54. (Examines Proudhon's most important intellectual debt.)

Ritter, A. (1969) *The Political Thought of Pierre-Joseph Proudhon*, Princeton, NJ: Princeton University Press. (A careful, critical, yet sympathetic analysis of Proudhon's central concepts.)

Waldron, J. (1988) *The Right to Private Property*, Oxford: Clarendon Press. (Contains an account of Proudhon's theory of property.)

Woodcock, G. (1956) *Pierre-Joseph Proudhon: His Life and Work*, New York: Schocken. (The standard English-language biography. Contains a bibliography.)

RICHARD VERNON

PROVABILITY LOGIC

Central to Gödel's second incompleteness theorem is his discovery that, in a sense, a formal system can talk about itself. Provability logic is a branch of modal logic specifically directed at exploring this phenomenon. Consider a sufficiently rich formal theory T. By Gödel's methods we can construct a predicate in the language of T representing the predicate 'is formally provable in T'. It turns out that T is able to prove statements of the form

(1) If A is provable in T, then it is provable in T that A is provable in T.

In modal logic, predicates such as 'it is unavoidable that' or 'I know that' are considered as modal operators, that is, as non-truth-functional propositional connectives. In provability logic, 'is provable in T' is similarly treated. We write $\Box A$ for 'A is provable in T'. This enables us to rephrase (1) as follows:

(1') $\Box A \to \Box\Box A$.

This is a well-known modal principle amenable to study by the methods of modal logic.

Provability logic produces manageable systems of modal logic precisely describing all modal principles for $\Box A$ that T itself can prove. The language of the modal system will be different from the language of the system T under study. Thus the provability logic of T (that is, the insights T has about its own provability predicate as far as visible in the modal language) is decidable and can be studied by finitistic methods. T, in contrast, is highly undecidable. The advantages of provability logic are: (1) it yields a very perspicuous representation of certain arguments in a formal theory T about provability in T; (2) it gives us a great deal of control of the principles for provability in so far as these can be formulated in the modal language at all; (3) it gives us a direct way to compare notions such as knowledge with the notion of formal provability; and (4) it is a fully worked-out syntactic approach to necessity in the sense of Quine.

1   The prehistory of the subject
2   What is provability logic?
3   What does provability logic achieve?

1   The prehistory of the subject

The history of provability logic proper starts with Kurt Gödel (1933), who, at the end of a discussion of the interpretation of intuitionistic propositional logic, briefly (in six lines!) discusses formal provability as a modal operator.

The next step was taken by Leon Henkin who, in 1952, asked a seemingly frivolous question:

If Σ is any standard formal system adequate for recursive number theory, a formula (having a certain integer q as its Gödel number) can be constructed which expresses the proposition that the formula with Gödel number q is provable in Σ. Is this formula provable or independent in Σ?

(1952: 180)

In short, is a sentence that 'says' 'I am provable in Σ' provable in Σ? Note that $\underline{0} = \underline{0}$ is a fixed point of $\mathrm{Prov}_T(x)$: $\underline{0} = \underline{0}$ is provable in T and so is $\mathrm{Prov}_T(\#(\underline{0} = \underline{0}))$; hence, by classical logic, $(\underline{0} = \underline{0} \leftrightarrow \overline{\mathrm{Prov}_T(\#(\underline{0} = \underline{0}))})$ is provable in T. (See §2 below for an explanation of the notation.) $\underline{0} = \underline{0}$ is, however, not a *literal* Henkin sentence: it is not built explicitly to say of itself 'I am provable' in the way that Gödel's sentence is built to say 'I am not provable'. In 1953, G. Kreisel published a noteworthy paper answering Henkin's question with a resounding 'It depends...'. Kreisel constructed two extensionally correct provability predicates where for the one the literal Henkin sentence ('I am provable in Σ') is provably true, but for the other it is provably false.

It might have ended there. Kreisel's result might have discouraged everyone from thinking further about Henkin's 'frivolous' question. Happily for the subject, a second paper, by M.H. Löb, appeared in 1955. Löb shows that under certain natural assumptions (the ones codified by (L1)–(L3) below) on the provability predicate, the answer to Henkin's question is that the literal Henkin sentence is true. In fact, under these conditions every solution to the 'Henkin equation' is provably true. With the formulation of the Löb conditions the modal study of provability could begin. For a good part of the subsequent story the reader is referred to Boolos and Sambin (1991).

2   What is provability logic?

Provability logic is best described as the sustained investigation of formal provability and related notions as modal operators. Consider the language $\mathfrak{L}$ of modal propositional logic (see MODAL LOGIC). Let $\mathfrak{A}$ be a language of predicate logic and let T be a theory in $\mathfrak{A}$. T should satisfy a number of conditions, which we will specify later. For the moment let us simply pretend that $\mathfrak{A}$ is the language of arithmetic and that T is Peano arithmetic (PA). An 'interpretation' $(.)\sigma$ of $\mathfrak{L}$ in $\mathfrak{A}$ with respect to T is given by a mapping σ of the propositional variables to sentences of $\mathfrak{A}$. This mapping is extended to a full interpretation via the following clauses:

$$(p)\sigma = \sigma(p),$$
$$(\bot)\sigma = \bot, \ (\top)\sigma = \top,$$
$$(A \wedge B)\sigma = (A)\sigma \wedge (B)\sigma,$$
$$(A \vee B)\sigma = (A)\sigma \vee (B)\sigma,$$
$$(A \to B)\sigma = (A)\sigma \to (B)\sigma,$$
$$(\Box A)\sigma = \mathrm{Prov}_T(\#((A)\sigma)).$$

Only the last clause deserves comment. Prov_T is the arithmetized provability predicate for T. $(A)\sigma$ is a sentence of $\mathfrak{A}$. $\#((A)\sigma)$ is the Gödel number of $(A)\sigma$. Finally, $\overline{\#((A)\sigma)}$ is the numeral of $\#((A)\sigma)$. Thus $\overline{\#((A)\sigma)}$ is a closed term of $\mathfrak{A}$ denoting $\#((A)\sigma)$ under the standard interpretation. For example, $(\neg\Box\bot)\sigma$ translates to $\neg\mathrm{Prov}_T(\#(\bot))$, the sentence expressing the consistency of T. $\overline{\#((A)\sigma)}$ is, in a sense, the obvious way available to T to talk about $(A)\sigma$.

The meaning of '$(.)\sigma$' depends on the given T. Strictly speaking we should write '$(.)(\sigma, T)$', or something similar, to make the dependence on T

visible. However, to avoid too heavy a notational burden, we 'hide' T.

In the definition of $(A)\sigma$ a subformula occurrence of B in A can 'go to' two different things. If the occurrence is not in the scope of a '$\Box$', then B translates to a formula of $\mathfrak{A}$. If the occurrence is in the scope of a '$\Box$', then the translation of B contributes to the value of a term in $(A)\sigma$. This difference in treatment leads to the existence of modalized fixed points. Let us remind ourselves of the Gödel fixed point lemma (see GÖDEL'S THEOREMS). For any formula $C(x)$ of $\mathfrak{A}$ with at most x free, there is a sentence D of $\mathfrak{A}$, such that $T \vdash D \leftrightarrow C(\overline{\#(D)})$. Observe that D 'occurs' in two different ways in the fixed point statement – as a formula and as a term. The fixed point lemma has the 'fixed point theorem' (1) below as a correlate in the modal language.

To formulate (1) we first give a definition. We say that p occurs 'only modalized' in A if all occurrences of p in A are in the scope of a box. For example, p occurs only modalized in $\Box(p \to \Box\Box p)$; p does not occur only modalized in $p \wedge \Box p$. Note that if p does not occur in A at all, then it occurs only modalized in A.

(1)   Suppose that p occurs only modalized in A. Consider any σ from the propositional atoms to the sentences of $\mathfrak{A}$. We can find a D in $\mathfrak{A}$ such that if τ is the function such that $\tau(q) = \sigma(q)$ for $q \neq p$ and $\tau(p) = D$, then we have $T \vdash (p \leftrightarrow A)\tau$.

For example, we can find a τ such that $T \vdash (p \leftrightarrow \neg\Box p)\tau$. Note that this is just a reformulation of the most celebrated application of the Gödel fixed point lemma: the proof of the existence of a Gödel sentence G such that

$$T \vdash G \leftrightarrow \neg\mathrm{Prov}_T(\overline{\#(G)}).$$

Note that if we were to drop the 'guardedness condition', that p must be only modalized, then we would immediately get the liar paradox by taking $A = \neg p$. We will see below that (1) has an unexpected improvement in (4).

Let Γ be a finite set of $\mathfrak{L}$-formulas. We write $(\Gamma)\sigma$ for $\{(A)\sigma | A \in \Gamma\}$. We define $\Gamma \models_T A$ (pronounced 'A is a T-consequence of Γ') to mean that for all σ,

$$T + (\Gamma)\sigma \vdash (A)\sigma.$$

'$\models_T$' is a relation of arithmetical validity (with respect to T) for the modal language. Interpretations take the place of semantics in this definition. The dependence on T in the definition is two-fold: first, we are considering principles derivable in T; second, the interpretation of '□' under the (.)σ is the arithmetization of the predicate 'is provable in T'.

We have, for example, $\Box p \models_T \Box\Box p$. Translating this back we find that it means that, for all sentences A of the language of T,

$$T + \mathrm{Prov}_T(\#(A)) \vdash \mathrm{Prov}_T(\#(\mathrm{Prov}_T(\#(A)))).$$

You could say that $\Box p \models_T \Box\Box p$ expresses the validity of a schematic step with respect to T. The unusual thing is that the schema is formulated in a different kind of language: the language of modal propositional logic, which contains a logical operator not occurring in the language of T.

The relation '$\models_T$' can be axiomatized by a theory called Löb's logic (L or PrL for provability logic, or GL for Gödel–Löb logic) with the following rules of proof:

(L1) $\vdash A \Rightarrow \vdash \Box A$

(L2) $\vdash \Box(A \to B) \to (\Box A \to \Box B)$

(L3) $\vdash \Box A \to \Box\Box A$

(L4) $\vdash \Box(\Box A \to A) \to \Box A$.

(L4) is also known as Löb's principle. In view of the fact that in classical logic an implication follows from its consequent, Löb's principle tells us that an instance of the reflection principle $\vdash \Box A \to A$ is *only* provable if its consequent is already provable. In other words, T 'knows' that it can prove only trivial instances of reflection.

The soundness of L was, in effect, proved by M.H. Löb (1955). Completeness was proved by R. Solovay (1976). 'Solovay's completeness theorem' is as follows:

(2)   Under appropriate conditions on the theory T (see below), $L + \Gamma \vdash A \Leftrightarrow \Gamma \models_T A$.

L has a Kripke-type completeness theorem with respect to transitive models with an upwardly well-founded accessibility relation. (The accessibility relation is upwardly well-founded if there are no infinite ascending chains.) Since the logic has the finite model property, we have Kripke completeness also with respect to finite, transitive, irreflexive models. The logic is not compact for the Kripke semantics: one can produce an infinite set X of modal formulas that cannot be valid on any transitive, upwardly well-founded model. On the other hand, for every finite subset X_0 of X one can find such a model on which X_0 is valid.

There are two major results about what L can prove. The first (due to Bernardi, de Jongh and Sambin) is the fact that fixed points of modalized formulas are unique. The theorem says that if p and q are truly and provably fixed points of A, then they are truly and provably equivalent. We write $A(B/p)$ for the result of substituting B for p in A. Define $\Box^+ A := A \wedge \Box A$.

(3) Suppose that p occurs only modalized in A and that q does not occur in A. Then

$$\Box^+(p \leftrightarrow A), \Box^+(q \leftrightarrow A(q/p)) \vdash \Box^+(p \leftrightarrow q).$$

The second major result (due to de Jongh and Sambin) is the existence of explicit fixed points. The theorem says that the language $\mathfrak{L}$ is rich enough to contain explicit definitions of the fixed points of formulas (with respect to propositional variables which occur only modalized in them).

(4)   Suppose that p occurs only modalized in A. Then there is a B in $\mathfrak{L}$ containing only variables occurring in A, but not containing p, such that $\vdash B \leftrightarrow A(B/p)$.

The proof of (4) yields an algorithm for computing B from A and p.

To illustrate (1), (3) and (4), consider $\neg\Box p$. (1) tells us that in the arithmetical interpretation this formula has a fixed point: precisely the celebrated Gödel sentence G. (3) tells us that, modulo provable equivalence in T, this sentence is unique. (4) tells us that we can find an explicit equivalent of G in the modal language. If we apply the algorithm associated to (4), we find that the explicit fixed point is $\neg\Box\bot$, the sentence expressing the consistency of T. Thus (4) links the unprovable sentence of Gödel's first incompleteness theorem to the unprovable sentence of Gödel's second incompleteness theorem (see GÖDEL'S THEOREMS).

The difference between (1) and (4) is as follows. (1) tells us that for all interpretations of the propositional variables (except p) of A (with p modalized), we can assign a sentence to p yielding the fixed point property. *Prima facie* this sentence need not be expressible in the modal language. (4) tells us that the modal language is rich enough to define the fixed point explicitly.

We close this section with some remarks about the precise choice of the theory T and $\mathfrak{A}$, the language of T. To make the results above work, T must be rich enough to do arithmetization in. This means that a sufficiently rich theory of arithmetic must be interpretable in T. The most natural choice for this theory is Buss' S_2^1, a theory far weaker than such well-known theories as primitive recursive arithmetic, $I\Sigma_1^0$ or PA. The theory S_2^1 is not contained in $I\Delta_0$. S_2^1 has induction restricted to the Σ_1^b-formulas, a class connected to the logical study of feasible algorithms (see COMPLEXITY, COMPUTATIONAL). $I\Delta_0$ has induction restricted to the Δ_0-formulas. In S_2^1 some functions are provably total which are not provably total in $I\Delta_0$. It turns out that the presence of S_2^1 is sufficient to verify the validity of L. However, to prove Solovay's completeness theorem (2) we seem to need more. Inspection of Solovay's proof shows that the theory we (*prima facie*) need is $I\Delta_0 + \text{Exp}$. Here Exp is an axiom expressing that the exponentiation function is total. It is consistent with everything we know that S_2^1 has a provability logic that is stronger than L! We can now give the first condition that the theory T should satisfy to be sound and complete for Löb's logic.

Condition 1: $I\Delta_0 + \text{Exp}$ is interpretable in T.

We do not demand that $I\Delta_0 + \text{Exp}$ be literally a subtheory of T, since we want the results of provability logic to be applicable to such theories as ZF (see SET THEORY) in which arithmetic is present only via a translation of the arithmetical language into the language of set theory.

A second condition on the theory is that it be sufficiently sound. For example, by the second incompleteness theorem $U := \text{PA} + \text{Prov}_{\text{PA}}(\#(\perp))$ is consistent. As is easily seen, $U \vdash \text{Prov}_U(\#(\perp))$. So $\models_U \square\perp$ and, hence, Solovay's completeness theorem cannot hold for U. We exclude such theories as U by demanding that T is Σ_1-sound, that is, the Σ_1-sentences T proves are all true. (A somewhat sharper condition is possible, but space does not permit its introduction here.)

Condition 2: T is Σ_1-sound.

3 What does provability logic achieve?

We end with some comments on the usefulness of provability logic. First the mathematical side. Clearly the modal presentation of arithmetical arguments makes them very perspicuous. So provability logic achieves Kreisel's excellent aim of 'saying simple things simply'. Also, by Solovay's theorem, provability logic completely describes the arithmetically valid modal provability principles. Moreover, it enables us to study these principles using the tools of modal logic (for example, Kripke semantics). Thus, by switching to the modal language, we gain control.

Now for philosophical relevance. Provability logic offers a fully worked-out syntactic treatment of modality (in the sense of Quine 1953). Since its principles are quite different from what one would ordinarily expect of notions of knowledge, necessity and so on, one way of viewing what is achieved is to conclude that syntactic treatments of such notions are not possible (for a brief discussion, see Thomason 1980). Moreover, comparing intuitively plausible

modal principles for notions such as knowledge, human provability and the like with the principles satisfied by formal provability gives some sense of how these notions differ from formal provability. The reflection principle $\vdash \square A \rightarrow A$ is built into or internal to the ordinary notions of knowledge and (human) provability. In contrast, formal provability satisfies Löb's principle ($\vdash \square(\square A \rightarrow A) \rightarrow \square A$). We can 'see' that the difference between human and formal provability is not simply one of *strength* (but, I would suggest, one of *kind*). (The popularity of the view that the difference is one of strength can be seen, for example, in the discussion concerning minds and machines, where it is sometimes claimed on the ground of Gödel's incompleteness theorems that humans can beat machines in a theorem-producing game.)

See also: LOGICAL AND MATHEMATICAL TERMS, GLOSSARY OF

References and further reading

Boolos, G. (1993) *The Logic of Provability*, New York and Cambridge: Cambridge University Press. (A very readable textbook; includes an up-to-date introduction to predicate provability logic.)

* Boolos, G. and Sambin, G. (1991) 'Provability: The Emergence of a Mathematical Modality', *Studia Logica* 50 (1): 1–23. (A brief history of the subject for roughly the period 1933–80.)

* Gödel, K. (1933) 'Eine Interpretation des intuitionistischen Aussagenkalküls', *Ergebnisse eines Mathematischen Kolloquiums* 4: 39–40; trans. 'An Interpretation of the Intuitionistic Propositional Calculus', in *Collected Works*, ed. S. Feferman, J.W. Dawson, W. Goldfarb, C.D. Parsons and R.M. Solovay, Oxford and New York: Oxford University Press, 1995, vol. 3, 296–302. (Includes a thorough discussion by A.S. Troelstra.)

* Henkin, L. (1952) 'A Problem concerning Provability', *Journal of Symbolic Logic* 17: 160, problem 3. (The paper in which Henkin posed the crucial question 'Is a sentence that "says" "I am provable in Σ" provable in Σ?'.)

* Kreisel, G. (1953) 'On a Problem of Henkin's', *Indagationes Mathematicae* 15: 405–6. (Kreisel's answer to Henkin: 'It depends...'.)

* Löb, M.H. (1955) 'Solution of a Problem of Leon Henkin', *Journal of Symbolic Logic* 20: 115–18. (As the title of this paper suggests, Löb answered Henkin's problem, and also proved the soundness of Löb's logic.)

* Quine, W.V. (1953) 'Three Grades of Modal Involvement', in *Proceedings of the 11th International*

Congress of Philosophy 14, Amsterdam: North Holland, 65–81. (Quine shows that provability logic offers a fully worked-out syntactic treatment of modality.)

Smorynski, C. (1985) Self-Reference and Modal Logic, New York: Springer. (A well-written and elegant textbook; includes good discussions of multi-modal provability logic and of non-extensional self-reference.)

* Solovay, R.M. (1976) 'Provability Interpretations of Modal Logic', Israel Journal of Mathematics 25: 287–304. (A proof of the completeness of Löb's logic.)

* Thomason, R.H. (1980) 'A Note on Syntactical Treatments of Modality', Synthèse 44: 391–5. (Presents the view that syntactic treatments of knowledge, necessity and so on are not possible.)

ALBERT VISSER

PROVIDENCE

Divine providence is God's care, provision, foresight and direction of the universe in such a way that the universe as a whole and individual creatures within it fulfil God's purposes. Belief in providence was affirmed by some Greek philosophers (especially the Stoics), and is a fundamental tenet of Judaism, Christianity and Islam. In modern times, questions have arisen about the possibility of divine intervention in worldly affairs; this creates a difficulty for belief in providence, because it makes it hard to see how God can shape events so as to carry out his providential purposes.

Theories of providence differ with regard to the extent to which God has direct and specific control over earthly events, as opposed to guiding the course of affairs in a general way towards his overall goals. The strongest affirmation of divine control comes from Calvinism, which accepts a compatibilist view of free will (that is, that free will is compatible with determinism) and affirms God's absolute control over everything that happens. Other views affirm libertarian free will for creatures; some place limitations on God's knowledge of the future, and process theology places stringent limits on God's power to affect worldly events. These limitations tend to give creatures a limited degree of independence over against God, and lessen God's direct and specific control over events.

1 A brief history of providence
2 Post-Enlightenment issues and problems
3 The resources of providence: five options
4 Assessing the options

1 A brief history of providence

Belief in a personal or quasi-personal deity has often been virtually synonymous with belief in some kind of divine providential governance of the world. Among the Homeric Greeks, to be sure, fate was an uncanny, impersonal destiny, taking precedence even over the will of the gods. But in HESIOD, the supreme governance of the universe is in the hands of Zeus, who awards both prosperity and punishments in accordance with the law of justice. Plato, in the *Laws*, wrote that 'It is a matter of no small consequence, in some way or other to prove that there are Gods, and that they are good, and regard justice more than men do' (Laws 10). Thus Plato rejected the prevalent mythology because it attributed moral defect to the gods, and the Demiurge of the *Timaeus* 'being without jealousy... desired that all things should come as near as possible to being like himself' (*Timaeus* 29e).

The most serious account of divine providence among the Greek philosophers came from the Stoics. According to them, the ruling power of the universe – God, or the Logos – orders all things for the best in accordance with a universal law of causation. Suffering and calamities are no exception to this. Thus, the path of wisdom is to accept whatever circumstances befall as divinely ordained; one should not complain about the part in the cosmic drama one has been assigned, but rather concern oneself with playing that part in the best way possible. One's inner response to circumstances is to some degree in one's own control; the circumstances themselves are not. It is not surprising that this first attempt to state a rigorous and thoroughgoing account of providence also generated the first major encounter with the problem of evil (see STOICISM §20).

The scriptures of all three major monotheistic religions place great emphasis on divine providence. The Hebrew Bible expresses strongly the belief in God's presence, activity, and direction of all things: 'The Lord is good to all, and his compassion is over all that he has made' (Psalms 145: 9). God's providential rule is seen especially in the history of the Hebrew people: 'For I brought you up from the land of Egypt, and redeemed you from the house of bondage; and I sent before you Moses, Aaron, and Miriam' (Micah 6: 4). But God's hand is not absent from the affairs of other nations: '"Are you not like the Ethiopians to me, O people of Israel?" says the Lord. "Did I not bring up Israel from the land of Egypt, and the Philistines from Caphtor and the Syrians from Kir?"' (Amos 9: 7). Similar themes are maintained in the Talmud: 'The Holy One sits and nourishes both the horns of the wild ox and the ova of lice' (*Shabbat* 107b). And with regard to human affairs, 'He is occupied in making ladders, casting down the one and elevating the other' (*Genesis Rabbah* 68.4).

The New Testament similarly attests God's intimate involvement in all aspects of existence. Best known, perhaps, are the words of Jesus: 'Are not two sparrows sold for a penny? And not one of them will fall to the ground without your Father's will. But even the hairs of your head are all numbered' (Matthew 10: 29–30). God's reign extends over worldly authorities: 'Let every person be subject to the governing authorities. For there is no authority except from God, and those that exist have been instituted by God' (Romans 13: 1). And Christ, as 'Lord of Lords and King of Kings' (Revelation 17: 14), will in the end subject all nations to himself.

The Qur'an, too, emphasizes God's universal providential activity:

Allah is He Who raised up the heavens without any pillars that you can see.... He it is Who spread out the earth and made therein firmly fixed mountains and rivers, and of fruits of every kind He has made pairs. He causes the night to cover the day. In all this, verily, are Signs for a people who reflect.

(13: 2–5)

The theme of providence is taken up, in varying degrees, by the early Fathers and theologians of the Christian Church. Their reflections are mainly inspired by Scriptural testimony, but also include themes and references derived from the Greek philosophers. According to Irenaeus, for example:

God does... exercise a providence over all things.... And, for this reason, certain of the Gentiles, ... being moved, though slightly, by His providence, were nevertheless convinced that they should call the Maker of this universe the Father, who exercises a providence over all things, and arranges the affairs of our world.

(*Against Heresies*, 3.25.1)

Augustine, however, gives by far the fullest account of providence to be found in the ancient Church. In *The City of God*, he paints a grand picture of the cosmic drama, beginning with the creation and the Fall, first of Satan and his angels, then of Adam and Eve, and culminating in the new heavens and the new earth, as the City of God and the earthly city each attain their appointed destinies in heaven and hell respectively. While the main emphasis is on God's redemption of humanity through Israel, Jesus Christ and the Christian Church, God's providence is involved in the affairs of pagan nations as well:

The one true God, who never permits the human race to be without the working of His wisdom and His power, granted to the Roman people an empire, when He willed it and as long as He willed it. It was the same God who gave kingdoms to the Assyrians and even to the Persians.

(*The City of God*, bk 5, ch. 21)

The main themes of Augustine's treatment survived intact through the Middle Ages and into the post-Reformation period, though his doctrines of grace and predestination remained controversial (see AUGUSTINE §§6, 10). Providence was often considered under the three headings of conservation (or 'sustenance'), concurrence and governance. The first two of these represent metaphysical aspects of God's support of his creatures; he both sustains them in existence and 'concurs' (or cooperates) with all of their activities, so that nothing in the world takes place without the exercise of divine power (see CREATION AND CONSERVATION, RELIGIOUS DOCTRINE OF §5). Governance, on the other hand, has to do with God's specific direction of worldly events to serve his purposes; it is primarily on this topic that problems arose in the modern era.

2 Post-Enlightenment issues and problems

For a variety of reasons, the Enlightenment was characterized by a general aversion to the miraculous, sometimes supported by philosophical arguments purporting to show either that miracles are impossible or that it is impossible in principle for human beings to ascertain that a miracle has occurred. Given this aversion, which found expression first in deism and then in various forms of liberal theology, it became quite problematic to speak of divine intervention in worldly affairs. This in turn makes it very difficult to see divine providence as manifested in particular occurrences. God's conservation and concurrence are entirely general in nature, and cannot serve to pick out some events as providential in contrast with others. So if God cannot in any way intervene to shape the course of events in one direction rather than another, there is a genuine question about the significance of any claim to 'see God at work' in specific events. Religious faith, on the other hand, cannot well be sustained without some sense of the active working of God. But with a ban on 'realistic' talk of divine intervention, identifying 'God's work in the world' tends to become an entirely subjective matter, lacking not only in public verification but even in publicly accessible meaning.

A second development is found in the tendency during the eighteenth and nineteenth centuries for the doctrine of providence to be closely associated or even identified with the belief in historical optimism and inevitable progress. This may be in part a reflex from the first development mentioned above. If we cannot with any confidence identify specific events as manifestations of divine governance, where else can we hope to see providence except in the shape and direction of the human story as a whole? But the tendency was also nourished by the general optimism of the Enlightenment, and later by the growth of evolutionary interpretations of history. Doctrines of historical optimism and inevitable progress, however, have nearly enough been refuted by the empirical facts of history in the twentieth century. And to the extent that belief in divine providence was associated with these doctrines, it suffered a blow from which it has not yet recovered.

Yet a third development in recent thought about providence is the increased concern, among both critics of religion and believers, with the problem of evil (see EVIL, PROBLEM OF). The problem of evil is certainly not a new one; it was used against the Stoics by the Epicureans and against the early Christians by the Marcionites and later by the Manicheans (see MANICHEISM). Nevertheless, it is undeniable that the preoccupation with this problem has increased, though the reasons for the increase are not entirely clear. No doubt the tendency noted in the previous paragraph to identify belief in providence with historical optimism, has played a part. The horrendous evils of the twentieth century – the two World Wars and the Holocaust, in particular – have also played a role, though it is not clear that human life on average has been worse for people of this century than for those of earlier epochs. It may be, also, that our perception of the real possibilities, through technology and medicine, of a better life for human beings has made us less tolerant of the deplorable conditions in which very many human beings have lived and still live today. In any case, it is evident that many appeal to the world's evil as a demonstration that belief in God and in providence – at least, as traditionally conceived – is no longer viable. Many theologians and philosophers of religion are more willing than their counterparts in earlier times to consider limitations on God's control over worldly events in order to lessen the directness of his involvement in and responsibility for evil.

3 The resources of providence: five options

A crucial question for any doctrine of providence concerns the resources that are available to God as he exercises his controlling oversight. The key variables here are the power of God, God's knowledge (especially his knowledge of the future), and the nature of human freedom. The views of providence that adhere generally to traditional Western theism, however, do not differ significantly concerning the power of God. (Process theism, as we shall see, is an exception here.) All the major views accept that God's power is limited only by what is logically possible, and perhaps by ethical constraints inherent in the divine nature (see OMNIPOTENCE §§1–3). This means that none of these views finds the notion of divine intervention in the world fundamentally problematic, though theologies will differ with respect to the sorts of divine interventions that actually occur. But there are serious disagreements concerning the nature of human freedom and divine knowledge (see OMNISCIENCE §§3–4). Here we survey five different views, beginning with the one which affords the highest degree of divine control over the world.

Theological determinism, or 'Calvinism' (so called because of its association with CALVIN (§§3–4), though it was held already by Augustine and probably also by Aquinas), holds that everything that happens, with no exceptions, is efficaciously determined by God in accordance with his eternal decrees. This means that God's control over events is absolute; there is no non-logical limitation on the states of affairs God is able to bring about. Calvinists do usually affirm human freedom, but only in a compatibilist sense. And God is able to know the future comprehensively simply by knowing his own intentions.

The theory of divine middle knowledge is also known as Molinism, after Luis de MOLINA (§§1–3), who first propounded it (see MOLINISM). The key idea of Molinism is the attribution to God of the knowledge of a certain class of propositions, now usually called 'counterfactuals of freedom'. Such counterfactual propositions state, concerning a particular free creature, what that creature would do in a particular situation of (libertarian) free choice with which it might be confronted. According to Molinism, God knows all the counterfactuals of freedom concerning all actual and possible free creatures. Thus, the fact that the creature is endowed with libertarian freedom constitutes no limitation on God's ability to anticipate the creature's actions; God merely consults his knowledge of the relevant counterfactuals in order to know exactly what the creature would do in any circumstance in which it might find itself. And this is of immense benefit with regard to God's providential governance of the world: God can survey in advance all of the possible scenarios for creation (all the 'possible worlds'), and select the very one which best fulfils his creative purposes. And once the decision is made, the exact fulfilment of God's plan is guaranteed; the necessity for any risk-taking on God's part is eliminated entirely. God's control is not as absolute as with Calvinism, for God is limited by the counterfactuals of freedom, which are not under his control. But given the counterfactuals, God is able to guarantee the actualization of the very best 'feasible world'.

The theory of 'simple foreknowledge' agrees with Molinism that human beings possess libertarian free will, and also that God has comprehensive knowledge of the future. But it does not accept that God possesses middle knowledge, knowledge of the counterfactuals of freedom. (Many adherents of simple foreknowledge deny that there are any true counterfactuals of freedom.) God's knowledge of the actual future is usually regarded as a kind of 'direct vision' – God 'sees' it as if in a telescope or a crystal ball.

The view that is coming to be known as 'free-will theism' differs from the simple foreknowledge theory by denying that God has comprehensive knowledge of the future. Free-will theism leans heavily on the arguments purporting to show that infallible fore-knowledge of future free actions is impossible. God, however, has comprehensive knowledge of the world's past and present, as well as knowledge of the dispositions, tendencies and so on of free agents. Furthermore, God is able to know many important things about the future on the basis of his own intentions, which in key respects are not contingent on the decisions of creatures. Nevertheless, God is not always able to guarantee in advance the results that will follow from his own actions and the situations he chooses to create; thus, for free-will theism, provi-dence involves a genuine element of divine risk-taking.

The final option to be considered is process theism, a contemporary view which draws heavily on the philosophy of A.N. Whitehead (see PROCESS THEISM; WHITEHEAD, A.N. §4). Process theism agrees with free-will theism that divine foreknowledge is necessa-rily limited by creaturely freedom. But it deviates sharply from all versions of traditional theism in its conception of God's power and activity. The process view of divine power may be summarized succinctly by saying that such power is always persuasive and never coercive. God is at all times attempting to persuade humans and other creatures to follow his way, by presenting to them his 'initial aim' for them, the 'direction' in which he wants them to go so as to realize rich and intense values in a harmonious fashion. But he does not, because he cannot, compel any created being to do his will, and so the actual course of events depends on how finite beings respond to God's persuasion. This means that God's ability to secure the fulfilment of his plan is actually very limited in comparison with that posited by all the other theories considered – and also in comparison with what seems to be presupposed in the Jewish, Christian and Muslim Scriptures.

4 Assessing the options

Clearly Calvinism affords God the maximal degree of control over worldly affairs. (It is noteworthy, how-ever, that it does not in fact accord to God any greater power than he possesses according to Molinism, simple foreknowledge, or free-will theism.) The price to be paid for this absolute control is extreme difficulty in accounting for the world's evil. If God has by his own decree ensured the existence of all the evil and sin that there is, how can human beings justly be held responsible for it? And how can God himself avoid being responsible for evil? How, indeed, is it intelligible that God has chosen to bring about sin and moral evil, and has then assumed towards what he has knowingly and deliberately chosen an attitude of utter, implacable hostility? It seems likely that there is no rationally comprehensible answer to these questions; Calvinists themselves frequently say that the relationship between God and evil is an impene-trable mystery.

Molinism, unlike Calvinism, accepts the existence of libertarian freedom and thus avoids the most severe of Calvinism's difficulties over evil. At the same time, it manages to ascribe to God a degree of providential control that is second only to Calvinism and is probably the greatest control possible if determinism is rejected. There are, however, serious metaphysical difficulties involved in the postulation of counter-factuals of freedom and middle knowledge. And Molinism does not remove all the sting of the problem of evil, for each instance of evil that occurs is one that God has specifically 'planned, ordered, and provided for' (Freddoso 1988: 3; in Molina 1592). So one is led to the difficult assertion (though one that is often enough made) that each and every instance of evil that exists is necessary for the existence of a 'greater good' (or the prevention of a greater evil) that God could not bring about without the evil in question.

The arguments concerning the compatibility of comprehensive divine foreknowledge and libertarian free will are well known and highly controversial. Somewhat surprisingly, these arguments do not have any important bearing on divine providence once middle knowledge has been given up. The reason for this is that simple foreknowledge does not contribute anything to God's providential control over the world beyond what he would have without it. To see this, consider the following argument: suppose God possesses comprehensive knowledge of the state of the earth as of some future time t. The state of the earth at t presupposes the entire causally relevant past history leading up to t. Now suppose that God decides, on the basis of his knowledge of the earth at t, to intervene in the earth's history at some earlier time $t - n$. A little reflection shows this scenario to be incoherent. For what God knows is, by hypothesis, the actual history of the earth leading up to t; to suppose that, on the basis of that knowledge, God intervenes in such a way that the actual history consequent upon the intervention is different from the history God knows to be actual makes no sense. We may conclude from this that it is impossible that God should use foreknowledge derived from the actual occurrence of future events to determine his own prior actions in the providential governance of the world. If simple foreknowledge did exist, it would be useless. (The same argument applies to divine timeless knowledge of the future, where this is not accompanied by middle knowledge (see ETERNITY).)

So free-will theism, simple foreknowledge, and divine timelessness can be treated together. All these views entail what may be termed a 'risk-taking' view of providence; they entail that when God makes decisions that depend for their outcomes on the responses of free creatures, his making of those decisions is not guided by a prior knowledge of the outcomes. This does something to mitigate the problem of evil, in that it need not be assumed that God has specifically 'planned, ordered, and provided for' each instance of evil that actually occurs. It also, to be sure, means that God's control over events is somewhat less direct and pervasive than theology has often assumed. Whether these consequences are acceptable is an important question for theology.

The chief appeal of a process view of providence (over and above the possible attractiveness of a God who is wholly non-coercive) lies in the fact that it virtually disposes of the problem of evil: God cannot properly be said to permit the world's evil, because he has no power to prevent it from occurring. The price of this is a virtual abandonment of the view (central to all historic conceptions of providence) that God is in control of what happens in the world. Whether this is acceptable is, once again, an important question, of fundamental religious as well as theological import.

See also: ALEXANDER OF APHRODISIAS §4; DEISM; ESCHATOLOGY; GRACE; MIRACLES; PREDESTINATION; REPROBATION; REVELATION §1

References and further reading

* Augustine (413–27) *The City of God*, trans. G.G. Walsh, D.B. Zema, G. Monahan and D.J. Honan, Garden City, NY: Image Books, 1958. (Classic account of the Christian drama of salvation from creation to final judgment.)

Bartholomew, D.J. (1984) *God of Chance*, London: SCM Press. (Examination of the issues posed for theology by the supposition that the physical world is fundamentally indeterministic.)

Berkouwer, G.C. (1950) *De Voorversiening Gods*, Kampen: J.H. Kok; trans. L.B. Smedes, *The Providence of God*, Grand Rapids, MI: Eerdmans, 1952. (The doctrine of providence from the perspective of Reformed theology.)

Farley, B.W. (1988) *The Providence of God*, Grand Rapids, MI: Baker Book House. (A useful historical discussion of the doctrine of providence, informed by a Reformed theological perspective.)

Flint, T.P. (1988) 'Two Accounts of Providence', in T.V. Morris (ed.) *Divine and Human Action: Essays in the Metaphysics of Theism*, Ithaca, NY: Cornell University Press, 147–81. (A finely crafted comparison of Thomism (= 'Calvinism') and Molinism.)

Griffin, D.R. (1991) *Evil Revisited: Responses and Reconsiderations*, Albany, NY: State University of New York Press. (A defence of the claim that process theism represents the best response to the problem of evil.)

Hasker, W. (1989) *God, Time and Knowledge*, Ithaca, NY: Cornell University Press. (A sustained argument against Molinism and simple foreknowledge, and in favour of free-will theism.)

—— (1992) 'Providence and Evil: Three Theories', *Religious Studies* 28: 91–105. (Expansion of material in §3 and §4.)

Helm, P. (1994) *The Providence of God*, Downers Grove, IL: InterVarsity Press. (Argues for theological determinism and against Molinist and risk-taking views of providence.)

* Irenaeus (180s) *Against Heresies*, in A. Roberts and J. Donaldson (eds and trans.) *The Ante-Nicene Fathers*, vol. 1, New York: The Christian Literature Co., 1896. (Defence of the Christian faith against the Gnostic heresies of the second century.)

Lanford, M.J. (1981) *Providence*, London: SCM Press. (Good general introduction to the topic in the light of current issues and problems.)

* Molina, L. de (1592) *On Divine Foreknowledge (Part IV of the Concordia)*, trans. with introduction by A.J. Freddoso, Ithaca, NY: Cornell University Press, 1988. (The classic source for Molinism; the introduction is an outstanding exposition and

defence of Molinism against the background of contemporary analytic philosophy.)

* Plato (*c.*366–360 BC) *Timaeus*, trans. F.M. Cornford, Indianapolis, IN: Library of Liberal Arts, 1959. (Plato's 'likely story' concerning the origin and structure of the cosmos.)

WILLIAM HASKER

PRUDENCE

The word 'prudence' is used in several ways in contemporary English, and its different philosophical senses to some extent reflect that variety. Traditionally, prudence is the ability to make morally discerning choices in general; but the term is also used to denote a habit of cautiousness in practical affairs; most recently, attempts have also been made to identify prudence with practical rationality, perhaps even with the pursuit of the agent's own interests, without any specifically moral implications.

1 **Prudence as a cardinal virtue, and contrasted with rashness**
2 **Possible nonmoral senses**

1 Prudence as a cardinal virtue, and contrasted with rashness

In its most traditional sense, 'prudence' translated the Latin *prudentia*, which in turn was the technical translation of Aristotle's *phronēsis* (*Nicomachean Ethics*) (see ARISTOTLE §23). Most contemporary English-speaking philosophers translate *phronēsis* as 'practical wisdom', and discussion of this latter topic will reveal much that traditionally was meant by 'prudence'.

Prudence was considered a virtue of the practical intellect (see VIRTUES AND VICES §3). That is to say, it consisted in an admirable intellectual skill in practical, as distinct from theoretical, matters. The details of this, in Aristotle and in Aquinas, are a matter of controversy, but in general it can be said that the prudent person has to have both an understanding of what human fulfilment is and an ability to perceive which action, here and now, can contribute to living a life of human fulfilment (see EUDAIMONIA).

The intellectual virtue of prudence presupposes other intellectual skills. A successful doctor needs good diagnostic abilities in order to see what is wrong with a patient, a practical knowledge of the treatment appropriate to this patient here and now, and perhaps also the ability to plan ahead for various stages of a long-term treatment. These skills in themselves were thought to be morally neutral; they might equally well characterize a doctor intent on making a fortune as a highly effective practitioner. Specific to prudence is the ability to see how these medical skills can fit into a fulfilled human life, and hence how their use can be morally significant, not simply technically or financially successful (see MORALITY AND ETHICS §2).

Prudence was traditionally contrasted with three other virtues: justice, fortitude and temperance. The latter two were thought to be 'moral' virtues, as distinct from prudence, which is an intellectual virtue. The term 'moral virtue' is confusing, since prudence, too, is concerned with the moral significance of what one does. The phrase 'moral virtue' reflects Aristotle's term *ēthikēaretē*, which referred to admirable emotional dispositions in the realms of aggressiveness and desire (see MORALITY AND EMOTIONS §3). Justice, on the other hand, was thought to reside not in the emotions (as the moral virtues do), nor in the intellect (as prudence does), but in the will. The prudent person would understand what is morally required in each situation; the just person is habitually willing to do what is morally required in giving each person their due.

These four virtues were called 'cardinal' virtues (from the Latin *cardo*, meaning 'hinge') because it was held that possession of all the more specific virtues, such as loyalty, kindness, courage and honesty, turned on the possession of these four. Indeed, Aquinas, like Aristotle, believed that one cannot have prudence without fortitude and temperance, because inappropriate emotional reactions to a particular situation would cloud one's intellectual grasp of what was morally required (*Summa theologiae* IIaIIae.47, IIaIIae.56).

The ability to grasp what is morally required in individual situations is sometimes explained as the ability to reason from general moral principles to particular cases. But the classical writers rather took the view that seeing which principle applies, and how it applies, is not a matter of argument, but, as Aristotle put it, a kind of perception (see VIRTUE ETHICS §6). Critics of a rationalistic bent have objected to this form of moral intuitionism.

Sometimes, rather than being considered as a cardinal virtue of great generality, prudence is conceived of as a particular virtue, contrasted with rashness. Thus, it might be prudent to insure one's house against fire, and prudent for the managers of a trust fund to invest in such a way that the participants in the fund were not exposed to speculative risks. Seen in this way, prudence is a particular virtue, and still belongs to the realm of ethics. On the other hand, 'prudent' is occasionally used in a more critical sense:

to insist on prudence is to insist on playing safe on every possible occasion. If it is thought that some risks are reasonable, or even that it is morally required on occasion to take some risk, prudence in this last sense might even be a vice rather than a virtue.

2 Possible nonmoral senses

More recently, philosophers have used the term 'prudence' in ways which are quite different from those already discussed. Two separate contrasts are involved, which unfortunately are often confused. The first is that between the moral and the nonmoral; and the second is that between the agent's own interests and the interests of other people (see EGOISM AND ALTRUISM). Invoking the first contrast, prudential reasons for doing something are held to be different in kind from moral reasons. Invoking the second contrast, prudential reasons are said to be those involving the agent's own interests, rather than those of others. On these grounds, it is sometimes argued that egoism does not count as a theory of morality at all, since the reasons egoists would give in support of an action are reasons connected either immediately or in the longer term with the furtherance of their own interests, and hence are 'merely prudential'. Moreover, it does seem to be the case that we are inclined to criticize people more severely for failing in their duties towards others, even if these duties are duties of prudence, than we are to criticize for failure in prudence in respect of oneself. This thought leads to the suggestion that failure in prudence with respect to oneself, though it may be irrational, is not properly a moral fault at all.

There are problems with this overall view. First, it is not at all clear that prudential considerations are properly thought of as nonmoral. If to insure one's house is prudent, is that not a moral reason in favour of doing so? And in general, there might be some risks which it is simply morally wrong to take. Second, it is not clear that prudential considerations are restricted to the interests only of the agent. The trust fund manager has prudential duties to the participants in the trust, and it is surely reasonable to suppose that these are moral duties. Third, it is not obvious that one is subject to moral requirements only towards other people and not towards oneself as well; Kant, for example, held that one has moral duties to oneself just as much as to others, as indeed do most theories which lay stress on impartiality as an important feature of the moral (see IMPARTIALITY; KANTIAN ETHICS). But if this is so, then the distinction between self-regarding and other-regarding considerations does not coincide with the distinction between the nonmoral and the morally significant. At least part of

the difficulty may stem from the fact that we ordinarily use the term 'prudence' in a variety of senses according to context, some closer to the older usage, others much less so.

Be that as it may, 'prudence' is often used in contemporary philosophy as equivalent to 'practical rationality', without any implications about moral significance. The prudent choice is that which, broadly speaking, furthers the agent's ends. The qualification is necessary because many writers have considered that we have to assume that agents formulate their decisions on the basis of full information, and do so without being influenced by such things as bias, malice or emotional stress. So it might appear that moral considerations have been reintroduced into the concept, thus bringing it closer to *phronēsis* and the medieval *prudentia*. Moreover, in default of an adequate characterization of the information and state of mind required for prudent choice, the practical usefulness of the concept is much lessened. For this reason other writers have been prepared to say simply that the only empirical basis for assessing persons' interests is to be found in the choices they actually make (see RATIONAL CHOICE THEORY). In this way, particular decisions may be assessed as irrational, and hence as imprudent, on formal grounds such as inconsistency, or being self-defeating, or being ill-adapted to stated ends; but criticism aimed directly at the content of such choices is excluded.

Theories of nonmoral rational choice themselves present problems, especially in relation to political philosophy, in which consideration has to be given to the different preferences of different individuals. This part of the modern discussion of prudence touches on some of the issues dealt with in older discussions of justice. The traditional definition, 'a willingness to give each person their due', of course does not answer the question how one is to discover what is due to different people, nor the further question whether it is possible to give a rational account of the 'best' way of reconciling conflicting preferences. These are just the problems which recent accounts of rational choice theory try to investigate.

References and further reading

* Aquinas, T. (1266–73) *Summa theologiae* (Synopsis of Theology), ed. T. Gilby, Cambridge: Blackfriars, 1965, vol. 36, IIaIIae.47, IIaIIae.56. (Based on Aristotle, these questions on prudence are a systematic account of the Western Christian understanding of prudence.)

* Aristotle (*c.* mid 4th century BC) *Nicomachean Ethics*, trans. with notes by T. Irwin, Indianapolis, IN:

Hackett Publishing Company, 1985, book VI, esp. chaps 1, 2, 5, 13. (The text on which most classic discussions of prudence interpreted as practical wisdom are based.)

Broadie, S. (1991) *Ethics with Aristotle*, Oxford: Oxford University Press, ch. 4. (A modern reading of Aristotle's *Nicomachean Ethics*, excellent for drawing out the implications of the text.)

Falk, W.D. (1963) 'Morality, self and others', in H-N. Castañeda and G. Nakhnikian (eds) *Morality and the Language of Conduct*, Detroit, IL: Wayne State University Press. (Though difficult to find, this valuable article assesses some recent attempts to interpret prudence in a nonmoral way.)

Gauthier, D.P. (1967) 'Morality and Advantage' *Philosophical Review* 74: 460–75, repr. in J. Raz (ed.) *Practical Reasoning*, Oxford: Oxford University Press, 1978, 185–97. (A modern theory of the relationship between morality and self-interest.)

Nagel, T. (1970) 'Desires, Prudential Motives, and the Present', in *The Possibility of Altruism*, Oxford: Clarendon Press; repr. in J. Raz (ed.) *Practical Reasoning*, Oxford: Oxford University Press, 1978, 153–67. (A modern account of prudence interpreted as rational choice.)

Sen, A. and Williams, B. (eds) (1982) *Utilitarianism and Beyond*, Cambridge: Cambridge University Press. (A valuable collection of articles on utilitarianism and other theories of rational choice. The editorial introduction gives a quick and helpful overview.)

Woods, M. (1986) 'Intuition and Perception in Aristotle's Ethics', in J. Annas (ed.) *Oxford Studies in Ancient Philosophy*, vol. IV, Oxford: Clarendon Press. (A discussion of some of the difficulties in interpreting Aristotle's account.)

GERARD J. HUGHES

PSEUDO-DIONYSIUS
(*fl. c.* AD 500)

'Pseudo-Dionysius' was a Christian Neoplatonist who wrote in the late fifth or early sixth century and who presented himself as Dionysius the Areopagite, an Athenian converted by St Paul. This pretence – or literary device – was so convincing that Pseudo-Dionysius acquired something close to apostolic authority, giving his writings tremendous influence throughout the Middle Ages and into the Renaissance.

The extant four treatises and ten letters articulate a metaphysical view of the cosmos, as well as a religious path of purification and perfection, that are grounded in the Neoplatonism developed in the Platonic Academy in Athens. Although this strand of Neoplatonist thought, in contrast to that developed at the school in Alexandria, was deliberately pagan in its religious orientation, Pseudo-Dionysius used its conceptual resources (drawing especially on Proclus) to give precision and depth to the philosophical principles of a Christian world view. Cardinal points of Pseudo-Dionysius' thought are the transcendence of a first cause of the universe, the immediacy of divine causality in the world and a hierarchically ordered cosmos.

1　**The works: character and origin**
2　**Doctrine and context**
3　**Philosophical influence**

1　The works: character and origin

Pseudo-Dionysius' works clearly reflect the late Neoplatonism of the fifth and sixth centuries, creatively modified in accordance with fifth-century Christian ideas and commitments. These facts belie the author's claim to be the disciple of Saint Paul who is described in Acts 17: 16–34 as an instantly converted member of an Athenian judicial body (*areopagos*) asked, by certain Epicurean and Stoic philosophers, among others, to judge the acceptability of Paul's preaching in Athens. The scholarly case against Pseudo-Dionysius' assumed identity was first made by Lorenzo Valla in 1457 and was publicized by Erasmus in 1504. Pseudo-Dionysius' real identity, however, remains unknown, despite continued debate during the sixteenth and seventeenth centuries and renewed scholarly investigation since the end of the nineteenth century.

The range of possible dates for authorship of the corpus is bounded at its early end by the conclusion of Proclus' career in AD 485. This dating is confirmed by Pseudo-Dionysius' appeal to parts of the Christian liturgy and to certain doctrinal formulae current in the late fifth century, and by his adaptation of late fifth-century Neoplatonist religious rites. The latest possible date is set by the earliest unmistakable citation of Pseudo-Dionysius' works, by Severus of Antioch between AD 518 and 528.

A translation into Syriac by Sergius of Reshaina (d. AD 536) made possible the rapid spread of Pseudo-Dionysius' ideas throughout the Syrian Christian centres of learning. Armenian and Arabic translations have also been found, and there is some evidence for Pseudo-Dionysius' influence in the Islamic realm. Despite these successes, however, the pseudonymous philosopher's claims to authority were not uncontroversial; nor was it clear that his views about the Trinity or the nature of Christ were orthodox.

Eventual acceptance on both counts required repeated defences, for example by John of Scythopolis and by Maximus Confessor.

Despite a florid or seemingly even obscurantist style, Pseudo-Dionysius shows himself in his works to be a serious philosopher, struggling against limitations of language and wrestling with the paradoxicality of metaphysical propositions about God, creation, cosmic order and so on. His systematic intent shows not only in his philosophically most important work, *Peri theiōn onomatōn* (On the Divine Names; Latin, *De divinis nominibus*), but also in his grand project. As he explains, this project commences with some treatments of the nature of God and the supra-sensible order insofar as they are accessible to us only with the aid of revelation. (These works are not extant and may never have been finished.) Then, relying more on human reason and thereby descending, as it were, in the cosmic hierarchy, Pseudo-Dionysius undertakes to treat God metaphysically in *Peri theiōn onomatōn*. From this standpoint he descends still further, treating God and the cosmic order insofar as they can be understood through sensible creatures, more distant manifestations of God that allow a kind of metaphoric understanding of their divine cause. Such objects Pseudo-Dionysius thinks of as symbols, and the two extant treatises *Peri tēs ouraniās hierarchiās* (On the Celestial Hierarchy; Latin, *De coelesti hierarchia*) and *Peri tēs ekklēsiastikēs hierarchiās* (On the Ecclesiastical Hierarchy; Latin, *De ecclesiastica hierarchia*) can be considered partial presentations of what he calls 'symbolical theology'.

Having reached the lowest point in the cosmic order, physical things and human religious institutions (whose rituals facilitate the metaphoric understanding of God), Pseudo-Dionysius now tries to recapitulate and complete the cognitive endeavour to reach God. He does this by exposing the limitations of the various sorts of positive knowledge he has outlined in the foregoing treatises. In this way he means to insure his reader's return to God after the descent to the level of creatures. He describes the method by which this perspective is achieved in his *Peri mystikēs theologiās* (On Mystical Theology; Latin, *De mystica theologia*).

2 Doctrine and context

The outline of Pseudo-Dionysius' philosophical project indicates a basic Neoplatonist principle on which his system rests: all finite things 'proceed from' (that is, are caused by) a being that is transcendent, infinite and perfect, and they eventually 'return to' this being since their fulfillment lies in closeness to it

and they are sustained by it for this end. This cosmic cycle of procession and return is the pattern according to which the first cause, or God, exercises its originative capacity and, so to speak, manifests itself through a world of creatures (see NEOPLATONISM).

According to its classic presentation by Neoplatonists from PLOTINUS through PROCLUS, the cosmic cycle actually involves three stages. Prior to the stages of procession and return, there is a first stage of 'immanence' in which the effects abide in their cause, being in a certain sense contained in the cause prior to their being caused. In line with that traditional theory, Pseudo-Dionysius speaks of things in the world as being 'contained beforehand' in their cause 'in a higher way', that is, as initially undifferentiated. However, by focusing on and developing the idea of the first stage, he makes one of his most original contributions to Neoplatonist metaphysics.

To understand this, one must first note two problems within Neoplatonism. First, there is a tension between the claim that the first cause is absolutely simple, containing its effects in some wholly undifferentiated way, and the claim that it does in some way really contain these effects. Second, if the first cause is radically different from its effects in virtue of its simplicity and perfection, and if its causality consists in making things like itself (bringing things to 'participate' in its perfection), how can it actually give rise to effects in the world, since they are quite different from it in nature? Exponents of classical Neoplatonism tend, to one degree or another, to meet these difficulties by supposing intermediate levels of reality between the first cause and its ultimate effects in the world. These 'hypostases' are causally prior to things in the world of nature but are causally dependent on the first cause, and they are supposed to mediate causally between the first cause and its ultimate effects. Pseudo-Dionysius reverses this multiplication of intermediary hypostases, which, one might argue, reaches excessive proportions in later Neoplatonists such as IAMBLICHUS and PROCLUS. He does so by further developing the notion of the first cause's precontainment of its effects. In *Peri theiōn onomatōn*, he argues that the predicates that would be construed in classical Neoplatonism as signifying intermediate hypostases in fact simply designate the first cause itself, considered with respect to effects that it is capable of producing in virtue of its intrinsic perfection.

This account of how the first cause causes things in the world is connected with two other salient Dionysian doctrines. Classical Neoplatonism had generally characterized the first, completely simple and perfect cause as 'the One', and had claimed that this cause of all things in some radical sense transcended being itself. Though Pseudo-Dionysius has often been taken to adhere to this claim that the first cause is 'beyond being', he in fact contends that the first cause is beyond the being of anything finite, even beyond the general sort of being that it can bestow on finite things; but it itself is perfect, infinite being. Pseudo-Dionysius seems to think that this characterization, in contrast to the classical Neoplatonist characterization, accords the first cause a kind of richness that explains how it can indeed be transcendently simple and yet in some sense contain all its effects. Second, Pseudo-Dionysius develops the Platonist idea that the first cause is the good itself. His famous principle, 'The good is such as to diffuse itself', indicates that it is in the very nature of the first cause, on account of its intrinsic perfection, to give rise to the variety and plurality of finite things in the world.

With regard to the return of finite beings to their source, Pseudo-Dionysius complements the ontological conception of a comprehensive hierarchy of beings of various degrees of perfection with an epistemology that stresses gradual cognitive ascent. The finite mind approaches the infinite source by climbing from an understanding of one level in the hierarchy to an understanding of the next. This ascent, which both requires and furthers moral and spiritual purification, finally ends in a state of unification with God that Pseudo-Dionysius describes as an 'inactivity of all knowledge', or a 'knowing beyond the mind', since in this state all particular knowledge must be left behind. Progressive illumination thus culminates, paradoxically, in the 'mysterious darkness of unknowing'. Achieving this state requires ultimately a kind of radical psychic break with ordinary ways of thinking and acting – a spiritual ecstasy.

3 Philosophical influence

Pseudo-Dionysius had a substantial influence on Christian spirituality as well as on medieval and Renaissance philosophy. The influence of his ideas about the spiritual life can be seen most clearly in the writings of medieval and Renaissance mystics who echo some of his pronouncements about the soul's union with God (see MYSTICISM, HISTORY OF). His method of apprehending God by negating positive knowledge – and ultimately seeing God as beyond both affirmation and negation – has appealed to the mystical temper. This method (*via negativa*) must be distinguished, however, from a mystical approach to God, if by that is meant either some sort of actual convergence of the enraptured soul with divinity or a non-intellectual approach (see MYSTICISM, NATURE AND ASSESSMENT OF; NEGATIVE THEOLOGY).

Pseudo-Dionysius' particular philosophical influence is especially marked and important in the Latin West. Its first phase comprises his entry into Western thought in the Carolingian period, via a translation into Latin by Hilduin in 832, and his appropriation by ERIUGENA, who retranslated the works in 862 and extended his ideas in the direction of metaphysical monism. The second phase of influence occurs as part of the rebirth of learning in the twelfth century, and can be seen in such diverse philosophers as HUGH OF ST VICTOR, ISAAC OF STELLA and Peter LOMBARD. His aesthetics (a chapter of *Peri theiōn onomatōn* is devoted to the predicate 'beauty') made its mark by inspiring, directly or indirectly, Abbot Suger's programme for a new architecture, the Gothic, that would lead the soul upward via sensible reality.

The third phase of influence lies in Pseudo-Dionysius' formative effect on some of the greatest philosophers of the thirteenth century: Robert GROSSETESTE, ALBERT THE GREAT, Thomas AQUINAS and BONAVENTURE. These philosophers (except Bonaventure) wrote substantial commentaries on Pseudo-Dionysius; Albert and Aquinas especially used their detailed knowledge of Dionysian texts to assimilate and then develop Platonist principles, making them foundational for their metaphysical systems. Finally, Pseudo-Dionysius' influence appears in the Renaissance as a factor in the revival of interest in Platonism in general. PICO DELLA MIRANDOLA and Marsilio FICINO, affirming the genuineness of Pseudo-Dionysius' claims to authority, see him as the exemplary Christian Platonist and hence as the exemplary philosopher.

In general, Pseudo-Dionysius appeals to medieval and Renaissance philosophers because he seems to them to be leading the way in regard to a common enterprise: the adaptation of Platonist philosophy to the purposes of monotheistic metaphysics. His ideas of creative goodness, creation against the backdrop of nothingness, the metaphysical primacy of being, the nature of evil as privation and the orderliness of the cosmos in terms of a hierarchy of perfection give his writings exceptional philosophical importance, an importance far beyond what they could have had merely by virtue of their presumed authority.

See also: BEING; CREATION AND CONSERVATION, RELIGIOUS DOCTRINE OF; NEOPLATONISM; PLATONISM, MEDIEVAL; ULRICH OF STRASBOURG

List of works

Pseudo-Dionysius (*c.* AD 500) Editions of the Complete Works: G. Heil, A. Ritter and B. Suchla (eds) *Corpus Dionysiacum*, Berlin: de Gruyter, 1990–1, 2 vols; trans. C. Lubheid and P. Rorem, *Pseudo-Dionysius: The Complete Works*, London: Society for the Promotion of Christian Knowledge, 1987; trans. M. de Gandillac, *Pseudo-Denys l'Aréopagite. Oeuvres complètes. Traduction, préface et note*, Paris: Aubier, 1980. (Heil, Ritter and Suchla is a very thorough, collaborative critical edition in two volumes, with a detailed introduction to the whole edition and an extensive bibliography in Volume 1. Lubheid and Rorem is the English reader's best introduction, with accessible, fairly accurate translations with helpful notes. De Gandillac serves as a valuable resource complementing English scholarship.)

—— (*c.* AD 500) *Peri theiōn onomatōn* (On the Divine Names; Latin, *De divinis nominibus*), in *Corpus Dionysiacum*, vol. 1, Berlin: de Gruyter, 1990; trans. C. Lubheid and P. Rorem, *Pseudo-Dionysius: The Complete Works*, London: Society for the Promotion of Christian Knowledge, 1987; trans. M. de Gandillac, *Pseudo-Denys l'Aréopagite. Oeuvres complètes*, Paris: Aubier, 1980. (Other translations of importance are B. Suchla, *Pseudo-Dionysius Areopagita. Die Namen Gottes*, Stuttgart: Hiersemann, 1988; and J. Jones, *Pseudo-Dionysius: The Divine Names and Mystical Theology*, Milwaukee, WI: Marquette University Press, 1980. Jones is an interesting if somewhat idiosyncratic rendering, with helpful references to relevant texts of Aquinas.)

—— (*c.* AD 500) *Peri tēs ouraniās hierarchiās* (On the Celestial Hierarchy; Latin, *De coelesti hierarchia*), in *Corpus Dionysiacum*, vol. 2, Berlin: de Gruyter, 1990; trans. C. Lubheid and P. Rorem, *Pseudo-Dionysius: The Complete Works*, London: Society for the Promotion of Christian Knowledge, 1987; trans. M. de Gandillac, *Pseudo-Denys l'Aréopagite. Oeuvres complètes*, Paris: Aubier, 1980. (A further translation is G. Heil, *Pseudo-Dionysius Areopagita. Uber die himmlische Hierarchie. Über die kirchliche Hierarchie*, Stuttgart: Hiersemann, 1986. This is an up-to-date, accurate translation.)

—— (*c.* AD 500) *Peri tēs ekklēsiastikēs hierarchiās* (On the Ecclesiastical Hierarchy; Latin, *De ecclesiastica hierarchia*), in *Corpus Dionysiacum*, vol. 2, Berlin: de Gruyter, 1990; trans. C. Lubheid and P. Rorem, *Pseudo-Dionysius: The Complete Works*, London: Society for the Promotion of Christian Knowledge, 1987; trans. M. de Gandillac, *Pseudo-Denys l'Aréopagite. Oeuvres complètes*, Paris: Aubier, 1980. (A further up-to-date translation is G. Heil, *Pseudo-Dionysius Areopagita. Über die himmlische Hierarchie. Über die kirchliche Hierarchie*, Stuttgart: Hiersemann, 1986.)

—— (*c.* AD 500) *Peri mystikēs theologiās* (On Mystical Theology; Latin, *De mystica theologia*), in *Corpus Dionysiacum*, vol. 2, Berlin: de Gruyter, 1990; trans. C. Lubheid and P. Rorem, *Pseudo-Dionysius: The Complete Works*, London: Society for the Promotion of Christian Knowledge, 1987; trans. M. de Gandillac, *Pseudo-Denys l'Aréopagite. Oeuvres complètes*, Paris: Aubier, 1980. (Further translations include A. Ritter, *Pseudo-Dionysius Areopagita. Über die mystische Theologie und Briefe*, Stuttgart: Hiersemann, 1994; and J. Jones, *Pseudo-Dionysius: The Divine Names and Mystical Theology*, Milwaukee, WI: Marquette University Press, 1980. Ritter's translation is supplemented by an informative introductory essay on Dionysian philosophical scholarship. Jones' edition contains useful links to relevant texts of Aquinas.)

References and further reading

Patristic and medieval commentaries

Albert the Great (*c.*1250–60) *Super Dionysium de divinis nominibus* (Commentary on *De divinis nominibus*), ed. P. Simon in *Opera omnia*, vol. 37, part 1, Münster: Aschendorff, 1972. (A critical edition of Albert's commentary; supplements that were found in the 1892 edition of the *Opera omnia*, edited by A. Borgnet, Paris: Vives, 1892.)

Aquinas, Thomas (*c.*1265–8) *In librum beati Dionysii De divinis nominibus expositio* (Commentary on Dionysius' *De divinis nominibus*), ed. C. Pera, Turin: Marietti, 1950. (A helpful study-edition, to be complemented by the Leonine critical edition in preparation. H. Jarka-Sellers (trans.) *Commentary on the Blessed Dionysius' On the Divine Names, Thomas Aquinas in Translation*, Washington, DC: Catholic University Press, forthcoming, is an accessible translation with introduction and notes.)

Chevallier, P. (ed.) (1937–50) *Dionysiaca: Receuil donnant l'ensemble des traditions latines des ouvrages attribués au Denys de l'Aréopagite*, Bruges: Desclée de Brouwer, 2 vols; repr. Stuttgart, 1989. (A valuable scholarly accomplishment, comprising translations by Hilduin, Eriugena, John Sarracenus, Grosseteste, Ficino and others.)

Eriugena, Johannes Scottus (*c.*860–70) *Expositiones in Ierarchiam coelestem* (Commentaries on Dionysius' *De coelesti hierarchia*), ed. J. Barbet, Corpus Christianorum, Continuatio Mediaevalis 31, Turnhout: Brepols, 1975. (Commentaries by the most creative philosopher of the early Middle Ages.)

Gallus, Thomas (1242) *Thomas Gallus: Grand commentaire sur la Théologie mystique* (Commentary on Dionysius' *De mystica theologia*), ed. G. Thery, Paris: Haloua, 1934. (A philosophically interesting commentary by a little-known contemporary of Aquinas and Bonaventure.)

Hugh of St Victor (*c.*1220–30) *Commentariorum in Hierarchima coelestem Sancti Dionysii Areopagitae* (Commentary on the *De coelesti hierarchia* of Dionysius the Areopagite), Patrologia Cursus Completus, Series Latinus 175, Paris: Migne, 1844–80. (A reflection of an important philosophical school's indebtedness to Platonic sources.)

John of Scythopolis *et al.* (*c.*530) *Scholia*, ed. P. Corderius, Patrologia Cursus Completus, Series Graeca 4, Paris: Migne 1857–91. (Annotations from Patristic period, whose philosophical importance is still being assessed.)

Secondary sources

Brons, B. (1976) *Gott und die Seienden. Untersuchungen zum Verhältnis von neuplatonischer Metaphysik und christlicher Tradition bei Dionysius Areopagita* (God and Beings: An Examination of the Relationship between Neoplatonist Metaphysics and Christian Tradition in Dionysius the Areopagite), Göttingen: Vandenhoeck & Ruprecht. (A stimulating and systematic study of Pseudo-Dionysius' thought and a careful examination of the texts.)

Gersh, S. (1978) *From Iamblichus to Eriugena: An Investigation of the Prehistory and Evolution of the Pseudo-Dionysian Tradition*, Leiden: Brill. (A learned study elucidating Pseudo-Dionysius' place in the Platonist tradition.)

Koch, J. (1956–7) 'Augustinischer und Dionysischer Neuplatonismus und das Mittelalter' (Augustinian and Dionysian Neoplatonism in the Middle Ages), *Kantstudien* 48: 117–33; repr. in W. Beierwaltes, *Platonismus in der Philosophie des Mittelalters*, Darmstadt: Wissenschaftliche Buchgesellschaft, 1969, 317–42. (A seminal analysis of different strands of Platonist thought in the Middle Ages.)

O'Daly, G. (1981) 'Dionysius Areopagita', *Theologische Realenzyklopädie* 8: 772–80. (An informative, judicious overview.)

O'Rourke, F. (1992) *Pseudo-Dionysius and the Metaphysics of Aquinas*, Leiden: Brill. (A suggestive study of an important topic.)

Roques, R. (1954) *L'univers Dionysien. Structure hierarchique du monde selon le Pseudo-Denys* (The Dionysian Universe: The Hierarchical Structure of the World According to Pseudo-Dionysius), Paris: Aubier; repr. Paris: Éditions du Cerf, 1983. (The classic systematic study.)

Roques, R. *et al.* (1954) 'Denys l'Areopagite (le

Pseudo-)', *Dictionnaire de spiritualité ascétique et mystique doctrine et histoire*, vol. 3, 244–429. (A highly informative treatment by one of the leaders of Dionysian scholarship, followed by discussions by an array of well-known scholars of various aspects of Pseudo-Dionysius' influence.)

Rorem, P. (1993) *Pseudo-Dionysius: A Commentary on the Texts and an Introduction to their Influence*, Oxford: Oxford University Press. (The most accessible and informative general introduction to Pseudo-Dionysius in English, with considerable attention to theological dimensions of Pseudo-Dionysius' thought. Extensive bibliography.)

Saffrey, H.-D. (1982) 'New Objective Links between the Pseudo-Dionysius and Proclus', in D.J. O'Meara (ed.) *Neoplatonism and Christian Thought*, Norfolk, VA: International Society for Neoplatonic Studies, 65–74. (A methodologically astute inquiry into the philosophical background of Pseudo-Dionysius.)

Sheldon-Williams, I.P. (1970) 'The Pseudo-Dionysius', in A.H. Armstrong (ed.) *The Cambridge History of Later Greek and Early Medieval Philosophy*, Cambridge: Cambridge University Press. (A good introduction by an eminent scholar.)

HANNES JARKA-SELLERS

PSEUDO-GROSSETESTE (*fl. c.*1265–75)

'Pseudo-Grosseteste' is the name given to the unidentified author of a philosophic encyclopedia written in England in the third quarter of the thirteenth century. Like other encyclopedias of that time, the Summa philosophiae *(Summa of Philosophy) marshals an astonishing array of facts, principles and arguments in every field of philosophic interest, from accounts of truth or cosmologies through analyses of rational and animal souls to the properties of minerals. The* Summa *is distinguished not by its range of interests, but by its clear sense of its own purposes. The author intends to arrange the history and the particular doctrines of philosophy within a hierarchy built according to Augustinian principles.*

To Robert GROSSETESTE, as to many other ancient or medieval authors, medieval scribes attributed a number of works that modern scholarship now judges spurious. Among works falsely attributed to Grosseteste there are a complete exposition of the Gospels, fragments of a summa of theology and two large-scale summaries of philosophy, one entitled *Summa philo-*

sophiae (Summa of Philosophy) and the other *Compendium philosophiae* (Compendium of Philosophy). The *Compendium* was quickly returned to its real author, the twelfth-century polymath Dominicus Gundissalinus, but the *Summa* has found no other author, and so it is still assigned to a 'Pseudo-Grosseteste'. It is the author of this work, and only of this work, who is treated here.

The *Summa philosophiae* cannot be by Grosseteste because it refers to an event, the death of Simon de Montfort, that occurred twelve years after Grosseteste's own death. There is little other evidence to place it precisely. It seems on internal evidence to have been written during the third quarter of the thirteenth century, probably between 1265 and 1275. Most scholars find traces of English authorship. There are citations to Alfred of Shareshill and perhaps to JOHN OF SALISBURY, if it is he who is named 'John the Peripatetic'. More significantly, the *Summa* shows striking affinities with the *Opus majus* of Roger BACON, to whom it defers on some disputed points of physical doctrine. Curiously, the *Summa* does not mention Grosseteste himself. It should also be noticed that the genre of the naturalist's encyclopedia was quite popular with English authors in the thirteenth century, attracting such notables as Alexander NECKHAM, Bartholomew the Englishman and THOMAS OF YORK.

The *Summa* also invokes a large number of other authors, ancient, patristic, and medieval. The largest number of references is to Aristotle, followed at some distance by Plato, Averroes, Avicenna and Augustine, but a simple count of citations is misleading. The principal philosophical authority here is not Aristotle, but AUGUSTINE. On any number of disputed points, the *Summa* sides with Augustine against Aristotle or the Aristotelians. For example, the proofs for the existence of God are not proofs from motion or causality, but from the necessity for an eternal first truth. The pattern of argument here is to be found in Augustine's *Soliloquia* (Soliloquies) and *De libero arbitrio* (On Free Choice of the Will). Again, in its division of matter the *Summa* allows for spiritual matter as an individuating principle in immaterial beings. At these and other points, the author of the *Summa* shows himself on the side of contemporary Augustinians. This is confirmed in the references to medieval authors. The *Summa* cites approvingly ALEXANDER OF HALES and ALBERT THE GREAT, both of whom it includes in its history of 'philosophy'. Alexander is the great authority among the Franciscans, and he relies throughout his work on Augustine. Albert is taken by the *Summa* either as a teacher of natural philosophy or as an eclectic thinker open to Neoplatonic doctrines. There are allusions to the teachings of Thomas AQUINAS, but they are hardly approving. Indeed, the author of the *Summa* singles out distinctively Thomist positions on several occasions for sharp criticism.

The *Summa* is divided into nineteen Books, a number also adopted by other encyclopedias of the thirteenth century. The Books may be arranged thematically into four groups: an introduction on the nature of philosophy and its relation to theology (Book 1); the principles of being and knowledge (Books 2–6); God and the creation in general (Books 7–9); and specific creatures, from the immaterial to the most material (Books 10–19). The last group is by far the longest and most detailed. It offers, for example, careful analyses of the types of soul, the operations of light, the properties of the elements, meteorological phenomena and minerals.

See also: AUGUSTINIANISM; GROSSETESTE, R.; PLATONISM, MEDIEVAL

List of works

Pseudo-Grosseteste (1265–75) *Summa philosophiae* (Summa of Philosophy) ed. L. Baur, Beiträge zur Geschichte des Philosophie und Theologie des Mittelalters, Münster: Aschendorff, 275–643; Books 2–3 trans. R.P. McKeon, *Selections from the Medieval Philosophers*, New York: Scribner's, 1929–30, vol. 1: 290–314. (A careful edition with helpful if limited annotation.)

References and further reading

McKeon, C.G. (1948) *A Study of the Summa Philosophiae of the Pseudo-Grosseteste*, New York: Columbia University Press. (A detailed retelling of the *Summa*'s doctrine according to the order of the original, with frequent comparisons to other thirteenth-century authors.)

MARK D. JORDAN

PSYCHĒ

Conventionally translated 'soul', psychē is the standard word in classical Greek for the centre of an animal's, and especially a human being's, 'life'. In its earliest usage (in Homer) psychē is a breath-like material persisting after death as a mere ghost. Its precise reference to the locus of thought and emotion only began under the influence of philosophy. From the beginning of the fourth century BC it became normal to pair and contrast psychē with 'body' (soma). The term generated sophisticated discussions. Leading questions include: Is psychē *immortal? Is it corporeal or incorporeal? What are its parts or functions?*

Before philosophy there was no single Greek term for the mind or for the body. In HOMER *psychē* refers to the life or ghost of a person rather than to the mind as such. Homer uses other terms for the location of thought and emotion, probably because *psychē* was taken to comprise *all* the powers a living person loses at death: Homer's disembodied shades retain the characters and histories of their embodied lives. By 500 BC PYTHAGORAS had become famous for rejecting the Homeric Hades and for teaching the transmigration of the same *psychē* into a succession of bodies, animal as well as human. Around the same time HERACLITUS treated *psychē* not only as the source of life but also as something to which the predicates 'wisest and best' can apply. Gradually the term gained wider currency as a way of referring to the self or personality. Socrates invokes this usage in Plato's *Apology* when he exhorts the Athenians to subordinate concern for their bodies to the care of their *psychē*.

Sustained reflection on *psychē* began with PLATO. In his *Phaedo*, although the *psychē* animates the body, that is not its best or primary function. Incorporeal and immortal, the *psychē* is unavoidably tainted by incarnation. The task of philosophers is to detach themselves from the distractions of the body in preparation at death for a return of the *psychē* to a discarnate state of purity and wisdom. In this dialogue sensual desires originate only in the body but a thoroughly impure *psychē* will identify with the body instead of valuing intellectual goods (see PLATO §13). Plato subsequently modified this doctrine. In his *Republic* IV, and repeatedly thereafter, he divides the *psychē* into three components – rational, spirited or competitive, and appetitive; this last component (and not the body itself) is the drive for instant sensual gratification. Plato's principal ground for this tripartition is the need to explain how a person can be simultaneously subject to conflicting desires. On this model of the *psychē*, each component has its own objectives. In a well-integrated *psychē*, the subordinate components perform their proper functions (of facilitating a person's embodied life) under the rule of reason (see PLATO §14).

Plato's moral psychology had a decisive influence on all the subsequent philosophical tradition. Later philosophers, however, paid closer attention to the biological functions of *psychē*. For Epicureans and Stoics, the *psychē* is a physical part of the living being, centred in the chest and distributed from there to the organs of the body (see EPICUREANISM §§12–13;

STOICISM §3). For ARISTOTLE (§§17–19), it is not a physical part but the 'form' or 'active functioning' of the body's organs, except in the case of intellect (see NOUS) which has no bodily organ. Plato had located the rational component of *psychē* in the head, but most philosophers, mistaking the functions of the cardiovascular system, favoured the chest or heart as its location. These errors continued even after the nervous system was identified in the third century BC. The first theorist to relate psychology to the most up-to-date physiology was GALEN (§2), writing in the second century AD.

In spite of these errors post-Platonic philosophers did work of lasting value in theorizing about *psychē*. Taking the human *psychē* to be an assemblage of vital functions, Aristotle analysed these, starting with the 'nutritive' (common to all living beings including plants) and ending with the 'intellectual' (peculiar to human beings). He is at his most effective, perhaps, in identifying the causal components of action: desire is stimulated by sense perception or 'imagination' (*phantasia*), and then intellect (in its practical function) works out the means to achieve the desired end (see ARISTOTLE §§20, 23–4).

Epicurus' theory of *psychē* is grounded in his physics. Being an aggregate of fine and highly mobile atoms, the *psychē* depends upon embodiment in order to exist, and cannot survive the body's dissolution. Although the motions of atoms underlie all mental phenomena, Epicurus saw no difficulty in ascribing causal agency to thought and desire. According to LUCRETIUS, Epicureans held that the random swerve of a mind's atoms frees it from mechanistic determinism.

The Stoic doctrine of *psychē* is also anchored to basic physical postulates. The 'active principle' of the Stoic universe is 'breath' (see PNEUMA) permeating everything, and the 'breath' permeating animals and human beings is their *psychē*. Unlike Aristotle, the Stoics did not attribute *psychē* to plants. In their philosophy *psychē* is the life principle of animals (creatures capable of perception and purposive motion) and more particularly of human beings, who have the additional faculties of reason and 'assent' (saying yes or no to their occurrent thoughts and impressions). In contrast with other philosophers, the Stoics ascribed rationality to the human *psychē* in its entirety. But a rational *psychē* can act irrationally through error, and it can experience conflict of desires by oscillating between one judgment and another (see STOICISM §19).

In the Neoplatonism of PLOTINUS (§4), *psychē* is a principle that mediates between the higher reality of 'intelligible being' and the physical world ('nature'). This doctrine applies both to the *psychē* of individual beings and to that of the world. The world-soul generates the physical world by its apprehension of intelligible reality. The souls of human individuals, even when embodied, do not 'descend' completely to the physical world. They live at two levels, one contemplative and immortal, the other mortal and engaged with embodied life. Apart from these ideas Plotinus treated numerous mental phenomena with great subtlety in his long treatise, *Problems of the Soul (Enneads)* IV.

Although discussions of *psychē* centre primarily on the vital powers of human beings, Plato and the Stoics as well as Plotinus attributed *psychē* to the world at large. Aristotle did not adopt this view in *On the Soul*, but he agreed with them in making the heavenly bodies ensouled. Only Epicurus restricted the scope of *psychē* to terrestrial creatures.

See also: ALEXANDER OF APHRODISIAS §2; ALCMAEON; ANAXIMENES §2; DEMOCRITUS §3; IAMBLICHUS; NEOPLATONISM §3; NEO-PYTHAGOREANISM; ORPHISM; PLATONISM, EARLY AND MIDDLE §5; PLUTARCH OF CHAERONEA §4; POSIDONIUS §5; PROCLUS §5; SOUL, NATURE AND IMMORTALITY OF THE; STRATO §5; THALES §2

References and further reading

* Aristotle (*c.* mid 4th century BC) *On the Soul*, trans. H. Lawson-Tancred, Harmondsworth: Penguin, 1986. (Book I discusses and criticizes Aristotle's predecessors; Books II–III present his own doctrines.)

Claus, D.B. (1981) *Toward the Soul*, New Haven, CN: Yale University Press. (Careful study of the meaning of *psychē* before Plato.)

Long, A.A. (1973) 'Psychological Ideas in Antiquity', in P.P. Wiener (ed.) *Dictionary of the History of Ideas*, New York: Scribner's, vol. IV, 1–9. (Encyclopaedic survey.)

Long, A.A. and Sedley, D.N. (1987) *The Hellenistic Philosophers*, Cambridge: Cambridge University Press. (Translation with commentary of Epicurean and Stoic texts in volume 1, 65–77, 313–22, 410–22.)

* Plato (*c.*386–380 BC) *Phaedo*, trans. D. Gallop, Oxford: Clarendon Press, 1975. (Includes notes; Plato's classic dialogue on the soul's immortality.)

* —— (*c.*380–367 BC) *Republic*, trans. R. Waterfield, Oxford: Oxford University Press, 1993. (On the soul; see Books IV and VIII–X.)

—— (*c.*366–360 BC) *Phaedrus*, trans. R. Hackforth, Cambridge: Cambridge University Press, 1952. (Includes commentary; the soul's nature and destiny are mythologically described at 245–56.)

—— (*c.*366–360 BC) *Timaeus*, trans. H.D.P. Lee,

Harmondsworth: Penguin, 1965. (Explains the tripartition of the soul from a largely physical viewpoint.)

* Plotinus (*c.*250–66) *Problems of the Soul (Enneads)* IV; trans. A.H. Armstrong, *Plotinus*, vol. 4, Loeb Classical Library, Cambridge, MA: Harvard University Press and London: Heinemann, 1984. (The entire book is an exploration of problems concerning *psychē*; Greek text with facing translation.)

A.A. LONG

PSYCHOANALYSIS AND FEMINISM *see* FEMINISM AND PSYCHOANALYSIS

PSYCHOANALYSIS, METHODOLOGICAL ISSUES IN

Philosophers have subjected psychoanalysis to an unusual degree of methodological scrutiny for several interconnected reasons. Even a cursory look at the Freudian corpus reveals a slender base of evidence: eleven 'case histories', including those published jointly with Breuer. On the other hand, the theoretical claims have broad scope: all psychopathology can be traced to repressed sexuality. Further, Freud and his followers have disdained the most widely accepted means of establishing theories – experimental confirmation – while allowing themselves to appeal to such apparently dubious sources of support as dream interpretation, literature and everyday life. Together, these factors conjure a picture of a 'science' with a large gap between theory and evidence that has not and cannot be filled by solid data.

The central methodological question about psychoanalysis is whether there is now or ever has been any evidence supporting its truth. Popper rejected psychoanalysis as a science on the grounds that there could be no possible evidence against it which could test its truth. More recently, Grünbaum has objected that there are serious logical difficulties with appealing to cures as evidence of truth. Grünbaum and others have attacked both the theory of dreams and the use of dream interpretation as evidence. Sulloway and Kitcher have argued that several tenets of psychoanalysis were supported by their nineteenth-century scientific context, particularly certain aspects of Darwinian biology, but that those crucial supports have been eroded by later scientific developments. Eysenck and Wilson have examined experimental results that have been offered in support of various claims of psychoanalysis and rejected them as inadequate to establish any specifically psychoanalytic claims. By contrast, Glymour (and others) have explained how even single case histories could provide evidence in favour of psychoanalysis. Other philosophers have argued that psychoanalysis is continuous with 'common-sense' psychology and is supported by the continual reaffirmation of the essential correctness of common-sense psychological prediction and explanation.

1   **Popper and Grünbaum**
2   **Statistical and experimental evidence**
3   **Dream and symptom interpretation**
4   **The foundation in nineteenth-century science**
5   **Single case histories as evidence**
6   **Scientifically informed common sense**

1   Popper and Grünbaum

Two influential critics of psychoanalytic methodology have been Sir Karl Popper and Adolf Grünbaum. Although POPPER did not publish his objections to psychoanalysis until 1962 (see Popper 1963), they were well-known in philosophical and psychoanalytic circles for many years before that. Dissatisfied with attempts to distinguish sciences as 'speculative' versus 'observational', he proposed a different approach to the question of demarcating the 'scientific' from other types of theories. In his view, what distinguished theoretical systems, dividing them into the 'scientific' and the 'pseudoscientific', was their 'refutability' or 'falsifiability'. For any scientific theory, there must be some possible, but not actual, observation that would be inconsistent with the claims of that theory; if a 'theory' is compatible with any possible observation whatsoever, then that theory is mere 'pseudoscience'.

Along with Marxism, psychoanalysis was Popper's prime example of a theory that is immune to refutation by any possible observation. Despite the seeming inaccessibility of unconscious motivations, however, in succeeding years philosophers and psychologists pointed out that psychoanalysis is vulnerable to refutation and that Freud took account of this vulnerability. So Fancher (1973), among others, has noted that Freud modified his theories in light of disconfirming evidence, and Grünbaum has observed that many of Freud's claims about the involvement of repressed homosexuality in paranoia are eminently capable of refutation.

Grünbaum (1984) defended psychoanalysis against Popper only to offer his own alternative critique.

From Freud onwards Grünbaum believes that the most important evidence in favour of the claims of psychoanalysis has come from alleged cures. For example, in 1930 the Berlin Psychoanalytic Institute issued a report on 721 analyses, 363 of which had been concluded by the time of the report. Of these, 111 patients were classified as cured, 89 as much improved, 116 as improved, and 47 as uncured (cited in Bergin and Lambert 1978). In Grünbaum's view, psychoanalysis presents a causal account of psychopathology: various symptoms are caused by repressed memories or desires; psychoanalytic treatment lifts these repressions, which removes the symptoms; hence, when patients are cured or improved, that testifies to the correctness of the causal hypotheses offered by the analyst.

The problems with treating therapeutic success as evidence for the truth of psychoanalytic claims are threefold. First, until recently, there have been no attempts to measure success rates objectively, by using observers who are unaware of the history of treatment. Second, any successes achieved must be compared with spontaneous 'cure' rates, to show that treatment makes a difference. Finally, many different conditions obtain in therapy sessions, including support from the therapist, personal factors in treatment and, most problematically, suggestions about the causes of the patient's illness. Grünbaum argues that, since any one of these factors might be responsible for patient improvement, the inference from partial cure to the correctness of any psychoanalytic hypothesis is invalid. Of particular concern is the therapist's suggestion that the cause of the illness has now been found and hence improvement is to be expected. Grünbaum argues that the therapist's words can act as a placebo and lead to substantial improvement, simply because patients believe that they will improve.

2   Statistical and experimental evidence

In recent years, a growing number of 'outcome' studies have compared psychoanalysis with other forms of treatment, with no treatment, and with placebo conditions. Although the results are sometimes inconsistent, a review by Bergin and Lambert (1978) concludes that psychoanalysis and a number of other therapies appear to have better results than no treatment, placebos and pseudotherapies. The problem is that it is not clear what such studies prove. They appear to support the claims of psychoanalysis to therapeutic success. As Grünbaum notes, however, they simultaneously raise serious questions about the *causal claims* of psychoanalysis. For, if the basic outlines of psychoanalysis are correct, and psychopathology is a result of repressed (sexual) memories and desires, then how is it possible to account for the successes of non-analytic therapies (especially behavioural therapies), which also exceed spontaneous 'cure' rates? Since the patients have not had their repressions lifted, there should be no improvement. Other therapies might ameliorate psychological conditions without truly curing them, so the argument is not conclusive. Still, as Hume noted long ago, if apparently different causes have a common effect, it is reasonable to look for unnoticed common factors (see CAUSATION). And Bergin and Lambert suggest that what accounts for improvement is not so much the truth of the theories underlying the different therapies, but the common placebo factors they share, such as the understanding and support of the therapist.

Comparing treatment outcomes with different therapies is an attempt to apply J.S. Mill's methods to causal hypotheses in psychotherapy. According to Mill, the way to establish that *A* (a particular treatment) is the cause of *B* (a cure) is to show that *A* reliably produces *B* in a variety of circumstances that differ in other respects and that *B* will not occur in the absence of *A* despite the presence of other circumstances (see SCIENTIFIC METHOD). Although recent studies are more sophisticated, the work just canvassed suggests what Mill fully anticipated: in complex cases, it may not be possible to disentangle all the possible causal factors and so apply his methods. Freud's defenders often object that methodological critiques of psychoanalysis suffer from exactly this flaw. Critics complain that psychoanalysis is unable to meet particular tests of scientific proof, when the real problem may be that the types of proof available are inadequate to handle the complexities encountered in psychopathology.

Similar problems have hindered attempts to find experimental evidence for or against central theories of psychoanalysis about, for example, the three phases of sexuality, the origin of the super-ego in the resolution of the Oedipal complex, or the sexual basis for the repression of unconscious ideas. Psychoanalytic claims about the causation of symptoms are complex, but only relatively simple factors can be observed or manipulated in experiments. The gap between 'experimental confirmation' and the theory to be confirmed is evident in Eysenck and Wilson's review of this literature (1973). One study was designed to test Freud's hypothesis of oral sexuality. Although the results confirmed thumb-sucking as a substitute form of oral activity, that claim is a rather bland surrogate for Freud's rich views about the oral phase of sexuality. Another study attempted to confirm Freud's claims about the Oedipal complex by looking at the proportion of male and female

strangers in dreams. Again, the results were positive. More strangers in dreams were males than females and this was true to a higher degree in the dreams of males. As Eysenck and Wilson note, however, these results are compatible with many hypotheses besides Freud's very specific claim about fear of the father in response to incestuous wishes about the mother. To take an obvious example, men may dream more about men, because they are more often in the company of men; all subjects may dream more about men, because men are more salient in our society. More recent attempts to provide experimental support for psychoanalysis by using subliminal or supraliminal stimuli may well be subject to the same criticism. Establishing that there is unconscious, but active ideation in human brains is a pale substitute for Freud's rich claims about the sexual aetiology of repression (see UNCONSCIOUS MENTAL STATES).

3 Dream and symptom interpretation

The study just mentioned appeals only to the 'manifest' or actual, reported content of dreams. One recurring methodological debate in psychoanalysis concerns the use of interpretations of dreams and symptoms in explaining psychopathology. Probably more than any other single issue, the question of dream and symptom interpretation reveals a huge gulf between the supporters and detractors of psychoanalysis. Dream and symptom interpretation are critical to psychoanalysis, because, along with 'free association', these are the primary methods by which diagnosis and remedy are possible. According to standard psychoanalytic theory, the true causes of psychopathology are hidden. They are repressed memories or desires. Hence, the analyst must find some indirect means of uncovering those causes, and dream and symptom interpretation, interpretations of particular actions or remarks, and free association are the distinctively psychoanalytic tools for accomplishing this task.

Critics have raised a host of objections. Grünbaum and others have argued that the theory that dreams are wish-fulfilments is false. Indeed, as Grünbaum observes, some of Freud's own reports of his patients' dreams cast serious doubts on this hypothesis. For example, a young woman dreamed that she was going on a summer holiday with her mother-in-law, something that she did not wish to do. Freud's explanation, that she had this dream to fulfil her wish to disprove his theory of dreams as wish-fulfilments, seems to be blatantly *ad hoc*. The more standard objection to dream and symptom interpretation is that this is either an enterprise with no rules at all or with one question-begging rule: find some interpretation that relates the symptom or manifest content to a hidden sexual wish. Echoing Popper, critics object that since, given sufficient imagination, some connection to sexual wishes is always possible, the ability of therapists to make these connections has no probative value.

More recently, Fancher, Sulloway (1991) and Kitcher (1992) have argued that the theory of dreams is not an autonomous part of psychoanalysis, but follows from some of Freud's early, but persisting views about the organization of the nervous system. If this view is correct, then it fundamentally alters the evidentiary status of the theory of dreams. Contrary to Freud's own position and that of many of his followers, the theory would be capable of confirmation outside the clinical setting. Although it provides the theory of dreams with an alternative source of evidence, this new understanding of the place of the dream theory in psychoanalysis leads quickly to disaster. For, if the real source of support for the dream theory is Freudian neurology, then that theory should be rejected along with its outmoded neurophysiological basis.

4 The foundation in nineteenth-century science

As QUINE has argued, theories can be supported both 'from below' (by experimental results) and 'from above' (by more general theoretical considerations). In considering experimental testing and therapeutic success rates – the experimental and therapeutic 'predictions' of psychoanalysis – we have considered only how the theory might be confirmed from below. Analysts have not tried to provide support from above for the obvious reason. Even if Freud's views were well supported by nineteenth-century science, so much has changed that that support has long ago eroded. In fact, some analysts have taken the opposite tack and attempted to detach a 'clinical' part of psychoanalysis from its 'metapsychological' foundations, especially Freud's claims about the flows of energy through the 'mental apparatus' (Klein 1976). One problem with this approach is that it makes the enterprise of psychoanalysis entirely dependent on 'confirmation from the couch', which is highly problematic (see §§2, 5). It also leaves psychoanalysis vulnerable to the charge that not only is it not well supported now, it never was a plausible scientific theory, but only some type of pseudoscience.

Frank Sulloway (1979) has argued that many of the basic tenets of Freud's theory derived from important work in nineteenth-century biology. So, for example, the prominence of sexual factors in psychopathology and mental life generally would be a plausible hypothesis, given Darwin's claims for the importance of sex in evolution. The view that psychopathology was a result of excess neural energy, or excitation, or libido – energy that was released in dreams, symptoms, jokes and slips – seems more plausible if the nervous system is understood as a reflex mechanism that seeks to rid itself of energy that has intruded into the system. Sulloway also provides great detail about the work in 'sexology' that preceded Freud, which was incorporated into some of the best-known claims of psychoanalysis about infantile sexuality and psychosexual development. Although Sulloway's research deflates some claims for the originality of psychoanalysis, it provides a powerful reply to critics who dismiss the theory as wild speculation made up on the basis of a handful of not very successful case histories.

Looking back to nineteenth-century work in linguistics, anthropology and psychology also provides some grounding for methodological strategies of psychoanalysis that have been subject to withering criticisms. Several of Freud's least popular interpretive principles were suggested by then contemporary work in linguistics. For example, the claim that the manifest verbal content of dreams often represented the exact opposite latent content (for example, 'strength' represented 'weakness'), was consonant with Abel's hypothesis that early concepts were formed by comparison and so indicated both sides of the comparison, 'strength' and 'weakness'. The equation of the infantile with the primitive was firmly supported by anthropology and by some biologists, who maintained a 'biogenetic law' (ontogeny is the rapid recapitulation of phylogeny). Most importantly, perhaps, the method of free association itself reflects the widespread psychological assumption that different thoughts or ideas are held together by bonds of association and that it is possible to uncover these associations by asking subjects to provide lists of associates. Although much has changed in biology and the social sciences, in so far as psychology still accepts associationism, and evolutionary theory still speaks to the importance of sexual factors in human life, some parts of psychoanalysis can still receive some mild support from above (see EVOLUTIONARY THEORY AND SOCIAL SCIENCE; LEARNING).

5 Single case histories as evidence

Although Freud offered many theoretical discussions of psychoanalysis, he often presented his ideas through the medium of the case history. Are these cases simply meant to illustrate the principles of psychoanalysis or can they be regarded as evidence in favour of one or another of its doctrines? Seemingly, case histories can provide evidence for psychoanalysis in one of two ways: a psychoanalytic claim would be confirmed either if the diagnosis produced a cure or if patients acknowledged that they did harbour the unconscious memory or desire inferred by the analyst. The problems with arguments from cures have already been noted. Patient confirmations of analysts' hypotheses are subject to some of the same difficulties, and more besides. Even more than in the case of cures, it seems that analysts' suggestions that patients have certain unconscious desires might lead patients to assume that they do have these desires, either because they wish to please the analyst or because they assume that analysts are knowledgeable in these matters. Further, a patient's confirmation of a particular unconscious desire is evidence of the analyst's correctness only if there is good reason to believe that patients, or the population as a whole, are generally reliable about the psychological states that cause their beliefs and actions. Recent work in psychology suggests that this crucial assumption may be false (see Nisbett and Wilson 1977; INTROSPECTION, PSYCHOLOGY OF).

Despite the serious difficulties with using single case histories as evidence for psychoanalysis, both Erwin (1988) and Glymour (1982) have argued that this is possible at least in theory. Erwin notes that a single case or intrasubject design can provide evidence, if the change in the patient is sufficiently dramatic. If a patient suddenly recovers from a physical illness after unsuccessful treatment by other medications, that is strong evidence of the efficacy of the new medicine. In the same way, if a patient who has been in different psychotherapies for some time with no improvement were suddenly to improve upon being offered a psychoanalytic hypothesis about the cause of the illness, that would suggest some causal connection. Although spontaneous remission cannot be ruled out, such a case would still have probative value.

Glymour has developed a very different approach to establishing the possible use of case histories as evidence. He notes that it is possible to test hypotheses in other non-experimental sciences, such as astronomy, by making inferences from observations via particular claims of the theory to further possible observations. The observations might provide evidence only when supported by other theoretical claims, but so long as these are independent of the claims to be tested, testing is still possible. This type of 'pincers' movement can be illustrated by the well-known Rat Man case. From the Rat Man's symptoms and various principles of psychoanalysis, Freud inferred that he had an unconscious wish for his father's death. But such a wish is unobservable. Given other claims of psychoanalysis, however, he inferred that this unconscious wish must have arisen from an early conflict over sexual matters. Hence he expected to find that the Rat Man had been punished for early sexual behaviour. Had this 'observation' been made, it would have offered some confirmation that the Rat Man wished for his father's death, because the evidence and assumptions supporting the inference to this wish would be independent of the evidence and assumptions that originally led Freud to infer such an unconscious wish. In opposition to Popper (see §1), Glymour notes that when Freud concluded that no episode of sexual misconduct occurred, he also recognized that his original theory was false. Although Popper might disapprove of how Freud then modified his theory, by allowing sexual fantasies as well as actual sexual encounters to be causes of psychoneuroses, from a logical point of view, the case is an example of negative evidence leading to the rejection of an early psychoanalytic hypothesis (see SCIENTIFIC METHOD).

The use of the Rat Man, the Wolf Man, and other well-known cases in presenting psychoanalysis has led Sulloway and others to investigate their accuracy. In a recent study, Sulloway argues that Freud's case histories were not particularly accurate representations of his case notes, and that in the case of the Rat Man and, especially, the Wolf Man, they exaggerated the degree to which a cure had been achieved.

6 Scientifically informed common sense

Richard Wollheim (1971), Donald Davidson (1982), Adam Morton (1982) and others suggest a different way of regarding Freud's theories, which provides a different source of possible evidence. On their view, psychoanalytic hypotheses about the causation of behaviour are of a piece with ordinary, common-sense explanations of behaviour (see FOLK PSYCHOLOGY). The standard view of 'common-sense' psychology, which dates back at least to Hume, is that actions are caused by the agent's beliefs and desires. Although this has sometimes been debated, the general view today is that, in discovering the beliefs and desires that led to a particular action, we are discovering both the cause of the action and the reasons for which it was done (see REASONS AND CAUSES). It is the latter feature that is distinctive of psychological explanation, for it permits actions to be understood in terms of their rational justification (see EXPLANATION).

According to these philosophers, the best way to understand psychoanalysis is by seeing it as extending common-sense psychological explanation to the realm of psychopathology or the irrational. At first, this seems paradoxical, because it suggests that Freud and his followers are trying to provide rational explanations of the apparently irrational. Although this is true, it becomes more plausible if we consider exactly why certain actions are regarded by psychoanalysis as pathological. According to psychoanalysis, pathology results when the cause or causes of actions or dreams are unconscious wishes or desires. If a wish is unconscious, then it is beyond the realm of rational control. Since the unconscious tolerates contradictions, no presumptively relevant evidence about the inappropriateness of a wish can be brought to bear on it (see UNCONSCIOUS MENTAL STATES). So, if a young man's belief that his father despises him is unconscious, then it cannot be undermined by words or gestures indicating quite a different attitude on the part of the father. Even though the belief is irrational in this sense, however, it can still rationalize the man's behaviour by explaining why he takes certain defensive measures to ward off possible aggression from his father. Hence, although unconscious wishes and desires are irrational in the sense that they cannot be touched by reasons, they are rational in that they can provide reasons for action. If this is the correct understanding of psychoanalytic explanation, as an extension of common-sense psychological explanation, then it can be argued that the basic approach of psychoanalysis is supported by the continuing successes of common-sense psychology. Common-sense psychology can provide no support for any particular psychoanalytic claims, such as the homosexual aetiology of paranoia, but it can lend credence to the general enterprise of looking for conscious or unconscious beliefs and desires that will make the agent's actions comprehensible in terms of reasons. Conversely, psychoanalysis can make common sense more scientific, by delineating the true scope of rational explanation.

Supporting psychoanalysis by appeal to common-sense psychology is highly controversial, for several reasons. At one extreme, some philosophers will deny that common-sense psychology can provide useful support, because it is itself an unscientific attempt to understand human behaviour. In particular, critics note that it is far from clear exactly what counts as an adequate rational justification of an action (see RATIONALITY, PRACTICAL). Even those willing to allow the acceptability of common-sense psychological explanations in straightforward cases would object that complex cases, especially those involving pathology, are too tangled to permit any degree of confidence in a particular belief–desire explanation. Finally, assimilating psychoanalytic hypotheses to common-sense psychological explanations is possible only if the latent content of dreams, slips, actions and so forth can be fathomed by the interpretive methods of psychoanalysis and, as we have seen, many critics find these methods objectionable.

See also: FREUD, S.; PSYCHOANALYSIS, POST-FREUDIAN; UNCONSCIOUS MENTAL STATES

References and further reading

* Bergin, A.E. and Lambert, M.J. (1978) 'The Evaluation of Therapeutic Outcomes', in S.L. Garfield and A.E. Bergin (eds) *Handbook of Psychotherapy and Behavior Change*, New York: Wiley & Sons, 2nd edn. (An important review of 'cure' rates.)
* Davidson, D. (1982) 'Paradoxes of Irrationality', in R. Wollheim and J. Hopkins (eds) *Philosophical Essays on Freud*, Cambridge: Cambridge University Press. (Discussion of an important problem by a well-known philosopher.)
* Erwin, E. (1988) 'Psychoanalysis: Clinical versus Experimental Evidence', in P. Clark and C. Wright (eds) *Mind, Psychoanalysis and Science*, Oxford: Blackwell. (A useful collection of essays by leading Freud scholars.)
* Eysenck, H.J. and Wilson, G.D. (1973) *The Experimental Study of Freudian Theories*, London: Methuen. (Still the best review of attempts to verify psychoanalysis experimentally.)
* Fancher, R.E. (1973) *Psychoanalytic Psychology*, New York: Norton. (A clear survey of Freud's views.)
* Glymour, C. (1982) 'Freud, Kepler, and the Clinical Evidence', in R. Wollheim and J. Hopkins (eds) *Philosophical Essays on Freud*, Cambridge: Cambridge University Press. (A classic, if somewhat difficult, essay on the methodology of testing.)
* Grünbaum, A. (1984) *The Foundations of Psychoanalysis*, Los Angeles, CA: University of California Press. (One of the most important studies of Freud's methodology.)
—— (1993) *Validation in the Clinical Theory of Psychoanalysis*, Madison, CT: International Universities Press. (A collection of essays that extends many of the arguments of Grünbaum (1984).)
* Kitcher, P. (1992) *Freud's Dream: A Complete Interdisciplinary Theory of Mind*, Cambridge, MA: MIT Press. (Analysis of the foundations of Freud's theories in a variety of nineteenth-century sciences.)
* Klein, G. (1976) 'Freud's Two Theories of Sexuality', in M. Gill and P. Holzman (eds) *Psychological Issues*, vol. 9, no. 4, *Psychology and Metapsychology*, New York: International Universities Press. (A classic discussion of Freud's metapsychology.)
* Morton, A. (1982) 'Freudian Commonsense', in R. Wollheim and J. Hopkins (eds) *Philosophical Essays on Freud*, Cambridge: Cambridge University Press. (A clear essay that argues for continuity

between Freud's ways of explaining behaviour and our everyday explanations.)

* Nisbett, R. and Wilson, T. (1977) 'Telling More Than We Can Know: Verbal Reports on Mental Processes', *Psychological Review* 84 (3): 231–59. (An important discussion of the illusion that we know what is going on in our minds.)
* Popper, K.R. (1963) *Conjectures and Refutations*, New York: Basic Books. (A classic book by one of the best-known philosophers of the twentieth century.)
* Sulloway, F. (1979) *Freud: Biologist of the Mind*, New York: Basic Books. (A brilliant and detailed account of the biological foundations of psychoanalysis.)
* —— (1991) 'Reassessing Freud's Case Histories', *Isis* 82: 245–75. (A critical and well-documented look at Freud's clinical 'successes'.)
* Wollheim, R. (1971) *Freud*, London: Fontana. (A clear introduction to the development of Freud's views.)

PATRICIA KITCHER

PSYCHOANALYSIS, POST-FREUDIAN

The basic concepts of psychoanalysis are due to Sigmund Freud. After establishing psychoanalysis Freud worked in Vienna until he and other analysts fled the Nazi occupation. Post-Freudian psychoanalysis has evolved in distinct ways in different countries, often in response to influential analysts who settled there.

Freud's patients were mainly adults who suffered from neurotic rather than psychotic disturbances. He found their psychological difficulties to be rooted in conflict between love and hate, caused by very disparate, often fantastic, images deriving from the same parental figure. These images provided the basic representations of the self and others, formed by processes of projection (representing the other via images from the self) and introjection (representing the self via images from the other). The internalized image of a parent could be used to represent the self as related to some version of the other, as in the formation of the punitive super-ego, or as like the other, as in the identification with the parent of the same sex through which the Oedipus complex was dissolved.

Later analysts, including Anna Freud and Melanie Klein, observed that the uninhibited play of children could be seen to express fantasies involving such images, often with striking clarity. This made it possible to analyse children, and to see that their representations of

the self were regularly coordinated with fantastic representations of others, with both organized into systematically interacting systems of good and bad. Emotional disturbance was marked by a fantasy world in which the self and idealized good figures engaged in conflict with hateful bad objects, unmitigated by any sense that all derived from the same self and parental figures.

Such observations made it possible to confirm, revise and extend Freud's theories. Klein saw that symptoms, character and personality could be understood in terms of relations to internalized fantasy-figures, laid down in early childhood; and this extended to psychotic disturbances, such as schizophrenia and manic-depressive illness, which turned on the particular nature of the figures involved. This gave rise to the British object-relations approach to psychoanalysis. It also influenced the development of ego-psychology and self-psychology by Hartmann, Kohut and others in the United States, and Lacan's attempt to relate psychoanalysis to language, in France.

1 **Melanie Klein, object-relations and the British school**
2 **Ego- and self-psychology in the United States**
3 **Psychoanalysis and language in France**
4 **Comparisons**

1 Melanie Klein, object-relations and the British school

The first, major post-Freudian innovations, and the most controversial, stemmed from the work of Melanie Klein. Klein realized that psychic structure and function could be understood in terms of relations to fantastic unconscious figures, which she called 'internal objects', and focused psychoanalytic investigation on them. For example, a little girl who suffered obsessional symptoms as well as depression played at being a queen who was getting married. When she

> had celebrated her marriage to the king, she lay down on the sofa and wanted me, as the king, to lie down beside her. As I refused to do this, I had to sit on a little chair by her side, and knock at the sofa with my fist. This she called 'churning' . . . immediately after this she announced that a child was creeping out of her, and she represented the scene in a quite realistic way, writhing about and groaning. Her imaginary child then had to share its parents' bedroom and had to be a spectator of sexual intercourse between them. If it interrupted, it was beaten. . . . If she, as the mother, put the child to bed, it was only in order to get rid of it

and to be able to be united with the father all the sooner.

(1975, vol. 2: 40)

FREUD had noted that the parents are frequently symbolized in adult dreams by the figures of king and queen. The play described above could be seen to use the same symbolism, and so to represent the child's unconscious fantasies about her parents (whom in real life she treated with excessive but demanding fondness). Here the child's representation of adult sexuality is partly symbolic (for example, in terms of 'churning' or something knocking something); but the referent of the symbolism can none the less be inferred from the context (the activity takes place after the wedding, with the parents lying together in bed, and is followed by the birth of a child).

The fantasies expressed in this game were repeated in many others, and in many related psychological constellations. Hence it was possible to understand the little girl's obsessions and depression by reference to what she felt to be happening between herself and the fantastic unconscious versions of her parents represented in her play (see UNCONSCIOUS MENTAL STATES).

How was it possible to understand the establishment of the fantastic *bad* internal objects central to conflict and psychopathology? Klein found *envy* to be particularly important in this process. This can be acute in children and infants, since they are particularly small, helpless and dependent. According to Klein, little children therefore seek relief from envy, as well as other emotions felt as bad, by both projection and introjection. In the former they try to locate in others whatever is felt as bad in the self, including envy and other forms of aggression; and in the latter to locate in themselves whatever is felt as good in others. This produces both *splitting of the self* and *splitting of the object*, in which the former is represented as good but lacking aggression, and the latter as bad and lacking goodness, both unrealistically.

These processes explained the structural features of children's fantasies, in which 'good' figures, identified with the self and sharing its goals, are systematically menaced by 'bad' figures which oppose them. Despite being kept out of consciousness, or represented as distant or alien, the 'bad' figures threaten to confront the self, or impinge upon or invade it, with mirroring directness. This is because such figures contain split-off aspects of the self, and so relate to those from which they are split with uncanny precision. Thus the little girl above dealt with aggressive envy of her parents' sexuality by such projection, and so unconsciously represented them as having sexual relations to make her envious. Hence she felt herself powerless

and surrounded by bad figures, and so sought to imagine herself in an idealized way, as a rich, powerful and enviable queen.

Since such projection creates images of the other unconsciously identified with disowned aspects of the self, Klein called it 'projective identification'. (Anna Freud described a comparable mechanism as 'identification with the aggressor'; Klein's description applies where the image of the aggressor is itself formed by projection.) This mechanism could be seen as basic to both individual and social thinking, ordering human relations on primitive patterns of idealized 'us' versus bad 'them'.

Klein also proposed far-reaching hypotheses about infancy. She held that object-relations had an innate basis, and began almost from birth. Thus the infant related to the mother and to parts of her, especially her breast, before coming to understand her as a single enduring object. The disparate images of 'good' and 'bad' objects shown in analysis were laid down before the infant formed an integrated conception of the human body, or realized that the parental figures it felt as very bad or very good were in fact the same (see COGNITION, INFANT; COGNITIVE DEVELOPMENT; NATIVISM).

In the first three or four months of life, Klein hypothesized, the infant made sense of its experience by building up concepts of episodic objects, which were anatomically incomplete, modelled on various parts of the body, and liable to be extremely good or bad, depending on the nature of the experience in which they were involved. During the fourth month, however, the infant began to unify its conception of the mother, and so to regard her as a single person, who was anatomically whole, complete and enduring.

Recent experiments seem partly to illustrate these ideas. For example, Campos observed that a 4-month-old infant made angry by someone's taking something away will direct expressions of anger towards the depriving hand, whereas by 7 months the infant will direct anger at the offending agent's face (see Campos *et al.* 1983). Bower (1982) used mirrors to display to infants three simultaneous images of the mother. Infants of 3 or 4 months are undisturbed by the apparent presence of three 'mothers', and interact with them in turn, preferring each to (images of) women not their mothers. Past 5 months, however, the sight of three 'mothers' becomes intensely disturbing. It seems that the infant does not specifically prefer enduring singularity to episodic multiplicity until this time.

Klein thought that the formation of the image of the mother as psychologically and physically unified was of particular importance. She called the pre-objective phase of life the 'paranoid-schizoid position', the term 'paranoid' indicating the extremity of the baby's potential for anxiety, and 'schizoid' the fragmentary way it represents itself and its objects. In acknowledging the mother as a single enduring object, the infant must begin to endow her with complex and apparently contradictory characteristics shown over a variety of episodes. In particular, it must recognize that she is the frustrating object towards which it feels anger and hatred, as well as the gratifying object towards which it feels love. This more complex object must now also be seen as distinct from the self, capable of absence, unique and irreplaceable. (This may explain why infants who have not before protested at their mother's leaving may at 6 or 7 months develop intense anxiety at separation; according to Klein, the infant is then consolidating the realization that the mother leaving is the only mother it has.)

In response to these changes the infant begins to dread the loss of the object, and becomes concerned to care for it, protect it and repair the harm inflicted on it in fantasy. This Klein called the 'depressive position', so named because unification entails liability to depression about damaging the object (principally the feeding, caring mother). The dialectic of projection and introjection correlates these more realistic and complex attitudes to the object with complementary changes in the self. This unification constitutes the emotional aspect of the establishing of the reality principle (see FREUD, S. §7), and so coincides with a diminution in the role of wish-fulfilling fantasy, splitting and projection.

According to Klein a range of psychic disturbances can be understood in terms of failure to achieve this Kantian synthesis. The worst case is schizophrenic illness, in which the infant is liable to particularly violent splitting and projection, and so cannot, in Hume's phrase, 'unite the broken appearances' of self and other (see HUME, D; MIND, BUNDLE THEORY OF). At deep levels the object remains represented as a multiplicity of episodic presences housing projected aspects of the self, which is therefore radically fragmented, depleted and threatened by persecution. In the less severe cases of manic and depressive illness, the object consists of partly integrated bad (hated) and good (idealized) parts. In mania the subject fantasizes triumphing over the bad and possessing the good of such an object, and in depression destroying the good together with the bad.

Klein's ideas were extended by Bion (1961) to groups and by Segal (1990) and Bion (1989) to the infantile origins of symbolism and thought. Many analysts, however, have tended to accept and extend Klein's descriptions of relations to real and fantasized objects, while disagreeing with her hypotheses about

infancy. Winnicott (1958) formulated further striking conceptions, such as the 'transitional object' and the 'true' and 'false' self, and Fairbairn (1954) attempted a full-scale restatement of psychoanalysis in terms of object-relations. Such accounts have now been elaborated by all schools, including that of ego-psychology (see Kernberg 1995). An ethological account of early object-relations by Bowlby (1969, 1973) fostered extensive empirical study of attachment (Ainsworth 1985).

2 Ego- and self-psychology in the United States

Freud introduced the ego and the super-ego as functional systems mediating between the individual's innate instinctual drives and the external world. This theory was elaborated by Anna Freud (1936) and developed more systematically by Heinz Hartmann and his colleagues in the United States.

Hartmann (1939) distinguished clearly between a person's conscious and unconscious representations of the self, and the ego as a system whose working could be described in impersonal terms. This system developed out of an 'undifferentiated matrix' present at birth and prior to both ego and id, and could be seen as having the general function of *adaptation*, that is, of relating the organism to the physical and social environment. Hence study of the ego could form a bridge between biology and the social sciences, rendering psychoanalysis a more general psychology.

Hartmann held that a main achievement of the ego was the attainment of *autonomy*, that is, the capacity to function with a degree of independence and self-sufficiency; and he linked this with normally conflict-free functions such as locomotion, which had received little attention in psychoanalytic theory. He related autonomy in object-relations to 'object constancy', the ability to represent self and other consistently, despite absence and changes in emotion (see COGNITION, INFANT).

This notion was carried into empirical research by Renée Spitz (1965), who made a number of pioneering efforts to study ego-development in infancy, including film studies of infants and mothers, focusing on smiling, anxiety at separation or encountering strangers, grief at loss of contact, and the like. Spitz thought that the development of object-relations could be detected in a number of features of overt infantile behaviour: the way the infant related the mother's breast and face, subsequently following her face with its eyes; the smiling response, followed by social smiling, which he took to indicate the inception of social relations; the onset of 6- to 8-month 'stranger anxiety', which indicated recognition of the mother as a specific individual; and the capacity to gesture (or verbalize) 'No!', which he took to show both identification with the mother as one who refuses, and a distinctive form of communication.

More detailed hypotheses about the development of the ego and object constancy were set out in work by Edith Jackobson (1964) and by Margaret Mahler (1968) and her associates. Mahler held with Spitz that in early life the mother serves as an 'external ego' for the infant; she argued that the infant first experiences the mother in a phase of *symbiosis*, during which it feels itself blissfully to merge with her, and imagines the two as a 'dual unity' with a common boundary, or what Jackobson called a 'self-object'. As the infant forms a more distinct image of the mother it develops a sense of basic trust, conveyed in smiling and eye contact; then, beginning to distinguish more clearly between itself and the mother, it enters the phase of 'separation-individuation', not completed until the third year. In this phase the infant builds up representations of 'good' and 'bad' self and objects, and finally unifies these into more stable and realistic representations, in which the characteristics of the self are fully distinguished from those of its objects.

Mahler divided this process into three sub-phases, marked by discernible patterns of infantile behaviour. The first is that of *differentiation*, lasting (roughly) from 5 to 9 months, during which the infant 'hatches' from the dual unity and focuses perception and action on the world. This is followed by a period of *practising*, in which the infant increasingly turns away from the mother to explore the environment, first by crawling and then by walking. As the child's enjoyment of its own capacities conflicts with its increasingly realistic sense of dependence on the mother there follows a phase of *rapprochement*, during which the child seeks to reconcile desires to remain in union with the mother with desires to become a separate and autonomous individual.

This conflict can show in a number of ways: new anxieties about separation; alternating 'shadowing' the mother, allowing no separation, and darting away, requiring her to prevent it; ignoring the mother's presence or departure, to deny her importance; 'becoming' the mother in her absence, and so creating a pseudo-independent false self; attempting to control or coerce the mother, to deny her autonomy; and so forth. In the ensuing 'rapprochement crisis' the child feels both longing and anger towards the absent mother, but directs the longing to an idealized 'good mother', while projecting the image of the 'bad mother' onto some resented substitute. The resolution of this phase, similar in structure and outcome to Klein's depressive position, is marked by diminution in splitting of this kind, so that the child approaches object constancy (see COGNITIVE DEVELOPMENT).

Much of the clinical work of ego-psychologists was concerned with feelings about the self linked to failures in individuation and autonomy. This set the stage for Heinz Kohut (1977) to argue that the development of a new psychoanalytic theory, 'self-psychology', was required to explain the pathology of the 'fragmented' and 'depleted' self. In attempting to frame such a theory Kohut re-employed Jackobson's term 'self-object', to designate another who is *experienced* as performing a psychological function essential to the self, and so as part of the self. This restored the phenomenological aspect of Freud's notion of an ego partly constituted by relations to its objects, lost in Hartmann's disambiguation.

In early life the primary self-objects are the parents – for example, the mother in her role as 'eternal ego' to the infant – and later versions inherit their significance from these. The 'primary psychological configuration' for self-psychology is thus the experience of the relation between the self and the self-object, and in particular that of the 'empathy', or degree of attuned adequacy, with which the self-object responds to the needs of the self. When the self-object responds appropriately to expressions of need, the infant's anxiety is replaced by an experience of merging with a powerful and calming self-object, whose functions, given repeated experience, can ultimately be internalized.

Kohut argued that two basic self-object functions show themselves in particular forms of transference to the analyst. There is an 'idealizing transference', in which the analyst is represented as embodying the kind of perfection with which the patient wishes to merge; and a 'mirror transference' in which the analyst is represented as having the function of responding empathically to the patient's narcissistic and grandiose displays, so as to sustain the patient's self-assertion through approval, mirroring and echoing. These transferences are best explained on the hypothesis that it is especially important for the infant's primary self-objects to provide both empathic mirroring for the infant's self-assertive, exhibitionistic and grandiose self, and embodiments of idealizable functioning with whom the infant can feel it merges. If these requirements are met, then the infant's grandiose self-assertions can develop towards realistic ambitions and goals, and its notions of ideal perfection towards realistic ideals and values.

Since the cohesion of the self depends upon these functions, the child (or the analytic patient in whom such infantile needs are re-activated) responds to the parent's (or analyst's) failures in performing them with an overwhelming hatred and desire to hurt, which Kohut calls 'narcissistic rage'. The infant seeks total control over the self-object's responses, which it cannot achieve. If it remains without adequate empathic mirroring or opportunity for idealization and merging, it may become convinced that the environment is hostile, a situation Kohut compares to Klein's paranoid-schizoid position.

3 Psychoanalysis and language in France

A main tenet of all psychoanalytic approaches is that desires from infancy are constantly re-symbolized, so as to secure representational pacification throughout life. Analysis seeks to trace the constantly evolving modes of representation of the self and the objects of its desires; and this is done through language, a particular form of symbolic representation. In seminars from 1953 to the 1970s, Jacques LACAN attempted a re-presentation of Freudian theory centred on symbolism and the relation of psychoanalysis to language.

A main theme in Lacan's work, like that of Klein and Kohut, is a lack of unity in the self, which Lacan takes as an ineliminable consequence of the processes that provide representation for the self and the objects of desire (see ALTERITY AND IDENTITY, POSTMODERN THEORIES OF §2). As a first example, he considers the infant's recognition of its own image in a mirror. The infant joyfully assumes this external image, which represents it as possessing a wholeness, permanence and unity which it feels itself to lack, and which anticipates and facilitates its ability to move and relate to others. Paradoxically, however, this enabling identification is also an alienation; for the infant identifies itself with something it feels itself *not actually to be* and which it *may yet fail to become*. Identifications with others are alienating in the same way, so that the self is constituted by images that threaten to confront it as reminders of its own lack of being. The subject is thus formed in a potentially rivalrous and aggressive relation with its own self, and thence with others.

Lacan describes these alienating self-images, as well as others created in projection, introjection and fantasy generally, as constituting an order of representations which he terms 'the imaginary'. This he contrasts with the 'symbolic order', which encompasses the personal and social systems of signs whose elements are intrinsically constrained by rules of combination and substitution like those of natural language (see SYNTAX). Freud's discussions of dreams and symptoms, he argues, shows them to be constructed in accordance with such rules; so, the combinations and substitutions of (representations of) objects in dreams and symptoms, or again in the course of development, can be seen as instances of metaphor, metonymy and other linguistic forms. The

unconscious is thus structured like a language, and representations of the subject and objects of desire are products of symbolic substitution, and shaped to fit the elements and rules of the combinatory systems through which they are articulated and satisfied.

This account extends to society, for Lacan regards structures of kinship and social exchange as further symbolic systems. In particular, the prohibition of incest, characteristic of all human societies, can be seen as a law regulating the relations (combinations) of men and women, taken as elements partly constituted by their role in exchanges among groups which compose society. Thus, according to Lacan, the resolution of the Oedipus complex is a development in which the boy forgoes an imaginary relation with the mother to occupy a place in a larger order, which is symbolic, social and constitutive of human culture. As in the prior instance of the mirror, the child secures a potentially fulfilling identity via the enabling but alienating assumption of an image – in this case that of the symbolic father, who embodies the social laws which regulate sexual desire and provide for its procreative satisfaction.

4 Comparisons

The diversity of psychoanalytic theories may conceal their underlying convergence. For example, Lacanian criticisms of ego-psychology assume a common basic account of the formation of the self, and an interest in symbol-formation is common to all schools. Again, Lacan's mirror stage illustrates a particular aspect of Klein's depressive position – namely, identification with something felt to be whole because seen as having spatial unity and permanence, and enviable on that account.

The main disagreements among the other approaches sketched above concern the first year of life. Klein hypothesized that envious projective identification was active from early infancy, whereas Kohut and the ego-psychologists regarded symbiotic unity as prior to envy and aggression, ego-weakening splitting and fantasies of relating to good and bad objects generally. Studies of infant cognition, imitation and communication (see Stern 1985; Mehler and Dupoux 1994) suggest that even very young babies might engage in psychological exchanges comparable to projective identification, which can also be seen as the establishing of object- and self-object relations (see COGNITION, INFANT; MIND, CHILD'S THEORY OF). In addition, empirical studies of attachment suggest that patterns of object-relations formed in infancy can be traced throughout life, and from one generation to the next (see Bretherton and Waters 1985; Cichetti and Cummings 1990). Some of these patterns coincide with psychoanalytic accounts, and recent work in the United States (Kumin 1996) relates them to both Klein and Kohut. Whether a conceptual and empirical synthesis along these lines will prove successful remains to be seen.

See also: FEMINISM AND PSYCHOANALYSIS; FREUD, S.; PSYCHOANALYSIS, METHODOLOGICAL ISSUES IN

References and further reading

* Ainsworth, M.D.S. (1985) 'I. Patterns of Infant–Mother Attachment: Antecedents and Effects on Development' and 'II. Attachment across the Life Span', *Bulletin of the New York Academy of Medicine* 6: 771–812. (Use of significant research paradigm for studying relationships between parents and infants.)
Anderson, R. (ed.) (1992) *Clinical Lectures on Klein and Bion*, London and New York: Tavistock/ Routledge. (Essays introducing and discussing Bion's work.)
Benvenuto, B. and Kennedy, R. (1986) *The Works of Jacques Lacan: An Introduction*, London: Free Associations Books. (Clear introductory discussion of Lacan.)
* Bion, W.R. (1961) *Experiences in Groups*, London: Tavistock and New York: Basic Books. (Extension of Klein's concepts to the mental functioning of groups.)
* —— (1989) *Second Thoughts: Selected Papers on Psychoanalysis*, London: Heinemann. (Advances in Kleinian thinking on symbolism and mental function, partly produced through work with schizophrenic patients. Emphasis on the mother's mental containment of the infant's projective identifications, and the infant's introjection of this function. Bion's work is discussed in Anderson (1992) and compared with Kohut's in Kumin (1996); Segal links her work on symbolism with Bion's on mental functioning in Segal (1990).)
Blank, G. and Blank, R. (1974) *Ego-Psychology: Theory and Practice*, New York: Columbia University Press. (Survey of ego-psychology.)
* Bower, T.R.G. (1982) *Development in Infancy*, San Francisco, CA: W.H. Freeman. (Experiments and discussions concerned with the abilities of infants; on this topic see also Mehler and Dupoux (1994).)
* Bowlby, J. (1969, 1973, 1980) *Attachment and Loss*, vol. 1, *Attachment*, London: Hogarth Press; vol. 2, *Separation*, New York: Basic Books; vol. 3, *Loss*, New York: Basic Books. (Series of books on early relation between infant and caretakers influenced by ethology and British object-relations theorists; gave rise to the empirical study of attachment by Ainsworth (1985) and others. See also Bretherton and Waters (1985); Cichetti and Cummings (1990).)
* Bretherton, I. and Waters, E. (1985) *Growing Points in Attachment Theory and Research*, Monographs of the Society for Research in Child Development no. 209, Chicago, IL: University of Chicago Press. (Empirical study of early object-relations.)
* Campos, J.J., Barrett, K.C., Lamb, M.E., Goldsmith, H.H. and Stenberg, C. (1983) 'Socioemotional Development', in Mussen (ed.) *Handbook of Child Psychology*, vol. 3, New York: Wiley & Sons. (Discussion of emotion and object-relations in infancy.)
* Cichetti, D. and Cummings, E.M. (eds) (1990) *Attachment in the Preschool Years: Theory, Research, and Intervention*, Chicago, IL: University of Chicago Press. (Empirical study of early object-relations.)
* Fairbairn, W.R.D. (1954) *An Object-Relations Theory of the Personality*, New York: Basic Books. (Attempted reformulation of Freudian theory in terms of object-relations.)
Feldstein, R., Fink, B. and Jaanus, M. (1996) *Reading Seminars I and II: Lacan's Return to Freud*, Albany, NY: State University of New York Press. (Essays discussing concepts introduced in Lacan's seminars.)
* Freud, A. (1936) *The Ego and the Mechanisms of Defense*, London: Hogarth Press; repr. in *The Writings of Anna Freud*, New York: International Universities Press, 1966. (Anna Freud's account of her father's late work which provided the starting point of ego-psychology.)
—— (1966) *The Writings of Anna Freud*, New York: International Universities Press. (Collected works of Freud's daughter, who influenced both child analysis and ego-psychology.)
* Hartmann, H. (1939) *Ego Psychology and the Problem of Adaptation*, New York: International Universities Press, 1958. (Influential attempt to set ego-psychology in unified biological and social context.)
Hinshelwood, R.D. (1990) *A Dictionary of Kleinian Thought*, London: Free Associations Books. (Explanations of terms and concepts in Kleinian theory.)
* Jackobson, E. (1964) *The Self and the Object World*, New York: International Universities Press. (Influential account of the self in ego-psychological terms.)
* Klein, M. (1975) *The Writings of Melanie Klein*, vol. 1, *Love, Guilt and Reparation and Other Works 1921–45*; vol. 2, *The Psychoanalysis of Children*; vol. 3, *Envy and Gratitude and Other Works*

1946–63; vol. 4, *Narrative of a Child Analysis*, London: Karnac Books and the Institute of Psychoanalysis; repr. New York: Delta Press, 1977; repr. London: Virago, 1989. (Volume 1 includes essays on the analysis of children, including initial descriptions of the depressive position, and Klein's seminal paper on symbolism, derived from the analysis of an autistic boy (discussed in Segal 1986; Lacan 1988). The first essays in this volume are both the easiest to read, and essential for understanding the rest. Volume 2 includes Klein's most comprehensive description of her technique and views. Volume 3 has later essays elaborating the paranoid-schizoid position and the role of envy and projective identification. Volume 4 gives a session-by-session account of an analysis of a 10-year-old boy.).

* Kernberg, O. (1995) 'Psychoanalytic Object Relations Theories', in B. Moore and B. Fine (eds) *Psychoanalysis: The Major Concepts*, New Haven, CT and London: Yale University Press. (Clear, accurate and comprehensive overview of object-relations approaches of various schools; includes bibliography.)

* Kohut, H. (1977) *The Restoration of the Self*, New York: International Universities Press. (First statement of self-psychology, relating his new ideas clearly to the ego-psychology he is revising.)

—— (1984) *How Does Analysis Cure?*, ed. A. Goldberg and P. Stepansky, Chicago, IL: University of Chicago Press. (Kohut's last exposition of self-psychology: fuller but less explicitly related to other schools than Kohut (1977).)

* Kumin, I. (1996) *Pre-Object Relatedness: Early Attachment and the Psychoanalytic Situation*, New York: Guilford Press. (Attempt to integrate Kleinian, Kohutian and ego-psychological thinking about early object-relations with infant research and attachment theory. The synthesis may be premature, but illustrates genuine connections among the basic ideas.)

Lacan, J. (1977) *Ecrits*, London: Tavistock and New York: Norton. (Partial translation of the French edition of Lacan's collected essays. Deliberately difficult, and only partly understood by many enthusiastic commentators. Best approached together with a guide such as Benvenuto and Kennedy (1986) and via the texts of the Seminars (1988), in which many points are discussed more fully.)

—— (1988) *The Seminars of Jaques Lacan*, book 1, *Freud's Papers on Technique, 1953–1954*, Cambridge: Cambridge University Press. (First volume of Lacan's seminars, notable for the way he begins by contrasting Anna Freud and ego-psychology with Melanie Klein, and uses Klein's work on symbolism and containment, later to be articulated by Bion, as the basis for his discussion of the opposition between the imaginary and the symbolic. This can be read with Feldstein, Fink and Jaanus (1996).)

Laplanche, J. and Pontalis, J.B. (1973) *The Language of Psycho-Analysis*, London: Hogarth Press. (Clear and scholarly exposition of basic psychoanalytic concepts, including some of Lacan's.)

* Mahler, M.S. (1968) *On Human Symbiosis and the Vicissitudes of Individuation*, New York: International Universities Press. (Mahler's account of early development; includes interesting clinical material.)

Mahler, M.S., Pine, F. and Bergman, A. (1975) *The Psychological Birth of the Human Infant*, New York: Basic Books. (Study of children's behaviour via Mahler's approach; some patterns observed are closely related to those studied via attachment theory, as in Bretherton and Waters (1985); Cichetti and Cummings (1990).)

* Mehler, J. and Dupoux, E. (1994) *What Infants Know: New Cognitive Science of Early Development*, Oxford: Blackwell. (Review of recent work on infant cognition.)

Moore, B. and Fine, B. (1990) *Psychoanalytic Terms and Concepts*, New Haven, CT and London: Yale University Press. (Short introductory discussions of main terms and concepts; briefer and clearer than Moore and Fine (1995). Includes discussions of Klein, Bion, Winnicott, Fairbairn and Kohut ('Self-Psychology'), all from the perspective of ego-psychology. Can be used together with Laplanche and Pontalis (1973) which is more rooted in Freud.)

—— (1995) *Psychoanalysis: The Major Concepts*, New Haven, CT and London: Yale University Press. (Introductions by various authors to important concepts, from ego-psychological perspective.)

Mussen, P. (ed.) (1983) *Handbook of Child Psychology*, vol. 3, New York: Wiley & Sons. (Includes Campos *et al.* (1983).)

Segal, H. (1986) *The Work of Hanna Segal: A Kleinian Approach to Clinical Practice*, London: Free Associations Books. (Exposition and development of Kleinian ideas, including influential discussion of concrete symbolism and symbol-formation, which has proven important in the analysis of psychotic states.)

—— (1989) *Klein*, London: Fontana Modern Masters. (Lucid introduction to Klein's work.)

* —— (1990) *Dream, Phantasy, and Art*, London and New York: Tavistock/Routledge. (Discussion of fantasy and art which includes clear exposition of Freud on dreams and Segal's own work on dreams and symbolism, relating them to Bion's work on

mental functioning. Includes a discussion of a recent analysis of an autistic child.)

* Spitz, R. (1965) *The First Year of Life: A Psychoanalytic Study of Normal and Deviant Development of Object Relations*, New York: International Universities Press. (Pioneering ego-psychological discussion of early development; some claims require revision in light of more recent research, as in Mehler and Dupoux (1994).)
* Stern, D. (1985) *The Interpersonal World of the Infant: A View from Psychoanalysis and Developmental Psychology*, New York: Basic Books. (Discussion of the infant's capacities to relate to others; attempts to integrate psychoanalytic theory with recent experimental work on infant cognition.)
* Winnicott, D. (1958) *Collected Papers: Through Pediatrics to Psychoanalysis*, New York: Basic Books; repr. London: Karnac Books and the Institute of Psychoanalysis, 1992. (Essays elaborating such influential notions as the transitional object, the value of illusion, and the true and false selves.)

JAMES HOPKINS

PSYCHOLOGY, PHILOSOPHY OF *see* MIND, PHILOSOPHY OF

PSYCHOLOGY, THEORIES OF

The object of study in psychology is the experience and behaviour of organisms, particularly human organisms. Psychology resembles the other sciences in employing methods appropriate to material phenomena but, unlike them, the mind (sometimes held to be immaterial) is among its objects of study. If the mind were immaterial it is difficult to see how psychology could proceed. Psychology differs from the other sciences in that understanding may not permit prediction and/or control of the phenomena. This is a consequence of the fact that human organisms may become aware of causal factors that would otherwise have determined their experience or behaviour. Being aware, they have a choice. (This is not, of course, to deny that the choice may itself be determined by more remote factors.)

In the seventeenth century, Descartes proposed that the mind (or soul), though immaterial, was nevertheless capable of two-way causal interaction with the material body. It is often held that what is immaterial cannot interact with what is material but Descartes' proposal was, in its context, so valuable that it has ever since

exercised a profound influence on philosophy and on what most of us take for granted (for example, the unexamined belief that the mind/soul is, in some sense, immaterial but does, in some sense, interact with the body).

The possibility of scientific psychology was preserved by Leibniz's hypothesis of psycho-physical parallelism (according to which the deity keeps mind and body running in parallel, though there is no causal interaction between them). This view did not survive the passing of an era of universal (and largely unquestioned) religious belief. At the beginning of the twentieth century behaviourism tried to do without mind, it also tried to avoid surreptitious appeal to the lay person's unexamined 'mind' concept. In the 1960s, the cognitive revolution in psychology substantially broadened the range of phenomena under investigation but at the cost of allowing appeals to an unexamined 'mind of last resort'.

The headlong advance of the computer, which has taken over many functions previously reserved to members of the human species, leaves open the question whether it will, one day, take over all of them – or will be permitted to do so.

1   **Origins**
2   **The emergence of psychology**
3   **The establishment of a scientific psychology**
4   **The contemporary orthodoxy**
5   **Marginal influences**
6   **Theories of personality**

1   Origins

The belief is deep-seated that human persons are, by virtue of possessing conscious minds, beings of a different order from the bodies with which they are associated – which share material reality with the other physical objects in our universe. The belief is not unreasonable since each of us can validate it, so we think, from immediate experience. Until the seventeenth century it was generally agreed that the 'mind/soul' constituting the person was a substance resembling the body but with the matter taken out. Christian dogma held that, on judgment day, all souls would resume existence as physical bodies. In the seventeenth century, Descartes first proposed the more etiolated conception now current. The mind/soul remains immaterial (thus suffering none of the disabilities attached to material existence) but is no longer supposed to have the external form of the body. It is, however, still capable of two-way, causal interaction with the body. Descartes' proposal was, historically, of very great significance since it proved acceptable to the Church and allowed a distinction to be drawn between knowledge related to the soul (the prerogative of the Church) and knowledge related to the body (including the human body) which could freely be advanced by scientific investigation. Prior to Descartes no such distinction had been drawn and a scientist might be guilty of heresy for holding opinions that appear to us to have no religious content at all (for example, Galileo and the moons of Jupiter).

DESCARTES was aware of the physical existence and functions of the sense organs but, in his view, their purpose was to model objects in the real world for presentation to the mind/soul via the pineal gland. Collins (1973) draws attention to this radical change of emphasis. The old philosophy held, with Descartes, that objects in the real world cause changes in the perceiving organism. But what was perceived (according to the old philosophy) were objects in the real world. What was perceived according to Descartes were models of the objects, formed by the sensory systems of the perceiver. Descartes' substitution is rational for an avowed mind/body dualist but ceases to be rational if there is no postulated 'mind' to which the models may be presented. Why do we need models if we have the real things in our perceptual field? Surely all we need is information about the real things, enabling us to respond appropriately to them? The majority of contemporary theorists follow Descartes in rejecting this argument (for example, Marr 1982). They seek only to specify how the organism constructs its hypothetical internal models. Gibson (1979) is the exception; insisting that what we perceive are objects in the real world, not models of them (see DUALISM; PERCEPTION §1).

2 The emergence of psychology

Psychology was the last of the established sciences to break free from philosophy (the word 'psychology' is rarely used prior to the nineteenth century). But the change of emphasis to which Collins (1973) drew attention had profound effects on philosophy which have in turn influenced psychology. If Descartes' substitution is accepted, it becomes possible (perhaps obligatory) to adopt what Collins calls the 'egocentric, sceptical perspective' – to doubt the existence of the external world and even the continuity of the perceiving person. The models may, after all, have no material correlate; they may exist only in the immaterial mind that perceives them. Philosophers since Descartes have laboured mightily to prove the postulations of everyday thinking – that we exist and that a real world external to us exists – but without success.

Psychology cannot allow the possibility that an immaterial 'mind' that is not law-governed interacts causally with each material human body; the intervention of such a mind would put the body's behaviour beyond the reach of science; the behaviour would still be observable but no longer predictable, even in principle. At first, Leibniz's doctrine of preestablished harmony appeared to offer a way out of the dilemma, in the form of 'psycho-physical parallelism'. In a world in which dogmas of the Church were widely accepted it seemed legitimate to postulate that mind and body might not interact but might, by God's grace, run in parallel – like two ideal clocks, started at the same moment, that always show the same time though there is no connection between them. Psycho-physical parallelism was tacitly accepted during the greater part of the nineteenth century. It was compatible with the theories of memory and thinking then taken for granted according to which ideas/mental images could become associated by contiguity of time and place in individual experience, or as (apparent) cause and effect. The occurrence of one would then be likely to elicit others with which it had been associated in the past. A 'mind' was tacitly assumed to be available to draw appropriate inferences from the associations furnished by experience. At about the same time, mathematics moved on from concern with the development of new, useful mathematical techniques to worries (often associated with the problem of infinitesimals) about the validity of the techniques. They appeared to work, but could they be relied upon?

At the end of the nineteenth century the theoretical status of psychology was uncertain. There had been advances in neurophysiology sufficient to show that the brain was intimately involved in behaviour and one or two lone voices had been heard advocating a purely physiological psychology. Generally, however, physiologists were careful to keep their options open. Fritsch and Hitzig (1870: 96), for example, believed that 'some psychological functions and perhaps all of them, in order to enter matter or originate from it need certain circumscript centers of the cortex'. Wilhelm WUNDT opened the first psychological laboratory at Leipzig in 1879 but he held strong views on what might and might not be done in the laboratory. Basic sensory functions were investigated to establish what was the least perceptible stimulus, or the least perceptible difference between stimuli, using controlled introspections in which the subject reported verbally whether the stimulus was present or whether two stimuli differed (Wundt 1894). Wundt did not, however, regard the higher mental functions as suitable topics for the laboratory, they might only be studied by historical and/or descriptive methods.

He insisted on the mind/body distinction and succeeded (1907) in aborting a programme of laboratory investigation into higher mental functions begun in Würzburg a few years earlier (Humphrey 1951); not, however, before it had been established that many such functions proceed in the absence of introspectible mental content. This finding was important as a refutation of one central argument of associationism which maintained that associated ideas/images must necessarily be in consciousness, that is, they must be introspectible. Titchener studied in Wundt's laboratory but, on his return to the USA, he too conducted introspective investigations into 'higher mental functions'. He maintained that failure to find introspectible mental content showed only that the subject had not tried hard enough and once confessed himself 'not at all astonished to observe that the recognition of a (shade of) gray might consist of a quiver of the stomach' (1909: 179).

3 The establishment of a scientific psychology

At the beginning of the twentieth century, psychology was still obsessively concerned with the problem of consciousness. Animal psychology asked only whether or how far animals could be said to possess consciousness. But philosophical thinking on the subject had moved on. It is a relatively short step from psycho-physical parallelism (where the hand of the deity keeps mind and body on parallel courses) to epiphenomenalism where mind and body keep on parallel courses because mind has no independent causal status and simply reflects what is going on in body (see EPIPHENOMENALISM). Either way psychologists may legitimately proceed to the experimental investigation of behaviour but the latter view sheds surplus theological baggage that had become progressively less easy to accept. Consciousness does not need to be denied to man or animal and may continue to be employed as a means of access (via language) to human subjects. However, no separate account need be given of the functions of consciousness since it has none.

J.B. Watson, the founder of behaviourism, was a philosopher who had become interested in animal behaviour (see BEHAVIOURISM, METHODOLOGICAL AND SCIENTIFIC). Watson (1913) asserts that consciousness should rightfully play no greater role in psychology than it plays in chemistry or physics. He appears to mean that it should play only the role allotted to it in associationism, as an arena in which observed associations may be interpreted as evidence of the existence of laws governing the observed phenomena (for example, of physics or chemistry). This should not be an acceptable view in psychology,

since the psychologist includes in his remit the mind which does the interpreting, though it does well enough in the other sciences. Watson later advocated the study of observable behaviour only, without any reference to internal, unobservable 'minds'. (A point of view maintained even more strongly by B.F. SKINNER (for example, 1974).) Neither behaviourism nor associationism offers any satisfactory account of how or where theories (of which behaviourism and associationism are themselves examples) are constructed.

Watson believed at this time that 'thoughts' might be nothing more than sub-threshold movements of the speech organs and tried in his laboratory to obtain photographic records of such movements. Koch (1964) reports Lashley as having told him that Watson hoped to present the photographic evidence in his presidential address to the American Psychological Association (1915) but being unable to obtain any, adopted the work of his student, Lashley, on conditioning (with due acknowledgement). Thus was born the association between behaviourism and conditioning theory which occupied most US academic psychologists for the next half century. Lashley had encountered Pavlovian theory in Germany (Pavlov's work had been translated into German although no English translation appeared until 1927). Watson (and, subsequently, Clark L. Hull) developed Pavlov's theory into 'learning theory'. Something was lost in the transition, since the US theory was frankly mechanist whilst Russian theory, though materialist, was never mechanist. (Mechanism was politically unacceptable in the USSR; account had to be taken of consciousness since both Marx and Lenin had used the term.) US theorists avoided reference to 'mind' or 'consciousness' since the intellectual tradition to which they subscribed equated consciousness with mind and mind with inaccessibility in principle to scientific investigation. The fundamental unit of behaviour was, for them, the link between stimulus and observable response (the S–R bond). Hull (1930; 1935) tried to show how higher mental functions might be explained as sets or sequences of these fundamental units but the basic theoretical and experimental task was, in his view, to understand the unit. Hull and his followers are said to have obtained almost total hegemony over US academic departments of psychology in the period 1920–1950 but the hegemony did not survive Hull's death in 1952. (US behaviourism is critically evaluated in Rozeboom (1970); for Russian work over the same period see Payne (1968) and Razran (1971).)

4 The contemporary orthodoxy

The demise of behaviourism and its replacement by cognitive, 'information-processing' psychology in the so-called cognitive revolution of the 1960s, was motivated primarily by a desire among experimental psychologists to work on more interesting topics than Hull had permitted. But it must also be remembered that a generation of psychologists who possessed a degree of philosophical sophistication was dying off. The new generation had often studied nothing but psychology. Until the 1960s, most psychologists had recognized the desirability of a central, theoretical framework, performing the function in psychology that atomic theory performs in physics and the theory of complex molecules, in biology. They had also recognized the undesirability of referring unresolved issues upwards to an unspecified, higher supervisory level; that is, in effect, to the operations of a (possibly immaterial) mind. Since the 1960s neither of these restrictions have been observed. There has been an exponential increase in the range of topics investigated and the sophistication of the techniques employed but few significant advances in our understanding of psychological issues.

Sutherland (1979) despaired of experimental psychology using human or animal subjects since there are simply too many possible contaminating factors to allow rational interpretation of the results obtained. He recommended that efforts should be devoted either to cognitive science (that is, the computer simulation of behaviour) or to neuroscience (the micro- or macro-physiology of the brain). There has been no significant reduction in the flow of experimental papers but both cognitive science and neuroscience have succeeded in establishing themselves as independent disciplines. Cognitive science takes symbols for granted and has tried to develop ways of manipulating them by computer that approximate to various human mental functions. Recently, technological advance has brought in the possibility of 'connectionism' (Rumelhart and McLelland 1986), which has the advantage of employing analytic methods resembling those of the brain more closely than do the methods of symbolic computing. Proponents of symbol processing (or 'artificial intelligence') and of connectionism, often profess to see their respective disciplines as incompatible alternatives but since the latter appears to model symbol formation and the former takes symbols for granted, it is likely that an accommodation will be reached. It remains to be seen whether this will contribute substantially to our understanding of human psychological function (see ARTIFICIAL INTELLIGENCE).

At the beginning it was suggested that human beings had, by the seventeenth century, evolved a monistic conception of human nature, in a direct perceptual relationship with the natural world outside itself, that was fundamentally sound. Unfortunately this conception had, over the centuries, acquired encumbrances relating to many tangential issues of religion and metaphysics that rendered the whole a positive block to further progress in human knowledge. In the seventeenth century the block was broken; physical and biological scientists were then free to proceed unencumbered – whether the mind was material or immaterial was of no consequence. For the psychological scientist this is not, of course, the case. If mind is immaterial then psychology has, as we have seen, no obvious way to proceed. The response of many psychologists has been to insist that the mind is, of course, material but to act as if there existed nevertheless an immaterial 'mind of last resort' that perceives and manipulates the models supposed by cognitive psychologists (following Descartes) to comprise the furniture of the mind. The activities of this 'mind of last resort' should constitute a significant part of the subject matter of psychology but are often passed over.

5 Marginal influences

The Gestalt movement (Koffka 1935) was a legitimate reaction against the late nineteenth-century view that a theory of perception could be derived from data on subjects' responses to punctate stimuli – points of light or brief pure tones. The Gestaltists' fundamental observation (the 'phi' phenomenon) was that if two adjacent points of light are flashed in quick succession, what the subject sees is one point of light moving from the first location to the second. The experience is unequivocal and many related phenomena have been discovered. The Gestalt emphasis on perceptual holism was salutary but they have advanced no viable alternative theory of perception (see GESTALT PSYCHOLOGY).

The experimental work of Jean PIAGET on human developmental psychology was influential in the UK and in the USA but his theory was not. He devoted a long life to the elaboration of a biologically-based theory of human development which may yet prove to be significant (Gruber and Vonèche 1977).

Phenomenological psychology, stemming from BRENTANO (§2) and HUSSERL (Thinès 1977), has sometimes limited itself to detailed analysis of subjects' states of consciousness but more recently (for example, Harré and Gillett 1994) emphasis has been placed on discourse between persons and on the social construction of personality. There is, some believe, no necessary conflict between a structural psychology that sets out to achieve scientific understanding of the human organism – the evolved 'thing' that is capable of doing what we know human beings have done and can do – and a discursive psychology concerned only with what the organism does in its interaction with other organisms, but both have necessarily to confront the question of logic. There is something inherently odd about founding logic, as at present, outside psychology – though logicians are unanimous in rejecting what they call 'psychologism'. It may be worth noting that Husserl (who is often cited as the final authority for the rejection of psychologism) thought his views on that subject had been grossly misrepresented. Husserl (1929) makes it clear that he thought he had shown only that logic could not be founded in an associationist psychology of mental contents. He believed that it could and must be founded in a cognitive, structural psychology (see PHENOMENOLOGY, EPISTEMIC ISSUES IN).

6 Theories of personality

So far, this entry has been concerned with theories that try to answer the question 'what sort of thing is the human organism and how should it be studied scientifically?' As we have seen, another level of theorizing considers the person in interpersonal interaction, in the development of 'personality'. Such theorizing frequently starts out from the malfunctioning or neurotic personality, a theory of normal personality may or may not emerge. Sigmund FREUD remains the outstanding theorist at this level. He constructed a theory of normal human development with an associated therapeutic method to correct developmental anomalies. The former was the more important in his view; he never had much confidence that the latter would do more than alleviate a patient's worst difficulties. By 1914 he had already acquired a number of US disciples with whom he lost contact during the First World War. They were largely responsible for the growth of psychoanalysis as a medical speciality, offering to cure neuroses as the orthopaedic surgeon cures broken limbs. Freud regarded neurosis as the inescapable accompaniment of civilized living – since the latter is entirely unnatural to man. Both are consequences of the diversion of libidinal energy whose natural object is physical survival and reproductive success. By complex evolutionary processes man has civilized himself, using energy surplus to what was required for survival or could be dissipated in the struggle for reproductive success (since civilization usually demands at least the pretence of monogamy). Energy not dissipated in sexual activity or sublimated in the achievement of economic, artistic or other non-sexual goals, must inevitably issue in neurotic behaviour. The developmental process determines, for better or worse, how libidinal energy will be directed in each individual. This is an unflattering account of human nature but we should not look to science for flattery. The point is that Freud's theory calls on no forces that are not already active in the evolution of lower animal species. Anyone who does not accept his account has either to argue for an alternative, working within the same constraints, or to postulate new forces specific to the formation of human (as opposed to animal) nature. Today, not many people take the latter course. Freud proposed answers to questions that no one else has asked and some would prefer never to have been asked at all. There is no guarantee that genuine alternative answers would be more flattering to human *amour propre* than Freud's were.

Following Freud, personality theories proliferated (Maddi 1989). Freud believed that successful therapy required recall into awareness of forgotten traumas of early childhood development, to redirect libidinal energy that had been misdirected or had failed to achieve any direction. The therapy was long, expensive and frequently unsuccessful. Carl Rogers (1961) proposed as an alternative a form of 'non-directive' therapy. In ordinary discourse between persons, an opinion expressed by one party is conventionally met with agreement or disagreement by the other party. Where the opinion concerns a personal predicament of the one (who knows more about it than anyone else), it is unlikely that either agreement or disagreement will persuade them to change it. Non-directive (or 'client-centred') therapy encourages the client to express opinions but the therapist avoids expressing either agreement or disagreement. The clients, not receiving the usual reinforcement, may then be inclined to review and perhaps modify their opinions for themselves. Unfortunately, Rogers later reverted to a form of directive therapy, conducted in small groups, on the (possibly mistaken) assumption that most human beings have it in them to function as therapists.

A second major development was the attempt to apply learning-theory principles (that is, behaviourism) in a clinical context; in which the client's behaviour is modified by manipulation of reinforcement by the therapist. Alcoholism may be treated by administering a drug that makes patients violently sick if they subsequently take alcohol. Phobic anxiety may be treated by teaching the patient to relax completely (a physical state incompatible with anxiety) and introducing the feared object gradually over a number of therapy sessions. All these treatments try to extinguish the learned connection between some unwanted piece of behaviour and its present, painful or pleasurable, outcome.

Treatment of personality disorders is now almost always eclectic, drawing on more than one therapeutic tradition. Since the object is to benefit the client, any treatment that works is, in principle, justifiable. The age of grand, overarching theories of personality has perhaps passed. True or false, they turn out to have few useful consequences – human nature is simply too complex.

See also: JUNG, C.G.

References and further reading

Arnold, W.J. (1976) *Nebraska Symposium on Motivation, 1975: Conceptual Foundations of Psychology*, Lincoln, NE and London: University of Nebraska Press. (Everything in this volume is worth reading.)

* Collins, A. (1973) 'The Objects of Perceptual Consciousness in Philosophical Thought', *Social Research* 40: 153–76. (An invaluable brief account of the changes in world-view brought about by Descartes in the seventeenth century.)

Coulson, W.R. and Rogers, C.R. (1968) *Man and the Science of Man*, Columbus, OH: Charles E. Merrill. (Included because it contains a substantial contribution from Michael Polanyi whose work has so far had no impact on psychological theory but may do so in the future.)

* Fritsch, G. and Hitzig, E. (1870) 'On the Electrical Excitability of the Cerebrum', in G. Von Bonin, *The Cerebral Cortex*, Springfield, IL: Charles C. Thomas, 1960. (An early classic of neurophysiology, originally published in German.)

* Gibson, J.J. (1979) *The Ecological Approach to Visual Perception*, Boston, MA: Houghton Mifflin. (A modern classic on visual perception.)

* Gruber, H.E. and Vonèche, J.J. (1977) *The Essential Piaget*, London: Routledge & Kegan Paul. (A selection from Piaget with linking commentary.)

* Harré, R. and Gillett, G. (1994) *The Discursive Mind*, London: Sage. (Concerned with what they term the 'discursive turn' in psychological theory.)

* Hull, C.L. (1930) 'Knowledge and purpose as habit mechanisms', *Psychological Review* 37: 511–25. (Hull's attempt to account for 'knowledge' and 'purpose' in his own terms, that is, without reference to any higher 'mental function'.)

* Hull, C.L. (1935) 'The mechanism of the assembly of behavior segments in novel combinations suitable for problem solution', *Psychological Review* 42: 219–45. (Hull's attempt to explain 'problem solving' in his own terms.)

* Humphrey, G. (1951) *Thinking*, London: Methuen.

(Described by the author as 'an introduction to its experimental psychology' which it is. It is probably also the best single work on psychological theory.)

* Husserl, E. (1929) *Formal and Transcendental Logic*, trans. D. Cairns, The Hague: Martinus Nijhoff, 1969. (A late work of Husserl on logic, originally published in German.)

* Koch, S. (1964) 'Psychology and emerging conceptions of knowledge as unitary', in T.W. Wann (ed.) *Behaviorism and Phenomenology*, Chicago, IL and London: University of Chicago Press. (This book also contains much other matter of interest.)

* Koffka, K. (1935) *Principles of Gestalt Psychology*, New York: Harcourt Brace. (The standard account of Gestalt theory.)

* Maddi, S.R. (1989) *Personality Theories: A Comparative Analysis*, Homewood, IL: The Dorsey Press, 5th edn. (A standard work on personality theories in all their infinite variety.)

* Marr, D. (1982) *Vision*, San Francisco, CA: W.H. Freeman. (A standard work on the computational theory of vision.)

* Payne, T.R. (1968) *S.L. Rubinsteyn and the Philosophical Foundations of Soviet Psychology*, Dordrecht: Reidel. (An account of psychological theory in the USSR.)

* Razran, G. (1971) *Mind in Evolution*, Boston, MA: Houghton Mifflin. (A brilliant synthesis of US and Russian experimental work by a psychologist who was familiar with both.)

* Rogers, C.R. (1961) *On Becoming a Person*, Boston, MA: Houghton Mifflin. (Roger's own account of his earlier work.)

* Rozeboom, W.W. (1970) 'The Art of Metascience III', in J.R. Royce (ed.) *Towards Unification in Psychology*, Toronto, Ont.: University of Toronto Press. (A critique of behaviourist theory.)

* Rumelhart, D.E. and McLelland, J.L. (1986) *Parallel Distributed Processing*, Cambridge, MA: MIT Press, vols 1 and 2. (The foundational work on connectionism.)

* Skinner, B.F. (1974) *About Behaviorism*, New York: Knopf. (A statement of Skinner's position.)

* Sutherland, N.S. (1979) 'Neurosciences Versus Cognitive Science', *Trends in Neuro-Sciences* 2 (8): I–II. (Sutherland's rejection of experimental cognitive psychology, in favour of either 'cognitive science' (computer simulation of mental function) or 'neuroscience' (direct investigation of the central nervous system).)

* Thinès, G. (1977) *Phenomenology and the Science of Behaviour*, London: Allen & Unwin. (A valuable but little read work relating continental phenomenology to biology, neurophysiology and experimental psychology.)

* Titchener, E.B. (1909) *Lectures on the Experimental Psychology of the Thought Processes*, New York: Macmillan. (The most satisfactory introduction to Titchener's ideas.)

* Watson, J.B. (1913) 'Psychology as the Behaviorist Views It', *Psychological Review* 20: 158–77. (Watson's first statement of the behaviourist position.)

Wolman, B.B. (1980) *Contemporary Theories and Systems in Psychology*, New York and London: The Plenum Press, 2nd edn. (A detailed and critical account of movements in psychological theory in the first three-quarters of the twentieth century.)

* Wundt, W. (1894) *Lectures on Human and Animal Psychology*, London: Swan, Sonnenscheim & Co. (Lectures on his experimental work.)

* —— (1907) 'On the Ausfrage Experiments and on the Methods of the Psychology of Thinking', *Psychologische Studien* 3: 301–60. (Published in German and not available in translation. For a detailed account and critique see Humphrey (1951: 107–16).)

N.E. WETHERICK

PTOLEMY (*c.* AD 100–70)

The astronomer Ptolemy was one of the leading scientific figures of Graeco-Roman antiquity. His contributions to philosophy lie in his reflections on scientific activity. In knowledge, he distinguishes a perceptual stage, which provides the natural link between knowledge and things, from a further, rational stage, governing the transition to science. The move towards science consists of the progressive distinction between concepts, initially acquired through experience and methodical observation. Many components of his thought are derived from earlier philosophy, but he excludes those aspects which bear on more general philosophical issues.

Ptolemy – Claudius Ptolemaeus – probably lived at Alexandria. His *Mathematical Composition*, better known under its Arabic title the *Almagest*, offered a complete treatment of celestial phenomena, based on the assumption of geocentricism and employing mathematical models founded on uniform circular motions. It is one of the greatest works in the history of science. In addition, he wrote monographs on astronomical themes and comprehensive treatments of nearly every science with a high mathematical content: optics, harmonics, geography, astrology. In all these areas his writings remained standard reference works for centuries.

His philosophical work, *On the Criterion and Commanding-Faculty*, concentrates on the act by which one attains knowledge of real objects – primarily sensible ones. The act consists of two stages: (1) by means of the sensory apparatus the soul is affected and perceives this; (2) the intellect reads the perception, translating it into the terms of reason (see LOGOS). This distinction between a perceptual and a rational stage does not make the translation artificial or arbitrary. The sensory apparatus is a set of *natural* tools, each with a proper, normal and natural mode of application which already contains a rational and conceptualizable principle. As a result, the perception yields a determinate reading, translatable into rational terms.

This theory is located within a general epistemology. The intellectual and perceptual faculties (the latter subdivided into five senses) both deal with the same domain – things and their properties. Intellect (see NOUS) develops only in human beings and is later than the perceptual faculty. Starting from the data of individual perceptions, intellect comes to grasp both the functioning of the senses and aspects of external things. By means of memory, these aspects are detached from the original perceptual encounter, to form the stock of concepts used in the reading of percepts. Subsequently they become the object of separate reflection by the intellect, as by progressively articulating them it classifies things, through genera and species, all the way down to indivisible particulars. Underlying this task are certain concepts – same/different, equal/unequal, similar/dissimilar – which Ptolemy calls the intellect's proper objects, not derived from perceptual activity at all. Anyone who does not progress beyond the stage of focusing on objects in isolation remains at the level of 'opinion'. The scientific frame of mind is achieved by incorporating one's opinions into the rational order.

While perception is incontrovertible regarding effects on the soul, being a direct awareness of these, it can nevertheless be deceptive regarding its own external cause. It indicates this cause, without being the judge of the indication's correctness. However, that does not reduce perceptions of things to mere subjective experiences, because (1) the natural basis of cognitive activity guarantees that in normal conditions it functions correctly, and (2) it is the intellect's role, through its capacity for rational translation, to act as the judge. When in doubt, the intellect can have recourse to repetition of the cognitive act. Moreover, it can organize systematic observation, and this, combined with the refinement of concepts, constitutes the path from opinion to knowledge.

If perceptions can be judged by the intellect, they must be analysable. Here Ptolemy adopts the Aristotelian distinction between special and common sensibles (see ARISTOTLE §18), and his *Optics* (partially extant in a Latin translation of an Arabic translation) offers an analysis of vision. 'In reality' vision perceives condensed illuminated surfaces; 'immediately' it perceives the special sensibles, that is, colours; 'derivatively' the common sensibles, that is, body, size, shape, position and motion. Structurally, vision is treated in geometrical terms as a cone with its apex at the eye. Ptolemy establishes the limits of vision's powers, and its internal interrelations in perceiving its different objects. And he produces a complete typology of optical illusions, both those due to natural external conditions and those due to inadequate understanding of vision's workings. The *Optics* perfectly illustrates how Ptolemy's overall conceptual framework can encase a scientific inquiry combining empirical observation, conceptual analysis and mathematics.

Ptolemy rarely invokes earlier philosophical discussions. Nevertheless, his thought and terminology include elements from every preceding major philosophy. His strategy is to extract from the tradition whatever he needs in order to define his scientific activity in its various aspects. But his principal philosophical hallmark is his way of ranking the perceptual and rational stages in knowledge, which enables him to build out of natural cognitive processes a path which, under the guidance of reason, leads to science. For any science to travel this path (as distinct from an individual's acquisition of a scientific disposition) takes longer than a human life span. He can thus, in the *On the Criterion and Commanding-Faculty*, deliberately ignore the classic Stoic–Academic debate (see ARCESILAUS §2; STOICISM §§12–13) on the criterion (despite frequently drawing material from it): he may take it to bear only on practical philosophy, not philosophy of science.

According to P. Duhem's (1913) classic thesis, Ptolemy assigned a purely instrumental value to the mathematical models used in his scientific work: they helped him organize his observations and derive predictions from them, without any pretence of referring to physical fact (see DUHEM, P.M.M. §4). In the *Almagest* Ptolemy certainly sometimes *uses* his models in that way. Nevertheless, his explicit defences of them do not sound instrumentalist, but normally rest on physical presuppositions. Moreover, in his *Planetary Hypotheses* he constructs an intricate system of nested corporeal spheres, and these match the components of the *Almagest*'s models. Finally, instrumentalism seems scarcely compatible with his theoretical pronouncements in the *On the Criterion and Commanding-Faculty* and the *Optics*. We may say that Ptolemy took a realist view, but that, given the absence in his day of a clearly formulated instrumentalist position, his implicit realism is not so rigorously defined as to prevent his adopting a more dismissive tone when it suits him.

List of works

Ptolemy (*c*. AD early 150s) *Almagest*, trans. G.J. Toomer, London: Duckworth, 1984. (English translation which includes notes.)

—— (*c*. AD 140–70) *On the Criterion and Commanding-Faculty*, trans. various authors in P. Huby and G. Neale (eds) *The Criterion of Truth*, Liverpool: Liverpool University Press, 1989, 179–230. (Parallel text and English translation, including notes.)

—— (*c*. AD 150s or 160s) *Optics*, in A. Lejeune (ed.) *L'Optique de Claude Ptolémée* (The Optics of Claude Ptolemy), Leiden: Brill, 1989. (Annotated Latin text with French translation.)

—— (*c*. AD 150s or 160s) *Harmonics*, in A. Barker (trans. and ed.) *Greek Musical Writings*, vol. 2, Cambridge: Cambridge University Press, 1989, 275–391. (With extensive notes.)

—— (*c*. AD 150s or 160s) *Tetrabiblos*, trans. F.E. Robbins, Loeb Classical Library, Cambridge, MA: Harvard University Press and London: Heinemann, 1980. (Greek text with facing translation.)

—— (*c*. AD 160s) *Planetary Hypotheses*, in J.L. Heiberg (ed.) *Claudii Ptolemaei Opera astronomica minora*, Leipzig: Teubner, 1907. (Greek text and German translation of the first (and the only extant in Greek) part of Book I, and German translation, by L.Nix, of an Arabic translation of Book II. There is an English translation of the Arabic translation of the second part of Book I (missing in Heiberg's edition) in B. Goldstein, 'The Arabic Version of Ptolemy's Planetary Hypotheses', in *Transaction of the American Philosophical Society*, n.s. 57: 3–55.)

References and further reading

* Duhem, P. (1913) *Le Système du monde I* (The World System), Paris: Hermann. (Proposes the instrumentalist interpretation of Ptolemy's mathematical astronomy.)

Lejeune, A. (1948) *Euclide et Ptolémée: Deux stades de l'optique géometrique grecque* (Euclid and Ptolemy: Two Stages of Greek Geometrical Optics), Louvain: Université de Louvain. (The standard work on the *Optics*.)

Long, A.A. (1988) 'Ptolemy on the Criterion: An Epistemology for the Practising Scientist', in J.M. Dillon and A.A. Long (eds) *The Question of*

'Eclecticism', Berkeley and Los Angeles, CA: University of California Press, 176–207. (A careful evaluation of Ptolemy's philosophical debts in *On the Criterion*.)

Lloyd, G.E.R. (1978) 'Saving the Appearances', *Classical Quarterly* 28: 202–22. (Refutation of Duhem's (1913) thesis.)

Taub, L.C. (1993) *Ptolemy's Universe*, La Salle, IL: Open Court. (Readable treatment of the philosophical motivations underlying Ptolemy's astronomy.)

FERRUCCIO FRANCO REPELLINI

PUBLIC INTEREST

The concept of the public interest can be used in a wide variety of ways, and this has led many to say that it is devoid of meaning. However, the concept enables us to evaluate the tendency of policies and institutions to promote the interests of the members of a society considered in their broadest relations, for example in connection with policies to promote public health. In this sense it has significance. Historically, the concept of the public interest has drawn upon three main traditions of thought: the utilitarian idea of utility maximization; the tradition of civic republicanism; and Rousseau's idea of the general will. Nowadays, three main ways of meeting the public interest are distinguishable: the supply of certain indivisible goods like clean air; the preservation of identity-conferring social goods like a distinctive language; and the balancing of competing considerations in the making of public policy. Although the provision of goods in the public interest may be associated with injustice, there is no reason in general to think that justice and the public interest must conflict.

1 The concept of the public interest
2 Three traditions
3 Modern conceptions of the public interest
4 The public interest and reducibility
5 Justice and the public interest

1 The concept of the public interest

The principle of the public interest is a broad one. Moreover, it is related to other ideas like 'common advantage', 'common good', 'public good', 'public benefit' and 'general will'. Given this wide range, it is tempting to say that the idea of the public interest is so indeterminate as to be virtually meaningless.

Despite these doubts, it is possible to identify a core sense to the term. The root idea seems to be that a policy, practice or institution is in the public interest if it is to the interest, advantage, benefit or good of some group or set of persons considered to be members of the same society. Thus, a well-functioning legal system together with an uncorrupt system of public administration will be in the public interest, by facilitating a wide range of civil and individual activities in a society.

It may turn out that a policy or practice that is in the public interest, so defined, will not be to the advantage of some subgroup in society. Does this show that all we mean by the concept is a collection of private interests? Not at all. If it would be more profitable for the Mafia to have a corrupt system of law and public administration, we may still quite properly say that there is a public interest to the contrary, since there is no way in which the minority interest could serve a more general good. For this reason, Bentham, with typical verve, called subgroups whose existence depended upon subverting the public interest 'sinister interests'.

2 Three traditions

An important influence in defining the concept of public interest has been the utilitarian tradition, in particular that strand stemming from the philosophic radicals at the beginning of the nineteenth century (see UTILITARIANISM). The philosophic radicals made the concept of the public interest central to their political philosophy and defined it in terms of the aggregate interests of the members of a society.

Within the tradition known as civic republicanism, by contrast, the principle of the public interest is associated with virtuous citizens upholding the institutions of a free republic, including the practices of participation in public affairs and the performance of military service (see REPUBLICANISM).

Rousseau's use of the term 'general will' forms a third tradition. According to Rousseau, the policies and practices of a society should be determined by a vote of a majority of citizens. Provided that all citizens are voting with an awareness that their choices will affect them in all the roles they occupy, the result of a majority vote will constitute the general will. In voting, citizens do not identify a pre-existing public interest, but instead define that interest in the process of choice. In this way, Rousseau hoped to combine a republican sense of virtue with a modern notion of moral autonomy (see GENERAL WILL §1; ROUSSEAU, J.-J. §§1–3).

3 Modern conceptions of the public interest

The traditions listed above intermingle in modern thought in defining three varieties of meaning for the public interest.

The first sense owes much to utilitarianism and draws upon the economist's notion of a public good. Within economics a pure public good is defined as being non-rival, so that one person's consumption does not diminish the consumption of others, and non-excludable, so that if one person in a society consumes the good, then others will as well. An example of a public good in this sense is clean air. Person A's consumption of clean air does not detract from anybody else's consumption, and if clean air is available to A it will also be available to anyone else in the society. Goods having these properties include: environmental amenity, public order, good government, a sense of fairness and obligation in contractual relations, tolerance and civic mindedness.

A familiar difficulty in the provision of such public goods is the so-called 'free rider' problem or problem of collective action (see RATIONAL CHOICE THEORY). The difficulty arises because, although it may be in everyone's interest that a public good is supplied, it may be in no particular person's interest to bear a share of the costs of supply. Since the good is non-rival and non-excludable, each individual will benefit from the existence of the good, whether or not they have made a contribution to its costs. Self-interested persons would therefore be tempted to free ride on the contributions of others, hoping that they could gain the benefit without incurring the costs. But free riding, when generalized, is collectively self-defeating, since if no one incurs the costs, the public good will not be supplied.

Various suggestions have been made for overcoming the free rider problem. A Hobbesian line of argument is that it provides a justification for the state to have coercive authority, so that it can enforce individual contributions to the supply of public goods in the public interest (Hobbes 1947). This line of argument also has affinities with Rousseau's idea that in the social contract people are 'forced to be free' in implementing the general will. Other suggestions for overcoming the free rider problem rely upon the consequences of repeated interaction among small numbers of people, in which norms of cooperation can emerge, or upon a moral education that will encourage people to internalize Kantian principles of fairness.

Public goods in this sense are instrumental, since they are compatible with widely divergent personal conceptions of the good. By contrast, the public interest may include the idea of a common good.

Drawing its inspiration both from the tradition of civic republicanism and from Rousseauian/Hegelian notions of community and social identity, this formulation identifies certain irreducibly social goods that are constitutive of central human interests: a language and the cultural traditions that go with it; a sense of place and landscape for a people; the continuation of a people's identity; or popular participation in the shaping of a common political life.

The specification of the concept of a common good in this sense is central to debates between liberals and communitarians, and therefore to debates about the virtues of patriotism and the obligations of citizenship. Communitarians contest the idea that individuals in a society are bound together solely by their subscription to a common set of rules constraining the exercise of their freedom. They argue that a common social life exists prior to the formation of individuals and that notions of the right and justice have to be conceptualized so that they are consistent with a society's common good. In practice, such a view would presumably licence policies and practices that would inculcate certain patriotic virtues, for example a willingness to defend one's country in time of attack (see COMMUNITY AND COMMUNITARIANISM).

The third modern notion of the public interest is more formal than the previous two, although common in everyday political argument. Here the public interest is a balance between competing, but incompatible, goods. For example, freedom from police constraint is a good and so is personal security. To ensure personal security, it may be necessary to give the police general powers to stop people on suspicion of carrying concealed weapons. In this case two incompatible goods are set against one another, and it is sometimes said that the public interest is best promoted where a suitable balance is struck between them.

Can one define how this balancing might take place? Two methods have sought to give substance to the idea of balancing: Benthamite utilitarianism, in which the balance is struck at the point at which aggregate utility is maximized, and Rousseau's notion of the social contract, in which the balance is struck at the point of majority decision on the general will.

Both approaches are beset with difficulties, however. It is not clear that Benthamite utilitarianism can provide a weighting of utilities that does not beg the question about the value of different outcomes. The Rousseauian approach can provide little independent evidence about the terms of a social contract. In practice, despite these limitations, public policy is often made by some form of balancing, either by decision makers weighing the supposed advantages or disadvantages of various alternatives or by popular decision. Thus, the principle of the public interest as a balancing of goods has some significance, even if its meaning is difficult to state precisely.

4 The public interest and reducibility

Who or what might be the bearer of a public interest? In speaking of the public interest, it may seem as though we are identifying an entity over and above the individuals who make up a society. Methodological individualists, who assert that there is no such entity, baulk at this thought.

In the first and the third modern senses of the public interest, however, it is not necessary to abandon methodological individualism, provided we are allowed to identify the interests of non-assignable individuals. This means that the ascription of interests cannot rest solely upon the expressed preferences of actual individuals, but must instead presuppose that there are certain interests sufficiently widely shared to ascribe them to a wide range of persons whoever they might be (see NEEDS AND INTERESTS §1).

The second sense of the public interest, involving the notion of a common good, raises more complicated questions. Languages and cultures are themselves non-reducible entities. Their preservation and advancement may therefore seem to require a non-reducible sense of the public interest. However, this appearance is misleading if we think that the reason why such entities should be preserved is to advance the wellbeing of those individuals who will be members of a certain society.

5 Justice and the public interest

The notion of the public interest is distinct from that of justice, since we can quite sensibly say that a practice is in the public interest but that the costs of maintaining it are unfairly distributed among the population. For example, a population might need to save water in a drought, but it might be unfair not to exempt market gardeners, whose livelihood depends upon a ready supply of water, from the restrictions.

In recent discussions of justice, it has been common to contrast justice and utilitarian conceptions of the public interest (see JUSTICE §3). Thus, it has been urged that a commitment to an impartial consideration of the public interest cuts across the special moral obligations that individuals owe to one another in justice, and can give weight to illegitimate preferences based upon prejudice that would discriminate against classes of individuals.

It is certainly true that without some principle of

equality an appeal to aggregate interests can disadvantage particular individuals. However, some aggregate balancing seems called for where general interests of similar importance are set against one another, for example freedom of movement and freedom from arbitrary attack. In these contexts, the concept of the public interest seems central to our ability to balance interests without being opposed to justice.

See also: WELFARE

References and further reading

Axelrod, R. (1990) *The Evolution of Cooperation*, Harmondsworth: Penguin. (A clear account of the problem of collective action and an original attempt to show how repeated interaction over time will lead to a solution.)

Barry, B.M. (1967) 'The Public Interest', in A. Quinton (ed.) *Political Philosophy*, Oxford: Oxford University Press, 112–26. (A clear outline of a want-based theory of interests with a connection to the public interest via Rousseau.)

Bentham, J. (1789) *An Introduction to the Principles of Morals and Legislation*, ed. J. Burns and H.L.A. Hart, London: Athlone Press, 1970. (The best statement of the traditional utilitarian view of the public interest as an aggregate of individual interests.)

Hargreaves Heap, S., Hollis, M., Lyons, B., Sugden, R. and Weale, A. (1992) *The Theory of Choice*, Oxford: Blackwell. (Provides an account of public goods, the free rider problem and references for further reading.)

Hart, H.L.A. (1983) *Essays in Jurisprudence and Philosophy*, Oxford: Clarendon Press. (Part IV contains a brilliant series of essays on the relationship of individual rights to ideas of general welfare.)

Hobbes, T. (1651) *Leviathan*, ed. M Oakeshott, Oxford: Blackwell, 1947. (The principal source of the argument that coercion is necessary to provide the public good of security.)

Kymlicka, W. (1990) *Contemporary Political Philosophy: An Introduction*, Oxford: Clarendon Press. (Chapter 2 contains a useful discussion of utilitarianism and unfairness.)

Mill, J.S. (1992) *Utilitarianism*, in J. Gray (ed.) *John Stuart Mill On Liberty and Other Essays*, Oxford and New York: Oxford University Press. (Chapter 5 contains the classic attempt to reconcile the ideas of justice and the maximization of social utility.)

Pocock, J.G.A. (1975) *The Machiavellian Moment*, Princeton, NJ, and London: Princeton University

Press. (Classic account of civic republican tradition in the history of political thought.)

Raz, J. (1986) *The Morality of Freedom*, Oxford: Clarendon Press. (Develops the idea that certain collective goods, like living in a tolerant society, are essential for individual freedom.)

Skinner, Q. (1992) 'On Justice, the Common Good and the Priority of Liberty', in C. Mouffe (ed.) *Dimensions of Radical Democracy*, London and New York: Verso. (A clear statement of the civic republican argument.)

Taylor, C. (1990) *Sources of the Self*, Cambridge: Cambridge University Press. (Advocates the view that individual wellbeing is tied to certain common social goods.)

ALBERT WEALE

PUFENDORF, SAMUEL (1632–94)

Pufendorf was the first university professor of the law of nature and nations. His De iure naturae et gentium *(On the Law of Nature and Nations) (1672) and* De officio hominis et civis iuxta legem naturalem *(On the Duty of Man and Citizen according to Natural Law) (1673) greatly influenced the handling of that subject in the eighteenth century. As a result Pufendorf has been recognized as an important figure in the development of the conception of international law as a body of norms commonly agreed to have universal validity by sovereign states. He regarded himself as an exponent of a new moral science founded by Hugo Grotius which transformed the natural law tradition by starting from identifiable traits of human nature rather than ideas about what human beings ought to be.*

Pufendorf began his higher education by enrolling to study theology at the University of Leipzig in 1650. He soon found philosophy, history and law more to his taste. Moving to Jena in 1656, he discovered the brand of philosophy that interested him most in the works of GROTIUS, DESCARTES and HOBBES. In 1658 he was made tutor to the family of the Swedish ambassador in Copenhagen, only to be imprisoned when war recommenced between Sweden and Denmark. The ambassador escaped to Holland, where Pufendorf eventually joined him, taking the opportunity to further his studies at the University of Leiden. In 1661 he accepted a chair at Heidelberg, moving in 1668 to a new appointment at Lund. When the Danes besieged Lund in 1676 Pufendorf was called to Stockholm by Charles XI and made a privy

councillor, secretary of state and Swedish historiographer royal. A decade later he received similar appointments in Prussia. He died after a brief visit to Sweden in 1694.

The parallels between the lives of Pufendorf and Grotius are striking: both became engaged in public service, particularly on Sweden's behalf; both took advantage of a period of imprisonment to develop their ideas; both wrote on a range of subjects – legal, historical and religious as well as philosophical. Where their paths most clearly diverged, however, was in Pufendorf's pursuit of a career as a university teacher. Though his *Elementa iurisprudentiae universalis* (The Elements of Universal Jurisprudence) (1660) was written after his connection with a Swedish embassy had resulted in his incarceration, it built on his earlier studies at Jena and secured his later appointment at Heidelberg. Both there and at Lund Pufendorf was employed as Professor of the Law of Nature and Nations to teach the doctrines adumbrated in Grotius' *De iure belli ac pacis* (The Law of War and Peace) (1625). Pufendorf produced a further exposition of those doctrines in his major work *De iure naturae et gentium* (On the Law of Nature and Nations) (1672) and its hugely influential epitome *De officio hominis et civis iuxta legem naturalem* (On the Duty of Man and Citizen according to Natural Law) (1673).

It is on these three treatises that his reputation as a philosopher rests. He has been hailed with Grotius as an early theorist of a new international order in which a society of sovereign states was formed by the common recognition of rules governing their relations with each other. More recently his own perception of himself as an exponent of a new moral science founded by Grotius has been revived. There can be little doubt that Pufendorf's widely disseminated works contributed greatly to the impact of this modern, post-sceptical, version of natural law theory on philosophers of the eighteenth century. Problematic is the extent to which he made a significant contribution to the substantial development of the theory.

Pufendorf was more conscious than Grotius of his role as an exponent of a distinctive discipline. Hitherto the study of universal jurisprudence had been the preserve of two academic elites: lawyers and theologians. Pufendorf insisted that the discipline of law was properly concerned with the civil laws regulating the conduct of citizens in specific states. Those laws turned on the legislator's will and, unlike natural laws, could not be ascertained by unaided reason. Similarly, the divine laws with which moral theologians were properly concerned had to be learned through revelation of the legislator's will.

They regulated the thoughts as well as the deeds of Christians whose citizenship was celestial. By contrast, Pufendorf's discipline used reason to discover the laws that governed the deeds of people of all creeds in earthly societies (see LEGAL POSITIVISM; SOVEREIGNTY).

If Pufendorf was led to this clearer demarcation of the provinces of ethics, law and theology by his involvement in university teaching, the altered circumstances of public life in his time may explain a second way in which he went beyond Grotius. Writing against a background of devastating warfare, Grotius had tried to discover a basic moral consensus from which it could be shown how human beings might achieve peace and security through the formation of societies. Writing after the Peace of Westphalia brought relative stability to Europe, Pufendorf was able to proceed beyond Grotius' minimalist account of natural law and to specify more fully the duties people owed to each other once they had formed societies. His exposition was therefore more extensive than Grotius' and more obviously relevant to readers who could take for granted the peace and security Grotius had sought. Later natural law theorists were to develop this trend further (see NATURAL LAW §5).

Both in defining the scope of his discipline and in exploring its contents, Pufendorf made significant adjustments to its conceptual apparatus. Grotius had still written in an Aristotelian way about human beings having an innate tendency towards life in society. In place of this essentialism Hobbes had depicted humans as beings entirely motivated by self-interest. Both authors had identified in each person's interest in self-preservation a natural right to do what each person saw fit for their own preservation. Pufendorf agreed with Grotius that human beings were sociable, but followed Hobbes in basing his claim on identifiable traits imposed on human nature by God rather than on any innate disposition in humans. Having done so, he was able to take human sociability as the foundation of all the duties of humanity and to talk more in terms of duties than of rights. For Pufendorf all rights were simply correlative to duties.

See also: DESCARTES, R.; HOBBES, T.; HOHFELD, W.N.; LAW, PHILOSOPHY OF; STAIR, J.D.

List of works

Pufendorf, S. (1660) *Elementorum iurisprudentiae universalis libri duo* (The Elements of Universal Jurisprudence), trans. W.O. Oldfather, Oxford: Clarendon Press, 1931. (An early 'geometrical' synthesis of natural law theory.)
—— (1672) *De iure naturae et gentium* (On the Law of Nature and Nations), trans. C.H. Oldfather and W.O. Oldfather, Oxford: Clarendon Press, 1934. (Pufendorf's major work on natural law theory.)
—— (1673) *De officio hominis et civis iuxta legem naturalem* (On the Duty of Man and Citizen according to Natural Law), trans. F.G. Moore, New York: Clarendon Press, 1927. (A highly influential epitome of Pufendorf's major work.)

References and further reading

Dufour, A. (1991) 'Pufendorf', in J.H. Burns and M. Goldie (eds) *The Cambridge History of Political Thought, 1450-1700*, Cambridge: Cambridge University Press, 561. (Links Pufendorf's philosophical works with his writings on history and public law.)
Krieger, L. (1969) *The Politics of Discretion*, Chicago, IL: University of Chicago Press. (The only book-length study of Pufendorf's life and thought in English.)
Seidler, M. (ed.) (1990) *Samuel Pufendorf's 'On the Natural State of Man'*, Lewiston, NY: Edwin Mellen Press. (Contains a helpful 'Introductory Essay'.)
Tuck, R. (1987) 'The "Modern" Theory of Natural Law', in A. Pagden (ed.), *The Languages of Political Theory in Early-Modern Europe*, Cambridge: Cambridge University Press, 99. (Revives Pufendorf's own assessment of his place in the history of moral theory.)

J.D. FORD

PUNISHMENT *see* CRIME AND PUNISHMENT

PURGATORY

According to Roman Catholic teaching, purgatory is the place or state of purification after death in which those who die in a state of grace (and hence are assured of being saved) make expiation for unforgiven venial sins or endure temporal punishment for mortal and venial sins already forgiven. The concept evolved to resolve the theological confusion about the state of souls between personal death and the general resurrection and Last Judgment, to explain what happens to those persons who repent before death but do not live long enough to do penance for their sins, and to make intelligible the widespread practice of praying for the souls of the departed. The doctrine developed in conjunction with a 'high' Eucharistic theology, according to which all the faithful departed take part in the liturgy of the Church. The idea of purgatory is therefore intimately connected with Christian ideas of sin, judgment, retributive punishment, the communion of saints and the idea that salvation occurs in history. It was rejected by the Reformers and, in the second half of the twentieth century, interest from Catholic theologians has waned. Nevertheless, some modern Protestant thinkers have defended the concept as an intermediate phase in salvation.

1   The development of the idea of purgatory
2   The emergence of the doctrine and its decline

1   The development of the idea of purgatory

Purgatory is not explicitly mentioned in the Bible, but its supporters have thought it is implied in the apocryphal 2 Maccabees 12: 39–45, where Judas Maccabaeus makes propitiation for the sins of those in his army who died in battle upon discovering that they had worn pagan amulets. Several New Testament texts have also been interpreted as indirectly referring to purgatory; an example is Matthew 12: 31–2, which refers to the sin 'which will not be forgiven either in this world or in the world to come', perhaps implying that expiation is still possible after death.

The custom of offering prayers for the dead in the early Church was widespread and quickly became established practice in the liturgy. With the exception of Aerius, a fourth-century presbyter of Pontus mentioned by Augustine as a heretic, there is no evidence of dissent or hesitation on the matter of prayers for the baptized dead. Hints of the belief in a place for which expiation for sin can be made after death probably appear first in the writings of Tertullian. His contemporary, Clement of Alexandria, more explicitly refers to a place where those who have repented on their deathbed but have not had time to do penance will be sanctified after death by purifying fire. Basil, active in the third to fourth centuries, wrote in a homily on Psalm VII that those with 'any stains or relics of sin' after death 'should be detained'. At the end of the fourth century, Jerome wrote to his friend, the senator Pammachius, on the death of the latter's wife, praising him for venerating her by giving alms, 'knowing that it is written: as water extinguishes fire, so does alms, sin' (Letter LXVI).

The views of Augustine are important, because his subtlety and clarity of thought have carried his influence on Christian philosophy into the present era, but his position on purgatory is not unequivocal. Upon the death of his mother, St Monica, Augustine offered prayers for the repose of her soul, but he is reticent on the question of the nature of purgatory and of a purgatorial fire and treats it tentatively in the *Enchiridion* (chaps 69–70). However, he appears more confident in *De civitate Dei* (*The City of God*):

> But temporary punishments are suffered by some in this life only, by others after death, by others both now and then; but all of them before that last and strictest judgment. But of those who suffer temporary punishments after death, all are not doomed to those everlasting pains which are to follow that judgment; for to some, as we have already said, what is not remitted in this world is remitted in the next, that is, they are not punished with the eternal punishment of the world to come.
> (XII: 13)

More importantly for the later development of the doctrine of purgatory, Augustine, in the *Enchiridion*, lays down rules for the use of suffrages, as prayers and alms offered for the dead were called. The first rule is that suffrages benefit not all the dead, but only those who are neither damned nor already in heaven; it is too late for the former, and the latter do not need it. The second rule is that a person qualifies for suffrages only in life. Bernstein (1993) says that these two rules came to guide the Church in regulating devotion of the living for the dead. As time went on they were interpreted as permitting the dedication of good works as well as prayers to expiate the sins of the deceased. Thus believers endowed charitable institutions and houses of prayer, and upon this basis the practice of indulgences arose.

2   The emergence of the doctrine and its decline

Atwell (1987) argues that important changes in the Church during the sixth century augmented the development of the idea of purgatory into a full doctrine in the work of Pope Gregory the Great. These developments included the systematic ordering of the penitential system within the Church, the differentiation of mortal and venial sins, and the emergence of a Eucharistic theology in which the faithful departed were commemorated and the saints petitioned for intercession. These liturgical practices were linked with the doctrine of the communion of saints, whereby the Church was understood as involving fellowship between the living and those among the dead who are saved and who therefore remain part of the Church.

Le Goff (1981) claims that the doctrine was really born in the twelfth century, when a great intellectual and moral revolution changed the way people thought about sin and profoundly altered penitential practices. This revolution started with ANSELM OF CANTERBURY (§8), whose investigation into the voluntariness necessary for sin in the *Cur Deus homo* (completed 1098) led to an era of examination of the notions of personal responsibility, guilt and punishment. This gave rise to the distinction between guilt (*culpa*) and the debt of punishment (*poena*), a distinction at the heart of the logic of purgatory. *Culpa* can be pardoned through contrition and confession, but *poena* is effaced only by 'satisfaction', that is, by completing a penance. This distinction appears in Aquinas, who says that if a soul has repented and been forgiven, but owes a debt to divine justice at death, this delays the soul's flight to heaven and makes a prior purgation obligatory (*Summa theologiae* IIIa, q.69, a.2, corpus). Aquinas maintained that souls in purgatory accept their suffering voluntarily, understanding that they are in the last stage of preparation for the beatific vision (see HEAVEN §3).

The official teaching of the Roman Catholic Church was defined at the Councils of Lyons (1274) and Florence (1439) with the intent of reconciling the Greek Christians, who objected to the idea of material fire and the distinction between *culpa* and *poena*. These councils avoid the term *purgatorium* for the sake of the Greeks, but speak of a purification after death for those souls 'who died truly penitent in the love of God before satisfying for their sins through worthy fruits of penance' (Denzinger and Schoenmetzer 1967: 464). There is no mention of fire. Even within the Latin Church there were disagreements on the nature of the pains of purgatory, with some emphasizing the pain of loss – the consciousness of being separated from God, albeit temporarily (and some even maintaining that such pain constitutes the entire pain of purgatory), while others emphasized the pain of sense – physical pain. Aquinas maintained that the pain of sense in purgatory comes from actual fire which is more painful than the greatest sufferings of this world, but later scholastics such as Suárez were inclined to doubt any comparison between the sensory pains of this world and those of purgatory. While the suffering in purgatory was often vividly described in imaginative literature, sometimes the hopefulness of purgatory was stressed instead. In the *Il Purgatorio* of Dante's *Divina Commedia*, purgatory is a mountain that reaches up to heaven. Dante describes how the desire for heaven makes souls fly towards God, causing the mountain to tremble constantly with a joyful thunderclap marking the arrival of each soul into paradise.

The existence of purgatory was denied by the Reformers, such as Luther, who usually also questioned the utility of prayers for the dead. In reply, the Council of Trent in 1562 proclaimed the propitiatory value of the sacrifice of the Mass even for the dead, but otherwise said only that 'Purgatory exists, and the souls detained there are helped by the prayers of the faithful' (Denzinger and Schoenmetzer 1967: 998, 983). No mention was made of the place or duration of purgatory, or of the nature of purgatorial punishment.

Interest in purgatory has declined during the latter half of the twentieth century, accompanied by a decline in interest in most of the concepts with which purgatory has been associated. The documents of Vatican II, the ecumenical council called by Pope John XXIII in the 1960s, do not mention purgatory at all, although prayers for the dead continue to be offered in liturgical services. Occasionally, however, Protestant theologians have offered defences of the existence of purgatory. Hick (1976) speaks approvingly of an intermediate state between death and heaven, but rejects many of the traditional elements of purgatory, believing that the person-making process can continue beyond the grave (see EVIL, PROBLEM OF §4). Brown (1985) has argued that there are conceptual problems with the idea that a human being makes an abrupt transition between a state of moral imperfection at death and a state of moral perfection in heaven. He argues that we know and identify ourselves only through continuity with our past, but a person who is suddenly morally perfected would have no reasonable grounds for believing themselves to be the same person whose past they 'remember'. Brown concludes that if there is a heaven, there must also be a purgatory that provides a gradual transition to a perfected state. Walls (1992) is another Protestant theologian who accepts the idea of purgatory as part of the logic of the Christian conception of salvation.

See also: HELL; LIMBO; SALVATION

References and further reading

* Anselm (completed 1098) *Cur Deus homo* (Why God Became a Man), in *St Anselm: Basic Writings*, trans. S.N. Deane, La Salle, IL: Open Court, 1966. (An account of the reasons for the Incarnation.)
* Aquinas, T. (1266–73) *Summa theologica*, trans. Fathers of the English Dominican Province, Westminster, MD: Christian Classics, 1981, IIIa, qq.69–70. (Essential reading on the traditional doctrine of purgatory.)
* —— (mid 13th century) *Comm. in lib. IV. sent.*, dist. xxi, q.1., Paris: Moos, 1933, 1947. (No English translation. Essential reading on the traditional

doctrine of purgatory; see also *Quaestiones disputatae de malo* (On Evil).)

Arendzen, J.P. (1951) *Purgatory and Heaven*, New York: Sheed & Ward. (A short and simple summary of traditional Roman Catholic teaching on judgment, the resurrection of the body, heaven and purgatory.)

* Atwell, R.R. (1987) 'From Augustine to Gregory the Great: An Evaluation of the Emergence of the Doctrine of Purgatory', *Journal of Ecclesiastical History* 38 (2): 173–86. (A historical treatment of the beginnings of the idea of purgatory in the early centuries of the Church.)

* Augustine (354–430) *Enchiridion theologicum*, Madrid: La editoria Catolica, 1961, chaps 67–70, 109–10. (An important source for the emergence of the idea of purgatory.)

* —— (413–27) *De civitate Dei*, trans. M. Dods, *The City of God*, New York: Modern Library, 1950, chaps 21, 24, 26. (An important source for the emergence of the idea of purgatory.)

* Bernstein, A.E. (1993) *The Formation of Hell*, Ithaca, NY: Cornell University Press. (Mostly about hell, but is up to date and contains some references to purgatory.)

* Brown, D. (1985) 'No Heaven Without Purgatory', *Religious Studies* 21 (4): 447–56. (A contemporary defence of the idea of purgatory by a Protestant theologian.)

* Denzinger, H. and Schoenmetzer, A. (1967) *Enchiridion symbolorum*, 34th edn, Barcelona, Freiburg im Breisgau, Rome, New York: Herder; 30th edn, trans. R.J. Deferrari, *The Sources of Catholic Dogma*, St Louis, MO and London: Herder, 1957. (A handbook in excerpt form of the sources and texts upon which Catholic dogmatic teachings are based. Texts are arranged chronologically.)

Garrigou-Lagrange, R. (1952) *Life Everlasting*, trans. P. Cummins, St Louis, MO and London: Herder. (A good explanation of Roman Catholic theology on death, judgment, heaven, hell and purgatory.)

* Hick, J. (1976) *Death and Eternal Life*, New York: Harper & Row. (An influential book, which discusses both Western and Eastern eschatologies.)

* Le Goff, J. (1981) *The Birth of Purgatory*, trans. A. Goldhammer, Chicago, IL: University of Chicago Press. (An important book on the historical development of the concept of purgatory; includes a discussion of Dante's *Il Purgatorio*.)

* Walls, J.L. (1992) *Hell: The Logic of Damnation*, Notre Dame, IN: University of Notre Dame Press. (This book is an examination of the Christian conception of hell, but includes a brief defence of the idea of purgatory on page 169.)

LINDA ZAGZEBSKI

PURPOSE IN NATURE
see TELEOLOGY

PŪRVA MĪMĀṂSĀ *see* MĪMĀṂSĀ

PUTNAM, HILARY (1926–)

Putnam's work spans a broad spectrum of philosophical interests, yet nonetheless reflects thematic unity in its concern over the question of realism. A critic of logical positivism, Putnam opposed verificationism and conventionalism, arguing for a realist understanding of scientific theories. He rejected the traditional conception of meaning according to which speakers' mental states determine meaning and consequently, reference, and put forward a conception of meaning on which external reality, for example, what one talks about, contributes essentially to meaning. Further, citing what he called the division of linguistic labour, Putnam saw the conferring of meaning as a social rather than an individual enterprise. In response to the relativistic challenge that the incommensurability of different theories precludes any possibility of intertheoretical dialogue, Putnam invoked a causal theory of reference construing reference as relatively insensitive to theoretical variation, so that the continuity and rationality of science and communication are upheld. The Copenhagen interpretation of quantum mechanics posed yet another difficulty for realism. Putnam saw quantum logic as an alternative which was compatible with realism, and argued that logic, like geometry, can be revised on the basis of empirical considerations. In the philosophy of mind, Putnam proposed functionalism, the view that mental states are characterized by function rather than material constitution. Putnam also made a substantial contribution to mathematics through his work on the insolvability of Hilbert's tenth problem.

In 1976, Putnam launched an attack on the coherence of the view he termed 'metaphysical realism'. Arguing that relativism and scepticism are disguised forms of metaphysical realism, and likewise incoherent, he suggested an alternative, referred to as 'internal realism'. Clarification of this position and its viability as a third way between realism and relativism is the focus of Putnam's later writings, and of much of the criticism they have incurred.

1 Life

Born in Chicago in 1926, Putnam spent his early years in France. His father, Samuel Putnam, was a well-known writer and translator, an active communist, and a columnist for the *Daily Worker*. Along with Noam Chomsky, Putnam majored in the emerging field of linguistic analysis at the University of Pennsylvania (and also in philosophy and German). His graduate studies were divided between Harvard, where he studied with Quine, Hao Wang, C.I. Lewis and Morton White, and UCLA, where he wrote his Ph.D. dissertation on the concept of probability under the supervision of Reichenbach. In 1953 he moved to Princeton, made the acquaintance of Carnap and, receiving informal instruction from Kreisel, worked intensively on mathematical logic. He has been at Harvard since 1965. Putnam actively protested against the Vietnam War, and was also active in Students for a Democratic Society (SDS) and The Progressive Labour Party, a Maoist group. Around 1972 he became disillusioned with communism. Since Putnam saw his early realism as embodying some of Engels' insights, it seems plausible that this turn affected his philosophical development. Later, he became interested in the study and practice of his Jewish heritage.

2 Realism

Putnam criticized such basic elements of logical positivism as the verificationist theory of meaning, reductionism and conventionalism, while sharing the positivists' interest in and respect for natural science (see LOGICAL POSITIVISM §2). He maintained that realism is the only philosophy that does not render the success of science a miracle (see REALISM AND ANTIREALISM; SCIENTIFIC REALISM AND ANTIREAL-ISM §3). His argument from success is presented as structurally similar to hypothetico-deductive arguments within science: realism provides the best explanation for the success of science in the same way atoms and genes provide explanations for observable phenomena. However, this analogy is problematic in that it is purely formal. Realism has no empirical import beyond that of its alternatives, a desideratum scientific hypotheses must meet.

Putnam's criticism of conventionalism is developed in *An Examination of Grünbaum's Philosophy of Geometry* and *The Refutation of Conventionalism*. On the Reichenbach–Grünbaum conception, the core of the transition from Newtonian to relativistic mechanics is a new definition of the spacetime metric. The definition chosen is a matter of convenience, not of truth (see CONVENTIONALISM §1). According to Putnam, however, meaning change is only part of the story; theoretical concepts have explanatory import, and must be anchored in a theory that meets both empirical and non-empirical constraints. There is, therefore, much less freedom than the conventionalist alleges. Putnam raises a similar objection to Quine's celebrated indeterminacy of translation thesis (see QUINE, W.V. §9). Here, as in the case of convention-alism, underdetermination is an illusion created by considering an unreasonably limited set of constraints. Once we recognize coherence, simplicity, and so on, as constraints on translation or theory-construction, conventionality and indeterminacy vanish.

3 The meaning of meaning

Putnam faults the traditional theory of meaning for being individualistic rather than social, and for neglecting the contribution of external reality to meaning. He construes the standard theory as based on the two assumptions that to know a term's intension is to be in a particular psychological state and that intension determines extension. Hence, it is argued, speakers who are in the same mental state when uttering a word share both its intension and its extension.

Putnam uses the twin earth (TE) thought experi-ment to attack this theory. TE resembles earth down to the smallest detail except that the liquid function-ing as water, and called 'water', on TE is not H_2O, but a different chemical compound. Since there is no reason to ascribe different mental states to a person using 'water' on earth, and their counterpart on TE, or, at least, there was no such difference prior to the emergence of chemistry as a science, this constitutes an example of people using the same word when in identical mental states, but ascribing different mean-ings to it: one refers to water, the other to the TE equivalent. One need not, however, travel as far as TE to find examples of similar mental states differing in extension. Putnam testifies that he is unable to tell a beech from an elm: his mental image of the two is the same, yet the extensions, and the meanings, of 'elm' and 'beech' are quite different in his idiolect. Can Putnam refer to an elm though unable to identify one? His answer introduces the concept of the division of linguistic labour: it is sufficient that experts can distinguish an elm from a beech, and unnecessary that each member of the linguistic community be able to do so.

The assumption underlying the TE example is that words like 'water' always refer to the stuff we call 'water' in the actual world. Though it is neither analytic nor even irrevisable that water is H_2O, the extensions of 'water' on TE and on earth cannot be identical. To complete the account of meaning, one has to address the question of how extension is actually fixed. These aspects of Putnam's conception are related to Kripke's work on reference and rigid designation (see KRIPKE, S.A.; PROPER NAMES; REFERENCE §2), but while Kripke was thinking mainly of proper names, Putnam's concern is the meaning of scientific terms. If the extensions of these terms are fixed by the theories in which they figure, then extensions will be liable to change with theoretical change. This argument can be taken as an encapsulation of Kuhn's relativism: different theories refer to different entities, and are therefore incommensurable (see INCOMMENSURABILITY). Viewing it as a *reductio ad absurdum* of the theory of meaning on which it rests, Putnam recommends replacement of this theory with a variant of Kripke's causal theory of reference that emphasizes not only the causal relation between speakers and what they refer to, but also such social and pragmatic factors as shared stereotypes, reliance on experts, discretion and charity (see CONTENT: WIDE AND NARROW).

4 The philosophy of quantum mechanics

Heisenberg's uncertainty principle imposes a limit on the precision with which the values of certain pairs of physical parameters, such as position and momentum, or two spin components, can be measured simultaneously. On the Copenhagen interpretation, this principle implies that it is meaningless to ascribe simultaneous sharp values to such pairs of physical parameters, whether or not they are actually being measured. Since, however, when any one magnitude is measured separately, a sharp value is obtained, it appears that it is measurement itself which creates the transition, better known as the collapse, from the indeterminate to the well-defined state. If so, measurement does not reflect a state objectively existing prior to measurement, but points to a state of its own creation (see QUANTUM MEASUREMENT PROBLEM). Both the inference from the impossibility of measurement to the meaninglessness of concepts

and the non-classical understanding of measurement, offend the realist. In *The Logic of Quantum Mechanics*, Putnam proposed overcoming these difficulties by adopting a nonclassical logic first suggested in the context of quantum mechanics (QM) by Birkhoff and von Neumann in 1936, and developed by Finkelstein in the 1960s. The suggested logic is non-distributive – from $p \cdot (q_1 \vee q_2)$ we cannot, in general, conclude that $p \cdot q_1 \vee p \cdot q_2$. If p states that the system has a well-defined value p, of a physical magnitude P, and $q_1, q_2, \ldots, q_n$ describe all possible values of an incompatible quantity Q, then the uncertainty principle entails that $p \cdot q_i$ is false for any i. Yet, assuming that p obtains, (ascertained by measurement, say) we cannot conclude, as we classically would, that $q_1 \vee q_2 \vee \ldots q_n$ is false. In fact, while $p \cdot q_i$ is a quantum logical contradiction, $q_1 \vee q_2 \vee \ldots q_n$ is a quantum logical tautology. The magnitude Q always has a well-defined value, which its measurement will reveal, and no collapse is called for (see QUANTUM MECHANICS, INTERPRETATION OF; QUANTUM LOGIC).

In light of the traditional gulf between factual and logical truth, the idea that logic can be revised on the basis of empirical considerations is revolutionary. Putnam saw this situation as analogous to the merging of physics and geometry into an interdependent whole in the framework of general relativity.

Quantum logic raises several questions. First, it is not clear that it is a logic, a way of reasoning, rather than a calculus that happens to fit the structure of the Hilbert space of QM. Second, the idea that one can save realism by rejecting classical logic, generally seen as constitutive of realism, seems paradoxical. Though intended to strengthen the analogy with logic, Putnam's operational definition of the quantum-logical operators obscures the connection to realism. Third, work on the foundations of QM by theorists such as Kochen and Specker, and Bell, put unbearable strain on the realist interpretation of QM (see BELL'S THEOREM). Indeed, in *Quantum Mechanics and the Observer*, when Putnam had already moved away from his early realism, he assumed a verificationist understanding of quantum logic. The main point of that paper, however, is to argue for yet another interpretation of QM – perspectivism, attributed by Putnam to von Neumann. Like quantum logic, perspectivism is a way of avoiding the collapse of the wave-function upon measurement. Collapse, on this interpretation, is not a physical process but an epiphenomenon created by the shift from one perspective to another. Thus, when a system M performs a measurement on another system S, we can either view M as interfering with S from without, inducing a collapse of the wave-function of S, or view

S and M as a unified system obeying QM, and the external observer as interfering with it and making its wave-function collapse. Ultimately, Putnam argues, different perspectives are empirically equivalent and congruent with the predictions of QM; hence, they are equally legitimate. But perspectives exclude each other in the sense that statements belonging to different perspectives cannot be combined to form a quantum state. Realism can be sustained within each perspective, but not across perspectives. Though this seemed an attractive way to retain 'internal' realism while forgoing metaphysical realism, upon realizing that, in some cases, different perspectives are not empirically equivalent Putnam became dissatisfied with perspectivism.

5 Mathematics and necessary truth

Putnam did significant work in mathematics, collaborating with Martin Davis and Julia Robinson in the late 1950s on proving the unsolvability of Hilbert's tenth problem, which sought an algorithm deciding the solvability of diophantine equations. The proof was completed by Yuri Matiyasevich in 1970.

The nature of logical and mathematical truth has been one of Putnam's ongoing concerns, yielding several different positions. Throughout, he rejects the standard alternatives, platonism and conventionalism. The former, is, he maintains, given twentieth-century physics, obsolete; the latter, empty: as Carroll, Wittgenstein and Quine pointed out, conventions cannot ground logic because logic is required for their application (see MATHEMATICS, FOUNDATIONS OF). In 'It Ain't Necessarily So', Putnam proposed replacing necessary truth with the more flexible, context-dependent notion of relative necessity, in line with his suggestion, raised regarding QM, that logic is empirical. Later, in 'Analyticity and Apriority', he argued that at least some logical truths are constitutive of rationality and, as such, cannot be rationally criticized or revised. This view is further elaborated in *Rethinking Mathematical Necessity*, where Putnam represents logical truths as 'formal presuppositions of thought' rather than as truths in the ordinary sense (see ANALYTIC AND SYNTHETIC).

6 Functionalism

In a series of papers beginning in 1960, Putnam proposed a fresh approach to the philosophy of mind, functionalism, seeking to secure the autonomy of mind without positing a non-physical mind-substance. 'The question of the autonomy of our mental life does not hinge on and has nothing to do with that all too popular...question about matter or soul-stuff.

We could be made of Swiss cheese and it wouldn't matter' (1975b: 291). What matters, Putnam argued, is functional organization. Putnam's guiding analogy for functional organization was the computer (Turing machine). Evidently, different machines need not share the same hardware to carry out the same computation. Similarly, Putnam claimed, pain-states, or jealousy-states, can be functionally alike though physically different. In other words, each pain-token has a physico-chemical realization, but no reduction of the type, pain, to a given physico-chemical state is assumed. The computer analogy suggested that mental states are computational states, characterized syntactically, the projected research programme being to provide the 'software' for their interaction.

In the late 1970s, Putnam began to reconsider this proposal. First, there were considerations of meaning (§3). Thinking of something seems like a simple enough example of a mental state, but if, as Putnam argued, 'meanings just ain't in the head', then meanings cannot be identified with internal computational states. The response of some theorists, notably Fodor and Block, was to use the distinction between narrow and wide content, presented by Putnam in The Meaning of Meaning, to save the computational picture. While acknowledging the contribution of physical and cultural environment to meaning in the wide sense, they held on to computationalism with respect to meaning in the narrow sense. Putnam's concern over intentionality led him to reject this solution. As he argued in *Representation and Reality*, narrow-content computationalism is still an attempt to reduce the intentional to the non-intentional. But since even the ascription of meaning in the narrow sense involves interpretation, the attribution of beliefs, charity and reasonableness, eliminating intentionality is untenable. Functionalism had conceived the computational level as autonomous, that is, irreducible to, even if supervenient on, the physico-chemical level. Putnam's critique of functionalism makes an analogous point with regard to the autonomy of the mental *vis-à-vis* the computational (see COMPUTATIONAL THEORIES OF MIND; FUNCTIONALISM; REDUCTIONISM IN THE PHILOSOPHY OF THE MIND).

7 The incoherence of metaphysical realism

In 1976 Putnam's philosophy underwent a major shift; rejecting what he referred to as 'metaphysical' realism, he adopted 'internal' realism in its stead. The attack on metaphysical realism, first presented in the final chapter of *Meaning and the Moral Sciences* (1978) is elaborated on in *Models and Reality* and in *Reason, Truth and History* (1981).

Just as establishing the objectivity of reference was central to Putnam's earlier realism, the dispersion of reference into a plurality of possible relations is at the heart of his later criticism. The argument draws on model-theoretic considerations. The Löwenheim–Skolem theorem entails that a first-order theory, rich enough to contain arithmetic, does not determine its models up to isomorphism (see LÖWENHEIM–SKOLEM THEOREMS AND NON-STANDARD MODELS). Putnam extrapolates: even an ideal theory of the world, complying with all empirical and theoretical constraints, will not define a unique model, that is, a unique reference relation. In particular, causality, previously seen as anchoring language in reality, now becomes just another relation, and hence open to interpretation.

Putnam's point is not to embrace scepticism. His argument is that both the metaphysical realist who purports to have a theory of everything, including the 'correct' reference relation, and the sceptic who undertakes to refute that theory, are making the same mistake – they are assuming a non-existent vantage point external to any language or description-scheme. From the internal perspective, questions about reference cannot arise, 'chair' refers to chairs, 'cherry' to cherries. 'To speak as if *this* were my problem, "I know how to use my Language, but, now, how shall I single out an interpretation?" is to speak nonsense. Either the use *already* fixes the "interpretation" or *nothing* can' (1983: 24).

Another argument against scepticism is found in *Reason, Truth and History* (1981), where considerations of reference and intentionality lead Putnam to conclude that the sceptic's favourite fantasy – that we are all brains in a vat – is self-refuting (see SCEPTICISM). The repudiation of scepticism is a recurrent theme uniting Putnam's earlier and later work. The strategy, however, changes; Putnam's responses to Quine, who has also invoked the Löwenheim–Skolem theorem, illustrate these. Whereas Putnam initially tried to reduce indeterminacy by increasing the number of constraints on an adequate translation, he later came to see the problem itself as a sceptical variation on a misguided metaphysics.

8 Internal realism

Internal realism is also referred to by Putnam as 'pragmatic' or 'natural' realism. Like the American pragmatists, Putnam holds that commonsense realism, which he respects, requires no 'deeper' philosophical foundation. He also follows pragmatism in rejecting the fact/value dichotomy, and opposes moral relativism as firmly as he opposes cognitive relativism (see PRAGMATISM). A critic of reductionism and naturalism, he maintains that there are forms of nonscientific knowledge and that reason and morality cannot be naturalized. He distances himself from 'end of philosophy' philosophies, and seeks to renew philosophy so as to reconnect it with human challenges and aspirations.

Internal realism is meant to avoid the pitfalls of both metaphysical realism and relativism, but Putnam has been accused of slipping back into these polar positions. At one point he was close to identifying internal realism with verificationism, with long-term warranted assertibility replacing the notion of truth. Later he rejected this view, as well as other attempts to eliminate truth.

While a long philosophical tradition sees realism and antirealism as exhaustive alternatives, Kant, the American pragmatists, and Wittgenstein, all strove to overcome this dichotomy. Putnam identifies with the latter camp. In his earlier writings, he represented realism as a kind of explanatory hypothesis, on a par with scientific theories. Internal realism, however, is not intended to play an explanatory role. Wittgenstein's influence, and particularly, his suspicion of philosophical theories, is perceptible here, not only in the subtle similarity between the extended Löwenheim–Skolem theorem and the rule-following paradox, but also in the change of perspective that constitutes the response to these related problems. When we realize that internal realism is not an alternative theory but a call for a change of perspective, it emerges that much of Putnam's earlier work, far from being undermined by his later philosophy, finds its proper place within it.

See also: REFERENCE §§3–4

List of works

Most of Putnam's papers, and all of those cited in the text, are included in the collections – *Philosophical Papers, volumes I–III* and the two volumes edited by J. Conant. Where the title has been changed, the text cites the title appearing in these volumes.

Putnam, H. and Benacerraf, P. (eds) (1964) *Philosophy of Mathematics: Selected Readings*, New Jersey: Prentice Hall. (Introduction by the editors. Includes classic works in the foundations of mathematics and the philosophy of mathematics by leading mathematicians such as Hilbert, Brouwer and Gödel.)

Putnam, H. (1971) *Philosophy of Logic*, New York: Harper & Row. (Putnam argues for a realist position on the problem of the existence of mathematical objects.)

—— (1975a) *Philosophical Papers*, vol. I, *Mathematics, Matter and Method*, Cambridge and New York: Cambridge University Press. (This volume contains papers on the philosophy of mathematics and the philosophy of science. It includes 'It Ain't Necessarily So', which develops the notion of relative necessity, 'An Examination of Grünbaum's Philosophy of Geometry', which argues against a conventionalist interpretation of the theory of relativity, and 'The Logic of Quantum Mechanics', advocating quantum logic.)

—— (1975b) *Philosophical Papers*, vol. II, *Mind, Language and Reality*, Cambridge, and New York: Cambridge University Press. (This volume includes one of Putnam's major contributions to the philosophy of language, 'The Meaning of Meaning', as well as 'Explanation and Reference' and 'The Refutation of Conventionalism', all of which expound a realist conception of meaning. It also includes papers in the philosophy of mind, in particular papers introducing functionalism, such as 'Philosophy and Our Mental Life' and 'The Mental Life of Some Machines'.)

—— (1978) *Meaning and the Moral Sciences*, London: Routledge & Kegan Paul. (Part One contains the John Locke Lectures, Oxford 1976, which explore the interconnections between explanation, theories of truth, and realism. Part Two marks the change in Putnam's position from realism to 'internal realism'.)

—— (1981) *Reason, Truth and History*, Cambridge, and New York: Cambridge University Press. (The book propounds 'internal realism', arguing that it avoids the difficulties of metaphysical realism on the one hand, and scepticism on the other.)

—— (1983) *Philosophical Papers*, vol. III, *Realism and Reason*, Cambridge, and New York: Cambridge University Press. (This volume reworks many of the themes previously dealt with by Putnam in the light of his new position. It includes 'Models and Reality', which pursues the implications of the Löwenheim–Skolem theorem; 'Analyticity and Apriority: Beyond Wittgenstein and Quine', which rejects some sceptical consequences of Quine's and Wittgenstein's positions; 'Why Reason Can't Be Naturalized', which argues against naturalism; and 'Quantum Mechanics and the Observer', which argues for perspectivism, and abandons the earlier realist interpretation of quantum mechanics in terms of quantum logic.)

—— (1987) *The Many Faces of Realism*, La Salle, IL: Open Court. (The Paul Carus Lectures, Washington 1985. Putnam's 'internal realism' is examined here in the context of American pragmatism, in particular Peirce's philosophy.)

—— (1988) *Representation and Reality*, Cambridge, MA: MIT Press. (Putnam reconsiders functionalism, his early philosophy of mind, in the light of his views on meaning, and his critique of naturalism.)

—— (1990) *Realism with a Human Face*, ed. J. Conant, Cambridge, MA: Harvard University Press. (A collection of essays by Putnam, selected and introduced by the editor. The essays in this volume are divided into three groups: metaphysics; ethics and aesthetics; studies in American philosophy. The rejection of the fact/value dichotomy is a central theme of this collection.)

—— (1992) *Renewing Philosophy*, Cambridge, MA: Harvard University Press. (This book grew out of the Gifford Lectures, St Andrews 1990. It takes issue with scientism in several areas such as artificial intelligence and ethics, while maintaining the possibility of a cognitive relation to reality.)

—— (1994) *Words and Life*, ed. J. Conant, Cambridge, MA: Harvard University Press. (A collection of essays by Putnam, selected and introduced by the editor. Some of the essays in this volume, such as 'Rethinking Mathematical Necessity' reflect Putnam's growing attraction to the later Wittgenstein. Others discuss pragmatism, logical positivism, the philosophy of mind and the role of philosophy in our lives.)

—— (1995) *Pragmatism*, Cambridge, MA, and Oxford: Blackwell. (First published in Italian as *Il Pragmatismo: Una Questione Aperta*, Rome, Bari: Gius Laterza & Figli Spa, 1992. Putnam's version of pragmatism. Includes a bibliography.)

References and further reading

Hill, C.S. (ed.) (1992) 'The Philosophy of Hilary Putnam', *Philosophical Topics* 20 (1). (Essays by D.A. Anderson, A. Bilgrami, N. Chomsky, J. Conant, B. Dreben, G. Ebbs, R. Healey, G.J. Massey, J. McDowell, R.W. Miller, and A. Sidelle, and replies by Putnam.)

Clark, P. and Hale, B. (eds) (1994) *Reading Putnam*, Oxford: Blackwell. (Essays by S. Blackburne, G. Boolos, M. Dummett, M. Hallett, C. Fuhl and C. Glymour, M. Redhead, T. Ricketts, D. Wiggins, and C. Wright, and replies by Putnam.)

YEMIMA BEN-MENAHEM

PYRRHO (*c.*365–*c.*275 BC)

The Greek philosopher Pyrrho of Elis gave his name first to the most influential version of ancient scepticism

(*Pyrrhonism*), *and later to scepticism as such (pyrrhonism). Like Socrates, he wrote nothing, despite which – or thanks to which – he too became one of the great figures of philosophy. Although he has vanished behind his own legend, he must have helped nurture that legend: his unique personality palpably exercised an unequalled fascination on his acquaintances, and through them, on many others. We possess, thanks especially to Sextus Empiricus, extensive documentation of what can be called 'Neo-Pyrrhonian' scepticism, because from the time of Aenesidemus (first century BC) it invoked Pyrrho as its patron saint. But Pyrrho's own thought is hard to recover. The documentary evidence for him is mainly anecdotal, and the principal doxography is more or less directly dependent on his leading disciple Timon of Phlius, who managed to present himself as Pyrrho's mere 'spokesman', but who was in fact perhaps rather more than that. The main question, which is still unanswered, is whether Pyrrho was primarily or even solely a moralist, the champion of an ethical outlook based on indifference and insensibility, or whether he had already explicitly set up the weaponry of the sceptical critique of knowledge which underlies the epistemological watchword 'suspension of judgment'.*

1　Life
2　The legends
3　The key testimony

1　Life

According to Diogenes Laertius (IX 61–70), who is following a life of Pyrrho written around 225 BC by Antigonus of Carystus, Pyrrho had been an obscure painter before his studies, which were first with Bryson (probably the Megarian philosopher of that name), then with ANAXARCHUS. Anaxarchus was a companion to Alexander the Great on his Asian campaign, and brought Pyrrho along too. Alexander's biographers speak quite often of Anaxarchus, but never of Pyrrho. On his return to Greece, Pyrrho lived in the countryside near Elis, surrounded by a group of admirers, but hardly seeming a head of school.

The numerous anecdotes about him reveal a split between two concurrent images. On the one hand we hear of Pyrrho as an eccentric: indifferent towards himself as towards others, he leaves himself entirely unprotected, taking account neither of sensations nor of the beliefs which guide practical life (fr. 6). He behaves as a fakir (fr. 16) who recalls his encounters with the 'gymnosophists' or 'naked sages' of India (frs 1A, 10). He thus personifies a 'rustic' kind of scepticism, which subjects to 'suspension of judg-

ment' not only learned doctrines but also beliefs found in ordinary life.

A second image, endorsed by AENESIDEMUS, is of a Pyrrho who suspends judgment when philosophizing but does not lack foresight in his practical life (fr.7). He lives in a manner which is modest, peaceful and relatively conformist (fr. 14), along with his sister and his farmyard animals, highly esteemed by his fellow citizens (fr. 11). He thus stands for an 'urbane' scepticism, which outlaws all doctrinal assertions but leaves intact the instinctive beliefs of everyday life.

This duality no doubt nurtured the debate as to what was the Pyrrhonists' chief good (*telos*) (Diogenes Laertius IX 108): insensibility (*apatheia*) according to some, gentleness (*praotēs*) according to others. It is possible, moreover, that both the 'rustic' and the 'urbane' image had their roots in the complexity of one and the same personality, as illustrated by some anecdotes. For example, the story goes that Pyrrho once fled from a vicious dog, and, reproached for violating his own principles of indifference, replied 'It is difficult to strip yourself completely of being human' (fr. 15A–B). We should take it that his ambition really was to escape the human condition, but that he knew himself incapable of unfailingly achieving this.

2　The legends

More by his personality than by his ideas, no doubt, Pyrrho created a sensation: he gave the impression of having found a new way of being happy. A disciple, TIMON, asks him the secret of his superhuman serenity (frs 60–1). Another, Nausiphanes, reported that one of his own pupils used to question him eagerly about Pyrrho's conduct (fr. 28); the pupil's name was EPICURUS (§1). When Cicero speaks of Pyrrho, he never describes him as a sceptical critic of knowledge (despite having the opportunity to do so), but always as an absurdly rigorous moralist (frs 69A–M), even more radical than the extremist Stoics ARISTON OF CHIOS (§2) and Herillus. Pyrrho must, nevertheless, have cared as little about the difference between knowledge and ignorance as about anything else; Timon contrasts his tranquil lack of curiosity to 'the empty wisdom of the sophists' (fr. 60). Later, his condemnation of the branches of knowledge as useless could be presented as a way of condemning knowledge itself as impossible.

His chronological position inevitably favoured this metamorphosis. Aristotle's junior by twenty years, Pyrrho was still in his forties when Aristotle and his former pupil Alexander the Great both died (322 and 323 BC), that is, at the start of the Hellenistic age. He was a generation older than Epicurus and the Stoic

ZENO OF CITIUM, the founders of the two great new schools of this era (see EPICUREANISM; STOICISM). And he was two generations older than ARCESILAUS, who restored scepticism to the Platonic Academy. He was therefore perfectly placed to appear a pivotal thinker in the eyes of posterity. Just before him, Aristotle seemed to have brought to completion an era of intellectual audacity, in which thinkers had vied in cognitive ambitions without necessarily considering their multiple disagreements a fatal drawback; when they had discussed knowledge, they had tended to suppose that its existence and possibility went without saying, and instead set themselves the task of analysing its nature, its tools and its methods. After Pyrrho, on the other hand, and throughout Hellenistic philosophy, there was a concern as to whether we really do have cognitive access to the world: the new schools placed the problem of the 'criterion of truth' at the head of their agenda, and their solutions to it marked the crucial distinction between dogmatists and sceptics (HELLENISTIC PHILOSOPHY). It looks as if, in the intervening time, a radical new challenge to the very possibility of knowledge had been thrown down. When the author of this challenge is sought, Pyrrho emerges as the perfect candidate. One might even speak of a duel fought between Aristotle and Pyrrho. When Aristotle (*Metaphysics* IV) speaks of the manner of speech, thought and action to which those who deny the law of non-contradiction are condemned, he uses expressions which recur in the reports of Pyrrho's behaviour and in the formulas which he recommends using. It is as if Pyrrho had found a way to show that one could perfectly well live, speak and think in just the way Aristotle had said one could not (unless these coincidences were a later imposition designed to make Pyrrho look like the hero of an unprecedented philosophical rebellion.)

To correct this exaggerated portrayal, it is enough to notice that Pyrrho's contemporaries and successors, even the most enthusiastic of them, do not present him as an innovative theorist. Timon, despite doing more than anyone else to place him on a pedestal, nevertheless does not make him stand altogether alone: it is he who first assembles that gallery of ancestors (the Eleatics, Democritus, Protagoras and, above all, Xenophanes) which is thereafter associated with Pyrrho by the doxographers and authors of 'successions' (see DOXOGRAPHY).

Much later, from Aenesidemus to SEXTUS EMPIRICUS, Pyrrho's name reappeared in the titles of sceptical works (*Pyrrhonian Discourses, Pyrrhonian Sketches*) as emblematic of a scepticism senior to that of Arcesilaus and altogether uncontaminated by the New Academy: after long neglect, it became a prestigious flag to wave. In this late era little was still known about Pyrrho. It was in any case sensible for a Pyrrhonist to disavow that name, as did Theodosius (second century AD), who remarked that 'given that the movement of someone else's thought is undiscoverable, we will never know what Pyrrho's mental disposition was; and not knowing that, we could not label ourselves Pyrrhonists' (fr. 41). It is notable that Sextus' only response to this objection is the mild one that scepticism can be called Pyrrhonism 'owing to the fact that Pyrrho seems to us to have devoted himself to the activity of sceptical inquiry (*skepsis*) more solidly and manifestly than his predecessors' (fr. 40) (see PYRRHONISM).

One may wonder, in the circumstances, whether Pyrrho's posthumous fate does not result from a sort of collage: the overwhelming originality of his ethical message, immediately recognized and celebrated, seemed to demand as its complement a radical critique of epistemology. This latter may have been bestowed on him retrospectively, in the way that philosophers often get saddled with the real or imagined consequences, or premises, of their ideas.

3 The key testimony

It would clearly be presumptuous, and would perhaps make little sense, to pretend to reconstitute the 'real' Pyrrho behind, or in front of, his multiple reflections. Reale (1981) has distinguished no fewer than eight defensible types of interpretation of Pyrrho's philosophy. Some separate him only narrowly, others widely, from the epistemological and phenomenalist scepticism of the neo-Pyrrhonists. For some he is above all an ascetic proponent of indifference; for others a nihilistic theorist of pure appearance and radical critic of all ontology. Such diversity is all the more surprising given the existence of a text (fr. 53) universally considered the centrepiece of Pyrrho's doxography, and respectable as much for its pedigree (it is cited by Eusebius from the late first century BC philosopher Aristocles, who himself drew its substance, if not its letter, from Timon) as for its content: an overview of Pyrrho's philosophical project. Clear and instructive in appearance, at a first reading this text seems to attest that Pyrrhonism does indeed have a fundamentally ethical goal, and that there are two closely linked means to its achievement: practical indifference and abstention from judgment, the latter going hand in hand with a complete disqualification of the ordinary instruments of knowledge. But the articulation of these different elements raises difficulties; and by scrutiny of the text we may be able to perform a task widely judged by interpreters to be impossible or useless: to separate Pyrrho's original message from Timon's own contribution.

Anyone who is on the verge of being happy, says Timon, should consider three questions: what the nature of things is, how we should be disposed towards them, and what benefit those who adopt this attitude will derive from it. The sequence of these three questions is itself puzzling: no latter-day sceptic would inquire about 'the nature of things' before asking himself whether we can know it. Pyrrho nevertheless does ask this; and he replies – in the one phrase of the text which Timon expressly attributes to him – that 'things are entirely undifferentiated, undetermined and undecided'. This no doubt means that it is we who introduce the differences which appear to us to distinguish them (fr. 64). But what differences? He might mean all differences, including those of colour and so on as much as those between values. Or he might mean only these latter. Another summary (fr. 1A) has Pyrrho saying 'that nothing is fair or foul, just or unjust, and that likewise in every case nothing is really (this or that), and that it is by custom and habit that people do everything they do; for nothing is any more this than that'. These generalizations seem restricted to the sphere of practical ethics.

Aristocles' summary, after characterizing 'things' as 'undifferentiated', strangely adds that 'for this reason, our sensations and beliefs are neither true nor false'. Here again, a latter-day sceptic would say otherwise, indeed the reverse: that our sensations and beliefs are untrustworthy, and that therefore 'things' are in their nature undifferentiated. Some have even emended the text to make it say this. However, once we notice that the grammar of the text attributes this bizarre inference to Timon, not to Pyrrho himself, we may prefer not to emend it, but to see in its very incongruity the traces of Timon's own intervention, a somewhat clumsy epistemological graft onto the original Pyrrhonian trunk.

The second point on the Pyrrhonian agenda admittedly does not help much with testing this hypothesis. In the face of undifferentiated 'things', the attitude that we should take is that of respecting their non-differentiation: we must be 'unopinionated, uninclined, undisturbed' either positively or negatively towards anything. These expressions can be interpreted as describing a refusal to affirm, just as much as a refusal to choose. And the same equivocation between theory and practice persists in the description of the discourse that goes with this behaviour: it is appropriate to say, of each thing, that 'it is no more (this or that) than it is not it', or again (no doubt with the implication 'if it is necessary at all costs to say something positive or negative') that it is appropriate immediately to negate our assertion, saying that 'it is (this or that) and at the same time that it is not it', or

that 'it neither is (this or that) nor is not it'. These expressions are remarkable; but they do not make it clear whether 'this or that' covers all possible predicates, or only those which, like 'desirable' and 'undesirable', concern the sphere of action.

One who is 'on the verge of being happy' must last consider – and this is the final phase of the Pyrrhonian programme – 'what will happen to those who are disposed thus' (that is, 'without opinions' and so on, as already defined). Whoever is reformed by Pyrrhonian training, says Timon, will achieve first *aphasia* (not in its modern sense of mutism, but a sort of non-assertive, non-committal use of language), then *ataraxia* (complete lack of disturbance, perfect unworriedness). It is worth noticing that the attainment of this benefit is here described as predictable. In later Pyrrhonism (Sextus Empiricus, *Outlines of Pyrrhonism* I 28–9), and already in Timon (Diogenes Laertius IX 107), there was to be on the contrary an insistence that *ataraxia* results unexpectedly, by a happy chance, from suspension of judgment. Might this difference not be the result of the epistemological graft hypothesized above? That *ataraxia* should result from practical indifference makes sense: freed of all preferences, we will no longer undergo the feelings which upset us. But that *ataraxia* should result from suspension of judgment makes less sense: the renunciation of all certainty might seem, on the contrary, to condemn us to everlasting anxiety. The appeal to 'happy chance', an innovation on the rational planning offered by Pyrrho's programme, may therefore reflect the new complexity introduced into the sceptic's itinerary by the epistemological detour. If this analysis of the key testimony in Aristocles is correct, we are entitled to say, even more firmly than before, that Pyrrho was not the first of the Pyrrhonists.

References and further reading

Ausland, H.W. (1989) 'On the Moral Origin of the Pyrrhonian Philosophy', *Elenchos* 10: 359–434. (A strongly ethical interpretation of Pyrrho's thought.)

Bett, R. (1994) 'Aristocles on Timon on Pyrrho: the text, its logic, and its credibility', *Oxford Studies in Ancient Philosophy* 12: 137–81. (An acute reading of the key testimony, contemporary and independent from Brunschwig (1994).)

Brochard, V. (1887) *Les Sceptiques grecs*, Paris: Alcan; repr. 1923. (A classic which has aged well; includes the first systematically presented ethical interpretation of Pyrrho.)

Brunschwig, J. (1994) 'Once Again on Eusebius on Aristocles on Timon on Pyrrho', in *Papers in Hellenistic Philosophy*, Cambridge: Cambridge University Press, 190–211. (Defends the interpretation favoured in §3 of the entry.)

* Diogenes Laertius (c. early 3rd century BC) *Lives of the Philosophers*, trans. R.D. Hicks, *Diogenes Laertius' Lives of Eminent Philosophers*, Loeb Classical Library, Cambridge, MA: Harvard University Press and London: Heinemann, 1925, 2 vols. (See IX 61–108 for a life of Pyrrho, which includes an extensive doxography on neo-Pyrrhonism.)

Flintoff, E. (1980) 'Pyrrho and India', *Phronesis* 25: 88–108. (Investigates possible Indian philosophical influences on Pyrrho.)

Giannantoni, G. (ed.) (1981) *Lo scetticismo antico* (Ancient Scepticism), Naples: Bibliopolis, 2 vols. (Important collection of articles, with a full bibliography on ancient scepticism, 1880–1978.)

Hankinson, R.J. (1995) *The Sceptics*, London and New York: Routledge. (The best modern book-length study.)

Long, A.A. and Sedley, D.N. (1987) *The Hellenistic Philosophers*, Cambridge: Cambridge University Press, 2 vols. (Volume 1 contains translations of the principal sources, with philosophical commentary (Early Pyrrhonism, pages 13–24). Volume 2 contains Greek and Latin texts with notes and bibliography (Early Pyrrhonism, pages 1–17). An outstanding work in all respects.)

* Pyrrho (c.365–c.275 BC) Fragments, ed. F. Decleva Caizzi, *Pirrone – Testimonianze*, Naples: Bibliopolis, 1981. (Standard edition of the testimonies on Pyrrho from which his fragments are cited; includes Italian translation and valuable commentary.)

* Reale, G. (1981) 'Ipotesi per una rilettura della filosofia di Pirrone di Elide' (Hypothesis on a Rereading of the Philosophy of Pyrrho of Elis), in G. Giannantoni (ed.), *Lo scetticismo antico*, Naples: Bibliopolis, 1981, vol. 1, 243–336. (Useful critical survey of interpretations, with an attempted genealogy of the paradoxes of a Janus-faced Pyrrho who is both dogmatic moralist and sceptic.)

Robin, L. (1944) *Pyrrhon et le scepticisme grec* (Pyrrho and Greek Scepticism), Paris: Presses Universitaires de France; repr. New York: Garland, 1980. (Careful and balanced study.)

Stopper, M.R. (1983) 'Schizzi pirroniani' (Pyrrhonist Sketches), *Phronesis* 28: 265–97. (Important review of Giannantoni (1981), in English, with powerful defence of the traditional 'neo-Pyrrhonian' interpretation of Pyrrho.)

JACQUES BRUNSCHWIG

PYRRHONISM

Pyrrhonism was the name given by the Greeks to one particular brand of scepticism, that identified (albeit tenuously) with Pyrrho of Elis, who was said (by his disciple Timon of Phlius) to have declared that everything was indeterminable and accordingly to have suspended judgment about the reality of things – in particular whether they were really good or bad. After Timon's death Pyrrhonism lapsed, until revived by Aenesidemus. Aenesidemus held that it was inadmissible either to affirm or to deny that anything was really the case, and in particular to hold, with the Academic sceptics, that certain things really were inapprehensible. Instead, the Sceptic (the capital letter denotes the Pyrrhonists, who adopted the term, literally 'inquirer', as one of the designations for their school) should only allow that things were no more the case than not, or only so under certain circumstances and not under others. Aenesidemean Scepticism took the form of emphasizing the disagreement among both lay people and theoreticians as to the nature of things, and the fact that things appear differently under different circumstances (the various ways of doing this were systematized into the Ten Modes of Scepticism); the result was meant to be suspension of judgment about such matters, which would in turn lead to tranquillity of mind. Thus 'Scepticism' denotes a particular philosophical position, not simply, as in modern usage, that of any philosopher inclined towards doubt. Later Pyrrhonists, notably Agrippa, refined the Sceptical method and concentrated on undermining the dogmatic (that is, anti-Sceptical) notion of the criterion – there is no principled way to settle such disputes without resorting to mere assertion, infinite regress or circularity. We owe to Sextus Empiricus our most complete account of Pyrrhonian argument and the clearest exposition of the Pyrrhonian attitude. Faced with endemic dispute, Sceptics reserve judgment; but this does not render life impossible for them, since they will still react to the way things appear to be, although without believing in any strong sense that things really are as they seem. Furthermore, when Pyrrhonians describe their affective states, they do so undogmatically – and the Sceptical slogans ('I determine nothing', 'nothing is apprehended', and so on) are to be understood in a similar way, as merely reporting a state of mind and not expressing a commitment. Thus the slogans apply to themselves, and like cathartic drugs are themselves purged along with the noxious humour of dogmatism.

1 History
2 The Ten Modes of Scepticism
3 The Sceptical slogans

1   History

Greek scepticism is inextricably associated with the name of Pyrrho; the ancients themselves dubbed the most enduring and interesting form of scepticism of their times 'Pyrrhonism' after its eponymous origin. Yet surprisingly little is known about Pyrrho the man, and it is possible that he was not even a Sceptic (in the strict sense of the term) at all (see PYRRHO §3). He lived from *c.*365 to *c.*275 BC, and his name became a byword for philosophical detachment from the ordinary concerns of life. Legend has it that his friends had to prevent him from walking over cliffs and under passing traffic; this and other amusing if apocryphal stories are recorded in the biography by Diogenes Laertius. He wrote nothing, and most of what we know of him derives from the writings of his disciple and amanuensis TIMON. According to Timon, Pyrrho held that to be happy we must confront three questions: How are things by nature? What attitude should we adopt towards them? What will be the outcome for those who have this attitude? He answered that all things were equally indifferent, unmeasurable and undecidable, and that our perceptions told us neither truths nor falsehoods about the way things really are. The upshot of this is that we should be free of all opinion and commitment. The proper attitude to anything is to suppose that it no more (*ou mallon*) is the case than not. As a result we should simply acquiesce in the way things appear without having any strong beliefs concerning the way they actually are.

These remained the characteristic attitudes of Pyrrhonism throughout its history. However, original though Pyrrho undoubtedly was (even if the tradition suggests that he learned philosophical detachment from Indian philosophers while following Alexander the Great's expedition with ANAXARCHUS), his scepticism was not entirely without precedent. Ever since XENOPHANES (§5), Greek thinkers had puzzled over the nature and scope of human knowledge, and whether it was genuinely possible. Some fragments of DEMOCRITUS in particular suggest a cautious attitude to the possibility of human understanding, and DEMOCRITUS (§3) employed the formula 'no more' on occasion to indicate a sceptical refusal to commit himself one way or the other on some question. Moreover, Aristotle is clearly aware of sceptical challenges to our ability to rely upon our senses (*Metaphysics* IV 4–5), although he dismisses them as mere captiousness (it is possible that he knew of Pyrrho's scepticism).

There is no hint of a concerted and systematic attempt to question our justification for belief in the natures of things before Pyrrho, however. Indeed Pyrrho himself may not have mounted a general assault on the reliability of the senses (although Timon evidently did), so much as a limited attack on our pretensions to ethical knowledge, or, more generally, knowledge of matters of value; in later antiquity, Pyrrho's name was certainly associated primarily with ethical (in the broad Greek sense) issues; and it was principally as a role model for a certain way of life, one in which tranquillity is to be achieved by a refusal to allow oneself strong commitments of any kind, that Pyrrho's fame was maintained in later antiquity.

After Timon's death Pyrrhonism as such died out, although the New Academy of ARCESILAUS and CARNEADES kept alive the sceptical tradition for the next two centuries, in the course of their long and tortuous epistemological conflict with the Stoics. The latter held that empirical certainty was attainable, on the basis of 'apprehensive' impressions whose clarity and distinctness were assurances of their truth (see STOICISM §12); the Academic sceptics countered by arguing that there was no true impression that was such that there could not be a false one indistinguishable from it in all internal characteristics: consequently, there was no criterion by which to judge whether or not an impression was indeed apprehensive.

By the first century BC both sides had so modified their positions as a result of the dialectical sparring that it was becoming increasingly difficult to tell the two schools apart, so much so that when (a little after 90 BC) PHILO OF LARISSA relaxed Academic strictures against the possibility of knowledge, ANTIOCHUS seceded from the Academy altogether and adopted a position very similar to the Stoics. Reacting against this dilution of the pure sceptical spirit, AENESIDEMUS re-founded Pyrrhonism. Aenesidemus' works are all lost, but a ninth-century summary of his eight-volume *Pyrrhonian Discourses* by Photius survives, which allows us to recreate something of its flavour. The target of his attack was the belief that apprehension, or secure knowledge of the nature of things, was ever attainable. Nobody really knows how things are, yet everybody but the Pyrrhonists claims to do so, wasting their time in futile, dogmatic bickering. Indeed, from this time on 'dogmatic' as applied to a philosopher or philosophical view, carries the connotation 'non-Sceptical': a dogmatist is anyone who professes belief in *dogmata*; and a *dogma* is, according to SEXTUS EMPIRICUS, an 'assent to one of the non-evident objects of scientific inquiry' (*Outlines of Pyrrhonism* I 13). Such matters are 'non-evident' precisely because they go beyond what is strictly contained in the appearances, the *phainomena*, themselves.

Aenesidemus apparently held that there was as a matter of fact no apprehension of things. He sought to distinguish this position from that of the sceptical Academy on the grounds that they (according to him) were prepared actually to affirm certain things absolutely, notably that apprehension was impossible; by contrast Aenesidemus' position is provisional – he has no apprehension *now*, but apprehension might yet be possible. Even so, the appropriate Pyrrhonian attitude to things is to say that they are no more so than not so, or sometimes so and sometimes not so, or so for some people and not for others. Thus Aenesidemus appears to allow a form of relativism. Relativism and Pyrrhonism are incompatible however: relativism positively asserts that there is no genuine fact of the matter, a relativist in ethics appealing to the facts of cultural divergence (as indeed will the Pyrrhonist); but while the relativist will conclude that there is no such thing as an objective good, or right and wrong, the Pyrrhonist will simply infer that we do not know whether any things are genuinely good, and, if any, which. The Pyrrhonist makes no metaphysical claims about the ontological status of such 'objects'; and hence when Aenesidemus says that some things are one way for some people and otherwise for others, he is not asserting that things *really* are that way – this is simply a report of how things seem to be.

2 The Ten Modes of Scepticism

Fundamental to the Pyrrhonists' method was the collection of cases in which things seem different under different circumstances. They appear differently to people as opposed to animals (muddy water appeals to pigs but not to us: Sextus Empiricus, *Outlines of Pyrrhonism* I 56), to different groups of people ('Indians enjoy different things from us': I 80), to different sense-modalities ('Paintings seem bumpy to vision, smooth to touch': I 92), and to the same sense-modality on different occasions ('Honey seems sweet to the healthy, bitter to the jaundiced': I 101). These are examples of the first four of the Ten Modes of Scepticism. Many of the examples retailed in the modes are Greek commonplaces, deriving from much earlier times (some may be found in Aristotle; and one of Sextus' examples of the first mode – that sea water is poisonous to humans but nourishing to fish – is drawn from HERACLITUS (§3)). What is important is the systematic way in which they are collected, and

the use to which they are put. Aenesidemus may well have been the first to collect the material and organize it into ten separate modes (although this is controversial); in any event, a generation or so later, in the time of Philo of Alexandria (one of our major sources for the modes; see PHILO OF ALEXANDRIA §1), they were firmly associated with Pyrrhonian Scepticism.

A mode (*tropos*) in this sense is a general pattern of argument, for which any number of specific instances may be found. The basic structure of all of the modes is simple and lucid. Sextus describes Pyrrhonism as a 'capacity for opposition' (*Outlines of Pyrrhonism* I 8): arguments are opposed to arguments, appearances to appearances, and arguments to appearances (I 8–9, 31–3). Whenever the issue goes beyond how things seem to particular individuals (that is, the way things *really* are), there is, the Pyrrhonists note, an 'undecidable disagreement' about the matter. Moreover, that dispute is undecidable because of the unavailability of any generally accepted means of resolving it, any criterion in the technical Greek sense (see §5). And in default of that, the Pyrrhonist urges, there is no reason to prefer one of the appearances to another, and hence we should not commit ourselves to any of them: we should suspend judgment about them (see §4). All the modes, then, share the following basic form:

(1) *x* appears *F* relative to *a*

(2) *x* appears *F** relative to *b*

(3) at most one of '*x* is *F*' and '*x* is *F**' can be (objectively) true

(4) no uncontroversial decision procedure tells decisively either for '*x* is *F*' or for '*x* is *F**' so

(5) we should suspend judgment as to what *x* is really like.

The range of *x* (for example, 'sea water' in the Heraclitus case) is broad and varies from mode to mode, as do the predicates covered by the variables *F* and *F**; what substitutes for *a* and *b* is determined by the particular nature of each mode (thus in the first mode '*a*' will be humans, '*b*' other animals, fish for example; in the second *a* and *b* will be different individuals or groups of humans; and so on for the other modes). The substituends for *F* and *F** must be incompatible predicates (for example, 'poisonous' and 'nourishing'), and since they are incompatible, (3) follows trivially. Then, on the supposition that (4) can be made good, (5) follows on reasonable assumptions about rationality.

Sextus Empiricus, our main source for the modes, spends most of his time collecting examples of (1) and (2) for each of his different modes. The first four he labels 'modes from the judger': that is, the various types of opposition are to do with variations in the individuals observing them. Modes 'from both judger and judged' include the fifth, which notes that the appearance of things varies according to the distance and standpoint from which they are viewed (this is the source of the hardy philosophical perennial that a straight oar looks bent in water: *Outlines of Pyrrhonism* I 119), and the ninth notes that our appreciation of things differs according to how familiar we are with them (naked bodies become unexciting after a while: I 142). The seventh and tenth modes are labelled 'from the thing judged' (although in the latter case it is hard to see why); the seventh is to do with supposed variations in the constitutions of things which are observed under various conditions (thus the filings of black horn look white: I 129), and it is very hard to see what Sceptical leverage such considerations might have; the tenth is the mode 'mainly concerned with ethics, having to do with ways of life, habits, laws, mythical beliefs and dogmatic suppositions' (I 145), in which Sextus collects with evident enthusiasm examples of cultural diversity ('Indians copulate in public': I 143; 'Persians marry their mothers': I 152). These examples are multiplied in a later, more general treatment of ethics (I 3 168–238).

The tenth mode in particular emphasizes an important issue. The proper Pyrrhonian conclusion from the facts of ethical diversity is, according to Sextus at least, that we cannot know whether or not anything is good or bad by nature (I 163, III 235); yet the ethical relativist will equally appeal to precisely the same examples in order to ground the different and incompatible conclusion that *nothing* is good or bad *by nature*: there simply are no fundamental facts about value. The Pyrrhonist avoids this move because it too is a species of dogmatism, albeit negative in form. Different people disagree; and that is all there is to it. For all we know there may be actual absolute values. The relativist, negative conclusion is just as unwarranted as its positive dogmatic opponent. Just as the Pyrrhonists will not say that everything is inapprehensible (although allowing that nothing actually seems to be apprehended: see §1), neither will they absolutely deny the existence of objective values.

Similarly, when propounding the eighth mode, the 'mode of relativity', the Pyrrhonist only affirms that everything *appears* to be relative (I 135), although (as Sextus notes elsewhere: I 39), relativity is in fact at the core of all of the modes' procedures (as (1) and (2) above make clear). Thus there is no second-order commitment to the *truth* of the claim that everything is relative; even that is a matter of appearances.

3 The Sceptical slogans

This is the core of the Pyrrhonian position. Pyrrhonists liked to sum up their philosophy in pithy slogans (such as 'I determine nothing': *Outlines of Pyrrhonism* I 197): but this merely means 'I am now so affected as neither to affirm nor deny dogmatically any of the subjects under investigation'. Equally, 'Everything is inapprehensible' only means 'All the non-evident subjects of dogmatic inquiry which I have investigated seem to me inapprehensible' (I 200), and similar caveats apply to 'to each argument an equal argument is opposed' (I 202–3), and *ou mallon*: 'the phrase "no more this than that" expresses our affection, by which we end up in equipoise because of the equal strength of opposing matters' (I 120). The end result is suspension of judgment, or *epochē* (stage (5) see §2 above); even then, the Pyrrhonist is careful to say only that matters *appear* equally balanced (I 196), while Sceptical *aphasia*, or non-assertion, is 'an affection of ours because of which we neither affirm nor deny anything' (I 192); moreover, its scope covers only 'what is said dogmatically in regard to things non-evident, since we yield to those things which move us affectively and force us necessarily to assent' (I 193).

Pyrrhonists, then, can say how things seem to be to them, and report the way they are affected; they live their lives according to those appearances, but 'undogmatically', that is, without any commitment to their underlying truth. Furthermore, the 'Sceptical expressions' such as 'I determine nothing' apply to themselves; for the Pyrrhonist, unlike some varieties of relativist, there is no privileged meta-language in which unalloyed second-order truths can be expressed: it is Scepticism all the way down. Thus Pyrrhonism manages to avoid being (at least in any damaging sense) self-refuting, precisely, if paradoxically, because the Sceptical slogans apply to themselves: Sextus compares them to purgative drugs which eliminate themselves along with the 'noxious humours' which are their object (I 206).

4 The criterion, signs and proof

The Ten Modes of Scepticism are ascribed by Sextus to 'the older Sceptics' (*Outlines of Pyrrhonism* I 36). By contrast, a set of five modes, more general in scope, is attributed by him to 'the more recent Sceptics' (I 164). Although in Sextus' presentation each of the ten modes concludes with suspension of judgment, the arguments by which that is supposed to commend itself are not spelled out in detail; the final steps of the basic schema outlined in §2 still require elucidation.

The modes of Agrippa organize the Sceptical material rather differently: two modes emphasize, in general terms, disagreement and the relativity of appearances, while the other three aver that any attempt to resolve the dispute will result either in mere assertion, infinite regress or circularity (see AGRIPPA). These three formal modes are in evidence throughout Sextus' presentation of Pyrrhonian argument; and they ultimately give the reasons why oppositions of the sort collected by the ten modes result in *epochē*. But, as Sextus was well aware, this is tricky, since elsewhere Pyrrhonists cast doubt on the validity of argument itself. If proof is doubtful, why imagine that (1)–(4) should entail (5)? Crucially, Sextus nowhere relies on the success of that entailment. Rather, perfectly consistently, he simply describes his own affective states. Persistent disputes of the sort gathered by the ten modes, and the persistent appearance that everything is relative, cause him to suspend judgment about things; but that too is simply an appearance, albeit an appearance of his own mental states, which he is at perfect liberty (non-dogmatically) to express.

Moreover, Pyrrhonian arguments are dialectical, directed against the various schools of dogmatists. If dogmatists believe in such things as proof, then they must, by their own lights, accept the Sceptics' arguments (if they are valid). The Sceptics, by contrast, are not obliged to accept them, and do not do so (although they do not reject them either); but since they do not suffer from dogmatic belief they have no need of them. The bulk of book II of *Outlines of Pyrrhonism* is taken up with such issues – and Sextus opens the argument with a vigorous defence of the salubrity of the Sceptic's procedure of investigating dogmatic doctrines on their own terms (II 1–12): the Sceptic can understand the content of the dogmatist's claims without being committed to it, and can thus point out what should (to the dogmatist) appear to be inconsistencies; and if there are such apparent inconsistencies, dogmatists themselves should abandon their own positions. All of the argument here concerns the criterion.

A criterion is, literally, something that judges: a touchstone. Criteria are standardly, in Hellenistic philosophy and after, divided into criteria of truth (means of judging true from false propositions) and criteria of action (ways to decide how best to behave). The Academics, in their battle with the Stoics (see §1), had denied the existence of the former, while allowing that the latter were still available. Sextus seeks to cast doubt on all of the former, by the standard Pyrrhonian means of contrasting what differing dogmatic schools (primarily the Stoics and the Epicureans) had to say about the issue, as well as by

pointing to internal difficulties in their several accounts. Thus Academic arguments are retailed against the Stoic criterion of the 'apprehensive impression', but not in order to show positively that there is no such thing (II 79).

Perhaps most characteristic is the claim that, since the existence of a criterion is itself a matter of dispute, it too requires a criterion to resolve it: but none is available, except on pain of infinite regress or circularity (II 20, 34–5). Given ubiquitous dispute, we might look for majority agreement, but that is hardly to be found, and even if it were would be no guarantee of the truth (you can fool almost all of the people some of the time, as the Stoics themselves allowed): Sextus employed similar considerations in discussion of the second of the ten modes (I 87–9); and elsewhere he refuses even to allow that universal agreement on an assertion is enough to show that it is true, since present consensus is no guarantee that future disagreements will not crop up (I 33–4).

Here an earlier issue resurfaces. What is wrong with adopting the Protagorean position that everyone is judge and jury in their own case? (See PROTAGORAS §3.) Exactly that, Sextus thinks: criteria should be independent. But why? Once again it is vital to place Sextus' argumentation in its dialectical context. Again and again, he will claim that some dispute, or opposition among arguments, or disagreement about appearances, is sufficient to induce *epochē* 'concerning how things are absolutely and in their real nature' (for example, *Outlines of Pyrrhonism* I 135). He is here relying upon what had become a commonplace of non-Sceptical metaphysics, namely that if something possesses a property essentially, it must do so under all circumstances and in all conditions; but surely the irremediable variability of appearances casts doubt upon our ability to infer to such properties; and if that commonplace is to be given a strong construal, the mere fact that nothing appears the same under all circumstances is enough to show that none of its apparent properties is, in this sense, real. Once more, that conclusion is presented as being something the dogmatist is forced, willy-nilly, to accept; the Pyrrhonist, of course, simply suspends judgment.

All of this is powerful and pointed; and it is backed up by the Sceptical attack on signs in general and proofs in particular. In the latter case, Sextus seeks to show that, on their own account, dogmatic conceptions of proof are self-stultifying (his principal target here is Stoic logic, his method to show that, on the Stoics' own account of the truth-conditions for the conditional, every proof will contain a redundant conditional premise; and yet redundancy is, on the Stoics' own account, invalidating) (II 159). More generally, Sextus argues that the dogmatists' 'indicative sign' cannot fulfil its supposed function (Sextus is however, perfectly happy to allow the existence of commemorative signs, whereby one evident phenomenon serves as a sign of some other, temporarily non-evident, phenomenon, on the basis of past experience). An indicative sign was defined as 'an antecedent in a sound conditional which serves to reveal the consequent' (II 101), where the consequent is something by nature non-evident (as sweating, in the dogmatists' stock example, is supposed to reveal the existence of invisible pores in the skin). But, the Sceptics urge, if what is signified is such as never to be evident, how can we know that it has been so revealed?

5 Cause and explanation: Sceptical physics

Dogmatists may reply that perhaps the phenomena are such that there is only one possible set of underlying circumstances which could account for them (as is alleged in the sweating-pores case). The atomists held that it was only on the assumption that the world was fundamentally composed of atoms and the void that evident facts of experience (such as the existence of motion) could be explained (see ATOMISM, ANCIENT; DEMOCRITUS §2; EPICUREANISM §2): perhaps such quasi-transcendental inferences really can take us indubitably to the heart of things. But the Sceptics simply respond that there is no reason to think that there are any such valid inferences – after all, most physical theorists reject the atomist inference from motion to the void.

Such considerations formed the core of a set of eight modes against the aetiologists, attributed to Aenesidemus. These modes consist of a set of general Sceptical reflections on the limitations of explanation: 'The first is that according to which... aetiology in general, being concerned with non-evident things, has no agreed confirmation'; 'The second shows that frequently when there are many ways of assigning an explanation to what is being investigated, some of them account for it one way only' (*Outlines of Pyrrhonism* I 181). That is, there is no general way in which we can determine the truth (if any) of non-evident matters, since they tend to be susceptible to different interpretations. The fourth mode further notes that dogmatists assume, unfoundedly, that the micro-mechanisms to which they 'infer' will be, in general, much like their phenomenal counterparts; furthermore, all theorists are inclined to overlook awkward recalcitrant facts, as well as contradicting the evidence and sometimes themselves, and in general begging the question in favour of their own position.

Aenesidemus' eight modes attack dogmatic scientific methodology. Elsewhere (III 13–30) Sextus retails more general arguments designed to cast doubt on the coherence of the notions of cause and explanation (some of these arguments mirror those against signs from the previous book). Causes must either precede their effects, or be concurrent with them, or succeed them. The last option is absurd; and cause and effect are relative, so one cannot precede the other; yet a cause is supposed to be productive of something, and hence must precede what it is productive of. This is just one of a battery of arguments Sextus rehearses here and elsewhere (for example, *Against the Professors* IX 210–51): he also urges that causes should invariably bring about their effects, and yet everything dogmatists refer to as a cause is defeasible; thus not even fire can really be of a nature to burn since it will not burn everything under all circumstances). Sextus then uses the apparent results of the attack on causation to undermine the rest of dogmatic physics: body is that which can act and be acted upon (*Outlines of Pyrrhonism* III 38), so if there is no agency, there is no body either (and out with it go a host of related notions such as limit, surface and solidity); and equally doomed are the nest of concepts relating to change (motion, increase, rest, and so on), while if these go, so do the ideas of addition and subtraction, and with them arithmetic and the concepts of part and whole.

6 The Sceptical end

Most of Sextus' argument is devoted to attacking dogmatic concepts, yet he never loses sight of the overall goal of the Pyrrhonian procedure of constructing a dispute – it is just that the vast majority of people (and not just dogmatic theorists) believe in the existence of bodies, motion, and so on, and consequently that arm of the disagreement needs little support. Thus, first appearances notwithstanding, all of this is consistent with the general aim of Pyrrhonism. None the less, the question remains: why bother? Why should Pyrrhonists concern themselves at such length with refuting dogmatists, not to mention the views of ordinary people? The latter case is in fact particularly pointed, since Sextus frequently says that he has no quarrel with ordinary views and that he sides with life. Why, then, try to argue that motion is non-existent? Furthermore, while Sextus will on occasion argue that not even fire is warm by nature, elsewhere he will contrast the case of fire with that of ethical values, saying that the latter would have to be like fire if they were to be natural properties (*Outlines of Pyrrhonism* III 179); surely that is simple inconsistency?

The answers to these questions are controversial, but the following account seems at least coherent. Sextus does not conceive of argument in the ordinary philosophical way as entailing (or at the very least rationally buttressing) conclusions. As seen in §5, he is perfectly happy to argue against argument. Rather arguments affect us in just the same way as phenomenal appearances do; and we may, non-dogmatically, report those effects. Thus, when confronted with an equally balanced pile of considerations on both sides of an issue, I do not *conclude* that it is *rational* to suspend judgment: rather *epochē* just happens to me. Furthermore, Sextus characterizes Sceptics as perpetual investigators: why should they need to go on investigating once they have attained *epochē*? The answer is precisely that *epochē* is not rationally inferred by argument: rather it is a state, and one that is in constant need of replenishment; moreover the Sceptic goes on investigating in response to the way things seem.

Sceptics of all stripes were greatly concerned to evade the charge that life without belief (at least dogmatic belief that things *really* are thus and so) was impossible, since belief is a necessary condition for action. Dogmatic belief, Sceptics claim, is not necessary: they act on the basis of their impressions, but with none of the commitment to the truth of those impressions characteristic of ordinary people's behaviour. This characterization of the Sceptic's attitude implies a position on a much discussed question (see Barnes 1982; Burnyeat 1983; Frede 1987): namely, just what is the scope of the *dogmata* the Sceptic rejects, an answer to which is of capital importance to the associated question of whether life can be lived without them. Are *dogmata* merely *scientific* beliefs, beliefs involving explicit commitment to theory (as *Outlines of Pyrrhonism* I 13 suggests, the line adopted by Frede)? Or are they any and every non-epistemic appearance (Burnyeat's view)? More probably what makes an appearance into a *dogma* is not its content, but one's attitude to it: any appearance can, on this view, be a *dogma*, but only if its recipient accepts it as *really* true. And such commitments are not prerequisites of all action.

The upshot of this rejection of *dogmata* is *epochē*: the payoff, Sextus claims, is tranquillity, *ataraxia*, the state of being untroubled by things in general (*Outlines of Pyrrhonism* I 25–30). Distress is caused by strong evaluations – get rid of those, and life will be simpler. Of course, as a Sceptic he cannot claim certainty for his prescription; this is just the way things seem to him. But he is moved by that appearance and his general philanthropy to offer these arguments to others as well. Indeed, in a famous passage at the very end of *Outlines of Pyrrhonism*, Sextus compares Sceptical arguments to drugs: their business is to effect a cure for morbid dogmatism. How they do so is no part of the Pyrrhonist's concern.

References and further reading

Annas, J. and Barnes, J. (1985) *The Modes of Scepticism*, Cambridge: Cambridge University Press. (Translation and detailed philosophical study of our sources for the Ten Modes of Scepticism.)

* Barnes, J. (1982) 'The Beliefs of a Pyrrhonist', *Proceedings of the Cambridge Philological Society* 28: 1–28. (Important contribution to the debate on the liveability of scepticism; see §6.)

Brochard, V. (1887) *Les Sceptiques grecs*, Paris: Alcan; repr. 1923. (Old but still useful general treatment.)

* Burnyeat, M.F. (ed.) (1983) *The Skeptical Tradition*, Los Angeles, CA: University of California Press. (Very useful collection of articles on the history of scepticism from the Greeks to Kant; includes Burnyeat's own seminal article 'Can the Skeptic Live his Skepticism?')

Dal Pra, M. (1975) *Lo scetticismo greco*, Rome and Bari: La Terza, 2nd edn. (Very good historical survey.)

* Diogenes Laertius (*c.* early 3rd century AD) *Lives of the Philosophers*, trans. R.D. Hicks, *Diogenes Laertius Lives of Eminent Philosophers*, Loeb Classical Library, Cambridge, MA: Harvard University Press and London: Heinemann, 1925, 2 vols. (Greek text with facing translation: IX 69–116 is devoted to Pyrrhonism.)

* Frede, M. (1987) *Essays in Ancient Philosophy*, Oxford: Oxford University Press. (Contains several essays pertaining to scepticism, including 'The Skeptic's Beliefs'.)

Hankinson, R.J. (1995) *The Sceptics*, London: Routledge. (Full philosophical treatment of the history and development of Greek scepticism.)

* Sextus Empiricus (*c.* AD 200) *Outlines of Pyrrhonism*, trans. J. Annas and J. Barnes, *Outlines of Scepticism*, Cambridge: Cambridge University Press, 1994. (Fine translation with introduction and notes.)

* —— (*c.* AD 200) *Against the Professors*, trans. R.G. Bury, *Against the Logicians, Against the Physicists, Against the Ethicists and Against the Professors*, Loeb Classical Library, Cambridge, MA: Harvard University Press and London: Heinemann, 3 vols, 1935, 1936, 1949. (Parallel Greek text and English translation with minimal notes.)

Stough, C.L. (1969) *Greek Skepticism*, Los Angeles, CA: University of California Press. (Brief survey, somewhat dated.)

R.J. HANKINSON

PYTHAGORAS (*c.*570–*c.*497 BC)

Pythagoras of Samos was an early Greek sage and religious innovator. He taught the kinship of all life and the immortality and transmigration of the soul. Pythagoras founded a religious community of men and women in southern Italy that was also of considerable political influence. His followers, who became known as Pythagoreans, went beyond these essentially religious beliefs of the master to develop philosophical, mathematical, astronomical, and musical theories with which they tended to credit Pythagoras himself. The tradition established by Pythagoras weaves through much of Greek philosophy, leaving its mark particularly on the thought of Empedocles, Plato, and later Platonists.

1 Life and deeds
2 Teachings
3 Legacy

1 Life and deeds

Pythagoras, son of Mnesarchus, was born on the island of Samos. For the first half of his life Pythagoras travelled widely, not only in Greece but supposedly also in Egypt, Phoenicia and Babylonia, where he is reputed to have acquired much of his knowledge and religious wisdom. Perhaps to escape the rule of Polycrates, the tyrant of Samos, he emigrated to Croton in southern Italy. His moral stature and eloquence gained him many adherents. With his followers, both men and women, Pythagoras practised a simple, communal life whose goal was to live in harmony with the divine. To that end he prescribed a regimen of purification that included dietary restrictions, periods of silence and contemplation, and other ascetic practices. In addition to the religious and monastic aspects of the Pythagorean society, we hear of Pythagorean political associations (*hetaireiai*) that played an important role in the public affairs of Croton and other southern Italian cities (it appears they initiated social reforms and supported aristocratic constitutions). After a time their dominance came to be resented and a 'Pythagorean revolt' ensued, in the course of which many Pythagoreans were killed or scattered abroad. Pythagoras himself, possibly as a result of this upheaval, moved to Metapontum where he died.

Already during his lifetime Pythagoras was regarded with near religious veneration. It is therefore not surprising that the stories told about him after his death should turn into hagiology and include many fantastic elements: that Pythagoras was the Hyperborean Apollo and had a golden thigh to prove it; that

he was seen in two places at one time; that he could converse with animals and control natural phenomena. Pythagoras' wonder-working clearly belongs to the realm of legend, although it reinforces the picture of him as a 'shaman'. A more difficult matter is to establish what Pythagoras actually taught, since the oral and then the written traditions attribute to him not only miracles but also sophisticated mathematical and philosophical achievements. This habit of tracing all things back to the master, coupled with evidence of the quasi-religious avoidance of uttering his name, is typified in the expression common among Pythagoreans: 'he himself said' (*autos epha*; Latin *ipse dixit*). However, because Pythagoras wrote nothing and shrouded his lectures in secrecy, it is impossible to verify all that is ascribed to him. What remains certain is that he was a highly influential religious teacher whose main tenets dealt with the soul and the rites required for its purification and salvation. This made the Pythagorean movement especially popular in Magna Graecia, a fertile soil for mystery cults of all kinds. Pythagoras is also connected with certain 'Orphic' writings, since these share eschatological concerns similar to his oral teachings (see ORPHISM). For these reasons the following account will emphasize those doctrines that accord with Pythagoras' reputation as an early Greek sage and religious innovator (for the philosophical and scientific theories traditionally associated with his name, see PYTHAGOREANISM).

2 Teachings

Pythagoras believed that the world was animate and that the planets were gods. This view of the universe as living and divine was characteristic of early Greek thought (see THALES §2), but what appears unique with Pythagoras is the corollary he drew on an anthropological level: there is an element in human beings that is related to the universe and that, like the universe in which events recur in eternal cycles, is eternal. This divine, immortal element is the soul (see PSYCHĒ). With the death of the body the soul passes into another body, human or animal. An early witness to Pythagoras' belief in transmigration (or *metempsychōsis*) is the poet-philosopher XENOPHANES (§1), who satirizes him for claiming to recognize the soul of a friend when he heard the voice of a puppy that was being beaten. Pythagoras asserted of himself, as is typical of a religious figure who draws on personal experience, that he had once been the Homeric hero Euphorbus, and he exhorted his disciples to recall their own past lives.

The immortality of the soul underlies many of Pythagoras' practical teachings, for the soul, as the most important element within a person, required nurture to ensure not only equanimity in this life but also a better incarnation in the life to come. These ends could be achieved by bringing the soul into harmony with the divine, cosmic order (according to a disputed doxography, Pythagoras was the first to pronounce the world a *kosmos*, a term that in Greek combines the ideas of adornment, beauty and order). In so far, however, as the soul resided in a body, it needed to be freed from the turmoils and corrupting influences of the body. Hence Pythagoras preached a strict way of life that centred on purification (see KATHARSIS) and asceticism. Furthermore, he practised a form of musical therapy for both body and soul. He valued friendship highly as a means of promoting equality and concord; the love of friends was a specific instance of the universal sympathy existing in the cosmos.

The rules of Pythagoras found expression in short, pithy sayings known as *akousmata*, a term that implies oral transmission, or, more frequently, as *symbola*. The latter most likely functioned as secret passwords for Pythagorean initiates but, as the name suggests and their often esoteric and oracular nature prompted, they were also subjects for 'symbolic' interpretation. The *symbola* range from primitive religious taboos to simple moral precepts and various dietary prohibitions (abstinence from certain parts of animals and the famous ban on eating beans).

3 Legacy

Pythagoras, according to Plato (*Republic* X 600b), handed down to his followers a distinctive way of life (*bios*) 'they call Pythagorean to this day'. By Plato's day the Pythagorean life meant, besides purifications of the soul, inquiries in philosophy, mathematics, astronomy and music. Did Pythagoras bequeath these enterprises as well? EMPEDOCLES (§2), who was greatly influenced by Pythagoras, praised him as a man of surpassing knowledge, with a vast wealth of understanding, capable of all kinds of wise works. HERACLITUS (§1), while agreeing that Pythagoras 'practised inquiry beyond all other men', saw the result as a peculiar wisdom consisting of polymathy and evil artifice. From both witnesses, however, Pythagoras emerges as a figure active in a wide variety of fields and therefore likely at least to have dabbled in those studies for which Pythagoreans were known in Plato's time. Still, the only sure legacy of Pythagoras is the immortality of the soul. Although this was primarily a religious belief, it carried philosophical import. By singling out the immortal soul as the essential element of life Pythagoras foreshadowed the Parmenidean/Platonic distinction between eternal being and changeable

becoming and, in general, the dualism of mind and matter that informs so much of Western philosophy.

See also: ARCHYTAS; IAMBLICHUS; NEO-PYTHAGOREANISM; PHILOLAUS; PRESOCRATIC PHILOSOPHY

References and further reading

Burkert, W. (1972) *Lore and Science in Ancient Pythagoreanism*, trans. E.L. Minar, Jr, Cambridge, MA: Harvard University Press. (A scholarly and critical examination of the sources; Pythagoras the religious figure is sharply distinguished from Pythagorean philosophy and science which become identifiable only in the late fifth century BC.)

Diogenes Laertius (first half of the third century AD) *Lives of the Philosophers*, trans. R.D. Hicks, *Diogenes Laertius' Lives of Eminent Philosophers*, Loeb Classical Library, Cambridge, MA: Harvard University Press and London: Heinemann, 1925. (VIII 1–50 is a life of Pythagoras.)

Guthrie, W.K.C. (1962–78) *A History of Greek Philosophy*, Cambridge: Cambridge University Press, 6 vols. (A comprehensive and readable discussion of Pythagoras and early Pythagoreanism can be found in volume 1 pages 146–340.)

—— (1987) *The Pythagorean Sourcebook and Library*, Grand Rapids, MI: Phanes Press. (Conveniently collects the main ancient sources.)

Iamblichus (*c.* AD 290–300) *On the Pythagorean Way of Life*, trans. J. Dillon and J. Hershbell, Atlanta, GA: Scholars Press, 1991. (A Neoplatonic account of the Pythagorean life in which Pythagoras appears as the philosopher *par excellence*; the most exhaustive ancient source that survives. The edition contains text, translation and notes.)

Kingsley, P. (1995) *Ancient Philosophy, Mystery, and Magic: Empedocles and Pythagorean Tradition*, Oxford: Oxford University Press. (Includes *passim* critical, yet sympathetic, discussions of the figure of Pythagoras and the Pythagoras legends.)

Navia, L.E. (1990) *Pythagoras: An Annotated Bibliography*, New York and London: Garland. (Covers the literature up to 1989 on all aspects of Pythagoras and Pythagoreanism.)

—— (1993) *The Presocratic Philosophers: An Annotated Bibliography*, New York and London: Garland. (At pages 591–7, gives an updated bibliography of works on Pythagoras and Pythagoreanism since 1988.)

Porphyry (*c.* AD 250–269) *The Life of Pythagoras*, trans. M. Smith, in M. Hadas and M. Smith, *Heroes and Gods: Spiritual Biographies in Antiquity*, New York: Harper & Row, 1965, 105–28. (The only surviving part of Porphyry's *Philosophic History*, it combines legendary material with historical information.)

HERMANN S. SCHIBLI

PYTHAGOREANISM

Pythagoreanism refers to a Greek religious-philosophical movement that originated with Pythagoras in the sixth century BC. Although Pythagoreanism in its historical development embraced a wide range of interests in politics, mysticism, music, mathematics and astronomy, the common denominator remained a general adherence among Pythagoreans to the name of the founder and his religious beliefs. Pythagoras taught the immortality and transmigration of the soul (reincarnation) and recommended a way of life that through ascetic practices, dietary rules and ethical conduct promised to purify the soul and bring it into harmony with the surrounding universe. Thereby the soul would become godlike since Pythagoras believed that the cosmos, in view of its orderly and harmonious workings and structure, was divine. Pythagoreanism thus has from its beginnings a cosmological context that saw further evolution along mathematical lines in the succeeding centuries. Pythagorean philosophers, drawing on musical theories that may go back to Pythagoras, expressed the harmony of the universe in terms of numerical relations and possibly even claimed that things are numbers. Notwithstanding a certain confusion in Pythagorean number philosophy between abstract and concrete, Pythagoreanism represents a valid attempt, outstanding in early Greek philosophy, to explain the world by formal, structural principles. Overall, the combination of religious, philosophical and mathematical speculations that characterizes Pythagoreanism exercised a significant influence on Greek thinkers, notably on Plato and his immediate successors as well as those Platonic philosophers known as Neo-Pythagoreans and Neoplatonists.

1 History
2 Music, mathematics and cosmology
3 Soul and ethics

1 History

In the second half of the sixth century BC, Pythagoras founded a community in the southern Italian city of Croton whose members were united by the belief in the transmigration of the soul, an ascetic way of life that centred on the purification of the soul, and a political outlook that aimed at social reform along aristocratic lines. Pythagorean associations (*hetaireiai*), which also formed in other cities of Magna Graecia, acquired considerable political authority, but their dominance eventually met with opposition, both during the lifetime of Pythagoras and later again about 450 BC. In the wake of these anti-Pythagorean movements the followers of Pythagoras were scattered throughout the Greek world, so that by the time of Plato there is little evidence of formal Pythagorean societies. Individual Pythagoreans, however, continued to be recognized, some by their distinctive lifestyle in matters of food, dress and purificatory practices, others by the additional pursuit of various philosophical, mathematical and musical theories with which they credited Pythagoras. Later tradition refers to these two types of Pythagoreans as 'hearers' (*akousmatikoi*) and 'learners' (*mathēmatikoi*). The distinction supposedly goes back to the original society in which some members were only fit to accept the oral teachings of Pythagoras without arguments and proofs, while those with more leisure and perhaps philosophical ability were further instructed in the rational foundations of the master's teachings. Whatever differences there may have been between groups of Pythagoreans, and even among individual *mathēmatikoi*, all professed allegiance to Pythagoras.

From the time of Pythagoras to Plato there were several famous Pythagoreans – Hippasus, PHILOLAUS and ARCHYTAS. Aristotle, in his extant works, speaks only generally of the Pythagoreans ('some Pythagoreans say...'); his special treatise on Pythagorean beliefs unfortunately no longer survives. In the third and second centuries BC we do not hear of philosophers who were known as or called themselves Pythagoreans, but interest in 'Pythagoreanism' continued, as is evidenced by the wealth of apocryphal writings in prose and verse on Pythagorean themes that mostly date from this period. The actual practice of Pythagoreanism experienced a revival in the Roman world from the first century BC to the first century AD; Latin writers such as Cicero, Ovid and Seneca testify to its popularity. In the first two centuries AD the theoretical side of Pythagoreanism marked certain philosophers to the extent that they may be called Neo-Pythagoreans (see NEO-PYTHAGOREANISM) and these in turn influenced later Platonic philosophers (see NEOPLATONISM).

2 Music, mathematics, and cosmology

PLATO says of the true philosopher, whose mind is on the higher realities (that is, the Platonic Forms):

he looks unto the fixed and eternally immutable realm where...all is orderly and according to reason, and he imitates this realm and, as much as possible, assimilates himself to it...and by association with the divine order becomes himself orderly and divine as far as a human being can...

(*Republic* VII 500c)

Plato's philosophic ideal, as well as one of the methods he prescribed to achieve it – namely mathematics – owes much to Pythagoreanism. Pythagoras had taught that life should be in harmony with the divine cosmos (see PYTHAGORAS §2). In Pythagoreanism harmony (*harmonia*) became a central tenet and was explained through numerical relations, possibly in connection with musical theory. For example, the Pythagoreans thought that the motions of the orbiting planets produced a sound which, given the belief that the intervals between the heavenly bodies corresponded to musical ratios, was harmonious. So Aristotle explains the 'music of the spheres' – one of several explanations offered for this famous Pythagorean image. Of seminal importance for illustrating the coherence of music and number was the discovery of musical ratios – that music should result when the first four integers of the numerical system, used as components in the harmonic ratios of the octave (2 : 1), the fifth (3 : 2) and the fourth (4 : 3), were imposed upon the continuum of sound. Whether or not Pythagoras, as tradition holds, was the 'discoverer' of the musical concords, the Pythagoreans fixed upon the first four numbers as the building blocks of nature. These four sufficed to give extension and shape to bodies in the sequence of point–line–surface–solid:

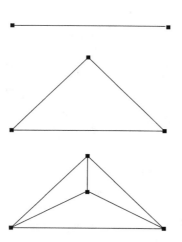

Moreover, the first four integers add up to ten, which the Pythagoreans considered a perfect number and represented in a figure called the *tetraktys*.

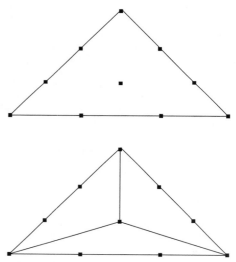

From whatever angle one approached the *tetraktys* in counting, the addition always resulted in ten, the basis of the decimal system. The *tetraktys* also produced an equilateral triangle, the simplest plane figure, and a pyramid, the simplest three-dimensional shape.

The Pythagoreans viewed the *tetraktys* as a sacred symbol and used it in the following oath: 'By him [Pythagoras] who handed down to us the *tetraktys*, source and root of everlasting nature'. In short, the Pythagoreans supposed the nature of things could be understood numerically; indeed, some of them apparently went so far as to say that things *are* numbers: '...they assumed the elements of numbers to be the elements of all things that exist, and the whole universe to be *harmonia* and number' (Aristotle, *Metaphysics* 986a2).

Since numbers functioned as the constituent elements of the cosmos, it is important to see how the Pythagoreans understood the nature and generation of number itself. Aristotle again offers the best starting-point:

> The elements of number are the even and the odd, the latter limited, the former unlimited. The One is composed of both of these (for it is both even and odd) and number comes from the one; and numbers...are the whole universe.
>
> (*Metaphysics* 986a17)

How the One can be both odd and even is best explained in the sense that the One, as the first number, is the principle of both odd and even numbers (zero was unknown in Greek mathematics). Thus 'number comes from the One', and the generation of number was simultaneously a cosmogonical process since 'numbers...are the whole universe'. Although in its origin the Pythagoreans viewed the One as both odd and even, limited and unlimited, in its practical application, that is, in its interaction with other numbers, they treated it as odd and limiting. This can be seen in the schema by which the Pythagoreans illustrated the correspondence of odd/even to limited/unlimited. Gnomons (carpenter squares) were placed around an arrangement of points (or pebbles) as follows:

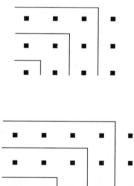

When a gnomon is placed around one point, and the process is continued in sequence, the resulting figure is always of 'limited' shape, that is, always a square, whereas when it is placed around two points, the result is a series of oblongs whose sides stand in an 'unlimited', that is, an infinite variation to each other. In this scheme the One, as a single unit or point, is equated with the odd. The One is also ranked with limited and odd in the Pythagorean table of ten opposites:

limited	unlimited
odd	even
one	many
right	left
male	female
rest	motion
straight	crooked
light	darkness
good	bad
square	oblong

The position of limited/unlimited at the beginning is not accidental, for their opposition, embodied in the original composition of the One, was considered primal and basic to the development of number and the universe, while the opposition between odd and even can be generally subsumed under this fundamental distinction. The connection of the One with the limited reappears in another Pythagorean text (Aristotle, *Metaphysics* 1091a17), where it is said that the limited (tantamount to the One) 'breathes in' and is thus penetrated by the unlimited. In this cosmological fragment the unlimited is equated with the void, to be thought of as infinite space and serving as a dividing principle. The One now becomes a Two (reminiscent of the mythological separation of heaven and earth), which in effect marks the beginning of number, plurality and the existence of discrete physical bodies. The cosmogonic process is sometimes put the other way round: the unlimited is limited (or penetrated) by the limit. This way of stating it brings to the fore the characteristic Greek feeling that what is unlimited, without bounds, is without order and somehow evil (hence 'bad' is listed under the unlimited in the above table) and therefore needs to be curtailed and bounded by limit and measure (as the limits of harmonic ratios must be imposed upon the limitless range of sound to produce music). The result, in cosmological terms, is then precisely a *kosmos*, an orderly and structured universe. In so far as the perfected and integral cosmos represents a *harmonia*, a unity stemming from a reconciliation of opposites, Pythagoreanism has a monistic aspect, yet in its source theory it remains essentially dualistic: number comes from the One, and the One is composed of limited and unlimited. From these first two principles everything derives, even though the One, when identified with limit, odd, male, and so on, was felt to be the 'good' element in this cosmic dualism. (There can be no question of positing the One as the sole ultimate principle without imposing

Platonic and Neo-Pythagorean notions upon early Pythagoreanism.)

Limited und unlimited are the principles of number. Numbers do not merely express the substance, shape and quantitative differences of things but actually appear to constitute bodies of physical dimension. The identification of things with numbers confuses physical bodies with abstractions, or, in Aristotelian terms, the material causes of things with their formal causes. Here Pythagoreanism connects with much of Presocratic thought according to which the source and informing element of the universe was thought of as some kind of matter, be it water, air, fire, earth, or a combination of these (see ARCHĒ). At the same time the numerical theories of the Pythagoreans represent a true advance in the history of Greek philosophy: the attempt to explain the nature of things by numbers is a valid philosophical striving to understand the world by its formal or structural principles, even if the Pythagoreans then equated these with the things themselves. And while the Pythagoreans' interest in numbers was often infused with a mystical element (their solemn veneration of the *tetraktys*) and a primitive number symbolism that blurred distinctions between abstract and concrete (a moral concept such as justice was considered the embodiment of four, a square number of 'just', that is, equal reciprocity), no less an authority than Aristotle acknowledged that the Pythagoreans were pioneers and made advances in the mathematical fields (arithmetic, astronomy, harmonics and some geometry). For the 'Pythagorean theorem', although long known to Babylonian mathematicians, the Pythagoreans are generally considered to have found the proofs and, although in the wake of this theorem they discovered that the ratios of geometrical figures to each other cannot simply be expressed by a series of rational integers – the discovery of irrational numbers and the principle of incommensurability upset the Pythagorean notion that the world is harmony and number – their very setbacks contributed to subsequent work in Greek mathematics. Plato valued mathematics as a useful discipline to train the philosopher in the perception of eternal and transcendent truth, since in his mind it dealt essentially with invisible and eternally valid realities. By divorcing number from physical substance Plato transforms Pythagorean mathematics, yet few doubt that his interest in number, arithmetic and measure largely rests upon Pythagorean foundations (consider the mathematical model of the universe in his *Timaeus* (see PLATO §16). Plato's immediate successors in the Academy were steeped in Pythagorean number theory (see SPEUSIPPUS §2; XENOCRATES §2).

3 Soul and ethics

Perhaps in no other ancient Greek philosophy is the human being as intimately linked to the cosmos as in Pythagoreanism. Although the correspondence between microcosm and macrocosm, the individual and the universe, is found in much of Greek thought, it received a particularly sharp outline in the Pythagorean view that by assimilation to the divine cosmos the self would come to reflect the cosmic order and harmony. The true self of every person was the soul (see PSYCHĒ), the essential element in the partnership of body and soul. Pythagoras' teaching that the soul survived the dissolution of the body and reappeared in other bodies was steadfastly adhered to throughout the history of Pythagoreanism, even if it was sometimes eclipsed by other interests. The doctrine of the immortality and transmigration of the soul translated into a practical and clearly defined way of life that combined ritual purity with high ethical standards and whose precepts were embodied in sayings known as *akousmata* and *symbola* (see PYTHAGORAS §2). The belief in the kinship of all life, as a corollary to the belief in transmigration, imposed a great moral responsibility towards parents, children, friends and fellow citizens, and generally entailed a respectful attitude towards all forms of life in which soul may be embodied; hence the Pythagoreans were, to varying degrees, vegetarians. Their dietary laws were also intended to free them from bodily pollution. The body was seen as a prison, even as a grave (Plato, *Gorgias* 493a) from which the soul was to rise, ever achieving superior reincarnations and culminating in a state of divinity. Thus the Pythagoreans postulated three kinds of rational creatures: 'gods, men, and such as Pythagoras'. Pythagoras was thought to have achieved semi-divine status, which in Greek could be expressed by 'daemon'. It is in a Pythagorean vein that EMPEDOCLES (§2) proclaims human beings to be fallen 'daemons'. (A complex 'daemonology' was to become an ingredient of Neo-Pythagoreanism.) The recognition of the religious and moral mandates of the Pythagorean life and of its eschatological meaning constituted wisdom (*sophia*) and the lover of such a life was a *philosophos*, a term that in this sense, as certain traditions report, was first coined in Pythagorean circles.

See also: MYSTICAL PHILOSOPHY IN ISLAM §2; ORPHISM; PRESOCRATIC PHILOSOPHY

References and further reading

* Aristotle (*c.* mid 4th century BC) *Metaphysics*, trans. in J. Barnes (ed.) *The Complete Works of Aristotle*,

Princeton, NJ: Princeton University Press, 1984. (A primary source on early Pythagoreanism.)

Burkert, W. (1972) *Lore and Science in Ancient Pythagoreanism*, trans. E.L. Minar, Jr, Cambridge, MA: Harvard University Press. (A scholarly examination of the sources of Pythagoreanism and a critical analysis of Pythagorean teachings; a prerequisite for all serious work on the subject.)

Diels, H and Kranz, W. (eds) (1952) *Die Fragmente der Vorsokratiker* (Fragments of the Presocratics), Berlin: Weidmann, 6th edn, vol. 1, 96–113 and 375–480. (The standard collection of the ancient sources containing the main sources on Pythagoreanism.)

Guthrie, W.K.C. (1962–78) *A History of Greek Philosophy*, Cambridge: Cambridge University Press, 6 vols. (A comprehensive and readable discussion of early Pythagoreanism can be found in volume 1, pages 146–340; emphasizes the harmony between its religious and philosophical-scientific elements.)

Huffman, C.A. (1993) *Philolaus of Croton: Pythagorean and Presocratic*, Cambridge: Cambridge University Press. (Examines the fragments of a notable Pythagorean; pages 57–64 argue that 'all things are number' was not an actual claim of the Pythagoreans but rather Aristotle's summary of their number theory.)

Kahn, C.H. (1974) 'Pythagorean Philosophy before Plato', in A.P.D. Mourelatos (ed.) *The Pre-Socratics*, Garden City, NY: Doubleday; repr. 1993. (A short but useful introduction.)

Kingsley, P. (1995) *Ancient Philosophy, Mystery and Magic: Empedocles and Pythagorean Tradition*, Oxford: Oxford University Press. (Examines Pythagoreanism against the background of Greek mystery and magic; also discusses the influence of Pythagoreans on the myths in Plato.)

Navia, L.E. (1990) *Pythagoras: An Annotated Bibliography*, New York and London: Garland. (Includes the literature, up to 1989, not only on Pythagoras but also on all aspects of Pythagoreanism.)

Philip, J.A. (1966) *Pythagoras and Early Pythagoreanism*, Toronto, Ont.: Toronto University Press. (An examination, based principally on Aristotle, of the major doctrines of Pythagoreanism; in regard to cosmology, holds that the Pythagorean opposites are not the first principles of a dualistic cosmos, but rather, given a creation in time, the constituents of one *physis*, one world-nature.)

* Plato (*c*.380–367 BC) *Republic*, trans. P. Shorey, *Plato: Republic*, Loeb Classical Library, Cambridge, MA: Harvard University Press and London: Heinemann, 1930, 2 vols. (Much Pythagorean influence in books VI–VII.)

HERMANN S. SCHIBLI

Q

QI

A difficult term to contextualize within Western conceptual frameworks, qi *is variously rendered as 'hylozoistic vapours', 'psychophysical stuff', 'the activating fluids in the atmosphere and body', and, perhaps most appropriately, 'vital energizing field'. In the earlier texts, before the notion came to be adapted to the speculative constructions of the Han cosmologists, it had a significance not unlike the Greek* pneuma *('breath' or 'animating fluid'). In the 'cosmological' speculations of the Han dynasty (206 BC–AD 220),* qi *came to be understood as the vital stuff constitutive of all things and was characterized in terms of the active and passive dynamics of* yang *and* yin.

Most individual Western interpretations of the vital and spiritual character of things operated with a physical–spiritual dichotomy; the animating principle was largely distinguishable from the animated things (see PNEUMA). In China, the animating fluid is conceptualized in terms of what we would today call an 'energy field'. This field not only pervades all things, but in some sense is the means or process of the constitution of all things. That is to say, there are no separable 'things' to be animated; there is only the field and its focal manifestations. During the period of the Han cosmologists, the notions of *yin* and *yang* came to be used to characterize the dynamics of the transformations which constituted the field of *qi*.

The energizing field as the 'reality' of things precludes the existence of forms or ideas or categories or principles which allow for the existence of 'natural kinds'. Thus, discriminations in the field of *qi* were made in terms of observed and conventionalized classifications associated with diurnal and seasonal changes, directions, colours, body parts and so forth. Processes associated with these correlative classifications were then charted in accordance with the rhythms of the *yang* and *yin*, or active and passive forces (see YIN–YANG).

Perhaps the most important areas in Chinese culture influenced by the notion of *qi* have to do with health, medicine and exercises leading to self-realization. Techniques such as acupuncture and the use of herbal medicines are based upon the understanding of *qi* as that fluid medium which manifests itself in the operations of the human body as well as in

the bodily environs. The term 'body' must of course be used advisedly; everything is a continuous field of *qi* manifesting itself as both 'body' and 'environs'. The purpose of acupuncture and medicine is to balance the flow of the *qi* such that environs and body are productively continuous one with the other. This productive continuity is achieved by considering the nature of the *qi* manifestation of the human body in terms of the *yin* and *yang* dynamics that are understood to be required for its health. The health of the body is, of course, dependent upon the 'health' of the environs. Adjustments of the *yin* and *yang* characteristics through the techniques of acupuncture or the administration of herbals serve to increase or retard the transformations of the *qi* in body and environs.

The *Huangdi neijing* (Inner Classic of the Yellow Emperor) is a pre-Han medical text which employs the sorts of correlative classifications mentioned above to promote a healthy regimen. Among many other advices, it suggests the behaviours associated with the proper response to the particular *qi* of each season. Further, each season is correlated to a part of the body. Inappropriate response to the *qi* of a particular season will harm the bodily organ associated with that season. For example, the *qi* of Spring is 'coming to life'. In this season one must 'sleep at night and rise early...relax the body [and] allow intent to come to life.' Failure to respond thus to the *qi* of Spring will damage the liver and cause one to suffer chills in summer.

Techniques of self-realization have a long history in China, dating from the earliest period of Chinese written records. A fourth century BC meditative piece, 'Inward Training', which appears as a chapter in an eclectic work called the *Guanzi* (see GUANZI), contains techniques associated with correct posture, diet and breath control aimed at bringing individuals into harmony with the Way and thereby allowing them to achieve health and long life. Later, MENCIUS interpreted the field of *qi* in terms of moral energy and offered advice on the attainment of true virtue. Mencius speaks of his ability to nourish his 'flood-like *qi*'. He describes this *qi* as that which is 'most vast' and 'most firm' (*Mencius* 2A2). His meaning seems to be, in Western philosophical parlance, that 'flood-like *qi*' has the greatest 'extensive' and 'intensive' magnitude. The language of (extensive) 'field' and (intensive) 'focus' allows us to understand Mencius as saying that one may nourish one's *qi* most successfully by making of oneself the most intense focus of the most extensive field of *qi*. In this manner one gains greatest virtue (excellence, potency) in relation to the most far-reaching elements of one's environs: 'The myriad things are here in me. There is no joy greater than to discover integrity in oneself and to seek virtue through action which persistently mirrors others (*Mencius* 7A4).

The meaning of this familiar passage from the Mencius is that 'all things are in me and I am with and in all things'. Recalling the meaning of *qi* as a continuous field, a better rendition might be 'The field of *qi* is focused by me, and thus all *qi* is here in me.'

See also: CHINESE PHILOSOPHY; GUANZI; MEDICINE, PHILOSOPHY OF; MENCIUS; PNEUMA; SELF-CULTIVATION, IN CHINESE PHILOSOPHY; WANG FUZHI; YIN–YANG; ZHANG ZAI

References and further reading

* *Guanzi* (*c.* 4th century BC–1st century AD?), trans. A. Rickett, Princeton, NJ: Princeton University Press, 1985. (An eclectic text with important chapters on psychology.)

Huangdi neijing (The Yellow Emperor's Classic of Internal Medicine) (*c.*220–200 BC?), trans. I. Veith, Baltimore, MD: Williams & Wilkins, 1949. (A translation, dated, but all that is available.)

Major, J.S. (1993) *Heaven and Earth in Early Han Thought: Chapters Three, Four, and Five of the Huainanzi*, Albany, NY: State University of New York Press. (An authoritative translation and interpretation of the technical chapters of *Huainanzi*, a Han dynasty Daoist text.)

* *Mengzi* (*c.*4th century BC?), trans. D.C. Lau, *Mencius*, Harmondsworth: Penguin Classics, 1970. (An authoritative translation.)

DAVID L. HALL
ROGER T. AMES

QUALIA

The terms 'quale' and 'qualia' (plural) are most commonly understood to mean the qualitative, phenomenal or 'felt' properties of our mental states, such as the throbbing pain of my current headache, or the peculiar blue of the afterimage I am experiencing now. Though it seems undeniable that at least some of our mental states have qualia, their existence raises a number of philosophical problems.

The first problem regards their nature or constitution. Many theorists have noted great differences between our intuitive conceptions of qualia and those of typical physical properties such as mass or length, and have asked whether qualia could nonetheless be identical with physical properties. Another problem regards our knowledge of qualia, in particular, whether our beliefs about them can be taken to be infallible, or at least to have some kind of special authority.

1   Anti-physicalist arguments
2   Physicalist responses
3   Our knowledge of qualia and other issues

1   Anti-physicalist arguments

The terms 'quale' and 'qualia' (plural) are most commonly used to characterize what may be called the qualitative, phenomenal or 'felt' properties of our mental states, such as the throbbing pain of my current headache, or the peculiar blue of the afterimage I am experiencing now. Qualitative properties can be more or less specific: the state I am in at the moment can be an example of a migraine, a headache, a pain, or, even more generally, a bodily sensation. Briefly, a mental state is considered to have qualitative properties just in case there is something it is like to be in it.

It seems undeniable that our sensations and perceptions have qualitative properties. However, many philosophers have claimed that the distinctive feels of pains, after-images and other sensations are so radically different from objective properties such as mass or length that they could not be identical with any physical or functional properties of the brain and nervous system. (Indeed, some theorists reserve the term qualia to denote those mental properties, if any, that are irreducibly qualitative: this is why disputes about the metaphysical nature of qualitative properties are sometimes characterized as disputes about whether there are qualia, rather than about what kind of properties qualia, in the metaphysically neutral sense introduced above, could be.) The view that qualitative properties are metaphysically unique has been supported by powerful argument, and may seem to be reinforced by common sense and introspection. If this view is true, however, the existence of qualia will be incompatible with a fully naturalistic account of the mind.

Anti-physicalists have argued against the identity of qualitative with physical (or functional) properties throughout the history of the philosophy of mind, but three arguments have been especially influential since the mid-1970s. The first, modelled upon Descartes' well-known argument for the 'real distinction' between mind and body in the *Sixth Meditation*, (see DESCARTES, R. §8; DUALISM) proposes that one could, under ideal epistemic circumstances, imagine or conceive of the qualitative features of one's pains or perceptions in the absence of any specific physical or functional properties (and vice versa), and that properties that can be so conceived or imagined must be distinct. The second argument proposes that there are qualitative properties of mental states that one could not know about before actually experiencing states of that (or similar) kind, no matter how much knowledge one had about the physical and functional properties of brains and nervous systems: for example, despite having comprehensive knowledge of the relevant sciences, a person raised in an entirely black and white environment would not know what it is like to see red, and despite years of studying bat neuropsychology, we could not know what it is like to be a bat. Moreover, the argument continues, properties that do not afford this sort of knowledge could not be part of the subject matter of any of the objective sciences. The third argument states that no physical or functional characterization of sensations or perceptions could adequately explain why they feel the way they do, and that such an explanatory gap raises doubts about the identification of the properties in question. The conclusion of the first two arguments, of course, is that qualia could not be identical with physical or functional properties, and the conclusion of the third argument is that, at the very least, we have no reason to believe that these identities hold.

Although there are interesting differences between them, these arguments are linked (and can profitably be treated together) in that the first premise of each appears to depend upon the thesis (1) that there is no conceptual connection between qualitative terms or concepts and physicalistic terms or concepts. If there were such a connection, then it would be impossible, if one was fully educated and attentive, to conceive (for example) of a pain existing apart from the relevant physical or functional property, and it would be possible, at least in principle, to know all there is to know about pain without ever having experienced pain oneself; it would also be easy to explain why it feels a certain way to have the associated physical or functional property. The second premise also appears to depend upon a common thesis, namely, (2) that given this lack of connection, our use of qualitative terms or concepts commits us to (or, at the very least, suggests) the existence of irreducibly qualitative properties.

2 Physicalist responses

Physicalists, in turn, have attempted to deny both (1) and (2). Those denying (1) have argued that, on the contrary, there is a conceptual or epistemic connection between qualitative concepts and physicalist concepts. The candidates here are usually causal, functional or otherwise topic neutral concepts that have at least some claim to be part of our common-sense understanding of these states, since it seems quite implausible to think that physical, neurophysiological or other scientific characterizations could serve as explications of our qualitative concepts (see MIND, IDENTITY THEORY OF §3). For example, the concept throbbing headache might be characterized in terms such as 'the state typically caused by a certain range of physical syndromes, and which produces certain desires and (perhaps) behaviour directed towards the abatement of that state', and the concept appearing blue might be characterized in terms such as 'the state typically caused by certain visual stimulations and which typically results in certain similarity judgments and sorting behaviour' (see FUNCTIONALISM).

Other theorists, however, have doubted that these common-sense causal or functional characterizations could be necessary or sufficient to capture qualitative concepts. The problem with sufficiency is that the attribution of such a characterization to an individual does not seem to close the question of whether they have the quale in question; this is often referred to as the 'absent qualia' objection. The problem with necessity is that some sensations or sensory features of perception seem to have no distinctive causal or functional roles that are sufficiently accessible to be part of our common sense concepts of those states: consider, for example, the strange, though mild, twinge in one's scalp that one felt for the first time yesterday. This leaves two alternatives for physicalists who accept premise (2) and thus wish to argue that there is some sort of conceptual connection between physicalistic and qualitative concepts: they can weaken the constraints on conceptual analysis, so that information from the sciences that may help to individuate sensations and perceptions can make a contribution to the explication of qualitative concepts, or they can deny that there is determinate, coherent content to our qualitative concepts over and above that which can be explicated by classical functionalist or topic neutral characterizations, and thus maintain that there are no corresponding qualitative properties at all (see ELIMINATIVISM).

The problem for the first alternative is that it is difficult to make a principled distinction between information that is relevant to conceptual explication and that which is not; defenders of this alternative respond that an important goal of explication in this case is to preserve the intuitive distinctions we make among our mental states, and that any additions to our common lore that enable us to do this (while preserving the bulk of our other commonly held beliefs about these states) will count as relevant to this project. The problem for the second alternative is that it seems counterintuitive to ignore (what seem to be) intuitively evident distinctions among qualitative states just because they cannot be captured in functional or topic-neutral terms that are part of our common knowledge. Defenders of this alternative counsel that we must be wary of judging the worth of a theory in the light of our current intuitions, since intuitions are at least partially shaped by theory and can change over time; they also point to the counterintuitive consequences of accepting a non-physicalist account of the qualitative features of our mental states, and argue that it is not clear which side has the greater burden.

On the other hand, there are many physicalists who agree that at least some qualitative concepts are ineffable, in that they cannot be captured by physical or functional descriptions, or anything other than a demonstrative such as 'feels like that' or 'seems this way to me now'. Nonetheless, they argue, one cannot draw the anti-physicalist conclusion, since the irreducibility of qualitative to physicalistic concepts does not entail the irreducibility of qualitative to physicalistic properties; that is, while accepting premise (1) of the argument against the identity of qualitative and physical or functional properties, they reject premise (2).

Physicalists using this strategy deny the Cartesian claim that our modes of conception can, even under special circumstances, be definitive guides to the nature of things. Properties exist, and are distinct or identical, by virtue of mind-independent facts about the world; the ways we conceive of properties, even clearly and distinctly, have little to do with these facts. So stated, the argument denies that our conceptualizing has significant metaphysical import. It can be responded, however, that premise (2) is a consequence of the very possibility of reference: that non-equivalent concepts can denote the same item only by picking out different, irreducible, properties of it, and thus that even if 'pain' and 'C-fibre stimulation' did indeed denote the same property, it could only be by virtue of introducing higher-order properties that were themselves distinct. This view of how reference is determined has been considered as received wisdom since its introduction by Frege. But the argument can be countered by challenging the picture of reference it presupposes, and suggesting that the reference of qualitative concepts is determined directly, much as current causal or historical theories of reference propose for the cases of demonstratives, natural kind terms, and proper names (see REFERENCE §4; PROPER NAMES). Anti-physicalists, in response, can mount a general challenge to these current theories of direct reference. They can also argue that qualitative concepts are a special case, one in which there is a tighter link between the concepts and the properties they pick out, but such a claim must be argued carefully, so as not to seem *ad hoc*. Alternatively, anti-physicalists can argue that, without some link between concepts (or at least clear and distinct conceptions) and the properties they denote, it would be impossible to have knowledge of metaphysical necessity and possibility at all, and thus, to preserve such knowledge, we must concede that there is at least some presumption that properties clearly and distinctly conceived to exist apart really do so.

Though all physicalists are committed to giving a physicalistic account of sensations and perceptions, those who deny that there are conceptual connections between physicalistic and qualitative concepts can concede that there is something in the realm of the qualitative that may be ineffable or irreducibly subjective, namely, the content of those qualitative concepts. In their view, however, the conceptual irreducibility of qualitative concepts implies neither the ontological irreducibility of the properties they denote nor of the concepts, as mental states, themselves; thus, this conceptual ineffability does not conflict with the physicalist requirement that all mental states and properties be fully describable in the vocabulary of the objective sciences.

Sometimes, in the post-1970s literature on this topic, anti-physicalists claim that it is only by having certain experiences that one can learn new facts about the mental. If this claim is taken to mean that experience alone provides access to a special realm of qualitative properties, then no physicalist can accept it; however, if it is taken to mean that experience affords qualitative concepts with novel content, then physicalists who accept the irreducibility of qualitative to physicalistic concepts can agree. On the other hand, physicalists who believe that qualitative concepts can be given a functional explication maintain that any knowledge we gain uniquely from experience is merely a kind of practical knowledge, or knowing how – a matter of gaining new imaginative or recognitional abilities, rather than concepts that one previously lacked.

3 Our knowledge of qualia and other issues

It is often argued that we have special epistemic access

to the qualitative properties of our own mental states: it is claimed that our knowledge of them is infallible, or at least that our beliefs about them have a kind of special authority, and also that these properties are transparent or self-intimating to the minds that experience them. To have infallible knowledge of a class of properties is for it to be logically or conceptually impossible for our (sincere) beliefs about them to be false; to have special authority about a class of properties is for it to be logically or conceptually necessary for most of our (sincere) beliefs about them to be true. A property is transparent or self-intimating if an individual (with adequate conceptual sophistication) cannot help but form accurate beliefs about it whenever it is present. Insofar as they bear these special epistemic relations to those (and only those) who experience them, qualitative properties are importantly different from physical (and classically objective) properties such as shape, temperature and length, about which beliefs may be both mildly and radically fallible. The question naturally arises whether qualitative properties, if they have the above-described epistemic features, could be physical, functional or otherwise objective nonetheless.

Functionalists can accommodate infallibility or special authority and transparency, since according to (at least some versions of) this doctrine, states with qualitative properties and the beliefs they produce are interdefined. Thus, as a matter of conceptual necessity, no state will count (for example) as an instance of pain unless it produces (either always or for the most part) the belief that one is in pain, and, conversely, no state will count as a belief that one is in pain unless it is actually produced by pain.

Nonfunctionalist physicalists, on the other hand, cannot point to a definitional connection between qualitative properties and an individual's beliefs about them. Thus, some theorists merely reject infallibility and transparency, arguing that we can and do make sincere and unambiguous errors about our experiences (and fail to notice some of their properties) when we are tired and inattentive, or when misinformation skews our expectations about the experiences we are soon to have. It is more difficult, however, to argue that one can make such mistakes in the absence of these mitigating factors. Thus, many physicalists have attempted to show that at least some sort of special epistemic access to qualia is compatible with their metaphysical views.

For example, some philosophers have argued that a certain sort of introspective accuracy is insured by the proper operation of our cognitive faculties, and thus that, as a matter of law, we cannot be mistaken about (or fail to notice certain properties of) our mental states. On a view such as this, the claim that we are infallible about our mental states (or that they are transparent to us) will be nomologically necessary, but not necessary in any stronger sense. However, on nonfunctionalist physicalist views that treat qualitative concepts as demonstrative, certain statements of infallibility can be logically or conceptually necessary, in that one cannot be wrong, on any particular occasion, to think that one's current mental state feels like that. Even so, one cannot be sure, on these views, that all states that appear to be of the same phenomenal type are in fact of that same phenomenal – that is, physical – type. Since this sort of infallibility does not guarantee that one has re-identified a single phenomenal type on different occasions, it cannot provide any substantive assurances about the nature or reality of our mental states.

There are other interesting issues about qualia which are worth mentioning, though their full discussion is beyond the scope of this entry. One involves the range or extent of their occurrence. Bodily sensations and perceptions, the most common examples of states with qualia, are often contrasted with beliefs and desires, in that the former are taken to be essentially qualitative, the latter essentially intentional (that is, purporting to be about items or events in the world) (see BODILY SENSATIONS; PERCEPTION; INTENTIONALITY; PROPOSITIONAL ATTITUDES). Some theorists dispute this distinction, arguing that true intentional states must have qualitative properties as well. But whether or not intentional states must also be qualitative, it certainly seems (for occurrent beliefs and desires) that there is something it is like for us, if not all creatures, to have them. If so, then the issues raised in giving a physicalistic account of sensations and perceptions will be relevant for intentional states as well.

A related issue is whether all sensations and perceptions are indeed essentially qualitative, or whether, instead, there could be perception without qualia; that is, whether there could be bona fide perceptual states that are unconscious, such that there is nothing it is like to be in them at all.

Yet another question is whether (and if so, how) the myriad qualia we seem to experience at any given time are bound together at a given moment, and continuous with our experiences at previous and subsequent times, or whether the common sense view that we enjoy a unity of consciousness and a stream of consciousness is rather an illusion to be dispelled.

See also: CONSCIOUSNESS; SENSE-DATA; COLOUR AND QUALIA

References and further reading

Block, N. (1978) 'Troubles with Functionalism', repr. in D. Rosenthal (ed.) *The Nature of Mind*, New York: Oxford University Press, 1991. (Describes and raises objections to functionalism; home of the 'absent qualia' objection.)

Dennett, D. (1991) *Consciousness Explained*, Boston, MA: Little, Brown. (Argues for eliminativism about qualia, and challenges the view that there is a unified stream of consciousness.)

Hill, C. (1991) *Sensations: A Defense of Type Materialism*, New York: Cambridge University Press. (Argues for a type-identity thesis for sensations.)

Jackson, F. (1982) 'Epiphenomenal Qualia', repr. in W.G. Lycan, *Mind and Cognition*, Cambridge, MA: Blackwell, 1990. (Develops a version of the knowledge argument against a physicalistic reduction of qualia; see §2.)

Kripke, S. (1970) from 'Naming and Necessity', repr. in D. Rosenthal (ed.) *The Nature of Minds*, New York: Oxford University Press. (Presents the neo-Cartesian argument against a physicalist reduction of qualia mentioned in §2.)

Levin, J. (1991) 'Analytic Functionalism and the Reduction of Phenomenal States', in *Philosophical Studies* 61: 211–38. (Expands on the material in §2.)

Levine, J. (1983) 'Materialism and Qualia: The Explanatory Gap', *Pacific Philosophical Quarterly* 64: 4. (Introduces the explanatory gap argument, discussed in §2.)

Lewis, D. (1972) 'Psychophysical and Theoretical Identifications', repr. in D. Rosenthal (ed.) *The Nature of Minds*, New York: Oxford University Press, 1991. (Argues for the equivalence of qualitative and functional concepts; see §2.)

Lewis, D. (1988) 'What Experience Teaches', repr. in W.G. Lycan, *Mind and Cognition*, Cambridge, MA: Blackwell. (Develops the view that what is gained by having new experiences are new abilities rather than knowledge of facts; see §2.)

Loar, B. (1990) 'Phenomenal States', in J. Tomberlin, (ed.) *Philosophical Perspectives*, vol. 4, Atascadero, CA: Ridgeview. (Introduces and develops the view discussed in §2.)

Nagel, T. (1974) 'What is it Like to Be a Bat?', repr. in D. Rosenthal (ed.) *The Nature of Mind*, New York: Oxford University Press, 1991. (Develops a version of the knowledge argument against physicalism, discussed in §2.)

Rosenthal, D. (ed.) (1991) *The Nature of Mind*, New York: Oxford University Press. (Anthology includes a number of articles in this list, and many others relevant to these issues.)

Searle, J. (1992) *The Rediscovery of the Mind*, Cambridge, MA: MIT. (Argues that intentional states must have qualitative character.)

Shoemaker, S. (1990) 'First-Person Access', in J. Tomberlin (ed.) *Philosophical Perspectives*, vol. 4, Atascadero, CA: Ridgeview. (Develops views about self-knowledge discussed in §3.)

JANET LEVIN

QUANTIFICATION AND INFERENCE

Quantificational reasoning in natural languages contains occurrences of expressions which, though name-like from a syntactic perspective, intuitively seem to be importantly different from ordinary names. For example, in attempting to argue that every F is G, we might consider an 'arbitrary' F, give 'it' the 'name' 'n', and go on to argue that n is G. That such an occurrence of 'n' is somehow different from occurrences of ordinary names can be seen by noting, for example, that arguing from the claim that Bertrand Russell is F to the claim that Bertrand Russell is G in general does not suffice for drawing the conclusion that every F is G. Similarly, given that some F is G, in general we do not think it legitimate to assert that Bertrand Russell is F and G, and continue reasoning from that claim. It seems that such occurrences of 'n' differ semantically from similar occurrences of ordinary names. Thus the question arises as to the semantics of occurrences of such expressions. An adequate semantic account must justify appropriate inferences to and from sentences containing these terms.

1   **Condition of adequacy**
2   **Three semantic theories of instantial terms**

1   Condition of adequacy

Natural languages contain quantificational reasoning employing expressions which function syntactically, but not semantically, as proper names. For example, in attempting to argue that every *F* is *G*, we might consider an 'arbitrary' *F*, give 'it' the 'name' '*n*', and go on to argue that *n* is *G*. Or, having been given that some *F* is *G*, we give the 'name' '*n*' to an arbitrary *F* that is *G*, and go on to draw further conclusions concerning *n*. It will help to shed light on these terms in natural language arguments if we turn our attention to systems of natural deduction for first-order logic (see NATURAL DEDUCTION, TABLEAU AND SEQUENT SYSTEMS). For such systems contain rules which more or less mimic these natural language forms. Though formulations vary significantly, many systems have a 'universal generalization' (UG) rule which licenses the inference of '$(\forall x)\phi(x)$' from '$\phi(a)$' subject to certain restrictions, and an 'existential instantiation' (EI) rule which allows one to infer '$\phi(a)$' from '$(\exists x)\phi(x)$', again subject to restrictions. We shall call singular terms in systems of natural deduction which play the role played by 'a' above 'instantial terms'. Instead of discussing terms such as 'n' in our natural language examples, we can ask about the proper semantic treatment of instantial terms in systems of natural deduction. The regimentation and explicitness of structure of natural deduction will enable us to state conditions of adequacy precisely and to see whether those conditions are met by particular semantic theories.

As in natural language, instantial terms in natural deduction appear to behave differently from names or 'individual constants'. Both UG and EI fail to be truth-preserving if the instantial term is an individual constant. Of course, in many formulations of natural deduction, expressions from the syntactic category of individual constant (or individual variable) are pressed into service as instantial terms in applications of UG and EI. However, this probably results more from the desire not to have an additional category of singular terms than from any view about the appropriate semantics for instantial terms.

Before discussing conditions of adequacy for semantic theories of instantial terms, let us consider the view that there can be no semantic theory for instantial terms, because occurrences of formulas in applications of UG and EI which contain instantial terms should not be thought of as having any meaning. On this view, UG and EI have a certain utility in that they allow us to move from meaningful formulas to other meaningful formulas (and soundness and completeness results for systems employing these rules justify their use), but it is a mistake to think that formulas containing instantial terms in applications of UG and EI themselves have any meaning. Whatever attraction this view may have as an account of formulas containing instantial terms in formal systems, it seems quite implausible as an account of natural language sentences containing the analogues of these terms. For surely sentences containing such terms in natural language arguments are meaningful: as we read an argument containing these terms, we understand the claims made by the sentences containing them.

In an adequate semantics all allowable inferences must be truth-preserving. That is, the truth-conditions assigned to a formula must be such that, should they obtain, then so will the truth-conditions of any formula properly inferred from it. So in so far as we

provide a semantics for instantial terms and the formulas containing them, it ought to account for the inferential relations such formulas manifest. Let us call this property of a semantics 'inferential adequacy'. It is important to appreciate the difference between inferential adequacy and classical completeness and soundness results. Quine's system of deduction ([1950] 1982) is illustrative. Quine defines a 'finished derivation' as a derivation whose last line neither contains an instantial term (a 'flagged variable', in his terminology) nor depends on a premise which contains an instantial term. He then proves what he calls soundness; that the premises imply the last line of a finished derivation. However, Quine provides no semantics for instantial terms that is inferentially adequate. As he himself remarks, UG and EI are not 'implicative' relative to the only semantics he gives (which essentially treats instantial terms as names).

An inferentially adequate semantics must assign distinct truth-conditions to occurrences of the same formula in different derivations. For suppose '$(\forall x)\phi(x)$' is correctly inferred from '$\phi(a)$' in some derivation. Inferential adequacy requires the truth-conditions of this occurrence of '$\phi(a)$' to be such that it entails '$(\forall x)\phi(x)$'. On the other hand, an occurrence of '$\phi(a)$' in a derivation where it is correctly inferred from '$(\exists x)\phi(x)$' must be assigned truth-conditions such that it is entailed by the latter. Thus '$\phi(a)$' must have different truth-conditions in the two derivations.

There are different sorts of cases in which a given formula must be assigned different truth-conditions as it occurs in different derivations. Consider the following example.

(A)	(B)
$(1)(\forall x)(\exists y)Fxy$	$(1)(\exists y)(\forall x)Fxy$
$(2)(\exists y)Fay$	$(2)(\forall x)Fxb$
$(3)Fab$	$(3)Fab$
$(4)(\exists w)Faw$	$(4)(\forall z)Fzb$
$(5)(\forall z)(\exists w)Fzw$	$(5)(\exists w)(\forall z)Fzw$

In derivation (A), inferential adequacy requires that 'Fab' is logically equivalent to '$(\forall x)(\exists y)Fxy$', from which it is inferred. In (B) it must be logically equivalent to '$(\exists y)(\forall x)Fxy$'. Note that this is unlike the previous case in that it is not simply a matter of (for example) '$\phi(a)$' being inferred from '$(\exists x)\phi(x)$' in one case and having '$(\forall x)\phi(x)$' inferred from it in another. In both (A) and (B) a formula containing 'a' has a universal generalization (on the place occupied by 'a') inferred from it.

2 Three semantic theories of instantial terms

Three semantic accounts of instantial terms have been shown to satisfy the requirement of inferential adequacy. Though other inferentially adequate accounts can be imagined, we shall consider only these three. The first holds that in addition to individual people, numbers and so on there are 'arbitrary' people, numbers and so on. (An arbitrary number has every property common to all numbers, and so on.) Instantial terms are names of these arbitrary or indefinite objects. Prior to Frege's attack on such views (1904), they were widely held and are still sometimes suggested by informal comments accompanying the introduction of UG and EI in logic textbooks. Kit Fine (1985a) has made the view respectable by formulating a precise and powerful version that is inferentially adequate. On Fine's formulation, which arbitrary object a given instantial term names is determined by features of the derivation in which it occurs. An arbitrary object is associated with a range of individual objects (an arbitrary number is associated with a range of individual numbers, and so on), and a predicate is true of the arbitrary object just in case it is true of each individual object in the range. It is this which allows '$\phi(a)$' to entail '$(\forall x)\phi(x)$' under the appropriate conditions.

A second account of the semantics of instantial terms holds that they are actually quantifiers. On this view, instantial terms are expressions of generality just like ordinary quantifiers except that the quantifications they express and the scope relations they have to each other are determined by linguistic context. So, for example, in (A) and (B) above, features of the derivations determine whether 'a' and 'b' express universal or existential quantifications, and whether 'a' or 'b' has wider scope ('a' has wide scope in (A) and narrow scope in (B) relative to 'b'). On this view, suggested in Wilson (1984) and formulated as inferentially adequate in King (1991), we might say that instantial terms are 'context-dependent quantifiers', thus emphasizing both that they express quantifications and that the quantifications they express and the relative scopes of those quantifications vary with the linguistic context. On such a view, '$\phi(a)$' entails '$(\forall x)\phi(x)$' (under the appropriate conditions) because '$\phi(a)$' itself expresses a quantified claim.

The third view is that instantial terms are to be thought of as ε-terms. Hilbert introduced the ε-operator as a variable-binding operator used to form terms: if 'ϕ' is a formula (some presentations require 'ϕ' to contain free 'x'), then '$\varepsilon x\phi$' is a singular term. Though Hilbert provided no explicit semantics for singular terms formed using the ε-operator, he remarked that '$\varepsilon x\phi$' should be thought of as denoting an arbitrary element in the domain satisfying 'ϕ' if anything does (if nothing satisfies 'ϕ', the term can be thought of as denoting any element in the domain). Further, Hilbert provided the following axiom to govern ε-terms: $(\exists x)\phi(x) \rightarrow \phi(\varepsilon x\phi)$. This axiom justifies the following rules of inference for ε-terms: (1) infer '$\phi(\varepsilon x\phi)$' from '$(\exists x)\phi(x)$'; and (2) infer '$(\forall x)\phi(x)$' from '$\phi(\varepsilon x{\sim}\phi)$'. Thus Hazen (1987) considers constructing a system of natural deduction in which (1) and (2) replace EI and UG respectively, but in which we abbreviate the ε-terms used in applications of (1) and (2) by single letters. Derivations using such abbreviations would be indistinguishable from those in Quine's (1950) system. A semantics for ε-terms of the sort given in Leisenring (1969) would result in an inferentially adequate theory.

Which of the three views discussed above is ultimately preferable appears to depend on philosophical and methodological considerations. In fact, it is not clear how different the views really are. One might well complain that arbitrary objects are unnecessary intermediaries, and that the ranges of individuals with which they are associated do all the real semantic work. But when arbitrary objects are eliminated from the first view and instantial terms are directly associated with ranges of individuals, the first and second views begin to look quite similar. In addition, since, following Hilbert, we can use ε-terms to 'define' the quantifiers $((\forall x)\phi(x) \leftrightarrow \phi(\varepsilon x{\sim}\phi))$ and $(\exists x)\phi(x) \leftrightarrow \phi(\varepsilon x\phi))$, it is unclear whether the difference between the second view (instantial terms are quantifiers) and the third view (instantial terms are ε-terms) is substantive.

See also: LOGICAL AND MATHEMATICAL TERMS, GLOSSARY OF

References and further reading

Fine, K. (1983) 'A Defence of Arbitrary Objects', *Proceedings of the Aristotelian Society*, supplementary vol. 57: 55–77. (An informal introduction to Fine's theory of arbitrary objects. The least technical of Fine's writings on the subject.)

* —— (1985a) *Reasoning with Arbitrary Objects*, Oxford: Blackwell. (Fine's definitive and most technical work on arbitrary objects.)

—— (1985b) 'Natural Deduction and Arbitrary Objects', *Journal of Philosophical Logic* 14: 57–107. (A fairly technical work which presents some highlights of Fine (1985a).)

* Frege, G. (1904) 'Was ist eine Funktion?', trans. 'What is a Function?', in *Translations from the*

Philosophical Writings of Gottlob Frege, ed. P.T. Geach and M. Black, Oxford: Blackwell, 1977. (An attack on the view that instantial terms name indefinite objects.)

* Hazen, A. (1987) 'Natural Deduction and Hilbert's ε-Operator', *Journal Of Philosophical Logic* 16: 411–21. (An outline of the view that instantial terms can be thought of as abbreviations of ε-terms. Informally written, but presupposes significant exposure to first-order logic and Fine (1985).)

King, J.C. (1987) 'Pronouns, Descriptions and the Semantics of Discourse', *Philosophical Studies* 51: 341–63. (Introduction to the view that instantial terms are contextually sensitive quantifier-like expressions of generality; very accessible.)

* —— (1991) 'Instantial Terms, Anaphora and Arbitrary Objects', *Philosophical Studies* 61: 239–65. (Compares the account of instantial terms as context-dependent quantifiers to the account of Fine (1983, 1985). The presentation is informal; technical material in the appendix.)

* Leisenring, A.C. (1969) *Mathematical Logic and Hilbert's ε-Symbol*, New York: Gordon & Breach. (The best English introduction to formal systems containing ε-terms; technical, but self-contained.)

* Quine, W.V. (1950) *Methods of Logic*, New York: Holt; repr., Cambridge, MA: Harvard University Press, 4th edn, 1982. (System of natural deduction discussed in both Hazen (1987) and Fine (1985). The 1950 and 1982 editions differ significantly.)

* Wilson, G. (1984) 'Pronouns and Pronominal Descriptions: A New Semantical Category', *Philosophical Studies* 45: 1–30. (The first paper to suggest that instantial terms are quantifier-like expressions of generality; very accessible.)

JEFFREY C. KING

QUANTIFIERS

The quantifiers 'some' and 'every' were the object of the very first logical theory, Aristotelian syllogistic. An example of a syllogism is 'Every Spartan is Greek, every Greek is European, therefore every Spartan is European'. In such inferences, no quantifier is governed by another one. Contrast this with 'Everybody loves somebody'. Modern logic is often taken to have begun when Frege systematized for the first time the logic of quantifiers, including such dependent ones. In general, much of what has passed as logic over the centuries is in effect the study of quantifiers. This is especially clear with the area of logic variously known as quantification theory, lower predicate calculus or elementary logic.

Some philosophers have even sought to limit the scope of logic to such a study of quantifiers. Yet the nature of quantifiers is a delicate matter which is captured incompletely by the logic initiated by Frege and Russell.

1 **Interpretation of the quantifiers**
2 **The game-theoretic approach**

1 Interpretation of the quantifiers

Traditionally, quantifiers have been taken to be those expressions which somehow indicate the size of the extension of a predicate (see LOGIC, ANCIENT §§1–3; PREDICATE CALCULUS), for example, expressions such as 'some' (the existential quantifier), 'every' (the universal quantifier), the numerical quantifiers 'one', 'two', 'three', ..., 'many', 'few' and so on. The logical properties of the existential and universal quantifiers are studied in quantification theory or first-order logic. The numerical quantifiers are definable in terms of the existential and universal quantifiers, unlike quantifiers such as 'many' and 'few'. For this reason the latter are sometimes called nonstandard quantifiers. Here we shall be concerned mainly with the standard quantifiers 'some' and 'every'. When such quantifiers are applied to higher-order entities (predicates, relations, functions, predicates, relations and functions of predicates, relations and functions and so on), we are dealing with higher-order quantifiers (see SECOND- AND HIGHER-ORDER LOGICS).

The formulas of a first-order language L are built out of a set of nonlogical constants and individual variables by means of propositional connectives, the identity symbol and quantifiers. Typically, the formation rules for quantifiers allow us to take a formula with a free variable x and to prefix to it the existential quantifier '$\exists x$' or the universal quantifier '$\forall x$'. The formula is then called the 'scope' of the quantifier in question (see SCOPE). In the resulting formula – for example, $(\exists x)(\ldots x \ldots)$ – the variable x is said to be 'bound' by the quantifier '$\exists x$'. The nonlogical constants can be predicates, function symbols or individual constants.

A first-order formal language allows us to systematize the laws of quantification. Usually, a number of logically true (valid) formulas are assumed as logical axioms and a number of rules of inference are used to derive other logical truths (ideally, all of them) as theorems. A complete axiomatization of ordinary quantification theory was first given by Gödel in 1929. A theoretically more illuminating completeness proof was given by Henkin in 1949.

Quantification theory must be considered semantically, not only as a purely formal system. To specify the meaning of an interpreted first-order sentence is to specify its truth-conditions. Usually, such a specification of truth-conditions is done step by step, starting from inside, and at each step indicating how the truth or falsity of an expression depends on the truth or falsity of its component expressions. Such specifications of meaning are said to satisfy the principle of 'compositionality' (see COMPOSITIONALITY).

Any specification of truth-values must be relative to a model of the underlying language. The set of elements (individuals) of this model is called its domain. A quantifier is often said to range over this domain.

The truth-value of an interpreted and quantified sentence, say, $(\forall x)(\ldots x \ldots)$, cannot be specified in terms of the truth-value of the formula $(\ldots x \ldots)$, for the latter contains a free variable and hence does not have a truth-value. The truth-value of $(\forall x)(\ldots x \ldots)$ therefore has to be defined as a function of all the substitution instances of $(\ldots x \ldots)$ or else through the other semantic attributes of $(\ldots x \ldots)$. Tarski, who was the first to formulate an explicit truth-definition for quantificational languages (1933), chose the latter course and defined truth for first-order languages via the notion of satisfaction, so preserving the compositionality of his procedure (see TARSKI'S DEFINITION OF TRUTH).

Tarski's truth-definition is a formal specification of truth-conditions of sentences containing quantifiers, not yet a genuine interpretation of quantifiers. There are three main interpretations of quantifiers in the literature.

(A) *Quantifiers as higher-order predicates.* On this view, what, for example, the existential quantifier does in a sentence such as

(1) $(\exists x)S(x)$

is to say that the complex or simple predicate $S(x)$ is not empty. This is the approach we described above and is *prima facie* quite natural. It goes back to Frege. Its most important systematization and further development is the theory of so-called generalized quantifiers, currently the dominant trend in the study of quantifiers among theoretical linguists (see QUANTIFIERS, GENERALIZED).

(B) *Substitutional interpretations of quantifiers.* On such an interpretation, the import of a sentence such as (1) is explained in terms of the set of different substitution-instances of the open formula S(x) (see QUANTIFIERS, SUBSTITUTIONAL AND OBJECTUAL).

(C) *Quantifiers as choice terms.* The basic idea can be explained by example. A natural interpretation of the sentence

(2)   Every man owns a dog

is to say that for any man given to one, one can

choose a dog such that the given man owns the chosen dog. In the formal counterpart of (2),

(3) $(\forall x)(\exists y)O(x,y)$,

we would say that, for every value of x, one can find a value of y such that $O(x, y)$. We can say that on this view quantifiers codify suitable choice terms. This way of interpreting quantifiers is systematized and generalized in Hintikka's game-theoretic semantics (see Hintikka and Sandu 1996).

2   The game-theoretic approach

In this game-theoretic treatment, a sentence such as (3) above is interpreted via a semantic game played by 'myself' (the initial verifier) against 'nature' (the initial falsifier), the former trying to produce true sentences while the latter is striving for the contrary. The universal quantifier '$\forall x$' in (3) marks a move by 'nature', who must choose an individual, say d, from the universe of the model in which (3) is evaluated, and the existential quantifier '$\exists y$' marks a move by 'myself', who must also choose an individual, say e. The sentence (3) is defined to be true if 'myself' has a method (usually codified by a mathematical function f) which, for every individual d chosen by 'nature' gives him the 'right' choice e, that is, $O(d,e)$ holds. More precisely, $O(d,f(d))$ holds (see SEMANTICS, GAME-THEORETIC).

The central notion involved in interpretation (C) is that of a strategy, that is, a rule which specifies which move a player is to make in any possible situation which might come up in the game. The idea of an 'independent' quantifier is captured by that of an informationally independent choice. For instance, in (3) the choice of a value of y depends on the choice of a value of x in the sense that the choice connected with y is made on the basis of the player's knowledge of the value that was chosen for x, but not vice versa. In the jargon of game-theory, a game associated with a sentence of ordinary first-order language is one of perfect information.

In the usual formal (but interpreted) first-order languages, the three interpretations (A)–(C) assign the same truth-value to each sentence. Nevertheless, several things distinguish (C) from (A) and (B).

First, only interpretation (C) does justice to the fact that the expressive power of first-order languages lies in the dependence of quantifiers on each other. To understand first-order logic is, in this sense, to understand the idea of a dependent quantifier. In contrast, in (A) and (B), quantifiers are considered in isolation from each other. Interpretations of type (C) guided the work of David Hilbert and his school in the 1920s and 1930s (see Hilbert and Bernays 1934) and similar views have enjoyed a widespread albeit inconspicuous currency in mathematical practice.

Second, (C), unlike (A), yields a non-compositional interpretation of the standard quantifiers. An existential quantifier '$\exists y$' is interpreted in (C) by a choice function whose arguments are certain universally quantified variables. Which ones they are depends on the context.

Interpretation (C) offers an interesting possibility of generalizing quantification theory (first-order logic). If one understands the idea of a dependent quantifier as illustrated by (3), one *ipso facto* understands the idea of an independent quantifier. What often passes unnoticed is that the usual nested ordering of scopes for first-order logic rules out certain perfectly possible and understandable patterns of mutual dependence and independence between quantifiers, in that it is required that the scopes of two different quantifiers are either exclusive or nested, that is, that their scopes do not overlap only partially.

But what happens when this arbitrary restriction is given up? As an example, consider the first-order formula

(4) $(\forall x)(\exists y)(\forall z)(\exists w)S(x,y,z,w)$.

The question is what happens if in (4) we require '$\exists w$' to be within the scope of '$\forall z$' but not in that of '$\forall x$'? There is no way of expressing this complex of dependencies in the usual linear notation of first-order logic. For that purpose, a different notation has to be introduced. A special kind of informational independence has been studied by logicians under the title of 'branching quantifiers'. They were introduced by Henkin in 1959. A more general way of indicating independence is to use a slash notation:

(5) $(\forall x)(\exists y)(\forall z)(\exists w/\forall x)S(x,y,z,w)$.

The idea here is that the last existential quantifier does not depend on '$\forall x$'.

What can be said of quantifiers can also be said, *mutatis mutandis*, of disjunctions and conjunctions: the independence indicator slash can be applied to them too. The languages using the slash notation are called independence-friendly first-order languages.

Neither approach (A) nor approach (B) works for independence-friendly first-order languages. The reason is that such a language involves context dependencies which make a compositional interpretation unrealistic. For a compositional interpretation requires that the meaning of an expression be specified in terms of its component parts. This is not the case with the expression $(\exists w/\forall x)S(x,y,z,w)$ in (5), for its interpretation makes reference to an element '$\forall x$' which occurs outside it.

In contrast, interpretation (C) extends naturally to cover this new language. All we need is to drop the requirement that the semantic game associated with a sentence such as (5) is one of perfect information.

What has been said has a number of consequences not usually noted in the study of quantifiers.

(1) The meaning of quantifiers is often explained in terms of their 'ranging over' a set of entities. Such an explanation presupposes an interpretation along the lines of (A) or (B) and hence is not a general explanation of the meaning of quantifiers.

(2) The notion of quantifier scope is ambiguous. The usual formal scope notation indicates two different things. On the one hand, it indicates the relative logical priority of different quantifiers (and connectives); on the other, it indicates the segment of a formula (or a discourse) in which a variable is bound by a given quantifier. There is no reason to expect that these two always go together, and in natural languages they seem to involve entirely different mechanisms.

(3) Certain types of quantifiers, namely informationally independent ones, do not admit of a natural compositional truth-definition, but have to be treated in other ways semantically.

(4) A general theory of quantification will have to comprise more than is currently known as quantification theory or ordinary first-order logic.

(5) Since independence-friendly first-order logic is not axiomatizable, it is unrealistic to expect the logic of quantifiers to admit of a complete systematization.

(6) The logical behaviour of quantifiers in natural languages seems to differ more radically from ordinary formal first-order logic than has usually been recognized.

See also: LOGICAL CONSTANTS; LOGICAL AND MATHEMATICAL TERMS, GLOSSARY OF; QUANTIFICATION AND INFERENCE

References and further reading

Frege, G. (1879) *Begriffsschrift, eine der arithmetischen nachgebildete Formelsprache des reinen Denkens*, Halle: Nebert; trans. J. van Heijenoort, '*Begriffsschrift*, a Formula Language, Modelled Upon That of Arithmetic, for Pure Thought', in J. van Heijenoort (ed.) *From Frege to Gödel: A Source Book in Mathematical Logic 1879–1931*, Cambridge, MA: Harvard University Press, 1967. (First explicit logic of quantifiers.)

* Gödel, K. (1929) 'Über die Vollständigkeit des Logikkalküls' (doctoral dissertation, University of Vienna), in *Kurt Gödel: Collected Works*, vol. 1, *Publications 1929–1936*, ed. S. Feferman, J.W. Dawson Jr, S.C. Kleene, G.H. Moore, R.M.

Solovay and J. van Heijenoort, Oxford: Oxford University Press, 1986, 60–101. (First completeness proof for ordinary first-order logic of quantifiers.)

Goldfarb, W. (1979) 'Logic in the Twenties: The Nature of the Quantifier', *Journal of Symbolic Logic* 44: 351–68. (Changing conceptions of quantifiers from Frege to Hilbert.)

* Henkin, L. (1949) 'Completeness in the Theory of Types', *Journal of Symbolic Logic* 14: 159–66. (Greatly improved completeness proof.)

* —— (1959) 'Some Remarks on Infinitely Long Formulas', in *Infinitistic Methods*, Oxford: Pergamon, 167–83. (First use of informationally independent quantifiers.)

* Hilbert, D. and Bernays, P. (1934) *Grundlagen der Mathematik I–II*, Berlin: Springer. (Quantifiers and choice functions.)

* Hintikka, J. and Sandu, G. (1996) 'Game-Theoretical Semantics', in J. van Benthem and A. ter Meulen (eds) *Handbook of Logic and Language*, Amsterdam: Elsevier. (A survey of game-theoretic semantics.)

Hintikka, J. and Kulas, J. (1985) *Anaphora and Definite Descriptions*, Dordrecht: Reidel. (Quantifiers in natural languages.)

Kripke, S.A. (1976) 'Is There a Problem about Substitutional Quantification?', in G. Evans and J. McDowell (eds) *Truth and Meaning*, Oxford: Oxford University Press, 325–419. (A spirited defence of the substitutional interpretation.)

* Tarski, A. (1933) *Pojęcie prawdy w językach nauk dedukcyjnych*, Warsaw; trans. J.H. Woodger (1956), 'On the Concept of Truth in Formalized Languages', in *Logic, Semantics, Metamathematics*, ed. J. Corcoran, Indianapolis, IN: Hackett Publishing Company, 2nd edn, 1983, 152–278. (The classic work on the concept of truth.)

Westerståhl, D. (1989) 'Quantifiers in Formal and Natural Languages', in D. Gabbay and F. Guenthner (eds) *Handbook of Philosophical Logic*, Dordrecht: Reidel, vol. 4, 1–131. (A survey of the theory of generalized quantifiers.)

JAAKKO HINTIKKA
GABRIEL SANDU

QUANTIFIERS, GENERALIZED

Generalized quantifiers are logical tools with a wide range of uses. As the term indicates, they generalize the ordinary universal and existential quantifiers from first-order logic, '$\forall x$' and '$\exists x$', which apply to a formula $A(x)$, binding its free occurrences of x. $\forall x A(x)$ says that $A(x)$ holds for all objects in the universe and $\exists x A(x)$ says that $A(x)$ holds for some objects in the universe, that is, in each case, that a certain condition on $A(x)$ is satisfied. It is natural then to consider other conditions, such as 'for at least five', 'at most ten', 'infinitely many' and 'most'. So a quantifier Q stands for a condition on $A(x)$, or, more precisely, for a property of the set denoted by that formula, such as the property of being non-empty, being infinite, or containing more than half of the elements of the universe. The addition of such quantifiers to a logical language may increase its expressive power.

A further generalization allows Q to apply to more than one formula, so that, for example, $Qx(A(x), B(x))$ states that a relation holds between the sets denoted by $A(x)$ and $B(x)$, say, the relation of having the same number of elements, or of having a non-empty intersection. One also considers quantifiers binding more than one variable in a formula. $Qxy,zu(R(x,y), S(z,u))$ could express, for example, that the relation (denoted by) $R(x,y)$ contains twice as many pairs as $S(z,u)$, or that $R(x,y)$ and $S(z,u)$ are isomorphic graphs.

In general, then, a quantifier (the attribute 'generalized' is often dropped) is syntactically a variable-binding operator, which stands semantically for a relation between relations (on individuals), that is, a second-order relation. Quantifiers are studied in mathematical logic, and have also been applied in other areas, notably in the semantics of natural languages. This entry first presents some of the main logical facts about generalized quantifiers, and then explains their application to semantics.

1   **The general concept**
2   **Quantifiers in logic**
3   **Quantifiers and natural language**

1   The general concept

A (generalized) quantifier is a relation between relations on individuals (in other words, a second-order relation). Its *type*, a finite sequence of positive numbers, indicates how many relations and of what degree. For example, a quantifier of type $\langle 2, 1, 1, 4 \rangle$ is a relation between one binary relation (that is, a relation of order 2), two sets and one four-place relation. Let M be a non-empty universe. Then define a (local) quantifier of type $\langle 2, 1, 1, 4 \rangle$ *on* M to be any relation between a binary relation on M, two subsets of M and a four-place relation on M. Then a (global) quantifier Q of type $\langle 2, 1, 1, 4 \rangle$ is a function which associates with each universe M a quantifier Q_M of the same type on M.

The quantifiers '$\forall$' and '$\exists$' are thus of type $\langle 1 \rangle$.

Below are definitions of these and some other type $\langle 1 \rangle$ quantifiers, with M any universe, A any subset of M, and $|A|$ the cardinality of A (Q^R is called the Rescher quantifier):

$$\forall_M A \Leftrightarrow A = M$$
$$\exists_M A \Leftrightarrow A$$
$$(\exists_{\geq 5})_M A \Leftrightarrow |A| \geq 5$$
$$(\exists_{\leq 10})_M A \Leftrightarrow |A| \leq 10$$
$$(Q_0)_M A \Leftrightarrow A$$
$$(Q^R)_M A \Leftrightarrow |A| > |M - A|$$

Here are some more examples of quantifiers (types are written to the left):

$\langle 1,1 \rangle$ $I_M AB \Leftrightarrow |A| = |B|$ (the Härtig quantifier)

$\langle 1,1,1 \rangle$ *more...than*$_M ABC \Leftrightarrow |A \cap C| > |B \cap C|$

$\langle 2 \rangle$ $W_M R \Leftrightarrow R$ is a well-order of M

$\langle 2,2 \rangle$ $IG_M RS \Leftrightarrow R$ and S are isomorphic graphs

The notion of a type $\langle 1 \rangle$ quantifier was introduced by Andrzej Mostowski (1957), and extended to arbitrary types by Per Lindström (1966). Aristotle's syllogisms (see LOGIC, ANCIENT §§1–3) involve type $\langle 1,1 \rangle$ quantifiers, a natural class, as will be seen in §3. The general notion of quantifiers as variable-binding operators denoting second-order relations was in fact explicit in Frege's work, except that Frege did not relativize to an arbitrary universe (see FREGE, G. §6).

The quantifiers above share an important property, closure under isomorphism (or ISOM). We use the following notation: a function f from a set X to a set Y is 'lifted' to subsets A of X, or to (for example) ternary relations R on X, by $f(A) = \{f(a) : a \in A\}$ and $f(R) = \{(f(a), f(b), f(c)) : (a,b,c) \in R\}$. Now for a quantifier Q of type $\langle 2,1,1,4 \rangle$, say, define Q to be *closed under isomorphism* if whenever f is a bijection from M to M' (a one-one function from M onto M'), and R, A, B, S are appropriate arguments for Q_M,

$$Q_M RABS \Leftrightarrow Q_{M'} f(R) f(A) f(B) f(S).$$

ISOM says that Q does not care about the individual elements of a universe, only about their 'structure' with respect to the relational arguments. This allows quantifiers to be treated as logical constants (see §2 below; LOGICAL CONSTANTS §3). ISOM has a particularly clear meaning for quantifiers which relate sets, so-called 'monadic' quantifiers (that is, of type $\langle 1,1,\ldots,1 \rangle$). It then says that Q only cares about the cardinalities of these sets (and sets that can be formed from them by taking unions, intersections and complements), not the sets themselves. For example, for a type $\langle 1,1 \rangle$ quantifier, ISOM is equivalent to the following condition:

If $A, B \subseteq M$, $A', B' \subseteq M'$, $|A \cap B| = |A' \cap B'|$, $|A - B| = |A' - B'|$, $|B - A| = |B' - A'|$, and $|M - (A \cup B)| = |M' - (A' \cup B')|$, then $Q_M AB \Leftrightarrow Q_{M'} A'B'$.

Thus, in the monadic case, ISOM quantifiers deal with *quantities*, as the name suggests they should. Indeed, such a quantifier can be redefined as a relation between numbers; the examples above provide illustrations.

2 Quantifiers in logic

Generalized quantifiers are easy to add as new logical constants to first-order logic, FO. For example, 'A is finite' cannot be expressed in FO, but if we add the quantifier Q_0 above, the sentence $\neg Q_0 xPx$ expresses precisely that the denotation of P is finite. If Q is a quantifier of type $\langle 2,1,1 \rangle$, say, the logic FO(Q) is formed from FO by adding a formation rule allowing formulas of the form

(1) $Qxy, z, u(A(x,y), B(z), C(u)),$

where $A(x,y)$, $B(z)$ and $C(u)$ are formulas. Free occurrences of the indicated variables become bound in (1). To interpret (1) in a model $\mathbf{M}$ with universe M, note that relative to $\mathbf{M}$ and the variables x, y (and a variable assignment which we suppress here), $A(x,y)$ denotes a binary relation $A(x,y)^{\mathbf{M}}$ on M, namely, the set of pairs (a,b) such that $A(a,b)$ holds in $\mathbf{M}$. Then, (1) is defined to be true in $\mathbf{M}$ if and only if $Q_M A(x,y)^{\mathbf{M}} B(z)^{\mathbf{M}} C(u)^{\mathbf{M}}$. This generalizes the usual clauses for $\forall x A(x)$ and $\exists x A(x)$ in the truth-definition for FO. Logical consequence in FO(Q) is defined as usual (the conclusion must be true in every model of the premises – see MODEL THEORY). And just as FO can be used to formulate theories, like arithmetic or group theory (first-order theories), so can FO(Q). The properties of these theories, and of the consequence relation, will of course depend on Q.

Similarly, one defines logics of the form FO($Q_1, \ldots, Q_n$). This is a model-theoretic conception of a logic as given roughly by a class of sentences, a class of models and a truth-relation between them (in contrast, a proof-theoretic conception would emphasize a formal inference system). Some basic constraints apply; for example, only ISOM quantifiers are considered.

Abstract model theory studies the properties of model-theoretic logics in general, logics with generalized quantifiers being prime examples. Among interesting properties of a logic L are axiomatizability (existence of a formal inference system proving precisely the valid sentences of L), compactness (if every finite subset of a set Φ of L-sentences has a model then the whole of Φ has a model) and the Löwenheim property (if an L-sentence has an infinite model it has a denumerable model; see LÖWENHEIM–SKOLEM THEOREMS AND NONSTANDARD MODELS §§2, 3). FO has these properties and several stronger properties as well, and a celebrated result of abstract model theory is that such properties in fact characterize FO. To state this one needs a way to compare the expressive power of various logics. A logic L' is said to be an extension of a logic L, $L \leqslant L'$, if everything that can be said in L can also be said in L', in other words if for every L-sentence there is a logically equivalent L'-sentence (one with the same models). Also, $L \equiv L'$ if $L \leqslant L'$ and $L' \leqslant L$. Note that if L is a logic with generalized quantifiers, FO $\leqslant L$. Given a simple assumption about these quantifiers, one can prove the following result (Lindström's theorem):

> If L is either compact or axiomatizable, and has the Löwenheim property, then FO $\equiv L$.

Thus, increase of expressive power entails loss of some of FO's properties. For example, if 'A is finite' is expressible in L, it can be seen that L can be neither compact nor axiomatizable. But there do exist compact and axiomatizable proper extensions of FO (hence the Löwenheim property fails for them), the simplest example being FO(Q_1), where Q_1 is the quantifier 'there exist uncountably many'. Extending FO should be done with care, to strike a balance between expressive power and model-theoretic behaviour.

How many different quantifiers (of a given type) are there? Locally, the rough answer is: many times more than the size of the universe (see Westerståhl 1989: §4.6 for more detail). For example, if M has n elements, then there are 2^{4^n} type $\langle 1, 1 \rangle$ quantifiers on M. So there are $2^{16} = 65,536$ type $\langle 1, 1 \rangle$ quantifiers on a universe with 2 elements! Counting only ISOM quantifiers the number is 1,024, still large compared to 2. As to global quantifiers, even if we restrict attention to finite universes there are uncountably many ISOM quantifiers of each type.

Some of these different quantifiers will have the same expressive power. For example, $\exists_{\geqslant 5}$ is definable in FO, so FO($\exists_{\geqslant 5}$) $\equiv$ FO. In general, a quantifier Q is said to be definable in a logic L if it is defined by some L-sentence whose nonlogical symbols match the type of Q. So for a Q of type $\langle 2, 1, 1 \rangle$ to be definable in L there must exist an L-sentence with nonlogical symbols P_1, P_2, and P_3, with P_1 binary and P_2, P_3 unary, which is logically equivalent to $Qxy, z, u(P_1xy, P_2z, P_3u)$. We have FO($Q_1, \ldots, Q_n$) $\leqslant L$ if and only if each Q_i is definable in L.

The number of non-equivalent logics of the form

FO(Q) is still uncountable, for each type of Q. Moreover, the types yield a strict hierarchy of expressive power. Types can be compared with respect to the largest degree of the relation arguments. For example, $\langle 2, 1, 1, 3, 3 \rangle$ is lower than $\langle 2, 4 \rangle$. A more fine-grained (partial) order also takes into account the number of arguments of each degree. Then $\langle 3, 1, 2, 3 \rangle$ is lower than $\langle 2, 1, 1, 3, 3 \rangle$ since it has fewer unary arguments but the same number of binary and ternary arguments. It can be proved that in each type there are quantifiers not definable in any logic FO($Q_1, \ldots, Q_n$) with $Q_1, \ldots, Q_n$ of lower types (in the more fine-grained order). Again this holds even if only finite models are considered.

The study of quantifiers in mathematical logic has either been in the direction of abstract model theory or focused on logics with particular quantifiers (and theories formulated in such logics), a prominent case being FO(Q_1) and certain of its extensions. Quantifiers have also found applications outside mathematics. Restricted to finite models, they have turned up in computer science, in attempts to find extensions of FO 'capturing' certain complexity classes from the theory of computational complexity. They have been applied to modal logic, and to the study of conditionals. But perhaps the most striking application concerns the semantics of natural languages, to which we now turn.

3 Quantifiers and natural language

Consider the following sentence form, common to many languages.

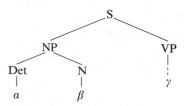

The sentence (S) consists of a noun phrase (NP) and a verb phrase (VP), and the NP in turn consists of a determiner (Det) and a noun (N). A simple English example is

(2)   No student smokes

but Det, N and VP could be complex expressions. Now, given a universe M, N typically denotes a subset A of M, and VP another subset, B. Thus, Det is most straightforwardly taken to denote a binary relation between subsets of M, that is, a type $\langle 1, 1 \rangle$ quantifier on M. Varying M, Det denotes a global type $\langle 1, 1 \rangle$ quantifier.

In (2), this quantifier is $no_M AB \Leftrightarrow A \cap B = \emptyset$. Other Dets denote other quantifiers:

$$all_M AB \Leftrightarrow A \subseteq B$$
$$at\ least\ five_M AB \Leftrightarrow |A \cap B| \geqslant 5$$
$$most_M AB \Leftrightarrow |A \cap B| > |A - B|$$
$$all\ but\ three_M AB \Leftrightarrow |A - B| = 3$$
$$more\ than\ two\text{-}thirds\ of\ the_M AB \Leftrightarrow |A \subseteq B| > \tfrac{2}{3}|A|$$
$$all \ldots except\ John_M AB \Leftrightarrow A - B = \{j\}$$

The last example comes from a 'discontinuous' Det, as in, for example, 'All students except John smoke'. A few Dets take more than one noun argument, as in

More students than teachers smoke,

which involves the type $\langle 1,1,1 \rangle$ quantifier 'more ...than' mentioned in §1.

Furthermore, NPs naturally denote type $\langle 1 \rangle$ quantifiers: 'at least five students' denotes the set of subsets of M containing at least five students. In general one obtains such NP denotations from Det denotations by fixing a particular noun. Also NPs without Dets, such as 'John', or 'Bill and Sue', may be taken to denote type $\langle 1 \rangle$ quantifiers:

$$John_M B \Leftrightarrow j \in B$$
$$Bill\ and\ Sue_M B \Leftrightarrow b \in B \,\&\, s \in B$$

This treatment of proper names may seem complex, but has the advantage of allowing all NPs to be interpreted in the same way.

Thus, generalized quantifiers appear in a linguistic context not by means of some technical trick or invention, but rather as the most straightforward way to treat the semantics of noun phrases.

Still, is it really necessary to bring in generalized quantifiers here? After all, 'all' can be defined in FO by $\forall x(Ax \rightarrow Bx)$ and, similarly, quantifiers such as 'at least five'. Nevertheless, sticking to FO is not advisable. First, the use of type $\langle 1,1 \rangle$ quantifiers respects the syntactic form of sentences whereas a translation into FO does not. So generalized quantifiers facilitate a compositional semantics for natural language (see COMPOSITIONALITY). Second, in important cases a translation into FO is simply impossible. For example, proportional quantifiers such as 'most' or 'more than two thirds of the' are undefinable in FO. That is, there is no sentence in first-order logic, however complex, which adequately accounts for the truth-conditions of, say, 'Most students smoke'. In fact, one can even prove that there is no such sentence in any logic $FO(Q_1, \ldots, Q_n)$ with $Q_1, \ldots, Q_n$ of type $\langle 1 \rangle$. So type $\langle 1,1 \rangle$ quantifiers are crucial also with respect to expressive power.

Most Dets have ISOM denotations, with putative exceptions including 'every...but John' or 'John's'. If 'John' denotes a fixed individual ISOM will fail, but there are various strategies for avoiding such Dets. The salient property of Det denotations, however, is the special role played by the first argument, coming from the noun: it restricts the domain of quantification. Formally this is reflected in two constraints, called 'conservativity' and 'extension': for all M, $A, B \subseteq M$ and $M \subseteq M'$,

CONS $\quad Q_M AB \Leftrightarrow Q_M A\ A \cap B$

EXT $\quad Q_M AB \Leftrightarrow Q_{M'} AB$

CONS says that only that part of the verb argument matters which is common to the noun argument. Indeed, 'All but three students smoke' is equivalent to 'All but three students are students which smoke'. CONS predicts, for example, that the Härtig quantifier $rmI_M AB \Leftrightarrow |A| = |B|$ (for which CONS fails) is not the denotation of any Det. EXT implies that the rest of the universe – the part lying outside the noun denotation – is irrelevant. It predicts, for example, that there can be no Det meaning 'some' on universes with, say, fewer than ten elements, and meaning 'most' on other universes.

Discounting a few marginal (and debatable) exceptions, all Det denotations appear to satisfy CONS and EXT. Other properties single out subclasses of quantifiers. Call Q 'intersective' if only the intersection of the noun and the verb argument matters; $A \cap B = A' \cap B'$ implies $Q_M AB \Leftrightarrow Q_M A'B'$. Examples are 'some', 'at least five', 'exactly three' and 'only finitely many'. This turns out to be related to the acceptability of the corresponding Dets in 'there'-constructions: 'There are some/at least five/no cows in the barn' is fine, but 'There are all but five/most/all cows in the barn', with non-intersective Dets, is not.

Monotonicity properties are also significant. Q is 'right monotone increasing' (or decreasing) if $Q_M AB$ and $B \subseteq B'$ (or $B' \subseteq B$) implies $Q_M AB'$. Similarly for monotonicity in the left argument. Many Dets denote right monotone quantifiers. For example, 'more than two thirds of the' is right monotone increasing, and 'at most one third of the' is right monotone decreasing (neither is left monotone). And many non-monotone cases, such as '(exactly) five', 'between three and five' and 'ten per cent of', are conjunctions of a decreasing and an increasing quantifier. Right monotonicity has been related to various linguistic phenomena, in particular so-called 'negative polarity items'. Left monotonicity is more scarce among Det denotations. It may be shown that, over finite models and assuming CONS and EXT, all left monotone quantifiers are first-order definable. Left monotone Det denotations are usually also right monotone. The four possible kinds of 'double monotonicity' are exemplified in the Aristotelian square of opposition:

Indeed, given CONS and a certain uniformity requirement, it can be proved that these are the *only* doubly monotone quantifiers (without this requirement there are other examples: 'at most ten', 'all but at most three', 'infinitely many').

NP and Det denotations are normally monadic: they relate sets. But sentences can combine several NPs with a transitive verb:

(3) tab; Most students know at least three teachers.

The truth-conditions of (3) are an *iteration* of the two type $\langle 1,1 \rangle$ quantifiers involved: formally (with A the set of students, B the set of teachers and R the relation of knowing), $most_M A\{a \text{ at least three}_M B\{b\ Rab\}\}$. However, other seemingly similar sentences combine the quantifiers differently, for example:

(4) tab; 1,200 philosophers wrote 2,000 entries for the Encyclopedia,

which does *not* mean that each of the 1,200 philosophers wrote 2,000 entries, as an iterated reading would have it, but rather that each of them wrote *some* entry, and that each of the 2,000 entries was written by *some* one (or more) of them. This mode of combination has been called 'cumulation'. Another suggested mode is 'branching':

(5) tab; Most of the students and most of the teachers all know each other

appears to have the reading that there is a large subset X of the set of students (containing more than half of them) and a large subset Y of the set of teachers such that every student in X and every teacher in Y know each other. Again this is not an iterated reading. But note that (3), (4) and (5) can be accounted for by quantifiers of type $\langle 1,1,2 \rangle$, taking two set arguments from the nouns and one relation argument from the verb. For (3) and (4) this quantifier is definable from the monadic Det denotations, but not so for (5). More precisely, it can be shown that the branching of 'most' as in (5) is not definable in FO('most'). Examples like this indicate a possible use also for polyadic (non-monadic) quantifiers in the semantics of natural languages.

See also: LOGICAL AND MATHEMATICAL TERMS, GLOSSARY OF

References and further reading

Barwise, J. and Feferman, S. (eds) (1985) *Model-Theoretic Logics*, Berlin: Springer. (Classical, handbook-style reference for abstract model theory and the mathematics of quantifiers.)

Benthem, J. van (1986) *Essays in Logical Semantics*, Dordrecht: Reidel. (Includes some of the papers that initiated the subject of generalized quantifiers and natural language.)

Benthem, J. van and Westerståhl, D. (1995) 'Directions in Generalized Quantifier Theory', *Studia Logica* 55: 389–419. (A quick survey of work on generalized quantifiers at the time of writing.)

Keenan, E.L. and Westerståhl, D. (1997) 'Generalized Quantifiers in Linguistics and Logic', in J. van Benthem and A. ter Meulen (eds) *Handbook of Logic and Language*, Amsterdam: Elsevier, 837–93. (Updates the exposition in Westerståhl (1989), from a more linguistic perspective.)

Krynicki, M., Mostowski, M. and Szczerba, L.W. (eds) (1995) *Quantifiers: Logics, Models and Computation*, vol. 1, *Surveys*, Dordrecht: Kluwer. (Surveys mathematical work on quantifiers between the time of appearance of Barwise and Feferman (1985) and 1992.)

* Lindström, P. (1966) 'First-Order Predicate Logic with Generalized Quantifiers', *Theoria* 32: 186–95. (The extension to arbitrary types of the notion of a type $\langle 1 \rangle$ quantifier.)

* Mostowski, A. (1957) 'On a Generalization of Quantifiers', *Fundamenta Mathematicae* 44: 12–36. (The introduction of the notion of a type $\langle 1 \rangle$ quantifier.)

* Westerståhl, D. (1989) 'Quantifiers in Formal and Natural Languages', in D. Gabbay and F. Guenthner (eds) *Handbook of Philosophical Logic*, vol. 4, Dordrecht: Reidel, 1–131. (Detailed exposition of much of the material in this entry.)

DAG WESTERSTÅHL

QUANTIFIERS, SUBSTITUTIONAL AND OBJECTUAL

Understood substitutionally, 'Something is F' is true provided one of its substitution instances (a sentence of the form 'a is F') is true. This contrasts with the objectual understanding, on which it is true provided 'is F' is true of some object in the domain of the quantifier. Substitutional quantifications have quite different truth-conditions from objectual ones. For instance,

'Something is a mythological animal' is true if understood substitutionally, since the substitution instance 'Pegasus is a mythological animal' is true. But understood objectually, the sentence is not true, since there are no mythological creatures to make up a domain for the quantifier.

Since substitutional quantifiers do not need domains over which they range, it is easy to introduce substitutional quantifiers which bind predicate or sentential variables, even variables within quotation marks. One reason for interest in substitutional quantification is the hope that it may provide a way to understand discourse which appears to be about numbers, properties, propositions and other 'troublesome' sorts of entities as being free of exceptional ontological commitments. Whether natural language quantification is sometimes plausibly construed as substitutional is not, however, clear.

1 **Objectual and substitutional quantification**
2 **Interpreting natural language quantifiers**
3 **Logic and semantics**

1 **Objectual and substitutional quantification**

The existential quantification

(1) $\exists x\, x$ is a logician

is true if 'x is a logician' is true in at least one case; the universal quantification

(2) $\forall x\, x$ is a logician

is true if 'x is a logician' is true in every case. Two accounts may be given of what it is for 'x is a logician' to be true for some or all cases. These yield two kinds of quantification: 'objectual' and 'substitutional'.

In an objectual account, the quantifier has a domain of objects; sentences such as 'x is a logician' are related to the contents of the quantifier's domain by the 'true of' relation. The sentence 'x is a logician' is true of a member of the domain if and only if that member is a logician; 'x taught y' is true of a pair $\langle u, v\rangle$ drawn from the domain just in case u taught v, and so on. Understood objectually, (1) is true if 'x is a logician' is true of at least one thing in the domain; (2) is true if 'x is a logician' is true of everything in the domain.

An objectual quantifier is tied directly to the domain of objects over which it quantifies. A substitutional quantifier does not have a domain; it is not a device whose semantics is explained in terms of the 'true of' relation. Instead, a substitutional quantifier has a 'substitution class', a collection of expressions which may be substituted for the variables the substitutional quantifier binds. The 'substitution instances' of a quantified sentence such as (1) or (2)

are the results of removing the initial quantifier and replacing what is bound with some member of the substitution class. For instance, if the substitution class consists of the names 'Frege' and 'Russell' (the names, not the people), the substitution instances of (1) and (2) are the sentences

Frege is a logician.

Russell is a logician.

In substitutional quantification the cases to be considered are substitution instances. Read substitutionally, (1) is true provided at least one of its substitution instances is true; (2) is true provided they all are.

In order to avoid confusion, it is best to use distinct notations for the two kinds of quantifiers. Hereafter '∃' and '∀' are the objectual quantifiers, 'x' and 'y' their variables; 'Σ' is the substitutional existential, 'Π' the substitutional universal quantifier, and 'X' and 'S' their variables.

How different are $\exists x \phi x$ and $\Sigma X \phi X$? Suppose the domain of '∃' contains things not named by anything in the substitution class of 'Σ'. For example, say the domain of '∃' is the set of all animals, and let the substitution class for 'Σ' be the proper names of animals. Not every horse has a name (proper or otherwise), so '∃x x is a horse and x has no name' is true. But 'ΣX X is a horse and X has no name' is false. If it were true, then

α is a horse and α has no name,

where α is a proper name of a horse, would be true. But if α names something, then 'α has no name' is clearly false.

Another difference arises because there can (apparently) be true sentences containing empty (non-referring) names, such as 'Pegasus is only a mythological animal'. If the animal name 'Pegasus' does not name anything, *a fortiori* it does not name anything in the domain of an objectual quantifier. So, if the domain of '∃' is all animals, the sentence '∃x x is only a mythological animal' is false: there is not any animal which is only mythological. But the sentence 'ΣX X is only a mythological animal' is true, as one of its substitution instances is true.

The quantifiers of (1) and (2) are 'nominal' quantifiers – their variables occupy only the positions of names or singular terms. To further appreciate the difference between substitutional and objectual quantifiers, let us consider how we might introduce *non-nominal* quantifiers into a language. To introduce a substitutional quantifier whose variables can occupy, say, the positions of predicates or whole sentences, all one needs to do is to specify a substitution class, add new variables and define 'substitution instance'. For example, if we take expressions such as 'is Greek' to comprise the substitution class, we can introduce a substitutional quantifier which, like that of

(1′) ΣX (Socrates X and Plato X),

binds predicate variables. (Examples of substitution instances thereof would be 'Socrates is wise and Plato is wise' and 'Socrates snores and Plato snores'.) If sentences make up the substitution class, we can write, for example,

(2′) ΠS (Dick said that $S \rightarrow$ it is false that S),

with a quantifier binding sentential variables. The truth-conditions of these sentences are exactly as before: (1′) is true provided at least one substitution instance is true; (2′) is true provided all are. Provided all the instances already had truth-values, such substitutional quantifications automatically have truth-values.

To introduce objectual quantifiers whose variables can occupy the positions of predicates or sentences requires one to assign domains to such quantifiers and to explain what it is for something such as 'Socrates X' or 'Dick said that X' to be true of something in the domain of the quantifier. One can do this only if there are objects to make up the domain. Since appropriate domains for predicate and sentential variables seem to be, respectively, sets (or, perhaps, universals) and propositions, someone with doubts about their existence ought to have doubts about the objectual analogues of (1′) and (2′) (see NOMINALISM §4). No such worries attach to (1′) and (2′) themselves.

Some have hoped that substitutional quantification would provide an innocuous means of interpreting non-nominal natural language quantifications, such as 'Bill did all that John did' and 'There's something Socrates is that Plato is too'. Some hope it will interpret apparently nominal quantifications ('Whatever Dick said is false') and numerical quantification, whose domains seem to some ontologically suspect.

Another reason for interest in substitutional quantification is worries about the coherence of using an objectual quantifier to 'quantify into' positions like that occupied by 'Jane' in

It is possible that Jane is happy.

Nancy thinks that Jane is happy.

The position of 'Jane' in these sentences is 'opaque' (it is a position for which substitution of terms which pick out the same thing can lead from truth to falsehood; see PROPOSITIONAL ATTITUDE STATEMENTS §2; MODAL LOGIC, PHILOSOPHICAL ISSUES

IN §3). Quine has argued repeatedly that an objectual quantifier cannot bind a variable in opaque position (see Quine 1951). Now, many perfectly good English sentences, for example,

(3) Some unhappy woman could have been happy.

There's someone [such that] Nancy thinks [that she] is happy.

seem to involve quantification into opaque position. Since there is no problem with a substitutional quantifier binding a variable in opaque position, one might conclude that sentences such as in (3) involve substitutional quantification.

In the author's opinion, it is implausible that English quantification into opaque positions as in (3) can or should be interpreted substitutionally. For one thing, Quine's arguments that an objectual quantifier cannot bind a variable in opaque position are unsound (see Kaplan 1986). Furthermore, the way we mix quantifiers and expressions such as 'believes' prohibits a substitutional reading of the quantifier. Consider

(4) Twain is Clemens; Sal believes that Twain is sad; Sal does not believe that Clemens is sad.

This does not imply

(5) Twain is something such that Sal believes that it is sad and Twain is something such that Sal does not believe that it is sad,

since (4) could be true, but (5) ascribes contradictory properties to Twain. Now (5) seems to have the form

(6) $(Ex)(x = \text{Twain \& Sal believes that x is sad}) \&$
$(Ex)(x = \text{Twain \& Sal does not believe that x is sad}).$

If the existential quantifier 'E' in (6) is objectual, (4) does not imply (6), since no object in the domain could make both conjuncts true. But if it is substitutional, (4) does imply (6), and hence (5). But we have already said that (4) does not imply (5). So the quantifier is not substitutional. (Incidentally, this shows that when a substitutional quantifier binds variables in opaque positions, $\exists x \phi x$ and $\Sigma X \phi X$ may have different truth-values even if the substitution class for 'Σ' consists only of names of objects in the domain of '$\exists$', and every such object is named by a member of the class.)

The above is not meant to suggest that one cannot substitutionally quantify into opaque positions, but only that English quantification into such positions is not substitutional. In fact, substitutional quantifiers are very useful when one wants to bind variables in positions, such as those inside quotation marks, where it is indeed impossible in English to bind a referential variable. A formula along the lines of

(7) ΠS: 'S' is true if and only if S

is perfectly intelligible, and may even, in certain cases, be looked upon as 'defining truth' (see Kripke 1976 and Grover 1992 for discussion).

2 Interpreting natural language quantifiers

Natural language quantifiers cannot in general be plausibly understood as substitutional. Is quantification in English (or other natural languages; the disjunct is dropped hereafter) ever plausibly taken to be substitutional? If so, what, if anything, might this say about the 'ontological commitments' of speakers?

Some philosophers (Gottlieb, for example) have suggested that English quantifiers are ambiguous, between substitutional and objectual ones. Others (Marcus 1993, for example) have suggested that substitutional quantifiers provide, in some sense, the primary interpretation of English idioms of quantification, the objectual interpretation being a limiting or special case.

Arguments for the ambiguity thesis often turn on intuitions about what (the use of) a sentence ontologically commits one to. Roughly speaking, a sentence S ontologically commits one to there being an F provided that, as a matter of logic, one cannot consistently hold that S is true but there is not an F. (More precisely, let F be a singular English noun and let s name the English sentence S. 's ontologically commits one to there being an F' is true if the sentence 'If S, then there is an F' is logically true, when 'there is' is understood objectually. To say 's commits one to a' is to say that 'a exists' follows from S. See Ontological commitment.)

One particular argument for the ambiguity thesis runs as follows: 'Quine believes that there are no propositions' is true; and 'If Quine believes that there are no propositions, then there is a thing Quine believes' is a logical truth, and thus a truth. So 'There is a thing Quine believes' is true. But Quine is not ontologically committed to the existence of things believed (propositions) since he says that he does not think there are any. So in English 'there is' is not always an objectual quantifier. So, presumably, it is sometimes a substitutional one. Another argument observes that to explain why

(8) If there are exactly as many boys as girls, then if there are 5 boys, there are 5 girls

is logically true, one must interpret its antecedent as involving numerical quantification; but asserting its antecedent surely does not commit one to the existence of numbers (see Gottlieb 1980). The arguments depend on the neutrality thesis: a substitutional quantification ΣXFX does not commit one to there being an F if none of its instances do. Given the definition of ontological commitment, the neutrality thesis is trivially true, since any substitution instance of ΣXFX logically implies it.

Such arguments must be evaluated on a case-by-case basis. As for the first, one might simply note that existential generalization (the move from something whose syntactic form is 'a is F' to 'Something is F') is not valid without restriction. The second argument seems inconclusive, at least given that what is at issue is the commitments of one who embraces the range of quantitative inferences commonly held valid in English, and accepts arithmetic practice as well as standard use of numerical talk for measurement, counting, estimating, and so on.

Even if the evidence for the ambiguity thesis is at best equivocal, the project of attempting to see how much of a stretch of a discourse (about, say, numbers, or properties, or propositions) can be interpreted substitutionally is often of interest. Even if we are most plausibly understood to be committed to existence of a sort, we might welcome the news that we need not be. In evaluating the claim that a stretch of discourse can be interpreted substitutionally, one needs to consider several questions.

First, how satisfactory is the account provided of the truth of substitution instances? If 'Some numbers are prime' is substitutional, the truth of '7 is prime' is not explained by saying that 'is prime' is true of 7. We then need an account of what makes '7 is prime' true but '8 is prime' false.

Second, how much apparently true discourse does a substitutional account render problematic or false? It is not altogether clear how much conventional mathematics can be accepted when its quantifiers are read substitutionally. (For one thing, substitutional quantification seems to require limits on expressibility akin to those in predicative logic.) It is not clear how a substitutional interpretation of 'Katya said something' can explain its truth as a report of Katya's assertive utterance of a sentence untranslatable into English. (One could say that some set theory or talk of Katya's assertions is false but useful fiction.)

Third, to what extent do the terms of a substitutional account undercut its motivation? For nominalists, substitutional quantification is of interest because it may offer a way to re-interpret a theory (without requiring significant change in the way it is used) so that it can be adopted by the ontologically scrupulous. Such nominalists need to be careful about what they themselves (objectually) quantify over, in giving a substitutional account of a theory. For example, the natural understanding of the substitution class for 'Π' for a language for arithmetic will identify it with an infinite set of expression 'types'; to give an adequate substitutional account of a language as strong as second-order arithmetic seems to require quantifying over sequences. But types and sequences are not objects acceptable to most nominalists (see Parsons 1971 and 1982).

Quine has claimed that substitutional quantification is irrelevant to questions of ontology, saying that 'the question of the ontological commitment of a theory does not properly arise' (1969) unless the theory is formulated in an objectual first-order language or translated into such. But surely this is not so. If quantifier-free expressions of English number theory do not in fact contain names of numbers, and English numerical quantification is substitutional, then English numerical discourse is free of commitment to numbers. In fact, if this is so, it is presumably untranslatable into objectual idiom, since such translation would involve wrongly ascribing such commitment.

3 Logic and semantics

There are many interesting issues in the logic and semantics of substitutional languages. The reader is directed to Kripke, Parsons and Grover for a sampling. Here we confine ourselves to mention of two fundamental facts about substitutional languages.

First, $\Sigma X \phi X$ is true provided one of its substitution instances is. Thus, if one is to define truth inductively for a language in which substitutional quantifiers occur, with the definition assigning a truth-value to every sentence, the substitution class for the quantifiers cannot contain expressions in which those very quantifiers are used. Kripke suggests that it is best to think of substitutional quantifiers as being introduced by extending a given (interpreted) language to a new language. The extension is achieved by introducing new variables for the quantifiers, defining a substitution class C thereof (consisting of some expressions of the original language) and taking the atomic sentences of the new language to be all the sentences of the old language along with results of replacing members of C in the base language with variables. (Call the last, following Kripke, 'forms'. Strictly, forms are those results, of replacing members of C with variables, which always return a sentence of the base language when the new variables are replaced with members of C.) As Kripke (and, earlier, Marcus) observe, provided the quantifiers are introduced in this way, one can formulate 'truth-definitions' along the lines of (7) without paradox.

Second, in the case of first-order languages (with-

out identity), choosing between objectual and substitutional quantifiers need not affect what we say about validity or satisfiability. (Again we rely on Kripke's work.) Consider the first-order substitutional and first-order objectual predicate calculi, which differ only in their quantifiers and variables. Think of an interpretation of the substitutional calculus (SC) as being given by specifying an interpreted language L and (non-empty) substitution class C therein, assigning members of C to SC's constants, forms (of appropriate number of argument places) of L to the predicate letters of SC. If validity for SC is truth in any such interpretation, and validity for the objectual predicate calculus is truth in any (objectual) interpretation, then a sentence of SC is valid if and only if its objectual analogue (the result of trading substitutional quantifiers and variables for objectual ones) is.

See also: LOGICAL AND MATHEMATICAL TERMS, GLOSSARY OF; ONTOLOGICAL COMMITMENT

References and further reading

* Gottlieb, D. (1980) *Ontological Economy: Substitutional Quantification and Mathematics*, Oxford: Oxford University Press. (Expounds and defends a substitutional interpretation of number theory. Includes a useful discussion of ontological commitment.)
* Grover, D. (1992) *A Prosentential Theory of Truth*, Princeton, NJ: Princeton University Press. (Uses substitutional quantification in characterizing truth for various languages.)
* Kaplan, D. (1986) 'Opacity', in P. Schlipp (ed.) *The Philosophy of W.V. Quine*, La Salle, IL: Open Court. (An important discussion of quantification and opacity.)
* Kripke, S.A. (1976) 'Is There a Problem about Substitutional Quantification?', in G. Evans and J. McDowell (eds) *Truth and Meaning*, Oxford: Oxford University Press. (Gives what has become the paradigmatic elementary account of substitutional quantification.)
* Marcus, R.B. (1993) *Modalities: Philosophical Essays*, Oxford: Oxford University Press. (Collected essays. Numbers 1, 5 and 8 defend the substitutional understanding of English quantification as well as its ontological importance.)
* Parsons, C. (1971) 'A Plea for Substitutional Quantification', *Journal of Philosophy* 68: 231–7. (Argues that substitutional quantification is not ontologically neutral.)
* —— (1982) 'Substitutional Quantification and

Mathematics', *British Journal for the Philosophy of Science* 33: 409–21. (A review of Gottlieb 1980.)

* Quine, W.V. (1951) 'Reference and Modality', in *From a Logical Point of View: Nine Logico-Philosophical Essays*, Cambridge, MA: Harvard University Press, 1980; repr. in L. Linsky (ed.) *Reference and Modality*, Oxford: Oxford University Press, 1971. (One source of Quine's objections to objectual quantification into opaque positions.)

* —— (1969) 'Existence and Quantification', in *Ontological Relativity and Other Essays*, New York: Columbia University Press, 1977. (Gives Quine's objections to the relevance of substitutional quantification to ontology.)

—— (1973) *The Roots of Reference*, La Salle, IL: Open Court. (Contains a subtle discussion of substitutional quantification, mathematical discourse and the conceptual priority of substitutional quantification.)

Richard, M. (1995) 'Propositional Quantification', in J. Copeland (ed.) *Logic and Reality: Essays in Pure and Applied Logic*, Oxford: Oxford University Press. (Includes a critical discussion of substitutional accounts of propositional quantification.)

MARK RICHARD

QUANTUM FIELD THEORY

see FIELD THEORY, QUANTUM

QUANTUM LOGIC

The topic of quantum logic was introduced by Birkhoff and von Neumann (1936), who described the formal properties of a certain algebraic system associated with quantum theory. To avoid begging questions, it is convenient to use the term 'logic' broadly enough to cover any algebraic system with formal characteristics similar to the standard sentential calculus. In that sense it is uncontroversial that there is a logic of experimental questions (for example, 'Is the particle in region R?' or 'Do the particles have opposite spins?') associated with any physical system. Having introduced this logic for quantum theory, we may ask how it differs from the standard sentential calculus, the logic for the experimental questions in classical mechanics. The most notable difference is that the distributive laws fail, being replaced by a weaker law known as orthomodularity.

All this can be discussed without deciding whether quantum logic is a genuine logic, in the sense of a system of deduction. Putnam argued that quantum logic was indeed a genuine logic, because taking it as such solved various problems, notably that of reconciling the wave-like character of a beam of, say, electrons, as it passes through two slits, with the thesis that the electrons in the beam go through one or other of the two slits. If Putnam's argument succeeds this would be a remarkable case of the empirical defeat of logical intuitions. Subsequent discussion, however, seems to have undermined his claim.

1   **The logic of experimental questions**
2   **The nonclassical character of quantum logic**
3   **An alternative approach to quantum logic**
4   **The logical reformulation of quantum theory**
5   **The status of quantum logic**

1   The logic of experimental questions

Idealizing physics somewhat, we can think of repeatable experiments as types of observation and the results as values of the corresponding observable. Given any set of possible results, R, for a type of observable, O, there is an experimental question, namely: 'Will the observation of O produce a value in the set R?'

If experiments are repeatable, then there must be some significance to the results of repeating them on systems in – idealizing again – the same state. For theories such as classical mechanics and quantum theory, therefore, we may take the statistics resulting from repetition to be manifestations of probabilities. In our idealized treatment, we then assign a precise numerical probability $u(a)$ to the 'yes' result for a given experimental question a when asked of a system in a state u. This connection between experimental questions and states imposes a logic on the experimental questions.

First we say that two experimental questions are 'equivalent' if they are assigned the same probability by every state. It is then convenient to talk as if equivalent experimental questions were identical. Next we define an entailment-like partial ordering, '$\leqslant$', on experimental questions: $a \leqslant b$ if, for all states u, $u(a) \leqslant u(b)$. The intuitive idea is that if a fails to 'entail' b then there is some state in which a 'yes' answer for a is more probable than a 'yes' for b. We define a maximum element 1 and a minimum element 0 corresponding to the trivial experimental questions which always give a 'yes' answer, or a 'no' answer, respectively. Moreover, there is a negation-like complement operator, where $a^{\perp}$, the complement of a, has a 'yes' answer precisely when a has a 'no' answer. Hence $(a^{\perp})^{\perp} = a$ for any experimental question a. Also for any experimental question a and any state u, $u(a) + u(a^{\perp}) = 1$. From this it follows that the logic is 'orthocomplemented', that is, $a \leqslant b$ implies $b^{\perp} \leqslant a^{\perp}$. We may then define the 'orthogonality' relation $a \perp b$ ('a is orthogonal to b') to hold if $a \leqslant b^{\perp}$, or, equivalently, $b \leqslant a^{\perp}$. In standard logic two propositions are 'inconsistent' just in case one entails the negation of the other. Orthogonality is the analogue of inconsistency.

The 'meet' $a \wedge b$, if it exists, is the greatest (with respect to '$\leqslant$') experimental question less than or equal to both a and b. It is analogous to the conjunction $p \& q$ of two propositions, which is the meet with respect to the ordering of entailment. Likewise the 'join' $a \vee b$, if it exists, is the least experimental question greater than or equal to both a and b. It is analogous to the disjunction, p or q of two propositions, which is the join with respect to the ordering of entailment. Because the logic is orthocomplemented, De Morgan's laws hold.

$$(a \wedge b)^{\perp} = a^{\perp} \vee b^{\perp}$$
$$(a \vee b)^{\perp} = a^{\perp} \wedge b^{\perp}$$

Thus far we have been exploring a priori the consequences of characterizing physics as having to do with idealized repeatable experiments on systems. The logic of experimental questions may be further developed by means of a constraint which, although inspired by quantum theory and not merely the result of conceptual analysis, seems antecedently plausible. This is 'postulate M': given any pairwise orthogonal set of experimental questions $\{a_i\}$ there is an experimental question b such that, for any state u, $u(b) + u(a_1) + u(a_2) + \ldots = 1$ (see Hughes 1989: 198). This is plausible because it amounts to there being an experimental question b which has the 'yes' answer just in case all the a_i have the 'no' answer. It may be inferred from postulate M by the Mackey–Maczynski theorem that the logic of experimental questions is 'orthomodular' (see Hughes 1989: 198), a weakened form of 'distributive'. That is, every pairwise orthogonal countable subset has a join and the orthomodular property holds: for any experimental questions a and b such that $a \leqslant b$, $b = a \vee (b \wedge a^{\perp})$.

We might expect the analogue of the material conditional, (not-p) or q, to be $a^{\perp} \vee b$, but since the material conditional could also be characterized as (not-p) or (p and q), another analogue is $a^{\perp} \vee (a \wedge b)$, which I abbreviate to $a \to b$. In fact it is the latter which is appropriate, because we require the analogue of *modus ponens*, namely $a \wedge (a \to b) \leqslant b$ (see Gibbins 1987: 139). The orthomodular property may then be stated succinctly: for any experimental questions a and b such that $a \leqslant b$, $b = a^{\perp} \to b$.

2 The nonclassical character of quantum logic

It is plausible, then, but not the result of pure conceptual analysis, that the logic of experimental questions forms an orthomodular partially ordered set.

For classical physics this logic is in addition a distributive lattice and so a Boolean algebra. (To say it is 'distributive' is to say that the familiar distributive laws hold.

$$a \wedge (b \vee c) = (a \wedge b) \vee (a \wedge c)$$
$$a \vee (b \wedge c) = (a \vee b) \wedge (a \vee c)$$

To say it is a 'lattice' is to say that every pair of experimental questions has a join and a meet.) The logic of experimental questions for quantum theory is not, however, a Boolean algebra. Instead it is usually taken to be isomorphic to an orthocomplemented partially ordered set which occurs naturally in an infinite-dimensional Hilbert space.

Without loss of generality we may think of a vector $\mathbf{v}$ in this Hilbert space as an infinite sequence of (complex) numbers $\langle v_1, v_2, v_3, \ldots \rangle$. Given numbers s and t, we can form the linear combination $\mathbf{z} = s\mathbf{v} + t\mathbf{w}$ of vectors $\mathbf{v}$ and $\mathbf{w}$, with $z_i = sv_i + tw_i$ for all i. More generally, given any set e of vectors we can consider those vectors which are finite or infinite linear combinations of members of e. This is the (closed) 'span' of e, which we shall write as '$[e]$'. (That it is closed with respect to the appropriate topology follows from the inclusion of infinite linear combinations.) A (closed) linear subspace is then any nonempty set a of vectors such that $[a] = a$.

These vectors are analogues of coordinate triples in three-dimensional Euclidean space. In this example, the linear subspaces, which are all closed, comprise (1) the coordinates of the origin, O, (2) lines through O, (3) planes through O, and (4) the whole of space. (1) and (4) correspond, respectively, to the elements 0 and 1 in the lattice, which is ordered by inclusion. So, for instance, if a is the set of coordinates for a line through O and b for a plane through O, then $a \leqslant b$ just in case the line is in the plane. The meet of two members of the lattice of closed linear subspaces is just their intersection. The join is not, however, the union, for the union is not in general a linear subspace (for example, the union of two lines is not a plane). Instead, the join is the *span* of the union (for instance, the set of coordinates of the plane containing the two lines).

Now some pairs of vectors in Hilbert space are orthogonal. This enables us to define the 'orthogonal complement' $e^{\perp}$ of a set of vectors e as the set of all vectors orthogonal to all vectors in e. This provides an alternative characterization of the span as $[e] = (e^\perp)^\perp$. Hence if a is a closed linear subspace, then $(a^\perp)^\perp = a$.

The lattice of closed linear subspaces of a Hilbert space is not a Boolean algebra, for the distributive laws fail to hold. The reason for this is easily seen in the case of the coordinate triples. Consider three different sets of coordinate triples a, b and c corresponding to three lines OA, OB and OC all in the one plane. Then $b \vee c$ corresponds to the plane they lie in, so $a = a \wedge (b \vee c)$. But $a \wedge b$ is the intersection of a and b and is therefore $\{\langle 0,0,0 \rangle\}$. Hence $a \wedge b = 0$. Likewise $a \wedge c = 0$. So $(a \wedge b) \vee (a \wedge c) = 0 \vee 0 = 0$. The orthomodular law, a weakening of the distributive laws, does hold.

The claim that quantum logic is a lattice could be justified either by the convenience of the standard representation using closed linear subspaces of a Hilbert space, or on the basis that we should depart as little as possible from the classical case. It is not, however, easy to find any other reasons (see Hughes 1989: 200).

The nonclassical character of quantum logic is also exhibited by its valuations. Consider the following weakening of the requirements for a valuation of the standard sentential calculus: $\text{Val}(1) = 1$ and if $a \perp b$ then $\text{Val}(a \vee b) = \text{Val}(a) + \text{Val}(b)$, from which it follows that $\text{Val}(0) = 0$. Any (pure or mixed) quantum state may be thought of as such a valuation with $\text{Val}(a)$ being the probability assigned by the state to the experimental question a. It can be shown that such a valuation must take all the values between 0 and 1. (In particular, there is no two-valued or three-valued valuation. That there is no two-valued valuation is Kochen and Specker's theorem.) Following Kochen and Specker, consider a spin 1 system in which the spin component in any direction takes the values -1, 0 and $+1$ (see Kochen and Specker 1967; Hughes 1989: 164–70). So for any direction p we have the experimental question o_p which has the 'yes' answer just in case the spin component in that direction is 0. For any three orthogonal p, q and r directions, the triad o_p, o_q and o_r are pairwise orthogonal experimental questions and their join is 1. Hence we would have $\text{Val}(o_p) + \text{Val}(o_q) + \text{Val}(o_r) = 1$. Gleason's theorem then tells us that $\text{Val}(o_p)$ is a quadratic function of the coordinates of p. Hence it is continuous and takes all values between the minimum, 0, and the maximum, 1.

3 An alternative approach to quantum logic

The presentation so far has been in the tradition of the paper by Birkhoff and von Neumann (1936) and the work of Mackey (1963). But there is an alternative approach to quantum logic due to Kochen and Specker (1965). The idea is to think of the logic as a family $\{B_i\}$ of overlapping Boolean algebras, each, intuitively, consisting of a family of experimental questions which can be answered without interfering with each other. We require the B_i to share the same maximum and minimum elements 0 and 1 (the two trivial questions) and to be such that the operations '$\wedge_i$', '$\vee_i$' and '$\perp_i$' agree on the overlaps. The family $\{B_i\}$ is called a 'partial Boolean algebra' if a 'coherence condition' holds. Call members of the logic 'neighbours' if there is some B_i to which they all belong. Coherence then says that if a, b and c are pairwise neighbours then they are neighbours. The set of closed linear subspaces of a Hilbert space is a partial Boolean algebra in which the Boolean subalgebras consist of sets of subspaces which make angles of either $0°$ or $90°$ with each other. For the case of the lattice of coordinate triples, each Boolean subalgebra contains eight members and is specified by a choice of three perpendicular lines OP, OQ and OR through O. The subalgebra then consists of the coordinate sets for (1) the origin, O, (2) the lines OP, OQ and OR (3) the planes OQR, ORP and OPQ, and (4) the whole of three-dimensional space (see Hughes 1989: 192–4).

The natural way of defining a valuation for a partial Boolean algebra would be one which satisfied the usual truth-functional constraints on each Boolean subalgebra. But such a valuation would have to satisfy the constraint that $\text{Val}(1) = 1$ and that if $a \perp b$ then $\text{Val}(a \vee b) = \text{Val}(a) + \text{Val}(b)$. As we have seen, such valuations must take all values between 0 and 1.

4 The logical reformulation of quantum theory

The fact that one important difference between quantum and classical physics can be expressed as a purely algebraic difference in the corresponding logics has inspired the programme of formulating quantum theory in terms of its logic of experimental questions. There is no obstacle to this provided the logic is assumed to be that of the closed linear subspaces of a Hilbert space. Given that assumption, the first step is to classify the states, which are identified with the probability measures on the logic. Assuming postulate M (see §1 above) this amounts merely to taking the states to be valuations which assign values in the range 0 to 1. Gleason's theorem tells us that, for any Hilbert space of dimension greater than two, the states thus characterized are all the mixtures (in positive proportions adding up to 100 per cent) of the standard pure states of quantum theory, which correspond to vectors in the Hilbert space. (The state represented by vector $\mathbf{v}$ assigns to a closed linear subspace a the square of the cosine of the angle between $\mathbf{v}$ and a.)

The next step is to consider the dynamics by which states change over time. The results of Mackey and Kadison show that we may represent the vectors in the Hilbert space as suitable functions on ordinary (that is, three-dimensional Euclidean) space in such a way that the dynamics is given by the familiar Schrödinger equation (see Beltrametti and Cassinelli 1981: 252–4). The difficulty with the programme, however, is in providing simple algebraic constraints which ensure that the logic of experimental questions is indeed represented by the set of closed subspaces of a Hilbert space (1981: ch. 21).

5 The status of quantum logic

What is the status of quantum logic? There seem to be three sorts of answer: the neoclassical, the quantum ontologists' and the quantum logicians'. The neoclassical answer is that quantum logic is more a mathematical curiosity than anything of great significance in understanding the physical world. Its non-Boolean character is the result of constraints on the questions it is physically possible for us human beings to answer, so that we might think of God as knowing the answers to two questions whose meet is the null question but which are not classically inconsistent (for example, the questions: 'Is the particle in bounded region R?' and 'Does it have momentum in bounded set S?'). Hence the meet, '$\wedge$', would not be a genuine conjunction even though it has analogous properties. For that reason the partial Boolean algebra formulation might be judged more perspicuous because the '$\wedge_i$' of a given Boolean subalgebra could be treated as a classical conjunction (see Garden 1984; Forrest 1988; Garola 1992).

The quantum ontologists' answer is that quantum logic tells us something important about the structure of the physical world, but that 'logic' is a misnomer, for it should not be interpreted as a theory of deductive reasoning. On this view the best way to describe the physical world is by specifying the 'logic' (better 'algebra') of experimental questions and specifying the states as probability measures on this logic (see §4). This is arguably implicit in the Copenhagen interpretation, and it would seem to be the position of van Fraassen (1991: ch. 5) and, in a more radical version, of Hughes (1989: ch. 10).

The quantum logicians' answer is that quantum logic holds because it is in fact the correct deductive logic for all thought, and we made a mistake in assuming classical logic, which we should abandon, not merely when considering quantum theory, but quite generally. This was Putnam's position and it has also been advocated by Stairs (see Putnam 1969; Stairs 1982).

How might we decide between these answers? While logic might well be empirically defeasible it does not seem to be initially derived from experience. Hence there is a burden of argument on the quantum logicians. Putnam (1969) took up this burden by arguing that abandoning the distributive law enables us to resolve various problems without abandoning a realist interpretation of quantum theory. If so, then indeed a case would have been made for the empirical defeat of classical logic, comparable to the empirical defeat of Euclidean geometry. Unfortunately, Putnam's claims are open to serious criticism. For example, Putnam noted that in the two-slit thought-experiment we might have expected the probability of a particle hitting the screen in a given region when both slits are open to be the mean of the two probabilities with one slit closed. But that result violates quantum theory. It seemed that we could, by rejecting distributivity, retain an interpretation in which particles really do pass through one slit or the other, without allowing action at a distance. The objection to this, made forcibly by Gibbins, is that even given quantum logic, realism about particles which pass through one rather than another slit, combined with the rejection of action at a distance, still gives us a result contrary to quantum theory, namely that the probability of a particle hitting the screen in a certain region should be at least as great as the mean of the probabilities with one slit closed. But in fact, for some regions that inequality does not hold (see Gibbins 1987: ch. 10).

If we reject the quantum logicians' answer then that of the quantum ontologists would be plausible enough, especially given the discovery of simple constraints on the logic which ensured it could be represented by the closed subspaces of a Hilbert space. Presumably, however, the choice between the neoclassical and the quantum ontologists' answers will depend on the overall advantages and disadvantages of their interpretations of quantum theory (see QUANTUM MECHANICS, INTERPRETATION OF).

See also: LOGICAL AND MATHEMATICAL TERMS, GLOSSARY OF

References and further reading

Bell, J.L. (1986) 'A New Approach to Quantum Logic', *British Journal for Philosophy of Science*, 37: 83–99. (Quantum logic is interpreted as a system of 'manifestations' of attributes in regions of a 'proximity space'.)

* Beltrametti, E. and Cassinelli, G. (1981) *The Logic of Quantum Mechanics*, Reading, MA: Addison-Wesley. (A comprehensive guide to the mathemati-

cal foundations, especially useful for a discussion of the 'coordinatization problem', that is, the problem of representing quantum logic using Hilbert space.)

Beltrametti, E. and Fraassen, B.C. van (eds) (1981) *Current Issues in Quantum Logic*, New York: Plenum. (A fairly up-to-date, though technical, survey, with useful introductions to the topic by Mittelstadt and van Fraassen.)

* Birkhoff, G. and Neumann, J. von (1936) 'The Logic of Quantum Mechanics', *Annals of Mathematics* 37: 823–43. (Of historical interest.)

Dummett, M.E. (1976) 'Is Logic Empirical?', in H.D. Lewis (ed.) *Contemporary British Philosophy*, London: Allen & Unwin, 45–68. (A critique of Putnam's claim that logic is empirical.)

* Forrest, P. (1988) *Quantum Metaphysics*, Oxford: Blackwell. (Defence of the neoclassical position on quantum logic.)

* Fraassen, B.C. van (1991) *Quantum Mechanics: An Empiricist View*, Oxford: Clarendon Press. (Careful and not too technical introduction to, among other things, quantum logic, with a case against the quantum logicians' position.)

* Garden, R.W. (1984) *Modern Logic and Quantum Mechanics*, Bristol: Hilger. (Argues that the peculiarities of quantum theory are features of our own description rather than of the microscopic world.)

* Garola, C. (1992) 'Truth Versus Testability in Quantum Logic', *Erkenntnis* 37: 197–221. (Shows how quantum logic can be obtained as the testable fragment of the standard sentential calculus.)

* Gibbins, P. (1987) *Particles and Paradoxes: The Limits of Quantum Logic*, Cambridge: Cambridge University Press. (Lucid introduction to quantum logic, with an incisive critique of Putnam.)

Hallam, N. (1987) 'Logic and Indeterminacy', *Philosophical Papers* 16: 53–8. (The most recent paper in a debate between Harrison and Hallam, in which Harrison argues against the quantum logicians' position. See also their papers in *Analysis* of 1983–5.)

Holdsworth, D.G. and Hooker, C.A. (1983) 'A Critical Survey of Quantum Logic', in M.L. dalla Chiara *et al.*, *Logic in the 20th Century: A Series of Papers on the Present State and Tendencies of Studies*, Aalen: Scientia, 127–246. (Useful survey of quantum logic with critical comments.)

Hooker, C. (ed.) (1975) *The Logico-Algebraic Approach to Quantum Mechanics*, Dordrecht: Reidel. (Anthology of papers, some hard to obtain in the original.)

* Hughes, R. (1989) *The Structure and Interpretation of Quantum Mechanics*, Cambridge, MA: Harvard University Press. (An excellent introduction to quantum theory and its interpretation, including

a not-too-technical discussion of quantum logic generally and the partial Boolean algebra approach in particular.)

* Kochen, S. and Specker, E. (1965) 'Logical Structures Arising in Quantum Theory', in J. Addison, L. Henkin and A. Tarski (eds) *The Theory of Models*, Amsterdam: North Holland; repr. in C. Hooker (ed.) *The Logico-Algebraic Approach to Quantum Mechanics*, Dordrecht: Reidel, 1975, 263–76. (The paper introducing the partial Boolean algebra approach to quantum logic.)

* —— (1967) 'The Problem of Hidden Variables in Quantum Mechanics', *Journal of Mathematics and Mechanics* 17: 59–87; repr. in C. Hooker (ed.) *The Logico-Algebraic Approach to Quantum Mechanics*, Dordrecht: Reidel, 1975, 293–328. (The original statement and proof of Kochen and Specker's theorem.)

Ludwig, G. (1983) *Foundations of Quantum Mechanics*, vol. 1, Berlin: Springer. (An operational approach to quantum theory.)

* Mackey, G. (1963) *The Mathematical Foundations of Quantum Mechanics*, New York: Benjamin. (A historically important, but technical, treatment.)

Mittelstadt, P. (1986) 'Empiricism and Apriorism in the Foundations of Quantum Logic', *Synthèse* 67: 497–525. (A discussion of the extent to which quantum logic has an empirical justification.)

* Putnam, H. (1969) 'Is Logic Empirical?', in R. Cohen and M. Wartofsky (eds) *Boston Studies in the Philosophy of Science*, vol. 5, Dordrecht: Reidel; repr. in C. Hooker (ed.) *The Logico-Algebraic Approach to Quantum Mechanics*, Dordrecht: Reidel, 1975, 181–206. (Best-known philosophical case for the quantum logicians' position.)

—— (1981) 'Quantum Mechanics and the Observer', *Erkenntnis* 16: 193–219. (This paper reflects some changes in Putnam's position.)

Redhead, M. (1987) *Incompleteness, Nonlocality, and Realism: A Prolegomenon to the Philosophy of Quantum Mechanics*, Oxford: Clarendon Press. (Careful and not-too-technical introduction to, among other things, quantum logic, with a discussion of Putnam's argument.)

* Stairs, A. (1982) 'Quantum Logic and the Luders' Rule', *Philosophy of Science* 49: 422–36. (Argument for the quantum logicians' position.)

PETER FORREST

QUANTUM MEASUREMENT PROBLEM

In classical mechanics a measurement process can be represented, in principle, as an interaction between two systems, a measuring instrument M and a measured system S, during which the classical states of M and S evolve dynamically, according to the equations of motion of the theory, in such a way that the 'pointer' or indicator quantity of M becomes correlated with the measured quantity of S. If a similar representation is attempted in quantum mechanics, it can be shown that, for certain initial quantum states of M and S, the interaction will result in a quantum state for the combined system in which neither the pointer quantity of M nor the measured quantity of S has a determinate value. On the orthodox interpretation of the theory, propositions assigning ranges of values to these quantities are neither true nor false. Since we require that the pointer readings of M are determinate after a measurement, and presumably also the values of the correlated S-quantities measured by M, it appears that the orthodox interpretation cannot accommodate the dynamical representation of measurement processes. The problem of how to do so is the quantum measurement problem.

1   States in classical and quantum mechanics
2   The source of the problem
3   Proposed solutions

1   States in classical and quantum mechanics

Classical mechanics describes model universes in which the state of the universe can be specified by an assignment of values to the positions and momenta of the systems in the universe, hence to all dynamical quantities, which are defined as functions of positions and momenta. The equations of motion yield rates of change for positions and momenta in terms of the Hamiltonian, a function of positions and momenta, and generate a possible history of the universe from the position and momentum values specified at some particular time. So we can understand a classical universe as consisting of separable classical systems interacting under the influence of forces encoded in the Hamiltonian. The evolution of the universe over time – a history of the universe – is given by a particular dynamical evolution of its state (see MECHANICS, CLASSICAL; MODELS).

The state of a model classical universe plays two distinct roles: a *diachronic* role as the carrier of the dynamics over time, and a *synchronic* role as the specification of a 'possible world' at a particular time; that is, the selection of a set of determinate values for the dynamical quantities as one of the possible sets of values for these quantities, equivalently the selection of a set of properties for the systems in the universe as one of the possible sets of properties.

The dynamical quantities, represented by real-valued functions on the classical state space or 'phase space' coordinated by the positions and momenta (not to be confused with real space), form a commutative algebra with respect to addition and multiplication. Properties in classical mechanics are represented by subsets of phase space (or, equivalently, by functions that take the values 1 on the subset and 0 elsewhere). The property that the value of a dynamical variable A lies in a certain range R is represented by the subset of classical states (phase space points) for which this property holds, via the functional relationship between A and positions and momenta. The properties form a Boolean algebra, isomorphic to a set of subsets of phase space. Classical states correspond to singleton subsets, minimal non-zero elements, or atoms in this algebra. The collection of properties represented by subsets of phase space containing the state is selected as the possible world associated with the state in the synchronic sense.

Quantum mechanics is derived as a generalization of classical mechanics in which certain 'canonically conjugate' quantities (like position and momentum) fail to commute with respect to multiplication. We obtain a non-commutative algebra of dynamical quantities that is representable as an algebra of operators on a Hilbert space, a linear vector space over the complex numbers. The dynamical quantities correspond to operators that can be decomposed into linear sums or integrals of projection operators, with real coefficients (the 'eigenvalues' of the operators) that represent the possible values of the quantities. Each projection operator has eigenvalues 0 and 1, and maps the Hilbert space onto a subspace that is the range of the operator. Properties are represented by subspaces or the corresponding projection operators and form a non-Boolean algebra, isomorphic to the algebra of projection operators or subspaces of Hilbert space. The one-dimensional subspaces or rays are atoms in this algebra and represent states in the diachronic sense; that is, they represent dynamical states that evolve over time according to the linear equation of motion of the theory (see QUANTUM LOGIC §2).

On the *orthodox* interpretation of quantum mechanics, the rays (or unit vectors along the rays) are also taken to represent states in the synchronic sense. The collection of properties determined by a ray in Hilbert space as obtaining in a model quantum mechanical universe is taken as the collection of subspaces containing the ray, just as the collection of properties belonging to a classical state in the synchronic sense is the collection of properties represented by subsets of phase space containing the state as a point in phase space. Properties represented by subspaces orthogonal to the ray are taken as not obtaining in the model universe, while properties represented by subspaces that are neither orthogonal to the ray nor contain the ray are regarded as indeterminate.

2 The source of the problem

The orthodox decision to take the ray representing a quantum state as defining a state in the synchronic sense has the consequence that we can no longer apply quantum mechanics to model quantum mechanical universes in the same way that classical mechanics is applied to model classical universes. In addition to selecting properties that obtain, properties that do not obtain, and properties that are indeterminate, the ray representing the quantum state is interpreted as assigning *probabilities* to *all* the properties represented by subspaces of the Hilbert space: probability 1 to properties represented by subspaces that contain the ray; probability 0 to properties represented by subspaces orthogonal to the ray; and non-zero probabilities to all other properties. These probabilities are not representable in the usual way as measures over different possible worlds, one of which is actual, defined by the orthodox interpretation of quantum states in the synchronic sense. So a non-zero probability assigned to the property that the value of a dynamical variable A lies in a certain range R is said to be 'the probability of finding the value of the dynamical quantity in the range R on measurement'. This means that the application of quantum mechanics is restricted to providing probabilities for the results of measurements on model quantum mechanical universes by some agent or device *external* to these universes. To mark this distinction between classical and quantum mechanics, dynamical quantities in quantum mechanics are referred to as 'observables', where an observable is understood to have no determinate value unless the ray representing the quantum state lies in one of the subspaces associated with the projection operators of the observable, a circumstance that is presumed to occur when the observable is measured.

This notion of 'measurement' is undefined dynamically, as is the notion of an observable having no determinate value at one time and coming to have a determinate value at some other time as the outcome of a 'measurement'. As Bell put it (1987), one would like to have an interpretation of quantum mechanics, our most fundamental theory of motion, in terms of 'beables' instead of 'observables'. What we want is an *internal* account of measurement in quantum mechanics, and this appears to be excluded by the orthodox interpretation of quantum states and the linear dynamics of the theory.

To see what goes wrong with an internal account of measurement on the orthodox interpretation, consider a model quantum mechanical universe consisting of a measuring instrument M and a measured system S. Suppose that the initial quantum state of $S + M$ is such that, according to the orthodox interpretation, an observable A of S has some determinate value and a 'pointer' or indicator observable R of M has a determinate zero value. Then there exists a dynamical evolution that results in a final quantum state for $S + M$ in which both A and R are determinate and R has some non-zero value that depends on the initial value of A. In this case, the dynamical evolution can be taken as representing a measurement of A via the pointer R in this model universe. But now it follows from the linearity of the dynamics of the theory that if the initial quantum state of $S + M$ is a state in which S has no determinate A-value, and R has the determinate zero value, then the final state of $S + M$ must be a state in which both A and R are indeterminate. So the dynamical evolution cannot be taken as representing a measurement in this case.

Schrödinger (1935) pointed out that if M represents a cat and R takes two possible values, associated with the cat being alive and dead, and the cat interacts with a microsystem S, such as an atom that can either decay or not decay in a certain time (where these events are associated with the two possible values of A), the decay event triggering a device that kills the cat, then the cat will be neither alive nor dead after the measurement interaction, according to the orthodox interpretation.

3 Proposed solutions

States represented by rays in Hilbert space are referred to as 'pure' states in quantum mechanics. The theory also introduces 'mixed' states or 'mixtures', which can be decomposed into probability distributions over pure states and interpreted epistemically (subject to certain qualifications introduced by the nonuniqueness of this decomposition). In terms of this distinction, the measurement problem arises because the final state of the instrument M and, measured system S, after a dynamical interaction representing a measurement, is a pure state associated with a ray that does not lie in any of the subspaces representing pointer properties of M or measured properties of S. What we appear to require after a measurement interaction is a mixed state for the combined system $S + M$, in which pure states that are determinate for different possible measurement outcomes occur with the appropriate probabilities.

There is a series of impossibility theorems by Wigner (1963), Fine (1970), Shimony (1974), and others that show, under very general constraints on what counts as a measurement interaction, that no evolution of the combined system $S + M$ governed by the linear dynamics of the theory can result in a final state for $S + M$ that is a mixture over pure states in which the pointer properties of M are determinate, on the orthodox interpretation of pure states.

Standard formulations of quantum mechanics invoke two modes of dynamical evolution for the pure state of a quantum system: the usual deterministic linear evolution, described by the equation of motion of the theory, that occurs when the system does not undergo measurement; and a second stochastic evolution that occurs when the system is measured and transforms the pure state into the required mixture. This measurement evolution is characterized by a 'projection postulate' as the projection or 'collapse' of the pure state onto one of the pure states in the mixture, with the appropriate probability.

Von Neumann's justification for this duality was that a measurement divides the world into two parts: the observed system and the observer (1932). We can follow all physical processes in the observed system with arbitrary precision, in principle, but not in the observer. The linear dynamics describes systems in the observed part of the world, so long as they do not interact with the observing part. When such an interaction occurs, the projection postulate applies. Consider the measurement of S by an instrument M and observer M'. The boundary between the observed system and the observer can be drawn between S and $M + M'$ or between $S + M$ and M'. Von Neumann showed that the application of the projection postulate directly to the system S is consistent with its application to the system $S + M$, after a suitable dynamical interaction between S and M governed by the linear equation of motion of the theory.

Von Neumann's argument for two distinct dynamical processes in quantum mechanics is hardly convincing, if only because classical mechanics requires no such duality. Indeed, the measurement problem is often formulated as the problem of reconciling these two modes of evolution in some way. Proposed solutions to the problem are restricted by the impossibility theorems and either (i) accept the orthodox interpretation and modify the linear dynamics of the theory; or (ii) accept the linear dynamics and modify the orthodox interpretation; or (iii) accept both the orthodox interpretation and the dynamics, and attempt to show that the difference between the mixture required by the orthodox interpretation and the pure state obtained on the basis of the linear dynamics can be ignored for all practical purposes, if certain relevant features of real measurement interactions are taken into account.

An example of a type (i) or 'collapse' proposal is the theory of Ghirardi, Rimini and Weber (1986). This theory introduces a modified dynamics for the quantum state that results in the occasional spontaneous localization of individual microsystems – so infrequently that the time evolution of a single particle follows the usual linear dynamics over long time intervals with high probability. For macrosystems, which consist of enormously large numbers of particles, the modified dynamics results in the almost instantaneous transition of pure states to mixed states for which macroscopically distinct position properties are determinate. The underlying claim is that all measurements can be characterized as ultimately involving macroscopic changes in the position of something that can function as a macroscopic pointer.

Type (ii) or 'no collapse' proposals include Bohm's hidden variable theory (1952), Everett's (1957) 'relative state' or 'many worlds' interpretation, and 'modal' interpretations, which interpret the pure quantum state as a dynamical state specifying probabilities only, and reject the orthodox interpretation in favour of alternative specifications for what collections of properties are determinate that are intended to support a purely internal account of measurement (see van Fraassen 1991).

Finally, type (iii) proposals include 'decoherence' theories and various other attempts to exploit the large number of degrees of freedom of the amplifying recording device, or the environment of the system, as the source of a dissipative process that effectively renders a final pure state, after a measurement process, empirically indistinguishable from the required mixture. Such proposals work only if we suppose that properties that are indeterminate in the pure state can somehow be regarded as determinate, because certain further measurements that would distinguish the pure state from the mixture are in practice impossible to perform. This can hardly be regarded as satisfactory for a fundamental theory of mechanics.

See also: QUANTUM MECHANICS, INTERPRETATION OF

References and further reading

With the exception of the book by van Fraassen, which is addressed to a philosophical audience, all these items involve a certain amount of technicality, and in most cases a great deal.

* Bell, J.S. (1987) *Speakable and Unspeakable in Quantum Mechanics*, Cambridge: Cambridge University Press. (A collection of influential papers on foundational problems of quantum mechanics. Bell's discussion of 'beables' is in chapter 19.)
* Bohm, D. (1952) 'A Suggested Interpretation of the Quantum Theory in Terms of Hidden Variables, I and II', *Physical Review* 85: 166–79, 180–93; repr. in J.A. Wheeler and W.H. Zurek (eds) *Quantum Theory and Measurement*, Princeton, NJ: Princeton University Press, 1983, 369–96. (The second paper deals with measurement.)
* Everett, H., III (1957) 'Relative State Formulation of Quantum Mechanics', *Reviews of Modern Physics* 29: 454–62; repr. in J.A. Wheeler and W.H. Zurek (eds) *Quantum Theory and Measurement*, Princeton, NJ: Princeton University Press, 1983, 315–23.
* Fine, A. (1970) 'Insolubility of the Quantum Measurement Problem', *Physical Review D* 2: 2783–7. (Fine's original proof that the measurement problem is insoluble, under very general constraints on what counts as a measurement interaction.)
* Fraassen, B. van (1991) *Quantum Mechanics: An Empiricist View*, Oxford: Clarendon Press. (A discussion of the conceptual problems of the theory and a development of the original version of the modal interpretation.)
* Ghirardi, G.C., Rimini, A. and Weber, T. (1986) 'Unified Dynamics for Microscopic and Macroscopic Systems', *Physical Review D* 34: 470–91. (The original paper of the 'GRW theory' – a proposed solution to the measurement problem involving a modification of the linear dynamics of quantum mechanics.)
* London, F. and Bauer, E. (1939) *La théorie de l'observation en mécanique quantique*, Paris: Hermann; trans. 'The Theory of Observation in Quantum Mechanics', in J.A. Wheeler and W.H. Zurek (eds) *Quantum Theory and Measurement*, Princeton, NJ: Princeton University Press, 1983, 217–59. (An early discussion of the measurement problem that is still an excellent introduction to the topic.)
* Neumann, J. von (1932) *Mathematische Grundlagen der Quantenmechanik*, Berlin: Springer; trans. R.T. Beyer, *Mathematical Foundations of Quantum Mechanics*, Princeton, NJ: Princeton University Press, 1955. (The first mathematically rigorous formulation of quantum mechanics. Chapter VI deals with the measurement problem and is reprinted in J.A. Wheeler and W.H. Zurek (eds) *Quantum Theory and Measurement*, Princeton, NJ: Princeton University Press, 1983, 619–56.)
* Schrödinger, E. (1935) 'Die Gegenwärtige Situation in der Quantenmechanik', *Naturwissenschaften* 23: 807–18, 823–8, 844–9; trans. J.D. Trimmer, in J.A. Wheeler and W.H. Zurek (eds) *Quantum Theory and Measurement*, Princeton, NJ: Princeton University Press, 1983, 152–67 (Contains Schrödinger's careful discussion of the measurement problem and his 'cat paradox' referred to in §2.)
* Shimony, A. (1974) 'Approximate Measurements in Quantum Mechanics', *Physical Review D* 9: 2,321–3. (Shimony's insolubility theorem for the measurement problem.)
* Wheeler, J.A. and Zurek, W.H. (eds) (1983) *Quantum Theory and Measurement*, Princeton, NJ: Princeton University Press. (A reference work, containing key papers on quantum mechanics as it relates to measurement.)
* Wigner, E.P. (1963) 'The Problem of Measurement', *American Journal of Physics* 31: 6–15; repr. in J.A. Wheeler and W.H. Zurek (eds) *Quantum Theory and Measurement*, Princeton, NJ: Princeton University Press, 1983, 324–41.

JEFFREY BUB

QUANTUM MECHANICS, INTERPRETATION OF

Quantum mechanics developed in the early part of the twentieth century in response to the discovery that energy is quantized, that is, comes in discrete units. At the microscopic level this leads to odd phenomena: light displays particle-like characteristics and particles such as electrons produce wave-like interference patterns. At the level of ordinary objects such effects are usually not evident, but this generalization is subject to striking exceptions and puzzling ambiguities.

The fundamental quantum mechanical puzzle is 'superposition of states'. Quantum states can be added together in a manner that recalls the superposition of waves, but the effects of quantum superposition show up only probabilistically in the statistics of many measurements. The details suggest that the world is indefinite in odd ways; for example, that things may not always have well-defined positions or momenta or energies. However, if we accept this conclusion, we have difficulty making sense of such straightforward facts as that measurements have definite results.

Interpretations of quantum mechanics are, in one way or another, attempts to understand the superposition of quantum states. The range of interpretations stretches from the metaphysically daring to the seemingly innocuous. But, so far, no single interpretation has commanded anything like universal agreement.

1 **Superposition of states**
2 **Superposition and the eigenvalue–eigenstate link**
3 **Interpretations of quantum theory**

1 Superposition of states

The *two-slit experiment* provides a vivid introduction to the concept of quantum superposition. Imagine a barrier with two slits, placed in front of a light source. On the other side of the barrier is a photographic plate. The intensity of the light can be made so low that photons (light quanta) hit the plate like particles, one at a time in definite though unpredictable locations. If we close the right slit, a narrow band of 'hits' will accumulate in front of the left slit. A similar result occurs if we close the left slit and keep the right one open. Now suppose both slits are left open. If photons were ordinary particles, we would predict two narrow bands of hits. What actually happens is *very* different: we get an array of bands, forming an interference pattern. If light were simply waves, this would not be mysterious: waves interfere. But individual photons are not waves. This leaves us wondering how the effect occurs and whether the individual photons even follow well-defined paths.

What does quantum theory say? Each of the one-slit experiments is associated with a particular *quantum state*. When we leave both slits open, the state becomes an odd amalgam – a *superposition* – of these. From the superposition we can derive a probability distribution for individual 'hits', a distribution that embodies the interference pattern. To say more than this, however, is to interpret quantum theory rather than simply to apply it.

Another example will make the notion of superposition more precise. Electrons have a directional property called *spin*. If we pick a direction and measure spin, we will always get one of two results: $+1$ or -1 ('up' or 'down'). Suppose we prepare a batch of electrons so that each would display spin up in measurement of spin in some specific direction x. It is usual to represent quantum states by abstract vectors in an abstract mathematical space called *Hilbert space* (see QUANTUM LOGIC §2): in this instance, we will denote the quantum state of the electrons by the vector $|x+\rangle$. Suppose now that instead of measuring x-spin we measure spin in a direction z at right-angles to x. We can use the rules of

quantum theory to write $|x+\rangle$ as a vector sum – a superposition – of z-spin states:

$$|x+\rangle = \frac{1}{\sqrt{2}}|z+\rangle + \frac{1}{\sqrt{2}}|z-\rangle.$$

The numerical coefficients are used to calculate the probabilities of observing z-spin up or down in any given measurement. We get the probabilities by squaring these coefficients, in this case yielding a probability of 1/2 for each possible outcome.

Superpositions are not the same as mixtures. Suppose we prepare a batch of electrons of which half are in state $|z+\rangle$ and half are in state $|z-\rangle$. This is not a case of superposition. No matter what direction we choose for our spin measurement, the probabilities of spin up and spin down will be 1/2. This is very different to what we see in a superposition, for example, the state $|x+\rangle$ discussed above. In this case, the probabilities depend on what direction we choose: for any direction in the x–z plane, the closer the direction to x the higher the probability of spin up will be, until the probability reaches certainty at x.

2 Superposition and the eigenvalue–eigenstate link

The example of spin illustrates some characteristic features of quantum mechanics. Quantum states are represented by vectors of length one in Hilbert space (an abstract mathematical shape). If we want to measure some quantity R (x-spin and z-spin being two examples of such quantities) on a system in state $|s\rangle$, our predictions typically involve probabilities. To find these, we write $|s\rangle$ as an appropriate sum of perpendicular vectors

$$|s\rangle = c_1|r_1\rangle + c_2|r_2\rangle + \ldots$$

For each possible measured value r_i of R, there is one vector $|r_i\rangle$. The measurable values r_i are called the *eigenvalues* of R, and the corresponding vectors r_i are the *eigenvectors* or *eigenstates* of R. If $|s\rangle$ happens to be one of the $|r_i\rangle$ – if c_i equals one and all the other c_i are zero – we predict the outcome r_i (the measurement of x-spin in the first system is an example of this: we predict that x-spin will be up, since $|s\rangle = |x\rangle$). If $|s\rangle$ is a superposition of the states $|r_i\rangle$, the probability of observing r_i in any given measurement is $|c_i|^2$. (As we saw when we measured z-spin in the first system for which $|s\rangle = (1/\sqrt{2})|z+\rangle + (1/\sqrt{2})|z-\rangle$). This rule is often referred to as the Born rule, after the physicist Max Born.

The conventional wisdom is that when $|s\rangle$ is a superposition of eigenstates of R, R has no definite value: so, for example, the electrons prepared with up x-spin have no definite z-spin. This principle is often called the *eigenvalue–eigenstate link*. Among other things, it would imply that the photons in the two-slit experiment do not go through either hole. To the uninitiated the principle might seem gratuitous, and in fact there is a classic argument that seems to undermine it. The modern formulation goes like this: we can produce a pair of electrons in a state called the *singlet state*:

$$| s \rangle = \frac{1}{\sqrt{2}} (| x_1 + \rangle \otimes | x_2 - \rangle - | x_1 - \rangle \otimes | x_2 + \rangle).$$

Here $| x_1 + \rangle \otimes | x_2 - \rangle$ is a state in which electron #1 has x-spin up and electron #2 has x-spin down. $| x_1 - \rangle \otimes | x_2 + \rangle$ is read similarly. What this means is that, if we measure x-spin on electron #1, then an x-spin measurement on electron #2 *must* yield the opposite result no matter how well-separated #1 and #2 are. Furthermore, this holds for *all* directions: in the singlet state, parallel spin measurements *always* have opposite results. Therefore, we can predict the spin of particle #2 *in any direction we choose* by measuring particle #1. We cannot measure spin on electron #1 in two directions at once, and after the first measurement the correlation is broken: consequently, we cannot continue to accumulate information about electron #2 by repeated measurement on electron #1. But the correlation will hold for the first measurement of electron #1 that we make. Now, our measurement on electron #1 presumably does not *create* the spin of electron #2. Therefore, it apparently must have been there all along. The tempting conclusion is that electron #2 (and, by symmetry, electron #1) has a definite spin in each direction, even though *no* quantum state could tell us all those spins. If so, the eigenvalue–eigenstate link cannot hold.

This argument has its origins in the reasoning of Einstein, Podolsky and Rosen (1935), though it is not the version Einstein preferred (see EINSTEIN, A. §5). Unfortunately, it is seriously flawed. Parallel spin measurements yield perfect anti-correlation. If the measurements are not parallel, the strength of the correlation varies with the angle. Suppose we assume that all spins are definite and that measurements on one electron do not affect the other. Can all the quantum predictions be captured consistently with the ordinary rules of probability? John Bell (1987) proved, roughly, that they cannot, and subsequent experiments have supported quantum theory's predictions. There are some loopholes here, but most physicists and philosophers agree that these results spell trouble for any wholesale rejection of the eigenvalue–eigenstate link (see BELL'S THEOREM).

Unfortunately, retaining the eigenvalue–eigenstate link seems at least as bad. For one thing, we seem to accept that our measurement of electron #1 *does* create the spin of electron #2. Worse still, if the

electrons are well separated their instantaneous 'communication' would seem to require faster-than-light signals, something which special relativity is usually held to forbid. There are more problems. Suppose we have an electron in the state $| x+ \rangle$ and we decide to measure its z-spin. We would like the result to be a state in which the pointer indicates spin up or else a state in which the pointer indicates spin down. But Schrödinger's equation, the fundamental dynamical law of quantum mechanics, says that at the end of the measurement, we will get a superposition of such states, precisely because the state $| x+ \rangle$ is not an eigenstate of the quantity (z-spin) which we are measuring. If we accept the eigenvalue–eigenstate link, this implies, absurdly, that the measurement will fail to have a result in the oddest way possible: the pointer will not point anywhere at all (see QUANTUM MEASUREMENT PROBLEM)!

3 Interpretations of quantum theory

Clearly quantum mechanics is puzzling. Interpretations of the theory usually focus on one or more specific puzzles, the measurement problem being the most notable. In what follows, we will look at a handful of interpretations and principles.

The most venerable is the Copenhagen interpretation, due to Niels BOHR (1935). Bohr maintains that physical concepts can only be applied in experimental contexts. This is not mere instrumentalism. Consider position and momentum. Both concepts are essential to quantum theory, but the experimental arrangements for measuring them are physically incompatible. Furthermore, the Heisenberg uncertainty relations guarantee that the more the state says about one, the less it says about the other. Bohr concludes that these concepts are *complementary*, and that each can be sensibly applied only within the appropriate experimental context.

On this view, the measurement problem is misconceived. It is a given that experiments have results. The function of quantum theory is not to tell a tale about how this comes to be, but to give an account of how the various possible experimental situations are related to one another.

A review of the literature reveals that the interpretation of the Copenhagen interpretation is no straightforward matter. Bohr may have been profound; few would claim he was clear. However, the stress on the need to ground physical concepts in experimental arrangements shows up in a different guise in a controversial principle called the projection postulate, first made explicit by von Neumann (1932). Schrödinger's equation tells us that quantum states change smoothly and deterministically, but we have noted that this makes measurement puzzling. The projection postulate says that when we measure a quantity *R*, the state 'projects' or 'collapses' abruptly and unpredictably (but with probabities determined by its coefficients, as above) on to one of *R*'s eigenstates, thereby leading to a definite measurement result.

One would like to know more. Does projection occur *only* during measurements? If so, what makes measurement special? Or does projection occur when a conscious observer enters the picture, as some interpreters claim? More recently, detailed physical theories of collapse have been offered. These amount to modifying quantum theory rather than merely interpreting it. The hope is that experiments will be able to settle the matter of whether collapses really occur.

Collapse theories deny that Schrödinger's equation always holds. The most notorious approach that upholds Schrödinger's equation is the many-worlds interpretation, which originated in Hugh Everett III's relative state interpretation (1957) and was further developed by Bryce deWitt (1970). This account claims that when certain sorts of interactions occur, measurement being one of them, the universe divides into separate branches, one for each component of the superposition. This means that observers branch too, and that each observer on each branch sees one of the possible measurement results.

This approach strikes many people as metaphysically extravagant. If it fails, however, it will more likely be for technical reasons having to do with the rules governing branching (the so-called 'basis problem') and the treatment of experimental probabilities.

Quantum logic is another scheme that seems to incorporate drastic measures. In fact, many different approaches, some quite harmless, fall under this rubric. Hilary Putnam made the most striking claims (1969). He maintained that quantum mechanics demands that we revise the laws of logic, notably the distributive law ('A and [B or C]' is equivalent to '[A and B] or [A and C]'). Putnam claimed that if we adopt quantum logic, all quantum paradoxes will vanish because it will be impossible to derive the apparent contradictions. He also maintained that, because statements like '*x*-spin is up or down' come out true on quantum logic, all quantities have values at all times, even though every attempt to list the values of all quantities would be inconsistent.

This is hard to understand, let alone believe, so much so that more or less no one believes it any more. However, a certain more general approach grew out of quantum logic, one that focuses on the mathematical structures underlying quantum mechanics. The hope is that by understanding the role of these structures in

the theory, it will be possible to see quantum mechanics as providing explanations and not mere predictions (see QUANTUM LOGIC; PUTNAM, H. §4).

Finally, there are some important approaches that begin by rejecting the eigenvalue– eigenstate link, but do so in a carefully-limited way. One such is due to David Bohm (1952), but has its roots in deBroglie's 'pilot wave' interpretation. According to Bohm, particle positions are always definite. They evolve deterministically under the guidance of a 'quantum potential' operating in a space of 3*n* dimensions (*n* being the number of particles). This is the most well-worked out example of a hidden variable theory. Hidden variable theories have often been 'proved' impossible, but such proofs deal with theories that make *all* quantities definite or that deny faster-than-light causation. Bohm's theory accepts superluminal causation and takes functions thereof to be the *only* hidden variables. An oft-cited virtue of this approach is that it describes detailed processes underlying such cases as the two-slit experiment. The odd relationship to relativity is troublesome to many, but Bohm's theory continues to be an active area of research.

There are many other approaches to interpreting quantum mechanics and many issues that have not been raised here. For example, ensemble interpretations, which deny that the quantum state characterizes individual systems at all, are important. So-called 'modal' interpretations – a term introduced by van Fraassen – distinguish between what the state necessitates and what may actually be true in addition. Modal interpretations reject the eigenvalue–eigenstate link and have a certain kinship both with the many-worlds view (though without the extravagant metaphysics) and with hidden variables. The investigation of Bell's result led to much debate about whether there is any useful content to the idea that quantum mechanics incorporates some form of holism. And more recently, philosophers have turned their attention to foundational problems in quantum field theory (see FIELD THEORY, QUANTUM).

The interpretation of quantum theory makes for an intriguing intersection between science and philosophy. The safest prediction is that the various controversies will not be settled soon.

References and further reading

Ballentine, L.E. (1970) 'The Statistical Interpretation of Quantum Mechanics', *Reviews of Modern Physics* 42: 358–81. (Ballentine defends the view that quantum states do not describe individual quantum systems but refer instead to ensembles.)

* Bell, J.S. (1987) *Speakable and Unspeakable in*

Quantum Mechanics, Cambridge: Cambridge University Press. (A collection of papers by Bell on various issues in foundations of quantum mechanics. His celebrated theorem was first proved in the paper reprinted as chapter 2.)

* Bohm, D. (1952) 'A Suggested Interpretation of the Quantum Theory in Terms of Hidden Variables, I and II', *Physical Review* 85: 166–79, 180–93. (These papers were the first to offer a detailed hidden variable interpretation of quantum theory and inaugurated a programme that is still vigorously pursued by some researchers.)

* Bohr, N. (1935) 'Can Quantum-Mechanical Description of Reality Be Considered Complete?', *Physical Review* 48: 696–702. (Bohr's reply to Einstein, Podolsky and Rosen (1935), and as good a place as any to get a sense of Bohr's understanding of complementarity.)

Bub, J. (1974) *The Interpretation of Quantum Mechanics*, Dodrecht: Reidel. (An extended development of a quantum-logical approach to the foundations of quantum mechanics.)

Cohen, R.S. and Wartofsky, M.W. (eds) (1969) *Boston Studies in the Philosophy of Science*, vol. 5, Dodrecht: Reidel. (An important collection of papers on the foundations of quantum theory and relativity.)

Cushing, J.T. and McMullin, E. (eds) (1989) *Philosophical Consequences of Quantum Theory: Reflections on Bell's Theorem*, Notre Dame, IN: University of Notre Dame Press. (A watershed collection of essays on Bell's theorem, covering a broad range of interpretive issues. On the issue of holism and quantum mechanics, the papers by Fine, Howard, Hughes, Teller and van Fraassen are especially relevant.)

* deWitt, B.S. (1970) 'Quantum Mechanics and Reality', *Physics Today* 23: 30–55. (A 'many worlds' version of the relative-state interpretation developed by Hugh Everett III.)

* Einstein, A., Podolsky, B. and Rosen, N. (1935) 'Can Quantum Mechanical Description of Reality Be Considered Complete?', *Physical Review* 47: 777–80. (A touchstone for the foundations of quantum mechanics, though not the version of the argument that Einstein himself preferred.)

* Everett, H., III (1957) 'Relative State Formulation of Quantum Mechanics', *Reviews of Modern Physics* 29: 454–62. (The paper from which the 'many-worlds' interpretation was developed. Everett's own view, as the title indicates, relies on the notion of a 'relative state' – a concept that applies to coupled systems, of which the measuring device and the measured system form an example. It is arguable that the relative state interpretation avoids

certain of the difficulties of the many-worlds interpretation, though it also lacks the relative intuitive clarity of the many-worlds view.)

Fine, A. (1986) *The Shaky Game: Einstein, Realism and the Quantum Theory*, Chicago, IL: University of Chicago Press. (A collection of essays. Chapter two makes a convincing case that the argument actually found in the EPR paper was not written by Einstein and was importantly different from the version that he favoured.)

* Fraassen, B. van (1991) *Quantum Mechanics: An Empiricist View*, Oxford: Clarendon Press. (Includes a development of the modal interpretation, which van Fraassen first introduced in the 1970s.)

Ghirardi, G.C., Rimini, A. and Weber, T. (1986) 'Unified Dynamics for Microscopic and Macroscopic Systems', *Physical Review D* 34: 470–91. (A detailed physical proposal for augmenting Schrödinger's equation with a process of collapse.)

Healey, R. (1989) *The Philosophy of Quantum Mechanics: An Interactive Interpretation*, Cambridge: Cambridge University Press. (An extended development of a modal interpretation of quantum theory. Healey refers to his view as an interactive approach.)

Hughes, R.I.G. (1989) *The Structure and Interpretation of Quantum Mechanics*, Cambridge, MA: Harvard University Press. (A pedagogically impressive introduction to the fundamentals of quantum mechanics in Hilbert space, as well as an interpretation of quantum mechanics in the tradition growing out of quantum logic.)

Jammer, M. (1974) *The Philosophy of Quantum Mechanics*, New York: John Wiley & Sons. (Still one of the most comprehensive introductions to the foundations of quantum mechanics.)

* Neumann, J. von (1932) *Mathematische Grundlagen der Quantenmechanik*, Berlin: Springer; trans. R.T. Beyer, *Mathematical Foundations of Quantum Mechanics*, Princeton, NJ: Princeton University Press, 1955. (The first rigorous Hilbert space formulation of quantum mechanics.)

* Putnam, H. (1969) 'Is Logic Empirical?', in R.S. Cohen and M.W. Wartofsky (eds) *Boston Studies in the Philosophy of Science*, Dodrecht: Reidel, vol. 5, 181–206. (In this seminal paper, Putnam attempts to argue for a realist interpretation of quantum mechanics by an appeal to so-called 'quantum logic', arguing that if we give up the principle that 'and' distributes over 'or', we will be able to claim that every quantum-mechanical quantity has a definite value.)

Zurek, W.H. (1991) 'Decoherence and the Transition from Quantum to Classical', *Physics Today* October: 36–44. (The decoherence programme attempts to give a *quantum mechanical* explanation of why the world normally appears classical. The account begins with the fact that virtually all the systems we encounter are *open systems*, that is, are in interaction with the environment. It goes on to argue rigorously that the result is a so-called 'reduced density matrix' (crudely, a restriction of the total state to a subsystem) that is a stable mixture of appropriate states. In the case of a measuring device, this would be a mixture of appropriate indicator states. Zurek is one of the main proponents of this approach and his article, though technical, is relatively accessible. The 'Letters' portion of the April 1993 issue of the same journal includes a number of reactions to Zurek's essay, with replies by Zurek.)

ALLEN STAIRS